S0-EQS-712

WHO'S WHERE

A

Aagaard, Chris ... (519) 894-2231
Cambridge Civic/General Reporter
Record, Kitchener, ON
Aamidor, Abe ... (317) 633-1240
Health/Fitness Writer
Indianapolis Star/News, Indianapolis, IN
Aamoth, Nila ... (616) 792-2271
ED, Penasee Globe, Wayland, MI
Aardema, Harold ... (712) 726-3313
PUB, ED, Doon Press, Doon, IA
Aaron, Charlotte ... (210) 225-7411
ADV MGR-CLASS
San Antonio Express-News, San Antonio, TX
Aaronson, H J ... (706) 724-0851
PROD DIR, Augusta Chronicle, Augusta, GA
Aarvig, David ... (701) 780-1100
PROD DIR
Grand Forks Herald, Grand Forks, ND
Abadie, Chuck ... (601) 582-4321
Sports ED
Hattiesburg American, Hattiesburg, MS
Aban, Debra ... (916) 321-1000
MGR-EDU SRV
Sacramento Bee, Sacramento, CA
Abate, Carl ... (315) 253-5311
PROD FRM-PR, Citizen, Auburn, NY
Abatemarco, Kathleen ... (908) 922-6000
ASSOC DIR-Human Resources
Asbury Park Press, Neptune, NJ
Abbey, Alan D ... (518) 454-5694
EX BUS ED, Times Union, Albany, NY
Abbey, Harlan C ... (716) 854-2192
ED, Buffalo Jewish Review, Buffalo, NY
Abbot, Bob ... (208) 664-8176
Automotive ED
Coeur d'Alene Press, Coeur d'Alene, ID
Abbott, Brian Patrick ... (616) 527-2100
MAN ED, Sentinel-Standard, Ionia, MI
Abbott, Charles ... (405) 363-3370
Cartoonist, DIR-Photography, Sports ED
Blackwell Journal-Tribune, Blackwell, OK
Abbott, Dean ... (619) 293-1818
NTL Sales DIR
Copley News Service, San Diego, CA
Abbott, Frank ... (202) 334-6000
PROD SUPT-PR (NW)
Washington Post, Washington, DC
Abbott, Greg ... (507) 625-4451
News DIR-Production/Design
Free Press, Mankato, MN
Abbott, Jack ... (714) 835-1234
PROD DIR-Pre Press
Orange County Register, Santa Ana, CA
Abbott, Jeanne ... (515) 284-8000
Features ED
Des Moines Register, Des Moines, IA
Abbott, Jim D ... (601) 887-2222
PUB, ED, Enterprise-Tocsin, Indianola, MS
Abbott, Keith ... (919) 446-5161
PROD SUPV
Rocky Mount Telegram, Rocky Mount, NC
Abbott, Loren C ... (916) 541-3880
PUB
Tahoe Daily Tribune, South Lake Tahoe, CA
Abbott, Thomas ... (610) 622-8800
ADV MGR-CLASS
Delaware County Daily Times, Primos, PA
Abcarian, Robin ... (213) 237-5000
COL, Los Angeles Times, Los Angeles, CA
Abdon, Jim ... (520) 453-4237
CIRC MGR
Today's News-Herald, Lake Havasu City, AZ
Abdou, Johnna ... (306) 692-6441
Accountant
Moose Jaw Times-Herald, Moose Jaw, SK
Abel, Jananne ... (914) 939-6864
ED, Westmore News, Port Chester, NY
Abel, Richard ... (914) 939-6864
PUB, America Latina, Port Chester, NY
Abell, Gene ... (606) 231-3100
Sports ED
Lexington Herald-Leader, Lexington, KY
Abell, Kathy ... (573) 468-6511
PUB, ED
Sullivan Independent News, Sullivan, MO
Abeln Sr, Richard E ... (816) 258-7237
PUB/GM, PA, ADV MGR, PROD SUPT
Daily News-Bulletin, Brookfield, MO
Abeln, Terry ... (605) 996-5514
PROD FRM-PR, Daily Republic, Mitchell, SD
Abels, Debbie ... (704) 358-5000
VP, DIR-Human Resources
Charlotte Observer, Charlotte, NC

The following is an alphabetical list of abbreviations used in this personnel directory.

ADM	Administration
ADTX	Audiotex
ADV	Advertising
ASSOC	Associate
ASST	Assistant
BC	Board Chairman
BM	Business Manager
BU	Bureau
BUS	Business
CEO	Chief Executive Officer
CFO	Chief Financial Officer
CIO	Chief Information Officer
CIRC	Circulation
CIS	Customer Information Service
CLASS	Classified
CNR	Coordinator
COB	Chairman of the Board
COL	Columnist
COMP	Composing
CONT	Controller
COO	Chief Operating Officer
CORP	Corporate
CR	Credit
DEPT	Department
DIR	Director
ED	Editor
EDL	Editorial
EDU	Education
EIC	Editor in Chief
ENG	Engineer
EPE	Editorial Page Editor
EVP	Executive Vice President
EX	Executive
FIN	Financial
FRM	Foreman
GEN	General
GM	General Manager
INFO SRV	Information Service
INFO SYS	Information System
MAN	Managing
MET	Metropolitan
MGR	Manager
MGT	Management
MIS	Management Information Service
MKTG	Marketing
MR	Mailroom
NIE	Newspapers in Education
NTL	National
OFF	Officer
OPER	Operations
PA	Purchasing Agent
PR	Pressroom
PRES	President
PROD	Production
PROM	Promotion
PUB	Publisher
PSL	Personnel
RE	Real Estate
RES	Research
RT	Retail
SCI	Science
SEC	Secretary
SRV	Service
SUB	Subscriptions
SUPT	Superintendent
SUPV	Supervisor
SYS	System
TELEMKTG	Telemarketing
TREAS	Treasurer
VBC	Vice Board Chairman
VIS	Voice Information Service
VP	Vice President

Aben, Elizabeth Rice ... (705) 789-5541
PUB, Huntsville Forester, Huntsville, ON
Aberbach, Jeff ... (916) 756-0800
BUS/FIN ED, City/MET ED, EPE, NTL ED,
News ED, Davis Enterprise, Davis, CA
Abercrombie, Karen W ... (205) 252-3672
ED, Alabama Messenger, Birmingham, AL
Abernathy, Dorothy L ... (502) 222-7183
PUB, Oldham Era, La Grange, KY
Abernathy, Michael ... (804) 358-0825
PUB, Style Weekly, Richmond, VA
Abernathy, Penelope Muse ... (212) 556-1234
Senior VP-Planning & Human Resources
New York Times, New York, NY
Abiro, Emmanuel ... (210) 686-4343
CIRC MGR-Home Delivery
Monitor, McAllen, TX
Abner, Dave ... (417) 345-2224
ED, Buffalo Reflex, Buffalo, MO
Abolafia, David ... (516) 739-6400
ED, Baldwin Citizen, Baldwin, NY
Abouhalkah, Yael ... (816) 234-4141
EDL Writer, Star, Kansas City, MO
Abraham, George ... (716) 374-5400
ED, Green Thumb, Naples, NY
Abraham, Katherine ... (716) 374-5400
ASST ED, Green Thumb, Naples, NY
Abraham Sr, Nat ... (803) 256-4015
ED, Carolina Panorama, Columbia, SC
Abraham Jr, Nat ... (803) 256-4015
PUB, Carolina Panorama, Columbia, SC
Abraham, Tim ... (715) 833-9200
MGR-MKTG/PROM
Leader-Telegram, Eau Claire, WI
Abrahamian, Emil V ... (716) 688-0902
PRES, Abrahamian Feature Syndicate,
Williamsville, NY
Abrahamian, Viken ... (617) 926-3974
ED, Armenian Weekly, Watertown, MA
Abrahamson, Gloria ... (701) 756-6363
PUB, ED, Renville County Farmer, Mohall, ND
Abramo, Patricia ... (914) 534-7771
ED, Cornwall Local, Cornwall, NY
Abramowitz, Roxanne ... (412) 628-2000
City ED, Daily Courier, Connellsville, PA
Abrams, Elliot ... (814) 234-9601
Sr. VP, AccuWeather Inc., State College, PA
Abrams, Joan ... (208) 743-9411
Entertainment/Amusements ED
Lewiston Morning Tribune, Lewiston, ID
Abramson, Elaine Sandra ... (817) 292-1855
PRES, A & A, Ft. Worth, TX
Abramson, Ronna ... (415) 348-4321
Transportation ED
San Mateo County Times, San Mateo, CA
Abramson, Stan ... (817) 292-1855
Senior VP, A & A, Ft. Worth, TX

Abramson, William ... (508) 586-7200
Sports ED, Enterprise, Brockton, MA
Abrego, Rick ... (210) 383-2705
CIRC MGR, PROD SUPT-PR
Edinburg Daily Review, Edinburg, TX
Abria, Jasmina ... (718) 899-8603
GM, Resumen Newspaper, Woodside, NY
Abruzzese, Leo ... (212) 837-7000
ED-Washington, Journal of Commerce &
Commercial, New York, NY
Absher, Kim ... (423) 246-8121
Librarian
Kingsport Times-News, Kingsport, TN
Abshier, Dan ... (360) 424-3251
News ED, Wire ED
Skagit Valley Herald, Mount Vernon, WA
Abssi, Michel B ... (213) 469-4354
PUB, ED, Beirut Times, Los Angeles, CA
Acchione III, John B ... (215) 592-1713
ED, Sons of Italy Times, Philadelphia, PA
Acevedo, Apolinar ... (408) 423-4242
PROD DIR
Santa Cruz County Sentinel, Santa Cruz, CA
Achatz, Carol ... (360) 754-5400
DIR-Human Resources
Olympian, Olympia, WA
Achenbach, Renate ... (204) 774-1883
ED, Kanada Kurier, Winnipeg, MB
Acheson, Dean ... (715) 356-5236
GM, Lakeland Times, Minocqua, WI
Achhorner, Dawn ... (303) 660-2360
PUB, Parker Trail, Castle Rock, CO
Achor, Pat ... (504) 826-3279
PROD ASST MGR
Times-Picayune, New Orleans, LA
Acker, Anne ... (806) 647-3123
MAN ED, Castro County News, Dimmitt, TX
Acker, Todd ... (937) 498-2111
Photo ED, Sidney Daily News, Sidney, OH
Ackerman, Bonnie ... (419) 492-2133
MAN ED, Herald, New Washington, OH
Ackerman, Irene ... (212) 455-4000
Domestic Licensing MGR, North America
Syndicate/King Features Syndicate, NY, NY
Ackerman, Jeff ... (702) 882-2111
PUB, Nevada Appeal, Carson City, NV
Ackermann, Baldwin ... (604) 270-2923
ED, Pazifische Rundschau, Richmond, BC
Ackert, Kristie ... (209) 578-2000
EDU Writer, Modesto Bee, Modesto, CA
Ackerwold, Robert ... (612) 442-4414
GM, Waconia Patriot, Waconia, MN
Ackley, Michael ... (916) 885-5656
ED, EPE, Auburn Journal, Auburn, CA
Acklin, Alisha ... (310) 230-3400
Account EX SUPV, Allsport Photography
USA, Pacific Palisades, CA

Acklin, Joe ... (309) 426-2255
PUB, Roseville Independent, Roseville, IL
Ackroyd, Carson ... (403) 250-4200
DIR-MKTG/PROM, Calgary Sun, Calgary, AB
Acohido, Byron ... (206) 464-2111
Aerospace Reporter
Seattle Times, Seattle, WA
Acosta, Anthony ... (507) 235-3303
Wire ED, Sentinel, Fairmont, MN
Acri, Robert J ... (412) 834-1151
TREAS/CONT
Tribune-Review, Greensburg, PA
Acuna, Armando ... (213) 237-5000
Sacramento BU
Los Angeles Times, Los Angeles, CA
Acuna, Lupe T ... (619) 357-3214
PUB, Calexico Chronicle, Calexico, CA
Adair, Dick ... (808) 525-8000
Cartoonist, Honolulu Advertiser, Honolulu, HI
Adair, Jim ... (417) 532-9131
Sports ED
Lebanon Daily Record, Lebanon, MO
Adair, Larry ... (918) 456-8833
PROD MGR
Tahlequah Daily Press, Tahlequah, OK
Adair, Mark ... (205) 325-2222
CIRC MGR-Northeast Zone
Birmingham News, Birmingham, AL
Adair, Wayne ... (208) 788-3444
MAN ED, Wood River Journal, Hailey, ID
Adam, Ren L ... (805) 646-1476
PUB, Ojai Valley News, Ojai, CA
Adami, David ... (217) 788-1300
BM, State Journal-Register, Springfield, IL
Adamis, Tony ... (914) 331-5000
Regional ED, Daily Freeman, Kingston, NY
Adamo, Kim ... (412) 628-2000
CIRC MGR, Daily Courier, Connellsville, PA
Adamopoulos, Robin ... (410) 749-0272
ED
Salisbury News & Advertiser, Salisbury, MD
Adams, Albert ... (817) 390-7400
PROD MGR-Pre Press
Fort Worth Star-Telegram, Fort Worth, TX
Adams, Amy Ann ... (419) 281-0581
EDU ED, Teen-Age/Youth ED
Ashland Times-Gazette, Ashland, OH
Adams, Anne ... (603) 298-8711
Arts/Entertainment ED, EDU/Books ED
Valley News, White River Jct., VT
Adams, April ... (801) 776-4951
ED, Lakeside Review, Layton, UT
Adams, Arthur J ... (504) 383-1111
Sunday ED, Advocate, Baton Rouge, LA
Adams, Bart ... (910) 891-1234
PRES, PUB/GM, BM, ED, ADTX MGR
Daily Record, Dunn, NC
Adams, Beth ... (504) 826-3279
PSL MGR, Times-Picayune, New Orleans, LA
Adams, Bobbi ... (304) 436-3144
Food/Home Furnishings ED, Society ED
Welch Daily News, Welch, WV
Adams, Bonnie ... (904) 294-1210
ED, Mayo Free Press, Mayo, FL
Adams, Bonniejean ... (412) 664-9161
City ED, Daily News, McKeesport, PA
Adams, Brent ... (910) 891-1234
VP, Daily Record, Dunn, NC
Adams, Charles ... (912) 283-2244
PROD ASST FRM-COMP
Waycross Journal-Herald, Waycross, GA
Adams, Chris ... (708) 336-7000
MAN ED, News-Sun, Waukegan, IL
Adams, Denise ... (713) 232-3737
Religion ED, Herald-Coaster, Rosenberg, TX
Adams, Earnest ... (918) 335-8200
CIRC Distribution Clerk
Examiner-Enterprise, Bartlesville, OK
Adams, Elizabeth ... (706) 724-0851
Features ED, Augusta Chronicle, Augusta, GA
Adams, Eric D ... (307) 765-4485
PUB, ED
Greybull Standard & Tribune, Greybull, WY
Adams Jr, Floyd ... (912) 232-4505
PUB, Savannah Herald, Savannah, GA
Adams, Fred ... (601) 226-4321
GM, CIRC MGR
Daily Sentinel-Star, Grenada, MS
Adams, Genetta ... (941) 335-0200
Features ED, News-Press, Fort Myers, FL
Adams, Glenn W ... (610) 820-6500
MGR-CR, Morning Call, Allentown, PA
Adams, Hoover ... (910) 891-1234
BUS/FIN ED, COL, EDL Writer, Radio/Television ED, Daily Record, Dunn, NC

Copyright ©1997 by the Editor & Publisher Co.

Ada Who's Where-4

Adams, Jackie .... (406) 755-7000
News ED, Daily Inter Lake, Kalispell, MT
Adams, James .... (603) 668-4321
Farm ED, Music ED, Radio/Television ED
Union Leader, Manchester, NH
Adams, James .... (416) 585-5000
Arts DIR, Globe and Mail, Toronto, ON
Adams, Jeff .... (719) 336-2266
CIRC MGR, Lamar Daily News, Lamar, CO
Adams, Jerry .... (504) 826-3279
MGR-CR, Times-Picayune, New Orleans, LA
Adams, Jo .... (520) 753-6397
MGR-OPER
Kingman Daily Miner, Kingman, AZ
Adams, John .... (904) 526-3614
PROD SUPT
Jackson County Floridan, Marianna, FL
Adams, Joni .... (573) 335-6611
MAN ED
Southeast Missourian, Cape Girardeau, MO
Adams, Joseph H .... (540) 669-2181
DIR-Sales, Herald-Courier Virginia Tennessean, Bristol, VA
Adams, Joseph H .... (334) 774-2715
PUB, ED, Southern Star, Ozark, AL
Adams, Julie .... (503) 363-0006
GM, Community News, Salem, OR
Adams, Kathryn .... (201) 428-6200
News ED, Daily Record, Parsippany, NJ
Adams, Kathy .... (204) 877-3321
GM, Reston Recorder, Reston, MB
Adams, Kelly .... (517) 835-7171
EDU Writer
Midland Daily News, Midland, MI
Adams, Ken .... (801) 829-3451
PUB, ED, Morgan County News, Morgan, UT
Adams, Kenneth .... (414) 224-2000
Senior VP-Printing
Milwaukee Journal Sentinel, Milwaukee, WI
Adams, Kenneth .... (912) 232-4505
ED, Savannah Herald, Savannah, GA
Adams, Kevin .... (803) 785-4293
Sports ED, Island Packet, Hilton Head, SC
Adams, Kim Edward .... (515) 737-2119
PUB, ED, Monitor Review, Stacyville, IA
Adams, Laura .... (419) 522-3311
CIRC MGR-Customer SRV
News Journal, Mansfield, OH
Adams, Linda M .... (307) 568-2458
PUB, Basin Republican Rustler, Basin, WY
Adams, Marie .... (801) 829-3451
PUB, Morgan County News, Morgan, UT
Adams, Marvin I .... (717) 291-8811
News ED, Lancaster Intelligencer Journal/New Era/Sunday News, Lancaster, PA
Adams, Melissa .... (508) 343-6911
City ED
Sentinel & Enterprise, Fitchburg, MA
Adams, Mellicent .... (910) 891-1234
VP/SEC/TREAS, Films/Theater ED, Travel ED
Daily Record, Dunn, NC
Adams, Michael .... (410) 332-6000
Perspective ED, Sun, Baltimore, MD
Adams, Mike .... (910) 323-4848
City ED
Fayetteville Observer-Times, Fayetteville, NC
Adams, Nancy J .... (503) 623-2373
PUB
Polk County Itemizer-Observer, Dallas, OR
Adams, Nelson D .... (919) 747-3883
PUB
Snow Hill Standard Laconic, Snow Hill, NC
Adams, Pam .... (316) 456-2232
ED, Norwich News, Conway Springs, KS
Adams, Ray .... (904) 359-4111
PROD SUPT-Bldg Mech
Florida Times-Union, Jacksonville, FL
Adams, Regina .... (910) 891-1234
Home Furnishings ED
Daily Record, Dunn, NC
Adams, Robert .... (319) 984-6179
PUB, ED, Forum, Denver, IA
Adams, Robert .... (507) 582-3542
PUB, Adams Monitor Review, Adams, MN
Adams, Robert .... (209) 674-2424
MAN ED, BUS/FIN ED, EPE
Madera Tribune, Madera, CA
Adams, Robert Hugo .... (516) 486-4211
PUB, ED, Economic Forum, Hempstead, NY
Adams, Robin .... (941) 687-7000
Health/Medical ED, Ledger, Lakeland, FL
Adams, Rodgers .... (612) 673-4000
DIR-News Budget
Star Tribune, Minneapolis, MN
Adams, San .... (606) 329-1717
Environmental ED
Daily Independent, Ashland, KY
Adams, Sarah .... (412) 981-6100
News ED, Herald, Sharon, PA
Adams, Sherry .... (713) 220-7171
Librarian, Houston Chronicle, Houston, TX
Adams, Stephen .... (602) 468-6565
VP/COO, VP PROD
Daily Racing Form, Phoenix, AZ
Adams, Tarena .... (616) 469-1100
GM, New Buffalo Times, New Buffalo, MI
Adams, Todd .... (414) 224-2000
Senior VP-FIN
Milwaukee Journal Sentinel, Milwaukee, WI
Adams, Todd .... (208) 743-9411
BUS/FIN ED, Graphics ED/Art DIR, Travel ED
Lewiston Morning Tribune, Lewiston, ID
Adams, Tony .... (706) 571-8574
ED, Benning Leader, Columbus, GA
Adams, Trish .... (504) 748-7156
ED, Amite Tangi-Digest, Amite, LA
Adams, Walt .... (309) 686-3000
PROD FRM-MR, Journal Star, Peoria, IL
Adams, Wanda .... (808) 525-8000
Fashion/Features ED
Honolulu Advertiser, Honolulu, HI
Adams-Mizelle, Pauline .... (805) 650-2900
ADV MGR-CLASS
Ventura County Star, Ventura, CA
Adams-Warren, Gerri .... (619) 266-2233
MAN ED, Voice & Viewpoint, San Diego, CA
Adamson, Deborah .... (404) 526-5151
CIRC MGR-Sales/PROM
Atlanta Journal-Constitution, Atlanta, GA
Adamson, Jan .... (903) 962-4275
ED, Grand Saline Sun, Grand Saline, TX
Adamson, Ned .... (616) 832-5566
ED, Reed City Herald News, Reed City, MI
Adamson, Scott .... (205) 362-1000
Sports ED, Daily Home, Talladega, AL
Adamson-Bray, Mari .... (612) 375-9222
PUB, Skyway News and Freeway News, Minneapolis, MN
Adcock, Joe .... (206) 448-8000
Theater ED, Post-Intelligencer, Seattle, WA
Adcock, Kelly .... (501) 268-8621
News ED, Daily Citizen, Searcy, AR
Addington, Larry .... (910) 727-7211
PROD MGR-Pre Press
Winston-Salem Journal, Winston-Salem, NC
Addison, Ellen M .... (423) 272-7325
PUB, ED, Rogersville Review, Rogersville, TN
Adelman, Caryn Rosen .... (212) 643-1890
PRES, Jewish Telegraphic Agency, NY, NY
Adelman, Matt .... (307) 358-2965
PUB, ED, Douglas Budget, Douglas, WY
Adelsman, Jean .... (310) 540-5511
MAN ED, Daily Breeze, Torrance, CA
Adema, Shirley .... (813) 689-7764
ED, Temple Terrace News, Brandon, FL
Adeshina, Tony .... (216) 999-4500
PROD CNR-Quality Assurance
Plain Dealer, Cleveland, OH
Adix, Dan .... (319) 472-2311
ED, Cedar Valley Daily Times, Vinton, IA
Adkins, James .... (512) 445-3500
CIRC MGR-OPER
Austin American-Statesman, Austin, TX
Adkins, Kenneth .... (304) 348-5140
PROD MGR-MR
Charleston Newspapers, Charleston, WV
Adkins, Melvin E .... (561) 562-2315
ADV MGR, MGR-Display Advertising
Vero Beach Press-Journal, Vero Beach, FL
Adkins, Ruth .... (304) 526-4000
ADV MGR-CLASS
Herald-Dispatch, Huntington, WV
Adkins, S Mark .... (412) 772-3900
PRES/PUB
North Hills News Record, Warrendale, PA
Adkins, Sam .... (520) 573-4400
ADV MGR-Major Accounts, TNI Partners dba Tucson Newspapers, Tucson, AZ
Adkisson, Gary D .... (817) 325-4465
PUB/GM
Mineral Wells Index, Mineral Wells, TX
Adler, Alan .... (313) 222-6400
Automotive Writer, Free Press, Detroit, MI
Adler, Allan P .... (810) 627-2843
ED, Reminder Newspapers, Ortonville, MI
Adler, Andrew .... (502) 582-4011
Music ED, Courier-Journal, Louisville, KY
Adler, Helmut .... (206) 455-2222
CIRC VP/DIR, Eastside Journal, Bellevue, WA
Adler, Larry .... (405) 772-3301
ED, EPE, News/Religion ED
Weatherford Daily News, Weatherford, OK
Adler, Ross .... (954) 356-4000
CIRC MGR-South Broward
Sun-Sentinel, Fort Lauderdale, FL
Adolph, Geraldine .... (810) 985-7171
CONT, Times Herald, Port Huron, MI
Adomeit, Bruce .... (612) 673-4000
CNR-Electronic News SYS
Star Tribune, Minneapolis, MN
Adone, Vincent .... (610) 820-6500
VP-Newspaper Sales/MKTG
Morning Call, Allentown, PA
Adrianson, Doug .... (213) 237-5000
Commitments ED, Laugh Lines ED
Los Angeles Times, Los Angeles, CA
Adsett, Dave .... (519) 843-5410
ED, Wellington Advertiser, Fergus, ON
Adwan, Alex .... (918) 581-8300
Senior ED, Tulsa World, Tulsa, OK
Aebly, Bill .... (815) 232-1171
ADV MGR-RT, Journal-Standard, Freeport, IL
Aeschliman, Theresa .... (419) 784-5441
Farm/Agribusiness ED
Crescent-News, Defiance, OH
Afflerbach, Libby .... (817) 390-7400
City ED-Night
Fort Worth Star-Telegram, Fort Worth, TX
Ager, Susan .... (313) 222-6400
COL-Features, Detroit Free Press, Detroit, MI
Aggergaard, Steve .... (218) 723-5281
City ED, Features ED
Duluth News-Tribune, Duluth, MN
Aggerholm, Barb .... (519) 894-2231
General Assignment Reporter
Record, Kitchener, ON
Agner, Wayne .... (805) 925-2691
MAN ED, Automotive ED, EPE, Travel ED
Santa Maria Times, Santa Maria, CA
Agnew, David .... (519) 255-5711
MAN ED, Windsor Star, Windsor, ON
Agnew, Ronny .... (601) 582-4321
MAN ED
Hattiesburg American, Hattiesburg, MS
Agnew, Tim .... (319) 754-8461
ADV CNR-Major Accounts
Hawk Eye, Burlington, IA
Agostino, K C .... (412) 794-6857
ED, Tri-County News, Slippery Rock, PA
Agosto, Tomas .... (520) 783-3333
CIRC DIR, Yuma Daily Sun, Yuma, AZ
Agren, Edwin .... (609) 845-3300
PROD SUPT
Gloucester County Times, Woodbury, NJ
Agres, Ted .... (202) 636-3000
ASST MAN ED, Online Contact
Washington Times, Washington, DC
Agris, A A .... (508) 820-9700
PUB, Hellenic Chronicle, Framingham, MA
Agryris, Eileen .... (905) 355-2843
ED, Colborne Chronicle, Colborne, ON
Aguero, Bidal .... (806) 763-3841
PUB, ED, El Editor-Lubbock, Lubbock, TX
Aguiar, Lourenco Costa .... (510) 537-9503
PUB, ED, Voz de Portugal, Hayward, CA
Aguilar, Carmen .... (312) 522-0288
PUB, Momento, Cicero, IL
Aguilar, Julia S .... (805) 781-7800
PRES/GM
Telegram-Tribune, San Luis Obispo, CA
Aguilar, Luis .... (516) 486-6457
ED, La Tribuna Hispana-NY/NJ, Westbury, NY
Aguilar, Melissa .... (713) 220-7171
Entertainment ED
Houston Chronicle, Houston, TX
Aguilar, Peter .... (505) 648-2333
PUB, Lincoln County News, Carrizozo, NM
Aguilar, Robert .... (408) 424-2221
ADV DIR, Californian, Salinas, CA
Aguina, Steven .... (312) 222-3232
PROD MGR-Newsprint OPER
Chicago Tribune, Chicago, IL
Aguirre, Alejandro J .... (305) 633-3341
ASST PUB, Diario Las Americas, Miami, FL
Aguirre, Amanda .... (210) 775-1551
BM, Del Rio News-Herald, Del Rio, TX
Aguirre, Horacio .... (305) 633-3341
PUB, ED, Diario Las Americas, Miami, FL
Aguirre, Johnny .... (308) 632-0670
ADV DIR, Star-Herald, Scottsbluff, NE
Aguirre, Louis G .... (504) 850-3132
PUB, Bayou Catholic, Schriever, LA
Aguirre, Roy .... (520) 364-3424
PROD SUPT, Daily Dispatch, Douglas, AZ
Agurkis, Leanne .... (805) 945-5634
ED, Aerotech News & Review, Lancaster, CA
Ahearn, William E .... (212) 621-1500
VP/EX ED, Associated Press, New York, NY
Ahern, Harry .... (603) 352-1234
ADV MGR-Co-op, Keene Sentinel, Keene, NH
Ahern, Mary Ellen .... (401) 277-7000
MGR-Community Affairs, CIRC MGR-NIE
Providence Journal-Bulletin, Providence, RI
Ahern, Tony .... (541) 475-2275
PUB, Madras Pioneer, Madras, OR
Ahillen, Steve .... (423) 523-3131
Sports ED
Knoxville News-Sentinel, Knoxville, TN
Ahle, Dorothy .... (617) 321-8302
Artist/Owner
Ahle, Dorothy Caricatures, Malden, MA
Ahlquist, Bev .... (320) 796-2945
ED, New London, New London, MN
Ahlrich, Jerry .... (502) 583-4471
MGR, Daily Record, Louisville, KY
Ahlstrom, Richard A .... (518) 439-4949
PUB, ED, Spotlight, Delmar, NY
Ahmad Syed, Hasanat .... (416) 481-7793
PUB, GM, ED, New Canada, Toronto, Ontario
Ahmann, Noel N .... (712) 786-1196
PUB, ED, Bell-Enterprise, Remsen, IA
Ahmed, F .... (416) 362-0304
PUB, ED, Dalil Al Arab, Toronto, ON
Ahmed, Safir .... (314) 231-6666
ED, Riverfront Times, St. Louis, MO
Ahrendes, Vern .... (509) 782-3781
ED, Cashmere Valley Record, Cashmere, WA
Ahrens, Bob .... (219) 933-3200
Graphics ED/Art DIR, Times, Munster, IN
Ahrens, Kimberly A .... (616) 722-3161
CONT, Muskegon Chronicle, Muskegon, MI
Ahrens, Tracey .... (815) 937-3300
Health/Medical ED
Daily Journal, Kankakee, IL
Ai, Nobuo .... (212) 603-6600
Office MGR
Kyodo News Service, New York, NY
Aiello, John .... (423) 981-1100
Sports ED, Daily Times, Maryville, TN
Aiello, Thom .... (414) 684-4433
Sports ED
Herald Times Reporter, Manitowoc, WI
Aiena, Frank .... (409) 833-3311
PROD SUPT-PR
Beaumont Enterprise, Beaumont, TX
Aikins, Glenda .... (316) 365-2111
MGR-Office, Iola Register, Iola, KS
Ailes, David .... (412) 834-1151
Sports ED, Tribune-Review, Greensburg, PA
Ainsley, P Steven .... (805) 564-5200
PUB, News-Press, Santa Barbara, CA
Ainsley, Spencer .... (914) 454-2000
Graphics ED, Photo ED
Poughkeepsie Journal, Poughkeepsie, NY
Ainsworth, Jim .... (707) 226-3711
PROD FRM-PR/Platemaking
Napa Valley Register, Napa, CA
Ainsworth, Wanda K .... (904) 252-1511
CIRC MGR-Home Delivery/Single Copy/Customer SRV, Daytona Beach News-Journal, Daytona Beach, FL
Aird, Malcolm .... (519) 894-2231
Travel ED, Record, Kitchener, ON
Airing, Todd .... (716) 798-1400
CIRC MGR, Journal-Register, Medina, NY
Akers, Corwan .... (816) 254-8600
PROD FRM-PR
Examiner, Independence, MO
Akers, Lee Anne .... (765) 762-3322
ED, Williamsport Review-Republican, Williamsport, IN
Akers, Mary Ann .... (765) 762-3322
PUB, Williamsport Review-Republican, Williamsport, IN
Akers, Shawn .... (803) 317-6397
NTL ED, News ED
Florence Morning News, Florence, SC
Akers, Steve .... (941) 992-2110
GM, Bonita Banner, Bonita Springs, FL
Akhavein, Hadi .... (414) 235-7700
CIRC MGR-Single Copy
Oshkosh Northwestern, Oshkosh, WI
Akins, Roger C .... (203) 789-5200
CIRC DIR, Register, New Haven, CT
Alabiso, Vincent .... (212) 621-1500
VP/EX Photo ED
Associated Press, New York, NY
Alagna, Ace .... (201) 485-6000
PUB, Italian Tribune News, Newark, NJ
Alagna, Joan .... (201) 485-6000
ED, Italian Tribune News, Newark, NJ
Alaks, Kathleen .... (541) 474-3700
Amusements/Books ED, Religion ED, Grants Pass Daily Courier, Grants Pass, OR
Alambar, Becky .... (915) 773-3621
GM, Stamford American, Stamford, TX
Alambar, Lewis .... (915) 773-3621
PUB, Stamford American, Stamford, TX
Alan, Frank .... (219) 772-2101
PUB, Leader, Knox, IN
Alanis, Veronica .... (312) 762-2266
ED, Lawndale News/Su Noticiero Bilingue, Chicago, IL
Alary, Etienne .... (306) 347-0481
ED, Journal L'eau Vive, Regina, SK
Alba, Harry .... (215) 557-2300
VP-Sales
Legal Intelligencer, Philadelphia, PA
Alba, Miguel .... (312) 252-3534
ED, Logan Square-Buckton Extra, Chicago, IL
Albanese, Anne E .... (312) 787-5396
PUB, North Loop News, Chicago, IL
Albanese, Ellen .... (508) 528-2600
MAN ED, Country Gazette, Franklin, MA
Albanese, Jim .... (408) 424-2221
News ED, Californian, Salinas, CA
Albanese, Michelle C .... (312) 787-5396
ED, North Loop News, Chicago, IL
Albano, George .... (203) 846-3281
ASST Sports ED, Hour, Norwalk, CT

Copyright ©1997 by the Editor & Publisher Co.

WHO'S WHERE
PART 2 OF THE 1997 INTERNATIONAL YEAR BOOK®

Published annually by **EDITOR & PUBLISHER**, the oldest publishers' and advertisers' periodical in the United States

With which has been merged: **The Journalist**, established March 22, 1884; **Newspaperdom**, March 22, 1892; **The Fourth Estate**, March 1, 1894; **Editor & Publisher**, June 29, 1901; **Advertising**, January 22, 1925.

James Wright Brown
Publisher, Chairman of the Board, 1912-1959

Robert U. Brown
President and Editor Emeritus

Year Book Staff

Editor
Ian E. Anderson

Research Staff
Shilpa Chatlani, Jaimie Frank, Myrna Gabriel, Nat Ives, David Maddux, Brooke Martinsen, Brian Switalski, Jessica Zonana, Seth Zupnik

Publishers
D. Colin Phillips
Christopher Phillips

Advertising Vice President
Michael Dardano

Advertising Production Manager
Carol Blum

Art Director
Hector W. Marrero

Production Staff
Lery Chan, Tatiana Sindalovskaia

Circulation Marketing Director
David Williams

Circulation Fulfillment Manager
Marlene Hazzard

Promotion Manager
Lawrence J. Burnagiel

CD-Rom Sales
Paul Arata, Greg Lawner

General Office

New York: 11 West 19th St., New York, NY 10011. Phone: (212) 675-4380; FAX: Editorial (212) 691-7287; Advertising (212) 929-1259; Circulation (212) 691-6939. James F. Hoos, Joanne Koenigsberg, Betsy Maloney — sales representatives

Offices

Chicago: 8 South Michigan Ave., Suite 1601, Chicago, IL 60603. Phone: (312) 641-0041; FAX: (312) 641-0043. Mark Fitzgerald — editor; Anthony R. George — central regional advertising manager; Richard H. Henrichs — sales representative

Palo Alto: 101 Alma Street, #405, Palo Alto, CA 94301. Phone: (415) 322-7178; FAX: (415) 322-7178. M.L. Stein — editor

San Francisco: 20993 Foothill Blvd., Suite 719, Hayward, CA 94541; Phone: (510) 888-9640; FAX (510) 886-4095. Michael Rogers — western regional advertising manager

Washington, DC: National Press Building, Suite 1128, Washington, DC 20045. Phone: (202) 662-7234; FAX: (202) 662-7223.

Copyright ©1997 by the Editor & Publisher Co. All rights reserved. Printed in the United States of America. No part of this publication may be reproduced or distributed in any form or by any means or stored in a data base or retrieval system, without the prior written permission of the publisher.
ISBN 0-9646364-2-5 (Part 2)
ISBN 0-9646364-0-9 (2 Part Set)

The Editor & Publisher Co. has employed reasonable precautions against errors in the development of this data but does not assume, and hereby disclaims, any liability to any person for any loss or damage caused by errors or omissions whether such errors or omissions result from negligence, accidents, or any other cause.

Editor & Publisher INTERNATIONAL YEAR BOOK®
WHO'S WHERE® 1997

PART 2

The Directory of Newspaper Industry Professionals

• "Who's Where," Part 2 of the Editor & Publisher International Year Book®, is an alphabetical listing of all U.S. and Canadian daily and weekly newspaper personnel listed in Part 1 of the Year Book. It also includes personnel from U.S. and Canadian newspaper groups as well as all personnel from News and Syndicate Services listings in Part 1 of the Year Book.

• Each name is followed by a phone number to reach that person, the person's title, name of newspaper or company, city and state.

• If a person is listed under more than one newspaper, "Who's Where" lists him or her under the daily paper with the highest circulation and the newspaper group name will appear at the end of the listing.

Index

A	3-10	N	166-170
B	10-34	O	170-174
C	34-53	P	174-186
D	53-65	Q	186-187
E	65-70	R	187-200
F	70-79	S	200-226
G	79-92	T	226-235
H	92-111	U	235
I	111-112	V	235-238
J	112-118	W	238-254
K	118-129	X	254
L	129-141	Y	254-255
M	141-166	Z	255-256

E&P HAS THE ANSWERS TO YOUR NEWSPAPER INDUSTRY QUESTIONS!

EDITOR & PUBLISHER
The authoritative weekly newsmagazine for the newspaper industry and related businesses. Covers editorial, business and production areas. Published Saturdays.
One-year subscription, 52 issues: $65.

SPECIAL EDITIONS OF E&P
Available Separately, $8.00 each.
(Included at no extra charge with annual subscriptions.)

Annual Directory of Syndicated Services (published August.)

Annual Directory of Interactive Products and Services (published September.)

Journalism Awards and Fellowships Directory (published December.)

FREE PAPER PUBLISHER
The comprehensive monthly trade publication for free community newspapers and shoppers. One-year subscription, $24.

EDITOR & PUBLISHER INTERNATIONAL YEAR BOOK
Annual, worldwide encyclopedia of the newspaper industry (Part I) and "Who's Where" directory (Part II). Published April, softbound.
Parts I & II, $125.
Part I only, $115.
Part II only, $35.

EDITOR & PUBLISHER INTERNATIONAL YEAR BOOK CD-ROM
Complete Year Book database and application. Annual, available May. With listing capabilities, $895.
Without listing capabilities, $495.
(Price includes softbound copy.)

EDITOR & PUBLISHER/FREE PAPER PUBLISHER COMMUNITY, SPECIALTY & FREE PUBLICATIONS YEAR BOOK
Annual guide to community paid and nonpaid weeklies, shoppers and total market coverage publications in the U.S. and Canada. Published October, softbound. $99.

MARKET GUIDE
Annual reference to U.S. and Canadian newspaper markets, with latest census and one-year projection. Published November, softbound. $100.

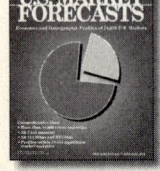

U.S. MARKET FORECASTS
In-depth profiles of every U.S. city with 2,500 residents or more, every county, MSA and state. Annual reference, published November, softbound. $269.

EDITOR & PUBLISHER MARKET GUIDE AND U.S. MARKET FORECASTS CD-ROM
Complete Market Guide AND U.S. Market Forecasts databases and application. Annual, available December. $795
(Including softbound books.)

E&P MEMBERS NETWORK
Online service for international newspaper professionals.
Membership, $150 per year.

CONFERENCES AND EXHIBITS
E&P organizes or sponsors annual interactive publishing conferences for the newspaper industry, including: Interactive Newspapers '98, February 4-7, 1998, Seattle, WA, USA; Interactive Publishing, held in November in Europe; Medios Interactivos, held in November in Latin America.

To order, or for more information, phone:
(212) 675-4380
Mon.-Fri., 9 a.m. to 5 p.m. EST.

Fax: **(212) 691-6939**

E-mail: **edpub@mediainfo.com**

Details and additional industry information also available on our Web site, Editor & Publisher Interactive:

Editor&Publisher INTERACTIVE — THE MEDIA INFO SOURCE

http://www.mediainfo.com

Editor & Publisher, 11 W. 19th Street,
New York, NY 10011-4234

All prices in U.S. dollars.

5-Who's Where **All**

Albanowski, James .... (609) 989-5454
MGR-DP, Times, Trenton, NJ
Albarado, Sonny .... (901) 529-2211
Sunday MET ED
Commercial Appeal, Memphis, TN
Albaugh, Jack .... (814) 723-8200
ADV MGR-CLASS
Warren Times-Observer, Warren, PA
Albee, Bonnie .... (607) 936-4651
Religion ED, Leader, Corning, NY
Albee, Terry .... (802) 334-6568
MAN ED, Daily Express, Newport, VT
Albers, Brenda .... (815) 937-3300
BM, Daily Journal, Kankakee, IL
Albers, Gwen .... (412) 981-6100
Environmental ED, Herald, Sharon, PA
Albert, Beverly .... (319) 472-2311
CIRC MGR
Cedar Valley Daily Times, Vinton, IA
Albert, G Claude .... (860) 241-6200
Deputy MAN ED-Sunday
Hartford Courant, Hartford, CT
Albert, Richard .... (860) 241-6200
PROD MGR-Press (Nights)
Hartford Courant, Hartford, CT
Albert, Ursula .... (207) 784-5411
Features ED, Living Page ED, Travel ED
Sun-Journal, Lewiston, ME
Albertson, Joe .... (616) 279-7488
GM, MAN ED, Three Rivers Commercial-News, Three Rivers, MI
Albertson, Judy .... (208) 436-4201
ED, Minidoka County News, Rupert, ID
Albertson, Keith .... (770) 532-1234
Sports ED, Times, Gainesville, GA
Albertson, Ron .... (905) 526-3333
Chief Photographer, Spectator, Hamilton, ON
Albi, Gina .... (213) 237-5000
CIRC DIR-ADM/FIN
Los Angeles Times, Los Angeles, CA
Albino, Silvio .... (860) 489-3121
ED, Register Citizen, Torrington, CT
Albion, Marla .... (810) 332-8181
PROD MGR-Engraving
Oakland Press, Pontiac, MI
Albom, Mitch .... (313) 222-6400
COL-Sports, Detroit Free Press, Detroit, MI
Albrecht, Arlin .... (612) 388-8235
COB
Red Wing Publishing Co., Red Wing, MN
Albrecht, Bill .... (218) 723-5281
ADV DIR-Sales & MKTG
Duluth News-Tribune, Duluth, MN
Albrecht, K Doug .... (517) 895-8551
Farm/Agriculture ED
Bay City Times, Bay City, MI
Albrecht, Marilyn .... (612) 388-8235
SEC/DIR
Red Wing Publishing Co., Red Wing, MN
Albrecht-Poss, Rebecca .... (612) 388-8235
VP, MGR-PROM
Republican Eagle, Red Wing, MN
Albright, Max .... (806) 376-4488
BUS/FIN ED, RE ED, Amarillo Daily News/ Globe Times, Amarillo, TX
Albright, Meredyth .... (715) 365-6397
MAN ED, Daily News, Rhinelander, WI
Albright, Susan .... (612) 673-4000
EPE, Star Tribune, Minneapolis, MN
Albuerne, Jose .... (213) 388-4639
MAN ED, LA Voz Libre, Los Angeles, CA
Alcala, Michael .... (316) 356-1201
MAN ED, Ulysses News, Ulysses, KS
Alcan, Peter .... (310) 337-7003
Sales EX
Creators Syndicate, Los Angeles, CA
Alcorn, Randy A .... (805) 564-5200
CONT, Santa Barbara News-Press, Santa Barbara, CA
Aldam, Mark E .... (860) 241-6200
VP-ADV & MKTG
Hartford Courant, Hartford, CT
Alden, Brad .... (604) 444-3451
PUB, Burnaby Now, Burnaby, BC
Alderdice, Barham .... (214) 775-3322
PUB, Midlothian Mirror, Midlothian, TX
Alderdice, Sunny .... (214) 775-3322
ED, Midlothian Mirror, Midlothian, TX
Alderman, Edward .... (318) 433-3000
Music ED, Lake Charles American Press, Lake Charles, LA
Alderman, Larry .... (601) 453-5312
ADV MGR
Greenwood Commonwealth, Greenwood, MS
Alderson, Mary .... (519) 683-4485
ED, North Kent Leader, Dresden, ON
Alderton, Jan .... (301) 722-4600
EPE
Cumberland Times-News, Cumberland, MD
Aldred, Katherine .... (819) 684-4755
ED, Aylmer Bulletin D'Alymer, Aylmer, QC
Aldrich, Anne .... (805) 273-2700
BUS/FIN ED
Antelope Valley Press, Palmdale, CA
Aldrich, Arthur R .... (201) 327-1212
PUB, Home And Store News, Ramsey, NJ
Aldrich, Hope .... (505) 988-5541
PUB, Santa Fe Reporter, Santa Fe, NM
Aldrich, Lawrence J .... (520) 573-4400
PRES-TNI Partners, TNI Partners dba Tucson Newspapers, Tucson, AZ
Aldridge, John .... (541) 776-4411
PROD MGR-PR, Mail Tribune, Medford, OR
Aldridge, Leon .... (210) 249-2441
PUB, ED, Boerne Star, Boerne, TX
Aldridge, Linda .... (717) 762-2151
CIRC MGR, Record Herald, Waynesboro, PA
Aleccia, JoNel .... (541) 776-4411
Fashion ED, Mail Tribune, Medford, OR
Aleff, Andrea .... (954) 356-4000
MGR-Media
Sun-Sentinel, Fort Lauderdale, FL
Aleks, Patricia .... (508) 758-9055
GM, Wanderer, Mattapoisett, MA
Aleman, Lazaro .... (904) 997-3568
ED, Monticello News, Monticello, FL
Aleshire, Ilene .... (808) 525-8000
BUS/FIN ED, Money ED
Honolulu Advertiser, Honolulu, HI
Alessandri, Rick .... (201) 309-1200
VP/GM, ESPN/SportsTicker, Jersey City, NJ
Alewel, Roger .... (816) 826-1000
PROD Commercial Sales
Sedalia Democrat, Sedalia, MO
Alexander, A B .... (405) 475-3311
PROD CNR
Daily Oklahoman, Oklahoma City, OK
Alexander, Andrew .... (202) 331-0900
Deputy BU Chief, Cox Newspapers Washington Bureau, Washington, DC
Alexander, Ann .... (316) 438-2370
ED, Cowley County Reporter, Burden, KS
Alexander, Anne .... (403) 468-0100
COL, Edmonton Sun, Edmonton, AB
Alexander, Brian .... (701) 225-8111
Sports ED, Dickinson Press, Dickinson, ND
Alexander, Carol .... (217) 429-5151
ADV Special Projects ED
Herald & Review, Decatur, IL
Alexander, Connie .... (317) 622-1212
ADV MGR, Herald Bulletin, Anderson, IN
Alexander, D A .... (214) 371-3986
SEC, Religious Drawings Inc., Dallas, TX
Alexander, Daniel E .... (518) 873-6368
PUB, Times of Ti, Ticonderoga, NY
Alexander, Dave .... (616) 722-3161
BUS/FIN ED
Muskegon Chronicle, Muskegon, MI
Alexander, David .... (202) 898-8254
Regional ED-Europe
United Press International, Washington, DC
Alexander, Debbie .... (412) 772-3900
DIR-Human Resources
North Hills News Record, Warrendale, PA
Alexander, Don .... (913) 682-0305
ADV Major Accounts Representative
Leavenworth Times, Leavenworth, KS
Alexander, Don .... (317) 773-3970
ED, Noblesville Times, Noblesville, IN
Alexander, Don V .... (903) 984-2593
ADV MGR, Kilgore News Herald, Kilgore, TX
Alexander, Ed .... (202) 334-6000
PROD MGR-Post Press (NW), PROD MGR-Plant (SE), Washington Post, Washington, DC
Alexander, J D .... (206) 448-8000
PUB/ED
Seattle Post-Intelligencer, Seattle, WA
Alexander, James G .... (919) 419-6500
VP/TREAS/BM, Herald-Sun, Durham, NC
Alexander, Jerry .... (864) 878-2453
PUB, Pickens Sentinel, Pickens, SC
Alexander, Ken .... (604) 392-2331
ED, Tribune, Williams Lake, BC
Alexander, Kerrie .... (519) 255-5711
DIR-FIN/Human Resources
Windsor Star, Windsor, ON
Alexander, Larry .... (317) 747-5700
CIRC DIR, Star Press, Muncie, IN
Alexander, Louis .... (408) 920-5000
ADV MGR-CLASS/Auto/RE
San Jose Mercury News, San Jose, CA
Alexander, Martin .... (219) 925-2611
ADV MGR, Evening Star, Auburn, IN
Alexander, Mary S .... (901) 847-6354
PUB, ED, News-Leader, Parsons, TN
Alexander, Max .... (213) 857-6600
EX ED, Daily Variety, Los Angeles, CA
Alexander, Nanine .... (503) 221-8327
EDL Writer, Oregonian, Portland, OR
Alexander, Norman .... (905) 845-3824
ED, Oakville Beaver, Oakville, ON
Alexander, Rebecca .... (941) 335-0200
ADV MGR-GEN/Co-op
News-Press, Fort Myers, FL
Alexander, Richard .... (401) 849-3300
ED, Newport Navalog, Newport, RI
Alexander, Rick .... (360) 754-5400
PROD MGR-PR, Olympian, Olympia, WA
Alexander, Robin .... (360) 377-3711
MGR-CR, Sun, Bremerton, WA
Alexander, Sandra S .... (816) 359-2212
VP, Republican-Times, Trenton, MO
Alexander, Steve .... (213) 237-5000
CIRC DIR-CIRC Sales/Distribution
Los Angeles Times, Los Angeles, CA
Alexander, Tim .... (317) 962-1575
CIRC DIR, Palladium-Item, Richmond, IN
Alexieff, Mike .... (512) 884-2011
News ED, Corpus Christi Caller-Times, Corpus Christi, TX
Alfieri, Denise .... (516) 751-7744
ED, Port Times-Record, Setauket, NY
Alfieri, Irene .... (941) 335-0200
ASST to PUB, News-Press, Fort Myers, FL
Alfonso, Melene .... (818) 713-3000
ADV MGR-CLASS
Daily News, Woodland Hills, CA
Alford Jr, A L .... (208) 882-5561
PRES
Moscow-Pullman Daily News, Moscow, ID
Alford, Carolyn .... (910) 353-1171
EDU ED, Fashion ED, Health/Medical ED, Religion ED, Daily News, Jacksonville, NC
Alford, George .... (404) 526-5151
PSL DIR
Atlanta Journal-Constitution, Atlanta, GA
Alford, Melissa .... (517) 377-1000
PSL DIR, Lansing State Journal, Lansing, MI
Alfred, Cheryl .... (409) 295-5407
CIRC MGR, Huntsville Item, Huntsville, TX
Algie, George D .... (310) 329-6351
PUB, Gardena Valley News, Gardena, CA
Algier, Angela J .... (401) 596-7791
City ED, Westerly Sun, Westerly, RI
Ali, Umm .... (416) 493-4374
ED, Al-Hilal, Willowdale, ON
Aliberti, Julie .... (203) 333-0161
ADV MGR-RT
Connecticut Post, Bridgeport, CT
Alin, Francois .... (514) 285-7272
ADM ASST, La Presse, Montreal, QC
Alison, Charlie .... (501) 751-6200
MET ED, Morning News of Northwest Arkansas, Springdale, AR
Alison, Dale .... (319) 754-8461
MAN ED, Hawk Eye, Burlington, IA
Alka, Carol .... (703) 276-3400
CIRC GM-Atlanta, USA Today, Arlington, VA
Alkire, Bill .... (918) 335-8200
CIRC Distribution Clerk
Examiner-Enterprise, Bartlesville, OK
Allain, Michael H .... (508) 586-7200
News ED, Enterprise, Brockton, MA
Allam, S .... (416) 362-0304
PUB, Canada & Arab World, Toronto, ON
Allan, Lon .... (805) 466-2585
ED, Atascadero News, Atascadero, CA
Allan, William A .... (412) 242-2332
COL, Allan, William A., Pittsburgh, PA
Allard, Debbie .... (614) 353-3101
ED, Portsmouth Daily Times, Portsmouth, OH
Allbritton, Joe L .... (413) 562-4181
PRES, Westfield Evening News, Westfield, MA
Allee, Rod .... (201) 646-4000
COL, Record, Hackensack, NJ
Allegretti, Anthony A .... (815) 432-6066
PRES/CEO
Independent Media Group Inc., Watseka, IL
Allen, Angela .... (360) 694-3391
Fashion/Style ED, Food ED
Columbian, Vancouver, WA
Allen, Annette .... (409) 245-5555
PROD SUPT, Daily Tribune, Bay City, TX
Allen, Bert .... (208) 323-0805
MAN ED, Diversity News, Boise, ID
Allen, Betty .... (901) 427-3333
MGR-CR, Jackson Sun, Jackson, TN
Allen, Bill .... (705) 789-5578
GM, Huntsville Herald, Huntsville, ON
Allen, Bill .... (314) 340-8000
SCI, St. Louis Post-Dispatch, St. Louis, MO
Allen, Chester .... (360) 754-5400
EDU Reporter, Olympian, Olympia, WA
Allen, Chris .... (910) 625-2101
ADV Senior EX, Courier-Tribune, Asheboro, NC
Allen, Chris .... (206) 842-6613
PUB, Bainbridge Review, Bainbridge Isle, WA
Allen, Cindy .... (909) 684-1200
PROM MGR, Press-Enterprise, Riverside, CA
Allen, Cindy .... (316) 231-2600
MAN ED, Morning Sun, Pittsburg, KS
Allen, Connie .... (517) 354-3111
Environmental ED, Farm/Agriculture ED
Alpena News, Alpena, MI
Allen, Craig .... (704) 249-3981
Graphics ED, Special Sections ED
Dispatch, Lexington, NC
Allen, Craig .... (203) 964-2200
VP/CIRC DIR, Stamford Advocate, Stamford, CT, Times Mirror Co.
Allen, Dale .... (330) 996-3000
ED, Akron Beacon Journal, Akron, OH
Allen, Danny L .... (540) 885-7281
CIRC DIR, Daily News Leader, Staunton, VA
Allen, David .... (201) 877-4141
BUS ED, Star-Ledger, Newark, NJ
Allen, David .... (515) 784-6397
PUB, ED, Lamoni Chronicle, Lamoni, IA
Allen, Diane .... (941) 687-7000
Teen-Age/Youth ED, Ledger, Lakeland, FL
Allen, Dirk .... (513) 863-8200
Opinion Page ED
Journal-News, Hamilton, OH
Allen, Doug .... (912) 923-6432
ADV MGR, Daily Sun, Warner Robins, GA
Allen, Ed .... (208) 377-6200
PROD MGR-Distribution Center
Idaho Statesman, Boise, ID
Allen, Ed .... (512) 327-2990
ED, Westlake Picayune, Austin, TX
Allen, F Ashley .... (407) 420-5000
VP/DIR-BUS Development
Orlando Sentinel, Orlando, FL
Allen, Gary .... (503) 538-2181
MAN ED, Newberg Graphic, Newberg, OR
Allen, Gordon .... (315) 376-3525
ED, Journal and Republican, Lowville, NY
Allen, Howard .... (307) 283-3411
PUB, ED, Sundance Times, Sundance, WY
Allen, James Preston .... (310) 519-1442
PUB, Random Lengths/Harbor Independent News, San Pedro, CA
Allen, James W .... (919) 556-3182
MAN ED, Wake Weekly, Wake Forest, NC
Allen, Jeanne .... (217) 223-5100
ADTX MGR, Quincy Herald-Whig, Quincy, IL
Allen, Jennifer .... (614) 532-1441
PRES, PUB, Ironton Tribune, Ironton, OH
Allen, Joel .... (606) 231-3100
PROD MGR-MR
Lexington Herald-Leader, Lexington, KY
Allen, Joseph .... (508) 775-1200
PROD MGR-MR
Cape Cod Times, Hyannis, MA
Allen, Kathleen .... (520) 573-4561
Visual Arts ED, Tucson Citizen, Tucson, AZ
Allen, Kirk .... (514) 987-2222
ADV MGR-RT, Gazette, Montreal, QC
Allen, Leah .... (405) 223-2200
Amusements/Books ED, Features ED, Films/Theater ED, Music/Society ED, Women's ED, Daily Ardmoreite, Ardmore, OK
Allen, Leslie .... (215) 854-2000
ED-Philadelphia BUS Section
Philadelphia Inquirer, Philadelphia, PA
Allen, Liz .... (814) 870-1600
MAN ED-Features, Travel ED
Morning News/Erie Daily Times, Erie, PA
Allen, Lois .... (616) 696-3655
PUB, Cedar Springs Post, Cedar Springs, MI
Allen, Lori .... (618) 382-4176
Society/Women's ED, Carmi Times, Carmi, IL
Allen, Lucie Santiago .... (972) 386-9120
GM, El Sol de Texas, Dallas, TX
Allen, Lynn .... (502) 582-4011
MGR-MKTG Communications
Courier-Journal, Louisville, KY
Allen, M .... (604) 562-2441
City ED
Prince George Citizen, Prince George, BC
Allen, Margaret G .... (919) 556-3182
ED, Wake Weekly, Wake Forest, NC
Allen, Martha .... (612) 673-4000
Religion/Spiritual Reporter
Star Tribune, Minneapolis, MN
Allen, Melica .... (205) 486-9461
MAN ED
Northwest Alabamian, Haleyville, AL
Allen, Mitch .... (330) 996-3000
ADV VP, Akron Beacon Journal, Akron, OH
Allen, Monica .... (401) 245-6000
ED, Barrington Times, Barrington, RI
Allen, Newell .... (205) 345-0505
ADV MGR-CLASS
Tuscaloosa News, Tuscaloosa, AL
Allen, Patty .... (405) 332-4433
Accountant, Ada Evening News, Ada, OK
Allen, Paul .... (208) 678-2201
Political ED, South Idaho Press, Burley, ID
Allen, R W .... (919) 556-3182
PUB, Wake Weekly, Wake Forest, NC
Allen, Richard .... (808) 244-3981
DP MGR/Online Contact
Maui News, Wailuku, HI
Allen, Rob .... (509) 926-8341
PUB, ED
Spokane Valley News, Spokane, WA
Allen Sr, Robert W .... (919) 556-3182
PUB, Wake Weekly, Wake Forest, NC
Allen, Roger C .... (616) 866-4465
PUB, Rockford Squire, Rockford, MI

All Who's Where-6

Allen, Ron .... (208) 467-9251
CIRC DIR, Idaho Press-Tribune, Nampa, ID

Allen, Scott .... (304) 788-3333
Sports ED
Mineral Daily News-Tribune, Keyser, WV

Allen, Teddy .... (318) 459-3200
COL, Times, Shreveport, LA

Allen, Thomas K .... (562) 498-0707
PUB, ED, Signal, Signal Hill, CA

Allen, Tim .... (207) 873-3341
ED-Waterville, Central Maine Morning Sentinel, Waterville, ME
Guy Gannett Communications

Allen, Tim .... (919) 829-4500
ADV MGR-RT, News & Observer, Raleigh, NC

Allen, Tim .... (619) 375-4481
Sports ED
Daily Independent, Ridgecrest, CA

Allen, W Dale .... (330) 996-3000
Senior VP, Akron Beacon Journal, Akron, OH

Allen III, William Prescott .... (970) 249-3444
PRES, PUB/GM, CIRC DIR
Montrose Daily Press, Montrose, CO

Allen, WM Fletcher .... (615) 371-2003
ED, Baptist & Reflector, Brentwood, TN

Allen-Evans, Carolynn .... (717) 421-3000
PRES/PUB, Pocono Record, Stroudsburg, PA

Allengham, S .... (213) 876-1668
ED, Communication International/National News, Los Angeles, CA

Alles, George .... (315) 253-5311
CIRC DIR, NIE Community Projects ED
Citizen, Auburn, NY

Alley, David G .... (602) 271-8000
ADV DIR
Phoenix Newspapers Inc., Phoenix, AZ

Alley, Rick .... (901) 529-2211
Art DIR, Commercial Appeal, Memphis, TN

Alleyne, Stan .... (919) 778-2211
EDU ED, Health/Medical ED
Goldsboro News-Argus, Goldsboro, NC

Alligood, Cara .... (915) 445-5475
ADV CNR, Pecos Enterprise, Pecos, TX

Alligood, John .... (919) 946-2144
PROD FRM-COMP
Washington Daily News, Washington, NC

Allis, Eve J .... (716) 892-5323
PUB, Cheektowaga Times, Cheektowaga, NY

Allison, Bill .... (315) 470-0011
ADV MGR-CLASS, Post-Standard/Syracuse Herald-Journal/American, Syracuse, NY

Allison, Bryan .... (702) 385-3111
Online Publishing ED
Las Vegas Sun, Las Vegas, NV

Allison, Don .... (419) 636-1111
County ED, Bryan Times, Bryan, OH

Allison, Garran .... (913) 295-1111
CIRC MGR, Capital-Journal, Topeka, KS

Allison, Garry .... (403) 328-4411
Outdoors ED
Lethbridge Herald, Lethbridge, AB

Allison, Lane .... (316) 624-2541
News ED, Southwest Daily Times, Liberal, KS

Allison, Larry .... (562) 435-1161
ED, EPE, Press-Telegram, Long Beach, CA

Allison, Mark .... (203) 846-3281
MAN ED, Hour, Norwalk, CT

Allison, Michael .... (410) 822-1500
PROD MGR, Star-Democrat, Easton, MD

Allison, Mike .... (713) 488-1108
PUB, Citizen, Webster, TX

Allison, Paul .... (210) 225-7411
PROD MGR-Facilities
San Antonio Express-News, San Antonio, TX

Allison, Peggy .... (409) 245-5555
CIRC MGR, Daily Tribune, Bay City, TX

Allison, Randall .... (313) 222-6400
DIR-Worker's Comp/Safety
Detroit Newspapers, Detroit, MI

Allison, Stanley .... (205) 755-5747
GM, Clanton Advertiser, Clanton, AL

Allman, Frank .... (904) 252-1511
PROD MGR, Daytona Beach News-Journal, Daytona Beach, FL

Allman, Robert L .... (219) 636-2727
PUB, Albion New Era, Albion, IN

Allnutt, Alan .... (514) 987-2222
ED, Gazette, Montreal, QC

Allon, Tom .... (212) 268-8600
PUB, ED
Our Town Newspaper, New York, NY

Allport, Richard T .... (904) 359-4111
EX ED, Florida Times-Union, Jacksonville, FL

Allred, Darrin .... (817) 665-5511
Sports ED
Gainesville Daily Register, Gainesville, TX

Allred, David .... (405) 233-6600
PROD SUPT-COMP
Enid News & Eagle, Enid, OK

Allred, Fran .... (304) 526-4000
City ED, Herald-Dispatch, Huntington, WV

Allsop, Susie .... (541) 269-1222
ADV MGR-CLASS, World, Coos Bay, OR

Allsopp, Craig O .... (212) 416-2414
VP, Dow Jones Financial News Services, New York, NY

Allston, Tom .... (806) 376-4488
Automotive ED, Amarillo Daily News/Globe Times, Amarillo, TX

Almeida, Alcino G .... (860) 442-2200
EVP, SEC/TREAS, GM, Day, New London, CT

Almen, Theodore J .... (320) 847-3130
PUB, Clara City Herald, Clara City, MN

Almirall, Sharon .... (218) 723-5281
DIR-MKTG/PROM
Duluth News-Tribune, Duluth, MN

Almond, Carey .... (706) 724-0851
ADV MGR-CLASS (Outside)
Augusta Chronicle, Augusta, GA

Almond, Kevin .... (316) 283-1500
PROD MGR-Press, Kansan, Newton, KS

Almond, Tammy .... (306) 825-5522
PROD DIR, Times, Lloydminster, SK

Almquist, Terese .... (218) 262-1011
GM, Daily Tribune, Hibbing, MN

Aloi, Dan .... (607) 734-5151
Films/Theater ED, Star-Gazette, Elmira, NY

Aloia, Karen .... (508) 626-3800
ADV MGR-Major Accounts
Middlesex News, Framingham, MA

Aloy, Chichi .... (305) 633-3341
Society ED, Diario Las Americas, Miami, FL

Alpert, Brian F .... (212) 924-8123
MAN ED
Keystone Press Agency Inc., New York, NY

Alpher, David A .... (716) 849-3434
ADV MGR-RT, Buffalo News, Buffalo, NY

Alps, Bernado .... (310) 832-0221
Photo ED, News-Pilot, San Pedro, CA

Alquist, Dan .... (913) 455-3466
PUB, Clifton News-Tribune, Clifton, KS

Alsobrook, Bruce .... (903) 885-8663
News ED, Sulphur Springs News-Telegram, Sulphur Springs, TX

Alsop, Caesar .... (215) 854-2000
Deputy Sports ED
Philadelphia Daily News, Philadelphia, PA

Alsop, Jonathon .... (617) 731-3593
Self-Syndicator
Alsop, Jonathon, Brookline, MA

Alston, M Elizabeth .... (912) 924-2751
ED, COL
Americus Times-Recorder, Americus, GA

Alston, Michael .... (757) 446-2000
Online MGR, Virginian-Pilot, Norfolk, VA

Altavilla, Mark .... (717) 821-2091
ADV DIR, Citizens' Voice, Wilkes-Barre, PA

Alten, Rocky .... (216) 245-6901
MGR-PROM, Morning Journal, Lorain, OH

Altepeter, Twylla .... (218) 281-2730
ED, Crookston Daily Times, Crookston, MN

Alter, Larry .... (419) 422-5151
Sports ED, Courier, Findlay, OH

Althaus, Robert .... (313) 222-6400
Senior VP-Circulation
Detroit Newspapers, Detroit, MI

Althoff, George .... (217) 429-5151
ED, Herald & Review, Decatur, IL

Althouse, Donald .... (717) 786-2992
PUB, Sun-Ledger, Quarryville, PA

Altine, Kenn .... (702) 788-6200
ASST MAN ED
Reno Gazette-Journal, Reno, NV

Altman, Dave .... (918) 273-2446
ED, Nowata Star, Nowata, OK

Altman, Ramsey .... (404) 526-5151
DIR-Purchasing
Atlanta Journal-Constitution, Atlanta, GA

Altman, Scott .... (414) 235-7700
TREAS, Oshkosh Northwestern, Oshkosh, WI

Altonen, Charles .... (216) 576-9115
ED, Sentinel, Jefferson, OH

Altonn, Helen .... (808) 525-8000
Health Writer, SCI/Technology Writer
Honolulu Star-Bulletin, Honolulu, HI

Altschiller, Howard .... (718) 834-9161
ED, Brooklyn Paper, Brooklyn, NY

Altuvilla, Mary .... (612) 222-5011
ADV VP, St. Paul Pioneer Press, St. Paul, MN

Alvarez, Alicia .... (505) 242-3010
ED, Health City Sun, Albuquerque, NM

Alvernaz, David .... (619) 766-4785
PUB, Sandpaper, Jacumba, CA

Alvey, Dan .... (210) 693-7152
PUB, Picayune, Marble Falls, TX

Alvey, Lee .... (210) 693-7152
PUB, Picayune, Marble Falls, TX

Alvey, Tina A .... (304) 645-1206
MAN ED, Society ED
West Virginia Daily News, Lewisburg, WV

Alvine, Ken .... (605) 336-9434
Owner/MGR
Creative Comic Syndicate, Sioux Falls, SD

Alvord, Judd .... (303) 820-1010
CIRC DIR, Denver Post, Denver, CO

Alward, Debra .... (412) 263-1100
DIR-MKTG
Pittsburgh Post-Gazette, Pittsburgh, PA

Alyward, Terry .... (918) 825-3292
ED, Daily Times, Pryor, OK

Amachree, Edison S .... (217) 446-1000
PROD DIR, Commercial News, Danville, IL

Amadio, Joseph .... (716) 693-1000
Fashion/Food ED, Films/Theater ED, Home ED, Tonawanda News, North Tonawanda, NY

Aman, Joe E .... (208) 337-4681
PUB, ED, Owyhee Avalanche, Homedale, ID

Amann, John .... (212) 930-8000
CIRC VP-OPER
New York Post, New York, NY

Amarante, Joseph .... (203) 789-5200
Radio/Television ED
New Haven Register, New Haven, CT

Amari, Jane .... (816) 234-4141
MAN ED-Features & Design, ADTX MGR
Kansas City Star, Kansas City, MO

Ambelang, Jerry .... (608) 252-6400
Area News Chief
Capital Times, Madison, WI

Amberg Jr, Richard H .... (334) 262-1611
PRES, PUB
Montgomery Advertiser, Montgomery, AL

Ambor, Brian .... (414) 435-4411
PROD DIR
Green Bay Press-Gazette, Green Bay, WI

Ambro, David .... (516) 265-2100
ED, Smithtown News, Smithtown, NY

Ambrose, Beth .... (201) 383-1500
Features ED, New Jersey Herald, Newton, NJ

Ambrose, David .... (217) 839-2130
PUB, ED, Area News, Gillespie, IL

Ambrose, Jim .... (705) 745-4641
PUB, GM, Examiner, Peterborough, ON
Hollinger Inc. (Sterling Newspapers)

Ambrose, Patricia .... (216) 951-0000
Features ED, Living/ Lifestyle ED
News-Herald, Willoughby, OH

Ambrose, Patty .... (217) 839-2130
PUB, Area News, Gillespie, IL

Ambrosini, Chris .... (202) 636-3000
DIR-OPER
Washington Times, Washington, DC

Amdur, Nancy .... (773) 878-7333
ED, Inside Publications, Chicago, IL

Amdur, Neil .... (212) 556-1234
Sports ED, New York Times, New York, NY

Ames, Darlene J .... (219) 567-2221
ED, Francesville Tribune, Francesville, IN

Ames, Donald H .... (219) 567-2221
PUB, Francesville Tribune, Francesville, IN

Ames, Jeff .... (616) 683-2100
PROD FRM-PR, Niles Daily Star, Niles, MI

Ames, Joe .... (714) 835-1234
Team Leader-Government/Politics
Orange County Register, Santa Ana, CA

Amestoy, Louis .... (909) 487-2200
Sports ED, Hemet News, Hemet, CA

Amey, Herb .... (614) 592-6612
ASST MAN ED, BUS/FIN ED, City ED
Athens Messenger, Athens, OH

Amland, Rod .... (507) 433-8851
MAN ED, EPE
Austin Daily Herald, Austin, MN

Ammarito, Thom .... (201) 438-8700
ED, North Arlington Leader, Lyndhurst, NJ

Ammenheuser, David .... (410) 848-4400
MAN ED
Carroll County Times, Westminster, MD

Ammerata, Carla .... (705) 472-3200
EDU, North Bay Nugget, North Bay, ON

Ammermann, Steve .... (320) 235-1150
BM, West Central Tribune, Willmar, MN

Ammons, Patricia .... (207) 623-3811
ED-Augusta, City ED
Kennebec Journal, Augusta, ME

Amo, Gary .... (310) 377-6877
ED, Palos Verdes Peninsula News, Palos Verdes Peninsula, CA

Amodeo, Gino .... (815) 232-1171
CIRC MGR, Journal-Standard, Freeport, IL

Amole, Gene .... (303) 892-5000
COL, Rocky Mountain News, Denver, CO

Amoroso, Mary .... (201) 646-4000
COL, Record, Hackensack, NJ

Amos, Allen .... (915) 869-3561
PUB, Eden Echo, Eden, TX

Amos, Jim .... (604) 287-7464
MAN ED, Campbell River Courier Islander, Campbell River, BC

Amos, Kathy .... (915) 869-3561
ED, Eden Echo, Eden, TX

Amos, Robert .... (410) 332-6000
DIR-Purchasing, Sun, Baltimore, MD

Amoss, Jim .... (504) 826-3279
ED, Times-Picayune, New Orleans, LA

Amsden, Harry .... (407) 420-5000
ASST CONT, Orlando Sentinel, Orlando, FL

Amundson, Dirk .... (319) 532-9113
PUB, ED, Ossian Bee, Ossian, IA

Amundson, Ken .... (970) 669-5050
MAN ED, EDL Writer
Loveland Daily Reporter-Herald, Loveland, CO

Amundson, Marlys .... (319) 532-9113
GM, Ossian Bee, Ossian, IA

Anaesy, Lisa Paulo .... (508) 674-4656
ED, Spectator, Somerset, MA

Anagnostos, George .... (508) 820-9700
MAN ED
Hellenic Chronicle, Framingham, MA

Anastasi, Michael .... (818) 713-3000
Sports ED, Daily News, Woodland Hills, CA

Ancona, John .... (212) 930-8000
ADV VP, New York Post, New York, NY

Anderberg, Howard .... (217) 788-1300
PROD FRM-Camera/Platemaking
State Journal-Register, Springfield, IL

Anderegg, Richard .... (212) 247-0459
ED, Swiss American Review, New York, NY

Anderloh, Deborah .... (916) 321-1000
EDU Writer
Sacramento Bee, Sacramento, CA

Anders, Clarice .... (309) 341-0737
MAN ED
Arcadia Feature Syndicate, Galesburg, IL

Anders, Corrie .... (415) 777-2424
RE ED
San Francisco Examiner, San Francisco, CA

Anders, John .... (214) 977-8222
COL-Today, Dallas Morning News, Dallas, TX

Anders, Kathy M .... (910) 372-5490
MAN ED, Blue Ridge Sun, Sparta, NC

Anders, Mike .... (502) 769-2312
PUB, News Enterprise, Elizabethtown, KY

Andersen, Carol .... (515) 295-3535
ED, Algona Upper Des Moines, Algona, IA

Andersen, Cynthia .... (914) 454-2000
DIR-MKTG SRV
Poughkeepsie Journal, Poughkeepsie, NY

Andersen, Deb .... (810) 332-8181
Radio/Television ED
Oakland Press, Pontiac, MI

Andersen, Denise .... (402) 729-6141
ED, Fairbury Journal-News, Fairbury, NE

Andersen, Dennies D .... (316) 582-2101
PUB, ED, Western Star, Coldwater, KS

Andersen, Elizabeth .... (816) 932-6600
ASSOC ED
Universal Press Syndicate, Kansas City, MO

Andersen, Elmer L .... (612) 464-4601
PUB, Times, Forest Lake, MN

Andersen, Erin .... (605) 394-8300
EDU ED, Rapid City Journal, Rapid City, SD

Andersen, Gary .... (507) 235-3303
PUB, ADV MGR, DIR-MKTG
Sentinel, Fairmont, MN

Andersen, John O .... (814) 870-1600
ADV DIR
Morning News/Erie Daily Times, Erie, PA

Andersen, Judy .... (818) 845-7300
PUB, Bien, Burbank, CA

Andersen, Kathryn R .... (320) 255-8700
CIRC ASST MGR
St. Cloud Times, St. Cloud, MN

Andersen, M J .... (401) 277-7000
EDL Writer
Providence Journal-Bulletin, Providence, RI

Andersen PhD, P Andrew .... (630) 377-6676
Author/Owner/PRES
Sports Adviser Features, St. Charles, IL

Andersen, Poul Dalby .... (818) 845-7300
PUB, ED, Bien, Burbank, CA

Andersen, Robert .... (319) 245-1311
ED, Clayton County Register, Elkader, IA

Andersen, Soren .... (206) 597-8742
Films Critic, News Tribune, Tacoma, WA

Anderson, Al .... (941) 748-0411
Photo Chief, Herald, Bradenton, FL

Anderson, Alice .... (605) 673-2217
ED, Custer County Chronicle, Custer, SD

Anderson, Amanda .... (617) 426-3000
CIRC MGR-MKTG
Boston Herald, Boston, MA

Anderson, Mrs. Andy .... (502) 754-3000
PUB, Leader-News, Central City, KY

Anderson, Angelene .... (615) 374-3556
ED, Hartsville Vidette, Hartsville, TN

Anderson, Beth .... (415) 924-8582
ED, Twin Cities Times, Sausalito, CA

Anderson, Betty .... (541) 836-2241
PUB, Drain Enterprise, Drain, OR

Anderson, Bill .... (905) 358-5711
ADV Sales MGR-RT
Niagara Falls Review, Niagara Falls, ON

Anderson, Bill .... (905) 857-3433
PUB, Bolton Enterprise, Bolton, ON

Anderson, Billie .... (415) 289-4040
GM, MAN ED, Newspointer, Sausalito, CA

Anderson, Bob .... (209) 358-5311
ED, Winton Times, Winton, CA

Anderson, Bob .... (330) 264-1125
ADV DIR, Daily Record, Wooster, OH

Copyright ©1997 by the Editor & Publisher Co.

7-Who's Where **And**

Anderson, Bob ... (573) 985-5531
PUB, ED, Ralls County Herald-Enterprise, New London, MO
Anderson, Brett ... (317) 473-6641
Sports ED, Peru Tribune, Peru, IN
Anderson, Bruce ... (707) 895-3016
PUB, ED
Anderson Valley Advertiser, Boonville, CA
Anderson, Carla ... (618) 234-1000
Librarian
Belleville News-Democrat, Belleville, IL
Anderson, Carol ... (540) 374-5000
Food ED
Free Lance-Star, Fredericksburg, VA
Anderson, Carol ... (402) 873-3334
MAN ED
Nebraska City News-Press, Nebraska City, NE
Anderson, Carol ... (573) 985-5531
PUB, Ralls County Herald-Enterprise, New London, MO
Anderson, Carolyn ... (218) 238-6872
ED, Lake Park Journal, Lake Park, MN
Anderson, Carolyn ... (210) 683-3130
PUB, ED
Texas Mohair Weekly, Rocksprings, TX
Anderson, Charles M ... (910) 343-2000
EX ED, COL, Morning Star/Sunday Star-News, Wilmington, NC
Anderson, Christine ... (309) 829-9411
Farm ED
Bloomington Pantagraph, Bloomington, IL
Anderson, Dale ... (209) 924-3488
PUB, ED, Lemoore Advance, Lemoore, CA
Anderson, Dan ... (715) 833-9200
PROD FRM-PR
Leader-Telegram, Eau Claire, WI
Anderson, Dan ... (605) 341-0011
ED, Indian Country Today, Rapid City, SD
Anderson, David ... (202) 463-8777
NTL Correspondent
Religion News Service, Washington, DC
Anderson, David ... (601) 961-7000
CIRC MGR-State
Clarion-Ledger, Jackson, MS
Anderson, David ... (413) 323-5999
GM, Sentinel, Belchertown, MA
Anderson, David ... (707) 441-0500
Political ED, Times-Standard, Eureka, CA
Anderson, Dennis ... (607) 798-1234
MET ED
Press & Sun Bulletin, Binghamton, NY
Anderson, Diana ... (814) 723-8200
Family/Fashion ED, Food ED, Women's ED
Warren Times-Observer, Warren, PA
Anderson, Don ... (540) 669-2181
PROD SUPT-PR, Herald-Courier Virginia Tennessean, Bristol, VA
Anderson, Donald C ... (603) 668-4321
DIR-Community Relations, Cooking School DIR, Union Leader, Manchester, NH
Anderson, Donna ... (520) 425-0355
PUB, ED, Copper Country News, Globe, AZ
Anderson, Dorin ... (218) 253-2594
ED, Gazette, Red Lake Falls, MN
Anderson, Doug ... (905) 668-6111
PUB, Whitby Free Press, Whitby, ON
Anderson, Earl L ... (218) 478-2210
PUB, ED, Messenger Banner, Stephen, MN
Anderson, Earl ... (406) 657-1200
DP MGR, Billings Gazette, Billings, MT
Anderson, Ellena ... (701) 862-3515
ED, Mountrail County Record, Parshall, ND
Anderson, Eric ... (518) 374-4141
BUS/FIN ED, Daily Gazette, Schenectady, NY
Anderson, Erik ... (217) 586-2512
PUB, ED, Mahomet Citizen, Mahomet, IL
Anderson, Evelyn ... (605) 365-5145
GM, West River Progress, Dupree, SD
Anderson, Frank T ... (912) 236-9511
PUB, Morning News, Savannah, GA
Anderson, Fritz ... (303) 820-1010
VP-FIN/CFO, Denver Post, Denver, CO
Anderson, Gail E ... (717) 687-7721
ED, Strasburg Weekly News, Strasburg, PA
Anderson, Garth ... (907) 456-6661
PROD SUPT-Equipment
Fairbanks Daily News-Miner, Fairbanks, AK
Anderson, Gary L ... (313) 222-6400
EVP/CFO
Detroit Newspapers, Detroit, MI
Anderson, Gerald W ... (701) 448-2649
PUB, ED
McLean County Journal, Turtle Lake, ND
Anderson, Gloria Brown ... (212) 499-3334
VP/EX ED, New York Times Syndication Sales Corp., New York, NY
Anderson, Greg ... (206) 597-8742
Online MGR, News Tribune, Tacoma, WA
Anderson, Greg ... (561) 287-1550
ADV DIR, Online MGR, ADTX MGR
Stuart News, Stuart, FL
Anderson, Guy ... (520) 425-0355
PUB, Copper Country News, Globe, AZ

Anderson, Holly ... (701) 284-6333
ED, Walsh County Press, Park River, ND
Anderson, Hugh ... (304) 845-2660
ED
Moundsville Daily Echo, Moundsville, WV
Anderson Jr, Ivan V ... (803) 577-7111
PRES
Evening Post Publishing Co., Charleston, SC
Anderson, Jack ... (612) 222-5011
PROD MGR-Electric Shop
St. Paul Pioneer Press, St. Paul, MN
Anderson, Jack ... (703) 764-0496
ED, Associated Features Inc., Burke, VA
Anderson, Jan ... (616) 527-2100
PUB, MGR-MKTG/PROM
Sentinel-Standard, Ionia, MI
Anderson, Jan ... (406) 287-5301
ED, Whitehall Ledger, Whitehall, MT
Anderson, Jeanne ... (208) 354-8101
ED, Teton Valley News, Driggs, ID
Anderson, Jeff ... (360) 736-3311
PROD DIR, Chronicle, Centralia, WA
Anderson, Jenny L ... (517) 835-7171
GM, ADV DIR
Midland Daily News, Midland, MI
Anderson, Jerry ... (913) 672-3228
PUB, Oakley Graphic, Oakley, KS
Anderson, Jim ... (573) 683-3351
ED, Enterprise-Courier, Charleston, MO
Anderson, Jim ... (906) 774-2772
City/MET ED, News ED
Daily News, Iron Mountain, MI
Anderson, Jim ... (605) 673-2217
ED, Custer County Chronicle, Custer, SD
Anderson, Jim L ... (406) 467-2334
PUB, ED, Sun Times, Fairfield, MT
Anderson, Joe ... (705) 435-6228
PUB, Herald Courier, Alliston, ON
Anderson, John ... (205) 532-4000
Political ED, Huntsville Times, Huntsville, AL
Anderson, John ... (317) 622-1212
DP MGR, Herald Bulletin, Anderson, IN
Anderson III, John A ... (508) 697-2881
PUB
Bridgewater Independent, Bridgewater, MA
Anderson, John N ... (901) 529-2211
MGR-MKTG SRV
Commercial Appeal, Memphis, TN
Anderson, Juanita ... (406) 363-3300
CIRC MGR, Ravalli Republic, Hamilton, MT
Anderson, Judith ... (520) 573-4220
Food ED, Arizona Daily Star, Tucson, AZ
Anderson, Julia ... (360) 694-3391
BUS ED, Community ED
Columbian, Vancouver, WA
Anderson, Julie ... (402) 444-1000
Environmental/Ecology ED
Omaha World-Herald, Omaha, NE
Anderson, K Gary ... (540) 574-6200
CIRC DIR
Daily News-Record, Harrisonburg, VA
Anderson, Karen ... (218) 723-5281
ADV SUPV-CLASS (Telephone)
Duluth News-Tribune, Duluth, MN
Anderson, Keith ... (612) 442-4414
ED, Waconia Patriot, Waconia, MN
Anderson, Keith ... (704) 652-3313
ADV DIR, McDowell News, Marion, NC
Anderson, Kelly ... (507) 526-7324
GM, Faribault County Register, Blue Earth, MN
Anderson, Kevin ... (320) 676-3123
GM, Mille Lacs Messenger, Isle, MN
Anderson, Kim M ... (507) 831-3455
PUB, Cottonwood County Citizen, Windom, MN
Anderson, Kirk ... (316) 855-3902
ED, Cimarron Jacksonian, Cimarron, KS
Anderson, Kitty ... (218) 865-6265
PUB, ED, Biwabik Times, Biwabik, MN
Anderson, Larry ... (912) 764-9031
Ed, Statesboro Herald, Statesboro, GA
Anderson, Lee S ... (423) 756-6900
PUB, ED, EPE
Chattanooga Free Press, Chattanooga, TN
Anderson, Les ... (316) 755-0821
PUB, ED, Ark Valley News, Valley Center, KS
Anderson, Linda ... (401) 849-3300
ADV MGR-CLASS
Newport Daily News, Newport, RI
Anderson, Linda ... (937) 652-1331
PUB, Urbana Daily Citizen, Urbana, OH
Anderson, Lisa ... (612) 673-4000
DIR-Circulation, PROD MGR-Pre Press
Star Tribune, Minneapolis, MN
Anderson, Lisa ... (212) 986-0970
BU Chief, Chicago Tribune Press Service Inc., New York, NY
Anderson, Liz ... (573) 683-3351
ED, Enterprise-Courier, Charleston, MO
Anderson, Loraine ... (616) 946-2000
Regional ED, Record-Eagle, Traverse City, MI
Anderson, Lorena ... (501) 442-1777
COL, ASST News ED
Northwest Arkansas Times, Fayetteville, AR

Anderson, Louise ... (508) 586-7200
Fashion/Style ED, Food ED, Women's ED
Enterprise, Brockton, MA
Anderson, Manley ... (716) 487-1111
BUS/FIN ED, Post-Journal, Jamestown, NY
Anderson, Mark ... (316) 357-8316
PUB, Jetmore Republican, Jetmore, KS
Anderson, Marlene ... (509) 459-5000
ADV MGR-CLASS
Spokesman-Review, Spokane, WA
Anderson, Matt ... (605) 296-3181
PUB, ED, Canistota Clipper, Canistota, SD
Anderson III, N Christian ... (719) 632-5511
PUB, Gazette, Colorado Springs, CO
Anderson, Nancy ... (316) 755-0821
PUB, ED, Ark Valley News, Valley Center, KS
Anderson, Nick ... (502) 582-4011
Cartoonist, Courier-Journal, Louisville, KY
Anderson, O D ... (210) 683-3130
PUB, ED
Texas Mohair Weekly, Rocksprings, TX
Anderson, Pamela ... (213) 525-2000
CIRC Fulfillment MGR
Hollywood Reporter, Los Angeles, CA
Anderson, Patty ... (318) 322-5161
ADV MGR-NTL, News-Star, Monroe, LA
Anderson, Paul ... (415) 289-4040
PUB, Newspointer, Sausalito, CA
Anderson, Paul E ... (217) 379-4313
PUB, Paxton Daily Record, Paxton, IL
Anderson, Paula Lea ... (520) 445-3333
BM, Daily Courier, Prescott, AZ
Anderson, Peter T ... (218) 568-8521
PUB, Lake Country Echo, Pequot Lakes, MN
Anderson, Philip S ... (501) 378-3400
ASST SEC
Wehco Media Inc., Little Rock, AR
Anderson, Randy ... (405) 354-5264
GM, Yukon Review, Yukon, OK
Anderson, Richard F ... (541) 926-2211
PRES Pacific-Northwest Group
Albany Democrat-Herald, Albany, OR
Anderson, Rick ... (360) 532-4000
Sports ED, Daily World, Aberdeen, WA
Anderson, Rick ... (513) 761-1188
Senior Critic
Critic's Choice Reviews, Cincinnati, OH
Anderson, Robert ... (512) 293-5266
PUB, GM Herald-Times, Yoakum, TX
Anderson Sr, Robert A ... (601) 285-6248
PUB, Choctaw Plaindealer, Ackerman, MS
Anderson, Rosemary ... (519) 822-4310
Fashion/Women's ED
Daily Mercury, Guelph, ON
Anderson, Ross ... (206) 464-2111
EDU Writer, Seattle Times, Seattle, WA
Anderson, Ruth ... (605) 456-2585
GM, Valley Irrigator, Newell, SD
Anderson, Ruth Nathan ... (847) 546-6557
Author/Owner
VIP Medical Grapevine, Round Lake, IL
Anderson, Sally Cook ... (704) 692-0505
Community ED, Lifestyle ED
Times-News, Hendersonville, NC
Anderson, Sandy ... (417) 926-5148
GM, Mountain Grove News-Journal, Mountain Grove, MO
Anderson, Scott ... (517) 835-7171
Environmental Writer, Farm/Agriculture ED
Midland Daily News, Midland, MI
Anderson, Scott ... (506) 632-8888
MAN ED (Telegraph Journal)
Telegraph-Journal/Saint John Times Globe, Saint John, NB
Anderson, Scott ... (306) 773-3116
ED, Swift Current Sun, Swift Current, SK
Anderson, Scott ... (954) 356-4000
EX Producer
Sun-Sentinel, Fort Lauderdale, FL
Anderson, Steve ... (213) 237-5000
ADV DIR-Orange County Edition
Los Angeles Times, Los Angeles, CA
Anderson, Sue ... (541) 836-2241
ED, Drain Enterprise, Drain, OR
Anderson, Suzanne Fish ... (908) 922-6000
DP MGR, Asbury Park Press, Neptune NJ
Anderson, Ted ... (705) 435-6228
GM, Herald Courier, Alliston, ON
Anderson, Thom ... (803) 394-3571
ED, News & Post, Lake City, SC
Anderson, Thomas J ... (561) 746-7815
PUB, American Way Features, Jupiter, FL
Anderson, Ticorral ... (217) 423-2231
GM, African-American Voice, Decatur, IL
Anderson, Tim ... (937) 225-2000
ADV MGR-CLASS
Dayton Daily News, Dayton, OH
Anderson, Tommy ... (409) 297-6512
PUB, ED, Brazorian News, Lake Jackson, TX
Anderson, Trent ... (403) 235-7100
PROD VP-Manufacturing
Calgary Herald, Calgary, AB
Anderson, Vanessa ... (540) 980-5220
CIRC DIR, Southwest Times, Pulaski, VA

Anderson, Virginia ... (208) 397-4440
ED, Aberdeen Times, Aberdeen, ID
Anderson, Walter ... (212) 450-7000
ED, Parade Publications Inc., New York, NY
Anderson, William C ... (814) 938-8740
PUB, GM, ADV MGR
Spirit, Punxsutawney, PA
Anding, Bettye ... (504) 826-3279
Features/Lifestyle ED
Times-Picayune, New Orleans, LA
Andorko, Elliott ... (909) 987-6397
MGR-Human Resources
Inland Valley Daily Bulletin, Ontario, CA
Andrade, Franklin G ... (408) 729-6397
PUB, La Oferta Review, San Jose, CA
Andrade, Mary J ... (408) 729-6397
ED, La Oferta Review, San Jose, CA
Andrade, Melissa ... (219) 772-2101
ED, Leader, Knox, IN
Andre, Marilyn ... (913) 367-0583
Accountant
Atchison Daily Globe, Atchison, KS
Andreasen, Dale D ... (916) 842-5777
GM/EX ED/PUB, EPE
Siskiyou Daily News, Yreka, CA
Andreossi, Ann ... (401) 277-7000
CIRC MGR-BUS
Providence Journal-Bulletin, Providence, RI
Andrepont, Al ... (318) 942-4971
ADV MGR-CLASS
Daily World, Opelousas, LA
Andres, Bob ... (904) 599-2100
DIR-Photography
Tallahassee Democrat, Tallahassee, FL
Andresen, Scott ... (816) 753-7880
MAN ED
Kansas City New Times, Kansas City, MO
Andrew, Bernadine ... (423) 482-1021
Entertainment ED, Films ED, Food ED, Religion ED, Oak Ridger, Oak Ridge, TN
Andrew, Bob ... (562) 435-1161
Librarian, Press-Telegram, Long Beach, CA
Andrews, Alyssa ... (414) 542-2501
Amusements/Features/Radio/Television ED
Waukesha County Freeman, Waukesha, WI
Andrews, Angela ... (601) 961-7000
Comptroller, Clarion-Ledger, Jackson, MS
Andrews, Bernie ... (314) 340-8000
CIRC MGR
St. Louis Post-Dispatch, St. Louis, MO
Andrews, Brenda H ... (804) 543-6531
PUB, Journal and Guide, Norfolk, VA
Andrews, Caesar ... (914) 694-9300
Senior MAN ED, Reporter Dispatch, White Plains, NY, Gannett Co. Inc.
Andrews, Chet ... (860) 241-6200
MGR-Publishing SYS
Hartford Courant, Hartford, CT
Andrews, Clara Padilla ... (503) 736-9878
PUB, El Hispanic News, Portland, OR
Andrews, Connie ... (610) 371-5000
NIE, Reading Times/Eagle, Reading, PA
Andrews, Danny ... (806) 296-1300
ED, EPE, Daily Herald, Plainview, TX
Andrews, Debbie ... (319) 524-8300
MGR-TELEMKTG, Daily Gate City, Keokuk, IA
Andrews, Dwight ... (409) 265-7411
Photo ED, Brazosport Facts, Clute, TX
Andrews, Gary ... (601) 489-3511
PUB, Pontotoc Progress, Pontotoc, MS
Andrews, Gene ... (712) 762-4188
PUB, ED, Anita Tribune, Anita, IA
Andrews, Herb ... (800) 924-9041
PUB, Limelite, Presque Island, ME
Andrews, Jack ... (919) 829-4500
VP, News & Observer, Raleigh, NC
Andrews, Julie ... (719) 632-5511
RE/Automotive ED
Gazette, Colorado Springs, CO
Andrews, Kathleen ... (816) 932-6600
VP/Co-Chairman
Universal Press Syndicate, Kansas City, MO
Andrews, Lyle ... (309) 686-3000
CIRC MGR, Journal Star, Peoria, IL
Andrews, Marshall ... (901) 427-3333
CIRC DIR, Jackson Sun, Jackson, TN
Andrews, Martin ... (812) 944-6481
CIRC MGR
Tribune/Ledger & Tribune, New Albany, IN
Andrews, Richard ... (412) 664-9161
PROD FRM-COMP
Daily News, McKeesport, PA
Andrews, Tammy ... (712) 362-2622
CIRC DIR, Daily News, Estherville, IA
Andrews, Tom ... (601) 798-4766
ADV DIR, Picayune Item, Picayune, MS
Andrews, Valerie ... (613) 962-9171
ADV MGR, Intelligencer, Belleville, ON
Andriacco, Dan ... (513) 352-2000
BUS ED, Cincinnati Post, Cincinnati, OH

And Who's Where-8

Andriesen, Marilyn .... (217) 429-5151
ADTX MGR-New Ventures
Herald & Review, Decatur, IL

Andrisevic, Kathy .... (206) 464-2111
Pacific Magazine ED
Seattle Times, Seattle, WA

Andrist, John E .... (509) 826-1110
PUB, ED
Omak-Okanogan County Chronicle, Omak, WA

Andrist, Steve .... (701) 965-6088
PUB, ED, Journal, Crosby, ND

Andrus II, John H .... (609) 399-5411
ED, Sentinel-Ledger, Ocean City, NJ

Andruskevich, Greg .... (603) 668-4321
EPE, Union Leader, Manchester, NH

Anfinson, Reed W .... (320) 843-4111
PUB, ED
Swift County Monitor & News, Benson, MN

Angaza, Maitefa .... (718) 624-5959
MAN ED, City Sun, Brooklyn, NY

Angel, Jerry .... (207) 368-2028
PUB, Rolling Thunder Express, Newport, ME

Angel, Stephanie .... (217) 446-1000
News ED, Commercial News, Danville, IL

Angel, Sylvia .... (207) 368-2028
PUB, Rolling Thunder Express, Newport, ME

Angeli, Burt .... (906) 774-2772
Sports ED, Daily News, Iron Mountain, MI

Angell, Allen .... (800) 999-3534
MKTG, Another Way, Harrisonburg, VA

Angelo, Andrew .... (616) 222-5400
City ED
Grand Rapids Press, Grand Rapids, MI

Angelo, Phil .... (815) 937-3300
MAN ED, City/MET ED
Daily Journal, Kankakee, IL

Angelo, Tony .... (904) 264-3200
PROD FRM-Press
Clay Today, Orange Park, FL

Angelopoulos, Aris .... (630) 766-2955
ED, Greek Press, Wood Dale, IL

Anger, Paul .... (305) 350-2111
ED-Broward, Miami Herald, Miami, FL

Angers, Gilles .... (418) 686-3233
RE, Le Soleil, Quebec, QC

Angle, Carol .... (405) 596-3344
ED, Cherokee Messenger & Republican, Cherokee, OK

Anglea, Marilyn .... (803) 775-6331
Action Line ED, Item, Sumter, SC

Anglin, Debbie .... (601) 762-1111
EDU ED, Religion ED, Teen-Age/Youth ED
Mississippi Press, Pascagoula, MS

Anglin, Tobey .... (714) 832-9601
GM, Tustin Weekly, Tustin, CA

Angus, Scott W .... (608) 754-3311
ED, Janesville Gazette, Janesville, WI

Angus-Smith, Meg .... (607) 432-1000
ED, EPE, Daily Star, Oneonta, NY

Anischik, Thomas J .... (860) 241-6200
PROD DIR, Hartford Courant, Hartford, CT

Ankrom, Shawn .... (505) 356-4481
ED, Portales News-Tribune, Portales, NM

Annan, Bruce .... (905) 853-8888
PUB, Newmarket-Aurora Era-Banner, Newmarket, ON

Annas, Ray .... (704) 484-7000
PROD SUPT-COMP, Shelby Star, Shelby, NC

Annett, Graham P .... (330) 454-5611
CIRC DIR, Repository, Canton, OH

Annett, Lesley .... (416) 947-2222
DIR-PROM, Toronto Sun, Toronto, ON

Anobile, Marilyn .... (330) 841-1600
Religion ED, Tribune Chronicle, Warren, OH

Ansberry, Clare .... (212) 416-2000
BU Chief-Pittsburgh
Wall Street Journal, New York, NY

Anson, Karen .... (405) 382-1100
ED, BUS/FIN ED, City/MET ED, Librarian, News ED, Women's/Society ED
Seminole Producer, Seminole, OK

Anson, Peter .... (518) 374-4141
PROD FRM-Camera/Platemaking
Daily Gazette, Schenectady, NY

Ansorge, Claudia .... (908) 219-5788
PUB, Two River Times, Red Bank, NJ

Anstaett, Douglas J .... (316) 283-1500
PUB, ED, EPE, EDL Writer
Newton Kansan, Newton, KS

Anstett, Patricia .... (313) 222-6400
Medical Writer
Detroit Free Press, Detroit, MI

Antal, Roy .... (306) 565-8211
Photo DEPT MGR, Leader-Post, Regina, SK

Antenbouck, John .... (219) 456-2824
ED, Todays Catholic, Fort Wayne, IN

Anthan, George .... (515) 284-8000
Washington BU Chief
Des Moines Register, Des Moines, IA

Anthony, David .... (517) 278-2318
PROD FRM-PR
Daily Reporter, Coldwater, MI

Anthony, Frank .... (423) 756-6900
PROD DIR-OPER
Chattanooga Free Press, Chattanooga, TN

Anthony, Gwenda .... (901) 427-3333
News ED, Jackson Sun, Jackson, TN

Anthony, Kate .... (919) 829-4500
Design/Features
News & Observer, Raleigh, NC

Anthony, Marcella .... (805) 395-7500
ADV MGR-Display
Bakersfield Californian, Bakersfield, CA

Anthony, Michael .... (612) 673-4000
Music Reporter-Classical
Star Tribune, Minneapolis, MN

Anthony, Richard J .... (607) 432-1000
PRES/PUB, Daily Star, Oneonta, NY

Anthony, Robert S .... (718) 797-0210
ED/COL
Stadium Circle Features, Brooklyn, NY

Anthony, Susan .... (717) 255-8100
DIR-Community SRV, MGR-EDU SRV
Patriot-News, Harrisburg, PA

Antinoro, Suzanne .... (970) 879-1502
PUB, Today, Steamboat Springs, CO

Antle, Joe .... (757) 446-2000
ADV DIR, Virginian-Pilot, Norfolk, VA

Anton Sr, Karl V .... (516) 747-8282
PUB
Oyster Bay Enterprise Pilot, Mineola, NY

Anton Jr, Karl V .... (516) 747-8282
PUB, Port Washington News, Mineola, NY

Anton, Mike .... (303) 892-5000
State ED, Rocky Mountain News, Denver, CO

Antonich, Suzanne .... (561) 461-2050
ADV DIR-MKTG, Tribune, Fort Pierce, FL

Antonishyn, Susan .... (306) 795-2412
ED, Ituna News, Ituna, SK

Antonovich, Darren .... (209) 369-2761
Graphics ED/Art DIR, Photo ED
Lodi News-Sentinel, Lodi, CA

Antony, Larry .... (414) 922-4600
PUB/GM, Reporter, Fond du Lac, WI

Antosiewicz, Joseph D .... (603) 352-1234
CONT, Keene Sentinel, Keene, NH

Antosy, Patrick S .... (610) 371-5000
PROD SUPT-Engraving
Reading Times/Eagle, Reading, PA

Antunes, Xana .... (212) 930-8000
BUS ED, New York Post, New York, NY

Anundsen, John .... (319) 382-4221
PUB, Decorah Journal, Decorah, IA

Anuszkiewicz, Laurie .... (304) 255-4400
ADV MGR-RT, Register Herald, Beckley, WV

Anya, Tom .... (816) 826-1000
CIRC MGR, Sedalia Democrat, Sedalia, MO

Anzalone, Arthur .... (504) 826-3279
CONT, Times-Picayune, New Orleans, LA

Anzalone, Charles .... (716) 849-3434
Magazine ED, Buffalo News, Buffalo, NY

Anziano, Daniel .... (203) 235-1661
PROD MGR-SYS
Record-Journal, Meriden, CT

Anzoategui, Marcela .... (408) 272-9394
ED, Alianza Metropolitan News, San Jose, CA

Apfelbaum, Marianne .... (802) 878-0051
PUB, ED, Williston Whistle, Williston, VT

Apfelbaum, Paul .... (802) 878-0051
PUB, ED, Williston Whistle, Williston, VT

Apicella, Charles .... (413) 772-0261
CIRC DIR, Recorder, Greenfield, MA

Apolinaro, Lynn .... (201) 584-7176
ED, Star Journal, Ledgewood, NJ

Appel, Adrienne .... (413) 447-7311
Boston BU, Berkshire Eagle, Pittsfield, MA

Appell, Howard W .... (716) 243-2211
ED, Livingston County Leader, Geneseo, NY

Appelman, Carolyn .... (505) 384-2744
PUB, Estancia Valley Citizen, Estancia, NM

Appen, Ray .... (770) 442-3278
PUB, Revue & News, Alpharetta, GA

Apperley, Richard E .... (512) 445-3500
DIR-INFO & Technology Services
Austin American-Statesman, Austin, TX

Apperson, Rainey .... (502) 753-1916
Fashion/Style ED, Ledger & Times, Murray, KY

Apperson, Walter L .... (502) 753-1916
PRES, PUB, ED, BUS/FIN ED, EPE, NTL ED
Murray Ledger & Times, Murray, KY

Apple, Barbara .... (708) 336-7000
Librarian, News-Sun, Waukegan, IL

Apple Jr, R W .... (212) 556-1234
Washington BU Chief
New York Times, New York, NY

Applebaum, David .... (212) 556-1234
Group DIR-Administrative SYS
New York Times, New York, NY

Appleby, Kristi .... (716) 372-3121
ADV MGR-CLASS
Olean Times-Herald, Olean, NY

Appleby, Larry .... (602) 271-8000
PROD Unit MGR-PR (Deer Valley)
Phoenix Newspapers Inc., Phoenix, AZ

Applegate, Malcolm W .... (317) 633-1240
PRES/GM, Star/News, Indianapolis, IN

Applegreen, Sandy .... (212) 535-6811
ED/VP, Megalo Media, Syosset, NY

Aquaro, Paul .... (908) 247-8700
MAN ED, Somerset Spectator, Somerset, NJ

Aquije, David .... (914) 939-6864
ED, America Latina, Port Chester, NY

Aquilina, Anne .... (212) 930-8000
Administrative ED, Post, New York, NY

Aquino, Andres .... (802) 767-9341
Owner, Aquino International, Rochester, VT

Arambula, Odie .... (210) 728-2500
ASST GM, ED, Sunday ED
Laredo Morning Times, Laredo, TX

Aramini, John .... (201) 646-4000
ADV MGR-Consumer Sales
Record, Hackensack, NJ

Arango, German .... (713) 774-4686
ED, Semana Newspaper, Houston, TX

Aranow, Zedra .... (413) 788-1000
COL, Union-News, Springfield, MA

Araujo, Richard .... (212) 807-4600
Sports ED, El Diario La Prensa, New York, NY

Arax, Mark .... (213) 237-5000
Fresno BU
Los Angeles Times, Los Angeles, CA

Arbaugh, Joyce .... (304) 645-1206
PROD MGR-Camera
West Virginia Daily News, Lewisburg, WV

Arber, Myles .... (303) 349-6114
PUB, Crested Butte Chronicle & Pilot, Crested Butte, CO

Arbing, Vince .... (902) 667-5102
SEC/TREAS
Amherst Daily News, Amherst, NS

Arce, Luis .... (216) 999-4500
MGR-Purchasing/ASST CONT
Plain Dealer, Cleveland, OH

Arceneaux, Alex .... (318) 734-2891
ED, Welsh Citizen, Welsh, LA

Archbold, Richard .... (562) 435-1161
VP/MAN ED
Press-Telegram, Long Beach, CA

Archer, Bill .... (304) 327-2811
ED-VA
Bluefield Daily Telegraph, Bluefield, WV

Archer, Carmen .... (423) 246-8121
Food ED
Kingsport Times-News, Kingsport, TN

Archer, Carol .... (313) 963-5522
MAN ED, Michigan Chronicle, Detroit, MI

Archer, Greg .... (605) 783-3636
PUB, ED, Herald-Enterprise, Hayti, SD

Archer, Lee Anne .... (605) 873-2475
GM, Estelline Journal, Estelline, SD

Archer, Pattye .... (601) 323-1642
MAN ED
Starkville Daily News, Starkville, MS

Archer, Ray .... (602) 271-8000
EDL Writer, Arizona Republic, Phoenix, AZ

Archer, T J .... (406) 755-7000
PROD FRM-MR
Daily Inter Lake, Kalispell, MT

Archibald, Bill .... (505) 388-1576
GM, Silver City Daily Press & Independent, Silver City, NM

Archibald, Ed .... (614) 439-3531
ADV DIR, ADTX MGR
Daily Jeffersonian, Cambridge, OH

Archibald, John .... (905) 729-2287
PUB, GM, Beeton-Schomberg Record Sentinel, Beeton, ON

Archibald, John .... (501) 623-7711
Religion ED
Sentinel-Record, Hot Springs, AR

Archuleta, Tony .... (505) 894-2143
ED, Herald, Truth or Consequences, NM

Arciero, Grace .... (915) 546-6100
MGR-CR, El Paso Times, El Paso, TX

Arcuate, Francisco .... (312) 252-3534
ED, Extra Bilingual Community Newspapers, Chicago, IL

Ard, Scott .... (510) 208-6300
BUS ED, Oakland Tribune, Oakland, CA
MediaNews Inc. (Alameda Newspapers)

Arden, Patrick .... (312) 828-0350
MAN ED, Chicago Reader, Chicago, IL

Arden-Hopkins, Christina .... (716) 968-2580
PUB, Cuba Patriot & Free Press, Cuba, NY

Arden-Hopkins, John .... (716) 968-2580
ED, Cuba Patriot & Free Press, Cuba, NY

Ardoin, Bernice .... (318) 363-2103
ED, Mamou Acadian Press, Mamou, LA

Ardoin, John .... (214) 977-8222
Music Critic
Dallas Morning News, Dallas, TX

Arduin, Luba .... (604) 886-7077
PUB, Gibsons Coastlife, Gibsons, BC

Aregood, Richard .... (201) 877-4141
EPE, Star-Ledger, Newark, NJ

Arenberg, Tom .... (205) 325-2222
Sports ED
Birmingham News, Birmingham, AL

Arend, Rolf .... (617) 929-2000
CIRC MGR-Planning/Market Development
Boston Globe, Boston, MA

Arends, Hank .... (503) 399-6611
Religion ED, Statesman Journal, Salem, OR

Arends, Jack .... (206) 282-0900
ED, Queen Anne News, Seattle, WA

Arens, Pam .... (414) 748-3017
ED, Ripon Commonwealth Press, Ripon, WI

Argabright, Joyce .... (540) 981-3100
MGR-CR, Roanoke Times, Roanoke, VA

Argo, Betty .... (405) 924-4388
PROD SUPT-COMP
Durant Daily Democrat, Durant, OK

Ariail, Robert .... (803) 771-6161
EDL Cartoonist, State, Columbia, SC

Arias, Euseuio .... (209) 674-2424
Photo DEPT, Madera Tribune, Madera, CA

Arie, Mike .... (405) 238-6464
Sports ED
Pauls Valley Daily Democrat, Pauls Valley, OK

Ariff, Mitch .... (601) 335-1155
Sports ED
Delta Democrat Times, Greenville, MS

Ariola, David .... (512) 352-8535
ADV MGR-RT, Taylor Daily Press, Taylor, TX

Arkens, Michelle .... (414) 657-1000
Librarian, Kenosha News, Kenosha, WI

Arkin, Judy .... (312) 616-3282
BM, Dodge Construction News Chicago, Chicago, IL

Arlofski, William A .... (203) 235-1661
Online Contact, Record-Journal, Meriden, CT

Armand, Dan .... (303) 820-1010
PROD MGR-PR, Denver Post, Denver, CO

Armantrout, Janet .... (510) 447-8700
ED, Independent, Livermore, CA

Armao, Jo-Ann .... (202) 334-6000
ASST MAN ED-MET
Washington Post, Washington, DC

Armband, Robert .... (312) 525-6285/9400
PUB, La Raza Newspaper, Chicago, IL

Armbruster, William .... (212) 837-7000
Specials ED, Journal of Commerce & Commercial, New York, NY

Armellini, Chris .... (213) 465-8792
BM, City News Service Inc., Los Angeles, CA

Armendariz, Billy .... (505) 546-2611
Sports ED, Deming Headlight, Deming, NM

Armendariz, Grant .... (213) 237-5485
Sales EX/Midwest & Southwest, Los Angeles Times Syndicate, Los Angeles, CA

Armenia, Joseph P .... (716) 693-1000
PUB, Tonawanda News, North Tonawanda, NY

Armenio, John .... (603) 882-2741
ADV ASST MGR, ADTX MGR
Telegraph, Nashua, NH

Armerding, Taylor .... (508) 739-1300
ED, North Shore Sunday, Danvers, MA

Armesto, Eladio Jose .... (305) 530-8787
PUB, El Nuevo Patria, Miami, FL

Armfield, Jack .... (910) 888-3500
PROD SUPT-PR
High Point Enterprise, High Point, NC

Armistead, Dr John .... (601) 842-2611
Religion ED, Northeast Mississippi Daily Journal, Tupelo, MS

Armon, Rick .... (419) 522-3311
City/MET ED, News Journal, Mansfield, OH

Armstrong, Bill .... (918) 224-5185
PROD MGR
Sapulpa Daily Herald, Sapulpa, OK

Armstrong, Cathy .... (714) 835-1234
Team Leader-S Calif Culture
Orange County Register, Santa Ana, CA

Armstrong, Charity .... (918) 542-5533
Bookkeeper, Miami News-Record, Miami, OK

Armstrong, Dave .... (412) 981-6100
ADV DIR-MKTG, Herald, Sharon, PA

Armstrong, David .... (415) 777-2424
Media Writer
San Francisco Examiner, San Francisco, CA

Armstrong, David .... (705) 647-6791
PUB, Temiskaming Speaker, New Liskeard, ON

Armstrong, Gene .... (217) 223-5100
ADV MGR-CLASS
Quincy Herald-Whig, Quincy, IL

Armstrong, Jack .... (317) 584-4501
PUB, News-Gazette, Winchester, IN

Armstrong, John .... (864) 298-4100
DP MGR, Greenville News, Greenville, SC

Armstrong, John .... (510) 935-2525
VP/EX ED
Contra Costa Times, Walnut Creek, CA

Armstrong, Julian .... (514) 987-2222
Food ED, Gazette, Montreal, QC

Armstrong, Larry .... (213) 237-5000
DIR-Photography
Los Angeles Times, Los Angeles, CA

Armstrong, Roger F .... (409) 776-4444
DIR-FIN, Eagle, Bryan, TX

Armstrong, Scott .... (617) 450-2000
NTL/News ED
Christian Science Monitor, Boston, MA

9-Who's Where **Atk**

Armstrong, Scott .... (610) 933-8926
BM, Phoenix, Phoenixville, PA
Armstrong, Shell .... (504) 758-2795
ED, St. Charles Herald-Guide, Boutte, LA
Armstrong, Sue .... (613) 829-9100
CIRC VP-Reader Sales & SRV
Ottawa Citizen, Ottawa, ON
Armstrong, William .... (614) 852-1616
ADV MGR, Madison Press, London, OH
Arn, Debra J .... (608) 365-8811
MGR-Office, Beloit Daily News, Beloit, WI
Arn Jr, John .... (606) 564-9091
PROD SUPV
Ledger Independent, Maysville, KY
Arndt, Rosann .... (715) 423-7200
Librarian
Daily Tribune, Wisconsin Rapids, WI
Arnett, Alison .... (617) 929-2000
Restaurant ED, Boston Globe, Boston, MA
Arnett, John A .... (203) 333-0161
DIR-MKTG, Connecticut Post, Bridgeport, CT
Arnett, Lary .... (412) 263-1100
ADV MGR-Sales NTL
Pittsburgh Post-Gazette, Pittsburgh, PA
Arney, Melanie L .... (803) 577-7111
ADV MGR-Local/RT
Post and Courier, Charleston, SC
Arney, Sarah .... (360) 435-5757
ED, Times, Arlington, WA
Arnholt, Michael .... (910) 323-4848
MAN ED
Fayetteville Observer-Times, Fayetteville, NC
Arno, Jim .... (218) 385-2275
ED, Contact, New York Mills, MN
Arnoczky, Jim .... (419) 342-4276
PROD MGR, Daily Globe, Shelby, OH
Arnold, Allison .... (810) 985-7171
Librarian, Times Herald, Port Huron, MI
Arnold, Chris .... (515) 933-4241
GM, Fremont Gazette, Fremont, IA
Arnold, Doug .... (909) 987-6397
Automotive ED, Travel ED
Inland Valley Daily Bulletin, Ontario, CA
Arnold, Ed .... (705) 745-4641
MAN ED, Examiner, Peterborough, ON
Arnold, Elin A .... (815) 339-2321
PUB, ED
Putnam County Record, Granville, IL
Arnold, F A .... (402) 729-6141
PUB, Fairbury Journal-News, Fairbury, NE
Arnold, George .... (501) 862-6611
MAN ED
El Dorado News-Times, El Dorado, AR
Arnold, Gord .... (204) 697-7000
Special Sections ED
Winnipeg Free Press, Winnipeg, MB
Arnold, Jack .... (515) 637-2632
PUB, New Sharon Star, New Sharon, IA
Arnold, Jerry L .... (817) 778-4444
SEC, Temple Daily Telegram, Temple, TX
Frank Mayborn Enterprises Inc.
Arnold, Jill .... (504) 383-1111
Librarian, Advocate, Baton Rouge, LA
Arnold, Jim .... (315) 635-3921
MAN ED, Messenger, Baldwinsville, NY
Arnold, Joe .... (573) 265-3321
PUB, ED
St. James Leader-Journal, St. James, MO
Arnold, John .... (540) 669-2181
CIRC MGR-Distribution, Herald-Courier
Virginia Tennessean, Bristol, VA
Arnold, John C .... (515) 856-6336
PRES, PUB, CIRC DIR, MAN ED
Ad Express & Daily Iowegian, Centerville, IA
Arnold, Judy .... (573) 335-6611
PROD FRM-COMP
Southeast Missourian, Cape Girardeau, MO
Arnold, Kate .... (513) 863-8200
ADV MGR-CLASS
Journal-News, Hamilton, OH
Arnold, Kelly .... (423) 753-3136
ED, Herald and Tribune, Jonesborough, TN
Arnold, Kirby .... (206) 339-3000
Sports ED, Herald, Everett, WA
Arnold, Lonnie .... (913) 263-1000
CIRC MGR
Abilene Reflector-Chronicle, Abilene, KS
Arnold, Lori .... (619) 442-4404
Religion ED, Zone ED
Daily Californian, El Cajon, CA
Arnold, Matthew .... (330) 747-1471
Sports ED, Vindicator, Youngstown, OH
Arnold, Michael .... (312) 321-3000
ASST FIN ED
Chicago Sun-Times, Chicago, IL
Arnold, Pete .... (937) 498-2111
PROD FRM-MR
Sidney Daily News, Sidney, OH
Arnold, Richard .... (212) 416-2000
PROD Senior MGR (Sharon PA)
Wall Street Journal, New York, NY
Arnold, Rodney W .... (802) 885-2246
PUB, ED
Springfield Reporter, Springfield, VT
Arnold, Roxane .... (213) 237-5000
State/Specialists ED
Los Angeles Times, Los Angeles, CA
Arnold, Ruth .... (515) 652-7612
ED, Beacon Forum, Eldon, IA
Arnold, S Lynn .... (541) 885-4410
PROD SUPV
Herald and News, Klamath Falls, OR
Arnold, Sam .... (715) 723-5515
CIRC MGR
Chippewa Herald, Chippewa Falls, WI
Arnold, Scott .... (330) 264-1125
Regional ED, Daily Record, Wooster, OH
Arnold, Troy .... (901) 885-0744
CIRC MGR, Daily Messenger, Union City, TN
Arnold, Van .... (601) 582-4321
News ED
Hattiesburg American, Hattiesburg, MS
Arnold, Vince .... (203) 789-5200
DP MGR
New Haven Register, New Haven, CT
Arnold, Wiley .... (901) 529-2211
PROD MGR-MR
Commercial Appeal, Memphis, TN
Arnold, William .... (206) 448-8000
Films ED
Seattle Post-Intelligencer, Seattle, WA
Arnsdorff, Janice .... (903) 887-4511
ED, Monitor/Leader, Mabank, TX
Arnt, Larry .... (805) 395-7500
PROD MGR
Bakersfield Californian, Bakersfield, CA
Aronson, Marvin .... (907) 456-6661
Chief Copy ED/Weekend ED, News/Wire ED
Fairbanks Daily News-Miner, Fairbanks, AK
Arpaio, Sherry .... (602) 898-5680
EDU ED
Tempe Daily News Tribune, Mesa, AZ
Arredondo, Imara .... (504) 456-6122
PUB, ED, Aqui New Orleans, Kenner, LA
Arrenius, Carl .... (309) 686-3000
ADV DIR, Journal Star, Peoria, IL
Arrigo, Mary .... (617) 326-9240
Sales MGR
White, Leo Productions, Westwood, MA
Arrigoni, Patricia .... (415) 454-0876
PRES, Arrigoni Travel Syndication, Fairfax, CA
Arrington, Debbie .... (562) 435-1161
Food ED, Press-Telegram, Long Beach, CA
Arrington, Jamie .... (601) 765-8275
PUB, ED, News-Commercial, Collins, MS
Arrington, Kim .... (202) 334-6375
Permissions ED, Washington Post Writers Group, Washington, DC
Arrington, Shelley .... (360) 694-3391
ASST to PUB, Columbian, Vancouver, WA
Arrington, Willie L .... (334) 624-8323
MAN ED
Greensboro Watchman, Greensboro, AL
Arritola, Madeleine Garcia ...... (954) 356-4000
MGR-Community Relations (South Broward)
Sun-Sentinel, Fort Lauderdale, FL
Arroyo, Blanca .... (213) 622-8332
TV Guide ED, La Opinion, Los Angeles, CA
Arsenault, Jocelyn .... (514) 985-3333
DIR-INFO SRV, DP MGR, PROD DIR
Le Devoir, Montreal, QC
Arsenault, Seth .... (415) 495-4200
Sales Representative
Daily Pacific Builder, San Francisco, CA
Arseneau, Terry M .... (604) 442-2191
ED, Gazette, Grand Forks, BC
Arter, Kerry .... (317) 747-5700
Deputy MAN ED, Star Press, Muncie, IN
Artero, Stephanie .... (561) 820-4100
Medical Section ED
Palm Beach Post, West Palm Beach, FL
Arth, Shelly .... (816) 886-2233
PUB, Marshall Democrat-News, Marshall, MO
Arthur, Allan .... (505) 863-6811
Sports ED, Gallup Independent, Gallup, NM
Arthur, Allison .... (206) 463-9195
ED, Vashon-Maury Island Beachcomber, Vashon Island, WA
Arthur, Allyn .... (515) 674-3591
PUB, ED, Jasper County Tribune, Colfax, IA
Arthur, Barry .... (501) 378-3400
Photo ED
Arkansas Democrat-Gazette, Little Rock, AR
Arthur, Debbie .... (423) 472-5041
ADV MGR-CLASS
Cleveland Daily Banner, Cleveland, TN
Arthur, John .... (213) 237-5000
ED-San Fernando Valley Edition
Los Angeles Times, Los Angeles, CA
Arthur, Marvin C .... (702) 228-3731
PRES, Arthur's International, Las Vegas, NV
Arthur, Stephen .... (717) 637-3736
CFO, DP MGR, Evening Sun, Hanover, PA
Arthur, Steve .... (909) 797-9101
PUB, Yucaipa & Calimesa News-Mirror, Yucaipa, CA
Artuso, Donna Marie .... (403) 468-0100
COL, Edmonton Sun, Edmonton, AB
Arundel, Arthur W .... (703) 437-5400
PUB, Springfield Times Courier, Reston, VA
Arundel, Peter .... (703) 437-5400
GM, Springfield Times Courier, Reston, VA
Arvayo, Ana Maria .... (520) 364-3424
ADV DIR, Daily Dispatch, Douglas, AZ
Arvia, Phil .... (773) 586-8800
Sports COL, Daily Southtown, Chicago, IL
Arwady, George E .... (616) 345-3511
PUB, Kalamazoo Gazette, Kalamazoo, MI
Asbach, Jeff .... (218) 741-5544
DIR-PROD, Mesabi Daily News, Virginia, MN
Asbach, Richard M .... (808) 329-9311
PUB, West Hawaii Today, Kailua-Kona, HI
Asbach, Scott .... (218) 741-5544
GM, Mesabi Daily News, Virginia, MN
Asbury, Barbara .... (423) 523-3131
Arts ED, Theater ED
Knoxville News-Sentinel, Knoxville, TN
Asbury, Timothy E .... (970) 586-3356
MAN ED, Trail-Gazette, Estes Park, CO
Aschaver, Kiersten .... (203) 876-6800
ED, West Haven News, Milford, CT
Ascher, Evelyn .... (609) 927-1842
SEC/TREAS, Ascher Features Syndicate, Egg Harbor Twp., NJ
Ascher, Marc .... (908) 246-5500
Photo ED
Home News & Tribune, East Brunswick, NJ
Ascher, Sidney .... (609) 927-1842
PRES, Ascher Features Syndicate, Egg Harbor Twp., NJ
Ascioti, Joseph A .... (413) 788-1000
ADV MGR-GEN, Union-News, Springfield, MA
Ash, Cathy .... (610) 932-2444
MAN ED, Chester County Press, Oxford, PA
Ash, Doreen .... (250) 380-5211
Librarian, Times Colonist, Victoria, BC
Ash, Jeff .... (414) 435-4411
Fashion ED, Food ED, Topics ED-Lifestyle
Green Bay Press-Gazette, Green Bay, WI
Ash, Miriam .... (812) 367-2041
PUB, GM, Ferdinand News, Ferdinand, IN
Ash, Paul .... (812) 367-2041
PUB, Ferdinand News, Ferdinand, IN
Ashby, Craig .... (801) 722-5131
PUB, Uintah Basin Standard, Roosevelt, UT
Ashby, Kevin .... (801) 637-0732
PUB, Sun Advocate, Price, UT
Ashby, Linnell .... (814) 665-8291
ADV MGR, Corry Evening Journal, Corry, PA
Ashby, William .... (903) 657-2501
ADV MGR, Daily News, Henderson, TX
Ashcroft, Wayne T .... (801) 752-2121
ADV DIR, Herald Journal, Logan, UT
Ashe, Barbara .... (912) 423-9331
MAN ED, Herald-Leader, Fitzgerald, GA
Ashe, John .... (517) 772-2971
MAN ED (Alma)
Morning Sun, Mount Pleasant, MI
Ashe, Reid .... (813) 259-7711
ASSOC PUB
Tampa Tribune and Times, Tampa, FL
Ashe, Sam .... (704) 864-3291
CIRC DIR, Gaston Gazette, Gastonia, NC
Ashenfelder, Dennis .... (717) 784-2121
DP MGR, Press Enterprise, Bloomsburg, PA
Asher, Donald G .... (219) 933-3200
MAN ED-Porter County, Times, Munster, IN
Asher, Jim .... (317) 342-3311
ASST MAN ED
Daily Reporter, Martinsville, IN
Asher, Jim .... (410) 332-6000
ED-City, Sun, Baltimore, MD
Asher, Mike .... (757) 247-4600
DIR-Technology
Daily Press, Newport News, VA
Ashfield, Cliff .... (306) 735-2230
PUB, ED, Whitewood Herald, Whitewood, SK
Ashfield, Elaine .... (306) 735-2230
PUB, Whitewood Herald, Whitewood, SK
Ashhock, Ronnie .... (501) 239-8562
Religion ED, Daily Press, Paragould, AR
Ashley, Albert .... (864) 223-1411
CIRC MGR-City
Index-Journal, Greenwood, SC
Ashley, Charles .... (817) 552-5454
PROD MGR, Vernon Daily Record, Vernon, TX
Ashley, Jim .... (423) 756-6900
Religion ED, Free Press, Chattanooga, TN
Ashley, Joyce .... (817) 552-5454
Fashion/Food ED, Society ED
Vernon Daily Record, Vernon, TX
Ashley, Karen .... (970) 345-2296
ED, Akron News-Reporter, Akron, CO
Ashley, Pamela .... (517) 278-2318
GM, PA, Daily Reporter, Coldwater, MI
Ashley, Phil .... (214) 977-8222
PROD MGR-Pre Press
Dallas Morning News, Dallas, TX
Ashley, Randall .... (404) 526-5151
Foreign ED, Journal-Constitution, Atlanta, GA
Ashley, Robert .... (502) 926-0123
ED, Messenger-Inquirer, Owensboro, KY
Ashley, Valerie .... (317) 584-4501
ADV MGR, News-Gazette, Winchester, IN
Ashley-Ward, Amelia .... (415) 931-5778
ED, San Francisco Metro Reporter Group, San Francisco, CA
Ashlock, Elaine .... (903) 583-2124
ADV MGR, Favorite, Bonham, TX
Ashmore, Sandy .... (805) 763-3171
DIR-MKTG, Daily Midway Driller, Taft, CA
Ashton, Jean .... (508) 764-4325
ADV Representative, Books ED, News, Southbridge, MA
Ashworth, Alan .... (216) 951-0000
Copy Desk Chief
News-Herald, Willoughby, OH
Ashworth, Ruck .... (334) 222-2402
ADV MGR
Andalusia Star-News, Andalusia, AL
Asiff, Fisal .... (403) 623-4221
PUB, ED
Lac La Biche Post, Lac La Biche, AB
Askew, Linda .... (602) 271-8000
CIRC MGR-Support
Phoenix Newspapers Inc., Phoenix, AZ
Askew-Hahn, Allison .... (757) 446-2000
GM-Voice INFO SYS
Virginian-Pilot, Norfolk, VA
Asleson, Becky .... (507) 625-4451
ADV MGR-NTL, Free Press, Mankato, MN
Asleson, Glen .... (507) 625-4451
PROD DIR, Free Press, Mankato, MN
Asman, David .... (212) 416-2000
Features ED
Wall Street Journal, New York, NY
Asmus, Rhonda .... (320) 324-2405
GM, ED, Chokio Review, Chokio, MN
Aspan Esq, Moses .... (212) 869-7038
PUB, Folha do Brasil, New York, NY
Aspenson, Sherron .... (815) 544-9811
ADV DIR
Belvidere Daily Republican, Belvidere, IL
Astbury, Carroll .... (207) 990-8000
BUS ED, Bangor Daily News, Bangor, ME
Aston, John A .... (513) 489-7227
TREAS/Comptroller
Brown Publishing Co., Cincinnati, OH
Aston, Timothy .... (860) 241-6200
MGR-Desktop Services
Hartford Courant, Hartford, CT
Asturias, Corinne .... (408) 298-8000
MAN ED, Metro, San Jose, CA
Aswege, Scott .... (309) 764-4344
BM, Dispatch, Moline, IL
Small Newspaper Group Inc.
Aswell, W Roy .... (334) 792-3141
CFO, Dothan Eagle, Dothan, AL
Atanay, Reginaldo .... (212) 807-4600
Community ED
El Diario La Prensa, New York, NY
Atencio, Jane .... (617) 450-2000
PROD MGR
Christian Science Monitor, Boston, MA
Athanasiades, Costas .... (718) 278-3014
PUB, ED, Campana, Astoria, NY
Atherton, Maryann .... (617) 245-0080
ADV MGR
Wakefield Daily Item, Wakefield, MA
Atherton, Tony .... (613) 829-9100
COL, Ottawa Citizen, Ottawa, ON
Atienza, Orlando .... (213) 483-4890
GM, 20 De Mayo, Los Angeles, CA
Atkeisson, Betty .... (903) 872-3931
ADV SUPV-CLASS, Corsicana Daily Sun, Corsicana, TX
Atkerson, Teresa .... (918) 423-1700
Entertainment/Amusements ED, Lifestyle ED, Society ED, Women's ED, McAlester News-Capital & Democrat, McAlester, OK
Atkin, Dennis .... (503) 221-8327
ADV DIR, Oregonian, Portland, OR
Atkin, Glenn .... (517) 787-2300
ED, News Advertiser, Jackson, MI
Atkin, Ross .... (617) 450-2000
Sports Writer
Christian Science Monitor, Boston, MA
Atkins, Bob .... (615) 452-2561
PUB, News-Examiner, Gallatin, TN
Atkins, Freddie .... (919) 708-9000
ADV ASST DIR, Sanford Herald, Sanford, NC
Atkins, Jim .... (610) 622-8800
Wire ED, Delaware County Daily Times, Primos, PA
Atkins, Jim .... (416) 367-2000
Star Week ED, Toronto Star, Toronto, ON
Atkins, Kathy .... (816) 532-4444
GM, Smithville Lake Democrat-Herald, Smithville, MO
Atkins, Patsy .... (504) 345-2333
CIRC MGR, Daily Star, Hammond, LA

Atk Who's Where-10

Atkins, Roy (541) 776-4411
CONT, Mail Tribune, Medford, OR

Atkins, Sandra M (802) 254-2311
DP MGR, PROD FRM-COMP
Brattleboro Reformer, Brattleboro, VT

Atkins, Thomas J (213) 237-5000
PROD DIR-Orange County OPER
Los Angeles Times, Los Angeles, CA

Atkins, Tom (314) 340-8000
PROD MGR-Inserting Facility
St. Louis Post-Dispatch, St. Louis, MO

Atkinson, Carole (408) 458-1100
PUB, Good Times, Santa Cruz, CA

Atkinson, Dave (913) 823-6363
PROD DIR-Safety, PROD MGR, Salina Journal, Salina, KS

Atkinson, Gerry (360) 532-4000
CIRC MGR, Daily World, Aberdeen, WA

Atkinson, Larry (605) 845-3646
PUB, ED, Mobridge Tribune, Mobridge, SD

Atkinson, M L (504) 826-3279
Women's ED
Times-Picayune, New Orleans, LA

Atkinson, Mark (715) 833-9200
VP, Leader-Telegram, Eau Claire, WI

Atkinson, Paul (212) 416-2600
VP-ADV-WSJ
Dow Jones & Co. Inc., New York, NY

Atkinson, Rollie (707) 823-7845
PUB
Sonoma West Times & News, Sebastopol, CA

Atkisson, Randy (618) 234-1000
VP/CFO
Belleville News-Democrat, Belleville, IL

Atseff, Timothy (315) 470-0011
MAN ED, Post-Standard/Syracuse Herald-Journal/ American, Syracuse, NY

Attala, Robert (514) 987-2222
ADV VP, Gazette, Montreal, QC

Atterbury, R (604) 723-8171
PA, PROD MGR, PROD FRM-COMP
Alberni Valley Times, Port Alberni, BC

Attig, Rick (541) 382-1811
EX ED, Bulletin, Bend, OR

Atwell, Kit K (520) 753-6397
PUB, Kingman Daily Miner, Kingman, AZ

Atwell, Tom (207) 791-6650
Travel ED
Portland Press Herald, Portland, ME

Atwill, Barbara (502) 236-2726
GM, Hickman Courier, Hickman, KY

Atwill, Kevin (770) 382-4545
GM, MAN ED
Herald-Tribune, Cartersville, GA

Atwood, Mike (319) 398-8211
PROD Administrator
Gazette, Cedar Rapids, IA

Aube, Bob (705) 567-5321
PROD FRM-COMP/PR
Northern Daily News, Kirkland Lake, ON

Aubespin, Mervin (502) 582-4011
ASSOC ED-Development
Courier-Journal, Louisville, KY

Aubin, Robert (514) 285-7272
ADV MGR-RT, La Presse, Montreal, QC

Aubry, R N (613) 933-0014
PUB, GM, Seaway News, Cornwall, ON

Auclair, Jean-Paul (514) 646-3333
ED, Le Courrier du Sud/South Shore Courier, Longueuil, QC

Auclair, Michel (514) 692-8552
PUB, St. Lawrence Sun, Chateauguay, QC

Auclair, Tom (603) 352-1234
Local News ED, Keene Sentinel, Keene, NH

Aud, Rosemary (618) 382-4176
PROD MGR, Carmi Times, Carmi, IL

Audet, Diane (418) 695-2601
PUB/ED
Le Reveil a Chicoutimi, Jonquiere, QC

Audsley, Barbara (816) 338-2195
MAN ED, Glasgow Missourian, Glasgow, MO

Audy, Valere (514) 375-4555
EPE, La Voix de l'Est, Granby, QC

Auer, Dave (309) 686-3000
ADV MGR-RT, Journal Star, Peoria, IL

Auer, James (414) 224-2000
Art Critic
Milwaukee Journal Sentinel, Milwaukee, WI

Auerbach, Jonathan (212) 930-8000
Deputy BUS ED
New York Post, New York, NY

Aufill, Twila (806) 762-8844
CONT-Division
Lubbock Avalanche-Journal, Lubbock, TX

Augare, Marlene (406) 338-2090
GM, Glacier Reporter, Browning, MT

Auge, Mike (405) 772-3301
CIRC MGR
Weatherford Daily News, Weatherford, OK

Aughenbaugh, Cindy (814) 765-5581
CIRC MGR, Progress, Clearfield, PA

Augspurger, Mike (319) 754-8461
BUS/Agriculture ED
Hawk Eye, Burlington, IA

Augstein, Tom (518) 792-3131
PROD Officer-Safety & Training
Post-Star, Glens Falls, NY

Augur, Marilyn (501) 378-3400
SEC, Wehco Media Inc., Little Rock, AR

August III, Albert T (804) 649-6000
PRES/GM
Richmond Times-Dispatch, Richmond, VA

August, Bob (216) 951-0000
COL, News-Herald, Willoughby, OH

Augustine, Diana (215) 855-8440
ADV MGR-CLASS, Reporter, Landsdale, PA

Auitabile, Karen (860) 347-3331
ED, Middletown Press, Middletown, CT

Aukerman, Charles (216) 524-0830
ED, Sun Banner Pride, Cleveland, OH

Aulino, Peggy (608) 754-3311
EPE, Janesville Gazette, Janesville, WI

Aultman, William J (803) 385-3177
PUB, News & Reporter, Chester, SC

Auman, Richard D (610) 371-5000
CIRC DIR
Reading Times/Eagle, Reading, PA

Aumann, Mark (919) 446-5161
Sports ED, Rocky Mount Telegram, Rocky Mount, NC

Aungst, Vern (313) 994-6989
PROD SUPV-Press Plate
Ann Arbor News, Ann Arbor, MI

Ausanka III, John J (203) 235-1661
VP, CONT, Record-Journal, Meriden, CT

Ausband, Jerry (803) 626-8555
EPE, Sun News, Myrtle Beach, SC

Ausenbaugh, E Terry (402) 444-1000
Chief PA, Omaha World-Herald, Omaha, NE

Ausherman, Donna (301) 662-1177
ADV MGR-NTL, Frederick Post/News, Frederick, MD

Auslander, Edith (520) 573-4400
VP-Human Resources, TNI Partners dba Tucson Newspapers, Tucson, AZ

Auslander, Steve (520) 573-4220
ED, Arizona Daily Star, Tucson, AZ

Ausley, Judy (704) 484-7000
Features ED, Shelby Star, Shelby, NC

Austen, Garnet (902) 681-2121
PUB, Advertiser, Kentville, NS

Auster, Elizabeth (216) 999-4500
ASSOC ED, Plain Dealer, Cleveland, OH

Austin, Amy (202) 332-2100
GM, Washington City Paper, Washington, DC

Austin, April (617) 450-2000
Theater/Arts ED
Christian Science Monitor, Boston, MA

Austin, Danforth W (212) 416-2600
VP/GM, Dow Jones & Co. Inc., New York, NY

Austin, Dave (701) 780-1100
ADV MGR-Display
Grand Forks Herald, Grand Forks, ND

Austin, David (810) 469-4510
PROD FRM-COMP
Macomb Daily, Mount Clemens, MI
Independent Newspapers Inc. (MI)

Austin, Gene (215) 854-2000
Residential RE Writer
Philadelphia Inquirer, Philadelphia, PA

Austin, Guy L (423) 928-4151
ED, DP MGR, Online MGR
Elizabethton Star, Elizabethton, TN

Austin, James (716) 366-3000
PUB/GM, Evening Observer, Dunkirk, NY
Ogden Newspapers

Austin, John (909) 672-8459
DIR
Hollywood Inside Syndicate, Los Angeles, CA

Austin, Judi (703) 276-5800
Regional ED/West
Gannett News Service, Arlington, VA

Austin, Karen (510) 734-8600
MGR-Human Resources
Tri-Valley Herald, Pleasanton, CA

Austin, Linda (215) 854-2000
BUS ED
Philadelphia Inquirer, Philadelphia, PA

Austin, Liuanne (540) 574-6200
Religion ED
Daily News-Record, Harrisonburg, VA

Austin, Natalie (540) 885-7281
Special Sections/ETC ED
Daily News Leader, Staunton, VA

Austin, Norma (509) 525-3300
PSL MGR
Walla Walla Union-Bulletin, Walla Walla, WA

Austin, Randi (313) 222-6400
VP-Human Resources
Detroit Newspapers, Detroit, MI

Austin, Randy (919) 419-6500
PROD MGR-Dayside Pre Press
Herald-Sun, Durham, NC

Austin, Sandi (970) 474-3388
PUB, GM, ED, Advocate, Julesburg, CO

Austin, Steve (423) 756-6900
CIRC DIR
Chattanooga Free Press, Chattanooga, TN

Austin, Steve (502) 827-2000
PUB, Gleaner, Henderson, KY

Auth, Tony (215) 854-2000
EDL Cartoonist
Philadelphia Inquirer, Philadelphia, PA

Authement, Marty (504) 850-1100
EDU ED, Features ED, Health/Medical ED, Women's ED, Courier, Houma, LA

Authur, Janelle (419) 245-6000
MGR-Human Resources, Blade, Toledo, OH

Autrey, Dan L (407) 846-7600
PUB, GM
Osceola News-Gazette, Kissimmee, FL

Autry, Al (209) 578-2000
ADV MGR-CLASS, Modesto Bee, Modesto, CA

Autry, Brett (915) 625-4128
PUB, ED
Chronicle & Democrat-Voice, Coleman, TX

Autz, H R (510) 783-6111
ADV DIR, ADV MGR-RT
Daily Review, Hayward, CA

Auyer, Jerry (541) 473-3377
ED, Malheur Enterprise, Vale, OR

Auyer, ZaDean (541) 473-3377
PUB, Malheur Enterprise, Vale, OR

Avalon, Janna (601) 969-1880
ED, Mississippi Today, Jackson, MS

Avalos, Carol (281) 422-8302
PROD FRM-COMP, Sun, Baytown, TX

Avalos, Joe (719) 846-3311
CIRC DIR, Chronicle-News, Trinidad, CO

Avelleyra, Lisa (608) 221-1544
ED, Community Herald, Monona, WI

Avendano, Manuel (212) 807-4600
MAN ED, El Diario La Prensa, New York, NY

Avent, Jan (423) 523-3131
Books ED
Knoxville News-Sentinel, Knoxville, TN

Avera-Roth, Susan (409) 265-7411
Health/Medical ED, Travel ED
Brazosport Facts, Clute, TX

Averett, Karla (541) 575-0710
GM, Blue Mountain Eagle, John Day, OR

Averill, David (918) 581-8300
EDL Writer, Tulsa World, Tulsa, OK

Averill, Ellen (918) 581-8300
RE ED, Tulsa World, Tulsa, OK

Avery, Carol Ann (210) 625-9144
CIRC DIR, PROD FRM-COMP, New Braunfels Herald-Zeitung, New Braunfels, TX

Avery, Ivan (419) 352-4611
CIRC DIR
Sentinel-Tribune, Bowling Green, OH

Avery, Jim (907) 786-4187
Self-Syndicator
Advertising Workshop, Anchorage, AK

Avery, Judy (919) 638-8101
ADV DIR, DIR-MKTG, PROD MGR-Graphics
Sun-Journal, New Bern, NC

Avery, Paul (908) 362-6161
ED, Blairstown Press, Blairstown, NJ

Avery, Rick (303) 892-5000
ADV DIR-RT
Rocky Mountain News, Denver, CO

Avery, Robert (713) 477-0221
Sports ED, Pasadena Citizen, Pasadena, TX

Avery, Steve (706) 778-2400
ED, Northeast Georgian, Cornelia, GA

Avey, George (860) 423-8466
PROD MGR, Chronicle, Willimantic, CT

Avey, Jim (816) 726-3997
ED, Albany Ledger, Albany, MO

Avila, Ingrid (408) 424-2221
DP MGR, Californian, Salinas, CA

Avins, Mimi (213) 237-5000
Fashion ED
Los Angeles Times, Los Angeles, CA

Avis, Gloria J (705) 856-2267
ED, Algoma News Review, Wawa, ON

Avis, W R (705) 856-2267
PUB, Algoma News Review, Wawa, ON

Avitable, Karen (860) 621-6751
ED, Observer, Southington, CT

Avok, Mike (402) 564-2741
News ED, Telegram, Columbus, NE

Awad, Joe (812) 537-0063
ED
Dearborn County Register, Lawrenceburg, IN

Axelson, Kitty (413) 781-1900
ED, Springfield Advocate, Springfield, MA

Axford, Bob (807) 727-2618
PUB, ED, District News, Red Lake, ON

Axline, Connie (419) 468-1117
ADV Administrator, Inquirer, Galion, OH

Axtman, Genny (916) 926-5214
PUB
Mount Shasta Herald, Mount Shasta, CA

Axvig, Keith O (218) 843-2868
PUB, Kittson County Enterprise, Hallock, MN

Ayala, Elaine (210) 225-7411
Lifestyle ED
San Antonio Express-News, San Antonio, TX

Ayala, Pam (909) 684-1200
ADV MGR-CLASS AUTO
Press-Enterprise, Riverside, CA

Ayala, Ruth (210) 565-2425
GM, Mercedes Enterprise, Mercedes, TX

Ayars, Paul (217) 732-2101
Church ED, Courier, Lincoln, IL

Aycock, James E (704) 669-8727
PUB, ED
Black Mountain News, Black Mountain, NC

Aycock, Jarvis (919) 243-5151
PROD FRM-PR
Wilson Daily Times, Wilson, NC

Aydelotte, Rod (817) 757-5757
Chief Photographer
Waco Tribune-Herald, Waco, TX

Aydlette, Larry (561) 820-4100
Music ED-Rock
Palm Beach Post, West Palm Beach, FL

Ayer, Richard (508) 532-5880
PUB, Peabody & Lynnfield Weekly News, Peabody, MA

Ayers, H Brandt (205) 236-1551
PUB/ED
Consolidated Publishing Co., Anniston, AL

Ayers, J Min (352) 463-7135
PUB, ED
Gilchrist County Journal, Trenton, FL

Ayers, Jere C (706) 783-2553
PUB, ED, Comer News, Comer, GA

Ayers, Teresa (423) 581-5630
Automotive ED, BUS ED, City ED, Travel ED
Citizen Tribune, Morristown, TN

Ayers, Terri L (800) 223-2154
ADV VP-West Coast
Investor's Business Daily, Los Angeles, CA

Aylesworth, J H (519) 876-2809
PUB, ED
Watford Guide-Advocate, Watford, ON

Aylmer, Kevin (330) 424-9541
PRES, Morning Journal, Lisbon, OH

Aylward, Terry (918) 825-3292
ED, Pryor Publishing Co., Pryor, OK

Aylworth, Roger (916) 533-3131
ED, Oroville Mercury Register, Oroville, CA

Ayotte, Chris (716) 247-9200
GM, Gates-Chili News, Rochester, NY

Ayre, Miller H (709) 364-6300
PUB/GEN MGR
Evening Telegram, St. John's, NF

Ayres, Linda (806) 546-2320
PUB/ED, Gaines County News, Seagraves, TX

Ayvazian, William (212) 210-2100
ASST BUS ED
New York Daily News, New York, NY

Azar, Lee Dickson (804) 446-2750
GM, Flagship, Norfolk, VA

Azeredo, Louis (617) 929-2000
PROD ASST MGR-Plants
Boston Globe, Boston, MA

Azuaje, Luis (202) 898-8254
Regional ED-Latin America
United Press International, Washington, DC

Azzara, Mike (203) 574-3636
Automotive ED, Waterbury Republican-American, Waterbury, CT

Azzato, Barbara (814) 371-4200
Lifestyle ED, Women's ED, Courier-Express/Tri-County Sunday, Du Bois, PA

Azzopardi, Susan Kellas (519) 756-2020
MGR-MKTG & PROM, CIRC MGR
Expositor, Brantford, ON

B

Baakko, Lori (906) 482-1500
ADV MGR-NTL, Daily Mining Gazette, Houghton, MI

Baar, Haward (804) 649-6000
ADV MGR-Creative SRV
Richmond Times-Dispatch, Richmond, VA

Baaron, Richard R (405) 332-4433
Photo ED, Ada Evening News, Ada, OK

Babad, Michael (416) 585-5000
NTL ED, Globe and Mail, Toronto, ON

Babb, Andrew M (803) 583-2907
VP, Mid-South Management Co. Inc., Spartanburg, SC

Babb, Jim (805) 781-7800
PROD FRM-PR
Telegram-Tribune, San Luis Obispo, CA

Babb, Larry (512) 445-3500
ADV MGR-Creative Services
Austin American-Statesman, Austin, TX

Babb, William (706) 724-0851
Outdoors ED
Augusta Chronicle, Augusta, GA

Babcock, Barbara (316) 442-4200
CIRC MGR
Arkansas City Traveler, Arkansas City, KS

Babcock, Ed (402) 444-1000
PROD DIR, Omaha World-Herald, Omaha, NE

Copyright ©1997 by the Editor & Publisher Co.

11-Who's Where **Bak**

Babcock, Huguette .... (613) 342-4441
Librarian, Brockville Recorder and Times, Brockville, ON

Babcock Jr, John .... (213) 525-2000
PRES/CEO
Hollywood Reporter, Los Angeles, CA

Babcock, Nick .... (509) 663-5161
Sports ED, Wenatchee World, Wenatchee, WA

Babcock, Robert .... (508) 744-0600
ADV MGR, Salem Evening News, Beverly, MA

Babczak, John .... (815) 673-3771
CIRC MGR, Streator Times-Press, Streator, IL

Baber, Fred .... (606) 744-3123
PROD SUPT-Plant
Winchester Sun, Winchester, KY

Babick, Donald .... (416) 445-6641
PRES/COO, Southam Inc., Don Mills, ON

Babigan, S John .... (213) 628-4384
GM, Metropolitan News-Enterprise, Los Angeles, CA

Babigan, Vahn .... (213) 628-4384
ASST MGR, Metropolitan News-Enterprise, Los Angeles, CA

Babin, Norris .... (504) 392-1619
PUB, Placquemines Gazette
Belle Chasse, LA

Babin, Rex .... (518) 454-5694
EDL Cartoonist, Times Union, Albany, NY

Bablak, Jane .... (330) 264-1125
Agriculture ED, BUS ED
Daily Record, Wooster, OH

Babler, Jason .... (414) 235-7700
Graphics Artist
Oshkosh Northwestern, Oshkosh, WI

Baca, Nancy .... (505) 823-7777
Fashion/Style ED, Food/Garden ED
Albuquerque Journal, Albuquerque, NM

Bacall, Cortland B .... (617) 245-0080
TREAS
Wakefield Daily Item, Wakefield, MA

Bacallao, Josie .... (305) 350-2111
VP-MKTG Services, DIR-MKTG/PROM
Miami Herald, Miami, FL

Bach, Jean .... (606) 283-6270
MAN ED, Messenger, Erlanger, KY

Bacha, Diane .... (414) 224-2000
Senior ED-Entertainment
Milwaukee Journal Sentinel, Milwaukee, WI

Bachar, Ray .... (815) 937-3300
News ED, Daily Journal, Kankakee, IL

Bachelder, Maryemma .... (941) 687-7000
Radio/Television ED, Religion ED
Ledger, Lakeland, FL

Bachellor, John .... (540) 949-8213
Farm ED, Police Beat ED
News Virginian, Waynesboro, VA

Bachetti, Bruce .... (707) 441-0500
PROD FRM-COMP
Times-Standard, Eureka, CA

Bachev, Yavor .... (408) 659-1845
Self-Syndicator/Owner
Cannery Row Creations, Carmel Valley, CA

Bachman, Bart .... (603) 356-3456
City ED, Conway Daily Sun, North Conway, NH

Bachman, Mary .... (517) 851-7833
GM, Town Crier, Stockbridge, MI

Bachman, Sarah .... (408) 920-5000
EDL Writer
San Jose Mercury News, San Jose, CA

Bachmeier, Bev .... (701) 662-2127
PROD SUPT
Devils Lake Daily Journal, Devils Lake, ND

Bachtell, James A .... (515) 432-1234
MAN ED, Boone News-Republican, Boone, IA

Backe, John D .... (757) 787-1200
PUB, Eastern Shore News, Onley, VA

Backer, Cathy .... (847) 486-9200
ED, Glenview Announcements, Glenview, IL

Backman, Dave .... (414) 657-1000
Building ED, BUS ED, Kenosha News, Kenosha, WI

Backman, Henry R .... (906) 224-9561
PUB, ED, Wakefield News, Wakefield, MI

Backstrom, Terry .... (218) 262-1011
ADV DIR, Daily Tribune, Hibbing, MN

Backus, Mark H .... (315) 963-7813
PUB, Independent Mirror, Mexico, NY

Backus Sr, Marty .... (606) 432-0148
PUB, Appalachian News-Express
Pikeville, KY

Backus Jr, Marty .... (501) 637-4161
PUB, ED, Waldron News, Waldron, AR

Bacon, Jack .... (303) 750-7555
ED, Aurora Sentinel, Aurora, OH

Bacon, Rick .... (704) 765-2071
PUB, Mitchell News-Journal
Spruce Pine, NC

Bacque, Peter .... (804) 649-6000
Aviation ED
Richmond Times-Dispatch, Richmond, VA

Baden, James .... (320) 676-3123
ED, Mille Lacs Messenger, Isle, MN

Baden, Thomas .... (717) 255-8100
MAN ED, Patriot-News, Harrisburg, PA

Bader, Andy .... (519) 348-8431
ED, Mitchell Advocate, Mitchell, ON

Bader, Laura .... (908) 722-8800
ADV MGR-Display
Courier-News, Bridgewater, NJ

Bader, Tim .... (614) 461-5000
PROD MGR-Quality Assurance
Columbus Dispatch, Columbus, OH

Badger, Gordon .... (705) 322-1871
PUB, Creemore Star, Creemore, ON

Badgley, Jim .... (613) 735-3141
PUB, Pembroke Daily News, Pembroke, ON

Badoud, John J .... (810) 733-2239
PUB, GM, Suburban News, Flint, MI

Baer, Ed .... (404) 526-5151
DIR-Computer SRV, Computer SRV DIR
Atlanta Journal-Constitution, Atlanta, GA

Baer, John .... (215) 854-2000
Harrisburg BU, Daily News, Philadelphia, PA

Baer, Rena .... (864) 582-4511
BUS ED, Herald-Journal, Spartanburg, SC

Baer, Sam .... (606) 672-3399
ED, Leslie County News, Hyden, KY

Baert, Bruce .... (562) 698-0955
Librarian, Whittier Daily News, Whittier, CA

Baeza, P A .... (713) 232-3737
Sports ED, Herald-Coaster, Rosenberg, TX

Baggerly, Beth .... (502) 821-6833
ADV DIR, Messenger, Madisonville, KY

Baggett, Debbie .... (916) 741-2345
ADV MGR-NTL, Appeal-Democrat
Marysville, CA

Baggett, Donnis .... (409) 776-4444
PUB/ED, Eagle, Bryan, TX

Baggett, Joe .... (770) 428-9411
ED, Douglas Neighbor, Marietta, GA

Baggs, Norman .... (770) 963-9205
ED, Gwinnett Daily Post, Lawrenceville, GA

Bagley, Catherine .... (907) 747-3219
ADV MGR, Daily Sitka Sentinel, Sitka, AK

Bagley, Mark .... (202) 347-2770
Contact, US Newswire, Washington, DC

Bagley, Pat .... (801) 237-2031
Cartoonist
Salt Lake Tribune, Salt Lake City, UT

Bagnaturo, Vincent .... (201) 309-1200
MGR/Media Sales
ESPN/SportsTicker, Jersey City, NJ

Bagwell, Jo .... (806) 376-4488
MGR-MKTG/PROM, Amarillo Daily News/Globe Times, Amarillo, TX

Bagwell, Joe .... (864) 582-4511
DIR-MIS, Herald-Journal, Spartanburg, SC

Bagwell, Keith .... (520) 573-4220
Environmental ED
Arizona Daily Star, Tucson, AZ

Bagwell, Steven K .... (541) 382-1811
MAN ED, Bulletin, Bend, OR

Bahash, Robert J .... (212) 208-8000
EX VP/CFO, Corporation Records, Daily News, New York, NY

Baier, Miriam .... (937) 592-3060
Librarian, Radio/Television ED, EDU ED
Bellefontaine Examiner, Bellefontaine, OH

Bahr, Tricia Brennan .... (518) 454-5694
MGR-New Venture/Media
Times Union, Albany, NY

Baier, Rick A .... (815) 457-2245
PUB, ED
Cissna Park News, Cissna Park, IL

Bailey, Andrew .... (519) 583-0112
ED, Port Dover Maple Leaf, Port Dover, ON

Bailey, Andrew C .... (407) 656-2121
PUB, West Orange Times, Winter Garden, FL

Bailey, Betty .... (712) 275-4229
PUB, ED, Schaller Herald, Schaller, IA

Bailey, Carolyn .... (415) 327-6397
ADV MGR-MET
Palo Alto Daily News, Palo Alto, CA

Bailey, Chris .... (847) 888-7800
EDL Writer, Courier-News, Elgin, IL

Bailey, David .... (501) 378-3400
City ED
Arkansas Democrat-Gazette, Little Rock, AR

Bailey, David M .... (405) 728-8000
VP, F.A.C.—P.A.C. Inc., Oklahoma City, OK

Bailey, Debbie .... (903) 396-2261
ED, Richland Chambers Progress, Kerens, TX

Bailey, Don .... (919) 708-9000
DP MGR, PROD SUPT/MGR, PROD FRM-Camera, Sanford Herald, Sanford, NC

Bailey, Don .... (912) 236-9511
ADV DIR
Savannah Morning News, Savannah, GA

Bailey, George .... (205) 345-0505
DIR-PROD Technology
Tuscaloosa News, Tuscaloosa, AL

Bailey, Howard .... (601) 627-2201
Sports ED, Press Register, Clarksdale, MS

Bailey, J June .... (405) 728-8000
SEC/TREAS
F.A.C.—P.A.C. Inc., Oklahoma City, OK

Bailey, Jim .... (317) 622-1212
COL, Herald Bulletin, Anderson, IN

Bailey, John .... (503) 221-8327
PROD ASST MGR-Ad SRV
Oregonian, Portland, OR

Bailey, Kathleen Feindt .... (904) 249-9033
ED
Beaches Leader, Jacksonville Beach, FL

Bailey, Kathy .... (608) 251-5627
GM, Isthmus, Madison, WI

Bailey, Marilyn .... (206) 455-2222
Entertainment ED, Features ED, Travel ED
Eastside Journal, Bellevue, WA

Bailey, Mark .... (804) 385-5400
Graphics/Art DIR
News & Advance, Lynchburg, VA

Bailey, Mike .... (309) 686-3000
ASSOC ED, Journal Star, Peoria, IL
Copley Press Inc.

Bailey, Mike .... (406) 657-1200
PROD MGR-Distribution
Billings Gazette, Billings, MT

Bailey, Mitch .... (815) 634-2102
GM, Coal City Courant, Coal City, IL

Bailey, Patrica .... (508) 222-7000
ADV ASST MGR-CLASS
Sun Chronicle, Attleboro, MA

Bailey, R Mike .... (360) 694-3391
Travel ED, Columbian, Vancouver, WA

Bailey, Robert M .... (208) 543-4335
PUB, Buhl Herald, Buhl, ID

Bailey, Roger .... (701) 477-6495
PUB, ED, Turtle Mountain Star, Rolla, ND

Bailey, Roger .... (513) 294-2662
GM, Oakwood Register, Dayton, OH

Bailey, Roxanne .... (419) 245-6000
ADV ASST MGR-CLASS, Blade, Toledo, OH

Bailey, Sandra S .... (770) 532-1234
PUB, Times, Gainesville, GA

Bailey, Sheridan R .... (815) 634-2102
PUB, ED, Coal City Courant, Coal City, IL

Bailey, Tammy .... (770) 428-9411
Accounting MGR
Marietta Daily Journal, Marietta, GA

Bailey, Tom .... (205) 325-2222
ADTX MGR
Birmingham Post-Herald, Birmingham, AL

Bailey Sr, Wayne .... (207) 791-6650
PROD OPER Ad Build SUPV-Days
Portland Press Herald, Portland, ME

Bailey, William .... (601) 429-6397
PUB, ED, DeSoto Times, Hernando, MS

Bailey, William F .... (904) 312-5200
CIRC DIR, Daily News, Palatka, FL

Baillargeon, Martha .... (413) 562-4181
ADV DIR, Evening News, Westfield, MA

Baillaut, Jacques .... (604) 730-9575
PUB, Le Soleil de Colombie, Vancouver, BC

Baillie, Peter .... (250) 380-5211
PUB, Times Colonist, Victoria, BC

Bailon, Gilbert .... (214) 977-8222
Deputy MAN ED-Hard News
Dallas Morning News, Dallas, TX

Baily, Peg .... (614) 373-2121
ADV Team Leader-West Virginia
Marietta Times, Marietta, OH

Baim, Tracy .... (773) 871-7610
PUB, ED, Outlines, Chicago, IL

Bain, Cheryl .... (702) 358-8061
PROD FRM-Press/Camera
Daily Sparks Tribune, Sparks, NV

Bain, Grisson .... (910) 323-4848
PROD ASST MGR
Fayetteville Observer-Times, Fayetteville, NC

Bain, Ian .... (416) 367-2000
ADV MGR-Travel, Toronto Star, Toronto, ON

Bain, Jeffrey W .... (406) 755-7000
MGR-EDU SRV, CIRC DIR
Daily Inter Lake, Kalispell, MT

Bain, Joyce .... (617) 444-1706
ED, Natick Bulletin, Needham, MA

Bain, Michael .... (414) 657-1000
PROD MGR-SYS, Kenosha News, Kenosha, WI

Bainbridge, Jean (Mitzi) .... (914) 454-2000
DIR-SYS, Poughkeepsie Journal, Poughkeepsie, NY

Bainbridge, Leesa .... (313) 222-6400
Deputy City ED, Detroit Free Press
Detroit, MI

Baine, Wallace .... (408) 423-4242
Entertainment ED, Films/Theater ED
Santa Cruz County Sentinel, Santa Cruz, CA

Baines, Donnie .... (757) 446-2000
PROD MGR-Press OPER
Virginian-Pilot, Norfolk, VA

Baines, Tom .... (919) 752-6166
Community News ED
Daily Reflector, Greenville, NC

Bains, Pauline .... (360) 577-2500
EDU ED, Daily News, Longview, WA

Bair, John .... (915) 653-1221
ADV DIR, Standard-Times, San Angelo, TX

Bair, Scott .... (412) 654-6651
PROD MGR-Press
New Castle News, New Castle, PA

Baird, Bruce .... (707) 226-3711
Features ED, Health ED, Living/Lifestyle ED, Women's ED, Napa Valley Register, Napa, CA

Baird, Dorothy .... (305) 350-2111
PROD ASST MGR-COMP
Miami Herald, Miami, FL

Baird, Ian M .... (709) 634-4348
PUB, Western Star, Corner Brook, NF

Baird, Moira .... (709) 364-6300
ASSOC ED/EPE
Evening Telegram, St. John's, NF

Baird, Myrna .... (505) 894-3088
PUB, Sierra County Sentinel, Truth or Consequences, NM

Baird, Nancy .... (901) 427-3333
ADV MGR-CLASS, Jackson Sun, Jackson, TN

Baird, Pam .... (813) 893-8111
ADV MGR-Co-op
St. Petersburg Times, St. Petersburg, FL

Baird, R .... (604) 562-2441
PROD FRM-PR
Prince George Citizen, Prince George, BC

Bairstow, Paul .... (704) 692-0505
PUB, Times-News, Hendersonville, NC

Bajares, Fernando .... (202) 745-7692
BU Chief, Agencia Efe/Efe News Services, Washington, DC

Bajic, G .... (905) 549-4079
ED, Kanadski Srbobran, Hamilton, ON

Bajraktari, Harry .... (718) 220-2000
PUB, Illyria, Bronx, NY

Bakan, George .... (206) 324-4297
PUB, Seattle Gay News, Seattle, WA

Bakarich, Michele .... (212) 416-2000
PROD MGR (Charlotte NC)
Wall Street Journal, New York, NY

Baker, A Charles .... (619) 337-3400
SEC, ADV MGR-CLASS
Imperial Valley Press, El Centro, CA

Baker, Alan L .... (207) 667-2576
PUB, Ellsworth American, Ellsworth, ME

Baker III, Alton F .... (541) 485-1234
PRES, PUB, ED, Register-Guard, Eugene, OR

Baker, Barbara L .... (330) 833-2631
ADV SUPV-TELEMKTG
Independent, Massillon, OH

Baker, Ben .... (912) 567-3655
PUB, ED, Wiregrass Farmer, Ashburn, GA

Baker, Betsy .... (315) 265-2068
MAN ED
North Country This Week, Potsdam, NY

Baker, Betty Jo .... (504) 383-1111
MGR-Human Resources
Advocate, Baton Rouge, LA

Baker, Bridget D .... (541) 485-1234
SEC, Register-Guard, Eugene, OR

Baker, Bruce .... (419) 422-5151
ADTX MGR, Courier, Findlay, OH

Baker, Carl .... (909) 793-3221
MAN ED
Redlands Daily Facts, Redlands, CA

Baker, Carolyn .... (417) 358-2191
BM, Carthage Press, Carthage, MO

Baker, Charles W .... (410) 848-4400
SEC, ADV DIR
Carroll County Times, Westminster, MD

Baker, Chris .... (505) 864-4472
PUB
Valencia County News-Bulletin, Belen, NM

Baker, Chris .... (604) 732-2222
PROD VP, Province, Vancouver, BC
Southam Inc.

Baker, Connie .... (619) 373-4812
ED, Mojave Desert News, California City, CA

Baker, Craig .... (815) 223-3200
MGR-CR, News-Tribune, La Salle, IL

Baker, Daleen .... (916) 527-2151
BM, Daily News, Red Bluff, CA

Baker, Dardre Cox .... (319) 355-2644
MAN ED, Bettendorf News, Bettendorf, IA

Baker, Dave .... (502) 227-4556
Automotive ED, State Journal, Frankfort, KY

Baker, David .... (541) 485-1234
ASST MAN ED-News
Register-Guard, Eugene, OR

Baker, Deb .... (704) 252-5611
CNR-Database SYS
Asheville Citizen-Times, Asheville, NC

Baker, Diane P .... (212) 556-1234
Sr VP/CFO
New York Times Co., New York, NY

Baker, Don .... (513) 422-3611
BUS ED, Journal, Middletown, OH

Baker, Edwin M .... (541) 485-1234
COB, Register-Guard, Eugene, OR

Baker, Francis .... (613) 732-3691
City ED, Observer, Pembroke, ON

Baker, Graham .... (512) 237-4655
ED, Smithville Times, Smithville, TX

Bak Who's Where-12

Baker, Helen .... (307) 682-9306
CIRC MGR, News-Record, Gillette, WY
Baker, James E .... (207) 828-8100
VP-FIN/CFO
Guy Gannett Communications, Portland, ME
Baker, Janet Campbell .... (317) 633-1240
MGR-MKTG
Indianapolis Star/News, Indianapolis, IN
Baker, Jennie .... (914) 454-2000
ADV MGR-RT
Poughkeepsie Journal, Poughkeepsie, NY
Baker, Jim .... (617) 426-3000
Sports COL, Boston Herald, Boston, MA
Baker, Joe .... (618) 483-6176
PUB, ED, Altamont News, Altamont, IL
Baker, Karen .... (208) 377-6200
MAN ED, Idaho Statesman, Boise, ID
Baker, Karen .... (612) 375-9222
ED, Skyway News and Freeway News, Minneapolis, MN
Baker, Kenneth .... (415) 777-1111
Arts ED
San Francisco Chronicle, San Francisco, CA
Baker, Leroy .... (937) 498-2111
PROD FRM-PR
Sidney Daily News, Sidney, OH
Baker, Mark .... (715) 723-5515
PUB, Music Critic
Chippewa Herald, Chippewa Falls, WI
Baker, Marv .... (701) 256-5311
PUB, ED
Cavalier County Republican, Langdon, ND
Baker, Melony .... (812) 231-4200
CONT, Tribune-Star, Terre Haute, IN
Baker, Mike .... (415) 495-4200
PROD MGR, Daily Pacific Builder, San Francisco, CA, McGraw-Hill
Baker, Paul .... (717) 272-5611
City ED, Government ED, News ED
Daily News, Lebanon, PA
Baker, Peter .... (616) 222-5400
DIR-OPER
Grand Rapids Press, Grand Rapids, MI
Baker, Reba .... (606) 672-3399
PUB, Thousandsticks News, Hyden, KY
Baker, Rebecca .... (330) 841-1600
EDU Reporter
Tribune Chronicle, Warren, OH
Baker, Renee .... (608) 348-3006
GM, Platteville Journal, Platteville, WI
Baker Jr, Richard A .... (541) 485-1234
ASST SEC, DP MGR
Register-Guard, Eugene, OR
Baker, Robert .... (304) 348-5140
COL, Charleston Gazette, Sunday Gazette-Mail, Charleston, WV
Baker, Robert .... (717) 265-2151
Sports ED, Daily Review, Towanda, PA
Baker, Rod .... (817) 594-7447
ADV MGR
Weatherford Democrat, Weatherford, TX
Baker, Sarah .... (910) 373-7000
BM, News & Record, Greensboro, NC
Baker, Steven .... (701) 857-1900
ADV DIR, Minot Daily News, Minot, ND
Baker, Terrie .... (217) 935-3171
PUB, PA, ADV DIR
Clinton Daily Journal, Clinton, IL
Baker, Tom .... (817) 665-5511
PROD SUPT-PR
Gainesville Daily Register, Gainesville, TX
Baker, Vernon .... (606) 672-3399
PUB, Leslie County News, Hyden, KY
Baker, William K .... (317) 664-5111
PROD DIR, Chronicle-Tribune, Marion, IN
Baker-Nantz, Jamie .... (606) 824-3343
ED, Grant County Express, Williamstown, KY
Bakke, Dave .... (217) 698-8500
ED, Catholic Times, Springfield, IL
Bakke, Elaine .... (509) 493-2112
PUB, Enterprise, White Salmon, WA
Bakke, Sam E .... (915) 682-5311
ADV DIR-Sales & MKTG, DIR-MKTG
Midland Reporter-Telegram, Midland, TX
Bakken, Peggy .... (612) 425-3323
MAN ED
Osseo-Maple Grove Press, Osseo, MN
Bakken, Ryan .... (701) 780-1100
EX Sports ED
Grand Forks Herald, Grand Forks, ND
Bako, Carl .... (330) 753-1068
MAN ED, Barberton Herald, Barberton, OH
Bakotich, Sam .... (360) 736-3311
Sports ED, Chronicle, Centralia, WA
Bakoyannis, George .... (514) 978-9999
GM, Nouvelles Chomedey News, Laval, QC
Bakst, M Charles .... (401) 277-7000
Political/Government COL
Providence Journal-Bulletin, Providence, RI

Balabon, Michael J .... (908) 349-3000
BM, DP MGR
Ocean County Observer, Toms River, NJ
Balandran, Tony .... (970) 352-0211
ASST City ED, Greeley Tribune, Greeley, CO
Balcar, Dan .... (409) 776-4444
ASST MAN ED, Eagle, Bryan, TX
Balch, John L .... (501) 285-2723
ED
Murfreesboro Diamond, Murfreesboro, AR
Balch, Melvin R .... (334) 433-1551
PROD DIR, Press Register, Mobile, AL
Balcom, David .... (507) 451-2840
VP, Owatonna People's Press, Owatonna, MN
Huckle Publishing Inc.
Balcomb, Terrie F .... (405) 735-2526
ED, Harper County Journal, Buffalo, OK
Baldacci, Leslie .... (312) 321-3000
ASST MAN ED-Sunday
Chicago Sun-Times, Chicago, IL
Baldt, David .... (215) 854-2000
COL, Philadelphia Inquirer, Philadelphia, PA
Balducci, Rachel .... (706) 724-0851
MGR-NIE, Augusta Chronicle, Augusta, GA
Baldus, Chris .... (612) 439-3130
News ED, Sports ED
Stillwater Evening Gazette, Stillwater, MN
Baldus, Sue .... (310) 230-3400
DIR-Sales & MKTG, Allsport Photography USA, Pacific Palisades, CA
Baldwin, Bill .... (972) 424-6565
PROD DIR, Plano Star Courier, Plano, TX
Baldwin, Bill .... (501) 442-1777
PROD FRM-PR, Northwest Arkansas Times, Fayetteville, AR
Baldwin, Bill .... (212) 686-6850
ASSOC ED
Black Press Service Inc. (BPS), New York, NY
Baldwin, Chad .... (307) 856-2244
ED, Desk/Wire ED, EDU ED, Fashion/Food ED
Riverton Ranger, Riverton, WY
Baldwin, Edward A .... (314) 938-4486
PUB
Creative Syndication Services, Eureka, MO
Baldwin, Frank .... (330) 332-4601
CIRC DIR, Salem News, Salem, OH
Baldwin, Jason .... (816) 747-3135
ED, Standard-Herald, Warrensburg, MO
Baldwin, Kate .... (907) 257-4200
PROD ASST DIR
Anchorage Daily News, Anchorage, AK
Baldwin, Mary .... (717) 836-2123
ED, New Age-Examiner, Tunkhannock, PA
Baldwin, Matt .... (303) 892-5000
DIR-RES, Rocky Mountain News, Denver, CO
Baldwin, Rachel .... (505) 546-2611
ADV Representative
Deming Headlight, Deming, NM
Baldwin, Ralph C .... (423) 745-5664
PUB/GM, Daily Post-Athenian, Athens, TN
Baldwin, Steve .... (803) 524-3183
PROD MGR, Beaufort Gazette, Beaufort, SC
Baldwin, William B .... (609) 396-2200
CORP CONT
Journal Register Co., Trenton, NJ
Bale, Les .... (613) 829-9100
ADV MGR-Local Sales
Ottawa Citizen, Ottawa, ON
Balek, Terry .... (515) 421-0500
DP MGR, Globe-Gazette, Mason City, IA
Bales, Mike .... (407) 420-5000
Online MGR, Orlando Sentinel, Orlando, FL
Bales, Richard .... (317) 633-1240
PROD OPER SUPT-PR (Day)
Indianapolis Star/News, Indianapolis, IN
Bales, Steve .... (512) 552-9788
PUB, ED
Calhoun County Wave Extra, Port Lavaca, TX
Bales, V J .... (307) 742-2176
Living/Lifestyle ED, Women's ED
Laramie Daily Boomerang, Laramie, WY
Balfe, Bob .... (561) 820-4100
PROD MGR
Palm Beach Post, West Palm Beach, FL
Baliff, Amanda .... (801) 674-6200
Features ED, Films/Theater ED, Living/Lifestyle ED, Spectrum, St. George, UT
Balisciano, Robert .... (203) 789-5200
CIRC MGR-Home Delivery
New Haven Register, New Haven, CT
Balkenbush, Cheri .... (307) 672-2431
ADV MGR-Local/NTL, Sheridan Press Sheridan, WY
Ball, Carol L .... (937) 548-3330
PUB, GM, Early Bird, Greenville, OH
Ball, Diana .... (816) 647-2121
MAN ED, Windsor Review, Windsor, MO
Ball, Donald .... (573) 642-7272
GM, Fulton Sun, Fulton, MO
Ball, Ellen .... (317) 747-5700
Fashion/Society ED, Garden ED, Home Furnishings ED, Star Press, Muncie, IN
Ball, Helen E .... (403) 664-3622
ED, Oyen Echo, Oyen, AB

Ball, Kevin .... (815) 459-4040
Sports ED, Northwest Herald, Crystal Lake, IL
Ball, Lee .... (318) 365-6773
Photo ED, Daily Iberian, New Iberia, LA
Ball, Millie .... (504) 826-3279
Travel ED, Times-Picayune, New Orleans, LA
Ball, Reggie .... (907) 257-4200
PROD MGR-Machine Maintenance
Anchorage Daily News, Anchorage, AK
Ball, Richard L .... (706) 935-2621
ED, Catoosa County News, Ringgold, GA
Ball, Steve .... (334) 262-1611
Environmental ED, Political/Government ED
Montgomery Advertiser, Montgomery, AL
Ball, Steven .... (415) 252-0500
MAN ED, Daily Journal, San Francisco, CA
Ball, Vince .... (519) 756-2020
EDU, Expositor, Brantford, ON
Ballanfant, Kathleen .... (713) 668-9293
PUB, GM, ED
Southwest News/Village News, Bellaire, TX
Ballantine, Morley C .... (970) 247-3504
BC, ED, Durango Herald, Durango, CO
Ballantine, Richard G .... (970) 247-3504
PUB, Durango Herald, Durango, CO
Ballantyne, Beth .... (864) 488-1016
GM, Cherokee Chronicle, Gaffney, SC
Ballard, Dorothy .... (812) 936-9630
PUB, Springs Valley Herald, French Lick, IN
Ballard, Gloria .... (615) 259-8000
Weekend ED-Features
Tennessean, Nashville, TN
Ballard, Larry .... (319) 291-1400
Teen-Age/Youth ED
Waterloo Courier, Waterloo, IA
Ballard, Lea .... (304) 645-1206
PROD MGR-Press
West Virginia Daily News, Lewisburg, WV
Ballard, Perry .... (334) 749-6271
COL, Sports ED
Opelika-Auburn News, Opelika, AL
Ballard, Peter .... (604) 738-1411
PUB, Vancouver Courier, Vancouver, BC
Ballard, Tim .... (502) 348-9003
ED, Kentucky Standard, Bardstown, KY
Ballenger, Jerry .... (810) 469-4510
ADV DIR-MKTG, Macomb Daily, Mount Clemens, MI, Independent Newspapers (MI)
Ballenger, Jerry .... (810) 731-1000
GM, Source, Utica, MI
Ballentine, Wallace .... (501) 623-7711
GM, Sentinel-Record, Hot Springs, AR
Ballestrini, Janet M .... (860) 442-2200
CIRC ASST MGR, Day, New London, CT
Ballew, Coco .... (915) 546-6100
Religion ED, El Paso Times, El Paso, TX
Ballew, Dan .... (405) 924-4388
PROD SUPT-Press
Durant Daily Democrat, Durant, OK
Ballhagen, Lloyd .... (316) 694-5830
COB, Harris Enterprises Inc., Hutchinson, KS
Balli, Celia .... (405) 363-3370
PROD FRM-COMP
Blackwell Journal-Tribune, Blackwell, OK
Ballou, Cathy .... (804) 732-3456
Books/School ED, Wire ED
Progress-Index, Petersburg, VA
Ballou, Rich .... (208) 232-4161
ADV MGR-CLASS
Idaho State Journal, Pocatello, ID
Balls, Sheryl .... (208) 547-3260
MAN ED
Caribou County Sun, Soda Springs, ID
Ballschmiede, Richard .... (847) 888-7800
ADV DIR-Sales, Courier-News, Elgin, IL
Balmaseda, Liz .... (305) 350-2111
COL, Miami Herald, Miami, FL
Balme, Robert .... (704) 894-3220
ED
Polk County News Journal, Columbus, NC
Balow, Jim .... (304) 348-5140
BUS/FIN ED, RE ED, Charleston Gazette, Sunday Gazette-Mail, Charleston, WV
Baltake, Joe .... (916) 321-1000
Films Critic, Sacramento Bee, Sacramento, CA
Balter, Joni .... (206) 464-2111
EDU Writer, Seattle Times, Seattle, WA
Baltrusaitis, Irene .... (816) 254-8600
ADV DIR, Examiner, Independence, MO
Morris Communications Corp.
Balusik, Chris .... (517) 265-5111
BUS/FIN ED, Daily Telegram, Adrian, MI
Balzano, Mark R .... (518) 725-8616
CIRC DIR/PROM MGR
Leader-Herald, Gloversville, NY
Balzer, Robert .... (818) 962-8811
VP MKTG, San Gabriel Valley Tribune, West Covina, CA, MediaNews Inc.
Bambauer, Rick .... (602) 271-8000
PROD CNR-SYS
Phoenix Newspapers Inc., Phoenix, AZ
Bamford, John .... (207) 729-3311
ADV DIR, Times Record, Brunswick, ME

Bammel, Jerome G .... (908) 722-8800
DIR-FIN, Courier-News, Bridgewater, NJ
Ban Alstyn, Mark .... (605) 394-8300
DP MGR, Rapid City Journal, Rapid City, SD
Banaszek, Jane .... (314) 831-4645
MAN ED, Independent News, Florissant, MO
Banaszynski, Jacqui .... (503) 221-8327
Senior ED-Enterprise
Oregonian, Portland, OR
Banbury, Jim .... (704) 358-5000
MGR-PROM
Charlotte Observer, Charlotte, NC
Banderob, Rollin .... (916) 243-2424
DIR-Photography
Record Searchlight, Redding, CA
Bandler, Kenneth .... (212) 643-1890
MAN ED, Jewish Telegraphic Agency, NY, NY
Bandy, Steven .... (318) 334-3186
GM, ED, Rayne-Acadian Tribune, Rayne, LA
Bangert, Dave .... (317) 423-5511
Enterprise ED, Food ED
Journal and Courier, Lafayette, IN
Bangert, Randall .... (970) 352-0211
City ED, Greeley Tribune, Greeley, CO
Bangs, Rich .... (303) 688-3128
ED, Elbert County News, Kiowa, CO
Banguis, Chris .... (317) 636-0200
ED
Court & Commercial Record, Indianapolis, IN
Banich, James .... (312) 644-7800
TREAS, Daily Law Bulletin, Chicago, IL
Banks, Adelle .... (202) 463-8777
NTL Correspondent
Religion News Service, Washington, DC
Banks, Barbara .... (716) 897-0442
PUB, ED, Buffalo Challenger, Buffalo, NY
Banks, Betty C .... (205) 372-2232
PUB, Greene County Independent, Eutaw, AL
Banks, James C .... (919) 708-9000
VP, ADV DIR, Sanford Herald, Sanford, NC
Banks, Joe .... (613) 525-2020
PUB, Glengarry News, Alexandria, ON
Banks, Ken .... (515) 898-7554
PUB, Seymour Herald, Seymour, IA
Banks, Lacy .... (312) 321-3000
Bulls/NBA Writer, Sun-Times, Chicago, IL
Banks, Liz .... (617) 444-1706
MAN ED, Needham Times, Needham, MA
Banks, Michael .... (502) 389-1833
ED, Union County Advocate, Morganfield, KY
Banks, Nancy .... (510) 540-7400
PUB, East Bay Express, Berkeley, CA
Bankston, Norman .... (912) 226-2400
ADV MGR, Thomasville Times-Enterprise, Thomasville, GA
Banman, Jim .... (303) 820-1010
VP-Human Resources
Denver Post, Denver, CO
Banning, Barbara .... (217) 895-2234
GM, Neoga News, Neoga, IL
Bannister, Barbara .... (906) 228-2500
News ED, Mining Journal, Marquette, MI
Bannister, Denise H .... (703) 284-6000
Group PRES-Gulf Coast Newspaper Group
Gannett Co. Inc., Arlington, VA
Bannon, Brian .... (519) 255-5711
COL-Wine, Windsor Star, Windsor, ON
Bannon, Dean .... (317) 622-1212
DIR-FIN, Herald Bulletin, Anderson, IN
Bannon, James .... (317) 622-1212
COL, EPE, Herald Bulletin, Anderson, IN
Banqerter, Lara .... (801) 373-5050
Wire ED, Daily Herald, Provo, UT
Banse, Tim .... (319) 398-8211
Automotive COL
Gazette, Cedar Rapids, IA
Banser, Robert .... (765) 768-6022
ED, Dunkirk News and Sun, Dunkirk, IN
Banville, Janet .... (508) 343-6911
ADV DIR-Sales/MKTG
Sentinel & Enterprise, Fitchburg, MA
Bany, Michael L .... (757) 247-4600
CIRC MGR-Production
Daily Press, Newport News, VA
Baottey, Sam .... (540) 935-2123
GM, Virginia Mountaineer, Grundy, VA
Baptista, Nicholas .... (702) 831-4666
GM, North Lake Tahoe Bonanza, Incline Village, NV
Baquet, Dean .... (212) 556-1234
NTL ED, New York Times, New York, NY
Barac, LaVonne .... (612) 448-2650
ED, Chaska Herald, Chaska, MN
Barada, Minoru .... (206) 623-0100
GM, Hokubei Hochi, Seattle, WA
Barajas, Ted .... (818) 962-8811
DIR-Human Resources, San Gabriel Valley Tribune, West Covina, CA, MediaNews Inc.
Barak, Jeff .... (212) 599-3666
MAN ED, Jerusalem Post International Edition, New York, NY
Barakat, Matthew .... (301) 662-1177
Health/Medical ED, SCI/Technology ED
Frederick Post/The News, Frederick, MD

Copyright ©1997 by the Editor & Publisher Co.

13-Who's Where **Bar**

Barancotta, Philip .... (716) 439-9222
CIRC MGR
Union-Sun & Journal, Lockport, NY

Baranczyk, Mary Kay .... (719) 539-6691
SEC/TREAS, Mountain Mail, Salida, CO

Baranczyk, Merle .... (719) 539-6691
PUB, ED, Mountain Mail, Salida, CO

Baranowski, Wayne .... (815) 937-3300
Photo ED, Picture ED
Daily Journal, Kankakee, IL

Barash, Andrea .... (914) 694-9300
DIR-MKTG Communications, Reporter Dispatch, White Plains, NY, Gannett Co. Inc.

Barash, Andrew .... (914) 358-2200
DIR-MKTG Communications
Rockland Journal-News, West Nyack, NY

Barbaro, Nick .... (512) 454-5766
PUB, Austin Chronicle, Austin, TX

Barbee, Chris F .... (409) 543-3363
MAN ED, Leader-News, El Campo, TX

Barbee Jr, Fred V .... (409) 543-3363
PUB, El Campo Leader-News, El Campo, TX

Barbee, Phil .... (573) 815-1500
PROD FRM-MR
Columbia Daily Tribune, Columbia, MO

Barber, Beth .... (216) 999-4500
ASSOC ED, Plain Dealer, Cleveland, OH

Barber, Beth .... (213) 237-5485
DIR-Acct. Relations & Article Sales, Los Angeles Times Syndicate, Los Angeles, CA

Barber, Cathy .... (214) 977-8222
Food ED, Dallas Morning News, Dallas, TX

Barber, Cindy .... (216) 321-2300
ED, Cleveland Free Times, Cleveland, OH

Barber, Dave .... (212) 715-2100
VP/Newspaper Relations
USA Weekend, New York, NY

Barber, Dean .... (205) 325-2222
BUS ED, BUS/FIN ED, RE ED
Birmingham News, Birmingham, AL

Barber, Donna .... (405) 286-3321
CIRC MGR
McCurtain Daily Gazette, Idabel, OK

Barber, Doug .... (308) 728-3262
ED, Ord Quiz, Ord, NE

Barber, Ed .... (904) 454-1297
PUB, High Springs Herald, High Springs, FL

Barber, Jeffrey A .... (315) 470-0011
CIRC DIR, Post-Standard/Syracuse Herald-Journal/ American, Syracuse, NY

Barber, Julie .... (401) 821-7400
DP MGR
Kent County Daily Times, West Warwick, RI

Barber, Mary .... (608) 754-3311
Entertainment/YouthPage ED
Janesville Gazette, Janesville, WI

Barber, Murri .... (212) 666-2300
Reporter, Basch, Buddy Feature Syndicate, New York, NY

Barber, Phil .... (702) 788-6200
Police ED, Reno Gazette-Journal, Reno, NV

Barbero, Rick .... (304) 255-4400
Photo ED, Register Herald, Beckley, WV

Barbieri, Barbara .... (219) 824-0224
Society ED, News-Banner, Bluffton, IN

Barbieri, James C .... (219) 824-0224
PRES/TREAS, PUB/GM, PA, ED
News-Banner, Bluffton, IN

Barbieri, Tony .... (410) 332-6000
ASST MAN ED-News, Sun, Baltimore, MD

Barbosa Jr, Nicholas .... (212) 416-2000
PROD MGR-OPER
Wall Street Journal, New York, NY

Barcikowski, Tom .... (614) 773-2111
PROD DIR
Chillicothe Gazette, Chillicothe, OH

Barclay, Becky .... (919) 778-2211
Food/Home Furnishings ED, Society/Women's ED, Goldsboro News-Argus, Goldsboro, NC

Barclay, James L .... (801) 625-4200
ADV MGR-Major/NTL
Standard-Examiner, Ogden, UT

Barden, Gregory R .... (860) 347-3331
GM, Middletown Press, Middletown, CT

Bardon, Tammy .... (205) 695-7029
MAN ED, Lamar Democrat, Vernon, AL

Bardwell, Jim .... (972) 636-4351
PUB, Big Sandy & Hawkins Journal and Tri-Area News, Big Sandy, TX

Bare, Leslie .... (208) 785-1100
ADV DIR, PROD MGR
Morning News, Blackfoot, ID

Barebo, Mark .... (316) 268-6000
ADV MGR-Display
Wichita Eagle, Wichita, KS

Barefield, Nicole .... (904) 747-5000
DIR-MKTG/PROM
News Herald, Panama City, FL

Barefoot, Jo .... (212) 210-2100
Picture Assignment ED
New York Daily News, New York, NY

Barfield, W Toland .... (919) 419-6500
VP/SEC, DIR-Sales/MKTG
Herald-Sun, Durham, NC

Bargas, Robert .... (817) 634-2125
PROD FRM-Press/Stereo
Killeen Daily Herald, Killeen, TX

Barger, Dan .... (314) 426-2222
ED, North County Journal West, Woodson Terrace, MO

Barger, Paul .... (520) 524-6203
PUB, ED
Holbrook Tribune-News, Holbrook, AZ

Barham, Marv .... (509) 663-5161
Regional ED
Wenatchee World, Wenatchee, WA

Barhorst, Kenneth .... (937) 498-2111
Sports ED, Sidney Daily News, Sidney, OH

Baril, Larry .... (207) 784-5411
ADV MGR-RT Sales
Sun-Journal, Lewiston, ME

Bark, Ed .... (214) 977-8222
Radio/Television ED
Dallas Morning News, Dallas, TX

Bark, Kathleen Dombhart .... (901) 523-1561
MAN ED, Daily News, Memphis, TN

Barker, Brian .... (614) 387-0400
CIRC DIR, Marion Star, Marion, OH

Barker, Bruce .... (616) 222-5400
Newspaper in Classroom ED
Grand Rapids Press, Grand Rapids, MI

Barker, Carol .... (803) 245-5204
GM, MAN ED
Advertizer-Herald, Bamberg, SC

Barker, Chris .... (770) 942-6571
Tri-County News ED
Douglas County Sentinel, Douglasville, GA

Barker, David L .... (513) 721-2700
PROD MGR-Quality/Night CNR
Cincinnati Enquirer, Cincinnati, OH

Barker, Doug .... (360) 532-4000
Radio/Television ED
Daily World, Aberdeen, WA

Barker, JoAnn .... (405) 256-2200
CIRC DIR, Woodward News, Woodward, OK

Barker, M Dale .... (210) 374-3465
PUB, ED
Zavala County Sentinel, Crystal City, TX

Barker, Marilyn .... (616) 723-3592
ADV MGR
Manistee News-Advocate, Manistee, MI

Barker, Marlys .... (515) 382-2161
ED, Nevada Journal, Nevada, IA

Barker, Nina .... (316) 456-2232
ED
South Haven New Era, Conway Spring, KS

Barker, Onyx .... (301) 662-1177
PROD MGR-PR (Day & Night)
Frederick Post/The News, Frederick, MD

Barker, Paul .... (614) 446-2342
CIRC MGR, Gallipolis Daily Tribune/Sunday Times-Sentinel, Gallipolis, OH
Gannett Co. Inc.

Barker, Rene .... (417) 532-9131
ADV MGR-Display
Lebanon Daily Record, Lebanon, MO

Barker, Richard A .... (518) 843-1100
PUB/CORP SEC, Recorder, Amsterdam, NY

Barker, Rocky .... (208) 377-6200
Environmental ED
Idaho Statesman, Boise, ID

Barker, Wayne .... (210) 225-7411
PROD SUPT-Engraving
San Antonio Express-News, San Antonio, TX

Barker, William .... (804) 649-6000
PROD DIR
Richmond Times-Dispatch, Richmond, VA

Barkin, Dan .... (919) 829-4500
BUS ED, News & Observer, Raleigh, NC

Barkley, Ben .... (318) 239-3444
Sports ED
Leesville Daily Leader, Leesville, LA

Barkley, Tom .... (510) 465-3121
ED, Inter-City Express, Oakland, CA

Barkovich, Joe .... (905) 732-2411
City ED, Tribune, Welland, ON

Barksdale, Martha .... (404) 363-8484
ED, South Fulton Neighbor, Forest Park, GA

Barkus, Sherry .... (916) 678-5594
ED, Dixon Tribune, Dixon, CA

Barlow, Doyle .... (918) 456-8833
Sports ED
Tahlequah Daily Press, Tahlequah, OK

Barlow, Jim .... (713) 220-7171
COL-BUS, Houston Chronicle, Houston, TX

Barlow, John .... (610) 272-2500
PROD DIR, Times Herald, Norristown, PA

Barlow, John .... (803) 317-6397
PROD DIR
Florence Morning News, Florence, SC

Barlow, John R .... (208) 667-3431
SEC, Hagadone Corp., Coeur d'Alene, ID

Barlow, Keith .... (912) 452-0567
PROD DIR-Creative/Technical SRV
Union-Recorder, Milledgeville, GA

Barlow, Michael .... (203) 964-2200
BUS ED, EX News ED, Stamford Advocate, Stamford, CT, Times Mirror Co.

Barlow, Rhonda .... (320) 255-8700
ADV DIR, St. Cloud Times, St. Cloud, MN

Barlow, Steve .... (406) 628-4412
ED, Laurel Outlook, Laurel, MT

Barmettler, Beth .... (804) 358-0825
ED, Style Weekly, Richmond, VA

Barna, John .... (609) 451-1000
MAN ED, EPE, Features ED, Films/Theater ED, Bridgeton Evening News, Bridgeton, NJ

Barnacle, Bob .... (218) 246-8533
PUB, ED
Western Itasca Review, Deer River, MN

Barnard, Ken .... (416) 585-5000
CONT, Globe and Mail, Toronto, ON

Barnard, Royal W .... (802) 422-2399
PUB, ED, Mountain Times, Killington, VT

Barnard, Veronica .... (802) 422-2399
GM, Mountain Times, Killington, VT

Barnard, William C .... (216) 999-4500
DIR-Public Affairs
Plain Dealer, Cleveland, OH

Barnekov, Kent .... (202) 334-6000
PROD SUPT-PR (VA)
Washington Post, Washington, DC

Barnes, Andrew .... (813) 893-8111
PRES/CEO/ED
St. Petersburg Times, St. Petersburg, FL

Barnes, Becky .... (606) 234-1035
ED, Cynthiana Democrat, Cynthiana, KY

Barnes, Betty .... (704) 249-3981
ADV DIR, Dispatch, Lexington, NC

Barnes, Beverly .... (208) 377-6200
CIRC MGR-Transportation
Idaho Statesman, Boise, ID

Barnes, Bob .... (518) 891-2600
CIRC DIR, Adirondack Daily Enterprise, Saranac Lake, NY

Barnes, Brian .... (317) 552-3355
ASST PUB, Elwood Call-Leader, Elwood, IN
Ray Barnes Newspapers Inc.

Barnes, Carol .... (904) 623-3616
GM, Santa Rosa Press Gazette, Milton, FL

Barnes, Charles G .... (419) 674-4066
PRES, Kenton Times, Kenton, OH
Ray Barnes Newspapers Inc.

Barnes, Clive .... (212) 930-8000
Drama/Dance ED
New York Post, New York, NY

Barnes, Cynthia .... (408) 920-5000
ADV MGR-RT/Major Accounts
San Jose Mercury News, San Jose, CA

Barnes, David H .... (909) 685-6191
PUB, ED
Riverside County Record, Riverside, CA

Barnes, Denise Rolark .... (202) 561-4100
ED, Washington Informer, Washington, DC

Barnes, Donnamaria .... (212) 779-6300
PROD ED, Gamma-Liaison Inc., New York, NY

Barnes, Greg .... (910) 323-4848
State ED, Observer-Times, Fayetteville, NC

Barnes, Greg .... (816) 665-2808
CIRC MGR, Kirksville Daily Express & News, Kirksville, MO

Barnes, Harper .... (314) 340-8000
Film ED
St. Louis Post-Dispatch, St. Louis, MO

Barnes, Jack L .... (317) 552-3355
COB, Ray Barnes Newspapers Inc., Elwood, IN

Barnes Jr, James T .... (208) 467-9251
PUB/PRES, Idaho Press-Tribune, Nampa, ID

Barnes, Jeff .... (419) 674-4066
PUB, GM/PA, Kenton Times, Kenton, OH

Barnes, Jim .... (915) 646-2541
MGR-BUS
Brownwood Bulletin, Brownwood, TX

Barnes, Judith K .... (317) 552-3355
SEC, Elwood Call-Leader, Elwood, IN
Ray Barnes Newspapers Inc.

Barnes, Larry .... (502) 769-2312
ED, Inside the Turrett, Elizabethtown, KY

Barnes, Marti .... (903) 757-3311
ADV MGR-RT
Longview News-Journal, Longview, TX

Barnes, Nancy .... (919) 829-4500
Deputy MET ED-Durham
News & Observer, Raleigh, NC

Barnes, Pete .... (903) 757-3311
PROD ASST DIR
Longview News-Journal, Longview, TX

Barnes, Richard .... (213) 237-5000
RE ED, Los Angeles Times, Los Angeles, CA

Barnes, Ruth Ann .... (317) 664-5111
CIRC Office MGR
Chronicle-Tribune, Marion, IN

Barnes, Thomas A .... (210) 772-3672
PUB, ED, Medina Valley Times, Lytle, TX

Barnet, Bruce .... (213) 857-6600
CEO, Daily Variety, Los Angeles, CA

Barnett, Betty .... (513) 721-2700
Readers Representative
Cincinnati Enquirer, Cincinnati, OH

Barnett, Catherine .... (707) 546-2020
City ED, EDU ED
Press Democrat, Santa Rosa, CA

Barnett, Galen .... (503) 221-8327
Team Leader-Presentation
Oregonian, Portland, OR

Barnett, Joclyn .... (219) 223-2111
ADV MGR-CLASS
Rochester Sentinel, Rochester, IN

Barnett, Kim .... (217) 578-3213
ED, Atwood Herald, Atwood, IL

Barnett, Linda .... (417) 836-1100
MGR-BUS SYS
Springfield News-Leader, Springfield, MO

Barnett, Lisa .... (212) 930-8000
DIR-PROM, New York Post, New York, NY

Barnett, Lorraine .... (814) 773-3161
ADV MGR, Ridgway Record, Ridgway, PA

Barnett, Ned .... (919) 829-4500
MET ED, News & Observer, Raleigh, NC

Barnett, Ronny .... (501) 633-3130
CIRC DIR, Times-Herald, Forrest City, AR

Barnett, Simon P .... (310) 230-3400
Senior MAN ED, Allsport Photography USA, Pacific Palisades, CA

Barnett, Terry .... (405) 789-1962
GM, Tribune, Bethany, OK

Barnett, Thomas .... (937) 667-2214
ED, Tipp City Herald, Tipp City, OH

Barnett, Wanda .... (314) 340-8000
Senior MGR-Data Communications
St. Louis Post-Dispatch, St. Louis, MO

Barney, Diane .... (707) 448-6401
MAN ED, Reporter, Vacaville, CA

Barney, Jerry .... (218) 583-2935
ED, Henning Advocate, Henning, MN

Barnhardt, Kathi .... (604) 426-5201
ADV DIR, Daily Townsman, Cranbrook, BC

Barnhardt, M .... (604) 426-5201
PROD MGR, Daily Townsman, Cranbrook, BC

Barnhart, Marlo .... (301) 733-5131
Religion ED
Morning Herald, Hagerstown, MD

Barnhart, Ted .... (614) 439-3531
City ED, Daily Jeffersonian, Cambridge, OH

Barnhill, Carol .... (616) 842-6400
CIRC MGR
Grand Haven Tribune, Grand Haven, MI

Barnhill, Joe .... (904) 435-8500
PROD MGR-MR
Pensacola News Journal, Pensacola, FL

Barnhill, Josh .... (360) 384-1411
ED, Record-Journal, Ferndale, WA

Barnhill, Mark .... (818) 713-3000
ASST MAN ED, Online MGR
Daily News, Woodland Hills, CA

Barnick, Florence R .... (540) 374-5000
DIR-Human Resources
Free Lance-Star, Fredericksburg, VA

Barnum, Beverly .... (512) 884-2011
DIR-MKTG/PROM, Corpus Christi Caller-Times, Corpus Christi, TX

Baron, Eric E .... (207) 990-8000
PROD FRM-MR
Bangor Daily News, Bangor, ME

Baron, Jed .... (212) 223-1821
Contact, Entertainment News Syndicate, New York, NY

Baron, Linda .... (508) 685-1000
Librarian, Eagle-Tribune, North Andover, MA

Barone, Paul .... (609) 663-6000
News ED, Courier-Post, Cherry Hill, NJ

Barr, Andrew .... (218) 583-2935
PUB, Henning Advocate, Henning, MN

Barr, Brian .... (209) 835-3030
EDU ED, Tracy Press, Tracy, CA

Barr, Debra .... (218) 583-2935
PUB, Henning Advocate, Henning, MN

Barr, Diana .... (217) 347-7151
CIRC MGR, Daily News, Effingham, IL

Barr, J Peter .... (705) 382-3843
PUB, Burks Falls/Powassan/Almaguin News, Burks Falls, ON

Barr, Jeff .... (618) 529-5454
ADV MGR
Southern Illinoisan, Carbondale, IL

Barr, Jim .... (717) 326-1551
Environmental ED
Williamsport Sun-Gazette, Williamsport, PA

Barr, Marie .... (403) 653-2222
PUB, ED, Cardston Chronicle, Cardston, AB

Barr, Thomas .... (502) 543-2288
PUB, ED, Pioneer News, Shepherdsville, KY

Barr, Vernon .... (360) 855-1641
PUB, Courier Times, Sedro-Woolley, WA

Barra, Mark .... (309) 467-3314
PUB, Woodford County Journal, Eureka, IL

Barrasso, Jean .... (860) 241-6200
MGR-Strategic Planning/ADM & Advertising OPER, Hartford Courant, Hartford, CT

Barrelet, Denise .... (514) 248-3353
ED, Journal des Rivieres, Bedford, QC

Copyright ©1997 by the Editor & Publisher Co.

Bar Who's Where-14

Barresi, Peter (315) 792-5000
CIRC MGR, Observer-Dispatch, Utica, NY
Barrett, Beth (818) 713-3000
Government/Politics ED
Daily News, Woodland Hills, CA
Barrett, David S (860) 241-6200
ED/VP, Hartford Courant, Hartford, CT
Barrett, Donna (812) 283-6636
ADV MGR, Evening News, Jeffersonville, IN
Barrett, Ed (617) 426-3000
Art/Graphics ED, Boston Herald, Boston, MA
Barrett, Leila (912) 924-2751
Society/Women's ED
Americus Times-Recorder, Americus, GA
Barrett, Mary (540) 885-7281
ADV Support SUPV
Daily News Leader, Staunton, VA
Barrett, Paul (601) 428-0551
PUB, Laurel Leader-Call, Laurel, MS
Barrett, Vicki (601) 896-2100
ADV MGR-RT, Sun Herald, Biloxi, MS
Barrett, William (617) 444-1706
PUB, Needham Times, Needham, MA
Barretta, Karen (860) 537-2341
ED, Regional Standard, Colchester, CT
Barrette, John (402) 475-4200
Police Reporter, Journal Star, Lincoln, NE
Barrick, Fran (519) 894-2231
Police, Record, Kitchener, ON
Barrick, Rhonda (803) 775-6331
Amusements ED, EDU ED, Fashion/Society ED, Food ED, Item, Sumter, SC
Barron, Cate (717) 255-8100
Features ED, Patriot-News, Harrisburg, PA
Barron, Darcey (817) 387-3811
DIR-MKTG/PROM
Denton Record-Chronicle, Denton, TX
Barron, John (312) 321-3000
Manufacturing/Telecommunications, Media/Advertising/Entertainment/Sports BUS
Chicago Sun-Times, Chicago, IL
Barron, Matt (413) 562-4181
BUS ED
Westfield Evening News, Westfield, MA
Barron, Robert (215) 854-2000
VP-Production
Philadelphia Inquirer, Philadelphia, PA
Barron-Fury, Linda (915) 337-4661
CIRC MGR-Single Copy/NIE
Odessa American, Odessa, TX
Barrow, Clyde B (716) 849-3434
CIRC ASST DIR, Buffalo News, Buffalo, NY
Barrows, Frank (704) 358-5000
MAN ED, Charlotte Observer, Charlotte, NC
Barrows, John M (406) 683-2331
PUB, ED
Dillon Tribune Examiner, Dillon, MT
Barrows, R Nathaniel W (207) 367-2200
PUB, ED
Island Ad-Vantages, Stonington, ME
Barrs, Denise (307) 334-2867
GM, Lusk Herald, Lusk, WY
Barrs, Rick (310) 477-0403
ED, Los Angeles New Times, Los Angeles, CA
Barry, Elizabeth T (319) 398-8211
SEC, Gazette, Cedar Rapids, IA
Barry, Jay (906) 265-9927
GM, Reporter, Iron River, MI
Barry, Joseph (201) 798-7800
PUB, North Bergen/North Hudson Reporter, Hoboken, NJ
Barry, Kevin J (210) 829-9000
VP, Harte-Hanks Communications Inc., San Antonio, TX
Barry, Nancy (214) 977-8222
VP-Community SRV
Dallas Morning News, Dallas, TX
Barry III, Richard F (757) 446-2000
VBC, Virginian-Pilot, Norfolk, VA
Barry, Sue (909) 684-1200
ADV MGR-CLASS
Press-Enterprise, Riverside, CA
Barry, William (401) 277-7000
ADV Sales DIR-Professional Services
Providence Journal-Bulletin, Providence, RI
Barry, William H (818) 551-0077
MAN ED
Adventure Feature Syndicate, Glendale, CA
Barry, William M (305) 294-6641
PUB, Key West Citizen, Key West, FL
Barseghien, Tina (415) 692-9406
ED
Millbrae/San Bruno Sun, Burlingame, CA
Barsony, Louis (908) 722-3000
PUB, Hills-Bedminster Press, Somerville, NJ
Bart, John (413) 788-1000
MET ED, Union-News, Springfield, MA
Bart, Peter (213) 857-6600
EIC/VP, Daily Variety, Los Angeles, CA
Barta, Linda (509) 663-5161
Librarian, Radio/Television ED
Wenatchee World, Wenatchee, WA
Bartee, Dean R (408) 920-5000
Senior VP-Sales & MKTG
San Jose Mercury News, San Jose, CA
Bartel, Roger (414) 542-2501
MAN ED, EPE
Waukesha County Freeman, Waukesha, WI
Bartel, Tom (612) 375-1015
PUB, City Pages, Minneapolis, MN
Bartell, Jack (204) 697-7000
PROD FRM-MR
Winnipeg Free Press, Winnipeg, MB
Bartelli, Michael (607) 936-4651
ADV DIR, Leader, Corning, NY
Bartels, Barbara (207) 729-3311
Amusements ED, Arts/Entertainment ED, Fashion/Style ED, Features ED, Travel ED
Times Record, Brunswick, ME
Bartels, Patricia A (219) 357-4123
ED, Garrett Clipper, Garrett, IN
Bartels, R Wayne (219) 357-4123
PUB, Garrett Clipper, Garrett, IN
Barter, Mae (204) 857-3427
DP MGR
Daily Graphic, Portage la Prairie, MB
Barth, Bill (608) 365-8811
ED, Beloit Daily News, Beloit, WI
Barth, Bob (541) 382-1811
CIRC DIR, Bulletin, Bend, OR
Barth, David (419) 734-3141
GM, ADV DIR, News-Herald, Port Clinton, OH
Barth, Erv (701) 225-8111
ADV MGR, Dickinson Press, Dickinson, ND
Barth, Janis (315) 470-0011
City ED, Post-Standard/Syracuse Herald-Journal/American, Syracuse, NY
Barth, Mary Ann (419) 542-7764
PUB, ED, News Tribune, Hicksville, OH
Barth, Michael G (419) 542-7764
PUB, ED, News Tribune, Hicksville, OH
Barthel, Bill (502) 827-2000
DP MGR, Gleaner, Henderson, KY
Barthel, Patrick (330) 454-5611
ADV MGR-NTL/Co-op
Repository, Canton, OH
Barthel, William J (502) 827-2000
CONT, Gleaner, Henderson, KY
Barthet, Ron (504) 892-2323
ED, St. Tammany Farmer, Covington, LA
Bartholomay, Lucy (617) 929-2000
ASST MAN ED-Design
Boston Globe, Boston, MA
Bartholomew, David (901) 885-0744
EPE
Union City Daily Messenger, Union City, TN
Bartholomew, Edward (802) 863-3441
CONT, PA
Burlington Free Press, Burlington, VT
Bartholomew, Glenda M (308) 423-2337
PUB, Benkelman Post and News-Chronicle, Benkelman, NE
Bartholomew, Joanne (619) 241-7744
Community ED, Daily Press, Victorville, CA
Bartizek, Ronald A (717) 587-1148
PUB, ED
Abington Journal, Clarks Summit, PA
Bartkowski, Anna (615) 259-8000
ADV MGR-CLASS, Tennessean, Nashville, TN
Bartle, Patty Wood (701) 493-2261
PUB, ED, Edgeley Mail, Edgeley, ND
Bartleman, Bill (502) 443-1771
Political/Government ED
Paducah Sun, Paducah, KY
Bartles, DeWayne (309) 263-2211
ED, Tazewell News/Tazewell News Extra, Morton, IL
Bartlett, C R (317) 832-2443
ADV MGR, Daily Clintonian, Clinton, IN
Bartlett, David W (315) 369-3747
PUB, Adirondack Echo, Old Forge, NY
Bartlett, Gary (403) 468-0100
Photo DEPT MGR
Edmonton Sun, Edmonton, AB
Bartlett, Jeane (806) 376-4488
PSL DIR, Amarillo Daily News/Globe Times, Amarillo, TX
Bartlett, Robert J (520) 573-4220
Outdoors ED, Sports ED
Arizona Daily Star, Tucson, AZ
Bartlett, Tom (901) 529-2211
DP MGR, Commercial Appeal, Memphis, TN
Bartley, Cari Dawson (702) 635-2230
PUB
Battle Mountain Bugle, Battle Mountain, NV
Bartley, Charity (812) 254-0480
Food/Society ED
Washington Times-Herald, Washington, IN
Bartley, Randon W (814) 849-5339
ED, Jeffersonian Democrat, Brookville, PA
Bartley, Robert (702) 635-2230
PUB, ED
Battle Mountain Bugle, Battle Mountain, NV
Bartley, Robert L (212) 416-2600
VP/ED-WSJ
Dow Jones & Co. Inc., New York, NY
Bartlick, Walt (816) 826-1000
DP MGR, Sedalia Democrat, Sedalia, MO
Bartlow, Dennis (217) 446-1000
Farm ED, Commercial News, Danville, IL
Bartman, Thurman R (610) 371-5000
ADV MGR-NTL/Co-op
Reading Times/Eagle, Reading, PA
Bartner, Martin (201) 877-4141
PUB, Star-Ledger, Newark, NJ
Bartoldson, Carl A (716) 366-3000
ADV DIR, Evening Observer, Dunkirk, NY
Barton, Bob (512) 268-7862
PUB, ED, Hays County Free Press, Buda, TX
Barton, Brett (916) 321-1000
BUS Applications Administrator
Sacramento Bee, Sacramento, CA
Barton, Bruce (415) 948-9000
ED, Los Altos Town Crier, Los Altos, CA
Barton, Doug (970) 949-0555
PROD FRM-Press, Vail Daily News, Vail, CO
Swift Newspapers
Barton, Joanne (409) 347-2322
PUB, ED, Garrison In The News, Garrison, TX
Barton, John (937) 773-2721
Sports ED, Piqua Daily Call, Piqua, OH
Barton Jr, John S (919) 829-4500
SEC/CONT, News & Observer, Raleigh, NC
Barton, Len (705) 753-2930
PUB, Tribune, Sturgeon Falls, ON
Barton Jr, Richard L (409) 968-3155
PUB, ED
Fayette County Record, La Grange, TX
Barton, Robert E (318) 747-7900
PUB
Bossier Press Tribune, Bossier City, LA
Barton, Tom (912) 236-9511
EPE, Savannah Morning News, Savannah, GA
Barton, Trish (970) 949-0555
CIRC MGR, Vail Daily News, Vail, CO
Swift Newspapers
Bartosek, John (561) 820-4100
ASST MAN ED
Palm Beach Post, West Palm Beach, FL
Bartow, Martin J (516) 843-2020
PROD DIR-Packaging
Newsday, Melville, NY
Bartscher, Larry (402) 371-1020
ADV DIR, Norfolk Daily News, Norfolk, NE
Bartsky, James (518) 828-1616
PROD MGR-SYS, Register-Star, Hudson, NY
Barwick, Bruce (410) 332-6000
VP/BM, Sun, Baltimore, MD
Basan, David (219) 474-5532
ED, Newton County Enterprise, Kentland, IN
Basbanes, Constance V (508) 839-4404
PRES, Literary Features Syndicate, North Grafton, MA
Basbanes, Nicholas A (508) 839-4404
MAN ED/Principal COL, Literary Features Syndicate, North Grafton, MA
Basch, Buddy (212) 666-2300
PUB, Basch, Buddy Feature Syndicate, New York, NY
Base, Buster (913) 823-6363
PROD FRM-PR, Salina Journal, Salina, KS
Bash, Steve (614) 345-4053
ADV MGR-RT, Advocate, Newark, OH
Basham, Barbara (609) 871-8000
ADV MGR-RT
Burlington County Times, Willingboro, NJ
Basham, Melvin J (814) 676-7444
CIRC MGR, Derrick, Oil City, PA
Basic, Carl (330) 747-1471
Regional ED-Trumbull Edition
Vindicator, Youngstown, OH
Basile, Colleen (609) 272-7000
ADV MGR-Ad Processing
Press of Atlantic City, Pleasantville, NJ
Basile, John (609) 989-7800
PROD FRM-MR, Trentonian, Trenton, NJ
Basile, Paul (630) 782-4440
ED, Fra Noi, Elmhurst, IL
Baskin, Mike (941) 953-7755
ADV MGR-RT
Sarasota Herald-Tribune, Sarasota, FL
Basler, Bob (202) 898-8300
News ED, Reuters, Washington, DC
Basler, George (607) 798-1234
EDU ED
Press & Sun Bulletin, Binghamton, NY
Bason, Darl (814) 445-9621
DP MGR, Daily American, Somerset, PA
Bass, Elissa (860) 442-2200
City ED-Night, Day, New London, CT
Bass, Inga (601) 693-1551
PROD FRM-COMP
Meridian Star, Meridian, MS
Bass, J Andy (803) 329-4000
ADV MGR-CLASS, Herald, Rock Hill, SC
Bass, James (910) 739-4322
EDU ED, Robesonian, Lumberton, NC
Bass, Lisa (713) 477-0221
MAN ED, Pasadena Citizen, Pasadena, TX
Bass, Mike (201) 646-4000
SWAT/General Assignment ED
Record, Hackensack, NJ
Bassel, Wilma Jo (405) 633-2376
PUB, ED, Eldorado Courier, El Dorado, OK
Bassett, Mike (715) 588-9272
ED, Lac du Flambeau News, Lac du Flambeau, WI
Bassin, Arthur (518) 792-9914
PRES/CEO, TV Data, Queensbury, NY
Bast, Phil (519) 894-2231
Entertainment ED, Music ED
Record, Kitchener, ON
Bastel, Joan (215) 345-3000
MAN ED
Intelligencer/Record, Doylestown, PA
Bastien, Francis (502) 678-5171
Society ED, Daily Times, Glasgow, KY
Basy, Rehka (515) 284-8000
Local COL
Des Moines Register, Des Moines, IA
Batcha, Becky (215) 854-2000
Food ED, Fresh Ink ED
Philadelphia Daily News, Philadelphia, PA
Batchelder, Margaret (719) 655-2620
MAN ED, Saguache Crescent, Saguache, CO
Batdorff, John (Jack) A (616) 796-4831
PRES/CEO, Pioneer Group, Big Rapids, MI
Batdorff II, John (616) 796-4831
GM, Pioneer Group, Big Rapids, MI
Bateman, Dennis R (712) 374-2251
ED, Sidney Argus-Herald, Sidney, IA
Bateman, G Earl (905) 372-0131
CEO, Cobourg Daily Star, Cobourg, ON
Bateman, Scott (937) 225-2000
Online MGR, ADTX MGR
Dayton Daily News, Dayton, OH
Bateman, Thomas R (908) 793-0147
GM
Ocean County Review, Seaside Heights, NJ
Bateman, Tom (972) 436-5551
MAN ED, Lewisville News, Lewisville, TX
Bates, Carl (205) 325-2222
ADV MGR-CLASS
Birmingham News, Birmingham, AL
Bates, David (819) 684-4755
GM, Aylmer Bulletin D'Alymer, Aylmer, QC
Bates, Donna (516) 843-2020
EDL SYS Group MGR, Newsday, Melville, NY
Bates, Doug (541) 382-1811
EPE, Bulletin, Bend, OR
Bates, James (213) 237-5000
Entertainment Reporter-Film
Los Angeles Times, Los Angeles, CA
Bates, Jim (303) 820-1010
EX News ED, Denver Post, Denver, CO
Bates, Karen (614) 373-2121
Community ED, Marietta Times, Marietta, OH
Bates, Karl Leif (313) 222-2300
SCI/Technology ED, Detroit News, Detroit, MI
Bates, Ralph (407) 242-3500
EDL Writer, Florida Today, Melbourne, FL
Bath, Tim (317) 459-3121
Photo ED, Kokomo Tribune, Kokomo, IN
Bathke, Joe (913) 776-2200
News ED
Manhattan Mercury, Manhattan, KS
Bathke, Nylin (314) 340-8000
PA, St. Louis Post-Dispatch, St. Louis, MO
Batie, Steve (402) 475-4200
Special Sections ED
Lincoln Journal Star, Lincoln, NE
Batson, Beth (864) 298-4100
ADV MGR-RT
Greenville News, Greenville, SC
Batson, Edwin (213) 237-5000
ADV DIR-MKTG RES
Los Angeles Times, Los Angeles, CA
Battagello, Dave (519) 255-5711
EDU ED, Windsor Star, Windsor, ON
Battagler, Randall E (816) 781-1044
PUB, Northland News, Liberty, MO
Battaglia, Joe (212) 208-8369
ED, Standard & Poor's Dividend Record, New York, NY
Battaglia, Pat (716) 285-6105
PRES, International Puzzle Features, Niagara Falls, NY
Battaglia, Tony (814) 837-6000
Sports ED, Kane Republican, Kane, PA
Batteast, Bill (219) 235-6161
CIRC MGR-Home Delivery
South Bend Tribune, South Bend, IN
Batten, Brent (941) 262-3161
City ED, Health/Medical ED
Naples Daily News, Naples, FL
Batten, Frank (757) 446-2010
COB
Landmark Communications Inc., Norfolk, VA
Batten Jr, Frank (757) 446-2010
EVP
Landmark Communications Inc., Norfolk, VA

Copyright ©1997 by the Editor & Publisher Co.

15-Who's Where **Bea**

Battersby, Mark E .... (215) 747-6684
ED
Cricket Communications Inc., Ardmore, PA

Batterson, Mark .... (860) 347-3331
BUS ED, Middletown Press, Middletown, CT

Battilana, Dan .... (209) 369-2761
ADV MGR, Lodi News-Sentinel, Lodi, CA

Battin, Al .... (319) 398-8211
CIRC MGR-City, Gazette, Cedar Rapids, IA

Battin, Richard .... (219) 461-8222
MAN ED, News-Sentinel, Fort Wayne, IN

Battin, Sandy .... (505) 864-4472
ED
Valencia County News-Bulletin, Belen, NM

Battle, Emily .... (903) 597-8111
Youth ED, Tyler Morning Telegraph, Tyler, TX

Battles, Sheila .... (508) 793-9100
PSL MGR
Telegram & Gazette, Worcester, MA

Batts, Lisa .... (919) 243-5151
Lifestyle ED, Wilson Daily Times, Wilson, NC

Bauder, Don .... (619) 299-3131
Senior COL-BUS
San Diego Union-Tribune, San Diego, CA

Bauer, Alan .... (208) 377-6200
EPE, Idaho Statesman, Boise, ID

Bauer, Alice .... (715) 568-3100
PUB, Bloomer Advance, Bloomer, WI

Bauer, Angela .... (502) 781-1700
Entertainment/Amusements ED,Lifestyle ED, Daily News, Bowling Green, KY

Bauer, Dave .... (305) 350-2111
VP-SYS & Technology, VP-DP
Miami Herald, Miami, FL

Bauer, David .... (502) 781-1700
EX ED/MAN ED
Daily News, Bowling Green, KY

Bauer, Deborah D .... (402) 887-4840
PUB, ED, Clearwater Record-Ewing News, Clearwater, NE

Bauer, Eric .... (508) 626-3800
Online ED, Technology ED
Middlesex News, Framingham, MA

Bauer, Eric .... (409) 245-5555
PRES, PUB, Daily Tribune, Bay City, TX

Bauer, Frank .... (503) 399-6611
ADV DIR, Statesman Journal, Salem, OR

Bauer, Gerri .... (904) 252-1511
Travel/Arts ED, Daytona Beach News-Journal, Daytona Beach, FL

Bauer, James R .... (814) 781-1596
CIRC MGR, DP MGR
Daily Press, St. Marys, PA

Bauer, John .... (910) 739-4322
GM, Robesonian, Lumberton, NC

Bauer, Linda .... (217) 351-5252
MGR-INFO Technology
News-Gazette, Champaign, IL

Bauer, Michael .... (415) 777-1111
Food ED
San Francisco Chronicle, San Francisco, CA

Bauer, Rich .... (618) 283-3374
MAN ED, Leader-Union, Vandalia, IL

Bauer, Terry .... (219) 533-2151
CIRC DIR, Goshen News, Goshen, IN

Bauer, Wayne .... (814) 781-1596
GM, MAN ED, Daily Press, St. Marys, PA

Bauerlein, Monika .... (612) 375-1015
MAN ED, City Pages, Minneapolis, MN

Baugess, Marsha .... (405) 341-2121
ADV DIR, Edmond Evening Sun, Edmond, OK

Baughan, Jeff .... (304) 485-1891
Music/Religion ED, Photo DEPT MGR,Parkersburg News & Sentinel, Parkersburg, WV

Baughman, Jon D .... (814) 635-2851
PUB, ED, Broad Top Bulletin, Saxton, PA

Bault, Thomas .... (419) 738-2128
CIRC MGR, Daily News, Wapakoneta, OH

Baum, Charles W .... (215) 257-6839
PUB, Perkasie News-Herald, Perkasie, PA

Baum, Michelle .... (423) 756-1234
Religion ED
Chattanooga Times, Chattanooga, TN

Bauman, Joseph .... (801) 237-2188
Health/Medical Writer, SCI ED
Deseret News, Salt Lake City, UT

Bauman, Michael .... (414) 224-2000
COL
Milwaukee Journal Sentinel, Milwaukee, WI

Bauman, Paula .... (218) 835-4211
GM, American, Blackduck, MN

Baumann, Daniel E .... (847) 427-4300
PRES/COO
Daily Herald, Arlington Heights, IL

Baumann, J Bruce .... (408) 372-3311
ASST MAN ED
Monterey County Herald, Monterey, CA

Baumann, James .... (847) 427-4300
ED-Fox Valley
Daily Herald, Arlington Heights, IL

Baumbaugh, Sharon G .... (717) 597-2164
ED, Echo Pilot, Greencastle, PA

Baumbaugh, Wayne E .... (717) 597-2164
PUB, Echo Pilot, Greencastle, PA

Baumer, Ben .... (619) 322-8889
PROD MGR-Building
Desert Sun, Palm Springs, CA

Baumer, Greg .... (614) 452-4561
ADV DIR, Times Recorder, Zanesville, OH

Baumgarten, Jim .... (502) 926-0123
SYS ED, Messenger-Inquirer, Owensboro, KY

Baumgartner, Anne .... (305) 350-2111
Action Line ED, Miami Herald, Miami, FL

Baumgartner, Della .... (219) 658-4111
PUB, Paper, Milford, IN

Baumgartner, Ron .... (219) 658-4111
GM, Paper, Milford, IN

Baur, David .... (618) 234-1000
ADV DIR
Belleville News-Democrat, Belleville, IL

Baur, Herbert H .... (614) 461-5000
CIRC MGR-MKTG/Training
Columbus Dispatch, Columbus, OH

Baures, Monica .... (414) 435-4411
DP MGR
Green Bay Press-Gazette, Green Bay, WI

Bausch, Jannell .... (612) 388-8235
ADV MGR-CLASS
Republican Eagle, Red Wing, MN

Bauslaugh, Cheryl .... (519) 426-5710
Fashion/Music ED, Food ED, Women's/Society ED, Simcoe Reformer, Simcoe, ON

Bauslaugh, Mike .... (519) 426-5710
BUS/FIN ED, Simcoe Reformer, Simcoe, ON

Bausman, Chuck .... (609) 663-6000
Sports ED, Courier-Post, Cherry Hill, NJ

Bausman, Dick .... (805) 736-2313
ADV MGR, Lompoc Record, Lompoc, CA

Baver, Terry .... (513) 748-2550
ED, Star Press, Springboro, OH

Bawden, Jim .... (416) 367-2000
Radio/Television Writer
Toronto Star, Toronto, ON

Baxley, Allen .... (352) 374-5000
PROD MGR-Pre Press
Gainesville Sun, Gainesville, FL

Baxley, Cindy .... (601) 776-3726
ED, Clarke Co. Tribune, Quitman, MS

Baxley, Larry M .... (816) 388-6131
PUB, GM
Salisbury Press-Spectator, Salisbury, MO

Baxley, Royce .... (903) 984-2593
PROD FRM-Camera/Press
Kilgore News Herald, Kilgore, TX

Baxley, Susan K .... (816) 388-6131
PUB
Salisbury Press-Spectator, Salisbury, MO

Baxter, Davette Baker .... (502) 732-4261
PUB, News-Democrat, Carrollton, KY

Baxter, Emme .... (615) 259-8000
Regional ED/BUS ED
Tennessean, Nashville, TN

Baxter, Gary .... (519) 735-2080
PUB, Shoreline Week, Tecumseh, ON

Baxter III, George W .... (517) 793-8070
ED, Saginaw Press, Saginaw, MI

Baxter, Gregg .... (209) 943-6397
PROD DIR, Record, Stockton, CA

Baxter, James .... (919) 829-0181
PUB, Front Page, Raleigh, NC

Baxter, Julie .... (970) 867-5651
Political/Government ED
Fort Morgan Times, Fort Morgan, CO

Baxter, Lisa .... (412) 224-4321
PROD MGR-SRV
Valley News Dispatch, Tarentum, PA

Baxter, Malcolm .... (604) 632-6144
MAN ED, Northern Sentinel, Kitimat, BC

Baxter, Richard .... (601) 961-7000
PSL MGR, Clarion-Ledger, Jackson, MS

Baxter, Robert .... (609) 663-6000
Theater/Music ED
Courier-Post, Cherry Hill, NJ

Baxter, Sally .... (813) 349-4949
GM, Pelican Press, Sarasota, FL

Baxter Jr, William A .... (860) 887-9211
ADV DIR, Norwich Bulletin, Norwich, CT

Baye, Betty .... (502) 582-4011
EDL Writer, Courier-Journal, Louisville, KY

Baye, Lori .... (605) 331-2200
ADV MGR-Sales
Argus Leader, Sioux Falls, SD

Bayer, Holly .... (619) 322-8889
ADV MGR-NTL
Desert Sun, Palm Springs, CA

Bayer, Stephen .... (410) 749-7171
PROD MGR-PR, Daily Times, Salisbury, MD

Bayless, Susanna .... (505) 325-4545
ADV SUPV-Display
Daily Times, Farmington, NM

Bayley, Nancy Cahalen .... (508) 793-9100
ADV ASST DIR
Telegram & Gazette, Worcester, MA

Bayne, John .... (214) 977-8222
Health/Fitness ED
Dallas Morning News, Dallas, TX

Bazinet, Jamison C .... (508) 764-4325
DIR-Photography, News, Southbridge, MA

Bazzell, Thomas L .... (410) 766-3700
GM, Maryland Gazette, Glen Burnie, MD

Bazzy, Jared .... (802) 254-2311
EDU ED, Reformer, Brattleboro, VT

Beach, Doug .... (319) 398-8211
News ED
Cedar Rapids Gazette, Cedar Rapids, IA

Beach, Joe .... (219) 936-3101
PUB, GM, Pilot-News, Plymouth, IN

Beach, John .... (213) 237-5000
DIR-Financial OPER
Los Angeles Times, Los Angeles, CA

Beach, Michael .... (818) 713-3000
CIRC MGR-Sales & MKTG
Daily News, Woodland Hills, CA

Beacom, Jack .... (209) 441-6111
PROD MGR-Packaging/Distribution
Fresno Bee, Fresno, CA

Beadle, Richard .... (906) 632-2235
ADV MGR
Evening News, Sault Ste. Marie, MI

Beagan, Joyce .... (401) 821-7400
BM
Kent County Daily Times, West Warwick, RI

Beager, Laurel .... (218) 285-7411
City/MET ED
Daily Journal, International Falls, MN

Beagle, Ben .... (716) 343-8000
Living/Lifestyle ED
Daily News, Batavia, NY

Beagle, Ben .... (540) 981-3100
COL, Roanoke Times, Roanoke, VA

Beagle, Linda .... (402) 487-2218
GM, Leigh World, Leigh, NE

Beagle, William .... (419) 636-1111
PROD FRM-PR, Bryan Times, Bryan, OH

Beal, Barbara .... (916) 527-2151
News ED, Daily News, Red Bluff, CA

Beal, Bruce .... (409) 725-9595
PUB, ED, Weimar Mercury, Weimar, TX

Beale, John .... (412) 263-1100
Chief Photographer
Pittsburgh Post-Gazette, Pittsburgh, PA

Beall, Robert L .... (910) 373-7000
Librarian, News & Record, Greensboro, NC

Beals, Gregg .... (316) 694-5700
PROD FRM-MR
Hutchinson News, Hutchinson, KS

Beals, Ray J .... (316) 342-4800
GM, Emporia Gazette, Emporia, KS

Beam Jr, Calvin .... (205) 325-2222
News ED, Online Contact
Birmingham Post-Herald, Birmingham, AL

Beam, Eric .... (704) 758-7381
Lifestyle ED, Lenoir News-Topic, Lenoir, NC

Beam, James .... (509) 663-5161
CONT, Wenatchee World, Wenatchee, WA

Beam, James C .... (318) 433-3000
ED, Lake Charles American Press, Lake Charles, LA

Beam, Lee .... (616) 781-3943
GM, Marshall Chronicle, Marshall, MI

Beam, Lee .... (800) 646-6397
PUB
Portland Review and Observer, Portland, MI

Beamguard, James .... (813) 259-7711
EDL Writer
Tampa Tribune and Times, Tampa, FL

Beamist, Jeff .... (604) 572-0064
ED, Surrey/North Delta Now, Surrey, BC

Bean, Brenda .... (909) 849-4586
Vice Chairman/CORP SEC
Record-Gazette, Banning, CA

Bean, Deborah .... (601) 684-2421
ADV DIR, ADV MGR-Local
Enterprise-Journal, McComb, MS

Bean, Gerald .... (909) 849-4586
PRES, Record-Gazette, Banning, CA

Bean, Gregory .... (908) 254-7000
ED, Sentinel, East Brunswick, NJ

Bean, Lana .... (304) 822-3871
MAN ED, Hampshire Review, Romney, WV

Bean, Michelle .... (618) 993-2626
ADV DIR
Marion Daily Republican, Marion, IL

Bean, Pat .... (801) 625-4200
Environmental ED
Standard-Examiner, Ogden, UT

Bean, R R .... (705) 472-3200
CIRC MGR
North Bay Nugget, North Bay, ON

Bean, Rick .... (919) 492-4001
PUB
Henderson Daily Dispatch, Henderson, NC

Bean, Susan .... (207) 784-5411
Automotive ED, Farm/Agriculture ED, Films/Theater ED, Special Sections ED
Sun-Journal, Lewiston, ME

Bean, Vern .... (352) 374-5000
PROD DIR, Gainesville Sun, Gainesville, FL

Bean, Wayne .... (520) 573-4400
PROD VP-OPER, TNI Partners dba Tucson Newspapers, Tucson, AZ

Bearce, Paul .... (505) 823-7777
Photo ED
Albuquerque Journal, Albuquerque, NM

Beard, Brucie .... (502) 756-2109
PUB, Breckinridge County Herald-News, Hardinsburg, KY

Beard, Cleo .... (501) 337-7523
ED, News ED, Daily Record, Malvern, AR

Beard, Michael .... (770) 532-1234
Entertainment/Amusements ED, Features ED, Television/Film ED, Times, Gainesville, GA

Beard, Nancy .... (502) 756-2109
MAN ED, Breckinridge County Herald-News, Hardinsburg, KY

Beard, Randy .... (864) 224-4321
Sports ED
Anderson Independent-Mail, Anderson, SC

Bearden, Claudia .... (360) 532-4000
Office MGR, Daily World, Aberdeen, WA

Bearden, Kathi .... (505) 393-2123
PUB, Hobbs Daily News-Sun, Hobbs, NM

Bearder, Don .... (414) 248-4444
PUB, Lake Geneva Regional News, Lake Geneva, WI

Bearder, Douglas A .... (414) 248-4444
GM, Lake Geneva Regional News, Lake Geneva, WI

Beardsley, Mark .... (706) 335-2927
GM, ED, Commerce News, Commerce, GA

Bears, Mike .... (403) 235-7100
PROD FRM-Plate Making
Calgary Herald, Calgary, AB

Beas, Richard .... (915) 546-6100
DIR-FIN, El Paso Times, El Paso, TX

Beasby, Truman .... (818) 713-3229
GM, Vecinos Del Valle, Woodland Hills, CA

Beasley, Alex .... (407) 420-5000
Health/SCI ED, Orlando Sentinel, Orlando, FL

Beasley, David .... (615) 444-3952
ADV MGR, Lebanon Democrat, Lebanon, TN

Beasley, Guy .... (334) 793-9586
PUB, Dothan Progress, Dothan, AL

Beasley, Jerry .... (910) 786-4141
PROD FRM-PR
Mount Airy News, Mount Airy, NC

Beasley, Kay .... (912) 744-4200
ADV MGR-ACS, Macon Telegraph, Macon, GA

Beasley, Larry T .... (818) 713-3000
PRES/CEO, PUB
Daily News, Woodland Hills, CA

Beasley, Lone .... (505) 356-4481
PUB, PUB Emeritus/Special Projects CNR
Portales News-Tribune, Portales, NM

Beasley, Rebecca .... (334) 775-3254
MAN ED, Clayton Record, Clayton, AL

Beasley, Robert A .... (804) 649-6000
DIR-PROM, Times-Dispatch, Richmond, VA

Beasley, Steve .... (806) 376-4488
ADV DIR, Amarillo Daily News/Globe Times, Amarillo, TX

Beasley, T L .... (205) 773-1953
PUB, Hartselle Enquirer, Hartselle, AL

Beasley, Truman .... (818) 713-3000
ADV MGR-OPER
Daily News, Woodland Hills, CA

Beason, Susan .... (904) 599-2100
Health/Medical ED, Travel ED
Tallahassee Democrat, Tallahassee, FL

Beattie, Bruce .... (904) 252-1511
EDL Cartoonist, Daytona Beach News-Journal, Daytona Beach, FL

Beattie, David A .... (905) 732-2411
PUB/GM, Tribune, Welland, ON

Beattie, Gerald .... (405) 475-3311
CIRC DIR
Daily Oklahoman, Oklahoma City, OK

Beatty, Chadwick M .... (610) 933-8926
PUB, Phoenix, Phoenixville, PA

Beatty, Doug .... (416) 367-2000
PROD SUPT-Mailing
Toronto Star, Toronto, ON

Beatty Jr, J Guy .... (423) 756-1234
SEC, Chattanooga Times, Chattanooga, TN

Beatty, James .... (206) 455-2222
VP-INFO SYS
Eastside Journal, Bellevue, WA

Beatty, Michael .... (312) 321-3000
ADV DIR-Display
Chicago Sun-Times, Chicago, IL

Beatty, Robert R .... (508) 793-9100
DIR-FIN
Telegram & Gazette, Worcester, MA

Beatty, S William .... (540) 374-5000
PROD FRM-PR
Free Lance-Star, Fredericksburg, VA

Beatty, Thomas J .... (800) 245-6536
Sales MGR-TMS TV Listings TMS Stocks & TMS Weather Serv.
Tribune Media Services Inc., Chicago, IL

Bea Who's Where-16

Beaty, J Rick .... (904) 747-5000
CIRC DIR, News Herald, Panama City, FL

Beaty, James .... (918) 423-1700
Area ED, McAlester News-Capital & Democrat, McAlester, OK

Beaty, Mark .... (423) 523-3131
PROD OPER MGR-Night CNR
Knoxville News-Sentinel, Knoxville, TN

Beauchamp, Debbi .... (250) 762-4445
Office MGR, Daily Courier, Kelowna, BC

Beauchamp, Ken .... (701) 873-4381
GM, Beulah Beacon, Beulah, ND

Beaudette, Dan .... (403) 632-2861
PUB, ED
Vegreville News Advertiser, Vegreville, AB

Beaudin, Michel .... (705) 726-6537
MAN ED, Examiner, Barrie, ON

Beaulieu, L Bart .... (610) 323-3000
CIRC DIR, Mercury, Pottstown, PA

Beaulieu, Pierre .... (514) 985-3333
City ED, Le Devoir, Montreal, QC

Beaumong, Shelley .... (406) 446-2222
ED, Carbon County News, Red Lodge, MT

Beaupre, Jean-Pascal .... (418) 686-3233
Arts/Entertainment ED, Music ED-Classical, Music ED-Popular, Le Soleil, Quebec, QC

Beaupre, Lawrence K .... (513) 721-2700
VP/ED, Cincinnati Enquirer, Cincinnati, OH

Beauregard, Claude .... (514) 985-3333
DIR-Information, Le Devoir, Montreal, QC

Beaushine, Dana .... (414) 432-2941
ADV MGR-CLASS
Green Bay News-Chronicle, Green Bay, WI

Beaver, Anita .... (937) 328-0300
Librarian
Springfield News-Sun, Springfield, OH

Beaver, Elizabeth .... (206) 324-0552
PUB, ED, Facts News, Seattle, WA

Beaver, Jerry .... (717) 286-5671
PROD SUPV-Pre Press
Daily Item, Sunbury, PA

Beaver, Lavonne .... (206) 324-0552
MAN ED, Facts News, Seattle, WA

Beavers, Bill .... (918) 335-8200
PROD FRM-Mark-up/Dispatch
Examiner-Enterprise, Bartlesville, OK

Beavers, Elizabeth .... (304) 788-3333
ED, City ED
Mineral Daily News-Tribune, Keyser, WV

Beavers, Larry W .... (405) 728-8000
PRES
F.A.C.—P.A.C. Inc., Oklahoma City, OK

Beavers, Roxanne .... (210) 225-7411
ADV MGR-Telephone Sales MGR
San Antonio Express-News, San Antonio, TX

Bebermeyer, Maxine .... (405) 327-2200
ADV MGR, Alva Review-Courier, Alva, OK

Bebout, Theresa .... (402) 873-3334
BM, PA
Nebraska City News-Press, Nebraska City, NE

Bebrowsky, Lynda .... (502) 926-0123
DIR-Community Relations/MKTG
Messenger-Inquirer, Owensboro, KY

Bechard, Gilles .... (819) 379-1490
GM, ED
L' Hebdo Journal, Cap-de-la-Madeleine, QC

Bechtel, Julie .... (913) 843-1000
CIRC MGR, Journal-World, Lawrence, KS

Bechtel, Samuel J .... (412) 465-5555
EX ED, Indiana Gazette, Indiana, PA

Bechtel, W D .... (412) 465-5555
Photo DEPT MGR
Indiana Gazette, Indiana, PA

Bechtholdt, Larry E .... (307) 634-3361
PROD FRM-PR
Wyoming Tribune-Eagle, Cheyenne, WY

Bechtol, Linda .... (512) 729-1828
ED, Herald, Rockport, TX

Bechtold, Dan .... (605) 842-1481
ED, Winner Advocate, Winner, SD

Bechtold, Rick .... (317) 482-4650
CIRC DIR, Reporter, Lebanon, IN

Beck, Brent .... (507) 694-1246
PUB, ED, Ivanhoe Times, Ivanhoe, MN

Beck Jr, Carl E .... (864) 582-4511
EX ED, Herald-Journal, Spartanburg, SC

Beck, Cory R .... (505) 622-7710
PUB, PA, Roswell Daily Record, Roswell, NM

Beck, Daniel .... (518) 374-4141
ADV DIR/MGR-CLASS
Daily Gazette, Schenectady, NY

Beck, David .... (408) 920-5000
Entertainment ED
San Jose Mercury News, San Jose, CA

Beck, Douglas J .... (910) 343-2000
PROD DIR, Morning Star/Sunday Star-News, Wilmington, NC

Beck, Ed .... (207) 791-6650
CIRC ASST DIR-Single Copy
Portland Press Herald, Portland, ME

Beck, Ellen .... (507) 694-1246
PUB, GM, Ivanhoe Times, Ivanhoe, MN

Beck, Gayle .... (330) 454-5611
Living Section ED, Repository, Canton, OH

Beck, Jim .... (408) 920-5000
CIRC MGR-Home Delivery
San Jose Mercury News, San Jose, CA

Beck, Joe .... (618) 529-5454
EPE, Southern Illinoisan, Carbondale, IL

Beck, John .... (217) 351-5252
EX ED, News-Gazette, Champaign, IL

Beck, John M .... (314) 421-1880
BM, St. Louis Countain, St. Louis, MO
ABC Inc. (Legal Communications Corp.)

Beck, Julie .... (912) 744-4200
PROD Administrative ASST
Macon Telegraph, Macon, GA

Beck, Kathy .... (308) 785-2251
ED, Elwood Bulletin, Elwood, NE

Beck, Lori .... (316) 694-5700
ADV DIR, Hutchinson News, Hutchinson, KS

Beck, Michael .... (319) 337-3181
MAN ED, Press-Citizen, Iowa City, IA

Beck, Patricia .... (518) 725-8616
PUB, Leader-Herald, Gloversville, NY

Beck, Randell .... (909) 889-9666
ASST MAN ED-MET
Sun, San Bernardino, CA

Beck, Robert H .... (505) 622-7710
PRES, Roswell Daily Record, Roswell, NM

Beck, Stuart R .... (505) 425-6796
PRES, PUB, ED, Books ED, EPE
Las Vegas Optic, Las Vegas, NM

Beck, Susan .... (415) 749-5400
EX ED, Recorder, San Francisco, CA

Beck, Tobin .... (202) 898-8254
ED-North America
United Press International, Washington, DC

Beck, Tom .... (515) 856-6336
PROD SUPT
Ad Express & Daily Iowegian, Centerville, IA

Beck III, William H .... (404) 521-1227
Printing DIR, Daily Report, Atlanta, GA

Becken, Bernice .... (507) 439-6214
ED, Hanska Herald, Hanska, MN

Becken, N Ross .... (507) 439-6214
MAN ED, Hanska Herald, Hanska, MN

Becken, Norman L .... (507) 439-6214
PUB, Hanska Herald, Hanska, MN

Becker, Alina .... (605) 897-6636
PUB, ED, Times-Record, Turton, SD

Becker, Carol .... (607) 272-2321
ADV DIR, Ithaca Journal, Ithaca, NY

Becker, David .... (403) 429-5400
VP-FIN, Edmonton Journal, Edmonton, AB

Becker, Don C .... (212) 837-7000
PRES, Journal of Commerce & Commercial, New York, NY

Becker, H Lyle .... (405) 628-2532
PUB, ED, Tonkawa News, Tonkawa, OK

Becker, Henry .... (212) 416-2000
EX VP/COO-Dow Jones Telerate
Wall Street Journal, New York, NY

Becker, James M .... (612) 388-8235
TREAS, BM, DP MGR
Republican Eagle, Red Wing, MN

Becker, Ken .... (319) 547-3601
ED, Times-Plain Dealer, Cresco, IA

Becker, Ken .... (615) 893-5860
Wire ED
Daily News Journal, Murfreesboro, TN

Becker, Pete .... (612) 388-8235
PA, Republican Eagle, Red Wing, MN

Becker, Rob .... (715) 735-6611
Presentation ED, EagleHerald, Marinette, WI

Becker, Robert .... (616) 222-5400
Sports ED
Grand Rapids Press, Grand Rapids, MI

Becker, Tom .... (209) 441-6111
Amusements/Entertainment ED, Travel ED
Fresno Bee, Fresno, CA

Beckett, Jim .... (519) 235-1331
PUB, ED, Times Advocate, Exeter, ON

Beckett, Stu .... (218) 723-5281
PROD FRM-PR (Night)
Duluth News-Tribune, Duluth, MN

Beckham, Heather .... (501) 372-4719
GM, Little Rock Free Press, Little Rock, AR

Beckley, Jan .... (706) 549-0123
Graphics ED/Art DIR, Athens Daily News/Banner-Herald, Athens, GA

Beckley, Jeffrey .... (214) 977-8222
CIRC DIR-ADM, Morning News, Dallas, TX

Beckley, Philip .... (315) 789-3333
ED, Finger Lakes Times, Geneva, NY

Becklund, Jack .... (218) 387-1025
PUB, ED
Cook County News-Herald, Grand Marais, MN

Becklund, Patti .... (218) 387-1025
PUB
Cook County News-Herald, Grand Marais, MN

Beckman, Linda .... (818) 962-8811
EDL Page Writer
San Gabriel Valley Tribune, West Covina, CA

Beckman, Rick .... (561) 820-4100
ADV MGR-RT
Palm Beach Post, West Palm Beach, FL

Beckmann, Dan .... (402) 341-7323
PUB, Reader, Omaha, NE

Becknell, Jennifer .... (803) 329-4000
Women's ED, Herald, Rock Hill, SC

Becknell, Kathleen Hill .... (903) 473-2653
PUB, ED, Rains County Leader, Emory, TX

Beckner, Larry .... (915) 337-4661
Photo DEPT MGR
Odessa American, Odessa, TX

Beckner, William T .... (334) 222-2402
PRES, PUB
Andalusia Star-News, Andalusia, AL

Beckwith, Barbara .... (817) 872-2247
ED, Bowie News, Bowie, TX

Beckwith, Charles .... (902) 893-9405
Assignment ED, Daily News, Truro, NS

Beckwith, Cynthia .... (307) 332-2323
ED, Wyoming State Journal, Lander, WY

Beckwith, Don .... (501) 425-6301
CIRC MGR, Daily News, Mountain Home, AR

Becnel Jr, George .... (504) 850-1100
Sports ED, Courier, Houma, LA

Bedard, Claude .... (418) 683-1573
Sports ED
Le Journal de Quebec, Ville Vanier, QC

Bedard, Joe .... (802) 863-3441
PROD MGR-COMP (Night)
Burlington Free Press, Burlington, VT

Bedard, William P .... (802) 257-7771
PUB, Brattleboro Town Crier, Brattleboro, VT

Beddies, Lynda .... (937) 426-5263
CIRC MGR, News-Current, Beavercreek, OH

Bedell, Barbara .... (914) 341-1100
COL, Times Herald-Record, Middletown, NY

Bedell, Mary .... (815) 933-1131
MAN ED
Herald/Country Market, Bourbonnais, IL

Bedford, Amy Aldrich .... (541) 276-2211
SEC, MGR-EDU SRV, MGR-PROM
East Oregonian, Pendleton, OR

Bedient, Paul .... (616) 842-6400
ADV MGR
Grand Haven Tribune, Grand Haven, MI

Bednar, Mark .... (330) 296-9657
Wire ED, Record-Courier, Kent-Ravenna, OH

Bednarz, Brenda .... (701) 662-2127
CIRC MGR
Devils Lake Daily Journal, Devils Lake, ND

Bedway, Nick .... (304) 233-0100
Sports ED, Intelligencer/Wheeling News-Register, Wheeling, WV

Beebe, Doris .... (419) 647-4981
PUB, Journal News, Spencerville, OH

Beebe, Richard .... (419) 647-4981
ED, Journal News, Spencerville, OH

Beecher, Cookson .... (360) 855-1641
ED, Courier Times, Sedro-Woolley, WA

Beeching, Diane .... (404) 521-1227
ADV DIR-Legal, CIRC DIR
Daily Report, Atlanta, GA

Beecken, Lenore .... (941) 687-7000
City ED, Ledger, Lakeland, FL

Beecroft, Stephen .... (905) 523-5800
ED, Stoney Creek News, Stoney Creek, ON

Beeland, Tim .... (601) 283-1131
PUB, ED, Winona Times, Winona, MS

Beeler, Monique .... (209) 369-2761
Television/Film ED, Theater/Music ED
Lodi News-Sentinel, Lodi, CA

Beem, Don .... (616) 946-2000
ADV MGR-RT
Record-Eagle, Traverse City, MI

Beeman, Perry .... (515) 284-8000
Environmental Reporter
Des Moines Register, Des Moines, IA

Beemer, Richard .... (219) 356-8400
MAN ED, Our Sunday Visitor, Huntington, IN

Beene, Charles .... (719) 275-7565
Sports ED, Daily Record, Canon City, CO

Beene, Richard .... (805) 395-7500
EX ED
Bakersfield Californian, Bakersfield, CA

Beer, Bob .... (970) 728-9788
ED, Telluride Daily Planet, Telluride, CO

Beer, Devon .... (937) 498-2111
PROD MGR, Sidney Daily News, Sidney, OH

Beers, Chris .... (330) 833-2631
Religion ED, Independent, Massillon, OH

Beers, Jonah .... (507) 836-8726
GM, Murray County Herald, Slayton, MN

Beers, Randy .... (507) 836-8726
ED, Murray County Herald, Slayton, MN

Beers, Will .... (507) 836-8726
PUB, Murray County Herald, Slayton, MN

Beery, David L .... (847) 427-4300
EPE, Daily Herald, Arlington Heights, IL

Beesley, Paul .... (416) 585-5000
CFO, Globe and Mail, Toronto, ON

Beesley, Tom .... (615) 384-3567
ED, Robertson County Times, Springfield, TN

Beeson, Dan .... (520) 445-3333
Sports ED, Daily Courier, Prescott, AZ

Beeson, Donna .... (520) 445-3333
PSL MGR, Daily Courier, Prescott, AZ

Beeson, Frank .... (330) 264-1125
GM, Daily Record, Wooster, OH

Beeson, Kimberley .... (415) 252-0500
BUS MGR, San Francisco Daily Journal, San Francisco, CA

Beeson, Michael A .... (810) 541-3000
ED, BUS ED, Daily Tribune, Royal Oak, MI

Beetham, George .... (215) 483-7300
ED, Review, Philadelphia, PA

Beets, Katrina .... (423) 472-5041
EDU ED
Cleveland Daily Banner, Cleveland, TN

Beevers, Jefferson .... (209) 854-6333
ED, Gustine Press-Standard, Gustine, CA

Befferman, Barbara .... (412) 687-1000
GM, Jewish Chronicle, Pittsburgh, PA

Begassi, Wayne .... (860) 442-2200
Photo ED, Day, New London, CT

Begert, Jane N .... (207) 828-8100
VP-Human Resources
Guy Gannett Communications, Portland, ME

Beggs, Bruce .... (816) 380-3228
MAN ED, Cass County Democrat-Missourian, Harrisonville, MO

Begley, Bill .... (937) 335-5634
COL, Sports ED, Troy Daily News/Miami Valley Sunday News, Troy, OH

Begley, Chris .... (617) 643-7900
ED, Belmont Citizen-Herald, Arlington, MA

Begnoche, Stephen .... (616) 845-5181
ADV MGR, Wire ED, COL, Features ED, News ED, Daily News, Ludington, MI

Begue, Mike .... (904) 359-4111
PROD DIR-ADV/Customer SRV, PROD MGR-Scheduling/Make-up, Florida Times-Union, Jacksonville, FL

Behan, Michael .... (807) 274-5373
ED
Fort Frances Daily Bulletin, Fort Frances, ON

Behling, Donald .... (608) 365-8811
PROD MGR, Beloit Daily News, Beloit, WI

Behm, Don .... (414) 224-2000
Environmental Reporter
Milwaukee Journal Sentinel, Milwaukee, WI

Behnke, Clifford .... (608) 252-6100
MAN ED
Wisconsin State Journal, Madison, WI

Behr, Soma Golden .... (212) 556-1234
ASST MAN ED
New York Times, New York, NY

Behren, Rick .... (708) 383-3200
ED, Elm Leaves, Oak Park, IL

Behrens, Daniel E .... (937) 644-9111
PRES, BM, PA, ED, EPE
Marysville Journal-Tribune, Marysville, OH

Behrens, David G .... (937) 644-9111
SEC, PUB
Marysville Journal-Tribune, Marysville, OH

Behrens, Eric .... (309) 686-3000
Photo ED, Journal Star, Peoria, IL

Behrens-LeRoy, Julie .... (937) 644-9111
VP
Marysville Journal-Tribune, Marysville, OH

Behrens-Miller, Mary .... (937) 644-9111
VP
Marysville Journal-Tribune, Marysville, OH

Behringer, Fred D .... (610) 896-9555
ED, Main Line Life, Ardmore, PA

Beidler, George A .... (412) 834-1151
VP, EX ED, Tribune-Review, Greensburg, PA

Beifuss, John .... (901) 529-2211
Films Reporter
Commercial Appeal, Memphis, TN

Beihoff, David .... (419) 245-6000
VP/GM, Blade, Toledo, OH

Beilhart, Terry L .... (610) 371-5000
ADV ASST DIR
Reading Times/Eagle, Reading, PA

Beilue, Jon Mark .... (806) 376-4488
Sports ED, Amarillo Daily News/Globe Times, Amarillo, TX

Beimer, Scott .... (541) 474-3700
DP MGR
Grants Pass Daily Courier, Grants Pass, OR

Beirne, Coite Charles .... (540) 962-2121
Automotive ED
Virginian Review, Covington, VA

Beirne, Elizabeth .... (540) 962-2121
Books ED, Films/Theater ED, Radio/Television ED, Virginian Review, Covington, VA

Beirne, Horton P .... (540) 962-2121
PRES, GM, ED, EDU ED, Entertainment ED, Features ED, Graphics ED/Art DIR, Health/Medical ED, NTL ED, News ED, Photo ED, Virginian Review, Covington, VA

Beirne, John .... (804) 649-6000
CIRC MGR-Subscriber Relations
Richmond Times-Dispatch, Richmond, VA

Copyright ©1997 by the Editor & Publisher Co.

17-Who's Where **Ben**

Beirne, Rose S .... (540) 962-2121
VP, Virginian Review, Covington, VA
Beirne, Tina .... (810) 766-6100
Photo ED, Flint Journal, Flint, MI
Beissenherz, Gary L .... (816) 463-7522
PUB, ED, Concordian, Concordia, MO
Beitler, Paul .... (219) 824-0224
Sports ED, News-Banner, Bluffton, IN
Bekins, Hillary .... (213) 876-1668
PRES, Communication International/National News, Los Angeles, CA
Belair, Michel .... (514) 985-3333
Cultural Pages, Le Devoir, Montreal, QC
Belanger, Ann .... (617) 321-8000
ADV MGR-Sales
Daily News-Mercury, Malden, MA
Belanger, Denis .... (514) 285-7272
ADV DIR-RT, La Presse, Montreal, QC
Belasco, Donald J .... (610) 820-6500
CIRC DIR, Morning Call, Allentown, PA
Belcher, Alethia .... (423) 581-5630
State ED, Citizen Tribune, Morristown, TN
Belcher, Ellen .... (937) 225-2000
COL, EDL Writer, Daily News, Dayton, OH
Belcher, Roy .... (508) 222-7000
BM, Sun Chronicle, Attleboro, MA
Belcher, Steve .... (405) 323-5151
News ED, Clinton Daily News, Clinton, OK
Belcher, Walt .... (813) 259-7711
Radio ED, Television ED
Tampa Tribune and Times, Tampa, FL
Belden, David .... (419) 485-3113
ED
Montpelier Leader-Enterprise, Montpelier, OH
Belden, John .... (501) 673-8533
Sports ED
Stuttgart Daily Leader, Stuttgart, AR
Belden, Roxy .... (913) 823-6363
DP MGR, Salina Journal, Salina, KS
Beldz, Colin .... (701) 572-2165
Sports ED
Williston Daily Herald, Williston, ND
Belehrad, Tim .... (504) 383-1111
Amusements ED, Radio/Television ED
Advocate, Baton Rouge, LA
Belew, James R .... (816) 263-4123
Sports ED, Moberly Monitor-Index & Democrat, Moberly, MO
Belew, Jim .... (409) 826-3361
PUB, ED
Waller County News-Citizen, Hempstead, TX
Belich, Jack .... (813) 893-8111
ASST to PRES
St. Petersburg Times, St. Petersburg, FL
Belisle, Guy .... (902) 564-5451
PROD MGR-Press
Cape Breton Post, Sydney, NS
Belislie, Syl .... (705) 268-5050
PUB/GM, Daily Press, Timmins, ON
Beliveau, Jules .... (514) 285-7272
Religion ED, La Presse, Montreal, QC
Bell, Aaron .... (812) 265-3641
PROD FRM-Camera/Press
Madison Courier, Madison, IN
Bell, Alan .... (714) 553-9292
Sr VP/PRES-Broadcast Division
Freedom Communications Inc., Irvine, CA
Bell, Alberta .... (508) 632-8000
PRES/PUB, Gardner News, Gardner, MA
Bell, Barbara .... (508) 626-3800
DP MGR, Middlesex News, Framingham, MA
Bell, Belva M .... (309) 924-1871
PUB
Henderson County Quill, Stronghurst, IL
Bell, Betty .... (518) 359-2166
GM
Tupper Lake Free Press, Tupper Lake, NY
Bell, Bill .... (562) 698-0955
MAN ED, Whittier Daily News, Whittier, CA
Bell, Bruce .... (307) 362-3736
PROD FRM-PR/MR
Daily Rocket-Miner, Rock Springs, WY
Bell, Carolyn .... (712) 328-1811
Accountant, PA, DP MGR
Daily Nonpareil, Council Bluffs, IA
Bell, Clark .... (518) 584-4242
Chief Photographer
Saratogian, Saratoga Springs, NY
Bell, Craig .... (704) 864-3291
Photo ED, Gaston Gazette, Gastonia, NC
Bell, Dave .... (613) 732-3691
CIRC MGR, Observer, Pembroke, ON
Bell, David .... (44-0171) 873-3000
Chief EX, Financial Times, London, England
Bell, David R .... (618) 283-3374
PUB, Leader-Union, Vandalia, IL
Bell, Diane .... (619) 299-3131
COL-City
San Diego Union-Tribune, San Diego, CA
Bell, Doe .... (219) 461-8444
MGR-Purchasing
Fort Wayne Newspapers Inc., Fort Wayne, IN
Bell, Doug .... (403) 667-6285
PUB, Yukon News, Whitehorse, YT
Bell, Ed .... (360) 694-3391
PROD MGR-Packaging Center
Columbian, Vancouver, WA
Bell, Elizabeth .... (415) 921-5100
ED, France Today, San Francisco, CA
Bell, Elizabeth .... (315) 287-2100
GM, Tribune-Press, Gouverneur, NY
Bell, Elma .... (205) 325-2222
Garden ED
Birmingham News, Birmingham, AL
Bell, Frank J .... (217) 486-7321
PUB, ED, Illiopolis Sentinel, Illiopolis, IL
Bell, Gary .... (904) 359-4111
ED-Night
Florida Times-Union, Jacksonville, FL
Bell, Gene .... (619) 299-3131
PRES/CEO
San Diego Union-Tribune, San Diego, CA
Bell, Grange .... (616) 781-3943
ADV MGR, Marshall Chronicle, Marshall, MI
Bell, James .... (301) 722-4600
PROD FRM-PR
Cumberland Times-News, Cumberland, MD
Bell, James E .... (406) 523-5200
PUB, Missoulian, Missoula, MT
Bell, Jeffery .... (610) 367-6041
ED, Boyertown Area Times, Boyertown, PA
Bell, Jennifer .... (706) 884-7311
ADV MGR, Daily News, La Grange, GA
Bell, Jim .... (715) 537-3117
PUB, County News-Shield, Barron, WI
Bell, June .... (904) 359-4111
Courts ED
Florida Times-Union, Jacksonville, FL
Bell, Linda .... (907) 283-7551
PA/CONT, Peninsula Clarion, Kenai, AK
Bell, Norman .... (909) 684-1200
ASST MAN ED-MET
Press-Enterprise, Riverside, CA
Bell, Phyllis .... (913) 389-6631
ED, Lebanon Times, Lebanon, KS
Bell, Randy .... (417) 395-4131
PUB, ED, Mining Review, Rich Hill, MO
Bell, Rick .... (360) 754-5400
CIRC DIR, Olympian, Olympia, WA
Bell, Ron .... (504) 383-1111
Photo DEPT MGR
Advocate, Baton Rouge, LA
Bell, Ronnie .... (501) 785-7700
ADV DIR
Southwest Times Record, Fort Smith, AR
Bell, Roy E .... (619) 454-0411
VP, Copley Press Inc., La Jolla, CA
Bell, Stephen D .... (205) 325-2222
MET ED
Birmingham Post-Herald, Birmingham, AL
Bell, Steve .... (716) 849-3434
City ED, Buffalo News, Buffalo, NY
Bell, Steve .... (913) 628-1081
ASST Sports ED, Hays Daily News, Hays, KS
Bell, T D .... (715) 532-5591
PUB, Ladysmith News, Ladysmith, WI
Bell, Thomas N .... (316) 431-4100
PRES, PUB, PA, ED, EPE
Chanute Tribune, Chanute, KS
Bell, Tom .... (609) 871-8000
EDL ED
Burlington County Times, Willingboro, NJ
Bell, Vance .... (919) 946-2144
PROD FRM-PR
Washington Daily News, Washington, NC
Bell, Wayne D .... (208) 852-0155
PUB, Preston Citizen, Preston, ID
Bellamy, Cindy .... (423) 246-8121
ADV MGR-NTL
Kingsport Times-News, Kingsport, TN
Bellan, Matt .... (204) 694-3332
ED, Jewish Post & News, Winnipeg, MB
Bellanti, Beth .... (617) 426-3000
ADV MGR-CLASS, Boston Herald
Boston, MA
Bellatti, James R .... (405) 372-5000
PUB, ED, News Press, Stillwater, OK
Bellatti, L F .... (405) 372-5000
PUB, News Press, Stillwater, OK
Bellatti, Rick .... (405) 372-5000
PA/ASSOC PUB, News Press, Stillwater, OK
Bellavance, Claude .... (418) 723-4800
PUB, ED
Le Progres-Echo-Dimanche, Rimouski, QC
Belle, Charles E .... (415) 931-5778
ED, Sun Reporter, San Francisco, CA
Bellefontaine, George .... (902) 485-8014
PUB, Pictou Advocate, Pictou, NS
Bellerose, Carmen .... (508) 458-7100
CONT, Sun, Lowell, MA
Belles, Ed .... (517) 799-3200
PUB, Township Times, Saginaw, MI
Belles, Mike .... (619) 241-7744
CIRC MGR, Daily Press, Victorville, CA
Freedom Communications Inc.
Belleville, Ronald C .... (616) 775-6565
TREAS, MGR-BUS/PSL, MGR-CR/PA, DP MGR, Cadillac News, Cadillac, MI
Bellinger, Janice .... (618) 943-2331
Agriculture ED, EDU ED
Daily Record, Lawrenceville, IL
Bello, Mike .... (617) 426-3000
EX City ED, Boston Herald, Boston, MA
Bellor, Beth .... (517) 835-7171
Online MGR, Daily News, Midland, MI
Bellune, Jerry .... (803) 359-7633
ED
Lexington County Chronicle, Lexington, SC
Bellune, MacLeod .... (803) 359-7633
PUB
Lexington County Chronicle, Lexington, SC
Belluomini, Peter .... (312) 321-3000
DIR-Distribution
Chicago Sun-Times, Chicago, IL
Belman, Felice .... (603) 224-5301
EPE, Concord Monitor, Concord, NH
Belmont, John .... (708) 336-7000
MGR-MKTG & PROM, News-Sun
Waukegan, IL
Belo, A H .... (502) 926-0123
BC, Messenger-Inquirer, Owensboro, KY
Belshaw, Jim .... (505) 823-7777
COL, Albuquerque Journal, Albuquerque, NM
Belt, Deb .... (515) 961-2511
ED, Record-Herald and Indianola Tribune, Indianola, IA
Belt, Molley Finch .... (214) 651-7066
PUB, Dallas Examiner, Dallas, TX
Belton, Jennifer .... (202) 334-6000
DIR-INFO SRV (Library), DIR-INFO Services
Washington Post, Washington, DC
Belton, Shane .... (912) 273-2277
ADV DIR, Cordele Dispatch, Cordele, GA
Beltrone, Jan A .... (210) 896-7000
CONT, Kerrville Daily Times, Kerrville, TX
Beltz, Margaret .... (304) 233-0100
ED-City, BUS/FIN ED, Intelligencer/Wheeling News-Register, Wheeling, WV
Belyea, Jim .... (905) 852-9141
MAN ED
Uxbridge Times-Journal, Uxbridge, ON
Beman, Don .... (507) 223-5303
PUB, ED, Canby News, Canby, MN
Beman, Ellie .... (507) 223-5303
PUB, Canby News, Canby, MN
Bemis, Jay .... (913) 242-4700
MAN ED, Automotive ED, City ED, Features ED, News ED, Ottawa Herald, Ottawa, KS
Bemis, Larry .... (765) 569-2033
ED, Parke County Sentinel, Rockville, IN
Ben-Dat, Mordechai .... (416) 422-2331
ED, Canadian Jewish News, Don Mills, ON
Benack, Walter .... (610) 258-7171
MGR-EDL/Production SYS, MGR-Communications, Express-Times, Easton, PA
Benanti, Mary .... (970) 493-6397
City ED
Fort Collins Coloradoan, Fort Collins, CO
Benazeski, Gayle .... (715) 842-2101
ADV MGR-CLASS/NTL
Wausau Daily Herald, Wausau, WI
Bencini, Gaye .... (502) 653-3381
ED, Hickman County Gazette, Clinton, KY
Benda, David .... (916) 243-2424
Sports ED, Record Searchlight, Redding, CA
Bendall, Gordon .... (910) 694-4145
ED, Caswell Messenger, Yanceyville, NC
Bender, Bud .... (330) 264-1125
MGR-SYS, Daily Record, Wooster, OH
Bender, Craig .... (703) 368-3101
ADV DIR, Journal Messenger, Manassas, VA
Bender, David .... (509) 459-5000
Online/Web Site MGR
Spokesman-Review, Spokane, WA
Bender, Gregg .... (219) 235-6161
Graphics CNR
South Bend Tribune, South Bend, IN
Bender, Sharon .... (215) 848-4300
MAN ED
Germantown Courier, Philadelphia, PA
Bender, Valerie .... (302) 324-2500
MAN ED, News Journal, Wilmington, DE
Bendily, Phil .... (517) 275-5100
ED, Roscommon County Herald-News, Roscommon, MI
Bendycki, Tom .... (419) 245-6000
ASST MAN ED, Blade, Toledo, OH
Benedict, Jim .... (201) 877-4141
MGR-CR, Star-Ledger, Newark, NJ
Benedict, Kim .... (316) 442-4200
PUB, ED
Arkansas City Traveler, Arkansas City, KS
Benedict, Monica .... (305) 350-2111
ADV VP, Miami Herald, Miami, FL
Benedict, Olin .... (607) 432-1000
PROD SUPV-COMP/Day FRM
Daily Star, Oneonta, NY
Benedict, T M .... (313) 428-8173
GM, Manchester Enterprise, Manchester, MI
Benetti, John .... (715) 842-2101
ADV MGR-RT
Wausau Daily Herald, Wausau, WI
Benevento, Michael A .... (716) 849-3434
CIRC ASST DIR, Buffalo News, Buffalo, NY
Benevento, Paul .... (419) 332-5511
PROD MGR-MR, News-Messenger
Fremont, OH
Benevides, William .... (508) 676-8211
PROD FRM-COMP
Herald News, Fall River, MA
Benfield, Richard .... (201) 646-4000
ASST MAN ED-EDL Pages
Record, Hackensack, NJ
Benge, George .... (317) 423-5511
EX ED/Chief News EX
Journal and Courier, Lafayette, IN
Benhk, Regina .... (613) 446-5196
ED, Star, Orleans, ON
Beni, John J .... (212) 450-7000
PRES/COO, React, Parade Publications Inc., New York, NY
Benitez, Victor .... (213) 881-6515
MAN ED, Novedades, Los Angeles, CA
Benjamin, Alvan R .... (802) 496-3928
PUB, ED, Valley Reporter, Waitsfield, VT
Benjamin, Brenda .... (717) 888-9643
CIRC MGR, Evening Times, Sayre, PA
Benjamin, Christianne .... (514) 521-4545
CIRC MGR
Le Journal de Montreal, Montreal, QC
Benjamin, Cynthia .... (716) 232-7100
ASST MAN ED-Outreach & Training
Rochester Democrat and Chronicle; Times-Union, Rochester, NY
Benjamin, Lawrence .... (908) 922-6000
Staff Development ED
Asbury Park Press, Neptune, NJ
Benjamin, Robert .... (716) 366-3000
CIRC MGR, Evening Observer, Dunkirk, NY
Benjamin, Robert .... (410) 332-6000
ED-Howard Sun, Sun, Baltimore, MD
Benjamin, Sonia .... (415) 921-5100
MAN ED
Journal Francais, San Francisco, CA
Benjamin, Timothy .... (408) 920-5000
PROD MGR-Publishing SYS
San Jose Mercury News, San Jose, CA
Benjamin, Wayne .... (504) 826-3279
PA, Times-Picayune, New Orleans, LA
Benko, Rick .... (607) 798-1234
CIRC MGR-Fleet
Press & Sun Bulletin, Binghamton, NY
Bennack Jr, Frank A .... (206) 448-8000
PRES/CEO (Hearst Corp), Seattle Post-Intelligencer, Seattle, WA
Hearst Newspapers
Bennati, John .... (412) 684-5200
ADV MGR
Valley Independent, Monessen, PA
Benner, Richard .... (860) 241-6200
ADV MGR-BUS Development
Hartford Courant, Hartford, CT
Bennet, J M .... (904) 427-1000
Sports ED
Observer, New Smyrna Beach, FL
Bennett, Allen .... (910) 227-0131
PROD FRM-PR
Times News Publishing Co., Burlington, NC
Bennett, Amanda .... (212) 416-2000
BU Chief-Atlanta
Wall Street Journal, New York, NY
Bennett, Bill .... (614) 773-2111
PROD MGR-PR, Gazette, Chillicothe, OH
Bennett, Brad .... (541) 485-1234
PROD FRM-Plate/Camera
Register-Guard, Eugene, OR
Bennett, Bruce S .... (508) 793-9100
PUB, Telegram & Gazette, Worcester, MA
Bennett, Carol .... (970) 522-1990
Women's ED, Journal-Advocate, Sterling, CO
Bennett, Carter J .... (201) 376-1200
ED
Item of Millburn & Short Hills, Millburn, NJ
Bennett, Chris .... (206) 627-1103
PUB, Seattle Medium, Seattle, WA
Bennett, David .... (803) 626-8555
News ED, Sun News, Myrtle Beach, SC
Bennett, David .... (860) 241-6200
CIRC MGR-Home Delivery
Hartford Courant, Hartford, CT
Bennett, Dena .... (319) 754-8461
Weekend ED, Hawk Eye, Burlington, IA
Bennett, Don .... (908) 349-3000
Environmental ED
Ocean County Observer, Toms River, NJ
Bennett, Don .... (913) 295-1111
PROD FRM-PR (Day)
Topeka Capital-Journal, Topeka, KS
Bennett, Doug .... (812) 275-3355
BUS/FIN ED, Political/Government ED
Times-Mail, Bedford, IN

Ben Who's Where-18

Bennett, Ed .... (502) 582-4011
EDL ED, Courier-Journal, Louisville, KY
Bennett, Gerald A .... (816) 279-9315
PRES/Cartoon ED, American International Syndicate, St. Joseph, MO
Bennett, Greg .... (206) 464-2111
ADV MGR-Display
Seattle Times, Seattle, WA
Bennett, Hannah .... (516) 569-4000
ED, Meadowbrook Times, Lawrence, NY
Bennett, Herbert R .... (307) 634-3361
PROD SUPT-COMP
Wyoming Tribune-Eagle, Cheyenne, WY
Bennett, Herman .... (817) 734-2410
ED, Gorman Progress, Gorman, TX
Bennett, Jack .... (423) 472-5041
ADV DIR, MGR-PROM
Cleveland Daily Banner, Cleveland, TN
Bennett, James .... (503) 399-6611
Sports ED, Statesman Journal, Salem, OR
Bennett, James R .... (803) 648-2311
PROD Head, Aiken Standard, Aiken, SC
Bennett, Jeff .... (901) 427-3333
BUS ED, Jackson Sun, Jackson, TN
Bennett, Jerry .... (520) 573-4400
PROD MGR-Special Section/Quality, TNI Partners dba Tucson Newspapers, Tucson, AZ
Bennett, Judith .... (904) 252-1511
MGR-CR, Daytona Beach News-Journal, Daytona Beach, FL
Bennett, Keith .... (403) 932-3500
PUB, Cochrane This Week, Cochrane, AB
Bennett, Ken .... (709) 634-4348
PROD FRM, Western Star, Corner Brook, NF
Bennett, Kerry .... (541) 276-2211
Food ED, East Oregonian, Pendleton, OR
Bennett, Kirk .... (803) 771-6161
ADV MGR-Coop, State, Columbia, SC
Bennett, Laurie .... (313) 222-6400
DIR-Free Press Plus-Web Page
Detroit Free Press, Detroit, MI
Bennett, Linda .... (816) 279-9315
EVP, American International Syndicate, St. Joseph, MO
Bennett, Liz .... (405) 227-4439
ED, Fairview Republican, Fairview, OK
Bennett, Lonnie Joe .... (817) 734-2410
PUB, Gorman Progress, Gorman, TX
Bennett, Mark .... (812) 231-4200
Sports ED, Tribune-Star, Terre Haute, IN
Bennett, Mary .... (540) 962-2121
Society ED, Virginian Review, Covington, VA
Bennett, Michael .... (216) 999-4500
Living ED, Plain Dealer, Cleveland, OH
Bennett, Patricia .... (219) 938-6962
VP, Listening Inc., Gary, IN
Bennett, Philip .... (617) 929-2000
Foreign ED, Boston Globe, Boston, MA
Bennett, Ralph .... (812) 847-4487
PROD FRM, Linton Daily Citizen, Linton, IN
Bennett, Rebecca .... (814) 238-5000
News ED
Centre Daily Times, State College, PA
Bennett, Rhonda .... (515) 872-1234
PUB, Corydon Times Republican, Corydon, IA
Bennett, Richard .... (518) 374-4141
Fashion ED, Food ED, Life/Leisure ED
Daily Gazette, Schenectady, NY
Bennett, Richard .... (219) 938-6962
PRES, Listening Inc., Gary, IN
Bennett, Robert .... (315) 363-5100
PROD DIR
Oneida Daily Dispatch, Oneida, NY
Bennett, Ron .... (904) 747-5000
MGR-MIS, News Herald, Panama City, FL
Bennett, Steve .... (518) 792-3131
MAN ED, Post-Star, Glens Falls, NY
Bennight, Ken .... (512) 445-3500
PROD MGR-Pre Press
Austin American-Statesman, Austin, TX
Benninghoff, Chris .... (219) 235-6161
Action Line ED
South Bend Tribune, South Bend, IN
Benoit, Dale .... (504) 392-1619
PUB, ED
Placquemines Gazette, Belle Chasse, LA
Bensheimer, Virginia .... (402) 444-1000
EDL Writer
Omaha World-Herald, Omaha, NE
Bensley, Carl .... (912) 764-9031
CIRC MGR-District
Statesboro Herald, Statesboro, GA
Benson Jr, A Ted .... (814) 870-1600
ADV MGR-CLASS
Morning News/Erie Daily Times, Erie, PA
Benson, Anne .... (970) 532-3715
ED, Old Berthoud Recorder, Berthoud, CO
Benson, Cliff .... (510) 748-1666
PUB, Alameda Journal, Alameda, CA
Benson, Clyde .... (719) 632-5511
MGR-Pre Press SYS
Gazette, Colorado Springs, CO
Benson, Darren .... (916) 842-5777
MAN ED, Siskiyou Daily News, Yreka, CA
Benson, David .... (609) 272-7000
Production ED, SCI/Technology ED
Press of Atlantic City, Pleasantville, NJ
Benson, Heidi .... (415) 777-2424
Arts/Features ED, Book Review ED, Style ED
San Francisco Examiner, San Francisco, CA
Benson, Jeff .... (318) 255-4353
MAN ED, EPE, NTL ED, Political/Government ED, Ruston Daily Leader, Ruston, LA
Benson, Larry .... (919) 829-4500
PROD MGR-Electronic SRV
News & Observer, Raleigh, NC
Benson, Larry .... (605) 665-7811
BM, DP MGR
Yankton Daily Press & Dakotan, Yankton, SD
Benson, Pat .... (213) 237-5000
MGT/Trends
Los Angeles Times, Los Angeles, CA
Benson, Steve .... (602) 271-8000
EDL Cartoonist
Arizona Republic, Phoenix, AZ
Benson, Ted .... (209) 578-2000
DIR-Photography, Modesto Bee, Modesto, CA
Benson, Ted .... (814) 870-1600
ADTX MGR
Morning News/Erie Daily Times, Erie, PA
Bent, Kevin .... (613) 829-9100
ADV VP, Ottawa Citizen, Ottawa, ON
Benteau, Steve .... (506) 452-6671
ED, EPE, Daily Gleaner, Fredericton, NB
Benter, Doris .... (217) 784-4244
ED, Gibson City Courier, Gibson City, IL
Benth, Dennis .... (520) 458-9440
ADV DIR, Sierra Vista Herald, Sierra Vista, AZ
Wick Communications
Benthall, Dot .... (919) 537-2505
Living/Lifestyle ED, Society ED, Women's ED
Daily Herald, Roanoke Rapids, NC
Bentley, Cecil .... (912) 744-4200
VP, EX ED, Macon Telegraph, Macon, GA
Bentley, Clyde H .... (541) 276-2211
GM, East Oregonian, Pendleton, OR
Bentley, Don .... (405) 353-0620
Co-PUB, Co-ED
Lawton Constitution, Lawton, OK
Bentley, Holly .... (604) 344-5251
PUB, Golden Star, Golden, BC
Bentley, James .... (219) 461-8444
PSL DIR
Fort Wayne Newspapers Inc., Fort Wayne, IN
Bentley, Kate .... (800) 355-9500
PROD MGR, News USA Inc., Vienna, VA
Bentley, Nora .... (601) 429-6397
MAN ED, DeSoto Times, Hernando, MS
Bentley, Robert .... (864) 223-1411
CEO, Index-Journal, Greenwood, SC
Bentley, Robert .... (812) 254-0480
CIRC DIR
Washington Times-Herald, Washington, IN
Bentley, Sara .... (703) 284-6000
Group PRES-Northwest Newspaper Group
Gannett Co. Inc., Arlington, VA
Bentley, Stephen .... (405) 353-0620
PUB, Cannonneer, Lawton, OK
Benton, David .... (704) 289-1541
PROD FRM-PR
Enquirer-Journal, Monroe, NC
Benton, Jackie .... (604) 997-6675
PUB, ED, Times, Mackenzie, BC
Benton, Jane .... (904) 526-3614
PUB/GM
Jackson County Floridan, Marianna, FL
Benton III, Nelson K .... (508) 744-0600
EPE, Salem Evening News, Beverly, MA
Benton, Nicholas F .... (703) 532-3267
PUB, ED, News-Press, Falls Church, VA
Bentt, Brian .... (403) 464-0033
GM
Sherwood Park News, Sherwood Park, AB
Bentz, Lynn .... (414) 235-7700
PROD MGR-COMP
Oshkosh Northwestern, Oshkosh, WI
Bentzen-Bilkvist, Claire .... (905) 526-3333
CONT, Spectator, Hamilton, ON
Benz, Mark .... (501) 442-1777
CIRC MGR
Northwest Arkansas Times, Fayetteville, AR
Benz, Twila .... (701) 225-8111
PROD FRM-COMP
Dickinson Press, Dickinson, ND
Benza, A J .... (212) 210-2100
Gossip COL
New York Daily News, New York, NY
Benzinger, Jeff .... (209) 537-5032
GM, Ceres Courier, Ceres, CA
Beqari, Shkelqim .... (617) 269-5192
ED, Liria, South Boston, MA
Bequette, Bill .... (509) 582-1500
COL, Tri-City Herald, Tri-Cities, WA
Beranak, Diane .... (319) 627-2814
GM, ED, West Liberty Index, West Liberty, IA
Berard, Pamela .... (401) 762-3000
Sunday ED, Call, Woonsocket, RI
Berardi, Tony .... (312) 222-3232
Photographer-Tribune Magazine
Chicago Tribune, Chicago, IL
Bercellos, Robert .... (508) 997-7411
Religion ED
Standard Times, New Bedford, MA
Berckman, Juliann .... (910) 727-7211
Garden ED
Winston-Salem Journal, Winston-Salem, NC
Bercowetz, Cynthia .... (860) 646-0500
Consumer COL
Journal Inquirer, Manchester, CT
Berdan, Kathy .... (515) 284-8000
Entertainment ED
Des Moines Register, Des Moines, IA
Berdowitz, David .... (305) 669-2355
ED, South Dade News, South Miami, FL
Berenger, Pam .... (309) 764-4344
Agriculture ED, Dispatch, Moline, IL
Small Newspaper Group Inc.
Berens, Tom .... (909) 684-1200
CIRC MGR-Transportation
Press-Enterprise, Riverside, CA
Berenson, Kay .... (413) 772-0261
PUB, EDL Board, Recorder, Greenfield, MA
Berentson, Dan .... (360) 336-6555
PUB, Skagit Argus, Mount Vernon, WA
Berezowski, David .... (403) 852-3620
ED, Jasper Booster, Jasper, AB
Berg, Barry .... (714) 835-1234
PROD DIR-MR/Transportation
Orange County Register, Santa Ana, CA
Berg, Barry .... (210) 225-7411
CIRC VP-Distribution
San Antonio Express-News, San Antonio, TX
Berg, Jim .... (210) 675-4500
PUB, Kelly Observer, San Antonio, TX
Berg, Larry .... (206) 464-2111
PROD MGR-Day OPER (North Creek), PROD MGR-Platemaking
Seattle Times, Seattle, WA
Bergen, Terry .... (319) 398-8211
MGR-PROM/Public Affairs
Gazette, Cedar Rapids, IA
Bergen, Werner .... (705) 745-4641
District ED, Examiner, Peterborough, ON
Berger, Bob .... (213) 237-5000
Op-Ed ED
Los Angeles Times, Los Angeles, CA
Berger, Dan .... (213) 237-5000
Wine COL
Los Angeles Times, Los Angeles, CA
Berger, Doug .... (417) 926-5148
ED, Mountain Grove News-Journal, Mountain Grove, MO
Berger, George .... (312) 321-3000
DIR-Special Events
Chicago Sun-Times, Chicago, IL
Berger, Jeff .... (210) 426-3346
PUB, Hondo Anvil Herald, Hondo, TX
Berger, Knute .... (206) 623-0500
ED, Seattle Weekly, Seattle, WA
Berger, Robert .... (209) 441-6111
CONT, Fresno Bee, Fresno, CA
McClatchy Newspapers
Berger, Tim .... (818) 962-8811
Photo ED, San Gabriel Valley Tribune, West Covina, CA, MediaNews Inc.
Berger, Tom .... (715) 842-2101
EPE, Wausau Daily Herald, Wausau, WI
Berger, William E .... (210) 426-3346
PUB, Hondo Anvil Herald, Hondo, TX
Bergeron, Francois .... (905) 465-2107
ED, L'Express, Toronto, ON
Bergeron, Paul .... (703) 560-4000
Sports ED, Fairfax Journal, Fairfax, VA
Journal Newspapers Inc.
Bergeron, Pierre .... (613) 562-0111
PUB/GM, Le Droit, Ottawa, ON
Bergeron, Richard R .... (603) 668-4321
PROD FRM-PR
Union Leader, Manchester, NH
Berggren, Dave .... (913) 632-2127
Sports ED, Dispatch, Clay Center, KS
Bergh, H Theodore .... (513) 721-2700
VP-FIN, Cincinnati Enquirer, Cincinnati, OH
Bergia, Fred L .... (309) 686-3000
VP/TREAS
Peoria Journal Star Inc., Peoria, IL
Bergin, Jeff .... (941) 335-0200
ADV MGR-RT, News-Press, Fort Myers, FL
Bergin, Mary .... (608) 274-8925
Founder/ED
Midwest Features, Madison, WI
Berglund, Florence J .... (715) 255-8531
PUB, Tribune Record-Gleaner, Loyal, WI
Berglund, Robert E .... (715) 255-8531
PUB, Tribune Record-Gleaner, Loyal, WI
Bergman, Kim B .... (330) 454-5611
ADV MGR-CLASS, Repository, Canton, OH
Bergman, Rollin .... (218) 436-2157
PUB, North Star News, Karlstad, MN
Bergmann, Horst A .... (213) 237-3700
VP/Chairman/PRES/CEO-Jeppesen Sanderson, Times Mirror Co., Los Angeles, CA
Bergmann, Randy .... (609) 924-3244
ED, Princeton Packet, Princeton, NJ
Bergmeier, Dave .... (913) 263-1000
MAN ED
Abilene Reflector-Chronicle, Abilene, KS
Bergonzi, Lou .... (718) 981-1234
Sports ED, Staten Island Advance, Staten Island, NY
Bergstedt, Elizabeth .... (217) 824-2233
Features ED, Taylorville Daily Breeze-Courier, Taylorville, IL
Bergstrand, Thomas W .... (508) 793-9100
Sunday News ED
Telegram & Gazette, Worcester, MA
Bergstresser, Charles E .... (216) 696-3322
TREAS, Daily Legal News and Cleveland Recorder, Cleveland, OH
Bergstrom, Mike .... (805) 395-7500
PROD MGR-Packaging/Distribution
Bakersfield Californian, Bakersfield, CA
Bergum, Judy .... (608) 767-3655
GM, News-Sickle-Arrow, Black Earth, WI
Beringer, Chris .... (206) 448-8000
ASST MAN ED
Seattle Post-Intelligencer, Seattle, WA
Berkeley, Gail .... (510) 763-1120
ED, Post Group, Oakland, CA
Berkeley, Thomas L .... (510) 763-1120
PUB, Post Group, Oakland, CA
Berkeley, Velda .... (510) 763-1120
PUB, Post Group, Oakland, CA
Berkenbosch, Kevin .... (705) 759-3030
MGR-MKTG/PROM
Sault Star, Sault Ste. Marie, ON
Berkley, Gary .... (618) 234-1000
PRES/PUB
Belleville News-Democrat, Belleville, IL
Berkley, Thomas L .... (510) 287-8200
PUB, El Mundo, Oakland, CA
Berkowitz, David .... (909) 793-3221
ADV DIR
Redlands Daily Facts, Redlands, CA
Berkowitz, David .... (305) 669-7355
ED, Aventura News, South Miami, FL
Berkowitz, Lana .... (713) 220-7171
TV Book ED, Houston Chronicle, Houston, TX
Berkowitz, Mark .... (315) 789-3333
CONT, CIRC DIR
Finger Lakes Times, Geneva, NY
Berlier, Nancy .... (513) 721-2700
Suburban ED
Cincinnati Enquirer, Cincinnati, OH
Berling, J Patrick .... (941) 262-3161
ADV DIR, Naples Daily News, Naples, FL
Berlinquette, Ron .... (807) 343-6200
PROD FRM-PR
Chronicle-Journal, Thunder Bay, ON
Berlow, Bill .... (904) 599-2100
EDU (Secondary/Higher)
Tallahassee Democrat, Tallahassee, FL
Berlyn, Steven .... (715) 423-7200
CONT, Daily Tribune, Wisconsin Rapids, WI
Berman, Audrey .... (805) 965-5205
MAN ED, Santa Barbara Independent, Santa Barbara, CA
Berman, Dan .... (203) 964-2200
Features ED
Stamford Advocate, Stamford, CT
Berman, Karen .... (212) 807-6622
Picture ED, Impact Visuals Photo & Graphics Inc., New York, NY
Bermingham, Raymond .... (501) 315-8228
PROD FRM-PR, Benton Courier, Benton, AR
Bermudez, Armando .... (201) 217-2475
ED, El Nuevo Hudson, Jersey City, NJ
Bern, Bill .... (540) 981-3100
Sports ED, Roanoke Times, Roanoke, VA
Bernard, Dan .... (218) 723-5281
Political Writer
Duluth News-Tribune, Duluth, MN
Bernard, Max .... (513) 422-3611
PROD MGR-COMP
Middletown Journal, Middletown, OH
Bernard, Michel G .... (212) 779-6300
PRES, Gamma-Liaison Inc., New York, NY
Bernard, Roy .... (815) 937-3300
BUS/FIN ED, Daily Journal, Kankakee, IL
Bernard, Sonya .... (616) 964-7161
Religion ED
Battle Creek Enquirer, Battle Creek, MI
Bernardin, Cardinal Joseph ..... (312) 243-1300
PUB, New World, Chicago, IL
Bernardini, Denise .... (415) 431-4792
ED
San Francisco Beacon, San Francisco, CA
Bernasconi, Fideie .... (603) 880-1516
PUB, Hudson-Litchfield News, Hudson, NH
Bernatchez, Raymond .... (514) 285-7272
Theater ED, La Presse, Montreal, QC

Copyright ©1997 by the Editor & Publisher Co.

19-Who's Where **Bie**

Bernatki-Byrd, Tess .... (204) 697-7000
DIR-PROM
Winnipeg Free Press, Winnipeg, MB
Berndt, John .... (308) 382-1000
Graphics ED/Art DIR
Grand Island Independent, Grand Island, NE
Berner, Fred A .... (715) 623-4191
GM, ED, MAN ED, Teen-Age/Youth ED
Antigo Daily Journal, Antigo, WI
Berner, M F .... (715) 623-4191
PUB, CIRC MGR
Antigo Daily Journal, Antigo, WI
Bernet, George .... (602) 468-6565
ED, Daily Racing Form, Phoenix, AZ
Bernett, Greg .... (206) 448-8000
ADV MGR-Display
Seattle Post-Intelligencer, Seattle, WA
Bernhagen, Marshall .... (414) 326-5151
PUB, Advance, Randolph, WI
Bernhard, Andy .... (801) 649-9014
PUB, Park Record, Park City, UT
Bernhard, Peter .... (510) 208-6300
PRES/PUB, Oakland Tribune, Oakland, CA
MediaNews Inc. (Alameda Newspapers)
Bernheim, Fred .... (719) 634-1593
PRES
Daily Transcript, Colorado Springs, CO
Bernheim, John .... (719) 634-1593
PUB, Mountaineer, Colorado Springs, CO
Bernick Jr, Bob .... (801) 237-2188
Political ED
Deseret News, Salt Lake City, UT
Berninger, Jack .... (804) 649-6000
Sports ED
Richmond Times-Dispatch, Richmond, VA
Bernini, Grace .... (801) 433-6933
ED, Eureka Reporter, Eureka, UT
Bernsee, Eric .... (317) 653-5151
ED, EPE, Radio/Television
Banner-Graphic, Greencastle, IN
Bernsen, Charles .... (901) 529-2211
MET ED, Commercial Appeal, Memphis, TN
Bernstein, Dan .... (909) 684-1200
COL, Press-Enterprise, Riverside, CA
Bernstein, Ellen Joy .... (413) 458-9000
PUB, Advocate/South Advocate, Williamstown, MA
Bernstein, Henry .... (312) 649-5464
ED, Crain News Service, Chicago, IL
Bernstein, Leonard .... (213) 237-5000
Orange County MAN ED
Los Angeles Times, Los Angeles, CA
Bernstein, Michelle .... (312) 750-4000
ADV MGR-CLASS, Wall Street Journal-Central Edition, Chicago, IL
Bernstein, Nell .... (415) 243-4364
Youth Outlook ED
Pacific News Service, San Francisco, CA
Bernstein, Sanford .... (718) 634-4000
GM
Wave of Long Island, Rockaway Beach, NY
Berreth, James D .... (612) 442-4414
PUB, Waconia Patriot, Waconia, MN
Berrier, David .... (910) 373-7000
CIRC MGR, News & Record, Greensboro, NC
Berry, Abel .... (908) 352-6654
PUB, ED, La Voz, Elizabeth, NJ
Berry, Allen W .... (501) 378-3400
CONT, Wehco Media Inc., Little Rock, AR
Berry, Bill .... (715) 344-6100
ED, Farm/Outdoor ED, Picture ED
Stevens Point Journal, Stevens Point, WI
Berry, Bob .... (561) 820-4100
ADV MGR-NTL
Palm Beach Post, West Palm Beach, FL
Berry, Cary .... (307) 532-2184
ED, Torrington Telegram, Torrington, WY
Berry, Charles A .... (501) 534-3400
PUB
Pine Bluff Commercial, Pine Bluff, AR
Berry, Dave .... (903) 597-8111
MAN ED, Tyler Morning Telegraph, Tyler, TX
Berry, Dave .... (417) 326-7636
PUB, Herald-Free Press, Bolivar, MO
Berry, Dave .... (814) 946-7411
CIRC MGR-MKTG
Altoona Mirror, Altoona, PA
Berry, John .... (309) 829-9411
EDU Writer, Pantagraph, Bloomington, IL
Berry, Karin .... (215) 854-2000
New Jersey ED
Philadelphia Daily News, Philadelphia, PA
Berry, Ken .... (808) 235-5881
PUB, Midweek Magazine, Kaneohe, HI
Berry, Linda .... (316) 225-4151
MGR-CR, PSL MGR, DP MGR
Dodge City Daily Globe, Dodge City, KS
Berry, Lynn .... (505) 763-3431
CIRC MGR, Clovis News Journal, Clovis, NM
Berry, Mark .... (513) 422-3611
Sports ED
Middletown Journal, Middletown, OH
Berry, Melody .... (913) 352-6235
ED, Linn County News, Pleasanton, KS

Berry, Mike .... (309) 852-2181
City/EDU ED, Photo DEPT MGR
Star-Courier, Kewanee, IL
Berry, Pat .... (405) 235-3100
Office MGR
Journal Record, Oklahoma City, OK
Berry, Peter .... (602) 468-6565
News ED, Daily Racing Form, Phoenix, AZ
Berry, Peter L .... (717) 421-3000
ADV DIR, Pocono Record, Stroudsburg, PA
Berry, Roy .... (918) 581-8300
ADV MGR-NTL, Tulsa World, Tulsa, OK
Berry, Ryan .... (937) 548-3330
MAN ED, Early Bird, Greenville, OH
Berry, Shelly .... (619) 442-4404
CIRC CNR-NIE
Daily Californian, El Cajon, CA
Berry, Stan .... (573) 785-1414
ED, Agriculture ED
Daily American Republic, Poplar Bluff, MO
Berry, Steve .... (770) 532-1234
DIR-Human Resources
Times, Gainesville, GA
Berry, Tracey .... (573) 581-1111
BUS ED, City ED, Features ED, News ED, Television/Film ED, Theater/Music ED
Mexico Ledger, Mexico, MO
Berry, Warren .... (516) 843-2020
Special Sections ED
Newsday, Melville, NY
Berry, William .... (419) 625-5500
ADV MGR-RT
Sandusky Register, Sandusky, OH
Berry, William .... (613) 829-9100
CIRC MGR-Reader Sales & SRV-Single Copy Sales, Ottawa Citizen, Ottawa, ON
Berry-Hawes, Jennifer .... (864) 298-4100
Health/Medical ED
Greenville News, Greenville, SC
Berryman, Betty .... (606) 744-3123
EVP, PUB, Winchester Sun, Winchester, KY
Berryman, Eric .... (704) 289-1541
PROD MGR, Enquirer-Journal, Monroe, NC
Berryman, Steve .... (606) 744-3123
PROD MGR-Pre Press
Winchester Sun, Winchester, KY
Berryman, Thomas H .... (815) 747-3171
ED
East Dubuque Register, East Dubuque, IL
Berryman, Tina .... (209) 441-6111
ADV MGR-OPER, Fresno Bee, Fresno, CA
Bersen, Misha .... (206) 464-2111
Theater Critic, Seattle Times, Seattle, WA
Bert, John N .... (904) 539-6586
PUB, ED, Havana Herald, Havana, FL
Berthiaume, Ed .... (414) 733-4411
Entertainment ED, Features ED, Films/Theater ED, Food ED, Lifestyle ED, Music ED, Travel ED, Post-Crescent, Appleton, WI
Berthiaume, Johanne .... (514) 743-8466
PUB, GM, ED, Journal La Voix, Sorel, QC
Berthiaume, Roland .... (418) 686-3233
Cartoonist, Le Soleil, Quebec, QC
Berti, Vince .... (609) 691-5000
PROD MGR-PR, Daily Journal, Vineland, NJ
Berto, Deborah L .... (206) 392-6434
PUB, Issaquah Press, Issaquah, WA
Bertrand, Frank .... (541) 485-1234
CIRC MGR-OPER
Register-Guard, Eugene, OR
Bertrand, Ross .... (815) 937-3300
PROD FRM-COMP
Daily Journal, Kankakee, IL
Berube, Andre .... (418) 683-1573
CONT
Le Journal de Quebec, Ville Vanier, QC
Berube, Gerard .... (514) 985-3333
Economic ED, Le Devoir, Montreal, QC
Berzanskis, Cheryl .... (806) 669-2525
Society ED, Pampa News, Pampa, TX
Beshears, Kathy .... (316) 694-5700
Human Resources DIR
Hutchinson News, Hutchinson, KS
Besougloff, Neil .... (941) 748-0411
Deputy City ED
Bradenton Herald, Bradenton, FL
Bess, Caralyn .... (407) 420-5000
ADV MGR-RT, Orange/Seminole Division
Orlando Sentinel, Orlando, FL
Bessel, Richard .... (203) 744-5100
ADV MGR, ADTX MGR
News-Times, Danbury, CT
Bessenyei, Laszlo .... (416) 221-6195
ED, Magyar Elet, Willowdale, ON
Besser, David .... (847) 966-3900
PUB, Bugle, Niles, IL
Bessette, B Jean .... (508) 997-7411
CNR-Educational Services
Standard Times, New Bedford, MA
Best, Brooks .... (919) 752-6166
PROD MGR-Press/Post Press
Daily Reflector, Greenville, NC
Best, Jonathan .... (610) 820-6500
VP/CFO, Morning Call, Allentown, PA

Best, Marion E .... (217) 728-7381
PUB, News-Progress, Sullivan, IL
Best, Mark .... (414) 457-7711
CIRC DIR-Sales/MKTG
Sheboygan Press, Sheboygan, WI
Bestgen, Connie .... (573) 796-2135
ED, California Democrat, California, MO
Bestor, Mary Jane .... (608) 328-4202
News ED, Monroe Times, Monroe, WI
Betbeze, Philip .... (615) 794-4564
MAN ED, Williamson Leader, Franklin, TN
Betcher, Robert J .... (561) 287-1550
Television/Film ED, Theater/Music ED
Stuart News, Stuart, FL
Betchkal, Paul .... (414) 634-3322
PROD SUPV-PR, Journal Times, Racine, WI
Bethel, Brian .... (915) 673-4271
EDU ED-Higher
Abilene Reporter-News, Abilene, TX
Bethel, Judith .... (706) 324-5526
Food ED, Ledger-Enquirer, Columbus, GA
Bethel, Karen .... (405) 372-5000
ADV MGR-NTL, News Press, Stillwater, OK
Bethke, James .... (507) 454-6500
PROD MGR-PR
Winona Daily News, Winona, MN
Betros, Ronald E .... (914) 454-2000
CIRC DIR
Poughkeepsie Journal, Poughkeepsie, NY
Betsi, Helen .... (209) 634-9141
BM, Turlock Journal, Turlock, CA
Bett, Daniel J .... (515) 522-7155
GM, Free Press, Brooklyn, IA
Bettelheim, Adriel .... (303) 820-1010
Washington BU Chief
Denver Post, Denver, CO
Bettis, Mitch .... (316) 624-2541
ADV MGR
Southwest Daily Times, Liberal, KS
Betts, Stephen .... (207) 594-4401
MAN ED, Courier-Gazette, Rockland, ME
Betwee, Pat .... (616) 345-3511
Radio/Television ED
Kalamazoo Gazette, Kalamazoo, MI
Betz, Ava .... (719) 336-2266
ED, Lamar Daily News, Lamar, CO
Betz, Gail .... (614) 345-4053
MGR-CR, Advocate, Newark, OH
Betz, Jacob P .... (717) 648-4641
MAN ED, News-Item, Shamokin, PA
Betz, Sharon .... (510) 208-6300
Features ED, Oakland Tribune, Oakland, CA
MediaNews Inc. (Alameda Newspapers)
Betz, Tom .... (719) 336-2266
PUB/PA, MAN ED
Lamar Daily News, Lamar, CO
Beucke, Dan .... (516) 843-2020
Daily BUS ED, Newsday, Melville, NY
Beumer, Roger .... (970) 824-7031
PROD MGR
Northwest Colorado Daily Press, Craig, CO
Beuter, Marietta .... (319) 644-2233
ED, Solon Economist, Solon, IA
Beutler, Patty .... (402) 475-4200
Teens/Features Reporter
Lincoln Journal Star, Lincoln, NE
Beveridge, James M .... (309) 473-2414
PUB, ED, Heyworth Star, Heyworth, IL
Beverley, Mrs Perry S Grant .... (613) 342-4441
Co-PUB, EIC, Brockville Recorder and Times, Brockville, ON
Beverly, Ginny .... (972) 542-2631
Women's ED
McKinney Courier-Gazette, McKinney, TX
Bevier, Ellen .... (619) 299-3131
MET ED-Day
San Diego Union-Tribune, San Diego, CA
Bevil, Bob .... (501) 667-2136
PUB, Spectator, Ozark, AR
Bevilacqua, Cardinal Anthony . (215) 587-3660
PUB
Catholic Standard & Times, Philadelphia, PA
Bevins, Doug .... (203) 235-1661
SYS ED, Record-Journal, Meriden, CT
Bewick, Frank H .... (313) 584-4000
PUB, Dearborn Times-Herald, Dearborn, MI
Bewkey, Bernie .... (423) 246-8121
PROD FRM-COMP
Kingsport Times-News, Kingsport, TN
Beyer, Mike .... (517) 752-7171
Political ED, Saginaw News, Saginaw, MI
Beyers, Becky .... (320) 255-8700
Topics ED, St. Cloud Times, St. Cloud, MN
Beyette, Beverly .... (213) 237-5000
COL, Los Angeles Times, Los Angeles, CA
Beyrau, Caroline .... (704) 358-5000
EDU ED, Charlotte Observer, Charlotte, NC
Bezgela, Sandra .... (910) 891-1234
DP MGR, Daily Record, Dunn, NC
Bezio, Lyman .... (518) 561-2300
ADV MGR-CLASS
Press-Republican, Plattsburgh, NY
Bezore, Buz .... (408) 457-9000
ED, Metro Santa Cruz, Santa Cruz, CA

Bezzano, Jack .... (317) 459-3121
ADTX MGR, Kokomo Tribune, Kokomo, IN
Bezzant, Brett R .... (801) 756-7669
PUB, Citizen, American Fork, UT
Bhatia, Peter .... (503) 221-8327
MAN ED, Oregonian, Portland, OR
Bhugaloo, Nariz .... (416) 441-1405
Africa Photographer, Fotopress Independent News Service International, Toronto, ON
Bialasiewicz, Wojciech .... (312) 763-3343
ED, Dziennik Zwaizkowy, Chicago, IL
Bialek, Nancy .... (414) 778-5000
ED, Brookfield News, Wauwatosa, WI
Bialick, Florence .... (516) 739-6400
ED, Oceanside-Rockville Centre Beacon, Mineola, NY
Bialka, Mike .... (218) 829-4705
Sports ED
Brainerd Daily Dispatch, Brainerd, MN
Bianchi, Jack .... (937) 328-0300
MAN ED
Springfield News-Sun, Springfield, OH
Bianci, Bob .... (908) 722-8800
PROD MGR-Maintenance
Courier-News, Bridgewater, NJ
Bianco, Robert .... (412) 263-1100
Radio/Television ED
Pittsburgh Post-Gazette, Pittsburgh, PA
Biancolli, Amy .... (518) 454-5694
Film Writer, Times Union, Albany, NY
Biano, Carmen .... (916) 533-3131
City ED
Oroville Mercury Register, Oroville, CA
Bias, Joan .... (304) 765-5555
ED, Braxton Democrat-Central, Sutton, WV
Bibb, David .... (816) 234-4141
PROD MGR-PR
Kansas City Star, Kansas City, MO
Bibbee, Mac .... (304) 348-5140
ADV MGR-RT
Charleston Newspapers, Charleston, WV
Bibisi, Susan .... (203) 574-3636
MET ED, Waterbury Republican-American, Waterbury, CT
Bible Sr, R H .... (423) 581-5630
BC, Citizen Tribune, Morristown, TN
Bibler, Steve .... (219) 294-1661
MET ED, Elkhart Truth, Elkhart, IN
Bibs, Tom .... (806) 376-4488
CIRC DIR, Amarillo Daily News/Globe Times, Amarillo, TX
Biccum, Dwayne .... (306) 233-4325
PUB, ED, Wakaw Recorder, Wakaw, SK
Bicker, Gary .... (319) 242-7101
ADV DIR, Clinton Herald, Clinton, IA
Bickert, Tom .... (412) 775-3200
ASSOC ED, Beaver County Times, Beaver, PA
Bickert, Tony .... (907) 835-2211
MAN ED, Valdez Vanguard, Valdez, AK
Bickford, Andrew T .... (610) 527-6330
VP, Independent Publications Inc., Bryn Mawr, PA
Bickford, Brice .... (913) 764-2211
PROD MGR-COMP
Olathe Daily News, Olathe, KS
Bickford, Charles .... (501) 751-6200
Photo DEPT MGR, Morning News of Northwest Arkansas, Springdale, AR
Bickler, Robert .... (509) 248-1251
ADV DIR
Yakima Herald-Republic, Yakima, WA
Bickley, Claire .... (416) 947-2222
Television ED, Toronto Sun, Toronto, ON
Bickley, Dan .... (312) 321-3000
Baseball Writer
Chicago Sun-Times, Chicago, IL
Biddle, Frederick M .... (617) 929-2000
Radio/Television ED
Boston Globe, Boston, MA
Biddle, Joe .... (615) 259-8800
Sports ED, Nashville Banner, Nashville, TN
Bides, Ed .... (904) 599-2100
ADTX MGR, Tallahassee Democrat, Tallahassee, FL
Bidnik, Alex .... (201) 773-8300
PUB, North Jersey Prospector, Clifton, NJ
Bidnik Jr, Alex .... (201) 773-8300
MAN ED
North Jersey Prospector, Clifton, NJ
Bidwell, Ann .... (415) 435-2652
GM, Ark, Tiburon, CA
Bidwell, Sharon .... (502) 582-4011
Librarian, Courier-Journal, Louisville, KY
Bieberich, John R .... (410) 268-5000
CIRC DIR, Capital, Annapolis, MD
Biederman, Howard .... (717) 821-2091
BUS/FIN ED, Wire ED
Citizens' Voice, Wilkes-Barre, PA

Copyright ©1997 by the Editor & Publisher Co.

Bie Who's Where-20

Bieger, Michael (814) 946-7411
City ED, Altoona Mirror, Altoona, PA

Biehn, Steve (405) 223-2200
Photo DEPT MGR
Daily Ardmoreite, Ardmore, OK

Bielawski, Esther (419) 695-0015
MAN ED, Delphos Daily Herald, Delphos, OH

Bielik, Craig (801) 625-4200
MGR-Creative
Standard-Examiner, Ogden, UT

Bielser, Jeffrey (308) 872-2471
ED, Custer County Chief, Broken Bow, NE

Bielss, Gayle (817) 527-4424
PUB, ED, Granger News, Bartlett, TX

Bien, Larry (817) 390-7400
ADV MGR-NTL
Fort Worth Star-Telegram, Fort Worth, TX

Bienveno, Patrick (318) 289-6300
MGR-SYS, Advertiser, Lafayette, LA

Bienvenu, Dee (318) 365-6773
CIRC DIR, Daily Iberian, New Iberia, LA

Bienvenu, Henri C (318) 394-6232
PUB, ED
Breaux Bridge Banner, St. Martinville, LA

Bier, Jerry (209) 441-6111
Medical Writer, Fresno Bee, Fresno, CA

Bierbaum, Debra (410) 228-3131
ADV MGR, ED, Daily Banner, Cambridge, MD

Bieringer, Connie (603) 742-4455
Features ED, Foster's Democrat, Dover, NH

Bierman, Noah (218) 723-5281
EDU Writer
Duluth News-Tribune, Duluth, MN

Biermann, Tom (414) 235-7700
CIRC MGR
Oshkosh Northwestern, Oshkosh, WI

Biernacki, Bernie (630) 257-1090
ED, Lemont Reporter, Downers Grove, IL

Biesen, Jeff Den (604) 256-4219
PUB, ED, Bridge River News, Lillooet, BC

Biesen, Robin (219) 933-3200
Health/Medical ED, Times, Munster, IN

Biesterfield, Jack (847) 888-7800
Travel ED, Courier-News, Elgin, IL

Bigelow, Bill (541) 382-1811
Sports ED, Bulletin, Bend, OR

Bigelow, Bob (503) 635-8811
PUB, Lake Oswego Review, Lake Oswego, OR

Bigelow, Susan (816) 271-8500
ADV MGR-CLASS
St. Joseph News-Press, St. Joseph, MO

Biggers, Donnie (704) 333-1718
Sports ED
Independent Tribune, Concord, NC

Biggers, Douglas (520) 792-3630
PUB, ED, Tucson Weekly, Tucson, AZ

Biggers, George (407) 645-5888
GM, Weekly, Winter Park, FL

Biggerstaff, Jim (915) 676-6765
ED, Dyess Peacemaker, Abilene, TX

Biggs, Anthony H (219) 294-1661
VP/PUB, Federated Media Corp., Elkhart, IN

Biggs, Betty N (806) 537-3634
ED, Panhandle Herald, Panhandle, TX

Biggs, Charles (812) 546-6113
ED, Hope Star-Journal, Hope, IN

Biggs, Dinah (219) 883-4903
MAN ED, Gary American, Gary, IN

Biggs, John H (601) 423-2211
PUB, Tishomingo County News, Iuka, MS

Biggs, Rick (408) 920-5000
CIRC MGR-Single Copy
San Jose Mercury News, San Jose, CA

Bigham, T C (205) 345-0505
PROD MGR-MR
Tuscaloosa News, Tuscaloosa, AL

Bigras, Bernard (514) 521-4545
ADV MGR-NTL
Le Journal de Montreal, Montreal, QC

Bilak, Victor W (814) 532-5199
CONT, Tribune-Democrat, Johnstown, PA

Bilbao, Gerard (212) 930-8000
CIRC SUPT-Delivery
New York Post, New York, NY

Bilby, Marg (209) 847-3021
ED, Riverbank News, Riverbank, CA

Bilderback, Ken (360) 694-3391
ADTX MGR, New Media MGR
Columbian, Vancouver, WA

Biles, Jan (913) 843-1000
Entertainment ED
Journal-World, Lawrence, KS

Bilinski, Bill (219) 235-6161
Sports ED
South Bend Tribune, South Bend, IN

Bilinski, James (607) 277-7000
PUB, Ithaca Times, Ithaca, NY

Billeter, Robert (304) 269-1600
PUB, Weston Democrat, Weston, WV

Billiel, Jeffrey (937) 498-2111
MAN ED, EPE, Graphics ED/Art DIR, Television/Film ED, Theater/Music ED
Sidney Daily News, Sidney, OH

Billig, Eve (703) 276-3796
ED, Kids Today, Arlington, VA

Billings, Brian (304) 675-1333
ADV MGR
Point Pleasant Register, Point Pleasant, WV

Billings, Denny (816) 234-4141
PROD MGR-CNR
Kansas City Star, Kansas City, MO

Billings, Ed (601) 453-5312
PROD MGR, Commonwealth, Greenwood, MS

Billings, Emily (702) 383-0211
ADV MGR-Sales Development
Las Vegas Review-Journal, Las Vegas, NV

Billings, Jerry (707) 448-6401
ADV DIR, Reporter, Vacaville, CA

Billingsley, Anna (540) 374-5000
Fashion ED, Lifestyle ED
Free Lance-Star, Fredericksburg, VA

Billingsley, Sharon (317) 831-0280
PUB, Times, Mooresville, IN

Billington, Linda (907) 257-4200
Community News ED, Films/Theater ED
Anchorage Daily News, Anchorage, AK

Billitteri, Tom (202) 463-8777
News ED
Religion News Service, Washington, DC

Billmyer, Steve (315) 470-0011
Religion ED, Post-Standard/Syracuse Herald-Journal/ American, Syracuse, NY

Billow, Pam (702) 383-0211
MGR-CR, Review-Journal, Las Vegas, NV

Bills, Steve (912) 744-4200
Online Contact, Macon Telegraph, Macon, GA

Bilmes, David (203) 744-5100
Sports ED, News-Times, Danbury, CT

Bilodeau, Andre (514) 375-4555
Sports ED, La Voix de l'Est, Granby, QC

Bilodeau, Katherine (802) 524-9771
NTL News ED
St. Albans Messenger, St. Albans, VT

Bilotti, Richard (609) 989-5454
PRES/PUB, Times, Trenton, NJ

Bilyeu, Hank (804) 458-8511
Sports ED, News, Hopewell, VA

Bind, Barbara (203) 964-2200
MGR-PROM/Public Affairs, ADTX MGR
Stamford Advocate, Stamford, CT
Times Mirror Co.

Binder, Mary (301) 921-2800
ED, Eagle, Gaithersburg, MD

Binder, Tom (414) 457-7711
ADTX MGR, Sheboygan Press, Sheboygan, WI

Bindler, Donald E (516) 283-4100
GM, Southampton Press, Southampton, NY

Bindokas, Danute (312) 585-9500
ED, Draugas, Chicago, IL

Binford, Tammy (615) 259-8800
Features ED, Nashville Banner, Nashville, TN

Bingham, Elesha (405) 884-2424
GM, Geary Star, Geary, OK

Bingham, Fred (405) 884-2424
PUB, ED, Geary Star, Geary, OK

Bingham, Janet (303) 820-1010
EDU Reporter, Denver Post, Denver, CO

Bingham, Maren (602) 271-8000
Features ED, Arizona Republic, Phoenix, AZ

Binghman, Ruthanne (714) 527-8210
GM, News-Enterprise, Los Alamitos, CA

Bingle, Patrick A (412) 775-3200
ADTX MGR
Beaver County Times, Beaver, PA

Bingley, Phil (416) 367-2000
ADTX MGR, Toronto Star, Toronto, ON

Binkerd, Brenda (406) 222-2000
Films/Theater ED, Food/Women's ED, Music ED, Radio/Television ED
Livingston Enterprise, Livingston, MT

Binkley, Judi (208) 783-1107
ADV DIR, Shoshone News-Press, Kellogg, ID

Binkley, Robert J (304) 255-4400
CIRC DIR, Register Herald, Beckley, WV

Binz, Larry (501) 338-9181
ED, Daily World, Helena, AR

Binz, Paul (210) 686-4343
MAN ED, Monitor, McAllen, TX

Biondi, Roy D (405) 332-4433
PUB/GM, Ada Evening News, Ada, OK

Bir, Glenes J (702) 738-3119
ADV MGR, Elko Daily Free Press, Elko, NV

Birbari, John (307) 856-2244
ADV DIR, DIR-MKTG/PROM
Riverton Ranger, Riverton, WY

Birch, Don (509) 684-4567
PUB, Statesman-Examiner, Colville, WA

Birch, Donna (209) 578-2000
Health/Medical Reporter
Modesto Bee, Modesto, CA

Birch, Edward J (215) 949-4000
TREAS, Bucks County Courier Times, Levittown, PA, Calkins Newspapers

Birch, Timothy J (215) 949-4000
ADV DIR
Bucks County Courier Times, Levittown, PA

Birckhead, Wanda J (804) 978-7200
ADV DIR, Daily Progress, Charlottesville, VA

Bird, Anita (309) 852-2181
GM, ED, Star-Courier, Kewanee, IL

Bird, Darrell (502) 769-2312
ASST ED
News Enterprise, Elizabethtown, KY

Bird, Ernie (210) 625-9144
PROD FRM-Press, New Braunfels Herald-Zeitung, New Braunfels, TX

Bird, Henry (317) 747-5700
VP, PUB, Star Press, Muncie, IN

Bird, Johnny (972) 937-3310
PROD FRM-PR
Waxahachie Daily Light, Waxahachie, TX

Biringer, Timothy (609) 272-7000
ADV MGR-City Sales
Press of Atlantic City, Pleasantville, NJ

Birkelo, Rochelle (608) 754-3311
Women's ED
Janesville Gazette, Janesville, WI

Birkenhauer, Tracy (517) 377-1000
Health/Medical ED
Lansing State Journal, Lansing, MI

Birkland, Marilyn (320) 235-1150
ADV DIR, West Central Tribune, Willmar, MN

Birks, Dennis (805) 395-7500
PROD MGR-Technical SRV
Bakersfield Californian, Bakersfield, CA

Birks, Melissa (901) 427-3333
Features ED, Jackson Sun, Jackson, TN

Birmingham, Laura (360) 754-5400
ADV MGR-RT, Olympian, Olympia, WA

Birner, Linda D (916) 441-6397
PUB, ED, Mom Guess What Newspaper, Sacramento, CA

Birnie, Peter (604) 732-2111
Movies Critic, Vancouver Sun, Vancouver, BC

Biron, Justin (819) 376-2501
DIR, Le Nouvelliste, Trois-Rivieres, QC

Bisbee, Rebecca (512) 445-3500
BUS ED
Austin American-Statesman, Austin, TX

Bischof, Greg (903) 794-3311
Farm ED, Texarkana Gazette, Texarkana, TX

Bischoff, Susan (713) 220-7171
ASST MAN ED
Houston Chronicle, Houston, TX

Biscorner, Jane (810) 985-7171
DP MGR, Times Herald, Port Huron, MI

Bisher, Furman (404) 526-5151
Sports ED (Journal)
Atlanta Journal-Constitution, Atlanta, GA

Bisher, Nanette (714) 835-1234
Deputy ED-New Media
Orange County Register, Santa Ana, CA

Bishoff, Murray (417) 235-3135
MAN ED, Times, Monett, MO

Bishop, Arlene E (504) 647-4569
GM, ED, Gonzales Weekly, Gonzales, LA

Bishop, Chris (609) 451-1000
Music ED
Bridgeton Evening News, Bridgeton, NJ

Bishop, Crawford A (504) 647-4569
PUB, Gonzales Weekly, Gonzales, LA

Bishop, David (313) 994-6989
ASSOC ED/Ombudsman
Ann Arbor News, Ann Arbor, MI

Bishop, Eric (507) 433-8851
ADV MGR, Austin Daily Herald, Austin, MN

Bishop, James (512) 575-1451
MAN ED, Victoria Advocate, Victoria, TX

Bishop, John (207) 990-8000
DIR-INFO Services
Bangor Daily News, Bangor, ME

Bishop, Kathy (212) 930-8000
Women's ED, New York Post, New York, NY

Bishop, Kevin (618) 529-5454
MGR-MKTG/PROM
Southern Illinoisan, Carbondale, IL

Bishop, Melody O (864) 967-9580
GM, Tribune-Times, Simpsonville, SC

Bishop, Randy (214) 977-8222
ELS Illustrator
Dallas Morning News, Dallas, TX

Bishop, Sam (907) 456-6661
EPE, EDL Writer
Fairbanks Daily News-Miner, Fairbanks, AK

Bishop, Tim (906) 786-2021
Graphics ED/Art DIR
Daily Press, Escanaba, MI

Bishop, Tom (603) 882-2741
PROD FRM-MR, Telegraph, Nashua, NH

Bishop, Wayne (918) 258-7171
ED, Broken Arrow Ledger, Broken Arrow, OK

Bishop II, Donald F (607) 746-2176
PUB, Delaware County Times, Delhi, NY

Bissell, Chas O (615) 259-8000
Cartoonist, Tennessean, Nashville, TN

Bissen, Joe (218) 723-5281
Sports ED, Duluth News-Tribune, Duluth, MN

Bisset, Mark (705) 325-1355
NTL News ED, Packet & Times, Orillia, ON

Bissett, Colleen (519) 442-7866
ED, Paris Star, Paris, ON

Bisson, Steve (912) 236-9511
Photo DEPT MGR
Savannah Morning News, Savannah, GA

Bissonette, Paul (518) 483-4700
PROD MGR-OPER
Malone Telegram, Malone, NY

Bissonnette, Brenda (203) 574-3636
Yes Desk MGR, Waterbury Republican-American, Waterbury, CT

Bissonnette, Lise (514) 985-3333
PUB, Le Devoir, Montreal, QC

Bite-Dickson, Guna (212) 210-2100
Travel ED, Daily News, New York, NY

Bitnery, Tim (612) 673-4000
Technology ED
Star Tribune, Minneapolis, MN

Bitolas, Christina (915) 445-5475
ADV DIR, Pecos Enterprise, Pecos, TX

Bittner-Mills, Sharon (304) 292-6301
ADTX MGR, Morgantown Dominion Post, Morgantown, WV

Bitzer Jr, John F (609) 272-7000
PRES/CEO
Press of Atlantic City, Pleasantville, NJ

Bivens, Mark (501) 337-7523
Sports ED
Malvern Daily Record, Malvern, AR

Bivens, Paula (317) 622-1212
Wire ED
Anderson Herald Bulletin, Anderson, IN

Bixler, Norma (615) 444-3952
CIRC DIR, Lebanon Democrat, Lebanon, TN

Bjerregaard, Wayne J (412) 263-1100
DIR-Human Resources
Pittsburgh Post-Gazette, Pittsburgh, PA

Bjoin, Bob (712) 755-3111
ED, News-Advertiser, Harlan, IA

Bjork, Becky (608) 782-9710
ADV DIR-CLASS
La Crosse Tribune, La Crosse, WI

Black, Ben E (903) 427-5616
ED, Clarksville Times, Clarksville, TX

Black, Buddy (913) 371-4300
PROD FRM-PR
Kansas City Kansan, Kansas City, KS

Black, Conrad M (416) 363-8721
COB, Hollinger Inc., Toronto, ON

Black, Craig (609) 845-3300
Farm/Energy ED
Gloucester County Times, Woodbury, NJ

Black, Dan (406) 755-7000
MAN ED, EPE, Daily Inter Lake, Kalispell, MT, Hagadone Corp.

Black, David (403) 468-0100
GM, Edmonton Sun, Edmonton, AB

Black, Debbie (317) 348-0110
CIRC MGR, News-Times, Hartford City, IN

Black, Don (208) 232-4161
MAN ED, EPE
Idaho State Journal, Pocatello, ID

Black, Donetta (505) 393-5141
GM, Hobbs Flare, Hobbs, NM

Black, Gordon R (503) 382-1811
PRES
Western Communications Inc., Bend, OR

Black, Grant (519) 255-5711
Photo ED, Windsor Star, Windsor, ON

Black, J Thomas (757) 857-1212
ED, Booster, Norfolk, VA

Black, Jackie (803) 551-1551
PUB, Lake Edition, Irmo, SC

Black, John (713) 471-1234
PUB, ED, Bay Shore Sun, La Porte, TX

Black, Liz (504) 345-2333
ADV MGR, Daily Star, Hammond, LA

Black, Louis (512) 454-5766
ED, Austin Chronicle, Austin, TX

Black, Marty (619) 299-3131
PROD MGR-Pre Press
San Diego Union-Tribune, San Diego, CA

Black, Robert (970) 669-5050
PROD SUPT-Composition
Loveland Daily Reporter-Herald, Loveland, CO

Black, Roberta (814) 445-9621
Farm/Food ED, Society ED
Daily American, Somerset, PA

Black, Rosemary (212) 210-2100
Food ED
New York Daily News, New York, NY

Black, Virginia (219) 235-6161
Features ED
South Bend Tribune, South Bend, IN

Blackburix, Chris (817) 937-2525
ED, Childress Index, Childress, TX

Blackburn, Carol (301) 831-0047
PUB, ED
Mt. Airy Courier-Gazette, Mt. Airy, MD

Blackburn, Connie (573) 759-2127
GM, Dixon Pilot, Dixon, MO

Copyright ©1997 by the Editor & Publisher Co.

21-Who's Where **Blo**

Blackburn, Gary .... (812) 385-2525
PRES, PUB
Princeton Daily Clarion, Princeton, IN

Blackburn, Paul .... (514) 659-8881
PUB, Le Reflet, Delsom, QC

Blackburn, Rick .... (573) 759-2127
PUB, Dixon Pilot, Dixon, MO

Blacker, Pamela .... (317) 962-1575
Accountant/MGR
Palladium-Item, Richmond, IN

Blackerby, Cheryl .... (561) 820-4100
Travel ED
Palm Beach Post, West Palm Beach, FL

Blackerby, Mike .... (423) 482-1021
Sports ED, Oak Ridger, Oak Ridge, TN

Blackford, Linda .... (304) 348-5140
EDU ED, Charleston Gazette, Sunday Gazette-Mail, Charleston, WV

Blackman, Billy .... (904) 539-6586
MAN ED, Havana Herald, Havana, FL

Blackman, Kay .... (609) 935-1500
ADV VP, Today's Sunbeam, Salem, NJ

Blackman, Michael .... (817) 390-7400
VP-EDL DIR, Star-Telegram, Fort Worth, TX

Blackman, Susan .... (403) 986-2271
ED, Leduc Representative, Leduc, AB

Blackmon, Cleretta T .... (334) 479-0629
ED, Mobile Beacon and Alabama Citizen, Mobile, AL

Blackmon, Kay .... (609) 845-3300
ADV VP
Gloucester County Times, Woodbury, NJ

Blackmon, Louis .... (713) 485-2785
PUB, Alvin Journal, Pearland, TX

Blackmon, Lyn .... (903) 794-3311
Features/Films ED, Radio/Television ED
Texarkana Gazette, Texarkana, TX

Blackshear, Bill .... (315) 792-5000
PROD MGR-Post Press
Observer-Dispatch, Utica, NY

Blackshear, Sonya M .... (405) 928-3372
GM, MAN ED, Sayre Journal, Sayre, OK

Blackstock, Patricia .... (540) 981-3100
ADV MGR-GEN, Roanoke Times, Roanoke, VA

Blackstone, Kevin .... (214) 977-8222
COL-SportsDay
Dallas Morning News, Dallas, TX

Blackstone, Renee .... (604) 732-2222
Living ED, Province, Vancouver, BC

Blackwell, J R .... (704) 692-0505
PROD FRM-PR
Times-News, Hendersonville, NC

Blackwell, Joe M .... (318) 487-6397
PROD DIR
Alexandria Daily Town Talk, Alexandria, LA

Blackwell, L .... (203) 846-3281
PROD FRM-PR, Hour, Norwalk, CT

Blackwell, Mike .... (805) 650-2900
Sports ED, Ventura County Star, Ventura, CA

Blackwell, Sam .... (573) 335-6611
Entertainment/Amusements ED
Southeast Missourian, Cape Girardeau, MO

Blackwood, David .... (800) 424-4747
Regional Accounts MGR, Tribune Media Services-Television Listings, Glens Falls, NY

Blackwood, Marti .... (918) 756-3600
Society ED
Okmulgee Daily Times, Okmulgee, OK

Blackwood, Mike .... (509) 925-1414
PROD DIR-PR, Daily Record, Ellensburg, WA

Bladine, Jon E .... (503) 472-5114
PUB, ED, News-Register, McMinnville, OR

Blaesing, Geoffrey .... (414) 224-2000
Senior ED-Graphics
Milwaukee Journal Sentinel, Milwaukee, WI

Blaesser, Mike .... (408) 423-4242
News ED
Santa Cruz County Sentinel, Santa Cruz, CA

Blagg, Brenda .... (501) 751-6200
Political ED, Morning News of Northwest Arkansas, Springdale, AR

Blagg, Timothy A .... (413) 772-0261
ED, EDL Board, Recorder, Greenfield, MA

Blaha, Joseph .... (503) 255-2142
PUB, Daily Shipping News, Portland, OR

Blaha, Marvin A .... (605) 589-3242
PUB, Tribune & Register, Tyndall, SD

Blain, Joel .... (909) 684-1200
EPE, Press-Enterprise, Riverside, CA

Blaine, James G .... (610) 444-6590
PUB, Kennett Paper, Kennett Square, PA

Blaine, Marilou .... (603) 352-1234
Living ED, Keene Sentinel, Keene, NH

Blair, Allen .... (606) 723-5161
ED, Citizen Voice & Times, Irvine, KY

Blair, Becky .... (719) 531-3304
Contact
Briargate Media, Colorado Springs, CO

Blair, Bill .... (704) 245-6431
SEC/TREAS, PUB/GM
Daily Courier, Forest City, NC

Blair, Billie .... (505) 983-3303
ASSOC PUB
Santa Fe New Mexican, Santa Fe, NM

Blair, Bruce .... (619) 299-3131
CIRC MGR-Sales
San Diego Union-Tribune, San Diego, CA

Blair, Charles M .... (317) 924-5143
GM, Indianapolis Recorder, Indianapolis, IN

Blair, Gary .... (419) 245-6000
VP/TREAS, VP-ADM, Blade, Toledo, OH

Blair, Janet .... (614) 654-1321
ADV MGR-RT
Lancaster Eagle-Gazette, Lancaster, OH

Blair, JoNell .... (915) 453-2433
ED, Observer Enterprise, Robert Lee, TX

Blair, Karen .... (209) 532-7151
MGR-Office, Union Democrat, Sonora, CA

Blair, Kirk .... (903) 794-3311
ADV DIR
Arkansas-Texas Comic Group, Texarkana, TX

Blair, Linda .... (815) 842-1153
BM, Daily Leader, Pontiac, IL

Blair, Nancy .... (914) 694-9300
ASST MAN ED-BUS
Reporter Dispatch, White Plains, NY

Blair, Paula .... (405) 255-5354
ADV MGR-CLASS
Duncan Banner, Duncan, OK

Blair, Randall .... (604) 853-1144
PUB, News, Abbotsford, BC

Blair, Seabury .... (360) 377-3711
Travel/Outdoors Writer, Sun, Bremerton, WA

Blais, Jacques .... (819) 776-1063
PUB, ED, Le Regional de Hull, Hull, QC

Blais, Lillian .... (401) 849-3300
MGR-CR, Newport Daily News, Newport, RI

Blaisdale, Chris .... (619) 792-3820
GM, Del Mar/Solana Beach/Carmel Valley/ Rancho Santa Fe Sun, Del Mar, CA

Blaisdell, Lynn .... (509) 427-8444
ED
Skamania County Pioneer, Stevenson, WA

Blaisdell-Bannon, Alicia .... (508) 775-1200
News Desk Chief
Cape Cod Times, Hyannis, MA

Blake, Alison .... (204) 857-3427
PROD SUPV-COMP
Daily Graphic, Portage la Prairie, MB

Blake, Carolyn .... (802) 334-6568
ADV DIR
Newport Daily Express, Newport, VT

Blake, George R .... (513) 721-2700
VP-Community Affairs
Cincinnati Enquirer, Cincinnati, OH

Blake, Harriet .... (214) 977-8222
High Profile ED
Dallas Morning News, Dallas, TX

Blake, Jeannie .... (504) 826-3279
Action Line ED
Times-Picayune, New Orleans, LA

Blake, Jim .... (519) 354-2000
ED, MAN ED, Books ED, EPE
Chatham Daily News, Chatham, ON

Blake, Kim .... (616) 696-3655
GM, Cedar Springs Post, Cedar Springs, MI

Blake, Nancy .... (509) 935-8422
PUB, Chewelah Independent, Chewelah, WA

Blake, Paula .... (316) 775-2218
ADV DIR, Augusta Daily Gazette, Augusta, KS

Blake, Peter .... (303) 892-5000
Political COL
Rocky Mountain News, Denver, CO

Blake, Philip .... (608) 252-6200
PRES, PUB (Wisconsin State Journal)
Madison Newspapers Inc., Madison, WI

Blake, Simon .... (204) 857-3427
MAN ED
Daily Graphic, Portage la Prairie, MB

Blake, William C .... (607) 936-4651
PUB, Leader, Corning, NY

Blake, Wilton .... (513) 961-3331
PUB, Cincinnati Herald, Cincinnati, OH

Blakeley, Eddie .... (409) 985-5541
GM, PROD MGR
Port Arthur News, Port Arthur, TX

Blakeley, Gary .... (719) 632-5511
DIR-OPER, Gazette, Colorado Springs, CO

Blakely, M K .... (330) 725-4166
ED-City, Medina County Gazette, Medina, OH

Blakeman, Royal E .... (914) 331-5000
SEC, Daily Freeman, Kingston, NY

Blakeman, William S .... (606) 744-3123
ED, EDL Writer
Winchester Sun, Winchester, KY

Blakemore, Brad .... (903) 785-8744
ADV DIR, Paris News, Paris, TX

Blakeslee, David .... (703) 204-2800
PUB, Sun Gazette, Merrifield, VA

Blakesley, Cynthia .... (307) 324-3411
Entertainment/Amusements ED, Living/Lifestyle ED, Television/Film ED, Women's ED
Rawlins Daily Times, Rawlins, WY

Blakey, Bob .... (403) 235-7100
Radio/Television Reporter
Calgary Herald, Calgary, AB

Blakley, Paula .... (205) 232-2720
ADV DIR-CLASS, News Courier, Athens, AL

Blalock, Barbara .... (205) 739-1351
PUB, Cullman Tribune, Cullman, AL

Blalock, Bob .... (205) 325-2222
EDL Writer
Birmingham News, Birmingham, AL

Blalock, Delton .... (205) 739-1351
PUB, ED, Cullman Tribune, Cullman, AL

Blalock, Randy .... (912) 382-4321
ADV MGR-Display, ADV MGR-CLASS
Tifton Gazette, Tifton, GA

Blanc, Grand .... (810) 751-2855
PUB, Italian American, Warren, MI

Blanchard, Alan D .... (616) 754-9301
ED, Daily News, Greenville, MI

Blanchard, Douglas J .... (603) 543-3100
CIRC DIR, Eagle Times, Claremont, NH

Blanchard, Phillip .... (706) 863-6165
PUB, Columbia News Times, Martinez, GA

Blanchard, Scott .... (410) 848-4400
Sports ED
Carroll County Times, Westminster, MD

Blanchard, Shelly .... (916) 361-1234
ED
Grapevine Independent, Rancho Cordova, CA

Blanchette, Jean .... (819) 293-4551
ED, Courrier-Sud, Nicolet, QC

Blanchflower, John C .... (330) 424-9541
VP, PUB, Morning Journal, Lisbon, OH

Blanco, Ana M .... (215) 557-2300
DIR-MKTG, CIRC DIR
Legal Intelligencer, Philadelphia, PA

Blanco, Rich .... (714) 835-1234
PROD GM-Anaheim Print Facility
Orange County Register, Santa Ana, CA

Bland, Alvin .... (334) 335-3541
PUB, ED, Luverne Journal, Luverne, AL

Bland, Dorothy M .... (970) 493-6397
PRES, PUB, Coloradoan, Fort Collins, CO

Bland, James E .... (212) 416-2000
PROD Senior MGR (Dallas TX)
Wall Street Journal, New York, NY

Bland, John A .... (501) 886-2464
PUB, ED, Times Dispatch, Walnut Ridge, AR

Bland, Murrel .... (913) 788-5565
PUB, ED, Wyandotte West, Kansas City, KS

Bland, Paul C .... (804) 862-9611
PUB, Southside Virginia Star, Petersburg, VA

Blank, Robert S .... (212) 582-2300
Co-COB, Whitcom Partners, New York, NY

Blank, Steven .... (718) 229-0300
PUB, ED, Bayside Times, Bayside, NY

Blankenburg, Dick .... (805) 489-4206
PUB, ED, Five Cities Times-Press-Recorder, Arroyo Grande, CA

Blankenship, Kelvin .... (408) 920-5000
ADV MGR-GEN
San Jose Mercury News, San Jose, CA

Blankenship, Lorrie .... (334) 683-6318
GM, Marion Times-Standard, Marion, AL

Blankenship, Mike .... (913) 295-1111
PROD MGR-Technical SRV
Topeka Capital-Journal, Topeka, KS

Blankenship, Murry .... (601) 447-5501
PUB, ED, Okolona Messenger, Okolona, MS

Blansett, Brian .... (817) 757-5757
Online ED, Waco Tribune-Herald, Waco, TX

Blansett, Joe .... (412) 834-1151
PROD MGR-Pre Press
Tribune-Review, Greensburg, PA

Blanton, Mike .... (704) 733-2448
PUB, Avery Journal, Newland, NC

Blaschko, Charles E .... (608) 323-3366
PUB, Arcadia News-Leader, Arcadia, WI

Blaser, Chris .... (509) 582-1500
CIRC DIR, Tri-City Herald, Tri-Cities, WA

Blaser, Randy .... (708) 383-3200
ED, Oak Leaves, Oak Park, IL

Blaskey, Larry .... (520) 428-2560
MAN ED
Eastern Arizona Courier, Safford, AZ

Blatchford, Barbara .... (604) 368-8551
Office MGR, Trail Daily Times, Trail, BC

Blauvelt, Bill .... (402) 879-3291
PUB, ED, Superior Express, Superior, NE

Blauvett, Keith .... (937) 328-0300
PROD SUPT-Platemaking
Springfield News-Sun, Springfield, OH

Blaylock, Jim .... (706) 724-0851
DIR-Photography
Augusta Chronicle, Augusta, GA

Blaylock, Linda .... (317) 636-0200
Administrative ASST
Court & Commercial Record, Indianapolis, IN

Blaylock, Peggy .... (423) 756-6900
MGR-CR
Chattanooga Free Press, Chattanooga, TN

Blazek, Terri .... (414) 363-4045
PUB, Mukwonago Chief, Mukwonago, WI

Blazer, Jamia .... (423) 581-5630
Amusements ED, EPE, Entertainment ED, Television/Film ED, Theater/Music ED
Citizen Tribune, Morristown, TN

Bleakley, Bill .... (405) 528-6000
PUB, Oklahoma Gazette, Oklahoma City, OK

Blecha, Mike .... (414) 435-4411
Reader Contact ED
Green Bay Press-Gazette, Green Bay, WI

Bledsoe, Bruce .... (702) 788-6200
EPE, Reno Gazette-Journal, Reno, NV

Bledsoe, Ken .... (606) 236-2551
Copy ED, Danville Advocate-Messenger, Danville, KY

Bledsoe, N Ray .... (201) 309-1200
MGR/NTL Accounts
ESPN/SportsTicker, Jersey City, NJ

Bledsoe, Wayne .... (423) 523-3131
Music ED
Knoxville News-Sentinel, Knoxville, TN

Bleezarde, Richard G .... (518) 756-2030
PUB, News-Herald, Ravena, NY

Blegen, Dale .... (605) 854-3331
PUB, ED, De Smet News, De Smet, SD

Bleich, Melvin E .... (810) 752-3524
PUB, ED, Countryman, Romeo, MI

Bleier, Marcia .... (210) 423-5511
GEN ADV MGR
Rio Grande Valley Group, Harlingen, TX

Bleiweiss, Susan .... (508) 626-3800
ADV Analyst
Middlesex News, Framingham, MA

Bleker, M A .... (404) 526-5151
ADV MGR-NTL/Sales
Atlanta Journal-Constitution, Atlanta, GA

Blesener, Paula .... (817) 757-5757
News ED, Waco Tribune-Herald, Waco, TX

Blessing, Gene S .... (817) 478-4661
PUB, ED, Everman Times, Everman, TX

Blessing, William E .... (817) 478-4661
GM, Everman Times, Everman, TX

Blethen, F A .... (206) 464-2111
BC, PUB/CEO, Seattle Times, Seattle, WA
Seattle Times Co.

Blethen, Robert C .... (206) 464-2111
DIR-MKTG, Seattle Times, Seattle, WA

Blethen, W K .... (206) 464-2111
TREAS, Seattle Times, Seattle, WA

Bletzer, Robert .... (617) 929-2000
PROD SUPT-COMP
Boston Globe, Boston, MA

Blevins, James D .... (616) 743-2481
PUB, ED, Marion Press, Marion, MI

Blevins, Lucille .... (805) 725-0600
GM, Delano Record, Delano, CA

Blevins, Peggy .... (510) 208-6300
ADV DIR-CLASS, Oakland Tribune, Oakland, CA, MediaNews Inc. (Alameda Newspapers)

Blexrud, John H .... (407) 420-5000
VP/DIR-MKTG, DIR-MKTG/PROM
Orlando Sentinel, Orlando, FL

Bliss, Gil .... (508) 586-7200
Environmental ED, Enterprise, Brockton, MA

Bliss, Linda .... (617) 786-7000
City Edition ED, Patriot Ledger, Quincy, MA

Bliss, Ron .... (423) 246-8121
EX Sports ED
Kingsport Times-News, Kingsport, TN

Bliss, Sidney H .... (608) 754-3311
PRES/CEO
Bliss Communications Inc., Janesville, WI

Blix, Curt .... (218) 723-5281
PROD FRM-MR/Night SUPV
Duluth News-Tribune, Duluth, MN

Blixhaun, Marj .... (907) 257-4200
MGR-MKTG
Anchorage Daily News, Anchorage, AK

Blixt, Sharon .... (916) 321-1000
MGR-PROM
Sacramento Bee, Sacramento, CA

Blizzard, Andy .... (937) 225-2000
ADV MGR-RT, Daily News, Dayton, OH

Blizzard, Nick .... (937) 294-7000
ED, Kettering-Oakwood Times, Kettering, OH

Bloch, Susan .... (415) 777-1111
DIR-HR
San Francisco Chronicle, San Francisco, CA

Block, Alex Ben .... (213) 525-2000
ED, Hollywood Reporter, Los Angeles, CA

Block, Allan .... (419) 245-6000
Vice Chairman, Blade, Toledo, OH

Block, Bernard .... (502) 582-4011
EVP, Courier-Journal, Louisville, KY

Block, David .... (908) 732-3000
ED, Highland Park Herald, Somerville, NJ

Block, Herbert .... (202) 334-6000
Cartoonist, Washington Post, Washington, DC

Block, John Robinson .... (419) 245-6000
Co-PUB
Blade Communications Inc., Toledo, OH

Block, Kim .... (705) 726-6537
ADV MGR-CLASS, Examiner, Barrie, ON

Block, Verna .... (306) 764-4276
MKTG/PROM MGR
Prince Albert Daily Herald, Prince Albert, SK

Blo Who's Where-22

Block Sr, William .... (412) 263-1100
Chairman, Pittsburgh Post-Gazette, Pittsburgh, PA, Blade Communications Inc.
Block Jr, William .... (419) 245-6000
Co-PUB/PRES
Blade Communications Inc., Toledo, OH
Blocker, Carol .... (817) 665-5511
CIRC MGR
Gainesville Daily Register, Gainesville, TX
Blocker, Rhonda .... (916) 885-5656
ADV MGR-RT, Auburn Journal, Auburn, CA
Blodgett, Carol .... (541) 753-2641
MGR-MKTG, ADTX MGR
Corvallis Gazette-Times, Corvallis, OR
Blodgett, Sandra T .... (203) 235-1661
DIR-MKTG SRV, Record-Journal, Meriden, CT
Blom, Bernice .... (712) 362-2622
Social ED
Estherville Daily News, Estherville, IA
Blom, Dan .... (219) 933-3200
DIR-OPER, Times, Munster, IN
Blomberg, Marina .... (352) 374-5000
Garden Ed, Gainesville Sun, Gainesville, FL
Blome, Paul .... (812) 886-9955
PROD FRM-COMP
Vincennes Sun-Commercial, Vincennes, IN
Blomquist, David .... (201) 646-4000
Polls ED, Television Programming ED
Record, Hackensack, NJ
Blomster, Mel .... (617) 593-7700
PROD FRM-Stereo
Daily Evening Item, Lynn, MA
Blonde, Scott .... (941) 574-1110
DP MGR
Cape Coral Daily Breeze, Cape Coral, FL
Blondin, Yves .... (819) 568-7736
PUB, ED
La Revue de Gatineau, Gatineau, QC
Bloodworth, Bryan .... (309) 829-9411
Sports ED, Pantagraph, Bloomington, IL
Bloom, David .... (573) 243-3515
ED, Cash-Book Journal, Jackson, MO
Bloom, Eugene A .... (712) 647-2821
PUB, ED, Woodbine Twiner, Woodbine, IA
Bloom, Gerald D .... (712) 644-2705
ED, Logan Herald-Observer, Logan, IA
Bloom, Hilda .... (415) 777-7212
Permissions ED
Chronicle Features, San Francisco, CA
Bloom, James E .... (316) 275-8500
PRES, PUB, ED, EPE
Garden City Telegram, Garden City, KS
Bloom, Karen J .... (712) 644-2705
PUB, Logan Herald-Observer, Logan, IA
Bloom, Larry .... (860) 241-6200
Magazine ED, Hartford Courant, Hartford, CT
Bloom, Larry L .... (319) 383-2100
VP-FIN/TREAS/CFO
Lee Enterprises Inc., Davenport, IA
Bloom, Merideth .... (970) 668-3998
Weekend ED, Summit Daily News, Frisco, CO
Bloom, William .... (609) 272-7000
MGR-Applications SYS
Press of Atlantic City, Pleasantville, NJ
Bloomfield, Ellis .... (715) 962-3535
PUB, ED, Colfax Messenger, Colfax, WI
Bloomfield, Patricia .... (606) 845-9211
GM, Flemingsburg Gazette, Flemingsburg, KY
Bloomquist, John F .... (218) 837-5558
PUB, Review Messenger, Sebeka, MN
Bloomquist, Timothy M .... (218) 837-5558
ED, Review Messenger, Sebeka, MN
Blose, F Len .... (330) 841-1600
CIRC VP, Tribune Chronicle, Warren, OH
Bloss, David .... (401) 277-7000
Sports ED
Providence Journal-Bulletin, Providence, RI
Blossom, Clif .... (317) 622-1212
CIRC DIR, Online MGR
Herald Bulletin, Anderson, IN
Blotzer, Jane .... (412) 263-1100
ASSOC ED
Pittsburgh Post-Gazette, Pittsburgh, PA
Blouin, Melissa .... (501) 442-1777
Amusements ED, Food ED, Religion ED
Northwest Arkansas Times, Fayetteville, AR
Blount, Thomas L .... (910) 888-3500
ED, COL
High Point Enterprise, High Point, NC
Blow, Steve .... (214) 977-8222
COL-MET, Dallas Morning News, Dallas, TX
Blower, Betsy .... (810) 541-3000
CIRC MGR, Daily Tribune, Royal Oak, MI
Blubitz, Donnel .... (218) 285-7411
CIRC MGR
Daily Journal, International Falls, MN
Blue, Gayle .... (954) 356-4000
ADV MGR-Display
Sun-Sentinel, Fort Lauderdale, FL

Blue, Gerald H .... (319) 422-3888
PUB, ED
Fayette County Union, West Union, IA
Blue, Mary Anne .... (919) 829-4500
PROD MGR-Programming
News & Observer, Raleigh, NC
Blue, Robert .... (317) 736-7101
CIRC DIR, Daily Journal, Franklin, IN
Bluesten, Dan .... (954) 457-8029
GM, Hallandale Digest, Hallandale, FL
Bluesten, Peter .... (954) 457-8029
PUB, ED, Hallandale Digest, Hallandale, FL
Bluford, Lucille H .... (816) 842-3804
PUB, ED, Call, Kansas City, MO
Blum, C Ken .... (330) 674-1811
MAN ED
Holmes County Hub, Millersburg, OH
Blum, Chuck .... (972) 298-4211
ED, Lancaster Today, Duncanville, TX
Blum, Deborah .... (916) 321-1000
SCI/Technology Writer
Sacramento Bee, Sacramento, CA
Blum MD, Jon H .... (810) 553-2900
PRES, Skintalk, Farmington Hills, MI
Blum, Ken .... (330) 264-1125
Weekly Division MGR
Daily Record, Wooster, OH
Blum, Mark .... (315) 792-5000
CONT, Observer-Dispatch, Utica, NY
Blum, Peter .... (219) 881-3000
EPE, Post-Tribune, Gary, IN
Blumel, William W .... (402) 444-1000
PROD ASST DIR
Omaha World-Herald, Omaha, NE
Blumenshine, David .... (907) 586-3740
PROD MGR, Juneau Empire, Juneau, AK
Blumenshine, Thomas L .... (307) 634-3361
PROD ASST DIR
Wyoming Tribune-Eagle, Cheyenne, WY
Blumenthal, Karen .... (212) 416-2000
BU Chief-Dallas
Wall Street Journal, New York, NY
Blumenthal, Les .... (206) 597-8742
Washington Reporter
News Tribune, Tacoma, WA
Blundo, Joseph .... (614) 461-5000
Home/RE ED
Columbus Dispatch, Columbus, OH
Bluner, Lelani .... (714) 835-1234
ADTX MGR
Orange County Register, Santa Ana, CA
Blurton, Bill .... (901) 427-3333
PROD DIR-Building/Safety
Jackson Sun, Jackson, TN
Blurton, Debbie .... (316) 331-3550
CONT/CR MGR, Independence Daily Reporter, Independence, KS
Blust, Steve .... (916) 321-1000
Sports ED, Sacramento Bee, Sacramento, CA
Blyth, David .... (816) 296-3412
ED, Lawson Review, Lawson, MO
Blyth, Jeffrey .... (212) 832-2839
US ED, Chief ED, Interpress of London and New York, Gemini News Service, Features International of London, New York, NY
Boales, Lloyd .... (817) 634-2125
PROD FRM-COMP, Daily Herald, Killeen, TX
Boals, Patty .... (616) 845-5181
Agriculture ED
Daily News, Ludington, MI
Boans, Barbara .... (505) 746-3524
ADV MGR-CLASS
Artesia Daily Press, Artesia, NM
Board, Kjersti .... (212) 583-2550
ED, Swedish Information Service (Consulate General of Sweden), New York, NY
Board, Wayne .... (806) 762-8844
Farm ED
Lubbock Avalanche-Journal, Lubbock, TX
Boardman, Arlen .... (414) 733-4411
BUS/Labor ED
Post-Crescent, Appleton, WI
Boardman, Beth .... (219) 362-2161
EPE, Political ED
La Porte Herald-Argus, La Porte, IN
Boardman, Dale .... (501) 785-7700
PROD SUPT-MR
Southwest Times Record, Fort Smith, AR
Boardman, Dave .... (206) 464-2111
Regional ED, Seattle Times, Seattle, WA
Boardman, Donna .... (717) 265-2151
ADV MGR-CLASS
Daily Review, Towanda, PA
Boardman, Edward .... (717) 265-2151
Photo ED, Daily Review, Towanda, PA
Boas, Phil .... (602) 898-6500
City ED, MET ED, Mesa Tribune, Mesa, AZ
Boates, Stephen R .... (902) 765-1494
ED, Aurora Newspaper, Greenwood, NS
Boatman, Jack .... (309) 686-3000
PA, Journal Star, Peoria, IL
Boatright, George .... (804) 649-6000
CONT
Richmond Times-Dispatch, Richmond, VA

Boatright, Marge .... (972) 392-0888
VP-Sales
Wieck Photo DataBase Inc., Dallas, TX
Boatwright, Larry .... (912) 244-1880
ADV MGR, Daily Times, Valdosta, GA
Boaz, Mike .... (910) 343-2000
Sports ED, Morning Star/Sunday Star-News, Wilmington, NC
Bobbin, Jay .... (800) 424-4747
Features ED, Tribune Media Services-Television Listings, Glens Falls, NY
Bobbitt, Eugene S .... (919) 419-6500
ADV DIR, Herald-Sun, Durham, NC
Bobblitt, Larry .... (606) 286-4201
ED, Olive Hill Times, Olive Hill, KY
Bobby, Kate .... (201) 791-8400
MAN ED, Shopper News, Fair Lawn, NJ
Bobeck, Dawn .... (717) 829-7100
ADV MGR-CLASS
Times Leader, Wilkes-Barre, PA
Boberg, James .... (701) 253-7311
ADV DIR, ADTX MGR, Forum, Fargo, ND
Bobic, Gene .... (517) 752-7171
ADV DIR, Saginaw News, Saginaw, MI
Boblitt, Larry .... (606) 474-5101
MAN ED, Journal-Enquirer, Grayson, KY
Bobo, Barbara .... (205) 662-4296
ED, West Alabama Gazette, Millport, AL
Bobo, Jeff .... (606) 573-4510
City/MET ED
Harlan Daily Enterprise, Harlan, KY
Bobo, L Peyton .... (205) 662-4296
PUB, West Alabama Gazette, Millport, AL
Boccardi, Louis D .... (212) 621-1500
PRES/CEO, Associated Press, New York, NY
Boccolini, Ejvind .... (908) 475-1848
ED, News, Belvidere, NJ
Boccone, Bud .... (201) 728-0591
Artist
Sports Biofile & Bio-Toons, West Milford, NJ
Bock, Allan .... (709) 454-2191
ED, Northern Pen, St. Anthony, NF
Bock, Corey .... (541) 382-1811
DP MGR, Bulletin, Bend, OR
Bock, Jill .... (573) 471-1137
MAN ED, Standard Democrat, Sikeston, MO
Bock, Michael L .... (207) 828-8100
VP-Television
Guy Gannett Communications, Portland, ME
Bockelman, George .... (419) 245-6000
Computer OPER MGR, Blade, Toledo, OH
Bockrath, Dan .... (513) 665-4700
PUB, GM
Cincinnati Citybeat, Cincinnati, OH
Bockskopf, Charles R .... (314) 261-5555
GM, ED, Community News, St. Louis, MO
Bodalski, Ann .... (610) 272-2500
CONT, Times Herald, Norristown, PA
Bode, Ron .... (319) 398-8211
ADV MGR-RT, Gazette, Cedar Rapids, IA
Boden, Curtis .... (304) 526-4000
CIRC MGR-Home Delivery
Herald-Dispatch, Huntington, WV
Bodenhorn, Tim .... (937) 498-2111
DP MGR, Sidney Daily News, Sidney, OH
Bodette Jr, John L .... (320) 255-8700
MAN ED, St. Cloud Times, St. Cloud, MN
Bodiford, Vincent .... (303) 279-5541
PUB, Golden Transcript, Golden, CO
Bodkin, Tom .... (212) 556-1234
ASSOC MAN ED-Art
New York Times, New York, NY
Bodley, Peter .... (612) 421-4444
ED, Anoka County Union, Coon Rapids, MN
Bodnar, Jo-Jo .... (412) 567-5656
ED, Leechburg Advance, Vandergrift, PA
Bodnar, Ted .... (404) 688-5623
GM, Creative Loafing, Atlanta, GA
Bodner, Sherman .... (914) 694-9300
DIR-SYS/Technology, Reporter Dispatch, White Plains, NY, Gannett Co. Inc.
Bodouvrian, Matt .... (916) 273-9561
ADV DIR, Union, Grass Valley, CA
Boe, Tom .... (605) 331-2200
PROD DIR, Argus Leader, Sioux Falls, SD
Boeck, David .... (701) 572-2165
CIRC MGR
Williston Daily Herald, Williston, ND
Boeckman, Ronald P .... (614) 522-8566
PUB, Ace News, Heath, OH
Boeding, Bill .... (561) 562-2315
Sports ED
Vero Beach Press-Journal, Vero Beach, FL
Boehler, Judy .... (937) 644-9111
Society ED
Marysville Journal-Tribune, Marysville, OH
Boehler, Mark .... (601) 287-6111
EX ED, Daily Corinthian, Corinth, MS
Boehm, Steve .... (210) 379-5402
Photo ED
Seguin Gazette-Enterprise, Seguin, TX
Boehme, Robert .... (509) 459-5000
ADV MGR-RT Sales
Spokesman-Review, Spokane, WA

Boesch, Markus .... (310) 230-3400
Overseas MGR, Allsport Photography USA, Pacific Palisades, CA
Boeselager, Patrick .... (414) 733-4411
MGR-CR, Post-Crescent, Appleton, WI
Boffey, Phillip M .... (212) 556-1234
Deputy EPE, New York Times, New York, NY
Bogar, Tom .... (304) 235-4242
Sports ED, Daily News, Williamson, WV
Bogda, Lori .... (616) 279-7488
ADV DIR, Three Rivers Commercial-News, Three Rivers, MI
Boger, David M .... (501) 238-2375
PUB, East Arkansas News Leader, Wynne, AR
Boger, Sandra .... (501) 238-2375
GM, East Arkansas News Leader, Wynne, AR
Bogert, John .... (310) 540-5511
COL, Daily Breeze, Torrance, CA
Bogert, William R .... (808) 525-8000
VP-Production, PROD VP
Hawaii Newspaper Agency Inc., Honolulu, HI
Boggs, Larry .... (318) 289-6300
CIRC MGR, Advertiser, Lafayette, LA
Boggs, Linda .... (703) 276-3400
CIRC GM-Nashville
USA Today, Arlington, VA
Boggs, Steve .... (405) 332-4433
MAN ED, EPE, NTL ED
Ada Evening News, Ada, OK
Boghosian, Sylva A .... (718) 380-1200
ED, Armenian Reporter International, Fresh Meadows, NY
Bogin, Mike .... (561) 562-2315
Features ED, Press-Journal, Vero Beach, FL
Bohannan, Denis .... (209) 582-0471
Entertainment ED, SCI/Technology ED
Hanford Sentinel, Hanford, CA
Bohannan, Joyce .... (619) 244-0021
MAN ED, Hesperia Resorter, Hesperia, CA
Bohannon, John .... (916) 527-2151
Sports ED, Daily News, Red Bluff, CA
Bohl, Debbie .... (308) 632-0670
BM, DP MGR, Star-Herald, Scottsbluff, NE
Bohl, John .... (601) 693-1551
GM, Meridian Star, Meridian, MS
Bohling, Tim .... (712) 792-3573
PROD FRM-Press
Daily Times Herald, Caroll, IA
Bohn, Brenda .... (904) 435-8500
ADV DIR-Sales, Pensacola News Journal, Pensacola, FL, Gannett Co. Inc.
Bohn, Claudia .... (402) 759-3117
ED, Nebraska Signal, Geneva, NE
Bohn, Dean .... (517) 673-3181
ED, Tuscola County Advertiser, Caro, MI
Bohn, Sandra .... (419) 695-0015
PROD MGR-Graphic Arts
Delphos Daily Herald, Delphos, OH
Bohnaker, Lisa .... (757) 247-4600
DIR-BUS Development
Daily Press, Newport News, VA
Bohnet, Charles .... (701) 235-7311
VP, Forum Communications Co., Fargo, ND
Bohrer, Craig .... (304) 263-8931
PROD MGR, Journal, Martinsburg, WV
Bohrer, Dave .... (607) 798-1234
Sports ED
Press & Sun Bulletin, Binghamton, NY
Bohs, Tom .... (901) 427-3333
EPE, Jackson Sun, Jackson, TN
Boice, Jennifer .... (520) 573-4561
BUS ED, Tucson Citizen, Tucson, AZ
Boies, Elaine .... (718) 981-1234
Fashion ED
Staten Island Advance, Staten Island, NY
Boig, Becky .... (306) 445-7261
ED, MAN ED
Riverbend Review, North Battleford, SK
Boike, Gloria .... (713) 477-0221
BM, Pasadena Citizen, Pasadena, TX
Boiko, Joan .... (619) 775-4200
ED, Palm Desert Post, Indio, CA
Boise, Leonard .... (216) 236-8982
PUB, GM, ED
Rural-Urban Record, Columbia Station, OH
Boisson, Robert .... (909) 889-9666
DIR-MKTG SRV, Sun, San Bernardino, CA
Boissy, Paul .... (413) 788-1000
PROD SUPV-Press
Union-News, Springfield, MA
Boisvert, Denise M .... (203) 235-1661
PROD MGR, Record-Journal, Meriden, CT
Boisvert, Paul .... (306) 648-3479
ED, Gravelbourg Tribune, Gravelbourg, SK
Boito, Tony .... (717) 272-5611
ADTX MGR, Daily News, Lebanon, PA
Bok, L Chip .... (330) 996-3000
EDL Cartoonist
Akron Beacon Journal, Akron, OH
Bolack, Charles N .... (508) 839-2259
PUB, ED, Grafton News, North Grafton, MA
Bolan, Patrick .... (405) 238-6464
PROD FRM-Press
Pauls Valley Daily Democrat, Pauls Valley, OK

23-Who's Where **Bor**

Boland, Ryan (573) 642-7272
Sports ED, Fulton Sun, Fulton, MO

Bolander, Noel (713) 220-7171
CIRC MGR-Sales/MKTG
Houston Chronicle, Houston, TX

Bolas, Rich (602) 977-8351
Sports ED, Daily News-Sun, Sun City, AZ

Bolch, Judy (919) 829-4500
MAN ED-Enterprise
News & Observer, Raleigh, NC

Bold, Mike (916) 321-1000
NTL ED, Sacramento Bee, Sacramento, CA

Bolden, Bonnie (330) 996-3000
Community News ED
Akron Beacon Journal, Akron, OH

Bolden, Don (910) 227-0131
EX ED, EPE
Times News Publishing Co., Burlington, NC

Bolden, Michael (305) 757-6333
ED, TWN News Magazine, Miami, FL

Boldig, Gordy (715) 253-2737
ED, Enterprise & News, Wittenberg, WI

Boldman, Craig (513) 761-1188
Senior Critic
Critic's Choice Reviews, Cincinnati, OH

Bolduc, Jean (919) 933-8883
ED/PUB
Public Education Monthly, Hillsbourgh, NC

Bolduc, Michael (860) 241-6200
MGR-Publishing Services Pre Press News
Hartford Courant, Hartford, CT

Bole, William (802) 254-6167
ASSOC ED
American News Service, Brattleboro, VT

Bolei, Heather (408) 920-5000
PROD MGR-Ad SRV
San Jose Mercury News, San Jose, CA

Bolejack, Scott (919) 934-2176
MAN ED, Smithfield Herald, Smithfield, NC

Bolender, Jack (309) 829-9411
PROD SUPV-PR
Pantagraph, Bloomington, IL

Bolerjack, Bob (206) 339-3000
ASST MAN ED-Editing & Production
Herald, Everett, WA

Boles, Charles (703) 276-3400
CIRC GM-Dallas, USA Today, Arlington, VA

Boles, Jean (915) 365-3501
GM, Ballinger Ledger, Ballinger, TX

Boles, Roeneal (915) 365-3501
ED, Ballinger Ledger, Ballinger, TX

Bolet, Rick (905) 526-3333
DIR-Human Resources
Spectator, Hamilton, ON

Boley, Gary W (912) 888-9300
PUB, Albany Herald, Albany, GA

Bolger, Bill (317) 633-1240
PROD OPER DIR
Indianapolis Star/News, Indianapolis, IN

Boliek, Brooks (213) 525-2000
Washington DC BU Chief
Hollywood Reporter, Los Angeles, CA

Bolin, Adrian (Stretch) (901) 529-2211
PROD MGR
Commercial Appeal, Memphis, TN

Bolin, Cheryl (601) 961-7000
ADV MGR-CLASS
Clarion-Ledger, Jackson, MS

Bolin, Mark D (406) 222-2000
CIRC DIR
Livingston Enterprise, Livingston, MT

Boline, Larry (415) 348-4321
ADV MGR-NTL/Major Accounts
San Mateo County Times, San Mateo, CA

Boling, Jobi (614) 345-4053
ADV MGR-CLASS, Advocate, Newark, OH

Bollinger, Vickie (423) 523-3131
MGR-CR, News-Sentinel, Knoxville, TN

Bolitho, Tom (405) 436-2603
PUB, ED, Chickasaw Times, Ada, OK

Boll, Bob (510) 462-4160
BUS ED, Valley Times, Pleasanton, CA

Bolleau, Andre (613) 829-9100
CIRC MGR-Reader Sales/SRV-Subscription
Ottawa Citizen, Ottawa, ON

Bolling, Charles (316) 223-1460
PROD FRM-PR
Fort Scott Tribune, Fort Scott, KS

Bolling, Susan (540) 669-2181
City ED, Herald-Courier Virginia Tennessean, Bristol, VA

Bollinger, Brad (707) 546-2020
BUS/FIN ED, RE ED
Press Democrat, Santa Rosa, CA

Bollinger, Cory (815) 729-6161
ADV MGR-Sales, Herald-News, Joliet, IL

Bollinger, John (212) 268-2552
PUB, Westsider, New York, NY

Bollinger, Mike (804) 848-2114
ED
Brunswick Times-Gazette, Lawrenceville, VA

Bollman, Bill (814) 870-1600
MGR-CR
Morning News/Erie Daily Times, Erie, PA

Bologna, Michael (516) 569-4000
GM, Nassau Herald, Lawrence, NY

Bolone, Robert (813) 893-8111
CIRC Deputy DIR
St. Petersburg Times, St. Petersburg, FL

Bolt, Brian (519) 344-3641
City ED, Observer, Sarnia, ON

Bolt, Greg (541) 382-1811
Environmental ED, Bulletin, Bend, OR

Bolten, Kathy (515) 284-8000
EDU Reporter-De Moines Schools
Des Moines Register, Des Moines, IA

Bolton, Bo (334) 575-3282
PUB, Monroe Journal, Monroeville, AL

Bolton, John (520) 573-4220
BUS ED, Arizona Daily Star, Tucson, AZ

Bolton, Lorne F (519) 271-2220
PROD MGR
Stratford Beacon-Herald, Stratford, ON

Bolton, Steve (405) 439-6500
PUB, ED, Comanche Times, Comanche, OK

Bolton, Tom (805) 564-5200
MAN ED, BUS ED, Santa Barbara News-Press, Santa Barbara, CA

Bolton, Tracy (405) 439-6500
PUB, Comanche Times, Comanche, OK

Bolyard, Frank J (304) 624-6411
PROD FRM-PR/Camera, Clarksburg Exponent/Telegram, Clarksburg, WV

Bolyard, Gary A (304) 329-0090
PUB, Preston County Journal, Kingwood, WV

Bolyard, Mark (614) 373-2121
PROD MGR-PR
Marietta Times, Marietta, OH

Bolyard, Tina M (304) 329-0090
ED, Preston County Journal, Kingwood, WV

Bolzner, Fal A (914) 694-9300
VP-OPER, Reporter Dispatch, White Plains, NY, Gannett Co. Inc.

Boman, Holly (515) 232-2160
ADTX MGR, Daily Tribune, Ames, IA

Bomberger, Phyllis (913) 367-0583
Women's ED
Atchison Daily Globe, Atchison, KS

Bommarito, Sal (416) 675-4390
ED, Etobicoke Guardian, Etobicoke, ON

Bonaccorso, Gary (207) 729-3311
Photo ED, Times Record, Brunswick, ME

Bonardi, Ford (804) 978-7200
BM, Daily Progress, Charlottesville, VA

Bonavita, Colette (716) 487-1111
News ED, Post-Journal, Jamestown, NY

Bonavita, Dennis (814) 371-4200
MAN ED, EPE, Photo DEPT MGR, Courier-Express/Tri-County Sunday, Du Bois, PA

Bond, Ben (601) 896-2100
PROD MGR-PR, Sun Herald, Biloxi, MS

Bond, Carol (502) 259-9622
GM, ED, Grayson County News-Gazette, Leitchfield, KY

Bond, Christopher (504) 447-4055
PUB, Daily Comet, Thibodaux, LA

Bond, Hank (502) 756-2109
GM, Breckinridge County Herald-News, Hardinsburg, KY

Bond, Sandy (605) 649-7866
ED, Selby Record, Selby, SD

Bond, Tom (804) 649-6000
Graphics ED
Richmond Times-Dispatch, Richmond, VA

Bondurant, Janet R (817) 926-5351
CIRC MGR
Commercial Recorder, Fort Worth, TX

Bondurant, Jay (540) 586-8612
GM, Bedford Bulletin, Bedford, VA

Bondurant, Sarah (601) 562-4414
ED, Democrat, Senatobia, MS

Bone, David (205) 236-1551
Graphics ED/Art DIR
Anniston Star, Anniston, AL

Bonekamp, Gerald (604) 530-9446
PUB, ED, De Hollandse Krant, Langley, BC

Bonelli, Judy (218) 262-1011
ADV MGR-NTL, DP MGR
Daily Tribune, Hibbing, MN

Bonenti, Charles (413) 447-7311
Features ED, Berkshire Eagle, Pittsfield, MA

Bonetti, David (415) 777-2424
Art Critic
San Francisco Examiner, San Francisco, CA

Boney Jr, Thomas E (910) 228-7851
PUB, ED, Alamance News, Graham, NC

Bonfield, David (617) 433-6700
EVP-Sales & MKTG
Community Newspaper Co., Needham, MA

Bonfietti, Thomas (970) 728-4488
PUB, Telluride Times-Journal, Telluride, CO

Bonfiglio, Dawn (219) 461-8333
DP MGR, Journal Gazette, Fort Wayne, IN

Bonham, Bruce (613) 925-4265
ED, Prescott Journal, Prescott, ON

Bonham, David (812) 231-4200
PROD FRM-COMP
Tribune-Star, Terre Haute, IN

Bonham, Harley (504) 826-3279
PROD MGR-Facility
Times-Picayune, New Orleans, LA

Boni, Nicole (717) 689-2595
ED, Villager, Moscow, PA

Bonilla, Herbert (718) 762-8833
PUB, GM
De Norte A Sur, Fresh Meadows, NY

Bonilla, Pablo Santiago (718) 762-8833
ED, De Norte A Sur, Fresh Meadows, NY

Bonino, Richard (509) 459-5000
Food ED, Spokesman-Review, Spokane, WA

Bonito, Gloria (603) 436-1800
ADV DIR
Portsmouth Herald, Portsmouth, NH

Bonko, Larry (757) 446-2000
Television COL, Virginian-Pilot, Norfolk, VA

Bonner, Al (317) 962-1575
ADV DIR, Palladium-Item, Richmond, IN

Bonner, Dave (307) 754-2221
PUB, Powell Tribune, Powell, WY

Bonner, Dee (317) 398-6631
ADV DIR, MGR-MKTG/PROM, Cartoonist
Shelbyville News, Shelbyville, IN

Bonnie, Debbie (412) 654-6651
Environmental ED
New Castle News, New Castle, PA

Bonnin, Rosetta (409) 744-3611
BM
Galveston County Daily News, Galveston, TX

Bonokoski, Mark (613) 739-7000
ED, Ottawa Sun, Ottawa, ON

Bonomo, Denise D (814) 946-7411
DIR-Human Resources/Community SRV
Altoona Mirror, Altoona, PA

Bonomo, Mike (360) 377-3711
MGR-SYS, Sun, Bremerton, WA

Bonora, Elizabeth A (516) 749-1000
ED, Shelter Island Reporter, Shelter Island Heights, NY

Bonordon, Lee (507) 433-8851
Reporter, SCI
Austin Daily Herald, Austin, MN

Bonta, Margie J (402) 266-5161
ED, Fillmore County News, Exeter, NE

Bonta, W A (402) 266-5161
PUB, Fillmore County News, Exeter, NE

Bonvegna, Diana L (954) 356-4000
DIR-Human Resources
Sun-Sentinel, Fort Lauderdale, FL

Boody, Michael (505) 823-7777
CIRC DIR, Albuquerque Publishing Co., Albuquerque, NM

Boody, Peter B (516) 283-4100
ED, Southampton Press, Southampton, NY

Booe, Charles (316) 231-2600
PROD SUPT, Morning Sun, Pittsburg, KS

Booher, Julie (904) 435-8500
PROD MGR-COMP/Graphic Arts
Pensacola News Journal, Pensacola, FL

Booher, Steve (405) 596-3344
GM, Cherokee Messenger & Republican, Cherokee, OK

Booher, Wes (810) 985-7171
Graphics ED, Times Herald, Port Huron, MI

Booken, Robin (912) 923-6432
MAN ED, Action Line ED, Automotive ED, City/MET ED, EPE
Daily Sun, Warner Robins, GA

Booker, Dan (206) 464-2111
PROD MGR-Color/Camera
Seattle Times, Seattle, WA

Booker, Darla (405) 278-6005
ED, Tinker Take-Off, Oklahoma City, OK

Booker, Vicki (916) 885-5656
Office MGR, DP MGR
Auburn Journal, Auburn, CA

Books, Kenneth (717) 587-1148
ED, Abington Journal, Clarks Summit, PA

Boon, Arie (616) 842-6400
PROD SUPT
Grand Haven Tribune, Grand Haven, MI

Boone, Edwin M (912) 946-2218
ED, Wilkinson County News, Irwinton, GA

Boone Jr, James B (205) 752-3381
COB, Boone Newspapers Inc., Tuscaloosa, AL

Boone, Jan (704) 633-8950
Films/Theater ED
Salisbury Post, Salisbury, NC

Boone, Joe (912) 946-2218
PUB, Wilkinson County News, Irwinton, GA

Boone, Julian F (217) 223-5100
PROD DIR-OPER
Quincy Herald-Whig, Quincy, IL

Boone, Kenneth S (601) 442-9101
PRES, PUB, Natchez Democrat, Natchez, MS

Boone, Lyle (515) 284-8000
ASST MAN ED-Graphics
Des Moines Register, Des Moines, IA

Boone, Michael (514) 987-2222
Radio/Television COL
Gazette, Montreal, QC

Boone, Raymond H (804) 644-0496
PUB, ED, Free Press, Richmond, VA

Boone, Robert H (860) 646-0500
News ED, Journal Inquirer, Manchester, CT

Boone, Tom (214) 739-2244
MAN ED, Park Cities People, Dallas, TX

Booraem, Ellen (207) 367-2200
MAN ED
Island Ad-Vantages, Stonington, ME

Booth, Barbara (910) 343-2000
Automotive ED, RE ED, Morning Star/Sunday Star-News, Wilmington, NC

Booth, Claudia (414) 224-2000
VP-CONT
Milwaukee Journal Sentinel, Milwaukee, WI

Booth, Colin (416) 367-2000
PROD SUPT-COMP
Toronto Star, Toronto, ON

Booth, Edward R (505) 983-3303
PROD DIR
Santa Fe New Mexican, Santa Fe, NM

Booth, Herb (817) 695-0500
ED, Grand Prairie News, Arlington, TX

Booth, Kyle (941) 953-7755
EX News ED
Sarasota Herald-Tribune, Sarasota, FL

Booth, Michael (908) 870-9338
PUB, Atlanticville, Long Branch, NJ

Booth, Phillip (813) 259-7711
Records ED-Pop
Tampa Tribune and Times, Tampa, FL

Booth, Ray H (614) 439-3531
Special Projects
Daily Jeffersonian, Cambridge, OH

Booth, Robert B (706) 342-2424
PUB, ED, Madisonian, Madison, GA

Booth, Sally (313) 426-8433
SEC, Schwadron Cartoon & Illustration Service, Ann Arbor, MI

Booth, Shannon (908) 870-9338
GM, Atlanticville, Long Branch, NJ

Boothe, Charles (540) 963-1081
ED, Richlands News-Press, Richlands, VA

Boots, John (416) 947-2222
TREAS/CORP CONT
Sun Media Corp., Toronto, ON

Boozer, David (803) 771-6161
PROD MGR, State, Columbia, SC

Bope, Jeffrey (312) 644-7800
EX VP
Chicago Daily Law Bulletin, Chicago, IL

Bopp, David (308) 497-2153
PUB, ED, Spalding Enterprise, Spalding, NE

Bopp, John (617) 929-2000
PROD DIR, Boston Globe, Boston, MA

Borak, Jeffrey (413) 447-7311
Entertainment ED
Berkshire Eagle, Pittsfield, MA

Borchardt, Jason (409) 836-7956
ASST to PUB
Brenham Banner-Press, Brenham, TX

Borchardt, Jerry (715) 842-2101
PROD MGR-Maintenance
Wausau Daily Herald, Wausau, WI

Borden, Jim (541) 485-1234
News ED, Register-Guard, Eugene, OR

Borden, Kenneth (508) 775-1200
ADV MGR-SRV
Cape Cod Times, Hyannis, MA

Borden, Margaret (505) 546-2611
PROD MGR-Layout
Deming Headlight, Deming, NM

Borden, Robert C (409) 776-4444
EPE, Eagle, Bryan, TX

Borders, Gary (409) 564-8361
PUB, ED, COL
Daily Sentinel, Nacogdoches, TX

Borders, Nan (313) 961-3949
ADV MGR, Detroit Legal News, Detroit, MI

Borders, William (212) 556-1234
Senior ED-News
New York Times, New York, NY

Bordner, Robert L (419) 492-2133
ED, Herald, New Washing-ton, OH

Boreman, Maggie (407) 366-9181
MAN ED, Oviedo Voice, Oviedo, FL

Boren, Ben (806) 658-4732
PUB, ED, Booker News, Booker, TX

Boren, James (209) 441-6111
EPE, Fresno Bee, Fresno, CA

Boren, Julie (217) 285-2191
PUB, ED, Pike Press, Pittsfield, IL

Borg Esq, Jennifer A (201) 646-4000
PUB, ED, Pike Press, Pittsfield, IL

Borg, Malcolm A (201) 646-4000
VP-Human Resources
Record, Hackensack, NJ

Borgaard, Cheryll (360) 636-3636
ED, Kelso-Longview Advocate, Longview, WA

Borgedalin, Angie (816) 454-9660
ED, Liberty Tribune-News, Kansas City, MO

Bor Who's Where-24

Borgen, Garry (507) 775-6180
PUB, Byron Review, Byron, MN

Borges, Craig (508) 880-9000
City ED, Taunton Daily Gazette, Taunton, MA

Borghese, Lorna (813) 893-8111
PROD MGR-Imaging
St. Petersburg Times, St. Petersburg, FL

Borghi, Dick (702) 383-0211
PROD ASST MGR
Las Vegas Review-Journal, Las Vegas, NV

Borland, Jack (303) 820-1010
CIRC MGR-Retention
Denver Post, Denver, CO

Borle, Brian A (403) 783-3311
PUB, Ponoka News & Advertiser, Ponoka, AB

Borlik, Kathy (219) 235-6161
Religion Writer
South Bend Tribune, South Bend, IN

Bormann, Brenda L (303) 454-3466
GM, North Weld Herald, Eaton, CO

Bormann, Bruce J (303) 454-3466
PUB, North Weld Herald, Eaton, CO

Born, Janet (316) 275-8500
BM, DP MGR
Garden City Telegram, Garden City, KS

Bornak, Mary Ellen (215) 949-4000
BUS/Health ED
Bucks County Courier Times, Levittown, PA

Borneman, Angela (410) 337-2400
ED, Jeffersonian, Towson, MD

Borneman, Bill (414) 834-4242
GM, ED, Oconto County Reporter, Oconto, WI

Bornemann, Everett (414) 733-4411
PROD FRM-PR
Appleton Post-Crescent, Appleton, WI

Borner, Barbara (901) 427-3333
Librarian, Jackson Sun, Jackson, TN

Bornfeld, Steve (423) 756-1234
Entertainment ED
Chattanooga Times, Chattanooga, TN

Bornhoft, Stephen (904) 747-5000
ED, EPE, Panama City News Herald, Panama City, FL

Borns, Dean (605) 886-6901
PROD MGR-Press
Watertown Public Opinion, Watertown, SD

Bornstein, Lisa (219) 235-6161
Films/Theater Writer, Music ED
South Bend Tribune, South Bend, IN

Borody, Dave (519) 344-3641
Sports ED, Observer, Sarnia, ON

Boroson, Rebecca (201) 837-8818
ED, Jewish Standard, Teaneck, NJ

Borowicz, Jeff (612) 972-6171
MAN ED, Delano Eagle, Delano, MN

Borowski, Greg (517) 377-1000
Political/Government ED
Lansing State Journal, Lansing, MI

Borrego, James (408) 761-7300
PROD MGR
Register-Pajaronian, Watsonville, CA

Borsellino, Rob (515) 284-8000
City/MET ED
Des Moines Register, Des Moines, IA

Borseth, Mary (406) 482-2403
ED, Sidney Herald, Sidney, MT

Borsi, Dianna (502) 926-0123
ASST ED-City
Messenger-Inquirer, Owensboro, KY

Borst, Charles (202) 383-6080
DIR-Photo SRV, Knight-Ridder/Tribune Information Services, Washington, DC

Borton, Robert E (318) 322-3161
PUB, Ouachita Citizen, West Monroe, LA

Borton, Sara Johnson (803) 785-4293
PUB, Island Packet, Hilton Head, SC

Bortvit, Michael (912) 985-4545
ADV Market DIR, Observer, Moultrie, GA

Borza, Paul (562) 435-1161
MGR-SYS & Technology, PROD MGR-Publishing SYS
Press-Telegram, Long Beach, CA

Bosak, Maria (204) 589-5871
ED, Ukrainsky Holos, Winnipeg, MB

Bosakowski, Jo (201) 327-1212
GM, Home And Store News, Ramsey, NJ

Bosanko, Tom (707) 464-2141
PROD SUPV-Press
Triplicate, Crescent City, CA

Bosarge, Les (334) 222-2402
CIRC DIR
Andalusia Star-News, Andalusia, AL

Bosau, Robert D (312) 222-3237
EVP-EDU, Tribune Co., Chicago, IL

Boscia, Jen (717) 389-4825
EX ED, Spectrum Features, Bloomsburg, PA

Bosco, Most Rev Anthony G (412) 834-4010
PUB, Catholic Accent, Greensburg, PA

Bose, Doug (407) 872-1870
PUB, Navigator, Delray Beach, FL

Boshart, Eric (406) 846-2424
PUB, Silver State Post, Deer Lodge, MT

Boshart, Kathryn (406) 846-2424
PUB, ED, Silver State Post, Deer Lodge, MT

Boshell, J H (205) 221-2840
CIRC MGR, Daily Mountain Eagle, Jasper, AL

Bosley, J Scott (219) 881-3000
PRES, PUB, Post-Tribune, Gary, IN

Bosse, Joyce (603) 464-3388
ED, New Hampshire Week In Review, Hillsboro, NH

Bosse, Leigh (603) 464-3388
PUB, New Hampshire Week In Review, Hillsboro, NH

Boster, Steve (619) 939-3354
PUB, Rocketeer, Ridgecrest, CA

Bostian, Kelly (907) 456-6661
ED
Fairbanks Daily News-Miner, Fairbanks, AK

Bostick, Alan (615) 259-8000
Arts/Fashion DIR, Tennessean, Nashville, TN

Bostick, Beverly (405) 273-4200
City ED, Shawnee News-Star, Shawnee, OK

Boston, Ernie (410) 366-3900
ED, Baltimore Times, Baltimore, MD

Bostwick, Bernadette (954) 345-1822
GM, Broward Times, Coral Springs, FL

Bostwick, Jane (317) 459-3121
EDU ED, Kokomo Tribune, Kokomo, IN

Bosveld, Calvin (905) 628-6313
PUB, Dundas Star, Dundas, ON

Bosveld, Ken (519) 763-3333
PUB, Guelph Tribune, Guelph, ON

Boswell, Thomas (202) 334-6000
COL-Sports
Washington Post, Washington, DC

Bosworth Jr, Henry W (617) 471-3100
PUB, Quincy Sun, Quincy, MA

Bosworth Jr, R S (401) 683-1000
PUB, Sakonnet Times, Portsmouth, RI

Bosworth, Robert H (617) 471-3100
ED, Quincy Sun, Quincy, MA

Boswyk, Marilyn (604) 534-8641
PUB, Langley Advance, Langley, BC

Botelho, Thomas (303) 820-1010
VP-MKTG, Denver Post, Denver, CO

Bothun, Brian (415) 327-6397
Features ED
Palo Alto Daily News, Palo Alto, CA

Bothun, Don (612) 222-5011
VP/DIR-Finance
St. Paul Pioneer Press, St. Paul, MN

Bothwell, Jim (903) 597-8111
ADTX MGR
Tyler Morning Telegraph, Tyler, TX

Bott, Alice W (419) 625-5500
VP/TREAS, Sandusky Register, Sandusky, OH

Bott, Mary (605) 331-2200
CIRC ASST DIR
Argus Leader, Sioux Falls, SD

Botta, Michael (212) 887-8550
EIC, American Metal Market, New York, NY

Botti, Deborah (914) 341-1100
Fashion/Style ED, Living/Lifestyle ED, Religion ED, SCI/Technology ED, Women's ED, Times Herald-Record, Middletown, NY

Botti, James A (914) 341-1100
DIR-Facilities
Times Herald-Record, Middletown, NY

Bottomly, Therese (503) 221-8327
Senior ED-Spot News
Oregonian, Portland, OR

Botton, Keith (315) 782-1000
BUS ED
Watertown Daily Times, Watertown, NY

Bouchard, Marielle (514) 739-3302
PUB, ED, Town of Mt. Royal Weekly Post/Le Post de Ville Mt. Royal, Mount Royal, QC

Bouchard, Ronald (717) 421-3000
EPE, Pocono Record, Stroudsburg, PA

Bouchards, Doug (860) 241-6200
PROD MGR-Packaging
Hartford Courant, Hartford, CT

Bouchelle, Charles (609) 989-5454
PROD MGR-MR, Times, Trenton, NJ

Boucher, Blake (516) 843-2020
PROD GEN FRM-Electric Shop
Newsday, Melville, NY

Boucher, Jean Pierre (506) 735-5575
PUB, ED, Le Madawaska, Edmundston, NB

Boucher, Marnie (519) 756-2020
ADV MGR, PROD MGR
Expositor, Brantford, ON

Boucher, Mike (316) 321-1120
ED, EDL Writer
El Dorado Times, El Dorado, KS

Boudreau, Len (906) 786-2021
PROD FRM-COMP, Daily Press, Escanaba, MI

Boudreaux, Chuck (504) 384-8370
DP MGR, Daily Review, Morgan City, LA

Boudreaux, Glen (318) 783-3450
ADV DIR, Crowley Post-Signal, Crowley, LA

Boudreaux, Lani (504) 384-8370
CIRC MGR, Morgan City Newspapers Inc., Morgan City, LA

Boudreaux, Laraine (601) 896-2100
ADV MGR-CLASS, Sun Herald, Biloxi, MS

Bougard, Peggy (504) 850-1100
ADV MGR-CLASS, ADTX MGR
Courier, Houma, LA

Bough, Helene (517) 725-5136
News ED, Argus-Press, Owosso, MI

Boughner PhD, Terry (414) 372-2773
ED, Wisconsin Light, Milwaukee, WI

Boughton, Kathryn (860) 435-9873
MAN ED, Lakeville Journal, Lakeville, CT

Bougie, Andre (514) 562-8593
MAN ED, Tribune/Le Progres/The Watchman, Lachute, QC

Boulanger, Jacques (514) 581-5120
ED, L'Artisan, Repentigny, QC

Boulay, Patrick (612) 333-4244
ASSOC PUB
Finance and Commerce, Minneapolis, MN

Bouldin, Bille G (409) 396-3391
PUB, Normangee Star, Normangee, TX

Bouldin, James F (816) 637-6155
PUB, Daily Standard, Excelsior Springs, MO

Boule, Margie (503) 221-8327
COL, Oregonian, Portland, OR

Boulet, Ben (318) 893-4223
CIRC MGR
Abbeville Meridional, Abbeville, LA

Boultbee, J A (416) 363-8721
VP-FIN & Treasury
Hollinger Inc., Toronto, ON

Boultinghouse, Chris (816) 442-5423
PUB, ED, Mound City News, Mound City, MO

Boultinghouse, Linda (816) 442-5423
PUB, ED, Mound City News, Mound City, MO

Boundurant, John M (817) 926-5351
ADV MGR
Commercial Recorder, Fort Worth, TX

Bouquet, Terry (516) 587-5612
ED, Beacon, Babylon, NY

Bouraem, Ellen (207) 374-2341
MAN ED, Weekly Packet, Blue Hill, ME

Bourassa, Don (508) 458-7100
PROD FRM-COMP, Sun, Lowell, MA

Bourassa, Shauna (306) 869-2202
GM, Radville Star, Radville, SK

Bourdette, Margaret J (716) 892-5323
GM, ED, Times, Cheektowaga, NY

Bourdow, Paula (517) 752-7171
MGR-CR, Saginaw News, Saginaw, MI

Bourjaily III, M F (540) 635-3229
ED/ASSOC PUB
Globe Syndicate, Strasburg, VA

Bourjaily Jr, Monte (540) 635-3229
ED/PUB, Globe Syndicate, Strasburg, VA

Bourjot, Frank (416) 367-2000
ADV DIR, Toronto Star, Toronto, ON

Bourke, Dale Hanson (202) 463-8777
PUB, Religion News Service, Washington, DC

Bourne, Jody (815) 584-3007
ED, Dwight Star & Herald, Dwight, IL

Bourque, David (207) 729-3311
Sports ED, Times Record, Brunswick, ME

Bourque, Jocelyn (418) 683-1573
Auto/Books ED, Entertainment ED, Food ED, Music ED, Radio/Television ED, RE, Women's ED, Le Journal de Quebec, Ville Vanier, QC

Bourret, Suzanne (905) 526-3333
Food ED, Spectator, Hamilton, ON

Bouska, Sue (619) 934-3929
GM, Mammoth Times Weekly, Mammoth Lakes, CA

Bouslog, Julie (510) 757-2525
ADV MGR, Ledger Dispatch, Antioch, CA

Bousquet, James (860) 584-0501
PROD MGR-Pre Press
Bristol Press, Bristol, CT

Bousu, Peter (906) 482-1500
Sports ED
Daily Mining Gazette, Houghton, MI

Bouthillette, Dennis (401) 277-7000
PROD MGR-PR
Providence Journal-Bulletin, Providence, RI

Boutilier, Fran (508) 764-4325
ADV DIR, News, Southbridge, MA

Boutilier, Lloyd (519) 756-2020
PROD CNR-Technology
Expositor, Brantford, ON

Boutwell, Wayne (334) 433-1551
CIRC MGR-City
Mobile Press Register, Mobile, AL

Bove, Tony (905) 358-5711
ADV DIR
Niagara Falls Review, Niagara Falls, ON

Bovee, Leonard (914) 331-5000
PROD FRM-COMP
Daily Freeman, Kingston, NY

Bovia, Steven (419) 668-3771
CIRC MGR, Norwalk Reflector, Norwalk, OH

Bovin, Jim (906) 786-2021
Photo ED, Daily Press, Escanaba, MI

Bowden, Bob (813) 259-7711
Food ED
Tampa Tribune and Times, Tampa, FL

Bowden, Dennis (906) 786-2021
CIRC MGR, Daily Press, Escanaba, MI

Bowden, J Earle (904) 435-8500
VP/ED, Cartoonist
Pensacola News Journal, Pensacola, FL

Bowden, Mark (319) 398-8211
MAN ED, Gazette, Cedar Rapids, IA

Bowden, Vicki (501) 968-5252
ADV MGR, Courier, Russellville, AR

Bowder, Mark (541) 942-3325
ED
Cottage Grove Sentinel, Cottage Grove, OR

Bowdon, Bill (615) 879-4040
PUB, ED, Fentress Courier, Jamestown, TN

Bowell, Steve (604) 875-8313
MAN ED, Community Digest, Vancouver, BC

Bowen, Anne (715) 723-5515
Women's ED
Chippewa Herald, Chippewa Falls, WI

Bowen, Barry T (717) 348-9100
MGR-Office, PA, DP MGR
Tribune & Scranton Times, Scranton, PA

Bowen, Dale (757) 446-2000
ADV MGR-CLASS/GEN
Virginian-Pilot, Norfolk, VA
Landmark Communications Inc.

Bowen Jr, Ed (912) 868-6015
ED, Telfair Enterprise, McRae, GA

Bowen, Greg (512) 575-1451
City ED, Victoria Advocate, Victoria, TX

Bowen, Mel (408) 423-4242
Travel ED
Santa Cruz County Sentinel, Santa Cruz, CA

Bowen, Melorie (408) 423-4242
DP MGR, ADTX MGR
Santa Cruz County Sentinel, Santa Cruz, CA

Bowen, Michael (705) 674-5271
Accountant, Sudbury Star, Sudbury, ON

Bowen, Reva (801) 225-1340
ED, Orem-Geneva Times, Orem, UT

Bowen, Sarah J (912) 868-6015
PUB, Telfair Enterprise, McRae, GA

Bowen, Susan Eagling (517) 354-3111
NTL ED, News ED, Political/Government ED, Religion ED, Alpena News, Alpena, MI

Bower, Betsy (330) 264-1125
Food ED, Daily Record, Wooster, OH

Bower, Sandy (717) 784-2121
ADV MGR-RT
Press Enterprise, Bloomsburg, PA

Bowerman, Dan (716) 282-2311
EX ED, Niagara Gazette, Niagara Falls, NY

Bowers, Carl (405) 255-5354
GM, EX ED, Duncan Banner, Duncan, OK

Bowers, John (401) 277-7000
VP/Human Resources
Providence Journal-Bulletin, Providence, RI

Bowers Jr, Marcus R (601) 825-8333
PUB, ED, Rankin County News, Brandon, MS

Bowers, Rick (202) 785-6629
MAN ED
Maturity News Service, Washington, DC

Bowers, Scott (216) 923-2397
GM, Scrambl-Gram Inc., Cuyahoga Falls, OH

Bowers, Suzanne G (610) 371-5000
Special Sections ED
Reading Times/Eagle, Reading, PA

Bowie, Jack (201) 428-6200
MAN ED, Daily Record, Parsippany, NJ

Bowker, Jim (913) 899-2338
PROD DIR
Goodland Daily News, Goodland, KS

Bowker, Todd A (517) 895-8551
PROD FRM-MR
Bay City Times, Bay City, MI

Bowlby, Allan W (304) 233-0100
CIRC DIR, Intelligencer/Wheeling News-Register, Wheeling, WV

Bowler, Larry C (406) 487-5303
PUB, ED, Daniels County Leader, Scobey, MT

Bowles, Susan (561) 820-4100
BUS ED
Palm Beach Post, West Palm Beach, FL

Bowlin, Brad (208) 733-0931
Sports ED, Times-News, Twin Falls, ID

Bowlin, Larry (815) 625-3600
PROD FRM-Press, Daily Gazette, Sterling, IL

Bowling, Mark (304) 255-4400
CIRC DIR-Single Copy Sales
Register Herald, Beckley, WV

Bowling, Vernon T (937) 236-4990
PUB, Huber Heights Courier, Dayton, OH

Bowlus, Charles H (307) 324-3411
MAN ED, City/MET ED, EPE, NTL ED, News ED, Photo ED, SCI/Technology ED, DP MGR
Rawlins Daily Times, Rawlins, WY

Bowman, Bobbi (315) 792-5000
MAN ED, Observer-Dispatch, Utica, NY

Bowman, Brian (316) 283-1500
EDU/Features ED
Newton Kansan, Newton, KS

Copyright ©1997 by the Editor & Publisher Co.

25-Who's Where **Bra**

Bowman, David .... (910) 888-3500
CONT, DP MGR
High Point Enterprise, High Point, NC

Bowman, Donald .... (330) 364-5577
CIRC DIR
Times Reporter, New Philadelphia, OH

Bowman, Elena .... (614) 224-4835
ADV Display, Daily Reporter, Columbus, OH

Bowman, Joan C .... (317) 398-6631
SEC, Shelbyville News, Shelbyville, IN

Bowman, Joseph J .... (305) 350-2111
VP-OPER, PROD VP
Miami Herald, Miami, FL

Bowman, Lois .... (419) 674-4066
ADV Bookkeeper, Kenton Times, Kenton, OH

Bowman, Nancy .... (937) 335-5634
MAN ED, BUS ED, Environmental ED, NTL ED, Political/Government ED, Troy Daily News/Miami Valley Sunday News, Troy, OH

Bowman, Philip M .... (803) 724-8375
ED, New Catholic Miscellany, Charleston, SC

Bowman, Rebecca .... (314) 340-8000
ADTX MGR
St. Louis Post-Dispatch, St. Louis, MO

Bowman, Rita .... (513) 422-3611
ADV MGR-CLASS
Middletown Journal, Middletown, OH

Bowman, Roger .... (413) 772-0261
Books ED, Entertainment ED
Recorder, Greenfield, MA

Bowman, Steve .... (423) 523-3131
ADV MGR-Sales
Knoxville News-Sentinel, Knoxville, TN

Bowser, Terry .... (814) 643-4040
Sports ED
Huntingdon Daily News, Huntingdon, PA

Bowyer, John F .... (304) 348-5140
DIR-Human Resources
Charleston Newspapers, Charleston, WV

Box, Alan .... (901) 285-4091
PROD MGR-Press
State Gazette, Dyersburg, TN

Box, James M .... (310) 540-5511
EX ED, Daily Breeze, Torrance, CA
Copley Press Inc.

Boxley Jr, John .... (501) 358-2993
PUB, ED, Tri-City Tribune, Marked Tree, AR

Boxmeyer, Don .... (612) 222-5011
COL, St. Paul Pioneer Press, St. Paul, MN

Boyan, Brian .... (516) 725-1700
ED, Sag Harbor Express, Sag Harbor, NY

Boyarsky, Bill .... (213) 237-5000
COL-Local
Los Angeles Times, Los Angeles, CA

Boyce, Ed .... (617) 426-8246
ED, In Newsweekly, Boston, MA

Boyce, Shawn .... (317) 653-5151
CONT, Banner-Graphic, Greencastle, IN

Boyd, Alda .... (316) 326-3326
ADV EX
Wellington Daily News, Wellington, KS

Boyd, Bruce .... (513) 498-2111
PRES, Amos Press, Sidney, OH

Boyd, Donald F .... (912) 686-3523
PUB, ED, Berrien Press, Nashville, GA

Boyd, G Andrew .... (504) 826-3279
Chief Photographer
Times-Picayune, New Orleans, LA

Boyd, Gerald .... (212) 556-1234
ASST MAN ED
New York Times, New York, NY

Boyd, Helen .... (619) 745-6611
ADV MGR-CLASS/Inside
North County Times, Escondido, CA

Boyd, Jack .... (519) 786-5242
PUB, ED, Forest Standard, Forest, ON

Boyd, James .... (615) 259-8000
CIRC DIR
Nashville Tennessean, Nashville, TN

Boyd, Janet .... (716) 328-2144
Correspondent
Syndicated News Service, Rochester, NY

Boyd, Jim .... (612) 673-4000
Deputy EPE, Star Tribune, Minneapolis, MN

Boyd, Kevin .... (408) 920-5000
Art DIR, Mercury News, San Jose, CA

Boyd, Kim M .... (630) 365-6446
MAN ED, Elburn Herald, Elburn, IL

Boyd, L M .... (206) 285-1888
PRES, Crown Syndicate Inc., Seattle, WA

Boyd, Larry .... (913) 877-3361
CIRC MGR-Bookkeeping
Norton Daily Telegram, Norton, KS

Boyd, Micah .... (210) 625-9144
EPE, New Braunfels Herald-Zeitung, New Braunfels, TX

Boyd, Ollette .... (313) 222-6400
CIRC DIR-ADM
Detroit Newspapers, Detroit, MI

Boyd, Patricia .... (206) 285-1888
VP, Crown Syndicate Inc., Seattle, WA

Boyd, R Scott .... (601) 726-4747
PUB, ED, Macon Beacon, Macon, MS

Boyd, Richard D .... (913) 877-3361
PRES, PUB, ED, EPE
Norton Daily Telegram, Norton, KS

Boyd, Rick .... (301) 862-2111
ED, Lexington Park Enterprise, Lexington Park, MD

Boyd, Robert .... (318) 322-5161
DP MGR, PROD MGR-Computer SYS
News-Star, Monroe, LA

Boyd, Robert .... (913) 674-5700
PUB, Hill City Times, Hill City, KS

Boyd, Robert David .... (770) 253-5355
PRES, Mark-Morgan Inc., Newnan, GA

Boyd, Rosalyn M .... (770) 253-5355
SEC/TREAS, Mark-Morgan Inc., Newnan, GA

Boyd, Sue .... (541) 485-1234
Librarian
Eugene Register-Guard, Eugene, OR

Boyd, Vickey Nexsen .... (803) 354-7454
PUB, News, Kingstree, SC

Boyd, Wendell .... (615) 388-6464
PROD MGR, Daily Herald, Columbia, TN

Boyer, Barb .... (605) 765-2464
ED, Potter County News, Gettysburg, SD

Boyer, Barbara .... (312) 222-3232
PROD DIR-Technical OPER/Pre Press
Chicago Tribune, Chicago, IL

Boyer, Dave .... (360) 424-3251
PROD FRM-PR
Skagit Valley Herald, Mount Vernon, WA

Boyer, Larry L .... (614) 446-2342
GM, ADV MGR, Gallipolis Daily Tribune/Sunday Times-Sentinel, Gallipolis, OH, Gannett Co. Inc.

Boyer, Rev Mark G .... (417) 866-0841
ED, Mirror, Springfield, MO

Boyer, Mary K .... (937) 548-3151
ADV DIR, DIR-MKTG OPER
Daily Advocate, Greenville, OH

Boyer, Richard .... (617) 786-7000
PROD MGR-COMP
Patriot Ledger, Quincy, MA

Boyer, Richard .... (204) 694-2022
VP, Winnipeg Sun, Winnipeg, MB

Boyer, Ron .... (316) 775-2218
CIRC MGR
Augusta Daily Gazette, Augusta, KS

Boyes, Scott .... (306) 425-3344
PUB, ED, Northerner, La Ronge, SK

Boyett, Frank .... (502) 827-2000
NTL ED, Political/Government ED, Religion ED, Gleaner, Henderson, KY

Boykin, Don .... (404) 526-5151
ASST MAN ED-Sports
Atlanta Journal-Constitution, Atlanta, GA

Boykin, Jayne .... (405) 353-0620
Copy ED, Lawton Constitution, Lawton, OK

Boykin, Karen .... (919) 243-5151
ADV MGR-CLASS
Wilson Daily Times, Wilson, NC

Boyle, Bill .... (212) 210-2100
Sunday ED
New York Daily News, New York, NY

Boyle, Bill .... (801) 587-2277
PUB, ED, San Juan Record, Monticello, UT

Boyle, E Michael .... (814) 676-7444
EVP, TREAS, Derrick, Oil City, PA

Boyle, E P .... (814) 676-7444
BC, PUB, Derrick, Oil City, PA

Boyle, Gerard .... (207) 873-3341
COL, News ED, Central Maine Morning Sentinel, Waterville, ME

Boyle, Jody .... (908) 349-3000
PROD DIR-COMP
Ocean County Observer, Toms River, NJ

Boyle, Joseph .... (773) 476-4800
ED, Southwest News-Herald, Chicago, IL

Boyle, Kevin .... (718) 634-4000
ED
Wave of Long Island, Rockaway Beach, NY

Boyle, Michelle .... (908) 349-3000
PROD MGR
Ocean County Observer, Toms River, NJ

Boyle, Patrick C .... (814) 676-7444
PRES, ED, Derrick, Oil City, PA

Boyle, Peter T .... (814) 676-7444
SEC, Derrick, Oil City, PA

Boyle, Robert W .... (215) 893-4050
PUB, Philadelphia Tribune, Philadelphia, PA

Boyle, Scott .... (902) 426-2811
CIRC MGR, Chronicle-Herald, Halifax, NS

Boyne, William C .... (507) 285-7600
PUB, ED
Rochester Post-Bulletin, Rochester, MN

Boynton, Cynthia Wolfe .... (203) 876-6800
MAN ED, Milford Reporter, Milford, CT

Boysick, Gail .... (607) 798-1234
ADV MGR-CLASS
Press & Sun Bulletin, Binghamton, NY

Bozarth, A J .... (316) 456-2232
PUB
South Haven New Era, Conway Spring, KS

Bozeman, Maurice G .... (334) 578-1492
PUB, Evergreen Courant, Evergreen, AL

Bozeman III, Robert .... (334) 578-1492
ED, Evergreen Courant, Evergreen, AL

Bozeman, Wells .... (334) 636-2214
PUB, Thomasville Times, Thomasville, AL

Brabender, Vic .... (502) 582-4011
ADV DIR, Courier-Journal, Louisville, KY

Bracamontes, Ramon .... (915) 546-6100
City/MET ED, El Paso Times, El Paso, TX

Brace, Bob .... (403) 743-8186
ADV MGR-RT
Fort McMurray Today, Fort McMurray, AB

Bracey, Robert N .... (412) 588-5000
PRES/CEO, PUB/GM
Record-Argus, Greenville, PA

Bracht, Randy .... (509) 754-4636
MAN ED, Grant County Journal, Ephrata, WA

Brackenbury, Mark .... (203) 789-5200
MET ED, Religion ED
New Haven Register, New Haven, CT

Brackett, Earl K .... (704) 864-3291
ADV DIR, Gaston Gazette, Gastonia, NC

Brackett, Sean .... (617) 593-7700
ADV MGR-RT, Daily Evening Item, Lynn, MA

Brackner, Darla .... (218) 751-3740
ADV MGR-CLASS
Daily Pioneer, Bemidji, MN

Bracy, Monte .... (804) 732-3456
ADV MGR, Progress-Index, Petersburg, VA

Bradbury, Cathrin .... (416) 585-5000
Features ED, Globe and Mail (Canada's National Newspaper), Toronto, ON

Bradbury, Dieter .... (207) 791-6650
Environmental ED
Portland Press Herald, Portland, ME

Bradbury, Janet .... (701) 427-9472
PUB, ED, Teller, Milnor, ND

Bradbury, Randy .... (701) 780-1100
Political ED
Grand Forks Herald, Grand Forks, ND

Bradbury, Richard .... (701) 427-9472
PUB, ED, Teller, Milnor, ND

Braddock, Hugh B .... (615) 384-3567
PUB
Robertson County Times, Springfield, TN

Braddock, Linda .... (360) 694-3391
CIRC MGR-PROM/TELEMKTG
Columbian, Vancouver, WA

Braden, Lou .... (970) 352-0211
ADV DIR, Greeley Tribune, Greeley, CO

Braden, Randall C .... (316) 625-2181
PUB, ED
Yates Center News, Yates Center, KS

Braden, Tyra .... (610) 820-6500
Lehighton ED, Morning Call, Allentown, PA

Bradford, Chris .... (915) 646-2541
CIRC MGR
Brownwood Bulletin, Brownwood, TX

Bradford, Christina .... (313) 222-2300
MAN ED, Detroit News, Detroit, MI

Bradford, Frances M .... (912) 468-5433
PUB, ED, Ocilla Star, Ocilla, GA

Bradford, Gigi .... (404) 526-5151
ADV MGR-CLASS/Telephone Sales
Atlanta Journal-Constitution, Atlanta, GA

Bradford, Mary .... (541) 474-3700
Librarian
Grants Pass Daily Courier, Grants Pass, OR

Bradford, Robert .... (507) 645-5615
PUB, Northfield News, Northfield, MN

Bradford, Robert G .... (412) 222-2200
DP MGR, PROD SUPV-SYS
Observer-Reporter, Washington, PA

Bradford, Timothy .... (904) 285-2915
PUB, Ponte Vedra Recorder, Ponte Vedra, FL

Bradham, Harry E .... (618) 456-8808
PUB, ED
West Salem Times Advocate, West Salem, IL

Bradham, Kelly .... (417) 667-3344
Sports ED, Nevada Daily Mail, Nevada, MO

Bradigan, Bret .... (619) 379-3667
PUB, ED, Kern Valley Sun, Lake Isabella, CA

Bradlee, Benjamin C .... (202) 334-6000
VP at Large
Washington Post, Washington, DC

Bradlee, Thomas F .... (212) 582-2300
PRES, Whitcom Partners, New York, NY

Bradley, Barbara .... (901) 529-2211
Fashion ED
Commercial Appeal, Memphis, TN

Bradley, Bernice .... (715) 384-3131
MGR-EDU SRV
Marshfield News-Herald, Marshfield, WI

Bradley Jr, David R .... (816) 271-8500
PRES, PUB, ED
St. Joseph News-Press, St. Joseph, MO

Bradley, Deanna .... (506) 328-8863
ED, Bugle, Woodstock, NB

Bradley, Debra .... (715) 344-6100
City ED
Stevens Point Journal, Stevens Point, WI

Bradley, Doris .... (514) 987-2222
ADV MGR-CLASS, Gazette, Montreal, QC

Bradley, Ed .... (810) 766-6100
Films/Theater ED, Flint Journal, Flint, MI

Bradley, George A .... (401) 849-3300
PROD FRM-PR
Newport Daily News, Newport, RI

Bradley, Hank .... (816) 271-8500
BC/TREAS, News-Press, St. Joseph, MO

Bradley, Jack .... (901) 529-2211
ASST MAN ED-Nights
Commercial Appeal, Memphis, TN

Bradley, James .... (573) 336-3711
MAN ED, City ED
Daily Guide, Waynesville, MO

Bradley, Janell .... (319) 426-5591
PUB, ED, Elgin Echo, Elgin, IA

Bradley, Jeanette .... (904) 829-6562
City ED, Record, St. Augustine, FL

Bradley, Jeff .... (303) 820-1010
Critic-at-Large, Denver Post, Denver, CO

Bradley, Jim .... (515) 993-4233
GM
Dallas County News & Roundup, Adel, IA

Bradley, Jo-Ann .... (941) 335-0200
DIR-Human Resources
News-Press, Fort Myers, FL

Bradley, Kent .... (360) 577-2500
PROD SUPV-Pre Press
Daily News, Longview, WA

Bradley, Mark .... (319) 653-2191
PROD MGR, Washington Evening Journal, Washington, IA, Inland Industries Inc.

Bradley, Melanie .... (815) 877-4044
MAN ED, Pecatonica/Winnebago Gazette, Loves Park, IL

Bradley, Ned J .... (812) 379-5612
PRES
Home News Enterprises, Columbus, IN

Bradley, R Bruce .... (757) 446-2000
PRES/PUB, Virginian-Pilot, Norfolk, VA

Bradley, Richard .... (303) 820-1010
CIRC MGR-City, Denver Post, Denver, CO

Bradley, Steve .... (716) 394-0770
Sports ED, Daily Messenger/The Sunday Messenger, Canandaigua, NY

Bradner, Rebecca .... (808) 525-8000
ADV DIR-CLASS
Hawaii Newspaper Agency Inc., Honolulu, HI

Bradow, Bill .... (501) 255-4538
MAN ED, Grand Prairie Herald, Hazen, AR

Bradshaw, Dennis E .... (703) 368-3101
GM, ED, Journal Messenger, Manassas, VA

Bradshaw, Don .... (709) 634-4348
Sports ED, Western Star, Corner Brook, NF

Bradshaw, Fred .... (301) 921-2800
ED, Tester, Gaithersburg, MD

Bradshaw, Jim .... (318) 289-6300
Action Line/Action Corner ED, City ED, Oil News ED, Advertiser, Lafayette, LA

Bradshaw, Josh .... (309) 692-4910
ED, Observer, Peoria, IL

Brady, Anne Vaccaro .... (914) 939-1164
ED, Port Chester Guide, Port Chester, NY

Brady, Carolyn .... (310) 832-0221
Maritime ED, News-Pilot, San Pedro, CA

Brady, Charles F .... (417) 235-3135
Sports ED, Times, Monett, MO

Brady, Charlotte .... (417) 235-3135
DP MGR, Times, Monett, MO

Brady, Denise .... (301) 662-1177
ADV ASST MGR-Display
Frederick Post/The News, Frederick, MD

Brady, Eileen .... (910) 353-1171
Automotive ED, BUS/FIN ED, Features ED, Living/Lifestyle ED, Daily News, Jacksonville, NC

Brady, Elaine .... (301) 921-2800
PUB, Pentagram, Gaithersburg, MD

Brady, Evelyn .... (417) 623-3480
ADV MGR-CLASS, Joplin Globe, Joplin, MO

Brady, Jerry M .... (208) 522-1800
PRES, PUB/ED
Post Register, Idaho Falls, ID

Brady, Joy .... (619) 442-4404
DP MGR, Daily Californian, El Cajon, CA

Brady, Karen .... (716) 849-3434
EDU ED, Buffalo News, Buffalo, NY

Brady, Karen .... (316) 697-4716
PUB, ED, Elkhart Tri-State News, Elkhart, KS

Brady, Kevin .... (954) 698-6397
ED, Delray Beach Times, Deerfield Beach, FL

Brady, Michael .... (401) 722-4000
PROD SUPT, Times, Pawtucket, RI

Brady, Terry .... (610) 323-3000
News ED, Mercury, Pottstown, PA

Brady, W .... (519) 679-6666
Group VP/CORP SEC
London Free Press, London, ON

Braeske, Arnold .... (201) 877-4141
Telegraph ED, Star-Ledger, Newark, NJ

Bragdon, Mark .... (207) 791-6650
PROD OPER SUPV-PR/Platemaking
Portland Press Herald, Portland, ME

Bra Who's Where-26

Bragg, Bob .... (403) 235-7100
EDL Writer, Calgary Herald, Calgary, AB

Bragg, Jeanine .... (313) 242-1100
ADTX MGR
Monroe Evening News, Monroe, MI

Bragg, Kelley .... (709) 535-6910
ED, Pilot, Lewisporte, NF

Bragg, Lois A .... (816) 332-4431
PUB, ED, Home Press, La Plata, MO

Braid, Don .... (403) 235-7100
COL, Calgary Herald, Calgary, AB

Braine, Barbara .... (516) 843-2020
Letter to the ED, Newsday, Melville, NY

Braithwaite, Chris .... (802) 525-3531
PUB, Chronicle, Barton, VT

Brake, Neil .... (205) 345-0505
Photo DEPT MGR
Tuscaloosa News, Tuscaloosa, AL

Braknis, Greg .... (419) 245-6000
BUS/RE ED, Blade, Toledo, OH

Braly, James .... (408) 920-5000
Commentary Page ED
San Jose Mercury News, San Jose, CA

Bramble, Joy .... (410) 366-3900
PUB, Baltimore Times, Baltimore, MD

Bramlett, Anthony .... (702) 383-0211
MIS MGR
Las Vegas Review-Journal, Las Vegas, NV

Bramlett, William .... (770) 382-4545
PROD SUPT
Daily Tribune News, Cartersville, GA

Branagh, Mae .... (209) 358-5311
MAN ED, Demair Dispatch, Winton, CA

Branam, Jud .... (313) 994-6989
School ED, Ann Arbor News, Ann Arbor, MI

Brancaccio, Lou .... (310) 829-6811
MAN ED, Outlook, Santa Monica, CA

Branch, David .... (903) 597-8111
Photo DEPT MGR
Tyler Morning Telegraph, Tyler, TX

Branch, Eleanor .... (718) 636-9119
ED, New American, Brooklyn, NY

Branch, John .... (210) 225-7411
Cartoonist
San Antonio Express-News, San Antonio, TX

Brand, Charles J .... (212) 666-2300
Reporter, Basch, Buddy Feature Syndicate, New York, NY

Brand, Sandra .... (501) 563-2615
ED, Osceola Times, Osceola, AR

Brandel, Alice .... (810) 727-3745
GM, Chesterfield Review/The Review/Independent Press, Richmond, MI

Brandenberger, George .... (516) 843-2020
CIRC DIR-Transportation
Newsday, Melville, NY

Brandenburg, Bobby .... (205) 325-2222
MGR-Direct MKTG
Birmingham Post-Herald, Birmingham, AL

Brandenburg, Daniel S .... (715) 754-5444
PUB, Marion Advertiser, Marion, WI

Brandenburg, Mike .... (317) 462-5528
PROD MGR-Post Press
Daily Reporter, Greenfield, IN

Brandenburg, Patsy R .... (715) 754-5444
ED, Marion Advertiser, Marion, WI

Brander, Don .... (902) 629-6000
PUB/GM
Charlottetown Guardian, Charlottetown, PEI

Brandes, Heidi .... (405) 255-5354
EDU ED, Duncan Banner, Duncan, OK

Brandlon, Jennifer .... (503) 635-8811
ED, Lake Oswego Review, Lake Oswego, OR

Brandner, Cheryl .... (507) 346-7365
ED, Spring Valley Tribune, Spring Valley, MN

Brandon, Kitty .... (919) 563-3555
ED, Mebane Enterprise, Mebane, NC

Brandon, Phyllis .... (501) 378-3400
Women's ED
Arkansas Democrat-Gazette, Little Rock, AR

Brandt, Brenda .... (970) 854-2811
ED, Holyoke Enterprise, Holyoke, CO

Brandt, Evan .... (914) 763-3200
MAN ED, Patent Trader, Cross River, NY

Brandt, Jane .... (701) 878-4494
PUB, Hebron Herald, Hebron, ND

Brandt, Linda .... (941) 953-7755
Food ED, SCI ED
Sarasota Herald-Tribune, Sarasota, FL

Brandt, Randolph D .... (317) 664-5111
MAN ED, Chronicle-Tribune, Marion, IN

Brandt, Robert .... (516) 843-2020
MAN ED-OPER, Newsday, Melville, NY

Brandt, Steven R .... (864) 298-4100
PUB, Greenville News, Greenville, SC

Brandvold, Ken .... (712) 279-5019
BM/CR MGR
Sioux City Journal, Sioux City, IA

Branen, Robert .... (414) 763-3511
PUB
Burlington Standard Press, Burlington, WI

Branham, Lorraine .... (904) 599-2100
Senior VP, EX ED
Tallahassee Democrat, Tallahassee, FL

Branham, Mary .... (502) 227-4556
Wire ED, State Journal, Frankfort, KY

Branham, Mason .... (606) 473-9851
ED, Greenup News, Greenup, KY

Branham, Phyllis .... (405) 479-5757
PUB, ED, Big Pasture News, Grandfield, OK

Branick, Robert .... (847) 888-7800
PROD FRM-COMP, Courier-News, Elgin, IL

Branigan, Mike .... (318) 487-6397
PROD SUPT-COMP
Alexandria Daily Town Talk, Alexandria, LA

Brann, June K .... (210) 585-4893
PUB, ED, Progress Times, Mission, TX

Brannan, Dan .... (864) 882-2375
ED, Seneca Journal/Tribune, Seneca, SC

Brannan, David .... (309) 829-9411
PROD SUPV-MR
Pantagraph, Bloomington, IL

Branning, Charles .... (512) 884-2011
People ED, Corpus Christi Caller-Times, Corpus Christi, TX

Brannon, Edward .... (814) 676-7444
Sports ED, Derrick, Oil City, PA

Brannon, Genevieve .... (606) 987-1870
PUB, GM, MAN ED
Bourbon County Citizen, Paris, KY

Brannon, Jimmy .... (606) 987-1870
ED, Bourbon County Citizen, Paris, KY

Brannon, Sue .... (904) 752-1293
CONT, Lake City Reporter, Lake City, FL

Brannon, Ted .... (501) 785-7700
CIRC DIR
Southwest Times Record, Fort Smith, AR

Branscome, James G .... (212) 208-8000
Senior VP-Equity Info Services, Corporation Records, Daily News, New York, NY

Bransdorfer, Alfred R .... (517) 386-9937
PUB, ED, Clare Sentinel, Clare, MI

Bransdorfer, Mary C .... (517) 386-9937
GM, Clare Sentinel, Clare, MI

Branson, Paul .... (913) 776-2200
Fashion/Home Furnishings ED, Living/Life-style ED, Society ED
Manhattan Mercury, Manhattan, KS

Branstiter, Dennis .... (612) 673-4000
ASST Features Section ED
Star Tribune, Minneapolis, MN

Brant, Lee .... (916) 273-9561
PROD SUPV-Printing
Union, Grass Valley, CA

Brant, Patty .... (941) 657-6000
ED, Caloosa Belle, La Belle, FL

Brant, Randall .... (808) 525-8000
ADV MGR-Display
Hawaii Newspaper Agency Inc., Honolulu, HI

Brantingham, Barney .... (805) 564-5200
COL, Santa Barbara News-Press, Santa Barbara, CA

Brantley, Dave .... (214) 977-8222
PROD MGR-Maintenance
Dallas Morning News, Dallas, TX

Brantley, Sandra .... (919) 243-5151
PROD FRM-COMP
Wilson Daily Times, Wilson, NC

Branum, Diana .... (901) 427-3333
EDU ED, Jackson Sun, Jackson, TN

Branyon, Faye .... (864) 456-7772
ED, Observer, Ware Shoals, SC

Branyon, S Daniel .... (864) 456-7772
PUB, Observer, Ware Shoals, SC

Brashears, Bob .... (301) 662-1177
PROD SUPV-COMP (Night)
Frederick Post/News, Frederick, MD

Brasier, John .... (803) 626-8555
Sports ED
Myrtle Beach Sun News, Myrtle Beach, SC

Brasier, Ken .... (401) 596-7791
PROD MGR-OPER
Westerly Sun, Westerly, RI

Brassard, Raymond .... (514) 987-2222
MAN ED, Gazette, Montreal, QC

Braswell, Bill .... (501) 946-3241
PUB, De Witt Era-Enterprise, De Witt, AR

Braswell, James .... (501) 946-3241
PUB, De Witt Era-Enterprise, De Witt, AR

Braswell, James .... (408) 920-5000
SYS ED
San Jose Mercury News, San Jose, CA

Braswell, Robert .... (915) 337-4661
DP MGR, PROD DIR-OPER
Odessa American, Odessa, TX

Braswell II, William H .... (601) 853-4222
MAN ED
Madison County Journal, Ridgeland, MS

Bratcher, Mark .... (405) 332-4433
Farm/Agriculture ED
Ada Evening News, Ada, OK

Bratcher, Sue .... (309) 962-4441
ED, Le Roy Journal, Le Roy, IL

Bratetic, Dan .... (573) 756-8927
Sports ED
Daily Press Leader, Farmington, MO

Bratigam, Kevin .... (306) 948-3344
MAN ED, Independent, Biggar, SK

Brauchli, Marcus .... (212) 416-2000
Reporter-in-Charge (Hong Kong)
Wall Street Journal, New York, NY

Brauckman, Diane .... (512) 884-2011
ADV MGR-Territory Sales, Corpus Christi Caller-Times, Corpus Christi, TX

Brauer, Mary .... (406) 587-4491
ADTX MGR, Daily Chronicle, Bozeman, MT

Brauer, Susanne A .... (812) 424-7711
BM/CONT
Evansville Courier Co. Inc., Evansville, IN

Braught, Diana .... (541) 753-2641
PSL CNR
Corvallis Gazette-Times, Corvallis, OR

Brault, Michael .... (413) 788-1000
MET ED, Union-News, Springfield, MA

Braun, Bob .... (717) 784-2121
PROD MGR-Color Division
Press Enterprise, Bloomsburg, PA

Braun, Gerry .... (619) 299-3131
Political Writer
San Diego Union-Tribune, San Diego, CA

Braun, Jonathan .... (310) 230-3400
RES, Allsport Photography USA, Pacific Palisades, CA

Braun, Michael A .... (330) 747-1471
Garden ED, Outdoors ED, Sunday ED, Travel ED, Vindicator, Youngstown, OH

Braun, Robert .... (201) 877-4141
COL, Star-Ledger, Newark, NJ

Braun, Stephen .... (213) 237-5000
Chicago BU
Los Angeles Times, Los Angeles, CA

Braun, Walter .... (913) 776-2200
EPE, Manhattan Mercury, Manhattan, KS

Brauner, Cathy .... (617) 235-4000
ED, Wellesley Townsman, Wellesley, MA

Braunschweig, Thomas E .... (717) 348-9100
PROD MGR
Tribune & The Scranton Times, Scranton, PA

Brautigam, Susan .... (414) 276-0273
CIRC DIR, Daily Reporter, Milwaukee, WI

Braverman, Alan N .... (212) 456-7777
Sr VP/GEN Counsel, ABC Inc., New York, NY

Brawdy, Bob .... (509) 582-1500
Chief Photographer
Tri-City Herald, Tri-Cities, WA

Brawn, Mike .... (808) 244-3981
Sports ED, Maui News, Wailuku, HI

Brawn, Paul .... (207) 791-6650
PROD OPER MGR-Printing & Distribution/Plant Maintenance
Portland Press Herald, Portland, ME

Brawner, Steve .... (501) 315-8228
MAN ED, Benton Courier, Benton, AR

Braxton, Greg .... (213) 237-5000
Television Industry Writer
Los Angeles Times, Los Angeles, CA

Bray, Keith .... (307) 875-3103
PUB, ED, Green River Star, Green River, WY

Bray, Thomas J .... (313) 222-2300
EPE, Detroit News, Detroit, MI

Bray, Tom .... (209) 734-5821
MAN ED, Visalia Times-Delta, Visalia, CA

Brayan, Don .... (507) 334-1853
CIRC ASSOC MGR
Faribault Daily News, Faribault, MN

Braymen, Pauline .... (541) 573-2022
ED, Burns Times-Herald, Burns, OR

Brazaitis, Tom .... (216) 999-4500
Washington BU Chief
Plain Dealer, Cleveland, OH

Brazeau, A .... (519) 344-3641
PROD FRM-PR, Observer, Sarnia, ON

Brazee, Rodney .... (517) 772-2971
Photo ED (Mt Pleasant)
Morning Sun, Mount Pleasant, MI

Brazsky, Rich .... (619) 299-3131
PROD MGR-Special Projects and Scheduling
San Diego Union-Tribune, San Diego, CA

Brazzell, Jennifer .... (219) 347-0400
ADV DIR-Inserts
News-Sun, Kendallville, IN

Breakfield, Louis .... (601) 794-2765
ED, Lamar County News, Purvis, MS

Brean, Henry .... (702) 727-5102
MAN ED
Pahrump Valley Times, Pahrump, NV

Breault, Rich .... (805) 273-2700
Features ED, Health/Medical ED, Living/Lifestyle ED, People/Outdoor ED
Antelope Valley Press, Palmdale, CA

Breaux, Nona .... (215) 855-8440
City ED, Teen-Age/Youth ED
Reporter, Landsdale, PA

Brebner, Roderick (Rod) .... (519) 538-1421
PUB, Express, Meaford, ON

Brecher, John .... (212) 416-2000
Page One ED
Wall Street Journal, New York, NY

Brechlin, Earl .... (207) 667-5514
ED, Ellsworth Weekly, Ellsworth, ME

Breckenridge, John .... (610) 279-5473
BM
Mullich Communications, Norristown, PA

Breckenridge, Patti .... (813) 259-7711
ASST MAN ED-Electronic Publishing, Online Services MGR
Tampa Tribune and Times, Tampa, FL

Breckner, Gene .... (805) 273-2700
Photo ED
Antelope Valley Press, Palmdale, CA

BreDahl, Clark .... (515) 745-3161
ED, Fontanelle Observer, Fontanelle, IA

Bredehoft, Jean .... (719) 765-4466
GM, Flagler News, Flagler, CO

Bredehoft, Thomas E .... (719) 765-4466
PUB, ED, Flagler News, Flagler, CO

Bredemeier, Kenneth .... (202) 334-6000
RE ED (BUS/FIN)
Washington Post, Washington, DC

Bredesen, Brian .... (250) 782-4888
ADV DIR
Peace River Block News, Dawson Creek, BC

Breed, David .... (918) 663-1414
ED, Southwest Tulsa News, Tulsa, OK

Breeden, Bill .... (423) 929-3111
ADV DIR, Press, Johnson City, TN

Breeden, Dan .... (808) 329-9311
ASST ED
West Hawaii Today, Kailua-Kona, HI

Breeden, Linda L .... (812) 332-4401
ASST SEC, Herald-Times Inc, Bloomington, IN, Schurz Communications Inc.

Breeden, Tami .... (712) 279-5019
MGR-MKTG/PROM, Online Contact
Sioux City Journal, Sioux City, IA

Breeding, Cindy .... (817) 387-3811
Features ED, Religion ED, Women's ED
Denton Record-Chronicle, Denton, TX

Breeding, Rob .... (406) 363-3300
MAN ED, Ravalli Republic, Hamilton, MT

Breedlove, Dan .... (302) 674-3600
PROD MGR-PR
Delaware State News, Dover, DE

Breedlove, Gary .... (704) 252-5611
CIRC MGR-Single Copy Sales
Asheville Citizen-Times, Asheville, NC

Breedlove, Michael M .... (334) 246-4494
PUB, South Alabamian, Jackson, AL

Breedlove, Ronald .... (541) 269-1222
PROD FRM-PR, World, Coos Bay, OR

Breen, Angi .... (250) 427-5333
CIRC DIR, Daily Bulletin, Kimberley, BC

Breen, Dan .... (718) 981-1234
Television ED, Travel ED
Staten Island Advance, Staten Island, NY

Breen, Ed .... (219) 461-8333
Graphics ED
Journal Gazette, Fort Wayne, IN

Breen, Steve .... (209) 847-3021
ED, Oakdale Leader, Oakdale, CA

Brehm, Jackie .... (334) 670-6324
ED, Troy Progress, Troy, AL

Brehm, Karen A .... (915) 546-6340
Features ED, Living/Life-style ED, Society ED, El Paso Herald-Post, El Paso, TX

Brehm, Mona M .... (812) 385-2525
TREAS, Princeton Daily Clarion, Princeton, IN, Brehm Communications Inc.

Brehm, Rita .... (406) 657-1200
ADV MGR-CLASS
Billings Gazette, Billings, MT

Brehm, W J .... (619) 451-6200
COB
Brehm Communication Inc., San Diego, CA

Brehm Jr, William .... (619) 451-6200
PRES
Brehm Communication Inc., San Diego, CA

Breig, Barry B .... (716) 849-3434
VP, DIR-MIS, ADTX MGR
Buffalo News, Buffalo, NY

Breig, James P .... (518) 453-6688
ED, Evangelist, Albany, NY

Breindel, Eric .... (212) 930-8000
EPE/COL, New York Post, New York, NY

Breise, Ronald .... (573) 431-2010
PROD MGR, PROD FRM-PR
Daily Journal, Park Hills, MO

Breister, Peggy .... (414) 922-4600
EDU ED
Fond du Lac Reporter, Fond du Lac, WI

Breite, Thea .... (401) 277-7000
ASST MAN ED-Visuals
Providence Journal-Bulletin, Providence, RI

Brekken, Jahelle .... (218) 281-2730
Women's ED, Daily Times, Crookston, MN

Breland, Bob Ann .... (504) 732-2565
COL-Consumerism, Librarian, Religion/Society ED, Daily News, Bogalusa, LA

Copyright ©1997 by the Editor & Publisher Co.

27-Who's Where **Bri**

Brem, Miki ... (416) 585-5000
CIRC Regional MGR-S.W. Ont.
Globe and Mail , Toronto, ON

Brem, Ralph ... (304) 292-6301
ED, Dominion Post, Morgantown, WV

Bremer, Patrice ... (612) 222-5011
DIR-MKTG Services
St. Paul Pioneer Press, St. Paul, MN

Bremner, Faith ... (702) 788-6200
Water/Washoe County ED
Reno Gazette-Journal, Reno, NV

Bremner, John E ... (314) 340-8000
EDL Writer, Post-Dispatch, St. Louis, MO

Brendel, Dale ... (816) 229-9161
MAN ED, Sports ED
Blue Springs Examiner, Blue Springs, MO

Brendza, Anna Lee ... (330) 364-5577
Action Line/Hot Line ED
Times Reporter, New Philadelphia, OH

Brengren, Helen ... (515) 993-4233
MAN ED
Dallas County News & Roundup, Adel, IA

Breniman, Glenn ... (503) 221-8327
ADV MGR-RT/OPER
Oregonian, Portland, OR

Breninghouse, Myron ... (860) 887-9211
PROD DIR, Norwich Bulletin, Norwich, CT

Brennan, Alice F ... (617) 444-8244
VP/ASSOC ED, Brenfeatures, Needham, MA

Brennan, Bill ... (308) 382-1000
EX ED, EPE
Grand Island Independent, Grand Island, NE

Brennan, Charles ... (352) 563-6363
MAN ED, EPE
Citrus County Chronicle, Crystal River, FL

Brennan, Eileen ... (516) 747-8282
ED, Manhasset Press, Mineola, NY

Brennan, Frederick W ... (914) 534-7771
ED, Cornwall Local, Cornwall, NY

Brennan, Jim ... (716) 849-3434
Television Topics ED
Buffalo News, Buffalo, NY

Brennan, Jim ... (201) 365-3000
Sports ED
North Jersey Herald & News, Passaic, NJ

Brennan, John ... (203) 846-3281
CIRC DIR, Hour, Norwalk, CT

Brennan, John ... (617) 444-8244
PRES/ED, Brenfeatures, Needham, MA

Brennan, John ... (505) 546-2611
ED, Deming Headlight, Deming, NM

Brennan, Pat ... (613) 829-9100
PROD VP-Manufacturing
Ottawa Citizen, Ottawa, ON

Brennan, Robert ... (516) 843-2020
CIRC DIR, Newsday, Melville, NY

Brennan, Tom ... (419) 522-3311
EX ED, News Journal, Mansfield, OH

Brennan, William ... (708) 336-7000
ADV MGR-Sales, News-Sun, Waukegan, IL

Brenneman, Susan ... (213) 237-5000
Deputy Arts ED
Los Angeles Times, Los Angeles, CA

Brenner, Bari ... (510) 208-6300
Travel ED, Oakland Tribune, Oakland, CA
MediaNews Inc. (Alameda Newspapers)

Brenner, Betty ... (810) 766-6100
Religion ED, Flint Journal, Flint, MI

Brenner, Bill ... (707) 963-2731
PUB, St. Helena Star, St. Helena, CA

Brenner, Chris ... (708) 336-7000
City ED, EDU ED, News-Sun, Waukegan, IL

Brenner, Elizabeth F ... (360) 377-3711
PRES/PUB, Sun, Bremerton, WA

Brenner, Kit ... (210) 695-3613
ED, Echo, Helotes, TX

Brenner, R B ... (941) 953-7755
City ED, Herald-Tribune, Sarasota, FL

Brenner, Virginia ... (618) 683-3531
PUB, ED, Herald-Enterprise, Golconda, IL

Brennglass, Ed ... (213) 738-7778
PUB, Jewish Journal of Greater Los Angeles, Los Angeles, CA

Brent, A J ... (813) 259-7711
SEC, Tampa Tribune and Times, Tampa, FL

Bresette, Jim ... (402) 444-1000
Books ED, Entertainment ED
Omaha World-Herald, Omaha, NE

Breslauer, Irwin ... (202) 408-1484
NTL Sales MAN, Scripps Howard News Service, Washington, DC

Bresnahan, Dennis ... (318) 433-3000
PROD FRM-MR, Lake Charles American Press, Lake Charles, LA

Bressoud, Steve ... (818) 962-8811
CFO, San Gabriel Valley Tribune, West Covina, CA, MediaNews Inc.

Breton, Brigitte ... (418) 686-3233
EDU, Le Soleil, Quebec, QC

Breton, Linda ... (207) 873-3341
PROD SUPV-COMP, Central Maine Morning Sentinel, Waterville, ME
Guy Gannett Communications

Bretsch, Stacy Seaman ... (605) 329-2538
ED
Brown County Independent, Frederick, SD

Brett, Kimberley ... (709) 489-2161
ED, Advertiser, Grand Falls, NF

Brett, Kristin ... (813) 893-8111
MGR-Creative Services
St. Petersburg Times, St. Petersburg, FL

Brett, Regina ... (330) 996-3000
COL-Local, Akron Beacon Journal, Akron, OH

Brett, Wilber R ... (519) 776-8511
PUB, ED, Free Press, Essex, ON

Brett-Beumer, Carol ... (970) 824-7031
PUB, GM, ADV MGR
Northwest Colorado Daily Press, Craig, CO

Brettingen, Tom ... (212) 621-1500
DIR-BUS Development
Associated Press, New York, NY

Brettman, Alan ... (360) 577-2500
News ED, Daily News, Longview, WA

Bretzias, Hunter ... (704) 864-3291
Art DIR, Graphics ED
Gaston Gazette, Gastonia, NC

Bretzius, Jim ... (704) 864-3291
ADTX MGR, Gaston Gazette, Gastonia, NC

Breunig, John ... (203) 625-4400
Sports ED, Greenwich Time, Greenwich, CT

Brew, Christine ... (717) 264-6161
CONT, Public Opinion, Chambersburg, PA

Brewer, Bert ... (915) 586-2561
MAN ED, Winkler County News, Kermit, TX

Brewer, Beth A ... (315) 866-2220
PUB, CIRC MGR
Evening Telegram, Herkimer, NY

Brewer, Byron ... (502) 863-1111
MAN ED, News-Graphic, Georgetown, KY

Brewer, Cherly ... (312) 222-3232
CIRC MGR-Customer SRV
Chicago Tribune, Chicago, IL

Brewer, Dale ... (616) 429-2400
City ED, Herald-Palladium, St. Joseph, MI

Brewer, Fred ... (717) 348-9100
PROD FRM-MR
Tribune & The Scranton Times, Scranton, PA

Brewer, Heather ... (803) 785-4293
Leisure ED, Island Packet, Hilton Head, SC

Brewer, Jim ... (419) 994-4166
ED, Loudonville Times, Loudonville, OH

Brewer, Joe ... (604) 344-5251
ED, Golden Star, Golden, BC

Brewer, John ... (212) 499-3334
PRES/EIC, New York Times Syndication Sales Corp., New York, NY

Brewer, John ... (419) 547-9194
ED, Clyde Enterprise, Clyde, OH

Brewer, Juanita ... (918) 224-5185
ADV MGR
Sapulpa Daily Herald, Sapulpa, OK

Brewer, Kay ... (501) 378-3400
PSL MGR
Arkansas Democrat-Gazette, Little Rock, AR

Brewer, Kelly ... (505) 823-7777
ASST MAN ED-News
Albuquerque Tribune, Albuquerque, NM

Brewer, Leslye ... (904) 863-1111
DP MGR, Northwest Florida Daily News, Fort Walton Beach, FL

Brewer, Linda ... (423) 986-6581
ED, News-Herald, Lenoir City, TN

Brewer, Mary D ... (207) 633-4620
MAN ED
Boothbay Register, Boothbay Harbor, ME

Brewer, Sharon ... (707) 964-5642
PUB
Fort Bragg Advocate-News, Fort Bragg, CA

Brewer, Steve ... (505) 823-7777
EDU (Higher)
Albuquerque Journal, Albuquerque, NM

Brewis, Cathy J ... (206) 597-8742
ADV DIR, News Tribune, Tacoma, WA

Brewster, Anna ... (419) 399-4015
PUB, ED, Paulding Progress, Paulding, OH

Brewster, David ... (206) 623-0500
PUB, Seattle Weekly, Seattle, WA

Brewster, Louis ... (909) 987-6397
Sports ED
Inland Valley Daily Bulletin, Ontario, CA

Brewster, Peter ... (416) 947-2222
ASST MAN ED, Toronto Sun, Toronto, ON

Brezina, A ... (416) 530-4222
PUB, ED, Satellite 1416, Toronto, ON

Brezina, Jack ... (705) 286-1288
PUB, ED, Times, Minden, ON

Brezina, Mike ... (520) 774-4545
CIRC MGR, Arizona Daily Sun, Flagstaff, AZ

Brezinski, Ken ... (715) 344-6100
ADV DIR, ADV MGR-NTL
Stevens Point Journal, Stevens Point, WI

Brian, Eric ... (316) 331-3550
EDU ED, School ED, Independence Daily Reporter, Independence, KS

Briand, Paul ... (508) 744-0600
ASST to the PUB
Salem Evening News, Beverly, MA

Briant, Maryjane ... (609) 272-7000
MAN ED
Press of Atlantic City, Pleasantville, NJ

Brice, Michael ... (419) 475-6000
ED, West Toledo Herald, Toledo, OH

Brice, Owen B ... (941) 676-3467
PUB, ED, Lake Wales News, Lake Wales, FL

Brick, Judy ... (608) 437-5553
ED, Mount Horeb Mail, Mount Horeb, WI

Bricker, Craig ... (210) 686-4343
PROD MGR-MR, Monitor, McAllen, TX

Bricker, Don ... (419) 223-1010
PROD OPER DIR, Lima News, Lima, OH

Bricker, Karen ... (419) 223-1010
DIR-MKTG, Lima News, Lima, OH

Bricker, Linda ... (804) 649-6000
ADV MGR-Ad SRV
Richmond Times-Dispatch, Richmond, VA

Brickey, Dean ... (541) 523-3673
ED, COL, EPE, Political ED
Baker City Herald, Baker City, OR

Brictingham, Tamara ... (302) 422-1200
PUB, Milford Chronicle, Milford, DE

Bridge, Bob ... (812) 275-3355
Sports ED, Times-Mail, Bedford, IN

Bridgeman, Ron ... (423) 482-1021
ED, Oak Ridger, Oak Ridge, TN

Bridges, Barry ... (704) 864-3291
News ED, Wire ED
Gaston Gazette, Gastonia, NC

Bridges, Frank ... (915) 648-2244
PUB, ED, Goldthwaite Eagle, Goldthwaite, TX

Bridges, Jackie ... (704) 484-7000
Living/Lifestyle ED, News ED, Society ED, Shelby Star, Shelby, NC

Bridges, Jonathan Pat ... (561) 287-1550
ADV MGR-RT, Stuart News, Stuart, FL

Bridges, Richard ... (719) 634-1593
ED, Mountaineer, Colorado Springs, CO

Bridgewater, Frank ... (808) 525-8000
ASST MAN ED
Honolulu Star-Bulletin, Honolulu, HI

Bridgewater, Jeff ... (317) 653-5151
CIRC MGR, Banner-Graphic, Greencastle, IN

Bridgewater, Kevin ... (317) 633-1240
ADV MGR-Major
Indianapolis Star/News, Indianapolis, IN

Bridson, Susan ... (516) 751-1550
ED, Three Village Herald, East Setauket, NY

Bridson, Tom ... (913) 295-1111
PROD FRM-COMP (Day)
Topeka Capital-Journal, Topeka, KS

Bridwell, Harlan ... (972) 377-2141
PUB, Frisco Enterprise, Frisco, TX

Bridwell, John ... (405) 223-2200
MAN ED, EPE, EDL Writer/Sunday ED
Daily Ardmoreite, Ardmore, OK

Briel, Joe ... (815) 433-2000
PROD CNR, Daily Times, Ottawa, IL

Brigandisi, Ben ... (717) 748-6791
Sports ED, Express, Lock Haven, PA

Briggeman, Beverly ... (812) 254-0480
ADV MGR-CLASS
Washington Times-Herald, Washington, IN

Briggs, Ardis ... (970) 587-4525
ED, Johnstown Breeze, Johnstown, CO

Briggs, Barbara ... (704) 859-9151
DP MGR, PROD SUPT
Tryon Daily Bulletin, Tryon, NC

Briggs, Chandler ... (408) 372-3311
PROD MGR-Pre Press
Monterey County Herald, Monterey, CA

Briggs, Cindy ... (515) 856-6336
ADV DIR
Ad Express & Daily Iowegian, Centerville, IA

Briggs, Clyde ... (970) 587-4525
PUB, Johnstown Breeze, Johnstown, CO

Briggs, Francesca ... (403) 235-7100
ADV VP-Sales, Calgary Herald, Calgary, AB

Briggs, Jack ... (509) 582-1500
PUB, Tri-City Herald, Tri-Cities, WA

Briggs, Mark ... (206) 888-9435
GM, ED
Snoqualmie Valley Reporter, North Bend, WA

Briggs, Michael ... (312) 321-3000
Washington BU
Chicago Sun-Times, Chicago, IL

Briggs, Mildred ... (607) 756-5665
ADV MGR-CLASS
Cortland Standard, Cortland, NY

Briggs, Roy ... (609) 663-6000
ADV MGR-RT, Courier-Post, Cherry Hill, NJ

Briggs, Stacy ... (215) 345-3000
BUS ED
Intelligencer/Record, Doylestown, PA

Briggs, Steve ... (619) 299-3131
MGR-MKTG Creative Service
San Diego Union-Tribune, San Diego, CA

Briggs, Tony ... (904) 252-1511
Political ED, Daytona Beach News-Journal, Daytona Beach, FL

Brigham, John R ... (614) 461-5000
CIRC DIR
Columbus Dispatch, Columbus, OH

Bright, Bob ... (208) 522-1800
PROD FRM-COMP
Post Register, Idaho Falls, ID

Bright, Fred ... (705) 759-3030
FIN MGR/MGR-Human Resources
Sault Star, Sault Ste. Marie, ON

Bright, Gary ... (815) 284-2222
ADV MGR-RT, Telegraph, Dixon, IL

Bright, Steve ... (918) 581-8300
ADV MGR-Sales Development
Tulsa World, Tulsa, OK

Brightbill, Earl ... (717) 272-5611
Photo ED, Daily News, Lebanon, PA

Brightman, Jeanne ... (607) 334-3276
VP, Lifestyle ED
Evening Sun, Norwich, NY

Brighton, Jim ... (717) 348-9100
SYS MGR
Tribune & Scranton Times, Scranton, PA

Brigit, Kroon ... (810) 641-9944
ED, Nordamerikaniche Wochenpost, Troy, MI

Brigman, Bobbie ... (912) 985-4545
CONT, Observer, Moultrie, GA

Briley, Thomas C ... (717) 546-8555
PUB
Williamsport Sun-Gazette, Williamsport, PA

Brill, Frank ... (910) 727-7211
BUS/FIN ED
Winston-Salem Journal, Winston-Salem, NC

Brill, Jimmy ... (212) 210-2100
CIRC VP/DIR
New York Daily News, New York, NY

Brill, Ken ... (315) 470-0011
ADV MGR-RT, Post-Standard/Syracuse Herald-Journal/American, Syracuse, NY

Brill, Rob ... (518) 454-5694
City ED, Times Union, Albany, NY

Brilliant, Ashleigh ... (805) 682-0531
PRES, Ashleigh Brilliant, Santa Barbara, CA

Brilliant, Dorothy ... (805) 682-0531
VP, Ashleigh Brilliant, Santa Barbara, CA

Brim, Donna ... (540) 638-8801
Food/Women's ED, Religion ED
Martinsville Bulletin, Martinsville, VA

Brimeyer, Jack ... (309) 686-3000
MAN ED, Journal Star, Peoria, IL

Brimley, Wendy ... (810) 766-6100
ADV MGR-Display Sales
Flint Journal, Flint, MI

Brin, Dale ... (250) 372-2331
CIRC MGR
Kamloops Daily News, Kamloops, BC

Brin, Dan ... (213) 737-2122
ED, Central California Jewish Heritage, Los Angeles, CA

Brin, Herb ... (213) 737-2122
PUB, Central California Jewish Heritage, Los Angeles, CA

Brincefield, Robert ... (507) 373-1411
PRES, PUB
Albert Lea Tribune, Albert Lea, MN

Brinda-Praus, Cathy ... (701) 225-8111
ADV MGR-CLASS
Dickinson Press, Dickinson, ND

Brindle, Gari ... (215) 854-2000
DIR-PROM, Philadelphia Inquirer, Philadelphia, PA, Knight-Ridder Inc.

Brindle, Laurie ... (619) 745-6611
MGR-MKTG/PROM
North County Times, Escondido, CA

Brinker, Darlene ... (317) 664-5111
Human Resources
Chronicle-Tribune, Marion, IN

Brinkmann, Martha ... (210) 734-2620
ED, Today's Catholic, San Antonio, TX

Brinley, Jeff ... (805) 781-7800
CIRC DIR
Telegram-Tribune, San Luis Obispo, CA

Brinsom, Robert P ... (707) 226-3711
CONT, Napa Valley Register, Napa, CA

Brinson, Claudia ... (803) 771-6161
ASSOC ED, State, Columbia, SC

Brinson, Karen ... (919) 446-5161
Fashion/Food ED, Features ED, Women's ED
Rocky Mount Telegram, Rocky Mount, NC

Brinson, Ray ... (403) 227-3477
PUB, ED, Innisfail Booster, Innisfail, AB

Brinson, Robert P ... (520) 573-4220
CONT, Arizona Daily Star, Tucson, AZ
Pulitzer Publishing Co.

Brinton, Byron C ... (541) 523-5353
PUB, ED
Baker City Record-Courier, Baker City, OR

Brisbane, Arthur S ... (816) 234-4141
VP/ED, Kansas City Star, Kansas City, MO

Brisbin, Ron ... (218) 723-5281
PROD MGR-Environmental, PROD SUPV-Building, Duluth News-Tribune, Duluth, MN

Bri Who's Where-28

Brisco, Robert N .... (213) 237-5000
Senior VP-MKTG/New BUS Development
Los Angeles Times, Los Angeles, CA
Briscoe, James .... (815) 729-6161
CIRC MGR, Herald-News, Joliet, IL
Briscoe, Janice .... (915) 236-6677
ADV MGR-CLASS
Sweetwater Reporter, Sweetwater, TX
Briscoe, Keith .... (303) 776-2244
MAN ED, Daily Times-Call, Longmont, CO
Brisendine, Lynn .... (806) 637-4535
PUB, ED, Brownfield News, Brownfield, TX
Briseno, Rosie M .... (210) 383-2705
DIR-FIN, Daily Review, Edinburg, TX
Brison, Kathy .... (615) 722-5429
MAN ED
Wayne County News, Waynesboro, TN
Brissette-Mata, Brenda .... (810) 766-6100
COL, Flint Journal, Flint, MI
Brissey, Violet .... (706) 724-0851
ADV MGR-CLASS (Inside)
Augusta Chronicle, Augusta, GA
Brisson, Daniel .... (705) 272-4363
PUB, Northland Post, Cochrane, ON
Brisson, Luc .... (418) 587-2090
PUB
Journal Haute Cote-Nord, Forestville, QC
Brisson, Paul .... (418) 665-6121
PUB
Plein Jour de Charlevoix, La Malbaie, QC
Bristol, Ned .... (508) 222-7000
MAN ED, Sun Chronicle, Attleboro, MA
Britt, Annie .... (903) 668-3090
MAN ED, Hallsville Herald, Hallsville, TX
Britt, Anthony .... (912) 273-2277
Reporter, Cordele Dispatch, Cordele, GA
Brittain, Paul S .... (412) 547-5722
ED
Mount Pleasant Journal, Mount Pleasant, PA
Britten, William H .... (515) 487-7661
PUB, ED, Tri-County News, Zearing, IA
Brittingham, Tamra .... (800) 426-4192
PRES-Delmarva, Independent Newspapers Inc. (DE), Dover, DE
Britton, Charles .... (310) 540-5511
Amusements/Arts ED, Entertainment ED, Music ED, Daily Breeze, Torrance, CA
Copley Press Inc.
Britton, Dennis A .... (303) 820-1010
EVP/EIC, Denver Post, Denver, CO
Britton, Edward .... (705) 645-8771
PUB
Bracebridge Examiner, Bracebridge, ON
Britton, Lynn .... (214) 977-8222
ADV MGR-Dallas Life
Dallas Morning News, Dallas, TX
Britton, Mary .... (712) 262-6610
PROD MGR, Daily Reporter, Spencer, IA
Britton, Teresa .... (541) 269-1222
MGR-Office, World, Coos Bay, OR
Britton, Toi .... (206) 597-8742
Chief Librarian, News Tribune, Tacoma, WA
Britton, Zac .... (517) 354-3111
Sports ED, Alpena News, Alpena, MI
Britz, OSB, Fr. Andrew .... (306) 682-1770
ED, Prairie Messenger, Muenster, Sk
Broach, Ann .... (901) 642-1162
Society ED
Paris Post-Intelligencer, Paris, TN
Broadus, Donald R .... (601) 762-1111
Political ED
Mississippi Press, Pascagoula, MS
Broadwell, Charles .... (910) 323-4848
ED
Fayetteville Observer-Times, Fayetteville, NC
Broadwell, Charlotte L .... (910) 323-4848
VP
Fayetteville Observer-Times, Fayetteville, NC
Broberg, Brad .... (206) 839-0700
ED, Federal Way News, Federal Way, WA
Brock, Brightman .... (334) 365-6739
ED, Prattville Progress, Prattville, AL
Brock, Chris .... (315) 343-3800
Regional ED, Palladium-Times, Oswego, NY
Brock, Darin .... (512) 756-6136
PUB, ED, Burnet Bulletin, Burnet, TX
Brock, Deborah .... (405) 326-8353
GM, Choctaw County Times, Hugo, OK
Brock, Gary .... (937) 372-4444
MAN ED, Xenia Daily Gazette, Xenia, OH
Brock, Gordon .... (705) 647-6791
ED
Temiskaming Speaker, New Liskeard, ON
Brock, Harvey .... (605) 352-6401
CIRC DIR, Huron Plainsman, Huron, SD
Brock, James A .... (209) 896-1976
PUB, Selma Enterprise, Selma, CA
Brock, Julia .... (205) 848-5574
PUB, McClellan News, Ft. McClellan, AL
Brock, R Buckman .... (515) 964-9375
PUB, ED, Ankeny Today, Ankeny, IA
Brock, Steve .... (303) 786-7375
Book Reviewer, Brock, Steve Book Reviews On The Internet, Boulder, CO
Brockel, Fritz .... (250) 423-4222
PUB, Elk Valley Miner, Sparwood, BC
Brockenborough, Pat .... (502) 443-1771
Food ED, Paducah Sun, Paducah, KY
Brockett, Budd .... (209) 638-2244
ED, Reedley Exponent, Reedley, CA
Brockish, Ted .... (605) 394-8300
Features ED, Sports ED
Rapid City Journal, Rapid City, SD
Brockling, Esther .... (319) 935-3027
PUB, ED, Winthrop News, Winthrop, IA
Brockman, Marion F .... (414) 775-4431
PUB, Valders Journal, Valders, WI
Brockman, Richard .... (608) 348-3006
PUB, ED, Platteville Journal, Platteville, WI
Brockmann, Marina .... (410) 453-0092
PUB, Times-Herald, Timonium, MD
Brockus, Lewis .... (702) 623-5011
PROD MGR
Humboldt Sun, Winnemucca, NV
Brockus, Susan M .... (702) 623-5011
TREAS, PUB
Humboldt Sun, Winnemucca, NV
Brockway, Babs .... (770) 532-1234
Environmental ED, Times, Gainesville, GA
Brockway, Laurie Sue .... (212) 631-3520
ED/Owner
Goddess Communications, New York, NY
Brockwell, Kay .... (501) 735-1010
ED, Evening Times, West Memphis, AR
Brodbeck, Mary .... (419) 636-1111
Radio/Television ED, Bryan Times, Bryan, OH
Brodeen, Clair R .... (605) 286-3919
MAN ED, Avon Clarion, Avon, SD
Brodeen, Jackson S .... (605) 286-3919
PUB, ED, Avon Clarion, Avon, SD
Broder, David .... (202) 334-6000
COL-Politics
Washington Post, Washington, DC
Broder, Eric .... (216) 321-2300
MAN ED
Cleveland Free Times, Cleveland, OH
Broderick, Christopher .... (303) 892-5000
EDU ED, Rocky Mountain News, Denver, CO
Broderick, Howard .... (716) 394-0770
PROD SUPT-Press, Daily Messenger/The Sunday Messenger, Canandaigua, NY
Broderick, Jim .... (209) 369-2761
DP MGR, Lodi News-Sentinel, Lodi, CA
Broderick, Pam .... (212) 416-2000
PROD MGR (Bowling Green OH)
Wall Street Journal, New York, NY
Broderick, Robert .... (412) 834-1151
ASST Sunday ED
Tribune-Review, Greensburg, PA
Brodeur, Chris .... (403) 874-6577
PUB, ED, Hub, Hay River, NT
Brodeur, Maura .... (401) 277-7000
ADV Senior Sales DIR
Providence Journal-Bulletin, Providence, RI
Brodeur, Nicole .... (919) 829-4500
COL, News & Observer, Raleigh, NC
Brodeur, Peggy .... (701) 780-1100
ADV SUPV-CLASS Phone Room
Grand Forks Herald, Grand Forks, ND
Brodeur, Real .... (819) 478-8171
GM, ED, L'Express, Drummondville, QC
Brodin, Eric .... (910) 891-1234
COL, Daily Record, Dunn, NC
Brodnax, Ken .... (915) 337-4661
COL, EPE, Odessa American, Odessa, TX
Brodt, Duane .... (317) 462-5528
News ED, Daily Reporter, Greenfield, IN
Brodt, Jay .... (360) 376-4500
PUB, Islands' Sounder, Eastsound, WA
Brody, Hal .... (816) 561-6061
PUB, PitchWeekly, Kansas City, MO
Brody, Jeff .... (360) 377-3711
Books ED, ASST Community ED, Living/Lifestyle ED, Sun, Bremerton, WA
Broeckelman, Roxanne K .... (913) 754-3651
PUB, Gove County Advocate, Quinter, KS
Broeckelman, Tom W .... (913) 754-3651
PUB, ED, Gove County Advocate, Quinter, KS
Brohawn, Raye .... (410) 228-3131
PROD MGR, Daily Banner, Cambridge, MD
Broi, Fred Dal .... (206) 464-2111
PROD MGR-Plant (North Creek)
Seattle Times, Seattle, WA
Brokke, Roger .... (605) 225-4100
ADV DIR
Aberdeen American News, Aberdeen, SD
Brolhorst, David .... (402) 475-4200
PROD MGR
Lincoln Journal Star, Lincoln, NE
Brom, Bishop Robert H .... (619) 490-8266
PUB, Southern Cross, San Diego, CA
Bromley, Bernard .... (709) 454-2191
PUB, Northern Pen, St. Anthony, NF
Bromley, Jan .... (409) 883-3571
PUB, ADV DIR, Orange Leader, Orange, TX
Bronner, Ethan .... (617) 929-2000
BU Chief-Jerusalem
Boston Globe, Boston, MA
Bronson, Brian .... (913) 295-1111
PROD FRM-Photo/Plate (Night)
Topeka Capital-Journal, Topeka, KS
Bronson, Daniel P .... (315) 337-4000
MGR-Applications
Daily Sentinel, Rome, NY
Bronson, James G .... (810) 766-6100
ADV MGR-CLASS, Flint Journal, Flint, MI
Bronson, Kenneth C .... (317) 473-3091
EX VP/COO, Nixon Newspapers Inc., Peru, IN
Bronson, Peter W .... (513) 721-2700
EPE, Cincinnati Enquirer, Cincinnati, OH
Bronson, W Howard .... (334) 433-1551
PRES, PUB, Mobile Press Register, Mobile, AL, Advance Publications
Bronstein, Phil .... (415) 777-2424
EX ED
San Francisco Examiner, San Francisco, CA
Brook, Steve .... (803) 771-6161
Fashion/Food ED, Living/Lifestyle ED, News ED-Advance Sections, State, Columbia, SC
Brooke, Carol A .... (504) 748-7156
PUB, Amite Tangi-Digest, Amite, LA
Brooke, Maryann .... (207) 623-3811
Books ED, Kennebec Journal, Augusta, ME
Brooker, Vicki .... (403) 724-4087
ED, Elk Point Review, Elk Point, AB
Brookins, Gary .... (804) 649-6000
Cartoonist
Richmond Times-Dispatch, Richmond, VA
Brooks, Al .... (540) 720-6300
Cartoonist/COL
Humor Books Syndicate, Stafford, VA
Brooks, B V .... (203) 255-4561
PUB, Fairfield Citizen-News, Fairfield, CT
Brooks, Ben .... (540) 667-3200
Sports ED, Winchester Star, Winchester, VA
Brooks, Ben .... (210) 943-5545
PUB, Port Isabel-South Padre Press, Port Isabel, TX
Brooks, Betty .... (202) 745-7858
PUB, ED, Capitol Spotlight, Washington, DC
Brooks, Bubba .... (205) 549-2000
PROD FRM-PR, Gadsden Times
Gadsden, AL
Brooks, Charles .... (601) 762-1111
Amusements ED, Books ED, Films/Theater ED, Radio/Television ED, Wire ED
Mississippi Press, Pascagoula, MS
Brooks, Eddie .... (912) 233-1281
CFO, Morris Newspaper Corp., Savannah, GA
Brooks, Fred .... (615) 452-2561
GM
Gallatin News-Examiner, Gallatin, TN
Brooks, Gary .... (815) 379-9290
PUB, Walnut Leader, Walnut, IL
Brooks, Geof .... (910) 574-2555
Cartoonist, Toonsmith Newspaper Features, Greensboro, NC
Brooks, Hubby .... (912) 244-1880
PROD DIR
Valdosta Daily Times, Valdosta, GA
Brooks, Jim .... (310) 540-5511
Radio/Television ED
Daily Breeze, Torrance, CA
Brooks, Karen .... (503) 221-8327
Entertainment ED, Oregonian, Portland, OR
Brooks, Kathy .... (901) 529-2211
NTL ED
Memphis Commercial Appeal, Memphis, TN
Brooks, Kathy .... (416) 947-2222
Entertainment ED, Toronto Sun, Toronto, ON
Brooks, Kevin .... (519) 894-2231
PROD MGR-Distribution
Record, Kitchener, ON
Brooks, Larry .... (606) 231-3100
ADV MGR-Display
Lexington Herald-Leader, Lexington, KY
Brooks, Linda .... (815) 379-9290
ED, Walnut Leader, Walnut, IL
Brooks, Lynn .... (919) 563-3555
GM, Mebane Enterprise, Mebane, NC
Brooks, Mary Lou .... (403) 641-3636
PUB, GM, ED, Bassano Times, Bassano, AB
Brooks, Mike .... (603) 882-2741
Online MGR, Telegraph, Nashua, NH
Brooks, O T .... (405) 569-2684
PUB, ED
Kiowa County Democrat, Snyder, OK
Brooks, Randy .... (618) 532-5604
CIRC DIR, Centralia Sentinel, Centralia, IL
Brooks, Rich .... (941) 953-7755
Venice BU Chief
Sarasota Herald-Tribune, Sarasota, FL
Brooks, Ron .... (704) 633-8950
CIRC DIR, Salisbury Post, Salisbury, NC
Brooks, Scott .... (410) 332-6000
ADV MGR-CLASS, Sun, Baltimore, MD
Brooks, Steve .... (317) 462-5528
Sports ED, Daily Reporter, Greenfield, IN
Brooks, Susan .... (317) 622-1212
Distribution MGR
Herald Bulletin, Anderson, IN
Brooks, Sylvia .... (614) 461-5000
Religion ED, Dispatch, Columbus, OH
Brooks, Tim .... (618) 544-2101
Sports ED, Daily News, Robinson, IL
Brophy, John .... (314) 340-8000
Newsroom ADM
St. Louis Post-Dispatch, St. Louis, MO
Brophy, Michael .... (416) 585-5000
VP-Human Resources, Globe and Mail (Canada's National Newspaper), Toronto, ON
Brophy, Peter .... (609) 272-7000
News ED
Press of Atlantic City, Pleasantville, NJ
Brose, Donald .... (605) 934-2640
PUB, Alcester Union, Alcester, SD
Brose, Mary Etta .... (605) 934-2640
ED, Alcester Union, Alcester, SD
Bross, James .... (360) 577-2500
EPE, EDL Writer, Daily News, Longview, WA
Brossart, Mike .... (909) 987-6397
MAN ED
Inland Valley Daily Bulletin, Ontario, CA
Brossart, Thomas L .... (520) 282-7795
ED, Sedona Red Rock News, Sedona, AZ
Brosseau, Guy .... (819) 564-5450
PROD FRM-COMP
La Tribune, Sherbrooke, QC
Brosseau, Michel .... (514) 692-8552
MAN ED
St. Lawrence Sun, Chateauguay, QC
Brosseau, Peter .... (403) 235-7100
Photo ED, Calgary Herald, Calgary, AB
Brosterhous, Dennis .... (909) 657-1967
ED, Perris Valley News, Sun City, CA
Brotheron, Velda .... (501) 839-2771
ED
Washington County Observer, West Fork, AR
Brothers, Dawn J .... (615) 592-2781
PUB, ED
Grundy County Herald, Tracy City, TN
Brothers, Erin .... (217) 864-4212
ED, Mt. Zion Region News, Mt. Zion, IL
Brothers, Gary .... (518) 725-8616
PA, Leader-Herald, Gloversville, NY
Brothers, Mike .... (217) 864-4212
PUB, Mt. Zion Region News, Mt. Zion, IL
Brotherton, Darrell .... (703) 276-3400
CIRC GM-South Florida
USA Today, Arlington, VA
Brotman, Barbara .... (312) 222-3232
COL-WomaNews
Chicago Tribune, Chicago, IL
Broucek, Brian .... (206) 455-2222
CONT, Eastside Journal, Bellevue, WA
Brouchard, Stacy .... (209) 582-0471
BUS ED, Hanford Sentinel, Hanford, CA
Brouillard, Dwight L .... (413) 788-1000
ADV DIR, Union-News, Springfield, MA
Broussard, Gwen .... (318) 893-4223
MAN ED, Abbeville Meridional, Abbeville, LA
Broussard, Sharon .... (216) 999-4500
ASSOC ED, Plain Dealer, Cleveland, OH
Brousseau, Francois .... (514) 985-3333
International ED, Le Devoir, Montreal, QC
Brouwer, Mark N .... (419) 683-3355
PUB, Crestline Advocate, Crestline, OH
Brower, Celeste .... (360) 694-3391
MGR-CR, Columbian, Vancouver, WA
Brower, Debora .... (910) 227-0131
PROD FRM-COMP
Times News Publishing Co., Burlington, NC
Brower, Don .... (714) 782-7701
PUB, Beacon, Riverside, CA
Brower, Eleanor .... (518) 584-4242
Librarian, Saratogian, Saratoga Springs, NY
Brower, Patrick .... (303) 887-3334
PUB, ED, Sky-Hi News, Granby, CO
Brower, Tom .... (405) 475-3311
CIRC MGR-MKTG
Daily Oklahoman, Oklahoma City, OK
Browing, Renee .... (316) 788-2835
PROD MGR, Daily Reporter, Derby, KS
Brown, A A .... (541) 269-1222
CIRC MGR, World, Coos Bay, OR
Brown, Aldon .... (817) 767-8341
Religion ED, Wichita Falls Times Record News, Wichita Falls, TX
Brown, Alton .... (912) 452-0567
ADV DIR-MKTG, CIRC DIR-MKTG
Union-Recorder, Milledgeville, GA
Brown, Arthur W .... (810) 387-2300
PUB, Yale Expositor, Yale, MI
Brown, Barbara A .... (814) 486-3711
PUB, Cameron County Echo, Emporium, PA
Brown, Bill .... (209) 592-3171
PUB, Sun, Exeter, CA
Brown, Bill .... (515) 284-8000
PROD MGR-Facility
Des Moines Register, Des Moines, IA

Copyright ©1997 by the Editor & Publisher Co.

29-Who's Where **Bro**

Brown, Bill ... (402) 773-5576
ED, Clay County News, Sutton, NE
Brown, Billie F ... (918) 968-2581
PUB, ED, Stroud American, Stroud, OK
Brown, BJ ... (918) 684-2828
EDU Writer, Muskogee Daily Phoenix & Times Democrat, Muskogee, OK
Brown, Bob ... (614) 461-5000
PROD ASST DIR, Dispatch, Columbus, OH
Brown, Bob ... (916) 321-1000
ADV MGR-Local RT
Sacramento Bee, Sacramento, CA
Brown, Bob ... (813) 259-7711
CIRC MGR-Distribution
Tampa Tribune and Times, Tampa, FL
Brown, Bonnie ... (810) 387-2300
ED, Yale Expositor, Yale, MI
Brown, Bruce ... (318) 289-6300
Sports ED, Advertiser, Lafayette, LA
Brown, Carole ... (601) 896-2100
DP MGR
Biloxi Sun Herald, Biloxi, MS
Brown, Casper ... (709) 896-3341
GM, Labradorian, Happy Valley, NF
Brown, Cathy ... (907) 586-3740
Entertainment/Amusements ED, Television/Film ED, Theater/Music ED, Juneau Empire, Juneau, AK
Brown, Cathy ... (812) 275-3355
CIRC MGR, Times-Mail, Bedford, IN
Brown, Cheryl ... (909) 682-6070
PUB, ED, Black Voice News, Riverside, CA
Brown, Cindy ... (618) 393-2931
MGR-Office, Olney Daily Mail, Olney, IL
Brown, Cindy ... (206) 597-8742
EDU Reporter (Higher)
News Tribune, Tacoma, WA
Brown, Clarence J ... (513) 489-7227
COB, Brown Publishing Co., Cincinnati, OH
Brown, Cliff ... (804) 649-6000
PROD MGR-PR
Richmond Times-Dispatch, Richmond, VA
Brown, Connie ... (316) 421-2000
Fashion/Food ED, Religion ED
Parsons Sun, Parsons, KS
Brown, Dan ... (319) 337-3181
DIR-MKTG SRV
Iowa City Press-Citizen, Iowa City, IA
Brown, Dan ... (618) 281-7691
MAN ED
Cahokia-Dupo Journal, Columbia, IL
Brown, Dan ... (505) 662-4185
PROD FRM-PR
Los Alamos Monitor, Los Alamos, NM
Brown, Dar ... (562) 430-7555
PUB, Sun, Seal Beach, CA
Brown, Darrell ... (212) 759-5571
PRES/EX ED
Sipa News Service, New York, NY
Brown, Dave ... (616) 429-2400
EPE, St. Joseph Herald-Palladium, St. Joseph, MI
Brown, Dave ... (613) 829-9100
COL, Ottawa Citizen, Ottawa, ON
Brown, David ... (941) 385-6155
ED, News-Sun, Sebring, FL
Brown, David ... (417) 836-1100
CIRC DIR
Springfield News-Leader, Springfield, MO
Brown, David ... (619) 745-6611
City ED-Poway/Rancho Bernardo
North County Times, Escondido, CA
Brown, David A ... (814) 486-3711
ED, Cameron County Echo, Emporium, PA
Brown, Denis ... (206) 622-8272
PRES, Seattle Daily Journal of Commerce, Seattle, WA
Brown, Dennis ... (606) 796-6182/2331
PUB, Lewis County Herald, Vanceburg, KY
Brown, Diane ... (717) 248-6741
ADV DIR, Sentinel, Lewistown, PA
Brown, Don ... (541) 269-1222
PUB, ED, World, Coos Bay, OR
Brown, Donald ... (812) 254-0480
ADV DIR, ADV MGR-RT, Radio/Television ED
Washington Times-Herald, Washington, IN
Brown, Dotty ... (215) 854-2000
Health/SCI ED
Philadelphia Inquirer, Philadelphia, PA
Brown, Doug ... (219) 244-5153
PROD MGR, Post & Mail, Columbia City, IN
Brown, Dwight ... (713) 220-7171
ADV VP, Houston Chronicle, Houston, TX
Brown, Eila ... (907) 257-4200
Wire ED
Anchorage Daily News, Anchorage, AK
Brown, Eileen ... (360) 675-6611
ED, Crosswind, Oak Harbor, WA
Brown, Fred ... (303) 820-1010
Political ED, Denver Post, Denver, CO
Brown, Gail B ... (206) 727-2727
CFO/TREAS
Buckner News Alliance, Seattle, WA

Brown, Garry P ... (413) 788-1000
COL
Springfield Union-News, Springfield, MA
Brown, Gary ... (941) 748-0411
News ED, Bradenton Herald, Bradenton, FL
Brown, Gary R ... (320) 732-2151
PUB, Long Prairie Leader, Long Prairie, MN
Brown, Geoff ... (312) 222-3232
Entertainment ED
Chicago Tribune, Chicago, IL
Brown, George ... (403) 352-2231
ED, Times-Advertiser, Wetaskiwin, AB
Brown, Gerald ... (314) 340-8000
Librarian, Post-Dispatch, St. Louis, MO
Brown, Gina ... (541) 963-3161
Farm ED, Observer, La Grande, OR
Brown, Glenn A ... (405) 942-3800
GM, ED
Baptist Messenger, Oklahoma City, OK
Brown, Gloria G ... (405) 336-2222
ED, Books/Music ED, Family Living ED
Perry Daily Journal, Perry, OK
Brown, Gordon ... (510) 935-2525
PROD MGR, Contra Costa Times, Walnut Creek, CA, Knight-Ridder Inc.
Brown, Greg ... (412) 775-3200
City ED, Beaver County Times, Beaver, PA
Brown, Greg ... (561) 820-4100
PROD SUPT-MR
Palm Beach Post, West Palm Beach, FL
Brown, Hardy ... (909) 682-6070
PUB, Black Voice News, Riverside, CA
Brown, Harold ... (419) 352-4611
City ED, RE ED
Sentinel-Tribune, Bowling Green, OH
Brown, Harry ... (204) 697-7000
CIRC DIR
Winnipeg Free Press, Winnipeg, MB
Brown, Herman ... (918) 756-3600
News ED
Okmulgee Daily Times, Okmulgee, OK
Brown, Hershel M ... (609) 298-7111
PUB, Register-News, Bordentown, NJ
Brown, Howard J ... (414) 657-1000
PRES, United Communications Corp., Wilmington, DE
Brown, Ida ... (601) 693-1551
Teen-Age/Youth ED, Travel ED
Meridian Star, Meridian, MS
Brown, Irene ... (914) 782-4000
ED, Pointer View, Monroe, NY
Brown, J C ... (309) 827-8555
PUB
Twin City Community News, Bloomington, IL
Brown Jr, J O ... (502) 932-4381
ED
Greensburg Record-Herald, Greensburg, KY
Brown, Jackie ... (423) 523-3131
DIR-Public SRV
Knoxville News-Sentinel, Knoxville, TN
Brown, Jacqueline Bedford ... (541) 276-2211
VP, MGR-Human Resources
East Oregonian, Pendleton, OR
Brown, James ... (410) 268-5000
CFO, Capital, Annapolis, MD
Brown, James ... (318) 462-0616
CIRC MGR
Beauregard Daily News, De Ridder, LA
Brown, James R ... (419) 668-3771
PUB, ED, Norwalk Reflector, Norwalk, OH
Brown, Jamie ... (757) 562-3187
ED, Tidewater News, Franklin, VA
Brown, Jan ... (919) 829-4500
PROD CNR (Night)
News & Observer, Raleigh, NC
Brown, Jay ... (719) 632-5511
Senior MGR INFO Services
Gazette, Colorado Springs, CO
Brown, Jay A ... (914) 692-4572
ED, Cineman Syndicate, Middletown, NY
Brown, Jeff ... (847) 223-8161
ED, Great Lakes Bulletin, Grayslake, IL
Brown, Jeff ... (215) 854-2000
COL-BUS
Philadelphia Inquirer, Philadelphia, PA
Brown, Jeffrey N ... (812) 379-5612
VP, Home News Enterprises, Columbus, IN
Brown, Jerry ... (607) 739-3001
GM, Chemung Valley Reporter
Horseheads, NY
Brown, Jim ... (215) 854-2000
PROD ASST DIR-Printing, Inquirer, Philadelphia, PA, Knight-Ridder Inc.
Brown, Jimmy ... (318) 239-3444
CIRC DIR
Leesville Daily Leader, Leesville, LA
Brown, Joan ... (519) 537-2341
DP MGR, Sentinel-Review, Woodstock, ON
Brown, Joe ... (813) 259-7711
EDL Writer
Tampa Tribune and Times, Tampa, FL
Brown, John ... (610) 272-2500
MGR-SYS, Times Herald, Norristown, PA

Brown, John Pat ... (601) 849-3434
PUB, GM, ED, Magee Courier, Magee, MS
Brown, Joseph ... (617) 933-3700
Photo DEPT MGR
Daily Times Chronicle, Woburn, MA
Brown, Joseph ... (757) 446-2000
CIRC MGR-State, Virginian-Pilot, Norfolk, VA
Brown, Joyce ... (912) 744-4200
CIRC MGR-H/P Market
Macon Telegraph, Macon, GA
Brown, Joyce ... (517) 592-2122
ED, Exponent, Brooklyn, MI
Brown, Joyce E ... (513) 489-7227
SEC, Brown Publishing Co., Cincinnati, OH
Brown, Judith W ... (860) 225-4601
ED, Herald, New Britain, CT
Brown, Karen ... (816) 234-4141
Sunday ED/EPE
Kansas City Star, Kansas City, MO
Brown, Karen ... (303) 426-6000
MAN ED, Northglenn-Thornton Sentinel, Westminster, CO
Brown, Karen ... (419) 738-2128
ADV MGR
Wapakoneta Daily News, Wapakoneta, OH
Brown, Kathleen ... (402) 444-1000
Fashion ED
Omaha World-Herald, Omaha, NE
Brown, Kathy ... (307) 682-9306
Sports ED, News-Record, Gillette, WY
Brown, Kathy ... (317) 664-5111
ADV MGR-Outside Sales
Chronicle-Tribune, Marion, IN
Brown, Ken ... (718) 769-4400
ED, Harbor Watch (Metro New York), Brooklyn, NY
Brown, Ken ... (815) 284-2222
MAN ED, Automotive/Aviation ED, BUS/FIN ED, City ED, Telegraph, Dixon, IL
Brown, Ken ... (403) 468-0100
ADV DIR, Edmonton Sun, Edmonton, AB
Brown, Kevin ... (515) 276-0265
PUB, Urbandale News, Urbandale, IA
Brown, Kevin ... (360) 424-3251
Sports ED
Skagit Valley Herald, Mount Vernon, WA
Brown, Kim R ... (619) 379-3667
MAN ED, Kern Valley Sun, Lake Isabella, CA
Brown, Lana ... (509) 525-3300
Food ED, Radio/Television ED
Walla Walla Union-Bulletin, Walla Walla, WA
Brown, Larry W ... (317) 462-5528
PUB, Daily Reporter, Greenfield, IN
Brown, Laura Varon ... (313) 222-6400
Graphics DIR, Detroit Free Press, Detroit, MI
Brown, Laurie Ezzell ... (806) 323-5321
ED, Canadian Record, Canadian, TX
Brown, Leon ... (713) 266-5481
EVP, Southern Newspapers Inc., Houston, TX
Brown, Lillian ... (707) 459-4643
ED, Willits News, Willits, CA
Brown, Linda ... (702) 358-8061
GM, Daily Sparks Tribune, Sparks, NV
Brown, Linda ... (803) 354-7454
ED, News, Kingstree, SC
Brown, Linda ... (903) 567-4000
ED, Canton Herald, Canton, TX
Brown, Linn ... (816) 454-9660
ED, Dispatch-Tribune/Press Dispatch, Kansas City, MO
Brown, Lisa ... (601) 428-0551
BM, Laurel Leader-Call, Laurel, MS
Brown, Lisa ... (360) 424-3251
ADTX MGR
Skagit Valley Herald, Mount Vernon, WA
Brown, Liz ... (317) 633-1240
Suburban ED
Indianapolis Star/News, Indianapolis, IN
Brown, Lloyd ... (904) 359-4111
EPE, Florida Times-Union, Jacksonville, FL
Brown, Lois ... (972) 234-3199
ED, Richardson News, Richardson, TX
Brown, Lonnie ... (941) 687-7000
ASSOC EPE, Ledger, Lakeland, FL
Brown, M E ... (206) 622-8272
VP, Seattle Daily Journal of Commerce, Seattle, WA
Brown, M Eileen ... (847) 427-4300
Travel ED
Daily Herald, Arlington Heights, IL
Brown, Marc ... (915) 546-6100
Entertainment ED, Fashion ED, Features ED, Health/Medical ED, Living/Lifestyle ED, El Paso Times, El Paso, TX
Brown, Marcela ... (712) 225-5111
PUB, ADV MGR-MKTG
Cherokee County's Daily Times, Cherokee, IA
Brown, Margaret A ... (816) 594-3712
ED, Norborne Democrat-Leader
Norborne, MO
Brown, Mark A ... (330) 747-1471
VP/SEC/ASST TREAS, GM
Vindicator, Youngstown, OH

Brown, Martha ... (904) 599-2100
Religion ED
Tallahassee Democrat, Tallahassee, FL
Brown, Mary Lou ... (901) 529-2211
DIR-EDL PROM
Commercial Appeal, Memphis, TN
Brown, Max S ... (614) 847-3800
PUB, Other Paper, Columbus, OH
Brown, Melanie ... (417) 235-3135
Society ED, Times, Monett, MO
Brown, Michael ... (905) 358-5711
MAN ED
Niagara Falls Review, Niagara Falls, ON
Brown, Michael ... (312) 225-2400
MAN ED
Chicago Daily Defender, Chicago, IL
Brown, Michael ... (609) 845-3300
PROD FRM-PR
Gloucester County Times, Woodbury, NJ
Brown, Michael ... (401) 272-1010
ED, Providence Visitor, Providence, RI
Brown, Michael ... (423) 523-3131
Online Sales & MKTG
Knoxville News-Sentinel, Knoxville, TN
Brown, Mike ... (818) 762-1707
Contact, Family Matters Publications, North Hollywood, CA
Brown, Mike ... (501) 271-3700
PUB, ADV MGR
Benton County Daily Record, Bentonville, AR
Brown, Mike ... (502) 582-4011
Washington BU
Courier-Journal, Louisville, KY
Brown, Neil ... (813) 893-8111
MAN ED
St. Petersburg Times, St. Petersburg, FL
Brown, Nelson ... (757) 446-2000
Deputy MAN ED-Presentation
Virginian-Pilot, Norfolk, VA
Brown, Obrey ... (909) 793-3221
Sports ED
Redlands Daily Facts, Redlands, CA
Brown, Oby ... (912) 744-4200
Families ED, Macon Telegraph, Macon, GA
Brown, Pat ... (318) 462-0616
PROD MGR
Beauregard Daily News, De Ridder, LA
Brown, Patricia ... (517) 377-1000
ADV MGR-Local Sales
Lansing State Journal, Lansing, MI
Brown, Patrick ... (510) 208-6300
ASST to PUB/VP ADM
Oakland Tribune, Oakland, CA
MediaNews Inc. (Alameda Newspapers)
Brown, Patty ... (515) 724-3224
PUB, ED, Moravia Union, Moravia, IA
Brown, Paul ... (919) 829-4500
MET ED-Day, News & Observer, Raleigh, NC
Brown, Paul B ... (908) 240-5330
PRES
Urner Barry's Price-Current, Toms River, NJ
Brown Jr, Paul B ... (908) 240-5330
VP
Urner Barry's Price-Current, Toms River, NJ
Brown, Paul K ... (619) 765-2231
ED, Julian News, Julian, CA
Brown, Phil ... (206) 622-8272
PUB, Seattle Daily Journal of Commerce, Seattle, WA
Brown, Phillip ... (412) 439-7500
ASSOC ED, Herald-Standard, Uniontown, PA
Brown, R D ... (970) 565-8527
PUB, Montezuma Valley Journal, Cortez, CO
Brown, Ramona ... (918) 885-2101
GM, Hominy News/Progress, Hominy, OK
Brown, Randy ... (520) 573-4400
PROD MGR-Packaging Center, TNI Partners dba Tucson Newspapers, Tucson, AZ
Brown, Randy ... (316) 268-6000
EPE, Wichita Eagle, Wichita, KS
Brown, Ray ... (205) 325-2222
Graphics ED/Art DIR, News, Birmingham, AL
Brown, Richard ... (514) 987-2222
PROD Building MGR, Gazette, Montreal, QC
Brown, Richard D ... (919) 335-0841
PUB, Elizabeth City Daily Advance, Elizabeth City, NC
Brown, Rick ... (908) 240-5330
TREAS
Urner Barry's Price-Current, Toms River, NJ
Brown, Rick ... (905) 684-7251
DP MGR, Standard, St. Catharines, ON
Brown, Rick J ... (913) 764-2211
ADV DIR, ADV MGR-CLASS
Olathe Daily News, Olathe, KS
Brown, Robert ... (970) 949-0555
PUB, Vail Daily News, Vail, CO
Swift Newspapers

Bro Who's Where-30

Brown, Robert F .... (806) 364-2030
VP, Hereford Brand, Hereford, TX
Brown, Robert N .... (812) 379-5612
COB, Home News Enterprises, Columbus, IN
Brown, Rodney .... (508) 343-6911
PROD DIR
Sentinel & Enterprise, Fitchburg, MA
Brown, Roger .... (616) 897-9261
PUB, Lowell Ledger, Lowell, MI
Brown, Ron .... (910) 372-8999
GM, MAN ED, Alleghany News, Sparta, NC
Brown, Ronald M .... (307) 634-3361
VP/SEC
Wyoming Tribune-Eagle, Cheyenne, WY
Brown, Ronda .... (316) 723-2115
GM, Kiowa County Signal, Greensburg, KS
Brown, Ronnie .... (864) 223-1411
PROD FRM-PR
Index-Journal, Greenwood, SC
Brown, Scott .... (901) 427-3333
PUB/PRES, Jackson Sun, Jackson, TN
Brown, Scott M .... (412) 782-2121
PUB, Herald, Aspinwall, PA
Brown, Sherri .... (912) 744-4200
CIRC MGR-Sales/MKTG
Macon Telegraph, Macon, GA
Brown, Stephen .... (312) 644-7800
MAN ED, Daily Law Bulletin, Chicago, IL
Brown, Stephen .... (604) 263-5643
PUB, Vancouver Herald, Vancouver, BC
Brown, Steve .... (214) 977-8222
RE ED, Dallas Morning News, Dallas, TX
Brown, Steve .... (805) 736-2313
News ED, Lompoc Record, Lompoc, CA
Brown, Steve .... (216) 329-7000
Entertainment/Amusements ED, Television/Music ED, Chronicle-Telegram, Elyria, OH
Brown, Steve .... (401) 273-6397
PUB, Providence Phoenix, Providence, RI
Brown, Steven .... (416) 441-1405
Accounts Administrator,
Fotopress Independent News Service International (FPINS), Toronto, ON
Brown, Stew .... (905) 526-3333
Theater Writer, Spectator, Hamilton, ON
Brown, Sue S .... (803) 648-2311
PROD MGR, Aiken Standard, Aiken, SC
Brown, Suzanne .... (919) 829-4500
Arts/Entertainment ED
News & Observer, Raleigh, NC
Brown, Suzanne .... (303) 892-5000
Style/Fashion ED
Rocky Mountain News, Denver, CO
Brown, Suzanne L .... (847) 669-5621
PUB, Huntley Farmside, Huntley, IL
Brown, Teresa .... (800) 521-5232
MAN ED, Post-Searchlight, Bainbridge, GA
Brown, Terry .... (214) 977-8222
PROD DIR-Pre Press
Dallas Morning News, Dallas, TX
Brown, Terry .... (312) 222-3232
EDL Writer, Chicago Tribune, Chicago, IL
Brown, Thomas F .... (610) 820-6500
CONT
Allentown Morning Call, Allentown, PA
Brown, Tim .... (704) 245-6431
Sports ED, Daily Courier, Forest City, NC
Brown, Bishop Tod David .... (208) 342-1311
PUB, Idaho Catholic Register, Boise ID
Brown, Tom .... (334) 433-1551
ADV MGR-NTL, Press Register, Mobile, AL
Brown, Tom .... (904) 252-1511
BUS ED, Daytona Beach News-Journal, Daytona Beach, FL
Brown, Tom .... (937) 773-2721
PROD MGR, Piqua Daily Call, Piqua, OH
Brown, Tom C .... (603) 224-5301
PUB, Concord Monitor, Concord, NH
Brown, Tony .... (704) 358-5000
Theater/Dance Critic
Charlotte Observer, Charlotte, NC
Brown, Tressi .... (502) 274-4949
GM
Ohio County Messenger, Beaver Dam, KY
Brown, Troy .... (409) 265-7411
BUS/FIN ED, Religion/Society ED
Brazosport Facts, Clute, TX
Brown, Vernon .... (515) 284-8000
Newsroom ADM
Des Moines Register, Des Moines, IA
Brown, Vince .... (817) 778-4444
PROD DIR-Technical/Pre Press
Temple Daily Telegram, Temple, TX
Brown, W James .... (864) 984-2586
PUB, Laurens County Advertiser, Laurens, SC
Brown, Wallace .... (315) 822-3001
PUB, ED
West Winfield Star, West Winfield, NY
Brown, Warren .... (202) 334-6000
Automotive ED
Washington Post, Washington, DC
Brown, Warren A (Chip) .... (510) 339-8777
PUB, Montclarion, Oakland, CA
Brown, Wendy .... (208) 365-6066
ED, Messenger-Index, Emmett, ID
Brown, William B .... (334) 262-1611
VP-News
Montgomery Advertiser, Montgomery, AL
Browne, Arthur .... (212) 210-2100
MAN ED
New York Daily News, New York, NY
Browne, David .... (717) 255-8100
SYS ED, Patriot-News, Harrisburg, PA
Browne, Joseph A .... (609) 871-8000
ADV DIR
Burlington County Times, Willingboro, NJ
Browne, Maggie .... (805) 650-2900
CIRC MGR-Single Copy
Ventura County Star, Ventura, CA
Brownell, Malcolm .... (601) 961-7000
CIRC MGR-Sales
Clarion-Ledger, Jackson, MS
Browning, Ann .... (804) 793-2311
ADV MGR-RT
Danville Register & Bee, Danville, VA
Browning, Bruce .... (770) 834-6631
EX ED, Times-Georgian, Carrollton, GA
Browning, Dick .... (501) 378-3400
ADV MGR-NTL
Arkansas Democrat-Gazette, Little Rock, AR
Browning, Joe R .... (619) 442-4404
PRES/PUB
Daily Californian, El Cajon, CA
Browning, Lori .... (618) 234-1000
EPE, Belleville News-Democrat, Belleville, IL
Browning, Michael .... (804) 793-2311
PROD MGR
Danville Register & Bee, Danville, VA
Browning, Pamela J .... (970) 493-6397
ADV DIR
Fort Collins Coloradoan, Fort Collins, CO
Browning, Robert .... (519) 336-1100
ED, Gazette, Sarnia, ON
Browning, Wilt .... (704) 252-5611
Sports ED
Asheville Citizen-Times, Asheville, NC
Brownlee, Bill .... (318) 942-4971
ADV DIR
Opelousas Daily World, Opelousas, LA
Brownlee, Harry .... (501) 968-5252
PROD MGR
Russellville Courier, Russellville, AR
Brownlee, Larry .... (417) 876-2500
PUB, ED, Star, El Dorado Springs, MO
Brownlee, Patsy .... (417) 876-2500
PUB, Star, El Dorado Springs, MO
Brownrout, Todd .... (215) 854-2000
VP-Advertising, Philadelphia Inquirer, Philadelphia, PA, Knight-Ridder Inc.
Brownstein, Ronald .... (213) 237-5000
Political Writer-D.C.
Los Angeles Times, Los Angeles, CA
Broxholm, Keith .... (517) 787-2300
PROD MGR-PR
Jackson Citizen Patriot, Jackson, MI
Broyhill, Kent .... (402) 494-4264
PUB
South Sioux City Star, South Sioux City, NE
Broz, Kathy .... (308) 286-3325
ED, Hayes Center Times-Republican, Hayes Center, NE
Brubaker, Becky .... (954) 356-4000
PROD MGR-PR
Sun-Sentinel, Fort Lauderdale, FL
Brubaker, Linda .... (313) 222-2300
Budget MGR, Detroit News, Detroit, MI
Brubaker, Moe .... (419) 592-5055
Sports ED
Northwest Signal, Napoleon, OH
Brubaker, Pat .... (415) 749-5400
CIRC DIR, Recorder, San Francisco, CA
Bruce, Barry .... (701) 857-1900
PROD FRM-PR, Minot Daily News, Minot, ND
Bruce, Bob .... (501) 735-1010
ADV DIR, Evening Times, West Memphis, AR
Bruce, Bob .... (915) 673-4271
Oil ED, Travel ED
Abilene Reporter-News, Abilene, TX
Bruce, Carol .... (417) 256-9191
NTL ED, News ED, Photo ED
West Plains Daily Quill, West Plains, MO
Bruce, Colin J .... (807) 343-6200
PUB/GM
Chronicle-Journal, Thunder Bay, ON
Bruce, Eric .... (616) 964-7161
CIRC MGR-Single Copy/Transportation
Battle Creek Enquirer, Battle Creek, MI
Bruce, Gary .... (807) 343-6200
ADV DIR
Chronicle-Journal, Thunder Bay, ON
Bruce, James .... (519) 255-5711
PUB, Windsor Star, Windsor, ON
Bruce, Jeffrey C .... (602) 898-6500
EX ED, Mesa Tribune, Mesa, AZ
Thomson Newspapers
Bruce, Paul .... (902) 468-1222
PROD MGR, Daily News, Halifax, NS
Bruce, Robert .... (707) 643-1706
ED, Benicia Herald, Vallejo, CA
Bruce, Sam .... (803) 551-1551
PUB, Lake Edition, Irmo, SC
Bruce-Thomann, Janeen .... (608) 328-4202
PROD MGR, Monroe Times, Monroe, WI
Bruch, Laura .... (215) 854-2000
EDU Writer
Philadelphia Inquirer, Philadelphia, PA
Bruckner, Charlotte .... (212) 455-4000
Administrative ASST
North America Syndicate, King Features Syndicate Inc., New York, NY
Bruder, Mary .... (208) 935-0838
GM, Clearwater Progress, Kamiah, ID
Brudney, Stan .... (915) 625-4128
PUB, ED
Chronicle & Democrat-Voice, Coleman, TX
Bruett, Ray .... (419) 245-6000
CIRC DIR, Blade, Toledo, OH
Bruffy, Ann .... (561) 820-4100
ADV MGR-TMC/Commercial Printing
Palm Beach Post, West Palm Beach, FL
Bruggman, Vickie .... (515) 736-4541
GM, MAN ED
St. Ansgar Enterprise Journal, St. Ansgar, IA
Brugmann, Bruce B .... (415) 255-3100
PUB, ED, Bay Guardian, San Francisco, CA
Bruington, Doris .... (601) 328-2424
TREAS, Commercial Dispatch, Columbus, MS
Brumas, Michael .... (205) 325-2222
Washington Correspondent
Birmingham News, Birmingham, AL
Brumbaugh, Dave .... (360) 354-4444
ED, Lynden Tribune, Lynden, WA
Brumbelow, Jim .... (770) 963-9205
CIRC DIR, Gwinnett Daily Post, Lawrenceville, GA, Gray Communications
Brumby Jr, Otis A .... (770) 428-9411
PUB, Marietta Daily Journal, Marietta, GA
Brumett, John .... (501) 378-3400
COL
Arkansas Democrat-Gazette, Little Rock, AR
Brumfield, Barbara .... (313) 961-3949
CIRC MGR
Detroit Legal News, Detroit, MI
Brumfield, Charles .... (804) 793-2311
PROD MGR-OPER/Building SUPT
Danville Register & Bee, Danville, VA
Brumley, Roger .... (501) 935-5525
PROD FRM-COMP
Jonesboro Sun, Jonesboro, AR
Brummer, Tim .... (616) 683-2100
CIRC DIR, Niles Daily Star, Niles, MI
Boone Newspapers Inc.
Brunais, Andrea .... (904) 599-2100
EPE, Tallahassee Democrat, Tallahassee, FL
Brunble, Melody .... (903) 756-7396
ED, Cass County Sun, Linden, TX
Brundage, Robert .... (208) 232-4161
Sports ED, Idaho State Journal, Pocatello, ID
Brunel, Cindy .... (604) 423-4666
PUB, Free Press, Fernie, BC
Brunell, Jerry .... (212) 873-7400
PUB, Aufbau, New York, NY
Bruner, Jeffrey .... (515) 232-2160
MAN ED, Daily Tribune, Ames, IA
Bruner, Sara .... (803) 532-6203
PUB, Twin City-News, Batesburg, SC
Brunet, Alain .... (514) 285-7272
Music ED-Pop, La Presse, Montreal, QC
Brunetti, Michelle .... (609) 272-7000
Action Line
Press of Atlantic City, Pleasantville, NJ
Brunetto, Joseph .... (518) 454-5694
PROD MGR, Times Union, Albany, NY
Bruney, Sandra Z .... (704) 694-2161
ED, Anson Record, Wadesboro, NC
Brungardt, Tom J .... (316) 275-8500
ASST SEC/TREAS, CIRC MGR
Garden City Telegram, Garden City, KS
Brunjes, Robert (Bob) .... (561) 287-1550
ADV MGR-CLASS, Stuart News, Stuart, FL
Brunk, Rick .... (314) 336-3435
ED, Essayons, St. Robert, MO
Brunkow, Helen .... (320) 677-2229
MAN ED, Herman Review, Herman, MN
Brunner, Bruce .... (330) 454-5611
PROD MGR-Computer OPER
Repository, Canton, OH
Brunner, Dennis .... (801) 644-2900
PUB, Southern Utah News, Kanab, UT
Brunner, Dixie .... (801) 644-2900
PUB, ED, Southern Utah News, Kanab, UT
Brunner, Pamela S .... (609) 358-6171
PUB, ED, Elmer Times, Elmer, NJ
Bruno, Andy .... (408) 920-5000
Action Line ED
San Jose Mercury News, San Jose, CA
Bruno, John .... (718) 981-1234
PROD FRM-COMP Room
Staten Island Advance, Staten Island, NY
Bruno, John .... (419) 625-5500
Radio/Television ED
Sandusky Register, Sandusky, OH
Bruno, John R .... (716) 243-2211
PUB, Livingston County Leader, Geneseo, NY
Bruno, Susan Q .... (804) 220-1736
MAN ED, Virginia Gazette, Williamsburg, VA
Bruns, Andrew S .... (715) 723-5515
ADV MGR
Chippewa Herald, Chippewa Falls, WI
Bruns, Bill .... (310) 454-1321
MAN ED
Palisadian-Post, Pacific Palisades, CA
Bruns Jr, Herb .... (419) 394-7414
PROD SUPT/MGR
Evening Leader, St. Marys, OH
Bruns, Sandy .... (419) 628-2369
PUB, Community Post, Minster, OH
Brunson, Charlie .... (803) 771-6161
PROD MGR-Distribution
State, Columbia, SC
Brunson, Drew .... (904) 359-4111
PROD MGR-Technical SRV Software
Florida Times-Union, Jacksonville, FL
Brunson, James .... (210) 585-4893
GM, Progress Times, Mission, TX
Brunswick, Cary .... (607) 432-1000
MAN ED, Features ED
Daily Star, Oneonta, NY
Brunt, Charles .... (505) 523-4581
City ED, Sun-News, Las Cruces, NM
Brusic, Ken .... (714) 835-1234
EX ED
Orange County Register, Santa Ana, CA
Bruskeitz, Most Rev Fabian ..... (402) 488-0090
PUB
Southern Nebraska Register, Lincoln, NE
Bruskotter, Jim .... (616) 796-4831
MAN ED, Pioneer Group, Big Rapids, MI
Bruso, William .... (413) 663-3741
PROD FRM-PR
North Adams Transcript, North Adams, MA
Brussat, David .... (401) 277-7000
EDL Writer
Providence Journal-Bulletin, Providence, RI
Brust, Pam .... (304) 485-1891
Society ED, Parkersburg News & Sentinel, Parkersburg, WV
Brutlag, Harold .... (320) 963-3813
PUB, ED
Maple Lake Messenger, Maple Lake, MN
Bruton, Bill .... (716) 343-8000
Sports ED, Daily News, Batavia, NY
Bruty, Simon .... (310) 230-3400
Senior Photographer, Allsport Photography USA, Pacific Palisades, CA
Bruzelius, Nils .... (617) 929-2000
SCI/Technology ED
Boston Globe, Boston, MA
Bruzzese, Len .... (360) 754-5400
MAN ED, Olympian, Olympia, WA
Bryan, Barbara F .... (605) 662-7201
PUB, ED
Edgemont Herald Tribune, Edgemont, SD
Bryan, Betty .... (205) 734-2131
SEC/TREAS, Cullman Times, Cullman, AL
Bryan Newspapers
Bryan, Bob .... (937) 498-2111
PA, Sidney Daily News, Sidney, OH
Bryan, Bob .... (318) 459-3200
MAN ED, Times, Shreveport, LA
Bryan, Craig .... (612) 338-8155
MKTG DIR, HomeStyles Publishing and Marketing Inc., Minneapolis, MN
Bryan, D Tennant .... (804) 649-6000
Chairman-EX Committee
Richmond Times-Dispatch, Richmond, VA
Bryan, Don .... (910) 353-1171
Photo ED, Daily News, Jacksonville, NC
Bryan, Fred .... (909) 684-1200
CIRC MGR-Customer SRV
Press-Enterprise, Riverside, CA
Bryan, Harry .... (502) 582-4011
Sports ED, Courier-Journal, Louisville, KY
Bryan, Henry .... (215) 854-2000
EDL Writer
Philadelphia Inquirer, Philadelphia, PA
Bryan III, J Stewart .... (804) 649-6000
COB/PRES/CEO
Media General Inc., Richmond, VA
Bryan, Jeffrey .... (312) 644-7800
ADV Sr DIR-Sales/MKTG
Chicago Daily Law Bulletin, Chicago, IL
Bryan, Jim .... (904) 863-1111
BM, Northwest Florida Daily News, Fort Walton Beach, FL
Bryan, Kathleen .... (202) 234-8787
Office MGR
Photopress Washington, Washington, DC
Bryan, Kathleen .... (305) 743-8766
GM, Keys Advertiser, Marathon, FL

31-Who's Where **Bum**

Bryan, Kelly .... (409) 883-3571
ADV MGR-CLASS, Orange Leader, Orange, TX
Bryan, La Mar .... (502) 886-4444
ASSOC ED-News, Farm ED
Kentucky New Era, Hopkinsville, KY
Bryan, Mark V .... (307) 634-3361
CIRC DIR
Wyoming Tribune-Eagle, Cheyenne, WY
Bryan, Robert .... (919) 419-6500
ADV MGR-CLASS, Herald-Sun, Durham, NC
Bryan, Robert C .... (205) 734-2131
PUB, Bryan Newspapers, Cullman, AL
Bryan, Thelma .... (816) 277-3211
ED, Randolph County Times-Herald, Huntsville, MO
Bryan, Tommy A .... (615) 444-6008
PUB, ED, Wilson World, Lebanon, TN
Bryan, William .... (916) 741-2345
PROD FRM-MR
Appeal-Democrat, Marysville, CA
Bryant, Arlene .... (206) 464-2111
Local/Suburban ED
Seattle Times, Seattle, WA
Bryant, Bill .... (402) 792-2255
PUB, GM, ED, Voice, Hickman, NE
Bryant Jr, Charles A .... (609) 272-7000
ASST TREAS, DIR-FIN/ADM
Press of Atlantic City, Pleasantville, NJ
Bryant, Cherie .... (805) 273-2700
ADV DIR-NTL, DIR-MKTG/PROM
Antelope Valley Press, Palmdale, CA
Bryant, Dale .... (408) 354-3110
ED, Los Gatos Weekly-Times, Los Gatos, CA
Bryant, Ed .... (212) 626-6801
Sr VP/Newspaper Relations
Print Marketing Concepts Inc., New York, NY
Bryant, Eric .... (518) 439-4949
MAN ED, Loudonville Weekly, Delmar, NY
Bryant, George .... (757) 446-2000
ASST to EX Administrator
Virginian-Pilot, Norfolk, VA
Bryant, James .... (609) 989-5454
PROD ASST MGR, Times, Trenton, NJ
Bryant, Jim .... (423) 472-5041
GM, Cleveland Daily Banner, Cleveland, TN
Bryant, Joe .... (910) 888-3500
PROD MGR-Technical SRV/Imaging
High Point Enterprise, High Point, NC
Bryant, Linda .... (402) 792-2255
PUB, GM, ED, Voice, Hickman, NE
Bryant, Mark .... (601) 762-1111
City ED, Mississippi Press, Pascagoula, MS
Bryant, Mary .... (317) 923-8291
MAN ED, Indiana Herald, Indianapolis, IN
Bryant, Miranda .... (218) 631-2561
ED, Wadena Pioneer Journal, Wadena, MN
Bryant, Paula .... (804) 376-2795
ED, Union Star, Brookneal, VA
Bryant, Richard L .... (919) 752-6166
CIRC DIR, Daily Reflector, Greenville, NC
Bryant, Sue .... (405) 482-1221
PROD SUPT, Altus Times, Altus, OK
Bryant, Ted .... (205) 325-2222
Political ED, Post-Herald, Birmingham, AL
Bryant, Teri F .... (717) 421-3000
ADV MGR-Sales
Pocono Record, Stroudsburg, PA
Bryce, Lee Ann .... (318) 222-0213
ED, Daily Legal News Inc., Shreveport, LA
Brydges, Douglas S .... (807) 854-1919
PUB, ED
Geraldton-Longlac Times Star, Geraldton, ON
Bryson, Andy .... (615) 563-2512
PUB, ED, Cannon Courier, Woodbury, TN
Bryson, George .... (907) 257-4200
Magazine ED, Weekend ED
Anchorage Daily News, Anchorage, AK
Bryson, Jerry .... (334) 644-1101
PROD FRM-PR
Valley Times-News, Lanett, AL
Bryson, Peggy .... (906) 786-2021
MAN ED, EDL Writer
Daily Press, Escanaba, MI
Bryson, Pete .... (713) 220-7171
PROD MGR/CNR (Night)
Houston Chronicle, Houston, TX
Bryson, Susan .... (615) 563-2512
PUB, ED, Cannon Courier, Woodbury, TN
Bubello, Paula .... (508) 626-3800
DIR-PROM, Middlesex News
Framingham, MA
Bubil, Harold .... (941) 953-7755
RE ED, Herald-Tribune, Sarasota, FL
Bublitz, Alan .... (406) 791-1444
PROD DIR
Great Falls Tribune, Great Falls, MT
Bucci, Greg J .... (520) 753-6397
News ED, Kingman Daily Miner, Kingman, AZ
Bucci, Paul .... (604) 792-1931
ED, Chilliwack Progress Weekender, Chilliwack, BC
Bucciero, Gary .... (203) 789-5200
ADV MGR-RT
New Haven Register, New Haven, CT

Buchan, Cliff .... (612) 464-4601
ED, Times, Forest Lake, MN
Buchan, Jim .... (509) 525-3300
Sports ED
Walla Walla Union-Bulletin, Walla Walla, WA
Buchanan, Bill .... (707) 425-4646
MAN ED, EPE
Daily Republic, Fairfield, CA
Buchanan, Bruce .... (316) 694-5700
PRES, PUB, ED, News, Hutchinson, KS
Buchanan, Dan .... (360) 659-1300
ED, Globe, Marysville, WA
Buchanan, Doug .... (518) 483-4700
Sports ED, Malone Telegram, Malone, NY
Buchanan, John .... (519) 482-3443
PUB, Clinton News-Record, Clinton, ON
Buchanan, Ken .... (912) 462-6776
PUB, Brantley Enterprise, Nahunta, GA
Buchanan, Margaret .... (815) 987-1200
ADV DIR
Rockford Register Star, Rockford, IL
Buchanan, Margaret E .... (607) 734-5151
PRES, PUB, Star-Gazette, Elmira, NY
Buchanan, Opal L .... (805) 324-9466
MAN ED
Bakersfield News Observer, Bakersfield, CA
Buchanan, Robert .... (334) 433-1551
News ED, Mobile Press Register, Mobile, AL
Bucher, Craig .... (715) 822-4469
PUB, Cumberland Advocate, Cumberland, WI
Bucher, Sharon .... (715) 822-4469
PUB, ED
Cumberland Advocate, Cumberland, WI
Buchheit, Bob .... (219) 933-3200
CIRC DIR, Times, Munster, IN
Buchholz, Harley .... (414) 922-4600
ASSOC ED, EPE, NTL ED, Fond du Lac, WI
Buchholz, Norman .... (701) 857-1900
PROD FRM-MR, Daily News, Minot, ND
Buchholz, Pam .... (605) 263-3339
PUB, ED, Tri-County News, Irene, SD
Buchhotz, Don .... (510) 783-6111
City ED, Daily Review, Hayward, CA
Buchiere, Stephen P .... (315) 597-6655
ED, Courier-Journal, Palmyra, NY
Buchinger, Elizabeth .... (904) 435-8500
TV Tab ED
Pensacola News Journal, Pensacola, FL
Buchner, John E .... (541) 926-2211
PUB, ADTX CNR
Albany Democrat-Herald, Albany, OR
Bucholtz, Aharon .... (216) 356-0920
MAN ED, Westlaker Times, Rocky River, OH
Bucholtz, Tom .... (810) 985-7171
PROD MGR-PR
Times Herald, Port Huron, MI
Buchta, Cheryl .... (801) 625-4200
EDU ED, Standard-Examiner, Ogden, UT
Buck, Charles W .... (719) 263-5311
PUB, Fowler Tribune, Fowler, CO
Buck, Howard .... (541) 474-3700
EDU ED
Grants Pass Daily Courier, Grants Pass, OR
Buck Jr, Maynard .... (330) 627-5591
PUB, Free Press Standard, Carrollton, OH
Buckaloo, Sondra .... (405) 661-3525
ED, Thomas Tribune, Thomas, OK
Buckel, Bob .... (817) 237-1184
PUB, ED, Azle News, Azle, TX
Buckel, Walter .... (915) 573-5486
SEC/TREAS, Snyder Daily News, Snyder, TX
Buckey, Dave .... (805) 781-7800
CONT
Telegram-Tribune, San Luis Obispo, CA
Buckingham, Tom .... (941) 953-7755
BUS ED, Farm/Agriculture ED
Sarasota Herald-Tribune, Sarasota, FL
Buckland, Fred .... (902) 426-2811
ADV MGR, Chronicle-Herald, Halifax, NS
Buckland, Rex .... (514) 987-2222
ASST to the PUB, Gazette, Montreal, QC
Buckles, Kent .... (618) 529-5454
PROD SUPV-Distribution
Southern Illinoisan, Carbondale, IL
Buckley, Dan .... (520) 573-4561
Music Critic, Tucson Citizen, Tucson, AZ
Buckley, Dawn .... (504) 826-3279
ADV MGR-Special Sections
Times-Picayune, New Orleans, LA
Buckley, J Stephen .... (910) 227-0131
PUB
Times News Publishing Co., Burlington, NC
Buckley, Karen .... (508) 626-3800
Features/Special Sections ED
Middlesex News, Framingham, MA
Buckley, M R F .... (617) 433-7839
ED, Needham Chronicle, Needham, MA
Buckley, Maria .... (919) 829-4500
CIRC MGR-MKTG
News & Observer, Raleigh, NC
Buckley, Mary Louise .... (405) 255-5354
Books ED, Duncan Banner, Duncan, OK
Buckley, Meg .... (508) 458-7100
MGR-Community Relations, Sun, Lowell, MA

Buckley, Ronnie L .... (601) 785-6525
PUB
Smith County Reformer, Taylorsville, MS
Buckley, Steve .... (617) 426-3000
Sports COL, Boston Herald, Boston, MA
Buckman, Ivan .... (816) 376-3508
PUB, Marceline Press, Marceline, MO
Buckmaster, Michael .... (317) 584-4501
MAN ED, Wire ED
News-Gazette, Winchester, IN
Bucknam, Don R .... (812) 372-7811
PUB, Republic, Columbus, IN
Buckner, Bobby J .... (423) 986-6581
PUB, News-Herald, Lenoir City, TN
Buckner, Donna .... (405) 224-2600
PROD FRM-COMP Room
Chickasha Daily Express, Chickasha, OK
Buckner, Jennie .... (704) 358-5000
VP, ED, Charlotte Observer, Charlotte, NC
Buckner, Joe Don .... (806) 762-8844
Photo DEPT MGR
Lubbock Avalanche-Journal, Lubbock, TX
Buckner, Philip F .... (206) 727-2727
PRES, Buckner News Alliance, Seattle, WA
Buckner, Walter L .... (915) 247-4433
PUB, ED, Llano News, Llano, TX
Buckner, Wanda .... (910) 592-8137
PROD SUPT-COMP
Sampson Independent, Clinton, NC
Buckner, Zach .... (803) 626-8555
CIRC MGR-Sales & MKTG
Sun News, Myrtle Beach, SC
Buckwalter, John M .... (717) 291-8811
PRES/CEO, Lancaster Intelligencer Journal/New Era/Sunday News, Lancaster, PA
Bucmys, Rev Dr Cornelius .... (718) 827-1352
ED, Darbininkas, Brooklyn, NY
Buczkowski, John .... (419) 245-6000
PROD SUPT-PR, Blade, Toledo, OH
Budai, Mr .... (514) 279-4536
PUB, Corriere Italiano, Montreal, QC
Buday, Ken .... (919) 638-8101
Sports ED, Sun-Journal, New Bern, NC
Budd, Bernadette .... (516) 929-8882
PUB, ED
Community Journal, Wading River, NY
Budde, Neil .... (212) 416-2000
ED-Interactive Edition
Wall Street Journal, New York, NY
Budge, Rose Mary .... (210) 225-7411
Fashion ED
San Antonio Express-News, San Antonio, TX
Budgick, Barbara .... (610) 622-8800
Librarian
Delaware County Daily Times, Primos, PA
Budihas, Stephen .... (610) 820-6500
DIR-Human Resources
Morning Call, Allentown, PA
Budke, Barry .... (209) 441-6111
CIRC MGR-Distribution
Fresno Bee, Fresno, CA
Budris, William .... (412) 775-3200
CIRC MGR, Beaver County Times, Beaver, PA
Budrys, Ignas .... (312) 585-9500
GM, Draugas, Chicago, IL
Budzisz, Russ .... (414) 684-4433
ED, COL, EPE, Fashion/Food ED
Herald Times Reporter, Manitowoc, WI
Buechlein, Daniel Mark .... (317) 236-1570
PUB, Criterion, Indianapolis, IN
Buege, Mary .... (414) 733-4411
ADV MGR-RT, Post-Crescent, Appleton, WI
Buehler, Ingrid A .... (423) 338-2818
ED, Polk County News/Citizen Advance, Benton, TN
Buehler Sr, Randolph E .... (423) 338-2818
PUB, Polk County News/Citizen Advance, Benton, TN
Buel, Bobbie Jo .... (520) 573-4220
MAN ED, Arizona Daily Star, Tucson, AZ
Buell, Duane .... (360) 694-3391
CIRC MGR-Dispatch
Columbian, Vancouver, WA
Buell, Harold G .... (212) 621-1500
ASST to the PRES for Electronic Darkroom & PhotoStream, Associated Press, NY, NY
Buendo, Christopher .... (413) 525-6661
GM, Reminder, East Longmeadow, MA
Buendo, Daniel .... (413) 525-6661
PUB, Reminder, East Longmeadow, MA
Buening, Diane .... (419) 586-2371
CIRC MGR, Daily Standard, Celina, OH
Buerck, Dave .... (573) 431-2010
BM, Daily Journal, Park Hills, MO
Buerer, Danni Jo .... (501) 673-8533
ADV MGR
Stuttgart Daily Leader, Stuttgart, AR
Buerger, Andrew A .... (604) 689-1520
PUB, Jewish Bulletin, Vancouver, BC
Buerger, Charles A .... (410) 752-3504
PUB, Jewish Times, Baltimore, MD
Buergi, Roy .... (505) 823-7777
Online MGR
Albuquerque Tribune, Albuquerque, NM

Buettner, Mike .... (419) 586-2371
MAN ED, EPE, Daily Standard, Celina, OH
Buffett, Warren E .... (716) 849-3434
BC, Buffalo News, Buffalo, NY
Buffington, Herman .... (706) 367-5233
PUB, Jackson Herald, Jefferson, GA
Buffington, Mike .... (706) 367-5233
GM, ED, Jackson Herald, Jefferson, GA
Buffington, Tracy .... (319) 263-2331
News ED, Muscatine Journal, Muscatine, IA
Bufkin, Celine .... (334) 749-6271
Photo DEPT MGR
Opelika-Auburn News, Opelika, AL
Bugbee, Tom .... (520) 445-3333
PROD DIR, Daily Courier, Prescott, AZ
Bugner, Mike .... (334) 262-1611
PROD MGR-Pre Press
Montgomery Advertiser, Montgomery, AL
Buhasz, Laszlo .... (416) 585-5000
Travel ED, Globe and Mail, Toronto, ON
Buhr, Richard .... (207) 282-1535
City ED, Journal Tribune, Biddeford, ME
Buhrmester, Myra .... (501) 935-5525
Society ED, Jonesboro Sun, Jonesboro, AR
Buice, Jeff .... (770) 428-9411
PROD DIR
Marietta Daily Journal, Marietta, GA
Buiso, Maria .... (716) 232-6920
PUB, Daily Record, Rochester, NY
Buitrago, Carlos .... (312) 525-6285/9400
GM, La Raza Newspaper, Chicago, IL
Buitrago, Rapael .... (213) 622-8332
EDL ED, La Opinion, Los Angeles, CA
Bujalski, Henry .... (814) 870-1600
ASST CONT
Morning News/Erie Daily Times, Erie, PA
Bukala, James .... (508) 458-7100
CIRC DIR, Sun, Lowell, MA
Buker, Lori .... (360) 754-5400
Librarian, Olympian, Olympia, WA
Bukowski, Lorraine .... (203) 268-6234
MAN ED, Stratford Star, Trumbull, CT
Bukro, Casey .... (312) 222-3232
Environmental Writer
Chicago Tribune, Chicago, IL
Bulat, Jennifer .... (312) 573-3800
ED, CoverStory, Chicago, IL
Buley, Bill .... (208) 263-9534
MAN ED
Bonner County Daily Bee, Sandpoint, ID
Bull, John V R .... (215) 854-2000
ASST to ED
Philadelphia Inquirer, Philadelphia, PA
Bullard, George .... (313) 222-2300
ASST MAN ED-MET News
Detroit News, Detroit, MI
Bullard, Marcia .... (212) 715-2100
CEO/PRES/ED, USA Weekend, New York, NY
Bullard, Mark .... (916) 756-0800
Online Contact
Davis Enterprise, Davis, CA
Bullas, Diane .... (503) 226-1311
PROD SUPT
Daily Journal of Commerce, Portland, OR
Bulling, Keith D .... (208) 377-6200
DIR-Personnel, Idaho Statesman, Boise, ID
Bullington, Stan .... (615) 526-9715
PROD MGR, Herald-Citizen, Cookeville, TN
Bullman, Tisha .... (913) 682-1334
ED, Lansing Chronicle, Leavenworth, KS
Bullmore, Lisa .... (916) 336-6262
GM, Mountain Echo, Fall River Mills, GA
Bullock, Michael L .... (719) 395-8621
ED, Chaffee County Times, Buena Vista, CO
Bullock, Paul .... (309) 686-3000
PROD MGR, Journal Star, Peoria, IL
Bullock, Phil .... (541) 963-3161
Photo ED, Observer, La Grande, OR
Bullock Jr, Robert H .... (804) 359-8442
ED, Presbyterian Outlook, Richmond, VA
Bullock, Bishop William H .... (608) 233-8060
PUB, Catholic Herald-Madison Edition, Madison, WI
Bulmahn, Lynn .... (817) 757-5757
Health/Medical ED
Waco Tribune-Herald, Waco, TX
Bulman, Robin .... (212) 837-7000
Senior Correspondent-Portland, OR, Trade ED
Journal of Commerce & Commercial, New York, NY
Bumgardner, Shirley .... (616) 345-3511
Travel ED
Kalamazoo Gazette, Kalamazoo, MI
Bumgarner, Chris .... (704) 873-1451
Sports ED, Statesville Record & Landmark, Statesville, NC
Bump, Rick .... (716) 693-1000
CIRC MGR
Tonawanda News, North Tonawanda, NY

Bum Who's Where-32

Bumpus, Brian .... (419) 522-3311
CIRC DIR
Mansfield News Journal, Mansfield, OH
Bunch, Ann .... (816) 457-3707
PUB, ED
Lancaster Excelsior, Lancaster, MO
Bunch, Beth .... (601) 842-2611
Automotive ED, Fashion/Style ED, Food ED, Health/Medical ED, Lifestyle ED, Northeast Mississippi Daily Journal, Tupelo, MS
Bunch, Charlene .... (817) 694-3713
PUB, Whitney Messenger, Whitney, TX
Bunch, Fred .... (713) 220-7171
Picture ED
Houston Chronicle, Houston, TX
Bunch Jr, George N .... (706) 635-4313
ED, Times-Courier, Ellijay, GA
Bunch III, George N .... (706) 635-4313
PUB, Times-Courier, Ellijay, GA
Bunch, Thomas .... (616) 946-2000
CIRC MGR
Record-Eagle, Traverse City, MI
Buncher, Alan .... (414) 634-3322
ED, Journal Times, Racine, WI
Bundick, Ahmed .... (614) 387-0400
Political ED, Marion Star, Marion, OH
Bundy, Beverly .... (817) 390-7400
Food ED
Fort Worth Star-Telegram, Fort Worth, TX
Bundy, Dan .... (701) 572-2165
PROD MGR
Williston Daily Herald, Williston, ND
Bundy, David .... (601) 582-4321
Photo ED
Hattiesburg American, Hattiesburg, MS
Bundy, David .... (317) 529-1111
BM, Courier-Times, New Castle, IN
Bundy, Floyd .... (217) 351-5252
PROD FRM-MR, News-Gazette
Champaign, IL
Bunge, Martin .... (515) 582-2112
PUB, Forest City Summit, Forest City, IA
Bunge, Paul .... (515) 732-3721
PUB, ED
Mitchell County Press-News, Osage, IA
Bunke, Joan .... (515) 284-8000
Books ED, Films/Theater ED
Des Moines Register, Des Moines, IA
Bunn, Timothy D .... (315) 470-0011
EX ED, Post-Standard/Syracuse Herald-Journal/American, Syracuse, NY
Bunner, John D .... (419) 495-2696
ED, Photo Star, Willshire, OH
Bunner, Judith .... (419) 495-2696
PUB, Photo Star, Willshire, OH
Bunting, Brenda .... (561) 996-4404
PUB, ED
Belle Glade Sun, Belle Glade, FL
Bunting, Dean .... (618) 445-2355
ED, Journal-Register, Albion, IL
Bunting, Kenneth F .... (206) 448-8000
MAN ED
Seattle Post-Intelligencer, Seattle, WA
Bunton, Larry .... (913) 295-1111
PROD MGR-SYS
Topeka Capital-Journal, Topeka, KS
Buntsma, John .... (712) 546-7031
News ED
Le Mars Daily Sentinel, Le Mars, IA
Buoen, Roger .... (612) 673-4000
Team Leader
Star Tribune, Minneapolis, MN
Buonauro, Gabe .... (201) 646-4000
ASST MAN ED-Sports
Record, Hackensack, NJ
Buoncuore, Robin .... (609) 935-1500
Fashion/Food ED, Religion ED, Society ED, Women's ED, Today's Sunbeam, Salem, NJ
Buonpane, Guy .... (212) 930-8000
PROD FRM-Machinist
New York Post, New York, NY
Buoy, Jean .... (203) 744-5100
Amusements ED, Films/Theater ED, Food ED, Garden/Home Furnishings ED, Music ED, Society/Fashion ED, Travel ED, Women's ED
News-Times, Danbury, CT
Burbage, John .... (803) 577-7111
MET ED
Charleston Post and Courier, Charleston, SC
Burbine, James .... (617) 929-2000
CIRC MGR-Data MGT
Boston Globe, Boston, MA
Burbrink, Bettie R .... (812) 379-5612
EX ASST
Home News Enterprises, Columbus, IN
Burch, Becky .... (918) 335-8200
Photo ED
Examiner-Enterprise, Bartlesville, OK
Burch, Cathalena .... (716) 282-2311
Community News ED
Niagara Gazette, Niagara Falls, NY
Burch, David .... (206) 872-6600
MAN ED, South County Journal, Kent, WA
Burch, Deanna .... (417) 532-9131
CIRC DIR, Daily Record, Lebanon, MO
Burch, Jack .... (604) 437-7030
PUB, Vancouver Echo, Vancouver, BC
Burch, Jim .... (817) 757-5757
PROD MGR-Pre Press
Waco Tribune-Herald, Waco, TX
Burch, Larry .... (315) 337-4000
PROD FRM-COMP, Daily Sentinel, Rome, NY
Burch, Leland E .... (864) 877-2076
PUB, ED, Greer Citizen, Greer, SC
Burch, Walter M .... (864) 877-2076
PUB, Greer Citizen, Greer, SC
Burch, William .... (419) 625-5500
PROD ENG-Maintenance
Sandusky Register, Sandusky, OH
Burcham, David .... (330) 841-1600
Sports ED, Tribune Chronicle, Warren, OH
Burcham, Lucy .... (614) 385-2107
PROD MGR, Logan Daily News, Logan, OH
Burcham, Rich .... (614) 385-2107
CIRC DIR, Logan Daily News, Logan, OH
Burchett, Wally .... (918) 647-3188
PUB, PROD MGR, News & Sun, Poteau, OK
Burchette, Bob .... (910) 627-1781
ED, Ledger, Eden, NC
Burchik, James .... (717) 272-5611
MAN ED, EPE, Political ED
Daily News, Lebanon, PA
Burckel, Floyd .... (504) 892-7980
PUB, News-Banner, Covington, LA
Burckhard, John .... (605) 225-4100
PROD MGR-COMP
Aberdeen American News, Aberdeen, SD
Burd, Susan .... (412) 663-7742
GM, Weekly Recorder, Claysville, PA
Burdett, Bruce .... (401) 683-1000
ED, Sakonnet Times, Portsmouth, RI
Burdett, Patty .... (412) 772-3900
DP MGR
North Hills News Record, Warrendale, PA
Burdette, Denise .... (818) 241-4141
Librarian
Glendale News-Press, Glendale, CA
Burdette, Roger .... (810) 332-8181
CIRC MGR-Distribution
Oakland Press, Pontiac, MI
Burdick, Eric .... (805) 781-7800
Sports ED
Telegram-Tribune, San Luis Obispo, CA
Burdick, Robert W .... (303) 892-5000
ED, Rocky Mountain News, Denver, CO
Burdine, Mike .... (606) 678-8191
PROD MGR
Commonwealth-Journal, Somerset, KY
Burdis, Mack .... (719) 384-4475
EX SEC
La Junta Tribune-Democrat, La Junta, CO
Burdon, Robert W .... (703) 560-4000
ASSOC PUB, Fairfax Journal, Fairfax, VA
Journal Newspapers Inc.
Burenga, Kenneth L .... (212) 416-2600
PRES/COO
Dow Jones & Co. Inc., New York, NY
Burfeind, David S .... (207) 828-8100
VP-Planning & Development
Guy Gannett Communications, Portland, ME
Burford, Lei-Launi .... (360) 332-6397
PUB, Banner, Blaine, WA
Burford, Tom .... (218) 694-6265
GM, ED, Farmers Independent, Bagley, MN
Burgamy, Debbie .... (770) 867-7557
PUB, Winder News, Winder, GA
Burgar, Jeff .... (403) 837-2585
PUB, Smoky River Express, Falher, AB
Burgard, David .... (605) 225-4100
CIRC DIR
Aberdeen American News, Aberdeen, SD
Burgard, Steve .... (213) 237-5000
EPE-Orange County
Los Angeles Times, Los Angeles, CA
Burgarella, Bob .... (203) 789-5200
PROD MGR-COMP
New Haven Register, New Haven, CT
Burge, Terry .... (713) 686-8494
PUB, Leader, Houston, TX
Burger, Christine A .... (610) 371-5000
Lifestyle ED
Reading Times/Eagle, Reading, PA
Burger, Don .... (814) 723-8200
ADV MGR-RT
Warren Times-Observer, Warren, PA
Burger, Fred .... (205) 236-1551
BUS/FIN ED, Anniston Star, Anniston, AL
Burgeson, Beth .... (203) 846-3281
Travel/Women's ED, Hour, Norwalk, CT
Burgess, Beth .... (403) 235-7100
Homes/Travel ED
Calgary Herald, Calgary, AB
Burgess, David .... (608) 782-9710
MGR-Financial Services, DP MGR
La Crosse Tribune, La Crosse, WI
Burgess, Everett A .... (519) 354-2000
MGR-PROM
Chatham Daily News, Chatham, ON
Burgess, Fred .... (717) 243-2611
City ED, Sentinel, Carlisle, PA
Burgess, Mike .... (360) 754-5400
Sports ED, Olympian, Olympia, WA
Burgess, Phyllis D .... (218) 753-3170
ED, Tower News, Tower, MN
Burgess, Robert .... (617) 245-0080
ASST ED
Wakefield Daily Item, Wakefield, MA
Burgess, Rodney .... (903) 794-3311
City ED, Texarkana Gazette, Texarkana, TX
Burgess, Scott .... (954) 752-7474
ED, Margate/Coconut Creek Forum, Coral Springs, FL
Burgess, William .... (610) 688-3000
PUB, Suburban Advertiser, Wayne, PA
Burghardt, Jacob J .... (603) 569-3126
PUB, Granite State News, Wolfeboro, NH
Burghardt, Joanne .... (905) 579-4400
ED, Oshawa-Whitby This Week, Oshawa, ON
Burgin, David .... (510) 208-6300
Senior VP/EIC, Oakland Tribune, Oakland, CA
MediaNews Inc. (Alameda Newspapers)
Burk, Kimberly .... (806) 376-4488
Religion ED, Amarillo Daily News/Globe Times, Amarillo, TX
Burke, Allan C .... (701) 254-4537
PUB, ED
Emmons County Record, Linton, ND
Burke, Audrey .... (416) 367-2000
DIR-OPER-Planning/Control
Toronto Star, Toronto, ON
Burke, Doug .... (214) 977-8222
ADV MGR-RT
Dallas Morning News, Dallas, TX
Burke, James .... (206) 324-4297
ED, Seattle Gay News, Seattle, WA
Burke, John .... (912) 236-9511
Outdoors ED
Savannah Morning News, Savannah, GA
Burke, Judy .... (802) 748-8121
CIRC ASST MGR
Caledonian-Record, St. Johnsbury, VT
Burke, Kathleen .... (202) 414-0535
MKTG/Sales MGR
Agence France-Presse, Washington, DC
Burke, Leah P .... (701) 254-4537
PUB, Emmons County Record, Linton, ND
Burke, Linda .... (508) 922-1234
ADV MGR, Gloucester Times, Beverly, MA
Burke, Maureen .... (802) 447-7567
Fashion/Food ED
Bennington Banner, Bennington, VT
Burke, Michael .... (301) 722-4600
Sports ED
Cumberland Times-News, Cumberland, MD
Burke, Michael J .... (715) 246-6881
PUB, News, New Richmond, WI
Burke, Paul .... (208) 664-8176
ADV DIR, MGR-PROM
Coeur d'Alene Press, Coeur d'Alene, ID
Burke, Bishop Raymond .... (608) 788-1524
PUB, Times Review, La Crosse, WI
Burke, Rhonda .... (847) 223-8161
MAN ED, Fox Lake Press, Grayslake, IL
Burke, Robert L .... (717) 348-9100
MAN ED, SCI/Travel ED
Tribune & The Scranton Times, Scranton, PA
Burke, Sheryl .... (317) 664-5111
ADV MGR-OPER
Chronicle-Tribune, Marion, IN
Burke, Terence J .... (619) 295-5432
MAN ED
Uptown San Diego Examiner, San Diego, CA
Burke, Terri .... (505) 823-7777
MAN ED
Albuquerque Tribune, Albuquerque, NM
Burke, Tim .... (561) 820-4100
Graphics ED, Sports ED
Palm Beach Post, West Palm Beach, FL
Burke, Tom .... (512) 258-4127
ED, Hill Country News, Cedar Park, TX
Burkeen, Jo B .... (502) 753-1916
Living/Lifestyle ED, Religion ED, Society ED
Murray Ledger & Times, Murray, KY
Burkes, Daisy .... (352) 365-8200
CIRC DIR, Daily Commercial, Leesburg, FL
Burkett, Deryck .... (520) 573-4400
PROD MGR-Plate/Camera, TNI Partners dba Tucson Newspapers, Tucson, AZ
Burkett, Eric .... (334) 541-3902
ED, Eclectic Observer, Eclectic, AL
Burkett, Ken .... (419) 332-5511
PROD MGR-SRV
News-Messenger, Fremont, OH
Burkett, Lynnell .... (210) 225-7411
EDL DIR
San Antonio Express-News, San Antonio, TX
Burkett, Rebecca .... (616) 429-2400
BUS ED, Herald-Palladium, St. Joseph, MI
Burkhammer, Victor .... (304) 348-5140
News ED, Charleston Gazette, Sunday Gazette-Mail, Charleston, WV
Burkhardt, Andrew .... (401) 277-7000
City ED
Providence Journal-Bulletin, Providence, RI
Burkhardt, Ann .... (612) 673-4000
Food ED, Star Tribune, Minneapolis, MN
Burkhardt, Charles .... (717) 767-6397
DP MGR, York Newspaper Company, York, PA
Burkhardt, D C Jesse .... (509) 493-2112
ED, Enterprise, White Salmon, WA
Burkhardt, Karl .... (501) 271-3700
ED
Benton County Daily Record, Bentonville, AR
Burkhardt, Marc .... (415) 692-9406
MAN ED, San Mateo Weekly, Burlingame, CA
Burkhardt, Nancy .... (913) 295-1111
DIR-MKTG SRV
Topeka Capital-Journal, Topeka, KS
Burkhardt, Tim .... (320) 384-6188
ED, Hinckley News, Hinckley, MN
Burkhart, Don .... (308) 532-6000
ED, North Platte Telegraph, North Platte, NE
Burkhart, Regina .... (203) 926-2080
PUB, Valley Gazette, Shelton, CT
Burkhead, Jeff A .... (316) 624-2541
PRES, PUB
Southwest Daily Times, Liberal, KS
Burkholder, James .... (412) 654-6651
PROD MGR-COMP
New Castle News, New Castle, PA
Burkholder, Jean .... (970) 240-4900
ADV DIR, Morning Sun, Montrose, CO
Burkley, Gerald .... (716) 849-3434
PROD OPER FRM-Machinist
Buffalo News, Buffalo, NY
Burklow, James .... (312) 321-3000
PROD ASST MGR
Chicago Sun-Times, Chicago, IL
Burlage, Tod .... (419) 238-2285
Sports ED
Van Wert Times-Bulletin, Van Wert, OH
Burleigh, William R .... (513) 977-3000
PRES/CEO
E W Scripps Co., Cincinnati, OH
Burleson, Barry .... (601) 256-5647
PUB, Amory Advertiser, Amory, MS
Burleson, Bertie .... (704) 733-2448
ED, Avery Journal, Newland, NC
Burleson, John L .... (216) 376-0917
PRES/PUB, Akron Legal News, Akron, OH
Burleson, Kevin .... (716) 945-1644
PUB, ED, Salamanca Press, Salamanca, NY
Burleson, Leslie .... (409) 265-7411
Fashion ED, Features ED, Living/Lifestyle ED, Women's ED, Brazosport Facts, Clute, TX
Burleson, W D .... (916) 846-3661
PUB, Gridley Herald, Gridley, CA
Burlingame, Mike .... (219) 461-8333
CIRC DIR, Journal Gazette, Fort Wayne, IN
Burman, Kathleen .... (515) 259-2708
PUB, ED, Monroe Legacy, Monroe, IA
Burmeister, Bruce .... (810) 332-8181
PROD FRM-COMP
Oakland Press, Pontiac, MI
Burmeister, Tim .... (406) 622-3311
ED, River Press, Fort Benton, MT
Burnagiel, Patricia A .... (516) 843-2020
ADV DIR-CLASS, Newsday, Melville, NY
Burnell, Gary .... (508) 626-3800
CIRC MGR-Transportation
Middlesex News, Framingham, MA
Burner, Dell .... (360) 577-2500
City ED, Daily News, Longview, WA
Burnett, Barbara .... (315) 393-1000
PROD SUPT, Courier-Observer Journal & The Advance-News, Ogdensburg, NY
Burnett, Bryan .... (919) 419-6500
DIR-New Media, Herald-Sun, Durham, NC
Burnett Jr, Carl W .... (614) 342-4121
ED
Perry County Tribune, New Lexington, OH
Burnett, Dan .... (717) 421-3000
City ED, Pocono Record, Stroudsburg, PA
Burnett, Helen .... (405) 225-3000
Travel ED, Elk City Daily News, Elk City, OK
Burnett, Helen A .... (540) 981-3100
CIRC DIR, Roanoke Times, Roanoke, VA
Burnett, Jim .... (402) 444-1000
Photo DEPT DIR
Omaha World-Herald, Omaha, NE
Burnett, Jim .... (601) 287-6111
ADV MGR, ADTX MGR
Daily Corinthian, Corinth, MS
Burnett, Patty .... (303) 794-7877
MAN ED
Highlands Ranch Herald, Littleton, CO
Burnett, R Morris .... (804) 793-2311
CIRC DIR
Danville Register & Bee, Danville, VA

Copyright ©1997 by the Editor & Publisher Co.

33-Who's Where **But**

Burnett, Raymond N .... (412) 263-1100
DIR-Labor Relations
Pittsburgh Post-Gazette, Pittsburgh, PA

Burnett, Robbie .... (904) 973-6361
ED
Madison Enterprise-Recorder, Madison, FL

Burnett, Sandra .... (415) 348-4321
Health/Medical ED
San Mateo County Times, San Mateo, CA

Burnett, Sheneace .... (706) 724-0851
CIRC CNR-CMS
Augusta Chronicle, Augusta, GA

Burnett, Sondra .... (912) 924-2751
PA, Americus Times-Recorder, Americus, GA

Burnett, Wayne .... (712) 225-5111
CIRC MGR-PROM
Cherokee County's Daily Times, Cherokee, IA

Burnett, Wesley W .... (806) 495-2816
PUB, ED, Post Dispatch, Post, TX

Burnette, Doug .... (770) 382-4545
CIRC DIR
Daily Tribune News, Cartersville, GA

Burnette, Lynell .... (704) 652-3313
PROD MGR-COMP, McDowell News
Marion, NC

Burnette, Russell .... (409) 295-5407
Sports ED
Huntsville Item, Huntsville, TX

Burney, Wayne .... (915) 573-5486
ADV DIR, Snyder Daily News, Snyder, TX

Burnham, Kevin G .... (207) 633-4620
ED, Boothbay Register, Boothbay Harbor, ME

Burnham, Sally .... (916) 321-1000
MGR-Accounts Services
Sacramento Bee, Sacramento, CA

Burns, Bob .... (704) 358-5000
PROD DIR-OPER
Charlotte Observer, Charlotte, NC

Burns, Bobby .... (919) 792-1181
MAN ED, Enterprise, Williamston, NC

Burns, Carolyn .... (515) 448-4745
ED, Eagle Grove Eagle, Eagle Grove, IA

Burns, Cheryl .... (412) 588-5000
VP, Record-Argus, Greenville, PA

Burns, Chris .... (406) 523-5200
PROD MGR-Distribution
Missoulian, Missoula, MT

Burns, David S .... (330) 747-1471
ADV MGR-RT, Vindicator, Youngstown, OH

Burns, Ed .... (201) 653-1000
ADV MGR-RT
Jersey Journal, Jersey City, NJ

Burns, Edward .... (602) 898-6500
CONT, Mesa Tribune, Mesa, AZ
Thomson Newspapers

Burns, Elizabeth Murphy .... (218) 741-5544
VP, Mesabi Daily News, Virginia, MN
Murphy McGinnis Media

Burns, Gary .... (719) 632-5511
News ED, Gazette, Colorado Springs, CO

Burns, Howard .... (213) 525-2000
MAN ED
Hollywood Reporter, Los Angeles, CA

Burns, James .... (407) 242-3500
PROD ASST DIR
Florida Today, Melbourne, FL

Burns, Jennifer .... (719) 632-5511
DIR-Human Resources
Gazette, Colorado Springs, CO

Burns, Jerry .... (704) 295-7522
ED, Blowing Rocket, Blowing Rock, NC

Burns, Jo Ann .... (406) 755-7000
BM, Daily Inter Lake, Kalispell, MT

Burns, Joe .... (707) 226-3711
ADV MGR-Display
Napa Valley Register, Napa, CA

Burns, Joel E .... (508) 997-7411
Manager-Human Resources
Standard Times, New Bedford, MA

Burns, John .... (415) 892-1516
PUB, Novato Advance, Novato, CA

Burns, John .... (610) 820-6500
DIR-Technology
Morning Call, Allentown, PA

Burns, Judith M .... (864) 223-1411
VP/SEC, Index-Journal, Greenwood, SC

Burns, Kevin .... (216) 524-0830
ED, West Side Sun News, Cleveland, OH

Burns, Kitty .... (302) 324-2500
ADV MGR-NTL
News Journal, Wilmington, DE

Burns, Laura .... (208) 678-2201
BM, DP MGR
South Idaho Press, Burley, ID

Burns, Marianne .... (301) 459-3131
CIRC MGR
Prince George's Journal, Lanham, MD

Burns, Mike .... (714) 835-1234
PROD DIR-Distribution
Orange County Register, Santa Ana, CA

Burns, Nancy Sue .... (607) 563-3526
ED, Tri-Town News, Sidney, NY

Burns, Patrick .... (412) 664-9161
PROD FRM-PR, Daily News, McKeesport, PA

Burns, Ramona W .... (412) 664-9161
BM, Daily News, McKeesport, PA

Burns, Ron .... (913) 295-1111
ADV DIR, ADTX MGR
Topeka Capital-Journal, Topeka, KS

Burns, Scott .... (214) 977-8222
COL-BUS News
Dallas Morning News, Dallas, TX

Burns, Stacy .... (937) 335-5634
Television ED, Troy Daily News/Miami Valley
Sunday News, Troy, OH

Burns, Tony .... (501) 862-6611
Sports ED
El Dorado News-Times, El Dorado, AR

Burnside, Sharon .... (613) 829-9100
MAN ED, Ottawa Citizen, Ottawa, ON

Burnstein, John .... (412) 488-1212
PUB
In Pittsburgh Newsweekly, Pittsburgh, PA

Burr, Bill .... (914) 341-1100
Sports ED
Times Herald-Record, Middletown, NY

Burr, Charles E .... (860) 423-8466
CIRC MGR, Chronicle, Willimantic, CT

Burr, John .... (904) 359-4111
News ED
Florida Times-Union, Jacksonville, FL

Burr, Richard .... (313) 222-2300
EDL Writer, Detroit News, Detroit, MI

Burr, Robert J .... (573) 883-2222
PUB
Ste. Genevieve Herald, Ste. Genevieve, MO

Burrell, Winston A .... (305) 743-8766
PUB, Keys Advertiser, Marathon, FL

Burress, Annie R .... (864) 582-4511
Fashion/Society ED, Women's ED
Herald-Journal, Spartanburg, SC

Burress, Chuck .... (540) 236-5178
PUB, Gazette, Galax, VA

Burridge, Gordon .... (206) 625-1448
ED & PRES
Pacific Rim News Service Inc., Seattle, WA

Burris, Gayle Jones .... (317) 622-1212
ADV MGR-Major Accounts
Herald Bulletin, Anderson, IN

Burris, Jerry .... (808) 525-8000
EPE, Honolulu Advertiser, Honolulu, HI

Burris, Jim .... (904) 793-6222
ED, Sumter Journal, Lake Panasoffkee, FL

Burris, Keith .... (860) 646-0500
EPE, Journal Inquirer, Manchester, CT

Burris, Nancy .... (504) 826-3279
Librarian, Times-Picayune, New Orleans, LA

Burris, Robert .... (316) 331-3550
PROD SUPT, Independence Daily Reporter,
Independence, KS

Burriss, Andy .... (803) 329-4000
Photo ED, Herald, Rock Hill, SC

Burrough, Christine .... (908) 922-6000
ADV MGR-CLASS Telephone
Asbury Park Press, Neptune, NJ

Burrough, Larry .... (714) 835-1234
Deputy ED-Days
Orange County Register, Santa Ana, CA

Burroughs, Park .... (412) 222-2200
MAN ED, Observer-Reporter, Washington, PA

Burrow, Melissa .... (501) 337-7523
Reporter, Malvern Daily Record, Malvern, AR

Burrows, Derek .... (604) 732-2944
CR MGR
Pacific Press Limited, Vancouver, BC

Burrows, Edward (Ted) .... (561) 287-1550
EPE, Stuart News, Stuart, FL

Burrows, Jim .... (417) 451-1520
Political/Government ED
Neosho Daily News, Neosho, MO

Burrows, Kenda .... (309) 764-4344
EPE, Dispatch, Moline, IL

Burrus, Bill .... (601) 453-5312
Sports ED
Greenwood Commonwealth, Greenwood, MS

Burson, C K .... (601) 627-2201
PUB, GM, ED
Press Register, Clarksdale, MS

Burson, Dan .... (800) 424-4747
Regional Accounts MGR, Tribune Media
Services-Television Listings, Glens Falls, NY

Burt, Henry .... (205) 345-0505
ADV MGR-RT
Tuscaloosa News, Tuscaloosa, AL

Burt, Jeff .... (508) 997-7411
Suburban ED
Standard Times, New Bedford, MA

Burtchell, Susan .... (413) 447-7311
ADV MGR-CLASS
Berkshire Eagle, Pittsfield, MA

Burtoff, Barbara .... (202) 966-6570
ED/PUB, Barbara Burtoff Syndicated Features, Washington, DC

Burton, David L .... (804) 649-6000
Deputy MAN ED-City/State/Suburban News
Richmond Times-Dispatch, Richmond, VA

Burton, Donna .... (806) 248-7333
ED, Groom News, Groom, TX

Burton, George .... (407) 420-5000
PROD MGR-Center/RPC/Lake
Orlando Sentinel, Orlando, FL

Burton, Greg .... (208) 882-5561
Environmental ED, School ED, SCI ED,
Moscow-Pullman Daily News, Moscow, ID

Burton, Jack D .... (913) 492-9050
EVP, Inland Industries Inc., Lenexa, KS

Burton, Kathryn .... (517) 354-3111
MGR-BUS Office, DP MGR
Alpena News, Alpena, MI

Burton, Kelly .... (804) 385-5400
ADTX MGR, News & Advance, Lynchburg, VA

Burton, Mary .... (410) 778-2011
GM, Kent County News, Chestertown, MD

Burton, Phil .... (812) 265-3641
Books ED, Madison Courier, Madison, IN

Burton, Roger .... (864) 223-1411
PROD MGR, Index-Journal, Greenwood, SC

Burton, Ruth .... (423) 447-2996
ED, Bledsonian-Banner, Pikeville, TN

Burton, Saundra .... (317) 552-3355
MAN ED, Elwood Call-Leader, Elwood, IN

Burton, Steven .... (317) 736-7101
CIRC MGR-Home Delivery
Daily Journal, Franklin, IN

Burton, Tom .... (608) 252-6100
News ED
Wisconsin State Journal, Madison, WI

Bury, Charles .... (819) 569-9526
EX ED, Record, Sherbrooke, QC

Buryk, Alexis .... (212) 556-1234
VP-ADV, New York Times Co., New York, NY

Burzynski, Susan .... (313) 222-2300
ASST MAN ED-Training & Recruitment
Detroit News, Detroit, MI

Busack, David L .... (313) 994-6989
MGR-Administrative Services
Ann Arbor News, Ann Arbor, MI

Busath, Nancy .... (502) 582-4011
ADV MGR-NTL
Courier-Journal, Louisville, KY

Busby, Charles .... (601) 896-2100
BUS ED, Sun Herald, Biloxi, MS

Busby, Jeanette .... (804) 732-3456
MGR-Accounting
Progress-Index, Petersburg, VA

Busby, Julie .... (215) 854-2000
ASST to ED
Philadelphia Inquirer, Philadelphia, PA

Busby, Lauri .... (714) 642-4321
Arts/Entertainment ED, Television/Film ED,
Theater/Music ED, Daily Pilot
Costa Mesa, CA

Buscaglia, Marti .... (562) 435-1161
DIR-MKTG/PROM
Press-Telegram, Long Beach, CA

Busch, Kristi .... (520) 774-4545
MGR-CR, Arizona Daily Sun, Flagstaff, AZ

Busch, Melaine .... (918) 581-8300
EDU ED, Tulsa World, Tulsa, OK

Busch, Wesley .... (713) 485-2785
ED, Alvin Journal, Pearland, TX

Busche, Edith .... (817) 767-8341
Librarian, Wichita Falls Times Record News,
Wichita Falls, TX

Busche, Linda .... (217) 446-1000
EDU ED
Danville Commercial News, Danville, IL

Busemeyer, Steve .... (970) 824-7031
ED, EPE
Northwest Colorado Daily Press, Craig, CO

Bush, Dan .... (405) 475-3311
Automotive ED, BUS ED
Daily Oklahoman, Oklahoma City, OK

Bush, Don .... (812) 522-4871
PROD SUPT, Tribune, Seymour, IN

Bush, Fred .... (614) 592-6612
TREAS, ASST PUB
Athens Messenger, Athens, OH

Bush, G Kenner .... (614) 592-6612
PRES, PUB, Athens Messenger, Athens, OH

Bush, Jennie Ray .... (614) 592-6612
SEC, Athens Messenger, Athens, OH

Bush, Jim .... (317) 482-4650
City ED, Reporter, Lebanon, IN

Bush, Kent .... (405) 224-2600
MAN ED
Chickasha Daily Express, Chickasha, OK

Bush, Lillie Cates .... (903) 537-2228
ED
Mt. Vernon Optic-Herald, Mount Vernon, TX

Bush, Michael .... (405) 782-3321
PUB, ED, Mangum Star-News, Mangum, OK

Bush, Mike .... (505) 622-7710
MAN ED
Roswell Daily Record, Roswell, NM

Bush, Richard .... (803) 771-6161
Sports ED, State, Columbia, SC

Bush, Susan A .... (504) 635-3366
ED
St. Francisville Democrat, St. Francisville, LA

Bush, Suzanne .... (215) 855-8440
PRES, PUB, Reporter, Landsdale, PA

Bush, Toebe .... (909) 793-3221
PUB, Redlands Daily Facts, Redlands, CA

Busha, Mary .... (505) 325-4545
MAN ED, Daily Times, Farmington, NM

Bushaw, Julie .... (719) 254-3351
News ED
Rocky Ford Daily Gazette, Rocky Ford, CO

Bushee, Ward .... (702) 788-6200
EX ED, Reno Gazette-Journal, Reno, NV

Bushey, Ed .... (516) 843-2020
PROD MGR-Electronic SYS
Newsday, Melville, NY

Bushey, Pat .... (541) 885-4410
MAN ED
Herald and News, Klamath Falls, OR

Bushman, Ed .... (815) 625-3600
ADV DIR, Daily Gazette, Sterling, IL

Bushman, Larry D .... (515) 573-2141
PUB/GM, Messenger, Fort Dodge, IA

Bushnell, Cheryl Cross .... (520) 297-1107
ED, Inside Tucson Business, Tucson, AZ

Busick, Ron .... (818) 962-8811
ADV MGR-CLASS, San Gabriel Valley
Tribune, West Covina, CA, MediaNews Inc.

Busk, Celeste .... (312) 321-3000
Features Reporter, Sun-Times, Chicago, IL

Busler, Joe .... (609) 663-6000
BUS Writer, Courier-Post, Cherry Hill, NJ

Buss, Ted .... (817) 767-8341
BUS/Oil ED, Wichita Falls Times Record
News, Wichita Falls, TX

Buss, Tim .... (205) 766-3434
Graphics ED
Florence Times Daily, Florence, AL

Bussam, Joseph .... (212) 210-2100
PROD MGR-Security
New York Daily News, New York, NY

Busser, Jerry .... (219) 933-3200
PROD FRM-SYS ADM, Times, Munster, IN

Bussey, Bill .... (864) 224-4321
PROD MGR-INFO SYS
Anderson Independent-Mail, Anderson, SC

Bussey, Evan Z .... (803) 577-7111
ASST to EX ED
Post and Courier, Charleston, SC

Bussey, John .... (212) 416-2000
ED-Foreign
Wall Street Journal, New York, NY

Bustamante, John .... (216) 791-7600
PUB, Call and Post, Cleveland, OH

Bustamante, Kamala .... (614) 224-8123
GM, Columbus Call and Post, Columbus, OH

Bustard III, Clarke .... (804) 649-6000
Music Writer
Richmond Times-Dispatch, Richmond, VA

Bustos, Aida .... (619) 299-3131
MET ED-Night
San Diego Union-Tribune, San Diego, CA

Bustos, Tony .... (602) 271-8000
Art DIR, Arizona Republic, Phoenix, AZ

Bustraan, James .... (954) 356-4000
VP-Circulation, CIRC VP/DIR
Sun-Sentinel, Fort Lauderdale, FL

Butala, Rebecca .... (310) 230-3400
Library CNR, Allsport Photography USA,
Pacific Palisades, CA

Butcher, Diana .... (801) 237-2800
ADV MGR-CLASS/Display
Newspaper Agency Corp., Salt Lake City, UT

Butcher, Jack .... (813) 259-7711
PUB/Chairman, Tampa Tribune and Times,
Tampa, FL, Media General Inc.

Butcher, Jim .... (918) 335-8200
BUS/FIN ED
Examiner-Enterprise, Bartlesville, OK

Butcher, Len .... (702) 871-6780
ED, CityLife, Las Vegas, NV

Butcher, Stuart .... (316) 431-4100
MAN ED, BUS/FIN ED, News ED, Travel ED
Chanute Tribune, Chanute, KS

Butera, Lesa .... (717) 829-7100
ADV MGR-RT, Times Leader, Wilkes-Barre, PA

Butler, A L .... (213) 487-7514
PUB
B'nai B'rith Messenger, Los Angeles, CA

Butler, Bettye .... (703) 878-8000
ADV MGR-CLASS
Potomac News, Woodbridge, VA

Butler, Bob .... (213) 857-6600
PROD MGR, Daily Variety, Los Angeles, CA

Butler, Carolyn .... (704) 375-2121
PUB, Creative Loafing, Charlotte, NC

Butler, Charles .... (207) 791-6650
PROD OPER Camera MGR-Nights
Portland Press Herald, Portland, ME

Butler, Charles I .... (814) 371-4200
PROD FRM-COMP, Courier-Express/Tri-County Sunday, Du Bois, PA

But Who's Where-34

Butler, Chuck .... (916) 885-5656
Automotive ED, RE ED
Auburn Journal, Auburn, CA
Butler, David A .... (704) 588-2453
PRES, RMS Syndication, Charlotte, NC
Butler, Elizabeth .... (912) 244-1880
Society ED
Valdosta Daily Times, Valdosta, GA
Butler, Gary .... (816) 271-8500
ADTX MGR, PROD SUPT-Pre Press
St. Joseph News-Press, St. Joseph, MO
Butler, Jim .... (409) 776-4444
Entertainment/Amusements ED, Radio/
Television ED, Eagle, Bryan, TX
Butler, Jim .... (318) 487-6397
MAN ED
Alexandria Daily Town Talk, Alexandria, LA
Butler, Jonathan .... (919) 732-2171
ED
News of Orange County, Hillsborough, NC
Butler, Kate .... (619) 299-3131
BUS ED-Day
San Diego Union-Tribune, San Diego, CA
Butler, Kateri .... (213) 465-9909
MAN ED, LA Weekly, Los Angeles, CA
Butler, Laura .... (604) 426-5201
CIRC DIR, Daily Townsman, Cranbrook, BC
Butler, Lisa .... (509) 925-1414
Reporter, Daily Record, Ellensburg, WA
Butler Jr, Lorenza P .... (713) 527-8261
PUB, Houston Informer & Texas Freeman,
Houston, TX
Butler, Melissa .... (501) 234-5130
MAN ED, Banner-News, Magnolia, AR
Butler, Robert W .... (816) 234-4141
Films/Theater ED
Kansas City Star, Kansas City, MO
Butler, Ross .... (403) 235-7100
VP-FIN, Calgary Herald, Calgary, AB
Butler, Ruth .... (616) 222-5400
Television ED
Grand Rapids Press, Grand Rapids, MI
Butler, Scott .... (864) 224-4321
City ED
Anderson Independent-Mail, Anderson, SC
Butler, Sharon .... (602) 386-4426
PUB, ED
Buckeye Valley News, Buckeye, AZ
Butler, Sharon .... (904) 435-8500
ADV MGR-Inside Sales, ADTX MGR
Pensacola News Journal, Pensacola, FL
Butler, Shaun M .... (617) 426-3000
VP-Advertising, Boston Herald, Boston, MA
Butler, Stan .... (613) 342-4441
CIRC MGR, Brockville Recorder and Times,
Brockville, ON
Butrum, Carol .... (317) 633-1240
CIRC MGR-State
Indianapolis Star/News, Indianapolis, IN
Butson, Elizabeth .... (212) 229-1890
PUB, Villager, New York, NY
Butson, Thomas G .... (212) 229-1890
ED, Villager, New York, NY
Butt, Debbye .... (501) 836-8192
DP MGR, Camden News, Camden, AR
Butt, Michael .... (317) 462-5528
ADV MGR-Commercial Sales
Daily Reporter, Greenfield, IN
Buttars, Lori .... (801) 237-2031
Radio/Television ED
Salt Lake Tribune, Salt Lake City, UT
Buttel, Tom .... (312) 222-3232
CIRC DIR-Consumer Sales/SRV
Chicago Tribune, Chicago, IL
Butters, Brian .... (250) 372-2331
PUB/PRES
Kamloops Daily News, Kamloops, BC
Butters, John .... (409) 722-0479
PUB, Mid County Chronicle, Nederland, TX
Butterworth, John .... (541) 929-3043
ED, Benton Bulletin, Philomath, OR
Butterworth, Leah .... (609) 935-1500
Environmental ED, Health/Medical ED
Today's Sunbeam, Salem, NJ
Butterworth, Steve .... (334) 347-9533
Sports ED
Enterprise Ledger, Enterprise, AL
Buttgen, Bob .... (219) 894-3102
ED, Advance-Leader, Ligonier, IN
Button, Don .... (604) 826-6221
PUB, ED, Mission City Record, Mission, BC
Button, Janet .... (818) 234-4368
GM, Community Herald, Cobleskill, NY
Button, Margaret .... (413) 663-3741
City ED
North Adams Transcript, North Adams, MA
Button, Scott .... (416) 494-4990
ED, Daily Commercial News and Construction
Record, N. York, ON

Butts, Kenny .... (919) 419-6500
PROD MGR-Nightside Press
Herald-Sun, Durham, NC
Butts, Willie .... (919) 708-9000
Librarian, Sanford Herald, Sanford, NC
Buxie, Ann .... (520) 445-3333
TREAS, Daily Courier, Prescott, AZ
Buxton, Bob .... (541) 382-1811
News ED, Bulletin, Bend, OR
Buxton, Chuck .... (707) 546-2020
ASST MAN ED
Press Democrat, Santa Rosa, CA
Buxton, Jerry .... (316) 357-8316
GM, ED, Jetmore Republican, Jetmore, KS
Buxton, Steve .... (719) 336-2266
PROD FRM-PR, Daily News, Lamar, CO
Buyer, Robert .... (716) 849-3434
Farm ED, Buffalo News, Buffalo, NY
Buys, Michelle .... (517) 278-2318
CONT, Daily Reporter, Coldwater, MI
Buys, Richard M .... (801) 654-1471
PUB, Wasatch Wave, Heber City, UT
Buys, Susan F .... (801) 336-5501
PUB, Summit County Bee, Coalville, UT
Buzinski, Jim .... (562) 435-1161
Sports ED, Press-Telegram, Long Beach, CA
Buzzerd, James S .... (301) 678-6255
PUB, Hancock News, Hancock, MD
Buzzerd, James Warren ..... (304) 258-1800
PUB, ED
Morgan Messenger, Berkeley Springs, WV
Buzzerd, Sandy .... (301) 678-6255
GM, Hancock News, Hancock, MD
Buzzetta, John .... (903) 567-4000
PUB, Canton Herald, Canton, TX
Byans, Bill .... (815) 937-3300
Outdoors ED, Daily Journal, Kankakee, IL
Byar, Rob .... (403) 429-5400
ADV MGR-RT Sales/Territory Accounts
Edmonton Journal, Edmonton, AB
Byard, Wayde .... (540) 667-3200
ASST MAN ED
Winchester Star, Winchester, VA
Byars, Thad .... (817) 634-2125
ADV DIR, Killeen Daily Herald, Killeen, TX
Bybee, Rick .... (309) 647-5100
CIRC MGR, Daily Ledger, Canton, IL
Bydalek, Leonard .... (815) 937-3300
PROD FRM-Press (Day)
Daily Journal, Kankakee, IL
Bye, Cheri .... (847) 888-7800
ADV SUPV-CLASS, Courier-News, Elgin, IL
Bye, Jimmy .... (812) 424-7711
DIR-Photography/Color Graphic Input
Evansville Courier, Evansville, IN
Byerly, David C .... (406) 538-3401
PUB, Lewistown News-Argus, Lewistown, MT
Byerly, Hanes .... (757) 562-3187
PUB, Tidewater News, Franklin, VA
Byers, Abbe .... (704) 245-6431
Living/Lifestyle ED, Religion ED, Society/
Women's ED, Daily Courier, Forest City, NC
Byers, Fritz .... (419) 245-6000
SEC, Blade, Toledo, OH
Byers, Josh .... (505) 622-7710
BUS/FIN ED, Farm/Agriculture ED
Roswell Daily Record, Roswell, NM
Byers, Karma .... (316) 792-1211
PROD FRM-COMP
Great Bend Tribune, Great Bend, KS
Byers, Larry .... (913) 258-2211
PUB, ED, Herington Times, Herington, KS
Byers, Leslie .... (402) 444-1000
INFO Services MGR-Publishing SYS
Omaha World-Herald, Omaha, NE
Byers, Russell .... (215) 854-2000
COL-News
Philadelphia Daily News, Philadelphia, PA
Byington, Joc Stacy .... (904) 389-4293
ED, Kings Bay Periscope, Jacksonville, FL
Bykofsky, Stuart D .... (215) 854-2000
COL-Features
Philadelphia Daily News, Philadelphia, PA
Byland, John .... (816) 562-2424
BM, Maryville Daily Forum, Maryville, MO
Bynum, Anita .... (205) 259-1020
PRES, PUB, Daily Sentinel, Scottsboro, AL
Bynum, Chris .... (504) 826-3279
Fashion ED
Times-Picayune, New Orleans, LA
Bynum, Larry .... (719) 632-5511
CIRC MGR-Packaging/Distribution
Gazette, Colorado Springs, CO
Bynum, R L .... (910) 227-0131
Copy Desk Chief
Times News Publishing Co., Burlington, NC
Bynum, William .... (205) 259-1020
ED, Daily Sentinel, Scottsboro, AL
Byork, Michelle .... (215) 854-2000
Pagination ED
Philadelphia Daily News, Philadelphia, PA
Byrd, Allen .... (757) 446-2000
PROD MGR-Distribution
Virginian-Pilot, Norfolk, VA

Byrd Jr, Harry F .... (540) 574-6200
PRES, Byrd Newspapers, Harrisonburg, VA
Byrd, Jeffrey .... (601) 843-4241
Sports ED
Bolivar Commercial, Cleveland, MS
Byrd, Jeffrey A .... (704) 859-9151
PUB, GM, Tryon Daily Bulletin, Tryon, NC
Byrd, Joann .... (206) 448-8000
EPE, Seattle Post-Intelligencer, Seattle, WA
Byrd, Thomas T .... (540) 667-3200
PUB, Winchester Star, Winchester, VA
Byrd, Tom .... (704) 333-1718
CIRC MGR
Independent Tribune, Concord, NC
Byrd, Warren .... (501) 968-5252
Sports ED, Courier, Russellville, AR
Byrn, Ann .... (615) 259-8000
Food ED, Tennessean, Nashville, TN
Byrne, A R .... (215) 836-4900
PUB, Irish Edition, Wyndmoor, PA
Byrne, Carol .... (612) 673-4000
Washington Correspondent
Star Tribune, Minneapolis, MN
Byrne, Dennis .... (312) 321-3000
EDL Board Member/EDL Writer
Chicago Sun-Times, Chicago, IL
Byrne, Donald J .... (208) 232-4161
PRES/PUB
Idaho State Journal, Pocatello, ID
Byrne, Eugene .... (419) 238-2285
PROD DIR, Times-Bulletin, Van Wert, OH
Byrne, Gerard A .... (213) 857-6600
PUB, Daily Variety, Los Angeles, CA
Byrne, Jay .... (719) 852-3531
PUB, Monte Vista Journal, Monte Vista, CO
Byrne, Jennifer .... (509) 459-5000
MGR-Community Affairs
Spokesman-Review, Spokane, WA
Byrne, John J .... (619) 873-3535
PUB, Inyo Register, Bishop, CA
Byrne, Rick .... (810) 437-2011
ED, South Lyon Herald, South Lyon, MI
Byrne, Robert A .... (304) 457-2222
PUB, ED, Barbour Democrat, Philippi, WV
Byun, Tom .... (213) 487-5323
ED, Korea Times, Los Angeles, CA
Bzdek, Vince .... (303) 820-1010
Deputy MAN ED-Sunday
Denver Post, Denver, CO

C

Caballero, Raul .... (972) 386-9120
ED, El Sol de Texas, Dallas, TX
Caban, Carlos .... (703) 527-7860
ED, El Tiempo Latino, Arlington, VA
Cabanatuan, Michael .... (209) 578-2000
Automotive ED, Modesto Bee, Modesto, CA
Cabe, Amy .... (406) 587-4491
DIR-MKTG/PROM
Bozeman Daily Chronicle, Bozeman, MT
Cabezas, Alex .... (408) 637-5566
PROD MGR-Packaging Center
Free Lance, Hollister, CA
Cable, Darrell .... (405) 756-4461
GM, Lindsay News, Lindsay, OK
Cable, Dot .... (910) 276-2311
Lifetimes ED, Exchange, Laurinburg, NC
Cable, Meredon .... (405) 756-4461
PUB, ED, Lindsay News, Lindsay, OK
Cable, Merry .... (704) 758-7381
PROD FRM-COMP
Lenoir News-Topic, Lenoir, NC
Cable, Phyllis .... (423) 981-1100
City/MET ED, News ED
Daily Times, Maryville, TN
Cabral, Doug .... (508) 693-6100
PUB, ED, Martha's Vineyard Times, Vineyard
Haven, MA
Cabral, Kim A .... (508) 997-7411
PROD MGR-Distribution
Standard Times, New Bedford, MA
Caccavaro, Dan .... (413) 781-1900
MAN ED
Springfield Advocate, Springfield, MA
Cadden, Ann .... (717) 821-2091
Librarian, Citizens' Voice, Wilkes-Barre, PA
Caddle, Sam .... (707) 546-2020
PROD MGR-Press/Plate
Press Democrat, Santa Rosa, CA
Cadogan, David .... (506) 622-2600
PUB, Miramichi Weekend, Newcastle, NB
Cadogan, Joanne .... (506) 622-2600
MAN ED, Miramichi Weekend
Newcastle, NB
Cady, Dick .... (317) 633-1240
COL
Indianapolis Star/News, Indianapolis, IN
Cady, Jan M .... (308) 423-2337
ED, Benkelman Post and News-Chronicle,
Benkelman, NE
Cady, Tara M .... (206) 597-8742
CIRC ASST DIR, News Tribune, Tacoma, WA
Caen, Herb .... (415) 777-1111
COL
San Francisco Chronicle, San Francisco, CA

Cafaro, Vera .... (860) 442-2200
CONT, Day, New London, CT
Cagle, Charles E .... (918) 258-7171
GM, Broken Arrow Ledger, Broken Arrow, OK
Cagle, Erik .... (609) 451-1000
Sports ED
Bridgeton Evening News, Bridgeton, NJ
Cagle, Frank .... (423) 523-3131
MAN ED, Aviation ED
Knoxville News-Sentinel, Knoxville, TN
Cagle, Shirley .... (817) 387-3811
ADV MGR
Denton Record-Chronicle, Denton, TX
Cagle, Steve .... (313) 994-6989
Fashion/Food ED, Travel ED
Ann Arbor News, Ann Arbor, MI
Cahalan, Bill .... (507) 235-3303
Agriculture Reporter, Religion Reporter
Sentinel, Fairmont, MN
Cahalan, Steve .... (406) 496-5500
City ED, Montana Standard, Butte, MT
Cahalane, T Ray .... (307) 634-3361
TREAS
Wyoming Tribune-Eagle, Cheyenne, WY
Cahill, Greg .... (707) 527-1200
ED
Sonoma County Independent, Santa Rosa, CA
Cahill, Jo Ann .... (540) 669-2181
MGR-CR, PA, Herald-Courier Virginia
Tennessean, Bristol, VA
Cahow, Steve .... (617) 929-2000
CIRC DIR, Boston Globe, Boston, MA
Caimano, Nick .... (518) 792-3131
ADV MGR-Display, Post-Star, Glens Falls, NY
Cain, Chad .... (509) 633-1350
ED, Star, Grand Coulee, WA
Cain, Charles .... (313) 222-2300
Lansing BU Chief, Detroit News, Detroit, MI
Cain, Damon .... (919) 829-4500
Design/News, News & Observer, Raleigh, NC
Cain, Elisabeth .... (415) 777-1111
CONT
San Francisco Chronicle, San Francisco, CA
Cain, Gretchen .... (813) 397-5563
ED, Seminole Beacon, Largo, FL
Cain, Joe H .... (405) 298-3314
PUB, ED, Antlers American, Antlers, OK
Cain, John .... (419) 422-5151
CIRC MGR, Courier, Findlay, OH
Cain, Lewis .... (318) 527-7075
SEC/CONT, Southwest Daily News, Sulphur,
LA, News Leader Inc.
Cain, Linda .... (405) 298-3314
PUB, Antlers American, Antlers, OK
Cain, Lonny .... (815) 433-2000
MAN ED, Daily Times, Ottawa, IL
Cain, Louise .... (405) 889-3319
PUB, Atoka County Times, Atoka, OK
Cain, Steve .... (313) 994-6989
Higher EDU ED
Ann Arbor News, Ann Arbor, MI
Caine, Barry .... (510) 208-6300
Films ED, Oakland Tribune, Oakland, CA
MediaNews Inc. (Alameda Newspapers)
Caines, Isis .... (219) 874-7211
ADV MGR-CLASS
News Dispatch, Michigan City, IN
Caison, Peter .... (919) 829-4500
PROD MGR-Mechanical/Electrical SRV
News & Observer, Raleigh, NC
CaJacob, Peter .... (916) 321-1855
VP-Human Resources
McClatchy Newspapers, Sacramento, CA
Calabrese, Robin .... (941) 574-1110
ADTX MGR
Cape Coral Daily Breeze, Cape Coral, FL
Calabro, Samuel .... (412) 439-7500
CIRC MGR-Distribution
Herald-Standard, Uniontown, PA
Calafati, James M .... (610) 820-6500
PROD MGR-Facilities
Morning Call, Allentown, PA
Calaiacovo, William .... (216) 999-4500
DIR-Labor Relations/Human Resources
Plain Dealer, Cleveland, OH
Calaiacovo Jr, William .... (216) 999-4500
PROD ASST MGR
Plain Dealer, Cleveland, OH
Calame, Byron .... (212) 416-2000
Deputy MAN ED
Wall Street Journal, New York, NY
Calame, Kathleen .... (210) 665-2211
GM, Devine News, Devine, TX
Calcado, Jack .... (516) 843-2020
PROD MGR-Electronic Pre Press
Newsday, Melville, NY
Calchi, Joe .... (609) 691-5000
ADV DIR, Daily Journal, Vineland, NJ
Calder, Ferguson .... (207) 454-3561
PUB, ED, Calais Advertiser, Calais, ME
Calder, Mark .... (613) 342-4441
Farm ED, Brockville Recorder and Times,
Brockville, ON

Copyright ©1997 by the Editor & Publisher Co.

35-Who's Where **Cam**

Calderhead, Robert ... (705) 759-3030
DP MGR, Sault Star, Sault Ste. Marie, ON

Caldwell, Andrew ... (904) 752-1293
ADV DIR, Lake City Reporter, Lake City, FL

Caldwell, Bill ... (417) 623-3480
Librarian, Joplin Globe, Joplin, MO

Caldwell, Bob ... (619) 299-3131
Sunday Insight Section ED
San Diego Union-Tribune, San Diego, CA

Caldwell, Brian ... (519) 894-2231
COL, Record, Kitchener, ON

Caldwell, Don L ... (904) 752-1293
PUB, Lake City Reporter, Lake City, FL

Caldwell, Douglas S ... (219) 866-5111
PUB, Remington Press, Rensselaer, IN

Caldwell, Harold ... (919) 778-2211
ADV MGR-NTL
Goldsboro News-Argus, Goldsboro, NC

Caldwell, Joe ... (615) 259-8800
Auto Racing ED
Nashville Banner, Nashville, TN

Caldwell, Richard ... (573) 335-6611
BM
Southeast Missourian, Cape Girardeau, MO

Caldwell, Robert J ... (503) 221-8327
EPE, Public ED, Oregonian, Portland, OR

Caldwell, Scott ... (972) 542-2631
Sports ED
McKinney Courier-Gazette, McKinney, TX

Caldwell, Thomas ... (603) 934-6560
PUB, ED
Franklin-Tilton Telegram, Franklin, NH

Caldwell, Walt ... (916) 336-6262
PUB, ED
Mountain Echo, Fall River Mills, GA

Cale, Alan ... (919) 823-3106
CIRC MGR, Daily Southerner, Tarboro, NC

Caleca, Vic ... (317) 633-1240
ASST MAN ED-Local News
Indianapolis Star/News, Indianapolis, IN

Calek, Roselyn ... (414) 878-1300
ED, Westine Report, Union Grove, WI

Calender, Jody ... (908) 922-6000
Deputy EX ED
Asbury Park Press, Neptune, NJ

Calhoun, Ken ... (510) 208-6300
DIR-MKTG/PROM SRV, Oakland Tribune, Oakland, CA, MediaNews Inc. (Alameda Newspapers)

Calhoun, Kim ... (770) 287-3798
Graphic Arts
Community Features, Oakwood, GA

Calhoun, Patricia ... (303) 296-7744
ED, Denver Westword, Denver, CO

Calhoun, Rodney ... (209) 734-5821
PROD MGR-PR
Visalia Times-Delta, Visalia, CA

Calhoun, Scott ... (205) 236-1551
MGR-CR, Anniston Star, Anniston, AL

Calis, Raphael ... (202) 898-8254
EX ED
United Press International, Washington, DC

Calka, Charles A ... (410) 822-1500
Chairman, Star-Democrat, Easton, MD

Calkins, Geoff ... (901) 529-2211
Sports COL
Commercial Appeal, Memphis, TN

Calkins, M Teresa ... (810) 766-6100
DIR-MKTG, Flint Journal, Flint, MI

Call, David E ... (801) 835-4241
GM, Manti Messenger, Manti, UT

Call, Max E ... (801) 835-4241
PUB, ED, Manti Messenger, Manti, UT

Call, Mike ... (801) 882-0050
ED, Tooele Transcript-Bulletin, Tooele, UT

Callahan, Bill ... (518) 792-9914
ASST VP-Sales, TV Data, Queensbury, NY

Callahan, David ... (614) 461-5000
PROD MGR-Packaging
Columbus Dispatch, Columbus, OH

Callahan, Jeff ... (918) 581-8300
PROD SUPV-Electrical Maintenance
Tulsa World, Tulsa, OK

Callahan, John ... (704) 437-2161
EDU ED, News Herald, Morganton, NC

Callahan, Loretta ... (360) 694-3391
Environmental ED, SCI/Technology ED
Columbian, Vancouver, WA

Callahan, Patrick ... (212) 944-7744
Chief Photographer, Wagner International Photos Inc., New York, NY

Callahan, Ralph W ... (205) 236-1551
Consultant, Anniston Star, Anniston, AL

Callan, Michael ... (619) 232-4381
ADV MGR-Commercial
San Diego Daily Transcript, San Diego, CA

Callaway, Karen ... (906) 482-1500
ADV MGR-RT
Daily Mining Gazette, Houghton, MI

Callaway, Karen ... (312) 222-3232
Sections ED
Chicago Tribune, Chicago, IL

Callaway, Roy ... (808) 245-8825
PUB, ED, Kauai Times, Lihue, Kauai, HI

Callaway, Wilbur ... (903) 873-2525
ED, Wills Point Chronicle, Wills Point, TX

Callea, Donna ... (904) 252-1511
Television ED, Daytona Beach News-Journal, Daytona Beach, FL

Callen, Bill ... (301) 733-5131
Sports ED, Morning Herald, Hagerstown, MD

Callicott, Blair ... (909) 987-6397
Graphics ED/Art DIR, Photo ED
Inland Valley Daily Bulletin, Ontario, CA

Callinan, Thomas E ... (716) 232-7100
ED/VP, Rochester Democrat and Chronicle; Rochester, NY Times-Union, Rochester, NY

Callow, John ... (615) 893-5860
County Government ED
Daily News Journal, Murfreesboro, TN

Calloway, Larry ... (505) 823-7777
COL, Albuquerque Journal, Albuquerque, NM

Calnan, Christopher ... (540) 949-8213
EDU ED, Religion/School ED
News Virginian, Waynesboro, VA

Calos, Ann ... (716) 439-9222
Women's ED
Union-Sun & Journal, Lockport, NY

Calouette, Tari ... (616) 347-2544
ADV MGR-RT
Petoskey News-Review, Petoskey, MI

Calsbeek, Doug ... (712) 737-4266
ED, Sioux County Capital-Democrat, Orange City, IA

Calsyn, Jamie ... (310) 230-3400
Account EX (East), Allsport Photography USA, Pacific Palisades, CA

Caltabiano, Marcia ... (210) 686-4343
ASST MAN ED, Monitor, McAllen, TX

Calus, Jenifer ... (716) 671-1533
ED, Wayne County Mail, Webster, NY

Calvano, Phyllis ... (212) 556-1234
ASST CONT, New York Times, New York, NY

Calvert, A R ... (306) 692-6441
PUB/GM
Moose Jaw Times-Herald, Moose Jaw, SK

Calvert, Ab ... (306) 692-6441
ADV MGR
Moose Jaw Times-Herald, Moose Jaw, SK

Calvert, Ann ... (619) 487-5757
GM, Rancho Bernardo News-Journal, San Diego, CA

Calvert, Bob ... (306) 565-8211
PUB, Leader-Post, Regina, SK

Calvert, David W ... (619) 487-5757
PUB, Rancho Bernardo News-Journal, San Diego, CA

Calvert, Monty ... (518) 792-3131
DIR-Photography
Post-Star, Glens Falls, NY

Calvert, Rick ... (502) 223-1736
Contact
Community Press Service, Frankfort, KY

Camacho, George ... (800) 995-8626
GM, El Popular - Bakersfield, Bakersfield, CA

Camacho Jr, Raul M ... (888) 588-2272
PUB, ED, El Popular-Fresno, Bakersfield, CA

Camara, Christine ... (360) 452-2345
ASST News ED
Peninsula Daily News, Port Angeles, WA

Cambell, Colin ... (404) 526-5151
COL
Atlanta Journal-Constitution, Atlanta, GA

Cambpell, David ... (219) 933-3200
Sports ED, Times, Munster, IN

Cambra, Tim ... (707) 546-2020
CIRC DIR, Press Democrat, Santa Rosa, CA

Cameron, Allan ... (250) 372-2331
News/Sports ED
Kamloops Daily News, Kamloops, BC

Cameron, Connie ... (206) 627-1103
ED, Seattle Medium, Seattle, WA

Cameron, Dave ... (519) 245-2370
ED, Age Dispatch, Strathroy, ON

Cameron, Helen ... (605) 895-2505
ED, Lyman County Herald, Presho, SD

Cameron, John ... (334) 433-1551
ASST MAN ED-Sports, Sports ED
Mobile Press Register, Mobile, AL

Cameron, Michael ... (802) 388-6366
ED, Valley Voice, Middlebury, VT

Cameron, Mindy ... (206) 464-2111
EPE, Seattle Times, Seattle, WA

Cameron, Neil ... (604) 287-7464
PUB, Campbell River Courier Islander, Campbell River, BC

Cameron, Richard ... (808) 244-3981
PUB, Maui News, Wailuku, HI

Cameron, Robert ... (605) 895-2505
PUB, Lyman County Herald, Presho, SD

Cameron, Shawn ... (315) 393-1000
PROD MGR, Courier-Observer Journal & Advance-News, Ogdensburg, NY

Camfield, Janis ... (806) 376-4488
CIRC MGR-City, Amarillo Daily News/Globe Times, Amarillo, TX

Camilleri, J ... (905) 526-3333
Purchasing, Spectator, Hamilton, ON

Caminita, Michael ... (504) 826-3279
PROD MGR-Pre Press
Times-Picayune, New Orleans, LA

Cammack, Charles ... (219) 881-3000
DIR-Human Resources
Post-Tribune, Gary, IN

Cammack, Charles L ... (208) 527-3038
MAN ED, Arco Advertiser, Arco, ID

Cammack, Donald L ... (208) 527-3038
PUB, ED, Arco Advertiser, Arco, ID

Cammarata, Frank ... (814) 674-3666
PUB, Union Press Courier, Patton, PA

Cammel, Ron ... (330) 699-7051
ED, Lake Leader, Uniontown, OH

Cammuso, Frank ... (315) 470-0011
Cartoonist, Post-Standard/Syracuse Herald-Journal/American, Syracuse, NY

Camp, Becky ... (806) 364-2030
Amusements ED, Brand, Hereford, TX

Camp, Charles ... (214) 977-8222
BUS ED, Dallas Morning News, Dallas, TX

Camp, Charlotte ... (517) 851-7833
PUB, Town Crier, Stockbridge, MI

Camp, Cindy ... (504) 748-7156
ED, Hammond Vindicator, Hammond, LA

Camp, Jim ... (814) 870-1600
Sports ED
Morning News/Erie Daily Times, Erie, PA

Camp, Keith ... (515) 672-2581
CIRC MGR, Herald, Oskaloosa, IA

Camp, Phillip C ... (802) 457-1313
PUB, Vermont Standard, Woodstock, VT

Camp, Ralph ... (330) 747-1471
PROD FRM-COMP
Vindicator, Youngstown, OH

Camp, Robert A ... (205) 734-2131
ADV DIR, Cullman Times, Cullman, AL

Camp, Roya ... (408) 424-2221
ASST City ED, Californian, Salinas, CA

Camp, Tommy ... (706) 884-7311
Sports ED, Daily News, La Grange, GA

Camp, William P ... (209) 847-3021
GM, Oakdale Leader, Oakdale, CA

Campanelli, John ... (216) 245-6901
News ED, Morning Journal, Lorain, OH

Campanie, Ann ... (315) 363-5100
PUB, Oneida Daily Dispatch, Oneida, NY

Campanini, James ... (508) 458-7100
EX News ED, Sun, Lowell, MA

Campassi, Mike ... (706) 278-1011
PROD FRM-COMP
Daily Citizen-News, Dalton, GA

Campbell, Alan C ... (810) 634-8219
PUB, ED, Northwest Oakland County Herald Advertiser, Holly, MI

Campbell, Bill ... (904) 863-1111
COL, Northwest Florida Daily News, Fort Walton Beach, FL

Campbell, Blanche ... (573) 882-5700
CIRC MGR, Missourian, Columbia, MO

Campbell, Bob ... (313) 222-6400
Environmental ED
Detroit Free Press, Detroit, MI

Campbell, Bob ... (419) 245-6000
PROD SUPT-Pre Press, Blade, Toledo, OH

Campbell, Bob ... (407) 242-3500
PROD MGR-PR, Florida Today, Melbourne, FL

Campbell, Bryan ... (716) 328-2144
EX ASST
Syndicated News Service, Rochester, NY

Campbell, Cam ... (915) 387-2507
PUB, Devil's River News, Sonora, TX

Campbell, Carol ... (405) 475-3311
Librarian
Daily Oklahoman, Oklahoma City, OK

Campbell, Charles ... (719) 544-3520
EPE, Radio/Television ED
Pueblo Chieftain, Pueblo, CO

Campbell, Charles ... (602) 257-9300
PUB, Arizona Informant, Phoenix, AZ

Campbell, Charles ... (604) 730-7000
MAN ED, Georgia Straight, Vancouver, BC

Campbell, Charles S ... (319) 285-8111
ED, North Scott Press, Eldridge, IA

Campbell, Chris ... (617) 933-3700
CONT, Daily Times Chronicle, Woburn, MA

Campbell, Chris ... (604) 463-2281
ED, Maple Ridge/Pitt Meadow Times, Maple Ridge, BC

Campbell Sr, Clovis ... (602) 257-9300
ED, Arizona Informant, Phoenix, AZ

Campbell Jr, Clovis ... (602) 257-9300
GM, Arizona Informant, Phoenix, AZ

Campbell, Cole C ... (314) 340-8000
ED, St. Louis Post-Dispatch, St. Louis, MO

Campbell, Coleen ... (403) 345-3081
PUB, Sunny South News, Coaldale, AB

Campbell, Cynthia ... (303) 666-6576
MAN ED, Louisville Times, Louisville, CO

Campbell, Dalmar J ... (209) 966-2500
PUB, Mountain Life, Mariposa, CA

Campbell, Danna ... (319) 372-6421
ADV DIR, Daily Democrat, Fort Madison, IA

Campbell, David ... (715) 365-6397
CIRC DIR, Daily News, Rhinelander, WI

Campbell, Dell ... (816) 234-4141
VP-Circulation
Kansas City Star, Kansas City, MO

Campbell, Don ... (360) 694-3391
Chairman, Columbian, Vancouver, WA

Campbell, Don ... (918) 473-2313
ED
McIntosh County Democrat, Checotah, OK

Campbell, Doug ... (609) 871-8000
CIRC MGR-Distribution
Burlington County Times, Willingboro, NJ

Campbell, Gary ... (705) 759-3030
ADTX MGR, Sault Star, Sault Ste. Marie, ON

Campbell, George ... (520) 573-4220
Copy Chief, Arizona Daily Star, Tucson, AZ

Campbell, Herman ... (615) 259-8000
Cartoonist, Tennessean, Nashville, TN

Campbell, James ... (713) 220-7171
EDL Writer, Houston Chronicle, Houston, TX

Campbell, James B ... (618) 576-2244
PUB, ED, Calhoun News, Hardin, IL

Campbell, Jay ... (404) 843-5000
VP-CIRC, Cox Newspapers Inc., Atlanta, GA

Campbell, Jim ... (360) 377-3711
Automotive Writer, EPE, Religion Writer
Sun, Bremerton, WA

Campbell, John ... (705) 653-3684
ED, Campbellford Herald, Campbellford, ON

Campbell, Judy ... (601) 842-2611
Librarian, Northeast Mississippi Daily Journal, Tupelo, MS

Campbell, Keith ... (214) 977-8222
Universal Desk ED
Dallas Morning News, Dallas, TX

Campbell, Kim ... (918) 335-8200
CIRC District MGR
Examiner-Enterprise, Bartlesville, OK

Campbell, Kristy ... (501) 793-2383
CIRC DIR, Batesville Guard, Batesville, AR

Campbell, Linda ... (561) 820-4100
CIRC MGR-Customer INFO SRV
Palm Beach Post, West Palm Beach, FL

Campbell, Linda ... (573) 336-3711
CIRC MGR, Daily Guide, Waynesville, MO

Campbell, Mark ... (812) 265-3641
ED-Kentucky, Madison Courier, Madison, IN

Campbell, Michael ... (907) 257-4200
ASST MAN ED
Anchorage Daily News, Anchorage, AK

Campbell, Michelle ... (312) 321-3000
Suburban Writer
Chicago Sun-Times, Chicago, IL

Campbell, Mike ... (319) 398-8211
CONT, Gazette, Cedar Rapids, IA

Campbell, Myrna ... (405) 338-3355
ADV MGR-CLASS
Guymon Daily Herald, Guymon, OK

Campbell, Nicole ... (805) 259-1234
EDU Writer, Signal, Santa Clarita, CA

Campbell, Paul ... (423) 756-6900
PROD MGR-PR
Chattanooga Free Press, Chattanooga, TN

Campbell, Paul D ... (816) 858-5154
PUB, Platte County Citizen, Platte City, MO

Campbell, R M ... (206) 448-8000
Classical Music/Dance ED
Seattle Post-Intelligencer, Seattle, WA

Campbell, Ray ... (573) 336-3711
Sports ED, Daily Guide, Waynesville, MO

Campbell, Rebecca K ... (816) 858-5154
PUB, Platte County Citizen, Platte City, MO

Campbell, Rich ... (601) 582-4321
EPE, Hattiesburg American, Hattiesburg, MS

Campbell, Richard E ... (517) 725-5136
PRES/TREAS, PUB, ED, BUS/FIN ED, EPE, NTL ED, Photo ED, Political/Government ED
Argus-Press, Owosso, MI

Campbell, Rick ... (519) 886-2830
PUB, Waterloo Chronicle, Waterloo, ON

Campbell, Robert ... (201) 877-4141
Films Critic, Star-Ledger, Newark, NJ

Campbell, Robert G ... (717) 733-6397
GM, Ephrata Review, Ephrata, PA

Campbell, Ross ... (403) 782-3498
PUB, Lacombe Globe, Lacombe, AB

Campbell, Ruth ... (209) 966-2500
ED, Mountain Life, Mariposa, CA

Campbell, Ruth ... (864) 582-4511
ADV MGR-RT
Herald-Journal, Spartanburg, SC

Campbell, Scott ... (360) 694-3391
PRES, PUB, Columbian, Vancouver, WA

Campbell, Stephanie ... (915) 387-2507
ED, Devil's River News, Sonora, TX

Campbell, Sue ... (612) 222-5011
Senior ED
St. Paul Pioneer Press, St. Paul, MN

Campbell, Susan ... (860) 241-6200
COL, Hartford Courant, Hartford, CT

Cam Who's Where-36

Campbell, Talmage A .... (216) 951-0000
EX ED, News-Herald, Willoughby, OH
Campbell, Terry .... (509) 248-1251
Entertainment ED, Films/ Theater ED, Food ED, Yakima Herald-Republic, Yakima, WA
Campbell, Theresa .... (317) 622-1212
Fashion ED, Herald Bulletin, Anderson, IN
Campbell, Thomas E .... (517) 725-5136
VP/SEC, GM, Argus-Press, Owosso, MI
Campbell, Tom .... (317) 423-5511
Chief Photographer
Journal and Courier, Lafayette, IN
Campbell, Tommy J .... (205) 459-2836
PUB, ED, Choctaw Advocate, Butler, AL
Campbell, Wayne .... (604) 492-3636
ED, Penticton Western News, Penticton, BC
Campbell, Wayne .... (705) 526-5431
PUB, Free Press, Midland, ON
Campi, John G .... (212) 210-2100
VP-PROM/Public Relations
New York Daily News, New York, NY
Campo, Charles .... (207) 990-8000
Librarian, Bangor Daily News, Bangor, ME
Campodonico, Renato .... (562) 235-2902
GM
Europa Press News Service, Santiago, Chile
Campos, Chris .... (510) 783-6111
ED, Daily Review, Hayward, CA
MediaNews Inc. (Alameda Newspapers)
Canaan, Jed .... (212) 223-1821
Sports ED, Entertainment News Syndicate, New York, NY
Canaan, Lee .... (212) 223-1821
ED, Hospitality ED, Entertainment News Syndicate, New York, NY
Canaday, Dick .... (352) 377-2444
ED, Record/Farm d'Ranch, Gainesville, FL
Canaday, Durwood .... (919) 829-4500
ADV MGR-CLASS
News & Observer, Raleigh, NC
Canaday, Tess .... (509) 257-2928
PUB, ED, Sprague Advocate, Sprague, WA
Canady, Hoyt .... (423) 523-3131
EPE, Knoxville News-Sentinel, Knoxville, TN
Canale, Edward .... (916) 321-1000
DIR-MKTG
Sacramento Bee, Sacramento, CA
Canavan, Thomas .... (908) 686-7700
ED, News-Record of Maplewood & South Orange, Maplewood, NJ
Cancino, Phyllis .... (713) 869-5434
Legal ADV DIR
Daily Court Review, Houston, TX
Candor, Andy .... (219) 461-8444
DIR-MKTG SRV
Fort Wayne Newspapers Inc., Fort Wayne, IN
Candy, Joan .... (301) 662-1177
News ED (News)
Frederick Post/The News, Frederick, MD
Caneles, Christopher .... (209) 441-6111
DIR-INFO SYS, Fresno Bee, Fresno, CA
Canepa, Nick .... (619) 299-3131
COL-Sports
San Diego Union-Tribune, San Diego, CA
Canfield, Candida .... (914) 694-9300
ADV DIR-CLASS, Reporter Dispatch, White Plains, NY, Gannett Co. Inc.
Canfield, Monte .... (316) 355-6162
PUB, Lakin Independent, Lakin, KS
Cangi, David .... (201) 945-5597
ED, Bergen Free Press, Ridgefield, NJ
Cangiano, Salvatore .... (201) 945-5597
PUB, Bergen Free Press, Ridgefield, NJ
Cann, Carolyn .... (706) 283-3100
ED, Elberton Star, Elberton, GA
Cannady, Bruce .... (909) 889-9666
CONT, Sun, San Bernardino, CA
Canning, Ming .... (310) 540-5511
Human Resources CNR
Daily Breeze, Torrance, CA
Cannizzaro, Ben .... (201) 646-4000
PROD DIR, Record, Hackensack, NJ
Cannon, Angela .... (615) 893-5860
EDU ED
Daily News Journal, Murfreesboro, TN
Cannon, Bryon .... (317) 664-5111
News ED, Chronicle-Tribune, Marion, IN
Cannon, Carl N .... (904) 359-4111
PUB, Florida Times-Union, Jacksonville, FL
Cannon, Frank .... (423) 246-8121
Senior ED-News, Times-News, Kingsport, TN
Cannon, Joe .... (541) 935-1882
PUB, West-Lane News, Veneta, OR
Cannon, John .... (606) 329-1717
EPE, Daily Independent, Ashland, KY
Cannon, Lisa S .... (504) 926-8882
ADV MGR, Baton Rouge Daily Legal News, Baton Rouge, LA
Cannon, Louise .... (541) 935-1882
PUB, West-Lane News, Veneta, OR
Cannon, Ron .... (202) 334-6000
PROD SUPT-PR (SE)
Washington Post, Washington, DC
Cannon, Russell .... (619) 365-3315
PUB, ED, Hi-Desert Star, Yucca Valley, CA
Cannon, Sue .... (806) 285-2631
PUB, ED, Olton Enterprise, Olton, TX
Cannon, Terry .... (903) 597-8111
Films/Theater ED
Tyler Morning Telegraph, Tyler, TX
Cannon, Theodore B .... (610) 259-4141
ED, Ridley Press, Drexel Hill, PA
Cannon-Sherlock, Robert .... (519) 376-2250
ADV DIR, Sun Times, Owen Sound, ON
Canny, Thomas .... (607) 798-1234
CIRC MGR-Regional
Press & Sun Bulletin, Binghamton, NY
Canody, Tony .... (804) 793-2311
ADV MGR-MIS, MGR-INFO SRV
Danville Register & Bee, Danville, VA
Canright, David .... (219) 926-1131
ED, Chesterton Tribune, Chesterton, IN
Canright, Warren H .... (219) 926-1131
PRES, PUB, Chesterton Tribune
Chesterton, IN
Cantella, Sean .... (702) 788-6200
Market Development
Reno Gazette-Journal, Reno, NV
Canter, Judy .... (415) 777-2424
Head Librarian, Examiner, San Francisco, CA
Cantero, Araceli M .... (305) 758-3399
ED, La Voz Catolica, Miami, FL
Cantiello, Nicholas .... (518) 374-4141
City ED, Daily Gazette, Schenectady, NY
Cantin, Omer .... (705) 372-1233
PUB, ED, Le Nord, Hearst, ON
Cantine, Pete .... (800) 544-4094
GM, Clinton County News, St. Johns, MI
Cantler, Elizabeth G .... (803) 577-7111
ASST MAN ED-Features, Travel ED
Post and Courier, Charleston, SC
Cantler, Mary .... (413) 584-5000
ADV MGR-Ad Production
Daily Hampshire Gazette, Northampton, MA
Cantor, George .... (313) 222-2300
COL, Detroit News, Detroit, MI
Cantor, Steve .... (860) 347-3331
CIRC DIR, Middletown Press, Middletown, CT
Cantrell, Bob .... (334) 262-1611
ADV MGR-Creative Services
Montgomery Advertiser, Montgomery, AL
Cantrell, Jon .... (906) 774-2772
ADV DIR, Daily News, Iron Mountain, MI
Cantrell, Joseph D .... (312) 222-3237
EVP-Publishing, Tribune Co., Chicago, IL
Cantrell, Scott .... (816) 234-4141
Music COL-Classical
Kansas City Star, Kansas City, MO
Cantwell, Josiah .... (910) 343-2000
BUS ED, Morning Star, Wilmington, NC
Canty, Patrick S .... (210) 423-5511
ED, Valley Morning Star, Harlingen, TX
Canty, William .... (502) 597-3115
PUB, ED, Edmonson News, Brownsville, KY
Caouette, Barbara .... (207) 324-5986
GM, Sanford News, Sanford, ME
Capaldini, Mark L .... (202) 898-2300
PRES, Legi-Slate, Washington, DC
Caparell, Tina .... (219) 235-6161
CIRC MGR-Special Publications
South Bend Tribune, South Bend, IN
Capece, Victor .... (202) 334-6000
CIRC DIR-Sales
Washington Post, Washington, DC
Capella, Jaime .... (813) 893-8111
ADV Deputy DIR-Advertising ADM
St. Petersburg Times, St. Petersburg, FL
Capers, Averil .... (508) 793-9100
DIR-RES, Telegram & Gazette, Worcester, MA
Caperton, Frank .... (317) 633-1240
EX ED, Star/News, Indianapolis, IN
Capillo, Joe .... (508) 764-4325
ASSOC ED-News, News, Southbridge, MA
Capitani, Randy .... (802) 464-3388
PUB, Deerfield Valley News, West Dover, VT
Caplan, Irwin J .... (503) 226-1311
ADV MGR-Bid Calls/Public Notices
Daily Journal of Commerce, Portland, OR
Caplan, Jeff .... (817) 387-3811
Sports ED
Denton Record-Chronicle, Denton, TX
Caple, Dean .... (203) 789-5200
Electronic Publishing Graphics ED
New Haven Register, New Haven, CT
Caplinger, Pat .... (417) 256-9191
PA, PROD MGR
West Plains Daily Quill, West Plains, MO
Caplinger, Shelly .... (541) 276-2211
DP MGR, East Oregonian, Pendleton, OR
Capobianco, Patricia .... (508) 626-3800
Design DIR, Middlesex News
Framingham, MA
Capoccia PhD, Victor .... (617) 527-1549
PRES, Twenty First Century Family Syndicate, Newton, MA
Capon, R J .... (902) 426-2811
VP/PSL MGR, Chronicle-Herald, Halifax, NS
Capone, M T .... (516) 798-5100
ED, Massapequa Post, Massapequa Park, NY
Cappellini, Lin .... (412) 439-7500
ADV MGR-RT
Herald-Standard, Uniontown, PA
Cappello, Mary J .... (312) 616-3282
PROD SUPV, Dodge Construction News Chicago, Chicago, IL
Capps, Ian .... (800) 832-5522
PRES, PR Newswire, New York, NY
Capretta, Ronald .... (941) 335-0200
ADV DIR, News-Press, Fort Myers, FL
Capriolio, Carolyn .... (860) 347-3331
Entertainment/Society ED
Middletown Press, Middletown, CT
Caputo, John .... (403) 468-0100
ADV MGR-RT, Edmonton Sun, Edmonton, AB
Caputo, Roland .... (212) 556-1234
PROD Group DIR/Plant MGR-Edison
New York Times, New York, NY
Caputo, Sal .... (602) 271-8000
Music ED-Popular
Arizona Republic, Phoenix, AZ
Caraccio, David .... (619) 442-4404
MAN ED, EPE
Daily Californian, El Cajon, CA
Caraganis, Nicholas .... (508) 458-7100
Travel ED, Sun, Lowell, MA
Caranfa, Dominic .... (806) 762-8844
PROD MGR-OPER
Lubbock Avalanche-Journal, Lubbock, TX
Caravan, Vincent R .... (315) 598-6397
PUB, ED, Valley News, Fulton, NY
Carberry, John .... (716) 343-8000
Farm/Agriculture ED
Daily News, Batavia, NY
Carberry, Mary Margaret .... (708) 799-6360
Author/Owner
Carberry Columns, Flossmoor, IL
Carbone, John .... (518) 374-4141
DP MGR, Daily Gazette, Schenectady, NY
Carbonelli, Larry .... (616) 754-9301
PRES, Daily News, Greenville, MI
Card, Charles L .... (605) 448-2281
PUB, ED, Britton Journal, Britton, SD
Card, Irene C .... (201) 492-2828
Author
Medical Insurance Claims, Kinnelon, NJ
Carda, Carla .... (402) 462-2131
PROD Ad Services
Hastings Tribune, Hastings, NE
Carden, Barry .... (502) 926-0123
CIRC MGR-OPER
Messenger-Inquirer, Owensboro, KY
Carden, Virgil .... (212) 416-2000
PROD DIR-Communications Network SRV
Wall Street Journal, New York, NY
Cardenas, Alfredo .... (512) 527-3261
MAN ED, Enterprise, Hebbronville, TX
Cardenas, Brigido .... (210) 775-1551
PROD SUPV-COMP Room
Del Rio News-Herald, Del Rio, TX
Cardenas, Susie D .... (210) 736-4450
Accountant
Daily Commercial Recorder, San Antonio, TX
Cardinale, John .... (510) 462-4160
Sports ED, Valley Times, Pleasanton, CA
Cardinali, Jose .... (212) 684-5656
ED, Noticias del Mundo, New York, NY
Cardon, Frank .... (716) 232-7100
News ED-Times-Union
Rochester Democrat and Chronicle; Rochester, NY Times-Union, Rochester, NY
Cardoza, Clifford A .... (408) 637-6300
GM, Pinnacle, Hollister, CA
Cardwell, Eric .... (604) 378-4241
PUB
Weekend News Advertiser, Merritt, BC
Cardwell, Jewell .... (330) 996-3000
COL-Local
Akron Beacon Journal, Akron, OH
Cardwell, Joel .... (803) 577-7111
ADV MGR-NTL/Major Accounts
Post and Courier, Charleston, SC
Careins, Danny .... (765) 674-0070
MAN ED
Twin City Journal-Reporter, Gas City, IN
Carew, Robert .... (414) 922-8640
PUB, Action Advertiser/Action Sunday, Fond du Lac, WI
Carey, Bob .... (403) 343-2400
ADV MGR-RT
Red Deer Advocate, Red Deer, AB
Carey, George B .... (317) 832-2443
VP, BM, PA, PROD FRM-COMP, PROD FRM-PR, Daily Clintonian, Clinton, IN
Carey, George L .... (317) 832-2443
PRES, PUB, COL
Daily Clintonian, Clinton, IN
Carey, James M .... (802) 863-3441
PRES, PUB
Burlington Free Press, Burlington, VT
Carey, Jay .... (937) 382-2574
ED, Wilmington News Journal
Wilmington, OH
Carey, Jinanne S .... (317) 832-2443
ED, Daily Clintonian, Clinton, IN
Carey, Kim .... (860) 489-3121
ADV MGR-RT
Register Citizen, Torrington, CT
Carey, Michael J .... (907) 257-4200
EPE, Anchorage Daily News, Anchorage, AK
Carey, Mike .... (914) 341-1100
Chief Photographer
Times Herald-Record, Middletown, NY
Carey, Patty .... (605) 692-6271
CIRC MGR
Brookings Register, Brookings, SD
Carey, Renee .... (614) 532-1441
MAN ED, Ironton Tribune, Ironton, OH
Carey, Susan .... (312) 750-4000
Deputy News BU Chief, Wall Street Journal-Central Edition, Chicago, IL
Carey, Tom .... (317) 459-3121
Living Section ED, Travel ED
Kokomo Tribune, Kokomo, IN
Carey, Vince .... (215) 855-8440
Sports ED, Reporter, Landsdale, PA
Cargill, Mrs J P .... (501) 793-2383
VP, Batesville Guard, Batesville, AR
Caricaburn, Linda .... (406) 791-1444
City ED, Great Falls Tribune, Great Falls, MT
Carillo, Maria .... (540) 374-5000
City ED, Free Lance-Star, Fredericksburg, VA
Carini, Frank .... (617) 395-3680
ED, Medford Citizen, Medford, MA
Carlberg, Don .... (219) 235-6161
PROD MGR-Press OPER
South Bend Tribune, South Bend, IN
Carlderg, Stan .... (209) 634-9141
Sports ED, Turlock Journal, Turlock, CA
Carle, Jack .... (419) 352-4611
Sports ED
Sentinel-Tribune, Bowling Green, OH
Carle, Jack .... (201) 838-9000
ED, Suburban Trends, Butler, NJ
Carle, Julie .... (419) 352-4611
Farm/Agriculture ED
Sentinel-Tribune, Bowling Green, OH
Carleton, Elizabeth .... (916) 397-2601
PUB, ED
Butte Valley-Lost River Star, Dorris, CA
Carletta, Dennis .... (212) 210-2100
CIRC MGR-Home Delivery
New York Daily News, New York, NY
Carley, Thomas .... (212) 556-1234
DIR-Database MKTG
New York Times, New York, NY
Carli, Gilles .... (514) 985-3333
SEC, Le Devoir, Montreal, QC
Carlic, Steve .... (315) 470-0011
Sports ED, Post-Standard/Syracuse Herald-Journal/American, Syracuse, NY
Carlile, Amy .... (602) 271-8000
Specialty Publications MGR
Arizona Republic, Phoenix, AZ
Carlile, Olga Gize .... (815) 232-1171
ASST MAN ED
Journal-Standard, Freeport, IL
Carlin, David .... (603) 882-2741
CIRC MGR-Home Delivery
Telegraph, Nashua, NH
Carlin, Joan .... (505) 823-7777
Visuals (Photo and Graphics)
Albuquerque Tribune, Albuquerque, NM
Carlin, Karol .... (814) 827-3634
CIRC MGR, DP MGR
Titusville Herald, Titusville, PA
Carlin, Marge .... (303) 892-5000
Books ED, Rocky Mountain News, Denver, CO
Carlin, Sandi .... (519) 537-2341
CIRC MGR, Sentinel-Review, Woodstock, ON
Carlinsky, Dan .... (212) 861-2526
DIR, Carlinsky Features, New York, NY
Carlisle, Donald .... (601) 684-2421
PROD SUPT
Enterprise-Journal, McComb, MS
Carlisle, Kate .... (202) 334-6173
MAN ED-Washington, MAN ED-Washington DC, Los Angeles Times-Washington Post News Service, Washington, DC
Carlisle, Tamsin .... (212) 416-2000
BU MGR-Calgary
Wall Street Journal, New York, NY
Carlone, Gary .... (520) 573-4400
CIRC MGR, TNI Partners dba Tucson Newspapers, Tucson, AZ
Carlos, Liam .... (212) 556-1234
Group DIR-FIN SRV
New York Times, New York, NY
Carlsen, Folmer .... (507) 634-7503
PUB
Dodge County Independent, Kasson, MN

37-Who's Where **Car**

Carlsen, Randy .... **(507) 634-7503**
ED, Dodge County Independent, Kasson, MN

Carlson, Brett .... **(206) 584-5818**
PUB, Northwest Guardian, Tacoma, WA

Carlson, Carol .... **(617) 933-3700**
MGR-CR
Daily Times Chronicle, Woburn, MA

Carlson, Cliff .... **(708) 445-0700**
PUB, Irish American News, Oak Park, IL

Carlson, Deborah .... **(415) 777-5700**
ADV DIR-CLASS, San Francisco Newspaper Agency, San Francisco, CA

Carlson, Fred .... **(203) 789-5200**
ADV MGR-Co-op, ADTX MGR
New Haven Register, New Haven, CT

Carlson, Gunnar .... **(616) 722-3161**
ED, Muskegon Chronicle, Muskegon, MI

Carlson, Jerry .... **(209) 441-6111**
PROD MGR-Pre Press
Fresno Bee, Fresno, CA

Carlson, Jill .... **(810) 985-7171**
Features ED
Times Herald, Port Huron, MI

Carlson, John .... **(317) 747-5700**
Aviation ED, COL, Star Press, Muncie, IN

Carlson, Joyce .... **(604) 485-5313**
PUB, Powell River Peak, Powell River, BC

Carlson, Katie .... **(904) 252-1511**
DIR-PROM, Daytona Beach News-Journal, Daytona Beach, FL

Carlson, Laurie V .... **(808) 528-1475**
PUB, Honolulu Weekly, Honolulu, HI

Carlson, Leigh .... **(508) 586-7200**
Automotive ED, Enterprise, Brockton, MA

Carlson, Linda .... **(315) 337-4000**
ADV MGR-CLASS, Daily Sentinel, Rome, NY

Carlson, Lori .... **(815) 942-3221**
CIRC MGR, Daily Herald, Morris, IL

Carlson, Louis .... **(715) 394-4411**
PROD FRM-PR, Daily Telegram, Superior, WI

Carlson, Lowell .... **(319) 872-4159**
ED, Bellevue Herald-Leader, Bellevue, IA

Carlson, Lynn Sweatt .... **(910) 754-6890**
ED, Brunswick Beacon, Shallotte, NC

Carlson, Mark L .... **(701) 776-5252**
PUB, ED, Pierce County Tribune, Rugby, ND

Carlson, Mary .... **(414) 542-2501**
ADV SUPV-CLASS
Waukesha County Freeman, Waukesha, WI

Carlson, Patricia W .... **(320) 255-8700**
DIR-Human Resources
St. Cloud Times, St. Cloud, MN

Carlson, Robert C .... **(313) 222-6400**
ADV VP, Detroit Newspapers, Detroit, MI

Carlson, Roger .... **(714) 642-4321**
Sports ED, Daily Pilot, Costa Mesa, CA

Carlson, Ron .... **(616) 792-2271**
PUB, Penasee Globe, Wayland, MI

Carlson, Stuart .... **(414) 224-2000**
Cartoonist
Milwaukee Journal Sentinel, Milwaukee, WI

Carlton, A C .... **(318) 559-2750**
PUB, ED
Banner-Democrat, Lake Providence, LA

Carlton, Bob .... **(205) 325-2222**
Films/Theater ED
Birmingham News, Birmingham, AL

Carlton, Flint .... **(614) 345-4053**
Photo ED, Advocate, Newark, OH

Carlton, Natalie .... **(619) 324-1503**
PRES
BONAT's Diversified, Palm Springs, CA

Carlton, Teresa .... **(619) 324-1503**
VP/SEC
BONAT's Diversified, Palm Springs, CA

Carman, Diane .... **(303) 820-1010**
Entertainment ED, Denver Post, Denver, CO

Carman, John .... **(415) 777-1111**
Radio/Television ED
San Francisco Chronicle, San Francisco, CA

Carmean, Michael .... **(330) 996-3000**
PROD DIR-Converging Technologies
Akron Beacon Journal, Akron, OH

Carmen, Angela .... **(703) 276-3400**
CIRC GM-San Francisco, USA Today, Arlington, VA

Carmen, Diane .... **(603) 436-1800**
PROD FRM-COMP Room
Portsmouth Herald, Portsmouth, NH

Carmen, Krystal .... **(918) 335-8200**
Religion ED
Examiner-Enterprise, Bartlesville, OK

Carmichael, Carole .... **(206) 464-2111**
ASST MAN ED-News
Seattle Times, Seattle, WA

Carmichael, Susan .... **(501) 234-5130**
ADV DIR, Banner-News, Magnolia, AR

Carmicino, Maria .... **(212) 455-4000**
MAN ED, North America Syndicate, King Features Syndicate Inc., New York, NY

Carmines, Daniel .... **(210) 896-7000**
CIRC MGR
Kerrville Daily Times, Kerrville, TX

Carmody, John .... **(202) 334-6000**
Television COL (Style)
Washington Post, Washington, DC

Carmody, Kevin .... **(773) 586-8800**
Health/Environment Writer
Daily Southtown, Chicago, IL

Carnahan, John .... **(937) 878-3993**
ADV DIR, Daily Herald, Fairborn, OH

Carnes, Gayle .... **(520) 385-2266**
ED, San Manuel Miner, San Manuel, AZ

Carnes, George .... **(702) 289-4491**
PUB, Ely Daily Times, Ely, NV

Carnes, James .... **(520) 385-2266**
PUB, San Manuel Miner, San Manuel, AZ

Carnes, Mindy .... **(614) 446-2342**
ED, Tri-County News, Mason, WV

Carnes, Toni .... **(417) 472-3100**
GM, Newton County News, Granby, MO

Carnevale, Carol .... **(561) 820-3800**
News ED
Palm Beach Daily News, Palm Beach, FL

Carney, Greg .... **(617) 786-7000**
PROD FRM-PR, Patriot Ledger, Quincy, MA

Carney, Henry .... **(601) 892-2581**
PUB, ED, Meteor, Crystal Springs, MS

Carney Jr, John H .... **(601) 587-2781**
PUB, ED
Lawrence County Press, Monticello, MS

Carney, Marilyn J .... **(402) 786-2344**
PUB, ED, News, Waverly, NE

Carney, Tom .... **(515) 284-8000**
Health/Medical Reporter
Des Moines Register, Des Moines, IA

Carney, Zean E .... **(402) 367-3054**
PUB, ED, Banner-Press, David City, NE

Carnicelli, Teri .... **(602) 972-6101**
MAN ED
Arrowhead Ranch Independent, Sun City, AZ

Carnot, Karen .... **(408) 423-4242**
ADV DIR
Santa Cruz County Sentinel, Santa Cruz, CA

Carnot, Rosa .... **(210) 225-7411**
ADV MGR-RT
San Antonio Express-News, San Antonio, TX

Carolan, Kevin .... **(520) 458-9440**
Sports ED
Sierra Vista Herald, Sierra Vista, AZ
Wick Communications

Carolla, Tony .... **(209) 943-6397**
DP MGR, Record, Stockton, CA

Caron, Glen .... **(507) 537-1551**
CIRC MGR, Independent, Marshall, MN

Carothers, Robert .... **(812) 372-7811**
CONT, Republic, Columbus, IN

Carothers, Tim .... **(206) 448-8000**
CIRC MGR-Home Delivery
Seattle Post-Intelligencer, Seattle, WA

Carpenter, Bryan .... **(815) 625-3600**
Photo ED, Daily Gazette, Sterling, IL

Carpenter, Carol .... **(561) 820-4100**
ADTX MGR
Palm Beach Post, West Palm Beach, FL

Carpenter, Cheryl .... **(704) 358-5000**
Deputy MAN ED-Content
Charlotte Observer, Charlotte, NC

Carpenter, Chris .... **(616) 964-7161**
PROD SUPV-Design
Battle Creek Enquirer, Battle Creek, MI

Carpenter, D R .... **(757) 446-2000**
CIRC DIR, Virginian-Pilot, Norfolk, VA

Carpenter, Edwina .... **(601) 365-3232**
GM, ED, Baldwyn News, Baldwyn, MS

Carpenter, Harold G .... **(618) 539-3320**
PUB, ED, Freeburg Tribune, Freeburg, IL

Carpenter, James D .... **(717) 326-1551**
Sports ED
Williamsport Sun-Gazette, Williamsport, PA

Carpenter, John .... **(312) 321-3000**
Suburban Writer
Chicago Sun-Times, Chicago, IL

Carpenter, John .... **(423) 775-6111**
ED, Herald-News, Dayton, TN

Carpenter, Kenneth .... **(904) 747-5000**
ADV DIR, News Herald, Panama City, FL

Carpenter, Kent .... **(409) 985-5541**
CIRC DIR
Port Arthur News, Port Arthur, TX

Carpenter, Maile .... **(910) 343-2000**
Entertainment/Amusements ED, Films/Theater ED, Radio/Television ED, Morning Star/Sunday Star-News, Wilmington, NC

Carpenter, Michael .... **(402) 475-4200**
MGR-MKTG & PROM, ADTX MGR
Lincoln Journal Star, Lincoln, NE

Carpenter, Paul .... **(815) 433-2000**
Farm ED, Photo DEPT MGR, Wire ED
Daily Times, Ottawa, IL

Carpenter, Renee .... **(808) 935-6621**
ADV MGR, Hawaii Tribune-Herald, Hilo, HI

Carpenter, Richard D .... **(719) 742-5591**
PUB, ED
La Veta/Cuchara Signature, La Veta, CO

Carpenter, Ronald .... **(616) 345-3511**
CONT, Kalamazoo Gazette, Kalamazoo, MI

Carpenter, Steve .... **(609) 871-8000**
SUPV-DP, ADTX MGR
Burlington County Times, Willingboro, NJ

Carpenter, Steve .... **(316) 694-5700**
Sports ED, News, Hutchinson, KS

Carpenter, Steve .... **(814) 946-7411**
EPE, Altoona Mirror, Altoona, PA

Carpenter, Todd H .... **(334) 382-3111**
PUB, Greenville Advocate, Greenville, AL

Carpenter, Tom .... **(717) 272-5611**
PROD FRM-COMP, Daily News, Lebanon, PA

Carpenter, Wayne .... **(716) 366-3000**
PROD MGR-SYS/Pre Press
Evening Observer, Dunkirk, NY

Carpentieri, Bob .... **(352) 374-5000**
CIRC MGR-OPER
Gainesville Sun, Gainesville, FL

Carper, Kathy .... **(616) 745-4635**
ED, Lake County Star, Baldwin, MI

Carr, Arthur .... **(617) 593-7700**
Comptroller, Daily Evening Item, Lynn, MA

Carr, Betty .... **(416) 493-4400**
PUB, North York Mirror, Willowdale, ON

Carr, Billy .... **(615) 444-3952**
PROD MGR, Lebanon Democrat
Lebanon, TN

Carr, Bryan .... **(716) 849-3434**
PROD OPER FRM-PR/Paper Handlers
Buffalo News, Buffalo, NY

Carr, Carol .... **(316) 542-3111**
GM, Times Sentinel, Cheney, KS

Carr, Dale .... **(303) 776-2244**
PROD VP/MGR
Daily Times-Call, Longmont, CO

Carr, Danny .... **(212) 930-8000**
CIRC MGR, New York Post, New York, NY

Carr, David .... **(202) 332-2100**
ED, Washington City Paper, Washington, DC

Carr, David B .... **(609) 895-2600**
COO/Sr VP
Goodson Newspaper Group, Lawrenceville, NJ

Carr, David S .... **(218) 435-1313**
ED, Thirteen Towns, Fosston, MN

Carr, Howie .... **(617) 426-3000**
Political COL, Boston Herald, Boston, MA

Carr, Jeff .... **(915) 546-6100**
Design ED, Graphics ED/Art DIR
El Paso Times, El Paso, TX

Carr, Jim .... **(817) 552-5454**
ED, EPE, News ED, Teen-Age/Youth ED
Vernon Daily Record, Vernon, TX

Carr, Ken .... **(208) 745-8701**
PUB, Jefferson Star, Rigby, ID

Carr, Kimberly .... **(403) 986-0860**
ED, Leduc & County This Week, Leduc, AB

Carr, Mark .... **(419) 522-3311**
DP MGR, News Journal, Mansfield, OH

Carr, Mike .... **(704) 864-3291**
Farm/Agriculture ED
Gaston Gazette, Gastonia, NC

Carr, Neil .... **(816) 234-4141**
PROD MGR-Whitepaper
Kansas City Star, Kansas City, MO

Carr, Richard .... **(954) 356-4000**
Stamps/Coins ED
Sun-Sentinel, Fort Lauderdale, FL

Carr, Rob .... **(706) 549-0123**
Photo DEPT MGR, Athens Daily News/Banner-Herald, Athens, GA

Carr, Robert .... **(407) 242-3500**
MGR Training
Florida Today, Melbourne, FL

Carr, Ruth .... **(816) 263-4123**
ED, EPE, Farm ED, News ED, Religion ED, Society ED, Moberly Monitor-Index & Democrat, Moberly, MO

Carr, Steve .... **(360) 676-2600**
PROD MGR-COMP
Bellingham Herald, Bellingham, WA

Carr, Terry .... **(208) 357-7661**
PUB, Shelley Pioneer, Shelley, ID

Carr UASAF, TSgt True .... **(805) 945-5634**
ED, Desert Wings, Lancaster, CA

Carr, Vickie .... **(208) 882-5561**
CIRC MGR
Moscow-Pullman Daily News, Moscow, ID

Carr-Elsing, Debra .... **(608) 252-6400**
Food ED, Capital Times, Madison, WI

Carranco, Rita .... **(915) 653-1221**
ADV SUPV-Inside Sales
Standard-Times, San Angelo, TX

Carrano, Ralph .... **(718) 389-6067**
PUB, ED, Greenpoint Gazette & Advertiser, Brooklyn, NY

Carraway, Larry .... **(407) 242-3500**
PROD MGR-Distribution Center
Florida Today, Melbourne, FL

Carre, Karen .... **(518) 483-4700**
ADV SUPV, Malone Telegram, Malone, NY

Carrelli, Jean .... **(614) 522-8566**
ED, Ace News, Heath, OH

Carreno, Richard D .... **(610) 873-8946**
MAN DIR
Writers Clearinghouse, Downingtown, PA

Carrico, Linda .... **(405) 621-3578**
PUB, ED, Freedom Call, Freedom, OK

Carrico, Loretta .... **(916) 365-2797**
ED, Valley Post, Anderson, CA

Carrier, Jacques R .... **(418) 686-3233**
ADV MGR-NTL CLASS, Le Soleil, Quebec, QC

Carrier, Jerry .... **(215) 854-2000**
News ED-Night
Philadelphia Daily News, Philadelphia, PA

Carrier, Lynne .... **(619) 232-4381**
Government ED
San Diego Daily Transcript, San Diego, CA

Carriere, Denise .... **(819) 449-2233**
PUB, La Gazette de Maniwaki, Maniwaki, QC

Carrillo, Carlos G .... **(212) 505-0288**
PUB, Impacto, New York, NY

Carrillo, David .... **(505) 823-7777**
Presentation (Design & Copydesk)
Albuquerque Tribune, Albuquerque, NM

Carrillo-Rivera, Hildy .... **(619) 357-3214**
ED, Calexico Chronicle, Calexico, CA

Carringer, Weaver .... **(704) 837-5122**
PUB, Cherokee Scout, Murphy, NC

Carrington, James .... **(218) 751-3740**
Sports ED, Daily Pioneer, Bemidji, MN

Carrington, Nick .... **(704) 664-5554**
GM, Mooresville Tribune, Mooresville, NC

Carrol, Jimmy .... **(910) 888-3500**
Home Furnishings ED
High Point Enterprise, High Point, NC

Carrol, Joanna .... **(601) 833-6961**
Women's ED, Daily Leader, Brookhaven, MS

Carrol, Mike .... **(310) 540-5511**
EPE, Daily Breeze, Torrance, CA

Carroll, Chris .... **(715) 842-2101**
Environmental ED, Farm/Food ED
Wausau Daily Herald, Wausau, WI

Carroll, Crawford C .... **(504) 826-3279**
DIR-MKTG
Times-Picayune, New Orleans, LA

Carroll, Doug .... **(703) 276-3400**
BUS/Travel ED, USA Today, Arlington, VA

Carroll, Edward .... **(908) 276-6000**
ED, Westfield Record, Cranford, NJ

Carroll, Edward .... **(804) 633-5005**
PUB, Caroline Progress, Bowling Green, VA

Carroll, Gerald J .... **(319) 539-4300**
PUB, Monona Billboard, Monona, IA

Carroll, James .... **(403) 872-2784**
ED, Slave River Journal, Fort Smith, NT

Carroll, Jennifer .... **(802) 863-3441**
EX ED, Burlington Free Press, Burlington, VT

Carroll, John .... **(910) 891-1234**
PROD FRM-PR, Daily Record, Dunn, NC

Carroll, John .... **(410) 332-6000**
Senior VP/ED, Sun, Baltimore, MD

Carroll, Jon .... **(415) 777-1111**
COL
San Francisco Chronicle, San Francisco, CA

Carroll, Marcia .... **(319) 539-4300**
GM, ED, Monona Billboard, Monona, IA

Carroll, Nancy .... **(504) 826-3279**
ADV MGR-RT, Times-Picayune
New Orleans, LA

Carroll, Noel G .... **(412) 981-6100**
EPE, Herald, Sharon, PA

Carroll, Roger .... **(603) 543-3100**
ADV DIR, DIR-MKTG
Eagle Times, Claremont, NH

Carroll, Sandi .... **(904) 427-1000**
Community ED
Observer, New Smyrna Beach, FL

Carroll, Tamela .... **(423) 482-1021**
ADV DIR, ADTX MGR
Oak Ridger, Oak Ridge, TN

Carroll, Vincent .... **(303) 892-5000**
EPE, Rocky Mountain News, Denver, CO

Carron, Ron .... **(913) 742-2111**
CIRC MGR
Hiawatha Daily World, Hiawatha, KS

Carruthers, Stanley .... **(607) 756-5665**
PROD FRM-COMP
Cortland Standard, Cortland, NY

Carson, Christine .... **(206) 597-8742**
BUS ED, News Tribune, Tacoma, WA

Carson, Clay .... **(501) 378-3400**
ASST MAN ED-SYS
Arkansas Democrat-Gazette, Little Rock, AR

Carson, Don .... **(414) 922-4600**
Graphics ED/Art DIR, Photo DEPT MGR
Reporter, Fond du Lac, WI

Carson, L Pierce .... **(707) 226-3711**
EntertainmentED, Radio/Television ED, Napa Valley Register, Napa, CA

Carson, Richard W .... **(614) 461-5000**
EPE, Columbus Dispatch, Columbus, OH

Carson, Ronald .... **(519) 271-2220**
MAN ED
Stratford Beacon-Herald, Stratford, ON

Car Who's Where-38

Carstens, Rick .... (806) 376-4488
PROD SUPT-Press, Amarillo Daily News/ Globe Times, Amarillo, TX
Carstens, Scott .... (402) 462-2131
PROD MGR-Press
Hastings Tribune, Hastings, NE
Carswell, Shirley .... (202) 334-6000
ASST MAN ED-ADM/Planning
Washington Post, Washington, DC
Carswell, Steve .... (904) 829-6562
ADTX MGR, PROD DIR
St. Augustine Record, St. Augustine, FL
Cart, Doug .... (318) 783-3450
BM, Crowley Post-Signal, Crowley, LA
Cart, Jo .... (318) 334-2128
PUB, ED, Rayne Independent, Rayne, LA
Cart, Walter T .... (318) 334-2128
GM, Rayne Independent, Rayne, LA
Carte, Jamie .... (770) 428-9411
EDU ED, Marietta Daily Journal, Marietta, GA
Carten, Fr, Thomas .... (717) 821-2091
Religion ED
Citizens' Voice, Wilkes-Barre, PA
Carter, A J .... (516) 843-2020
Deputy Sports ED, Newsday, Melville, NY
Carter, Art .... (540) 981-3100
PROD MGR-Distribution
Roanoke Times, Roanoke, VA
Carter, Arthur L .... (212) 755-2400
PUB, New York Observer, New York, NY
Carter, Bob .... (816) 646-2411
Sports ED
Constitution-Tribune, Chillicothe, MO
Carter, Brian .... (508) 632-8000
Sports ED, Gardner News, Gardner, MA
Carter, Brian .... (913) 776-2200
PROD CNR-SYS
Manhattan Mercury, Manhattan, KS
Carter, Calvin .... (214) 428-8958
MAN ED, Dallas Weekly, Dallas, TX
Carter, Catherine .... (817) 390-7400
PROD DIR-OPER (Administrative & Newsprint), Fort Worth Star-Telegram, Fort Worth, TX
Carter, Cathy .... (803) 524-3183
Action Line ED
Beaufort Gazette, Beaufort, SC
Carter, Charles .... (404) 521-1227
MAN ED, Daily Report, Atlanta, GA
Carter, Christine .... (605) 886-6901
DIR-MKTG
Watertown Public Opinion, Watertown, SD
Carter, Cynthia A .... (515) 582-2112
ED, Forest City Summit, Forest City, IA
Carter, Danny .... (912) 888-9300
City ED, Albany Herald, Albany, GA
Carter, Deedie .... (334) 566-4270
ADV DIR, Messenger, Troy, AL
Carter, Dick .... (618) 529-5454
Photo ED
Southern Illinoisan, Carbondale, IL
Carter, Donnie .... (912) 283-2244
BM, MGR-CR, MGR-PROM
Waycross Journal-Herald, Waycross, GA
Carter, Earl .... (423) 246-8121
Photo DEPT MGR
Kingsport Times-News, Kingsport, TN
Carter, Gary .... (800) 424-4747
Technical OPER MGR, Tribune Media Services-Television Listings, Glens Falls, NY
Carter, Gwen Bogh .... (702) 273-7245
PUB, GM, ED
Lovelock Review-Miner, Lovelock, NV
Carter, Howard .... (209) 943-6397
PROD MGR-MR, Record, Stockton, CA
Carter, James E .... (207) 363-4343
PUB, ED, York Weekly, York, ME
Carter, John .... (212) 509-4444
European ED
Market News Service, New York, NY
Carter, Keith .... (619) 322-8889
EPE, Desert Sun, Palm Springs, CA
Carter, Kelly .... (401) 539-0100
ED, Chariho Times, Wyoming, RI
Carter, Ken .... (907) 257-4200
PROD DIR
Anchorage Daily News, Anchorage, AK
Carter, Ken .... (706) 549-0123
CIRC DIR, Athens Daily News/Banner-Herald, Athens, GA
Carter, Kenneth .... (518) 792-9914
VP-BUS Development/CFO
TV Data, Queensbury, NY
Carter, Larry .... (419) 245-6000
PROD FRM-Paperhandler, Blade, Toledo, OH
Carter, Lee .... (419) 625-5500
CIRC DIR, Sandusky Register, Sandusky, OH
Sandusky-Norwalk Newspapers
Carter, Lenora .... (713) 526-4727
PUB, Houston Metro, Houston, TX
Carter, Lucy .... (615) 433-6151
PUB, ED, Elk Valley Times/Observer & News, Fayetteville, TN
Carter, Mark .... (505) 396-2844
Sports ED, Lovington Daily Leader, Lovington, NM
Carter, Matt .... (805) 736-2313
Political ED, Lompoc Record, Lompoc, CA
Carter, Nancy .... (908) 922-6000
CIRC MGR-OPER
Asbury Park Press, Neptune, NJ
Carter, Nickie .... (912) 283-2244
Fashion ED, Food/Garden ED, Society/ Women's ED, Journal-Herald, Waycross, GA
Carter, Ric .... (919) 946-2144
Photo DEPT MGR, Picture ED
Washington Daily News, Washington, NC
Carter, Rich .... (815) 459-4040
News ED, Northwest Herald, Crystal Lake, IL
Carter, Robert C .... (502) 886-4444
PRES, PUB, PA
Kentucky New Era, Hopkinsville, KY
Carter, Rosella .... (904) 634-1993
MAN ED
Jacksonville Free Press, Jacksonville, FL
Carter, Ryan .... (205) 234-4281
CIRC MGR
Alexander City Outlook, Alexander City, AL
Carter, Sammie W .... (910) 285-2178
ED, Wallace Enterprise, Wallace, NC
Carter, Sue .... (540) 638-8801
Librarian
Martinsville Bulletin, Martinsville, VA
Carter, Sue .... (701) 225-8111
Farm ED, Dickinson Press, Dickinson, ND
Carter, Susan .... (423) 472-5041
DP MGR, PROD FRM-COMP
Cleveland Daily Banner, Cleveland, TN
Carter, Tammy .... (504) 826-3279
Radio/Television ED
Times-Picayune, New Orleans, LA
Carter, Tim .... (513) 531-9229
PRES, Carter, Tim, Cincinnati, OH
Carter, W Horace .... (910) 653-3153
PUB, Tabor City Tribune, Tabor City, NC
Carter, Yvonne .... (910) 888-3500
ADV MGR-Major Accounts
High Point Enterprise, High Point, NC
Cartrette, Marti .... (803) 756-1447
GM, ED, Loris Scene, Loris, SC
Cartun, David S .... (520) 432-4400
PUB, GM, Bisbee News, Bisbee, AZ
Cartwright, Caroline .... (505) 983-3303
ADV MGR-CR
Santa Fe New Mexican, Santa Fe, NM
Cartwright, Judy .... (516) 843-2020
Features ED, Newsday, Melville, NY
Carty, Paul .... (814) 238-5000
EPE, Centre Daily Times, State College, PA
Caruba, Alan .... (201) 763-6392
PRES, Caruba Organization, Maplewood, NJ
Caruso, Mark .... (412) 664-9161
ADV DIR, Daily News, McKeesport, PA
Caruso, Michael .... (617) 929-2000
CONT, Boston Globe, Boston, MA
Caruso, Tom .... (203) 333-0161
BUS ED, Connecticut Post, Bridgeport, CT
Caruthers, Theresa .... (561) 287-1550
CONT, Stuart News, Stuart, FL
Carvalhido, Michael .... (212) 930-8000
VP-FIN, New York Post, New York, NY
Carvalho, Deborah .... (510) 935-2525
Radio/Television ED
Contra Costa Times, Walnut Creek, CA
Carvalho, Joe .... (609) 691-5000
PROD MGR-Litho
Daily Journal, Vineland, NJ
Carver, Ann .... (413) 525-6661
ED, Reminder, East Longmeadow, MA
Carver, Linda .... (205) 345-0505
ADV MGR-NTL
Tuscaloosa News, Tuscaloosa, AL
Carver, Louise .... (540) 546-1210
MAN ED
Powell Valley News, Pennington Gap, VA
Cary, Annette .... (509) 582-1500
Arts/Entertainment ED
Tri-City Herald, Tri-Cities, WA
Cary, Bob .... (218) 365-3141
ED, Ely Echo, Ely, MN
Casady, Rita G .... (401) 277-7000
CIRC MGR-MKTG Services
Providence Journal-Bulletin, Providence, RI
Casanova, Joseph E .... (210) 334-3644
ED, Frio-Nueces Current, Pearsall, TX
Casanova de Toro, Dora .... (407) 767-0070
ED, La Prensa, Longwood, FL
Casati, Christopher .... (907) 543-3500
PUB, Tundra Drums, Bethel, AK
Casciano, Debra .... (315) 363-5100
CIRC DIR
Oneida Daily Dispatch, Oneida, NY
Case, Bill .... (360) 694-3391
MGR-Purchasing, Columbian, Vancouver, WA
Case, Ken .... (616) 845-5181
COL, Daily News, Ludington, MI
Case, Lloyd G .... (701) 235-7311
VP, Forum Communications Co., Fargo, ND
Case, Marvin F .... (360) 687-5151
PUB, ED, Reflector, Battle Ground, WA
Case, Phillip .... (502) 227-4556
Amusements ED, EDU ED, Films/Theater ED, Women's ED, State Journal, Frankfort, KY
Casebeer, Michelle .... (402) 645-3344
ED, Wymore Arbor State, Wymore, NE
Casebeer, Sue .... (219) 724-2121
MGR-EDU SRV
Decatur Daily Democrat, Decatur, IN
Casebolt, Barry J .... (319) 566-2687
ED, Lime Springs Herald, Lime Springs, IA
Casebolt, Sara G .... (319) 566-2687
PUB, Lime Springs Herald, Lime Springs, IA
Casell, Robert J .... (716) 849-3434
Senior VP, PROD OPER DIR
Buffalo News, Buffalo, NY
Casella, Billie .... (316) 231-2600
CIRC MGR, Morning Sun, Pittsburg, KS
Casey, Alicia .... (414) 235-7700
ADV Special Sections
Oshkosh Northwestern, Oshkosh, WI
Casey, Carol .... (205) 532-4000
MGR-PROM/RES
Huntsville Times, Huntsville, AL
Casey, Denise .... (209) 688-0521
CIRC SUPV, Advance-Register, Tulare, CA
Casey, Don R .... (320) 255-8700
VP, EX ED, St. Cloud Times, St. Cloud, MN
Casey, Edward D .... (410) 268-5000
EX ED, Capital, Annapolis, MD
Casey, Harry F .... (408) 678-2660
PUB, Soledad Bee, Soledad, CA
Casey, Jay .... (815) 987-1200
PROD CNR, Register Star, Rockford, IL
Casey, Jim .... (312) 321-3000
Police Beat-Days
Chicago Sun-Times, Chicago, IL
Casey, Lola .... (352) 867-4010
ADV MGR-Display
Ocala Star-Banner, Ocala, FL
Casey, Mary Alice .... (614) 373-2121
Copy Desk Chief
Marietta Times, Marietta, OH
Casey, Maura .... (860) 442-2200
ASSOC EPE, Day, New London, CT
Casey, Ron .... (205) 325-2222
EPE, Birmingham News, Birmingham, AL
Casey, Steve .... (216) 999-4500
ADV MGR-Display
Plain Dealer, Cleveland, OH
Casey, Tom .... (219) 726-8141
MAN ED, Farm Supplement ED
Commercial Review, Portland, IN
Casey, William .... (212) 416-2000
CIRC VP, Wall Street Journal, New York, NY
Cash, David .... (541) 276-2211
ED, EPE, East Oregonian, Pendleton, OR
Cash, Margene .... (913) 446-2201
PUB, ED, Clyde Republican, Clyde, KS
Cash, Rick .... (405) 332-4433
ADV MGR, Ada Evening News, Ada, OK
Cash, Wanda .... (704) 859-9151
CIRC DIR, Tryon Daily Bulletin, Tryon, NC
Cash, Wanda Garner .... (409) 265-7411
MAN ED, News ED
Brazosport Facts, Clute, TX
Cashin, Patrick .... (715) 344-6100
VP, Stevens Point Journal, Stevens Point, WI
Cashman, Chris .... (708) 336-7000
ASST MAN ED-SYS/ADM
News-Sun, Waukegan, IL
Cashman III, Louis P .... (601) 636-4545
PRES, PUB, ED, Vicksburg Post
Vicksburg, MS
Casimir, Judy .... (717) 286-5671
Sunday ED, Daily Item, Sunbury, PA
Casner, Charles L .... (616) 429-2400
PUB, Herald-Palladium, St. Joseph, MI
Cason, Ben .... (614) 841-1781
ED, Westerville This Week, Columbus, OH
Cason, Wade H .... (904) 359-4111
PROD DIR
Florida Times-Union, Jacksonville, FL
Casper, Robert .... (313) 222-6400
MGR-HRIS/Compensation
Detroit Newspapers, Detroit, MI
Cassal, Rosemary .... (509) 787-4511
GM, Quincy Valley Post Register, Quincy, WA
Cassavoy, Ed .... (519) 822-4310
MAN ED, Daily Mercury, Guelph, ON
Cassel, William D .... (541) 266-6831
PUB, Canby Herald/Wilsonville Spokesman, Canby, OR
Casselberry, Dick .... (941) 763-3134
ASSOC ED
Daily Okeechobee News, Okeechobee, FL
Cassell, Dana K .... (603) 922-8338
ED, Business Features Syndicate, North Stratford, NH
Cassell, Phillip .... (972) 542-2631
PROD SUPT
McKinney Courier-Gazette, McKinney, TX
Casselton, Valerie .... (604) 732-2111
Life ED, Vancouver Sun, Vancouver, BC
Cassens, Henry .... (815) 756-4841
News ED, Daily Chronicle, De Kalb, IL
Casserly, Joan .... (707) 938-2111
MAN ED, Index-Tribune, Sonoma, CA
Cassidy, Edward L .... (615) 259-8000
DIR-MKTG & Development
Tennessean, Nashville, TN
Cassidy Jr, John H .... (203) 574-3636
SEC, Waterbury Republican-American, Waterbury, CT
Cassidy, Marcia .... (508) 458-7100
City ED, Sun, Lowell, MA
Cassidy, Suzanne .... (717) 255-8100
Religion ED, Patriot-News, Harrisburg, PA
Cassie, Steven .... (508) 249-3535
CIRC MGR, Athol Daily News, Athol, MA
Cassone, Joe .... (360) 754-5400
CIRC MGR-Home Delivery
Olympian, Olympia, WA
Casstevens, David .... (602) 271-8000
Sports COL, Arizona Republic, Phoenix, AZ
Cast, Michael .... (216) 999-4500
PROD Chief ENG
Plain Dealer, Cleveland, OH
Castagneto, Stephen .... (203) 622-1547
DIR-ADM
Cartoonews Inc., Greenwich, CT
Castagnier, Andre .... (514) 264-5364
GM, Gleaner, Huntingdon, QC
Castaneda, Elena .... (360) 377-3711
EDU Writer, Sun, Bremerton, WA
Castaneda, Jaime A .... (619) 740-9561
ED, Hispanos Unidos, Escondido, CA
Castaneda, Lawrence .... (505) 863-6811
PROD SUPT, Independent, Gallup, NM
Castaneda, Tonja .... (303) 659-1141
ED, Brighton Standard Blade, Brighton, CO
Castellano, Gene .... (215) 854-2000
ASSOC ED
Philadelphia Daily News, Philadelphia, PA
Castellano, Peggy .... (714) 835-1234
VP-Human Resources
Orange County Register, Santa Ana, CA
Castelletti, Midic .... (610) 258-7171
Photo DEPT MGR, Express-Times, Easton, PA
Castelli Jr, Edward .... (203) 789-5200
PROD MGR-PR, PROD MGR-Commercial Printing, Register, New Haven, CT
Castellini, Daniel J .... (513) 977-3000
Sr VP-FIN/ADM, E W Scripps Co.
Cincinnati, OH
Casterline, Len .... (610) 622-8800
Automotive ED
Delaware County Daily Times, Primos, PA
Castile, Gordon .... (515) 755-2115
GM, Guthrie County Vedette, Panora, IA
Castillo, Darragh .... (409) 985-5541
Books ED, Music ED, Radio/Television ED
Port Arthur News, Port Arthur, TX
Castillo, Frank .... (505) 622-7710
PROD DIR
Roswell Daily Record, Roswell, NM
Castillo, Lucio .... (210) 423-5511
Sports ED, Valley Morning Star
Harlingen, TX
Castillo, Michael .... (210) 728-2500
PROD MGR-SYS
Laredo Morning Times, Laredo, TX
Castle, Charlie .... (417) 334-3161
Sports ED
Branson Tri-Lakes Daily News, Branson, MO
Castle, John .... (423) 929-3111
MGR-Facilities
Johnson City Press, Johnson City, TN
Casto, James E .... (304) 526-4000
EPE, Herald-Dispatch, Huntington, WV
Castonguay, Bertrand .... (514) 562-2494
GM, L'Argenteuil, Lachute, QC
Castor, Stephen R .... (313) 563-0360
ED, World Press, Dearborn, MI
Castren, Blaise .... (408) 920-5000
Online ED
San Jose Mercury News, San Jose, CA
Castro, Greg .... (619) 322-8889
CIRC MGR-Sales
Desert Sun, Palm Springs, CA
Castro, Kathleen B .... (508) 675-0321
PUB, ED, O Jornal, Fall River, MA
Castro, Lillian .... (352) 374-5000
BUS ED, Gainesville Sun, Gainesville, FL
Castro, Martin .... (209) 582-0471
Environmental ED, Farm ED
Hanford Sentinel, Hanford, CA
Castro, Tony .... (213) 263-5743
MAN ED, Eastern Group, Los Angeles, CA
Castro-Genao, Ceasar .... (904) 264-3200
PROD FRM-COMP, Clay Today
Orange Park, FL

Copyright ©1997 by the Editor & Publisher Co.

39-Who's Where **Cha**

Casuscelli, Michael C .... (317) 664-5111
ADV DIR
Marion Chronicle-Tribune, Marion, IN

Caswell, Bob .... (318) 433-3000
ADV MGR-RT/NTL, Lake Charles American Press, Lake Charles, LA

Caswell, Daniel .... (716) 439-9222
ADV MGR, ADTX MGR
Union-Sun & Journal, Lockport, NY

Catalano, Grace .... (814) 781-1596
ADV MGR-RT, Home Furnishings ED
Daily Press, St. Marys, PA

Catalano, Larry D .... (307) 634-3361
CONT
Wyoming Tribune-Eagle, Cheyenne, WY

Catalini, Jon .... (508) 764-4325
Sports ED, News, Southbridge, MA

Catambay, Anne .... (408) 920-5000
MGR-MKTG Innovations
San Jose Mercury News, San Jose, CA

Catania, Meribeth .... (608) 782-9710
MGR-Human Resources
La Crosse Tribune, La Crosse, WI

Catchings, Bill .... (504) 683-5195
ED, Watchman, Clinton, LA

Cate, Steve .... (617) 929-2000
PROD MGR-Plant (Boston)
Boston Globe, Boston, MA

Cater, Karen .... (206) 464-2111
Copy Desk Chief
Seattle Times, Seattle, WA

Cates, Karl .... (801) 237-2188
Environmental Writer
Deseret News, Salt Lake City, UT

Cates, Max .... (501) 895-3207
ED, News, Salem, AR

Cates, Rich .... (215) 587-4400
PRES, MediaStream, Philadelphia, PA

Catherincchia, Mike .... (810) 332-8181
MGR-CR, Oakland Press, Pontiac, MI

Catherwood, Charles E .... (610) 527-6330
VP/TREAS, Independent Publications Inc., Bryn Mawr, PA

Cativiela, Jean-Pierre .... (916) 458-2121
ED, Colusa County Sun-Herald, Colusa, CA

Catlett, Betty P .... (502) 835-7521
PUB, Sebree Banner, Sebree, KY

Catlett, Robert .... (501) 442-1777
MGR-PROM
Northwest Arkansas Times, Fayetteville, AR

Catlett III, Robert .... (765) 362-1200
CIRC DIR
Journal Review, Crawfordsville, IN

Catlett, Sandra .... (505) 393-2123
CONT, Hobbs Daily News-Sun, Hobbs, NM

Catlett, Tony .... (502) 835-7521
ED, Sebree Banner, Sebree, KY

Cato, James .... (803) 524-3183
ED, EPE, EDL Writer
Beaufort Gazette, Beaufort, SC

Catron, Jim .... (407) 420-5000
PROD MGR-PR/OPC
Orlando Sentinel, Orlando, FL

Catron, Melinda .... (918) 335-8200
CIRC District MGR
Examiner-Enterprise, Bartlesville, OK

Catsimatidis, John .... (212) 986-6881
PUB, Hellenic Times, New York, NY

Catterall, Lee .... (808) 525-8000
EDL Writer
Honolulu Star-Bulletin, Honolulu, HI

Cattles, Sue .... (307) 324-3411
CIRC DIR
Rawlins Daily Times, Rawlins, WY

Caudill, Susan .... (614) 363-1161
PROD FRM-COMP
Delaware Gazette, Delaware, OH

Caudill, Tom .... (606) 231-3100
ASST MAN ED-Local News
Lexington Herald-Leader, Lexington, KY

Caudle, Bob .... (501) 751-6200
Sports ED, Morning News of Northwest Arkansas, Springdale, AR

Caudle, Deena .... (702) 385-3111
DP MGR, Las Vegas Sun, Las Vegas, NV

Caufield, William M .... (610) 696-1775
ED, West Chester Daily Local News, West Chester, PA

Caughey, Bernard W .... (617) 786-7000
ASSOC ED, Patriot Ledger, Quincy, MA

Caughey, Joyce .... (218) 829-4705
DP MGR, Brainerd Daily Dispatch
Brainerd, MN

Caukins, Ann .... (817) 390-7400
ADV MGR-RT
Fort Worth Star-Telegram, Fort Worth, TX

Caulfield, Susan .... (609) 845-3300
News ED, Sunday ED
Gloucester County Times, Woodbury, NJ

Caulkins, David .... (205) 766-3434
CONT, Times Daily, Florence, AL

Caulkins, Jackie .... (309) 647-5100
ADV MGR, Daily Ledger, Canton, IL

Causey, Ron .... (501) 337-7523
PUB, ADV MGR
Malvern Daily Record, Malvern, AR

Cauthen, Marita .... (508) 343-3822
ED, Raivaaja, Fitchburg, MA

Cauthon, Sherri .... (517) 787-2300
TV Magazine, Citizen Patriot, Jackson, MI

Cauthorn, Robert .... (520) 573-4220
Online Contact
Arizona Daily Star, Tucson, AZ

Cavalier, Theresa .... (504) 473-3101
GM, Donaldsonville Chief, Donaldsonville, LA

Cavaliere, Phyllis .... (212) 689-8200
PRES/CEO, Sunday Magazine Network, Metro-Puck Comics Network, New York, NY

Cavanagh, Kevin .... (905) 684-7251
MAN ED, Standard, St. Catharines, ON

Cavanaugh, Douglas J .... (614) 461-5000
MGR-RES, Columbus Dispatch
Columbus, OH

Cavanaugh, Sean .... (303) 776-2244
CIRC MGR-Single Copy Sales
Daily Times-Call, Longmont, CO

Cavanaugh, T Pat .... (805) 237-6060
PUB, ED, County News-Press
Paso Robles, CA

Cavaness, John .... (770) 942-6571
CIRC DIR
Douglas County Sentinel, Douglasville, GA

Cavazos, R Daniel .... (210) 686-4343
ED, Monitor, McAllen, TX

Cavell, William C .... (705) 232-4081
PUB, Enterprise, Iroquois Falls, ON

Cavender, Charlotte .... (304) 348-5140
Fashion ED
Charleston Daily Mail, Charleston, WV

Cavett, Van .... (610) 820-6500
Comment Page ED
Morning Call, Allentown, PA

Cavner, Dixie .... (402) 733-7300
PUB, Bellevue Leader, Bellevue, NE

Cavness, Gayle .... (901) 285-4091
Sports CNR, State Gazette, Dyersburg, TN

Cavone, Joseph .... (908) 922-6000
MGR-PROM, Asbury Park Press, Neptune, NJ

Cavrich, J D .... (814) 946-7411
Photo ED, Altoona Mirror, Altoona, PA

Caw, Margaret .... (614) 927-2991
GM, Pataskala Standard, Pataskala, OH

Caw, T W .... (614) 927-2991
PUB, ED, Pataskala Standard, Pataskala, OH

Cawley, Donald .... (860) 442-2200
Sports ED, Day, New London, CT

Cawley, Kraig .... (412) 834-1151
ADV DIR, Tribune-Review, Greensburg, PA

Cawley, Nancy M .... (314) 426-2222
GM, North County Journal West, Woodson Terrace, MO

Cawley, William O .... (972) 722-5191
ED, Rockwall Journal-Success, Rockwall, TX

Cawood, Hap .... (937) 225-2000
EPE, Dayton Daily News, Dayton, OH

Cawood, Neil .... (541) 485-1234
Television ED
Register-Guard, Eugene, OR

Cawthon, W Herman .... (770) 775-3107
PUB, Jackson Progress-Argus, Jackson, GA

Caylor, Lee .... (703) 276-3400
CIRC GM-Pittsburgh
USA Today, Arlington, VA

Cayon, Jose C .... (718) 507-0832
PUB, ED
El Tiempo de Nueva York, New York, NY

Cazabon, Roger .... (705) 674-5271
MAN ED, Sudbury Star, Sudbury, ON

Cazalet Jr, David J .... (502) 866-3191
PUB, ED
Russell County News, Russell Springs, KY

C Corley, Dan .... (405) 379-5411
MAN ED
Holdenville Daily News, Holdenville, OK

Cearnal, Lee .... (713) 220-7171
City ED-Night
Houston Chronicle, Houston, TX

Ceasar, Brian .... (717) 762-2151
PROD SUPT, Record Herald, Waynesboro, PA

Cease, Don .... (918) 786-9051
MAN ED, Grove Sun, Grove, OK

Cebalt, Steve .... (219) 461-8333
DIR-MKTG/PROM
Journal Gazette, Fort Wayne, IN

Cebula, Judith .... (317) 633-1240
Religion Writer
Indianapolis Star/News, Indianapolis, IN

Cecil, Charles F .... (605) 997-3725
PUB, ED
Moody County Enterprise, Flandreau, SD

Cecil, Jill .... (615) 792-4230
ED, Ashland City Times, Ashland City, TN

Cedar, Diane .... (612) 388-8235
CIRC DIR, Republican Eagle, Red Wing, MN

Cedo, Alex .... (810) 544-0470
Sales MGR, Feature Service Syndicate, Madison Heights, MI

Celek, Chris .... (219) 881-3000
ASST MAN ED, Post-Tribune, Gary, IN

Celeste, Eric .... (817) 390-7400
Life ED, Star-Telegram, Fort Worth, TX

Celino, Joe .... (403) 468-0100
PROD MGR, Edmonton Sun, Edmonton, AB

Celizic, Mike .... (201) 646-4000
COL, Record, Hackensack, NJ

Cellucci, Rita .... (610) 933-8926
ED, Phoenix, Phoenixville, PA

Cembal, Darryl .... (613) 389-8884
PUB, Heritage, Kingston, ON

Cembal, Joseph .... (613) 472-2431
PUB, Land O'Lakes Sun, Marmora, ON

Cembeliste, Basil .... (416) 234-1212
ED, Svitlo, Etobicoke, ON

Centeno, Lourdes .... (212) 807-4600
MET ED, El Diario La Prensa, New York, NY

Center, Bridgett .... (970) 925-2220
ADV MGR-Sales
Aspen Daily News, Aspen, CO

Centers, Joe .... (419) 668-3771
Sports ED, Norwalk Reflector, Norwalk, OH

Centi, Lori .... (814) 643-4040
COL, Daily News, Huntingdon, PA

Centineo, Pete .... (904) 526-3614
Sports ED
Jackson County Floridan, Marianna, FL

Ceppos, Jerry M .... (408) 920-5000
Senior VP/EX ED, EX ED/Senior VP
San Jose Mercury News, San Jose, CA

Cepuch, Martha .... (905) 892-6022
PUB, Pelham Herald, Fonthill, ON

Ceraso, John .... (201) 646-4000
ADV MGR-Co-op, ADTX MGR
Record, Hackensack, NJ

Ceravolo, Thomas N .... (716) 439-9222
GM, Union-Sun & Journal, Lockport, NY

Cerbin, Carolyn .... (800) 245-6536
Special Sections ED
US/Express, Chicago, IL

Cerenzia, Judith .... (509) 765-4561
BM, Columbia Basin Herald, Moses Lake, WA

Cerny, Keith R .... (719) 589-2553
PUB, ADV DIR, Valley Courier, Alamosa, CO

Certain, Geni .... (205) 236-1551
Automotive ED, MET ED, SCI/Technology ED
Anniston Star, Anniston, AL

Cesario, Sergio R .... (212) 869-7038
ED, Folha do Brasil, New York, NY

Cessna, Allen .... (316) 331-3550
CIRC DIR, Independence Daily Reporter, Independence, KS

Cessna, Robert .... (409) 776-4444
Sports ED, Eagle, Bryan, TX

Cevesque, John .... (206) 448-8000
Television ED
Seattle Post-Intelligencer, Seattle, WA

Chaban, Irene .... (212) 674-5508
ED, Nashe Zhyttia, New York, NY

Chabek, Herb .... (864) 224-4321
PROD MGR-Distribution
Anderson Independent-Mail, Anderson, SC

Chace, Carla .... (802) 254-2311
MGR-Office
Brattleboro Reformer, Brattleboro, VT

Chachkes, Karen .... (206) 441-4553
GM, Jewish Transcript, Seattle, WA

Chadwick, Ian .... (705) 445-4611
ED, Enterprise-Bulletin, Collingwood, ON

Chadwick, Sharon R .... (405) 369-2807
PUB, ED, Davis News, Davis, OK

Chaffee, Kevin .... (909) 987-6397
EPE, Inland Valley Daily Bulletin, Ontario, CA

Chaffee, Paul C .... (517) 752-7171
ED, Saginaw News, Saginaw, MI

Chaffee, William H .... (712) 845-4541
PUB, Laurens Sun, Laurens, IA

Chaffee, Mrs William H .... (712) 845-4541
ED, Laurens Sun, Laurens, IA

Chaffin, Cleo .... (405) 229-0132
PUB, MAN ED
Healdton Herald, Healdton, OK

Chaffin, Ken .... (405) 229-0132
PUB, ED, Healdton Herald, Healdton, OK

Chafin, Kathy .... (304) 752-6950
ADV MGR, Logan Banner, Logan, WV

Chagolla, Raymond .... (916) 444-2355
CIRC DIR-Los Angeles CORP Office
Daily Recorder, Sacramento, CA

Chaiken, Michael .... (860) 283-4355
ED, Thomaston Express, Thomaston, CT

Chaimowitz, Ann .... (914) 477-2575
PUB, Greenwood Lake News and West Milford News, Greenwood Lake, NY

Chairez, Margaret .... (619) 337-3400
Cartoonist, Graphics ED
Imperial Valley Press, El Centro, CA

Chalat-Noaker, Nan .... (801) 649-9014
ED, Park Record, Park City, UT

Chalker, Karleen .... (770) 887-3126
ED, Forsyth County News, Cumming, GA

Chalker Jr, Roy F .... (706) 554-2111
PUB, Sentinel, Waynesboro, GA

Chaloner, Clayton .... (204) 773-2069
PUB, GM, ED, MAN ED, Banner, Russell, MB

Chaloner, Jim T .... (204) 546-2555
PUB, ED
Grandview Exponent, Grandview, MB

Chamberlain, Adrian .... (250) 380-5211
Arts/Entertainment Reporter
Times Colonist, Victoria, BC

Chamberlain, D J .... (818) 551-0077
BM
Adventure Feature Syndicate, Glendale, CA

Chamberlain, Don .... (810) 731-1000
ED, Source, Utica, MI

Chamberlain, Jackie .... (909) 684-1200
Librarian, Press-Enterprise, Riverside, CA

Chamberlain, Laura .... (212) 268-2552
GM, Westsider, New York, NY

Chamberlain, Scott .... (602) 271-8000
PROD Unit MGR-Platemaking (Mesa)
Phoenix Newspapers Inc., Phoenix, AZ

Chamberlin, Pam .... (803) 359-3195
ED, Dispatch-News, Lexington, SC

Chambers, Atsuko .... (808) 591-0656
GM, ED, Japanese Beach Press, Honolulu, HI

Chambers, Becky .... (513) 352-2000
ASST MET ED
Cincinnati Post, Cincinnati, OH

Chambers, Bud .... (405) 223-2200
BUS/FIN ED, Political/Government ED
Daily Ardmoreite, Ardmore, OK

Chambers, Fred .... (409) 335-4014
ED, East Bernard Tribune, East Bernard, TX

Chambers, J Gene .... (810) 469-4510
PRES/PUB/CEO, Independent Newspapers Inc. (MI), Mt Clemens, MI

Chambers, Jerry .... (813) 259-7711
News Technology DIR
Tampa Tribune and Times, Tampa, FL

Chambers, Jesse .... (209) 665-5751
PUB, GM, ED
Chowchilla News, Chowchilla, CA

Chambers, Mike .... (815) 625-3600
Lifestyle ED
Daily Gazette, Sterling, IL

Chambers, Patricia .... (301) 662-1177
MGR-VIS, Frederick Post/News Frederick, MD

Chambers, Peter F .... (401) 762-3000
PROD FRM-PR, Call, Woonsocket, RI

Chambers, Steve .... (201) 877-4141
Religion ED, Star-Ledger, Newark, NJ

Chambless, John .... (610) 696-1775
Television/Film ED, Theater/Music ED
Daily Local News, West Chester, PA

Chambliss, Betty .... (941) 748-0411
CNR-MKTG RES
Bradenton Herald, Bradenton, FL

Champ, Vic .... (860) 241-6200
PROD MGR-MR
Hartford Courant, Hartford, CT

Champagne, Karma .... (318) 276-5171
ED, Jeanerette Enterprise, Jeanerette, LA

Champer, Stan .... (606) 329-1717
Wire ED, Daily Independent, Ashland, KY

Champion, Charles F .... (215) 854-2000
Senior VP-Circulation (Inquirer & Daily News), VP-MKTG, Philadelphia Daily News, Philadelphia, PA

Champion, Jenn .... (312) 573-3800
MKTG DIR, CoverStory, Chicago, IL

Champion, Lee .... (205) 234-4281
PROD MGR
Alexander City Outlook, Alexander City, AL

Champion, Scott .... (309) 734-3176
Senior VP, Daily Review Atlas, Monmouth, IL

Champoux, Bernard .... (819) 376-2501
Chief ED, Le Nouvelliste, Trois-Rivieres, QC

Chan, Mei Mei .... (208) 522-1800
EX ED, Post Register, Idaho Falls, ID

Chance, Amy .... (916) 321-1000
Capitol BU Chief
Sacramento Bee, Sacramento, CA

Chance, Billy .... (316) 667-2697
PUB, Mount Hope Clarion, Mount Hope, KS

Chance, Carla .... (712) 328-1811
Features ED
Daily Nonpareil, Council Bluffs, IA

Chance, George .... (501) 675-4455
PUB, Booneville Democrat, Booneville, AR

Chance, Wes .... (706) 278-1011
News ED, Wire ED
Daily Citizen-News, Dalton, GA

Chancellor, Carl .... (330) 996-3000
COL-Local, Akron Beacon Journal, Akron, OH

Chandler, Ben .... (606) 873-4131
PUB, Woodford Sun, Versailles, KY

Chandler, Chuck .... (334) 875-2110
MAN ED, Selma Times-Journal, Selma, AL

Chandler, Craig .... (319) 383-2200
Photo ED, Quad-City Times, Davenport, IA

Cha Who's Where-40

Chandler, Don .... (360) 694-3391
Sports/Leisure ED
Columbian, Vancouver, WA

Chandler, Doris .... (352) 374-5000
Consumer Writer, Health Writer
Gainesville Sun, Gainesville, FL

Chandler, Helen .... (205) 259-1020
PROD FRM-PR
Daily Sentinel, Scottsboro, AL

Chandler, Joseph .... (215) 854-2000
VP-Circulation ADM
Philadelphia Inquirer, Philadelphia, PA

Chandler, Joyce .... (704) 245-6431
CIRC DIR, Daily Courier, Forest City, NC

Chandler, Ken .... (212) 930-8000
ED, New York Post, New York, NY

Chandler, Linda .... (812) 689-6364
PUB, Versailles Republican, Versailles, IN

Chandler, Mary Jean .... (541) 382-1811
SEC, Bulletin, Bend, OR
Western Communications Inc.

Chandler, Robert W .... (541) 382-1811
Chief EDL OFF, Bulletin, Bend, OR
Western Communications Inc.

Chandler Jr, Robert W .... (541) 382-1811
TREAS, Bulletin, Bend, OR
Western Communications Inc.

Chandler, Ross .... (910) 623-2155
MAN ED, Automotive ED, City/MET ED, EPE, NTL ED, News ED, Daily News, Eden, NC

Chandwani, Ashok .... (514) 987-2222
ASST MAN ED, Gazette, Montreal, QC

Chaney, Becky .... (817) 767-8341
Photo DEPT MGR, Wichita Falls Times Record News, Wichita Falls, TX

Chaney, Kenneth .... (515) 622-3110
PUB, Sigourney News-Review, Sigourney, IA

Chang, Ching-Tao .... (718) 746-8889
GM, World Journal, Whitestone, NY

Chang, Diane .... (808) 525-8000
Senior ED/EPE, Star-Bulletin, Honolulu, HI

Chang, Howard .... (312) 463-1050
MAN ED, Korea Times, Chicago, IL

Chang, Jae Min .... (213) 487-5323
PUB, Korea Times, Los Angeles, CA

Chang, Jenny .... (303) 442-1202
DP DIR, Daily Camera, Boulder, CO

Channing, Charlotte .... (616) 345-3511
Political ED
Kalamazoo Gazette, Kalamazoo, MI

Channing, Deirdre .... (203) 964-2200
ED, Stamford Advocate, Stamford, CT

Channon, Ethel .... (903) 794-3311
EPE, Texarkana Gazette, Texarkana, TX

Chao, Frank S .... (303) 722-8268
PUB, Colorado Chinese News, Denver, CO

Chao, Wendy Y .... (303) 722-8268
GM, MAN ED
Colorado Chinese News, Denver, CO

Chapa, John .... (512) 664-6588
CIRC MGR, Alice Echo-News, Alice, TX

Chapelle, Andy .... (313) 994-6989
Graphics ED/Art DIR, NTL ED, News ED, Political/Government ED, Ann Arbor News, Ann Arbor, MI

Chapelli Jr, Armando .... (703) 527-7860
PUB, El Tiempo Latino, Arlington, VA

Chapin, Mark .... (706) 724-0851
PROD DIR-Pre Press
Augusta Chronicle, Augusta, GA

Chapin, Michael W .... (630) 844-5844
MAN ED, Beacon-News, Aurora, IL

Chapleau, Serge .... (514) 285-7272
Cartoon ED, La Presse, Montreal, QC

Chaplin, George .... (808) 525-8000
ED-at-Large
Honolulu Advertiser, Honolulu, HI

Chapman, Barry .... (502) 582-4011
VP-Human Resources
Courier-Journal, Louisville, KY

Chapman, Cindy .... (313) 242-1100
Local ED
Monroe Evening News, Monroe, MI

Chapman, Cindy Cullen .... (319) 398-8211
Films/Theater ED, Radio/Television ED
Gazette, Cedar Rapids, IA

Chapman, Cy .... (613) 475-0255
ED, Brighton Independent, Brighton, ON

Chapman, Darlene .... (903) 757-3311
Photo DEPT MGR
Longview News-Journal, Longview, TX

Chapman, Don .... (310) 540-5511
Travel ED, Daily Breeze, Torrance, CA

Chapman, Don .... (808) 235-5881
ED, Midweek Magazine, Kaneohe, HI

Chapman, Geoff .... (416) 367-2000
Theater Writer, Toronto Star, Toronto, ON

Chapman, Gloria .... (305) 361-3333
GM, Islander News, Key Biscayne, FL

Chapman, Jennifer .... (912) 744-4200
MGR-PROM, Macon Telegraph, Macon, GA

Chapman, Jim .... (604) 732-2944
ADV MGR-OPER
Pacific Press Limited, Vancouver, BC

Chapman, John .... (205) 353-4612
CIRC MGR, Decatur Daily, Decatur, AL

Chapman, Keiron .... (250) 352-3552
PROD FRM-PR
Nelson Daily News, Nelson, BC

Chapman, Linda .... (617) 786-7000
MGR-Electronic Library INFO SYS, Online MGR, Patriot Ledger, Quincy, MA

Chapman, Mike .... (815) 625-3600
EX ED, Daily Gazette, Sterling, IL
Shaw Newspapers

Chapman, Nancy .... (757) 363-2400
ED, Port Folio, Virginia Beach, VA

Chapman, Paul .... (705) 472-3200
PROD MGR, PROD FRM-MR
North Bay Nugget, North Bay, ON

Chapman, Peggy .... (619) 745-6611
PSL MGR
North County Times, Escondido, CA

Chapman, Rick .... (601) 582-4321
ADV DIR, American, Hattiesburg, MS

Chapman, Sharon .... (503) 399-6611
Travel ED, Statesman Journal, Salem, OR

Chapman, Sherwood W .... (607) 756-5665
News ED, Cortland Standard, Cortland, NY

Chapman, Steve .... (312) 222-3232
EDL Writer/COL
Chicago Tribune, Chicago, IL

Chapman, Stuart .... (901) 465-4042
MAN ED, East Shelby Review
Sommerville, TN

Chapman, Will .... (318) 365-6773
PUB, COL, Daily Iberian, New Iberia, LA

Chapnick, Ben .... (212) 679-3288
PRES, Black Star Pub. , New York, NY

Chapnick, John P .... (212) 679-3288
EVP, Black Star Pub. Co. Inc., New York, NY

Chappel, George .... (860) 423-8466
Suburban ED, Chronicle, Willimantic, CT

Chappel, Thomas .... (415) 883-8600
SEC, Marin Independent Journal, Novato, CA

Chappell, Bruce .... (604) 674-3343
PUB, North Thompson Times, Clearwater, BC

Chappell, Fred .... (615) 388-6464
CIRC MGR, Daily Herald, Columbia, TN

Chappell, Nancy .... (604) 674-3343
ED, North Thompson Times, Clearwater, BC

Chappelle, Carolyn .... (918) 582-7124
ED, Oklahoma Eagle, Tulsa, OK

Chapple, Thomas L .... (615) 259-8000
SEC, Tennessean, Nashville, TN
Gannett Co. Inc.

Charbonneau, Chad .... (306) 682-2561
PUB, Humboldt Journal, Humboldt, SK

Charest, Robert .... (603) 668-4321
Features ED, Union Leader, Manchester, NH

Charf, Cindy .... (402) 887-4840
PUB, ED, Neligh News and Leader
Neligh, NE

Charf, Sid .... (402) 358-5220
GM, Creighton News, Creighton, NE

Charles, Ann K .... (316) 421-2000
PRES, PUB, ED, Parsons Sun, Parsons, KS

Charles, Gordon .... (616) 946-2000
Outdoors ED
Record-Eagle, Traverse City, MI

Charles, Jeff .... (414) 542-2501
CIRC MGR-Distribution
Waukesha County Freeman, Waukesha, WI

Charles, Mickey .... (215) 942-7890
PRES, Sports Network (Div. of Computer Info. Network), Southampton, PA

Charles, Randolph R .... (516) 843-2020
VP-MKTG/New BUS Development
Newsday, Melville, NY

Charles Jr, Roy F .... (706) 724-2122
PUB, Fort Gordon Signal, Waynesboro, GA

Charlet, Bob .... (504) 826-3279
ADV MGR-RT
Times-Picayune, New Orleans, LA

Charley, Amy .... (606) 283-0404
ED, Boone County Recorder, Florence, KY

Charlier, Tom .... (901) 529-2211
Environmental Reporter
Commercial Appeal, Memphis, TN

Charlton, Chuck .... (304) 485-1891
PROD SUPT-PR, Parkersburg News & Sentinel, Parkersburg, WV

Charlton, Jacquie .... (403) 882-4044
GM, Castor Advance, Castor, AB

Charlton, William .... (217) 788-1300
ADV MGR-CLASS
State Journal-Register, Springfield, IL

Charnley, Blair .... (714) 835-1234
News ED-Wires
Orange County Register, Santa Ana, CA

Charpentier, Colley .... (504) 447-4055
MAN ED, BUS/Farm ED
Daily Comet, Thibodaux, LA

Charpentier, Jeff .... (913) 371-4300
CIRC MGR
Kansas City Kansan, Kansas City, KS

Charrey, Martha .... (409) 628-6851
ED, San Jacinto News-Times, Shepherd, TX

Chartier, Benoit .... (514) 773-6028
PUB, Le Courrier de Saint-Hyacinthe, Saint-Hyacinthe, QC

Chartrand, M .... (313) 428-8173
MAN ED, Enterprise, Manchester, MI

Chasanow-Richman, Phyllis .... (202) 334-6000
Restaurant Critic
Washington Post, Washington, DC

Chase, Al .... (608) 252-6200
PROD MGR-Technical SRV
Madison Newspapers Inc., Madison, WI

Chase, Belinda .... (907) 225-3157
ED, Ketchikan Daily News, Ketchikan, AK

Chase, Bruce .... (207) 873-3341
CIRC MGR-Home Delivery, Central Maine Morning Sentinel, Waterville, ME
Guy Gannett Communications

Chase, Charlie .... (415) 588-5990
EX ED, Yossarian Universal News Service, Millbrae, CA

Chase, Jennifer .... (508) 249-3535
Women's ED
Athol Daily News, Athol, MA

Chase, Kelly L .... (508) 249-3535
Food ED, Librarian, Women's ED
Athol Daily News, Athol, MA

Chase, Kevin .... (506) 452-6671
CIRC MGR, PROD FRM-MR
Daily Gleaner, Fredericton, NB

Chase Jr, Richard J .... (508) 249-3535
PRES, PUB, GM, PA, DIR-MKTG/PROM, Radio/Television ED, RE ED, Athol Daily News, Athol, MA

Chase, Stephen F .... (508) 249-3535
TREAS, Athol Daily News, Athol, MA

Chase, Trevor .... (802) 863-3441
PROD MGR-Technical SRV
Burlington Free Press, Burlington, VT

Chatelain, Steve .... (308) 237-2152
PRES, PUB, ED
Kearney Hub, Kearney, NE

Chatenever, Rick .... (808) 244-3981
Entertainment ED, Features ED
Maui News, Wailuku, HI

Chatham, Betty .... (501) 234-5130
GM, PA, Banner-News, Magnolia, AR

Chatlosh, Jeff .... (803) 317-6397
Graphics ED/Art DIR, Photo DEPT MGR/Picture ED, Florence Morning News Florence, SC

Chatterley, Matthew .... (515) 284-8000
Art DIR, Des Moines Register, Des Moines, IA

Chau, Katie .... (212) 334-2061
MAN ED, Herald Monthly, New York, NY

Chaulk, Tim .... (520) 783-3333
ADV MGR-Display
Yuma Daily Sun, Yuma, AZ

Chavarria, Jessie .... (805) 564-5200
City ED, Santa Barbara News-Press, Santa Barbara, CA

Chavers, Janice .... (317) 622-1212
Health/Medical ED, Teen-Age/Youth ED, Travel ED, Herald Bulletin, Anderson, IN

Chavers, Karen .... (334) 222-2402
CIRC DIR-Safety
Andalusia Star-News, Andalusia, AL

Chavez, Augustine J .... (909) 793-3221
PROD DIR
Redlands Daily Facts, Redlands, CA

Chavez, Harturo .... (516) 352-6009
ED, Nueva Americana, Franklin Square, NY

Chavez, Jeanette .... (303) 820-1010
ASSOC ED, Denver Post, Denver, CO

Chavez, Lori .... (505) 242-3010
MAN ED, Health City Sun, Albuquerque, NM

Chavez, Manuel .... (505) 823-7777
PROD MGR, Albuquerque Publishing Co., Albuquerque, NM

Chavez, Margarita .... (516) 352-6009
PUB, Nueva Americana, Franklin Square, NY

Chavez, Neal .... (915) 653-1221
PROD MGR-Press/Distribution
Standard-Times, San Angelo, TX

Chavez-Sitters, Sylvia .... (210) 225-7411
ADV MGR-MKTG
San Antonio Express-News, San Antonio, TX

Chavira, Ricardo .... (214) 977-8222
Foreign ED, Dallas Morning News, Dallas, TX

Chavonne, Anthony G .... (910) 323-4848
ASST SEC, GM
Fayetteville Observer-Times, Fayetteville, NC

Chavoya, Maria .... (520) 783-3333
ED, Bajo El Sol, Yuma, AZ

Chawkins, Steve .... (805) 650-2900
Writing Coach
Ventura County Star, Ventura, CA

Chaykowsky, John .... (304) 233-0100
DP MGR, Intelligencer/Wheeling News-Register, Wheeling, WV

Chaytor, L .... (709) 364-6300
PROD FRM-PR
Evening Telegram, St. John's, NF

Cheadle, Judy .... (804) 649-6000
PROD MGR-Commercial Ventures
Richmond Times-Dispatch, Richmond, VA

Cheak, Connie J .... (502) 583-4471
PUB, Daily Record, Louisville, KY

Cheaney, Mark .... (573) 546-3917
ED, Mountain Echo, Ironton, MO

Cheater, Glenn .... (204) 694-2022
MAN ED, Winnipeg Sun, Winnipeg, MB

Chebuhar, Cheryl .... (402) 986-1777
ED, Howells Journal, Howells, NE

Chebuhar, Chris .... (402) 986-1777
PUB, Howells Journal, Howells, NE

Checchi, Tom .... (718) 981-1234
City ED, Features ED
Staten Island Advance, Staten Island, NY

Checkosky, Anne .... (315) 422-8153
GM, ED, Catholic Sun, Syracuse, NY

Cheek, Billie .... (217) 732-2101
PA, Office MGR, Courier, Lincoln, IL

Cheek, John .... (519) 354-2000
PUB/GM, Chatham Daily News, Chatham, ON

Cheek, Kip .... (815) 539-9396
ED, Mendota Reporter, Mendota, IL

Cheek, Larry .... (910) 323-4848
COL
Fayetteville Observer-Times, Fayetteville, NC

Cheek, Pat .... (606) 248-1010
ADV DIR, Daily News, Middlesboro, KY

Cheek, Tammy .... (423) 272-7325/7422
MAN ED, Rogersville Review, Rogersville, TN

Cheesman, James .... (605) 331-2200
Sports ED, Argus Leader, Sioux Falls, SD

Cheevers, Jack .... (310) 477-0403
MAN ED
Los Angeles New Times, Los Angeles, CA

Cheffey, Mark .... (573) 769-3111
PUB, ED, Palmyra Spectator, Palmyra, MO

Chehanske, Jim .... (908) 922-6000
PROD ASST MGR-Distribution
Asbury Park Press, Neptune, NJ

Chehubar, Cheryl .... (402) 652-8312
PUB, ED, North Bend Eagle, North Bend, NE

Chehubar, Chris .... (402) 652-8312
PUB, ED, North Bend Eagle, North Bend, NE

Chelette, Tommy .... (601) 762-1111
ADV DIR-MKTG
Mississippi Press, Pascagoula, MS

Chen, C Ti .... (718) 461-7668
MAN ED, Pacific Times, Flushing, NY

Chen, Kathy .... (212) 416-2000
Reporter-in-Charge (Beijing)
Wall Street Journal, New York, NY

Chen, Laura .... (317) 659-4622
EDU ED, Times, Frankfort, IN

Chenaille, Wendy .... (802) 447-7567
MGR-SYS
Bennington Banner, Bennington, VT

Chenault, Ernie .... (757) 539-3437
ADV DIR, Suffolk News-Herald, Suffolk, VA

Chendester, Jeff .... (916) 321-1000
PROD MGR-Trucking
Sacramento Bee, Sacramento, CA

Cheney, LaRue .... (208) 678-2201
Books/EDU ED, Food ED, Librarian, Radio/Television ED, Society/Women's ED, Youth ED, South Idaho Press, Burley, ID

Chergotis, Pam .... (914) 252-7414
ED, River Reporter, Narrowsburg, NY

Cheriel, Sally .... (503) 221-8327
Team Leader-Health
Oregonian, Portland, OR

Cherneski, John .... (306) 652-9200
Community Notes ED
StarPhoenix, Saskatoon, SK

Chernin, Lynne .... (403) 672-4421
PUB, Camrose Canadian, Camrose, AB

Chernock, Nick .... (206) 455-2222
VP-Human Resources
Eastside Journal, Bellevue, WA

Cherry, Brice .... (409) 836-7956
Sports ED
Brenham Banner-Press, Brenham, TX

Cherry Sr, Charles W .... (904) 253-0321
PUB, Daytona Times, Daytona Beach, FL

Cherry Jr, Charles W .... (904) 253-0321
ED, Daytona Times, Daytona Beach, FL

Cherry, Thomas V .... (757) 247-4600
CIRC MGR-Sales
Daily Press, Newport News, VA

Cherwa, John .... (312) 222-3232
Sports ED, Chicago Tribune, Chicago, IL

Chesar, Chris .... (201) 653-1000
CIRC DIR
Jersey Journal, Jersey City, NJ

Cheshire, Steve .... (706) 724-0851
CIRC MGR-OPER
Augusta Chronicle, Augusta, GA

Cheski, Steve .... (904) 359-4111
ADTX MGR
Florida Times-Union, Jacksonville, FL

41-Who's Where **Chr**

Chesley, Lois .... (757) 898-7225
ED, York Town Crier, Yorktown, VA

Chesney, Mike .... (601) 961-7000
MGR-Creative/PROM
Clarion-Ledger, Jackson, MS

Chesnut, Helen .... (250) 380-5211
Garden ED, Times Colonist, Victoria, BC

Chessman, Chet .... (207) 873-3341
CIRC MGR-Distribution, Central Maine Morning Sentinel, Waterville, ME
Guy Gannett Communications

Chesteen, Gloria .... (901) 885-0744
ADV MGR-RT
Union City Daily Messenger, Union City, TN

Chester, Bill .... (204) 727-2451
PROD MGR, Brandon Sun, Brandon, MB

Chester, Tom .... (423) 523-3131
ASST MAN ED-News
Knoxville News-Sentinel, Knoxville, TN

Chester Jr, Kenneth J .... (515) 270-6782
PRES
ABP Writers Syndicate, Urbandale, Iowa

Cheverton, Richard .... (714) 835-1234
Deputy Ed-Sunday
Orange County Register, Santa Ana, CA

Chewning, Sue .... (352) 498-3312
MAN ED
Dixie County Advocate, Cross City, FL

Cheyne, Kathryn T .... (501) 892-4451
ED, Pocahontas Star Herald, Pocahontas, AR

Chianca, Peter .... (617) 395-3680
MAN ED, Medford Citizen, Medford, MA

Chiantelli, Lisa .... (408) 372-3311
CFO, Monterey County Herald, Monterey, CA

Chiarella, Debby .... (910) 592-8137
GM, MAN ED
Sampson Independent, Clinton, NC

Chiasson, JoAnn .... (504) 826-3279
ADV MGR-CLASS
Times-Picayune, New Orleans, LA

Chiavaro, Ron .... (516) 843-2020
PROD MGR-Quality Assurance & Electric Pre Press, Newsday, Melville, NY

Chichester, Duane L .... (352) 544-5200
PUB/GM, Hernando Today, Brooksville, FL

Chick, Richard E .... (941) 748-0411
PROD DIR-OPER
Bradenton Herald, Bradenton, FL

Chick-Whiteside, Mary Ann .... (810) 766-6100
New Media MGR, Online MGR, ADTX MGR
Flint Journal, Flint, MI

Chickering, Pam .... (414) 478-2188
MAN ED, Courier, Waterloo, WI

Chidell, Beverly .... (301) 921-2800
ED, Stripe, Gaithersburg, MD

Chidlow, Carol .... (904) 454-1297
GM, High Springs Herald, High Springs, FL

Chiecchi, Dino .... (210) 225-7411
BUS ED
San Antonio Express-News, San Antonio, TX

Chiger, Norman .... (407) 242-3500
ADV MGR-CLASS, ADTX MGR
Florida Today, Melbourne, FL

Chihak, Michael A .... (408) 424-2221
PRES, PUB, Californian, Salinas, CA

Childers, Bobby .... (601) 636-4545
PROD FRM-PR
Vicksburg Post, Vicksburg, MS

Childers, Tony .... (618) 393-2931
PROD FRM-Press
Olney Daily Mail, Olney, IL

Childress, Greg .... (919) 419-6500
EDU ED, Herald-Sun, Durham, NC

Childress, Jerry M .... (517) 895-8551
CONT, Bay City Times, Bay City, MI

Childress, John .... (806) 762-8844
News ED, Avalanche-Journal, Lubbock, TX

Childress, Robert L .... (423) 428-0746
PUB, Mountain Press, Sevierville, TN

Childress, Sabrina .... (704) 249-3981
Youth ED, Dispatch, Lexington, NC

Childs, Betty .... (316) 278-2114
ED, Sterling Bulletin, Sterling, KS

Childs, Harvey .... (412) 588-5000
VP, Record-Argus, Greenville, PA

Childs, Joe .... (813) 893-8111
MAN ED-Clearwater
St. Petersburg Times, St. Petersburg, FL

Childs, Julian .... (212) 416-2000
EVP-Dow Jones Telerate
Wall Street Journal, New York, NY

Childs, Mike .... (706) 549-0123
City ED (Banner-Herald), Athens Daily News/Banner-Herald, Athens, GA

Childs, Sam .... (904) 863-1111
ADV DIR, Northwest Florida Daily News, Fort Walton Beach, FL

Chiles, Nick .... (201) 877-4141
EDU ED, Star-Ledger, Newark, NJ

Chiles-Wheeler, Heidi .... (201) 428-6200
ADV DIR, Daily Record, Parsippany, NJ

Chillianis, Janet C .... (212) 208-8369
PUB, Standard & Poor's Dividend Record, New York, NY

Chilton, Dan .... (417) 836-1100
ADTX MGR
Springfield News-Leader, Springfield, MO

Chilton, Elizabeth E .... (304) 348-5140
PRES, Charleston Gazette, Sunday Gazette-Mail, Charleston, WV

Chimelis, Ron .... (413) 788-1000
COL, Union-News, Springfield, MA

Chimner, Dennis .... (616) 964-7161
PROD MGR-Pre Press
Battle Creek Enquirer, Battle Creek, MI

Chin, Christine M .... (619) 322-8889
DIR-MKTG, Desert Sun, Palm Springs, CA

Chin, Dianne .... (617) 426-3000
ADV MGR-MKTG RES/ADM
Boston Herald, Boston, MA

Chin, Lucy .... (212) 556-1234
DIR-Pre Press
New York Times, New York, NY

Chinappi, Anna .... (401) 762-3000
MAN ED, EPE, FIN ED
Call, Woonsocket, RI

Ching, Richard A .... (602) 977-8351
CONT, Daily News-Sun, Sun City, AZ

Ching, Val .... (310) 230-3400
RES, Allsport Photography USA, Pacific Palisades, CA

Chinigo, Marajen Stevick .... (217) 485-4010
PUB, County Star, Tolono, IL

Chiodo, Daniel P .... (417) 623-3480
PUB, Joplin Globe, Joplin, MO

Chionsini, Brandi .... (713) 331-4421
MAN ED, Sun, Alvin, TX

Chionsini, Jim .... (512) 352-8535
PRES, Taylor Daily Press, Taylor, TX

Chiott, Larry .... (716) 372-3121
ADV DIR
Olean Times-Herald, Olean, NY

Chipello, Christopher .... (212) 416-2000
BU Chief-Montreal
Wall Street Journal, New York, NY

Chipkin, Robert .... (413) 788-1000
COL, MET ED
Union-News, Springfield, MA

Chipman, Peter L .... (617) 593-7700
PROD DIR, Daily Evening Item, Lynn, MA

Chirgwin, Andrew .... (518) 792-9914
ASST MAN ED, Pagination Services
TV Data, Queensbury, NY

Chirie, Kevin .... (504) 643-4918
ED, Slidell Sentry-News, Slidell, LA

Chisler, Matt .... (412) 222-2200
ADV MGR-RT
Observer-Reporter, Washington, PA

Chism, Beth .... (417) 532-9131
VP-OPER, PUB
Lebanon Daily Record, Lebanon, MO

Chism, David M .... (501) 758-2571
PUB, Times, North Little Rock, AR

Chism, Eric J .... (417) 532-9131
MAN ED
Lebanon Daily Record, Lebanon, MO

Chism, Kitty .... (501) 758-2571
ED, Times, North Little Rock, AR

Chiszar, Sean .... (219) 583-5121
Sports ED, Herald Journal, Monticello, IN

Chittam, Neil .... (205) 232-2720
Sports ED, News Courier, Athens, AL

Chittick, Ted .... (561) 820-4100
MGR-CR
Palm Beach Post, West Palm Beach, FL

Chittock, Steve .... (707) 464-2141
PROD SUPV-MR
Triplicate, Crescent City, CA

Chitwood, Carol .... (913) 755-4151
ED, Osawatomie Graphic, Osawatomie, KS

Chitwood, Pat .... (706) 324-5526
CIRC MGR-Distribution
Columbus Ledger-Enquirer, Columbus, GA

Chitwood, Tim .... (706) 324-5526
COL
Columbus Ledger-Enquirer, Columbus, GA

Chivers, Gayle .... (505) 325-4545
SEC, Daily Times, Farmington, NM

Choate, Alan .... (409) 265-7411
Entertainment/Amusements ED, SCI/Technology ED, Television/Film ED, Theater/Music ED, Brazosport Facts, Clute, TX

Choate, Charles .... (217) 788-1300
ADV MGR-Display
State Journal-Register, Springfield, IL

Choate, John .... (318) 487-6397
PROD DIR-Engineering Maintenance
Alexandria Daily Town Talk, Alexandria, LA

Choate, Willis .... (405) 276-3255
PUB, Marietta Monitor, Marietta, OK

Choate, Wilma .... (405) 276-3255
ED, Marietta Monitor, Marietta, OK

Chodan, Lucinda .... (514) 987-2222
Entertainment ED, Gazette, Montreal, QC

Chodos, Barbara .... (412) 263-1100
ADV ASST DIR
Pittsburgh Post-Gazette, Pittsburgh, PA

Chogi, L .... (403) 328-4411
PROD FRM-PR
Lethbridge Herald, Lethbridge, AB

Choi, K J .... (212) 582-5205
PUB, ED, Korea Herald/U.S.A., New York, NY

Choice, Harriet .... (816) 932-6600
VP/EDL Special Services
Universal Press Syndicate, Kansas City, MO

Choiniere, Paul .... (860) 442-2200
Environmental ED, Health/Medical ED, SCI/Technology ED, Day, New London, CT

Chola, Mulenga .... (416) 441-1405
Africa Journalist, Fotopress Independent News Service International, Toronto, ON

Chomokovski, Irene .... (403) 624-2591
ED, Record-Gazette, Peace River, AB

Choney, Suzanne .... (619) 299-3131
Features ED
San Diego Union-Tribune, San Diego, CA

Chong, Pin Chek .... (416) 441-1405
Indochina Journalist, Fotopress Independent News Service International, Toronto, ON

Chong, Tim .... (520) 783-3333
Television/Film ED, Theater/Music ED
Yuma Daily Sun, Yuma, AZ

Choruzy, Nick .... (302) 324-2500
MGR-CR, News Journal, Wilmington, DE

Chote, Randy .... (903) 657-2501
MAN ED
Henderson Daily News, Henderson, TX

Chotkowski, L A .... (203) 828-5016
Author/Owner
What's New In Medicine, Kensington, CT

Choucair, Salwa .... (210) 736-4450
ED
Daily Commercial Recorder, San Antonio, TX

Chouinard, Jacqueline .... (306) 731-3143
PUB, ED, Waterfront Press, Lumsden, SK

Chouinard, Lucien .... (306) 731-3143
PUB, ED, Waterfront Press, Lumsden, SK

Choulis, Gary .... (410) 268-5000
DP MGR, Capital, Annapolis, MD

Chovenac, Daniel .... (404) 352-2400
PUB, Atlanta Jewish Times, Atlanta, GA

Chow, Crystal .... (408) 920-5000
Celebrations ED
San Jose Mercury News, San Jose, CA

Chow, Tyler .... (601) 895-6220
ED, DeSoto County Tribune
Olive Branch, MS

Choyke, Bill .... (615) 259-8000
Regional ED-Day
Tennessean, Nashville, TN

Chretien, Louis .... (418) 683-1573
DP MGR, Le Journal de Quebec, Ville Vanier, QC

Chrisman, Dorothy .... (712) 729-3201
PUB, ED, Sanborn Pioneer, Sanborn, IA

Chrismer, Ellen .... (209) 369-2761
Fashion/Style ED, Features ED, Lifestyle ED, Women's ED, Lodi News-Sentinel, Lodi, CA

Chriss, Catherine .... (510) 208-6300
Food ED, Oakland Tribune, Oakland, CA
MediaNews Inc. (Alameda Newspapers)

Christensen, Annmarie .... (603) 298-8711
News ED, Valley News, White River Jct., VT

Christensen, Bente .... (941) 366-2169
BM, Editor's Copy Syndicate, Sarasota, FL

Christensen, Bill .... (515) 484-2841
GM, Toledo Chronicle, Tama, IA

Christensen, Bill .... (906) 228-2500
CIRC MGR, Mining Journal, Marquette, MI

Christensen, Chris .... (562) 435-1161
COL, Press-Telegram, Long Beach, CA

Christensen, Dennis .... (800) 678-8135
Western Representative, Better Homes & Gardens Features Syndicate, Des Moines, IA

Christensen, Dick .... (218) 723-5281
PROD FRM-PR (Gen)
Duluth News-Tribune, Duluth, MN

Christensen, Doug .... (801) 373-5050
ADV MGR-CLASS, Daily Herald, Provo, UT

Christensen, Gary .... (912) 888-9300
PROD DIR-OPER, Albany Herald, Albany, GA

Christensen, Jim .... (507) 625-4451
CIRC DIR, Free Press, Mankato, MN

Christensen, Morris .... (719) 539-6691
PROD FRM-Press, Mountain Mail, Salida, CO

Christensen, Rod .... (715) 526-2121
PROD MGR, Shawano Leader, Shawano, WI

Christensen, Steven .... (213) 237-5485
VP/GM, Los Angeles Times Syndicate, Los Angeles, CA

Christenson, D Jeff .... (501) 741-2325
PUB, Harrison Daily Times, Harrison, AR

Christenson, Diana .... (602) 468-6565
Financial Officer
Daily Racing Form, Phoenix, AZ

Christenson, Gary .... (318) 462-0616
Sports ED
Beauregard Daily News, De Ridder, LA

Christenson, Jane Dunlap .... (501) 741-2325
Fashion/Style ED, Food ED
Harrison Daily Times, Harrison, AR

Christenson, Jeff .... (501) 741-2325
PUB, Boone County Headlight, Harrison, AR

Christian, Bruce .... (602) 898-6500
Radio/Television ED, Mesa Tribune, Mesa, AZ
Thomson Newspapers

Christian, Chris .... (518) 561-2300
CIRC MGR
Press-Republican, Plattsburgh, NY

Christian, Darrell L .... (212) 621-1500
MAN ED, Associated Press, New York, NY

Christian, Felicia .... (912) 272-5522
Society/Women's ED
Courier Herald, Dublin, GA

Christian, Judy .... (414) 261-4949
ADV DIR-RT & NTL
Watertown Daily Times, Watertown, WI

Christian, Pat .... (801) 373-5050
EDU ED, Daily Herald, Provo, UT

Christiansen, Barbara .... (801) 756-7669
ED, Citizen, American Fork, UT

Christiansen, Becky .... (702) 788-6200
ASST CONT, Reno Gazette-Journal, Reno, NV

Christiansen, Cheryl .... (908) 922-6000
MGR-CORP RES & Planning
Asbury Park Press, Neptune, NJ

Christiansen, Norm .... (218) 285-7411
PROD FRM
Daily Journal, International Falls, MN

Christiansen, Richard .... (312) 222-3232
Chief Critic
Chicago Tribune, Chicago, IL

Christie, Agnes .... (416) 979-9588
Sales MGR
Miller Features Syndicate Inc., Toronto, ON

Christie, Alan .... (416) 367-2000
NTL ED, Toronto Star, Toronto, ON

Christie, Bob .... (954) 356-4000
PROD MGR
Sun-Sentinel, Fort Lauderdale, FL

Christie, Cam .... (905) 372-0131
MAN ED, Cobourg Daily Star, Cobourg, ON

Christie, Casey .... (805) 395-7500
Photo DIR
Bakersfield Californian, Bakersfield, CA

Christie, Cindi .... (510) 758-8400
Photo ED, West County Times, Pinole, CA

Christie, Derwood .... (303) 820-1010
PROD MGR-MR, Denver Post, Denver, CO

Christie, Jim .... (317) 459-3121
PROD FRM-COMP, Tribune, Kokomo, IN

Christie, John .... (954) 356-4000
GM (South Broward)
Sun-Sentinel, Fort Lauderdale, FL

Christie, Joyce .... (520) 783-3333
Farm/Agriculture ED, Daily Sun, Yuma, AZ

Christie, Judy Pace .... (407) 242-3500
EX ED, Florida Today, Melbourne, FL

Christie, Rebecca .... (541) 382-1811
Health/Medical ED, Bulletin, Bend, OR

Christine, Ed .... (717) 275-3235
MGR-BUS, Danville News, Danville, PA

Christine, Pamela S .... (717) 275-3235
GM, ED, Danville News, Danville, PA

Christinidis, Jim .... (817) 390-7400
CIRC MGR-Northeast
Fort Worth Star-Telegram, Fort Worth, TX

Christner, Fred .... (217) 563-2115
ED, Free Press-Progress, Nokomis, IL

Christner, Rex .... (316) 694-5700
SEC/TREAS, BUS Office MGR, SYS DIR
Hutchinson News, Hutchinson, KS

Christo, Van .... (617) 269-5192
MAN ED, Liria, South Boston, MA

Christoff, Robert .... (330) 996-3000
MGR-Human Resources
Akron Beacon Journal, Akron, OH

Christofides, Aris .... (513) 761-1188
EIC, Critic's Choice Reviews, Cincinnati, OH

Christofides, Lori .... (513) 761-1188
Senior Critic
Critic's Choice Reviews, Cincinnati, OH

Christopher, Amy .... (814) 643-4040
Food ED, Women's ED
Daily News, Huntingdon, PA

Christopher, Carl .... (717) 455-3636
ED-Sunday, BUS ED
Standard-Speaker, Hazleton, PA

Christopher, Phillip .... (718) 626-7676
PUB, Proini, Long Island City, NY

Christopherson, Brad .... (712) 279-5019
PROD FRM-MR
Sioux City Journal, Sioux City, IA

Christy, Carol M .... (815) 432-5227
GM, PROD MGR, Iroquois County's Times-Republic, Watseka, IL

Christy, David .... (405) 758-3255
ED, Oklahoma Hornet, Waukomis, OK

Christy Jr, R Jack .... (405) 758-3255
PUB, Oklahoma Hornet, Waukomis, OK

Chr Who's Where-42

Christy, Susan (505) 267-3546
ED, Courier, Hatch, NM
Chronister, Dale (573) 238-2821
GM, Banner-Press, Marble Hill, MO
Chronister, Janet (501) 239-8562
BUS/Office MGR, DP MGR
Paragould Daily Press, Paragould, AR
Chrostowski, Edmond J (203) 966-9541
ED, New Canaan Advertiser, New Canaan, CT
Chrus, Dimitri (416) 585-5000
CIRC DIR, Globe and Mail (Canada's National Newspaper), Toronto, ON
Chu, Emerson (713) 498-4310
GM, Southern Chinese Daily News
Houston, TX
Chu, Mr (212) 349-4778
PUB, China Tribune, New York, NY
Chu, Patrick (503) 221-8327
BUS ED, Oregonian, Portland, OR
Chua, Linus (561) 820-4100
RE ED
Palm Beach Post, West Palm Beach, FL
Chubb, Anne T (610) 371-5000
ADV MGR-RT Sales
Reading Times/Eagle, Reading, PA
Chubb, Ken (913) 764-2211
PROD MGR, Olathe Daily News, Olathe, KS
Chudy, Susan (203) 333-0161
ADV MGR-RT
Connecticut Post, Bridgeport, CT
Chuisano, Bill (912) 923-6432
PUB, Daily Sun, Warner Robins, GA
Chulski, Thomas (313) 242-1100
EPE, Monroe Evening News, Monroe, MI
Chun, Diane (352) 374-5000
Family/Food ED, Features ED, Religion ED, Travel ED, Gainesville Sun, Gainesville, FL
Chun-Ming, Holly (808) 525-8000
MGR-Safety
Hawaii Newspaper Agency Inc., Honolulu, HI
Chung, Eva (415) 982-6206
ED, Chinese Times, San Francisco, CA
Chung, Julien (514) 285-7272
Art DIR, Photography ED
La Presse, Montreal, QC
Chuparkoff, Karen (330) 996-3000
Milestones ED
Akron Beacon Journal, Akron, OH
Church, Allan S (203) 235-1661
EPE, Record-Journal, Meriden, CT
Church, Beth (419) 448-3200
NTL ED, Political/Government ED
Advertiser-Tribune, Tiffin, OH
Church, Dave (707) 226-3711
PROD FRM-COMP
Napa Valley Register, Napa, CA
Church, Dean (415) 777-1111
DIR-PROM
San Francisco Chronicle, San Francisco, CA
Church, Ellen (910) 739-4322
Farm ED, Robesonian, Lumberton, NC
Church, Harrison Leon (618) 537-4498
PUB, Lebanon Advertiser, Lebanon, IL
Church, Helen S (618) 537-4498
ED, Lebanon Advertiser, Lebanon, IL
Church, Johanna (610) 272-2500
ED-Sunday, BUS ED
Times Herald, Norristown, PA
Church, Roy (219) 563-2131
News ED, Wabash Plain Dealer, Wabash, IN
Church, William (616) 964-7161
MAN ED
Battle Creek Enquirer, Battle Creek, MI
Churchill, Bonnie (213) 876-1668
Lead COL, Communication International/National News, Los Angeles, CA
Churchill, Dave (507) 433-8851
PUB, GM, Austin Daily Herald, Austin, MN
Churchill, Lisa (408) 287-4866
PROD Design, San Jose Post-Record, San Jose, CA, Daily Journal Corp.
Churchill, Theresa (217) 429-5151
Lifestyle ED, Herald & Review, Decatur, IL
Chyz, Ken (306) 783-7355
PUB, GM, News, Yorkton, SK
Ciampa, Gail (401) 277-7000
Fashion/Style ED
Providence Journal-Bulletin, Providence, RI
Cianciola, Fran (703) 276-3400
CIRC GM-N Central Florida
USA Today, Arlington, VA
Ciani, Ron (816) 271-8500
ADV DIR
St. Joseph News-Press, St. Joseph, MO
Ciaravino, Trish (801) 674-6200
City ED-Night, Spectrum, St. George, UT
Ciarimboli, Michael (615) 259-8000
DIR-Special Projects/Planning, ADTX MGR
Tennessean, Nashville, TN
Ciarochi, Michael (412) 439-7500
Sports ED
Herald-Standard, Uniontown, PA
Ciccantelli, Steve (414) 887-0321
ADV DIR, Daily Citizen, Beaver Dam, WI
Cicchetti, Geri (814) 870-1600
ADV MGR-Telesales
Morning News/Erie Daily Times, Erie, PA
Ciccone, F Richard (312) 222-3232
ASSOC ED, Chicago Tribune, Chicago, IL
Cicconetti, Charles (330) 264-1125
News ED, Daily Record, Wooster, OH
Ciccotelli, Patty (505) 546-2611
Office MGR, Deming Headlight, Deming, NM
Cicero, Kimberly (508) 793-9100
CIRC ASST DIR
Telegram & Gazette, Worcester, MA
Cicero, Vito T (609) 272-7000
DIR-Circulation, CIRC DIR
Press of Atlantic City, Pleasantville, NJ
Cichiowski, Lorraine (703) 276-3400
Online MGR, USA Today, Arlington, VA
Cichon, Ron (904) 997-3568
PUB, Monticello News, Monticello, FL
Cichowski, Gary (360) 736-3311
Photo MGR, Chronicle, Centralia, WA
Ciechon, Sharon (603) 668-4321
DIR-Human Resources
Union Leader, Manchester, NH
Cillarear, Lisa (909) 381-9898
ED, Rialto Record, San Bernardino, CA
Cillo, Joseph (216) 999-4500
DIR-INFO SYS
Plain Dealer, Cleveland, OH
Cimburek, James (605) 665-7811
Sports ED
Yankton Daily Press & Dakotan, Yankton, SD
Cincotta, G T (914) 331-5000
MGR-OPER, Daily Freeman, Kingston, NY
Cincotta, Patsy (515) 856-6336
Society ED
Ad Express & Daily Iowegian, Centerville, IA
Cincotta, Ruth (561) 820-3800
Chief Photographer
Palm Beach Daily News, Palm Beach, FL
Cindrich, John (412) 664-9161
EDU ED, Daily News, McKeesport, PA
Cipollo, John J (518) 454-5694
PROD SUPT-MR, Times Union, Albany, NY
Cipriano, Joan (516) 751-7744
ED, Village Times, Setauket, NY
Cipriano, Marianne (203) 488-2535
ED, Branford Review, Branford, CT
Circh, Steve (716) 394-0770
Automotive ED, News ED, Daily Messenger/The Sunday Messenger, Canandaigua, NY
Ciria Jr, Mario (201) 864-9505
ED, Continental Newspaper, Union City, NJ
Cisneros, Cynthia (512) 575-1451
ADV MGR-Voice Line, ADTX MGR
Victoria Advocate, Victoria, TX
Cisneros, Juanita (970) 669-5050
Librarian
Loveland Daily Reporter-Herald, Loveland, CO
Cissell, Bill (605) 642-2761
City ED, Black Hills Pioneer, Spearfish, SD
Cissell, Mary (573) 783-3366
PUB, Democrat News, Fredericktown, MO
Cissna, Gail (301) 662-1177
Food ED, Religion ED
Frederick Post/The News, Frederick, MD
Citrano, Sal (516) 393-9250
BUS MGR, Professional Communications Group, Hicksville, NY
Claassen, Dwight (316) 283-1500
Online MGR, Newton Kansan, Newton, KS
Clabes, Gene A (606) 283-0404
PUB, Boone County Recorder, Florence, KY
Clader, Fran (707) 448-6401
City ED, Reporter, Vacaville, CA
Claflin, Blair (716) 232-7100
EDU ED, Public Affairs ED
Rochester Democrat and Chronicle; Times-Union, Rochester, NY
Claggett, Jim (403) 346-3356
ED, Central Alberta Adviser, Red Deer, AB
Clairemont, Sharon (714) 835-1234
News DIR-RES
Orange County Register, Santa Ana, CA
Clancy, Douglas (201) 646-4000
ASST to ED, Record, Hackensack, NJ
Clancy, Frederick (207) 791-6650
PROD OPER Camera MGR-Days
Portland Press Herald, Portland, ME
Clancy, Lou (416) 367-2000
MAN ED, Toronto Star, Toronto, ON
Clancy, Sean (501) 268-8621
BUS/FIN ED, Farm/Agriculture ED
Daily Citizen, Searcy, AR
Clap, Allen (415) 692-9406
ED, Belmont & San Carlos Enquirer Bulletin, Burlingame, CA
Clapper, Frank H (330) 875-5610
ED, Louisville Herald, Louisville, OH
Clapper, Jacqueline (715) 365-6397
BM, Daily News, Rhinelander, WI
Clapper, Paul M (330) 875-5610
PUB, Louisville Herald, Louisville, OH
Clare, Tammy (505) 523-4581
ADV DIR/MGR-RT/Display
Las Cruces Sun-News, Las Cruces, NM
Claridge, Allan (519) 925-2832
ED, Free Press & Economist, Shelburne, ON
Claridge, Pamela A (519) 941-2230
PUB, Orangeville Citizen, Orangeville, ON
Claridge, Thomas (519) 925-2832
PUB
Free Press & Economist, Shelburne, ON
Clarin, Paul (540) 981-3100
CONT, Roanoke Times, Roanoke, VA
Clark, Abby (317) 633-1240
ADV MGR-RT
Indianapolis Star/News, Indianapolis, IN
Clark, Al (919) 752-6166
EX ED, Daily Reflector, Greenville, NC
Clark, Alex (505) 622-7710
CIRC MGR-OPER, Daily Record, Roswell, NM
Clark, Anne (406) 755-7000
Society ED, Daily Inter Lake, Kalispell, MT
Clark, Art (916) 741-2345
DP MGR, PROD DIR
Appeal-Democrat, Marysville, CA
Clark, Barbara (416) 367-2000
PROD MGR-Pre-Press/ADM
Toronto Star, Toronto, ON
Clark, Beth (541) 753-2641
PUB, Corvallis Gazette-Times, Corvallis, OR
Clark, Bill (215) 949-4000
DIR-INFO SRV, Bucks County Courier Times, Levittown, PA, Calkins Newspapers
Clark, Bob (516) 747-8282
ED, Three Village Times, Mineola, NY
Clark, Brian (612) 333-4244
CIRC MGR
Finance and Commerce, Minneapolis, MN
Clark, Brian (519) 894-2231
Photo CNR, Record, Kitchener, ON
Southam Inc.
Clark, C Lee (540) 981-3100
ADV MGR-CLASS
Roanoke Times, Roanoke, VA
Clark, Charles (405) 353-0620
Books ED, Fashion ED, Films/ Theater ED, Lifestyle ED, Music ED, Women's ED, Lawton Constitution, Lawton, OK
Clark, Cheri (352) 563-6363
PROD MGR-COMP Room
Citrus County Chronicle, Crystal River, FL
Clark, Cheryl (619) 299-3131
Medical Writer
San Diego Union-Tribune, San Diego, CA
Clark, Chris (519) 763-3333
ED, Guelph Tribune, Guelph, ON
Clark, Cliff (919) 482-4418
ED, Chowan Herald, Edenton, NC
Clark, Colin (703) 560-4000
BU ED, Arlington Journal, Fairfax, VA
Journal Newspapers Inc.
Clark, Craig (607) 798-1234
PROD MGR-T/S & Building
Press & Sun Bulletin, Binghamton, NY
Clark, Curtiss (203) 426-3141
MAN ED, Newtown Bee, Newtown, CT
Clark, Debbie (408) 424-2221
ADV MGR-RT/CLASS
Californian, Salinas, CA
Clark, Denise (816) 932-6600
MGR-MKTG ADM
Universal Press Syndicate, Kansas City, MO
Clark, Dennis (910) 373-7000
PROD MGR-PR, PROD MGR-Platemaking
News & Record, Greensboro, NC
Clark, Diane (308) 665-2310
MAN ED
Crawford Clipper/Harrison Sun, Crawford, NE
Clark, Don (512) 865-3510
ED, Flatonia Argus, Flatonia, TX
Clark, Donna (813) 893-8111
MGR-Community Events
St. Petersburg Times, St. Petersburg, FL
Clark, Donna (541) 573-2022
PUB, Burns Times-Herald, Burns, OR
Clark, Dorie (352) 374-5000
ADV CNR-NTL
Gainesville Sun, Gainesville, FL
Clark, Doug (910) 888-3500
ASSOC ED, EPE
High Point Enterprise, High Point, NC
Clark, Doug (619) 337-3400
Music ED
Imperial Valley Press, El Centro, CA
Clark, Eric (314) 533-8000
ED, St. Louis American, St. Louis, MO
Clark, Gary R (216) 999-4500
MAN ED, Plain Dealer, Cleveland, OH
Clark, Grayson (205) 532-4000
PROD MGR-Distribution Center
Huntsville Times, Huntsville, AL
Clark, Greg (916) 622-1255
Online Contact
Mountain Democrat, Placerville, CA
Clark, Gregory (916) 243-2424
MAN ED, Record Searchlight, Redding, CA
Clark, Herbert E (319) 886-2131
PUB, Tipton Conservative and Advertiser, Tipton, IA
Clark, James (414) 224-2000
Senior VP-Circulation, CIRC Senior VP
Milwaukee Journal Sentinel, Milwaukee, WI
Clark, James L (304) 265-3333
GM, MAN ED
Mountain Statesman, Grafton, WV
Clark, Jane (707) 448-6401
ADV MGR-CLASS, Reporter, Vacaville, CA
Clark, Jay (407) 242-3500
DIR-Human Resources
Florida Today, Melbourne, FL
Clark, Jayne (412) 263-1100
Travel ED
Pittsburgh Post-Gazette, Pittsburgh, PA
Clark, Jeff (810) 469-4510
DP MGR, Macomb Daily, Mount Clemens, MI
Clark, Jerry (540) 261-8000
PUB, ED, Rockbridge Weekly
Buena Vista, VA
Clark, Jill (704) 252-5611
MGR-Database MKTG, Online MGR
Asheville Citizen-Times, Asheville, NC
Clark, Jim (604) 763-3212
PUB, Kelowna Capital News, Kelowna, BC
Clark, Jim (508) 343-6911
Sports ED
Sentinel & Enterprise, Fitchburg, MA
Clark, Jim (407) 420-5000
Staff Development ED
Orlando Sentinel, Orlando, FL
Clark, John (216) 999-4500
ASSOC ED, Plain Dealer, Cleveland, OH
Advance Publications
Clark, John (607) 798-1234
PROD MGR-PR
Press & Sun Bulletin, Binghamton, NY
Clark, John (918) 962-2075
ED, Spiro Graphic, Spiro, OK
Clark, John (414) 682-5231
PUB, Lakeshore Chronicle, Manitowoc, WI
Clark, Joyce (816) 279-9315
MKTG DIR, American International Syndicate, St. Joseph, MO
Clark, Ken (817) 390-7400
DIR-INFO SYS
Fort Worth Star-Telegram, Fort Worth, TX
Clark, Kevin (360) 694-3391
Photo ED, Columbian, Vancouver, WA
Clark, Kevin (209) 784-5000
PROD MGR
Porterville Recorder, Porterville, CA
Clark, L Brian (716) 343-8000
PROD MGR-SYS, Daily News, Batavia, NY
Clark, Larry (804) 793-2311
News ED
Danville Register & Bee, Danville, VA
Clark, Larry (317) 459-3121
PROD FRM-PR, Kokomo Tribune
Kokomo, IN
Clark, Larry D (704) 322-4510
ED, Hickory Daily Record, Hickory, NC
Clark, Lisa (412) 224-4321
ASST Lifestyles ED
Valley News Dispatch, Tarentum, PA
Clark, Margaret (604) 624-6781
CIRC MGR, Daily News, Prince Rupert, BC
Clark, Mark (219) 235-6161
CIRC MGR-Transportation
South Bend Tribune, South Bend, IN
Clark, Matthew (412) 782-2121
ED, Herald, Aspinwall, PA
Clark, Most Rev Matthew H (716) 328-4340
PUB, Catholic Courier, Rochester, NY
Clark, Michael (513) 352-2000
EDU ED, Cincinnati Post, Cincinnati, OH
Clark, Mike (212) 416-2000
PROD MGR (Denver CO)
Wall Street Journal, New York, NY
Clark, Mike (904) 359-4111
Reader Advocate
Florida Times-Union, Jacksonville, FL
Clark, Mike (405) 376-4571
ED, Mustang News, Mustang, OK
Clark, Nancy (937) 644-9111
PROD FRM-COMP
Marysville Journal-Tribune, Marysville, OH
Clark, Neil (847) 427-4300
PROD MGR-Newspaper Processing Center
Daily Herald, Arlington Heights, IL
Clark, Patricia A (802) 496-3928
GM, Valley Reporter, Waitsfield, VT
Clark, R V (405) 547-2411
PUB, ED, Perkins Journal, Perkins, OK
Clark, Richard (716) 232-7100
DP MGR, Rochester Democrat and Chronicle; Rochester, NY Times-Union, Rochester, NY

Copyright ©1997 by the Editor & Publisher Co.

43-Who's Where **Cli**

Clark, Rick .... (519) 679-6666
PROD SUPV-Building Maintenance
London Free Press, London, ON

Clark, Rick K .... (806) 669-2525
ADV MGR, Pampa News, Pampa, TX

Clark, Rob .... (309) 932-2103
ED, Galva News, Galva, IL

Clark, Robert .... (310) 829-6811
Photo DEPT MGR
Outlook, Santa Monica, CA

Clark, Robin .... (904) 359-4111
BUS ED
Florida Times-Union, Jacksonville, FL

Clark, Roger .... (954) 963-4000
PUB, Community News, Hollywood, FL

Clark, Ron .... (502) 443-1771
City/MET ED, Farm/Agriculture ED, Home Furnishings ED, Paducah Sun, Paducah, KY

Clark, Ron .... (604) 732-2944
VP-Advertising
Pacific Press Limited, Vancouver, BC

Clark, Ronald D .... (612) 222-5011
EPE, St. Paul Pioneer Press, St. Paul, MN

Clark, Sandy Thorn .... (219) 461-8333
ASST MAN ED-Features, Food ED
Journal Gazette, Fort Wayne, IN

Clark, Scott .... (713) 220-7171
BUS ED, Houston Chronicle, Houston, TX

Clark, Shirley .... (606) 528-2464
ADV MGR, Times-Tribune, Corbin, KY

Clark, Steve .... (613) 342-4441
ADTX MGR, Brockville Recorder and Times, Brockville, ON

Clark, Steve .... (804) 649-6000
COL, Times-Dispatch, Richmond, VA

Clark, Steve .... (503) 684-0360
PUB, Beaverton Valley Times, Beaverton, OR

Clark, Stuart .... (319) 886-2131
GM, ED, Tipton Conservative and Advertiser, Tipton, IA

Clark, Tim .... (505) 887-5501
Government ED, News ED
Current-Argus, Carlsbad, NM

Clark, Tina .... (717) 255-8100
PSL MGR
Harrisburg Patriot-News, Harrisburg, PA

Clark, Tom .... (703) 878-8000
Sports ED, Potomac News, Woodbridge, VA

Clark, Wayne L .... (607) 756-5665
BM, Cortland Standard, Cortland, NY

Clark, Wes .... (816) 279-9315
VP/Art DIR, American International Syndicate, St. Joseph, MO

Clark-Johnson, Susan .... (703) 284-6000
Sr Group PRES-Pacific Newspaper Group
Gannett Co. Inc., Arlington, VA

Clarke, Bob .... (516) 569-4000
ED, Lynbrook Herald, Lawrence, NY

Clarke, Brad .... (812) 332-4401
PROD SUPT, Herald-Times Inc
Bloomington, IN

Clarke, Byron .... (423) 472-5041
Films/Theater ED
Cleveland Daily Banner, Cleveland, TN

Clarke, Dave .... (309) 852-2181
Regional ED
Kewanee Star-Courier, Kewanee, IL

Clarke, Dawn .... (705) 472-3200
Radio/Television ED, Religion/Lifestyle ED
North Bay Nugget, North Bay, ON

Clarke, Debbie .... (508) 546-2448
ASST, 5th Wave, Rockport, MA

Clarke, Joan .... (808) 525-8000
Food ED, Honolulu Advertiser, Honolulu, HI

Clarke, John .... (913) 798-2213
PUB, ED, Ness County News, Ness City, KS

Clarke, John .... (212) 779-6300
Sales & MKTG DIR
Liaison International, New York, NY

Clarke, John P .... (217) 732-2101
PUB, Courier, Lincoln, IL

Clarke, Mike .... (408) 920-5000
PROD MGR-Platemaking
San Jose Mercury News, San Jose, CA

Clarke, Mitch .... (912) 744-4200
Houston & Peach ED
Macon Telegraph, Macon, GA

Clarke, Norm .... (303) 892-5000
Sports COL
Rocky Mountain News, Denver, CO

Clarke, Norma Jean .... (418) 985-2100
GM, First Informer, Grosse Ile., Magdalen Islands, QC

Clarke, Robert .... (516) 747-8282
ED, Garden City Life, Mineola, NY

Clarke, Ron .... (405) 475-3311
ADV MGR-Creative SRV
Daily Oklahoman, Oklahoma City, OK

Clarke, Tad .... (914) 694-9300
MAN ED-Lifestyles, Reporter Dispatch, White Plains, NY, Gannett Co. Inc.

Clarke, Tricia .... (516) 747-8282
ED, Hicksville Illustrated News, Mineola, NY

Clarksmith, Vicky .... (503) 399-6611
DP MGR, Statesman Journal, Salem, OR

Clarkson, Keith .... (402) 645-3344
PUB, Wymore Arbor State, Wymore, NE

Clarkson, Maggie .... (210) 379-5402
BM, Seguin Gazette-Enterprise, Seguin, TX

Clasen, Denise .... (616) 796-4831
ADV MGR, Pioneer, Big Rapids, MI

Clasen, Richard W .... (316) 583-5721
PUB, ED, Eureka Herald, Eureka, KS

Clasgens, Brad .... (520) 573-4220
ADV MGR-Major Accounts
Arizona Daily Star, Tucson, AZ

Clatch, Joseph .... (717) 455-3636
PROD SUPT-PR
Standard-Speaker, Hazleton, PA

Claus, Marty .... (305) 376-3800
VP-News, Knight-Ridder Inc., Miami, FL

Clausen, Chris .... (409) 833-3311
BUS ED, Enterprise, Beaumont, TX

Clausen, Ron .... (614) 773-2111
ADV DIR, Gazette, Chillicothe, OH

Clausing, Robert .... (316) 775-2218
EDU ED, Augusta Daily Gazette, Augusta, KS

Clawson, Doug .... (207) 784-5411
Sports ED, Sun-Journal, Lewiston, ME

Claxton, John .... (317) 825-0581
PRES, GM, News-Examiner, Connersville, IN

Clay, B K .... (803) 577-7111
PROD DIR-OPER
Post and Courier, Charleston, SC

Clay, Daniel H .... (612) 894-1111
PUB, Dakota County Tribune, Burnsville, MN

Clay, Jac .... (330) 364-5577
ADV SUPV-RT
Times Reporter, New Philadelphia, OH

Clay, Joseph R .... (612) 894-1111
PUB, Dakota County Tribune, Burnsville, MN

Clay, Nancy L .... (517) 895-8551
MGR-PROM, Bay City Times, Bay City, MI

Clay, Patty .... (304) 526-4000
Librarian, Herald-Dispatch, Huntington, WV

Clay, Robert S .... (806) 249-4511
PUB, BM, PA (Shop), COL
Dalhart Daily Texan, Dalhart, TX

Clay, Stanley Bennett .... (213) 733-5611
PUB, ED, SBC, Los Angeles, CA

Clay, Sue .... (616) 222-5400
SYS Leader
Grand Rapids Press, Grand Rapids, MI

Clay, Vicki .... (540) 980-5220
ADV MGR, Southwest Times, Pulaski, VA

Claybaugh, Charles C .... (801) 723-3471
PUB
Box Elder News Journal, Brigham City, UT

Claybaugh, Tom .... (518) 584-4242
ADV DIR, Saratogian, Saratoga Springs, NY

Clayborne, Keith A .... (954) 755-2090
PUB
Coral Springs City News, Coral Springs, FL

Claybourn, David .... (903) 455-4220
Sports ED
Greenville Herald-Banner, Greenville, TX

Claydon, Dave .... (905) 358-5711
EDL Writer
Niagara Falls Review, Niagara Falls, ON

Clayman, Arthur J .... (518) 374-4141
EPE, Daily Gazette, Schenectady, NY

Clayman, Darrell .... (209) 634-9141
ADV DIR, Turlock Journal, Turlock, CA

Clayton, Darlene .... (909) 684-1200
ADV ASST MGR-CLASS TELEMKTG
Press-Enterprise, Riverside, CA

Clayton, Janet .... (213) 237-5000
VP/EPE, EPE/VP
Los Angeles Times, Los Angeles, CA

Clayton, Jerry M .... (910) 599-0162
PUB, Courier-Times, Roxboro, NC

Clayton, Kathryn .... (801) 237-2188
Action Line ED, Travel ED
Deseret News, Salt Lake City, UT

Clayton, Kim .... (403) 429-5400
ADV MGR-RT Sales/Territory Accounts
Edmonton Journal, Edmonton, AB

Clayton, Richard .... (509) 525-3300
EDU ED
Walla Walla Union-Bulletin, Walla Walla, WA

Clayton, Ward .... (706) 724-0851
Sports ED
Augusta Chronicle, Augusta, GA

Cleary, C Patrick .... (970) 242-5050
BUS Writer
Daily Sentinel, Grand Junction, CO

Cleary, John .... (317) 622-1212
Photo, Herald Bulletin, Anderson, IN

Cleary, Kate .... (919) 829-4500
CIRC DIR, News & Observer, Raleigh, NC

Cleary, Mary C .... (315) 841-4105
PUB, ED, Waterville Times, Waterville, NY

Cleary, Patrick J .... (815) 727-4811
PUB, ED, Farmers Weekly Review, Joliet, IL

Cleary, William E .... (609) 456-1199
PUB, ED
Gloucester City News, Gloucester City, NJ

Cleaton, Stephannia .... (718) 981-1234
ASST News ED
Staten Island Advance, Staten Island, NY

Cleaton, W A .... (804) 443-2200
PUB, Rappahannock Times
Tappahannock, VA

Cleaveland, Janet .... (360) 694-3391
Graphics ED, News ED
Columbian, Vancouver, WA

Cleek, Ellen .... (805) 324-9466
ED, News Observer, Bakersfield, CA

Clegg, Chris .... (403) 523-4484
ED, South Peace News, High Prairie, AB

Clegg, Ellen .... (617) 929-2000
MET ED, Boston Globe, Boston, MA

Clegg, Sheri .... (204) 638-4420
ED, Dauphin Herald, Dauphin, MB

Clelan, Gary .... (916) 273-9561
PROD SUPV, Union, Grass Valley, CA

Cleland, J David .... (405) 353-0620
CIRC DIR, Lawton Constitution, Lawton, OK

Cleland, Robert S .... (202) 334-6173
MKTG MGR, Los Angeles Times-Washington Post News Service, Washington, DC

Clem, Molly .... (334) 222-8541
ED, Covington Times Courier, Andalusia, AL

Clemence, Crystal .... (306) 652-9200
Librarian, StarPhoenix, Saskatoon, SK

Clemens, Dave .... (206) 464-2111
PROD MGR-Receiving
Seattle Times, Seattle, WA

Clemens, Joyce .... (505) 396-2844
ADV MGR
Lovington Daily Leader, Lovington, NM

Clement, Douglas .... (203) 355-4141
MAN ED
Litchfield County Times, New Milford, CT

Clement, John .... (613) 267-1100
PUB, Perth Courier, Perth, ON

Clement, Lonnie .... (713) 477-0221
PUB, CIRC DIR
Pasadena Citizen, Pasadena, TX

Clement, Sandy .... (817) 665-5511
ADV MGR
Gainesville Daily Register, Gainesville, TX

Clementelli, Ron .... (516) 843-2020
PROD MGR-Nightside OPER
Newsday, Melville, NY

Clements, Bernie .... (330) 966-1121
GM, Sun Journal, North Canton, OH

Clements, Betty .... (903) 794-3311
PROD MGR-MR
Texarkana Gazette, Texarkana, TX

Clements, Cliff .... (409) 744-3611
ADV MGR-CLASS
Galveston County Daily News, Galveston, TX

Clements, Don .... (918) 581-8300
PROD SUPT-MR, Tulsa World, Tulsa, OK

Clements, Linda .... (504) 732-2565
ADV DIR, Daily News, Bogalusa, LA

Clements, Tyler .... (403) 349-3033
PUB, Westlock News, Westlock, AB

Clemons, Alan .... (205) 532-4000
Outdoors ED
Huntsville Times, Huntsville, AL

Clemons, Harold .... (904) 359-4111
PROD SUPT-Engraving
Florida Times-Union, Jacksonville, FL

Clemons, John .... (606) 231-3100
PROD MGR-SYS OPER
Lexington Herald-Leader, Lexington, KY

Clendaniel, Don .... (302) 674-3600
PROD MGR-Camera Room/MR
Delaware State News, Dover, DE

Clendaniel, Ed .... (408) 920-5000
Perspective ED
San Jose Mercury News, San Jose, CA

Clerks, Peter .... (941) 953-7755
CIRC MGR-County
Sarasota Herald-Tribune, Sarasota, FL

Clermont, Lois .... (518) 561-2300
News ED, Press-Republican, Plattsburgh, NY

Clester, William Sam .... (316) 488-2234
PUB, Belle Plaine News, Belle Plaine, KS

Cleveland, Barry .... (618) 382-4176
PUB, ED, Carmi Times, Carmi, IL

Cleveland, David J .... (603) 352-1234
PROD MGR, Keene Sentinel, Keene, NH

Cleveland, Gary .... (706) 549-0123
PROD MGR, Athens Daily News/Banner-Herald, Athens, GA

Cleveland, Judy .... (402) 634-2332
ED, Meadow Grove News, Meadow Grove, NE

Cleveland, Ken .... (508) 343-6911
MAN ED, Sentinel & Enterprise
Fitchburg, MA

Cleveland, Margaret .... (716) 945-1644
Features ED
Salamanca Press, Salamanca, NY

Clevenger, David .... (318) 893-4223
PUB, Abbeville Meridional, Abbeville, LA

Clevenger, Lewis .... (520) 763-2505
EDU ED, Features ED, Living/Lifestyle ED
Mohave Valley Daily News, Bullhead City, AZ

Clevenson, Laurie J .... (518) 459-8455
ED, Jewish World, Albany, NY

Clevenson, Sam S .... (518) 459-8455
PUB, Jewish World, Albany, NY

Cliche, Louise .... (207) 791-6650
PROD OPER SUPV-Control Point
Portland Press Herald, Portland, ME

Click, Kay .... (937) 878-3993
Family ED
Fairborn Daily Herald, Fairborn, OH

Cliff, Debra .... (406) 665-1008
ED, Big Horn County News, Hardin, MT

Clifford, Andy .... (519) 537-2341
CIRC MGR, Sentinel-Review, Woodstock, ON

Clifford, Frank .... (213) 237-5000
Environmental Writer
Los Angeles Times, Los Angeles, CA

Clifford, James M .... (414) 261-4949
PRES, PUB/ED
Watertown Daily Times, Watertown, WI

Clifford, Jeremiah .... (716) 232-7100
PROD MGR-Pre Press, Rochester Democrat and Chronicle; Rochester, NY Times-Union, Rochester, NY

Clifford, Patricia L .... (414) 261-4949
VP, Watertown Daily Times, Watertown, WI

Clifford, Patrick A .... (213) 237-3700
Sr VP/Chairman & CEO-Mosby-Year Book Inc.
Times Mirror Co., Los Angeles, CA

Clifford, Tom .... (407) 242-3500
Amusements ED, Fashion/Features ED, News Features ED, Florida Today, Melbourne, FL

Clifford, William .... (860) 567-5336
Owner/ED
White Castle Communications, Morris, CT

Clifton, Bill .... (318) 339-7242
PUB, Catahoula News Booster, Jonesville, LA

Clifton, Doug .... (305) 350-2111
Senior VP/EX ED, Miami Herald, Miami, FL

Clifton, Gary .... (512) 251-5574
PUB, Pflugerville Pflag, Pflugerville, TX

Clifton, Harold F .... (805) 395-7500
SEC, Bakersfield Californian, Bakersfield, CA

Clifton, Jean B .... (609) 396-2200
EVP/CFO/TREAS
Journal Register Co., Trenton, NJ

Clifton, Jim .... (405) 275-1000
PUB, Shawnee American, Shawnee, OK

Clifton, Laurie .... (916) 891-1234
Lifestyle ED
Chico Enterprise-Record, Chico, CA

Clifton, Liz .... (718) 372-1920
Correspondent
Graham News Syndicate, Brooklyn, NY

Clifton, Marguerite .... (405) 275-1000
ED, Shawnee American, Shawnee, OK

Clifton, Michael .... (219) 563-8326
ED, Paper, Wabash, IN

Clifton, Wayne .... (416) 367-2000
ADV DIR-Group, Toronto Star, Toronto, ON

Climer, David .... (615) 259-8000
Senior Writer-Sports
Tennessean, Nashville, TN

Cline, Cathy .... (317) 962-1575
DIR-MKTG, Palladium-Item, Richmond, IN

Cline, Charles .... (304) 732-6060
PUB, Independent Herald, Pineville, WV

Cline, Elizabeth .... (864) 298-4100
MGR-PROM
Greenville News, Greenville, SC

Cline, Lee Ann .... (216) 951-0000
PROD MGR-Pre Press
News-Herald, Willoughby, OH

Cline, M Andrew .... (860) 646-0500
CIRC VP, Journal Inquirer, Manchester, CT

Cline, Mike .... (317) 664-5111 (Prod/Comm)
EPE, Chronicle-Tribune, Marion, IN

Cline, Raymond J .... (316) 456-2473
PUB, ED, Conway Springs Star and The Argonia Argosy, Conway Springs, KS

Cline, Susan .... (401) 596-7791
ADV MGR-CLASS, Westerly Sun, Westerly, RI

Cline, William C .... (804) 385-5400
EX ED, News & Advance, Lynchburg, VA

Clingenpeel, Michael J .... (804) 672-1973
ED, Religious Herald, Richmond, VA

Clinger, Bob .... (316) 268-6000
ADV MGR-CLASS
Wichita Eagle, Wichita, KS

Clinton Jr, John H .... (415) 348-4321
PRES, San Mateo County Times
San Mateo, CA

Clinton, Mary Jane .... (415) 348-4321
Fashion ED, Home Furnishings ED, Living/Lifestyle ED, "Time Out" ED, Women's ED, San Mateo County Times, San Mateo, CA

Clinton, Sharon .... (601) 843-4241
PROD FRM-COMP
Bolivar Commercial, Cleveland, MS

Cli Who's Where-44

Clinton, Tom .... (502) 821-6833
ED, EPE, Messenger, Madisonville, KY
Clobes, Terri .... (719) 632-5511
CIRC MGR-Subscriber Services
Gazette, Colorado Springs, CO
Clodfelter, Mary Rob .... (614) 967-2045
ED, Johnstown Independent, Johnstown, OH
Cloe, Kevin .... (520) 684-5454
PUB, Wickenburg Sun, Wickenburg, AZ
Clohessy, Craig .... (360) 834-2141
MAN ED
Camas-Washougal Post Record, Camas, WA
Cloos, Edward .... (716) 232-7100
MGR-Computer Publishing SYS, Rochester Democrat and Chronicle; Times-Union, Rochester, NY
Cloos, Paul .... (334) 433-1551
City ED, Mobile Press Register, Mobile, AL
Cloos, Susie Spear .... (334) 433-1551
Society ED
Mobile Press Register, Mobile, AL
Clopper, Ed .... (301) 733-5131
PROD FRM-MR
Morning Herald, Hagerstown, MD
Close, Sandy .... (415) 243-4364
EX ED
Pacific News Service, San Francisco, CA
Cloud, Bob .... (912) 226-2400
Wire ED, Thomasville Times-Enterprise, Thomasville, GA
Cloud, Curt .... (806) 376-4488
ADV MGR-RT, Amarillo Daily News/Globe Times, Amarillo, TX
Clough, Peter .... (604) 732-2222
Showcase ED, Province, Vancouver, BC
Clouse, H Kenneth .... (603) 668-4321
ADV DIR, Union Leader, Manchester, NH
Clouse, Paul G .... (614) 461-5000
ADV MGR-Customer SRV
Columbus Dispatch, Columbus, OH
Clouse, Tom .... (208) 377-6200
EDU ED, Idaho Statesman, Boise, ID
Cloutier, Nancy S .... (805) 658-2244
PUB, ED, Ventura County & Coast Reporter, Ventura, CA
Cloutier, Norman .... (508) 997-7411
SYS ED, Standard Times, New Bedford, MA
Cloutier, Roland .... (514) 285-7272
PROD DIR, La Presse, Montreal, QC
Clover, Kenneth .... (313) 222-6400
ASST MAN ED-ADM, Free Press, Detroit, MI
Clow, Steve .... (213) 237-5000
Deputy Sunday Calendar ED
Los Angeles Times, Los Angeles, CA
Clowater, Dana .... (506) 452-6671
ADV MGR, Daily Gleaner, Fredericton, NB
Cluck, Chris .... (417) 667-3344
RE ED, Nevada Daily Mail, Nevada, MO
Cluett, Rick .... (902) 625-1900
PUB, Scotia Sun, Port Hawkesbury, NS
Clugston, Patty .... (717) 264-6161
PROD MGR-COMP/Camera
Public Opinion, Chambersburg, PA
Clurman, Michael .... (202) 334-6000
PROD VP, Washington Post, Washington, DC
Clutter, Brian .... (614) 452-4561
ADV MGR, Times Recorder, Zanesville, OH
Clutter, Dan .... (419) 562-3333
Sports ED, Telegraph-Forum, Bucyrus, OH
Clutter, Mike .... (616) 651-5407
Sports ED, Sturgis Journal, Sturgis, MI
Clyburn, James E .... (803) 723-5318
PUB, Coastal Times, Charleston, SC
Clyburn, Karen .... (561) 562-2315
ADV MGR-CLASS
Vero Beach Press-Journal, Vero Beach, FL
Clyburn, Mignon .... (803) 723-5318
GM, Coastal Times, Charleston, SC
Clyde, Andrew .... (903) 597-8111
PROD MGR-OPER
Tyler Morning Telegraph, Tyler, TX
Clyde III, Nelson .... (903) 597-8111
PRES, Tyler Morning Telegraph, Tyler, TX
Clyde IV, Nelson .... (903) 597-8111
ADV DIR, Tyler Morning Telegraph, Tyler, TX
Clyde, Thomas .... (903) 597-8111
CFO, Tyler Morning Telegraph, Tyler, TX
Coady, Jane Howard .... (250) 492-4002
PUB/GEN MGR
Penticton Herald, Penticton, BC
Coady, Michael .... (212) 630-4000
PRES, Women's Wear Daily, New York, NY
Coakley, Bill .... (212) 715-2100
VP/OPER, USA Weekend, New York, NY
Coakley, John .... (209) 441-6111
ADV MGR-Display, Fresno Bee, Fresno, CA
Coate, John .... (415) 777-1111
DIR-VIS/Online Contact
San Francisco Chronicle, San Francisco, CA

Coates, Al .... (519) 894-2231
ASSOC ED, Record, Kitchener, ON
Coates, Deb .... (704) 289-1541
Society ED, Enquirer-Journal, Monroe, NC
Coates, Dorothea J .... (813) 788-1998
Owner/GM, Smith, Al Feature Service Inc., Zephyrhills, FL
Coates, James K .... (860) 442-2200
PROD MGR-PR, Day, New London, CT
Coates, Michael .... (818) 962-8811
News ED, San Gabriel Valley Tribune, West Covina, CA, MediaNews Inc.
Coates, R Duane .... (701) 845-0463
ED, Valley City Times-Record, Valley City, ND
Coats, Edward .... (802) 985-2400
PUB, Vermont Times, Shelburne, VT
Coats, Erin .... (512) 445-3500
ADV MGR-CLASS
Austin American-Statesman, Austin, TX
Coats, Ronald L .... (909) 889-9666
PROD ASST DIR, Sun, San Bernardino, CA
Coats, Royce .... (817) 767-8341
PROD MGR-Distribution Center, Wichita Falls Times Record News, Wichita Falls, TX
Cobb, Amy .... (303) 296-7744
PUB, Denver Westword, Denver, CO
Cobb, Brent .... (308) 345-4500
MAN ED, Entertainment ED
McCook Daily Gazette, McCook, NE
Cobb, Daniel .... (512) 575-1451
EPE, EDL Writer
Victoria Advocate, Victoria, TX
Cobb, Dawn E .... (972) 436-5551
ED, Lewisville News, Lewisville, TX
Cobb, Ian .... (604) 342-9216
ED, Valley Echo, Invermere, BC
Cobb, Kim .... (501) 777-8841
PROD SUPT, Hope Star, Hope, AR
Cobb, Mark .... (205) 345-0505
Entertainment/Amusements ED, Television/Film ED, Theater/Music ED
Tuscaloosa News, Tuscaloosa, AL
Cobb, Price .... (303) 279-5541
GM, Golden Transcript, Golden, CO
Cobb, Robert E .... (816) 535-4313
PUB, ED, Tri-County News, King City, MO
Cobb, Thomas T .... (904) 252-1511
VP, Daytona Beach News-Journal, Daytona Beach, FL
Cobler, Chris .... (970) 352-0211
ED, Greeley Tribune, Greeley, CO
Coburn, James .... (405) 341-2121
Photo DEPT MGR
Edmond Evening Sun, Edmond, OK
Coburn, Patrick .... (217) 788-1300
PUB, State Journal-Register, Springfield, IL
Coburn, Tom .... (413) 736-1587
PUB, ED, West Springfield Record, West Springfield, MA
Coccagna, Tom .... (717) 264-6161
Sports ED, Public Opinion
Chambersburg, PA
Coccaro, Joe .... (757) 446-2000
BUS/FIN ED, RE ED
Virginian-Pilot, Norfolk, VA
Cochelin, Cathy .... (804) 374-2451
MAN ED, News-Progress, Clarksville, VA
Cochran, Bill .... (540) 981-3100
Outdoors ED, Roanoke Times, Roanoke, VA
Cochran, Elizabeth .... (770) 382-4545
Society ED, Women's ED
Daily Tribune News, Cartersville, GA
Cochran, Mick .... (401) 277-7000
MAN ED-Technology
Providence Journal-Bulletin, Providence, RI
Cochran, Scott .... (706) 549-0123
ADTX MGR, Athens Daily News/Banner-Herald, Athens, GA
Cochran, Terry .... (316) 225-4151
PUB, Dodge City Daily Globe, Dodge City, KS
Cochrane, Bill .... (409) 744-3611
PROD SUPT
Galveston County Daily News, Galveston, TX
Cochrane Jr, Charles .... (509) 248-1251
PUB, Yakima Herald-Republic, Yakima, WA
Cochrane, Mike .... (403) 235-7100
PROD SUPV-SYS Support
Calgary Herald, Calgary, AB
Cochrum, Glenn .... (502) 443-1771
Entertainment/Amusements ED, Radio/Television ED, Paducah Sun, Paducah, KY
Cockburn, Ed .... (905) 632-4444
GM, Burlington Post, Burlington, ON
Cockburn, Roy M .... (609) 895-2600
CFO/Sr VP
Goodson Newspaper Group, Lawrenceville, NJ
Cocke, Larry .... (409) 945-3441
ADV DIR, Texas City Sun, Texas City, TX
Cocke, Nan .... (816) 747-8123
News ED
Daily Star-Journal, Warrensburg, MO
Cockerham Jr, Bryce .... (706) 724-0851
ADV MGR-Major/NTL
Augusta Chronicle, Augusta, GA

Cockerham, Sean .... (907) 747-3219
Sports ED
Daily Sitka Sentinel, Sitka, AK
Cockerill, Bill .... (210) 278-3335
ED, Uvalde Leader-News, Uvalde, TX
Cockrell, Les .... (817) 488-8561
ED, Grapevine Sun, Grapevine, TX
Cockrell, Ruth .... (303) 292-5158
GM, Denver Weekly News, Denver, CO
Coco, Benjamin J .... (610) 371-5000
MGR-Accounting/CR
Reading Times/Eagle, Reading, PA
Cocoles, Chris .... (209) 674-2424
Sports ED, Madera Tribune, Madera, CA
Cocozzo, Joseph A .... (216) 951-0000
PUB, News-Herald, Willoughby, OH
Cocte, Randy .... (519) 354-2000
Amusements ED, Films/Theater ED, Music ED, NTL News ED, Teen-Age Youth ED
Chatham Daily News, Chatham, ON
Coda, Roger .... (814) 725-4557
ED, North East Breeze, North East, PA
Coddington, Kathleen .... (860) 241-6200
ADV MGR-RT
Hartford Courant, Hartford, CT
Coddington, Richard M .... (330) 996-3000
PROD MGR-Building/Facilities
Akron Beacon Journal, Akron, OH
Coder, Tim .... (505) 823-7777
State ED
Albuquerque Journal, Albuquerque, NM
Coderre C A, Raymond .... (514) 759-3664
PUB, ED, L'Action, Joliette, QC
Codner, Mark A .... (405) 795-3355
PUB, Madill Record, Madill, OK
Codner, Sherry .... (405) 795-3355
GM, Madill Record, Madill, OK
Cody, Don .... (864) 427-1234
CIRC MGR, Union Daily Times, Union, SC
Cody, Gordon .... (815) 432-6066
CONT
Independent Media Group Inc., Watseka, IL
Cody, Kevin .... (310) 372-4611
PUB, ED, Easy Reader, Hermosa Beach, CA
Cody, Lucille E .... (317) 664-5111
ASST SEC/TREAS
Chronicle-Tribune, Marion, IN
Cody, Martin .... (520) 763-2505
PRES, PRES/PUB
Mohave Valley Daily News, Bullhead City, AZ
Cody, Ruth .... (360) 377-3711
ADV MGR-Display, Sun, Bremerton, WA
Cody, William H .... (717) 291-8811
ED (Intelligencer Journal)
Lancaster Intelligencer Journal/New Era/Sunday News, Lancaster, PA
Coe, Michelle .... (717) 265-2151
PROD SUPT (Day)
Daily Review, Towanda, PA
Coe, Richard .... (205) 236-1551
Environmental ED
Anniston Star, Anniston, AL
Coe, Terry .... (713) 624-1400
PUB, Houston Press, Houston, TX
Coe, Tom .... (414) 473-3363
PUB, Whitewater Register, Whitewater, WI
Coehrs, David .... (419) 738-2128
Agriculture BUS ED
Wapakoneta Daily News, Wapakoneta, OH
Coffeen, Steve .... (702) 383-0211
CIRC DIR
Las Vegas Review-Journal, Las Vegas, NV
Coffey, Cathy B .... (404) 843-5000
VP-ADV, Cox Newspapers Inc., Atlanta, GA
Coffey, Charles .... (317) 898-3728
Contact Person
Leaning Tree Features, Indianapolis, IN
Coffey, Gloria .... (312) 346-8123
GM, Tri-City Journal, Chicago, IL
Coffey, J Wallace .... (540) 669-2181
DIR-MKTG, Herald-Courier Virginia Tennessean, Bristol, VA
Coffey, Kevin D .... (330) 833-2631
MAN ED, EPE, Independent, Massillon, OH
Coffey, Laura .... (206) 622-8272
Environmental ED, Seattle Daily Journal of Commerce, Seattle, WA
Coffey, Lisa .... (317) 633-1240
EDL Writer
Indianapolis Star/News, Indianapolis, IN
Coffey, Raymond .... (312) 321-3000
COL-GEN, Chicago Sun-Times, Chicago, IL
Coffey, Richard A .... (320) 245-2368
PUB, ED, Pine County Courier
Sandstone, MN
Coffey III, Shelby .... (213) 237-3700
VP/ED & EX VP-Los Angeles Times
Times Mirror Co., Los Angeles, CA
Coffield, Connie .... (303) 776-2244
MGR-PROM, Daily Times-Call, Longmont, CO
Coffin, Jonetta .... (206) 339-3000
Librarian, Herald, Everett, WA
Coffman, Linda K .... (937) 498-2111
PUB, Sidney Daily News, Sidney, OH

Coffman, Rick .... (406) 587-4491
PUB, Daily Chronicle, Bozeman, MT
Coffman, Steven .... (315) 789-3333
News ED, Finger Lakes Times, Geneva, NY
Cofiel, Tricia .... (610) 622-8800
Entertainment ED, Fashion/Style ED, Youth ED, Delaware County Daily Times, Primos, PA
Cogdell, Tom .... (423) 745-5664
CIRC MGR, Daily Post-Athenian, Athens, TN
Coggins, Mike .... (806) 935-4111
PUB, ED
Moore County News-Press, Dumas, TX
Cognetta, Gary V .... (718) 981-1234
ADV MGR
Staten Island Advance, Staten Island, NY
Cogswell, Dennis .... (616) 429-2400
Regional ED, Herald-Palladium
St. Joseph, MI
Cogswell, George .... (719) 632-5511
CIRC MGR-Subscriber Acquisition
Gazette, Colorado Springs, CO
Cogswell, Ken .... (616) 345-3511
CIRC MGR, Gazette, Kalamazoo, MI
Cogswell, Phil .... (503) 221-8327
EDL Writer, Oregonian, Portland, OR
Cohen, Aaron .... (312) 357-4848
ED, JUF (Jewish United Fund), Chicago, IL
Cohen, Al .... (310) 829-6811
PROD FRM-MR, Outlook, Santa Monica, CA
Cohen, Amir .... (201) 887-3900
GM, Metrowest Jewish News, Whippany, NJ
Cohen, Carla L .... (516) 775-2700
PUB, ED, Gateway, Floral Park, NY
Cohen, Carol L .... (717) 236-9555
ED, Community Review, Harrisburg, PA
Cohen, Daniel H .... (212) 556-1234
VP-ADV, New York Times Co., New York, NY
Cohen, David .... (408) 298-8000
PUB, Metro, San Jose, CA
Cohen, Fred .... (561) 820-3800
City ED, Palm Beach Daily News, Palm Beach, FL
Cohen, Gabriel .... (317) 972-7800
PUB, ED, National Jewish Post & Opinion, Indianapolis, IN
Cohen, Greg .... (503) 397-0116
ED
Chronicle and Sentinel-Mist, St. Helens, OR
Cohen, Hal .... (215) 587-4400
DIR of Technology
MediaStream, Philadelphia, PA
Cohen, Ira .... (603) 668-4321
PROD FRM-Platemaking
Union Leader, Manchester, NH
Cohen, Jeff .... (518) 454-5694
ED, Times Union, Albany, NY
Cohen, Lori .... (217) 788-1300
MGR-MKTG RES
State Journal-Register, Springfield, IL
Cohen, Martin .... (202) 334-6000
VP, Washington Post Co., Washington, DC
Cohen, Murray .... (419) 695-0015
PRES, TREAS, PUB
Delphos Daily Herald, Delphos, OH
Cohen, Richard .... (202) 334-6000
COL, Washington Post, Washington, DC
Cohen, Robert .... (201) 877-4141
Washington BU, Star-Ledger, Newark, NJ
Cohen, Ron .... (703) 276-5800
NTL ED
Gannett News Service, Arlington, VA
Cohen, Shelly .... (617) 426-3000
EPE, Boston Herald, Boston, MA
Cohen, William .... (201) 947-5000
PUB
Bergen News Palisades, Palisades Park, NJ
Cohn, Douglas A .... (703) 764-0496
PRES/ED/GEN MGR
Associated Features Inc., Burke, VA
Cohn, Heather .... (954) 963-4000
ED, Community News, Hollywood, FL
Cohn, Lowell .... (707) 546-2020
COL-Sports, Press Democrat, Santa Rosa, CA
Cohn, Robert .... (314) 432-3353
PUB, Saint Louis Jewish Light, St. Louis, MO
Coit, Valerie .... (701) 436-4241
ED, Hillsboro Banner, Hillsboro, ND
Coker, Don .... (706) 324-5526
Graphics ED/Art DIR
Columbus Ledger-Enquirer, Columbus, GA
Coker, Erik .... (607) 432-1000
Arts ED, Daily Star, Oneonta, NY
Colander, Pat .... (219) 933-3200
MAN ED, Times, Munster, IN
Colantoni, Alfred D .... (908) 922-6000
VP-CORP Services/CFO
New Jersey Press Inc., Neptune, NJ
Colas, Faith .... (414) 449-4860
PUB, Milwaukee Courier, Milwaukee, WI
Colbenson, Peter .... (701) 252-3120
CIRC MGR, Jamestown Sun, Jamestown, ND
Colbert, Harley .... (415) 777-7212
PROD MGR
Chronicle Features, San Francisco, CA

45-Who's Where **Col**

Colbert, J D (405) 275-3121
ED, How-Ni-Kan, Shawnee, OK
Colbert, Neil (405) 938-2533
PUB, ED
Northwest Oklahoman, Shattuck, OK
Colbert-Martin, Angie (319) 372-6421
City Government
Daily Democrat, Fort Madison, IA
Colburn, A Loren (315) 472-7825
PUB, Onondaga Valley News, Syracuse, NY
Colby, Anne (305) 372-0933
Writer, Legal & Word Briefs, Miami, FL
Colby, Charles (818) 713-3000
MGR-MIS, MGR-Telecommunications
Daily News, Woodland Hills, CA
Colclasure, Lela (618) 548-3330
ED, Salem Times-Commoner, Salem, IL
Coldwell Sr, Kenneth C (410) 687-7775
PUB, Avenue News, Baltimore, MD
Cole, Asa (508) 626-3800
PUB, Middlesex News, Framingham, MA
Cole, Bettyann (419) 245-6000
Publishing SYS MGR, Blade, Toledo, OH
Cole, Brian (204) 697-7000
EPE, Winnipeg Free Press, Winnipeg, MB
Cole, Brian D (304) 292-6301
CONT, Dominion Post, Morgantown, WV
Cole, C E (817) 995-2586
ED, Saint Jo Tribune, Saint Jo, TX
Cole, Carol (918) 335-8200
Living/Lifestyle ED
Examiner-Enterprise, Bartlesville, OK
Cole, Carrie (805) 763-3171
PROD SUPV
Daily Midway Driller, Taft, CA
Cole, Christy (910) 323-4848
CIRC MGR-Sales
Fayetteville Observer-Times, Fayetteville, NC
Cole, Dee (817) 995-2586
MAN ED, Saint Jo Tribune, Saint Jo, TX
Cole, Diane (801) 237-2031
EDL Writer
Salt Lake Tribune, Salt Lake City, UT
Cole, Don (412) 567-5656
PUB, Leechburg Advance, Vandergrift, PA
Cole, John (919) 419-6500
Graphics ED, Herald-Sun, Durham, NC
Cole, John G (216) 245-6901
ED, Morning Journal, Lorain, OH
Cole, K C (213) 237-5000
SCI Writer
Los Angeles Times, Los Angeles, CA
Cole, Kevin (617) 426-3000
DIR-Photography
Boston Herald, Boston, MA
Cole, Marge (805) 781-7800
CIRC MGR-Customer SRV
Telegram-Tribune, San Luis Obispo, CA
Cole, Maxine (405) 475-3311
Television ED
Daily Oklahoman, Oklahoma City, OK
Cole, Michelle (208) 377-6200
Political ED, Idaho Statesman, Boise, ID
Cole, Nelle Bailey (615) 722-5429
PUB, ED
Wayne County News, Waynesboro, TN
Cole, Patty (919) 829-4500
Newsroom Asst
News & Observer, Raleigh, NC
Cole, Preston J (816) 748-3266
ED, Post-Telegraph, Princeton, MO
Cole, Richard (308) 532-6783
VP-ADM & FIN
Western Publishing Co., North Platte, NE
Cole, Ronald (330) 747-1471
EDU ED, School ED
Vindicator, Youngstown, OH
Cole, Sherry (201) 646-4000
MGR-EDU SRV, Record, Hackensack, NJ
Cole, Stanley (817) 560-2396
PUB, Carswell Sentinel, Fort Worth, TX
Cole, Thomas F X (508) 793-9100
DIR-MKTG SRV
Telegram & Gazette, Worcester, MA
Cole, Tink (912) 236-9511
PROD SUPV-Building
Savannah Morning News, Savannah, GA
Cole, Trevor (416) 585-5000
ED (Broadcast Week Mag), Globe and Mail (Canada's National Newspaper), Toronto, ON
Coleburn, Doug (804) 292-3019
PUB, ED, Courier-Record, Blackstone, VA
Coleman, Alice (318) 443-7664
ED, Alexandria News Weekly, Alexandria, LA
Coleman, Barbara (757) 539-3437
BUS ED, Suffolk News-Herald, Suffolk, VA
Coleman, Bebe (919) 528-2393
MAN ED
Butner-Creedmoor News, Creedmoor, NC
Coleman, Christopher (716) 662-0001
PUB, ED, Southtowns Citizen
Orchard Park, NY
Coleman, Dan (615) 259-8800
EPE, Nashville Banner, Nashville, TN
Coleman, Darrell (816) 932-6600
ASST ED
Universal Press Syndicate, Kansas City, MO
Coleman, Darrell G (512) 884-2011
CFO, Caller-Times, Corpus Christi, TX
Coleman, Dave (202) 636-3000
PROD MGR-Pre Press OPER
Washington Times, Washington, DC
Coleman, Don (614) 446-2342
PROD FRM-Press/Camera, Gallipolis Daily Tribune/Sunday Times-Sentinel, Gallipolis, OH, Gannett Co. Inc.
Coleman, Elaine (817) 643-4141
ED, Rising Star, Rising Star, TX
Coleman, Eugene (210) 224-0706
PUB, Snap News, San Antonio, TX
Coleman, Frances (334) 433-1551
EPE, Mobile Press Register, Mobile, AL
Coleman, George (423) 246-8121
ADV DIR
Kingsport Times-News, Kingsport, TN
Coleman, Harry R (919) 528-2393
PUB, ED
Butner-Creedmoor News, Creedmoor, NC
Coleman, Jane (707) 464-2141
PROD SUPV-COMP
Triplicate, Crescent City, CA
Coleman, John (519) 255-5711
EPE, Windsor Star, Windsor, ON
Coleman, Judith L (541) 963-3161
ASST SEC, Observer, La Grande, OR
Coleman, Kate (408) 920-5000
ADV DIR-Creative/MKTG SRV, MGR-Product Development
San Jose Mercury News, San Jose, CA
Coleman, Ken (204) 727-2451
Life/Style ED, Brandon Sun, Brandon, MB
Coleman, Kevin (573) 815-1500
CONT, Daily Tribune, Columbia, MO
Coleman, L Dan (509) 248-1251
ED, Yakima Herald-Republic, Yakima, WA
Coleman, Michael J (703) 284-6000
Sr Group PRES-South Newspaper Group
Gannett Co. Inc., Arlington, VA
Coleman, Milton (202) 334-6000
Deputy MAN ED
Washington Post, Washington, DC
Coleman, Murray (919) 419-6500
BUS ED, Herald-Sun, Durham, NC
Coleman, Nancy (717) 265-2151
Features ED, Living/Lifestyle ED, Television/Film ED, Theater/Music ED, Women's ED
Daily Review, Towanda, PA
Coleman, Pam (210) 686-4343
ASST MET ED, Monitor, McAllen, TX
Coleman, Rachel (316) 624-2541
Features ED
Southwest Daily Times, Liberal, KS
Coleman, Robert (903) 794-3311
Photo ED, Texarkana Gazette, Texarkana, TX
Coleman, Robert F (815) 784-5138
PUB
Genoa-Kingston-Kirkland News, Sycamore, IL
Coleman, Roger F (630) 232-9222
PUB, Kane County Chronicle, Geneva, IL
Coleman, Scott (334) 875-2110
CIRC MGR, Selma Times-Journal, Selma, AL
Coleman, Tammy (712) 328-1811
Films/Theater ED, Music ED
Daily Nonpareil, Council Bluffs, IA
Coleman, Terri (573) 888-4505
ADV MGR
Daily Dunklin Democrat, Kennett, MO
Coleman, William (209) 875-2511
ED, Sanger Herald, Sanger, CA
Coleman, Yvonne (502) 772-2591
ED, Louisville Defender, Louisville, KY
Coleman Sr, Leon (318) 443-7664
PUB
Alexandria News Weekly, Alexandria, LA
Coles, Hartley (519) 357-2320
PUB
Wingham Advance-Times, Wingham, ON
Coles, Linda (719) 348-5913
ED, Stratton Spotlight, Stratton, CO
Coles, Timothy R (330) 454-5611
CIRC MGR
Canton Repository, Canton, OH
Coletta Jr, Edmund (617) 284-2400
MAN ED
East Boston Sun Transcript, Revere, MA
Coley, Jerry (214) 977-8222
ADV DIR-RT
Dallas Morning News, Dallas, TX
Coley, Jim (202) 334-6000
PROD MGR-Springfield Plant
Washington Post, Washington, DC
Coley, Joseph (805) 324-9466
PUB, GM
Bakersfield News Observer, Bakersfield, CA
Coley, Roger (318) 459-3200
Graphics ED
Shreveport Times, Shreveport, LA
Colfer, Susan (207) 873-3341
ADV MGR-CLASS, Central Maine Morning Sentinel, Waterville, ME
Guy Gannett Communications
Colindres, Adriana (309) 686-3000
NTL ED, Political/Government ED
Journal Star, Peoria, IL
Coll, Steve (202) 334-6000
Washington Post Magazine ED & PUB
Washington Post, Washington, DC
Collado, A B (505) 243-6161
PUB, El Hispano News, Albuquerque, NM
Collado, Francisco (505) 243-6161
MAN ED
El Hispano News, Albuquerque, NM
Collado, Lizette (505) 243-6161
GM, El Hispano News, Albuquerque, NM
Collar, Mike (518) 725-8616
Sports ED, Leader-Herald, Gloversville, NY
Collard, Marcel (418) 686-3233
Auto ED, Le Soleil, Quebec, QC
Collazo, Jasmin J (212) 807-4600
ASST to ED
El Diario La Prensa, New York, NY
Collett, Ritter (937) 225-2000
Sports COL, Dayton Daily News, Dayton, OH
Colletta Jr, Edmund (617) 846-3700
ED, Winthrop Sun-Transcript, Winthrop, MA
Collette, Kenneth (203) 574-3636
CIRC ASST DIR, CIRC CNR-NIE, Waterbury Republican-American, Waterbury, CT
Colley, Tom (304) 327-2811
EX ED
Bluefield Daily Telegraph, Bluefield, WV
Colleyn, Dave (419) 522-3311
Photo ED, News Journal, Mansfield, OH
Collica, Ken (313) 994-6989
ADV MGR-CLASS
Ann Arbor News, Ann Arbor, MI
Collicutt, Richard (250) 423-4222
ED, Elk Valley Miner, Sparwood, BC
Collier, Buck (573) 624-4545
ED, Daily Statesman, Dexter, MO
Collier, Carol (910) 343-2000
Graphics ED/Art DIR, Morning Star/Sunday Star-News, Wilmington, NC
Collier, Gene (412) 263-1100
Sports COL
Pittsburgh Post-Gazette, Pittsburgh, PA
Collier, Joelle (714) 634-1567
ED, Orange City News, Anaheim, CA
Collier, Kristen (619) 270-3103
MAN ED, Peninsula Beacon, San Diego, CA
Collier, Steve (541) 926-2211
Asst News ED
Albany Democrat-Herald, Albany, OR
Collier, Terry (210) 997-2155
GM, ED, Fredericksburg Standard Radio Post, Fredericksburg, TX
Collin, Dan D (402) 362-4478
PUB, ED, York News-Times, York, NE
Colling, Dennis J (715) 735-6611
VP, PUB/GM, EagleHerald, Marinette, WI
Colling, Ronald A (712) 653-3854
PUB, ED, Manning Monitor, Manning, IA
Collins, Allie (615) 823-1274
ED, Livingston Enterprise, Livingston, TN
Collins, Alvin (615) 444-3952
PROD FRM-PR, Lebanon Democrat, Lebanon, TN
Collins, Arian (619) 459-4201
MAN ED, La Jolla Light, La Jolla, CA
Collins, Barry T (513) 863-8200
CIRC MGR-Sales
Journal-News, Hamilton, OH
Collins, Bill (803) 572-0511
PUB, Goose Creek Gazette, Goose Creek, SC
Collins, Bob (609) 663-4200
PUB, Courier Post/This Week, Cherry Hill, NJ
Collins, Brenda (505) 542-3471
ED, Lordsburg Liberal, Lordsburg, NM
Collins, Brian (905) 684-7251
Entertainment ED, Family/Society, Fashion Music ED, Standard, St. Catharines, ON
Collins, Calvin (407) 841-3052
PUB, ED, Orlando Times, Orlando, FL
Collins, Cameron (615) 452-2561
MAN ED, News-Examiner, Gallatin, TN
Collins, Christine (541) 523-3673
EDU ED, Health/Medical ED
Baker City Herald, Baker City, OR
Collins, Danny (919) 829-4500
PROD DIR-OPER
News & Observer, Raleigh, NC
Collins, Dave (907) 224-8070
MAN ED, Seward Phoenix Log, Seward, AK
Collins, Dave (904) 829-6562
Travel ED
St. Augustine Record, St. Augustine, FL
Collins, Dennis (616) 347-2544
PROD CNR
Petoskey News-Review, Petoskey, MI
Collins, Diane (417) 776-2236
PUB, ED, News-Dispatch, Seneca, MO
Collins, Elizabeth (318) 281-4421
CIRC MGR
Bastrop Daily Enterprise, Bastrop, LA
Collins, Fred (706) 278-1011
PROD FRM-MR
Daily Citizen-News, Dalton, GA
Collins, Greg A (903) 984-2593
MAN ED, Travel ED, Women's ED
Kilgore News Herald, Kilgore, TX
Collins, J B (423) 756-6900
Urban Affairs ED
Chattanooga Free Press, Chattanooga, TN
Collins, James (212) 930-8000
CIRC MGR-MET
New York Post, New York, NY
Collins, James K (216) 951-0000
ED, EPE, News-Herald, Willoughby, OH
Collins, James W (217) 223-5100
VP-Newspaper OPER
Quincy Newspapers Inc., Quincy, IL
Collins, Janelle (864) 465-3311
ED, McCormick Messenger, McCormick, SC
Collins, Janet (509) 525-3300
Librarian
Walla Walla Union-Bulletin, Walla Walla, WA
Collins, Jean Ann (972) 542-2631
MAN ED
McKinney Courier-Gazette, McKinney, TX
Collins, Jennifer L (609) 298-7111
ED, Register-News, Bordentown, NJ
Collins, Jerry (520) 783-3333
ADV DIR, Yuma Daily Sun, Yuma, AZ
Collins, Jim (805) 945-8671
PUB, Desert Mailer News, Lancaster, CA
Collins, John (609) 396-2200
VP-Budgets & Planning
Journal Register Co., Trenton, NJ
Collins, Judy (417) 256-9191
BM, West Plains Daily Quill, West Plains, MO
Collins, Judy (914) 341-1100
Wire ED
Times Herald-Record, Middletown, NY
Collins, L H (407) 841-3052
GM, Orlando Times, Orlando, FL
Collins, Linda (618) 262-5144
CIRC MGR
Daily Republican Register, Mount Carmel, IL
Collins, Linda (310) 322-1830
ED, El Segundo Herald, El Segundo, CA
Collins, Martha (770) 428-9411
Books Writer, Fashion/Style ED, Features ED, Food ED, Living/Lifestyle ED, Travel ED
Marietta Daily Journal, Marietta, GA
Collins, Mary (319) 398-8211
DIR-Human Resources
Gazette, Cedar Rapids, IA
Collins, Mary Ann (423) 992-3392
GM, Union News Leader, Maynardville, TN
Collins, Monica (617) 426-3000
Television COL, Boston Herald, Boston, MA
Collins, Neil P (617) 284-2400
PUB, Revere Journal, Revere, MA
Collins, Pat (919) 829-4500
CIRC MGR-CLASS
News & Observer, Raleigh, NC
Collins, Pat (905) 526-3333
PUB, Spectator, Hamilton, ON
Collins, Paul (910) 969-6076
ED, Weekly Independent, Rural Hall, NC
Collins, Phyllis (208) 743-9411
Librarian
Lewiston Morning Tribune, Lewiston, ID
Collins, Richard (972) 298-4211
PUB, Duncanville Today, Duncanville, TX
Collins, Robert C (212) 581-4640
MAN ED, America, New York, NY
Collins, Robert T (609) 663-6000
PRES, PUB, Courier-Post, Cherry Hill, NJ
Collins, S John (541) 523-3673
Photo ED
Baker City Herald, Baker City, OR
Collins, Sandy (505) 325-4545
ADV CNR-Design
Daily Times, Farmington, NM
Collins, Steve (860) 584-0501
Political ED, Bristol Press, Bristol, CT
Collins, Terrell (415) 327-6397
ADV MGR-CLASS
Palo Alto Daily News, Palo Alto, CA
Collins, Tracy (412) 263-1100
ASSOC ED-Graphics
Pittsburgh Post-Gazette, Pittsburgh, PA
Collins, Trevor (502) 781-1700
ADV MGR-CLASS
Daily News, Bowling Green, KY
Collins, Valerie (409) 642-1726/1891
ED, Groveton News, Groveton, TX
Collins, Voletta (409) 985-5541
Librarian, Port Arthur News, Port Arthur, TX

Col Who's Where-46

Collins, William (216) 999-4500
PROD ASST MGR
Plain Dealer, Cleveland, OH
Collins, William A (864) 223-1411
EX ED, Amusements/Automotive ED, EPE, NTL ED, Radio/Television ED, RE ED
Index-Journal, Greenwood, SC
Collins, William C (803) 873-9424
PUB, ED, Journal-Scene, Summerville, SC
Collinson, Thomas H (316) 231-2600
PUB, Morning Sun, Pittsburg, KS
Collis, Judith A (501) 246-5525
PUB, ADV MGR
Arkadelphia Siftings Herald, Arkadelphia, AR
Collison, Cathy (313) 222-6400
Yak! ED, Detroit Free Press, Detroit, MI
Collum, Peter (403) 429-5400
BUS ED, Edmonton Journal, Edmonton, AB
Colmar, Susan (770) 963-9205
DIR-Financial
Gwinnett Daily Post, Lawrenceville, GA
Colmore, Perry C (508) 475-5731
ED, Andover Townsman, Andover, MA
Colon, Bob (405) 475-3311
Sports ED
Daily Oklahoman, Oklahoma City, OK
Colosant, Chuck (541) 482-3456
CIRC MGR, Daily Tidings, Ashland, OR
Colquitt, Ron (334) 433-1551
Automotive ED
Mobile Press Register, Mobile, AL
Colquitt, Steve (706) 549-0123
Sports ED, Athens Daily News/Banner-Herald, Athens, GA
Colson, Mark (316) 431-4100
Picture ED, Chanute Tribune, Chanute, KS
Colston, J Willard (207) 828-8100
VP-New Media Strategies
Guy Gannett Communications, Portland, ME
Colt, Patsy J (816) 748-3266
GM, Post-Telegraph, Princeton, MO
Coltharp, Nick (501) 268-8621
ADV DIR, Daily Citizen, Searcy, AR
Coltharp, Richard (505) 437-7120
ED, Alamogordo Daily News, Alamogordo, NM
Colton, Dave (717) 265-2151
Graphics ED/Art DIR, PROD MGR
Daily Review, Towanda, PA
Coltrain, Dallas F (919) 792-1181
PUB, GM, Enterprise, Williamston, NC
Colucci, Marie Anne (514) 987-2222
ADV MGR-Special Sections/PROM
Gazette, Montreal, QC
Colucci, Robert (401) 277-7000
CORP CONT, Journal-Bulletin, Providence, RI
Colunil, Bill (610) 562-7515
GM, Hamburg Item, Hamburg, PA
Colurso, Mary (203) 789-5200
Arts/Travel ED
New Haven Register, New Haven, CT
Colville, Warren T (716) 849-3434
Senior VP, ADV DIR
Buffalo News, Buffalo, NY
Colvin, Leonard (804) 543-6531
ED, Journal and Guide, Norfolk, VA
Colvin, Richard (213) 237-5000
EDU Writer (K-12)
Los Angeles Times, Los Angeles, CA
Colvin Jr, T L (318) 259-2551
PUB, ED, Jackson Independent, Jonesboro, LA
Colvin III, T L (318) 259-2551
MAN ED
Jackson Independent, Jonesboro, LA
Colvin, W A (913) 776-2200
Senior ED
Manhattan Mercury, Manhattan, KS
Colwell, Jack (219) 235-6161
Political Writer
South Bend Tribune, South Bend, IN
Colwell, Lyn (519) 756-2020
Librarian, Expositor, Brantford, ON
Colwell, Steve (318) 539-3511
PUB, ED, Springhill Press & News-Journal, Springhill, LA
Comacho Sr, Raul R (800) 995-8626
PUB, ED
El Popular - Bakersfield, Bakersfield, CA
Combest, Craig (210) 829-9000
VP, Harte-Hanks Communications Inc., San Antonio, TX
Combs, Bill (606) 573-4510
ADV MGR
Harlan Daily Enterprise, Harlan, KY
Combs, Billy A (806) 259-2441
PUB, ED, Memphis Democrat, Memphis, TX
Combs, Clara (903) 364-2276
GM, ED, Whitewright Sun, Whitewright, TX
Combs, Dennis (903) 364-2276
PUB, Whitewright Sun, Whitewright, TX
Combs, Erin (416) 367-2000
Picture ED, Toronto Star, Toronto, ON
Combs, Sara B (812) 738-4552
ED, Clarion News, Corydon, IN
Combs, Veronica (541) 269-1222
MAN ED, World, Coos Bay, OR
Combs, Wanda (540) 745-2127
ED, Floyd Press, Floyd, VA
Comden, David (916) 498-1234
GM, News & Review, Sacramento, CA
Comely, Richard (519) 622-1520
ED/PUB
Semple Comics Features, Cambridge, ON
Comer, Harriet (912) 744-4200
Librarian, Macon Telegraph, Macon, GA
Comer, John (903) 597-8111
PROD FRM-MR (Day)
Tyler Morning Telegraph, Tyler, TX
Comer, Mary (913) 462-3963
ADV MGR, Colby Free Press, Colby, KS
Comfort, Jane (803) 577-7111
MGR-Market RES
Post and Courier, Charleston, SC
Comia-Hoffman, Nancy S (314) 421-1880
CIRC MGR, St. Louis Countain, St. Louis, MO
ABC Inc. (Legal Communications Corp.)
Comins, Linda (304) 233-0100
Fashion/Women's ED, Intelligencer/Wheeling News-Register, Wheeling, WV
Comiskey, James (630) 232-9222
PROD DIR
Kane County Chronicle, Geneva, IL
Comiskey, Nancy (317) 633-1240
MAN ED-Features/Photo/Graphics
Indianapolis Star/News, Indianapolis, IN
Commons, Dave (423) 376-3481
PUB, Roane County News, Kingston, TN
Como, Edward (Ted) (423) 246-8121
MAN ED, Books/Films ED, SCI/Technology ED, Kingsport Times-News, Kingsport, TN
Compion, Maureen (707) 643-1706
PROD MGR, Benicia Herald, Vallejo, CA
Compton, Bob (214) 977-8222
Books ED
Dallas Morning News, Dallas, TX
Compton, Brian (307) 266-0500
PROD FRM-PR, Star-Tribune, Casper, WY
Compton, Mrs Joe R (903) 822-3511
PUB, ED, Mount Enterprise Progress, Mount Enterprise, TX
Compton, Kelly (517) 437-7351
CIRC CNR, Daily News, Hillsdale, MI
Compton, Lodge (540) 935-2123
PUB, ED, Virginia Mountaineer, Grundy, VA
Comrie, Marilyn J (401) 596-7791
Entertainment ED, Features ED
Westerly Sun, Westerly, RI
Comstock, Jay (304) 846-2666
PUB
Nicholas County News Leader, Richwood, WV
Comstock, Paul (614) 363-1161
BUS ED, City/County ED, Farm/Agriculture ED, Delaware Gazette, Delaware, OH
Conaboy, Jack (410) 332-6000
CIRC MGR-Packaging OPER
Sun, Baltimore, MD
Conant, Colleen C (941) 262-3161
VP, ED, Naples Daily News, Naples, FL
Conant, Rendy (573) 336-3711
ADV DIR, Daily Guide, Waynesville, MO
Conarroe, Douglas E (303) 666-6576
PUB, Louisville Times, Louisville, CO
Conarroe, Percy A (303) 665-6515
ED, Lafayette News, Lafayette, CO
Conary, Bob (903) 786-4051
PUB, Pottsboro Press, Pottsboro, TX
Conary, Lori (903) 786-4051
PUB, Pottsboro Press, Pottsboro, TX
Conaty, John (401) 277-7000
DIR-TELEMKTG
Providence Journal-Bulletin, Providence, RI
Conaway, Darla (409) 265-7411
EPE, Political/Government ED
Brazosport Facts, Clute, TX
Conboy, John (212) 416-2000
PROD MGR-Construction & Facilities
Wall Street Journal, New York, NY
Concannon, James T (617) 929-2000
NTL ED, Boston Globe, Boston, MA
Conchel, Anthony (937) 652-1331
MAN ED, Urbana Daily Citizen, Urbana, OH
Brown Publishing Co.
Condon, Bob (518) 792-3131
Regional ED, Post-Star, Glens Falls, NY
Condon, Kevin (765) 362-1200
Entertainment ED, Environmental ED, Farm/Agriculture ED, Films/Theater ED, Music ED, Radio/ Television ED, Travel ED
Journal Review, Crawfordsville, IN
Condon, Pat (701) 253-7311
Political ED (ND), Forum, Fargo, ND
Condon, Tom (860) 241-6200
COL-Urban Affairs
Hartford Courant, Hartford, CT
Condra, Edward (609) 989-7800
ADV DIR, Trentonian, Trenton, NJ
Condren, Dave (716) 849-3434
Religion ED, Buffalo News, Buffalo, NY
Condy, William (408) 423-4242
City ED
Santa Cruz County Sentinel, Santa Cruz, CA
Cone, E Christopher (201) 992-1771
PUB, ED, West Essex Tribune, Livingston, NJ
Cone, Marla (213) 237-5000
Environmental Writer
Los Angeles Times, Los Angeles, CA
Confiant, Wendy (905) 358-5711
ADV SUPV-CLASS
Niagara Falls Review, Niagara Falls, ON
Congdon, Sharon (906) 482-1500
ADV CNR
Daily Mining Gazette, Houghton, MI
Conger, Philip (816) 425-6325
PUB, ED
Bethany Republican-Clipper, Bethany, MO
Conidi, Frank (614) 654-1321
CIRC MGR
Lancaster Eagle-Gazette, Lancaster, OH
Conidi, Joseph (330) 364-5577
PROD FRM-COMP
Times Reporter, New Philadelphia, OH
Conkis, Bill (630) 368-1100
ED, Suburban Life Citizen, Oak Brook, IL
Conklin, C L (515) 435-4151
PUB, ED
Nashua Reporter & Weekly Post, Nashua, IA
Conklin, Hugh (616) 582-6761
PUB, ED, Boyne Citizen, Boyne City, MI
Conklin, Jon (330) 364-5577
Photo ED, Times Reporter, New Philadelphia, OH
Conklin, Mike (312) 222-3232
COL, Chicago Tribune, Chicago, IL
Conklin, Susan (616) 582-6761
MAN ED, Boyne Citizen, Boyne City, MI
Conkling, Jennifer (607) 756-5665
Society/Women's ED
Cortland Standard, Cortland, NY
Conley, Cathy (617) 843-2937
ED, Braintree Forum, Braintree, MA
Conley Jr, James E (414) 887-0321
PRES, PUB, Daily Citizen, Beaver Dam, WI
Conley, Larry (404) 526-5151
Perspective ED
Atlanta Journal-Constitution, Atlanta, GA
Conley, Michael (618) 224-9422
PUB, ED, Trenton Sun, Trenton, IL
Conley, Patti (412) 775-3200
Food ED, Beaver County Times, Beaver, PA
Conley, Rev Peter V (617) 482-4316
ED, Pilot, Boston, MA
Conley, Richard (716) 439-9222
ADV MGR-RT
Union-Sun & Journal, Lockport, NY
Conley, Steve (606) 329-1717
PROD MGR-MR
Daily Independent, Ashland, KY
Conlin, Bill (215) 854-2000
COL-Sports
Philadelphia Daily News, Philadelphia, PA
Conlin, Marilyn (518) 658-2777
ED, Taconic Valley Echo, Berlin, NY
Conlon, Jean E (201) 226-8900
ED, Progress, Caldwell, NJ
Conly, Michael J (210) 829-9000
Sr VP/PRES & GM-KENS-TV, Harte-Hanks Communications Inc., San Antonio, TX
Conn, Lesley (904) 435-8500
EDU, Pensacola News Journal, Pensacola, FL
Conn, Merv (330) 264-1125
CIRC MGR, Daily Record, Wooster, OH
Connaghan, William B (314) 421-1880
ED, St. Louis Countain, St. Louis, MO
ABC Inc. (Legal Communications Corp.)
Connell, Helen (519) 679-6666
ASSOC ED, London Free Press, London, ON
Connell, Joan (202) 463-8777
ED, Religion News Service, Washington, DC
Connell, Lise (203) 226-8877
ED, Westport Minuteman, Westport, CT
Connell, Mike (810) 985-7171
EX ED, Times Herald, Port Huron, MI
Connell, Susan (901) 427-3333
PROD MGR-Commercial Print Shop
Jackson Sun, Jackson, TN
Connell, Tara (703) 276-3400
MAN ED-Page One
USA Today, Arlington, VA
Connelly, Chris (617) 933-3700
News ED, Daily Times Chronicle
Woburn, MA
Connelly, Joel (206) 448-8000
NTL Correspondent
Seattle Post-Intelligencer, Seattle, WA
Connelly, Mike (303) 820-1010
EX Sports ED, Denver Post, Denver, CO
Connelly, Mike (410) 332-6000
Regional ED, Sun, Baltimore, MD
Connelly, Ross (802) 472-6521
PUB, ED, Hardwick Gazette, Hardwick, VT
Connelly, Scott (510) 339-8777
GM, Montclarion, Oakland, CA
Connelly, Tom (212) 686-1266
ED, Irish Echo, New York, NY
Connelly, William (219) 463-2166
PUB, LaGrange Standard, LaGrange, IN
Conner, Charles (901) 529-2211
Farm/Agriculture Reporter
Commercial Appeal, Memphis, TN
Conner, Fred (209) 734-5821
PROD DIR, Visalia Times-Delta, Visalia, CA
Gannett Co. Inc.
Conner, Gary D (804) 649-6000
ADV MGR-Display
Richmond Times-Dispatch, Richmond, VA
Conner, James (504) 383-1111
ADV MGR-CLASS, Advocate
Baton Rouge, LA
Conner, Keith (614) 385-2107
ADV MGR, Logan Daily News, Logan, OH
Conner, Kevin (202) 334-6000
PROD MGR-Quality Assurance
Washington Post, Washington, DC
Conner, Loretta W (803) 583-2907
SEC/TREAS, Mid-South Management Co. Inc., Spartanburg, SC
Conner, Nancy (612) 222-5011
Reader Advocate
St. Paul Pioneer Press, St. Paul, MN
Conner, Olga (305) 350-2111
Viernes ED-El Nuevo
Miami Herald, Miami, FL
Conner, Patricia (518) 692-2266
ED, Journal-Press, Greenwich, NY
Conner, Tom (904) 863-1111
ED, Northwest Florida Daily News, Fort Walton Beach, FL
Connery, Michael (508) 997-7411
Environmental ED
Standard Times, New Bedford, MA
Connolly, Brent M (508) 922-1234
ADV DIR-Sales/MKTG
Daily News of Newburyport, Beverly, MA
Ottaway Newspapers Inc.
Connolly, Daphne (902) 436-2121
Accountant
Journal-Pioneer, Summerside, PEI
Connolly, Jack (513) 721-2700
ADV CNR-Co-op
Cincinnati Enquirer, Cincinnati, OH
Connolly, John (403) 429-5400
ADV VP-Sales
Edmonton Journal, Edmonton, AB
Connolly, Kathleen (604) 498-3711
ED, Oliver Chronicle, Oliver, BC
Connolly, Mary (203) 744-5100
EPE, EDL Writer, News-Times, Danbury, CT
Connolly, Patrick (615) 259-8000
Deputy MAN ED-Features
Tennessean, Nashville, TN
Connolly Jr, William F (617) 929-2000
TREAS, Boston Globe, Boston, MA
Connor, Don (615) 552-1808
ASSOC PUB, DIR-MKTG
Leaf-Chronicle, Clarksville, TN
Connor, Gary (903) 872-3931
PUB, Corsicana Daily Sun, Corsicana, TX
Connor, Mike (315) 470-0011
EX ED, Post-Standard/Syracuse Herald-Journal American, Syracuse, NY
Connor, Richard L (817) 390-7400
PRES/PUB
Fort Worth Star-Telegram, Fort Worth, TX
Connor, Terry (334) 792-3141
MAN ED, Dothan Eagle, Dothan, AL
Connors, James (304) 263-8931
ADV DIR, Journal, Martinsburg, WV
Connors, Joanna (216) 999-4500
Films ED, Plain Dealer, Cleveland, OH
Connors, Capt John (520) 783-3333
ED, Cactus Comet, Yuma, AZ
Connors, Mary Jean (305) 376-3800
Sr VP-Human Resources
Knight-Ridder Inc., Miami, FL
Connors, Thomas J (617) 426-3000
PROD DIR-OPER, Boston Herald, Boston, MA
Connors, Thomas J (212) 837-7000
Senior Correspondent-DC, Journal of Commerce & Commercial, New York, NY
Conolly, Simon (807) 622-8588
ED, Thunder Bay Post, Thunder Bay, ON
Conolly, Stasha (613) 475-0255
PUB, East Northumberland, Brighton, ON
Conover, Dan (803) 577-7111
State ED, Post and Courier, Charleston, SC
Conover, Joseph I (217) 223-5100
ED, Online Contact
Quincy Herald-Whig, Quincy, IL
Conover, M Craig (801) 489-5651
GM, Springville Herald, Springville, UT
Conover, Martin W (801) 489-5651
PUB, Springville Herald, Springville, UT

Copyright ©1997 by the Editor & Publisher Co.

47-Who's Where **Coo**

Conover, Pat .... (801) 489-5651
ED, Springville Herald, Springville, UT

Conquergood, Tom .... (403) 545-2258
PUB, 40-Mile County Commentator, Bow Island, AB

Conrad, Dale .... (316) 421-2000
PROD FRM-PR, Parsons Sun, Parsons, KS

Conrad, Dave .... (902) 893-9405
DP MGR, PROD MGR
Truro Daily News, Truro, NS

Conrad, Eric .... (207) 791-6650
City Ed-Day
Portland Press Herald, Portland, ME

Conrad, James .... (212) 803-8200
PROD CNR, Bond Buyer, New York, NY

Conrad, Jan .... (330) 264-1125
Specialty Publications MGR
Daily Record, Wooster, OH

Conrad, John .... (541) 485-1234
Sports ED
Eugene Register-Guard, Eugene, OR

Conrad, Laurie .... (215) 949-4000
Enterprise ED
Bucks County Courier Times, Levittown, PA

Conrad, Linda .... (409) 245-5555
ADV MGR-PROM
Daily Tribune, Bay City, TX

Conrad, Mark .... (330) 364-5577
ADV DIR
Times Reporter, New Philadelphia, OH

Conrad, Pete .... (513) 863-8200
Sports ED, Journal-News, Hamilton, OH

Conrad, Richard .... (203) 789-5200
SYS ED
New Haven Register, New Haven, CT

Conrad, Willa .... (704) 358-5000
Music Critic
Charlotte Observer, Charlotte, NC

Conrad, William .... (614) 592-6612
PROD MGR, Athens Messenger, Athens, OH

Conron, Kevin .... (410) 535-1214
ED, Recorder, Prince Frederick, MD

Conrow, Carol .... (816) 230-5311
ED, Odessan, Odessa, MO

Conroy, Jerry .... (412) 834-1151
ADV MGR-RT
Tribune-Review, Greensburg, PA

Conroy, Wensel .... (504) 826-3279
ADV MGR-RT
Times-Picayune, New Orleans, LA

Consello-Brandes, Diane .... (914) 255-7000
GM, Herald, New Paltz, NY

Constantino, Diane .... (813) 893-8111
PROD MGR-Packaging
St. Petersburg Times, St. Petersburg, FL

Constine, Bill .... (517) 723-1118
ED, Sunday Independent, Owosso, MI

Consuegra, Jorge .... (305) 633-3341
MGR-CR, Diario Las Americas, Miami, FL

Content, Tom .... (414) 435-4411
RE ED, Topics ED-Money
Green Bay Press-Gazette, Green Bay, WI

Contini, Nora .... (415) 263-7200
GM, Jewish Bulletin of Northern California, San Francisco, CA

Contreras, John .... (719) 336-2266
Sports ED, Lamar Daily News, Lamar, CO

Contreras, Mark .... (717) 829-7100
PUB/PRES, Times Leader, Wilkes-Barre, PA

Converse, John E .... (209) 834-2535
ED, Fowler Ensign, Fowler, CA

Convey, Kevin .... (617) 426-3000
MAN ED-Sunday Features
Boston Herald, Boston, MA

Conway, Bill .... (606) 672-3399
ED, Thousandsticks News, Hyden, KY

Conway, Bob .... (713) 220-7171
ADV MGR-RE
Houston Chronicle, Houston, TX

Conway, Daniel .... (317) 236-1570
PUB, Criterion, Indianapolis, IN

Conway, Gloria S .... (617) 241-9511
PUB, ED, Charlestown Patriot & Somerville Chronicle, Charlestown, MA

Conway, John .... (602) 932-5555
ED, West Valley View, Avondale, AZ

Conway, Kevin .... (561) 287-1550
Sports ED, Stuart News, Stuart, FL

Conway, Mike .... (209) 722-1511
EPE, Merced Sun-Star, Merced, CA

Conway, Nancy .... (510) 208-6300
EX ED, Oakland Tribune, Oakland, CA
MediaNews Inc. (Alameda Newspapers)

Conway, Russ .... (508) 685-1000
Sports ED
Eagle-Tribune, North Andover, MA

Conyers, Ashley M .... (904) 267-2461
PRES, Pythia Press, Santa Rosa Beach, FL

Conyers, Steve .... (706) 724-0851
CIRC Senior SUPV
Augusta Chronicle, Augusta, GA

Cook, A J .... (901) 754-8925
Author/Owner, Cook, A.J., Memphis, TN

Cook, Allen .... (901) 454-1411
GM, ED
Triangle Journal News, Memphis, TN

Cook, Amy .... (308) 532-6000
BM, DP MGR
North Platte Telegraph, North Platte, NE

Cook, Andrea .... (605) 859-2516
ED, Pioneer-Review, Philip, SD

Cook, Andy .... (905) 526-3333
ADV VP-Sales, Spectator, Hamilton, ON

Cook, Burl .... (605) 537-4276
PUB, Rosholt Review, Rosholt, SD

Cook, Carey Orr .... (415) 854-3132
PRES/Cartoon ED
Sam Mantics Enterprise, Menlo Park, CA

Cook, Chelsea C .... (918) 652-3311
News ED, Daily Free-Lance, Henryetta, OK

Cook, Cynthia .... (801) 237-2800
ADV MGR-MKTG/PROM
Newspaper Agency Corp., Salt Lake City, UT

Cook, Dave .... (320) 632-2345
MAN ED
Morrison County Record, Little Falls, MN

Cook, David T .... (617) 450-2000
ED, Christian Science Monitor, Boston, MA

Cook, Donald .... (716) 798-1400
Photo ED, Journal-Register, Medina, NY

Cook, Doug .... (901) 285-4091
CIRC DIR, State Gazette, Dyersburg, TN

Cook, Elizabeth G .... (704) 633-8950
ED, Salisbury Post, Salisbury, NC

Cook, George .... (941) 335-0200
CIRC MGR-Customer Affairs
News-Press, Fort Myers, FL

Cook, Glenn .... (910) 349-4331
Environmental ED, Women's ED
Reidsville Review, Reidsville, NC

Cook, James .... (704) 864-3291
PROD FRM-PR
Gaston Gazette, Gastonia, NC

Cook, James A .... (847) 427-4300
MGR-MKTG/PROM
Daily Herald, Arlington Heights, IL

Cook, Jim .... (316) 421-2000
MAN ED, Parsons Sun, Parsons, KS

Cook, Jon .... (816) 665-2808
ADV DIR, Kirksville Daily Express & News, Kirksville, MO

Cook, Karla .... (201) 877-4141
Food Critic, Star-Ledger, Newark, NJ

Cook, Kathleen .... (605) 537-4276
ED, Rosholt Review, Rosholt, SD

Cook, Kylie .... (415) 854-3132
Internet/WWW ED
Sam Mantics Enterprise, Menlo Park, CA

Cook, Layman .... (804) 458-8511
PROD SUPT-PR, News, Hopewell, VA

Cook, Loyd .... (903) 396-2261
ED, Kerens Tribune, Kerens, TX

Cook, Lynne .... (713) 220-7171
DIR-Advertising SRV/New BUS
Houston Chronicle, Houston, TX

Cook, Margaret .... (972) 442-5515/2623
ED, Wylie News, Wylie, TX

Cook, Maryl .... (209) 688-0521
DIR-MKTG/PROM
Tulare Advance-Register, Tulare, CA

Cook, Nancy .... (318) 747-7900
ED, Bossier Press Tribune, Bossier City, LA

Cook, Neil .... (602) 468-6565
EIC, Daily Racing Form, Phoenix, AZ

Cook, Peter J .... (308) 324-5511
PUB, Clipper-Herald, Lexington, NE

Cook, Ray .... (601) 693-1551
Photo DEPT MGR
Meridian Star, Meridian, MS

Cook, Rob .... (912) 272-5522
Sports ED, Courier Herald, Dublin, GA

Cook, Ron .... (412) 263-1100
Sports COL
Pittsburgh Post-Gazette, Pittsburgh, PA

Cook, Sam .... (218) 723-5281
Outdoors Writer
Duluth News-Tribune, Duluth, MN

Cook, Stanley L .... (209) 847-3021
PUB, Oakdale Leader, Oakdale, CA

Cook, Stephen .... (415) 777-2424
ASST MAN ED-Enterprise, MET ED (Acting)
San Francisco Examiner, San Francisco, CA

Cook, Susan .... (864) 298-4100
Online MGR
Greenville News, Greenville, SC

Cook, Suzette .... (412) 224-4321
DIR-MKTG
Valley News Dispatch, Tarentum, PA
Gannett Co. Inc.

Cooke, Bill .... (905) 526-3333
PROD MGR-Electronic PROD
Spectator, Hamilton, ON

Cooke, Bryan .... (408) 920-5000
PROD SUPV-PR
San Jose Mercury News, San Jose, CA

Cooke, David .... (501) 763-4461
Sports ED, Courier News, Blytheville, AR

Cooke, Ian .... (209) 722-1511
ADV MGR, Merced Sun-Star, Merced, CA

Cooke, J C .... (202) 882-1021
PUB, ED, Washington Sun, Washington, DC

Cooke, J W .... (512) 446-5838
PUB, ED, Rockdale Reporter & Messenger, Rockdale, TX

Cooke, Jack Kent .... (818) 713-3000
BC, Daily News, Woodland Hills, CA

Cooke, John Warren .... (804) 693-3101
PUB, Gloucester Mathews Gazette-Journal, Gloucester, VA

Cooke, Julie .... (801) 237-2800
MGR-CR
Newspaper Agency Corp., Salt Lake City, UT

Cooke, Kevin .... (408) 920-5000
MGR-Software Development (Webmaster)
San Jose Mercury News, San Jose, CA

Cooke, Lynne .... (941) 687-7000
Automotive ED, BUS/RE ED, Farm/ Agriculture ED, Ledger, Lakeland, FL

Cooke, Michael .... (604) 732-2222
EIC, Province, Vancouver, BC

Cooke, Russell .... (215) 854-2000
EDL Writer
Philadelphia Inquirer, Philadelphia, PA

Cooke, Thomas .... (303) 820-1010
PROD MGR-Newsprint
Denver Post, Denver, CO

Cooksey, Bill .... (318) 459-3200
BUS Writer, Times, Shreveport, LA

Cooksey, Jack .... (803) 775-6331
Graphics ED/Art DIR, Item, Sumter, SC

Cooksey, Lynette .... (601) 693-1551
EDU ED, Meridian Star, Meridian, MS

Cooley, James R .... (308) 824-3582
PUB, ED, Oxford Standard, Oxford, NE

Cooley, Maria H .... (308) 824-3582
PUB, Oxford Standard, Oxford, NE

Cooley, Ronald .... (765) 362-1200
PROD FRM-PR
Journal Review, Crawfordsville, IN

Coombs, Dean I .... (719) 655-2620
PUB, Saguache Crescent, Saguache, CO

Coombs Jr, Francis .... (202) 636-3000
ASST MAN ED
Washington Times, Washington, DC

Coombs, Marie O .... (719) 655-2620
ED, Saguache Crescent, Saguache, CO

Coomer, Terry .... (317) 598-6397
CIRC DIR
Noblesville Daily Ledger, Noblesville, IN

Coon, Connie .... (702) 727-5102
GM, Pahrump Valley Times, Pahrump, NV

Coon, Fred .... (501) 735-1010
DP MGR, PROD FRM-PR
Evening Times, West Memphis, AR

Coon, Laura Summer .... (219) 461-8444
ADV MGR-OPER
Fort Wayne Newspapers Inc., Fort Wayne, IN

Coon, Sheila .... (607) 734-5151
DIR-Market Development
Star-Gazette, Elmira, NY

Coon, Steve .... (517) 772-2971
News ED (Mt Pleasant)
Morning Sun, Mount Pleasant, MI

Cooney, Charles T .... (914) 341-1100
MGR-SYS/DP
Times Herald-Record, Middletown, NY

Cooney, Mary .... (203) 964-2200
DIR-Photography
Stamford Advocate, Stamford, CT

Cooney, Peter .... (514) 987-2222
ASST MAN ED, EDL SYS MGR
Gazette, Montreal, QC

Cooney, Robert B .... (202) 638-0444
EX ED
Press Associates Inc., Washington, DC

Cooney, Roman .... (403) 235-7100
City & Life ED
Calgary Herald, Calgary, AB

Coons, Sherry .... (717) 248-6741
Lifestyle/EDU ED, Teen-Age/Youth ED
Sentinel, Lewistown, PA

Coop, Barb .... (515) 684-4611
PROD FRM-COMP
Ottumwa Courier, Ottumwa, IA

Coop, Ruth .... (615) 684-1200
ADV MGR
Shelbyville Times-Gazette, Shelbyville, TN

Cooper, Al .... (816) 826-1000
PROD FRM-Day
Sedalia Democrat, Sedalia, MO

Cooper, Andy .... (306) 565-8211
City ED, Leader-Post, Regina, SK

Cooper, Bonnie .... (804) 793-2311
EX ED, Danville Register & Bee, Danville, VA

Cooper, Brenda J .... (540) 374-5000
PROD FRM-Pre Press, PROD FRM-Packaging
Free Lance-Star, Fredericksburg, VA

Cooper, Brian .... (319) 588-5611
EX ED, EPE
Telegraph Herald, Dubuque, IA

Cooper, Brian G .... (404) 843-5000
Sr VP, Cox Newspapers Inc., Atlanta, GA

Cooper, Carol .... (316) 275-8500
ED, La Semana en el suroeste de Kansas, Garden City, KS

Cooper, Charles .... (201) 877-4141
MAN ED-Production
Star-Ledger, Newark, NJ

Cooper, Connie .... (513) 721-2700
ADV MGR-Sales
Cincinnati Enquirer, Cincinnati, OH

Cooper, D P .... (804) 649-6000
ASST SEC/DIR-Employee Benefits
Media General Inc., Richmond, VA

Cooper, Dave .... (209) 688-0521
MGR-OPER, MAN ED
Tulare Advance-Register, Tulare, CA

Cooper, David .... (423) 756-6900
News ED
Chattanooga Free Press, Chattanooga, TN

Cooper, David .... (330) 996-3000
ASSOC ED
Akron Beacon Journal, Akron, OH

Cooper, David .... (219) 235-6161
Photo ED
South Bend Tribune, South Bend, IN

Cooper, Desiree .... (313) 961-4060
ED, Metro Times, Detroit, MI

Cooper, Diane .... (561) 461-2050
PROD FRM-COMP (Day)
Tribune, Fort Pierce, FL

Cooper, Don .... (309) 343-7181
PUB, Register-Mail, Galesburg, IL

Cooper, Donald .... (405) 654-1443
PUB, Carnegie Herald, Carnegie, OK

Cooper, Donald M .... (903) 645-3940
PUB, ED, Bee, Daingerfield, TX

Cooper, Evan .... (908) 922-6000
PROD MGR-Process Engineering
Asbury Park Press, Neptune, NJ

Cooper, Gary .... (207) 892-1166
PUB, Suburban News, Windham, ME

Cooper, Jack .... (402) 862-2200
PUB, ED, Humboldt Standard, Humboldt, NE

Cooper, James A .... (404) 843-5000
VP-OPER
Cox Newspapers Inc., Atlanta, GA

Cooper, James F .... (217) 824-2233
PRES, PUB, Taylorville Daily Breeze-Courier, Taylorville, IL

Cooper, Jean T .... (315) 589-4421
PUB, ED
Williamson Sun & Sentinel, Williamson, NY

Cooper, Jeff .... (860) 584-0501
PROD MGR-SYS, Bristol Press, Bristol, CT

Cooper, Jim .... (304) 927-2360
ED, Times Record, Spencer, WV

Cooper, Jimmy .... (903) 794-3311
PROD MGR-Press
Texarkana Gazette, Texarkana, TX

Cooper, John Robert .... (217) 824-2233
SEC, PSL MGR, ED, City ED, News ED, Taylorville Daily Breeze-Courier, Taylorville, IL

Cooper, Julie .... (210) 225-7411
Travel ED
San Antonio Express-News, San Antonio, TX

Cooper, Kara K .... (520) 836-7461
SEC, ADV DIR, ADV DIR-PROM/MKTG
Casa Grande Dispatch, Casa Grande, AZ

Cooper, Kate .... (706) 724-0851
MGR-MKTG/PROM
Augusta Chronicle, Augusta, GA

Cooper, Lon .... (805) 395-7500
MGR-Publishing SYS
Bakersfield Californian, Bakersfield, CA

Cooper, Lori .... (405) 654-1443
PUB, ED, Carnegie Herald, Carnegie, OK

Cooper, Lorne .... (306) 445-7261
ED, Regional Optimaist/Advertiser Post, North Battleford, SK

Cooper, Louise B .... (630) 365-6446
ED, Elburn Herald, Elburn, IL

Cooper, Mark .... (502) 477-2239
GM, ED, Spencer Magnet, Taylorsville, KY

Cooper, Mary Ann .... (201) 790-1582
Writer, Speaking of Soaps Inc., Totowa, NJ

Cooper, Michael .... (610) 828-4600
GM, Recorder, Conshohocken, PA

Cooper, Norma .... (606) 236-2551
SEC, Advocate-Messenger, Danville, KY

Cooper, Pat .... (770) 461-6317
ED, Fayette County News, Fayetteville, GA

Cooper, Paulette .... (212) 744-4623
PUB
National Press Syndicate, New York, NY

Cooper, Ralph J .... (609) 399-5411
PUB, Sentinel-Ledger, Ocean City, NJ

Cooper, Richard L .... (630) 365-6446
PUB, Elburn Herald, Elburn, IL

Coo Who's Where-48

Cooper, Rose (937) 783-2421
ED, Blanchester Star-Republican, Blanchester, OH

Cooper, Roy (915) 446-2610
ED, Junction Eagle, Junction, TX

Cooper, Steve (937) 328-0300
Films/Theater ED
Springfield News-Sun, Springfield, OH

Cooper, Steven (513) 721-2700
CIRC DIR-Sales
Cincinnati Enquirer, Cincinnati, OH

Cooper, Terri (318) 255-4353
CIRC MGR, Publications MGR
Ruston Daily Leader, Ruston, LA

Cooper, Terri (910) 997-3111
ADV MGR-GEN, Richmond County Daily Journal, Rockingham, NC

Cooper, Thomas R (334) 262-1611
Market Development DIR
Montgomery Advertiser, Montgomery, AL

Cooper, Tony (915) 337-4661
ADV DIR
Odessa American, Odessa, TX

Cooper, Whittemore (915) 446-2610
PUB, Junction Eagle, Junction, TX

Cooper, Wilda Quinn (217) 824-2233
EVP, Taylorville Daily Breeze-Courier, Taylorville, IL

Cooper, Yasmin (407) 833-4511
PUB, ED, Florida Photo News and Image, West Palm Beach, FL

Cooperrider, Sara (202) 636-3000
DIR-Computer SRV, DP MGR
Washington Times, Washington, DC

Coots, John (508) 764-4325
PRES, News, Southbridge, MA

Coover, Roger W (561) 395-8300
PRES, PUB
Boca Raton News, Boca Raton, FL

Cope, Christopher S (414) 657-1000
MGR-CR, Kenosha News, Kenosha, WI

Cope, Debra (212) 803-8200
EXEC ED, American Banker, New York, NY

Cope, Lewis (612) 673-4000
Health/SCI ED
Star Tribune, Minneapolis, MN

Cope, Randy W (501) 442-1777
PUB
Northwest Arkansas Times, Fayetteville, AR

Cope, Renae (302) 674-3600
ADV MGR-CLASS
Delaware State News, Dover, DE

Copelan, Harry (800) 336-0007
PUB, High Desert Advocate, Wendover, NV

Copelan, Howard (800) 336-0007
ED, High Desert Advocate, Wendover, NV

Copeland, Arlette (912) 744-4200
Food Writer
Macon Telegraph, Macon, GA

Copeland, Denise (201) 653-1000
DP MGR, Jersey Journal, Jersey City, NJ

Copeland, Dennis (305) 350-2111
DIR of Photography
Miami Herald, Miami, FL

Copeland, Joan (419) 738-2128
ADTX MGR
Wapakoneta Daily News, Wapakoneta, OH

Copeland, Joe (206) 339-3000
EPE, Herald, Everett, WA

Copeland, Julie (701) 780-1100
Ag Week ED, Farm ED
Grand Forks Herald, Grand Forks, ND

Copeland, Mike (817) 757-5757
BUS/FIN ED
Waco Tribune-Herald, Waco, TX

Copeland, Peter (202) 408-1484
ASST MAN ED-News, Scripps Howard News Service, Washington, DC

Copeland, Rick (803) 626-8555
CIRC MGR-Single Copy
Sun News, Myrtle Beach, SC

Copeland, Tim (757) 539-3437
ED, Suffolk News-Herald, Suffolk, VA

Copeland, Zell S (205) 362-1000
ASST GM
Talladega Daily Home, Talladega, AL

Copely, Sarah (919) 335-0841
PROD MGR, PROD SUPT-COMP
Daily Advance, Elizabeth City, NC

Copen, David E (937) 236-4990
GM, Huber Heights Courier, Dayton, OH

Coplan, Alvin M (904) 737-6996
PUB, ED
Syrian-Lebanese Star, Jacksonville, FL

Copler, Lori (320) 328-4444
ED, Brownton Bulletin, Brownton, MN

Copley, David C (619) 454-0411
PRES, Copley Press Inc., La Jolla, CA

Copley, Frank J (219) 866-5111
PUB, ADV DIR, Republican, Rensselaer, IN

Copley, Helen K (619) 454-0411
COB/CEO, Copley Press Inc., La Jolla, CA

Copley, Lynnette (817) 562-2868
ADV DIR-RT, Mexia Daily News, Mexia, TX

Copley, Renee (304) 235-4242
ADV MGR-CLASS
Williamson Daily News, Williamson, WV

Copley, Rich (706) 549-0123
Features ED, Radio/Television ED, Athens Daily News/Banner-Herald, Athens, GA

Coppedge-Martin, Lin (202) 898-8254
DIR-Human Resources
United Press International, Washington, DC

Copper, Andrew W (718) 624-5959
PUB, City Sun, Brooklyn, NY

Coppinger, James (616) 345-3511
ADV DIR-Sales & MKTG
Kalamazoo Gazette, Kalamazoo, MI

Copple, Julie (618) 532-5604
MGR-Office, Sentinel, Centralia, IL

Coppock, Sharon (616) 258-4600
ED
Kalkaska Leader & Kalkaskian, Kalkaska, MI

Coppola, Elio (613) 232-5689
ED, L'Ora Di Ottawa, Ottawa, ON

Coppola, Renata (613) 232-5689
GM, L'Ora Di Ottawa, Ottawa, ON

Corbari, Tom (608) 873-6671
PUB, Stoughton Courier-Hub, Stoughton, WI

Corbett, Mary Ellen (520) 432-8003
MAN ED
Little, Lew Enterprises Inc., Bisbee, AZ

Corbett, Michael (507) 454-6500
ADV MGR-RT, Daily News, Winona, MN

Corbett, Neil (717) 821-2091
Sports ED, Citizens' Voice, Wilkes-Barre, PA

Corbett, Neil (604) 869-2421
ED, Hope Standard Publications, Hope, BC

Corbett, Rebecca (410) 332-6000
ASST MAN ED-Projects, Sun, Baltimore, MD

Corbett, Steve (717) 829-7100
COL, Times Leader, Wilkes-Barre, PA

Corbin, Andy H (307) 634-3361
MGR-BUS Office
Wyoming Tribune-Eagle, Cheyenne, WY

Corbin, Dennis (715) 394-4411
PROD FRM-COMP
Daily Telegram, Superior, WI

Corbin, Don (770) 478-5753
Sports ED
Clayton News/Daily, Jonesboro, GA

Corbin, Gail S (908) 232-4407
GM, Westfield Leader, Westfield, NJ

Corbin, Horace R (908) 232-4407
PUB, Westfield Leader, Westfield, NJ

Corbin, John (334) 222-2402
PROD SYS Operator
Andalusia Star-News, Andalusia, AL

Corbin, Will (757) 247-4600
VP/ED
Newport News Daily Press, Newport News, VA

Corbitt, Paul (419) 522-3311
News ED, News Journal, Mansfield, OH

Corbran, Paul (814) 870-1600
BUS ED, City ED
Morning News/Erie Daily Times, Erie, PA

Corby, Marshall (937) 328-0300
Photo ED
Springfield News-Sun, Springfield, OH

Corcoran, Charles (352) 374-5000
CIRC MGR-Sales
Gainesville Sun, Gainesville, FL

Corcoran, David H (304) 462-7309
PUB, ED
Glenville Democrat, Glenville, WV

Corder, Dinah (618) 544-2101
ADV MGR-CLASS
Robinson Daily News, Robinson, IL

Cordes, Keith (614) 532-1441
ADV Representative
Ironton Tribune, Ironton, OH

Cordes, Rob (630) 844-5844
PROD FRM-Camera, Beacon-News
Aurora, IL

Cordsen, John (915) 336-2281
PUB, ED, Fort Stockton Pioneer, Fort Stockton, TX

Cordts, Michael (312) 321-3000
Deputy MET ED
Chicago Sun-Times, Chicago, IL

Corduck, James (617) 933-3700
PROD FRM-COMP
Daily Times Chronicle, Woburn, MA

Corell, Cindy (540) 885-7281
City ED, Daily News Leader, Staunton, VA

Corella, Marie (505) 887-5501
ADV MGR-CLASS
Current-Argus, Carlsbad, NM

Corey, Steve (401) 274-2149
VP/GM
Whitegate Features Syndicate, Providence, RI

Corie, Sue (717) 265-2151
Society ED
Towanda Daily Review, Towanda, PA

Corkery, Dan (217) 351-5252
News ED, News-Gazette, Champaign, IL

Corkum-Greek, Susan (902) 634-8863
ED, Progress Enterprise, Bridgewater, NS

Corley, Pat (406) 356-2149
ED, Independent Enterprise, Forsyth, MT

Corley, Stephanie (409) 787-2172
PUB, ED
Sabine County Reporter, Hemphill, TX

Corliss, Bryan (509) 525-3300
RE ED, Union-Bulletin, Walla Walla, WA

Cormack, Mary R (405) 363-3370
MGR-CR, ADV MGR-CLASS
Blackwell Journal-Tribune, Blackwell, OK

Cormier, Jerry (318) 527-7075
Sports ED
Southwest Daily News, Sulphur, LA

Cormier, Nancy J (318) 734-2891
PUB, Welsh Citizen, Welsh, LA

Corn, Donna (706) 745-6343
GM, North Georgia News, Blairsville, GA

Corn, Mike (913) 628-1081
Regional ED, Hays Daily News, Hays, KS

Cornatzer, Mary (919) 829-4500
Entertainment ED-Day, Lifestyle ED
News & Observer, Raleigh, NC

Cornelio, Paula (207) 729-3311
CIRC ASST MGR
Times Record, Brunswick, ME

Cornelius, Brenda S (402) 374-2225
MAN ED
Burt County Plaindealer, Tekamah, NE

Cornelius, Chuck (703) 284-6000
DIR-ADV Sales Development
Gannett Co. Inc., Arlington, VA

Cornelius, Ellen (410) 848-4400
Lifestyle ED
Carroll County Times, Westminster, MD

Cornelius, Karen (216) 967-5268
ED, Vermilion Photojournal, Vermilion, OH

Cornelius, Michael (414) 224-2000
ADV DIR-Display
Milwaukee Journal Sentinel, Milwaukee, WI

Cornell, John (914) 358-2200
Art DIR
Rockland Journal-News, West Nyack, NY

Cornell, Michael (250) 372-2331
City ED, Daily News, Kamloops, BC

Cornell, Robert C (315) 782-1000
ADV DIR
Watertown Daily Times, Watertown, NY

Cornell, Susan (519) 679-6666
CIRC Sales MGR
London Free Press, London, ON

Cornely, Deborah (410) 288-6060
MAN ED, Dundalk Eagle, Dundalk, MD

Cornett, Phyllis (502) 223-1736
Contact
Community Press Service, Frankfort, KY

Cornette, Paula (606) 329-1717
ADV MGR-NTL CNR
Daily Independent, Ashland, KY

Cornils, Mary (516) 378-5320
GM, Merrick Life, Merrick, NY

Cornish, Mike (314) 340-8000
PROD CNR-Environmental
St. Louis Post-Dispatch, St. Louis, MO

Cornish, Scott (212) 556-1234
DIR-Quality Assurance
New York Times, New York, NY

Cornute, Bob (518) 584-4242
PROD FRM-COMP
Saratogian, Saratoga Springs, NY

Cornwall, Bill (409) 265-7411
PUB, ED, Brazosport Facts, Clute, TX

Cornwall, Dave (909) 684-1200
ADV DIR, Press-Enterprise, Riverside, CA

Cornwell, Brenda (812) 723-2572
MAN ED, Paoli Republican, Paoli, IN

Cornwell, Gary (770) 461-6317
GM, Fayette County News, Fayetteville, GA

Corona, Xavier (619) 585-6300
GM, Frontera San Diego, Chula Vista, CA

Coronado, John (318) 322-5161
PROD MGR-MR, News-Star, Monroe, LA

Corr, Angie (515) 636-2309
ED, Keota Eagle, Keota, IA

Corr, Gregory R (605) 745-4170
PUB, ED, Hot Springs Star, Hot Springs, SD

Correa, Richard (505) 388-1576
News ED, Silver City Daily Press & Independent, Silver City, NM

Correge, Patricia (212) 286-0123
Spanish Division DIR, Inter Press Service, New York, NY

Correll, Harold (407) 482-6271
Author-Legislation
Demko Publishing, Boca Raton, FL

Corrigan, Sara (812) 424-7711
Food ED, Evansville Press, Evansville, IN

Corrigan, Tom (910) 373-7000
MET ED, News & Record, Greensboro, NC

Corrins, Leslie (306) 297-4144
PUB, GM
Shaunavon Standard, Shaunavon, SK

Corriveau, Claire (418) 248-8820
GM, L'Oie Blance, Montmagny, QC

Corriveau, Ronald G (508) 793-9100
PROD SUPT-Plant (Night)
Telegram & Gazette, Worcester, MA

Corro, Frank (702) 649-8553
ED, El Mundo, Las Vegas, NV

Corsair, Gary (352) 753-1119
ED, Tri-County Sun, Lady Lake, FL

Corsaro, Kim (415) 227-0800
PUB, ED, Bay Times, San Francisco, CA

Corsoe, Frank (860) 646-0500
EX Sports ED
Journal Inquirer, Manchester, CT

Corson, Ed (912) 744-4200
Training/Reader Advocate
Macon Telegraph, Macon, GA

Corson, Madeleine (207) 791-6650
COB/PUB
Portland Press Herald, Portland, ME

Corson, Wendy (717) 326-1551
Farm ED
Williamsport Sun-Gazette, Williamsport, PA

Corstange, Duane (616) 345-3511
CIRC MGR-Packaging/Distribution, PROD FRM-MR, Kalamazoo Gazette, Kalamazoo, MI

Cortez, Ernie (210) 686-4343
PROD MGR-COMP/Ad SRV
Monitor, McAllen, TX

Cortez, Genie (512) 884-2011
MGR-CR, Corpus Christi Caller-Times, Corpus Christi, TX

Cortez, Marjorie (801) 237-2188
EDU Writer, Deseret News, Salt Lake City, UT

Cortus, Bill (909) 987-6397
DIR-MKTG/PROM
Inland Valley Daily Bulletin, Ontario, CA

Corty, Andrew P (813) 893-8111
VP-Affiliates and Planning
St. Petersburg Times, St. Petersburg, FL

Corum, Mike (423) 523-3131
MGR-SYS
Knoxville News-Sentinel, Knoxville, TN

Corus, Lorraine (717) 762-2151
Entertainment/Amusements ED
Record Herald, Waynesboro, PA

Corvi, Lawrence (918) 684-2828
PRES, PUB, Muskogee Daily Phoenix & Times Democrat, Muskogee, OK

Corwin, Laura J (212) 556-1234
SEC, New York Times Co., New York, NY

Corwin, Scott (941) 629-2855
PROD MGR-OPER
Sun Herald, Port Charlotte, FL

Cosby, Jerry L (317) 788-4554
PUB, ED, Spotlight, Indianapolis, IN

Coscarelli, Tom (216) 999-4500
ASST MAN ED, Plain Dealer, Cleveland, OH

Cosgrove, Mike (505) 983-3303
News ED
Santa Fe New Mexican, Santa Fe, NM

Cosgrove, Wally (813) 259-7711
PROD MGR-PR
Tampa Tribune and Times, Tampa, FL

Cosky, Kelly (601) 842-2611
CIRC MGR, Northeast Mississippi Daily Journal, Tupelo, MS

Cosner, Patti Farris (619) 371-4301
ED, News Review, Ridgecrest, CA

Costa, John A (208) 377-6200
EX ED, Idaho Statesman, Boise, ID

Costa, Ken (415) 348-4321
Automotive ED
San Mateo County Times, San Mateo, CA

Costa-Landers, Rhonda (702) 882-2111
Entertainment/Amusements ED, Television/Film ED, Theater/Music ED
Nevada Appeal, Carson City, NV

Costanzo, Bob (401) 277-7000
ADV Sales DIR-Travel
Providence Journal-Bulletin, Providence, RI

Costanzo, Joe (801) 237-2188
EDU Writer
Deseret News, Salt Lake City, UT

Costello, Alexander (508) 458-7100
PRES, ASSOC ED, EPE, Sun, Lowell, MA

Costello Jr, Andrew F (617) 426-3000
ED, Boston Herald, Boston, MA

Costello, Art (312) 222-3232
PROD MGR-OPER (Night)
Chicago Tribune, Chicago, IL

Costello, Brian (504) 638-7155
ED, Pointe Coupee Banner, New Roads, LA

Costello, David (207) 784-5411
PROD MGR-Pre Press
Sun-Journal, Lewiston, ME

Costello, Edwin (212) 210-2100
ADV VP-OPER
New York Daily News, New York, NY

Copyright ©1997 by the Editor & Publisher Co.

49-Who's Where **Cox**

Costello Sr, James R .... (207) 784-5411
PUB/GM, Sun-Journal, Lewiston, ME
Costello Jr, James R .... (207) 784-5411
PROD MGR-Press
Sun-Journal, Lewiston, ME
Costello Jr, John H .... (508) 458-7100
PUB, ED, Sun, Lowell, MA
Costello, Stephen M .... (207) 784-5411
ADV DIR, DIR-MKTG
Sun-Journal, Lewiston, ME
Costello, Steve .... (815) 987-1200
CIRC MGR-Single Copy Sales
Rockford Register Star, Rockford, IL
Costello, Thomas .... (508) 458-7100
VP, PROD DIR, Sun, Lowell, MA
Costello, Tim .... (219) 874-7211
COL, Sports ED
News Dispatch, Michigan City, IN
Costigan, Tom .... (509) 276-5043
ED, Tribune, Deer Park, WA
Cota, Karen .... (419) 352-4611
Fashion ED, Society/ Women's ED, Sentinel-Tribune, Bowling Green, OH
Cote, Gaetan .... (514) 987-2222
PROD MGR-Pre Press, Gazette, Montreal, QC
Cote, Len .... (810) 332-8181
DP MGR, Oakland Press, Pontiac, MI
Cote, Lisa .... (705) 268-5050
Accountant, Daily Press, Timmins, ON
Cote, Maria .... (941) 262-3161
Entertainment/Amusements ED, Features ED
Naples Daily News, Naples, FL
Cote, Marie .... (401) 762-3000
Librarian, Call, Woonsocket, RI
Cote, Rene .... (204) 857-3427
PROD SUPV-Press
Daily Graphic, Portage la Prairie, MB
Cote, Serge .... (418) 683-1573
Chief ED
Le Journal de Quebec, Ville Vanier, QC
Cote, Sylvie .... (819) 758-6211
MAN ED, Journal L'Union, Victoriaville, QC
Cote, Tim .... (705) 726-6537
ADV DIR, Examiner, Barrie, ON
Cote, Tony .... (613) 829-9100
Action Line, Ottawa Citizen, Ottawa, ON
Cothran, Justin .... (913) 631-2550
GM, Journal Herald, Shawnee, KS
Cotliar, Sharon .... (312) 321-3000
Suburban Writer
Chicago Sun-Times, Chicago, IL
Cotter, Betty .... (401) 789-9744
ED, Narragansett Times, Wakefield, RI
Cotter, Daniel M .... (314) 340-8000
VP-Marketing, St. Louis Post-Dispatch, St. Louis, MO, Pulitzer Publishing Co.
Cotter, Pamela Reinsal .... (412) 664-9161
MAN ED, Daily News, McKeesport, PA
Cotter, Peter .... (902) 564-5451
City ED, Cape Breton Post, Sydney, NS
Cotter, Tim .... (860) 442-2200
News ED-Night, Day, New London, CT
Cottingham, Ed .... (912) 452-0567
Photo ED, Union-Recorder, Milledgeville, GA
Cottingham, James .... (405) 353-0620
BM, DP MGR
Lawton Constitution, Lawton, OK
Cotton, Crosbie .... (403) 235-7100
EIC, Calgary Herald, Calgary, AB
Cotton, George .... (505) 393-2123
CIRC DIR, Daily News-Sun, Hobbs, NM
Cottone, Vincent .... (508) 685-1000
ADV DIR, Eagle-Tribune, North Andover, MA
Cottos, Scott .... (419) 435-6641
Sports ED, Review Times, Fostoria, OH
Cottrill, Harry .... (609) 272-7000
PROD MGR-Mechanical OPER
Press of Atlantic City, Pleasantville, NJ
Cottrill, Jack .... (330) 841-1600
PROD MGR-Technical SRV
Tribune Chronicle, Warren, OH
Couch, Jeff .... (910) 323-4848
ASST MAN ED
Fayetteville Observer-Times, Fayetteville, NC
Couch, Shari .... (941) 748-0411
ADV MGR-RT
Bradenton Herald, Bradenton, FL
Coudret, Rebecca .... (812) 424-7711
Television ED
Evansville Courier, Evansville, IN
Coughenour, Dean .... (913) 539-7558
PUB, Grass & Grain, Manhattan, KS
Coughlin, Kathy .... (904) 252-1511
ADV DIR, Daytona Beach News-Journal, Daytona Beach, FL
Coulbourn, John .... (416) 947-2222
Theater ED, Toronto Sun, Toronto, ON
Coulby, Susan .... (609) 935-1500
EDU ED, Entertainment/Amusements ED, Features ED, Senior Reporter, Travel ED
Today's Sunbeam, Salem, NJ
Coulombe, Roger .... (315) 470-0011
PROD MGR-PR, Post-Standard/Syracuse Herald-Journal/American, Syracuse, NY
Coulombe, Trevor .... (306) 236-5265
ED
Meadow Lake Progress, Meadow Lake, SK
Coulson, Arthur .... (716) 232-7100
Deputy EPE-Democrat and Chronicle
Rochester Democrat and Chronicle; Times-Union, Rochester, NY
Coulson, Joan .... (217) 773-3371
PUB, Democrat Message, Mt. Sterling, IL
Coulson, Warren .... (217) 773-3371
GM, MAN ED
Democrat Message, Mt. Sterling, IL
Coulson, Wright (Bud) .... (913) 492-9050
Vice Chairman
Inland Industries Inc., Lenexa, KS
Coulter, Alexander .... (501) 735-1010
PUB, Evening Times, West Memphis, AR
Coulter, Charles .... (423) 756-6900
ADTX MGR
Chattanooga Free Press, Chattanooga, TN
Coulter, David .... (717) 421-3000
Photo DEPT MGR
Pocono Record, Stroudsburg, PA
Coulter, Don .... (510) 208-6300
Sports ED, Oakland Tribune, Oakland, CA
MediaNews Inc. (Alameda Newspapers)
Coulter, Keith .... (306) 652-9200
PROD FRM-PR, StarPhoenix, Saskatoon, SK
Coulter, Michael F .... (904) 362-1734
PUB, Suwannee Democrat, Live Oak, FL
Coulter, Phyllis .... (519) 537-2341
Features ED, Food ED, Home ED, Lifestyle ED, Medical/Health ED, RE ED, Women's ED
Sentinel-Review, Woodstock, ON
Coulthard, Carl .... (803) 763-1800
PUB, Airlift Spirit, Charleston, SC
Coulton, Dave .... (712) 328-1811
Weekend ED
Daily Nonpareil, Council Bluffs, IA
Counce, Tom .... (518) 792-9914
Regional Sales DIR
TV Data, Queensbury, NY
Council, Kim .... (703) 560-4000
PROD DIR, Fairfax Journal, Fairfax, VA
Journal Newspapers Inc.
Council, Wanda .... (904) 879-2727
GM, Nassau County Record, Callahan, FL
Counihan, Schuyler .... (941) 748-0411
ADV MGR-Commercial Print
Bradenton Herald, Bradenton, FL
Countiss, Susan .... (603) 298-8711
ADV ASST MGR
Valley News, White River Jct., VT
Countryman Jr, Albert .... (609) 753-4500
ED, Record-Breeze, Berlin, NJ
Countryman, Ernest .... (315) 823-3680
CIRC MGR
Evening Times, Little Falls, NY
Counts, Huey .... (816) 254-8600
Sports ED, Examiner, Independence, MO
Counts, Judy .... (205) 353-4612
PROD FRM-Camera, Daily, Decatur, AL
Coupe, Debbie .... (916) 741-2345
ADV MGR-CLASS
Appeal-Democrat, Marysville, CA
Courogen, Chris .... (717) 622-3456
Sports ED, Pottsville Republican & Evening Herald, Pottsville, PA
Coursey, Rick .... (907) 488-0669
PUB, Goldpanner, North Pole, AK
Courson, Shirley .... (904) 747-5000
Entertainment ED
News Herald, Panama City, FL
Courter, Kenneth .... (703) 560-4000
ADV DIR, Fairfax Journal, Fairfax, VA
Journal Newspapers Inc.
Courter, Tammy .... (515) 872-1234
ED, Corydon Times Republican, Corydon, IA
Courtner, Marvin .... (618) 939-3814
ED, Waterloo Republic-Times, Waterloo, IL
Courtney, James .... (814) 445-9621
SEC, Daily American, Somerset, PA
Courtney, Jamie .... (616) 445-2656
ED, Cassopolis Vigilant, Cassopolis, MI
Courtney, Kevin .... (707) 226-3711
BUS ED, Napa Valley Register, Napa, CA
Courtney, Ron .... (712) 262-6610
CIRC MGR, Daily Reporter, Spencer, IA
Courtright, Peter .... (202) 636-3000
DIR-MKTG
Washington Times, Washington, DC
Courtright, Sharon .... (405) 336-2222
City ED, Perry Daily Journal, Perry, OK
Courtwright, Anthony .... (509) 459-5000
CIRC MGR-MKTG/Sales Development
Spokesman-Review, Spokane, WA
Coury, Bruce E .... (618) 656-4700
VP, PUB, Intelligencer, Edwardsville, IL
Cousineau, Louise .... (514) 285-7272
Radio/Television ED
La Presse, Montreal, QC
Cousineau, Paul .... (212) 416-2000
PROD MGR (Chickopee MA)
Wall Street Journal, New York, NY
Cousins, Bruce .... (250) 758-4917
CIRC MGR
Nanaimo Daily Free Press, Nanaimo, BC
Cousins, David .... (802) 479-0191
ADV DIR, Times Argus, Barre, VT
Cousland, Harold .... (505) 523-4581
ED, Las Cruces Sun-News, Las Cruces, NM
Couteau, Greg .... (703) 642-7330
MAN ED, Defense News, Springfield, VA
Couto, Tony .... (803) 329-4000
PROD MGR-Camera/Plate/Press
Herald, Rock Hill, SC
Couton, Bill .... (203) 333-0161
ADV MGR-RT
Connecticut Post, Bridgeport, CT
Coutts, Kathy .... (403) 938-6397
ED, Okotoks Western Wheel, Okotoks, AB
Couture, Gail .... (508) 997-7411
Librarian
Standard Times, New Bedford, MA
Couture, Marc .... (418) 683-1573
CIRC MGR
Le Journal de Quebec, Ville Vanier, QC
Couture, Pierre .... (902) 742-9119
ED, Le Courrier de la Nouvelle-Ecosse, Yarmouth, NS
Covaleskie, Vince .... (717) 348-9100
BUS/FIN ED, RE ED
Tribune & The Scranton Times, Scranton, PA
Cove, Lou .... (800) 584-6758
PRES, Syndicate X, Northampton, MA
Coven, David .... (937) 667-2214
GM, Tipp City Herald, Tipp City, OH
Coveney, Tom .... (617) 929-2000
PROD MGR, Boston Globe, Boston, MA
Coventry, Duane .... (603) 224-5301
DP MGR, Concord Monitor, Concord, NH
Cover, James T .... (330) 747-7777
PRES, Co-PUB, Co-ED
Daily Legal News, Youngstown, OH
Cover, Lyz .... (802) 863-3441
PROD MGR-COMP (Day)
Burlington Free Press, Burlington, VT
Covert, Colin .... (612) 673-4000
GEN Assignment Reporter
Star Tribune, Minneapolis, MN
Covert, Steve .... (317) 633-1240
PROD OPER MGR
Indianapolis Star/News, Indianapolis, IN
Covert, Tom .... (412) 654-6651
MGR-Computer SRV
New Castle News, New Castle, PA
Covey, Greg .... (808) 329-9311
PROD SUPV-Press
West Hawaii Today, Kailua-Kona, HI
Covington, John .... (910) 997-3111
PROD FRM-PR, Richmond County Daily Journal, Rockingham, NC
Covington, Pam .... (405) 326-3311
ED, Hugo Daily News, Hugo, OK
Covington, Terry .... (616) 695-3878
MAN ED
Berrien County Record, Buchanan, MI
Cowan, Alison .... (212) 556-1234
Sunday BUS ED
New York Times, New York, NY
Cowan, Bruce .... (705) 472-3200
City ED, EDL Writer
North Bay Nugget, North Bay, ON
Cowan, Dave .... (916) 891-1234
PROD FRM-COMP
Chico Enterprise-Record, Chico, CA
Cowan, Ilana .... (409) 744-3611
ADV DIR
Galveston County Daily News, Galveston, TX
Cowan, Jack .... (915) 653-1221
EPE, Standard-Times, San Angelo, TX
Cowan, Marylouise .... (207) 633-4620
PUB
Boothbay Register, Boothbay Harbor, ME
Cowan, Ned .... (704) 692-0505
CIRC DIR, Times-News, Hendersonville, NC
Cowan, Ron .... (503) 399-6611
Television/Film ED, Theater/Music ED
Statesman Journal, Salem, OR
Cowan, Ted .... (416) 869-4991
Sales, Toronto Star Syndicate, Toronto, ON
Cowan-Smith, Cindy .... (505) 325-4545
DP MGR, PROD ASST SUPT
Daily Times, Farmington, NM
Coward, Doug .... (613) 342-4441
EPE, EDL Writer, Brockville Recorder and Times, Brockville, ON
Coward, Marty .... (919) 269-6101
ED, Zebulon Record, Zebulon, NC
Cowart, Edward B .... (814) 676-7444
ADV DIR, Derrick, Oil City, PA
Cowart, Kathy .... (334) 262-1611
ADV MGR-CLASS
Montgomery Advertiser, Montgomery, AL
Cowart, Lawton .... (334) 644-1101
SEC/TREAS, Valley Times-News, Lanett, AL
Cowbrough, Chris K .... (509) 684-4567
ED, Statesman-Examiner, Colville, WA
Cowell, Fuller A .... (907) 257-4200
PUB, Anchorage Daily News, Anchorage, AK
Cowen, Jenelle .... (913) 263-1000
Lifestyle ED
Abilene Reflector-Chronicle, Abilene, KS
Cowger, R D .... (405) 395-2212
PUB, ED, Medford Patriot-Star and Grant County Journal, Medford, OK
Cowger, Rose .... (405) 395-2212
PUB, Medford Patriot-Star and Grant County Journal, Medford, OK
Cowgill, Gene .... (304) 636-2121
CIRC MGR, Inter-Mountain, Elkins, WV
Cowgill, Mary Ann .... (816) 265-4244
MAN ED, Milan Standard, Milan, MO
Cowherd, Kevin .... (410) 332-6000
COL-Features, Sun, Baltimore, MD
Cowhig, Vincent .... (718) 981-1234
ADV MGR-Ad SRV
Staten Island Advance, Staten Island, NY
Cowie, Reginald .... (815) 987-1200
ADV MGR-CLASS/NTL
Rockford Register Star, Rockford, IL
Cowles, Gardner .... (516) 725-1700
PUB, Sag Harbor Express, Sag Harbor, NY
Cowles III, Gardner .... (516) 751-1550
PUB, Three Village Herald, East Setauket, NY
Cowles, James P .... (509) 459-5000
PRES, Spokesman-Review, Spokane, WA
Cowles, Roger .... (409) 985-5541
ED, EDL Writer
Port Arthur News, Port Arthur, TX
Cowles, Stephen .... (757) 539-3437
MAN ED, Suffolk News-Herald, Suffolk, VA
Cowles, William Stacey .... (509) 459-5000
VP/PUB, Spokesman-Review, Spokane, WA
Cowless III, John .... (612) 673-4000
COB, Star Tribune, Minneapolis, MN
Cowley, Ed .... (403) 942-2023
PUB, Review, Redwater, AB
Cowley, Wanda .... (403) 942-2023
GM, Review, Redwater, AB
Cowman, Colette .... (208) 342-1311
ED, Idaho Catholic Register, Boise, ID
Cox, Ann .... (501) 946-3241
ED, De Witt Era-Enterprise, De Witt, AR
Cox, Becky .... (205) 698-8148
GM, Lamar Leader, Sulligent, AL
Cox, Beverly .... (706) 549-0123
EDU ED, Athens Daily News/Banner-Herald, Athens, GA
Cox, Christine .... (905) 526-3333
EDU, Spectator, Hamilton, ON
Cox, Clark .... (910) 997-3111
ED, EDL Writer, Sunday ED, Richmond County Daily Journal, Rockingham, NC
Cox, David .... (501) 257-2417
PUB, ED
Cherokee Villager, Cherokee Village, AR
Cox, David C .... (612) 673-4000
PRES/CEO, Star Tribune, Minneapolis, MN
Cox, David H .... (812) 231-4200
ED, Tribune-Star, Terre Haute, IN
Cox, Eric M .... (765) 345-2111
ED, Tri-County Banner, Knightstown, IN
Cox, Ezell .... (209) 943-6397
VP-MKTG, ADTX MGR, Record, Stockton, CA
Cox, George .... (210) 542-4301
ED, Photo DEPT MGR
Brownsville Herald, Brownsville, TX
Freedom Communications Inc.
Cox, J William .... (214) 977-8222
Senior VP-ADM/OPER
Dallas Morning News, Dallas, TX
Cox, James B .... (205) 247-5565
PUB, ED
East Lauderdale News, Rogersville, AL
Cox, Jere .... (972) 392-0888
DIR-MKTG
Wieck Photo DataBase Inc., Dallas, TX
Cox, Jim .... (360) 694-3391
CIRC MGR-Sales/Home Delivery
Columbian, Vancouver, WA
Cox, Jim .... (606) 792-2831
PUB
Lancaster Central Record, Lancaster, KY
Cox, Jimmy .... (817) 325-4465
PROD MGR-PR
Mineral Wells Index, Mineral Wells, TX
Cox, Joel .... (804) 649-6000
PROD CNR-Quality
Richmond Times-Dispatch, Richmond, VA
Cox, John Ferrin .... (334) 897-2823
PUB, Elba Clipper, Elba, AL
Cox, Keith .... (416) 367-2000
PROD SUPT-PR, Toronto Star, Toronto, ON
Cox, Len .... (757) 539-3437
PROD FRM-PR, PROD SUPV
Suffolk News-Herald, Suffolk, VA

Copyright ©1997 by the Editor & Publisher Co.

Cox Who's Where-50

Cox, Linda ... (508) 676-8211
Entertainment ED
Herald News, Fall River, MA

Cox, Mary ... (213) 237-5000
Letters ED
Los Angeles Times, Los Angeles, CA

Cox, Mike ... (912) 744-4200
DIR-INFO SYS, Macon Telegraph, Macon, GA

Cox, Mike ... (402) 475-4200
PROD MGR-MR
Lincoln Journal Star, Lincoln, NE

Cox, Patrick ... (203) 574-3636
ADV MGR, Waterbury Republican-American, Waterbury, CT

Cox, Paul ... (904) 234-6990
GM, ED
Beach-Bay News, Panama City Beach, FL

Cox, Phyllis D ... (205) 247-5565
PUB, ED
East Lauderdale News, Rogersville, AL

Cox, Rich ... (602) 271-8000
VP-OPER & Product Management
Phoenix Newspapers Inc., Phoenix, AZ

Cox, Rich ... (219) 722-5000
PROD MGR, Pharos-Tribune, Logansport, IN

Cox, Robert E ... (303) 239-9890
PUB, Jefferson Sentinel, Lakewood, CO

Cox, Robert G ... (540) 638-8801
ADV MGR, Bulletin, Martinsville, VA

Cox, Robert J ... (803) 577-7111
ASST ED, Post and Courier, Charleston, SC

Cox, Sean ... (212) 210-2100
PROD GEN FRM-COMP
New York Daily News, New York, NY

Cox, Sharon ... (817) 390-7400
ED-Class Acts
Fort Worth Star-Telegram, Fort Worth, TX

Cox, Steve ... (205) 221-2840
MGR-EDU SRV, MAN ED
Daily Mountain Eagle, Jasper, AL

Cox, Steve ... (540) 885-7281
Sports ED, Daily News Leader, Staunton, VA

Cox, Theodore J ... (847) 427-4300
Television ED
Daily Herald, Arlington Heights, IL

Cox, Therese ... (304) 348-5140
Health/Medical ED
Charleston Daily Mail, Charleston, WV

Cox, Tony ... (606) 885-5381
PUB, Jessamine Journal, Nicholasville, KY

Cox, William J ... (412) 664-9161
Chairman, Daily News, McKeesport, PA

Coxwell, Alan ... (613) 395-3015
ED, Community Press, Stirling, ON

Coy, Sharon ... (913) 243-2424
City/People ED, Women's ED
Blade-Empire, Concordia, KS

Coya, T Alicia ... (305) 377-3721
ASSOC PUB
Miami Daily Business Review, Miami, FL

Coyle, Hugh ... (802) 864-6399
ED, Out in the Mountains, Burlington, VT

Coyle, Sandy ... (914) 694-9300
ASST MAN ED, Herald Statesman, Yonkers, NY, Gannett Co. Inc.

Coyne, Daniel ... (919) 752-6166
PROD MGR-Press
Daily Reflector, Greenville, NC

Coyne, Larry ... (901) 529-2211
DIR-Photography
Commercial Appeal, Memphis, TN

Coyne, Ryland ... (613) 257-1303
ED
Carleton Place Canadian, Carleton Place, ON

Cozart, Gary ... (216) 329-7000
CIRC MGR, Chronicle-Telegram, Elyria, OH

Crabill, Michele ... (817) 634-2125
Personnel MGR
Killeen Daily Herald, Killeen, TX

Crabill, Steve ... (201) 646-4000
Arts/Architecture ED, YourTime ED
Record, Hackensack, NJ

Crabtree, James ... (405) 475-3311
PROD SUPT-PR
Daily Oklahoman, Oklahoma City, OK

Crabtree, Larry L ... (817) 552-5454
PRES, PUB/GM
Vernon Daily Record, Vernon, TX

Crabtree, Peggy S ... (317) 664-5111
CONT, Chronicle-Tribune, Marion, IN

Crabtree, Sharlene ... (541) 382-1811
MGR-Human Resources, Bulletin, Bend, OR

Craddock, Gary ... (540) 981-3100
PROD MGR-Quality Control/PR
Roanoke Times, Roanoke, VA

Craddock, Kathryn ... (901) 925-6397
PUB, Courier, Savannah, TN

Craddock, Pat ... (409) 825-6484
MAN ED, Navasota Examiner, Navasota, TX

Craft, Dan ... (309) 829-9411
COL, Entertainment Writer
Pantagraph, Bloomington, IL

Craft, Michael ... (318) 459-3200
PRES, PUB, Times, Shreveport, LA

Craft, Mike ... (805) 650-2900
ED-Oxnard Edtion
Ventura County Star, Ventura, CA

Craft, Robert ... (318) 433-3000
PROD FRM-PR, American Press, Lake Charles, LA

Craig, Angie ... (901) 529-2211
EDU Reporter
Commercial Appeal, Memphis, TN

Craig, Bill ... (812) 331-0963
PUB, Bloomington Voice, Bloomington, IN

Craig, Brian A ... (941) 335-0200
CONT, News-Press, Fort Myers, FL

Craig, Bruce ... (613) 829-9100
PROD MGR-Manufacturing-Pre Press (Night)
Ottawa Citizen, Ottawa, ON

Craig, Darla ... (316) 275-8500
ADV MGR
Garden City Telegram, Garden City, KS

Craig, Frank ... (419) 245-6000
ASST MAN ED, Blade, Toledo, OH

Craig, Jayne ... (806) 669-2525
BM, Pampa News, Pampa, TX

Craig, Jeff ... (403) 468-0100
Express ED, Edmonton Sun, Edmonton, AB

Craig, Jennifer ... (915) 537-2251
PUB, ED
Jones County Journal, Hawley, TX

Craig, Jerry ... (206) 622-8272
City ED, Seattle Daily Journal of Commerce, Seattle, WA

Craig, Jim ... (205) 325-2222
CIRC MGR-South Zone
Birmingham News, Birmingham, AL

Craig, Jim ... (407) 242-3500
PROD MGR-COMP
Florida Today, Melbourne, FL

Craig Jr, John G ... (412) 263-1100
VP, ED
Pittsburgh Post-Gazette, Pittsburgh, PA

Craig, Kacey ... (619) 232-4381
MGR-SYS
San Diego Daily Transcript, San Diego, CA

Craig, Kevin ... (707) 644-1141
CIRC DIR
Vallejo Times-Herald, Vallejo, CA

Craig, Lloyd ... (316) 221-1050
BM, ADV MGR, ADV MGR-CLASS
Winfield Daily Courier, Winfield, KS

Craig, Louise ... (514) 458-5482
GM, Hudson Gazette, Hudson, QC

Craig, M Joseph ... (712) 328-1811
PUB/GM
Daily Nonpareil, Council Bluffs, IA

Craig, Marge ... (209) 239-3531
ADV MGR-CLASS
Manteca Bulletin, Manteca, CA

Craig, Marilyn ... (615) 759-7302
PUB, ED
Moore County News, Lynchburg, TN

Craig, Maureen ... (910) 623-2155
ADV MGR, Daily News, Eden, NC

Craig, Michael ... (202) 334-6000
GM, Washington Post, Washington, DC

Craig, Morris G ... (903) 897-2281
PUB, ED, Monitor, Naples, TX

Craig, Rick ... (915) 576-3606
PUB, ED, Hamlin Herald, Hamlin, TX

Craig, Sharon ... (970) 242-5050
PROD FRM-COMP
Daily Sentinel, Grand Junction, CO

Craig, Sonja Sorensen ... (320) 255-8700
PRES, PUB
St. Cloud Times, St. Cloud, MN

Craig, Terry ... (316) 326-3326
PROD SUPT
Wellington Daily News, Wellington, KS

Craig, Terry ... (615) 455-4545
PUB
Tullahoma News & Guardian, Tullahoma, TN

Craig, Tim ... (515) 573-2141
ADV DIR, MGR-MKTG/PROM
Messenger, Fort Dodge, IA

Craigie, Barbara ... (518) 943-2100
ADV CNR-Legal, Daily Mail, Catskill, NY

Craigo, Kar ... (419) 674-4066
Society ED, Kenton Times, Kenton, OH

Crain, Danny ... (520) 573-4400
PROD MGR-Production Maintenance, TNI Partners dba Tucson Newspapers, Tucson, AZ

Cramer, Daniel ... (517) 752-7171
PROD MGR-MR, Saginaw News, Saginaw, MI

Cramer, Larry ... (815) 987-1200
PROD MGR-PR
Rockford Register Star, Rockford, IL

Cramer, Mark ... (402) 274-3185
PUB, Auburn Press-Tribune, Auburn, NE

Cramer, Rodger ... (972) 418-9999
ED, Metrocrest News, Carrollton, TX

Cramer, Sally ... (419) 422-5151
ADV MGR-Office
Findlay Courier, Findlay, OH

Cramer, Wayne ... (317) 342-3311
ADTX CNR
Martinsville Daily Reporter, Martinsville, IN

Cramton, Donn E ... (517) 752-7171
MGR-MKTG SRV
Saginaw News, Saginaw, MI

Crandall, L E ... (313) 533-1846
MGR/MAN ED
Specialty Features Syndicate, Detroit, MI

Crandall, Robert ... (407) 420-5000
PROD MGR-Quality Assurance
Orlando Sentinel, Orlando, FL

Crane, Ann ... (407) 242-3500
MGR-MKTG Communications
Florida Today, Melbourne, FL

Crane, Charlotte ... (904) 435-8500
BUS/FIN ED
Pensacola News Journal, Pensacola, FL

Crane, Ernest ... (541) 672-3321
PROD FRM-PR, News-Review, Roseburg, OR

Crane, Gerald W ... (404) 292-3536
PUB
Decatur-De Kalb News/Era, Decatur, GA

Crane, Kevin ... (304) 526-4000
DP MGR, PROD MGR-SYS
Herald-Dispatch, Huntington, WV

Crane, Sally ... (614) 221-2449
PUB, ED, Columbus Alive, Columbus, OH

Cranfill, John ... (214) 977-8222
PROD DIR-Publishing Technology
Dallas Morning News, Dallas, TX

Cranford, Bill ... (864) 582-4511
ADV DIR, ADV MGR-GEN
Herald-Journal, Spartanburg, SC

Cranford, Jane ... (504) 643-4918
PROD MGR, Slidell Sentry-News, Slidell, LA

Crann, Alice ... (904) 435-8500
Religion ED
Pensacola News Journal, Pensacola, FL

Cranson, Jeff ... (616) 222-5400
Community Editions ED
Grand Rapids Press, Grand Rapids, MI

Cranston, Alice ... (609) 272-7000
Books ED, Features ED, Films/Theater ED, Health/Medical ED, Lifestyle ED, Religion ED
Press of Atlantic City, Pleasantville, NJ

Cranston, Valerie ... (505) 887-5501
Food/Women's ED, Religion ED
Current-Argus, Carlsbad, NM

Crapson, G B ... (308) 334-5226
PUB, ED
Hitchcock County News, Trenton, NE

Crass, Stephen L ... (417) 235-3135
PUB, ED, COL, Times, Monett, MO

Crater, Michael ... (208) 743-9411
Wire ED
Lewiston Morning Tribune, Lewiston, ID

Cratty, Glenn ... (310) 230-3400
Photo ED, Allsport Photography USA, Pacific Palisades, CA

Crausse, Henry ... (210) 542-4301
City ED, Brownsville Herald, Brownsville, TX

Craven, Allan ... (914) 341-1100
PROD SUPT-PR
Times Herald-Record, Middletown, NY

Craven, Eric ... (716) 282-2311
Graphics ED
Niagara Gazette, Niagara Falls, NY

Craven, Glenn ... (316) 251-3300
City ED, Coffeyville Journal, Coffeyville, KS

Cravens, Clement ... (573) 748-2120
PUB, ED, Weekly Record, New Madrid, MO

Crawford, Bill ... (405) 379-5411
News ED
Holdenville Daily News, Holdenville, OK

Crawford, Bobby ... (615) 762-2222
MAN ED
Democrat-Union, Lawrenceburg, TN

Crawford, Brenda G ... (573) 888-4505
CIRC MGR
Daily Dunklin Democrat, Kennett, MO

Crawford, Brian ... (613) 258-3451
ED, Weekly Advance, Kemptville, ON

Crawford, Charlie ... (615) 762-2222
ED, Democrat-Union, Lawrenceburg, TN

Crawford, Dale ... (308) 367-4144
PUB, Hi-Line Enterprise, Curtis, NE

Crawford, Darryl ... (318) 255-4353
PROD MGR, Ruston Daily Leader, Ruston, LA

Crawford, Debbie ... (502) 769-2312
ADV MGR
News Enterprise, Elizabethtown, KY

Crawford, E ... (412) 758-5573
CIRC MGR
Ellwood City Ledger, Ellwood City, PA

Crawford, F Steven ... (513) 977-3000
Sr VP-Cable Television
E W Scripps Co., Cincinnati, OH

Crawford, Franklin ... (607) 272-2321
COL, Ithaca Journal, Ithaca, NY

Crawford, Garnet ... (613) 258-3451
PUB, Weekly Advance, Kemptville, ON

Crawford, Gerald J ... (505) 823-7777
Senior ED
Albuquerque Journal, Albuquerque, NM

Crawford Jr, Jim ... (615) 762-2222
PUB, Democrat-Union, Lawrenceburg, TN

Crawford, Joanne ... (607) 798-1234
CIRC MGR-Customer SRV
Press & Sun Bulletin, Binghamton, NY

Crawford, Joe ... (503) 221-8327
PROD SUPT-Plant, Oregonian, Portland, OR

Crawford, Joe ... (616) 222-5400
EPE/Writer
Grand Rapids Press, Grand Rapids, MI

Crawford, John ... (334) 262-1611
PSL DIR
Montgomery Advertiser, Montgomery, AL

Crawford, Karen ... (517) 772-2971
Librarian, Morning Sun, Mount Pleasant, MI

Crawford, Kevin ... (209) 582-0471
ADV MGR-CLASS
Hanford Sentinel, Hanford, CA

Crawford, Michael ... (913) 352-6235
PUB, Linn County News, Pleasanton, KS

Crawford, Michael ... (417) 646-2211
ED, St. Clair Co. Courier, Osceola, MO

Crawford, Phil ... (209) 734-5821
PROD MGR-Distribution/MR
Visalia Times-Delta, Visalia, CA

Crawford, Richard ... (320) 587-5000
ED, Hutchinson Leader, Hutchinson, MN

Crawford, Tom ... (218) 894-1112
ED, Staples World, Staples, MN

Crawford-Whitehead, Estelle ... (205) 383-8471
MAN ED
Colbert County Reporter, Tuscumbia, AL

Crawley, Bill ... (902) 564-5451
ADTX MGR, Cape Breton Post, Sydney, NS

Crawley, Laura ... (412) 488-1890
ED, Narodne Noviny, Pittsburgh, PA

Cray, Chris ... (910) 276-2311
ADV DIR, Exchange, Laurinburg, NC

Crays, Duane ... (618) 662-2108
City ED
Daily Clay County Advocate-Press, Flora, IL

Crea, Joe ... (419) 245-6000
Food ED, Blade, Toledo, OH

Crea, John ... (412) 684-5200
PROD SUPT
Valley Independent, Monessen, PA

Creacy, Dan ... (703) 276-3400
CIRC GM-Denver, USA Today, Arlington, VA

Creagh, David ... (617) 450-2000
MGR-BUS Development
Christian Science Monitor, Boston, MA

Creamer, Charles ... (304) 233-0100
News ED, Religion ED, Intelligencer/Wheeling News-Register, Wheeling, WV

Creamer, Dennis ... (910) 373-7000
PROD MGR-MR
News & Record, Greensboro, NC

Creasman, Vickie ... (704) 321-4271
PUB, Andrews Journal, Andrews, NC

Creech, David ... (419) 394-7414
PUB, ADV MGR-Commercial Sales, MGR-PROM, Evening Leader, St. Marys, OH

Creech, Jerome ... (919) 823-3106
PUB, Daily Southerner, Tarboro, NC

Creech, Laura ... (812) 689-6364
ED, Versailles Republican, Versailles, IN

Creed, Gary ... (404) 526-5151
PROD MGR-OPER
Atlanta Journal-Constitution, Atlanta, GA

Creedon, Dan ... (303) 442-1202
Sports ED, Daily Camera, Boulder, CO

Creer, John Dennis ... (330) 332-4601
ED, Salem News, Salem, OH

Crees, Jim ... (616) 734-5587
ED, Evart Review, Evart, MI

Cregar, Heather ... (302) 674-3600
MGR-MKTG, Delaware State News, Dover, DE

Creger, Gary ... (614) 532-1441
PROD FRM-MR
Ironton Tribune, Ironton, OH

Creighton, Don ... (613) 739-7000
DIR-PROM, Ottawa Sun, Ottawa, ON

Creighton, E Donald ... (203) 574-3636
PROD SUPT-COMP, Waterbury Republican-American, Waterbury, CT

Creighton, John P ... (309) 343-5617
ED, Galesburg Post, Galesburg, IL

Creighton, Mary A ... (309) 343-5617
PUB, Galesburg Post, Galesburg, IL

Creighton, Ned ... (602) 258-7026
PUB, Arizona Capitol Times, Phoenix, AZ

Creitz, Sandy ... (317) 459-3121
CIRC MGR-Sales
Kokomo Tribune, Kokomo, IN

Cremer, Diane ... (610) 258-7171
PA, Express-Times, Easton, PA

Crenshaw, George ... (408) 637-9795
PRES, Post/Dispatch Features, Hollister, CA

51-Who's Where **Cro**

Crenshaw, Richard .... (601) 842-2611
ADV DIR, Northeast Mississippi Daily Journal, Tupelo, MS
Crepeau, Kim .... (207) 282-1535
ADV MGR-CLASS
Journal Tribune, Biddeford, ME
Crerar, John .... (250) 380-5211
CIRC MGR-Sales
Times Colonist, Victoria, BC
Cresenzo, Bill .... (910) 623-2155
Television/Film ED, Theater/Music ED, Travel ED, Women's ED, Daily News, Eden, NC
Creskey, Jim .... (613) 237-8226
PUB, ED, Ottawa XPress, Ottawa, ON
Creson, Marilyn .... (619) 299-3131
DIR-FIN, Union-Tribune, San Diego, CA
Cretella, Louis .... (203) 333-0161
CIRC MGR, Connecticut Post, Bridgeport, CT
Crevier, Glen .... (206) 597-8742
Senior ED-Sports, Sports ED
News Tribune, Tacoma, WA
Creviere, Marie .... (414) 336-4221
ED, De Pere Journal, De Pere, WI
Creviere, Paul J .... (414) 336-4221
PUB, De Pere Journal, De Pere, WI
Crews, Donald R .... (210) 829-9000
Sr VP/Legal SEC, Harte-Hanks Communications Inc., San Antonio, TX
Crews, William L .... (601) 842-2611
EVP, PUB, Northeast Mississippi Daily Journal, Tupelo, MS
Cribb, Edwin .... (912) 244-1880
PROD FRM-PR
Valdosta Daily Times, Valdosta, GA
Cribb, Vince .... (912) 226-2400
PROD FRM-PR, Thomasville Times-Enterprise, Thomasville, GA
Cribbs, Jim .... (919) 419-6500
CIRC MGR-EDU SRV
Herald-Sun, Durham, NC
Crichton, Howie .... (613) 273-8000
PUB, ED, Rideau Valley Mirror, Westport, ON
Criddle, Sandy .... (304) 235-4242
SEC/TREAS, BM
Williamson Daily News, Williamson, WV
Crider, Bob .... (509) 525-3300
News ED
Walla Walla Union-Bulletin, Walla Walla, WA
Crider, Dennis .... (417) 256-9191
Farm ED, Sports ED
West Plains Daily Quill, West Plains, MO
Crider, Kitty .... (512) 445-3500
Food ED
Austin American-Statesman, Austin, TX
Crile, Jeffrey .... (515) 472-4129
CIRC MGR, Fairfield Ledger, Fairfield, IA
Crilley, Timothy J .... (207) 791-6650
CIRC ASST DIR-Home Delivery
Portland Press Herald, Portland, ME
Crim, Don .... (217) 223-5100
News ED, Quincy Herald-Whig, Quincy, IL
Criminger, Ronnie .... (910) 323-4848
PROD ASST MGR
Fayetteville Observer-Times, Fayetteville, NC
Crimmin, Stephen F .... (802) 463-9591
GM, ED
Bellows Falls Town Crier, Bellows Falls, VT
Crinite, Tina .... (208) 882-5561
EDU ED-Higher, Farm ED
Moscow-Pullman Daily News, Moscow, ID
Crisalli, Al .... (805) 822-6828
GM, Tehachapi News, Tehachapi, CA
Criscoe, Ray .... (910) 625-2101
ED, Courier-Tribune, Asheboro, NC
Crisler Jr, Edgar T .... (601) 437-5103
PUB, ED
Port Gibson Reveille, Port Gibson, MS
Crisp, Bob .... (205) 362-1000
Photo ED, Daily Home, Talladega, AL
Crisp, Dan .... (909) 889-9666
PROD DIR, Sun, San Bernardino, CA
Crisp Jr, Fred .... (919) 829-4500
PRES, PUB, News & Observer, Raleigh, NC
Crispo, Gio .... (705) 268-5050
CIRC MGR, Daily Press, Timmins, ON
Crist, William .... (915) 646-2541
ADV DIR-MKTG
Brownwood Bulletin, Brownwood, TX
Crist-Flanagan, Irene .... (901) 529-2211
DIR-EDU SRV
Commercial Appeal, Memphis, TN
Criswell, Ann .... (713) 220-7171
Food ED, Houston Chronicle, Houston, TX
Critcher, Charles .... (919) 693-2646
PUB, Oxford Public Ledger, Oxford, NC
Critchlow Sr, Dave .... (901) 885-0744
PUB/GM, Photo MGR
Union City Daily Messenger, Union City, TN
Critchlow Jr, David .... (901) 885-0744
ED, News ED
Union City Daily Messenger, Union City, TN
Crittendon, Jules .... (617) 426-3000
Environmental ED
Boston Herald, Boston, MA
Croan, Robert .... (412) 263-1100
Music ED, Post-Gazette, Pittsburgh, PA
Crocco, Robert M .... (410) 332-6000
PROD DIR, Sun, Baltimore, MD
Croce, Jon .... (715) 623-4191
ADV DIR, Antigo Daily Journal, Antigo, WI
Crock, Duane .... (319) 398-8211
Graphics DIR, Gazette, Cedar Rapids, IA
Crockatt, Joan .... (403) 235-7100
MAN ED, Calgary Herald, Calgary, AB
Crocker, Joy .... (607) 798-1234
Features ED, Food ED, Garden ED, Press & Sun Bulletin, Binghamton, NY
Crocker, Matt .... (210) 423-5511
Graphics ED/Art DIR
Valley Morning Star, Harlingen, TX
Crockett, Caren .... (360) 754-5400
ASST MAN ED, Olympian, Olympia, WA
Crockett, David .... (907) 257-4200
CIRC ASST DIR, Daily News, Anchorage, AK
Crockett, Hank .... (352) 753-1119
PUB, Tri-County Sun, Lady Lake, FL
Crockett, Jim .... (312) 616-3282
Sr ED, Dodge Construction News Chicago, Chicago, IL
Crockett, Lane .... (318) 459-3200
Amusements ED, Films/Theater ED
Times, Shreveport, LA
Crockett, Mary .... (803) 577-7111
Librarian, Post and Courier, Charleston, SC
Crockett, Walter .... (508) 799-0511
ED, Worcester Magazine, Worcester, MA
Crockford, Dick .... (406) 563-5283
ED, Anaconda Leader, Anaconda, MT
Croessman, John H .... (618) 542-2133
MAN ED, Action Line ED, BUS/FIN ED, EPE, EDU/Travel ED, NTL ED, SCI/Technology ED, Television/Film ED, Theater/Music ED
Du Quoin Evening Call, Du Quoin, IL
Croft, Charles .... (334) 433-1551
Farm/Agriculture ED
Mobile Press Register, Mobile, AL
Croft, David .... (801) 237-2188
SYS MGR, DP MGR
Deseret News, Salt Lake City, UT
Croft, Margaret .... (318) 322-5161
Photo DEPT MGR, News-Star, Monroe, LA
Crofton, Richard .... (517) 354-3111
MAN ED, BUS/FIN ED, Graphics ED/Art DIR, SCI/Technology ED, Alpena News, Alpena, MI
Croke, Cindi .... (317) 622-1212
ADV MGR-NTL
Herald Bulletin, Anderson, IN
Croley, Tina .... (313) 222-6400
The Way We Live ED, Free Press, Detroit, MI
Crombie, Greg .... (416) 947-2222
ADV MGR-NTL, Toronto Sun, Toronto, ON
Cromer, Ed .... (615) 259-8800
Political ED
Nashville Banner, Nashville, TN
Cromer, Wendy .... (937) 652-1331
PROD FRM-COMP
Urbana Daily Citizen, Urbana, OH
Cromley, Ray .... (703) 765-4184
PRES
Cromley News-Features, Alexandria, VA
Crompton, Brett .... (208) 226-5294
GM, ED
Power County Press, American Falls, ID
Crompton, Erma .... (208) 226-5294
PUB, Power County Press, American Falls, ID
Cromwell, William .... (937) 652-1331
MGR-Commercial
Urbana Daily Citizen, Urbana, OH
Cron, Walter .... (313) 242-1100
PROD FRM-PR
Monroe Evening News, Monroe, MI
Cronbaugh, Craig .... (319) 664-3237
ED, North English Record, North English, IA
Crone, Greg .... (519) 894-2231
Queen's Park, Record, Kitchener, ON
Croneis, James F .... (419) 562-3333
PUB, BM, PA
Telegraph-Forum, Bucyrus, OH
Cronin, Anthony .... (860) 442-2200
Deputy MAN ED, BUS/FIN ED
Day, New London, CT
Cronin, Archbishop Daniel A .... (860) 527-1175
PUB, Catholic Transcript, Hartford, CT
Cronin, Dennis .... (402) 444-1000
CIRC MGR-Transportation
Omaha World-Herald, Omaha, NE
Cronin, Mary .... (206) 464-2111
Fashion Writer, Seattle Times, Seattle, WA
Cronin, Ray .... (618) 943-2331 ext. 100
Books ED, Films/Theater ED, Political ED
Daily Record, Lawrenceville, IL
Cronin, Sylvia .... (305) 376-6057
VP/Author, Cronin Feature Syndicating Inc., Hallandale, FL
Cronk, Alan .... (910) 727-7211
DIR-MKTG/PROM
Winston-Salem Journal, Winston-Salem, NC
Cronk, Donna .... (317) 529-1111
Society ED, Courier-Times, New Castle, IN
Crook, Deborah .... (804) 746-1235
GM
Mechanicsville Local, Mechanicsville, VA
Crook, Jack .... (515) 842-2155
PUB, Knoxville Journal-Express, Knoxville, IA
Crook, Jay D .... (719) 738-1720
PUB, ED, Huerfano World, Walsenburg, CO
Crooks, Bill .... (717) 455-3636
Sports ED, Standard-Speaker, Hazleton, PA
Crookston, David .... (330) 833-2631
Radio/Television ED
Independent, Massillon, OH
Croom Jr, Larry D .... (619) 241-7744
EX ED, Daily Press, Victorville, CA
Croome, Richard .... (512) 575-1451
Sports ED, Victoria Advocate, Victoria, TX
Crosbie, Grant .... (416) 585-5000
VP/GM, Globe and Mail, Toronto, ON
Crosbie, Kevin B .... (860) 423-8466
SEC, PUB, GM, PA, Automotive/Aviation ED
Chronicle, Willimantic, CT
Crosbie, Lucy B .... (860) 423-8466
PRES/TREAS, Chronicle, Willimantic, CT
Crosby, Ann .... (541) 889-5387
EDU ED, Argus Observer, Ontario, OR
Crosby, Bruce .... (308) 345-4500
ED, McCook Daily Gazette, McCook, NE
Crosby, Cherrill .... (801) 237-2031
BUS/FIN ED
Salt Lake Tribune, Salt Lake City, UT
Crosby, Karen .... (403) 235-7100
Librarian, Calgary Herald, Calgary, AB
Crosby, Scot .... (541) 889-5387
ASST ED, BUS/FIN ED, City/MET ED, Outdoors ED, Argus Observer, Ontario, OR
Crosby, Steve .... (517) 377-1000
ED, Lansing State Journal, Lansing, MI
Crosby, T J .... (904) 359-4111
PROD ASST DIR
Florida Times-Union, Jacksonville, FL
Crosier, Sean .... (970) 867-5651
Photo ED
Fort Morgan Times, Fort Morgan, CO
Crosina, Gary .... (604) 392-2331
PUB, Tribune, Williams Lake, BC
Crosley, Michael E .... (812) 254-7322
GM, ED, Hoosier Express, Washington, IN
Cross, Al .... (502) 582-4011
Political/Government ED
Courier-Journal, Louisville, KY
Cross, Alan .... (515) 792-3121
Sports ED, Newton Daily News, Newton, IA
Cross Jr, C B .... (334) 227-4411
PUB, Lowndes Signal, Fort Deposit, AL
Cross, C J .... (614) 654-1321
BUS/FIN ED
Lancaster Eagle-Gazette, Lancaster, OH
Cross, C Thomas .... (815) 562-4171
PUB, Rochelle News-Leader, Rochelle, IL
Cross, Cheryl .... (814) 734-1234
ED
Independent Enterprise News, Edinboro, PA
Cross, Dale .... (909) 849-4586
ADV DIR, Record-Gazette, Banning, CA
Cross, Daryl .... (405) 323-5151
ADV MGR-CLASS
Clinton Daily News, Clinton, OK
Cross, Duane .... (601) 728-6214
ED, Banner-Independent, Booneville, MS
Cross, F B .... (334) 227-4411
ED, Lowndes Signal, Fort Deposit, AL
Cross, Greg .... (541) 382-1811
Graphics ED, Bulletin, Bend, OR
Cross, Karen .... (519) 756-2020
ADV SUPV-Customer SRV
Expositor, Brantford, ON
Cross, Michael .... (405) 353-0620
PROD SUPT-PR
Lawton Constitution, Lawton, OK
Cross, Pam .... (815) 244-2411
GM, Mirror-Democrat, Mt. Carroll, IL
Cross, Pete .... (561) 820-4100
Photo DEPT DIR
Palm Beach Post, West Palm Beach, FL
Cross, Robert .... (804) 649-6000
PROD DIR-Engineering
Richmond Times-Dispatch, Richmond, VA
Cross, Roy .... (614) 592-6612
Senior Writer, Athens Messenger, Athens, OH
Cross, Virgil .... (518) 561-2300
PROD FRM-Press
Press-Republican, Plattsburgh, NY
Cross-Bushnell, Cheryl .... (520) 294-1200
EX ED, Daily Territorial, Tucson, AZ
Crossman, Dianne .... (407) 420-5000
CIRC MGR-Planning/SYS
Orlando Sentinel, Orlando, FL
Crossman, Timothy .... (800) 281-3802
MAN ED, Rutland Tribune, Rutland, VT
Crosson, Stephen .... (908) 657-8936
ED, Advance News, Lakehurst, NJ
Crosthwaite, Fred .... (916) 891-1234
ADV MGR-RT/NTL
Chico Enterprise-Record, Chico, CA
Crothers, Carl .... (910) 727-7211
MAN ED
Winston-Salem Journal, Winston-Salem, NC
Crotser, F Max .... (423) 981-1100
PUB, Daily Times, Maryville, TN
Crouch, Amy .... (316) 542-3111
PUB, Times Sentinel, Cheney, KS
Crouch, Chuck .... (706) 324-5526
News ED, Ledger-Enquirer, Columbus, GA
Crouch, Dannye .... (901) 285-4091
EX ED, EPE
Dyersburg State Gazette, Dyersburg, TN
Crouch, David L .... (405) 924-4388
PUB, EPE
Durant Daily Democrat, Durant, OK
Crouch, Jerry .... (704) 252-5611
MGR-PROM
Asheville Citizen-Times, Asheville, NC
Crouch, Mary .... (317) 736-7101
ADV MGR-Ad Sales
Daily Journal, Franklin, IN
Crouch, Rod .... (702) 738-3119
PROD MGR
Elko Daily Free Press, Elko, NV
Crouch, Sue .... (219) 461-8444
ADV Senior MGR-Product Development
Fort Wayne Newspapers Inc., Fort Wayne, IN
Crouse, Greg .... (910) 623-2155
CIRC MGR, Daily News, Eden, NC
Crouse, Robert J .... (308) 764-2402
PUB, Arthur Enterprise, Arthur, NE
Crouse, Sharon .... (717) 637-3736
PROD SUPV-Pre Press
Evening Sun, Hanover, PA
Crout, Kathy .... (405) 376-4571
PUB, Mustang News, Mustang, OK
Crout, Robert .... (405) 376-4571
GM, Mustang News, Mustang, OK
Crout, Sharon .... (864) 847-7361
ED, Journal, Williamston, SC
Croutch, Paul .... (604) 782-9424
PUB, GM, ED, Mirror, Dawson Creek, BC
Crow, Matthew D .... (630) 232-9222
MGR-MKTG/PROM
Kane County Chronicle, Geneva, IL
Crow, Tommy .... (409) 849-8581
ED, Angleton Times, Angleton, TX
Crowcroft, Melinda .... (607) 272-2321
News ED, Ithaca Journal, Ithaca, NY
Crowder, Cindy .... (972) 937-3310
ADV MGR-CLASS
Waxahachie Daily Light, Waxahachie, TX
Crowe, Daniel L .... (972) 272-6591
PUB, Garland News, Garland, TX
Crowe, Donna .... (502) 384-6471
PUB, Adair Progress, Columbia, KY
Crowe, J D .... (619) 582-2769
Self-Syndicator, Crowe, J.D., San Diego, CA
Crowe, John .... (916) 243-2424
Religion ED
Record Searchlight, Redding, CA
Crowe, Judy .... (601) 896-2100
ADV MGR-RT, Sun Herald, Biloxi, MS
Crowe, Martin A .... (912) 868-5776
PUB, Telfair Times, Helena, GA
Crowe Jr, Reese J .... (610) 356-6664
PUB, County Press, Newtown Square, PA
Crowe, Richard L .... (610) 356-6664
PUB, County Press, Newtown Square, PA
Crowel, Denise K .... (219) 294-1661
DIR-MKTG SRV, Elkhart Truth, Elkhart, IN
Crowell, Amanda .... (304) 348-5140
EDU ED
Charleston Daily Mail, Charleston, WV
Crowell, Bob .... (219) 724-2121
CIRC MGR
Decatur Daily Democrat, Decatur, IN
Crowell, Charles .... (316) 236-7591
PUB, Chetopa Advance, Chetopa, KS
Crowell, Charles R .... (316) 784-5722
PUB, Altamont Journal, Oswego, KS
Crowell, Ed .... (512) 445-3500
Entertainment/Amusements ED, Fashion/Style ED, Features ED, Living/Lifestyle ED
Austin American-Statesman, Austin, TX
Crowell, John .... (203) 574-3636
Litchfield County ED, Waterbury Republican-American, Waterbury, CT
Crowell, Mike .... (619) 299-3131
Entertainment/Amusements ED
San Diego Union-Tribune, San Diego, CA
Crowell, Robert O .... (316) 236-7591
PUB, ED, Chetopa Advance, Chetopa, KS
Crowley, Brian .... (561) 820-4100
Political/Government ED
Palm Beach Post, West Palm Beach, FL
Crowley, Kevin .... (519) 894-2231
Municipal Goverment Reporter
Record, Kitchener, ON

Cro Who's Where-52

Crowley, M J .... (215) 854-2000
Librarian
Philadelphia Inquirer, Philadelphia, PA
Crowley, Mark .... (812) 886-9955
Graphics ED
Vincennes Sun-Commercial, Vincennes, IN
Crowley, Stephen .... (717) 243-2611
ADV DIR, Sentinel, Carlisle, PA
Crowner, Neil .... (301) 662-1177
News ED (Post)
Frederick Post/News, Frederick, MD
Crowson, Bruz .... (803) 775-6331
Photo DEPT MGR, Item, Sumter, SC
Crowson, Scott .... (604) 624-6781
ED, Daily News, Prince Rupert, BC
Crowther, Thomas .... (506) 452-6671
PRES, Summit Publishing, Fredericton, NB
Crozier, Jim .... (306) 692-6441
PROD FRM-COMP
Moose Jaw Times-Herald, Moose Jaw, SK
Crozier, Lesley .... (201) 428-6200
Graphics ED, Daily Record, Parsippany, NJ
Crubtree, Larry .... (817) 852-5232
PUB, ED, Valley News, Chillicothe, TX
Cruden, Alex .... (313) 222-6400
Copy Desk Chief
Detroit Free Press, Detroit, MI
Cruger, Jack .... (630) 834-0900
PUB, Lombard Spectator, Elmhurst, IL
Cruger, Peter C .... (630) 834-0900
PUB, Lombard Spectator, Elmhurst, IL
Cruickshank, John .... (604) 732-2111
EIC, Vancouver Sun, Vancouver, BC
Cruikshank, L Alan .... (602) 837-1931
PUB
Times of Fountain Hills, Fountain Hills, AZ
Crum, Karen .... (909) 849-4586
PROD MGR, Record-Gazette, Banning, CA
Crum, Steve .... (817) 757-5757
PROD MGR-PR
Waco Tribune-Herald, Waco, TX
Crumm, David .... (313) 222-6400
Religion Writer, Free Press, Detroit, MI
Crumbacker, Richard .... (410) 651-1600
GM, ED
Somerset Herald, Princess Anne, MD
Crump, James F .... (306) 463-4611
PUB
West Central Crossroads, Kindersley, SK
Crump, Steve .... (208) 733-0931
Society ED, Times-News, Twin Falls, ID
Crump, Stewart .... (306) 463-4611
GM, West Central Crossroads, Kindersley, SK
Crump B A, Tim .... (306) 463-4611
ED, West Central Crossroads, Kindersley, SK
Crupi, Joann M .... (518) 454-5694
Opinion Pages ED, Times Union, Albany, NY
Crupper, Carol .... (316) 275-8500
SEC/TREAS, MAN ED, Photo DEPT MGR
Garden City Telegram, Garden City, KS
Cruse, Gary .... (512) 884-2011
ADV MGR-CLASS, Corpus Christi Caller-Times, Corpus Christi, TX
Crutcher, Deanna .... (360) 754-5400
PROD MGR-Pre Press
Olympian, Olympia, WA
Crutchfield, James .... (562) 435-1161
Senior VP/EX ED
Press-Telegram, Long Beach, CA
Crutchfield, Nancy .... (804) 946-7195
ED, Amherst New Era Progress, Amherst, VA
Cruz, Joe .... (415) 872-3000
GM
Philippine News, South San Francisco, CA
Cruz, Manny .... (619) 232-4381
FIN ED, News ED
San Diego Daily Transcript, San Diego, CA
Cruze Jr, George R .... (410) 268-5000
BM, Capital, Annapolis, MD
Cruzen, Nelda M .... (719) 784-6383
PUB, Florence Citizen, Florence, CO
Cruzen, Robert B .... (719) 784-6383
PUB, Florence Citizen, Florence, CO
Cryderman, Becky .... (316) 775-2218
DP MGR, Augusta Daily Gazette, Augusta, KS
Cryser, Julie R .... (304) 348-5140
BUS ED, Charleston Gazette, Sunday Gazette-Mail, Charleston, WV
Cuba, Andrea .... (512) 352-8535
CIRC DIR, Taylor Daily Press, Taylor, TX
Cubarrubia, Eydie .... (941) 748-0411
Features Reporter
Bradenton Herald, Bradenton, FL
Cubbal, Kayleen .... (412) 654-6651
Sports ED, New Castle News, New Castle, PA
Cubbison, Chris .... (303) 892-5000
Projects ED
Rocky Mountain News, Denver, CO
Cubitt, Babette .... (864) 582-4511
ADTX MGR, Herald-Journal, Spartanburg, SC
Cuddihy, Edward L .... (716) 849-3434
Deputy MAN ED, Buffalo News, Buffalo, NY
Cuddy, Bob .... (510) 783-6111
EPE, Daily Review, Hayward, CA
MediaNews Inc. (Alameda Newspapers)
Cudmore, Dana .... (518) 234-4368
ED, Daily Editor, Cobleskill, NY
Cuenca, Peter N .... (617) 541-2222
PUB, ED, La Semana, Dorchester, MA
Cueva, Hector .... (405) 233-6600
CIRC DIR, Enid News & Eagle, Enid, OK
Cuevas, Ellis .... (601) 467-5473
PUB, ED, Sea Coast Echo, Bay St. Louis, MS
Cuffee, Shelley .... (410) 332-6000
PROD MGR-Graphics, Sun, Baltimore, MD
Culbertson, Kay H .... (614) 397-5333
PUB
Mount Vernon News, Mount Vernon, OH
Culbertson, Shawnee Lee .... (412) 628-2000
MAN ED
Connellsville Daily Courier, Connellsville, PA
Culbertson, Todd .... (804) 649-6000
Chief EDL Writer
Richmond Times-Dispatch, Richmond, VA
Culhane, Ed .... (414) 733-4411
Outdoors ED, Post-Crescent, Appleton, WI
Cull, Robin .... (812) 265-3641
ADTX MGR, Madison Courier, Madison, IN
Cullen, Art .... (712) 732-4991
ED, Storm Lake Times, Storm Lake, IA
Cullen, Carmen .... (352) 365-8200
ADV DIR, PROD SUPV-COMP
Daily Commercial, Leesburg, FL
Cullen, John .... (712) 732-4991
PUB, Storm Lake Times, Storm Lake, IA
Cullen, John .... (401) 722-4000
News ED, Times, Pawtucket, RI
Cullen, Laura .... (408) 761-7300
Amusements/Entertainment ED, News ED
Register-Pajaronian, Watsonville, CA
Cullen, Mark .... (334) 347-9533
PUB, Army Flier, Enterprise, AL
Culley, Leslie .... (509) 582-1500
CNR-MKTG, ADTX MGR
Tri-City Herald, Tri-Cities, WA
Culley, Tanis .... (604) 533-4157
PUB, Langley Times, Langley, BC
Culley, Wayne .... (913) 632-2127
ED, Clay Center Dispatch, Clay Center, KS
Cullinan, Thomas .... (209) 441-6111
CIRC DIR, Fresno Bee, Fresno, CA
Cullis, Christopher .... (419) 636-1111
PRES, PROD MGR
Bryan Times, Bryan, OH
Cullis, Ford .... (419) 485-3113
PUB
Montpelier Leader-Enterprise, Montpelier, OH
Cullum, Barbara .... (501) 268-8621
Fashion/Style ED, Health/Medical ED, Living/Lifestyle ED, Religion ED, Women's/Society ED, Daily Citizen, Searcy, AR
Cullum, Lee .... (703) 764-0496
Dallas & Texas Correspondent
Associated Features Inc., Burke, VA
Culp Ph.D., Mildred L .... (206) 285-0800
DIR, Passage Media, Seattle, WA
Culver, Janet .... (706) 724-0851
ADV MGR-Delivery
Augusta Chronicle, Augusta, GA
Culver, Roger .... (970) 864-7425
PUB, ED
San Miguel Basin Forum, Nucla, CO
Culver, Russ .... (202) 334-6000
PROD MGR-Maintenance (NW)
Washington Post, Washington, DC
Culver, Virginia .... (303) 820-1010
Religion Reporter, Denver Post, Denver, CO
Cumbo, John .... (716) 232-7100
MGR-Computer Digital SYS
Rochester Democrat and Chronicle; Rochester, NY Times-Union, Rochester, NY
Cumbridge, Connie .... (304) 369-1165
MAN ED, Coal Valley News, Madison, WV
Cumiskey, Gail .... (904) 829-6562
PROD SUPT-COMP
St. Augustine Record, St. Augustine, FL
Cumming, Doland G .... (807) 274-5373
GM, PROD MGR
Fort Frances Daily Bulletin, Fort Frances, ON
Cumming, Gordon .... (514) 987-2222
PROD MGR-Press, Gazette, Montreal, QC
Cumming, James R .... (807) 274-5373
PUB, Fort Frances Times, Fort Frances, ON
Cumming, Tim .... (519) 527-0240
ED, Huron Expositor, Seaforth, ON
Cummings, Art .... (860) 354-2261
ED, New Milford Times, New Milford, CT
Cummings, Barney B .... (508) 249-3535
ED, City ED, EDL Writer, Sports ED, Wire ED
Athol Daily News, Athol, MA
Cummings, Dale .... (204) 697-7000
Cartoonist
Winnipeg Free Press, Winnipeg, MB
Cummings, Darron .... (812) 372-7811
Photo ED, Republic, Columbus, IN
Cummings, Ellen .... (609) 845-3300
MGR-CR
Gloucester County Times, Woodbury, NJ
Cummings, Janet .... (203) 655-7476
ED, Darien News-Review, Darien, CT
Cummings, Joan .... (713) 485-7501
ED
Friendswood Reporter News, Pearland, TX
Cummings, Joseph D .... (603) 924-3333
PUB
Peterborough Transcript, Peterborough, NH
Cummings, Joseph E .... (717) 348-9100
Community Relations DIR
Tribune & Scranton Times, Scranton, PA
Cummings, Katherine .... (912) 864-3528
ED, Wrightsville Headlight, Wrightsville, GA
Cummings, Kevin .... (902) 597-3731
PUB
Springhill & Parrsboro Record, Springhill, NS
Cummings, Stephen .... (617) 969-0340
PUB, Newton TAB, Newton, MA
Cummings III, William S .... (704) 264-3612
PUB, Watauga Democrat, Boone, NC
Cummins, Erik H .... (707) 545-1166
BUS News ED, Sonoma County Daily Herald-Recorder, Santa Rosa, CA
Cummins, Fredd .... (916) 891-1234
Community Relations DIR
Chico Enterprise-Record, Chico, CA
Cummins, Gregg .... (618) 544-2101
PROD FRM-Press
Robinson Daily News, Robinson, IL
Cummins, John .... (310) 540-5511
MGR-Technical SRV, Daily Breeze, Torrance, CA, Copley Press Inc.
Cummins, Kandy .... (520) 753-6397
CIRC MGR
Kingman Daily Miner, Kingman, AZ
Cummins, Mike .... (419) 784-5441
Automotive ED
Crescent-News, Defiance, OH
Cummins, Robert M .... (419) 784-5441
ED; Crescent-News, Defiance, OH
Cunard, Gary R .... (919) 496-6503
PUB, ED, Franklin Times, Louisburg, NC
Cundey, Carol Lee .... (607) 798-1234
MGR-PROM
Press & Sun Bulletin, Binghamton, NY
Cuneo, Kevin .... (814) 870-1600
MAN ED-Supplements/Sports, Films/Theater ED, Morning News/Erie Daily Times, Erie, PA
Cunha, Carlos .... (508) 997-7411
Travel ED, New Bedford Standard Times, New Bedford, MA
Cuningham, Henry .... (910) 323-4848
Military Affairs ED
Fayetteville Observer-Times, Fayetteville, NC
Cunis Jr, Frank M .... (717) 821-2091
TREAS, CONT/CFO
Citizens' Voice, Wilkes-Barre, PA
Cunniff, Mike .... (815) 433-2000
Sports ED, Daily Times, Ottawa, IL
Cunning, Shanna .... (208) 232-4161
PROD SUPV
Idaho State Journal, Pocatello, ID
Cunning, Tonia .... (702) 788-6200
MAN ED, Reno Gazette-Journal, Reno, NV
Cunningham, Bernard R .... (508) 249-3535
ADV DIR, Automotive ED
Athol Daily News, Athol, MA
Cunningham, Billy G .... (816) 279-3441
PRES/PUB
St. Joseph Daily Courier, St. Joseph, MO
Cunningham, Bob .... (816) 263-4123
PUB, NTL ED, Political/Government ED, Television/Film ED, Travel ED, Moberly Monitor-Index & Democrat, Moberly, MO
Cunningham, Chuck .... (615) 728-7577
PUB, Manchester Times, Manchester, TN
Cunningham, Dan .... (713) 220-7171
ASST MAN ED
Houston Chronicle, Houston, TX
Cunningham, Don .... (423) 581-5630
CIRC DIR, Citizen Tribune, Morristown, TN
Cunningham, Eldon .... (515) 432-1234
PROD MGR
Boone News-Republican, Boone, IA
Cunningham, George .... (860) 875-3366
GM, Reminder, Vernon, CT
Cunningham, Judith .... (203) 846-3281
SEC, Hour, Norwalk, CT
Cunningham, Linda G .... (815) 987-1200
EX ED, Rockford Register Star, Rockford, IL
Cunningham, Lloyd .... (605) 331-2200
Photo Chief, Argus Leader, Sioux Falls, SD
Cunningham, Lynn .... (504) 826-3279
ASST to ED
Times-Picayune, New Orleans, LA
Cunningham, Mark .... (800) 223-2154
Senior ED
Investor's Business Daily, Los Angeles, CA
Cunningham, Norbert .... (506) 859-4900
EDL Writer, Times-Transcript, Moncton, NB
Cunningham, Richard .... (602) 271-8000
MGR-INFO SRV
Phoenix Newspapers Inc., Phoenix, AZ
Cunningham, Rob .... (209) 634-9141
EDU/School ED, Teen-Age/Youth ED, Travel ED, Turlock Journal, Turlock, CA
Cunningham, Robert .... (201) 646-4000
ASST MAN ED-Production & Technology
Record, Hackensack, NJ
Cunningham, Ron .... (352) 374-5000
EPE, Gainesville Sun, Gainesville, FL
Cunningham, Rusty .... (515) 684-4611
ED, Ottumwa Courier, Ottumwa, IA
Cunningham, Sandra .... (716) 652-0320
GM, East Aurora Advertiser, East Aurora, NY
Cunningham, Tanya .... (817) 778-4444
Women's ED
Temple Daily Telegram, Temple, TX
Cunningham, Tim .... (812) 847-4487
ADV DIR, Linton Daily Citizen, Linton, IN
Cunningham, William .... (805) 273-2700
ADV DIR-CLASS
Antelope Valley Press, Palmdale, CA
Cuozzo, Steve .... (212) 930-8000
EX ED, New York Post, New York, NY
Cupolo, Shawn .... (201) 691-9530
MAN ED
Sussex County Chronicle, Stanhope, NJ
Cuprionis, M Denise .... (916) 243-2424
SEC, Record Searchlight, Redding, CA
Cuprisin, Tim .... (414) 224-2000
Radio/Television Reporter
Milwaukee Journal Sentinel, Milwaukee, WI
Cupstid, Ronnie .... (501) 777-8841
VP, PUB, Hope Star, Hope, AR
Curatolo, Fred .... (403) 468-0100
Cartoonist, Edmonton Sun, Edmonton, AB
Curci, Paul .... (215) 735-8444
PUB, City Paper, Philadelphia, PA
Curd, Steve .... (816) 234-4141
ADV MGR-Magazine
Kansas City Star, Kansas City, MO
Curd, Tom .... (905) 526-3333
PROD MGR, Spectator, Hamilton, ON
Cureton, Jzonn .... (800) 760-3100
Motor Sports ED/Orlando
Williams Syndications Inc., Holiday, FL
Cureton, Russell .... (713) 220-7171
PROD MGR-Technical SRV
Houston Chronicle, Houston, TX
Curl, M Hollis .... (334) 682-4422
PUB, ED
Wilcox Progressive Era, Camden, AL
Curlee, Tim .... (310) 230-3400
Archive SUPV, Allsport Photography USA, Pacific Palisades, CA
Curley, John .... (415) 777-1111
Outdoors ED, Sports ED
San Francisco Chronicle, San Francisco, CA
Curley, John J .... (703) 284-6000
COB/PRES/CEO
Gannett Co. Inc., Arlington, VA
Curley, Rob .... (515) 753-6611
PROD MGR-Press
Times-Republican, Marshalltown, IA
Curley, Thomas .... (703) 276-3400
PRES/PUB, USA Today, Arlington, VA
Curmi, Charles .... (212) 447-1450
Sales-Europe, Middle East, Near East & Africa, Los Angeles Times Syndicate International, New York, NY
Curnane, Joseph A .... (617) 387-4570
PUB, Everett Leader Herald News Gazette, Everett, MA
Curnane Jr, Joseph .... (617) 387-4570
ED, Everett Leader Herald News Gazette, Everett, MA
Curphey, Robert .... (416) 367-2000
CIRC MGR-Single Copy Sales
Toronto Star, Toronto, ON
Curran, David .... (203) 846-3281
Environmental ED, Hour, Norwalk, CT
Curran, Jeanne .... (207) 990-8000
Maine Style ED, Daily News, Bangor, ME
Curran, Michael .... (613) 830-3005
PUB, ED
Orleans Weekly Journal, Orleans, ON
Curran, Peter .... (617) 933-3700
CIRC MGR, PROD FRM-MR
Daily Times Chronicle, Woburn, MA
Curran, Robert .... (716) 849-3434
COL-GEN, Buffalo News, Buffalo, NY
Curran, Steve .... (406) 447-4000
PROD SUPV-PR
Helena Independent Record, Helena, MT
Curran, Tom .... (201) 877-4141
ASST MAN ED, Star-Ledger, Newark, NJ
Currey, Brownlee O .... (615) 259-8800
Chairman, Nashville Banner, Nashville, TN
Currey, Donna .... (318) 459-3200
ADV MGR-CLASS, Times, Shreveport, LA
Curridan, Mark .... (423) 756-1234
Crimes & Courts ED
Chattanooga Times, Chattanooga, TN

Copyright ©1997 by the Editor & Publisher Co.

53-Who's Where **Dal**

Currie, Carole (704) 252-5611
Women's ED
Asheville Citizen-Times, Asheville, NC

Currie, Don (503) 399-6611
BUS/FIN ED, Statesman Journal, Salem, OR

Currie, John E (206) 448-8000
BM, Seattle Post-Intelligencer, Seattle, WA

Currie, Mark (715) 394-4411
PROD FRM-MR, Daily Telegram, Superior, WI

Currie, Phil (703) 284-6000
Sr VP/News-Newspaper Division
Gannett Co. Inc., Arlington, VA

Curry, Angela (816) 234-4141
Consumer COL
Kansas City Star, Kansas City, MO

Curry, Chris (409) 632-6631
Photo ED, Lufkin Daily News, Lufkin, TX

Curry, Chuck (941) 262-3161
News ED, Naples Daily News, Naples, FL

Curry, Dale (504) 826-3279
Food ED, Times-Picayune, New Orleans, LA

Curry, Drake (864) 298-4100
CIRC MGR, Greenville News, Greenville, SC

Curry, Gaylen (541) 889-5387
CIRC MGR, Argus Observer, Ontario, OR

Curry, J E (417) 683-4181
PUB, Douglas County Herald, Ava, MO

Curry, Jerry (417) 667-3344
ED, Nevada Herald, Nevada, MO

Curry, Jim (317) 664-5111
CIRC DIR, Chronicle-Tribune, Marion, IN

Curry, John (613) 836-1357
PUB, ED, Stittsville News, Stittsville, ON

Curtin, Barbara (541) 753-2641
City ED-Day, Gazette-Times, Corvallis, OR

Curtin, Christine (212) 210-2100
DIR/VP-MKTG
New York Daily News, New York, NY

Curtin, Jack (407) 420-5000
ADV MGR-Ad Delivery/OPER Division
Orlando Sentinel, Orlando, FL

Curtin, Michael (614) 461-5000
ED, Columbus Dispatch, Columbus, OH

Curtin, Robert (508) 532-5880
ED, Peabody & Lynnfield Weekly News, Peabody, MA

Curtin, Thomas (212) 803-8200
PUB, Bond Buyer, New York, NY

Curtin, Tim (405) 542-6644
PUB, ED, MAN ED
Hinton Record, Hinton, OK

Curtis, Dan (908) 922-6000
ADV MGR-Regional
Asbury Park Press, Neptune, NJ

Curtis, Dean (417) 836-1100
Photo ED
Springfield News-Leader, Springfield, MO

Curtis, James (717) 532-4101
ED, News-Chronicle, Shippensburg, PA

Curtis, Jasper (903) 597-8111
ADV MGR-CLASS
Tyler Morning Telegraph, Tyler, TX

Curtis, Mary (704) 358-5000
Features ED
Charlotte Observer, Charlotte, NC

Curtis, Pat (605) 331-2200
DIR-Human Resources
Argus Leader, Sioux Falls, SD

Curtis, Richard (703) 276-3400
MAN ED-Graphics/Photography, Photo ED
USA Today, Arlington, VA

Curtis, Shirley (501) 741-2325
Photo ED, Harrison Daily Times, Harrison, AR

Curtis, Susan (330) 996-3000
ASST MAN ED-Design & Graphics
Akron Beacon Journal, Akron, OH

Curtis, Wayne (800) 286-6601
ED, Casco Bay Weekly, Portland, ME

Curtiss, Aaron (213) 237-5000
EPE-SF Valley
Los Angeles Times, Los Angeles, CA

Curtiss, Most Rev Elden F (402) 558-6611
PUB, Catholic Voice, Omaha, NE

Curtner, Roger (512) 575-1451
Chief Photographer
Victoria Advocate, Victoria, TX

Cusack, Jack (604) 692-7526
PUB, Lakes District News, Burns Lake, BC

Cusack, Thomas (201) 877-4141
PROD DIR-Pre Press
Star-Ledger, Newark, NJ

Cusack, William (513) 523-4139
PUB, Oxford Press, Oxford, OH

Cushing, Cindy (207) 873-3341
ADTX MGR, Central Maine Morning Sentinel, Waterville, ME, Guy Gannett Communications

Cushing, Michael (800) 424-4747
MAN ED, Tribune Media Services-Television Listings, Glens Falls, NY

Cushman, Kathleen (508) 456-8122
PUB, Harvard Post, Harvard, MA

Cushman, Margaret C (541) 963-3161
VBC, Observer, La Grande, OR
Western Communications Inc.

Cushman, Tom (619) 299-3131
Senior COL-Sports
San Diego Union-Tribune, San Diego, CA

Cusick, Steve (802) 933-4375
ED, County Courier, Enosburg Falls, VT

Cusimano, Chris (954) 356-4000
CIRC MGR-Alternate Distribution
Sun-Sentinel, Fort Lauderdale, FL

Custard, Dan (303) 892-5000
PROD MGR-Technical SRV
Rocky Mountain News, Denver, CO

Custer, Jim (516) 264-0077
ED, Amityville Record, Amityville, NY

Custer, Rod (219) 461-8444
MGR-Programming
Fort Wayne Newspapers Inc., Fort Wayne, IN

Cusumano, John (810) 332-8181
Senior ED, Oakland Press, Pontiac, MI

Cutie, James A (212) 556-1234
Sr VP-MKTG
New York Times Co., New York, NY

Cutler, Dan (515) 749-5317
PUB, ED, Advertiser, Nora Springs, IA

Cutler, David (508) 764-4325
PUB, EX ED, News, Southbridge, MA

Cutler, John Henry (617) 934-2811
PUB, ED, Duxbury Clipper, Duxbury, MA

Cutler, Ted (718) 624-0536
ADV MGR, Daily Bulletin, Brooklyn, NY

Cutlip, Teresa (304) 327-2811
BUS ED, RE ED
Bluefield Daily Telegraph, Bluefield, WV

Cutrell, Harleen (812) 372-7811
MGR-Human Resources
Republic, Columbus, IN

Cutrer, Angela H (417) 667-3344
ED, EPE, Nevada Daily Mail, Nevada, MO

Cutright, Jane (217) 632-2236
PUB, ED
Petersburg Observer, Petersburg, IL

Cutshall, Bill (601) 287-6111
PROD FRM-PR, Daily Corinthian, Corinth, MS

Cutshall, Carol A (814) 643-4040
ADV DIR, Daily News, Huntingdon, PA

Cutter, Elizabeth A (415) 777-5700
PSL MGR, San Francisco Newspaper Agency, San Francisco, CA

Cutting, Robert (617) 929-2000
Special Sections ED
Boston Globe, Boston, MA

Cvelbar, Chris K (317) 398-6631
CIRC DIR, Shelbyville News, Shelbyville, IN

Cypert, Vickie (806) 762-8844
PROD MGR-Dispatch
Lubbock Avalanche-Journal, Lubbock, TX

Cyphers, Robert (903) 657-2501
PROD SUPT/FRM-PR
Henderson Daily News, Henderson, TX

Cyran, William (216) 245-6901
ADV DIR, Morning Journal, Lorain, OH

Cyril, David (352) 867-4010
Online MGR, Ocala Star-Banner, Ocala, FL

Czarnecki, John (509) 525-3300
ADTX MGR, Union-Bulletin, Walla Walla, WA

Czarny, Gene (916) 321-1000
CIRC DIR, Sacramento Bee, Sacramento, CA

Czeczot, Mike (904) 252-1511
ASST MAN ED, Daytona Beach News-Journal, Daytona Beach, FL

Czuchan-Pasinski, Gloria (412) 439-7500
MAN ED, Living Section ED, Sunday ED
Herald-Standard, Uniontown, PA

D

Dable, Perry (618) 393-2931
ED, Olney Daily Mail, Olney, IL

Dabney, Bailey (904) 599-2100
CIRC DIR
Tallahassee Democrat, Tallahassee, FL

Dabrowa, Michael (757) 247-4600
Art DIR, Daily Press, Newport News, VA

D'Adamo, Gene (602) 271-8000
Deputy DIR-Public Affairs
Phoenix Newspapers Inc., Phoenix, AZ

Daddona, Patricia (860) 489-3121
News ED, Register Citizen, Torrington, CT

Dadisman, Carrol (904) 599-2100
PRES, PUB
Tallahassee Democrat, Tallahassee, FL

Dadson, Elizabeth (519) 485-3631
ED, Ingersoll Times, Ingersoll, ON

Daffron, Andy (423) 756-1234
Sports ED
Chattanooga Times, Chattanooga, TN

Dafnis, Bill (407) 420-5000
CIRC MGR-Distribution Development
Orlando Sentinel, Orlando, FL

Dafoe, Dave (807) 343-6200
PROD FRM-COMP Room
Chronicle-Journal, Thunder Bay, ON

Dagar, Jim (318) 487-6397
Amusements ED, Fashion/Focus ED, Living ED, SCI ED, Travel ED, Women's ED
Alexandria Daily Town Talk, Alexandria, LA

Daggett, Frank (705) 268-6252
ED, Enterprise, Iroquois Falls, ON

Daggett, Joy (716) 394-0770
PROD DIR-Pre Press, Daily Messenger/ The Sunday Messenger, Canandaigua, NY

D'Agosta, Bob (402) 444-1000
PROD ASST DIR (Night)
Omaha World-Herald, Omaha, NE

D'Agosta, Mike (402) 444-1000
PROD MGR-COMP (Night)
Omaha World-Herald, Omaha, NE

D'Agostino, John (716) 487-1111
City ED, Post-Journal, Jamestown, NY

DaHarb, Marifrank (505) 622-7710
Fashion/Food ED, Women's/Society ED
Roswell Daily Record, Roswell, NM

Dahel, Annie (512) 398-4886
ED, Lockhart Post-Register, Lockhart, TX

Dahl, Carol (317) 633-1240
CIRC MGR-Recruiting & Training
Indianapolis Star/News, Indianapolis, IN

Dahl, Jerry (319) 242-7101
Photo DEPT MGR, Clinton Herald, Clinton, IA

Dahl, Jim (906) 482-1500
DP MGR, Daily Mining Gazette, Houghton, MI

Dahl, Jonathan (212) 416-2000
Travel ED, Wall Street Journal, New York, NY

Dahl, Kurt (206) 464-2111
VP-INFO Technology, DP MGR
Seattle Times, Seattle, WA

Dahl, Nancy (218) 723-5281
PROD Ad MGR, News-Tribune, Duluth, MN

Dahl, Virgil (319) 291-1400
CIRC EX DIR, Waterloo Courier, Waterloo, IA

Dahlburg, John-Thor (213) 237-5000
Paris BU, Los Angeles Times, Los Angeles, CA

Dahlen, Nancy (509) 663-5161
PA/CR MGR, World, Wenatchee, WA

Dahlmeier, Phil (605) 692-6271
ADV MGR, Brookings Register, Brookings, SD

Dahm, Mary Dolores (219) 456-2824
GM, Todays Catholic, Fort Wayne, IN

Dahms, Heidi (520) 775-4440
ED, Prescott Valley Tribune, Prescott Valley, AZ

Dahms, Paul (609) 989-7800
CIRC DIR, Trentonian, Trenton, NJ

Dahnke, Ellen (615) 259-8000
EDL Writer, Tennessean, Nashville, TN

Daib, Jolene (402) 475-4200
Farm/Agribusiness Reporter
Lincoln Journal Star, Lincoln, NE

Daigle, Diana (318) 684-5711
ED, Church Point News, Church Point, LA

Daigle, Marco (506) 735-5575
GM, Le Madawaska, Edmundston, NB

Dail, Bobby (919) 736-0447
NTL Representative
Dail Advertising Service, Goldsboro, NC

Dailey, Marc (360) 694-3391
CIRC VP, Columbian, Vancouver, WA

Dailey, Pat (312) 222-3232
Food Writer, Chicago Tribune, Chicago, IL

Dailey, Richard R (617) 944-4444
PUB, Suburban News, Reading, MA

Daily, Vivian (717) 546-8555
ED, Luminary, Muncy, PA

Dakers, Diane (250) 380-5211
RE Reporter, Times Colonist, Victoria, BC

Dakin, David (209) 734-5821
ADV DIR, Visalia Times-Delta, Visalia, CA

Dakota, Clair (706) 635-4313
MAN ED, Times-Courier, Ellijay, GA

Dakroob, Michael (805) 650-2900
CIRC MGR-Sales/PROM
Ventura County Star, Ventura, CA

Dalbey, Beth (515) 472-4129
ED, Fairfield Ledger, Fairfield, IA

Dal Broi, Fred (602) 271-8000
PROD Deputy DIR
Phoenix Newspapers Inc., Phoenix, AZ

Dalby, Nick (208) 232-4161
Entertainment ED
Idaho State Journal, Pocatello, ID

Dalck, Richard (810) 541-3000
PROD FRM-PR
Daily Tribune, Royal Oak, MI

Dalco-Nixon, Chela (313) 222-6400
ADV DIR-CLASS
Detroit Newspapers, Detroit, MI

Dal Corobbo, Rick (219) 663-4212
MAN ED, Lake County Star, Crown Point, IN

Dale, Curtis (210) 222-1721
GM, San Antonio Register, San Antonio, TX

Dale, Kevin (817) 390-7400
MAN ED-Sports, BUS, Features, Design
Fort Worth Star-Telegram, Fort Worth, TX

Dale, Larry D (704) 322-4510
EPE, Hickory Daily Record, Hickory, NC

Dale, Paul W (205) 927-5037
ED, Cherokee County Herald, Centre, AL

Dale, Peggy (619) 337-3400
Books ED, Couples ED, Features ED, Food/Home ED, Life Page ED
Imperial Valley Press, El Centro, CA

Dale, Steve (613) 829-9100
PROD SUPT-Manufacturing-PR
Ottawa Citizen, Ottawa, ON

Daleo, Sam A (914) 331-5000
MAN ED, Daily Freeman, Kingston, NY

D'Alessandro, G S (914) 225-7735
VP/Photo ED
All-Sports Publications, Carmel, NY

D'Alessandro, George (914) 225-7735
VP/Sr. ED, All-Sports Publications, Carmel, NY

D'Alessio, Jeff (502) 769-2312
Sports ED, News Enterprise, Elizabethtown, KY

D'Alessio, Lisa (502) 769-2312
MGR-BUS Office
News Enterprise, Elizabethtown, KY

Daley, Kathy (914) 737-7747
ED, Peekskill Herald, Peekskill, NY

Daley, Nancy (518) 792-9914
MAN, Print & Information Services
TV Data, Queensbury, NY

Daley, Patrick (905) 660-9556
PUB, King Vaughan Weekly, Concord, ON

Daley, Ray (954) 356-4000
ADV MGR-CLASS
Sun-Sentinel, Fort Lauderdale, FL

Daley, Ron (606) 785-5134
PUB, ED
Troublesome Creek Times, Hindman, KY

Daley, Steve (312) 222-3232
COL, Chicago Tribune, Chicago, IL

D'Alio, Cindy (717) 622-3456
ASST News ED, Farm/Garden ED, Fashion/ Society ED, Music ED, Teen-Age/Youth ED, Travel ED, Weekender ED, Pottsville Republican & Evening Herald, Pottsville, PA

Dall'Acqua, Charles R (210) 829-9000
VP, Harte-Hanks Communications Inc., San Antonio, TX

Dallas, Cal (403) 346-3356
GM, Central Alberta Adviser, Red Deer, AB

Dallas, Danette (706) 291-6397
ADV MGR-GEN, Rome News-Tribune, Rome, GA

Dallman, Raymond P (904) 359-4111
ADV DIR-Sales/MKTG
Florida Times-Union, Jacksonville, FL

Dalney, M (416) 767-4840
ED, Nowi Dni, Toronto, ON

Dalpra, Robert (906) 875-6633
ED, Diamond Drill, Crystal Falls, MI

Dalpra, Rudolph (906) 875-6633
PUB, Diamond Drill, Crystal Falls, MI

Dalsis, Gus (209) 943-6397
PROD MGR-PR, Record, Stockton, CA

Dalton, Amy (423) 756-6900
ADV MGR-NTL
Chattanooga Free Press, Chattanooga, TN

Dalton, Bob (704) 692-0505
Sports ED, Hendersonville Times-News, Hendersonville, NC

Dalton, Dan (816) 932-6600
ASST VP/Sales MGR
Universal Press Syndicate, Kansas City, MO

Dalton, David (415) 777-2424
DIR-SYS, Online MGR
San Francisco Examiner, San Francisco, CA

Dalton, G Richard (507) 263-3991
PUB, ED, Beacon, Cannon Falls, MN

Dalton, Rex (619) 299-3131
Medical Writer
San Diego Union-Tribune, San Diego, CA

Dalton, Sarah Pritchett (304) 425-8191
ED, Princeton Times, Princeton, WV

Daly, Dan (605) 394-8300
BUS ED, Rapid City Journal, Rapid City, SD

Daly, Dan (517) 265-5111
Outdoors/Sports ED
Daily Telegram, Adrian, MI

Daly, John (212) 556-1234
CIRC DIR-Home Delivery Expansion Team
New York Times, New York, NY

Daly, John J (212) 208-8000
ED, Corporation Records
Daily News, New York, NY

Daly, Katherine (415) 588-5990
EDL DIR, Yossarian Universal News Service, Millbrae, CA

Daly, Michael (212) 210-2100
COL, New York Daily News, New York, NY

Daly, Michael (203) 333-0161
MAN ED, Connecticut Post, Bridgeport, CT

Daly, Nancy (513) 923-3111
ED, Western Hills Press, Cincinnati, OH

Daly, Russ (801) 756-7669
ED, Lehi Free Press, American Fork, UT

Dalzell, Scott (815) 459-4040
Photo ED, Northwest Herald, Crystal Lake, IL

Dalziel, Graham (403) 468-0100
MAN ED, Edmonton Sun, Edmonton, AB

Copyright ©1997 by the Editor & Publisher Co.

Dam Who's Where-54

D'Amato, Luisa .... (519) 894-2231
COL, Record, Kitchener, ON
D'Amico, Rob .... (210) 249-2441
MAN ED, Boerne Star, Boerne, TX
Damish, Stephen .... (508) 586-7200
City ED, Enterprise, Brockton, MA
Damme, Lawrence .... (805) 237-6060
CIRC MGR
County News-Press, Paso Robles, CA
Dammeier, John .... (206) 597-8742
DP MGR, News Tribune, Tacoma, WA
Dana, Claire .... (315) 363-5100
ADV DIR, Oneida Daily Dispatch, Oneida, NY
Danaceau, Kyle .... (352) 867-4010
Photo ED, Ocala Star-Banner, Ocala, FL
Danahay, Barbara .... (504) 892-7980
MAN ED, News-Banner, Covington, LA
Dance, Robert .... (203) 625-4400
CIRC MGR, Greenwich Time, Greenwich, CT
Dance, Wayne .... (514) 987-2222
ADV MGR-National, Gazette, Montreal, QC
Dancis, Bruce .... (916) 321-1000
Entertainment ED
Sacramento Bee, Sacramento, CA
Danciu, Tami .... (905) 526-3333
Librarian/Senior INFO Technician
Spectator, Hamilton, ON
Danehart, Cheryl .... (304) 233-0100
Food/Women's ED, Intelligencer/Wheeling News-Register, Wheeling, WV
Daneliuk, Randy .... (204) 687-7339
PRES, PUB, CIRC MGR, ED, PROD FRM-PR
Reminder, Flin Flon, MB
Danford, Roy .... (803) 524-3183
CIRC MGR, Beaufort Gazette, Beaufort, SC
Danforth, David N .... (603) 356-3456
PRES, Conway Daily Sun, North Conway, NH
Dang, Bao N .... (202) 334-6173
TREAS, Los Angeles Times-Washington Post News Service, Washington, DC
d'Angelini, Regis .... (215) 885-1345
MAN ED, Times Chronicle, Jenkintown, PA
D'Angelo, Chris .... (412) 654-6651
ADV DIR, New Castle News, New Castle, PA
D'Angelo, Joseph F .... (212) 455-4000
PRES, North America Syndicate, King Features Syndicate Inc., New York, NY
Daniel, Carole .... (205) 766-3434
ADV MGR-CLASS, Times Daily, Florence, AL
Daniel, Diane .... (617) 786-7000
Living/Lifestyle ED
Patriot Ledger, Quincy, MA
Daniel, Jackson .... (912) 994-2358
PUB, ED
Monroe County Reporter, Forsyth, GA
Daniel, Jennifer .... (561) 562-2315
Local News ED
Vero Beach Press-Journal, Vero Beach, FL
Daniel, Keith .... (904) 312-5200
CONT, DP MGR, Daily News, Palatka, FL
Daniel, Kris .... (614) 633-1131
BUS ED, Times Leader, Martins Ferry, OH
Daniel, Lucille .... (508) 369-2800
ED, Concord Journal, Concord, MA
Daniel, Parker .... (703) 560-4000
Chief Photographer
Fairfax Journal, Fairfax, VA
Danieli, Michael C .... (518) 454-5694
ADV MGR-CLASS, Times Union, Albany, NY
Daniell, Parker .... (703) 560-4000
Chief Photographer, Arlington Journal, Fairfax, VA, Journal Newspapers Inc.
Daniels, Barbara .... (913) 682-0305
CIRC MGR
Leavenworth Times, Leavenworth, KS
Daniels, Calvin .... (306) 782-2465
ED
Yorkton This Week & Enterprise, Yorkton, SK
Daniels, Diana M .... (202) 334-6000
VP/GEN Counsel/SEC
Washington Post Co., Washington, DC
Daniels, Don .... (330) 264-1125
CIRC ASST MGR-MR
Daily Record, Wooster, OH
Daniels, Glenn .... (937) 498-2111
Environmental ED
Sidney Daily News, Sidney, OH
Daniels, Leah .... (864) 224-4321
News ED
Anderson Independent-Mail, Anderson, SC
Daniels, Michael .... (207) 824-2444
ED, Bethel Oxford County Citizen, Bethel, ME
Daniels, Peter F .... (816) 827-2425
ED, Central Missouri News, Sedalia, MO
Daniels, Richard J .... (617) 929-2000
VP-Strategic Planning
Boston Globe, Boston, MA
Daniels, Ted .... (317) 633-1240
MAN ED-News
Indianapolis Star/News, Indianapolis, IN
Daniels, Velma .... (941) 294-7731
Books ED, News Chief, Winter Haven, FL
Danielsen, Dick .... (518) 234-4368
ED, Community Herald, Cobleskill, NY
Danielski, Deborah .... (815) 436-2431
ED, Enterprise, Plainfield, IL
Danielson, Lon .... (561) 820-4100
EVP/GM
Palm Beach Post, West Palm Beach, FL
Danielson, Rich .... (904) 359-4111
Television ED, Weekend ED
Florida Times-Union, Jacksonville, FL
Danison, Paul .... (714) 564-7072
ED, Tustin News, Santa Ana, CA
Daniszewski, John .... (213) 237-5000
Cairo BU
Los Angeles Times, Los Angeles, CA
Dankenbring, Sharon .... (816) 254-8600
ADV MGR-CLASS
Examiner, Independence, MO
Danko, Dennis .... (212) 455-4000
TELEMKTG Sales MGR, North America Syndicate, King Features Syndicate, NY, NY
Dann, Lori .... (205) 234-4281
Sports ED
Alexander City Outlook, Alexander City, AL
D'Anna, John .... (602) 271-8000
MET ED, Arizona Republic, Phoenix, AZ
Danneker, Paul .... (407) 420-5000
CIRC MGR-Consumer Sales/SRV
Orlando Sentinel, Orlando, FL
Danner, Ed .... (906) 524-6194
PUB, L'Anse Sentinel, L'Anse, MI
Dantzler, Frank .... (504) 383-1111
PROD SUPT-PR, Advocate, Baton Rouge, LA
Dantzler, Gayle .... (219) 235-6161
ASSOC ED
South Bend Tribune, South Bend, IN
Danuloff, Ann .... (419) 522-3311
ADV Representative
News Journal, Mansfield, OH
Danze, Richard .... (215) 854-2000
PROD DIR-Printing
Philadelphia Inquirer, Philadelphia, PA
Knight-Ridder Inc.
Danzer, Paul .... (503) 325-3211
Sports ED, Daily Astorian, Astoria, OR
Danzig, Robert J .... (212) 649-2000
VP/GM, Hearst Newspapers, New York, NY
Danziger, Ian .... (918) 335-8200
ASST MAN ED, Entertainment/Amusements ED, Features ED, Society/Women's ED
Examiner-Enterprise, Bartlesville, OK
Danziger, Jeff .... (617) 450-2000
EDL Cartoonist
Christian Science Monitor, Boston, MA
Dar, Gayle .... (512) 575-1451
Graphics ED, Victoria Advocate, Victoria, TX
Daranyi, Tony .... (970) 641-1414
PUB, Gunnison Country Times, Gunnison, CO
Darbonne, Nissa .... (318) 289-6300
BUS ED, Advertiser, Lafayette, LA
Darby, Harry .... (501) 763-4461
CIRC MGR
Blytheville Courier News, Blytheville, AR
Darby, Jim .... (505) 823-7777
ADV MGR-GEN, Albuquerque Publishing Co., Albuquerque, NM
Darby, Richard .... (618) 993-2626
MAN ED, Marion Daily Republican, Marion, IL
Darby, Stacy .... (573) 581-1111
ADV MGR-CLASS, Mexico Ledger, Mexico, MO
D'Arc Germain, Jeanne .... (514) 692-8552
ED, St. Lawrence Sun, Chateauguay, QC
Darch, Melody .... (404) 526-5151
CONT, Atlanta Journal-Constitution, Atlanta, GA
D'Arconte, Oreste P .... (508) 222-7000
GM, Sun Chronicle, Attleboro, MA
Darcy, Jeff .... (216) 999-4500
Cartoonist, Plain Dealer, Cleveland, OH
D'Arcy, John Michael .... (219) 456-2824
PUB, Todays Catholic, Fort Wayne, IN
Dardarian, Suki .... (206) 597-8742
Senior ED, News Tribune, Tacoma, WA
Darden, Richard E .... (407) 420-5000
VP/DIR-ADM, Orlando Sentinel, Orlando, FL
Dardenne, Tom .... (706) 724-0851
News ED, Augusta Chronicle, Augusta, GA
Dare, Ken .... (618) 643-2387
ED
McLeansboro Times Leader, McLeansboro, IL
D'Arienzo, Elaine .... (610) 622-8800
ADV MGR-RT
Delaware County Daily Times, Primos, PA
D'Arienzo, Michael .... (610) 622-8800
PROD DIR
Delaware County Daily Times, Primos, PA
D'Aries, Dawn .... (908) 223-0076
MAN ED, Coast Star, Manasquan, NJ
Darkis, Donald D .... (207) 990-8000
PROD MGR, Bangor Daily News, Bangor, ME
Darling, Ed .... (601) 693-1551
PUB, ED, EDL Writer
Meridian Star, Meridian, MS
Darling, Ian .... (519) 894-2231
BUS ED, Record, Kitchener, ON
Darling, Juanita .... (213) 237-5000
San Salvador BU
Los Angeles Times, Los Angeles, CA
Darling, Steve .... (508) 793-9100
CIRC MGR-OPER
Telegram & Gazette, Worcester, MA
Darmofal, Nancy .... (520) 763-2505
DIR-Production
Mohave Valley Daily News, Bullhead City, AZ
Darmondy, George .... (508) 676-8211
Sports ED, Herald News, Fall River, MA
Darnall, Michael .... (210) 625-9144
Photo ED, New Braunfels Herald-Zeitung, New Braunfels, TX
Darnay, Keith .... (701) 223-2500
BUS/FIN Reporter
Bismarck Tribune, Bismarck, ND
Darnell, Jack A .... (330) 758-2658
PUB, Boardman News, Youngstown, OH
Darnell, John A .... (330) 758-2658
ED, Boardman News, Youngstown, OH
Darnell, Mike .... (330) 454-5611
MGR-RT/CR MGR, Repository, Canton, OH
Darnton, Jack .... (360) 825-2555
PUB, Enumclaw Courier-Herald/Buckley News Banner, Enumclaw, WA
Da Rosa, Alison .... (619) 299-3131
Travel ED
San Diego Union-Tribune, San Diego, CA
Darr, Jim .... (216) 999-4500
Deputy MET ED
Plain Dealer, Cleveland, OH
Darragh, Dan .... (513) 746-3691
ED, Franklin Chronicle, Franklin, OH
Darrow, Katharine P .... (212) 556-1234
Sr VP, New York Times Co., New York, NY
Darst, Guy .... (617) 426-3000
Chief EDL Writer
Boston Herald, Boston, MA
Darst, Vicky .... (318) 539-3511
MAN ED, Springhill Press & News-Journal, Springhill, LA
Darstein, Michele .... (716) 632-4700
ED, East Aurora Bee, Buffalo, NY
Dasher, Anthony .... (912) 764-9031
Sports ED, Statesboro Herald, Statesboro, GA
Daskatothanasis, Harry .... (718) 784-5255
ED, National Herald, Long Island City, NY
Datta, Frank .... (406) 795-2218
PUB, ED, Wibaux Pioneer-Gazette, Wibaux, MT
Dattoma, Doug .... (516) 843-2020
PROD GEN FRM-Platemaking
Newsday, Melville, NY
Daubel, James F .... (419) 332-5511
PRES, PUB, News-Messenger, Fremont, OH
Gannett Co. Inc.
Daubel, Philip F .... (614) 272-5422
GM, Eastside Messenger, Columbus, OH
D'Aubin, Bill .... (408) 372-3311
PROD FRM-COMP
Monterey County Herald, Monterey, CA
Dauber, Carol .... (203) 333-0161
ADTX MGR, Connecticut Post, Bridgeport, CT
Daugherty, Barbara .... (708) 946-2151
ED, Manhattan American, Peotone, IL
Daugherty, Carolyn .... (540) 981-3100
Travel ED, Roanoke Times, Roanoke, VA
Daugherty, Patrick .... (607) 272-2321
CIRC DIR, Ithaca Journal, Ithaca, NY
Daughtridge, Angela .... (919) 446-5161
PA, Rocky Mount Telegram, Rocky Mount, NC
Daughtry, Beverly .... (512) 285-3333
PUB, ED, Elgin Courier, Elgin, TX
Daughtry Sr, Leslie P .... (409) 744-3611
PRES
Galveston County Daily News, Galveston, TX
Daughtry Jr, Leslie P .... (409) 945-3441
PRES, PUB, ED, Texas City Sun, Texas City, TX
Dauler, Karla A .... (804) 843-2282
MAN ED, Tidewater Review, West Point, VA
D'Aurizio, Elaine .... (201) 646-4000
COL, Record, Hackensack, NJ
Davant, Jeanne .... (719) 685-9201
MAN ED
Pikes Peak Journal, Manitou Springs, CO
Davaz, Carl .... (541) 485-1234
ASST MAN ED-Graphics & Technology, Register-Guard, Eugene, OR
Davenport, Dale .... (717) 255-8100
EPE, Patriot-News, Harrisburg, PA
Davenport, Dave .... (414) 435-4411
News ED
Green Bay Press-Gazette, Green Bay, WI
Davenport, Debra .... (209) 734-5821
ADV MGR-RT, Visalia Times-Delta, Visalia, CA
Davenport, Frank .... (610) 623-6088
PUB, ED, Yeadon Times, Yeadon, PA
Davenport, Janet .... (860) 241-6200
EDL Writer, Hartford Courant, Hartford, CT
Davenport, John .... (214) 977-8222
Special ASST to MAN ED
Dallas Morning News, Dallas, TX
Davenport Jr, John F .... (540) 374-5000
ADV MGR-RT
Free Lance-Star, Fredericksburg, VA
Davenport, Kristin .... (505) 863-6811
MAN ED, Gallup Independent, Gallup, NM
Davenport, Reginald .... (212) 556-1234
EVP-OPER, New York Times, New York, NY
New York Times Co.
Davenport, Tony .... (914) 358-2200
Local News ED
Rockland Journal-News, West Nyack, NY
Daves, Rob .... (612) 673-4000
News RES DIR
Star Tribune, Minneapolis, MN
Davey, Joanne .... (707) 546-2020
ADV MGR-Sales
Press Democrat, Santa Rosa, CA
D'Avey, Micky .... (706) 846-3188
ED, Star-Mercury, Manchester, GA
David, Brian .... (412) 458-5010
ED, Allied News, Grove City, PA
David, Cynthia .... (416) 947-2222
Food ED, Toronto Sun, Toronto, ON
David, Dan .... (515) 782-2141
PROD MGR-Press/Darkroom
Creston News-Advertiser, Creston, IA
David, Gabrielle .... (520) 387-7688
ED, Ajo Copper News, Ajo, AZ
David, Hollister .... (520) 387-7688
PUB, Ajo Copper News, Ajo, AZ
David, Jeff M .... (504) 665-5176
PUB, Denham Springs-Livingston Parish News, Denham Springs, LA
David, Marie .... (519) 364-2001
PUB, GM, Weekender, Hanover, ON
David, Therese .... (514) 521-4545
MGR, Le Journal de Montreal, Montreal, QC
Davidheiser, James H .... (610) 367-6041
GM, Boyertown Area Times, Boyertown, PA
Davidson, Ann .... (401) 884-4665
ED, East Greenwich Pendulum, East Greenwich, RI
Davidson, Bob .... (913) 823-6363
Sports ED, Salina Journal, Salina, KS
Davidson, Bruce .... (210) 225-7411
Political ED
San Antonio Express-News, San Antonio, TX
Davidson, Craig .... (770) 834-6631
BM, Times-Georgian, Carrollton, GA
Davidson Jr, Herbert M .... (904) 252-1511
PRES, PUB, Co-ED, Daytona Beach News-Journal, Daytona Beach, FL
Davidson, Iver .... (402) 475-4200
Wire ED
Lincoln Journal Star, Lincoln, NE
Davidson, Joanne .... (303) 820-1010
Society Reporter, Denver Post, Denver, CO
Davidson, John .... (214) 977-8222
ASST MAN ED-Visuals
Dallas Morning News, Dallas, TX
Davidson, John B .... (813) 349-4949
PUB, Pelican Press, Sarasota, FL
Davidson, Keay .... (415) 777-2424
SCI/Technology Writer
San Francisco Examiner, San Francisco, CA
Davidson, Kent .... (318) 289-6300
Radio/Television ED, Advertiser, Lafayette, LA
Davidson, Leonard .... (215) 848-7864
MAN ED
Philadelphia Sunday Sun, Philadelphia, PA
Davidson, Marc L .... (904) 252-1511
ASST SEC, Daytona Beach News-Journal, Daytona Beach, FL
Davidson, Neil .... (416) 364-0321
GEN Sports ED, Canadian Press & Broadcast News, Toronto, ON
Davidson, Peter W .... (212) 807-4600
PRES, El Diario La Prensa, New York, NY
Davidson, Randy .... (210) 423-5511
EPE, Valley Morning Star, Harlingen, TX
Davidson, Ronald .... (316) 268-6000
VP-MKTG, ADV VP-MKTG
Wichita Eagle, Wichita, KS
Davidson, Scott .... (970) 240-4900
PROD MGR-OPER,
Morning Sun, Montrose, CO
Davidson, Sheila .... (312) 222-3232
CIRC MGR-South MET
Chicago Tribune, Chicago, IL
Davidson, Susan .... (512) 445-3500
DIR-Human Resources
Austin American-Statesman, Austin, TX
Davidson, Tippen .... (904) 437-2491
PUB, Flagler/Palm Coast News-Tribune, Bunnell, FL
Davidson, Tom .... (310) 519-1442
MAN ED, Random Lengths/Harbor Independent News, San Pedro, CA
Davidson, Tom .... (954) 356-4000
City/MET ED (Broward)
Sun-Sentinel, Fort Lauderdale, FL
Davidson, Wade .... (405) 341-2121
PROD FRM-Press
Edmond Evening Sun, Edmond, OK

Copyright ©1997 by the Editor & Publisher Co.

55-Who's Where **Daw**

Davidson, Wayne (807) 343-6200
ADV MGR
Chronicle-Journal, Thunder Bay, ON

Davidson, Wendy (510) 462-4160
ADV MGR, Valley Times, Pleasanton, CA

Davies, Delmar (306) 642-5901/5902
ED, Assiniboia Times, Assiniboia, SK

Davies, Harold (562) 435-1161
DIR-Production, PROD DIR
Press-Telegram, Long Beach, CA

Davies, Hugh (800) 367-8313
Correspondent
Daily Telegraph, London, England

Davies, Jerry (316) 345-6353
PUB, Ledger, Moundridge, KS

Davies, Jim (612) 222-5011
PROD MGR-MR, Pioneer Press, St. Paul, MN

Davies, Julie (808) 525-8000
MGR-Human Resources
Hawaii Newspaper Agency Inc., Honolulu, HI

Davies, Mary-Anne (519) 756-2020
Fashion/Women's ED, Food ED, Teenage Youth ED, Expositor, Brantford, ON

Davis, Aaron (213) 237-5000
Involvement Opportunities Writer, Pets Reporter, Los Angeles Times, Los Angeles, CA

Davis, Adrienne (304) 292-6301
ADV MGR-RT
Dominion Post, Morgantown, WV

Davis, Anita (619) 241-7744
ADV MGR-Major Accounts/NTL
Daily Press, Victorville, CA

Davis, Barbara (717) 265-2151
MGR-Customer SRV
Daily Review, Towanda, PA

Davis, Bev (304) 255-4400
Features ED, Women's ED
Register Herald, Beckley, WV

Davis, Beverly (614) 397-5333
Lifestyle ED
Mount Vernon News, Mount Vernon, OH

Davis, Bill (901) 642-1162
BM, DP MGR
Paris Post-Intelligencer, Paris, TN

Davis, Bill (817) 594-7447
CIRC MGR
Weatherford Democrat, Weatherford, TX

Davis, Boyce R (501) 839-2771
PUB
Washington County Observer, West Fork, AR

Davis, Brian (213) 237-5000
CIRC DIR-Customer Service
Los Angeles Times, Los Angeles, CA

Davis, Bruce (904) 312-5200
ADV DIR, Daily News, Palatka, FL

Davis, Carolyn (803) 785-4293
CIRC MGR, Island Packet, Hilton Head, SC

Davis, Cathy (602) 271-8000
Senior VP-MKTG & Development
Phoenix Newspapers Inc., Phoenix, AZ

Davis, Cecil (812) 446-2216
Sports ED, Brazil Times, Brazil, IN

Davis, Chad (806) 659-3434
PUB, ED, Hansford County Reporter-Statesman, Spearman, TX

Davis, Clarke (913) 945-3257
ED, Valley Falls Vindicator, Valley Falls, KS

Davis, Dan (601) 762-1111
ED, EPE
Mississippi Press, Pascagoula, MS

Davis, Dan (812) 522-4871
ED, Tribune, Seymour, IN

Davis, David H (813) 942-2883
ASST SEC
Fackelman Newspapers, Tarpon Springs, FL

Davis, Deb (970) 824-7031
Society ED
Northwest Colorado Daily Press, Craig, CO

Davis, Debbie (916) 756-0800
ED, Arts ED, News ED, Television/Music ED, Theater/Film ED, Travel ED
Davis Enterprise, Davis, CA

Davis, Dennis (307) 754-2221
MAN ED, Powell Tribune, Powell, WY

Davis, Diane (607) 734-5151
MET ED, Star-Gazette, Elmira, NY

Davis, Donald P (610) 371-5000
ADM ED, Reading Times/Eagle, Reading, PA

Davis, Donn M (312) 222-3237
PRES-Tribune Ventures
Tribune Co., Chicago, IL

Davis, Douglas D (417) 682-5529
PUB, ED, Lamar Democrat, Lamar, MO

Davis, Douglas R (904) 252-1511
CORP DIR-Circulation/Human Resources, CIRC DIR, Daytona Beach News-Journal, Daytona Beach, FL

Davis, Drew (912) 427-3757
ED, Press-Sentinel, Jesup, GA

Davis, Eddie Mae (616) 429-2400
CIRC MGR-Single Copy
Herald-Palladium, St. Joseph, MI

Davis, Eileen (419) 468-1117
ADV MGR-CLASS, Galion Inquirer, Galion, OH

Davis, Elbra (423) 992-3392
ED, Union News Leader, Maynardville, TN

Davis, Emilie (703) 276-5800
Copy Desk Chief
Gannett News Service, Arlington, VA

Davis, Eric (614) 387-0400
Sports ED, Marion Star, Marion, OH

Davis, Evelyn (914) 429-2000
PUB, Rockland County Times, Haverstraw, NY

Davis, F Keith (304) 369-1165
PUB, ED, Coal Valley News, Madison, WV

Davis, F T (770) 428-9411
SEC, Marietta Daily Journal, Marietta, GA

Davis, Gregory T (207) 364-7893
ED, Rumford Falls Times, Rumford, ME

Davis, H Denny (816) 248-2235
PUB, ED, Democrat-Leader, Fayette, MO

Davis, Harry C (330) 996-3000
CIRC VP, Akron Beacon Journal, Akron, OH

Davis, Henry (716) 849-3434
Health/Medical ED
Buffalo News, Buffalo, NY

Davis, Jack (417) 358-2191
PROD FRM-PR
Carthage Press, Carthage, MO

Davis Jr, Jack W (312) 222-3237
PRES/PUB/CEO-Daily Press
Tribune Co., Chicago, IL

Davis, James (954) 356-4000
Religion ED, Sun-Sentinel, Fort Lauderdale, FL

Davis, James E (330) 833-2631
ED, Independent, Massillon, OH

Davis Jr, James R (806) 828-6201
PUB, ED, Slatonite, Slaton, TX

Davis, James S (847) 427-4300
ED-DuPage, Daily Herald, Arlington Heights, IL

Davis, Janis (210) 907-3882
PUB, ED
Times Guardian/Chronicle, Canyon Lake, TX

Davis, Jay (334) 875-2110
BM, Selma Times-Journal, Selma, AL

Davis, Jill (905) 632-4444
ED, Burlington Post, Burlington, ON

Davis, Jim (817) 390-7400
TV Star ED
Fort Worth Star-Telegram, Fort Worth, TX

Davis, Jim (604) 738-1411
GM, Vancouver Courier, Vancouver, BC

Davis, Jim (713) 220-7171
PROD MGR-MR
Houston Chronicle, Houston, TX

Davis, Jim (616) 796-4831
ED, Pioneer East, Big Rapids, MI

Davis, Jim (615) 893-5860
Photo DEPT MGR, Photographer
Daily News Journal, Murfreesboro, TN

Davis, Jim (423) 428-0746
Sports ED, Mountain Press, Sevierville, TN

Davis, Jim (303) 892-5000
PROD MGR-Dispatch
Rocky Mountain News, Denver, CO

Davis, Joan (504) 345-2333
Society ED, Daily Star, Hammond, LA

Davis, John (717) 455-3636
ADV ASST DIR
Standard-Speaker, Hazleton, PA

Davis, John (716) 849-3434
Graphics ED, Buffalo News, Buffalo, NY

Davis, John (770) 227-3276
PROD SUPT, Griffin Daily News, Griffin, GA

Davis, John T (606) 236-2551
VP/EX ED, Advocate-Messenger, Danville, KY

Davis, Joseph P (504) 345-2333
BUS Office MGR, Daily Star, Hammond, LA

Davis, Joy (609) 935-1500
Political/Government
Today's Sunbeam, Salem, NJ

Davis, Joyce (303) 776-2244
Features ED, Daily Times-Call, Longmont, CO

Davis, Julia (405) 795-3355
ED, Madill Record, Madill, OK

Davis, Karl T (716) 366-3000
DIR-MKTG/PROM
Evening Observer, Dunkirk, NY

Davis, Kay (915) 676-6765
GM, Dyess Peacemaker, Abilene, TX

Davis, Kelly (501) 268-8621
BM, DP MGR, Daily Citizen, Searcy, AR

Davis, Ken (501) 935-5525
CIRC DIR, Jonesboro Sun, Jonesboro, AR

Davis, Kerry (810) 332-8181
ADV MGR-RT, Oakland Press, Pontiac, MI

Davis, Kirk (508) 528-2600
PUB, Country Gazette, Franklin, MA

Davis, Lance D (406) 566-2471
PUB, Judith Basin Press, Stanford, MT

Davis, Larry (615) 292-9150
PUB, Nashville Pride, Nashville, TN

Davis, Larry (801) 381-2431
ED, Emery County Progress, Castle Dale, UT

Davis, Lisa (817) 390-7400
Features ED
Fort Worth Star-Telegram, Fort Worth, TX

Davis, Lorna (705) 458-4434
ED, Innisfil Scope, Beeton, ON

Davis, Lowe (904) 435-8500
Books ED, Fashion ED, Life/Features ED
Pensacola News Journal, Pensacola, FL

Davis, Lynn (302) 324-2500
CIRC MGR-Single Copy
News Journal, Wilmington, DE

Davis, Marilee (305) 253-4339
GM, Cutler Courier, Miami, FL

Davis, Mark E (304) 472-2800
PUB, Record Delta, Buckhannon, WV

Davis, Marsha (503) 221-8327
ADTX MGR, Oregonian, Portland, OR

Davis, Martha (912) 283-2244
EDU/Religion ED, School/SCI ED
Waycross Journal-Herald, Waycross, GA

Davis, Mary Lou (210) 542-4301
ADV MGR-CLASS
Brownsville Herald, Brownsville, TX

Davis, Melanie (704) 358-5000
ADV MGR-Display, Observer, Charlotte, NC

Davis, Melodie M (800) 999-3534
Self-Syndicator
Another Way, Harrisonburg, VA

Davis, Melvin (618) 656-4700
PROD FRM-Press/Camera
Edwardsville Intelligencer, Edwardsville, IL

Davis, Michael (410) 752-3504
ED, Jewish Times, Baltimore, MD

Davis, Mickey (937) 225-2000
COL, Dayton Daily News, Dayton, OH

Davis, Mike (915) 236-6677
PUB, Sweetwater Reporter, Sweetwater, TX

Davis, Mike (313) 222-6400
Design DIR, Detroit Free Press, Detroit, MI

Davis, Murdoch (403) 429-5400
EIC, Edmonton Journal, Edmonton, AB

Davis, Natalie (601) 833-6961
ADV DIR, Daily Leader, Brookhaven, MS

Davis, O DeWayne (804) 649-6000
MGR-Special Events/Community Relations
Richmond Times-Dispatch, Richmond, VA

Davis, O K (318) 255-4353
Sports ED, Ruston Daily Leader, Ruston, LA

Davis, Pamela (405) 822-4401
ED, Okeene Record, Okeene, OK

Davis, Paul (773) 487-7700
MAN ED, Chicago Citizen, Chicago, IL

Davis, Paul (801) 752-2121
DP MGR, PROD SUPT
Herald Journal, Logan, UT

Davis, Paul R (334) 727-3020
PUB, Tuskegee News, Tuskegee, AL

Davis, Paula (501) 731-2561
PUB, Woodruff Monitor-Leader-Advocate, McCrory, AR

Davis, Philip (508) 752-2512
PUB, Jewish Chronicle, Worcester, MA

Davis, Pula (719) 632-5511
Web Master
Gazette, Colorado Springs, CO

Davis, Ray (501) 449-4257
GM, ED, Mountain Echo, Yellville, AR

Davis, Richard (205) 549-2000
BUS SYS MGR, Gadsden Times, Gadsden, AL

Davis, Rick (412) 282-8000
Sports ED, Butler Eagle, Butler, PA

Davis, Robert (509) 459-5000
MGR-Computer SRV, DP MGR
Spokesman-Review, Spokane, WA

Davis, Robert (360) 274-6663
ED, New Rainier Review, Castle Rock, WA

Davis, Robert E (509) 476-3602
PUB, Okanogan Valley Gazette-Tribune, Oroville, WA

Davis, Rodney (705) 472-3200
VP-FIN/SEC, Nugget, North Bay, ON

Davis, Roger (318) 487-6397
DIR-DP, DP MGR
Alexandria Daily Town Talk, Alexandria, LA

Davis, Roger (423) 246-8121
News ED, Wire ED
Kingsport Times-News, Kingsport, TN

Davis, Ron (517) 787-3018
GM, ED, Blazer News, Jackson, MI

Davis, Ronald (330) 841-1600
ADV MGR-CLASS
Tribune Chronicle, Warren, OH

Davis, Russ (315) 792-5000
ASST MAN ED, Observer-Dispatch, Utica, NY

Davis, Sandi (405) 475-3311
Films/Theater ED
Daily Oklahoman, Oklahoma City, OK

Davis, Scott (601) 961-7000
MGR-SYS, Clarion-Ledger, Jackson, MS
Gannett Co. Inc.

Davis, Scott (501) 723-5445
ED, Westville Reporter, Westville, OK

Davis, Sheila (816) 254-8600
MAN ED, Examiner, Independence, MO

Davis, Stam (352) 867-4010
ADV MGR-Special Projects/NTL
Ocala Star-Banner, Ocala, FL

Davis, Stella (505) 887-5501
Farm/Agriculture ED
Current-Argus, Carlsbad, NM

Davis, Steve (717) 264-6161
EX ED, Public Opinion, Chambersburg, PA

Davis, Steve (803) 626-8555
CIRC DIR, Sun News, Myrtle Beach, SC

Davis, Steve (613) 739-7000
ADV Sales MGR, Ottawa Sun, Ottawa, ON

Davis, Susan (617) 444-1706
ED, Medfield Suburban Press, Needham, MA

Davis, Tim (352) 374-5000
Photo ED, Gainesville Sun, Gainesville, FL

Davis, Tim (804) 432-2791
ED, Star-Tribune, Chatham, VA

Davis, Tom (334) 687-3506
MAN ED, Eufaula Tribune, Eufaula, AL

Davis, Tom (912) 732-2731
ED, Cuthbert Times and News Record, Cuthbert, GA

Davis, Tracey (805) 395-7500
Network Analyst Programmer
Bakersfield Californian, Bakersfield, CA

Davis, Tricia (614) 452-4561
News ED, Times Recorder, Zanesville, OH

Davis, Verlaine (505) 523-4581
ASST CONT
Las Cruces Sun-News, Las Cruces, NM

Davis, Vernon (802) 479-2582
ED, World, Barre, VT

Davis, Wayne (916) 321-1000
Features ED
Sacramento Bee, Sacramento, CA

Davis-Cluck, Christina (316) 223-1460
Living/Lifestyle ED, Women's ED
Fort Scott Tribune, Fort Scott, KS

Davison, Jim (903) 564-3565
PUB, ED, News-Record, Whitesboro, TX

Davison, Rick (604) 788-2246
MAN ED, Chetwynd Echo, Chetwynd, BC

Davitt, Mark (515) 594-4488
PUB, ED, Diamond Trail News, Sully, IA

Davolt, Christi (816) 258-7237
Society ED
Daily News-Bulletin, Brookfield, MO

Davy, Dean (916) 685-3945
GM, Elk Grove Citizen, Elk Grove, CA

Davy, James L (714) 498-0833
Owner, Davy Associates Media Features, San Clemente, CA

Davy, Jimmy (615) 259-8000
Senior Writer-Sports
Tennessean, Nashville, TN

Davy, John (715) 394-4411
Sports ED, Daily Telegram, Superior, WI

Davy, Kent (619) 745-6611
ED, North County Times, Escondido, CA

D'Avy, Micky (706) 846-3188
ED, Talbotton New Era, Talbotton, GA

Daw, Bruce (613) 829-9100
PROD FRM-Manufacturing-PR
Ottawa Citizen, Ottawa, ON

Dawes, Donald (915) 823-3253
PUB, ED, Western Observer, Anson, TX

Dawkins, Jim (813) 535-4400
PUB, Jewish Press, Clearwater, FL

Dawkins, Karen (813) 535-4400
MAN ED, Jewish Press, Clearwater, FL

Dawn, Keith (609) 272-7000
ADV MGR
Press of Atlantic City, Pleasantville, NJ

Dawson, Chris (707) 546-2020
PROD ASST DIR
Press Democrat, Santa Rosa, CA

Dawson, Dave (705) 325-1355
Sports ED, Packet & Times, Orillia, ON

Dawson, Dave (610) 820-6500
NTL ED, Morning Call, Allentown, PA

Dawson, Dudley E (501) 442-1777
Sports ED
Northwest Arkansas Times, Fayetteville, AR

Dawson, Ed (704) 252-5611
MAN ED
Asheville Citizen-Times, Asheville, NC

Dawson, Eric (403) 235-7100
Entertainment ED, Music ED
Calgary Herald, Calgary, AB

Dawson, Johnette (770) 382-4545
MGR-Office
Daily Tribune News, Cartersville, GA

Dawson, Mark (905) 468-3283
GM, Niagara Advance, Virgil, ON

Dawson, Richard (317) 633-1240
PROD OPER ASST to DIR
Indianapolis Star/News, Indianapolis, IN

Dawson, Stephanie A (402) 678-2771
PUB, ED
St. Edward Advance, St. Edward, NE

Dawson, Sue (614) 461-5000
Food ED, Columbus Dispatch, Columbus, OH

Dawson, Walter .... (408) 372-3311
MAN ED, Political ED
Monterey County Herald, Monterey, CA

Dawson, William R .... (916) 243-2424
ADV DIR-MKTG
Record Searchlight, Redding, CA

Day, Barbara .... (501) 378-3400
ADV MGR-RT Sales
Arkansas Democrat-Gazette, Little Rock, AR

Day, Bill .... (313) 222-6400
EDL Cartoonist, Detroit Free Press, Detroit, MI

Day, Bryan .... (573) 888-4505
Sports ED
Daily Dunklin Democrat, Kennett, MO

Day, Chris .... (334) 566-4270
ED, PROD MGR, Messenger, Troy, AL

Day, Chris .... (501) 239-8562
EPE, Paragould Daily Press, Paragould, AR

Day, Diane .... (616) 345-3511
ADV MGR-CLASS/ADM
Kalamazoo Gazette, Kalamazoo, MI

Day, Jeannie .... (501) 297-8300
PUB, ED
White River Current, Calico Rock, AR

Day, Jeff .... (705) 325-1355
MAN ED, EPE, Packet & Times, Orillia, ON

Day, Jerry .... (937) 328-0300
PROD MGR-COMP
Springfield News-Sun, Springfield, OH

Day, Jim .... (510) 935-2525
Wire ED
Contra Costa Times, Walnut Creek, CA

Day, Kathy .... (606) 735-2198
PUB, Bracken County News, Brooksville, KY

Day, Marshall .... (817) 865-5212
PUB, Gatesville Messenger and Star-Forum, Gatesville, TX

Day, Melanie .... (901) 686-1632
GM, MAN ED, Mirror-Exchange, Milan, TN

Day, Michele .... (606) 292-2600
Features ED, Kentucky Post, Covington, KY

Day, Norman .... (815) 625-3600
PROD FRM-COMP, Daily Gazette, Sterling, IL
Shaw Newspapers

Day, Ramona .... (707) 263-5636
CIRC DIR
Lake County Record-Bee, Lakeport, CA

Day, Richard E .... (970) 249-3444
MAN ED, Montrose Daily Press, Montrose, CO

Day, T C .... (501) 534-3400
PROD FRM-PR
Pine Bluff Commercial, Pine Bluff, AR

Dayberry, John .... (704) 322-4510
Lifestyle ED
Hickory Daily Record, Hickory, NC

Dayley, Darold .... (541) 963-3161
CIRC MGR, Observer, La Grande, OR

Daylor, Dennis .... (610) 688-3000
ED, King of Prussia Courier, Wayne, PA

Days, Michael .... (215) 854-2000
ASST MAN ED
Philadelphia Daily News, Philadelphia, PA

Dayton, Dave .... (415) 777-2424
Entertainment ED
San Francisco Examiner, San Francisco, CA

Deacon, Beth .... (919) 419-6500
ADV GM-Chapel Hill Herald
Herald-Sun, Durham, NC

Deak, Michael .... (908) 722-3000
ED
Somerset Messenger-Gazette, Somerville, NJ

Deal, Charles H .... (704) 328-6164
PUB, ED, Hickory News, Hickory, NC

Deal, Douglas D .... (218) 245-1422
PUB, ED, Scenic Range News, Bovey, MN

Deal, Ethel .... (218) 245-1422
PUB, Scenic Range News, Bovey, MN

Deal, Jennifer .... (707) 374-6431
GM, River News-Herald & Isleton Journal, Rio Vista, CA

Deal, Jerry .... (210) 423-5511
MAN ED
Valley Morning Star, Harlingen, TX

Deal, Teri .... (217) 526-3323
ED, Morrisonville Times, Morrisonville, IL

Dean, Bill .... (941) 687-7000
Films/Theater ED, Ledger, Lakeland, FL

Dean, Billy .... (352) 374-5000
PROD MGR-Plant
Gainesville Sun, Gainesville, FL

Dean, Charles .... (205) 325-2222
EDU ED, Birmingham News, Birmingham, AL

Dean, Gail .... (410) 228-0222
ED, Dorchester Star, Cambridge, MD

Dean, J William .... (508) 880-9000
CIRC MGR
Taunton Daily Gazette, Taunton, MA

Dean, James .... (203) 574-3636
Graphics ED, Waterbury Republican-American, Waterbury, CT

Dean, Janet .... (206) 339-3000
PROD MGR-Packaging/Distribution
Herald, Everett, WA

Dean, Karen .... (813) 893-8111
SYS ED
St. Petersburg Times, St. Petersburg, FL

Dean, Mark .... (901) 645-5346
ED, Independent Appeal, Selmer, TN

Dean, Rob .... (505) 983-3303
MAN ED, New Mexican, Santa Fe, NM

Dean, Wally .... (618) 544-2101
ADV DIR, Robinson Daily News, Robinson, IL

Dean, William .... (941) 335-0200
PROD MGR-Distribution
News-Press, Fort Myers, FL

Dean-Simmons, Barbara .... (709) 466-2243
ED, Packet, Clarenville, NF

Deane, Barbara .... (318) 459-3200
DIR-Human Resources
Times, Shreveport, LA

DeAngelis, Bernard .... (215) 855-8440
TREAS, PA, CONT, Reporter, Landsdale, PA

DeAngelis, Steven .... (401) 277-7000
DIR-RES
Providence Journal-Bulletin, Providence, RI

DeAngelo, Joseph .... (216) 999-4500
DIR-Building/Transportation SRV
Plain Dealer, Cleveland, OH

Deans, Susan C .... (803) 626-8555
VP/ED, Sun News, Myrtle Beach, SC

Dear, Clare .... (519) 679-6666
Homes ED, London Free Press, London, ON

Dear Jr, David R .... (703) 356-3320
PUB, ED, McLean Providence Journal & Fairfax Herald, McLean, VA

Dear, Martha C .... (502) 827-2000
SEC/TREAS, Gleaner, Henderson, KY

Dear, Walter .... (502) 389-1833
PUB, Union County Advocate, Morganfield, KY

Dear II, Walter M .... (502) 827-2000
PRES, Gleaner, Henderson, KY

Dearman, Mildred .... (601) 267-4501
ED, Carthaginian, Carthage, MS

Dearman, Stanley .... (601) 656-4000
PUB, ED
Neshoba Democrat, Philadelphia, MS

Dearman, Tim .... (704) 873-1451
PUB, PA, Statesville Record & Landmark, Statesville, NC

De Armond, Rob .... (504) 384-8370
Sports ED, Daily Review, Morgan City, LA

Dearrington, John .... (423) 756-6900
PROD MGR-COMP
Chattanooga Free Press, Chattanooga, TN

Dearth, Terri .... (513) 422-3611
ADV MGR-RT
Middletown Journal, Middletown, OH

Deason, B Randy .... (912) 244-1880
CIRC DIR
Valdosta Daily Times, Valdosta, GA

Deason, Gene .... (915) 646-2541
MAN ED, Brownwood Bulletin, Brownwood, TX

Deason, Shirley .... (916) 741-2345
MGR-MKTG/PROM
Appeal-Democrat, Marysville, CA

Deatherage, Marilyn .... (805) 273-2700
SEC/TREAS
Antelope Valley Press, Palmdale, CA

De Atley, Richard .... (909) 684-1200
Entertainment ED, Friday Entertainment ED, Music ED, Press-Enterprise, Riverside, CA

Deaton, Bruce .... (417) 836-1100
DIR-Market Development
Springfield News-Leader, Springfield, MO
Gannett Co. Inc.

Deaton, Marcia .... (601) 323-1642
BM, Starkville Daily News, Starkville, MS

Deaton, Mike .... (706) 291-6397
DP MGR, Rome News-Tribune, Rome, GA

Deaton, Sherri .... (607) 272-2321
ADV MGR-CLASS
Ithaca Journal, Ithaca, NY

DeAugustine, John .... (412) 523-6588
CIRC MGR
Standard Observer, Greensburg, PA

Deaver, Mitch .... (601) 794-2765
ED, Lamar County News, Purvis, MS

Deaver, Rick .... (903) 757-3311
CIRC DIR
Longview News-Journal, Longview, TX

Deavers, Richard .... (502) 754-2331
MAN ED, Times-Argus, Central City, KY

DeBarras, Dana .... (508) 880-9000
MGR-MKTG/PROM
Taunton Daily Gazette, Taunton, MA

DeBarros, Anthony .... (914) 454-2000
Technology ED
Poughkeepsie Journal, Poughkeepsie, NY

DeBell, Jeff .... (540) 981-3100
MET ED, Roanoke Times, Roanoke, VA

DeBerry, Mina S .... (316) 378-4415
MAN ED, Wilson County Citizen, Fredonia, KS

DeBettignies, Daniel J .... (319) 642-5506
GM, Marengo Pioneer-Republican, Marengo, IA

Debevec, James V .... (216) 431-0628
ED, Ameriska Domovina, Cleveland, OH

Debnam, Carol M .... (910) 762-1337
GM, Challenger, Wilmington, NC

DeBoer, Melvin .... (507) 442-6161
PUB, ED, Edgerton Enterprise, Edgerton, MN

DeBolt, Carol Ann .... (904) 863-1111
MGR-EDU SRV, Northwest Florida Daily News, Fort Walton Beach, FL

DeBolt, Lyle .... (210) 423-5511
PUB, Rio Grande Valley Group, Harlingen, TX

DeBolt, Marvin .... (904) 863-1111
PUB, Books ED, Northwest Florida Daily News, Fort Walton Beach, FL

Debolt, Nancy .... (510) 661-2600
MAN ED, Argus, Fremont, CA

DeBolt Jr, Vernon Lyle .... (210) 423-5511
PUB, Books ED, Golf ED
Valley Morning Star, Harlingen, TX

DeBolt III, Vernon Lyle .... (601) 335-1155
PUB, Delta Democrat Times, Greenville, MS

DeBonte, Johanna .... (703) 276-3400
ADV VP-Midwest Sales
USA Today, Arlington, VA

DeBoth, James R .... (800) 509-INFO
Writer/PRES, Mortgage Market Information Services, Villa Park, IL

Debrow, Agatha Hudson .... (706) 682-3346
ED, Bayonet, Columbus, GA

DeBrux, Scott .... (414) 432-2941
CIRC DIR
Green Bay News-Chronicle, Green Bay, WI

Debth, Jim .... (319) 398-8211
VP/GM-Interactive Media Inc.
Gazette, Cedar Rapids, IA

DeBus, Bill .... (216) 951-0000
Automotive ED, BUS/FIN ED
News-Herald, Willoughby, OH

DeBuse, Nikki .... (503) 981-3441
ED, Woodburn Independent, Woodburn, OR

Decherd, Robert W .... (214) 977-6606
COB/PRES/CEO
A H Belo Corp., Dallas, TX

Deck, Andrew .... (701) 857-1900
PROD FRM-COMP
Minot Daily News, Minot, ND

Deckard, Joe .... (541) 386-1234
GM, Hood River News, Hood River, OR

Deckard, Stephen A .... (812) 247-2828
PUB, ED, Shoals News, Shoals, IN

Deckelnick, Gary .... (908) 922-6000
Legal Affairs ED
Asbury Park Press, Neptune, NJ

Decker, Barbara .... (770) 382-4545
ADV MGR-CLASS
Daily Tribune News, Cartersville, GA

Decker, Cathleen .... (213) 237-5000
Political Writer
Los Angeles Times, Los Angeles, CA

Decker, Dave .... (414) 457-7711
PUB, Sheboygan Press, Sheboygan, WI

Decker, David .... (815) 937-3300
PROD FRM-Press (Night)
Daily Journal, Kankakee, IL

Decker, Edith .... (541) 474-3700
Films/Theater ED, Food ED, Women's ED
Grants Pass Daily Courier, Grants Pass, OR

Decker, Lisa .... (315) 393-1000
MGR-CR, Courier-Observer Journal & Advance-News, Ogdensburg, NY

Decker, Matt .... (417) 532-9131
BUS/FIN ED, EDU ED
Lebanon Daily Record, Lebanon, MO

Decker, Patty .... (913) 462-3963
PUB, Colby Free Press, Colby, KS

Decker, Robert .... (201) 428-6200
Sports ED, Daily Record, Parsippany, NJ

Deckert, Dick .... (814) 870-1600
News ED
Morning News/Erie Daily Times, Erie, PA

Deckert, Mary .... (505) 823-7777
DIR-MKTG/PROM, Albuquerque Publishing Co., Albuquerque, NM

Deckert, Rod .... (505) 823-7777
MAN ED
Albuquerque Journal, Albuquerque, NM

DeClue, Marlene .... (417) 637-2712
ED, Greenfield Vedette & Advocate, Greenfield, MO

de Cordoba, Jose .... (212) 416-2000
BU Chief-Miami
Wall Street Journal, New York, NY

Decosse, Rene C .... (705) 864-0640
PUB, ED, Sentinel, Chapleau, ON

DeCosta, Steven .... (508) 997-7411
Automotive ED, Books ED, Features ED, Health/Medical ED, Lifestyle ED, SCI/Technology ED, Sports ED
Standard Times, New Bedford, MA

Decoste, Jean-Claude .... (514) 285-7272
PROD SUPT-PR, La Presse, Montreal, QC

Decuir, Loretta .... (504) 343-2540
PUB, West Side Journal, Port Allen, LA

DeCuir, Randy .... (318) 253-5413
PUB, ED, Avoyelles Journal, Marksville, LA

Dedolf, Bob .... (509) 837-4500
ADV DIR, Daily Sun News, Sunnyside, WA

Dee, Michael J .... (202) 898-8254
Strategic BUS Planning
United Press International, Washington, DC

Deeds, Michael .... (208) 377-6200
Entertainment/Amusements ED, Fashion/Features ED, SCI/Technology ED
Idaho Statesman, Boise, ID

Deegan, Jim .... (610) 258-7171
City ED, Express-Times, Easton, PA

Deegan, Suzanne .... (719) 632-5511
ADV DIR-Major/NTL
Gazette, Colorado Springs, CO

Deeks, Gordon .... (403) 429-5400
ADV MGR-Sales Planning
Edmonton Journal, Edmonton, AB

Deeley, Jonathan .... (210) 761-9341
PUB, Coastal Current, South Padre Island, TX

Deemer, Mary .... (616) 637-1104
GM, ADV MGR-CLASS
South Haven Daily Tribune, South Haven, MI

Deemer, Nancy .... (412) 834-1151
MGR-PROM, Tribune-Review, Greensburg, PA

Deemer, Robin .... (562) 435-1161
Radio/Television ED
Press-Telegram, Long Beach, CA

Deer, Freddie .... (601) 684-2421
CIRC DIR, Enterprise-Journal, McComb, MS

Deere, Vicki .... (601) 684-2421
ADV MGR-CLASS
Enterprise-Journal, McComb, MS

Deering, John .... (501) 378-3400
Cartoonist
Arkansas Democrat-Gazette, Little Rock, AR

Deering, Roy .... (405) 332-4433
City/MET ED, News ED, Political/Government ED, Ada Evening News, Ada, OK

Deese, David .... (704) 982-2121
ED, Stanly News and Press, Albemarle, NC

Defalco, Jane .... (613) 829-9100
Travel ED, Ottawa Citizen, Ottawa, ON

Defendorf, Richard .... (510) 208-6300
ASST Features ED,
Oakland Tribune, Oakland, CA
MediaNews Inc. (Alameda Newspapers)

Defeo, Tom .... (303) 892-5000
Deputy MAN ED-Graphics
Rocky Mountain News, Denver, CO

Deferia, Tony .... (404) 526-5151
ASST MAN ED-Graphics and Photo
Atlanta Journal-Constitution, Atlanta, GA

DeFoy, Margaret P .... (318) 222-0213
SEC/TREAS, MAN ED
Daily Legal News Inc., Shreveport, LA

DeFrance, Lloyd .... (813) 259-7711
DIR-Human Resources
Tampa Tribune and Times, Tampa, FL

De Francesco, Frank .... (207) 282-1535
MGR-MKTG/PROM
Journal Tribune, Biddeford, ME

DeFrancis, Robert .... (304) 233-0100
GM, Intelligencer/Wheeling News-Register, Wheeling, WV

DeFrange, Ann .... (405) 475-3311
Books ED
Daily Oklahoman, Oklahoma City, OK

DeFries, Bill .... (210) 780-3924
PUB, ED, Karnes Citation, Karnes City, TX

DeGard Knox, Neoma .... (407) 886-2777
GM, Planter, Apopka, FL

Degener, Craig .... (520) 526-3881
ED, Navajo Hopi Observer, Flagstaff, AZ

Degenhart, Hazel H .... (812) 784-2341
ED, White River News, Hazleton, IN

DeGeorge, Janet .... (602) 898-6500
ADV MGR-CLASS Sales, Mesa Tribune, Mesa, AZ, Thomson Newspapers

DeGette, Cara .... (719) 577-4545
MAN ED, Colorado Springs Independent, Colorado Springs, CO

Deggendorf, Steve .... (319) 754-8461
PROD MGR-MR, Hawk Eye, Burlington, IA

Degginger, Craig .... (206) 441-4553
ED, Jewish Transcript, Seattle, WA

DeGiso, Patrick J .... (617) 786-7000
GM, Patriot Ledger, Quincy, MA

DeGolyer, Larry J .... (970) 242-5050
TREAS, GM
Daily Sentinel, Grand Junction, CO

de Graci, Jim .... (954) 356-4000
News ED, Sun-Sentinel, Fort Lauderdale, FL

DeGrado, Mari Jo .... (515) 792-3121
PROD FRM-COMP
Newton Daily News, Newton, IA

DeGraff, George .... (770) 227-3276
CIRC DIR, Griffin Daily News, Griffin, GA

DeGraw, Ed .... (330) 364-5577
Farm/Agriculture ED
Times Reporter, New Philadelphia, OH

DeGroff, Judy .... (315) 343-3800
Accountant, Palladium-Times, Oswego, NY

57-Who's Where **Den**

De Groff, Raymond .... (315) 343-3800
PROD FRM-Press
Palladium-Times, Oswego, NY

DeGuilio-Fox, Kathy .... (219) 881-3000
CIRC CNR-NIE, Post-Tribune, Gary, IN

DeGuire, Andre .... (514) 263-5288/5488
PUB, ED
Le Guide de Cowansville, Cowansville, QC

DeGurse, Carl .... (306) 692-6441
ED, Moose Jaw Times-Herald, Moose Jaw, SK

De Haan, Eloise .... (610) 820-6500
BUS ED, Morning Call, Allentown, PA

DeHaven, Carol .... (202) 414-0535
Regional MKTG/Sales DIR, North America
Agence France-Presse, Washington, DC

Dehning, James .... (503) 648-1131
GM, Hillsboro Argus, Hillsboro, OR

Deibler, William .... (412) 263-1100
Senior ED, Post-Gazette, Pittsburgh, PA

Deighan, Gertrude .... (902) 436-2121
ASST ED, Journal-Pioneer, Summerside, PEI

Deintzelman, Andrew .... (717) 622-3456
ASST News ED, Pottsville Republican & Evening Herald, Pottsville, PA

Deis, James E .... (507) 237-2476
PUB, ED, Gaylord Hub, Gaylord, MN

Deitz, Charles E .... (618) 242-0117
GM, Register-News, Mount Vernon, IL

Deitz, Harry J .... (610) 371-5000
ASST MAN ED-Graphics
Reading Times/Eagle, Reading, PA

Deitz, Robert D .... (618) 242-0117
PROD MGR
Register-News, Mount Vernon, IL

Deiwert, Mona .... (812) 663-3111
ADV MGR-RT
Greensburg Daily News, Greensburg, IN

DeJean, Stella .... (602) 898-6500
Religion ED, Mesa Tribune, Mesa, AZ
Thomson Newspapers

Dejoie, Bertel .... (504) 524-5563
GM, Louisiana Weekly, New Orleans, LA

Dejoie Sr, Henry B .... (504) 524-5563
PUB, Louisiana Weekly, New Orleans, LA

DeJong, Gary .... (605) 874-2499
PUB, ED, Clear Lake Courier, Clear Lake, SD

De Jong, Stan .... (905) 682-8311
GM, Christian Courier, St. Catharines, ON

Dekett, Ron .... (864) 298-4100
Regional ED, Greenville News, Greenville, SC

Dekeyser, Hal .... (602) 941-2300
ED, Scottsdale Progress Tribune, Mesa, AZ

Dekeyser, Jill .... (319) 383-2200
PSL MGR, Quad-City Times, Davenport, IA

de la Bastide, Ken .... (317) 622-1212
City Government ED, Political
Herald Bulletin, Anderson, IN

Delacoma, Wynne .... (312) 321-3000
Music ED-Classical
Chicago Sun-Times, Chicago, IL

DeLaConcepcion, Jonathan ..... (913) 628-1081
PROD MGR-MR, Hays Daily News, Hays, KS

De la Cruz, Ralph .... (562) 435-1161
COL, Press-Telegram, Long Beach, CA

De La Fuente, Charles .... (518) 270-1200
ED, Record, Troy, NY

de Lafuente, Della .... (312) 321-3000
Health Care/Computers
Chicago Sun-Times, Chicago, IL

de Lama, George .... (312) 222-3232
ASSOC MAN ED-NTL & Foreign News
Chicago Tribune, Chicago, IL

Delancy, Jimmy .... (910) 349-4331
PROD SUPT, Reidsville Review, Reidsville, NC

DeLand, David .... (320) 255-8700
Sports ED, St. Cloud Times, St. Cloud, MN

Deland, James .... (517) 895-8551
Sports ED, Bay City Times, Bay City, MI

Delaney, Charles .... (508) 458-7100
PROD FRM-PR, Sun, Lowell, MA

Delaney, Constance .... (941) 465-2522
ED, Lake Placid Journal, Lake Placid, FL

Delaney, Bishop Joseph P .... (817) 560-3300
PUB, North Texas Catholic, Ft. Worth, TX

Delaney, Mathew .... (941) 465-2522
PUB, Lake Placid Journal, Lake Placid, FL

Delaney, Michael .... (401) 277-7000
Chief Photographer
Providence Journal-Bulletin, Providence, RI

Delaney, Monte .... (941) 465-2522
GM, Lake Placid Journal, Lake Placid, FL

Delaney, Robert .... (334) 749-6271
CONT, Opelika-Auburn News, Opelika, AL

Delaney, Robin .... (319) 372-6421
ED, Daily Democrat, Fort Madison, IA

Delaney, Ted .... (417) 334-3161
PUB
Branson Tri-Lakes Daily News, Branson, MO

Delano, Norman .... (919) 894-3331
GM, Four Oaks-Benson News in Review, Benson, NC

Delano, Ralph E .... (919) 894-3331
PUB, Four Oaks-Benson News in Review, Benson, NC

DeLapa, Sue .... (805) 564-5200
Librarian, Santa Barbara News-Press, Santa Barbara, CA

DeLaPaz, Brent T .... (509) 773-3777
GM, Goldendale Sentinel, Goldendale, WA

Delaplaine Jr, George B .... (301) 662-1177
PRES/PUB, ED
Frederick Post/News, Frederick, MD

DeLapp, James M .... (910) 349-4331
PRES, PUB, PA, ED, EPE
Reidsville Review, Reidsville, NC

DeLapp, Phyllis B .... (803) 583-2907
COB/PRES, Mid-South Management Co. Inc., Spartanburg, SC

Delascasas, Elvira .... (305) 856-5664
ED, Viva Semanal, Miami, FL

DeLashmutt, Steve .... (308) 346-4504
PUB, Burwell Tribune, Burwell, NE

DeLatte, Joe .... (757) 446-2000
DIR-MKTG, Virginian-Pilot, Norfolk, VA

DeLauter, Lori .... (412) 775-3200
EDU ED, Beaver County Times, Beaver, PA

Delco, Virginia .... (541) 296-2141
MGR-CR
Dalles Daily Chronicle, The Dalles, OR

DeLee, Donna .... (504) 229-8607
MAN ED
Kentwood News-Ledger, Kentwood, LA

DeLege, Jaime .... (218) 783-6875
ED, Northern Light, Williams, MN

De Leon, John .... (206) 464-2111
ASST Local ED, Seattle Times, Seattle, WA

de Leon, Ralph .... (518) 658-2777
PUB, Taconic Valley Echo, Berlin, NY

Del Favero, Albie .... (615) 244-7989
PUB, Nashville Scene, Nashville, TN

Delfin, Jon .... (516) 795-8823
VP/Senior ED, American Crossword Federation, Massapequa Park, NY

Delgado, Rosa .... (210) 775-1551
ED, Del Rio News-Herald, Del Rio, TX

Delgado, Vincent .... (616) 964-7161
Political/Government Reporter
Battle Creek Enquirer, Battle Creek, MI

Delhomme, Ron .... (813) 394-7592
ED, Marco Island Eagle, Marco Island, FL

DeLisle, Doug .... (518) 270-1200
Entertainment ED, Focus/Fashion ED
Record, Troy, NY

Delker, Valerie .... (972) 424-6565
EPE, Plano Star Courier, Plano, TX

Dell, Laura .... (412) 834-1151
Radio/Television ED
Tribune-Review, Greensburg, PA

Dellafacoma, Glenn .... (212) 930-8000
CIRC GEN FRM-MR
New York Post, New York, NY

Dellavechia, Richard .... (518) 828-1616
PROD MGR-PR, Register-Star, Hudson, NY

Dello Russo, Christopher .... (617) 321-8000
CIRC MGR, PROD FRM-PR
Daily News-Mercury, Malden, MA

Delmont, George .... (716) 823-8222
MAN ED
South Buffalo News, Lackawanna, NY

Delmont, Jim .... (402) 444-1000
Film/Theater ED, Restaurants ED
Omaha World-Herald, Omaha, NE

Delmont, William .... (716) 823-8222
PUB, ED
Lackawanna Front Page, Lackawanna, NY

Delo, Patricia .... (413) 788-1000
EPE, Union-News, Springfield, MA

DeLoach, Ron .... (901) 427-3333
DIR-OPER, PROD DIR-OPER
Jackson Sun, Jackson, TN

DeLoache, Frank .... (704) 633-8950
MAN ED, Area News ED
Salisbury Post, Salisbury, NC

del Olmo, Frank .... (213) 237-5000
ASST to ED
Los Angeles Times, Los Angeles, CA

DeLonge, Ray .... (541) 885-4410
PROD SUPV-Printing
Herald and News, Klamath Falls, OR

DeLorey, Paul D .... (617) 786-7000
CIRC DIR, Patriot Ledger, Quincy, MA

DeLost, William D .... (319) 524-8300
PRES, PUB, Daily Gate City, Keokuk, IA

Delp, Barb .... (215) 855-8440
MAN ED, Reporter, Landsdale, PA

Delperdang, Judy .... (515) 421-0500
Librarian, Globe-Gazette, Mason City, IA

Delposen, Patty .... (412) 775-3200
PROD SUPV-Computer SYS
Beaver County Times, Beaver, PA

Del Rio, J .... (212) 348-8200
ED, La Voz Hispana, New York, NY

Del Rocco, Joseph P .... (407) 420-5000
ADV MGR-CLASS, Advertising Division
Orlando Sentinel, Orlando, FL

Del Santo, John .... (606) 329-1717
PRES, PUB, Daily Independent, Ashland, KY

Delsol, Christine .... (415) 348-4321
Travel/Weekend ED
San Mateo County Times, San Mateo, CA

Delson, Donald W .... (610) 543-0900
PUB, Swarthmorean, Swarthmore, PA

Delson, Sam .... (510) 783-6111
Political/Government ED, BU Chief-Sacramento, Daily Review, Hayward, CA

del Toro, Peggy .... (909) 987-6397
ADV DIR-CLASS
Inland Valley Daily Bulletin, Ontario, CA

De Luca, Don .... (215) 854-2000
Music Critic-Popular
Philadelphia Inquirer, Philadelphia, PA

Deluca, Michael J .... (508) 473-1111
PROD FRM-COMP
Milford Daily News, Milford, MA

DeLucia, Lynne .... (860) 241-6200
Deputy CT ED, Hartford Courant, Hartford, CT

Del Vecchio, Mark .... (860) 241-6200
GM-Electronic Publishing
Hartford Courant, Hartford, CT

Delworth, Brock .... (607) 387-3181
ED, Newfield News, Trumansburg, NY

DeMaagd, Pete .... (616) 222-5400
COL, Grand Rapids Press, Grand Rapids, MI

Demaree, Bob .... (812) 265-3641
Sports ED, Madison Courier, Madison, IN

Demaree, Virginia .... (540) 374-5000
City ED
Free Lance-Star, Fredericksburg, VA

Demarinis, Michael .... (413) 788-1000
Purchasing MGR
Union-News, Springfield, MA

Dematte, Dave .... (609) 691-5000
DP MGR, Daily Journal, Vineland, NJ

Dembski, Barbara .... (414) 224-2000
Senior ED-ADM
Milwaukee Journal Sentinel, Milwaukee, WI

Demchinsky, Bryan .... (514) 987-2222
Books ED, Gazette, Montreal, QC

DeMeer, Andrea .... (519) 442-7866
GM, Paris Star, Paris, ON

DeMeglio, Linda .... (610) 622-8800
MAN ED
Delaware County Daily Times, Primos, PA

Dement, Betty .... (615) 455-4545
MAN ED
Tullahoma News & Guardian, Tullahoma, TN

DeMers, Alisa .... (507) 359-2911
Farm/Agriculture ED, Regional Reporter
Journal, New Ulm, MN

Demers, Gilbert H .... (810) 756-8800
PUB, Warren Weekly, Warren, MI

Demers, Gregg .... (810) 756-8800
MAN ED, Warren Weekly, Warren, MI

Demers, Paula .... (508) 997-7411
Teen-Age/Youth ED
Standard Times, New Bedford, MA

Demers, Roland A .... (508) 222-7000
ADV MGR-RT, Sun Chronicle, Attleboro, MA

DeMetrotion, Brendt .... (816) 932-6600
ASST VP/Sales MGR/Southwest Div.
Universal Press Syndicate, Kansas City, MO

Demeyer, Trace .... (715) 634-4881
ED, Sawyer County Record, Hayward, WI

Demick, Barbara .... (215) 854-2000
Berlin BU
Philadelphia Inquirer, Philadelphia, PA

Demings, John .... (902) 245-4715
ED, Courier, Digby, NS

Demitroulas, Deborah M .... (812) 332-4401
VP, Herald-Times Inc, Bloomington, IN

Demjanik, Dan .... (770) 834-6631
CIRC DIR, Times-Georgian, Carrollton, GA

Demko PhD, David J .... (407) 482-6271
ED-in-Chief, Aging America News Net
Demko Publishing, Boca Raton, FL

Demko, Richard F .... (330) 747-7777
SEC/TREAS, Co-PUB, Co-ED
Daily Legal News, Youngstown, OH

Demma, Joe .... (516) 843-2020
ED-Investigations, Newsday, Melville, NY

Demontigny, Rhonda .... (941) 574-1110
PROD MGR-Commercial Printing
Cape Coral Daily Breeze, Cape Coral, FL

DeMorro, Al .... (203) 789-5200
PROD MGR-MR
New Haven Register, New Haven, CT

DeMoss, Bud .... (614) 224-4835
ADV Display, Daily Reporter, Columbus, OH

Dempsey, Jennifer .... (902) 667-5102
ED, Citizen, Amherst, NS

Dempsey, Kristi .... (602) 898-6500
BUS/FIN ED, Mesa Tribune, Mesa, AZ
Thomson Newspapers

Dempsey, Laura .... (937) 225-2000
Books ED, Dayton Daily News, Dayton, OH

Dempsey, W R .... (403) 532-1110
PRES
Daily Herald-Tribune, Grande Prairie, AB

Dempsey, Warren .... (618) 594-3131
PUB, ED, Union Banner, Carlyle, IL

Dempsey, William .... (416) 947-2222
VP-Community Newspaper Div/PRES & CEO-Bowes Pub Ltd
Sun Media Corp., Toronto, ON

Dempster, Lisa .... (403) 235-7100
EDU Reporter, Calgary Herald, Calgary, AB

Denato, Pat .... (515) 284-8000
Travel Reporter
Des Moines Register, Des Moines, IA

Denault, Sylvain .... (514) 375-4555
ADV Sales MGR
La Voix de l'Est, Granby, QC

Deneau, Jonathan .... (519) 255-5711
DIR-MKTG/PROM, Windsor Star, Windsor, ON

Denerstein, Robert .... (303) 892-5000
Films Critic
Rocky Mountain News, Denver, CO

Dengler, John .... (417) 836-1100
Graphics CNR
Springfield News-Leader, Springfield, MO

Denious, Jon .... (970) 387-5477
PUB, ED, Silverton Standard and The Miner, Silverton, CO

Denious, Sharon .... (970) 387-5477
PUB, Silverton Standard and The Miner, Silverton, CO

Denison, Paul .... (541) 485-1234
Entertainment/Amusements ED, Theater/Music ED, Register-Guard, Eugene, OR

Denison, R G .... (701) 968-3223
PUB, ED
Towner County Record Herald, Cando, ND

Denk, Jon .... (414) 542-2501
ADV ASST MGR
Waukesha County Freeman, Waukesha, WI

Denk, Sherry .... (912) 923-6432
CIRC MGR, Daily Sun, Warner Robins, GA

Denley, Gerald H .... (601) 675-2446
PUB, Coffeeville Courier, Coffeeville, MS

Denley, James H .... (205) 325-2222
PRES/PUB, ED
Birmingham Post-Herald, Birmingham, AL

Denley, Joanne .... (601) 983-2570
ED, Calhoun County Journal, Bruce, MS

Denley, Lisa .... (601) 983-2570
ED, Calhoun County Journal, Bruce, MS

Denley, S Gale .... (601) 983-2570
PUB, Calhoun County Journal, Bruce, MS

Denlinger, Kenneth .... (202) 334-6000
COL-Sports, Washington Post, Washington, DC

Denman, James .... (508) 793-9100
PROD MGR-Facilities
Telegram & Gazette, Worcester, MA

Denmark, Lee .... (615) 794-2555
PUB, Review Appeal, Franklin, TN

Dennan, John F .... (415) 777-5700
VP-Production, San Francisco Newspaper Agency, San Francisco, CA

Dennen, Rusty .... (540) 374-5000
BUS ED, Free Lance-Star, Fredericksburg, VA

Denneny, Joe .... (704) 358-5000
MGR-RES, Charlotte Observer, Charlotte, NC

Dennert, Rudi .... (415) 777-5700
MGR-Advertising Accounts Receivable
San Francisco Newspaper Agency, San Francisco, CA

Denney, Linda .... (504) 826-3279
VP/TREAS, GM
Times-Picayune, New Orleans, LA

Denney, Jim .... (513) 863-8200
Photo ED, Journal-News, Hamilton, OH

Denney, Rick .... (817) 757-5757
PROD ASST SUPV-Mail
Waco Tribune-Herald, Waco, TX

Denney, Sharon .... (405) 225-3000
ADV DIR, Automotive ED
Elk City Daily News, Elk City, OK

Dennie, Debbie .... (606) 654-3333
PUB, ED, Falmouth Outlook, Falmouth, KY

Denning, Charles .... (615) 526-9715
EX ED, Herald-Citizen, Cookeville, TN

Denning, W Mitchel .... (904) 359-4111
CONT-Division, DP MGR
Florida Times-Union, Jacksonville, FL

Dennis, Allan .... (705) 382-3843
ED, Burks Falls/Powassan/Almaguin News, Burks Falls, ON

Dennis, Andy .... (502) 781-1700
ASST MAN ED, News/Wire ED
Daily News, Bowling Green, KY

Dennis, Brett .... (614) 363-1161
Internet Service MGR
Delaware Gazette, Delaware, OH

Dennis, Craig .... (206) 242-0100
PUB
Highline News/Des Moines News, Burien, WA

Dennis, Don .... (714) 261-2435
ED, Irvine World News, Irvine, CA

Dennis, G W .... (902) 426-2811
CEO, PUB, Chronicle-Herald, Halifax, NS

Copyright ©1997 by the Editor & Publisher Co.

Den Who's Where-58

Dennis, Helen .... (805) 269-1169
MAN ED, Acton-Agua Dulce News, Acton, CA
Dennis, Jan .... (309) 829-9411
MAN ED-News, Pantagraph, Bloomington, IL
Dennis, Joe .... (509) 754-4636
ED, Grant County Journal, Ephrata, WA
Dennis, Joe Wayne .... (903) 665-2462
PUB, Jefferson Jimplecute, Jefferson, TX
Dennis, Larry .... (417) 924-3226
GM, ED, Mansfield Mirror/Wright Co. Republican, Mansfield, MO
Dennis, Laura .... (915) 337-4661
Living/Lifestyle ED, Television/Film ED, Travel ED, Odessa American, Odessa, TX
Dennis, Nancy .... (334) 262-1611
MET ED, Advertiser, Montgomery, AL
Dennis, Pat .... (402) 444-1000
CIRC MGR-MSA
Omaha World-Herald, Omaha, NE
Dennis, Rhonda .... (605) 837-2259
ED, Kadoka Press, Kadoka, SD
Dennis, Robert .... (573) 756-8927
GM, Daily Press Leader, Farmington, MO
Dennis, Sarah .... (902) 426-2811
VP, Chronicle-Herald, Halifax, NS
Dennis, Sharon .... (614) 373-2121
PROD DIR, Marietta Times, Marietta, OH
Dennis, Tom .... (717) 829-7100
EDL Writer, Times Leader, Wilkes-Barre, PA
Dennison, John .... (612) 673-4000
VP-Labor Relations
Star Tribune, Minneapolis, MN
Denniston, John .... (604) 732-2222
Photo ED, Province, Vancouver, BC
Denny, Jack .... (303) 892-5000
CIRC MGR-Consumer Sales and SRV
Rocky Mountain News, Denver, CO
Denny, Kevin .... (503) 221-8327
CIRC MGR-Sales, Oregonian, Portland, OR
Denny, Sharon .... (703) 642-7330
ED, Defense News, Springfield, VA
Denny, Victor .... (507) 285-7600
MGR-MIS, Post-Bulletin, Rochester, MN
Denny Jr, W M .... (505) 622-7710
TREAS, Roswell Daily Record, Roswell, NM
Denson, Anita .... (405) 885-7788
PUB, Ellis County Capital, Arnett, OK
Denson, David .... (219) 885-4357
GM, Gary Crusader, Gary, IN
Denson, Jerry L .... (405) 885-7788
PUB, ED, Ellis County Capital, Arnett, OK
Denton, Frank .... (608) 252-6100
ED, Wisconsin State Journal, Madison, WI
Denton, Jean R .... (606) 845-9211
PUB, Flemingsburg Gazette, Flemingsburg, KY
Denton, Joy .... (770) 461-1136
ED, Fayette Neighbor, Marietta, GA
Denton, Lowell O .... (606) 845-9211
PUB, ED
Flemingsburg Gazette, Flemingsburg, KY
Denton, Patti .... (317) 633-1240
Food ED
Indianapolis Star/News, Indianapolis, IN
Denton, Tommy .... (817) 390-7400
Senior EDL Writer
Fort Worth Star-Telegram, Fort Worth, TX
Dentry, Ed .... (303) 892-5000
Outdoors ED
Rocky Mountain News, Denver, CO
Denty, Eric .... (803) 359-3195
PUB, Dispatch-News, Lexington, SC
Denuet, Dick .... (212) 689-1340
BU Chief, Globe Photos Inc., New York, NY
DeOre, Bill .... (214) 977-8222
EDL Cartoonist
Dallas Morning News, Dallas, TX
de Padua, M Z .... (415) 465-3121
MKTG DIR,Inter-City Express, Oakland, CA
Depalma, Sam .... (609) 758-2112
ED, New Egypt Press, New Egypt, NJ
DePaola, Kenneth .... (312) 321-3000
VP-Advertising, ADV VP
Chicago Sun-Times, Chicago, IL
De Pasqua, Carl A .... (412) 537-3351
PRES, Latrobe Bulletin, Latrobe, PA
DePaul, Jeanne .... (208) 743-9411
Books ED, Fashion/Style ED, Food ED, Garden ED, Radio/Television ED, Religion ED, Women's ED
Lewiston Morning Tribune, Lewiston, ID
DePew, Renee .... (317) 598-6397
MAN ED, Castleton Banner, Noblesville, IN
De Phillips, Jeanne .... (301) 670-1400
News ED, Montgomery Journal, Rockville, MD
De Pietro, Mary .... (815) 459-4040
Features ED
Northwest Herald, Crystal Lake, IL
Deppe, Jackie F .... (317) 241-7363
PUB
West Side Community News, Indianapolis, IN

DePrez, John .... (317) 398-6631
PUB, Extra, Shelbyville, IN
DePrez Jr, John C .... (317) 398-6631
PRES/PUB, Shelbyville News, Shelbyville, IN
DePrez, Peter G .... (317) 398-6631
VP/TREAS, Shelbyville News, Shelbyville, IN
Deptula, T .... (212) 594-2266
MAN ED, Nowy Dziennik, New York, NY
Depui, Desiree .... (209) 358-5311
ED, Delhi Express, Delhi, CA
Depuy, Bill .... (212) 930-8000
PROD FRM-Electrical
New York Post, New York, NY
Derby, Bill .... (605) 347-2503
PUB
Meade County Times-Tribune, Sturgis, SD
Derby, John M .... (209) 358-5311
PUB, ED, Merced County Times, Winton, CA
Derby, Robert .... (419) 625-5500
News ED, Sandusky Register, Sandusky, OH
Derby Sr, Terrence .... (808) 525-8000
PROD MGR-Commercial
Hawaii Newspaper Agency Inc., Honolulu, HI
Deremer, Charles .... (304) 263-8931
CONT, Journal, Martinsburg, WV
DeRemer, William .... (717) 821-2091
City ED-Day, Citizens' Voice, Wilkes-Barre, PA
Derfel, Aaron .... (514) 987-2222
Environment Reporter, Gazette, Montreal, QC
Derfler, Joe .... (805) 259-1234
CIRC DIR, Signal, Santa Clarita, CA
Dergarabedian, Paul .... (310) 657-2005
EVP, Exhibitor Relations Co., Los Angeles, CA
Derge, Ed .... (415) 348-4321
DP MGR, MGR-INFO SYS
San Mateo County Times, San Mateo, CA
Deringer, Rick .... (937) 548-3151
CIRC MGR, Daily Advocate, Greenville, OH
Derk, Roseann .... (812) 424-7711
Librarian, Evansville Courier, Evansville, IN
Derksen, Rick .... (204) 326-3421
PUB, Carillon, Steinbach, MB
Dermody, Jack .... (319) 242-7101
PUB, Clinton Herald, Clinton, IA
Derneau, Patricia .... (941) 369-2191
PUB, News-Star, Lehigh Acres, FL
DeRose, Charles W .... (413) 584-5000
VP, Co-PUB
Daily Hampshire Gazette, Northampton, MA
DeRose, Peter L .... (413) 584-5000
PRES, Co-PUB
Daily Hampshire Gazette, Northampton, MA
DeRosier, Joe .... (630) 368-1100
MAN ED, Suburban Life Citizen, Oak Brook, IL
DeRosier, Joseph .... (630) 368-1100
MAN ED, Suburban Life, Oak Brook, IL
DeRossett, Dennis M .... (402) 223-5233
PUB, Beatrice Daily Sun, Beatrice, NE
De Rossi, Giuseppe .... (514) 328-2062
ED, Insieme, Montreal-North, QC
Derouin, Gord .... (204) 727-2451
ADV MGR-Sales, Brandon Sun, Brandon, MB
DeRousse, June .... (817) 461-6397
ADV DIR, Morning News, Arlington, TX
Derr Jr, Robert M .... (910) 625-5576
PUB, Randolph Guide, Asheboro, NC
Derrick, Liz .... (212) 803-8200
ADV DIR, Bond Buyer, New York, NY
Derrickson, G Eugene .... (573) 674-2412
PUB, ED, Licking News, Licking, MO
Derrickson, Tom .... (405) 327-2200
PROD MGR, Alva Review-Courier, Alva, OK
Derry, Mark .... (408) 842-6400
EX ED, Dispatch, Gilroy, CA
Derry, Randy .... (519) 832-9001
ED, Beacon Times, Port Elgin, ON
Derry, Ross .... (705) 472-3200
ADV MGR-CLASS
North Bay Nugget, North Bay, ON
DeRungs, Jerry .... (218) 485-4406
PUB, ED, Star Gazette, Moose Lake, MN
Derusha, Afred N .... (810) 332-8181
ADTX MGR, Oakland Press, Pontiac, MI
Derusha, Alfred .... (810) 332-8181
ADV DIR, Oakland Press, Pontiac, MI
Dery, Matthew R .... (860) 442-2200
CIRC MGR-Sales, Day, New London, CT
DeSalvo, James .... (617) 426-3000
CIRC ASST DIR, Boston Herald, Boston, MA
De Sanctis, Joe .... (941) 748-4140
GM, Weekly, Bradenton, FL
DeSantis, Guy .... (403) 532-1110
BUS ED, City ED, Features ED, Food ED, Local Goverment ED, Medical/Health ED
Daily Herald-Tribune, Grande Prairie, AB
DeSantis, Russ .... (908) 922-6000
Photo Assignment ED
Asbury Park Press, Neptune, NJ
De Santo, John .... (610) 696-1775
Sports ED
Daily Local News, West Chester, PA
DeSarno, Bonnie .... (908) 246-5500
ADV MGR
Home News & Tribune, East Brunswick, NJ

Desautels, Kurt .... (970) 949-0555
PROD MGR, Vail Daily News, Vail, CO
des Becquets, Jacques .... (705) 673-3377
ED, Le Journal Le Voyageur, Sudbury, ON
DeSchriver, Tom .... (717) 421-3000
Sports ED, Pocono Record, Stroudsburg, PA
Descoteaux, Bernard .... (514) 985-3333
EIC, Le Devoir, Montreal, QC
DeSelle, Stanley .... (318) 487-6397
PROD SUPT-MR
Alexandria Daily Town Talk, Alexandria, LA
Deselms, Jen .... (512) 884-2011
City ED-Day, Corpus Christi Caller-Times, Corpus Christi, TX
DeSeno, Jim .... (773) 586-8800
MGR-CIRC MKTG
Daily Southtown, Chicago, IL
Desgroseilliers, Lise .... (613) 739-7000
ADV DIR-Sales, Ottawa Sun, Ottawa, ON
Deshaney, Ginger .... (708) 336-7000
Sports ED, News-Sun, Waukegan, IL
DeShong, Martha .... (716) 282-2311
CONT, Niagara Gazette, Niagara Falls, NY
DeSilva, Rita .... (808) 245-3681
MAN ED, Garden Island, Lihue, HI
DeSimas, Jerry .... (860) 225-4601
Sports ED, Herald, New Britain, CT
DeSimone, James .... (401) 277-7000
PROD MGR-Packing Delivery
Providence Journal-Bulletin, Providence, RI
Desjardins, Jean-Guy .... (418) 562-4040
ED, La Voix Gaspesienne, Matane, QC
DesJardins, Marc .... (415) 726-4424
MAN ED, Review, Half Moon Bay, CA
Desjardins, Marcel .... (514) 285-7272
MAN ED, La Presse Plus Magazine ED, News ED, La Presse, Montreal, QC
Desjardins, Rob .... (403) 645-3342
ED, St. Paul Journal, St. Paul, AB
Deskin, Ruthe .... (702) 385-3111
SEC, Las Vegas Sun, Las Vegas, NV
des Lauriers, Donald U .... (815) 937-3300
VP-ADM, Daily Journal, Kankakee, IL
Des Marais, Paul G .... (819) 564-5450
BC, La Tribune, Sherbrooke, QC
Des Marais II, Pierre .... (418) 686-3233
BC/PRES/CEO, Le Soleil, Quebec, QC
Desmarteau, Charles .... (514) 641-4844
PUB, GM, La Releve, Boucherville, QC
De Smit, Scott .... (716) 343-8000
COL, Daily News, Batavia, NY
Desmond, Kevin .... (316) 268-6000
VP-OPER, PROD OPER DIR
Wichita Eagle, Wichita, KS
Desmond, Pat .... (617) 837-3500
ED, Cohasset Mariner, Marshfield, MA
Desormeau, Gerry .... (705) 472-3200
Sports ED, North Bay Nugget, North Bay, ON
deSouza, Bertram .... (330) 747-1471
EDL Writer, Vindicator, Youngstown, OH
DeSpain, Karen .... (520) 445-3333
MAN ED/MET ED, Daily Courier, Prescott, AZ
DeSpain, Margery .... (307) 455-2525
ED, Dubois Frontier, Dubois, WY
Despard, Joanne .... (413) 592-1400
ED, Chicopee Herald Weekly, Chicopee, MA
Despatis, Aime .... (514) 964-4444
ED, La Revue, Terrebonne, QC
Despatis, Marie-France .... (514) 964-4444
PUB, La Revue, Terrebonne, QC
DesRochers, Carl .... (207) 729-3311
PROD MGR-PR/Post Press
Times Record, Brunswick, ME
Desrosiers, Francis .... (418) 775-4381
PUB, L'Information, Mont Joli, QC
Desrosiers, Mike .... (905) 526-3333
ADV MGR-Local Accounts
Spectator, Hamilton, ON
DeStefano, Tony .... (516) 826-0333
MAN ED, Bellmore Life, Bellmore, NY
De Stephano, Elton .... (513) 761-1188
Contributing Critic
Critic's Choice Reviews, Cincinnati, OH
Deter, Janelle .... (916) 685-3945
ED, Elk Grove Citizen, Elk Grove, CA
Deterding, Gene .... (319) 472-2311
PROD MGR
Cedar Valley Daily Times, Vinton, IA
Detiege Sr, Frank .... (318) 387-3001
PUB, Monroe Dispatch, Monroe, LA
Detiege, Irma .... (318) 387-3001
ED, Monroe Dispatch, Monroe, LA
Dettelback, Cynthia .... (216) 991-8300
ED, Cleveland Jewish News, Cleveland, OH
Dettmar, Eddie .... (910) 623-2155
GM, ED, Daily News, Eden, NC
Deupree, Mike .... (319) 398-8211
COL, Gazette, Cedar Rapids, IA
Deuriarte, Richard .... (602) 271-8000
Reader Advocate
Arizona Republic, Phoenix, AZ
Deuschle, Anne .... (941) 946-0511
ED, Glades County Democrat, Clewiston, FL
Deutsch, Harley E .... (605) 698-7642
PUB, ED, Sisseton Courier, Sisseton, SD

Deutsch, Paul .... (307) 672-2431
ADV MGR-CLASS
Sheridan Press, Sheridan, WY
Deutsch, Rabbi Sender .... (718) 797-3900
ED, Der Yid, Brooklyn, NY
Deutsch, Sylvia .... (307) 672-2431
CIRC MGR, Sheridan Press, Sheridan, WY
Devall, Candy .... (505) 763-3431
ADV DIR, Clovis News Journal, Clovis, NM
DeValois, Dave .... (515) 964-0639
ED, Ankeny Press Citizen, Ankeny, IA
DeVarenne, Maria .... (909) 889-9666
Arts ED, Sun, San Bernardino, CA
DeVarrenne, Maria .... (909) 889-9666
ASST MAN ED-Features
Sun, San Bernardino, CA
DeVassie, Terry L .... (614) 461-5000
CIRC ASST DIR, Dispatch, Columbus, OH
DeVaul, Franklin .... (360) 264-2500
PUB, Tenino Independent, Tenino, WA
DeVaul, Judith .... (360) 264-2500
PUB, Tenino Independent, Tenino, WA
DeVeau, Carol .... (517) 893-6344
GM, Bay City Democrat & Bay County Legal News, Bay City, MI
DeVeau, Scott E .... (517) 893-6344
PUB, ED, Bay City Democrat & Bay County Legal News, Bay City, MI
De Venney, Sharon .... (717) 243-2611
ADTX MGR, Sentinel, Carlisle, PA
Dever, Ed .... (305) 674-9746
BUS DEPT
International News Agency, Miami Beach, FL
Dever, Roger .... (207) 784-5411
CIRC MGR-Home Delivery
Sun-Journal, Lewiston, ME
De Vera-Gougherty, Geny .... (916) 444-2355
PUB, Daily Recorder, Sacramento, CA
Devers, Carol .... (937) 773-2721
Accountant, Piqua Daily Call, Piqua, OH
Devier, Eve .... (916) 257-5321
MAN ED, Lassen County Times, Susanville, CA
DeView, Lucille .... (714) 835-1234
Writing Coach
Orange County Register, Santa Ana, CA
Devincenzi, Robert John .... (408) 262-2454
ED, Milpitas Post, Milpitas, CA
Devine, James .... (212) 837-7000
Senior VP-Advertising, Journal of Commerce & Commercial, New York, NY
Devine, Jerald .... (401) 849-3300
CIRC MGR, Newport Daily News, Newport, RI
Devine, Larry .... (313) 222-6400
Theater Writer, Detroit Free Press, Detroit, MI
Devine, Lawrence .... (712) 792-3573
News ED, Daily Times Herald, Caroll, IA
Devine, P .... (902) 426-2811
VP/SEC, Chronicle-Herald, Halifax, NS
Devine, Susan .... (209) 722-1511
BM, Merced Sun-Star, Merced, CA
DeVine, Terry .... (701) 253-7311
MAN ED, Sunday ED, Forum, Fargo, ND
Deviney, Jim .... (704) 245-6431
ADV DIR, Daily Courier, Forest City, NC
Devish, Mary J .... (605) 331-2200
DIR-FIN, Argus Leader, Sioux Falls, SD
DeVita-Gee, Antoinette .... (619) 442-4404
PROD MGR, Daily Californian, El Cajon, CA
Devlin, James P .... (718) 821-7500
MAN ED, Times Newsweekly, Ridgewood, NY
Devlin, Paula .... (504) 826-3279
Page One ED
Times-Picayune, New Orleans, LA
Devlin, Russ .... (218) 894-1112
PUB, Staples World, Staples, MN
Devlin, Sean P .... (414) 634-3322
EPE, Journal Times, Racine, WI
Devlin, William R .... (701) 524-1640
PUB, ED, Steele County Press, Finley, ND
Devoe, Norma .... (208) 934-4449
GM, Gooding County Leader, Gooding, ID
DeVoge, Edward R .... (412) 222-2200
VP, GM, Observer-Reporter, Washington, PA
DeVon, Gary A .... (509) 476-3602
ED, Okanogan Valley Gazette-Tribune, Oroville, WA
DeVore, Holly .... (515) 753-6611
EDU ED, Living/Lifestyle ED, Religion ED
Times-Republican, Marshalltown, IA
Devore, Steve .... (208) 377-6200
CIRC MGR-State, Idaho Statesman, Boise, ID
Devoti, Lori .... (406) 496-5500
ADV MGR-RT, ADTX MGR
Montana Standard, Butte, MT
Devoy, Linda .... (618) 382-4176
ADV MGR, Carmi Times, Carmi, IL
DeVries, Dean .... (417) 926-5148
PUB, News-Journal, Mountain Grove, MO
DeVries, Jim .... (701) 642-8585
ASST PUB, CIRC MGR
Daily News, Wahpeton, ND
De Wall, Tricia .... (515) 684-4611
ASST City ED, Ottumwa Courier, Ottumwa, IA
Dewalt, Gregg .... (205) 766-3434
Sports ED, Times Daily, Florence, AL

Copyright ©1997 by the Editor & Publisher Co.

59-Who's Where **Dil**

Dewar, Timothy .... (805) 646-1476
ED, Ojai Valley News, Ojai, CA

Dewberry, Beatrice O'Quinn .... (413) 788-1000
Religion ED, Union-News, Springfield, MA

Dewberry, Randy .... (205) 353-4612
PROD FRM-PR, Decatur Daily, Decatur, AL

DeWeese, Jerri .... (918) 663-1414
ED, Mannford Eagle, Tulsa, OK

Dewey, Jan .... (914) 454-2000
ADV MGR-CLASS
Poughkeepsie Journal, Poughkeepsie, NY

Dewey, Mike .... (330) 264-1125
Entertainment ED, Daily Record, Wooster, OH

Dewig, Robert .... (812) 897-2330
ED, Boonville Standard, Boonville, IN

DeWitt, Blake .... (520) 783-3311
VP/COO, Western Newspapers Inc., Yuma, AZ

De Witt, Carlton .... (715) 265-4646
PUB, ED
Glenwood City Tribune, Glenwood City, WI

Dewitt, Malcolm .... (803) 577-7111
Sports ED, Post and Courier, Charleston, SC

De Witt, Shawn .... (715) 265-4646
MAN ED
Glenwood City Tribune, Glenwood City, WI

DeWolfe, Owen .... (614) 461-5000
Insight ED
Columbus Dispatch, Columbus, OH

Dexter, Jere .... (607) 756-5665
Sports ED, Cortland Standard, Cortland, NY

Dey, Jim .... (217) 351-5252
EDL Writer, News-Gazette, Champaign, IL

Dey, Ken .... (406) 363-3300
Sports ED, Ravalli Republic, Hamilton, MT

Deyo, Steve .... (612) 339-7571
EIC, ComputerUser, Minneapolis, MN

De Young, Bill .... (352) 374-5000
Entertainment/Amusements ED, Radio/Television ED, Gainesville Sun, Gainesville, FL

DeYoung, Karen .... (202) 334-6000
ASST MAN ED-NTL
Washington Post, Washington, DC

Deysher, Dennis V .... (610) 371-5000
City ED, Reading Times/Eagle, Reading, PA

Dezort, Jeff .... (501) 741-2325
City/MET ED, EDU ED, Farm/Agriculture ED, NTL ED, Political/Government ED
Harrison Daily Times, Harrison, AR

Dhiri, Manju .... (0171) 411-3111
Deputy ED, Newslink Africa Ltd., London

D'Hooge, Edward .... (520) 774-4545
PROD MGR-COMP
Arizona Daily Sun, Flagstaff, AZ

Diadium, Ted .... (216) 999-4500
ASST MAN ED, Plain Dealer, Cleveland, OH

Dial, John .... (608) 782-9710
Online MGR, ADTX MGR
La Crosse Tribune, La Crosse, WI

Dial, Kent N .... (619) 457-5920
Market Development MGR
Trade Service Corp., San Diego, CA

Dial, Mark .... (407) 420-5000
PROD MGR-Pre Press
Orlando Sentinel, Orlando, FL

Dial, Marla .... (915) 653-1221
Health/Medical ED
Standard-Times, San Angelo, TX

Dial, Royce .... (913) 295-1111
PROD FRM-PR (Night)
Topeka Capital-Journal, Topeka, KS

Diamandis, Alyce .... (813) 259-7711
Archive & RES Center MGR
Tampa Tribune and Times, Tampa, FL

Diamataris, Anthony H .... (718) 784-5255
PUB, National Herald, Long Island City, NY

Diamond, G William .... (207) 892-1166
PUB, Suburban News, Windham, ME

Diamond, Keith .... (970) 493-6397
PROD MGR-PR
Fort Collins Coloradoan, Fort Collins, CO

Diamond, Richard .... (609) 989-5454
ASST to the PUB, Times, Trenton, NJ

Diamond, Richard E .... (503) 221-8327
ASST TREAS, Oregonian, Portland, OR
Advance Publications

Diamond, Tom .... (406) 587-4491
PROD SUPT
Bozeman Daily Chronicle, Bozeman, MT

Dianda, Mario .... (510) 208-6300
ASST MAN ED-Regional
Oakland Tribune, Oakland, CA

Diano, Annette .... (516) 736-1617
MAN ED
MDA Management Co. Inc., Coram, NY

Dias, Kathy .... (303) 776-2244
CIRC ASST MGR
Daily Times-Call, Longmont, CO

Diaz, Arthur .... (312) 283-7900
PUB, GM, Spotlight Chicago, Chicago, IL

Diaz, Carlos Julio .... (212) 807-4600
Night ED, El Diario La Prensa, New York, NY

Diaz, Hector A .... (407) 659-1833
MAN ED
La Voz Hispana, West Palm Beach, FL

Diaz, James .... (612) 673-4000
Senior VP-Marketer Customer Unit, GM-Marketer Customer Unit, ADV DIR
Star Tribune, Minneapolis, MN

Diaz CPA, Jenise .... (210) 686-4343
BM, Monitor, McAllen, TX

Diaz, Jesus .... (305) 350-2111
VP/CFO, Miami Herald, Miami, FL

Diaz, John .... (415) 777-1111
EPE
San Francisco Chronicle, San Francisco, CA

Diaz, Octavio .... (407) 242-3500
Graphics ED/Art DIR
Florida Today, Melbourne, FL

Diaz, Samuel .... (941) 687-7000
CIRC DIR, Ledger, Lakeland, FL

Dibble, Glenn E .... (810) 544-0470
EVP/Senior ED, Feature Service Syndicate, Madison Heights, MI

Dibble, Marcia .... (904) 599-2100
Radio/Television ED
Tallahassee Democrat, Tallahassee, FL

DiBenedetto, Bill .... (212) 837-7000
BU Chief-Seattle, Journal of Commerce & Commercial, New York, NY

DiBlasio, Sheilah .... (518) 374-4141
PROD MGR-Ad SRV
Daily Gazette, Schenectady, NY

Dible, Dennis D .... (412) 775-3200
EX ED, Beaver County Times, Beaver, PA

Dible, James .... (814) 870-1600
VP/GM
Morning News/Erie Daily Times, Erie, PA

Dible, Jim .... (814) 870-1600
VP/GEN MGR
Times Publishing Inc., Erie, PA

Dicampo, Marie .... (508) 473-1111
MGR-Office
Milford Daily News, Milford, MA

DiCarlo, John .... (213) 881-6515
PUB, Novedades, Los Angeles, CA

Dice, Janis .... (916) 624-9713
ED, Placer Herald, Rocklin, CA

DiCenso, Emily .... (718) 769-4400
MAN ED, Harbor Watch (Metro New York), Brooklyn, NY

DiChiara, Tom .... (516) 843-2020
ADV MGR-NTL, Newsday, Melville, NY

Dick, Brad .... (607) 334-3276
CIRC MGR, Evening Sun, Norwich, NY

Dick, Denise .... (614) 654-1321
Political/Government ED, Religion ED
Lancaster Eagle-Gazette, Lancaster, OH

Dick, Elaine .... (613) 432-3655
ED, Renfrew Mercury, Renfrew, ON

Dick, Gregory .... (416) 585-5000
PROD Building MGR-Facilities
Globe and Mail (Canada's National Newspaper), Toronto, ON

Dick, William .... (209) 441-6111
MGR-Creative SRV, Fresno Bee, Fresno, CA

Dickason, Glen .... (360) 264-2500
ED, Tenino Independent, Tenino, WA

Dickens, Bill .... (619) 442-4404
Sports ED, Daily Californian, El Cajon, CA

Dickens, David .... (502) 769-2312
PROD MGR-Post Press
News Enterprise, Elizabethtown, KY

Dickens, Tom .... (561) 562-2315
CIRC DIR, PROD DIR
Vero Beach Press-Journal, Vero Beach, FL

Dickerman, Margaret .... (919) 243-5151
VP, Wilson Daily Times, Wilson, NC

Dickerman III, Morgan Paul .... (919) 243-5151
PRES, PUB
Wilson Daily Times, Wilson, NC

Dickerson, Amy .... (864) 298-4100
Librarian, Greenville News, Greenville, SC

Dickerson, Brian .... (313) 222-6400
Projects ED, Detroit Free Press, Detroit, MI

Dickerson, Den .... (919) 446-5161
PUB/GM
Rocky Mount Telegram, Rocky Mount, NC

Dickerson, Gary S .... (502) 582-4011
ADV OPER DIR, Courier-Journal, Louisville, KY

Dickerson, James E .... (402) 843-5500
PUB, ED, Elgin Review, Elgin, NE

Dickerson, James R .... (816) 647-2121
PUB, Windsor Review, Windsor, MO

Dickerson, Julianne K .... (402) 843-5500
PUB, ED, Elgin Review, Elgin, NE

Dickerson, Lee .... (219) 461-8444
MGR-OPER
Fort Wayne Newspapers Inc., Fort Wayne, IN

Dickerson, Lynn .... (972) 424-6565
PUB, Plano Star Courier, Plano, TX

Dickerson, Suzanne .... (615) 836-3284
PUB, ED, Sparta Expositor, Sparta, TN

Dickey, Arden .... (305) 350-2111
VP-Circulation, CIRC VP
Miami Herald, Miami, FL

Dickey, Bob .... (619) 775-4200
PUB, Palm Desert Post, Indio, CA

Dickey, Geraldine .... (219) 235-6161
SEC, South Bend Tribune, South Bend, IN

Dickey, Glenn .... (415) 777-1111
COL-Sports
San Francisco Chronicle, San Francisco, CA

Dickey, James .... (602) 977-8351
PROD MGR-Press
Daily News-Sun, Sun City, AZ

Dickey, Richard .... (910) 727-7211
PROD MGR
Winston-Salem Journal, Winston-Salem, NC

Dickey, Robert J .... (619) 322-8889
PRES, PRES/PUB
Desert Sun, Palm Springs, CA

Dickie, David L .... (412) 465-5555
CIRC MGR, Indiana Gazette, Indiana, PA

Dickinson, Brian .... (401) 277-7000
EDL COL
Providence Journal-Bulletin, Providence, RI

Dickinson, David .... (416) 441-1405
Indochina Photographer
Fotopress Independent News Service International (FPINS), Toronto, ON

Dickinson, Steven Y .... (804) 649-6000
CONT, Media General Inc., Richmond, VA

Dickman, Blaine .... (702) 358-8061
CIRC MGR, Daily Sparks Tribune, Sparks, NV

Dickman, Ed .... (406) 755-7000
PROD FRM-PR
Daily Inter Lake, Kalispell, MT

Dickman, Jack .... (703) 276-3400
ADV VP/ASSOC DIR
USA Today, Arlington, VA

Dickman, Pamela .... (970) 867-5651
Farm/Agriculture ED
Fort Morgan Times, Fort Morgan, CO

Dickman, Sharon .... (716) 232-7100
Deputy EPE-Times-Union
Rochester Democrat and Chronicle; Rochester, NY Times-Union, Rochester, NY

Dickon, Richard .... (201) 759-3200
ED, Belleville Times, Belleville, NJ

Dickover, Jeff .... (618) 654-2366
ED, Highland News Leader, Highland, IL

Dicks, Rudy .... (216) 329-7000
Sports ED, Chronicle-Telegram, Elyria, OH

Dickson, Carolyn .... (801) 237-2188
NIE ED, Deseret News, Salt Lake City, UT

Dickson, Dan .... (423) 929-3111
PROD FRM-COMP
Johnson City Press, Johnson City, TN

Dickson, Gary .... (970) 945-8515
ED/PUB
Glenwood Post, Glenwood Springs, CO

Dickson, Heather .... (819) 647-2204
PUB, GM, Equity, Shawville, QC

Dickson, Joe .... (205) 251-6523
PUB, Birmingham World, Birmingham, AL

Dickson, John .... (810) 766-6100
ASST MAN ED, Flint Journal, Flint, MI

Dickson, Kate B .... (573) 324-2222
PUB, ED
Bowling Green Times, Bowling Green, MO

Dickson, Ross .... (613) 237-8226
PUB, Ottawa XPress, Ottawa, ON

Dicus, Howard .... (202) 898-8254
GEN MGR, Broadcast
United Press International, Washington, DC

DiDonna, Cindy .... (630) 232-9222
Entertainment ED
Kane County Chronicle, Geneva, IL

Diebel, Craig .... (817) 390-7400
VP/Advertising DIR, ADV DIR
Fort Worth Star-Telegram, Fort Worth, TX

Diebel, Joyce .... (847) 696-3133
ED, Des Plaines Times, Park Ridge, IL

Diebold, Robert .... (207) 827-4451
MAN ED, Penobscot Times, Old Town, ME

Diebolt, Judy .... (313) 222-2300
City ED, Detroit News, Detroit, MI

Diefenbach, Thomas .... (814) 870-1600
CONT
Morning News/Erie Daily Times, Erie, PA

Dieffenbacher, Steve .... (541) 776-4411
Special Section Graphics ED
Mail Tribune, Medford, OR

Diehl, Dan .... (913) 336-2175
PUB, ED, Seneca Courier-Tribune, Seneca, KS

Diehl, Darlene .... (515) 547-2811
PUB, Dayton Review, Dayton, IA

Diehl, Don .... (918) 224-5185
MAN ED
Sapulpa Daily Herald, Sapulpa, OK

Diehl, Jackson .... (202) 334-6000
ASST MAN ED-Foreign
Washington Post, Washington, DC

Diehl, James A .... (515) 547-2811
PUB, ED, Dayton Review, Dayton, IA

Diehl, Matt .... (913) 336-2175
MAN ED, Seneca Courier-Tribune, Seneca, KS

Diehl, Pat .... (509) 427-8444
PUB
Skamania County Pioneer, Stevenson, WA

Diehl, Robert .... (804) 649-6000
Copy Desk Chief
Richmond Times-Dispatch, Richmond, VA

Diehl, Robert .... (304) 233-0100
ADV DIR, Intelligencer/Wheeling News-Register, Wheeling, WV

Diehl, Robert .... (616) 796-4831
EDL DIR, Pioneer Group, Big Rapids, MI

Diehl, Scott .... (541) 485-1234
CONT, Register-Guard, Eugene, OR

Diem, Nancy .... (810) 293-8401
PUB, ED, Newberry News, Newberry, MI

Diener, Seymour .... (613) 829-9100
Online MGR, ADTX MGR
Ottawa Citizen, Ottawa, ON

Dierzbicki, Thomas .... (314) 340-8000
PROD MGR-Downtown Plant
St. Louis Post-Dispatch, St. Louis, MO

Diestel, Chet .... (209) 582-0471
Features ED, Hanford Sentinel, Hanford, CA

Dietl, J G .... (507) 752-7181
PUB, ED, Lamberton News, Lamberton, MN

Dietrich, Bill .... (206) 464-2111
SCI Reporter, Seattle Times, Seattle, WA

Dietrich, Doris .... (407) 322-2611
People ED, Society ED
Sanford Herald, Sanford, FL

Dietrich, Matt .... (217) 788-1300
Radio/Television ED
State Journal-Register, Springfield, IL

Dietrich, Tamara .... (518) 792-3131
Features ED, Post-Star, Glens Falls, NY

Dietterle, Dusty A M .... (603) 742-3700
PUB, Tri-Town Transcript, Dover, NH

Dietterle, Paul (Buzz) .... (207) 324-5986
ED, Sanford News, Sanford, ME

Dietz Sr, Bill .... (814) 870-1600
PROD SYS MGR
Morning News/Erie Daily Times, Erie, PA

Dietz, Debbie .... (316) 792-1211
ADV MGR, ADTX MGR
Great Bend Tribune, Great Bend, KS

Dietz, Diane .... (503) 399-6611
EDU ED, Statesman Journal, Salem, OR

Dietz, Laura .... (360) 424-3251
Books/Films ED, Features/Travel ED, Food/Women's ED, Living/Lifestyle ED, Television/Film ED
Skagit Valley Herald, Mount Vernon, WA

Dietz, Robert .... (814) 643-4040
PROD MGR, Daily News, Huntingdon, PA

Dietz, Sharon .... (701) 225-8111
MAN ED, EPE, Religion ED, School ED
Dickinson Press, Dickinson, ND

Dietz, Susan .... (605) 352-6401
MGR-MKTG/PROM
Huron Plainsman, Huron, SD

Dieu, Gary .... (307) 856-2244
PROD FRM-COMP
Riverton Ranger, Riverton, WY

Dievendorf, Steve .... (315) 470-0011
PA, Post-Standard/Syracuse Herald-Journal/American, Syracuse, NY

Difurio, Elspeth .... (609) 871-8000
BUS ED
Burlington County Times, Willingboro, NJ

DiGeronimo, S .... (508) 343-6911
Arts ED, Entertainment/Amusements ED, Fashion/Style ED, Living/Lifestyle ED, Television/Film ED, Theater/Music ED
Sentinel & Enterprise, Fitchburg, MA

Diggins, Nancy .... (514) 987-2222
MGR-PROM, Gazette, Montreal, QC

Diggle Sr, Charles P .... (803) 849-1778
PUB, Moultrie News, Mt. Pleasant, SC

Diggle, Chuck .... (803) 849-1778
GM, ED, Moultrie News, Mt. Pleasant, SC

Diggs, Angel .... (203) 789-5200
Librarian, New Haven Register, New Haven, CT

Diggs, George .... (816) 932-6600
VP-Creative
Universal Press Syndicate, Kansas City, MO

Diggs, Mitchell .... (205) 325-2222
Magazine/Music ED
Birmingham Post-Herald, Birmingham, AL

DiGioia, Robert .... (203) 333-0161
MGR-PROM
Connecticut Post, Bridgeport, CT

DiGiovanni, Nick .... (908) 996-4047
ED, Delaware Valley News, Frenchtown, NJ

Digon, Polly D .... (717) 436-8206
ED, Juniata Sentinel, Mifflintown, PA

Diioia, Anthony .... (212) 327-0998
CEO, Animagic Syndication, New York, NY

Dikeman, Neil .... (316) 223-1460
Features ED, Fort Scott Tribune, Fort Scott, KS

DiLauro Sr, Paul .... (518) 270-1200
PROD DIR, Record, Troy, NY

Diles, Harriett H .... (312) 225-2400
ADV DIR, Chicago Defender, Chicago, IL

Dill, Cecil .... (409) 744-3611
PROD FRM-PR
Galveston County Daily News, Galveston, TX

Dil Who's Where-60

Dill, Joe .... (414) 235-7700
Features ED, News ED
Oshkosh Northwestern, Oshkosh, WI
Dill, Joseph .... (701) 253-7311
ED, Forum, Fargo, ND
Dill, Sheri .... (316) 268-6000
VP/ASSOC PUB, Wichita Eagle, Wichita, KS
Dillaby, Donald .... (603) 889-1590
ED, 1590 Broadcaster, Nashua, NH
Dillard, Dorothy .... (954) 523-5115
GM, Westside Gazette, Fort Lauderdale, FL
Dillard, Lataine Wright .... (512) 394-7402
PUB, ED, Freer Press, Freer, TX
Dillard, Sandra .... (303) 820-1010
Drama Critic, Denver Post, Denver, CO
Dille, John .... (219) 294-1661
PRES, Federated Media Corp., Elkhart, IN
Dille III, John F .... (219) 294-1661
PRES, Elkhart Truth, Elkhart, IN
Dille, Penny .... (303) 776-2244
ADV MGR-CLASS
Daily Times-Call, Longmont, CO
Diller, Bill .... (412) 224-4321
PROD MGR-Distribution Center
Valley News Dispatch, Tarentum, PA
Diller, Brad .... (304) 348-5140
Music ED, Daily Mail, Charleston, WV
Dillin, John .... (617) 450-2000
MAN ED
Christian Science Monitor, Boston, MA
Dillingham, Jed .... (502) 797-3271
PUB, ED, Progress, Dawson Springs, KY
Dillingham, Russel .... (207) 784-5411
Photo ED, Sun-Journal, Lewiston, ME
Dillingham, Scott N .... (502) 797-3271
PUB, MAN ED, Dawson Springs Progress, Dawson Springs, KY
Dillman, Terry .... (814) 447-5506
ED, Valley Log, Orbisonia, PA
Dillon, Carolyn .... (601) 876-5111
PUB, ED, Tylertown Times, Tylertown, MS
Dillon, David .... (214) 977-8222
Architecture Critic
Dallas Morning News, Dallas, TX
Dillon, Jay .... (770) 428-9411
MET ED, Marietta Daily Journal, Marietta, GA
Dillon, Joe .... (617) 929-2000
PROD MGR, Boston Globe, Boston, MA
Dillon, John .... (208) 467-9251
ADV ASST DIR, ADTX MGR
Idaho Press-Tribune, Nampa, ID
Dillon, John A .... (804) 649-6000
Deputy MAN ED-ADM/Photo/Copy Desk
Richmond Times-Dispatch, Richmond, VA
Dillon, Kathy .... (707) 441-0500
Features/Food ED, Women's ED
Times-Standard, Eureka, CA
Dillon, Kim .... (219) 722-5000
MGR-BUS Office
Pharos-Tribune, Logansport, IN
Dillon, Marilyn .... (908) 722-8800
ASST MAN ED
Courier-News, Bridgewater, NJ
Dillon, Mike .... (206) 282-0900
PUB, Queen Anne News, Seattle, WA
Dillon, Patty .... (317) 598-6397
DP MGR, Daily Ledger, Noblesville, IN
Dillon, Roger .... (573) 226-3335
PUB, ED, Current Wave, Eminence, MO
Dillworth, Brock .... (607) 387-3181
ED, Free Press, Trumansburg, NY
DiMaiolo, John .... (908) 922-6000
CONT, Asbury Park Press, Neptune, NJ
DiMambro, John .... (904) 435-8500
ADV DIR, News Journal, Pensacola, FL
DiManno, Susan .... (617) 929-2000
DIR-RES, Boston Globe, Boston, MA
Dimarco, S .... (519) 679-6666
CR MGR, London Free Press, London, ON
DiMaria, Mike .... (312) 321-3000
CIRC MGR-Single Copy Sales & MKTG
Chicago Sun-Times, Chicago, IL
DiMarino, Joe .... (215) 587-4400
VP-Sales & MKTG
MediaStream, Philadelphia, PA
DiMartini, Mark .... (908) 349-3000
City/MET ED, News ED
Ocean County Observer, Toms River, NJ
DiMascio, Debbie .... (330) 688-0088
ED, Hudson Hub-Times, Stow, OH
DiMassa, Mike .... (203) 789-5200
PROD MGR-Preprint Packaging/Distribution
New Haven Register, New Haven, CT
DiMassimo, Debra A .... (413) 447-7311
City ED, Berkshire Eagle, Pittsfield, MA
Dimmitt, James L .... (916) 891-1234
PUB, Chico Enterprise-Record, Chico, CA
Dimond, Dennis .... (309) 686-3000
EDL SYS ED, Online Contact
Journal Star, Peoria, IL
Dimsdale, Sandra .... (315) 792-5000
Features ED, Observer-Dispatch, Utica, NY
Dinar, Nancy B .... (201) 992-1771
MAN ED, West Essex Tribune, Livingston, NJ
DiNardo, Debbie .... (716) 232-7100
MGR-MKTG Projects, Rochester Democrat and Chronicle; Times-Union, Rochester, NY
Dinenger, Rick .... (937) 773-2721
CIRC MGR, Piqua Daily Call, Piqua, OH
Dinger, David .... (208) 377-6200
PROD MGR-Technichal SRV
Idaho Statesman, Boise, ID
Dinger, Mike .... (405) 278-6005
GM, Tinker Take-Off, Oklahoma City, OK
Dingman, Carolyn .... (519) 271-2220
EDU SRV MGR, MGR-MKTG/PROM
Stratford Beacon-Herald, Stratford, ON
Dingman, Charles W .... (519) 271-2220
VP, Co-PUB, GM
Stratford Beacon-Herald, Stratford, ON
Dingman, Stanford H .... (519) 271-2220
PRES, Co-PUB, ED
Stratford Beacon-Herald, Stratford, ON
Dingrando, Joey .... (817) 757-5757
ADV MGR-NTL, Tribune-Herald, Waco, TX
DiNicola, Dan .... (518) 374-4141
Films/Theater ED
Daily Gazette, Schenectady, NY
DiNicola, Tony .... (608) 754-3311
Graphics ED/Art DIR
Janesville Gazette, Janesville, WI
Dinkel, John .... (814) 946-7411
ADV MGR-Outside Sales
Altoona Mirror, Altoona, PA
Dinnerstein, Madelyn .... (216) 329-7000
EDU ED, Chronicle-Telegram, Elyria, OH
Dinnes, Richard .... (705) 472-3200
EDU SRV MGR, ADV MGR, ADV MGR-GEN
North Bay Nugget, North Bay, ON
Dinsmore, Dan .... (805) 273-2700
Sports ED
Antelope Valley Press, Palmdale, CA
Dinsmore, Pam .... (916) 321-1000
EX News ED
Sacramento Bee, Sacramento, CA
Dinville, Julia .... (712) 246-3097
News ED, Valley News Today, Shenandoah, IA
Diodato, Fred .... (313) 222-6400
PROD OPER MGR
Detroit Newspapers, Detroit, MI
Diog, Becky .... (306) 445-7261
ED, Maidstone Mirror, North Battleford, SK
Dion, Jacques .... (514) 667-4360
ED, Contact Laval, Laval Des Rapides, QC
Dion, Jill .... (203) 926-2080
ED, Milford Mirror, Monroe, CT
Dionne, Joseph L .... (212) 208-8000
COB/CEO, Corporation Records, Daily News, New York, NY
Diorio, Ralph .... (610) 696-1775
PROD SUPT-PR
Daily Local News, West Chester, PA
Diotte, Rob .... (604) 723-8171
MAN ED
Alberni Valley Times, Port Alberni, BC
Di Paolo, Carolyn .... (219) 461-8222
ASST MAN ED, News-Sentinel, Fort Wayne, IN
DiPaolo, Roger .... (330) 296-9657
MGR-EDU SRV, EX ED, Building Pages ED, EPE, Religion ED
Record-Courier, Kent-Ravenna, OH
Diperi, Sal .... (516) 265-3500
PUB, ED, Messenger, Smithtown, NY
Di Pietro, Sylvia .... (212) 255-4059
Self-Syndicator
Di Pietro, Sylvia, New York, NY
Dippel, Carolyn .... (941) 294-7731
ADV MGR, News Chief, Winter Haven, FL
Dippold, Jude .... (814) 723-8200
MAN ED, BUS/FIN ED, EPE
Warren Times-Observer, Warren, PA
DiPreta, Mike .... (212) 930-8000
ADV MGR-RES, New York Post, New York, NY
DiPrima, Pat .... (815) 338-5096
MKTG DIR
Spectrum Syndicate, Woodstock, IL
Dir, James .... (602) 488-3436
ED, Foothills Sentinel, Cave Creek, AZ
Diricco, Heloise C .... (707) 643-1706
SEC, Benicia Herald, Vallejo, CA
DiSalvo, Tony .... (813) 259-7711
ADV DIR, Tribune and Times, Tampa, FL
Di Sandro, Deb .... (847) 639-1232
Author/Owner, Slightly Off, Cary, IL
Disante, Linda .... (412) 775-3200
Librarian, Beaver County Times, Beaver, PA
DiSanto, Gary .... (609) 663-6000
CIRC DIR, Courier-Post, Cherry Hill, NJ
Dischler, Kenneth P .... (715) 762-4940
PUB, ED, Park Falls Herald, Park Falls, WI
Disco, Connie .... (308) 345-4500
Lifestyle ED
McCook Daily Gazette, McCook, NE
Dise, Alan .... (716) 849-3434
Graphics ED, Buffalo News, Buffalo, NY
Dishman, Matt .... (804) 793-2311
ADV MGR-PROM, DIR-PROM
Danville Register & Bee, Danville, VA
Disney, Walt .... (405) 321-1800
ADV DIR, Norman Transcript, Norman, OK
DiStaso, John .... (603) 668-4321
COL, Union Leader, Manchester, NH
DiStaulo, Tony .... (514) 987-2222
Purchasing MGR, Gazette, Montreal, QC
Distelheim, Joe .... (205) 532-4000
ED, Huntsville Times, Huntsville, AL
DiTommaso, Lois .... (201) 646-4000
ASST MAN ED-Special Sections, Features ED
Record, Hackensack, NJ
Ditter, Lori .... (414) 922-4600
ADTX MGR, Reporter, Fond du Lac, WI
Ditterline, Sue .... (215) 949-4000
Librarians
Bucks County Courier Times, Levittown, PA
Dittmann, James .... (414) 887-0321
PROD MGR, Daily Citizen, Beaver Dam, WI
Dittmer, Dawn .... (816) 254-8600
DP MGR, Examiner, Independence, MO
Ditto, Brian .... (410) 876-4670
ED, Community Times, Westminster, MD
Ditzel, Al .... (908) 349-3000
Sports ED
Ocean County Observer, Toms River, NJ
DiUbaldi, Mario G .... (212) 803-8200
PUB, American Banker, New York, NY
Divelbiss, David R .... (814) 938-8740
ED, City ED, EPE, Photo DEPT MGR
Spirit, Punxsutawney, PA
Divelbiss, Judy .... (614) 397-5333
City ED, News, Mount Vernon, OH
Divibiss, Wick .... (814) 938-8740
ED, Jefferson County Neighbors, Punxsutawney, PA
DiVito, Allyn .... (813) 259-7711
Photo DIR, Tribune and Times, Tampa, FL
Dix, Albert E .... (330) 264-1125
PRES, Daily Record, Wooster, OH
Dix Communications
Dix Jr, Charles C .... (330) 264-1125
VP, Dix Communications, Wooster, OH
Dix, Christopher Scorell .... (415) 348-4321
PUB
San Mateo County Times, San Mateo, CA
Dix, David E .... (330) 264-1125
VP, Dix Communications, Wooster, OH
Dix II, G Charles .... (330) 264-1125
TREAS, Dix Communications, Wooster, OH
Dix, Grady T .... (804) 793-2311
Day ED, Register & Bee, Danville, VA
Dix, Natalie .... (904) 252-1511
EPE, News-Journal, Daytona Beach, FL
Dix, R C .... (614) 435-3531
PUB
New Concord Area Leader, Cambridge, OH
Dix, Raymond Victor .... (330) 264-1125
VP, Dix Communications, Wooster, OH
Dix, Robert .... (603) 668-4321
Cartoonist, Union Leader, Manchester, NH
Dix, Robert .... (614) 425-1912
PUB, Barnesville Enterprise, Barnesville, OH
Dix Jr, Robert C .... (330) 264-1125
SEC, Dix Communications, Wooster, OH
Dix, Robert Victor .... (330) 264-1125
VP, Dix Communications, Wooster, OH
Dix, Troy .... (502) 227-4556
PUB, State Journal, Frankfort, KY
Dix Maenza, Ann .... (502) 227-4556
PUB, ADTX MGR, State Journal, Frankfort, KY
Dixon, Al .... (334) 262-5026
PUB, ED, Montgomery/Tuskegee Times, Montgomery, AL
Dixon, Bill .... (616) 946-2000
PROD MGR-PR
Record-Eagle, Traverse City, MI
Dixon, Brandi .... (405) 326-3311
CIRC DIR, Hugo Daily News, Hugo, OK
Dixon, Chris .... (419) 448-3200
ADV DIR, Advertiser-Tribune, Tiffin, OH
Dixon, Claude .... (914) 331-5000
Religion ED, Daily Freeman, Kingston, NY
Dixon, David .... (502) 827-2000
MAN ED, Gleaner, Henderson, KY
Dixon, Ellie .... (802) 748-8121
MAN ED, Caledonian-Record, St. Johnsbury, VT
Dixon, Frank .... (303) 820-1010
VP-Production, PROD VP
Denver Post, Denver, CO
Dixon, Pam .... (704) 245-6431
PROD MGR/FRM-COMP
Daily Courier, Forest City, NC
Dixon, Phil .... (215) 854-2000
ASSOC MAN ED
Philadelphia Inquirer, Philadelphia, PA
Dixon, Robert J .... (207) 791-6650
ASST MAN ED-Copy Desk Chief
Portland Press Herald, Portland, ME
Dixon, Rod .... (816) 646-2411
ADV MGR
Constitution-Tribune, Chillicothe, MO
Dixon, Schuyler .... (915) 653-1221
Sports ED, Standard-Times, San Angelo, TX
Dixon, Ted E .... (360) 532-4000
PUB, Daily World, Aberdeen, WA
Dlugoborski, Robert .... (416) 531-2491
ED, Zwiazkowiec, Toronto, ON
Dmoch, Tim .... (810) 360-6397
ED
Spinal Column Newsweekly, Union Lake, MI
Dmuchowski, Edward .... (516) 223-6514
MAN ED, Polish American World, Baldwin, NY
Do, Yen .... (714) 892-9414
PUB, Nguoi Viet Daily News, Westminster, CA
Doak, Richard .... (515) 284-8000
EPE, Des Moines Register, Des Moines, IA
Doak, William .... (860) 289-6468
ED, Gazette, East Hartford, CT
Doan, Mary .... (904) 312-5200
News ED, Daily News, Palatka, FL
Doane, Chris .... (770) 227-3276
PROD SUPV-Pre Press
Griffin Daily News, Griffin, GA
Doane, Darlene .... (970) 842-5516
PUB, ED, Brush News-Tribune, Brush, CO
Dobbins, Gary L .... (805) 684-4428
PUB, Coastal View, Carpinteria, CA
Dobbins, Kathy .... (219) 461-8444
PROD MGR-Budget/Warehouse
Fort Wayne Newspapers Inc., Fort Wayne, IN
Dobbins, Keith .... (864) 224-4321
PROD MGR-PR
Anderson Independent-Mail, Anderson, SC
Dobbs, Gary M .... (281) 422-8302
PUB, ED, Baytown Sun, Baytown, TX
Dobbs, Sherri .... (913) 462-3963
BM, Colby Free Press, Colby, KS
Dobbyn, Karen .... (617) 786-7000
DIR-ADM, Patriot Ledger, Quincy, MA
Dobie, Bruce .... (615) 244-7989
ED, Nashville Scene, Nashville, TN
Dobrow, Mark .... (908) 722-8800
News ED, Courier-News, Bridgewater, NJ
Dobs, Gerald .... (717) 255-8100
Graphics ED, Patriot-News, Harrisburg, PA
Dobson, Barbara .... (803) 572-0511
GM, Goose Creek Gazette, Goose Creek, SC
Dobson PhD, James C .... (719) 531-3304
Author
Briargate Media, Colorado Springs, CO
Dobson, Joe .... (501) 425-6301
ED, Daily News, Mountain Home, AR
Dobson, Larry .... (507) 794-3511
PUB, ED, Herald-Dispatch, Sleepy Eye, MN
Dobson, Richard .... (414) 224-2000
Senior VP-Advertising, ADV VP
Milwaukee Journal Sentinel, Milwaukee, WI
Dobson, Valdean R .... (423) 638-4181
Copy ED, Greeneville Sun, Greeneville, TN
Dockeney Jr, Edward W .... (304) 725-2046
ED, Spirit of Jefferson Advocate, Charles Town, WV
Dockery, Bill .... (423) 522-5399
ED, Metro Pulse, Knoxville, TN
Dockery, Sherrie .... (910) 888-3500
News ED, Wire ED
High Point Enterprise, High Point, NC
Dockham, Janice .... (306) 565-8211
MGR-Human Resources
Leader-Post, Regina, SK
Dockstader, Dan .... (307) 886-5727
PUB, ED, Star Valley Independent, Afton, WY
Doctor, Kenneth .... (612) 222-5011
MAN ED, St. Paul Pioneer Press, St. Paul, MN
Doctorian, Sonya .... (813) 893-8111
Photo ED
St. Petersburg Times, St. Petersburg, FL
Doctorow, Daniel .... (718) 624-0536
ADV MGR-Legal
Daily Bulletin, Brooklyn, NY
Dodd, Donald D .... (573) 729-4126
MAN ED, Salem News, Salem, MO
Dodd, J David .... (312) 321-3000
EVP/CFO, Chicago Sun-Times, Chicago, IL
Dodd III, J Edward .... (334) 585-2331
PUB, ED, Abbeville Herald, Abbeville, AL
Dodd, Monroe .... (816) 234-4141
News ED, Kansas City Star, Kansas City, MO
Dodd, Robert .... (910) 343-2000
PROD FRM-PR, Morning Star/Sunday Star-News, Wilmington, NC
Dodd, Rusty .... (912) 744-4200
PROD Senior SUPV-Pre Press
Macon Telegraph, Macon, GA
Dodder, Joanna .... (505) 257-4001
ED, Ruidoso News, Ruidoso, NM
Dodds, Don .... (408) 920-5000
PROD CNR (Night)
San Jose Mercury News, San Jose, CA
Dodds, Donald .... (913) 742-2111
PROD MGR
Hiawatha Daily World, Hiawatha, KS
Dodds, John T .... (518) 792-9914
DIR-Newspaper Sales & Interactive Services
TV Data, Queensbury, NY

Copyright ©1997 by the Editor & Publisher Co.

61-Who's Where **Dor**

Dodds, Richard (504) 826-3279
Films/Theater ED
Times-Picayune, New Orleans, LA

Dodds, Stuart (415) 777-7212
ED/GM
Chronicle Features, San Francisco, CA

Dodds, Tracy (512) 445-3500
Sports ED, American-Statesman, Austin, TX

Dodge, John (360) 754-5400
Environmental Reporter
Olympian, Olympia, WA

Dodge, Larry R (313) 994-6989
ADV DIR-Sales & MKTG
Ann Arbor News, Ann Arbor, MI
Advance Publications (Booth Newspapers)

Dodge, Rose (603) 752-5858
MAN ED, Berlin Daily Sun, Berlin, NH

Dodson, Barb (219) 294-1661
Home Furnishings ED
Elkhart Truth, Elkhart, IN

Dodson, Dave (704) 358-5000
ADV MGR-Sales Development/Special Sections, Charlotte Observer, Charlotte, NC

Dodson, Don (217) 351-5252
BUS ED, News-Gazette, Champaign, IL

Dodson, Jennifer (573) 333-4336
ED
Tuesday Democrat-Argus, Caruthersville, MO

Dodson, Julie (519) 255-5711
Administrative ASST
Windsor Star, Windsor, ON

Dodson, Martha W (901) 784-2531
ED, Chronicle, Humboldt, TN

Dodson, Shae (806) 376-4488
Health/Medical ED, Amarillo Daily News/Globe Times, Amarillo, TX

Doeden, Dennis (701) 253-7311
ASST MAN ED, Graphics ED
Forum, Fargo, ND

Doerfler, Ronald J (212) 456-7777
Sr VP/CFO, ABC Inc., New York, NY

Doering, Ed (204) 937-8377
ED, Roblin Review, Roblin, MB

Dogali, Mike (203) 846-3281
DP MGR, PROD DIR-DP, Hour, Norwalk, CT

Dogan, Reggie (904) 435-8500
Environmental ED, ASST MET ED
Pensacola News Journal, Pensacola, FL

Dogg-Fulton, Susan (613) 739-7000
ADV ASSOC DIR, Ottawa Sun, Ottawa, ON

Doheny, Kathy (213) 237-5000
Health Writer (freelance contributor)
Los Angeles Times, Los Angeles, CA

Doherty, Brad (210) 542-4301
Photo ED
El Heraldo de Brownsville, Brownsville, TX

Doherty, Jayne (609) 272-7000
ADV MGR-CLASS
Press of Atlantic City, Pleasantville, NJ

Doherty, Martin (519) 822-4310
CIRC MGR, Daily Mercury, Guelph, ON

Dohrer, Kim (605) 996-5514
State ED, Daily Republic, Mitchell, SD

Dohrman, Kathryn (816) 529-2888
PUB, Slater News-Rustler, Slater, MO

Dohy, Mike (403) 250-4200
INFO SRV MGR, Calgary Sun, Calgary, AB

Doig, Becky (306) 445-7261
ED
Northwest Neighbors, North Battleford, SK

Doke, Mike (541) 386-1234
ED, Hood River News, Hood River, OR

Dolan, Beth (813) 259-7711
RE ED, Tampa Tribune and Times, Tampa, FL

Dolan, Christopher (301) 459-3131
City/MET ED
Prince George's Journal, Lanham, MD

Dolan, Dallas (913) 843-1000
PROD MGR, Journal-World, Lawrence, KS

Dolan, James P (414) 276-0273
PRES/CEO, Daily Reporter, Milwaukee, WI

Dolan, Jim (612) 333-4244
PRES/CEO
Finance and Commerce, Minneapolis, MN

Dolan, Jim P (405) 235-3100
COB, Journal Record, Oklahoma City, OK

Dolan, Maura (213) 237-5000
Legal Affairs Writer
Los Angeles Times, Los Angeles, CA

Doland, Ross (317) 962-1575
PROD DIR, Palladium-Item, Richmond, IN

Dolata, Al (609) 691-5000
PRES, PUB, Daily Journal, Vineland, NJ

Dolbeabe, James R (617) 245-0080
PROD FRM
Wakefield Daily Item, Wakefield, MA

Dolbeare, Glenn D (617) 245-0080
PRES, GM, CONT/PSL MGR, CIRC MGR
Wakefield Daily Item, Wakefield, MA

Dolbeare, Robert P (617) 245-0080
PUB, Wakefield Daily Item, Wakefield, MA

Dolbee, Sandi (619) 299-3131
Religion/Ethics ED
San Diego Union-Tribune, San Diego, CA

Dolce, Steven P (401) 722-4000
CIRC DIR, Times, Pawtucket, RI

Dold, R Bruce (312) 222-3232
COL, Deputy EPE
Chicago Tribune, Chicago, IL

Dolen, Christine (305) 350-2111
Drama Critic, Miami Herald, Miami, FL

Dolen, John (954) 356-4000
Arts/Features ED
Sun-Sentinel, Fort Lauderdale, FL

Doler, Kathleen (800) 223-2154
Silicon Valley BU Chief
Investor's Business Daily, Los Angeles, CA

Dolezal, Melinda (303) 820-1010
MGR-CR, Denver Post, Denver, CO

Doll, Julie (914) 454-2000
City ED
Poughkeepsie Journal, Poughkeepsie, NY

Dollar, Don (205) 698-8148
PUB, ED, Lamar Leader, Sulligent, AL

Dollar, Rob (502) 886-4444
ASSOC ED-News OPER
Kentucky New Era, Hopkinsville, KY

Dolphens, Tom (816) 234-4141
Design DIR
Kansas City Star, Kansas City, MO

Dolye, Patrick (414) 542-2501
PUB
Waukesha County Freeman, Waukesha, WI

Domain, Edward V (847) 427-4300
PROD MGR-PR/MR
Daily Herald, Arlington Heights, IL

Domaingue II, Edward C (603) 668-4321
ED-Night
Manchester Union Leader, Manchester, NH

Doman, Lacy (407) 322-2611
Assignment ED, Sanford Herald, Sanford, FL

Dombrowski, Ed (517) 895-8551
MGR-MKTG/Creative
Bay City Times, Bay City, MI

Dombrowski, Jim (313) 242-1100
PROD MGR-Pre Press
Monroe Evening News, Monroe, MI

Domeyer, Debra S (213) 237-3700
VP-Information SYS
Times Mirror Co., Los Angeles, CA

Domico, Patrick P (814) 765-5581
ADV EX-MKTG
Clearfield Progress, Clearfield, PA

Domingue, Dawn (318) 824-3011
Family/Living ED
Jennings Daily News, Jennings, LA

Domingue, Roland (318) 783-3450
PROD SUPT, Crowley Post-Signal, Crowley, LA

Dominick, Beverly (803) 771-6161
ASST to EX ED, State, Columbia, SC

Dominick, Linda (813) 397-5563
PUB, Seminole Beacon, Largo, FL

Domotor, Sharon (306) 682-2561
MAN ED, Humboldt Journal, Humboldt, SK

Domres, William (701) 537-5610
GM, ED, Mouse River Journal, Towner, ND

Domyan, Karen (618) 939-3814
GM, Waterloo Republic-Times, Waterloo, IL

Donadio, Bruce (518) 374-4141
PROD MGR, Daily Gazette, Schenectady, NY

Donadio, Edward (203) 789-5200
MGR-CR
New Haven Register, New Haven, CT

Donahoo, M (508) 343-6911
NTL ED, News ED
Sentinel & Enterprise, Fitchburg, MA

Donahue, Jim (907) 257-4200
MGR-CR
Anchorage Daily News, Anchorage, AK

Donahue Jr, John L (520) 573-4561
ASST SEC, Tucson Citizen, Tucson, AZ

Donahue, Lisa (619) 270-3103
MAN ED, Beach & Bay Press, San Diego, CA

Donahue, Michael (901) 529-2211
Society Reporter
Commercial Appeal, Memphis, TN

Donahue, Thomas (716) 372-3121
MAN ED, Olean Times-Herald, Olean, NY

Donald, David (912) 236-9511
Environmental ED, Health/EDU ED
Savannah Morning News, Savannah, GA

Donald, Wendy (404) 526-5151
ADTX MGR
Atlanta Journal-Constitution, Atlanta, GA

Donaldson, Dusty (910) 888-3500
Automotive ED
High Point Enterprise, High Point, NC

Donaldson, Ernest R (412) 222-2200
PROD FRM (Night)
Observer-Reporter, Washington, PA

Donaldson, Fred (215) 885-4111
PUB, Leader, Philadelphia, PA

Donaldson, George (416) 367-2000
PROD MGR-Electrical DEPT
Toronto Star, Toronto, ON

Donaldson, John (608) 767-3655
ED, News-Sickle-Arrow, Black Earth, WI

Donaldson, Nancy (501) 534-3400
ADV DIR
Pine Bluff Commercial, Pine Bluff, AR

Donaldson, Pat (423) 246-8121
ADV MGR-CLASS
Kingsport Times-News, Kingsport, TN

Donaldson, William (402) 444-1000
Sr VP, Omaha World-Herald Co., Omaha, NE

Donati, Richard (410) 332-6000
CIRC MGR-Distribution & Fleet
Sun, Baltimore, MD

Donato, Andrew (416) 947-2222
CORP Art DIR, Toronto Sun, Toronto, ON

Doncevic, Lois (610) 820-6500
Library DIR, Morning Call, Allentown, PA

Doncsecz, Steve (610) 820-6500
PROD FRM-Packaging
Morning Call, Allentown, PA

Dondoneau, Dave (701) 857-1900
Sports ED, Minot Daily News, Minot, ND

Donegan, Brenda (614) 387-0400
Food ED, Religion ED
Marion Star, Marion, OH

Donelly, Lucille (216) 576-9115
ED, Gazette, Jefferson, OH

Doner, Robert A (517) 857-2500
PUB, ED, Springport Signal, Springport, MI

Dones, M Ofelia (201) 864-9505
GM, Continental Newspaper, Union City, NJ

Doney, Gerald G (519) 271-2220
CIRC MGR, Beacon-Herald, Stratford, ON

Donham, James B (508) 793-9100
ASST MAN ED
Telegram & Gazette, Worcester, MA

Donily, Barbara (970) 625-3245
GM, MAN ED, Citizen Telegram, Rifle, CO

Donivan, Jim (703) 276-3400
CIRC GM-Detroit, USA Today, Arlington, VA

Donley, Paul E (417) 678-2115
PUB, Aurora Advertiser, Aurora, MO

Donley, Reba (405) 323-5151
ADV MGR-NTL
Clinton Daily News, Clinton, OK

Donlon, Chris (315) 637-3121
ED, Fayetteville-Manilus Eagle Bulletin, Fayetteville, NY

Donna, James M (212) 621-1500
VP/SEC/DIR of Human Resources
Associated Press, New York, NY

Donnally, Trish (415) 777-1111
Fashion ED
San Francisco Chronicle, San Francisco, CA

Donnaruma, Pamela (617) 227-8929
PUB, ED, Boston Post Gazette, Boston, MA

Donnell, Megan (501) 785-7700
BUS/FIN ED
Southwest Times Record, Fort Smith, AR

Donnellon, William (201) 428-6200
ED, Daily Record, Parsippany, NJ

Donnelly, Cheryl (704) 252-5611
PROD CNR
Asheville Citizen-Times, Asheville, NC

Donnelly, Christine (808) 525-8000
EDU Reporter
Honolulu Star-Bulletin, Honolulu, HI

Donnelly, Dave (707) 468-3500
Sports ED, Ukiah Daily Journal, Ukiah, CA

Donnelly, Dave (808) 525-8000
COL, Honolulu Star-Bulletin, Honolulu, HI

Donnelly, Edward (718) 981-1234
News ED
Staten Island Advance, Staten Island, NY

Donnelly, George (617) 433-8200
ED, Boston TAB, Needham, MA

Donnelly, Jim (609) 871-8000
ASSOC ED, Automotive ED
Burlington County Times, Willingboro, NJ

Donnelly, John (312) 222-3232
CIRC DIR-OPER
Chicago Tribune, Chicago, IL

Donnelly, John R (609) 871-8000
PROD DIR
Burlington County Times, Willingboro, NJ

Donnelly, Joseph L (412) 465-5555
Chairman, Co-PUB
Indiana Gazette, Indiana, PA

Donnelly, Michael J (412) 465-5555
PRES, Co-PUB, Indiana Gazette, Indiana, PA

Donnelly, Mindy (954) 356-4000
Palm Beach ED
Sun-Sentinel, Fort Lauderdale, FL

Donnelly, Patty (816) 932-6600
EDL Services MGR
Universal Press Syndicate, Kansas City, MO

Donnelly, Shannon (561) 820-3800
Society ED
Palm Beach Daily News, Palm Beach, FL

Donnelly, Tom (601) 762-1111
BUS ED, Mississippi Press, Pascagoula, MS

Donney, Frank J (807) 868-2701
PUB, ED, Bear News, Hornepayne, ON

D'Onofrio, John (401) 277-7000
ADV MGR-Plans/Statistics
Providence Journal-Bulletin, Providence, RI

D'Onofrio, Ralf (212) 930-8000
ADV DIR-CLASS, New York Post, New York, NY

Donoghue, Jack (308) 995-4441
Sports ED
Holdrege Daily Citizen, Holdrege, NE

Donoghue, Marge (317) 473-6641
Agriculture ED, Peru Tribune, Peru, IN

Donoghue, Peter (908) 922-6000
Night ED, Asbury Park Press, Neptune, NJ

Donohue, Jerry (501) 935-5525
ADV DIR, Jonesboro Sun, Jonesboro, AR

Donohue, Maureen L (513) 721-2700
VP-Labor Relations
Cincinnati Enquirer, Cincinnati, OH

Donohue, Mike (703) 276-3400
CIRC GM-Seattle, USA Today, Arlington, VA

Donohue, Peter (703) 276-3400
CIRC GM-New York
USA Today, Arlington, VA

Donohue, Roberta (310) 454-1321
PUB, Palisadian-Post, Pacific Palisades, CA

Donovan, Betty (715) 842-2101
DIR-Human Resources
Wausau Daily Herald, Wausau, WI

Donovan, Bill (506) 653-6806
MAN ED
New Freeman Catholic, Saint John, NB

Donovan, Brian (607) 734-5151
CIRC DIR, Star-Gazette, Elmira, NY

Donovan, Donna M (315) 792-5000
PUB, Observer-Dispatch, Utica, NY

Donovan, Helen W (617) 929-2000
EX ED, Boston Globe, Boston, MA

Donovan, Lauren (701) 748-2255
ED, Hazen Star, Hazen, ND

Donovan, Liz (305) 350-2111
RES MGR, Miami Herald, Miami, FL

Donovan, Mark (919) 419-6500
Body/Mind (Health) ED, Books ED
Herald-Sun, Durham, NC

Donovan, Michael (617) 426-3000
PROD ASST MGR,
Boston Herald, Boston, MA

Donovan, Phyllis (203) 235-1661
Community News ED
Record-Journal, Meriden, CT

Donovan, Rhonda (415) 777-5700
MGR-Payroll, San Francisco Newspaper Agency, San Francisco, CA

Donovan, Tom (317) 633-1240
ADV MGR-CLASS
Indianapolis Star/News, Indianapolis, IN

Donze, Elmo L (573) 547-8005
PUB, Perryville Sun Times, Perryville, MO

Doo, Jack (209) 578-2000
Wine Writer, Modesto Bee, Modesto, CA

Doody, Cheryl (506) 433-1070
GM, Kings County Record, Sussex, NB

Doogan, Mike (907) 257-4200
COL, Anchorage Daily News, Anchorage, AK

Doolen, Dina (520) 723-5441
ED, Coolidge Examiner, Casa Grande, AZ

Dooley, Jim (516) 843-2020
Photo DIR, Newsday, Melville, NY

Dooley, Michael (401) 277-7000
VP-Circulation, CIRC VP
Providence Journal-Bulletin, Providence, RI

Dooley, Pat (757) 446-2000
Food/Home Furnishings ED
Virginian-Pilot, Norfolk, VA

Dooley, Richard (519) 822-4310
EDU, Daily Mercury, Guelph, ON

Doolittle, Lucinda (208) 377-6200
Radio/Television ED
Idaho Statesman, Boise, ID

Doornenbal, Bob (403) 835-4925
PUB, Fairview Post, Fairview, AB

Dopf, R Stuart (208) 257-3515
PUB, ED, Upper Country News-Reporter, Cambridge, ID

DoRais, Michel (514) 546-3271
PUB, ED, La Penseede Bagot, Acton Vale, QC

Doram, D R (403) 328-4411
PUB/GM, Lethbridge Herald, Lethbridge, AB

Doran, Gary (519) 255-5711
DP MGR, Windsor Star, Windsor, ON

Doran, Terry (716) 849-3434
Entertainment ED
Buffalo News, Buffalo, NY

Doran, Thomas C (815) 584-3007
GM, Dwight Star & Herald, Dwight, IL

Dore, Marc (514) 285-7272
MET ED, SCI/Technology ED, Sunday ED
La Presse, Montreal, QC

Dorge, Gerald L (204) 949-6100
PUB, Metro, Winnipeg, MB

Dorksen, Bob (216) 999-4500
Picture ED, Plain Dealer, Cleveland, OH

Dorman, Brenda (812) 283-6636
EDU ED, Evening News, Jeffersonville, IN

Dor Who's Where-62

Dorman, Jay .... (713) 220-7171
City ED-Weekend
Houston Chronicle, Houston, TX

Dormann, Henry O .... (212) 759-5571
Chairman/EIC
Sipa News Service, New York, NY

Dorn, Daryl .... (817) 390-7400
DIR Technology
Fort Worth Star-Telegram, Fort Worth, TX

Dorn, Lowell .... (706) 724-0851
ADTX MGR, Augusta Chronicle, Augusta, GA

Dornbusch, Jane .... (617) 426-3000
Food ED, Boston Herald, Boston, MA

Dorner, Lorrie .... (903) 496-7297
PUB, ED, Wolfe City Mirror, Wolfe City, TX

Dorney, Matt .... (219) 881-3000
Sports ED, Post-Tribune, Gary, IN

Dornfeld, Steven .... (612) 222-5011
EDL Writer
St. Paul Pioneer Press, St. Paul, MN

Doroff, Ronald .... (320) 251-1971
PUB, ED
Sauk Rapids Herald, Sauk Rapids, MN

Doron, Meir .... (818) 783-3090
GM, ED, Shalom L.A., Van Nuys, CA

Doroz, Bob .... (204) 694-2022
GM, Winnipeg Sun, Winnipeg, MB

Dorr, Joe .... (217) 824-2233
ADV DIR, Daily Breeze-Courier, Taylorville, IL

Dorr, Luther J .... (612) 389-1222
ED, Princeton Union-Eagle, Princeton, MN

Dorr, Richard .... (503) 221-8327
PROD SUPT-COMP, Oregonian, Portland, OR

Dorrance, Saundra .... (303) 773-8313
GM, Villager, Greenwood Village, CO

Dorrance, Warren L .... (715) 234-2121
PUB, Rice Lake Chronotype, Rice Lake, WI

Dorrell, Karen .... (405) 321-1800
News ED, Norman Transcript, Norman, OK

Dorris, Barbara .... (601) 335-1155
DP MGR, PROD FRM-COMP
Delta Democrat Times, Greenville, MS

Dorschner, Larry .... (330) 629-6200
PUB, Boardman Town Crier, Youngstown, OH

Dorsett, Greg .... (616) 722-3161
Photo ED, Muskegon Chronicle, Muskegon, MI

Dorsey, Barbara A .... (515) 532-2871
PUB, ED
Clarion Wright County Monitor, Clarion, IA

Dorsey, Chris .... (515) 462-2101
ED, Winterset Madisonian, Winterset, IA

Dorsey, Dean .... (308) 784-3644
PUB, Tri-City Trib, Cozad, NE

Dorsey, George .... (301) 662-1177
Courts Reporter
Frederick Post/The News, Frederick, MD

Dorsey, Helen .... (310) 273-2245
CEO
Dorsey Communications, Los Angeles, CA

Dorsey, Most Rev Norbert M .... (407) 660-9141
PUB, Florida Catholic, Orlando, FL

Dorsey, R Meade .... (304) 725-2046
GM, Spirit of Jefferson Advocate, Charles Town, WV

Dorsey, Tom .... (502) 582-4011
Radio/Television ED
Courier-Journal, Louisville, KY

Dosik, Duke .... (602) 468-6565
MAN ED, Daily Racing Form, Phoenix, AZ

Doss, Dennis .... (410) 749-7171
PROD DIR, Daily Times, Salisbury, MD

Doss, George .... (913) 295-1111
PROD FRM-COMP (Night)
Topeka Capital-Journal, Topeka, KS

Doss, Jill .... (704) 249-3981
Political ED, Dispatch, Lexington, NC

Doss, Lisa .... (910) 623-2155
Graphics ED/Art DIR
Daily News, Eden, NC

Doss, Rick .... (410) 749-7171
PROD MGR-Commercial Print
Daily Times, Salisbury, MD

Doss, Rod .... (412) 481-8302
GM, New Pittsburgh Courier, Pittsburgh, PA

Dostal, Nancy .... (515) 484-2841
ED, Toledo Chronicle, Tama, IA

Dotine, Larry .... (360) 779-4464
MAN ED
Kitsap County Herald, Poulsbo, WA

Dotson Jr, D Boyd .... (304) 847-5828
PUB, ED
Webster Echo, Webster Springs, WV

Dotson, Gary .... (618) 234-1000
City ED
Belleville News-Democrat, Belleville, IL

Dotson Jr, John L .... (330) 996-3000
PRES, PUB
Akron Beacon Journal, Akron, OH

Dotson, Roger .... (706) 554-2111
ED, Sentinel, Waynesboro, GA

Dottavio, Peggy .... (330) 833-2631
Living/Society ED
Independent, Massillon, OH

Doty, Deborah A .... (402) 845-2728
PUB, ED, Doniphan Herald, Doniphan, NE

Doty, Timothy P .... (614) 461-5000
ADV MGR-RT
Columbus Dispatch, Columbus, OH

Douan, Crystalee .... (250) 427-5333
ED, Daily Bulletin, Kimberley, BC

Doubek, Madeleine L .... (847) 427-4300
Political ED
Daily Herald, Arlington Heights, IL

Doucet, Dany .... (514) 375-4555
Newsroom MGR, News ED
La Voix de l'Est, Granby, QC

Doucet, Janet .... (318) 783-3450
Features ED, Post-Signal, Crowley, LA

Doucet, Nicole .... (601) 442-9101
BM, Natchez Democrat, Natchez, MS

Doucet, Thomas .... (864) 582-4511
MGR-TELEMKTG
Herald-Journal, Spartanburg, SC

Doucette, Bob .... (405) 794-5555
ED, Moore American, Moore, OK

Doud, Don .... (209) 578-2000
ADV MGR-RT, Modesto Bee, Modesto, CA

Doud, Kathy .... (616) 345-3511
Music ED
Kalamazoo Gazette, Kalamazoo, MI

Douga, Billy .... (318) 527-7075
MGR-MKTG/PROM, CIRC MGR
Southwest Daily News, Sulphur, LA

Dougall, Elizabeth .... (807) 622-8588
PUB, Thunder Bay Post, Thunder Bay, ON

Dougan, Dan .... (219) 461-8444
MGR-CR
Fort Wayne Newspapers Inc., Fort Wayne, IN

Dougdale, Gail .... (816) 468-5999
GM, Sun Chronicle, Kansas City, MO.

Dougherty, Chuck .... (305) 350-2111
PROD MGR-Electrical
Miami Herald, Miami, FL

Dougherty, Dick .... (215) 949-4000
EX Sports ED
Bucks County Courier Times, Levittown, PA

Dougherty, Kathleen .... (310) 540-5511
Political ED, Daily Breeze, Torrance, CA

Dougherty, Patrick .... (907) 257-4200
MAN ED
Anchorage Daily News, Anchorage, AK

Dougherty, Robert C .... (970) 464-5614
ED, Palisade Tribune, Palisade, CO

Dougherty, Robin .... (305) 350-2111
Television Critic
Miami Herald, Miami, FL

Doughton, James .... (941) 953-7755
ADV DIR-MKTG/Advertising
Sarasota Herald-Tribune, Sarasota, FL

Doughton, Sandi .... (206) 597-8742
Environmental Reporter
News Tribune, Tacoma, WA

Doughty, Frank .... (616) 222-5400
PROD FRM-Paper Storage
Grand Rapids Press, Grand Rapids, MI

Doughty, Rickey .... (334) 433-1551
PROD MGR-Distribution/MR
Mobile Press Register, Mobile, AL

Doughty, Steve .... (405) 282-2222
Sports ED, Guthrie News Leader, Guthrie, OK

Douglas, Andrea .... (705) 887-2940
PUB, Fenelon Falls Gazette, Fenelon Falls, ON

Douglas, Bob .... (561) 820-4100
BUS COL
Palm Beach Post, West Palm Beach, FL

Douglas, Chuck .... (614) 592-6612
ADV MGR, Athens Messenger, Athens, OH

Douglas, Cleon .... (802) 863-3441
PROD MGR-MR
Burlington Free Press, Burlington, VT

Douglas, Donnie .... (910) 739-4322
ED, Robesonian, Lumberton, NC

Douglas, Heather .... (705) 789-5578
ED, Huntsville Herald, Huntsville, ON

Douglas, John .... (616) 222-5400
COL, Films COL
Grand Rapids Press, Grand Rapids, MI

Douglas, John .... (204) 697-7000
BUS ED, City ED
Winnipeg Free Press, Winnipeg, MB

Douglas, Margaret .... (818) 713-3000
Chief Librarian
Daily News, Woodland Hills, CA

Douglas, Michael .... (330) 996-3000
Chief EDL Writer
Akron Beacon Journal, Akron, OH

Douglas, Ray .... (212) 556-1234
VP-SYS/Technology
New York Times, New York, NY

Douglas, Tim .... (320) 564-2126
PUB, Granite Falls-Clarkfield Advocate-Tribune, Granite Falls, MN

Douglas, Tom .... (812) 829-2255
ED, Spencer Evening World, Spencer, IN

Douglas, Vasin .... (512) 445-3500
Graphics DIR
Austin American-Statesman, Austin, TX

Douglas, Vicki .... (905) 358-5711
Payroll Clerk
Niagara Falls Review, Niagara Falls, ON

Douglass, Mardi Browning ...... (408) 423-4242
CIRC MGR
Santa Cruz County Sentinel, Santa Cruz, CA

Doup, Cathy .... (614) 397-5333
ADV MGR-CLASS
Mount Vernon News, Mount Vernon, OH

Dourlet, John .... (970) 728-9788
ADV DIR, ADTX MGR/Online Contact
Telluride Daily Planet, Telluride, CO

Doussard, John .... (714) 835-1234
Topics ED-EDU/SCI/Health/Technology
Orange County Register, Santa Ana, CA

Doussard, Robin .... (714) 835-1234
Deputy ED-Features
Orange County Register, Santa Ana, CA

Douthit, Evelyn .... (915) 378-3251
PUB, ED
Sterling City News-Record, Sterling City, TX

Douthit III, Harold K .... (419) 836-2221
PUB
Suburban Press & Metro Press, Millbury, OH

Dovalina, Fernando .... (713) 220-7171
ASST MAN ED
Houston Chronicle, Houston, TX

Dove, Andrea .... (212) 210-2100
ADV VP-Group Sales
New York Daily News, New York, NY

Dove, Jim .... (510) 208-6300
CIRC DIR, Oakland Tribune, Oakland, CA
MediaNews Inc. (Alameda Newspapers)

Dove, Joe M .... (601) 961-7000
DIR-BUS Development
Clarion-Ledger, Jackson, MS

Dover, Marjorie .... (402) 376-3742
PUB, Valentine Newspaper, Valentine, NE

Dover, Ray K .... (402) 376-3742
PUB, ED, Valentine Newspaper, Valentine, NE

Dovi, Marc .... (703) 257-4600
Sports ED
Prince William Journal, Manassas, VA

Dovichi, Larry .... (209) 578-2000
ADV MGR-NTL, Modesto Bee, Modesto, CA

Dow, Cynthia .... (418) 752-5400
ED
Gaspe Peninsula SPEC, New Carlisle, QC

Dow, Evelyn .... (716) 352-3411
ED, Suburban News, Spencerport, NY

Dow, M Gene .... (915) 758-3667
PUB, Seminole Sentinel, Seminole, TX

Dow, William .... (602) 468-6565
PRES/CEO, Daily Racing Form, Phoenix, AZ

Dowd, Bill .... (518) 454-5694
Technology ED, Times Union, Albany, NY

Dowd, Jeannette .... (201) 365-3000
ADV MGR-CLASS
North Jersey Herald & News, Passaic, NJ

Dowd, Joe .... (717) 348-9100
ASST MAN ED, Garden ED
Tribune & The Scranton Times, Scranton, PA

Dowd, Mike .... (207) 990-8000
BUS ED, Bangor Daily News, Bangor, ME

Dowd, Tim .... (614) 387-0400
PUB, Marion Star, Marion, OH

Dowd, William M .... (518) 454-5694
ASSOC ED, Times Union, Albany, NY

Dowdell, Kenneth L .... (414) 657-1000
VP, ADV DIR-Public SRV, ADTX MGR
Kenosha News, Kenosha, WI

Dowdle, Don L .... (901) 465-4042
PUB, ED
East Shelby Review, Sommerville, TN

Dowdle, James C .... (312) 222-3237
EVP-Media OPER, Tribune Co., Chicago, IL

Dowdy, Judy .... (304) 645-1206
ADV MGR
West Virginia Daily News, Lewisburg, WV

Dowell, Ken .... (800) 832-5522
EDL DIR, PR Newswire, New York, NY

Dowell, Sharon .... (405) 475-3311
Food ED, Daily Oklahoman, Oklahoma City, OK

Dower, Bobby .... (318) 433-3000
News ED, Lake Charles American Press, Lake Charles, LA

Dowlen, Carla .... (817) 767-8341
ADV CNR-NTL, Wichita Falls Times Record News, Wichita Falls, TX

Dowling, Robert J .... (213) 525-2000
PUB/EXEC VP, EIC
Hollywood Reporter, Los Angeles, CA

Down, Steve .... (519) 245-2370
PUB, Age Dispatch, Strathroy, ON

Downer, Brett .... (318) 433-3000
MAN ED, Lake Charles American Press, Lake Charles, LA

Downer, Chuck .... (360) 577-2500
Outdoors ED, Daily News, Longview, WA

Downey, Debra .... (905) 628-6313
ED, Dundas Star, Dundas, ON

Downey, Denis .... (715) 526-2121
Sports ED, Shawano Leader, Shawano, WI

Downey, Joe .... (716) 372-3121
Religion ED, Times-Herald, Olean, NY

Downey, Kevin .... (814) 665-8291
GM, Corry Evening Journal, Corry, PA

Downey, Meg .... (914) 454-2000
EPE, Poughkeepsie Journal, Poughkeepsie, NY

Downey, Sara .... (847) 329-2000
ED, Morton Grove/Niles Life, Lincolnwood, IL

Downey, Shirley .... (705) 567-5321
CIRC MGR
Northern Daily News, Kirkland Lake, ON

Downie, Alison .... (519) 537-2341
MAN ED, EPE, News ED
Sentinel-Review, Woodstock, ON

Downie, Leonard .... (202) 334-6000
EX ED, Washington Post, Washington, DC

Downing, Bob .... (330) 996-3000
Environmental Writer
Akron Beacon Journal, Akron, OH

Downing, Catherine .... (205) 236-1551
Features ED, Living/Lifestyle ED, Travel ED, Women's ED, Anniston Star, Anniston, AL

Downing, Charles .... (541) 485-1234
CIRC DIR, Register-Guard, Eugene, OR

Downing, Helen .... (302) 674-3600
ADV MGR, Delaware State News, Dover, DE

Downing, John .... (416) 947-2222
ED, Toronto Sun, Toronto, ON

Downing, Kathryn M .... (213) 237-3700
VP/PRES & CEO-Matthew Bender & Co. Inc.
Times Mirror Co., Los Angeles, CA

Downing, Margaret .... (601) 961-7000
MAN ED, Clarion-Ledger, Jackson, MS

Downing, Roger .... (210) 225-7411
Sunday ED
San Antonio Express-News, San Antonio, TX

Downing, Suzanne .... (907) 586-3740
MAN ED, Juneau Empire, Juneau, AK

Downing, Terry .... (508) 586-7200
BUS/FIN ED, RE ED
Enterprise, Brockton, MA

Downs, Harry .... (406) 653-2222
GM, Herald-News, Wolf Point, MT

Downs, Jean .... (703) 276-3400
CIRC GM-Phoenix
USA Today, Arlington, VA

Downs, John .... (518) 561-2300
Design ED
Press-Republican, Plattsburgh, NY

Downs, Mamie .... (406) 653-2222
PUB, Herald-News, Wolf Point, MT

Downs, Shelby J .... (916) 662-5421
MGR-Office, Daily Democrat, Woodland, CA

Downs, Sue .... (705) 268-5050
ADV MGR, Daily Press, Timmins, ON

Dowty, JoAnn .... (618) 936-2212
GM, ED, Sumner Press, Sumner, IL

Dowty, Mike .... (504) 665-5176
ED, Denham Springs-Livingston Parish News, Denham Springs, LA

Doyle, Ann .... (617) 786-7000
Health/Medical ED, Religion ED, SCI/Technology ED, Patriot Ledger, Quincy, MA

Doyle, Barbara .... (318) 335-0635
ED, Oakdale Journal, Oakdale, LA

Doyle, Candy .... (414) 778-5000
ED, Cudahy-St. Francis Reminder-Enterprise, Wauwatosa, WI

Doyle, Christopher .... (716) 487-1111
CIRC DIR, Post-Journal, Jamestown, NY

Doyle, Donald .... (717) 253-3055
PUB, Wayne Independent, Honesdale, PA

Doyle, Jim .... (618) 269-3147
PUB, ED
Gallatin Democrat, Shawneetown, IL

Doyle, Joan .... (705) 466-3431
ED, Elmvale Lance, Creemore, ON

Doyle, Judy .... (904) 599-2100
BUS ED, Technology ED
Tallahassee Democrat, Tallahassee, FL

Doyle, Kevin .... (508) 922-1234
Sports ED
Daily News of Newburyport, Beverly, MA

Doyle, Kevin .... (414) 733-4411
ED, Post-Crescent, Appleton, WI

Doyle, Rick .... (509) 525-3300
MAN ED
Walla Walla Union-Bulletin, Walla Walla, WA

Doyle, Steve .... (407) 420-5000
Deputy MAN ED-News Features
Orlando Sentinel, Orlando, FL

Doyle, Tim .... (905) 526-3333
Sports ED, Spectator, Hamilton, ON

Doyle, Tim .... (814) 946-7411
Librarian, Altoona Mirror, Altoona, PA

Doyle, Wayne D .... (407) 322-2611
EX ED, Sanford Herald, Sanford, FL

Doyon, Michel .... (819) 564-5450
PROD FRM-MR (Night)
La Tribune, Sherbrooke, QC

Dozbaba, Jeff .... (602) 271-8000
ASST MAN ED, Arizona Republic, Phoenix, AZ

63-Who's Where **Duf**

Dozier, Pam .... (408) 372-3311
ADV MGR-RT
Monterey County Herald, Monterey, CA
Dozier Jr, William E .... (210) 334-3644
PUB, Frio-Nueces Current, Pearsall, TX
Draeger, Arden A .... (219) 722-5000
PUB, Pharos-Tribune, Logansport, IN
Draeger, Jay .... (414) 634-3322
PROD SUPV-Maintenance
Journal Times, Racine, WI
Drago, Terrie Lafferty .... (619) 431-4850
ED, Carlsbad Sun, Carlsbad, CA
Drahan, Ken .... (915) 546-6100
ADV MGR-CLASS, El Paso Times, El Paso, TX
Drahn, Sharon .... (319) 864-3333
ED, Postville Herald-Leader, Postville, IA
Drain, Rick .... (864) 427-1234
PROD MGR, Union Daily Times, Union, SC
Drake, Anita I .... (608) 849-5227
PUB, Waunakee Tribune, Waunakee, WI
Drake, Arthur M .... (608) 849-5227
PUB, ED, Waunakee Tribune, Waunakee, WI
Drake, Carolyn .... (902) 629-6000
Features ED, Guardian, Charlottetown, PEI
Drake, Jeff .... (816) 561-6061
MAN ED, PitchWeekly, Kansas City, MO
Drake, Shannon .... (219) 724-2121
ADV MGR-CLASS
Decatur Daily Democrat, Decatur, IN
Drake, Susan .... (619) 241-7744
ADV MGR-CLASS
Daily Press, Victorville, CA
Drake, Tamara F .... (414) 224-2000
VP-INFO Technologies, DP MGR
Milwaukee Journal Sentinel, Milwaukee, WI
Drane, Raymond .... (412) 224-4321
PROD MGR-PR
Valley News Dispatch, Tarentum, PA
Draper, Charles L .... (507) 825-3333
PUB, Pipestone County Star, Pipestone, MN
Draper, Doug .... (905) 684-7251
Environment ED
Standard, St. Catharines, ON
Draper, Electa .... (970) 247-3504
MAN ED, Acting, Regional ED
Durango Herald, Durango, CO
Draper, Margaret .... (216) 999-4500
ADV MGR-CLASS
Plain Dealer, Cleveland, OH
Draper, Marlow L .... (801) 438-2891
ED, Beaver Press, Beaver, UT
Draper, Miriam .... (405) 594-2440
PUB, ED, Wakita Herald, Wakita, OK
Draper, Monte .... (218) 751-3740
EDU ED, Photo ED
Daily Pioneer, Bemidji, MN
Draper, Robert L .... (801) 438-2891
PUB, Beaver Press, Beaver, UT
Drasner, Fred .... (212) 210-2100
CEO/Co-PUB
New York Daily News, New York, NY
Draughon, Dennis .... (717) 348-9100
Cartoonist
Tribune & The Scranton Times, Scranton, PA
Dreher, Rod .... (954) 356-4000
Motion Pictures ED
Sun-Sentinel, Fort Lauderdale, FL
Dreifuerst, Brian .... (715) 365-6397
PROD FRM-Press/Plate
Daily News, Rhinelander, WI
Dreiling, Janell .... (316) 241-2422
PROD SUPT
McPherson Sentinel, McPherson, KS
Dreiling, Thomas .... (307) 672-2431
MAN ED, EDL Writer
Sheridan Press, Sheridan, WY
Drell, Adrienne .... (312) 321-3000
Museums/Libraries/Cultural Institutions
Chicago Sun-Times, Chicago, IL
Dresner, Edward Wallace .... (305) 376-6057
Sales MGR, Cronin Feature Syndicating Inc., Hallandale, FL
Dresser, Trish K .... (609) 396-2200
VP-MKTG & PROM
Journal Register Co., Trenton, NJ
Dressler, James .... (812) 446-2216
MAN ED, EPE, Seen 'n Heard ED
Brazil Times, Brazil, IN
Dressman, Dennis .... (303) 892-5000
VP-Labor/Human Resources
Rocky Mountain News, Denver, CO
Drew, Frederick C .... (904) 627-7649
PUB, Gadsden County Times, Quincy, FL
Drew, Kenneth .... (718) 264-1500
PUB, New York Voice, Fresh Meadows, NY
Drew, Steve D .... (937) 836-2610
ED, Englewood Independent, Englewood, OH
Drew, Tommy .... (757) 446-2000
ADV MGR-BUS Development/GEN Sales
Virginian-Pilot, Norfolk, VA
Drewen, Karen Jolley .... (410) 838-4409
ED, APG News, Bel Air, MD
Drewry, Dan .... (208) 783-1107
PUB, Shoshone News-Press, Kellogg, ID
Drewry, Elizabeth .... (516) 843-2020
VP-Employee, Labor & Public Affairs
Newsday, Melville, NY
Drews, Chris .... (317) 787-3291
PUB, Perry Township Weekly, Beech Grove, IN
Dreyer, Evan .... (619) 745-6611
City ED-Vista
North County Times, Escondido, CA
Dreyer, Steve .... (619) 487-5757
ED, Rancho Bernardo News-Journal, San Diego, CA
Dreyfuss-Tuchman, Deborah .... (312) 573-3800
PUB, CoverStory, Chicago, IL
Dribben, Melissa .... (215) 854-2000
COL, Philadelphia Inquirer, Philadelphia, PA
Drier, Michele .... (209) 239-3531
EX ED, Manteca Bulletin, Manteca, CA
Dries, Joseph .... (717) 622-3456
CIRC DIR, Pottsville Republican & Evening Herald, Pottsville, PA
Driggs, Helen .... (609) 663-6000
Graphics ED/Art DIR
Courier-Post, Cherry Hill, NJ
Drillen, Ron .... (519) 822-4310
ADV MGR-CLASS, Daily Mercury, Guelph, ON
Dring, Neil .... (905) 765-4441
PUB, Grand River Sachem, Caledonia, ON
Dring, Wayne E .... (318) 894-6397
PUB, Ringgold Progress, Ringgold, LA
Dring, Wayne R .... (318) 894-6397
PUB, ED, Ringgold Record, Ringgold, LA
Drinker, Nick .... (617) 450-2000
ADV MGR
Christian Science Monitor, Boston, MA
Drinkwater, Joyce .... (912) 625-7722
PUB, News & Farmer & Wadely Herald, Louisville, GA
Drinkwater, Marcus .... (706) 547-6629
PUB, Jefferson Reporter, Wrens, GA
Drinnan, Greg .... (306) 565-8211
Sports ED, Leader-Post, Regina, SK
Driscoll, Joan .... (201) 383-1500
ADV MGR, New Jersey Herald, Newton, NJ
Driscoll, Lori .... (810) 985-7171
ADV MGR-CLASS
Times Herald, Port Huron, MI
Driscoll, Michelle .... (619) 232-4381
PROD DIR
San Diego Daily Transcript, San Diego, CA
Driscoll, Robert .... (403) 777-2345
ED, Calgary Mirror, Calgary, AB
Driscoll, Todd .... (603) 543-3100
ED, Eagle Times, Claremont, NH
Driskill, Ken .... (316) 283-1500
PROD SUPV-Press
Newton Kansan, Newton, KS
Driver, Ann .... (918) 567-2390
ED, Talihina American, Wilburton, OK
Driver, Michael J .... (904) 456-3121
PUB, Escambia Sun Press, Pensacola, FL
Driver, R Sonny .... (215) 236-2945
PUB, ED, Scoop USA, Philadelphia, PA
Drobner, Terry .... (518) 828-1616
MGR-BUS/PSL, Register-Star, Hudson, NY
Droege, Peter .... (303) 388-4411
ED, Denver Catholic Register, Denver, CO
Droegemeier, Howard K .... (913) 628-1081
PROD MGR-SYS, Hays Daily News, Hays, KS
Droeger, Linda .... (303) 892-5000
Sunday ED
Rocky Mountain News, Denver, CO
Droegmiller, John .... (515) 573-2141
CIRC DIR, Messenger, Fort Dodge, IA
Drogin, Bob .... (213) 237-5000
Johannesburg BU
Los Angeles Times, Los Angeles, CA
Drohan, Glenn .... (802) 254-2311
MAN ED, EPE
Brattleboro Reformer, Brattleboro, VT
Drolet, Kevin E .... (818) 713-3000
ADV DIR, Daily News, Woodland Hills, CA
Dromgoole, Glenn .... (915) 673-4271
ED, Abilene Reporter-News, Abilene, TX
Drosendahl, Glenn .... (206) 448-8000
Sports ED
Seattle Post-Intelligencer, Seattle, WA
Drouin, Guy .... (403) 645-3342
PUB, St. Paul Journal, St. Paul, AB
Drown, Stuart .... (330) 996-3000
BUS ED, Akron Beacon Journal, Akron, OH
Drozd, Darrell .... (306) 652-9200
PROD MGR-Distribution
StarPhoenix, Saskatoon, SK
Druckenmiller, John .... (770) 532-1234
MAN ED, Times, Gainesville, GA
Drudge, Mark .... (970) 945-8515
CIRC MGR
Glenwood Post, Glenwood Springs, CO
Drue, Barry .... (906) 524-6194
ED, L'Anse Sentinel, L'Anse, MI
Drueke, Lisa .... (508) 368-0176
MAN ED, Item, Clinton, MA
Druga, Carol .... (219) 362-2161
EDU ED, La Porte Herald-Argus, La Porte, IN
Drumeller, Barbara .... (540) 885-7281
ADV MGR-RT
Daily News Leader, Staunton, VA
Drummer, Randyl .... (909) 987-6397
BUS/FIN ED
Inland Valley Daily Bulletin, Ontario, CA
Drummond, Jim .... (619) 299-3131
Online Contact
San Diego Union-Tribune, San Diego, CA
Drummond, Jon .... (708) 336-7000
ASST MAN ED-News, News-Sun, Waukegan, IL
Drummond, Mike .... (916) 272-7176
Author/Self-Syndicator/PUB
Clear Creek Features, Rough & Ready, CA
Drummy, Mike .... (402) 444-1000
Art DIR, Omaha World-Herald, Omaha, NE
Drury, Lorne .... (905) 454-4344
ED, Brampton Guardian, Brampton, ON
Drury, Richard .... (419) 352-4611
PROD FRM-COMP
Sentinel-Tribune, Bowling Green, OH
Druzak, Joe .... (910) 739-4322
PROD MGR-COMP
Robesonian, Lumberton, NC
Dryer, Ruth .... (616) 222-5400
Librarian, Press, Grand Rapids, MI
Drysdale, M Dickey .... (802) 728-3232
PUB, ED
Herald of Randolph, Randolph, VT
Dubail, Jean .... (216) 999-4500
ASSOC ED, Plain Dealer, Cleveland, OH
Dubay, Mike .... (603) 752-1200
CIRC MGR, Berlin Reporter, Berlin, NH
Dubberly, Debbie .... (507) 359-2911
BM, MGR-MIS, Journal, New Ulm, MN
Dube, Alberta .... (902) 426-2811
Online MGR, Chronicle-Herald, Halifax, NS
Dube, Christiane .... (514) 285-7272
CIRC DIR, La Presse, Montreal, QC
Dube, Denise .... (207) 282-1535
PROD SUPV-COMP
Journal Tribune, Biddeford, ME
Dube, Martine .... (514) 985-3333
ADV MGR, DIR-PROM, CIRC MGR
Le Devoir, Montreal, QC
Dubik, Janine .... (717) 821-2091
City ED-Night
Citizens' Voice, Wilkes-Barre, PA
Dubilier, Alison .... (802) 933-4375
PUB, County Courier, Enosburg Falls, VT
Dubilier, Mathias .... (802) 933-4375
PUB, County Courier, Enosburg Falls, VT
Dubill, Robert .... (703) 276-3400
EX ED, USA Today, Arlington, VA
Duble, Ann .... (301) 921-2800
ED, Fort Detrick Standard, Gaithersburg, MD
Dubnanski, David .... (914) 341-1100
PROD MGR-Pre Press
Times Herald-Record, Middletown, NY
Du Bois, Paul Martin .... (802) 254-6167
PUB, American News Service, Brattleboro, VT
Dubois, Paul R .... (401) 762-3000
City ED, Call, Woonsocket, RI
Dubois, Pierre .... (819) 564-5450
CIRC MGR, La Tribune, Sherbrooke, QC
DuBois, Tessie .... (603) 436-1800
Lifestyle ED
Portsmouth Herald, Portsmouth, NH
DuBos, Clancy .... (504) 486-5900
ED, Gambit-New Orleans Weekly, New Orleans, LA
DuBos, Margo .... (504) 486-5900
PUB, Gambit-New Orleans Weekly, New Orleans, LA
DuBose, Charlie Pat .... (210) 665-2211
PUB, Devine News, Devine, TX
DuBose, L Kitty .... (210) 665-2211
ED, Devine News, Devine, TX
Dubose, Lou .... (512) 477-0746
ED, Texas Observer, Austin, TX
DuBose, Shel .... (904) 599-2100
PROD MGR-Commercial SRV
Tallahassee Democrat, Tallahassee, FL
DuBuisson, David .... (910) 373-7000
EPE, News & Record, Greensboro, NC
Dubuisson, Philippe .... (514) 285-7272
International Politics, NTL & Provincial Politics, La Presse, Montreal, QC
Dubus, Tim .... (303) 820-1010
PROD MGR-Creative Services
Denver Post, Denver, CO
Dubyn, Kathy .... (805) 945-8671
ED, Desert Mailer News, Lancaster, CA
Duca, John .... (201) 646-4000
CIRC MGR-Product SRV/Distribution/Fleet OPER, Record, Hackensack, NJ
Ducas, Isabelle .... (514) 375-4555
BUS/FIN ED, La Voix de l'Est, Granby, QC
Ducceschi, Frank D .... (360) 452-2345
PUB, Peninsula Daily News, Port Angeles, WA
Ducharme, Cora .... (613) 829-9100
ADV MGR-Category Sales
Ottawa Citizen, Ottawa, ON
Ducharme, Doug .... (601) 636-4545
CIRC MGR, Vicksburg Post, Vicksburg, MS
Ducharme, Jeff .... (709) 695-3671
ED, Gulf News, Port aux Basques, NF
DuCharme, Linda .... (802) 254-2311
Religion ED
Brattleboro Reformer, Brattleboro, VT
Duchek, David .... (330) 629-6210
ED, Poland Town Crier, Youngstown, OH
Duchek, Dennis .... (541) 276-2211
PROD Mechanical SUPV
East Oregonian, Pendleton, OR
Duchin, Susan .... (303) 892-5000
MGR-NTL/New BUS
Rocky Mountain News, Denver, CO
Ducick, Mark .... (714) 634-1567
ED, Brea Progress, Anaheim, CA
Duck, Barbara .... (904) 427-1000
GM, Observer, New Smyrna Beach, FL
Duck, Carlos .... (904) 427-1000
PROD MGR
Observer, New Smyrna Beach, FL
Duck, Terry .... (702) 383-0211
PROD DIR-OPER
Las Vegas Review-Journal, Las Vegas, NV
Ducker, Delight .... (606) 231-3100
CIRC MGR-MKTG
Lexington Herald-Leader, Lexington, KY
Ducker, Penny .... (914) 331-5000
ADV MGR-CLASS
Daily Freeman, Kingston, NY
Duckett, Steve .... (941) 953-7755
Graphics ED
Sarasota Herald-Tribune, Sarasota, FL
Dudderar, Conrad .... (405) 354-5264
ED, Yukon Review, Yukon, OK
Duddy, Curt .... (604) 564-0005
PUB, GM
Prince George Free Press, Prince George, BC
Dudek, Duane .... (414) 224-2000
Film Critic
Milwaukee Journal Sentinel, Milwaukee, WI
Dudek, Jerry .... (330) 852-4634
ED, Budget, Sugarcreek, OH
Dudek, Matt .... (716) 232-7100
ASST MAN ED-ADM
Rochester Democrat and Chronicle; Rochester, NY Times-Union, Rochester, NY
Dudek, Patricia .... (312) 321-3000
MGR-Community/Client SRV
Chicago Sun-Times, Chicago, IL
Dudgeon, Thom .... (334) 433-1551
Graphics ED, Mobile Press Register, Mobile, AL
Dudley, Bonnie J .... (619) 457-5920
MAN ED, Trade Service Corp., San Diego, CA
Dudley, Brier .... (509) 248-1251
BUS/FIN ED
Yakima Herald-Republic, Yakima, WA
Dudley, Gary .... (712) 469-3381
PUB, Manson Journal, Manson, IA
Dudley, Lynette .... (803) 626-8555
PROD MGR, Sun News, Myrtle Beach, SC
Dudley, Mary H .... (806) 435-3631
ED, Perryton Herald, Perryton, TX
Dudley, Rob .... (808) 525-8000
Graphics ED
Honolulu Advertiser, Honolulu, HI
Dudruch, Darian .... (719) 384-4475
Sports ED
La Junta Tribune-Democrat, La Junta, CO
Dueber, Daniel S .... (719) 632-5511
DIR-FIN, Gazette, Colorado Springs, CO
Dueker, Craig .... (319) 732-2029
ED, Wilton-Durant Advocate News, Wilton, IA
Duenas, Mario G .... (713) 774-4686
PUB, Semana Newspaper, Houston, TX
Duenas, Raul .... (713) 774-4686
MAN ED, Semana Newspaper, Houston, TX
Duerksen, Susan .... (619) 299-3131
Medical Writer
San Diego Union-Tribune, San Diego, CA
Duerr, Joseph E .... (502) 636-0296
ED, Record, Louisville, KY
Duerr, Sandra .... (502) 582-4011
ASST MAN ED-News
Courier-Journal, Louisville, KY
Dueweke, Gerald P .... (517) 895-8551
DP MGR, PROD MGR-SYS
Bay City Times, Bay City, MI
Duewell, Jeff .... (541) 474-3700
Sports ED, Daily Courier, Grants Pass, OR
Duff, Carol .... (612) 388-8235
VP, Republican Eagle, Red Wing, MN
Duff, Kathleen .... (970) 493-6397
EPE, Coloradoan, Fort Collins, CO
Duff, Philip N .... (612) 388-8235
VP, Republican Eagle, Red Wing, MN
Duff, Sean .... (970) 493-6397
Sports ED
Fort Collins Coloradoan, Fort Collins, CO

Copyright ©1997 by the Editor & Publisher Co.

Duf Who's Where-64

Duffett, Michael (707) 374-6431
ED, River News-Herald & Isleton Journal, Rio Vista, CA
Duffey, Dan (601) 896-2100
Features ED, Sun Herald, Biloxi, MS
Duffield, Bill (937) 372-4444
Sports ED, Xenia Daily Gazette, Xenia, OH
Duffield, Ken (916) 321-1000
DIR-Production, PROD DIR
Sacramento Bee, Sacramento, CA
Duffield, Linda (301) 733-5131
MAN ED (Herald)
Morning Herald, Hagerstown, MD
Duffield, Virginia (573) 392-5658
ED, Eldon Advertiser, Eldon, MO
Duffin, Jane M (215) 836-4900
ED, Irish Edition, Wyndmoor, PA
Duffon, Monte (704) 864-3291
Automotive ED
Gaston Gazette, Gastonia, NC
Duffy, Beverley (319) 398-8211
Religion ED, Gazette, Cedar Rapids, IA
Duffy, Brian (515) 284-8000
Cartoonist
Des Moines Register, Des Moines, IA
Duffy, Jim (704) 287-3327
PUB
County News Enterprise, Rutherfordton, NC
Duffy, Robert (816) 932-6600
VP-Sales & New Media
Universal Press Syndicate, Kansas City, MO
Duffy, Robert (314) 340-8000
Arts ED, St. Louis Post-Dispatch, St. Louis, MO
Duffy, Sean (609) 737-3379
ED, Pennington Post, Pennington, NJ
Duffy, Traci (803) 775-6331
Living/Lifestyle ED, Teen-Age/Youth ED, Women's ED, Item, Sumter, SC
Dufner, Edward (214) 977-8222
NTL ED, Dallas Morning News, Dallas, TX
Duford, Mary (616) 946-2000
Food ED, Record-Eagle, Traverse City, MI
Dufour, Kris (413) 663-3741
Sports ED
North Adams Transcript, North Adams, MA
Dufour, Liz (513) 721-2700
DIR-Photography
Cincinnati Enquirer, Cincinnati, OH
DuFour, Susan (941) 953-7755
ADV MGR-NTL/Co-op
Sarasota Herald-Tribune, Sarasota, FL
Dufrain, Roy W (707) 459-4643
GM, Willits News, Willits, CA
Dufrain Jr, Roy (707) 263-5636
PROD DIR
Lake County Record-Bee, Lakeport, CA
Dufresne, Bethe (860) 442-2200
Arts ED, Entertainment/Amusements ED, Films/Theater ED, Day, New London, CT
DuFresne, Kelly (619) 934-8544
ED, Review Herald, Mammoth Lakes, CA
Dugan, Annelle (903) 984-2593
EDU ED, Kilgore News Herald, Kilgore, TX
Dugan, Barry (707) 823-7845
ED
Sonoma West Times & News, Sebastopol, CA
Dugan, Charles (718) 981-1234
PROD FRM-Camera DEPT
Staten Island Advance, Staten Island, NY
Dugan, Dick (405) 475-3311
MGR-PROM
Daily Oklahoman, Oklahoma City, OK
Dugan, Fred (812) 332-4401
PROD SUPT-MR
Herald-Times Inc, Bloomington, IN
Dugan, Judy (213) 237-5000
Voices ED
Los Angeles Times, Los Angeles, CA
Dugan, Kevin P (402) 447-6012
PUB, ED
Newman Grove Reporter, Newman Grove, NE
Dugan, Reese (412) 222-2200
PROD ASST SUPV-SYS
Observer-Reporter, Washington, PA
Dugan, Tom (608) 356-4808
ADV MGR, ADV DIR, News-Republic/South Central Wisconsin News, Baraboo, WI
Dugdale, Sandra (604) 632-6144
PUB, Northern Sentinel, Kitimat, BC
Duggan, Joe (402) 475-4200
Outdoors/Recreation Reporter, Regional Reporter, Lincoln Journal Star, Lincoln, NE
Duggan, Kevin (303) 239-9890
MAN ED, Jefferson Sentinel, Lakewood, CO
Duggan, Mike (202) 383-6080
MAN ED-News SRV & KRT Kids, Knight-Ridder/Tribune Information Services, Washington, DC
Duggan, Natalie (912) 888-9300
CONT, Albany Herald, Albany, GA
Duggan, Tom (201) 877-4141
Sunday ED, Star-Ledger, Newark, NJ
Duguay, Denise (204) 694-2022
Radio/Television ED
Winnipeg Sun, Winnipeg, MB
Duhame, Yves L (514) 985-3333
PRES, Le Devoir, Montreal, QC
Duhamel, Maurice (514) 768-2544
PUB, Verdun Messenger, Verdun, QC
Duhamel, Monique (603) 893-4356
ED, Salem Observer, Salem, NH
Duhe, Ken (504) 383-1111
News ED, Advocate, Baton Rouge, LA
Duhon, Krista (318) 462-0616
Photo ED
Beauregard Daily News, De Ridder, LA
Duhon, Shannon (318) 239-3444
ED, Leesville Daily Leader, Leesville, LA
Duin, Steve (503) 221-8327
COL, Oregonian, Portland, OR
Dujardin, Richard C (401) 277-7000
Religion Writer
Providence Journal-Bulletin, Providence, RI
Duke, Beth (806) 376-4488
City ED (Globe-Times & News), Amarillo Daily News/Globe Times, Amarillo, TX
Duke, Frank (618) 234-1000
VP/DIR-MKTG
Belleville News-Democrat, Belleville, IL
Duke, James (619) 337-3400
News ED, Imperial Valley Press, El Centro, CA
Duke, Kerry (513) 352-2000
Deputy MET ED, Cincinnati Post, Cincinnati, OH, Scripps Howard
Duke, Marion (519) 291-1660
ED, Listowel Banner, Listowel, ON
Duke, Oak (716) 593-5300
PUB, ADV DIR, Daily Reporter, Wellsville, NY
Duke, Sharyon (417) 667-3344
Religion ED, Nevada Daily Mail, Nevada, MO
Duke, Steve (312) 321-3000
BUS ED, Chicago Sun-Times, Chicago, IL
Duke, Tom (757) 446-2000
ADV MGR-OPER, Virginian-Pilot, Norfolk, VA
Dukelow, Lynn (406) 363-3300
DP MGR, Ravalli Republic, Hamilton, MT
Dukeman, Kelly (219) 881-3000
CIRC MGR-MKTG, Post-Tribune, Gary, IN
Dukes, Mark (319) 398-8211
Sports ED, Gazette, Cedar Rapids, IA
Dulac, Donald T (412) 664-9161
ASSOC ED, EPE
Daily News, McKeesport, PA
Dulen, Jackie (847) 427-4300
Food ED, Daily Herald, Arlington Heights, IL
Duley, Jim (919) 829-0181
ED, Front Page, Raleigh, NC
Duley, Joseph (304) 292-6301
CIRC MGR-OPER
Dominion Post, Morgantown, WV
Duley, Marsha (716) 394-0770
Religion ED, Daily Messenger/Sunday Messenger, Canandaigua, NY
Dulhanty, Ron (317) 482-4650
Photo ED, Reporter, Lebanon, IN
Dulin, Ed (800) 426-4192
PRES-Arizona, Independent Newspapers Inc. (DE), Dover, DE
Dull, Mary Ann (419) 281-0581
Fashion ED, Times-Gazette, Ashland, OH
Dulley, James T (513) 231-6034
PRES
Starcott Media Services, Cincinnati, OH
Dullum, Randall (414) 563-5553
City ED, Daily Jefferson County Union, Fort Atkinson, WI
Duman, Jill (408) 394-5656
ED, Coast Weekly, Seaside, CA
Dumas, Maurice (418) 686-3233
Sports DIR, Le Soleil, Quebec, QC
Dumont, Andre (418) 686-3233
ADV RT-Group Head, Le Soleil, Quebec, QC
Dump, Rob (402) 254-3997
PUB, ED
Cedar County News, Hartington, NE
Dunagan, Christopher (360) 377-3711
Environmental Writer, Sun, Bremerton, WA
Dunagin, Charles M (601) 684-2421
TREAS, PUB, ED
Enterprise-Journal, McComb, MS
Dunaief, Leah S (516) 751-7744
PUB, Village Times, Setauket, NY
Dunavan, Tom (918) 456-8833
CIRC MGR
Tahlequah Daily Press, Tahlequah, OK
Dunbar, Bethany M (802) 525-3531
ED, Chronicle, Barton, VT
Dunbar, Henry T (703) 204-2800
ED, Sun Gazette, Merrifield, VA
Dunbar, Maria (317) 482-4650
Farm ED, Reporter, Lebanon, IN
Duncan, Amy (515) 967-4224
GM, Altoona Herald-Mitchellville Index, Altoona, IA
Duncan, Archie W (517) 895-8551
ADV DIR, Bay City Times, Bay City, MI
Duncan, Charley (901) 529-2211
PROD MGR-PR
Commercial Appeal, Memphis, TN
Duncan, Dale (810) 332-8181
PRES, PUB, Oakland Press, Pontiac, MI
Duncan, Debra (412) 224-4321
EPE, Valley News Dispatch, Tarentum, PA
Duncan, Grace (847) 888-7800
CIRC MGR-Home Delivery
Courier-News, Elgin, IL
Duncan, James (Pat) (604) 492-3636
PUB, Penticton Western News, Penticton, BC
Duncan, Jeff (502) 753-1916
CIRC MGR, Ledger & Times, Murray, KY
Duncan, Jim (916) 985-2581
ED, Folsom Telegraph, Folsom, CA
Duncan, Joel (205) 532-4000
News ED, Huntsville Times, Huntsville, AL
Duncan, Kim (704) 437-2161
City/MET ED, Films/Theater ED, Music ED
News Herald, Morganton, NC
Duncan, Michael (415) 777-5700
CIRC Analyst/Financial Planning, San Francisco Newspaper Agency, San Francisco, CA
Duncan, Ruby (719) 589-2553
CIRC MGR, Valley Courier, Alamosa, CO
Duncan, Sheila (519) 941-2230
ED, Orangeville Citizen, Orangeville, ON
Duncan, Susan (217) 347-7151
MAN ED
Effingham Daily News, Effingham, IL
Dundas, Bob (970) 963-3211
PUB, Valley Journal, Carbondale, CO
Dundas, Jim (908) 922-6000
SYS ED, Asbury Park Press, Neptune, NJ
Dundas, Tim (905) 871-3100
PUB, Fort Erie Times, Fort Erie, ON
Dungen Jr, Raymond L (409) 992-3351
PUB, ED, New Ulm Enterprise, New Ulm, TX
Dunham, Chuck V (515) 522-9288
PUB, ED, Brooklyn Chronicle, Brooklyn, IA
Dunham, Grant (719) 486-0641
GM, ED
Leadville Herald Democrat, Leadville, CO
Dunham, Mike (907) 257-4200
Arts ED, Books ED
Anchorage Daily News, Anchorage, AK
Dunham, Randy (419) 522-3311
MAN ED, News Journal, Mansfield, OH
Dunham, Sandy (206) 597-8742
Central/Tacoma ED
News Tribune, Tacoma, WA
Dunham, Sharon (406) 434-5171
ED, Shelby Promoter, Shelby, MT
Dunham, Tim (412) 263-1100
Technology SYS ED
Pittsburgh Post-Gazette, Pittsburgh, PA
Dunkel, Dick (904) 252-1511
Author/Owner, Dunkel Sports Research Service, Daytona Beach, FL
Dunkin, Zoch (317) 633-1240
Arts/Entertainment ED
Indianapolis Star/News, Indianapolis, IN
Dunkle, Amy (605) 692-6271
MAN ED, Brookings Register, Brookings, SD
Dunlap, Doris (904) 599-2100
Senior VP, Senior VP/GM
Tallahassee Democrat, Tallahassee, FL
Dunlap, Edward B (814) 634-8321
PUB, New Republic, Meyersdale, PA
Dunlap, James (912) 244-1880
PROD FRM-COMP
Valdosta Daily Times, Valdosta, GA
Dunlap, Jon (309) 686-3000
MGR-CR, Journal Star, Peoria, IL
Dunlap, Joy (402) 444-1000
CIRC MGR-Sales/MKTG
Omaha World-Herald, Omaha, NE
Dunlap, Leslie (614) 654-1321
BM, Lancaster Eagle-Gazette, Lancaster, OH
Dunlap, Pam (815) 937-3300
ADV DIR, Daily Journal, Kankakee, IL
Dunlap, Russ (412) 282-8000
PROD FRM-Electronics/Computers
Butler Eagle, Butler, PA
Dunn, Bill (612) 673-4000
Visual Content ED
Star Tribune, Minneapolis, MN
Dunn, Bill (407) 420-5000
ASSOC MAN ED-Planning/Design
Orlando Sentinel, Orlando, FL
Dunn, Byrne K (615) 796-3191
PUB, ED
Lewis County Herald, Hohenwald, TN
Dunn, Carol (212) 327-0998
SEC/TREAS
Animagic Syndication, New York, NY
Dunn, Dana T (334) 636-2214
ED, Thomasville Times, Thomasville, AL
Dunn, Dave (520) 573-4400
PROD MGR-Technical SRV, TNI Partners dba Tucson Newspapers, Tucson, AZ
Dunn, Dennis (765) 423-2624
PUB, Lafayette Leader, Lafayette, IN
Dunn, Dennis (706) 324-5526
CIRC MGR-MKTG
Columbus Ledger-Enquirer, Columbus, GA
Dunn, Edward J (860) 887-9211
EPE, Norwich Bulletin, Norwich, CT
Dunn, Gary (209) 688-0521
DIR-Technical SRV
Tulare Advance-Register, Tulare, CA
Dunn, Glen (405) 353-0620
PROD SUPT-COMP
Lawton Constitution, Lawton, OK
Dunn, James W (316) 842-5129
PUB, ED
Anthony Republican & Bulletin, Anthony, KS
Dunn, Janine G (860) 887-9211
DIR-Human Resources
Norwich Bulletin, Norwich, CT
Dunn, Jerry (909) 684-1200
ADV MGR-New BUS Development
Press-Enterprise, Riverside, CA
Dunn, Jim (517) 724-6384
PUB, Klaxon, Wurtsmith, MI
Dunn, Jim (815) 284-2222
Farm ED, Telegraph, Dixon, IL
Dunn, John (Chip) (561) 287-1550
PROD MGR-Press, Stuart News, Stuart, FL
Dunn, Ken (416) 367-2000
PROD MGR-Maintenance Planning
Toronto Star, Toronto, ON
Dunn, Lon (402) 444-1000
Facilities MGR
Omaha World-Herald, Omaha, NE
Dunn, Michelle (717) 275-3235
ADV MGR-CLASS, News, Danville, PA
Dunn, Phil (847) 329-2000
MAN ED, Lerner News Star, Lincolnwood, IL
Dunn, Raymond (613) 544-5000
DIR-Manufacturing & Computer SYS
Kingston Whig-Standard, Kingston, ON
Dunn, Rick (617) 426-8246
MAN ED, In Newsweekly, Boston, MA
Dunn, Scott (801) 882-0050
PUB, Tooele Transcript-Bulletin, Tooele, UT
Dunn, Steve (515) 856-6336
ED
Ad Express & Daily Iowegian, Centerville, IA
Dunn, Tim (702) 788-6200
DIR-Photography
Reno Gazette-Journal, Reno, NV
Dunn, Vera L (316) 842-5129
GM, Republican & Bulletin, Anthony, KS
Dunn-Rankin, Debbie (941) 629-2855
DP MGR, Sun Herald, Port Charlotte, FL
Dunn-Rankin, Derek (941) 629-2855
PRES, PUB, Sun Herald, Port Charlotte, FL
Dunn-Rankin, Jeff (941) 629-2855
MAN ED, Sun Herald, Port Charlotte, FL
Dunne, Freda (504) 383-1111
News/Features ED
Advocate, Baton Rouge, LA
Dunne, Mike (916) 321-1000
Food ED, Sacramento Bee, Sacramento, CA
Dunning, Jerry (303) 892-5000
ADV VP-Advertising
Rocky Mountain News, Denver, CO
Dunphy, Sarah J (607) 798-1234
PA, PROD PA
Press & Sun Bulletin, Binghamton, NY
Dunsmore, Pam (817) 767-8341
Arts/Amusements ED, Wichita Falls Times Record News, Wichita Falls, TX
Duplaga, Michael (304) 636-2121
ADV DIR, Inter-Mountain, Elkins, WV
Duplantie, Roger (613) 938-1433
PUB, ED
Le Journal de Cornwall, Cornwall, ON
Dupont, David (419) 352-4611
Religion ED
Sentinel-Tribune, Bowling Green, OH
Dupont Jr, Ronald (941) 629-2855
Online Contact
Sun Herald, Port Charlotte, FL
Dupont-Smith, Alice (904) 627-7649
ED, Gadsden County Times, Quincy, FL
Dupratt, Lynn (805) 273-2700
ASSOC MAN ED
Antelope Valley Press, Palmdale, CA
Dupre, Crystal (601) 428-0551
ADV MGR, Laurel Leader-Call, Laurel, MS
Dupre, Wayne (504) 850-1100
CONT, PA, Courier, Houma, LA
DuPre', Mike (608) 754-3311
Automotive ED
Janesville Gazette, Janesville, WI
Dupree, Jimmy (919) 419-6500
Sports ED, Herald-Sun, Durham, NC
DuPree, Leslie (309) 764-4344
Online MGR, Dispatch, Moline, IL
Small Newspaper Group Inc.
Dupuis, Robert P (508) 793-9100
PROD MGR-Pre Press
Telegram & Gazette, Worcester, MA

65-Who's Where **Ebe**

Dupuy, Benjamin .... (718) 434-8100
PUB, Haiti Progres, Brooklyn, NY
Duquette, Catherine A .... (518) 561-2300
CONT, Press-Republican, Plattsburgh, NY
Duquette, Clair S .... (715) 682-2313
MAN ED, Area News ED
Daily Press, Ashland, WI
Duquette, John .... (315) 789-3333
PROD MGR, Finger Lakes Times, Geneva, NY
Dura, Gary .... (319) 588-5611
Food ED, Telegraph Herald, Dubuque, IA
Duran, Art .... (505) 823-7777
Data SYS DIR, Albuquerque Publishing Co., Albuquerque, NM
Duran, Luis .... (213) 622-8332
ADV DIR-Display
La Opinion, Los Angeles, CA
Duran, Robert A .... (505) 523-4581
CIRC MGR
Las Cruces Sun-News, Las Cruces, NM
Duran, Tino .... (210) 242-7900
PUB
La Prensa De San Antonio, San Antonio, TX
Durban, Jim .... (614) 852-0809
GM, Madison Messenger, London, OH
Durbin, Debra .... (918) 423-1700
PROD SUPV, McAlester News-Capital & Democrat, McAlester, OK
Durbin, Greg .... (217) 351-5252
PROD FRM-COMP
News-Gazette, Champaign, IL
Durbin, Joan .... (954) 428-9045
ED, Deerfield Beach-Lighthouse Point Observer, Deerfield Beach, FL
Durbin, Rich .... (914) 562-1218
GM, Sentinel, Vails Gate, NY
Durda, Robbin .... (330) 792-7729
GM, ED
Austintown Leader, Austintown, OH
Durden, Douglas .... (804) 649-6000
Radio/Television Writer
Richmond Times-Dispatch, Richmond, VA
Duren, Crad .... (713) 529-8490
PUB, Houston Voice, Houston, TX
Durfey, Jim .... (406) 222-2000
ADV DIR
Livingston Enterprise, Livingston, MT
Durham, Anne .... (317) 462-5528
EDU ED, Daily Reporter, Greenfield, IN
Durham, Charlotte .... (901) 529-2211
Travel ED, Commercial Appeal, Memphis, TN
Durham, Cindy .... (317) 552-3355
CIRC DIR, Elwood Call-Leader, Elwood, IN
Ray Barnes Newspapers Inc.
Durham, Darrell D .... (614) 461-5000
DIR-MKTG Services
Columbus Dispatch, Columbus, OH
Durham, Jim .... (606) 231-3100
Community ED
Lexington Herald-Leader, Lexington, KY
Durham, Mark N .... (910) 276-2311
ED, Exchange, Laurinburg, NC
Durham, Marshall .... (901) 529-2211
PROD MGR-Engraving
Commercial Appeal, Memphis, TN
Durham, Ron .... (915) 653-1221
EDU Writer, Standard-Times, San Angelo, TX
Durichen, Pauline .... (519) 894-2231
Religion/Classical Music Reporter
Record, Kitchener, ON
Durkee, Dennis .... (561) 562-2315
News ED-Night
Vero Beach Press-Journal, Vero Beach, FL
Durkin, Barbara .... (914) 694-9300
Health/Medical ED, Reporter Dispatch, White Plains, NY, Gannett Co. Inc.
Durkin, Jim .... (701) 780-1100
MAN ED-Content
Grand Forks Herald, Grand Forks, ND
Durman, Louise G .... (423) 523-3131
Food ED
Knoxville News-Sentinel, Knoxville, TN
Durocher, Claudette .... (603) 882-2741
EPE, Telegraph, Nashua, NH
Durrance, Martha .... (813) 259-7711
Features ED
Tampa Tribune and Times, Tampa, FL
Durrell, Brad .... (203) 926-2080
ED, Bridgeport News, Monroe, CT
Durreman, Carl .... (417) 532-9131
PROD MGR
Lebanon Daily Record, Lebanon, MO
Durrett, Craig .... (318) 459-3200
ASST MAN ED, Times, Shreveport, LA
Durrett, Rachel .... (205) 345-0505
Librarian
Tuscaloosa News, Tuscaloosa, AL
Durst, John .... (715) 693-2300
PUB, ED, Mosinee Times, Mosinee, WI
Duskey, Gaylen .... (318) 487-6397
Sports ED
Alexandria Daily Town Talk, Alexandria, LA
Dussault, Rosemary .... (508) 675-7151
GM, Anchor, Fall River, MA
Dutcher, Jeri Hird .... (701) 786-3281
ED, Traill County Tribune, Mayville, ND
Dutcher, Tom .... (701) 786-3281
PUB, Traill County Tribune, Mayville, ND
Dute, Jeff .... (540) 825-0771
MAN ED
Culpeper Star-Exponent, Culpeper, VA
Dutka, Elaine .... (213) 237-5000
Movie Industry Writer
Los Angeles Times, Los Angeles, CA
Dutruch, Toni .... (601) 896-2100
DIR-Human Relations
Sun Herald, Biloxi, MS
Dutson, Susan B .... (801) 864-2400
PUB, ED, Millard County Chronicle Progress, Fillmore, UT
Dutton, David .... (360) 532-4000
MGR-SYS
Aberdeen Daily World, Aberdeen, WA
Dutton, George .... (205) 353-4612
PROD FRM-MR, Decatur Daily, Decatur, AL
Dutton, Tim .... (818) 962-8811
Sports ED, San Gabriel Valley Tribune, West Covina, CA, MediaNews Inc.
D'Uva, Robert .... (401) 821-7400
EX Sales DIR
Kent County Daily Times, West Warwick, RI
DuVal, Dalton .... (209) 943-6397
CIRC MGR-Home Delivery
Record, Stockton, CA
Duval, Linda .... (719) 632-5511
Books ED, Travel ED
Gazette, Colorado Springs, CO
Duvall, Connie .... (816) 263-4123
EDU ED, Photo ED, Moberly Monitor-Index & Democrat, Moberly, MO
Duvall, Doug .... (812) 283-6636
PROD FRM-COMP
Evening News, Jeffersonville, IN
Duvall, Todd .... (502) 227-4556
Books/RE ED, COL, EPE
State Journal, Frankfort, KY
Dvorak, Terry .... (916) 321-1000
California Life ED
Sacramento Bee, Sacramento, CA
Dwelle, Dan .... (903) 675-5626
PUB, Athens Daily Review, Athens, TX
Dwelle, R E .... (903) 675-5626
EDL Writer
Athens Daily Review, Athens, TX
Dwight, Arthur R .... (603) 224-5301
ADV MGR-RT/Training
Concord Monitor, Concord, NH
Dwight, Donald R .... (603) 224-5301
COB
Newspapers of New England, Concord, NH
Dwinell, Joe .... (508) 626-3800
Sunday ED
Middlesex News, Framingham, MA
Dwyer, Dean P .... (619) 454-0411
VP-FIN & Treasure
Copley Press Inc., La Jolla, CA
Dwyer, Douglas J .... (617) 929-2000
DIR-ADM SRV, Boston Globe, Boston, MA
Dwyer, Kerry .... (413) 458-9000
MAN ED, Advocate/The South Advocate, Williamstown, MA
Dwyer, Kevin .... (360) 377-3711
BUS/FIN ED, Sun, Bremerton, WA
Dwyer, Leo .... (770) 428-9411
ADV DIR
Marietta Daily Journal, Marietta, GA
Dwyer, Robert T .... (603) 668-4321
DP MGR, Union Leader, Manchester, NH
Dwyer, Tim .... (215) 854-2000
COL-Sports
Philadelphia Inquirer, Philadelphia, PA
Dwyer, Tina .... (602) 488-3436
PUB, Foothills Sentinel, Cave Creek, AZ
Dwyre, Bill .... (213) 237-5000
Sports ED
Los Angeles Times, Los Angeles, CA
Dyboloski, Marcin .... (847) 581-1132
MAN ED, Kobieta, Morton Grove, IL
Dyck, Peter .... (204) 326-3421
ED, Carillon, Steinbach, MB
Dyck, R Bruce .... (306) 665-9605
ASST News ED, Western Producer Newsfeature Service, Saskatoon, SK
Dyckman, Martin .... (813) 893-8111
ASSOC ED
St. Petersburg Times, St. Petersburg, FL
Dye, Charles .... (713) 780-7055
PRES, Print Marketing Concepts, Houston, TX
Dye, John .... (419) 332-5511
EX ED, News-Messenger, Fremont, OH
Gannett Co. Inc.
Dye, Robert .... (414) 224-2000
VP-Communications
Milwaukee Journal Sentinel, Milwaukee, WI
Dye, Robert .... (972) 937-3310
CIRC MGR
Waxahachie Daily Light, Waxahachie, TX
Dye, Susie .... (419) 864-6046
ED
Morrow County Independent, Cardington, OH
Dyer, Bob .... (330) 996-3000
COL-Local
Akron Beacon Journal, Akron, OH
Dyer, Eileen .... (214) 977-8222
ADV DIR-CLASS
Dallas Morning News, Dallas, TX
Dyer, Joel .... (303) 494-5511
ED, Boulder Weekly, Boulder, CO
Dyer, Ray T .... (405) 262-5180
PUB, ED, El Reno Tribune, El Reno, OK
Dyer, Richard .... (617) 929-2000
Music ED-Classical
Boston Globe, Boston, MA
Dyer, Richard H .... (602) 982-7799
ED
East Mesa Independent, Apache Junction, AZ
Dyer, Sean E .... (405) 262-5180
PUB, GM, El Reno Tribune, El Reno, OK
Dyer-Zinner, Joan .... (313) 729-4000
ED, Westland Eagle, Wayne, MI
Dyess, Clarajane .... (806) 756-4402
PUB, ED, Borden Star, Gail, TX
Dygert, James H .... (513) 671-3000
PUB, ED, Suburban Press/West Chester Press, Sharonville, OH
Dykema, C Kevin .... (517) 895-8551
PUB, Bay City Times, Bay City, MI
Dykes, D R .... (423) 246-4800
SEC/TREAS, PA, CIRC MGR
Daily News, Kingsport, TN
Dykes, David .... (706) 324-5526
MET ED
Columbus Ledger-Enquirer, Columbus, GA
Dykes, J Steven .... (423) 246-4800
VP, PUB, ADV MGR
Daily News, Kingsport, TN
Dykes, Pete .... (423) 246-4800
PRES, ED, Daily News, Kingsport, TN
Dykk, Lloyd .... (604) 732-2111
Drama Critic, Vancouver Sun, Vancouver, BC
Dynan, Joe .... (603) 742-4455
BUS ED, Foster's Democrat, Dover, NH
Dynko, James .... (518) 561-2300
ED, Press-Republican, Plattsburgh, NY
Dyson, Harry .... (401) 277-7000
TREAS/SEC
Providence Journal-Bulletin, Providence, RI
Dyson, James D .... (717) 226-4547
PUB, News Eagle, Hawley, PA
Dyson Jr, John C .... (717) 226-4547
ED, News Eagle, Hawley, PA
Dzierzek, Jeanne .... (606) 666-2451
PUB, Jackson Times, Jackson, KY
Dziublenski, Joe .... (201) 646-4000
Home & Family ED, Record, Hackensack, NJ
Dzubay, Steve .... (715) 386-9333
PUB, Hudson Star-Observer, Hudson, WI
Dzuro, Joan E .... (805) 650-2900
DIR-Human Resources
Ventura County Star, Ventura, CA
Dzwonczyk, Florence .... (609) 396-2200
DIR-Human Resources
Journal Register Co., Trenton, NJ
Dzwonkowski, Ron .... (313) 222-6400
Projects ED, Detroit Free Press, Detroit, MI

E

Eades, Jennifer .... (812) 265-3641
Teen-Age/Youth ED, Women's ED
Madison Courier, Madison, IN
Eagan, Margery .... (617) 426-3000
News COL, Boston Herald, Boston, MA
Eagan, Pat .... (810) 469-4510
PROD DIR-Press OPER
Macomb Daily, Mount Clemens, MI
Independent Newspapers Inc. (MI)
Eagan, Trudy A .... (416) 947-2222
VP-CORP Affairs/CORP SEC
Sun Media Corp., Toronto, ON
Eagle, Avis Little .... (605) 341-0011
ED, Indian Country Today, Rapid City, SD
Eagles, Dana .... (407) 420-5000
Deputy MAN ED-Topics
Orlando Sentinel, Orlando, FL
Eakin, David .... (706) 846-3188
ED, MAN ED
Harris County Journal, Hamilton, GA
Eanes, Jim R .... (804) 645-7534
PUB, ED
Crewe-Burkeville Journal, Crewe, VA
Earehart, C L .... (540) 459-4078
ED
Shenandoah Valley-Herald, Woodstock, VA
Earheart, Janice .... (423) 523-3131
DIR-FIN
Knoxville News-Sentinel, Knoxville, TN
Earl, Carl .... (503) 325-3211
PROD MGR-SYS
Daily Astorian, Astoria, OR
Earl, Cesarina A .... (201) 942-2814
PUB, ED, Italian Voice, Totowa, NJ
Earle, Rosalie .... (304) 348-5140
MAN ED, Charleston Gazette, Sunday Gazette-Mail, Charleston, WV
Earle, Samuel L .... (609) 799-6601
PUB, ED, West Windsor-Plainsboro Chronicle, Princeton Junction, NJ
Earley, Brenda .... (937) 393-3456
CIRC MGR, Times-Gazette, Hillsboro, OH
Earls, Terry .... (209) 674-2424
BM, Madera Tribune, Madera, CA
Early, Chris .... (541) 276-2211
Farm ED, East Oregonian, Pendleton, OR
Earlywine, Larry .... (206) 339-3000
PROD MGR-Press, Herald, Everett, WA
Earnest, Jon .... (209) 582-0471
Sports ED, Hanford Sentinel, Hanford, CA
Earnest, Tawana .... (316) 624-2541
PA, Southwest Daily Times, Liberal, KS
Earnhardt, Jim .... (334) 262-1611
Action Line ED, Books ED, ASST EPE
Montgomery Advertiser, Montgomery, AL
Easley, James K .... (908) 922-6000
ADV MGR-CLASS
Asbury Park Press, Neptune, NJ
Easley, Jimmy .... (404) 526-5151
CIRC MGR-Bulk Distribution
Atlanta Journal-Constitution, Atlanta, GA
Easley, Rick .... (409) 564-8361
CIRC MGR, Daily Sentinel, Nacogdoches, TX
Eason, Ben .... (813) 286-1600
PUB, Weekly Planet, Tampa, FL
Eason, Deborah .... (404) 688-5623
PUB, Creative Loafing, Atlanta, GA
Eason, Thomas A .... (810) 766-6100
ADV DIR, Flint Journal, Flint, MI
Eason, Tom .... (219) 461-8444
ADV Senior MGR-Sales
Fort Wayne Newspapers Inc., Fort Wayne, IN
East, Robert .... (203) 744-5100
Photo ED, News-Times, Danbury, CT
Eastburn, Kathryn C .... (719) 577-4545
ED, Colorado Springs Independent, Colorado Springs, CO
Easter, Russ .... (614) 345-4053
CIRC DIR, Advocate, Newark, OH
Easterby, Terry .... (519) 344-3641
Auto ED, Observer, Sarnia, ON
Easterday, Conrad .... (316) 672-5511
ED, Pratt Tribune, Pratt, KS
Easterling, Denise .... (716) 897-0442
MAN ED, Buffalo Challenger, Buffalo, NY
Easterling, Mike .... (405) 528-6000
ED, Oklahoma Gazette, Oklahoma City, OK
Easterly, David E .... (404) 843-5000
PRES/COO-Cox Enterprises Inc.
Cox Newspapers Inc., Atlanta, GA
Eastman, Kim .... (513) 863-8200
ADV MGR-RT, Journal-News, Hamilton, OH
Eastman, R Stephen .... (603) 447-6336
PUB, ED, Mt. Washington Valley Mountain Ear, Conway, NH
Easton Jr, Karl J .... (561) 585-9387
PUB, Lake Worth Herald and Coastal Observer, Lake Worth, FL
Eastwood, Brian .... (204) 949-6100
ED, Metro, Winnipeg, MB
Eastwood, Wayne A .... (413) 447-7311
DIR-SYS, Berkshire Eagle, Pittsfield, MA
Eaton, Daryle .... (210) 736-4450
CIRC MGR
Daily Commercial Recorder, San Antonio, TX
Eaton, Janice .... (512) 392-2458
ADV DIR, Daily Record, San Marcos, TX
Eaton, John .... (303) 820-1010
Automotive Reporter
Denver Post, Denver, CO
Eaton, Roy J .... (817) 627-5987
PUB, Wise County Messenger, Decatur, TX
Eaton-Hopper, Susie .... (612) 673-4000
Features Section ED
Star Tribune, Minneapolis, MN
Ebbets, John .... (413) 584-5000
ADV DIR
Daily Hampshire Gazette, Northampton, MA
Ebensberger, Jerry T .... (817) 473-4451
PUB, ED
Mansfield News-Mirror, Mansfield, TX
Eberhart, Paul G .... (212) 455-4000
DIR-OPER, North America Syndicate, King Features Syndicate Inc., New York, NY
Eberle, Terry .... (941) 335-0200
EX ED, News-Press, Fort Myers, FL
Ebersold, Tom .... (203) 926-2080
ED, Trumbull Times, Monroe, CT
Ebert, Pam .... (202) 659-1921
ED, Global Horizons, Washington, DC
Ebert, Roger .... (312) 321-3000
Movie Critic, Chicago Sun-Times, Chicago, IL
Ebert, Russell .... (319) 293-3197
PUB, ED, Van Buren Register, Keosauqua, IA

Ebe Who's Where-66

Eberth, Beth .... (716) 372-3121
Lifestyle ED, Olean Times-Herald, Olean, NY
Eberts, Marge .... (317) 844-1188
Owner/ED, Compass Syndicate, Carmel, IN
Ebrahim, Nazir .... (604) 875-8313
PUB, Community Digest, Vancouver, BC
Ebright, Cheryl .... (409) 776-4444
ADV DIR-Sales & MKTG, Eagle, Bryan, TX
Ebright, Cheryl .... (209) 578-2000
ADV DIR, Modesto Bee, Modesto, CA
Eby, Gay A .... (219) 294-1661
ADV DIR, Elkhart Truth, Elkhart, IN
Eby, John .... (616) 782-2101
MAN ED
Dowagiac Daily News, Dowagiac, MI
Echlin, Bill .... (616) 946-2000
BUS ED, Record-Eagle, Traverse City, MI
Echols, Nita .... (540) 343-0720
GM, Vinton Messenger, Vinton, VA
Eck, Elizabeth .... (410) 337-2400
ED, Owings Mills Times, Towson, MD
Eckard, Eric .... (919) 446-5161
Automotive ED
Rocky Mount Telegram, Rocky Mount, NC
Eckdahl, Joe .... (213) 237-5000
San Fernando Valley EX News ED
Los Angeles Times, Los Angeles, CA
Eckelberry, Steve .... (630) 830-4145
MAN ED, Bartlett Examiner, Bartlett, IL
Ecken, Steven .... (304) 526-4000
CIRC DIR, Herald-Dispatch, Huntington, WV
Eckenrod, Nancy .... (515) 228-3211
PROD FRM-COMP
Charles City Press, Charles City, IA
Eckenrode, Ray .... (814) 946-7411
News ED, Altoona Mirror, Altoona, PA
Eckerman, Melodee A .... (715) 924-4118
PUB, ED, Chetek Alert, Chetek, WI
Eckert, Diane .... (212) 455-4000
Weekly SRV MAN ED
North America Syndicate, King Features Syndicate Inc., New York, NY
Eckert, Florence .... (717) 823-8876
ED, Mic Garsas, Wilkes-Barre, PA
Eckert III, John .... (412) 684-5200
PROD CNR-Commercial Printing
Valley Independent, Monessen, PA
Eckert, Laura .... (609) 989-7800
Sports ED, Trentonian, Trenton, NJ
Eckhardt, D Reed .... (318) 322-5161
MAN ED, News-Star, Monroe, LA
Eckhardt, Mary .... (414) 457-7711
Community ED
Sheboygan Press, Sheboygan, WI
Eckhardt, Vera .... (618) 459-3655
GM, ED
Madison County Chronicle, Worden, IL
Eckhart, Ray .... (407) 420-5000
MGR-Advertiser MKTG
Orlando Sentinel, Orlando, FL
Eckland, Brian .... (360) 577-2500
MGR-SYS, Daily News, Longview, WA
Eckles, Chuck .... (912) 374-0360
ED, Dodge County News, Eastman, GA
Eckles, Cindy .... (912) 374-0360
PUB, GM, Dodge County News, Eastman, GA
Eckstein, Florence .... (602) 870-9470
PUB, ED
Jewish News of Greater Phoenix, Phoenix, AZ
Eckstrom, Ron .... (608) 365-8811
CIRC MGR, Beloit Daily News, Beloit, WI
Eddings, Christopher A .... (409) 756-6671
PUB, Conroe Courier, Conroe, TX
Eddins, James T .... (803) 577-7111
CIRC DIR, Post and Courier, Charleston, SC
Eddins, Jim .... (417) 836-1100
PROD DIR
Springfield News-Leader, Springfield, MO
Eddleman, Burman P .... (618) 827-4353
PUB, ED
Dongola Tri-County Record, Dongola, IL
Eddleman, Marleen .... (501) 378-3582
GM, Air Scoop, Little Rock, AR
Edds, Carolyn .... (864) 582-4511
Librarian, Herald-Journal, Spartanburg, SC
Eddy, Bill .... (402) 475-4200
ASST City ED
Lincoln Journal Star, Lincoln, NE
Eddy, Colleen .... (860) 241-6200
Customer SRV MGR
Hartford Courant, Hartford, CT
Eddy, Gerald .... (608) 654-7330
PUB, Cashton Record, Cashton, WI
Eddy, John (Jack) .... (209) 835-3030
News ED, Tracy Press, Tracy, CA
Eddy, Kristina .... (603) 298-8711
Health/SCI ED
Valley News, White River Jct., VT
Eddy, Merrill .... (317) 736-7101
PROD DIR, Daily Journal, Franklin, IN
Eddy, Rose .... (608) 654-7330
GM, ED, Cashton Record, Cashton, WI
Eddy, Ruth .... (717) 248-6741
BM, Sentinel, Lewistown, PA
Edelen, James .... (502) 633-2526
PUB, Sentinel-News, Shelbyville, KY
Edelman, Andy .... (215) 546-8088
VP, National News Bureau, Philadelphia, PA
Edelman, Lawrence .... (617) 929-2000
BUS ED, Boston Globe, Boston, MA
Edelson, Allan .... (212) 456-7777
VP/CONT/Asst SEC, ABC Inc., New York, NY
Edelstein, Robert .... (914) 692-4572
ASSOC ED
Cineman Syndicate, Middletown, NY
Eden, Carol .... (415) 495-4200
ED, Daily Pacific Builder, San Francisco, CA
Eden, Troy .... (815) 842-1153
PROD FRM-Press/Camera DEPT
Daily Leader, Pontiac, IL
Edenloff, Al .... (320) 763-3133
ED, Echo-Press, Alexandria, MN
Eder, Richard .... (213) 237-5000
Books Critic
Los Angeles Times, Los Angeles, CA
Edey, Noel D .... (403) 827-3539
PUB, Grande Cache Mountaineer, Grande Cache, AB
Edgar, Robert G .... (313) 882-0294
PUB, Connection, Grosse Pointe, MI
Edge, Lisa .... (334) 864-8885
GM, LaFayette Sun, LaFayette, AL
Edge, Malcolm .... (419) 245-6000
DIR-Information SYS, Blade, Toledo, OH
Edgecombe, Jan .... (402) 723-5861
PUB, Henderson News, Henderson, NE
Edgecombe, JoAnn .... (308) 832-2220
PUB, Minden Courier, Minden, NE
Edgecombe, John .... (308) 832-2220
PUB, Minden Courier, Minden, NE
Edgecombe Jr, John .... (402) 759-3117
PUB, Nebraska Signal, Geneva, NE
Edgerton, Scott .... (561) 395-8300
VP-OPER, DP MGR, PROD VP-OPER
News, Boca Raton, FL
Edgren, Charles .... (915) 546-6340
Books ED, COL, EPE
El Paso Herald-Post, El Paso, TX
Edie, Scott .... (301) 834-7722
ED, Brunswick Citizen, Brunswick, MD
Edinger, William J .... (803) 329-4000
ADV DIR, Herald, Rock Hill, SC
Edington, Connie .... (219) 824-0224
ADV DIR, News-Banner, Bluffton, IN
Edison, Randy .... (709) 673-3721
ED, Nor'Wester, Springdale, NF
Edleman, Mary Ann .... (610) 323-3000
ADV MGR-CLASS, Mercury, Pottstown, PA
Edlin, Bill .... (509) 488-3342
PUB, GM, Outlook, Othello, WA
Edman, Louis S .... (860) 928-3500
Author/Owner, Edman Co., Putnam, CT
Edminster, Jean .... (313) 222-6400
MGR-Communications
Detroit Newspapers, Detroit, MI
Edmond, Susan .... (520) 836-7461
Valley Life ED
Casa Grande Dispatch, Casa Grande, AZ
Edmonds, John .... (909) 987-6397
News ED
Inland Valley Daily Bulletin, Ontario, CA
Edmonds, Kenneth W .... (919) 682-2913
GM, Carolina Times, Durham, NC
Edmonds, Vivian Austin .... (919) 682-2913
PUB, ED, Carolina Times, Durham, NC
Edmondson, Susan .... (719) 632-5511
Entertainment ED
Gazette, Colorado Springs, CO
Edmondson II, John .... (941) 484-2611
ED, Venice Gondolier, Venice, FL
Edmonson, George .... (404) 526-5151
ASST MAN ED-Nation/Local
Atlanta Journal-Constitution, Atlanta, GA
Edmund, J Linden .... (208) 377-6200
CONT, Idaho Statesman, Boise, ID
Edmunds, Donald .... (715) 258-5546
GM, Wisconsin State Farmer, Waupaca, WI
Edmunds, George A .... (603) 927-4028
MAN ED
InterTown RECORD, North Sutton, NH
Edmunds, James .... (318) 237-3560
ED, Times of Acadiana, Lafayette, LA
Edmunds, Lorraine F .... (603) 927-4028
GM, InterTown RECORD, North Sutton, NH
Edmundson, Fay .... (770) 428-9411
ED, Northside-Sandy Springs Neighbor, Marietta, GA
Edson, Jennifer .... (212) 416-2000
Art DIR-Interactive Edition
Wall Street Journal, New York, NY
Edson, Nick .... (616) 946-2000
Sports ED, Record-Eagle, Traverse City, MI
Edstrom, David .... (716) 945-1644
Sports ED, Salamanca Press, Salamanca, NY
Edstrom, Frances .... (507) 452-1262
ED, Winona Post & Shopper, Winona, MN
Edstrom, John .... (507) 452-1262
PUB, Winona Post & Shopper, Winona, MN
Edward, Tom .... (416) 367-2000
DP MGR, Toronto Star, Toronto, ON
Edwards, Bernard .... (604) 732-2944
PROD GEN FRM-Mailing
Pacific Press Limited, Vancouver, BC
Edwards, Bob L .... (864) 882-3272
PRES, Edwards Publications, Seneca, SC
Edwards, Bruce .... (802) 747-6121
BUS ED, Rutland Herald, Rutland, VT
Edwards, Byron .... (615) 325-9241
MAN ED, Portland Leader, Portland, TN
Edwards, Caroline .... (210) 796-3718
ED, Bandera Bulletin, Bandera, TX
Edwards, Chris .... (717) 854-1575
Photo ED, Chief Photographer
York Dispatch/York Sunday News, York, PA
Edwards, David .... (906) 228-2500
MAN ED, Mining Journal, Marquette, MI
Edwards, Donald A .... (616) 222-5400
ADV DIR-CLASS
Grand Rapids Press, Grand Rapids, MI
Edwards, Doug .... (408) 920-5000
MGR-MKTG Communication, MGR-MKTG Communications
San Jose Mercury News, San Jose, CA
Edwards, Doug .... (307) 672-2431
DIR-OPER, DP MGR
Sheridan Press, Sheridan, WY
Edwards, E J .... (212) 476-0802
VP/BU Chief, International BusinessMan News Bureau, New York, NY
Edwards, Frank .... (818) 508-6400
ED, Fotos International, Studio City, CA
Edwards, Geoffrey .... (202) 636-3000
VP/GM, Washington Times, Washington, DC
Edwards, Greg .... (618) 234-1000
PUB-Sunday Magazine, ED
Belleville News-Democrat, Belleville, IL
Edwards, Hal .... (801) 896-5476
ED, Richfield Reaper, Richfield, UT
Edwards II, Harold .... (219) 267-3111
PROD DIR, Times-Union, Warsaw, IN
Edwards, J J .... (212) 476-0802
Chairman/CEO/EIC, International Business Man News Bureau, New York, NY
Edwards, Jeff .... (704) 873-1451
PROD MGR, Statesville Record & Landmark, Statesville, NC
Edwards, Jerry .... (864) 882-3272
VP, Edwards Publications, Seneca, SC
Edwards, Jim .... (909) 684-1200
DIR-Photography
Press-Enterprise, Riverside, CA
Edwards, Jim .... (501) 862-6611
City ED, News-Times, El Dorado, AR
Edwards, Joe .... (706) 245-7351
ED, News Leader, Royston, GA
Edwards, Joe .... (808) 525-8000
Sports ED
Honolulu Star-Bulletin, Honolulu, HI
Edwards, John .... (212) 755-4363
Contributing Writer
Punch In Travel & Entertainment News Syndicate, New York, NY
Edwards, John B .... (757) 357-3288
PUB, ED, Times, Smithfield, VA
Edwards, Jon .... (510) 935-2525
ADV MGR-NTL
Contra Costa Times, Walnut Creek, CA
Edwards, Joseph H .... (918) 335-8200
PUB, Examiner-Enterprise, Bartlesville, OK
Edwards, Joyce L .... (864) 882-3272
SEC/TREAS
Edwards Publications, Seneca, SC
Edwards, Kathy .... (410) 268-5000
Entertainment/Amusements ED, Features ED, Living/Lifestyle ED, SCI/Technology ED
Capital, Annapolis, MD
Edwards, Ken .... (919) 638-8101
DP MGR, Sun-Journal, New Bern, NC
Edwards, L J .... (408) 920-5000
ADV Sales MGR-NTL
San Jose Mercury News, San Jose, CA
Edwards, Liz .... (613) 774-2524
ED, Winchester Press, Winchester, ON
Edwards, Lori .... (815) 223-3200
City ED, News-Tribune, La Salle, IL
Edwards, Mary Ann .... (614) 461-5000
EDL Writer, Columbus Dispatch, Columbus, OH
Edwards, Mary Morgan .... (614) 461-5000
School ED
Columbus Dispatch, Columbus, OH
Edwards, Mike .... (704) 859-9151
ADV MGR, Tryon Daily Bulletin, Tryon, NC
Edwards, Mike .... (541) 753-2641
PROD SUPV-Distribution
Corvallis Gazette-Times, Corvallis, OR
Edwards, Moya .... (941) 953-7755
ADV MGR-CLASS
Sarasota Herald-Tribune, Sarasota, FL
Edwards, Nancy .... (360) 577-2500
Religion ED, Daily News, Longview, WA
Edwards, Pat .... (910) 739-4322
ADV MGR-CLASS, Robesonian, Lumberton, NC
Edwards, R Jeffery .... (314) 340-8402
VP, Pulitzer Publishing Co., St. Louis, MO
Edwards, Rachael .... (802) 863-3441
CIRC MGR-PROM
Burlington Free Press, Burlington, VT
Edwards, Ray .... (417) 836-1100
MGR-Technical SRV
Springfield News-Leader, Springfield, MO
Edwards, Roger .... (304) 526-4000
PROD MGR-Pre Press
Herald-Dispatch, Huntington, WV
Edwards, Sgt Robert .... (803) 782-2554
ED, Fort Jackson Leader, Columbia, SC
Edwards, Steve .... (864) 882-3272
VP, Edwards Publications, Seneca, SC
Edwards, T O .... (212) 476-0802
Software Review ED, International Business-Man News Bureau, New York, NY
Edwards, Thomas J .... (313) 584-4000
ED, Dearborn Times-Herald, Dearborn, MI
Edwards, Thomas M .... (419) 358-8010
PUB, Bluffton News, Bluffton, OH
Edwards, Verne .... (614) 363-1161
ASST to PUB
Delaware Gazette, Delaware, OH
Edwards, Victoria .... (212) 727-8170
DIR
Sovfoto-Eastfoto Agency Inc., New York, NY
Edwards, Victoria .... (757) 547-4571
ED, Chesapeake Post, Chesapeake, VA
Edwards, William .... (912) 764-9031
PROD SUPV-Camera
Statesboro Herald, Statesboro, GA
Edwin, Elizabeth .... (915) 682-5311
Fashion/Style ED, Features ED
Midland Reporter-Telegram, Midland, TX
Eedy, Lars .... (519) 843-1310
ED, Fergus-Elora News Express, Fergus, ON
Eedy, R Lorne .... (519) 284-2440
PUB, Journal Argus, St. Marys, ON
Efchak, Edward J .... (201) 646-4000
VP-Strategic Development
Record, Hackensack, NJ
Effinger, Linda .... (954) 356-4000
CIRC MGR-Consumer MKTG
Sun-Sentinel, Fort Lauderdale, FL
Effingham, Larry .... (410) 822-1500
PUB, Star-Democrat, Easton, MD
Effren, Gary .... (305) 376-3800
VP/CONT, Knight-Ridder Inc., Miami, FL
Efren, Gary .... (303) 442-1202
ASST TREAS, Daily Camera, Boulder, CO
Egan, Alexandra .... (402) 475-4200
News ED, Lincoln Journal Star, Lincoln, NE
Egan, Dan .... (516) 843-2020
MGR-Production SYS Software
Newsday, Melville, NY
Egan, Deb .... (701) 252-3120
PA, Jamestown Sun, Jamestown, ND
Egan, Terence F .... (508) 947-1111
ED, Capeway News, Middleboro, MA
Egdish, Len .... (816) 454-9660
GM, Dispatch-Tribune/Press Dispatch, Kansas City, MO
Egenberger, Deb .... (308) 532-6000
Features ED
North Platte Telegraph, North Platte, NE
Egerton, Judy .... (502) 582-4011
Theater ED
Courier-Journal, Louisville, KY
Eggeman, Donna .... (219) 925-2611
CIRC MGR, Evening Star, Auburn, IN
Eggensperger, Bina .... (406) 827-3421
PUB
Sanders County Ledger, Thompson Falls, MT
Eggensperger, Tom .... (406) 827-3421
PUB, ED
Sanders County Ledger, Thompson Falls, MT
Egger, C Z .... (314) 340-8000
GM, St. Louis Post-Dispatch, St. Louis, MO
Egger, Jim .... (503) 255-2142
ADV Sales Representative, ED
Daily Shipping News, Portland, OR
Egger, Terrance C Z .... (314) 340-8402
VP, Pulitzer Publishing Co., St. Louis, MO
Eggleston, Buzz .... (209) 532-7151
MAN ED, Union Democrat, Sonora, CA
Eggleton, R J .... (904) 634-1993
GM, Jacksonville Free Press, Jacksonville, FL
Egler Jr, Frederick N .... (412) 261-6255
EIC, Pittsburgh Legal Journal, Pittsburgh, PA
Egner, Diane .... (813) 259-7711
EDL Writer, Tribune and Times, Tampa, FL
Egolf, Tom .... (610) 622-8800
PROD FRM-PR
Delaware County Daily Times, Primos, PA
Egyir, William .... (212) 932-7400
MAN ED, Amsterdam News, New York, NY

Copyright ©1997 by the Editor & Publisher Co.

67-Who's Where EII

Ehingeo, John ... (205) 532-4000
EPE, Parkston Advance, Parkston, SD

Ehler, Scott ... (605) 935-6015
PUB, ED, Tripp Star Ledger, Tripp, SD

Ehlert, Eugene ... (603) 788-4939
ED, Coos County Democrat, Lancaster, NH

Ehn, Jack ... (505) 823-7777
EPE, Albuquerque Tribune, Albuquerque, NM

Ehoff, Larry ... (320) 632-2345
ED, Morrison County Record, Little Falls, MN

Ehrenberg, Leslie ... (320) 734-4458
GM
Milan Standard-Watson Journal, Milan, MN

Ehrhardt, Dave ... (541) 582-1707
PUB, ED, Rogue River Press, Rogue River, OR

Ehrlich, Fred ... (618) 234-1000
BUS ED
Belleville News-Democrat, Belleville, IL

Ehrlich, Rhona Bayer ... (212) 807-4600
ADV DIR, El Diario La Prensa, New York, NY

Ehrlich, Willie ... (614) 474-3131
ED, Herald, Circleville, OH

Ehrman, Susan ... (210) 225-7411
VP-Human Resources
San Antonio Express-News, San Antonio, TX

Eichberger, Steve ... (502) 582-4011
PROD SUPT-MR
Courier-Journal, Louisville, KY

Eichenberger, Bill ... (330) 996-3000
Sports ED
Akron Beacon Journal, Akron, OH

Eichenberger, Bob ... (406) 587-4491
MGR-Office
Bozeman Daily Chronicle, Bozeman, MT

Eichenlaub, Frank J ... (810) 685-1507
PUB, ED, Milford Times, Milford, MI

Eichmeyer, Mabel ... (314) 433-2223
PUB, ED
Marthasville Record, Marthasville, MO

Eichmeyer, Rueben ... (314) 433-2223
PUB, ED
Marthasville Record, Marthasville, MO

Eichwald, Stan ... (206) 622-8272
Graphics ED/Art DIR, Seattle Daily Journal of Commerce, Seattle, WA

Eick, Andy ... (508) 685-1000
CIRC ASST DIR
Eagle-Tribune, North Andover, MA

Eickhoff, Robert W ... (407) 420-5000
VP/DIR-Circulation, CIRC VP/DIR
Orlando Sentinel, Orlando, FL

Eiden, John ... (419) 668-3771
PROD MGR-SYS
Norwalk Reflector, Norwalk, OH

Eierdam, Don ... (817) 295-0486
ED, Joshua Tribune, Joshua, TX

Eierdan, Tony ... (903) 657-2501
Sports ED
Henderson Daily News, Henderson, TX

Eighmy, Kevin ... (918) 335-8200
CIRC Distribution Clerk
Examiner-Enterprise, Bartlesville, OK

Eikamp, Cindy ... (605) 225-4100
VP, EX ED
Aberdeen American News, Aberdeen, SD

Eikenberry, Kent ... (501) 751-6200
ADV DIR, Morning News of Northwest Arkansas, Springdale, AR

Eilts, Ardis ... (712) 278-2092
ED, Ireton Examiner, Ireton, IA

Einstein, Donald ... (607) 775-0472
PUB, Country Courier, Conklin, NY

Einstein, Elizabeth ... (607) 775-0472
ED, Country Courier, Conklin, NY

Eirich, Dennis ... (414) 457-7711
PROD FRM-PR
Sheboygan Press, Sheboygan, WI

Eisele, Sandy ... (313) 994-6989
MGR-PROM/Community Relations
Ann Arbor News, Ann Arbor, MI

Eisen, Marc ... (608) 251-5627
ED, Isthmus, Madison, WI

Eisenbeiss, William C ... (804) 857-1212
PUB, Soundings, Norfolk, VA

Eisenberg, Chris ... (310) 230-3400
Picture Desk MGR, Allsport Photography USA, Pacific Palisades, CA

Eisenberg, Paul ... (217) 483-2614
ED, Chatham Clarion, Chatham, IL

Eisenhoth, Daniel A ... (610) 642-4300
ED, Main Line Times, Ardmore, PA

Eisman, Amy ... (212) 715-2100
EX ED, USA Weekend, New York, NY

Eisner, Jane R ... (215) 854-2000
EPE, Philadelphia Inquirer, Philadelphia, PA

Eisner, Robert ... (516) 843-2020
Design DIR, Newsday, Melville, NY

Eitzen, James ... (303) 922-0589
PUB, ED, Colorado Leader, Denver, CO

Eklund, Jane ... (603) 924-7172
ED, Monadnock Ledger, Peterborough, NH

Elam, Jim ... (210) 399-2436
PUB, San Benito News, San Benito, TX

Elam, Joe S ... (304) 624-6411
PROD DIR, Clarksburg Exponent/Telegram, Clarksburg, WV

Elbers II, John ... (517) 265-5111
Photo ED, Daily Telegram, Adrian, MI

Elbert, Joe ... (202) 334-6000
ASST MAN ED-Photo
Washington Post, Washington, DC

Elchel, Larry ... (215) 854-2000
NTL ED
Philadelphia Inquirer, Philadelphia, PA

Elchert, John ... (906) 482-1500
PUB, Daily Mining Gazette, Houghton, MI

Elchert, Keith ... (219) 461-8333
ASST MAN ED-News
Journal Gazette, Fort Wayne, IN

Elder, Kevin ... (815) 459-4040
PROD MGR
Northwest Herald, Crystal Lake, IL

Elder, Peggy ... (210) 423-5511
PROD ASST SUPT
Valley Morning Star, Harlingen, TX

Elder, Rob ... (408) 920-5000
VP-EDL Pages, EPE
San Jose Mercury News, San Jose, CA

Elder, Teri ... (573) 815-1500
PROD MGR-Computer
Columbia Daily Tribune, Columbia, MO

Elderton, Linda ... (417) 548-3311
PUB, ED, Sarcoxie Record, Sarcoxie, MO

Eldred, Kevin ... (541) 382-1811
PROD SUPV-MR, Bulletin, Bend, OR

Eldred, Kris ... (209) 441-6111
News ED, Fresno Bee, Fresno, CA

Eldredge, Charles ... (701) 324-4646
PUB, Herald-Press, Harvey, ND

Eldredge, Don ... (903) 893-8181
ED, Herald Democrat, Sherman, TX

Eldreth, Lisa ... (423) 246-8121
EDU ED, Kingsport Times-News, Kingsport, TN

Eldridge, Chris ... (864) 855-0355
ED, Easley Progress, Easley, SC

Eldridge, Dave ... (502) 845-2858
PUB, Henry County Local, New Castle, KY

Eldridge, David ... (281) 422-8302
MAN ED, EPE, EDL Writer
Baytown Sun, Baytown, TX

Eldridge, Janine ... (805) 564-5200
MGR-CR, News-Press, Santa Barbara, CA

Eldridge, Kelly ... (601) 693-1551
City/MET ED, Meridian Star, Meridian, MS

Eldridge, Steve ... (601) 693-1551
CIRC MGR, Meridian Star, Meridian, MS

Eley, Bob ... (907) 456-6661
Sports ED
Fairbanks Daily News-Miner, Fairbanks, AK

Eley, Rob ... (802) 863-3441
MET ED, Burlington Free Press, Burlington, VT

Elfers, Bill ... (617) 433-6700
COB/CEO
Community Newspaper Co., Needham, MA

Elgsaer, John P ... (402) 345-1303
ED, Daily Record, Omaha, NE

Elhard, Kathryn E ... (218) 897-5278
PUB, ED, Northome Record and Mizpah Message, Northome, MN

Elhart, Maurice D ... (307) 266-0500
CIRC DIR, Star-Tribune, Casper, WY

Eli, Carol ... (316) 251-3300
Women's ED
Coffeyville Journal, Coffeyville, KS

Elias, Gayle ... (815) 433-2000
MGR-BUS, Daily Times, Ottawa, IL

Elias, Ken ... (701) 663-6823
PUB
Morton Co. & Mandan News, Mandan, ND

Elias, Thomas ... (213) 452-3918
Author
Southern California Focus, Santa Monica, CA

Elie, Lolis ... (504) 826-3279
COL, Times-Picayune, New Orleans, LA

Elizondo, Ernie ... (210) 728-2500
CIRC DIR
Laredo Morning Times, Laredo, TX

Elkins, Andrew ... (501) 534-3400
PROD FRM-MR
Pine Bluff Commercial, Pine Bluff, AR

Elkins, Charles ... (910) 727-7211
News ED
Winston-Salem Journal, Winston-Salem, NC

Elkins, Ken ... (205) 236-1551
Photo ED, Anniston Star, Anniston, AL

Elkins, Ken ... (803) 329-4000
BUS ED, Herald, Rock Hill, SC

Elkins, Ken J ... (314) 340-8402
Sr VP-Broadcasting OPER
Pulitzer Publishing Co., St. Louis, MO

Elkins, Rick ... (209) 784-5000
MAN ED, Recorder, Porterville, CA

Elkins, Rita ... (407) 242-3500
Religion ED
Florida Today, Melbourne, FL

Elkins, Steve ... (310) 540-5511
ADV DIR, Daily Breeze, Torrance, CA
Copley Press Inc.

Elkins, Steve ... (317) 622-1212
DIR-MKTG, Herald Bulletin, Anderson, IN

Ell, Flynn J ... (701) 764-5312
PUB, ED, Dunn County Herald, Killdeer, ND

Elleby, David ... (206) 622-8272
PROD FRM-PR, Seattle Daily Journal of Commerce, Seattle, WA

Elledge, Flora Jean ... (501) 734-1056
PUB, Brinkley Argus, Brinkley, AR

Elledge, Franklin H ... (501) 747-3373
PUB, Monroe County Sun, Clarendon, AR

Ellefsen, Terri ... (801) 237-2031
Data Center
Salt Lake Tribune, Salt Lake City, UT

Ellenbecker, Phil ... (913) 371-4300
Sports ED
Kansas City Kansan, Kansas City, KS

Eller, Charles ... (718) 981-1234
PROD ASST-COMP Room
Staten Island Advance, Staten Island, NY

Eller, Claudia ... (213) 237-5000
COL-The Biz , Entertainment Reporter-Company Town
Los Angeles Times, Los Angeles, CA

Eller, Donnelle ... (319) 588-5611
ASST City ED
Telegraph Herald, Dubuque, IA

Eller, J David ... (954) 428-9045
PUB, Deerfield Beach-Lighthouse Point Observer, Deerfield Beach, FL

Ellerbach, Susan ... (918) 581-8300
MAN ED, Tulsa World, Tulsa, OK

Ellerbee, Tim ... (504) 826-3279
Sports MAN ED
Times-Picayune, New Orleans, LA

Ellerbrock, Tom ... (619) 229-0500
PUB, Update, San Diego, CA

Ellerin, Michael B ... (415) 255-3100
GM, Bay Guardian, San Francisco, CA

Ellerton, Glenda ... (308) 345-4500
CIRC MGR
McCook Daily Gazette, McCook, NE

Ellie, Beth ... (715) 597-3313
MAN ED, Tri-County News, Osseo, WI

Elliman, D T ... (802) 253-2101
PUB, Stowe Reporter, Stowe, VT

Ellinghouse, Cletis R ... (573) 222-3243
PUB, ED, Weekly Press, Puxico, MO

Ellinghouse, Harold T ... (573) 223-7122
PUB, ED
Wayne County Journal-Banner, Piedmont, MO

Ellingsworth, Tom ... (816) 465-7016
PUB, ED, Memphis Democrat, Memphis, MO

Ellington, Kay ... (805) 395-7500
MGR-MKTG
Bakersfield Californian, Bakersfield, CA

Ellington, Lori ... (817) 767-8341
ADV DIR, Wichita Falls Times Record News, Wichita Falls, TX

Ellington, Ray ... (910) 891-1234
PROD FRM, Daily Record, Dunn, NC

Elliot, Billy ... (214) 977-8222
PROD Paperhandle GEN FRM
Dallas Morning News, Dallas, TX

Elliot, Dan ... (918) 684-2828
EX ED
Muskogee Daily Phoenix & Times Democrat, Muskogee, OK

Elliot, David ... (512) 476-0576
MAN ED, Texas Triangle, Austin, TX

Elliot, Douglas ... (414) 248-4444
ED, Lake Geneva Regional News, Lake Geneva, WI

Elliot, Jean ... (812) 546-6113
GM, Hope Star-Journal, Hope, IN

Elliot, Lisa ... (316) 283-1500
Reporter, Newton Kansan, Newton, KS

Elliot, Scott ... (937) 335-5634
News ED, Troy Daily News/Miami Valley Sunday News, Troy, OH

Elliot House, Karen ... (212) 416-2600
PRES-International
Dow Jones & Co. Inc., New York, NY

Elliott, Angela ... (717) 389-4825
BM, Spectrum Features, Bloomsburg, PA

Elliott, Carroll ... (330) 364-5577
PROD FRM-Distribution
Times Reporter, New Philadelphia, OH

Elliott, Charles E ... (937) 335-5634
VP-OPER, Troy Daily News/Miami Valley Sunday News, Troy, OH

Elliott, Cindy ... (912) 236-9511
ADV MGR-RT Display
Savannah Morning News, Savannah, GA

Elliott, David ... (619) 299-3131
Films ED
San Diego Union-Tribune, San Diego, CA

Elliott, David ... (301) 733-5131
PSL DIR, Morning Herald, Hagerstown, MD

Elliott, David ... (519) 756-2020
CIRC SUPV-Sales
Expositor, Brantford, ON

Elliott, Donna ... (716) 343-8000
MGR-BUS DEPT, Daily News, Batavia, NY

Elliott, Glenda ... (316) 268-6000
News ASSOC ED
Wichita Eagle, Wichita, KS

Elliott, Henry ... (614) 532-1441
PROD FRM-Press
Ironton Tribune, Ironton, OH

Elliott, James ... (217) 645-3033
PUB, Liberty Bee-Times, Liberty, IL

Elliott, Jeffrey A ... (312) 222-3232
CIRC DIR-Alternate Delivery
Chicago Tribune, Chicago, IL

Elliott, John ... (206) 622-8272
Online MGR, Seattle Daily Journal of Commerce, Seattle, WA

Elliott, John T ... (815) 265-7332
PUB, ED, Gilman Star, Gilman, IL

Elliott, Karen ... (219) 925-2611
ADV DIR-Inserts
Evening Star, Auburn, IN

Elliott, Kathy ... (519) 822-4310
CR MGR, PA, Daily Mercury, Guelph, ON

Elliott, Marcia ... (217) 645-3033
ED, Liberty Bee-Times, Liberty, IL

Elliott, Marion ... (864) 298-4100
City ED, EDU ED, Environmental ED, Farm/Agriculture ED, Religion ED
Greenville News, Greenville, SC

Elliott, Mark ... (807) 274-5373
BUS/EDU ED
Fort Frances Daily Bulletin, Fort Frances, ON

Elliott, Mark ... (802) 254-2311
ADV MGR
Brattleboro Reformer, Brattleboro, VT

Elliott, Michael G ... (606) 236-2551
ADV MGR-NTL
Advocate-Messenger, Danville, KY

Elliott, Pat ... (415) 777-5700
CIRC MGR-Customer SRV, San Francisco Newspaper Agency, San Francisco, CA

Elliott, Sam ... (913) 449-7272
PUB, ED
Flint Hills Independent, Eskridge, KS

Elliott, Teressa L ... (513) 761-1188
Senior Critic
Critic's Choice Reviews, Cincinnati, OH

Elliott, Tom ... (619) 322-8889
Sports ED, Desert Sun, Palm Springs, CA

Elliott, Vondell ... (806) 998-4888
PUB, GM, ED
Lynn County News, Tahoka, TX

Ellis, Bill ... (901) 529-2211
Music Reporter
Commercial Appeal, Memphis, TN

Ellis, Bill ... (806) 247-2211
PUB, ED, Friona Star, Friona, TX

Ellis, Bob ... (618) 932-2146
ED, Daily American, West Frankfort, IL

Ellis, Carlton D ... (330) 773-4196
ED, Akron Reporter, Akron, OH

Ellis, Chip ... (304) 348-5140
Photo DEPT MGR
Charleston Daily Mail, Charleston, WV

Ellis, Dorris ... (713) 524-4474
PUB, ED, Houston Sun, Houston, TX

Ellis, Elizabeth S ... (860) 646-0500
PRES, PUB
Journal Inquirer, Manchester, CT

Ellis, Eric ... (541) 889-5387
Farm/Garden ED
Argus Observer, Ontario, OR

Ellis, Frank X ... (770) 459-5166
ED, Villa Rican, Villa Rica, GA

Ellis, Harold D ... (610) 622-8800
Harrisburg BU ED
Delaware County Daily Times, Primos, PA

Ellis, Harriette R ... (310) 595-5543
ED, Jewish Community Chronicle, Long Beach, CA

Ellis, James ... (417) 623-3480
ED Emeritus, Joplin Globe, Joplin, MO

Ellis, Jane ... (719) 632-5511
ADV DIR-RT
Gazette, Colorado Springs, CO

Ellis, Jill ... (330) 296-9657
MAN ED, Automotive/Aviation ED, Books ED
Record-Courier, Kent-Ravenna, OH

Ellis, Jim ... (918) 542-5533
Sports ED, Miami News-Record, Miami, OK

Ellis, Jim ... (409) 744-3611
CIRC MGR
Galveston County Daily News, Galveston, TX

Ellis, Kristen ... (804) 446-2750
ED, Flagship, Norfolk, VA

Ellis, Lorraine ... (603) 352-1234
ADV MGR-CLASS, Keene Sentinel, Keene, NH

Ellis, Mark ... (614) 461-5000
City ED, Columbus Dispatch, Columbus, OH

Ellis, Mary ... (705) 726-6537
BM, Examiner, Barrie, ON

Ellis, Michael C ... (412) 439-7500
ED (Herald)
Herald-Standard, Uniontown, PA

Ellis, Mickey ... (205) 532-4000
Food ED, Huntsville Times, Huntsville, AL

Ellis, Milton ... (902) 564-5451
PUB/GM, Cape Breton Post, Sydney, NS

EII Who's Where-68

Ellis, Paula .... (803) 771-6161
ASST to PUB, State, Columbia, SC
Ellis, Peggy .... (517) 629-3984
PROD MGR-COMP, Recorder, Albion, MI
Ellis, Peter .... (605) 331-2200
MAN ED, Argus Leader, Sioux Falls, SD
Ellis, Ray .... (714) 768-3631
PUB, Flight Jacket, Mission Viejo, CA
Ellis, Roger .... (519) 255-5711
PROD FRM-MR, Windsor Star, Windsor, ON
Ellis, Sheryl .... (502) 886-4444
Personnel MGR
Kentucky New Era, Hopkinsville, KY
Ellis, Shirley C .... (215) 949-4000
VP/SEC, Bucks County Courier Times, Levittown, PA, Calkins Newspapers
Ellis, Stanley M .... (215) 949-4000
VP, Bucks County Courier Times, Levittown, PA, Calkins Newspapers
Ellis, Steve .... (616) 345-3511
ADV DIR, Kalamazoo Gazette, Kalamazoo, MI
Ellis, Steve .... (912) 888-9300
Sports ED, Albany Herald, Albany, GA
Ellis, Stone .... (601) 896-2100
ADV DIR, Sun Herald, Biloxi, MS
Ellis, Tim .... (520) 458-9440
Sunday News ED
Sierra Vista Herald, Sierra Vista, AZ
Ellis Jr, William R .... (330) 773-4196
PUB, Akron Reporter, Akron, OH
Ellison, Aaron .... (918) 786-9002
ADV DIR, Grove Daily News, Grove, OK
Ellison, Alva .... (409) 833-3311
CONT, Beaumont Enterprise, Beaumont, TX
Ellison Jr, B F .... (864) 338-6124
PUB, News-Chronicle, Honea Path, SC
Ellison, David .... (713) 220-7171
ASST City ED
Houston Chronicle, Houston, TX
Ellison, Fred .... (205) 353-4612
ADV MGR, Decatur Daily, Decatur, AL
Ellison, William .... (502) 582-4011
Deputy MAN ED
Courier-Journal, Louisville, KY
Ellison-Rider, Elaine .... (864) 338-6124
ED, News-Chronicle, Honea Path, SC
Ellsworth, A Whitney .... (860) 435-9873
PUB, Lakeville Journal, Lakeville, CT
Ellsworth, Barry .... (613) 392-6501
MAN ED
Trentonian & Tri-County News, Trenton, ON
Ellsworth, Dennis .... (915) 653-1221
ED, Standard-Times, San Angelo, TX
Ellwood, N Suzanne .... (313) 222-6400
VP-Market Development
Detroit Newspapers, Detroit, MI
Ellzey, Don .... (504) 386-6537
PUB, ED, Enterprise, Ponchatoula, LA
Elman, Merlyn R .... (515) 562-2606
PUB, ED
Buffalo Center Tribune, Buffalo Center, IA
El Masri, E .... (416) 362-0304
ED, Akbar El-Arab El-Dawlah, Toronto, ON
Elmendorf, Jim .... (310) 519-1442
ED, Random Lengths/Harbor Independent News, San Pedro, CA
Elmore, Barbara .... (817) 757-5757
MAN ED, Waco Tribune-Herald, Waco, TX
Elmore, Dannie .... (205) 586-3188
GM, Arab Tribune, Arab, AL
Elmore, Johnny .... (770) 787-6397
GM, Covington News, Covington, GA
Elmore, Ken .... (205) 532-4000
ADV CNR-GEN
Huntsville Times, Huntsville, AL
Elmore, Lori .... (817) 645-2441
Amusements ED, City/MET ED
Cleburne Times-Review, Cleburne, TX
Elmore, Nancy .... (816) 637-6155
CONT, DP MGR
Daily Standard, Excelsior Springs, MO
Elmore, Sherry L .... (605) 756-4200
PUB, ED
South Shore Gazette, South Shore, SD
Elmstrom, David .... (612) 333-4244
ED
Finance and Commerce, Minneapolis, MN
Elpel, Tricia .... (406) 322-5212
GM, ED
Stillwater County News, Columbus, MT
Elrich, Matthew .... (360) 736-3311
News ED, Chronicle, Centralia, WA
Elrod, Sam .... (612) 222-5011
Food ED, Travel ED
St. Paul Pioneer Press, St. Paul, MN
Elsasser, Ron .... (610) 820-6500
PROD SUPT-PR
Morning Call, Allentown, PA
Elsberry, James T .... (713) 266-5481
VP/Group MGR
Southern Newspapers Inc., Houston, TX

Elsea, Jerry .... (319) 398-8211
EPE, EDL Writer
Gazette, Cedar Rapids, IA
Elsen, William .... (202) 334-6000
DIR-Recruiting/News
Washington Post, Washington, DC
Elsessor, David .... (815) 223-3200
Sports ED, News-Tribune, La Salle, IL
Elsken, Katrina .... (941) 763-3134
ED
Daily Okeechobee News, Okeechobee, FL
Elson, Bradley .... (212) 455-4000
Weekly SRV Sales MGR, North America Syndicate, King Features Syndicate, NY, NY
Elson, Craig .... (613) 933-3160
ED, Photo DEPT MGR, SCI/Sports ED
Standard-Freeholder, Cornwall, ON
Elson, Stuart .... (306) 297-4144
MAN ED
Shaunavon Standard, Shaunavon, SK
Elswick, Carolyn .... (816) 562-2424
Lifestyle ED
Maryville Daily Forum, Maryville, MO
Elswick, Mike .... (903) 668-3090
PUB, ED
Hallsville Herald, Hallsville, TX
Elsworthy, Tom .... (403) 468-0100
Features ED, Edmonton Sun, Edmonton, AB
Elterman, Brad .... (310) 587-0025
CEO
Online USA, Beverly Hills, CA
Eltringham, Norma .... (614) 283-4711
BUS MGR, Herald-Star, Steubenville, OH
Ogden Newspapers
Elum, Charles R .... (216) 923-2397
PRES
Scrambl-Gram Inc., Cuyahoga Falls, OH
Elving, Belle .... (202) 334-6000
Deputy ED
Washington Post, Washington, DC
Elwell, Patty .... (219) 824-0224
ADV MGR-GEN/CLASS
News-Banner, Bluffton, IN
Elwood, Aimee .... (903) 935-7914
CIRC MGR
Marshall News Messenger, Marshall, TX
Elwood, Scott L .... (218) 879-6761
PUB, ED, Pine Knot, Cloquet, MN
Elworthy, Ted .... (541) 474-3700
CIRC MGR
Grants Pass Daily Courier, Grants Pass, OR
Ely, Becky .... (816) 254-8600
BM, PSL MGR, Examiner, Independence, MO
Morris Communications Corp.
Ely, Betty J .... (505) 388-1576
Co-PUB, Silver City Daily Press & Independent, Silver City, NM
Ely, Christina .... (505) 542-3471
PUB, Lordsburg Liberal, Lordsburg, NM
Ely-Dubiskas, Christina B .... (505) 388-1576
Co-PUB, ADV DIR, Silver City Daily Press & Independent, Silver City, NM
Elze, Olaf .... (509) 837-4500
Opinion ED
Daily Sun News, Sunnyside, WA
Emanuel, Richard .... (607) 936-4651
ADV MGR, Leader, Corning, NY
Embree, Charles .... (816) 263-4123
City/MET ED, Environmental ED, Moberly Monitor-Index & Democrat, Moberly, MO
Embry, Pat .... (615) 259-8800
MAN ED, Nashville Banner, Nashville, TN
Emenegger, Sharon .... (541) 753-2641
CONT, DP MGR
Corvallis Gazette-Times, Corvallis, OR
Emens, Ed .... (423) 775-6111
PUB, Herald-News, Dayton, TN
Emerick, Laura .... (312) 321-3000
ASST Features ED
Chicago Sun-Times, Chicago, IL
Emerle, Mark .... (518) 374-4141
PROD FRM-MR
Daily Gazette, Schenectady, NY
Emerson, Bob .... (219) 235-6161
CIRC MGR-Customer SRV
South Bend Tribune, South Bend, IN
Emerson, Craig .... (910) 323-4848
ADV MGR-CLASS
Fayetteville Observer-Times, Fayetteville, NC
Emerson, Ellen F .... (540) 347-5522
PUB, Fauquier Citizen, Warrenton, VA
Emerson, Floyd .... (501) 623-7711
ADV DIR
Sentinel-Record, Hot Springs, AR
Emerson, John .... (573) 888-4505
PROD FRM-PR
Daily Dunklin Democrat, Kennett, MO
Emerson, Lawrence K .... (540) 347-5522
PUB, ED, Fauquier Citizen, Warrenton, VA
Emerson, Molly .... (608) 635-2565
PUB, Poynette Press, Poynette, WI
Emerson, Paul .... (208) 743-9411
MAN ED, Automotive ED, Environmental ED
Lewiston Morning Tribune, Lewiston, ID
Emerson, Richard .... (608) 635-2565
ED, Poynette Press, Poynette, WI

Emert, Rich .... (412) 834-1151
Scholastic Sports ED
Tribune-Review, Greensburg, PA
Emery, Frank E .... (316) 223-1460
PRES, PUB
Fort Scott Tribune, Fort Scott, KS
Emery, Mike .... (317) 598-6397
Sports ED
Noblesville Daily Ledger, Noblesville, IN
Emery, Randy .... (306) 764-4276
CIRC MGR
Prince Albert Daily Herald, Prince Albert, SK
Emery, Sherry .... (509) 582-1500
Graphics ED, Tri-City Herald, Tri-Cities, WA
Emig, John .... (909) 866-3456
ED, Big Bear Grizzly, Big Bear Lake, CA
Emigh, Susan .... (905) 526-3333
DIR-New Media/INFO Technology, ADTX MGR, Spectator, Hamilton, ON
Emke, Bert .... (502) 582-4011
Chief EDL Writer
Courier-Journal, Louisville, KY
Emmerich, Celia .... (601) 453-5312
COL, Commonwealth, Greenwood, MS
Emmerich, J Wyatt .... (601) 957-1122
PRES/CEO
Emmerich Enterprises Inc., Jackson, MS
Emmerthal, Ronald .... (203) 333-0161
PROD MGR-Pre Print
Connecticut Post, Bridgeport, CT
Emmons, Laura .... (713) 485-7501
PUB, MAN ED
Friendswood Reporter News, Pearland, TX
Emmons, Lyle .... (306) 528-2020
PUB, ED, Last Mountain Times, Nokomis, SK
Emmons, Mark .... (313) 222-6400
Fun & Fitness Writer
Detroit Free Press, Detroit, MI
Emmons, Matt .... (614) 363-1161
Chief Photographer
Delaware Gazette, Delaware, OH
Emmons, Shirley .... (306) 528-2020
PUB, ED, Last Mountain Times, Nokomis, SK
Emond, Gilles .... (418) 686-3233
CIRC DIR, Le Soleil, Quebec, QC
Emord-Netzley, Gary .... (502) 926-0123
Photo ED
Messenger-Inquirer, Owensboro, KY
Emory, John .... (318) 377-1866
ADV MGR-RT
Minden Press-Herald, Minden, LA
Emple, Jim .... (207) 990-8000
News ED, Bangor Daily News, Bangor, ME
Emrick, Cindy .... (217) 824-2233
ADTX MGR, Taylorville Daily Breeze-Courier, Taylorville, IL
Emrick, Larry .... (604) 732-2111
NTL ED, Vancouver Sun, Vancouver, BC
Emro, Kathleen .... (573) 756-8927
ED, Daily Press Leader, Farmington, MO
Emry, Big Dee .... (515) 653-2344
ED, Hedrick Journal, Hedrick, IA
Emsley, Bruce .... (415) 883-8600
CIRC DIR
Marin Independent Journal, Novato, CA
Emslie, T David .... (519) 482-3443
ED, Clinton News-Record, Clinton, ON
Emsweller, Jeff .... (812) 663-3111
ED, Greensburg Times, Greensburg, IN
Encounter, Rich .... (415) 854-3132
Graphic Artist
Sam Mantics Enterprise, Menlo Park, CA
Enda, Jodi .... (215) 854-2000
Washington BU
Philadelphia Inquirer, Philadelphia, PA
Ende, Lori .... (507) 283-2333
ED, Rock County Star Herald, Luverne, MN
Enderle, Jerry .... (606) 283-6270
GM, ED, Messenger, Erlanger, KY
Enderle, Marvin .... (910) 997-3111
PUB, Richmond County Daily Journal, Rockingham, NC
Endicott, William .... (916) 321-1000
ASST MAN ED-Capitol/Politics/ADM
Sacramento Bee, Sacramento, CA
Endress, Jay .... (317) 873-6397
PUB, Zionsville Times Sentinel, Zionsville, IN
Endress, Paula .... (317) 873-6397
ED, Zionsville Times Sentinel, Zionsville, IN
Endries, Bruce .... (607) 432-1000
DP MGR, Daily Star, Oneonta, NY
Endrst, James .... (860) 241-6200
Television Writer
Hartford Courant, Hartford, CT
Ends, Tony .... (608) 754-3311
Special Sections ED, Wire ED
Janesville Gazette, Janesville, WI
Endsley, Lyle .... (419) 245-6000
CIRC MGR-Home Delivery
Blade, Toledo, OH
Enea, James .... (610) 258-7171
PROD MGR-MR, Express-Times, Easton, PA
Enersen, Judy .... (515) 847-2592
PUB, ED, World Journal, Ackley, IA

Enfinger, Adrian .... (904) 435-8500
PROD MGR-SYS
Pensacola News Journal, Pensacola, FL
Eng, Daniel .... (203) 574-3636
ASST TREAS, CONT, Waterbury Republican-American, Waterbury, CT
Eng, Donald .... (203) 926-2080
ED, Amity Observer, Monroe, CT
Eng, Rick .... (215) 854-2000
Wire ED
Philadelphia Daily News, Philadelphia, PA
Engberg MD, Karen M .... (805) 682-8844
Self-Syndicator
Karen M Engberg MD, Santa Barbara, CA
Engbrock, Chad .... (972) 442-5515/2623
PUB, Wylie News, Wylie, TX
Engdahl, Todd .... (303) 820-1010
New Media ED, ADTX MGR
Denver Post, Denver, CO
Engebrecht, Julie .... (513) 721-2700
Sports ED
Cincinnati Enquirer, Cincinnati, OH
Engel, Chris .... (800) 426-4192
CFO, Independent Newspapers, Dover, DE
Engel, Duane .... (913) 222-2555
PUB, ED, Rush County News, La Crosse, KS
Engel, Jane .... (520) 573-4400
VP-FIN/TREAS, TNI Partners dba Tucson Newspapers, Tucson, AZ
Engel, Mary .... (913) 222-2555
PUB, MAN ED
Rush County News, La Crosse, KS
Engel, Paul .... (517) 864-3630
PUB, ED
Minden City Herald, Minden City, MI
Engelhardt, Thomas A .... (314) 340-8000
EDL Cartoonist
St. Louis Post-Dispatch, St. Louis, MO
Engelke, Roseann .... (561) 287-1550
DP DIR, Stuart News, Stuart, FL
Engelman, Tom .... (609) 663-4200
ED, Courier Post/This Week, Cherry Hill, NJ
Engels, David .... (414) 657-1000
EDU ED, Kenosha News, Kenosha, WI
Engelstad, Bobbie .... (406) 523-5200
DIR-Human Resources
Missoulian, Missoula, MT
Engen, John .... (406) 523-5200
PROD MGR-Pre Press/Commercial
Missoulian, Missoula, MT
Enger, Timothy J .... (612) 389-1222
GM, Princeton Union-Eagle, Princeton, MN
Engesser, Margaret A .... (507) 465-8112
PUB, ED
New Richland Star, New Richland, MN
Engh, Rohn .... (715) 248-3800
DIR, Photosource International, Osceola, WI
England, Millard .... (216) 999-4500
INFO SYS MGR-Ad SRV
Plain Dealer, Cleveland, OH
Engle, Genevive .... (308) 472-3217
ED, Bertrand Herald, Bertrand, NE
Engle, J Michael .... (610) 371-5000
PROD SUPT-PR
Reading Times/Eagle, Reading, PA
Engle, Kathy .... (520) 625-5511
ED
Green Valley News & Sun, Green Valley, AZ
Engle, Robert .... (518) 843-1100
PROD SUPV, Recorder, Amsterdam, NY
Engle, Robert .... (308) 472-3217
PUB, ED, Bertrand Herald, Bertrand, NE
Englehart, Bob .... (860) 241-6200
EDL Cartoonist
Hartford Courant, Hartford, CT
Engleman, Chas E .... (405) 323-5151
PRES, PUB, ED
Clinton Daily News, Clinton, OK
Engleman, Jean .... (405) 323-5151
SEC, Clinton Daily News, Clinton, OK
Engleman, Kenneth .... (503) 822-3358
PUB, McKenzie River Reflections, McKenzie Bridge, OR
Engleman, Louise .... (503) 822-3358
MAN ED, McKenzie River Reflections, McKenzie Bridge, OR
Engleman, Steve .... (405) 323-5151
VP, Clinton Daily News, Clinton, OK
Engler, Daniel .... (520) 634-2241
ED, Verde Independent, Cottonwood, AZ
Engler, Edward .... (603) 569-3126
GM, Granite State News, Wolfeboro, NH
Englert, Jim .... (717) 767-6397
PROD MGR-PR
York Newspaper Company, York, PA
Engles, Matt .... (803) 785-4293
DP MGR, ADTX MGR
Island Packet, Hilton Head, SC
Engleton, Terre T .... (217) 429-5151
CONT, Herald & Review, Decatur, IL
English, Alan .... (910) 323-4848
Photo ED
Fayetteville Observer-Times, Fayetteville, NC
English, Bobby .... (304) 327-2811
CIRC DIR
Bluefield Daily Telegraph, Bluefield, WV

Copyright ©1997 by the Editor & Publisher Co.

69-Who's Where **Est**

English, Christy (506) 452-6671
Fashion/Women's ED
Daily Gleaner, Fredericton, NB

English, Dewey (334) 433-1551
ASST MAN ED
Mobile Press Register, Mobile, AL

English, Doug (519) 679-6666
Travel ED, London Free Press, London, ON

English, Susan (509) 459-5000
Entertainment ED
Spokesman-Review, Spokane, WA

Englund, Eric (201) 791-8400
ED, Shopper News, Fair Lawn, NJ

Englund, Gail (906) 228-2500
ADV MGR, Mining Journal, Marquette, MI

Engram, Sara (410) 332-6000
EDL Page DIR, Sun, Baltimore, MD

Engstrom, Darlene (360) 694-3391
CIRC MGR-Customer SRV/Office MGR
Columbian, Vancouver, WA

Engstrom, John (206) 448-8000
Lifestyle ED, Post-Intelligencer, Seattle, WA

Enlow, Clair (206) 622-8272
Architectural/Engineering ED, Seattle Daily Journal of Commerce, Seattle, WA

Enlow, Roger (817) 573-7066
ED, Hood County News, Granbury, TX

Enman, Marcia (902) 436-6005
PUB, ED
La Voix Acadienne, Summerside, PE

Enman, Maureen (416) 585-5000
Consumer Relations, Globe and Mail, Toronto, ON

Ennis, Dave (910) 343-2000
City ED, Morning Star/Sunday Star-News, Wilmington, NC

Ennis, Paul (304) 348-5140
PROD MGR-PR
Charleston Newspapers, Charleston, WV

Ennis, Ron (709) 256-4371
MAN ED, Gander Beacon, Gander, NF

Ennis-Reddick, Tara D (403) 783-3074
ED, Ponoka Herald, Ponoka, AB

Enns, Kurt (204) 697-7000
CR MGR, Free Press, Winnipeg, MB

Enoch, David (319) 383-2200
CIRC MGR, Quad-City Times, Davenport, IA

Enoch, Vicki (502) 781-1700
MGR-EDU SRV
Daily News, Bowling Green, KY

Enomoto, Catherine (808) 525-8000
Food ED
Honolulu Star-Bulletin, Honolulu, HI

Enos, John (508) 997-7411
MGR-Production SYS
Standard Times, New Bedford, MA

Enrich, Ann (719) 676-3304
PUB, ED
Greenhorn Valley News, Colorado City, CO

Enrietto, John (614) 283-4711
Sports ED, Herald-Star, Steubenville, OH

Enright, James P (301) 662-1177
CORP DIR-ADV/MKTG
Frederick Post/News, Frederick, MD

Enright, Jeffery R (612) 777-8800
PUB, South-West Review, North St. Paul, MN

Enright, Judy (617) 837-3500
ED, Hanover Mariner, Marshfield, MA

Enright, Sherri (319) 242-7101
ADV MGR-CLASS
Clinton Herald, Clinton, IA

Enriquez, Alberto (541) 776-4411
EDU ED, Mail Tribune, Medford, OR

Enriquez, Bertha V (305) 633-3341
ADV MGR-NTL
Diario Las Americas, Miami, FL

Ens, Rhonda J (306) 784-2422
PUB, Herald, Herbert, SK

Enser, Dennis (716) 849-3434
Photo ED, Buffalo News, Buffalo, NY

Ensley, Debbie (219) 347-0400
ADV MGR, News-Sun, Kendallville, IN

Ensley, Ron (219) 925-2611
ADV DIR-MKTG, Evening Star, Auburn, IN
Witwer Newspapers

Ensor, Deborah (505) 758-2241
ED, Taos News, Taos, NM

Enstad, David J (901) 529-2211
ADV DIR, Commercial Appeal, Memphis, TN

Enstrom, Nancy (812) 665-3145
PUB, ED
Jasonville Leader, Jasonville, IN

Enters, Antonia (415) 692-9406
ED, San Mateo Weekly, Burlingame, CA

Enwright, Thomas (715) 423-7200
ED, EPE, Daily Tribune, Wisconsin Rapids, WI

Enyart, Jeanie (215) 854-2000
ADV DIR-CLASS
Philadelphia Inquirer, Philadelphia, PA

Epler, Frank J (717) 255-8100
ASST TREAS, CONT
Patriot-News, Harrisburg, PA

Epling, Jerry (304) 526-4000
PROD DIR
Herald-Dispatch, Huntington, WV

Epp, Dan M (316) 376-4264
PUB, ED
Greeley County Republican, Tribune, KS

Epp, Jan (316) 376-4264
PUB, ED
Greeley County Republican, Tribune, KS

Epp, Peter (519) 683-4485
ED, Bothwell Times, Bothwell, ON

Epperheimer, Bill (509) 248-1251
News ED
Yakima Herald-Republic, Yakima, WA

Epperheimer, William (913) 371-4300
PRES, PUB
Kansas City Kansan, Kansas City, KS

Epperly, Dianna (419) 738-2128
PUB, Daily News, Wapakoneta, OH

Epperly, Jeffrey S (617) 266-6670
ED, Bay Windows, Boston, MA

Epple, Earl R (812) 482-2424
PROD MGR, Herald, Jasper, IN

Epple, Janet (812) 482-2424
People ED, Herald, Jasper, IN

Epplett, R W (519) 825-4541
PUB, ED, Wheatley Journal, Wheatley, ON

Epps, Mel (706) 353-9300
ED, Athens Observer, Athens, GA

Epstein, George (510) 428-2000
PUB, ED, Bay Area Press, Oakland, CA

Epstein, Noel (202) 334-6000
PUB/NTL Weekly
Washington Post, Washington, DC

Epstein, Richard (216) 999-4500
CIRC DIR, Plain Dealer, Cleveland, OH

Epstein, Rick (908) 782-4747
MAN ED
Hunterdon County Democrat, Flemington, NJ

Epstein, Ronni (702) 732-0556
GM, Jewish Reporter, Las Vegas, NV

Epstein, Shelley (309) 686-3000
ASSOC ED, Journal Star, Peoria, IL

Epstein, Warren (719) 632-5511
Radio/Television ED
Gazette, Colorado Springs, CO

Epton, Jeff (937) 275-8855
PUB, GM, Dayton Voice, Dayton, OH

Eramo, Michael (508) 922-1234
ADV MGR
Daily News of Newburyport, Beverly, MA

Eranstiter, LaReta (402) 857-3737
ED, Niobrara Tribune, Niobrara, NE

Erb, Fannie (330) 852-4634
MAN ED, Budget, Sugarcreek, OH

Erb, Susan (717) 533-2900
ED, Hershey Chronicle, Hershey, PA

Erbeck, Bruce (904) 599-2100
PROD MGR-Press
Tallahassee Democrat, Tallahassee, FL

Erbsen, Claude E (212) 621-1500
VP/DIR of World SRV
Associated Press, New York, NY

Ercolino, Jill (717) 762-2151
Fashion/Style ED, Home Furnishings/Society ED, Living/Lifestyle ED, Television/Film ED, Theater/Music ED, Women's ED
Record Herald, Waynesboro, PA

Erdman, David (610) 820-6500
City ED, Morning Call, Allentown, PA

Erdman, Katie (320) 392-5527
ED, Hancock Record, Hancock, MN

Erichsen, Gerald (360) 424-3251
Religion ED
Skagit Valley Herald, Mount Vernon, WA

Ericksen, Charles (202) 234-0280
PUB
Hispanic Link News Service, Washington, DC

Erickson, Ann (715) 833-9200
Librarian, Leader-Telegram, Eau Claire, WI

Erickson, Beth (503) 221-8327
Team Leader-North
Oregonian, Portland, OR

Erickson, Beth (617) 821-4418
PUB, ED, Canton Citizen, Canton, MA

Erickson, Brenda (414) 684-4433
Religion/Society ED, Women's ED
Herald Times Reporter, Manitowoc, WI

Erickson, Bryan (313) 222-6400
Deputy Design DIR-Features
Detroit Free Press, Detroit, MI

Erickson, Chris (212) 268-8600
ED, Manhattan Spirit, New York, NY

Erickson, Chuck (612) 673-4000
PROD MGR-Electric Shop
Star Tribune, Minneapolis, MN

Erickson, Eric (715) 373-5500
PUB, GM, County Journal, Washburn, WI

Erickson, James (520) 573-4220
SCI/Technology ED
Arizona Daily Star, Tucson, AZ

Erickson, John (312) 321-3000
ASST MET ED
Chicago Sun-Times, Chicago, IL

Erickson, Kurt (309) 829-9411
Political Writer
Pantagraph, Bloomington, IL

Erickson, LaVonne (701) 756-6363
GM, Renville County Farmer, Mohall, ND

Erickson, Lisa (715) 623-4191
Home Furnishings/Society ED
Antigo Daily Journal, Antigo, WI

Erickson, Lois (701) 253-7311
Human Resources, Forum, Fargo, ND

Erickson, Mark (507) 662-5555
ED, Lakefield Standard, Lakefield, MN

Erickson, Nancy G (360) 424-3251
EX ED, Opinion Page ED
Skagit Valley Herald, Mount Vernon, WA

Erickson, Randy (773) 286-6100
ED
Chicago's Northwest Side Press, Chicago, IL

Erickson, Randy (305) 294-6641
ADV MGR, Key West Citizen, Key West, FL

Erickson, Robert (613) 342-4441
ASST GM, Brockville Recorder and Times, Brockville, ON

Erickson, Stanford (212) 837-7000
PRES-Magazine Division, Journal of Commerce & Commercial, New York, NY

Erickson, Terri (405) 335-2188
ED, Amusements ED, Military/Religion ED, Society ED, Women's Interests ED
Frederick Leader, Frederick, OK

Erickson, Tom (316) 624-2541
Sports ED
Southwest Daily Times, Liberal, KS

Ericson, Lee J (814) 723-8200
BM/PA, Warren Times-Observer, Warren, PA

Ericson, William (213) 682-1412
PUB, Review, South Pasadena, CA

Erikson III, Ed (906) 265-9927
MAN ED, Reporter, Iron River, MI

Erikson, Jane (520) 573-4220
Health/Medical ED
Arizona Daily Star, Tucson, AZ

Erikson, John (937) 225-2000
Environmental ED, Fashion/Style ED, Health/Medical ED, SCI/Technology ED
Dayton Daily News, Dayton, OH

Erikson, Steven A (508) 793-9100
PROD MGR-Transportation/Warehouse
Telegram & Gazette, Worcester, MA

Erikson, Tom (702) 882-2111
CIRC DIR, Nevada Appeal, Carson City, NV

Erives, Manny (513) 721-2700
ADV DIR-CLASS
Cincinnati Enquirer, Cincinnati, OH

Erksine, Germaine R (714) 527-8210
PUB, News-Enterprise, Los Alamitos, CA

Erlam, Robert (403) 668-2063
PRES/PUB
Whitehorse Star, Whitehorse, YT

Erlandson, Greg (219) 356-8400
GM, Our Sunday Visitor, Huntington, IN

Erlewine, Meredith (614) 592-6612
Radio/Television ED
Athens Messenger, Athens, OH

Ernde, Sue (717) 762-2151
ED, BUS/FIN ED, City/MET ED, EPE, Features ED, NTL ED, News ED, Photo ED
Record Herald, Waynesboro, PA

Ernest, David (803) 283-1133
PUB, Lancaster News, Lancaster, SC

Ernesto, John M (610) 371-5000
DIR-MKTG/PROM
Reading Times/Eagle, Reading, PA

Ernst, Doug (707) 226-3711
MAN ED, EPE, NTL ED, SCI/Technology ED
Napa Valley Register, Napa, CA

Ernst, Eric (941) 953-7755
COL-Charlotte
Sarasota Herald-Tribune, Sarasota, FL

Ernst, Joe (561) 820-4100
ADV DIR-OPER
Palm Beach Post, West Palm Beach, FL

Ernst, Mark (714) 553-9292
VP-Human Resources
Freedom Communications Inc., Irvine, CA

Erramouspe, Pedro (56-2) 235-2902
EX DIR
Europa Press News Service, Santiago

Errera, Joseph F (814) 368-3173
PROD MGR, Bradford Era, Bradford, PA

Erskine, Chris (213) 237-5000
Deputy Graphics ED
Los Angeles Times, Los Angeles, CA

Ersland, Bruce (515) 753-6611
Sports ED, Times-Republican, Marshalltown, IA

Ertolahti, Aarre (807) 344-1611
MAN ED, Canadan Uutiset, Thunder Bay, ON

Ervin, Bonnie (812) 829-2255
CIRC MGR
Spencer Evening World, Spencer, IN

Ervin, Kenneth Scott (515) 827-5931
PUB, ED
South Hamilton Record-News, Jewell, IA

Ervin, Lee (303) 349-6114
ED, Crested Butte Chronicle & Pilot, Crested Butte, CO

Ervolino, Bill (201) 646-4000
COL, Record, Hackensack, NJ

Erwin, David (613) 342-4441
Photo DEPT MGR, PROD Photo Lab
Recorder and Times, Brockville, ON

Erwin, Diana Griego (916) 321-1000
COL, Sacramento Bee, Sacramento, CA

Erwin, Sheila (615) 569-8351
PUB, Scott County News, Oneida, TN

Erwin, Tanyalee (206) 597-8742
CIRC MGR-Direct Delivery
News Tribune, Tacoma, WA

Esan, Kelly (613) 829-9100
Valley Reporter
Ottawa Citizen, Ottawa, ON

Escalon, Marsha (505) 546-2611
ADV Representative
Deming Headlight, Deming, NM

Esclamado, Alex A (415) 872-3000
PUB, ED
Philippine News, South San Francisco, CA

Escobar, Ted (509) 865-4055
ED, Toppenish Review, Toppenish, WA

Escobedo Sr, Eddie (702) 649-8553
PUB, El Mundo, Las Vegas, NV

Escobedo Jr, Eddie (702) 649-8553
GM, El Mundo, Las Vegas, NV

Escobedo, Frank (210) 728-2500
ADV DIR-NTL, PROD DIR
Laredo Morning Times, Laredo, TX

Eshleman, Tina (804) 978-7200
City ED, Daily Progress, Charlottesville, VA

Eskil, Rick (509) 525-3300
EPE
Walla Walla Union-Bulletin, Walla Walla, WA

Eskridge, David (713) 220-7171
Copy Desk Chief
Houston Chronicle, Houston, TX

Esmond, Mary (410) 332-6000
ADV MGR-PROM, Sun, Baltimore, MD

Esmont, Erin (717) 771-2000
MET ED, York Daily Record, York, PA

Esola, Lyn (714) 642-4321
ADV MGR-Display, Daily Pilot, Costa Mesa, CA

Espe, Erik (702) 324-4440
ED, Reno News & Review, Reno, NV

Espenson, Barry (208) 783-1107
MAN ED, BUS/Mining ED, COL, EDU ED, News ED, Shoshone News-Press, Kellogg, ID

Espetia, Tony (305) 350-2111
MAN ED-El Nuevo, Miami Herald, Miami, FL

Espino, Herb (305) 633-3341
ADV DIR, Diario Las Americas, Miami, FL

Espinosa, Bobbie (619) 299-3131
DIR-Human Resources
San Diego Union-Tribune, San Diego, CA

Espinosa, Rusurreccion (203) 933-8118
Writer, Amanda y Rocinante, West Haven, CT

Espinosa, Vivian (561) 395-8300
TREAS/CFO, News, Boca Raton, FL

Espinoza, Leon (206) 464-2111
News ED-Night, Seattle Times, Seattle, WA

Espinoza, Veronica (408) 287-4866
ADV MGR-Legal, CIRC MGR
San Jose Post-Record, San Jose, CA

Esposito, Anne N (508) 793-9100
BUS ED, Telegram & Gazette, Worcester, MA

Esposito, Carl E (513) 422-3611
PUB/GM
Middletown Journal, Middletown, OH

Esposito, Gina (610) 272-2500
EPE, Times Herald, Norristown, PA

Espy, David (706) 857-2494
GM, Summerville News, Summerville, GA

Espy, Jimmy (941) 574-1110
EDL DIR, Daily Breeze, Cape Coral, FL

Espy, Winston Eugene (706) 857-2494
PUB, ED, Summerville News, Summerville, GA

Esselstyn, Van (561) 820-4100
ADV DIR-CLASS
Palm Beach Post, West Palm Beach, FL

Esser, Jacob R (610) 683-7343
PUB, Patriot, Kutztown, PA

Esser, Lynn (417) 836-1100
DIR-INFO SYS
Springfield News-Leader, Springfield, MO

Esser, Pete (423) 482-1021
PUB, Oak Ridger, Oak Ridge, TN

Esses, Mike (410) 730-3620
GM, Howard County Times, Columbia, MD

Essory, Gordon (806) 762-8844
DIR-Online Services
Lubbock Avalanche-Journal, Lubbock, TX

Estep, Darin (603) 668-4321
Books ED, Sunday ED
Union Leader, Manchester, NH

Estep, Don (606) 528-9767
PUB, GM, News Journal, Corbin, KY

Ester, Bob (816) 254-8600
CIRC MGR, Examiner, Independence, MO

Esterline, Warren (714) 832-9601
ED, Tustin Weekly, Tustin, CA

Estes, Ashley (205) 353-4612
EDU ED, Decatur Daily, Decatur, AL

Estes, Bruce (607) 272-2321
ASST MAN ED, Ithaca Journal, Ithaca, NY

Est Who's Where-70

Estes, Carolyn .... (918) 443-2428
MAN ED, Oologah Lake Leader, Oologah, OK
Estes, Donna .... (501) 239-8562
ADV DIR, Daily Press, Paragould, AR
Estes, Doug .... (409) 985-5541
DP MGR, PROD MGR-COMP
Port Arthur News, Port Arthur, TX
Estes III, John F .... (757) 446-2000
VP-ADM/FIN, Virginian-Pilot, Norfolk, VA
Estill, Libby .... (606) 735-2198
ED, Bracken County News, Brooksville, KY
Estlack, Roger A .... (806) 874-2259
PUB, ED, Clarendon Enterprise, Clarendon, TX
Estrada, Rich .... (209) 578-2000
Agriculture Writer, Farm/Agriculture Writer
Modesto Bee, Modesto, CA
Estrada, Richard .... (214) 977-8222
ASSOC ED-EDL Page
Dallas Morning News, Dallas, TX
Estridge, John L .... (765) 647-4221
ED, Brookville Democrat, Brookville, IN
Estrin, Richard .... (941) 953-7755
ASST MAN ED
Sarasota Herald-Tribune, Sarasota, FL
Ethelston, Ray .... (705) 848-7195
PUB, Standard, Elliot Lake, ON
Etherington, Frank .... (519) 894-2231
City ED, Record, Kitchener, ON
Ethier, Dick .... (941) 335-0200
DP MGR, News-Press, Fort Myers, FL
Ethier, Rolly .... (613) 472-2431
ED, Campbellford Courier, Marmora, ON
Ethridge, Edie .... (810) 784-5551
ED, Armada Times, Armada, MI
Ethridge, Tim .... (812) 464-7614
Sports ED, Evansville Press, Evansville, IN
Etnyre, Geoff .... (202) 636-3000
News ED, Washington Times, Washington, DC
Ettenhofer, C .... (906) 786-2021
CONT, Daily Press, Escanaba, MI
Etter, Gerald .... (215) 854-2000
Food ED
Philadelphia Inquirer, Philadelphia, PA
Ettinger, Amy .... (602) 271-8000
ADTX MGR, Arizona Republic, Phoenix, AZ
Central Newspapers Inc.
Ettinger, Stewart .... (609) 663-6000
Television/Film ED
Courier-Post, Cherry Hill, NJ
Etzel, Herman .... (503) 221-8327
PROD ASST SUPT-PR
Oregonian, Portland, OR
Eubank, Clay .... (916) 662-5421
CIRC MGR, Daily Democrat, Woodland, CA
Eubank, Rodney .... (901) 476-7116
ED, Covington Leader, Covington, TN
Eubanks, Johnny .... (904) 643-3333
PUB, Calhoun Liberty Journal, Bristol, FL
Eubanks, Kathy .... (513) 352-2000
DIR-Community SRV
Cincinnati Post, Cincinnati, OH
Eubanks, Teresa .... (904) 643-3333
ED, Calhoun Liberty Journal, Bristol, FL
Eure, Julian .... (919) 335-0841
MAN ED
Daily Advance, Elizabeth City, NC
Eurle, Dorothy .... (203) 876-6800
ED, Stratford Bard, Milford, CT
Eutz, L .... (314) 531-2101
GM, St. Louis Metro Sentinel, St. Louis, MO
Euvino, Steve .... (219) 942-0521
ED, Hobart Gazette, Merrillville, IN
Evan, Laurie .... (919) 829-4500
Home/Travel ED
News & Observer, Raleigh, NC
Evangelisti, Karen .... (717) 784-2121
ADTX MGR
Press Enterprise, Bloomsburg, PA
Evanoff, Mel .... (217) 223-5100
ADV MGR, Quincy Herald-Whig, Quincy, IL
Evans, Akwasi .... (512) 499-8713
PUB, ED, Nokoa-The Observer, Austin, TX
Evans, Alfred R .... (507) 324-5325
MAN ED, Le Roy Independent, Le Roy, MN
Evans, Allan D .... (913) 483-2116
PRES, PUB/GM, ADV DIR
Russell Daily News, Russell, KS
Evans, Betty .... (501) 367-5325
ED, Advance-Monticellonian, Monticello, AR
Evans, Bill .... (818) 584-1500
ED, MAN ED, Pasadena Weekly, Pasadena, CA
Evans, Bill .... (816) 376-3508
GM, Marceline Press, Marceline, MO
Evans, Charles .... (814) 870-1600
DP MGR
Morning News/Erie Daily Times, Erie, PA
Evans, Cherran .... (201) 877-4141
DIR-Human Resources
Star-Ledger, Newark, NJ
Evans, Chris .... (502) 965-3191
ED, Crittenden Press, Marion, KY
Evans, Christine .... (610) 258-7171
ADV Inside SUPV-CLASS
Express-Times, Easton, PA
Evans, David .... (614) 732-2341
PUB, ED, Journal & Noble County Leader, Caldwell, OH
Evans, David .... (403) 429-5400
DP MGR, Edmonton Journal, Edmonton, AB
Evans, David A .... (913) 483-2116
ASSOC PUB, Russell Daily News, Russell, KS
Evans, David B .... (413) 788-1000
TREAS, CONT, Union-News, Springfield, MA
Evans, David G .... (218) 596-8813
PUB, ED, Ulen Union, Ulen, MN
Evans, Debbie .... (815) 796-2271
GM, ED, Flanagan Home Times, Flanagan, IL
Evans, Deborah .... (915) 263-7331
ADV MGR-CLASS
Big Spring Herald, Big Spring, TX
Evans, Deborah .... (912) 452-0567
MAN ED, Union-Recorder, Milledgeville, GA
Evans, Diane .... (330) 996-3000
COL-BUS, Akron Beacon Journal, Akron, OH
Evans, Donita .... (505) 393-2123
Graphics ED/Art DIR
Hobbs Daily News-Sun, Hobbs, NM
Evans, Doug .... (208) 522-1800
DIR-Production, Online MGR, DP MGR, PROD DIR, Post Register, Idaho Falls, ID
Evans, Doyle H .... (713) 220-7171
DIR-Packaging and Distribution
Houston Chronicle, Houston, TX
Evans, Eileen M .... (507) 324-5325
PUB, ED, Le Roy Independent, Le Roy, MN
Evans, Ellen .... (509) 582-1500
ADV DIR, DIR-MKTG
Tri-City Herald, Tri-Cities, WA
Evans, Evelyn M .... (913) 483-2116
ASSOC PUB, Daily News, Russell, KS
Evans, Fran .... (516) 569-4000
MAN ED, Nassau Herald, Lawrence, NY
Evans, Francesca .... (910) 343-2000
Religion ED, Morning Star/Sunday Star-News, Wilmington, NC
Evans, Gary .... (561) 820-4100
CIRC MGR-Sales/MKTG
Palm Beach Post, West Palm Beach, FL
Evans, Gary .... (910) 472-9500
ED, MAN ED
Thomasville Times, Thomasville, NC
Evans, Gary .... (800) 424-4747
SYS MGR, Tribune Media Services-Television Listings, Glens Falls, NY
Evans, George .... (909) 487-2200
PROD MGR-Press/Camera
Hemet News, Hemet, CA
Evans, Harlan B .... (410) 332-6000
ADV MGR-NTL & Major RT Accounts
Sun, Baltimore, MD
Evans, Helen .... (402) 892-3544
GM, Colfax County Press, Clarkson, NE
Evans, Hilton A .... (607) 467-2191
PUB, ED, Deposit Courier, Deposit, NY
Evans, James .... (813) 259-7711
Vice Chairman
Tampa Tribune and Times, Tampa, FL
Evans, James S .... (804) 649-6000
Vice Chairman
Media General Inc., Richmond, VA
Evans, Jared Z .... (318) 222-0213
PRES, Daily Legal News Inc., Shreveport, LA
Evans, Jeff .... (860) 887-9211
Photo ED, Norwich Bulletin, Norwich, CT
Evans, Jeffrey .... (317) 747-5700
PROD DIR-OPER, Star Press, Muncie, IN
Evans, Jim .... (512) 335-5959
Self-Syndicator, Academy of Professional Umpiring, Austin, TX
Evans, Joe .... (209) 223-1767
MAN ED
Amador Ledger-Dispatch, Jackson, CA
Evans, John .... (416) 367-2000
BC, Toronto Star, Toronto, ON
Evans, Joyce .... (414) 224-2000
COL
Milwaukee Journal Sentinel, Milwaukee, WI
Evans, Judy .... (314) 340-8000
Food ED
St. Louis Post-Dispatch, St. Louis, MO
Evans, Karen .... (520) 634-2241
MAN ED, Verde Independent, Cottonwood, AZ
Evans, Kevin .... (319) 291-1400
Sports ED, Waterloo Courier, Waterloo, IA
Evans, Lanita .... (308) 546-2242
PUB, ED, Hooker County Tribune, Mullen, NE
Evans, Larry .... (918) 335-8200
CIRC Distribution Clerk
Examiner-Enterprise, Bartlesville, OK
Evans, Larry .... (702) 786-3178
Author/Owner, Chesstours, Reno, NV
Evans, Larry R .... (540) 374-5000
EPE, Free Lance-Star, Fredericksburg, VA
Evans, Lori .... (907) 283-7551
EX ED, Peninsula Clarion, Kenai, AK
Evans, Louis .... (502) 582-4011
PROD SUPT-PR
Courier-Journal, Louisville, KY
Evans, Mark A .... (614) 461-5000
VP-Human Resources
Columbus Dispatch, Columbus, OH
Evans, Mark L .... (520) 458-3340
PUB, Huachuca Scout, Sierra Vista, AZ
Evans, Molly .... (617) 593-7700
DIR-MKTG, Daily Evening Item, Lynn, MA
Evans, Morris .... (308) 282-0118
PUB, Gordon Journal, Gordon, NE
Evans, Nancy F .... (217) 788-1300
MGR-PROM
State Journal-Register, Springfield, IL
Evans, Paul .... (203) 744-5100
ADV MGR, News-Times, Danbury, CT
Evans, Randy .... (515) 284-8000
ASST MAN ED
Des Moines Register, Des Moines, IA
Evans, Rebekah .... (318) 738-5642
GM, Kinder Courier News, Kinder, LA
Evans, Robbie .... (803) 775-6331
Automotive/Aviation ED, Sports ED
Item, Sumter, SC
Evans, Robert D .... (501) 787-5300
ED, Gravette News Herald, Gravette, AR
Evans, Robert L .... (918) 543-8786
PUB, Inola Independent, Inola, OK
Evans, Robin .... (510) 758-8400
City ED, West County Times, Pinole, CA
Evans, Stan .... (716) 849-3434
ASST MAN ED-Local News
Buffalo News, Buffalo, NY
Evans, Suzanne .... (308) 282-0118
ED, Gordon Journal, Gordon, NE
Evans, T A .... (402) 892-3544
PUB, ED, Colfax County Press, Clarkson, NE
Evans, Tim .... (317) 839-5129
ED, Hendricks County Flyer, Plainfield, IN
Evans, Tom .... (908) 722-8800
ASST MET ED
Courier-News, Bridgewater, NJ
Evans, Yvonne M .... (918) 543-8786
ED, Inola Independent, Inola, OK
Evarts, Eric .... (617) 450-2000
Natural Science ED, SCI/Technology ED
Christian Science Monitor, Boston, MA
Evavold, Ross .... (715) 723-5515
MAN ED, Books ED
Chippewa Herald, Chippewa Falls, WI
Eveld, Jo .... (501) 667-2136
ED, Spectator, Ozark, AR
Evely, Ron .... (902) 564-5451
PROD MGR-COMP
Cape Breton Post, Sydney, NS
Evens, Kyle .... (317) 747-5700
Photo ED, Star Press, Muncie, IN
Evensen, Jay .... (801) 237-2188
EPE, EDL Writer
Deseret News, Salt Lake City, UT
Evenson, Bill .... (507) 376-9711
News ED, Daily Globe, Worthington, MN
Evenson, O J .... (715) 985-3815
PUB, ED, News-Wave, Independence, WI
Everest, Christine Gaylord .... (405) 475-3311
VP, Daily Oklahoman, Oklahoma City, OK
Everett, Eileen Burns .... (904) 734-4622
MAN ED, DeLand Beacon/West Volusia Beacon, DeLand, FL
Everett, Ginny .... (404) 526-5151
DIR-News RES
Atlanta Journal-Constitution, Atlanta, GA
Everett, Julie .... (501) 268-8621
EDL Writer, Daily Citizen, Searcy, AR
Everett, Paulette .... (954) 356-4000
TV Book ED, Sun-Sentinel, Fort Lauderdale, FL
Everett, Polly .... (405) 786-2224
MAN ED, Weleetkan, Weleetka, OK
Everett, Rick .... (201) 877-4141
MAN ED-News, Star-Ledger, Newark, NJ
Everhart, Ann .... (212) 210-2100
CIRC DIR/VP-Sales & Communications
New York Daily News, New York, NY
Everhart, Bill .... (413) 447-7311
EPE, Berkshire Eagle, Pittsfield, MA
Everidge, Frank .... (541) 963-3161
PROD FRM-PR, Observer, La Grande, OR
Western Communications Inc.
Everingham, Guy .... (503) 472-5114
GM, News-Register, McMinnville, OR
Everitt, Kelly .... (208) 587-3331
ED, Pipeline, Mountain Home, ID
Everitt, Tammy .... (317) 622-1212
Action Line ED, Radio/Television ED
Herald Bulletin, Anderson, IN
Everly, Debra .... (219) 874-7211
GM, ADV MGR-RT
News Dispatch, Michigan City, IN
Evers, Charles (Chuck) H .... (806) 762-8844
ADV MGR-RT
Lubbock Avalanche-Journal, Lubbock, TX
Everson, Diane .... (608) 884-3367
PUB, Edgerton Reporter, Edgerton, WI
Everson, Helen V .... (608) 884-3367
PUB, ED, Edgerton Reporter, Edgerton, WI
Ewald, Patti .... (216) 329-7000
Graphics ED, Chronicle-Telegram, Elyria, OH
Eward, Tom .... (416) 367-2000
MGR-Data Centre, Toronto Star, Toronto, ON
Eways, Kamal P .... (303) 933-2233
PUB
Columbine Community Courier, Littleton, CO
Ewen, Kathy .... (360) 532-4000
Photo DEPT MGR
Daily World, Aberdeen, WA
Ewig, Steve S .... (414) 457-7711
CIRC MGR-Distribution
Sheboygan Press, Sheboygan, WI
Ewing, Bernadine .... (903) 455-4220
BM, Greenville Herald-Banner, Greenville, TX
Hollinger International Inc.
Ewing, Bill .... (619) 248-7878
ED, Lucerne Leader, Lucerne Valley, CA
Ewing, Cynthia R .... (603) 352-1234
VP, Keene Sentinel, Keene, NH
Ewing Sr, George M .... (716) 394-0770
COB/TREAS, ED, Daily Messenger/Sunday Messenger, Canandaigua, NY
Ewing Jr, George M .... (716) 394-0770
PRES, PUB, Daily Messenger/Sunday Messenger, Canandaigua, NY
Ewing, James .... (603) 352-1234
PUB Emeritus, Keene Sentinel, Keene, NH
Ewing, John M .... (609) 451-1000
PUB, CIRC MGR
Bridgeton Evening News, Bridgeton, NJ
Ewing, Larry .... (614) 446-2342
MAN ED, Gallipolis Daily Tribune/Sunday Times-Sentinel, Gallipolis, OH
Ewing, M M .... (716) 394-0770
VP/SEC, Daily Messenger/Sunday Messenger, Canandaigua, NY
Ewing, Margaret L .... (716) 394-0770
SEC, Daily Messenger/Sunday Messenger, Canandaigua, NY
Ewing, Thomas M .... (603) 352-1234
PUB, Keene Sentinel, Keene, NH
Exstrom, Lyle M .... (405) 482-1221
PUB, Altus Times, Altus, OK
Exum, Helen .... (423) 756-6900
EVP, Books ED, Food/Garden ED
Chattanooga Free Press, Chattanooga, TN
Exum, Roy .... (423) 756-6900
VP, EX Sports ED
Chattanooga Free Press, Chattanooga, TN
Eybers, Ed .... (813) 259-7711
PROD MGR-Quality Assurance
Tampa Tribune and Times, Tampa, FL
Eyerly III, Paul R .... (717) 784-2121
PRES, PUB
Press Enterprise, Bloomsburg, PA
Eykyn, James .... (906) 786-2021
PUB, Daily Press, Escanaba, MI
Eyman, Scott .... (561) 820-4100
Books ED
Palm Beach Post, West Palm Beach, FL
Eymann, Kent D .... (608) 365-8811
PUB, Beloit Daily News, Beloit, WI
Eymer, Rick .... (415) 348-4321
Books ED
San Mateo County Times, San Mateo, CA
Eyring, Donna .... (407) 420-5000
Deputy MAN ED-Sports
Orlando Sentinel, Orlando, FL
Ezell, Wayne .... (941) 294-7731
ED/PUB, News Chief, Winter Haven, FL
Ezzell, Jimmy .... (706) 554-2111
ED, True Citizen, Waynesboro, GA
Ezzell, Nancy .... (806) 323-5321
PUB, ED, Canadian Record, Canadian, TX

F

Fabia, Michael .... (508) 775-1200
PROD MGR-PR
Cape Cod Times, Hyannis, MA
Fabian, Amos .... (209) 582-0471
EDU ED, Political ED, Teen-Age/Youth ED
Hanford Sentinel, Hanford, CA
Fabris, James A .... (216) 999-4500
Deputy MAN ED, Plain Dealer, Cleveland, OH
Fabris, Paul .... (217) 935-3171
PROD MGR, Daily Journal, Clinton, IL
Fabrizio, Linda .... (860) 225-4601
Regional Human Resources MGR
Herald, New Britain, CT
Fackelman, Ann .... (318) 255-4353
SEC, Ruston Daily Leader, Ruston, LA
Fackelman Newspapers
Faddis, Jim .... (308) 382-1000
News ED
Grand Island Independent, Grand Island, NE
Fader, Carole .... (904) 359-4111
A-1 ED, Florida Times-Union, Jacksonville, FL
Fadness, Gene .... (208) 522-1800
Political ED, Post Register, Idaho Falls, ID
Fagan, J Stephen .... (217) 788-1300
ED, State Journal-Register, Springfield, IL
Fageol, Mark .... (712) 279-5019
Photo DEPT MGR
Sioux City Journal, Sioux City, IA

71-Who's Where **Fay**

Fagerstorm, Scot .... (419) 522-3311
Sports ED, News Journal, Mansfield, OH
Fagiano, Chris .... (304) 263-8931
CIRC MGR, Journal, Martinsburg, WV
Fagin, Steve .... (860) 442-2200
Travel ED, Day, New London, CT
Fagler, Ruby .... (912) 237-9971
ED, Blade, Swainsboro, GA
Faherty, Diane .... (218) 723-5281
EX ED-City
Duluth News-Tribune, Duluth, MN
Faherty, Pat .... (218) 262-1011
MAN ED, EPE, Daily Tribune, Hibbing, MN
Faherty, Tim .... (609) 272-7000
Graphics ED
Press of Atlantic City, Pleasantville, NJ
Fahey, Richard .... (413) 772-0261
ADV DIR, Recorder, Greenfield, MA
Fahrenbacher, C J .... (605) 775-2612
PUB, ED, Burke Gazette, Burke, SD
Faile Jr, Jim .... (803) 393-3811
ED, News and Press, Darlington, SC
Fain, Ferris H .... (409) 632-6631
PROD DIR, Lufkin Daily News, Lufkin, TX
Cox Newspapers Inc.
Fain, George R .... (804) 732-3456
PUB, Progress-Index, Petersburg, VA
Fain, Victor B .... (409) 564-8361
COL, Daily Sentinel, Nacogdoches, TX
Fair, Gloria .... (864) 582-4511
News ED, Herald-Journal, Spartanburg, SC
Fair, Jim .... (864) 582-4511
Sports ED, Herald-Journal, Spartanburg, SC
Fairbanks, Jeff .... (805) 781-7800
ED, Telegram-Tribune, San Luis Obispo, CA
Fairbridge, Jerry .... (416) 364-3172
Sales/MKTG MGR
Broadcast News Limited, Toronto, ON
Fairchild, Jim .... (419) 935-0184
MAN ED
Willard Times-Junction, Willard, OH
Fairchild, John B .... (212) 630-4000
COB, Women's Wear Daily, New York, NY
Fairchild, Kathy S .... (417) 466-2185
PUB, ED
Lawrence County Record, Mount Vernon, MO
Fairchild, Steve .... (417) 466-2185
PUB, GM
Lawrence County Record, Mount Vernon, MO
Faircloth, Billy .... (706) 324-5526
PROD MGR-AM
Columbus Ledger-Enquirer, Columbus, GA
Fairfield, Cindy .... (616) 722-3161
Sports ED, Chronicle, Muskegon, MI
Fairgrieve, Gordon .... (506) 375-4458
PUB, ED, Observer, Hartland, NB
Fairlie, Dave .... (918) 581-8300
ADV MGR-CLASS, Tulsa World, Tulsa, OK
Fairweather, Joan .... (416) 367-2000
DIR-FIN, Toronto Star, Toronto, ON
Faison, Glenn .... (209) 924-3488
ED, Lemoore Advance, Lemoore, CA
Falardeau, Michelle .... (518) 584-4242
EDU ED, Saratogian, Saratoga Springs, NY
Falcone, Don .... (573) 581-1111
CIRC MGR, Mexico Ledger, Mexico, MO
Falcone, Steve .... (702) 788-6200
BUS ED, Reno Gazette-Journal, Reno, NV
Falda, Wayne .... (219) 235-6161
Farm/Agriculture Writer
South Bend Tribune, South Bend, IN
Falk, Steven B .... (415) 777-5700
PRES/CEO, San Francisco Newspaper Agency, San Francisco, CA
Falk, Thomas G .... (607) 432-1000
CIRC MGR, Daily Star, Oneonta, NY
Falkenberg, Barth .... (614) 461-5000
DIR-Photography
Columbus Dispatch, Columbus, OH
Falkenhagen, Chris .... (410) 535-1575
MAN ED
Calvert Independent, Prince Frederick, MD
Falkenstein, Sophie .... (609) 663-6000
ADV MGR-NTL
Courier-Post, Cherry Hill, NJ
Faller, Carol .... (402) 362-4478
ADTX MGR, York News-Times, York, NE
Faller, Mark .... (203) 333-0161
Sports ED, Connecticut Post, Bridgeport, CT
Fallon, Elena .... (816) 932-6600
VP-FIN
Universal Press Syndicate, Kansas City, MO
Fallon, Karen .... (519) 728-1082
ED, North Essex News, Belle River, ON
Fallon, Peter .... (603) 524-3800
CIRC DIR, Citizen, Laconia, NH
Fallstrom, Robert .... (217) 429-5151
Community News ED
Herald & Review, Decatur, IL
Faloon, R A (Rube) .... (216) 923-2397
Sales Development
Scrambl-Gram Inc., Cuyahoga Falls, OH
Falter, Leslie D .... (402) 329-4665
PUB, Pierce County Leader, Pierce, NE
Falter, Randee D .... (402) 329-4665
ED, Pierce County Leader, Pierce, NE

Faltz, Mary .... (608) 297-2424
ED, Marquette County Tribune, Montello, WI
Falvey, Nora .... (303) 442-1202
ADTX MGR, Daily Camera, Boulder, CO
Falzarano, Jim .... (802) 479-0191
EPE, Times Argus, Barre, VT
Famulary, John .... (908) 957-0070
PUB, Courier, Middletown, NJ
Fancher Jr, Charles B .... (215) 854-2000
VP-Communications/Public Affairs
Philadelphia Inquirer, Philadelphia, PA
Fancher, Michael R .... (206) 464-2111
Senior VP-EX ED, VP/EX ED
Seattle Times, Seattle, WA
Fancy, James W .... (810) 360-6397
PUB
Spinal Column Newsweekly, Union Lake, MI
Fandell, Elaine .... (847) 486-9200
ED, Wilmette Life, Glenview, IL
Fanelli, Damian .... (518) 561-2300
Sunday ED
Press-Republican, Plattsburgh, NY
Fang, James .... (713) 498-4310
MAN ED
Southern Chinese Daily News, Houston, TX
Fang, Ted .... (415) 826-1100
PUB, ED, San Francisco Independent, San Francisco, CA
Fang, Yin Cheng .... (713) 498-4310
ED
Southern Chinese Daily News, Houston, TX
Fanlund, Paul .... (608) 252-6100
ASST MAN ED
Wisconsin State Journal, Madison, WI
Fann, Marcus .... (404) 526-5151
DIR-Training/Development
Atlanta Journal-Constitution, Atlanta, GA
Fantin, Linda .... (307) 733-2430
MAN ED, Jackson Hole Guide, Jackson, WY
Fantini, Frank A .... (302) 674-3600
VP, Delaware State News, Dover, DE
Independent Newspapers Inc. (DE)
Fantl, Brian .... (505) 823-7777
DIR-OPER, Albuquerque Publishing Co., Albuquerque, NM
Fanto, Clarence .... (413) 447-7311
News ED, Berkshire Eagle, Pittsfield, MA
Fanucchi, Rosemarie .... (805) 684-4428
PUB, ED, Coastal View, Carpinteria, CA
Farabee, Sherrie .... (334) 847-2599
MAN ED
Washington County News, Chatom, AL
Farah, J G .... (819) 564-5450
CONT, La Tribune, Sherbrooke, QC
Fararo, Kim .... (907) 257-4200
Environmental Reporter, Oil Reporter
Anchorage Daily News, Anchorage, AK
Farber, Arthur .... (510) 208-6300
Senior VP-Circulation
Oakland Tribune, Oakland, CA
MediaNews Inc. (Alameda Newspapers)
Farber, Jim .... (310) 540-5511
Theater ED, Daily Breeze, Torrance, CA
Fargnoli, Everett .... (401) 762-3000
DP MGR, Call, Woonsocket, RI
Fargo, Charlyn .... (217) 788-1300
Food ED
State Journal-Register, Springfield, IL
Faricy, Bob .... (318) 459-3200
DIR-MKTG SRV, ADTX MGR
Times, Shreveport, LA
Farina, Robert .... (414) 457-7711
MAN ED-Presentation/Features
Sheboygan Press, Sheboygan, WI
Farinella, Mark .... (508) 222-7000
Sunday Sports ED
Sun Chronicle, Attleboro, MA
Farkas, Beth .... (914) 454-2000
ASST CONT
Poughkeepsie Journal, Poughkeepsie, NY
Farkas, Tom .... (207) 621-6000
MAN ED, Capital Weekly, Augusta, ME
Farkas, Tony .... (505) 763-3431
EPE, News ED
Clovis News Journal, Clovis, NM
Farley, Austin .... (918) 581-8300
Librarian, Tulsa World, Tulsa, OK
Farley, Bob .... (614) 286-2187
ED
Jackson-Vinton Journal-Herald, Jackson, OH
Farley, Catherine .... (416) 463-3824
EDL MGR, Graphics Syndicate, Toronto, ON
Farley, Cory .... (702) 788-6200
COL, Reno Gazette-Journal, Reno, NV
Farley, David .... (219) 881-3000
PROD ENG-Plant, Post-Tribu ne, Gary, IN
Farley, Don .... (410) 523-2300
PUB, Baltimore City Paper, Baltimore, MD
Farley, Eileen .... (914) 294-6111
ED, Independent Republican, Goshen, NY
Farley, Jim G .... (417) 358-2191
PUB/GM, ADV DIR
Carthage Press, Carthage, MO
Farley, Maggie .... (213) 237-5000
Hong Kong BU
Los Angeles Times, Los Angeles, CA

Farley Jr, Tony .... (757) 247-4600
CIRC MGR-Production OPER
Daily Press, Newport News, VA
Farley, Wes .... (402) 475-4200
CIRC MGR-Division
Lincoln Journal Star, Lincoln, NE
Farley-Villalobos, Robbie .... (915) 546-6340
BUS ED, RE ED, Herald-Post, El Paso, TX
Farlow, Fran .... (704) 864-3291
Librarian, Gaston Gazette, Gastonia, NC
Farmer, Jack .... (618) 463-2500
City ED, Telegraph, Alton, IL
Farmer, John .... (201) 877-4141
COL, Star-Ledger, Newark, NJ
Farmer, Kaye .... (919) 778-2211
Photo DEPT MGR
Goldsboro News-Argus, Goldsboro, NC
Farmer, Marilyn .... (816) 744-6245
PUB, ED
Atchison County Mail, Rock Port, MO
Farmer, Mervin E .... (204) 347-8402
PUB, Selkirk Journal, Stonewall, MB
Farmer, Michael P .... (816) 744-6245
GM, Atchison County Mail, Rock Port, MO
Farmer, Regina .... (818) 713-3000
CIRC MGR-Customer Relations
Daily News, Woodland Hills, CA
Farmer, Roger .... (912) 265-8320
PROD FRM-COMP
Brunswick News, Brunswick, GA
Farmer, Sue .... (320) 732-2151
ED, Long Prairie Leader, Long Prairie, MN
Farmer, Susan .... (360) 694-3391
Agriculture ED, Columbian, Vancouver, WA
Farmer, W D .... (770) 934-7380
PRES, Farmer, W.D. Residence Designer Inc., Atlanta, GA
Farmer, William W .... (816) 744-6245
PUB, ED
Atchison County Mail, Rock Port, MO
Farmier, Virginia N .... (907) 456-6661
DIR-FIN
Fairbanks Daily News-Miner, Fairbanks, AK
Farmington, Jim .... (201) 877-4141
DIR-News OPER, Star-Ledger, Newark, NJ
Farnell, Bob .... (212) 499-3334
Sales EX-North America
New York Times Syndication Sales Corp., New York, NY
Farnell, Jeffrey .... (212) 556-4204
ASST DIR, NYT Photo Service, NYT Graphics, New York, NY
Farnelli, Anthony J .... (630) 782-4440
PUB, Fra Noi, Elmhurst, IL
Farnetti, Judy M .... (205) 926-9769
ED, Centreville Press, Centreville, AL
Farney, Dennis .... (212) 416-2000
Reporter-in-Charge (Kansas City)
Wall Street Journal, New York, NY
Farnsworth, Jack .... (602) 468-6565
PUB, Daily Racing Form, Phoenix, AZ
Farquharson, Duart .... (403) 429-5400
EDL BC, Edmonton Journal, Edmonton, AB
Farr, Carolyn .... (864) 427-1234
Food/Society ED, Women's ED
Union Daily Times, Union, SC
Farr, Susie .... (406) 447-4000
PROD SUPV-Pre Press
Helena Independent Record, Helena, MT
Farrah, Lyndell .... (573) 581-1111
PROD FRM, Mexico Ledger, Mexico, MO
Farrand, Scott .... (803) 771-6161
Graphics ED, State, Columbia, SC
Farrar Jr, Fletcher F .... (217) 753-2226
PUB, ED, Illinois Times, Springfield, IL
Farrar, LuAnn .... (606) 231-3100
Chief Librarian
Lexington Herald-Leader, Lexington, KY
Farrar, Stanley .... (206) 464-2111
ASST MAN ED-Graphics
Seattle Times, Seattle, WA
Farrell, Al .... (215) 949-4000
PROD FRM-MR, PROD FRM-Press/Plate
Bucks County Courier Times, Levittown, PA
Farrell, Bill .... (315) 792-5000
Health/Medical Writer
Observer-Dispatch, Utica, NY
Farrell, David .... (205) 325-2222
DP MGR
Birmingham Post-Herald, Birmingham, AL
Farrell, Ed .... (516) 843-2020
MGR-RES, Newsday, Melville, NY
Farrell, James .... (301) 459-3131
Senior ED
Prince George's Journal, Lanham, MD
Farrell, Laura .... (909) 987-6397
MET ED-Los Angeles Co.
Inland Valley Daily Bulletin, Ontario, CA
Farrell, LaVonne .... (913) 292-4726
PUB, ED, Frankfort Area News, Frankfort, KS
Farrell, Pamela .... (518) 943-2100
ADV MGR-MKTG/PROM
Daily Mail, Catskill, NY
Farrell, Paul M .... (508) 626-3800
ADV DIR-Sales/MKTG
Middlesex News, Framingham, MA

Farrell, R Douglas .... (616) 429-2400
ADV DIR, Herald-Palladium, St. Joseph, MI
Farrell, Richard .... (330) 364-5577
ED, Times Reporter, New Philadelphia, OH
Farrell, Sharon .... (418) 752-5400
PUB, Gaspe Peninsula SPEC, New Carlisle, QC
Farren, Jeffrey A .... (630) 553-7034
PUB, Kendall County Record, Yorkville, IL
Farren, Kathleen M .... (630) 553-7034
ED, Kendall County Record, Yorkville, IL
Farrer, Fran .... (704) 376-0496
MAN ED, Charlotte Post, Charlotte, NC
Farrier, Donald .... (301) 670-1400
ADV MGR-CLASS
Montgomery Journal, Rockville, MD
Farrington, John .... (613) 933-3160
PUB/GM, PA
Standard-Freeholder, Cornwall, ON
Farris, Marzet .... (908) 922-6000
ADV MGR-Telesales
Asbury Park Press, Neptune, NJ
Farris, Patricia .... (619) 371-4301
PUB, News Review, Ridgecrest, CA
Farris, Terry .... (918) 756-3600
ASST News ED
Okmulgee Daily Times, Okmulgee, OK
Farrow, Kaye .... (501) 561-4634
GM
Northeast Arkansas Town Crier, Manila, AR
Farruggia, Steve .... (217) 351-5252
PROD SUPT-Building
News-Gazette, Champaign, IL
Farrugia, Joe .... (703) 522-9898
MAN ED, Arlington Courier, Arlington, VA
Farstad, Alice A .... (605) 374-3751
PUB, ED, Lemmon Leader, Lemmon, SD
Farus, Bruce .... (605) 987-2631
PUB, Sioux Valley News, Canton, SD
Farwell, Scott .... (619) 375-4481
MAN ED, Daily Independent, Ridgecrest, CA
Fasang, Matthew J .... (810) 541-3000
ADV MGR, Daily Tribune, Royal Oak, MI
Fashona, Ray .... (518) 325-4400
MAN ED, Independent, Hillsdale, NY
Fasnaght, Andrew .... (717) 733-6397
ED, Ephrata Review, Ephrata, PA
Fast, Becky .... (417) 667-3344
BM, Nevada Daily Mail, Nevada, MO
Fatemi, Erik .... (301) 670-1400
City ED, Montgomery Journal, Rockville, MD
Fatla, Sharon A .... (719) 539-6691
VP, Mountain Mail, Salida, CO
Fattig, Paul .... (541) 776-4411
COL, Mail Tribune, Medford, OR
Faulk, John .... (502) 821-6833
PROD FRM-PR, Messenger, Madisonville, KY
Faulk, Kenneth R .... (205) 532-4000
CONT, Huntsville Times, Huntsville, AL
Faulk, Marty .... (360) 754-5400
CIRC MGR-Sales, Olympian, Olympia, WA
Faulkenberry, Mike .... (803) 684-9903
ED, Clover Herald, Clover, SC
Faulkenberry, Roy .... (501) 474-5215
ED, Van Buren Press Argus-Courier, Van Buren, AR
Faulkner, Chris .... (319) 372-6421
Sports ED
Daily Democrat, Fort Madison, IA
Faulkner, Donna .... (501) 725-3131
GM, ED, Smackover Journal, Smackover, AR
Faulkner, Fred .... (312) 644-7800
PROD MGR-Print SRV
Chicago Daily Law Bulletin, Chicago, IL
Faulkner, Max .... (817) 390-7400
DIR-Photography
Fort Worth Star-Telegram, Fort Worth, TX
Faulmann, Bruce .... (941) 748-0411
ADV DIR, Bradenton Herald, Bradenton, FL
Faunce, Kerry .... (941) 763-3134
ASSOC ED
Daily Okeechobee News, Okeechobee, FL
Faust, Andy .... (717) 264-6161
ADV MGR-Sales
Public Opinion, Chambersburg, PA
Faust, Michele .... (616) 722-3161
ADV SUPV-NTL
Muskegon Chronicle, Muskegon, MI
Faust, Scott .... (815) 987-1200
ASST MAN ED, Register Star, Rockford, IL
Faveere, Ron .... (314) 340-8000
PROD GEN FRM-COMP Room
St. Louis Post-Dispatch, St. Louis, MO
Favre, Gregory E .... (916) 321-1855
VP-News
McClatchy Newspapers, Sacramento, CA
Fawer, Lyle .... (309) 343-7181
PROD MGR, Register-Mail, Galesburg, IL
Fay, Michael P .... (413) 788-1000
CIRC DIR, Union-News, Springfield, MA
Fay, Stephen .... (207) 667-2576
MAN ED, Ellsworth American, Ellsworth, ME

Faz Who's Where-72

Fazendin, B J .... (715) 644-3319
PUB, ED, Stanley Republican, Stanley, WI
Fazio, Dawn .... (507) 625-4451
CONT, Free Press, Mankato, MN
Fazza, R A Bob .... (404) 539-2200
PUB, GM, MAN ED
Montgomery County Bulletin, Conroe, TX
Fazzari, Ken .... (906) 632-2235
ED, Evening News, Sault Ste. Marie, MI
Feagler, Dale .... (406) 265-6795
Photo ED, Havre Daily News, Havre, MT
Fear, Jon .... (519) 894-2231
ASST City ED, Record, Kitchener, ON
Fear, Rebecca .... (540) 949-8213
ADV MGR-RT, News Virginian, Waynesboro, VA
Fearing, Jeannine .... (409) 234-5521
PUB, ED
Eagle Lake Headlight, Eagle Lake, TX
Fears, Diane .... (504) 384-8370
Fashion/Style ED, Women's ED
Daily Review, Morgan City, LA
Feather, Carl .... (216) 994-3241
Lifestyle ED, Star-Beacon, Ashtabula, OH
Feather Jr, Dan .... (915) 396-2243
PUB, Menard News & Messenger, Menard, TX
Feaver, Bob .... (705) 745-4641
Sports ED, Examiner, Peterborough, ON
Febriby, Ron .... (512) 884-2011
PROD MGR-PR, Corpus Christi Caller-Times, Corpus Christi, TX
Fecht, Steve .... (313) 222-2300
DIR-Photography
Detroit News, Detroit, MI
Fedder, Elmer .... (217) 374-2871
PUB, Greene Prairie Press, White Hall, IL
Fedder, Merrilyn .... (217) 374-2871
ED, Greene Prairie Press, White Hall, IL
Feddern, Jason .... (402) 371-1020
PROD FRM-MR
Norfolk Daily News, Norfolk, NE
Feder, Don .... (617) 426-3000
EDL COL, Boston Herald, Boston, MA
Feder, Robert .... (312) 321-3000
Radio/Television COL
Chicago Sun-Times, Chicago, IL
Federspiel, Jack .... (810) 332-8181
VP-FIN/Production
Oakland Press, Pontiac, MI
Fedesco, Fred .... (805) 395-7500
CIRC DIR, PROD DIR-OPER
Bakersfield Californian, Bakersfield, CA
Fedler, Lorene A .... (319) 837-6722
MAN ED, West Point Bee, West Point, IA
Fedor, John .... (905) 684-7251
Sports, Standard, St. Catharines, ON
Fee, Gayle .... (617) 426-3000
The Inside Track COL
Boston Herald, Boston, MA
Feeback, Michael .... (573) 346-2132
ED, BUS/FIN ED, City/MET ED, EPE, Features ED, Graphics ED/Art DIR, News ED, Photo ED, Sports ED, Lake Sun Leader, Camdenton, MO
Feeley, Cathleen .... (705) 674-5271
DIR-MKTG/PROM
Sudbury Star, Sudbury, ON
Feely, Martin R .... (213) 525-2000
EX VP, Hollywood Reporter, Los Angeles, CA
Feeney, Joe .... (706) 769-5175
MAN ED, Oconee Enterprise, Watkinsville, GA
Feeney, Michael .... (910) 434-2716
ED, Archdale Trinity News, Archdale, NC
Feeney, Mike .... (714) 835-1234
PROD Senior Administrative MGR-MR/Transportation
Orange County Register, Santa Ana, CA
Feeney, Richard S .... (860) 241-6200
ASSOC PUB-Eastern Connecticut, CIRC Acting DIR, Hartford Courant, Hartford, CT
Fees, Gary .... (800) 678-8135
BUS/Customer SRV MGR
Better Homes & Gardens Features Syndicate, Des Moines, IA
Fegley, Billy G .... (402) 684-3771
PUB, ED, Rock County Leader, Bassett, NE
Fegley, Tom .... (610) 820-6500
Outdoors ED, Morning Call, Allentown, PA
Fehler, Rick .... (306) 565-8211
PROD MGR-Pre Press/Sys
Leader-Post, Regina, SK
Fehnel, Jay .... (800) 245-6536
GM/Electronic INFO Services
Tribune Media Services Inc., Chicago, IL
Fehr, Fred .... (405) 273-4200
Sports ED, Shawnee News-Star, Shawnee, OK
Fehr-Snyder, Kerry .... (602) 271-8000
Technology Writer
Arizona Republic, Phoenix, AZ
Fehrnstrom, Larry .... (909) 793-3221
CIRC MGR
Redlands Daily Facts, Redlands, CA
Feibish, Pamela .... (804) 649-6000
BUS/FIN ED
Richmond Times-Dispatch, Richmond, VA
Feider, Gary .... (414) 994-9244
GM, ED, Sounder, Random Lake, WI
Feidler, Eric .... (203) 846-3281
PROD FRM-COMP, Hour, Norwalk, CT
Feigenbaum, Harriet .... (516) 829-4000
MAN ED
Long Island Jewish World, Great Neck, NY
Feigenbaum, Lynn .... (757) 446-2000
Public ED, Virginian-Pilot, Norfolk, VA
Feigl, Rita Hendren .... (773) 586-8800
ADV MGR-CLASS
Daily Southtown, Chicago, IL
Feiler, Mike .... (208) 664-8176
ED, City ED, EPE
Coeur d'Alene Press, Coeur d'Alene, ID
Fein, Geoff .... (408) 287-4866
ED, San Jose Post-Record, San Jose, CA
Feinberg, Ron .... (404) 526-5151
Religion ED
Atlanta Journal-Constitution, Atlanta, GA
Feinman, Myke .... (815) 673-3771
City ED, Streator Times-Press, Streator, IL
Feist, Joe Michael .... (409) 776-4444
ED, Eagle, Bryan, TX
Feist, Paul .... (209) 943-6397
MET ED, Record, Stockton, CA
Felbab, Joseph J .... (714) 835-1234
CIRC DIR-MKTG, DIR-Consumer MKTG
Orange County Register, Santa Ana, CA
Felber, Bill .... (913) 776-2200
EX ED, Manhattan Mercury, Manhattan, KS
Feld, Karen .... (202) 337-2044
COL, Capital Connections, Washington, DC
Feldberg, Robert .... (201) 646-4000
Theater ED, Record, Hackensack, NJ
Felder, Lynn .... (910) 727-7211
Arts ED, Books ED, Entertainment/Travel ED, Food ED, Sunday/Women's ED
Winston-Salem Journal, Winston-Salem, NC
Feldhiser, Andrew .... (517) 354-3111
PROD MGR, Alpena News, Alpena, MI
Feldkamp, Karen .... (704) 358-5000
VP, TREAS/ASST SEC, DIR-FIN/ADM
Charlotte Observer, Charlotte, NC
Feldman, Dave .... (312) 321-3000
Horse Racing
Chicago Sun-Times, Chicago, IL
Feldman, Ed .... (617) 786-7000
ADV DIR-Advertising
Patriot Ledger, Quincy, MA
Feldman, Joseph .... (312) 842-5883
PUB, Bridgeport News, Chicago, IL
Feldman, Karen .... (941) 335-0200
Travel ED, News-Press, Fort Myers, FL
Feldman, Mary .... (310) 477-0403
PUB
Los Angeles New Times, Los Angeles, CA
Feliciano, Arnold .... (904) 863-1111
Sports ED, Northwest Florida Daily News, Fort Walton Beach, FL
Felicissimo, Paul .... (914) 694-9300
CIRC DIR, Reporter Dispatch, White Plains, NY, Gannett Co. Inc.
Felix-Jayes, Billy .... (513) 381-2606
MAN ED, Everybody's News, Cincinnati, OH
Felke, Joe .... (219) 267-3111
Films/Theater ED, Music ED, Radio/Television ED, Times-Union, Warsaw, IN
Felkel, Jean S .... (803) 496-3242
GM, Observer, Holly Hill, SC
Fell, Jared .... (970) 352-0211
Farm/Agriculture ED
Greeley Tribune, Greeley, CO
Fellers, Steve .... (501) 246-5525
News ED
Arkadelphia Siftings Herald, Arkadelphia, AR
Fellone, Frank .... (501) 378-3400
Deputy MAN ED, COL
Arkansas Democrat-Gazette, Little Rock, AR
Fellows, George .... (505) 758-2241
PUB, Taos News, Taos, NM
Fellows, Robert .... (508) 775-1200
PROD MGR-COMP
Cape Cod Times, Hyannis, MA
Felps, Paula .... (817) 387-3811
Entertainment/Amusements ED, Music ED, Radio/Television ED
Denton Record-Chronicle, Denton, TX
Felsberg, Jay .... (334) 684-2280
ED, Geneva County Reaper, Geneva, AL
Felser, Larry .... (716) 849-3434
COL-Sports, Sports ED
Buffalo News, Buffalo, NY
Felsheim, Louis L .... (541) 332-2361
PUB, Port Orford News, Port Orford, OR
Felter, Mary .... (410) 268-5000
Society ED, Women's ED
Capital, Annapolis, MD
Feltman, Linda .... (412) 772-3900
DIR-FIN
North Hills News Record, Warrendale, PA
Felts, David .... (618) 532-5604
MAN ED, Centralia Sentinel, Centralia, IL
Fenimore, Warren .... (908) 922-6000
CIRC MGR-Single Copy Sales
Asbury Park Press, Neptune, NJ
Fenison, Brad .... (218) 736-7511
ADV DIR, Daily Journal, Fergus Falls, MN
Fenley, Don .... (423) 246-8121
ASST MAN ED-EDL/Features, EPE
Kingsport Times-News, Kingsport, TN
Fennell, Jan .... (817) 390-7400
Librarian, Star-Telegram, Fort Worth, TX
Fennessey, Mary .... (212) 930-8000
CIRC MGR-OPER
New York Post, New York, NY
Fenoff, Linda .... (518) 828-1616
Sunday ED, Register-Star, Hudson, NY
Fenrich, John L .... (916) 533-3131
PUB, Oroville Mercury Register, Oroville, CA
Fensin, Lee .... (414) 542-2501
Automotive ED, Sports ED
Waukesha County Freeman, Waukesha, WI
Fenske, Bob .... (515) 684-4611
Sports ED, Ottumwa Courier, Ottumwa, IA
Fenske, Bruce .... (507) 359-2911
PUB, GM, Journal, New Ulm, MN
Fenster, Bob .... (602) 271-8000
Films/Theater Writer, Movie Critic
Arizona Republic, Phoenix, AZ
Fenstermaker, Sue .... (415) 777-7212
EDL PROD MGR
Chronicle Features, San Francisco, CA
Fenton, Joe .... (509) 459-5000
City ED, Spokesman-Review, Spokane, WA
Fenton, Lois .... (914) 698-0721
COL, Male Call, Mamaroneck, NY
Fentress, Mark .... (910) 373-7000
CIRC DIR, News & Record, Greensboro, NC
Fenyes, Maria .... (213) 463-3473
PUB, ED
Californiai Magyarsag, Los Angeles, CA
Feola, Christopher .... (203) 574-3636
BUS ED, Waterbury Republican-American, Waterbury, CT
Feorino, Lu .... (413) 788-1000
MET ED, Union-News, Springfield, MA
Ferdula, Tammy-Jo .... (860) 442-2200
Librarian, Day, New London, CT
Ferguson, Alan .... (561) 820-4100
ADV VP
Palm Beach Post, West Palm Beach, FL
Ferguson, Bill .... (217) 357-2149
PUB
Hancock County Journal-Pilot, Carthage, IL
Ferguson, Carol .... (903) 455-4220
Fashion/Society ED
Greenville Herald-Banner, Greenville, TX
Ferguson, Chad .... (409) 732-6243
PUB, Banner Press Newspaper, Columbus, TX
Ferguson, D Jo .... (918) 762-2552
PUB, ED, Pawnee Chief, Pawnee, OK
Ferguson, Diane .... (410) 822-1500
ADV MGR-CLASS
Star-Democrat, Easton, MD
Ferguson, Don K .... (615) 688-3400
Author, Grammar Gremlins, Knoxville, TN
Ferguson, Evelyn .... (716) 882-9570
MAN ED, Buffalo Criterion, Buffalo, NY
Ferguson, Fred .... (800) 832-5522
Features CNR, PR Newswire, New York, NY
Ferguson, J Gray .... (804) 295-0124
PUB, Charlottesville Albemarle Observer, Charlottesville, VA
Ferguson, Jim .... (419) 522-3311
PROD FRM-PR, News Journal, Mansfield, OH
Ferguson, Jon .... (801) 674-6200
NTL ED, News ED-Local, Political/Government ED, Spectrum, St. George, UT
Ferguson, Karen .... (619) 322-8889
CIRC DIR, Desert Sun, Palm Springs, CA
Ferguson, Larry .... (719) 687-3006
MAN ED
Ute Pass Courier, Woodland Park, CO
Ferguson, Larry .... (918) 885-2101
PUB, Hominy News/Progress, Hominy, OK
Ferguson, Lesa .... (507) 451-2840
BM, DP MGR
Owatonna People's Press, Owatonna, MN
Huckle Publishing Inc.
Ferguson, Michael .... (909) 987-6397
PUB, Inland Valley Daily Bulletin, Ontario, CA
Ferguson, Mike .... (419) 435-6641
CIRC MGR, Review Times, Fostoria, OH
Ferguson, Paul .... (716) 328-2144
ASST ED
Syndicated News Service, Rochester, NY
Ferguson, Shelby .... (804) 946-7195
GM, Amherst New Era Progress, Amherst, VA
Ferguson, Terri .... (601) 226-4321
MAN ED, BUS/FIN ED, City/MET ED, EPE, Entertainment/Amusements ED, Graphics ED/Art DIR, NTL ED, News ED, Photo ED
Daily Sentinel-Star, Grenada, MS
Ferguson, William .... (419) 245-6000
Travel ED, Blade, Toledo, OH
Fericano, Paul .... (415) 588-5990
ED, Yossarian Universal News Service, Millbrae, CA
Fern Jr, Michael .... (413) 663-3741
CIRC DIR
North Adams Transcript, North Adams, MA
Fern, Tammy .... (719) 544-3520
ADV MGR-CLASS
Pueblo Chieftain, Pueblo, CO
Fernandes, Alcido .... (508) 997-7411
PROD FRM-Press/Plate
Standard Times, New Bedford, MA
Fernandes, Donna .... (860) 241-6200
MGR-Employment
Hartford Courant, Hartford, CT
Fernandez, Abel .... (210) 686-4343
ADV DIR, Monitor, McAllen, TX
Fernandez, Eduardo .... (215) 457-6999
ED, Al Dia, Philadelphia, PA
Fernandez, Ellen .... (304) 624-6411
Webmaster, Clarksburg Exponent/Telegram, Clarksburg, WV
Fernandez, Hugo .... (416) 441-1405
South America Journalist
Fotopress Independent News Service International (FPINS), Toronto, ON
Fernandez, Pamela .... (505) 983-3303
CONT, Santa Fe New Mexican, Santa Fe, NM
Fernandez, Phil .... (407) 420-5000
Osceola County ED
Orlando Sentinel, Orlando, FL
Fernando, S H .... (602) 468-6565
Bloodstock ED
Daily Racing Form, Phoenix, AZ
Fero, Debbie .... (717) 265-2151
CIRC MGR, Daily Review, Towanda, PA
Ferone, George A .... (800) 424-4747
OPER MGR, Tribune Media Services-Television Listings, Glens Falls, NY
Ferra, Charles .... (814) 773-3161
Sports ED, Ridgway Record, Ridgway, PA
Ferra, Dory .... (814) 371-4200
ADV MGR-CLASS, Courier-Express/Tri-County Sunday, Du Bois, PA
Ferrano, Ken .... (519) 255-5711
PROD FRM-Engraving, Star, Windsor, ON
Ferrante, Domenic .... (617) 426-3000
PROD SUPT-COMP
Boston Herald, Boston, MA
Ferrante, Joe .... (516) 843-2020
PROD GEN FRM-PR, Newsday, Melville, NY
Ferrara, Cheryl .... (813) 394-7592
PUB, Marco Island Eagle, Marco Island, FL
Ferrara, Geri .... (609) 691-5000
EPE, Daily Journal, Vineland, NJ
Ferrara, Philip M .... (717) 767-6397
CIRC VP, York Newspaper Company, York, PA
Ferrari, Barry .... (954) 356-4000
PROD MGR-Packaging
Sun-Sentinel, Fort Lauderdale, FL
Ferrario, Most Rev Joseph A .... (808) 533-1791
PUB, Hawaii Catholic Herald, Honolulu, HI
Ferraro, Lynn .... (561) 461-2050
PROD MGR, Tribune, Fort Pierce, FL
Ferrarone, Aida .... (818) 713-3229
ED, Vecinos Del Valle, Woodland Hills, CA
Ferrebee, Cheryl .... (614) 373-2121
DIR-Market Services
Marietta Times, Marietta, OH
Ferreira, Richard E .... (508) 586-7200
ADV MGR, Enterprise, Brockton, MA
Ferrell, Bob .... (601) 833-6961
PROD MGR, Daily Leader, Brookhaven, MS
Ferrell, David .... (205) 325-2222
DP MGR, News, Birmingham, AL
Ferrell, Garry .... (904) 362-1734
MAN ED, Suwannee Democrat, Live Oak, FL
Ferrell, Lisa .... (504) 850-1100
ADV DIR-RT, ADV MGR-PROM
Courier, Houma, LA
Ferrier, Dan M .... (330) 454-5611
PROD DIR, Repository, Canton, OH
Ferrier, Pat .... (303) 776-2244
Local News ED
Daily Times-Call, Longmont, CO
Ferrier, Patricia .... (615) 552-1808
City ED, Leaf-Chronicle, Clarksville, TN
Ferrington, Fred .... (318) 339-7242
ED, Catahoula News Booster, Jonesville, LA
Ferris, Lesly .... (860) 927-4621
ED, Kent Good Times Dispatch, Kent, CT
Ferris, Linda .... (765) 724-4469
ED, Alexandria Times-Tribune, Alexandria, IN
Ferris, Myrna .... (519) 822-4310
Wire ED, Daily Mercury, Guelph, ON
Ferris, Paul .... (519) 364-2001
ED, Weekender, Hanover, ON
Ferris, Richard J .... (517) 377-1000
CIRC DIR, Lansing State Journal, Lansing, MI
Ferriter, Ellie .... (603) 668-4321
Fashion/Food ED, Garden ED, Health/Medical ED, Home Furnishings ED, Women's ED
Union Leader, Manchester, NH
Ferriter, Jim .... (603) 668-4321
Automotive ED, RE ED
Union Leader, Manchester, NH
Ferriter, Thomas .... (207) 791-6650
ASST MAN ED-Special Projects
Portland Press Herald, Portland, ME

73-Who's Where **Fis**

Ferro, Nick .... (717) 767-6397
PROD MGR-MR
York Newspaper Company, York, PA

Ferson, Jerome .... (507) 285-7600
PROD MGR-Distribution Center
Post-Bulletin, Rochester, MN

Fertado, Frank .... (702) 383-0211
Features ED, Review-Journal, Las Vegas, NV

Fertig, Mike .... (515) 832-4350
PUB/GM
Daily Freeman-Journal, Webster City, IA

Feru Jr, Michael .... (413) 447-7311
CIRC DIR, Berkshire Eagle, Pittsfield, MA

Ferziger, Jonathan .... (202) 898-8254
Regional ED-Asia/Pacific
United Press International, Washington, DC

Fessier, Bruce .... (619) 322-8889
Entertainment ED, Society ED
Desert Sun, Palm Springs, CA

Feterl, Mary Ann .... (605) 296-3181
GM, Canistota Clipper, Canistota, SD

Fetsch, Jim .... (914) 694-9300
CIRC MGR-Single Copy, Reporter Dispatch, White Plains, NY, Gannett Co. Inc.

Fetsch, Jim .... (701) 780-1100
CIRC DIR, Herald, Grand Forks, ND

Fetsch, Kathy .... (219) 461-8333
CIRC MGR
Journal Gazette, Fort Wayne, IN

Fette, Dave .... (817) 759-4311
PUB, ED, Muenster Enterprise, Muenster, TX

Fetter, Julie .... (717) 738-1151
GM, Shopping News, Ephrata, PA

Fetzer, Doug .... (814) 946-7411
ADV MGR-Commercial Printing
Altoona Mirror, Altoona, PA

Fetzer, Jeff .... (717) 724-2287
ED, Wellsboro Gazette, Wellsboro, PA

Feuling, Daniel T .... (515) 394-2111
PUB
New Hampton Economist, New Hampton, IA

Fey, J T .... (605) 886-6901
Sports ED
Watertown Public Opinion, Watertown, SD

Fey, Martin .... (508) 943-4800
ED, Times, Webster, MA

Fey, Shari .... (409) 833-3311
Books/TV Scope ED, Records ED
Beaumont Enterprise, Beaumont, TX

Fey, Susanne .... (213) 881-6515
GM, Novedades, Los Angeles, CA

Feyerabend, Troy .... (818) 241-4141
PROD DIR
Glendale News-Press, Glendale, CA

Ficara, Ken .... (212) 416-2000
Webmaster
Wall Street Journal, New York, NY

Ficarra, Elaine K .... (203) 333-0161
Magazine/Food ED
Connecticut Post, Bridgeport, CT

Ficarro, Charles .... (717) 853-3134
PUB, ED, Susquehanna County Transcript, Susquehanna, PA

Fichtner, Margaria .... (305) 350-2111
Books ED, Miami Herald, Miami, FL

Ficke, Laura .... (206) 597-8742
EX SEC, News Tribune, Tacoma, WA

Ficklin, Thomas R .... (203) 387-0354
ED, Inner-City, New Haven, CT

Fidler, Julie .... (501) 793-2383
City ED, EDU/Women's Fashion ED, Home Furnishings ED
Batesville Guard, Batesville, AR

Fiedelman, Dave .... (703) 276-3400
CIRC GM-Chicago
USA Today, Arlington, VA

Fiedler, Frank .... (541) 382-1811
City ED, Bulletin, Bend, OR

Fiedler, John .... (305) 350-2111
DIR-Advanced SYS
Miami Herald, Miami, FL

Field, Dan .... (515) 322-3161
PUB, ED
Adams County Free Press, Corning, IA

Field, John D .... (712) 382-1234
PUB, ED, Hamburg Reporter, Hamburg, IA

Field, Victor .... (818) 781-2605
PUB, ED, Variedades HTMC, Van Nuys, CA

Fielder, Bill .... (912) 888-9390
CFO, Gray Communications, Albany, GA

Fielder, Mary .... (712) 246-3097
PROD MGR-COMP
Valley News Today, Shenandoah, IA

Fielder, Sandy .... (805) 781-7800
ADV MGR-CLASS
Telegram-Tribune, San Luis Obispo, CA

Fielder, Virginia .... (305) 376-3800
VP-RES, Knight-Ridder Inc., Miami, FL

Fielding, Howard .... (203) 574-3636
News SYS ED, ADTX MGR, Waterbury Republican-American, Waterbury, CT

Fielding, Todd .... (315) 458-4406
ED, Star-News, North Syracuse, NY

Fields, Archie .... (910) 323-4848
PROD ADM-PR
Fayetteville Observer-Times, Fayetteville, NC

Fields, August .... (407) 242-3500
CIRC DIR, Florida Today, Melbourne, FL

Fields, Connie .... (412) 775-3200
MGR-EDU SRV
Beaver County Times, Beaver, PA

Fields, Debbie .... (937) 652-1331
PROD FRM-Distribution
Urbana Daily Citizen, Urbana, OH

Fields, Gary .... (704) 252-5611
Photo DEPT MGR
Asheville Citizen-Times, Asheville, NC

Fields, Helen B .... (415) 465-3121
PUB, Inter-City Express, Oakland, CA

Fields, Howard .... (812) 385-2525
PROD MGR
Princeton Daily Clarion, Princeton, IN

Fields, Nell .... (213) 229-5300
ADV DIR
Los Angeles Daily Journal, Los Angeles, CA
Daily Journal Corp.

Fields, Pete .... (910) 373-7000
Online MGR
News & Record, Greensboro, NC

Fields, Steve .... (317) 653-5151
Sports ED
Banner-Graphic, Greencastle, IN

Fields, Vicki .... (812) 275-3355
BM, Times-Mail, Bedford, IN

Fienup, Jim .... (918) 962-2075
PUB, Spiro Graphic, Spiro, OK

Fierst, Mark .... (812) 482-2424
CONT, Herald, Jasper, IN

Fierstos, Edward L .... (706) 724-0851
ADV DIR-Display
Augusta Chronicle, Augusta, GA

Fietsam, James J .... (210) 393-2111
GM
Floresville Chronicle-Journal, Floresville, TX

Fietsam, Joe H .... (210) 393-2111
PUB
Floresville Chronicle-Journal, Floresville, TX

Fietsam, Mrs Joe H .... (210) 393-2111
ED
Floresville Chronicle-Journal, Floresville, TX

Fife, Buck .... (313) 222-6400
PROD MGR-Special Projects
Detroit Newspapers, Detroit, MI

Figert, Margaret .... (605) 856-4469
PUB, ED, Todd County Tribune, Mission, SD

Figueroa, Angelo .... (408) 920-5000
Nuevo Mundo ED
San Jose Mercury News, San Jose, CA

Figueroa, Maria .... (413) 788-4668
PUB, La Nueva Era, Springfield, MA

Figura, David .... (914) 341-1100
Regional ED
Times Herald-Record, Middletown, NY

Figy, Norman .... (919) 446-5161
Accountant, DP MGR
Rocky Mount Telegram, Rocky Mount, NC

Fijor, Grazyna .... (847) 581-1132
PUB, Kobieta, Morton Grove, IL

Fijor, Jan M .... (847) 581-1132
ED, Kobieta, Morton Grove, IL

Fike, Bob .... (304) 355-2381
ED, Piedmont Herald, Piedmont, WV

Fike, Brenda .... (573) 581-1111
Entertainment/Amusements ED, Fashion/Style ED, Home Furnishings ED, Living/Lifestyle ED
Mexico Ledger, Mexico, MO

Fike, David .... (410) 822-1500
ADV DIR, Star-Democrat, Easton, MD

Fike, Jeff .... (502) 247-5223
CIRC MGR
Mayfield Messenger, Mayfield, KY

Fikes, Brad .... (619) 232-4381
Bio Medical ED
San Diego Daily Transcript, San Diego, CA

Files, James .... (602) 982-7799
ED, Apache Junction Independent, Apache Junction, AZ

Filiaggi, Jim .... (319) 383-2200
DP MGR, Quad-City Times, Davenport, IA

Filichia, Peter .... (201) 877-4141
Drama Critic (New Jersey)
Star-Ledger, Newark, NJ

Filkins, Ron .... (812) 547-3424
PUB, Perry County News, Tell City, IN

Filla, Peter .... (608) 323-3366
ED, Arcadia News-Leader, Arcadia, WI

Fillaglia, Jennifer .... (716) 394-0770
News ED, Daily Messenger/The Sunday Messenger, Canandaigua, NY

Filler, Les .... (205) 549-2000
PROD DIR, Gadsden Times, Gadsden, AL

Filoe, Virginia .... (606) 845-9211
MAN ED
Flemingsburg Gazette, Flemingsburg, KY

Finazzo, Sam .... (715) 234-2121
ED, Rice Lake Chronotype, Rice Lake, WI

Finberg, Alan R .... (206) 339-3000
VP/SEC, Herald, Everett, WA

Finberg, Howard .... (602) 271-8000
DIR-INFO Technology, Senior ED-Information Technology
Phoenix Newspapers Inc., Phoenix, AZ

Finch, Bill .... (334) 433-1551
Growth/Environmental ED
Mobile Press Register, Mobile, AL

Finch, Cindy .... (218) 723-5281
MGR-PROM
Duluth News-Tribune, Duluth, MN

Finch, Michael C .... (502) 265-2439
PUB, ED, Todd County Standard, Elkton, KY

Finch, Paul .... (212) 499-3334
VP-Central & South America, New York Times Syndication Sales Corp., New York, NY

Finch, Robert E .... (847) 427-4300
Graphics ED
Daily Herald, Arlington Heights, IL

Fincher, Amanda .... (501) 442-1777
EDU ED
Northwest Arkansas Times, Fayetteville, AR

Finck, Donald .... (212) 580-8559
DIR, Journal Press Syndicate, New York, NY

Findelle Esq, Stann .... (310) 441-0565
VP, California Features International Inc., Beverly Hills, CA

Finder-Koziol, Sally .... (515) 684-4611
EPE, News ED
Ottumwa Courier, Ottumwa, IA

Findlay, W R (Bill) .... (519) 756-2020
PUB, Expositor, Brantford, ON

Findley, Edwin .... (903) 586-2236
CIRC MGR
Jacksonville Daily Progress, Jacksonville, TX

Findley, Jack A .... (304) 348-5140
PRES/GM
Charleston Newspapers, Charleston, WV

Fine, Arnold .... (718) 330-1100
ED, Jewish Press, Brooklyn, NY

Fine, Boni .... (312) 321-3000
VP-ADM, Chicago Sun-Times, Chicago, IL

Fine, Marshall .... (617) 786-7000
DIR-FIN SRV, Patriot Ledger, Quincy, MA

Fine, Meredith .... (508) 922-1234
ED, Gloucester Times, Beverly, MA

Finebaum, Paul .... (205) 325-2222
COL, Post-Herald, Birmingham, AL

Finefrock, Jim .... (415) 777-2424
EPE
San Francisco Examiner, San Francisco, CA

Finefrock, Ray .... (540) 825-0771
News ED
Culpeper Star-Exponent, Culpeper, VA

Fineman, Mark .... (213) 237-5000
Mexico City BU
Los Angeles Times, Los Angeles, CA

Fingal, Jerry .... (916) 741-2345
News ED, Appeal-Democrat, Marysville, CA

Finger, Ray .... (607) 734-5151
EPE, Star-Gazette, Elmira, NY

Fingeroot, Randy .... (770) 963-9205
Sports ED
Gwinnett Daily Post, Lawrenceville, GA

Finholm, Karl .... (406) 523-5200
CONT, Missoulian, Missoula, MT

Fink, David .... (860) 241-6200
Government ED
Hartford Courant, Hartford, CT

Fink, John F .... (317) 236-1570
ED, Criterion, Indianapolis, IN

Fink, Lorraine .... (912) 888-9300
ADV MGR-RT, Albany Herald, Albany, GA

Fink-Frazier, Susan .... (615) 259-8000
Wire ED, Tennessean, Nashville, TN

Finkelstein, Gary .... (508) 586-7200
EPE, Enterprise, Brockton, MA

Finkelstein, James A .... (212) 779-9200
PRES/PUB
New York Law Journal, New York, NY

Finkle, Tom .... (305) 571-7699
MAN ED, Miami New Times, Miami, FL

Finklea, Gaylon .... (512) 331-1144
ED, Jewish Outlook, Austin, TX

Finlay, Diana .... (512) 392-2458
Women's ED
San Marcos Daily Record, San Marcos, TX

Finlay, Steven .... (810) 541-3000
City ED, Political ED
Daily Tribune, Royal Oak, MI

Finlay, Terry .... (604) 368-8551
CIRC MGR, Trail Daily Times, Trail, BC

Finley, Betty .... (561) 820-4100
MGR-Purchasing
Palm Beach Post, West Palm Beach, FL

Finley, Denis .... (757) 446-2000
Features ED, Virginian-Pilot, Norfolk, VA

Finley, Don .... (210) 225-7411
Medical Writer
San Antonio Express-News, San Antonio, TX

Finley, Gary .... (864) 582-4511
CIRC MGR-PROM
Herald-Journal, Spartanburg, SC

Finley, Larry .... (312) 321-3000
RE Writer, Chicago Sun-Times, Chicago, IL

Finley, Laurie .... (204) 697-7000
ADV DIR
Winnipeg Free Press, Winnipeg, MB

Finley, Mark .... (405) 238-6464
ED
Pauls Valley Daily Democrat, Pauls Valley, OK

Finley, Nolan .... (313) 222-2300
BUS ED
Detroit News, Detroit, MI

Finn, Dan .... (206) 464-2111
PROD MGR-Facilities (North Creek)
Seattle Times, Seattle, WA

Finn, Judi .... (207) 563-3171
ED
Lincoln County News, Damariscotta, ME

Finn, Thomas .... (773) 586-8800
ASST MET ED
Daily Southtown, Chicago, IL

Finnegan, Ardith .... (403) 932-3500
ED, Cochrane This Week, Cochrane, AB

Finnegan, Cally .... (601) 328-2424
ADV MGR-PROM
Commercial Dispatch, Columbus, MS

Finnegan, Danny .... (804) 649-6000
ASST MAN ED-Night OPER
Richmond Times-Dispatch, Richmond, VA

Finnegan, Michael J .... (515) 357-2131
PUB, Clear Lake Reporter, Clear Lake, IA

Finnerty, John .... (814) 438-7666
ED
Union City Times-Leader, Union City, PA

Finney, Michael .... (402) 444-1000
EX ED, Omaha World-Herald, Omaha, NE

Finney, Peter .... (504) 826-3279
Sports ED, Times-Picayune, New Orleans, LA

Finney Jr, Peter .... (504) 524-1618
GM, ED, Clarion Herald, New Orleans, LA

Finnigan, Philip .... (941) 687-7000
PROD MGR-Press, Ledger, Lakeland, FL

Finora, Joe .... (718) 220-2000
GM, MAN ED, Illyria, Bronx, NY

Finucane, William .... (508) 626-3800
Regional ED-South
Middlesex News, Framingham, MA

Fiorenza, Bishop Joseph A .... (713) 659-5461
PUB, Texas Catholic Herald, Houston, TX

Fioretti, Karen .... (508) 685-5128
ED
North Andover Citizen, North Andover, MA

Fiorilla, Paul .... (908) 254-7000
MAN ED, Independent, East Brunswick, NJ

Fiorini, Phillip .... (317) 423-5511
Local/Regional ED
Journal and Courier, Lafayette, IN

Fiorito, Greg .... (320) 255-8700
PROD DIR, St. Cloud Times, St. Cloud, MN

Firestone, JoAnna .... (313) 222-2300
State ED
Detroit News, Detroit, MI

Firpo, Jean .... (561) 793-7606
MAN ED, Town Crier, Wellington, FL

Firus, Cynthia .... (306) 784-2422
ED, Herald, Herbert, SK

Fiscalini, Monica .... (805) 781-7800
Entertainment/Amusements ED
Telegram-Tribune, San Luis Obispo, CA

Fisch, Deborah .... (712) 757-4055
PUB, ED
O'Brien County Bell, Primghar, IA

Fisch, Michael J .... (805) 395-7500
PRES/CEO
Bakersfield Californian, Bakersfield, CA

Fischels, Lori .... (515) 832-4350
CIRC MGR
Daily Freeman-Journal, Webster City, IA

Fischer, Aaron .... (315) 792-5000
PROD MGR-Post Press
Observer-Dispatch, Utica, NY

Fischer, Charles .... (910) 353-1171
PUB, Daily News, Jacksonville, NC

Fischer, Doug .... (613) 829-9100
Sports ED, Ottawa Citizen, Ottawa, ON

Fischer, Ed .... (507) 285-7750
Self-Syndicator
Fischer Production, Ed, Rochester, MN

Fischer, Jennifer .... (412) 222-2200
CIRC ASST DIR
Observer-Reporter, Washington, PA

Fischer, Judy .... (414) 733-4411
MGR-PROM, Post-Crescent, Appleton, WI

Fischer, Michelle .... (414) 684-4433
DP MGR
Herald Times Reporter, Manitowoc, WI

Fischer, Ryan .... (215) 855-8440
BUS/FIN ED, Reporter, Landsdale, PA

Fischer, Sarah .... (770) 963-9205
Food ED, Lifestyle ED
Gwinnett Daily Post, Lawrenceville, GA

Fischer, Scott .... (714) 553-9292
Sr VP/PRES-Western Newspaper Division
Freedom Communications Inc., Irvine, CA

Fischione-Donovan, Sandra .... (412) 775-3200
ED-Allegheny Times
Beaver County Times, Beaver, PA

Fischman, Gerald .... (410) 268-5000
EPE, Capital, Annapolis, MD

Fis Who's Where-74

Fiscus, Cheryl .... (812) 372-7811
Features ED, Republic, Columbus, IN

Fish, Ann .... (910) 349-4331
MAN ED, BUS/FIN ED, City/MET ED, Features ED, Graphics ED/Art DIR, NTL ED, News ED, Photo ED
Reidsville Review, Reidsville, NC

Fish, Dick .... (518) 843-1100
CIRC DIR, Recorder, Amsterdam, NY

Fish, John .... (706) 724-0851
MAN ED, Augusta Chronicle, Augusta, GA

Fish, Randy .... (704) 245-6431
PROD FRM-PR, Daily Courier, Forest City, NC

Fishbein, Jack .... (312) 407-0060
PUB, ED, Sentinel, Chicago, IL

Fisher, Ann .... (419) 245-6000
Columbus BU Chief, Blade, Toledo, OH

Fisher, Bart .... (860) 225-4601
Automotive ED, Herald, New Britain, CT

Fisher, Bob .... (405) 225-3000
Farm/Agriculture ED, Graphics ED/Art DIR, News ED, Photo ED, Religion ED
Elk City Daily News, Elk City, OK

Fisher, Bobbi S .... (219) 643-3165
ED, Royal Center Record, Royal Center, IN

Fisher, Brent .... (316) 856-2115
MAN ED
Baxter Springs Citizen, Baxter Springs, KS

Fisher, Coreen .... (419) 522-3311
ADV DIR, News Journal, Mansfield, OH

Fisher, Cory .... (509) 925-1414
Religion ED, Daily Record, Ellensburg, WA

Fisher, Dan .... (217) 835-4868
PUB, ED, Enterprise, Benld, IL

Fisher, Dave J .... (915) 758-3667
ED, Seminole Sentinel, Seminole, TX

Fisher, David .... (715) 682-2313
PROD SUPT, Daily Press, Ashland, WI

Fisher, David .... (360) 675-6611
ED, Whidbey News Times, Oak Harbor, WA

Fisher, Dennis A .... (717) 291-8811
Sports ED, Lancaster Intelligencer Journal/New Era/Sunday News, Lancaster, PA

Fisher, Eric .... (505) 887-5501
MAN ED, EPE, Current-Argus, Carlsbad, NM

Fisher, Eric D .... (815) 476-7966
MAN ED
Wilmington Free Press, Wilmington, IL

Fisher, Eunice .... (915) 728-3413
ED, Colorado City Record, Colorado City, TX

Fisher, Evelyn .... (915) 445-5475
BM, Pecos Enterprise, Pecos, TX

Fisher, George H .... (815) 476-7966
PUB, Wilmington Free Press, Wilmington, IL

Fisher, James .... (816) 234-4141
COL, Kansas City Star, Kansas City, MO

Fisher, James .... (208) 743-9411
EDL Writer
Lewiston Morning Tribune, Lewiston, ID

Fisher, Jerry .... (515) 832-4350
ADV MGR
Daily Freeman-Journal, Webster City, IA

Fisher, John .... (573) 564-2339
PUB, ED
Montgomery Standard, Montgomery City, MO

Fisher, Ken .... (212) 744-1867
MGR, Quaternary Features, New York, NY

Fisher, Larry .... (517) 772-2971
CIRC DIR
Morning Sun, Mount Pleasant, MI

Fisher, Leonard .... (201) 877-4141
ASSOC ED, Star-Ledger, Newark, NJ

Fisher, Mag .... (217) 835-4868
GM, Enterprise, Benld, IL

Fisher, Mark .... (614) 461-5000
EDL Writer
Columbus Dispatch, Columbus, OH

Fisher, Michael .... (304) 292-6301
Graphic Arts/Design ED
Dominion Post, Morgantown, WV

Fisher, Mike .... (704) 358-5000
Art DIR
Charlotte Observer, Charlotte, NC

Fisher, Nancy .... (704) 633-8950
Librarian, Salisbury Post, Salisbury, NC

Fisher, Patricia .... (408) 920-5000
EDL Writer
San Jose Mercury News, San Jose, CA

Fisher, R L .... (501) 754-2005
PUB, Johnson County Graphic, Clarksville, AR

Fisher, Raymond P .... (609) 396-2200
DIR-Taxes, Journal Register Co., Trenton, NJ

Fisher, Robert .... (405) 225-3000
MAN ED, Elk City Daily News, Elk City, OK

Fisher, Robert .... (514) 481-7510
PUB, Monitor, Montreal, QC

Fisher, Roy .... (250) 758-4917
ADV MGR
Nanaimo Daily Free Press, Nanaimo, BC

Fisher, Sam R .... (815) 875-4461
PUB
Bureau County Republican, Princeton, IL

Fisher, Scott .... (717) 854-1575
EPE, York Dispatch, York, PA

Fisher, Shana .... (970) 352-0211
DP MGR, Greeley Tribune, Greeley, CO

Fisher, Stephen E .... (219) 643-3165
PUB, Royal Center Record, Royal Center, IN

Fisher, Steve .... (618) 542-2133
PUB, GM, Du Quoin Evening Call, Du Quoin, IL

Fisher, Tammy .... (517) 772-2971
ADV MGR-Sales (Alma)
Morning Sun, Mount Pleasant, MI

Fisher, Tom .... (913) 843-1000
ADV DIR, ADV MGR-NTL
Journal-World, Lawrence, KS

Fisher, Val .... (715) 833-9200
DP MGR, Leader-Telegram, Eau Claire, WI

Fisher, Wade W .... (704) 633-8950
PROD FRM-PR
Salisbury Post, Salisbury, NC

Fisher-Polomski, Dawn .... (908) 722-8800
ASST FIN DIR
Courier-News, Bridgewater, NJ

Fishkin, Rebecca .... (717) 771-2000
Religion ED, York Daily Record, York, PA

Fishleigh, Sonja .... (216) 951-0000
ADV MGR-NTL
News-Herald, Willoughby, OH

Fishman, Jon .... (505) 287-4411
PUB, Cibola County Beacon, Grants, NM

Fishman, R Jack .... (423) 581-5630
PRES, PUB, ED
Citizen Tribune, Morristown, TN

Fishoff, Marty .... (313) 222-2300
ASST MAN ED, Detroit News, Detroit, MI

Fisk, Alan .... (313) 222-2300
Books ED, Detroit News, Detroit, MI

Fisk, Patricia .... (520) 763-2505
PROD SUPV-COMP
Mohave Valley Daily News, Bullhead City, AZ

Fiske, Fred .... (315) 470-0011
EPE Post-Standard,Post-Standard/Syracuse Herald-Journal/American, Syracuse, NY

Fiske, Heather .... (902) 752-3000
City ED, Evening News, New Glasgow, NS

Fissolo, Maureen .... (707) 425-4646
News ED, Daily Republic, Fairfield, CA

Fister, Donna .... (615) 259-8800
CFO, Nashville Banner, Nashville, TN

Fitch, Dan .... (408) 423-4242
Sports ED
Santa Cruz County Sentinel, Santa Cruz, CA

Fitch, Jeff .... (601) 234-4331
CIRC MGR, Oxford Eagle, Oxford, MS

Fitch, Mary .... (518) 374-4141
MGR-CR, Daily Gazette, Schenectady, NY

Fitch, Mike .... (707) 448-6401
BUS/FIN ED, Reporter, Vacaville, CA

Fitch, Rick .... (619) 427-3000
ED, Star-News, Chula Vista, CA

Fitchko, T R .... (614) 461-5000
Accent ED
Columbus Dispatch, Columbus, OH

Fite, Renae .... (918) 663-1414
ED, Bixby Bulletin, Tulsa, OK

Fithian, Sherry .... (314) 421-1880
ADV MGR
St. Louis Daily Record, St. Louis, MO

Fitts, Francis .... (212) 779-9200
ADV MGR-CLASS
New York Law Journal, New York, NY

Fitzgerald, Bill .... (201) 877-4141
PROD OPER MGR-Newark
Star-Ledger, Newark, NJ

Fitzgerald, Bonnie .... (414) 386-2421
ED
Dodge County Independent-News, Juneau, WI

Fitzgerald, Dennis .... (508) 473-1111
ADV MGR-CLASS
Milford Daily News, Milford, MA

Fitzgerald, Dennis .... (206) 461-1300
ED, North Central Outlook, Seattle, WA

Fitzgerald, James W .... (212) 556-1234
PRES/CEO-Sports/Leisure Magazine
New York Times, New York, NY

Fitzgerald, Joe .... (617) 426-3000
News COL, Boston Herald, Boston, MA

Fitzgerald, Joe .... (217) 788-1300
ADV MGR-GEN
State Journal-Register, Springfield, IL

Fitzgerald, Karen .... (540) 885-7281
Lifestyle ED
Daily News Leader, Staunton, VA

Fitzgerald, Martha H .... (318) 459-3200
ASST MAN ED, Times, Shreveport, LA

Fitzgerald, Mary .... (508) 685-1000
Features ED, Food ED
Eagle-Tribune, North Andover, MA

Fitzgerald, Nancy .... (802) 479-0191
ADV MGR-CLASS, Times Argus, Barre, VT

Fitzgerald, Rick .... (313) 994-6989
MET ED, Picture ED
Ann Arbor News, Ann Arbor, MI

Fitzgerald, Scott .... (414) 386-2421
PUB
Dodge County Independent-News, Juneau, WI

Fitzgerald, Steve .... (504) 383-1111
MGR-EDU SRV, Advocate, Baton Rouge, LA

FitzGerald, Susan .... (215) 854-2000
Medical Writer
Philadelphia Inquirer, Philadelphia, PA

Fitzgerald, Vicky .... (617) 786-7000
Food ED, Patriot Ledger, Quincy, MA

Fitzhenry, James .... (212) 556-1234
PROD Group DIR-Production
New York Times, New York, NY

Fitzler, Don .... (605) 996-5514
CIRC MGR, Daily Republic, Mitchell, SD

Fitzpatrick, Brendan .... (802) 479-0191
PROD CNR, Times Argus, Barre, VT

Fitzpatrick, Cathy .... (414) 224-2000
Fashion Reporter, Home Furnishings Reporter
Milwaukee Journal Sentinel, Milwaukee, WI

Fitzpatrick, Colleen .... (518) 454-5694
EX City ED, Times Union, Albany, NY

Fitzpatrick, Debbie .... (816) 263-4123
Women's ED, Moberly Monitor-Index & Democrat, Moberly, MO

Fitzpatrick, Edward .... (518) 584-4242
City ED, Saratogian, Saratoga Springs, NY

Fitzpatrick, Joanne .... (617) 786-7000
EPE, Patriot Ledger, Quincy, MA

Fitzpatrick, John .... (716) 372-3121
PROD FRM-PR
Olean Times-Herald, Olean, NY

Fitzpatrick, Sharon .... (410) 332-6000
DIR-Human Resources
Baltimore Sun, Baltimore, MD

Fitzpatrick, Tim .... (801) 237-2031
Environmental ED, Health/Medical ED, Political ED, Salt Lake Tribune, Salt Lake City, UT

Fitzpatrick, William B .... (716) 372-3121
BM, Olean Times-Herald, Olean, NY

FitzSimmons, Cal .... (509) 582-1500
Features ED, Sunday ED
Tri-City Herald, Tri-Cities, WA

Fitzsimmons, Helen .... (908) 349-3000
EPE, Ocean County Observer, Toms River, NJ

Fitzsimmons, Jim .... (609) 989-7800
BUS/FIN ED, Trentonian, Trenton, NJ

Fitzsimmons, Robert .... (619) 241-7744
BM, Daily Press, Victorville, CA
Freedom Communications Inc.

FitzSimons, Brendan .... (520) 281-9706
PUB, ED, Nogales International, Nogales, AZ

FitzSimons, Dennis J .... (312) 222-3237
EVP-Broadcasting, Tribune Co., Chicago, IL

Fitzwater, John .... (352) 374-5000
PUB, Gainesville Sun, Gainesville, FL

Fitzwater, Terence J .... (616) 723-3592
PUB, MGR-MKTG/PROM
Manistee News-Advocate, Manistee, MI

Fitzwater, Teresa .... (616) 781-3943
CONT, Marshall Chronicle, Marshall, MI

Fix, Charles .... (716) 849-3434
CIRC MGR-Single Copy
Buffalo News, Buffalo, NY

Flack, Bob .... (540) 981-3100
DP MGR, Roanoke Times, Roanoke, VA

Flack, Deborah .... (518) 792-9914
DIR Sales & MKTG, Entertainment & Features Syndicate, TV Data, Queensbury, NY

Flack, John T .... (217) 392-2715
PUB
Augusta Eagle/Tri-County Scribe, Augusta, IL

Flack, Lea A .... (217) 392-2715
PUB, MAN ED
Augusta Eagle/Tri-County Scribe, Augusta, IL

Fladung, Thom .... (313) 222-6400
News ED
Detroit Free Press, Detroit, MI

Flagan, Arthur S .... (208) 667-3431
TREAS, Hagadone Corp., Coeur d'Alene, ID

Flagg, James .... (610) 258-7171
EPE, Express-Times, Easton, PA

Flaherty, Dennis J .... (207) 282-1535
PUB, Journal Tribune, Biddeford, ME

Flaherty, Ed .... (603) 436-1800
Sports ED
Portsmouth Herald, Portsmouth, NH

Flaherty, Jim .... (414) 363-4045
ED, Mukwonago Chief, Mukwonago, WI

Flaherty, R .... (212) 947-7280
MAN DIR
Voter News Service, New York, NY

Flaherty, Roger .... (312) 321-3000
ASST MET ED
Chicago Sun-Times, Chicago, IL

Flaherty, Terri .... (203) 964-2200
DIR-Human Resources, Stamford Advocate, Stamford, CT, Times Mirror Co.

Flake, Gerald B .... (416) 814-4239
Sr VP-New Media Ventures
Thomson Newspapers, Toronto, ON

Flam, Faye .... (215) 854-2000
SCI Writer
Philadelphia Inquirer, Philadelphia, PA

Flanagan, Bernard T .... (212) 416-2600
VP-MKTG
Dow Jones & Co. Inc., New York, NY

Flanagan, David .... (916) 321-1000
DIR-Creative
Sacramento Bee, Sacramento, CA

Flanagan, John M .... (808) 525-8000
ED/PUB
Honolulu Star-Bulletin, Honolulu, HI

Flanagan, Mark .... (508) 222-7000
ASST MAN ED
Sun Chronicle, Attleboro, MA

Flanagan, Martha L .... (513) 721-2700
SEC/ASST to Publisher
Cincinnati Enquirer, Cincinnati, OH

Flanagan, R Joseph .... (507) 375-3161
PUB, Plaindealer, St. James, MN

Flanagan, Tara .... (303) 949-4004
MAN ED, Vail Trail, Vail, CO

Flanagan Jr, William .... (937) 878-3993
MAN ED, Fairborn Daily Herald, Fairborn, OH

Flanders, Danny .... (803) 771-6161
Home Furnishings ED, State, Columbia, SC

Flanders, Margie S .... (847) 427-4300
VP/ASST SEC/TREAS, ADV MGR-Legal
Daily Herald, Arlington Heights, IL

Flangan, John .... (808) 525-8000
PUB (Honolulu Star-Bulletin)
Hawaii Newspaper Agency Inc., Honolulu, HI

Flanigan, James .... (213) 237-5000
Senior Economics ED/FIN COL
Los Angeles Times, Los Angeles, CA

Flannery, Dan .... (414) 733-4411
News ED, Post-Crescent, Appleton, WI

Flannery, Joseph X .... (717) 348-9100
EPE
Tribune & The Scranton Times, Scranton, PA

Flansburg, James M .... (515) 284-8000
Local COL
Des Moines Register, Des Moines, IA

Flansburg, Jim .... (817) 387-3811
MAN ED
Denton Record-Chronicle, Denton, TX

Flaster, Michael .... (212) 666-2300
Photographer, Basch, Buddy Feature Syndicate, New York, NY

Flater, Rob T .... (414) 733-4411
PROD FRM-COMP (Night)
Post-Crescent, Appleton, WI

Flatland, Jon E .... (816) 542-0881
ED, Carrollton Democrat, Carrollton, MO

Flatt, Holly .... (406) 222-2000
Sports ED
Livingston Enterprise, Livingston, MT

Flatt, Steve .... (309) 764-4344
DIR-Special Projects/PROM, ADTX MGR
Dispatch, Moline, IL
Small Newspaper Group Inc.

Flattau, Edward .... (202) 659-1921
PRES, Global Horizons, Washington, DC

Flatten, Mark .... (602) 898-6500
Political/Government ED, Mesa Tribune, Mesa, AZ, Thomson Newspapers

Flatten, Shirley .... (616) 723-3592
PROD MGR
Manistee News-Advocate, Manistee, MI

Flaum, Randy .... (860) 584-0501
Graphics ED/Art DIR, Photo ED
Bristol Press, Bristol, CT

Flavell, John .... (606) 329-1717
Photo Dept MGR
Daily Independent, Ashland, KY

Fleck, Brian .... (319) 644-2233
PUB, Solon Economist, Solon, IA

Fleck, John .... (505) 823-7777
SCI/Technology ED
Albuquerque Journal, Albuquerque, NM

Fleck, Tim .... (419) 625-5500
Photo ED, Sandusky Register, Sandusky, OH

Fleener, Katherine .... (316) 223-1460
ADV DIR, Fort Scott Tribune, Fort Scott, KS

Fleet, William H .... (805) 259-1234
GM, Signal, Santa Clarita, CA

Fleet, Zeke M .... (616) 946-2000
GM, ADV MGR-NTL, MGR-MKTG
Record-Eagle, Traverse City, MI

Fleetwood, Chrystine .... (503) 226-1311
MGR-Accounting
Daily Journal of Commerce, Portland, OR

Fleetwood, Jean .... (352) 374-5000
News Graphic MGR
Gainesville Sun, Gainesville, FL

Flegel, Ralph .... (704) 484-7000
PROD SUPT-Press/Plate
Shelby Star, Shelby, NC

Fleischaker, Ted .... (317) 632-8840
PUB, Word, Indianapolis, IN

Fleischer, Karen .... (954) 356-4000
CIRC MGR (North/Central Broward)
Sun-Sentinel, Fort Lauderdale, FL

Fleischer, Richard .... (401) 732-3100
GM, Warwick Beacon, Warwick, RI

Fleischman, Bill .... (215) 854-2000
Automotive ED
Philadelphia Daily News, Philadelphia, PA

Fleischman, Tom .... (607) 272-2321
Sports ED, Ithaca Journal, Ithaca, NY

Fleming, Allan .... (702) 383-0211
GM, Las Vegas Review-Journal, Las Vegas, NV

Copyright ©1997 by the Editor & Publisher Co.

75-Who's Where **Fon**

Fleming, Becky (304) 348-5140
Environmental/Ecology ED
Charleston Daily Mail, Charleston, WV
Fleming, Bill (810) 469-4510
BUS/FIN ED, Religion ED, SCI/Technology ED, Macomb Daily, Mount Clemens, MI
Fleming, Dick (410) 749-7171
News ED, Daily Times, Salisbury, MD
Fleming, James (519) 756-2020
Auto ED, RE ED, Expositor, Brantford, ON
Fleming, John (813) 893-8111
Music ED-Classical
St. Petersburg Times, St. Petersburg, FL
Fleming, John (618) 684-5833
GM, Murphysboro American, Murphysboro, IL
Fleming, John (601) 326-2181
PUB, ED
Quitman County Democrat, Marks, MS
Fleming, Josephine (601) 326-2181
PUB, ED
Quitman County Democrat, Marks, MS
Fleming, Judy (912) 723-4376
GM, Early County News, Blakely, GA
Fleming, Kenneth S (918) 581-8300
PRES/COO, Tulsa World, Tulsa, OK
Fleming, Kim (519) 785-2455
GM, Chronicle, Rodney, ON
Fleming, Marjorie (519) 627-2243
PUB, Wallaceburg News, Wallaceburg, ON
Fleming, Mary (202) 334-6375
Sales MGR/International, Washington Post Writers Group, Washington, DC
Fleming, Phyllis (319) 398-8211
ASST MAN ED, Environmental ED, Health ED, SCI/Technology ED
Gazette, Cedar Rapids, IA
Fleming, Suzy (205) 345-0505
Travel ED, Women's ED
Tuscaloosa News, Tuscaloosa, AL
Fleming, Ted J (309) 692-4910
PUB, Observer, Peoria, IL
Fleming, Terri (719) 632-5511
MAN ED, Gazette, Colorado Springs, CO
Fleming, William W (912) 723-4376
PUB, Early County News, Blakely, GA
Flemington, Jan (816) 932-6600
Sales Administrator
Universal Press Syndicate, Kansas City, MO
Flemming, Deb (507) 625-4451
ED, Free Press, Mankato, MN
Flemming, M (902) 426-2811
Sports ED, Chronicle-Herald, Halifax, NS
Flemmons, Jerry (817) 390-7400
Travel ED
Fort Worth Star-Telegram, Fort Worth, TX
Flessner, David (423) 756-1234
BUS ED
Chattanooga Times, Chattanooga, TN
Fletcher, Carol B (412) 465-5555
ADV DIR-MKTG
Indiana Gazette, Indiana, PA
Fletcher, Chris (903) 586-2236
ED, Daily Progress, Jacksonville, TX
Fletcher, Cindy (504) 345-2333
News ED, Daily Star, Hammond, LA
Fletcher, Danny (405) 225-3000
Sports ED
Elk City Daily News, Elk City, OK
Fletcher, David (706) 324-5526
ADV DIR
Columbus Ledger-Enquirer, Columbus, GA
Fletcher, Denise (941) 687-7000
TREAS, Ledger, Lakeland, FL
Fletcher, Gary (318) 433-3000
PROD MGR-Computer, Lake Charles American Press, Lake Charles, LA
Fletcher, Gloria (405) 256-2200
PUB, Woodward News, Woodward, OK
Fletcher, Harrison (505) 823-7777
COL-News
Albuquerque Tribune, Albuquerque, NM
Fletcher, J Crisler (601) 487-1551
PUB, ED, Southern Reporter, Sardis, MS
Fletcher, Jean (423) 246-4800
City ED, Features ED, PROD FRM
Daily News, Kingsport, TN
Fletcher, Jeffrey G (509) 754-4636
PUB, Grant County Journal, Ephrata, WA
Fletcher, Jim (904) 623-2120
ED, MAN ED
Santa Rosa Press Gazette, Milton, FL
Fletcher, Larry (813) 259-7711
MET ED
Tampa Tribune and Times, Tampa, FL
Fletcher, Leroy (308) 382-1000
PROD MGR-Pre Press
Grand Island Independent, Grand Island, NE
Fletcher, Mary (502) 678-5171
ADV MGR-CLASS
Glasgow Daily Times, Glasgow, KY
Fletcher, Penny (813) 634-3007
ED, East Bay Breeze, Sun City Center, FL
Fletcher, Scott (802) 479-0191
City ED, Times Argus, Barre, VT
Fletcher, Susan (516) 843-2020
DIR-PROM, Newsday, Melville, NY
Fletcher, T R (203) 622-1547
PRES, Cartoonews Inc., Greenwich, CT
Fletcher, William N (213) 237-5000
PROD DIR-Technology Resource Group
Los Angeles Times, Los Angeles, CA
Flick, Bill (309) 829-9411
COL, Pantagraph, Bloomington, IL
Flick, Jim (910) 727-7211
CIRC DIR
Winston-Salem Journal, Winston-Salem, NC
Flick, Jon (520) 763-2505
Sports ED
Mohave Valley Daily News, Bullhead City, AZ
Flick, Linda (203) 789-5200
CIRC MGR-Single Copy
New Haven Register, New Haven, CT
Flickinger, Reed (808) 329-9311
ED, Agriculture ED, EPE
West Hawaii Today, Kailua-Kona, HI
Fliess, Claire (815) 433-2000
PROD DIR-Creative Services
Daily Times, Ottawa, IL
Flink, Dick (573) 657-2334
PUB, Boone County Journal, Ashland, MO
Flink, Jane (573) 657-2334
PUB, ED
Boone County Journal, Ashland, MO
Flinn, Albert (419) 422-5151
PROD MGR-SYS, Courier, Findlay, OH
Flinn, John (415) 777-2424
Travel ED
San Francisco Examiner, San Francisco, CA
Flint, Connie (608) 328-4202
MGR-Office, Monroe Times, Monroe, WI
Flint, James (509) 865-4055
PUB, Toppenish Review, Toppenish, WA
Flint, Jimmy (540) 638-8801
PROD FRM-PR
Martinsville Bulletin, Martinsville, VA
Flippin, James C (610) 371-5000
VP/SEC, Reading Times/Eagle, Reading, PA
Flippin, William S (610) 371-5000
VP/PRES, PUB
Reading Times/Eagle, Reading, PA
Fliss, Bishop Raphael M (715) 392-8268
PUB, Catholic Herald, Superior, WI
Floco, Richard (619) 634-1534
PUB, Encinitas Sun, Carlsbad, CA
Flom, Paula K (319) 337-3181
CONT, Iowa City Press-Citizen, Iowa City, IA
Flood, Carolyn (207) 883-5944
PUB, Scarborough Leader, Scarborough, ME
Flood, David (207) 282-4337
PUB, ED
Biddeford-Saco-OOB Courier, Biddeford, ME
Flood, Don (302) 678-3616
ED, Dover Post, Dover, DE
Flood Sr, Jim (302) 678-3616
PUB, Dover Post, Dover, DE
Flood Jr, Jim (302) 678-3616
GM, Dover Post, Dover, DE
Flood, Pat (352) 365-8200
Features ED
Daily Commercial, Leesburg, FL
Floore, Ken (601) 762-1111
ADV MGR-Sales/RT
Mississippi Press, Pascagoula, MS
Flora, Kenneth L (804) 793-2311
EPE, Danville Register & Bee, Danville, VA
Flora, Tim (573) 392-5658
GM, Eldon Advertiser, Eldon, MO
Flores, Alma R (210) 727-8507
GM, El Clamor, Laredo, TX
Flores, Christine (602) 285-1095
MAN ED, El Sol De Arizona, Phoenix, AZ
Flores, Diane (209) 578-2000
EDU (Higher), Environmental Writer
Modesto Bee, Modesto, CA
Flores, Dionicio (Don) (915) 546-6100
PUB, ED, El Paso Times, El Paso, TX
Flores, Jose Mario (210) 727-8507
PUB, El Clamor, Laredo, TX
Flores, Martha (312) 321-3000
Television Prevue
Chicago Sun-Times, Chicago, IL
Flores, Michael (517) 723-1118
PUB, Sunday Independent, Owosso, MI
Flores, Archbishop Patrick (210) 734-2620
PUB, Today's Catholic, San Antonio, TX
Flores, Ray (602) 285-1095
PUB, El Sol De Arizona, Phoenix, AZ
Flores, Raymond (915) 546-6100
PROD MGR-SYS, El Paso Times, El Paso, TX
Flores, Rosie (915) 445-5475
Food ED, Lifestyle ED
Pecos Enterprise, Pecos, TX
Flores, Terry (805) 273-2700
Design/Graphics ED
Antelope Valley Press, Palmdale, CA
Flores, Veronica (210) 225-7411
EDL Writer, Express-News, San Antonio, TX
Florian, Louis F (412) 222-2200
EPE, Observer-Reporter, Washington, PA
Floriana, Stacy (419) 332-5511
Technical Support
News-Messenger, Fremont, OH
Floro, Charles D (605) 938-4452
GM, MAN ED
Sota Iya Ye Ypai, Agency Village, SD
Floto, Edmond G (610) 371-5000
CIRC MGR-Single Copy
Reading Times/Eagle, Reading, PA
Flowe, Douglas (704) 245-6431
ADV MGR, Daily Courier, Forest City, NC
Flower, Kathy (717) 474-6397
MAN ED
Mountaintop Eagle, Mountaintop, PA
Flowers, Dayton O (404) 526-5151
PROD MGR-Reach OPER
Atlanta Journal-Constitution, Atlanta, GA
Flowers, Juanita (316) 251-3300
PROD SUPV-COMP
Coffeyville Journal, Coffeyville, KS
Flowers, Susan (409) 985-5541
Features ED, Teen-Age/Youth ED, Women's ED, Port Arthur News, Port Arthur, TX
Flowers, Tim (316) 251-3300
ED, Coffeyville Journal, Coffeyville, KS
Flowers, Tony (409) 755-4912
MAN ED
Hardin County News, Lumberton, TX
Flownoy, Katheryn (504) 383-1111
City ED, Advocate, Baton Rouge, LA
Floyd, Anita (501) 642-2111
VP/SEC
De Queen Daily Citizen, De Queen, AR
Floyd, Greg (704) 758-7381
Photo DEPT MGR
Lenoir News-Topic, Lenoir, NC
Floyd, Karl (601) 842-2611
Photo ED, Northeast Mississippi Daily Journal, Tupelo, MS
Floyd, Lewis (601) 961-7000
CIRC MGR-Single Copy
Clarion-Ledger, Jackson, MS
Fluharty, Tom (509) 248-1251
MAN ED-Production/ADM
Yakima Herald-Republic, Yakima, WA
Flury, Fred (219) 294-1661
Photo DEPT MGR
Elkhart Truth, Elkhart, IN
Flynn, Carolyn (505) 823-7777
ASST MAN ED-Photo/Design
Albuquerque Journal, Albuquerque, NM
Flynn, Charles A (608) 754-3311
VP-Technical Services
Bliss Communications Inc., Janesville, WI
Flynn, Gene (502) 227-4556
ADV MGR-CLASS
State Journal, Frankfort, KY
Flynn, Janie (501) 895-3207
GM, News, Salem, AR
Flynn, Joe (212) 556-1234
Group DIR-BUS SYS
New York Times, New York, NY
Flynn, Mandy (912) 888-9300
Features ED, Albany Herald, Albany, GA
Flynn, Pat (204) 697-7000
ASST MAN ED (Night)
Winnipeg Free Press, Winnipeg, MB
Flynn, Priscilla (401) 596-7791
CONT, Westerly Sun, Westerly, RI
Flynn, Thomas (701) 253-7311
PROD SUPT-PR, Forum, Fargo, ND
Flynn, Thomas P (716) 232-7100
VP-Communications
Rochester Democrat and Chronicle; Rochester, NY Times-Union, Rochester, NY
Flynn, Tillie (541) 947-3378
GM, Lake County Examiner, Lakeview, OR
Flynn, Tom (519) 396-2963
PUB, Kincardine News, Kincardine, ON
Flynn, Tony (360) 336-6555
ED, Skagit Argus, Mount Vernon, WA
Flynn, William (716) 849-3434
Aviation ED, BUS/FIN ED
Buffalo News, Buffalo, NY
Flynt, Patricia (205) 236-1551
ADV MGR-CLASS
Anniston Star, Anniston, AL
Flyr, Michelle (402) 564-2741
EDU Reporter
Columbus Telegram, Columbus, NE
Foard III, Edwin (410) 332-6000
PROD MGR-Press OPER, Sun, Baltimore, MD
Fobes, Jeff (704) 251-1333
PUB, ED, Mountain Xpress, Asheville, NC
Focht, Bob (360) 289-2441
GM, North Coast News, Ocean Shores, WA
Fode, Mark (507) 825-3333
ED, Pipestone County Star, Pipestone, MN
Foderaro, John (215) 483-7300
GM, Review, Philadelphia, PA
Foell, Earl (617) 450-2000
EPE, Christian Science Monitor, Boston, MA
Foerder, Steve (408) 424-2221
CIRC MGR-Single Copy Sales
Californian, Salinas, CA
Foerster, Mary (715) 445-3415
GM, Iola Herald, Iola, WI
Foerster, Trey (715) 445-3415
PUB, Iola Herald, Iola, WI
Fogarty, Steve (216) 329-7000
Films/Theater ED
Chronicle-Telegram, Elyria, OH
Fogg, Alan (703) 560-4000
EPE, Fairfax Journal, Fairfax, VA
Journal Newspapers Inc.
Fogg, Randy (316) 788-2835
ED, Daily Reporter, Derby, KS
Fogleman Jr, Louis H (910) 875-2121
PUB, News-Journal, Raeford, NC
Fogler, Jim (215) 855-8440
DIR-Market Development
Reporter, Landsdale, PA
Foglesong, Sam (814) 445-9621
CIRC MGR, PROD FRM-PR
Daily American, Somerset, PA
Foley, Billy (903) 729-0281
MGR-CR
Palestine Herald-Press, Palestine, TX
Foley, Carol Young (814) 238-5000
ADV ASST DIR-NTL/Major Accounts
Centre Daily Times, State College, PA
Foley, Dana (913) 989-4415
ED, Wathena Times, Wathena, KS
Foley, Doug (905) 526-3333
Entertainment ED
Spectator, Hamilton, ON
Foley, Edward J (954) 946-7277
ED, Pompano Ledger, Pompano Beach, FL
Foley, Eileen (419) 245-6000
ASSOC ED, Blade, Toledo, OH
Foley, Ellen (816) 234-4141
Lifestyle ED
Kansas City Star, Kansas City, MO
Foley, Ethel Mae (816) 858-2313
PUB, Landmark, Platte City, MO
Foley, Ivan (816) 858-2313
ED, Landmark, Platte City, MO
Foley, Jim (413) 788-1000
PROD DIR, Union-News, Springfield, MA
Folkes, Karen M (954) 946-7277
PUB, Pompano Ledger, Pompano Beach, FL
Foley, Kathy (210) 225-7411
INFO Services ED
San Antonio Express-News, San Antonio, TX
Foley, Kevin (607) 798-1234
CIRC MGR-Sales/MKTG USA Today
Press & Sun Bulletin, Binghamton, NY
Foley, Lisa (507) 373-1411
MGR-MIS
Albert Lea Tribune, Albert Lea, MN
Foley, Marietta (616) 222-5400
MGR-Employment
Grand Rapids Press, Grand Rapids, MI
Foley, Michael (360) 377-3711
ASST Community ED, Sun, Bremerton, WA
Foley, Michael F (813) 893-8111
VP-Community Relations
St. Petersburg Times, St. Petersburg, FL
Foley, Mike (415) 777-5700
MGR-MKTG, San Francisco Newspaper Agency, San Francisco, CA
Foley, Mike (803) 283-1133
ED, Lancaster News, Lancaster, SC
Foley, Pat (814) 445-9621
ADV MGR-CLASS
Daily American, Somerset, PA
Foley, Sharon (312) 644-7800
ADV CLASS
Chicago Daily Law Bulletin, Chicago, IL
Foley, Tere (208) 888-1941
PUB, Valley News, Meridian, ID
Foley, Terry (816) 234-4141
CIRC MGR-MET
Kansas City Star, Kansas City, MO
Foley, Thomas (716) 372-3121
CIRC MGR, Olean Times-Herald, Olean, NY
Foliart, Debbie (501) 785-7700
ADV MGR-RT
Southwest Times Record, Fort Smith, AR
Folker, James (706) 724-0851
MET ED, Augusta Chronicle, Augusta, GA
Folkers, Ron (719) 544-3520
ADV MGR-RT, Pueblo Chieftain, Pueblo, CO
Follett, Irma (419) 592-5055
Librarian, Northwest Signal, Napoleon, OH
Folmer, James (909) 676-4315
ED, Californian, Temecula, CA
Foltz, Dan (907) 456-6661
CIRC DIR
Fairbanks Daily News-Miner, Fairbanks, AK
Fong, Gary (415) 777-1111
Graphics Technology DIR
San Francisco Chronicle, San Francisco, CA
Fonseca, Nicholas P (313) 222-6400
DIR-Purchasing
Detroit Newspapers, Detroit, MI
Fontaine, John C (305) 376-3800
PRES, Knight-Ridder Inc., Miami, FL
Fontaine, Keith (860) 887-9211
EX ED, Norwich Bulletin, Norwich, CT

Copyright ©1997 by the Editor & Publisher Co.

Fon Who's Where-76

Fontaine, Pete .... (401) 821-7400
Sports ED
Kent County Daily Times, West Warwick, RI

Fontana, Cyndee .... (209) 441-6111
School Writer, Fresno Bee, Fresno, CA

Fontana, Tom .... (717) 282-3300
ED, Carbondale News, Carbondale, PA

Fontenot Jr, Horace .... (409) 985-5541
ADV DIR, News, Port Arthur, TX

Fontenot, Janet .... (801) 674-6200
MAN ED-COMP SRV, EPE
Spectrum, St. George, UT

Fontenot, Kenny .... (504) 383-1111
PROD SUPT-Platemaking
Advocate, Baton Rouge, LA

Foos, Bob .... (417) 673-2421
PUB, ED, Webb City Sentinel/Wise Buyer, Webb City, MO

Foos, Hank .... (405) 475-3311
PROD MGR-Publishing SYS
Daily Oklahoman, Oklahoma City, OK

Foote, Harry T .... (207) 854-2577
PUB, ED, American Journal, Westbrook, ME

Foote, Pat .... (206) 464-2111
ASST MAN ED-Features
Seattle Times, Seattle, WA

Foote, Raymond M .... (207) 854-2577
MAN ED, American Journal, Westbrook, ME

Foote, Russ .... (607) 334-3276
ADV MGR, Evening Sun, Norwich, NY

Forberg, Omar .... (218) 751-3740
GM, ED, Daily Pioneer, Bemidji, MN

Forbes, Elizabeth .... (716) 232-7100
Books/Arts ED, Rochester Democrat and Chronicle; Rochester, NY Times-Union, Rochester, NY

Forbes, Gerry .... (307) 787-3229
ED, Uinta County Pioneer, Lyman, WY

Forbes, James B .... (314) 340-8000
Photo DEPT MGR/Photo ED
St. Louis Post-Dispatch, St. Louis, MO

Forbes, Luba .... (202) 334-6000
ADV DIR-Advertising Services
Washington Post, Washington, DC

Forbes, Margaret .... (250) 782-4888
PUB
Peace River Block News, Dawson Creek, BC

Forbes, Mary Lou .... (202) 636-3000
ED-Commentary
Washington Times, Washington, DC

Forbes, Rob .... (204) 727-2451
PUB, Brandon Sun, Brandon, MB

Forbis, Barry .... (303) 892-5000
Sports ED
Rocky Mountain News, Denver, CO

Forbregd, Ila Mae .... (406) 787-5821
ED, Searchlight, Culbertson, MT

Force, Andrea .... (410) 752-3849
PROD MGR, Daily Record, Baltimore, MD

Force, Tammy .... (360) 424-3251
MGR-Office
Skagit Valley Herald, Mount Vernon, WA

Forcier, George .... (413) 772-0261
MAN ED, Recorder, Greenfield, MA

Ford, Alan .... (704) 484-7000
Sports ED, Shelby Star, Shelby, NC

Ford, Bruce .... (210) 225-7411
ADV ASST MGR-NTL
San Antonio Express-News, San Antonio, TX

Ford, Cynthia A .... (717) 334-1131
PRES/PUB
Gettysburg Times, Gettysburg, PA

Ford, George .... (319) 398-8211
BUS ED, Gazette, Cedar Rapids, IA

Ford, Greg .... (410) 641-4561
ED, Maryland Coast-Dispatch, Berlin, MD

Ford, Grover .... (904) 829-6562
ADV MGR
St. Augustine Record, St. Augustine, FL

Ford, James R .... (419) 422-5151
MGR-DP, DP MGR, Courier, Findlay, OH

Ford, Jerry .... (318) 322-5161
PROD MGR-PR, News-Star, Monroe, LA

Ford, John .... (304) 233-0100
ADV MGR-CLASS, Intelligencer/Wheeling News-Register, Wheeling, WV

Ford, Judy .... (303) 756-9995
Project News MGR, Daily Journal, Denver, CO

Ford, Lige B .... (409) 945-3441
PROD FRM-PR
Texas City Sun, Texas City, TX

Ford, Mary .... (617) 749-0031
ED, Hingham Journal, Hingham, MA

Ford, Nancy .... (315) 792-5000
Photo ED, Observer-Dispatch, Utica, NY

Ford, Patrick .... (918) 756-3600
Telecommunications MGR, PROD FRM-COMP, Okmulgee Daily Times, Okmulgee, OK

Ford, Ray .... (520) 445-3333
PROD ASST MGR
Daily Courier, Prescott, AZ

Ford, Rhonda L .... (513) 398-8856
PUB, Pulse-Journal, Mason, OH

Ford, Robert .... (213) 525-2000
PROD MGR
Hollywood Reporter, Los Angeles, CA

Ford, Robert D .... (860) 442-2200
CIRC MGR-Delivery Services
Day, New London, CT

Ford, Roland .... (209) 578-2000
PROD MGR-PR, Modesto Bee, Modesto, CA

Ford, Ronda .... (316) 492-6244
PUB, ED, Johnson Pioneer, Johnson, KS

Ford, Russell .... (703) 276-3400
CIRC VP, USA Today, Arlington, VA

Ford, Steve .... (502) 582-4011
ASSOC ED-Forum
Courier-Journal, Louisville, KY

Ford, Steven B .... (919) 829-4500
EPE, News & Observer, Raleigh, NC

Ford, Terry .... (901) 635-1771
GM
Lauderdale County Enterprise, Ripley, TN

Ford, Tom .... (717) 334-1131
DP MGR, Gettysburg Times, Gettysburg, PA

Fordham, Bill .... (770) 942-6571
ED
Douglas County Sentinel, Douglasville, GA

Forehand, Betty .... (219) 461-8444
PROD ASST DIR
Fort Wayne Newspapers Inc., Fort Wayne, IN

Foreman, Gene .... (215) 854-2000
Deputy ED/VP (Inquirer)
Philadelphia Inquirer, Philadelphia, PA

Foreman, Joe .... (712) 527-3191
ED, Opinion-Tribune, Glenwood, IA

Foreman, John R .... (217) 351-5252
ED/GM/VP-Newspapers
News-Gazette, Champaign, IL

Foreman, Mary .... (517) 752-7171
Food ED, Saginaw News, Saginaw, MI

Foreman, T E .... (909) 684-1200
Theater ED
Press-Enterprise, Riverside, CA

Foren, John .... (810) 766-6100
MET ED-PM, Flint Journal, Flint, MI

Forgay, Richard .... (610) 820-6500
CIRC MGR-MKTG
Morning Call, Allentown, PA

Forget, Marc .... (514) 620-0781
ED, Cites Nouvelles/City News, Ste. Genevieve, QC

Forgette, Michael .... (508) 222-7000
PROD MGR-Graphics
Sun Chronicle, Attleboro, MA

Forgey, Ben .... (202) 334-6000
Architecture ED (Style)
Washington Post, Washington, DC

Forgey, Gordon .... (509) 397-4333
PUB, Whitman County Gazette, Colfax, WA

Forgues, Andre .... (418) 686-3233
Newsroom DIR, Librarian, News ED, Political ED, Le Soleil, Quebec, QC

Forhan, William E .... (805) 273-2700
CONT, Antelope Valley Press, Palmdale, CA

Forman, Deborah .... (508) 775-1200
Features ED, Cape Cod Times, Hyannis, MA

Forman, Garland .... (318) 346-7251
ED, Bunkie Record, Bunkie, LA

Forman, Leonard P .... (212) 556-1234
Sr VP-Corp Development/News Ventures/Electronic BUS
New York Times Co., New York, NY

Forman, Mike .... (913) 295-1111
Online MGR
Topeka Capital-Journal, Topeka, KS

Fornek, Scott .... (312) 321-3000
GEN Assignment
Chicago Sun-Times, Chicago, IL

Forness, Roger R .... (716) 232-7100
DIR-INFO SYS, Rochester Democrat and Chronicle; Times-Union, Rochester, NY

Forney, Ada Lewis .... (407) 259-3822
PRES
Future Features Syndicate, Melbourne, FL

Forney, Jerome L .... (407) 259-3822
Creative DIR
Future Features Syndicate, Melbourne, FL

Fornof, David .... (520) 783-3333
DIR-Facility, Yuma Daily Sun, Yuma, AZ

Forrest, Ben .... (908) 870-9338
MAN ED, Atlanticville, Long Branch, NJ

Forrest, H Miles .... (504) 850-1100
PUB, EPE, Courier, Houma, LA

Forrest, Kevin M .... (802) 457-1313
ED, Vermont Standard, Woodstock, VT

Forrest, Tim .... (901) 642-1162
CIRC MGR, Paris Post-Intelligencer, Paris, TN

Forrestal, Steve .... (954) 356-4000
CIRC MGR-Circulation & Accounting
Sun-Sentinel, Fort Lauderdale, FL

Forrester, Eleanor A .... (541) 276-2211
TREAS, East Oregonian, Pendleton, OR

Forrester, J W .... (541) 276-2211
COB, East Oregonian, Pendleton, OR

Forrester, Michael A .... (541) 276-2211
PRES, East Oregonian, Pendleton, OR

Forrester, Stephen A .... (541) 276-2211
VP, East Oregonian, Pendleton, OR

Forry, Edward W .... (617) 436-1222
ED, Reporter, Dorchester, MA

Forry, Marc .... (617) 436-1222
PUB, Reporter, Dorchester, MA

Forsberg, Helen .... (801) 237-2031
Ballet/Dance ED
Salt Lake Tribune, Salt Lake City, UT

Forsberg, Myra .... (212) 556-1234
Weekend Section ED
New York Times, New York, NY

Forsberg, Paul .... (218) 829-4705
Wire ED, Daily Dispatch, Brainerd, MN

Forst, Don .... (212) 475-3333
ED, Village Voice, New York, NY

Forst, Donna R .... (501) 996-4494
ED, Greenwood Democrat, Greenwood, AR

Forster, Cathy .... (519) 679-6666
MKTG MGR-Sponsorship/PROM
London Free Press, London, ON

Forstner, Sandy .... (507) 533-4271
PUB, ED, Stewartville Star, Stewartville, MN

Forstrom, Tommy .... (503) 399-6611
Food ED, Statesman Journal, Salem, OR

Forsyth, Malcolm .... (504) 826-3279
ASSOC ED-EDL, EPE
Times-Picayune, New Orleans, LA

Forsyth, Scott .... (800) 521-5232
GM, Post-Searchlight, Bainbridge, GA

Forsyth, Virginia .... (816) 263-4123
PROD FRM-COMP, Moberly Monitor-Index & Democrat, Moberly, MO

Fort, Frankie .... (912) 236-9511
PSL MGR
Savannah Morning News, Savannah, GA

Forthun, Ben .... (701) 572-2165
GM, Plains Reporter, Williston, ND

Forthun, Beverly .... (701) 572-2165
BM, Williston Daily Herald, Williston, ND

Fortier, Claire .... (916) 541-3880
MAN ED, EPE, Online Contact
Tahoe Daily Tribune, South Lake Tahoe, CA

Fortin, Bernie .... (508) 343-6911
CIRC DIR
Sentinel & Enterprise, Fitchburg, MA

Fortner, Carie .... (817) 767-8341
Society/Women's ED, Wichita Falls Times Record News, Wichita Falls, TX

Fortney, Ed .... (419) 468-1117
CIRC MGR, Galion Inquirer, Galion, OH

Fortune, Mark .... (919) 446-5161
ADV DIR
Rocky Mount Telegram, Rocky Mount, NC

Fortune, Renee .... (401) 596-7791
PROD FRM-COMP
Westerly Sun, Westerly, RI

Forys, Marshall L .... (412) 887-6101
ED, Independent-Observer, Scottdale, PA

Foscalina, Dan .... (916) 346-2232
ED, Colfax Record, Colfax, CA

Foslin, Irene B .... (608) 754-3311
SEC
Bliss Communications Inc., Janesville, WI

Foss, Ed .... (916) 842-5777
COL, Siskiyou Daily News, Yreka, CA

Foster, Allen C .... (419) 475-6000
PUB, West Toledo Herald, Toledo, OH

Foster, Bernie .... (503) 287-3562
PUB, Skanner, Portland, OR

Foster, Beth .... (502) 866-3191
MAN ED
Russell County News, Russell Springs, KY

Foster, Bill .... (352) 867-4010
ADTX MGR (Advertising)
Ocala Star-Banner, Ocala, FL

Foster, Bill .... (918) 786-9002
Sports ED, Grove Daily News, Grove, OK

Foster, Bill C .... (817) 853-2801
PUB, Moody Courier, Moody, TX

Foster, Bobbie .... (503) 287-3562
ED, Skanner, Portland, OR

Foster, Brenda .... (919) 946-2144
ADV MGR-CLASS
Washington Daily News, Washington, NC

Foster, Carolyn .... (713) 356-6397
PUB, GM, Potpourri Newspaper, Magnolia, TX

Foster, Clay .... (601) 842-2611
DP MGR, PROD DIR, Northeast Mississippi Daily Journal, Tupelo, MS

Foster, Cliff .... (719) 632-5511
City ED, Gazette, Colorado Springs, CO

Foster, Crystal .... (208) 357-7661
GM, Shelley Pioneer, Shelley, ID

Foster, Dale .... (301) 627-2833
GM
Maryland Independent, Upper Marlboro, MD

Foster, Dan .... (864) 298-4100
Sports COL
Greenville News, Greenville, SC

Foster, Darrell .... (212) 416-2000
PROD MGR (La Grange GA)
Wall Street Journal, New York, NY

Foster, Dave .... (301) 733-5131
DP MGR, PROD MGR-DP
Morning Herald, Hagerstown, MD

Foster, Dean .... (919) 335-0841
CIRC MGR
Daily Advance, Elizabeth City, NC

Foster, Debbie .... (507) 235-3303
MGR-Office, Sentinel, Fairmont, MN

Foster, Eleanor Abercrombie ... (205) 252-3672
PUB, Alabama Messenger, Birmingham, AL

Foster, Frankie .... (405) 924-4388
ADV MGR-RT
Durant Daily Democrat, Durant, OK

Foster, Fred L .... (864) 224-4321
PRES, PUB
Anderson Independent-Mail, Anderson, SC

Foster, Greg .... (403) 939-7443
GM
Morinville & District Gazette, Morinville, AB

Foster, Harold .... (910) 353-1171
ADV MGR-RT, Daily News, Jacksonville, NC

Foster, Jason .... (909) 889-9666
Entertainment ED
Sun, San Bernardino, CA

Foster, Jeffrey .... (937) 222-6000
PRES/PUB
Daily Court Reporter, Dayton, OH

Foster, Judy .... (601) 961-7000
MGR-Public Affairs
Clarion-Ledger, Jackson, MS

Foster, Julianne .... (770) 537-2434
MAN ED
Haralson Gateway Beacon, Bremen, GA

Foster, Ken .... (814) 938-8740
PROD FRM-PR, Spirit, Punxsutawney, PA

Foster, Linda .... (919) 537-2505
ADV MGR-CLASS
Daily Herald, Roanoke Rapids, NC

Foster, Maria .... (619) 435-3141
ED, Coronado Journal, Coronado, CA

Foster, Marta .... (312) 455-0300
PUB, El Heraldo, Chicago, IL

Foster, Matt .... (352) 867-4010
PROD MGR-Pre Press
Ocala Star-Banner, Ocala, FL

Foster, Patrice .... (603) 742-4455
ASST to PUB
Foster's Democrat, Dover, NH

Foster, Pauline .... (918) 684-2828
Librarian, Muskogee Daily Phoenix & Times Democrat, Muskogee, OK

Foster, Randy .... (707) 226-3711
City ED, Napa Valley Register, Napa, CA

Foster, Rick .... (508) 222-7000
Wire ED, Sun Chronicle, Attleboro, MA

Foster, Robert H .... (603) 742-4455
PRES, PUB, Foster's Democrat, Dover, NH

Foster, Skip .... (704) 864-3291
MAN ED, Gaston Gazette, Gastonia, NC

Foster, Stephen .... (209) 578-2000
CIRC MGR-Single Copy Sales
Modesto Bee, Modesto, CA

Foster, Terry .... (313) 222-2300
COL, Detroit News, Detroit, MI

Foster, Therese D .... (603) 742-4455
VP, ASSOC PUB
Foster's Democrat, Dover, NH

Foster, Tom .... (315) 470-0011
Projects ED, Post-Standard/Syracuse Herald-Journal/American, Syracuse, NY

Foster, Tracie .... (864) 582-4511
ADM ASST
Herald-Journal, Spartanburg, SC

Foster, W David .... (707) 546-2020
CFO, Press Democrat, Santa Rosa, CA

Fostor, Matt .... (352) 867-4010
DP MGR, Ocala Star-Banner, Ocala, FL

Fotes, Jim .... (209) 441-6111
CIRC MGR-SYS, Fresno Bee, Fresno, CA

Fouch, Bill .... (304) 257-1844
ED, Grant County Press, Petersburg, WV

Foudy, James T .... (413) 584-5000
ED
Daily Hampshire Gazette, Northampton, MA

Fought, Tim .... (701) 780-1100
EPE, Grand Forks Herald, Grand Forks, ND

Foulsham, George .... (213) 237-5000
Orange County News ED
Los Angeles Times, Los Angeles, CA

Fountain, Clayton .... (912) 923-6432
Photo ED, Daily Sun, Warner Robins, GA

Fountain, Walter .... (601) 392-3307
ED, Biloxi-D'Iberville Press, Biloxi, MS

Fouquet, Francois .... (819) 564-5450
ADV MGR, La Tribune, Sherbrooke, QC

Fournier, Celine .... (418) 686-3233
MGR-PROM, Le Soleil, Quebec, QC

Fournier, Charles .... (509) 787-4511
PUB, Quincy Valley Post Register, Quincy, WA

Fournier Jr, John L .... (509) 786-1711
PUB, Prosser Record-Bulletin, Prosser, WA

Foust, Bobbie .... (502) 443-1771
Environmental ED, Sun, Paducah, KY

Foust, Carolyn Pugh .... (317) 633-1240
DIR-Community Relations
Indianapolis Star/News, Indianapolis, IN

Foust, Demi .... (910) 888-3500
ADV DIR
High Point Enterprise, High Point, NC

77-Who's Where **Fra**

Foutz, Fred .... (412) 224-4321
CIRC DIR
Valley News Dispatch, Tarentum, PA
Gannett Co. Inc.

Foutz, Keith .... (614) 532-1441
DIR-MKTG, Ironton Tribune, Ironton, OH

Foutz, Stanley .... (213) 237-3700
VP-Audit
Times Mirror Co., Los Angeles, CA

Fowler, Annie .... (541) 889-5387
Sports ED, Argus Observer, Ontario, OR

Fowler, B H (Berdie) .... (403) 672-3142
ED, Camrose Booster, Camrose, AB

Fowler, Butch .... (912) 744-4200
PROD MGR-PR
Macon Telegraph, Macon, GA

Fowler, Carol .... (510) 935-2525
Travel ED
Contra Costa Times, Walnut Creek, CA

Fowler, Charles .... (501) 271-3700
Photographer
Benton County Daily Record, Bentonville, AR

Fowler, Chris .... (905) 526-3333
ADV MGR-Burlington News
Spectator, Hamilton, ON

Fowler, Darran .... (402) 462-2131
Regional ED
Hastings Tribune, Hastings, NE

Fowler, Donna .... (800) 238-1133
DIR-Public Affairs DEPT, American Federation of Teachers, Washington, DC

Fowler Jr, Edgar L .... (205) 362-1000
PUB, ED, EPE, Daily Home, Talladega, AL

Fowler, Elaine S .... (802) 372-5600
PUB, Islander, South Hero, VT

Fowler, Frances .... (814) 965-2503
PUB, ED
Johnsonburg Press, Johnsonburg, PA

Fowler Jr, Gene .... (803) 785-4293
ADV MGR-CLASS
Island Packet, Hilton Head, SC

Fowler, George D .... (802) 372-5600
PUB, ED, Islander, South Hero, VT

Fowler, Gwen .... (803) 626-8555
Deputy MAN ED
Sun News, Myrtle Beach, SC

Fowler, Howard .... (908) 722-8800
CIRC MGR-Single Copy
Courier-News, Bridgewater, NJ

Fowler, John E .... (814) 965-2503
GM, Johnsonburg Press, Johnsonburg, PA

Fowler, Karl A .... (315) 232-4586
PUB, ED
Jefferson County Journal, Adams, NY

Fowler, Kim .... (573) 642-7272
Lifestyle ED, Fulton Sun, Fulton, MO

Fowler, Linda .... (201) 877-4141
Entertainment ED
Star-Ledger, Newark, NJ

Fowler, Michael C .... (716) 374-5260
PUB, ED, Naples Record, Naples, NY

Fowler, Rhonda .... (501) 935-5525
CONT, Jonesboro Sun, Jonesboro, AR

Fowler, Sam .... (903) 893-8181
CIRC DIR, Herald Democrat, Sherman, TX

Fowler, Sharon .... (408) 920-5000
PROD MGR-ADM
San Jose Mercury News, San Jose, CA

Fowler, Tracie .... (601) 582-4321
ADV MGR-CLASS
Hattiesburg American, Hattiesburg, MS

Fowler, Von .... (913) 877-3361
Society/Women's ED
Norton Daily Telegram, Norton, KS

Fowler, W Blain .... (403) 672-3142
PUB, Camrose Booster, Camrose, AB

Fowler, Wade .... (717) 582-4305
ED, Perry County Times, New Bloomfield, PA

Fowler-Nash, Linda .... (512) 664-6588
ADV DIR, Alice Echo-News, Alice, TX

Fox, Ashton L .... (910) 323-4848
SEC/TREAS
Fayetteville Observer-Times, Fayetteville, NC

Fox, Bob .... (618) 544-2101
CIRC MGR-PROM
Robinson Daily News, Robinson, IL

Fox, Carolyn .... (818) 986-8168
EIC
Hollywood News Calendar, Sherman Oaks, CA

Fox, Connie .... (913) 726-4583
MAN ED, Ellis Review, Ellis, KS

Fox, David .... (916) 321-1000
PROD MGR-Building/Purchasing
Sacramento Bee, Sacramento, CA

Fox, Doug .... (801) 373-5050
Sports ED, Daily Herald, Provo, UT

Fox, Elaine W .... (912) 384-9112
GM, Coffee County News, Douglas, GA

Fox, Harry M .... (412) 628-2000
PROD MGR
Daily Courier, Connellsville, PA

Fox, Janie .... (918) 647-3188
ADV DIR, Poteau News & Sun, Poteau, OK

Fox, Jeff .... (816) 254-8600
EX ED, EPE, Legislature ED
Examiner, Independence, MO

Fox, Jerry .... (219) 461-8333
SEC/CORP TREAS
Journal Gazette, Fort Wayne, IN

Fox, Jim .... (603) 298-8711
ED, Valley News, White River Jct., VT

Fox, John .... (918) 542-5533
MAN ED, NEWS ED
Miami News-Record, Miami, OK

Fox, John .... (513) 665-4700
PUB, ED, Citybeat, Cincinnati, OH

Fox, Julie .... (409) 265-7411
CIRC MGR, Brazosport Facts, Clute, TX

Fox, Kym .... (210) 225-7411
MET ED-Day, Express-News, San Antonio, TX

Fox, Mark .... (816) 331-5353
PUB, ED, Star-Herald, Belton, MO

Fox, Michael .... (519) 894-2231
Librarian, Record, Kitchener, ON

Fox, Michael J .... (801) 237-2800
ADV MGR-RT Sales/NTL
Newspaper Agency Corp., Salt Lake City, UT

Fox, Rhonda .... (573) 785-1414
BM/CONT
Daily American Republic, Poplar Bluff, MO

Fox, Rick .... (573) 756-8927
CIRC MGR
Daily Press Leader, Farmington, MO

Fox, Sara .... (910) 727-7211
DIR-Electronic Publishing
Winston-Salem Journal, Winston-Salem, NC

Fox, Sharon .... (607) 849-4555
ED
Cortland Democrat Sunday, Marathon, NY

Fox, Thomas C .... (816) 531-0538
ED
National Catholic Reporter, Kansas City, MO

Fox-Alston, Jeanne .... (202) 334-6000
DIR-Recruiting/News
Washington Post, Washington, DC

Fox-Davis, Susan .... (818) 986-8168
ED
Hollywood News Calendar, Sherman Oaks, CA

Fox-Tamblyn, Ellen .... (908) 396-4500
ED, Suburban News/Elizabeth City News, Westfield, NJ

Foxmeyer, Caroline .... (714) 835-1234
ADTX MGR-900 lines
Orange County Register, Santa Ana, CA

Foxworth, Ernie .... (941) 335-0200
PROD MGR-Pre Press/COMP
News-Press, Fort Myers, FL

Foy, Bill .... (715) 833-9200
Amusements/Books ED, Films/Theater ED, Music ED, Radio/Television ED
Leader-Telegram, Eau Claire, WI

Foy, David .... (805) 259-1234
City ED, Signal, Santa Clarita, CA

Frable, Merry .... (412) 342-5300
MAN ED
Minority Features Syndicate Inc., Farrel, PA

Fracassa, Anne .... (810) 573-2755
Executive ED
Avanti NewsFeatures, Warren, MI

Fracassa, Becca .... (810) 573-2755
Medical ED, Avanti NewsFeatures, Warren, MI

Fracassa, Filip .... (810) 573-2755
Travel ED, Avanti NewsFeatures, Warren, MI

Fracassa, Francesca .... (810) 573-2755
Food ED, Avanti NewsFeatures, Warren, MI

Fracassa, Hawke .... (810) 573-2755
Senior MAN ED
Avanti NewsFeatures, Warren, MI

Frachiseur, Arlie .... (501) 642-2111
PROD SUPT
De Queen Daily Citizen, De Queen, AR

Fracul, Scott .... (412) 654-6651
ADV MGR-CLASS
New Castle News, New Castle, PA

Fradkin, Linda .... (409) 744-3611
Food ED
Galveston County Daily News, Galveston, TX

Frahm, Robert .... (860) 241-6200
EDU Writer, Hartford Courant, Hartford, CT

Frahura, Ralph .... (916) 321-1000
MGR-New Media
Sacramento Bee, Sacramento, CA

Frailey, Fred .... (903) 885-8663
EVP, Sulphur Springs News-Telegram, Sulphur Springs, TX

Frailly, Ronald L .... (614) 345-4053
ADV DIR, Advocate, Newark, OH

Frain, Joyce L .... (304) 564-3131
PUB, ED, Hancock County Courier, New Cumberland, WV

Frair, John .... (903) 583-2124
PUB, ED, Favorite, Bonham, TX

Fraire, Gabe .... (707) 838-9211
MAN ED, Times, Windsor, CA

Frakes, Jason .... (502) 781-1700
Sports ED, Daily News, Bowling Green, KY

Frakes, Larry .... (303) 820-1010
PROD MGR-Maintenance
Denver Post, Denver, CO

Fralic, Shelley .... (604) 732-2111
Deputy MAN ED-Features & ADM
Vancouver Sun, Vancouver, BC

Frame, Earle E .... (815) 246-6911
PUB, Earlville Leader, Earlville, IL

Franceschini, Antoinette .... (302) 324-2500
PROD DIR, News Journal, Wilmington, DE

Franchine, Phil .... (312) 321-3000
Suburban Writer
Chicago Sun-Times, Chicago, IL

Francis, David R .... (617) 450-2000
BUS/FIN ED, Economy ED
Christian Science Monitor, Boston, MA

Francis, Deanna .... (219) 235-6161
Living/Lifestyle ED
South Bend Tribune, South Bend, IN

Francis, Dennis E .... (808) 525-8000
VP-Circulation, CIRC VP
Hawaii Newspaper Agency Inc., Honolulu, HI

Francis, Don .... (608) 754-3311
PROD SUPV-ADV
Janesville Gazette, Janesville, WI

Francis, Fred .... (412) 263-1100
PROD MGR-Post Press
Pittsburgh Post-Gazette, Pittsburgh, PA

Francis, Garth .... (941) 335-0200
Photo ED, News-Press, Fort Myers, FL

Francis, Mark .... (716) 282-2311
PRES, PUB
Niagara Gazette, Niagara Falls, NY

Francis, Tim .... (604) 672-5611
PUB
North Thompson Star/Journal, Barriere, BC

Francisco, Brian .... (317) 747-5700
BUS/FIN ED, RE ED
Star Press, Muncie, IN

Francisco, Karen .... (317) 747-5700
EDL Writer, Star Press, Muncie, IN

Franck, Kurt .... (954) 356-4000
EX ED-News
Sun-Sentinel, Fort Lauderdale, FL

Franck, Lynn .... (954) 356-4000
ADV MGR-Display (Palm Beach)
Sun-Sentinel, Fort Lauderdale, FL

Franck, Matt .... (423) 246-8121
Political ED
Kingsport Times-News, Kingsport, TN

Franco, Jose .... (864) 582-4511
Features ED, Food ED
Herald-Journal, Spartanburg, SC

Franco, Scott .... (717) 248-6741
Films/Theater ED, Radio/Television ED, Sports ED, Sentinel, Lewistown, PA

Francoeur, Pierre .... (514) 521-4545
PUB, Le Journal de Montreal, Montreal, QC

Franconeri, Louis J .... (813) 893-8111
VP-OPER, PROD VP-OPER
St. Petersburg Times, St. Petersburg, FL

Francouer, Anne .... (403) 662-4046
PUB, ED, Tofield Mercury, Tofield, AB

Franczyk, Walter .... (705) 568-6397
ED
Kirkland Lake Gazette, Kirkland Lake, ON

Frandsen, M Olaf .... (916) 741-2345
ASST PUB
Appeal-Democrat, Marysville, CA

Frandson, Charles .... (414) 563-5553
ADV MGR, DIR-MKTG, Daily Jefferson County Union, Fort Atkinson, WI

Frangenberg, Rosanna .... (402) 345-1303
CIRC MGR, Daily Record, Omaha, NE

Frank, A C .... (606) 236-8541
ED, MAN ED, Danville Examiner, Danville, KY

Frank, Chuck .... (403) 235-7100
EDL Writer, Calgary Herald, Calgary, AB

Frank, Donald H .... (414) 733-4411
PA, PROD MGR
Post-Crescent, Appleton, WI

Frank, Ed .... (814) 946-7411
Wire ED, Altoona Mirror, Altoona, PA

Frank, J Peter .... (606) 236-8541
PUB, Danville Examiner, Danville, KY

Frank, Jeff .... (313) 994-6989
PROD MGR, Ann Arbor News, Ann Arbor, MI

Frank, Kathryn .... (607) 734-5151
Features ED, Star-Gazette, Elmira, NY

Frank, Kay .... (904) 934-1200
ED, Whiting Tower, Gulf Breeze, FL

Frank, Lynn .... (408) 920-5000
MGR-Telecommunications
San Jose Mercury News, San Jose, CA

Frank, Marian .... (602) 271-8000
BUS ED, Arizona Republic, Phoenix, AZ

Frank, Martin .... (603) 298-8711
EPE, Valley News, White River Jct., VT

Frank, Robert .... (818) 962-8811
City ED
San Gabriel Valley Tribune, West Covina, CA

Frank, Russell .... (814) 238-5000
Features ED
Centre Daily Times, State College, PA

Frank, Scott .... (503) 842-7535
ED, Headlight-Herald, Tillamook, OR

Frank, Susan .... (310) 377-6877
PUB, Palos Verdes Peninsula News, Palos Verdes Peninsula, CA

Franke, Dana .... (954) 356-4000
MGR-RES SRV
Sun-Sentinel, Fort Lauderdale, FL

Frankel, Barbara .... (908) 246-5500
DIR-EDL Pages
Home News & Tribune, East Brunswick, NJ

Frankel, Janette .... (515) 232-2160
ADV DIR, Daily Tribune, Ames, IA

Frankeny, Kelly .... (415) 777-2424
ASST MAN ED-Design
San Francisco Examiner, San Francisco, CA

Franklin, Carolyn .... (812) 424-7711
MGR-PROM/RES
Evansville Courier Co. Inc., Evansville, IN

Franklin, Douglas E .... (937) 225-2000
EVP/GM, Dayton Daily News, Dayton, OH

Franklin, Ellie .... (704) 252-5611
CIRC CNR-NIE
Asheville Citizen-Times, Asheville, NC

Franklin, John .... (603) 924-3333
ED
Peterborough Transcript, Peterborough, NH

Franklin, Jonathan .... (506) 859-4900
PUB/GM, Times-Transcript, Moncton, NB

Franklin, Joy .... (704) 692-0505
ED, Times-News, Hendersonville, NC

Franklin, Judith P .... (614) 337-2055
MAN ED, Ohio Jewish Chronicle, Columbus, OH

Franklin, Karen .... (305) 757-1147
GM, Miami Times, Miami, FL

Franklin, Larry .... (210) 829-9000
PRES/CEO, Harte-Hanks Communications Inc., San Antonio, TX

Franklin, Larry .... (864) 833-1900
PUB, Clinton Chronicle, Clinton, SC

Franklin, Leada D .... (205) 669-3131
MAN ED
Shelby County Reporter, Columbiana, AL

Franklin, Marcia .... (316) 268-6000
PROD OPER MGR-Composing
Wichita Eagle, Wichita, KS

Franklin, Mark .... (717) 637-3736
City ED, Evening Sun, Hanover, PA

Franklin, Michael .... (619) 299-3131
Photo DIR
San Diego Union-Tribune, San Diego, CA

Franklin, Sammy J .... (318) 649-7136
PUB, News Journal, Columbia, LA

Franklin, T Craig .... (318) 649-7136
ED, News Journal, Columbia, LA

Franklin, Teryl .... (608) 754-3311
News ED, Janesville Gazette, Janesville, WI

Franklin, Tom .... (901) 968-6397
PUB, Lexington Progress, Lexington, TN

Franklin, Vicki .... (330) 996-3000
PROD ASST MGR
Akron Beacon Journal, Akron, OH

Franklin, Most Rev William .... (319) 323-9959
PUB, Catholic Messenger, Davenport, IA

Franko, Todd .... (402) 564-2741
EX ED, MAN ED, Political/Government ED
Columbus Telegram, Columbus, NE

Frankovic, Dave .... (415) 348-4321
PROD MGR-Technical SRV/Facilities
San Mateo County Times, San Mateo, CA

Franks, Arlene .... (309) 467-3314
ED, Woodford County Journal, Eureka, IL

Franks, Debbie .... (316) 268-6000
PROD OPER MGR-Assembly & Distribution
Wichita Eagle, Wichita, KS

Franks, Linda .... (972) 424-6565
CIRC DIR, Plano Star Courier, Plano, TX

Franovich, James .... (317) 962-1575
BM, Palladium-Item, Richmond, IN

Franscell, Ann .... (307) 682-9306
PUB, News-Record, Gillette, WY

Franscell, Ron .... (307) 682-9306
VP, PUB, ED, News-Record, Gillette, WY

Fransen, Donna E .... (207) 990-8000
MGR-EDU SRV
Bangor Daily News, Bangor, ME

Franson, Bertel .... (617) 933-3700
PROD FRM-PR
Daily Times Chronicle, Woburn, MA

Fransz, Kip .... (250) 762-4445
Photo ED, Daily Courier, Kelowna, BC

Frantz, Ann Connery .... (508) 343-6911
EX ED, Sentinel & Enterprise, Fitchburg, MA

Frantz, Elizabeth (Pat) T .... (406) 791-1444
PRES, PUB
Great Falls Tribune, Great Falls, MT

Frantz, Jim .... (316) 384-5640
PUB, Syracuse Journal, Syracuse, KS

Frantz, Linda .... (316) 384-5640
GM, ED, Syracuse Journal, Syracuse, KS

Frantzen, Scott .... (612) 222-5011
VP-Consumer MKTG
St. Paul Pioneer Press, St. Paul, MN

Franz, Beverley .... (803) 775-6331
CNR-NIE, Item, Sumter, SC

Franz, Bill .... (718) 447-4700
ED, Staten Island Register, Staten Island, NY

Franz, James .... (608) 365-8811
Sports ED, Beloit Daily News, Beloit, WI

Fra Who's Where-78

Franz, Janet (312) 222-3232
ASSOC MAN ED-Features
Chicago Tribune, Chicago, IL

Franz, John (405) 363-3370
PROD SUPT-PR
Blackwell Journal-Tribune, Blackwell, OK

Franz, Karen M (716) 328-4340
GM, ED, Catholic Courier, Rochester, NY

Frasch, Kristen (610) 696-1775
Features ED
Daily Local News, West Chester, PA

Fraser, Charles (506) 632-8888
ADV DIR-Sales/MKTG
Telegraph-Journal/Saint John Times Globe, Saint John, NB

Fraser, Georges (418) 862-1774
PUB, MAN ED
Le Saint-Laurent Echo du Grand-Po, Riviere-du-Loup, QC

Fraser, Jack (408) 335-5321
PUB, ED
Scotts Valley Banner, Felton, CA

Fraser, James R (501) 269-3841
PUB, ED
Stone County Leader, Mountain View, AR

Fraser, Jan (619) 322-8889
BUS ED, Desert Sun, Palm Springs, CA

Fraser, Judy (413) 788-1000
PSL DIR, Union-News, Springfield, MA

Fraser, Rob (817) 645-2441
MAN ED, BUS/FIN ED, EPE, Features ED, Graphics ED/Art DIR
Cleburne Times-Review, Cleburne, TX

Frasher, Steve (604) 395-2219
ED, 100 Mile House Free Press, 100 Mile House, BC

Frassinelli, Bruce (315) 343-3800
PUB, Palladium-Times, Oswego, NY

Frates, Tim (919) 537-2505
ADV DIR, DIR-MKTG/PROM
Daily Herald, Roanoke Rapids, NC

Fratti, Kathleen (215) 788-1682
ED, Bristol Pilot, Bristol, PA

Frattura, Ralph (916) 321-1000
Online Contact
Sacramento Bee, Sacramento, CA

Fraze, Kathleen (330) 996-3000
Copy Desk Chief
Akron Beacon Journal, Akron, OH

Frazee, Brent (816) 234-4141
Outdoors ED
Kansas City Star, Kansas City, MO

Frazer, David K (504) 345-2333
VP, PUB, MGR-PROM
Daily Star, Hammond, LA

Frazer, Kaye (319) 283-2144
Fashion/Food ED, Radio/Television ED, Society/Women's ED, Teen-Age/Youth ED
Register, Oelwein, IA

Frazer, Patricia (334) 262-1611
CNR-NIE
Montgomery Advertiser, Montgomery, AL

Frazier, B J (203) 846-3281
PUB, Hour, Norwalk, CT

Frazier, Dan (715) 526-2121
CIRC MGR, Shawano Leader, Shawano, WI

Frazier, Duncan (360) 293-3122
PUB, ED
Anacortes American, Anacortes, WA

Frazier, George (217) 774-2161
PUB, Daily Union, Shelbyville, IL

Frazier, Jennifer (601) 226-4321
Creative Services MGR
Daily Sentinel-Star, Grenada, MS

Frazier, John (517) 635-2435
ED, Marlette Leader, Marlette, MI

Frazier, Lynne (316) 268-6000
CIRC MGR-State
Wichita Eagle, Wichita, KS

Frazier, Sandra (614) 532-1441
ADV Representative
Ironton Tribune, Ironton, OH

Frazier, Terry (818) 962-8811
DIR-MIS, San Gabriel Valley Tribune, West Covina, CA, MediaNews Inc.

Frea, Diane (803) 771-6161
PROD MGR, State, Columbia, SC

Freake, Ross (250) 762-4445
MET ED, Daily Courier, Kelowna, BC

Freakley, Ed (804) 385-5400
PRES, News & Advance, Lynchburg, VA

Frear, Edward K (814) 623-1151
PRES, PUB, ED
Bedford Gazette, Bedford, PA

Frear, M L (814) 623-1151
SEC, Bedford Gazette, Bedford, PA

Freck, Tammy (614) 224-4835
ADV Classified
Daily Reporter, Columbus, OH

Frede, Edward (203) 744-5100
EX ED, News-Times, Danbury, CT

Fredel, Jill (302) 324-2500
Features ED
News Journal, Wilmington, DE

Frederich, Judy (573) 722-5322
GM, Advance Statesman, Advance, MO

Frederick, Eric (919) 829-4500
ED-Night, News & Observer, Raleigh, NC

Frederick, George (201) 877-4141
Art/Graphic DIR, Star-Ledger, Newark, NJ

Frederick, Henry (914) 358-0222
PUB, Rockland Review, West Nyack, NY

Frederick, James M (419) 245-6000
PROD DIR, Blade, Toledo, OH

Frederick, Karl (414) 657-1000
News ED, Kenosha News, Kenosha, WI

Frederick, Kelly (573) 888-4505
ADV MGR, PROD FRM-COMP
Daily Dunklin Democrat, Kennett, MO

Frederick, Michele (573) 785-1414
Lifestyle ED
Daily American Republic, Poplar Bluff, MO

Frederick, Sandra (914) 358-0222
ED, Rockland Review, West Nyack, NY

Frederick, Sherman (702) 383-0211
PUB, Review-Journal, Las Vegas, NV

Fredericks, Jim (909) 487-2200
PUB, Hemet News, Hemet, CA

Fredericks, Jim (409) 756-6671
ED, Conroe Courier, Conroe, TX

Fredericks, John (904) 252-1511
CORP Sales DIR, Daytona Beach News-Journal, Daytona Beach, FL

Frederickson, David (904) 747-5000
ADV MGR-CLASS
News Herald, Panama City, FL

Frederickson, Joe (909) 684-1200
DIR-MKTG, Press-Enterprise, Riverside, CA

Fredette, Bob (802) 747-6121
Sports ED, Rutland Herald, Rutland, VT

Fredrick, Mike (519) 426-5710
PUB, Simcoe Reformer, Simcoe, ON

Fredrick, Richard J (816) 327-4192
PUB, Monroe Co. Appeal, Paris, MO

Fredricks, Bob (203) 574-3636
Local News ED, Waterbury Republican-American, Waterbury, CT

Free, Mitchell J (800) 583-6056
VP-Sales & Development
Name Game Co. Inc., Plantation, FL

Freeborn, Lorraine (201) 383-1500
PROD FRM-MR
New Jersey Herald, Newton, NJ

Freed, Catherine (419) 898-5361
PUB, Exponent, Oak Harbor, OH

Freed, Donna (213) 237-5000
ADV DIR-Entertainment/TV/Media/Department Stores, Los Angeles Times, Los Angeles, CA

Freed, Linda (419) 636-1111
MAN ED, Home Furnishings ED, News ED
Bryan Times, Bryan, OH

Freedman, Donna (907) 257-4200
Home Reporter
Anchorage Daily News, Anchorage, AK

Freedman, Josephine (516) 226-2636
ED, South Bay's Official Shopping Newspaper, Lindenhurst, NY

Freedman, Lew (907) 257-4200
SCI/Technology ED, Sports ED
Anchorage Daily News, Anchorage, AK

Freedman, Phil (215) 855-8440
News ED, Reporter, Landsdale, PA

Freedman, Richard A (516) 226-2636
PUB, South Bay's Official Shopping Newspaper, Lindenhurst, NY

Freehling, Kris (616) 756-2421
ED, Southcounty Gazette & Shopper, Three Oaks, MI

Freeland, Dennis (901) 521-9000
ED, Memphis Flyer, Memphis, TN

Freeland, Jim (304) 485-1891
PROD MGR, Parkersburg News & Sentinel, Parkersburg, WV

Freels, Larry W (816) 665-2808
PUB/BM, MAN ED, Kirksville Daily Express & News, Kirksville, MO

Freeman, Barbara (717) 648-4641
ADV MGR-CLASS, News-Item, Shamokin, PA

Freeman, Bill (613) 472-2431
ED, Norwood Register, Marmora, ON

Freeman, Carol (602) 271-8000
CIRC MGR-Sales
Phoenix Newspapers Inc., Phoenix, AZ

Freeman, Chris (606) 734-2726
GM, Harrodsburg Herald, Harrodsburg, KY

Freeman, Darrel (505) 472-5454
PUB, ED, Santa Rosa News, Santa Rosa, NM

Freeman, Don (619) 299-3131
COL-Television/Radio
San Diego Union-Tribune, San Diego, CA

Freeman, Duane (907) 486-3227
Co-Owner
Kodiak Daily Mirror, Kodiak, AK

Freeman, E L (334) 433-1551
PROD SUPT-Pre Press
Mobile Press Register, Mobile, AL

Freeman, Hazel (501) 578-2121
PUB, Modern News, Harrisburg, AR

Freeman, Henry M (908) 722-8800
PRES, PUB, Courier-News, Bridgewater, NJ

Freeman, Jane (707) 468-3500
Chief Photographer
Ukiah Daily Journal, Ukiah, CA

Freeman, John (619) 299-3131
Television/Radio Writer
San Diego Union-Tribune, San Diego, CA

Freeman, Keith (860) 584-0501
Sports ED, Bristol Press, Bristol, CT

Freeman, Kirk (403) 527-1101
ADV DIR-Sales/SRV, MGR-MKTG
Medicine Hat News, Medicine Hat, AB

Freeman, Lisa Lee (800) 223-2154
New York BU Chief
Investor's Business Daily, Los Angeles, CA

Freeman, Lynn (919) 938-7467
PUB, Globe, Jacksonville, NC

Freeman, Mark (541) 776-4411
Outdoors ED, Mail Tribune, Medford, OR

Freeman, Meda (209) 943-6397
ASST MET ED, Record, Stockton, CA

Freeman, Mike (501) 451-1196
PUB, ED, Times of Northeast Benton County, Pea Ridge, AR

Freeman, Mike (541) 382-1811
BUS ED, Bulletin, Bend, OR

Freeman, Muriel (520) 783-3333
DIR-PSL, Yuma Daily Sun, Yuma, AZ

Freeman, Nancy L (907) 486-3227
Co-Owner, PUB
Kodiak Daily Mirror, Kodiak, AK

Freeman, Neil (905) 684-7251
PROD FRM-COMP
Standard, St. Catharines, ON

Freeman, Rebecca K (561) 287-1550
BM, Stuart News, Stuart, FL

Freeman, Rick (717) 296-6641
MAN ED
Pike County Dispatch, Milford, PA

Freeman, Scott (505) 393-2123
Political/Government ED
Hobbs Daily News-Sun, Hobbs, NM

Freeman, Teresa E (315) 942-4449
GM, Boonville Herald & Adirondack Tourist, Boonville, NY

Freeman, Rev Tom (910) 891-1234
COL, Daily Record, Dunn, NC

Freemyer, Reg (405) 224-2600
PUB, Daily Express, Chickasha, OK

Freeze, Lori (501) 269-3841
MAN ED
Stone County Leader, Mountain View, AR

Freider, Neil (216) 994-3241
ED, Star-Beacon, Ashtabula, OH

Freiman, Jane (212) 210-2100
Deputy Features ED
New York Daily News, New York, NY

Freindlich, Mark (561) 395-8300
ADV MGR-NTL, News, Boca Raton, FL

Freire, Dr Joaquin (407) 659-1833
ED, La Voz Hispana, West Palm Beach, FL

Freireich, Elliott (602) 932-5555
PUB, West Valley View, Avondale, AZ

Freitag, Duane (414) 224-2000
News SYS ED
Milwaukee Journal Sentinel, Milwaukee, WI

Freivogel, Margaret (314) 340-8000
International/NTL News ED
St. Louis Post-Dispatch, St. Louis, MO

Freker, Stephen (617) 321-8000
ED, Daily News-Mercury, Malden, MA

Fremgen, Jim (707) 546-2020
News ED, Press Democrat, Santa Rosa, CA

French, Arthur M (308) 848-2511
PUB, Arnold Sentinel, Arnold, NE

French, Audrey (308) 587-2433
ED, Tryon Graphic, Tryon, NE

French, Brenda (206) 461-1300
PUB, North Central Outlook, Seattle, WA

French, Christine (603) 436-1800
Sunday ED, Herald, Portsmouth, NH

French Sr, James J (803) 723-2785
PUB, ED
Charleston Chronicle, Charleston, SC

French, Jeff (908) 647-0412
MAN ED, Echoes-Sentinel, Sterling, NJ

French, Mark (610) 258-7171
ADV MGR-RT, Express-Times, Easton, PA

French, Mike (606) 986-0959
PUB, ED, Berea Citizen, Berea, KY

French, Nell (903) 763-4522
PUB, Wood County Democrat, Quitman, TX

French, Sean (210) 796-3718
PUB, Bandera Bulletin, Bandera, TX

French, Sherry (317) 664-5111
DIR-MKTG/PROM
Chronicle-Tribune, Marion, IN

French, Suzan (802) 747-6121
PROD FRM-ADV Design SRV
Rutland Herald, Rutland, VT

French-Smalls, Nanette (803) 723-2785
PUB, ED
Charleston Chronicle, Charleston, SC

Frenette, Claude (819) 845-2705
PUB, L'Etincelle, Windsor, QC

Frennea, Rick (205) 325-2222
Sunday ED
Birmingham News, Birmingham, AL

Frenya, James (518) 561-2300
PROD SUPV-Distribution
Press-Republican, Plattsburgh, NY

Fressola, Michael (718) 981-1234
Arts ED
Staten Island Advance, Staten Island, NY

Frets, Cindy Rolain (612) 629-6771
ED, Pine City Pioneer, Pine City, MN

Freudenberg, Ellen (970) 493-6397
CONT
Fort Collins Coloradoan, Fort Collins, CO

Freudenheim, Susan (213) 237-5000
Arts ED, Los Angeles Times, Los Angeles, CA

Freudmann, Aviva (212) 837-7000
EDL DIR, Journal of Commerce & Commercial, New York, NY

Freumbl, Ed (517) 531-4542
ED, West County Press, Parma, MI

Frey, Bob (602) 271-8000
MGR-SYS Platform Support
Phoenix Newspapers Inc., Phoenix, AZ

Frey, Jackie (508) 369-8313
ED, Carlisle Mosquito, Carlisle, MA

Frey, John (201) 383-1500
PROD FRM-COMP
New Jersey Herald, Newton, NJ

Frey, Mary Cameron (312) 321-3000
COL-Society, Features Reporter
Chicago Sun-Times, Chicago, IL

Frey, Mike (815) 937-3300
Sports ED, Daily Journal, Kankakee, IL

Frey, Richard N (916) 321-1000
DIR-OPER, Sacramento Bee, Sacramento, CA

Freyer, Felice (401) 277-7000
Health/Medical Writer
Providence Journal-Bulletin, Providence, RI

Frezell, M (519) 255-5711
ASST MET ED, Windsor Star, Windsor, ON

Frick, Bob (716) 232-7100
Automotive ED, Farm/Agriculture ED
Rochester Democrat and Chronicle; Rochester, NY Times-Union, Rochester, NY

Frick, Kelly Adrian (517) 895-8551
Automotive ED, BUS ED
Bay City Times, Bay City, MI

Friday, Donald (715) 344-6100
Sports ED
Stevens Point Journal, Stevens Point, WI

Friday, Rufus (815) 987-1200
CIRC DIR
Rockford Register Star, Rockford, IL

Friddell, Guy (757) 446-2000
COL, Virginian-Pilot, Norfolk, VA

Friecke, Lillian (815) 433-5595
MAN ED, Town and Country, Seneca, IL

Fried, Fran (203) 789-5200
Entertainment ED
New Haven Register, New Haven, CT

Friedberg, Ruth (505) 393-2123
Entertainment/Amusements ED, Fashion/Style ED, Radio/Television ED
Hobbs Daily News-Sun, Hobbs, NM

Friedeck, Sheila (409) 833-3311
Features ED
Beaumont Enterprise, Beaumont, TX

Friedel, Duke (615) 552-1808
PROD MGR-OPER
Leaf-Chronicle, Clarksville, TN

Friedel, Harve (306) 734-2313
PUB, ED, Weekly News, Craik, SK

Frieden, Kit (713) 220-7171
State ED, Houston Chronicle, Houston, TX

Friedland, Jonathan (212) 416-2000
Reporter-in-Charge (Buenos Aires)
Wall Street Journal, New York, NY

Friedland, Michelle (207) 443-6241
ED, Coastal Journal, Bath, ME

Friedman, Aron (718) 797-3900
GM, Der Yid, Brooklyn, NY

Friedman, Barry (941) 687-7000
Action Line ED, Amusements/Books ED, Features ED, SCI/Technology ED, Travel ED
Ledger, Lakeland, FL

Friedman, Dan (352) 374-5000
CONT, Gainesville Sun, Gainesville, FL

Friedman, Dorothy (203) 625-4400
Arts ED, Greenwich Time, Greenwich, CT

Friedman, Janice (201) 384-0998
ED, Twin-Boro News, Bergenfield, NJ

Friedman, Robert (813) 893-8111
Deputy EPE, Times, St. Petersburg, FL

Friedman, Shirley (201) 877-4141
Home Furnishings ED
Star-Ledger, Newark, NJ

Friedmann, Ariela (604) 689-1520
ED, Jewish Bulletin, Vancouver, BC

Friedrich, Katherine (518) 454-5694
EX Photo ED, Times Union, Albany, NY

Friedrichs, George (415) 777-5700
PROD MGR-Engineering, San Francisco Newspaper Agency, San Francisco, CA

79-Who's Where **Gab**

Friel, Mike .... (304) 255-4400
News ED, Register Herald, Beckley, WV

Friend, Barbara .... (208) 753-0203
GM, Idaho News Observer, Wallace, ID

Friend, Chuck .... (304) 348-5140
CIRC MGR-OPER
Charleston Newspapers, Charleston, WV

Friend, Grover J .... (215) 949-4011
PRES, Calkins Newspapers, Levittown, PA

Friend, Lenore .... (716) 394-0770
BUS/FIN ED, Sunday ED, Television/Music ED, Travel ED, Daily Messenger/The Sunday Messenger, Canandaigua, NY

Friend, Nanya .... (304) 348-5140
City/MET ED, Daily Mail, Charleston, WV

Friend, Paul .... (208) 753-0203
PUB, ED, Idaho News Observer, Wallace, ID

Frier Jr, Thomas .... (912) 384-2323
ED, Douglas Enterprise, Douglas, GA

Fries, George .... (718) 981-1234
ADV MGR-CLASS
Staten Island Advance, Staten Island, NY

Fries, Paula .... (319) 398-8211
CIRC MGR-Office
Gazette, Cedar Rapids, IA

Fries, Ted .... (319) 398-8211
CIRC MGR-OPER, Gazette, Cedar Rapids, IA

Friesch, David .... (419) 448-3200
PUB, Advertiser-Tribune, Tiffin, OH

Friesen, George .... (316) 694-5700
PROD FRM-COMP
Hutchinson News, Hutchinson, KS

Friesen, Glen .... (204) 325-4772
PUB, Winkler Times, Winkler, MB

Frieze, Roger .... (417) 581-3541
PUB
Christian County Headliner News, Ozark, MO

Frink, Clayton .... (608) 252-6100
PRES, Wisconsin State Journal, Madison, WI

Frisbie IV, S L .... (813) 533-4183
PUB, ED
Polk County Democrat, Bartow, FL

Frisby, Mark .... (609) 663-6000
PROD DIR, Courier-Post, Cherry Hill, NJ

Frisch, David A .... (701) 857-1900
GM, Minot Daily News, Minot, ND

Frisch, Kevin M .... (716) 394-0770
MAN ED, Daily Messenger/The Sunday Messenger, Canandaigua, NY

Frisch, R C .... (801) 237-2031
GEN MGR
Kearns-Tribune Corp., Salt Lake City, UT

Frischkorn, Jeff .... (216) 951-0000
Environmental Writer
News-Herald, Willoughby, OH

Friskup, Judy .... (405) 279-2363
PUB, Meeker News, Meeker, OK

Friskup, Kent .... (405) 279-2363
ED, Meeker News, Meeker, OK

Fristoe, Susie .... (404) 521-1227
DIR-Display & Classified
Daily Report, Atlanta, GA

Fritschner, Sarah .... (502) 582-4011
Food ED, Courier-Journal, Louisville, KY

Fritts, Barbara .... (918) 456-8833
BUS ED
Tahlequah Daily Press, Tahlequah, OK

Fritts, Donald H .... (805) 395-7500
PUB-Emeritus
Bakersfield Californian, Bakersfield, CA

Fritz, David C .... (412) 772-3900
MAN ED
North Hills News Record, Warrendale, PA

Fritz, John .... (904) 359-4111
Military ED
Florida Times-Union, Jacksonville, FL

Fritz, Keith A .... (610) 371-5000
ADTX MGR
Reading Times/Eagle, Reading, PA

Fritz, Louise F .... (412) 537-3351
Religion ED, Women's ED
Latrobe Bulletin, Latrobe, PA

Fritz, Marsha .... (606) 564-9091
CIRC MGR
Ledger Independent, Maysville, KY

Frizzell, Anisha .... (706) 549-0123
ED, Suburban Review, Athens, GA

Frizzi, Andrea .... (812) 231-4200
CIRC MGR-Sales & SRV
Tribune-Star, Terre Haute, IN

Frizzo, Jay .... (502) 443-1771
VP-Newspapers
Paxton Media Group Inc., Paducah, KY

Frizzo, John .... (616) 754-9301
News ED, Daily News, Greenville, MI

Frocts, Janenne .... (616) 547-6558
ED, Charlevoix Courier, Charlevoix, MI

Froelich, Joe .... (701) 462-8126
ED, Leader-News, Washburn, ND

Froelich, John .... (608) 372-4123
MAN ED, Tomah Journal, Tomah, WI

Froelich, Mark .... (419) 784-5441
Entertainment/Amusements ED, Features ED, Health/Medical ED, Television/Film ED, Theater/Music ED
Crescent-News, Defiance, OH

Froese, Anne .... (204) 326-6790
GM, Mennonitische Post, Steinbach, MB

Froese, Lisa .... (316) 442-4200
ADV MGR, Traveler, Arkansas City, KS

Frohm, Stu .... (517) 835-7171
BUS ED, Midland Daily News, Midland, MI

Froio, Etta .... (212) 630-4000
Sr VP-WWD/EXEC ED-W
Women's Wear Daily, New York, NY

Frol, Deborah D .... (509) 525-3300
PUB, Union-Bulletin, Walla Walla, WA

Fromm, Richard M .... (319) 382-4221
ED, Decorah Journal, Decorah, IA

Froseth, Terry .... (701) 385-4275
PUB, ED, Kenmare News, Kenmare, ND

Frost, James .... (616) 845-5181
ADTX MGR, Daily News, Ludington, MI

Frost, Jim .... (307) 682-9306
News ED, News-Record, Gillette, WY

Frost, Mark .... (518) 792-1126
ED, Chronicle, Glens Falls, NY

Frost, Stan .... (905) 732-2411
PROD SUPV-PR, Tribune, Welland, ON

Fruits, Hadley .... (402) 694-2131
ED, Aurora News-Register, Aurora, NE

Frungillo, John .... (607) 324-1425
ADV DIR, Evening Tribune, Hornell, NY

Frustere, James .... (216) 951-0000
CONT, News-Herald, Willoughby, OH

Fry, Donn .... (206) 464-2111
Books ED, Seattle Times, Seattle, WA

Fry Jr, Fran .... (814) 870-1600
MAN ED-Bureaus, COL
Morning News/Erie Daily Times, Erie, PA

Fry, Kristi .... (918) 684-2828
ASST MAN ED, Muskogee Daily Phoenix & Times Democrat, Muskogee, OK

Fry, Melvin .... (317) 552-3355
PROD FRM, Elwood Call-Leader, Elwood, IN
Ray Barnes Newspapers Inc.

Fry, Richard F .... (901) 658-3691
PUB, Bolivar Bulletin-Times, Bolivar, TN

Fry, Rupert .... (416) 367-2000
CIRC DIR, Toronto Star, Toronto, ON

Fryar, Ron .... (615) 893-5860
PUB, Daily News Journal, Murfreesboro, TN

Fryar, William R .... (615) 473-2191
PUB, Southern Standard, McMinnville, TN

Fryday, Donald J .... (717) 724-2287
PUB, Wellsboro Gazette, Wellsboro, PA

Frydendall, Marion .... (541) 485-1234
PROD FRM-PR, Register-Guard, Eugene, OR

Frye, Laura .... (806) 273-5611
ED, BUS/FIN ED, News-Herald, Borger, TX

Frye, Ray .... (606) 528-2464
PROD FRM-COMP
Times-Tribune, Corbin, KY

Frye, Roger .... (501) 271-3700
Online MGR
Benton County Daily Record, Bentonville, AR

Frye, William E .... (217) 379-4313
PRES, PROD SUPT
Paxton Daily Record, Paxton, IL

Fryer, Bob .... (412) 224-4321
City ED
Valley News Dispatch, Tarentum, PA

Fryer, Dorothy .... (402) 371-1020
City ED, Norfolk Daily News, Norfolk, NE

Fryer, Marilynn .... (517) 437-7351
MAN ED
Hillsdale Daily News, Hillsdale, MI

Fryette, Michael .... (203) 574-3636
PROD MGR-PR, Waterbury Republican-American, Waterbury, CT

Fryor, Jim .... (417) 623-3480
Sports ED, Joplin Globe, Joplin, MO

Fryxell, David .... (612) 222-5011
Senior ED-BUS & Technology
St. Paul Pioneer Press, St. Paul, MN

Fuchs, Holly .... (219) 546-2941
ED, Bremen Enquirer, Bremen, IN

Fuchs, Nancy .... (414) 634-3322
CONT, Journal Times, Racine, WI

Fucito, Karen .... (201) 428-6200
Chief Photographer
Daily Record, Parsippany, NJ

Fudge, Karla .... (314) 336-3435
PUB, Essayons, St. Robert, MO

Fuellenbach, Mark G .... (801) 896-5476
PUB, Richfield Reaper, Richfield, UT

Fuentes, Diana .... (210) 225-7411
Regional ED
San Antonio Express-News, San Antonio, TX

Fuersich, Larry .... (212) 279-7000
PUB, Retail News Bureau (Div. of Retail Reporting Corp.), New York, NY

Fugate, Larry .... (501) 935-5525
ASSOC ED, Jonesboro Sun, Jonesboro, AR

Fuhr, Bruce .... (250) 352-3552
Sports ED, Nelson Daily News, Nelson, BC

Fuhrman, Mike .... (904) 829-6562
Sports ED
St. Augustine Record, St. Augustine, FL

Fujimoto, Lila .... (808) 525-8000
ASST City ED
Honolulu Star-Bulletin, Honolulu, HI

Fukatsu, Jan .... (202) 636-3000
DIR-Accounting
Washington Times, Washington, DC

Fuke, Richard .... (808) 525-8000
VP-FIN
Hawaii Newspaper Agency Inc., Honolulu, HI

Fulbright, Jon .... (915) 445-5475
MAN ED, Sports ED, Enterprise, Pecos, TX

Fulks, Bobby .... (606) 231-3100
CIRC MGR-Home Delivery (City)
Lexington Herald-Leader, Lexington, KY

Fullenkamp, Ray .... (319) 837-6722
PUB, Donnellson Star, West Point, IA

Fullenwider, Karen .... (602) 977-8351
ED, Prospector, Glendale, AZ

Fuller, Brenda .... (319) 334-2557
ED, Bulletin-Journal, Indepen-dence, IA

Fuller, David .... (416) 493-4400
ED, North York Mirror, Willowdale, ON

Fuller, Deborah .... (407) 242-3500
ASST CONT, Florida Today, Melbourne, FL

Fuller, Dick .... (937) 225-2000
CIRC DIR-Home Delivery
Dayton Daily News, Dayton, OH

Fuller, Dustin .... (307) 347-3241
ADV MGR
Northern Wyoming Daily News, Worland, WY

Fuller, Glenn E .... (714) 553-9292
VP/GEN Counsel
Freedom Communications Inc., Irvine, CA

Fuller, Gregg .... (334) 382-3111
MAN ED, Greenville Advocate, Greenville, AL

Fuller, Harry .... (801) 237-2031
EPE, Salt Lake Tribune, Salt Lake City, UT

Fuller, Jack .... (312) 222-3237
PRES/PUB/CEO-Chicago Tribune Co.
Tribune Co., Chicago, IL

Fuller, James .... (864) 582-4511
PROD DIR-OPER
Herald-Journal, Spartanburg, SC

Fuller, Joe .... (601) 693-1551
PROD SUPT-PR, Star, Meridian, MS

Fuller, Kevin .... (503) 221-8327
CIRC MGR-NIE, Oregonian, Portland, OR

Fuller, Lawrence R .... (808) 525-8000
PRES/CEO, PUB
Honolulu Advertiser, Honolulu, HI

Fuller, Mike .... (907) 257-4200
PROD MGR-PR, Daily News, Anchorage, AK

Fuller, Myron F .... (508) 586-7200
PRES, Enterprise, Brockton, MA

Fuller, Richard .... (937) 328-0300
CIRC MGR, News-Sun, Springfield, OH

Fuller, Shir .... (518) 523-4401
ED, Lake Placid News, Lake Placid, NY

Fullerton, Joe .... (705) 645-8771
ED, Bracebridge Examiner, Bracebridge, ON

Fullwood, Janet .... (916) 321-1000
Travel ED, Sacramento Bee, Sacramento, CA

Fulmer, Marcia .... (219) 294-1661
Radio/Television ED, Truth, Elkhart, IN

Fulp, Sean .... (907) 486-3227
Sports ED, Kodiak Daily Mirror, Kodiak, AK

Fulps, Janice .... (502) 422-2155
ED
Meade County Messenger, Brandenburg, KY

Fulton, Ben .... (801) 575-7003
MAN ED
Private Eye Weekly, Salt Lake City, UT

Fulton, Charlotte .... (205) 232-2720
Librarian, News Courier, Athens, AL

Fulton, Dennis .... (214) 977-8222
Deputy BUS ED
Dallas Morning News, Dallas, TX

Fulton, Gene .... (541) 753-2641
ADV MGR-RT
Corvallis Gazette-Times, Corvallis, OR

Fulton, Ron .... (903) 729-0281
CIRC MGR
Palestine Herald-Press, Palestine, TX

Fumo, Paige .... (708) 366-0600
ED, Forest Park Review, Oak Park, IL

Funderburk, Jaby .... (864) 298-4100
ADTX MGR, Greenville News, Greenville, SC

Fung, Liza .... (213) 237-5000
ASST BUS ED-Technology/Telecommunica-tions, Los Angeles Times, Los Angeles, CA

Funk, Allen .... (206) 339-3000
GM, Herald, Everett, WA

Funk, Deane .... (619) 934-8544
PUB, Review Herald, Mammoth Lakes, CA

Funk, Doug .... (303) 677-2214
PUB, Dove Creek Press, Dove Creek, CO

Funk, Fran .... (860) 423-8466
Photo DEPT MGR, Chronicle, Willimantic, CT

Funk, Jeff .... (308) 382-1000
MAN ED
Grand Island Independent, Grand Island, NE

Funk, Larry .... (306) 652-9200
PROD MGR-Pre Press
StarPhoenix, Saskatoon, SK

Funk, Larry .... (913) 776-2200
PROD FRM-PR/Stereo
Manhattan Mercury, Manhattan, KS

Funk, Linda .... (303) 677-2214
ED, Dove Creek Press, Dove Creek, CO

Funk, Rhesa .... (405) 372-5000
ADV DIR, News Press, Stillwater, OK

Funk, Steve .... (616) 964-7161
ADV MGR-RT, Enquirer, Battle Creek, MI

Funk, Warren C .... (901) 529-2211
PSL DIR/General Counsel
Commercial Appeal, Memphis, TN

Funke, Kelly .... (807) 737-3209
MAN ED, Bulletin, Sioux Lookout, ON

Funkhouser, David .... (203) 789-5200
Sunday ED, Travel ED
New Haven Register, New Haven, CT

Funsten, Ted .... (860) 347-3331
Copy ED, Middletown Press, Middletown, CT

Fuqua, Craig .... (405) 372-5000
EDU ED, News Press, Stillwater, OK

Fuqua, Randall G .... (502) 726-8394
PUB
News Democrat & Leader, Russellville, KY

Furber, Ken .... (604) 567-9258
ED, Omineca Express, Vanderhoof, BC

Furcron, Betty .... (312) 225-2400
PROD MGR, Chicago Defender, Chicago, IL

Furgason, Marge .... (517) 265-5111
Theater/Music ED
Daily Telegram, Adrian, MI

Furlong, Tom .... (213) 237-5000
Deputy BUS ED
Los Angeles Times, Los Angeles, CA

Furlow, Darilynn .... (213) 237-5000
Food MAN ED
Los Angeles Times, Los Angeles, CA

Furnari, Jack .... (718) 981-1234
ADV MGR-MKTG
Staten Island Advance, Staten Island, NY

Furnari, Mike .... (304) 292-6301
PROD MGR-Post Press
Dominion Post, Morgantown, WV

Furness, Richard .... (604) 445-2233
PUB, Boundary Creek Times, Greenwood, BC

Furrer, Carol .... (914) 694-9300
MGR-Advertising MKTG, Reporter Dispatch, White Plains, NY, Gannett Co. Inc.

Furry, George .... (330) 841-1600
PROD FRM-PR
Tribune Chronicle, Warren, OH

Furry, William .... (217) 753-2226
MAN ED, Illinois Times, Springfield, IL

Furse, Ronald L .... (402) 694-2131
PUB, Aurora News-Register, Aurora, NE

Furst, Jay .... (507) 285-7600
City ED, Post-Bulletin, Rochester, MN

Furstenau, Bill .... (208) 743-9411
News ED, Morning Tribune, Lewiston, ID

Fursteneau, Dan .... (208) 522-1800
PROD FRM-PR, Post Register, Idaho Falls, ID

Furtak, John .... (805) 395-7500
News ED, Californian, Bakersfield, CA

Furukawa, Ross .... (970) 925-2220
GM, Aspen Daily News, Aspen, CO

Fusco, Robert .... (330) 424-9541
News ED, Morning Journal, Lisbon, OH

Fuselier, David .... (319) 263-2331
PUB, Muscatine Journal, Muscatine, IA

Fuselier, Herman .... (318) 942-4971
Sports ED, Daily World, Opelousas, LA

Fusfeld, Ira .... (914) 331-5000
PUB, Daily Freeman, Kingston, NY

Fusie, Robert A .... (319) 383-2200
PUB, Quad-City Times, Davenport, IA

Fuson Jr, Harold W .... (619) 454-0411
VP-Legal Affairs/SEC
Copley Press Inc., La Jolla, CA

Futch, John .... (561) 395-8300
VP/ED, News, Boca Raton, FL

Futrell Sr, Ashley B .... (919) 946-2144
PUB-Emeritus, Daily News, Washington, NC

Futrell Jr, Ashley B .... (919) 946-2144
PRES, PUB
Washington Daily News, Washington, NC

Futrell, Rachel F .... (919) 946-2144
TREAS, Daily News, Washington, NC

Futrell, Susan B .... (919) 946-2144
VP, Washington Daily News, Washington, NC

Futterman, Ellen .... (314) 340-8000
Get Out ED
St. Louis Post-Dispatch, St. Louis, MO

Fyffe, Tony .... (606) 789-5315
ED, Paintsville Herald, Paintsville, KY

G

Gaal, Csaba .... (416) 233-3131
ED, Kanadai Magyarsag, Etobicoke, ON

Gaarder, Nancy .... (402) 444-1000
School ED, Omaha World-Herald, Omaha, NE

Gaasterland, Jim .... (303) 442-1202
VP-OPER, Daily Camera, Boulder, CO

Gabarik, Mindi .... (216) 232-4055
ED, Bedford Times-Register, Bedford, OH

Gable, C Allen .... (603) 279-4516
PUB, Meredith News, Meredith, NH

Gab Who's Where-80

Gaboden, Cliff (617) 536-5390
MAN ED, Boston Phoenix, Boston, MA
Gabordi, Robert (304) 526-4000
EX ED, Herald-Dispatch, Huntington, WV
Gabrele, Arlene (518) 943-2100
ADV MGR-CLASS, Daily Mail, Catskill, NY
Gabrenya, Frank (614) 461-5000
Films ED
Columbus Dispatch, Columbus, OH
Gabriel, Cyn (415) 327-6397
PROD MGR, Daily News, Palo Alto, CA
Gabriele, Frank (508) 586-7200
PROD MGR-SYS/COMP
Enterprise, Brockton, MA
Gabriele, Judy (517) 437-7351
DIR-MKTG/PROM, Daily News, Hillsdale, MI
Gabrielson, Charles (212) 715-2100
PUB, USA Weekend, New York, NY
Gabrion, Patrick (207) 873-3341
Fashion/Food ED, Central Maine Morning Sentinel, Waterville, ME
Gackle, Donald C (701) 463-2201
PUB
McLean County Independent, Garrison, ND
Gackle, Jill (701) 463-2201
MAN ED
McLean County Independent, Garrison, ND
Gackle, Michael W (701) 463-2201
GM
McLean County Independent, Garrison, ND
Gaddy, Becky (719) 541-2288
GM, Ranchland News, Simla, CO
Gaddy, Bennie (505) 393-2123
PROD MGR, Daily News-Sun, Hobbs, NM
Gaddy, Monty (719) 541-2288
PUB, ED, Ranchland News, Simla, CO
Gadulka, Stan (517) 377-1000
PROD MGR-PR
Lansing State Journal, Lansing, MI
Gaff, Doug (815) 987-1200
Features ED
Rockford Register Star, Rockford, IL
Gaffney, Eva (508) 880-9000
MAN ED
Taunton Daily Gazette, Taunton, MA
Gaffney, James B (619) 483-3412
NTL Affairs/Health ED
Mature Life Features, San Diego, CA
Gaford, Alan (310) 377-6877
MAN ED, Palos Verdes Peninsula News, Palos Verdes Peninsula, CA
Gage, Carolyn Cole (712) 826-2142
PUB, ED
Villisca Review & Stanton Viking, Villisca, IA
Gage, Don (519) 326-4434
PUB, Leamington Post, Leamington, ON
Gage, Frederick H (608) 252-6400
TREAS, Capital Times, Madison, WI
Gage, Gwen (617) 426-3000
VP-PROM, Boston Herald, Boston, MA
Gage, Larry (713) 220-7171
EDL Writer
Houston Chronicle, Houston, TX
Gage, Nancy B (608) 252-6400
ASST SEC, Capital Times, Madison, WI
Gage, Ralph (913) 843-1000
GM, Journal-World, Lawrence, KS
Gage Jr, Ralph D (505) 546-2611
Owner, Deming Headlight, Deming, NM
Gage, Tim (573) 276-5148/4523
ED, Delta News Journal & Press Merit, Malden, MO
Gager, Wilma W (719) 263-5311
PUB, ED, Fowler Tribune, Fowler, CO
Gagley, Perry (403) 527-1101
CIRC MGR-Readers Sales/SRV
Medicine Hat News, Medicine Hat, AB
Gagli, Rich (201) 646-4000
DIR-Photography, Record, Hackensack, NJ
Gagliardi, Alfred (514) 279-4536
ED, Corriere Italiano, Montreal, QC
Gagne, Gilles (506) 727-4444
PUB, L'Acadie Nouvelle, Caraquet, NB
Gagnier, Mary (610) 820-6500
Quakertown ED
Morning Call, Allentown, PA
Gagnon, Ben (970) 242-5050
Political Writer
Daily Sentinel, Grand Junction, CO
Gagnon, Bud (207) 873-3341
PROD SUPV-PR, Central Maine Morning Sentinel, Waterville, ME
Guy Gannett Communications
Gagnon, Claude (418) 545-4474
PRES & ED, GM
Le Quotidien, Chicoutimi, QC
Gagnon, Suzanne (514) 455-7955
MAN ED, 1ere Edition du Sud-Quest, Vandreuil-Dorion, QC
Gagon, David (801) 237-2188
Art ED, Deseret News, Salt Lake City, UT
Gahagan, Chris (717) 248-6741
Obit ED, Sentinel, Lewistown, PA
Gahagan, Jack (517) 787-2300
PROD MGR-Commercial Printing
Jackson Citizen Patriot, Jackson, MI
Gahan, Bobbie (402) 685-5624
PUB, Oakland Independent, Oakland, NE
Gahan, Dewaine (402) 685-5624
PUB, ED, Oakland Independent, Oakland, NE
Gaida, Rev Dr Pranas (905) 275-4672
ED, Teviskes Ziburiai, Mississauga, ON
Gaidziunas, B (216) 431-6344
ED, Dirva, Cleveland, OH
Gail, Richard (612) 598-7521
PUB, ED, Western Guard, Madison, MN
Gailey, Philip (813) 893-8111
EPE, St. Petersburg Times, St. Petersburg, FL
Gaines, Dan (213) 237-5000
ASST BUS ED-Markets
Los Angeles Times, Los Angeles, CA
Gaines, Jack (937) 225-2000
DIR-INFO/Technical SRV
Dayton Daily News, Dayton, OH
Gaines, John (319) 754-8461
Photo DEPT MGR, Hawk Eye, Burlington, IA
Gaines, John B (502) 781-1700
PRES/TREAS, PUB
Daily News, Bowling Green, KY
Gaines, Mark (219) 347-0400
CIRC MGR, News-Sun, Kendallville, IN
Gaines, Mary (502) 781-1700
ADV MGR-NTL
Daily News, Bowling Green, KY
Gaines, Michael (305) 370-6009
GM, Broward Informer, Sunrise, FL
Gaines, Nancy (816) 686-2741
PUB, ED, Fairfax Forum, Fairfax, MO
Gaines, Pipes (502) 781-1700
VP/SEC, Co-PUB
Daily News, Bowling Green, KY
Gaines, Stephen (315) 782-1000
CIRC MGR-Office
Watertown Daily Times, Watertown, NY
Gaines-Riffel, Beth (913) 539-7558
ED, Grass & Grain, Manhattan, KS
Gaitens, Phil (314) 340-8000
MET ED
St. Louis Post-Dispatch, St. Louis, MO
Gajdos, Andrew (416) 531-2055
ED, Kanadsky Slovak, Toronto, ON
Gajilan, Arlyn Tobias (201) 434-1114
MAN ED, Filipino Express, Jersey City, NJ
Gajilan Jr, Lito A (201) 434-1114
PUB, Filipino Express, Jersey City, NJ
Galabrese, Ross (614) 283-4711
News ED, Herald-Star, Steubenville, OH
Galands, John N (412) 458-5010
GM, Allied News, Grove City, PA
Galanos, Sally (352) 374-5000
ADV MGR-RT
Gainesville Sun, Gainesville, FL
Galant, Richard (516) 843-2020
ASSOC MAN ED, Newsday, Melville, NY
Galante, Italo (617) 933-3700
PROD FRM-Ad COMP
Daily Times Chronicle, Woburn, MA
Galanti, Marie (415) 921-5100
PUB, Journal Francais, San Francisco, CA
Galarneau, Mike (303) 622-4417
PUB, ED
Eastern Colorado News, Strasburg, CO
Galassini, Chris (212) 416-2000
PROD Senior MGR (Beaumont TX)
Wall Street Journal, New York, NY
Galati, K J (610) 258-7171
ADV SUPV-Special Sections, Automotive ED, RE ED, Express-Times, Easton, PA
Galati, Mike (708) 834-0900
ED, Lemont Metropolitan, Elmhurst, IL
Galbecka, Julian (604) 792-1931
PUB, Chilliwack Progress Weekender, Chilliwack, BC
Galbincea, Barbara (216) 999-4500
State ED, Plain Dealer, Cleveland, OH
Galbraith, Joe (203) 574-3636
Wire ED, Waterbury Republican-American, Waterbury, CT
Galbreth, John (412) 282-8000
PROD FRM-COMP, Butler Eagle, Butler, PA
Gale, Kevin (954) 356-4000
BUS/FIN ED
Sun-Sentinel, Fort Lauderdale, FL
Gale, P Douglas (805) 229-1520
ED, Marathon Mercury, Marathon, ON
Gale, Paul (815) 625-3600
Lifestyle ED, Daily Gazette, Sterling, IL
Gale, Reg (516) 843-2020
SCI ED, Newsday, Melville, NY
Gale, Tony (919) 419-6500
PROD MGR-Quality Assurance
Herald-Sun, Durham, NC
Gale, William K (401) 277-7000
Theater Writer
Providence Journal-Bulletin, Providence, RI
Gale, Zona (509) 582-1500
Librarian, Tri-City Herald, Tri-Cities, WA
Galer, John M (217) 532-3933
PUB, Hillsboro Journal, Hillsboro, IL
Galer, Phillip C (217) 532-3933
ED, Hillsboro Journal, Hillsboro, IL
Galetano, James J (847) 427-4300
VP-Circulation, CIRC DIR
Daily Herald, Arlington Heights, IL
Galewski, Jim (507) 454-6500
MAN ED, EPE, News ED
Winona Daily News, Winona, MN
Galka, Dennis (810) 469-4510
ADV MGR-RT
Macomb Daily, Mount Clemens, MI
Gall, Bob (419) 245-6000
CIRC MGR-OPER, Blade, Toledo, OH
Gall, Steve (218) 723-8000
MKTG DIR
Murphy McGinnis Media, Duluth, MN
Gallacher, John J (413) 447-7311
ADV MGR-Sales
Berkshire Eagle, Pittsfield, MA
Gallagher, Beth (519) 894-2231
Social Service Reporter
Record, Kitchener, ON
Gallagher, Charles M (610) 371-5000
MAN ED
Reading Times/Eagle, Reading, PA
Gallagher, Dan (619) 232-4381
Legal ED
San Diego Daily Transcript, San Diego, CA
Gallagher, Dave (707) 441-0500
Films/Theater ED, Radio/Television ED
Times-Standard, Eureka, CA
Gallagher, David (716) 873-2594
PUB, West Side Times, Buffalo, NY
Gallagher, Dennis (716) 873-2594
MAN ED, Buffalo Rocket, Buffalo, NY
Gallagher, Don (617) 482-9447
MAN ED
BPI Entertainment News Wire, Boston, MA
Gallagher, Ed (405) 925-3187
GM, ED, Konawa Leader, Konawa, OK
Gallagher, Max (405) 925-3187
PUB, Konawa Leader, Konawa, OK
Gallagher, Michael (408) 424-2221
PC Specialist, Californian, Salinas, CA
Gallagher, Michael F (517) 895-8551
ADV MGR-Sales
Bay City Times, Bay City, MI
Gallagher, Mike (360) 834-2141
PUB
Camas-Washougal Post Record, Camas, WA
Gallagher, Robert S (414) 338-0622
PUB, Daily News, West Bend, WI
Gallagher, Tim (805) 650-2900
ED, Ventura County Star, Ventura, CA
Gallagher, Valerie (206) 622-8272
ADV MGR-Legal, Seattle Daily Journal of Commerce, Seattle, WA
Gallagher, W Clark (541) 926-2211
GM/Sales
Albany Democrat-Herald, Albany, OR
Gallaher, Mark (605) 331-2200
ADV MGR, Argus Leader, Sioux Falls, SD
Gallant, Joseph H (508) 775-1200
ADV MGR-RT, Cape Cod Times, Hyannis, MA
Gallant, Sherri (403) 328-4411
City ED
Lethbridge Herald, Lethbridge, AB
Gallaudet, Bruce (707) 448-6401
MGR-MKTG & PROM, CIRC MGR
Reporter, Vacaville, CA
Gallaway, Mike (405) 224-2600
CIRC DIR
Chickasha Daily Express, Chickasha, OK
Galle, Roger (817) 582-3431
PUB, ED, Reporter, Hillsboro, TX
Gallego, Julie (562) 435-1161
City ED (Night)
Press-Telegram, Long Beach, CA
Gallegos, Russell J (801) 237-2188
SEC/TREAS
Deseret News, Salt Lake City, UT
Galleguillos, Orestes (817) 626-8624
ED
El Informador Hispano, Fort Worth, TX
Gallert, Hans (208) 783-1107
CIRC MGR
Shoshone News-Press, Kellogg, ID
Galli, James (214) 977-8222
DIR-BUS Development
Dallas Morning News, Dallas, TX
Gallian, Wally (318) 281-4421
PRES/PUB
Bastrop Daily Enterprise, Bastrop, LA
Gallihugh, Charlotte (540) 672-1266
GM, Orange County Review, Orange, VA
Gallivan, J W (801) 237-2031
COB, Salt Lake Tribune, Salt Lake City, UT
Gallmeister, Eugene (618) 542-2133
PROD MGR
Du Quoin Evening Call, Du Quoin, IL
Gallo, Barbara (607) 798-1234
CIRC DIR
Press & Sun Bulletin, Binghamton, NY
Gallo, Bill (212) 210-2100
ASSOC Sports ED
New York Daily News, New York, NY
Gallo, Greg (212) 930-8000
Sports ED, New York Post, New York, NY
Gallo, Rocco A (609) 989-7800
PROD DIR, Trentonian, Trenton, NJ
Gallo Jr, William J (609) 935-1500
NTL ED, News ED
Today's Sunbeam, Salem, NJ
Gallo-Farrell, Barbara (914) 225-3633
MAN ED
Putnam Courier-Trader, Carmel, NY
Gallont, Grant (902) 436-2121
CIRC MGR
Journal-Pioneer, Summerside, PEI
Galloway, Debra (904) 599-2100
Librarian, Democrat, Tallahassee, FL
Galloway, Mike (813) 893-8111
PROD MGR-Distribution
St. Petersburg Times, St. Petersburg, FL
Galloway, Paul (312) 222-3232
Religion Writer
Chicago Tribune, Chicago, IL
Galloway, Randy (214) 977-8222
COL-SportsDay
Dallas Morning News, Dallas, TX
Galloway, Rusty (505) 356-4481
CIRC MGR, News-Tribune, Portales, NM
Galloway, Wiley (210) 225-7411
PA
San Antonio Express-News, San Antonio, TX
Galloway, William (603) 863-1776
PUB, Argus-Champion, Newport, NH
Gallup, Larry (414) 733-4411
Sports ED, Post-Crescent, Appleton, WI
Galperin, Ron (213) 937-5255
Author/ASSOC
Real Estate News Group, Beverly Hills, CA
Galuim, William (508) 945-2220
MAN ED, Cape Cod Chronicle, Chatham, MA
Galusha, Diane (914) 586-2601
ED
Catskill Mountain News, Margaretville, NY
Galusha, Mike (303) 892-5000
PROD FRM-PR
Rocky Mountain News, Denver, CO
Galvacky, Steve (201) 748-9700
ED, Bloomfield Life, Bloomfield, NJ
Galvan, Jimmy (409) 885-3562
MAN ED, Sealy News, Sealy, TX
Galvan, Rudy (805) 925-2691
PROD FRM-COMP
Santa Maria Times, Santa Maria, CA
Galvin, Martin (212) 947-7022
ED, Irish People, New York, NY
Galway, Linda (207) 784-5411
Advocate ED, Sun-Journal, Lewiston, ME
Galyean, Marie (208) 467-9251
Women's ED
Idaho Press-Tribune, Nampa, ID
Gamage, Peter H (617) 593-7700
PRES/TREAS, VP/ASST TREAS
Daily Evening Item, Lynn, MA
Gambardella, Edward P (806) 762-8844
ADV MGR-CLASS
Lubbock Avalanche-Journal, Lubbock, TX
Gambell, Gregg A (315) 422-7011
GM, Syracuse New Times, Syracuse, NY
Gambill, George (Buzz) (619) 251-2401
Creator/Owner/Artist, Gambill Arts & Graphix Syndicate, Desert Hot Springs, CA
Gambill, Suzanne (619) 251-2401
Feature ED, Gambill Arts & Graphix Syndicate, Desert Hot Springs, CA
Gamble, Camille (901) 523-1561
Copy ED, Daily News, Memphis, TN
Gamble, Ed (904) 359-4111
EDL Cartoonist
Florida Times-Union, Jacksonville, FL
Gamble, Harry (219) 933-3200
MAN ED-Illinois, Times, Munster, IN
Gamble, Paul (415) 749-5400
ASSOC PUB, Recorder, San Francisco, CA
Gamble, Phonda (937) 225-2000
CIRC MGR, Dayton Daily News, Dayton, OH
Gamble, Stephen (630) 844-5844
PROD FRM-COMP, Beacon-News, Aurora, IL
Gamboa, Renee (408) 372-3311
MGR-CR
Monterey County Herald, Monterey, CA
Gambrel, David (606) 236-2551
ED, Lincoln Ledger, Danville, KY
Gammage, Jeff (215) 854-2000
Pittsburgh BU
Philadelphia Inquirer, Philadelphia, PA
Gammage, Jennifer (618) 632-3643
MAN ED, O'Fallon Progress, O'Fallon, IL
Gammage, Randy (614) 345-4053
Automotive ED, Advocate, Newark, OH
Gammill, Don (405) 475-3311
Farm ED
Daily Oklahoman, Oklahoma City, OK

Copyright ©1997 by the Editor & Publisher Co.

81-Who's Where **Gar**

Gammon, Ralph .... (412) 588-5000
Sports ED, Record-Argus, Greenville, PA
Gammon, Suzanne .... (705) 753-2930
ED, Tribune, Sturgeon Falls, ON
Gammond, Karen .... (941) 629-2855
ADV MGR-Regional Sales
Sun Herald, Port Charlotte, FL
Gander, Ron .... (541) 672-3321
PROD MGR-COMP
News-Review, Roseburg, OR
Gandhi, Ketan .... (607) 798-1234
CONT
Press & Sun Bulletin, Binghamton, NY
Gandolfo, A .... (314) 638-3446
ED, Il Pensiero, St. Louis, MO
Gandy, Mell Rose .... (512) 394-7402
MAN ED, Freer Press, Freer, TX
Gandy, Peggy .... (405) 475-3311
Society ED
Daily Oklahoman, Oklahoma City, OK
Gandy, Terry E .... (801) 625-4200
DIR-MKTG/SALES, DIR MKTG/Sales
Standard-Examiner, Ogden, UT
Gang, Christine Arpe .... (901) 529-2211
Food Reporter
Commercial Appeal, Memphis, TN
Gange, Phil .... (301) 662-1177
PROD SUPV-PR (Night)
Frederick Post/News, Frederick, MD
Gann, Perry .... (904) 359-4111
PROD MGR-PR
Florida Times-Union, Jacksonville, FL
Gannett, John H .... (207) 828-8100
Vice Chairman
Guy Gannett Communications, Portland, ME
Gannon, Kate .... (915) 546-6100
Technology SYS ED
El Paso Times, El Paso, TX
Gannon, Mike .... (916) 321-1000
CIRC MGR-MKTG
Sacramento Bee, Sacramento, CA
Gannon, Thomas .... (773) 586-8800
PROD DIR, Daily Southtown, Chicago, IL
Ganote, Mark .... (317) 529-1111
CIRC DIR, Courier-Times, New Castle, IN
Gant, Kelly .... (541) 672-3321
ADV DIR, News-Review, Roseburg, OR
Ganta, Jayaprada .... (860) 241-6200
MGR-BUS SYS Applications
Hartford Courant, Hartford, CT
Gantenbein, Janelle .... (913) 263-1000
ADV MGR, Reflector-Chronicle, Abilene, KS
Gantt, Leon .... (706) 884-7311
TMC ED, Daily News, La Grange, GA
Ganz, Tom .... (708) 383-3200
ED, Maywood Herald, Oak Park, IL
Ganzi, Victor F .... (212) 649-2000
Sr VP/CFO
Hearst Newspapers, New York, NY
Gapen, Tom .... (818) 241-4141
Chief Photographer
Glendale News-Press, Glendale, CA
Garabedian, Lisa .... (209) 441-6111
MGR-Special Sections
Fresno Bee, Fresno, CA
Garabiedian, H .... (617) 924-4420
ED
Baikar-Armenian Monthly, Watertown, MA
Garai, Joseph .... (212) 254-0397
GM, ED
Amerikai Magyar Szo, New York, NY
Garber, Anna .... (423) 428-0746
ED, EPE, Mountain Press, Sevierville, TN
Garber, J Mark .... (541) 746-1671
PUB, Springfield News, Springfield, OR
Garber, Phil .... (201) 691-8181
ED, Mount Olive Chronicle, Budd Lake, NJ
Garceau, Becky .... (613) 544-5000
Features ED, Whig-Standard, Kingston, ON
Garcia, Arnold .... (512) 445-3500
EPE, Austin American-Statesman, Austin, TX
Garcia, Astrid .... (414) 224-2000
Senior VP-OPER
Milwaukee Journal Sentinel, Milwaukee, WI
Garcia, Beatrice .... (305) 350-2111
EX BUS ED, Miami Herald, Miami, FL
Garcia, Carolina .... (414) 224-2000
ASST MAN ED
Milwaukee Journal Sentinel, Milwaukee, WI
Garcia, Daniel .... (908) 352-6654
GM, La Voz, Elizabeth, NJ
Garcia, Dawn .... (408) 920-5000
City ED
San Jose Mercury News, San Jose, CA
Garcia, Dennis .... (910) 625-2101
Sports ED, Courier-Tribune, Asheboro, NC
Garcia, Diane .... (209) 688-0521
ADV SUPV
Tulare Advance-Register, Tulare, CA
Garcia, Frank .... (210) 675-4500
ED, Kelly Observer, San Antonio, TX
Garcia, Frederick L .... (817) 626-8624
PUB, El Informador Hispano, Fort Worth, TX
Garcia, Gerald .... (860) 225-4601
PUB, Herald, New Britain, CT
Garcia, Gil .... (213) 622-8332
CFO, La Opinion, Los Angeles, CA
Garcia, Gina .... (512) 664-6588
Bookkeeper, Alice Echo-News, Alice, TX
Garcia, Hermie .... (416) 461-8694
PUB, Phillipine Reporter, Toronto, ON
Garcia, Jennifer Dokes .... (602) 271-8000
EDL Writer, Arizona Republic, Phoenix, AZ
Garcia, Joe .... (520) 573-4561
City ED, Tucson Citizen, Tucson, AZ
Garcia, Juan G .... (714) 541-6007
PUB, ED, Union Hispana, Santa Ana, CA
Garcia, Martha .... (916) 652-7939
GM, Loomis News, Loomis, CA
Garcia, Norma .... (210) 728-2500
MGR-Office
Laredo Morning Times, Laredo, TX
Garcia, Peter .... (415) 777-5700
PROD MGR-MR, San Francisco Newspaper Agency, San Francisco, CA
Garcia, Peter .... (512) 664-6588
Sports ED, Alice Echo-News, Alice, TX
Garcia, Renee .... (501) 534-3400
ADV MGR-CLASS
Pine Bluff Commercial, Pine Bluff, AR
Garcia, Robert .... (970) 242-5050
Graphics ED/Art DIR
Daily Sentinel, Grand Junction, CO
Garcia, Rosie .... (210) 775-1551
CIRC MGR
Del Rio News-Herald, Del Rio, TX
Garcia, Sara .... (505) 243-6161
ED, El Hispano News, Albuquerque, NM
Garcia, Shirley .... (970) 493-6397
ADV MGR-Inside Sales
Fort Collins Coloradoan, Fort Collins, CO
Garcia-Villalta, Oscar .... (202) 898-8254
GEN MGR-Latin America
United Press International, Washington, DC
Gard, Bill .... (202) 334-6000
PROD DIR-Engineering
Washington Post, Washington, DC
Gard, Robert L .... (608) 676-4111
ED, Clinton Topper, Clinton, WI
Gard, Roger .... (419) 332-5511
PROD DIR, News-Messenger, Fremont, OH
Gard Jr, S Richard .... (404) 521-1227
PUB, ED, Daily Report, Atlanta, GA
Gardener Jr, Wayne .... (540) 885-7281
PROD FRM-PR
Daily News Leader, Staunton, VA
Gardiner, Hugh .... (404) 526-5151
ADV MGR-Supplements/OPER
Atlanta Journal-Constitution, Atlanta, GA
Gardiner, John .... (718) 624-0536
ED, Brooklyn Heights Press & Cobble Hill News, Brooklyn Heights, NY
Gardner, Ann .... (913) 843-1000
EPE, Journal-World, Lawrence, KS
Gardner, Barbara .... (715) 796-2355
PUB, ED
Central St. Croix News, Hammond, WI
Gardner, Barbara E .... (316) 397-5347
PUB, ED, Dighton Herald, Dighton, KS
Gardner, Bill .... (614) 596-5393
PUB, ED
Vinton County Courier, McArthur, OH
Gardner, Bob .... (704) 358-5000
PROD MGR-MR
Charlotte Observer, Charlotte, NC
Gardner, Brian .... (510) 208-6300
News ED, Oakland Tribune, Oakland, CA
Gardner, Bruce .... (502) 443-1771
BUS/FIN ED, Paducah Sun, Paducah, KY
Gardner, Chris .... (513) 761-1188
Contributing Critic
Critic's Choice Reviews, Cincinnati, OH
Gardner, Dale .... (614) 286-2187
PUB
Jackson-Vinton Journal-Herald, Jackson, OH
Gardner, Ellen .... (314) 340-8000
Lifestyle ED
St. Louis Post-Dispatch, St. Louis, MO
Gardner, Frank .... (513) 977-3000
Sr VP-Broadcasting
E W Scripps Co., Cincinnati, OH
Gardner, George .... (704) 252-5611
PROD MGR, Citizen-Times, Asheville, NC
Gardner, Helen .... (912) 367-2468
PUB, ED, Baxley News-Banner, Baxley, GA
Gardner, J Charles .... (610) 371-5000
Photo MGR
Reading Times/Eagle, Reading, PA
Gardner, James E .... (518) 861-6641
PUB, Altamont Enterprise and Albany County Post, Altamont, NY
Gardner, Jamie .... (912) 367-2468
MAN ED, Baxley News-Banner, Baxley, GA
Gardner, Jerry L .... (518) 251-3012
PUB, ED, North Creek News-Enterprise, North Creek, NY
Gardner, Jim W .... (316) 397-5347
PUB, ED, Dighton Herald, Dighton, KS
Gardner, Joe .... (618) 393-2931
CIRC MGR, Olney Daily Mail, Olney, IL
Gardner, Kent .... (612) 673-4000
ADM ED, Star Tribune, Minneapolis, MN
Gardner, Lyne .... (405) 789-1962
ED, Tribune, Bethany, OK
Gardner, Malcomb .... (512) 445-3500
CIRC MGR-MKTG
Austin American-Statesman, Austin, TX
Gardner, Marilyn .... (617) 450-2000
COL, Christian Science Monitor, Boston, MA
Gardner, Mary Ann .... (415) 348-4321
SEC
San Mateo County Times, San Mateo, CA
Gardner, Max .... (912) 367-2468
PUB, ED, Baxley News-Banner, Baxley, GA
Gardner, Michael .... (916) 891-1234
Farm ED, Enterprise-Record, Chico, CA
Gardner, Otis .... (910) 353-1171
DP MGR, Daily News, Jacksonville, NC
Gardner, P Dale .... (614) 384-6786
PUB, Wellston Sentry, Wellston, OH
Gardner Jr, P Dale .... (614) 947-2149
PUB, News Watchman, Waverly, OH
Gardner, Sheila .... (702) 782-5121
MAN ED, Record-Courier, Gardnerville, NV
Gardner, Terry .... (805) 781-7800
PROD MGR-MR
Telegram-Tribune, San Luis Obispo, CA
Gardner, Warren F .... (203) 235-1661
COL, Record-Journal, Meriden, CT
Gardner-Howell, Sherri .... (423) 523-3131
Fashion/Features ED, Health ED, Radio/Television ED, Society/Women's ED
Knoxville News-Sentinel, Knoxville, TN
Gardon, Mary Ann .... (715) 582-4541
PUB, Peshtigo Times, Peshtigo, WI
Gareau, Ed .... (212) 416-2000
PROD Senior MGR (Orlando FL)
Wall Street Journal, New York, NY
Gareau, Michel .... (514) 229-6664
GM, Le Journal des Pays D'en Haut, Sainte-Adele, QC
Garfield, Reed .... (802) 748-8121
PROD MGR
Caledonian-Record, St. Johnsbury, VT
Gargano, Frank .... (609) 845-3300
VP/CONT
Gloucester County Times, Woodbury, NJ
MediaNews Inc. (Garden State Newspapers)
Gargano, James .... (515) 332-2514
PUB, Humboldt Independent, Humboldt, IA
Gargano, Jeffrey .... (515) 332-2514
ED, Humboldt Independent, Humboldt, IA
Gargasz, Steve .... (412) 588-5000
ADV DIR, DIR-MKTG
Record-Argus, Greenville, PA
Garhart, Rosemary T .... (217) 351-5252
EPE, News-Gazette, Champaign, IL
Gariety Sr., John .... (307) 265-3870
PUB, Casper Journal, Casper, WY
Gariky, Frank .... (212) 755-4363
Contributing Writer
Punch In Travel & Entertainment News Syndicate, New York, NY
Garlick, Emory W .... (313) 428-8173
PUB, ED
Manchester Enterprise, Manchester, MI
Garlington, Doug .... (505) 325-4545
BM, Daily Times, Farmington, NM
Garlock, Dale .... (712) 272-4417
ED
Buena Vista County Journal, Newell, IA
Garlock, John .... (414) 224-2000
PROD FRM-PR
Milwaukee Journal Sentinel, Milwaukee, WI
Garmon, Michelle .... (317) 675-2115
Sports ED
Tipton County Tribune, Tipton, IN
Garnatz-Harriman, Judy .... (813) 893-8111
Action Line ED
St. Petersburg Times, St. Petersburg, FL
Garneau, Gilles .... (418) 686-3233
DP DIR, DP MGR, PROD DIR
Le Soleil, Quebec, QC
Garner, Brian .... (864) 878-2453
MAN ED, Pickens Sentinel, Pickens, SC
Garner, Bruce .... (904) 747-5000
PROD DIR, PROD MGR-OPER
News Herald, Panama City, FL
Garner, Carol .... (903) 729-0281
PROD SUPV-COMP
Palestine Herald-Press, Palestine, TX
Garner, Cecil .... (501) 785-7700
CIRC MGR-OPER
Southwest Times Record, Fort Smith, AR
Garner, Deb .... (814) 684-4000
ADV MGR-RT, Daily Herald, Tyrone, PA
Garner, Frazier .... (618) 271-0468
MAN ED
East St. Louis Monitor, East St. Louis, IL
Garner, Gary .... (817) 778-4444
ADV DIR
Temple Daily Telegram, Temple, TX
Garner, Jack .... (716) 232-7100
Movies/Videos Critic, Rochester Democrat and Chronicle; Times-Union, Rochester, NY
Garner, James .... (501) 752-3675
ED, Gentry Courier-Journal, Gentry, AR
Garner, Jennifer .... (203) 226-6311
MAN ED, Westport News, Westport, CT
Garner, Jim .... (520) 445-3333
ED, COL, EPE, EDL Writer, Political ED
Daily Courier, Prescott, AZ
Garner, Jolyn .... (201) 438-8700
ED, Commercial Leader, Lyndhurst, NJ
Garner, Ray .... (205) 532-4000
BUS ED, Huntsville Times, Huntsville, AL
Garner, Shea .... (814) 684-4000
CIRC MGR, Daily Herald, Tyrone, PA
Garner, Stuart .... (508) 880-9000
COO, Taunton Daily Gazette, Taunton, MA
Garner, Stuart .... (330) 454-5611
COO, Repository, Canton, OH
Thomson Newspapers
Garner, Stuart M .... (416) 814-4239
PRES/CEO-Canadian OPER, EVP/COO
Thomson Newspapers, Toronto, ON
Garner, Warren .... (604) 368-8551
PROD FRM-COMP
Trail Daily Times, Trail, BC
Hollinger Inc. (Sterling Newspapers)
Garnett, Craig K .... (210) 278-3335
PUB, Uvalde Leader-News, Uvalde, TX
Garnos, Gordon R .... (605) 886-6901
ED, Amusements ED, EPE
Watertown Public Opinion, Watertown, SD
Garred, Frank W .... (360) 385-2900
PUB, ED, Port Townsend Jefferson County Leader, Port Townsend, WA
Garren, Danny .... (813) 259-7711
PROD MGR-MR
Tampa Tribune and Times, Tampa, FL
Garren, Michael .... (303) 349-6114
MAN ED, Crested Butte Chronicle & Pilot, Crested Butte, CO
Garren, Ralph .... (719) 544-3520
PROD FRM-PR
Pueblo Chieftain, Pueblo, CO
Garrett, Alexander .... (212) 631-3520
ASST ED
Goddess Communications, New York, NY
Garrett, Cathy .... (901) 427-3333
DIR-MKTG/PROM, Jackson Sun, Jackson, TN
Garrett, Celeste .... (312) 321-3000
ASST MET ED
Chicago Sun-Times, Chicago, IL
Garrett, Dana .... (512) 398-4886
PUB, Lockhart Post-Register, Lockhart, TX
Garrett, Elizabeth .... (912) 868-5776
ED, Telfair Times, Helena, GA
Garrett, Gini .... (515) 622-3110
ED, Sigourney News-Review, Sigourney, IA
Garrett, Harriet .... (215) 848-7864
GM
Philadelphia Sunday Sun, Philadelphia, PA
Garrett, Harry L .... (864) 223-1411
ADV DIR, MGR-Sales/PROM
Index-Journal, Greenwood, SC
Garrett, John .... (909) 684-1200
Sports ED, Press-Enterprise, Riverside, CA
Garrett, Nancy .... (217) 465-6424
MAN ED
Paris Daily Beacon-News, Paris, IL
Garrett, Rickey .... (205) 362-1000
CIRC MGR, Daily Home, Talladega, AL
Garrett, Robert .... (912) 552-3161
GM, ED
Sandersville Progress, Sandersville, GA
Garrett, Rusty .... (501) 442-1777
Political ED
Northwest Arkansas Times, Fayetteville, AR
Garrett, Rusty .... (619) 745-6611
PROD MGR-Pre Press
North County Times, Escondido, CA
Garrett, Shari .... (810) 469-4510
Automotive ED
Macomb Daily, Mount Clemens, MI
Garrett, Sherrye D .... (717) 291-8811
CNR-NIE, Lancaster Intelligencer Journal/New Era/Sunday News, Lancaster, PA
Garrett, Shirley .... (618) 662-2108
ADV MGR
Daily Clay County Advocate-Press, Flora, IL
Garrett, Suzanne .... (816) 932-6600
Sales Administrator/International
Universal Press Syndicate, Kansas City, MO
Garrett, Terry .... (813) 286-1600
PUB, Weekly Planet, Tampa, FL

Gar Who's Where-82

Garrett, William (Bill) ... (405) 338-3355
ADV MGR
Guymon Daily Herald, Guymon, OK

Garrick, Charles ... (803) 533-5500
PROD FRM-PR
Times and Democrat, Orangeburg, SC

Garriga, Julio ... (305) 350-2111
MGR-CR, Miami Herald, Miami, FL

Garris, Kevin ... (910) 727-7211
PROD MGR-Packaging
Winston-Salem Journal, Winston-Salem, NC

Garris, Thomas C ... (352) 867-4010
DIR-OPER, Ocala Star-Banner, Ocala, FL

Garris, Tom ... (352) 867-4010
DIR-INFO SYS, PROD DIR
Ocala Star-Banner, Ocala, FL

Garrison, Carol ... (618) 393-2931
ADV MGR, Olney Daily Mail, Olney, IL

Garrison, Dennis ... (316) 283-1500
ADV MGR, Newton Kansan, Newton, KS

Garrison, Elaine ... (816) 826-1000
Living/Lifestyle ED
Sedalia Democrat, Sedalia, MO

Garrison, Greg ... (205) 325-2222
Religion ED
Birmingham News, Birmingham, AL

Garrison, Jacque ... (800) 223-2154
DIR (Finadco Agency)
Investor's Business Daily, Los Angeles, CA

Garrison, Peter ... (518) 374-4141
PROD MGR-Pre Press
Daily Gazette, Schenectady, NY

Garrison, Ron ... (607) 734-5151
PROD MGR-MR, Star-Gazette, Elmira, NY

Garrison, Virginia ... (516) 324-0002
MAN ED
East Hampton Star, East Hampton, NY

Garron, Barry ... (816) 234-4141
Radio/Television ED
Kansas City Star, Kansas City, MO

Garron, Chet ... (207) 282-1535
PA, PROD MGR
Journal Tribune, Biddeford, ME

Garson, Arnold ... (605) 331-2200
PRES, PUB, Argus Leader, Sioux Falls, SD

Garst Jr, J F ... (916) 629-2811
PUB, ED, Kourier, Willow Creek, CA

Gart, Mary Claire ... (312) 243-1300
MAN ED, New World, Chicago, IL

Garten, Michael P ... (916) 371-8030
PUB, News-Ledger, West Sacramento, CA

Garth, Janice ... (773) 487-7700
GM, Chicago Citizen, Chicago, IL

Garth, William A ... (773) 487-7700
PUB, Chicago Citizen, Chicago, IL

Gartlen, Paul ... (519) 679-6666
PROD MGR, London Free Press, London, ON

Gartman, Susan ... (318) 649-6411
ED
Caldwell Watchman Progress, Columbia, LA

Gartner, Michael G ... (515) 232-2160
Chairman, ED, Daily Tribune, Ames, IA

Garvan, Michael ... (508) 775-1200
MGR-EDU SRV
Cape Cod Times, Hyannis, MA

Garven, Chuck ... (216) 999-4500
PROD SUPT-Newsprint Handling
Plain Dealer, Cleveland, OH

Garvey, C H ... (305) 674-9746
BU Chief
International News Agency, Miami Beach, FL

Garvey, Gary ... (415) 777-5700
ADV MGR-Co-op, San Francisco Newspaper Agency, San Francisco, CA

Garvey, John ... (212) 450-7000
VP/Manufacturing, React, Parade Publications Inc., New York, NY

Garvey, Richard C ... (413) 788-1000
ASSOC PUB, Union-News, Springfield, MA

Garwood, Marti ... (812) 663-3111
ADV MGR-CLASS
Greensburg Daily News, Greensburg, IN

Garwood, Susan ... (616) 582-6761
GM, Boyne Citizen, Boyne City, MI

Gary, Carl ... (817) 387-3811
PROD FRM-PR
Denton Record-Chronicle, Denton, TX

Gary, Richard N ... (415) 777-5700
SEC (SFNA), San Francisco Newspaper Agency, San Francisco, CA

Garza, Celina ... (719) 544-3520
ADV MGR-Co-op
Pueblo Chieftain, Pueblo, CO

Garza, Jose Luis B ... (210) 631-5628
PUB, ED, El Periodico USA, McAllen, TX

Garza, Leo ... (210) 225-7411
Cartoonist
San Antonio Express-News, San Antonio, TX

Garza, Malita Marie ... (312) 222-3232
Ethic Affairs Writer
Chicago Tribune, Chicago, IL

Garza, Oscar ... (213) 237-5000
Daily Calendar ED
Los Angeles Times, Los Angeles, CA

Garza, Sylvia ... (313) 222-6400
MGR-Benefits
Detroit Newspapers, Detroit, MI

Gasbarre, Ann ... (330) 264-1125
Family/Fashion ED, Women's ED
Daily Record, Wooster, OH

Gasho, Lawrence P ... (320) 255-8700
TREAS/CORP, St. Cloud Times, St. Cloud, MN, Gannett Co. Inc.

Gaskell, Michele ... (913) 742-2111
Lifestyle ED
Hiawatha Daily World, Hiawatha, KS

Gaskill, Allan ... (308) 697-3326
PUB, ED
Cambridge Clarion, Cambridge, NE

Gaskill, Robert L ... (312) 243-1300
GM, New World, Chicago, IL

Gaskins, Betty Lee ... (804) 435-1701
PUB, Rappahannock Record, Kilmarnock, VA

Gaskins, Frederick A ... (804) 435-1701
PUB, GM
Rappahannock Record, Kilmarnock, VA

Gaspard, Bill ... (619) 299-3131
Senior ED-Visuals
San Diego Union-Tribune, San Diego, CA

Gasper, Bill ... (913) 675-3321
PUB, ED, Hoxie Sentinel, Hoxie, KS

Gass, Bridget ... (716) 343-8000
ADV CNR-NTL, Daily News, Batavia, NY

Gassaway, Melinda ... (501) 623-7711
EX ED, COL, EPE
Sentinel-Record, Hot Springs, AR

Gasseling, Julienne ... (308) 832-2220
ED, Minden Courier, Minden, NE

Gast, Michael ... (541) 753-2641
ED, Corvallis Gazette-Times, Corvallis, OR

Gastler, Debra A ... (213) 237-3700
VP-Taxes
Times Mirror Co., Los Angeles, CA

Gaston, Dorothy A ... (913) 472-3103
PUB, Ellsworth Reporter, Ellsworth, KS

Gaston, Karl K ... (913) 456-7838
PUB, Wamego Times, Wamego, KS

Gaston, Robert B ... (360) 577-2500
SEC, MAN ED, Daily News, Longview, WA

Gaston, Robert C ... (304) 624-6411
CIRC MGR (Acting), Clarksburg Exponent/Telegram, Clarksburg, WV

Gately, Helen ... (201) 779-7500
ED, Passaic Citizen, Passaic, NJ

Gateman, Mel ... (519) 986-3151
ED, Markdale Standard, Markdale, ON

Gates, Brenda ... (918) 793-3841
PUB, Shidler Review, Shidler, OK

Gates Jr, Charles M ... (712) 328-1811
MAN ED
Daily Nonpareil, Council Bluffs, IA

Gates, Ernie ... (757) 247-4600
News Gathering ED
Daily Press, Newport News, VA

Gates, George ... (716) 849-3434
EDL Writer, Buffalo News, Buffalo, NY

Gates, Harley ... (617) 450-2000
CONT
Christian Science Monitor, Boston, MA

Gates, J Danielle ... (317) 482-4650
EDU ED, Lifestyle ED
Reporter, Lebanon, IN

Gates II, James K ... (717) 326-1551
ADV MGR-NTL
Williamsport Sun-Gazette, Williamsport, PA

Gates, John ... (910) 727-7211
EPE
Winston-Salem Journal, Winston-Salem, NC

Gates, Robert J ... (508) 374-0321
MAN ED, Haverhill Gazette, Haverhill, MA

Gatewood, Sondra ... (503) 843-4555
EX DIR/EDL DIR
Acme Features Syndicate, Sheridan, OR

Gathen, Richard ... (201) 428-6200
CIRC DIR, Daily Record, Parsippany, NJ

Gatherwright, Michael ... (716) 849-3434
PROD OPER FRM-MR
Buffalo News, Buffalo, NY

Gati, Bobbi ... (913) 738-3537
Sports ED, Beloit Daily Call, Beloit, KS

Gatlin, Tommi ... (360) 532-4000
Religion ED, Daily World, Aberdeen, WA

Gatling, Sarah ... (501) 793-2383
Food/Garden ED
Batesville Guard, Batesville, AR

Gatti, Carlo ... (514) 769-5711
PUB
La Vace Degli (Italo Canadesi), Montreal, QC

Gatti, Frank R ... (212) 556-1234
VP-Financial MGT
New York Times Co., New York, NY

Gatti, James ... (808) 525-8000
ED (Honolulu Advertiser)
Hawaii Newspaper Agency Inc., Honolulu, HI

Gatti, Vicky ... (514) 769-5711
ED
La Vace Degli (Italo Canadesi), Montreal, QC

Gatzak, Rev John P ... (860) 527-1175
MAN ED
Catholic Transcript, Hartford, CT

Gaudet, Belinda ... (602) 898-6500
VP, GM, Mesa Tribune, Mesa, AZ
Thomson Newspapers

Gauer, Lawrence ... (605) 285-6101
PUB, Bowdle Pioneer, Bowdle, SD

Gauer, Mary Lou ... (605) 285-6101
ED, Bowdle Pioneer, Bowdle, SD

Gauert, Mark ... (954) 356-4000
Sunshine Magazine ED
Sun-Sentinel, Fort Lauderdale, FL

Gauf, Michael ... (810) 443-1753
Self-Syndicator
Midwest Journal, Lathrup Village, MI

Gauger, Charles A ... (715) 538-4765
GM, Whitehall Times, Whitehall, WI

Gauger, Jeff ... (509) 548-5286
PUB, Leavenworth Echo, Leavenworth, WA

Gauger, Jim ... (609) 989-5454
EX Sports ED, Times, Trenton, NJ

Gauger, Liz ... (509) 548-5286
PUB, Leavenworth Echo, Leavenworth, WA

Gauger, Robert O ... (715) 538-4765
PUB, Whitehall Times, Whitehall, WI

Gaugh, Catherine ... (818) 962-8811
Features ED, Health/Medical ED
San Gabriel Valley Tribune, West Covina, CA
MediaNews Inc.

Gaul, Allan ... (914) 341-1100
News ED
Times Herald-Record, Middletown, NY

Gaul, Connie S ... (614) 773-2111
PSL/ADM SEC, Gazette, Chillicothe, OH

Gaul, Lou ... (609) 871-8000
Entertainment ED
Burlington County Times, Willingboro, NJ

Gaulden, Sid ... (803) 577-7111
State Government
Post and Courier, Charleston, SC

Gauldin, April ... (303) 820-1010
CIRC MGR-OPER, Denver Post, Denver, CO

Gaulding, Jerry ... (318) 462-0616
News ED
Beauregard Daily News, De Ridder, LA

Gaultney, Bruce ... (352) 867-4010
EX ED, Ocala Star-Banner, Ocala, FL

Gauntt, Tom ... (503) 786-1996
ED, Clackamas Review, Milwaukie, OR

Gaur, Krishna ... (219) 933-3200
EPE, Times, Munster, IN

Gauriglia, Carol ... (212) 779-9200
ADV PROD MGR
New York Law Journal, New York, NY

Gause, Kay ... (509) 248-1251
DIR-Human Resources
Yakima Herald-Republic, Yakima, WA

Gause, Scott ... (317) 598-6397
ADV DIR, Daily Ledger, Noblesville, IN

Gausnell, Eric ... (970) 925-2220
PROD MGR, Aspen Daily News, Aspen, CO

Gauthier, Daniel ... (819) 564-5450
PROD MGR, La Tribune, Sherbrooke, QC

Gauthier, Deborah E ... (508) 234-5686
ED
Blackstone Valley Tribune, Whitinsville, MA

Gauthier, Michel ... (613) 562-0111
Sports ED, Le Droit, Ottawa, ON

Gauthier, Michel ... (819) 752-6718
PUB, La Nouvelle, Victoriaville, QC

Gauthier, Tom ... (508) 458-7100
CIRC MGR-Alternate Delivery
Sun, Lowell, MA

Gauvin, Yvon ... (514) 375-4555
DIR-FIN/ADM
La Voix de l'Est, Granby, QC

Gaver, Jerry ... (402) 564-2741
PROD MGR
Columbus Telegram, Columbus, NE

Gaver, Joe ... (402) 564-2741
PROD ASST MGR
Columbus Telegram, Columbus, NE

Gavin, Kelley ... (308) 237-2152
Food/Women's ED, Religion ED
Kearney Hub, Kearney, NE

Gavin, Richard T ... (509) 682-2213
PUB, ED, Lake Chelan Mirror, Chelan, WA

Gawel, Maureen Saltzer ... (619) 241-7744
PUB, Daily Press, Victorville, CA

Gawlak, Sue ... (403) 460-5500
ED, St. Albert Gazette, St. Albert, AB

Gay, Charlie ... (360) 426-4412
MAN ED
Shelton-Mason County Journal, Shelton, WA

Gay, Cheryl ... (912) 272-5522
CIRC MGR, Courier Herald, Dublin, GA

Gay, Henry ... (360) 426-4412
PUB, ED
Shelton-Mason County Journal, Shelton, WA

Gay, William A ... (619) 337-3400
VP, GM, Imperial Valley Press, El Centro, CA

Gaydos, Robert ... (914) 341-1100
EPE, Times Herald-Record, Middletown, NY

Gaydou, Danny R ... (616) 222-5400
PRES/PUB
Grand Rapids Press, Grand Rapids, MI

Gayle, Sam ... (518) 792-3131
CIRC MGR-Electronic Edition, PROD MGR
Post-Star, Glens Falls, NY

Gayles, Yolonda ... (312) 783-3333
COL/Writer Seminars
Gayles, Yolonda & Associates, Chicago, IL

Gaylord II, Edward K ... (405) 475-3311
PRES, Daily Oklahoman, Oklahoma City, OK

Gaylord, Edward L ... (405) 475-3311
COB/PUB, ED
Daily Oklahoman, Oklahoma City, OK

Gaylord-Harper, Edith ... (405) 475-3311
SEC-Emerita
Daily Oklahoman, Oklahoma City, OK

Gaymon, Maxie ... (803) 317-6397
PROD FRM-PR
Florence Morning News, Florence, SC

Gaynor, Dan ... (905) 684-7251
PRES/PUB, Standard, St. Catharines, ON

Gazaway, Paul ... (415) 348-4321
CIRC ASST MGR
San Mateo County Times, San Mateo, CA

Gazy, Dick ... (619) 775-4200
ED, Indio Post, Indio, CA

Gearhart, Tom ... (419) 245-6000
Features/Entertainment ED
Blade, Toledo, OH

Geary, Carole ... (414) 449-4860
PUB, Milwaukee Courier, Milwaukee, WI

Geary, John ... (250) 785-5631
Sports ED, Alaska Highway Daily News, Fort St. John, BC

Geary, Joseph L ... (412) 465-5555
GM, Indiana Gazette, Indiana, PA

Geary, Marie ... (502) 582-4011
News ED-Night
Courier-Journal, Louisville, KY

Geary, Ray ... (419) 695-0015
ASST TREAS, BM
Delphos Daily Herald, Delphos, OH

Gebeloff, Rob ... (201) 646-4000
Technology ED, Record, Hackensack, NJ

Gebensleben, Rick ... (703) 276-3400
CIRC GM-Cleveland/Columbus
USA Today, Arlington, VA

Geberer, Ron ... (718) 624-0536
MAN ED, Daily Bulletin, Brooklyn, NY

Gebis, Wayne S ... (847) 427-4300
CIRC MGR-PROM
Daily Herald, Arlington Heights, IL

Geddes, Duane ... (604) 588-4313
PUB, Surrey/North Delta Leader, Surrey, BC

Geddes, John ... (212) 556-1234
BUS/FIN ED, New York Times, New York, NY

Geddings, Jerry ... (205) 221-2840
ADV DIR
Daily Mountain Eagle, Jasper, AL

Gee, Barbara ... (806) 762-8844
ADV MGR-CLASS TELEMKTG
Lubbock Avalanche-Journal, Lubbock, TX

Gee, John C ... (406) 563-5283
MAN ED, Anaconda Leader, Anaconda, MT

Gee, Michael ... (617) 426-3000
Sports COL, Boston Herald, Boston, MA

Geer, Eulalie A ... (701) 780-1100
TREAS/ASST SEC
Grand Forks Herald, Grand Forks, ND

Geer, Rhonda J ... (419) 281-0581
ADV DIR
Ashland Times-Gazette, Ashland, OH

Geere, Allen ... (250) 762-4445
ED, MAN ED-News
Daily Courier, Kelowna, BC

Geerlinks, Diane ... (519) 426-5710
ADV MGR, Simcoe Reformer, Simcoe, ON

Geers, George ... (603) 882-2741
ED, Telegraph, Nashua, NH

Geese, Terry ... (618) 242-0117
MAN ED, Register-News, Mount Vernon, IL

Geffry, Anita ... (701) 780-1100
CONT/CFO, Herald, Grand Forks, ND

Geggus, Jacqi ... (330) 364-5577
Sunday Weekend ED
Times Reporter, New Philadelphia, OH

Gehle, Janice ... (941) 953-7755
News RES MGR
Sarasota Herald-Tribune, Sarasota, FL

Gehring, Brian ... (605) 734-6360
ED, Chamberlain Register, Chamberlain, SD

Gehringer, John ... (610) 323-3000
ADV MGR-Sales, Mercury, Pottstown, PA

Gehrke, David ... (507) 874-3440
PUB, Alden Advance, Alden, MN

Copyright ©1997 by the Editor & Publisher Co.

83-Who's Where **Gia**

Gehrke, Jim .... (507) 874-3440
ED, Alden Advance, Alden, MN

Geibel, Paul L .... (607) 756-5665
PRES/TREAS
Cortland Standard, Cortland, NY

Geiger, Christy .... (616) 765-8511
PUB, ED, Freeport News, Freeport, MI

Geiger, David .... (508) 626-3800
ADV MGR-RT
Middlesex News, Framingham, MA

Geiger, Jennifer .... (207) 729-3311
ADV MGR, Times Record, Brunswick, ME

Geiger, Laura .... (706) 567-3446
PUB, ED, Pike County Journal and Reporter, Zebulon, GA

Geiger, Richard .... (415) 777-1111
Librarian
San Francisco Chronicle, San Francisco, CA

Geiger, Robert .... (281) 422-8302
Sports ED, Baytown Sun, Baytown, TX

Geiger, Robert W .... (912) 888-9300
ADV DIR, Albany Herald, Albany, GA

Geiger, Ron .... (616) 765-8511
PUB, ED, Freeport News, Freeport, MI

Geiger, Walter B .... (912) 836-3195
PUB, ED, Georgia Post, Roberta, GA

Geiger Jr, Walter B .... (770) 358-0754
PUB, ED
Barnesville Herald-Gazette, Barnesville, GA

Geigle, Waynette .... (605) 889-2320
ED, Prairie Pioneer, Pollock, SD

Geinger, Viola .... (561) 820-4100
EDU ED
Palm Beach Post, West Palm Beach, FL

Geis, Larry .... (419) 245-6000
PROD SUPT-Maintenance, Blade, Toledo, OH

Geise, George .... (406) 791-1444
Sports ED
Great Falls Tribune, Great Falls, MT

Geiser, Dan .... (319) 398-8211
Sunday ED, Gazette, Cedar Rapids, IA

Geisinger, Pam .... (360) 694-3391
Wire ED, Columbian, Vancouver, WA

Geisler, Jennie .... (216) 232-4055
ED, News Leader, Bedford, OH

Geiss, Mike .... (308) 382-1000
CIRC MGR
Grand Island Independent, Grand Island, NE

Geist, Linda .... (573) 735-4538
PUB, ED, Monroe City News, Monroe, MO

Geist, Richard .... (419) 586-2371
City ED/Wire ED
Daily Standard, Celina, OH

Gelb, Adele .... (330) 452-6444
GM, Stark Jewish News, Canton, OH

Gelestia, Judy .... (614) 283-4711
ADV DIR, Herald-Star, Steubenville, OH

Gelfand, Larry .... (212) 679-1850
PUB, Upper West Side Resident, New York City, NY

Gelfand, Lou .... (612) 673-4000
Reader Representative
Star Tribune, Minneapolis, MN

Gelhausen, Marvin .... (304) 265-3333
ED, Mountain Statesman, Grafton, WV

Gelik, Robert .... (717) 348-9100
City ED
Tribune & The Scranton Times, Scranton, PA

Gelineau, Most Rev Louis E .... (401) 272-1010
PUB, Providence Visitor, Providence, RI

Gellene, Denise .... (213) 237-5000
Consumer Affairs/ADV/MKTG
Los Angeles Times, Los Angeles, CA

Gelman, Bernard .... (718) 434-6050
Owner/ED
Gelman Feature Syndicate, Brooklyn, NY

Gels, James V .... (218) 723-5281
PRES, PUB
Duluth News-Tribune, Duluth, MN

Gelsen, Greg .... (507) 375-3161
ED, Plaindealer, St. James, MN

Gelzinis, Peter .... (617) 426-3000
News COL, Boston Herald, Boston, MA

Gemmer, Jane .... (219) 533-2151
PRES/TREAS, Goshen News, Goshen, IN

Gemmer, John .... (219) 533-2151
EVP/SEC, PUB, Goshen News, Goshen, IN

Gemondo, Kim .... (304) 592-1030
PUB, Shinnston News & Harrison County Journal, Shinnston, WV

Gemoules, Craig .... (218) 723-5281
MAN ED, Duluth News-Tribune, Duluth, MN

Gemperlein, Joyce .... (408) 920-5000
Food ED
San Jose Mercury News, San Jose, CA

Genco, Joseph .... (716) 693-1000
Sports ED
Tonawanda News, North Tonawanda, NY

Gendelman, George J .... (45) 633344
PRES, International Press Syndicate, Paris

Gendelman, Paul O .... (45) 633344
Chairman
International Press Syndicate, Paris,

Gendrom, Greg .... (412) 834-1151
Online MGR
Tribune-Review, Greensburg, PA

Generotti, A J .... (215) 855-8440
PROD DIR, Reporter, Landsdale, PA

Genest, Bertrand .... (418) 545-4474
EPE, Le Quotidien, Chicoutimi, QC

Gengenbach, Laurie .... (919) 638-8101
Life ED, Sun-Journal, New Bern, NC

Gengenbach, William .... (815) 259-2131
ED, Carroll County Review, Thomson, IL

Gengo, Lorraine .... (203) 406-2406
ED, Fairfield County Weekly, Stamford, CT

Geniec, Steven .... (317) 398-6631
SYS Administrator, PROD MGR-Pre Press
Shelbyville News, Shelbyville, IN

Genna, Chris .... (206) 872-6600
BUS/FIN ED
South County Journal, Kent, WA

Gennarelli, W Frank .... (508) 685-1000
CIRC DIR
Eagle-Tribune, North Andover, MA

Gensheimer, Al .... (318) 527-7075
PRES, News Leader Inc., Sulphur, LA

Gensheimer, E C .... (318) 239-3444
PRES, Leesville Daily Leader, Leesville, LA
News Leader Inc.

Gensmer, Bruce J .... (207) 791-6650
PRES, Portland Press Herald, Portland, ME

Gentele, Jeanette .... (803) 775-6331
PA, Item, Sumter, SC

Gentieu, Robert .... (609) 845-3300
BUS ED, SCI/Technology ED
Gloucester County Times, Woodbury, NJ

Gentile, Nick .... (314) 340-8000
PROD MGR-Northwest Plant
St. Louis Post-Dispatch, St. Louis, MO

Gentrup, Gene .... (816) 628-6010
MAN ED, Kearney Courier, Kearney, MO

Gentry, Bradley G .... (417) 967-2000
PUB, MAN ED, Houston Herald, Houston, MO

Gentry, Charles E .... (972) 875-3801
PRES, PUB/GM, ED, BUS ED
Ennis Daily News, Ennis, TX

Gentry II, Charles E .... (972) 875-3801
VP, Ennis Daily News, Ennis, TX

Gentry, Dale .... (423) 475-2081
PUB, ED, Jefferson Standard Banner, Jefferson City, TN

Gentry, David .... (608) 356-4808
PUB, News-Republic/South Central Wisconsin News, Baraboo, WI

Gentry, Jeff .... (410) 398-3311
Sports ED, Cecil Whig, Elkton, MD

Gentry, Leah .... (312) 222-3232
ED-Web Edition
Chicago Tribune, Chicago, IL

Gentry, Mary Helen .... (972) 875-3801
SEC/TREAS, Lifestyle ED
Ennis Daily News, Ennis, TX

Gentry, Pam .... (972) 424-6565
DIR-MKTG, Plano Star Courier, Plano, TX

Gentry, Phil .... (423) 638-4181
PROD MGR-Quality, Sun, Greeneville, TN

Gentry, Robert .... (318) 256-3495
PUB, Sabine Index, Many, LA

Gentry, Roger N .... (972) 875-3801
ADV DIR, Ennis Daily News, Ennis, TX

Gentry, Sanford .... (812) 275-3355
PROD FRM-Electronic Pre Press
Times-Mail, Bedford, IN

Genung, Jack .... (908) 246-5500
Sports ED
Home News & Tribune, East Brunswick, NJ

Genung, Jeff .... (607) 334-3276
MAN ED, Evening Sun, Norwich, NY

Genung, Sharon .... (702) 788-6200
Religion ED
Reno Gazette-Journal, Reno, NV

Geoghan, Brian .... (717) 854-1575
Health/Medical ED
York Dispatch/York Sunday News, York, PA

Geonnotti, Tom .... (215) 855-8440
ADV DIR, Reporter, Landsdale, PA

George, Anthony .... (312) 573-3800
Sales MGR, CoverStory, Chicago, IL

George, Beverly .... (540) 465-5137
CIRC MGR
Northern Virginia Daily, Strasburg, VA

George, Cindy .... (330) 841-1600
ADV DIR-MKTG
Tribune Chronicle, Warren, OH

George, David C .... (602) 271-8000
PROD Unit MGR-PR (Mesa)
Phoenix Newspapers Inc., Phoenix, AZ

George, Gary .... (317) 462-5528
PROD DIR, Daily Reporter, Greenfield, IN

George, Geoffrey S .... (501) 378-3400
MGR-DP/Typeset, Online Contact
Arkansas Democrat-Gazette, Little Rock, AR

George, Gloria .... (301) 733-5131
EX ED, Morning Herald, Hagerstown, MD

George, Hunter .... (941) 687-7000
MAN ED, Ledger, Lakeland, FL

George, J P .... (416) 654-0431
PUB, Kerala Express, Toronto, ON

George, James .... (808) 525-8000
VP-Market Development
Hawaii Newspaper Agency Inc., Honolulu, HI

George, John N .... (412) 775-3200
PROD MGR-Control
Beaver County Times, Beaver, PA

George, Lenn .... (208) 342-1311
GM, Idaho Catholic Register, Boise, ID

George, Nancy .... (607) 798-1234
Library CNR
Press & Sun Bulletin, Binghamton, NY

George, Stephanie .... (212) 630-4000
Sr VP/Group PUB
Women's Wear Daily, New York, NY

George, Tom .... (304) 272-3433
PUB, ED, Wayne County News, Wayne, WV

George, V P .... (416) 654-0431
ED, Kerala Express, Toronto, ON

Georgette, David .... (914) 694-9300
ASST MAN ED-Sports, Reporter Dispatch, White Plains, NY, Gannett Co. Inc.

Georgia, Dave .... (419) 245-6000
ADV MGR-Ad SRV DEPT, Blade, Toledo, OH

Gephart, Glenda .... (607) 535-2711
ED
Watkins Review & Express, Watkins Glen, NY

Gerace, Steve .... (916) 926-5214
ED, Mount Shasta Herald, Mount Shasta, CA

Geracie, Bud .... (408) 920-5000
Sports COL, Mercury News, San Jose, CA

Geracimos, Ann .... (202) 636-3000
Fashion/Style ED
Washington Times, Washington, DC

Gerard, Gary .... (219) 267-3111
MAN ED, EPE, Times-Union, Warsaw, IN

Gerard, Steve .... (513) 721-2700
MGR-CR, Cincinnati Enquirer, Cincinnati, OH

Gerardi, Charles J .... (214) 977-8222
ADV DIR, Dallas Morning News, Dallas, TX

Gerber, Dale E .... (330) 264-1125
Comptroller, Dix Communications, Wooster, OH

Gerber, Dawn .... (717) 272-5611
ADV MGR-CLASS, Daily News, Lebanon, PA

Gerber, Kathy .... (516) 747-8282
ED, Syosset/Jericho Tribune, Mineola, NY

Gerber, Most Rev Eugene J ..... (316) 269-3965
PUB, Catholic Advance, Wichita, KS

Gerdauskas, Walter .... (203) 744-5100
PROD FRM-PR, News-Times, Danbury, CT

Gerdes, Carol .... (706) 324-2404
ED, Columbus Times, Columbus, GA

Gerdes, Dean .... (312) 222-3232
PROD MGR-OPER SRV
Chicago Tribune, Chicago, IL

Gerdes, Galen .... (512) 575-1451
DP MGR, Victoria Advocate, Victoria, TX

Gerdes, Helmet .... (706) 324-2404
MAN ED, Columbus Times, Columbus, GA

Gerdes, Jennifer .... (618) 656-4700
PROD DIR-Advertising Design SRV
Edwardsville Intelligencer, Edwardsville, IL

Gerdes, Jerry .... (517) 787-2300
ADV DIR, ADV MGR-NTL
Jackson Citizen Patriot, Jackson, MI

Gerding, Barry .... (604) 444-3451
ED, Burnaby Now, Burnaby, BC

Gerding, Phil .... (309) 426-2255
ED, Roseville Independent, Roseville, IL

Gerds, Warren .... (414) 435-4411
Films/Theater ED, Radio/ Television ED
Green Bay Press-Gazette, Green Bay, WI

Gereau, John .... (518) 873-6368
ED, Times of Ti, Ticonderoga, NY

Gerhart, Lori E .... (610) 371-5000
ADV MGR-CLASS
Reading Times/Eagle, Reading, PA

Geringer, Dan .... (215) 854-2000
COL-News
Philadelphia Daily News, Philadelphia, PA

Gerken, Don .... (605) 574-2538
ED, Pennington County Prevalier-News, Hill City, SD

Gerken, Robert .... (402) 444-1000
ADV MGR-Advertising Development
Omaha World-Herald, Omaha, NE

Gerkens Jr, Frank E .... (609) 779-7788
PUB, ED, Mount Laurel Progress Press, Maple Shade, NJ

Gerlach, Gary G .... (515) 232-2160
PRES, PUB, Daily Tribune, Ames, IA

Gerlach, Kendra .... (910) 592-8137
Lifestyle/Religion ED, Travel ED
Sampson Independent, Clinton, NC

Gerlach, Kingsley .... (520) 453-4237
ADV MGR, DIR-MKTG
Today's News-Herald, Lake Havasu City, AZ

Gerlach, Michele Cox .... (334) 368-2123
PUB, ED, Atmore Advance, Atmore, AL

Germain, Chuck .... (612) 222-5011
PROD MGR-Machine Shop
St. Paul Pioneer Press, St. Paul, MN

Germain, Jeanne D'Arc .... (514) 692-8552
GM
Le Soleil du St-Laurent, Chateauguay, QC

German, Glenn R .... (316) 364-5325
PUB, Coffey County Today, Burlington, KS

German, William .... (415) 777-1111
ED
San Francisco Chronicle, San Francisco, CA

Germann, George .... (814) 643-4040
BUS/FIN ED, COL
Daily News, Huntingdon, PA

Germond, Tom .... (407) 846-7600
MAN ED
Osceola News-Gazette, Kissimmee, FL

Gerner, John A .... (215) 257-6839
ED, Perkasie News-Herald, Perkasie, PA

Gerome, John .... (423) 756-1234
City Life ED
Chattanooga Times, Chattanooga, TN

Gerraughty, David R .... (713) 220-7171
NTL ED, Houston Chronicle, Houston, TX

Gerrie, Lonnie .... (217) 235-5656
PROD FRM-Press
Mattoon Journal-Gazette, Mattoon, IL

Gerry, Kristy .... (402) 475-4200
PROD MGR-COMP
Lincoln Journal Star, Lincoln, NE

Gersten, Alan .... (212) 837-7000
Senior Correspondent-NY, Journal of Commerce & Commercial, New York, NY

Gerstenslager, Dale E .... (540) 949-8213
PUB/GM, ED
News Virginian, Waynesboro, VA

Gerszewski, Matthew .... (701) 857-1900
News ED, Minot Daily News, Minot, ND

Gert, Beth .... (309) 274-2185
GM, ED
Illinois Valley Advertiser, Chillicothe, IL

Gertner, James J .... (716) 671-1533
PUB, ED, Webster Herald, Webster, NY

Gertz, Debbie .... (217) 223-5100
Farm ED, Quincy Herald-Whig, Quincy, IL

Gertzen, Ian .... (317) 664-5111
ASST City ED
Chronicle-Tribune, Marion, IN

Gervais, Leonard .... (514) 481-7510
ED, Monitor, Montreal, QC

Gervais, Marty .... (519) 255-5711
Books ED, Windsor Star, Windsor, ON

Gervais, Ron .... (713) 485-2785
PUB, Friendswood Journal, Friendswood, TX

Gerwin, Carol .... (617) 786-7000
EDU ED, Patriot Ledger, Quincy, MA

Gess, Joe .... (813) 259-7711
ADV MGR-GEN
Tampa Tribune and Times, Tampa, FL

Gett Jr, Samuel R .... (602) 977-8351
ASST GM, Daily News-Sun, Sun City, AZ

Gettelfinger, Most Rev Gerald .. (812) 424-5536
PUB, Message, Evansville, IN

Gettinger, Nancy Pierce .... (812) 268-6356
PRES, PUB, Sullivan Daily Times, Sullivan, IN

Gettinger, Tom P .... (812) 268-6356
TREAS, GM/MAN ED, PA
Sullivan Daily Times, Sullivan, IN

Gettner, Ken .... (402) 462-2131
ADV DIR, Hastings Tribune, Hastings, NE

Getts, Matt .... (219) 347-0400
Sports ED, News-Sun, Kendallville, IN

Getty, Lori .... (717) 784-2121
Graphics ED/Art DIR
Press Enterprise, Bloomsburg, PA

Getz, Dennis A .... (717) 291-8811
VP/SEC, Lancaster Intelligencer Journal/New Era/Sunday News, Lancaster, PA

Getzfred, Mark S .... (212) 837-7000
MAN ED, Journal of Commerce & Commercial, New York, NY

Getzloff, Mike .... (701) 228-2605
PUB, Bottineau Courant, Bottineau, ND

Getzug, Steve .... (818) 713-3000
Courts/Police ED
Daily News, Woodland Hills, CA

Gevalt, Geoff .... (330) 996-3000
ASST MAN ED-News
Akron Beacon Journal, Akron, OH

Geyer, Debby .... (419) 245-6000
CNR-NIE, Blade, Toledo, OH

Geyer, Linda .... (316) 375-2631
ED, Leoti Standard, Leoti, KS

Geyer, Melva .... (903) 455-4220
ED, EPE
Greenville Herald-Banner, Greenville, TX

Geyer, Thomas P .... (201) 428-6200
PUB, Daily Record, Parsippany, NJ

Ghianni, Suzanne .... (615) 893-5860
Arts/Books ED, Entertainment/Music ED, Fashion/Society ED, Features ED, Food ED, Home Furnishings ED
Daily News Journal, Murfreesboro, TN

Ghianni, Tim .... (615) 259-8800
INFO Services ED
Nashville Banner, Nashville, TN

Gholson, Nick .... (817) 767-8341
Sports ED, Wichita Falls Times Record News, Wichita Falls, TX

Giaco, Annette .... (302) 324-2500
PROD MGR-Pre Press
News Journal, Wilmington, DE

Gia Who's Where-84

Giago, Tim .... (605) 341-0011
PUB, Indian Country Today, Rapid City, SD
Giallombardo, Leslie .... (615) 259-8000
ADV VP/DIR, Tennessean, Nashville, TN
Giambalvo, Joe .... (561) 562-2315
PROD MGR-Press
Vero Beach Press-Journal, Vero Beach, FL
Giambelluca, Robert .... (513) 863-8200
CIRC DIR, Journal-News, Hamilton, OH
Giametta, Jim .... (903) 597-8111
EX ED, Tyler Morning Telegraph, Tyler, TX
Giampietro, Joe .... (330) 841-1600
Design ED, News ED
Tribune Chronicle, Warren, OH
Gianchetti, Marie .... (413) 562-4181
BM, Westfield Evening News, Westfield, MA
Gianelloni, Philip .... (504) 369-7153
PUB, Assumption Pioneer, Napoleonville, LA
Giangreco, Michael .... (707) 226-3711
PUB, Napa Valley Register, Napa, CA
Giannakos, George .... (216) 999-4500
MGR-Credit, Plain Dealer, Cleveland, OH
Giannamore, Paul .... (614) 283-4711
EPE, Herald-Star, Steubenville, OH
Giannnettino, Judy .... (505) 823-7777
MET ED
Albuquerque Journal, Albuquerque, NM
Giardino, Laurette .... (914) 227-7456
PUB, In-The-Life, Wappinger Falls, NY
Gibb, Robert W .... (306) 764-4276
PUB/GM, ADV MGR
Prince Albert Daily Herald, Prince Albert, SK
Gibb, Steve .... (306) 652-9200
ED, StarPhoenix, Saskatoon, SK
Gibbens, Mark .... (605) 394-8300
PROD FRM-MR, Journal, Rapid City, SD
Gibboney, Tom .... (415) 854-2626
PUB, Country Almanac, Menlo Park, CA
Gibbons, Eleanor .... (309) 346-1111
ADV DIR, ADV MGR-NTL
Pekin Daily Times, Pekin, IL
Gibbons, Gerald .... (708) 388-2425
ED, Oak Lawn Independent, Midlothian, IL
Gibbons, Jack .... (410) 332-6000
ASST MAN ED-Sports, Sun, Baltimore, MD
Gibbons, James .... (713) 220-7171
EDL Writer
Houston Chronicle, Houston, TX
Gibbons, James .... (913) 456-2602
GM, Wamego Smoke Signal, Wamego, KS
Gibbons, Jim .... (203) 789-5200
ADV MGR-NTL
New Haven Register, New Haven, CT
Gibbons, Kathy .... (616) 946-2000
Fashion ED, Section ED
Record-Eagle, Traverse City, MI
Gibbons, Martha .... (209) 532-7151
PROD MGR, Union Democrat, Sonora, CA
Gibbons, Patti C .... (615) 259-8000
DIR-Customer INFO Program
Tennessean, Nashville, TN
Gibbons, Paul .... (518) 454-5694
NTL ED, Times Union, Albany, NY
Gibbons, Rick .... (613) 739-7000
ASSOC ED, Ottawa Sun, Ottawa, ON
Gibbons, Sandy .... (415) 749-5400
CIRC Legal MGR
Recorder, San Francisco, CA
Gibbons, Terry .... (604) 395-2219
PUB, 100 Mile House Free Press, 100 Mile House, BC
Gibbs, Al .... (206) 597-8742
Maritime Reporter
News Tribune, Tacoma, WA
Gibbs, Cindy .... (517) 275-5100
MAN ED, Roscommon County Herald-News, Roscommon, MI
Gibbs, Connie .... (319) 588-5611
DIR-PROM, Telegraph Herald, Dubuque, IA
Gibbs, Darrell .... (812) 944-6481
PROD FRM-PR
Tribune/Ledger & Tribune, New Albany, IN
Gibbs, Joe .... (716) 849-3434
ASST MAN ED-Graphics/Photo
Buffalo News, Buffalo, NY
Gibbs, Larry .... (614) 363-1161
MAN ED, EPE
Delaware Gazette, Delaware, OH
Gibbs, Lawrence .... (405) 372-5000
MAN ED, News Press, Stillwater, OK
Giberson, Art .... (904) 438-5421
ED, Gosport, Pensacola, FL
Gibilaro, Pete .... (212) 455-4000
MGR-PROD & Shipping, MGR-Product & Shiping, North America Syndicate, King Features Syndicate Inc., New York, NY
Giblak, Rob .... (604) 949-6225
ED, North Island Gazette, Port Hardy, BC
Gibney, Charles W .... (201) 646-4000
Senior VP/CFO/TREAS
Record, Hackensack, NJ
Gibney, Juanita .... (604) 494-5406
PUB, Summerland Review, Summerland, BC
Gibon, Grant .... (414) 922-4600
CIRC MGR, Reporter, Fond du Lac, WI
Gibson, Alan B .... (606) 387-5144
PUB, ED, Clinton County News, Albany, KY
Gibson, Allan R .... (801) 623-0525
PUB, Times News, Nephi, UT
Gibson, Bob .... (406) 657-1200
ADTX MGR, PROD MGR
Billings Gazette, Billings, MT
Gibson, Charles .... (717) 829-7100
ADV MGR-NTL
Times Leader, Wilkes-Barre, PA
Gibson, Cindy .... (715) 926-4970
ED, Mondovi Herald-News, Mondovi, WI
Gibson, D E .... (605) 426-6471
PUB, Ipswich Tribune, Ipswich, SD
Gibson, David .... (202) 541-3250
Features ED
Catholic News Services, Washington, DC
Gibson, David .... (201) 646-4000
Religion COL, Record, Hackensack, NJ
Gibson, Dawn .... (618) 253-7146
CIRC DIR, Daily Register, Harrisburg, IL
Hollinger International Inc.
Gibson, Elise .... (413) 584-5000
Books/Films ED, Entertainment ED, Music ED, Women's ED
Daily Hampshire Gazette, Northampton, MA
Gibson, Ellen .... (954) 356-4000
ADV MGR-MKTG Services RT/NTL Zone
Sun-Sentinel, Fort Lauderdale, FL
Gibson, Frank .... (615) 259-8000
Regional ED-Day, Tennessean, Nashville, TN
Gibson, Fred E .... (513) 748-2550
PUB, Star Press, Springboro, OH
Gibson, Hugh .... (215) 735-8444
GM, Philadelphia City Paper, Philadelphia, PA
Gibson, J L (Skip) .... (360) 676-2600
PROD DIR, Herald, Bellingham, WA
Gibson, Jack .... (204) 476-2309
PUB, ED, Neepawa Press, Neepawa, MB
Gibson, Jaime .... (306) 697-2722
ED, Grenfell Sun, Grenfell, SK
Gibson, Jean .... (812) 283-6636
MGR-BUS
Evening News, Jeffersonville, IN
Gibson, Jeffrey .... (406) 496-5500
EPE, Montana Standard, Butte, MT
Gibson, Jim .... (250) 380-5211
COL, Times Colonist, Victoria, BC
Gibson, John .... (905) 526-3333
MAN ED, Spectator, Hamilton, ON
Gibson, Lorie .... (306) 398-4901
MAN ED
Highway 40 Courier, Cut Knife, SK
Gibson, Mariann C .... (801) 623-0525
ED, Times News, Nephi, UT
Gibson, Marx .... (815) 729-6161
GM, Herald-News, Joliet, IL
Gibson, Pat .... (713) 220-7171
ADV MGR-Sales
Houston Chronicle, Houston, TX
Gibson, Preston .... (212) 887-8550
ADV DIR
American Metal Market, New York, NY
Gibson, Robin .... (317) 747-5700
School ED, Star Press, Muncie, IN
Gibson, Shirley .... (616) 347-2544
ADV MGR-CLASS
Petoskey News-Review, Petoskey, MI
Gibson, Tena .... (605) 426-6471
ED, Ipswich Tribune, Ipswich, SD
Gibson, Thomas .... (618) 271-0468
ED
East St. Louis Monitor, East St. Louis, IL
Gibson, Will .... (403) 939-7443
ED, Morinville & District Gazette, Morinville, AB
Gibson, William .... (954) 356-4000
BU Chief-Washington
Sun-Sentinel, Fort Lauderdale, FL
Gice, Francis .... (601) 833-6961
ADV MGR-RT, Daily Leader, Brookhaven, MS
Giddens, Neil .... (813) 259-7711
CIRC MGR-ADM
Tampa Tribune and Times, Tampa, FL
Giddings, Charles .... (609) 272-7000
PROD MGR-Quality Control
Press of Atlantic City, Pleasantville, NJ
Gideon, Kevin .... (317) 584-4501
Sports ED, News-Gazette, Winchester, IN
Gidley, Mark .... (219) 461-8444
CIRC MGR-ADM
Fort Wayne Newspapers Inc., Fort Wayne, IN
Gidney, Norman .... (250) 380-5211
BUS/FIN Reporter
Times Colonist, Victoria, BC
Giedgaudas, Rev Francis .... (718) 827-1352
GM, Darbininkas, Brooklyn, NY
Gielczyk, Greg .... (616) 723-3592
Sports ED
Manistee News-Advocate, Manistee, MI
Gierber, Kathy .... (516) 747-8282
ED
Plainview/Old Bethpage Herald, Mineola, NY
Gierke, Jim .... (314) 486-5418
PUB, Advertiser-Courier, Hermann, MO
Giesbert, Franz Olivier .... (33-1) 4087-4245
EIC, Le Figaro, Levallois-Perret,
Giffin, Glenn .... (303) 820-1010
Music Critic, Denver Post, Denver, CO
Gifford, Boots .... (406) 265-6795
Sports ED, Havre Daily News, Havre, MT
Gifford, Mike .... (405) 382-1100
ADV MGR-RT
Seminole Producer, Seminole, OK
Gifford, Rich .... (515) 228-3211
ADV MGR
Charles City Press, Charles City, IA
Gifford, William E .... (706) 657-6182
PUB, ED
Dade County Sentinel, Trenton, GA
Gift, Laura .... (515) 993-4233
ED
Dallas County News & Roundup, Adel, IA
Giglio, Jan .... (954) 698-6501
GM, Jewish Journal Palm Beach South, Deerfield Beach, FL
Giglio, Sheri .... (617) 444-1706
ED
Westwood Suburban Press, Needham, MA
Giguere, Lee .... (860) 646-0500
ASSOC ED
Journal Inquirer, Manchester, CT
Giguere, Lisa .... (207) 784-5411
BUS/FIN ED, Sun-Journal, Lewiston, ME
Gilbert, Anne .... (305) 491-5368
PRES/Writer, Antique Detective Syndicate, Ft. Lauderdale, FL
Gilbert, Cecelia .... (573) 588-2133
PUB, ED, Shelbina Democrat, Shelbina, MO
Gilbert, Garry .... (810) 332-8181
MAN ED, Oakland Press, Pontiac, MI
Gilbert, Glenn .... (216) 951-0000
MAN ED, News-Herald, Willoughby, OH
Gilbert, Guy .... (514) 467-1821
PUB, ED, L'Oeil Regional, Beloeil, QC
Gilbert, Jasmin .... (418) 686-3233
ADV DIR, DIR-MKTG, Le Soleil, Quebec, QC
Gilbert, June .... (601) 684-2421
Women's ED
Enterprise-Journal, McComb, MS
Gilbert, Karl D .... (610) 437-4982
PRES
Golf Publishing Syndicate, Allentown, PA
Gilbert, Keith .... (519) 534-1560
GM, ED, Wiarton Echo, Wiarton, ON
Gilbert, Kevin .... (301) 733-5131
Photo DEPT MGR
Morning Herald, Hagerstown, MD
Gilbert, Michael .... (206) 597-8742
Political ED, News Tribune, Tacoma, WA
Gilbert, Susan .... (704) 358-5000
DIR-Photography
Charlotte Observer, Charlotte, NC
Gilbert, Tisha .... (903) 794-3311
EDU ED, Texarkana Gazette, Texarkana, TX
Gilbert, Walt .... (573) 754-5566
PUB, ED
Louisiana Press-Journal, Louisiana, MO
Gilberti, Terry .... (516) 265-3500
MAN ED
Smithtown Messenger, Smithtown, NY
Gilbertson, Linda .... (904) 262-5076
ED, Mandarin News & St. Johns River Pilot, Mandarin, FL
Gilbreath, J A .... (915) 345-2442
PUB, ED, Sanderson Times, Sanderson, TX
Gilbreth, Mary M .... (803) 577-7111
ASST SEC
Evening Post Publishing Co., Charleston, SC
Gilchriest, Linda .... (713) 220-7171
ASST City ED
Houston Chronicle, Houston, TX
Gilchrist, David .... (208) 522-1800
ADV DIR, Post Register, Idaho Falls, ID
Gilchrist, Phyliss .... (561) 395-8300
MAN ED, News, Boca Raton, FL
Gilday, Jim .... (413) 774-7226
ED, Athol/Orange Town Crier, Greenfield, MA
Gildea, James .... (413) 774-7226
ED, Greenfield Town Crier, Greenfield, MA
Gildner Jr, Frank H .... (608) 882-5220
PUB, Evansville Review, Evansville, WI
Gildner, M Vivian .... (608) 882-5220
ED, Evansville Review, Evansville, WI
Giles, Bruce E .... (205) 345-0505
EX ED, Tuscaloosa News, Tuscaloosa, AL
Giles Jr, Charles E .... (757) 247-4600
ADV MGR-Commercial Printing
Daily Press, Newport News, VA
Giles, Jackie .... (715) 833-9200
CNR-NIE, Leader-Telegram, Eau Claire, WI
Giles, Joseph .... (216) 999-4500
PROD MGR-Printing
Plain Dealer, Cleveland, OH
Giles, Kevin .... (701) 223-2500
ED, Bismarck Tribune, Bismarck, ND
Giles, Robert H .... (313) 222-2300
PUB, ED, Detroit News, Detroit, MI
Giles, Tammi .... (405) 379-5411
ADV MGR
Holdenville Daily News, Holdenville, OK
Gilette, Christine .... (603) 436-1800
BUS ED
Portsmouth Herald, Portsmouth, NH
Gilger, Kristin .... (503) 399-6611
MAN ED, Statesman Journal, Salem, OR
Gilhooly, Brenda .... (914) 341-1100
Sunday ED
Times Herald-Record, Middletown, NY
Gilje, Shelby .... (206) 464-2111
Action Line/Troubleshooter ED
Seattle Times, Seattle, WA
Gilkey, John .... (812) 283-6636
ED, Clark County Journal, Jeffersonville, IN
Gill, Ann .... (815) 458-6246
ED, Braidwood Journal, Braidwood, IL
Gill, Bruce .... (414) 224-2000
Senior ED-Waukegka
Milwaukee Journal Sentinel, Milwaukee, WI
Gill, David .... (414) 733-4411
CIRC MGR-Home Delivery
Post-Crescent, Appleton, WI
Gill, Dee .... (601) 961-7000
BUS ED, Clarion-Ledger, Jackson, MS
Gill, Earle .... (416) 585-5000
EX ED, Globe and Mail (Canada's National Newspaper), Toronto, ON
Gill, James .... (504) 826-3279
COL, Times-Picayune, New Orleans, LA
Gill, James .... (423) 523-3131
Librarian
Knoxville News-Sentinel, Knoxville, TN
Gill, Jim .... (607) 936-4651
Photo ED, Leader, Corning, NY
Gill, John .... (508) 685-1000
Political ED
Eagle-Tribune, North Andover, MA
Gill, Joseph .... (914) 534-7771
PUB, Cornwall Local, Cornwall, NY
Gill, Joseph V .... (914) 446-4519
GM
News of the Highlands, Highland Falls, NY
Gill, Pam Wier .... (803) 577-7111
PA, Post and Courier, Charleston, SC
Gill, Peter .... (815) 459-4040
ED-Woodstock
Northwest Herald, Crystal Lake, IL
Gill, T M (Ted) .... (308) 452-3411
PUB, Ravenna News, Ravenna, NE
Gill, Tina .... (757) 446-2000
ADV MGR-MKTG
Virginian-Pilot, Norfolk, VA
Gillaspy, John A .... (812) 829-2255
PUB, ASST GM
Spencer Evening World, Spencer, IN
Gillaspy, John T .... (812) 876-2254
PUB, Journal, Elletsville, IN
Gillaspy, Philip .... (812) 829-2255
PROD MGR
Spencer Evening World, Spencer, IN
Gillaspy, Tom .... (812) 829-2255
DIR-Publication
Spencer Evening World, Spencer, IN
Gillen, Doug .... (516) 298-3200
GM, Suffolk Times, Mattituck, NY
Gillen, James .... (413) 788-1000
MET ED, Union-News, Springfield, MA
Gillentine, Cathy .... (409) 945-3441
Amusements ED, EDU/Fashion ED, Food/Garden ED, Society/Women's ED, Teen-Age/Youth ED, Texas City Sun, Texas City, TX
Gillenwater, Kelso .... (206) 597-8742
PUB/PRES, News Tribune, Tacoma, WA
Giller, Susan .... (619) 337-3400
ASST SEC, MAN ED, EDL Writer
Imperial Valley Press, El Centro, CA
Gilles, Hache .... (506) 727-4444
ADV MGR, L'Acadie Nouvelle, Caraquet, NB
Gillespie, Ben .... (806) 675-2881
PUB, ED, Crosby County News & Chronicle, Crosbyton, TX
Gillespie, Don .... (219) 726-8141
ADV MGR-RT
Commercial Review, Portland, IN
Gillespie, Doug .... (419) 281-0581
PROD FRM-Press
Ashland Times-Gazette, Ashland, OH
Gillespie, Jack .... (541) 327-2241
PUB, ED, Jefferson Review, Jefferson, OR
Gillespie, Johanne .... (506) 473-3083
GM, Cataracte Weekly, Grand Falls, NB
Gillespie, Mary Helen .... (617) 426-3000
ASST MAN ED-BUS
Boston Herald, Boston, MA
Gillespie, Mike .... (613) 829-9100
Photo DIR, Ottawa Citizen, Ottawa, ON
Gillespie, Russell C .... (717) 291-8811
ADV MGR-CLASS, Lancaster Intelligencer Journal/New Era/Sunday News, Lancaster, PA
Gillespie, Steve .... (573) 888-4505
ED, Daily Dunklin Democrat, Kennett, MO
Gillespie, Tony .... (906) 632-2235
CIRC MGR
Evening News, Sault Ste. Marie, MI

Copyright ©1997 by the Editor & Publisher Co.

85-Who's Where **Glo**

Gillespie, William .... (307) 362-3736
Sports ED
Daily Rocket-Miner, Rock Springs, WY
Gillett, Keith .... (618) 632-3643
MAN ED, Base News, O'Fallon, IL
Gillette, Mary Beth .... (319) 372-6421
PROD FRM-COMP
Daily Democrat, Fort Madison, IA
Gillette, P Joseph .... (630) 844-5844
EPE, Beacon-News, Aurora, IL
Gillette, Richard .... (937) 548-3151
MAN ED, Daily Advocate, Greenville, OH
Gillgannon, Michael .... (306) 665-9605
MAN ED, Western Producer Newsfeature Service, Saskatoon, SK
Gilliam, Chris .... (501) 234-5130
Sports ED, Banner-News, Magnolia, AR
Gilliam, Larry .... (419) 522-3311
MGR-CR, News Journal, Mansfield, OH
Gilliam, Rick .... (409) 945-3441
Sports ED, Texas City Sun, Texas City, TX
Gilligan, Amy .... (319) 588-5611
City ED, Telegraph Herald, Dubuque, IA
Gilligan, Thomas .... (910) 891-1234
CIRC DIR, Daily Record, Dunn, NC
Gilliland, Janet .... (316) 724-4426
MAN ED, Girard Press, Girard, KS
Gilliland, Pat .... (405) 475-3311
Religion ED
Daily Oklahoman, Oklahoma City, OK
Gilliland, Robert .... (520) 445-3333
CEO, PUB, Daily Courier, Prescott, AZ
Gilliland, Sharon K .... (519) 876-2809
GM, Watford Guide-Advocate, Watford, ON
Gilliland, Steve .... (319) 383-2200
PROD SUPV-MR
Quad-City Times, Davenport, IA
Gilliland, William A .... (717) 436-8206
PUB, Juniata Sentinel, Mifflintown, PA
Gillin, Beth .... (215) 854-2000
Features ED, Lifestyle ED
Philadelphia Inquirer, Philadelphia, PA
Gillis, Andy .... (902) 825-3457
ED, Mirror-Examiner, Middleton, NS
Gillis, D L .... (902) 863-4370
PUB, Casket, Antigonish, NS
Gillis, David .... (601) 636-4545
ADV MGR, MGR-MKTG/PROM
Vicksburg Post, Vicksburg, MS
Gillis, Janet .... (813) 782-1558
PUB, Zephyrhills News, Zephyrhills, FL
Gillis, Joe .... (613) 962-9171
Accountant, Intelligencer, Belleville, ON
Gillis, Lilah .... (605) 665-7811
EDU ED
Yankton Daily Press & Dakotan, Yankton, SD
Gillis, Sandy .... (803) 785-4293
ADV MGR-RT Sales
Island Packet, Hilton Head, SC
Gillispie, Jay .... (319) 754-8461
CIRC DIR, Hawk Eye, Burlington, IA
Gill PhD, Robert .... (616) 243-0082
PRES, National Features Syndicate, Grand Rapids, MI
Gilluly, Bob .... (406) 791-1444
Regional ED
Great Falls Tribune, Great Falls, MT
Gilman, Frances .... (316) 437-2433
PUB, Madison News, Madison, KS
Gilman, Leah .... (406) 447-4000
Cooking ED, Films/Theater ED, Music ED, Radio/Television ED
Helena Independent Record, Helena, MT
Gilman, Mary .... (515) 284-8000
MGR-CR, Des Moines Register, Des Moines, IA
Gilman, Richard H .... (212) 556-1234
Senior VP-OPER
New York Times, New York, NY
Gilman, Stephen .... (316) 437-2433
ED, Madison News, Madison, KS
Gilmartin, David .... (610) 272-2500
ED, Times Herald, Norristown, PA
Gilmer, Maribel .... (320) 275-2192
MAN ED
Enterprise & Dispatch, Dassel, MN
Gilmore, Guy L .... (503) 221-8327
CIRC DIR, Oregonian, Portland, OR
Gilpatrick, Kristin .... (608) 356-4808
Lifestyle ED, News-Republic/South Central Wisconsin News, Baraboo, WI
Gilreath, Tommy .... (601) 842-2611
CFO, Northeast Mississippi Daily Journal, Tupelo, MS
Gilroy, Alice Towery .... (806) 983-3737
PUB, ED, Floyd County Hesperian-Beacon, Floydada, TX
Gilroy, Herb .... (814) 870-1600
Human Resources
Morning News/Erie Daily Times, Erie, PA
Gilroy, Joe .... (717) 421-3000
PROD FRM-MR
Pocono Record, Stroudsburg, PA
Gilroy, Robert .... (306) 865-2771
PUB, Post-Review, Hudson Bay, SK
Gilroy, Robert F .... (204) 734-3858
PUB, Star & Times, Swan River, MB
Gilson, Debbie .... (816) 565-2401
ED, Hale Tribune, Hale, MO
Gilstrap, Kathleen .... (509) 663-5161
Food ED, Religion ED
Wenatchee World, Wenatchee, WA
Gilzow, James .... (501) 623-7711
City ED, Sentinel-Record, Hot Springs, AR
Ginapp, Patricia .... (515) 923-2684
ED, Garner Leader/Signal, Hancock, IA
Gindlesperger, Linda A .... (814) 634-8321
GM, New Republic, Meyersdale, PA
Ginest, Donya .... (512) 445-3500
DIR-MKTG, American-Statesman, Austin, TX
Gingles, Keenan C .... (318) 872-4120
PUB, Mansfield Enterprise, Mansfield, LA
Gingras, Claude .... (514) 285-7272
Music ED-Classical
La Presse, Montreal, QC
Ginnetti, Toni .... (312) 321-3000
Baseball Writer, College Sports
Chicago Sun-Times, Chicago, IL
Ginnings, Don .... (417) 745-6404
ED, Index, Hermitage, MO
Ginter, Barry .... (414) 457-7711
Outdoors ED
Sheboygan Press, Sheboygan, WI
Gintoft, Ethel M .... (414) 769-3500
PUB, ED, Catholic Herald, Milwaukee, WI
Gioioso, Joseph .... (201) 365-3000
EVP, DIR-OPER
North Jersey Herald & News, Passaic, NJ
Giombetti, Gary .... (218) 262-1011
Sports ED, Daily Tribune, Hibbing, MN
Giordano, Basilio .... (514) 253-2332
PUB, Il Cittadino Canadese, Montreal, QC
Giordano, Carl .... (310) 274-0848
MAN ED, Olshan's, Mort Sports Features, Los Angeles, CA
Giorella, Sibella .... (804) 649-6000
Fashion Writer
Richmond Times-Dispatch, Richmond, VA
Giorgianni, Anthony .... (860) 241-6200
Consumer Affairs Writer
Hartford Courant, Hartford, CT
Giosio, Joe .... (201) 784-0266
PUB, Suburbanite, Closter, NJ
Giovinelli, Barbara .... (603) 668-4321
ADV MGR-Ad SRV
Union Leader, Manchester, NH
Giovo, Jack .... (318) 824-3011
ED, Jennings Daily News, Jennings, LA
Gipp, Dave .... (406) 587-4491
DP MGR
Bozeman Daily Chronicle, Bozeman, MT
Gipson, Hoot .... (504) 383-1111
PROD Co-MGR-Creative SRV
Advocate, Baton Rouge, LA
Girard, Keith .... (410) 752-3849
ED, Daily Record, Baltimore, MD
Girard, P A .... (610) 259-4141
ED, MAN ED
Marcus Hook Press, Drexel Hill, PA
Girard, Philippe A .... (610) 259-4141
ED, Upper Darby Press, Drexel Hill, PA
Girard, Yvon .... (418) 545-4474
ADV MGR (Le Quotidien)
Le Quotidien, Chicoutimi, QC
Gire, Dann P .... (847) 427-4300
Films ED
Daily Herald, Arlington Heights, IL
Girion, Lisa Pope .... (818) 713-3000
Features ED
Daily News, Woodland Hills, CA
Giroux, Joan .... (819) 569-9526
PROD MGR-Graphics
Record, Sherbrooke, QC
Giroux, Raymond .... (418) 686-3233
EDL Writer, Le Soleil, Quebec, QC
Gish, Ben .... (606) 633-2252
MAN ED, Mountain Eagle, Whitesburg, KY
Gish, Patricia .... (606) 633-2252
GM, Mountain Eagle, Whitesburg, KY
Gish, Thomas .... (606) 633-2252
PUB, ED, Mountain Eagle, Whitesburg, KY
Gisler, Peggy .... (317) 844-1188
Owner/ED, Compass Syndicate, Carmel, IN
Gist, Francis .... (716) 882-9570
GM, Buffalo Criterion, Buffalo, NY
Gist, Karen Taylor .... (504) 826-3279
Entertainment/Amusements ED
Times-Picayune, New Orleans, LA
Gittens, James .... (717) 821-2091
EPE, Citizens' Voice, Wilkes-Barre, PA
Gittings, Larry .... (405) 255-5354
MAN ED, EDL Writer
Duncan Banner, Duncan, OK
Giuca, Linda .... (860) 241-6200
Food ED, Hartford Courant, Hartford, CT
Giuffrida, Tom .... (561) 820-4100
PUB, Palm Beach Post, West Palm Beach, FL, Cox Newspapers Inc.
Giuliani, Diane .... (218) 624-3349
GM, Proctor Journal, Proctor, MN
Gius, Gary .... (210) 216-4519
MAN ED
Wilson County News, Floresville, TX
Giusti, George .... (403) 468-0100
INFO SRV MGR
Edmonton Sun, Edmonton, AB
Givan, John .... (320) 269-2156
ED, American-News, Montevideo, MN
Given, Ed .... (304) 765-5193
PUB, Braxton Citizens' News, Sutton, WV
Given, Gordon .... (219) 461-8444
ADTX MGR
Fort Wayne Newspapers Inc., Fort Wayne, IN
Givens, David .... (314) 340-8000
PROD DIR
St. Louis Post-Dispatch, St. Louis, MO
Givens, Deborah .... (502) 526-4151
ED, Green River Republican & The Butler County Banner, Morgantown, KY
Givens, Murphy .... (512) 884-2011
EDL Writer, Corpus Christi Caller-Times, Corpus Christi, TX
Givens, Roger .... (502) 526-4151
PUB, Green River Republican & The Butler County Banner, Morgantown, KY
Givens, Ron .... (212) 210-2100
Arts/Entertainment ED
New York Daily News, New York, NY
Givens, Theresa M .... (520) 774-4545
ADV DIR, Arizona Daily Sun, Flagstaff, AZ
Givhan, Robin .... (202) 334-6000
Fashion ED (Style)
Washington Post, Washington, DC
Givler, Michael .... (717) 367-7152
ED
Elizabethtown Chronicle, Elizabethtown, PA
Glackin, Bill .... (916) 321-1000
Theater ED, Sacramento Bee, Sacramento, CA
Gladding, William J .... (519) 655-2341
PUB, ED, Gazette, Tavistock, ON
Gladsick, Merek .... (518) 943-2100
CIRC MGR, Daily Mail, Catskill, NY
Gladstone, David .... (210) 423-5511
PROD FRM-COMP
Valley Morning Star, Harlingen, TX
Gladu, Richard .... (401) 762-3000
CONT, Call, Woonsocket, RI
Glaeser, Paul F .... (415) 777-5700
CIRC MGR-Sales & Home Delivery, San Francisco Newspaper Agency, San Francisco, CA
Glain, Steven .... (212) 416-2000
Reporter-in-Charge (Seoul)
Wall Street Journal, New York, NY
Glancey, Paula .... (918) 786-9002
EDU Writer, News Reporter
Grove Daily News, Grove, OK
Glanville, Kathleen .... (503) 221-8327
Team Leader-East, Oregonian, Portland, OR
Glanzer, Rhonda .... (605) 729-2251
GM, Bridgewater Tribune, Bridgewater, SD
Glarrow, Jack .... (304) 263-8931
PUB, Journal, Martinsburg, WV
Glaser, Ken .... (913) 888-3800
MGR-Media & Member SRV, Family Features Editorial Services Inc., Shawnee Mission, KS
Glaser, Mark .... (818) 713-3000
PROD MGR-MR
Daily News, Woodland Hills, CA
Glasier, David S .... (216) 951-0000
Radio/Television Writer
News-Herald, Willoughby, OH
Glass, Andrew J .... (202) 331-0900
BU Chief, Cox Newspapers Washington Bureau, Washington, DC
Glass, Diane .... (515) 284-8000
VP-MKTG
Des Moines Register, Des Moines, IA
Glass, Donna .... (915) 468-3611
PUB, ED, Miles Messenger, Miles, TX
Glass, Nick .... (310) 540-5511
PROD Electronic Technician
Daily Breeze, Torrance, CA
Glasser, Selma .... (818) 769-4774
PRES/ED
Glasserfide Directory, Toluca Lake, CA
Glasson, Larry .... (915) 546-6100
PROD MGR-MR, El Paso Times, El Paso, TX
Glasson, Richard .... (909) 889-9666
PROD MGR-MR, Sun, San Bernardino, CA
Glatfelter, Phil .... (717) 637-3736
Sports ED, Evening Sun, Hanover, PA
Glatter, Crystal .... (308) 237-2152
CNR-MKTG/PROM
Kearney Hub, Kearney, NE
Glavanic, Charles D .... (519) 685-2292
ED, Trumpeter, London, ON
Glaves, Michelle .... (907) 283-7551
ADV DIR, Peninsula Clarion, Kenai, AK
Glaze, Ellen .... (816) 657-2222
ED, Drexel Star, Drexel, MO
Glazer, Charles .... (802) 222-5281
MAN ED, Journal Opinion, Bradford, VT
Glazier, Cynthia .... (616) 796-4831
Community ED
Big Rapids Pioneer, Big Rapids, MI
Gleason, Cindy .... (218) 843-2868
ED, Kittson County Enterprise, Hallock, MN
Gleason, Harold .... (405) 661-3525
PUB, Thomas Tribune, Thomas, OK
Gleason, Randy .... (309) 829-9411
EDU Writer, Pantagraph, Bloomington, IL
Gleason, Steve .... (309) 829-9411
Features ED, Radio/Television ED
Pantagraph, Bloomington, IL
Gleba, Rich .... (573) 642-7272
ED, News ED, Political/Government ED
Fulton Sun, Fulton, MO
Gledhill, Paul .... (303) 892-5000
VP-OPER, Rocky Mountain News, Denver, CO
Gleeson, John .... (204) 347-8402
ED, Selkirk Journal, Stonewall, MB
Gleim, James C .... (414) 733-4411
PUB/GM, Post-Crescent, Appleton, WI
Gleim, Jim .... (414) 722-4243
PUB, News-Record, Neenah, WI
Gleiss, William V .... (608) 269-3186
PUB, ED
Monroe County Democrat, Sparta, WI
Gleiter, Dan .... (717) 248-6741
Photo DEPT ED, Sentinel, Lewistown, PA
Glen, Eddie .... (918) 456-8833
Photographer
Tahlequah Daily Press, Tahlequah, OK
Glendening, Ron .... (330) 996-3000
DP MGR, Akron Beacon Journal, Akron, OH
Glenn, Anita .... (219) 235-6161
ADTX MGR
South Bend Tribune, South Bend, IN
Glenn, Barry .... (407) 420-5000
Arts/Entertainment ED
Orlando Sentinel, Orlando, FL
Glenn, Curt .... (319) 291-1400
Food/Garden ED, Radio/Television ED
Waterloo Courier, Waterloo, IA
Glenn, Dr Earl D .... (404) 284-4010
GM, Champion, Decatur, GA
Glenn, Jane .... (913) 823-6363
MGR-Human Resources
Salina Journal, Salina, KS
Glenn, Joline .... (505) 823-7777
Arts/Entertainment ED, Consumer News, COL-Restaurant
Albuquerque Tribune, Albuquerque, NM
Glenn, Shirley .... (208) 935-0838
PUB, Clearwater Progress, Kamiah, ID
Glenn, Steven L .... (308) 468-5393
PUB, Gibbon Reporter, Gibbon, NE
Glennie, Fred P .... (410) 268-5000
DIR-Technology, Capital, Annapolis, MD
Glennie, Rich .... (320) 864-5518
ED, McLeod County Chronicle, Glencoe, MN
Glenz, Val .... (412) 834-1151
Style ED, Tribune-Review, Greensburg, PA
Glessner, Debbie .... (913) 762-5000
PROD FRM-COMP
Daily Union, Junction City, KS
Glines, Sara .... (203) 789-5200
ED-Electronic Publishing
New Haven Register, New Haven, CT
Glines, Walt .... (408) 779-4106
ED, Morgan Hill Times, Morgan Hill, CA
Glink, Ilyce R .... (847) 835-3450
PUB
Real Estate Matters Syndicate, Glencoe, IL
Glinka, H R .... (516) 223-6514
PUB, Polish American World, Baldwin, NY
Glisch, John .... (407) 242-3500
SCI/Technology ED
Florida Today, Melbourne, FL
Glissmann, Robert .... (402) 444-1000
City ED-Night
Omaha World-Herald, Omaha, NE
Gloger, Peggy .... (770) 532-1234
ADV MGR-Creative, Times, Gainesville, GA
Gloman, Chas .... (717) 455-3636
ED-Day, Standard-Speaker, Hazleton, PA
Glonka, Mary Jo .... (313) 961-3949
OPER MGR
Detroit Legal News, Detroit, MI
Glosson, Edwin .... (210) 222-1721
PUB, ED
San Antonio Register, San Antonio, TX
Gloster, Steve .... (613) 732-3691
PUB/GM, Observer, Pembroke, ON
Glouner, Douglas R .... (717) 291-8811
DP MGR, Lancaster Intelligencer Journal/New Era/Sunday News, Lancaster, PA
Glover, Aaron .... (606) 678-8191
CIRC MGR
Commonwealth-Journal, Somerset, KY
Glover, Anne .... (813) 893-8111
ASST MAN ED-Copy Desk
St. Petersburg Times, St. Petersburg, FL
Glover, Barbara .... (913) 672-3228
ED, Oakley Graphic, Oakley, KS
Glover, L D .... (717) 888-9643
EPE, Evening Times, Sayre, PA
Glover, Laura .... (512) 575-1451
ADV MGR-NTL
Victoria Advocate, Victoria, TX

Glo Who's Where-86

Glover, Melanie .... (312) 649-5464
Administrative ASST
Crain News Service, Chicago, IL

Glover, Mindy .... (317) 932-2222
CIRC MGR, Republican, Rushville, IN

Glover, Paul .... (501) 793-2383
Outdoors/Sports ED
Batesville Guard, Batesville, AR

Glover, Paula .... (719) 687-3006
ED, Gold Rush, Woodland Park, CO

Glowinski, Judy .... (908) 722-8800
PROD MGR-Pre Press
Courier-News, Bridgewater, NJ

Glowner, Dwayne .... (205) 766-3434
PROD MGR-MR, Times Daily, Florence, AL

Gluvna Sr, Jos .... (216) 329-7000
News ED, Chronicle-Telegram, Elyria, OH

Glynn, Steve .... (215) 854-2000
News ED
Philadelphia Inquirer, Philadelphia, PA

Glynn, Tom .... (508) 230-7964
ED, Easton Journal, Sharon, MA

Gnau, Joanna .... (502) 582-4011
MGR-Public Affairs
Courier-Journal, Louisville, KY

Gnau, Thomas .... (937) 878-3993
Reporter, Fairborn Daily Herald, Fairborn, OH

Gnerre, Sam .... (310) 540-5511
Librarian, Daily Breeze, Torrance, CA

Gniewek, Ray .... (703) 276-3400
Senior ED, USA Today, Arlington, VA

Gnoss, Barbara .... (415) 435-2652
PUB, ED, Ark, Tiburon, CA

Goad, Gary .... (305) 350-2111
PROD MGR-Mechanical
Miami Herald, Miami, FL

Goasterland, Jim .... (303) 466-3636
GM, Enterprise Sentinel, Broomfield, CO

Gobeil, Pierre .... (514) 375-4555
PRES/ED, La Voix de l'Est, Granby, QC

Gobel, Tim .... (812) 283-6636
Farm/Agriculture ED
Evening News, Jeffersonville, IN

Goble, Ronald D .... (310) 540-5511
PROD DIR, Daily Breeze, Torrance, CA
Copley Press Inc.

Goch, Alan .... (954) 698-6501
MAN ED, Jewish Journal Palm Beach South, Deerfield Beach, FL

Gocken, Deborah .... (303) 892-5000
MET ED, Rocky Mountain News, Denver, CO

Gocking, JoAnn .... (217) 283-5111
ED, Chronicle, Hoopeston, IL

Goda, Terri .... (919) 446-5161
ADV MGR-NTL
Rocky Mount Telegram, Rocky Mount, NC

Godbold, James .... (541) 485-1234
MAN ED, Register-Guard, Eugene, OR

Godbold, Lisa .... (803) 626-8555
ADV MGR-CLASS
Sun News, Myrtle Beach, SC

Godbout, Jocelyn .... (819) 564-5450
ADV ASST MGR, La Tribune, Sherbrooke, QC

Goddard, Art .... (803) 329-4000
ADV MGR-RT, Herald, Rock Hill, SC

Goddard, Carol .... (604) 632-6144
ED, News Advertiser, Kitimat, BC

Goddard, Carol .... (847) 317-0500
ED, Highland Park News, Bannockburn, IL

Goddard, Joe .... (312) 321-3000
Baseball Writer
Chicago Sun-Times, Chicago, IL

Goddard, William T .... (614) 461-5000
ADV MGR-CLASS
Columbus Dispatch, Columbus, OH

Godden, Jean .... (206) 464-2111
COL, Seattle Times, Seattle, WA

Godfrey, Caroly .... (315) 824-2150
ED, Mid-York Weekly, Hamilton, NY

Godfrey, Clark .... (919) 419-6500
ADV MGR-RT, ADV MGR-NTL
Herald-Sun, Durham, NC

Godfrey Esq, G .... (212) 666-2300
Attorney, Basch, Buddy Feature Syndicate, New York, NY

Godfrey, Gary L .... (937) 473-2028
PUB, ED
Stillwater Valley Advertiser, Covington, OH

Godfrey, Paul V .... (416) 947-2222
PRES/CEO, Sun Media Corp., Toronto, ON

Godfrey, Peter .... (604) 624-6781
PUB, Daily News, Prince Rupert, BC

Godfrey, Robbie .... (805) 781-7800
ADV MGR-SRV
Telegram-Tribune, San Luis Obispo, CA

Godfrey, Ron .... (805) 781-7800
PROD DIR
Telegram-Tribune, San Luis Obispo, CA

Godmer, Michel .... (33-1) 4087-4245
Copyrights MGR
Le Figaro, Levallois-Perret,

Godoy, Gustavo .... (305) 442-2462
PUB, Vista - The Hispanic Magazine, Coral Gables, FL

Godoy, Dr Ramon .... (806) 371-7084
ED, El Mensajero, Amarillo, TX

Godoy, Virginia .... (305) 633-3341
Food ED, Diario Las Americas, Miami, FL

Godsey, Sharon .... (317) 529-1111
City ED, Courier-Times, New Castle, IN

Godwin, David .... (912) 265-8320
BUS ED, Religion ED
Brunswick News, Brunswick, GA

Godzyk, Robert .... (603) 668-4321
PROD FRM-COMP
Union Leader, Manchester, NH

Goebel, Julie .... (208) 232-4161
MGR-MKTG, ADTX MGR
Idaho State Journal, Pocatello, ID

Goemaat, Darrell .... (847) 888-7800
Photo ED, Courier-News, Elgin, IL

Goens, Mike .... (913) 682-0305
Sports ED
Leavenworth Times, Leavenworth, KS

Goering, Donald .... (316) 544-4321
PUB, Hugoton Hermes, Hugoton, KS

Goering, Pete .... (913) 295-1111
MAN ED-Sports
Topeka Capital-Journal, Topeka, KS

Goering, Sherill .... (316) 544-4321
ED, Hugoton Hermes, Hugoton, KS

Goerz, Gay .... (310) 829-6811
Society ED, Outlook, Santa Monica, CA

Goethals, Thomas .... (716) 232-7100
PROD FRM-Camera/Platemaking (Times-Union), Rochester Democrat and Chronicle; Rochester, NY Times-Union, Rochester, NY

Goette, Jo Ann .... (605) 886-6901
Wire ED
Watertown Public Opinion, Watertown, SD

Goetz, Bob .... (518) 561-2300
Sports ED, Press-Republican, Plattsburgh, NY

Goetz, Devon .... (805) 781-7800
ADV MGR-RT
Telegram-Tribune, San Luis Obispo, CA

Goetz, Diane .... (606) 283-0404
ED, Kenton County Recorder, Florence, KY

Goetz, Mary .... (916) 662-5421
News ED, Daily Democrat, Woodland, CA

Goetz, Tom .... (601) 833-6961
Sports ED, Daily Leader, Brookhaven, MS

Goff, Royce .... (919) 243-5151
PROD DIR, Wilson Daily Times, Wilson, NC

Goff, Susan .... (317) 459-3121
Entertainment/Amusements ED, Radio/Television ED, Kokomo Tribune, Kokomo, IN

Goff, Tom .... (208) 365-6066
MAN ED, Messenger-Index, Emmett, ID

Goffin, Janet .... (208) 733-0931
ADV MGR-Sales, Times-News, Twin Falls, ID

Gogerty, Terry .... (303) 659-1141
PUB, Brighton Standard Blade, Brighton, CO

Goggins, Gerard E .... (508) 757-6387
GM, ED
Catholic Free Press, Worcester, MA

Goin, Philip .... (412) 684-5200
PROD FRM-PR
Valley Independent, Monessen, PA

Goins, Tammie .... (423) 472-5041
Garden ED
Cleveland Daily Banner, Cleveland, TN

Gokie, Mike .... (308) 237-2152
News ED, Kearney Hub, Kearney, NE

Golas, Matt .... (215) 854-2000
New Jersey ED
Philadelphia Inquirer, Philadelphia, PA

Golbeck, Christopher L .... (815) 459-4040
ADV DIR, Northwest Herald, Crystal Lake, IL

Gold, Fran .... (908) 654-0077
ED, Jewish Horizon, Westfield, NJ

Goldberg, Bob .... (212) 944-7744
PRES
Feature Photo Service Inc., New York, NY

Goldberg, Elliot .... (609) 845-3300
NTL ED, Political/Government ED
Gloucester County Times, Woodbury, NJ

Goldberg, Gerald .... (716) 849-3434
ASST MAN ED-Sunrise
Buffalo News, Buffalo, NY

Goldberg, Rabbi Hiller .... (303) 861-2234
ED, Intermountain Jewish News, Denver, CO

Goldberg, Irwin M .... (702) 831-4666
MAN ED, North Lake Tahoe Bonanza, Incline Village, NV

Goldberg, James M .... (212) 456-7777
VP-Taxes, ABC Inc., New York, NY

Goldberg, Marc .... (607) 724-2360
PUB, Reporter, Vestal, NY

Goldberg, Miriam .... (303) 861-2234
PUB, Intermountain Jewish News, Denver, CO

Goldberg, Nan .... (201) 646-4000
Books ED, Record, Hackensack, NJ

Goldberg, Nick .... (516) 843-2020
Mid-East Correspondent
Newsday, Melville, NY

Goldberg, Randy S .... (916) 877-4413
PUB, Paradise Post, Paradise, CA

Goldberg, Sidney .... (212) 293-8500
Sr VP/GM-Syndication, United Media, United Feature Syndicate, Newspaper Enterprise Association, New York, NY

Goldberg, Stan .... (301) 662-1177
Sports ED
Frederick Post/News, Frederick, MD

Goldberger, Herman I .... (901) 763-2215
PUB, ED, Hebrew Watchman, Memphis, TN

Goldberger, Richard .... (801) 355-3336
MAN ED, FNA News, Salt Lake City, UT

Goldbloom, Michael .... (514) 987-2222
PUB, Gazette, Montreal, QC

Goldblum, Robert .... (212) 921-7822
MAN ED, Jewish Week, New York, NY

Golden, Arthur .... (619) 299-3131
Mexico/Latin America Writer
San Diego Union-Tribune, San Diego, CA

Golden, Dwayne .... (219) 235-6161
PROD MGR-Training
South Bend Tribune, South Bend, IN

Golden, Jill .... (814) 781-1596
ED, Daily Press, St. Marys, PA

Golden, Louis J .... (860) 241-6200
VP-New BUS, Hartford Courant, Hartford, CT

Golden, Michael .... (212) 556-1234
VP-OPER Development
New York Times Co., New York, NY

Golden, Russell J .... (330) 747-1471
PROD FRM-MR, Vindicator, Youngstown, OH

Golden, Stephen .... (212) 556-1234
VP-Forest Products
New York Times Co., New York, NY

Golden, Thomas R .... (402) 444-1000
ADV DIR, Omaha World-Herald, Omaha, NE

Goldfarb, Alexander .... (212) 387-0299
GM, Novoye Russkoye Slovo, New York, NY

Goldie, Diane .... (212) 210-2100
News ED-NTL
New York Daily News, New York, NY

Golding, Nancy J .... (207) 990-8000
ADV MGR-CLASS, Daily News, Bangor, ME

Goldman, Henry .... (215) 854-2000
New York BU
Philadelphia Inquirer, Philadelphia, PA

Goldman, John .... (213) 237-5000
New York BU
Los Angeles Times, Los Angeles, CA

Goldsbury, Timothy .... (212) 416-2000
PROD MGR (Highland IL)
Wall Street Journal, New York, NY

Goldsmith, Sarah Sue .... (504) 383-1111
Books ED, Advocate, Baton Rouge, LA

Goldsmith, Thomas .... (615) 259-8000
City ED, Tennessean, Nashville, TN

Goldstein, Elyce Small .... (800) 245-6536
Licensing DIR
Tribune Media Services Inc., Chicago, IL

Goldstein, Martha H .... (213) 237-3700
VP-CORP Communications
Times Mirror Co., Los Angeles, CA

Goldstein, Norm .... (212) 621-1821
DIR/APN Special Projects
Associated Press, AP Newsfeatures, New York, NY

Goldstein, Steve .... (215) 854-2000
Washington BU
Philadelphia Inquirer, Philadelphia, PA

Goldstrom III, Morton .... (914) 341-1100
DIR-Sales/MKTG
Times Herald-Record, Middletown, NY

Goldwire, Mark .... (912) 236-9511
PROD SUPV-Electronics
Savannah Morning News, Savannah, GA

Golem, Mary .... (519) 363-2414
GM, ED, Enterprise, Chesley, ON

Goley, Jay .... (941) 953-7755
MET ED
Sarasota Herald-Tribune, Sarasota, FL

Golias, Paul L .... (717) 821-2091
SEC, MAN ED
Citizens' Voice, Wilkes-Barre, PA

Golightly, Kelly .... (573) 683-3351
GM, Enterprise-Courier, Charleston, MO

Golin, Karen T .... (717) 255-8100
MGR-MKTG/PROM
Patriot-News, Harrisburg, PA

Golis, Peter .... (707) 546-2020
Books ED, EDL DIR, EPE
Press Democrat, Santa Rosa, CA

Goll, Bob .... (510) 935-2525
BUS ED
Contra Costa Times, Walnut Creek, CA

Gollop, Howard .... (216) 245-6901
Entertainment/Amusements ED
Morning Journal, Lorain, OH

Golnick, Linda .... (517) 348-6811
GM, Crawford County Avalanche, Grayling, MI

Golo, Jim .... (209) 943-6397
MAN ED, Record, Stockton, CA

Golomboski, Art .... (610) 272-2500
PROD FRM-PR
Times Herald, Norristown, PA

Golub, Mitch .... (954) 356-4000
GM-Interactive SRV
Sun-Sentinel, Fort Lauderdale, FL

Golum, Robert .... (800) 223-2154
Senior ED
Investor's Business Daily, Los Angeles, CA

Golzman, Ita .... (212) 455-4000
Sr. DIR-Domestic Licensing, North America Syndicate, King Features Syndicate, NY, NY

Gombossy, George .... (860) 241-6200
BUS ED, Hartford Courant, Hartford, CT

Gomes, Ruth .... (209) 582-0471
Films/Theater ED, Music ED, Radio/Television ED, Hanford Sentinel, Hanford, CA

Gomez, Carla .... (415) 334-2061
ED, El Latino, San Francisco, CA

Gomez, Carmen R .... (708) 484-1188
MAN ED, El Imparcial, Chicago, IL

Gomez, Kim .... (915) 570-0405
GM, El Editor Permian Basin, Midland, TX

Gomez, Mayra .... (714) 498-7227
ASSOC ED
Singer Media Corp., San Clemente, CA

Gomez, Nancy .... (715) 528-3276
PUB, ED, Florence Mining News, Florence, WI

Gomez, Philip .... (405) 247-3331
CIRC MGR, Daily News, Anadarko, OK

Gomez, Vitterbo .... (915) 546-6100
CIRC MGR-Transportation
El Paso Times, El Paso, TX

Gompers, Theadiane .... (304) 233-0100
ED-City, Entertainment ED, Intelligencer/Wheeling News-Register, Wheeling, WV

Gonnering, James .... (813) 259-7711
CONT, Tampa Tribune and Times, Tampa, FL

Gonsalves, Ann Marie .... (610) 838-2066
PUB, Valley Voice, Hellertown, PA

Gonsalves, Chris .... (508) 997-7411
MET ED, Standard Times, New Bedford, MA

Gonsalves, Susan .... (508) 992-1522
ED, Chronicle, South Dartmouth, MA

Gonser, James .... (808) 235-5881
MAN ED, Windward Sun Press, Kaneohe, HI

Gonyaw, Mike .... (802) 748-8121
ADV MGR
Caledonian-Record, St. Johnsbury, VT

Gonynor, John .... (508) 793-9100
CIRC MGR-Single Copy Sales
Telegram & Gazette, Worcester, MA

Gonyo, R M .... (414) 361-1515
PUB, Berlin Journal, Berlin, WI

Gonyo, T Y .... (414) 361-1515
GM, Berlin Journal, Berlin, WI

Gonzales, Bryan .... (970) 925-3414
Graphics ED/Art DIR
Aspen Times, Aspen, CO

Gonzales, Carlos .... (915) 263-7331
CIRC MGR
Big Spring Herald, Big Spring, TX

Gonzales, Carol .... (505) 863-6811
MGR-MKTG/PROM
Gallup Independent, Gallup, NM

Gonzales, Diana .... (409) 985-5541
Wire ED
Port Arthur News, Port Arthur, TX

Gonzales, Eloy .... (512) 445-3500
PROD MGR-COMP
Austin American-Statesman, Austin, TX

Gonzales, Harold .... (318) 783-3450
ED, Action Line/Hot Line ED, COL
Crowley Post-Signal, Crowley, LA

Gonzales, John .... (805) 736-2313
PROD SUPV-PR
Lompoc Record, Lompoc, CA

Gonzales, Juan .... (415) 252-5957
ED, El Tecolote, San Francisco, CA

Gonzales, Marcelino .... (210) 542-4301
ED-El Heraldo
El Heraldo de Brownsville, Brownsville, TX

Gonzales, Patricia E .... (619) 293-1818
VP/BM
Copley News Service, San Diego, CA

Gonzales, Randy .... (913) 628-1081
Sports ED, Hays Daily News, Hays, KS

Gonzales, Ray .... (330) 821-1200
PROD FRM-COMP
Alliance Review, Alliance, OH

Gonzales, Rudy .... (916) 541-3880
CIRC MGR
Tahoe Daily Tribune, South Lake Tahoe, CA

Gonzales, Scott P .... (515) 747-2297
PUB, ED
Guthrie Center Times, Guthrie Center, IA

Gonzalez, Amado .... (909) 487-2200
CIRC DIR, Hemet News, Hemet, CA

Gonzalez, Armando .... (305) 350-2111
PROD DIR-Engineering
Miami Herald, Miami, FL

Gonzalez, Bertha Alicia .... (619) 428-2277
PUB, Ahora Now, San Diego, CA

Gonzalez, Jacqueline .... (212) 265-8054
VP, Stevens, Gary Associates, New York, NY

Gonzalez, John .... (616) 222-5400
Music Critic-Popular
Grand Rapids Press, Grand Rapids, MI

Gonzalez, Linda .... (210) 686-4343
ADV MGR-CLASS, Monitor, McAllen, TX

Gonzalez, Luis .... (305) 633-3341
Home ED, Diario Las Americas, Miami, FL

87-Who's Where **Gou**

Gonzalez, Miriam .... (305) 530-8787
GM, El Nuevo Patria, Miami, FL

Gonzalez, Sam .... (209) 578-2000
DIR-MKTG, Modesto Bee, Modesto, CA

Gooch, F Wendall .... (812) 254-7322
PUB, Hoosier Express, Washington, IN

Gooch, Helen M .... (812) 723-2572
PUB, Paoli Republican, Paoli, IN

Good, Cathy .... (907) 895-5115
ED, Delta Wind, Delta Junction, AK

Good, Claude .... (219) 356-6700
ADV MGR, Herald-Press, Huntington, IN

Good, Dale .... (619) 749-1112
PUB, Valley Roadrunner, Valley Center, CA

Good, David .... (313) 222-2300
Deputy Features ED/Theater ED
Detroit News, Detroit, MI

Good, Duane E .... (717) 692-4737
ED, Upper Dauphin Sentinel, Millersburg, PA

Good, Joe .... (219) 653-2101
PUB, Observer, Kewanna, IN

Good, Karen .... (219) 653-2101
ED, Observer, Kewanna, IN

Good, Linda .... (419) 784-5441
DP MGR, Crescent-News, Defiance, OH

Good, Michael .... (330) 996-3000
DIR-Photography
Akron Beacon Journal, Akron, OH

Good IV, R Fletcher .... (910) 835-1513
PUB, Tribune, Elkin, NC

Good, Robin L .... (713) 780-7055
VP-NTL Sales
Print Marketing Concepts, Houston, TX

Goode Jr, A D .... (205) 325-2222
CIRC MGR-West Zone
Birmingham News, Birmingham, AL

Goode, Kenny .... (601) 837-8111
MAN ED, Southern Sentinel, Ripley, MS

Goode, Ovid .... (501) 798-2236
PUB, ED
South Arkansas Accent, Hampton, AR

Gooden, Ronda .... (513) 961-3331
MAN ED, Cincinnati Herald, Cincinnati, OH

Goodfellow, William .... (801) 237-2188
Music ED-Classical
Deseret News, Salt Lake City, UT

Goodge, Marcia .... (904) 964-6305
ED, Bradford County Telegraph, Starke, FL

Goodhines, Tom .... (315) 363-5100
Sports ED
Oneida Daily Dispatch, Oneida, NY

Gooding, Stace .... (701) 223-2500
Online MGR, PROD SUPV-Graphic Services
Bismarck Tribune, Bismarck, ND

Goodlett, Gary .... (415) 931-5778
PUB, San Francisco Metro Reporter Group, San Francisco, CA

Goodlin, Lori .... (717) 854-1575
EDU ED, Living/Lifestyle ED, MET ED
York Dispatch/York Sunday News, York, PA

Goodlove, Dawn .... (319) 398-8211
Family ED, Fashion/Home Furnishings ED, Growing Older ED, RE ED, Travel/Leisure ED
Gazette, Cedar Rapids, IA

Goodman, Allen .... (815) 987-1200
MGR-Data SYS
Rockford Register Star, Rockford, IL

Goodman, Ed .... (203) 574-3636
Deputy MAN ED, Waterbury Republican-American, Waterbury, CT

Goodman, Ellen .... (617) 929-2000
ASSOC ED, Boston Globe, Boston, MA

Goodman, Henry L .... (918) 825-3292
GM, Pryor Publishing Co., Pryor, OK

Goodman, Howard .... (215) 854-2000
EDU Writer-Higher
Philadelphia Inquirer, Philadelphia, PA

Goodman, Joey .... (405) 353-0620
Sports ED, Lawton Constitution, Lawton, OK

Goodman, Lisa .... (219) 461-8333
ADV DIR, Journal Gazette, Fort Wayne, IN

Goodman, Mike .... (919) 335-0841
EX ED, Automotive ED, EPE
Daily Advance, Elizabeth City, NC

Goodman, Wallace .... (912) 226-2400
PUB, Thomasville Times-Enterprise, Thomasville, GA

Goodrich, Charles F .... (508) 739-1300
PUB, North Shore Sunday, Danvers, MA

Goodrich, Dan .... (401) 762-3000
PUB, Call, Woonsocket, RI

Goodridge, Joel .... (573) 336-3711
PUB, Daily Guide, Waynesville, MO

Goodridge, Paula .... (603) 882-2741
ADV MGR-Inside Sales
Telegraph, Nashua, NH

Goodsell, Greg .... (888) 588-2272
MAN ED
El Popular-Fresno, Bakersfield, CA

Goodson, Bill .... (803) 259-3501
GM, People-Sentinel, Barnwell, SC

Goodson, Kelly .... (409) 265-7411
PROD Camera, Brazosport Facts, Clute, TX

Goodson, Ken .... (214) 977-8222
PROD MGR-Quality Assurance
Dallas Morning News, Dallas, TX

Goodson, Lori .... (919) 752-6166
Features ED, Daily Reflector, Greenville, NC

Goodson, Sabrina .... (305) 350-2111
ADV DIR-CLASS, Miami Herald, Miami, FL

Goodspeed, Peter .... (416) 367-2000
Foreign ED, Toronto Star, Toronto, ON

Goodstein, Les .... (212) 210-2100
EVP/ASSOC PUB
New York Daily News, New York, NY

Goodwin, Barbara .... (806) 257-3314
PUB, Earth Weekly News, Earth, TX

Goodwin, Carol .... (519) 894-2231
Labor Reporter, Record, Kitchener, ON

Goodwin, Clair .... (417) 623-3480
Books ED, EPE, Joplin Globe, Joplin, MO

Goodwin, Conn .... (405) 476-2525
PUB, Rush Springs Gazette, Rush Springs, OK

Goodwin, Danny .... (614) 461-5000
ASST MAN ED-Nights
Columbus Dispatch, Columbus, OH

Goodwin, Dave .... (305) 531-0071
Author/Owner
Goodwin, Dave & Associates, Surfside, FL

Goodwin, Donna .... (513) 381-2606
PUB, Everybody's News, Cincinnati, OH

Goodwin, Edward L .... (918) 582-7124
PUB, Oklahoma Eagle, Tulsa, OK

Goodwin, George .... (806) 227-2183
PUB, Sudan Beacon News, Sudan, TX

Goodwin, Glendora .... (812) 275-3355
Religion ED, Times-Mail, Bedford, IN

Goodwin, James O .... (918) 582-7124
PUB, Oklahoma Eagle, Tulsa, OK

Goodwin, Karen .... (405) 476-2525
PUB, ED
Rush Springs Gazette, Rush Springs, OK

Goodwin, Michael .... (212) 210-2100
EPE, New York Daily News, New York, NY

Goodwin, Pat .... (615) 552-1808
Human Resources
Leaf-Chronicle, Clarksville, TN

Goodwin, Sherry Posnick .... (415) 348-4321
Music ED
San Mateo County Times, San Mateo, CA

Goodwin, Tina .... (203) 789-5200
ADV MGR-RES
New Haven Register, New Haven, CT

Goodwin, Wanda .... (416) 947-2191
Photo Sales, Canada Wide Feature Service Ltd., Toronto, ON

Goodyear, Barry .... (208) 785-1100
CIRC DIR, Morning News, Blackfoot, ID

Goodyear, Bill .... (916) 527-2151
ED, Daily News, Red Bluff, CA

Goodyear, E D .... (614) 461-5000
ASST TREAS
Columbus Dispatch, Columbus, OH

Goodyear, Robert F .... (319) 465-3555
PUB, Monticello Express, Monticello, IA

Goold, Russ .... (712) 439-1075
ED, Sioux County Index-Reporter, Hull, IA

Goolsby, Nina B .... (601) 234-4331
ED, Oxford Eagle, Oxford, MS

Goossen, John D .... (308) 382-1000
PUB
Grand Island Independent, Grand Island, NE

Gopffarth, Sue .... (512) 575-1451
ADV MGR-CLASS
Victoria Advocate, Victoria, TX

Goralka, Martha .... (510) 757-2525
CIRC DIR, Ledger Dispatch, Antioch, CA

Gordan, Lee .... (330) 332-4601
PUB/GM, Salem News, Salem, OH

Gordanier, Tim .... (613) 544-5000
Sports ED, Online MGR
Kingston Whig-Standard, Kingston, ON

Gordobil, Gene Garay .... (209) 734-5821
City ED, Visalia Times-Delta, Visalia, CA

Gordon, Andy .... (613) 829-9100
PROD SUPT-Manufacturing-MR
Ottawa Citizen, Ottawa, ON

Gordon, Anne .... (216) 999-4500
Sunday Magazine ED
Plain Dealer, Cleveland, OH

Gordon, Barbara A .... (706) 724-6556
PUB, ED, Metro Courier, Augusta, GA

Gordon, Charles .... (613) 829-9100
Books ED, COL
Ottawa Citizen, Ottawa, ON

Gordon, Chuck .... (818) 892-9433
MAN ED
Science Features Service, North Hills, CA

Gordon, Chuck .... (704) 289-1541
Sports ED, Enquirer-Journal, Monroe, NC

Gordon, David M .... (507) 665-3332
PUB, News-Herald, Le Sueur, MN

Gordon, Don .... (502) 443-1771
EPE, Paducah Sun, Paducah, KY

Gordon, Donna .... (704) 358-5000
ADV MGR-Display/Co-op
Charlotte Observer, Charlotte, NC

Gordon, F Wallace .... (412) 775-3200
VP, PUB, Beaver County Times, Beaver, PA

Gordon, Frank .... (707) 226-3711
Farm ED, Wire ED
Napa Valley Register, Napa, CA

Gordon, Garry .... (613) 392-6501
PUB
Trentonian & Tri-County News, Trenton, ON

Gordon, Gerald H .... (216) 524-0830
PUB, Parma Sun Post, Cleveland, OH

Gordon, Gillian .... (610) 630-6200
ED, Colonial, King of Prussia, PA

Gordon, Gregory L .... (206) 863-8171
PUB, News Review, Sumner, WA

Gordon, Heather .... (916) 444-2355
PROD ED, Daily Recorder, Sacramento, CA

Gordon, James .... (540) 949-8213
Sports ED, News Virginian, Waynesboro, VA

Gordon, Jean .... (704) 245-6431
Features ED
Daily Courier, Forest City, NC

Gordon, Jim .... (410) 453-0092
ED, Times-Herald, Timonium, MD

Gordon, Joe E .... (937) 833-2545
PUB, Brookville Star, Brookville, OH

Gordon, Laine .... (713) 220-7171
MGR-Public Affairs
Houston Chronicle, Houston, TX

Gordon, Margaret H .... (419) 422-5151
SEC, Courier, Findlay, OH

Gordon, Nancy .... (309) 829-9411
Food ED, Pantagraph, Bloomington, IL

Gordon, Nancy .... (813) 259-7711
Commentary Writer
Tampa Tribune and Times, Tampa, FL

Gordon, Patricia .... (915) 337-4661
City ED, Odessa American, Odessa, TX

Gordon, Paul .... (309) 686-3000
Automotive ED, BUS ED, Farm/Agriculture ED, Journal Star, Peoria, IL

Gordon, Rich .... (305) 350-2111
Online Contact, Miami Herald, Miami, FL

Gordon, Rick .... (705) 745-4641
CIRC MGR, Examiner, Peterborough, ON
Hollinger Inc. (Sterling Newspapers)

Gordon, Robert J .... (705) 869-2860
PUB, MAN ED
Mid-North Monitor, Espanola, ON

Gordon, Robert L .... (419) 422-5151
VP, CONT, BM, Courier, Findlay, OH

Gordon, Ronni .... (413) 788-1000
Theater ED, Union-News, Springfield, MA

Gordon, Scott .... (816) 632-6543
GM, Citizen Observer, Cameron, MO

Gordon, Steve .... (603) 298-8711
Sunday ED, Valley News, White River Jct., VT

Goreham Jr, W J .... (815) 427-6734
PUB, St. Anne Record, Saint Anne, IL

Gorell, LeRoy .... (501) 253-9719
PUB, Eureka Springs Times-Echo, Eureka Springs, AR

Goretti, John .... (908) 859-4444
GM, Free Press, Phillipsburg, NJ

Gorgas, Jeanne .... (419) 522-3311
Wire ED, News Journal, Mansfield, OH

Gorham, Dan .... (208) 788-3444
GM, ED, Wood River Journal, Hailey, ID

Gorham, David L .... (212) 556-1234
Sr VP/Deputy COO
New York Times Co., New York, NY

Gorin, Walter C .... (502) 932-4381
PUB
Greensburg Record-Herald, Greensburg, KY

Gorlewski, Eugene L .... (860) 225-4601
Amusements ED, City ED, EDU ED
Herald, New Britain, CT

Gorley, Cindy .... (404) 526-5151
EDU ED
Atlanta Journal-Constitution, Atlanta, GA

Gorman, Duane C .... (320) 255-8700
MGR-SYS, DP MGR, ADTX MGR
St. Cloud Times, St. Cloud, MN

Gorman, Fred .... (604) 531-1711
PUB, Peace Arch News, White Rock, BC

Gorman, James .... (203) 574-3636
PROD FRM-MR, Waterbury Republican-American, Waterbury, CT

Gorman, James M .... (412) 263-1100
CIRC MGR-Transportation
Pittsburgh Post-Gazette, Pittsburgh, PA

Gorman, Jamie .... (970) 925-3414
Online Contact, Aspen Times, Aspen, CO

Gorman, John .... (602) 271-8000
CIRC MGR-Single Copy Sales
Phoenix Newspapers Inc., Phoenix, AZ

Gorman, Peter E .... (210) 829-9000
Sr VP/PRES & CEO-Harte-Hanks Shoppers
Harte-Hanks Communications Inc., San Antonio, TX

Gorman, Shirley .... (915) 573-5486
News ED, Snyder Daily News, Snyder, TX

Gorman, Ted C .... (515) 462-2101
PUB, Winterset Madisonian, Winterset, IA

Gorman, Tom .... (213) 237-5000
San Bernardino/Riverside BU
Los Angeles Times, Los Angeles, CA

Gormley, John .... (207) 791-6650
BUS ED, Portland Press Herald, Portland, ME

Gormus Jr, P A .... (804) 649-6000
Photo DEPT MGR
Richmond Times-Dispatch, Richmond, VA

Gorrell, Bob .... (804) 649-6000
Cartoonist
Richmond Times-Dispatch, Richmond, VA

Gorrell, Cathy .... (206) 872-6600
BM, South County Journal, Kent, WA

Gorrell, LeRoy .... (501) 423-6636
PUB, Star Progress, Berryville, AR

Gorsich, Mike .... (330) 833-2631
CIRC DIR, Independent, Massillon, OH

Gorson, Madeleine G .... (207) 828-8100
COB
Guy Gannett Communications, Portland, ME

Gorum, Kim .... (817) 757-5757
Sports ED, Waco Tribune-Herald, Waco, TX

Gosier, Elijah .... (813) 893-8111
COL, St. Petersburg Times, St. Petersburg, FL

Goslin, Jo Ann .... (301) 459-3131
EPE, Prince George's Journal, Lanham, MD

Gossard, Dale .... (419) 223-1010
PROD OPER SUPT-Facilities
Lima News, Lima, OH

Gosselin, Denis .... (312) 222-3232
Magazine ED, Sunday Magazine ED
Chicago Tribune, Chicago, IL

Gosselin, Joanne .... (806) 376-4488
ADV MGR-RT, Amarillo Daily News/Globe Times, Amarillo, TX

Gosselin, Richard .... (514) 375-4555
Court House
La Voix de l'Est, Granby, QC

Gosselin, Serge .... (418) 683-1573
Features ED, News ED, Political ED
Le Journal de Quebec, Ville Vanier, QC

Gosselin, Van A .... (954) 698-6501
MAN ED, Tamarac/North Lauderdale Forum, Deerfield Beach, FL

Gossen, Rich .... (403) 963-2291
ED, Stony Plain Reporter, Stony Plain, AB

Gossert, Shirley .... (717) 762-2151
ADV MGR-CLASS
Record Herald, Waynesboro, PA

Gossett, Dave .... (512) 884-2011
CIRC VP-Distribution, Corpus Christi Caller-Times, Corpus Christi, TX

Gossett, Gary .... (210) 658-7424
ED, Herald, Universal City, TX

Gossett, Wade R .... (513) 761-1188
Contributing Critic
Critic's Choice Reviews, Cincinnati, OH

Gossie, Jan .... (607) 734-5151
ADV MGR-RT, Star-Gazette, Elmira, NY

Gossie, Mike .... (607) 936-4651
MAN ED, Leader, Corning, NY

Gossman, Bishop F Joseph ...... (919) 821-9720
PUB, North Carolina Catholic, Raleigh, NC

Goth, Brian .... (614) 345-4053
News ED, Advocate, Newark, OH

Gothie, Frank .... (610) 622-8800
PUB
Delaware County Daily Times, Primos, PA

Gottbrath, Paul .... (606) 329-1717
City ED, Daily Independent, Ashland, KY

Gottesman, Jan .... (508) 835-4865
MAN ED, Banner, West Boylston, MA

Gottfredson, Stacie D .... (412) 465-5555
TREAS, Indiana Gazette, Indiana, PA

Gottfried, Jay .... (360) 676-2600
ADV MGR-CLASS
Bellingham Herald, Bellingham, WA

Gottlieb, Carole .... (212) 715-2100
PSL, USA Weekend, New York, NY

Gottlieb, Maria .... (212) 887-8550
Group CIRC Director
American Metal Market, New York, NY

Gottlieb, Martin .... (937) 225-2000
EDL Writer/COL
Dayton Daily News, Dayton, OH

Gottlieb, Melinda .... (718) 981-1234
Librarian
Staten Island Advance, Staten Island, NY

Gottlieb, Richard D .... (319) 383-2100
PRES/CEO
Lee Enterprises Inc., Davenport, IA

Gottschalk, Arthur .... (212) 837-7000
Energy Reporter, Journal of Commerce & Commercial, New York, NY

Gottschalk, Eleanor J .... (216) 356-0920
PUB, ED, Westlaker Times, Rocky River, OH

Gottschalk, John E .... (402) 444-1000
CEO, Omaha World-Herald Co., Omaha, NE

Gottschalk, V .... (913) 689-4339
PUB, ED, Logan Republican, Logan, KS

Gouch, John .... (864) 224-4321
MAN ED, Independent-Mail, Anderson, SC

Gouchie, Earl J .... (902) 667-5102
PRES, GM, Amherst Daily News, Amherst, NS

Gouchie, Jeff .... (902) 667-5102
VP, Amherst Daily News, Amherst, NS

Goudreau, Rosemary .... (757) 446-2000
Deputy MAN ED-Sports/Features
Virginian-Pilot, Norfolk, VA

Gou Who's Where-88

Gouger, Garry .... (307) 362-3736
ADV DIR, ADV MGR-RT
Daily Rocket-Miner, Rock Springs, WY
Gougherty, Dan .... (916) 444-2355
ADV Legal Sales, Daily Recorder, Sacramento, CA, Daily Journal Corp.
Gould, Carolyne .... (817) 594-7447
MAN ED, Democrat, Weatherford, TX
Gould, Dave .... (406) 791-1444
ADV DIR
Great Falls Tribune, Great Falls, MT
Gould, Harriet .... (617) 929-2000
DIR-Employee Relations
Boston Globe, Boston, MA
Gould, Herb .... (312) 321-3000
College Sports
Chicago Sun-Times, Chicago, IL
Gould, Marie .... (504) 391-3385
Owner/Author
Coyote Inc., New Orleans, LA
Gould, Robert .... (419) 223-1010
PROD OPER MGR-Distribution
Lima News, Lima, OH
Goulden, Joseph C .... (202) 364-4401
DIR-Media Analysis, AIM (Accuracy in Media) Report, Washington, DC
Gouldie, R .... (204) 727-2451
PROD FRM-COMP
Brandon Sun, Brandon, MB
Goulet, Russell .... (419) 674-4066
Photo DEPT MGR, Sports ED
Kenton Times, Kenton, OH
Goupil, Mario .... (819) 564-5450
Sports ED, La Tribune, Sherbrooke, QC
Gourley, J Leland .... (405) 755-3311
PUB, ED, Friday, Oklahoma City, OK
Gourley, Vicki .... (405) 755-3311
GM, Friday, Oklahoma City, OK
Gouvellis, Jim .... (941) 629-2855
EX ED, Sun Herald, Port Charlotte, FL
Gove, Ken C .... (419) 752-3854
PUB, ED
Greenwich Enterprise Review, Greenwich, OH
Gove, Scott M .... (419) 342-4276
PUB, Daily Globe, Shelby, OH
Gover, Raymond L .... (717) 255-8100
VP, PUB, Patriot-News, Harrisburg, PA
Govey, Charles W .... (330) 385-4545
PUB, ED, Review, East Liverpool, OH
Gowdy, Kerri .... (707) 441-0500
ADV MGR-NTL Representative
Times-Standard, Eureka, CA
Gowen, Bill .... (847) 427-4300
Music-Classical
Daily Herald, Arlington Heights, IL
Gowen, Samantha .... (804) 732-3456
BUS/FIN ED, City ED
Progress-Index, Petersburg, VA
Gower, Mike .... (219) 933-3200
DP MGR, Times, Munster, IN
Gower, Phil .... (618) 262-5144
ED
Daily Republican Register, Mount Carmel, IL
Gower, Ron .... (610) 377-2051
RE ED, SCI/Technology ED, Television/Film ED, Theater/Music ED
Times News, Lehighton, PA
Gowler, Vicki .... (218) 723-5281
VP, EX ED
Duluth News-Tribune, Duluth, MN
Goyan, David .... (515) 386-4161
GM, Bee, Jefferson, IA
Goyette, Regean .... (514) 435-6537
ED, Le Nord-Info, Sainte-Therese, QC
Graaf, Randy .... (715) 384-3131
PUB
Marshfield News-Herald, Marshfield, WI
Graaskamp, Charles .... (715) 833-9200
PRES, Leader-Telegram, Eau Claire, WI
Graaskamp, John .... (715) 833-9200
SEC/TREAS, CONT
Leader-Telegram, Eau Claire, WI
Graaskamp, Pieter .... (715) 833-9270
PUB, Country Today, Eau Claire, WI
Grabbe, Nick .... (413) 549-2000
ED, Amherst Bulletin, Amherst, MA
Graber, Kyp .... (509) 725-0101
PUB, Davenport Times, Davenport, WA
Graberek, Larry .... (713) 220-7171
MGR-RES
Houston Chronicle, Houston, TX
Grabowski, Chester .... (201) 473-5414
ED, Post Eagle, Clifton, NJ
Grabowski, Jerry .... (419) 245-6000
ADV DIR, Blade, Toledo, OH
Grabowski, Ken .... (616) 723-3592
ED, Manistee Observer, Manistee, MI
Grace, Buddy .... (817) 767-8341
PROD MGR-PR, Wichita Falls Times Record News, Wichita Falls, TX
Grace, Debbie .... (717) 854-1575
Religion ED
York Dispatch/York Sunday News, York, PA
Grace, Frances K .... (888) BIG RED H
Self-Syndicator
Big Red Hen Productions, New York, NY
Grace, Jo-Ann W .... (213) 628-4384
Co-PUB, Metropolitan News-Enterprise, Los Angeles, CA
Grace, Keith .... (815) 987-1200
Graphics ED, Register Star, Rockford, IL
Grace, Mary .... (405) 662-2221
MAN ED, Ringling Eagle, Ringling, OK
Grace, Melissa .... (405) 662-2221
PUB, ED, Ringling Eagle, Ringling, OK
Grace, Rodger M .... (213) 628-4384
Co-PUB, Metropolitan News-Enterprise, Los Angeles, CA
Gracey, Linda T .... (814) 946-7411
Features/Women's ED, Living/Lifestyle ED
Altoona Mirror, Altoona, PA
Gracida, Most Rev Rene H ...... (512) 289-1752
PUB
South Texas Catholic, Corpus Christi, TX
Graczyk, Mark .... (716) 343-8000
MAN ED, Religion ED, Teen-Age/Youth ED
Daily News, Batavia, NY
Grad, Peter .... (201) 646-4000
Computers ED, Record, Hackensack, NJ
Gradillas, John .... (520) 783-3333
DP MGR, Yuma Daily Sun, Yuma, AZ
Grady, C Daniel .... (509) 459-5000
ADV DIR, Spokesman-Review, Spokane, WA
Grady, James .... (704) 437-2161
CIRC MGR, News Herald, Morganton, NC
Grady, Marie .... (413) 788-1000
MET ED, Union-News, Springfield, MA
Grady, Robert .... (518) 561-2300
MAN ED, Press-Republican, Plattsburgh, NY
Grady, Sandy .... (215) 854-2000
COL-Washington
Philadelphia Daily News, Philadelphia, PA
Graf, Barbara .... (330) 821-1200
Living/Lifestyle ED, Women's ED
Alliance Review, Alliance, OH
Graf, Daniel .... (715) 423-7200
Sports ED
Daily Tribune, Wisconsin Rapids, WI
Graf, John .... (608) 582-2330
PUB, Galesville Republican, Galesville, WI
Graf, Randy .... (715) 423-7200
PUB, Daily Tribune, Wisconsin Rapids, WI
Graf, Vicky .... (419) 352-4611
ADV DIR
Sentinel-Tribune, Bowling Green, OH
Graff, David A .... (217) 223-5100
CONT/ASST TREAS
Quincy Newspapers Inc., Quincy, IL
Graff, Tim .... (509) 837-4500
GM, PROD MGR
Daily Sun News, Sunnyside, WA
Graff, William .... (412) 465-5555
ASST ED, Indiana Gazette, Indiana, PA
Graffam, Judith .... (909) 684-1200
Garden ED, Lifestyle ED
Press-Enterprise, Riverside, CA
Graggs, Tuseda .... (510) 758-8400
Religion ED, West County Times, Pinole, CA
Graglia, Ray F .... (414) 261-4949
ADV MGR-CLASS
Watertown Daily Times, Watertown, WI
Graham, Barbara .... (910) 739-4322
Lifestyle ED, Robesonian, Lumberton, NC
Graham, Barry .... (208) 783-1107
Sports ED
Shoshone News-Press, Kellogg, ID
Graham, Bob .... (604) 525-6397
PUB, Sunday News, Port Coquitlam, BC
Graham, Charles D .... (520) 573-4561
Theater Critic, Tucson Citizen, Tucson, AZ
Graham, Charlotte .... (601) 961-7000
Religion ED, Clarion-Ledger, Jackson, MS
Graham, Clarence .... (937) 783-2421
PUB, Star-Republican, Blanchester, OH
Graham, David .... (619) 299-3131
SCI Writer
San Diego Union-Tribune, San Diego, CA
Graham, Diane .... (515) 284-8000
MAN ED
Des Moines Register, Des Moines, IA
Graham, Donald .... (202) 334-6000
COB/CEO, PUB-Washington Post
Washington Post Co., Washington, DC
Graham, Dorothy .... (515) 981-0406
PUB, North Warren Town and County News, Norwalk, IA
Graham, Douglas E .... (609) 396-2200
Information Services DIR
Journal Register Co., Trenton, NJ
Graham, Frank .... (401) 351-8860
PUB, ED
Providence American, Providence, RI
Graham, Gary .... (316) 268-6000
ASST MAN ED, Wichita Eagle, Wichita, KS
Graham, Gene .... (803) 684-9903
ED, Yorkville Enquirer, York, SC
Graham, J Tom .... (303) 688-3128
PUB, Elbert County News, Kiowa, CO
Graham, Janice .... (407) 420-5000
ADTX CNR-SRV (Marketing)
Orlando Sentinel, Orlando, FL
Graham, Jean .... (516) 569-4000
ED, Long Island Graphic, Lawrence, NY
Graham, Jeanne .... (505) 396-2844
ED, Lovington Daily Leader, Lovington, NM
Graham, John .... (847) 427-4300
Online MGR
Daily Herald, Arlington Heights, IL
Graham, John G .... (719) 685-9201
PUB, ED
Pikes Peak Journal, Manitou Springs, CO
Graham, John R .... (919) 638-8101
PUB, Sun-Journal, New Bern, NC
Graham, Keith .... (540) 981-3100
DIR-Photo, Roanoke Times, Roanoke, VA
Graham, Larry .... (613) 732-3691
ADV MGR, Observer, Pembroke, ON
Graham, Larry .... (501) 378-3400
CIRC DIR
Arkansas Democrat-Gazette, Little Rock, AR
Graham, Li .... (410) 752-3849
ASSOC PUB, Daily Record, Baltimore, MD
Graham, Margaret .... (806) 273-5611
CIRC DIR, Borger News-Herald, Borger, TX
Graham, Mike .... (561) 461-2050
Sports ED, Tribune, Fort Pierce, FL
Graham, Mollie .... (908) 922-6000
Librarian, Asbury Park Press, Neptune, NJ
Graham, Pat .... (817) 778-4444
CIRC MGR, Daily Telegram, Temple, TX
Graham, Patricia .... (604) 732-2111
EPE, Vancouver Sun, Vancouver, BC
Graham, Patrick .... (205) 845-2550
ED, Times Journal, Fort Payne, AL
Graham, Paula Royce .... (718) 372-1920
PRES/EIC
Graham News Syndicate, Brooklyn, NY
Graham, Penny .... (604) 837-4667
PUB, Revelstoke Times-Review, Revelstoke, BC
Graham, Pete .... (712) 642-2791
MAN ED
Valley Times-News, Missouri Valley, IA
Graham, Phyllis .... (812) 268-6356
CIRC MGR, Daily Times, Sullivan, IN
Graham, Rob .... (908) 722-8800
PROD DIR, Courier-News, Bridgewater, NJ
Graham, Robert .... (415) 777-1111
Arts ED
San Francisco Chronicle, San Francisco, CA
Graham Jr, Robert A .... (215) 557-2300
VP-Finance/CFO
Legal Intelligencer, Philadelphia, PA
Graham, Robin .... (416) 869-4991
Sales, Toronto Star Syndicate, Toronto, ON
Graham, Sandy .... (405) 482-1221
CIRC MGR-Subscriber SRV
Altus Times, Altus, OK
Graham, Tim .... (510) 208-6300
ED, Oakland Tribune, Oakland, CA
Graham, Tom .... (410) 730-3620
ED, Columbia Flier, Columbia, MD
Graham, William .... (217) 465-6424
PROD FRM-Press
Paris Daily Beacon-News, Paris, IL
Graham, Worth .... (910) 739-4322
MGR-Accounting
Robesonian, Lumberton, NC
Grahl, Arnold .... (847) 317-0500
MAN ED, Deerfield Review, Bannockburn, IL
Grahmann, Most Rev Charles ... (214) 528-8792
PUB, Texas Catholic, Dallas, TX
Grahn, Jim .... (507) 625-4451
ADV MGR, Free Press, Mankato, MN
Grahnke, Lon .... (312) 321-3000
Television Critic
Chicago Sun-Times, Chicago, IL
Grainger, Steven .... (517) 652-3246
PUB, Frankenmuth News, Frankenmuth, MI
Grall, Dennis .... (906) 786-2021
Sports ED, Daily Press, Escanaba, MI
Graman, Kevin .... (509) 459-5000
News ED, Spokesman-Review, Spokane, WA
Gramblin, Garth .... (502) 821-6833
Farm/Agriculture ED
Messenger, Madisonville, KY
Gramer, Bob .... (810) 573-2755
Music ED, Avanti NewsFeatures, Warren, MI
Gramling, Sue .... (309) 764-4344
DP MGR, Dispatch, Moline, IL
Small Newspaper Group Inc.
Grams, Margaret Ann .... (619) 372-4747
ED, Trona Argonaut, Trona, CA
Granat, David J .... (312) 222-3237
VP/TREAS, Tribune Co., Chicago, IL
Granatino, John .... (401) 277-7000
DIR-Electronic Publishing, Online MGR
Providence Journal-Bulletin, Providence, RI
Grand, Jeannie .... (310) 540-5511
Design ED, Daily Breeze, Torrance, CA
Grande, Jackqueline .... (203) 729-2228
PROD SUPT
Naugatuck Daily News, Naugatuck, CT
Grande, Marcella .... (216) 933-5100
ED, Press, Avon Lake, OH
Grandinan, Dave .... (617) 444-1706
ED, Norfolk Suburban Press, Needham, MA
Grandson, Frank .... (218) 723-5281
PROD FRM-MR (Gen)
Duluth News-Tribune, Duluth, MN
Grandstaff, Scott .... (515) 832-4350
MGR-MKTG/PROM
Daily Freeman-Journal, Webster City, IA
Grandy, Ernest R .... (518) 374-4141
TREAS, Daily Gazette, Schenectady, NY
Grandy, Wayne .... (912) 985-4545
MAN ED, Observer, Moultrie, GA
Granfield, Linda .... (402) 375-2600
GM, Wayne Herald, Wayne, NE
Grangenois, Mireille .... (215) 854-2000
ADV DIR-RT
Philadelphia Inquirer, Philadelphia, PA
Granger, Helen .... (517) 725-5136
Fashion/Style ED, Living/Lifestyle ED, Women's ED, Argus-Press, Owosso, MI
Granier, Frank .... (208) 664-8176
BM, PA
Coeur d'Alene Press, Coeur d'Alene, ID
Graning, Stacy .... (601) 442-9101
MAN ED, Natchez Democrat, Natchez, MS
Gransbery, James .... (406) 657-1200
Farm/Agriculture ED, Political/Government ED, Billings Gazette, Billings, MT
Grant, Barbara .... (701) 642-8585
MAN ED, Daily News, Wahpeton, ND
Grant, Bruce .... (916) 321-1000
Automotive ED
Sacramento Bee, Sacramento, CA
Grant, Dennis .... (312) 222-3232
VP-Advertising, ADV DIR
Chicago Tribune, Chicago, IL
Grant, Faith K .... (603) 437-7000
GM, Derry News, Derry, NH
Grant, Gene H .... (916) 321-1000
ADV DIR, Sacramento Bee, Sacramento, CA
Grant, Glenn .... (803) 684-9903
GM, Yorkville Enquirer, York, SC
Grant, Hunter S .... (613) 342-4441
PRES, Co-PUB, GM, Brockville Recorder and Times, Brockville, ON
Grant, Jeff .... (712) 324-5347
MAN ED, N'West Iowa Review, Sheldon, IA
Grant, Joan .... (207) 563-5006
ED
Lincoln County Weekly, Damariscotta, ME
Grant, Kathleen .... (707) 546-2020
DIR-Human Resources
Press Democrat, Santa Rosa, CA
Grant, Lawson .... (804) 793-2311
PRES, Danville Register & Bee, Danville, VA
Grant, Lee .... (619) 299-3131
Arts ED
San Diego Union-Tribune, San Diego, CA
Grant, Newell C .... (701) 642-8585
PUB/ED, Daily News, Wahpeton, ND
Grant, Ron .... (318) 487-6397
ASST MAN ED
Alexandria Daily Town Talk, Alexandria, LA
Grant, Stephan S .... (954) 356-4000
MGR-Purchasing
Sun-Sentinel, Fort Lauderdale, FL
Grant, Tom .... (301) 948-3120
ED
Damascus Courier-Gazette, Gaithersburg, MD
Grant, Tracy .... (202) 334-6000
Washington BUS ED
Washington Post, Washington, DC
Grantham, Colin .... (519) 679-6666
PROD Electronic Pre Press Team Leader
London Free Press, London, ON
Grantham, Jennifer .... (205) 352-4775
PUB, ED, Herald, Hanceville, AL
Grantham, Michelle .... (519) 679-6666
MGR-Customer SRV
London Free Press, London, ON
Grantner, Mary .... (219) 862-2179
PUB, Wakarusa Tribune, Wakarusa, IN
Granville, Kari .... (516) 843-2020
Food ED, Newsday, Melville, NY
Granville, Kevin .... (201) 646-4000
Health ED, Record, Hackensack, NJ
Grass, Bill .... (306) 482-3252
PUB, ED, Gazette-Post News, Carnduff, SK
Grass, Lori .... (812) 332-4401
ADV DIR, ADV MGR-NTL
Herald-Times Inc, Bloomington, IN
Grass, Shirley .... (306) 482-3252
PUB, Gazette-Post News, Carnduff, SK
Grasso, Lou .... (516) 369-0800
MAN ED
Suffolk Life Newspapers, Riverhead, NY
Gratch, Kathleen O'Mara .... (315) 337-4000
MGR-PROM/MKTG, Daily Sentinel, Rome, NY
Grau, Maryann .... (212) 447-1450
Sales-Europe, Middle East, Near East & Africa, Los Angeles Times Syndicate International, New York, NY
Grau, Rawley .... (410) 235-3401
ED, Baltimore Alternative, Baltimore, MD

Copyright ©1997 by the Editor & Publisher Co.

89-Who's Where **Gre**

Grauel, James .... (419) 674-4066
ADV DIR, ADV MGR-GEN/PROM, ADV MGR-RT, Kenton Times, Kenton, OH
Grauel, Rusty .... (219) 235-6161
Librarian
South Bend Tribune, South Bend, IN
Grauerholz, Mary .... (508) 775-1200
Lifestyle ED, Cape Cod Times, Hyannis, MA
Graul, Mel .... (209) 734-5821
CIRC DIR, Visalia Times-Delta, Visalia, CA
Gannett Co. Inc.
Graustark, Barbara .... (212) 556-1234
Home Section ED
New York Times, New York, NY
Gravdahl, Michael .... (218) 732-9242
GM, Park Rapids Enterprise, Park Rapids, MN
Gravel, Pierre .... (514) 285-7272
EDL Writer, La Presse, Montreal, QC
Gravel, Thane .... (203) 226-8877
MAN ED, Westport Minuteman, Westport, CT
Gravel, Vaughn .... (717) 421-3000
PROD DIR, Pocono Record, Stroudsburg, PA
Gravelle, Marie .... (503) 399-6611
Farm/Agriculture ED
Statesman Journal, Salem, OR
Graves, Craig .... (610) 696-1775
CONT, Daily Local News, West Chester, PA
Graves, Dave .... (605) 692-6271
News ED, Brookings Register, Brookings, SD
Graves, Ed .... (904) 435-8500
CIRC DIR
Pensacola News Journal, Pensacola, FL
Graves, Gary .... (614) 773-2111
PROD MGR-Pre Press
Chillicothe Gazette, Chillicothe, OH
Graves, Harriette .... (915) 646-2541
Features ED
Brownwood Bulletin, Brownwood, TX
Graves, Louie .... (501) 845-2010
PUB, ED, Nashville News, Nashville, AR
Graves, Lyle .... (615) 259-8800
Info ED, Nashville Banner, Nashville, TN
Graves, Marcia .... (816) 932-6600
Sales Administrator
Universal Press Syndicate, Kansas City, MO
Graves, Randy .... (573) 785-1414
PROD FRM-PR
Daily American Republic, Poplar Bluff, MO
Graves, Susan .... (518) 439-4949
MAN ED, Spotlight, Delmar, NY
Graves, Tom .... (619) 634-1534
ED, Encinitas Sun, Carlsbad, CA
Graves, Valerie .... (404) 363-8484
ED, Henry Neighbor, Forest Park, GA
Gravois, John .... (817) 390-7400
Government Affairs ED
Fort Worth Star-Telegram, Fort Worth, TX
Gravunder, Wally .... (612) 439-3130
PROD FRM-COMP, PROD FRM-PR
Stillwater Evening Gazette, Stillwater, MN
Graxiola, Michael D .... (903) 785-8744
PUB, Paris News, Paris, TX
Gray, Andy .... (330) 841-1600
Entertainment/Amusements Reporter
Tribune Chronicle, Warren, OH
Gray, Barry .... (514) 987-2222
Photo ED, Gazette, Montreal, QC
Gray, Bill .... (913) 242-9200
ED, Ottawa Times, Ottawa, KS
Gray, Bob .... (909) 684-1200
ADV ASST DIR/MGR-Display
Press-Enterprise, Riverside, CA
Gray, Channing .... (401) 277-7000
Music Writer-Classical
Providence Journal-Bulletin, Providence, RI
Gray, DeWayne .... (330) 747-1471
PROD MGR, Vindicator, Youngstown, OH
Gray, Ellen .... (215) 854-2000
Television ED
Philadelphia Daily News, Philadelphia, PA
Gray, Frank .... (219) 461-8333
BUS ED, Journal Gazette, Fort Wayne, IN
Gray, Gary W .... (317) 633-1240
MGR-CR
Indianapolis Star/News, Indianapolis, IN
Gray, Glenn .... (606) 598-2319
PUB, Manchester Enterprise, Manchester, KY
Gray, Helen T .... (816) 234-4141
Religion ED
Kansas City Star, Kansas City, MO
Gray, J A .... (704) 586-2611
PUB, Sylva Herald & Ruralite, Sylva, NC
Gray, James R .... (817) 549-7800
PUB, Graham Leader, Graham, TX
Gray, Jean .... (970) 774-6118
PUB, ED, Haxtun Herald, Haxtun, CO
Gray, Jim .... (403) 786-2602
PUB, Freelancer, Mayerthorpe, AB
Gray, Jim .... (505) 662-4185
CIRC DIR
Los Alamos Monitor, Los Alamos, NM
Gray, Katherine W .... (803) 771-6161
ASSOC ED, State, Columbia, SC
Gray, Kathy .... (541) 296-2141
ASSOC ED
Dalles Daily Chronicle, The Dalles, OR
Gray, Larry .... (502) 582-4011
VP-Circulation, CIRC DIR
Courier-Journal, Louisville, KY
Gray, Lee .... (816) 353-5545
PUB, ED, Raytown Post, Raytown, MO
Gray, Linda .... (806) 273-5611
Home Furnishings/Lifestyles ED
Borger News-Herald, Borger, TX
Gray, Lloyd .... (601) 842-2611
ED, EDL Writer, Northeast Mississippi Daily Journal, Tupelo, MS
Gray, Mark .... (504) 850-1100
DP MGR, PROD DIR-OPER
Courier, Houma, LA
Gray, Matthew .... (609) 935-1500
MAN ED, EPE, Today's Sunbeam, Salem, NJ
Gray, O D .... (318) 487-6397
ADV MGR-CLASS
Alexandria Daily Town Talk, Alexandria, LA
Gray, Pete .... (919) 335-0841
PROD SUPT-PR
Daily Advance, Elizabeth City, NC
Gray, Pete .... (918) 335-8200
PROD FRM-Camera/Platemaking
Examiner-Enterprise, Bartlesville, OK
Gray, Rhonda .... (402) 444-1000
MKTG MGR-Sales PROM
Omaha World-Herald, Omaha, NE
Gray, Stephen T .... (313) 242-1100
PRES, ED, Evening News, Monroe, MI
Gray, Steve .... (704) 586-2611
GM, Sylva Herald & Ruralite, Sylva, NC
Gray, Steven F .... (815) 433-5595
PUB, ED, Town and Country, Seneca, IL
Gray, Thomas S .... (800) 223-2154
Senior ED
Investor's Business Daily, Los Angeles, CA
Gray, Walling E .... (419) 625-5500
ADV DIR, Sandusky Register, Sandusky, OH
Graybeal, Kathy .... (540) 669-2181
ASST DIR-MKTG, Herald-Courier Virginia Tennessean, Bristol, VA
Grayson, Barth .... (501) 724-0398
PUB, Bald Knob Banner, Bald Knob, AR
Grayson, Mark .... (606) 298-4612
PUB, ED, Martin County Sun, Inez, KY
Grayson, Mike .... (219) 722-5000
ADTX MGR, Pharos-Tribune, Logansport, IN
Graziano, Art .... (504) 345-2333
PROD MGR, Daily Star, Hammond, LA
Graziano, Pat .... (815) 842-1153
MAN ED, Daily Leader, Pontiac, IL
Graziano, Patti .... (216) 999-4500
Head Librarian, Online MGR
Plain Dealer, Cleveland, OH
Graziano, Raymond .... (416) 947-2222
PROD SUPV-Maintenance
Toronto Sun, Toronto, ON
Graziano, Rick .... (510) 935-2525
CONT, Contra Costa Times, Walnut Creek, CA
Graziano, Sallie .... (908) 782-4747
MAN ED
Hunterdon Observer, Flemington, NJ
Grazier, Jack .... (814) 870-1600
SCI/Technology ED
Morning News/Erie Daily Times, Erie, PA
Grear, Kathy .... (910) 762-1337
PUB, Challenger, Wilmington, NC
Greary, Carol .... (414) 449-4860
PUB, Milwaukee Courier, Milwaukee, WI
Greathead, Jamie S .... (717) 485-4513
PUB
Fulton County News, McConnellsburg, PA
Greaves, Harry .... (214) 977-8222
VP-FIN, Dallas Morning News, Dallas, TX
Grecco, Joseph A .... (814) 371-4200
SEC, ADTX MGR, Courier-Express/Tri-County Sunday, Du Bois, PA
Grech, Joe .... (313) 994-6989
ADV DIR, ADTX MGR
Ann Arbor News, Ann Arbor, MI
Greco, John .... (602) 468-6565
National DIR-Communications
Daily Racing Form, Phoenix, AZ
Greco, Pete .... (208) 377-6200
PROD MGR-SYS, Idaho Statesman, Boise, ID
Greeley, Benita P .... (203) 574-3636
VP/ASST TREAS/ASST SEC, Waterbury Republican-American, Waterbury, CT
Greeley, Mary .... (702) 383-0211
News ED
Las Vegas Review-Journal, Las Vegas, NV
Green, Alan .... (864) 582-4511
CONT, Herald-Journal, Spartanburg, SC
Green, Allen .... (208) 377-6200
CIRC MGR-Home Delivery
Idaho Statesman, Boise, ID
Green, Amanda .... (501) 337-7523
Lifestyle/Religion Ed
Malvern Daily Record, Malvern, AR
Green, Ann .... (864) 298-4100
Political ED, State ED
Greenville News, Greenville, SC
Green, Bartley C .... (415) 777-5700
VP-Advertising, San Francisco Newspaper Agency, San Francisco, CA
Green, Billy Joe .... (806) 669-2525
PROD FRM-PR, Pampa News, Pampa, TX
Green, Brian .... (815) 232-1171
Sports ED
Journal-Standard, Freeport, IL
Green, Chris .... (972) 937-3310
Sports ED, Daily Light, Waxahachie, TX
Green, Connie .... (404) 526-5151
Travel ED
Atlanta Journal-Constitution, Atlanta, GA
Green, Cooper .... (205) 532-4000
ADTX MGR/Online Contact
Huntsville Times, Huntsville, AL
Green, Sgt Darrell .... (301) 921-2800
ED, Beam, Gaithersburg, MD
Green, David .... (615) 259-8000
MAN ED-Days, Tennessean, Nashville, TN
Green, David E .... (201) 383-1500
MGR-OPER, New Jersey Herald, Newton, NJ
Green, David G .... (517) 458-6811
PUB, ED, Morenci Observer, Morenci, MI
Green, Denise .... (806) 762-8844
MGR-CR
Lubbock Avalanche-Journal, Lubbock, TX
Green, Dennis .... (801) 237-2031
Art DEPT MGR
Salt Lake Tribune, Salt Lake City, UT
Green, Don .... (512) 445-3500
PROD MGR, PROD MGR-Commercial Print
Austin American-Statesman, Austin, TX
Green, Eve .... (401) 274-2149
Talent MGR/Special Sales
Whitegate Features Syndicate, Providence, RI
Green, G David .... (618) 932-2146
PUB, Daily American, West Frankfort, IL
Green, Gerald .... (405) 323-5151
City ED, Clinton Daily News, Clinton, OK
Green, Harry .... (805) 781-7800
VP, Telegram-Tribune, San Luis Obispo, CA
Green Sr, Hurley L .... (773) 783-1040
PUB, ED
Chicago Independent Bulletin, Chicago, IL
Green, Jack .... (804) 644-9060
PUB, ED, Richmond Voice, Richmond, VA
Green, Jacqui .... (619) 789-1350
PUB, Ramona Sentinel, Ramona, CA
Green, James .... (916) 321-1000
MGR-Strategic Resources
Sacramento Bee, Sacramento, CA
Green, James R .... (606) 231-3100
DIR-Human Resources
Lexington Herald-Leader, Lexington, KY
Green, Jamie .... (704) 289-1541
BM, DP MGR, Enquirer-Journal, Monroe, NC
Green, Janice .... (561) 287-1550
PSL DIR, Stuart News, Stuart, FL
Green, Jeannie .... (410) 535-1214
GM, Recorder, Prince Frederick, MD
Green, Jeffrey .... (813) 259-7711
VP/MKTG
Tampa Tribune and Times, Tampa, FL
Green, Jim .... (502) 442-7380
ED, West Kentucky News, Paducah, KY
Green, Joan .... (316) 497-6448
ED, Record, Turon, KS
Green, Joe .... (812) 967-3176
PUB, Banner-Gazette, Pekin, IN
Green, John .... (805) 273-2700
ASSOC MAN ED, City ED
Antelope Valley Press, Palmdale, CA
Green, John C .... (914) 694-9300
VP/PRES-Advertising
Reporter Dispatch, White Plains, NY
Gannett Co. Inc.
Green, Johnny .... (903) 794-3311
Sports ED
Texarkana Gazette, Texarkana, TX
Green, Joy .... (912) 272-5522
ADV DIR, Courier Herald, Dublin, GA
Green, Judy .... (561) 395-8300
ADV MGR-CLASS/MKTG
News, Boca Raton, FL
Green, Judy .... (352) 867-4010
Books ED, Ocala Star-Banner, Ocala, FL
Green, Judy .... (904) 526-3614
MAN ED
Jackson County Floridan, Marianna, FL
Green, Karen .... (408) 920-5000
CIRC MGR-Accounting
San Jose Mercury News, San Jose, CA
Green, Karen .... (810) 573-2755
Arts & Crafts ED
Avanti NewsFeatures, Warren, MI
Green, Karen .... (405) 273-4200
Society/Women's ED
Shawnee News-Star, Shawnee, OK
Green, Keith .... (505) 257-4001
PUB, Ruidoso News, Ruidoso, NM
Green, Ken .... (312) 225-2400
City ED, Chicago Defender, Chicago, IL
Green, Kristy L .... (412) 543-1303
PUB/GM, Leader Times, Kittanning, PA
Green, Larry .... (312) 321-3000
EX ED, Chicago Sun-Times, Chicago, IL
Green, Larry .... (316) 497-6448
PUB, Record, Turon, KS
Green, Linda .... (360) 754-5400
City ED, Olympian, Olympia, WA
Green, Lisa .... (615) 259-8000
Database ED, Tennessean, Nashville, TN
Green, Lois .... (406) 279-3719
PUB, ED, Valierian, Valier, MT
Green, Lynn .... (608) 365-5521
ED, Stateline Shopping News, Beloit, WI
Green, Marcia H .... (401) 658-1234
ED
Cumberland Valley Breeze, Cumberland, RI
Green, Mark .... (941) 687-7000
ASST EPE, Ledger, Lakeland, FL
Green, Melinda .... (970) 882-4486
ED, Dolores Star, Dolores, CO
Green, Neville .... (813) 893-8111
MAN ED-Tampa
St. Petersburg Times, St. Petersburg, FL
Green, R A .... (519) 679-6666
PRES/PUB, London Free Press, London, ON
Green, Ray .... (904) 599-2100
PROD DIR
Tallahassee Democrat, Tallahassee, FL
Green, Rhonda .... (901) 642-1162
ADV MGR-CLASS
Paris Post-Intelligencer, Paris, TN
Green, Richard .... (812) 446-2216
News ED, Brazil Times, Brazil, IN
Green, Russ .... (816) 776-5454
Sports ED
Richmond Daily News, Richmond, MO
Green, Sam .... (970) 882-4486
PUB, Dolores Star, Dolores, CO
Green, Susan .... (561) 820-3800
Fashion ED
Palm Beach Daily News, Palm Beach, FL
Green, Susan .... (515) 623-5116
ED, Montezuma Republican, Montezuma, IA
Green, Tom .... (316) 268-6000
Nation/World ED, Wichita Eagle, Wichita, KS
Green, Walt .... (505) 746-3524
PRES/TREAS, Artesia Daily Press, Artesia, NM
Green, Wayne .... (918) 581-8300
MET ED, Tulsa World, Tulsa, OK
Green, Wayne .... (619) 789-1350
PUB, Ramona Sentinel, Ramona, CA
Green, William B .... (210) 728-2500
VP, PUB, Laredo Morning Times, Laredo, TX
Greenbank, Fern .... (907) 442-3213
ED, Arctic Sounder, Kotzebue, AK
Greenbaum, Kurt .... (954) 356-4000
ED-Interactive Media
Sun-Sentinel, Fort Lauderdale, FL
Greenberg, Bonnie .... (309) 686-3000
ASST MAN ED, Journal Star, Peoria, IL
Greenberg, Catherine .... (540) 981-3100
DIR-MKTG, Roanoke Times, Roanoke, VA
Greenberg, Elicia .... (201) 653-1000
DIR-MKTG
Jersey Journal, Jersey City, NJ
Greenberg, Howard .... (954) 356-4000
VP-Development
Sun-Sentinel, Fort Lauderdale, FL
Greenberg, Joel .... (213) 237-5000
SCI/Medicine ED
Los Angeles Times, Los Angeles, CA
Greenberg, Paul .... (501) 378-3400
COL, EPE
Arkansas Democrat-Gazette, Little Rock, AR
Greenberg, Steve .... (317) 633-1240
ASST MAN ED-Sports
Indianapolis Star/News, Indianapolis, IN
Greenberg, Steven .... (206) 448-8000
EDL Cartoonist
Seattle Post-Intelligencer, Seattle, WA
Greenberg, Terry .... (415) 348-4321
MAN ED
San Mateo County Times, San Mateo, CA
Greenberg, Terry .... (219) 294-1661
MAN ED, Elkhart Truth, Elkhart, IN
Greenberger, Sheldon L .... (954) 356-4000
VP-Advertising, ADV DIR
Sun-Sentinel, Fort Lauderdale, FL
Greene, Andrea .... (713) 220-7171
EDL Writer
Houston Chronicle, Houston, TX
Greene, Bob .... (312) 222-3232
COL, Chicago Tribune, Chicago, IL
Greene, Cynthia .... (205) 353-4612
Graphics ED/Art DIR
Decatur Daily, Decatur, AL
Greene, Donna .... (606) 248-1010
Automotive/Books ED, Farm/Food ED, Fashion ED, Teen-Age/Youth ED
Daily News, Middlesboro, KY
Greene, Donna .... (508) 388-2406
ED, Merrimack Valley Sunday, Amesbury, MA
Greene, Ginny .... (719) 632-5511
DIR-New Media
Gazette, Colorado Springs, CO

Copyright ©1997 by the Editor & Publisher Co.

Gre Who's Where-90

Greene, Glen .... (606) 498-2222
ED, Mt. Sterling Advocate, Mt. Sterling, KY
Greene, Hal .... (404) 526-5151
ADV MGR-RT/Territory Sales
Atlanta Journal-Constitution, Atlanta, GA
Greene, Harvey .... (904) 973-4141
ED, Madison County Carrier, Madison, FL
Greene, Jody .... (216) 647-3171
ED, Wellington Enterprise, Wellington, OH
Greene, Kelly .... (803) 648-2311
City ED, Aiken Standard, Aiken, SC
Greene, Leonard .... (617) 426-3000
News COL, Boston Herald, Boston, MA
Greene, Peggy .... (919) 747-3883
ED, Standard Laconic, Snow Hill, NC
Greene, Richard .... (817) 390-7400
ADV MGR-OPER
Fort Worth Star-Telegram, Fort Worth, TX
Greene, Richard .... (716) 232-7100
VP-Human Resources
Rochester Democrat and Chronicle; Rochester, NY Times-Union, Rochester, NY
Greene, Robert K .... (219) 235-6161
MGR-PROM
South Bend Tribune, South Bend, IN
Greene, Sarah L .... (903) 843-2503
PUB, ED, Gilmer Mirror, Gilmer, TX
Greene, Shirley .... (803) 577-7111
ASST MET ED
Post and Courier, Charleston, SC
Greene, Tommy .... (601) 842-2611
CIRC DIR, Northeast Mississippi Daily Journal, Tupelo, MS
Greene, Tommy .... (904) 973-4141
PUB, Madison County Carrier, Madison, FL
Greene, Tracy R .... (508) 676-8211
PUB, Herald News, Fall River, MA
Greene, William R .... (903) 843-2503
GM, Gilmer Mirror, Gilmer, TX
Greene-Comm, Deborah .... (561) 461-2050
MGR-EDU Services, Tribune, Fort Pierce, FL
Greeneberg, Weldon .... (815) 937-3300
CIRC DIR, Daily Journal, Kankakee, IL
Greener, Morris .... (416) 367-2000
CIRC MGR-Home Delivery
Toronto Star, Toronto, ON
Greenfield, David .... (304) 348-5140
ED/PUB
Charleston Daily Mail, Charleston, WV
Greenfield, Meg .... (202) 334-6000
EPE, Washington Post, Washington, DC
Greenhalgh, Kent .... (602) 271-8000
PROD Unit MGR-Platemaking (Deer Valley)
Phoenix Newspapers Inc., Phoenix, AZ
Greenhoe, Kurt .... (517) 368-0365
PUB, Camden Publications, Camden, MI
Greenia, Dennis .... (706) 549-9523
PUB, Flagpole Magazine, Athens, GA
Greening, Mike .... (541) 382-1811
PROD MGR-OPER, Bulletin, Bend, OR
Greenlee, Charles E .... (308) 367-4144
ED, Hi-Line Enterprise, Curtis, NE
Greenlee, Steve .... (207) 791-6650
City ED-Night
Portland Press Herald, Portland, ME
Greenman, John F .... (706) 324-5526
PRES, PUB
Columbus Ledger-Enquirer, Columbus, GA
Greenspun, Barbara .... (702) 385-3111
TREAS, PUB, Las Vegas Sun, Las Vegas, NV
Greenspun, Brian .... (702) 385-3111
PRES, ED, Las Vegas Sun, Las Vegas, NV
Greenspun, Daniel .... (702) 385-3111
VP, Las Vegas Sun, Las Vegas, NV
Greenstein, Bill .... (541) 776-4411
ADTX MGR, Mail Tribune, Medford, OR
Greenstein, Mike .... (315) 422-7011
ED, Syracuse New Times, Syracuse, NY
Greenup, Rhoda .... (701) 377-2626
PUB, ED
Burke County Tribune, Bowbells, ND
Greenwald, John .... (508) 458-7100
ASST MAN ED-Sunday, Sun, Lowell, MA
Greenway, H D S .... (617) 929-2000
EPE, Boston Globe, Boston, MA
Greenwell, Randy .... (812) 464-7614
Photo ED, Evansville Press, Evansville, IN
Greenwood, Alan .... (603) 882-2741
Sports ED, Telegraph, Nashua, NH
Greenwood, Donald .... (608) 588-2508
ED, Weekly Home News, Spring Green, WI
Greenwood, Emily .... (508) 626-3800
MGR-INFO SRV
Middlesex News, Framingham, MA
Greer, Angela .... (316) 331-3550
Fashion/Food ED, Home Furnishings ED/Librarian, Society/Women's ED, Independence Daily Reporter, Independence, KS
Greer, Bill .... (561) 820-4100
News ED
Palm Beach Post, West Palm Beach, FL
Greer, David .... (502) 769-2312
ED, News Enterprise, Elizabethtown, KY
Greer, Gregg .... (606) 231-3100
CIRC DIR
Lexington Herald-Leader, Lexington, KY
Greer, Jim .... (403) 934-3021
ED, Strathmore Standard, Strathmore, AB
Greer, Thomas H .... (216) 999-4500
VP/Senior ED, Plain Dealer, Cleveland, OH
Greer, Wayne .... (915) 652-3312
PUB, ED, McCamey News, McCamey, TX
Gref, Barbara .... (914) 341-1100
EDU Writer
Times Herald-Record, Middletown, NY
Greg, Greg .... (404) 526-5151
MGR-Advertising SRV
Atlanta Journal-Constitution, Atlanta, GA
Gregerson, Nancy .... (319) 462-3511
ED, Anamosa Journal-Eureka, Anamosa, IA
Gregg, Ann .... (408) 920-5000
DIR-MKTG
San Jose Mercury News, San Jose, CA
Gregg, Frances .... (512) 884-2011
ADV MGR-CLASS MKTG, Corpus Christi Caller-Times, Corpus Christi, TX
Gregg, Gary .... (214) 977-8222
PROD MGR-PR
Dallas Morning News, Dallas, TX
Gregg, Michael .... (416) 585-5000
EDL Art DIR, Globe and Mail (Canada's National Newspaper), Toronto, ON
Gregg, Randa .... (304) 659-2441
GM, Pennsboro News, Pennsboro, WV
Gregg, Tim .... (219) 824-0224
PROD SUPT, News-Banner, Bluffton, IN
Gregonian, Alin .... (508) 369-2800
ED, Bedford Minuteman, Concord, MA
Gregor-North, Cheryl .... (510) 661-2600
COL, Argus, Fremont, CA
Gregory, Allen .... (540) 762-7671
PUB, Clinch Valley Times, St. Paul, VA
Gregory, Ann Y .... (540) 762-7671
PUB, ED, Clinch Valley Times, St. Paul, VA
Gregory, Barbara .... (719) 632-5511
DIR-MKTG, Gazette, Colorado Springs, CO
Gregory, Becky .... (817) 757-5757
City ED, Waco Tribune-Herald, Waco, TX
Gregory, David .... (508) 458-7100
DIR-Photography, Sun, Lowell, MA
Gregory, Gary .... (937) 845-3861
ED, New Carlisle Sun, New Carlisle, OH
Gregory, Jim .... (510) 462-4160
CIRC MGR, Valley Times, Pleasanton, CA
Gregory, John .... (508) 685-1000
DP MGR, Eagle-Tribune, North Andover, MA
Gregory, John .... (619) 270-3103
ED, Beach & Bay Press, San Diego, CA
Gregory, Kathy .... (606) 678-8191
ADV MGR, MGR-MKTG & PROM
Commonwealth-Journal, Somerset, KY
Gregory, Leonard .... (719) 544-3520
MAN ED, Pueblo Chieftain, Pueblo, CO
Gregory, Linda B .... (301) 662-1177
Entertainment/Amusements ED, Family ED, Features ED, Travel ED
Frederick Post/The News, Frederick, MD
Gregory, Mark .... (501) 623-7711
Environmental ED, Farm/Agriculture ED, Graphics ED/Art DIR, Health/Medical ED, Political ED, SCI/Technology ED
Sentinel-Record, Hot Springs, AR
Gregory, Marketta .... (918) 684-2828
ASST City ED, Muskogee Daily Phoenix & Times Democrat, Muskogee, OK
Gregory, Mike .... (816) 885-2281
PROD MGR
Clinton Daily Democrat, Clinton, MO
Gregory, Patricia .... (212) 362-9256
ASST ED-BUS Special Sales, Cartoonists & Writers Syndicate, New York, NY
Gregory, Scott .... (330) 385-4545
PROD FRM-PR, Review, East Liverpool, OH
Greider, Gary .... (209) 369-2761
CIRC MGR, Lodi News-Sentinel, Lodi, CA
Greiling, Dave .... (970) 493-6397
EX ED
Fort Collins Coloradoan, Fort Collins, CO
Grein, Thomas .... (703) 437-5886
PUB, ED, Observer, Herndon, VA
Greiner, Jodelle .... (817) 665-5511
Living/Lifestyle ED, Women's ED
Gainesville Daily Register, Gainesville, TX
Greiner, Vickie K .... (507) 776-2751
PUB, ED, Truman Tribune, Truman, MN
Greiwe, Linda R .... (414) 435-4411
ADV MGR-CLASS
Green Bay Press-Gazette, Green Bay, WI
Greklek, John M .... (914) 331-5000
ADV MGR-MKTG
Daily Freeman, Kingston, NY
Grenesko, Donald C .... (312) 222-3237
Sr VP-FIN & ADM
Tribune Co., Chicago, IL
Grenier, Gaston .... (819) 564-5450
PROD FRM-Engraving
La Tribune, Sherbrooke, QC
Grenier, Meredith .... (310) 540-5511
Garden ED, Daily Breeze, Torrance, CA
Grennan, Dave .... (204) 727-2451
BM, Brandon Sun, Brandon, MB
Gresham, Michael .... (972) 563-6476
Sports ED, Terrell Tribune, Terrell, TX
Gresham, Sallie .... (601) 335-1155
MAN ED
Delta Democrat Times, Greenville, MS
Gress, Allen .... (419) 946-3010
ED
Morrow County Sentinel, Mount Gilead, OH
Gress, Karol .... (717) 272-5611
NTL ED, Daily News, Lebanon, PA
Gressard, Bill .... (330) 296-9657
Outdoors ED
Record-Courier, Kent-Ravenna, OH
Gressette, Felicia .... (919) 829-4500
Features ED, News & Observer, Raleigh, NC
Greto, Victor .... (719) 632-5511
RES Center MGR
Gazette, Colorado Springs, CO
Gretsky, Joanne .... (717) 622-3456
Librarian, Pottsville Republican & Evening Herald, Pottsville, PA
Greve, Dutch .... (619) 745-6611
PROD DIR
North County Times, Escondido, CA
Grewe, Amy .... (502) 273-3287
MAN ED, McLean County News, Calhoun, KY
Grewenig, Hilma .... (815) 544-9811
CIRC MGR
Belvidere Daily Republican, Belvidere, IL
Grey, Gene .... (607) 798-1234
Amusements/Books ED, Films/Theater ED, Press & Sun Bulletin, Binghamton, NY
Grey, Jane .... (616) 845-5181
Food ED, Daily News, Ludington, MI
Gribble, Beth .... (334) 262-1611
News ED
Montgomery Advertiser, Montgomery, AL
Grice, Joseph .... (803) 317-6397
ADTX MGR
Florence Morning News, Florence, SC
Griden, Jeanette .... (918) 423-1700
ADV MGR, McAlester News-Capital & Democrat, McAlester, OK
Grider, Phil .... (701) 223-2500
CIRC DIR, Bismarck Tribune, Bismarck, ND
Grider, William R .... (317) 633-1240
PROD OPER MGR
Indianapolis Star/News, Indianapolis, IN
Griebel, David F .... (402) 444-1000
DIR-MKTG
Omaha World-Herald, Omaha, NE
Grieff, Edward .... (717) 622-3456
PROD FRM-PR, Pottsville Republican & Evening Herald, Pottsville, PA
Griego, Christine K .... (707) 545-1166
PUB, ADV Legal Notices, Sonoma County Daily Herald-Recorder, Santa Rosa, CA
Grieman, John .... (612) 673-4000
VP/CFO, Star Tribune, Minneapolis, MN
Griendstaff, Sharon .... (501) 229-2250
GM, ED
Dardanelle Post-Dispatch, Dardanelle, AR
Griep, Charles .... (619) 375-4481
CIRC DIR, Daily Independent, Ridgecrest, CA
Grier, Patricia E .... (616) 243-0577
PUB
Afro-American Gazette, Grand Rapids, MI
Grieser, Jeff .... (217) 732-2101
Sports ED, Courier, Lincoln, IL
Griess, Karen .... (402) 475-4200
EDU Reporter (Higher)
Lincoln Journal Star, Lincoln, NE
Griess, Ken .... (619) 745-6611
MGR-Purchasing
North County Times, Escondido, CA
Grieve, Michael .... (507) 867-3870
PUB, ED, Chatfield News, Chatfield, MN
Griff, Martin .... (609) 989-5454
DIR-Photography, Times, Trenton, NJ
Griffey, Jan .... (616) 683-2100
ED, News ED, Niles Daily Star, Niles, MI
Griffin, Barbara .... (412) 263-1100
ASST MAN ED-News
Pittsburgh Post-Gazette, Pittsburgh, PA
Griffin, Bernard M .... (607) 798-1234
PRES, PUB
Press & Sun Bulletin, Binghamton, NY
Griffin, Cari .... (209) 578-2000
ADTX CNR, Modesto Bee, Modesto, CA
Griffin, Cary L .... (972) 552-3121
PUB, ED, Forney Messenger, Forney, TX
Griffin, Christy .... (706) 444-5330
GM, Sparta Ishmaelite, Sparta, GA
Griffin, Danny J .... (205) 325-2222
CIRC ASST DIR
Birmingham News, Birmingham, AL
Griffin, Dick .... (941) 953-7755
MGR-CR
Sarasota Herald-Tribune, Sarasota, FL
Griffin, Donald .... (704) 289-1541
PROD FRM-Camera
Enquirer-Journal, Monroe, NC
Griffin, Gary .... (912) 283-2244
MAN ED, Films/Theater ED
Waycross Journal-Herald, Waycross, GA
Griffin, George J .... (301) 722-4600
GM, CIRC DIR
Cumberland Times-News, Cumberland, MD
Griffin, Howard L .... (808) 525-8000
Senior VP-MKTG, ADV Senior VP
Hawaii Newspaper Agency Inc., Honolulu, HI
Griffin, J Frank .... (718) 238-6600
PUB, Home Reporter and Sunset News, Brooklyn, NY
Griffin, Jack .... (540) 825-0771
PROD FRM-COMP, PROD FRM-PR
Culpeper Star-Exponent, Culpeper, VA
Griffin, Most Rev James A .... (614) 224-5195
PUB, Catholic Times, Columbus, OH
Griffin, Jean Latz .... (312) 222-3232
Public Health Writer
Chicago Tribune, Chicago, IL
Griffin, Johnnie .... (601) 442-9101
PROD FRM-PR
Natchez Democrat, Natchez, MS
Griffin, Keith .... (203) 314-3439
ED, West Hartford News, Bristol, CT
Griffin Jr, Lee Roy .... (512) 564-2242
PUB, ED, Yorktown News, Yorktown, TX
Griffin Jr, Leslie F .... (617) 929-2000
DIR-Public Affairs
Boston Globe, Boston, MA
Griffin, Linda Gillan .... (713) 220-7171
Fashion ED
Houston Chronicle, Houston, TX
Griffin, Mark .... (912) 368-0526
GM, Patriot, Hinesville, GA
Griffin, Martha .... (903) 757-3311
Travel ED
Longview News-Journal, Longview, TX
Griffin, Michelle .... (317) 633-1240
ADTX MGR
Indianapolis Star/News, Indianapolis, IN
Griffin, Mike .... (203) 574-3636
Copy Desk Chief, Waterbury Republican-American, Waterbury, CT
Griffin Jr, S M .... (800) 521-5232
PUB, Post-Searchlight, Bainbridge, GA
Griffis, Linda .... (904) 964-6305
ED, Union County Times, Starke, FL
Griffis, Richard .... (219) 461-8222
Sports ED, News-Sentinel, Fort Wayne, IN
Griffith, Amy .... (302) 645-2265
ADV DIR, Daily Whale, Lewes, DE
Griffith, B .... (204) 748-3931
ED, Virden Empire-Advance, Virden, MB
Griffith, Bill .... (608) 786-1950
PUB, La Crosse County Countryman, West Salem, WI
Griffith, Eddie .... (706) 724-0851
CONT-Division
Augusta Chronicle, Augusta, GA
Griffith, Greg .... (409) 632-6631
PROD FRM-PR
Lufkin Daily News, Lufkin, TX
Griffith, John .... (216) 999-4500
Special Projects ED
Plain Dealer, Cleveland, OH
Griffith, Margi .... (712) 279-5019
ADV MGR-PROM
Sioux City Journal, Sioux City, IA
Griffith, Patricia .... (412) 263-1100
Washington BU
Pittsburgh Post-Gazette, Pittsburgh, PA
Blade Communications Inc.
Griffith, Ray .... (619) 322-8889
MAN ED, Desert Sun, Palm Springs, CA
Griffith, Robert P .... (319) 245-1311
PUB, Clayton County Register, Elkader, IA
Griffith, Steve .... (712) 279-5019
ADV MGR, Sioux City Journal, Sioux City, IA
Griffith, Van .... (910) 888-3500
ADV MGR-CLASS
High Point Enterprise, High Point, NC
Griffiths, Dave .... (207) 784-5411
City ED, Sun-Journal, Lewiston, ME
Griffiths, Donald .... (902) 667-5102
CIRC MGR
Amherst Daily News, Amherst, NS
Griffiths, Patti .... (352) 867-4010
EPE, Ocala Star-Banner, Ocala, FL
Griffiths, Ruth .... (306) 764-4276
City ED
Prince Albert Daily Herald, Prince Albert, SK
Griffiths, Tom .... (213) 237-5485
Sales EX/West & South, Los Angeles Times Syndicate, Los Angeles, CA
Griffone, Betts .... (909) 889-9666
Graphics DIR, Sun, San Bernardino, CA
Grigg, Maxine .... (250) 762-4445
ADV MGR-SUPV CLASS
Daily Courier, Kelowna, BC
Griggs, Laurie .... (508) 885-9402
ED, New Leader, Spencer, MA
Griggs, Mark D .... (573) 756-8927
PUB, Daily Press Leader, Farmington, MO
Griggs, Red .... (219) 874-7211
COL, News Dispatch, Michigan City, IN

91-Who's Where **Gue**

Grigsby, Alan S .... (802) 479-0191
VP/GM, Times Argus, Barre, VT
Grigsby, Karen .... (405) 354-5264
PUB, Yukon Review, Yukon, OK
Grigsby, Mark .... (812) 967-3176
ED, Banner-Gazette, Pekin, IN
Grigsby, Randel .... (405) 354-5264
PUB, Yukon Review, Yukon, OK
Grilli, Thomas .... (603) 882-2741
News ED, Telegraph, Nashua, NH
Grillo, Thomas P .... (205) 325-2222
PROD ASST DIR-OPER
Birmingham News, Birmingham, AL
Grilly, Eric .... (916) 321-1000
MGR-Newsroom Sales
Sacramento Bee, Sacramento, CA
Grim, George E .... (517) 828-6360
PUB, Shepherd Argus, Shepherd, MI
Grim, Geraldine .... (517) 828-6360
ED, Shepherd Argus, Shepherd, MI
Grim, John A .... (517) 828-6360
GM, Shepherd Argus, Shepherd, MI
Grim, John .... (610) 820-6500
ASST MAN ED-News (Night)
Morning Call, Allentown, PA
Grim, Mark .... (509) 488-3342
ED, Outlook, Othello, WA
Grimaldi, Nicholas .... (415) 777-5700
PROD MGR, San Francisco Newspaper Agency, San Francisco, CA
Grimes, Claire .... (212) 686-1266
PUB, Irish Echo, New York, NY
Grimes, David .... (941) 953-7755
COL, Sarasota Herald-Tribune, Sarasota, FL
Grimes, Deb .... (419) 245-6000
CIRC MGR-Zone South, Blade, Toledo, OH
Grimes, Jeanne .... (405) 353-0620
Farm ED, Lawton Constitution, Lawton, OK
Grimes, Jim .... (409) 885-3562
PUB, Sealy News, Sealy, TX
Grimes, Joe .... (208) 263-9534
PUB
Bonner County Daily Bee, Sandpoint, ID
Grimes, John .... (816) 826-1000
PROD FRM-PR (Day)
Sedalia Democrat, Sedalia, MO
Grimes, Mary Anne .... (212) 293-8500
PROM MGR, United Media, United Feature Syndicate, Newspaper Enterprise Association, New York, NY
Grimes, Ray .... (573) 796-2135
PUB, California Democrat, California, MO
Grimes, Richard .... (304) 348-5140
COL, Political ED
Charleston Daily Mail, Charleston, WV
Grimes, Steve .... (704) 484-7000
BUS/FIN ED, Shelby Star, Shelby, NC
Grimes, Teri .... (941) 748-0411
Agriculture/Garden ED, Features ED, Lifestyle ED, Bradenton Herald, Bradenton, FL
Grimes, Terry .... (334) 693-3326
ED, Headland Observer, Headland, AL
Grimley, Janet .... (206) 448-8000
ASST MAN ED
Seattle Post-Intelligencer, Seattle, WA
Grimm, Joseph .... (313) 222-6400
Recruiting & Development ED
Detroit Free Press, Detroit, MI
Grimm-Richardson, Anne .... (360) 484-7722
Author/CIO
Tiptoe Literary Service, Naselle, WA
Grimmer, Steve .... (313) 222-6400
SCI ED, Detroit Free Press, Detroit, MI
Grimsley, Edward .... (804) 649-6000
Op-Ed/COL
Richmond Times-Dispatch, Richmond, VA
Grimsley, Judy .... (407) 420-5000
MGR-Library Resources
Orlando Sentinel, Orlando, FL
Grimsrud, David A .... (507) 732-7617
PUB, ED, News Record, Zumbrota, MN
Grinde, Kevin .... (701) 780-1100
News ED
Grand Forks Herald, Grand Forks, ND
Grindle, Russ .... (219) 356-1107
PUB
Huntington County TAB, Huntington, IN
Grindstaff, Robb .... (903) 586-2236
PUB
Jacksonville Daily Progress, Jacksonville, TX
Grineager, Merle .... (541) 474-3700
PROD FRM-COMP
Grants Pass Daily Courier, Grants Pass, OR
Grinstead, Jeanne .... (813) 893-8111
Campaign ED
St. Petersburg Times, St. Petersburg, FL
Grippi, Vince .... (509) 459-5000
Graphics ED
Spokesman-Review, Spokane, WA
Grisso, James L .... (517) 732-1111
PUB, Gaylord Herald Times, Gaylord, MI
Grissom, Becky .... (812) 849-2075
PUB, Mitchell Tribune, Mitchell, IN
Grissom, Norman .... (812) 849-2075
PUB, ED, Mitchell Tribune, Mitchell, IN
Grizzard, Kim Jones .... (919) 752-6166
Special Sections ED
Daily Reflector, Greenville, NC
Grizzard, Mike .... (919) 752-6166
Sports News ED
Daily Reflector, Greenville, NC
Grizzle, Sandra .... (512) 268-7862
GM, Hays County Free Press, Buda, TX
Grnak, Robert .... (517) 799-3200
MAN ED, Township Times, Saginaw, MI
Groccia, Louis .... (413) 584-5000
MAN ED, Wire ED
Daily Hampshire Gazette, Northampton, MA
Grochala, Joe .... (515) 284-8000
CIRC MGR-Single Copy Sales
Des Moines Register, Des Moines, IA
Grochow, Tom .... (714) 835-1234
DIR-Facilities
Orange County Register, Santa Ana, CA
Grochowski, Mitchell .... (717) 344-1513
ED, Straz, Scranton, PA
Grodsky, Dawn .... (941) 482-7111
ED, Fort Myers Observer, Fort Myers, FL
Groebner, Marie .... (507) 243-3031
PUB, ED
Lake Region Times, Madison Lake, MN
Groene, Janet .... (904) 736-0313
Writer, Groene & Groene, DeLand, FL
Groenenberg, Henry J .... (307) 266-0500
BM, Star-Tribune, Casper, WY
Groeneveld, Bob .... (604) 534-8641
ED, Langley Advance, Langley, BC
Groening, Tom .... (207) 338-3333
ED, Republican Journal, Belfast, ME
Groff, Robert .... (717) 421-3000
Features ED, RE ED
Pocono Record, Stroudsburg, PA
Grogan, Paula .... (404) 526-5151
VP/BM
Atlanta Journal-Constitution, Atlanta, GA
Groglio, Marcia .... (203) 964-2200
ADV MGR-NTL, Stamford Advocate, Stamford, CT, Times Mirror Co.
Grollmus, Cindy .... (937) 225-2000
ADV GM-ADS
Dayton Daily News, Dayton, OH
Gronemann, Linda .... (602) 497-0048
ED, Chandler/Sun Lakes Independent, Chandler, AZ
Gronning, Don .... (360) 374-2281
ED
Forks Forum & Peninsula Herald, Forks, WA
Grooms, Cristy .... (515) 421-0500
ADV DIR, Globe-Gazette, Mason City, IA
Grooms, John .... (704) 375-2121
ED, Creative Loafing, Charlotte, NC
Grooms, Larry .... (805) 273-2700
ED, EPE
Antelope Valley Press, Palmdale, CA
Grooms, Michelle .... (615) 388-6464
Picture ED, Daily Herald, Columbia, TN
Grooms, West .... (319) 524-8300
ADV DIR, Daily Gate City, Keokuk, IA
Grooters, Eric .... (916) 842-5777
ADV DIR, Siskiyou Daily News, Yreka, CA
Groppa, Carlos .... (213) 654-6268
ED
La Prensa de Los Angeles, Los Angeles, CA
Grosam, Steve .... (507) 359-2911
MGR-MKTG/PROM, CIRC MGR
Journal, New Ulm, MN
Groshans, Garth .... (864) 224-4321
CIRC DIR
Anderson Independent-Mail, Anderson, SC
Groshart, Craig .... (206) 455-2222
EPE, Eastside Journal, Bellevue, WA
Groshong, Robert .... (715) 537-3117
ED, County News-Shield, Barron, WI
Groshong, Warren .... (805) 781-7800
EPE, Telegram-Tribune, San Luis Obispo, CA
Gross, Beth .... (610) 543-0900
PUB, ED, Swarthmorean, Swarthmore, PA
Gross, Deena .... (717) 854-1575
MAN ED
York Dispatch/York Sunday News, York, PA
Gross, Dennis .... (505) 325-4545
ADV DIR, Daily Times, Farmington, NM
Gross, Don .... (718) 981-1234
Health/Medical ED
Staten Island Advance, Staten Island, NY
Gross, Eric .... (614) 654-1321
PROD FRM-COMP
Lancaster Eagle-Gazette, Lancaster, OH
Gross, George .... (416) 947-2222
CORP Sports ED, Toronto Sun, Toronto, ON
Gross, Joe .... (410) 268-5000
Sports ED, Capital, Annapolis, MD
Gross, Leslie .... (410) 268-5000
EDU ED, Capital, Annapolis, MD
Grossberg, Michael .... (614) 461-5000
Theater ED
Columbus Dispatch, Columbus, OH
Grossfeld, Stanley .... (617) 929-2000
ASSOC ED, Boston Globe, Boston, MA
Grossman, Cathy .... (703) 276-3400
Religion Reporter, USA Today, Arlington, VA
Grossman, Gary .... (410) 749-7171
EX ED, Daily Times, Salisbury, MD
Grossman, Jo .... (330) 629-6200
ED, Austintown Town Crier, Youngstown, OH
Grossman, Rodger J .... (812) 883-3281
PUB, Your Advantage, Salem, IN
Grossman, Roger .... (510) 208-6300
Senior VP-Advertising
Oakland Tribune, Oakland, CA
MediaNews Inc. (Alameda Newspapers)
Grossman, Ted .... (360) 376-4500
ED, Islands' Sounder, Eastsound, WA
Grossmann, Mary Ann .... (612) 222-5011
Books ED
St. Paul Pioneer Press, St. Paul, MN
Grosso, Jorge .... (305) 858-9613
DIR, Colombian Comics Syndicate, Miami, FL
Grosso, William .... (305) 858-9613
Representative for U.S. & Canada
Colombian Comics Syndicate, Miami, FL
Grote, Glenn .... (603) 298-8711
PROD MGR-Pre Press
Valley News, White River Jct., VT
Grote, Tom .... (208) 634-2123
PUB, ED, Star-News, McCall, ID
Groteboer, Audrey .... (507) 285-7600
ADV MGR-Display
Post-Bulletin, Rochester, MN
Grotte, Joe .... (817) 665-5511
PROD SUPT-COMP
Gainesville Daily Register, Gainesville, TX
Groucutt, Paul .... (814) 870-1600
News ED, Wire ED
Morning News/Erie Daily Times, Erie, PA
Grove, Ben .... (702) 788-6200
EDU ED, Reno Gazette-Journal, Reno, NV
Grove, Elaine .... (423) 675-6397
PUB, Press Enterprise, Knoxville, TN
Grove, Harriet .... (301) 722-4600
MGR-CR
Cumberland Times-News, Cumberland, MD
Grove-White, Pat .... (250) 372-2331
PROD MGR
Kamloops Daily News, Kamloops, BC
Grover, Michael .... (505) 983-3303
ADV MGR-CLASS
Santa Fe New Mexican, Santa Fe, NM
Groves, Al .... (864) 224-4321
ADV MGR-Display
Anderson Independent-Mail, Anderson, SC
Groves, Bill .... (804) 649-6000
CIRC MGR-Transportation
Richmond Times-Dispatch, Richmond, VA
Groves, Don .... (601) 928-4802
PUB, ED
Stone County Enterprise, Wiggins, MS
Groves, Karen .... (904) 224-3805
MAN ED, Tallahassean, Tallahassee, FL
Groves, Martha .... (213) 237-5000
MGT/Trends/Agriculture/GEN Assignment
Los Angeles Times, Los Angeles, CA
Groves, Richard H .... (410) 752-3849
PRES/PUB, Daily Record, Baltimore, MD
Groves, Todd .... (419) 448-3200
CIRC MGR, Advertiser-Tribune, Tiffin, OH
Grubaugh, Dennis .... (618) 463-2500
BUS/FIN ED, Environmental/Ecology ED, RE ED, Telegraph, Alton, IL
Grubbs, Sherman .... (904) 252-1511
PROD FRM-PR, Daytona Beach News-Journal, Daytona Beach, FL
Gruber, Bob .... (352) 867-4010
ADV DIR, Ocala Star-Banner, Ocala, FL
Gruber, James .... (937) 328-0300
PROD SUPV-Building/Post Press
Springfield News-Sun, Springfield, OH
Gruber, William .... (312) 222-3232
COL, Chicago Tribune, Chicago, IL
Grubert, Stephanie .... (717) 474-6397
PUB, ED
Mountaintop Eagle, Mountaintop, PA
Gruda, Agnes .... (514) 285-7272
EDL Writer, La Presse, Montreal, QC
Gruehr, Jenny L .... (317) 861-4242
MAN ED
New Palestine Press, New Palestine, IN
Gruenberg, Mark J .... (202) 638-0444
ED, Press Associates Inc., Washington, DC
Grueter, Frank .... (617) 786-7000
CFO, Patriot Ledger, Quincy, MA
Gruetze, Mark .... (412) 224-4321
News ED, Valley News Dispatch, Tarentum, PA, Gannett Co. Inc.
Gruman, Sue .... (218) 935-5296
ED, Mahnomen Pioneer, Mahnomen, MN
Grunder, Eric .... (209) 943-6397
BUS/FIN ED, Record, Stockton, CA
Grundstrom Jr, Frank E .... (617) 929-2000
VP-Human Resources
Boston Globe, Boston, MA
Grunwald, Dolores A .... (937) 855-2300
PUB, ED, Press, Germantown, OH
Grutho, Allan .... (306) 236-5265
PUB, GM, Progress, Meadow Lake, SK
Gruwell, Ed .... (941) 748-0411
CIRC DIR, Bradenton Herald, Bradenton, FL
Gryder, Sherry .... (202) 334-6000
PROD SUPT-COMP
Washington Post, Washington, DC
Gryman, Laura .... (918) 456-8833
RE ED
Tahlequah Daily Press, Tahlequah, OK
Grzella, Paul .... (908) 722-8800
Features ED, Courier-News, Bridgewater, NJ
Grzych, Lesly .... (812) 522-4871
Television/Wire ED, Tribune, Seymour, IN
Grzywacz, Jackie .... (810) 469-4510
PROD ASST, Macomb Daily, Mount Clemens, MI, Independent Newspapers Inc. (MI)
Gstalder, Herbert .... (212) 777-6200
PRES, Bettmann Archive/Bettman Newsphotos, New York, NY
Guadagnini, Bill .... (501) 741-2325
CIRC DIR-MKTG
Harrison Daily Times, Harrison, AR
Guadalupe, Patricia .... (202) 234-0280
ED
Hispanic Link News Service, Washington, DC
Guajardo, Louie .... (210) 728-2500
ADV MGR-RT
Laredo Morning Times, Laredo, TX
Guaracao, Hernan .... (215) 457-6999
PUB, Al Dia, Philadelphia, PA
Guaratillo, Frank .... (603) 224-5301
Regional ED, Concord Monitor, Concord, NH
Guardado, Elena .... (408) 295-4272
GM, El Observador, San Jose, CA
Guarini, Maurice J .... (508) 793-9100
ADV MGR-NTL
Telegram & Gazette, Worcester, MA
Guarini, Michael .... (908) 370-1441
Author
Interior Design Teacher, Lakewood, NJ
Guarino, Fred .... (205) 669-3131
ED, Childersburg Extra, Columbiana, AL
Guay, Dave .... (518) 792-3131
PROD FRM-Press, Post-Star, Glens Falls, NY
Gubiotti, Amy .... (716) 394-0770
MGR-Human Resources, Daily Messenger/The Sunday Messenger, Canandaigua, NY
Gubitosi, Pamela A .... (212) 556-1234
Deputy BM-News
New York Times, New York, NY
Guckert, Linda .... (203) 846-3281
ADV MGR-CLASS, Hour, Norwalk, CT
Gudas, Linda .... (607) 739-3001
MAN ED
Chemung Valley Reporter, Horseheads, NY
Gudmundsen, Lance .... (801) 237-2031
Music ED-Classical
Salt Lake Tribune, Salt Lake City, UT
Guenin, Greg .... (218) 829-4705
CIRC MGR, Daily Dispatch, Brainerd, MN
Guenther, Anne .... (213) 237-5000
TV Times Managing ED
Los Angeles Times, Los Angeles, CA
Guenther, Bob .... (602) 271-8000
DIR-Property Facilities
Phoenix Newspapers Inc., Phoenix, AZ
Guenther, Mary Clarke .... (423) 756-1234
ASST MAN ED
Chattanooga Times, Chattanooga, TN
Guenther, Richard .... (937) 498-2111
CONT, Sidney Daily News, Sidney, OH
Guenther, Rosalie .... (402) 721-5000
MGR-CR, Fremont Tribune, Fremont, NE
Guerbe, Gwen .... (302) 645-2265
ED, Daily Whale, Lewes, DE
Guerin, J P .... (213) 229-5300
Vice-COB, Daily Journal, Los Angeles, CA
Guerra, Arnulfo .... (210) 849-1757
PUB, South Texas Reporter, Roma, TX
Guerra, Patty .... (209) 634-9141
Lifestyle ED, Music ED
Turlock Journal, Turlock, CA
Guerra, Raul .... (210) 849-1757
ED, South Texas Reporter, Roma, TX
Guerrein, Bob .... (814) 870-1600
Books ED, EPE
Morning News/Erie Daily Times, Erie, PA
Guerrero, Anthony W .... (810) 573-2755
Motorcycle ED
Avanti NewsFeatures, Warren, MI
Guerrero, Elena V .... (210) 849-1757
GM, South Texas Reporter, Roma, TX
Guerrero, Richard .... (915) 653-1221
ADV MGR-RT
Standard-Times, San Angelo, TX
Guerrettaz, Don .... (317) 888-3376
PUB, ED, Greenwood and Southside Challenger, Greenwood, IN
Guerringue, Mark .... (603) 356-3456
PUB, CIRC MGR
Conway Daily Sun, North Conway, NH
Guerry, Gill .... (803) 577-7111
Graphics ED/Art DIR
Post and Courier, Charleston, SC

Gue Who's Where-92

Guersch, Michael .... (408) 920-5000
Reporter/ED
San Jose Mercury News, San Jose, CA

Guesman, Tim .... (310) 540-5511
ADV MGR-CLASS, Daily Breeze, Torrance, CA
Copley Press Inc.

Guessler, Kurt .... (815) 756-4841
Lifestyle ED, Daily Chronicle, De Kalb, IL

Guest, Larry .... (407) 420-5000
Senior COL-Sports
Orlando Sentinel, Orlando, FL

Guevara Vasquez, Rey .... (210) 542-4301
City ED
El Heraldo de Brownsville, Brownsville, TX

Guezewich, Dan .... (315) 866-2220
MAN ED, Evening Telegram, Herkimer, NY

Guffey, Tom .... (918) 335-8200
PROD FRM-PR
Examiner-Enterprise, Bartlesville, OK

Guggi, Ros .... (613) 236-0491
MGR, Southam Syndicate, Ottawa, ON

Gugliotta, Bill .... (803) 771-6161
Photo ED, State, Columbia, SC

Gugliotta, Guy .... (202) 334-6000
Congress Reporter
Washington Post, Washington, DC

Gugliotto, Mike .... (303) 776-2244
GM, Daily Times-Call, Longmont, CO

Guido, Nick .... (718) 981-1234
DP MGR
Staten Island Advance, Staten Island, NY

Guidry, Joe .... (813) 259-7711
Books ED, Deputy EPE
Tampa Tribune and Times, Tampa, FL

Guilfoyle, Don .... (616) 964-7161
PROD MGR-Distribution
Battle Creek Enquirer, Battle Creek, MI

Guillaud, Betty .... (504) 826-3279
COL, Times-Picayune, New Orleans, LA

Guillerault, Richard R .... (207) 729-3311
VP/CONT, PA, Times Record, Brunswick, ME

Guillet, Sherry .... (705) 232-4081
GM, Enterprise, Iroquois Falls, ON

Guin, W R .... (916) 243-2424
PROD FRM-COMP
Record Searchlight, Redding, CA

Guinivan Jr, Paul .... (617) 593-7700
MGR-CR, Daily Evening Item, Lynn, MA

Guinn, Frances .... (210) 426-3346
ED, Hondo Anvil Herald, Hondo, TX

Guinnup, Carol .... (812) 735-2222
GM, ED, North Knox News, Bicknell, IN

Guinto, Joseph .... (214) 696-2900
ED, Met, Dallas, TX

Guiremand, Rich .... (805) 925-2691
Sports ED, Times, Santa Maria, CA

Guittar, Lee J .... (212) 649-2000
VP/Group EX
Hearst Newspapers, New York, NY

Gulbranson, Karen .... (804) 366-5224
Principal, Gulbranson Communications Group, Virginia Beach, VA

Gulick, Joe .... (806) 762-8844
EDL Writer/COL
Lubbock Avalanche-Journal, Lubbock, TX

Gulig, Joseph .... (414) 457-7711
City ED, State ED
Sheboygan Press, Sheboygan, WI

Gulino, Denis .... (212) 509-4444
Washington BU Chief
Market News Service, New York, NY

Gulla, Richard P .... (617) 929-2000
DIR-Public Relations
Boston Globe, Boston, MA

Gullberg, Ron .... (307) 266-0500
Sports ED, Star-Tribune, Casper, WY

Gulledge, Bill R .... (210) 829-9000
VP, Harte-Hanks Communications Inc., San Antonio, TX

Gulledge, Michael .... (319) 383-2200
ADV MGR-NTL, ADV MGR-RT Sales, MGR-Database, ADTX MGR
Quad-City Times, Davenport, IA

Gullett, Larry .... (618) 544-2101
ADV MGR-NTL
Robinson Daily News, Robinson, IL

Gullett, Mike .... (417) 623-3480
Photo DEPT MGR, Joplin Globe, Joplin, MO

Gullian, Donald .... (317) 747-5700
PROD MGR-Mailroom, Star Press, Muncie, IN

Gullickson, Darlene .... (701) 579-4530
GM, Herald, New England, ND

Gullickson, Lucille .... (701) 462-8126
ED, Center Republican, Washburn, ND

Gullixson, Paul .... (415) 326-8210
ED, Palo Alto Weekly, Palo Alto, CA

Gullotta, Bernard .... (860) 241-6200
PROD MGR-Engineering
Hartford Courant, Hartford, CT

Gully, Andrew .... (617) 426-3000
MAN ED-News, Boston Herald, Boston, MA

Gumbel, Peter .... (212) 416-2000
BU Chief-Los Angeles
Wall Street Journal, New York, NY

Gumm, Benjamin W .... (203) 268-6234
PUB, Stratford Star, Trumbull, CT

Gummere, Jeff .... (510) 783-6111
CONT, Daily Review, Hayward, CA

Gump, Debbie .... (415) 883-8600
News Desk ED
Marin Independent Journal, Novato, CA

Gumz, Jondi .... (408) 423-4242
EDU ED
Santa Cruz County Sentinel, Santa Cruz, CA

Gun, Eleanor .... (617) 969-4102
PRES/CEO, Travel & Leisure Features, New England News Service Inc., Newton, MA

Gun, Milton J .... (617) 969-4102
BU Chief
New England News Service Inc., Newton, MA

Gunderson, Marsha .... (701) 780-1100
ADV CNR-MKTG RES
Grand Forks Herald, Grand Forks, ND

Gunderson, Tom .... (414) 432-2941
News ED
Green Bay News-Chronicle, Green Bay, WI

Gunn, Paula .... (601) 287-6111
BM, Daily Corinthian, Corinth, MS

Gunn, Pete .... (904) 435-8500
PROD MGR-PR
Pensacola News Journal, Pensacola, FL

Gunn, Rick .... (702) 882-2111
Photo ED, Nevada Appeal, Carson City, NV

Gunst, Carla .... (715) 258-5546
ED, Wisconsin State Farmer, Waupaca, WI

Gunter, Dave .... (208) 664-8176
RE ED
Coeur d'Alene Press, Coeur d'Alene, ID

Gunter, John Michael .... (970) 669-5050
CIRC MGR
Loveland Daily Reporter-Herald, Loveland, CO

Gunter, Rebecca Comer .... (205) 699-2214
ED, Leeds News, Leeds, AL

Gunter, Rene .... (813) 259-7711
MGR-EDU SRV
Tampa Tribune and Times, Tampa, FL

Gunter, Rick .... (540) 885-7281
EX ED, EPE
Daily News Leader, Staunton, VA

Gunther III, Arthur .... (914) 358-2200
EPE
Rockland Journal-News, West Nyack, NY

Gunther, Sally .... (613) 591-3060
MAN ED
Kanata Kourier-Standard, Kanata, ON

Gunzelmann, Donald .... (610) 323-3000
PROD MGR-Pre Press
Mercury, Pottstown, PA

Guralski, Gary .... (608) 328-4202
ADV MGR-RT, ADV MGR-CLASS
Monroe Times, Monroe, WI

Guregian, Elaine .... (330) 996-3000
Music ED-Classical
Akron Beacon Journal, Akron, OH

Gurgone, Joseph .... (312) 750-4000
ADV MGR, Wall Street Journal-Central Edition, Chicago, IL

Gurian, Joel .... (813) 893-8111
ADV MGR-GEN
St. Petersburg Times, St. Petersburg, FL

Gurly, George .... (816) 234-4141
Books ED, Kansas City Star, Kansas City, MO

Gurse, Carl De .... (306) 692-2325
MAN ED
Moose Jaw This Week, Moose Jaw, SK

Gusewelle, C W .... (816) 234-4141
COL, Kansas City Star, Kansas City, MO

Gushard, Keith .... (814) 724-6370
BUS ED, Meadville Tribune, Meadville, PA

Gushee, Steve .... (561) 820-4100
Religion ED
Palm Beach Post, West Palm Beach, FL

Guski, Pete .... (218) 741-5544
PROD FRM-PR
Mesabi Daily News, Virginia, MN

Guss, Sandra .... (203) 964-2200
MGR-MKTG SRV, Stamford Advocate, Stamford, CT, Times Mirror Co.

Gust, Steve .... (405) 341-2121
City ED, Edmond Evening Sun, Edmond, OK

Gustafson, Barb .... (306) 764-4276
MAN ED, EPE
Prince Albert Daily Herald, Prince Albert, SK

Gustafson, Craig .... (612) 388-8235
Sports ED, Republican Eagle, Red Wing, MN

Gustafson, Denise .... (320) 325-5152
MAN ED, Northern Star, Ortonville, MN

Gustafson, Pat .... (707) 226-3711
Office MGR, Napa Valley Register, Napa, CA

Gustavson, Eric .... (716) 232-7100
PROD FRM-Camera/Platemaking (Democrat and Chronicle), Rochester Democrat and Chronicle; Times-Union, Rochester, NY

Gustavson, Joan .... (516) 298-3200
PUB, Suffolk Times, Mattituck, NY

Gustavson, Troy .... (516) 298-3200
PUB, Suffolk Times, Mattituck, NY

Gustin, Bob .... (812) 424-7711
MAN ED, MET ED
Evansville Press, Evansville, IN

Gustin, Carol .... (319) 242-7101
ED, Clinton Herald, Clinton, IA

Gustin, Chris .... (812) 424-7711
Books ED, Evansville Press, Evansville, IN

Guthard, Lori .... (308) 237-2152
ADV MGR-Sales, Kearney Hub, Kearney, NE

Guthrie, Sgt .... (301) 921-2800
ED, Capital Flyer, Gaithersburg, MD

Guthrie, Charles .... (704) 252-5611
City ED, Citizen-Times, Asheville, NC

Guthrie, Jim .... (360) 452-2345
Entertainment/Amusements ED
Peninsula Daily News, Port Angeles, WA

Guthrie, Jim .... (814) 238-5000
DIR-Technology
Centre Daily Times, State College, PA

Guthrie, Patricia R .... (307) 362-3736
SEC, Daily Rocket-Miner, Rock Springs, WY

Guthrie, Robert .... (404) 526-5151
PROD MGR-Gwinnett Printing Facility
Atlanta Journal-Constitution, Atlanta, GA

Guthrie, Troy .... (812) 275-3355
Health/Medical ED, Times-Mail, Bedford, IN

Gutierrer, Lena .... (305) 551 3292
ED, La Prensa Centroamericana, Miami, FL

Gutierrez, Barbara .... (305) 350-2111
ED-El Nuevo, Miami Herald, Miami, FL

Gutierrez Jr, E G .... (210) 423-5511
ADV MGR-Local
Valley Morning Star, Harlingen, TX

Gutierrez, Enrique .... (209) 835-3030
Photo ED, Tracy Press, Tracy, CA

Gutierrez, George .... (512) 445-3500
ADV DIR
Austin American-Statesman, Austin, TX

Gutierrez, Joel .... (305) 350-2111
City ED-El Nuevo, Miami Herald, Miami, FL

Gutierrez, Lisa .... (716) 232-7100
Fashion Reporter, Rochester Democrat and Chronicle; Times-Union, Rochester, NY

Gutierrez, Omar .... (313) 841-0100
ED, El Central, Detroit, WI

Gutierrez, Rudy .... (915) 546-6100
Chief Photographer, Photo ED
El Paso Times, El Paso, TX

Gutierrez, Santana .... (210) 727-8507
ED, El Clamor, Laredo, TX

Gutridge, Jeff .... (617) 438-1660
ED, Stoneham Independent, Stoneham, MA

Guttman, Jeannine .... (207) 791-6650
MAN ED
Portland Press Herald, Portland, ME

Guttman, Lorrie .... (904) 599-2100
Food ED
Tallahassee Democrat, Tallahassee, FL

Gutz, Fred .... (519) 255-5711
PROD MGR-Plant Services/DP
Windsor Star, Windsor, ON

Guy, Chris .... (410) 332-6000
ED-Carroll Sun, Sun, Baltimore, MD

Guy, Dave .... (613) 829-9100
ASST City ED, News ED
Ottawa Citizen, Ottawa, ON

Guy, Eilene .... (419) 625-5500
ASST MAN ED, Area ED
Sandusky Register, Sandusky, OH

Guy, Gerald .... (912) 244-1880
ED, Valdosta Daily Times, Valdosta, GA

Guy, Jeff .... (316) 442-4200
Farm/City ED
Arkansas City Traveler, Arkansas City, KS

Guy, Kingsley .... (954) 356-4000
EPE, Sun-Sentinel, Fort Lauderdale, FL

Guyette, Greg .... (802) 479-0191
CIRC ASST DIR, Times Argus, Barre, VT

Guynn, Sue .... (301) 662-1177
Fashion/Style ED
Frederick Post/The News, Frederick, MD

Guzek, Maureen .... (906) 884-2826
PUB, ED, Ontonagon Herald, Ontonagon, MI

Guzior, Betsey .... (847) 888-7800
Entertainment/Amusements ED, Features ED, Living/Lifestyle ED, Women's ED
Courier-News, Elgin, IL

Guzmas, George S .... (514) 978-9999
PUB, Nouvelles Chomedey News, Laval, QC

Guzzo, Glenn .... (330) 996-3000
MAN ED, Akron Beacon Journal, Akron, OH

Gwartney, Debra .... (503) 484-0519
ED, Eugene Weekly, Eugene, OR

Gwathney, Arnold .... (501) 633-3130
PROD SUPT, Times-Herald, Forrest City, AR

Gwin, Gary .... (308) 632-0670
MGR-MKTG/PROM
Star-Herald, Scottsbluff, NE

Gwinn, Earl .... (817) 888-2616
PUB, ED, Baylor County Banner, Seymour, TX

Gwinner, Joe .... (573) 221-2800
PROD FRM-PR
Hannibal Courier-Post, Hannibal, MO

Gwynn, Patti .... (910) 694-4145
GM, Caswell Messenger, Yanceyville, NC

Gyger, Cindi .... (319) 337-3181
ADV MGR-CLASS
Iowa City Press-Citizen, Iowa City, IA

Gyllenhaal, Anders .... (919) 829-4500
Senior MAN ED
News & Observer, Raleigh, NC

H

Haag, Jim .... (913) 823-6363
ASST ED, Amusements ED, Books ED, Films/Theater ED, Radio/Television ED
Salina Journal, Salina, KS

Haar, Dan .... (312) 782-8100
City ED (night)
City News Bureau of Chicago, Chicago, IL

Haas, Al .... (215) 854-2000
Automotive Writer
Philadelphia Inquirer, Philadelphia, PA

Haas, George .... (773) 586-8800
Features/Entertainment ED
Daily Southtown, Chicago, IL

Haas, Greg .... (805) 237-6060
City ED, County News-Press, Paso Robles, CA

Haas, Herbert O .... (814) 587-2033
PUB, Conneautville Courier, Springboro, PA

Haas, James .... (717) 784-2121
CIRC MGR, Press Enterprise, Bloomsburg, PA

Haas, Jessie .... (814) 587-2033
GM, ED
Conneautville Courier, Springboro, PA

Haas, Jim .... (309) 346-1111
Sports ED, Pekin Daily Times, Pekin, IL

Haas, Lemont R .... (603) 668-4321
PROD MGR, Union Leader, Manchester, NH

Haas, Mark .... (715) 833-9200
CIRC MGR-Sales PROM & Training
Leader-Telegram, Eau Claire, WI

Haas, Michael H .... (913) 628-1081
ADV DIR, Hays Daily News, Hays, KS

Haas, Wally .... (815) 987-1200
ASST MAN ED-OPER
Rockford Register Star, Rockford, IL

Haase, Roald .... (630) 232-9222
BUS ED, Kane County Chronicle, Geneva, IL

Haase, Stephanie .... (206) 872-6600
PROD MGR-Pre Press
South County Journal, Kent, WA

Haase, Walter F .... (618) 635-2000
PUB, ED, Staunton Star-Times, Staunton, IL

Haaven, Jon .... (320) 763-3133
PUB, Echo-Press, Alexandria, MN

Habayeb, Jody .... (219) 461-8333
News Technology DIR
Journal Gazette, Fort Wayne, IN

Haberman, Margaret .... (360) 676-2600
City ED, Bellingham Herald, Bellingham, WA

Haberman, Ronnie .... (219) 362-2161
PROD FRM-COMP
La Porte Herald-Argus, La Porte, IN

Habetz, Edward .... (318) 289-6300
PROD FRM-PR, Advertiser, Lafayette, LA

Habich, John .... (612) 673-4000
Team Leader, Star Tribune, Minneapolis, MN

Hablin, Tim .... (805) 237-6060
ADV DIR, County News-Press
Paso Robles, CA

Habrick, Maryann .... (517) 456-4100
PUB, ED, Clinton Local, Clinton, MI

Hachadorian, Andrew .... (610) 323-3000
MAN ED, Mercury, Pottstown, PA

Hache, Claudine .... (506) 727-4444
PROD MGR, L'Acadie Nouvelle
Caraquet, NB

Hachman, JoAnn .... (520) 453-4237
PROD MGR
Today's News-Herald, Lake Havasu City, AZ

Hack, Joel .... (707) 875-3574
PUB, GM
Bodega Bay Navigator, Bodega Bay, CA

Hack, Marjorie .... (718) 981-1234
EDU ED
Staten Island Advance, Staten Island, NY

Hackenmiller, Chuck .... (515) 432-1234
Sports ED, News-Republican, Boone, IA

Hacker, Tom .... (307) 733-2430
ED, Jackson Hole Guide, Jackson, WY

Hackert, Verna .... (515) 594-4488
GM, Diamond Trail News, Sully, IA

Hackett, David .... (317) 736-7101
MAN ED, Daily Journal, Franklin, IN

Hackett, Jim .... (212) 715-2100
ADV DIR/East Coast
USA Weekend, New York, NY

Hackett, Larry .... (212) 210-2100
Features ED
New York Daily News, New York, NY

Hackett, Raymond .... (860) 887-9211
City ED, Norwich Bulletin, Norwich, CT

Hackett, Regina .... (206) 448-8000
Fine Arts ED
Seattle Post-Intelligencer, Seattle, WA

Hackleman, Kathy .... (316) 241-2422
ED, McPherson Sentinel, McPherson, KS

Hackman, Randy .... (909) 889-9666
PROD MGR-PR, Sun, San Bernardino, CA

Copyright ©1997 by the Editor & Publisher Co.

93-Who's Where **Hal**

Hackney, Richard A .... (941) 629-2855
VP OPER, Sun Herald, Port Charlotte, FL
Hackney, William .... (414) 684-4433
CIRC MGR
Herald Times Reporter, Manitowoc, WI
Hadar, Mary .... (202) 334-6000
ASST MAN ED-Features, Features ED
Washington Post, Washington, DC
Haddad, Annette .... (213) 237-5000
ASST BUS ED-Wires/People/Earnings
Los Angeles Times, Los Angeles, CA
Haddad, Bob .... (303) 820-1010
ADV MGR-CLASS, Denver Post, Denver, CO
Haddad, David .... (803) 317-6397
ADV MGR, Morning News, Florence, SC
Hadden, Jeff .... (313) 222-2300
EPE, Detroit News, Detroit, MI
Haddix, Doug .... (217) 446-1000
City ED, Features ED
Commercial News, Danville, IL
Haddix, Doug .... (717) 348-9100
City ED
Tribune & The Scranton Times, Scranton, PA
Haddock, Marc .... (801) 756-7669
MAN ED, Citizen, American Fork, UT
Haddock Sr, Roy .... (212) 837-7000
CIRC DIR, Journal of Commerce & Commercial, New York, NY
Haddy, Frank .... (603) 356-3456
PROD MGR
Conway Daily Sun, North Conway, NH
Hadland, Stephen .... (310) 313-6733
PUB, ED
Hawthorne Community News, Culver City, CA
Hadley, Stephen .... (409) 945-3441
MAN ED, Texas City Sun, Texas City, TX
Hadnot, Ira J .... (214) 977-8222
TODAY ED, Dallas Morning News, Dallas, TX
Hadnott, William .... (713) 527-8261
GM, Houston Informer & Texas Freeman, Houston, TX
Hadzewycz, Romana .... (201) 434-0237
ED, Ukrainian Weekly, Jersey City, NJ
Haeberlein, George .... (212) 455-4000
DIR-Sales, North America Syndicate, King Features Syndicate Inc., New York, NY
Haenel, Bob .... (713) 232-3737
MAN ED, News ED
Herald-Coaster, Rosenberg, TX
Haenlein, Joy .... (203) 964-2200
EPE, Stamford Advocate, Stamford, CT
Haerle, David .... (408) 372-3311
Sports ED
Monterey County Herald, Monterey, CA
Haessly, Michael .... (414) 922-4600
MGR-Special Products, ADV MGR
Reporter, Fond du Lac, WI
Haezebroeck, Kevin .... (217) 429-5151
ADV MGR-RT, Herald & Review, Decatur, IL
Hafdahl, Gregory .... (941) 335-0200
CIRC DIR, News-Press, Fort Myers, FL
Haferd, Theresa .... (419) 468-1117
Family ED, Women's ED
Galion Inquirer, Galion, OH
Hafermehl, John H .... (519) 367-2681
PUB, ED
Town and Country Crier, Mildmay, ON
Hagadone, Bradley D .... (208) 667-3431
VP, Hagadone Corp., Coeur d'Alene, ID
Hagadone, Duane B .... (208) 667-3431
PRES, Hagadone Corp., Coeur d'Alene, ID
Hagaman, James .... (201) 877-4141
ADV MGR-RT, Star-Ledger, Newark, NJ
Hagan, Gay .... (573) 684-2929
ED, Optic-News, Wellsville, MO
Hagan, Mike .... (360) 378-4191
ED, Journal of the San Juan Islands, Friday Harbor, WA
Hagar, Jim .... (208) 785-1100
Online Contact
Morning News, Blackfoot, ID
Hage, Jeff .... (320) 983-6111
MAN ED
Mille Lacs County Times, Milaca, MN
Hagedorn, Charles G .... (212) 679-1234
PUB, New York Town & Village
New York, NY
Hagedorn, Christopher G .... (914) 636-7400
PUB, Co-op City News, Bronx, NY
Hagel, Keith .... (203) 846-3281
EDU ED, Hour, Norwalk, CT
Hagel, Roger .... (309) 263-7414
PUB, ED, Courier, Morton, IL
Hageman, Teri .... (419) 784-5441
Area ED, Crescent-News, Defiance, OH
Hagemeyer, Seanne .... (515) 573-2141
Entertainment ED, Television/Film ED, Theater/Music ED, Messenger, Fort Dodge, IA
Hagen, Angela .... (520) 573-4561
Food ED, Tucson Citizen, Tucson, AZ
Hagen, Bill .... (217) 788-1300
Chief Photographer
State Journal-Register, Springfield, IL
Hagen, Daniel .... (217) 728-7381
ED, News-Progress, Sullivan, IL
Hagen, Mary Ann .... (208) 934-4449
ED, Gooding County Leader, Gooding, ID
Hagen, Phil .... (702) 385-3111
Features ED, Las Vegas Sun, Las Vegas, NV
Hager Sr, Clark E .... (509) 924-2440
PUB, Valley Herald, Spokane, WA
Hager, David .... (919) 537-2505
PROD FRM-PR
Daily Herald, Roanoke Rapids, NC
Hager, Don .... (304) 348-5140
COL, Sports ED, Daily Mail, Charleston, WV
Hager, Phil .... (604) 738-1411
PUB, Vancouver Courier, Vancouver, BC
Hager, Philip D .... (415) 252-0500
ED, San Francisco Daily Journal, San Francisco, CA
Hager, Ray .... (702) 788-6200
Sports ED, Reno Gazette-Journal, Reno, NV
Hager, Robert .... (405) 282-2222
PUB, Food ED, News Leader, Guthrie, OK
Hager, Terry .... (541) 938-0702
PUB, Valley Times, Milton-Freewater, OR
Hager, William .... (501) 963-2901
PUB, Paris Express-Progress, Paris, AR
Hagert, Mary Lee .... (612) 777-8800
MAN ED
South-West Review, North St. Paul, MN
Hagerty, Marilyn .... (701) 780-1100
Food ED
Grand Forks Herald, Grand Forks, ND
Hagerty, Vaughn .... (512) 884-2011
Chief INFO Officer, Corpus Christi Caller-Times, Corpus Christi, TX
Hagg, Norman L .... (219) 267-3111
GM, EIC, Automotive/Travel ED, SCI ED
Times-Union, Warsaw, IN
Haggart, Peter .... (807) 343-6200
MAN ED
Chronicle-Journal, Thunder Bay, ON
Haggerty, Brenda .... (403) 532-1110
PROD SUPT
Daily Herald-Tribune, Grande Prairie, AB
Haggerty III, James D .... (617) 933-3700
TREAS, ED, Action Line ED, Books ED, BUS/FIN ED, EPE, Features ED, Health/Medical ED, NTL ED, Political/Government ED, Radio/Television ED, RE ED, Travel ED
Daily Times Chronicle, Woburn, MA
Haggerty IV, James D .... (617) 933-3700
MAN ED, City ED, News ED
Daily Times Chronicle, Woburn, MA
Haggerty Esq, James J .... (717) 265-2151
VP, Daily Review, Towanda, PA
Haggerty, Jay M .... (617) 933-3700
PROD MGR
Daily Times Chronicle, Woburn, MA
Haggerty, Jefferey .... (207) 784-5411
ADV MGR-RT Sales
Sun-Journal, Lewiston, ME
Haggerty, Joel .... (617) 933-3700
SEC, Daily Times Chronicle, Woburn, MA
Haggerty, Laurie .... (617) 933-3700
Amusements ED, Garden ED, Graphics ED/Art DIR, Home Furnishings ED, Music ED
Daily Times Chronicle, Woburn, MA
Haggerty, Mark .... (617) 933-3700
MGR-PROM
Daily Times Chronicle, Woburn, MA
Haggerty, Mary .... (617) 933-3700
ADV MGR-CLASS
Daily Times Chronicle, Woburn, MA
Haggerty, Mike .... (305) 350-2111
ASST MAN ED-Administration
Miami Herald, Miami, FL
Haggerty, Peter M .... (617) 933-3700
PRES, PUB, PSL MGR, PA
Daily Times Chronicle, Woburn, MA
Haggerty, Phil .... (219) 461-8333
PROD DIR, Journal Gazette, Fort Wayne, IN
Haggerty, Richard P .... (617) 933-3700
BM, Daily Times Chronicle, Woburn, MA
Haggerty, Thomas F .... (413) 788-1000
MAN ED-Production
Union-News, Springfield, MA
Haggstrom, Ron .... (218) 741-5544
Sports ED, Mesabi Daily News, Virginia, MN
Hagihara, Randy .... (213) 237-5000
Orange County City ED
Los Angeles Times, Los Angeles, CA
Hagin, Lawrence R .... (510) 228-7821
PRES/GM, Pacheco Automotive News Service, Concord, CA
Hagley, Robert .... (216) 999-4500
Database/Market RES MGR
Plain Dealer, Cleveland, OH
Hagstrom, Ed .... (503) 221-8327
PROD MGR, Oregonian, Portland, OR
Hagwood, Rod .... (954) 356-4000
Fashion ED
Sun-Sentinel, Fort Lauderdale, FL
Hagy, Ervin .... (301) 662-1177
CIRC DIR
Frederick Post/The News, Frederick, MD
Hahn, Arthur .... (409) 836-7956
MAN ED, EDL Writer
Brenham Banner-Press, Brenham, TX
Hahn, Carol .... (606) 292-2600
ADV DIR, Kentucky Post, Covington, KY
Hahn, Jon .... (206) 448-8000
COL-Features
Seattle Post-Intelligencer, Seattle, WA
Hahn, Laurie .... (219) 267-3111
Farm ED, Times-Union, Warsaw, IN
Hahn, Pat .... (613) 732-3691
PSL MGR, PA, Observer, Pembroke, ON
Hahn, Robert .... (513) 352-2000
Librarian, Cincinnati Post, Cincinnati, OH
Hahn, Terri .... (308) 382-1000
BUS ED, Features ED, Women's ED, Grand Island Independent, Grand Island, NE
Hahn, Tim .... (317) 633-1240
MGR-Safety
Indianapolis Star/News, Indianapolis, IN
Haider, Ted .... (607) 272-2321
MAN ED, Ithaca Journal, Ithaca, NY
Haidvogel, Lois .... (607) 734-5151
PSL DIR, Star-Gazette, Elmira, NY
Haigh, Sherri .... (905) 358-5711
City ED
Niagara Falls Review, Niagara Falls, ON
Haight, Donna G .... (515) 347-8721
PUB, ED, Afton Star-Enterprise, Afton, IA
Haight, Frank .... (816) 254-8600
Community News ED
Examiner, Independence, MO
Haight, Steven .... (908) 722-8800
PROD MGR-PR
Courier-News, Bridgewater, NJ
Haile, L John .... (407) 420-5000
VP/ED, Orlando Sentinel, Orlando, FL
Hailey, Prisilla .... (206) 627-1103
GM, Seattle Medium, Seattle, WA
Haines, Adelle .... (718) 389-6067
PUB, ED, Greenpoint Gazette & Advertiser, Brooklyn, NY
Haines, Olin .... (505) 823-7777
DP DIR, Albuquerque Publishing Co., Albuquerque, NM
Haines, Rosalee .... (330) 877-9345
ED, Hartville News, Hartville, OH
Haines, Tom .... (215) 949-4000
Entertainment/Television ED, Theater/Music ED, Bucks County Courier Times, Levittown, PA
Hainline, Kalyn .... (309) 652-3328
ED
Blandinsville Star-Gazette, Blandinsville, IL
Hainsworth, Jeremy .... (250) 782-4888
ED
Peace River Block News, Dawson Creek, BC
Hainworth, Ted .... (306) 652-9200
Books ED, Features ED
StarPhoenix, Saskatoon, SK
Haire, Bruce R .... (905) 857-6626
PUB, Caledon Citizen, Bolton, ON
Haire, Clarke .... (517) 872-2010
GM, Cass City Chronicle, Cass City, MI
Haire, John .... (517) 872-2010
PUB, Cass City Chronicle, Cass City, MI
Hairston, James (Hap) .... (212) 210-2100
ASST MAN ED
New York Daily News, New York, NY
Haitz III, Henry .... (814) 238-5000
CFO, Centre Daily Times, State College, PA
Hajna, Larry .... (609) 663-6000
Environmental ED
Courier-Post, Cherry Hill, NJ
Hakeman, Keith .... (605) 256-4555
PROD FRM-PR
Madison Daily Leader, Madison, SD
Hakowski, Maryann .... (757) 247-4600
Presentation ED
Daily Press, Newport News, VA
Halberstadt, Alan .... (519) 735-2080
ED, Shoreline Week, Tecumseh, ON
Halbfinger, Andrea S .... (516) 739-6400
ED, Valley Stream Maileader, Mineola, NY
Halbfoerster, David W .... (610) 837-0107
GM, Home News, Bath, PA
Halbfoerster, William J .... (610) 837-0107
PUB, ED, Home News, Bath, PA
Halblaub, Amy .... (614) 345-4053
Food ED, Advocate, Newark, OH
Halbreich, Jeremy L .... (214) 977-8222
PRES/GM, Dallas Morning News, Dallas, TX
Hale, Amy Sue .... (423) 447-2996
PUB, Bledsonian-Banner, Pikeville, TN
Hale, Barbara .... (209) 722-1511
Features ED, Merced Sun-Star, Merced, CA
Hale, Bert .... (815) 756-4841
PROD FRM-COMP
Daily Chronicle, De Kalb, IL
Hale, David .... (405) 353-0620
EPE, Lawton Constitution, Lawton, OK
Hale, David .... (209) 441-6111
Arts Writer, Fresno Bee, Fresno, CA
Hale, Don .... (613) 829-9100
EDU SRV MGR, Ottawa Citizen, Ottawa, ON
Hale, John .... (330) 385-4545
CIRC MGR, Review, East Liverpool, OH
Hale, Judy .... (616) 796-4831
MAN ED, Big Rapids Pioneer, Big Rapids, MI
Hale, Leon .... (713) 220-7171
COL, Houston Chronicle, Houston, TX
Hale, Marjorie P .... (606) 638-4581
GM, Big Sandy News, Louisa, KY
Hale, Mary Flora .... (508) 597-5465
PUB, Main Street Trilogy, Townsend, MA
Hale, Mike .... (706) 846-3188
GM, Star-Mercury, Manchester, GA
Hale, Monte .... (615) 893-5860
Sports ED
Daily News Journal, Murfreesboro, TN
Hale, Nancy .... (419) 636-1111
ADTX MGR, Bryan Times, Bryan, OH
Hale, Paul .... (715) 687-4112
PUB, ED, Stratford Journal, Stratford, WI
Hale, Peggy .... (330) 296-9657
Food ED, Society ED
Record-Courier, Kent-Ravenna, OH
Hale, Robert O .... (770) 267-8371
PUB, ED, Walton Tribune, Monroe, GA
Hale, Sue .... (405) 475-3311
Online MGR
Daily Oklahoman, Oklahoma City, OK
Hale, Terri .... (304) 327-2811
ADV DIR
Bluefield Daily Telegraph, Bluefield, WV
Hale, Todd .... (417) 623-3480
MGR-Telecommunications
Joplin Globe, Joplin, MO
Hale, Vip .... (209) 943-6397
PROD MGR-COMP, Record, Stockton, CA
Hale, Warren .... (313) 439-8118
ED, Milan Area Leader, Milan, MI
Hale, William S .... (608) 723-2151
PUB, Grant County Herald Independent, Lancaster, WI
Hale, Zan .... (215) 557-2300
ED, Legal Intelligencer, Philadelphia, PA
Hales, Linda .... (202) 334-6000
Washington Home ED
Washington Post, Washington, DC
Hales, William R .... (860) 522-1462
PUB, Inquirer Group, Hartford, CT
Haley, Dan .... (708) 524-8300
PUB, Wednesday Journal of Oak Park & River Forest, Oak Park, IL
Haley, Douglas F .... (219) 946-6628
PUB, Pulaski County Journal, Winamac, IN
Haley, Eric .... (501) 378-3400
PROD MGR-Remote Plant
Arkansas Democrat-Gazette, Little Rock, AR
Haley, Jean .... (816) 234-4141
Letters ED/EPE
Kansas City Star, Kansas City, MO
Haley, Laura .... (219) 946-6628
GM, Pulaski County Journal, Winamac, IN
Haley, Laura .... (506) 466-3220
ED, Saint Croix Courier, St. Stephen, NB
Halfman, Linda .... (515) 421-0500
ADV MGR-NTL/Co-op Sales
Globe-Gazette, Mason City, IA
Halfrey, Linda .... (617) 444-1706
ED, Millis Suburban Press, Needham, MA
Halgrimson, Andrea .... (701) 253-7311
Food ED, Librarian, Forum, Fargo, ND
Hall, Andy .... (904) 312-5200
Sports ED, Daily News, Palatka, FL
Hall, Annette .... (757) 857-1212
ED, Jet Observer, Norfolk, VA
Hall, Arthur R .... (609) 886-8600
PUB, Herald Newspapers, Rio Grande, NJ
Hall, Bill .... (816) 385-3121
PUB, Macon Chronicle-Herald, Macon, MO
Hall, Bill .... (208) 743-9411
EPE, Lewiston Morning Tribune, Lewiston, ID
Hall, Bill .... (407) 420-5000
PROD MGR-Building OPER
Orlando Sentinel, Orlando, FL
Hall, Bob .... (812) 424-7711
Television ED
Evansville Press, Evansville, IN
Hall, Bonnie .... (219) 356-6700
CIRC MGR
Huntington Herald-Press, Huntington, IN
Hall, Britt .... (409) 336-3611
MAN ED, Liberty Vindicator, Liberty, TX
Hall, Charlie .... (919) 446-5161
City ED, Telegram, Rocky Mount, NC
Hall, Charlotte H .... (516) 843-2020
DIR-MKTG, Newsday, Melville, NY
Hall, Cheryl .... (214) 977-8222
FIN ED, Dallas Morning News, Dallas, TX
Hall, Cody .... (205) 236-1551
Books ED, Anniston Star, Anniston, AL
Hall, David .... (216) 999-4500
ED, Plain Dealer, Cleveland, OH
Hall, Dennis W .... (507) 376-9711
PUB, Daily Globe, Worthington, MN
Hall, Don .... (605) 225-4100
Amusements ED, Music ED
Aberdeen American News, Aberdeen, SD

Hal Who's Where-94

Hall, Don .... (307) 347-3241
MAN ED, EPE, EDU ED
Northern Wyoming Daily News, Worland, WY

Hall, Don .... (914) 628-8400
PUB, ED, Brewster Times, Mahopac, NY

Hall, Don .... (519) 376-2250
CNR-Computer Services
Sun Times, Owen Sound, ON

Hall, Donna .... (610) 377-2051
ADV DIR-NTL, Times News, Lehighton, PA

Hall, Elaine .... (610) 820-6500
ADV MGR-CLASS
Morning Call, Allentown, PA

Hall, Fred .... (209) 875-2511
PUB, Sanger Herald, Sanger, CA

Hall, Fred M .... (417) 723-5248
GM, MAN ED, Crane Chronicle/Stone County Republican, Crane, MO

Hall, Gabriel .... (904) 359-4111
PROD SUPT-Newsprint Handling
Florida Times-Union, Jacksonville, FL

Hall, Gary .... (905) 526-3333
EPE, Spectator, Hamilton, ON

Hall, Gene .... (316) 788-2835
VP, Daily Reporter, Derby, KS

Hall, Gene A .... (515) 228-3211
PUB, Charles City Press, Charles City, IA

Hall, Glen .... (306) 642-5901
PUB, GM, Assiniboia Times, Assiniboia, SK

Hall, Gordon .... (517) 835-7171
PUB/CEO, Midland Daily News, Midland, MI

Hall, H .... (902) 426-2811
Comptroller, Chronicle-Herald, Halifax, NS

Hall, Jane .... (812) 886-9955
Women's ED
Vincennes Sun-Commercial, Vincennes, IN

Hall, Jane .... (213) 237-5000
Television Industry Writer-NY Bureau
Los Angeles Times, Los Angeles, CA

Hall, Janet G .... (502) 886-4444
ADV MGR-GEN Sales
Kentucky New Era, Hopkinsville, KY

Hall, Janice .... (813) 259-7711
BayLife ED
Tampa Tribune and Times, Tampa, FL

Hall, Jayne A Thomas .... (319) 352-3334
PUB, Bremer County Independent
Waverly, IA

Hall, Jeff .... (206) 455-2222
News ED, Eastside Journal, Bellevue, WA

Hall, Jeff .... (405) 228-2316
GM, ED, News-Democrat, Waurika, OK

Hall, Joe .... (416) 367-2000
Weekend ED, Toronto Star, Toronto, ON

Hall, John .... (912) 744-4200
CIRC ASST DIR
Macon Telegraph, Macon, GA

Hall, John .... (954) 356-4000
Graphics DIR
Sun-Sentinel, Fort Lauderdale, FL

Hall, John K .... (319) 547-3601
PUB, Times-Plain Dealer, Cresco, IA

Hall, Judy .... (916) 741-2345
MGR-CR, Appeal-Democrat, Marysville, CA

Hall, Julie .... (905) 372-0131
PROD SUPV
Cobourg Daily Star, Cobourg, ON

Hall, Karen .... (910) 323-4848
Controller
Fayetteville Observer-Times, Fayetteville, NC

Hall, Karen .... (519) 255-5711
EDL Writer, Windsor Star, Windsor, ON

Hall, Kelly .... (334) 670-6324
GM, Troy Progress, Troy, AL

Hall, Ken .... (616) 946-2000
EX ED, Record-Eagle, Traverse City, MI

Hall, Kevin .... (717) 255-8100
ADV SUPV-RT, Patriot-News, Harrisburg, PA

Hall, Kevin .... (212) 837-7000
BU Chief-Miami, Journal of Commerce & Commercial, New York, NY

Hall, Lane W .... (718) 372-1920
Correspondent
Graham News Syndicate, Brooklyn, NY

Hall, Larry .... (616) 429-2400
MGR-OPER
Herald-Palladium, St. Joseph, MI

Hall, Lawrence .... (201) 877-4141
COL, Star-Ledger, Newark, NJ

Hall, Lloyd R .... (704) 322-4510
CIRC MGR, Hickory Daily Record
Hickory, NC

Hall, Mark .... (810) 332-8181
PROD SUPT-PR, Oakland Press, Pontiac, MI

Hall, Mark .... (403) 235-7100
PROD MGR-Technical OPER
Calgary Herald, Calgary, AB

Hall, Marlene .... (918) 581-8300
Chief Accountant, Tulsa World, Tulsa, OK

Hall, Mary .... (907) 257-4200
CONT, Anchorage Daily News, Anchorage, AK

Hall, Matt .... (540) 638-8801
PROD MGR
Martinsville Bulletin, Martinsville, VA

Hall, Michael .... (619) 322-8889
PROD MGR, Desert Sun, Palm Springs, CA

Hall, Michael .... (403) 743-8186
Features ED
Fort McMurray Today, Fort McMurray, AB

Hall, Mike .... (505) 823-7777
Sports ED, Journal, Albuquerque, NM

Hall, Mike .... (502) 926-0123
Wire ED, Messenger-Inquirer, Owensboro, KY

Hall, Morrow .... (505) 384-2744
ED, Estancia Valley Citizen, Estancia, NM

Hall, Patricia .... (919) 829-4500
Newsroom Administrator
News & Observer, Raleigh, NC

Hall, Renette .... (504) 524-5563
ED, Louisiana Weekly, New Orleans, LA

Hall, Richard D .... (801) 237-2188
City ED, Deseret News, Salt Lake City, UT

Hall, Robert G .... (905) 768-3111
PUB, ED, Haldimand Press, Cayuga, ON

Hall, Robert J .... (215) 854-2000
PUB/Chairman, Philadelphia Inquirer, Philadelphia, PA, Knight-Ridder Inc.

Hall, Ron .... (903) 984-2593
CIRC MGR
Kilgore News Herald, Kilgore, TX

Hall, Ron .... (503) 363-0006
ED, Community News, Salem, OR

Hall, Rusty .... (217) 245-6121
CIRC MGR
Jacksonville Journal-Courier, Jacksonville, IL

Hall, Ruth .... (712) 328-1811
City ED, Daily Nonpareil, Council Bluffs, IA

Hall, Stan .... (816) 563-3606
PUB, ED
Knob Noster Item, Knob Noster, MO

Hall, Steve .... (334) 433-1551
ADV MGR-RT
Mobile Press Register, Mobile, AL

Hall, Steve .... (317) 633-1240
Television/Radio ED
Indianapolis Star/News, Indianapolis, IN

Hall, Steve .... (605) 394-8300
MGR-Human Resources
Rapid City Journal, Rapid City, SD

Hall, Steve .... (704) 873-1451
BM, Record & Landmark, Statesville, NC

Hall, Suzanne .... (423) 756-1234
Food ED
Chattanooga Times, Chattanooga, TN

Hall, Ted .... (616) 222-5400
PROD FRM-MR
Grand Rapids Press, Grand Rapids, MI

Hall, Terry L .... (804) 385-5400
VP, PUB, News & Advance, Lynchburg, VA

Hall, Trish .... (212) 556-1234
Living Section ED
New York Times, New York, NY

Hall, Wally .... (501) 378-3400
ASST MAN ED-Sports
Arkansas Democrat-Gazette, Little Rock, AR

Hall, William H .... (540) 963-1081
PUB, Richlands News-Press, Richlands, VA

Halla, Fred .... (718) 624-0528/3609
ED, Brooklyn Phoenix, Brooklyn Heights, NY

Hallameyer, John .... (410) 332-6000
PROD MGR-Sun Park, Sun, Baltimore, MD

Hallaron, Mike .... (404) 539-2200
ED, Montgomery County Bulletin, Conroe, TX

Hallas, Chuck .... (206) 455-2222
Photo DIR, Eastside Journal, Bellevue, WA

Hallas, James .... (860) 633-7691
PUB, ED
River East News Bulletin, Glastonbury, CT

Hallberg, Jeffrey .... (616) 533-8523
GM, Antrim County News, Bellaire, MI

Halle, Jean .... (410) 332-6000
VP-New BUS Development
Sun, Baltimore, MD

Halleck, Lonnie .... (612) 321-7300
GM, Twin Cities Reader, Minneapolis, MN

Hallenbeck, Terri .... (607) 432-1000
Night ED, Daily Star, Oneonta, NY

Haller, Catherine .... (705) 435-6228
ED, Herald Courier, Alliston, ON

Hallet, Kenneth .... (716) 328-2144
Correspondent
Syndicated News Service, Rochester, NY

Halliburton, Deanna .... (601) 843-4241
PROD FRM-PR
Bolivar Commercial, Cleveland, MS

Halliday, Nancy .... (617) 933-3700
Fashion/Women's ED, Food ED, Living/Lifestyle ED, SCI/Technology ED, Daily Times Chronicle, Woburn, MA

Halliday, Roland .... (616) 352-9659
ED
Benzie County Record-Patriot, Frankfort, MI

Halling, Gregory .... (913) 628-1081
MAN ED, EDL Writer
Hays Daily News, Hays, KS

Hallmark, Herrel .... (817) 559-5412
ED, American, Breckenridge, TX

Hallmark, Missy .... (915) 682-5311
News ED, Reporter-Telegram, Midland, TX

Hallmark, Pat .... (501) 935-5525
ADV MGR-CLASS
Jonesboro Sun, Jonesboro, AR

Hallock, John O .... (815) 889-4321
PUB, ED, Milford Herald-News, Milford, IL

Halloran, Dennis M .... (312) 616-3282
MAN ED, Dodge Construction News Chicago, Chicago, IL

Halloran, Paul .... (617) 593-7700
Sports ED, Daily Evening Item, Lynn, MA

Halloway, Beverly .... (816) 776-5454
CIRC MGR, PROD MGR
Daily News, Richmond, MO

Halls, Thom .... (209) 441-6111
Photo DIR, Fresno Bee, Fresno, CA

Hallyburton, Carole Anne .... (704) 633-8950
Radio/Television ED
Salisbury Post, Salisbury, NC

Halmo, Bruce .... (414) 457-7711
Photo Lab, Sheboygan Press, Sheboygan, WI

Halperen, Ian .... (972) 424-6565
Photo ED, Plano Star Courier, Plano, TX

Halperin, Naomi .... (610) 820-6500
Photo ED
Allentown Morning Call, Allentown, PA

Halpern, Joe .... (630) 844-5844
Sports ED, Beacon-News, Aurora, IL

Halpern, Robert L .... (915) 729-4342
PUB, ED, Big Bend Sentinel, Marfa, TX

Halpern, Rosario Salgado .... (915) 729-4342
GM, Big Bend Sentinel, Marfa, TX

Halsey, Ashley .... (215) 854-2000
Travel ED
Philadelphia Inquirer, Philadelphia, PA

Halsey, Linda .... (202) 334-6000
Travel ED (Style)
Washington Post, Washington, DC

Halstead, Ray .... (608) 356-4808
Sports ED, News-Republic/South Central Wisconsin News, Baraboo, WI

Halterman, Todd .... (616) 866-4465
ED, Rockford Squire, Rockford, MI

Halucha, John .... (705) 759-3030
ED, Sault Star, Sault Ste. Marie, ON

Halvorson, Barry .... (210) 379-5402
Sports ED, Gazette-Enterprise, Seguin, TX

Halvorson, Brenda .... (218) 894-1112
GM, Staples World, Staples, MN

Halvorson, Jeff .... (218) 751-3740
ADV DIR, Daily Pioneer, Bemidji, MN

Halvorson, Les .... (218) 281-2730
PROD MGR
Crookston Daily Times, Crookston, MN

Halvorson, Todd .... (407) 242-3500
Aerospace/Aviation ED
Florida Today, Melbourne, FL

Ham, C Mendel .... (910) 343-2000
CONT, Morning Star/Sunday Star-News, Wilmington, NC

Ham, Jeff .... (207) 791-6650
MET ED, Press Herald, Portland, ME

Ham, Jon C .... (919) 419-6500
MAN ED, COL
Durham Herald-Sun, Durham, NC

Ham, Larry .... (317) 462-5528
PROD MGR-Press/Plate
Daily Reporter, Greenfield, IN

Ham, Tom .... (919) 243-5151
Sports ED, Wilson Daily Times, Wilson, NC

Hamachek, Ross .... (202) 334-6000
VP-Planning/Development
Washington Post Co., Washington, DC

Hamaludin, Mohamed .... (305) 757-1147
ED, Miami Times, Miami, FL

Hamberger, Peter .... (519) 894-2231
BM, Record, Kitchener, ON

Hambke, Paul M .... (814) 226-7000
ED, Clarion News, Clarion, PA

Hamblett, Stephen .... (401) 277-7000
Chairman/PUB/CEO, PRES/COO
Providence Journal-Bulletin, Providence, RI

Hambrick, Randy .... (806) 762-8844
ADV DIR, Avalanche-Journal, Lubbock, TX

Hambrose, John .... (717) 348-9100
Automotive ED, Aviation ED, Religion ED
Tribune & The Scranton Times, Scranton, PA

Hamburger, Tom .... (612) 673-4000
BU Chief-Washington
Star Tribune, Minneapolis, MN

Hamel, Julie .... (913) 922-6856
ED, Chapman Advertiser and Enterprise Journal, Chapman, KS

Hamel, Maureen .... (860) 584-0501
Teen-Age/Youth ED, Women's ED
Bristol Press, Bristol, CT

Hamel, William B .... (217) 345-7085
PUB, Coles County Daily Times-Courier, Charleston, IL

Hamel Jr, William B .... (217) 235-5656
PUB, Mattoon Journal-Gazette, Mattoon, IL

Hamer, Jim .... (704) 252-5611
Sports ED
Asheville Citizen-Times, Asheville, NC

Hamer, Lori .... (815) 875-4461
ED, Bureau County Republican, Princeton, IL

Hamerly, David .... (210) 943-5545
MAN ED, Port Isabel-South Padre Press, Port Isabel, TX

Hamiel, Noel L .... (605) 996-5514
ED, Daily Republic, Mitchell, SD

Hamill, D .... (613) 933-3160
PROD FRM-COMP
Standard-Freeholder, Cornwall, ON

Hamill, Pete .... (212) 210-2100
EIC, New York Daily News, New York, NY

Hamill, Suzanne .... (617) 592-4601
ED, Lynn Sunday Post, Lynn, MA

Hamilton, Bill .... (204) 857-3427
ADV MGR
Daily Graphic, Portage la Prairie, MB

Hamilton, Bob .... (817) 592-4431
PUB, ED, Iowa Park Leader, Iowa Park, TX

Hamilton, Brian .... (313) 475-1371
GM, ED, Chelsea Standard, Chelsea, MI

Hamilton, C A .... (706) 886-9476
PUB, ED, Toccoa Record, Toccoa, GA

Hamilton, David .... (317) 962-1575
PROD MGR-Pre Press
Palladium-Item, Richmond, IN

Hamilton, Ed .... (317) 552-3355
Sports ED, Elwood Call-Leader, Elwood, IN

Hamilton, Floyd .... (810) 332-8181
CIRC MGR, Oakland Press, Pontiac, MI

Hamilton, Fred .... (360) 754-5400
PRES, PUB, Olympian, Olympia, WA

Hamilton, Gaildene .... (765) 362-1200
MAN ED, EPE
Journal Review, Crawfordsville, IN

Hamilton, Grant M .... (716) 652-0320
PUB, ED, Advertiser, East Aurora, NY

Hamilton, Harriet .... (501) 442-1777
Living Section Writer
Northwest Arkansas Times, Fayetteville, AR

Hamilton, Jack .... (707) 725-6166
ED, Humboldt Beacon, Fortuna, CA

Hamilton, James E .... (417) 345-2224
PUB, Buffalo Reflex, Buffalo, MO

Hamilton, Jimmy V .... (901) 529-2211
PROD DIR-OPER
Commercial Appeal, Memphis, TN

Hamilton, June .... (705) 472-3200
BM, PA, North Bay Nugget, North Bay, ON

Hamilton, Katy .... (717) 264-6161
Wire ED, Public Opinion, Chambersburg, PA

Hamilton, Kenneth .... (405) 889-3319
ED, Atoka County Times, Atoka, OK

Hamilton, Kevin .... (510) 208-6300
Online MGR, Oakland Tribune, Oakland, CA
MediaNews Inc. (Alameda Newspapers)

Hamilton, Linda .... (916) 321-1000
CIRC MGR-Home Delivery
Sacramento Bee, Sacramento, CA

Hamilton, Lynn .... (501) 378-3400
VP/OPER MGR, PROD VP/OPER MGR
Arkansas Democrat-Gazette, Little Rock, AR

Hamilton, Mark H .... (515) 648-2521
PUB, Times-Citizen, Iowa Falls, IA

Hamilton, Martin D .... (970) 668-3998
Sports ED, Summit Daily News, Frisco, CO

Hamilton, Nancy F .... (707) 545-1166
Recordings, Sonoma County Daily Herald-Recorder, Santa Rosa, CA

Hamilton, Patrick .... (210) 686-4343
Photo ED, Monitor, McAllen, TX

Hamilton, Penny .... (801) 462-2134
ED, Pyramid, Mount Pleasant, UT

Hamilton, Scott M .... (718) 296-2200
GM, Leader/Observer, Woodhaven, NY

Hamilton, Sherry L .... (501) 735-1010
VP, GM, Evening Times, West Memphis, AR

Hamilton, Terry .... (604) 478-9552
PUB, Goldstream News Gazette, Victoria, BC

Hamilton, Terry .... (716) 232-7100
PROD MGR-Press Production
Rochester Democrat and Chronicle; Rochester, NY Times-Union, Rochester, NY

Hamilton, Vernice .... (910) 765-5502
GM, Wilmington Journal, Wilmington, NC

Hamilton, William .... (409) 295-5407
Accountant, Huntsville Item, Huntsville, TX

Hamilton, William .... (202) 334-6000
NTL ED, Washington Post, Washington, DC

Hamler, Bobbi .... (610) 933-8926
PROD FRM-COMP Room
Phoenix, Phoenixville, PA

Hamler, Wayne .... (715) 833-9200
PROD FRM-COMP
Leader-Telegram, Eau Claire, WI

Hamlin, John .... (503) 221-8327
SYS DIR, Oregonian, Portland, OR

Hamlin, Richard A .... (812) 384-3501
ADV MGR, PROD SUPT
Evening World, Bloomfield, IN

Hamm, Andrew .... (209) 835-3030
City ED, Tracy Press, Tracy, CA

Hamm, Benjamin .... (864) 582-4511
City ED, Herald-Journal, Spartanburg, SC

Hamm, Catherine .... (909) 889-9666
MAN ED, Sun, San Bernardino, CA

Copyright ©1997 by the Editor & Publisher Co.

95-Who's Where **Han**

Hamm, Claus .... (603) 224-5301
BUS ED, Concord Monitor, Concord, NH
Hamm, Jack .... (214) 371-3986
Artist/DIR
Religious Drawings Inc., Dallas, TX
Hamm, Madeleine McDermott . (713) 220-7171
Home Furnishings ED
Houston Chronicle, Houston, TX
Hamm, Patricia .... (508) 458-7100
ADV CNR-NTL, Sun, Lowell, MA
Hamm, Sandy .... (800) 922-4655
MGR, Newsfinder, Milwaukee, WI
Hamm, Wanda .... (217) 446-1000
PROD FRM-MR
Commercial News, Danville, IL
Hammack, Carol .... (407) 242-3500
DIR-Customer Relations
Florida Today, Melbourne, FL
Hammer, Hoby .... (405) 227-4439
PUB, Fairview Republican, Fairview, OK
Hammer, Larry .... (405) 596-3344
PUB, Cherokee Messenger & Republican, Cherokee, OK
Hammer, Lisa .... (309) 944-2119
ED, Geneseo Republic, Geneseo, IL
Hammer, Randy .... (608) 754-3311
CIRC DIR
Janesville Gazette, Janesville, WI
Hammer, Randy .... (417) 836-1100
EX ED
Springfield News-Leader, Springfield, MO
Hammericksen, Randy .... (541) 776-4411
COL, Sports ED
Mail Tribune, Medford, OR
Hammersley, Clarke W .... (203) 272-5316
ED, Cheshire Herald, Cheshire, CT
Hammerstrom, Richard .... (540) 638-8801
MAN ED, EPE
Martinsville Bulletin, Martinsville, VA
Hammes, Daniel H .... (208) 245-4538
PUB
Saint Maries Gazette-Record, St. Maries, ID
Hammes, Robert M .... (208) 245-4538
ED
Saint Maries Gazette-Record, St. Maries, ID
Hammett, Glenn .... (805) 395-7500
Design ED
Bakersfield Californian, Bakersfield, CA
Hammett, John B .... (408) 920-5000
Senior VP-Employee/Community Relations
San Jose Mercury News, San Jose, CA
Hammock, Brian .... (918) 225-3333
ADV MGR, MGR-MKTG & PROM
Cushing Daily Citizen, Cushing, OK
Hammock, John .... (601) 961-7000
News ED, Clarion-Ledger, Jackson, MS
Hammock, Ralph .... (912) 452-0567
PROD DIR
Union-Recorder, Milledgeville, GA
Hammond, Bill .... (716) 366-3000
Entertainment/Amusements ED, News ED
Evening Observer, Dunkirk, NY
Hammond, Bruce .... (503) 221-8327
Team Leader-West, Oregonian, Portland, OR
Hammond, Gregg .... (516) 826-0812
MAN ED, Citizen, Bellmore, NY
Hammond, Ken .... (713) 220-7171
Texas Magazine ED
Houston Chronicle, Houston, TX
Hammond, Margo .... (813) 893-8111
Books ED
St. Petersburg Times, St. Petersburg, FL
Hammond, Marla .... (817) 390-7400
Online MGR
Fort Worth Star-Telegram, Fort Worth, TX
Hammond CPA, Philip W .... (301) 662-1177
TREAS
Frederick Post/The News, Frederick, MD
Hammond, Robert .... (307) 742-2176
Sports ED
Laramie Daily Boomerang, Laramie, WY
Hammond, Robert R .... (304) 255-4400
PUB, Register Herald, Beckley, WV
Hammond, Ruth .... (505) 648-2333
PUB, ED
Lincoln County News, Carrizozo, NM
Hammond, Todd .... (916) 756-0800
Photo ED, Davis Enterprise, Davis, CA
Hammond-Cuff, Eileen .... (510) 935-2525
PROD MGR-Pre Press
Contra Costa Times, Walnut Creek, CA
Hammonds, Don .... (412) 263-1100
ASSOC ED
Pittsburgh Post-Gazette, Pittsburgh, PA
Hammonds, Randy .... (901) 427-3333
PROD ASST DIR-OPER, PROD MGR-Technical SRV, Jackson Sun, Jackson, TN
Hammons, Kathy .... (706) 724-0851
MGR-CR, Augusta Chronicle, Augusta, GA
Hammons, Randy .... (601) 684-2421
Sports ED, Enterprise-Journal, McComb, MS
Hammontree, Chris .... (816) 234-4141
CIRC MGR-State CIRC
Kansas City Star, Kansas City, MO
Hammontree, Don .... (630) 834-0900
ED, Wood Dale Press, Elmhurst, IL
Hamory, June .... (352) 567-5639
ED, Pasco News, Dade City, FL
Hamp, Thomas W .... (517) 366-5341
PUB, ED
Houghton Lake Resorter, Houghton Lake, MI
Hampton, Arthur .... (812) 723-2572
GM, Paoli Republican, Paoli, IN
Hampton, Brett .... (317) 398-6631
Chief Photographer
Shelbyville News, Shelbyville, IN
Hampton, David .... (601) 961-7000
EDL DIR, Clarion-Ledger, Jackson, MS
Hampton, David .... (709) 634-4348
CIRC MGR, Western Star, Corner Brook, NF
Hampton, Denise .... (919) 829-4500
CIRC MGR-Development
News & Observer, Raleigh, NC
Hampton, Harold .... (612) 222-5011
VP-Pre Press & Technology
St. Paul Pioneer Press, St. Paul, MN
Hampton, Jim .... (305) 350-2111
ED, Miami Herald, Miami, FL
Hampton, John .... (501) 483-6317
GM, Trumann Democrat, Trumann, AR
Hampton, Pat .... (707) 942-6242
ED, Weekly Calistogan, Calistoga, CA
Hampton, Paul .... (601) 896-2100
News ED, Sun Herald, Biloxi, MS
Hampton, Randy .... (402) 475-4200
Photo MGR
Lincoln Journal Star, Lincoln, NE
Hampton, Walter P .... (954) 356-4000
TREAS, DIR-FIN
Sun-Sentinel, Fort Lauderdale, FL
Hampton, Will .... (512) 255-5827
ED, Round Rock Leader, Round Rock, TX
Hamrick, Rhonda .... (601) 896-2100
Librarian, Sun Herald, Biloxi, MS
Hamstra, Terri .... (317) 636-0200
CIRC DIR
Court & Commercial Record, Indianapolis, IN
Hanafin, John C .... (217) 324-2121
PUB, BM, News-Herald, Litchfield, IL
Hanafin, Teresa M .... (617) 929-2000
ASST MAN ED-MET
Boston Globe, Boston, MA
Hanan, Jeff .... (319) 524-8300
MAN ED, Daily Gate City, Keokuk, IA
Hance, Cheryl .... (717) 265-2151
PROD SUPT (Night)
Daily Review, Towanda, PA
Hanchett, Bonnie J .... (408) 374-9700
PUB, Campbell Express, Campbell, CA
Hanchett, Kathryn .... (408) 374-9700
ED, Campbell Express, Campbell, CA
Hancks, Murray .... (309) 786-6441
EPE, Rock Island Argus, Rock Island, IL
Hancock, Barbara .... (614) 363-1161
Lifestyle/Religion ED
Delaware Gazette, Delaware, OH
Hancock, Eric .... (907) 835-2211
GM, Valdez Vanguard, Valdez, AK
Hancock, Gina .... (502) 753-1916
MAN ED, EDL Writer
Murray Ledger & Times, Murray, KY
Hancock, Kevin .... (910) 227-0131
ADV DIR
Times News Publishing Co., Burlington, NC
Hancock, Marilyn .... (508) 586-7200
EDU ED, Enterprise, Brockton, MA
Hancock, Rhonda .... (770) 537-2434
ED, Haralson Gateway Beacon, Bremen, GA
Hancock, Stewart F .... (315) 635-3921
PUB, Messenger, Baldwinsville, NY
Hancock, Tina .... (804) 978-7200
ADV MGR-Sales
Daily Progress, Charlottesville, VA
Hancock, Todd .... (406) 654-2020
GM, MAN ED
Phillips County News, Malta, MT
Hancon, Leigh .... (847) 329-2000
MAN ED, Skokie Life, Lincolnwood, IL
Hancox, Mike .... (902) 629-6000
ADV MGR-RT, Guardian, Charlottetown, PEI
Hand, Earl .... (541) 672-3321
CIRC DIR, News-Review, Roseburg, OR
Hand, Gail Stewart .... (701) 780-1100
Family ED, Personal Issues ED
Grand Forks Herald, Grand Forks, ND
Hand, Michael D .... (334) 864-8885
PUB, ED, LaFayette Sun, LaFayette, AL
Handcock, Judy .... (606) 678-8191
BM, Commonwealth-Journal, Somerset, KY
Handel, Donna .... (508) 222-7000
PROD SUPV-Graphics
Sun Chronicle, Attleboro, MA
Handel, Jeremy .... (602) 497-0048
ED, Gilbert Independent, Chandler, AZ
Handel, Mary L .... (406) 791-1444
MGR-CR
Great Falls Tribune, Great Falls, MT
Handelman, Jay .... (941) 953-7755
Films/Theater ED
Sarasota Herald-Tribune, Sarasota, FL
Handeyside, Robert H .... (517) 752-7171
MET ED, Saginaw News, Saginaw, MI
Handley, Marilyn .... (334) 575-3282
ED, Monroe Journal, Monroeville, AL
Handley, Ruth .... (405) 341-2121
CIRC DIR, Edmond Evening Sun
Edmond, OK
Handrick, Denise .... (414) 435-4411
PROD MGR-Pre Press
Green Bay Press-Gazette, Green Bay, WI
Handwiche, Kenneth .... (414) 867-2158
ED, Weyauwega Chronicle, Weyauwega, WI
Handy, Carolyn .... (603) 742-3700
ED, Tri-Town Transcript, Dover, NH
Handy, Stephen G .... (801) 237-2188
DIR-MKTG
Deseret News, Salt Lake City, UT
Hanel, Joe .... (303) 776-2244
Graphics ED
Daily Times-Call, Longmont, CO
Haner, Francis .... (419) 294-2332
CIRC DIR
Daily Chief-Union, Upper Sandusky, OH
Hanes, Doug .... (714) 835-1234
ADV VP
Orange County Register, Santa Ana, CA
Hanes, Karen E .... (904) 747-5000
PUB, News Herald, Panama City, FL
Haney, Charles .... (816) 646-2411
PUB, PA
Constitution-Tribune, Chillicothe, MO
Haney, Kevin .... (816) 646-2411
ADV MGR-GEN, SCI/Technology ED, Television/Film ED, Theater/Music ED, Travel ED, Constitution-Tribune, Chillicothe, MO
Haney, Mark .... (810) 664-0811
ED, County Press, Lapeer, MI
Haney, Paul .... (908) 349-3000
ADV DIR, DIR-MKTG/PROM
Ocean County Observer, Toms River, NJ
Hanie, Retta .... (214) 327-9335
PUB, ED, White Rocker News, Dallas, TX
Hanif, C B .... (561) 820-4100
Reader Representative
Palm Beach Post, West Palm Beach, FL
Hanisek, Greg .... (203) 574-3636
News ED, Waterbury Republican-American, Waterbury, CT
Hank, Ron .... (312) 222-3232
PROD MGR-Printing OPER
Chicago Tribune, Chicago, IL
Hanka, Harold .... (860) 442-2200
ASST MAN ED-Photography/Graphics
Day, New London, CT
Hanke, Michael E .... (330) 454-5611
ED, Repository, Canton, OH
Hankin, Larry .... (303) 861-2234
MAN ED
Intermountain Jewish News, Denver, CO
Hankins, Bill .... (903) 785-8744
MAN ED, Paris News, Paris, TX
Hankins, Greg .... (910) 576-6051
GM, Montgomery Herald, Troy, NC
Hankins, R Guy .... (910) 576-6051
PUB, Montgomery Herald, Troy, NC
Hanks, Jeannie .... (915) 445-5475
CIRC MGR, Pecos Enterprise, Pecos, TX
Hanks, Linda .... (904) 359-4111
Fashion ED
Florida Times-Union, Jacksonville, FL
Hanks, Mechealle .... (606) 231-3100
DIR-Technology/INFO SYS, PROD DIR-Technology/INFO SRV, Lexington Herald-Leader, Lexington, KY
Hanley, James R .... (203) 846-3281
Wire ED, Hour, Norwalk, CT
Hanley, Joseph .... (312) 649-5464
Sales MGR, Crain News Service, Chicago, IL
Hanley, Mark .... (718) 981-1234
EPE/Books ED
Staten Island Advance, Staten Island, NY
Hanley, Robert .... (619) 299-3131
BUS ED-Night
San Diego Union-Tribune, San Diego, CA
Hanlon, Gary .... (409) 384-3441
ED, Jasper News-Boy, Jasper, TX
Hanlon, Leigh .... (847) 329-2000
MAN ED
Morton Grove/Niles Life, Lincolnwood, IL
Hann, Gale .... (503) 897-2772
PUB, ED, Mill City Enterprise, Mill City, OR
Hann, Rick .... (705) 726-6537
CIRC MGR, Examiner, Barrie, ON
Hanna, Barbara .... (509) 276-5043
PUB, Tribune, Deer Park, WA
Hanna, Christine .... (614) 654-1321
Accent Society ED, Features ED, Lifestyle ED, Television/Film ED, Travel ED, Women's ED, Lancaster Eagle-Gazette, Lancaster, OH
Hanna, Ivy .... (613) 478-2017
PUB, ED, Tweed News, Tweed, ON
Hanna, Jim .... (705) 746-2104
ED, North Star, Parry Sound, ON
Hanna, Pat .... (304) 255-4400
City ED, Register Herald, Beckley, WV
Hanna, Paul .... (605) 225-4100
PROD MGR-MR
Aberdeen American News, Aberdeen, SD
Hanna, S Dwight .... (410) 332-6000
ADV MGR-Local, Sun, Baltimore, MD
Hanna, Sam .... (318) 435-4521
PUB, ED, Franklin Sun, Winnsboro, LA
Hanna, William .... (218) 741-5544
ED, Mesabi Daily News, Virginia, MN
Hannaford, N .... (604) 723-8171
PUB/GM, CR MGR
Alberni Valley Times, Port Alberni, BC
Hannagan, A .... (619) 740-9561
PUB, Hispanos Unidos, Escondido, CA
Hannagan, Richard A .... (608) 339-7844
PUB, ED, Adams County Times/The Friendship Reporter, Adams, WI
Hannah, Jim .... (702) 383-0211
PSL MGR
Las Vegas Review-Journal, Las Vegas, NV
Hannah, Steve .... (319) 398-8211
VP-INFO Technologies
Gazette, Cedar Rapids, IA
Hannah, Ted .... (212) 455-4000
DIR-ADV & Public Relations, North America Syndicate, King Features Syndicate Inc., New York, NY
Hannahs, Kathy .... (541) 926-2211
ASST CONT
Albany Democrat-Herald, Albany, OR
Hannan, William .... (412) 775-3200
CIRC MGR-Distribution
Beaver County Times, Beaver, PA
Hanner, Carol .... (606) 231-3100
ASST MAN ED-Projects
Lexington Herald-Leader, Lexington, KY
Hanner, Gary .... (205) 884-2310
ED, St. Clair News-Aegis, Pell City, AL
Hanner, Ken .... (202) 636-3000
NTL ED, Washington Times, Washington, DC
Hanney, Brian .... (816) 885-2281
Sports ED
Clinton Daily Democrat, Clinton, MO
Hannibal, Edward W .... (415) 777-5700
Senior VP-ADM, San Francisco Newspaper Agency, San Francisco, CA
Hannigan, Mike .... (903) 489-0531
ED, Malakoff News, Malakoff, TX
Hannon, Bob .... (201) 935-1612
PUB, ED, Independent, Wood-Ridge, NJ
Hano, Randy .... (617) 426-3000
ADV MGR-NTL, Boston Herald, Boston, MA
Hans, Thomas R .... (412) 263-1100
PROD MGR-Press/Paper
Pittsburgh Post-Gazette, Pittsburgh, PA
Hanscom, Dennis .... (206) 339-3000
PROD MGR-Ad, Herald, Everett, WA
Hanselman, Cyndy .... (515) 637-2632
ED, New Sharon Star, New Sharon, IA
Hansen, Alice .... (907) 456-6661
ADV MGR-CLASS
Fairbanks Daily News-Miner, Fairbanks, AK
Hansen, Bill .... (307) 532-2184
PUB, Torrington Telegram, Torrington, WY
Hansen, Bob .... (317) 489-4035
PUB, ED, Main Event, Hagerstown, IN
Hansen, Debbie .... (206) 348-5598
Partner, Schwartz, Gary, Mukilteo, WA
Hansen, Don .... (319) 588-5611
PROD DIR-OPER
Telegraph Herald, Dubuque, IA
Hansen, George .... (509) 925-1414
Sports ED, Daily Record, Ellensburg, WA
Hansen, Glenn P .... (414) 766-4651
PUB, Kaukauna Times, Kaukauna, WI
Hansen, Jeff .... (205) 325-2222
SCI ED, Birmingham News, Birmingham, AL
Hansen, Jo .... (847) 381-9200
ED, Barrington Courier-Review, Barrington, IL
Hansen, John .... (919) 829-4500
Photo ED, News & Observer, Raleigh, NC
Hansen, Larry .... (402) 371-1020
PROD FRM-PR
Norfolk Daily News, Norfolk, NE
Hansen, Leonard J .... (970) 385-6999
COL/ED, Mature Market Editorial Services, Durango, CO
Hansen, Lyle J .... (414) 766-4651
GM, Kaukauna Times, Kaukauna, WI
Hansen, Marc .... (515) 284-8000
Local COL, Sports COL
Des Moines Register, Des Moines, IA
Hansen, Norvin .... (402) 385-3013
PUB, ED, Pender Times, Pender, NE
Hansen, Pat .... (765) 489-4035
PUB, MAN ED
Hagerstown Exponent, Hagerstown, IN
Hansen, Ramon D .... (315) 493-1270
PUB, ED, Republican Tribune, Carthage, NY
Hansen, Reed .... (800) 365-3020
PUB, Gunfighter, Boise, ID
Hansen, Trygg J .... (715) 239-6688
PUB
Cornell & Lake Holcombe Courier, Cornell, WI

Han Who's Where-96

Hansen, William (941) 953-7755
PUB-Manatee (AM)
Sarasota Herald-Tribune, Sarasota, FL
Hansen Cardona, Laurie (414) 769-3500
MAN ED, Catholic Herald, Milwaukee, WI
Hansford, Cheryl (705) 869-2860
ED, Mid-North Monitor, Espanola, ON
Hanshaw, Lynda (303) 892-5000
CIRC DIR-SYS Development
Rocky Mountain News, Denver, CO
Hanson, Bernard (517) 725-5136
PROD MGR, Argus-Press, Owosso, MI
Hanson, Bob (913) 837-4321
ED, Louisburg Herald, Louisburg, KS
Hanson, Christopher (206) 448-8000
Washington Correspondent
Seattle Post-Intelligencer, Seattle, WA
Hanson, Doug (507) 647-5357
PUB, Winthrop News, Winthrop, MN
Hanson, Gene (816) 637-6155
EX ED, Daily Standard, Excelsior Springs, MO
Hanson, Holly (313) 222-6400
Fashion Writer
Detroit Free Press, Detroit, MI
Hanson, Jean (916) 527-2151
ADV MGR, Daily News, Red Bluff, CA
Hanson, Jim (216) 994-3241
PROD DIR, Star-Beacon, Ashtabula, OH
Hanson, Karen (207) 282-1535
Sports ED, Journal Tribune, Biddeford, ME
Hanson, Keith (406) 265-6795
PROD FRM-PR, Havre Daily News, Havre, MT
Hanson, Kevin (509) 235-6184
ED, Cheney Free Press, Cheney, WA
Hanson, Larry L (206) 339-3000
PRES, PUB, Herald, Everett, WA
Hanson, Mark (701) 857-1900
ED, Minot Daily News, Minot, ND
Hanson, Marla (817) 754-3511
PUB, Waco Citizen, Waco, TX
Hanson, Melba (604) 426-6119
PUB, GM
Rocky Mountain Weekender, Cranbrook, BC
Hanson, Patty (803) 771-6161
City/MET ED, State, Columbia, SC
Hanson, Perry (913) 543-5242
ED, Phillips County Review, Phillipsburg, KS
Hanson, Robert (218) 485-8420
PUB, MAN ED
Arrowhead Leader, Moose Lake, MN
Hanson, Robert A (402) 746-3700
PUB, ED, Red Cloud Chief, Red Cloud, NE
Hanson, Sandy (970) 625-3245
ED, Citizen Telegram, Rifle, CO
Hanson, Sara (417) 836-1100
Suburban ED, News-Leader, Springfield, MO
Hanson, Tammy (517) 265-5111
CIRC MGR, Daily Telegram, Adrian, MI
Hanson II, V H (205) 325-2222
PRES, PUB
Birmingham News, Birmingham, AL
Hanson III, V H (205) 325-2222
VP, GM, Birmingham News, Birmingham, AL
Hanson, Worth (616) 222-5400
ADV MGR-Advertising Production
Grand Rapids Press, Grand Rapids, MI
Hanus OSB, Most Rev Jerome (319) 588-0556
PUB, Witness, Dubuque, IA
Hao, Sean (317) 423-5511
BUS Writer, Journal and Courier
Lafayette, IN
Happ, Tom (319) 398-8211
PROD Administrator
Gazette, Cedar Rapids, IA
Harabedian, Mark (212) 837-7000
VP/CONT, Journal of Commerce & Commercial, New York, NY
Harada, Wayne (808) 525-8000
Arts/Entertainment ED
Honolulu Advertiser, Honolulu, HI
Haraden, Christopher (617) 925-9266
ED, Hull Times, Hull, MA
Haram, Karen (210) 225-7411
Food ED
San Antonio Express-News, San Antonio, TX
Harasta, Cathy (214) 977-8222
COL-SportsDay
Dallas Morning News, Dallas, TX
Harayda, Janice (216) 999-4500
Books ED, Plain Dealer, Cleveland, OH
Harbaugh, Marg (704) 333-1718
BUS MGR
Independent Tribune, Concord, NC
Harbinson, Sandy (807) 887-3583
PUB
Nipigon-Red Rock Gazette, Nipigon, ON
Harbison, J Glenn (706) 632-2019
PUB, ED, News Observer, Blue Ridge, GA
Harbor, Frank (561) 461-2050
ADV MGR-Major Accounts
Tribune, Fort Pierce, FL
Harbour, Alison B (501) 623-7711
Books ED, Films/Theater ED, Radio/Television ED, Sentinel-Record, Hot Springs, AR
Hardee, Gary M (817) 390-7400
ED-Arlington
Fort Worth Star-Telegram, Fort Worth, TX
Hardee, Ricky A (803) 756-1447
PUB, Loris Scene, Loris, SC
Hardegree, Stan (770) 428-9411
ED, Paulding Neighbor, Marietta, GA
Harden, Bennie (910) 434-2716
PUB, Archdale Trinity News, Archdale, NC
Harden, David (209) 532-7151
MGR-SYS, Union Democrat, Sonora, CA
Harden, George (617) 929-2000
ADV MGR-Display, Boston Globe, Boston, MA
Harden, Jon B (860) 296-6128
PUB, ED, Hartford News, Hartford, CT
Harden, Kevin (503) 226-1311
ED, Portland Daily Journal of Commerce, Portland, OR
Harden, Mark (303) 820-1010
State ED, Denver Post, Denver, CO
Harden, Rubye Del (601) 862-3141
PUB, ED, Itawamba County Times
Fulton, MS
Harder, James (617) 329-5008
ED, West Roxbury Transcript, Dedham, MA
Hardgrave, Johnie (903) 885-8663
ADV DIR, Sulphur Springs News-Telegram, Sulphur Springs, TX
Hardie, Douglas (210) 542-4301
PUB, Brownsville Herald, Brownsville, TX
Freedom Communications Inc.
Hardie, Robert C (714) 553-9292
COB
Freedom Communications Inc., Irvine, CA
Hardie, Tom (612) 673-4000
PROD MGR, Star Tribune, Minneapolis, MN
Hardin, Bill (918) 684-2828
DP MGR-Accounting, Muskogee Daily Phoenix & Times Democrat, Muskogee, OK
Hardin, Carolyn (309) 764-4344
Environmental ED, Government ED, Health/Medical ED, SCI/Technology ED, Dispatch, Moline, IL, Small Newspaper Group Inc.
Hardin, David (813) 259-7711
ASST MAN ED
Tampa Tribune and Times, Tampa, FL
Hardin, James R (937) 456-5553
PUB, County Register, Eaton, OH
Hardin, John Thomas (804) 758-2328
MAN ED, Southside Sentinel, Urbanna, VA
Hardin, Rozella (423) 928-4151
Home Furnishings ED, Teen-Age/Youth ED
Elizabethton Star, Elizabethton, TN
Hardin, William C (318) 728-6467
ED, Richland Beacon-News, Rayville, LA
Hardin, Winn (904) 879-2727
ED, Nassau County Record, Callahan, FL
Harding, Adella (702) 738-3119
BUS ED, Elko Daily Free Press, Elko, NV
Harding, Barbara (910) 679-4900
ED, Enterprise, Yadkinville, NC
Harding, Gail M (540) 694-3101
PUB, Enterprise, Stuart, VA
Harding, Jennifer (803) 771-6161
CIRC MGR-Sales & MKTG
State, Columbia, SC
Harding, John (250) 762-4445
Sports ED, Daily Courier, Kelowna, BC
Harding, Laura (505) 983-3303
ADTX MGR, New Mexican, Santa Fe, NM
Harding, Ron (250) 762-4445
ADV MGR-Special Projects
Daily Courier, Kelowna, BC
Harding, Scott (303) 776-2244
MGR-District
Daily Times-Call, Longmont, CO
Hardister, Tina (501) 315-8228
Women's ED, Benton Courier, Benton, AR
Hardisty, Dianne (805) 395-7500
EPE, Bakersfield Californian, Bakersfield, CA
Hardman, Vera (504) 892-2323
GM, St. Tammany Farmer, Covington, LA
Hardy, Darrel (918) 224-5185
BM, Sapulpa Daily Herald, Sapulpa, OK
Hardy, Doug (860) 584-0501
News ED, Bristol Press, Bristol, CT
Hardy, Earl G (334) 792-3141
PROD MGR-COMP, Eagle, Dothan, AL
Hardy, Ian (416) 494-4990
PUB, Daily Commercial News and Construction Record, N. York, ON
Hardy, Judy (805) 650-2900
Retention MGR
Ventura County Star, Ventura, CA
Hardy, Marty (913) 227-3348
ED, Lindsborg News-Record, Lindsborg, KS
Hardy, Michael (334) 433-1551
Environmental Reporter
Mobile Press Register, Mobile, AL
Hardy, Sandra C (215) 949-4000
VP/SEC, Bucks County Courier Times, Levittown, PA, Calkins Newspapers
Hardy, Shawn (717) 762-2151
Religion ED
Record Herald, Waynesboro, PA
Hardy, Steve (705) 726-6537
Sports ED, Examiner, Barrie, ON
Hardy, Vivan (910) 343-2000
PROD FRM-COMP (Night), Morning Star/Sunday Star-News, Wilmington, NC
Hardy-Carranza, Joann (520) 573-4220
PROD MGR-SRV
Arizona Daily Star, Tucson, AZ
Hare, Doug (403) 352-2231
PUB, Times-Advertiser, Wetaskiwin, AB
Hare, Doug (403) 532-1110
ADV Sales MGR
Daily Herald-Tribune, Grande Prairie, AB
Hare, Kenneth (334) 262-1611
EPE, Advertiser, Montgomery, AL
Hare, Kevin (616) 964-7161
Photo DEPT MGR
Battle Creek Enquirer, Battle Creek, MI
Hare, Lowell A (505) 823-7777
VP-FIN
Albuquerque Journal, Albuquerque, NM
Hare, Mark (716) 232-7100
EPE-Times-Union, Rochester Democrat and Chronicle; Times-Union, Rochester, NY
Hare, Monica (419) 586-2371
Sports ED, Daily Standard, Celina, OH
Hare, Rabbit (918) 581-8300
Photo DEPT MGR, Tulsa World, Tulsa, OK
Hare, Tony (317) 473-6641
Photo DEPT MGR, Peru Tribune, Peru, IN
Haren, Pam (330) 454-5611
ADV MGR-SRV, Repository, Canton, OH
Harger, Jim (616) 222-5400
BUS ED
Grand Rapids Press, Grand Rapids, MI
Hargett, Delores (972) 542-2631
DP MGR
McKinney Courier-Gazette, McKinney, TX
Hargis, B J (812) 268-6356
Sports ED, Sullivan Daily Times, Sullivan, IN
Hargis, Don (606) 231-3100
CIRC MGR-Single Copy
Lexington Herald-Leader, Lexington, KY
Hargis, Karen (217) 732-2101
ADV DIR, Courier, Lincoln, IL
Hargrave, Randolph U (757) 446-2000
ADV MGR-Co-op
Virginian-Pilot, Norfolk, VA
Hargraves, Jason (409) 756-6671
Religion ED, Trends ED
Conroe Courier, Conroe, TX
Hargrove, Mary (501) 378-3400
ASSOC ED
Arkansas Democrat-Gazette, Little Rock, AR
Hargrove, Thomas (205) 325-2222
Washington Correspondent
Birmingham Post-Herald, Birmingham, AL
Haring, Loretta (410) 268-5000
News ED, Capital, Annapolis, MD
Harkavy, Mel (909) 242-7614
PUB, Valley Times, Moreno Valley, CA
Harke, Gary (315) 792-5000
Copy ED, Observer-Dispatch, Utica, NY
Harkless, Ernest (412) 664-9161
PROD MGR, Daily News, McKeesport, PA
Harkness, Bruce (614) 633-1131
DP MGR, Times Leader, Martins Ferry, OH
Harknett, Richard F (908) 396-4500
PUB, Suburban News/Elizabeth City News, Westfield, NJ
Harlan, Jerry (313) 961-3949
Legal ED, Detroit Legal News, Detroit, MI
Harles, Dave (605) 352-6401
ASSOC ED, Huron Plainsman, Huron, SD
Harless, Todd (304) 263-8931
Photo DEPT MGR, Journal, Martinsburg, WV
Harley, Cathy (904) 252-1511
Librarian, Daytona Beach News-Journal, Daytona Beach, FL
Harling, Lynne (716) 798-1400
Librarian, Journal-Register, Medina, NY
Harlow, Clyde T (502) 678-5171
CIRC MGR
Glasgow Daily Times, Glasgow, KY
Harman, Eleanor (201) 327-1212
ED, Home And Store News, Ramsey, NJ
Harmer, Mike (250) 762-4445
PROD FRM-Press, Daily Courier, Kelowna, BC
Harmer, William (212) 416-2000
PROD DIR-NTL
Wall Street Journal, New York, NY
Harmon, Amy (213) 237-5000
Technology/Multimedia
Los Angeles Times, Los Angeles, CA
Harmon, Brad (513) 721-2700
ADV MGR-Sales
Cincinnati Enquirer, Cincinnati, OH
Harmon, Bruce (202) 383-6150
Washington BU Chief
Bridge News, Washington, DC
Harmon, Dee (405) 475-3311
PROD MGR-Mechanical SRV
Daily Oklahoman, Oklahoma City, OK
Harmon, Gary (970) 242-5050
City ED, Environmental ED, Farm/Agriculture ED, Daily Sentinel, Grand Junction, CO
Harmon, James M (516) 432-6376
ED/PUB
Harmon Football Forecast, Long Beach, NY
Harmon, Jay (317) 633-1240
CIRC MGR-ADM
Indianapolis Star/News, Indianapolis, IN
Harmon, John (812) 372-7811
ED, EDL Page, Republic, Columbus, IN
Harmon, Rick (334) 262-1611
COL, Entertainment/Amusements ED, Television/Film ED, Montgomery Advertiser, Montgomery, AL
Harmon, Steve (317) 659-4622
Photographer, Times, Frankfort, IN
Harmon, Tom (505) 823-7777
Features ED, Travel ED
Albuquerque Journal, Albuquerque, NM
Harmond, Charles (601) 328-2424
PRES, GM
Commercial Dispatch, Columbus, MS
Harms, Barbara (217) 324-2121
ADV ASST MGR
News-Herald, Litchfield, IL
Harms, Joni (507) 376-9711
Accountant, Daily Globe, Worthington, MN
Harms, Krista (618) 445-2355
PUB, Journal-Register, Albion, IL
Harmsen, Scott (616) 345-3511
Graphics ED
Kalamazoo Gazette, Kalamazoo, MI
Harnage, Kristine (912) 226-2400
Lifestyle ED, Thomasville Times-Enterprise, Thomasville, GA
Harnett, Cindy E (604) 381-3484
ED, Victoria News, Victoria, BC
Harney, Harold (614) 452-4561
PROD MGR-COMP
Times Recorder, Zanesville, OH
Harney, Richard E (765) 569-2033
PUB, Parke County Sentinel, Rockville, IN
Harnisch, Eric (805) 259-1234
Entertainment/Amusements ED, Features ED, Television/Film ED, Theater/Music ED
Signal, Santa Clarita, CA
Harp, Dianne (405) 924-4388
ADV MGR-CLASS
Durant Daily Democrat, Durant, OK
Harp, Susan (601) 862-3141
MAN ED
Itawamba County Times, Fulton, MS
Harper, Amy (937) 767-7373
ED, Yellow Springs News, Yellow Springs, OH
Harper, Bill (918) 581-8300
PROD MGR-OPER, Tulsa World, Tulsa, OK
Harper, Bill (319) 377-7037
GM, ED, Marion Times, Marion, IA
Harper, Bruce G (303) 426-6000
GM, Northglenn-Thornton Sentinel, Westminster, CO
Harper, Darby (212) 777-6200
RES MGR, Bettmann Archive/Bettman Newsphotos, New York, NY
Harper, Denise (706) 724-0851
CIRC DIR-Technical Development
Augusta Chronicle, Augusta, GA
Harper, Ed (910) 457-4568
ED, State Port Pilot, Southport, NC
Harper, Howard (573) 471-1137
CIRC MGR
Standard Democrat, Sikeston, MO
Harper, James (813) 893-8111
EDU ED
St. Petersburg Times, St. Petersburg, FL
Harper, Jo Anne Hartley (316) 325-3000
PUB, ED, Neodesha Derrick, Neodesha, KS
Harper, Kent (702) 289-4491
ED, BUS/FIN ED, City/MET ED, EPE, NTL ED, News ED, Sports ED, Ely Daily Times, Ely, NV
Harper, Larry (317) 659-4622
CIRC MGR, Times, Frankfort, IN
Harper, Laydell (313) 222-6400
DIR-Community Affairs
Detroit Newspapers, Detroit, MI
Harper, Mark (219) 362-2161
BUS/FIN ED, City ED, RE ED
La Porte Herald-Argus, La Porte, IN
Harper, Marty (501) 747-3373
ED, Monroe County Sun, Clarendon, AR
Harper, Mary Jane (403) 556-3351
ED, Olds Gazette, Olds, AB
Harper, Nathan (608) 252-6100
Online MGR
Wisconsin State Journal, Madison, WI
Harper, Phyllis (601) 842-2611
Features ED, Northeast Mississippi Daily Journal, Tupelo, MS

Copyright ©1997 by the Editor & Publisher Co.

RED BLUE & GREEN

The Powerhouse Newspaper Directories from E&P.

GET THE FACTS!

Editor & Publisher International Year Book 1997 (77th edition)

Find all you need to know about US, Canadian and foreign newspapers. Includes: ad rates, circulations, contacts, installed equipment, associations, suppliers and loads more! Now in two easy–to–use, portable volumes!

❑ **YES!** Please ship me the 1997 edition of the **Editor & Publisher International Year Book**.

❑ Payment enclosed--payable to E&P Year Book. Only $125 (including postage and handling)

Bill my ❑ MC ❑ VISA: Acct. #_____

Signature_____ Exp. Date_____

My name_____

Company_____ Address_____

City_____ State_____ Zip_____

Payment must accompany orders. CA, NY, OH, D.C., and Canada residents must add applicable taxes. No delivery to P.O. boxes. All remittances must be in U.S. dollars.

YB7Y

GET THE MARKETS!

Editor & Publisher Market Guide 1997 (73rd Annual Edition)

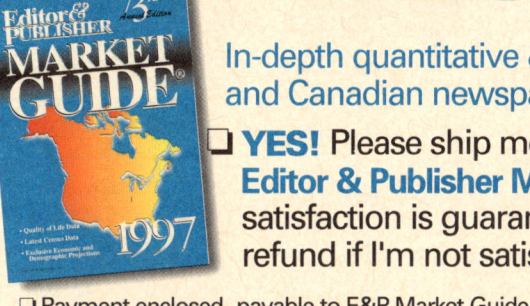

In-depth quantitative & qualitative data on over 1600 US and Canadian newspaper markets. **ONLY $100** postpaid!

❑ **YES!** Please ship me the current edition of the **Editor & Publisher Market Guide** to review. My satisfaction is guaranteed--I may return my copy for a full refund if I'm not satisfied.

❑ Payment enclosed--payable to E&P Market Guide.

Bill my ❑ MC ❑ VISA: Acct. #_____

Signature_____ Exp. Date_____

My name_____

Company_____ Address_____

City_____ State_____ Zip_____

Payment must accompany orders. CA, NY, OH, D.C., and Canada residents must add applicable taxes. No delivery to P.O. boxes. All remittances must be in U.S. dollars.

MB7Y

GET THE NEWEST!

Editor & Publisher/Free Paper Publisher Community, Specialty & Free Publications Year Book 1997 – A Media Buyers Guide

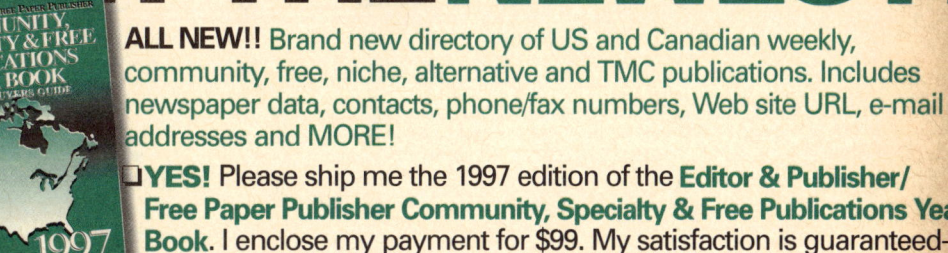

ALL NEW!! Brand new directory of US and Canadian weekly, community, free, niche, alternative and TMC publications. Includes newspaper data, contacts, phone/fax numbers, Web site URL, e-mail addresses and MORE!

❑ **YES!** Please ship me the 1997 edition of the **Editor & Publisher/Free Paper Publisher Community, Specialty & Free Publications Year Book**. I enclose my payment for $99. My satisfaction is guaranteed-- I may return my copy for a full refund if I'm not satisfied.

❑ Payment enclosed--payable to E&P/FPP Year Book.

Bill my ❑ MC ❑ VISA: Acct. #_____

Signature_____ Exp. Date_____

My name_____

Company_____ Address_____

City_____ State_____ Zip_____

Payment must accompany orders. CA, NY, OH, D.C., and Canada residents must add applicable taxes. No delivery to P.O. boxes. All remittances must be in U.S. dollars.

RECYCLED PAPER

BUSINESS REPLY MAIL
FIRST-CLASS MAIL   PERMIT NO.20   NEW YORK, NY

POSTAGE WILL BE PAID BY ADDRESSEE

EDITOR&PUBLISHER
YEAR BOOK®
CIRCULATION DEPARTMENT
11 W 19TH ST.
NEW YORK NY 10114-0741

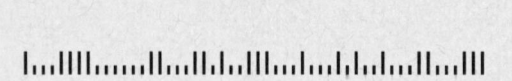

NO POSTAGE
NECESSARY
IF MAILED
IN THE
UNITED STATES

BUSINESS REPLY MAIL
FIRST-CLASS MAIL   PERMIT NO.20   NEW YORK, NY

POSTAGE WILL BE PAID BY ADDRESSEE

EDITOR&PUBLISHER
MARKET GUIDE®
CIRCULATION DEPARTMENT
11 W 19TH ST.
NEW YORK NY 10114-0741

NO POSTAGE
NECESSARY
IF MAILED
IN THE
UNITED STATES

BUSINESS REPLY MAIL
FIRST-CLASS MAIL   PERMIT NO.20   NEW YORK, NY

POSTAGE WILL BE PAID BY ADDRESSEE

EDITOR&PUBLISHER/FREE PAPER PUBLISHER
**COMMUNITY, SPECIALITY &
FREE PUBLICATIONS YEAR BOOK**
CIRCULATION DEPARTMENT
11 W 19TH ST.
NEW YORK NY 10114-0741

NO POSTAGE
NECESSARY
IF MAILED
IN THE
UNITED STATES

97-Who's Where **Har**

Harper, Robert ... (301) 662-1177
ASST MAN ED
Frederick Post/The News, Frederick, MD
Harper, Tom ... (330) 821-1200
Entertainment/Amusements ED
Alliance Review, Alliance, OH
Harper, William ... (812) 446-2216
PUB, ADV DIR, Brazil Times, Brazil, IN
Harpster, Charles ... (515) 284-8000
Wire ED
Des Moines Register, Des Moines, IA
Harpster, Jack ... (702) 383-0211
ADV DIR
Las Vegas Review-Journal, Las Vegas, NV
Harr, Brian ... (970) 522-1990
Agriculture ED
Journal-Advocate, Sterling, CO
Harr, Gregg ... (561) 820-4100
PROD MGR-Pre Press
Palm Beach Post, West Palm Beach, FL
Harr, Joyce ... (561) 820-3800
PUB, Daily News, Palm Beach, FL
Harral, Paul K ... (817) 390-7400
MAN ED-Special Projects
Fort Worth Star-Telegram, Fort Worth, TX
Harre, Kelly ... (402) 362-4478
MAN ED, York News-Times, York, NE
Harrell, Ann ... (402) 475-4200
City Hall Reporter
Lincoln Journal Star, Lincoln, NE
Harrell, Barry ... (501) 442-1777
COL, News ED
Northwest Arkansas Times, Fayetteville, AR
Harrell, Billy ... (919) 823-3106
PROD MGR, Daily Southerner, Tarboro, NC
Harrell, Carol M ... (605) 384-5616
PUB, ED
Wagner Post & Announcer, Wagner, SD
Harrell, Charles R ... (817) 778-4444
VP, GM, Temple Daily Telegram, Temple, TX
Harrell, Dale ... (941) 748-0411
DP MGR, Bradenton Herald, Bradenton, FL
Harrell, Donald ... (605) 384-5616
PUB, Post & Announcer, Wagner, SD
Harrell, Edward H ... (412) 834-1151
PRES, Tribune-Review Publishing, Greensburg, PA
Harrell, John ... (520) 445-3333
CIRC MGR, Daily Courier, Prescott, AZ
Harrell, Laura ... (919) 794-3185
PUB, ED
Bertie Ledger-Advance, Windsor, NC
Harrell, Scott ... (501) 524-5144
PUB, Herald-Leader, Siloam Springs, AR
Harrelson, Kathy ... (919) 752-6166
City ED, Daily Reflector, Greenville, NC
Harrigan, John D ... (603) 788-4939
PUB, Coos County Democrat, Lancaster, NH
Harrigan, Laura ... (908) 722-8800
MAN ED, Courier-News, Bridgewater, NJ
Harriman, Chap ... (409) 279-3411
PUB, Hearne Democrat, Hearne, TX
Harriman, Michelle ... (409) 279-3411
ED, Hearne Democrat, Hearne, TX
Harrington, Bradley ... (806) 655-7121
ED, Canyon News, Canyon, TX
Harrington, Brian ... (815) 987-1200
PROD MGR-Technical SRV
Rockford Register Star, Rockford, IL
Harrington, Craig ... (916) 335-4533
PUB, ED, Intermountain News, Burney, CA
Harrington, Janice ... (403) 335-3301
ED, Didsbury Review, Didsbury, AB
Harrington, Jeffery C ... (810) 686-3840
PUB
Genesee County Herald, Mount Morris, MI
Harrington, Mary T ... (401) 849-3300
City ED, Newport Daily News, Newport, RI
Harrington, Michael J ... (810) 686-3840
PUB
Genesee County Herald, Mount Morris, MI
Harrington, Ralph ... (713) 220-7171
ADV DIR-Display
Houston Chronicle, Houston, TX
Harrington, Richard J ... (416) 814-4239
PRES/CEO
Thomson Newspapers, Toronto, ON
Harrington, Rod ... (501) 862-6611
Entertainment ED
El Dorado News-Times, El Dorado, AR
Harrington, Steve ... (203) 964-2200
DIR-INFO Services, Stamford Advocate, Stamford, CT, Times Mirror Co.
Harris, Andrew ... (318) 631-6222
MAN ED, Shreveport Sun, Shreveport, LA
Harris, Ben ... (812) 231-4200
Photo/Graphics ED
Tribune-Star, Terre Haute, IN
Harris, Bonnie ... (317) 633-1240
EDL Writer
Indianapolis Star/News, Indianapolis, IN
Harris, Brent ... (765) 362-1200
DP MGR, Journal Review, Crawfordsville, IN
Harris, Bruce ... (317) 962-1575
PROD MGR-Commercial Sales
Palladium-Item, Richmond, IN
Harris, Bruce ... (210) 224-0706
ED, Snap News, San Antonio, TX
Harris, Cathy ... (319) 926-2626
ED, Delaware County Leader, Hopkinton, IA
Harris, Charlene ... (505) 763-3431
BM/CONT, DP MGR
Clovis News Journal, Clovis, NM
Harris, Dale ... (402) 444-1000
ADV MGR-CLASS
Omaha World-Herald, Omaha, NE
Harris, Dean ... (318) 783-3450
CIRC MGR, PROD FRM-MR
Crowley Post-Signal, Crowley, LA
Harris, Dean ... (209) 862-2222
ED, Tuesday Review, Newman, CA
Harris, Debbie ... (502) 754-2331
GM, Times-Argus, Central City, KY
Harris, Dennis (Chip) ... (540) 981-3100
PROD MGR-Maintenance/Support SRV
Roanoke Times, Roanoke, VA
Harris, Derrick ... (918) 335-8200
Cablevision ED, Radio/Television ED
Examiner-Enterprise, Bartlesville, OK
Harris, Donnie ... (706) 724-0851
PROD MGR-MR
Augusta Chronicle, Augusta, GA
Harris, Dorothy ... (407) 482-6271
Author-EDU
Demko Publishing, Boca Raton, FL
Harris, Douglas C ... (305) 376-3800
VP/SEC, Knight-Ridder Inc., Miami, FL
Harris, Ed ... (408) 920-5000
PROD MGR-Pre Press
San Jose Mercury News, San Jose, CA
Harris, F Cosmo ... (303) 292-5158
PUB, Denver Weekly News, Denver, CO
Harris, Frances K ... (409) 744-3611
Travel ED
Galveston County Daily News, Galveston, TX
Harris, Fred ... (219) 883-4903
PUB, ED, Gary American, Gary, IN
Harris, George H ... (502) 247-5223
EVP, Mayfield Messenger, Mayfield, KY
Haskell Newspapers
Harris, Gerald P ... (701) 883-5393
PUB, ED, La Moure Chronicle, La Moure, ND
Harris, Herm ... (315) 866-2220
PROD FRM-COMP
Evening Telegram, Herkimer, NY
Harris, Imogene ... (219) 882-5591
PUB, ED, Gary Info, Gary, IN
Harris, Jack ... (316) 421-2000
Sports ED, Parsons Sun, Parsons, KS
Harris, Jay T ... (408) 920-5000
Chairman/PUB
San Jose Mercury News, San Jose, CA
Harris, Jim ... (518) 725-8616
City ED, Leader-Herald, Gloversville, NY
Harris, Joanne ... (360) 694-3391
Radio/Television ED
Columbian, Vancouver, WA
Harris, John G ... (316) 694-5700
VP, Hutchinson News, Hutchinson, KS
Harris, Joseph ... (410) 289-6834
MAN ED
Maryland Beachcomber, Ocean City, MD
Harris, Kathleen ... (519) 537-2341
City ED, Political ED, Radio/Television ED, SCI ED, Sentinel-Review, Woodstock, ON
Harris, Kimberly ... (303) 442-1202
MGR-MKTG/PROM, Daily Camera
Boulder, CO
Harris, Marie ... (601) 896-2100
EDL DIR, Sun Herald, Biloxi, MS
Harris, Marsha ... (217) 824-2233
CIRC DIR, Taylorville Daily Breeze-Courier, Taylorville, IL
Harris, Michael ... (352) 365-8200
Sports ED, Daily Commercial, Leesburg, FL
Harris, Nick ... (716) 232-7100
PROD FRM-MR
Rochester Times-Union, Rochester, NY
Harris, Pat ... (501) 777-8841
Society/Women's ED, Hope Star, Hope, AR
Harris, Paul ... (310) 587-0025
Features Desk, Online USA, Beverly Hills, CA
Harris, Phil ... (941) 262-3161
ADTX MGR, Naples Daily News, Naples, FL
Harris, Phyllis Montague ... (315) 363-5100
MAN ED, Oneida Daily Dispatch, Oneida, NY
Harris, Rick ... (941) 953-7755
CIRC MGR-City
Sarasota Herald-Tribune, Sarasota, FL
Harris, Rick ... (219) 936-3101
MGR-Office, Pilot-News, Plymouth, IN
Harris, Robert ... (202) 383-6080
DIR-BUS News, Knight-Ridder/Tribune Information Services, Washington, DC
Harris, Rodney ... (910) 227-0131
PROD FRM-MR
Times News Publishing Co., Burlington, NC
Harris, Roger ... (201) 877-4141
Books Critic, Star-Ledger, Newark, NJ
Harris, Samuel ... (810) 766-6100
CIRC DIR, Flint Journal, Flint, MI
Harris, Sonya ... (405) 921-3391
ED, Laverne Leader Tribune, Laverne, OK
Harris, Susan ... (919) 426-5728
ED, Perquimans Weekly, Hertford, NC
Harris, Thomas D ... (423) 743-4112
PUB, ED, Erwin Record, Erwin, TN
Harris, Thomas N ... (501) 670-5555
PUB, Easy Living News, Horseshoe Bend, AR
Harris, Tom ... (904) 435-8500
PROD MGR-Platemaking
Pensacola News Journal, Pensacola, FL
Harris, Trevor P G ... (403) 354-2460
PUB, ED, Advertiser, Beaverlodge, AB
Harris, W Russell ... (619) 745-6611
ASST MAN ED
North County Times, Escondido, CA
Harrison, Bill ... (909) 381-9898
PUB, Rialto Record, San Bernardino, CA
Harrison, Bruce ... (815) 938-3320
ED, Forreston Journal, Forreston, IL
Harrison, Caroline D ... (717) 255-8100
GM, Patriot-News, Harrisburg, PA
Harrison, Carolyn ... (817) 325-4465
CIRC MGR, Index, Mineral Wells, TX
Harrison, David ... (909) 684-1200
EX BUS ED, Press-Enterprise, Riverside, CA
Harrison, David ... (303) 776-2244
Photo ED, Daily Times-Call, Longmont, CO
Harrison, David N ... (606) 623-1669
PUB, Richmond Register, Richmond, KY
Harrison, Eric ... (213) 237-5000
Atlanta BU
Los Angeles Times, Los Angeles, CA
Harrison, Gary W ... (540) 374-5000
DIR-Technical SRV
Free Lance-Star, Fredericksburg, VA
Harrison, Grady Joe ... (806) 271-3381
PUB, ED, Texas Spur, Spur, TX
Harrison Jr, Granville P ... (601) 224-6681
PUB, ED, Southern Advocate, Ashland, MS
Harrison, Janet ... (813) 254-5888
PUB, Free Press, Tampa, FL
Harrison, Jeff ... (619) 459-4201
GM, La Jolla Light, La Jolla, CA
Harrison, Jeff ... (614) 633-1131
Sports ED
Times Leader, Martins Ferry, OH
Harrison, John ... (813) 254-5888
GM, MAN ED, Free Press, Tampa, FL
Harrison, Judi ... (509) 925-1414
Office MGR, Daily Record, Ellensburg, WA
Harrison, Karl ... (502) 443-1771
EX ED, Paducah Sun, Paducah, KY
Harrison, Katie ... (202) 298-6920
Office MGR
Hearst News Service, Washington, DC
Harrison, Michael ... (516) 569-4000
ED, Long Beach Herald, Lawrence, NY
Harrison, Monique ... (601) 842-2611
EDU ED, Teen-Age/Youth ED, Northeast Mississippi Daily Journal, Tupelo, MS
Harrison, Patrick ... (815) 433-2000
City ED, Daily Times, Ottawa, IL
Harrison, Rick ... (614) 452-4561
Photo ED, Times Recorder, Zanesville, OH
Harrison, Robert F ... (309) 343-7181
ED, EPE, EDL Writer, Farm ED, Radio/Television ED, Register-Mail, Galesburg, IL
Harrison, Sarah ... (812) 829-2255
ADV DIR
Spencer Evening World, Spencer, IN
Harrison, Scott ... (604) 792-9117
ED, Chilliwack Times, Chilliwack, BC
Harrison, Sharon ... (801) 752-2121
Sports ED, Herald Journal, Logan, UT
Harrison, Stan ... (616) 722-3161
ASST News ED
Muskegon Chronicle, Muskegon, MI
Harrison, Stephan ... (609) 935-1500
Photo ED, Chief Photographer
Today's Sunbeam, Salem, NJ
Harrison, Thomas A ... (901) 529-2211
CIRC DIR, Commercial Appeal, Memphis, TN
Harrison, Tom ... (334) 262-1611
Religion ED
Montgomery Advertiser, Montgomery, AL
Harristod, Keith ... (202) 334-6000
MET City ED
Washington Post, Washington, DC
Harrod, Rodney ... (419) 522-3311
CIRC MGR-Distribution
News Journal, Mansfield, OH
Harrold, James ... (419) 422-5151
MAN ED, Courier, Findlay, OH
Harron, Steve ... (519) 941-1350
ED, Orangeville Banner, Orangeville, ON
Harrop, Froma ... (401) 277-7000
EDL Writer
Providence Journal-Bulletin, Providence, RI
Harryman, Roy ... (816) 524-2345
ED, Journal, Lee's Summit, MO
Harshaw, Jay ... (501) 785-7700
Entertainment/Amusements ED, Food ED
Southwest Times Record, Fort Smith, AR
Harshaw, Karla Garrett ... (937) 328-0300
ED, EPE
Springfield News-Sun, Springfield, OH
Harshaw, Wayne E ... (614) 461-5000
ASST DIR-MKTG Services
Columbus Dispatch, Columbus, OH
Harshbarger, J Richard ... (419) 332-5511
DIR-MKTG/PROM
News-Messenger, Fremont, OH
Harshman, Debra J ... (217) 335-2112
PUB, ED, Paper, Barry, IL
Harslip, Jeanette ... (202) 334-6000
MKTG MGR-Creative Services
Washington Post, Washington, DC
Hart, Andy ... (860) 296-6128
GM, MAN ED, Hartford News, Hartford, CT
Hart, Chuck ... (604) 886-2622
ED, Sunshine Coast News, Gibsons, BC
Hart, Don ... (316) 694-5700
EDU/School ED
Hutchinson News, Hutchinson, KS
Hart, Earnest ... (601) 961-7000
DIR-Graphics, Clarion-Ledger, Jackson, MS
Hart, Jack ... (503) 221-8327
Senior ED-Training, Oregonian, Portland, OR
Hart, Janet ... (801) 373-5050
Fashion/Style ED, Features ED, Health/Medical ED, Lifestyle ED, Society ED, Daily Herald, Provo, UT
Hart, Jason ... (606) 474-5101
GM, Grayson Journal-Enquirer, Grayson, KY
Hart, Jim ... (812) 265-3641
CIRC MGR, Madison Courier, Madison, IN
Hart, Jim ... (770) 394-4147
GM, Dunwoody Crier, Dunwoody, GA
Hart, Jim ... (503) 357-3181
ED
Forest Grove News Times, Forest Grove, OR
Hart, Jim ... (319) 588-5611
ADV DIR, Telegraph Herald, Dubuque, IA
Hart, Joe ... (608) 252-6400
Sports ED, Capital Times, Madison, WI
Hart, John ... (414) 261-4949
Photo ED
Watertown Daily Times, Watertown, WI
Hart, Jon ... (304) 367-2500
PROD MGR-SYS
Times-West Virginian, Fairmont, WV
Hart, Kenneth A ... (606) 329-1717
BUS/FIN ED
Daily Independent, Ashland, KY
Hart, Kevin M ... (814) 724-6370
News ED, Meadville Tribune, Meadville, PA
Hart Jr, Matthew J ... (715) 264-3481
PUB, ED, Glidden Enterprise, Glidden, WI
Hart, Michael G ... (602) 842-6000
ED, Glendale Star, Glendale, AZ
Hart, Nancy ... (405) 258-1818
ED, Lincoln County News, Chandler, OK
Hart, Patricia ... (518) 454-5694
Online Electronic News ED
Times Union, Albany, NY
Hart, Paul ... (317) 473-6641
CIRC MGR, Peru Tribune, Peru, IN
Nixon Newspapers Inc.
Hart, Phillip ... (812) 663-3111
PUB, DIR-MKTG/PROM
Greensburg Daily News, Greensburg, IN
Hart, Randy ... (704) 437-2161
ADV MGR, News Herald, Morganton, NC
Hart, Rayleen ... (616) 429-2400
ADV MGR-Advertising SRV
Herald-Palladium, St. Joseph, MI
Hart, Richard ... (919) 932-2000
MAN ED, Chapel Hill News, Chapel Hill, NC
Hart, Rodney ... (217) 223-5100
Sports ED, Quincy Herald-Whig, Quincy, IL
Hart, Roger ... (517) 265-5111
News ED, Travel ED
Daily Telegram, Adrian, MI
Harte, Houston H ... (210) 829-9000
COB, Harte-Hanks Communications Inc., San Antonio, TX
Hartel, Sandra ... (814) 870-1600
ADV CNR-Co-op
Morning News/Erie Daily Times, Erie, PA
Harter, Lee ... (803) 533-5500
ED, Times and Democrat, Orangeburg, SC
Harteveld, Andrew C ... (201) 877-4141
PROD OPER DIR, Star-Ledger, Newark, NJ
Hartfiel, Betty ... (713) 232-3737
CIRC MGR
Rosenberg Herald-Coaster, Rosenberg, TX

Copyright ©1997 by the Editor & Publisher Co.

Har Who's Where-98

Hartgen, Stephen (208) 733-0931
PUB, Times-News, Twin Falls, ID

Hartgrove, Tina (317) 398-6631
CONT, Shelbyville News, Shelbyville, IN

Hartig, Dennis (757) 446-2000
Deputy MAN ED-Local News
Virginian-Pilot, Norfolk, VA

Hartings, Pat (419) 586-2371
ADV DIR-NTL, Daily Standard, Celina, OH

Hartl, John (206) 464-2111
Films Critic, Seattle Times, Seattle, WA

Hartle, M L (219) 267-3111
VP, Times-Union, Warsaw, IN

Hartle, Molly (508) 374-0321
Lifestyle ED, Gazette, Haverhill, MA

Hartle, Richard (937) 225-2000
PROD ENG-Building/Facilities
Dayton Daily News, Dayton, OH

Hartley, A J (313) 222-6400
Newsroom Technology DIR
Detroit Free Press, Detroit, MI

Hartley, Donald L (614) 852-1616
PRES, PUB, CIRC MGR
Madison Press, London, OH

Hartley, Jeffrey (904) 599-2100
CIRC MGR-Sales
Tallahassee Democrat, Tallahassee, FL

Hartley, Peter (416) 367-2000
PROD MGR-Press Centre (Night)
Toronto Star, Toronto, ON

Hartley, W B (403) 527-1101
PROD MGR
Medicine Hat News, Medicine Hat, AB

Hartlieb, Douglas J (304) 233-0100
PROD MGR, Intelligencer/Wheeling News-Register, Wheeling, WV

Hartman, Barrie (303) 442-1202
ED, Daily Camera, Boulder, CO

Hartman, Bill (713) 232-3737
PRES, Herald-Coaster, Rosenberg, TX
Hartman Newspapers Inc.

Hartman, Darrell (352) 374-5000
MET ED-North
Gainesville Sun, Gainesville, FL

Hartman, Fred B (713) 342-8691
VP-Group OPER
Hartman Newspapers Inc., Rosenberg, TX

Hartman, J William (713) 342-8691
PRES
Hartman Newspapers Inc., Rosenberg, TX

Hartman, Jerry D (217) 459-2121
ED, Shelby County News-Gazette, Windsor, IL

Hartman, Laurie (612) 447-6669
PUB, Prior Lake American, Prior Lake, MN

Hartman, Leo L (419) 625-5500
PROD SUPV-Electronics, PROD FRM-COMP
Sandusky Register, Sandusky, OH

Hartman, Mark (614) 385-2107
ED, Logan Daily News, Logan, OH

Hartman, Peggy A (217) 459-2121
PUB
Shelby County News-Gazette, Windsor, IL

Hartman, Phil (908) 246-5500
ED-Sunday, Sunday ED
Home News & Tribune, East Brunswick, NJ

Hartman, Suzie (308) 237-2152
PROD FRM-COMP, Kearney Hub
Kearney, NE

Hartman, Tamara (718) 224-5863
ED, Queen Courier, Bayside, NY

Hartmann, Brad (403) 335-3301
GM, Didsbury Review, Didsbury, AB

Hartmann, Bruce R (423) 523-3131
GM, Knoxville News-Sentinel, Knoxville, TN

Hartmann, Frederick W (904) 359-4111
ED, Florida Times-Union, Jacksonville, FL

Hartmann, Gene (403) 335-3301
PUB, Didsbury Review, Didsbury, AB

Hartmann, Raymond P (314) 231-6666
PUB, Riverfront Times, St. Louis, MO

Hartmann, Robert H
PUB, Evansville Press, Evansville, IN

Hartnett Sr, Frank J (508) 772-0777
PUB, Times Free Press, Ayer, MA

Hartnett Jr, Frank J (508) 772-0777
ED, Times Free Press, Ayer, MA

Hartnett, Ken (508) 997-7411
ED, Standard Times, New Bedford, MA

Hartnett, Richard E (313) 222-6400
CIRC DIR-Home Delivery
Detroit Newspapers, Detroit, MI

Hartnett, Sherry (517) 377-1000
DIR-MKTG/PROM
Lansing State Journal, Lansing, MI

Hartseille, Kyle (505) 425-6796
CIRC MGR, Las Vegas Optic, Las Vegas, NM

Hartten, Richard (908) 735-4081
ED, Hunterdon Review, Clinton, NJ

Hartwell, Rusty (816) 732-5552
PUB, ED, Holden MH Progress, Holden, MO

Harty Jr, Robert (972) 782-6171
PUB, Farmersville Times, Farmersville, TX

Harty, Roger (701) 642-8585
ADV MGR, Daily News, Wahpeton, ND

Hartz, Deborah (954) 356-4000
Food ED, Sun-Sentinel, Fort Lauderdale, FL

Hartzell, Phil (814) 946-7411
ADTX MGR, Altoona Mirror, Altoona, PA

Hartzell, Ted (616) 429-2400
MET ED, Herald-Palladium, St. Joseph, MI

Hartzog, Carol (405) 341-2121
MAN ED, EPE, Evening Sun, Edmond, OK

Hartzog, Maj Gen William (913) 762-5000
PUB, Fort Riley Post, Junction City, KS

Harvall, Debra (608) 251-3252
MAN ED, Oregon Observer, Oregon, WI

Harvath III, Louis (Lou) P (706) 884-7311
PUB, La Grange Daily News, La Grange, GA

Harvey, Alec (205) 325-2222
Amusements ED, Books ED, Lively Arts/Music ED, Life/Style ED, Radio/Television ED
Birmingham News, Birmingham, AL

Harvey, Bev (810) 573-2755
Lifestyle ED
Avanti NewsFeatures, Warren, MI

Harvey, Carol (507) 451-2840
CIRC ASSOC MGR-Sales
Owatonna People's Press, Owatonna, MN

Harvey, Cec (306) 565-8211
PROD MGR-Distribution/Press
Leader-Post, Regina, SK

Harvey, David D (805) 564-5200
PROD MGR-Plant, Santa Barbara News-Press, Santa Barbara, CA

Harvey, Duston (206) 448-8000
Arts/Entertainment ED
Seattle Post-Intelligencer, Seattle, WA

Harvey, John (503) 221-8327
Senior ED-Production, Team Leader-Nation/World, Oregonian, Portland, OR

Harvey, Paul (905) 684-7251
Assignment ED, BUS ED, News ED
Standard, St. Catharines, ON

Harvey, Ray (903) 597-8111
PROD FRM-PR, Morning Telegraph, Tyler, TX

Harvey, Sam (205) 582-3232
PUB, ED, Advertiser-Gleam, Guntersville, AL

Harvieux, Gerry (519) 627-1488
ED, Courier Press, Wallaceburg, ON

Harvill, Jerry (717) 243-2611
DP MGR, PROD MGR-OPER
Sentinel, Carlisle, PA

Harville, Deborah (608) 845-9559
ED, Verona Press, Verona, WI

Harville, Kelly (407) 242-3500
DIR-Market Development
Florida Today, Melbourne, FL

Harville, Vic (501) 378-3400
Cartoonist
Arkansas Democrat-Gazette, Little Rock, AR

Harwell, Frank (334) 847-2599
ED, Washington County News, Chatom, AL

Harwell, Kim (214) 696-2900
MAN ED, Met, Dallas, TX

Harwood, Joe (509) 582-1500
EDU ED, Tri-City Herald, Tri-Cities, WA

Harwood, Michael (401) 277-7000
ADV Sales DIR-Local RT
Providence Journal-Bulletin, Providence, RI

Harwood, Skippy (561) 820-3800
Food ED
Palm Beach Daily News, Palm Beach, FL

Hasden, Wes (423) 756-1234
Books ED
Chattanooga Times, Chattanooga, TN

Hasein, Daryl (306) 948-3344
PUB, GM, Independent, Biggar, SK

Hasein, Margaret (306) 948-3344
PUB, ED, Independent, Biggar, SK

Haselden, Barry (407) 420-5000
ADV MGR-RT, GEN Division
Orlando Sentinel, Orlando, FL

Hasert, Linda (215) 854-2000
Popular Arts ED
Philadelphia Inquirer, Philadelphia, PA

Hashman, Larry (209) 532-7151
News ED, Union Democrat, Sonora, CA

Haskell, Antoinette M (540) 638-8801
COB, Martinsville Bulletin, Martinsville, VA

Haskell, Brenda (918) 256-6422
Lifestyle ED, Vinita Daily Journal, Vinita, OK

Haskell, Elizabeth H (502) 247-5223
VP, Mayfield Messenger, Mayfield, KY
Haskell Newspapers

Haskell, Robert (207) 990-8000
Sports ED, Bangor Daily News, Bangor, ME

Haskell, Robert H (540) 638-8801
PRES/TREAS, PUB
Martinsville Bulletin, Martinsville, VA

Haskell, Scott (207) 990-8000
Photo ED, Bangor Daily News, Bangor, ME

Haskins, Alan J (814) 870-1600
ADV MGR-RT
Morning News/Erie Daily Times, Erie, PA

Haskins, Cheryl E (508) 793-9100
ADTX MGR
Telegram & Gazette, Worcester, MA

Haskins, Hak (812) 482-2424
DIR-Electronic News SRV
Herald, Jasper, IN

Haskins, Ronda (303) 442-1202
Radio/Television ED, Special Sections ED, Women's ED, Daily Camera, Boulder, CO

Haskins, Scott (505) 823-7777
ADV DIR, Tribune, Albuquerque, NM

Haskins, Scott (403) 468-0100
Sports ED, Edmonton Sun, Edmonton, AB

Haslanger, Phil (608) 252-6400
ASSOC ED, EPE, Capital Times, Madison, WI

Hasler, Pat A (812) 384-3501
CIRC MGR, Evening World, Bloomfield, IN

Hasman, Edward (716) 232-7100
PROD FRM-PR, Times-Union, Rochester, NY

Hass, Gary (802) 479-2582
PUB, World, Barre, VT

Hass Jr, Paul (205) 345-0505
CIRC DIR, Tuscaloosa News, Tuscaloosa, AL

Hassania, Ali (503) 226-1311
PROD FRM-COMP
Daily Journal of Commerce, Portland, OR

Hasse, Ron (818) 713-3000
CIRC MGR-OPER
Daily News, Woodland Hills, CA

Hasselbrink, Karen (719) 539-6691
Office MGR, Mountain Mail, Salida, CO

Hasselmeier, John (817) 754-3511
ED, Waco Citizen, Waco, TX

Hasselwander, John E (334) 262-1611
City ED, EDU ED
Montgomery Advertiser, Montgomery, AL

Hasselwander, Mary (916) 256-2277
ED, Westwood Pinepress, Westwood, CA

Hassler, Kevin (405) 233-6600
Features ED, Enid News & Eagle, Enid, OK

Hassler, Rick (505) 746-3524
Sports ED, Artesia Daily Press, Artesia, NM

Hastie, Traci L (817) 567-2616
MAN ED
Jacksboro Gazette-News, Jacksboro, TX

Hastings, Dwight (916) 321-1000
CONT, Sacramento Bee, Sacramento, CA

Hastings, Frederick (207) 259-7751
PUB, ED
Downeast Coastal Press, Cutler, ME

Hastings, Jack E (316) 365-2111
SEC/TREAS, ADV MGR, Graphics ED/Art DIR
Iola Register, Iola, KS

Hastings, James (330) 821-1200
ED, EPE, Alliance Review, Alliance, OH

Hastings, Linda (216) 999-4500
ADV ASST DIR, Plain Dealer, Cleveland, OH

Hastings, Mark (316) 365-2111
ADV MGR-Display, Iola Register, Iola, KS

Hastings, Randy H (217) 253-2358
ED, Tuscola Review, Tuscola, IL

Hastings, Robert D (217) 253-2358
PUB, Tuscola Review, Tuscola, IL

Hastings, Stephen (604) 732-2111
CIRC MGR-Sales, Vancouver Sun, Vancouver, BC, Southam Inc.

Haston, Richard A (205) 772-8666
PUB, ED
Madison County Record, Madison, AL

Hasty, J D (718) 624-0536
PUB, Daily Bulletin, Brooklyn, NY

Haswell, Kathryn A (419) 352-4611
SEC/TREAS
Sentinel-Tribune, Bowling Green, OH

Haswell, T M (419) 352-4611
PRES, PUB
Sentinel-Tribune, Bowling Green, OH

Hatch, Jim (216) 999-4500
Chief Photographer
Plain Dealer, Cleveland, OH

Hatch, John (717) 265-2151
PROD FRM-PR (Day)
Daily Review, Towanda, PA

Hatch, Ken (509) 525-3300
CIRC MGR, DP MGR
Walla Walla Union-Bulletin, Walla Walla, WA

Hatch, Larry (801) 373-5050
CIRC DIR, Daily Herald, Provo, UT

Hatch, Shirley W (904) 935-1427
PUB, Branford News, Branford, FL

Hatch, William R (810) 544-0470
PRES, Feature Service Syndicate, Madison Heights, MI

Hatcher, Billie P (502) 237-3441
PUB, Citizen-Times, Scottsville, KY

Hatcher, Cole (216) 951-0000
City/MET ED, News-Herald, Willoughby, OH

Hatcher, Curtis (504) 383-1111
DIR-Accounting
Advocate, Baton Rouge, LA

Hatcher, John (716) 394-0770
City/MET ED, Environmental ED, Health/Medical ED, Daily Messenger/The Sunday Messenger, Canandaigua, NY

Hatcher, June (423) 756-6900
Films/Theater ED
Chattanooga Free Press, Chattanooga, TN

Hatcher, Sam (615) 444-3952
ED, Lebanon Democrat, Lebanon, TN

Hatcher, Tom (206) 464-2111
PROD ASST Plant MGR-Maintence
Seattle Times, Seattle, WA

Hatem, Shawn (614) 439-3531
Sports ED, Daily Jeffersonian, Cambridge, OH

Hatfield, C Donald (520) 573-4561
PRES/PUB, ED, Tucson Citizen, Tucson, AZ

Hatfield, Dan (510) 935-2525
MET ED
Contra Costa Times, Walnut Creek, CA

Hatfield, Fred (902) 742-7111
ED, Vanguard, Yarmouth, NS

Hatfield, Guy (606) 723-5161
PUB, Citizen Voice & Times, Irvine, KY

Hatfield, Ken (209) 441-6111
CIRC MGR, Fresno Bee, Fresno, CA

Hathaway, Bill (208) 522-1800
Special Sections ED
Post Register, Idaho Falls, ID

Hathaway, Emily (201) 877-4141
Entertainment ED, Star-Ledger, Newark, NJ

Hathaway, Les (619) 322-8889
PROD MGR-SYS
Desert Sun, Palm Springs, CA

Hathaway, Maureen (817) 390-7400
VP-Special Projects/New Media
Fort Worth Star-Telegram, Fort Worth, TX

Hathaway, Patrick (609) 272-7000
CIRC MGR-OPER
Press of Atlantic City, Pleasantville, NJ

Hathaway, Warren G (508) 674-4656
PUB, Spectator, Somerset, MA

Hathcock, Chuck (601) 226-4321
Sports ED, Daily Sentinel-Star, Grenada, MS

Hathcock, Darrell C (606) 878-7400
GM, ED, Sentinel-Echo, London, KY

Hatley, Donald (334) 213-7323
PUB
Montgomery Independent, Montgomery, AL

Hatley, Elton (901) 584-7200
GM, Camden Chronicle, Camden, TN

Hatley, Trip (423) 756-1234
ADV DIR-RT
Chattanooga Times, Chattanooga, TN

Hatten, Charles (318) 322-5161
PROD MGR-Camera/Platemaking
News-Star, Monroe, LA

Hatten, Jimmy (318) 322-5161
EPE, News-Star, Monroe, LA

Hatter, David (412) 628-2000
PROD FRM-PR
Daily Courier, Connellsville, PA

Hatter, Lou (540) 347-4222
ED, Fauquier Times-Democrat, Warrenton, VA

Hattfield, C Donald (520) 573-4400
SEC, TNI Partners dba Tucson Newspapers, Tucson, AZ

Hattock, Sandy (913) 684-5267
PUB, Fort Leavenworth Lamp, Lansing, KS

Hatton, Katherine (215) 854-2000
VP/GEN Counsel, Philadelphia Inquirer, Philadelphia, PA, Knight-Ridder Inc.

Hatton, Spencer (509) 248-1251
City ED, Political/RE ED
Yakima Herald-Republic, Yakima, WA

Hatza Jr, George L (610) 371-5000
Entertainment ED
Reading Times/Eagle, Reading, PA

Hauck, Ed J (405) 233-6600
PUB, Enid News & Eagle, Enid, OK

Hauenstein, Krista (612) 339-7571
MAN ED, ComputerUser, Minneapolis, MN

Haugen, Brenda (612) 894-1111
ED, Dakota County Tribune, Burnsville, MN

Haugen, Peter (916) 321-1000
Reviewer-Scene & Features
Sacramento Bee, Sacramento, CA

Hauger, Joseph (304) 233-0100
News ED, Intelligencer/Wheeling News-Register, Wheeling, WV

Hauger, Terry (517) 752-7171
ADV MGR-Co-op/NTL
Saginaw News, Saginaw, MI

Haugh, David (219) 235-6161
MAN ED-Irish Sports Report
South Bend Tribune, South Bend, IN

Haughey, Patricia E (609) 654-5000
PUB, Central Record, Medford, NJ

Haught, James A (304) 348-5140
ED, Charleston Gazette, Sunday Gazette-Mail, Charleston, WV

99-Who's Where **Hea**

Haughton, Natalie ... (818) 713-3000
Food ED, Daily News, Woodland Hills, CA

Haugland, Keith ... (402) 564-2741
VP, Columbus Telegram, Columbus, NE

Hauke, James ... (414) 657-1000
PROD FRM-PR, Kenosha News, Kenosha, WI

Haun, Carol ... (304) 372-2421
PUB, Jackson Herald, Ripley, WV

Haun, John ... (412) 654-6651
ADV DIR-Creative SRV
New Castle News, New Castle, PA

Haupt, Bill ... (608) 592-3261
PUB, ED, Lodi Enterprise, Lodi, WI

Haupt, Jan ... (608) 592-3261
PUB, Lodi Enterprise, Lodi, WI

Hauser, Dianne ... (608) 782-9710
ADV SUPV-CLASS
La Crosse Tribune, La Crosse, WI

Hauser, Jeanne ... (402) 444-1000
Librarian, Omaha World-Herald, Omaha, NE

Hauslohner, Amy ... (540) 236-5178
ED, Gazette, Galax, VA

Hausrath, Terry ... (716) 849-3434
PROD OPER FRM-Engineering
Buffalo News, Buffalo, NY

Hauswald, Virginia ... (910) 727-7211
Librarian
Winston-Salem Journal, Winston-Salem, NC

Hautanen, David ... (508) 775-1200
CONT, Cape Cod Times, Hyannis, MA

Havard, Bronson ... (214) 528-8792
ED, Texas Catholic, Dallas, TX

Havel, Charles ... (201) 646-4000
PROD MGR-Pre Press
Record, Hackensack, NJ

Havelka, Steve ... (914) 694-9300
ADV MGR-Display, Reporter Dispatch, White Plains, NY, Gannett Co. Inc.

Haven, Lee ... (770) 306-2175
MAN ED
Atlanta-News Leader, Union City, GA

Havener, Bob ... (219) 461-8444
PROD MGR-Building
Fort Wayne Newspapers Inc., Fort Wayne, IN

Havens, Lisa ... (309) 833-2114
ADV MGR, Macomb Journal, Macomb, IL

Havens, Vicki ... (317) 664-5111
PROD CNR-Commercial Print
Chronicle-Tribune, Marion, IN

Haverkoch, Vanessa ... (802) 447-7567
CIRC MGR, Banner, Bennington, VT

Havington, Jeanette ... (607) 272-2321
PROD FRM-COMP
Ithaca Journal, Ithaca, NY

Havlicek, Franklin J ... (202) 334-6000
VP-Industrial Relations/Environmental Services, Washington Post, Washington, DC

Havranek, Larry ... (402) 462-2131
PROD MGR-OPER
Hastings Tribune, Hastings, NE

Hawatmeh, Suletman ... (213) 469-4354
MAN ED, Beirut Times, Los Angeles, CA

Hawerson, John ... (414) 728-3411
GM, Delavan Enterprise, Delavan, WI

Hawes, Christine ... (941) 953-7755
EDU ED
Sarasota Herald-Tribune, Sarasota, FL

Hawes, Leland ... (813) 259-7711
COL, Tampa Tribune and Times, Tampa, FL

Hawes, Richard ... (202) 334-6000
PROD MGR-Packaging/Distribution (VA)
Washington Post, Washington, DC

Hawes, Steve ... (206) 339-3000
ADV DIR, Herald, Everett, WA

Hawk, David ... (219) 874-7211
MAN ED, News Dispatch, Michigan City, IN

Hawken, Charles ... (716) 232-7100
PROD FRM-MR, Rochester Democrat and Chronicle, Rochester, NY

Hawker, Fred J ... (515) 823-4525
PUB, Greene Recorder, Greene, IA

Hawker, Sylvia J ... (515) 823-4525
ED, Greene Recorder, Greene, IA

Hawkes, Arlys J ... (414) 648-2334
ED, Lake Mills Leader, Lake Mills, WI

Hawkes, Dennis L ... (414) 648-2334
PUB, Lake Mills Leader, Lake Mills, WI

Hawkes, Richard R ... (212) 930-8000
VP/GM, New York Post, New York, NY

Hawkins, Barbara ... (304) 327-2811
ED-WV, City ED, EDU ED
Bluefield Daily Telegraph, Bluefield, WV

Hawkins, Beth ... (313) 961-4060
MAN ED, Metro Times, Detroit, MI

Hawkins, Chuck ... (212) 318-2300
Washington BU Chief
Bloomberg Business News, New York, NY

Hawkins, Frank ... (918) 581-8300
SEC/TREAS, Tulsa World, Tulsa, OK

Hawkins, Frank ... (423) 929-3111
ADV MGR-RT
Johnson City Press, Johnson City, TN

Hawkins, Gina M ... (812) 876-2254
MAN ED, Journal, Elletsville, IN

Hawkins, Gladys ... (913) 837-4321
PUB, Louisburg Herald, Louisburg, KS

Hawkins, James ... (414) 657-1000
ADV MGR-RT, Kenosha News, Kenosha, WI

Hawkins, Lisa ... (910) 592-8137
ADV MGR
Sampson Independent, Clinton, NC

Hawkins, Parris ... (914) 694-9300
ADV DIR-BUS Development, Reporter Dispatch, White Plains, NY, Gannett Co. Inc.

Hawkins, Roger N ... (205) 549-2000
PUB, Gadsden Times, Gadsden, AL

Hawkins, Ross ... (415) 777-5700
MGR-CR, San Francisco Newspaper Agency, San Francisco, CA

Hawkins, Terry ... (501) 382-4925
ED, Dumas Clarion, Dumas, AR

Hawkins, Thomas E ... (817) 729-5103
PUB, ED, Groesbeck Journal, Groesbeck, TX

Hawkins, Thomas H ... (615) 359-1188
PUB, Lewisburg Tribune, Lewisburg, TN

Hawkins, Tom ... (937) 328-0300
Graphics ED/Art DIR
Springfield News-Sun, Springfield, OH

Hawkins, Webster ... (913) 755-4151
PUB, Osawatomie Graphic, Osawatomie, KS

Hawkins, William E N ... (919) 419-6500
VP/EX ED, Herald-Sun, Durham, NC

Hawkins, Yvonne ... (517) 377-1000
News ED, Lansing State Journal, Lansing, MI

Hawks, Jodi ... (417) 667-3344
ADV MGR, Nevada Daily Mail, Nevada, MO

Hawley, Catherine ... (503) 325-3211
EDU ED, Daily Astorian, Astoria, OR

Hawley, Glenda ... (802) 747-6121
ADV MGR-TELEMKTG SRV
Rutland Herald, Rutland, VT

Hawley, Peter ... (715) 684-2484
PUB, Baldwin Bulletin, Baldwin, WI

Hawley, Thomas ... (412) 543-1303
PROD FRM-PR, Leader Times
Kittanning, PA

Hawley, Thomas ... (715) 684-2484
ED, Baldwin Bulletin, Baldwin, WI

Hawley, Tom ... (605) 352-6401
PRES, PUB, Huron Plainsman, Huron, SD

Hawpe, David ... (502) 582-4011
ED/VP, Courier-Journal, Louisville, KY

Haws, William ... (716) 649-4040
PUB, Sun and Erie County Independent, Hamburg, NY

Hawthorne, Mary Anne ... (315) 363-5100
BM, Oneida Daily Dispatch, Oneida, NY

Haxton, Bill ... (615) 589-2169
GM, Buffalo River Review, Linden, TN

Hay, George ... (306) 869-2202
PUB, Radville Star, Radville, SK

Hay, Gerald ... (913) 764-2211
News ED, Olathe Daily News, Olathe, KS

Hay, Heather ... (704) 864-3291
Features ED, Films/Theater ED, Travel ED, Women's ED, Gaston Gazette, Gastonia, NC

Hay, Howard ... (312) 222-3232
VP-Circulation, CIRC DIR
Chicago Tribune, Chicago, IL

Hay, Johnson D ... (716) 232-6920
COB, Daily Record, Rochester, NY

Hay, Tom ... (203) 425-2500
Sr VP-OPER North
Thomson Newspapers, Stamford, CT

Hayakawa, Alan ... (717) 255-8100
ADTX MGR, Patriot-News, Harrisburg, PA

Haycox, Richard ... (501) 777-8841
ADV DIR, MGR-PROM, Hope Star, Hope, AR

Haydan, Richard ... (954) 698-6501
MAN ED, Sunrise Times, Deerfield Beach, FL

Hayden, Chaunce ... (201) 358-2929
ED, Collins Communications, Westwood, NJ

Hayden, Ed ... (305) 674-9746
Charity DEPT
International News Agency, Miami Beach, FL

Hayden, Jim ... (202) 636-3000
ADV MGR-NTL
Washington Times, Washington, DC

Hayden, Johnny L ... (360) 740-0445
PUB, Lewis County News, Chehalis, WA

Hayden, Joyce ... (937) 225-2000
ADV MGR-NTL
Dayton Daily News, Dayton, OH

Hayden, Julie ... (716) 773-7676
ED
Lewiston-Porter Sentinel, Grand Island, NY

Hayden, Nancy Oliver ... (916) 541-3880
Women's ED
Tahoe Daily Tribune, South Lake Tahoe, CA

Hayden, Richard M ... (810) 643-9150
GM, St. Ignace News, St. Ignace, MI

Hayden, Rod ... (541) 753-2641
PROD MGR
Corvallis Gazette-Times, Corvallis, OR

Hayden, Tom ... (941) 335-0200
Sports ED, News-Press, Fort Myers, FL

Hayes, Ben ... (813) 893-8111
PROD MGR-Packaging/Distribution
St. Petersburg Times, St. Petersburg, FL

Hayes, C ... (814) 723-8200
Environmental ED
Warren Times-Observer, Warren, PA

Hayes, Charlie ... (316) 624-2541
EPE, Southwest Daily Times, Liberal, KS

Hayes, Chris ... (319) 337-3181
PROD MGR-SRV
Iowa City Press-Citizen, Iowa City, IA

Hayes, Daniel K ... (319) 383-2200
ED, Quad-City Times, Davenport, IA

Hayes, Darlene ... (901) 885-0744
Fashion/Society ED, Women's ED, Union City Daily Messenger, Union City, TN

Hayes, Diane Aden ... (812) 331-0963
ED, Bloomington Voice, Bloomington, IN

Hayes, Edward J ... (914) 341-1100
CONT, Times Herald-Record, Middletown, NY

Hayes, Grace ... (904) 285-2915
ED, Ponte Vedra Recorder, Ponte Vedra, FL

Hayes, Gwendolyn ... (813) 248-1921
ED, Florida Sentinel-Bulletin, Tampa, FL

Hayes, Holly ... (408) 920-5000
Features ED
San Jose Mercury News, San Jose, CA

Hayes, J Todd ... (800) 227-6229
GM/ED, North American Auto Writers Syndicate, Houston, TX

Hayes, James P ... (207) 990-8000
CIRC ASST MGR, Daily News, Bangor, ME

Hayes, Jeff ... (812) 254-0480
RE/Sports ED
Washington Times-Herald, Washington, IN

Hayes, Jennifer ... (618) 529-5454
ADV CNR-NTL
Southern Illinoisan, Carbondale, IL

Hayes, Joeleene ... (912) 233-6128
GM, Savannah Tribune, Savannah, GA

Hayes, Larry ... (219) 461-8333
EPE, Journal Gazette, Fort Wayne, IN

Hayes, Margaret A ... (801) 237-2800
ADM DIR-Human Resources
Newspaper Agency Corp., Salt Lake City, UT

Hayes, Matthew D ... (401) 683-1000
GM, MAN ED
Sakonnet Times, Portsmouth, RI

Hayes, Michael ... (613) 283-3182
ED, Record News, Smiths Falls, ON

Hayes, Ophelia ... (318) 527-7075
VP, News Leader Inc., Sulphur, LA

Hayes, Paul B ... (502) 384-6471
ED, Adair Progress, Columbia, KY

Hayes, Reg ... (802) 863-3441
CIRC ASST DIR, Free Press, Burlington, VT

Hayes, Sandy ... (515) 432-1234
Fashion ED, Society/Women's ED
Boone News-Republican, Boone, IA

Hayes, Sharon ... (423) 246-8121
BUS ED
Kingsport Times-News, Kingsport, TN

Hayes, Taylor ... (502) 886-4444
VP-Development
Kentucky New Era, Hopkinsville, KY

Hayes, Tracy ... (214) 977-8222
Fashion! Dallas ED
Dallas Morning News, Dallas, TX

Hayes, Valerie ... (610) 820-6500
CIRC MGR-OPER
Morning Call, Allentown, PA

Hayes, Vance ... (304) 436-3144
ADV DIR, Welch Daily News, Welch, WV

Hayley, Randy ... (613) 739-7000
CIRC DIR, Ottawa Sun, Ottawa, ON

Hayner, Don ... (312) 321-3000
ASST MET ED
Chicago Sun-Times, Chicago, IL

Haynes, Andrea ... (508) 626-3800
ED, Middlesex News, Framingham, MA

Haynes, Bud ... (201) 877-4141
ADV MGR-CLASS, Star-Ledger, Newark, NJ

Haynes, Cynthia ... (913) 475-2206
PUB, Oberlin Herald, Oberlin, KS

Haynes, Dana ... (503) 635-8811
MAN ED
Lake Oswego Review, Lake Oswego, OR

Haynes, Dave ... (403) 235-7100
ADTX MGR, Calgary Herald, Calgary, AB

Haynes, George ... (219) 347-0400
Wire ED, News-Sun, Kendallville, IN

Haynes, John ... (601) 365-3232
PUB, Baldwyn News, Baldwyn, MS

Haynes, Lisa ... (414) 224-2000
CIRC MGR-FIN
Milwaukee Journal Sentinel, Milwaukee, WI

Haynes, Marilyn A ... (508) 355-4000
ED, Barre Gazette, Barre, MA

Haynes, Ron ... (514) 987-2222
ASST DIR, Gazette, Montreal, QC

Haynes, Steve ... (913) 475-2206
PUB, ED, Oberlin Herald, Oberlin, KS

Haynes, Vicky ... (417) 732-2525
GM, Republic Monitor, Republic, MO

Haynes, Wesley ... (913) 762-5000
Chief Photographer
Daily Union, Junction City, KS

Haynes-Hooks, Ella ... (912) 744-4200
TV Books ED, Macon Telegraph, Macon, GA

Hayon, Jack ... (212) 556-1234
VP-Internal Audit
New York Times Co., New York, NY

Hays, Arlan ... (409) 275-2181
PUB, ED
San Augustine Tribune, San Augustine, TX

Hays, Connie Gaines ... (317) 924-5143
MAN ED
Indianapolis Recorder, Indianapolis, IN

Hays, Debbie ... (412) 775-3200
MGR-CR, Beaver County Times, Beaver, PA

Hays, Helen C ... (909) 684-1200
SEC/TREAS, Press-Enterprise, Riverside, CA

Hays Jr, Howard H ... (909) 684-1200
BC, Press-Enterprise, Riverside, CA

Hays, Jonathan F ... (909) 684-1200
EVP, Press-Enterprise, Riverside, CA

Hays, Kristen ... (913) 295-1111
EDU ED, Topeka Capital-Journal, Topeka, KS

Hays, Pat ... (605) 734-6360
PUB, Chamberlain Register, Chamberlain, SD

Hays, Robert ... (610) 258-7171
Amusements ED, Books ED, Fashion/Food ED, Music ED, Radio/Television ED, Religion ED, Women's ED, Express-Times, Easton, PA

Hays, Rod ... (605) 734-6360
PUB, Chamberlain Register, Chamberlain, SD

Hays, William ... (219) 267-3111
ADV MGR, ADV DIR-Special Editions
Times-Union, Warsaw, IN

Hays, William M ... (913) 325-2219
PUB, ED
Washington County News, Washington, KS

Hayter, Bill ... (904) 752-1293
CIRC DIR, Lake City Reporter, Lake City, FL

Hayter, Carl ... (519) 294-6264
PUB, Parkhill Gazette, Parkhill, ON

Hayward, Nancy ... (207) 255-6561
MAN ED
Machias Valley News Observer, Machias, ME

Hayward, V M (Vicki) ... (204) 529-2342
PUB, ED
Southern Manitoba Review, Cartwright, MB

Haywood, Kamala ... (804) 862-9611
ED, Southside Virginia Star, Petersburg, VA

Haywood, Karl N ... (706) 863-6165
GM, ED, Columbia News Times, Martinez, GA

Haywood, R Allen ... (706) 444-5330
PUB, ED, Sparta Ishmaelite, Sparta, GA

Haywood, Tom ... (318) 459-3200
BUS/FIN ED, Health/ Medical ED, SCI/Technology ED, Times, Shreveport, LA

Hazard, Carol ... (706) 324-5526
BUS/FIN ED
Columbus Ledger-Enquirer, Columbus, GA

Hazard, Glenda ... (508) 485-5200
ED, Southborough Villager, Marlboro, MA

Hazard, John ... (401) 277-7000
DIR-Quality Improvement & Training
Providence Journal-Bulletin, Providence, RI

Hazarian, Tony ... (206) 851-9921
ED, Peninsula Gateway, Gig Harbor, WA

Hazelwood, Tom ... (319) 372-6421
PROD SUPT
Daily Democrat, Fort Madison, IA

Hazen, Deborah Steele ... (503) 728-3350
PUB, ED, Clatskanie Chief, Clatskanie, OR

Hazen, John ... (312) 222-3232
PROD DIR-Engineering
Chicago Tribune, Chicago, IL

Hazen, Pat ... (505) 325-4545
Online MGR, ADTX MGR
Daily Times, Farmington, NM

Hazlett, Curt ... (207) 791-6650
ASST MAN ED-News
Portland Press Herald, Portland, ME

Hazlett, Terry P ... (412) 222-2200
ASST MAN ED, Entertainment ED, Living/Lifestyle ED, Television/Film ED, Travel ED,, Observer-Reporter, Washington, PA

Hazzard, Jody ... (803) 626-8555
MGR-Specialty Publications
Sun News, Myrtle Beach, SC

He, Mike H ... (713) 498-4310
ED, U.S. Asia News, Houston, TX

Heaberun, Julie ... (817) 390-7400
Senior ED-Features
Fort Worth Star-Telegram, Fort Worth, TX

Head, Alison ... (707) 546-2020
Librarian, Press Democrat, Santa Rosa, CA

Head, Carol ... (213) 237-5000
ADV Group MGR-MKTG Services
Los Angeles Times, Los Angeles, CA

Head, John ... (507) 451-2840
MAN ED, People's Press, Owatonna, MN

Head, Pat ... (502) 926-0123
PROD MGR-PR
Messenger-Inquirer, Owensboro, KY

Head, Rick ... (912) 283-2244
Amusements ED, Wire ED
Waycross Journal-Herald, Waycross, GA

Head, Terry ... (314) 340-8000
PROD GEN FRM-PR
St. Louis Post-Dispatch, St. Louis, MO

Hea Who's Where-100

Headington, James R .... (306) 338-2231
PUB, ED, Wadena News, Wadena, SK
Headlee, Terry .... (301) 733-5131
City/MET ED
Morning Herald, Hagerstown, MD
Headley, James .... (913) 367-0583
ED, BUS/FIN ED
Atchison Daily Globe, Atchison, KS
Headley, Otis .... (601) 636-4545
GM, PA, Vicksburg Post, Vicksburg, MS
Headley, Rich .... (308) 762-3060
Sports ED, Times-Herald, Alliance, NE
Headley, William J .... (605) 387-5158
PUB, ED, Hutchinson Herald, Menno, SD
Headrick, Doug .... (423) 745-5664
ED, EDL Writer
Daily Post-Athenian, Athens, TN
Headrick, Gail P .... (801) 237-2800
ADV MGR-Major Accounts
Newspaper Agency Corp., Salt Lake City, UT
Healey, Ann L .... (303) 794-7877
ED, Highlands Ranch Herald, Littleton, CO
Healey, David .... (410) 398-3311
News ED, Cecil Whig, Elkton, MD
Healey, Gerard J .... (303) 794-7877
PUB, Highlands Ranch Herald, Littleton, CO
Healey, James R .... (703) 276-3400
Automotive ED, USA Today, Arlington, VA
Healing, Dan .... (403) 468-0100
BUS/FIN ED, Edmonton Sun, Edmonton, AB
Healy, Ann .... (305) 253-4339
PUB, Cutler Courier, Miami, FL
Healy, Bonnie .... (610) 622-8800
City ED
Delaware County Daily Times, Primos, PA
Healy, Diana .... (716) 282-2311
DIR-Market Development
Niagara Gazette, Niagara Falls, NY
Healy, Howard T .... (518) 454-5694
EPE, Times Union, Albany, NY
Healy, James D .... (305) 253-4339
PUB, MAN ED, Cutler Courier, Miami, FL
Healy, Jane .... (407) 420-5000
MAN ED, Orlando Sentinel, Orlando, FL
Healy, Mike .... (612) 673-4000
Photo ED, Star Tribune, Minneapolis, MN
Heaney, Dennis W .... (612) 291-4444
PUB, Catholic Bulletin, St. Paul, MN
Heaney, James .... (716) 849-3434
EDU ED, Buffalo News, Buffalo, NY
Heaphy, Janis .... (213) 237-5000
Senior VP-ADV
Los Angeles Times, Los Angeles, CA
Heard, Jeff .... (912) 244-1880
MGR-MKTG/PROM
Valdosta Daily Times, Valdosta, GA
Hearin, W J .... (334) 433-1551
COB, Mobile Press Register, Mobile, AL
Hearing, Carl C .... (608) 328-4202
VP, GM, Monroe Times, Monroe, WI
Hearkell, Sgt Renee E .... (617) 433-7900
ED, Hansconian, Framingham, MA
Hearst III, George R .... (518) 454-5694
DIR-OPER/Planning
Times Union, Albany, NY
Hearst, R A .... (415) 777-2424
Divisional PRES
San Francisco Examiner, San Francisco, CA
Hearst, Stephen T .... (415) 777-5700
VP-Circulation/MIS, San Francisco Newspaper Agency, San Francisco, CA
Heasley, Bill .... (810) 469-4510
CIRC DIR
Macomb Daily, Mount Clemens, MI
Independent Newspapers Inc. (MI)
Heasley, Jim .... (412) 543-1303
Lifestyle ED, Leader Times, Kittanning, PA
Heaster, Jerry .... (816) 234-4141
COL, Kansas City Star, Kansas City, MO
Heaston, Jean .... (402) 341-7323
GM, Reader, Omaha, NE
Heater, Jay .... (510) 758-8400
Sports ED, West County Times, Pinole, CA
Heath, George .... (508) 997-7411
Graphics ED
Standard Times, New Bedford, MA
Heath, Georgie .... (206) 872-6600
Human Resources MGR
South County Journal, Kent, WA
Heath, Geraldine .... (615) 292-9150
MAN ED, Nashville Pride, Nashville, TN
Heath, Jay .... (901) 635-1238
ED, Lauderdale Voice, Ripley, TN
Heath, Jean .... (907) 486-3227
CIRC MGR, Kodiak Daily Mirror, Kodiak, AK
Heath, Jeanne .... (308) 623-1322
PUB, ED, Index, Mitchell, NE
Heath, John .... (803) 524-3183
PUB, Beaufort Gazette, Beaufort, SC
Heath, Steve .... (317) 831-0280
ED, Times, Mooresville, IN
Heath, William .... (715) 384-3131
ED, Marshfield News-Herald, Marshfield, WI
Heatherly, Roy .... (318) 322-5161
ADV DIR, News-Star, Monroe, LA
Heaton, Betty Jo .... (619) 375-4481
PROD MGR
Daily Independent, Ridgecrest, CA
Heaton, Heather .... (518) 789-4401
ED, Millerton News, Millerton, NY
Heaton, Rick .... (316) 442-4200
Sports ED
Arkansas City Traveler, Arkansas City, KS
Heavens, Al .... (215) 854-2000
Residential RE Writer
Philadelphia Inquirer, Philadelphia, PA
Hebert, Chantal .... (514) 285-7272
Ottawa BU, La Presse, Montreal, QC
Hebert, David .... (517) 893-6507
PUB, Valley Farmer, Bay City, MI
Hebert, Ellie .... (504) 687-3288
ED, Plaquemine Post/South, Plaquemine, LA
Hebert, Joyce S .... (504) 687-3288
PUB
Plaquemine Post/South, Plaquemine, LA
Hebert, Mike .... (318) 643-8002
GM, Kaplan Herald, Kaplan, LA
Hebert, Terry .... (216) 999-4500
ADV DIR, Plain Dealer, Cleveland, OH
Hecht, Beth .... (319) 263-2331
PROD MGR-Photo Lab
Muscatine Journal, Muscatine, IA
Heck, Fred .... (604) 295-3535
PUB, ED, Princeton Similkameen Spotlight, Princeton, BC
Heck, Rose .... (201) 288-0333
ED, Observer, Hasbrouck Heights, NJ
Heckbert, Peter .... (902) 895-7947
ED, Weekly Record, Truro, NS
Hecke, Don .... (618) 783-2324
PUB, ED, Press-Mentor, Newton, IL
Heckel, Sherri .... (502) 926-0123
Librarian
Messenger-Inquirer, Owensboro, KY
Hecker, Tina .... (215) 675-3430
ED, Public Spirit, Hatboro, PA
Hector, John .... (773) 586-8800
Deputy MET ED
Daily Southtown, Chicago, IL
Hedberg, Charles A .... (573) 682-2133
ED, Centralia Fireside Guard, Centralia, MO
Hedberg, Janann .... (573) 682-2133
ED, Centralia Fireside Guard, Centralia, MO
Hedberg, Jeff .... (573) 682-2133
PUB, Centralia Fireside Guard, Centralia, MO
Hedden-Nicely, Andy .... (208) 344-2055
PUB, Boise Weekly, Boise, ID
Hedden-Nicely, Debi .... (208) 344-2055
PUB, Boise Weekly, Boise, ID
Hedes, Ed .... (610) 377-2051
Sports ED, Times News, Lehighton, PA
Hedgecock, Kathy .... (509) 725-0101
ED, Davenport Times, Davenport, WA
Hedgecoth, Roger .... (316) 225-4151
PROD FRM-MR
Dodge City Daily Globe, Dodge City, KS
Hedgepeth, Elizabeth .... (804) 732-3456
MAN ED, COL/EDL Writer, Sunday ED
Progress-Index, Petersburg, VA
Hedges, David J .... (304) 927-2360
PUB, Times Record, Spencer, WV
Hedges, Roger .... (501) 378-3400
State ED
Arkansas Democrat-Gazette, Little Rock, AR
Hedgpeth, Steve .... (201) 877-4141
Television Book (Scanner) ED
Star-Ledger, Newark, NJ
Hedstrom, P C .... (507) 723-4225
PUB
Springfield Advance-Press, Springfield, MN
Heegaard, Jeff .... (612) 338-8155
PRES, HomeStyles Publishing and Marketing Inc., Minneapolis, MN
Heegaard, Roger .... (612) 338-8155
PUB, HomeStyles Publishing and Marketing Inc., Minneapolis, MN
Heerwagen, Art .... (503) 543-6387
PUB, ED
South County Spotlight, Scappoose, OR
Heerwagen, Sally .... (503) 543-6387
PUB, South County Spotlight, Scappoose, OR
Heffelfinger, Jan .... (419) 542-7764
MAN ED, News Tribune, Hicksville, OH
Hefferan, Mary .... (616) 222-5400
Television Listing ED
Grand Rapids Press, Grand Rapids, MI
Heffernan, Jim .... (218) 723-5281
ASSOC EPE
Duluth News-Tribune, Duluth, MN
Heffley, Lynn .... (213) 237-5000
Children's Television Reporter
Los Angeles Times, Los Angeles, CA
Heffling, Joe .... (717) 253-3055
CIRC MGR
Wayne Independent, Honesdale, PA
Hefflinger, Bruce .... (419) 784-5441
Sports ED, Crescent-News, Defiance, OH
Heffner, James .... (704) 827-7526
MAN ED, Belmont Banner, Belmont, NC
Hefley, Cindy .... (520) 573-4400
ADV MGR-RT, TNI Partners dba Tucson Newspapers, Tucson, AZ
Hefley, Jim .... (405) 223-2200
CIRC MGR, Daily Ardmoreite, Ardmore, OK
Hefner, Paul .... (510) 462-4160
City ED, Valley Times, Pleasanton, CA
Hefron, Michael J .... (812) 332-4401
VP, GM, Herald-Times Inc, Bloomington, IN
Schurz Communications Inc.
Hefton, Richard R .... (405) 737-3050
PUB, ED, Sunday Sun, Midwest City, OK
Hegazy, M .... (416) 362-0304
ED, Canada & Arab World, Toronto, ON
Hegger, Susan .... (314) 340-8000
EDL Writer
St. Louis Post-Dispatch, St. Louis, MO
Hegland, Dennis .... (403) 835-4925
ED, Fairview Post, Fairview, AB
Hehm, Connie .... (307) 266-0500
PROD FRM-COMP, Star-Tribune, Casper, WY
Heiberg, Michele .... (320) 677-2229
PUB, Herman Review, Herman, MN
Heiberg, Owen .... (320) 324-2405
PUB, Chokio Review, Chokio, MN
Heick, Frank .... (215) 854-2000
SYS ED
Philadelphia Daily News, Philadelphia, PA
Heidbreder, Paul .... (207) 873-3341
ADV MGR-RT, Central Maine Morning Sentinel, Waterville, ME, Guy Gannett Communications
Heidbreder, Paul J .... (517) 486-2400
PUB, Blissfield Advance, Blissfield, MI
Heide, Ruth .... (719) 589-2553
Living/Lifestyle ED, Religion ED, Women's ED, Valley Courier, Alamosa, CO
Heide, Steve .... (907) 376-5225
GM, Valley Sun, Wasilla, AK
Heider Jr, Bill .... (609) 989-5454
PROD MGR-PR, Times, Trenton, NJ
Heidman, Fred .... (705) 746-2104
PUB, North Star, Parry Sound, ON
Heidrich, Betty .... (619) 299-3131
MGR-Telecommunications
San Diego Union-Tribune, San Diego, CA
Heifner, Barry .... (505) 325-4545
News ED, Daily Times, Farmington, NM
Heigelmann, Volker .... (904) 829-6562
PROD FRM-PR
St. Augustine Record, St. Augustine, FL
Heigl, Paul .... (202) 898-8254
CEO
United Press International, Washington, DC
Heikkila, Doug .... (612) 460-6606
PUB, ED
Farmington Independent, Farmington, MN
Heil, Jim .... (616) 347-2544
Wire ED
Petoskey News-Review, Petoskey, MI
Heilenman, Diane .... (502) 582-4011
Garden ED, Courier-Journal, Louisville, KY
Heilig, Bobby .... (910) 888-3500
PROD MGR-MR
High Point Enterprise, High Point, NC
Heilig, John .... (610) 965-4257
PRES, Auto Page Syndicate, Emmaus, PA
Heiling, Joe .... (409) 833-3311
Sports ED
Beaumont Enterprise, Beaumont, TX
Heiller, Cynthia .... (320) 838-3151
PUB, Askov American, Askov, MN
Heiller, David .... (320) 838-3151
PUB, ED, Askov American, Askov, MN
Heilprin, John .... (803) 577-7111
State Government
Post and Courier, Charleston, SC
Heim, Delores .... (810) 724-2615
PUB, Tri-City Times, Imlay City, MI
Heim, Martin .... (810) 724-2615
PUB, Tri-City Times, Imlay City, MI
Heim, Rueben .... (715) 698-2401
PUB, ED, Woodville Leader, Woodville, WI
Heiman, Roberta .... (812) 424-7711
Special Assignments ED
Evansville Courier, Evansville, IN
Heimbigner, Renda .... (907) 789-4144
PUB, Capital City Weekly, Juneau, AK
Heimburger, Sara .... (573) 431-2010
City/MET ED, EDU ED, Environmental ED, Fashion/Style ED, Features ED, SCI/Technology ED, Television/Film ED, Theater/Music ED, Travel ED, Daily Journal, Park Hills, MO
Heimer, Scott .... (215) 854-2000
Automotive ED
Philadelphia Daily News, Philadelphia, PA
Heimerman, Jon .... (619) 322-8889
CONT, Desert Sun, Palm Springs, CA
Heimlich, Richard .... (212) 455-4000
ASST Sales MGR, North America Syndicate, King Features Syndicate Inc., New York, NY
Heimsath, Peter .... (703) 451-9204
BU MGR, Photo International/Photo Associates News Service, Springfield, VA
Hein, Darin .... (317) 962-1575
ADV MGR-Sales
Palladium-Item, Richmond, IN
Hein, DeLane .... (816) 359-2212
ADV DIR, Republican-Times, Trenton, MO
Heine, Kult .... (215) 854-2000
ASST City ED
Philadelphia Daily News, Philadelphia, PA
Heine, Max .... (205) 345-0505
Automotive ED, BUS ED
Tuscaloosa News, Tuscaloosa, AL
Heinelein, Parker .... (406) 587-4491
Features ED
Bozeman Daily Chronicle, Bozeman, MT
Heinold, Bob .... (313) 994-6989
Religion ED, Ann Arbor News, Ann Arbor, MI
Heinrich, Peter .... (716) 328-2144
Features ED
Syndicated News Service, Rochester, NY
Heinritz, Joe .... (715) 842-2101
PROD MGR-Distribution Center
Wausau Daily Herald, Wausau, WI
Heinsen, Lindsay .... (713) 220-7171
Fine Arts ED
Houston Chronicle, Houston, TX
Heintz, Florence .... (608) 782-9710
CNR-MKTG, Tribune, La Crosse, WI
Heinz, Andrew .... (518) 792-9914
Technical Sales CNR
TV Data, Queensbury, NY
Heinzerling, Sherry .... (513) 294-2662
ED, Oakwood Register, Dayton, OH
Heinzman, Don .... (612) 441-3500
GM, ED, Elk River Star News, Elk River, MN
Heironimus, Mitchell O .... (540) 667-3200
PROD FRM-PR
Winchester Star, Winchester, VA
Heirtzler Jr, William C (Bill) .... (318) 487-6397
ADV MGR-GEN/RT, MGR-PROM/MKTG
Alexandria Daily Town Talk, Alexandria, LA
Heiser, Lorraine .... (573) 276-5148/4523
MAN ED, Delta News Journal & Press Merit, Malden, MO
Heishman, David .... (304) 538-2342
GM, Moorefield Examiner and Weekender, Moorefield, WV
Heishman, Phoebe F .... (304) 538-2342
PUB, ED, Moorefield Examiner and Weekender, Moorefield, WV
Heisler, Bob .... (516) 843-2020
Weekend ED, Newsday, Melville, NY
Heisse, Robert .... (717) 255-8100
City ED (Night), Patriot-News, Harrisburg, PA
Heissenberger, George .... (716) 232-7100
ADV MGR-Community Newspapers
Rochester Democrat and Chronicle; Rochester, NY Times-Union, Rochester, NY
Heist, Robert .... (814) 724-6370
Sports ED, Meadville Tribune, Meadville, PA
Heit, Elaine .... (702) 623-5011
ADV MGR, Humboldt Sun, Winnemucca, NV
Heithaus, Harriet .... (219) 461-8333
Travel/Arts ED
Journal Gazette, Fort Wayne, IN
Heitholt, Kent .... (573) 815-1500
Sports ED
Columbia Daily Tribune, Columbia, MO
Heitz, David .... (818) 241-4141
MAN ED, Glendale News-Press, Glendale, CA
Heitzman, Kay .... (213) 237-5000
CIRC DIR-Consumer PROM/MKTG
Los Angeles Times, Los Angeles, CA
Helberg, Todd .... (419) 784-5441
City/MET ED, EPE, Political/Government ED
Crescent-News, Defiance, OH
Helbig, Carl D .... (716) 394-0770
CIRC DIR-MKTG, Daily Messenger/The Sunday Messenger, Canandaigua, NY
Held, Jon .... (602) 271-8000
ASST SEC/TREAS, DIR-FIN
Phoenix Newspapers Inc., Phoenix, AZ
Held, K C .... (330) 938-2060
ED, Sebring Times, Sebring, OH
Heldenbrand, Charlotte .... (972) 636-4351
ED, Big Sandy & Hawkins Journal and Tri-Area News, Big Sandy, TX
Heldenfels, R D .... (330) 996-3000
Television Writer, Beacon Journal, Akron, OH
Helderman Jr, Frank .... (205) 766-3434
PUB, Times Daily, Florence, AL
Heldman, Cindy .... (817) 694-3713
ED, Whitney Messenger, Whitney, TX
Heldman, Lou .... (814) 238-5000
PUB/PRES
Centre Daily Times, State College, PA
Heldt, Diane .... (515) 232-2160
EDU ED, Daily Tribune, Ames, IA
Heldt, John .... (360) 452-2345
Sports ED
Peninsula Daily News, Port Angeles, WA
Helenthal, Mike .... (630) 739-2300
ED, Darien Metropolitan, Lemont, IL
Helfenstein, Carol .... (519) 392-6896
PUB, ED, Teeswater News, Teeswater, ON
Helfenstein, Harry .... (519) 392-6896
PUB, ED, Teeswater News, Teeswater, ON

Copyright ©1997 by the Editor & Publisher Co.

101-Who's Where **Hen**

Helicke, James .... (412) 222-2200
PROD FRM-PR
Observer-Reporter, Washington, PA

Helland, Jim .... (605) 331-2200
News ED, Argus Leader, Sioux Falls, SD

Hellar, Martin .... (316) 725-3176
PUB, Sedan Times-Star, Sedan, KS

Helle, Mary .... (319) 926-2626
PUB, Delaware County Leader, Hopkinton, IA

Helle, Roger .... (319) 926-2626
PUB, Delaware County Leader, Hopkinton, IA

Hellegaard, Marvel .... (406) 765-2190
GM, Plentywood Herald, Plentywood, MT

Hellems, Thomas M .... (310) 540-5511
ASST BM, Daily Breeze, Torrance, CA
Copley Press Inc.

Heller, Andrew .... (810) 766-6100
COL, Flint Journal, Flint, MI

Heller, Ann .... (937) 225-2000
Food ED, Dayton Daily News, Dayton, OH

Heller, Janice .... (412) 543-1303
City ED, Leader Times, Kittanning, PA

Heller, Jonathan .... (619) 745-6611
City ED-Carlsbad
North County Times, Escondido, CA

Heller, Marlene A .... (908) 432-7711
ED, Jewish Star, South River, NJ

Heller, Roberto .... (415) 334-2061
GM, El Latino, San Francisco, CA

Hellerman, Cynthia .... (908) 722-8800
RE ED, Courier-News, Bridgewater, NJ

Hellmann, Msgr Donald .... (606) 283-6270
PUB, Messenger, Erlanger, KY

Hellman, Mary .... (619) 299-3131
RE ED, Union-Tribune, San Diego, CA

Hellman, Rick .... (913) 648-4620
MAN ED, Kansas City Jewish Chronicle, Overland Park, KS

Hellmuth, Ann .... (407) 420-5000
News ED, Orlando Sentinel, Orlando, FL

Hellyer, Kevin .... (505) 823-7777
ASST MAN ED-Features Business/Sports
Albuquerque Tribune, Albuquerque, NM

Helm, Hunt .... (502) 582-4011
MET ED, Courier-Journal, Louisville, KY

Helm, Kathy .... (502) 769-2312
CIRC MGR
News Enterprise, Elizabethtown, KY

Helm, Leslie .... (213) 237-5000
Technology/Telecommunications-Seattle
Los Angeles Times, Los Angeles, CA

Helm, Marian .... (715) 423-7200
PROD FRM-COMP
Daily Tribune, Wisconsin Rapids, WI

Helm, Steve .... (816) 234-4141
CONT, Kansas City Star, Kansas City, MO

Helmchen, Scott .... (815) 459-4040
Sidetracks Copy ED
Northwest Herald, Crystal Lake, IL

Helmer, David .... (610) 377-2051
PROD DIR, Times News, Lehighton, PA

Helmick, Gene .... (423) 928-4151
CIRC MGR, Star, Elizabethton, TN

Helmling, J Gregory .... (517) 895-8551
Radio/Television ED, Sunday ED, Travel ED
Bay City Times, Bay City, MI

Helms, Arthur .... (203) 964-2200
Senior ED, Stamford Advocate, Stamford, CT

Helms, David .... (601) 489-3511
ED, Pontotoc Progress, Pontotoc, MS

Helms, Don .... (405) 321-1800
CIRC MGR, Norman Transcript, Norman, OK

Helms, Donna .... (501) 673-8533
PA, Stuttgart Daily Leader, Stuttgart, AR

Helms, Jack .... (540) 374-5000
PROD MGR
Free Lance-Star, Fredericksburg, VA

Helms, LaVerne E .... (605) 375-3228
GM, Nation's Center News, Buffalo, SD

Helms, Lois .... (712) 527-3191
PUB, Opinion-Tribune, Glenwood, IA

Helms, Mary Ann .... (704) 289-1541
ADV MGR-CLASS
Enquirer-Journal, Monroe, NC

Helms, Paul .... (909) 987-6397
COL-Sports
Inland Valley Daily Bulletin, Ontario, CA

Helms, Sammy .... (704) 358-5000
PROD MGR-Quality & Planning
Charlotte Observer, Charlotte, NC

Helms, Shirley .... (334) 847-2599
GM, Washington County News, Chatom, AL

Helsabeck, Michael .... (802) 479-0191
Sports ED, Times Argus, Barre, VT

Helsdon, Jeff .... (519) 582-2510
ED, Delhi News Record, Delhi, ON

Helsley, Robert .... (719) 275-7565
GM, ED, Daily Record, Canon City, CO

Helstoski, Henry .... (201) 779-7500
PUB, GM, Passaic Citizen, Passaic, NJ

Helton, Greg .... (941) 335-0200
PROD MGR-Computer SYS, News-Press, Fort Myers, FL

Helton, John .... (334) 262-1611
Graphics ED/Art DIR
Montgomery Advertiser, Montgomery, AL

Heltsley, Debbie .... (217) 465-6424
ADV MGR-GEN, Daily Beacon-News, Paris, IL

Heltzel, Ellen .... (503) 221-8327
Books ED, Oregonian, Portland, OR

Hembree, LaDonna .... (423) 523-3131
ADV MGR-Sales
Knoxville News-Sentinel, Knoxville, TN

Hemby, Tom .... (704) 758-7381
News ED, Lenoir News-Topic, Lenoir, NC

Hemenway, Laura .... (912) 744-4200
MGR-RES, Macon Telegraph, Macon, GA

Heminger, Edwin L .... (419) 422-5151
BC, PUB, Courier, Findlay, OH

Heminger, Karl .... (419) 422-5151
VP, ASSOC PUB, PROD MGR
Courier, Findlay, OH

Hemingway, V Rulon .... (302) 324-2500
DIR-FIN, News Journal, Wilmington, DE

Hemlepp, Catherine .... (212) 450-7000
DIR-Public Relations, React, Parade Publications, New York, NY

Hemman, Ray .... (316) 694-5700
Farm ED, Hutchinson News, Hutchinson, KS

Hemman, Thomas .... (414) 223-2180
ED, MAN ED, Italian Times, Milwaukee, WI

Hemmer Jr, R J .... (216) 933-5100
PUB, Press, Avon Lake, OH

Hempe, Rudy .... (401) 294-4576
ED, Standard-Times, North Kingstown, RI

Hempel, Kay L .... (612) 433-3845
PUB, ED, Country Messenger, Scandia, MN

Hempfling, Vickie .... (812) 424-7711
Online MGR
Evansville Courier, Evansville, IN

Hemphill, Lex .... (801) 237-2031
EDL Writer
Salt Lake Tribune, Salt Lake City, UT

Hemstreet, Wayne .... (520) 428-2560
PUB, ED
Eastern Arizona Courier, Safford, AZ

Henaghan, Robert .... (212) 930-8000
PROD FRM-Stereo
New York Post, New York, NY

Henderberg, Mary K .... (315) 946-9701
ED, Wayne County Star, Lyons, NY

Hendershot, Steve .... (317) 653-5151
GM, ADV DIR
Banner-Graphic, Greencastle, IN

Henderson, Al .... (904) 434-6963
MAN ED, Pensacola Voice, Pensacola, FL

Henderson, Anne .... (402) 444-1000
City ED-Day
Omaha World-Herald, Omaha, NE

Henderson, Beth .... (601) 453-5312
Women's Reporter
Greenwood Commonwealth, Greenwood, MS

Henderson, Brad .... (416) 367-2000
Deputy MAN ED-Prepress
Toronto Star, Toronto, ON

Henderson, Bruce .... (215) 949-4000
EPE
Bucks County Courier Times, Levittown, PA

Henderson, Charles A .... (502) 886-4444
SEC/TREAS, VP/GM
Kentucky New Era, Hopkinsville, KY

Henderson, Christine .... (937) 498-2111
Automotive ED, BUS/FIN ED, RE ED, SCI/Technology ED
Sidney Daily News, Sidney, OH

Henderson, Dave .... (607) 798-1234
COL-Sports
Press & Sun Bulletin, Binghamton, NY

Henderson, Edwina .... (914) 331-5000
Entertainment/Amusements ED, Fashion/Style ED, Living/Lifestyle ED
Daily Freeman, Kingston, NY

Henderson, Eric .... (604) 245-2277
ED, Ladysmith-Chemainus Chronicle, Ladysmith, BC

Henderson, Fred .... (330) 385-4545
PROD MGR, Review, East Liverpool, OH

Henderson, Guy .... (601) 968-3800
ED, Baptist Record, Jackson, MS

Henderson, Keith .... (617) 450-2000
Senior Writer
Christian Science Monitor, Boston, MA

Henderson, Lane .... (801) 798-9770
PUB, ED
Spanish Fork Press, Spanish Fork, UT

Henderson, Larry .... (205) 845-2550
CIRC MGR, Times Journal, Fort Payne, AL

Henderson, Linda .... (401) 277-7000
Librarian
Providence Journal-Bulletin, Providence, RI

Henderson, Mark .... (318) 322-5161
EX News ED, News-Star, Monroe, LA

Henderson, Randy .... (205) 325-2222
City ED, Health ED
Birmingham News, Birmingham, AL

Henderson, Richard L .... (919) 829-4500
VP, ADV DIR-Sales/MKTG
News & Observer, Raleigh, NC

Henderson, Robert .... (617) 929-2000
DIR-Training, Boston Globe, Boston, MA

Henderson, Robyn .... (210) 868-7181
PUB, ED, Record-Courier, Johnson City, TX

Henderson, Shirley M .... (601) 374-8318
ED, Gulf Pine Catholic, Biloxi, MS

Henderson, Tanya .... (616) 222-5400
MGR-MKTG/PROM
Grand Rapids Press, Grand Rapids, MI

Henderson, Terry .... (937) 382-2574
PROD MGR, News Journal, Wilmington, OH

Henderson, Virginia .... (503) 623-2373
MAN ED
Polk County Itemizer-Observer, Dallas, OR

Henderson-Watson, Adrienne .. (313) 869-0033
GM, MAN ED
Michigan Citizen, Highland Park, MI

Hendley, W E .... (903) 597-8111
BM, Tyler Morning Telegraph, Tyler, TX

Hendricks, Dan .... (909) 889-9666
Radio/Television ED
Sun, San Bernardino, CA

Hendricks, David .... (210) 225-7411
COL, Express-News, San Antonio, TX

Hendricks, Jane .... (310) 862-4880
GM, MAN ED
California Veckoblad, Downey, CA

Hendricks, Jim .... (912) 888-9300
MET ED, Albany Herald, Albany, GA

Hendricks, Julie .... (905) 648-4464
ED, Ancaster News, Ancaster, ON

Hendricks, Karen .... (717) 742-9671
Accountant
Milton Daily Standard, Milton, PA
Hollinger International Inc.

Hendricks, Lynne .... (813) 964-2728
ED, Gasparilla Gazette, Boca Grande, FL

Hendricks, Mary A .... (310) 862-4880
PUB, ED, California Veckoblad, Downey, CA

Hendricks, Rick .... (864) 833-1900
ED, Clinton Chronicle, Clinton, SC

Hendricks, Sara .... (512) 575-1451
Lifestyle ED, Victoria Advocate, Victoria, TX

Hendricks, Ted .... (410) 838-4400
ED, Weekender, Bel Air, MD

Hendrickson, Dyke .... (617) 937-8000
MAN ED, Woburn Advocate, Woburn, MA

Hendrickson, Nancy .... (712) 273-5681
ED, Chronicle, Early, IA

Hendrickson, Richard .... (216) 245-6901
EPE, Morning Journal, Lorain, OH

Hendrickson, Robert L .... (606) 564-9091
PUB, Ledger Independent, Maysville, KY

Hendrix, Anastasia .... (209) 441-6111
School Writer, Fresno Bee, Fresno, CA

Hendrix, Arnold .... (804) 793-2311
City ED, Register & Bee, Danville, VA

Hendrix, Charles .... (864) 298-4100
PROD FRM-COMP (Night)
Greenville News, Greenville, SC

Hendrix, Charlie Frank .... (704) 633-8950
DP MGR, PROD FRM-COMP
Salisbury Post, Salisbury, NC

Hendrix, Daryl .... (903) 597-8111
PROD FRM-MR (Night)
Tyler Morning Telegraph, Tyler, TX

Hendrix, Don .... (206) 339-3000
DIR-SYS/Technology, DP MGR
Herald, Everett, WA

Hendrix, Sharon .... (505) 823-7777
Northern BU ED
Albuquerque Journal, Albuquerque, NM

Hendry, Jim .... (705) 745-4641
City ED, Examiner, Peterborough, ON

Henecker, Tom .... (518) 891-2600
Television/Film ED, Theater/Music ED, Adirondack Daily Enterprise, Saranac Lake, NY

Henery, Gary .... (614) 363-1161
Sports ED, Delaware Gazette, Delaware, OH

Hengel, Michael T .... (501) 327-6621
PRES/PUB, Log Cabin Democrat, Conway, AR

Henistock, Kevin .... (561) 746-5111
MAN ED, Jupiter Courier, Jupiter, FL

Henke, Bradley F .... (206) 284-4424
GEN Counsel/VP
Pioneer Newspapers, Seattle, WA

Henke, Bruce .... (701) 252-3120
PUB, BM, Jamestown Sun, Jamestown, ND

Henke, Tate W .... (316) 886-5654
ED, Gyp Hill Premiere, Medicine Lodge, KS

Henkel, Cathy .... (206) 464-2111
Sports ED, Seattle Times, Seattle, WA

Henkel, Gretchen .... (201) 867-2071
PUB, ED, Home News, Secaucus, NJ

Henley, Brian .... (410) 268-5000
Graphics ED, Photo ED, ADTX MGR
Capital, Annapolis, MD

Henley, Dan .... (573) 221-2800
Sports ED
Hannibal Courier-Post, Hannibal, MO

Henley, David C .... (702) 423-6041
Co-PUB, Lahontan Valley News & Fallon Eagle Standard, Fallon, NV

Henley, David S .... (506) 328-8863
PUB, Bugle, Woodstock, NB

Henley, Deborah .... (502) 582-4011
MAN ED, Courier-Journal, Louisville, KY

Henley, Ludie .... (702) 423-6041
Co-PUB, Lahontan Valley News & Fallon Eagle Standard, Fallon, NV

Henly, Rick .... (219) 356-6700
Photo DEPT MGR
Huntington Herald-Press, Huntington, IN

Henn, Catherine E C .... (617) 929-2000
CORP Counsel/Clerk, VP-Corporate & Legal Affairs, Boston Globe, Boston, MA

Henneberry, Bart .... (902) 468-1222
VP-FIN, Daily News, Halifax, NS

Hennen, Scott .... (614) 345-4053
Sports ED, Advocate, Newark, OH

Hennen, Sue .... (505) 523-6464
ED, Missile Ranger, Las Cruces, NM

Hennessey, Chris .... (215) 948-4850
ED, Valley Item, Schwenksville, PA

Hennessey, James P .... (905) 372-0131
ADV DIR, Cobourg Daily Star, Cobourg, ON

Hennessey, Phil .... (602) 271-8000
Travel ED, Arizona Republic, Phoenix, AZ

Hennessey, Tom .... (207) 990-8000
Outdoors COL
Bangor Daily News, Bangor, ME

Hennessy, C P .... (212) 476-0802
VP/Food Editor, Test Kitchen, International BusinessMan News Bureau, New York, NY

Hennessy, Tom .... (562) 435-1161
COL, Press-Telegram, Long Beach, CA

Hennick, Tom .... (203) 574-3636
Regional ED, Waterbury Republican-American, Waterbury, CT

Hennig, Lou Ann .... (907) 257-4200
MGR-Human Resources
Anchorage Daily News, Anchorage, AK

Hennigan, David M .... (717) 291-8811
ED (Sunday News)
Lancaster Intelligencer Journal/New Era/Sunday News, Lancaster, PA

Hennigar, Deane .... (902) 468-1222
ADV MGR, Daily News, Halifax, NS

Hennigar, Lynn .... (902) 543-2457
GM, Lighthouse Log, Bridgewater, NS

Hennigar, Margaret .... (902) 543-2457
ED, Lighthouse Log, Bridgewater, NS

Henning, Daryl .... (912) 924-2751
PUB
Americus Times-Recorder, Americus, GA

Henning, Rick .... (209) 943-6397
DIR-SYS INFO, Record, Stockton, CA

Henning, Rita-Helen .... (805) 736-2313
ED, Lompoc Record, Lompoc, CA

Henninger, Don .... (602) 271-8000
MAN ED, Arizona Republic, Phoenix, AZ

Henningsen, Brian .... (402) 345-1303
PROD MGR, Daily Record, Omaha, NE

Henningsen, Lynda K .... (402) 345-1303
VP, ADV MGR, Daily Record, Omaha, NE

Henningsen, Michael .... (505) 268-8111
MAN ED, Weekly Alibi, Albuquerque, NM

Henningsen, Ronald A .... (402) 345-1303
PRES, PUB, Daily Record, Omaha, NE

Henrichs, Todd .... (308) 382-1000
Sports ED
Grand Island Independent, Grand Island, NE

Henricksen, Rev Francis .... (319) 323-9959
ED, Catholic Messenger, Davenport, IA

Henrikson, Lynn .... (815) 246-6911
ED, Earlville Leader, Earlville, IL

Henritze, Cosette .... (719) 846-3311
PUB, ADV DIR, MAN ED
Chronicle-News, Trinidad, CO

Henry, Barbara A .... (515) 284-8000
PRES/PUB
Des Moines Register, Des Moines, IA

Henry, Clifton .... (903) 729-0281
PROD MGR
Palestine Herald-Press, Palestine, TX

Henry, Ed .... (219) 235-6161
VP-ADM
South Bend Tribune, South Bend, IN

Henry, Eric .... (916) 583-3487
ED, Tahoe World, Tahoe City, CA

Henry, Fay W .... (713) 532-2145
EX DIR, Royal Features, Houston, TX

Henry, Gene .... (912) 236-9511
CIRC MGR-Alternate Delivery
Savannah Morning News, Savannah, GA

Henry, Jerry .... (501) 338-9181
PROD FRM-PR, Daily World, Helena, AR

Henry, Joe .... (802) 863-3441
News ED
Burlington Free Press, Burlington, VT

Henry, John .... (501) 534-3400
MAN ED, ED, Copy ED, Health/Medical ED, NTL ED, News ED, Radio/Television ED, Pine Bluff Commercial, Pine Bluff, AR

Henry, John .... (713) 220-7171
Political ED
Houston Chronicle, Houston, TX

Henry, Judy .... (205) 221-2840
MGR-CR, Daily Mountain Eagle, Jasper, AL

Henry, Kate .... (704) 479-3383
ED, Graham Star, Robbinsville, NC

Copyright ©1997 by the Editor & Publisher Co.

Hen Who's Where-102

Henry, Levi (954) 523-5115
PUB, Westside Gazette, Fort Lauderdale, FL
Henry, Lisa (310) 540-5511
DIR-Human Resources
Daily Breeze, Torrance, CA
Henry, Mark (512) 352-8535
ADV DIR, Taylor Daily Press, Taylor, TX
Henry, Marylyn (212) 599-3666
New York Correspondent, Jerusalem Post Foreign Service, New York, NY
Henry, Nancy (412) 628-2000
ADV DIR, Daily Courier, Connellsville, PA
Henry, Pat (806) 385-4481
PUB
Lamb County Leader News, Littlefield, TX
Henry, Scott (415) 883-8600
Photo ED
Marin Independent Journal, Novato, CA
Henry, Stephen A (806) 894-3121
PUB, ED, Levelland & Hockley County News-Press, Levelland, TX
Henry, Steve (210) 828-3321
MAN ED
North Side Recorder-Times, San Antonio, TX
Henry, Tedda (207) 623-3811
Social ED, Kennebec Journal, Augusta, ME
Henry, Tom (520) 625-5511
GM
Green Valley News & Sun, Green Valley, AZ
Henry, Tom (203) 926-2080
ED, Huntington Herald, Monroe, CT
Henschel, Gene (414) 457-7711
Features ED, Music/Drama ED
Sheboygan Press, Sheboygan, WI
Henschen, Mark (619) 745-6611
CIRC DIR
North County Times, Escondido, CA
Henseler, Kevin (402) 388-4355
PUB, Crofton Journal, Crofton, NE
Henseler, Tweeter (402) 388-4355
PUB, ED, Crofton Journal, Crofton, NE
Henshaw, Dave (250) 762-4445
BUS ED, Daily Courier, Kelowna, BC
Henshaw, David (508) 597-5465
ED, Main Street Trilogy, Townsend, MA
Hensley, Don (937) 592-3060
Sports ED, Examiner, Bellefontaine, OH
Hensley, Doug (806) 762-8844
Sports ED
Lubbock Avalanche-Journal, Lubbock, TX
Hensley, Glenn (606) 528-2464
PROD FRM-PR, Times-Tribune, Corbin, KY
Hensley, James C (320) 796-2945
PUB, New London, New London, MN
Hensley, Laura F (803) 626-8555
VP-FIN/ADM, VP-ADM/FIN
Sun News, Myrtle Beach, SC
Hensley, Merline (505) 546-2611
ADV MGR-CLASS
Deming Headlight, Deming, NM
Hensley, Phil (423) 929-3111
CIRC DIR
Johnson City Press, Johnson City, TN
Hensley, Randy (970) 493-6397
BUS SYS MGR
Fort Collins Coloradoan, Fort Collins, CO
Hensley, Richard (218) 736-7511
MAN ED, BUS/FIN ED
Fergus Falls Daily Journal, Fergus Falls, MN
Hensly, Jeannie (409) 632-6631
ADV MGR, Lufkin Daily News, Lufkin, TX
Henson, Irma (717) 265-2151
News ED, Daily Review, Towanda, PA
Henson, JoAnn (915) 236-6677
CIRC DIR
Sweetwater Reporter, Sweetwater, TX
Henson, John (606) 573-4510
EX ED, EPE
Harlan Daily Enterprise, Harlan, KY
Henson, Pamela (510) 935-2525
ADV VP
Contra Costa Times, Walnut Creek, CA
Henson, Stacey (517) 629-3984
MAN ED, Albion Recorder, Albion, MI
Henson, Steve (719) 544-3520
City ED, Pueblo Chieftain, Pueblo, CO
Hentman, Andrew (202) 334-6000
PROD SUPT-Engraving (NW)
Washington Post, Washington, DC
Hentschel, F William (508) 699-6755
PUB, Free Press, North Attleborough, MA
Hentz, Mike (305) 294-6641
Photo ED, Key West Citizen, Key West, FL
Henwood, Carolyn (704) 484-1047
GM, Cleveland Observer, Shelby, NC
Hephner, Norm (970) 945-8515
PROD MGR
Glenwood Post, Glenwood Springs, CO
Hepler, Todd (806) 935-4111
MAN ED
Moore County News-Press, Dumas, TX
Hepner, Thomas C (603) 536-1311
PUB, Record-Enterprise, Plymouth, NH
Heppner, Gary (402) 371-1020
CIRC MGR, Norfolk Daily News, Norfolk, NE
Hepworth, Harry (201) 877-4141
PROD DIR, Star-Ledger, Newark, NJ
Herauf, Brian (705) 745-4641
ADV MGR, Examiner, Peterborough, ON
Hollinger Inc. (Sterling Newspapers)
Herb, Kimra Traynor (419) 898-5361
ED,Exponent, Oak Harbor, OH
Herb, Raymond (419) 898-5361
GM, Exponent, Oak Harbor, OH
Herbert, Andy (318) 783-3450
Sports ED, Crowley Post-Signal, Crowley, LA
Herbert, Susan (415) 826-1100
MAN ED, San Francisco Independent, San Francisco, CA
Herbig, Donna (309) 764-4344
PSL OFF, Dispatch, Moline, IL
Small Newspaper Group Inc.
Herbig, Terry (309) 764-4344
Photo DIR, Dispatch, Moline, IL
Small Newspaper Group Inc.
Herbst, Cristie L (716) 487-1111
ED, EPE, Post-Journal, Jamestown, NY
Herburger, Roy (916) 685-3945
PUB, Elk Grove Citizen, Elk Grove, CA
Herder, Janet (616) 345-3511
EX SEC, Kalamazoo Gazette, Kalamazoo, MI
Herdt, Timm (805) 650-2900
EPE, Ventura County Star, Ventura, CA
Herendeen, Steve (510) 734-8600
Sports ED
Tri-Valley Herald, Pleasanton, CA
Herguth, Bob (312) 321-3000
Features Reporter
Chicago Sun-Times, Chicago, IL
Herick, Frank (609) 448-3005
ED, Windsor-Hights Herald, Hightstown, NJ
Hering, Hasso (541) 926-2211
ED, EDL Page, Democrat-Herald, Albany, OR
Herman, Brian (412) 684-5200
Sports ED
Valley Independent, Monessen, PA
Herman, Edna Mae (704) 437-2161
Fashion ED, Food/Garden ED, Living/Lifestyle ED, Society/Women's ED, News Herald, Morganton, NC
Herman, Florence (504) 524-1618
MAN ED, Clarion Herald, New Orleans, LA
Herman, Gary (609) 691-5000
PROD DIR, Daily Journal, Vineland, NJ
Herman, Jim (715) 842-2101
MAN ED, Wausau Daily Herald, Wausau, WI
Herman, Laura (616) 651-5407
PROD MGR-Publications
Sturgis Journal, Sturgis, MI
Herman, Sandra R (520) 529-1500
ED, Arizona Jewish Post, Tucson, AZ
Herman III, William A (706) 724-0851
SEC/TREAS
Morris Communications Corp., Augusta, GA
Hermans, Erik R (718) 788-0900
ED, Norden, Brooklyn, NY
Hermanson, Linda (701) 442-5535
ED
Underwood News, Underwood-Washburn, ND
Hermes, Sharon (970) 247-3504
ADV MGR-Sales/Display
Durango Herald, Durango, CO
Hermosillo, Esther (520) 364-3424
Bookkeeper, Daily Dispatch, Douglas, AZ
Hernandez, Alfredo (601) 582-4321
MGR-Production SYS, PROD MGR-SYS
Hattiesburg American, Hattiesburg, MS
Hernandez, Brian (717) 253-3055
PROD SUPV
Wayne Independent, Honesdale, PA
Hernandez, Fred (408) 372-3311
Alta Vista Magazine ED, Arts/Books ED
Monterey County Herald, Monterey, CA
Hernandez, Jesus (213) 622-8332
MET ED, La Opinion, Los Angeles, CA
Hernandez, Jonathan (408) 842-6400
CIRC MGR, Dispatch, Gilroy, CA
USMedia Inc. (Central Valley Publishing)
Hernandez, Karen (937) 767-7373
PUB
Yellow Springs News, Yellow Springs, OH
Hernandez, Tony (915) 263-7331
PROD MGR
Big Spring Herald, Big Spring, TX
Herndon, Cecil (502) 886-4444
COL, Kentucky New Era, Hopkinsville, KY
Herndon, Joe (409) 423-2696
PUB, East Texas Banner, Kirbyville, TX
Herndon, Lucia (215) 854-2000
COL-Lifestyle
Philadelphia Inquirer, Philadelphia, PA
Herndon, Mike (502) 886-4444
MAN ED, EPE
Kentucky New Era, Hopkinsville, KY
Hernes, Tom (219) 356-6700
Automotive ED, BUS ED
Huntington Herald-Press, Huntington, IN
Herning, Walter (610) 323-3000
ED, Mercury's Tri-County Marketplace, Pottstown, PA
Hernley, H Ralph (412) 547-5722
PUB, Journal, Mount Pleasant, PA
Herod, Doug (905) 684-7251
ASST MAN ED
Standard, St. Catharines, ON
Heroff, Todd (507) 285-7600
CIRC MGR, Post-Bulletin, Rochester, MN
Heron, Phil (610) 622-8800
ASSOC ED, News ED, Photo ED
Delaware County Daily Times, Primos, PA
Heronemus, Mike (502) 821-6833
BUS/FIN ED, City ED
Messenger, Madisonville, KY
Herr, Alicia (804) 625-0700
PUB, Our Own Community Press, Norfolk, VA
Herr, Bruce (505) 983-3303
SEC, Santa Fe New Mexican, Santa Fe, NM
Herr, Frank (212) 875-8914
ED, Staats-Zeitung Und Herold
New York, NY
Herr, Jeff (614) 633-1131
ADV DIR, Times Leader, Martins Ferry, OH
Herre, Bob (605) 225-4100
PROD DIR, American News, Aberdeen, SD
Herrell, Rick (360) 377-3711
ADV MGR-Co-op, Sun, Bremerton, WA
Herren, Rebecca (702) 732-0556
ED, Jewish Reporter, Las Vegas, NV
Herrera, Dan (505) 823-7777
Arts ED, Films/Theater ED, Music ED
Albuquerque Journal, Albuquerque, NM
Herrera, Estela (213) 622-8332
MGR-CORP Affairs
La Opinion, Los Angeles, CA
Herrichs, Bill (608) 252-6200
CIRC MGR-Single Copy
Madison Newspapers Inc., Madison, WI
Herrick, Dennis F (319) 895-6216
PUB, ED, Sun, Mount Vernon, IA
Herrick, Mark (201) 877-4141
ADV DIR, Star-Ledger, Newark, NJ
Herrin, Jeff (919) 446-5161
MAN ED, Action Line ED/Open Line, EPE
Rocky Mount Telegram, Rocky Mount, NC
Herrin, Jennie (417) 847-4475
ED, Barry County Advertiser, Cassville, MO
Herring, Don (502) 247-5223
PROD SUPT
Mayfield Messenger, Mayfield, KY
Herring, Joretta (405) 549-6045
ED, Fletcher Herald, Fletcher, OK
Herring, Kent (405) 549-6045
PUB, Fletcher Herald, Fletcher, OK
Herring, Margaret Ann (573) 898-2318
ED, Elsberry Democrat, Elsberry, MO
Herring, Robert A (918) 789-2331
PUB, ED, Chelsea Reporter, Chelsea, OK
Herring, Steve (919) 658-9456
ED, Mount Olive Tribune, Mount Olive, NC
Herring, Walter L (610) 323-3000
ED, Mercury, Pottstown, PA
Herrink, Ruth (540) 775-2024
PUB, ED, Journal, King George, VA
Herrmann, Andrew (312) 321-3000
Religion, Chicago Sun-Times, Chicago, IL
Herrmann, Jerry (520) 635-4426
ED, Williams-Grand Canyon News Inc., Williams, AZ
Herrmann, Virginia (315) 337-4000
Living/Lifestyle ED, Women's ED
Daily Sentinel, Rome, NY
Herron, Howard (317) 736-7101
PUB, Daily Journal, Franklin, IN
Herron, Larry (614) 474-3131
PROD MGR, Herald, Circleville, OH
Herron, Mike (757) 446-2000
ADV MGR-Sales Development/Training
Virginian-Pilot, Norfolk, VA
Herron, Ron (502) 227-4556
City ED, Radio/Television ED
State Journal, Frankfort, KY
Hersam, Marty (203) 966-9541
GM, New Canaan Advertiser, New Canaan, CT
Hersam Jr, V Donald (203) 966-9541
PUB
New Canaan Advertiser, New Canaan, CT
Herschberg, Dan (908) 362-6161
MAN ED, Blairstown Press, Blairstown, NJ
Herschell, Don (412) 222-2200
Farm/Agriculture ED, Religion ED
Observer-Reporter, Washington, PA
Hersh, James P (717) 291-8811
Sports ED, Lancaster Intelligencer Journal/New Era/Sunday News, Lancaster, PA
Hershberger, Margaret (318) 894-6397
GM, Ringgold Progress, Ringgold, LA
Hershey, Susan (617) 631-7700
ED, Swampscott Reporter, Marblehead, MA
Hersom, Terry (712) 279-5019
Sports ED, Sioux City Journal, Sioux City, IA
Herts, Kenneth (212) 416-2000
Senior VP-Dow Jones Telerate
Wall Street Journal, New York, NY
Hertter, William R (309) 829-9411
CIRC DIR, Pantagraph, Bloomington, IL
Hertz, David (818) 249-8090
MAN ED, Foothill Leader, Glendale, CA
Hertz, David (330) 996-3000
Deputy MET ED
Akron Beacon Journal, Akron, OH
Hertz, Kelly (605) 665-7811
ED, Daily Press & Dakotan, Yankton, SD
Hertz, Mike (306) 773-3116
PUB, Swift Current Sun, Swift Current, SK
Hertzberg, Mark (414) 634-3322
Photo DIR, Journal Times, Racine, WI
Hertzler, Gerry (219) 533-2151
ED, Goshen News, Goshen, IN
Herum, Jandell L W (330) 996-3000
ADV MGR-Display
Akron Beacon Journal, Akron, OH
Heryet, John (250) 380-5211
PROD FRM-Stereo
Times Colonist, Victoria, BC
Herzberg-Bender, Barbara (701) 223-2500
Librarian, Bismarck Tribune, Bismarck, ND
Herzfeld, Jim (414) 224-2000
INFO SRV/BUS SYS
Milwaukee Journal Sentinel, Milwaukee, WI
Herzig, Bill (419) 245-6000
CIRC MGR-RTZ, Blade, Toledo, OH
Herzig, Gary (607) 535-2711
PUB
Watkins Review & Express, Watkins Glen, NY
Herzog, Bob (516) 843-2020
ASST Sports ED, Newsday, Melville, NY
Herzog, Dennis (970) 242-5050
MAN ED, Daily Sentinel, Grand Junction, CO
Herzog, Garry (908) 879-4100
ED, Observer Tribune, Chester, NJ
Herzog, Karen (701) 223-2500
Religion Reporter
Bismarck Tribune, Bismarck, ND
Herzog, Susan (312) 321-3000
ADV DIR-Network Advertising
Chicago Sun-Times, Chicago, IL
Heskett, Walt (815) 459-4040
CIRC DIR, Northwest Herald, Crystal Lake, IL
Heslin, Tom (401) 277-7000
MAN ED-MET
Providence Journal-Bulletin, Providence, RI
Hespenhide, Melissa T (757) 247-4600
MGR-Public Relations
Daily Press, Newport News, VA
Hess, Dana (605) 224-7301
ED, Capital Journal, Pierre, SD
Hess, Diane (713) 686-8494
ED, Leader, Houston, TX
Hess, James D (717) 291-8811
MGR-CR, Lancaster Intelligencer Journal/New Era/Sunday News, Lancaster, PA
Hess, Paul (517) 772-2971
DIR-Sales/MKTG
Morning Sun, Mount Pleasant, MI
Hess, Robbie (716) 798-1400
Society ED, Journal-Register, Medina, NY
Hess, Roy (210) 686-4343
Sports ED, Monitor, McAllen, TX
Hess, Skip (317) 633-1240
Outdoors Life Writer
Indianapolis Star/News, Indianapolis, IN
Hess, Steven H (303) 776-2244
PROD MGR-Pre Press
Daily Times-Call, Longmont, CO
Hess, Susan (316) 342-4800
City ED, Emporia Gazette, Emporia, KS
Hess, Tim (352) 563-6363
MGR-OPER
Citrus County Chronicle, Crystal River, FL
Hess, Val (503) 648-1131
ED, Hillsboro Argus, Hillsboro, OR
Hesse, Robert (419) 422-5151
ED, Courier, Findlay, OH
Hesse, Steve (303) 820-1010
VP-Circulation, Denver Post, Denver, CO
Hessler, Mark (320) 255-8700
PROD MGR-Building SRV
St. Cloud Times, St. Cloud, MN
Hessling, Michelle (717) 253-3055
ADV MGR-Sales
Wayne Independent, Honesdale, PA
Hesson, Gary (915) 337-4661
PROD FRM-MR, Odessa American
Odessa, TX
Hester, Ashton (864) 638-5856
ED, Keowee Courier, Walhalla, SC
Hester, Craig (970) 493-6397
CIRC MGR-Sales
Fort Collins Coloradoan, Fort Collins, CO
Hester, David (817) 757-5757
CONT, Waco Tribune-Herald, Waco, TX
Hester, Robert (817) 634-2125
Sports ED, Killeen Daily Herald, Killeen, TX
Hester, Wayne (205) 325-2222
MET ED, Birmingham News, Birmingham, AL
Heth, Philip T (717) 282-3300
PUB, Carbondale News, Carbondale, PA
Hethcock, Bill (210) 423-5511
City ED, Valley Morning Star, Harlingen, TX

Copyright ©1997 by the Editor & Publisher Co.

103-Who's Where **Hil**

Hetherington, Bob .... (901) 529-2211
BUS/FIN ED
Commercial Appeal, Memphis, TN

Hetrick, Jean .... (814) 643-4040
BM, Daily News, Huntingdon, PA

Hettig, Rose .... (612) 523-2032
PUB, Olivia Times-Journal, Olivia, MN

Hetzel, Dennis R .... (717) 771-2000
PUB, York Daily Record, York, PA

Hetzler, John .... (203) 789-5200
ADV DIR-MKTG
New Haven Register, New Haven, CT

Heun, Dave .... (630) 232-9222
ED, Kane County Chronicle, Geneva, IL

Heupel, Dana .... (217) 788-1300
City ED
State Journal-Register, Springfield, IL

Heurdejs, Judy .... (312) 222-3232
COL, Chicago Tribune, Chicago, IL

Heuring, Andy .... (812) 354-8500
ED, Press-Dispatch, Petersburg, IN

Heuring, Frank .... (812) 354-8500
PUB, Press-Dispatch, Petersburg, IN

Heuring, Rachael .... (812) 354-8500
PUB, Press-Dispatch, Petersburg, IN

Heusel, Darren .... (405) 382-1100
Sports ED, Seminole Producer, Seminole, OK

Heuser, Billie .... (919) 638-8101
CIRC MGR, Sun-Journal, New Bern, NC

Hevenor, Steve .... (705) 472-3200
PROD FRM-PR, Nugget, North Bay, ON

Hewey, Elizabeth .... (904) 435-8500
DIR-Market Development
Pensacola News Journal, Pensacola, FL

Hewit, Greg .... (613) 448-2321
ED, Chesterville Record, Chesterville, ON

Hewitt, Brian .... (312) 321-3000
Notre Dame Sports/Golf
Chicago Sun-Times, Chicago, IL

Hewitt, C G Jim .... (416) 445-6641
VP, Southam Inc., Don Mills, ON

Hewitt, Edward D .... (410) 332-6000
Administrative ED, Sun, Baltimore, MD

Hewitt, Frank .... (508) 368-0176
PUB, Item, Clinton, MA

Hewitt, Howard .... (317) 659-4622
MAN ED, Times, Frankfort, IN

Hewitt, Marylynn .... (810) 332-8181
Entertainment ED
Oakland Press, Pontiac, MI

Hewitt, R Cress .... (816) 296-3412
PUB, Lawson Review, Lawson, MO

Hewitt, Roy .... (216) 999-4500
Sports ED, Plain Dealer, Cleveland, OH

Hewitt, W Rogers .... (573) 633-2261
PUB, ED
Shelby County Herald, Shelbyville, MO

Heyer, Marigrace .... (610) 377-2051
Action Line ED, Fashion/Style ED, Lifestyle ED, Society ED, Women's ED
Times News, Lehighton, PA

Heyers, Joan A .... (815) 433-2000
ASST GM, ADV DIR
Daily Times, Ottawa, IL
Small Newspaper Group Inc.

Heyl, Jack .... (419) 245-6000
ADV MGR-CLASS, Blade, Toledo, OH

Heymann, Paul .... (954) 356-4000
CIRC MGR-Alternate Products
Sun-Sentinel, Fort Lauderdale, FL

Heymen, Anne .... (904) 829-6562
Fashion/Style ED, Lifestyle ED, Religion ED, Society ED, Women's ED, St. Augustine Record, St. Augustine, FL

Heynes, Jim .... (814) 870-1600
Amusements ED
Morning News/Erie Daily Times, Erie, PA

Heyrend, M F .... (801) 355-3336
Legal Affairs ED
FNA News, Salt Lake City, UT

Heyward, Evelyn .... (212) 421-1370
BU Chief
Entertainment News Calendar, New York, NY

Heywood, D Michael .... (360) 694-3391
EPE, Columbian, Vancouver, WA

Heywood, Lucille F .... (603) 424-7610
ED, Village Crier, Merrimack, NH

Heywood, Seth .... (603) 424-7610
PUB, Village Crier, Merrimack, NH

Hiaasen, Carl .... (305) 350-2111
COL, Miami Herald, Miami, FL

Hiatt, Larry .... (913) 738-3537
PUB, ED, Beloit Daily Call, Beloit, KS

Hiatt, Sharon .... (913) 738-3537
ADV MGR, Beloit Daily Call, Beloit, KS

Hibbard, Ray .... (405) 341-2121
GM, Edmond Evening Sun, Edmond, OK

Hibbert, Barry .... (403) 887-2331
PUB, Sylvan Lake News, Sylvan Lake, AB

Hibbert, Charles .... (508) 775-1200
Copy Desk Chief
Cape Cod Times, Hyannis, MA

Hibbs, Therese .... (519) 679-6666
ADTX MGR, London Free Press, London, ON

Hibner, Lynn .... (517) 354-3111
EDU ED, Alpena News, Alpena, MI

Hick, Glendo .... (505) 523-4581
CONT
Las Cruces Sun-News, Las Cruces, NM

Hickam, Flo .... (816) 882-5335
PROD SUPT
Boonville Daily News, Boonville, MO

Hicken, Robb .... (707) 468-3500
ED, Ukiah Daily Journal, Ukiah, CA

Hickenlooper, Elizabeth .... (904) 312-5200
Copy ED, Daily News, Palatka, FL

Hickerson, Dawn .... (501) 623-7711
News ED/Wire ED
Sentinel-Record, Hot Springs, AR

Hickey, Bill .... (519) 255-5711
MET ED, Windsor Star, Windsor, ON

Hickey, Brian .... (803) 317-6397
BUS/FIN ED
Florence Morning News, Florence, SC

Hickey, Charles .... (315) 470-0011
ASST MAN ED-Shared DEPT, Post-Standard/Herald-Journal/American, Syracuse, NY

Hickey, Dave .... (320) 769-2497
PUB, ED, Dawson Sentinel, Dawson, MN

Hickey, Cardinal James A .... (301) 853-4599
PUB, Catholic Standard, Hyattsville, MD

Hickey, Madelyn .... (352) 746-4292
ED, Beverly Hills Visitor, Beverly Hills, FL

Hickey, Rex .... (423) 426-2220
ED, Town Crier, Lake City, TN

Hickey, Tom .... (815) 987-1200
PROD MGR-Distribution Center
Rockford Register Star, Rockford, IL

Hickling, Gary .... (403) 778-3977
ED, Whitecourt Star, Whitecourt, AB

Hickman, Albert .... (217) 465-6424
PROD FRM-COMP
Paris Daily Beacon-News, Paris, IL

Hickman, Bob .... (941) 748-0411
PROD MGR
Bradenton Herald, Bradenton, FL

Hickman, Gerald .... (412) 222-2200
CIRC MGR-Distribution, PROD SUPV-MR
Observer-Reporter, Washington, PA

Hickman, Sally .... (303) 776-2244
CIRC MGR-District
Daily Times-Call, Longmont, CO

Hicks, Alisa .... (619) 365-3315
MAN ED, Hi-Desert Star, Yucca Valley, CA

Hicks, Anissa .... (423) 745-5664
Lifestyle ED
Daily Post-Athenian, Athens, TN

Hicks, Bill .... (540) 669-2181
CIRC MGR, Herald-Courier Virginia Tennessean, Bristol, VA

Hicks, Brad .... (515) 456-2585
ED, Hampton Times, Hampton, IA

Hicks, Brian .... (310) 540-5511
ADV CNR-Co-op, Daily Breeze, Torrance, CA

Hicks, Carrie .... (816) 932-6600
Sales Administrator
Universal Press Syndicate, Kansas City, MO

Hicks, Chris .... (801) 237-2188
Entertainment ED, Films/Theater ED
Deseret News, Salt Lake City, UT

Hicks, D Paul .... (616) 429-2400
ADV MGR-CLASS
Herald-Palladium, St. Joseph, MI

Hicks, Dane .... (913) 448-3121
PUB, ED, Garnett Review, Garnett, KS

Hicks, Darryl K .... (561) 562-2315
PRES/GM
Vero Beach Press-Journal, Vero Beach, FL

Hicks, Doris .... (502) 298-7100
GM, Ohio County Times-News, Hartford, KY

Hicks, Earl .... (703) 878-8000
ED, Quantico Sentry, Woodbridge, VA

Hicks, Edward .... (757) 247-4600
ADV MGR-GEN
Daily Press, Newport News, VA

Hicks, Garold Dane .... (913) 448-3121
PUB, ED, Anderson Countian, Garnett, KS

Hicks, Gary K .... (405) 657-6492
PUB, Lone Grove Ledger, Lone Grove, OK

Hicks, Glenda .... (770) 834-6631
ADV DIR, Times-Georgian, Carrollton, GA

Hicks, Jeff .... (317) 962-1575
PROD MGR-PR
Palladium-Item, Richmond, IN

Hicks, Jim .... (307) 684-2223
PUB, ED, Buffalo Bulletin, Buffalo, WY

Hicks, L Marie .... (210) 249-9524
PUB, Hill Country Recorder, Boerne, TX

Hicks, Linda .... (501) 621-6397
MAN ED, Hometown News, Rogers, AR

Hicks, Linda .... (405) 657-6492
ED, Lone Grove Ledger, Lone Grove, OK

Hicks, Marie .... (210) 695-3613
PUB, Echo, Helotes, TX

Hicks, Nancy .... (402) 475-4200
EPE, Lincoln Journal Star, Lincoln, NE

Hicks, Paul .... (616) 429-2400
ADTX MGR
Herald-Palladium, St. Joseph, MI

Hicks, Phil .... (903) 597-8111
Sports ED
Tyler Morning Telegraph, Tyler, TX

Hicks, R Lee .... (509) 997-7011
PUB
Methow Valley News, Methow Valley, WA

Hicks, Robert .... (307) 746-2777
PUB, ED
News Letter Journal, Newcastle, WY

Hicks, Ron .... (217) 446-1000
ADV MGR-Ad SRV
Commercial News, Danville, IL

Hidlay, William C .... (609) 663-6000
MAN ED, Courier-Post, Cherry Hill, NJ

Hieggelke, Brian J .... (312) 243-8786
PUB, ED, New City, Chicago, IL

Hieggelke, Jan .... (312) 243-8786
PUB, GM, New City, Chicago, IL

Hiett, Joe .... (770) 957-9161
PUB, ED, Henry Herald, McDonough, GA

Higden, Ken .... (419) 245-6000
CIRC MGR-MKTG, Blade, Toledo, OH

Higdon, Bill .... (517) 787-2300
PROD MGR
Jackson Citizen Patriot, Jackson, MI

Higdon, Robert B .... (412) 263-1100
VP, GM
Pittsburgh Post-Gazette, Pittsburgh, PA

Higgin, Byron .... (715) 463-2341
PUB, ED
Burnett County Sentinel, Grantsburg, WI

Higgins, Christopher .... (405) 363-3370
MAN ED
Blackwell Journal-Tribune, Blackwell, OK

Higgins, Edward .... (314) 340-8000
EPE, St. Louis Post-Dispatch, St. Louis, MO

Higgins, Harold .... (303) 442-1202
PRES/PUB, Daily Camera, Boulder, CO

Higgins, Jack .... (312) 321-3000
EDL Cartoonist
Chicago Sun-Times, Chicago, IL

Higgins, Jim .... (313) 222-2300
Deputy BUS ED, Detroit News, Detroit, MI

Higgins, Jody .... (704) 682-2120
PUB, ED
Burnsville Times Journal, Burnsville, NC

Higgins, Pamm .... (213) 237-5000
Design ED
Los Angeles Times, Los Angeles, CA

Higgins, Ronald .... (201) 839-7200
PUB, Independent News, Pompton Lakes, NJ

Higgins, Shaun O'L .... (212) 626-6801
CEO
Print Marketing Concepts Inc., New York, NY

Higgins, Stephanie .... (207) 454-3561
GM, Calais Advertiser, Calais, ME

Higgins, William .... (508) 775-1200
Sports ED, Cape Cod Times, Hyannis, MA

Higginson, Cheryl .... (616) 845-5181
Amusements ED, Lifestyle ED
Daily News, Ludington, MI

Higginson, Chris .... (503) 843-2312
GM, Sun, Sheridan, OR

Higginson, William J .... (609) 396-2200
VP-PROD, Journal Register Co., Trenton, NJ

Higgs, Chuck .... (209) 943-6397
ADV MGR-RT, Record, Stockton, CA

Higgs, Janet .... (613) 342-4441
SEC, Brockville Recorder and Times, Brockville, ON

Higgs, Virginia .... (209) 369-2761
ADV MGR-CLASS
Lodi News-Sentinel, Lodi, CA

High, Georgia .... (316) 331-3550
VP, MAN ED, Amusements ED, Films/Theater ED, News ED, Religion ED, Independence Daily Reporter, Independence, KS

High, James C .... (910) 642-4104
PUB, ED, News Reporter, Whiteville, NC

High, Kristina .... (330) 725-4166
ADV DIR-Sales
Medina County Gazette, Medina, OH

High, Pam .... (972) 932-2171
ED, Kaufman Herald, Kaufman, TX

High, Richard .... (619) 745-6611
PRES South Coast Newspapers, PUB-Escondido, North County Times, Escondido, CA

Highfield, Thomas G .... (561) 820-3800
CIRC DIR
Palm Beach Daily News, Palm Beach, FL

Highland Jr, Cecil B .... (304) 624-6411
PRES/TREAS, PUB/GM, Clarksburg Exponent/Telegram, Clarksburg, WV

Hight, Joe .... (405) 475-3311
ASST MAN ED
Daily Oklahoman, Oklahoma City, OK

Hight, R V .... (919) 708-9000
City ED, EDL Writer, News ED
Sanford Herald, Sanford, NC

Hight, Theresa .... (317) 473-6641
PROD MGR-Pre Press
Peru Tribune, Peru, IN

Hightower, Geraldine H .... (318) 927-3541
PUB, Homer Guardian-Journal, Homer, LA

Hightower, Sam .... (512) 445-3500
DIR-OPER, PROD DIR-OPER
Austin American-Statesman, Austin, TX

Higi, Most Rev William L .... (317) 742-2050
PUB, Catholic Moment, Lafayette, IN

Higley, Morris .... (817) 937-2525
PUB, Childress Index, Childress, TX

Higley, Susan .... (913) 486-2512
GM, ED, Horton Headlight, Horton, KS

Higley, Tom .... (405) 928-3372
PUB, ED, Sayre Journal, Sayre, OK

Hignite, Edsel .... (614) 532-1441
CIRC ASST MGR
Ironton Tribune, Ironton, OH

Hilbert, Marianne .... (716) 232-7100
MGR-MKTG INFO
Rochester Democrat and Chronicle; Rochester, NY Times-Union, Rochester, NY

Hilbig, Beth .... (210) 225-7411
News ED
San Antonio Express-News, San Antonio, TX

Hilbun, Paul .... (318) 365-6773
Health/Medical ED
Daily Iberian, New Iberia, LA

Hilburn, Robert .... (213) 237-5000
Music Critic-Pop/Rock
Los Angeles Times, Los Angeles, CA

Hilburn, Van .... (903) 785-8744
Sports ED, Paris News, Paris, TX

Hildebrand, Bill .... (909) 889-9666
CIRC MGR-Division
Sun, San Bernardino, CA
ED, Record-Courier, Gardnerville, NV

Hildebrand, Kurt .... (702) 882-2111
News ED, Nevada Appeal, Carson City, NV

Hildebrand, Scott .... (414) 435-4411
Madison BU Chief
Green Bay Press-Gazette, Green Bay, WI

Hilderbrand, Ann .... (406) 232-0450
DP MGR, Miles City Star, Miles City, MT

Hilderbrand, Larry .... (503) 221-8327
EDL Writer, Oregonian, Portland, OR

Hildner, Jack .... (719) 544-3520
News ED, Pueblo Chieftain, Pueblo, CO

Hildner, Judy .... (719) 544-3520
Sports ED, Pueblo Chieftain, Pueblo, CO

Hildreth, Kara .... (515) 573-2141
Religion ED, Messenger, Fort Dodge, IA

Hile, Sally .... (816) 932-6600
Sales Administrator
Universal Press Syndicate, Kansas City, MO

Hileman, Maria .... (860) 442-2200
ASST MAN ED-Projects
Day, New London, CT

Hileman, Molly .... (561) 287-1550
MGR-Home Delivery
Stuart News, Stuart, FL

Hilfrink, Michael B .... (217) 223-5100
MAN ED, Sunday ED
Quincy Herald-Whig, Quincy, IL

Hill, Andy .... (906) 932-2211
MAN ED, Ironwood Daily Globe, Ironwood, MI

Hill, Barbara .... (573) 624-4545
PUB, Daily Statesman, Dexter, MO

Hill, Bruce .... (601) 834-1151
PUB, ED
Holmes County Herald, Lexington, MS

Hill, Charles .... (609) 691-5000
PROD MGR-MR, Daily Journal, Vineland, NJ

Hill, Charles .... (203) 789-5200
PROD MGR-Engineering SRV
New Haven Register, New Haven, CT

Hill, Charlie .... (757) 446-2000
VP-Human Resources
Virginian-Pilot, Norfolk, VA

Hill, D J .... (817) 390-7400
Neighborhood ED
Fort Worth Star-Telegram, Fort Worth, TX

Hill, Dan .... (515) 472-4129
Sports ED
Fairfield Ledger, Fairfield, IA

Hill, Dave .... (209) 578-2000
Weekend ED, Modesto Bee, Modesto, CA

Hill, David .... (607) 272-2321
BUS/FIN ED, Ithaca Journal, Ithaca, NY

Hill, Dawn .... (306) 825-5522
PUB/GM
Lloydminster Times, Lloydminster, SK

Hill, Debra .... (401) 277-7000
DIR-SYS, DP MGR
Providence Journal-Bulletin, Providence, RI

Hill, Draper .... (313) 222-2300
Cartoonist, Detroit News, Detroit, MI

Hill, Grace .... (202) 334-6375
Sales MGR/North America, Washington Post Writers Group, Washington, DC

Hill, Harvey .... (215) 854-2000
ADV DIR-NTL
Philadelphia Inquirer, Philadelphia, PA

Hill, Harvey D .... (603) 543-3100
PRES, PUB, Eagle Times, Claremont, NH

Hill, Heather .... (715) 239-6688
ED
Cornell & Lake Holcombe Courier, Cornell, WI

Hil Who's Where-104

Hill, James E (615) 864-3675
PUB, ED
Pickett County Press, Byrdstown, TN

Hill, Jeff (219) 866-5111
ED, Courier, Morocco, IN

Hill, Jerry (941) 748-0411
Outdoors ED
Bradenton Herald, Bradenton, FL

Hill, Jerry K (702) 788-6200
CIRC DIR, Reno Gazette-Journal, Reno, NV

Hill, Jimmie D (904) 623-2120
PUB, Santa Rosa Press Gazette, Milton, FL

Hill, Joan (517) 589-8228
GM, Leslie Local Independent, Leslie, MI

Hill, John (505) 823-7777
Environmental ED
Albuquerque Tribune, Albuquerque, NM

Hill, John (206) 339-3000
ADV MGR-RT, Herald, Everett, WA

Hill, Judy (717) 784-2121
Fashion/Style ED, Living ED
Press Enterprise, Bloomsburg, PA

Hill, Judy (813) 259-7711
COL, Tampa Tribune and Times, Tampa, FL

Hill, Justice (219) 461-8333
Sports ED, Journal Gazette, Fort Wayne, IN

Hill, Kristi (405) 772-3301
EDU/Lifestyle ED, Women's ED
Weatherford Daily News, Weatherford, OK

Hill, Libby (601) 834-1151
GM, Holmes County Herald, Lexington, MS

Hill, Marlene (601) 693-1551
DP MGR, Meridian Star, Meridian, MS

Hill, Matthew (619) 375-4481
ADV DIR
Daily Independent, Ridgecrest, CA

Hill, Melissa (903) 786-4051
ED, Pottsboro Press, Pottsboro, TX

Hill, Michael (330) 629-6200
ED, Canfield Town Crier, Youngstown, OH

Hill, Michelle (216) 999-4500
CIRC MGR-NIE
Plain Dealer, Cleveland, OH

Hill, Michelle (704) 739-7496
ED, Cleveland Times, Kings Mountain, NC

Hill, Pamela (501) 442-1777
Justice ED
Northwest Arkansas Times, Fayetteville, AR

Hill, Randy (403) 250-4200
Graphics ED, Calgary Sun, Calgary, AB

Hill, Rita (209) 239-3531
ADV MGR-RT
Manteca Bulletin, Manteca, CA

Hill, Robert (507) 285-7600
GM, Post-Bulletin, Rochester, MN

Hill, Rosa (541) 753-2641
MGR-CR
Corvallis Gazette-Times, Corvallis, OR

Hill, Roxie (405) 335-2188
ADV MGR-Local/NTL
Frederick Leader, Frederick, OK

Hill, Sandy (903) 962-4275
PUB, Grand Saline Sun, Grand Saline, TX

Hill, Scott (901) 529-2211
BU ED, Commercial Appeal, Memphis, TN

Hill, Shandra (770) 306-2175
ED, Atlanta-News Leader, Union City, GA

Hill, Steve (509) 765-4561
PUB, ADV DIR
Columbia Basin Herald, Moses Lake, WA

Hill, Steve (515) 753-6611
Television/Film ED
Times-Republican, Marshalltown, IA

Hill, Todd (718) 981-1234
BUS/FIN ED
Staten Island Advance, Staten Island, NY

Hill, Vernon (413) 788-1000
News ED, Union-News, Springfield, MA

Hill, Veronica (619) 241-7744
Entertainment/Amusements ED, Magazine ED, Television/Film ED, Theater/Music ED
Daily Press, Victorville, CA

Hill, W Les (619) 375-4481
PUB, Daily Independent, Ridgecrest, CA

Hill, Wade (941) 494-7600
ED, DeSoto Sun-Herald, Arcadia, FL

Hill, William (617) 450-2000
GM, Christian Science Monitor, Boston, MA

Hillan, Pete (408) 920-5000
EXEC BUS ED
San Jose Mercury News, San Jose, CA

Hillard, Carolyn (502) 754-3000
ED, Leader-News, Central City, KY

Hillard, Juli Cragg (941) 953-7755
Religion ED
Sarasota Herald-Tribune, Sarasota, FL

Hillberg, Dorris (508) 369-2800
ED, Beacon, Concord, MA

Hillemann, Gary (805) 650-2900
PROD FRM-PR
Ventura County Star, Ventura, CA

Hiller, David D (312) 222-3237
Sr VP-Development
Tribune Co., Chicago, IL

Hiller, Jonathan (415) 777-5700
DIR-MIS, San Francisco Newspaper Agency, San Francisco, CA

Hiller, Larry (913) 462-3963
PROD MGR, Colby Free Press, Colby, KS

Hilles, Jim (614) 773-2111
ADV MGR-Major Accounts
Chillicothe Gazette, Chillicothe, OH

Hillesheim, Milly (505) 356-4481
ADV DIR
Portales News-Tribune, Portales, NM

Hilliard, Ardith (213) 237-5000
San Fernando Valley MAN ED
Los Angeles Times, Los Angeles, CA

Hilliard, David R (717) 286-5671
News CNR, Daily Item, Sunbury, PA

Hilliard, James L (770) 479-1441
PUB, Cherokee Tribune, Canton, GA

Hillibish, James (330) 454-5611
New Media ED, ADTX MGR
Repository, Canton, OH

Hillig, Terry (618) 463-2500
EDL Writer, Telegraph, Alton, IL

Hillkirk, John (703) 276-3400
MAN ED-Money, USA Today, Arlington, VA

Hillman, Bernice (810) 346-2753
ED, Brown City Banner, Brown City, MI

Hillman, Debra (609) 272-7000
ADV MGR-Major/NTL
Press of Atlantic City, Pleasantville, NJ

Hillman, Douglas W (413) 772-0261
DIR-OPER, DP MGR
Recorder, Greenfield, MA

Hillman, Jacque (901) 427-3333
Books ED, Jackson Sun, Jackson, TN

Hillman, Tim (812) 438-2011
GM, ED, Rising Sun Recorder, Rising Sun, IN

Hillmer-Pierson, Kris (515) 573-2141
Fashion/Style ED, Lifestyle ED
Messenger, Fort Dodge, IA

Hillock, Darren (414) 656-1101
ED, Bulletin, Kenosha, WI

Hills, Jim (206) 775-7521
ED, Enterprise, Lynnwood, WA

Hills, Lee (313) 222-6400
PUB-Emeritus
Detroit Free Press, Detroit, MI

Hills, Stephen (202) 334-6000
VP-Advertising
Washington Post, Washington, DC

Hillsmith, Susan (803) 577-7111
EDU ED, Post and Courier, Charleston, SC

Hillwig, Chris (412) 543-1303
BM, Leader Times, Kittanning, PA

Hillyer, Delia (815) 673-3771
Women's ED, Times-Press, Streator, IL

Hilmer, Tammy (918) 684-2828
MGR-Technical SRV, Muskogee Daily Phoenix & Times Democrat, Muskogee, OK

Hilpert, Gayle (806) 376-4488
ADV MGR-CLASS, ADTX MGR, Amarillo Daily News/Globe Times, Amarillo, TX

Hilsen, Larry (412) 664-9161
CIRC DIR, PROD FRM-MR
Daily News, McKeesport, PA

Hilser, Bill (520) 573-4220
PROD MGR-OPER
Arizona Daily Star, Tucson, AZ

Hilstrom, Lea (204) 467-2421
MAN ED, Stonewall Argus/Teulon Times, Stonewall, MB

Hiltner, Mary (215) 855-8440
PROD ASST DIR, Reporter, Landsdale, PA

Hilton, Bob (316) 268-6000
CIRC MGR-Home Delivery
Wichita Eagle, Wichita, KS

Hilton, Calvin (713) 220-7171
PROD MGR-Night
Houston Chronicle, Houston, TX

Hilton, Ken (540) 885-7281
PROD MGR, PROD MGR-OPER
Daily News Leader, Staunton, VA

Hilton, Lynn (318) 281-4421
ADV DIR
Bastrop Daily Enterprise, Bastrop, LA

Hilton, Spud (707) 448-6401
Automotive ED, Reporter, Vacaville, CA

Hilts, Rod (519) 354-2000
City ED, News ED
Chatham Daily News, Chatham, ON

Hilty, Wyn (714) 708-8400
MAN ED, OC Weekly, Costa Mesa, CA

Hiltzik, Michael (213) 237-5000
Enterprise
Los Angeles Times, Los Angeles, CA

Hilwig, Brenda (716) 439-9222
PROD FRM-COMP
Union-Sun & Journal, Lockport, NY

Himebaugh, Eleanor (812) 275-3355
Fashion ED, Features ED, Lifestyle ED, Travel ED, Women's ED, Times-Mail, Bedford, IN

Himes, Dale (405) 372-5000
EPE, News Press, Stillwater, OK

Himes, Merle (217) 774-2161
ADV MGR, Daily Union, Shelbyville, IL

Hinch Jr, Richard (508) 626-3800
CIRC DIR, Middlesex News, Framingham, MA

Hinchey, Frank (614) 461-5000
State ED, Columbus Dispatch, Columbus, OH

Hinchey, Timothy (860) 442-2200
MGR-Credit, Day, New London, CT

Hinckley, David (212) 210-2100
Critic-At-Large
New York Daily News, New York, NY

Hinckley, Katy (307) 634-3361
MGR-PROM
Wyoming Tribune-Eagle, Cheyenne, WY

Hinderaker, Amy (605) 627-9471
ED, Volga Tribune, Volga, SD

Hinds, Peter J (517) 725-5136
DIR-MKTG/PROM, Argus-Press, Owosso, MI

Hinds, Robert (210) 565-2425
PUB, ED, Mercedes Enterprise, Mercedes, TX

Hine, Richard (415) 854-2626
ED, Country Almanac, Menlo Park, CA

Hine, Tom (215) 854-2000
Architectural Writer
Philadelphia Inquirer, Philadelphia, PA

Hineline, Theresa (619) 745-6611
City ED-Encinitas
North County Times, Escondido, CA

Hiner, John P (517) 895-8551
EDU ED, MET ED
Bay City Times, Bay City, MI

Hines, Cheryl (765) 354-2221
ED, Middletown News, Middletown, IN

Hines, Ernie (510) 734-8600
ED, Tri-Valley Herald, Pleasanton, CA

Hines, Gerald L (704) 322-4510
PROD FRM-PR
Hickory Daily Record, Hickory, NC

Hines, Greg (405) 353-0620
PROD FRM-MR, Constitution, Lawton, OK

Hines, Jennifer (801) 752-2121
City ED, Herald Journal, Logan, UT

Hines, Patricia (203) 255-4561
ED, Fairfield Citizen-News, Fairfield, CT

Hines, Patti (408) 920-5000
CIRC Office MGR
San Jose Mercury News, San Jose, CA

Hines, Paul W (540) 980-5220
PROD SUPT, Southwest Times, Pulaski, VA

Hines, Randy (704) 322-4510
PROD MGR, Daily Record, Hickory, NC

Hines, Scott (618) 253-7146
MAN ED, Daily Register, Harrisburg, IL
Hollinger International Inc.

Hines, William (717) 348-9100
Librarian
Tribune & Scranton Times, Scranton, PA

Hines, Willie (770) 478-5753
PROD FRM-PR
Clayton News/Daily, Jonesboro, GA

Hinick, Walter (406) 496-5500
Photo ED, Montana Standard, Butte, MT

Hinkle, Donn (509) 248-1251
PROD FRM-MR
Yakima Herald-Republic, Yakima, WA

Hinkley, Doug (937) 767-7373
GM
Yellow Springs News, Yellow Springs, OH

Hinkley, Gerry (414) 224-2000
Deputy MAN ED
Milwaukee Journal Sentinel, Milwaukee, WI

Hinkley, Scott (317) 962-1575
Features ED
Palladium-Item, Richmond, IN

Hinman, Pam (414) 457-7711
County Government
Sheboygan Press, Sheboygan, WI

Hinojosa, Mark (312) 222-3232
DIR-Photography
Chicago Tribune, Chicago, IL

Hinshaw, Lydia (904) 252-1511
Sports ED, Daytona Beach News-Journal, Daytona Beach, FL

Hinshaw, Richard (704) 331-4842
GM, ED, Leader, Charlotte, NC

Hinshaw, Wayne (704) 633-8950
Photo DEPT MGR
Salisbury Post, Salisbury, NC

Hinson, Doug (423) 246-8121
PROD DIR-OPER
Kingsport Times-News, Kingsport, TN

Hinson, Jay B (207) 255-6561
ED
Machias Valley News Observer, Machias, ME

Hinson, Kathy (310) 540-5511
News ED, Daily Breeze, Torrance, CA

Hinterberger, John (206) 464-2111
COL, Seattle Times, Seattle, WA

Hinterlong, Anne (815) 673-3771
ADV MGR-Sales
Streator Times-Press, Streator, IL

Hinton, Anna (317) 622-1212
PROD CNR, Herald Bulletin, Anderson, IN

Hinton, Chris (810) 469-4510
PROD DIR-Pre Press OPER
Macomb Daily, Mount Clemens, MI

Hinton, David (217) 379-4313
MAN ED, Paxton Weekly Record, Paxton, IL

Hinton, Earleen (815) 946-2364
GM, Tri-County Press, Polo, IL

Hinton, Jim (541) 485-1234
MGR-PROM, Register-Guard, Eugene, OR

Hinton, Peter (705) 325-1355
ADV MGR, Packet & Times, Orillia, ON

Hinton, Richard (701) 663-6823
ED, Morton Co. & Mandan News
Mandan, ND

Hinton, Rolf (972) 322-4248
ED, Buffalo Press, Buffalo, TX

Hintz, Doug (306) 825-5522
ED, Lloydminster Times, Lloydminster, SK

Hintz, Martin (414) 273-8132
PUB, Irish American Post, Milwaukee, WI

Hintzman, Judie (608) 328-4202
ED, Monroe Times, Monroe, WI

Hipp, Andy Lai (808) 525-8000
PROD MGR-COMP
Hawaii Newspaper Agency Inc., Honolulu, HI

Hipple, Brad (605) 224-7301
VP/BM, PROD SUPT
Capital Journal, Pierre, SD

Hipple, Kevin (605) 224-7301
BM, Capital Journal, Pierre, SD

Hipple, Saundra (206) 432-9696
PUB, ED
Voice of the Valley, Maple Valley, WA

Hipple, Terry J (605) 224-7301
PRES, PUB, ADV MGR, CIRC MGR, ADTX MGR, Capital Journal, Pierre, SD

Hippo, Ed (609) 989-5454
CIRC DIR, Times, Trenton, NJ

Hipps, John (605) 967-2161
PUB, ED, Faith Independent, Faith, SD

Hirahara, Naomi (213) 629-2231
ED, Rafu Shimpo, Los Angeles, CA

Hird, Livy (701) 349-3222
ED, Dickey County Leader, Ellendale, ND

Hirsch, Douglas P (916) 365-2797
PUB, Valley Post, Anderson, CA

Hirsch, Mark (319) 588-5611
Photo MGR, Telegraph Herald, Dubuque, IA

Hirsch, Mike (315) 470-0011
Travel ED, Post-Standard/Syracuse Herald-Journal/American, Syracuse, NY

Hirsch, Rod (908) 246-5500
News ED
Home News & Tribune, East Brunswick, NJ

Hirschfeld, John C (217) 351-5252
PRES/CEO, News-Gazette, Champaign, IL

Hirschler, Emery L (219) 235-6161
TREAS, VP-Advertising/MKTG
South Bend Tribune, South Bend, IN

Hirschman, David (901) 529-2211
Transportation Reporter
Commercial Appeal, Memphis, TN

Hirshan, Adam (603) 356-3456
EX ED, Conway Daily Sun, North Conway, NH

Hirshbeck, Fred (610) 820-6500
CIRC FRM-Trucking
Morning Call, Allentown, PA

Hirshberg, Dan (908) 852-1212
ED, Star Gazette, Hackettstown, NJ

Hirst, Desmond (334) 262-1611
PROD MGR-Press/Post Press
Montgomery Advertiser, Montgomery, AL

Hirt, Bob (909) 684-1200
TV Week ED, Press-Enterprise, Riverside, CA

Hirt, Danny (704) 245-6431
Amusements ED, Automotive/Aviation ED, Photo DEPT MGR, Radio/Television ED
Daily Courier, Forest City, NC

Hirt, Gary L (419) 523-5709
PUB, Putnam County Sentinel, Ottawa, OH

Hirten, Mickey (802) 863-3441
MAN ED, Burlington Free Press, Burlington, VT, Gannett Co. Inc.

Hirtzel, Susan (360) 694-3391
ADV MGR, Columbian, Vancouver, WA

Hisaw, Sue (505) 437-7120
PROD SUPV-COMP
Alamogordo Daily News, Alamogordo, NM

Hiscock, Derek (709) 673-3721
PUB, Nor'Wester, Springdale, NF

Hiscock, Kenneth (507) 462-3575
PUB, ED, Minnesota Lake Tribune, Minnesota Lake, MN

Hisle, Mark (816) 263-4123
PROD FRM-PR, Moberly Monitor-Index & Democrat, Moberly, MO

Hissom, Doug (414) 276-2222
PUB, ED, Shepherd Express Weekly News, Milwaukee, WI

Histed, William M (813) 425-3411
PUB, ED, Polk County Press, Mulberry, FL

Hitch, Jim (913) 628-1081
PUB, ED, EDL Writer
Hays Daily News, Hays, KS

Hitchcock, Bill (410) 289-6834
ED, Maryland Beachcomber, Ocean City, MD

Hitchens, Keith (219) 461-8222
DIR-Photography
News-Sentinel, Fort Wayne, IN

Copyright ©1997 by the Editor & Publisher Co.

105-Who's Where **Hoh**

Hite, Alice .... (864) 223-1411
Living/Lifestyle ED, Today's Living ED, Women's/Fashion ED
Index-Journal, Greenwood, SC
Hite, Ray .... (516) 481-5487
COL, Editorial Consultant Service, West Hempstead, NY
Hites, Jeanette .... (208) 882-5561
PROD MGR
Moscow-Pullman Daily News, Moscow, ID
Hitt, Bill .... (310) 540-5511
PROD SUPV-PR, Daily Breeze, Torrance, CA
Copley Press Inc.
Hitt, Mary L .... (513) 398-8856
ED, Pulse-Journal, Mason, OH
Hitt, Richard .... (800) 426-4192
PRES-Florida, Independent Newspapers Inc. (DE), Dover, DE
Hitt, Tom .... (913) 843-1000
DP MGR, Journal-World, Lawrence, KS
Hittle, H Todd .... (213) 525-2000
CFO, Hollywood Reporter, Los Angeles, CA
Hively, Jeff .... (916) 243-2424
VP, Record Searchlight, Redding, CA
Hixson, Angie .... (918) 266-3664
GM, Port of Catoosa Times-Herald
Catoosa, OK
Hjornevik, Elizabeth .... (608) 989-2531
PUB, Blair Press, Blair, WI
Hjornevik, Gerald R .... (608) 989-2531
PUB, ED, Blair Press, Blair, WI
Hladky, Greg .... (203) 789-5200
Capitol BU Chief, Political/Government ED
New Haven Register, New Haven, CT
Hladky, Joe .... (319) 398-8211
PRES, PUB, ED, Gazette, Cedar Rapids, IA
Hlas, Mike .... (319) 398-8211
Sports COL, Gazette, Cedar Rapids, IA
Hlavaty, Brian .... (517) 752-7171
News ED, Wire ED
Saginaw News, Saginaw, MI
Ho, Paula .... (416) 441-1405
North America Journalist, Fotopress Independent News Service International, Toronto, ON
Hoag, Charles .... (612) 673-4000
VP-Sales Leader, Marketer Customer Unit
Star Tribune, Minneapolis, MN
Hoard-Banks, Cynthia .... (412) 263-1100
ADTX MGR
Pittsburgh Post-Gazette, Pittsburgh, PA
Hoarty, John .... (617) 426-3000
CIRC VP, Boston Herald, Boston, MA
Hoban, Bill .... (702) 298-6090
ED, Laughlin Nevada Times, Laughlin, NV
Hoban, Irene .... (909) 657-2181
PUB, Perris Progress, Perris, CA
Hoban, John F .... (909) 657-2181
PUB, ED, Perris Progress, Perris, CA
Hobart, Sue .... (503) 221-8327
Travel ED, Oregonian, Portland, OR
Hobbs, Ann .... (205) 325-2222
Librarian
Birmingham News, Birmingham, AL
Hobbs, Carol .... (954) 356-4000
MGR-Public Relations
Sun-Sentinel, Fort Lauderdale, FL
Hobbs, Deb Saygers .... (616) 544-2345
ED, Torch, Central Lake, MI
Hobbs, Lin .... (606) 337-2333
PUB, Pineville Sun-Cumberland Courier, Pineville, KY
Hobbs, Ray .... (501) 378-3400
EX City ED
Arkansas Democrat-Gazette, Little Rock, AR
Hobbs, Scooter .... (318) 433-3000
Sports ED, Lake Charles American Press, Lake Charles, LA
Hobbs, Susan .... (606) 464-2444
ED, Beattyville Enterprise, Beattyville, KY
Hobbs, Tim .... (903) 757-3311
ADV DIR
Longview News-Journal, Longview, TX
Hoblitzell, Kenny .... (601) 456-3771
PUB, ED, Times Post, Houston, MS
Hoch, Bob .... (316) 268-6000
PROD OPER MGR-SYS
Wichita Eagle, Wichita, KS
Hochberger, Ruth S .... (212) 779-9200
EIC, New York Law Journal, New York, NY
Hochenauer, Kelly .... (405) 475-3311
Entertainment/Amusements ED, Features ED, Home Furnishings ED, Living/Lifestyle ED
Daily Oklahoman, Oklahoma City, OK
Hochhauser, Richard M .... (210) 829-9000
Sr VP/PRES & CEO-Harte-Hanks Direct MKTG, Harte-Hanks Communications Inc., San Antonio, TX
Hochman, Stan .... (215) 854-2000
COL-Sports
Philadelphia Daily News, Philadelphia, PA
Hochstedler, Mike .... (619) 256-2257
PROD MGR-COMP
Desert Dispatch, Barstow, CA
Hockaday, Laura .... (816) 234-4141
Society ED
Kansas City Star, Kansas City, MO
Hocker, Mark .... (219) 235-6161
CONT, South Bend Tribune, South Bend, IN
Hocking, John W .... (717) 738-1151
PUB, Shopping News of Lancaster County, Ephrata, PA
Hockley, Mike .... (307) 742-2176
CIRC MGR, Daily Boomerang, Laramie, WY
Hodapp, Mark .... (618) 532-5604
ASSOC ED, Political ED, West Counties ED
Centralia Sentinel, Centralia, IL
Hodder, Chris .... (709) 364-6300
CIRC MGR-Home Delivery Sales
Evening Telegram, St. John's, NF
Hoddinott, Patricia B .... (573) 882-5700
SEC/TREAS, GM
Columbia Missourian, Columbia, MO
Hodgden, Ken .... (414) 833-2517
GM, Times Press, Seymour, WI
Hodge, Carmi .... (619) 454-0411
VP-Human Resources/ASST SEC
Copley Press Inc., La Jolla, CA
Hodge, Charlotte .... (501) 354-2451
MAN ED, Conway County Petit Jean Country Headlight, Morrillton, AR
Hodge, Eddy .... (501) 354-2451
GM, Conway County Petit Jean Country Headlight, Morrillton, AR
Hodge, Jerry .... (704) 464-0221
PUB, GM, ADTX MGR
Observer-News-Enterprise, Newton, NC
Hodge, John .... (317) 529-1111
Sports ED, Courier-Times, New Castle, IN
Hodge, Kelly .... (423) 929-3111
Sports ED
Johnson City Press, Johnson City, TN
Hodge, Shelby .... (713) 220-7171
Society ED, Houston Chronicle, Houston, TX
Hodge, Tom .... (423) 929-3111
EDL DIR, EPE
Johnson City Press, Johnson City, TN
Hodges, Dianne .... (904) 230-6103
PUB, ED
Florida Monitor, Panama City Beach, FL
Hodges, Jeannie .... (910) 891-1234
Society/Women's ED
Daily Record, Dunn, NC
Hodges, Karen .... (209) 239-3531
News ED, Manteca Bulletin, Manteca, CA
Hodges, Laura .... (812) 265-3641
ED-Indiana, Madison Courier, Madison, IN
Hodges, Mary C .... (319) 523-4631
PUB, Wapello Republican, Wapello, IA
Hodges, Michael A .... (319) 523-4631
PUB, GM, Wapello Republican, Wapello, IA
Hodges, Regina .... (904) 778-6055
PUB, Airwinger, N.A.S. Cecil Field, FL
Hodges, Rick .... (208) 756-2221
PUB, ED, Recorder-Herald, Salmon, ID
Hodges, Sandra .... (601) 323-1642
PROD MGR
Starkville Daily News, Starkville, MS
Hodges, Vikki .... (704) 249-3981
BUS ED, Dispatch, Lexington, NC
Hodges Winburn, Rebecca .... (501) 315-8228
PUB, Benton Courier, Benton, AR
Hodgson, Bill .... (817) 594-7447
City ED
Weatherford Democrat, Weatherford, TX
Hodgson, Mike .... (805) 489-4206
MAN ED, Five Cities Times-Press-Recorder, Arroyo Grande, CA
Hodgson, William .... (604) 494-5406
ED, Summerland Review, Summerland, BC
Hodierne, Robert .... (202) 383-7800
NTL ED/Deputy BU Chief
Newhouse News Service, Washington, DC
Hodosko, William .... (419) 223-1010
PROD OPER MGR-SYS, Lima News
Lima, OH
Hodson, Jim .... (603) 668-4321
Travel ED, Union Leader, Manchester, NH
Hoeflich, Charlene .... (614) 992-2155
GM, News ED, Daily Sentinel/Sunday Times-Sentinel, Pomeroy, OH
Hoeft, Mike .... (414) 435-4411
Travel ED
Green Bay Press-Gazette, Green Bay, WI
Hoeft, Randy .... (520) 783-3333
MAN ED, Automotive ED, Graphics ED/Art DIR, Yuma Daily Sun, Yuma, AZ
Hoegl, Peter .... (516) 931-1400
PUB, East Meadow Beacon, Hicksville, NY
Hoegner, Jerry .... (216) 999-4500
DIR-MKTG Services
Plain Dealer, Cleveland, OH
Hoegnomann, Steve .... (302) 537-1881
ED, Wave, Bethany Beach, DE
Hoekstra, Dave .... (312) 321-3000
Music ED-Pop/Country
Chicago Sun-Times, Chicago, IL
Hoekstra, Mary .... (512) 729-9900
ED, Rockport Pilot, Rockport, TX
Hoel, Arne L .... (702) 333-7676
PRES/CEO, Swift Newspapers, Reno, NV
Hoelzel, William .... (860) 241-6200
MGR-RES, Hartford Courant, Hartford, CT
Hoemann, Darrell .... (217) 351-5252
Photo DEPT MGR
News-Gazette, Champaign, IL
Hoenig, Frank J .... (206) 455-2222
PROD DIR, Eastside Journal, Bellevue, WA
Hoenig, Lisa .... (518) 463-2500
GM, Metroland, Albany, NY
Hoerig, Dennis .... (937) 372-4444
ASST MAN ED, Daily Gazette, Xenia, OH
Hoey, John .... (508) 586-7200
Political/Government ED
Enterprise, Brockton, MA
Hofer, J Chuck .... (515) 421-0500
CONT, Globe-Gazette, Mason City, IA
Hofer, Jim .... (715) 735-6611
ADV MGR
Marinette Eagle Herald, Marinette, WI
Hoff III, Bernard C .... (410) 268-5000
ADV DIR, Capital, Annapolis, MD
Hoff, David .... (808) 244-3981
ED, Maui News, Wailuku, HI
Hoff, Steve .... (402) 444-1000
PSL MGR, Omaha World-Herald, Omaha, NE
Hoffer, Ron .... (805) 736-2313
PUB, Lompoc Record, Lompoc, CA
Hofferber, Don .... (307) 742-2176
PROD FRM-COMP
Laramie Daily Boomerang, Laramie, WY
Hoffert, Jamie .... (515) 792-3121
CIRC MGR, Newton Daily News, Newton, IA
Hoffman, Alicia .... (915) 337-4661
News ED, Odessa American, Odessa, TX
Hoffman, Ann .... (937) 225-2000
ASST MAN ED, Daily News, Dayton, OH
Hoffman, Denise .... (605) 331-2200
ADV MGR-Sales
Argus Leader, Sioux Falls, SD
Hoffman, Dirk .... (716) 343-8000
News ED, Regional News ED
Daily News, Batavia, NY
Hoffman, Doug .... (301) 733-5131
PROD FRM-PR
Morning Herald, Hagerstown, MD
Hoffman, Ed .... (410) 643-7770
GM, Kent Island Bay Times Extra, Stephensville, MD
Hoffman, Eric .... (502) 247-5223
PUB, Mayfield Messenger, Mayfield, KY
Hoffman, Fred .... (614) 446-2342
PROD MGR, Gallipolis Daily Tribune/Sunday Times-Sentinel, Gallipolis, OH, Gannett Co. Inc.
Hoffman, Gilbert .... (713) 266-3444
PUB, ED
Highlands Star/Crosby Courier, Highlands, TX
Hoffman, Heidi .... (707) 644-1141
ADV DIR
Vallejo Times-Herald, Vallejo, CA
Hoffman, Howard E .... (212) 450-7000
Southwestern MGR/Newspaper Relations, VP/Southwestern MGR/Newspaper Relations
React, Parade Publications, New York, NY
Hoffman, Most Rev James R .... (419) 243-4178
PUB, Catholic Chronicle, Toledo, OH
Hoffman, Jeff C .... (715) 823-3151
GM, Tribune-Gazette, Clintonville, WI
Hoffman, Jim .... (304) 636-2121
GM/PUB, Inter-Mountain, Elkins, WV
Hoffman, Jim .... (937) 833-2545
ED, Brookville Star, Brookville, OH
Hoffman, Joan J .... (616) 238-7362
PUB, Straitsland Resorter, Indian River, MI
Hoffman, John .... (415) 348-4321
MGR-Commercial Printing
San Mateo County Times, San Mateo, CA
Hoffman, John F .... (309) 829-9411
ADV MGR-Display
Pantagraph, Bloomington, IL
Hoffman, Larry .... (541) 889-5387
Photo DEPT MGR
Argus Observer, Ontario, OR
Hoffman, Lonna .... (817) 390-7400
CIRC DIR-Training
Fort Worth Star-Telegram, Fort Worth, TX
Hoffman, Marshall .... (612) 920-7000
ED, American Jewish World
Minneapolis, MN
Hoffman, Mary .... (605) 439-3131
PUB, ED
McPherson County Herald, Leola, SD
Hoffman, Michael .... (805) 650-2900
ED-Simi Valley Edition
Ventura County Star, Ventura, CA
Hoffman, Milton .... (914) 694-9300
EPE, Herald Statesman, Yonkers, NY
Hoffman, Nicholas R .... (712) 784-3575
PUB, ED, Walnut Bureau, Walnut, IA
Hoffman, Nick .... (814) 371-4200
BUS/FIN ED, MET ED, Courier-Express/Tri-County Sunday, Du Bois, PA
Hoffman, Paul .... (317) 398-6631
Sports ED, Shelbyville News, Shelbyville, IN
Hoffman, Roger .... (405) 475-3311
ADV MGR-CLASS
Daily Oklahoman, Oklahoma City, OK
Hoffman, Scott .... (308) 345-4500
City ED, McCook Daily Gazette, McCook, NE
Hoffman, Sharon .... (716) 232-7100
Weekend Magazine ED, Rochester Democrat and Chronicle; Times-Union, Rochester, NY
Hoffman, Steve .... (309) 928-2193
ED, Farmer City Journal, Farmer City, IL
Hoffman, Thomas .... (616) 222-5400
CIRC MGR-State, Press, Grand Rapids, MI
Hoffman, SSgt Timothy .... (805) 736-2313
MAN ED
Space & Missile Times, Lompoc, CA
Hoffman, Woody .... (312) 782-8100
Chief Copy ED
City News Bureau of Chicago, Chicago, IL
Hoffmann, Barbara .... (908) 922-6000
PROD ASST MGR-Distribution
Asbury Park Press, Neptune, NJ
Hoffmann, Pat .... (513) 352-2000
News ED, Cincinnati Post, Cincinnati, OH
Hoffmaster, Howard .... (507) 454-6500
PUB, Winona Daily News, Winona, MN
Hoffpauir, Jerry .... (318) 457-3061
ED, Eunice News, Eunice, LA
Hoflander, Heather .... (816) 584-3611
ED, Higginsville Advance, Higginsville, MO
Hofman, Lisa .... (815) 584-3007
ED, Gardner Chronicle, Dwight, IL
Hofmann, Carol .... (203) 846-3281
Photo ED, Religion ED, Television/Film ED, Theater/Music ED, Hour, Norwalk, CT
Hofmann, Ed .... (304) 485-1891
ADV DIR, ADV MGR-NTL/CLASS, Parkersburg News & Sentinel, Parkersburg, WV
Hofmann, Jim .... (419) 625-5500
VP, PUB, Sandusky Register, Sandusky, OH
Hofmann, Rich .... (215) 854-2000
COL-Sports
Philadelphia Daily News, Philadelphia, PA
Hofmann, Wally .... (619) 934-3929
PUB, Mammoth Times Weekly, Mammoth Lakes, CA
Hofmeister, Larry .... (618) 234-1000
PROD FRM-PR
Belleville News-Democrat, Belleville, IL
Hofmeister, Sallie .... (213) 237-5000
Entertainment Reporter-Broadcast
Los Angeles Times, Los Angeles, CA
Hofmeyer, Marlin J .... (715) 682-2313
GM, Daily Press, Ashland, WI
Hogan, Al .... (506) 859-4900
MAN ED, Times-Transcript, Moncton, NB
Hogan, Barbara .... (614) 353-3101
DP MGR, Daily Times, Portsmouth, OH
Hogan, Charles .... (518) 885-4341
PUB, ED, Ballston Journal, Ballston Spa, NY
Hogan, Gail .... (701) 252-3120
Food/Home ED, Religion ED, Teen-Age/Youth ED, Jamestown Sun, Jamestown, ND
Hogan, J Timothy .... (609) 989-7800
CONT, DP MGR, Trentonian, Trenton, NJ
Hogan, Jack .... (909) 889-9666
CIRC DIR, Sun, San Bernardino, CA
Hogan, Kathy .... (315) 697-7142
ED, Canastota Bee-Journal, Canastota, NY
Hogan, Laura .... (508) 586-7200
ADV CNR-NTL/Preprint
Enterprise, Brockton, MA
Hogan, Nat .... (914) 694-9300
PROD DIR, Reporter Dispatch, White Plains, NY, Gannett Co. Inc.
Hogan, Rex .... (405) 233-6600
City ED, Enid News & Eagle, Enid, OK
Hogan, Vickie .... (405) 863-2240
PUB, ED, Garber-Billings News, Garber, OK
Hoge, Alyson .... (501) 378-3400
ASST MAN ED-Night, Arkansas Democrat-Gazette, Little Rock, AR
Hogeboom, Larry .... (705) 745-4641
PROD SUPV, Examiner, Peterborough, ON
Hogens, Stephen .... (315) 470-0011
MGR-PROM, Post-Standard/Syracuse Herald-Journal/American, Syracuse, NY
Hogerty, Dianne S .... (913) 888-3800
PRES, Family Features Editorial Services Inc., Shawnee Mission, KS
Hoggatt, Terry .... (918) 225-3333
MAN ED, Cushing Daily Citizen, Cushing, OK
Hoghe, Tracy .... (419) 238-2285
ADV MGR-RT/CLASS/NTL, ADTX MGR, Times-Bulletin, Van Wert, OH
Hoglund, Louis .... (218) 568-8521
ED, Lake Country Echo, Pequot Lakes, MN
Hogstrom, Erik .... (541) 947-3378
MAN ED
Lake County Examiner, Lakeview, OR
Hogue, Bev .... (419) 257-2771
ED, News, North Baltimore, OH
Hoheisel, Carolyn .... (320) 632-2345
PUB
Morrison County Record, Little Falls, MN

Copyright ©1997 by the Editor & Publisher Co.

Hoh Who's Where-106

Hohenfeldt, R D (573) 364-2468
Society ED, Rolla Daily News, Rolla, MO

Hohlfeld, Kent (913) 762-5000
Sports ED, Daily Union, Junction City, KS

Hohlt, Rick (318) 255-4353
PUB, Ruston Daily Leader, Ruston, LA

Hohman, Eric (605) 987-2631
ED, Sioux Valley News, Canton, SD

Hohman, James (703) 471-2200
VP/Sales, Reuters America Inc. (NewMedia), Reston, VA

Hojanchi, Stan (704) 333-1718
MAN ED, Independent Tribune, Concord, NC

Hojnacki, Marisue (616) 756-2421
PUB, GM, Southcounty Gazette & Shopper, Three Oaks, MI

Hojnacki, Michael (616) 756-2421
PUB, Southcounty Gazette & Shopper, Three Oaks, MI

Hojnacki, Ron (419) 245-6000
PROD SUPT-MR, Blade, Toledo, OH

Hojnicki, Tom (312) 222-3232
PROD DIR-Printing OPER
Chicago Tribune, Chicago, IL

Hoke, Gerald (713) 266-5481
VP/CONT
Southern Newspapers Inc., Houston, TX

Holamon, Craig (817) 567-2616
ED, Jack County Herald, Jacksboro, TX

Holbert, Abby (770) 478-5753
Fashion/Women's ED
Clayton News/Daily, Jonesboro, GA

Holbert, Deb (307) 682-9306
BUS ED, News-Record, Gillette, WY

Holbert, Linda (405) 338-3355
MAN ED, Guymon Daily Herald, Guymon, OK

Holbrook, Vickie Schaffeld (208) 467-9251
MAN ED, Idaho Press-Tribune, Nampa, ID

Holcher, Molly (308) 382-1000
Office MGR, DP MGR
Grand Island Independent, Grand Island, NE

Holcomb, David (517) 437-7351
BM, Hillsdale Daily News, Hillsdale, MI

Holcomb, Kirk (701) 780-1100
ADV MGR-NTL Sales
Grand Forks Herald, Grand Forks, ND

Holcombe, Al (610) 622-8800
ADV MGR-CLASS Display
Delaware County Daily Times, Primos, PA

Holden, Bill (604) 732-2222
News ED, Province, Vancouver, BC

Holden, Tom (757) 446-2000
Medical ED, Virginian-Pilot, Norfolk, VA

Holdener, Ken (618) 234-1000
CIRC MGR
Belleville News-Democrat, Belleville, IL

Holder, Alan (816) 234-4141
Magazine ED
Kansas City Star, Kansas City, MO

Holder, Bill (903) 693-7888
PUB, Panola Watchman, Carthage, TX

Holder, Clara (717) 443-9131
PUB, Journal-Herald, White Haven, PA

Holder, Don (309) 346-1111
PROD MGR-SYS, Daily Times, Pekin, IL

Holder, Jay (717) 443-9131
PUB, Journal-Herald, White Haven, PA

Holder, Sam (816) 263-4123
CIRC DIR, Automotive ED, Moberly Monitor-Index & Democrat, Moberly, MO

Holder, Sue (520) 763-2505
MGR-BUS
Mohave Valley Daily News, Bullhead City, AZ

Holderfield, Avis (205) 878-1311
ED, Sand Mountain Reporter, Albertville, AL

Holdta, Andrew (604) 588-4313
ED, Surrey/North Delta Leader, Surrey, BC

Hole, Robert (218) 687-3775
PUB, ED, Erskine Echo, Erskine, MN

Holecek, Russell (813) 689-7764
ED, South Tampa News, Brandon, FL

Holeman, Bob (318) 628-2712
PUB, ED, Winn Parish Enterprise-News American, Winnfield, LA

Holiber, William D (212) 210-2100
Senior VP-Advertising
New York Daily News, New York, NY

Holien, Christina (609) 758-2112
GM, New Egypt Press, New Egypt, NJ

Holje, Carolyn H (320) 275-2192
PUB, ED, Enterprise & Dispatch, Dassel, MN

Holje, Dan (320) 275-2192
GM, Enterprise & Dispatch, Dassel, MN

Hollabaugh, Cindy (814) 723-8200
CIRC MGR-Office
Warren Times-Observer, Warren, PA

Holladay, Ruth (317) 633-1240
Lifestyle ED, Star/News, Indianapolis, IN

Holladay, Susan (408) 920-5000
VP/CFO
San Jose Mercury News, San Jose, CA

Holladay, Tisha (405) 584-6210
ED, Broken Bow News, Broken Bow, OK

Holland, Anne (915) 673-4271
Librarian
Abilene Reporter-News, Abilene, TX

Holland, Bill (402) 873-3334
PUB
Nebraska City News-Press, Nebraska City, NE

Holland, Dan (423) 246-8121
CIRC DIR
Kingsport Times-News, Kingsport, TN

Holland, Darrell (216) 999-4500
Religion ED, Plain Dealer, Cleveland, OH

Holland, Jim (402) 721-5000
PUB, Fremont Tribune, Fremont, NE

Holland, Joel (616) 669-2700
PUB, Grand Valley Advance, Jenison, MI

Holland, John (209) 532-7151
Environmental ED
Union Democrat, Sonora, CA

Holland, Lynn (765) 423-2624
ED, Lafayette Leader, Lafayette, IN

Holland, Marcia (212) 837-7000
VP-PROM & RES, Journal of Commerce & Commercial, New York, NY

Holland, Robert (703) 764-0496
Richmond Correspondent
Associated Features Inc., Burke, VA

Holland, Sheila K (603) 668-4321
ADV MGR-NTL/Co-op
Union Leader, Manchester, NH

Holland, Vicky (918) 684-2828
News ED, Muskogee Daily Phoenix & Times Democrat, Muskogee, OK

Hollander, Jeff (718) 526-9069
Entertainment/Sports ED
Press Photo Service, Flushing, NY

Hollander, Nicole (312) 943-4862
PRES, Sylvia Syndicate, Chicago, IL

Hollen, Phil (912) 744-4200
ADV MGR-RT, Macon Telegraph, Macon, GA

Hollenback, Lynda (501) 315-8228
ASSOC ED, Benton Courier, Benton, AR

Hollenbaugh, Pat (805) 945-5634
ED, Missile, Lancaster, CA

Hollenbeck, Jim (205) 532-4000
ADV MGR-CLASS
Huntsville Times, Huntsville, AL

Hollenbeck, Marie (314) 456-3481
MAN ED
Warrenton News-Journal, Warrenton, MO

Hollenbeck, Sandra (206) 339-3000
CIRC DIR, Herald, Everett, WA

Hollenberger, John (334) 262-1611
Senior VP-Circulation, CIRC DIR
Montgomery Advertiser, Montgomery, AL

Holleran, James (716) 232-7100
Sports ED, Rochester Democrat and Chronicle; Times-Union, Rochester, NY

Hollerbach, Brad (573) 335-6611
DIR-SYS, DP MGR
Southeast Missourian, Cape Girardeau, MO

Hollerman, Joey (803) 771-6161
NTL ED, State, Columbia, SC

Hollett, Michael (416) 461-0871
PUB, ED, NOW, Toronto, ON

Holley, Alvin (409) 327-4357
PUB, Polk County Enterprise, Livingston, TX

Holley, Jack (909) 684-1200
ASST MAN ED-News
Press-Enterprise, Riverside, CA

Holliday, Jeff (405) 286-3321
News ED
McCurtain Daily Gazette, Idabel, OK

Holliday, William (318) 239-3444
GM, ADV DIR, Daily Leader, Leesville, LA

Hollifield, Jim (423) 581-5630
EDU ED, Political/County Government ED
Citizen Tribune, Morristown, TN

Hollifield, Scott (704) 652-3313
PUB, MAN ED, McDowell News, Marion, NC

Hollihan, Michael (414) 432-2941
ADV MGR
Green Bay News-Chronicle, Green Bay, WI

Holling, Bill (519) 354-2000
ADV MGR, Daily News, Chatham, ON

Hollinger, Berni (320) 255-8700
CONT, St. Cloud Times, St. Cloud, MN

Hollings, Roger (206) 932-0300
GM, West Seattle Herald, Seattle, WA

Hollingshead, Wayne (208) 743-9411
GM, Lewiston Morning Tribune, Lewiston, ID

Hollingsworth, Christina (770) 287-3798
BM, Community Features, Oakwood, GA

Hollingsworth, David (414) 435-4411
DIR-Market Development
Green Bay Press-Gazette, Green Bay, WI

Hollingsworth, Jerry (402) 925-5411
PUB, ED, Atkinson Graphic, Atkinson, NE

Hollingsworth, Roxanne (402) 925-5411
GM, Atkinson Graphic, Atkinson, NE

Hollis, Bob (812) 967-3176
MAN ED, Giveaway, Pekin, IN

Hollis, Jim (803) 655-5619
Sales Agent
Star Watch, SpotLight, Winston-Salem, NC

Hollis, John (619) 868-3245
PUB, ED, Mountaineer Progress, Phelan, CA

Hollis, Larry (806) 669-2525
MAN ED, City ED, Pampa News, Pampa, TX

Hollis, Mike (205) 532-4000
Regional ED
Huntsville Times, Huntsville, AL

Hollis, Todd (203) 333-0161
OPER ED, Connecticut Post, Bridgeport, CT

Hollister, Mary Bormann (608) 637-3137
PUB, MAN ED
Vernon County Broadcaster, Viroqua, WI

Hollister, Peggy (609) 871-8000
ADV MGR-RT
Burlington County Times, Willingboro, NJ

Hollister, Peter (608) 637-3137
PUB
Vernon County Broadcaster, Viroqua, WI

Hollister, Scott (913) 764-2211
Sports ED, Olathe Daily News, Olathe, KS

Hollnagel, Gayda (608) 782-9710
Religion ED
La Crosse Tribune, La Crosse, WI

Holloman, Wendell (512) 251-5574
ED, Pflugerville Pflag, Pflugerville, TX

Hollon, Jay (419) 522-3311
CONT, News Journal, Mansfield, OH

Hollon, John (808) 525-8000
EX ED, Honolulu Advertiser, Honolulu, HI

Hollopeter, Cathy (941) 992-2110
MAN ED, Bonita Banner, Bonita Springs, FL

Hollow, Dan (406) 791-1444
News ED, Great Falls Tribune
Great Falls, MT

Holloway, Ardith (614) 461-5000
ADV CNR-Co-op
Columbus Dispatch, Columbus, OH

Holloway, Becky (816) 433-5721
ED, Tipton Times, Tipton, MO

Holloway, Ben (816) 776-5454
BM, Daily News, Richmond, MO

Holloway, Caren S (804) 649-6000
ASST CONT
Richmond Times-Dispatch, Richmond, VA

Holloway, Diane (512) 445-3500
Radio/Television ED
Austin American-Statesman, Austin, TX

Holloway, Jane (916) 233-2632
PUB, Modoc County Record, Alturas, CA

Holloway, Kenneth (615) 388-6464
Outdoors ED, Daily Herald, Columbia, TN

Holloway, Laurie E (414) 435-4411
MAN ED
Green Bay Press-Gazette, Green Bay, WI

Holloway, Rick (916) 233-2632
PUB, ED, Modoc County Record, Alturas, CA

Holloway, Rita J (508) 586-7200
CONT, Enterprise, Brockton, MA

Holloway, Terri (719) 275-7565
ADV MGR-Sales
Daily Record, Canon City, CO

Holloway, Vanessa (708) 594-9340
MAN ED
Des Plaines Valley News, Summit, IL

Hollway, Cameron (915) 337-4661
Sports ED, Odessa American, Odessa, TX

Holly, Kay (817) 645-2441
ADV MGR-CLASS
Cleburne Times-Review, Cleburne, TX

Hollyer, Bill (703) 560-4000
City/MET ED, Fairfax Journal, Fairfax, VA
Journal Newspapers Inc.

Holm, Bill (612) 472-1140
GM, ED, Laker, Mound, MN

Holm, Caroline (805) 763-3171
ADV MGR, Daily Midway Driller, Taft, CA

Holm, James W (630) 232-9222
ADV DIR, Kane County Chronicle, Geneva, IL

Holman, Beverly (541) 997-3441
PUB, Siuslaw News, Florence, OR

Holman, Denise L (502) 582-4011
VP-Advertising, ADV VP, Courier-Journal, Louisville, KY

Holman, Jim (619) 235-3000
PUB, ED, San Diego Reader, San Diego, CA

Holman, Paul R (541) 997-3441
PUB, Siuslaw News, Florence, OR

Holman, Steve (405) 372-5000
Photo ED, News Press, Stillwater, OK

Holmberg, A William (423) 756-1234
PRES, Chattanooga Times, Chattanooga, TN

Holmberg, Ruth S (423) 756-1234
COB, Chattanooga Times, Chattanooga, TN

Holmberg, Susan (604) 378-4241
ED, Weekend News Advertiser, Merritt, BC

Holmberg, Theodore (401) 821-7400
PRES, PUB, ED
Kent County Daily Times, West Warwick, RI

Holmes, Ann (403) 652-2034
ED, High River Times, High River, AB

Holmes, Bill (403) 652-2034
PUB, High River Times, High River, AB

Holmes, Bill (519) 679-6666
MGR-OPER, London Free Press, London, ON

Holmes, Donald W (616) 695-3878
PUB, Berrien County Record, Buchanan, MI

Holmes, Jeff (319) 472-2311
Sports ED
Cedar Valley Daily Times, Vinton, IA

Holmes, Jeffrey W (217) 832-4201
PUB, ED, Southern Champaign Co. Today, Villa Grove, IL

Holmes, John (910) 323-4848
DIR-Personnel
Fayetteville Observer-Times, Fayetteville, NC

Holmes, Mark (905) 732-2411
ADV MGR, Tribune, Welland, ON

Holmes, Maureen (518) 483-4700
CIRC MGR, Malone Telegram, Malone, NY

Holmes, Melvin (330) 996-3000
PROD MGR-MR
Akron Beacon Journal, Akron, OH

Holmes, Patrick (919) 638-8101
ED, Sun-Journal, New Bern, NC

Holmes, Peggy (317) 664-5111
PROD Television Data Input
Chronicle-Tribune, Marion, IN

Holmes, Richard C (403) 753-2564
PUB, ED, Provost News, Provost, AB

Holmes, Rick (508) 626-3800
Op-Ed/EPE
Middlesex News, Framingham, MA

Holmes, Roger (403) 842-4465
PUB, ED
Wainwright Star Chronicle, Wainwright, AB

Holmes, Ronald E (403) 664-3622
PUB, Oyen Echo, Oyen, AB

Holmes, Sharon (613) 342-4441
CR MGR, Brockville Recorder and Times, Brockville, ON

Holmes, Tom M (903) 989-2325
PUB, ED, Trenton Tribune, Trenton, TX

Holmquist, Jeff (715) 294-2314
PUB, Osceola Sun, Osceola, WI

Holmquist, Julie (715) 294-2314
PUB, ED, Osceola Sun, Osceola, WI

Holquist, Robert (916) 243-2424
Health/Medical ED
Record Searchlight, Redding, CA

Holsapple, Marilyn (501) 623-7711
Fashion/Style ED, Food ED, Travel ED, Women's ED, Sentinel-Record, Hot Springs, AR

Holscher, Rory (219) 942-0521
ED, Merrillville Herald, Merrillville, IN

Holschuh-Van Zeeland, Marion (414) 733-4411
PROD FRM-COMP (Day)
Post-Crescent, Appleton, WI

Holsington, Mary (316) 792-1211
MGR-CR
Great Bend Tribune, Great Bend, KS

Holste, Glenda (612) 222-5011
EDL Writer
St. Paul Pioneer Press, St. Paul, MN

Holston, Noel (612) 673-4000
TV Critic, Star Tribune, Minneapolis, MN

Holsworth, Dan (605) 256-4555
Sports ED
Madison Daily Leader, Madison, SD

Holt, Colleen (501) 327-6621
EPE, Log Cabin Democrat, Conway, AR

Holt, Dan (718) 769-4400
PUB, Harbor Watch (Metro New York), Brooklyn, NY

Holt, Donald (212) 837-7000
ED, Journal of Commerce & Commercial, New York, NY

Holt, Dyanne (540) 825-0771
ADV DIR
Culpeper Star-Exponent, Culpeper, VA

Holt, J Tim (919) 752-6166
ADV DIR, DIR-MKTG
Daily Reflector, Greenville, NC

Holt, Jon H (314) 340-8402
ASST TREAS
Pulitzer Publishing Co., St. Louis, MO

Holt, Kathryn (317) 342-3311
TREAS, Daily Reporter, Martinsville, IN

Holt, Mikel (414) 265-5300
ED, Community Journal, Milwaukee, WI

Holt, Patricia (415) 777-1111
Books ED
San Francisco Chronicle, San Francisco, CA

Holt, Ron (405) 372-5000
Sports ED
Stillwater News Press, Stillwater, OK

Holt, Ron (812) 886-9955
PROD FRM-PR
Vincennes Sun-Commercial, Vincennes, IN

Holt, Wendell (317) 342-3311
EVP, Daily Reporter, Martinsville, IN

Holthaus, Mark (216) 999-4500
INFO SYS MGR-Imaging
Plain Dealer, Cleveland, OH

Holtkamp, Christy (319) 837-6722
ED, West Point Bee, West Point, IA

Holtman, Roger (540) 981-3100
ASSOC ED, Roanoke Times, Roanoke, VA

Holton, Lisa (312) 321-3000
Personal FIN/Banking
Chicago Sun-Times, Chicago, IL

107-Who's Where **Hor**

Holton, Raymond B .... (610) 820-6500
MAN ED, Morning Call, Allentown, PA
Holtz, Richard L .... (317) 423-5511
PUB, Journal and Courier, Lafayette, IN
Holtzapple, Ali .... (315) 635-3921
ED, Review, Baldwinsville, NY
Holtzinger, Kenneth L .... (814) 652-5191
PUB, Guide, Everett, PA
Holwerk, David .... (606) 231-3100
MAN ED
Lexington Herald-Leader, Lexington, KY
Holzel, David .... (404) 352-2400
MAN ED, Atlanta Jewish Times, Atlanta, GA
Holzkamp, Debbie .... (305) 350-2111
ADV DIR-Display, Miami Herald, Miami, FL
Holzman, Jyll .... (212) 556-1234
VP-Sales, New York Times Co., New York, NY
Hom, Dana .... (415) 777-1111
DP MGR
San Francisco Chronicle, San Francisco, CA
Homan, Becky .... (314) 340-8000
Fashion ED
St. Louis Post-Dispatch, St. Louis, MO
Homan, John .... (618) 942-5000
ED, Spokesman, Herrin, IL
Homco, Mike .... (309) 343-7181
News ED, Register-Mail, Galesburg, IL
Homer, Doug .... (412) 981-6100
ADV MGR-CLASS, Herald, Sharon, PA
Honderich, John .... (416) 367-2000
PUB, Toronto Star, Toronto, ON
Honea, Bob .... (907) 283-7551
PROD MGR, Peninsula Clarion, Kenai, AK
Honebrink, Forrest .... (320) 235-1150
PROD FRM-Assembly
West Central Tribune, Willmar, MN
Honey, Charles .... (616) 222-5400
Religion ED
Grand Rapids Press, Grand Rapids, MI
Honeycutt, David .... (704) 252-5611
ADV MGR-RT
Asheville Citizen-Times, Asheville, NC
Honeycutt, George .... (713) 220-7171
Chief Photographer
Houston Chronicle, Houston, TX
Honeycutt, James .... (505) 863-6753
PUB, Gallup Weekly Paper, Gallup, NM
Honeycutt, Jay .... (770) 382-4545
Sports ED
Daily Tribune News, Cartersville, GA
Honeycutt, Tharon L .... (941) 687-7000
CONT, Ledger, Lakeland, FL
Honeysett, William L .... (916) 321-1855
Sr VP
McClatchy Newspapers, Sacramento, CA
Honeywell, Michael .... (517) 835-7171
Photo ED
Midland Daily News, Midland, MI
Honig, Tom .... (408) 423-4242
ED, EDL Writer
Santa Cruz County Sentinel, Santa Cruz, CA
Honigfeld, Neil .... (860) 347-3331
ADV DIR
Middletown Press, Middletown, CT
Honley, Jim .... (203) 846-3281
News ED, Hour, Norwalk, CT
Honsey, Harris D .... (515) 592-4222
PUB, ED, Lake Mills Graphic, Lake Mills, IA
Hood, Aileen .... (205) 766-3434
CIRC DIR, Times Daily, Florence, AL
Hood, Brian .... (205) 367-2217
PUB, Pickens County Herald, Carrollton, AL
Hood, Brian R .... (417) 934-2025
PUB, ED
Mountain View Standard, Mountain View, MO
Hood, Frank B .... (412) 465-5555
ED-Sunday, Indiana Gazette, Indiana, PA
Hood Jr, Ken .... (423) 638-4181
GM, Greeneville Sun, Greeneville, TN
Hood, Margaret J .... (304) 355-2381
PUB, ED, Piedmont Herald, Piedmont, WV
Hood, Marilyn .... (810) 766-6100
ADV Clerk-Pre Print
Flint Journal, Flint, MI
Hood, Marshall .... (614) 461-5000
Fashion ED
Columbus Dispatch, Columbus, OH
Hood, Mike .... (210) 828-7660
ED, San Antonio Current, San Antonio, TX
Hood, Orley .... (601) 961-7000
Senior ED, Clarion-Ledger, Jackson, MS
Hood, Pam .... (520) 445-3333
ADV DIR, MGR-MKTG/PROM
Daily Courier, Prescott, AZ
Hood, Rich .... (816) 234-4141
VP/EPE, Kansas City Star, Kansas City, MO
Hood, Susan .... (810) 332-8181
ASST MAN ED, Oakland Press, Pontiac, MI
Hood, William T .... (304) 355-2381
PUB, ED, Piedmont Herald, Piedmont, WV
Hoogendoorn, Jodie A .... (712) 472-2525
ED, Lyon County Reporter, Rock Rapids, IA
Hook, David .... (805) 763-3171
ED, Daily Midway Driller, Taft, CA
Hook, Kevin .... (712) 546-7031
ADV DIR, Le Mars Daily Sentinel, Le Mars, IA
Hook Jr, Larry .... (517) 589-8228
ED, Leslie Local Independent, Leslie, MI
Hooker, Edith .... (601) 328-2424
CIRC DIR, CIRC DIR-Promotion
Commercial Dispatch, Columbus, MS
Hooker, Karen .... (913) 899-2338
ADV MGR, Goodland Daily News
Goodland, KS
Hooks, Ellis .... (919) 823-3106
ADV MGR, Daily Southerner, Tarboro, NC
Hooks, James .... (912) 283-2244
Photo DEPT MGR, PROD SUPT/FRM-COMP,
Waycross Journal-Herald, Waycross, GA
Hooper, Brad .... (603) 752-1200
GM, ADV MGR, Berlin Reporter, Berlin, NH
Hooper, David .... (903) 885-8663
PROD MGR, Sulphur Springs News-Telegram,
Sulphur Springs, TX
Hooper, George .... (802) 863-3441
CIRC MGR-Single Copy
Burlington Free Press, Burlington, VT
Hooper, Jerry .... (318) 352-5501
CIRC MGR
Natchitoches Times, Natchitoches, LA
Hooper, Richard .... (817) 390-7400
PROD MGR-Warehouse
Fort Worth Star-Telegram, Fort Worth, TX
Hooper, Susan .... (808) 525-8000
Consumer Affairs ED
Honolulu Advertiser, Honolulu, HI
Hooper, Timothy J .... (207) 791-6650
ADV MGR-Group Sales
Portland Press Herald, Portland, ME
Hoopes, Cora .... (202) 737-1888
ASSOC ED, Roll Call Report Syndicate
(Thomas Reports Inc.), Washington, DC
Hoos, Jeff .... (815) 223-3200
PROD MGR-PR, News-Tribune, La Salle, IL
Hoover, Aaron .... (910) 343-2000
EDU Reporter, Morning Star/Sunday Star-
News, Wilmington, NC
Hoover, Andrew .... (814) 234-9601
MGR-Sales & MKTG
AccuWeather Inc., State College, PA
Hoover, Carl .... (817) 757-5757
Amusements ED, Books ED, Films/Theater
ED, Waco Tribune-Herald, Waco, TX
Hoover, Evelyn .... (612) 894-1111
MAN ED
Dakota County Tribune, Burnsville, MN
Hoover, George .... (704) 289-1541
ADV MGR, MGR-MKTG/PROM
Enquirer-Journal, Monroe, NC
Hoover, James G .... (617) 266-6670
PUB, Bay Windows, Boston, MA
Hoover, John .... (305) 350-2111
PROD MGR-Quality Assurance/OPER
Miami Herald, Miami, FL
Hoover, Kerwin .... (818) 799-0467
ED/MGR, Hometown Flavor, Pasadena, CA
Hoover, Lil .... (703) 560-4000
CIRC DIR, Fairfax Journal, Fairfax, VA
Journal Newspapers Inc.
Hoover, Rick .... (208) 882-5561
MAN ED
Moscow-Pullman Daily News, Moscow, ID
Hoover, Robert .... (412) 263-1100
Books ED, Post-Gazette, Pittsburgh, PA
Hoover, Scott .... (520) 645-8888
ED, Lake Powell Chronicle, Page, AZ
Hope, Doug .... (619) 299-3131
Senior ED-ADM
San Diego Union-Tribune, San Diego, CA
Hope, Sandra .... (501) 534-3400
City/MET ED
Pine Bluff Commercial, Pine Bluff, AR
Hope, William .... (410) 268-5000
PROD MGR, PROD SUPT-PR
Capital, Annapolis, MD
Hopey, Don .... (412) 263-1100
Environmental/Ecology ED
Pittsburgh Post-Gazette, Pittsburgh, PA
Hopf, Don .... (814) 623-1151
GM, Bedford Gazette, Bedford, PA
Hopkins, Carmel .... (702) 383-0211
RE ED
Las Vegas Review-Journal, Las Vegas, NV
Hopkins, Dusty .... (941) 964-2995
PUB, ED, Boca Beacon, Boca Grande, FL
Hopkins, Elaine .... (309) 686-3000
Environmental ED, Health/Medical ED
Journal Star, Peoria, IL
Hopkins, Elayne .... (410) 268-5000
Television/Film ED, Theater/Music ED
Capital, Annapolis, MD
Hopkins, Gary .... (202) 636-3000
Sports ED
Washington Times, Washington, DC
Hopkins, Harvey L .... (805) 650-2900
ADV DIR
Ventura County Star, Ventura, CA
Hopkins, James .... (219) 724-2121
Sports ED
Decatur Daily Democrat, Decatur, IN
Hopkins, Joe C .... (818) 798-3972
PUB, Pasadena Journal-News, Pasadena, CA
Hopkins, John .... (803) 577-7111
News ED, Post and Courier, Charleston, SC
Hopkins, Joseph .... (413) 788-1000
EPE, Union-News, Springfield, MA
Hopkins, Leslie .... (817) 684-1355
PUB, ED, Foard County News and Crowell
Index, Crowell, TX
Hopkins, Raymond P .... (508) 674-4656
GM, Spectator, Somerset, MA
Hopkins, Rich .... (619) 299-3131
ADV MGR-Sales Automotive
San Diego Union-Tribune, San Diego, CA
Hopkins, Ron .... (402) 444-1000
PROD MGR-PR
Omaha World-Herald, Omaha, NE
Hopkins, Ruthie .... (818) 798-3972
PUB, ED, Journal-News, Pasadena, CA
Hopkins, Susan .... (770) 942-6571
ADV MGR
Douglas County Sentinel, Douglasville, GA
Hopkins, Suzanne .... (818) 713-3000
Travel ED
Daily News, Woodland Hills, CA
Hopkins, Tammy .... (304) 436-3144
ADV MGR-CLASS
Welch Daily News, Welch, WV
Hopkins, Terry .... (410) 749-7171
PUB, Daily Times, Salisbury, MD
Hopkins, Tom .... (937) 225-2000
Television ED
Dayton Daily News, Dayton, OH
Hopp, Neil .... (815) 459-4040
MAN ED, Northwest Herald, Crystal Lake, IL
Hoppe, Arthur .... (415) 777-1111
COL
San Francisco Chronicle, San Francisco, CA
Hoppensteadt, Norm .... (508) 428-8900
GM, Otis Notice, Osterville, MA
Hopper, C Steve .... (941) 953-7755
PUB-Charlotte (AM)
Sarasota Herald-Tribune, Sarasota, FL
Hopper, Jim .... (810) 727-3745
ED, Chesterfield Review/The Review/
Independent Press, Richmond, MI
Hopper, William .... (330) 454-5611
EPE, Repository, Canton, OH
Hoppner, Gina .... (907) 456-6661
Graphics ED
Fairbanks Daily News-Miner, Fairbanks, AK
Hopson, Marcel .... (205) 251-6523
ED, Birmingham World, Birmingham, AL
Hopson, Sylvia .... (510) 208-6300
ADV DIR, Oakland Tribune, Oakland, CA
Hopwood, Barry .... (610) 323-3000
PUB, Mercury, Pottstown, PA
Hopwood, Erin M .... (610) 323-3000
ADTX MGR, Mercury, Pottstown, PA
Hopwood, Howard .... (770) 947-0117
Self-Syndicator
Media Maven, Douglasville, GA
Hora, Marcia R .... (308) 848-2511
ED, Arnold Sentinel, Arnold, NE
Horan Jr, John F .... (540) 465-5137
PRES, GM, ED
Northern Virginia Daily, Strasburg, VA
Horchak, David .... (412) 543-1303
CIRC MGR, Leader Times, Kittanning, PA
Hordt, Robert .... (908) 922-6000
BUS ED, Asbury Park Press, Neptune, NJ
Horgan, Daniel .... (617) 698-6563
PUB, ED
Milton Record Transcript, Milton, MA
Horgan, Denis .... (860) 241-6200
COL-Human Interest
Hartford Courant, Hartford, CT
Horgan, John .... (415) 348-4321
Sports ED
San Mateo County Times, San Mateo, CA
Horgan, Michael .... (201) 877-4141
PROD DIR-SYS, Star-Ledger, Newark, NJ
Horinek, Charity .... (316) 675-2204
ED, Haskell County Monitor-Chief
Sublette, KS
Horlbeck, Fred .... (803) 329-4000
News ED, Herald, Rock Hill, SC
Horman, Hope .... (202) 383-7800
Office MGR
Newhouse News Service, Washington, DC
Horn, David .... (918) 581-8300
PROD SUPT-Camera/Plate
Tulsa World, Tulsa, OK
Horn, Debra .... (414) 682-5231
ED, Lakeshore Chronicle, Manitowoc, WI
Horn, James .... (815) 756-4841
ADV MGR, Daily Chronicle, De Kalb, IL
Horn, Laurie .... (305) 350-2111
Dance Critic, Miami Herald, Miami, FL
Horn, Richard .... (915) 673-4271
Political/Government ED
Abilene Reporter-News, Abilene, TX
Horn, Rick .... (316) 442-4200
MAN ED, Society ED
Arkansas City Traveler, Arkansas City, KS
Horn, Virginia .... (619) 337-3400
Action Line/Probe ED, Consumer Interest ED,
Imperial Valley Press, El Centro, CA
Hornbeck, Don .... (561) 461-2050
CIRC DIR, Tribune, Fort Pierce, FL
Hornberger, Fred .... (512) 575-1451
ADV DIR-MKTG
Victoria Advocate, Victoria, TX
Horne, Allen .... (706) 324-5526
Photo ED
Columbus Ledger-Enquirer, Columbus, GA
Horne, Bennett .... (501) 741-2325
Sports ED
Harrison Daily Times, Harrison, AR
Horne, Bob .... (910) 323-4848
Live Wire (Consumer) ED
Fayetteville Observer-Times, Fayetteville, NC
Horne, Ceclia .... (417) 532-9131
Online MGR
Lebanon Daily Record, Lebanon, MO
Horne, Janet .... (206) 464-2111
ASST Local ED
Seattle Times, Seattle, WA
Horne, Jed .... (504) 826-3279
City ED, Times-Picayune, New Orleans, LA
Horne, Mike .... (904) 359-4111
PROD CNR-Color
Florida Times-Union, Jacksonville, FL
Horne, Richard .... (213) 237-5000
PROD DIR-San Fernando Valley OPER
Los Angeles Times, Los Angeles, CA
Horne, Robert .... (540) 669-2181
PROD MGR-Computer SRV, Herald-Courier
Virginia Tennessean, Bristol, VA
Horne, Robert .... (912) 226-2400
Sports ED, Thomasville Times-Enterprise,
Thomasville, GA
Horne, Terry .... (301) 722-4600
PUB
Cumberland Times-News, Cumberland, MD
Hornell, Patricia G .... (516) 739-6400
MAN ED, Baldwin Citizen, Baldwin, NY
Horner III, Bill .... (919) 708-9000
SEC, TREAS, GM, PA, MGR-MKTG/PROM,
Action Line ED, COL, Art DIR, Political ED
Sanford Herald, Sanford, NC
Horner, Charles .... (908) 322-8343
EDL DIR, Sidebar News International, Scotch
Plains, NJ
Horner, Grier .... (413) 447-7311
ASSOC ED, Berkshire Eagle, Pittsfield, MA
Horner, Joseph E .... (412) 263-1100
PROD DIR, Post-Gazette, Pittsburgh, PA
Horner, Marlene .... (705) 472-3200
Lifestyle ED
North Bay Nugget, North Bay, ON
Horner Jr, W E .... (919) 708-9000
PRES, PUB, Sanford Herald, Sanford, NC
Horner, Will .... (212) 416-2000
PROD MGR (White Oak MD)
Wall Street Journal, New York, NY
Horning, Clay .... (405) 223-2200
Sports ED, Daily Ardmoreite, Ardmore, OK
Horning, J D .... (320) 235-1150
Wire ED, West Central Tribune, Willmar, MN
Hornsby, Bob .... (816) 646-2411
PROD SUPT
Constitution-Tribune, Chillicothe, MO
Hornsby, Tommy .... (904) 752-1293
EX ED, Lake City Reporter, Lake City, FL
Hornung, Darlene .... (406) 778-3344
PUB, Fallon County Times, Baker, MT
Hornung, Mark .... (312) 321-3000
CIRC DIR-Distribution
Chicago Sun-Times, Chicago, IL
Hornung, Sandy .... (410) 848-4400
DP MGR
Carroll County Times, Westminster, MD
Hornyak, Joe .... (705) 324-2113
MAN ED, Lindsay Daily Post, Lindsay, ON
Hornyak, Kim .... (616) 946-2000
ADV MGR-CLASS
Record-Eagle, Traverse City, MI
Horowitz, Barton .... (718) 981-1234
Automotive ED
Staten Island Advance, Staten Island, NY
Horowitz, David .... (212) 688-7557
ED, World Union Press, New York, NY
Horowitz, Michael .... (718) 642-2718
ED, Spring Creek Sun, Brooklyn, NY
Horowitz, Rick .... (414) 963-9333
Self-Syndicator
Horowitz, Rick, Shorewood, WI
Horrell, Tim K .... (619) 431-1660
VP, Sun Features Inc., Cardiff, CA
Horsey, David .... (206) 448-8000
EDL Cartoonist
Seattle Post-Intelligencer, Seattle, WA
Horstmann, Peter H .... (508) 793-9100
DIR-Human Resources
Telegram & Gazette, Worcester, MA
Horton, Al .... (317) 462-5528
PROD MGR-Building Services
Daily Reporter, Greenfield, IN

Copyright ©1997 by the Editor & Publisher Co.

Hor Who's Where-108

Horton, Alan M (360) 377-3711
Senior VP-Newspaper Division, Sun, Bremerton, WA, Scripps Howard

Horton, Barbara (573) 785-1414
Religion ED
Daily American Republic, Poplar Bluff, MO

Horton, Bob (806) 762-8844
EDL Writer/COL
Lubbock Avalanche-Journal, Lubbock, TX

Horton, Debbie (501) 448-3321
ED, Marshall Mountain Wave, Marshall, AR

Horton, Don (907) 486-3227
PROD Pressman, Daily Mirror, Kodiak, AK

Horton, Ina L (540) 728-7311
PUB, Carroll News, Hillsville, VA

Horton, Jim (813) 259-7711
CIRC DIR
Tampa Tribune and Times, Tampa, FL

Horton, John (216) 951-0000
Community ED
News-Herald, Willoughby, OH

Horton, Marc (403) 429-5400
Films ED, Edmonton Journal, Edmonton, AB

Horton, Martha (607) 739-3001
ED
Chemung Valley Reporter, Horseheads, NY

Horton, Rick (509) 765-4561
PROD MGR-PR
Columbia Basin Herald, Moses Lake, WA

Horton, Stan (503) 221-8327
Television ED, Oregonian, Portland, OR

Horton, Sue (213) 465-9909
ED, LA Weekly, Los Angeles, CA

Horvath, Adam (516) 843-2020
EDU ED, Long Island Lifestyle
Newsday, Melville, NY

Horvath, Nick (717) 255-8100
Sports ED, Patriot-News, Harrisburg, PA

Horvathova, Alexandra (818) 508-6400
MGR, Fotos International, Studio City, CA

Horvitz, Peter A (206) 455-2222
CEO/PRES
Horvitz Newspapers Inc., Bellevue, WA

Horwell, Patricia G (516) 739-6400
MAN ED
Valley Stream Maileader, Mineola, NY

Horwich, Lee (410) 332-6000
NTL ED, Sun, Baltimore, MD

Horwitz, Adam (808) 525-8000
PROD MGR-Pre Press
Hawaii Newspaper Agency Inc., Honolulu, HI

Horwitz, Arthur (810) 354-6060
PUB, Detroit Jewish News, Southfield, MI

Horwitz, Karl (212) 499-3334
VP-International, New York Times Syndication Sales Corp., New York, NY

Horwitz, Richard (212) 944-7744
VP, Feature Photo Service Inc., New York, NY

Hoschouer, Charlene (308) 583-2241
PUB, ED
Wood River Sunbeam, Wood River, NE

Hoschouer, Douglas G (308) 583-2241
PUB, ED
Wood River Sunbeam, Wood River, NE

Hosek, Ron (404) 875-6572
Technology ED
Atlanta Bureau, Atlanta, GA

Hoselton, Patty (414) 623-3160
ED, Columbus Journal, Columbus, WI

Hosey, Thomas (717) 286-5671
PROD FRM-PR, Daily Item, Sunbury, PA

Hosick, Dave (815) 937-3300
EDU ED, Daily Journal, Kankakee, IL

Hosie, Ronald W (913) 762-5000
MAN ED, EPE
Daily Union, Junction City, KS

Hoskin, Christine (954) 356-4000
EX ASST
Sun-Sentinel, Fort Lauderdale, FL

Hoskins, Greg (618) 566-8282
PUB, Scott Flier, Mascoutah, IL

Hoskins, Mark (606) 598-2319
ED, Manchester Enterprise, Manchester, KY

Hoskins, Rachel (704) 765-2071
ED, Mitchell News-Journal, Spruce Pine, NC

Hoskins, Stan (213) 933-5518
ED, Beverly Press/Park LaBrea News, Los Angeles, CA

Hoskiws, Lonnie (606) 248-1010
CIRC SUPV, Daily News, Middlesboro, KY

Hospers, Garth (408) 372-3311
PROD DIR
Monterey County Herald, Monterey, CA

Host, Dennis (320) 255-8700
PROD MGR-Pre Press
St. Cloud Times, St. Cloud, MN

Hostein, Lisa (212) 643-1890
ED, Jewish Telegraphic Agency Inc., New York, NY

Hostetler, Les (618) 566-8282
MAN ED, Scott Flier, Mascoutah, IL

Hostetler, Minnette (800) 999-3534
CNR, Another Way, Harrisonburg, VA

Hostutler, Anna (316) 694-5700
Hospitals ED
Hutchinson News, Hutchinson, KS

Hotaling, Lynn (704) 586-2611
MAN ED, Sylva Herald & Ruralite, Sylva, NC

Hotchkiss, Heather (319) 283-2144
CIRC MGR, Register, Oelwein, IA

Hotchkiss, Peggy (616) 673-5534
GM, Allegan County News, Allegan, MI

Hotho, Eileen (716) 649-4040
ED, Sun and Erie County Independent, Hamburg, NY

Hottes, Doris (618) 542-2133
ADV DIR, Evening Call, Du Quoin, IL

Hotts, Mitch (810) 469-4510
Environmental ED
Macomb Daily, Mount Clemens, MI

Hotz, Robert Lee (213) 237-5000
SCI Writer
Los Angeles Times, Los Angeles, CA

Houck, Jim (712) 472-2525
PUB,Lyon County Reporter, Rock Rapids, IA

Houck, Most Rev William R (601) 969-1880
PUB, Mississippi Today, Jackson, MS

Houde, Daniel (418) 683-1573
ADV MGR
Le Journal de Quebec, Ville Vanier, QC

Hough, Brian K (803) 672-2358
PUB, ED
Pageland Progressive-Journal, Pageland, SC

Hough, Lorie (864) 223-1411
PROD FRM-COMP
Index-Journal, Greenwood, SC

Hough, Stan (717) 637-3736
ED, Evening Sun, Hanover, PA

Hough, William Henry (508) 548-4700
PUB, ED, Enterprise, Falmouth, MA

Houghton, Amory (207) 791-6650
PROD OPER MGR-Facilities (390 Congress St), Portland Press Herald, Portland, ME

Houghton, Howard (505) 983-3303
ASST City ED
Santa Fe New Mexican, Santa Fe, NM

Houghton, Sharon (607) 798-1234
DIR-Market Development
Press & Sun Bulletin, Binghamton, NY

Houk, Ed (813) 893-8111
PROD MGR-Dispatch
St. Petersburg Times, St. Petersburg, FL

Houle, Barbara (508) 793-9100
Food ED
Telegram & Gazette, Worcester, MA

Houle, D (604) 723-8171
PROD PR
Alberni Valley Times, Port Alberni, BC

Houle, Glen (306) 652-9200
PROD MGR-Press
StarPhoenix, Saskatoon, SK

Houle, Robin (219) 933-3200
PROD FRM-Press, Times, Munster, IN

Houlihan, Daniel (717) 348-9100
CONT
Tribune & The Scranton Times, Scranton, PA

Hounigringer, Tina (212) 210-2100
VP-RT Sales
New York Daily News, New York, NY

Hounshell, Allen (202) 334-6000
MGR-Labor Relations
Washington Post, Washington, DC

Hourston, Lois (604) 463-2281
PUB, Maple Ridge/Pitt Meadow Times, Maple Ridge, BC

Housare, Timothy (520) 868-5897
ED, Florence Reminder & Blade-Tribune, Casa Grande, AZ

House, David A (512) 884-2011
VP/EX ED, Corpus Christi Caller-Times, Corpus Christi, TX

House, Karen Elliott (212) 416-2000
PRES-International Group
Wall Street Journal, New York, NY

House, Mildred C (505) 437-7120
ADV DIR
Alamogordo Daily News, Alamogordo, NM

House, Myron (970) 522-1990
ADV DIR, Journal-Advocate, Sterling, CO

House, Ron (913) 295-1111
CIRC MGR-City
Topeka Capital-Journal, Topeka, KS

Housen, Judi (501) 785-7700
EDU ED
Southwest Times Record, Fort Smith, AR

Housen, Tim (330) 296-9657
Sports ED (Pro-Scholastic)
Record-Courier, Kent-Ravenna, OH

Houser, Marian (614) 283-4711
Features ED
Herald-Star, Steubenville, OH

Houser, Michael (208) 377-6200
CIRC MGR-Market Development
Idaho Statesman, Boise, ID

Houser, Troy L (704) 322-4510
BUS ED
Hickory Daily Record, Hickory, NC

Housh, David (918) 581-8300
Features ED, Tulsa World, Tulsa, OK

Housholder, Grace (219) 347-0400
COL, News-Sun, Kendallville, IN

Housholder, Terry (219) 347-0400
MAN ED, COL, EPE, Features ED
News-Sun, Kendallville, IN

Housley, Sharen (405) 335-3893
MAN ED, Frederick Press, Frederick, OK

Houston, Bob (318) 462-0616
ED, Beauregard Daily News, De Ridder, LA

Houston, Loretta (912) 985-4545
CIRC SUPV-Customer SRV
Observer, Moultrie, GA

Houston, Robert (716) 326-3163
ED, Chautauqua News, Westfield, NY

Houston, Steve (604) 525-6306
PUB
Royal City Record/Now, New Westminster, BC

Houston, Steve (905) 683-5110
MAN ED
Ajax/Pickering News Advertiser, Ajax, ON

Houtman, Jennifer (614) 373-2121
City ED, Marietta Times, Marietta, OH

Hov, Edward (701) 947-2417
ED
New Rockford Transcript, New Rockford, ND

Hovey, Art (402) 475-4200
ASST EPE
Lincoln Journal Star, Lincoln, NE

Hovind, Jeff (414) 887-0321
EX ED, EPE
Daily Citizen, Beaver Dam, WI

Hovis, Kathy (607) 272-2321
Local ED, Ithaca Journal, Ithaca, NY

Hovland Jr, Kenneth (860) 875-3366
PUB, ED, Reminder, Vernon, CT

Howald, Eric (519) 396-3111
PUB, ED, Independent, Kincardine, ON

Howard, Anthony (516) 589-6200
MAN ED, Suffolk County News, Sayville, NY

Howard, Barbara (605) 732-4555
PUB, ED, Stickney Argus, Stickney, SD

Howard, Carol (503) 221-8327
DIR-Computer SRV
Oregonian, Portland, OR

Howard, Clare (309) 686-3000
EDU ED, Journal Star, Peoria, IL

Howard, Dean (419) 298-2369
PUB, ED, Edgerton Earth, Edgerton, OH

Howard, Debbie (502) 753-1916
ADV MGR-CLASS
Murray Ledger & Times, Murray, KY

Howard, Ed (704) 689-4612
PUB, ED, Mountain Advisor, Mars Hill, NC

Howard, Ellen (508) 685-1000
PSL MGR, DIR-MKTG
Eagle-Tribune, North Andover, MA

Howard, Fred B (907) 586-3740
CIRC MGR, Juneau Empire, Juneau, AK

Howard, Freddie (410) 366-3900
GM, Baltimore Times, Baltimore, MD

Howard, Garry D (414) 224-2000
Senior ED-Sports
Milwaukee Journal Sentinel, Milwaukee, WI

Howard, Greg (970) 493-6397
PROD MGR-Pre Press
Fort Collins Coloradoan, Fort Collins, CO

Howard, Jan (203) 775-2533
MAN ED, Brookfield Journal, Brookfield, CT

Howard, Jeanne (408) 457-9000
PUB, Metro Santa Cruz, Santa Cruz, CA

Howard, Jenny (540) 949-8213
Fashion/Food ED, Garden ED, Home Furnishings ED, Living/Lifestyle ED, Society/Women's ED, News Virginian, Waynesboro, VA

Howard, Judy (309) 686-3000
Librarian, Journal Star, Peoria, IL

Howard, SSgt Kelly (904) 863-1111
ED, Eglin Eagle, Fort Walton Beach, FL

Howard, Lounita (615) 444-3952
News ED, Lebanon Democrat, Lebanon, TN

Howard, Mari (401) 274-2149
Office MGR
Whitegate Features Syndicate, Providence, RI

Howard, Mary (419) 298-2369
PUB, ED, Edgerton Earth, Edgerton, OH

Howard, Murray M (864) 298-4100
MGR-RES, Greenville News, Greenville, SC

Howard, Pat (814) 870-1600
Books ED, COL-BUS & Politics, EPE, Political ED
Morning News/Erie Daily Times, Erie, PA

Howard, Phoebe Wall (209) 441-6111
Political Writer, Fresno Bee, Fresno, CA

Howard, Robert S (619) 433-5771
PRES, Howard Publications, Oceanside, CA

Howard, Sherry (215) 854-2000
ASST to ED
Philadelphia Inquirer, Philadelphia, PA

Howard, Thomas W (619) 433-5771
VP, Howard Publications, Oceanside, CA

Howard, Tim (910) 373-7000
CIRC MGR-Distribution/Home Delivery
News & Record, Greensboro, NC

Howard, Tom (406) 657-1200
EDU ED, Billings Gazette, Billings, MT

Howard, W Stan (517) 377-1000
ADV DIR, Lansing State Journal, Lansing, MI

Howard, William (910) 274-6210
ED, Carolina Peacemaker, Greensboro, NC

Howard, William E (219) 933-3200
PRES, PUB, Times, Munster, IN

Howden, Gale (561) 820-4100
DIR-Community Relations/NIE
Palm Beach Post, West Palm Beach, FL

Howe, Ann G (607) 756-5665
VP, Cortland Standard, Cortland, NY

Howe IV, Arthur W (610) 896-9555
PUB, Main Line Life, Ardmore, PA

Howe, David (250) 352-3552
MAN ED, Nelson Daily News, Nelson, BC

Howe, Diane (352) 867-4010
News ED, Ocala Star-Banner, Ocala, FL

Howe, Don (607) 324-1425
PROD MGR, Evening Tribune, Hornell, NY

Howe, E B (608) 326-2441
PUB, Courier Press, Prairie du Chien, WI

Howe, G Woodson (402) 444-1000
Sr VP, Omaha World-Herald Co., Omaha, NE

Howe, Jack (319) 873-2210
PUB, North Iowa Times, McGregor, IA

Howe, John (603) 524-3800
EX ED, Citizen, Laconia, NH

Howe, Kevin R (607) 756-5665
SEC, PUB, ED
Cortland Standard, Cortland, NY

Howe, Randall (413) 447-7311
Berkshire Week ED
Berkshire Eagle, Pittsfield, MA

Howe, Russell Warren (202) 337-1560
Author, Arms & The World, Washington, DC

Howe, William H (608) 326-2441
ED, Courier Press, Prairie du Chien, WI

Howell, Andy (801) 625-4200
ASST MAN ED-Davis County
Standard-Examiner, Ogden, UT

Howell, Bill (209) 935-2906
ED, Coalinga Record, Coalinga, CA

Howell, Brian (608) 252-6100
Books ED, Fashion ED, Films/Theater ED, Food ED, Garden/Home Furnishings ED, Music ED, Religion ED, Society ED, Women's ED, Wisconsin State Journal, Madison, WI

Howell, Cynthia (501) 378-3400
EDU Writer
Arkansas Democrat-Gazette, Little Rock, AR

Howell, Deborah (202) 383-7800
Washington BU Chief/ED
Newhouse News Service, Washington, DC

Howell, Diane (317) 825-0581
ADV MGR-CLASS/RT
Connersville News-Examiner, Connersville, IN

Howell, Don (912) 273-2277
COL, Cordele Dispatch, Cordele, GA

Howell, Ed (205) 921-3104
ED, Journal Record, Hamilton, AL

Howell, Ed (316) 278-2114
PUB, Sterling Bulletin, Sterling, KS

Howell, Gus (704) 358-5000
CIRC DIR-Distribution
Charlotte Observer, Charlotte, NC

Howell, Jack (208) 263-9534
CIRC DIR
Bonner County Daily Bee, Sandpoint, ID

Howell, Jeff (704) 252-5611
ADTX MGR
Asheville Citizen-Times, Asheville, NC

Howell, Jeff (204) 825-2772
PUB, Sentinel-Courier, Pilot Mound, MB

Howell Jr, John I (401) 732-3100
PUB, Warwick Beacon, Warwick, RI

Howell, Lee N (706) 672-1753
PUB, ED
Meriwether Free Press, Greenville, GA

Howell, Leslie (716) 232-7100
PROD FRM-Paperhandler, Rochester Democrat and Chronicle; Rochester, NY Times-Union, Rochester, NY

Howell, Melissa (316) 278-2114
PUB, Sterling Bulletin, Sterling, KS

Howell, Mike (915) 653-1221
Photo DEPT MGR
Standard-Times, San Angelo, TX

Howell, Paula (405) 924-4388
ADV DIR, Durant Daily Democrat, Durant, OK

Howell, Penny (817) 965-3124
ADV MGR-CLASS, Stephenville Empire-Tribune, Stephenville, TX

Howell, Peter (410) 479-1800
ED, Times Record, Denton, MD

Howell, Ron (915) 236-6677
Sports ED
Sweetwater Reporter, Sweetwater, TX

Howell, Ron (403) 235-7100
BUS ED, Calgary Herald, Calgary, AB

Howell, Sheila L (204) 825-2772
ED, Sentinel-Courier, Pilot Mound, MB

Howell, Steve (512) 445-3500
PROD MGR-PR OPER
Austin American-Statesman, Austin, TX

Copyright ©1997 by the Editor & Publisher Co.

109-Who's Where **Hug**

Hower, Kurt (717) 255-8100
CIRC ASST DIR-Sales & MKTG
Patriot-News, Harrisburg, PA

Hower, Wendy (907) 456-6661
EDU Reporter, Teen-Age/Youth ED
Fairbanks Daily News-Miner, Fairbanks, AK

Howerton, Sally (419) 342-4276
CIRC DIR, Daily Globe, Shelby, OH

Howie, Bob (319) 852-3217
ED, Cascade Pioneer-Advertiser, Cascade, IA

Howie, David (212) 972-0460
PUB, Action, New York, NY

Howie, Teresa (306) 634-2654
GM, Mercury, Estevan, SK

Howitt, J (902) 426-2811
Night ED, Chronicle-Herald, Halifax, NS

Howland, Chick (417) 836-1100
City ED
Springfield News-Leader, Springfield, MO

Howley, Dan (518) 454-5694
EX Sports ED, Times Union, Albany, NY

Howley, Joe (616) 683-2100
Sports ED, Niles Daily Star, Niles, MI

Howley, Kay (619) 765-2231
GM, Julian News, Julian, CA

Howry, Joe (805) 650-2900
MAN ED, Ventura County Star, Ventura, CA

Howton, Elizabeth (805) 395-7500
Religion ED
Bakersfield Californian, Bakersfield, CA

Howze, Bishop Joseph L (601) 374-8318
PUB, Gulf Pine Catholic, Biloxi, MS

Howze, Lenora (410) 332-6000
ADV MGR-Division, Sun, Baltimore, MD

Hoye, Raymond (203) 789-5200
Automotive ED, News ED
New Haven Register, New Haven, CT

Hoyle, John (704) 484-7000
Entertainment ED, Television/Films ED, Travel ED, Shelby Star, Shelby, NC

Hoyle, Russ (860) 548-9300
ED, Hartford Advocate, Hartford, CT

Hoyles, Dixon (419) 448-3200
DP MGR, ADTX MGR
Advertiser-Tribune, Tiffin, OH

Hoyles, Monty (419) 448-3200
BM, Advertiser-Tribune, Tiffin, OH

Hoyt, Clark (305) 376-3800
VP-News, Knight-Ridder Inc., Miami, FL

Hoyt, Frank (208) 743-9411
MGR-CR
Lewiston Morning Tribune, Lewiston, ID

Hoyt, Jerry (501) 534-3400
CIRC DIR
Pine Bluff Commercial, Pine Bluff, AR

Hoyt, Linda (419) 245-6000
DIR-FIN, Blade, Toledo, OH

Hrim, Sandra (315) 942-4449
MAN ED, Boonville Herald & Adirondack Tourist, Boonville, NY

Hritz, Thomas (412) 263-1100
COL, Pittsburgh Post-Gazette, Pittsburgh, PA

Hromadka, Erik (317) 926-0204
Author
EH Communications, Indianapolis, IN

Hruby, Alexander J (405) 255-5354
PRES, PUB, ED, Duncan Banner
Duncan, OK

Hruby, John A (405) 255-5354
CIRC MGR, Duncan Banner, Duncan, OK

Hruby, Trish (914) 341-1100
ADV MGR
Times Herald-Record, Middletown, NY

Hruz, Judy (301) 948-3120
ED, Rockville Gazette, Gaithersburg, MD

Hryn, Nicholas (204) 589-5871
PUB, ED
Ukrainsky Holos, Winnipeg, MB

Hryhor, Edward (207) 990-8000
ADV MGR-Portland Office
Bangor Daily News, Bangor, ME

Hubach, Glynette (417) 732-2525
ED, Republic Monitor, Republic, MO

Hubartt, Kerry (219) 461-8222
EX News ED
News-Sentinel, Fort Wayne, IN

Hubbard, Allan (903) 785-8744
Web Page ED, Paris News, Paris, TX

Hubbard, Bruce (313) 822-7712
Author
Advisor Group, Grosse Pointe Farms, MI

Hubbard, Fred W (954) 356-4000
MGR-Facilities
Sun-Sentinel, Fort Lauderdale, FL

Hubbard, Holly A Olmsted (313) 822-7712
Author
Advisor Group, Grosse Pointe Farms, MI

Hubbard, Bishop Howard J (518) 453-6688
PUB, Evangelist, Albany, NY

Hubbard, Janet K (937) 592-3060
VP
Bellefontaine Examiner, Bellefontaine, OH

Hubbard, Janice (801) 259-9139
Self-Syndicator, Hubbard, Janice, Moab, UT

Hubbard Jr, JC (910) 838-4117
PUB, Journal-Patriot, North Wilkesboro, NC

Hubbard, John W (910) 838-4117
PUB, Journal-Patriot, North Wilkesboro, NC

Hubbard, Jon B (937) 592-3060
GM, Examiner, Bellefontaine, OH

Hubbard, Steve (503) 221-8327
DIR-MKTG SRV, Oregonian, Portland, OR

Hubbard, Thomas E (937) 592-3060
PRES, TREAS, Examiner, Bellefontaine, OH

Hubbell, John M (601) 328-2424
MAN ED
Commercial Dispatch, Columbus, MS

Hubbell, Linda (415) 252-0500
ADV MGR, San Francisco Daily Journal, San Francisco, CA

Hubble, Shawn (307) 789-6560
ED, Uinta County Herald, Evanston, WY

Hubenthal, James P (412) 654-6651
DIR-BUS, DP MGR
New Castle News, New Castle, PA

Huber, Curtis (360) 377-3711
CIRC DIR, Sun, Bremerton, WA

Huber, Dennis L (812) 738-4552
PUB, Clarion News, Corydon, IN

Huber, Kathy (713) 220-7171
Garden ED, Houston Chronicle, Houston, TX

Huber, Lee (407) 420-5000
EDL ADM Budget MGR
Orlando Sentinel, Orlando, FL

Huber, Mark (937) 382-2574
Sports ED
Wilmington News Journal, Wilmington, OH

Huber, Shannon (513) 721-2700
CONT, Cincinnati Enquirer, Cincinnati, OH

Huber, Tom (414) 338-0622
CIRC MGR-Sales
Daily News, West Bend, WI

Hubert, Achille (418) 986-2345
ED, Le Radar, Cap Aux Mueles, QC

Hubin, John (320) 833-2001
PUB, ED
Buffalo Lake News Mirror, Buffalo Lake, MN

Hubin, Ken (320) 833-2001
PUB, ED
Buffalo Lake News Mirror, Buffalo Lake, MN

Hubler, Paul (818) 843-8700
MAN ED, Burbank Leader, Burbank, CA

Hubred, Jonette (612) 469-2181
MAN ED
Lakeville Life & Times, Lakeville, MN

Huchanec, Gary (803) 317-6397
CIRC MGR
Florence Morning News, Florence, SC

Huchingson, Greg (409) 823-0088
PUB, GM, ED, Press, Bryan, TX

Huck, Michael (618) 295-2812
ED, Journal Messenger, Marissa, IL

Huckaby, John (717) 286-5671
Sports ED, Daily Item, Sunbury, PA

Huckle, Chris (616) 775-6565
ADV MGR-MKTG
Cadillac News, Cadillac, MI

Huckle, Diana (507) 451-2840
VP, Owatonna People's Press, Owatonna, MN
Huckle Publishing Inc.

Huckle, James (616) 929-3571
PRES
Huckle Publishing Inc., Traverse City, MI

Huckle, R Kaye (616) 775-6565
VP/SEC, Cadillac News, Cadillac, MI

Huckle, Thomas C (616) 775-6565
PRES, PUB/GM, ED, EPE, PROD MGR
Cadillac News, Cadillac, MI

Huculak, Ed (403) 250-4200
ADV DIR, Calgary Sun, Calgary, AB

Huddle, Cathie (402) 475-4200
ASST City ED, Lincoln Journal Star
Lincoln, NE

Huddleson, Pete (916) 622-1255
DIR-MIS, PROD DIR, Mountain Democrat, Placerville, CA, McNaughton Newspapers

Huddleson, Tom (308) 284-4046
MAN ED, Keith County News, Ogallala, NE

Huddleston, Dick (209) 441-6111
CIRC MGR-Sales, Fresno Bee, Fresno, CA

Huddleston, Norman (817) 757-5757
PROD DIR, Waco Tribune-Herald, Waco, TX

Huddleston, Steve (707) 448-6401
ASST PUB, EPE, Reporter, Vacaville, CA

Hudgins, Kenneth (704) 524-2010
PUB, Franklin Press, Franklin, NC

Hudgins, Michael (205) 878-1311
PUB
Sand Mountain Reporter, Albertville, AL

Hudler, Carol (912) 744-4200
PRES, PUB, Macon Telegraph, Macon, GA

Hudler, Martha C (317) 773-3970
PUB, Noblesville Times, Noblesville, IN

Hudler, Rol (303) 346-5381
PUB, ED
Burlington Record, Burlington, CO

Hudman, Jerry (334) 644-1101
PROD FRM-Engraving
Valley Times-News, Lanett, AL

Hudnutt, Arthur D (216) 329-7000
PRES, Lorain County Printing & Publishing Corp., Elyria, OH

Hudnutt, George D (330) 725-4166
PUB, Medina County Gazette, Medina, OH

Hudon, Joe (714) 676-5247
MAN ED, Rancho News, Temecula, CA

Hudson, Arlene (408) 842-6400
ADV MGR-RT, Dispatch, Gilroy, CA

Hudson, Bob (405) 353-0620
City ED, Lawton Constitution, Lawton, OK

Hudson, Bob (573) 221-2800
ADV MGR, Courier-Post, Hannibal, MO

Hudson, Chuck (613) 283-3182
PUB, Record News, Smiths Falls, ON

Hudson, Don (407) 420-5000
Orange County ED
Orlando Sentinel, Orlando, FL

Hudson, Fred (718) 643-1162
ADV DIR, Daily Challenge, Brooklyn, NY

Hudson, Jim (806) 435-3631
PUB, Perryton Herald, Perryton, TX

Hudson, Larry (814) 532-5199
MAN ED, Tribune-Democrat, Johnstown, PA

Hudson, Linda (901) 885-0744
ADV MGR-CLASS
Union City Daily Messenger, Union City, TN

Hudson, Linn (912) 882-4927
PUB, Camden County Tribune, St. Marys, GA

Hudson, Lou (817) 390-7400
ASST NTL ED
Fort Worth Star-Telegram, Fort Worth, TX

Hudson, Pam (918) 456-8833
ADV DIR
Tahlequah Daily Press, Tahlequah, OK

Hudson, Phillip K (203) 333-0161
CIRC DIR
Connecticut Post, Bridgeport, CT

Hudson, Terry (918) 225-3333
CIRC MGR
Cushing Daily Citizen, Cushing, OK

Hudzinski, John (908) 922-6000
Civic Journalism/Newsroom ADM
Asbury Park Press, Neptune, NJ

Huebner, Leandro (Lee) (318) 487-6397
Photo DEPT MGR
Alexandria Daily Town Talk, Alexandria, LA

Huebscher, Don (715) 833-9200
MAN ED, Leader-Telegram, Eau Claire, WI

Huelsman, Louise (419) 238-2285
CIRC SUPV-MR
Times-Bulletin, Van Wert, OH

Huerta, Melissa (407) 420-5000
EDL Art MGR
Orlando Sentinel, Orlando, FL

Huerto, Joel (818) 241-4141
Sports ED
Glendale News-Press, Glendale, CA

Hueston, Arthur (519) 773-3126
PUB, Aylmer Express, Aylmer, ON

Hueston, John (519) 773-3126
ED, Aylmer Express, Aylmer, ON

Huet, Linda (412) 224-4321
CONT, Valley News Dispatch, Tarentum, PA

Huether, Tim (702) 782-5121
PUB, Record-Courier, Gardnerville, NV

Huettmann, Theodore M (402) 529-3229
PUB, ED
Wisner News-Chronicle, Wisner, NE

Huey Jr, Ward L (214) 977-6606
Vice Chairman/PRES-Broadcast Division
A H Belo Corp., Dallas, TX

Huff, Christopher (803) 496-3242
MAN ED, Observer, Holly Hill, SC

Huff, Dan (520) 792-3630
MAN ED, Tucson Weekly, Tucson, AZ

Huff, Deborah M (317) 473-3091
SEC/CONT
Nixon Newspapers Inc., Peru, IN

Huff, Diane (520) 783-3311
Financial DIR
Western Newspapers Inc., Yuma, AZ

Huff, Donna (806) 537-3634
MAN ED, Panhandle Herald, Panhandle, TX

Huff, Doug (805) 524-0153
PUB, ED, Fillmore Herald, Fillmore, CA

Huff, Doug (304) 233-0100
Sports ED, Intelligencer/Wheeling News-Register, Wheeling, WV

Huff, James (301) 722-4600
PROD SUPV-Plant Maintenance
Cumberland Times-News, Cumberland, MD

Huff, Jerry (501) 785-7700
MAN ED
Southwest Times Record, Fort Smith, AR

Huff, John (407) 420-5000
ED-EDL Technology
Orlando Sentinel, Orlando, FL

Huff, Kelly (317) 598-6397
Picture ED
Daily Ledger, Noblesville, IN

Huff, Lisa (812) 663-3111
CIRC MGR
Greensburg Daily News, Greensburg, IN

Huff, Marge (520) 445-3333
ADTX MGR, Daily Courier, Prescott, AZ

Huff, Mary (706) 724-0851
ADV MGR-Sales
Augusta Chronicle, Augusta, GA

Huff, William B (617) 929-2000
CFO/EVP, Boston Globe, Boston, MA

Hufferd, Gary (317) 825-0581
Copy ED
Connersville News-Examiner, Connersville, IN

Huffines, Ronda (405) 224-2600
Fashion/Food ED, Home Furnishings/Society ED, Chickasha Daily Express, Chickasha, OK

Huffington, Richard J (706) 278-1011
PRES, Daily Citizen-News, Dalton, GA
Thomson Newspapers

Huffman, Arnold (905) 827-2244
PUB, GM, Free Press Journal, Oakville, ON

Huffman, Christine (815) 937-3300
PSL OFF, Daily Journal, Kankakee, IL

Huffman, Dale (937) 225-2000
COL, Dayton Daily News, Dayton, OH

Huffman, Donna (614) 387-0400
ADV DIR, Marion Star, Marion, OH

Huffman, E H (910) 353-1171
ADV MGR-CLASS
Daily News, Jacksonville, NC

Huffman, J Ford (703) 276-5800
MAN ED/Features/Graphics & Photography
Gannett News Service, Arlington, VA

Huffman, James A (201) 473-1927
ED, Messenger, Garfield, NJ

Huffman, Linda (901) 529-2211
MGR-CR, Commercial Appeal, Memphis, TN

Huffman, Mike (601) 961-7000
PROD MGR-Press
Clarion-Ledger, Jackson, MS

Huffman, Nancy C (201) 473-1927
PUB, Messenger, Garfield, NJ

Huffman, Rex (330) 364-5577
Entertainment/Amusements ED, Radio/Television ED, Times Reporter, New Philadelphia, OH

Huffman, Shari (913) 632-2127
CIRC DIR
Clay Center Dispatch, Clay Center, KS

Huffman, Sherry (313) 222-6400
MGR-Employee Relations
Detroit Newspapers, Detroit, MI

Hufford, Sharilyn (912) 236-9511
Online Contact
Savannah Morning News, Savannah, GA

Hug, Gerald (209) 441-6111
DIR-FIN, Fresno Bee, Fresno, CA

Hugg, Pat (212) 779-6300
CORP DIR
Liaison International, New York, NY

Huggett, Barbara (215) 379-5500
GM, Northeast Breeze, Rockledge, PA

Huggins, Kerry (803) 577-7111
ADTX MGR, Post and Courier, Charleston, SC

Hughes, Almena (540) 981-3100
Food ED, Roanoke Times, Roanoke, VA

Hughes, Andrew (219) 235-6161
Books ED, Tribune, South Bend, IN

Hughes, Barbara Wallace (515) 573-2141
BUS ED, Messenger, Fort Dodge, IA

Hughes, Bill (717) 784-2121
Photo ED, Press Enterprise, Bloomsburg, PA

Hughes, Bob (306) 565-8211
ED, Leader-Post, Regina, SK

Hughes, Butch (805) 781-7800
ADV DIR
Telegram-Tribune, San Luis Obispo, CA

Hughes, Carolyn Pictor (219) 461-8333
ADV VP-Sales/MKTG
Journal Gazette, Fort Wayne, IN

Hughes, Cathy (803) 533-5500
ADV DIR, ADTX MGR
Times and Democrat, Orangeburg, SC

Hughes, Debbye (501) 785-7700
City ED, Environmental ED
Southwest Times Record, Fort Smith, AR

Hughes, Dick (503) 399-6611
EPE, Statesman Journal, Salem, OR

Hughes, Edith (412) 856-7400
ED, Norwin Star, Monroeville, PA

Hughes, Frank (702) 945-2414
PUB, Mineral County Independent News, Hawthorne, NV

Hughes, Gary (915) 546-6100
PROD DIR, El Paso Times, El Paso, TX

Hughes, Gaynell (304) 752-6950
PROD FRM-COMP, Logan Banner, Logan, WV

Hughes, J Mike (410) 332-6000
CIRC ASST DIR-Home Delivery
Sun, Baltimore, MD

Hughes, Jim (501) 793-2383
PA, PROD MGR-PR
Batesville Guard, Batesville, AR

Hughes, Sgt Jim (906) 228-8920
ED, Northern Light, Marquette, MI

Hughes, Joe (806) 762-8844
EPE, Avalanche-Journal, Lubbock, TX

Hughes, John C (360) 532-4000
ED, Daily World, Aberdeen, WA

Copyright ©1997 by the Editor & Publisher Co.

Hug Who's Where-110

Hughes, Judy .... (905) 273-8111
ED, Mississauga News, Mississauga, ON
Hughes, Ken .... (513) 761-1188
Senior Critic
Critic's Choice Reviews, Cincinnati, OH
Hughes, Kenneth E .... (508) 458-7100
ADV MGR-Co-op/Special Projects
Sun, Lowell, MA
Hughes, Linda .... (403) 429-5400
PRES, PUB
Edmonton Journal, Edmonton, AB
Hughes, Martin J .... (717) 286-5671
ADV DIR, ADTX MGR
Daily Item, Sunbury, PA
Hughes, Martin S .... (717) 286-5671
PUB, Weekender, Sunbury, PA
Hughes, Mary Jo .... (517) 278-2318
ADV DIR, Daily Reporter, Coldwater, MI
Hughes, Melissa .... (405) 756-4461
MAN ED, Lindsay News, Lindsay, OK
Hughes, Michael .... (972) 563-6476
CIRC DIR, Terrell Tribune, Terrell, TX
Hughes, Mike .... (517) 377-1000
Entertainment/Amusements ED, Radio/ Television ED, Lansing State Journal, Lansing, MI
Hughes, Pamela .... (765) 563-3631
PUB, ED, Prairie Review, Brookston, IN
Hughes, Phyllis J .... (508) 746-5555
PUB, Old Colony Memorial, Plymouth, MA
Hughes, Richard A .... (908) 246-5500
ED
Home News & Tribune, East Brunswick, NJ
Hughes, Robert .... (904) 252-1511
ADV DIR-MKTG, Daytona Beach News-Journal, Daytona Beach, FL
Hughes, Robert M .... (408) 423-4242
CONT
Santa Cruz County Sentinel, Santa Cruz, CA
Hughes, Robert T .... (203) 964-2200
VP/DIR-Production/Facility, PROD VP/DIR, Stamford Advocate, Stamford, CT, Times Mirror Co.
Hughes, Ronnie J .... (904) 829-6562
PUB
St. Augustine Record, St. Augustine, FL
Hughes, Sheila .... (504) 732-2565
Action Line/Hot Line ED
Daily News, Bogalusa, LA
Hughes, Sue .... (315) 792-5000
DP MGR, Observer-Dispatch, Utica, NY
Hughes, Sue .... (219) 253-6234
PUB, ED, Monon News, Monon, IN
Hughes, Sylvia .... (919) 826-2111
ED
Commonwealth Progress, Scotland Neck, NC
Hughes, Ted .... (702) 945-2414
PUB, ED, Mineral County Independent News, Hawthorne, NV
Hughes, Todd .... (814) 773-3161
ED, Ridgway Record, Ridgway, PA
Hughes, Tony .... (702) 945-2414
PUB, Mineral County Independent News, Hawthorne, NV
Hughes Jr, William T .... (770) 468-6511
PUB, Monticello News, Monticello, GA
Hughey, Chris .... (918) 341-1101
PROD SUPT
Claremore Daily Progress, Claremore, OK
Hughey, David .... (919) 419-6500
PRES, PUB, Herald-Sun, Durham, NC
Hughey, J .... (918) 335-8200
PROD SUPT
Examiner-Enterprise, Bartlesville, OK
Hughey, John .... (812) 275-3355
Television/Film ED, Theater/Music ED
Times-Mail, Bedford, IN
Hughs, Maureen .... (717) 255-8100
Photo ED, Patriot-News, Harrisburg, PA
Hughs, Travis .... (972) 392-0888
Chairman/CEO
Wieck Photo DataBase Inc., Dallas, TX
Hugley, Jeanne .... (318) 527-7075
PROD MGR
Southwest Daily News, Sulphur, LA
News Leader Inc.
Huguley, Dick .... (404) 526-5151
VP-Circulation
Atlanta Journal-Constitution, Atlanta, GA
Huisgenga, Glo .... (712) 273-5681
GM, Chronicle, Early, IA
Huisman, Arvid E .... (515) 782-2141
PUB, Creston News-Advertiser, Creston, IA
Huizenga, Sharon .... (605) 337-3101
GM, Platte Enterprise, Platte, SD
Hule, Anna .... (505) 425-6796
ADV MGR, Las Vegas Optic, Las Vegas, NM
Hulin, Belinda .... (904) 359-4111
Food ED
Florida Times-Union, Jacksonville, FL
Hulin, Kelly .... (206) 339-3000
MGR-MKTG, Herald, Everett, WA
Hull, Bert .... (913) 542-2747
PUB, Eudora News, Eudora, KS
Hull, Fred .... (203) 574-3636
ADV DIR-MKTG, Waterbury Republican-American, Waterbury, CT
Hull, Jim .... (419) 592-5055
ADV MGR-NTL
Northwest Signal, Napoleon, OH
Hull, Kathy Lee .... (757) 898-7225
ED, Poquoson Post, Yorktown, VA
Hull, Lisa .... (501) 751-6200
ADV MGR-NTL/Co-op, Morning News of Northwest Arkansas, Springdale, AR
Hull, Mark .... (408) 920-5000
Online ED
San Jose Mercury News, San Jose, CA
Hull, Robert .... (705) 472-3200
PUB, COL, Nugget, North Bay, ON
Hull, Vickie .... (913) 542-2747
ED, Eudora News, Eudora, KS
Hullette, Ed .... (608) 356-4808
PROD MGR-COMP, News-Republic/South Central Wisconsin News, Baraboo, WI
Hulme, Etta .... (817) 390-7400
Cartoonist
Fort Worth Star-Telegram, Fort Worth, TX
Hulse, Loretto .... (509) 582-1500
Food ED, Tri-City Herald, Tri-Cities, WA
Hulsen, Ron .... (516) 843-2020
PROD MGR-Planning & Analysis
Newsday, Melville, NY
Hulstein, Bob .... (712) 737-4266
GM, Sioux County Capital-Democrat, Orange City, IA
Hultberg, Peter .... (212) 293-8500
Customer SRV MGR, United Feature Syndicate, Newspaper Enterprise Association, New York, NY
Hultgren, Randal .... (218) 281-2730
PUB/GM, Daily Times, Crookston, MN
Hultman, Mark .... (502) 443-1771
Health/Medical ED, News ED
Paducah Sun, Paducah, KY
Humbert, Mark .... (970) 669-5050
City ED
Loveland Daily Reporter-Herald, Loveland, CO
Humbert, Steve .... (910) 739-4322
Photo DEPT MGR
Robesonian, Lumberton, NC
Humble, Loretta .... (903) 489-0531
PUB, Malakoff News, Malakoff, TX
Humble, Rhonda .... (913) 856-7615
PUB, Spring Hill New Era, Gardner, KS
Hume, Bill .... (505) 823-7777
EPE
Albuquerque Journal, Albuquerque, NM
Hume, Brian .... (815) 756-4841
PROD FRM-Press
Daily Chronicle, De Kalb, IL
Hume, Fran .... (919) 638-8101
BUS ED, Sun-Journal, New Bern, NC
Hume III, John E N .... (518) 374-4141
PRES, PUB, MGR-EDU SRV, Outdoors ED
Daily Gazette, Schenectady, NY
Hume, Steve .... (604) 732-2111
COL, Vancouver Sun, Vancouver, BC
Hume, William S .... (518) 374-4141
SEC, Daily Gazette, Schenectady, NY
Humenik, John .... (513) 721-2700
Graphics ED
Cincinnati Enquirer, Cincinnati, OH
Humes, Jane .... (609) 845-3300
Radio/Television ED, Religion ED
Gloucester County Times, Woodbury, NJ
Huminski, Robert F .... (802) 222-5281
PUB, ED, Journal Opinion, Bradford, VT
Hummel, Jack .... (609) 451-1000
Wire ED
Bridgeton Evening News, Bridgeton, NJ
Hummel, Keith .... (304) 233-0100
PROD FRM-PR, Intelligencer/Wheeling News-Register, Wheeling, WV
Hummel, Susan .... (770) 963-9205
ADV MGR
Gwinnett Daily Post, Lawrenceville, GA
Hummell, Joseph A .... (212) 837-7000
EDL SYS MGR, Journal of Commerce & Commercial, New York, NY
Humphrey, Anne .... (508) 997-7411
Amusements ED, Fashion ED
Standard Times, New Bedford, MA
Humphrey, Betty .... (713) 232-3737
Fashion/Style ED, Living/Lifestyle ED, Travel ED, Women's ED, Herald-Coaster, Rosenberg, TX
Humphrey, Dave .... (508) 997-7411
MAN ED-News
Standard Times, New Bedford, MA
Humphrey, Les .... (904) 434-6963
PUB, Pensacola Voice, Pensacola, FL
Humphrey, Margaret .... (219) 874-7211
Consumer Interest ED, Food ED, Lifestyle ED
News Dispatch, Michigan City, IN
Humphrey, Russ .... (310) 540-5511
CIRC MGR-Distribution/Transportation
Daily Breeze, Torrance, CA
Humphrey, Vern .... (209) 578-2000
CIRC MGR-Fleet SRV
Modesto Bee, Modesto, CA
Humphreys, Charles .... (318) 487-6397
PROD SUPT-PR
Alexandria Daily Town Talk, Alexandria, LA
Humphreys, Cindy .... (618) 529-5454
Environmental ED, Health/Medical ED
Southern Illinoisan, Carbondale, IL
Humphreys, David .... (715) 842-2101
Photo DEPT MGR
Wausau Daily Herald, Wausau, WI
Humphreys, Tami .... (402) 462-2131
Wire ED, Hastings Tribune, Hastings, NE
Humphries, Dan .... (503) 281-1191
GM, Catholic Sentinel, Portland, OR
Hundley, R B .... (540) 483-5113
PUB, Franklin News-Post, Rocky Mount, VA
Huneke Jr, Robert J .... (314) 261-5555
PUB, Community News, St. Louis, MO
Hungerford, Steven E .... (308) 632-0670
PUB/VP, Star-Herald, Scottsbluff, NE
Hunhoff, Brian .... (605) 665-0484
PUB, ED
Missouri Valley Observer, Yankton, SD
Hunhoff, Randal .... (800) 833-4050
PUB, ED
La Villa News, Hot Springs Village, AR
Hunke, David L .... (513) 721-2700
ADV VP, Cincinnati Enquirer, Cincinnati, OH
Hunke, Lowell E .... (701) 223-2500
DP MGR, PROD MGR-SYS/Computers
Bismarck Tribune, Bismarck, ND
Hunkele, Michele .... (414) 224-2000
ADV MGR-CLASS
Milwaukee Journal Sentinel, Milwaukee, WI
Hunnell, Carl .... (937) 328-0300
Action Line ED, BUS ED, City ED, EDU ED, Features ED, Political ED, SCI/Technology ED
Springfield News-Sun, Springfield, OH
Hunnicutt, Ken .... (509) 663-5161
GM, Wenatchee World, Wenatchee, WA
Hunnicutt, Melvin .... (706) 291-6397
PROD DIR, Rome News-Tribune, Rome, GA
Hunsberger, William W .... (513) 721-2700
VP-Circulation, CIRC VP
Cincinnati Enquirer, Cincinnati, OH
Hunt, Alan .... (805) 736-2313
Sports ED, Lompoc Record, Lompoc, CA
Hunt, Albert R .... (212) 416-2000
EX ED-D.C.
Wall Street Journal, New York, NY
Hunt, April .... (616) 222-5400
Sunday ED
Grand Rapids Press, Grand Rapids, MI
Hunt, Bernard .... (305) 294-6641
ED, Key West Citizen, Key West, FL
Hunt, Brian .... (410) 289-6834
PUB
Maryland Beachcomber, Ocean City, MD
Hunt, Bud .... (573) 888-4505
PUB, MGR-MKTG/PROM, ADTX MGR
Daily Dunklin Democrat, Kennett, MO
Hunt, Charles R .... (507) 247-5502
PUB, ED, Tyler Tribute, Tyler, MN
Hunt, Chris .... (719) 539-6691
ED, Mountain Guide, Salida, CO
Hunt, Cortland .... (914) 454-2000
PROD DIR
Poughkeepsie Journal, Poughkeepsie, NY
Hunt, Dolores .... (201) 646-4000
CIRC MGR-Product SRV/Consumer Relations
Record, Hackensack, NJ
Hunt, Don .... (864) 878-2453
GM, Pickens Sentinel, Pickens, SC
Hunt, Donita .... (616) 857-2570
ED, Commercial Record, Saugatuck, MI
Hunt, Doug .... (765) 362-1200
EDU ED, Journal Review, Crawfordsville, IN
Hunt, George W .... (212) 581-4640
ED, America, New York, NY
Hunt, Gregory D .... (908) 775-0007
PUB, ED, Ocean Grove & Neptune Times, Ocean Grove, NJ
Hunt, Jack .... (419) 223-1010
PROD OPER SUPV-Press
Lima News, Lima, OH
Hunt, James D .... (814) 643-4040
ED, Automotive ED, EPE, Political ED, Wire ED, Daily News, Huntingdon, PA
Hunt, Jill .... (405) 255-5354
ADV MGR, DIR-MKTG/PROM
Duncan Banner, Duncan, OK
Hunt, Jon .... (904) 359-4111
ASSOC ED
Florida Times-Union, Jacksonville, FL
Hunt, Judy .... (541) 935-1882
ED, West-Lane News, Veneta, OR
Hunt, Pamela J .... (507) 247-5502
GM, Tyler Tribute, Tyler, MN
Hunt, Richard .... (810) 541-3000
Photo DEPT MGR
Daily Tribune, Royal Oak, MI
Hunt, Richard .... (402) 444-1000
MGR MKTG/RES
Omaha World-Herald, Omaha, NE
Hunt, Scot .... (209) 582-0471
Medical ED
Hanford Sentinel, Hanford, CA
Hunt, Susan .... (407) 420-5000
PROD MGR, Orlando Sentinel, Orlando, FL
Hunt, Tim .... (510) 734-8600
ASSOC PUB
Tri-Valley Herald, Pleasanton, CA
Hunt, Tracy .... (317) 462-5528
PROD MGR-Pre Press
Daily Reporter, Greenfield, IN
Hunt, Val .... (403) 532-1110
CIRC MGR
Daily Herald-Tribune, Grande Prairie, AB
Hunter, Betty .... (317) 473-6641
DP MGR, Peru Tribune, Peru, IN
Hunter, Beverly .... (605) 256-4555
VP/SEC, Madison Daily Leader, Madison, SD
Hunter, Bruce .... (203) 625-4400
City ED, Greenwich Time, Greenwich, CT
Hunter, Carol .... (908) 722-8800
ED, Courier-News, Bridgewater, NJ
Hunter, Chris .... (415) 359-6666
PUB, ED, Pacifica Tribune, Pacifica, CA
Hunter, David .... (904) 252-1511
Special Sections ED, Daytona Beach News-Journal, Daytona Beach, FL
Hunter, Ethel .... (919) 492-4001
Society ED
Henderson Daily Dispatch, Henderson, NC
Hunter, Fred .... (312) 222-3232
CIRC DIR-NTL
Chicago Tribune, Chicago, IL
Hunter, James .... (614) 461-5000
Librarian, MGR-INFO SRV
Columbus Dispatch, Columbus, OH
Hunter, Jeff .... (801) 752-2121
Sports ED, Herald Journal, Logan, UT
Hunter, Joan .... (814) 532-5199
PSL MGR, Tribune-Democrat, Johnstown, PA
Hunter, Jon M .... (605) 256-4555
PRES/TREAS, PUB/PA, GM, EDL Writer
Madison Daily Leader, Madison, SD
Hunter, Kathy .... (206) 464-2111
PROD MGR-COMP
Seattle Times, Seattle, WA
Hunter, Neale .... (352) 563-6363
PROM Team Leader
Citrus County Chronicle, Crystal River, FL
Hunter, Pete .... (423) 756-6900
Art ED, EDL Art DIR
Chattanooga Free Press, Chattanooga, TN
Hunter, Renee .... (501) 673-8533
ED, Stuttgart Daily Leader, Stuttgart, AR
Hunter, Robert .... (541) 776-4411
ED, Mail Tribune, Medford, OR
Hunter, Ross .... (403) 372-3608
GM, ED, Bashaw Star, Bashaw, AB
Hunter, Scott .... (509) 633-1350
PUB, Star, Grand Coulee, WA
Hunter, Scott B .... (803) 648-2311
PRES/PUB, ED, Aiken Standard, Aiken, SC
Hunter, Tony .... (312) 222-3232
CIRC MGR-North MET
Chicago Tribune, Chicago, IL
Hunter, William A .... (802) 228-8817
PUB, Black River Tribune, Ludlow, VT
Hunter, William R .... (503) 665-2181
PUB, Gresham Outlook, Gresham, OR
Huntington, Rebecca .... (208) 743-9411
EDU ED, Morning Tribune, Lewiston, ID
Huntley, Steven .... (312) 321-3000
ASST MAN ED-MET
Chicago Sun-Times, Chicago, IL
Huntley, Theodore G .... (607) 798-1234
PROD MGR-Distribution Center
Press & Sun Bulletin, Binghamton, NY
Hunton, Kaye .... (501) 442-1777
ADV MGR
Northwest Arkansas Times, Fayetteville, AR
Huntoon, Sally .... (515) 981-0406
ED, North Warren Town and County News, Norwalk, IA
Huntzinger, Roger .... (317) 284-2528
GM, Advertiser, Muncie, IN
Huot, Elaine .... (914) 694-9300
DIR-BUS Development, Reporter Dispatch, White Plains, NY, Gannett Co. Inc.
Huot, Mike .... (914) 694-9300
VP/DIR-Circulation, Reporter Dispatch, White Plains, NY, Gannett Co. Inc.
Hupp, James .... (412) 775-3200
CIRC MGR-Single Copy Sales
Beaver County Times, Beaver, PA
Hupp, Karen .... (401) 722-4000
MAN ED, Times, Pawtucket, RI
Hurd, Don L .... (219) 583-5121
PUB, Herald Journal, Monticello, IN
Hurd, Hatcher .... (770) 442-3278
ED, Revue & News, Alpharetta, GA
Hurd-Lof, Lu Ann .... (218) 732-9242
ED
Park Rapids Enterprise, Park Rapids, MN
Hurdle, Jon .... (212) 509-4444
London BU Chief
Market News Service, New York, NY

Copyright ©1997 by the Editor & Publisher Co.

111-Who's Where **Ing**

Hurford, Noel E .... (618) 287-2361
PUB, ED, Hardin County Independent, Elizabethtown, IL
Hurlbert, Dave .... (602) 258-7026
ED, Arizona Capitol Times, Phoenix, AZ
Hurlburt, Roger .... (954) 356-4000
Arts COL, Sun-Sentinel, Fort Lauderdale, FL
Hurless, Robin W .... (307) 266-0500
PUB, Star-Tribune, Casper, WY
Hurley, Charles E .... (770) 382-4545
VP, PUB, ED
Daily Tribune News, Cartersville, GA
Hurley, Garth .... (902) 629-6000
Sports ED
Charlottetown Guardian, Charlottetown, PEI
Hurley, Gordon P .... (704) 633-8950
PRES, Salisbury Post, Salisbury, NC
Hurley, Isabel .... (419) 342-4276
News ED, Daily Globe, Shelby, OH
Hurley III, J F .... (704) 633-8950
BC, SEC/TREAS, PUB
Salisbury Post, Salisbury, NC
Hurley, Paul .... (209) 734-5821
EPE, Visalia Times-Delta, Visalia, CA
Hurley, Sandra G .... (304) 235-4242
PRES, PUB
Williamson Daily News, Williamson, WV
Hurrle, Larry .... (541) 889-5387
ED, Graphics ED/Art DIR, News ED
Argus Observer, Ontario, OR
Hurst, Ann .... (408) 920-5000
Deputy MAN ED-Newsroom Innovation
San Jose Mercury News, San Jose, CA
Hurst, J T .... (606) 248-1010
PUB, PROD DIR
Daily News, Middlesboro, KY
Hurst, Jack .... (312) 222-3232
Music Critic-Country
Chicago Tribune, Chicago, IL
Hurst, Jeff .... (519) 651-2390
ED, Cambridge Times, Cambridge, ON
Hurst, Leslie .... (941) 335-0200
DIR-Market Development
News-Press, Fort Myers, FL
Hurst, Mary .... (318) 255-4353
GM-CR, DP MGR
Ruston Daily Leader, Ruston, LA
Hurst, Mary .... (904) 261-3696
MAN ED, New-Leader, Fernandina Beach, FL
Hurst, Rose Ann .... (304) 624-6411
Society ED-Telegraph, Clarksburg Exponent/ Telegram, Clarksburg, WV
Hurst, T C .... (903) 872-3931
ADV DIR, Corsicana Daily Sun, Corsicana, TX
Hurwitt, Robert .... (415) 777-2424
Theater Critic
San Francisco Examiner, San Francisco, CA
Hurwitz, David N .... (609) 895-2600
PRES
Goodson Newspaper Group, Lawrenceville, NJ
Husar, John .... (312) 222-3232
COL, Chicago Tribune, Chicago, IL
Huse, Jerry .... (402) 371-1020
PRES, PUB, Norfolk Daily News, Norfolk, NE
Huse Jr, W H .... (402) 371-1020
VP, GM, Norfolk Daily News, Norfolk, NE
Husers, Stephanie .... (504) 343-2540
GM, West Side Journal, Port Allen, LA
Husfeldt, Lee .... (630) 232-9222
MAN ED, Kane County Chronicle, Geneva, IL
Husman, John R .... (419) 245-6000
MGR-Human Resources, Blade, Toledo, OH
Huson, Kim .... (905) 765-4441
ED, Grand River Sachem, Caledonia, ON
Hussar, John .... (619) 322-8889
RE ED, Desert Sun, Palm Springs, CA
Hussein, Iman M A .... (313) 868-2266
PUB, ED
American-Arab Message, Detroit, MI
Hussey, Victor W .... (317) 664-5111
PUB, Chronicle-Tribune, Marion, IN
Hussey, Yvonne .... (408) 920-5000
DIR-FIN
San Jose Mercury News, San Jose, CA
Hussie, Andrew .... (215) 675-3430
ED, Willow Grove Guide, Fort Washington, PA
Hussman, Gary .... (307) 266-0500
ADV DIR, Star-Tribune, Casper, WY
Hussman Jr, Walter E .... (501) 378-3400
PRES/CEO
Wehco Media Inc., Little Rock, AR
Hussmann, Peter .... (515) 792-3121
ED, EDL Writer, Picture ED
Newton Daily News, Newton, IA
Hust, Charles .... (502) 667-2068
GM, MAN ED
Journal Enterprise, Providence, KY
Hust, Edd .... (502) 667-2068
PUB, Journal Enterprise, Providence, KY
Huston, John .... (360) 452-2345
ADV DIR
Peninsula Daily News, Port Angeles, WA
Hutchens, Hal .... (915) 693-2873
ED, Rankin News, Rankin, TX
Hutchens, Katie .... (915) 693-2873
PUB, Rankin News, Rankin, TX
Hutchens, Mike .... (901) 885-0744
Sports ED, Daily Messenger, Union City, TN
Hutcherson, Jackie .... (914) 454-2000
ASST Features ED
Poughkeepsie Journal, Poughkeepsie, NY
Hutcheson, Earl .... (812) 446-2216
CIRC DIR, PROD MGR
Brazil Times, Brazil, IN
Hutcheson III, J S .... (502) 365-5588
PUB, ED, Times Leader, Princeton, KY
Hutcheson, Ron .... (817) 390-7400
BU Chief-Washington
Fort Worth Star-Telegram, Fort Worth, TX
Hutching, Shawnie .... (709) 535-6910
GM, Pilot, Lewisporte, NF
Hutchings, Mary .... (610) 444-6590
MAN ED, Kennett Paper, Kennett Square, PA
Hutchings, Rhonda .... (918) 456-8833
Food ED, Daily Press, Tahlequah, OK
Hutchins, David N .... (804) 732-3456
PROD MGR-PR
Progress-Index, Petersburg, VA
Hutchins, Lee .... (904) 829-6562
CIRC DIR
St. Augustine Record, St. Augustine, FL
Hutchinson, Cam .... (306) 652-9200
MAN ED, StarPhoenix, Saskatoon, SK
Hutchinson, Faye V .... (517) 752-7171
CONT, Saginaw News, Saginaw, MI
Hutchinson, John .... (816) 826-1000
MAN ED, Sedalia Democrat, Sedalia, MO
Hutchinson, Joseph .... (410) 332-6000
ASST MAN ED-Graphics, Sun, Baltimore, MD
Hutchinson, Linda .... (412) 684-5200
CIRC MGR
Valley Independent, Monessen, PA
Hutchinson, Turner .... (615) 259-8800
Chief Photographer
Nashville Banner, Nashville, TN
Hutchison, A C .... (802) 479-0191
MAN ED, Times Argus, Barre, VT
Hutchison, Edward .... (517) 631-2333
Author/Owner
From the Ground Up, Midland, MI
Hutchison, James .... (903) 586-2236
ADV MGR
Jacksonville Daily Progress, Jacksonville, TX
Hutchison, Jim .... (705) 472-3200
COL, North Bay Nugget, North Bay, ON
Hutchison, John .... (406) 759-5355
GM, Liberty County Times, Chester, MT
Hutchison, Patricia .... (403) 429-5400
VP-MKTG, Edmonton Journal, Edmonton, AB
Hutchison, Ron .... (304) 348-5140
COL, Television
Charleston Daily Mail, Charleston, WV
Hutley, Trip .... (423) 756-6900
ADV MGR-RT
Chattanooga Free Press, Chattanooga, TN
Hutner, Gary .... (909) 659-2145
PUB, ED, Idyllwild Town Crier, Idyllwild, CA
Hutson, Ronald .... (617) 929-2000
RE ED, Boston Globe, Boston, MA
Hutson, Thomas E .... (309) 833-2114
GM, ED, Macomb Journal, Macomb, IL
Hutter, Janet .... (319) 283-2144
MGR-CR, Librarian, Register, Oelwein, IA
Hutton, Brian .... (417) 623-3480
Amusements ED, Films ED
Joplin Globe, Joplin, MO
Hutton, Carole Leigh .... (313) 222-6400
MAN ED, Detroit Free Press, Detroit, MI
Hutton, Diana .... (905) 523-5800
ED
Hamilton Mountain News, Stoney Creek, ON
Hutton, Patty .... (410) 398-3311
PROD MGR-Printing, Cecil Whig, Elkton, MD
Hutzell, Rick .... (410) 268-5000
BUS/FIN ED, Capital, Annapolis, MD
Huus, William .... (718) 981-1234
MAN ED, Production ED
Staten Island Advance, Staten Island, NY
Huxley, Fred .... (519) 759-5550
PUB, Brant News, Brantford, ON
Huyett, David H .... (610) 371-5000
PROD SUPT-COMP
Reading Times/Eagle, Reading, PA
Huysman, Frederick .... (412) 263-1100
ASST MAN ED-Sports
Pittsburgh Post-Gazette, Pittsburgh, PA
Hvalek, Beth .... (812) 446-2216
Women's ED, Brazil Times, Brazil, IN
Hvezdos, Mike .... (903) 757-3311
Action Line ED, EPE, EDL Writer
Longview News-Journal, Longview, TX
Hvidsten, J Peter .... (905) 985-7383
PUB
Port Perry Weekend Star, Port Perry, ON
Hvidston III, Colburn .... (701) 253-7311
Photo DEPT MGR, Picture ED
Forum, Fargo, ND
Hyatt, Beenea .... (423) 837-6312
MAN ED
South Pittsburg Hustler, South Pittsburg, TN
Hyatt, Daniel R .... (719) 384-8121
PUB, Arkansas Valley Journal, La Junta, CO
Hyatt, David .... (914) 331-5000
PROD MGR-SYS
Daily Freeman, Kingston, NY
Hyatt, Mary .... (212) 529-2255
MGR, Downtown, New York, NY
Hyatt, Steven .... (302) 324-2500
DIR-Human Resources
News Journal, Wilmington, DE
Hyde, Dave .... (954) 356-4000
COL, Sun-Sentinel, Fort Lauderdale, FL
Hyde, Paul .... (864) 224-4321
EPE, Independent-Mail, Anderson, SC
Hyde, Peter .... (860) 449-3514
ED, Dolphin, Groton, CT
Hyde, Richard .... (419) 562-3333
PROD FRM-Pre Press
Telegraph-Forum, Bucyrus, OH
Hyde, Rodney .... (541) 926-2211
PROD FRM-PR/Safety CNR
Albany Democrat-Herald, Albany, OR
Hyde, Rollie .... (806) 296-1300
PUB, Plainview Daily Herald, Plainview, TX
Hyde, Tabitha .... (573) 888-4505
Bookkeeper
Daily Dunklin Democrat, Kennett, MO
Hyde, Tom .... (360) 289-2441
ED, North Coast News, Ocean Shores, WA
Hydomako, Marvin .... (306) 652-9200
DP MGR, PROD MGR-Systems
StarPhoenix, Saskatoon, SK
Hyland, Mary Pat .... (607) 757-0753
MAN ED, Valley News, Endwell, NY
Hyland, Patrick .... (216) 696-6525
ED
Catholic Universe Bulletin, Cleveland, OH
Hyland-Savage, Gail .... (213) 237-5000
ADV Recruitment Sales MGR
Los Angeles Times, Los Angeles, CA
Hyman, Ann .... (904) 359-4111
Books ED
Florida Times-Union, Jacksonville, FL
Hyman, Debbie .... (573) 346-2132
CIRC MGR, Lake Sun Leader
Camdenton, MO
Hynds, Tim .... (515) 573-2141
Photo ED, Messenger, Fort Dodge, IA
Hynes, Leslie .... (360) 568-4121
ED
Snohomish County Tribune, Snohomish, WA
Hynum, James B .... (405) 633-2376
PUB, ED, Eldorado Courier, Eldorado, OK
Hynum, Rick .... (601) 842-2611
Entertainment/Amusements ED, Films/ Theater ED, Northeast Mississippi Daily Journal, Tupelo, MS
Hyora, Henry C .... (508) 945-2220
PUB, ED, Cape Cod Chronicle, Chatham, MA
Hypse, Harold .... (913) 295-1111
PROD FRM-Photo/Plate (Day)
Topeka Capital-Journal, Topeka, KS
Hyska, Blaine .... (906) 774-2772
MAN ED, EPE, Entertainment/Amusements ED, Daily News, Iron Mountain, MI
Hyska, Carrie .... (906) 774-2772
ADV MGR-CLASS
Daily News, Iron Mountain, MI
Hyson, Bernadine .... (902) 893-9405
Accountant, Daily News, Truro, NS

I

Iacoboni, John .... (603) 882-2741
BUS ED, Telegraph, Nashua, NH
Iacometti, Marlene .... (702) 788-6200
DIR-MIS, Reno Gazette-Journal, Reno, NV
Iacona, Carl .... (914) 694-9300
ADTX MGR, Reporter Dispatch, White Plains, NY, Gannett Co. Inc.
Iacona, Thomas R .... (717) 264-6161
CIRC DIR, Public Opinion, Chambersburg, PA
Iacuessa, Mark .... (603) 882-2741
ADV MGR, Telegraph, Nashua, NH
Iams, David .... (215) 854-2000
COL-Society
Philadelphia Inquirer, Philadelphia, PA
Ibarguen, Alberto .... (305) 376-3535
PUB, El Nuevo Herald, Miami, FL
Icart, Melodye Hecht .... (800) 583-6056
PRES, Name Game Co. Inc., Plantation, FL
Icen, Richard .... (217) 429-5151
Opinion Writer, Herald & Review, Decatur, IL
Icenhour, David .... (704) 632-2532
ED, Taylorsville Times, Taylorsville, NC
Icenogle, Alan .... (217) 322-3321
ED, Rushville Times, Rushville, IL
Ickes, Dave .... (304) 636-2121
PROD FRM-PR, Inter-Mountain, Elkins, WV
Ickler, Glenn H .... (413) 967-3505
ED, Ware River News, Ware, MA
Iddings, John .... (619) 241-7744
MAN ED, Daily Press, Victorville, CA
Ide, Michael A .... (617) 929-2000
VP-Production, PROD VP
Boston Globe, Boston, MA
Ide, Teresa .... (901) 427-3333
ADV MGR-RT, Jackson Sun, Jackson, TN
Iezzi, Don .... (412) 523-6588
ADV MGR
Standard Observer, Greensburg, PA
Ifft, Bill .... (509) 235-6184
PUB, Cheney Free Press, Cheney, WA
Igarouen, Alberto .... (305) 350-2111
PUB/El Nuevo Herald
Miami Herald, Miami, FL
Iger, Robert A .... (212) 456-7777
PRES, ABC Inc., New York, NY
Iglesias, Jose .... (305) 350-2111
Photo ED-El Nuevo, Miami Herald, Miami, FL
Ignatiou, Michael .... (718) 626-7676
ED, Proini, Long Island City, NY
Ignatius, David .... (202) 334-6000
ASST MAN ED-FIN, BUS/FIN ED
Washington Post, Washington, DC
Igo, Michael .... (419) 281-0581
CIRC MGR
Ashland Times-Gazette, Ashland, OH
Igoe, Rev John T .... (205) 838-8305
PUB, One Voice, Birmingham, AL
Igou, Jerrod .... (507) 847-3771
ED, Jackson County Pilot, Jackson, MN
Ihejrika, Maudlyn .... (312) 321-3000
Foundation/Charities/Social SRV
Chicago Sun-Times, Chicago, IL
Ihne, Susan .... (904) 435-8500
Deputy MAN ED
Pensacola News Journal, Pensacola, FL
Ikirt, Glen A .... (814) 724-6370
DP MGR, PROD DIR
Meadville Tribune, Meadville, PA
Illman, Art .... (508) 626-3800
Photo DEPT MGR
Middlesex News, Framingham, MA
Imada, Lee .... (808) 244-3981
News ED, Maui News, Wailuku, HI
Imai, Lili .... (520) 783-3333
ADV CNR-NTL, Yuma Daily Sun, Yuma, AZ
Imai, Masaru .... (212) 603-6600
Deputy BU Chief
Kyodo News Service, New York, NY
Imbrogno, Doug .... (304) 348-5140
Amusements ED, Films/Theater ED, Living/ Lifestyle ED, Travel ED, Women's ED
Charleston Gazette, Sunday Gazette-Mail, Charleston, WV
Imel, Joe .... (502) 781-1700
Photo ED, Daily News, Bowling Green, KY
Imes Jr, Birney .... (601) 328-2424
PUB, ED
Commercial Dispatch, Columbus, MS
Imes III, Birney .... (601) 328-2424
EPE, Commercial Dispatch, Columbus, MS
Imes, Nancy M .... (601) 328-2424
COB, Commercial Dispatch, Columbus, MS
Imhof, Ralph .... (619) 299-3131
DIR-Operations
San Diego Union-Tribune, San Diego, CA
Imhoff, Joan .... (418) 752-5400
GM
Gaspe Peninsula SPEC, New Carlisle, QC
Imman, Judy .... (903) 845-2235
ED, Gladewater Mirror, Gladewater, TX
Inabinet, Paulette .... (404) 875-6572
ASST MAN ED, Atlanta Bureau, Atlanta, GA
Inabinett, Mark .... (919) 946-2144
MAN ED, City ED, News ED
Washington Daily News, Washington, NC
Inerassia, Paul .... (212) 416-2000
Exec Editor-Dow Jones News Service
Wall Street Journal, New York, NY
Infante, Esme .... (808) 525-8000
Family Reporter
Honolulu Advertiser, Honolulu, HI
Infield, Leslie .... (803) 626-8555
ADV MGR-RT, Sun News, Myrtle Beach, SC
Ingalls, Charlotte .... (603) 224-5301
ADV SUPV-CLASS Telephone
Concord Monitor, Concord, NH
Ingalls, John .... (315) 792-5000
SYS MGR, Observer-Dispatch, Utica, NY
Ingalls, Larry .... (605) 345-3356
PUB, ED, Reporter and Farmer, Webster, SD
Ingalls, Paul .... (707) 546-2020
Political ED, Press Democrat, Santa Rosa, CA
Inge, Carolyn .... (208) 263-9534
MGR-CR
Bonner County Daily Bee, Sandpoint, ID
Ingebritsen, John D .... (608) 723-2151
ED, Grant County Herald Independent, Lancaster, WI
Ingebritson, Rick .... (505) 393-2123
Sports E
Hobbs Daily News-Sun, Hobbs, NM
Ingegneri, Paul .... (520) 573-4400
ADV VP, TNI Partners dba Tucson Newspapers, Tucson, AZ

Ing Who's Where-112

Ingells, Norris ... (517) 377-1000
Environmental ED
Lansing State Journal, Lansing, MI
Ingels, J Mark ... (317) 659-4622
PUB, Times, Frankfort, IN
Ingeneri, Paul ... (520) 573-4220
ADV MGR-CLASS
Arizona Daily Star, Tucson, AZ
Ingham, Darrell ... (310) 230-3400
New York Representative, Allsport Photography USA, Pacific Palisades, CA
Ingham, Stephen S ... (423) 756-1234
VP/TREAS, GM, Times, Chattanooga, TN
Ingle, Anne ... (901) 658-3691
ED, Bolivar Bulletin-Times, Bolivar, TN
Ingle, Robert ... (609) 663-6000
EPE, Courier-Post, Cherry Hill, NJ
Ingoglia, Arthur A ... (516) 481-5487
EDL DIR, Editorial Consultant Service, West Hempstead, NY
Ingraham, Vern ... (916) 321-1000
MGR-Neighbors (Advertising)
Sacramento Bee, Sacramento, CA
Ingram, Bob ... (334) 262-1611
COL, Advertiser, Montgomery, AL
Ingram, Denise ... (301) 733-5131
ADTX MGR, Morning Herald, Hagerstown, MD
Ingram, Don ... (915) 523-2085
ED, Andrews County News, Andrews, TX
Ingram, Floyd ... (601) 494-1422
MAN ED
Daily Times Leader, West Point, MS
Ingram, Joyce ... (757) 446-2000
Deputy MAN ED-ADM/Community/Metro
Virginian-Pilot, Norfolk, VA
Ingram, Mary ... (815) 729-6161
MGR-EDU SRV, MGR-MKTG/PROM
Herald-News, Joliet, IL
Ingram, Ragan ... (334) 262-1611
Sports ED
Montgomery Advertiser, Montgomery, AL
Ingram, Ron ... (415) 777-1111
GEN Counsel
San Francisco Chronicle, San Francisco, CA
Ingram, Ruth ... (601) 961-7000
ASST MET ED, Clarion-Ledger, Jackson, MS
Ingram, Talmadge ... (919) 829-4500
CIRC MGR-State
News & Observer, Raleigh, NC
Ingrao, Charles ... (415) 777-5700
CIRC MGR-MET Home Delivery, San Francisco Newspaper Agency, San Francisco, CA
Ingrassia, Larry ... (212) 416-2000
BU Chief-London
Wall Street Journal, New York, NY
Ingrassia, Leonard M ... (717) 286-5671
ED, Daily Item, Sunbury, PA
Inks, Bill ... (815) 625-3600
BUS/FIN ED, Daily Gazette, Sterling, IL
Inman, Bradley ... (510) 658-9252
Owner, Inman News Features, Oakland, CA
Inman, Laura ... (812) 332-4401
MGR-MKTG
Herald-Times Inc, Bloomington, IN
Inman, Richard ... (817) 767-8341
BM, Wichita Falls Times Record News, Wichita Falls, TX
Inman, Tom ... (864) 298-4100
EPE, Greenville News, Greenville, SC
Innerst, P E ... (202) 636-3000
Deputy MAN ED
Washington Times, Washington, DC
Inscoe, Robin ... (905) 873-0301
ED, Georgetown Independent/Acton Free Press, Georgetown, ON
Inscore, Angela ... (816) 882-5335
ADV MGR
Boonville Daily News, Boonville, MO
Inskeep, Richard G ... (219) 461-8333
PRES, PUB, Journal Gazette, Fort Wayne, IN
Inskeep, Stephen S ... (219) 461-8333
VP-FIN, Journal Gazette, Fort Wayne, IN
Interrante, Daniel ... (609) 589-5957
MAN ED, News & World Report, Pitman, NJ
Inzer, Dennis ... (812) 944-6481
ADV MGR-New Products
Tribune/Ledger & Tribune, New Albany, IN
Iparra, Susan ... (316) 672-5511
ADV MGR-CLASS, Pratt Tribune, Pratt, KS
Ippen, Dirk ... (603) 543-3100
VP, Eagle Times, Claremont, NH
Irby, Chris ... (401) 423-3200
MAN ED, Jamestown Press, Jamestown, RI
Irby, John ... (818) 962-8811
EX ED/VP, San Gabriel Valley Tribune, West Covina, CA, MediaNews Inc.
Ireland, Barbara ... (716) 849-3434
EPE, Buffalo News, Buffalo, NY
Ireland, Corydon ... (716) 232-7100
Environmental Reporter, Rochester Democrat and Chronicle; Times-Union, Rochester, NY
Ireland, Lee ... (615) 552-1808
ADV MGR, Leaf-Chronicle, Clarksville, TN
Ireland, Marianne ... (207) 784-5411
ADV MGR-CLASS, Sun-Journal, Lewiston, ME
Ireland, Sean ... (770) 382-4545
BUS/FIN ED
Daily Tribune News, Cartersville, GA
Irish, George B ... (212) 649-2000
VP/Group EX
Hearst Newspapers, New York, NY
Iritani, Evelyn ... (213) 237-5000
Pacific Rim BUS/International Trade
Los Angeles Times, Los Angeles, CA
Irons, Kenneth ... (910) 888-3500
MAN ED
High Point Enterprise, High Point, NC
Irsik, Linda ... (316) 225-4151
ADV DIR, ADV MGR-RT, ADV MGR-MKTG, ADTX MGR
Dodge City Daily Globe, Dodge City, KS
Irvin, Rick ... (937) 382-2574
ADV DIR
Wilmington News Journal, Wilmington, OH
Irvine, Carole ... (941) 335-0200
PROD MGR-Ad SRV
News-Press, Fort Myers, FL
Irvine, Cathryn ... (213) 237-5485
PROM MGR, Los Angeles Times Syndicate, Los Angeles, CA
Irvine, Dale T ... (360) 424-3251
CIRC DIR
Skagit Valley Herald, Mount Vernon, WA
Irvine, Dennis ... (717) 265-2151
MAN ED, EPE, Travel ED
Daily Review, Towanda, PA
Irvine, Donald K ... (202) 364-4401
EX SEC, AIM (Accuracy in Media) Report, Washington, DC
Irvine, Doris ... (905) 526-3333
ADV MGR-CLASS, Spectator, Hamilton, ON
Irvine, Frances ... (915) 337-4661
BM, Odessa American, Odessa, TX
Irvine, Harry ... (941) 335-0200
PROD ENG-Plant
News-Press, Fort Myers, FL
Irvine, Reed J ... (202) 364-4401
Chairman, AIM (Accuracy in Media) Report, Washington, DC
Irving, Gordon ... (416) 441-1405
United Kingdom Journalist
Fotopress Independent News Service International (FPINS), Toronto, ON
Irwin, Anna ... (423) 981-1100
Photo ED, Daily Times, Maryville, TN
Irwin, Dan ... (412) 654-6651
ASST ED, Layout ED, News ED
New Castle News, New Castle, PA
Irwin, Deborah ... (407) 420-5000
CIRC MGR-Consumer Distribution
Orlando Sentinel, Orlando, FL
Irwin, Gloria ... (330) 996-3000
Deputy MET ED
Akron Beacon Journal, Akron, OH
Irwin, John ... (541) 926-2211
CONT, Albany Democrat-Herald, Albany, OR
Irwin, Lee ... (520) 783-3333
NTL ED, News ED
Yuma Daily Sun, Yuma, AZ
Irwin, Matt ... (501) 327-6621
Wire ED, Log Cabin Democrat, Conway, AR
Irwin, Peter ... (416) 445-6641
PRES-Southam New Media
Southam Inc., Don Mills, ON
Isaac, Ed ... (401) 274-2149
PRES
Whitegate Features Syndicate, Providence, RI
Isaacs, Bob ... (954) 356-4000
Librarian, Sun-Sentinel, Fort Lauderdale, FL
Isabel, Lonnie ... (516) 843-2020
NTL ED, Newsday, Melville, NY
Isakson, Robert ... (212) 930-8000
PROD SUPT-Mechanical
New York Post, New York, NY
Isbell, Tim ... (601) 896-2100
Photo ED, Sun Herald, Biloxi, MS
Iselin, Diane ... (212) 293-8500
DIR-Communications
United Media, New York, NY
Isely, Judy ... (215) 345-3000
ADV MGR-RT
Intelligencer/Record, Doylestown, PA
Isenberg, Ruth ... (717) 443-9131
ED, Journal-Herald, White Haven, PA
Isenberg, Seth ... (717) 443-9131
GM, Journal-Herald, White Haven, PA
Isenhart, Laura ... (541) 572-2717
PUB, ED
Myrtle Point Herald, Myrtle Point, OR
Isert, Joedy ... (904) 435-8500
EPE, Pensacola News Journal, Pensacola, FL
Isgur, David ... (860) 548-9300
MAN ED, Hartford Advocate, Hartford, CT
Isham, Richard D ... (810) 541-3000
PUB, Daily Tribune, Royal Oak, MI
Ishkanian, Ellen ... (617) 398-8000
ED, Newton Graphic, Waltham, MA
Isinger, William R ... (213) 237-5000
Senior VP-FIN
Los Angeles Times, Los Angeles, CA
Isley, Keith ... (515) 774-2137
PUB, Chariton Leader, Chariton, IA
Ismon, Ilana ... (204) 697-7000
Food ED, Winnipeg Free Press, Winnipeg, MB
Ismonde, Donn ... (716) 849-3434
COL-Local, Buffalo News, Buffalo, NY
Isom, Rebecca ... (804) 458-8511
ED, News, Hopewell, VA
Ison, Robert ... (304) 367-2500
PROD FRM-PR
Times-West Virginian, Fairmont, WV
Israelson, Consuelo ... (909) 849-4586
ED, Amusements/Books ED, Automotive/Aviation ED, COL, Sports ED
Record-Gazette, Banning, CA
Itano, Lori ... (330) 688-0088
ED, Stow Sentry, Stow, OH
Itterman, Darrell ... (403) 429-5400
ADV MGR-CLASS
Edmonton Journal, Edmonton, AB
Itughes, Trey ... (205) 755-5747
MAN ED, Clanton Advertiser, Clanton, AL
Iturri, Marilyn ... (714) 835-1234
News ED-Copy Desks
Orange County Register, Santa Ana, CA
Ivancic, Mark ... (513) 721-2700
BUS ED, Cincinnati Enquirer, Cincinnati, OH
Ivanis, Dan ... (206) 455-2222
Sports ED, Eastside Journal, Bellevue, WA
Iverson, Howard ... (508) 739-1300
ED, Danvers Herald, Danvers, MA
Iverson, Nina D ... (941) 262-3161
ASST SEC, Naples Daily News, Naples, FL
Iverson, Paul ... (512) 884-2011
Photo ED, Corpus Christi Caller-Times, Corpus Christi, TX
Ives, Kenneth ... (718) 434-8100
GM, Haiti Progres, Brooklyn, NY
Ivey, Mike ... (608) 252-6400
Environmental/Ecology ED
Capital Times, Madison, WI
Ivey, Roy ... (208) 238-3701
ED, Sho-Ban News, Fort Hall, ID
Ivins, Molly ... (817) 390-7400
COL-Political
Fort Worth Star-Telegram, Fort Worth, TX
Ivory, Bennie L ... (302) 324-2500
EX ED, News Journal, Wilmington, DE
Ivy, Carol ... (757) 898-7225
GM, By The Bay, Yorktown, VA
Ivy, Grady ... (319) 588-5611
TREAS, Telegraph Herald, Dubuque, IA
Iwasaki, Scott ... (801) 237-2188
Music ED-Pop
Deseret News, Salt Lake City, UT
Iweriebor, Obuse ... (909) 889-9666
CIRC MGR-Division
Sun, San Bernardino, CA
Izell, Booker ... (404) 526-5151
VP-Community Affairs/Work Force Diversity
Atlanta Journal-Constitution, Atlanta, GA
Izzo, Pat ... (313) 222-6400
PROD OPER DIR-Pre Press
Detroit Newspapers, Detroit, MI

J

Jablonski, Naheta ... (773) 476-4800
GM, Southwest News-Herald, Chicago, IL
Jacalone, Dan ... (517) 752-7171
Graphics ED, Saginaw News, Saginaw, MI
Jack, Cindy ... (508) 249-3535
MAN ED, Athol Daily News, Athol, MA
Jack, Dee ... (402) 444-1000
Sunday ED
Omaha World-Herald, Omaha, NE
Jacklin, Michele ... (860) 241-6200
EDL Writer, Hartford Courant, Hartford, CT
Jackman, Wallace ... (612) 827-4021
GM
Minneapolis Spokesman, Minneapolis, MN
Jackoway, Richard ... (805) 546-8208
MAN ED, New Times, San Luis Obispo, CA
Jackowiak, John ... (517) 354-3111
ADV DIR, Alpena News, Alpena, MI
Jacks, Jennifer ... (915) 673-4271
ADV MGR-CLASS
Abilene Reporter-News, Abilene, TX
Jackson, Andrea ... (709) 634-4348
PROD DIR-Art
Western Star, Corner Brook, NF
Jackson, April ... (901) 692-3506
ED, Tri-City Reporter, Dyer, TN
Jackson, Bart ... (604) 732-2111
Arts/Entertainment ED
Vancouver Sun, Vancouver, BC
Jackson, Bill D ... (812) 424-7711
PRES (Press)
Evansville Courier Co. Inc., Evansville, IN
Jackson, Bruce L ... (416) 947-2222
VP-FIN/CFO, Sun Media Corp., Toronto, ON
Jackson, Cathy ... (402) 362-4478
CIRC MGR, York News-Times, York, NE
Jackson, Charles D ... (904) 252-1511
ASST MET ED, Daytona Beach News-Journal, Daytona Beach, FL
Jackson, Chris ... (616) 222-5400
CIRC MGR-MET North
Grand Rapids Press, Grand Rapids, MI
Jackson, Christen ... (417) 451-1520
ED, BUS/ FIN ED, City/MET ED, EPE, Living/Lifestyle ED, NTL ED, News ED, Religion ED, SCI/Technology ED, Daily News, Neosho, MO
Jackson, Daniel E ... (712) 464-3188
PUB, ED, Lake City Graphic, Lake City, IA
Jackson, David R ... (616) 845-5181
PRES, PUB/GM, Daily News, Ludington, MI
Jackson, Dawn ... (573) 738-2604
MAN ED, Dunklin County Press, Senath, MO
Jackson, Debbie ... (918) 581-8300
Sunday ED, Tulsa World, Tulsa, OK
Jackson, Deborah ... (919) 419-6500
News ED, Herald-Sun, Durham, NC
Jackson, Delores A ... (606) 589-2588
GM, Tri-City News, Cumberland, KY
Jackson, Dick ... (800) 760-3100
Features ED/Orlando
Williams Syndications Inc., Holiday, FL
Jackson, Don ... (905) 957-3315
ED, West Lincoln Review, Smithville, ON
Jackson, Eddie ... (919) 829-4500
DIR-Human Resources
News & Observer, Raleigh, NC
Jackson, Elmo ... (706) 647-5414
GM, Thomaston Times, Thomaston, GA
Jackson, Frank ... (816) 565-2401
PUB, Hale Tribune, Hale, MO
Jackson, Fred ... (902) 564-5451
ED, Cape Breton Post, Sydney, NS
Jackson, Freida ... (817) 757-5757
SYS ED, Waco Tribune-Herald, Waco, TX
Jackson, Gordon ... (303) 292-5158
ED, Denver Weekly News, Denver, CO
Jackson, Grant ... (803) 771-6161
BUS/FIN ED, State, Columbia, SC
Jackson, Henry A ... (205) 463-2872
PUB, Cleburne News, Heflin, AL
Jackson, Herb ... (908) 922-6000
Online ED, Asbury Park Press, Neptune, NJ
Jackson, Hugh ... (307) 266-0500
ASST MAN ED, Star-Tribune, Casper, WY
Jackson, J W ... (505) 622-7710
VP, Roswell Daily Record, Roswell, NM
Jackson, Jay W ... (501) 745-5175
PUB, ED
Van Buren County Democrat, Clinton, AR
Jackson, Jerry ... (506) 859-4900
CIRC MGR, Times-Transcript, Moncton, NB
Jackson, Jerry ... (250) 380-5211
CIRC DIR, Times Colonist, Victoria, BC
Jackson, Jerry M ... (501) 842-3111
PUB, ED, England Democrat, England, AR
Jackson, Joan ... (408) 920-5000
Home/Garden ED
San Jose Mercury News, San Jose, CA
Jackson, John ... (415) 892-1516
ED, Novato Advance, Novato, CA
Jackson, John ... (312) 321-3000
Bulls/NBA Writer
Chicago Sun-Times, Chicago, IL
Jackson, John A ... (205) 463-2872
ED, Cleburne News, Heflin, AL
Jackson, John J ... (405) 643-2331
PUB, ED, Fort Cobb News, Fort Cobb, OK
Jackson, Joie ... (610) 740-0944
GM, East Penn Press, Allentown, PA
Jackson, Kim ... (541) 926-2211
News ED
Albany Democrat-Herald, Albany, OR
Jackson, Larry ... (409) 532-8840
GM, ED
Wharton Journal-Spectator, Wharton, TX
Jackson, Leon ... (706) 324-5526
PROD FRM-Platemaking
Columbus Ledger-Enquirer, Columbus, GA
Jackson, Letta ... (606) 986-0959
GM, Berea Citizen, Berea, KY
Jackson, Linda ... (613) 472-2431
ED, Land O'Lakes Sun, Marmora, ON
Jackson, Mabel ... (414) 736-4380
ED, Sharon Reporter, Sharon, WI
Jackson, Mailyn ... (617) 837-3500
ED, Scituate Mariner, Marshfield, MA
Jackson, Marg ... (209) 838-7043
ED, Escalon Times, Escalon, CA
Jackson, Margaret E ... (803) 537-5261
PUB, ED, Cheraw Chronicle, Cheraw, SC
Jackson, Martha ... (304) 348-5140
Religion ED
Charleston Daily Mail, Charleston, WV
Jackson, Miles ... (609) 451-1000
COL, News/Political ED
Bridgeton Evening News, Bridgeton, NJ
Jackson, Minnie R ... (205) 463-2872
GM, Cleburne News, Heflin, AL
Jackson, Naiomi ... (770) 478-5753
CIRC DIR, Clayton News/Daily, Jonesboro, GA
Jackson, Nancy ... (308) 452-3411
ED, Ravenna News, Ravenna, NE

Copyright ©1997 by the Editor & Publisher Co.

113-Who's Where **Jan**

Jackson, Neil A .... (617) 929-2000
PROD MGR-Plant (Billerica)
Boston Globe, Boston, MA
Jackson, Patrick .... (614) 452-4561
NTL ED, Political/Government ED
Times Recorder, Zanesville, OH
Jackson, Patsy .... (501) 745-5175
PUB
Van Buren County Democrat, Clinton, AR
Jackson, Paul .... (203) 789-5200
BUS/FIN ED
New Haven Register, New Haven, CT
Jackson, Philip A .... (614) 353-3101
ADV MGR-NTL, Daily Times, Portsmouth, OH
Jackson, Raymond .... (334) 792-3141
PROD MGR-PR, Dothan Eagle, Dothan, AL
Jackson, Rich .... (715) 842-2101
City ED, Wausau Daily Herald, Wausau, WI
Jackson, Richard .... (864) 223-1411
CONT, DP MGR
Index-Journal, Greenwood, SC
Jackson, Robert .... (217) 347-7151
PROD MGR, Daily News, Effingham, IL
Jackson, Robert D .... (712) 379-3313
ED, Essex Independent, Essex, IA
Jackson, Robyn .... (601) 582-4321
Religion ED
Hattiesburg American, Hattiesburg, MS
Jackson, Rosemary K .... (717) 566-3251
PUB, Sun, Hummelstown, PA
Jackson, Scott J .... (816) 882-5335
PUB, Boonville Daily News, Boonville, MO
Jackson, Steve .... (604) 732-2111
Foreign ED, Vancouver Sun, Vancouver, BC
Jackson, Teri .... (916) 533-3131
CIRC DIR
Oroville Mercury Register, Oroville, CA
Jackson, Thomas E .... (314) 340-8402
VP, Pulitzer Publishing Co., St. Louis, MO
Jackson, Tom .... (405) 353-0620
Political ED
Lawton Constitution, Lawton, OK
Jackson, Tommy .... (501) 268-8621
ED, COL, EPE, EDL Writer
Daily Citizen, Searcy, AR
Jackson, William R .... (616) 845-5181
VP, Daily News, Ludington, MI
Jackson, William S .... (717) 566-3251
ED, Sun, Hummelstown, PA
Jackson, Wister .... (704) 245-6431
EX ED, COL, EDL Writer, NTL ED, Political/Government ED, RE, State ED, Travel ED
Daily Courier, Forest City, NC
Jackson-Clause, Rebecca .... (540) 586-8612
ED, Bedford Bulletin, Bedford, VA
Jaco, Wayne .... (409) 297-6512
MAN ED, Brazorian News, Lake Jackson, TX
Jacob, Mark .... (312) 321-3000
MAN ED-Sunday
Chicago Sun-Times, Chicago, IL
Jacobi, Fredrick T (Fritz) .... (941) 335-0200
PRES, PUB, News-Press, Fort Myers, FL
Jacobitz, Jerry .... (402) 723-5861
ED, Henderson News, Henderson, NE
Jacobo, Joe .... (505) 887-5501
PROD SUPV-OPER
Current-Argus, Carlsbad, NM
Jacobs, Amy A .... (601) 833-6961
EVP, SEC/TREAS
Daily Leader, Brookhaven, MS
Jacobs, Chick .... (910) 323-4848
Features/Lifestyle ED, Travel ED
Fayetteville Observer-Times, Fayetteville, NC
Jacobs, Dori .... (406) 538-3401
ED, Lewistown News-Argus, Lewistown, MT
Jacobs, Doug .... (203) 789-5200
Sports ED
New Haven Register, New Haven, CT
Jacobs, Edwin E .... (209) 897-2993
ED, Kingsburg Recorder, Kingsburg, CA
Jacobs, Ellen B .... (602) 271-8000
MGR-RES
Phoenix Newspapers Inc., Phoenix, AZ
Jacobs, Frederic J .... (616) 948-8051
GM, Hastings Banner, Hastings, MI
Jacobs, George William .... (606) 234-1035
PUB, Cynthiana Democrat, Cynthiana, KY
Jacobs, Glenn .... (520) 333-2033
PUB, ED, MAN ED
Round Valley Paper, Eagar, AZ
Jacobs, Guy .... (505) 863-6811
Photo ED, Gallup Independent, Gallup, NM
Jacobs, H Robert .... (215) 423-1000
PUB, ED
Guide Newspapers, Philadelphia, PA
Jacobs, Jane W .... (812) 265-3641
PRES, PUB, Madison Courier, Madison, IN
Jacobs, JoAnn .... (517) 627-6085
PUB
Delta-Waverly News Herald, Grand Ledge, MI
Jacobs, Joanne .... (408) 920-5000
EDL COL
San Jose Mercury News, San Jose, CA
Jacobs, Jody .... (315) 782-1000
Books ED
Watertown Daily Times, Watertown, NY
Jacobs, Kristin .... (414) 224-2000
ADTX MGR
Milwaukee Journal Sentinel, Milwaukee, WI
Jacobs, Martha .... (515) 472-4129
Society ED, Fairfield Ledger, Fairfield, IA
Jacobs, Matt .... (316) 321-1120
Sports ED, El Dorado Times, El Dorado, KS
Jacobs, Maurice .... (802) 334-6568
Sports ED
Newport Daily Express, Newport, VT
Jacobs, Melvin F .... (616) 948-8051
PUB, Hastings Banner, Hastings, MI
Jacobs, Mike .... (701) 780-1100
VP, ED, Grand Forks Herald, Grand Forks, ND
Jacobs, Oron .... (406) 222-2000
PROD SUPT, Enterprise, Livingston, MT
Jacobs, Phil .... (810) 354-6060
ED, Detroit Jewish News, Southfield, MI
Jacobs, Rainer .... (213) 413-5500
MAN ED
California-Staats Zeitung, Los Angeles, CA
Jacobs, Ronda .... (717) 264-6161
PROD DIR
Public Opinion, Chambersburg, PA
Jacobs, Rusty .... (352) 867-4010
PROD MGR-PR
Ocala Star-Banner, Ocala, FL
Jacobs, Shery .... (501) 337-7523
CIRC MGR, Daily Record, Malvern, AR
Jacobs, Shirley .... (206) 872-6600
CIRC DIR, South County Journal, Kent, WA
Jacobs, Susan .... (562) 435-1161
Features ED, Travel ED
Press-Telegram, Long Beach, CA
Jacobs, Tom .... (201) 383-1500
Sports ED, New Jersey Herald, Newton, NJ
Jacobs, Wanda Heary .... (601) 762-1111
PUB, Mississippi Press, Pascagoula, MS
Jacobs, William O .... (601) 833-6961
PRES, PUB, BM, ED, Action Line ED (Generally Speaking), EPE
Daily Leader, Brookhaven, MS
Jacobsen, Bob .... (602) 271-8000
Sports COL, Arizona Republic, Phoenix, AZ
Jacobsen, David .... (360) 452-2345
CIRC MGR
Peninsula Daily News, Port Angeles, WA
Jacobsen, Fred .... (619) 299-3131
MGR-CR
San Diego Union-Tribune, San Diego, CA
Jacobsen, Gwen .... (701) 780-1100
MGR-Human Resources
Grand Forks Herald, Grand Forks, ND
Jacobsen, Jeff .... (913) 295-1111
MAN ED-Photo
Topeka Capital-Journal, Topeka, KS
Jacobson, Bryan .... (702) 358-8061
MAN ED, Daily Sparks Tribune, Sparks, NV
Jacobson, Carrie .... (410) 848-4400
ED, Carroll County Times, Westminster, MD
Jacobson, Gary .... (817) 461-6397
PUB, ED
Arlington Morning News, Arlington, TX
Jacobson, James E .... (205) 325-2222
ED, Birmingham News, Birmingham, AL
Jacobson, Linda .... (701) 780-1100
ADV MGR-Ad SRV/Commercial Print
Grand Forks Herald, Grand Forks, ND
Jacobson, Nancy .... (605) 256-4555
DP MGR, Madison Daily Leader, Madison, SD
Jacobson, Nancy .... (414) 723-2250
ED, Elkhorn Independent, Elkhorn, WI
Jacobson, Peter J .... (320) 243-3772
PUB, Paynesville Press, Paynesville, MN
Jacobson, Sebby .... (716) 232-7100
Special Projects ED, Rochester Democrat and Chronicle; Times-Union, Rochester, NY
Jacobus, Mary .... (719) 632-5511
DIR-Sales/MKTG
Gazette, Colorado Springs, CO
Jacoby, Dan .... (941) 262-3161
ADV MGR-MKTG & RES, Online MGR
Naples Daily News, Naples, FL
Jacoby, Dean .... (214) 977-8222
PROD ASST MGR
Dallas Morning News, Dallas, TX
Jacoby, Jayson .... (541) 523-3673
Environmental ED
Baker City Herald, Baker City, OR
Jaconia, Joe .... (609) 871-8000
PROD SUPT-PR
Burlington County Times, Willingboro, NJ
Jacovini, Ronald .... (609) 641-3100
PUB, Record Journal, Mays Landing, NJ
Jacowleff, Julie .... (212) 887-8550
PROD MGR
American Metal Market, New York, NY
Jacques, Kate .... (501) 734-1056
GM, Brinkley Argus, Brinkley, AR
Jacques, Mark .... (519) 255-5711
ADV MGR-NTL, Windsor Star, Windsor, ON
Jacques, Thomas .... (501) 734-1056
ED, Brinkley Argus, Brinkley, AR
Jadrnak, Jackie .... (505) 823-7777
Health/Medical ED
Albuquerque Journal, Albuquerque, NM
Jaeger, Gary .... (208) 377-6200
CIRC MGR-Single Copy
Idaho Statesman, Boise, ID
Jaeger, Harold J .... (605) 337-2571
PUB, ED
Charles Mix County News, Geddes, SD
Jaeger, Jan .... (319) 754-8461
MGR-Employee Relations
Hawk Eye, Burlington, IA
Jaeger, Mark .... (414) 375-5100
ED, News Graphic, Cedarburg, WI
Jaeschke, Robert .... (414) 224-2000
PROD FRM-MR
Milwaukee Journal Sentinel, Milwaukee, WI
Jaffe, Charles A .... (617) 383-9858
COL, J Features, Cohasset, MA
Jaffe, Phil .... (909) 336-3555
PUB, Mountain News & Mountaineer, Lake Arrowhead, CA
Jaffe, Rick .... (312) 321-3000
Graphics/Photo ED
Chicago Sun-Times, Chicago, IL
Jaffe, Susan Biddle .... (617) 383-9858
Syndicate MGR, J Features, Cohasset, MA
Jaffe, Vivienne .... (518) 658-2777
MAN ED, Taconic Valley Echo, Berlin, NY
Jagler, Steve .... (309) 786-6441
BUS/FIN ED, ASST MET ED
Rock Island Argus, Rock Island, IL
Jagnow, Betty H Brown .... (330) 747-1471
PRES/TREAS, PUB
Vindicator, Youngstown, OH
Jagnow, Paul C .... (330) 747-1471
MAN ED, Books/SCI ED
Vindicator, Youngstown, OH
Jahansoozi, Hormoz .... (707) 546-2020
DP MGR, PROD MGR-INFO SYS
Press Democrat, Santa Rosa, CA
Jahn, Kendra .... (319) 394-3174
ED, Mediapolis News, Mediapolis, IA
Jahn, Steven .... (414) 567-5511
PUB, Enterprise, Oconomowoc, WI
Jahnke, Fred .... (313) 994-6989
CIRC MGR
Ann Arbor News, Ann Arbor, MI
Jairell, N .... (307) 742-2176
PROD FRM-PR
Laramie Daily Boomerang, Laramie, WY
Jakle, Jeanne .... (210) 225-7411
Radio/Television ED
San Antonio Express-News, San Antonio, TX
Jaklewicz, Greg .... (915) 673-4271
Entertainment/Amusements ED, Weekend ED
Abilene Reporter-News, Abilene, TX
Jakubisyn, Joseph J .... (203) 272-5316
PUB, Cheshire Herald, Cheshire, CT
Jakubisyn, Maureen .... (203) 272-5316
GM, Cheshire Herald, Cheshire, CT
Jakubowski, Tom .... (308) 382-1000
PROD SUPT/PR
Grand Island Independent, Grand Island, NE
Jamal, Ahmad .... (404) 526-5151
CIRC MGR-Single Copy
Atlanta Journal-Constitution, Atlanta, GA
James, Alfred .... (516) 798-5100
PUB
Massapequa Post, Massapequa Park, NY
James, Bill .... (707) 425-4646
ED, Daily Republic, Fairfield, CA
James, Carolyn .... (516) 798-5100
PUB, MAN ED
Massapequa Post, Massapequa Park, NY
James, Clifford .... (619) 337-3400
PROD SUPT, PROD FRM-PR
Imperial Valley Press, El Centro, CA
James, Dolores .... (501) 965-7368
ED, Charleston Express, Charleston, AR
James, Gary .... (315) 463-8348
PRES, James, Gary, East Syracuse, NY
James, George .... (706) 549-0123
ADV MGR-SRV, Athens Daily News/Banner-Herald, Athens, GA
James, Glenn .... (405) 475-3311
PROD MGR-Packaging/Distribution
Daily Oklahoman, Oklahoma City, OK
James, Howard A .... (603) 752-1200
PRES/PUB, Berlin Reporter, Berlin, NH
James, Jesse .... (214) 977-8222
EDL Writer
Dallas Morning News, Dallas, TX
James, Jimmy .... (713) 220-7171
News ED, Houston Chronicle, Houston, TX
James, Judith V .... (603) 752-1200
Chairman, TREAS
Berlin Reporter, Berlin, NH
James, Judy .... (309) 659-2761
ED, Review, Port Byron, IL
James, Judy .... (207) 743-7011
GM, Advertiser Democrat, Norway, ME
James, Jyrl .... (330) 996-3000
VP-Human Resources/GEN Counsel
Akron Beacon Journal, Akron, OH
James, Kay .... (608) 254-8327
ED
Wisconsin Dells Events, Wisconsin Dells, WI
James, Lawrence .... (712) 279-5019
PROD FRM-Press
Sioux City Journal, Sioux City, IA
James, M L (Jess) .... (405) 273-4200
CIRC MGR
Shawnee News-Star, Shawnee, OK
James, Marty .... (707) 226-3711
Sports ED, Napa Valley Register, Napa, CA
James, Michael .... (205) 932-6271
GM, ED, Times-Record, Fayette, AL
James, Pam .... (610) 258-7171
ADV SUPV-SRV, Express-Times, Easton, PA
James, Rick .... (905) 623-3303
PUB, Bowmanville Canadian Statesman, Bowmanville, ON
James, Shirley .... (912) 233-6128
PUB, ED, Savannah Tribune, Savannah, GA
James, Terri .... (815) 673-3771
Photo DEPT MGR
Streator Times-Press, Streator, IL
James, Timothy R .... (601) 258-7532
PUB, GM
Webster Progress-Times, Eupora, MS
James, Tom .... (304) 469-3373
PUB, Fayette Tribune, Oak Hill, WV
James, Tracy .... (618) 529-5454
EDU ED
Southern Illinoisan, Carbondale, IL
James, Vickey .... (770) 532-1234
MGR-CR, Times, Gainesville, GA
James, William E .... (816) 380-3228
PUB, ED, Cass County Democrat-Missourian, Harrisonville, MO
James, William H .... (503) 630-3241
PUB, ED
Clackamas County News, Estacada, OR
James-Bosch, Murray .... (905) 433-5546
ED, Oshawa News, Courtice, ON
James-Lacey, Kristy .... (307) 362-3736
PROD FRM-COMP
Daily Rocket-Miner, Rock Springs, WY
Jameson, Barclay .... (719) 544-3520
GM, Pueblo Chieftain, Pueblo, CO
Jameson, Michael .... (608) 252-6200
VP/GM
Madison Newspapers Inc., Madison, WI
Jamieson, Brian .... (403) 235-7100
DP MGR, PROD MGR-Pre Press/INFO Technology, Calgary Herald, Calgary, AB
Jamieson, J H .... (604) 546-3121
PUB, Armstrong Advertiser, Armstrong, BC
Jamieson, Jamie .... (508) 927-2777
ED, Beverly Citizen, Beverly, MA
Jamison, Duff .... (403) 460-5500
PUB, St. Albert Gazette, St. Albert, AB
Jamison, Linda .... (207) 873-3341
CIRC MGR-OPER, Central Maine Morning Sentinel, Waterville, ME
Guy Gannett Communications
Jamrog, Joseph .... (616) 946-2000
PROD FRM-COMP
Record-Eagle, Traverse City, MI
Janacek, John E .... (512) 564-2122
PUB, ED, DeWitt County View, Yorktown, TX
Janacek, Mary .... (512) 564-2122
PUB, ED, DeWitt County View, Yorktown, TX
Jancek, Victoria .... (800) 355-9500
Media Relations, News USA Inc., Vienna, VA
Jancsura, Deb .... (216) 245-6901
ADV DIR-NTL, Morning Journal, Lorain, OH
Janecek, Karla .... (308) 645-2403
ED, Thomas County Herald, Thedford, NE
Janecek, W W .... (512) 729-1828
PUB, Herald, Rockport, TX
Janecka, Melvin .... (512) 575-1451
PROD FRM-COMP
Victoria Advocate, Victoria, TX
Janes, Melissa .... (413) 447-7311
CIRC MGR-Single Copy
Berkshire Eagle, Pittsfield, MA
Janicke, Tim .... (816) 234-4141
Photo ED
Kansas City Star, Kansas City, MO
Janiga, Jim .... (510) 208-6300
VP-Human Resources, MGR-Human Resources, Oakland Tribune, Oakland, CA
MediaNews Inc. (Alameda Newspapers)
Janisse, Daniel .... (519) 354-2000
Photo DEPT MGR, Picture ED
Chatham Daily News, Chatham, ON
Jankowski, Carol .... (519) 894-2231
Food ED, Health ED, Lifestyle ED
Record, Kitchener, ON
Jankowski, Deb .... (573) 815-1500
ADV MGR
Columbia Daily Tribune, Columbia, MO
Janner, Brian .... (409) 836-7956
CIRC MGR, Banner-Press, Brenham, TX
Janney, Cristina .... (913) 762-5000
EDU/Youth ED
Daily Union, Junction City, KS

Copyright ©1997 by the Editor & Publisher Co.

Jan Who's Where-114

Janning, Tom .... (941) 953-7755
CIRC MGR-County
Sarasota Herald-Tribune, Sarasota, FL
Janoff, James .... (201) 837-8818
PUB, Jewish Standard, Teaneck, NJ
Janos, John G .... (847) 427-4300
CIRC MGR
Daily Herald, Arlington Heights, IL
Janoski, Dave .... (717) 655-1418
ED, Sunday Dispatch, Pittston, PA
Janscura, Deb .... (216) 245-6901
ADV CNR-Co-op
Morning Journal, Lorain, OH
Jansen, Barbara .... (715) 526-2121
CONT, DP MGR
Shawano Leader, Shawano, WI
Jansen, Bart .... (410) 268-5000
City Government ED
Capital, Annapolis, MD
Jansen, Raymond A .... (213) 237-3700
VP/PUB & PRES-Newsday
Times Mirror Co., Los Angeles, CA
Jansen, Robert .... (612) 673-4000
Head Librarian
Star Tribune, Minneapolis, MN
Janssen, Anita H .... (913) 437-2935
PUB, ED, St. Marys Star, St. Marys, KS
Janssen, Mark .... (913) 776-2200
Sports ED
Manhattan Mercury, Manhattan, KS
Janssen, Roger .... (605) 997-3725
GM
Moody County Enterprise, Flandreau, SD
Jantzi, Karen .... (419) 223-1010
Night Charge ED, Lima News, Lima, OH
Janus, Bill .... (302) 324-2500
ADV MGR-CLASS
News Journal, Wilmington, DE
Janus, Bridget .... (319) 398-8211
Books ED, Librarian
Gazette, Cedar Rapids, IA
Janusonis, Michael .... (401) 277-7000
Films Writer
Providence Journal-Bulletin, Providence, RI
Januzzi, Frank .... (212) 556-1234
DIR-INFO Processing
New York Times, New York, NY
Janz, Bill .... (414) 224-2000
COL
Milwaukee Journal Sentinel, Milwaukee, WI
Janz, Tom .... (907) 283-7551
CIRC MGR, Peninsula Clarion, Kenai, AK
Janzen, Eva .... (708) 445-0700
ED, Irish American News, Oak Park, IL
Janzen, Howard .... (403) 343-2400
PUB, Red Deer Advocate, Red Deer, AB
Japp, Ron .... (409) 833-3311
Chief Photographer
Beaumont Enterprise, Beaumont, TX
Jaque, Don .... (403) 872-2784
PUB, Slave River Journal, Fort Smith, NT
Jaque, Sandra .... (403) 872-2784
PUB, MAN ED
Slave River Journal, Fort Smith, NT
Jaques, Damien .... (414) 224-2000
Drama Reporter
Milwaukee Journal Sentinel, Milwaukee, WI
Jaques, Fran .... (410) 268-5000
Religion ED, Capital, Annapolis, MD
Jaques, Michelle .... (250) 427-5333
PUB, ADV Salesperson
Daily Bulletin, Kimberley, BC
Jaquish, Jim .... (770) 382-4545
ASSOC MAN ED
Daily Tribune News, Cartersville, GA
Jaquish, Pauline .... (616) 864-3311
GM, ED, Manistee County Pioneer Press, Bear Lake, MI
Jaquith, Frank .... (712) 336-1211
ED, Spirit Lake Beacon, Spirit Lake, IA
Jaquith, William .... (603) 882-2741
CONT, Telegraph, Nashua, NH
Jarboe, Lori .... (317) 932-2222
PROD SUPT
Rushville Republican, Rushville, IN
Jarmakowski, Andrew .... (312) 283-1898
MAN ED
Dzlennik Chicagowski, Chicago, IL
Jarmusch, Ann .... (619) 299-3131
Architecture Critic
San Diego Union-Tribune, San Diego, CA
Jaroslvsky, Rich .... (212) 416-2000
MAN ED-Interactive Edition
Wall Street Journal, New York, NY
Jarrach, Robert .... (609) 989-5454
VP-Production, PROD DIR-OPER
Times, Trenton, NJ
Jarrell, Randy .... (910) 997-3111
PROD FRM-Engraving, Richmond County Daily Journal, Rockingham, NC
Jarrett, Donald .... (416) 364-3172
TREAS
Broadcast News Limited, Toronto, ON
Jarrett, Jason .... (512) 327-2990
PUB, Westlake Picayune, Austin, TX
Jarrett, Will D .... (214) 450-1717
PRES
Westward Communications Inc., Dallas, TX
Jarvi, Weikko .... (715) 394-4961
GM
Finnish-American Reporter, Superior, WI
Jarvis, Barbara .... (919) 752-6166
DIR-ADM/PSL
Daily Reflector, Greenville, NC
Jarvis, Charles .... (614) 283-4711
PUB, Herald-Star, Steubenville, OH
Jarvis, Jean M .... (213) 237-3700
VP-Investor Relations
Times Mirror Co., Los Angeles, CA
Jarvis, John .... (614) 387-0400
District ED, Marion Star, Marion, OH
Jarvis, Monique .... (860) 522-1462
ED, Inquirer Group, Hartford, CT
Jarvis, Rick .... (314) 426-2222
GM, County Star Journal East, St. Louis, MO
Jarvis, Tanya .... (219) 461-8444
PROD MGR-Press/Plate
Fort Wayne Newspapers Inc., Fort Wayne, IN
Jarzyna, Susan M .... (802) 472-6521
ED, Hardwick Gazette, Hardwick, VT
Jasek, Henry .... (512) 798-2481
ED, Lavaca County Tribune-Herald, Hallettsville, TX
Jasiek, Gary J .... (414) 367-3272
PUB
Lake Country Reporter, Hartland Lake, WI
Jasinek, Gary .... (206) 597-8742
Food ED, Living/Lifestyle ED
News Tribune, Tacoma, WA
Jasper, Jeff .... (417) 276-4211
PUB, Cedar County Republican/Stockton Journal, Stockton, MO
Jasper, Ron .... (612) 673-4000
PROD MGR-Graphics
Star Tribune, Minneapolis, MN
Jasper, Steve .... (916) 321-1000
Telecommunications Analyst
Sacramento Bee, Sacramento, CA
Jaster, Cheryl .... (817) 757-5757
CIRC MGR-Home Delivery
Waco Tribune-Herald, Waco, TX
Jastrab, Jerry .... (201) 664-2501
GM, Community Life, Westwood, NJ
Jaurigue, Tommy .... (505) 523-4581
PROD SUPT-PR
Las Cruces Sun-News, Las Cruces, NM
Jawanda, Marianne Onsrud ..... (212) 768-8228
MAN ED, Nordisk Tidende, New York, NY
Jaworowski, J Frank .... (412) 684-5200
MAN ED, Valley Independent, Monessen, PA
Jaworski, Charles .... (607) 798-1234
EX ED-Sports
Press & Sun Bulletin, Binghamton, NY
Jay Jr, Anthony J .... (202) 898-8254
CFO
United Press International, Washington, DC
Jaynes, Dwight .... (503) 221-8327
Sports COL, Oregonian, Portland, OR
Jaynes, Tim .... (573) 471-1137
Photo DEPT MGR
Standard Democrat, Sikeston, MO
Jean-Marie, Suzanne .... (819) 849-9846
PUB, ED
Le Progres de Coaticook, Coaticook, QC
Jeanice, Flo .... (504) 850-1100
PSL MGR, Courier, Houma, LA
Jeannin, Judy .... (201) 646-4000
Fashion ED, Record, Hackensack, NJ
Jedlicka, Dan .... (312) 321-3000
Auto Industry Writer
Chicago Sun-Times, Chicago, IL
Jeffcoat, Louise .... (817) 757-5757
DIR-Employee Relations
Waco Tribune-Herald, Waco, TX
Jefferies, Laverne .... (919) 492-4001
MAN ED, EPE
Henderson Daily Dispatch, Henderson, NC
Jeffers, Jay .... (817) 757-5757
Graphics ED/Art DIR
Waco Tribune-Herald, Waco, TX
Jefferson, Catherine .... (919) 492-4001
PROD FRM-COMP
Henderson Daily Dispatch, Henderson, NC
Jefferson, Roy .... (818) 962-8811
PROD MGR-PR
San Gabriel Valley Tribune, West Covina, CA
Jeffery, Estel .... (501) 378-3400
DIR-PROM
Arkansas Democrat-Gazette, Little Rock, AR
Jeffery, Mark .... (330) 841-1600
CIRC MGR-Home Delivery
Tribune Chronicle, Warren, OH
Jeffery, Michael .... (608) 356-4808
CIRC DIR, News-Republic/South Central Wisconsin News, Baraboo, WI
Jeffery, Ralph .... (864) 298-4100
News ED, Wire ED, News, Greenville, SC
Jeffrey, Donald F .... (717) 275-3235
MAN ED, Danville News, Danville, PA
Jeffreys, Mike .... (205) 232-2720
GM, News Courier, Athens, AL
Jeffreys, Raymond .... (205) 766-3434
PROD MGR-COMP, Times Daily, Florence, AL
Jeffries, C Wayne .... (209) 578-2000
MGR-Publishing SYS
Modesto Bee, Modesto, CA
Jeffries, Fran .... (502) 582-4011
Neighborhoods ED
Courier-Journal, Louisville, KY
Jeffries, Greg .... (317) 825-0581
PROD FRM-PR
Connersville News-Examiner, Connersville, IN
Jeffus, Jeff .... (409) 985-5541
PUB, Port Arthur News, Port Arthur, TX
Jekel, Tom .... (317) 598-6397
ED, Daily Ledger, Noblesville, IN
Jelenic, Robert M .... (609) 396-2200
PRES/CEO, Journal Register Co., Trenton, NJ
Jelley, Michael .... (909) 889-9666
CIRC MGR-Sales/MKTG
Sun, San Bernardino, CA
Jeneb, Lucille .... (409) 478-6412
ED, Wallis News-Review, Wallis, TX
Jenereaux, Joyce .... (313) 222-6400
ASST CONT, Detroit Newspapers, Detroit, MI
Jenison, Barbara .... (217) 465-6424
TREAS, Aviation ED
Paris Daily Beacon-News, Paris, IL
Jenison, Kevin .... (217) 465-6424
EVP/ASSOC PUB, GM, PA, Sports ED
Paris Daily Beacon-News, Paris, IL
Jenison, Ned .... (217) 465-6424
PRES, PUB, ED, News ED, Photo DEPT MGR, Paris Daily Beacon-News, Paris, IL
Jenkins, Bill .... (706) 324-5526
DIR-Electronic INFO SYS
Columbus Ledger-Enquirer, Columbus, GA
Jenkins, Bob .... (813) 893-8111
Travel ED
St. Petersburg Times, St. Petersburg, FL
Jenkins, Bruce .... (415) 777-1111
COL-Sports
San Francisco Chronicle, San Francisco, CA
Jenkins, Carolyn .... (918) 581-8300
Religion ED, Tulsa World, Tulsa, OK
Jenkins, Chris .... (517) 732-1111
ED, Gaylord Herald Times, Gaylord, MI
Jenkins, Chuck .... (814) 870-1600
CIRC DIR
Morning News/Erie Daily Times, Erie, PA
Jenkins, Earl .... (417) 745-6404
PUB, Index, Hermitage, MO
Jenkins, Eva .... (803) 329-4000
ADV MGR-NTL/Preprint
Herald, Rock Hill, SC
Jenkins, George .... (520) 294-1200
PROD SUPT, Daily Territorial, Tucson, AZ
Jenkins, Greg .... (919) 537-2505
Sports ED, Daily Herald, Roanoke Rapids, NC
Jenkins, James .... (919) 829-4500
EDL Writer, News & Observer, Raleigh, NC
Jenkins, James L .... (412) 775-3200
PROD MGR-MR/Insert
Beaver County Times, Beaver, PA
Jenkins, Jason .... (919) 946-2144
Sports ED
Washington Daily News, Washington, NC
Jenkins, Jay .... (919) 332-2123
MAN ED, News Herald, Ahoskie, NC
Jenkins, Jessica .... (803) 726-6161/6041
MAN ED, Jasper County Sun, Ridgeland, SC
Jenkins, Jim .... (712) 279-5019
News ED-Night
Sioux City Journal, Sioux City, IA
Jenkins, Joel .... (941) 463-4421
GM, Fort Myers Beach Bulletin, Fort Myers Beach, FL
Jenkins, John .... (319) 398-8211
PROD MGR-PR, PROD MGR-Processing/Packaging, Gazette, Cedar Rapids, IA
Jenkins, Judy .... (502) 827-2000
Health/Medical ED, Gleaner, Henderson, KY
Jenkins, Kathy .... (506) 452-6671
ASST MAN ED, City ED
Daily Gleaner, Fredericton, NB
Jenkins, Larry .... (416) 367-2000
PROD MGR-Platemaking
Toronto Star, Toronto, ON
Jenkins, Marshall W .... (407) 255-7300
PUB/Author
Quaylor Communications, Melbourne, FL
Jenkins, Maureen .... (312) 321-3000
Fashion, Chicago Sun-Times, Chicago, IL
Jenkins, Norma .... (937) 548-3330
ED, Early Bird, Greenville, OH
Jenkins, Patrick .... (360) 876-4414
ED
Port Orchard Independent, Port Orchard, WA
Jenkins, Phil .... (205) 236-1551
MAN ED, Anniston Star, Anniston, AL
Jenkins, Richard .... (415) 777-5700
CIRC MGR-Suburban/County, San Francisco Newspaper Agency, San Francisco, CA
Jenkins, Ron .... (502) 827-2000
ED, EPE, Gleaner, Henderson, KY
Jenkins, Sam .... (910) 227-0131
PROD DIR
Times News Publishing Co., Burlington, NC
Jenkins, Sarah .... (360) 736-3311
ED, Chronicle, Centralia, WA
Jenkins, William P .... (213) 469-2333
GM
World News Syndicate Ltd., Hollywood, CA
Jenkins Conyers, Laura .... (510) 757-2525
News ED, Ledger Dispatch, Antioch, CA
Jenkinson, Steve .... (604) 753-3277
ED, Nanaimo Times, Nanaimo, BC
Jenner, Mike .... (805) 395-7500
MAN ED
Bakersfield Californian, Bakersfield, CA
Jenney, Rob .... (419) 562-3333
CIRC MGR, Telegraph-Forum, Bucyrus, OH
Jennifer, Perry .... (601) 896-2100
ED, Keesler News, Biloxi, MS
Jennigan, Floyd .... (507) 373-1411
ED, Albert Lea Tribune, Albert Lea, MN
Jennings, Connie .... (713) 356-6397
ED, Potpourri Newspaper, Magnolia, TX
Jennings, David .... (502) 886-4444
Amusements ED
Kentucky New Era, Hopkinsville, KY
Jennings, Dennis .... (412) 981-6100
NTL ED, Herald, Sharon, PA
Jennings, Jeanne .... (202) 887-8500
Media Market MGR, Congressional Quarterly Service, Washington, DC
Jennings, Jerry .... (801) 237-2800
DIR-MIS
Newspaper Agency Corp., Salt Lake City, UT
Jennings, Jo .... (918) 663-1414
ED, Jenks Journal, Tulsa, OK
Jennings, Joe .... (954) 356-4000
South Broward ED
Sun-Sentinel, Fort Lauderdale, FL
Jennings, John .... (520) 573-4561
COL, Tucson Citizen, Tucson, AZ
Jennings, John M .... (412) 459-6100
GM, ED, Dispatch, Blairsville, PA
Jennings, Lisa .... (901) 529-2211
Food Reporter
Commercial Appeal, Memphis, TN
Jennings, Max .... (937) 225-2000
ED, Dayton Daily News, Dayton, OH
Jennings, Mike .... (502) 582-4011
EDU ED, Courier-Journal, Louisville, KY
Jennings, Ralph .... (916) 243-2424
Environmental ED
Record Searchlight, Redding, CA
Jennings, Stacy .... (912) 236-9511
MGR-MKTG SRV, ADTX MGR
Savannah Morning News, Savannah, GA
Jennings, Virginia .... (313) 222-6400
MGR-CR, Detroit Newspapers, Detroit, MI
Jensen, Andrew L .... (207) 695-3077
PUB, ED
Moosehead Messenger, Greenville, ME
Jensen, Brenda .... (808) 329-9311
BUS ED, Food ED, Home/Family ED, RE ED
West Hawaii Today, Kailua-Kona, HI
Jensen, Cheri .... (805) 259-1234
CNR-PROM, Fashion/Style ED
Signal, Santa Clarita, CA
Jensen, Chris .... (915) 546-6100
PRES, El Paso Times, El Paso, TX
Jensen, Christopher .... (216) 999-4500
Automotive ED, Plain Dealer, Cleveland, OH
Jensen, Clay .... (808) 935-6621
PROD FRM-PR
Hawaii Tribune-Herald, Hilo, HI
Jensen, Darren L .... (916) 891-1234
CIRC DIR
Chico Enterprise-Record, Chico, CA
Jensen, Hal .... (607) 849-4555
GM
Cortland Democrat Sunday, Marathon, NY
Jensen, Holger .... (303) 892-5000
International ED
Rocky Mountain News, Denver, CO
Jensen, Ian .... (604) 562-2441
CIRC DIR-Reader Sales & SRV
Prince George Citizen, Prince George, BC
Jensen, Judith .... (801) 547-9800
MAN ED, Kaysville Today, Layton, UT
Jensen, Lynda .... (605) 272-5731
MAN ED, Gary Interstate, Gary, SD
Jensen, Michael .... (307) 789-6560
PUB, Uinta County Herald, Evanston, WY
Jensen, Michael D .... (715) 597-3313
PUB, Tri-County News, Osseo, WI
Jensen, Michael L .... (573) 471-1137
PUB, Standard Democrat, Sikeston, MO
Jensen, Newell .... (703) 276-3400
CIRC GM-St Louis, USA Today, Arlington, VA

Copyright ©1997 by the Editor & Publisher Co.

115-Who's Where **Joh**

Jensen, Paul .... (319) 398-8211
Photo DEPT MGR, Picture ED
Gazette, Cedar Rapids, IA

Jensen, Randy .... (403) 328-4411
Sports ED, Lethbridge Herald, Lethbridge, AB

Jensen, Richard .... (315) 792-5000
ED, Observer-Dispatch, Utica, NY

Jensen, Robert M .... (308) 946-3081
PUB, ED
Republican-Nonpareil, Central City, NE

Jensen, Rosemary .... (414) 224-2000
Librarian
Milwaukee Journal Sentinel, Milwaukee, WI

Jensen, Teresa .... (405) 353-0620
ADTX MGR
Lawton Constitution, Lawton, OK

Jensen, Thomas L .... (801) 625-4200
PROD MGR-MR
Standard-Examiner, Ogden, UT

Jensen, Todd .... (414) 922-4600
Travel ED, Reporter, Fond du Lac, WI

Jensen, Tom .... (701) 282-2443
ED, West Fargo Pioneer, West Fargo, ND

Jensis, Annibar .... (518) 943-2100
MAN ED, Daily Mail, Catskill, NY

Jenson, Roland .... (306) 867-8262
PUB, Outlook, Outlook, SK

Jeong, Se-Yong .... (416) 537-3474
PUB, Minjoong Shinmoon, Toronto, ON

Jepsen, Irene .... (913) 483-2111
ED, Russell Record, Russell, KS

Jernick, Ruth .... (516) 298-3200
MAN ED, News-Review, Mattituck, NY

Jernigan, Floyd .... (918) 542-5533
PUB, Miami News-Record, Miami, OK

Jernigan-Glenn, Carolyn .... (404) 284-4010
PUB, ED, Champion, Decatur, GA

Jero, Nancy .... (608) 365-5521
ED, Stateline Shopping News, Beloit, WI

Jerome, Paul .... (813) 893-8111
Web PUB
St. Petersburg Times, St. Petersburg, FL

Jervay, W E .... (910) 765-5502
PUB, Wilmington Journal, Wilmington, NC

Jesmer, A .... (613) 933-3160
CIRC DIR
Standard-Freeholder, Cornwall, ON

Jessee, Glenn .... (703) 878-8000
PROD MGR-OPER
Potomac News, Woodbridge, VA

Jessee, Randy .... (757) 446-2000
DIR-SYS, Virginian-Pilot, Norfolk, VA

Jessel, Wayne .... (715) 735-6611
CIRC MGR, EagleHerald, Marinette, WI

Jessome, Shaun .... (403) 624-2591
PUB, Record-Gazette, Peace River, AB

Jesson, Kristin .... (609) 989-5454
Features ED, Times, Trenton, NJ

Jessop, Steve .... (507) 357-2233
PUB, Le Center Leader, Le Center, MN

Jesswein, Robert .... (804) 793-2311
BM, Danville Register & Bee, Danville, VA

Jester, Randy .... (812) 663-3111
PROD SUPT-PR
Greensburg Daily News, Greensburg, IN

Jestes, Chrissy .... (816) 449-2121
ED
DeKalb County Record-Herald, Maysville, MO

Jett, Jason .... (201) 877-4141
ASST MET ED, Star-Ledger, Newark, NJ

Jette, Rosemary .... (413) 663-3741
ASST MAN ED
North Adams Transcript, North Adams, MA

Jetton, Pat .... (970) 247-3504
PA/OPER MGR, ADV MGR-Class, PROD MGR
Durango Herald, Durango, CO

Jetton, Steve .... (713) 220-7171
MET ED, Houston Chronicle, Houston, TX

Jevens, Darel .... (312) 321-3000
ASST Features ED
Chicago Sun-Times, Chicago, IL

Jewell, Kirk .... (405) 475-3311
CONT, Daily Oklahoman, Oklahoma City, OK

Jewell, Steve .... (616) 429-2400
News ED, Herald-Palladium, St. Joseph, MI

Jewett, Dave .... (360) 694-3391
Books ED, Films ED, Radio/Television ED
Columbian, Vancouver, WA

Jewett, Jim .... (406) 285-3414
PUB, Three Forks Herald, Three Forks, MT

Jewett, Jo .... (406) 285-3414
ED, Three Forks Herald, Three Forks, MT

Jewett, Stephen E .... (520) 294-1200
PUB, Daily Territorial, Tucson, AZ

Jicha, Mark .... (912) 729-5231
PUB, ED, Southeast Georgian, Kingsland, GA

Jicha, Tom .... (954) 356-4000
Radio/Television ED
Sun-Sentinel, Fort Lauderdale, FL

Jiggins, Michael .... (613) 354-6641
ED, Napanee Beaver, Napanee, ON

Jimenez, D Miguel .... (714) 569-0156
ED, Excelsior, Santa Anna, CA

Jimenez, Gil .... (312) 321-3000
Housing, Chicago Sun-Times, Chicago, IL

Jimenez, Israel .... (210) 686-4343
CIRC DIR, Monitor, McAllen, TX

Jimenez, Nick .... (512) 884-2011
EPE, ADTX MGR, Corpus Christi Caller-Times, Corpus Christi, TX

Jimenez, Ramon .... (202) 667-8881
ED, Washington Hispanic, Washington, DC

Jimerson, Christy .... (316) 767-5123
CIRC MGR, Republican, Council Grove, KS

Jiminez, Roman .... (619) 229-0500
ED, Update, San Diego, CA

Jimison, Jon .... (704) 864-3291
City ED, Gaston Gazette, Gastonia, NC

Jimmar, Renita .... (205) 766-3434
ADV MGR-RT, ADTX MGR
Times Daily, Florence, AL

Jindra, Christine .... (216) 999-4500
ASST MAN ED-Features
Plain Dealer, Cleveland, OH

Jinks, George .... (318) 462-0616
GM, Beauregard Daily News, De Ridder, LA

Jobagy, Jean .... (403) 668-2063
ADV MGR, Whitehorse Star, Whitehorse, YT

Jobin, Michel .... (514) 339-1292
ED, Saint-Laurent News, Saint-Laurent, QC

Jochens, Donald .... (510) 935-2525
PROD DIR, Contra Costa Times, Walnut Creek, CA, Knight-Ridder Inc.

Jock, Lawrence J .... (412) 224-4321
PRES/PUB
Valley News Dispatch, Tarentum, PA

Jodell, Brandon .... (513) 761-1188
Senior Critic
Critic's Choice Reviews, Cincinnati, OH

Jodon, Robert .... (517) 265-5111
ED, EPE, Daily Telegram, Adrian, MI

Joenks, Laurinda .... (501) 751-6200
EDU ED, Lifestyle ED, Morning News of Northwest Arkansas, Springdale, AR

Joffe, Mark .... (212) 643-1890
PUB, Jewish Telegraphic Agency Daily News Bulletin, New York, NY

Johannes, Junita .... (970) 356-7176
ED, Voice, Kersey, CO

Johanning, Mark .... (219) 726-8141
BM, CIRC MGR
Commercial Review, Portland, IN

Johansen, Gary .... (402) 462-2131
MAN ED, Hastings Tribune, Hastings, NE

Johanson, Barry S .... (414) 893-6411
PUB, ED, Review, Plymouth, WI

Johanson, M Christine .... (414) 893-6411
PUB, ED, Review, Plymouth, WI

Johansson, Mike .... (716) 232-7100
Travel ED, Rochester Democrat and Chronicle; Times-Union, Rochester, NY

John, Frankie .... (308) 268-2205
PUB, Times-Tribune, Beaver City, NE

John, Gary .... (303) 776-2244
CIRC CORP DIR
Daily Times-Call, Longmont, CO

John, James .... (405) 622-2102
PUB, ED, Times-Democrat, Sulphur, OK

John, Jana .... (601) 961-7000
Southern Style ED
Clarion-Ledger, Jackson, MS

John, Kathy .... (405) 622-2102
GM, MAN ED
Sulphur Times-Democrat, Sulphur, OK

John, Lisa Stevens .... (316) 549-3201
ED, St. John News, St. John, KS

John, Roger .... (810) 332-8181
PROD SUPV-Building SRV
Oakland Press, Pontiac, MI

John, Ronald .... (717) 264-6161
PROD ASST DIR
Public Opinion, Chambersburg, PA

Johnansson, Kristy .... (505) 887-5501
ADV DIR, Current-Argus, Carlsbad, NM

Johnese, Karen Block .... (412) 263-1100
DIR-Community Affairs
Pittsburgh Post-Gazette, Pittsburgh, PA

Johngrass, Nancy .... (330) 424-9541
Community ED
Morning Journal, Lisbon, OH

Johns, Jennie .... (801) 674-6200
ADV DIR, Spectrum, St. George, UT

Johns, Pattie A .... (360) 466-3315
GM, MAN ED
Channel Town Press, LaConner, WA

Johns, Phil .... (619) 322-8889
DP MGR, ADTX MGR, PROD MGR-SYS/BUS
Desert Sun, Palm Springs, CA

Johns, Walter .... (713) 220-7171
ASST MAN ED
Houston Chronicle, Houston, TX

Johnsen, Rita .... (605) 225-4100
CONT
Aberdeen American News, Aberdeen, SD

Johnson, A W (Windy) .... (605) 886-6901
ADV MGR
Watertown Public Opinion, Watertown, SD

Johnson, Al .... (706) 324-5526
VP, EX ED, Ledger-Enquirer, Columbus, GA

Johnson, Alan .... (507) 373-1411
ADV MGR, Tribune, Albert Lea, MN

Johnson, Allen .... (910) 373-7000
Sports ED, News & Record, Greensboro, NC

Johnson, Andrew .... (414) 387-2211
PUB, Mayville News, Mayville, WI

Johnson, Ann .... (757) 446-2000
Librarian, Virginian-Pilot, Norfolk, VA

Johnson, Anne .... (813) 349-4949
ED, Pelican Press, Sarasota, FL

Johnson, Anne M .... (801) 394-9655
GM, Hill Top Times, Roy, UT

Johnson, Annysa Concoran .... (219) 461-8222
BUS ED, News-Sentinel, Fort Wayne, IN

Johnson, Aubrey .... (757) 247-4600
ADV MGR-CLASS
Daily Press, Newport News, VA

Johnson, Barry .... (515) 628-3882
ED, Pella Chronicle, Pella, IA

Johnson, Betsy .... (508) 222-7000
Lifestyle ED, Sun Chronicle, Attleboro, MA

Johnson, Bev .... (805) 546-8208
PUB, New Times, San Luis Obispo, CA

Johnson, Beverly .... (409) 632-6631
Society ED, Lufkin Daily News, Lufkin, TX

Johnson, Beverly .... (618) 943-2331
Food/Religion ED, Librarian/Music, Radio/Television ED, Women's ED, PROD MGR
Daily Record, Lawrenceville, IL

Johnson, Bill .... (770) 287-3798
PRES, Community Features, Oakwood, GA

Johnson, Bob .... (805) 395-7500
ASST to PRES
Bakersfield Californian, Bakersfield, CA

Johnson, Bob .... (704) 376-0496
GM, Charlotte Post, Charlotte, NC

Johnson, Bob .... (306) 272-3262
ED, Foam Lake Review, Foam Lake, SK

Johnson, Brooks .... (909) 889-9666
PRES, PUB, Sun, San Bernardino, CA

Johnson, Bruce .... (303) 892-5000
CIRC VP-Circulation
Rocky Mountain News, Denver, CO

Johnson, Bud .... (713) 526-4727
ED, Metro Weekender, Houston, TX

Johnson, C W .... (815) 987-1200
MAN ED
Rockford Register Star, Rockford, IL

Johnson, Carl A .... (306) 272-3262
PUB, Foam Lake Review, Foam Lake, SK

Johnson, Carol .... (812) 275-3355
MAN ED, City/MET ED, EPE, School ED
Times-Mail, Bedford, IN

Johnson, Carol .... (501) 623-7711
EDU ED, Teen-Age/Youth ED
Sentinel-Record, Hot Springs, AR

Johnson, Catherine C .... (315) 782-1000
VP/SEC
Johnson Newspaper Corp., Watertown, NY

Johnson, Cecil .... (817) 390-7400
EDL Writer
Fort Worth Star-Telegram, Fort Worth, TX

Johnson, Cedric .... (407) 242-3500
CIRC MGR, Florida Today, Melbourne, FL

Johnson, Charles R .... (218) 723-8000
VP, Murphy McGinnis Media, Duluth, MN

Johnson, Charley .... (812) 424-7711
DP MGR, Evansville Courier, Evansville, IN
Scripps Howard

Johnson, Cheryl .... (612) 673-4000
COL-Gossip, Star Tribune, Minneapolis, MN

Johnson, Chris .... (903) 586-2236
PROD MGR
Jacksonville Daily Progress, Jacksonville, TX

Johnson, Chris .... (334) 262-1611
MGR-PROM
Montgomery Advertiser, Montgomery, AL

Johnson, Chris .... (912) 924-2751
News ED
Americus Times-Recorder, Americus, GA

Johnson, Christopher .... (505) 268-8111
PUB, ED, Weekly Alibi, Albuquerque, NM

Johnson, Clarence .... (512) 392-2458
PROD FRM-PR
San Marcos Daily Record, San Marcos, TX

Johnson Jr, Cleveland .... (813) 896-2922
PUB, Weekly Challenger, St. Petersburg, FL

Johnson, Connie .... (503) 399-6611
MGR-CR, Statesman Journal, Salem, OR

Johnson, Curtis .... (320) 289-1323
PUB, Appleton Press, Appleton, MN

Johnson, D C .... (612) 222-5011
PROD MGR-COMP
St. Paul Pioneer Press, St. Paul, MN

Johnson, Dan .... (912) 564-2045
ED, Sylvania Telephone, Sylvania, GA

Johnson, Dan .... (709) 364-6300
ADV MGR, ADV MGR-RT Sales
Evening Telegram, St. John's, NF

Johnson, Darla .... (609) 272-7000
ADV MGR-Co-op
Press of Atlantic City, Pleasantville, NJ

Johnson, Dave .... (603) 668-4321
Sports ED-Sunday
Union Leader, Manchester, NH

Johnson, Dave .... (812) 424-7711
EX Sports ED
Evansville Courier, Evansville, IN

Johnson, David .... (208) 743-9411
COL, Lewiston Morning Tribune, Lewiston, ID

Johnson, David .... (617) 361-6500
ED, Hyde Park Tribune, Hyde Park, MA

Johnson, David .... (903) 587-3303
PUB, ED, Leonard Graphic, Leonard, TX

Johnson, David A .... (608) 754-3311
GM, Janesville Gazette, Janesville, WI

Johnson, David Asper .... (310) 822-1629
PUB, ED, Argonaut, Marina del Rey, CA

Johnson, David H .... (508) 793-9100
PROD SUPT-PR
Telegram & Gazette, Worcester, MA

Johnson, Dawn .... (612) 375-9222
MAN ED, Skyway News and Freeway News, Minneapolis, MN

Johnson, Dianna .... (815) 625-3600
Accountant, Daily Gazette, Sterling, IL

Johnson, Don .... (712) 476-2795
PUB, Rock Valley Bee, Rock Valley, IA

Johnson, Donald .... (717) 455-3636
PROD SUPT-COMP
Standard-Speaker, Hazleton, PA

Johnson, Donna .... (208) 377-6200
CIRC MGR-Customer INFO SYS
Idaho Statesman, Boise, ID

Johnson, Duane .... (573) 378-5441
ED
Versailles Leader-Statesman, Versailles, MO

Johnson, Earl .... (204) 535-2127
PUB, ED, Gazette-News, Baldur, MB

Johnson, Elaine .... (405) 224-2600
ADV MGR
Chickasha Daily Express, Chickasha, OK

Johnson, Elaine M .... (330) 833-2631
ADV MGR-NTL, ADV MGR-Co-op
Independent, Massillon, OH

Johnson, Elna .... (308) 882-4453
PUB, Imperial Republican, Imperial, NE

Johnson, Eugene D .... (612) 429-7781
PUB
White Bear Press, White Bear Lake, MN

Johnson, Eve .... (604) 732-2111
Food Writer, Vancouver Sun, Vancouver, BC

Johnson, Forrest .... (218) 834-2141
ED, Lake County News-Chronicle, Two Harbors, MN

Johnson, Foster .... (405) 765-3311
MAN ED, Ponca City News, Ponca City, OK

Johnson, Fred .... (913) 295-1111
MET ED
Topeka Capital-Journal, Topeka, KS

Johnson, Frederick H .... (212) 450-7000
VP/DIR Newspaper Relations, React, Parade Publications Inc., New York, NY

Johnson, George .... (304) 255-4400
PROD MGR-PR
Register Herald, Beckley, WV

Johnson, George Bud .... (713) 526-4727
ED, Houston Metro, Houston, TX

Johnson, Gerald D .... (507) 425-2303
PUB, ED, Fulda Free Press, Fulda, MN

Johnson, Gerald O .... (704) 376-0496
PUB, Charlotte Post, Charlotte, NC

Johnson, Glenn .... (204) 694-2022
Assignment ED
Winnipeg Sun, Winnipeg, MB

Johnson, Greg .... (502) 582-4011
Fashion/Style ED, Features ED, Living/Lifestyle ED, Scene ED, Women's ED
Courier-Journal, Louisville, KY

Johnson, Greg .... (719) 589-2553
ED, Action ED, Automotive ED, BUS/FIN ED, City/MET ED, EPE, EDU ED, Fashion/Style ED, Features/Travel ED, NTL ED, News ED, Photo ED, Political/Government ED, SCI/Technology ED, Valley Courier, Alamosa, CO

Johnson, Hank .... (706) 549-0123
COL, EPE, EDL Writer, Athens Daily News/Banner-Herald, Athens, GA

Johnson, Harold .... (352) 365-8200
ADTX MGR, Daily Commercial, Leesburg, FL

Johnson, Harold B .... (315) 782-1000
GM
Johnson Newspaper Corp., Watertown, NY

Johnson, Howard J .... (320) 346-2400
PUB, ED, Bonanza Valley Voice, Brooten, MN

Johnson, J J .... (912) 987-1823
PUB, ED, Houston Home Journal, Perry, GA

Johnson, Jack .... (918) 653-2425
PUB, ED, Heavener Ledger, Heavener, OK

Johnson, James A .... (918) 653-2425
PUB, Heavener Ledger, Heavener, OK

Joh Who's Where-116

Johnson, James A .... (512) 293-5266
ED, Herald-Times, Yoakum, TX
Johnson, Jan .... (617) 786-7000
MGR-Purchasing Communications
Patriot Ledger, Quincy, MA
Johnson, Janet .... (316) 326-3326
ED, BUS/FIN ED, EPE, Living/Lifestyle ED, News ED, Photo ED, Political/Government ED
Wellington Daily News, Wellington, KS
Johnson, Jeannie .... (903) 587-3303
PUB, ED, Leonard Graphic, Leonard, TX
Johnson, Jeff .... (520) 763-2505
ASST SEC/TREAS
Mohave Valley Daily News, Bullhead City, AZ
Johnson, Jeffrey M .... (407) 420-5000
VP/DIR-OPER, PROD DIR-OPER
Orlando Sentinel, Orlando, FL
Johnson, Jenelle .... (316) 365-2111
EDU ED, Entertainment/Amusements ED, Fashion/Style ED, Health/Medical ED, Society ED, Travel/Women's ED
Iola Register, Iola, KS
Johnson, Jerry .... (414) 372-2773
PUB, Wisconsin Light, Milwaukee, WI
Johnson, JoAnne D .... (316) 431-4100
ADV DIR, Chanute Tribune, Chanute, KS
Johnson, John .... (412) 222-2200
PROD FRM-Plate Prep
Observer-Reporter, Washington, PA
Johnson, John .... (334) 875-2110
PROD FRM-PR
Selma Times-Journal, Selma, AL
Johnson, John .... (309) 686-3000
PROD FRM-COMP, Journal Star, Peoria, IL
Johnson, John .... (916) 741-2345
Sports ED, Appeal-Democrat, Marysville, CA
Johnson, John .... (810) 727-3745
PUB, Chesterfield Review/The Review/Independent Press, Richmond, MI
Johnson, John B .... (315) 782-1000
PRES/TREAS
Johnson Newspaper Corp., Watertown, NY
Johnson Jr, John B .... (315) 782-1000
COO
Johnson Newspaper Corp., Watertown, NY
Johnson, John D .... (810) 648-4000
PUB, Sanilac County News, Sandusky, MI
Johnson, Jon .... (334) 792-3141
Sports ED, Dothan Eagle, Dothan, AL
Johnson, Joy L .... (816) 736-4111
PUB, ED, Tarkio Avalanche, Tarkio, MO
Johnson, Judith .... (617) 929-2000
PROD ASST MGR, Boston Globe, Boston, MA
Johnson, Judy .... (205) 236-1551
EDU ED, Anniston Star, Anniston, AL
Johnson, Judy .... (601) 896-2100
Local News ED, Sun Herald, Biloxi, MS
Johnson, Julie .... (518) 943-2100
DP MGR, Daily Mail, Catskill, NY
Johnson, Julie .... (541) 963-3161
BUS/FIN ED, Observer, La Grande, OR
Johnson, Karen .... (303) 750-7555
PUB, Aurora Sentinel, Aurora, CO
Johnson, Kathy .... (903) 586-2236
MGR-Office
Jacksonville Daily Progress, Jacksonville, TX
Johnson, Kathy .... (612) 222-5011
PROD CNR, St. Paul Pioneer Press, St. Paul, MN, Knight-Ridder Inc.
Johnson, Kelly .... (707) 441-0500
EDU ED, Times-Standard, Eureka, CA
Johnson, Ken .... (508) 685-1000
BUS/FIN ED
Eagle-Tribune, North Andover, MA
Johnson, Ken .... (617) 786-7000
South Edition ED
Patriot Ledger, Quincy, MA
Johnson, Kenneth P .... (214) 450-1717
COB
Westward Communications Inc., Dallas, TX
Johnson, Kent .... (414) 275-2166
ED, Times, Walworth, WI
Johnson, Kent L .... (847) 427-4300
ASST TREAS/CONT
Daily Herald, Arlington Heights, IL
Johnson, Kerry .... (901) 427-3333
ADV DIR, Jackson Sun, Jackson, TN
Johnson, Kerry .... (208) 232-4161
PROD FRM-PR
Idaho State Journal, Pocatello, ID
Johnson, Kevin .... (330) 996-3000
Music ED-Pop/Culture
Akron Beacon Journal, Akron, OH
Johnson, Kevin R .... (970) 493-6397
PROD DIR
Fort Collins Coloradoan, Fort Collins, CO
Johnson, Kim .... (402) 768-7214
PUB, ED
Hebron Journal-Register, Hebron, NE
Johnson, Kurt .... (605) 352-6401
EX ED, Huron Plainsman, Huron, SD
Johnson, LaCinda .... (805) 688-5522
GM
Santa Ynez Valley News/Extra, Solvang, CA
Johnson, Lana H .... (714) 642-4321
DIR-PROM, Daily Pilot, Costa Mesa, CA
Johnson, Lance .... (860) 442-2200
MAN ED, Day, New London, CT
Johnson, Larry W .... (501) 364-5186
PUB, Ashley News Observer, Crossett, AR
Johnson, Lawrence .... (313) 222-2300
Music Critic, Detroit News, Detroit, MI
Johnson, Leonard .... (910) 762-1337
ED, Challenger, Wilmington, NC
Johnson, Linda .... (423) 992-3392
MAN ED
Union News Leader, Maynardville, TN
Johnson, Linton .... (706) 283-8500
PUB, ED
Elbert County Examiner, Elberton, GA
Johnson, Loral .... (970) 854-2811
PUB, Holyoke Enterprise, Holyoke, CO
Johnson, Loren .... (320) 289-1323
ED, Appleton Press, Appleton, MN
Johnson, Lowell .... (414) 684-4433
ADV MGR-RT/CLASS, ADTX MGR
Herald Times Reporter, Manitowoc, WI
Johnson, Luke .... (770) 428-9411
Automotive Writer, Daily Journal, Marietta, GA
Johnson, Lynn W .... (707) 441-0500
CONT, DP MGR, Times-Standard, Eureka, CA
Johnson, Lynnda .... (801) 637-0732
ED, Sun Advocate, Price, UT
Johnson, Malcolm .... (860) 241-6200
Films/Theater Writer
Hartford Courant, Hartford, CT
Johnson, Mark .... (712) 243-2624
PROD FRM-COMP
Atlantic News-Telegraph, Atlantic, IA
Johnson, Mark .... (219) 362-2161
MAN ED, Books ED, SCI/Technology ED
La Porte Herald-Argus, La Porte, IN
Johnson, Mark I .... (904) 427-1000
ASSOC ED, Observer, New Smyrna Beach, FL
Johnson, Mary .... (812) 275-3355
Environmental ED
Times-Mail, Bedford, IN
Johnson, Mary Ann .... (540) 981-3100
Books ED, Roanoke Times, Roanoke, VA
Johnson, Mary Ellen .... (319) 398-8211
CIRC MGR-Sales, Gazette, Cedar Rapids, IA
Johnson, Matt .... (608) 822-3912
ED, Fennimore Times, Fennimore, WI
Johnson, Melinda .... (805) 564-5200
Home Furnishings ED, Lifestyle ED, Santa Barbara News-Press, Santa Barbara, CA
Johnson, Merle .... (614) 439-3531
MGR-MIS, Daily Jeffersonian, Cambridge, OH
Johnson, Metta R .... (512) 237-4655
PUB, Smithville Times, Smithville, TX
Johnson, Michael .... (207) 729-3311
PROD SYS Technician
Times Record, Brunswick, ME
Johnson, Michael .... (304) 526-4000
MAN ED, Herald-Dispatch, Huntington, WV
Johnson, Michael .... (219) 461-8222
MET ED, News-Sentinel, Fort Wayne, IN
Johnson, Michael .... (507) 553-3131
PUB, Wells Mirror, Wells, MN
Johnson, Mike .... (606) 231-3100
ASST MAN ED-Lifestyles/Sports/Newsroom Artist, Herald-Leader, Lexington, KY
Johnson, Mike .... (204) 827-2343
PUB, ED, Gazette, Glenboro, MB
Johnson, Nan .... (970) 945-8515
Special Publications ED, Online Contact
Glenwood Post, Glenwood Springs, CO
Johnson, Neil .... (317) 552-3355
ED, Elwood Call-Leader, Elwood, IN
Ray Barnes Newspapers Inc.
Johnson, Nila .... (318) 377-1866
BM, ADV MGR-CLASS
Minden Press-Herald, Minden, LA
Johnson, Pam .... (602) 271-8000
EX ED/VP-News, Arizona Republic, Phoenix, AZ, Central Newspapers Inc.
Johnson, Pam .... (501) 785-7700
CIRC MGR-Sales/PROM
Southwest Times Record, Fort Smith, AR
Johnson, Pat .... (702) 383-0211
MGR-BUS Office
Las Vegas Review-Journal, Las Vegas, NV
Johnson, Patricia .... (860) 442-2200
PROD MGR-COMP Room
Day, New London, CT
Johnson, Patricia .... (507) 483-2213
ED, Nobles County Review, Adrian, MN
Johnson, Paula .... (919) 446-5161
ADV ASST DIR, Telegram, Rocky Mount, NC
Johnson, Pearl .... (712) 476-2795
PUB, ED, Rock Valley Bee, Rock Valley, IA
Johnson, Peg .... (805) 688-5522
PUB, ED
Santa Ynez Valley News/Extra, Solvang, CA
Johnson, Penny .... (817) 427-2112
PUB, ED, Alvord Gazette, Alvord, TX
Johnson, Peter .... (513) 721-2700
MAN ED-Night
Cincinnati Enquirer, Cincinnati, OH
Johnson, Peter .... (603) 436-1800
DIR-MKTG/PROM
Portsmouth Herald, Portsmouth, NH
Johnson, Phil .... (605) 347-2503
ED, Black Hills Press, Sturgis, SD
Johnson, Phil .... (416) 947-2222
Wire ED, Toronto Sun, Toronto, ON
Johnson, Phyllis .... (423) 929-3111
BUS/FIN ED, RE ED
Johnson City Press, Johnson City, TN
Johnson, R Michael .... (614) 622-1122
ED, PROD MGR-COMP
Coshocton Tribune, Coshocton, OH
Johnson, R Michael .... (304) 788-3333
ED
Weekender-The Mountain Echo, Keyser, WV
Johnson, R William .... (219) 936-3101
PROD FRM-COMP, Pilot-News, Plymouth, IN
Johnson, Ralph .... (419) 245-6000
ASSOC ED, Blade, Toledo, OH
Johnson, Ralph .... (910) 274-6210
GM, Carolina Peacemaker, Greensboro, NC
Johnson, Ralph F .... (201) 801-0771
PUB, ED, Connection, Teaneck, NJ
Johnson, Randall .... (815) 877-4044
GM, Journal, Rockford, IL
Johnson, Randy .... (205) 549-2000
City ED, Religion ED
Gadsden Times, Gadsden, AL
Johnson, Ray .... (910) 888-3500
PROD MGR-MR
High Point Enterprise, High Point, NC
Johnson, Rebecca .... (770) 532-1234
DIR-MKTG, ADTX MGR
Times, Gainesville, GA
Johnson, Reg .... (203) 333-0161
New Haven County ED
Connecticut Post, Bridgeport, CT
Johnson, Rene .... (616) 345-3511
MGR-MKTG/PROM
Kalamazoo Gazette, Kalamazoo, MI
Johnson, Rene .... (818) 962-8811
Librarian
San Gabriel Valley Tribune, West Covina, CA
Johnson, Rheta Grimsley .... (404) 526-5151
COL
Atlanta Journal-Constitution, Atlanta, GA
Johnson, Richard .... (812) 332-4401
PROD FRM-COMP
Herald-Times Inc, Bloomington, IN
Johnson, Richard J V .... (713) 220-7171
Chairman/PUB
Houston Chronicle, Houston, TX
Johnson, Rick .... (904) 599-2100
PROD MGR-Building Services
Tallahassee Democrat, Tallahassee, FL
Johnson, Rita .... (573) 226-3335
GM, Current Wave, Eminence, MO
Johnson, Robert .... (617) 426-3000
PROD SUPT-MR, Boston Herald, Boston, MA
Johnson, Robert .... (810) 985-7171
DIR-MKTG Services
Times Herald, Port Huron, MI
Johnson, Robert .... (210) 225-7411
Weekender ED
San Antonio Express-News, San Antonio, TX
Johnson, Robert .... (906) 774-2772
PUB, Daily News, Iron Mountain, MI
Johnson, Ron .... (318) 459-3200
CONT, Times, Shreveport, LA
Johnson, Ron .... (501) 623-7711
ADV MGR-CLASS
Sentinel-Record, Hot Springs, AR
Johnson, Ruth .... (701) 436-4241
GM, Hillsboro Banner, Hillsboro, ND
Johnson, Sam .... (423) 981-1100
CIRC DIR, Daily Times, Maryville, TN
Johnson, Sandra .... (518) 891-2600
MGR-Sales, Adirondack Daily Enterprise, Saranac Lake, NY
Johnson, Scott .... (803) 771-6161
Online MGR, State, Columbia, SC
Johnson, Sean .... (816) 271-8500
Online MGR
St. Joseph News-Press, St. Joseph, MO
Johnson, Sharon M .... (918) 967-4655
ED, Stigler News-Sentinel, Stigler, OK
Johnson, Sherry .... (316) 268-6000
Kansas Roots ED, Wichita Eagle, Wichita, KS
Johnson, Sonya .... (719) 275-7565
EDU ED, Fashion/Style ED, Living/Lifestyle ED, News ED, Daily Record, Canon City, CO
Johnson, Steve .... (704) 633-8950
ADV MGR-GEN, Salisbury Post, Salisbury, NC
Johnson, Steve .... (205) 325-2222
PROD MGR-Packing/Distribution
Birmingham News, Birmingham, AL
Johnson, Steve .... (541) 776-4411
Photo ED, Mail Tribune, Medford, OR
Johnson, Steve .... (312) 222-3232
Television Critic
Chicago Tribune, Chicago, IL
Johnson, Tamara .... (501) 633-3130
MAN ED, Times-Herald, Forrest City, AR
Johnson, Tamara .... (406) 363-3300
ADV MGR, Ravalli Republic, Hamilton, MT
Johnson, Teresa .... (817) 757-5757
Brazos Living ED, Fashion/Food ED, Features ED, Waco Tribune-Herald, Waco, TX
Johnson, Thomas D .... (202) 898-8254
VP-Sales & MKTG
United Press International, Washington, DC
Johnson, Thomas H .... (714) 642-4321
PUB, Daily Pilot, Costa Mesa, CA
Johnson, Tim .... (317) 962-1575
MAN ED, Palladium-Item, Richmond, IN
Gannett Co. Inc.
Johnson, Tim .... (320) 564-2126
ED, Granite Falls-Clarkfield Advocate-Tribune, Granite Falls, MN
Johnson, Tim .... (914) 246-4985
ED, Old Dutch Post Star, Saugerties, NY
Johnson, Tim .... (770) 227-3276
PROD FRM-PR
Griffin Daily News, Griffin, GA
Johnson, Tom .... (714) 965-3030
PUB, Huntington Beach Independent, Huntington Beach, CA
Johnson, Tom .... (630) 844-5844
Automotive ED, Beacon-News, Aurora, IL
Johnson, Tom .... (319) 568-3431
PUB, Waukon Standard, Waukon, IA
Johnson, Tom .... (818) 241-4141
VP, Glendale News-Press, Glendale, CA
Johnson, Tony .... (304) 294-4144
PUB, Mullens Advocate, Mullens, WV
Johnson, Travis .... (204) 827-2343
PUB, ED, Gazette, Glenboro, MB
Johnson, W A .... (703) 344-2489
VP, Moffitt Newspapers, Roanoke, VA
Johnson, W James .... (402) 475-4200
ASST ED, Lincoln Journal Star, Lincoln, NE
Johnson, Wally .... (319) 627-2814
PUB, West Liberty Index, West Liberty, IA
Johnson, Walter .... (541) 269-1222
PROD MGR, World, Coos Bay, OR
Johnson, William .... (313) 222-2300
EDL Writer, Detroit News, Detroit, MI
Gannett Co. Inc.
Johnson, William .... (514) 987-2222
COL, Gazette, Montreal, QC
Johnson, William A .... (210) 736-4450
PRES
Daily Commercial Recorder, San Antonio, TX
Johnson, William S .... (415) 326-8210
PUB, Palo Alto Weekly, Palo Alto, CA
Johnson, William W .... (816) 736-4111
PUB, ED, Tarkio Avalanche, Tarkio, MO
Johnsred, Matt .... (319) 263-2331
CIRC MGR, Muscatine Journal, Muscatine, IA
Johnston, Al H .... (512) 575-1451
CIRC MGR, Victoria Advocate, Victoria, TX
Johnston, Betty .... (619) 728-6116
ED, Enterprise, Fallbrook, CA
Johnston, Bill .... (519) 449-5478
PUB, ED, Burford Times, Burford, ON
Johnston, Dallas K .... (219) 294-1661
CONT, DP MGR, Elkhart Truth, Elkhart, IN
Johnston, Florence .... (919) 419-6500
Religion ED, Herald-Sun, Durham, NC
Johnston, Glen .... (513) 721-2700
ADV MGR-Make-Up
Cincinnati Enquirer, Cincinnati, OH
Johnston, Grace E .... (802) 747-6121
ADV DIR, Rutland Herald, Rutland, VT
Johnston, Jackie .... (209) 734-5821
Lifestyle ED, Visalia Times-Delta, Visalia, CA
Johnston, Jeanne .... (423) 756-6900
SEC/TREAS, PA
Chattanooga Free Press, Chattanooga, TN
Johnston, Jerry .... (801) 237-2188
Books ED, Music ED-Vocal
Deseret News, Salt Lake City, UT
Johnston, Joan .... (757) 247-4600
Travel ED, Daily Press, Newport News, VA
Johnston, Ken .... (807) 852-3366
MAN ED
Rainy River Record, Rainy River, ON
Johnston, Larry .... (909) 684-1200
CIRC MGR-Single Copy
Press-Enterprise, Riverside, CA
Johnston, Lynn .... (316) 223-1460
EDU ED, Fort Scott Tribune, Fort Scott, KS
Johnston, Mark .... (864) 298-4100
ADV VP, Greenville News, Greenville, SC
Johnston, Marshall W .... (608) 754-3311
COB
Bliss Communications Inc., Janesville, WI
Johnston, Mike .... (509) 925-1414
City ED, Daily Record, Ellensburg, WA
Johnston, Patricia .... (913) 295-1111
Librarian
Topeka Capital-Journal, Topeka, KS

Copyright ©1997 by the Editor & Publisher Co.

117-Who's Where **Jon**

Johnston, Rebecca .... (770) 479-1441
MAN ED, Cherokee Tribune, Canton, GA
Johnston, Richard C .... (503) 221-8327
ASST ED, Oregonian, Portland, OR
Johnston, Richard R .... (618) 529-5454
PUB, Southern Illinoisan, Carbondale, IL
Johnston, Robert .... (801) 625-4200
CONT, Standard-Examiner, Ogden, UT
Johnston, Robert L .... (302) 573-3109
PUB, ED, Dialog, Wilmington, DE
Johnston, Roger .... (218) 741-5544
PROD FRM, Mesabi Daily News, Virginia, MN
Johnston, Susan .... (519) 756-2020
News ED, Expositor, Brantford, ON
Johnston, Virginia .... (503) 221-8327
Food ED, Oregonian, Portland, OR
Johnston, William H .... (410) 749-7171
CFO, Daily Times, Salisbury, MD
Johnston, William K .... (217) 429-5151
PUB, Herald & Review, Decatur, IL
Johnston, William R .... (908) 722-8800
CIRC DIR, Courier-News, Bridgewater, NJ
Johnstone, Bruce .... (306) 565-8211
FIN ED, Leader-Post, Regina, SK
Johnstone, Dolores .... (416) 869-4991
Sales, Toronto Star Syndicate, Toronto, ON
Johson, Jacquelin .... (416) 441-1405
North America Journalist, Fotopress Independent News Service International, Toronto, ON
Johston, Tyrone .... (614) 773-2111
Lifestyle ED
Chillicothe Gazette, Chillicothe, OH
Joiner, Melinda .... (205) 532-4000
MAN ED, Huntsville Times, Huntsville, AL
Joiner, Robert .... (314) 340-8000
EDL Writer, Post-Dispatch, St. Louis, MO
Joint, Penny .... (814) 870-1600
Librarian
Morning News/Erie Daily Times, Erie, PA
Jolicoeur, Guy .... (514) 722-7708
GM, Le Monde, Montreal, QC
Jolley, Bobby .... (704) 464-0221
PROD MGR
Observer-News-Enterprise, Newton, NC
Jolliff, Charlene .... (614) 943-2214
GM, Richwood Gazette, Richwood, OH
Jolly, Brad .... (423) 929-3111
City ED
Johnson City Press, Johnson City, TN
Jolly, Roger .... (910) 786-4141
CIRC MGR, Mount Airy News, Mount Airy, NC
Joly, John .... (206) 448-8000
DIR-Public Affairs
Seattle Post-Intelligencer, Seattle, WA
Jonaitis, Ramune .... (905) 275-4672
MAN ED, Teviskes Ziburiai, Mississauga, ON
Jonas, Christina .... (519) 621-3810
MAN ED
Cambridge Reporter, Cambridge, ON
Jonas, Victoria .... (513) 352-2000
CIRC DIR-Customer SRV
Cincinnati Post, Cincinnati, OH
Jonasson, Wes .... (416) 441-1405
Europe Journalist, Fotopress Independent News Service International, Toronto, ON
Jones, Adam .... (515) 276-0265
ED, Urbandale News, Urbandale, IA
Jones, Al .... (616) 345-3511
BUS/FIN ED, Consumer Interest ED, RE ED
Kalamazoo Gazette, Kalamazoo, MI
Jones, Al .... (601) 896-2100
Outdoors ED, Sun Herald, Biloxi, MS
Jones, Arthur .... (508) 676-8211
Lifestyle ED, Herald News, Fall River, MA
Jones, Barbara .... (818) 713-3000
ASST MAN ED
Daily News, Woodland Hills, CA
Jones, Bernie .... (619) 299-3131
Op-EPE
San Diego Union-Tribune, San Diego, CA
Jones, Bob .... (512) 658-7424
PUB, News Leader, Universal City, TX
Jones Jr, Boisfeuillit .... (202) 334-6000
PRES/GM, Washington Post, Washington, DC
Jones, Brian .... (613) 962-9171
PROD FRM-PR, Intelligencer, Belleville, ON
Jones, Bruce .... (918) 786-9002
GM, Photo ED, Grove Daily News, Grove, OK
Jones, Budd .... (915) 646-2541
Sports ED
Brownwood Bulletin, Brownwood, TX
Jones III, Carleton A .... (423) 929-3111
VP/TREAS
Carl A Jones Newspapers, Johnson City, TN
Jones, Carole .... (716) 496-5013
MAN ED, Arcade Herald, Arcade, NY
Jones, Charles .... (909) 684-1200
PROD MGR-Pre Press
Press-Enterprise, Riverside, CA
Jones, Charles E .... (217) 965-3355
PUB, Virden Recorder, Virden, IL
Jones, Cheryl .... (605) 256-4555
CIRC MGR
Madison Daily Leader, Madison, SD
Jones, Clay .... (617) 450-2000
International News ED
Christian Science Monitor, Boston, MA
Jones, Connie .... (816) 646-2411
ADV MGR-CLASS
Constitution-Tribune, Chillicothe, MO
Jones, D W .... (601) 895-6220
PUB
DeSoto County Tribune, Olive Branch, MS
Jones, Daniel .... (860) 241-6200
Environmental Writer
Hartford Courant, Hartford, CT
Jones, Daniel J .... (208) 467-9251
BM, Idaho Press-Tribune, Nampa, ID
Jones, Danny .... (901) 855-1711
ED, Herald Gazette, Trenton, TN
Jones, David .... (202) 636-3000
Foreign ED
Washington Times, Washington, DC
Jones, David .... (919) 732-2171
GM
News of Orange County, Hillsborough, NC
Jones, David R .... (212) 556-1234
ASST MAN ED, NTL Edition ED
New York Times, New York, NY
Jones, David W .... (216) 951-0000
Political ED, News-Herald, Willoughby, OH
Jones, Debra .... (912) 758-5549
MAN ED, Miller County Liberal, Colquitt, GA
Jones, Debra .... (541) 382-1811
CIRC MGR-Customer SRV
Bulletin, Bend, OR
Jones, Del .... (708) 336-7000
CIRC MGR, News-Sun, Waukegan, IL
Jones, Don F .... (713) 342-8691
VP/SEC/TREAS
Hartman Newspapers Inc., Rosenberg, TX
Jones, Donald .... (205) 362-1000
PROD FRM, Daily Home, Talladega, AL
Jones, Donna .... (408) 335-5321
ED, Valley Press, Felton, CA
Jones, Dorothy .... (217) 965-3355
PUB, Virden Recorder, Virden, IL
Jones Jr, Doward N .... (919) 793-2123
ED, Roanoke Beacon, Plymouth, NC
Jones, Durand .... (619) 322-8889
PROD MGR-COMP
Desert Sun, Palm Springs, CA
Jones, Eddie .... (615) 259-8800
ED, Nashville Banner, Nashville, TN
Jones, Edward W .... (540) 374-5000
MAN ED
Free Lance-Star, Fredericksburg, VA
Jones, Elizabeth .... (317) 348-0110
ED, News ED, News-Times, Hartford City, IN
Jones, Elvyn .... (913) 284-3300
ED, Sabetha Herald, Sabetha, KS
Jones, Emmett .... (501) 785-9404
PRES/COO
Donrey Media Group, Fort Smith, AR
Jones, Evan S .... (901) 253-6666
GM, ED, Lake County Banner, Tiptonville, TN
Jones, Floyd V .... (614) 461-5000
VP-Production
Columbus Dispatch, Columbus, OH
Jones, Frances .... (919) 527-3191
CIRC MGR, Free Press, Kinston, NC
Jones, Fred W .... (217) 324-2121
ADV DIR, News-Herald, Litchfield, IL
Jones, Gary .... (706) 485-3501
ED, Eatonton Messenger, Eatonton, GA
Jones, Gene .... (901) 427-3333
PROD MGR-Post Press
Jackson Sun, Jackson, TN
Jones, Gerald .... (573) 243-3515
PUB, Cash-Book Journal, Jackson, MO
Jones, Glenna .... (313) 439-8118
PUB, GM, MAN ED
Milan Area Leader, Milan, MI
Jones, Greg .... (219) 267-3111
Sports ED, Times-Union, Warsaw, IN
Jones, Greg .... (514) 458-5482
PUB, ED, Hudson Gazette, Hudson, QC
Jones, Gregg K .... (423) 638-4181
PRES, Media Services Group, Greeneville, TN
Jones Jr, H Carter .... (303) 776-2244
CIRC MGR-District
Daily Times-Call, Longmont, CO
Jones, Helena Z .... (423) 638-4181
Features ED
Greeneville Sun, Greeneville, TN
Jones, Herbert .... (904) 434-6963
ED, Pensacola Voice, Pensacola, FL
Jones, Hope G .... (919) 793-2123
PUB, Roanoke Beacon, Plymouth, NC
Jones, Howard F .... (919) 257-1200
ED, MAN ED, Warren Record, Warrenton, NC
Jones Jr, Howard .... (219) 724-2121
SYS MGR, Daily Democrat, Decatur, IN
Jones, J Ross .... (501) 793-2383
Photo ED, Batesville Guard, Batesville, AR
Jones, Jackie .... (414) 224-2000
Senior ED-Local News
Milwaukee Journal Sentinel, Milwaukee, WI
Jones, Jake .... (419) 245-6000
Art DIR, Blade, Toledo, OH
Jones, James .... (607) 936-4651
PROD FRM-PR, Leader, Corning, NY
Jones, James .... (414) 657-1000
CIRC MGR, Kenosha News, Kenosha, WI
Jones Jr, James A .... (904) 427-1000
ED, Observer, New Smyrna Beach, FL
Jones Jr, James E .... (205) 325-2222
DIR-Public SRV
Birmingham Post-Herald, Birmingham, AL
Jones, Jami .... (501) 524-5144
ED, Herald-Leader, Siloam Springs, AR
Jones, Jana .... (805) 395-7500
CONT
Bakersfield Californian, Bakersfield, CA
Jones, Jane .... (317) 473-6641
ADV MGR-NTL, Peru Tribune, Peru, IN
Jones, Janet K .... (541) 276-2211
CIRC DIR, East Oregonian, Pendleton, OR
Jones, Janice .... (818) 962-8811
ADV MGR-RT, San Gabriel Valley Tribune, West Covina, CA, MediaNews Inc.
Jones, Jenny .... (619) 244-0021
PUB, Hesperia Resorter, Hesperia, CA
Jones, Jerry .... (509) 397-4333
ED, Whitman County Gazette, Colfax, WA
Jones, Jim .... (817) 390-7400
Religion ED
Fort Worth Star-Telegram, Fort Worth, TX
Jones, Joe .... (618) 943-2331
Sports ED, Daily Record, Lawrenceville, IL
Jones, John .... (910) 323-4848
ADV MGR-RT
Fayetteville Observer-Times, Fayetteville, NC
Jones, John .... (518) 270-1200
SYS MGR, Record, Troy, NY
Jones, John A .... (423) 929-3111
PRES
Carl A Jones Newspapers, Johnson City, TN
Jones, John M .... (423) 638-4181
Chairman
Media Services Group, Greeneville, TN
Jones Jr, John M .... (423) 638-4181
SEC/TREAS, ED
Greeneville Sun, Greeneville, TN
Jones, John O .... (502) 236-2726
ED, Hickman Courier, Hickman, KY
Jones, Joyce .... (817) 864-2686
ED, Haskell Free Press, Haskell, TX
Jones, Juanell .... (806) 998-4888
PUB, ED, Lynn County News, Tahoka, TX
Jones, Judy .... (316) 257-2368
Home Furnishings/Society ED
Lyons Daily News, Lyons, KS
Jones, Julianne .... (910) 343-2000
ADV MGR-CLASS, Morning Star/Sunday Star-News, Wilmington, NC
Jones, June .... (616) 345-3511
Librarian, Kalamazoo Gazette, Kalamazoo, MI
Jones, Kathy .... (520) 763-2505
ADV SUPV-CLASS
Mohave Valley Daily News, Bullhead City, AZ
Jones, Kay .... (414) 657-1000
Amusements ED, Automotive ED, Films/Theater ED, Radio/Television ED, RE ED, Weekend ED, Kenosha News, Kenosha, WI
Jones, Keith .... (510) 783-6111
PROD DIR-News, Daily Review, Hayward, CA
Jones, Kellie .... (915) 263-7331
Lifestyle ED
Big Spring Herald, Big Spring, TX
Jones, Ken .... (810) 332-8181
News ED, Oakland Press, Pontiac, MI
Jones, Kenneth .... (601) 534-6321
GM, New Albany Gazette, New Albany, MS
Jones, Kent .... (508) 586-7200
Health/Medical ED, Enterprise, Brockton, MA
Jones, Klayton .... (415) 692-9406
ED, Redwood City Tribune, Burlingame, CA
Jones, Laddie .... (205) 372-3373
GM, Greene County Democrat, Eutaw, AL
Jones, Linda .... (216) 329-7000
DP MGR, Chronicle-Telegram, Elyria, OH
Jones, Linda .... (607) 746-2176
GM, ED, Delaware County Times, Delhi, NY
Jones, Maggie .... (212) 332-2540
North American Representative
Australian Broadcasting Corp., New York, NY
Jones, Marge .... (405) 286-3321
ADV MGR
McCurtain Daily Gazette, Idabel, OK
Jones, Marguerite .... (415) 252-0500
ASSOC PUB, CIRC MGR, San Francisco Daily Journal, San Francisco, CA
Jones, Marie Reinhart .... (215) 248-8800
ED, Chestnut Hill Local, Philadelphia, PA
Jones, Marvin E .... (614) 773-2111
PUB, Chillicothe Gazette, Chillicothe, OH
Jones, Matt .... (405) 475-3311
ADTX MGR
Daily Oklahoman, Oklahoma City, OK
Jones, Max .... (812) 231-4200
EPE, Tribune-Star, Terre Haute, IN
Jones, Melissa L .... (307) 634-3361
ED-Entertainment
Wyoming Tribune-Eagle, Cheyenne, WY
Jones, Michael .... (318) 433-3000
Books ED, Lake Charles American Press, Lake Charles, LA
Jones, Michelle .... (334) 222-2402
Lifestyle ED
Andalusia Star-News, Andalusia, AL
Jones, Mike .... (918) 581-8300
EDL Writer, Tulsa World, Tulsa, OK
Jones, Mike .... (918) 684-2828
Sports ED, Muskogee Daily Phoenix & Times Democrat, Muskogee, OK
Jones, Mike .... (912) 382-4321
MAN ED, Gazette Light, Tifton, GA
Jones, Mike .... (204) 727-2451
Sports ED, Brandon Sun, Brandon, MB
Thomson Newspapers
Jones, Mike .... (409) 756-6671
Sports ED, Conroe Courier, Conroe, TX
Jones, Nathan .... (217) 965-3355
GM, Virden Recorder, Virden, IL
Jones, Nora .... (415) 348-4321
ADV MGR-CLASS
San Mateo County Times, San Mateo, CA
Jones, Norris E .... (217) 229-4412
ED, Panhandle Press, Raymond, IL
Jones Jr, Dr O E .... (501) 793-2383
PUB, Batesville Guard, Batesville, AR
Jones, Owen .... (918) 297-2577
GM, Hartshorne Sun, Hartshorne, OK
Jones, Pat .... (501) 793-2383
GM, Batesville Guard, Batesville, AR
Jones, Pat .... (813) 259-7711
ADV MGR-CLASS, ADTX MGR
Tampa Tribune and Times, Tampa, FL
Jones, Patricia .... (907) 456-6661
BUS ED
Fairbanks Daily News-Miner, Fairbanks, AK
Jones, Paul .... (803) 774-3311
ED, Dillon Herald, Dillon, SC
Jones, Paul E .... (316) 257-2368
PUB, ADV DIR, Lyons Daily News, Lyons, KS
Jones, Pete .... (217) 351-5252
CIRC MGR, News-Gazette, Champaign, IL
Jones, Phil .... (912) 382-4321
CIRC MGR, Tifton Gazette, Tifton, GA
Jones, Philip M .... (717) 334-1131
COB, Gettysburg Times, Gettysburg, PA
Jones, Phyllis T .... (508) 366-1511
PUB, ED
Westborough News, Westboro, MA
Jones, Randy .... (601) 896-2100
PROD DIR, Sun Herald, Biloxi, MS
Jones, Randy .... (815) 432-5227
ADV MGR-CLASS, Iroquois County's Times-Republic, Watseka, IL
Jones, Richard .... (315) 337-4000
PROD MGR, Daily Sentinel, Rome, NY
Jones, Richard .... (215) 854-2000
COL, Philadelphia Inquirer, Philadelphia, PA
Jones, Richard S .... (901) 253-6666
PUB, Lake County Banner, Tiptonville, TN
Jones, Rick .... (513) 863-8200
Entertainment/Amusements ED, Fashion/Style ED, Lifestyle ED, Television/Film ED, Theater/Music ED, Travel ED
Journal-News, Hamilton, OH
Jones, Robbie .... (901) 529-2211
MGR-Purchasing
Commercial Appeal, Memphis, TN
Jones, Robert .... (918) 256-6422
PROD SUPT
Vinita Daily Journal, Vinita, OK
Jones, Robert .... (334) 433-1551
PROD MGR-PR
Mobile Press Register, Mobile, AL
Jones, Robert .... (206) 872-6600
EPE, South County Journal, Kent, WA
Jones, Robert A .... (213) 237-5000
COL-Local
Los Angeles Times, Los Angeles, CA
Jones, Rodger .... (214) 977-8222
State ED, Dallas Morning News, Dallas, TX
Jones, Roger .... (502) 781-1700
ADV MGR, Bowling Green Daily News, Bowling Green, KY
Jones, Roger .... (817) 896-2311
PUB, Riesel Rustler, Riesel, TX
Jones, Roger Ann .... (912) 336-5265
PUB, ED, Camilla Enterprise, Camilla, GA
Jones, Ross .... (305) 376-3800
Sr VP-FIN/CFO
Knight-Ridder Inc., Miami, FL
Jones, Roxi .... (802) 748-8121
Entertainment/Amusements ED
Caledonian-Record, St. Johnsbury, VT

Jon — Who's Where-118

Jones, Roy .... (915) 673-4271
Military ED, Religion ED
Abilene Reporter-News, Abilene, TX

Jones, Royce .... (915) 653-1221
Agriculture/Farm ED
Standard-Times, San Angelo, TX

Jones, Scott .... (505) 393-2123
Design ED, Daily News-Sun, Hobbs, NM

Jones, Seth E .... (212) 930-8000
Photo ED, New York Post, New York, NY

Jones, Sharon .... (619) 299-3131
EDU K-12 Writer
San Diego Union-Tribune, San Diego, CA

Jones, Shelley .... (903) 935-7914
EDL Writer
Marshall News Messenger, Marshall, TX

Jones, Shirley .... (801) 237-2031
ADM ASST
Salt Lake Tribune, Salt Lake City, UT

Jones, Skipper .... (352) 498-3312
PUB, ED
Dixie County Advocate, Cross City, FL

Jones, Stan .... (907) 257-4200
Political Reporter, Online Contact
Anchorage Daily News, Anchorage, AK

Jones, Steve .... (210) 225-7411
CONT
San Antonio Express-News, San Antonio, TX

Jones, Susan .... (304) 348-5140
Books ED, Graphics ED
Charleston Daily Mail, Charleston, WV

Jones, Terry B .... (504) 822-4433
PUB, New Orleans Data News Weekly, New Orleans, LA

Jones, Terry Lee .... (800) 223-2154
Senior ED
Investor's Business Daily, Los Angeles, CA

Jones, Tim .... (919) 752-6166
PROD MGR-Pre Press/SYS
Daily Reflector, Greenville, NC

Jones, Tim P .... (423) 929-3111
VP/SEC
Carl A Jones Newspapers, Johnson City, TN

Jones, Todd .... (614) 452-4561
CIRC MGR, Times Recorder, Zanesville, OH

Jones, Tony .... (518) 325-4400
PUB, Independent, Hillsdale, NY

Jones, Tricia .... (541) 672-3321
Radio/Television ED
News-Review, Roseburg, OR

Jones, Walter .... (414) 449-4860
GM, ED, Milwaukee Courier, Milwaukee, WI

Jones-Romero, Douglas ..... (609) 691-1148
GM, El Veterano, Vineland, NJ

Jones II, Robert L .... (210) 828-3321
PUB
North Side Recorder-Times, San Antonio, TX

Joo, Dong Moon .... (202) 636-3000
PRES, Washington Times, Washington, DC

Joos, Dennis .... (603) 237-5501
ED, News and Sentinel, Colebrook, NH

Jorawsky, Lori .... (403) 934-3021
PUB, Strathmore Standard, Strathmore, AB

Jordan, Anne .... (618) 271-0468
PUB
East St. Louis Monitor, East St. Louis, IL

Jordan, Annette .... (910) 625-2101
News ED, Courier-Tribune, Asheboro, NC

Jordan, Casey .... (714) 768-3631
ED, Preview, Lake Forest, CA

Jordan Jr, Clyde .... (618) 271-0468
GM
East St. Louis Monitor, East St. Louis, IL

Jordan, Dan .... (308) 995-4441
PROD MGR
Holdrege Daily Citizen, Holdrege, NE

Jordan, Denise .... (816) 531-5253
GM, Kansas City Globe, Kansas City, MO

Jordan, Diane .... (619) 299-3131
MGR-Purchasing/Facilities
San Diego Union-Tribune, San Diego, CA

Jordan, Donald .... (203) 964-2200
PROD MGR-PR, Stamford Advocate, Stamford, CT, Times Mirror Co.

Jordan, Doretha .... (913) 596-1008
ED, Kansas State Globe, Kansas City, KS

Jordan, Felicia .... (970) 669-5050
Valley Life ED
Loveland Daily Reporter-Herald, Loveland, CO

Jordan, Frank .... (402) 475-4200
PROD MGR-Plate/Press
Lincoln Journal Star, Lincoln, NE

Jordan, Jeanne .... (954) 356-4000
News ED, Sun-Sentinel, Fort Lauderdale, FL

Jordan, Jeff .... (509) 459-5000
Sports ED, Spokesman-Review, Spokane, WA

Jordan, Joe .... (573) 785-1414
ADV DIR
Daily American Republic, Poplar Bluff, MO

Jordan, Karen .... (214) 977-8222
Travel ED
Dallas Morning News, Dallas, TX

Jordan, Klonie .... (864) 489-1131
MAN ED, Gaffney Ledger, Gaffney, SC

Jordan, Lee B .... (907) 694-2727
PUB, ED, Chugiak-Eagle River Alaska Star, Eagle River, AK

Jordan, Linda .... (208) 448-2431
PUB, ED, Priest River Times, Priest River, ID

Jordan, Linda .... (808) 245-3681
MGR-Office/BM, Garden Island, Lihue, HI

Jordan, Marion .... (816) 531-5253
PUB, ED
Kansas City Globe, Kansas City, MO

Jordan, Mary .... (202) 334-6000
Foreign Correspondent (Tokyo)
Washington Post, Washington, DC

Jordan, Richard .... (415) 777-5700
VP-Employee Relations, San Francisco Newspaper Agency, San Francisco, CA

Jordan, Robert .... (912) 273-2277
BUS ED, Cordele Dispatch, Cordele, GA

Jordan, Sharon .... (319) 291-1400
ADV MGR-CLASS
Waterloo Courier, Waterloo, IA

Jordan, Steve .... (915) 673-4271
CIRC DIR, PROD DIR
Abilene Reporter-News, Abilene, TX

Jordan, Steve .... (402) 444-1000
PROD MGR-Quality Assurance
Omaha World-Herald, Omaha, NE

Jordan, Susan .... (716) 244-9030
ED, Empty Closet, Rochester, NY

Jordan, Sylvia .... (904) 224-3805
PUB, Tallahassean, Tallahassee, FL

Jordan, Tony .... (910) 592-8137
CIRC MGR
Sampson Independent, Clinton, NC

Jordan, William .... (972) 563-6476
PUB, ADV MGR
Terrell Tribune, Terrell, TX

Jordon, Carol .... (207) 791-6650
ADV MGR-Group Sales
Portland Press Herald, Portland, ME

Jordon, Mark A .... (817) 627-5987
GM, Wise County Messenger, Decatur, TX

Jordon, Steve .... (402) 444-1000
BUS/FIN ED
Omaha World-Herald, Omaha, NE

Jorgensen, Randy .... (810) 724-2615
GM, Tri-City Times, Imlay City, MI

Jorgensen, Steen O .... (902) 436-2121
PUB, Summerside Journal-Pioneer, Summerside, PEI

Jorgensen, Tricia .... (303) 892-5000
MGR-Malls/Special Sections
Rocky Mountain News, Denver, CO

Joseph, Dave .... (954) 356-4000
Horse Racing ED
Sun-Sentinel, Fort Lauderdale, FL

Joseph, Gar .... (215) 854-2000
Political ED
Philadelphia Daily News, Philadelphia, PA

Joseph, Larry R .... (419) 238-2285
PUB, Times-Bulletin, Van Wert, OH

Joseph, Michael .... (937) 225-2000
PROD DIR-OPER
Dayton Daily News, Dayton, OH

Joslyn, Heather .... (410) 523-2300
MAN ED
Baltimore City Paper, Baltimore, MD

Joslyn, Ken .... (217) 347-7151
PROD MGR-SYS
Effingham Daily News, Effingham, IL

Joslyn, Robert .... (414) 457-7711
MAN ED-News
Sheboygan Press, Sheboygan, WI

Jost, Irmintraud .... (212) 983-1983
BU Chief
Springer Foreign News Service, New York, NY

Jost, Rick .... (515) 284-8000
BUS/FIN ED
Des Moines Register, Des Moines, IA

Joudy, Rich .... (203) 744-5100
DP MGR, News-Times, Danbury, CT

Joule, Jim .... (913) 483-2116
ED, Russell Daily News, Russell, KS

Jovanovich, Joe .... (206) 597-8742
PROD MGR-Packaging
News Tribune, Tacoma, WA

Jowers, Jayne .... (601) 743-5760
GM, Kemper County Messenger, De Kalb, MS

Jowers, Jeff .... (601) 743-5760
ED, Kemper County Messenger, De Kalb, MS

Jowers, Marcia .... (334) 875-2110
ADV MGR-CLASS
Selma Times-Journal, Selma, AL

Joy, Bob .... (805) 650-2900
CONT, Ventura County Star, Ventura, CA

Joy, Judith .... (618) 532-5604
Farm ED, Features ED
Centralia Sentinel, Centralia, IL

Joyce, Denise .... (312) 222-3232
Lifestyle ED, Chicago Tribune, Chicago, IL

Joyce, Dennis .... (208) 377-6200
MET ED, Idaho Statesman, Boise, ID

Joyce, Jim .... (864) 223-1411
MAN ED, Automotive/Travel ED, City/MET ED, Farm/Garden ED, Photographer, SCI ED, Sports ED, Teen-Age/Youth ED
Index-Journal, Greenwood, SC

Joyce, John .... (805) 269-1169
PUB, Acton-Agua Dulce News, Acton, CA

Joyce, Kevin .... (518) 792-9914
Interactive & Online Services Product MGR
TV Data, Queensbury, NY

Joyce, M Gayle .... (805) 269-1169
ED, Acton-Agua Dulce News, Acton, CA

Joyce, Marion .... (914) 961-2020
PRES, Joyce, Marion, Bronxville, NY

Joyce, Michael .... (610) 272-2500
ADV DIR, Times Herald, Norristown, PA

Joyce, Tom .... (910) 786-4141
MAN ED, Mount Airy News, Mount Airy, NC

Joye, George .... (704) 873-1054
ED, Iredell County News, Statesville, NC

Joyner, Jim .... (410) 788-4500
ED, Catonsville Times, Baltimore, MD

Joyner Jr, William M .... (205) 532-4000
ADV DIR, Huntsville Times, Huntsville, AL

Judd, David .... (519) 756-2020
City ED, Expositor, Brantford, ON

Judd, Patsy .... (502) 864-3891
PUB
Cumberland County News, Burkesville, KY

Judge, Bernard .... (312) 644-7800
VP, ED
Chicago Daily Law Bulletin, Chicago, IL

Judge, Frank .... (716) 328-2144
ED/PUB
Syndicated News Service, Rochester, NY

Judge, Lee .... (816) 234-4141
Cartoonist, Kansas City Star, Kansas City, MO

Judge, Patrick .... (212) 930-8000
ADV DIR, New York Post, New York, NY

Judge, Pauline L .... (508) 428-8900
ED, Otis Notice, Osterville, MA

Judice, Mary .... (504) 826-3279
Energy ED, Times-Picayune, New Orleans, LA

Judson, Marcia .... (941) 687-7000
Music ED, Ledger, Lakeland, FL

Judson, Mary .... (512) 749-5131
PUB, ED
Port Aransas South Jetty, Port Aransas, TX

Judson, Murray .... (512) 749-5131
PUB, GM
Port Aransas South Jetty, Port Aransas, TX

Judson-Carr, Michael .... (619) 765-2231
PUB, Julian News, Julian, CA

Judy, Mark .... (330) 833-2631
PROD SUPT-Photo Comp
Independent, Massillon, OH

Juenger, Judy .... (507) 235-3303
Fashion/Food ED, Women's ED
Sentinel, Fairmont, MN

Juillard, R M .... (210) 423-5511
Consultant
Valley Morning Star, Harlingen, TX

Jukes, Stephen .... (202) 898-8300
ED-Reuters America/Sr. VP/News & TV
Reuters, Washington, DC

Julavits, Joe .... (904) 359-4111
Outdoors ED
Florida Times-Union, Jacksonville, FL

Juley, Mike .... (414) 224-2000
Suburban ED
Milwaukee Journal Sentinel, Milwaukee, WI

Julian, Sheryl .... (617) 929-2000
Food ED, Boston Globe, Boston, MA

Julien, Robert .... (514) 285-7272
CONT, La Presse, Montreal, QC

Jump, Jason .... (405) 323-5151
Sports ED, Clinton Daily News, Clinton, OK

Jumper, Kathy .... (334) 433-1551
RE ED, Mobile Press Register, Mobile, AL

Junck, Mary .... (410) 332-6000
PUB/CEO, Sun, Baltimore, MD

Juneau, Bill .... (318) 363-3939
ED, Ville Platte Gazette, Ville Platte, LA

Jung, Michael D .... (407) 242-3500
ADV DIR, Florida Today, Melbourne, FL

Jung, Thomas .... (423) 928-4151
PROD FRM-PR
Elizabethton Star, Elizabethton, TN

Jungers, Gary .... (712) 546-7031
CIRC MGR, PROD SUPT
Le Mars Daily Sentinel, Le Mars, IA

Jungwith, Helen .... (715) 423-7200
ADV DIR
Daily Tribune, Wisconsin Rapids, WI

Junker, Phil .... (812) 547-3424
GM, Perry County News, Tell City, IN

Junkins, Susan .... (601) 693-1551
ED, Skyline, Meridian, MS

Jurek, June .... (508) 586-7200
Action Line ED, Enterprise, Brockton, MA

Jurgena-Stamer, Barbara ... (618) 656-4700
CIRC MGR
Edwardsville Intelligencer, Edwardsville, IL

Jurgens, Barbara .... (402) 475-4200
PSL MGR, Lincoln Journal Star, Lincoln, NE

Jurgens, David .... (701) 253-7311
BUS ED, Forum, Fargo, ND

Jurgensen, Beverly .... (910) 343-2000
DIR-Human Resources, Morning Star/Sunday Star-News, Wilmington, NC

Jurgensen, Karen .... (703) 276-3400
EPE, USA Today, Arlington, VA

Jurkowitz, Mark .... (617) 929-2000
Ombudsman, Boston Globe, Boston, MA

Jussel, Rick M .... (970) 242-5050
Sports ED
Daily Sentinel, Grand Junction, CO

Justesen, David .... (805) 650-2900
PROD FRM-COMP
Ventura County Star, Ventura, CA

Justice, Clarence .... (605) 432-4516
GM, Grant County Review, Milbank, SD

Justice, Phyllis Dolan .... (605) 432-4516
PUB, ED, Grant County Review, Milbank, SD

Justice, Travis .... (501) 239-8562
EDU ED
Paragould Daily Press, Paragould, AR

Justus, Lavella .... (970) 675-5033
MAN ED, Rangely Times, Rangely, CO

Justus, Lewis .... (770) 382-4545
ASSOC ED, EPE
Daily Tribune News, Cartersville, GA

Juzwiak, Robert J .... (908) 349-3000
PUB, Ocean County Observer, Toms River, NJ

Juzwik, Chris .... (319) 383-2200
Sports ED, Quad-City Times, Davenport, IA

Jynes, Joyce .... (501) 483-6317
ED, Trumann Democrat, Trumann, AR

K

K-Turkel, Judi .... (608) 231-1003
PRES, P/K Associates Inc., Madison, WI

Kaas, Gale .... (701) 627-4829
ED, New Town News, New Town, ND

Kaba, Steve .... (573) 431-2010
CIRC MGR, Daily Journal, Park Hills, MO

Kabat, Bruce .... (817) 757-5757
ASST MAN ED
Waco Tribune-Herald, Waco, TX

Kachelriess, Henry .... (908) 922-6000
PROD CNR-Insert
Asbury Park Press, Neptune, NJ

Kacich, Tom .... (217) 351-5252
Amusements ED, Food ED, Women's ED
News-Gazette, Champaign, IL

Kaczmarczyk, Jeff .... (616) 222-5400
Music Critic-Classical
Grand Rapids Press, Grand Rapids, MI

Kaczmarek, Jackie .... (702) 623-5011
ASSOC ED, Humboldt Sun, Winnemucca, NV

Kaczmarek, Jim .... (317) 423-5511
ADV MGR-RT
Journal and Courier, Lafayette, IN

Kadel, Steve .... (907) 283-7551
News ED, Peninsula Clarion, Kenai, AK

Kadner, Phil .... (773) 586-8800
COL, Daily Southtown, Chicago, IL

Kadonsky, Charles .... (715) 344-6100
BM, CIRC MGR
Stevens Point Journal, Stevens Point, WI

Kadrich, Brad .... (810) 628-4801
ED, Oxford Leader, Oxford, MI

Kadzis, Peter .... (401) 273-6397
ED, Providence Phoenix, Providence, RI

Kaechele, Cheryl .... (616) 673-5534
PUB, Allegan County News, Allegan, MI

Kaemper, Michael .... (505) 753-2126
ED, Rio Grande Sun, Espanola, NM

Kaercher, James D .... (320) 839-6163
PUB, GM
Ortonville Independent, Ortonville, MN

Kaercher-Blake, Suzette .... (320) 839-6163
ED, Ortonville Independent, Ortonville, MN

Kaeser, Michael J .... (202) 334-6173
MAN ED-Los Angeles
Los Angeles Times-Washington Post News Service, Washington, DC

Kaffsack, Hanns-Jochen .... (202) 783-5097
Deputy BU Chief, Deutsche Presse-Agentur (dpa), Washington, DC

Kagay, Michael .... (212) 556-1234
News Surveys ED
New York Times, New York, NY

Kah, Kurt P .... (419) 422-5151
PRES, TREAS, GM, Courier, Findlay, OH

Kah, Terry .... (419) 422-5151
CIRC MGR-Sales, Courier, Findlay, OH

Kahlor, Robert A .... (414) 224-2000
COB/CEO
Milwaukee Journal Sentinel, Milwaukee, WI

Kahn, A David .... (810) 355-4100
ED, Kahn, A.D. Inc., Southfield, MI

Kahn, Brady .... (510) 540-7400
MAN ED, East Bay Express, Berkeley, CA

Copyright ©1997 by the Editor & Publisher Co.

119-Who's Where **Kat**

Kahnt, Joann .... (913) 349-5516
PUB, ED, Prairie Post, White City, KS
Kahoun, Jane .... (216) 999-4500
EDU ED, Plain Dealer, Cleveland, OH
Kahrel, Al .... (614) 387-0400
DP MGR, PROD SUPV-COMP
Marion Star, Marion, OH
Kaikai, Edwina .... (412) 263-1100
MET ED
Pittsburgh Post-Gazette, Pittsburgh, PA
Kaikowski, Geri Anne .... (717) 821-2091
Features/Food ED, Radio/Television ED
Citizens' Voice, Wilkes-Barre, PA
Kain, Roger C .... (804) 649-6000
ADV DIR-Sales/MKTG
Richmond Times-Dispatch, Richmond, VA
Kaiser, Cami .... (702) 788-6200
ADV MGR-Entertainment
Reno Gazette-Journal, Reno, NV
Kaiser, Dennis .... (562) 430-7555
ED, Sun, Seal Beach, CA
Kaiser, Howard A .... (906) 632-2235
PUB, Evening News, Sault Ste. Marie, MI
Kaiser, Kathy .... (303) 494-5511
MAN ED, Boulder Weekly, Boulder, CO
Kaiser, Martin .... (414) 224-2000
Senior VP/ED
Milwaukee Journal Sentinel, Milwaukee, WI
Kaiser, Mike .... (513) 352-2000
Neighbors ED
Cincinnati Post, Cincinnati, OH
Kaiser, Robert .... (202) 334-6000
MAN ED, Washington Post, Washington, DC
Kaiser, Tim .... (812) 424-7711
ASST Sports ED
Evansville Courier, Evansville, IN
Kakaty, Kenneth J .... (315) 337-4000
TREAS, CONT, Daily Sentinel, Rome, NY
Kalaydjian, Ara .... (617) 924-4420
PUB, ED
Armenian-Mirror Spector, Watertown, MA
Kalb, Loretta .... (916) 321-1000
RE Writer, Sacramento Bee, Sacramento, CA
Kalbaugh, James A .... (717) 253-9270
PUB, ED, Weekly Almanac, Honesdale, PA
Kalbaugh, Judie G .... (717) 253-9270
PUB, GM, Weekly Almanac, Honesdale, PA
Kalech, Marc .... (212) 930-8000
MAN ED, New York Post, New York, NY
Kaley, Jeff .... (405) 255-5354
Sports ED, Duncan Banner, Duncan, OK
Kaley, Kevin .... (813) 294-5603
ED, Carrollwood News, Tampa, FL
Kalich, Timothy A .... (601) 453-5312
PUB, ED, EPE
Greenwood Commonwealth, Greenwood, MS
Kalinowski, Tess .... (519) 679-6666
Arts/Entertainment ED, Our Times ED
London Free Press, London, ON
Kalk, Samara .... (608) 252-6400
Radio/Television ED
Capital Times, Madison, WI
Kall-Shewan, Phil .... (613) 342-4441
Picture ED, Radio/Television ED, Travel ED
Recorder and Times, Brockville, ON
Kallam, Clay .... (510) 757-2525
ASSOC ED/COL
Ledger Dispatch, Antioch, CA
Kallan, Vicky .... (603) 424-7610
GM, Village Crier, Merrimack, NH
Kallaugher, Kevin .... (410) 332-6000
EDL Cartoonist, Sun, Baltimore, MD
Kallenbach, Judy .... (417) 326-7636
ED, Herald-Free Press, Bolivar, MO
Kallet, Judith S .... (860) 241-6200
VP-INFO Technology
Hartford Courant, Hartford, CT
Kalmbach, Bruce .... (701) 475-2513
PUB, ED, Steele Ozone-Press, Steele, ND
Kaltenbach, Hubert L .... (310) 540-5511
Vice Chairman, Daily Breeze, Torrance, CA
Copley Press Inc.
Kaluza, Noreen .... (320) 255-8700
Topics ED, St. Cloud Times, St. Cloud, MN
Kalvelage, Jennifer .... (402) 462-2131
ASST News ED
Hastings Tribune, Hastings, NE
Kamberaj, Sinan .... (718) 220-2000
ED, Illyria, Bronx, NY
Kameen, John P .... (717) 785-3800
PUB, Forest City News, Forest City, PA
Kamen, Edward R .... (717) 291-8811
BUS ED, Lancaster Intelligencer Journal/New Era/Sunday News, Lancaster, PA
Kamerling, Lori .... (501) 968-5252
Society ED, Courier, Russellville, AR
Kamin, Blair .... (312) 222-3232
Architecture Critic
Chicago Tribune, Chicago, IL
Kaminski, David .... (352) 365-8200
News ED, News Features ED
Daily Commercial, Leesburg, FL
Kaminski, David .... (330) 454-5611
MAN ED, Repository, Canton, OH
Kaminski, John .... (717) 648-4641
ADV DIR, News-Item, Shamokin, PA
Kaminsky, Gregg .... (310) 453-0304
Artist/Author, Tuttle Comics, Irvine, CA
Kaminsky, Julie E .... (508) 775-1200
ADV MGR-CLASS
Cape Cod Times, Hyannis, MA
Kamm, Thomas .... (212) 416-2000
BU Chief-Paris
Wall Street Journal, New York, NY
Kamody, Ann .... (614) 592-6612
EPE, Athens Messenger, Athens, OH
Kampman, Kevin .... (918) 423-1700
PUB/GM, EPE, McAlester News-Capital & Democrat, McAlester, OK
Kampner, David .... (508) 626-3800
ADV MGR-Auto/RE, ADV MGR-Special Sections, Middlesex News, Framingham, MA
Kamula, Julia .... (905) 684-7251
ADV DIR, Standard, St. Catharines, ON
Kanaday, Cathy .... (502) 886-4444
Lifestyle ED
Kentucky New Era, Hopkinsville, KY
Kandarian, Paul .... (508) 880-9000
Suburban ED
Taunton Daily Gazette, Taunton, MA
Kandle, Terrence .... (415) 777-5700
CIRC MGR-City Single Copy, San Francisco Newspaper Agency, San Francisco, CA
Kane, Angelika .... (412) 263-1100
Librarian
Pittsburgh Post-Gazette, Pittsburgh, PA
Kane, Ben .... (910) 625-2101
PROD MGR-Press
Courier-Tribune, Asheboro, NC
Kane, Cindy .... (941) 953-7755
Manatee County BU Chief
Sarasota Herald-Tribune, Sarasota, FL
Kane, Craig .... (913) 295-1111
PROD SUPT-Press
Topeka Capital-Journal, Topeka, KS
Kane, Daniel V .... (716) 439-9222
MAN ED, EPE
Union-Sun & Journal, Lockport, NY
Kane, Eugene .... (414) 224-2000
COL
Milwaukee Journal Sentinel, Milwaukee, WI
Kane, Gregory .... (410) 332-6000
COL-Local, Sun, Baltimore, MD
Kane, James .... (847) 427-4300
BUS ED
Daily Herald, Arlington Heights, IL
Kane, James B .... (717) 622-3456
MAN ED, Automotive ED, Books ED, Special Sections ED, Pottsville Republican & Evening Herald, Pottsville, PA
Kane, Jane A .... (413) 772-0261
BM, Recorder, Greenfield, MA
Kane, Jerry .... (814) 948-6210
MAN ED, Barnesboro Star, Barnesboro, PA
Kane, Kate .... (215) 536-6820
MAN ED
Quakertown Free Press, Quakertown, PA
Kane, Marion .... (416) 367-2000
Food ED, Toronto Star, Toronto, ON
Kane, Michael .... (541) 567-6457
ED, Hermiston Herald, Hermiston, OR
Kane, Michael G .... (914) 694-9300
VP-MKTG, Reporter Dispatch, White Plains, NY, Gannett Co. Inc.
Kane, Tim .... (508) 667-2156
ED
Wilmington Advertiser, North Billerica, MA
Kanelis, John .... (806) 376-4488
EPE, Amarillo Daily News/Globe Times, Amarillo, TX
Kaney, Georgia M .... (904) 252-1511
VP, GM, Daytona Beach News-Journal, Daytona Beach, FL
Kaney Jr, Jonathan D .... (904) 252-1511
SEC, Daytona Beach News-Journal, Daytona Beach, FL
Kanhai, Nadia R .... (630) 830-4145
ED, Bartlett Examiner, Bartlett, IL
Kanick Jr, Robert W .... (412) 465-5555
CONT, Indiana Gazette, Indiana, PA
Kann, Peter R .... (212) 416-2600
COB/CEO
Dow Jones & Co. Inc., New York, NY
Kann, Roger .... (712) 279-5019
CIRC DIR, Sioux City Journal, Sioux City, IA
Kanne, Marvin G .... (314) 340-8402
VP/DIR-OPER
Pulitzer Publishing Co., St. Louis, MO
Kant, Anthony .... (604) 598-4123
PUB, ED, Oak Bay News, Victoria, BC
Kanthak, John .... (309) 786-6441
Medical ED
Rock Island Argus, Rock Island, IL
Kantowski, Ron .... (702) 385-3111
Sports ED, Las Vegas Sun, Las Vegas, NV
Kanzler, George .... (201) 877-4141
Music Critic-Jazz
Star-Ledger, Newark, NJ
Kapaun, Sue .... (507) 433-8851
MGR-CR
Austin Daily Herald, Austin, MN
Kapiloff, Lynn .... (301) 306-9500
PUB
Prince George's Sentinel, Seabrook, MD
Kaplan, Bernard .... (202) 298-6920
Paris BU Chief
Hearst Newspapers, Washington, DC
Kaplan, Neil .... (213) 237-5000
ADV Group MKTG MGR
Los Angeles Times, Los Angeles, CA
Kaplan, Peter .... (212) 755-2400
ED, New York Observer, New York, NY
Kaplan, Sis .... (704) 331-4842
MAN ED, Leader, Charlotte, NC
Kaplan, Stan .... (704) 331-4842
PUB, Leader, Charlotte, NC
Kaplan, Stephanie .... (609) 989-7800
ADV MGR-RT, Trentonian, Trenton, NJ
Kaplow, Larry .... (561) 820-4100
Capitol Reporter
Palm Beach Post, West Palm Beach, FL
Kappler, Brian .... (514) 987-2222
NTL, Gazette, Montreal, QC
Kappmeyer, Ron .... (507) 454-6500
PROD MGR-COMP
Winona Daily News, Winona, MN
Kapsalis, Chris .... (201) 646-4000
PROD MGR-Technology Support
Record, Hackensack, NJ
Kapsalis, Jimmy .... (212) 986-6881
ED, Hellenic Times, New York, NY
Kapsidelis, Tom .... (804) 649-6000
State ED
Richmond Times-Dispatch, Richmond, VA
Kapuscinski, Jeffrey A .... (716) 232-7100
VP-Market Development, Rochester Democrat and Chronicle; Times-Union, Rochester, NY
Kapusta, Joseph .... (412) 981-6100
City ED, Herald, Sharon, PA
Kapusta, Michael P .... (603) 224-5301
CONT
Newspapers of New England, Concord, NH
Kapyrka, Peter .... (250) 762-4445
PUB/GM, Daily Courier, Kelowna, BC
Karafa, Andy .... (330) 841-1600
CIRC MGR-Single Copy
Tribune Chronicle, Warren, OH
Karafin, Ron .... (609) 663-6000
Photo ED, Courier-Post, Cherry Hill, NJ
Karakashia, Vahakn .... (617) 926-3974
ED, Hairenik, Watertown, MA
Karalekas, Anne .... (202) 334-6000
ADV PUB Magazine/News
Washington Post, Washington, DC
Karangelen, George .... (757) 446-2000
PROD MGR-Quality Assurance
Virginian-Pilot, Norfolk, VA
Karavangelos, Anna .... (202) 334-6375
ASSOC ED, Washington Post Writers Group, Washington, DC
Karbonit, Judy .... (304) 255-4400
Entertainment/Amusements ED, Radio/Television ED, Register Herald, Beckley, WV
Karchella, Debra .... (702) 623-5011
Office MGR
Humboldt Sun, Winnemucca, NV
Karcher, Henry .... (419) 332-5511
PROD MGR-Commercial Sales
News-Messenger, Fremont, OH
Kardoes, Lanita .... (515) 928-2723
PUB, ED, Titonka Topic, Titonka, IA
Kardon, Fred .... (309) 829-9411
EX ED, Pantagraph, Bloomington, IL
Karikomi, Bradley .... (317) 423-5511
CIRC DIR, Journal and Courier, Lafayette, IN
Karis, Rebecca .... (715) 682-2313
CIRC MGR, Daily Press, Ashland, WI
Karius, Joseph .... (605) 692-6271
PUB, Brookings Register, Brookings, SD
Karkovack, Eric .... (717) 243-2611
Online MGR, Sentinel, Carlisle, PA
Karl, Catherine .... (813) 893-8111
VP-ADM/TREAS/SEC
St. Petersburg Times, St. Petersburg, FL
Karlon, Marty .... (603) 882-2741
Regional ED, Telegraph, Nashua, NH
Karlovec, Jeffrey B .... (216) 696-3322
ASST PUB, Daily Legal News and Cleveland Recorder, Cleveland, OH
Karlovec Jr, Lucien B .... (216) 696-3322
PUB, ED/MAN ED, Daily Legal News and Cleveland Recorder, Cleveland, OH
Karlovec, Richard .... (216) 696-3322
ADV Legal, CIRC MGR, Daily Legal News and Cleveland Recorder, Cleveland, OH
Karls, Olaf .... (705) 268-5050
PROD MGR-Creative Services
Daily Press, Timmins, ON
Karlson, Bruce .... (317) 633-1240
ADV MGR-GEN/Co-op
Indianapolis Star/News, Indianapolis, IN
Karlsson, Alvalene P .... (212) 944-0776
ED, Nordstjernan-Svea, New York, NY
Karmel, T C .... (860) 423-8466
Arts/Entertainment ED, Food ED
Chronicle, Willimantic, CT
Karnauchov, Val .... (203) 789-5200
ADV DIR-Art
New Haven Register, New Haven, CT
Karp, Gregory .... (610) 258-7171
Area ED (NJ), Express-Times, Easton, PA
Karpevych, Christine .... (212) 837-7000
Library MGR, Journal of Commerce & Commercial, New York, NY
Karpi, Dagmar .... (516) 747-8282
ED, Oyster Bay Enterprise Pilot, Mineola, NY
Karpinski, Kelly .... (414) 235-7700
EDU ED, Oshkosh Northwestern, Oshkosh, WI
Karst, Frederick A .... (219) 842-3229
PUB, Culver Citizen, Culver, IN
Karst, Judith L .... (219) 842-3229
ED, Culver Citizen, Culver, IN
Karstaedt, Stephen P .... (608) 365-5521
PUB, Stateline Shopping News, Beloit, WI
Karsten, Linda .... (315) 337-4000
PROD FRM-COMP, Daily Sentinel, Rome, NY
Karzin, Kevin .... (805) 259-1234
Photo ED, Signal, Santa Clarita, CA
Kaser, Tom .... (808) 525-8000
Labor ED, Honolulu Advertiser, Honolulu, HI
Kashner, Dean .... (717) 784-2121
MAN ED-News
Press Enterprise, Bloomsburg, PA
Kasich, Wayne .... (218) 285-7411
GM, Daily Journal, International Falls, MN
Kaskan, Mary .... (315) 782-1000
Radio/Television ED, Society ED
Watertown Daily Times, Watertown, NY
Kaskovich, Steve .... (817) 390-7400
Sunday ED
Fort Worth Star-Telegram, Fort Worth, TX
Kasniunas, Vytautas .... (212) 563-2210
ED, Tevyne, New York, NY
Kasold, Doris .... (703) 276-3400
CIRC VP, USA Today, Arlington, VA
Kasper, Richard .... (818) 713-3000
CFO, Daily News, Woodland Hills, CA
Kasperek, Larry .... (205) 325-2222
Graphics ED
Birmingham Post-Herald, Birmingham, AL
Kasperek, Marilyn J .... (716) 542-9615
PUB, ED, Akron Bugle, Akron, NY
Kasprzak, Thomas P .... (860) 442-2200
ADV DIR, Day, New London, CT
Kasselman, Russell .... (360) 332-6397
ED, Banner, Blaine, WA
Kasteen, Judy .... (941) 763-3134
ADV DIR
Daily Okeechobee News, Okeechobee, FL
Kaster, Dennis C .... (217) 892-9613
PUB, Rantoul Press, Rantoul, IL
Kastner, Ernie .... (864) 967-9580
ED, Tribune-Times, Simpsonville, SC
Kastner, John .... (519) 271-2220
Sports ED
Stratford Beacon-Herald, Stratford, ON
Katahara, Alvin .... (808) 525-8000
DIR-RES
Hawaii Newspaper Agency Inc., Honolulu, HI
Kates, Brian .... (212) 210-2100
Deputy EPE
New York Daily News, New York, NY
Kates, Doug .... (814) 665-8291
Sports ED, Corry Evening Journal, Corry, PA
Katete, Jacqueline Mure .... (514) 393-1010
GM, Montreal Mirror, Montreal, QC
Kathan, Keith .... (409) 267-6131
GM, MAN ED
Anahuac Progress, Anahuac, TX
Katin, Geraldine .... (508) 957-0007
ED, Dracut Dispatch, Dracut, MA
Katonak, Lynne .... (803) 648-2311
Books ED, Aiken Standard, Aiken, SC
Kattan, Eyal .... (514) 393-1010
PUB, Montreal Mirror, Montreal, QC
Katz, Abe .... (203) 789-5200
Environmental ED, Health/Medical ED, SCI/Technology ED
New Haven Register, New Haven, CT
Katz, Barry .... (315) 470-0011
News ED, Post-Standard/Syracuse Herald-Journal/American, Syracuse, NY
Katz, Diane .... (313) 222-2300
EDL Writer, Detroit News, Detroit, MI
Katz, Harry Jay .... (215) 546-8088
PUB
National News Bureau, Philadelphia, PA
Katz, Jesse .... (213) 237-5000
Houston BU
Los Angeles Times, Los Angeles, CA

Kat Who's Where-120

Katz, Larry .... (617) 426-3000
Music ED, Boston Herald, Boston, MA

Katz, Randy .... (513) 381-2606
ED, Everybody's News, Cincinnati, OH

Katz, Tonnie L .... (714) 835-1234
ED/VP
Orange County Register, Santa Ana, CA

Katzanek, Jack .... (805) 259-1234
BUS/FIN ED, Signal, Santa Clarita, CA

Katzcuback, Karen .... (937) 698-4451
ED, West Milton Record, West Milton, OH

Katzman, Carol .... (402) 334-6448
ED, Jewish Press, Omaha, NE

Kauffman, John .... (419) 448-3200
MAN ED, Action Line ED, EPE
Advertiser-Tribune, Tiffin, OH

Kauffman, Kermit .... (813) 259-7711
VP/BM
Tampa Tribune and Times, Tampa, FL

Kauffman, Larry .... (717) 275-3235
PROD SUPT, Danville News, Danville, PA

Kauffman, Tim .... (864) 223-1411
EDU ED, Index-Journal, Greenwood, SC

Kauffmann, Craig .... (508) 676-8211
CIRC MGR, Herald News, Fall River, MA

Kauffmann Jr, Godfrey W .... (617) 929-2000
VP-Circulation, CIRC VP
Boston Globe, Boston, MA

Kauffold, Kathy .... (402) 693-2415
PUB, ED, Dodge Criterion, Dodge, NE

Kauffold, Ken H .... (402) 693-2415
PUB, ED, Dodge Criterion, Dodge, NE

Kaufman, Jean .... (914) 341-1100
Action Line ED
Times Herald-Record, Middletown, NY

Kaufman, Kathy .... (402) 873-3334
ADV DIR, News-Press, Nebraska City, NE

Kaufman, Mark .... (937) 498-2111
ADV DIR, Sidney Daily News, Sidney, OH

Kaufman, Peter .... (215) 854-2000
Media ED
Philadelphia Inquirer, Philadelphia, PA

Kauh, Elaine .... (937) 328-0300
Environmental ED
Springfield News-Sun, Springfield, OH

Kaukas, Dick .... (502) 582-4011
Health/Medical ED
Courier-Journal, Louisville, KY

Kaul, Nikky .... (217) 452-3513
ED, Virginia Gazette, Virginia, IL

Kaup, Dave .... (913) 764-2211
Photo ED, Olathe Daily News, Olathe, KS

Kaup, Jean .... (402) 395-2115
PUB, ED, Albion News, Albion, NE

Kaupins, Pam .... (515) 684-4611
PROM MKTG Specialist
Ottumwa Courier, Ottumwa, IA

Kausler Jr, Donald .... (205) 325-2222
Sports ED
Birmingham Post-Herald, Birmingham, AL

Kauss, Jennifer .... (319) 337-3181
News ED
Iowa City Press-Citizen, Iowa City, IA

Kautz, Emogene .... (913) 367-0583
PROD FRM-Paste-Up
Atchison Daily Globe, Atchison, KS

Kautz, Richard .... (814) 368-3173
MGR-CR, CIRC DIR
Bradford Era, Bradford, PA

Kavanagh, Brian .... (406) 873-2201
PUB, Cut Bank Pioneer Press, Cut Bank, MT

Kavanagh, Keelin .... (212) 930-8000
ASST DIR-PROM
New York Post, New York, NY

Kavanagh, LeAnne .... (406) 873-2201
ED, Cut Bank Pioneer Press, Cut Bank, MT

Kavelman, Lynn .... (309) 686-3000
DP MGR, MGR-INFO SYS
Journal Star, Peoria, IL

Kavulich, Andrew P .... (716) 394-0770
EVP/GM, Daily Messenger/Sunday Messenger, Canandaigua, NY

Kawahara, Hitoshi .... (212) 603-6600
Correspondent
Kyodo News Service, New York, NY

Kawai, Shin .... (416) 593-1583
PUB, GM, New Canadian, Toronto, ON

Kay, Alan .... (608) 764-5515
ED, Independent, Deerfield, WI

Kay, Donald .... (619) 322-8889
PROD DIR, Desert Sun, Palm Springs, CA

Kay, Timothy C .... (614) 474-3131
PUB, Herald, Circleville, OH

Kaya, Beatrice .... (808) 525-8000
PROD Librarian
Hawaii Newspaper Agency Inc., Honolulu, HI

Kayata, Nicholas .... (401) 277-7000
PROD ASST to DIR of OPER
Providence Journal-Bulletin, Providence, RI

Kaye, Louis .... (313) 533-1846
BUS ED
Specialty Features Syndicate, Detroit, MI

Kaye, Ron .... (818) 713-3000
MAN ED, Daily News, Woodland Hills, CA

Kaye, William F .... (219) 866-5111
ED, Remington Press, Rensselaer, IN

Kayler, Francoise .... (514) 285-7272
Food ED, La Presse, Montreal, QC

Kaylor, Mike .... (205) 532-4000
Entertainment/Leisure ED, Television/Radio ED, Huntsville Times, Huntsville, AL

Kaylor, Steve .... (813) 259-7711
State ED
Tampa Tribune and Times, Tampa, FL

Kays, Lea .... (618) 438-5611
ADV MGR-CLASS
Benton Evening News, Benton, IL

Kayzer, Trevor .... (604) 624-6781
FRM, Daily News, Prince Rupert, BC

Kazanjian, Gary .... (209) 582-0471
Graphics ED, Photo ED
Hanford Sentinel, Hanford, CA

Kazmaier, David L .... (316) 659-2080
PUB, ED
Edwards County Sentinel, Kinsley, KS

Kazynski, Mona .... (715) 526-2121
Lifestyle ED, Religion ED
Shawano Leader, Shawano, WI

Keabouth, Houay .... (510) 465-3121
Support Staff
Inter-City Express, Oakland, CA

Keach, Sam F .... (512) 387-4511
PUB, ED
Nueces County Record-Star, Robstown, TX

Kealy, Dave .... (403) 429-5400
PROD FRM-PR
Edmonton Journal, Edmonton, AB

Keane, Kevin .... (609) 871-8000
ASSOC ED
Burlington County Times, Willingboro, NJ

Keane, Robert .... (516) 843-2020
EX ED, Newsday, Melville, NY

Keaney, David .... (401) 277-7000
CIRC MGR-SYS
Providence Journal-Bulletin, Providence, RI

Kearley, Rob .... (318) 459-3200
CIRC DIR, Times, Shreveport, LA

Kearly, Tammy .... (517) 377-1000
ADV MGR-SRV
Lansing State Journal, Lansing, MI

Kearney, Greg .... (319) 754-8461
Online Contact, Hawk Eye, Burlington, IA

Kearney, Janetta .... (501) 371-9991
PUB, ED
Arkansas State Press, Little Rock, AR

Kearney, Jess .... (619) 299-3131
Sports ED-ADM
San Diego Union-Tribune, San Diego, CA

Kearney, Kim .... (309) 527-8595
GM, ED, El Paso Journal, El Paso, IL

Kearney, Michael .... (317) 423-5511
DP MGR, Journal and Courier, Lafayette, IN

Kearney, Thomas .... (603) 352-1234
EX ED, Keene Sentinel, Keene, NH

Kearns, Charles .... (508) 922-1234
CIRC MGR, Gloucester Times, Beverly, MA

Kearns, Michael .... (306) 736-2535
PUB, ED, MAN ED, Citizen, Kipling, SK

Kearns, Mindy L .... (304) 675-1333
ED, EPE
Point Pleasant Register, Point Pleasant, WV

Kearns, Scott .... (864) 582-4511
MAN ED, Herald-Journal, Spartanburg, SC

Kearns, Scott .... (306) 736-2535
GM, Citizen, Kipling, SK

Kearny, Matt .... (509) 663-5161
ADV MGR-Display, ADTX MGR
Wenatchee World, Wenatchee, WA

Keasling, Edna .... (409) 348-3505
PUB, ED
Madisonville Meteor, Madisonville, TX

Keaten, James .... (770) 428-9411
BUS Writer
Marietta Daily Journal, Marietta, GA

Keating, Doug .... (215) 854-2000
Theater Critic
Philadelphia Inquirer, Philadelphia, PA

Keating, Jeff .... (541) 482-3456
MAN ED, BUS/FIN ED, News ED
Daily Tidings, Ashland, OR

Keating, Bishop John R .... (703) 841-2590
PUB, Arlington Catholic Herald, Arlington, VA

Keating, Kevin .... (415) 331-7700
Author
Silver Bird Travel Features, Sausalito, CA

Keating, Michael .... (612) 388-8235
ADTX MGR
Republican Eagle, Red Wing, MN

Keating, Terry .... (705) 745-4641
PROD FRM-COMP
Examiner, Peterborough, ON

Keaton, Susan .... (602) 821-7474
ED, Chandler Arizonan Tribune, Mesa, AZ

Keck, Nan E .... (915) 546-6340
ASST MAN ED, Graphics ED/Art DIR
El Paso Herald-Post, El Paso, TX

Keefe, Dan .... (206) 872-6600
PROD MGR-Commercial Printing
South County Journal, Kent, WA

Keefe, John McCarroll .... (937) 839-4733
PUB, ED
Twin Valley News, West Alexandria, OH

Keefe, Lauren .... (617) 979-5670
ED, Melrose Free Press, Melrose, MA

Keefe, Mike .... (303) 820-1010
Cartoonist, Denver Post, Denver, CO

Keefe, Pat .... (507) 376-9711
ADV MGR, Daily Globe, Worthington, MN

Keefe, Rich .... (208) 323-0805
ED, Diversity News, Boise, ID

Keefel, Karri .... (812) 886-9955
CIRC MGR, Sun-Commercial, Vincennes, IN

Keefer, Chuck .... (561) 820-4100
SYS ED
Palm Beach Post, West Palm Beach, FL

Keefer, Donna .... (717) 275-3235
ADV DIR, Danville News, Danville, PA

Keefer, Marsha .... (412) 775-3200
Amusements ED, Fashion/Style ED, Features ED, Leisure ED, Living/Lifestyle ED, Radio/Television ED, Women's ED
Beaver County Times, Beaver, PA

Keegan, Frank .... (610) 258-7171
ED, Express-Times, Easton, PA

Keegan, Michael .... (202) 334-6000
ASST MAN ED-Art
Washington Post, Washington, DC

Keegan, Theresa .... (510) 757-2525
EPE, Ledger Dispatch, Antioch, CA

Keele, Karen .... (805) 925-2691
BM, Santa Maria Times, Santa Maria, CA

Keeler, Lance .... (302) 856-0026
ED, Sussex Countian, Georgetown, DE

Keeler, Maureen .... (613) 544-5000
ADV ASST MGR-RT/NTL
Kingston Whig-Standard, Kingston, ON

Keeler, Nancy .... (717) 746-1217
GM, Rocket-Courier, Wyalusing, PA

Keeler, W David .... (717) 746-1217
PUB, Rocket-Courier, Wyalusing, PA

Keeler, Archbishop William H .. (410) 547-5380
PUB, Catholic Review, Baltimore, MD

Keeling, Dean .... (417) 451-1520
Sports ED, Neosho Daily News, Neosho, MO

Keely, Mary .... (609) 884-3466
ED, Cape May Star and Wave, Cape May, NJ

Keen, Lisa .... (202) 797-7000
ED, Washington Blade, Washington, DC

Keen, Paul .... (209) 441-6111
ADV MGR-CLASS, ADTX MGR
Fresno Bee, Fresno, CA

Keen, Russ .... (605) 225-4100
Farm/Agriculture ED
Aberdeen American News, Aberdeen, SD

Keena, Brian .... (813) 259-7711
CIRC MGR-SYS
Tampa Tribune and Times, Tampa, FL

Keenan, Cheryl .... (304) 469-3373
ED, Fayette Tribune, Oak Hill, WV

Keenan, Gerald .... (416) 441-1405
North America Reporter
Fotopress Independent News Service International (FPINS), Toronto, ON

Keenan, Robert .... (401) 277-7000
ADV Sales DIR-Major RT
Providence Journal-Bulletin, Providence, RI

Keene, Richard K .... (315) 635-3921
GM, Messenger, Baldwinsville, NY

Keeney, Jill .... (502) 582-4011
EDL Writer, Courier-Journal, Louisville, KY

Keeney, Michael .... (713) 449-9945
ED, Mercado Latino, Houston, TX

Keeny, Mike .... (608) 836-1601
ED, Middleton Times-Tribune, Middleton, WI

Keep, Paul M .... (517) 895-8551
ED, Bay City Times, Bay City, MI

Keep, R D .... (515) 672-2581
Sports ED, Oskaloosa Herald, Oskaloosa, IA

Keeton, Dana .... (615) 363-3544
ED, Giles Free Press, Pulaski, TN

Keffer, Ray .... (412) 654-6651
MGR-EDU SRV
New Castle News, New Castle, PA

Kegel, Scott R .... (412) 758-5573
GM, Ellwood City Ledger, Ellwood City, PA

Kegel, W C .... (412) 758-5573
PRES, Ellwood City Ledger, Ellwood City, PA

Kegel, W Ryan .... (412) 758-5573
PUB, Ellwood City Ledger, Ellwood City, PA

Kegley, Dan .... (540) 628-7101
ED, Washington County News, Abingdon, VA

Kegley, James G .... (614) 574-8494
PUB, ED, Scioto Voice, Wheelersburg, OH

Kehetian, Mitch .... (810) 469-4510
EPE, Macomb Daily, Mount Clemens, MI

Kehoe, Belinda .... (407) 242-3500
Online MGR, Florida Today, Melbourne, FL

Kehoe, Peter .... (519) 426-5710
Sports ED, Simcoe Reformer, Simcoe, ON

Kehrer, Jack .... (518) 828-1616
MAN ED, Register-Star, Hudson, NY

Keidan, Bruce .... (412) 263-1100
Sports COL
Pittsburgh Post-Gazette, Pittsburgh, PA

Keil, Beverly .... (202) 334-6000
VP-Human Resources
Washington Post Co., Washington, DC

Keil, Scott L .... (515) 454-2216
PUB, ED, Manly Signal, Manly, IA

Keim, Julie .... (716) 372-3121
ADV MGR-NTL
Olean Times-Herald, Olean, NY

Keine, Ellen .... (515) 284-8000
CIRC MGR-Sales
Des Moines Register, Des Moines, IA

Keirnan, Mindi .... (305) 376-3800
VP-OPER, Knight-Ridder Inc., Miami, FL

Keirsey, Karen L .... (609) 825-8811
ED, Cumberland Reminder, Millville, NJ

Keiser, Barbara .... (219) 773-3127
MAN ED
Nappanee Advance News, Nappanee, IN

Keiser, Gretchen .... (404) 888-7832
ED, Georgia Bulletin, Atlanta, GA

Keiser, Norm .... (937) 225-2000
PROD FRM-Imaging
Dayton Daily News, Dayton, OH

Keisman, Jim .... (405) 382-1100
BM, ADV DIR, DIR-MKTG/PROM
Seminole Producer, Seminole, OK

Keister, Hilda L .... (540) 465-5137
SEC, Northern Virginia Daily, Strasburg, VA

Keister, John D .... (540) 465-5137
VP, Northern Virginia Daily, Strasburg, VA

Keith, David .... (501) 327-6621
MAN ED, City ED, MET ED
Log Cabin Democrat, Conway, AR

Keith, Gary .... (407) 242-3500
MGR-CR, Florida Today, Melbourne, FL

Keith, Jack .... (206) 597-8742
Suburban ED, News Tribune, Tacoma, WA

Keith, James .... (217) 324-2121
PROD SUPT, News-Herald, Litchfield, IL

Keith, Janice .... (205) 362-1000
News ED, Daily Home, Talladega, AL

Keith, Jenetta .... (816) 646-2411
CIRC MGR
Constitution-Tribune, Chillicothe, MO

Keith, John .... (601) 267-4501
PUB, Carthaginian, Carthage, MS

Keith, Louis .... (706) 724-0851
CIRC DIR, Augusta Chronicle, Augusta, GA

Keith, Luther .... (313) 222-2300
ASST MAN ED-Sunday
Detroit News, Detroit, MI

Keith, R W .... (614) 439-3531
PROD MGR
Daily Jeffersonian, Cambridge, OH

Keith, Randy .... (617) 786-7000
City ED, Patriot Ledger, Quincy, MA

Keith, Steven .... (304) 348-5140
Films ED
Charleston Daily Mail, Charleston, WV

Keleher, Most Rev James P ..... (618) 235-9601
PUB, Messenger, Belleville, IL

Kelekolio, Gloria .... (808) 935-6621
PROD FRM-COMP
Hawaii Tribune-Herald, Hilo, HI

Kellagher, Robert .... (717) 829-7100
VP/DIR-MKTG
Times Leader, Wilkes-Barre, PA

Kellam, Mark .... (937) 294-7000
ED
Centerville-Bellbrook Times, Kettering, OH

Kellar, Mike .... (501) 879-5450
PUB, Pine Bluff News, Pine Bluff, AR

Kellar, Patrick .... (701) 845-0463
GM
Valley City Times-Record, Valley City, ND

Kellar, Wes .... (519) 941-2230
ED, Star & Vidette, Orangeville, ON

Kelleher, John .... (607) 936-4651
City ED, Leader, Corning, NY

Kelleher, John .... (800) 245-6536
DIR-Database Products
Tribune Media Services Inc., Chicago, IL

Kelleher, Timothy J .... (313) 222-6400
Senior VP-Labor Relations and Legal
Detroit Newspapers, Detroit, MI

Keller, Bassett .... (409) 544-2238
PUB, Houston County Courier, Crockett, TX

Keller, Bill .... (212) 556-1234
Foreign ED, New York Times, New York, NY

Keller, Carol .... (402) 564-2741
ADV MGR-RT
Columbus Telegram, Columbus, NE

Keller, Cindy .... (307) 742-2176
ADV MGR-CLASS
Laramie Daily Boomerang, Laramie, WY

Keller, Darin .... (701) 225-8111
CIRC DIR, Dickinson Press, Dickinson, ND

Copyright ©1997 by the Editor & Publisher Co.

121-Who's Where **Ken**

Keller, Dave .... (916) 283-0800
ED, Feather River Bulletin, Quincy, CA

Keller, Don .... (614) 962-3377
GM, ED
Morgan County Herald, McConnelsville, OH

Keller, Gene .... (701) 252-3120
ADV MGR, Jamestown Sun, Jamestown, ND

Keller, Jay .... (607) 734-5151
MGR-Telecommunications, PROD MGR-SYS
Star-Gazette, Elmira, NY

Keller, Jerry .... (812) 332-4401
DP MGR, PROD DIR-Technical
Herald-Times Inc, Bloomington, IN

Keller, Julia .... (614) 461-5000
Radio/Television ED
Columbus Dispatch, Columbus, OH

Keller, Mark J .... (419) 636-1111
CIRC MGR, Bryan Times, Bryan, OH

Keller, Martin .... (573) 581-1111
ADV DIR, Mexico Ledger, Mexico, MO

Keller, Pamela .... (513) 422-3611
Group CONT, Journal, Middletown, OH

Keller, Richard .... (765) 362-1200
PROD MGR
Journal Review, Crawfordsville, IN

Keller, Steven P .... (614) 384-6102
PUB, ED, Wellston Telegram, Wellston, OH

Kellerman, Pam .... (618) 529-5454
Graphics ED/Art DIR
Southern Illinoisan, Carbondale, IL

Kelleter, Robert A .... (207) 990-8000
EX ED, Bangor Daily News, Bangor, ME

Kelley Jr, Cecil B .... (864) 298-4100
PROD VP/DIR
Greenville News, Greenville, SC

Kelley, Chris .... (941) 953-7755
ADTX MGR
Sarasota Herald-Tribune, Sarasota, FL

Kelley, Don .... (901) 584-7200
ED, Camden Chronicle, Camden, TN

Kelley, Duane .... (715) 778-4395
PUB, ED
Spring Valley Sun, Spring Valley, WI

Kelley, Ed .... (405) 475-3311
MAN ED
Daily Oklahoman, Oklahoma City, OK

Kelley, Gary .... (812) 424-7711
MGR-CR
Evansville Courier Co. Inc., Evansville, IN

Kelley, Michael .... (203) 235-1661
Local News ED, Suburban ED
Record-Journal, Meriden, CT

Kelley, Michael J .... (773) 586-8800
ED, Daily Southtown, Chicago, IL

Kelley, Michael R .... (205) 755-5747
PUB, ED, Clanton Advertiser, Clanton, AL

Kelley, Mike .... (301) 948-1520
ED, Basecamp Briefs, Gaithersburg, MD

Kelley, Pat .... (330) 454-5611
BU Chief, Repository, Canton, OH

Kelley, Patrick S .... (316) 342-4800
MAN ED, Book Review ED
Emporia Gazette, Emporia, KS

Kelley, Retta .... (602) 898-6500
ADV DIR, Mesa Tribune, Mesa, AZ
Thomson Newspapers

Kelley, Scott .... (941) 574-1110
PROD MGR-Press
Cape Coral Daily Breeze, Cape Coral, FL

Kelley, Shirley .... (316) 257-2368
CIRC DIR, Lyons Daily News, Lyons, KS

Kelley, Steve .... (619) 299-3131
Cartoonist
San Diego Union-Tribune, San Diego, CA

Kelley, Steve .... (314) 340-8000
News ED
St. Louis Post-Dispatch, St. Louis, MO

Kelley, Teresa Maxwell .... (313) 869-0033
ED, Michigan Citizen, Highland Park, MI

Kelley, Terri .... (618) 532-5604
DP MGR, Centralia Sentinel, Centralia, IL

Kelley, Thomas .... (608) 782-9710
ADV DIR-RT
La Crosse Tribune, La Crosse, WI

Kelley, Tim .... (816) 234-4141
ADV MGR-CLASS
Kansas City Star, Kansas City, MO

Kelley, Tim .... (608) 252-6100
City ED, EDU ED, School ED
Wisconsin State Journal, Madison, WI

Kellner, Doug .... (719) 632-5511
MGR-BUS SYS
Gazette, Colorado Springs, CO

Kellogg, Jonathan .... (508) 458-7100
EX ED, Sun, Lowell, MA

Kellogg, Mike .... (716) 282-2311
ADV DIR, Niagara Gazette, Niagara Falls, NY

Kellum, Linda .... (601) 335-1155
CIRC DIR
Delta Democrat Times, Greenville, MS

Kelly Jr, Allan H .... (617) 267-1396
Creative DIR, Small Talk, Boston, MA

Kelly, Angie .... (701) 523-5623
ED, Bowman County Pioneer, Bowman, ND

Kelly, Barbara .... (810) 767-6525
ED, Catholic Times, Flint, MI

Kelly, Bill .... (617) 254-0334
ED, Boston Citizen Journal, Boston, MA

Kelly, Bob .... (913) 823-6363
PROD MGR-SYS, Salina Journal, Salina, KS

Kelly, Brian .... (218) 935-5296
GM, Mahnomen Pioneer, Mahnomen, MN

Kelly, Brian .... (206) 888-2311
ED
Snoqualmie Valley Record, Snoqualmie, WA

Kelly, Bryan .... (717) 767-6397
ADV MGR-Display CLASS
York Newspaper Company, York, PA

Kelly, Carolyn S .... (206) 464-2111
Senior VP/CFO, Seattle Times, Seattle, WA

Kelly, Charles .... (313) 869-0033
PUB, Michigan Citizen, Highland Park, MI

Kelly, Charles W .... (315) 393-1000
GM, ED, Courier-Observer Journal & Advance-News, Ogdensburg, NY

Kelly, Cheryl .... (701) 683-4128
GM, Ransom County Gazette, Lisbon, ND

Kelly, Chris .... (970) 963-8252
ED, Family Times Magazine, Active Times Publications Inc., Carbondale, CO

Kelly, Clark .... (815) 284-2222
EDU ED, Political ED, School ED
Telegraph, Dixon, IL

Kelly, Colleen .... (907) 842-5572
MAN ED, Bristol Bay Times, Dillingham, AK

Kelly, Debora .... (905) 881-3373
ED, Richmond Hill/Thornill/Vaughan Liberal, Richmond Hill, ON

Kelly, Dennis .... (703) 276-3400
EDU ED, USA Today, Arlington, VA

Kelly, Dennis K .... (701) 872-3755
PUB, Golden Valley News, Beach, ND

Kelly, Dick .... (515) 432-6694
ED, Boone Today, Boone, IA

Kelly, Frank .... (604) 438-6397
PUB, Burnaby and New Westminster News, Burnaby, BC

Kelly, Harry W .... (701) 284-6333
PUB, Walsh County Press, Park River, ND

Kelly, Jacques .... (410) 332-6000
COL-Local, Sun, Baltimore, MD

Kelly, James A .... (541) 386-1234
PUB, Hood River News, Hood River, OR

Kelly, Jim .... (941) 773-3255
PUB, ED, Herald-Advocate, Wauchula, FL

Kelly, John .... (601) 961-7000
ADV DIR, Clarion-Ledger, Jackson, MS

Kelly, John .... (706) 324-5526
VP-MKTG, MGR-BUS, CIRC DIR
Columbus Ledger-Enquirer, Columbus, GA

Kelly, Kathy .... (315) 823-3680
ADV MGR-NTL
Evening Times, Little Falls, NY

Kelly, Kathy .... (904) 252-1511
ASST MET ED, Daytona Beach News-Journal, Daytona Beach, FL

Kelly, Kevin .... (617) 593-7700
ADV DIR, Daily Evening Item, Lynn, MA

Kelly, Larry A .... (709) 364-6300
Comptroller
Evening Telegram, St. John's, NF

Kelly, LuAnn .... (937) 644-9111
CIRC MGR
Marysville Journal-Tribune, Marysville, OH

Kelly, Marilyn .... (509) 427-8444
PUB
Skamania County Pioneer, Stevenson, WA

Kelly, Mark .... (770) 532-1234
EDU Writer, Times, Gainesville, GA

Kelly, Maryann .... (207) 791-6650
DIR-Labor Relations
Portland Press Herald, Portland, ME

Kelly, Michael .... (507) 537-1551
Sports ED, Independent, Marshall, MN

Kelly, Michael .... (503) 684-0360
ED, Beaverton Valley Times, Beaverton, OR

Kelly, Michael J .... (908) 464-1025
PUB
Independent Press, New Providence, NJ

Kelly, Mike .... (201) 646-4000
COL, Record, Hackensack, NJ

Kelly, Mikkel .... (303) 466-3636
ED, Broomfield Enterprise Sentinel, Broomfield, CO

Kelly, Pat .... (318) 574-1404
ED, Madison Journal, Tallulah, LA

Kelly, Patricia .... (313) 222-6400
DIR-PROM
Detroit Newspapers, Detroit, MI

Kelly, Patrick D .... (218) 935-5296
PUB, Mahnomen Pioneer, Mahnomen, MN

Kelly, Paul .... (304) 348-5140
PROD MGR-COMP
Charleston Newspapers, Charleston, WV

Kelly, Pete .... (201) 791-8400
ED, News Beacon, Fair Lawn, NJ

Kelly, Philip W .... (216) 329-7000
SEC/TREAS, CONT
Chronicle-Telegram, Elyria, OH

Kelly, Phyllis .... (616) 469-1410
ED, Harbor County News, New Buffalo, MI

Kelly, Rob .... (905) 878-2341
ED, Canadian Champion, Milton, ON

Kelly, Robert A .... (304) 233-0100
EX ED, EPE, Intelligencer/Wheeling News-Register, Wheeling, WV

Kelly, Rod .... (403) 865-3115
ED, Parklander, Hinton, AB

Kelly, Ron .... (902) 629-6000
CONT, Guardian, Charlottetown, PEI

Kelly, Ronna .... (714) 835-1234
VP-Community Relations
Orange County Register, Santa Ana, CA

Kelly, Sandra .... (817) 387-3811
ADV DIR
Denton Record-Chronicle, Denton, TX

Kelly, Sandra .... (540) 981-3100
Medical ED, SCI ED
Roanoke Times, Roanoke, VA

Kelly, Sara .... (215) 563-7400
MAN ED
Philadelphia Weekly, Philadelphia, PA

Kelly, Sean W .... (701) 683-4128
PUB, ED
Ransom County Gazette, Lisbon, ND

Kelly, Shaun .... (701) 347-4493
PUB, Cass County Reporter, Casselton, ND

Kelly, Steve .... (206) 464-2111
COL, Seattle Times, Seattle, WA

Kelly, Teresa .... (616) 927-1527
ED, Citizen, Benton Harbor, MI

Kelly, Terri .... (618) 532-5604
PROD SUPV-COMP
Centralia Sentinel, Centralia, IL

Kelly, Tim .... (409) 833-3311
ED, Beaumont Enterprise, Beaumont, TX

Kelly, Tim .... (606) 231-3100
PRES, PUB
Lexington Herald-Leader, Lexington, KY

Kelly, Tim .... (516) 298-3200
MAN ED, Suffolk Times, Mattituck, NY

Kelly, Tom .... (402) 372-2461
PUB, West Point News, West Point, NE

Kelly, Tom .... (213) 237-5000
ADV DIR-Food/Electronics/Home Furnishings/Sporting Goods
Los Angeles Times, Los Angeles, CA

Kelsey, Gene .... (913) 242-4700
CIRC MGR, Ottawa Herald, Ottawa, KS

Kelsey, Lana .... (805) 395-7500
MGR/PA-Building SRV
Bakersfield Californian, Bakersfield, CA

Kelsey, Stephen W .... (801) 237-2031
CIRC DIR
Salt Lake Tribune, Salt Lake City, UT

Kelsh, James .... (414) 887-0321
City ED, Daily Citizen, Beaver Dam, WI

Kelso, Iris .... (504) 826-3279
COL, New Orleans Times-Picayune, New Orleans, LA

Kelstinsky, Lee .... (608) 221-1544
ED, Community Life, Monona, WI

Kemball, Terri .... (403) 464-0033
ED, Sherwood Park News, Sherwood Park, AB

Kemmeter, Gene .... (715) 344-6100
Wire ED
Stevens Point Journal, Stevens Point, WI

Kemp, Barbara .... (508) 456-8122
GM, Harvard Post, Harvard, MA

Kemp, Beverly .... (318) 828-3706
CIRC MGR
Franklin Banner-Tribune, Franklin, LA

Kemp, Jack .... (703) 764-0496
NTL Correspondent
Associated Features Inc., Burke, VA

Kemp, Julianne .... (304) 348-5140
Amusements ED, Features ED, Food/Home Furnishings ED, Lifestyle ED, Travel ED
Charleston Daily Mail, Charleston, WV

Kemp, Kathryn .... (205) 325-2222
Films/Theater ED
Birmingham Post-Herald, Birmingham, AL

Kemp, Kenny .... (304) 348-5140
Photo ED, Charleston Gazette, Charleston Sunday Gazette-Mail, Charleston, WV

Kemp, Mike .... (806) 376-4488
PROD SUPT-COMP, Amarillo Daily News/Globe Times, Amarillo, TX

Kemp, Nancy J .... (501) 561-4634
PUB, ED
Northeast Arkansas Town Crier, Manila, AR

Kemp, Randy .... (501) 362-2425
ED, Cleburne County Sun-Times, Heber Springs, AR

Kemp, Ronald E .... (501) 598-2201
PUB, ED, Piggott Times, Piggott, AR

Kemper, Kevin .... (405) 255-5354
Political ED, Duncan Banner, Duncan, OK

Kempf, Bruce .... (406) 791-1444
MGR-Technical Services
Great Falls Tribune, Great Falls, MT

Kempf, Cristi .... (312) 321-3000
Features ED
Chicago Sun-Times, Chicago, IL

Kempher, Susan .... (217) 852-3511
PUB, ED
Dallas City Enterprise, Dallas City, IL

Kempin, Paul .... (352) 563-6363
Online MGR
Citrus County Chronicle, Crystal River, FL

Kempkes, Ted .... (715) 339-3036
PUB, Bee, Phillips, WI

Kempley, Rita .... (202) 334-6000
Films ED (Style)
Washington Post, Washington, DC

Kenan, Charlotte .... (520) 573-4561
Librarian, Tucson Citizen, Tucson, AZ

Kendall, David R .... (904) 252-1511
CFO, Daytona Beach News-Journal, Daytona Beach, FL

Kendall, Don .... (604) 545-3322
PUB, Morning Star, Vernon, BC

Kendall, Dorothy .... (317) 342-3311
EVP, Daily Reporter, Martinsville, IN

Kendall, Howard .... (316) 548-2678
PUB, ED
Merchant's Directory, Mullinville, KS

Kendall, Jeanette .... (309) 444-2513
MAN ED, Washington Reporter, Morton, IL

Kendall, Josh .... (912) 923-6432
Sports ED, Daily Sun, Warner Robins, GA

Kendall, Judith B .... (818) 241-4141
VP/GM, Glendale News-Press, Glendale, CA

Kendall, Lois .... (314) 664-2700
ED, South Side Journal, St. Louis, MO

Kendall, Mark C .... (317) 342-3311
PRES, Daily Reporter, Martinsville, IN

Kendall, Pete .... (817) 645-2441
Sports ED
Cleburne Times-Review, Cleburne, TX

Kendall, Rick .... (941) 262-3161
ADV MGR-RT, Naples Daily News, Naples, FL

Kendall, Robert S .... (317) 342-3311
BC, COL, Daily Reporter, Martinsville, IN

Kendall, Wilbur C .... (317) 653-5151
PROD MGR, Banner-Graphic, Greencastle, IN

Kendell, Joel .... (405) 256-2200
ED, Woodward News, Woodward, OK

Kenditos, Y .... (416) 441-1405
Middle East Photographer
Fotopress Independent News Service International (FPINS), Toronto, ON

Kendle, Jeanine .... (330) 674-1811
ED, Holmes County Hub, Millersburg, OH

Kendle, John .... (204) 694-2022
Entertainment ED, Music ED
Winnipeg Sun, Winnipeg, MB

Kendrick, Ronald .... (615) 552-1808
PROD SUPT-COMP, PROD SUPT-Graphic Arts, Leaf-Chronicle, Clarksville, TN

Kendrick, Steve .... (512) 445-3500
ASST MGR-MIS
Austin American-Statesman, Austin, TX

Kening, Dan .... (847) 427-4300
Music-Contemporary
Daily Herald, Arlington Heights, IL

Kenitzer, Terri .... (502) 926-0123
MGR-CORE/INFO SRV
Messenger-Inquirer, Owensboro, KY

Kenna, Kathleen .... (416) 367-2000
Entertainment ED, Toronto Star, Toronto, ON

Kennebeck, Sue .... (217) 636-8453
ED, Menard County Review, Athens, IL

Kennedy, Basil .... (414) 684-4433
PROD FRM-COMP
Herald Times Reporter, Manitowoc, WI

Kennedy, Betty .... (307) 682-9306
PRES, News-Record, Gillette, WY

Kennedy, Brian M .... (406) 892-2151
PUB, ED
Hungry Horse News, Columbia Falls, MT

Kennedy, Bud .... (817) 390-7400
COL-Star
Fort Worth Star-Telegram, Fort Worth, TX

Kennedy, Dan .... (617) 933-3700
COL, Daily Times Chronicle, Woburn, MA

Kennedy, Dave .... (603) 742-4455
ADV MGR-CLASS
Foster's Democrat, Dover, NH

Kennedy, David .... (616) 722-3161
ADV MGR-Sales
Muskegon Chronicle, Muskegon, MI

Kennedy, Diana .... (616) 964-7161
CIRC DIR
Battle Creek Enquirer, Battle Creek, MI

Kennedy, Ed .... (808) 525-8000
Travel ED, Honolulu Advertiser, Honolulu, HI

Kennedy, George .... (573) 882-5700
MAN ED
Columbia Missourian, Columbia, MO

Kennedy, James .... (601) 335-1155
ADV DIR
Delta Democrat Times, Greenville, MS

Ken Who's Where-122

Kennedy, James C .... (404) 843-5000
COB/CEO-Cox Enterprises Inc.
Cox Newspapers Inc., Atlanta, GA
Kennedy, James M .... (212) 621-1500
DIR-Multimedia Services
Associated Press, New York, NY
Kennedy, Janice .... (613) 829-9100
Films/Theater ED
Ottawa Citizen, Ottawa, ON
Kennedy, Jay .... (212) 455-4000
Comics ED, North America Syndicate, King Features Syndicate Inc., New York, NY
Kennedy, Jim .... (318) 365-6773
ADV MGR, Daily Iberian, New Iberia, LA
Kennedy, Joey .... (205) 325-2222
EDL Writer
Birmingham News, Birmingham, AL
Kennedy, John W .... (704) 333-1718
PUB, Independent Tribune, Concord, NC
Kennedy, Jon .... (604) 732-2944
VP-MKTG
Pacific Press Limited, Vancouver, BC
Kennedy, Joyce Lain .... (619) 431-1660
PRES, Sun Features Inc., Cardiff, CA
Kennedy, Karen .... (212) 416-2000
PROD DIR-OPER Support
Wall Street Journal, New York, NY
Kennedy, Kevin .... (209) 875-8771
PUB, ED, El Sol de Valle, Sanger, CA
Kennedy, Kris .... (541) 459-2261
GM, Sun Tribune, Sutherlin, OR
Kennedy, Larry .... (817) 865-5212
ED, Gatesville Messenger and Star-Forum, Gatesville, TX
Kennedy, Lorry .... (972) 424-6565
EDU ED, Plano Star Courier, Plano, TX
Kennedy, Mac .... (305) 377-3721
MKTG DIR
Miami Daily Business Review, Miami, FL
Kennedy, Mark .... (423) 756-1234
Personal Life ED
Chattanooga Times, Chattanooga, TN
Kennedy, Matthew .... (412) 263-1100
ASST to ED
Pittsburgh Post-Gazette, Pittsburgh, PA
Kennedy, Michelle .... (501) 741-2325
ADV MGR, Daily Times, Harrison, AR
Kennedy, Morris .... (813) 259-7711
EDL Writer
Tampa Tribune and Times, Tampa, FL
Kennedy, Patrick .... (773) 586-8800
DP MGR, Daily Southtown, Chicago, IL
Kennedy, Pete .... (414) 542-2501
News ED
Waukesha County Freeman, Waukesha, WI
Kennedy, Randy .... (912) 244-1880
Sports ED, Daily Times, Valdosta, GA
Kennedy, Robert .... (203) 964-2200
Sports ED, Stamford Advocate, Stamford, CT
Kennedy, Sam .... (901) 847-6354
PUB, News-Leader, Parsons, TN
Kennedy, Susan .... (219) 235-6161
Copy Desk Chief
South Bend Tribune, South Bend, IN
Kennedy, Thomas C .... (304) 624-6411
BM/ASST TREAS, Clarksburg Exponent/Telegram, Clarksburg, WV
Kennedy, Wally .... (417) 623-3480
EDU ED, Joplin Globe, Joplin, MO
Kennedy, Will .... (330) 454-5611
ASST MAN ED, Repository, Canton, OH
Kennedy, William T .... (508) 997-7411
PUB, Standard Times, New Bedford, MA
Kennett, Carolyn .... (316) 421-2000
ADV DIR, ADV MGR-CLASS
Parsons Sun, Parsons, KS
Kenney, Cary .... (813) 893-8111
Librarian
St. Petersburg Times, St. Petersburg, FL
Kenney, Crane .... (312) 222-3237
VP/GEN Counsel/SEC
Tribune Co., Chicago, IL
Kenney, Fay .... (408) 287-4866
PUB, San Jose Post-Record, San Jose, CA
Kenney, Robert .... (609) 663-6000
Entertainment/Amusements ED, PROD MGR-Pre Press, Courier-Post, Cherry Hill, NJ
Kenney, Russle .... (816) 747-8123
CIRC DIR
Daily Star-Journal, Warrensburg, MO
Kennicoff, Phil .... (314) 340-8000
Music ED
St. Louis Post-Dispatch, St. Louis, MO
Kennon, J .... (504) 652-9545
PUB, ED
LaPlace L'Observateur, LaPlace, LA
Kennon, John .... (719) 336-2266
Agriculture ED
Lamar Daily News, Lamar, CO
Kenny, Ann .... (506) 859-4900
MGR-MKTG, Times-Transcript, Moncton, NB
Kenny, John R .... (608) 372-4123
PUB, ED, Tomah Journal, Tomah, WI
Kenny, Michael .... (219) 223-2111
Photo DEPT MGR
Rochester Sentinel, Rochester, IN
Kenny, Terry .... (517) 835-7171
ADV MGR-NTL, Daily News, Midland, MI
Kensik, Edward .... (201) 933-1166
ED, South Bergenite, Rutherford, NJ
Kensinger, Leah .... (316) 244-3371
PUB, ED, Erie Record, Erie, KS
Kent, Bob .... (215) 379-5500
ED, Northeast Breeze, Rockledge, PA
Kent, David .... (915) 673-4271
Photo ED, Reporter-News, Abilene, TX
Kent, Gaylon .... (619) 337-3400
EDU ED, Imperial Valley Press, El Centro, CA
Kent, Phil .... (706) 724-0851
EPE, Augusta Chronicle, Augusta, GA
Kent, Roy .... (505) 763-3431
Sports ED, Clovis News Journal, Clovis, NM
Kent, Rusty .... (419) 468-1117
Sports ED, Galion Inquirer, Galion, OH
Kent, Scott .... (912) 236-9511
EDL Writer
Savannah Morning News, Savannah, GA
Kent, Stephen M .... (402) 558-6611
ED, Catholic Voice, Omaha, NE
Kent, Stephen W .... (904) 678-1080
PUB, ED, Bay Beacon, Niceville, FL
Kentling, Fran .... (316) 268-6000
Administrative ED
Wichita Eagle, Wichita, KS
Kenyon, Henry S .... (202) 638-0444
ED, Press Associates Inc., Washington, DC
Kenyon, Judith A .... (604) 774-2357
PUB, ED, Fort Nelson News, Fort Nelson, BC
Kenyon, Kevin .... (803) 317-6397
CFO, Florence Morning News, Florence, SC
Kenyon, Maureen .... (304) 263-8931
Local Magazine ED, Journal, Martinsburg, WV
Kenyon, Ron .... (604) 749-3143
PUB, ED, Lake News, Lake Cowichan, BC
Kenyon, Sheila .... (604) 749-3143
PUB, GM, Lake News, Lake Cowichan, BC
Kenyon, Tim .... (515) 753-6611
Entertainment/Amusements ED
Times-Republican, Marshalltown, IA
Keogh, Jim .... (508) 829-5981
ED, Landmark, Holden, MA
Keogh, Mary E .... (309) 829-9411
ADV DIR, Pantagraph, Bloomington, IL
Keohan, Robert .... (617) 245-0080
School ED
Wakefield Daily Item, Wakefield, MA
Keosky, Donna .... (914) 694-9300
MGR-Community Relations, Reporter Dispatch, White Plains, NY, Gannett Co. Inc.
Kephart, Art .... (412) 282-8000
ADV DIR-RT, Butler Eagle, Butler, PA
Kepler, Peggy .... (814) 837-6000
CIRC DIR, Kane Republican, Kane, PA
Keplinger, Teresa .... (541) 776-4411
ADV MGR, Mail Tribune, Medford, OR
Kepple, Clifford .... (814) 532-5199
Art DIR, Tribune-Democrat, Johnstown, PA
Kerbin, Bill .... (410) 957-1700
GM, ED, Worcester County Messenger, Pocomoke City, MD
Kerby, James .... (606) 573-4510
PUB, Harlan Daily Enterprise, Harlan, KY
Keren-David, Nina .... (212) 599-3666
Electronic Publishing, Jerusalem Post Foreign Service, New York, NY
Kerkemeyer, Terra .... (618) 438-5611
ADV MGR-RT
Benton Evening News, Benton, IL
Kerkhoff, Cynthia S .... (712) 659-3144
GM, ED, Glidden Graphic, Glidden, IA
Kerley, Coye .... (915) 337-4661
ADV MGR-CLASS
Odessa American, Odessa, TX
Kerlin, Tom .... (770) 478-5753
MAN ED, EPE
Clayton News/Daily, Jonesboro, GA
Kern, Gerould .... (312) 222-3232
Deputy MAN ED-Features, City/MET ED
Chicago Tribune, Chicago, IL
Kern, Judy .... (614) 363-1161
ADV MGR-CLASS
Delaware Gazette, Delaware, OH
Kernen, A William .... (402) 444-1000
Sr VP/CFO
Omaha World-Herald Co., Omaha, NE
Kerner, Diane .... (212) 556-1234
Art DIR, New York Times, New York, NY
Kerner-Odgis, Carol .... (212) 715-2100
VP/New BUS Development
USA Weekend, New York, NY
Kerns, Bill .... (806) 762-8844
Amusements/Books ED, Music ED
Lubbock Avalanche-Journal, Lubbock, TX
Kerns, Dorothy .... (915) 396-2243
ED, Menard News & Messenger, Menard, TX
Kerns, Jo .... (419) 245-6000
DIR-Human Resources, Blade, Toledo, OH
Kerntopf, Willy .... (250) 492-4002
PROD FRM-PR
Penticton Herald, Penticton, BC
Kerr, Alan .... (401) 277-7000
Automotive ED
Providence Journal-Bulletin, Providence, RI
Kerr, Alan .... (215) 345-3000
EPE, Intelligencer/Record, Doylestown, PA
Kerr, Amy .... (304) 526-4000
MGR-MKTG/PROM
Herald-Dispatch, Huntington, WV
Kerr, Dick .... (815) 232-1171
PROD FRM-Press
Journal-Standard, Freeport, IL
Kerr, Don .... (303) 776-2244
PROD SUPV-Press
Daily Times-Call, Longmont, CO
Kerr Jr, Frederick J .... (908) 922-6000
MAN ED-News
Asbury Park Press, Neptune, NJ
Kerr, Gail .... (705) 325-1355
PA, Packet & Times, Orillia, ON
Kerr, James .... (610) 323-3000
City ED, Mercury, Pottstown, PA
Kerr, Jeff .... (606) 744-3123
Sports ED, Winchester Sun, Winchester, KY
Kerr, John .... (702) 383-0211
EPE
Las Vegas Review-Journal, Las Vegas, NV
Kerr, Kathy .... (403) 429-5400
City ED, Edmonton Journal, Edmonton, AB
Kerr, Mike .... (901) 529-2211
ASST MAN ED-Graphics
Commercial Appeal, Memphis, TN
Kerr, Pauline .... (519) 364-4597
ED, Saugeen City News, Hanover, ON
Kerr, Peter .... (519) 679-6666
Online MGR, London Free Press, London, ON
Kerr, R C .... (616) 256-9827
PUB, ED
Leelanau Enterprise and Tribune, Leland, MI
Kerr, Suzanne Myrick .... (901) 529-2211
EDL PROD ED
Commercial Appeal, Memphis, TN
Kerr, Thomas .... (908) 246-5500
Art DIR
Home News & Tribune, East Brunswick, NJ
Kerrigan, Jack .... (703) 642-7330
PUB, Defense News, Springfield, VA
Kerrigan, Paul J .... (209) 784-5000
CIRC MGR, Recorder, Porterville, CA
Kerrigan, Richard .... (617) 929-2000
PROD SUPT-MR, PROD MGR-Plant (Westwood), Boston Globe, Boston, MA
Kerrill, Tamara .... (312) 321-3000
Transportation
Chicago Sun-Times, Chicago, IL
Kerrison, Ray .... (212) 930-8000
COL, New York Post, New York, NY
Kersey, Sharon .... (937) 393-3456
ADV MGR, Times-Gazette, Hillsboro, OH
Kershner, Charles J .... (315) 853-3490
ED, Clinton Courier, Clinton, NY
Kershner, Cynthia Z .... (315) 853-3490
PUB, Clinton Courier, Clinton, NY
Kershner, James W .... (508) 775-1200
Production ED, Sunday ED
Cape Cod Times, Hyannis, MA
Kershner, Larry .... (515) 732-3721
MAN ED
Mitchell County Press-News, Osage, IA
Kersmarki, Mike .... (313) 994-6989
Automotive ED, BUS/FIN ED, RE ED
Ann Arbor News, Ann Arbor, MI
Kersten, Lori Anne .... (905) 689-4841
MAN ED
Flamborough Review, Waterdown, ON
Kerth, Gregory P .... (716) 798-1400
ADV MGR, Journal-Register, Medina, NY
Kerwin, Jackie .... (415) 883-8600
MAN ED
Marin Independent Journal, Novato, CA
Keskela, Mai-Lis .... (715) 394-4961
ED, Tyomies-Eteenpain, Superior, WI
Kesler, William .... (314) 340-8000
PROD ASST MGR-Color Graphics
St. Louis Post-Dispatch, St. Louis, MO
Kessel, Scott H .... (207) 443-6241
GM, Coastal Journal, Bath, ME
Kessinger, Howard .... (913) 562-2317
PUB, ED, Marysville Advocate, Marysville, KS
Kessinger, K Kurt .... (913) 654-3621
PUB, ED
Osage County Chronicle, Burlingame, KS
Kessinger, Sarah .... (210) 686-4343
Arts/Entertainment ED, Monitor, McAllen, TX
Kessinger, Sharon .... (913) 562-2317
PUB, Marysville Advocate, Marysville, KS
Kessler, John .... (303) 820-1010
Food Writer, Denver Post, Denver, CO
Kessler, Julie .... (219) 362-2161
Music ED, Radio/Television ED, Religion ED, Wire ED, La Porte Herald-Argus, La Porte, IN
Kessler, Larry .... (508) 222-7000
Local ED, Sun Chronicle, Attleboro, MA
Kessler, Marilyn .... (415) 435-2652
PUB, ED, Ark, Tiburon, CA
Kessler, Mary Elum .... (216) 923-2397
MKTG DIR
Scrambl-Gram Inc., Cuyahoga Falls, OH
Kessler, Fr Thomas .... (614) 224-5195
ED, Catholic Times, Columbus, OH
Kessler, Tim .... (501) 238-2375
MAN ED
East Arkansas News Leader, Wynne, AR
Kessler, Tom .... (214) 977-8222
Arts/Entertainment ED
Dallas Morning News, Dallas, TX
Kessler, Tony .... (615) 259-8800
News ED, Nashville Banner, Nashville, TN
Kessler-Rix, Judy .... (716) 496-5013
ED, Arcade Herald, Arcade, NY
Kessner, Larry .... (410) 332-6000
PUB-SunSpot, Sun, Baltimore, MD
Kester, Art .... (301) 662-1177
ADV MGR-Co-op/Special Sections
Frederick Post/The News, Frederick, MD
Kester, Eula .... (918) 673-1085
PUB, Tri-State Tribune, Picher, OK
Kester, John R .... (918) 673-1085
ED, Tri-State Tribune, Picher, OK
Kestler, Ed .... (409) 985-5541
ADV MGR-CLASS
Port Arthur News, Port Arthur, TX
Kestner, Laura .... (817) 796-4325
ED, Hico News-Review, Hico, TX
Ketcham, Janet .... (207) 791-6650
ADV MGR-CLASS Development
Portland Press Herald, Portland, ME
Ketchie, Kenneth .... (704) 264-6397
PUB, ED, Mountain Times, Boone, NC
Ketchum, Ben .... (520) 432-7254
PUB, Bisbee Observer, Bisbee, AZ
Ketchum, Chad .... (802) 254-2311
PROD MGR-PR (Night)
Brattleboro Reformer, Brattleboro, VT
Ketchum, James .... (810) 985-7171
Religion ED, Times Herald, Port Huron, MI
Ketchum, Jim .... (619) 299-3131
News ED-Night
San Diego Union-Tribune, San Diego, CA
Ketsdever, William .... (541) 347-2423
PUB, ED, Western World, Bandon, OR
Ketteman, Wanda .... (803) 547-2353
GM, Fort Mill Times, Fort Mill, SC
Ketter, William B .... (617) 786-7000
ED, Patriot Ledger, Quincy, MA
Ketterling, Ken .... (209) 943-6397
CONT, Record, Stockton, CA
Ketterman, Becky .... (301) 662-1177
CIRC MGR-Customer SRV
Frederick Post/News, Frederick, MD
Kettles, Harris S .... (770) 428-9411
VP/DIR-OPER
Marietta Daily Journal, Marietta, GA
Kettlewell, Bret .... (330) 364-5577
CONT, DP MGR
Times Reporter, New Philadelphia, OH
Keuer, Martin .... (573) 581-1111
MGR-MKTG/PROM
Mexico Ledger, Mexico, MO
Keul, James V .... (507) 847-3771
PUB, Jackson County Pilot, Jackson, MN
Keuning, Patty .... (515) 284-8000
ADV MGR-CLASS
Des Moines Register, Des Moines, IA
Keute, Todd .... (715) 394-4411
GM
Superior Daily Telegram, Superior, WI
Kevlin III, James C .... (717) 622-3456
ED, Pottsville Republican & Evening Herald, Pottsville, PA
Key, Kaycee .... (817) 387-3811
Automotive ED, RE ED
Denton Record-Chronicle, Denton, TX
Keyburn, Jack .... (609) 871-8000
PROD SUPT-Maintenance
Burlington County Times, Willingboro, NJ
Keyes, David .... (208) 267-5521
PUB, ED
Bonners Ferry Herald, Bonners Ferry, ID
Keyes, Saundra .... (510) 935-2525
MAN ED
Contra Costa Times, Walnut Creek, CA
Keyes, Thad .... (303) 442-1202
Special Projects ED
Daily Camera, Boulder, CO
Keys, Carolyn .... (903) 885-8663
SEC/TREAS, Sulphur Springs News-Telegram, Sulphur Springs, TX
Keys, Dawn .... (304) 255-4400
Health/Medical ED
Register Herald, Beckley, WV

123-Who's Where **Kin**

Keys, Kathi .... (910) 625-5576
GM, ED, Randolph Guide, Asheboro, NC
Keys, Scott .... (903) 885-8663
PRES, PUB, ED, Sulphur Springs News-Telegram, Sulphur Springs, TX
Keyser, Gene .... (218) 723-5281
PROD FRM-COMP (Gen)
Duluth News-Tribune, Duluth, MN
Keyser, Tom .... (403) 235-7100
COL, Calgary Herald, Calgary, AB
Kezmarsky, Tadd .... (412) 439-7500
PROD MGR-PR
Herald-Standard, Uniontown, PA
Kezziah Jr, William H .... (719) 481-3423
PUB, ED, Tribune, Monument, CO
Khan, Matin .... (613) 820-3126
PUB, ED, Nepean Clarion, Nepean, ON
Khankan, Ghazi .... (212) 972-0460
GM, Action, New York, NY
Khorey, John .... (401) 277-7000
MET Edition ED
Providence Journal-Bulletin, Providence, RI
Kiamie, Dennis .... (212) 930-8000
PROD GEN FRM-COMP
New York Post, New York, NY
Kibbey, William H .... (912) 384-9112
ED, Coffee County News, Douglas, GA
Kibodeaux, Syd M .... (540) 980-5220
PUB, MGR-Office
Southwest Times, Pulaski, VA
Kiczales, Ken .... (212) 930-8000
ADV MGR-NTL/Travel
New York Post, New York, NY
Kidd, Jim .... (315) 536-4422
ED
Penn Yan Chronicle-Express, Penn Yan, NY
Kidwell, David .... (919) 446-5161
Photo DEPT MGR
Rocky Mount Telegram, Rocky Mount, NC
Kieck, Ken .... (414) 224-2000
VP-PROD DIR
Milwaukee Journal Sentinel, Milwaukee, WI
Kieckhefer, Bob .... (202) 898-8254
GEN MGR-US/Canada
United Press International, Washington, DC
Kiefer, Francine .... (408) 920-5000
NTL/Foreign ED
San Jose Mercury News, San Jose, CA
Kiefer, Gary .... (614) 461-5000
MAN ED-Features
Columbus Dispatch, Columbus, OH
Kiefer, George J .... (313) 222-6400
ADV Sales DIR-NTL
Detroit Newspapers, Detroit, MI
Kieffer, C Dean .... (419) 435-6641
VP, GM, Review Times, Fostoria, OH
Kiefner, Pat .... (317) 636-0200
PROD DIR
Court & Commercial Record, Indianapolis, IN
Kielec, Greg .... (613) 525-2020
ED, Glengarry News, Alexandria, ON
Kiely, Eugene .... (201) 646-4000
Trenton BU Chief, Record, Hackensack, NJ
Kiely, Theresa .... (516) 843-2020
Library DIR, Newsday, Melville, NY
Kientz, Renee .... (713) 220-7171
Lifestyle ED, Houston Chronicle, Houston, TX
Kienzler, Mike .... (217) 788-1300
ASSOC City ED
State Journal-Register, Springfield, IL
Kier, Dwight .... (814) 238-5000
Sports ED
Centre Daily Times, State College, PA
Kier, Katherine .... (717) 829-7100
Librarian, Times Leader, Wilkes-Barre, PA
Kiernan, Steven .... (802) 863-3441
EPE, Burlington Free Press, Burlington, VT
Kies, Tom .... (203) 846-3281
ADV MGR-Sales, Hour, Norwalk, CT
Kiesewetter, John .... (513) 721-2700
Radio/Television ED
Cincinnati Enquirer, Cincinnati, OH
Kiesler, Chris .... (914) 694-9300
Graphics ED, Reporter Dispatch, White Plains, NY, Gannett Co. Inc.
Kiest, James .... (210) 225-7411
Arts ED, Entertainment ED
San Antonio Express-News, San Antonio, TX
Kieszek, Stanley .... (717) 821-2091
EDU ED, Citizens' Voice, Wilkes-Barre, PA
Kifner, Allan .... (217) 675-2461
GM, Franklin Times, Franklin, IL
Kilbourne, Chris .... (201) 646-4000
Online ED, Record, Hackensack, NJ
Kilburn, Lois .... (606) 464-2444
PUB, Beattyville Enterprise, Beattyville, KY
Kilcoyne, Joseph .... (518) 828-1616
City ED, Register-Star, Hudson, NY
Kilcrease, Monte .... (912) 273-2277
PROD Compositor
Cordele Dispatch, Cordele, GA
Kildee, Jennifer .... (810) 766-6100
People/Community Events ED
Flint Journal, Flint, MI
Kile, Dan .... (616) 279-7488
CIRC MGR, Three Rivers Commercial-News, Three Rivers, MI
Kilen, Donald .... (701) 628-2333
PUB, ED
Mountrail County Promoter, Stanley, ND
Kilen, Esther .... (209) 846-6689
GM, MAN ED, Kerman News, Kerman, CA
Kilen, Mark .... (209) 846-6689
PUB, ED, Kerman News, Kerman, CA
Kiley, Richard .... (516) 481-5487
VP, Editorial Consultant Service, West Hempstead, NY
Kilfoil, David .... (506) 452-6671
DP MGR, Daily Gleaner, Fredericton, NB
Kilgo, Dwayne .... (410) 749-7171
MGR-SYS, Daily Times, Salisbury, MD
Kilgore, James B .... (609) 924-3244
PUB, Princeton Packet, Princeton, NJ
Kilgore, Michael .... (813) 259-7711
DIR-PROM
Tampa Tribune and Times, Tampa, FL
Kilgore, Troy .... (205) 236-1551
PROD FRM-Camera Room
Anniston Star, Anniston, AL
Kilgore, Vickie .... (941) 335-0200
MAN ED, News-Press, Fort Myers, FL
Kilgus, Betty S .... (803) 245-5204
PUB, ED, Advertizer-Herald, Bamberg, SC
Kilian, Mary Lou .... (315) 393-2540
ED, North Country Catholic, Ogdenburg, NY
Kilian, Michael .... (312) 222-3232
COL-Washington Based
Chicago Tribune, Chicago, IL
Kilimanjaro, C Vickie .... (910) 274-6210
MAN ED
Carolina Peacemaker, Greensboro, NC
Kilimanjaro, John Marshall ..... (910) 274-6210
PUB, Carolina Peacemaker, Greensboro, NC
Kill, Gail M .... (507) 964-5547
PUB, Arlington Enterprise, Arlington, MN
Killackey, Jim .... (405) 475-3311
EDU ED
Daily Oklahoman, Oklahoma City, OK
Killebrew, Chad .... (704) 249-3981
EPE, Wire ED, Dispatch, Lexington, NC
Killeen Jr, Calhoun J .... (508) 922-1234
MAN ED
Daily News of Newburyport, Beverly, MA
Killen, John .... (503) 221-8327
Team Leader-City Life
Oregonian, Portland, OR
Killgore, Jack C .... (817) 583-7811
PUB, Rosebud News, Rosebud, TX
Killgore, John R .... (817) 583-7811
PUB, Rosebud News, Rosebud, TX
Killian, Greg .... (412) 224-4321
PROD MGR-Pre Press
Valley News Dispatch, Tarentum, PA
Killian, John .... (212) 455-4000
ASST Sales MGR, North America Syndicate, King Features Syndicate Inc., New York, NY
Killian, Michael F .... (203) 235-1661
VP-BUS Development
Record-Journal, Meriden, CT
Killian, Mike .... (315) 792-5000
MET ED, Observer-Dispatch, Utica, NY
Killin, J Blake .... (914) 679-2145
PUB, ED
Ulster County Townsman, Woodstock, NY
Killingsworth, Louise .... (505) 396-2844
Society ED, Daily Leader, Lovington, NM
Killion, Ann .... (408) 920-5000
Sports COL
San Jose Mercury News, San Jose, CA
Killion, Diane .... (815) 987-1200
DIR-Human Resources
Rockford Register Star, Rockford, IL
Killion, Larry R .... (317) 633-1240
MGR-Transportation
Indianapolis Star/News, Indianapolis, IN
Killion, Renee .... (605) 886-6901
Fashion/Neighbors ED, Women's ED
Watertown Public Opinion, Watertown, SD
Kilpatrick, Bill .... (941) 335-0200
Automotive Writer
News-Press, Fort Myers, FL
Kilpatrick, Kent .... (601) 335-1155
OPER DIR
Delta Democrat Times, Greenville, MS
Kilpatrick, Mark .... (707) 838-9211
PUB, ED, Times, Windsor, CA
Kilpatrick, Sharon .... (540) 675-3349
ED, Rappahannock News, Washington, VA
Kilroy, John .... (860) 225-4601
BUS ED, Herald, New Britain, CT
Kim, Doug .... (206) 464-2111
Arts/Entertainment ED
Seattle Times, Seattle, WA
Kim, Jae-Ha .... (312) 321-3000
Features Reporter
Chicago Sun-Times, Chicago, IL
Kim, Steve .... (312) 463-1050
GM, Korea Times, Chicago, IL
Kim, Sun D .... (213) 487-5323
MAN ED, Korea Times, Los Angeles, CA
Kim, Yong W .... (312) 463-1050
PUB, Korea Times, Chicago, IL
Kimantas, John .... (250) 758-4917
MAN ED, Daily Free Press, Nanaimo, BC
Kimball, Art .... (813) 259-7711
PROD ADM ASST
Tampa Tribune and Times, Tampa, FL
Kimball, George .... (617) 426-3000
Sports COL, Boston Herald, Boston, MA
Kimball, John E .... (201) 646-4000
VP-Sales, Record, Hackensack, NJ
Kimball, Ray .... (501) 642-2111
PRES, PUB, Daily Citizen, De Queen, AR
Kimball, Richard S .... (909) 889-9666
EPE, Sun, San Bernardino, CA
Kimball, Sandra .... (414) 467-6591
ED
Sheboygan Falls News, Sheboygan Falls, WI
Kimbel, John .... (813) 259-7711
ADV MGR-RT/Major Accounts
Tampa Tribune and Times, Tampa, FL
Kimber, Mark .... (209) 268-0941
PUB, California Advocate, Fresno, CA
Kimber, Pauline .... (209) 268-0941
ED, California Advocate, Fresno, CA
Kimberlin, Joanne .... (305) 294-6641
City Desk ED, Key West Citizen, Key West, FL
Kimberlini, Keith E .... (401) 596-7791
ASST Sports ED, Westerly Sun, Westerly, RI
Kimble, Marge .... (319) 868-7509
GM
Morning Sun News-Herald, Morning Sun, IA
Kimble, Mark .... (520) 573-4561
EPE, Tucson Citizen, Tucson, AZ
Kimble, Nora .... (304) 822-3871
GM, Hampshire Review, Romney, WV
Kimbro, Jeff N .... (901) 529-2211
CIRC MGR
Commercial Appeal, Memphis, TN
Kimbro, Judy .... (423) 756-6900
Automotive ED
Chattanooga Free Press, Chattanooga, TN
Kimbrough, Graham .... (205) 325-2222
CIRC MGR-PROM
Birmingham News, Birmingham, AL
Kime, Mark .... (515) 933-4241
ED, Fremont Gazette, Fremont, IA
Kimelman, Don .... (215) 854-2000
Suburban ED
Philadelphia Inquirer, Philadelphia, PA
Kimm, Todd .... (319) 668-1240
ED, Williamsburg Journal Tribune, Williamsburg, IA
Kimmel, Gary .... (219) 356-6700
PROD FRM
Huntington Herald-Press, Huntington, IN
Kimmel, Jon .... (219) 726-8141
ADV MGR-PROM
Commercial Review, Portland, IN
Kimmel, Steven K .... (219) 356-6700
VP-OPER/GEN MGR, DP MGR
Huntington Herald-Press, Huntington, IN
Kimmer, Laura .... (810) 985-7171
ADV MGR-RT, Times Herald, Port Huron, MI
Kimmey, Debbie .... (281) 422-8302
ADV MGR-CLASS, Baytown Sun, Baytown, TX
Kimsey, Don .... (912) 888-9300
PROD SUPV-COMP
Albany Herald, Albany, GA
Kimura, Nohiro .... (416) 441-1405
Japan Journalist, Fotopress Independent News Service International, Toronto, ON
Kinal, Brian .... (814) 870-1600
COL
Morning News/Erie Daily Times, Erie, PA
Kincaid, Don .... (205) 353-4612
DIR-MKTG/Sales, Decatur Daily, Decatur, AL
Kincaid, Kristine .... (360) 676-2600
ADV DIR
Bellingham Herald, Bellingham, WA
Kincaid, Linda .... (617) 426-3000
Design/Production ED
Boston Herald, Boston, MA
Kinch, Mel .... (214) 977-8222
DIR-Plant & Purchasing
Dallas Morning News, Dallas, TX
Kincy, Gene .... (501) 785-7700
PUB
Southwest Times Record, Fort Smith, AR
Kind, Mark .... (208) 733-0931
City ED, Times-News, Twin Falls, ID
Kinder, Bette M .... (513) 721-2700
DIR-SYS, PROD DIR-SYS
Cincinnati Enquirer, Cincinnati, OH
Kinder, Nancy .... (765) 825-2496
PUB, Centerville Crusader, Centerville, IN
Kinder, Peter .... (573) 335-6611
ASSOC PUB
Southeast Missourian, Cape Girardeau, MO
Kinder, Rita .... (606) 564-9091
ADV MGR-Advertising SRV
Ledger Independent, Maysville, KY
Kinderman, Patricia .... (303) 823-6625
ED, Old Lyons Recorder, Lyons, CO
Kinderman, Walter J .... (970) 532-3715
PUB, Old Berthoud Recorder, Berthoud, CO
Kindred, Ingrid .... (205) 325-2222
Fashion ED
Birmingham News, Birmingham, AL
Kindred, Jack .... (519) 736-2147
PUB, ED
Echo Community News, Amherstburg, ON
King, Alan .... (414) 224-2000
Senior ED-Photo
Milwaukee Journal Sentinel, Milwaukee, WI
King, Barbara .... (812) 346-3973
PUB, ED
North Vernon Plain Dealer, North Vernon, IN
King, Beckie .... (937) 498-2111
News ED, Religion ED
Sidney Daily News, Sidney, OH
King, Bob .... (561) 820-4100
Environmental ED
Palm Beach Post, West Palm Beach, FL
King, Bob .... (218) 723-5281
Chief Photographer, Photo ED
Duluth News-Tribune, Duluth, MN
King, Brenda .... (315) 393-1000
BM, Courier-Observer Journal & Advance-News, Ogdensburg, NY
King, Bruce .... (912) 744-4200
DIR-Human Resources
Macon Telegraph, Macon, GA
King, Buddy .... (903) 794-3311
GM, Texarkana Gazette, Texarkana, TX
King, Mrs C Raymond .... (912) 268-2096
ED, Vienna News-Observer, Vienna, GA
King, Carol .... (610) 258-7171
Librarian, Express-Times, Easton, PA
King, Carpenter .... (803) 484-9431
ED, Lee County Observer, Bishopville, SC
King, Cindy .... (910) 739-4322
ADV MGR, Robesonian, Lumberton, NC
King Jr, Clyde C .... (713) 342-8691
Sr VP
Hartman Newspapers Inc., Rosenberg, TX
King, D Ashley .... (313) 222-6400
PROD DIR
Detroit Newspapers, Detroit, MI
King, David .... (334) 867-4876
PUB, ED, Brewton Standard, Brewton, AL
King, David .... (540) 825-3232
GM, Culpeper News, Culpeper, VA
King, David .... (406) 222-2000
CONT, DP MGR
Livingston Enterprise, Livingston, MT
King, Dianne .... (604) 559-4680
GM, Islands Observer, Queen Charlotte, BC
King, Don .... (937) 652-1331
PROD FRM-PR
Urbana Daily Citizen, Urbana, OH
King, Edward R .... (601) 762-1111
PROD FRM-PR
Mississippi Press, Pascagoula, MS
King, Frank .... (416) 441-1405
North America Journalist
Fotopress Independent News Service International (FPINS), Toronto, ON
King, Gail E .... (413) 458-9000
GM
Advocate/South Advocate, Williamstown, MA
King, Gary B .... (715) 327-4236
ED, Inter-County Leader, Frederic, WI
King, Gene .... (919) 946-2144
ADV DIR, ADV MGR-PROM
Washington Daily News, Washington, NC
King, Glen .... (334) 262-1611
ADV MGR-Client Services
Montgomery Advertiser, Montgomery, AL
King Jr, Gorman .... (701) 436-4241
PUB, Hillsboro Banner, Hillsboro, ND
King, Gurney .... (409) 945-3441
CIRC MGR, Texas City Sun, Texas City, TX
King, H Dwight .... (308) 995-4441
PRES/TREAS, Daily Citizen, Holdrege, NE
King, Harrell .... (512) 847-2202
MAN ED, Wimberley View, Wimberley, TX
King, James .... (423) 745-5664
PROD SUPT-PR
Daily Post-Athenian, Athens, TN
King, Jane .... (208) 886-2740
ED, Lincoln County Journal, Shoshone, ID
King, Jean .... (520) 458-9440
Entertainment/Amusements ED
Sierra Vista Herald, Sierra Vista, AZ
King, Jeff .... (515) 232-2160
Sports ED, Daily Tribune, Ames, IA
King, Jeff .... (901) 285-4091
CONT, DP MGR
State Gazette, Dyersburg, TN

Kin Who's Where-124

King, Jim .... (630) 844-5844
ASSOC ED, Television/ Film ED, Theater/ Music ED, Travel/Women's ED
Beacon-News, Aurora, IL
King, Joe .... (403) 250-4200
CIRC DIR, Calgary Sun, Calgary, AB
King, John .... (416) 585-5000
Deputy MAN ED, Globe and Mail (Canada's National Newspaper), Toronto, ON
King, John P .... (864) 298-4100
CONT, Greenville News, Greenville, SC
King, Keith .... (352) 867-4010
CIRC DIR, Ocala Star-Banner, Ocala, FL
King, Ken .... (403) 235-7100
PUB/PRES, Calgary Herald, Calgary, AB
King, Kevin .... (312) 222-3232
CIRC MGR-Distribution
Chicago Tribune, Chicago, IL
King, Larry .... (860) 584-0501
CIRC DIR, Bristol Press, Bristol, CT
King, Larry .... (402) 444-1000
ASST MAN ED
Omaha World-Herald, Omaha, NE
King, Linda .... (208) 743-9411
PROD FRM-MR
Lewiston Morning Tribune, Lewiston, ID
King, Lonnie .... (910) 323-4848
ADV MGR-Regional Sales
Fayetteville Observer-Times, Fayetteville, NC
King, Marcia .... (419) 726-1037
ED/PUB
Green Grass Syndicated Features, Toledo, OH
King, Margaret .... (619) 299-3131
Food ED
San Diego Union-Tribune, San Diego, CA
King, Mark .... (613) 382-2156
ED, Reporter, Gananoque, ON
King, Marshall .... (219) 294-1661
EDU ED, Elkhart Truth, Elkhart, IN
King, Mary Beth .... (505) 892-8080
MAN ED, Observer, Rio Rancho, NM
King, Maxwell E P .... (215) 854-2000
EVP/ED, Philadelphia Inquirer, Philadelphia, PA, Knight-Ridder
King, Michael .... (512) 477-0746
MAN ED, Texas Observer, Austin, TX
King, Mike .... (404) 526-5151
City/MET ED
Atlanta Journal-Constitution, Atlanta, GA
King, Nick .... (617) 929-2000
Living ED, Boston Globe, Boston, MA
King, Nina .... (202) 334-6000
Book World ED
Washington Post, Washington, DC
King, Peggy .... (912) 268-2096
GM, Vienna News-Observer, Vienna, GA
King, Peter .... (213) 237-5000
COL-State
Los Angeles Times, Los Angeles, CA
King, Randall .... (204) 694-2022
Films ED, Winnipeg Sun, Winnipeg, MB
King, Richard A .... (610) 258-7171
ADV MGR-PROM, Express-Times, Easton, PA
King, Rob .... (502) 582-4011
Photo ED, Courier-Journal, Louisville, KY
King, Robert B .... (517) 895-8551
PROD FRM-PR, Bay City Times, Bay City, MI
King, Robert D .... (308) 995-4441
SEC, PUB, EDL Writer, Teen-Age/Youth ED
Holdrege Daily Citizen, Holdrege, NE
King, Ruth E .... (308) 995-4441
VP, Holdrege Daily Citizen, Holdrege, NE
King, Sylvia .... (516) 843-2020
Queens Sports ED, Newsday, Melville, NY
King, Tom .... (614) 592-6612
PROD FRM-MR
Athens Messenger, Athens, OH
King, Tom .... (916) 243-2424
ED, Record Searchlight, Redding, CA
King, Van .... (910) 373-7000
PRES, PUB, News & Record, Greensboro, NC
King, Vanda .... (817) 725-6111
ED, Cross Plains Review, Cross Plains, TX
King, W J .... (604) 559-4680
PUB, Islands Observer, Queen Charlotte, BC
King, Warren .... (206) 464-2111
Medical Reporter, Seattle Times, Seattle, WA
King, Wes .... (903) 893-8181
ADV DIR, Herald Democrat, Sherman, TX
King, Wesley .... (706) 595-1601
ED, McDuffie Progress, Thomson, GA
King, William .... (918) 581-8300
CIRC MGR-MET Area
Tulsa World, Tulsa, OK
Kingcade, Carolyn .... (314) 340-8000
ASST MAN ED-News
St. Louis Post-Dispatch, St. Louis, MO
Kingery, Tammy .... (317) 664-5111
Graphics ED, Chronicle-Tribune, Marion, IN
Kingman, Shelby .... (320) 235-1150
DP MGR, West Central Tribune, Willmar, MN
Kingsbury, Annette .... (810) 625-3370
ED, Clarkston News, Clarkston, MI
Kingsley, Diana .... (616) 782-2101
ADV MGR, Daily News, Dowagiac, MI
Kinison, Paul .... (805) 945-5634
PUB
Aerotech News & Review, Lancaster, CA
Kinkade, James R .... (609) 694-1600
PUB, ED, Sentinel, Franklinville, NJ
Kinnaird, Melinda .... (405) 255-5354
Librarian, Duncan Banner, Duncan, OK
Kinnamon, Kristen .... (360) 653-8000
ED, North Snohomish Weekly, Arlington, WA
Kinnas, Ronald T .... (413) 447-7311
PA, Berkshire Eagle, Pittsfield, MA
Kinnear, Randy .... (819) 569-9526
PUB/GM, Record, Sherbrooke, QC
Kinner Sr, Earl W .... (606) 738-5574
PUB, ED
Elliott County News, Sandy Hook, KY
Kinner Jr, Earl W .... (606) 743-3551
PUB, MAN ED
Licking Valley Courier, West Liberty, KY
Kinner, Sue .... (606) 743-3551
ED
Licking Valley Courier, West Liberty, KY
Kinney, Bill .... (770) 428-9411
COL, Marietta Daily Journal, Marietta, GA
Kinney, Bob .... (419) 245-6000
Sports ED, Blade, Toledo, OH
Kinney, John P .... (508) 744-0600
PRES/PUB, Salem Evening News, Beverly, MA, Ottaway Newspapers Inc.
Kinney, Pat .... (319) 291-1400
BUS/FIN ED, BUS ED, City ED
Waterloo Courier, Waterloo, IA
Kinney, Vickie .... (618) 463-2500
Wire ED, Telegraph, Alton, IL
Kinney Jr, W L .... (803) 479-3815
PUB, ED
Marlboro Herald-Advocate, Bennettsville, SC
Kinsella, James .... (508) 775-1200
BUS ED, Cape Cod Times, Hyannis, MA
Kinser, Melody .... (304) 327-2811
News ED, Photo ED
Bluefield Daily Telegraph, Bluefield, WV
Kinsey, Kathy .... (941) 335-0200
Radio/Television ED
News-Press, Fort Myers, FL
Kinsey, Linda .... (216) 524-0830
ED, Parma Sun Post, Cleveland, OH
Kinsey, Michelle .... (317) 747-5700
Amusements/Music ED
Star Press, Muncie, IN
Kinsey, Rob .... (903) 885-8663
CIRC MGR, Sulphur Springs News-Telegram, Sulphur Springs, TX
Kinsley, Emerald .... (904) 973-4141
GM, Madison County Carrier, Madison, FL
Kinslow, Gina .... (502) 487-5576
ED, Tompkinsville News, Tompkinsville, KY
Kinter, Hastie D .... (412) 465-5555
SEC, Indiana Gazette, Indiana, PA
Kintzel, Roger .... (404) 526-5151
PUB
Atlanta Journal-Constitution, Atlanta, GA
Kinzler, Ron .... (816) 947-2222
PUB, ED
Unionville Republican, Unionville, MO
Kiosses, Ellen .... (508) 632-8000
PROD MGR, Gardner News, Gardner, MA
Kiraly, Linda .... (505) 983-3303
MGR-MKTG/PROM
Santa Fe New Mexican, Santa Fe, NM
Kirby, Bill .... (706) 724-0851
Deputy MET ED
Augusta Chronicle, Augusta, GA
Kirby, Gordon .... (540) 885-7281
PROD SYS OPER
Daily News Leader, Staunton, VA
Kirby, Joe .... (505) 823-7777
Design DIR, Journal, Albuquerque, NM
Kirby, Marilyn .... (408) 372-3311
Radio/Television ED
Monterey County Herald, Monterey, CA
Kirby, Mary Ann .... (205) 766-3434
EPE, Times Daily, Florence, AL
Kirby, Mike .... (508) 222-7000
ASST MAN ED
Sun Chronicle, Attleboro, MA
Kirby, Peggy .... (630) 844-5844
GM, Beacon-News, Aurora, IL
Copley Press Inc.
Kirby, Rennie .... (415) 777-7212
Office MGR
Chronicle Features, San Francisco, CA
Kirby, William .... (410) 758-1400
ED, Queen Anne's Record-Observer, Centreville, MD
Kirchberg, Doug .... (317) 398-6631
Automotive/News ED, Farm ED
Shelbyville News, Shelbyville, IN
Kircher, Ralf .... (941) 472-1587
ED, Island Reporter, Sanibel, FL
Kircher, Steven .... (813) 893-8111
MGR-RES
St. Petersburg Times, St. Petersburg, FL
Kirchmeier, Jesse .... (970) 493-6397
PROD MGR-MR
Fort Collins Coloradoan, Fort Collins, CO
Kirchner, James .... (502) 582-4011
News ED-Day, Courier-Journal, Louisville, KY
Kirchner, Keith S .... (717) 291-8811
CIRC DIR, Lancaster Intelligencer Journal/ New Era/Sunday News, Lancaster, PA
Kirgan, Harlan .... (318) 942-4971
ED, Books/EDU ED, BUS/FIN ED, Religion ED, Daily World, Opelousas, LA
Kirgan, Jim .... (817) 562-2868
PROD FRM-Press
Mexia Daily News, Mexia, TX
Kirk, Allen .... (423) 942-2433
PUB, Jasper Journal, Jasper, TN
Kirk, Betty .... (503) 221-8327
MGR-CR, Oregonian, Portland, OR
Kirk, Bill .... (715) 273-4334
ED, Pierce County Herald, Ellsworth, WI
Kirk, Cary .... (616) 429-2400
CIRC MGR-Home Delivery
Herald-Palladium, St. Joseph, MI
Kirk, Malcom .... (604) 732-2222
Sports ED, Province, Vancouver, BC
Kirk, Ray .... (916) 891-1234
News ED, Chico Enterprise-Record, Chico, CA
Kirk, Snamira .... (509) 248-1251
DP MGR
Yakima Herald-Republic, Yakima, WA
Kirk, Thomas .... (617) 933-3700
ADV MGR
Daily Times Chronicle, Woburn, MA
Kirkam, Kari .... (817) 390-7400
ADTX MGR
Fort Worth Star-Telegram, Fort Worth, TX
Kirkbride, Rob .... (313) 453-6900
ED, Community Crier, Plymouth, MI
Kirkendall, Joyce .... (913) 776-2200
CIRC DIR
Manhattan Mercury, Manhattan, KS
Kirkhart, Ken .... (703) 276-3400
PROD VP, USA Today, Arlington, VA
Kirkland, Bruce .... (416) 947-2222
Films ED, Toronto Sun, Toronto, ON
Kirkland, Jack .... (423) 523-3131
Photo DEPT MGR, Picture ED
Knoxville News-Sentinel, Knoxville, TN
Kirkland, Kay .... (334) 393-2969
ED, Daleville Sun-Courier, Enterprise, AL
Kirkland, Nelson .... (941) 687-7000
ADV MGR-CLASS, Ledger, Lakeland, FL
Kirkland, Patsy W .... (912) 422-3824
PUB, ED
Atkinson County Citizen, Pearson, GA
Kirkman, David .... (919) 419-6500
CIRC DIR, Herald-Sun, Durham, NC
Kirkpatrick, Dale D .... (308) 894-3025
PUB, Palmer Journal, Palmer, NE
Kirkpatrick, Don W .... (816) 747-8123
ADV MGR, ADV MGR-PROM
Daily Star-Journal, Warrensburg, MO
Kirkpatrick, John A .... (717) 255-8100
ED, Patriot-News, Harrisburg, PA
Kirkpatrick, Kyle .... (308) 894-3025
GM, ED, Palmer Journal, Palmer, NE
Kirkpatrick, Terry .... (503) 399-6611
ASST MGR-Technical SRV
Statesman Journal, Salem, OR
Kirksey, Ron .... (330) 996-3000
Higher EDU Writer
Akron Beacon Journal, Akron, OH
Kirkwood, R Cort .... (540) 743-5123
GM, ED
Page News and Courier, Luray, VA
Kirn, Eric .... (202) 898-8254
DIR-OPS
United Press International, Washington, DC
Kirschbaum, Donald .... (414) 657-1000
PROD MGR, Kenosha News, Kenosha, WI
Kirschbaum, Michael .... (970) 668-3998
ADV MGR, Summit Daily News, Frisco, CO
Kirschenheiter, John J .... (419) 529-2847
GM, ED, Tribune Courier & Madison Tribune, Ontario, OH
Kirsh, Kevin .... (414) 398-2334
ED, Herald, Markesan, WI
Kirtley, Linda .... (303) 454-3466
ED, North Weld Herald, Eaton, CO
Kirvan, Thomas S .... (313) 429-7380
ED, Saline Reporter, Saline, MI
Kirzner, Ellie .... (416) 461-0871
MAN ED, NOW, Toronto, ON
Kiser, Debra .... (417) 836-1100
ADV MGR-Sales
Springfield News-Leader, Springfield, MO
Kiser, James M .... (520) 573-4220
EPE, Arizona Daily Star, Tucson, AZ
Kiser, Robert .... (330) 821-1200
PROD FRM-PR
Alliance Review, Alliance, OH
Kish, Ken .... (810) 469-4510
MAN ED-News, News ED
Macomb Daily, Mount Clemens, MI
Kish, Peter .... (203) 846-3281
CIRC MGR, Hour, Norwalk, CT
Kish, Selweski .... (810) 469-4510
NTL ED, Macomb Daily, Mount Clemens, MI
Kishbaugh, Jerry .... (717) 821-2091
Music ED, Weekend ED
Citizens' Voice, Wilkes-Barre, PA
Kishbaugh, Kim .... (312) 782-8100
News ED
City News Bureau of Chicago, Chicago, IL
Kiska, Tim .... (313) 222-2300
Radio/Television ED
Detroit News, Detroit, MI
Kislenko, Dan .... (905) 526-3333
Travel ED, Spectator, Hamilton, ON
Kislingbury, Graham .... (541) 926-2211
MAN ED, Democrat-Herald, Albany, OR
Kisor, Henry .... (312) 321-3000
Books ED
Chicago Sun-Times, Chicago, IL
Kiss, Tony .... (704) 252-5611
Radio/Television ED
Asheville Citizen-Times, Asheville, NC
Kissel, Cindy .... (409) 836-7956
ADV MGR-RT
Brenham Banner-Press, Brenham, TX
Kisselburg, Joseph .... (706) 864-3613
ED, Dahlonega Nugget, Dahlonega, GA
Kissin, G .... (416) 633-0202
ED, Toronto Jewish Press, Downsview, ON
Kissin, Mara .... (954) 345-1822
ED, Broward Times, Coral Springs, FL
Kissler, Donald L .... (402) 462-2131
SEC/TREAS, BM/CR MGR, DP MGR
Hastings Tribune, Hastings, NE
Kissman, Nancy .... (713) 780-7055
CONT
Print Marketing Concepts, Houston, TX
Kitchell, David .... (317) 459-3121
Sports ED, Kokomo Tribune, Kokomo, IN
Kite, Pat .... (510) 794-1446
Writer/ED
Science Communications, Newark, CA
Kitkowski, Dan .... (715) 735-6611
Regional ED, EagleHerald, Marinette, WI
Kitsch, Le Donna .... (319) 754-8461
BM, Hawk Eye, Burlington, IA
Kitsos, Joanne .... (312) 321-3000
MGR-CORP Communications
Chicago Sun-Times, Chicago, IL
Kittel, Tod .... (715) 842-2101
PROD MGR-Pre Press
Wausau Daily Herald, Wausau, WI
Kitten, Marcia Bleier .... (210) 423-5511
ADV MGR-NTL (Rio Grande Valley)
Valley Morning Star, Harlingen, TX
Kitterman, Dee .... (316) 251-3300
CIRC MGR
Coffeyville Journal, Coffeyville, KS
Kittle, Bob .... (619) 299-3131
EPE
San Diego Union-Tribune, San Diego, CA
Kittle, Joe .... (304) 636-2121
Sports ED, Inter-Mountain, Elkins, WV
Kitto, Tom .... (315) 782-1000
DP MGR
Watertown Daily Times, Watertown, NY
Kitts, Jeff .... (513) 761-1188
Contributing Critic
Critic's Choice Reviews, Cincinnati, OH
Kitzmiller, Shari .... (717) 248-6741
Government ED
Lewistown Sentinel, Lewistown, PA
Klaas, Gerald W .... (605) 796-4221
PUB, Woonsocket News, Woonsocket, SD
Klaas, Gloria K .... (605) 796-4221
ED, Woonsocket News, Woonsocket, SD
Klaes, Cathy .... (812) 372-7811
ADV MGR-Special Publications
Republic, Columbus, IN
Klamo, Lynne .... (812) 372-7811
CIRC DIR-OPER, Republic, Columbus, IN
Klapper, Fred .... (864) 582-4511
DIR-FIN SRV
Herald-Journal, Spartanburg, SC
Klasne, Nick .... (904) 252-1511
ASST MAN ED, Daytona Beach News-Journal, Daytona Beach, FL
Klass, Rabbi Sholom .... (718) 330-1100
PUB, Jewish Press, Brooklyn, NY
Klassen, Stacy .... (316) 947-3975
GM, Hillsboro Star-Journal, Hillsboro, KS
Klatt, Dan .... (414) 684-4433
ASST MAN ED
Herald Times Reporter, Manitowoc, WI
Klatt, Debra .... (402) 362-4478
CIRC MGR, York News-Times, York, NE

125-Who's Where **Kni**

Klatt, Maureen .... (403) 986-0860
PUB, Leduc & County This Week, Leduc, AB
Klaus, Steve .... (515) 284-8000
CIRC MGR-Customer SRV
Des Moines Register, Des Moines, IA
Klausner, Howard .... (201) 748-0700
ED, Glen Ridge Voice, Glen Ridge, NJ
Klear, Carol .... (800) 327-3378
ED, Press & Light, North Ridgeville, OH
Kleban, Rich .... (914) 694-9300
OPER ED, Reporter Dispatch, White Plains, NY, Gannett Co. Inc.
Kleber, Richard .... (507) 645-5615
GM, Northfield News, Northfield, MN
Kleczewski, Linda .... (815) 223-3200
MAN ED, News-Tribune, La Salle, IL
Kleffman, Edgar .... (717) 622-3456
CONT, Pottsville Republican & Evening Herald, Pottsville, PA
Kleiman, Carol .... (312) 222-3232
Careers Writer, Chicago Tribune, Chicago, IL
Klein, Dan .... (618) 542-2133
CIRC DIR
Du Quoin Evening Call, Du Quoin, IL
Klein, Dee .... (308) 532-6000
ADV MGR-Newspaper Sales
North Platte Telegraph, North Platte, NE
Klein, Fred .... (212) 416-2000
Sports ED
Wall Street Journal, New York, NY
Klein, Herbert G .... (619) 454-0411
VP, Copley Press Inc., La Jolla, CA
Klein, Jeffrey S .... (213) 237-5000
CIRC Senior VP-Consumer MKTG
Los Angeles Times, Los Angeles, CA
Klein, John .... (918) 581-8300
ASSOC Sports ED, Tulsa World, Tulsa, OK
Klein, Kevin .... (604) 562-2441
ADV DIR
Prince George Citizen, Prince George, BC
Klein, Linda .... (605) 996-5514
ADV DIR, Daily Republic, Mitchell, SD
Klein, Marc S .... (415) 263-7200
PUB, ED, Jewish Bulletin of Northern California, San Francisco, CA
Klein, Margaret A .... (914) 738-8717
PUB, ED, Pelham Weekly, Pelham, NY
Klein, Mark .... (404) 526-5151
DIR-MKTG/PROM
Atlanta Journal-Constitution, Atlanta, GA
Klein, Mike .... (715) 833-9200
BUS ED, RE ED
Leader-Telegram, Eau Claire, WI
Klein, Pamela .... (317) 633-1240
ASST MAN ED-BUS
Indianapolis Star/News, Indianapolis, IN
Klein, Richard .... (909) 849-4586
CIRC MGR, Record-Gazette, Banning, CA
Klein, Robert .... (515) 989-0525
PUB, Carlisle Citizen, Carlisle, IA
Klein, Tom .... (218) 285-7411
ED, EPE
Daily Journal, International Falls, MN
Klein, Willy .... (515) 843-3851
GM, ED, Britt News-Tribune, Britt, IA
Klein, Woody .... (203) 226-6311
ED, Westport News, Westport, CT
Kleindeinst, Linda .... (954) 356-4000
BU Chief-Tallahassee
Sun-Sentinel, Fort Lauderdale, FL
Kleinerman, Ellen .... (330) 841-1600
Features ED, Health/Medical Reporter, Lifestyle ED, Tribune Chronicle, Warren, OH
Kleinhenz, Nancy .... (419) 448-3200
Entertainment/Amusements ED, Fashion/Style ED, Features ED, Living/Lifestyle ED, Women's ED, Advertiser-Tribune, Tiffin, OH
Kleinklaus, James F .... (315) 470-0011
ADV DIR, Post-Standard/Syracuse Herald-Journal/American, Syracuse, NY
Kleinmaier, Judie .... (608) 252-6400
Copy Desk Chief, Capital Times, Madison, WI
Kleinmann, Leanne .... (901) 529-2211
ASST MAN ED-Features
Commercial Appeal, Memphis, TN
Kleinschmidt, William E .... (216) 883-0300
PUB, ED, Leader, Garfield Heights, OH
Klem, John .... (816) 932-6600
MAN DIR-International
Universal Press Syndicate, Kansas City, MO
Kleman, Kim .... (813) 893-8111
Suburban ED
St. Petersburg Times, St. Petersburg, FL
Klemann, Thomas L .... (315) 597-6655
GM, Courier-Journal, Palmyra, NY
Klement, David E .... (941) 748-0411
EPE, Bradenton Herald, Bradenton, FL
Kleppe, Jill L .... (815) 385-2231
ED, McHenry Star, McHenry, IL
Klepper, Cindy .... (219) 356-6700
Books/Music ED, EDU ED, Films/Theater ED, Radio/Television ED, Religion ED, Wire ED
Huntington Herald-Press, Huntington, IN

Kler, Marlene .... (704) 358-5000
PROD MGR-Pre Press
Charlotte Observer, Charlotte, NC
Kleske, Andrew .... (619) 232-4381
ASSOC ED, BUS ED, City ED, DIR-INFO SYS
San Diego Daily Transcript, San Diego, CA
Kletke, Walter E .... (209) 578-2000
DIR-FIN, Modesto Bee, Modesto, CA
Kletzing, Helen .... (219) 838-0717
PUB, MAN ED, Calumet Press, Highland, IN
Kletzing, Wayne .... (219) 838-0717
PUB, Calumet Press, Highland, IN
Kleveland, Shannon .... (402) 223-5233
CIRC MGR, Beatrice Daily Sun, Beatrice, NE
Kleven, Sandra .... (810) 332-8181
Accounting MGR, Oakland Press, Pontiac, MI
Klevin, Patricia R .... (330) 747-1471
EDL Writer, Vindicator, Youngstown, OH
Klicki, Richard .... (847) 427-4300
News ED, Daily Herald, Arlington Heights, IL
Kliebenstein, John .... (507) 373-1411
CIRC MGR
Albert Lea Tribune, Albert Lea, MN
Kliewer, Ken .... (702) 289-4491
ADV DIR, Ely Daily Times, Ely, NV
Kligerman, Anabel .... (609) 443-4012
Author, MarketPlace Project, Princeton, NJ
Klima, Karen .... (815) 729-6161
CONT, Herald-News, Joliet, IL
Klimek, Ken .... (219) 235-6161
ASST MAN ED-OPER
South Bend Tribune, South Bend, IN
Kline, Bill .... (812) 332-4401
ADTX MGR
Herald-Times Inc, Bloomington, IN
Kline, Dale .... (704) 333-1718
ED, Independent Tribune, Concord, NC
Kline, David A .... (916) 445-6336
EX ED
Capitol News Service, Sacramento, CA
Kline, Gene .... (219) 461-8444
PROD MGR-Packaging/Distribution
Fort Wayne Newspapers Inc., Fort Wayne, IN
Kline, Jeff .... (941) 687-7000
County ED, Ledger, Lakeland, FL
Kline, Jerry .... (919) 419-6500
PROD MGR-Nightside Pre Press
Herald-Sun, Durham, NC
Kline, Lawrence M .... (213) 237-5000
ADV DIR-CLASS/Regional
Los Angeles Times, Los Angeles, CA
Kline, Nancy J .... (419) 523-5709
ED, Putnam County Sentinel, Ottawa, OH
Kline, Sandy .... (941) 687-7000
Librarian, Ledger, Lakeland, FL
Kline, William .... (717) 421-3000
MAN ED, Pocono Record, Stroudsburg, PA
Klinec, Joe .... (216) 329-7000
Sunday ED, Travel ED
Chronicle-Telegram, Elyria, OH
Kling, Dusty .... (504) 383-1111
ASST DIR-INFO SYS
Advocate, Baton Rouge, LA
Kling, John .... (713) 220-7171
City ED-Sunday
Houston Chronicle, Houston, TX
Klingenberger, John .... (219) 356-6700
CNR-PROM, Herald-Press, Huntington, IN
Klinger, Gary .... (717) 455-3636
CIRC DIR, Standard-Speaker, Hazleton, PA
Klinger, Stephen .... (505) 524-8061
PUB, ED
Las Cruces Bulletin, Las Cruces, NM
Klink, J Bruce .... (716) 232-7100
VP-FIN, Rochester Democrat and Chronicle; Rochester, NY Times-Union, Rochester, NY
Klink, Teresa .... (908) 246-5500
MAN ED
Home News & Tribune, East Brunswick, NJ
Klinka, Karen .... (405) 475-3311
Health/Medical Reporter
Daily Oklahoman, Oklahoma City, OK
Klinnert, Yvonne .... (612) 896-4700
MAN ED
Burnsville Sun-Current, Bloomington, MN
Klint, Denny .... (408) 761-7300
DP MGR
Register-Pajaronian, Watsonville, CA
Klippenstein, Bryan .... (204) 242-2555
PUB, ED, Western Canadian, Manitou, MB
Klipsteine, Sandy .... (937) 773-2721
ADV DIR, Piqua Daily Call, Piqua, OH
Klitsch, Glen .... (320) 255-8700
PROD MGR-PR
St. Cloud Times, St. Cloud, MN
Klobuchar, Jim .... (612) 673-4000
COL-News, Star Tribune, Minneapolis, MN
Klobuchar, Mike .... (206) 597-8742
ADV MGR-RT, News Tribune, Tacoma, WA
Klocke, Mike .... (209) 943-6397
Sports ED, Record, Stockton, CA
Kloer, Phil .... (404) 526-5151
Television ED
Atlanta Journal-Constitution, Atlanta, GA

Klose, Ann .... (217) 732-2101
Photo ED, Courier, Lincoln, IL
Kloss, Ron .... (814) 368-3173
Sports ED, Bradford Era, Bradford, PA
Klott, Gary .... (502) 339-0334
ED/COL
National Newspaper Syndicate, Louisville, KY
Kluckhohn, Karl .... (716) 649-4040
PUB, Sun and Erie County Independent, Hamburg, NY
Kluever, Nancy .... (319) 383-2200
ADV MGR-CLASS
Quad-City Times, Davenport, IA
Kluewer, Jeff .... (516) 569-4000
ED, Rockville Centre Herald, Lawrence, NY
Kluger, Dara .... (717) 854-1575
Style ED
York Dispatch/York Sunday News, York, PA
Klugman, Craig .... (219) 461-8333
ED, Journal Gazette, Fort Wayne, IN
Klurfeld, Jim .... (516) 843-2020
EPE, Newsday, Melville, NY
Klutnick, Susan .... (213) 237-5000
PROD DIR-Olympic OPER
Los Angeles Times, Los Angeles, CA
Klutts, Charlotte .... (918) 756-3600
ADV DIR, MGR-MKTG/PROM
Okmulgee Daily Times, Okmulgee, OK
Klutts, William A .... (901) 635-1771
PUB, ED
Lauderdale County Enterprise, Ripley, TN
Kluver, Cheryl A .... (402) 751-2652
ED, Kenesaw Clarion, Kenesaw, NE
Klypka, Rich .... (201) 646-4000
CIRC MGR-Product SRV/Delivery SYS
Record, Hackensack, NJ
Kmiec, Most Rev Edward .... (615) 383-6393
PUB, Tennessee Register, Nashville, TN
Knaack, Mike .... (219) 294-1661
Society ED, Elkhart Truth, Elkhart, IN
Knaak, Jeff .... (913) 762-5000
PROD FRM-PR
Daily Union, Junction City, KS
Knaak, Michael .... (320) 255-8700
Assignment ED, Photo DEPT MGR
St. Cloud Times, St. Cloud, MN
Knaak, R Bruce .... (316) 342-4800
ADV MGR-Display, ADV MGR-NTL
Emporia Gazette, Emporia, KS
Knadler, David .... (406) 523-5200
News ED, Missoulian, Missoula, MT
Knape, Steve G .... (616) 392-2311
CIRC MGR, Holland Sentinel, Holland, MI
Knapek, Larry .... (817) 826-3718
ED, West News, West, TX
Knapik, Mark .... (330) 966-1121
ED, Sun Journal, North Canton, OH
Knapp, Connie .... (218) 736-7511
CIRC MGR
Fergus Falls Daily Journal, Fergus Falls, MN
Knapp, Fred .... (402) 475-4200
Environmental Reporter, State Government Reporter, Lincoln Journal Star, Lincoln, NE
Knapp, Gary .... (606) 678-8191
PRES, Commonwealth-Journal, Somerset, KY
Knapp, Gwen .... (415) 777-2424
Sports COL
San Francisco Examiner, San Francisco, CA
Knapp, Jamie .... (712) 732-3130
Sports ED, Pilot Tribune, Storm Lake, IA
Knapp, Kevin .... (773) 643-8533
ED, Hyde Park Herald, Chicago, IL
Knapp, Kim .... (315) 866-2220
CONT, Evening Telegram, Herkimer, NY
Knapp, Lee .... (520) 783-3333
BM, Yuma Daily Sun, Yuma, AZ
Knapp, Stephen .... (800) 424-4747
Regional Accounts MGR, Tribune Media Services-Television Listings, Glens Falls, NY
Knapp, Todd .... (408) 424-2221
CIRC DIR, Californian, Salinas, CA
Knapper, Phil .... (618) 253-7146
Sports ED, Daily Register, Harrisburg, IL
Hollinger International Inc.
Knarr Jr, Glenn A .... (717) 648-4641
Graphics ED, PROD FRM-COMP
News-Item, Shamokin, PA
Knarr, Tom .... (717) 248-6741
News ED, Wire ED, Sentinel, Lewistown, PA
Knauer, Carolyn .... (704) 892-8809
MAN ED
Mecklenburg Gazette, Davidson, NC
Knauf, Ronald .... (412) 282-8000
CONT, Butler Eagle, Butler, PA
Knauss, Sue .... (606) 231-3100
ADV MGR-Customer SRV
Lexington Herald-Leader, Lexington, KY
Knauth, Betty .... (815) 468-6397
MAN ED, Manteno News, Manteno, IL
Kneale, Michael .... (816) 271-8500
PROD SUPT-Camera/Plate/Press
St. Joseph News-Press, St. Joseph, MO
Knecht, Fred V .... (717) 385-3120
PUB, Call, Schuylkill Haven, PA

Knecht II, William K .... (717) 385-3120
GM, MAN ED, Call, Schuylkill Haven, PA
Kneer, Mark .... (573) 335-6611
DIR-MKTG/PROM, CIRC DIR, Online MGR
Southeast Missourian, Cape Girardeau, MO
Kneib, Bruce .... (816) 271-8500
CONT, DP MGR
St. Joseph News-Press, St. Joseph, MO
Kneip, Joyce .... (712) 546-7031
BM, DP MGR
Le Mars Daily Sentinel, Le Mars, IA
Knepp, Sheron .... (219) 342-5143
ED, Bourbon News-Mirror, Bourbon, IN
Knepper, Ken .... (913) 632-2127
ADV DIR, Automotive ED
Clay Center Dispatch, Clay Center, KS
Knepper, Lea .... (419) 738-2128
MGR-BUS Office, DP MGR
Wapakoneta Daily News, Wapakoneta, OH
Knepper, Pam .... (219) 356-6700
Fashion ED, Food ED, Women's ED
Huntington Herald-Press, Huntington, IN
Kniceley, Andrew B .... (412) 628-2000
PUB/GM
Connellsville Daily Courier, Connellsville, PA
Knickmeyer, Steve .... (602) 271-8000
Deputy MAN ED
Arizona Republic, Phoenix, AZ
Knierim, James .... (217) 429-5151
PROD MGR-Distribution
Herald & Review, Decatur, IL
Knight, Ann .... (912) 263-4615
GM, Quitman Free Press, Quitman, GA
Knight, Bob .... (713) 220-7171
PROD ENG-Safety
Houston Chronicle, Houston, TX
Knight, Bob .... (804) 649-6000
SYS ED
Richmond Times-Dispatch, Richmond, VA
Knight, Bridget .... (817) 767-8341
Fashion/Garden ED, Lifestyle ED, Radio/Television ED, Wichita Falls Times Record News, Wichita Falls, TX
Knight, C P .... (205) 773-1953
ED, Hartselle Enquirer, Hartselle, AL
Knight, Chic .... (419) 281-0581
Chief Photographer
Ashland Times-Gazette, Ashland, OH
Knight, Christopher .... (218) 741-5544
ADV DIR, Mesabi Daily News, Virginia, MN
Knight, Christopher .... (213) 237-5000
Art Critic
Los Angeles Times, Los Angeles, CA
Knight, Doug .... (416) 947-2222
PUB & CEO-Financial Post
Sun Media Corp., Toronto, ON
Knight, Ed .... (910) 739-4322
CIRC MGR, Robesonian, Lumberton, NC
Knight, Guyon .... (202) 334-6000
VP-Communications
Washington Post Co., Washington, DC
Knight, Hank .... (714) 642-4321
PROD DIR, Daily Pilot, Costa Mesa, CA
Knight, Helene .... (919) 357-0960
ED, Gates County Index, Gatesville, NC
Knight, Jim .... (517) 787-2300
Sports ED
Jackson Citizen Patriot, Jackson, MI
Knight, Keith .... (519) 627-2243
ED, Wallaceburg News/Weekender, Wallaceburg, ON
Knight, Laura .... (352) 867-4010
Automotive ED, BUS/RE ED
Ocala Star-Banner, Ocala, FL
Knight, Linda .... (713) 485-7501
GM
Friendswood Reporter News, Pearland, TX
Knight, Paula .... (219) 881-3000
ADV MGR-Customer SRV
Post-Tribune, Gary, IN
Knight, Peter .... (212) 686-6850
Sales MGR
Black Press Service Inc. (BPS), New York, NY
Knight, R B .... (704) 568-7804
PUB, Griffon, Charlotte, NC
Knight, Richard F .... (615) 823-1274
PUB, Livingston Enterprise, Livingston, TN
Knight, Robin .... (502) 821-6833
CIRC DIR, Madisonville Messenger, Madisonville, KY
Knight, Sande .... (505) 662-4185
ADV DIR, Monitor, Los Alamos, NM
Knight, Sharon .... (501) 239-8562
ED, Entertainment/Amusements ED, News ED, Paragould Daily Press, Paragould, AR
Knight, Skip .... (330) 996-3000
ADV MGR-CLASS
Akron Beacon Journal, Akron, OH

Copyright ©1997 by the Editor & Publisher Co.

Kni Who's Where-126

Knight, Tony .... (818) 713-3000
City ED
Los Angeles Daily News, Woodland Hills, CA

Knipe, Sandra .... (812) 424-7711
Amusements/Entertainment ED, Music/Radio ED, Evansville Press, Evansville, IN

Knipple, Kathy .... (301) 662-1177
ADV ASST MGR-CLASS
Frederick Post/The News, Frederick, MD

Knobbe, Steve .... (916) 891-1234
PROD FRM-PR
Chico Enterprise-Record, Chico, CA

Knoblasch, Mary .... (312) 222-3232
Writing Coach, Chicago Tribune, Chicago, IL

Knoblauch, Carl .... (504) 826-3279
PROD MGR-PR
Times-Picayune, New Orleans, LA

Knobler, Mike .... (601) 961-7000
Sports ED
Jackson Clarion-Ledger, Jackson, MS

Knoblich, Jerry .... (206) 339-3000
DIR-Labor Relations, CONT
Herald, Everett, WA

Knobloch, Jacqueline .... (315) 792-5000
PROD MGR
Utica Observer-Dispatch, Utica, NY

Knoop, Karin .... (770) 963-9205
PROD DIR, Gwinnett Daily Post, Lawrenceville, GA, Gray Communications

Knop, Bert .... (216) 951-0000
ADV MGR-CLASS
News-Herald, Willoughby, OH

Knopf, David .... (816) 454-9660
MAN ED
Wednesday Magazine, Kansas City, MO

Knopfler, Vicki .... (910) 888-3500
Amusements ED, Books ED, Films/Theater ED, Radio/Television ED
High Point Enterprise, High Point, NC

Knott, Dan .... (219) 362-2161
Sports ED
La Porte Herald-Argus, La Porte, IN

Knouff, Thomas N .... (614) 397-5333
PROD MGR
Mount Vernon News, Mount Vernon, OH

Knowles, Ellis .... (406) 791-1444
CIRC DIR
Great Falls Tribune, Great Falls, MT

Knowles, Francine .... (312) 321-3000
Manufacturing/Utilities
Chicago Sun-Times, Chicago, IL

Knowles, Gregg K .... (712) 246-3097
PRES, PUB, ADV DIR
Valley News Today, Shenandoah, IA

Knowles, John W .... (608) 489-2264
PUB, ED, Sentry-Enterprise, Hillsboro, WI

Knowles, Paul .... (519) 662-1240
PUB, ED, New Hamburg Independent, New Hamburg, ON

Knowles, Richard .... (800) 657-5889
PUB, Denison Review, Denison, IA

Knowles, Sarah .... (617) 396-1982
ED, Medford Transcript, Medford, MA

Knox, Aaron .... (801) 625-4200
Sports ED, Standard-Examiner, Ogden, UT

Knox, Allen .... (303) 949-4004
PUB, ED, Vail Trail, Vail, CO

Knox, Bill .... (806) 376-4488
News ED-Day, News ED-Night, Amarillo Daily News/Globe Times, Amarillo, TX

Knox, Brian Victor .... (414) 563-5553
PUB, Book Review ED, Daily Jefferson County Union, Fort Atkinson, WI

Knox, Cheri .... (912) 462-6776
GM, Brantley Enterprise, Nahunta, GA

Knox, Debbie .... (903) 856-6629
PUB, Pittsburg Gazette, Pittsburg, TX

Knox, Don .... (303) 892-5000
BUS ED, Rocky Mountain News, Denver, CO

Knox, Glenda .... (912) 985-4545
PROD FRM-COMP, Observer, Moultrie, GA

Knox, Jack .... (250) 380-5211
City ED, Times Colonist, Victoria, BC

Knox, James A .... (508) 997-7411
PROD DIR-OPER
Standard Times, New Bedford, MA

Knox, Ken .... (312) 222-3232
EDL Writer, Chicago Tribune, Chicago, IL

Knox, Kraig .... (915) 673-4271
INFO SYS MGR
Abilene Reporter-News, Abilene, TX

Knox, Marv .... (502) 244-6470
ED, Western Recorder, Louisville, KY

Knox, Mike .... (515) 228-3211
CIRC MGR
Charles City Press, Charles City, IA

Knox, Richard .... (617) 929-2000
Medical ED, Boston Globe, Boston, MA

Knox, W D .... (414) 563-5553
PRES, Daily Jefferson County Union, Fort Atkinson, WI

Knuckles, Wayne .... (423) 581-5630
MAN ED, Books ED
Citizen Tribune, Morristown, TN

Knudsen, Dr Alf L .... (206) 784-4617
PUB, ED, Western Viking, Seattle, WA

Knudsen, James J .... (904) 682-6524
PUB, MAN ED
North Okaloosa Bulletin, Crestview, FL

Knudson, Carl .... (715) 394-4411
Photo DEPT MGR, Religion ED
Daily Telegram, Superior, WI

Knudson, Lee .... (970) 867-5651
PA, PROD FRM
Fort Morgan Times, Fort Morgan, CO

Knudson, Max .... (801) 237-2188
Automotive ED, BUS/FIN ED
Deseret News, Salt Lake City, UT

Knue, Paul F .... (513) 352-2000
ED, Cincinnati Post, Cincinnati, OH
Scripps Howard

Knuth, Beth .... (810) 641-9944
PUB
Nordamerikaniche Wochenpost, Troy, MI

Knuth, Michael .... (414) 457-7711
Sports ED, Sheboygan Press, Sheboygan, WI

Knutson, William .... (414) 733-4411
MAN ED, Action Line ED
Post-Crescent, Appleton, WI

Kobar, Alex .... (903) 729-0281
ADV MGR-NTL
Palestine Herald-Press, Palestine, TX

Kober, Sherry .... (610) 258-7171
ADTX SUPV, Express-Times, Easton, PA

Koberg, Katherine .... (206) 623-0500
MAN ED, Seattle Weekly, Seattle, WA

Kocal, Lynn .... (815) 493-2560
ED, Prairie Advocate, Lanark, IL

Kocal, Thomas .... (815) 493-2560
PUB, Prairie Advocate, Lanark, IL

Koch, Dennis .... (307) 347-3241
CIRC DIR, Librarian
Northern Wyoming Daily News, Worland, WY

Koch, Mary .... (509) 826-1110
PUB, ED
Omak-Okanogan County Chronicle, Omak, WA

Koch, Mya .... (304) 292-6301
Lifestyle ED, Marquee ED
Dominion Post, Morgantown, WV

Koch, Stephen .... (501) 372-4719
ED, Little Rock Free Press, Little Rock, AR

Kochakian, Charles P .... (203) 789-5200
EPE, New Haven Register, New Haven, CT

Kocher, Ben L .... (717) 692-4737
PUB
Upper Dauphin Sentinel, Millersburg, PA

Kocher, Chris .... (717) 654-1260
MAN ED
Greater Pittston Gazette, Pittston, PA

Kochman, Gerald .... (414) 657-1000
MGR-Computer SRV, PROD ENG-SYS
Kenosha News, Kenosha, WI

Koczak, Steve .... (914) 856-5383
GM, Gazette, Port Jervis, NY

Kodama, Lester .... (808) 525-8000
CIRC MGR-Single Copy
Hawaii Newspaper Agency Inc., Honolulu, HI

Kodet, Rose .... (515) 753-6611
Features ED
Times-Republican, Marshalltown, IA

Koehl III, Edgar .... (419) 468-1117
PRES, TREAS, PUB, BM
Galion Inquirer, Galion, OH

Koehl, Fred .... (419) 468-1117
VP, SEC, Galion Inquirer, Galion, OH

Koehler, Darrel .... (701) 780-1100
Consumer Interest ED
Grand Forks Herald, Grand Forks, ND

Koehler, Dirk .... (519) 621-3810
PROD FRM-COMP
Cambridge Reporter, Cambridge, ON

Koehler, Gary .... (815) 899-6397
MAN ED, Sycamore News, Sycamore, IL

Koehler, John .... (516) 843-2020
MGR-BUS SYS Software
Newsday, Melville, NY

Koehler, Kevin .... (401) 821-7400
CIRC MGR
Kent County Daily Times, West Warwick, RI

Koehn, Lisa .... (417) 667-3344
CIRC MGR, Nevada Daily Mail, Nevada, MO

Koeller, Brian .... (419) 592-5055
Amusements ED
Northwest Signal, Napoleon, OH

Koelln, Georgann .... (612) 222-5011
Fashion ED
St. Paul Pioneer Press, St. Paul, MN

Koelz, W E .... (615) 259-8000
DIR-SYS, Tennessean, Nashville, TN

Koen, Frankie .... (817) 757-5757
CIRC MGR-Single Copy
Waco Tribune-Herald, Waco, TX

Koenders, Denny .... (712) 328-1811
ADV MGR
Daily Nonpareil, Council Bluffs, IA

Koenemann, Scott .... (217) 351-5252
City ED, Political ED
News-Gazette, Champaign, IL

Koenenn, Connie .... (213) 237-5000
Enviormental/Consumer Affairs Reporter
Los Angeles Times, Los Angeles, CA

Koenig, Bob .... (509) 663-5161
PROD DIR-Press/Packaging
Wenatchee World, Wenatchee, WA

Koenig, Linda .... (908) 574-1200
MAN ED, Atom Tabloid, Rahway, NJ

Koenig, Linda .... (505) 393-2123
ADV DIR, Hobbs Daily News-Sun, Hobbs, NM

Koenig, Lynn .... (505) 746-3524
Aviation/Travel ED, Books ED
Artesia Daily Press, Artesia, NM

Koenigsfeld, Pete .... (515) 421-0500
PROD MGR, Globe-Gazette, Mason City, IA

Koenninger, Tom .... (360) 694-3391
VP/ED, Columbian, Vancouver, WA

Koepp, Charlene J .... (612) 492-2224
ED, Jordan Independent, Jordan, MN

Koeppel, E Wilson .... (334) 875-2110
PRES, PUB, Selma Times-Journal, Selma, AL

Koeppel, Fredric .... (901) 529-2211
Books ED, Commercial Appeal, Memphis, TN

Koerselman, Cheryl .... (712) 475-3351
ED, Lyon County News, George, IA

Koester, Joan .... (814) 238-5000
MGR-PROM
Centre Daily Times, State College, PA

Koetting, Tom .... (316) 268-6000
Relationships ED, Wichita Eagle, Wichita, KS

Koetzle, Dottie .... (610) 544-6660
ED, Springfield Press, Springfield, PA

Koffler, Eugene .... (412) 439-7500
ADV MGR-Design
Herald-Standard, Uniontown, PA

Kofford, Bret .... (619) 337-3400
COL, MET ED, Political ED, SCI/Technology ED, Special Edition ED
Imperial Valley Press, El Centro, CA

Kohan, Mark A .... (716) 893-5771
ED, Polish-American Journal, Buffalo, NY

Kohanik, Eric .... (905) 526-3333
Radio/Television Writer
Spectator, Hamilton, ON

Kohatsu, Gary .... (310) 329-6351
ED, Gardena Valley News, Gardena, CA

Kohl, Bill .... (937) 225-2000
PROD MGR-PR, Daily News, Dayton, OH

Kohler, Jenny .... (510) 758-8400
ADV MGR, West County Times, Pinole, CA

Kohlman, Patricia W .... (520) 458-9440
ASST GM, DIR-MKTG, Sierra Vista Herald, Sierra Vista, AZ, Wick Communications

Kohlmeyer, James A .... (812) 985-7989
PUB, ED
Posey County News, Poseyville, IN

Kohls, Steve .... (218) 829-4705
Photo DEPT MGR
Brainerd Daily Dispatch, Brainerd, MN

Kohn, Dennis .... (209) 722-1511
CIRC MGR, Merced Sun-Star, Merced, CA

Kohn, Ed .... (314) 340-8000
MET Desk ED-Night
St. Louis Post-Dispatch, St. Louis, MO

Kohner, Jim .... (507) 454-6500
Sports ED, Daily News, Winona, MN

Kohutek, Rosalie .... (512) 352-8535
ADV MGR-CLASS
Taylor Daily Press, Taylor, TX

Kok, Jeff .... (803) 329-4000
DIR-FIN, Herald, Rock Hill, SC

Kokiko, Karen .... (702) 788-6200
DIR-MKTG, Reno Gazette-Journal, Reno, NV

Kolar, Christine .... (610) 696-1775
ADV MGR-CLASS
Daily Local News, West Chester, PA

Kolb, David .... (616) 722-3161
EPE, Muskegon Chronicle, Muskegon, MI

Kolb, Holly .... (317) 348-0110
ADV DIR, News-Times, Hartford City, IN

Kolberg, Christian .... (702) 383-0211
DIR-MKTG/PROM
Las Vegas Review-Journal, Las Vegas, NV

Kolega, Marsha .... (330) 854-4549
ED, Signal, Canal Fulton, OH

Koleski, J M .... (612) 541-9868
ED, Nowiny Minnescockie, St. Paul, MN

Kolhagen, Kelly .... (313) 222-2300
ASST MAN ED-Features
Detroit News, Detroit, MI

Kolkman, Richard .... (317) 858-0630
Cartoonist
Kolkman, Richard, Indianapolis, IN

Koll, Jaelene .... (402) 475-4200
DP MGR
Lincoln Journal Star, Lincoln, NE

Kollman, Kristi .... (602) 898-6500
ADV MGR-RT, Mesa Tribune, Mesa, AZ
Thomson Newspapers

Kolodziej, Elaine .... (210) 216-4519
PUB, Wilson County News, Floresville, TX

Kolodziej, Tim .... (412) 654-6651
ED, Television/Film ED
New Castle News, New Castle, PA

Kologie, Carl A .... (412) 465-5555
MAN ED, Indiana Gazette, Indiana, PA

Koloski, Paul .... (412) 834-1151
EPE, Tribune-Review, Greensburg, PA

Kolsti, Paul .... (207) 775-4211
PRES
Pen Tip International Features, Portland, ME

Kolthoff, Beverly .... (515) 394-2111
ED
New Hampton Economist, New Hampton, IA

Koltz, Bradley M .... (508) 744-0600
PROD DIR-SYS, Salem Evening News, Beverly, MA, Ottaway Newspapers Inc.

Kolynuk, Gerald .... (313) 222-6400
MGR-SYS Applications
Detroit Newspapers, Detroit, MI

Komai, Michael .... (213) 629-2231
PUB, Rafu Shimpo, Los Angeles, CA

Komar, Debbie .... (810) 469-4510
Entertainment/Amusements ED, Fashion/Style ED, Features/Travel ED, Health/Medical ED, Television/Film ED, Theater/Music ED
Macomb Daily, Mount Clemens, MI

Kominsky, Donald .... (307) 877-3347
ED, Kemmerer Gazette, Kemmerer, WY

Komlanc Jr, Anthony M .... (815) 772-7244
PUB, ED
Whiteside News-Sentinel, Morrison, IL

Komonicki, John .... (405) 235-3100
PUB, Journal Record, Oklahoma City, OK

Komosky, Dave .... (204) 694-2022
Sports ED, Winnipeg Sun, Winnipeg, MB

Koncos, Jim .... (609) 663-6000
SCI/Technology ED
Courier-Post, Cherry Hill, NJ

Kondel, Debbie .... (412) 523-6588
Lifestyle ED
Standard Observer, Greensburg, PA

Konder, Jerry .... (717) 829-7100
DIR-MKTG SRV
Times Leader, Wilkes-Barre, PA

Kondrak, Jerry .... (612) 673-4000
PROD MGR-Newsprint
Star Tribune, Minneapolis, MN

Konley, Patricia .... (415) 252-0500
News ED, San Francisco Daily Journal, San Francisco, CA

Konschuk, Tracy .... (604) 368-8551
MAN ED, Trail Daily Times, Trail, BC

Konte, Joe .... (415) 883-8600
Sunday ED
Marin Independent Journal, Novato, CA

Kontokosta, Emanuel .... (516) 765-3425
PUB, Traveler-Watchman, Southold, NY

Konz, Michael .... (308) 237-2152
MAN ED, EPE, Kearney Hub, Kearney, NE

Koo, Nancy .... (612) 673-4000
VP-Human Resources (Star Tribune)
Star Tribune, Minneapolis, MN

Kooiker, Peter J .... (614) 461-5000
ADV MGR-NTL
Columbus Dispatch, Columbus, OH

Koon, Bruce .... (408) 920-5000
MAN ED-Mercury Center
San Jose Mercury News, San Jose, CA

Koon, Scott .... (309) 647-5100
PUB, Daily Ledger, Canton, IL

Koonts, Danny .... (704) 249-3981
PROD FRM-PR, Dispatch, Lexington, NC

Koontz, Arv .... (812) 522-4871
Sports ED, Tribune, Seymour, IN

Koontz, Hal .... (302) 324-2500
PROD MGR-PR
News Journal, Wilmington, DE

Koontz, Hugh D .... (704) 649-2741
ED, MAN ED, News-Record, Marshall, NC

Koopersmith, Adrienne Sioux .. (312) 743-5341
Founder/CEO, Koopersmith's Kreative Kingdom & Kalendar, Chicago, IL

Koopman, John .... (510) 758-8400
Features ED, West County Times, Pinole, CA

Koors, Tim .... (602) 271-8000
Photo DIR, Arizona Republic, Phoenix, AZ

Kopczak, Mary .... (518) 792-9914
Program MAN, Consumer Online Services
TV Data, Queensbury, NY

Kopel, David .... (303) 279-6536
ED
Independence Feature Syndicate, Golden, CO

Koper, Terry .... (406) 496-5500
Sports ED, Montana Standard, Butte, MT

Koper, Vanessa .... (216) 994-3241
ADV MGR-Display, ADV MGR-CLASS
Star-Beacon, Ashtabula, OH

Kopitsky, Alan .... (573) 783-3366
ED, Democrat News, Fredericktown, MO

Kopke, Joel .... (609) 272-7000
CIRC MGR-Marketing
Press of Atlantic City, Pleasantville, NJ

127-Who's Where **Kra**

Kopp, Curt .... (314) 340-8000
PROD FRM-Job Printing
St. Louis Post-Dispatch, St. Louis, MO

Kopp, Dan .... (419) 522-3311
BUS Writer, News Journal, Mansfield, OH

Kopp, Darrell .... (609) 825-8811
PUB, Cumberland Reminder, Millville, NJ

Kopp, David .... (816) 747-8123
Picture ED, Sports ED
Daily Star-Journal, Warrensburg, MO

Kopp, Eric .... (913) 654-3621
MAN ED
Osage County Chronicle, Burlingame, KS

Koppa, Steve .... (715) 842-2101
DP MGR, Wausau Daily Herald, Wausau, WI

Koppelman, A Mitchell .... (703) 471-2200
DIR/News MKTG, Reuters America Inc. (NewMedia), Reston, VA

Koppelmann, Ken .... (317) 659-4622
PROD MGR, Times, Frankfort, IN

Koppen, Steve .... (415) 883-8600
CIRC MGR-Sales
Marin Independent Journal, Novato, CA

Koppenhofer, Tom .... (814) 445-9621
ADV MGR, Daily American, Somerset, PA

Koppleman, Glenn .... (609) 845-3300
Automotive ED
Gloucester County Times, Woodbury, NJ

Koppy, Carrie .... (406) 791-1444
Deputy News ED
Great Falls Tribune, Great Falls, MT

Kopsa, Helen .... (515) 366-2020
PUB, ED, Record, Conrad, IA

Korando, Donna .... (314) 340-8000
Commentary Page ED
St. Louis Post-Dispatch, St. Louis, MO

Korb, Marvin .... (406) 791-1444
CIRC MGR, Tribune, Great Falls, MT

Korch, Jody .... (715) 735-6611
Sports ED, EagleHerald, Marinette, WI

Kordalski, David .... (313) 222-2300
Graphics DIR, Detroit News, Detroit, MI

Kordel, Verdice .... (313) 533-1846
Food ED
Specialty Features Syndicate, Detroit, MI

Korff, Rabbi Dr Yitzchok A ...... (617) 367-9100
PUB, Jewish Advocate, Boston, MA

Korfhage, Stuart .... (219) 563-2131
Sports ED, Wabash Plain Dealer, Wabash, IN

Korik, Martin .... (609) 383-0999
PUB, Jewish Record, Pleasantville, NJ

Korinek, Kent M .... (402) 821-2586
PUB, ED, Wilber Republican, Wilber, NE

Korn, Beatriz .... (305) 442-2462
MKTG Services Coord., Vista - The Hispanic Magazine, Coral Gables, FL

Kornheiser, Tony .... (202) 334-6000
COL-Sports
Washington Post, Washington, DC

Kornmiller, Debbie .... (520) 573-4220
Books ED, Entertainment ED, Features ED, Radio/Television ED
Arizona Daily Star, Tucson, AZ

Korobanik, John .... (403) 429-5400
Food ED, Travel ED
Edmonton Journal, Edmonton, AB

Koropas, Nell .... (204) 589-5871
GM, Ukrainsky Holos, Winnipeg, MB

Korper, Jon .... (203) 235-1661
Copy Desk Chief
Record-Journal, Meriden, CT

Korstanje, Casey .... (905) 526-3333
Religion/Ethics Writer
Spectator, Hamilton, ON

Kort, Allan T .... (617) 593-7700
MAN ED, Daily Evening Item, Lynn, MA

Korte, Mike .... (507) 285-7600
MGR-Telecommunications
Post-Bulletin, Rochester, MN

Kortekaas, Sally .... (206) 339-3000
ADV MGR-CLASS, ADTX MGR
Herald, Everett, WA

Korten, Jean A .... (717) 291-8811
Magazine ED, Lancaster Intelligencer Journal/New Era/Sunday News, Lancaster, PA

Kosan, Lisa .... (508) 744-0600
MET ED, Salem Evening News, Beverly, MA

Kosel, Paul Irvin .... (605) 397-2676
PUB, ED
Groton Regional Independent, Groton, SD

Kosemund, Ron .... (423) 472-5041
ADV MGR-RT
Cleveland Daily Banner, Cleveland, TN

Koshan, Kaweem M .... (703) 922-6321
GM, Omaid Weekly, Hayward, CA

Koshan, Mohammad Q .... (703) 922-6321
PUB, ED, Omaid Weekly, Hayward, CA

Koshar, Kathleen .... (216) 988-2801
ED, Amherst News-Times, Amherst, OH

Kosik, Michael .... (320) 845-2700
ED, Stearns-Morrison Enterprise, Albany, MN

Kosinar, Sam .... (216) 951-0000
PROD MGR-Press OPER
News-Herald, Willoughby, OH

Koski, John A .... (815) 857-2311
PUB, ED, Amboy News, Amboy, IL

Koskie, Robert .... (306) 745-6669
PUB, ED
Potashville Miner-Journal, Esterhazy, SK

Kossen, Bill .... (206) 464-2111
ASST Suburban ED
Seattle Times, Seattle, WA

Koster, Darcy .... (209) 943-6397
MGR-PROM, Record, Stockton, CA

Kostes, Peter .... (916) 587-6061
ED, Sierra Sun, Truckee, CA

Kostich, Drago .... (212) 807-4600
PROD DIR
El Diario La Prensa, New York, NY

Kostrzewa, John .... (401) 277-7000
BUS/FIN ED
Providence Journal-Bulletin, Providence, RI

Kosut, Renee .... (414) 642-7451
ED, East Troy News, East Troy, WI

Kot, Greg .... (312) 222-3232
Music Critic-Rock
Chicago Tribune, Chicago, IL

Kotake, Shotaro .... (416) 441-1405
Japan Photographer, Fotopress Independent News Service International, Toronto, ON

Kothe, Paula .... (907) 456-6661
ADV MGR-PROM
Fairbanks Daily News-Miner, Fairbanks, AK

Kothenbeutel, A Ralph .... (319) 824-6958
PUB, Grundy Register, Grundy Center, IA

Kotrotsios, Paul .... (610) 446-1463
PUB
Hellenic News of America, Havertown, PA

Kotsch, John .... (352) 544-5200
Weekend ED
Hernando Today, Brooksville, FL

Kotula, Corinta .... (203) 661-3386
EX DIR, Newspaper Features Council Inc., Greenwich, CT

Kotulak, Ronald .... (312) 222-3232
SCI Writer, Chicago Tribune, Chicago, IL

Kotwasinski, Bob .... (602) 271-8000
PROD DIR
Phoenix Newspapers Inc., Phoenix, AZ

Kotz, Geraldine .... (904) 359-4111
ADV MGR-CLASS
Florida Times-Union, Jacksonville, FL

Kotz, Pete .... (515) 288-3336
ED, Cityview, Des Moines, IA

Kotzer, Peter .... (416) 947-2222
CR MGR, Toronto Sun, Toronto, ON

Kotznski, Tom .... (406) 791-1444
Features ED, Features/Travel ED
Great Falls Tribune, Great Falls, MT

Kough, Barry .... (208) 743-9411
Photo ED, Morning Tribune, Lewiston, ID

Koupal, Raymond A .... (860) 241-6200
VP/CFO, Hartford Courant, Hartford, CT

Kourajian, Chad .... (701) 223-2500
ADTX MGR, Bismarck Tribune, Bismarck, ND

Koutsis, James .... (516) 427-7000
PUB, Long-Islander, Huntington, NY

Kovac, Cynthia .... (810) 985-7171
DIR-Human Resources
Times Herald, Port Huron, MI

Kovac Jr, Ed .... (717) 944-6308
ED, Zornicka, Middletown, PA

Kovac, Marc .... (515) 232-2160
BUS ED, Daily Tribune, Ames, IA

Kovac, Tom .... (919) 444-1999
ED, Havelock News, Havelock, NC

Kovach, Carol .... (216) 524-0830
ED, Garfield-Maple Sun, Cleveland, OH

Kovacs, Peter .... (504) 826-3279
ASSOC ED-News, MET ED
Times-Picayune, New Orleans, LA

Kovacs, Rosemary .... (216) 999-4500
MAN ED-Production
Plain Dealer, Cleveland, OH

Kovaleski, Jeff .... (317) 664-5111
City ED, Chronicle-Tribune, Marion, IN

Kovalic, Robert .... (608) 222-5522
BM, Shetland Productions, Madison, WI

Kovalich, Jennifer .... (315) 655-3415
ED, Cazenovia Republican, Cazenovia, NY

Kovar, Dale .... (320) 485-2535
GM, ED
Winsted Lester Prairie Journal, Winsted, MN

Kovatch, John .... (219) 461-8444
CFO
Fort Wayne Newspapers Inc., Fort Wayne, IN

Kovener, Curt .... (812) 793-2188
PUB, ED
Crothersville Times, Crothersville, IN

Kowalczyk, Benjamin J .... (609) 895-2600
VP-FIN
Goodson Newspaper Group, Lawrenceville, NJ

Kowaleski, John .... (801) 625-4200
SYS MGR, Standard-Examiner, Ogden, UT

Kowalski, B J .... (212) 889-5155
Senior ED
World Press Review, New York, NY

Kowalski, Bettyann .... (414) 833-2517
ED, Times Press, Seymour, WI

Kowalski, Craig .... (608) 744-2107
ED, Tri-County Press, Cuba City, WI

Kowalski, Janice .... (562) 435-1161
Design ED, Press-Telegram, Long Beach, CA

Kowalski, Jay .... (419) 245-6000
ADV MGR-GEN Sales, Blade, Toledo, OH

Kowalski, Jean .... (513) 732-2511
ED, Clermont Sun, Batavia, OH

Kowaluk, Melanie .... (403) 743-8186
PROD CNR-COMP
Fort McMurray Today, Fort McMurray, AB

Kowert, Arthur H .... (210) 997-2155
PUB, Fredericksburg Standard Radio Post, Fredericksburg, TX

Kowsky, Frances Kosa .... (801) 394-9655
ED, Hill Top Times, Roy, UT

Kozak, Doreen .... (413) 663-3741
BM
North Adams Transcript, North Adams, MA

Kozak, Peter .... (416) 441-1405
Australia Photographer
Fotopress Independent News Service International (FPINS), Toronto, ON

Kozak, Robert J .... (717) 291-8811
ED, Lancaster New Era, Lancaster, PA

Kozen, Bernard .... (717) 421-3000
CIRC MGR, Pocono Record, Stroudsburg, PA

Koziarski, Ed .... (773) 586-8800
EPE, Daily Southtown, Chicago, IL

Kozin, Barbara .... (860) 423-8466
PROD FRM-COMP
Chronicle, Willimantic, CT

Kozin, Laura .... (308) 468-5393
ED, Gibbon Reporter, Gibbon, NE

Koziol, Timothy .... (406) 452-1665
MKTG DIR, Wally Pike's Outdoor Features, Great Falls, MT

Kozlovski, Toni .... (970) 728-9788
MGR-Office, Daily Planet, Telluride, CO

Kozlowski, Chris .... (313) 222-2300
ASST MAN ED-Graphics & Design
Detroit News, Detroit, MI

Kozlowski, Gary .... (818) 713-3000
PROD MGR-PR
Daily News, Woodland Hills, CA

Kozlowski, Richard .... (304) 263-8931
Sports ED, Journal, Martinsburg, WV

Kozlowski, Tony .... (970) 240-4900
BM, Morning Sun, Montrose, CO

Kraemer, Dave .... (414) 634-3322
City ED, Journal Times, Racine, WI

Kraemer, Wendy .... (717) 421-3000
PROD FRM-COMP
Pocono Record, Stroudsburg, PA

Kraft, Bob .... (606) 292-2600
MAN ED, Kentucky Post, Covington, KY

Kraft, Dave .... (509) 663-5161
Entertainment ED, Films/Theater ED
Wenatchee World, Wenatchee, WA

Kraft, Dennis .... (219) 294-1661
Sports ED, Elkhart Truth, Elkhart, IN

Kraft, Ken .... (903) 885-8663
Chairman, Sulphur Springs News-Telegram, Sulphur Springs, TX

Kraft, Ken J .... (805) 650-2900
BUS MGR, Ventura County Star, Ventura, CA

Kraft, Robert F .... (513) 352-2000
MAN ED, Cincinnati Post, Cincinnati, OH

Kraft, Scott .... (213) 237-5000
Deputy Foreign ED
Los Angeles Times, Los Angeles, CA

Kraft, Steve .... (610) 258-7171
BUS SYS MGR, Express-Times, Easton, PA

Krafve, Susan M .... (914) 341-1100
ADV DIR
Times Herald-Record, Middletown, NY

Kragthorpe, Kurt .... (801) 237-2031
Sports ED
Salt Lake Tribune, Salt Lake City, UT

Krahl, Cynthia .... (941) 773-3255
MAN ED, Herald-Advocate, Wauchula, FL

Krahn, Cathy .... (916) 624-9713
GM, Placer Herald, Rocklin, CA

Kraimer, Buzz .... (713) 477-0221
ADV DIR, Pasadena Citizen, Pasadena, TX

Krall, Martin .... (212) 210-2100
EVP/Chief Legal Officer
New York Daily News, New York, NY

Kralovetz, Jeff .... (414) 863-2154
ED, Denmark Press, Denmark, WI

Kralowetz, Jeff .... (717) 854-1575
BUS ED, Environmental ED, SCI/Tech. ED, York Dispatch/York Sunday News, York, PA

Kram, Jerry .... (701) 662-2127
Action Line ED
Devils Lake Daily Journal, Devils Lake, ND

Kramer, A J .... (415) 777-5700
CIRC MGR-Sales & Development, San Francisco Newspaper Agency, San Francisco, CA

Kramer, Becky .... (509) 525-3300
Political ED, Union-Bulletin, Walla Walla, WA

Kramer, Bob .... (407) 420-5000
PROD MGR-Technical OPER
Orlando Sentinel, Orlando, FL

Kramer, Bruce .... (312) 222-3232
DIR-MKTG RES/SRV
Chicago Tribune, Chicago, IL

Kramer, Chuck .... (520) 573-4220
Graphics ED/Art DIR
Arizona Daily Star, Tucson, AZ

Kramer Sr, Donovan M .... (520) 836-7461
PRES, PUB, ED
Casa Grande Dispatch, Casa Grande, AZ

Kramer Jr, Donovan M .... (520) 836-7461
TREAS, ASSOC PUB, MAN ED, EPE
Casa Grande Dispatch, Casa Grande, AZ

Kramer, Doris .... (815) 589-2424
PUB, Fulton Journal, Fulton, IL

Kramer, Elaine .... (860) 241-6200
ASST to the PUB
Hartford Courant, Hartford, CT

Kramer, Evelynne H .... (617) 929-2000
Sunday Magazine ED
Boston Globe, Boston, MA

Kramer, Henry .... (815) 589-2424
PUB, ED, Fulton Journal, Fulton, IL

Kramer, Jack .... (203) 789-5200
ED, New Haven Register, New Haven, CT

Kramer, Joann .... (904) 734-4622
GM, DeLand Beacon/West Volusia Beacon, DeLand, FL

Kramer, Joel .... (612) 673-4000
PUB/PRES, Star Tribune, Minneapolis, MN

Kramer, Jonathan .... (609) 989-5454
ADV MGR-GEN, Times, Trenton, NJ

Kramer, Keith .... (970) 879-1502
News ED
Steamboat Today, Steamboat Springs, CO

Kramer, Kristen .... (209) 835-3030
BUS ED, Tracy Press, Tracy, CA

Kramer, Marc .... (212) 210-2100
ASSOC GEN Counsel
New York Daily News, New York, NY

Kramer, Randy .... (918) 335-8200
Cable Newspaper EX
Examiner-Enterprise, Bartlesville, OK

Kramer, Ruth A .... (520) 836-7461
VP, Casa Grande Dispatch, Casa Grande, AZ

Kramer, Ted .... (541) 963-3161
ED, EDL Writer, Observer, La Grande, OR

Kramer, Wayne .... (317) 342-3311
ADV MGR, Daily Reporter, Martinsville, IN

Kramon, Glenn .... (212) 556-1234
Deputy BUS/FIN ED
New York Times, New York, NY

Krampota, Glenn .... (409) 265-7411
Sports ED, Brazosport Facts, Clute, TX

Krans, Michelle .... (408) 424-2221
DIR-MKTG Development
Californian, Salinas, CA

Krape, Angela .... (941) 434-5555
ASST, Strategist, Naples, FL

Krapesh, C .... (317) 832-2443
CIRC MGR, Daily Clintonian, Clinton, IN

Krasean, Bill .... (616) 345-3511
Environmental ED, Health/Medical ED, SCI ED, Kalamazoo Gazette, Kalamazoo, MI

Krasnowsky, Marc .... (402) 475-4200
ASST Features ED
Lincoln Journal Star, Lincoln, NE

Kratzer, Eleanor .... (412) 664-9161
Society ED, Daily News, McKeesport, PA

Kraus, Bill .... (919) 527-3191
BM, Free Press, Kinston, NC

Kraus, David .... (518) 374-4141
MGR-Photo DEPT
Daily Gazette, Schenectady, NY

Kraus, Dennis .... (308) 382-1000
PROD MGR
Grand Island Independent, Grand Island, NE

Kraus, Jim .... (716) 328-2144
Correspondent
Syndicated News Service, Rochester, NY

Kraus, Scott .... (701) 252-3120
Films/Theater ED, Picture ED, Political ED
Jamestown Sun, Jamestown, ND

Kraus, Thad .... (616) 897-9261
ED, Lowell Ledger, Lowell, MI

Krause, David .... (970) 669-5050
Sports ED
Loveland Daily Reporter-Herald, Loveland, CO

Krause, Don .... (812) 934-4343
ED, Herald Tribune, Batesville, IN

Krause, Faith .... (319) 385-3131
ADV DIR, ADV MGR-NTL
Mt. Pleasant News, Mount Pleasant, IA

Krause, Hanna .... (407) 242-3500
Food ED, Travel/Women's ED
Florida Today, Melbourne, FL

Krause, Marilyn .... (414) 224-2000
Health & Family ED
Milwaukee Journal Sentinel, Milwaukee, WI

Kra Who's Where-128

Krause, Shirley B .... (316) 983-2185
PUB, Gazette-Bulletin, Peabody, KS
Krause, William V .... (316) 983-2185
ED, Gazette-Bulletin, Peabody, KS
Krauss, Robert .... (808) 525-8000
COL, Honolulu Advertiser, Honolulu, HI
Krauter, Joan .... (817) 390-7400
ED/Northeast-Tarrant
Fort Worth Star-Telegram, Fort Worth, TX
Kravetz, Jay N .... (561) 585-9387
ED, Lake Worth Herald and Coastal Observer, Lake Worth, FL
Kravitz, Bob .... (303) 892-5000
Sports COL
Rocky Mountain News, Denver, CO
Kravitz, Lee .... (212) 450-7000
VP/ED, React, New York, NY
Krawczyk, Fred .... (416) 585-5000
ADV VP-Sales, Globe and Mail, Toronto, ON
Krayer, Michael D .... (717) 291-8811
PROD MGR-Quality, Lancaster Intelligencer Journal/New Era/Sunday News, Lancaster, PA
Kraza, Paul .... (307) 266-0500
State ED, Star-Tribune, Casper, WY
Krazit, Thomas .... (860) 241-6200
Town Editorials ED
Hartford Courant, Hartford, CT
Kreag, Mark .... (219) 362-2161
Farm ED, La Porte Herald-Argus, La Porte, IN
Krebs, Anna Mary .... (765) 869-5536
PUB, Boswell Enterprise, Boswell, IN
Krebs, Cecil .... (765) 869-5536
PUB, ED, Boswell Enterprise, Boswell, IN
Krebs, Gene .... (216) 329-7000
Photo ED, Chronicle-Telegram, Elyria, OH
Krebs, Margaret E .... (814) 765-5581
PRES, ASSOC PUB, MGR-CR, PA
Progress, Clearfield, PA
Krebs, Randy .... (320) 255-8700
Copy Desk Chief
St. Cloud Times, St. Cloud, MN
Krebs, Tamara .... (801) 625-4200
ADV MGR-CLASS
Standard-Examiner, Ogden, UT
Krecklow, Robert L .... (573) 221-2800
PUB, ED
Hannibal Courier-Post, Hannibal, MO
Kreeger, William W .... (419) 886-2291
PUB
Bellville Star & Tri-Forks Press, Bellville, OH
Kreger, Kevin .... (405) 765-3311
CIRC MGR, Ponca City News, Ponca City, OK
Krehl, Steve .... (907) 376-5225
GM, Valley Sun, Wasilla, AK
Kreiner, Judith .... (202) 636-3000
Features ED
Washington Times, Washington, DC
Kreiser, Mike .... (909) 684-1200
CIRC MGR, Press-Enterprise, Riverside, CA
Kreisler, Kevin .... (619) 322-8889
CIRC MGR-Home Delivery
Desert Sun, Palm Springs, CA
Kreiss, Randi .... (516) 569-4000
ED, Nassau Herald, Lawrence, NY
Kreitz, Gregory A .... (610) 371-5000
BUS/FIN ED
Reading Times/Eagle, Reading, PA
Kreitzman, Wendy .... (516) 747-8282
ED, Great Neck Record, Mineola, NY
Krekel, Thomas H .... (414) 938-5000
PUB, Whitefish Bay Herald, New Berlin, WI
Krekow, Russ .... (541) 776-4411
PROD SUPV, Mail Tribune, Medford, OR
Kremer, Michael P .... (320) 563-8146
MAN ED, Wheaton Gazette, Wheaton, MN
Kremer, William N .... (320) 563-8146
PUB, ED, Wheaton Gazette, Wheaton, MN
Krenek, Debby .... (212) 210-2100
EX ED, New York Daily News, New York, NY
Krengel, Ron .... (615) 259-8000
PROD DIR, Tennessean, Nashville, TN
Krentz, Gary .... (414) 224-2000
Senior ED-Day News
Milwaukee Journal Sentinel, Milwaukee, WI
Kreppert, Gary .... (217) 788-1300
ADV MGR
State Journal-Register, Springfield, IL
Kreps, Marilee .... (219) 244-5153
ASSOC ED, Post & Mail, Columbia City, IN
Kreps, Rick .... (219) 244-5153
GM, ADV MGR, MGR-MKTG/PROM
Post & Mail, Columbia City, IN
Kreska, Don .... (800) 245-6536
FIN DIR
Tribune Media Services Inc., Chicago, IL
Kresnak, William .... (808) 525-8000
Colleges ED
Honolulu Advertiser, Honolulu, HI

Kress, Ken .... (215) 345-3000
ADTX MGR
Intelligencer/Record, Doylestown, PA
Kress, Mary E .... (904) 359-4111
MAN ED
Florida Times-Union, Jacksonville, FL
Kresse, William .... (212) 580-8559
Art DIR
Journal Press Syndicate, New York, NY
Kretsch, Ellen .... (520) 425-7121
PUB, ED, Arizona Silver Belt, Globe, AZ
Kretschmer, Charles .... (517) 752-7171
ADV MGR-Sales, Saginaw News, Saginaw, MI
Kreutzer, Joseph .... (412) 282-8000
CIRC DIR, Butler Eagle, Butler, PA
Krewson, Jeanne .... (541) 382-1811
PROD SUPV-COMP, Bulletin, Bend, OR
Kridner, Suzy .... (904) 252-1511
Entertainment/Amusements ED, Daytona Beach News-Journal, Daytona Beach, FL
Kriebel-Bangert, Carol .... (317) 423-5511
MAN ED, Journal and Courier, Lafayette, IN
Krieger, Jenny .... (910) 574-2555
MKTG, Toonsmith Newspaper Features, Greensboro, NC
Krien, Karen .... (913) 332-3162
GM, ED
Saint Francis Herald, St. Francis, KS
Krier, David .... (608) 375-4458
ED, Boscobel Dial, Boscobel, WI
Krier, Jack .... (816) 747-3135
PUB, Standard-Herald, Warrensburg, MO
Krier, John .... (310) 657-2005
PRES
Exhibitor Relations Co., Los Angeles, CA
Krier, Kathy .... (816) 594-3712
PUB, Democrat-Leader, Norborne, MO
Krietemeyer, Daniel V .... (314) 340-8000
DIR-INFO SYS, DP MGR
St. Louis Post-Dispatch, St. Louis, MO
Kriewall, Garth .... (810) 985-7171
ASST MAN ED, Times Herald, Port Huron, MI
Krikac, Bill .... (605) 532-3654
ED, Clark County Courier, Clark, SD
Krim, Jonathan .... (408) 920-5000
ASST MAN ED-BUS/Projects
San Jose Mercury News, San Jose, CA
Krinock, Al .... (412) 537-3351
PROD SUPT, PROD FRM-COMP
Latrobe Bulletin, Latrobe, PA
Krisch, Robert .... (800) 678-8135
Northeast Representative, Better Homes & Gardens Features Syndicate, Des Moines, IA
Krisher, Tom .... (412) 772-3900
City/MET ED, Political/Government ED
North Hills News Record, Warrendale, PA
Kristiansen, Leigh Ann .... (618) 542-2133
ADV DIR-NTL CLASS
Du Quoin Evening Call, Du Quoin, IL
Kristof, Kathy .... (213) 237-5000
Personal FIN
Los Angeles Times, Los Angeles, CA
Kristofik, Joseph R .... (717) 944-0461
ED, Jednota, Middletown, PA
Krittle, Charles .... (215) 854-2000
News ED
Philadelphia Inquirer, Philadelphia, PA
Kritzer, Paul E .... (414) 224-2000
VP-Legal
Milwaukee Journal Sentinel, Milwaukee, WI
Krizman, Steve .... (303) 892-5000
Suburban ED
Rocky Mountain News, Denver, CO
Krizmanic, Phyllis .... (219) 933-3200
MGR-MKTG, Times, Munster, IN
Kroan, Darin .... (317) 342-3311
Sports ED, Daily Reporter, Martinsville, IN
Kroeger, Mark .... (812) 424-7711
MET ED, Evansville Courier, Evansville, IN
Kroeger, Terry J .... (209) 943-6397
PRES/PUB, Record, Stockton, CA
Omaha World-Herald Co.
Kroeker, Ben .... (204) 747-2249
PUB, ED
Deloraine Times and Star, Deloraine, MB
Kroemer, James D .... (219) 347-0400
PRES, Witwer Newspapers, Kendallville, IN
Kroemer, Pat .... (319) 944-5387
ED, Sun-News, Lowden, IA
Kroes, Matt .... (414) 634-3322
PROD SUPV-Pre Press
Journal Times, Racine, WI
Krogstad, Tom .... (415) 348-4321
Religion ED
San Mateo County Times, San Mateo, CA
Krokson, Janet I .... (715) 635-2181
PUB, Spooner Advocate, Spooner, WI
Krol, Eva .... (313) 222-6400
MGR-SYS OPER
Detroit Newspapers, Detroit, MI
Krolczyk, Clem .... (409) 836-7956
PROD FRM-PR
Brenham Banner-Press, Brenham, TX

Kroll, Keenen .... (209) 578-2000
CIRC MGR-Home Delivery
Modesto Bee, Modesto, CA
Krompocker, Pam .... (604) 485-4255
PUB, Powell River News/Town Crier, Powell River, BC
Kron, Roy .... (817) 431-2231
ED, Keller Citizen, Keller, TX
Krone, Jeff .... (906) 932-2211
CIRC MGR, Daily Globe, Ironwood, MI
Kronen, H B .... (413) 788-1000
Dance ED, Union-News, Springfield, MA
Kronert, Manfred .... (403) 826-3876
PUB, Bonnyville Nouvelle, Bonnyville, AB
Kropf, Cindy .... (937) 225-2000
CIRC DIR-ADM
Dayton Daily News, Dayton, OH
Krost, Margaret .... (562) 435-1161
VP-Advertising, ADV VP
Press-Telegram, Long Beach, CA
Krout, Robert L .... (517) 265-5111
PUB, Daily Telegram, Adrian, MI
Krueger, Jodie .... (207) 791-6650
CIRC ASST DIR-MKTG & Subscriber Services
Portland Press Herald, Portland, ME
Krueger, Kurt .... (715) 479-4421
ED
Vilas County News Review, Eagle River, WI
Krueger, Margaret A .... (414) 261-4949
SEC, Watertown Daily Times, Watertown, WI
Krueger, Margaret E .... (414) 457-7711
CONT, Sheboygan Press, Sheboygan, WI
Krueger, Mary .... (701) 845-0463
ADV MGR-CLASS
Valley City Times-Record, Valley City, ND
Krueger, Mike .... (402) 444-1000
PROD FRM-Paperhandling
Omaha World-Herald, Omaha, NE
Krueger, Paul .... (608) 328-4202
Sports ED, Monroe Times, Monroe, WI
Krueger, Ralph H .... (414) 261-4949
TREAS, BM
Watertown Daily Times, Watertown, WI
Krueger, Ron .... (810) 766-6100
Food ED, Flint Journal, Flint, MI
Kruger, Carol .... (409) 836-7956
ADV MGR-CLASS
Brenham Banner-Press, Brenham, TX
Kruger, Dara .... (717) 854-1575
Entertainment ED
York Dispatch/York Sunday News, York, PA
Kruger, Edward .... (304) 485-1891
PUB, Parkersburg News & Sentinel, Parkersburg, WV
Kruger, Jeanne .... (608) 938-4855
GM, Monticello Messenger, Monticello, WI
Kruger, R Gary .... (717) 348-9100
MGR-EDU SRV, CIRC DIR
Tribune & Scranton Times, Scranton, PA
Kruger, Terry .... (604) 485-4255
ED, Powell River News/Town Crier, Powell River, BC
Krugman, Milt .... (215) 949-4000
Topic ED
Bucks County Courier Times, Levittown, PA
Kruithof, Doug .... (812) 331-0963
MAN ED
Bloomington Voice, Bloomington, IN
Krumel, Jim .... (419) 223-1010
MAN ED, Lima News, Lima, OH
Kruming, Martin .... (619) 232-4381
ED/VP
San Diego Daily Transcript, San Diego, CA
Krumm, Robert M .... (419) 335-2010
PUB, Expositor, Wauseon, OH
Krupa, William .... (860) 489-3121
CONT, Register Citizen, Torrington, CT
Krupnick, Jerry .... (201) 877-4141
Television Critic, Star-Ledger, Newark, NJ
Kruse, Rick .... (507) 376-9711
PROD FRM-PR
Daily Globe, Worthington, MN
Kruz, Don .... (314) 486-5418
ED, Advertiser-Courier, Hermann, MO
Kruza, J A .... (508) 528-6211
Glass & Photo News Writer
Kruza Kaleidoscopix Inc., Franklin, MA
Krzsnow, Bruce .... (505) 983-3303
ASST City ED
Santa Fe New Mexican, Santa Fe, NM
Krzyzanowski, Rick K .... (818) 962-8811
MAN ED, Covina Highlander Press Courier, West Covina, CA
Kubat, Blanche .... (201) 773-8300
ED, North Jersey Prospector, Clifton, NJ
Kubiak, Kim .... (815) 899-6397
ED, Sycamore News, Sycamore, IL
Kubik, Jack R .... (708) 242-1234
PUB, Cicero-Berwyn-Stickney Forest View Life, Berwyn, IL
Kubik, John M .... (416) 441-1405
OPER DIR, Fotopress Independent News Service International (FPINS), Toronto, ON

Kubisek, Helena .... (203) 744-5100
PROD FRM-MR (Day)
News-Times, Danbury, CT
Kubissa, David .... (607) 734-5151
MAN ED, Star-Gazette, Elmira, NY
Kucera, Josef .... (708) 749-1891
PUB, ED, Denni Hlasatel, Berwyn, IL
Kuchejda, Michael .... (312) 283-1898
PUB, ED
Dzlennik Chicagowski, Chicago, IL
Kuchera Jr, Tom .... (701) 780-1100
ADV DIR
Grand Forks Herald, Grand Forks, ND
Kuchner, Elmer .... (717) 326-1551
CIRC DIR
Williamsport Sun-Gazette, Williamsport, PA
Kucifer, Dave .... (918) 341-1101
ADV MGR
Claremore Daily Progress, Claremore, OK
Kuczora, Jeff .... (630) 844-5844
ASSOC ED, NTL ED, News ED, Political/Government ED, Beacon-News, Aurora, IL
Kudeba, Wendy .... (519) 688-6397
ED, Tillsonburg News, Tillsonburg, ON
Kueck, Bruce .... (314) 965-9000
MAN ED, Reporter, St. Louis, MO
Kuehl, A R .... (414) 626-3312
MAN ED
Kewaskum Statesman, Kewaskum, WI
Kuehl, Cheyl A .... (414) 626-3312
GM, Kewaskum Statesman, Kewaskum, WI
Kuehl, Lana L .... (414) 626-3312
PUB, ED
Kewaskum Statesman, Kewaskum, WI
Kuehl, Mark D .... (414) 261-4949
CIRC DIR
Watertown Daily Times, Watertown, WI
Kuehling, Max .... (810) 766-6100
PROD MGR-PR, Flint Journal, Flint, MI
Kuehn, Bruce .... (904) 252-1511
Sunday ED, Daytona Beach News-Journal, Daytona Beach, FL
Kuehn, Jeff .... (810) 541-3000
Sports ED, Daily Tribune, Royal Oak, MI
Kuehn, Michael J .... (712) 336-1211
PUB, Spirit Lake Beacon, Spirit Lake, IA
Kuenzli, Ernie .... (407) 420-5000
PROD MGR-New Technology
Orlando Sentinel, Orlando, FL
Kueter, Dale .... (319) 398-8211
Writing/Editing Coach
Gazette, Cedar Rapids, IA
Kueter, Maricarrol .... (605) 331-2200
City ED, Argus Leader, Sioux Falls, SD
Kugelman, David .... (916) 741-2345
ADV DIR, Appeal-Democrat, Marysville, CA
Kuglin, Ernst .... (613) 475-0255
ED, East Northumberland, Brighton, ON
Kuhl, Pat .... (618) 234-1000
Lifestyle ED
Belleville News-Democrat, Belleville, IL
Kuhle, Terri .... (217) 429-5151
MGR-Human Resources
Herald & Review, Decatur, IL
Kuhlman, Fred G .... (308) 762-3060
EVP/SEC/TREAS, PUB
Alliance Times-Herald, Alliance, NE
Kuhlman, Tricia .... (409) 836-7956
Teen-Age/Youth ED, Women's ED
Brenham Banner-Press, Brenham, TX
Kuhn, Brian C .... (308) 487-3334
PUB, ED, Ledger, Hemingford, NE
Kuhn, Gene .... (360) 532-4000
PROD FRM-COMP
Daily World, Aberdeen, WA
Kuhn, Karen .... (317) 462-5528
Lifestyle ED, Daily Reporter, Greenfield, IN
Kuhn, Robert .... (313) 222-6400
VP/CONT, Detroit Newspapers, Detroit, MI
Kuhns, John B .... (603) 298-8711
PUB, Valley News, White River Jct., VT
Kuhns, Tom .... (316) 873-2118
ED, Meade County News, Meade, KS
Kuhr, Peggy .... (509) 459-5000
MAN ED-Content
Spokesman-Review, Spokane, WA
Kuisel, Johness Watts .... (516) 751-7744
GM, Village Times, Setauket, NY
Kujawa, Dawn .... (803) 771-6161
Travel ED, State, Columbia, SC
Kujawa, Michael .... (317) 633-1240
CIRC VP
Indianapolis Star/News, Indianapolis, IN
Kujichagulia, Kaman .... (609) 989-0285
PUB, Nubian News, Trenton, NJ
Kukielski, Philip .... (401) 277-7000
MAN ED-State, State ED
Providence Journal-Bulletin, Providence, RI
Kukla, Gloria .... (701) 764-5312
GM, Dunn County Herald, Killdeer, ND
Kuklenski, Valerie .... (202) 898-8254
Entertainment ED
United Press International, Washington, DC

129-Who's Where **Laf**

Kukowski, Edward M .... (201) 437-2460
PUB
Bayonne Community News, Bayonne, NJ
Kulhanek, Shelly .... (402) 475-4200
Wire ED, Lincoln Journal Star, Lincoln, NE
Kulik, Thomas E .... (519) 255-5711
PROD FRM-PR, Windsor Star, Windsor, ON
Kull Jr, F Thomas .... (212) 416-2000
PROD VP-OPER
Wall Street Journal, New York, NY
Kulow, Charles .... (512) 575-1451
PROD MGR, Victoria Advocate, Victoria, TX
Kulpinski, Diane .... (541) 382-1811
Photo ED, Bulletin, Bend, OR
Kult, Tim .... (904) 264-3200
PUB, ADV MGR
Clay Today, Orange Park, FL
Kumar, Sid .... (0171) 411-3111
Deputy ED
Newslink Africa Ltd., London, England
Kunerth, Bill .... (916) 587-6061
PUB, Sierra Sun, Truckee, CA
Kunke, George .... (307) 347-3241
Sports ED
Northern Wyoming Daily News, Worland, WY
Kunke, L James .... (817) 695-0560
ED, Mid-Cities News, Arlington, TX
Kunkel, Debbie .... (904) 747-5000
Fashion/Society ED, Food/Women's ED
News Herald, Panama City, FL
Kunkel, Karl L .... (206) 392-6434
ED, Issaquah Press, Issaquah, WA
Kunken, Darrell .... (916) 321-1000
MGR-RES
Sacramento Bee, Sacramento, CA
Kunkle, Deb .... (319) 283-2144
EDU ED, Register, Oelwein, IA
Kunkler, Russel .... (330) 725-4166
DP MGR
Medina County Gazette, Medina, OH
Kunosch, Mary .... (414) 787-3334
PUB, ED, Waushara Argus, Wautoma, WI
Kunsch, Bruce .... (815) 432-5227
CIRC DIR, Iroquois County's Times-Republic, Watseka, IL
Kuntz, Fred .... (416) 367-2000
City ED, Toronto Star, Toronto, ON
Kuntz, Karl .... (614) 461-5000
MAN ED-Graphics
Columbus Dispatch, Columbus, OH
Kunzman, Dorothy .... (308) 762-3060
Society ED
Alliance Times-Herald, Alliance, NE
Kunzman, Michael .... (402) 335-3394
PUB, Tecumseh Chieftain, Tecumseh, NE
Kuo, Jung-Ling .... (718) 746-8889
ED, World Journal, Whitestone, NY
Kupcinet, Irv .... (312) 321-3000
COL-GEN, Chicago Sun-Times, Chicago, IL
Kuper, Ronald W .... (314) 725-1515
PRES/PUB
St. Louis Watchman Advocate, Clayton, MO
Kuperstock, Steve .... (504) 839-9077
PUB, Era-Leader, Franklinton, LA
Kurapka, Val .... (202) 636-3000
ADV MGR-CLASS
Washington Times, Washington, DC
Kurdy, Tom .... (712) 279-5019
PUB, Sioux City Journal, Sioux City, IA
Kurenoff, Gord .... (604) 853-1144
ED, Abbotsford News, Abbotsford, BC
Kurie, John F .... (704) 377-6221
PUB, Mecklenburg Times, Charlotte, NC
Kurk, Jim .... (502) 827-2000
Sports ED, Gleaner, Henderson, KY
Kurklin, Richard .... (817) 442-2244
ED, Cisco Press, Cisco, TX
Kurowski, Paul .... (208) 733-0931
PROD FRM-Press
Times-News, Twin Falls, ID
Kurth, Sue .... (608) 365-8811
Society ED, Beloit Daily News, Beloit, WI
Kurtich, Mark H .... (860) 241-6200
VP-CIRC/PROD/Customer SRV
Hartford Courant, Hartford, CT
Kurtz, Ced .... (412) 263-1100
ASST MAN ED-News Production
Pittsburgh Post-Gazette, Pittsburgh, PA
Kurtz, Chuck .... (913) 764-2211
MAN ED, Olathe Daily News, Olathe, KS
Kurtz, Craig .... (503) 399-6611
Graphics ED/Art DIR
Statesman Journal, Salem, OR
Kurtz, Dave .... (219) 925-2611
MAN ED, Evening Star, Auburn, IN
Kurtz, David .... (318) 237-3560
MAN ED, Times of Acadiana, Lafayette, LA
Kurtz, Frederick W .... (716) 335-2271
PUB, Genesee Country Express, Dansville, NY
Kurtz, Karen .... (503) 399-6611
News ED, Statesman Journal, Salem, OR
Kurtz, Pat .... (319) 524-8300
CIRC DIR, Daily Gate City, Keokuk, IA
Kurtz, Tim .... (515) 684-4611
ADV DIR-RT, ADTX MGR
Ottumwa Courier, Ottumwa, IA
Kurtz, William .... (717) 272-5611
CIRC MGR, Daily News, Lebanon, PA
Kurz, Jeff .... (203) 235-1661
Online ED, Record-Journal, Meriden, CT
Kurzenberger, Karen A .... (402) 497-3651
PUB, GM, ED
Springview Herald, Springview, NE
Kusel, Denise .... (505) 983-3303
Arts ED, Entertainment ED
Santa Fe New Mexican, Santa Fe, NM
Kuser, Helen L .... (419) 592-5055
SEC/TREAS, Northwest Signal, Napoleon, OH
Kuser Sr, James K .... (419) 592-5055
PRES, Northwest Signal, Napoleon, OH
Kuser Jr, James K .... (419) 592-5055
PUB, City ED
Northwest Signal, Napoleon, OH
Kuser, Jamie .... (419) 592-5055
VP, GM, ED, Northwest Signal, Napoleon, OH
Kuser, John L .... (419) 592-5055
CIRC MGR, PROD FRM-MR
Northwest Signal, Napoleon, OH
Kushma, David .... (313) 222-6400
ASSOC ED, Detroit Free Press, Detroit, MI
Kushner, Barry .... (610) 272-2500
ADV MGR-Sales
Times Herald, Norristown, PA
Kushner, Cheryl .... (216) 999-4500
Entertainment ED
Plain Dealer, Cleveland, OH
Kushnier, Joanne .... (807) 343-6200
News ED
Chronicle-Journal, Thunder Bay, ON
Kuslich, Cynthia .... (409) 336-6416
PUB, Liberty Gazette, Liberty, TX
Kuslich, Lawrence J .... (409) 336-6416
PUB, Liberty Gazette, Liberty, TX
Kusper, John .... (415) 777-5700
PROD MGR-Pre Press, San Francisco Newspaper Agency, San Francisco, CA
Kuster, Steve .... (805) 564-5200
PROD MGR-MR, Santa Barbara News-Press, Santa Barbara, CA
Kustrup, Joseph .... (609) 989-5454
PROD MGR-Transportation
Times, Trenton, NJ
Kustyn, William A .... (315) 337-4000
CIRC DIR, Daily Sentinel, Rome, NY
Kusunose, Akiko .... (206) 623-0100
ED, Hokubei Hochi, Seattle, WA
Kuta, Carol .... (219) 362-2161
ADV MGR, ADV MGR-RT, MGR-PROM
La Porte Herald-Argus, La Porte, IN
Kuta, Dave .... (907) 257-4200
ADV DIR
Anchorage Daily News, Anchorage, AK
Kuth, Andy May .... (215) 854-2000
Johannesburg BU
Philadelphia Inquirer, Philadelphia, PA
Kutkus, Grace .... (803) 577-7111
ASST MAN ED-News
Post and Courier, Charleston, SC
Kutler, Jeff .... (212) 803-8200
EXEC ED, American Banker, New York, NY
Kutner, Janet .... (214) 977-8222
Art Critic, Dallas Morning News, Dallas, TX
Kutter, Elizabeth .... (319) 398-8211
Neighbors ED, Gazette, Cedar Rapids, IA
Kuttler, Hilley .... (212) 599-3666
Washington DC Correspondent, Jerusalem Post Foreign Service, New York, NY
Kutz, Ed .... (918) 684-2828
CIRC DIR, Muskogee Daily Phoenix & Times Democrat, Muskogee, OK
Kutz, K Don .... (316) 672-5511
PROD MGR, Pratt Tribune, Pratt, KS
Kuwasaki, Michelle .... (619) 232-4381
CIRC MGR
San Diego Daily Transcript, San Diego, CA
Kuykendall, Bill .... (573) 882-5700
Photo DEPT MGR
Columbia Missourian, Columbia, MO
Kuykendall, David L .... (714) 553-9292
Sr VP/CFO
Freedom Communications Inc., Irvine, CA
Kuykendall, Debra .... (209) 578-2000
ADV MGR-OPER, Modesto Bee, Modesto, CA
Kuyper, Jerry .... (815) 459-4040
Automotive ED
Northwest Herald, Crystal Lake, IL
Kuz, Martin .... (702) 871-6780
MAN ED, CityLife, Las Vegas, NV
Kuzel, Colleen .... (219) 874-7211
News ED, News Dispatch, Michigan City, IN
Kuzjak, Nick .... (715) 743-2600
ED, Clark County Press, Neillsville, WI
Kvidt, Dewey .... (701) 780-1100
MGR-INFO SYS
Grand Forks Herald, Grand Forks, ND
Kwiatkowski, Jim .... (613) 732-3691
Weekly MGR, Observer, Pembroke, ON
Kwolek, Michael .... (401) 722-4000
CONT, Times, Pawtucket, RI
Kwong, Betty .... (818) 713-3000
Lifestyle ED, Daily News, Woodland Hills, CA
Kyer, Bob .... (615) 455-4545
ED, News & Guardian, Tullahoma, TN
Kyle, Sharon .... (205) 845-2550
ADV MGR, Times Journal, Fort Payne, AL
Kyse, Bruce W .... (707) 546-2020
EX ED, Press Democrat, Santa Rosa, CA

L

LaBarca, Josephine .... (516) 589-6200
GM, Suffolk County News, Sayville, NY
Labarth, Len .... (610) 622-8800
City ED (Night), RE ED
Delaware County Daily Times, Primos, PA
Labat, Russell .... (507) 537-1551
GM, Independent, Marshall, MN
Labbe, Emery L .... (207) 728-3336
PUB, E
St. John Valley Times, Madawaska, ME
Labbe, J R (Jill) .... (817) 390-7400
City ED
Fort Worth Star-Telegram, Fort Worth, TX
L'Abbee, Jean Claude .... (418) 683-1573
ED/GM
Le Journal de Quebec, Ville Vanier, QC
Labedz, Luann .... (970) 493-6397
DIR-Market Development
Fort Collins Coloradoan, Fort Collins, CO
Labelee, Darquise .... (705) 272-4363
ED, Northland Post, Cochrane, ON
LaBell, Dave .... (941) 748-0411
CIRC MGR-PROM
Bradenton Herald, Bradenton, FL
Laberge, Michael .... (207) 791-6650
PROD OPER MGR-Publishing SYS
Portland Press Herald, Portland, ME
LaBonte, George R .... (508) 793-9100
Librarian, Telegram & Gazette, Worcester, MA
La Bran, Renee .... (213) 237-5000
ADV DIR-New BUS Development/Strategic Planning
Los Angeles Times, Los Angeles, CA
Labranche, Jean .... (418) 686-3233
ADV MGR-Telemarketing/Arts
Le Soleil, Quebec, QC
LaBreche, Paul A .... (508) 586-7200
VP, GM, Enterprise, Brockton, MA
Labs, Eugene .... (320) 695-2570
PUB, ED, Valley News, Browns Valley, MN
Lacaeyse, Joseph E .... (815) 937-3300
TREAS
Small Newspaper Group Inc., Kankakee, IL
LaCamp, Jerry .... (541) 485-1234
PROD MGR, Register-Guard, Eugene, OR
Lacasse, Denis .... (514) 774-5375
ED, Le Clairon, Saint-Hyacinthe, QC
Lacasse, Gilbert .... (418) 686-3233
PRES, PUB, GM, Le Soleil, Quebec, QC
Lacasse, Lionel .... (819) 629-2618
PUB, ED, Le Temiscamien, Ville-Marie, QC
Lacerte, Jean-Francois .... (204) 237-4823
PUB, GM, La Liberte, St. Boniface, MB
Lacey, Bruce .... (316) 321-1120
PROD SUPT, El Dorado Times, El Dorado, KS
Lacey, Daniel A .... (805) 395-7500
CFO/ASST SEC
Bakersfield Californian, Bakersfield, CA
Lachambre, Ray O .... (306) 554-2224
PUB, ED, Advance/Gazette, Wynyard, SK
LaChance, Earl .... (617) 786-7000
Sports ED, Patriot Ledger, Quincy, MA
LaChance, Joe .... (608) 754-3311
PROD FRM-PR
Janesville Gazette, Janesville, WI
LaChance, Renee .... (503) 236-1252
PUB, MAN ED, Just Out, Portland, OR
Lachowicz, Steve .... (509) 663-5161
City ED, Wenatchee World, Wenatchee, WA
Lachtman, Howard .... (209) 943-6397
Books ED, Record, Stockton, CA
Lacitis, Erik .... (206) 464-2111
COL, Seattle Times, Seattle, WA
Laciura, Phillip .... (313) 222-2300
EX Sports ED, Detroit News, Detroit, MI
Lack, David .... (818) 713-3000
CIRC MGR-Single Copy Sales
Daily News, Woodland Hills, CA
Lackey, Brad .... (616) 964-7161
ADV DIR
Battle Creek Enquirer, Battle Creek, MI
Lackey, Carol .... (915) 673-4271
Fashion ED, Features ED, Health/Medical ED, Life ED, Living/Lifestyle ED, Teen-Age/Youth ED, Abilene Reporter-News, Abilene, TX
Lackey, James .... (202) 541-3250
GEN News ED
Catholic News Services, Washington, DC
Lacock, Patti J .... (412) 222-2200
VP/SEC, DIR-Human Resources
Observer-Reporter, Washington, PA
LaCour, Claudette .... (213) 622-8332
VP-Sales & MKTG
La Opinion, Los Angeles, CA
LaCour, Mary .... (504) 638-7155
PUB, Pointe Coupee Banner, New Roads, LA
Lacourciere, Denise .... (819) 449-1725
GM, La Gatineau, Maniwaki, QC
Lacourse, Fernand .... (514) 285-7272
ADV DIR-NTL, La Presse, Montreal, QC
Lacy, Brian .... (617) 593-7700
CIRC DIR, Daily Evening Item, Lynn, MA
Lacy, Jay .... (316) 429-2773
BM, ADV MGR
Columbus Daily Advocate, Columbus, KS
Lacy-Pendleton, Stevie .... (718) 981-1234
Perspective ED
Staten Island Advance, Staten Island, NY
Ladd, Scott .... (201) 877-4141
MET ED-Night, Star-Ledger, Newark, NJ
Ladd, Terry .... (918) 341-1101
CIRC DIR
Claremore Daily Progress, Claremore, OK
Laddin, Michael .... (518) 792-9914
VP-MKTG/Product Development
TV Data, Queensbury, NY
Ladewski, Paul .... (773) 586-8800
Sports COL, Daily Southtown, Chicago, IL
Ladins, David .... (937) 225-2000
ADV MGR-Pre Press
Dayton Daily News, Dayton, OH
Ladner, Randy .... (601) 896-2100
PROD SUPV-Building SRV
Sun Herald, Biloxi, MS
Ladogana, Marguerite .... (352) 563-6363
Communications Leader
Citrus County Chronicle, Crystal River, FL
Ladowski, Casey .... (312) 321-3000
ADV DIR-Display Entertainment/Amusement
Chicago Sun-Times, Chicago, IL
Ladson, Sheon .... (919) 829-4500
State ED, News & Observer, Raleigh, NC
Lael, Sally .... (217) 323-1010
ED, Illinoian Star, Beardstown, IL
Lafady, Stephen A .... (360) 577-2500
MGR-Human Resources, CIRC MGR
Daily News, Longview, WA
Lafave, Dick .... (212) 455-4000
Southwest Sales, North America Syndicate, King Features Syndicate Inc., New York, NY
LaFave, Ken .... (602) 271-8000
Performing Arts Writer
Arizona Republic, Phoenix, AZ
LaFave, Vicki .... (906) 786-2021
EDU ED, Daily Press, Escanaba, MI
LaFave, Yvonne .... (203) 574-3636
EDU ED, Waterbury Republican-American, Waterbury, CT
Lafavers, Carol .... (606) 678-8191
DP MGR
Commonwealth-Journal, Somerset, KY
La Fee, Scott .... (619) 299-3131
SCI Writer
San Diego Union-Tribune, San Diego, CA
Lafemina, Michael .... (212) 930-8000
CONT, New York Post, New York, NY
LaFerrara, Charles .... (504) 643-4918
ADV DIR, Slidell Sentry-News, Slidell, LA
Laferriere, David .... (508) 586-7200
Graphics ED/Art DIR
Enterprise, Brockton, MA
Lafferty, Mike .... (407) 420-5000
Topics ED/Tourism
Orlando Sentinel, Orlando, FL
Lafferty, Walt T .... (201) 428-6200
GM, Daily Record, Parsippany, NJ
Lafferty-Drago, Terrie .... (619) 792-3820
MAN ED, Del Mar/Solana Beach/Carmel Valley/Rancho Santa Fe Sun, Del Mar, CA
Laffey, Mary Lu .... (815) 937-3300
Fashion/Style ED, Home Furnishings ED, Women's ED, Daily Journal, Kankakee, IL
Laffoon IV, Polk .... (305) 376-3800
VP-CORP Relations
Knight-Ridder Inc., Miami, FL
Laflamme, Fred .... (613) 544-5000
PUB (Interim), VP-Advertising & Reader Sales, Kingston Whig-Standard, Kingston, ON
LaFleche, Lyn .... (403) 777-2345
PUB, Calgary Mirror, Calgary, AB
LaFleur, Claire .... (203) 574-3636
Features ED, Waterbury Republican-American, Waterbury, CT
Lafoe, Lynn .... (601) 335-1155
Lifestyle ED
Delta Democrat Times, Greenville, MS
LaFolette, Jan .... (541) 266-6831
GM, Canby Herald/Wilsonville Spokesman, Canby, OR

Laf Who's Where-130

LaFontaine, Georges .... (819) 449-2233
ED, La Gazette de Maniwaki, Maniwaki, QC
Laforet, Gary .... (416) 422-2331
GM, Canadian Jewish News, Don Mills, ON
LaFreniere, Greg .... (207) 784-5411
MAN ED, Sun-Journal, Lewiston, ME
LaFreniere, Paulie .... (406) 791-1444
ADV MGR-RT
Great Falls Tribune, Great Falls, MT
Lafromboise, Mrs J R .... (360) 736-3311
PRES, Chronicle, Centralia, WA
La Ganga, Maria .... (213) 237-5000
San Francisco BU
Los Angeles Times, Los Angeles, CA
Lagarde, Jack D .... (504) 826-3279
ADV MGR-RT
Times-Picayune, New Orleans, LA
LaGasse, Mark J .... (715) 669-5525
PUB, ED, Thorp Courier, Thorp, WI
Lage, Wally .... (573) 335-6611
COO
Rust Communications, Cape Girardeau, MO
Lager, Thomas J .... (205) 325-2222
ADV DIR-Sales/MKTG
Birmingham News, Birmingham, AL
Lager, Tom .... (205) 325-2222
ADV DIR-Sales/MKTG
Birmingham Post-Herald, Birmingham, AL
Lagermey, Mark .... (616) 775-6565
MAN ED, Cadillac News, Cadillac, MI
Lago, Amy .... (212) 293-8500
MAN ED-Comic Art, United Media, United Feature Syndicate, Newspaper Enterprise Association, New York, NY
Lagow, Karen .... (706) 291-6397
Lifestyle ED, Rome News-Tribune, Rome, GA
LaGraffe, Arthur .... (315) 470-0011
PROD ASST MGR, Post-Standard/Syracuse Herald-Journal/American, Syracuse, NY
La Guire, Lannie .... (213) 237-5000
City ED, Los Angeles Times, Los Angeles, CA
Lahaise, Mark .... (701) 642-8585
PROD FRM-COMP
Daily News, Wahpeton, ND
Lahargoue, Lee .... (805) 564-5200
CIRC DIR, Santa Barbara News-Press, Santa Barbara, CA
Lahmers, Ken .... (330) 688-0088
ED, Aurora Advocate, Stow, OH
Lai, Tai .... (714) 835-1234
Team Leader-Graphics
Orange County Register, Santa Ana, CA
Laidman, Jenni .... (517) 895-8551
Environmental ED, Health/Medical ED
Bay City Times, Bay City, MI
Lail, Jack .... (423) 523-3131
MGR-Online Publishing
Knoxville News-Sentinel, Knoxville, TN
Laing, LaWanda .... (541) 963-3161
MGR-Office
La Grande Observer, La Grande, OR
Lair, Dwain .... (501) 741-2325
ED, EPE, News ED
Harrison Daily Times, Harrison, AR
Lair, Mary .... (601) 582-4321
PROD MGR-Camera/Platemaking
Hattiesburg American, Hattiesburg, MS
Lair, William .... (217) 235-5656
News ED
Mattoon Journal-Gazette, Mattoon, IL
Laird, Elizabeth .... (507) 235-3303
Court Reporter, Sentinel, Fairmont, MN
Laird, John .... (915) 546-6100
EPE, El Paso Times, El Paso, TX
Laird, Robert .... (212) 210-2100
Chief EDL Writer
New York Daily News, New York, NY
Laird, Stephen A .... (315) 782-1000
CIRC DIR
Watertown Daily Times, Watertown, NY
Laitala, Lynn Maria .... (715) 394-4961
ED
Finnish-American Reporter, Superior, WI
Lajeunesse, Jacques .... (418) 683-1573
MGR-MKTG/PROM
Le Journal de Quebec, Ville Vanier, QC
Lake, Charles S .... (918) 224-5185
GM, Sapulpa Daily Herald, Sapulpa, OK
Lake, Janelle .... (604) 785-5631
ED, North Peace Express, Fort St. John, BC
Lake, John .... (419) 586-2371
ADV MGR
Celina Daily Standard, Celina, OH
Lake, Marvin Leon .... (757) 446-2000
DIR-Recruiting
Virginian-Pilot, Norfolk, VA
Lake, S Hershel .... (615) 363-3544
PUB, Giles Free Press, Pulaski, TN

Lakin, Michael .... (217) 792-5557
PUB, ED, Weekly-News, Mt. Pulaski, IL
Lakshmann, Indira .... (617) 929-2000
BU Chief-Hong Kong
Boston Globe, Boston, MA
Lakus, Richard .... (617) 786-7000
CIRC DIR-Distribution, PROD DIR-Printing/Distribution, Patriot Ledger, Quincy, MA
Lalancette, Gilles .... (418) 545-4474
Features ED, Le Quotidien, Chicoutimi, QC
LaLande, Andre .... (705) 472-3200
ADV MGR-RT, Nugget, North Bay, ON
Laliberte, Kevin .... (403) 786-2602
ED, Freelancer, Mayerthorpe, AB
Laline, Brian .... (718) 981-1234
ED
Staten Island Advance, Staten Island, NY
Lalley, Kevin .... (203) 655-7476
GM, Darien News-Review, Darien, CT
Lally, Bill .... (814) 623-1151
CIRC MGR, Bedford Gazette, Bedford, PA
Lally, Luke P .... (508) 428-8900
PUB, Otis Notice, Osterville, MA
Lalonde, Claire-Anne .... (613) 739-7000
PROD DIR-Commercial Printing
Ottawa Sun, Ottawa, ON
Lalonde, Normand .... (514) 722-7708
ED, Le Monde, Montreal, QC
Lam, Andrew .... (415) 243-4364
ASSOC ED
Pacific News Service, San Francisco, CA
Lam, Betty .... (405) 273-4200
Religion ED, News-Star, Shawnee, OK
Lam, Leon .... (212) 513-1440
MAN ED, United Journal, New York, NY
Lamadeleine, Gilles .... (613) 562-0111
ADV MGR-CLASS, CIRC DIR
Le Droit, Ottawa, ON
Lamanna, Frank .... (814) 870-1600
CIRC MGR
Morning News/Erie Daily Times, Erie, PA
Lamar, Ron .... (501) 785-9404
VP/Outdoor/TV Group
Donrey Media Group, Fort Smith, AR
LaMarca, Maureen B .... (908) 534-1793
Author, KidSmarts, Whitehouse Station, NJ
LaMarche, Marie .... (360) 377-3711
DIR-Human Resources, Sun, Bremerton, WA
Lamarche, Serge .... (819) 983-2725
ED, La Petite Nation, Saint-Andre-Avellin, QC
LaMay, Colleen .... (208) 377-6200
Health/Medical ED
Idaho Statesman, Boise, ID
Lamb, Bill .... (903) 885-8663
MAN ED, Sulphur Springs News-Telegram, Sulphur Springs, TX
Lamb, Cory .... (801) 373-5050
CIRC ASST DIR, Daily Herald, Provo, UT
Lamb, Ginger .... (716) 232-6920
ED, Daily Record, Rochester, NY
Lamb, Gloria .... (502) 821-6833
PROD SUPV-MR
Messenger, Madisonville, KY
Lamb, Madelyn .... (504) 383-1111
Home Furnishings ED, Women's ED
Advocate, Baton Rouge, LA
Lamb, Mary .... (540) 962-2121
SEC/TREAS, Librarian
Virginian Review, Covington, VA
Lamb, Quincy .... (806) 762-8844
PROD SUPT-COMP
Lubbock Avalanche-Journal, Lubbock, TX
Lamb, Richard W .... (517) 734-2105
GM, ED
Presque Isle County Advance, Rogers City, MI
Lamb, Theresa .... (503) 226-1311
ASSOC ED
Daily Journal of Commerce, Portland, OR
Lamberg, Gary A .... (906) 932-2211
VP, GM, ED
Ironwood Daily Globe, Ironwood, MI
Lamberson, Carolyn .... (541) 382-1811
Food ED, Religion ED, Bulletin, Bend, OR
Lambert, Albert E .... (717) 326-1551
PROD SUPT-COMP
Williamsport Sun-Gazette, Williamsport, PA
Lambert, Brian .... (612) 222-5011
Television ED
St. Paul Pioneer Press, St. Paul, MN
Lambert, Carole .... (212) 803-8200
ASSOC PUB
American Banker, New York, NY
Lambert, Deborah .... (202) 364-4401
Public Affairs DIR, AIM (Accuracy in Media) Report, Washington, DC
Lambert Jr, James W .... (601) 894-3141
PUB, ED
Copiah County Courier, Hazlehurst, MS
Lambert, Jennie .... (704) 864-3291
ED, Gaston Gazette, Gastonia, NC
Lambert, Kellie .... (203) 574-3636
Fashion Writer, Waterbury Republican-American, Waterbury, CT

Lambert, Lois .... (406) 775-6245
ED, Ekalaka Eagle, Ekalaka, MT
Lambert, M Brice .... (406) 775-6245
PUB, Ekalaka Eagle, Ekalaka, MT
Lambert, Steve .... (914) 358-2200
MAN ED
Rockland Journal-News, West Nyack, NY
Lambert, Terry .... (812) 231-4200
PROD SUPT-Press
Tribune-Star, Terre Haute, IN
Lambert, Vickie .... (919) 335-0841
MGR-MKTG/PROM
Daily Advance, Elizabeth City, NC
Lambeth, Kathy .... (910) 373-7000
ADV DIR, News & Record, Greensboro, NC
Lambie, Cathy Hamilton .... (514) 987-2222
CIRC VP-Reader Sales & SRV
Gazette, Montreal, QC
Lambright, Teresa .... (505) 887-5501
EDU ED, Current-Argus, Carlsbad, NM
Lambuth, Mitch .... (601) 684-2421
PA, Enterprise-Journal, McComb, MS
Lamirand, Robert .... (219) 267-3111
BUS/FIN ED, RE ED, Religion ED, Wire ED
Times-Union, Warsaw, IN
Lamm, Greg .... (360) 424-3251
City ED
Skagit Valley Herald, Mount Vernon, WA
Lamm, James S .... (219) 881-3000
CIRC DIR, Post-Tribune, Gary, IN
Lamm, Tracey .... (319) 372-6421
School ED, Daily Democrat, Fort Madison, IA
Lammerding, Betsy .... (330) 996-3000
Travel ED, Akron Beacon Journal, Akron, OH
Lammers, Dale .... (501) 935-5525
PROD FRM-PR
Jonesboro Sun, Jonesboro, AR
Lamonski, Frank .... (209) 441-6111
MGR-Technical SRV, Fresno Bee, Fresno, CA
Lamont, Ian .... (509) 582-1500
GM, Tri-City Herald, Tri-Cities, WA
Lamont, James .... (202) 797-7000
GM, Washington Blade, Washington, DC
Lamont, Ray .... (540) 574-6200
City ED
Daily News-Record, Harrisonburg, VA
LaMont, Sanders .... (209) 578-2000
EX ED, Modesto Bee, Modesto, CA
Lamontagne, Gisele .... (207) 784-5411
DP MGR, Sun-Journal, Lewiston, ME
LaMore, Mary .... (815) 468-6397
GM, Manteno News, Manteno, IL
Lamoureux, Gilles .... (514) 521-4545
ADV MGR
Le Journal de Montreal, Montreal, QC
Lamoureux, Jean-Denis .... (514) 521-4545
News ED
Le Journal de Montreal, Montreal, QC
Lamoureux, Jocelyne .... (514) 844-3131
PUB, La Concorde, St. Eustache, QC
Lampe, Nelson .... (402) 444-1000
EX News ED
Omaha World-Herald, Omaha, NE
Lampert, C .... (604) 562-2441
PROD MGR-Manufacturing
Prince George Citizen, Prince George, BC
Lampert, Joseph .... (614) 633-1131
ED, Times Leader, Martins Ferry, OH
Lamphier Jr, Frank A .... (203) 235-1661
Cartoonist, Record-Journal, Meriden, CT
Lamphier, Gerald .... (315) 789-3333
PROD FRM-PR
Finger Lakes Times, Geneva, NY
Lampinen, John A .... (847) 427-4300
ASST VP/MAN ED
Daily Herald, Arlington Heights, IL
Lampinen, Lynda .... (501) 623-7711
Automotive ED, BUS/FIN ED, RE ED
Sentinel-Record, Hot Springs, AR
Lampkin, Bob .... (415) 348-4321
CIRC ASST MGR
San Mateo County Times, San Mateo, CA
Lampley, Myra .... (512) 594-3346
ED, Shiner Gazette, Shiner, TX
Lampmann, Jane .... (617) 450-2000
Features ED, Living/Lifestyle ED, Religion ED
Christian Science Monitor, Boston, MA
Lampson, Jeff .... (216) 576-9115
GM, Sentinel, Jefferson, OH
Lampson, John .... (216) 576-9115
PUB, Sentinel, Jefferson, OH
Lampton, Georgette .... (512) 884-2011
ADV MGR-Territory Sales, Corpus Christi Caller-Times, Corpus Christi, TX
Lamson, Leah .... (508) 793-9100
MAN ED-Local News
Telegram & Gazette, Worcester, MA
Lamson, Martha .... (512) 526-2397
PUB, ED
Refugio County Advantage Press, Refugio, TX
Lamun, Shirley .... (208) 377-6200
CIRC MGR-Customer SRV
Idaho Statesman, Boise, ID

Lanaris, Paul .... (201) 653-1000
ADTX MGR, Jersey Journal, Jersey City, NJ
Lancaster, Charles W .... (205) 543-3417
PRES
Lancaster Management Inc., Gadsden, AL
Lancaster, Dale .... (360) 694-3391
PROD MGR-PR, Columbian, Vancouver, WA
Lancaster, James D .... (205) 543-3417
COB
Lancaster Management Inc., Gadsden, AL
Lancaster Jr, James D .... (205) 543-3417
VP
Lancaster Management Inc., Gadsden, AL
Lancaster, Jimmy .... (417) 334-3161
Entertainment ED
Branson Tri-Lakes Daily News, Branson, MO
Lancaster, Lori .... (206) 339-3000
My Life ED, Herald, Everett, WA
Lancaster, Michele .... (207) 924-7402
GM, Eastern Gazette, Dexter, ME
Lancaster, Sue .... (513) 721-2700
News ED
Cincinnati Enquirer, Cincinnati, OH
Lance, Doris G .... (805) 945-5634
MAN ED, Seabee Coverall, Lancaster, CA
Lance, Gary .... (408) 920-5000
Library MGR
San Jose Mercury News, San Jose, CA
Lance, Tiffany .... (801) 373-5050
Entertainment/Amusements ED, Television ED, Daily Herald, Provo, UT
Lancia, Agostino .... (508) 473-1111
PROD FRM-PR, Daily News, Milford, MA
Lanctot, Tom .... (509) 837-4500
PUB, Daily Sun News, Sunnyside, WA
Land, Clint .... (318) 377-1866
Sports ED, Minden Press-Herald, Minden, LA
Land, Marilyn .... (317) 932-2222
ADV DIR, Rushville Republican, Rushville, IN
Land, Mark .... (914) 694-9300
ASST MAN ED-BUS, Herald Statesman, Yonkers, NY, Gannett Co. Inc.
Landenberger, Lee .... (813) 689-7764
MAN ED, Brandon News, Brandon, FL
Lander, Howard .... (213) 525-2000
EX VP, Hollywood Reporter, Los Angeles, CA
Lander, Paul .... (914) 454-2000
Features ED
Poughkeepsie Journal, Poughkeepsie, NY
Landers, Everetts .... (609) 663-6000
EX ED, Courier-Post, Cherry Hill, NJ
Landers, Rich .... (509) 459-5000
Outdoors ED
Spokesman-Review, Spokane, WA
Landers, Scott .... (702) 788-6200
CIRC MGR-OPER, Gazette-Journal, Reno, NV
Landes, Robert N .... (212) 208-8000
EX VP/General Counsel/SEC, Corporation Records, Daily News, New York, NY
Landesman, Stephen .... (607) 272-2321
Features ED, Ithaca Journal, Ithaca, NY
Landewee, Irvin .... (573) 335-6611
ADV MGR-Major Accounts/Preprints
Southeast Missourian, Cape Girardeau, MO
Landfried, Ron .... (919) 419-6500
State ED, Herald-Sun, Durham, NC
Landini, Leigh .... (502) 443-1771
Features ED, Women's ED
Paducah Sun, Paducah, KY
Landis, Keith .... (814) 623-1151
ADV DIR, PROD FRM-COMP
Bedford Gazette, Bedford, PA
Landis, Norm .... (315) 337-4000
Copy ED, Daily Sentinel, Rome, NY
Landis, Tim .... (217) 788-1300
BUS ED
State Journal-Register, Springfield, IL
Landman, Jonathan .... (212) 556-1234
Week in Review ED
New York Times, New York, NY
Landmann, Connie G .... (817) 547-4207
ED, Copperas Cove Leader-Press, Copperas Cove, TX
Landmann, David G .... (817) 547-4207
PUB, Copperas Cove Leader-Press, Copperas Cove, TX
Landolt, Elizabeth .... (802) 525-3531
ED, Chronicle, Barton, VT
Landon, Chuck .... (304) 348-5140
COL, Charleston Daily Mail, Charleston, WV
Landon, Gloria .... (608) 744-2107
GM, Tri-County Press, Cuba City, WI
Landon, Tim .... (312) 222-3232
VP-MKTG & Development
Chicago Tribune, Chicago, IL
Landrum, William .... (501) 675-4455
ED, Booneville Democrat, Booneville, AR
Landry, Arthur P .... (205) 766-3434
DIR-ITS/Pre Press SRV
Times Daily, Florence, AL
Landry, Berthold .... (418) 686-3233
City ED, Photo DEPT MGR
Le Soleil, Quebec, QC

131-Who's Where **Lar**

Landry, Chris .... (318) 365-6773
Sports ED, Daily Iberian, New Iberia, LA
Landry, Greg .... (902) 667-5102
PROD SUPT, PROD FRM-COMP
Amherst Daily News, Amherst, NS
Landry, John .... (902) 468-1222
CIRC VP-OPER, Daily News, Halifax, NS
Landry, Roger D .... (514) 285-6918
PRES, Les Journaux Trans-Canada (JTC), Montreal, QC
Landry, Serge .... (514) 644-3360
GM, ED, Le Seigneurie, Boucherville, QC
Landry, Sonya C .... (318) 631-6222
PUB, ED, Shreveport Sun, Shreveport, LA
Landry, Sue .... (813) 893-8111
Medical Section ED
St. Petersburg Times, St. Petersburg, FL
Landson, Amy .... (334) 566-4270
Features ED, Messenger, Troy, AL
Lane, Al .... (804) 649-6000
PROD MGR-Engraving
Richmond Times-Dispatch, Richmond, VA
Lane, Bill .... (213) 469-2333
PUB
World News Syndicate Ltd., Hollywood, CA
Lane, Bill .... (423) 246-8121
Sports ED, Times-News, Kingsport, TN
Lane, Brian .... (812) 231-4200
PROD DIR, Tribune-Star, Terre Haute, IN
Lane, Dottie .... (330) 296-9657
Fashion/Food ED, Home Furnishings ED, Society ED
Record-Courier, Kent-Ravenna, OH
Lane, Ed .... (804) 458-8511
PROD SUPT, News, Hopewell, VA
Lane, Edwin .... (817) 390-7400
PROD MGR-Press OPER
Fort Worth Star-Telegram, Fort Worth, TX
Lane, George .... (406) 447-4000
Photo DEPT MGR
Helena Independent Record, Helena, MT
Lane, James .... (814) 946-7411
Sports ED, Altoona Mirror, Altoona, PA
Lane, Jane .... (617) 837-3500
ED, Marshfield Mariner, Marshfield, MA
Lane, Michael J .... (410) 332-6000
EDL Cartoonist, Sun, Baltimore, MD
Lane, Polly .... (206) 464-2111
Aerospace Reporter
Seattle Times, Seattle, WA
Lane, Renee .... (910) 323-4848
MGR-MKTG SRV
Fayetteville Observer-Times, Fayetteville, NC
Lane, Sharon .... (206) 464-2111
Food ED, Seattle Times, Seattle, WA
Laner, Valerie .... (706) 278-1011
ED, Daily Citizen-News, Dalton, GA
Lanetot, Claire .... (519) 756-2020
SEC/TREAS, Expositor, Brantford, ON
Laney, Addie B .... (919) 946-2144
CONT
Washington Daily News, Washington, NC
Lang, Becky .... (608) 754-3311
Marketplace ED
Janesville Gazette, Janesville, WI
Lang, Dennis .... (405) 353-0620
MAN ED, Lawton Constitution, Lawton, OK
Lang, Ellen .... (515) 782-2141
PROD MGR-COMP
Creston News-Advertiser, Creston, IA
Lang, Greg .... (508) 685-1000
EX News ED
Eagle-Tribune, North Andover, MA
Lang, H D .... (508) 668-0243
PUB, Walpole Times, Walpole, MA
Lang, Lin J .... (513) 761-1188
Contributing Critic
Critic's Choice Reviews, Cincinnati, OH
Lang, Melvin .... (919) 752-6166
News ED, Daily Reflector, Greenville, NC
Lang, Rusty .... (918) 581-8300
Fashion/Style ED, Living/Lifestyle ED, Women's ED, Tulsa World, Tulsa, OK
Lang, Stew .... (250) 380-5211
BUS/FIN ED, Times Colonist, Victoria, BC
Lang, Terri .... (706) 359-3229
GM, Lincoln Journal, Lincolnton, GA
Lang, Thompson H .... (505) 823-7777
PRES/TREAS
Albuquerque Journal, Albuquerque, NM
Lang, Vicci .... (573) 568-3310
GM, Bloomfield Vindicator, Bloomfield, MO
Lang, William P .... (505) 823-7777
VP, Albuquerque Journal, Albuquerque, NM
Lang, Zelda .... (806) 249-4511
ED, Dalhart Daily Texan, Dalhart, TX
Langdale, Sandra .... (916) 321-1000
DIR-INFO SYS
Sacramento Bee, Sacramento, CA
Langdon, Chas .... (970) 247-3504
Arts/Entertainment ED, Religion ED
Durango Herald, Durango, CO
Langdon, Craig D .... (913) 525-6355
PUB, Lucas-Sylvan News, Lucas, KS
Langdon, Helen .... (405) 927-2355
GM, Coalgate Record-Register, Coalgate, OK
Langdon, Jerry .... (703) 276-5800
Sports ED
Gannett News Service, Arlington, VA
Lange, David .... (216) 247-5335
ED, Chagrin Valley Times, Chagrin Falls, OH
Lange, Henry .... (219) 874-7211
BUS/FIN ED, COL
News Dispatch, Michigan City, IN
Lange, James J .... (405) 475-3311
Cartoonist
Daily Oklahoman, Oklahoma City, OK
Lange, P James .... (414) 922-4600
CONT, Reporter, Fond du Lac, WI
Lange, Paul H .... (715) 924-4118
PUB, Chetek Alert, Chetek, WI
Lange, Tami .... (330) 264-1125
City ED, Daily Record, Wooster, OH
Lange-Kubick, Cindy .... (402) 475-4200
Entertainment/Features Reporter
Lincoln Journal Star, Lincoln, NE
Langen, Brian .... (716) 335-2271
ED, Genesee Country Express, Dansville, NY
Langen, Laurie .... (320) 255-8700
ADV MGR-Inside Sales
St. Cloud Times, St. Cloud, MN
Langen, Mark .... (403) 887-2331
ED, Sylvan Lake News, Sylvan Lake, AB
Langer, Bruce .... (519) 344-3641
BUS/FIN ED, Entertainment ED, Picture ED, Radio/Television ED, Travel ED, Wire ED
Observer, Sarnia, ON
Langer, Ralph .... (214) 977-8222
Senior VP/EX ED
Dallas Morning News, Dallas, TX
Langerlaan, Carolyn .... (817) 461-6397
ADV DIR-CLASS
Arlington Morning News, Arlington, TX
Langeveld, Martin C .... (413) 447-7311
EX VP/COO, PUB, Berkshire Eagle, Pittsfield, MA, MediaNews (New England Newspapers)
Langevin, Kelly .... (204) 467-2421
ED, Stonewall Argus/Teulon Times, Stonewall, MB
Langford, Charlie .... (601) 842-2611
Wire ED, Northeast Mississippi Daily Journal, Tupelo, MS
Langford, David .... (416) 585-5000
Sports ED, Globe and Mail, Toronto, ON
Langford, Debra .... (517) 843-6441
PUB, MAN ED
Mayville Monitor, Mayville, MI
Langford, Gale .... (517) 843-6441
PUB, ED, Mayville Monitor, Mayville, MI
Langford, George .... (312) 222-3232
Public ED, Chicago Tribune, Chicago, IL
Langford, Jane .... (217) 453-6771
PUB, Nauvoo News Independent, Nauvoo, IL
Langford, Ken .... (903) 893-8181
ADV MGR-CLASS
Herald Democrat, Sherman, TX
Langford, Vernon .... (970) 242-5050
PROD FRM-PR
Daily Sentinel, Grand Junction, CO
Langham, Mike .... (618) 594-3131
GM, Union Banner, Carlyle, IL
Langham, Phil .... (814) 623-1151
PROD FRM-PR
Bedford Gazette, Bedford, PA
Langlais, David .... (573) 815-1500
PROD FRM-PR
Columbia Daily Tribune, Columbia, MO
Langley, Catherine T .... (908) 782-4747
PUB, Hunterdon Observer, Flemington, NJ
Langley, Jay .... (908) 782-4747
ED
Hunterdon County Democrat, Flemington, NJ
Langley, Lynne .... (803) 577-7111
Medical ED, Post and Courier, Charleston, SC
Langlie, Mavis .... (507) 684-2315
ED, Our Community News, Ellendale, MN
Langlie, Orville .... (507) 684-2315
PUB, Our Community News, Ellendale, MN
Langlois, Jean Claude .... (514) 430-5111
ED
La Voix des Mille-Iles, Sainte-Therese, QC
Langlois, Keith .... (810) 332-8181
Sports ED, Oakland Press, Pontiac, MI
Langlois, Mark .... (203) 744-5100
Automotive ED, BUS/FIN ED, RE ED
News-Times, Danbury, CT
Langman, William .... (202) 636-3000
PROD DIR-Commercial Printing
Washington Times, Washington, DC
Langman Jr, William R .... (860) 442-2200
PROD DIR, Day, New London, CT
Langmann, Rudy .... (604) 856-8303
ED, Aldergrove Star, Aldergrove, BC
Langschied, James .... (317) 459-3121
Wire ED, Kokomo Tribune, Kokomo, IN
Langston, J Truett .... (615) 666-2440
PUB, ED
Macon County Times, Lafayette, TN
Langston, Scott .... (937) 526-9131
PUB, ED, Versailles Policy, Versailles, OH
Langston, Terry .... (573) 335-6611
PROD FRM-PR
Southeast Missourian, Cape Girardeau, MO
Langton, Trent .... (313) 242-1100
DP MGR, Monroe Evening News, Monroe, MI
Lanham, Fritz .... (713) 220-7171
Books ED, Houston Chronicle, Houston, TX
Lanier, David .... (405) 321-1800
Sports ED, Norman Transcript, Norman, OK
Lanier, Tony .... (617) 786-7000
Graphics ED, Patriot Ledger, Quincy, MA
Lank, Marshall .... (204) 694-2022
ADV MGR-National Sales
Winnipeg Sun, Winnipeg, MB
Lankford, John .... (805) 564-5200
EPE, News-Press, Santa Barbara, CA
Lanman, Pat .... (812) 427-2311
MAN ED
Vevay Reveille-Enterprise, Vevay, IN
Lanning, Roger .... (515) 782-2141
ADV DIR
Creston News-Advertiser, Creston, IA
Lannom, Pamela .... (630) 887-0600
MAN ED, Doings, Hinsdale, IL
Lannon, Linnea .... (313) 222-6400
Books ED, Detroit Free Press, Detroit, MI
Lannum, Harley .... (330) 296-9657
PROD FRM-Engraving
Record-Courier, Kent-Ravenna, OH
Lanpher, Katherine .... (612) 222-5011
COL, St. Paul Pioneer Press, St. Paul, MN
Lansden, Joe .... (405) 625-3241
PUB, ED, Herald-Democrat, Beaver, OK
Lansing, Jeffrey .... (507) 285-7600
PROD MGR-Press/Post Press
Post-Bulletin, Rochester, MN
Lansing, Mrs Livingston .... (315) 942-4449
PUB, ED, Boonville Herald & Adirondack Tourist, Boonville, NY
Lanteigne, Jacques .... (506) 727-4444
CIRC MGR, L'Acadie Nouvelle, Caraquet, NB
Lanterman, Ken .... (409) 744-3611
ASST MAN ED
Galveston County Daily News, Galveston, TX
Lanthier, Sylviane .... (204) 237-4823
ED, La Liberte, St. Boniface, MB
Lantis, Patricia .... (212) 621-1930
DIR, AP/Wide World Photos, New York, NY
Lantrip, Terry .... (817) 497-4141
PUB, ED, Argyle Sun, Lake Dallas, TX
Lantz, Angie .... (614) 633-1131
MGR-MKTG/PROM
Times Leader, Martins Ferry, OH
Lantz, Bruce .... (250) 785-5631
PUB, Alaska Highway Daily News, Fort St. John, BC
Lantz, Mark .... (916) 333-4481
PUB, ED, El Dorado Gazette, Georgetown Gazette & Town Crier, Georgetown, CA
Lanute, Dave .... (610) 696-1775
Special Sections ED
Daily Local News, West Chester, PA
LaOrange, Monte .... (208) 522-1800
Photo ED, Post Register, Idaho Falls, ID
Laosa, Michael .... (512) 445-3500
PUB, Austin American-Statesman, Austin, TX
Lapan, Wade .... (800) 424-4747
Desktop Publishing MGR, Tribune Media Services-Television Listings, Glens Falls, NY
Lapanja, Margie .... (916) 546-5995
ED, North Tahoe/Truckee Week Magazine, Tahoe Vista, CA
LaPann, Paul .... (304) 485-1891
ASST MAN ED, Parkersburg News & Sentinel, Parkersburg, WV
Lapcevic, Michael J .... (718) 981-1234
PROD MGR-SYS
Staten Island Advance, Staten Island, NY
LaPeter, Leonora .... (803) 785-4293
City ED, Island Packet, Hilton Head, SC
Lapham, Bob .... (915) 673-4271
Films/Theater ED, Television ED
Abilene Reporter-News, Abilene, TX
Lapham, Michael .... (206) 339-3000
PROD MGR-Pre Press Technical SRV
Herald, Everett, WA
LaPierre, Charlotte .... (508) 458-7100
DIR-Special SRV, Sun, Lowell, MA
LaPierre, Daniel .... (418) 986-2345
GM, Le Radar, Cap Aux Mueles, QC
LaPierre, Dexter .... (619) 299-3131
ADV DIR-CLASS/NTL
San Diego Union-Tribune, San Diego, CA
LaPierre, Robert .... (413) 774-7226
GM
Greenfield Town Crier, Greenfield, MA
Laping, Francis .... (610) 277-6342
PUB, ED
Montgomery County Observer, Blue Bell, PA
Lapinskie, Peter .... (613) 732-3691
MAN ED, Observer, Pembroke, ON
Laplante, Bob .... (416) 585-5000
CIRC Branch MGR-Montreal, Globe and Mail (Canada's National Newspaper), Toronto, ON
Laplante, Jean-Nil .... (514) 375-4555
CIRC DIR, La Voix de l'Est, Granby, QC
LaPoar, Maureen .... (402) 334-6448
MAN ED, Jewish Press, Omaha, NE
LaPointe, Kirk .... (905) 526-3333
EIC, Spectator, Hamilton, ON
LaPorte, John .... (970) 867-5651
Automotive ED, Entertainment/Amusements ED, Sports ED
Fort Morgan Times, Fort Morgan, CO
LaPorte, Margie .... (803) 626-8555
MGR-PROM, Sun News, Myrtle Beach, SC
LaPorte, Phil .... (803) 626-8555
ADV DIR
Myrtle Beach Sun News, Myrtle Beach, SC
Lapp, Susan .... (215) 721-9100
GM, Bucks-Mont Courier, Harleysville, PA
Lappä, Frances Moore .... (802) 254-6167
ED, American News Service, Brattleboro, VT
La Prade, Darel .... (302) 645-2265
MKTG MGR, Daily Whale, Lewes, DE
Lara, Adair .... (415) 777-1111
COL
San Francisco Chronicle, San Francisco, CA
Larabee, Laina .... (941) 748-0411
ADV SUPV-Inside Phone
Bradenton Herald, Bradenton, FL
Larcen, Donna .... (860) 241-6200
Fashion Writer
Hartford Courant, Hartford, CT
Larcom, Geoff .... (313) 994-6989
Sports ED, Ann Arbor News, Ann Arbor, MI
Lard, Eddie .... (205) 325-2222
EDL Writer
Birmingham News, Birmingham, AL
Lardomita, Jack .... (310) 540-5511
Chief Photographer
Daily Breeze, Torrance, CA
Larenas, Bel .... (916) 442-0267
ED, El Hispano, Sacramento, CA
Larence, Roger .... (508) 676-8211
CONT, Herald News, Fall River, MA
Largent, Charles .... (970) 352-0211
PROD MGR, Greeley Tribune, Greeley, CO
Larimer, Colleen .... (712) 523-2525
PUB, Bedford Times-Press, Bedford, IA
Larimer, Randall .... (712) 523-2525
PUB, Bedford Times-Press, Bedford, IA
Larimer, Tom .... (316) 792-1211
PUB, Great Bend Tribune, Great Bend, KS
Larimore, Ruth M .... (309) 244-7111
PUB, ED, Delavan Times, Delavan, IL
Laris, Jim P .... (818) 584-1500
PUB, Pasadena Weekly, Pasadena, CA
Laris-Eastin, Sue .... (213) 481-1448
PUB, ED, Los Angeles Downtown News, Los Angeles, CA
Larison, Dennis .... (509) 582-1500
Radio/Television ED
Tri-City Herald, Tri-Cities, WA
Lark, Jerry E .... (540) 889-2112
PUB, ED, Lebanon News, Lebanon, VA
Lark, Nigel .... (604) 426-5201
PUB, Daily Townsman, Cranbrook, BC
Larkee, Joann .... (417) 836-1100
CIRC MGR-Sales
Springfield News-Leader, Springfield, MO
Larkin Jr, Alfred S .... (617) 929-2000
MAN ED-ADM, Boston Globe, Boston, MA
Larkin, Brent .... (216) 999-4500
EDL DIR, EPE, Plain Dealer, Cleveland, OH
Larkin, Glenn .... (719) 632-5511
PROD Senior MGR
Gazette, Colorado Springs, CO
Larkin, Jack L .... (618) 253-7146
PROD MGR, Daily Register, Harrisburg, IL
Larkin, Jim .... (810) 766-6100
Suburban ED, Flint Journal, Flint, MI
Larkin, Michael .... (617) 929-2000
ASST MAN ED-Sunday
Boston Globe, Boston, MA
Larkin, Sherry .... (617) 925-9266
PUB, Hull Times, Hull, MA
Larkin, William .... (412) 224-4321
Photo DEPT MGR
Valley News Dispatch, Tarentum, PA
Larkins, Carrie .... (402) 426-2121
ED, Arlington Citizen, Blair, NE
LaRocca, Joseph P .... (330) 841-1600
FIN MGR, Tribune Chronicle, Warren, OH
LaRoche, Barry .... (508) 793-9100
CIRC DIR
Telegram & Gazette, Worcester, MA
Laroche, Etienne .... (514) 285-7272
ADV CLASS, La Presse, Montreal, QC

Lar Who's Where-132

LaRoche, Ken (419) 668-3771
PROD FRM-PR
Norwalk Reflector, Norwalk, OH
LaRocque, Paula (214) 977-8222
ASST MAN ED-PSL/Training
Dallas Morning News, Dallas, TX
Larouco, Armando (508) 473-1111
CIRC DIR, Milford Daily News, Milford, MA
Larrick, James (614) 461-5000
Cartoonist
Columbus Dispatch, Columbus, OH
Larsen, Bob (954) 356-4000
MGR-FIN, Sun-Sentinel, Fort Lauderdale, FL
Larsen, Carl (619) 299-3131
Homes ED
San Diego Union-Tribune, San Diego, CA
Larsen, Dana (712) 732-3130
MAN ED, Pilot Tribune, Storm Lake, IA
Larsen, Dave (937) 225-2000
Music ED, Dayton Daily News, Dayton, OH
Larsen, Don (205) 325-2222
MGR-CR
Birmingham News, Birmingham, AL
Larsen, Jeri (208) 232-4161
MGR-Office, DP MGR
Idaho State Journal, Pocatello, ID
Larsen, Jim (360) 221-5300
ED, South Whidbey Record, Langley, WA
Larsen, John (414) 657-1000
PROD SUPV-Pre Press
Kenosha News, Kenosha, WI
Larsen, Mark (937) 225-2000
CIRC MGR-TELEMKTG
Dayton Daily News, Dayton, OH
Larsen, Roger (605) 352-6401
Political ED, Huron Plainsman, Huron, SD
Larsen, Sharon (716) 343-8000
EPE, Daily News, Batavia, NY
Larsen, Sheila (616) 651-5407
CIRC DIR, Sturgis Journal, Sturgis, MI
Larsen, Steve (303) 820-1010
DIR-Photography, Denver Post, Denver, CO
Larsen, Ted (508) 741-3916
ED/PUB, Larsen, Ted Media, Salem, MA
Larsen, Tom (360) 377-3711
PROD DIR, Sun, Bremerton, WA
Larson, Albert (406) 759-5355
PUB, Liberty County Times, Chester, MT
Larson, Brenda (905) 853-8888
ED, Newmarket-Aurora Era-Banner, Newmarket, ON
Larson, Brenda (605) 889-2320
GM, Prairie Pioneer, Pollock, SD
Larson, Carole J (612) 425-3323
ED, Osseo-Maple Grove Press, Osseo, MN
Larson, Dale (319) 398-8211
VP, GM, Gazette, Cedar Rapids, IA
Larson, Dawn (201) 428-6200
PROD FRM-Pre Press
Daily Record, Parsippany, NJ
Larson, Don R (612) 425-3323
PUB, Osseo-Maple Grove Press, Osseo, MN
Larson, Gary (320) 983-6111
ED, Mille Lacs County Times, Milaca, MN
Larson, Gwen (316) 342-4800
Lifestyle ED, Emporia Gazette, Emporia, KS
Larson, Jan (419) 352-4611
County ED
Sentinel-Tribune, Bowling Green, OH
Larson, Jean (219) 838-0717
ED, Calumet Press, Highland, IN
Larson, Jeanne (406) 759-5355
ED, Liberty County Times, Chester, MT
Larson, Jonie (815) 625-3600
MAN ED, Daily Gazette, Sterling, IL
Larson, Ken (612) 673-4000
PROD MGR-MR
Star Tribune, Minneapolis, MN
Larson, Ken G (360) 653-8000
GM, North Snohomish Weekly, Arlington, WA
Larson, Kevin (402) 296-2141
ED, Plattsmouth Journal, Plattsmouth, NE
Larson, Lanny (209) 441-6111
Radio/Television Writer
Fresno Bee, Fresno, CA
Larson, Mary Lou (509) 674-2511
ED, Northern Kittitas County Tribune, Cle Elum, WA
Larson, Philip K (916) 541-3880
Chairman
Tahoe Daily Tribune, South Lake Tahoe, CA
Larson, Rahn (507) 831-3455
ED, Cottonwood County Citizen, Windom, MN
Larson, Renae (507) 962-3230
MAN ED, Hills Cresent, Hills, MN
Larson, Richard E (520) 634-2241
PUB, Bugle, Cottonwood, AZ
Larson, Richard K (702) 333-7676
COB, Swift Newspapers, Reno, NV
Larson, Rick (509) 582-1500
ASST MAN ED
Tri-City Herald, Tri-Cities, WA
Larson, Robert B (520) 282-7795
PUB, Sedona Red Rock News, Sedona, AZ
Larson, Robin (206) 339-3000
PROD DIR-OPER, Herald, Everett, WA
Larson, Roger (701) 780-1100
CIRC MGR-RT Zone
Grand Forks Herald, Grand Forks, ND
Larson, Ron (608) 252-6100
Librarian
Wisconsin State Journal, Madison, WI
Larson, Ron (402) 444-1000
ADV MGR-Creative SRV
Omaha World-Herald, Omaha, NE
Larson, Stephen (619) 356-2995
PUB, Imperial Valley Weekly, Holtville, CA
Larson, Tim (612) 467-2271
ED, Norwood-Young America Times, Norwood, MN
Larson, Vaughn (414) 893-6411
MAN ED, Review, Plymouth, WI
Larson, Virgil (402) 444-1000
City ED-Day, World-Herald, Omaha, NE
Larson, Walter R (509) 674-2511
PUB, Northern Kittitas County Tribune, Cle Elum, WA
Larson, Wanda (715) 463-2341
GM, Burnett County Sentinel, Grantsburg, WI
La Rue, Steve (619) 299-3131
Environmental Writer
San Diego Union-Tribune, San Diego, CA
LaRussa, Christina (310) 540-5511
School/EDU ED, Daily Breeze, Torrance, CA
Larzelere, David W (810) 766-6100
Librarian, Flint Journal, Flint, MI
Lasak, Ed (909) 684-1200
DIR-FIN, Press-Enterprise, Riverside, CA
Lasalandra, Mike (617) 426-3000
Health/Medical ED
Boston Herald, Boston, MA
Lasanen, Jeff (419) 784-5441
EDU ED, Crescent-News, Defiance, OH
Lashbrook, Kevin (219) 583-5121
ADV DIR, Herald Journal, Monticello, IN
Lashmit, Maere Kay (910) 891-1234
VP, ADV DIR, MGR-PROM, EPE, RE ED
Daily Record, Dunn, NC
Laska, Robert H (203) 333-0161
PUB, Connecticut Post, Bridgeport, CT
Laskowski, Joseph (602) 468-6565
VP-Track & Field OPER
Daily Racing Form, Phoenix, AZ
Laskowski, Mark E (814) 774-9648
GM, Cosmopolite Herald, Girard, PA
Lasky, Ed (904) 793-6222
PUB, Sumter Journal, Lake Panasoffkee, FL
Lasky, Shirley (904) 793-6222
GM, Sumter Journal, Lake Panasoffkee, FL
Lass, E Donald (908) 922-6000
PRES/CEO
New Jersey Press Inc., Neptune, NJ
Lass, Mark D (908) 922-6000
VP, New Jersey Press Inc., Neptune, NJ
Lasseter, Tim (205) 631-8716
ED, North Jefferson News, Gardendale, AL
Lassiter, Bonnie (903) 729-0281
ED, Palestine Herald-Press, Palestine, TX
Lassner, David (403) 532-1110
MAN ED, EPE
Daily Herald-Tribune, Grande Prairie, AB
Lasswell, Marylee C (217) 824-2233
TREAS, GM-TREAS, PA, Taylorville Daily Breeze-Courier, Taylorville, IL
Laster, Nanette (601) 833-6961
News ED, Daily Leader, Brookhaven, MS
Latanzio, George (201) 653-1000
MAN ED, Jersey Journal, Jersey City, NJ
Latcham Jr, Fred C (512) 358-2550
PUB, Beeville Bee-Picayune, Beeville, TX
Latcham III, Fred C (512) 358-2550
ED, Beeville Bee-Picayune, Beeville, TX
Latcham, George Geoffrey (512) 358-2550
GM, Beeville Bee-Picayune, Beeville, TX
Latcheran, Jeff (419) 245-6000
PROD MGR-Facilities, PROD ASST MGR
Blade, Toledo, OH
Latham, Art (505) 425-6796
MAN ED, Las Vegas Optic, Las Vegas, NM
Latham, Phil (409) 632-6631
ED, Lufkin Daily News, Lufkin, TX
Latham, Steve (817) 387-3811
CIRC ASST DIR
Denton Record-Chronicle, Denton, TX
Latham, Steve (205) 549-2000
Photo DEPT MGR, Times, Gadsden, AL
Latham, William C (937) 444-3441
PUB, Brown County Press, Mt. Orab, OH
Latimer, Bill (508) 779-5113
ED, Bolton Common, Bolton, MA
Latka, Lori (412) 834-1151
ADV MGR-TELEMKTG
Tribune-Review, Greensburg, PA
Latonis, Thomas R (217) 562-2113
ED, Pana News-Palladium, Pana, IL
Latoz, Mike (217) 446-1000
PROD FRM-Press
Commercial News, Danville, IL
Latshaw, Dick (330) 996-3000
PROD FRM-COMP
Akron Beacon Journal, Akron, OH
Latta, Bob (316) 327-4831
PUB, ED, Hesston Record, Hesston, KS
Latta, Loretta (316) 327-4831
PUB, ED, Hesston Record, Hesston, KS
Lattimer, Ed (519) 537-2341
PROD FRM-PR
Sentinel-Review, Woodstock, ON
Latulippe, Dennis (802) 863-3441
PROD MGR-PR, Free Press, Burlington, VT
Laub, Val J (412) 439-7500
PUB, CIRC DIR
Herald-Standard, Uniontown, PA
Laubach, Edward (610) 258-7171
Sports ED, Express-Times, Easton, PA
Laube, Leigh Ann (423) 246-8121
Fashion/Features ED
Kingsport Times-News, Kingsport, TN
Lauderdale, David (803) 785-4293
ED, Island Packet, Hilton Head, SC
Lauderdale, M Catherine (319) 257-6813
PUB, ED
Winfield Beacon/Wayland News, Winfield, IA
Laudick, Greg (919) 752-6166
Copy Desk Chief
Daily Reflector, Greenville, NC
Laue, Norbert (913) 823-6363
PROD FRM-MR, Salina Journal, Salina, KS
Laufenberg, DeAnn (414) 338-0622
News ED, Daily News, West Bend, WI
Laufer, John M (314) 340-8000
ADV MGR-CLASS
St. Louis Post-Dispatch, St. Louis, MO
Laughlin, Barbara (904) 599-2100
RE ED
Tallahassee Democrat, Tallahassee, FL
Laughlin, Nancy (313) 222-6400
Nation/World ED
Detroit Free Press, Detroit, MI
Laughon, Barbara (619) 934-8544
MAN ED
Review Herald, Mammoth Lakes, CA
Laukaitis, Al (402) 475-4200
Regional/Lancaster County Reporter
Lincoln Journal Star, Lincoln, NE
Laundrie, Carl (904) 437-2491
MAN ED, Flagler/Palm Coast News-Tribune, Bunnell, FL
Laundry, Cindy (807) 887-3583
ED, Nipigon-Red Rock Gazette, Nipigon, ON
Launius, Tony (205) 356-2148
ED, Red Bay News, Red Bay, AL
Laurelli, Jerry (904) 252-1511
PROD FRM-Camera/Platemaking, Daytona Beach News-Journal, Daytona Beach, FL
Laurence, Ann (606) 744-3123
ADV DIR, Winchester Sun, Winchester, KY
Laurence, Charles (800) 367-8313
BU Chief, Daily Telegraph, London
Laurence, Robert (619) 299-3131
Television Writer
San Diego Union-Tribune, San Diego, CA
Laurencio, Shelley (508) 458-7100
CIRC MGR-TELEMKTG/PROM
Sun, Lowell, MA
Laureno, Ben (703) 276-3400
ADV VP-Atlantic Sales
USA Today, Arlington, VA
Laurie, G S (Gord) (519) 676-3321
PUB, ED
Blenheim News-Tribune, Blenheim, ON
Laurie, Jim (702) 383-0211
Photo ED
Las Vegas Review-Journal, Las Vegas, NV
Laurie, William T (904) 698-1644
PUB, Putnam County Courier-Journal, Crescent City, FL
Laurin, Art (613) 543-2987
PUB, ED, Morrisburg Leader, Morrisburg, ON
Laurin, Beverly (716) 487-1111
ADV Clerk-NTL, Post-Journal, Jamestown, NY
Laurin, Bill (250) 380-5211
PROD MGR-Pre Press
Times Colonist, Victoria, BC
Laurin, John (514) 987-2222
PROD VP-Manufacturing
Gazette, Montreal, QC
Laurin, Ron (705) 726-6537
PUB/GM, Examiner, Barrie, ON
Laursen, Paul (516) 378-5320
ED, Merrick Life, Merrick, NY
Laut, Marvin (719) 544-3520
CIRC DIR, Pueblo Chieftain, Pueblo, CO
Lautens, Trevor (604) 732-2111
COL, Vancouver Sun, Vancouver, BC
Lautzenheiser, Libby (502) 827-2000
Action Line ED, Gleaner, Henderson, KY
Lauzier, Donald (207) 282-1535
ADV MGR-NTL/RT
Journal Tribune, Biddeford, ME
Lauzon, Jerry (207) 873-3341
Sports ED, Central Maine Morning Sentinel, Waterville, ME, Guy Gannett Communications
Lavallee, Stephane (819) 564-5450
Food ED, News ED, Religion ED, Society/Fashion ED, Women's ED
La Tribune, Sherbrooke, QC
LaValley, Jan (540) 825-0771
Community ED, Star-Exponent, Culpeper, VA
Lavan, Carolyn (305) 350-2111
MGR-Newspapers in Education
Miami Herald, Miami, FL
LaVecchia, Thomas (718) 845-3221
PUB, Forum of Queens, Ozone Park, NY
Lavelle, Chris (602) 271-8000
Online MGR, Arizona Republic, Phoenix, AZ
Lavelle, John J (914) 341-1100
ADV MGR-Direct MKTG/TMC
Times Herald-Record, Middletown, NY
Laven, Michele (602) 271-0040
PUB, New Times, Phoenix, AZ
Laventhol, David (213) 237-3700
ED-At-Large-Times Mirror
Times Mirror Co., Los Angeles, CA
Laverdure, Del (604) 562-2441
DIR-FIN
Prince George Citizen, Prince George, BC
Lavey, Kathleen (517) 377-1000
Features ED, Living/Lifestyle ED, Women's ED, Lansing State Journal, Lansing, MI
LaVigne, Jodie (405) 233-6600
Accountant, DP MGR
Enid News & Eagle, Enid, OK
Lavin, Chris (813) 893-8111
NTL ED, World ED
St. Petersburg Times, St. Petersburg, FL
Lavin, Steve (414) 435-4411
ADV MGR-RT
Green Bay Press-Gazette, Green Bay, WI
Lavin, Tim (360) 377-3711
DIR-FIN, Sun, Bremerton, WA
La Violette, Suzanne (206) 464-2111
BUS News ED, Seattle Times, Seattle, WA
La Vo, Carl (215) 949-4000
Fashion/Lifestyles ED, Life ED, Religion ED
Bucks County Courier Times, Levittown, PA
Lavoie, Basil (705) 325-1355
CIRC MGR, Packet & Times, Orillia, ON
Lavoie, Gilbert (418) 686-3233
EIC, MAN ED, Le Soleil, Quebec, QC
Lavoie, Jean-Louis (418) 545-4474
CIRC MGR, Le Quotidien, Chicoutimi, QC
Law, Ann K (814) 765-5581
SEC, ASST PUB/BM, Progress, Clearfield, PA
Law, Clair M (814) 765-5581
Photo DEPT MGR, Progress, Clearfield, PA
Law, Tom (706) 886-9476
MAN ED, Toccoa Record, Toccoa, GA
Lawfon, Kelly (409) 295-5407
ADV MGR, Huntsville Item, Huntsville, TX
Lawhead, Bonita (509) 284-5782
ED, Standard-Register, Tekoa, WA
Lawhon, Cathy (714) 768-3631
ED, Saddleback Valley News, Lake Forest, CA
Lawhorn, Chad (913) 749-0006
MAN ED, Baldwin Ledger, Lawrence, KS
Lawis, Kurt (573) 422-3441
PUB, ED
Maries County Gazette-Adviser, Vienna, MO
Lawitz, Jim (805) 650-2900
ASST MAN ED-News
Ventura County Star, Ventura, CA
Lawler, Jim (201) 646-4000
MGR-BUS SYS, Record, Hackensack, NJ
Lawler, Sylvia (610) 820-6500
Television ED, Morning Call, Allentown, PA
Lawless, Jim (515) 284-8000
FIN COL
Des Moines Register, Des Moines, IA
Lawrence, Beth (212) 715-2100
VP/ADV, USA Weekend, New York, NY
Lawrence, Betty (419) 586-2371
Society/Women's ED
Daily Standard, Celina, OH
Lawrence, Brent (612) 222-5011
ADV MGR-MKTG INFO
St. Paul Pioneer Press, St. Paul, MN
Lawrence, Burnis (915) 837-3334
PUB, ED, Alpine Avalanche, Alpine, TX
Lawrence, Curtis (414) 224-2000
EDU Reporter
Milwaukee Journal Sentinel, Milwaukee, WI
Lawrence, David (409) 564-8361
ADV MGR, Daily Sentinel, Nacogdoches, TX
Lawrence Jr, David (305) 350-2111
COB, PUB, Miami Herald, Miami, FL
Lawrence, Gary D (401) 849-3300
ADV DIR-MKTG
Newport Daily News, Newport, RI
Lawrence, Grant (604) 338-5811
PUB, Comox Valley Record, Courtenay, BC

Copyright ©1997 by the Editor & Publisher Co.

133-Who's Where **Lee**

Lawrence, Howard (607) 272-2321
PROD DIR, Ithaca Journal, Ithaca, NY
Lawrence, James (716) 232-7100
EPE, Rochester Democrat and Chronicle, Rochester, NY
Lawrence, Jim (209) 578-2000
Graphics DIR, Modesto Bee, Modesto, CA
Lawrence, John F (704) 894-3220
PUB
Polk County News Journal, Columbus, NC
Lawrence, Larry (915) 673-4271
Books ED
Abilene Reporter-News, Abilene, TX
Lawrence, Lee Roy (210) 225-7411
PROD SUPT-COMP
San Antonio Express-News, San Antonio, TX
Lawrence, Marie (419) 223-1010
BM, Lima News, Lima, OH
Lawrence, Mary (614) 387-0400
MAN ED, EPE, Marion Star, Marion, OH
Lawrence, Mike (502) 827-2000
Photo ED, Gleaner, Henderson, KY
Lawrence, Richard (212) 837-7000
Senior Correspondent-DC, Journal of Commerce & Commercial, New York, NY
Lawrence, Virginia (405) 475-3311
DP MGR
Daily Oklahoman, Oklahoma City, OK
Lawrence, William W (610) 356-6664
ED, County Press, Newtown Square, PA
Lawrenz, Lee (414) 487-2222
MAN ED, Algoma Record-Herald, Algoma, WI
Lawson, Barbara (219) 279-2167
GM, New Wolcott Enterprise, Wolcott, IN
Lawson, Brent (905) 526-3333
ED-Burlington, Spectator, Hamilton, ON
Lawson, Carol (501) 741-2325
BM, Harrison Daily Times, Harrison, AR
Lawson, Deborah (703) 204-2800
GM, Sun Gazette, Merrifield, VA
Lawson, Eric (902) 426-2811
ADV Sales MGR-Display
Chronicle-Herald, Halifax, NS
Lawson, George (914) 454-2000
ADV DIR
Poughkeepsie Journal, Poughkeepsie, NY
Lawson, James G (614) 461-5000
CIRC ASST DIR
Columbus Dispatch, Columbus, OH
Lawson, Laurie (212) 755-4363
Contributing Writer, Punch In Travel & Entertainment News Syndicate, NY, NY
Lawson, Michael (609) 989-5454
PROD MGR-Pre Press, Times, Trenton, NJ
Lawson, Ron (705) 325-1355
PROD SUPT, Packet & Times, Orillia, ON
Lawson, Tempsey (718) 264-1500
GM, New York Voice, Fresh Meadows, NY
Lawson, Terry (315) 470-0011
PROD MGR-COMP, Post-Standard/Syracuse Herald-Journal/American, Syracuse, NY
Lawson, Terry (313) 222-6400
Films Critic, Detroit Free Press, Detroit, MI
Lawson, Vern (805) 273-2700
MAN ED
Antelope Valley Press, Palmdale, CA
Lawstrom, Martha (207) 496-3251
ED, Aroostook Republican and News, Caribou, ME
Lawton, Wayne A (207) 990-8000
ADV DIR, Bangor Daily News, Bangor, ME
Laxineta, Michael A (213) 932-6397
PUB, Independent, Los Angeles, CA
Lay, Geoff (604) 732-2111
CIRC MGR-Single Copy, Vancouver Sun, Vancouver, BC, Southam Inc.
Lay, Julie (803) 648-2311
CIRC MGR-Sales/NIE
Aiken Standard, Aiken, SC
Lay, Pat (606) 573-4510
CIRC MGR, DP MGR
Harlan Daily Enterprise, Harlan, KY
Layana, Carol (310) 313-6727
GM, Westchester News, Culver City, CA
Laycox, Donald (416) 947-2222
PROD MGR-MR, Toronto Sun, Toronto, ON
Layden, Joseph (573) 431-2010
MAN ED, BUS/FIN ED, EPE, News ED, Wire ED, Daily Journal, Park Hills, MO
Layman, Judy Tetrick (304) 788-3333
SEC/Co-PUB, TREAS, Home Furnishings ED
Mineral Daily News-Tribune, Keyser, WV
Layman, Mark (540) 981-3100
MET ED, Roanoke Times, Roanoke, VA
Laymance, Reid (713) 220-7171
Sports ED, Houston Chronicle, Houston, TX
Laymon, Thomas L (765) 728-5322
PUB, ED, Montpelier Herald, Montpelier, IN
Laymond, Linda (502) 582-4011
Public ED, Courier-Journal, Louisville, KY
Layne, Frank (615) 526-9715
Sports ED, Herald-Citizen, Cookeville, TN
Layonc, Carol (310) 313-6733
GM, Culver City News, Culver City, CA
Layton, Dorothy (901) 427-3333
PROD MGR-Pre Press
Jackson Sun, Jackson, TN
Layton, Doug (972) 424-6565
Graphics ED/Art DIR, Star Courier, Plano, TX
Layton, Rodney E (716) 849-3434
TREAS, CONT, Buffalo News, Buffalo, NY
Layton, Tracey (972) 298-4211
ED, Midlothian Today, Duncanville, TX
Lazarus, George (312) 222-3232
COL, Chicago Tribune, Chicago, IL
Lazarus, Shelly (305) 977-7770
GM, Broward News, Margate, FL
Lazauskas, Grozvydas J (708) 543-8198
ED, Sandara, Addison, IL
Lazorko, Tony (314) 340-8000
Art DEPT DIR
St. Louis Post-Dispatch, St. Louis, MO
Lazrick, Len (410) 337-2400
MAN ED, Towson Times, Towson, MD
Lazure, Leonard J (508) 793-9100
Photo/Graphics ED
Telegram & Gazette, Worcester, MA
Lazzareschi, Carla (213) 237-5000
COL-"Money Talk"
Los Angeles Times, Los Angeles, CA
Lea, Bill (318) 322-3161
GM, Ouachita Citizen, West Monroe, LA
Lea, Daniel (517) 799-3200
PUB, Township Times, Saginaw, MI
Lea, Michael (416) 463-3824
GM, Graphics Syndicate, Toronto, ON
Lea, Patricia (423) 756-1234
Garden ED
Chattanooga Times, Chattanooga, TN
Leach, Chuck (812) 424-7711
EPE, Evansville Courier, Evansville, IN
Leach, Edward R (508) 228-8455
PUB, Nantucket Beacon, Nantucket, MA
Leach, Janet C (513) 721-2700
MAN ED
Cincinnati Enquirer, Cincinnati, OH
Leach, John (602) 271-8000
ASST MAN ED-News OPER
Arizona Republic, Phoenix, AZ
Leach, Leah M (209) 582-0471
MAN ED, Books ED
Hanford Sentinel, Hanford, CA
Leach, Ted (903) 693-7888
ED, Panola Watchman, Carthage, TX
League, John W (301) 733-5131
PRES, PUB, ED,
Morning Herald, Hagerstown, MD
Leahy, Frank W (715) 344-6100
PRES, PUB
Stevens Point Journal, Stevens Point, WI
Leahy, James P (715) 344-6100
SEC/TREAS, GM
Stevens Point Journal, Stevens Point, WI
Leahy, Michael (212) 556-1234
RE ED, New York Times, New York, NY
Leake, Sandra (601) 234-4331
ADV DIR, Oxford Eagle, Oxford, MS
Leal, Carolyn (408) 867-6397
ED, Saratoga News, Saratoga, CA
Leal, Maria C (510) 237-0888
MAN ED, Jornal Portugues, San Pablo, CA
Leaman, Kay (415) 348-4321
CIRC MGR-SYS/Office
San Mateo County Times, San Mateo, CA
Leap, Kevin (619) 745-6611
ADV MGR-RT
North County Times, Escondido, CA
Leard, David (864) 224-4321
PROD DIR
Anderson Independent-Mail, Anderson, SC
Leary, Kay (617) 593-7700
MGR-EDU SRV
Daily Evening Item, Lynn, MA
Leary, Mike (215) 854-2000
ASSOC EPE
Philadelphia Inquirer, Philadelphia, PA
Leary, Sean (309) 764-4344
Entertainment ED, Films/Music ED, Radio/Television ED, Travel ED, Dispatch, Moline, IL, Small Newspaper Group Inc.
Lease, Betty (916) 243-2424
Entertainment/Amusements ED, Family/Food ED, Fashion/Style ED, Features ED, Living/Lifestyle ED, Television/Film ED, Theater/Music ED, Record Searchlight, Redding, CA
Leasor, Lydia (502) 769-2312
ADV Graphic Design Team Leader
News Enterprise, Elizabethtown, KY
Leath, Bart (717) 248-6741
PUB, Sentinel, Lewistown, PA
Leath, O Scott (804) 649-6000
Senior VP/BM
Richmond Times-Dispatch, Richmond, VA
Leatham, Jim (941) 629-2855
ADV DIR, Sun Herald, Port Charlotte, FL
Leatherdale, Brian (403) 556-3351
PUB, Olds Gazette, Olds, AB
Leatherdale, Linda (416) 947-2222
BUS/FIN ED, Toronto Sun, Toronto, ON
Leatherdale, Monica (403) 638-3577
PUB, ED, Sundre Round-Up, Sundre, AB
Leatherdale, Neil (403) 638-3577
PUB, Sundre Round-Up, Sundre, AB
Leathers, Mike (618) 463-2500
Music ED, Telegraph, Alton, IL
Leathers, Susan (707) 546-2020
Features/Fashion ED, Food ED, Home Furnishings ED, Living/Lifestyle ED
Press Democrat, Santa Rosa, CA
Leavell, Dorothy R (312) 752-2500
PUB, ED, Chicago Crusader, Chicago, IL
Leavitt, Linda (914) 725-2500
ED, Scarsdale Inquirer, Scarsdale, NY
Leavy, Buff (912) 265-8320
MGR-Data Processing
Brunswick News, Brunswick, GA
Leavy III, C H (912) 265-8320
PRES/PUB, ED
Brunswick News, Brunswick, GA
Lebar, Bob (717) 421-3000
PROD FRM-PR
Pocono Record, Stroudsburg, PA
Lebar, Scott (916) 321-1000
ASST MAN ED-Features
Sacramento Bee, Sacramento, CA
LeBeau, Wade (815) 937-3300
DP MGR, Daily Journal, Kankakee, IL
Lebedoff, Randy Miller (612) 673-4000
VP/GEN Counsel
Star Tribune, Minneapolis, MN
Leberg, Bruce (715) 423-7200
PROD FRM-PR
Daily Tribune, Wisconsin Rapids, WI
LeBlanc, Carol (504) 384-8370
PROD MGR, Daily Review, Morgan City, LA
LeBlanc, Forrest (206) 872-6600
PROD MGR-MR
South County Journal, Kent, WA
LeBlanc, Gilles (519) 631-2790
PROD FRM-PR
St. Thomas Times-Journal, St. Thomas, ON
Leblanc, Maude (718) 434-8100
ED, Haiti Progres, Brooklyn, NY
LeBlanc, Maurice (514) 637-2381
PUB, ED, Lachine Messenger, Lachine, QC
Leblond, Francois (514) 521-4545
Sports ED
Le Journal de Montreal, Montreal, QC
LeBlue, Amelia (504) 732-2565
CIRC DIR, Daily News, Bogalusa, LA
Lebolt, Fred (312) 321-3000
Online Contact
Chicago Sun-Times, Chicago, IL
Lebowitz, Hal (216) 951-0000
COL, News-Herald, Willoughby, OH
LeBrun, Fred (518) 454-5694
COL, Times Union, Albany, NY
Lebzelter, Bob (216) 994-3241
City ED, Star-Beacon, Ashtabula, OH
Lechman, Don (310) 540-5511
Books ED, Daily Breeze, Torrance, CA
Lecius, Mark A (603) 668-4321
DIR-Accounting
Union Leader, Manchester, NH
Leckey, Andrew (312) 222-3232
COL, Chicago Tribune, Chicago, IL
Lecky, George (513) 352-2000
Crime ED, Cincinnati Post, Cincinnati, OH
LeClair, Kathy (561) 461-2050
BM, Tribune, Fort Pierce, FL
Leclair, Larry (403) 468-0100
CIRC DIR, Edmonton Sun, Edmonton, AB
LeClerc, Alaiu (819) 564-5450
ADV ASST MGR, La Tribune, Sherbrooke, QC
LeClerc, Chip (413) 562-4181
Sports ED, Evening News, Westfield, MA
Leclerc, Madeleine (506) 473-3083
ED, MAN ED
Cataracte Weekly, Grand Falls, NB
L'Ecluse, Cathy (707) 425-4646
City ED, Daily Republic, Fairfield, CA
LeComte, Michelle (330) 996-3000
Quick Response ED
Akron Beacon Journal, Akron, OH
LeCount, Joy Y (219) 636-2727
ED, Albion New Era, Albion, IN
Le Cours, Rudy (514) 285-7272
BUS ED, FIN ED, RE
La Presse, Montreal, QC
Ledbetter, Chris (313) 222-6400
Entertainment ED
Detroit Free Press, Detroit, MI
Ledbetter, David (903) 935-7914
PROD MGR
Marshall News Messenger, Marshall, TX
Ledbetter, George (605) 578-3305
ED
Lawrence County Centennial, Deadwood, SD
Ledbetter, Kay (806) 376-4488
Farm ED, Amarillo Daily News/Globe Times, Amarillo, TX
Leddy, Garth (403) 328-4411
CIRC MGR
Lethbridge Herald, Lethbridge, AB
Leddy, Peter E (201) 365-3000
VP-FIN
North Jersey Herald & News, Passaic, NJ
Leder, Michelle (914) 454-2000
BUS ED
Poughkeepsie Journal, Poughkeepsie, NY
Lederer, Thomas (609) 466-8650
ED, Lawrence Ledger, Hopewell, NJ
Ledford, David (801) 237-2031
Deputy ED-News
Salt Lake Tribune, Salt Lake City, UT
Ledford, Dennis (704) 484-1047
PUB, Cleveland Observer, Shelby, NC
Ledford, Don (816) 454-9660
ED
Raytown Dispatch-Tribune, Kansas City, MO
Ledford, Greg (704) 484-1047
PUB, Cleveland Observer, Shelby, NC
Ledford, Iris (318) 322-5161
ADV MGR-CLASS, News-Star, Monroe, LA
Ledford Sr, William F (912) 537-3131
PUB, Advance-Progess, Vidalia, GA
Ledford Jr, William F (912) 537-3131
GM, Advance-Progess, Vidalia, GA
Le Duc, Dan (215) 854-2000
Chicago BU
Philadelphia Inquirer, Philadelphia, PA
Lee, Barbara S (801) 328-8641
ED
Intermountain Catholic, Salt Lake City, UT
Lee, Bill (509) 248-1251
EPE, Yakima Herald-Republic, Yakima, WA
Lee, Brenda R (601) 226-4321
SEC/TREAS
Daily Sentinel-Star, Grenada, MS
Lee, Brian (520) 573-4561
Outdoors ED, Tucson Citizen, Tucson, AZ
Lee, Bryan (619) 337-3400
Sports ED
Imperial Valley Press, El Centro, CA
Lee, Carolyn (573) 471-1137
PROD FRM-COMP/Paste-Up
Standard Democrat, Sikeston, MO
Lee, Carolyn (212) 556-1234
ASST MAN ED
New York Times, New York, NY
Lee, Chao-ming (617) 426-9492
PUB, Sampan, Boston, MA
Lee, Charles (573) 471-1137
PROD FRM-Press/Camera/Platemaking
Standard Democrat, Sikeston, MO
Lee, Cindy (501) 879-5450
GM, Pine Bluff News, Pine Bluff, AR
Lee, Don (419) 625-5500
Automotive ED
Sandusky Register, Sandusky, OH
Lee, Don (213) 237-5000
Energy/Economy/Banking
Los Angeles Times, Los Angeles, CA
Lee, Donna (401) 277-7000
Food ED
Providence Journal-Bulletin, Providence, RI
Lee, Dorothy (214) 946-7678
MAN ED, Dallas Post Tribune, Dallas, TX
Lee, Edward (817) 757-5757
PROD SUPT-MR
Waco Tribune-Herald, Waco, TX
Lee, Edward (212) 513-1440
MAN ED, United Journal, New York, NY
Lee, Frank (517) 895-8551
Political/Government ED
Bay City Times, Bay City, MI
Lee, Frederick W (518) 234-4368
PUB, Daily Editor, Cobleskill, NY
Lee, George W (403) 783-3311
ED, Ponoka News & Advertiser, Ponoka, AB
Lee, Gerry (517) 787-2300
MGR-PROM
Jackson Citizen Patriot, Jackson, MI
Lee, Glenda (903) 896-4401
ED, Edgewood Enterprise, Edgewood, TX
Lee, Helen J (714) 498-7227
VP, Singer Media Corp., San Clemente, CA
Lee, Howard (718) 746-8889
PUB, World Journal, Whitestone, NY
Lee, Janet (517) 437-7351
Home Furnishings ED
Hillsdale Daily News, Hillsdale, MI
Lee, Jay (601) 226-4321
ASST to the PUB, ADV DIR
Daily Sentinel-Star, Grenada, MS
Lee, Jeff (810) 573-2755
Sports ED, Avanti NewsFeatures, Warren, MI
Lee, Jim (910) 227-0131
City ED
Times News Publishing Co., Burlington, NC

Lee Who's Where-134

Lee, Jim (715) 842-2101
Outdoors ED
Wausau Daily Herald, Wausau, WI

Lee, John (316) 694-5830
PRES
Harris Enterprises Inc., Hutchinson, KS

Lee, John F (904) 653-8868
GM, ED
Apalachicola Times, Apalachicola, FL

Lee, John H (406) 278-5561
PUB, Independent Observer, Conrad, MT

Lee III, Joseph B (601) 226-4321
PRES, PUB
Daily Sentinel-Star, Grenada, MS

Lee Jr, Joseph (908) 246-5500
Design ED
Home News & Tribune, East Brunswick, NJ

Lee, Kaijer (912) 744-4200
CIRC DIR, Macon Telegraph, Macon, GA

Lee, Kap S (213) 487-5323
ED, Korea Times, Los Angeles, CA

Lee, Katherine (707) 964-5642
MAN ED
Fort Bragg Advocate-News, Fort Bragg, CA

Lee, Kathryn C (916) 452-4781
GM, MAN ED
Observer Group, Sacramento, CA

Lee, Kee Young (718) 482-1111
ED, Korea Times, Long Island City, NY

Lee, Linda (805) 273-2700
EDU ED, SCI/Technology ED, Travel ED
Antelope Valley Press, Palmdale, CA

Lee, Louise Laval (418) 248-0415
PUB, Le Peuple de la Cote du Sud, Montmagny, QC

Lee, Mark (918) 581-8300
Farm ED, Tulsa World, Tulsa, OK

Lee, Mike (512) 884-2011
Sports ED, Corpus Christi Caller-Times, Corpus Christi, TX

Lee, Mike (805) 564-5200
CIRC MGR-Home Delivery, Santa Barbara News-Press, Santa Barbara, CA

Lee, Mike (219) 235-6161
CIRC DIR
South Bend Tribune, South Bend, IN

Lee, Mike (206) 883-7187
ED, Redmond Sammamish Valley News, Redmond, WA

Lee, Mitchell (817) 292-1855
VP-MKTG & Sales, A & A, Ft. Worth, TX

Lee, Nancy (212) 556-1234
Picture ED, New York Times, New York, NY

Lee, Nina (419) 738-2128
PROD MGR-COMP/Printing
Wapakoneta Daily News, Wapakoneta, OH

Lee, Otto C (803) 648-2311
CIRC DIR, Aiken Standard, Aiken, SC

Lee, Pat (319) 383-2200
PROD MGR, Quad-City Times, Davenport, IA

Lee, Pattikay (213) 857-6600
ADV DIR, Daily Variety, Los Angeles, CA

Lee, R Marilyn (213) 237-5000
VP-Public Affairs, CIRC VP-Public Affairs
Los Angeles Times, Los Angeles, CA

Lee, Rex (515) 573-2141
DP MGR, Messenger, Fort Dodge, IA

Lee, Rob (941) 687-7000
ADV MGR-RT, Ledger, Lakeland, FL

Lee, Sally (970) 669-5050
ADV DIR
Loveland Daily Reporter-Herald, Loveland, CO

Lee, Sandra (208) 743-9411
Farm/Agriculture ED
Lewiston Morning Tribune, Lewiston, ID

Lee, Scott (316) 788-2835
Sports ED, Daily Reporter, Derby, KS

Lee, Sharon (352) 374-5000
ADV CNR-Preprint/Co-op
Gainesville Sun, Gainesville, FL

Lee, Simon (501) 982-6506
ED, Jacksonville Patriot, Jacksonville, AR

Lee, Stephen (810) 686-3840
ED
Genesee County Herald, Mount Morris, MI

Lee, Steve (701) 780-1100
Religion ED
Grand Forks Herald, Grand Forks, ND

Lee Jr, Theodore (214) 946-7678
PUB, ED, Dallas Post Tribune, Dallas, TX

Lee, Thomas (405) 772-3301
Sports ED
Weatherford Daily News, Weatherford, OK

Lee, Thomas (406) 222-2000
Photo ED
Livingston Enterprise, Livingston, MT

Lee, Thomas P (414) 235-7700
EX ED/VP-News
Oshkosh Northwestern, Oshkosh, WI

Lee, Tomas (213) 782-8770
ED, Free China Journal, Los Angeles, CA

Lee, Wea H (713) 498-4310
PUB
Southern Chinese Daily News, Houston, TX

Lee, William H (916) 452-4781
PUB, ED, Observer Group, Sacramento, CA

Lee, Winkie (919) 778-2211
Amusements ED, Books ED, Features ED, Films/Theater ED, Teen-Age/Youth ED, Travel ED, Goldsboro News-Argus, Goldsboro, NC

Lee-Petri, Tracey (810) 573-2755
Parenting COL
Avanti NewsFeatures, Warren, MI

Leece, Curtis T (517) 752-7171
Photo, Saginaw News, Saginaw, MI

Leech Jr, Fred (814) 371-4200
PROD FRM-Press, Courier-Express/Tri-County Sunday, Du Bois, PA

Leech, Melissa (417) 235-3135
CIRC DIR, Times, Monett, MO

Leeds, Al (202) 334-6173
PRES/EDL DIR, Los Angeles Times-Washington Post News Service, Washington, DC

Leedy, Jerry G (704) 735-3031
PUB, ED
Lincoln Times-News, Lincolnton, NC

Leek, Jerry (608) 252-6200
PROD ASST MGR
Madison Newspapers Inc., Madison, WI

Leeman, Dana B (207) 990-8000
ADV MGR-RT
Bangor Daily News, Bangor, ME

Leeney, Robert J (203) 789-5200
ED-Emeritus
New Haven Register, New Haven, CT

Leeper, Susan (614) 943-2214
ED, Richwood Gazette, Richwood, OH

Leer, Steve (704) 864-3291
Political/Government ED
Gaston Gazette, Gastonia, NC

Lees, John (601) 442-9101
PROD MGR-SYS
Natchez Democrat, Natchez, MS

Lefebure, Therese (418) 589-5900
GM, Plein Jour sur Manicouagan, Baie Comeau, QC

Lefebvre, Juli (705) 472-3200
CR MGR, North Bay Nugget, North Bay, ON

Leferink, Tom (817) 390-7400
ASST News ED
Fort Worth Star-Telegram, Fort Worth, TX

Lefevers, Toby (915) 337-4661
ADTX MGR, Odessa American, Odessa, TX

Lefko, Jim (317) 423-5511
Sports ED, Journal and Courier, Lafayette, IN

Lefkovitz, Louise (505) 823-7777
Office MGR
Albuquerque Tribune, Albuquerque, NM

Lefkowitz, Michael (610) 696-1775
EPE, Daily Local News, West Chester, PA

Lefkowitz, Steve (203) 622-1547
Graphic ASST
Cartoonews Inc., Greenwich, CT

LeFort, Mikel (318) 459-3200
Sports ED, Times, Shreveport, LA

LeFort-Cintron, Debbie (609) 691-5000
ADV MGR-CLASS
Daily Journal, Vineland, NJ

Lefton, Hal (602) 898-6500
ADV MGR-RT/NTL, Mesa Tribune, Mesa, AZ
Thomson Newspapers

Lefton, Judy (520) 573-4561
ASST MAN ED, Tucson Citizen, Tucson, AZ

Lefton, Paul (219) 881-3000
Design ED, Post-Tribune, Gary, IN

Legatz, Alan (941) 434-5555
Proprietor, Strategist, Naples, FL

Legault, Francois (613) 632-0191
ED, La Tribune-Express, Hawkesbury, ON

Legault, Tracie (613) 739-7000
PROD MGR, Ottawa Sun, Ottawa, ON

Legenbauer, Heidi (518) 270-1200
Food ED, Record, Troy, NY

Legendre Sr, Earl P (504) 693-7229
PUB, GM, LaFourche Gazette, Larose, LA

Leger, Robert (417) 836-1100
EPE
Springfield News-Leader, Springfield, MO

Legg, Hal (716) 243-3530
MAN ED, Lake & Valley Clarion, Geneseo, NY

Legg, Linda (903) 729-0281
ADV MGR-CLASS
Palestine Herald-Press, Palestine, TX

Leggett, Jim (318) 487-6397
EPE
Alexandria Daily Town Talk, Alexandria, LA

Leggett, Kerry E (308) 728-3262
PUB, Ord Quiz, Ord, NE

LeGrand, Dick (209) 578-2000
ASSOC ED, Modesto Bee, Modesto, CA

LeGrand, William (903) 729-0281
SEC/TREAS
Palestine Herald-Press, Palestine, TX

Leheney, Mark (202) 383-6150
News Development MGR
Bridge News, Washington, DC

Lehew, Margaret (614) 446-2342
CONT, Daily Tribune/Sunday Times-Sentinel, Gallipolis, OH, Gannett Co. Inc.

Lehew, Ron (609) 935-1500
COL, Today's Sunbeam, Salem, NJ

Lehman, Beverly (515) 969-4846
ED, Eddyville Tribune, Eddyville, IA

Lehman, Dean G (303) 776-2244
PRES/ED, Daily Times-Call, Longmont, CO
Lehman Communications Corp.

Lehman, Edward (303) 776-2244
PUB, Lehman Communications Corp., Longmont, CO

Lehman, Jon L (617) 786-7000
Entertainment/Amusements ED, Features/TV Ledger ED, Patriot Ledger, Quincy, MA

Lehman, Julie (817) 387-3811
Librarian, Record-Chronicle, Denton, TX

Lehman, Karen D (937) 548-3151
MGR-CR, Daily Advocate, Greenville, OH

Lehman, Lauren R (303) 776-2244
DIR, Daily Times-Call, Longmont, CO
Lehman Communications Corp.

Lehman, Ruth G (303) 776-2244
VP/TREAS, ASSOC ED
Daily Times-Call, Longmont, CO
Lehman Communications Corp.

Lehmann, Dan (312) 321-3000
Criminal Courts
Chicago Sun-Times, Chicago, IL

Lehmann, Gene (903) 675-5626
ED, Religion/SCI ED
Athens Daily Review, Athens, TX

Lehnert, Eileen (517) 787-2300
MET ED, Jackson Citizen Patriot, Jackson, MI

Lehto, Oliver (705) 759-3030
Local COL, Sault Star, Sault Ste. Marie, ON

Leibengood, Lawrence A (219) 881-3000
ADV DIR, Post-Tribune, Gary, IN

Leibold, Kelly (707) 464-2141
CIRC DIR, Triplicate, Crescent City, CA

Leibowitz, David (602) 898-6500
COL, Mesa Tribune, Mesa, AZ
Thomson Newspapers

Leibson, Mark (318) 738-5642
PUB, ED, Kinder Courier News, Kinder, LA

Leichnitz, Peter E (613) 962-9171
PUB/GM, Intelligencer, Belleville, ON

Leicht, Dr Robert (416) 391-4196
ED, Die Zeit, Toronto, ON

Leifeld, Ellen (607) 272-2321
PRES, PUB, Ithaca Journal, Ithaca, NY

Leifeste, Alvin (817) 645-2441
CIRC DIR
Cleburne Times-Review, Cleburne, TX

Leifheit, Douglas M (408) 761-7300
PUB, Register-Pajaronian, Watsonville, CA

Leigh, John (212) 208-8000
ASSOC ED, Corporation Records, Daily News, New York, NY

Leigh, Penny (704) 692-0505
City ED, Times-News, Hendersonville, NC

Leightner, Donald (330) 296-9657
PROD FRM-PR
Record-Courier, Kent-Ravenna, OH

Leighton, Paul (508) 744-0600
Sports ED, Salem Evening News, Beverly, MA

Leimkuhler, Lyle (816) 271-8500
VP-FIN/SEC
St. Joseph News-Press, St. Joseph, MO

Leinbach, Richard (219) 533-2151
PROD SYS MGR, Goshen News, Goshen, IN

Leingang, Paul R (812) 424-5536
ED, Message, Evansville, IN

Leinhart, Ken (423) 457-2515
MAN ED, Courier-News, Clinton, TN

Leipzig, Richard H (414) 763-3511
GM
Burlington Standard Press, Burlington, WI

Leisch, Janet (217) 446-1000
Librarian, Commercial News, Danville, IL

Leishman, E Paul (416) 814-4239
CORP CONT
Thomson Newspapers, Toronto, ON

Leithty, Sandy (719) 336-2266
ADV DIR, Lamar Daily News, Lamar, CO

LeJeune, Darrel B (318) 432-6807
PUB, ED, Basile Weekly, Basile, LA

Leland, Timothy (617) 929-2000
VP/ASST to PUB, Boston Globe, Boston, MA

Leliaert Jr, Ray (219) 235-6161
BUS/FIN ED
South Bend Tribune, South Bend, IN

Leluika, Cheryl (419) 281-0581
PROD MGR-SYS
Ashland Times-Gazette, Ashland, OH

Lelyveld, Joseph (212) 556-1234
EX ED, New York Times, New York, NY

Lelyveld, Michael S (212) 837-7000
Senior Correspondent-Boston, Journal of Commerce & Commercial, New York, NY

Lemansky, Michael (860) 669-5727
ED, Clinton Recorder, Clinton, CT

Lemasters, Ronald (317) 747-5700
Automotive ED, Star Press, Muncie, IN

LeMay, Daniel (514) 285-7272
Arts/Entertainment ED
La Presse, Montreal, QC

LeMay, Konnie (715) 394-4411
ASST ED, EDU ED, SCI ED, Teen-Age/Youth ED, Daily Telegram, Superior, WI

Lemay, Raymond (514) 877-9777
EVP, Quebecor Communications Inc., Montreal, QC

LeMay, Robert H (319) 377-7037
PUB, Marion Times, Marion, IA

Lemieux, Guy (705) 673-3377
PUB, Le Journal Le Voyageur, Sudbury, ON

Lemieux, Sergie (514) 964-2655
GM, Courrier-des Moulins Mascouche/Laplaine, Terrebonne, QC

Lemik, Lester (315) 823-3680
PA, PROD MGR
Evening Times, Little Falls, NY

Leming, Mary Kate (561) 820-4100
Online Contact, ASST MAN ED-RES
Palm Beach Post, West Palm Beach, FL

Lemire, Don (609) 663-6000
CONT, Courier-Post, Cherry Hill, NJ

Lemke, Jami (414) 457-7711
Municipal Government ED
Sheboygan Press, Sheboygan, WI

Lemke, Michael C (206) 464-2111
VP-Advertising, ADV VP
Seattle Times, Seattle, WA

Lemley, Gail (207) 282-1535
EPE, Journal Tribune, Biddeford, ME

Lemm, Timothy (310) 832-0221
Automotive ED, City ED, Religion ED
News-Pilot, San Pedro, CA

Lemmon, Russ (619) 241-7744
Sports ED, Daily Press, Victorville, CA
Freedom Communications Inc.

Lemmons, Michael (218) 262-1011
Photographer
Daily Tribune, Hibbing, MN

Lemoi, Arthur (401) 724-0200
PUB
Rhode Island Jewish Herald, Providence, RI

Lemons, Blake (817) 458-7429
ED, Sanger Courier, Sanger, TX

Lemons, John (719) 275-7565
Environmental ED
Daily Record, Canon City, CO

Lemons, Roy L (817) 458-7429
PUB, Sanger Courier, Sanger, TX

Lemos, Alberto S (510) 237-0888
ED, Jornal Portugues, San Pablo, CA

Lempert, Barbara (609) 989-7800
City ED, Trentonian, Trenton, NJ

Leneave, Greg (502) 442-7380
GM, West Kentucky News, Paducah, KY

Lenehan, Art (201) 877-4141
ASST MAN ED
Star-Ledger, Newark, NJ

Lenerose, B E (806) 376-4488
PROD SUPT-MR, Amarillo Daily News/Globe Times, Amarillo, TX

Lenerville, Daniel (605) 331-2200
MGR-INFO SYS
Argus Leader, Sioux Falls, SD

Lengel, David (216) 999-4500
INFO SYS SUPV-Composing
Plain Dealer, Cleveland, OH

Lenhardt, Bridget D (716) 849-3434
ADV MGR-CLASS, Buffalo News, Buffalo, NY

Lenhart, Joe (217) 763-3541
PUB, ED, News-Record, Cerro Gordo, IL

Lenhart, Keith (610) 820-6500
CIRC MGR-Home Delivery
Morning Call, Allentown, PA

Lenhart, Wendell (816) 359-2212
PRES, SEC/TREAS, PA/PUB, MAN ED, DP MGR, Republican-Times, Trenton, MO

Lenhoff, Alan S (313) 222-6400
DIR-Strategic Planning
Detroit Newspapers, Detroit, MI

Lenius, Curtis (414) 887-0321
CIRC DIR, Daily Citizen, Beaver Dam, WI

Lenkersdorfer, Jay (208) 678-2201
GM/PUB, South Idaho Press, Burley, ID

Lenney, Michael (617) 341-1111
MAN ED, Chronicle (A Weekly News/Magazine), Stoughton, MA

Lennie, Al (905) 526-3333
CIRC MGR-Country, Spectator, Hamilton, ON

Lenno, Phil (516) 481-5487
COL, Editorial Consultant Service, West Hempstead, NY

Lennon, Gerry (613) 829-9100
CIRC ASST MGR-Reader Sales & SRV-Sales
Ottawa Citizen, Ottawa, ON

Lennon, John (217) 526-3323
PUB, Morrisonville Times, Morrisonville, IL

135-Who's Where **Lev**

Lennon, Julia .... (217) 526-3323
PUB, Morrisonville Times, Morrisonville, IL
LeNoir, Andy .... (215) 855-8440
CIRC DIR, Reporter, Landsdale, PA
Lensch, Darlene .... (937) 225-2000
CIRC MGR, Dayton Daily News, Dayton, OH
Lent, Jim .... (201) 377-2000
ED, Hanover Eagle/Regional Weekly News, Madison, NJ
Lent, Joanne .... (718) 447-4700
PUB
Staten Island Register, Staten Island, NY
Lentz, Betty Robbins .... (219) 461-8444
CIRC MGR-The News-Sentinel
Fort Wayne Newspapers Inc., Fort Wayne, IN
Lentz, Rebecca .... (701) 223-2500
EDU Reporter, Tribune, Bismarck, ND
Lenyk, Ron .... (905) 273-8111
PUB, Mississauga News, Mississauga, ON
Lenz, John .... (504) 345-2333
Sports ED, Daily Star, Hammond, LA
Lenz, Mark .... (702) 738-3119
Sports ED, Elko Daily Free Press, Elko, NV
Lenz, Scott .... (818) 566-4388
MAN ED, Entertainment Today, Burbank, CA
Leo, Peter .... (412) 263-1100
COL, Pittsburgh Post-Gazette, Pittsburgh, PA
Leon, Frank .... (609) 871-8000
CIRC DIR
Burlington County Times, Willingboro, NJ
Leon, Jacqueline .... (408) 297-1553
GM, ED, La Voz Latina, San Jose, CA
Leon, Raul .... (408) 297-1553
PUB, La Voz Latina, San Jose, CA
Leon, Stephen .... (518) 463-2500
PUB, ED, Metroland, Albany, NY
Leon, Tony .... (414) 922-4600
BUS ED, Reporter, Fond du Lac, WI
Leonard, Annette .... (910) 472-9500
GM, Thomasville Times, Thomasville, NC
Leonard, Brian .... (313) 994-6989
MGR-SYS, DP MGR
Ann Arbor News, Ann Arbor, MI
Leonard, Cathy .... (757) 539-3437
BM, Suffolk News-Herald, Suffolk, VA
Leonard, Christina .... (516) 747-8282
ED, Farmingdale Observer, Mineola, NY
Leonard, David .... (916) 321-1000
PROD MGR-OPER Maintenance
Sacramento Bee, Sacramento, CA
Leonard, Jack .... (713) 529-8490
GM, Houston Voice, Houston, TX
Leonard, John .... (805) 564-5200
ADV DIR-CLASS/NTL, ADTX MGR, Santa Barbara News-Press, Santa Barbara, CA
Leonard, Joseph .... (312) 222-3232
ASSOC ED-OPER
Chicago Tribune, Chicago, IL
Leonard, Kathleen J .... (609) 272-7000
DIR-Personnel
Press of Atlantic City, Pleasantville, NJ
Leonard, Kurt .... (419) 422-5151
City ED, Courier, Findlay, OH
Leonard, Kyle .... (847) 317-0500
MAN ED
Highland Park News, Bannockburn, IL
Leonard Jr, Lawrence H .... (603) 298-8711
PROD FRM-PR, PROD MGR-MR
Valley News, White River Jct., VT
Leonard, Lisa .... (916) 321-1000
ADV MGR-GEN
Sacramento Bee, Sacramento, CA
Leonard, Marsha .... (816) 254-8600
MGR-CR, Examiner, Independence, MO
Leonard, Michael .... (360) 754-5400
ADV MGR-CLASS, Olympian, Olympia, WA
Leonard, Michael C .... (704) 694-2161
PUB, Anson Record, Wadesboro, NC
Leonard Jr, Michael V .... (213) 525-2000
GM, Hollywood Reporter, Los Angeles, CA
Leonard, Pat .... (860) 241-6200
PROD MGR-Fleet Maintenance
Hartford Courant, Hartford, CT
Leonard, Richard .... (412) 224-4321
EX ED, Valley News Dispatch, Tarentum, PA
Gannett Co. Inc.
Leonard, Sherrie .... (219) 294-1661
State ED, Elkhart Truth, Elkhart, IN
Leonard, Teresa .... (919) 829-4500
News/RES DIR
News & Observer, Raleigh, NC
Leonard, Tim .... (330) 424-9541
Sports ED, Morning Journal, Lisbon, OH
Leonard, Tina .... (541) 926-2211
ADV SUPV-SRV
Albany Democrat-Herald, Albany, OR
Leone, David .... (406) 657-1200
CIRC MGR, Billings Gazette, Billings, MT
Leone-Schmidt, Curtis .... (914) 454-2000
Sports ED
Poughkeepsie Journal, Poughkeepsie, NY
Leong, Wilson Y .... (608) 754-3311
DIR-MKTG/PROM
Janesville Gazette, Janesville, WI

Leopard, Bailey .... (615) 794-4564
PUB, ED, Williamson Leader, Franklin, TN
Leopard, Richard F .... (614) 461-5000
CIRC MGR-Single Copy Sales
Columbus Dispatch, Columbus, OH
LePage, Norman .... (413) 562-4181
PROD FRM, Evening News, Westfield, MA
Lepelis, Frank .... (212) 416-2000
PROD DIR/ENG
Wall Street Journal, New York, NY
Lepien, Greg .... (601) 582-4321
CONT
Hattiesburg American, Hattiesburg, MS
LePine, Brian .... (604) 746-4451
ED, Pictorial, Duncan, BC
Lepley, Denny .... (615) 484-7510
PUB, ED, Cumberland Times, Crossville, TN
Lepore, Connie .... (203) 574-3636
EDL Writer, Waterbury Republican-American, Waterbury, CT
Leposky, George .... (305) 285-2200
ED, Ampersand Communications, Miami, FL
Leposky, Rosalie .... (305) 285-2200
MKTG DIR
Ampersand Communications, Miami, FL
Leppanen, Garry .... (508) 586-7200
NTL ED, Wire ED
Enterprise, Brockton, MA
LeQuear, Robert E .... (860) 442-2200
CIRC DIR, Day, New London, CT
Lerback, Larry .... (406) 523-5200
PROD MGR-Press, Missoulian, Missoula, MT
Lerner, Arthur .... (818) 781-2605
GM, Variedades HTMC, Van Nuys, CA
Lerner, Diane Flores .... (818) 781-2605
ED, Variedades HTMC, Van Nuys, CA
LeRoux, Leslee .... (715) 394-4411
EX ED, Books/BUS ED, EPE, FIN ED, News ED, Daily Telegram, Superior, WI
LeRoy-Herbert, Angelina .... (904) 432-8410
PUB, New American Press, Pensacola, FL
Lerseth, Mike .... (707) 644-1141
News ED, Vallejo Times-Herald, Vallejo, CA
Les, Mike .... (505) 823-7777
Copy Desk Chief/News ED
Albuquerque Journal, Albuquerque, NM
Lesar, Dean .... (715) 255-8531
ED, Tribune Record-Gleaner, Loyal, WI
Lescault, Debora .... (352) 374-5000
MGR-CR, Gainesville Sun, Gainesville, FL
Lescelius, Terri .... (715) 735-6611
ED, EagleHerald, Marinette, WI
Leschper, Lee .... (817) 965-3124
VP, PUB, Stephenville Empire-Tribune, Stephenville, TX
Lesco, Deana .... (409) 265-7411
ADV MGR-RT, Brazosport Facts, Clute, TX
Lescott, John .... (904) 359-4111
ADV MGR-NTL/Major Accounts
Florida Times-Union, Jacksonville, FL
Leseberg, Russell .... (813) 893-8111
Data Service DIR
St. Petersburg Times, St. Petersburg, FL
Leser, Lawrence A .... (513) 977-3000
Chairman, E W Scripps Co., Cincinnati, OH
Lesh, Greta .... (908) 722-8800
ADV MGR-Inside Sales, ADTX MGR
Courier-News, Bridgewater, NJ
Le Shane, Donald .... (603) 882-2741
PROD MGR-Technical SRV
Telegraph, Nashua, NH
Leshin, Arnie .... (954) 755-2090
ED
Coral Springs City News, Coral Springs, FL
Leshovsky, Karen .... (701) 242-7696
ED, Richland County News-Monitor, Hankinson, ND
Lesley, Bonnie .... (864) 855-0355
GM, Easley Progress, Easley, SC
Lesley, Jason R .... (704) 633-8950
ASSOC PUB, Salisbury Post, Salisbury, NC
Leslie, Clarence .... (502) 772-2591
GM, Louisville Defender, Louisville, KY
Leslie, Fern .... (501) 327-6621
CIRC MGR, Log Cabin Democrat, Conway, AR
Leslie, Marilyn .... (517) 278-2318
CIRC DIR, Daily Reporter, Coldwater, MI
Leslie, Tim .... (541) 753-2641
Online MGR
Corvallis Gazette-Times, Corvallis, OR
Lesniak, Peter .... (403) 667-6285
ED, Yukon News, Whitehorse, YT
Lesnick, Dave .... (406) 755-7000
Sports ED, Daily Inter Lake, Kalispell, MT
Lessard, Denis .... (514) 285-7272
Quebec Bureau, La Presse, Montreal, QC
Lessard, Jean .... (514) 276-9615
PUB, GM
L 'Express d 'Outremont, Montreal, QC
Lessard, M A .... (514) 521-4545
ADTX MGR-Services
Le Journal de Montreal, Montreal, QC
Lessard, Most Rev Raymond W (770) 554-3539
PUB, Southern Cross, Waynesboro, GA

Lessard, Richard .... (819) 569-9526
PROD MGR, Record, Sherbrooke, QC
Lessy, Harriet .... (215) 854-2000
COL-BUS
Philadelphia Daily News, Philadelphia, PA
Lester, Becky .... (903) 872-3931
DP MGR
Corsicana Daily Sun, Corsicana, TX
Lester, Betty .... (301) 662-1177
MGR-ADM Services, Automotive ED
Frederick Post/The News, Frederick, MD
Lester, Dave .... (509) 248-1251
Farm/Agriculture ED
Yakima Herald-Republic, Yakima, WA
Lester, Mary .... (408) 257-9567
PUB, Lester Syndicate, Cupertino, CA
Lester, Michelle .... (319) 588-5611
ADV MGR-CLASS
Telegraph Herald, Dubuque, IA
Lester, Rexanna .... (912) 236-9511
EX ED, Morning News, Savannah, GA
Lester, Roz .... (718) 229-0300
MAN ED, Fresh Meadows Times, Bayside, NY
Lester, William .... (408) 257-9567
EX ED, Lester Syndicate, Cupertino, CA
Lestrud, Howard D .... (612) 464-4601
GM, Times, Forest Lake, MN
Lestz, Gerald S .... (717) 687-7721
PUB, Strasburg Weekly News, Strasburg, PA
Leszcynski, Ray .... (972) 272-6591
ED, Garland News, Garland, TX
Leszczynski, Emily .... (312) 763-3343
GM, Dziennik Zwaizkowy, Chicago, IL
Letexier, Noel .... (701) 780-1100
ADV DIR-Sales (Ag Week)
Grand Forks Herald, Grand Forks, ND
Letheby, Pete .... (308) 382-1000
Agriculture ED
Grand Island Independent, Grand Island, NE
Leto, Frank .... (502) 926-0123
ADV DIR, Messenger-Inquirer, Owensboro, KY
Lett, Cory May .... (801) 237-2188
Online News ED
Deseret News, Salt Lake City, UT
Lettera, Larry .... (212) 944-7744
PRES, Wagner International Photos Inc., New York, NY
Letterman, Gretchen .... (813) 893-8111
SCI/Technology ED
St. Petersburg Times, St. Petersburg, FL
Lettunich, Sandy .... (970) 879-1502
ADV MGR
Steamboat Today, Steamboat Springs, CO
Leu, Al .... (201) 428-6200
PROD DIR
Parsippany Daily Record, Parsippany, NJ
Leu, Jon .... (712) 328-1811
News ED, Daily Nonpareil, Council Bluffs, IA
Leubsdorf, Carl .... (214) 977-8222
ASST MAN ED-Washington BU Chief
Dallas Morning News, Dallas, TX
Leuci, Phyllis .... (607) 798-1234
ADV MGR-Data/Co-op
Press & Sun Bulletin, Binghamton, NY
Leuschner, Paul .... (716) 232-7100
PROD FRM-COMP (Times-Union), Rochester Democrat and Chronicle; Rochester, NY
Times-Union, Rochester, NY
Leute, James .... (608) 754-3311
BUS ED, Janesville Gazette, Janesville, WI
Levac, Sandy .... (250) 785-5631
ADV MGR, Alaska Highway Daily News, Fort St. John, BC
Levak, Larry .... (304) 348-5140
VP-Advertising
Charleston Newspapers, Charleston, WV
LeValley, Norma .... (213) 682-1412
ED
South Pasadena Review, South Pasadena, CA
Levan, Janice .... (937) 644-9111
ADV MGR-CLASS
Marysville Journal-Tribune, Marysville, OH
Levasseur, Rick .... (207) 990-8000
Political ED, Bangor Daily News, Bangor, ME
Leveille, Lise .... (418) 365-6262
ED
Le Dynamique de la Maurice, Saint-Tite, QC
Levendosky, Charles .... (307) 266-0500
EPE, Star-Tribune, Casper, WY
Lever, Bill .... (352) 374-5000
News ED, Gainesville Sun, Gainesville, FL
Levert, Caroline .... (613) 830-3005
PUB, GM
Orleans Weekly Journal, Orleans, ON
Levesque, Don .... (207) 728-3336
GM, MAN ED
St. John Valley Times, Madawaska, ME
Levesque, Francine .... (807) 826-3788
MAN ED, Echo, Manitouwadge, ON
Levesque, Sonia .... (418) 775-4381
ED, L'Information, Mont Joli, QC
Levett, Ron .... (905) 526-3333
Wire ED, Spectator, Hamilton, ON

Levey, Bob .... (202) 334-6000
COL-Local
Washington Post, Washington, DC
Levey, Kelli .... (409) 776-4444
City ED, Eagle, Bryan, TX
Levey, Noam .... (218) 723-5281
EDU Writer
Duluth News-Tribune, Duluth, MN
Levi, Michael A .... (904) 837-2828
PUB, Destin Log, Destin, FL
Levin, Deborah .... (310) 392-5146
PRES, Levin Represents, Santa Monica, CA
Levin, John .... (540) 981-3100
Auto/Aviation ED, BUS/FIN ED, RE ED
Roanoke Times, Roanoke, VA
Levin, Martin .... (416) 585-5000
Books ED, Globe and Mail (Canada's National Newspaper), Toronto, ON
Levin, Sondra .... (718) 543-5200
ED, Bronx Press-Review, Bronx, NY
Levine, Bonnie .... (707) 546-2020
ADV MGR-OPER
Press Democrat, Santa Rosa, CA
Levine, David .... (617) 837-3500
MAN ED
Abington/Rockland Mariner, Marshfield, MA
Levine, Ed .... (201) 646-4000
Legal Affairs ED, Record, Hackensack, NJ
Levine, Eric .... (810) 648-4000
ED, Sanilac County News, Sandusky, MI
Levine, Jacki .... (352) 374-5000
ASST MAN ED
Gainesville Sun, Gainesville, FL
Levine, Jane .... (312) 828-0350
PUB, Chicago Reader, Chicago, IL
Levine, Jesse E .... (213) 237-5485
PRES/CEO, Los Angeles Times Syndicate, Los Angeles, CA
Levine, Jonathan .... (413) 443-2010
PUB, ED, Pittsfield Gazette, Pittsfield, MA
Levine, Larry A .... (330) 996-3000
VP/ASST TREAS/ASST SEC
Akron Beacon Journal, Akron, OH
LeVine, Marc .... (908) 922-6000
ASSOC DIR-Human Resources
Asbury Park Press, Neptune, NJ
Levine, Michael .... (310) 540-5511
CIRC MGR
Torrance Daily Breeze, Torrance, CA
Levine, Mike .... (914) 341-1100
City ED, COL
Times Herald-Record, Middletown, NY
Levine, Mort .... (408) 262-2454
PUB, Milpitas Post, Milpitas, CA
Levine, Richard J .... (212) 416-2000
MAN ED-News Services
Wall Street Journal, New York, NY
Levine, Sheldon .... (814) 234-9601
DIR-Sales
AccuWeather Inc., State College, PA
Levine, Susan .... (716) 849-3434
CIRC MGR-NIE, Buffalo News, Buffalo, NY
Levings, Darryl .... (816) 234-4141
Mid America/NTL ED
Kansas City Star, Kansas City, MO
Levins, Harry .... (314) 340-8000
Writing Coach
St. Louis Post-Dispatch, St. Louis, MO
Levinson, Linda .... (203) 314-3439
ED, Valley News, Bristol, CT
Levinson, Rick .... (619) 299-3131
Senior ED-Special Sections
San Diego Union-Tribune, San Diego, CA
Levison, Ann .... (508) 456-8122
ED, Harvard Post, Harvard, MA
Levitt, Barbara .... (203) 744-5100
MGR-Educational SRV
News-Times, Danbury, CT
Levitt, Leon .... (602) 271-8000
CIRC DIR
Phoenix Newspapers Inc., Phoenix, AZ
Levy, Al .... (219) 235-6161
CIRC MGR-OPER
South Bend Tribune, South Bend, IN
Levy, Charlie .... (508) 343-6911
ADTX MGR
Sentinel & Enterprise, Fitchburg, MA
Levy, Ed .... (800) 223-2154
CIRC MGR-NTL
Investor's Business Daily, Los Angeles, CA
Levy, Henry .... (212) 967-7313
PUB, Jewish Post of New York, New York, NY
Levy, Jay R .... (212) 686-6850
PRES
Black Press Service Inc. (BPS), New York, NY
Levy, Marc .... (508) 343-6911
Features ED, Health/Medical ED, Travel ED
Sentinel & Enterprise, Fitchburg, MA

Lev Who's Where-136

Levy, Marcel .... (702) 385-3111
Online Publishing Art DIR
Las Vegas Sun, Las Vegas, NV

Levy, Robert .... (212) 293-8500
EX ED-UFS & NEA, United Media, United Feature Syndicate, Newspaper Enterprise Association, New York, NY

Levy, Ronald N .... (800) 222-5551
PRES/EX ED, North American Precis Syndicate Inc., New York, NY

Levy, Yehuda .... (212) 599-3666
PUB, Jerusalem Post International Edition, New York, NY

LeWallen, Tim .... (501) 862-6611
GM, El Dorado News-Times, El Dorado, AR

Lewars, Donald .... (610) 258-7171
ADV MGR-Major Accounts/NTL
Express-Times, Easton, PA

Lewers, Jim .... (812) 231-4200
City ED, Tribune-Star, Terre Haute, IN

Lewey, Weston .... (501) 633-3130
ASSOC PUB, Times-Herald, Forrest City, AR

Lewin, Luis E .... (312) 222-3237
VP-Human Resources
Tribune Co., Chicago, IL

Lewis, Alfred E .... (614) 754-1608
PUB, ED, Dresden Transcript, Dresden, OH

Lewis, Andrew J .... (601) 888-4293
PUB, ED, Republican, Woodville, MS

Lewis, Barbara A .... (201) 746-1100
PUB, Montclair Times, Montclair, NJ

Lewis, Barry .... (765) 362-1200
Sports ED, Journal Review, Crawfordsville, IN

Lewis, Barry .... (203) 964-2200
City ED, Stamford Advocate, Stamford, CT

Lewis, Brenda .... (601) 267-4501
GM, Carthaginian, Carthage, MS

Lewis, Brian .... (213) 932-6397
ED, Independent, Los Angeles, CA

Lewis, Brian .... (319) 291-1400
PROD FRM-COMP
Waterloo Courier, Waterloo, IA

Lewis, Cameron .... (513) 761-1188
Contributing Critic
Critic's Choice Reviews, Cincinnati, OH

Lewis, Carol .... (757) 446-2000
MGR-CR, Virginian-Pilot, Norfolk, VA

Lewis, Carol Ann .... (308) 436-2222
PUB, ED, Gering Courier, Gering, NE

Lewis, Cathryn C .... (617) 929-2000
DIR-Benefits, Boston Globe, Boston, MA

Lewis, Cathy .... (409) 245-5555
BM, Daily Tribune, Bay City, TX

Lewis, Charles J .... (202) 298-6920
Washington BU Chief
Hearst News Service, Washington, DC

Lewis, Claude .... (215) 854-2000
COL, Philadelphia Inquirer, Philadelphia, PA

Lewis, Connie .... (318) 365-6773
BUS/FIN ED, Farm/Agriculture ED
Daily Iberian, New Iberia, LA

Lewis, Cue .... (972) 382-2341
PUB, ED, Celina Record, Celina, TX

Lewis, Dale .... (605) 685-6866
PUB, ED
Bennett County Booster II, Martin, SD

Lewis, David .... (317) 598-6397
PUB, Daily Ledger, Noblesville, IN

Lewis, David .... (972) 382-2341
PUB, ED, Celina Record, Celina, TX

Lewis, David .... (504) 732-2565
Sports ED, Daily News, Bogalusa, LA

Lewis, David A .... (802) 362-3535
ED
Vermont News Guide, Manchester Center, VT

Lewis, DeLancey B .... (206) 284-4424
SEC/TREAS
Pioneer Newspapers, Seattle, WA

Lewis, Dwight .... (615) 259-8000
ED-Night/Weekend
Tennessean, Nashville, TN

Lewis, Ed .... (706) 629-2231
GM, Calhoun Times and Gordon County News, Calhoun, GA

Lewis, Franca .... (301) 733-5131
Action Line ED
Morning Herald, Hagerstown, MD

Lewis, Frank .... (908) 922-6000
MGR-Customer Interface
Asbury Park Press, Neptune, NJ

Lewis, Jack D .... (308) 436-2222
GM, Gering Courier, Gering, NE

Lewis, James .... (610) 688-3000
ED, Suburban & Wayne Times, Wayne, PA

Lewis, James W .... (319) 291-1400
PUB/GM, Waterloo Courier, Waterloo, IA

Lewis, Jeanie .... (608) 987-2141
ED, Democrat Tribune, Mineral Point, WI

Lewis, Jerry .... (619) 299-3131
CIRC MGR-Single Copy
San Diego Union-Tribune, San Diego, CA

Lewis, Dr Jesse J .... (205) 251-5158
PUB, Birmingham Times, Birmingham, AL

Lewis, Joan .... (304) 645-1206
CIRC MGR
West Virginia Daily News, Lewisburg, WV

Lewis, John .... (405) 382-1100
PROD FRM-PR/Engraving
Seminole Producer, Seminole, OK

Lewis, Julie .... (607) 432-1000
Photo DEPT MGR, Daily Star, Oneonta, NY

Lewis, Kathy .... (618) 544-2101
SEC/TREAS, BM
Robinson Daily News, Robinson, IL

Lewis, Kevin .... (806) 296-1300
Sports ED
Plainview Daily Herald, Plainview, TX

Lewis, Kris .... (317) 736-7101
PROD MGR-Graphic Arts
Daily Journal, Franklin, IN

Lewis, Kurt J .... (573) 859-3328
PUB, Bland Courier, Belle, MO

Lewis, Larry H .... (502) 653-3381
PUB
Hickman County Gazette, Clinton, KY

Lewis, Laurie J .... (706) 846-3188
ED, Hogansville Herald, Hogansville, GA

Lewis, Lee .... (203) 574-3636
EX Sports ED, Waterbury Republican-American, Waterbury, CT

Lewis, Lisa Robert .... (518) 270-1200
MAN ED, Record, Troy, NY

Lewis, Marajane .... (409) 833-3311
PSL MGR
Beaumont Enterprise, Beaumont, TX

Lewis, Marcia .... (814) 532-5199
Regional ED
Tribune-Democrat, Johnstown, PA

Lewis, Mark .... (601) 961-7000
CIRC MGR-OPER
Clarion-Ledger, Jackson, MS

Lewis, Mark .... (810) 469-4510
ADV DIR, Macomb Daily, Mount Clemens, MI

Lewis, Mary .... (605) 685-6866
PUB, ED
Bennett County Booster II, Martin, SD

Lewis, Maryam .... (614) 754-1608
GM, Dresden Transcript, Dresden, OH

Lewis, Michael .... (305) 358-2663
PUB, ED, Miami Today, Miami, FL

Lewis, Michael .... (503) 399-6611
NTL ED, Statesman Journal, Salem, OR

Lewis, Michael .... (612) 222-0059
Mechanical SUPT
St. Paul Legal Ledger, St. Paul, MN

Lewis, Michael D .... (360) 354-4444
PUB, Lynden Tribune, Lynden, WA

Lewis, Michael S .... (812) 988-2221
GM, ED
Brown County Democrat, Nashville, IN

Lewis, Nancy .... (757) 446-2000
CIRC MGR-MKTG
Virginian-Pilot, Norfolk, VA

Lewis, Nick .... (614) 373-2121
CIRC DIR, Marietta Times, Marietta, OH

Lewis, Norman .... (406) 496-5500
PUB/ED, Montana Standard, Butte, MT

Lewis, Pamela .... (954) 523-5115
ED, Westside Gazette, Fort Lauderdale, FL

Lewis, Philip .... (941) 262-3161
MAN ED, Naples Daily News, Naples, FL

Lewis, Quentin .... (540) 669-2181
ADV MGR-RT, Herald-Courier Virginia Tennessean, Bristol, VA

Lewis, Ray .... (207) 791-6650
DP MGR-Hardware
Portland Press Herald, Portland, ME

Lewis, Richard .... (408) 423-4242
PROD FRM-PR
Santa Cruz County Sentinel, Santa Cruz, CA

Lewis, Robert .... (330) 996-3000
PROD ASST MGR
Akron Beacon Journal, Akron, OH

Lewis, Ron J .... (573) 859-3328
PUB, ED, Belle Banner, Belle, MO

Lewis, Ronnie .... (214) 977-8222
PROD MGR-Platemaking
Dallas Morning News, Dallas, TX

Lewis, Roy .... (613) 342-4441
RE ED, Brockville Recorder and Times, Brockville, ON

Lewis, Russell T .... (212) 556-1234
PRES/COO
New York Times Co., New York, NY

Lewis Jr, Samuel E .... (612) 222-0059
PRES/PUB, ED
St. Paul Legal Ledger, St. Paul, MN

Lewis, Sandi .... (407) 294-1385
GM, Florida Sun Review, Orlando, FL

Lewis, Sandra S .... (817) 431-2231
GM, Keller Citizen, Keller, TX

Lewis, Sharon .... (615) 259-8000
DIR-Human Resources
Tennessean, Nashville, TN

Lewis, Shirley .... (717) 297-3024
ED, Troy Gazette-Register, Troy, PA

Lewis, Sonja .... (602) 898-6500
EDU ED, Mesa Tribune, Mesa, AZ

Lewis, Wendi .... (334) 213-7323
ED
Montgomery Independent, Montgomery, AL

Lewis, William C .... (817) 431-2231
PUB, Keller Citizen, Keller, TX

Lewittes, Michael .... (212) 210-2100
Gossip COL
New York Daily News, New York, NY

Lewyckyj, Maryanna .... (416) 947-2222
Action Line, Toronto Sun, Toronto, ON

Lexa, Lauren .... (615) 371-6154
ED, Brentwood Journal, Brentwood, TN

Leyerle, Jocile .... (405) 387-5277
PUB, GM, Newcastle Pacer, Newcastle, OK

Leyerle, Marvin .... (405) 387-5277
PUB, ED, Newcastle Pacer, Newcastle, OK

Leyshon, Donald J .... (602) 977-8351
DP MGR, PROD DIR-OPER
Daily News-Sun, Sun City, AZ

Leyshon, Maryanne .... (602) 977-8351
ED, Daily News-Sun, Sun City, AZ

Leytham, Tommy .... (334) 928-2321
ED, Fairhope Courier, Fairhope, AL

L'Hommedieu, Jon .... (520) 445-3333
News/Wire ED, Daily Courier, Prescott, AZ

Li, Arthur .... (808) 525-8000
DIR-Analysis & Reporting
Hawaii Newspaper Agency Inc., Honolulu, HI

Li, Jesse .... (415) 982-6206
GM, Chinese Times, San Francisco, CA

Li, Simon K C .... (213) 237-5000
Foreign ED
Los Angeles Times, Los Angeles, CA

Li, Yong .... (212) 343-9717
ED, New Jersey China Times, Edison, NJ

Lias, David .... (605) 472-0822
ED, Redfield Press, Redfield, SD

Lias, W Dock .... (814) 371-4200
VP/PUB, PA, Courier-Express/Tri-County Sunday, Du Bois, PA

Libbon, Mark .... (315) 470-0011
Deputy MAN ED, Post-Standard/Syracuse Herald-Journal/American, Syracuse, NY

Libby, Tom .... (617) 426-3000
DIR-INFO Technology
Boston Herald, Boston, MA

Liberi, Judy .... (904) 252-1511
Fashion/Style ED, Daytona Beach News-Journal, Daytona Beach, FL

Libersat, Deacon Henry .... (407) 660-9141
GM, ED, Florida Catholic, Orlando, FL

Liberty, Fran .... (412) 834-1151
DP MGR, Tribune-Review, Greensburg, PA

Libis, Zoa .... (605) 369-2441
ED, Springfield Times, Springfield, SD

Licano, Adela .... (719) 384-4475
ADV MGR-CLASS
La Junta Tribune-Democrat, La Junta, CO

Licence, Terence K .... (970) 586-3356
PUB, ED
Estes Park Trail-Gazette, Estes Park, CO

Licht, A V .... (847) 446-4082
PRES
Los Angeles Features Syndicate, Winnetka, IL

Lichtenstein, Gene .... (213) 738-7778
ED, Jewish Journal of Greater Los Angeles, Los Angeles, CA

Lichtenwald, Larry .... (319) 263-2331
PROD MGR-PR
Muscatine Journal, Muscatine, IA

Licki, Christine .... (860) 225-4601
CONT, Herald, New Britain, CT

Licklider, Daniel A .... (320) 329-3324
PUB, ED, Renville County Star Farmer News, Renville, MN

Licklider, Deborah .... (215) 854-2000
Features ED, Health ED
Philadelphia Daily News, Philadelphia, PA

Liddell, Don .... (403) 250-4200
CONT, Calgary Sun, Calgary, AB

Liddle, Jerry .... (812) 424-7711
CIRC DIR
Evansville Courier Co. Inc., Evansville, IN

Lidestri, Dina .... (334) 749-6271
PROD FRM-COMP
Opelika-Auburn News, Opelika, AL

Lidstone, E .... (613) 933-3160
CONT/CR MGR
Standard-Freeholder, Cornwall, ON

Lidy, Paula .... (618) 783-2324
MAN ED, Press-Mentor, Newton, IL

Lieb, Bill .... (814) 238-5000
PROD MGR
Centre Daily Times, State College, PA

Lieb, Gene .... (209) 634-9141
Photo DEPT MGR, Picture ED
Turlock Journal, Turlock, CA

Lieberman, Andrew H .... (610) 932-2444
PUB, Chester County Press, Oxford, PA

Lieberman, Candace .... (800) 222-5551
EIC, North American Precis Syndicate Inc., New York, NY

Lieberman, Paul .... (213) 237-5000
EDU ED (Acting), Religion ED (Acting)
Los Angeles Times, Los Angeles, CA

Lieberman, Randall S .... (610) 932-2444
GM, Chester County Press, Oxford, PA

Liebhaber, Rabbi Marc .... (612) 920-7000
PUB
American Jewish World, Minneapolis, MN

Liebman, Steve .... (814) 532-5199
Travel ED, Tribune-Democrat, Johnstown, PA

Liefer, Richard .... (312) 222-3232
EDL Writer, Chicago Tribune, Chicago, IL

Liefeste, Alvin .... (817) 645-2441
PROD MGR
Cleburne Times-Review, Cleburne, TX

Liesen, Joe .... (217) 223-5100
Photo DEPT MGR
Quincy Herald-Whig, Quincy, IL

Liesman, Steve .... (212) 416-2000
BU Chief-Moscow
Wall Street Journal, New York, NY

Liezt, Lorrie .... (615) 552-1808
MGR-CR, Leaf-Chronicle, Clarksville, TN

Lifford, Brad .... (423) 246-8121
Religion ED, Teen-Age/Youth ED
Kingsport Times-News, Kingsport, TN

Lifka, Robert .... (708) 242-1234
ED, Cicero-Berwyn-Stickney Forest View Life, Berwyn, IL

Light, Jeff .... (714) 835-1234
Deputy ED-Cities
Orange County Register, Santa Ana, CA

Light, Murray B .... (716) 849-3434
Senior VP, ED, Buffalo News, Buffalo, NY

Lightfoot, Frank .... (501) 247-4700
PUB, ED, White Hall Journal, Pine Bluff, AR

Lightfoot, Linda .... (504) 383-1111
EX ED, Advocate, Baton Rouge, LA

Lightfoot, Linda .... (307) 672-2431
MGR-Office, Sheridan Press, Sheridan, WY

Likovic, Ron .... (815) 729-6161
PROD MGR-Pre Press
Herald-News, Joliet, IL

Liles, Jeffrey .... (606) 231-3100
DIR-Market RES
Lexington Herald-Leader, Lexington, KY

Liles, Vince .... (941) 382-1164
CIRC MGR, Highlands Today, Sebring, FL

Lillge, Jay .... (715) 842-2101
Sports ED, Wausau Daily Herald, Wausau, WI

Lilliberg, Jerry .... (218) 723-5281
PROD FRM-Maintenance
Duluth News-Tribune, Duluth, MN

Lillie, N T .... (612) 777-8800
PUB, East Side Review, North St. Paul, MN

Lillis, Karen .... (614) 387-0400
BUS ED, EDU ED, Marion Star, Marion, OH

Lillis, Mike .... (212) 930-8000
DIR-Technology
New York Post, New York, NY

Lillquist, Kathy .... (206) 339-3000
PROD MGR-Pre Press, Herald, Everett, WA

Lilly, Deborah .... (317) 584-4501
News ED, Radio/Television ED
News-Gazette, Winchester, IN

Lima, Christina .... (503) 399-6611
Health/Medical ED
Statesman Journal, Salem, OR

Lima, John .... (412) 981-6100
PUB, Herald, Sharon, PA

Limb, John .... (503) 281-1191
PUB, Catholic Sentinel, Portland, OR

Lime, Susan .... (419) 281-0581
ASST MAN ED
Ashland Times-Gazette, Ashland, OH

Limmer, Thomas .... (517) 787-2300
News ED
Jackson Citizen Patriot, Jackson, MI

Limoge, Bradley A .... (802) 888-2212
PUB, News & Citizen, Morrisville, VT

Limon, Michael .... (702) 788-6200
ASST MAN ED
Reno Gazette-Journal, Reno, NV

Limpert, Lynn S .... (301) 662-1177
PROD MGR-Art
Frederick Post/News, Frederick, MD

Limpf, Larry .... (419) 836-2221
MAN ED
Suburban Press & Metro Press, Millbury, OH

Lin, Ching-wen .... (213) 782-8770
MAN ED
Free China Journal, Los Angeles, CA

Lin, Jennifer .... (215) 854-2000
Beijing BU
Philadelphia Inquirer, Philadelphia, PA

Linam, Steve .... (918) 335-8200
MAN ED, EPE, EDU ED, News ED, MGR-Telecommunications
Examiner-Enterprise, Bartlesville, OK

137-Who's Where **Lit**

Linard, Greg (410) 848-4400
PROD DIR
Carroll County Times, Westminster, MD

Lincicome, Bernie (312) 222-3232
COL, Chicago Tribune, Chicago, IL

Lincir, Nick (562) 435-1161
PROD MGR-Maintenance
Press-Telegram, Long Beach, CA

Lincoln, Art (207) 873-3341
CIRC MGR-Single Copy, Central Maine Morning Sentinel, Waterville, ME
Guy Gannett Communications

Lincoln, David B (717) 291-8811
MGR-MKTG/Circ, Lancaster Intelligencer Journal/New Era/Sunday News, Lancaster, PA

Lincoln, Donald D (904) 584-5513
PUB, Taco Times, Perry, FL

Lincoln, H Gene (815) 472-2000
PUB, Progress-Reporter, Momence, IL

Lincoln, Ivan (801) 237-2188
Theater ED, Deseret News, Salt Lake City, UT

Lincoln, James C (517) 423-2174
PUB, Tecumseh Herald, Tecumseh, MI

Lincoln Jr, James L (517) 423-2174
ED, Tecumseh Herald, Tecumseh, MI

Lincoln, M Sue (815) 472-2000
ED
Momence Progress-Reporter, Momence, IL

Lincoln, Michelle (540) 949-8213
BUS/FIN ED, Features ED
News Virginian, Waynesboro, VA

Lincoln, Ray (504) 826-3279
News ED, Times-Picayune, New Orleans, LA

Lincoln, Steven (913) 899-2338
ED, Goodland Daily News, Goodland, KS

Lincoln, Susan H (904) 584-5513
GM, MAN ED, Taco Times, Perry, FL

Lind, Angus (504) 826-3279
COL, Times-Picayune, New Orleans, LA

Lind, Elizabeth L (518) 374-4141
VP, Daily Gazette, Schenectady, NY

Lind, Robin (804) 784-5025
MAN DIR
Hope Springs Press, Manakin-Sabot, VA

Lindahl-Urben, CA (612) 288-9008
PUB, ED, Focus Point, Minneapolis, MN

Lindau, Bill (910) 997-3111
Sports ED, Richmond County Daily Journal, Rockingham, NC

Lindberg, Dick (402) 654-2218
PUB, Rustler Sentinel, Hooper, NE

Lindberg, Tod (202) 636-3000
EPE, Washington Times, Washington, DC

Lindblom, Sandy (906) 482-1500
ADV MGR-CLASS, ADTX MGR
Daily Mining Gazette, Houghton, MI

Lindeman, David R (937) 335-5634
VP-News, EX ED, COL, EPE, Troy Daily News/Miami Valley Sunday News, Troy, OH

Lindemann, Steve (310) 540-5511
ADV MGR-NTL, Daily Breeze, Torrance, CA

Lindemeir-Burnell, Ruth (204) 774-1883
ED, Kanada Kurier, Winnipeg, MB

Linden, Michael (412) 981-6100
CIRC DIR, Herald, Sharon, PA

Lindenbaum, Sharon (816) 234-4141
VP-FIN, Kansas City Star, Kansas City, MO

Lindenmoyer, Marta (717) 421-3000
Food ED, Women's ED
Pocono Record, Stroudsburg, PA

Lindenmuth, Gary (609) 871-8000
Senior ASSOC ED
Burlington County Times, Willingboro, NJ

Lindenmuth, Jeff (610) 820-6500
Graphics DIR, Morning Call, Allentown, PA

Lindequist, J Peter (609) 597-3211
PUB, Beacon, Manahawkin, NJ

Linder, Aubry (504) 383-1111
PROD MGR-Blue Bonnet Plant
Advocate, Baton Rouge, LA

Lindermann, Bill (972) 424-6565
DP MGR, PROD MGR-DP
Plano Star Courier, Plano, TX

Lindgren, Kristi (541) 926-2211
Administrator-Employee Benefits
Albany Democrat-Herald, Albany, OR

Lindley, Don (904) 252-1511
MAN ED-News & EDL, Daytona Beach News-Journal, Daytona Beach, FL

Lindley, Doug (208) 232-4161
Photo DEPT MGR
Idaho State Journal, Pocatello, ID

Lindley, Jean Casey (804) 857-1212
PUB, Traveller, Norfolk, VA

Lindley, Leon (806) 762-8844
PROD SUPT-MR
Lubbock Avalanche-Journal, Lubbock, TX

Lindley Jr, Thomas H (810) 766-6100
ED, Flint Journal, Flint, MI

Lindley, Thomas M (904) 252-1511
PROD DIR-Creative SRV, Daytona Beach News-Journal, Daytona Beach, FL

Lindley III, Tom (812) 283-6636
GM, ED, Evening News, Jeffersonville, IN

Lindner, Doug (319) 472-2311
PUB, Cedar Valley Daily Times, Vinton, IA

Lindner, Ninnett (610) 932-2444
ED, Unidad Latina, Oxford, PA

Lindo, Roger (213) 622-8332
Assignment ED
La Opinion, Los Angeles, CA

Lindquist, Bruce (507) 642-3636
ED, Madelia Times-Messenger, Madelia, MN

Lindquist, David (219) 933-3200
Entertainment/Amusements ED, Fashion/Style ED, Living/Lifestyle ED, Television/Film ED, Theater/Music ED, Times, Munster, IN

Lindquist, Diane (619) 299-3131
Farm/Agriculture Writer
San Diego Union-Tribune, San Diego, CA

Lindquist, Larry G (703) 276-3400
CIRC Senior VP, USA Today, Arlington, VA

Lindquist, Peter J (609) 597-3211
PUB, Beacon Mailbag, Manahawkin, NJ

Lindquist, Rob (510) 783-6111
DIR-Photo/Graphics, PROD MGR
Daily Review, Hayward, CA
MediaNews Inc. (Alameda Newspapers)

Lindquist, Ron (612) 239-2244
PUB, ED, Starbuck Times, Starbuck, MN

Lindquist, Steve (616) 392-2311
PROD MGR, Holland Sentinel, Holland, MI

Lindsay, Alvie (209) 578-2000
Work & Money, Modesto Bee, Modesto, CA

Lindsay, Brenda (216) 329-7000
MGR-Human Resources
Chronicle-Telegram, Elyria, OH

Lindsay, Colin (213) 237-5000
DIR-Administrative Services
Los Angeles Times, Los Angeles, CA

Lindsay, Jean (804) 293-4709
Author, Keister-Williams Newspaper Services, Charlottesville, VA

Lindsay, John L (408) 423-4242
GM
Santa Cruz County Sentinel, Santa Cruz, CA

Lindsay, John P (213) 237-5000
EX Calendar ED/ASST ASSOC ED, Los Angeles Times Magazine ED
Los Angeles Times, Los Angeles, CA

Lindsay, Ky (804) 293-4709
Sales VP, Keister-Williams Newspaper Services, Charlottesville, VA

Lindsay, Larry (507) 454-6500
MGR-Direct MKTG
Winona Daily News, Winona, MN

Lindsay, Robert (518) 993-2321
ED
Courier-Standard-Enterprise, Fort Plain, NY

Lindsay, Robert A (904) 697-2222
PUB, Carrabelle Times, Carrabelle, FL

Lindsay, Virginia (916) 541-3880
ADV MGR-CLASS
Tahoe Daily Tribune, South Lake Tahoe, CA

Lindsey, Albert J (405) 424-4695
MAN ED
Black Chronicle, Oklahoma City, OK

Lindsey, Gary D (515) 446-4151
PUB, Leon Journal-Reporter, Leon, IA

Lindsey, Jim (602) 271-8000
MGR-Data/Applications Support
Phoenix Newspapers Inc., Phoenix, AZ

Lindsey, John L (212) 887-8550
PUB/Group VP
American Metal Market, New York, NY

Lindsey, Margaret (515) 446-4151
ED, Leon Journal-Reporter, Leon, IA

Lindsey, Mike (907) 376-5225
PUB, Valley Sun, Wasilla, AK

Lindsey, Nancy (540) 694-3101
ED, Enterprise, Stuart, VA

Lindsey, Pat (907) 376-5225
PUB, Valley Sun, Wasilla, AK

Lindsey, Paul (941) 382-1164
PUB, Highlands Today, Sebring, FL

Lindsey, Robert (314) 831-4645
PUB, ED, Independent News, Florissant, MO

Lindsey, Roland (817) 390-7400
Texas & Southwest ED
Fort Worth Star-Telegram, Fort Worth, TX

Lindsey, William R (515) 446-4151
PUB, Leon Journal-Reporter, Leon, IA

Lindstrom, Bill (360) 532-4000
City ED, Daily World, Aberdeen, WA

Lindus, Linda (520) 526-3881
PUB, Navajo Hopi Observer, Flagstaff, AZ

Lindwall, Rebecca (319) 398-8211
Music ED-Classical/Pop
Gazette, Cedar Rapids, IA

Linebarger, Les (972) 932-2171
GM, Kaufman Herald, Kaufman, TX

Lineberg, Don (602) 271-0040
GM, New Times, Phoenix, AZ

Lineberry, Patricia (757) 247-4600
Answer ED, Daily Press, Newport News, VA

Linehan, Gary (209) 532-7151
Television/Film ED, Theater/Music ED
Union Democrat, Sonora, CA

Linehan, James R (603) 668-4321
MAN ED, Union Leader, Manchester, NH

Liner, William R (205) 766-5542
PUB, ED
Florence Shoals News-Leader, Florence, AL

Lines, Jeff (360) 694-3391
CIRC MGR-Zone, Columbian, Vancouver, WA

Linford, Clark (801) 373-5050
MGR-BUS Office, Daily Herald, Provo, UT

Ling, Robert M (916) 361-1234
PUB
Grapevine Independent, Rancho Cordova, CA

Lingen, Ken (402) 223-5233
ADV MGR, Beatrice Daily Sun, Beatrice, NE

Lingenfelter, Kay (316) 342-4800
Copy ED, Emporia Gazette, Emporia, KS

Lingerman, Mark (508) 922-1234
CIRC MGR
Daily News of Newburyport, Beverly, MA

Lingg, Marilyn (308) 928-2143
PUB, Harlan County Journal, Alma, NE

Lingg, Wayne (308) 928-2143
PUB, ED, Harlan County Journal, Alma, NE

Lingruen, Kaye (419) 533-2401
ED, Liberty Press, Liberty Center, OH

Linhapt, Lettie (407) 366-9181
ED, Oviedo Voice, Oviedo, FL

Linhart, Sean (216) 576-9115
ED, Valley News, Jefferson, OH

Linhorst, Stan (315) 470-0011
DIR-New Media, Post-Standard/Syracuse Herald-Journal/American, Syracuse, NY

Link, John (918) 256-6422
PUB, Vinita Daily Journal, Vinita, OK

Link, Rod (604) 638-7283
PUB, ED, Terrace Standard, Terrace, BC

Link, Wendy (716) 326-3163
MAN ED, Republican, Westfield, NY

Linkkila, Peter (860) 423-8466
PROD FRM-PR, Chronicle, Willimantic, CT

Linn, Albert (913) 483-2116
City ED, Russell Daily News, Russell, KS

Linn, Betty E (209) 683-4464
PUB, Sierra Star, Oakhurst, CA

Linn, Rebecca (907) 747-3219
CIRC MGR, Daily Sitka Sentinel, Sitka, AK

Linn, Richard (906) 932-2211
PROD SUPT
Ironwood Daily Globe, Ironwood, MI

Linnenburger, Kenneth (573) 221-2800
PROD MGR-OPER
Hannibal Courier-Post, Hannibal, MO

Linonis, Linda (412) 981-6100
Enterprise ED, Fashion/Style ED, Features ED, Living/Lifestyle ED, Women's ED
Herald, Sharon, PA

Lint, Bea (619) 256-2257
ADV MGR-RT, Desert Dispatch, Barstow, CA

Linthicum Jr, Thomas (410) 332-6000
Administrative ED, Sun, Baltimore, MD

Linton, Marilyn (416) 947-2222
Lifestyle ED, News RES DEPT
Toronto Sun, Toronto, ON

Linz, Carla (609) 272-7000
EPE, Press of Atlantic City, Pleasantville, NJ

Lionetti, Tony (401) 596-7791
PROD FRM-PR, Westerly Sun, Westerly, RI

Lionts, Ira J (217) 675-2461
PUB, ED, Franklin Times, Franklin, IL

Lipack, Mike (212) 210-2100
Deputy DIR-Photography
New York Daily News, New York, NY

Lipe, Brad A (603) 332-2300
PUB, Rochester Times, Rochester, NH

Lipez, John (717) 923-1500
GM, Record, Renovo, PA

Lipinski, Ann Marie (312) 222-3232
MAN ED, Chicago Tribune, Chicago, IL

Lipker, Roger (970) 686-9646
PUB, Windsor Beacon, Windsor, CO

Lipker, Ruth (970) 686-9646
GM, Windsor Beacon, Windsor, CO

Lipman, Harvy (518) 454-5694
State ED, Times Union, Albany, NY

Lipman, Joann (212) 416-2000
Weekend ED
Wall Street Journal, New York, NY

Lipman, Larry (561) 820-4100
BU Chief-Washington
Palm Beach Post, West Palm Beach, FL

Lipp, Heather (616) 964-7161
DIR-MKTG SRV
Battle Creek Enquirer, Battle Creek, MI

Lippman, Darrell (213) 229-5300
ED, Daily Commerce, Los Angeles, CA

Lippman, Jerome W (212) 244-4949
PUB, Jewish Sentinel, New York, NY

Lippman, Naomi W (212) 244-4949
PUB, Jewish Sentinel, New York, NY

Lippman, Robert A (203) 406-2406
PUB, Fairfield County Weekly, Stamford, CT

Lippus, Mike (419) 625-5500
PROD FRM-MR
Sandusky Register, Sandusky, OH

Lipschutz, Neal (212) 416-2414
Deputy MAN ED, Dow Jones Financial News Services, New York, NY

Lipscomb, Most Rev Oscar H (334) 432-3529
PUB, Catholic Week, Mobile, AL

Lipsey, Jeff (601) 328-2424
DIR-OPER, PROD SUPT
Commercial Dispatch, Columbus, MS

Lipsey, Stanford (716) 849-3434
PRES, PUB, Buffalo News, Buffalo, NY

Lipsky, Seth (212) 889-8200
PUB, ED, Forward, New York, NY

Lipson, Jim (702) 788-6200
ADV MGR-RT
Reno Gazette-Journal, Reno, NV

Lipson, Larry (818) 713-3000
Restaurant Critic
Daily News, Woodland Hills, CA

Liptak, Adam (413) 562-4181
CIRC MGR, Evening News, Westfield, MA

Liptak, Cynthia J (815) 433-2000
CIRC DIR, Daily Times, Ottawa, IL

Liput, Joyce (847) 669-5621
ED, Huntley Farmside, Huntley, IL

Lira, Linda (520) 363-5554
GM, Superior Sun, Superior, AZ

LiRon, Sam (707) 643-1706
CIRC MGR, Benicia Herald, Vallejo, CA

Lishchyna, Leonid (416) 255-8604
ED, Moloda Ukraina, Toronto, ON

Liskai, Brian (419) 335-2010
ED, Expositor, Wauseon, OH

Lisowski, Peter (913) 899-2338
ED, Goodland Daily News, Goodland, KS

Lissauer, Michael (415) 986-4422
VP-MKTG & Creative Services
Business Wire, San Francisco, CA

Lisser, Robert J (608) 754-3311
VP/CFO
Bliss Communications Inc., Janesville, WI

Lisser, William (507) 285-7600
CIRC DIR, Post-Bulletin, Rochester, MN

List, Randy (618) 532-5604
Sports ED, Centralia Sentinel, Centralia, IL

List, Randy (765) 362-1200
ADV MGR-GEN, ADV DIR-Sales/MKTG
Journal Review, Crawfordsville, IN

Lister, Letitia (605) 642-2761
ADV MGR, Black Hills Pioneer, Spearfish, SD

Lister, Scott (605) 642-2761
PROD MGR
Black Hills Pioneer, Spearfish, SD

Liston, Lance (219) 461-8222
CIRC MGR-Single Copy Sales
News-Sentinel, Fort Wayne, IN

Liston, Roz (718) 229-0300
MAN ED, Bayside Times, Bayside, NY

Litchy, Alan (406) 755-7000
ADV DIR, Daily Inter Lake, Kalispell, MT

Lite, Dave (562) 435-1161
ADV MGR-RT
Press-Telegram, Long Beach, CA

Litowchak, Richard A (813) 849-7500
PUB, GM
Suncoast News, New Port Richey, FL

Litt, Larry (212) 614-1591
ED, Humornet, New York, NY

Litten, Allen (540) 574-6200
Photo/Graphics DEPT MGR
Daily News-Record, Harrisonburg, VA

Litterski, Pete (903) 757-3311
ED, Longview News-Journal, Longview, TX

Little, Bruce (207) 364-7893
GM, MAN ED
Rumford Falls Times, Rumford, ME

Little, David (320) 235-1150
Farm ED, West Central Tribune, Willmar, MN

Little, David (916) 243-2424
City ED, Record Searchlight, Redding, CA

Little, Greg (406) 653-2222
ED, Herald-News, Wolf Point, MT

Little, Jim (805) 643-5952
ED, Ventura Independent, Ventura, CA

Little, Jim (719) 783-2361
PUB, ED
Wet Mountain Tribune, Westcliffe, CO

Little, Lewis A (520) 432-8003
ED, Little, Lew Enterprises Inc., Bisbee, AZ

Little, Loyd (919) 726-7081
MAN ED, Carteret County News-Times, Morehead City, NC

Little, Patty (704) 837-5122
ED, Cherokee Scout, Murphy, NC

Little, R Fletcher (541) 485-1234
VP, GM, Register-Guard, Eugene, OR

Little, Scott (916) 885-5656
PUB/PRES, Auburn Journal, Auburn, CA

Little, Sybil (810) 332-8181
Fashion/Food ED, Oakland Press, Pontiac, MI

Lit Who's Where-138

Littlefair, John (801) 237-2800
PROD GEN FRM-PR
Newspaper Agency Corp., Salt Lake City, UT
Littlefield, Charlsea (817) 246-2473
MAN ED, White Settlement Bomber News, Fort Worth, TX
Littlefield, Robin (706) 549-9523
MAN ED, Flagpole Magazine, Athens, GA
Littlefield, Sue (207) 784-5411
Society ED, Sun-Journal, Lewiston, ME
Littlefield, Thomas (508) 458-7100
ADV MGR-CLASS, Sun, Lowell, MA
Littlejohn, Jeff (618) 463-2500
ADV DIR, Telegraph, Alton, IL
Littlemore Jr, Robert (613) 829-9100
CIRC MGR-Reader Sales & SRV-ADM
Ottawa Citizen, Ottawa, ON
Littlepage, Ron (904) 359-4111
COL, Florida Times-Union, Jacksonville, FL
Littlepaige, Maggie (812) 231-4200
CIRC MGR-Home Delivery
Tribune-Star, Terre Haute, IN
Littler, Janet (614) 773-2111
ADV MGR-Sales, Gazette, Chillicothe, OH
Littler Jr, W E (515) 742-3241
ED, Adair News, Adair, IA
Littler III, W E (515) 742-3241
PUB, Adair News, Adair, IA
Littler, William (416) 367-2000
Music Writer, Toronto Star, Toronto, ON
Littleton, Patty (503) 399-6611
PROD MGR-PROD SRV
Statesman Journal, Salem, OR
Littlewood, Sheila (905) 835-2411
PUB, Port Colborne News, Port Colborne, ON
Litton, MaryAnn (219) 726-8141
Society ED, Commercial Review, Portland, IN
Litton, Sharon (609) 272-7450
GM, Current, Pleasantville, NJ
Littwin, Mike (410) 332-6000
COL-Features, Sun, Baltimore, MD
Litwicki, Jim (573) 887-3636
GM, Scott County Signal, Chaffee, MO
Litzinger, Jim (701) 780-1100
PROD MGR-MR
Grand Forks Herald, Grand Forks, ND
Liu, George (206) 223-0623
GM, Northwest Asian Weekly, Seattle, WA
Liu, K K (808) 536-6883
ED, United Chinese Press, Honolulu, HI
Liu, Tally (305) 376-3800
VP-FIN & ADM
Knight-Ridder Inc., Miami, FL
Liuzzo, Joe R (716) 487-1111
Photo DEPT MGR
Post-Journal, Jamestown, NY
Lively, Russell (423) 756-6900
BM, DP MGR
Chattanooga Free Press, Chattanooga, TN
Livengood, Hilery (319) 398-8211
Interactive Media ED
Gazette, Cedar Rapids, IA
Livermore Sr, E K (405) 341-2121
COB, Livermore Newspapers, Edmond, OK
Livermore Jr, E K (405) 341-2121
PRES, Livermore Newspapers, Edmond, OK
Livermore, Marcia H (405) 341-2121
TREAS, CONT
Edmond Evening Sun, Edmond, OK
Livermore, Melba H (405) 341-2121
VP, Edmond Evening Sun, Edmond, OK
Livingston, Dean B (803) 533-5500
PUB, Times and Democrat, Orangeburg, SC
Livingston, Grover D (214) 977-8222
VP-INFO MGT
Dallas Morning News, Dallas, TX
Livingston Jr, Horace G (217) 423-2231
PUB, African-American Voice, Decatur, IL
Livingston, Leo (217) 423-2231
ED, African-American Voice, Decatur, IL
Livingston, Milt (334) 262-1611
ADV MGR-NTL
Montgomery Advertiser, Montgomery, AL
Livingston, Pat (519) 528-2822
ED, Lucknow Sentinel, Lucknow, ON
Livingston, Thad (402) 462-2131
News ED, Hastings Tribune, Hastings, NE
Livingston, Theresa (913) 325-2219
GM
Washington County News, Washington, KS
Lix, Doug (306) 692-6441
PROD MGR
Moose Jaw Times-Herald, Moose Jaw, SK
Lizotte, Bernard (514) 521-4545
ADTX MGR-Technical
Le Journal de Montreal, Montreal, QC
Lizotte, Tom (207) 564-8355
MAN ED
Piscataquis Observer, Dover-Foxcroft, ME

Llavona, Odalys (305) 377-3721
CIRC DIR
Miami Daily Business Review, Miami, FL
Llebelt, David (414) 457-7711
ADV DIR, Sheboygan Press, Sheboygan, WI
Llewellyn, James (800) 760-3100
Features ED/Chicago
Williams Syndications Inc., Holiday, FL
Llewellyn, William (423) 523-3131
PROD OPER SUPT-MR
Knoxville News-Sentinel, Knoxville, TN
Lloyd, Bob (315) 470-0011
ASST MAN ED, Post-Standard/Syracuse Herald-Journal/American, Syracuse, NY
Lloyd, C Sherry (912) 496-3585
GM, Charlton County Herald, Folkston, GA
Lloyd, Charles (501) 271-3700
PROD MGR
Benton County Daily Record, Bentonville, AR
Lloyd, Erwin (573) 379-5355
PUB, ED
Missourian-Review, Portageville, MO
Lloyd, Gary (205) 353-4612
Photo DEPT ED, Decatur Daily, Decatur, AL
Lloyd, Jim (520) 927-5402
PUB, ED, Gem, Quartzsite, AZ
Lloyd, Lem (612) 222-5011
ADTX/Online MGR
St. Paul Pioneer Press, St. Paul, MN
Lloyd, Michael S (616) 222-5400
ED, Grand Rapids Press, Grand Rapids, MI
Lloyd, Roger (304) 235-4242
PROD FRM-PR
Williamson Daily News, Williamson, WV
Lloyd, Sue Doty (717) 296-6641
PUB, ED, Pike County Dispatch, Milford, PA
Lloyd, Wanda (864) 298-4100
MAN ED-Features/ADM/Planning
Greenville News, Greenville, SC
Lo, Babacar (212) 286-0123
Technical ENG
Inter Press Service, New York, NY
Lo, John (212) 334-2061
ED, Herald Monthly, New York, NY
Loader, Fred (705) 759-3030
EPE, Sault Star, Sault Ste. Marie, ON
Lobaco, Julia (305) 442-2462
ED, Vista - The Hispanic Magazine, Coral Gables, FL
Lobanov, Igor (619) 483-3412
Travel ED
Mature Life Features, San Diego, CA
Lobas, James M (414) 435-4411
ADV DIR
Green Bay Press-Gazette, Green Bay, WI
Lobash, Michael (414) 457-7711
EDU ED, Sheboygan Press, Sheboygan, WI
Lobaugh, Charles T (937) 335-5634
TREAS, CFO, DIR-SYS/Technology, Troy Daily News/Miami Valley Sunday News, Troy, OH
Lobdell, Richard (603) 543-3100
PROD FRM-PR, Eagle Times, Claremont, NH
Lobdell, William S (714) 642-4321
ED, Daily Pilot, Costa Mesa, CA
Lobeck, Linda (906) 774-2772
BUS/FIN ED, Daily News, Iron Mountain, MI
Lobecker, William B (215) 345-3000
CIRC DIR
Intelligencer/Record, Doylestown, PA
Lobner, Diana (713) 592-2626
PUB, Cleveland Advocate, Cleveland, TX
Lobsinger, Robert W (405) 362-2140
PUB, ED
Newkirk Herald Journal, Newkirk, OK
Lobsinger, Susan M (405) 362-2140
MAN ED
Newkirk Herald Journal, Newkirk, OK
Locher, Barry J (217) 788-1300
MAN ED
State Journal-Register, Springfield, IL
Locher, Mark (215) 855-8440
Graphics ED/Art DIR
Reporter, Lansdale, PA
Locher, Paul (330) 264-1125
EDU ED, Daily Record, Wooster, OH
Locher, Richard (312) 222-3232
Cartoonist, Chicago Tribune, Chicago, IL
Lochridge, Lisa (407) 420-5000
Seminole County ED
Orlando Sentinel, Orlando, FL
Lochridge, Mick (407) 420-5000
Lifestyle ED
Orlando Sentinel, Orlando, FL
Locke, Deborah (612) 222-5011
EDL Writer
St. Paul Pioneer Press, St. Paul, MN
Locke, Leon S (718) 634-4000
PUB
Wave of Long Island, Rockaway Beach, NY
Locke, Margot (413) 667-3211
PUB, ED, Country Journal, Huntington, MA
Locke, Raymond (319) 352-3334
ED, Bremer County Independent, Waverly, IA

Locke, Sara Jane (423) 745-5664
ADV DIR, Daily Post-Athenian, Athens, TN
Lockett, Cheryl (606) 723-5161
GM, Citizen Voice & Times, Irvine, KY
Lockett, Julie (501) 741-2325
Graphics ED/Art DIR, PROD MGR-COMP
Harrison Daily Times, Harrison, AR
Lockhart, Gary (910) 625-2101
CIRC DIR, Courier-Tribune, Asheboro, NC
Lockhart, Jim (941) 262-3161
BUS ED, Naples Daily News, Naples, FL
Lockhart, Larry (319) 754-8461
Radio/Television ED
Hawk Eye, Burlington, IA
Lockhart, Lee (307) 347-3241
PRES, TREAS, PUB
Northern Wyoming Daily News, Worland, WY
Lockhart, Mary (908) 464-1025
GM, Independent Press, New Providence, NJ
Lockhart, Niki (606) 248-1010
News ED, Daily News, Middlesboro, KY
Lockhart, Susan (307) 347-3241
Special Projects ED
Northern Wyoming Daily News, Worland, WY
Locklear, David (405) 535-2166
GM, Granite Enterprise, Granite, OK
Locklear, Jan (405) 535-2166
MAN ED, Granite Enterprise, Granite, OK
Locklear, Patti (405) 535-2166
PUB, Granite Enterprise, Granite, OK
Locklear, Tena Hahn (405) 535-2166
ED, Granite Enterprise, Granite, OK
Locklin, Steve (802) 863-3441
Sports ED, Free Press, Burlington, VT
Locksley, Lila (212) 556-1927
ASSOC ED
New York Times News Service, New York, NY
Lockwood, Allison (970) 669-5050
MGR-MKTG/PROM
Loveland Daily Reporter-Herald, Loveland, CO
Lockwood, Everett (405) 765-3311
ADV MGR, Ponca City News, Ponca City, OK
Lockwood, James (608) 328-4202
Photo ED, Monroe Times, Monroe, WI
Lockwood, Robert P (219) 356-8400
PUB, Our Sunday Visitor, Huntington, IN
Lockwood, Rod (937) 328-0300
ASST City ED
Springfield News-Sun, Springfield, OH
Locorriere, Judith (201) 653-1000
ED, Jersey Journal, Jersey City, NJ
Lodge, Richard (508) 369-2800
ED, Lexington Minuteman, Concord, MA
Lodi, Rus (508) 626-3800
MAN ED, News ED
Middlesex News, Framingham, MA
Lodl, Kathy (402) 654-2218
GM, ED, Rustler Sentinel, Hooper, NE
Lodovic, Joseph (717) 854-1575
EVP/CFO
York Dispatch/York Sunday News, York, PA
Lodwick, Gary (204) 723-2542
PUB, ED, Times, Treherne, MB
Loeb, Nackey S (603) 668-4321
PRES/PUB, Union Leader, Manchester, NH
Loebach, J L (519) 679-6666
VP/GM, London Free Press, London, ON
Loeffel, Joyce (719) 539-6691
CIRC MGR, Mountain Mail, Salida, CO
Loerzel, Robert (847) 381-9200
ED, Palatine Countryside, Barrington, IL
Loesch, Anne (907) 772-9393
PUB, Petersburg Pilot, Petersburg, AK
Loesch, Jerry (907) 586-3740
PROD FRM-PR, Juneau Empire, Juneau, AK
Loesch, Ronald J (907) 772-9393
PUB, ED, Petersburg Pilot, Petersburg, AK
Loescher, Ed (562) 698-0955
ADV MGR-RT
Whittier Daily News, Whittier, CA
Loeschner, Bob (217) 935-3171
ED, Clinton Daily Journal, Clinton, IL
Loevy, Diana B (212) 293-8500
VP/EDL DIR, United Media, United Feature Syndicate, Newspaper Enterprise Association, New York, NY
Lofaro, Joe (901) 587-3144
MAN ED, Weakley County Press, Martin, TN
Lofgren, Lavonne (605) 823-4490
PUB, Corson County News, McLaughlin, SD
Lofgren, Merle E (605) 823-4490
ED, Corson County News, McLaughlin, SD
Lofgren, Myron L (605) 466-2258
PUB, Isabel Dakotan, Isabel, SD
Lofgren, Sarah A (605) 466-2258
ED, Isabel Dakotan, Isabel, SD
Lofholm, Nancy (970) 242-5050
Health/Medical ED
Daily Sentinel, Grand Junction, CO
Loft, Kurt (813) 259-7711
Records ED-Classical, SCI Writer
Tampa Tribune and Times, Tampa, FL
Loftin, Darrell W (805) 736-2313
EVP/CFO, Lompoc Record, Lompoc, CA

Loftin, Marsha (318) 932-4201
PUB, ED, Coushatta Citizen, Coushatta, LA
Loftin, Michael (423) 756-1234
EPE, Chattanooga Times, Chattanooga, TN
Loftis Jr, D E (804) 374-2451
ED, News-Progress, Clarksville, VA
Loftis, Jack (713) 220-7171
EVP/ED, Houston Chronicle, Houston, TX
Loftis, Randy (214) 977-8222
Environmental Writer
Dallas Morning News, Dallas, TX
Loftis, Scott (501) 534-3400
Sports ED
Pine Bluff Commercial, Pine Bluff, AR
Loftus, Bill (208) 743-9411
Outdoors ED
Lewiston Morning Tribune, Lewiston, ID
Loftus, Gary (308) 382-1000
ADV MGR
Grand Island Independent, Grand Island, NE
Loftus, George (501) 271-3700
CIRC MGR
Benton County Daily Record, Bentonville, AR
Logan, Brian (317) 348-0110
News ED, News-Times, Hartford City, IN
Logan, Cathy (918) 581-8300
Entertainment ED, Tulsa World, Tulsa, OK
Logan, D (807) 274-5373
ADV MGR
Fort Frances Daily Bulletin, Fort Frances, ON
Logan, David (416) 461-0871
GM, NOW, Toronto, ON
Logan, Harry (803) 771-6161
Deputy MAN ED, State, Columbia, SC
Logan, Nicki (806) 296-1300
Lifestyle ED
Plainview Daily Herald, Plainview, TX
Logan, Pat (519) 537-2341
PUB/GM, Sentinel-Review, Woodstock, ON
Logan, Paul (505) 823-7777
Religion ED
Albuquerque Journal, Albuquerque, NM
Logan, Richard (330) 747-1471
News ED, Vindicator, Youngstown, OH
Logan, Samuel (313) 963-5522
PUB, GM, Michigan Chronicle, Detroit, MI
Logback, James (913) 674-5700
ED, Hill City Times, Hill City, KS
Logsdon, Diane (309) 829-9411
Librarian, Pantagraph, Bloomington, IL
Logsdon, Mark (304) 526-4000
ADV DIR, ADV MGR-NTL
Herald-Dispatch, Huntington, WV
Logue, Ann Pell (218) 281-2730
ADV MGR
Crookston Daily Times, Crookston, MN
Lohman, John (701) 253-7311
ASSOC ED, Forum, Fargo, ND
Lohman, Wayne (317) 459-3121
PUB/GM, Kokomo Tribune, Kokomo, IN
Lohmeyer, Dick (410) 641-4561
PUB, Maryland Coast-Dispatch, Berlin, MD
Lohr, Lilah (305) 377-3721
EX ED
Miami Daily Business Review, Miami, FL
Lohr, Sandra (609) 989-5454
ADV DIR, Times, Trenton, NJ
Lohrenz, Randy (217) 245-6121
ADV DIR
Jacksonville Journal-Courier, Jacksonville, IL
Loignon, Pierre (514) 285-7272
Desk ED (Evening), La Presse, Montreal, QC
Lokeman, Rhonda (816) 234-4141
Op-Ed ED/EPE
Kansas City Star, Kansas City, MO
Loker, Elizabeth (202) 334-6000
VP-Engineering, VP-SYS/Engineering
Washington Post, Washington, DC
Lokey, Ann L (415) 986-4422
CORP SEC
Business Wire, San Francisco, CA
Lokey, Lorry I (415) 986-4422
PRES, Business Wire, San Francisco, CA
Lokey, Ray (405) 371-2356
PUB, ED, Johnston County Capital-Democrat, Tishomingo, OK
Lollis, Dean (864) 223-1411
News ED, Index-Journal, Greenwood, SC
Loman, Cindy (910) 373-7000
News ED, News & Record, Greensboro, NC
Lomas, Gord (705) 687-2259
PUB, Gravenhurst News, Gravenhurst, ON
Lomax, Debbie (305) 350-2111
PROD ASST MGR-Ad PROD
Miami Herald, Miami, FL
Lombardi, Bob (303) 660-2360
PUB, ED, Parker Trail, Castle Rock, CO
Lombardi, Gail (207) 474-0606
PUB, ED, Somerset Gazette, Skowhegan, ME
Lombardi, Rita (914) 454-2000
MGR-Office
Poughkeepsie Journal, Poughkeepsie, NY
Lombardo, Antonio (314) 638-3446
PUB, GM, Il Pensiero, St. Louis, MO

139-Who's Where **Low**

Lombardo, Barbara .... (518) 584-4242
MAN ED, Saratogian, Saratoga Springs, NY
Lombardo, L .... (314) 638-3446
MAN ED, Il Pensiero, St. Louis, MO
Lombardo, Lisa .... (610) 630-6200
ED, Post, Norristown, PA
Lombardo, Tom .... (212) 556-1234
PROD Group DIR/Plant MGR-College Point
New York Times, New York, NY
Lombardo, Tony .... (215) 625-8501
GM, Philadelphia Gay News, Philadelphia, PA
Lomenick, Rick .... (405) 482-1221
ED, Altus Times, Altus, OK
Lomenzo, Jim .... (213) 237-5485
Sales EX/East & Ohio, Los Angeles Times
Syndicate, Los Angeles, CA
Lomicky, Bob .... (914) 677-8241
ED, Harlem Valley Times, Millbrook, NY
LoMonte, Frank .... (404) 589-8424
BU Chief, Morris News Service, Atlanta, GA
Lomoriella, Gene .... (914) 677-8241
MAN ED, Voice-Ledger, Millbrook, NY
Loncki, Gary C .... (814) 824-1160
MAN ED, Lake Shore Visitor, Erie, PA
London, Paul E .... (320) 235-1150
EVP, PUB/GM, EPE
West Central Tribune, Willmar, MN
Londre, Larry .... (818) 282-5707
GM, San Marino Tribune, San Marino, CA
Loney, Bretton .... (709) 364-6300
News ED, Evening Telegram, St. John's, NF
Loney, Warren .... (717) 421-3000
PROD Technician-SYS
Pocono Record, Stroudsburg, PA
Long, Bill .... (303) 442-1202
BUS ED, FIN ED, Daily Camera, Boulder, CO
Long, Brian J .... (413) 788-1000
GM, Union-News, Springfield, MA
Long, Brian L .... (814) 532-5199
ADV DIR, Tribune-Democrat, Johnstown, PA
Long, Chris .... (423) 837-6312
GM
South Pittsburg Hustler, South Pittsburg, TN
Long, Dave .... (219) 722-5000
ED, Pharos-Tribune, Logansport, IN
Long, David .... (219) 294-1661
CIRC MGR, Elkhart Truth, Elkhart, IN
Long, David .... (409) 833-3311
City ED, Beaumont Enterprise, Beaumont, TX
Long, Donna .... (507) 285-7600
ADV MGR-CLASS
Post-Bulletin, Rochester, MN
Long, Fred .... (304) 466-0005
PUB, ED, Hinton News, Hinton, WV
Long, Janet .... (941) 434-5555
ASST, Strategist, Naples, FL
Long, Jim .... (360) 584-8080
PUB, Lakewood Journal, Tacoma, WA
Long, Joe .... (507) 285-7600
PROD MGR-Pre Press
Post-Bulletin, Rochester, MN
Long, John .... (937) 372-4444
PROD FRM-COMP
Xenia Daily Gazette, Xenia, OH
Long, Karen .... (813) 259-7711
Travel ED
Tampa Tribune and Times, Tampa, FL
Long, Kenneth H .... (512) 255-5827
PUB, Round Rock Leader, Round Rock, TX
Long, Kenneth J .... (609) 871-8000
CONT, Burlington County Times, Willingboro,
NJ, Calkins Newspapers
Long, Kenneth W .... (417) 876-3841
ED, El Dorado Springs Sun, El Dorado
Springs, MO
Long, Kimball S .... (417) 876-3841
PUB, El Dorado Springs Sun, El Dorado
Springs, MO
Long, Laverne .... (519) 343-2440
PUB, Palmerston Observer, Palmerston, ON
Long, Leon .... (508) 997-7411
CIRC MGR-Sales
Standard Times, New Bedford, MA
Long, Linda .... (503) 325-3211
CIRC MGR, Daily Astorian, Astoria, OR
Long, Lorna .... (219) 294-1661
PROD MGR-MR, Elkhart Truth, Elkhart, IN
Long, Nancy .... (314) 340-8000
MGR-Public Relations
St. Louis Post-Dispatch, St. Louis, MO
Long, Pam .... (334) 433-1551
Religion ED
Mobile Press Register, Mobile, AL
Long, Phil .... (609) 663-6000
PROD MGR-MR, Courier-Post, Cherry Hill, NJ
Long, Rob .... (615) 728-7577
ED, Manchester Times, Manchester, TN
Long, Robert .... (603) 668-4321
MGR-CR, Union Leader, Manchester, NH
Long, Robert M .... (216) 999-4500
EX VP, Plain Dealer, Cleveland, OH
Long, Ruth Anne .... (219) 267-3111
Features/Food ED, Living/Lifestyle ED,
Women's ED, Times-Union, Warsaw, IN
Long, Sandra .... (215) 854-2000
ASST MAN ED
Philadelphia Inquirer, Philadelphia, PA
Long, Sara .... (206) 597-8742
DIR-MKTG, News Tribune, Tacoma, WA
Long, Steven .... (330) 364-5577
EPE, Times Reporter, New Philadelphia, OH
Long, Sue A .... (706) 884-7311
MGR-PROM
La Grange Daily News, La Grange, GA
Long, William B .... (609) 845-3300
ED
Gloucester County Times, Woodbury, NJ
Longacre, Donald J .... (847) 427-4300
ADV MGR-CLASS
Daily Herald, Arlington Heights, IL
Longcope, Kay .... (512) 476-0576
PUB, ED, Texas Triangle, Austin, TX
Longman, Ellen West .... (712) 374-2251
PUB, GM, MAN ED
Sidney Argus-Herald, Sidney, IA
Longnus, Pierre .... (604) 730-9575
ED, Le Soleil de Colombie, Vancouver, BC
Longwill, Lynn .... (905) 526-3333
DIR-MKTG, Spectator, Hamilton, ON
Longwood, Denise .... (916) 321-1000
DIR-Human Resources
Sacramento Bee, Sacramento, CA
Lonkevich, Susan .... (215) 949-4000
EDU Writer
Bucks County Courier Times, Levittown, PA
Lonsdale, Jim .... (918) 473-2313
PUB
McIntosh County Democrat, Checotah, OK
Loock, Steve .... (941) 629-2855
PROD SUPT-PR
Sun Herald, Port Charlotte, FL
Looman, Ed .... (216) 994-3241
PUB, Star-Beacon, Ashtabula, OH
Loomis, Greg .... (419) 352-4611
PROD FRM-PR
Sentinel-Tribune, Bowling Green, OH
Loomis, Jay .... (205) 353-4612
BUS ED, Environmental ED, SCI/Technology
ED, Decatur Daily, Decatur, AL
Loomis, Lisa A .... (802) 496-3928
MAN ED, Valley Reporter, Waitsfield, VT
Loomis, Robert .... (619) 232-4381
GM
San Diego Daily Transcript, San Diego, CA
Looney, Ernest .... (501) 862-6611
PROD MGR
El Dorado News-Times, El Dorado, AR
Looney, Gus .... (501) 836-8192
PROD SUPT, Camden News, Camden, AR
Loose, James A .... (717) 291-8811
BUS ED, Lancaster Intelligencer Journal/New
Era/Sunday News, Lancaster, PA
Loper, Charles .... (219) 726-8141
PROD FRM-PR
Commercial Review, Portland, IN
Loper, Mary Lou .... (213) 237-5000
Writer-The Social City
Los Angeles Times, Los Angeles, CA
Lopes, Carlos .... (203) 744-5100
PROD FRM-MR (Night)
News-Times, Danbury, CT
Lopes, Jane .... (617) 947-1760
ED, Middleboro Gazette, Middleboro, MA
Lopes, Paul R .... (508) 758-9055
PUB, Wanderer, Mattapoisett, MA
Lopez, Aaron G .... (610) 789-5512
PUB, MAN ED, El Hispano, Upper Darby, PA
Lopez, Brandon .... (310) 230-3400
Picture Desk ED, Allsport Photography USA,
Pacific Palisades, CA
Lopez, Diane .... (209) 835-3030
ADV MGR, Tracy Press, Tracy, CA
Lopez, Elena .... (561) 287-1550
DIR-MKTG/PROM, Stuart News, Stuart, FL
Lopez, Elida .... (817) 626-8624
GM, El Informador Hispano, Fort Worth, TX
Lopez, Gerardo .... (213) 622-8332
ASSOC ED, La Opinion, Los Angeles, CA
Lopez, Joe .... (573) 756-8927
ADV DIR-MKTG
Daily Press Leader, Farmington, MO
Lopez, Kristi .... (502) 863-1111
ED
Georgetown News-Graphic, Georgetown, KY
Lopez, Larry .... (719) 544-3520
City ED, Pueblo Chieftain, Pueblo, CO
Lopez, Manuel .... (508) 775-1200
Graphics ED, Cape Cod Times, Hyannis, MA
Lopez, Pia .... (320) 255-8700
EPE, St. Cloud Times, St. Cloud, MN
Lopez, Richard .... (714) 835-1234
PROD DIR-PR
Orange County Register, Santa Ana, CA
Lopez, Sammy M .... (505) 887-5501
PUB, Current-Argus, Carlsbad, NM
Lopez, Sara .... (610) 789-5512
ED, El Hispano, Upper Darby, PA
Lopez, Sonny .... (915) 546-6340
EDU ED, El Paso Herald-Post, El Paso, TX
Lopez, Steve .... (215) 854-2000
COL
Philadelphia Inquirer, Philadelphia, PA
Lopiccolo, Ginny .... (803) 771-6161
DIR-NIE, State, Columbia, SC
LoPilato, Joseph J .... (617) 426-3000
ADV MGR-CLASS
Boston Herald, Boston, MA
Lopushinsky, Bonni .... (403) 468-0100
MGR-PROM, Edmonton Sun, Edmonton, AB
Loran, Tom .... (306) 652-9200
Outdoors ED, StarPhoenix, Saskatoon, SK
Loranger, Claude .... (819) 379-1490
ED, L'Hebdo Cap-de-La-Madeleine et Trois-
Rivieres, Cap de la Madeleine, QC
Lorberter, Daryl .... (715) 833-9200
PROD MGR, Leader-Telegram, Eau Claire, WI
Lord, Craig .... (310) 230-3400
Picture Desk ED, Allsport Photography USA,
Pacific Palisades, CA
Lord, David R .... (206) 284-4424
PRES, Pioneer Newspapers, Seattle, WA
Lord, Debbie .... (904) 863-1111
MAN ED, Women's ED, Northwest Florida
Daily News, Fort Walton Beach, FL
Lord, Jane P .... (207) 791-6650
Arts/Books ED, Entertainment/Amusements
ED, Living/Lifestyle ED, Music ED, Radio/
Television ED
Portland Press Herald, Portland, ME
Lord, Katie .... (415) 883-8600
DIR-MKTG/PROM
Marin Independent Journal, Novato, CA
Lord, Peter .... (401) 277-7000
Environmental Writer
Providence Journal-Bulletin, Providence, RI
Lord, Philip .... (803) 648-2311
Entertainment/Society ED, Sunday Morning
ED, Aiken Standard, Aiken, SC
Loregio, Joe .... (908) 722-8800
PROD MGR-MR
Courier-News, Bridgewater, NJ
Lorell, Monte .... (703) 276-3400
MAN ED-Sports, Sports ED
USA Today, Arlington, VA
Lorenca, Michael J .... (908) 922-6000
ASSOC DIR-Human Resources
Asbury Park Press, Neptune, NJ
Lorenson, Maria .... (304) 263-8931
ED, EPE, Journal, Martinsburg, WV
Lorenz, Paul .... (618) 242-0117
City ED, Register-News, Mount Vernon, IL
Lorenzo, Mario .... (212) 563-2252
VP, Editors Press Service Inc., New York, NY
Lorick, Jay .... (213) 237-5000
CIRC ASST to Senior VP-Consumer MKTG
Los Angeles Times, Los Angeles, CA
Lorimer, Andy .... (403) 998-7070
PUB, ED, Record, Fort Saskatchewan, AB
Loring, Elaine .... (515) 648-2521
MAN ED, Times-Citizen, Iowa Falls, IA
Lorsung, Thomas N .... (202) 541-3250
DIR/EIC
Catholic News Services, Washington, DC
Lorton, Robert E .... (918) 581-8300
COB, PUB, Tulsa World, Tulsa, OK
Lorton III, Robert E .... (918) 581-8300
VP-ADM/OPER, PROD VP-OPER
Tulsa World, Tulsa, OK
Lorton, William .... (309) 772-2129
PUB, ED
McDonough-Democrat, Bushnell, IL
Lortz, Merle .... (417) 673-2421
PUB, Webb City Sentinel/Wise Buyer, Webb
City, MO
LoScalzo, Mary Beth .... (412) 981-6100
CNR-EDU SRV, Herald, Sharon, PA
Losing, Rob .... (403) 468-0100
Online MGR, DP MGR/RES Analyst
Edmonton Sun, Edmonton, AB
Losness, Jon .... (507) 285-7600
MAN ED, Post-Bulletin, Rochester, MN
Lostrom, Martha M .... (207) 768-5431
ED
Presque Isle Star-Herald, Presque Isle, ME
Lott, Bob .... (817) 757-5757
ED, Waco Tribune-Herald, Waco, TX
Lott, Lori .... (515) 465-4666
GM, Perry Chief, Perry, IA
Louchheim, Donald H .... (516) 283-4100
PUB, Southampton Press, Southampton, NY
Loudermilk, Brigette .... (912) 923-6432
BUS/FIN ED, Features ED, News ED, Special
Sections ED, Daily Sun, Warner Robins, GA
Lougee, Kevin .... (603) 352-1234
CIRC ASST MGR
Keene Sentinel, Keene, NH
Lough, Larry .... (317) 747-5700
ED, COL, Star Press, Muncie, IN
Loumena, Jennine .... (510) 734-8600
ADV DIR, Tri-Valley Herald, Pleasanton, CA
Lound, Richard .... (616) 894-5356
PUB, White Lake Beacon, Whitehall, MI
Lourens, Karen .... (618) 375-3131
ED, Mercury-Independent, Grayville, IL
Louwsma, Robert .... (562) 435-1161
PROD ASST-PR
Press-Telegram, Long Beach, CA
Loux, Sharon .... (317) 482-4650
ADV DIR, Reporter, Lebanon, IN
Lovato, Sam .... (510) 783-6111
Telecommunications MGR
Daily Review, Hayward, CA
MediaNews Inc. (Alameda Newspapers)
Love, Beryl .... (319) 383-2200
News ED, Quad-City Times, Davenport, IA
Love, Charles .... (502) 769-2312
PROD Press Team Leader
News Enterprise, Elizabethtown, KY
Love, Ian .... (202) 898-8254
Sports ED
United Press International, Washington, DC
Love, Keith .... (509) 925-1414
PUB, EPE, Political ED
Daily Record, Ellensburg, WA
Love, Orlan .... (319) 398-8211
Outdoors ED, Gazette, Cedar Rapids, IA
Love, Susan .... (818) 713-3000
LA Life ED, Daily News, Woodland Hills, CA
Love, Tom .... (913) 242-4700
SEC/TREAS, ADV DIR
Ottawa Herald, Ottawa, KS
Lovejoy, Andrea .... (706) 884-7311
ED, City ED
La Grange Daily News, La Grange, GA
Lovejoy, Bill .... (408) 423-4242
Photo ED
Santa Cruz County Sentinel, Santa Cruz, CA
Lovejoy, Steven T .... (414) 634-3322
News ED, Journal Times, Racine, WI
Lovelace, Jack .... (913) 381-1010
ED, Sun Newspapers, Overland Park, KS
Lovell, Bill .... (954) 698-6501
ED, Sunrise Times, Deerfield Beach, FL
Lovell, John .... (207) 781-3661
ED, Forecaster, Falmouth, ME
Lovell, Michael .... (214) 969-0000
SEC
Texas Sunday Comic Section Inc., Dallas, TX
Lovely, Randy .... (941) 335-0200
Graphic Arts ED, News-Press, Fort Myers, FL
Lovern, Carl .... (609) 663-6000
DIR-MKTG, Courier-Post, Cherry Hill, NJ
Lovestone, Lon .... (709) 364-6300
CIRC MGR, Evening Telegram, St. John's, NF
Lovestone, Ron .... (604) 832-2131
PUB
Shuswap Market News, Salmon Arm, BC
Lovett, Don .... (205) 353-4612
PROD FRM-COMP
Decatur Daily, Decatur, AL
Lovett, Genia .... (419) 332-5511
ADV DIR, News-Messenger, Fremont, OH
Lovett, Griffin .... (912) 272-5522
PRES, PUB, Courier Herald, Dublin, GA
Lovett, Robert .... (505) 325-4545
ADV MGR-CLASS
Daily Times, Farmington, NM
Lovewell, Harold .... (616) 845-5181
PROD MGR/FRM, Daily News, Ludington, MI
Lovik, Thomas E .... (701) 288-3531
PUB, Ashley Tribune, Ashley, ND
Lovik, Wanda L .... (701) 288-3531
PUB, Ashley Tribune, Ashley, ND
Loving, Bob .... (502) 769-2312
PROD MGR
News Enterprise, Elizabethtown, KY
Lovinger, Bob .... (508) 997-7411
Films ED, Standard Times, New Bedford, MA
Lovins, Jason .... (614) 353-1151
ED, Community Common, Portsmouth, OH
Lovinski, Frank .... (313) 222-2300
Deputy MAN ED, Detroit News, Detroit, MI
LoVullo, Lisa .... (410) 332-6000
DIR-Electronic News/INFO SRV
Sun, Baltimore, MD
Lovvorn, Joella .... (806) 385-4481
ED
Lamb County Leader News, Littlefield, TX
Low, Brent .... (801) 674-6200
DIR-FIN/OPER, Spectrum, St. George, UT
Low, K Prescott .... (617) 786-7000
BC, PUB, Patriot Ledger, Quincy, MA
Lowdermilk, Al .... (540) 667-3200
CIRC DIR, Winchester Star, Winchester, VA
Lowdermilk, Amy .... (501) 996-4494
GM, Greenwood Democrat, Greenwood, AR
Lowe, Cody .... (540) 981-3100
Religion ED, Roanoke Times, Roanoke, VA

Low Who's Where-140

Lowe, Fred .... (512) 556-6262
PUB
Lampasas Dispatch Record, Lampasas, TX

Lowe, Hal .... (909) 845-9564
ED, Community Adviser, Beaumont, CA

Lowe, Harold .... (219) 235-6161
News ED, SCI/Technology ED
South Bend Tribune, South Bend, IN

Lowe, Jack L .... (719) 384-4475
GM, PROD MGR
La Junta Tribune-Democrat, La Junta, CO

Lowe, James .... (802) 479-0191
Courier ED, Times Argus, Barre, VT

Lowe, Jim .... (512) 556-6262
ED, Dispatch Record, Lampasas, TX

Lowe, John .... (614) 439-3531
Wire ED, Daily Jeffersonian, Cambridge, OH

Lowe, John B .... (719) 384-4475
PRES, PUB
La Junta Tribune-Democrat, La Junta, CO

Lowe, Ken .... (910) 353-1171
Online MGR, ADTX MGR
Daily News, Jacksonville, NC

Lowe, Kinsey .... (213) 857-6600
News ED, Daily Variety, Los Angeles, CA

Lowe, Lorri .... (614) 272-5422
ED, Southeast Messenger, Columbus, OH

Lowe, Mark .... (415) 749-5400
CONT, Recorder, San Francisco, CA

Lowe, Mark .... (510) 208-6300
ASST City ED, Oakland Tribune, Oakland, CA

Lowe, Marshall .... (213) 299-3800
ED, Los Angeles Sentinel, Los Angeles, CA

Lowe, Mike .... (208) 522-1800
DIR-Circulation, CIRC DIR
Post Register, Idaho Falls, ID

Lowe, Norval J .... (515) 877-3951
PUB, Humeston New Era, Humeston, IA

Lowe, Teresa .... (334) 376-2325
MAN ED, Butler County News, Georgiana, AL

Lowe, Wanda .... (719) 384-4475
ED, News ED, Society ED
La Junta Tribune-Democrat, La Junta, CO

Lowell, Art .... (913) 243-2424
VP, Blade-Empire, Concordia, KS

Lowell, Brad .... (913) 243-2424
PRES, PUB, ED
Blade-Empire, Concordia, KS

Lowell, David T .... (510) 447-8700
PUB, Independent, Livermore, CA

Lowell, Jim .... (913) 243-2424
Sports ED, Blade-Empire, Concordia, KS

Lowell, Joe .... (707) 644-1141
ED, Vallejo Times-Herald, Vallejo, CA

Lower, Ronald K .... (913) 543-5242
PUB
Phillips County Review, Phillipsburg, KS

Lowery, Bruce .... (205) 236-1551
Fashion/Style ED
Anniston Star, Anniston, AL

Lowery, Steve .... (502) 348-9003
PUB, Kentucky Standard, Bardstown, KY

Lowin, Julian R .... (212) 210-2100
VP-NTL Sales
New York Daily News, New York, NY

Lowis, Larry .... (305) 674-9746
MAN ED
International News Agency, Miami Beach, FL

Lowman, John .... (512) 758-5391
MAN ED
Aransas Pass Progress, Aransas Pass, TX

Lowman, John W .... (319) 372-6421
PRES, PUB
Daily Democrat, Fort Madison, IA

Lowman, John W .... (707) 994-6444
PUB
Clear Lake Observer-American, Clearlake, CA

Lowman, Pauline L .... (803) 249-3525
PUB, Times, North Myrtle Beach, SC

Lowman, Polly .... (803) 249-3525
ED, Times, North Myrtle Beach, SC

Lowman, Robert .... (818) 713-3000
Entertainment/Book ED
Daily News, Woodland Hills, CA

Lowrey, Roberto .... (913) 243-2424
Arts/Entertainment ED
Blade-Empire, Concordia, KS

Lowrie, John R .... (605) 886-6901
VP/TREAS, Action Line ED
Watertown Public Opinion, Watertown, SD

Lowrie, Steven W .... (605) 886-6901
SEC, PUB, MGR-SYS/Office
Watertown Public Opinion, Watertown, SD

Lowry, Brian .... (213) 237-5000
Television Industry Writer
Los Angeles Times, Los Angeles, CA

Lowry, Don .... (417) 836-1100
PROD MGR-PR
Springfield News-Leader, Springfield, MO

Lowry, Doug .... (706) 549-0123
DIR-MKTG/PROM, Athens Daily News/Banner-Herald, Athens, GA

Lowry Jr, Edward E .... (334) 624-8323
PUB, ED, Watchman, Greensboro, AL

Lowry, Patrick .... (913) 371-4300
ED, Kansas City Kansan, Kansas City, KS

Lowry, Robert .... (317) 231-9200
CONT, Central Newspapers, Indianapolis, IN

Lows, Melissa .... (602) 898-6500
DIR-Human Resources, Mesa Tribune, Mesa, AZ, Thomson Newspapers

Loxton, John .... (810) 985-7171
PROD MGR-SYS
Times Herald, Port Huron, MI

Lozano Jr, Ignacio E .... (213) 622-8332
Chairman/EIC, La Opinion, Los Angeles, CA

Lozano, Jose I .... (213) 622-8332
PRES/PUB, La Opinion, Los Angeles, CA

Lozano, Monica .... (213) 622-8332
ASSOC PUB/ED, La Opinion, Los Angeles, CA

Lozoya, Alma .... (915) 546-6100
Travel/Women's ED
El Paso Times, El Paso, TX

Lubrano, Gina .... (619) 299-3131
Ombudsman
San Diego Union-Tribune, San Diego, CA

Lubrano, Norlynne .... (609) 641-3100
ED, Record Journal, Mays Landing, NJ

Luby, John .... (704) 358-5000
Senior VP, GM
Charlotte Observer, Charlotte, NC

Lucas, Charlotte-Anne .... (210) 225-7411
BUS Writer
San Antonio Express-News, San Antonio, TX

Lucas, David .... (403) 343-2400
INFO SRV MGR
Red Deer Advocate, Red Deer, AB

Lucas, Diane .... (712) 673-2318
ED, Breda News, Breda, IA

Lucas, Donnie .... (915) 762-2201
PUB, ED, Albany News, Albany, TX

Lucas, Guy .... (910) 727-7211
State ED
Winston-Salem Journal, Winston-Salem, NC

Lucas, James .... (904) 863-1111
PROD MGR, Northwest Florida Daily News, Fort Walton Beach, FL

Lucas, Larry .... (360) 676-2600
CIRC DIR
Bellingham Herald, Bellingham, WA

Lucas, Marlene .... (319) 398-8211
Farm/Rural Affairs Writer
Gazette, Cedar Rapids, IA

Lucas, Melinda .... (915) 762-2201
MAN ED, Albany News, Albany, TX

Lucas, Merrilee .... (808) 525-8000
CIRC MGR-Customer SRV
Hawaii Newspaper Agency Inc., Honolulu, HI

Lucas, Mike .... (503) 829-2301
ED, Molalla Pioneer, Molalla, OR

Lucas, Phil .... (334) 749-6271
ED, Opelika-Auburn News, Opelika, AL

Lucas, Ron .... (864) 223-1411
ADV MGR, Index-Journal, Greenwood, SC

Lucas, Tom .... (816) 385-3121
PROD SUPT
Macon Chronicle-Herald, Macon, MO

Lucas, Tom .... (707) 425-4646
CIRC DIR-OPER
Daily Republic, Fairfield, CA

Lucca, Arthur .... (508) 473-1111
ADV MGR, Milford Daily News, Milford, MA

Luce, Scott .... (806) 298-2033
PUB, ED
Abernathy Weekly Review, Abernathy, TX

Lucente, Thomas .... (937) 878-3993
Reporter, Fairborn Daily Herald, Fairborn, OH

Lucero, John .... (360) 754-5400
News ED, Olympian, Olympia, WA

Lucero, Sam M .... (715) 392-8268
ED, Catholic Herald, Superior, WI

Lucey, David T .... (203) 235-1661
Senior VP, GM, Record-Journal, Meriden, CT

Lucey Jr, William F .... (508) 685-1000
VP, BM/PA
Eagle-Tribune, North Andover, MA

Lucey III, William F .... (401) 849-3300
PA, BM, Newport Daily News, Newport, RI

Lucht, Becky .... (918) 684-2828
DIR-MKTG/PROM, Muskogee Daily Phoenix & Times Democrat, Muskogee, OK

Lucht, Debra .... (712) 792-3573
ADV MGR-RT, Daily Times Herald, Caroll, IA

Lucht, Jane .... (618) 282-3803
ED, North County News, Red Bud, IL

Lucia, Sandra Santa .... (403) 762-2453
PUB, Banff Crag & Canyon, Banff, AB

Lucido, Teresa M .... (313) 222-6400
ADV Sales DIR-Agency & Automotive
Detroit Newspapers, Detroit, MI

Lucieer, Larry M .... (716) 663-0068
PUB
AdNet Community News, Rochester, NY

Lucier, Virginia .... (508) 626-3800
Fashion/Theater ED
Middlesex News, Framingham, MA

Luck, Linda .... (919) 778-2211
Religion ED
Goldsboro News-Argus, Goldsboro, NC

Luckovich, Mike .... (404) 526-5151
Cartoonist (Constitution)
Atlanta Journal-Constitution, Atlanta, GA

Luckring, Brian .... (309) 346-1111
PROD FRM-Press, Daily Times, Pekin, IL

Lucock, Christopher .... (401) 277-7000
ADV Creative DIR
Providence Journal-Bulletin, Providence, RI

Ludden, Michael .... (407) 420-5000
Sunday ED, Orlando Sentinel, Orlando, FL

Ludeman, Bob .... (573) 882-5700
PROD SUPT
Columbia Missourian, Columbia, MO

Ludemann, Donna L .... (402) 497-3651
MAN ED, Springview Herald, Springview, NE

Luder, Janice .... (818) 962-8811
MAN ED, Highlander, West Covina, CA

Ludington, Mark .... (517) 725-5136
ADV DIR, ADV MGR-NTL
Argus-Press, Owosso, MI

Ludlow, Greg .... (317) 659-4622
ADV DIR, Times, Frankfort, IN

Ludlow, Randy .... (513) 352-2000
Legislature ED
Cincinnati Post, Cincinnati, OH

Ludlum, Barron .... (817) 387-3811
Chief Photographer, Photo ED
Denton Record-Chronicle, Denton, TX

Ludlum, Brandy .... (812) 847-4487
Sports ED, Linton Daily Citizen, Linton, IN

Ludlum, Melissa .... (201) 646-4000
SEC/ASST TREAS, Record, Hackensack, NJ

Ludwig, Gerald J .... (517) 787-2300
CIRC MGR, Citizen Patriot, Jackson, MI

Ludwig, Rob .... (903) 872-3931
MAN ED, Corsicana Daily Sun, Corsicana, TX

Ludwig, Robert .... (508) 458-7100
PROD SUPT, Sun, Lowell, MA

Ludwig, Robert D .... (205) 532-4000
PUB, Huntsville Times, Huntsville, AL

Lue, Glen .... (416) 585-5000
CIRC Regional MGR-Toronto, Globe and Mail (Canada's National Newspaper), Toronto, ON

Luebbers, John .... (319) 263-2331
Sports ED, Muscatine Journal, Muscatine, IA

Luebke, Jason .... (815) 756-4841
CIRC MGR, Daily Chronicle, De Kalb, IL

Luecke, Pam .... (606) 231-3100
EPE, Lexington Herald-Leader, Lexington, KY

Luedecke, Wendy .... (210) 379-5402
ADV DIR
Seguin Gazette-Enterprise, Seguin, TX

Luedke, Pat .... (915) 546-6100
PROD ASST MGR
El Paso Times, El Paso, TX

Luedtke, Gene .... (515) 472-4129
ADV MGR, Fairfield Ledger, Fairfield, IA

Luengo, Kathy .... (216) 999-4500
INFO SYS MGR-Telecommunication
Plain Dealer, Cleveland, OH

Luethmers, Joseph M .... (309) 764-4344
CIRC DIR, Dispatch, Moline, IL
Small Newspaper Group Inc.

Lufkin, Liz .... (415) 777-1111
Entertainment ED
San Francisco Chronicle, San Francisco, CA

Luft, Judith .... (517) 725-5136
CIRC MGR, Argus-Press, Owosso, MI

Luginbill, James E .... (219) 726-8141
TREAS, Commercial Review, Portland, IN

Lugo, Cynthia .... (914) 636-7400
ED, Co-op City News, Bronx, NY

Lugo Jr, Nick .... (212) 348-8200
PUB, La Voz Hispana, New York, NY

Luhn, Harold .... (360) 577-2500
ADV MGR-NTL, ADV MGR-RT
Daily News, Longview, WA

Luicha, Bill .... (602) 977-8351
CIRC MGR, Daily News-Sun, Sun City, AZ

Lujan, Dr Carlos Diaz .... (305) 530-8787
ED, El Nuevo Patria, Miami, FL

Luken, Karen .... (712) 279-5019
MAN ED, Sioux City Journal, Sioux City, IA

Lukens, Mark P .... (610) 371-5000
INFO SYS MGR
Reading Times/Eagle, Reading, PA

Lukens, Robert .... (312) 927-7200
ED, Back of the Yards Journal/El Periodico, Chicago, IL

Luker, A Merle .... (409) 769-5428
PUB, Vidorian, Vidor, TX

Luker, Randall .... (409) 769-5428
MAN ED, Vidorian, Vidor, TX

Lukits, Steve .... (613) 544-5000
EPE, Kingston Whig-Standard, Kingston, ON

Luksa, Frank .... (214) 977-8222
COL-SportsDay
Dallas Morning News, Dallas, TX

Lum, Mr .... (212) 349-4778
ED, China Tribune, New York, NY

Lum, Stanford .... (808) 525-8000
PROD MGR-Camera/Quality
Hawaii Newspaper Agency Inc., Honolulu, HI

Lumbye, Betsy .... (803) 329-4000
MAN ED, Herald, Rock Hill, SC

Lummel, Oneva M .... (308) 262-0675
ED, Bridgeport News-Blade, Bridgeport, NE

Lummel, Wendelin P .... (308) 262-0675
PUB, Bridgeport News-Blade, Bridgeport, NE

Lumpkin, Ben .... (301) 459-3131
Sports ED
Prince George's Journal, Lanham, MD

Lumpkin, John .... (817) 387-3811
Environmental ED, Farm/Agriculture ED, Health/Medical ED, SCI/Technology ED
Denton Record-Chronicle, Denton, TX

Lumsden, Carolyn .... (860) 241-6200
Commentary ED
Hartford Courant, Hartford, CT

Lumsden, Lynne .... (860) 296-6128
PUB, Hartford News, Hartford, CT

Luna, Deni .... (206) 223-0623
ED, Northwest Asian Weekly, Seattle, WA

Luna, Judy .... (505) 523-4581
MGR-Human Resources
Las Cruces Sun-News, Las Cruces, NM

Lund, Brian A .... (608) 776-4425
PUB, Republican-Journal, Darlington, WI

Lund, Cindy .... (608) 776-4425
ED, Republican-Journal, Darlington, WI

Lund, Elizabeth .... (617) 450-2000
Home Forum ED (TMC)
Christian Science Monitor, Boston, MA

Lund, John .... (612) 439-3130
ADV DIR
Stillwater Evening Gazette, Stillwater, MN

Lund, Robert W .... (818) 713-3000
ED, Daily News, Woodland Hills, CA

Lund, Steve .... (414) 657-1000
City ED, Kenosha News, Kenosha, WI

Lund, Tom .... (317) 633-1240
PROD OPER FRM-Platemaking
Indianapolis Star/News, Indianapolis, IN

Lund-Seeden, Kathleen .... (562) 698-0955
City ED, Whittier Daily News, Whittier, CA

Lundahl, Mark .... (702) 788-6200
City ED, Reno Gazette-Journal, Reno, NV

Lunde, Anne .... (847) 696-3133
ED, Edison-Norwood Times Review, Park Ridge, IL

Lundeberg, Steve .... (541) 926-2211
Sports ED
Albany Democrat-Herald, Albany, OR

Lundgren, John .... (520) 573-4400
PROD MGR-PR, TNI Partners dba Tucson Newspapers, Tucson, AZ

Lundgren, Rich .... (903) 757-3311
BUS ED
Longview News-Journal, Longview, TX

Lundin, Marvin .... (218) 681-4450
ED, Northern Watch, Thief River Falls, MN

Lundquest, William C .... (518) 828-1616
PUB/GM, Register-Star, Hudson, NY

Lundquist, Jeff .... (712) 225-5111
ED
Cherokee County's Daily Times, Cherokee, IA

Lundstrom, Marje .... (916) 321-1000
ASST MAN ED-MET
Sacramento Bee, Sacramento, CA

Lundy, Harold .... (613) 829-9100
CIRC MGR-Reader Sales & SRV-Country
Ottawa Citizen, Ottawa, ON

Lundy, John .... (219) 874-7211
City ED, News Dispatch, Michigan City, IN

Lundy, Walker .... (612) 222-5011
Senior VP/ED
St. Paul Pioneer Press, St. Paul, MN

Lungren, Dennis .... (316) 421-2000
Photo ED, Parsons Sun, Parsons, KS

Lunsford, Teresa .... (802) 863-3441
ADV Sales EX-Regional/NTL
Burlington Free Press, Burlington, VT

Lupinacci, David .... (203) 333-0161
CFO, Connecticut Post, Bridgeport, CT

Lupo, Mike .... (313) 222-6400
City ED, Detroit Free Press, Detroit, MI

Lupton, John W H .... (204) 834-2153
PUB, ED
Carberry News Express, Carberry, MB

Luse, Daniel T .... (800) 760-3100
Features ED/Los Angeles
Williams Syndications Inc., Holiday, FL

Luse, Nancy .... (301) 662-1177
City ED, Frederick Post/News, Frederick, MD

Luse, Ruth P .... (609) 466-1190
ED, Hopewell Valley News, Hopewell, NJ

Lush, Gerald .... (502) 737-5585
PUB, ED, Hardin County Independent, Elizabethtown, KY

Lusk, Angela .... (415) 883-8600
DIR-Human Resources
Marin Independent Journal, Novato, CA

141-Who's Where **Mac**

Lusk, John .... (216) 696-3322
News ED, Daily Legal News and Cleveland Recorder, Cleveland, OH
Lusk, Larry .... (209) 239-3531
CIRC MGR, Manteca Bulletin, Manteca, CA
Lusk, Laurie .... (209) 239-3531
GM, Manteca Bulletin, Manteca, CA
Lussier, John H .... (608) 252-6100
SEC, Wisconsin State Journal, Madison, WI
Lussier, Pierre .... (514) 768-2544
ED, Verdun Messenger, Verdun, QC
Lussier, Rachel .... (819) 564-5450
Music ED, La Tribune, Sherbrooke, QC
Lust, Judy .... (419) 562-3333
PROD Creative SRV
Telegraph-Forum, Bucyrus, OH
Luster, Bill .... (502) 582-4011
Chief Photographer
Courier-Journal, Louisville, KY
Luster, Edward E .... (718) 769-4400
PUB, Kings Courier, Brooklyn, NY
Lustig, Harvey .... (305) 977-7770
PUB, Broward News, Margate, FL
Lustig, Jay .... (201) 877-4141
Music Critic-Pop/Rock
Star-Ledger, Newark, NJ
Lute, Tanya .... (402) 256-3200
ED, Advocate, Laurel, NE
Lutes, Greg .... (403) 343-2400
MGR-MKTG/PROM
Red Deer Advocate, Red Deer, AB
Lutgen, Robert .... (501) 378-3400
MAN ED
Arkansas Democrat-Gazette, Little Rock, AR
Lutgen, Tom .... (213) 237-5000
Library DIR
Los Angeles Times, Los Angeles, CA
Lutgens, Jim .... (507) 373-1411
Sports ED
Albert Lea Tribune, Albert Lea, MN
Luther, Claudia .... (213) 237-5000
Deputy Calendar ED
Los Angeles Times, Los Angeles, CA
Lutheran, Amy .... (812) 372-7811
ADV MGR-CLASS, Republic, Columbus, IN
Luttrell, Glenn W .... (217) 623-5523
PUB, ED, Herald-Star, Edinburg, IL
Luttrell, Leo .... (217) 223-5100
PROD FRM-COMP
Quincy Herald-Whig, Quincy, IL
Lutwick, Elizabeth .... (614) 397-5333
ASST PUB, News, Mount Vernon, OH
Lutz, Cheryl .... (419) 245-6000
CIRC ASST DIR, Blade, Toledo, OH
Lutz, Helen I .... (210) 736-4450
PUB
Daily Commercial Recorder, San Antonio, TX
Lutz, Susan .... (317) 747-5700
DIR-MKTG/Services, Online MGR
Star Press, Muncie, IN
Lutz, Ted .... (202) 334-6000
VP-CIRC/BM
Washington Post, Washington, DC
Lutz, W R .... (814) 676-7444
VP, CONT, Derrick, Oil City, PA
Luvison, Kelly .... (607) 324-1425
PUB, Evening Tribune, Hornell, NY
Lux, John .... (312) 222-3232
Online ED, Chicago Tribune, Chicago, IL
Luxner, Mort .... (305) 977-7770
ED, Broward News, Margate, FL
Luzarraga, Beba Llano .... (305) 350-2111
Community Relations MGR-Hispanic Market
Miami Herald, Miami, FL
Lyall, Dennis .... (209) 441-6111
PROD MGR-PR, Fresno Bee, Fresno, CA
Lyde, Leophus .... (334) 432-0356
PUB, ED, New Times, Mobile, AL
Lyden, Tobey .... (212) 715-2100
VP/FIN, USA Weekend, New York, NY
Lydia, C Ailene .... (615) 292-9150
ED, Nashville Pride, Nashville, TN
Lydon, Joyce .... (904) 264-3200
PUB, Clay County Crescent, Orange Park, FL
Lyghtle, Dave .... (209) 578-2000
Political/Government ED
Modesto Bee, Modesto, CA
Lyke, Dan .... (518) 584-4242
PROD DIR, Saratogian, Saratoga Springs, NY
Lyke, Tim .... (414) 748-3017
PUB, Ripon Commonwealth Press, Ripon, WI
Lyle, Colin R .... (603) 352-1234
ADV DIR, ADTX MGR
Keene Sentinel, Keene, NH
Lyle, Zannah .... (904) 599-2100
Books ED, Environmental ED
Tallahassee Democrat, Tallahassee, FL
Lyles, Jerry .... (502) 527-3162
PUB, Tribune-Courier, Benton, KY
Lyman, David .... (313) 222-6400
Art Writer, Detroit Free Press, Detroit, MI
Lyman, L Peter .... (315) 470-0011
EPE, Post-Standard/Syracuse Herald-Journal/American, Syracuse, NY
Lyman, Robert .... (209) 992-3115
PUB, Corcoran Journal, Corcoran, CA
Lyman, Shelby .... (212) 586-3700
PRES
Basic Chess Features, South Gibson, PA
Lymberopoulos, Diane .... (312) 878-7331
ED, Greek Star, Chicago, IL
Lynam, Ken .... (507) 451-2840
PUB/ED, People's Press, Owatonna, MN
Lynch, Alethea .... (610) 948-4850
MAN ED
Spring-Ford Reporter, Royersford, PA
Lynch, Andrew .... (604) 382-6188
PUB
Victoria's Monday Magazine, Victoria, BC
Lynch, Dan .... (219) 461-8333
Cartoonist, Journal Gazette, Fort Wayne, IN
Lynch, Daniel .... (518) 454-5694
COL, Times Union, Albany, NY
Lynch, Dean .... (806) 669-2525
CIRC DIR, Pampa News, Pampa, TX
Lynch, Ed .... (808) 525-8000
BUS ED, Star-Bulletin, Honolulu, HI
Lynch, J Frank .... (912) 236-9511
News Planning ED
Savannah Morning News, Savannah, GA
Lynch, Jack .... (218) 262-1011
News ED, Daily Tribune, Hibbing, MN
Lynch, Mrs James .... (915) 964-2426
PUB, ED, Hudspeth County Herald & Dell Valley Review, Dell City, TX
Lynch, Jodi .... (814) 946-7411
ADV MGR-Inside/CLASS Sales
Altoona Mirror, Altoona, PA
Lynch, John A .... (910) 343-2000
PUB, Morning Star, Wilmington, NC
Lynch, Kevin .... (608) 252-6400
Music ED, Capital Times, Madison, WI
Lynch, Lloyd .... (502) 227-4556
ADV DIR, State Journal, Frankfort, KY
Lynch, Lucy .... (215) 949-4000
PA
Bucks County Courier Times, Levittown, PA
Lynch, Marg .... (519) 822-4310
Librarian, Daily Mercury, Guelph, ON
Lynch, Martha .... (814) 765-5581
ADV MGR-CLASS, Progress, Clearfield, PA
Lynch, Maxine .... (216) 999-4500
MAN ED-PSL, Plain Dealer, Cleveland, OH
Lynch, Michael .... (510) 783-6111
Senior VP-Advertising
Daily Review, Hayward, CA
Lynch, Paul .... (610) 820-6500
PROD MGR-Manufacturing
Morning Call, Allentown, PA
Lynch, Paul .... (312) 222-3232
PROD MGR-Technical Training
Chicago Tribune, Chicago, IL
Lynch, Peter .... (410) 749-7171
ADV MGR-Sales, Daily Times, Salisbury, MD
Lynch, Robert M .... (707) 938-2111
PUB, Sonoma Index-Tribune, Sonoma, CA
Lynch, Russ .... (808) 525-8000
Automotive/Aviation ED
Honolulu Star-Bulletin, Honolulu, HI
Lynch, Thomas P .... (603) 772-6000
ED, Exeter News-Letter, Exeter, NH
Lynch, Tim .... (617) 471-8733
PRES
New Wave Syndication, North Quincy, MA
Lynch, William E .... (707) 938-2111
ED, Sonoma Index-Tribune, Sonoma, CA
Lyne, David .... (540) 374-5000
Wire ED, Fredericksburg Free Lance-Star, Fredericksburg, VA
Lynett Jr, Edward J .... (717) 348-9100
PUB, Times-Shamrock Communications, Scranton, PA
Lynett, George V .... (717) 348-9100
PUB, Times-Shamrock Communications, Scranton, PA
Lynett, William R .... (717) 348-9100
PUB, Times-Shamrock Communications, Scranton, PA
Lynker, John .... (212) 580-8559
MAN ED
Journal Press Syndicate, New York, NY
Lynn, Angelo S .... (802) 388-4944
PUB, ED
Addison County Independent, Middlebury, VT
Lynn, Cynthia .... (802) 524-9771
Co-PUB, BM/CONT
St. Albans Messenger, St. Albans, VT
Lynn, Don .... (501) 268-8621
ADV Office MGR/Bookkeeper
Daily Citizen, Searcy, AR
Lynn, Emerson .... (802) 524-9771
Co-PUB, ED, EPE
St. Albans Messenger, St. Albans, VT
Lynn Jr, Emerson E .... (316) 365-2111
PUB/GM, BUS/FIN ED, EPE, NTL ED, Political/Government ED, PROD SUPT
Iola Register, Iola, KS
Lynn, Linda .... (405) 475-3311
Community ED
Daily Oklahoman, Oklahoma City, OK
Lynn, Lisa .... (816) 826-1000
ADV DIR, Sedalia Democrat, Sedalia, MO
Lynn, Mae .... (202) 882-1021
MAN ED, Washington Sun, Washington, DC
Lynn, Mary Anne .... (405) 238-6464
PUB
Pauls Valley Daily Democrat, Pauls Valley, OK
Lynn, Michelle .... (360) 452-2345
CIRC ASST MGR
Peninsula Daily News, Port Angeles, WA
Lynn, Mickey J .... (316) 365-2111
PRES, Iola Register, Iola, KS
Lynn, Mike .... (310) 540-5511
MGR-MKTG/PROM, Daily Breeze, Torrance, CA, Copley Press Inc.
Lynn, Nora .... (916) 444-2355
ED, Daily Recorder, Sacramento, CA
Lynn, R J .... (219) 782-2345
PRES, Lynn, Richard Enterprises, Lagro, IN
Lynn, Ralph .... (502) 678-5171
PROD FRM-PR
Glasgow Daily Times, Glasgow, KY
Lynn, Robert .... (757) 446-2000
ASST MAN ED-Photo, Chief Photo ED
Virginian-Pilot, Norfolk, VA
Lynn, Ruth .... (309) 547-3055
ED, Fulton Democrat, Lewistown, IL
Lyon, Ann .... (616) 964-7161
ADV MGR-CLASS, ADTX MGR
Battle Creek Enquirer, Battle Creek, MI
Lyon, Bill .... (215) 854-2000
COL-Sports
Philadelphia Inquirer, Philadelphia, PA
Lyon, Darrin .... (219) 936-3101
News ED, Pilot-News, Plymouth, IN
Lyon, Edward M .... (712) 882-1101
PUB, ED, Mapleton Press, Mapleton, IA
Lyon, Frank .... (816) 826-1000
PUB, Sedalia Democrat, Sedalia, MO
Lyon, G W .... (915) 347-5757
PUB, ED, Mason County News, Mason, TX
Lyon, John .... (405) 225-3000
City/MET ED, Envrnmntl ED, Health/Medical ED, Elk City Daily News, Elk City, OK
Lyon, Kenneth .... (316) 223-1460
CIRC MGR
Fort Scott Tribune, Fort Scott, KS
Lyon, Peg .... (607) 734-5151
DIR-Graphics, Star-Gazette, Elmira, NY
Lyon, Rob .... (540) 297-1222
ED, Smith Mountain Eagle, Moneta, VA
Lyon, Robert D .... (805) 650-2900
ADV MGR-NTL
Ventura County Star, Ventura, CA
Lyon, Steve F .... (702) 635-2230
MAN ED
Battle Mountain Bugle, Battle Mountain, NV
Lyons, Barry .... (603) 224-5301
CONT, Concord Monitor, Concord, NH
Lyons, David .... (409) 295-5407
PUB, Huntsville Item, Huntsville, TX
Lyons, Dennis M .... (215) 855-8440
EX ED, Reporter, Landsdale, PA
Lyons, James L .... (209) 784-5000
PUB, Recorder, Porterville, CA
Lyons, Jim .... (517) 265-5111
Local News ED, Television/Film ED
Daily Telegram, Adrian, MI
Lyons, Joe .... (610) 867-5000
ED, Bethlehem Star, Bethlehem, PA
Lyons, Julie .... (214) 757-9000
ED, Dallas Observer, Dallas, TX
Lyons, Kathy .... (360) 496-5993
GM, Morton Journal, Morton, WA
Lyons, Pam .... (609) 663-6000
Fashion/Food ED
Courier-Post, Cherry Hill, NJ
Lyons, Roberta .... (707) 894-3339
MAN ED
Cloverdale Reveille, Cloverdale, CA
Lyons, Susan .... (302) 537-1881
GM, Wave, Bethany Beach, DE
Lyons, Tom .... (941) 953-7755
COL
Sarasota Herald-Tribune, Sarasota, FL
Lysen, Walter H .... (708) 388-2425
PUB, Oak Lawn Independent, Midlothian, IL
Lysko, Deanna .... (613) 342-4441
Films/Theater ED, Music ED, PROD Photographer, Brockville Recorder and Times, Brockville, ON
Lysko, Mark .... (613) 342-4441
PROD Photographer, Brockville Recorder and Times, Brockville, ON
Lyst, John H .... (317) 633-1240
ED (Star), EPE
Indianapolis Star/News, Indianapolis, IN
Lystra, Helen .... (616) 842-6400
ADTX MGR
Grand Haven Tribune, Grand Haven, MI
Lythcott, Marcia .... (312) 222-3232
ASSOC ED-Op-Ed Page
Chicago Tribune, Chicago, IL
Lythgoe, Dennis .... (801) 237-2188
Fashion ED
Deseret News, Salt Lake City, UT
Lytle, Jeffrey .... (941) 262-3161
EPE, Naples Daily News, Naples, FL
Lytle, Lisa .... (714) 835-1234
Fashion Writer
Orange County Register, Santa Ana, CA
Lytle, Ron .... (419) 223-1010
PROD OPER SUPV- COMP
Lima News, Lima, OH
Lytle, Tamara .... (203) 789-5200
Washington BU Chief
New Haven Register, New Haven, CT
Lyttle, Bill .... (417) 451-1520
Photo DEPT MGR, PROD MGR
Neosho Daily News, Neosho, MO

M

Maack, Dave .... (605) 279-2565
ED, Pennington County Courant, Wall, SD
Maag, Kathy .... (813) 893-8111
MGR-Internal Communications
St. Petersburg Times, St. Petersburg, FL
Maas, Larry .... (219) 933-3200
DIR-PROD/MGR-Plant
Times, Munster, IN
Maas, Rick .... (419) 245-6000
ASST MAN ED, Blade, Toledo, OH
Maas, Sally Ann .... (909) 684-1200
ASST MAN ED-Features/Arts
Press-Enterprise, Riverside, CA
Maasdam, Karl .... (503) 325-3211
Photo DEPT MGR, Daily Astorian, Astoria, OR
Maassen, Mark .... (816) 234-4141
ADV MGR-NTL
Kansas City Star, Kansas City, MO
Mabbs, Brenda .... (605) 394-8300
MGR-EDU SRV
Rapid City Journal, Rapid City, SD
Mabe, Allen .... (704) 633-8950
PROD FRM-MR
Salisbury Post, Salisbury, NC
Mabe, Chauncey .... (954) 356-4000
Books ED, Sun-Sentinel, Fort Lauderdale, FL
Maben, Scott .... (541) 548-2184
ED, Redmond Spokesman, Redmond, OR
Mabin, Butch .... (402) 475-4200
Courts/Corrections Reporter
Lincoln Journal Star, Lincoln, NE
Mabry, Drake .... (515) 232-2160
EPE, Daily Tribune, Ames, IA
Mabry, Paula .... (408) 842-6400
PUB, Dispatch, Gilroy, CA
USMedia Inc. (Central Valley Publishing)
Maby, Timothy .... (910) 727-7211
ADV DIR
Winston-Salem Journal, Winston-Salem, NC
MacAdam, Ron .... (330) 996-3000
PROD MGR
Akron Beacon Journal, Akron, OH
Macal, Andrea K .... (817) 583-7811
ED, Rosebud News, Rosebud, TX
MacAlpine, Andy .... (607) 324-1425
Sports ED, Evening Tribune, Hornell, NY
MacArthur, Kyle J .... (507) 526-7324
ED
Faribault County Register, Blue Earth, MN
MacAulay, Cindy .... (203) 876-6800
ED, Bulletin, Milford, CT
Macaulay, Pat .... (218) 485-8420
ED, Arrowhead Leader, Moose Lake, MN
MacCallum, Mary .... (910) 343-2000
Librarian, Morning Star, Wilmington, NC
MacCamdless, Marie .... (412) 537-3351
ED, Latrobe Bulletin, Latrobe, PA
MacCarthy, Leo .... (902) 629-6000
PROD MGR, Guardian, Charlottetown, PEI
Macchiusi, Lou .... (416) 367-2000
CIRC MGR-Home Delivery
Toronto Star, Toronto, ON
MacCluggage, Reid .... (860) 442-2200
PRES, PUB, ED, Day, New London, CT
MacDonald, Brenda .... (203) 333-0161
ADV DIR, Connecticut Post, Bridgeport, CT
MacDonald, C .... (617) 341-1111
MAN ED
East Bridgewater Citizen, Stoughton, MA
MacDonald, C Patrick .... (206) 464-2111
Music Critic-Rock/Popular
Seattle Times, Seattle, WA
MacDonald Jr, Charles H .... (609) 845-3300
MGR-MIS
Gloucester County Times, Woodbury, NJ
MacDonald, Christine .... (617) 944-4444
GM, Suburban News, Reading, MA

Mac Who's Where-142

MacDonald, Claire .... (604) 932-5131
PUB, Whistler Question, Whistler, BC
MacDonald, Dave .... (604) 334-8722
PUB, GM
Comox Valley Echo, Courtenay, BC
MacDonald, David .... (204) 697-7000
Washington DC Bureau
Winnipeg Free Press, Winnipeg, MB
MacDonald, Dean .... (805) 273-2700
RE ED, Antelope Valley Press, Palmdale, CA
MacDonald, Don .... (705) 674-5271
City ED, Sudbury Star, Sudbury, ON
MacDonald, Helen .... (315) 685-8338
ED, Marcellus Observer, Skaneateles, NY
MacDonald, J F .... (604) 992-2121
PUB, ED, Cariboo Observer, Quesnel, BC
Macdonald, John .... (206) 464-2111
Travel ED, Seattle Times, Seattle, WA
MacDonald, Karen .... (418) 650-1764
PUB, ED
Quebec Chronicle Telegraph, Ste-Foy, QC
MacDonald, Ken .... (910) 875-2121
GM, ED, News-Journal, Raeford, NC
MacDonald, Kirk .... (303) 820-1010
EVP/GM, Denver Post, Denver, CO
Macdonald, Nancy .... (514) 739-3302
GM, Town of Mt. Royal Weekly Post/Le Post de Ville Mt. Royal, Mount Royal, QC
MacDonald, Pat .... (502) 583-4471
TREAS, Daily Record, Louisville, KY
Macdonald, Sally .... (206) 464-2111
Religion Reporter, Seattle Times, Seattle, WA
MacDonald, Sandy .... (902) 468-1222
Entertainment ED
Halifax Daily News, Halifax, NS
MacDonald, Tom .... (517) 875-4151
PUB, Gratiot County Herald, Ithaca, MI
MacDonald, Vic .... (803) 276-0625
ED, Newberry Observer & Herald & News, Newberry, SC
MacDonald, Wayne .... (519) 894-2231
PUB, Record, Kitchener, ON
MacDonald, Will .... (704) 864-3291
Regional ED, Gaston Gazette, Gastonia, NC
MacDougall, Bruce .... (902) 436-2121
ADV MGR, Summerside Journal-Pioneer, Summerside, PEI
MacDougall, Gary J .... (902) 629-6000
MAN ED, Guardian, Charlottetown, PEI
MacDuff, Cassie .... (909) 889-9666
Political ED, Sun, San Bernardino, CA
Mace, Ben .... (302) 653-2083
ED, Smyrna/Clayton Sun-Times, Smyrna, DE
Mace, Eugene A .... (314) 937-5200
PRES, USMedia Group Inc., Crystal City, MO
Mace, Michael .... (518) 454-5694
PROD SUPT-Photoengraving
Times Union, Albany, NY
Mace, Tony .... (212) 509-4444
MAN ED
Market News Service, New York, NY
Macey, Richard .... (616) 627-7144
Sports ED
Cheboygan Daily Tribune, Cheboygan, MI
Macfarland, Brewster .... (312) 644-7800
VP, Chicago Daily Law Bulletin, Chicago, IL
Macfarland Jr, Lanning .... (312) 644-7800
PRES
Chicago Daily Law Bulletin, Chicago, IL
Macfarland III, Lanning .... (312) 644-7800
VP, Chicago Daily Law Bulletin, Chicago, IL
Macfayden, Bill .... (805) 564-5200
News ED, Santa Barbara News-Press, Santa Barbara, CA
MacGillivray, Thomas K .... (317) 231-9200
CFO
Central Newspapers Inc., Indianapolis, IN
MacGoohan, Brandon .... (513) 761-1188
Contributing Critic
Critic's Choice Reviews, Cincinnati, OH
MacGregor, Heather .... (201) 635-0639
ED, Chatham Courier, Chatham, NJ
MacGregor, Roy .... (613) 829-9100
COL, Ottawa Citizen, Ottawa, ON
Mach, David H .... (360) 568-4121
PUB
Snohomish County Tribune, Snohomish, WA
Machan, Randy .... (614) 439-3531
CIRC MGR
Daily Jeffersonian, Cambridge, OH
Machaskee, Alex .... (216) 999-4500
PRES/PUB, Plain Dealer, Cleveland, OH
Machcinski, Rhonda .... (313) 242-1100
TREAS
Monroe Evening News, Monroe, MI
Macher, Ralph .... (909) 684-1200
CIRC MGR-CIS SYS
Press-Enterprise, Riverside, CA
Machinski, Peggy .... (814) 774-9648
MAN ED, Cosmopolite Herald, Girard, PA
Machio, Robert .... (717) 637-3736
BUS ED, EPE, Evening Sun, Hanover, PA
Macias, Sandra .... (702) 788-6200
Food ED, Reno Gazette-Journal, Reno, NV
MacInnis, Dr Frank .... (604) 868-8603
Author
HFM Medical Publications, Kelowna, BC
MacIntosh, Calvin .... (506) 452-6671
PUB/GM, Daily Gleaner, Fredericton, NB
MacIntyre, Bruce .... (705) 325-1355
PUB/GM, Packet & Times, Orillia, ON
Macioce, Diane .... (301) 670-1400
ASSOC PUB
Montgomery Journal, Rockville, MD
Mack, Amy .... (815) 459-4040
ED-Crystal Lake Northwest Herald, Crystal Lake, IL
Mack, Ann Baker .... (541) 485-1234
TREAS, Register-Guard, Eugene, OR
Mack, Bedel .... (619) 299-3131
Production ED
San Diego Union-Tribune, San Diego, CA
Mack, Bernice T .... (419) 822-3231
PUB, ED, Delta Atlas, Delta, OH
Mack, David J .... (716) 232-7100
PRES/PUB
Rochester Democrat and Chronicle; Rochester, NY Times-Union, Rochester, NY
Mack, Dennis .... (541) 474-3700
PUB
Grants Pass Daily Courier, Grants Pass, OR
Mack, Edward J .... (908) 782-4747
GM
Hunterdon County Democrat, Flemington, NJ
Mack, Janet M .... (507) 534-3121
ED, Plainview News, Plainview, MN
Mack, Lloyd .... (403) 875-3362
ED, Lloydminster Meridian Booster, Lloydminster, AB
Mack, Millard .... (513) 621-3145
PUB, American Israelite, Cincinnati, OH
Mack, Patricia .... (201) 646-4000
Food ED, Record, Hackensack, NJ
Mack, Paul .... (617) 878-5100
PUB, South Shore News, Rockland, MA
Mack, Pete .... (605) 886-6901
PROD MGR-Pre Press
Watertown Public Opinion, Watertown, SD
Mack, Timothy M .... (507) 932-3663
PUB, St. Charles Press, St. Charles, MN
MacKay, Bonnie .... (630) 627-7010
ED, Lombardian, Lombard, IL
MacKay, Douglas .... (902) 468-1222
EIC, Daily News, Halifax, NS
MacKay, Scott D .... (630) 627-7010
PUB, Lombardian, Lombard, IL
Mackay-Smith, Janet .... (508) 412-1500
ED, Ipswich Chronicle, Ipswich, MA
Macke, Rich .... (915) 646-2541
PROD MGR
Brownwood Bulletin, Brownwood, TX
Mackenna, John .... (508) 744-0600
News ED, Salem Evening News, Beverly, MA
MacKenzie, Bruce .... (403) 429-5400
ADTX MGR
Edmonton Journal, Edmonton, AB
Mackenzie, Colin .... (416) 585-5000
MAN ED, Globe and Mail (Canada's National Newspaper), Toronto, ON
Mackenzie, Craig .... (209) 578-2000
CIRC MGR-Transportation
Modesto Bee, Modesto, CA
MacKenzie, Dick .... (807) 737-3209
PUB, Bulletin, Sioux Lookout, ON
MacKenzie, Ian .... (705) 759-3030
ADV MGR, Sault Star, Sault Ste. Marie, ON
Mackenzie, J Blair .... (416) 445-6641
VP/GEN Counsel/SEC
Southam Inc., Don Mills, ON
MacKenzie, Jo-Anne .... (802) 747-6121
City ED, Rutland Herald, Rutland, VT
MacKenzie, John E .... (603) 668-4321
VP-FIN, Union Leader, Manchester, NH
MacKenzie, Rob .... (519) 343-2440
ED, Palmerston Observer, Palmerston, ON
Mackenzie, Ross .... (804) 649-6000
EPE
Richmond Times-Dispatch, Richmond, VA
Mackey, Bob .... (405) 475-3311
PROD MGR-Building SRV
Daily Oklahoman, Oklahoma City, OK
Mackey, Howard .... (715) 394-4411
PROD DIR, Daily Telegram, Superior, WI
Mackie, Beverly .... (816) 584-3611
GM, Higginsville Advance, Higginsville, MO
Mackin, Randy .... (615) 589-2169
ED, Buffalo River Review, Linden, TN
MacKinnon, James .... (604) 382-6188
ED, Victoria's Monday Magazine, Victoria, BC
Mackintosh, Robert .... (603) 673-3100
ED, Milford Cabinet and Wilton Journal, Milford, NH
Macknicki, Jim .... (907) 257-4200
Copy Desk Chief
Anchorage Daily News, Anchorage, AK
Macko, Richard .... (802) 254-2311
PUB, Brattleboro Reformer, Brattleboro, VT
Mackzum, Mary .... (419) 245-6000
Librarian, Blade, Toledo, OH
MacLachlan, Don .... (604) 732-2944
DIR-Communications
Pacific Press Limited, Vancouver, BC
MacLaren, Barb .... (906) 495-5207
GM, Community Voice, Kincheloe, MI
MacLaren, Jim .... (906) 495-5207
PUB, ED, Community Voice, Kincheloe, MI
MacLaughlin, James .... (617) 426-3000
Deputy MAN ED-News
Boston Herald, Boston, MA
MacLean, Ray .... (562) 435-1161
VP/CFO, VP-ADM
Press-Telegram, Long Beach, CA
MacLean, Rick .... (506) 622-2600
ED, Miramichi Weekend, Newcastle, NB
MacLean, Tom .... (902) 895-7947
PUB, Weekly Record, Truro, NS
MacLean, Vicky .... (403) 468-0100
ED, Edmonton Sun, Edmonton, AB
MacLellan, Joey .... (516) 765-3425
ED, Traveler-Watchman, Southold, NY
MacLennan, Bruce .... (519) 364-4597
PUB, Saugeen City News, Hanover, ON
MacLeod, Alex .... (206) 464-2111
MAN ED, Seattle Times, Seattle, WA
MacLeod, Don .... (905) 985-7383
GM, Port Perry Weekend Star, Port Perry, ON
MacLeod, E A .... (519) 894-2231
CIRC MGR, Record, Kitchener, ON
MacLeod, G D .... (902) 354-3441
PUB, Advance, Liverpool, NS
MacLeod, Meredith .... (519) 268-7337
ED, Signpost, Dorchester, ON
MacMenamin, John .... (561) 287-1550
CIRC MGR-Single Copy
Stuart News, Stuart, FL
MacMillan, Kyle .... (402) 444-1000
Music ED (Fine Arts)
Omaha World-Herald, Omaha, NE
MacMillan, Wayne .... (416) 367-2000
PROD MGR-Photo Engraving
Toronto Star, Toronto, ON
MacMillin, Guy .... (603) 352-1234
EPE, Keene Sentinel, Keene, NH
Mac Monigle, Joyce .... (516) 378-3133
GM, Leader, Freeport, NY
MacNeil, Bert .... (617) 426-3000
EX ASST to ED, Boston Herald, Boston, MA
MacNeil, Doug .... (902) 752-3000
MAN ED, Evening News, New Glasgow, NS
MacNeil, Paul .... (306) 297-4144
ED, Shaunavon Standard, Shaunavon, SK
MacNeill, Jim .... (902) 853-3320
PUB, ED, West Prince Graphic, Alberton, PEI
MacNelly, Jeff .... (312) 222-3232
Cartoonist, Chicago Tribune, Chicago, IL
Macomber, Mystique .... (715) 423-7200
News ED
Daily Tribune, Wisconsin Rapids, WI
Macomber, Paul .... (541) 776-4411
Automotive ED, BUS ED
Mail Tribune, Medford, OR
Macomber, Sandy .... (503) 221-8327
Librarian, Oregonian, Portland, OR
Macon, James W .... (407) 294-1385
PUB, Florida Sun Review, Orlando, FL
Macor, Alida .... (908) 722-5676
PRES/Author, And Sew On, Martinsville, NJ
Macoy, Steve .... (203) 574-3636
EDL Writer, Waterbury Republican-American, Waterbury, CT
MacPhail, Angus Crane .... (614) 221-2449
PUB, GM, Columbus Alive, Columbus, OH
MacPherson, Don .... (514) 987-2222
COL, Gazette, Montreal, QC
MacPherson, Kitta .... (201) 877-4141
SCI ED, Star-Ledger, Newark, NJ
MacPherson, Rick .... (902) 468-1222
ADV VP-Sales, Daily News, Halifax, NS
Macsymic, Pat .... (306) 652-9200
Entertainment ED
StarPhoenix, Saskatoon, SK
Macumber, Penny .... (913) 762-5000
Features ED
Daily Union, Junction City, KS
MacVane, Marcia .... (207) 791-6650
Library MGR, Press Herald, Portland, ME
MacVicar, George .... (709) 279-3188
PUB, ED, Southern Gazette, Marystown, NF
Madarieta, Lon .... (208) 664-8176
CIRC MGR
Coeur d'Alene Press, Coeur d'Alene, ID
Madary, Madelyn .... (610) 789-5512
GM, El Hispano, Upper Darby, PA
Madden, Bill .... (914) 694-9300
MAN ED-ADM, Reporter Dispatch, White Plains, NY, Gannett Co. Inc.
Madden, Brenda .... (608) 489-2264
GM, Sentry-Enterprise, Hillsboro, WI
Madden, Curt .... (419) 435-6641
ADV MGR, MKTG MGR
Review Times, Fostoria, OH
Madden, Dave .... (415) 348-4321
BUS ED
San Mateo County Times, San Mateo, CA
Madden, David .... (704) 464-0221
CIRC MGR
Observer-News-Enterprise, Newton, NC
Madden, Deborah .... (312) 787-5396
MAN ED, North Loop News, Chicago, IL
Madden, Donald .... (502) 827-2000
PROD FRM-PR, Gleaner, Henderson, KY
Madden, Doreen .... (860) 388-3441
ED, Pictorial Gazette, Old Saybrook, CT
Madden, Edward J .... (508) 458-7100
ADV MGR-RT, Sun, Lowell, MA
Madden, Jeff .... (313) 222-2300
Deputy EPE, Detroit News, Detroit, MI
Madden, Kelly .... (250) 762-4445
ADV MGR, Daily Courier, Kelowna, BC
Madden, Tracy .... (507) 553-3131
ED, Wells Mirror, Wells, MN
Maddock, Mimi .... (803) 771-0219
ED, Star-Reporter, Columbia, SC
Maddock, Patricia .... (518) 792-1126
PUB, Chronicle, Glens Falls, NY
Maddocks, Phil .... (617) 444-1706
ED, Dover-Sherborn Suburban Press, Needham, MA
Maddox, Brendo C .... (502) 926-0123
TREAS, Messenger-Inquirer, Owensboro, KY
Maddox, Jean .... (912) 272-5522
BM, Courier Herald, Dublin, GA
Maddox, John .... (915) 682-5311
PROD DIR, Reporter-Telegram, Midland, TX
Maddox, Terry .... (504) 643-4918
PUB, COL, Slidell Sentry-News, Slidell, LA
Maddox, Tony .... (502) 926-0123
CIRC DIR-Packaging
Messenger-Inquirer, Owensboro, KY
Maddox, Troy .... (606) 236-2551
PROD FRM-Press
Advocate-Messenger, Danville, KY
Maddry, Lawrence .... (757) 446-2000
COL, Virginian-Pilot, Norfolk, VA
Maddux, Jason .... (614) 654-1321
NTL ED, Eagle-Gazette, Lancaster, OH
Maddux, Mike .... (903) 785-8744
PROD MGR-SYS, Paris News, Paris, TX
Madere, Brent .... (504) 447-4055
ADV MGR-CLASS
Daily Comet, Thibodaux, LA
Madewell, Rick .... (317) 622-1212
Art DIR, Graphics ED
Herald Bulletin, Anderson, IN
Madigan, John W .... (312) 222-3237
COB/PRES/CEO, Tribune Co., Chicago, IL
Madill, John .... (616) 429-2400
Photo ED, Herald-Palladium, St. Joseph, MI
Madison, Anne .... (770) 532-1234
Theater/Music Writer, Times, Gainesville, GA
Madison, Casey .... (206) 597-8742
DIR-Photography
News Tribune, Tacoma, WA
Madison, David .... (208) 344-2055
ED, Boise Weekly, Boise, ID
Madison, Deborah .... (937) 652-1331
ADV DIR, Urbana Daily Citizen, Urbana, OH
Madison, James A .... (407) 294-1385
ED, Florida Sun Review, Orlando, FL
Madison, Larry .... (801) 237-2800
Online MGR
Newspaper Agency Corp., Salt Lake City, UT
Madison, Rhonda .... (360) 577-2500
ADV MGR-CLASS, Daily News, Longview, WA
Madlock, Linda .... (918) 569-4741
MAN ED, Clayton Today, Clayton, OK
Madlom, Kim .... (706) 647-5414
MAN ED, Thomaston Times, Thomaston, GA
Madore, Daryl .... (207) 729-3311
Copy ED, Times Record, Brunswick, ME
Madrid, Michael .... (970) 493-6397
Chief Photographer
Fort Collins Coloradoan, Fort Collins, CO
Madrid, Peter .... (520) 573-4561
Sports ED, Tucson Citizen, Tucson, AZ
Madrzyk, Anna .... (847) 427-4300
Home Furnishings ED
Daily Herald, Arlington Heights, IL
Madsen, Aase .... (309) 346-1111
CIRC MGR, Pekin Daily Times, Pekin, IL
Madsen, Bob .... (712) 283-2500
PUB
Sioux Rapids Bulletin Press, Sioux Rapids, IA
Madsen, Clifford .... (609) 272-7000
ADV CNR-NTL
Press of Atlantic City, Pleasantville, NJ
Madsen, Howard .... (517) 348-6811
PUB
Crawford County Avalanche, Grayling, MI
Madsen, Jeff .... (317) 736-7101
Sports ED, Daily Journal, Franklin, IN

Copyright ©1997 by the Editor & Publisher Co.

143-Who's Where **Mal**

Madsen, Robert .... (712) 732-3130
PUB, Pilot Tribune, Storm Lake, IA
Madson, Anna Belle .... (817) 853-2801
GM, ED, Moody Courier, Moody, TX
Madson, Greg .... (801) 257-5182
PUB, Leader, Tremonton, UT
Madson, Jerry .... (218) 751-3740
Wire ED, Daily Pioneer, Bemidji, MN
Madson, Julie .... (414) 235-7700
MGR-INFO SYS
Oshkosh Northwestern, Oshkosh, WI
Madson, Lloyd O .... (515) 324-1051
PUB, Northwood Anchor, Northwood, IA
Madson, Stuart B .... (515) 324-1051
ED, Northwood Anchor, Northwood, IA
Madson, Vern .... (320) 693-3266
GM, Independent Review, Litchfield, MN
Maeglin, Kathy .... (608) 252-6400
Women's ED, Capital Times, Madison, WI
Maertens-Poole, Shari .... (403) 837-2585
ED, Smoky River Express, Falher, AB
Maffettone, Tom .... (954) 356-4000
MGR-Technology Development
Sun-Sentinel, Fort Lauderdale, FL
Maffitt, Robert .... (402) 444-1000
Automotive ED, World-Herald, Omaha, NE
Maganda, Kate .... (601) 896-2100
Sports ED, Sun Herald, Biloxi, MS
Magann, Tony .... (801) 237-2031
CONT, Salt Lake Tribune, Salt Lake City, UT
Magazine, Cheryl .... (860) 241-6200
ASSOC ED-Technology
Hartford Courant, Hartford, CT
Magazzu, Thomas V .... (205) 764-4268
ED, Courier Journal, Florence, AL
Magdefrau, Don E .... (319) 444-2520
PUB, Belle Plaine Union, Belle Plaine, IA
Magdefrau, James .... (319) 444-2520
ED, Belle Plaine Union, Belle Plaine, IA
Magdelinic, Robert .... (717) 348-9100
ADV MGR-Display
Tribune & The Scranton Times, Scranton, PA
Magdziuk, Patrick .... (315) 470-0011
PROD MGR-Camera/Platemaking
Post-Standard/Syracuse Herald-Journal/ American, Syracuse, NY
MaGee, Edward J .... (717) 767-6397
VP-FIN, York Newspaper Company, York, PA
Magee, Jim .... (415) 883-8600
ADV MGR-RT
Marin Independent Journal, Novato, CA
Magee, Michael .... (716) 232-7100
ADV MGR-NTL/Major RT/CLASS Automotive
Rochester Democrat and Chronicle; Rochester, NY Times-Union, Rochester, NY
Magee, Randy .... (913) 295-1111
BM, CNR-Human Resources
Topeka Capital-Journal, Topeka, KS
Mager, Esther Cohen .... (717) 821-2091
ADV MGR-NTL
Citizens' Voice, Wilkes-Barre, PA
Magers, Kathie .... (214) 943-7755
ED, Oak Cliff Tribune, Dallas, TX
Magers, Pat .... (419) 448-3200
Sports ED, Advertiser-Tribune, Tiffin, OH
Maggard, Debbie .... (513) 721-2700
ADV MGR-OPER
Cincinnati Enquirer, Cincinnati, OH
Maggard, Sharon .... (405) 567-3933
MAN ED, Times-Herald, Prague, OK
Magie, Betty .... (501) 982-6506
Co-PUB
Jacksonville Patriot, Jacksonville, AR
Magie, Cone .... (501) 676-2463
ED, Lonoke Democrat, Lonoke, AR
Magie, Mark .... (501) 982-6506
Co-PUB, GM
Jacksonville Patriot, Jacksonville, AR
Magie, Susie .... (501) 982-6506
ADV MGR
Jacksonville Patriot, Jacksonville, AR
Magiera, Frank .... (508) 793-9100
Arts ED, Telegram & Gazette, Worcester, MA
Magiera, Marilee .... (402) 444-1000
Travel ED, Omaha World-Herald, Omaha, NE
Magiera, Wieslaw .... (416) 533-9469
ED, Glos Polski, Toronto, ON
Magill, Eric .... (610) 932-8886
ED, Oxford Tribune, Oxford, PA
Magill, Keith .... (504) 850-1100
City ED, Courier, Houma, LA
Magill, Kerin D .... (610) 932-8886
ED, Oxford Tribune, Oxford, PA
Maginn, Thomas R .... (518) 454-5694
CONT-Resident, Times Union, Albany, NY
Maginnis, Bob .... (301) 733-5131
EPE, Morning Herald, Hagerstown, MD
Magliano, Edward M .... (513) 721-2700
PROD ENG-Plant
Cincinnati Enquirer, Cincinnati, OH
Maglio, Donna .... (219) 362-2161
ADV MGR-CLASS
La Porte Herald-Argus, La Porte, IN
Maglio, Tony .... (201) 646-4000
PROD MGR-PR, Record, Hackensack, NJ
Magliolt, Tammy .... (814) 781-1596
City ED, Daily Press, St. Marys, PA
Maglione, Heather .... (520) 445-3333
Teen-age/Youth ED
Daily Courier, Prescott, AZ
Magner, Jeff .... (919) 829-4500
PROD Press Trainer
News & Observer, Raleigh, NC
Magneson, Jane .... (712) 623-2566
PUB, Red Oak Express, Red Oak, IA
Magness, Diane .... (817) 866-3391
GM, Grandview Tribune, Grandview, TX
Magness Jr, Jack .... (817) 866-3391
PUB, Grandview Tribune, Grandview, TX
Magnier, Mark .... (212) 837-7000
Trade/Commodities, Journal of Commerce & Commercial, New York, NY
Magnuson, Karen .... (510) 462-4160
MAN ED, Valley Times, Pleasanton, CA
Magnuson, Robert .... (213) 237-5000
VP/PRES-Orange County Edition
Los Angeles Times, Los Angeles, CA
Magore, Angie .... (816) 529-2888
ED, Slater News-Rustler, Slater, MO
Magram, Jefferey .... (617) 426-3000
VP-Finance, Boston Herald, Boston, MA
Magruder II, James A .... (541) 926-2211
DIR-Internet, Democrat-Herald, Albany, OR
Maguire, Jeff .... (613) 257-1303
PUB
Carleton Place Canadian, Carleton Place, ON
Maguire, Maggie .... (916) 842-5777
ASST ED, Siskiyou Daily News, Yreka, CA
Maguire, Michael W .... (941) 687-7000
DIR-INFO Technology, DIR-INFO SYS
Ledger, Lakeland, FL
Maguire, Robert .... (800) 281-3802
PUB, Rutland Tribune, Rutland, VT
Magyar Jr, Richard .... (615) 569-8351
ED, Scott County News, Oneida, TN
Mah, Linda .... (616) 345-3511
EDU ED, Kalamazoo Gazette, Kalamazoo, MI
Mahai, Chris .... (612) 673-4000
Senior VP-Leader Strategic Integration Unit
Star Tribune, Minneapolis, MN
Mahal, Jennifer .... (305) 294-6641
News ED, Key West Citizen, Key West, FL
Mahan, Lee .... (916) 273-9561
CIRC MGR, Union, Grass Valley, CA
Mahanes, Jim .... (502) 753-1916
EDU ED, Murray Ledger & Times, Murray, KY
Mahaney, Timothy .... (412) 263-1100
PROD MGR-OPER
Pittsburgh Post-Gazette, Pittsburgh, PA
Mahannah, Willis .... (402) 372-2461
ED, West Point News, West Point, NE
Mahaskey, M Scott .... (515) 684-4611
Photo DEPT MGR
Ottumwa Courier, Ottumwa, IA
Maher, John .... (816) 234-4141
MGR-Database Marketing, Online MGR
Kansas City Star, Kansas City, MO
Maher, Philip N .... (716) 849-3434
ADV MGR-MKTG Services
Buffalo News, Buffalo, NY
Maher, Steve .... (509) 663-5161
BUS ED, RE ED
Wenatchee World, Wenatchee, WA
Maheras, TSgt Russ .... (302) 674-3600
ED, Airlifter, Dover, DE
Mahi, Mike .... (909) 987-6397
MAN ED-Online Services
Inland Valley Daily Bulletin, Ontario, CA
Mahin, Tim .... (203) 655-7476
MAN ED, Darien News-Review, Darien, CT
Mahlandt, Dave .... (618) 526-7211
ED, Breese Journal, Breese, IL
Mahlandt, Steve .... (618) 526-7211
PUB, Breese Journal, Breese, IL
Mahler, Donald .... (603) 298-8711
Sports ED, Valley News, White River Jct., VT
Mahler, Jonathan .... (212) 889-8200
MAN ED, Forward, New York, NY
Mahne, Ted .... (504) 826-3279
Music Writer-Classical
Times-Picayune, New Orleans, LA
Mahnke, Ronald .... (317) 398-6631
PROD MGR
Shelbyville News, Shelbyville, IN
Mahone, Rodney .... (706) 324-5526
ADV MGR-Sales
Columbus Ledger-Enquirer, Columbus, GA
Mahoney, Bill .... (604) 566-4425
PUB, Valley Sentinel, Valemount, BC
Mahoney, Buck .... (308) 237-2152
Sports ED, Kearney Hub, Kearney, NE
Mahoney, Dennis .... (614) 461-5000
News ED, Columbus Dispatch, Columbus, OH
Mahoney, George L .... (804) 649-6000
SEC/GEN Counsel
Media General Inc., Richmond, VA
Mahoney, John .... (619) 429-5533
PUB, ED
Imperial Beach Times, Imperial Beach, CA
Mahoney, Kent .... (913) 738-3537
PROD MGR, Beloit Daily Call, Beloit, KS
Mahoney, Louis .... (804) 649-6000
Food Writer
Richmond Times-Dispatch, Richmond, VA
Mahoney, Mark .... (518) 792-3131
City ED, Post-Star, Glens Falls, NY
Mahoney, Mike .... (612) 439-3130
PUB/PA
Stillwater Evening Gazette, Stillwater, MN
Mahoney, Richard .... (613) 678-3327
MAN ED, Review, Vankleek Hill, ON
Mahoney, Walter F .... (800) 245-6536
VP-Sales Syndicate & KRT Products
Tribune Media Services Inc., Chicago, IL
Mahoney-Moore, Patricia .... (619) 299-3131
CIRC MGR-N County Circulation
San Diego Union-Tribune, San Diego, CA
Mahony, Cardinal Roger M ..... (213) 251-3360
PUB, Tidings, Los Angeles, CA
Mahony, T Paul .... (401) 722-4000
PUB, Times, Pawtucket, RI
Mahr, Chris .... (619) 322-8889
EDU Writer, Desert Sun, Palm Springs, CA
Mahr, Kathy .... (319) 472-2311
ADV MGR
Cedar Valley Daily Times, Vinton, IA
Mahr, Michael R .... (202) 636-3000
ADV DIR, Washington Times, Washington, DC
Mahsman, Rev David .... (314) 965-9000
PUB, ED, Reporter, St. Louis, MO
Maida, Archbishop Adam J ...... (313) 244-8000
PUB, Michigan Catholic, Detroit, MI
Maidenberg, Michael .... (701) 780-1100
PRES, PUB
Grand Forks Herald, Grand Forks, ND
Maier, Francis .... (303) 388-4411
GM, Denver Catholic Register, Denver, CO
Maier, Frank .... (318) 433-3000
CIRC MGR, Lake Charles American Press, Lake Charles, LA
Maier, Sharon .... (306) 825-5522
ADV MGR-Sales, DIR-MKTG/PROM
Lloydminster Times, Lloydminster, SK
Maihos, John .... (508) 744-0600
DIR-Human Resources
Salem Evening News, Beverly, MA
Ottaway Newspapers Inc.
Maijala, Bert .... (807) 343-6200
BM, Chronicle-Journal, Thunder Bay, ON
Mailliard, Ed .... (814) 724-6370
Special Sections ED
Meadville Tribune, Meadville, PA
Mailloux, Toni .... (207) 338-5100
ED, Waldo Independent, Belfast, ME
Mailman, Allen J .... (609) 396-2200
VP-Technology
Journal Register Co., Trenton, NJ
Main, Fred .... (614) 654-1321
Sports ED
Lancaster Eagle-Gazette, Lancaster, OH
Main, Sandy .... (616) 754-9301
ASST News ED, Daily News, Greenville, MI
Mainquist, Colleen .... (913) 374-4428
PUB, ED
Courtland Journal-Empire, Courtland, KS
Mainquist, R .... (913) 374-4428
PUB
Courtland Journal-Empire, Courtland, KS
Maio, Rosemarie .... (908) 852-1212
PUB, Star Gazette, Hackettstown, NJ
Maisel, Todd .... (212) 679-1234
MAN ED
New York Town & Village, New York, NY
Maisonville, Maurice .... (910) 343-2000
PROD FRM-Distribution Center, Morning Star/Sunday Star-News, Wilmington, NC
Maitland, Gary E .... (941) 294-7731
EX ED, News Chief, Winter Haven, FL
Maitre, Michelle .... (209) 532-7151
EDU ED, Union Democrat, Sonora, CA
Majeri, Tony .... (312) 222-3232
Senior ED, Chicago Tribune, Chicago, IL
Majeste, Eddie .... (501) 425-3133
ADV MGR, DIR-MKTG
Baxter Bulletin, Mountain Home, AR
Majic, Rev Timothy .... (312) 268-2819
ED, Danica, Chicago, IL
Major, Edgar A .... (318) 322-5161
PUB, News-Star, Monroe, LA
Major, Jack .... (401) 277-7000
MAN ED-Features
Providence Journal-Bulletin, Providence, RI
Major, Jim .... (707) 644-1141
PROD FRM-Creative Services
Vallejo Times-Herald, Vallejo, CA
Major Sr, Lou .... (520) 458-3973
EVP, Wick Communications, Sierra Vista, AZ
Major Jr, Lou .... (504) 732-2565
GM, ED, Daily News, Bogalusa, LA
Major, Phil .... (972) 298-4211
MAN ED, Duncanville Today, Duncanville, TX
Major, Richard .... (918) 581-8300
DP MGR-BUS/Circulation
Tulsa World, Tulsa, OK
Major, Wayne .... (705) 335-2283
GM, ED, Northern Times, Kapuskasing, ON
Majors, Beverly .... (423) 482-1021
BUS ED, Oak Ridger, Oak Ridge, TN
Majors, Russell .... (706) 782-3312
PUB, Clayton Tribune, Clayton, GA
Majot, Joseph A .... (814) 274-8044
PUB
Potter Leader-Enterprises, Coudersport, PA
Mak, David .... (306) 565-8211
CIRC DIR, Leader-Post, Regina, SK
Maki, Allan .... (403) 235-7100
COL, Calgary Herald, Calgary, AB
Maki, Fred .... (715) 723-5515
Sports ED
Chippewa Herald, Chippewa Falls, WI
Makings, Vicki .... (303) 820-1010
EDL Librarian, Denver Post, Denver, CO
Makler, Justin .... (618) 656-4700
Online MGR, ADTX MGR, PROD MGR-SYS
Edwardsville Intelligencer, Edwardsville, IL
Makris, Steve .... (403) 429-5400
Photo ED, Edmonton Journal, Edmonton, AB
Malagrida, Rose .... (508) 885-9402
PUB, New Leader, Spencer, MA
Malan, Martie .... (612) 222-5011
Senior ED-Nation/World
St. Paul Pioneer Press, St. Paul, MN
Malato, Lucha M .... (201) 798-7800
GM, North Bergen/North Hudson Reporter, Hoboken, NJ
Malchow, Paul M .... (507) 248-3223
PUB
Henderson Independent, Henderson, MN
Malchow, Sarah Johnson .... (507) 248-3223
GM, ED
Henderson Independent, Henderson, MN
Maldonado, Cynthia .... (210) 423-5511
CIRC MGR
Valley Morning Star, Harlingen, TX
Maldonado, Jose .... (305) 350-2111
Sports News ED-El Nuevo
Miami Herald, Miami, FL
Maldonado, Mari .... (915) 445-5475
EDU ED, Pecos Enterprise, Pecos, TX
Maldonado, Paul .... (915) 546-6340
News ED, Wire ED
El Paso Herald-Post, El Paso, TX
Malek, Terri .... (814) 665-8291
CIRC MGR, Corry Evening Journal, Corry, PA
Malenfont, Christine .... (517) 354-3111
Photo ED, Alpena News, Alpena, MI
Maler, James R .... (512) 865-3131
PUB, ED, Bellville Times, Bellville, TX
Maley, Amy .... (912) 744-4200
TREAS, CFO, Macon Telegraph, Macon, GA
Maley, Dan .... (912) 744-4200
Arts/Entertainment Writer
Macon Telegraph, Macon, GA
Maley, Gary .... (210) 423-5511
PROD DIR-Quality Control, PROD SUPT
Valley Morning Star, Harlingen, TX
Maley, Mark .... (414) 224-2000
State ED
Milwaukee Journal Sentinel, Milwaukee, WI
Maley, Ron .... (913) 762-5000
PROD MGR, Daily Union, Junction City, KS
Malin, Janet .... (719) 846-3311
Features ED, Chronicle-News, Trinidad, CO
Malinowski, Mark .... (201) 728-0591
ED
Sports Biofile & Bio-Toons, West Milford, NJ
Malitz, Nancy .... (313) 222-2300
ASST MAN ED-Interactive News
Detroit News, Detroit, MI
Malkin, Michelle .... (206) 464-2111
EDL Writer, Seattle Times, Seattle, WA
Malkovich, Danny .... (618) 438-5611
PUB, MAN ED
Benton Evening News, Benton, IL
Malkovich, Jo Anne .... (618) 438-5611
Entertainment ED
Benton Evening News, Benton, IL
Mall, Janice .... (213) 237-5000
Family ED, Society News/Practical View/First Person ED
Los Angeles Times, Los Angeles, CA
Mall, Tom M .... (913) 348-5481
PUB, ED, Linn-Palmer Record, Linn, KS
Malleck, Bonnie .... (519) 894-2231
Radio/Television COL, Record, Kitchener, ON
Mallery, Jim .... (206) 464-2111
Wire News ED, Seattle Times, Seattle, WA

Copyright ©1997 by the Editor & Publisher Co.

Mal Who's Where-144

Mallery, Paul (601) 896-2100
MGR-MKTG Development
Sun Herald, Biloxi, MS

Mallet, Cynthia (508) 249-3535
ADV MGR-CLASS, Daily News, Athol, MA

Mallette, Karl (905) 729-4501
PUB, ED
Woodbridge Advertiser, Palgrave, ON

Malley, James (815) 433-2000
GM, Daily Times, Ottawa, IL

Mallick, Heather (416) 947-2222
Books ED, Toronto Sun, Toronto, ON

Mallinger, Scott (215) 790-1179
PUB, MAN ED
Pride Weekly, Philadelphia, PA

Mallon, Peter (212) 666-2300
RES, Buddy Basch Feature Syndicate, NY, NY

Mallory, James A (404) 526-5151
ASST MAN ED-Nights
Atlanta Journal-Constitution, Atlanta, GA

Mallory, R Mark (312) 222-3237
VP/CONT, Tribune Co., Chicago, IL

Malloy, Jeanie (316) 365-2111
ADV MGR-CLASS, Iola Register, Iola, KS

Malloy, Kate (613) 232-5925
MAN ED, Hill Times, Ottawa, ON

Malmgren, Jeanne (813) 893-8111
Garden ED
St. Petersburg Times, St. Petersburg, FL

Malmgren, Jeff (817) 634-2125
CNR-Telecommunications
Killeen Daily Herald, Killeen, TX

Malone, Brian S (609) 989-5454
ED, Times, Trenton, NJ

Malone, Don (703) 276-3400
CIRC GM-North Jersey
USA Today, Arlington, VA

Malone, JCL, Most Rev Francis (501) 664-0125
MAN ED, Arkansas Catholic, Little Rock, AR

Malone, George (407) 242-3500
PROD MGR-SYS
Florida Today, Melbourne, FL

Malone, Gina (704) 859-9151
ED, Tryon Daily Bulletin, Tryon, NC

Malone, Jann (804) 649-6000
COL
Richmond Times-Dispatch, Richmond, VA

Malone, Jim (508) 739-1300
MAN ED, North Shore Sunday, Danvers, MA

Malone, Patrick (719) 846-3311
Sports ED, Chronicle-News, Trinidad, CO

Malone, Richard H (954) 356-4000
VP-OPER, PROD VP/DIR
Sun-Sentinel, Fort Lauderdale, FL

Malone, Ryan (704) 859-9151
Community ED
Tryon Daily Bulletin, Tryon, NC

Malone, Susan (312) 927-7200
GM, MAN ED, Back of the Yards Journal/El Periodico, Chicago, IL

Maloney, Brown M (360) 683-3311
PUB, Sequim Gazette, Sequim, WA

Maloney, Charlie (941) 953-7755
PROD MGR-Pre Press
Sarasota Herald-Tribune, Sarasota, FL

Maloney Jr, E Mayer (619) 337-3400
PRES, PUB, ED
Imperial Valley Press, El Centro, CA

Maloney, Gary (716) 372-3121
Sports ED, Olean Times-Herald, Olean, NY

Maloney, James V (314) 340-8402
SEC, Pulitzer Publishing Co., St. Louis, MO

Maloney, Michelle (816) 385-3121
CIRC DIR
Macon Chronicle-Herald, Macon, MO

Maloney, Mick (604) 738-1411
ED, Vancouver Courier, Vancouver, BC

Maloney, Mike (212) 210-2100
PROD MGR-Press/Paper Handler
New York Daily News, New York, NY

Maloney, Mike (416) 947-2222
DIR-INFO SRV, Toronto Sun, Toronto, ON

Malott, Adele (702) 786-7419
ED/PUB, Mature Traveler, Reno, NV

Malott, Gene (702) 786-7419
ED/PUB, Mature Traveler, Reno, NV

Maloy, Foy (904) 261-3696
PUB, New-Leader, Fernandina Beach, FL

Malsbury, Art (913) 762-5000
PROD SUPT-Maintenance
Daily Union, Junction City, KS

Maltais, M (613) 562-0111
EPE, EDL Writer, Le Droit, Ottawa, ON

Maltby, Karin (250) 762-4445
Life ED, Daily Courier, Kelowna, BC

Malucci, Lou (705) 759-3030
CIRC MGR-Reader Sales
Sault Star, Sault Ste. Marie, ON

Maly, Ray (504) 826-3279
PROD DIR
Times-Picayune, New Orleans, LA

Mamis, Josh (203) 789-0010
ED, New Haven Advocate, New Haven, CT

Mammen, Larry (707) 425-4646
PROD FRM-PR, Daily Republic, Fairfield, CA

Mamoone, Cathy (716) 394-0770
ADV MGR, Daily Messenger/The Sunday Messenger, Canandaigua, NY

Manaher, Don J (219) 874-7211
PUB, News Dispatch, Michigan City, IN

Manas, Robert (212) 887-8550
MAN ED
American Metal Market, New York, NY

Manassah, Edward E (502) 582-4011
PRES, PUB, Courier-Journal, Louisville, KY

Mancher, Brooks (916) 865-4433
MAN ED, Orland Press-Register, Orland, CA

Manchester, Brad (607) 757-0753
PUB, Valley News, Endwell, NY

Manchester, John M (518) 642-1234
PUB, North Country Free Press, Granville, NY

Mancini, Francis (401) 277-7000
EDL Writer
Providence Journal-Bulletin, Providence, RI

Mancini, Jesse (304) 485-1891
COL, News & Sentinel, Parkers-burg, WV

Mancuso, Barbara (212) 556-1927
DIR-Consumer MKTG
New York Times News Service, New York, NY

Mancuso, Jo (415) 777-2424
Epicure ED, Habitat ED
San Francisco Examiner, San Francisco, CA

Mandelaro, Douglas (716) 232-7100
Religion Reporter, Rochester Democrat and Chronicle; Times-Union, Rochester, NY

Manders, Jim (360) 683-3311
ED, Sequim Gazette, Sequim, WA

Mandeville, Will (213) 622-8332
DIR-MKTG, La Opinion, Los Angeles, CA

Manegre, Roger (306) 398-4901
PUB, ED, Highway 40 Courier, Cut Knife, SK

Manes, George (517) 377-1000
MET ED, Lansing State Journal, Lansing, MI

Manes, Nancy G (207) 873-3341
DIR-Human Resources, Central Maine Morning Sentinel, Waterville, ME
Guy Gannett Communications

Maney, Robert (217) 379-4313
ED, Paxton Daily Record, Paxton, IL

Mang, Bill (717) 348-9100
Sunday ED
Tribune & The Scranton Times, Scranton, PA

Mangan, Dennis (330) 747-1471
EPE, Vindicator, Youngstown, OH

Mangan, Kevin (212) 684-3366
GM, Irish Voice, New York, NY

Manganiello, Robert (717) 821-2091
GM, Citizens' Voice, Wilkes-Barre, PA

Mangano, Edward P (516) 587-5612
PUB, Beacon, Babylon, NY

Mangano, John (516) 587-5612
PUB, Beacon, Babylon, NY

Mangano, Linda (516) 681-0442
PUB, ED, Bethpage Tribune, Bethpage, NY

Mangels, Darrel (316) 694-5700
PROD FRM-Press
Hutchinson News, Hutchinson, KS

Mangerian, Mayda (305) 370-6009
PUB, ED, Broward Informer, Sunrise, FL

Mangerian, Steve (305) 370-6009
PUB, ED, Broward Informer, Sunrise, FL

Manginelli, Pat (303) 892-5000
ADV DIR-CLASS
Rocky Mountain News, Denver, CO

Mangini, Andrew (330) 454-5611
PROD MGR-MR, Repository, Canton, OH

Mango, Terry (803) 626-8555
MGR-Customer SRV
Sun News, Myrtle Beach, SC

Mangone, Mark (813) 259-7711
CIRC MGR-Sales
Tampa Tribune and Times, Tampa, FL

Mangum, Jeffrey (914) 694-9300
ASST MAN ED-BUS
Daily Item, New Rochelle, NY

Mangus, Barbara (814) 532-5199
ADV MGR-CLASS
Tribune-Democrat, Johnstown, PA

Mangus, Karen (412) 772-3900
PROD MGR-Ad SRV
North Hills News Record, Warrendale, PA

Manhemer, Robert (516) 921-4611
ED, DANY News Service, Syosset, NY

Mani, Tom (301) 921-2800
ED, Pentagram, Gaithersburg, MD

Maniaci, John (715) 423-7200
Photo Chief
Daily Tribune, Wisconsin Rapids, WI

Maniaci, Manny (520) 289-2467
GM, Winslow Mail, Winslow, AZ

Manicias, Janice (805) 237-6060
BM, County News-Press, Paso Robles, CA

Manigan, Liz (212) 450-7000
Newspaper Relations Promotions DIR, React, Parade Publications Inc., New York, NY

Manigault, Peter (803) 577-7111
Chairman
Evening Post Publishing Co., Charleston, SC

Manikis, Christos (514) 272-6873
PUB, ED
Greek Canadian Tribune, Montreal, QC

Manilla, Kathy (312) 222-3232
DIR-PROM/Public Relations
Chicago Tribune, Chicago, IL

Manis, Michael (561) 287-1550
CIRC DIR, Stuart News, Stuart, FL

Maniscalco, Gina (617) 929-2000
ADTX MGR, Boston Globe, Boston, MA

Manley, Eric (412) 523-6588
PROD MGR
Standard Observer, Greensburg, PA

Manley, Frank P (603) 673-3100
PUB, Milford Cabinet and Wilton Journal, Milford, NH

Manley, Jerry (615) 259-8000
Close-up ED, Tennessean, Nashville, TN

Manley, John (619) 367-3577
ED, Desert Trail, Twenty-nine Palms, CA

Manley, Joy (519) 396-2963
ED, Kincardine News, Kincardine, ON

Manley, Rodney (912) 272-5522
MAN ED/BUS ED, Courier Herald, Dublin, GA

Manley, Tom (419) 422-5151
PROD FRM-MR, Courier, Findlay, OH

Mann, Amy (518) 792-9914
MAN ED, TV Data, Queensbury, NY

Mann, Bill (415) 777-2424
Television Critic
San Francisco Examiner, San Francisco, CA

Mann, Bill (306) 773-9321
PUB, Southwest Booster, Swift Current, SK

Mann, Carolyn (209) 578-2000
Entertainment/Amusements ED, Television/Film Writer, Modesto Bee, Modesto, CA

Mann, Corey (308) 237-2152
CIRC MGR, Kearney Hub, Kearney, NE

Mann, Dinn (816) 234-4141
Sports ED, Kansas City Star, Kansas City, MO

Mann, Helen (601) 582-4321
Features ED
Hattiesburg American, Hattiesburg, MS

Mann, Horst (810) 296-6007
ED, Detroit Monitor, Fraser, MI

Mann, James A (540) 374-5000
ASST MAN ED
Free Lance-Star, Fredericksburg, VA

Mann, Jim (213) 237-5000
COL-Foreign Affairs
Los Angeles Times, Los Angeles, CA

Mann, Jimmy (706) 324-5526
Chief Technician
Columbus Ledger-Enquirer, Columbus, GA

Mann, Judy (202) 334-6000
COL-Local, Washington Post, Washington, DC

Mann, Lester J (402) 375-2600
PUB, ED, Wayne Herald, Wayne, NE

Mann, Mark (412) 282-8000
MAN ED, Butler Eagle, Butler, PA

Mann, Mary Jane (401) 849-3300
ADV MGR-Sales
Newport Daily News, Newport, RI

Mann, Mike (904) 264-3200
MAN ED, Clay Today, Orange Park, FL

Mann, Nancy J (515) 284-8000
ADV MGR-OPER
Des Moines Register, Des Moines, IA

Mann, Ralph S (501) 868-4400
ADV MGR, ED, PROD MGR
Daily Record, Little Rock, AR

Mann, Rick (972) 424-6565
Sports ED, Plano Star Courier, Plano, TX

Mann, Ron (212) 941-1130
PUB, New York Press, New York, NY

Mann, Ron (213) 237-5000
ADV DIR-San Fernando Valley Edition
Los Angeles Times, Los Angeles, CA

Mann, Steve (519) 679-6666
PROD SUPV-Distribution
London Free Press, London, ON

Mann, Wesley F (800) 223-2154
EIC
Investor's Business Daily, Los Angeles, CA

Mann, William J (416) 445-6641
PRES-Southam Magazine & Information Group, Southam Inc., Don Mills, ON

Manna, John (412) 654-6651
Political ED
New Castle News, New Castle, PA

Manner, Jim (804) 946-7195
ED, Nelson County Times, Amherst, VA

Manners, Michael (860) 347-3331
DP MGR, PROD SUPT-COMP
Middletown Press, Middletown, CT

Mannes, George (212) 210-2100
Computers/Technology ED
New York Daily News, New York, NY

Mannex, John (503) 221-8327
ADV MGR-RT/Sales, Oregonian, Portland, OR

Manning, Ann (615) 259-8800
Newsroom Administrative Officer
Nashville Banner, Nashville, TN

Manning, Barry S (516) 739-6400
PUB, Valley Stream Maileader, Mineola, NY

Manning, Brian M (714) 832-9601
PUB, Tustin Weekly, Tustin, CA

Manning, Carl (307) 856-2244
CIRC MGR, SYS MGR
Riverton Ranger, Riverton, WY

Manning, E N (919) 482-4418
PUB, Chowan Herald, Edenton, NC

Manning, Gary (905) 732-2411
MAN ED, Tribune, Welland, ON

Manning, James (604) 381-3484
PUB, Victoria News, Victoria, BC

Manning, Jennifer L (812) 379-5612
Human Resources DIR
Home News Enterprises, Columbus, IN

Manning, Kay (219) 881-3000
MAN ED, Post-Tribune, Gary, IN

Manning, Robert (617) 929-2000
ADV DIR, Boston Globe, Boston, MA

Manning, Stan (714) 768-3631
PUB, Preview, Lake Forest, CA

Manning, T (203) 235-1661
Cartoonist, Record-Journal, Meriden, CT

Mannis, David (619) 270-3103
PUB, Beach & Bay Press, San Diego, CA

Mannis, Julie (619) 270-3103
PUB, Beach & Bay Press, San Diego, CA

Manno, Joseph (716) 849-3434
PROD OPER MGR-Facility, PROD OPER FRM-Plant Maintenance
Buffalo News, Buffalo, NY

Manns, Tony (219) 874-7211
PROD MGR-Distribution
News Dispatch, Michigan City, IN

Mannweiler, David (317) 633-1240
Travel/Books ED
Indianapolis Star/News, Indianapolis, IN

Mannweiler, Lyle (317) 633-1240
ASST MAN ED-ADM
Indianapolis Star/News, Indianapolis, IN

Manny, Bill (541) 776-4411
EPE, Mail Tribune, Medford, OR

Mansbach, Charles (617) 929-2000
Page One ED, Boston Globe, Boston, MA

Manser, James M (908) 223-0076
PUB, ED, Coast Star, Manasquan, NJ

Mansfield, Dennis (517) 345-0044
ED, Ogemaw County Herald, West Branch, MI

Mansfield, Gayle (406) 646-9719
ED, West Yellowstone News, West Yellowstone, MT

Mansfield, Jim (309) 685-3814
PUB, ED, Herald, Peoria Heights, IL

Mansfield, Mark P (609) 396-2200
GEN MGR-Supply Division
Journal Register Co., Trenton, NJ

Mansfield, Mary H (412) 664-9161
Vice Chairman, Daily News, McKeesport, PA

Mansfield, Matt (219) 933-3200
ASST EX ED, Times, Munster, IN

Mansfield, Sylvia (540) 949-8213
PROD MGR, News Virginian, Waynesboro, VA

Mansfield-Miles, Patricia J (412) 664-9161
PUB, Daily News, McKeesport, PA

Mansheffer, Peter S (607) 656-4511
ED, Chenango American/Whitney Point Reporter/Oxford Review-Times, Greene, NY

Manship, David C (504) 383-1111
PUB, Advocate, Baton Rouge, LA

Manship Jr, Doug (504) 383-1111
DIR-New Media, Advocate, Baton Rouge, LA

Manship Sr, Douglas L (504) 383-1111
PRES, Advocate, Baton Rouge, LA

Mansur, Michael (816) 234-4141
Environmental ED
Kansas City Star, Kansas City, MO

Manteiga, Patrick (813) 248-3921
PUB, ED, GM
Community Connections, Tampa, FL

Manteiga, Roland (813) 248-3921
PUB, Community Connections, Tampa, FL

Manteufel, Jim (415) 777-5700
DIR-Internal Audit, San Francisco Newspaper Agency, San Francisco, CA

Mantina, Lisa (517) 265-5111
Religion ED, Daily Telegram, Adrian, MI

Mantineo, Andrea (201) 358-6697
ED, America Oggi, Westwood, NJ

Mantle, John E (803) 547-2353
PUB, Fort Mill Times, Fort Mill, SC

Mantle, Linda Matz (314) 432-3353
ED, Saint Louis Jewish Light, St. Louis, MO

Mantooth, Rick (915) 653-1221
ADV SUPV-Outside Sales/CLASS
Standard-Times, San Angelo, TX

Mantua, Elaine (403) 429-5400
Librarian
Edmonton Journal, Edmonton, AB

145-Who's Where **Mar**

Manty, Kris .... (906) 482-1500
Regional ED
Daily Mining Gazette, Houghton, MI
Mantz-Drake, Barb .... (309) 686-3000
EPE, Journal Star, Peoria, IL
Manuel, Fredrick G .... (313) 246-0828
PUB
News-Herald Newspapers, Southgate, MI
Manugian, Rick .... (360) 377-3711
Presentation ED, Sun, Bremerton, WA
Manus, Tanya .... (520) 453-4237
Features ED
Today's News-Herald, Lake Havasu City, AZ
Manz, Kenneth W .... (212) 837-7000
VP/CFO, Senior VP-FIN/OPER, Journal of Commerce & Commercial, New York, NY
Manzano, Erlinda H .... (805) 323-9334
GM, El Mexicalo, Bakersfield, CA
Manzano, Esther H .... (805) 323-9334
PUB, El Mexicalo, Bakersfield, CA
Manzano, Tony H .... (805) 323-9334
ED, El Mexicalo, Bakersfield, CA
Manzi, Albert .... (717) 829-7100
CIRC VP/DIR-OPER
Times Leader, Wilkes-Barre, PA
Manzi, Robert .... (601) 961-7000
DIR-FIN, Clarion-Ledger, Jackson, MS
Manzie, Nick .... (312) 321-3000
CIRC MGR-Suburban, CIRC MGR-Home Delivery, Chicago Sun-Times, Chicago, IL
Mao, Xiao-Yin .... (212) 343-9717
GM, MAN ED
New Jersey China Times, Edison, NJ
Mapes, Chris .... (616) 845-5181
PROD SUPT, Daily News, Ludington, MI
Maqalhaes, Maria .... (203) 729-2228
CIRC MGR, Daily News, Naugatuck, CT
Mara, Jamie .... (715) 384-3131
City ED, Society ED
Marshfield News-Herald, Marshfield, WI
Marabell, Linda .... (802) 863-3441
DIR-MKTG SRV
Burlington Free Press, Burlington, VT
Marben, Don R .... (507) 726-2133
PUB, ED
Lake Crystal Tribune, Lake Crystal, MN
Marbert, Larry .... (305) 376-3800
VP-Technology
Knight-Ridder Inc., Miami, FL
Marbery, Amantha .... (515) 856-6336
Sports/City ED
Ad Express & Daily Iowegian, Centerville, IA
Marble, Steve .... (714) 642-4321
MAN ED, Daily Pilot, Costa Mesa, CA
Marbut, Dale .... (316) 792-1211
PROD FRM-PR
Great Bend Tribune, Great Bend, KS
Marcangelo, Frank .... (312) 321-3000
VP-Production, PROD VP
Chicago Sun-Times, Chicago, IL
Marcano, Sandra .... (315) 331-1000
ED, Courier-Gazette, Newark, NY
Marceau, Jean .... (418) 686-3233
PROD FRM-COMP, Le Soleil, Quebec, QC
Marcella, Carol .... (414) 877-2813
ED, Westosha Report, Twin Lakes, WI
Marcella, Dennis .... (519) 756-2020
Books ED, Features ED, Music ED, Radio/Television ED, Expositor, Brantford, ON
March, Bill .... (215) 854-2000
Design DIR
Philadelphia Inquirer, Philadelphia, PA
March, Lorraine .... (604) 836-2570
ED, Eagle Valley News, Sicamous, BC
March, William .... (813) 259-7711
Political Writer
Tampa Tribune and Times, Tampa, FL
Marchand, Chris .... (517) 772-2971
Sports, Mount Pleasant Morning Sun, Mount Pleasant, MI
Marchand, Dave .... (219) 726-8141
Photo DEPT MGR, PROD SUPT, PROD FRM-COMP, Commercial Review, Portland, IN
Marchand, Deborah .... (212) 556-4204
DIR Graphics/Photo, NYT Photo Service, NYT Graphics, New York, NY
Marchant, Glenn .... (902) 447-2051
PUB, Oxford Journal, Oxford, NS
Marchetti, Reesa .... (609) 935-1500
COL, SCI/Technology ED
Today's Sunbeam, Salem, NJ
Marchio, Bob .... (717) 637-3736
News ED, Evening Sun, Hanover, PA
Marchione, Robert L .... (617) 254-0334
PUB, Boston Citizen Journal, Boston, MA
Marciel, Bob .... (808) 525-8000
CIRC MGR-Sales
Hawaii Newspaper Agency Inc., Honolulu, HI
Marcil Jr, Bill .... (701) 253-7311
MGR-MKTG, Forum, Fargo, ND
Marcil, Jane B .... (701) 235-7311
SEC/TREAS
Forum Communications Co., Fargo, ND
Marcil, William C .... (701) 235-7311
PRES/CEO
Forum Communications Co., Fargo, ND
Marcille, Lorraine .... (800) 281-3802
GM, Rutland Tribune, Rutland, VT
Marciochi, Alan .... (520) 763-2505
Entertainment ED
Mohave Valley Daily News, Bullhead City, AZ
Marcks, Drew .... (512) 445-3500
ASST MAN ED
Austin American-Statesman, Austin, TX
Marcon, Paul .... (705) 674-5271
ADV MGR, Sudbury Star, Sudbury, ON
Marcotte, Duane .... (507) 454-6500
PROD MGR-Graphics/Pre Press
Winona Daily News, Winona, MN
Marcoux, Maurice .... (508) 222-7000
PROD FRM-PR
Sun Chronicle, Attleboro, MA
Marcoux-Prevost, Angele .... (514) 455-7955
ED, 1ere Edition du Sud-Quest, Vandreuil-Dorion, QC
Marcum, Dan .... (812) 663-3111
Sports ED
Greensburg Daily News, Greensburg, IN
Marcum, Ken .... (510) 208-6300
DP MGR, Oakland Tribune, Oakland, CA
MediaNews Inc. (Alameda Newspapers)
Marcum, Kim .... (410) 332-6000
Features ED, Sun, Baltimore, MD
Marcum, Lisa A .... (304) 235-4242
ADV MGR-RT, MGR-MKTG/PROM, PROD FRM-COMP
Williamson Daily News, Williamson, WV
Marcum, William .... (360) 577-2500
ADV DIR, MGR-MKTG/PROM
Daily News, Longview, WA
Marcus, Amy Dockser .... (212) 416-2000
Reporter-in-Charge (Tel Aviv)
Wall Street Journal, New York, NY
Marcus, David .... (508) 744-0600
ED, Salem Evening News, Beverly, MA
Marcus, Ruth .... (312) 407-0060
MAN ED, Sentinel, Chicago, IL
Marcy, Ann .... (405) 772-3301
City ED
Weatherford Daily News, Weatherford, OK
Mardenborough, Leslie A .... (212) 556-1234
VP-Human Resources
New York Times Co., New York, NY
Marder, Keith .... (818) 713-3000
Television COL
Daily News, Woodland Hills, CA
Mardis, Bill .... (606) 678-8191
MAN ED
Commonwealth-Journal, Somerset, KY
Marek, Cynthia M .... (307) 634-3361
ADV MGR-NTL
Wyoming Tribune-Eagle, Cheyenne, WY
Marek, Joseph M .... (847) 427-4300
CIRC MGR-Single Copy Sales
Daily Herald, Arlington Heights, IL
Marek, Joycelyn .... (713) 220-7171
VP-MKTG and New Media
Houston Chronicle, Houston, TX
Marek, Patrick .... (507) 452-1262
GM, Winona Post & Shopper, Winona, MN
Marelius, John .... (619) 299-3131
Political Writer
San Diego Union-Tribune, San Diego, CA
Mares, Nicholas .... (412) 263-1100
PROD MGR-SYS
Pittsburgh Post-Gazette, Pittsburgh, PA
Maret, Dee .... (813) 259-7711
News ED
Tampa Tribune and Times, Tampa, FL
Marez, JoAnne .... (360) 377-3711
Health/Medical Writer
Bremerton Sun, Bremerton, WA
Margolies, Peter .... (608) 524-4336
ED, Times-Press, Reedsburg, WI
Margolis, David .... (416) 441-1405
Southern Europe & Middle East Journalist
Fotopress Independent News Service International (FPINS), Toronto, ON
Margolis, Eleanor .... (617) 969-4102
VP, Travel & Leisure Features, Newton, MA
Margulies, Lee .... (213) 237-5000
TV Times ED
Los Angeles Times, Los Angeles, CA
Mariani, Gary .... (906) 932-2211
BM
Ironwood Daily Globe, Ironwood, MI
Maricich, Ruth .... (510) 935-2525
ADV MGR-RT
Contra Costa Times, Walnut Creek, CA
Marien, Ray .... (619) 241-7744
ADV MGR-RT, Daily Press, Victorville, CA
Maril, David .... (508) 473-1111
Sports ED
Milford Daily News, Milford, MA
Marimow, William .... (410) 332-6000
MAN ED, Sun, Baltimore, MD
Marin, David .... (408) 372-3311
ADV MGR-CLASS/RES, MGR-Audiotex Services, Monterey County Herald, Monterey, CA
Mariniello, Gabe .... (201) 646-4000
MGR-Purchasing, Record, Hackensack, NJ
Marino, Edward .... (908) 922-6000
Community ED
Asbury Park Press, Neptune, NJ
Marino, Eugene .... (716) 232-7100
Television/Radio ED, Rochester Democrat and Chronicle; Times-Union, Rochester, NY
Marino, Joe .... (416) 947-2191
GM, Canada Wide Feature Service Ltd., Toronto, ON
Marino, Louis .... (860) 347-3331
Wire ED, Middletown Press, Middletown, CT
Marino, Mike .... (801) 625-4200
Automotive ED, BUS/FIN ED, Farm/Agriculture ED, Standard-Examiner, Ogden, UT
Mario, Luis .... (305) 633-3341
News ED, Diario Las Americas, Miami, FL
Marion Jr, Harold F .... (717) 348-9100
GM, Times-Shamrock Communications Scranton, PA
Mariona, Sihanouk .... (212) 362-9256
ASST ED, Cartoonists & Writers Syndicate, New York, NY
Mark, Rick .... (812) 424-7711
Family/Leisure ED, News ED, Women's ED
Evansville Press, Evansville, IN
Markevicz, George .... (334) 433-1551
CIRC DIR, Mobile Press Register, Mobile, AL
Markey Jr, Bob .... (561) 793-7606
PUB, ED, Town Crier, Wellington, FL
Markey, Jonathan H .... (201) 646-4000
PRES, Record, Hackensack, NJ
Markey, Judy .... (312) 321-3000
COL-GEN, Chicago Sun-Times, Chicago, IL
Markgraf, Richard .... (619) 435-2514
Self-Syndicator
Markgraf, Richard, Coronado, CA
Markham, Dan .... (608) 897-2193
ED, Independent-Register, Brodhead, WI
Markham, Kim .... (608) 897-2193
PUB, Independent-Register, Brodhead, WI
Markham, Virginia .... (805) 273-2700
VP, Antelope Valley Press, Palmdale, CA
Markham, William C .... (805) 273-2700
PRES/PUB
Antelope Valley Press, Palmdale, CA
Markle, Ted .... (514) 521-4545
PROD MGR
Le Journal de Montreal, Montreal, QC
Marko, James .... (330) 841-1600
PROD FRM-MR
Tribune Chronicle, Warren, OH
Marko, Shaun .... (605) 428-5441
ED, Dell Rapids Tribune, Dell Rapids, SD
Markowitz, Andy .... (410) 523-2300
ED, Baltimore City Paper, Baltimore, MD
Markowski, Kevin .... (203) 235-1661
Cartoonist, Record-Journal, Meriden, CT
Marks, Charles W .... (219) 589-2101
PUB, Berne Tri Weekly News, Berne, IN
Marks, Doug .... (515) 832-4350
Sports ED
Daily Freeman-Journal, Webster City, IA
Marks, Edwin .... (215) 747-6684
PRES/PUB
Cricket Communications Inc., Ardmore, PA
Marks, Fred .... (201) 877-4141
ADV MGR-GEN, Star-Ledger, Newark, NJ
Marks, Linda .... (805) 650-2900
ADV MGR-RT
Ventura County Star, Ventura, CA
Marks, Marlene .... (213) 738-7778
MAN ED, Jewish Journal of Greater Los Angeles, Los Angeles, CA
Marks, Ted .... (860) 927-3948
PRES
Marks & Frederick Associates Inc., Kent, CT
Marks-Erickson, Jamie .... (218) 847-3151
ED
Becker County Record, Detroit Lakes, MN
Markstein, Gary .... (414) 224-2000
Cartoonist, Journal Sentinel, Milwaukee, WI
Markward, Phil .... (219) 925-2611
PROD MGR, Evening Star, Auburn, IN
Witwer Newspapers
Marlatt, Toby F .... (307) 326-8311
ED, Saratoga Sun, Saratoga, WY
Marlean, Lynn .... (510) 661-2600
ADV DIR, Argus, Fremont, CA
Marlette, Doug .... (516) 843-2020
Cartoonist, Newsday, Melville, NY
Marlow, David .... (701) 572-2165
ADV MGR
Williston Daily Herald, Williston, ND
Marlow, Ron .... (806) 376-4488
Photo DEPT MGR, Amarillo Daily News/Globe Times, Amarillo, TX
Marlow, Tim .... (712) 732-3130
PROD MGR-COMP
Pilot Tribune, Storm Lake, IA
Marlowe, Betty .... (423) 472-5041
Farm ED, Living/Lifestyle ED, Society ED, Women's ED
Cleveland Daily Banner, Cleveland, TN
Marlowe, Nancy .... (704) 252-5611
Lifestyle ED
Asheville Citizen-Times, Asheville, NC
Marmes, Loran .... (414) 338-0622
PROD MGR-PR, Daily News, West Bend, WI
Marocco, Nicholas J .... (602) 977-8351
PROD MGR-Distribution
Daily News-Sun, Sun City, AZ
Marocco, Sam L .... (602) 977-8351
PRES/PUB, Daily News-Sun, Sun City, AZ
Maroney, David .... (219) 583-5121
ED, Herald Journal, Monticello, IN
Maroney, Russell E .... (812) 944-6481
PUB
Tribune/Ledger & Tribune, New Albany, IN
Marose, Ron .... (608) 786-1950
ED, La Crosse County Countryman, West Salem, WI
Marowits, Ross .... (519) 756-2020
Political ED, Expositor, Brantford, ON
Marple, Deborah .... (520) 458-9440
BM, Sierra Vista Herald, Sierra Vista, AZ
Wick Communications
Marple, Ken .... (209) 441-6111
PROD MGR-Plant Engineering
Fresno Bee, Fresno, CA
Marquard, Bryan .... (603) 298-8711
News ED, Valley News, White River Jct., VT
Marquard, Jill .... (603) 298-8711
Wire ED, Valley News, White River Jct., VT
Marquardt, Tom .... (410) 268-5000
MAN ED, Capital, Annapolis, MD
Marques, Stuart .... (212) 930-8000
MET ED, New York Post, New York, NY
Marquez, Anthony .... (510) 758-8400
MAN ED, West County Times, Pinole, CA
Marquez, Manny .... (505) 393-2123
ED, EPE, Hobbs Daily News-Sun, Hobbs, NM
Marquez, Manuel .... (408) 920-5000
PROD SUPT-Mechanical
San Jose Mercury News, San Jose, CA
Marquez, Nick .... (970) 668-3998
DP MGR, PROD MGR
Summit Daily News, Frisco, CO
Marquez, Susan .... (909) 684-1200
DIR-Human Resources
Press-Enterprise, Riverside, CA
Marquis, Don .... (716) 232-7100
Photo ED
Rochester Democrat and Chronicle; Rochester, NY Times-Union, Rochester, NY
Marquis, Jennifer .... (716) 232-7100
ASST MAN ED-Local News
Rochester Democrat and Chronicle; Rochester, NY Times-Union, Rochester, NY
Marquis, Michele .... (714) 835-1234
ADV DIR-CLASS/TELEMKTG
Orange County Register, Santa Ana, CA
Marquis, Tom .... (714) 835-1234
ADV DIR-Major/NTL
Orange County Register, Santa Ana, CA
Marr, John .... (203) 333-0161
ADV MGR-CLASS
Connecticut Post, Bridgeport, CT
Marr, Robert L .... (401) 596-7791
Sports ED, Westerly Sun, Westerly, RI
Marr, Wendy .... (506) 375-4458
MAN ED, Observer, Hartland, NB
Marra, Eleanor .... (201) 947-5000
ED
Bergen News Palisades, Palisades Park, NJ
Marran, David .... (414) 657-1000
Sports ED, Kenosha News, Kenosha, WI
Marro, Anthony .... (516) 843-2020
ED/EVP, ED/Senior VP
Newsday, Melville, NY
Marrone, Sergio .... (705) 674-5271
CIRC MGR-Regional
Sudbury Star, Sudbury, ON
Marroni, Tony .... (864) 224-4321
ADV DIR
Anderson Independent-Mail, Anderson, SC
Marrow, Pat .... (816) 886-2233
CIRC MGR
Marshall Democrat-News, Marshall, MO
Marrs, Val .... (562) 698-0955
Community ED, Daily News, Whittier, CA
Marschel, C Thomas .... (803) 317-6397
PUB, Florence Morning News, Florence, SC
Marschke, Steve .... (916) 371-8030
ED, News-Ledger, West Sacramento, CA
Marsden, David .... (250) 762-4445
Westside ED, Daily Courier, Kelowna, BC
Marsh, Carolyn .... (207) 236-8511
ED, Camden Herald, Camden, ME

Mar Who's Where-146

Marsh, Janet (219) 235-6161
ASST MAN ED-News
South Bend Tribune, South Bend, IN

Marsh, John (770) 428-9411
ED, Clayton Neighbor, Forest Park, GA

Marsh Jr, John S (605) 331-2200
EX ED, Argus Leader, Sioux Falls, SD

Marsh, Mary (308) 364-2130
PUB, ED, Indianola News, Indianola, NE

Marsh, Richard (209) 943-6397
EPE, Record, Stockton, CA

Marshall III, Alexander F (614) 633-1131
PUB, Times Leader, Martins Ferry, OH

Marshall, Alice (213) 290-3000
ED
Central-News Wave Group, Los Angeles, CA

Marshall, Andy (403) 235-7100
EDU Reporter, Calgary Herald, Calgary, AB

Marshall, Brian (204) 727-2451
MAN ED, Brandon Sun, Brandon, MB

Marshall, Cynthia (520) 783-3333
ADV MGR-CLASS
Yuma Daily Sun, Yuma, AZ

Marshall, David (403) 429-5400
CR SUPV, Edmonton Journal, Edmonton, AB

Marshall, Gail (209) 441-6111
Lifestyle ED, Fresno Bee, Fresno, CA

Marshall, James G (518) 792-3131
VP, PUB, Post-Star, Glens Falls, NY

Marshall, Jane P (713) 220-7171
Features ED, Houston Chronicle, Houston, TX

Marshall, Janet (941) 687-7000
EDU ED, Ledger, Lakeland, FL

Marshall, John R (419) 659-2173
ED, Putnam County Vidette/Pandora Times, Columbus Grove, OH

Marshall, Jonathan (415) 777-1111
Economics ED
San Francisco Chronicle, San Francisco, CA

Marshall, Marilyn (713) 663-6996
MAN ED, Houston Defender, Houston, TX

Marshall, Marlon (306) 565-8211
MAN ED, Leader-Post, Regina, SK

Marshall, Michael (334) 433-1551
MAN ED, Mobile Press Register, Mobile, AL

Marshall, Phoebe (717) 888-9643
ADV MGR-CLASS, Evening Times, Sayre, PA

Marshall, Rich (209) 441-6111
Deputy MAN ED, Fresno Bee, Fresno, CA

Marshall, Ron (417) 836-1100
CIRC MGR-Single Copy
Springfield News-Leader, Springfield, MO

Marshall, Ruth (812) 936-9630
ED, Springs Valley Herald, French Lick, IN

Marshall, Sandi (304) 354-6917
GM, Calhoun Chronicle, Grantsville, WV

Marshall, Sherrie (612) 673-4000
News Content ED
Star Tribune, Minneapolis, MN

Marshall, Sue (306) 565-8211
Librarian, Leader-Post, Regina, SK

Marshall, Thom (713) 220-7171
COL, Houston Chronicle, Houston, TX

Marshall, Woody (910) 227-0131
DIR-Photography
Times News Publishing Co., Burlington, NC

Marshburn, Peggy (510) 935-2525
MGR-PROM
Contra Costa Times, Walnut Creek, CA

Marshburn, Roxann (708) 336-7000
ASST MAN ED-Lake County
News-Sun, Waukegan, IL

Marsolais, Daniel (514) 285-7272
Desk ED (Evening), La Presse, Montreal, QC

Marsten, Barbara (212) 223-1821
Fashion/Beauty ED, Entertainment News Syndicate, New York, NY

Martaindale, Steve (903) 893-8181
MAN ED, Herald Democrat, Sherman, TX

Martel, Joan (603) 742-4455
PA, Foster's Democrat, Dover, NH

Martens, David B (206) 727-2727
VP, Buckner News Alliance, Seattle, WA

Martens, Dick (612) 222-5011
ADV SUPV-Co-op
St. Paul Pioneer Press, St. Paul, MN

Martens, Margie (605) 594-6315
PUB, ED, Garretson Weekly, Garretson, SD

Martensson, Ulf E (212) 944-0776
PUB, Nordstjernan-Svea, New York, NY

Marter, Marilynn (215) 854-2000
Food CO
Philadelphia Inquirer, Philadelphia, PA

Martieau, David (519) 344-3641
ADV MGR, Observer, Sarnia, ON

Martin, Alan (941) 335-0200
CIRC MGR, News-Press, Fort Myers, FL

Martin, Alex (516) 843-2020
Long Island ED, Newsday, Melville, NY

Martin, Andre (250) 492-4002
ADV MGR, Penticton Herald, Penticton, BC

Martin, Barry (412) 222-2200
ADV DIR, Observer-Reporter, Washington, PA

Martin, Bill (903) 757-3311
PUB, Longview News-Journal, Longview, TX

Martin, Bob (606) 744-3123
CIRC DIR, Winchester Sun, Winchester, KY

Martin, Brad (615) 729-4282
ED, Hickman County Times, Centerville, TN

Martin, Brantley (601) 961-7000
ADV MGR-Preprint
Clarion-Ledger, Jackson, MS

Martin, Brenda (814) 870-1600
Radio/Television ED, RE ED
Morning News/Erie Daily Times, Erie, PA

Martin, Bruce (313) 994-6989
Entertainment/Amusements ED, Films/Theater ED
Ann Arbor News, Ann Arbor, MI

Martin, Carolyn (817) 387-3811
Graphics ED/Art DIR
Denton Record-Chronicle, Denton, TX

Martin, Cathy (319) 283-2144
ADV DIR, Register, Oelwein, IA

Martin, Celia (912) 836-3195
MAN ED, Georgia Post, Roberta, GA

Martin, Charles (615) 388-6464
ADV MGR, Daily Herald, Columbia, TN

Martin, Cheryl (502) 526-4151
MAN ED, Green River Republican & The Butler County Banner, Morgantown, KY

Martin, Chuck (513) 721-2700
Food ED, Cincinnati Enquirer, Cincinnati, OH

Martin, Craig (501) 968-5252
PUB, Courier, Russellville, AR

Martin, Craig (403) 468-0100
PUB, Edmonton Sun, Edmonton, AB

Martin, Dale (415) 348-4321
EDU ED
San Mateo County Times, San Mateo, CA

Martin, Danny A (417) 836-1100
PRES/PUB
Springfield News-Leader, Springfield, MO

Martin, Darrell (214) 977-8222
CIRC DIR, Dallas Morning News, Dallas, TX

Martin, Dave (913) 823-6363
BM, Salina Journal, Salina, KS

Martin, Dave (319) 291-1400
Copy ED, Waterloo Courier, Waterloo, IA

Martin, David (515) 288-3336
MAN ED, Cityview, Des Moines, IA

Martin, David (509) 925-1414
ADV DIR, Daily Record, Ellensburg, WA

Martin, David K (202) 737-1888
ASSOC ED, Roll Call Report Syndicate (Thomas Reports Inc.), Washington, DC

Martin, Dawn (419) 426-3491
ED, Attica Hub, Attica, OH

Martin, Deborah (915) 546-6340
Amusements/Films ED, Music ED-Classical, Music ED-Rock/Country, Radio/Television ED, Theater ED, El Paso Herald-Post, El Paso, TX

Martin, Deborah M (610) 371-5000
Assignment ED
Reading Times/Eagle, Reading, PA

Martin, Debra (604) 334-8722
ED, Comox Valley Echo, Courtenay, BC

Martin, Dennis (316) 285-3111
MAN ED, ADV MGR
Tiller & Toiler, Larned, KS

Martin, Dennis (414) 248-4444
MAN ED, Lake Geneva Regional News, Lake Geneva, WI

Martin, Diane (860) 442-2200
ADV CNR-Co-op, Day, New London, CT

Martin, Don (403) 235-7100
COL, Calgary Herald, Calgary, AB

Martin, Donna (816) 932-6600
VP/Contributing ED
Universal Press Syndicate, Kansas City, MO

Martin, Dorsey (706) 782-3312
ED, Clayton Tribune, Clayton, GA

Martin, Dotty (717) 287-8484
PUB, ED, West Side Weekly, Forty Fort, PA

Martin, Doug (604) 732-2944
PROD GEN FRM-PR
Pacific Press Limited, Vancouver, BC

Martin, Edmund O (405) 475-3311
VP, GM
Daily Oklahoman, Oklahoma City, OK

Martin, Edward C (540) 949-8213
CIRC DIR, News Virginian, Waynesboro, VA

Martin, Esther (815) 987-1200
CIRC MGR-Home Delivery
Rockford Register Star, Rockford, IL
Gannett Co. Inc.

Martin III, Frank L (417) 256-9191
PRES, SEC/TREAS, PUB, ED, EPE, Political/Government ED, SCI ED
West Plains Daily Quill, West Plains, MO

Martin, Fred (501) 378-3400
PROD MGR-MR
Arkansas Democrat-Gazette, Little Rock, AR

Martin, Gaston (418) 668-4548
GM, ED, Le Lac St. Jean, Alma, QC

Martin, George (608) 862-3224
PUB, ED, Albany Herald, Albany, WI

Martin Jr, George (518) 454-5694
CIRC DIR, Times Union, Albany, NY

Martin, Glenn A (305) 245-2311
PUB
South Dade News Leader, Homestead, FL

Martin, Greg (601) 323-1642
CIRC MGR, Daily News, Starkville, MS

Martin, Greg (417) 742-2539
ED, Cross Country Times, Willard, MO

Martin, Helen J (517) 269-6461
ADV MGR, Huron Daily Tribune, Bad Axe, MI

Martin, Holly (407) 242-3500
Radio/Television ED
Florida Today, Melbourne, FL

Martin, J E (515) 648-2521
GM, Times-Citizen, Iowa Falls, IA

Martin, James (609) 272-7000
PROD MGR-MR
Press of Atlantic City, Pleasantville, NJ

Martin, James W (803) 577-7111
TREAS
Evening Post Publishing Co., Charleston, SC

Martin, Jeanne (413) 772-0261
ADV MGR-CLASS, Recorder, Greenfield, MA

Martin, Jennifer (417) 358-2191
PROD SUPT, Carthage Press, Carthage, MO

Martin, Jessie (804) 385-5400
Entertainment/Amusements ED, Radio/Television ED, News & Advance, Lynchburg, VA

Martin, Jim (412) 981-6100
Farm/Agriculture ED, Herald, Sharon, PA

Martin, Joe (916) 894-2300
ED, Chico News & Review, Chico, CA

Martin, Joe (804) 649-6000
PROD MGR-Commercial Print Shop
Richmond Times-Dispatch, Richmond, VA

Martin, John (401) 277-7000
Radio/Television Writer
Providence Journal-Bulletin, Providence, RI

Martin, John (414) 435-4411
Sports ED
Green Bay Press-Gazette, Green Bay, WI

Martin, John (219) 881-3000
PROD MGR-PR, Post-Tribune, Gary, IN

Martin, John P (914) 331-5000
ADV DIR, Daily Freeman, Kingston, NY

Martin, Julia (718) 981-1234
Religion ED
Staten Island Advance, Staten Island, NY

Martin, Julie (203) 729-2228
Features/Ski ED
Naugatuck Daily News, Naugatuck, CT

Martin, Keith (202) 636-3000
PROD MGR-Printing OPER
Washington Times, Washington, DC

Martin, Kirk (601) 961-7000
PROD MGR-Tech SRV
Clarion-Ledger, Jackson, MS

Martin III, L Richmond (540) 981-3100
ASSOC ED, Roanoke Times, Roanoke, VA

Martin, Lance (919) 537-2505
BUS/FIN ED, News ED
Daily Herald, Roanoke Rapids, NC

Martin, Larry E (606) 789-5315
PUB, Paintsville Herald, Paintsville, KY

Martin, Larry T (520) 573-4400
CIRC VP, TNI Partners dba Tucson Newspapers, Tucson, AZ

Martin, Leonard C (208) 232-4161
ADV DIR, Idaho State Journal, Pocatello, ID

Martin, Les (202) 334-6000
PROD ASST MGR-Plant/MR (SE)
Washington Post, Washington, DC

Martin, Linda (206) 463-9195
PUB, Vashon-Maury Island Beachcomber, Vashon Island, WA

Martin, Lori D (707) 644-1141
DIR-MKTG/PROM
Vallejo Times-Herald, Vallejo, CA

Martin, Louise (907) 456-6661
ADV MGR-RT
Fairbanks Daily News-Miner, Fairbanks, AK

Martin, Lynn L (405) 327-2200
PUB, GM, Alva Review-Courier, Alva, OK

Martin, Margaret (318) 459-3200
Fashion ED, Times, Shreveport, LA

Martin, Marione (405) 327-2200
ED, Alva Review-Courier, Alva, OK

Martin, Matt (919) 708-9000
Sports ED, Sanford Herald, Sanford, NC

Martin, Mike (941) 953-7755
DIR-Publishing Technologies
Sarasota Herald-Tribune, Sarasota, FL

Martin, Nancy (941) 953-7755
CIRC MGR-County
Sarasota Herald-Tribune, Sarasota, FL

Martin Jr, Norman (209) 722-1511
MAN ED, Merced Sun-Star, Merced, CA

Martin, Patrick (416) 585-5000
Foreign ED, Globe and Mail, Toronto, ON

Martin, Patrick (409) 396-3391
ED, Normangee Star, Normangee, TX

Martin, Pete (864) 574-2777
ED, Your Paper, Spartanburg, SC

Martin, Ralph (301) 627-2833
PUB
Maryland Independent, Upper Marlboro, MD

Martin, Ralph J (315) 393-1000
VP-Newspapers, Courier-Observer Journal & Advance-News, Ogdensburg, NY
Park Communications Inc.

Martin, Ray (704) 864-3291
DP MGR, PROD MGR
Gaston Gazette, Gastonia, NC

Martin, Richard (408) 424-2221
Sports ED, Californian, Salinas, CA

Martin, Richard D (414) 657-1000
COL, Kenosha News, Kenosha, WI

Martin, Rick (504) 826-3279
ADV MGR-Copy/Art SRV
Times-Picayune, New Orleans, LA

Martin, Rick (334) 347-9533
GM, Enterprise Ledger, Enterprise, AL

Martin, Rita J (413) 788-1000
ADV MGR-Major Accounts
Union-News, Springfield, MA

Martin, Robert (202) 898-8254
ED-International
United Press International, Washington, DC

Martin, Robert (408) 424-2221
CIRC MGR, Californian, Salinas, CA

Martin, Robert E (904) 359-4111
GM, Florida Times-Union, Jacksonville, FL

Martin Jr, Robert L (309) 547-3055
PUB, Fulton Democrat, Lewistown, IL

Martin, Ron (404) 526-5151
ED, Atlanta Journal-Constitution, Atlanta, GA

Martin, Ron (502) 227-4556
PROD FRM-COMP
State Journal, Frankfort, KY

Martin, Ronald L (609) 871-8000
EX ED
Burlington County Times, Willingboro, NJ

Martin, Ryne R (315) 393-1000
MAN ED (Courier-Observer), Courier-Observer Journal & Advance-News, Ogdensburg, NY

Martin, Samuel P (302) 324-2500
ADV DIR, News Journal, Wilmington, DE

Martin Sr, Samuel (909) 889-7677
PUB, American News, San Bernardino, CA

Martin Jr, Samuel (909) 889-7677
ED, American News, San Bernardino, CA

Martin, Shirley (209) 943-6397
MGR-CR, Record, Stockton, CA

Martin, Stan (914) 782-4000
PUB, Pointer View, Monroe, NY

Martin, Stephen (602) 468-6565
National CIRC DIR
Daily Racing Form, Phoenix, AZ

Martin, Stephen (217) 852-3511
MAN ED
Dallas City Enterprise, Dallas City, IL

Martin, Steve (406) 657-1200
PROD MGR-Press
Billings Gazette, Billings, MT

Martin, Steve (409) 265-7411
PROD Press, Brazosport Facts, Clute, TX

Martin, Susan (716) 849-3434
Fashion ED, Buffalo News, Buffalo, NY

Martin, Susan Taylor (813) 893-8111
Deputy MAN ED
St. Petersburg Times, St. Petersburg, FL

Martin, Talmadge (502) 443-1771
ADV CNR-NTL, Paducah Sun, Paducah, KY

Martin, Terri (806) 653-2871
PUB, ED
Lipscomb County Limelight, Follett, TX

Martin, Thomas (937) 382-2574
CIRC DIR, News Journal, Wilmington, OH

Martin, Thomas E (419) 294-2332
PUB, GM/PA, ADV MGR, MGR-MKTG/PROM
Daily Chief-Union, Upper Sandusky, OH

Martin, Todd (915) 653-1221
BUS/FIN Writer
Standard-Times, San Angelo, TX

Martin, Tom (309) 833-2114
News ED, Macomb Journal, Macomb, IL

Martin, Tommy E (864) 488-1016
PUB, Cherokee Chronicle, Gaffney, SC

Martin, Tony (573) 624-4545
Sports ED, Daily Statesman, Dexter, MO

Martin, Travis (910) 623-2155
Sports ED, Daily News, Eden, NC

Martin, Wade H (501) 935-5525
GM, Jonesboro Sun, Jonesboro, AR

Martin, Wendy J (309) 543-3311
ED, Mason County Democrat, Havana, IL

Martin, William E (606) 329-1717
Graphics ED/Art DIR
Daily Independent, Ashland, KY

147-Who's Where **Mat**

Martin, Willie Mae .... (909) 889-7677
PUB, American News, San Bernardino, CA

Martin-Almy, James .... (360) 832-4411
PUB
South Pierce County Dispatch, Eatonville, WA

Martindale, Cathy A .... (806) 376-4488
EX ED, Amarillo Daily News/Globe Times, Amarillo, TX

Martine, Steven .... (208) 882-5561
Picture ED
Moscow-Pullman Daily News, Moscow, ID

Martineau, Janet I .... (517) 752-7171
Amusements ED, Films/Theater ED, Music ED, Radio/Television ED
Saginaw News, Saginaw, MI

Martinelli, Ralph R .... (914) 965-4000
PUB, Home News & Times, Yonkers, NY

Martinez, Al .... (213) 237-5000
COL-Local
Los Angeles Times, Los Angeles, CA

Martinez, Angela .... (305) 885-5111
PUB, ED, Sol de Hialeah, Hialeah, FL

Martinez, Art .... (201) 877-4141
Features/Entertainment ED
Star-Ledger, Newark, NJ

Martinez, Bobby .... (212) 807-4600
CIRC DIR, El Diario La Prensa, New York, NY

Martinez, Horacio .... (213) 622-8332
GM, La Opinion, Los Angeles, CA

Martinez, Irma .... (210) 849-7403
GM, Roma Star, Roma, TX

Martinez, James .... (915) 546-6340
City ED, El Paso Herald-Post, El Paso, TX

Martinez, Jim .... (415) 348-4321
PROD FRM-MR
San Mateo County Times, San Mateo, CA

Martinez, Jody .... (707) 468-3500
ASST ED, Ukiah Daily Journal, Ukiah, CA

Martinez, Jorge .... (212) 563-2252
Latin American Sales MGR
Editors Press Service Inc., New York, NY

Martinez, Jose M .... (213) 388-4639
GM, LA Voz Libre, Los Angeles, CA

Martinez, Julie .... (512) 387-4511
MAN ED
Nueces County Record-Star, Robstown, TX

Martinez, Karen .... (316) 694-5700
Lifestyle ED, Religion ED
Hutchinson News, Hutchinson, KS

Martinez, Larry .... (360) 225-8287
ED, Lewis River News/Kalama Bulletin, Woodland, WA

Martinez, Marino .... (305) 633-3341
Sports ED, Diario Las Americas, Miami, FL

Martinez, Mark .... (509) 787-4511
ED, Quincy Valley Post Register, Quincy, WA

Martinez, Nelson .... (203) 964-2200
Design DIR
Stamford Advocate, Stamford, CT

Martinez, Rick .... (215) 949-4000
Environmental Writer
Bucks County Courier Times, Levittown, PA

Martinez, Rick .... (219) 665-3117
ED, Herald-Republican, Angola, IN

Martinez, Vic .... (707) 468-3500
PROD MGR, Ukiah Daily Journal, Ukiah, CA

Martini, Dorothy .... (407) 242-3500
DIR-MIS, Florida Today, Melbourne, FL

Martins, John .... (207) 985-2961
ED, York County Coast Star, Kennebunk, ME

Martinsen, Jeffrey O .... (406) 466-2403
PUB, Choteau Acantha, Choteau, MT

Martinsen, Melody .... (406) 466-2403
ED, Choteau Acantha, Choteau, MT

Martinson, Suzanne .... (412) 263-1100
Food ED
Pittsburgh Post-Gazette, Pittsburgh, PA

Martinuk, Melodee .... (519) 886-2830
ED, Waterloo Chronicle, Waterloo, ON

Martoccia, Mike .... (812) 372-7811
City ED, Republic, Columbus, IN

Martonosi, Leo .... (616) 392-2311
Sports ED, Holland Sentinel, Holland, MI

Martslof-Miller, Marcia .... (717) 637-3736
ADV MGR, Evening Sun, Hanover, PA

Marty, John .... (213) 721-1735
PUB, ED
Montebello Messenger, Montebello, CA

Marty, Mary E .... (617) 929-2000
ASST TREAS, Boston Globe, Boston, MA

Martz, JoHanne Zerbey .... (717) 622-3456
ASST SEC/TREAS, Pottsville Republican & Evening Herald, Pottsville, PA

Martz, Larry .... (212) 889-5155
ED, World Press Review, New York, NY

Martz Jr, Uzal H .... (717) 622-3456
PRES, TREAS, PUB, Pottsville Republican & Evening Herald, Pottsville, PA

Marujo, David .... (508) 997-7411
DIR-MIS, PROD FRM-Pre Press
Standard Times, New Bedford, MA

Maruyama, Toru .... (212) 603-6600
Correspondent
Kyodo News Service, New York, NY

Marvel, Betsy .... (302) 645-2265
CIRC DIR, Daily Whale, Lewes, DE

Marx, Andy .... (501) 534-3400
Photo ED, Commercial, Pine Bluff, AR

Marx, Gary .... (618) 529-5454
News ED, Southern Illinoisan, Carbondale, IL

Marx, Hal .... (601) 428-0551
MAN ED, EPE, RE ED
Laurel Leader-Call, Laurel, MS

Marx, John .... (309) 786-6441
COL, Rock Island Argus, Rock Island, IL

Maryanski, Ken .... (510) 757-2525
City ED, Ledger Dispatch, Antioch, CA

Marymont, Mark .... (417) 836-1100
Music ED, News-Leader, Springfield, MO

Marymount, Kate .... (417) 836-1100
MAN ED, News-Leader, Springfield, MO

Maryniak, Paul .... (215) 854-2000
City ED-Enterprise
Philadelphia Daily News, Philadelphia, PA

Mascarella, Paul .... (213) 622-8332
DIR-MIS, La Opinion, Los Angeles, CA

Mascarenas, Steve .... (505) 325-4545
CIRC MGR, Daily Times, Farmington, NM

Mascaro, Mitch .... (801) 752-2121
Photo ED, Herald Journal, Logan, UT

Masenheimer, Fred L .... (610) 377-2051
GM, Times News, Lehighton, PA

Masenheimer, Scott .... (610) 377-2051
ADV MGR-PROM
Times News, Lehighton, PA

Masessa Jr, Michael A .... (508) 475-5731
GM, Andover Townsman, Andover, MA

Mashburn, Dan .... (423) 523-3131
CIRC DIR-Alternate Direct Delivery
Knoxville News-Sentinel, Knoxville, TN

Masingale, Bob .... (619) 745-6611
City ED-San Marcos
North County Times, Escondido, CA

Masingale, Jim .... (510) 935-2525
PROD MGR-Packaging Center
Contra Costa Times, Walnut Creek, CA

Maslar, John .... (413) 592-1400
PUB, Chicopee Herald Weekly, Chicopee, MA

Mason, Amy .... (614) 283-4711
CIRC DIR, Herald-Star, Steubenville, OH

Mason, Bob .... (214) 977-8222
PROD MGR-Technical Services
Dallas Morning News, Dallas, TX

Mason, Cathy .... (517) 354-3111
City/MET ED, EPE, Health/Medical ED
Alpena News, Alpena, MI

Mason, Charles .... (304) 652-4141
ED, Tyler Star News, Sistersville, WV

Mason, Christine .... (702) 383-0211
Weekend ED
Las Vegas Review-Journal, Las Vegas, NV

Mason, Delores .... (812) 424-7711
ADV MGR-Territory Sales
Evansville Courier Co. Inc., Evansville, IN

Mason, Dick .... (541) 963-3161
EDU ED, Outdoors ED
Observer, La Grande, OR

Mason, Dina .... (501) 239-8562
PUB, Paragould Daily Press, Paragould, AR

Mason, Don .... (713) 220-7171
Projects ED, Houston Chronicle, Houston, TX

Mason, F Dal .... (417) 751-2322
PUB, ED
Ash Grove Commonwealth, Ash Grove, MO

Mason, Mrs F Dal .... (417) 751-2322
PUB
Ash Grove Commonwealth, Ash Grove, MO

Mason, Felicia .... (757) 247-4600
Staff Development ED
Daily Press, Newport News, VA

Mason, Guy .... (918) 623-0123
PUB, ED
Okemah News Leader, Okemah, OK

Mason, Jim .... (937) 592-3060
ADTX MGR
Bellefontaine Examiner, Bellefontaine, OH

Mason, Jim .... (561) 461-2050
PROD FRM-PR, Tribune, Fort Pierce, FL

Mason Sr, Joe V .... (501) 628-4161
PUB, ED, Lincoln Ledger, Star City, AR

Mason, John .... (309) 686-3000
PROD FRM-Press, Journal Star, Peoria, IL

Mason, John .... (409) 985-5541
PROD ASST MGR-Press
Port Arthur News, Port Arthur, TX

Mason, Joseph .... (609) 663-6000
PROD ASST DIR
Courier-Post, Cherry Hill, NJ

Mason, Matthew .... (217) 732-2101
PROD FRM-Press, Courier, Lincoln, IL

Mason, Regina .... (208) 783-1107
BM, Shoshone News-Press, Kellogg, ID

Mason, Scott .... (518) 792-3131
PROD FRM-Shipping & Receiving
Post-Star, Glens Falls, NY

Mason, Sheila .... (515) 284-8000
CIRC MGR-OPER
Des Moines Register, Des Moines, IA

Masotto, Sharon .... (412) 981-6100
ADV CNR-RT Sales, Herald, Sharon, PA

Massa, Joe .... (504) 826-3279
EDL Writer
Times-Picayune, New Orleans, LA

Massaglia, Mark .... (715) 623-4191
Sports ED, Antigo Daily Journal, Antigo, WI

Massaro, Chuck .... (614) 283-4711
City ED, Herald-Star, Steubenville, OH

Masse, Lucie .... (514) 646-3333
PUB, Le Courrier du Sud/South Shore Courier, Longueuil, QC

Massek, Mike .... (913) 762-5000
CIRC DIR, Daily Union, Junction City, KS

Massett, Ray .... (504) 826-3279
VP/SEC, BM
Times-Picayune, New Orleans, LA

Massey, Craig .... (505) 523-4581
News ED
Las Cruces Sun-News, Las Cruces, NM

Massey, Ike .... (818) 962-8811
PUB/CEO, San Gabriel Valley Tribune, West Covina, CA, MediaNews Inc.

Massey, Jim .... (715) 833-9270
ED, Country Today, Eau Claire, WI

Massey, Lynette .... (308) 995-4441
CIRC MGR
Holdrege Daily Citizen, Holdrege, NE

Massey, Patricia .... (817) 739-2141
PUB, Teague Chronicle, Teague, TX

Massey, Paul J .... (907) 456-6661
PUB
Fairbanks Daily News-Miner, Fairbanks, AK

Massey, Rob .... (519) 822-4310
Sports ED, Daily Mercury, Guelph, ON

Massey, Sandra .... (205) 734-2131
ED, Cullman Times, Cullman, AL

Massey, Steve .... (817) 739-2141
ED, Teague Chronicle, Teague, TX

Massey, Thomas .... (201) 646-4000
MGR-Facilities, Record, Hackensack, NJ

Massi, Giselle .... (303) 820-1010
TV Week ED, Denver Post, Denver, CO

Massie, Linda .... (304) 845-2660
CIRC MGR
Moundsville Daily Echo, Moundsville, WV

Massie, P .... (613) 562-0111
Comptroller, Le Droit, Ottawa, ON

Massie, Steve .... (414) 733-4411
Graphics ED/Art DIR
Post-Crescent, Appleton, WI

Massing, Dana .... (814) 870-1600
EDU ED
Morning News/Erie Daily Times, Erie, PA

Masson, Claude .... (514) 285-7272
VP/ASST PUB, La Presse, Montreal, QC

Massoth, Michele .... (815) 987-1200
ADV MGR-RT
Rockford Register Star, Rockford, IL

Mast, Greg .... (913) 242-4700
Sports ED, Ottawa Herald, Ottawa, KS

Mast, Joel .... (937) 592-3060
Religion ED
Bellefontaine Examiner, Bellefontaine, OH

Mast, Robert .... (219) 294-1661
Wire ED, Elkhart Truth, Elkhart, IN

Master, Brian .... (416) 367-2000
CIRC MGR-Sales, Toronto Star, Toronto, ON

Master, Judy E .... (416) 367-2000
ADV MGR-MKTG/Planning/Sales Development/CLASS, Toronto Star, Toronto, ON

Masters, Cathy .... (509) 786-1711
ED, Prosser Record-Bulletin, Prosser, WA

Masters, Jeff .... (912) 924-2751
ADV MGR, PROD MGR
Americus Times-Recorder, Americus, GA

Masters, Jim .... (219) 762-9564
ED, Portage Journal-Press, Portage, IN

Masters, Rebecca .... (540) 669-2181
ED-Opinion, Herald-Courier Virginia Tennessean, Bristol, VA

Masters, Van .... (408) 637-9795
MAN ED
Post/Dispatch Features, Hollister, CA

Masterson Jr, Bill .... (605) 642-2761
EVP, PUB, Black Hills Pioneer, Spearfish, SD

Masterson, Mike .... (501) 442-1777
EX ED, COL, EDL Writer
Northwest Arkansas Times, Fayetteville, AR

Masterson, Steve .... (205) 734-2131
CONT, Cullman Times, Cullman, AL

Mastin, Dan .... (218) 723-5281
PROD MGR
Duluth News-Tribune, Duluth, MN

Maston, Tom .... (506) 452-6671
Comptroller, Daily Gleaner, Fredericton, NB

Mastro, Nicholas .... (941) 953-7755
PSL DIR
Sarasota Herald-Tribune, Sarasota, FL

Mastrobernardino, John .... (201) 309-1200
GM/News OPER
ESPN/SportsTicker, Jersey City, NJ

Mastroianni, Paula .... (330) 454-5611
DIR-MKTG, Repository, Canton, OH

Mastron, Bruce .... (904) 312-5200
Copy ED, Daily News, Palatka, FL

Mastrud, Harry .... (541) 382-1811
PROD MGR-SYS, Bulletin, Bend, OR

Mastumato, Sandy .... (408) 920-5000
CIRC MGR-MKTG/Regional Home Delivery
San Jose Mercury News, San Jose, CA

Masure, Patty .... (413) 584-5000
ADV MGR-Co-op, ADTX MGR
Daily Hampshire Gazette, Northampton, MA

Maszak, David .... (808) 525-8000
DIR-PROM
Hawaii Newspaper Agency Inc., Honolulu, HI

Mata, Toni .... (209) 369-2761
EDU ED, Health/Medical ED, SCI/Technology ED, Lodi News-Sentinel, Lodi, CA

Matal, Norman .... (913) 628-1081
PROD MGR-Pre Press
Hays Daily News, Hays, KS

Matalavage, Daniel .... (610) 323-3000
PROD MGR-PR, Mercury, Pottstown, PA

Matani, Sunnil .... (819) 569-9526
Chief Correspondent
Record, Sherbrooke, QC

Matanky, Arnie .... (312) 787-2677
PUB, ED, Near North News, Chicago, IL

Matassa, Mark .... (206) 464-2111
Political ED, Seattle Times, Seattle, WA

Matava, Mary Ellen .... (918) 581-8300
Health/Medical ED, Tulsa World, Tulsa, OK

Mateer, Mark .... (814) 238-5000
ADV DIR
Centre Daily Times, State College, PA

Mateja, James .... (312) 222-3232
Automotive Writer
Chicago Tribune, Chicago, IL

Matera, Robert D .... (757) 247-4600
CIRC MGR-Alternate Delivery SRV
Daily Press, Newport News, VA

Materise, Maurice .... (716) 849-3434
ADV MGR-Outside CLASS Sales
Buffalo News, Buffalo, NY

Matessa, Joe .... (561) 461-2050
ADV MGR-Display Sales
Tribune, Fort Pierce, FL

Mathe, Bill .... (219) 926-1131
ADV DIR, Chesterton Tribune, Chesterton, IN

Matheny, Keith .... (616) 533-8523
ED, Antrim County News, Bellaire, MI

Matheny, Susan .... (541) 475-2275
ED, Madras Pioneer, Madras, OR

Matheny, Wayne .... (712) 542-2181
PUB, ED
Clarinda Herald-Journal, Clarinda, IA

Mather, L B .... (814) 765-5581
EX ED, Progress, Clearfield, PA

Mathers, Henry .... (306) 764-4276
PROD FRM-PR
Prince Albert Daily Herald, Prince Albert, SK

Mathers, Mike .... (907) 456-6661
Photo DEPT MGR
Fairbanks Daily News-Miner, Fairbanks, AK

Mathes, Joe .... (414) 898-4276
PUB
New Holstein Reporter, New Holstein, WI

Mathes, Mark .... (800) 245-6536
ED-News & Features
Tribune Media Services Inc., Chicago, IL

Mathes, Mike E .... (414) 898-4276
PUB
New Holstein Reporter, New Holstein, WI

Mathesen, Carol .... (505) 887-5501
CIRC MGR, Current-Argus, Carlsbad, NM

Mathew, John .... (205) 752-3381
PRES, Boone Newspapers, Tuscaloosa, AL

Mathew, T J .... (212) 481-3110
GM, News India-Times, New York, NY

Mathews, Charles .... (937) 328-0300
PROD MGR-Pagination
Springfield News-Sun, Springfield, OH

Mathews, Dave .... (409) 744-3611
News ED
Galveston County Daily News, Galveston, TX

Mathews, Dena .... (409) 265-7411
ADV MGR-CLASS
Brazosport Facts, Clute, TX

Mathews, Garrett .... (812) 424-7711
COL, Evansville Courier, Evansville, IN

Mathews, George .... (419) 468-1117
PROD MGR, PROD FRM-Photocomp
Galion Inquirer, Galion, OH

Mathews, Jackie .... (800) 292-4308
ED, Puzzle Features Syndicate, Sun City, CA

Mathews, Kevin .... (205) 549-2000
ADV SUPV-RT, Gadsden Times, Gadsden, AL

Mathews, Ricky .... (601) 896-2100
DIR-MKTG, Sun Herald, Biloxi, MS

Mathews Jr, Thomas .... (618) 842-2662
PUB, ED, Wayne County Press, Fairfield, IL

Mat Who's Where-148

Mathewson, Bob .... (603) 298-8711
PROD MGR-OPER
Valley News, White River Jct., VT
Mathieson, Anne .... (312) 222-5168
Sales Rep., Tribune TV Log, Chicago, IL
Mathis, Brett .... (616) 754-9301
ADV DIR, Daily News, Greenville, MI
Mathis, Chandra .... (915) 773-3621
ED, Stamford American, Stamford, TX
Mathis, Charles .... (910) 679-2341
ED, Yadkin Ripple, Yadkinville, NC
Mathis, Cherri .... (910) 592-8137
ED, Sampson Independent, Clinton, NC
Mathis, David .... (502) 443-1771
CONT/ASST TREAS
Paducah Sun, Paducah, KY
Mathis, P Dawn .... (405) 258-1818
GM, Lincoln County News, Chandler, OK
Mathis, Pearl V .... (210) 383-2705
PRES, PUB
Edinburg Daily Review, Edinburg, TX
Mathis, Stephen E .... (405) 258-1818
PUB, Lincoln County News, Chandler, OK
Mathis Sr, Walter L .... (616) 243-0577
ED, Afro-American Gazette, Grand Rapids, MI
Matics, Gregory .... (304) 273-9333
PUB, ED
Jackson Star News, Ravenswood, WV
Matile, Roger A .... (630) 554-8573
ED, Ledger-Sentinel, Oswego, IL
Matinho, A S .... (201) 589-4600
PUB, ED, Luso Americano, Newark, NJ
Matlack, Thomas .... (401) 277-7000
VP-FIN
Providence Journal-Bulletin, Providence, RI
Matlock, Martha .... (318) 459-3200
Librarian, Times, Shreveport, LA
Matlow, Stephen .... (406) 222-2000
MAN ED
Livingston Enterprise, Livingston, MT
Matson, Cynthia A .... (507) 294-3400
PUB, ED, Courier-Sentinel, Kiester, MN
Matson, John .... (812) 332-4401
PROD SUPT-COMP
Herald-Times Inc, Bloomington, IN
Matson, Patricia J .... (212) 456-7777
VP-CORP Communications
ABC Inc., New York, NY
Matson, Robert .... (716) 394-0770
VP-News/EX ED, Daily Messenger/The Sunday Messenger, Canandaigua, NY
Matsumiya, S K .... (310) 519-1442
GM, Random Lengths/Harbor Independent News, San Pedro, CA
Matsumoto, Yasuki .... (212) 603-6600
Correspondent
Kyodo News Service, New York, NY
Matsune, Jon .... (209) 734-5821
Sports ED, Visalia Times-Delta, Visalia, CA
Matsuo, Akira .... (415) 567-7324
PUB, ED
Hokubei Mainichi, San Francisco, CA
Matsuse, Manabu .... (212) 603-6600
Correspondent
Kyodo News Service, New York, NY
Matsuzawa, Mick .... (206) 624-4169
GM, Northwest Nikkei, Seattle, WA
Matte, Jim .... (617) 426-3000
RE ED, Boston Herald, Boston, MA
Matteau, Michel .... (819) 537-5111
PUB, ED
Hebdo du St. Maurice, Shawinigan, QC
Mattei, Daniel .... (919) 829-4500
PROD MGR-Packaging
News & Observer, Raleigh, NC
Mattek, Mitch .... (405) 353-0620
Wire ED, Lawton Constitution, Lawton, OK
Matter, Kathy .... (317) 423-5511
Films/Theater ED
Journal and Courier, Lafayette, IN
Mattern, Hal .... (602) 271-8000
EDU ED, Arizona Republic, Phoenix, AZ
Matteson, Kris .... (406) 496-5500
PROD MGR-Delivery Services
Montana Standard, Butte, MT
Matteucci, Vince .... (216) 999-4500
Chief EDL Artist, Plain Dealer, Cleveland, OH
Matthews, Charles .... (408) 920-5000
MAN ED-West Magazine
San Jose Mercury News, San Jose, CA
Matthews, Christopher .... (415) 777-2424
COL
San Francisco Examiner, San Francisco, CA
Matthews, Holly .... (814) 827-3634
City ED, Titusville Herald, Titusville, PA
Matthews, John B .... (212) 293-8500
NTL Sales DIR, United Media, United Feature Syndicate, Newspaper Enterprise Association, New York, NY
Matthews, Kathy .... (770) 227-3276
Accountant, Griffin Daily News, Griffin, GA
Matthews, Lisa .... (912) 923-6432
Graphics ED/Art DIR
Daily Sun, Warner Robins, GA
Matthews, Lynn O .... (941) 953-7755
PUB, Sarasota Herald-Tribune, Sarasota, FL
Matthews, Mary .... (423) 472-5041
Librarian, Daily Banner, Cleveland, TN
Matthews, Richard .... (413) 625-9417
PUB, ED, Shelburne Falls and West County News, Shelburne Falls, MA
Matthews, Robert S .... (209) 835-3030
SEC, PUB, GM, Tracy Press, Tracy, CA
Matthews, Russell .... (919) 446-5161
PROD FRM-COMP
Rocky Mount Telegram, Rocky Mount, NC
Matthews, Samuel H .... (209) 835-3030
VP, ED, Tracy Press, Tracy, CA
Matthews, Steve .... (813) 259-7711
BUS/FIN ED
Tampa Tribune and Times, Tampa, FL
Matthews, Thomas F .... (209) 835-3030
PRES, Tracy Press, Tracy, CA
Matthews, Vicki .... (812) 385-2525
CIRC MGR
Princeton Daily Clarion, Princeton, IN
Matthias, Fred .... (314) 340-8402
VP/DIR-CIRC
Pulitzer Publishing Co., St. Louis, MO
Matties, Bernd .... (716) 232-7100
PROD FRM-COMP, Rochester Democrat and Chronicle, Rochester, NY
Mattingly, J Fred .... (317) 736-7101
ADV DIR, Daily Journal, Franklin, IN
Mattioli, Wendy .... (909) 684-1200
ADV MGR-Regional
Press-Enterprise, Riverside, CA
Mattis, Mike .... (916) 321-1000
TV Magazine ED
Sacramento Bee, Sacramento, CA
Mattison, Kevin .... (518) 843-1100
MAN ED, Films/Theater ED, Music ED, Radio/Television ED
Recorder, Amsterdam, NY
Mattison, Nancy S .... (815) 544-9811
PUB
Belvidere Daily Republican, Belvidere, IL
Mattison, Patrick .... (815) 544-9811
PRES, ASSOC PUB, EPE
Belvidere Daily Republican, Belvidere, IL
Mattner Jr, W E .... (813) 849-7500
ED, West Pasco Press, New Port Richey, FL
Mattocks, James .... (919) 638-8101
PROD FRM-PR, Sun-Journal, New Bern, NC
Mattos, Susan .... (209) 862-2222
GM, Tuesday Review, Newman, CA
Mattos, William H .... (209) 862-2222
PUB, Tuesday Review, Newman, CA
Mattson, Charles L R .... (719) 473-4370
PUB, ED
Black Forest News, Colorado Springs, CO
Mattson, E Neil .... (218) 463-1521
PUB, Roseau Times-Region, Roseau, MN
Mattson, Ed .... (216) 696-3322
PROD MGR, Daily Legal News and Cleveland Recorder, Cleveland, OH
Mattson, Elaine .... (800) 365-3020
ED, Gunfighter, Boise, ID
Mattson, Esley .... (810) 387-3282
PUB, Munising News, Munising, MI
Mattson, John P .... (218) 681-4450
PUB, Northern Watch, Thief River Falls, MN
Mattson, Marcia .... (810) 766-6100
Health/Medical Writer, Flint Journal, Flint, MI
Mattson, Roger A .... (517) 377-1000
PROD MGR-Platemaking
Lansing State Journal, Lansing, MI
Matturro, Richard .... (518) 454-5694
Librarian, Times Union, Albany, NY
Matus, John .... (614) 272-5422
MAN ED
Southeast Messenger, Columbus, OH
Matusiak, Vincent .... (718) 981-1234
PROD FRM-MR
Staten Island Advance, Staten Island, NY
Matuszak, Henry .... (601) 328-2424
Sports ED
Commercial Dispatch, Columbus, MS
Matuszak, John .... (614) 272-5422
ED, Eastside Messenger, Columbus, OH
Matuszek, Rebecca .... (401) 722-4000
ED-Night, Times, Pawtucket, RI
Matz, Mary Ann .... (602) 271-8000
DIR-Human Resources
Phoenix Newspapers Inc., Phoenix, AZ
Mauch, Rick .... (817) 594-7447
Sports ED
Weatherford Democrat, Weatherford, TX
Mauck, Debbie .... (812) 424-7711
Office Administrator
Evansville Press, Evansville, IN
Maucker, Earl .... (954) 356-4000
VP-EDL, Sun-Sentinel, Fort Lauderdale, FL
Mauder, Mickey .... (313) 222-6400
PROD OPER MGR-Quality Assurance
Detroit Newspapers, Detroit, MI
Maue, Kay .... (618) 654-2366
PUB, Highland News Leader, Highland, IL
Mauer, Rich .... (907) 257-4200
City ED, Daily News, Anchorage, AK
Maugh III, Thomas H .... (213) 237-5000
Medical Writer
Los Angeles Times, Los Angeles, CA
Maughan, Joe .... (618) 382-4176
PROD FRM, Carmi Times, Carmi, IL
Mauk, Phil .... (719) 632-5511
PROD OPER MGR-PR
Gazette, Colorado Springs, CO
Maulden, W R .... (912) 265-8320
GM, ADV DIR
Brunswick News, Brunswick, GA
Mauldin, Donna B .... (713) 449-9945
GM, Northeast News, Houston, TX
Mauldin, Tom .... (503) 738-5561
PUB, ED, Seaside Signal, Seaside, OR
Mauldin, V E .... (713) 449-9945
PUB, Mercado Latino, Houston, TX
Maulove, Jon .... (510) 935-2525
Photo/Graphics ED
Contra Costa Times, Walnut Creek, CA
Mauney, Paul .... (615) 893-5860
CIRC MGR
Daily News Journal, Murfreesboro, TN
Maupin, Deborah .... (804) 385-5400
CIRC MGR, News & Advance, Lynchburg, VA
Maupin, Sue .... (804) 385-5400
BM, News & Advance, Lynchburg, VA
Maurer, Gilbert C .... (206) 448-8000
EVP/COO (Hearst Corp)
Seattle Post-Intelligencer, Seattle, WA
Maurer, Jim .... (909) 684-1200
ADV MGR-Major Accounts
Press-Enterprise, Riverside, CA
Maurer, Patricia .... (517) 386-4414
PUB, ED, Clare County Review, Clare, MI
Maurer, Tom .... (805) 395-7500
MET ED
Bakersfield Californian, Bakersfield, CA
Maurer Jr, Wesley H .... (810) 643-9150
PUB, St. Ignace News, St. Ignace, MI
Maurice, Johanna .... (304) 348-5140
EPE, Charleston Daily Mail, Charleston, WV
Mauro, Judi .... (609) 989-7800
Automotive ED, Trentonian, Trenton, NJ
Mauro, Maria .... (717) 637-3736
Features ED, Evening Sun, Hanover, PA
Maury, Chip .... (317) 633-1240
DIR-Photography
Indianapolis Star/News, Indianapolis, IN
Maus, Phil .... (317) 633-1240
PROD OPER ASST
Indianapolis Star/News, Indianapolis, IN
Mauser, Ken .... (309) 686-3000
CONT, BM, Journal Star, Peoria, IL
Mauser, Robin .... (619) 922-3181
PUB, Palo Verde Valley Times, Blythe, CA
Maust, Melody .... (812) 254-0480
ED, EDL Writer, Farm/School ED, Fashion ED
Washington Times-Herald, Washington, IN
Mauter, Richard .... (516) 594-1000
MAN ED
Long Island Catholic, Rockville Center, NY
Mavro, Gil .... (813) 893-8111
CIRC MGR-OPER
St. Petersburg Times, St. Petersburg, FL
Mawhinney, Robert E .... (609) 272-7000
DIR-Sales/MKTG, ADV DIR-Sales/MKTG
Press of Atlantic City, Pleasantville, NJ
Mawson, David .... (508) 793-9100
Features ED
Telegram & Gazette, Worcester, MA
Maxam, David .... (518) 584-4242
CIRC MGR, Saratogian, Saratoga Springs, NY
Maxcy, Jane .... (201) 646-4000
CIRC MGR-Product SRV/SYS/ADM
Record, Hackensack, NJ
Maxex, Robin .... (405) 737-3050
MAN ED, Choctaw/Nicoma Park Free Press, Midwest City, OK
Maxey, Sandy .... (812) 268-6356
ADV MGR-CLASS
Sullivan Daily Times, Sullivan, IN
Maxfield, Dennis C .... (716) 396-0027
Senior ED, Trade News Service (Published by Parmax Inc.), Canandaigua, NY
Maximovich, Edward .... (419) 238-2285
CIRC MGR, Times-Bulletin, Van Wert, OH
Maxwell, Alberto .... (415) 641-6051
MAN ED, Horizontes, San Francisco, CA
Maxwell, Chip .... (402) 444-1000
EDL Writer
Omaha World-Herald, Omaha, NE
Maxwell, Daisy .... (910) 323-4848
Librarian
Fayetteville Observer-Times, Fayetteville, NC
Maxwell, Debbie C .... (540) 783-5121
PUB
Smyth County News & Messenger, Marion, VA
Maxwell, Doug .... (507) 376-9711
CIRC MGR, Daily Globe, Worthington, MN
Maxwell, Doug .... (601) 335-1155
PROD FRM-PR
Delta Democrat Times, Greenville, MS
Maxwell, Linda .... (619) 322-8889
City ED, Desert Sun, Palm Springs, CA
Maxwell, Lowanna .... (909) 674-1535
ED, Lake Elsinore Valley Sun-Tribune, Lake Elsinore Valley, CA
Maxwell, Ralph B .... (706) 743-5510/3111
PUB, Oglethorpe Echo, Lexington, GA
Maxwell Jr, Ralph B .... (706) 743-5510/3111
ED, Oglethorpe Echo, Lexington, GA
Maxwell, Ronald .... (207) 873-3341
Photo DEPT MGR, Central Maine Morning Sentinel, Waterville, ME
Maxwell, Sally .... (918) 775-4433
ED, Sequoyah County Times, Sallisaw, OK
Maxwell, Teri .... (512) 445-3500
ADV MGR-RT
Austin American-Statesman, Austin, TX
Maxwell, Tim .... (334) 749-6271
PROD FRM-PR
Opelika-Auburn News, Opelika, AL
May, Bill .... (214) 977-8222
PROD ASST MGR
Dallas Morning News, Dallas, TX
May, Cherry Fisher .... (318) 237-3560
PUB, Times of Acadiana, Lafayette, LA
May, Clifford .... (303) 892-5000
ASSOC ED
Rocky Mountain News, Denver, CO
May, David .... (972) 424-6565
City/MET ED, Plano Star Courier, Plano, TX
May, De Anna .... (317) 622-1212
MGR-MKTG Services
Herald Bulletin, Anderson, IN
May, Diane .... (903) 597-8111
Librarian, Tyler Morning Telegraph, Tyler, TX
May, Frank .... (817) 778-4444
PROD FRM-COMP
Temple Daily Telegram, Temple, TX
May, Frank .... (318) 459-3200
EPE, Times, Shreveport, LA
May, Gary .... (519) 679-6666
ASSOC ED, London Free Press, London, ON
May, Heather .... (709) 786-7014
ED, Compass, Carbonear, NF
May, Jennifer .... (318) 365-6773
Action Line ED, Fashion/Style ED, Features ED, Food ED, Living/Lifestyle ED, Women's ED, Daily Iberian, New Iberia, LA
May, Joe .... (573) 581-1111
PUB, ADV MGR-PROM
Mexico Ledger, Mexico, MO
May, Martha .... (502) 821-6833
Society/Women's ED
Messenger, Madisonville, KY
May, Mary .... (301) 662-1177
CIRC ASST DIR
Frederick Post/News, Frederick, MD
May, Miriam .... (601) 849-3434
MAN ED, Magee Courier, Magee, MS
May, Roger B .... (212) 416-2600
DIR-CORP Relations
Dow Jones & Co. Inc., New York, NY
May, Roy .... (318) 459-3200
ADV MGR-OPER, Times, Shreveport, LA
May, Stephen C .... (318) 237-3560
PUB, Times of Acadiana, Lafayette, LA
May, Thomas .... (334) 738-2360
PUB, ED
Union Springs Herald, Union Springs, AL
May, Thomas E .... (360) 736-3311
ADV DIR, Chronicle, Centralia, WA
Mayborn, Sue .... (817) 778-4444
PRES
Frank Mayborn Enterprises Inc., Temple, TX
Maycock, Brent D .... (316) 342-4800
Sports ED, Emporia Gazette, Emporia, KS
Mayden, Steve .... (417) 623-3480
CIRC MGR, Joplin Globe, Joplin, MO
Maye, Fran .... (717) 684-0687
ED, Columbia Public Ledger, Columbia, PA
Mayer, Allan .... (403) 429-5400
ASST MAN ED
Edmonton Journal, Edmonton, AB
Mayer, Bob .... (215) 345-3000
ASST GM, Outdoors ED, PROD DIR
Intelligencer/Record, Doylestown, PA
Mayer, Christopher M .... (617) 929-2000
DIR-INFO Services
Boston Globe, Boston, MA
Mayer, Larry .... (406) 657-1200
Photo ED, Billings Gazette, Billings, MT
Mayer, Pamela J .... (814) 532-5199
PUB, Tribune-Democrat, Johnstown, PA
Mayer, Rick .... (208) 377-6200
PROD MGR-PR, Idaho Statesman, Boise, ID
Mayer, Robert .... (505) 988-5541
ED, Santa Fe Reporter, Santa Fe, NM
Mayers, Allen .... (717) 255-8100
BUS ED, Patriot-News, Harrisburg, PA

149-Who's Where **Mcc**

Mayes, Cecil (817) 849-7951
PUB, ED
Throckmorton Tribune, Throckmorton, TX

Mayes, Joyce (817) 849-7951
PUB
Throckmorton Tribune, Throckmorton, TX

Mayes, Malcolm (403) 429-5400
EDL Cartoonist
Edmonton Journal, Edmonton, AB

Mayes, Mark (517) 377-1000
EDU ED, Lansing State Journal, Lansing, MI

Mayes, Warren (618) 463-2500
Sports ED, Telegraph, Alton, IL

Mayfield, Trevis (812) 231-4200
ASST ED, Tribune-Star, Terre Haute, IN

Mayhew, Arthur E (215) 949-4000
VP, PUB
Bucks County Courier Times, Levittown, PA

Mayhew, Catherine (615) 259-8000
ASST MAN ED-News
Tennessean, Nashville, TN

Maynard, Greg (317) 747-5700
Religion ED, Star Press, Muncie, IN

Maynard, Julie (301) 371-9399
ED
Middletown Valley Citizen, Middletown, MD

Maynard, Kevin (304) 752-6950
PROD FRM-PR, Logan Banner, Logan, WV

Maynard, Mark (619) 299-3131
Automotive ED
San Diego Union-Tribune, San Diego, CA

Maynard, Mark (606) 329-1717
Sports ED, Daily Independent, Ashland, KY

Maynard, Pete (301) 834-7722
PUB, Brunswick Citizen, Brunswick, MD

Maynard, Richard (607) 757-0753
GM, Valley News, Endwell, NY

Maynard, Steve (206) 597-8742
Religion Reporter
News Tribune, Tacoma, WA

Maynes, Paul (415) 777-5700
MGR-BUS Applications, San Francisco Newspaper Agency, San Francisco, CA

Mayo, James (918) 775-4433
PUB, Sequoyah County Times, Sallisaw, OK

Mayo, John (709) 634-4348
City ED, Western Star, Corner Brook, NF

Mayo, Larry (903) 729-0281
PRES, PUB, PA, Herald-Press, Palestine, TX

Mayo, Phyllis (206) 464-2111
DIR-Human Resources & Diversity
Seattle Times, Seattle, WA

Mayo, Terri (901) 529-2211
ADTX MGR
Commercial Appeal, Memphis, TN

Mayotte, Ernest A (508) 943-4800
PUB, Times, Webster, MA

Mays, Gary (309) 829-9411
Health/Medical Writer
Pantagraph, Bloomington, IL

Mays, Laura J (209) 727-5776
PUB
Lockeford-Clements News, Lockeford, CA

Mays, Patricia (501) 523-5855
ED, Newport Daily Independent, Newport, AR

Mays, Vivienne (910) 373-7000
ADV MGR-CLASS
News & Record, Greensboro, NC

Mays, William G (317) 924-5143
PUB, Indianapolis Recorder, Indianapolis, IN

Mayshark, Jesse (423) 523-3131
Lower EDU ED
Knoxville News-Sentinel, Knoxville, TN

Maza, Mike (214) 977-8222
Guide ED, Dallas Morning News, Dallas, TX

Mazare, Jean (905) 465-2107
PUB, L'Express, Toronto, ON

Mazen, Don (818) 790-8774
ED, La Canada Valley Sun, La Canada Flintridge, CA

Mazenauer, Arthur (Skip) (716) 773-7676
PUB, Niagara-Wheatfield Tribune, Grand Island, NY

Mazenko, Mary Ann (618) 463-2500
Family/Fashion ED, Medical/Hospital ED, Women's ED, Telegraph, Alton, IL

Mazleck, Ray (604) 368-8551
City ED, Trail Daily Times, Trail, BC

Maznaritz, Marguerite (541) 276-2853
PUB, Pendleton Record, Pendleton, OR

Maznaritz, Richard E (541) 276-2853
ED, Pendleton Record, Pendleton, OR

Mazur, Dawn (812) 482-2424
Farm ED, Wire ED, Herald, Jasper, IN

Mazur, Gene (860) 241-6200
MGR-Compensation, Benefits and SYS
Hartford Courant, Hartford, CT

Mazurosky, Rudy (203) 263-2116
PUB, Voices, Southbury, CT

Mazza, Brian L (403) 845-3334
ED, Mountaineer, Rocky Mountain House, AB

Mazza, E Carol (413) 562-4181
VP, PUB
Westfield Evening News, Westfield, MA

Mazza, Lawrence O (403) 845-3334
PUB
Mountaineer, Rocky Mountain House, AB

Mazzara, Sam (205) 734-2131
CIRC MGR, Cullman Times, Cullman, AL

Mazzarella, Dave (703) 276-3400
ED, USA Today, Arlington, VA

Mazzolini, Joan (216) 999-4500
Health/Medical ED
Plain Dealer, Cleveland, OH

McAdams, Ryan (403) 328-4411
ADV MGR, ADV MGR-NTL
Lethbridge Herald, Lethbridge, AB

McAden, Owen (Fitz) (803) 785-4293
EX ED, Island Packet, Hilton Head, SC

McAdow, Betty (614) 947-2149
ED, News Watchman, Waverly, OH

McAfee, Jack (509) 248-1251
DIR-OPER
Yakima Herald-Republic, Yakima, WA

McAlary, Mike (212) 210-2100
COL, New York Daily News, New York, NY

McAlexander, J E (800) 562-1041
PRES, Landmark Designs Inc., Eugene, OR

McAlexander, M J (800) 562-1041
TREAS, Landmark Designs Inc., Eugene, OR

McAlexander, W S (800) 562-1041
VP, Landmark Designs Inc., Eugene, OR

McAlister, Don (512) 352-8535
ED, Taylor Daily Press, Taylor, TX

McAllan, Robert (908) 922-6000
VP, New Jersey Press Inc., Neptune, NJ

McAllister, Duane (601) 924-7142
PUB, Clinton News, Clinton, MS

McAllister, Harry (423) 892-1336
GM
Hamilton County Herald, Chattanooga, TN

McAllister, Karen (501) 378-3400
Health/Medical Writer
Arkansas Democrat-Gazette, Little Rock, AR

McAllister, Marcia (703) 437-5400
ED, Springfield Times Courier, Reston, VA

McAllister, Natha (816) 684-6515
PUB, ED, Tri-County Weekly, Jamesport, MO

McAllister, Ray (804) 649-6000
COL
Richmond Times-Dispatch, Richmond, VA

McAnally, Keith (501) 623-7711
PROD FRM-PR
Sentinel-Record, Hot Springs, AR

McAndrew, Brian (416) 367-2000
Environment Writer
Toronto Star, Toronto, ON

McAndrews, Tom (970) 641-1414
PROD MGR-Press
Gunnison Country Times, Gunnison, CO

McArdle, David (508) 458-7100
NTL News ED, Sun, Lowell, MA

McArthur, Craig (403) 723-5787
PUB, Anchor, Edson, AB

McArthur, Dana (403) 723-5787
GM, Anchor, Edson, AB

McArthur, Dennis (508) 793-9100
PROD MGR-Equipment Maintenance
Telegram & Gazette, Worcester, MA

McArthur, Nancy (403) 632-2353
PUB, ED, Vegreville Observer, Vegreville, AB

McAuley, Davis (512) 321-2557
ED, Bastrop Advertiser & County News, Bastrop, TX

McAuley, Kathy (306) 862-4618
GM, Nipawin Journal, Nipawin, SK

McAuley, Robert (216) 999-4500
ASST MAN ED, Plain Dealer, Cleveland, OH

McAuliff, Steve (319) 588-5611
Online Contact
Telegraph Herald, Dubuque, IA

McAuliffe, Bishop Michael F (314) 635-9127
PUB, Catholic Missourian, Jefferson City, MO

McAuliffe, Paul (812) 424-7711
EX ED, Evansville Courier, Evansville, IN

McAvoy, Doug (616) 754-9301
CIRC MGR, Daily News, Greenville, MI

McBain, Roger (812) 424-7711
Entertainment ED
Evansville Courier, Evansville, IN

McBeath, Mrs A W (210) 773-2309
ED, Eagle Pass News-Guide & Sunday News, Eagle Pass, TX

McBeath, Rex S (210) 773-2309
PUB, Eagle Pass News-Guide & Sunday News, Eagle Pass, TX

McBeath, Sean C (817) 569-2191
PUB, ED, Informer Star, Burkburnett, TX

McBee, Susanna (202) 298-6920
ASST BU Chief/News ED
Hearst News Service, Washington, DC

McBride, Barb (519) 344-3641
ADV MGR-CLASS, Observer, Sarnia, ON

McBride, Bobbie (712) 832-3131
ED, Lake Park News, Lake Park, IA

McBride, Carolyn N (405) 247-3331
PRES, PUB, Travel ED
Anadarko Daily News, Anadarko, OK

McBride, Dave (502) 298-7100
ED, Ohio County Times-News, Hartford, KY

McBride, Don (813) 893-8111
SYS ED
St. Petersburg Times, St. Petersburg, FL

McBride, Faye (205) 259-1020
BM, Daily Sentinel, Scottsboro, AL

McBride, Jim (806) 376-4488
NTL ED, Political/Government ED, SCI/Technology ED, Amarillo Daily News/Globe Times, Amarillo, TX

McBride Jr, Joe W (405) 247-3331
SEC/TREAS, PUB
Anadarko Daily News, Anadarko, OK

McBride, Marjory (613) 623-6571
PUB, Arnprior Chronicle-Guide, Arnprior, ON

McBride, Maureen (520) 458-9440
Sunday News ED
Sierra Vista Herald, Sierra Vista, AZ

McBride, Michael (208) 743-9411
CIRC MGR, Morning Tribune, Lewiston, ID

McBride, Roland (716) 372-3121
Comptroller, Olean Times-Herald, Olean, NY
Hollinger International Inc.

McBride, Steve (316) 331-3550
VP, ADV MGR, MGR-PROM, Independence Daily Reporter, Independence, KS

McBride-Alexander, Carla (405) 247-3331
Entertainment/Amusements ED, Films/Theater ED, Television/Music ED
Anadarko Daily News, Anadarko, OK

McBride-Savage, Paula L (405) 247-3331
ASST ED, News ED, Weekender ED
Anadarko Daily News, Anadarko, OK

McBride-Thomas, JoNell (405) 247-3331
PROD SUPT
Anadarko Daily News, Anadarko, OK

McBryde, Andrew (601) 453-5312
CIRC MGR
Greenwood Commonwealth, Greenwood, MS

McCabe, Fred A (307) 733-2430
PUB, Jackson Hole Guide, Jackson, WY

McCabe, Ken (306) 695-3565
ED
Indian Head-Wolseley News, Indian Head, SK

McCabe, Serge (503) 221-8327
Photo DIR, Oregonian, Portland, OR

McCadams, Steve (901) 642-1162
Outdoors ED
Paris Post-Intelligencer, Paris, TN

McCaffrey, Ed (801) 237-2031
ADV DIR
Salt Lake Tribune, Salt Lake City, UT

McCaffrey, Joseph (540) 825-3232
PUB, Culpeper News, Culpeper, VA

McCain, Anita (205) 532-4000
ASST CONT, Huntsville Times, Huntsville, AL

McCain, Terry (405) 282-2222
CIRC MGR
Guthrie News Leader, Guthrie, OK

McCall, Katrina (803) 549-2586
ED, Press & Standard, Walterboro, SC

McCall, LW (812) 847-4487
PUB, Linton Daily Citizen, Linton, IN

McCall, Sheila (501) 763-4461
ED, Entertainment/Amusements ED, Environmental ED, Food ED, Health/Medical ED, Living/Lifestyle ED, Religion ED, SCI/Technology ED, Society/Women's ED
Blytheville Courier News, Blytheville, AR

McCall-Bogan, Margo (805) 259-1234
News ED, Signal, Santa Clarita, CA

McCallister, Duane K (601) 961-7000
PRES, PUB, Clarion-Ledger, Jackson, MS

McCallum, Kevin (509) 773-3777
ED, Goldendale Sentinel, Goldendale, WA

McCambridge, James J (847) 427-4300
ADV MGR-Division Sales
Daily Herald, Arlington Heights, IL

McCan, Jennifer (906) 786-2021
Entertainment/Amusements ED, Fashion/Style ED, Features ED, Lifestyle ED, Religion ED, Women's ED, Daily Press, Escanaba, MI

McCance, McGregor (804) 746-1235
ED, Mechanicsville Local, Mechanicsville, VA

McCandless, Iris (703) 368-3101
BM, Journal Messenger, Manassas, VA

McCandless, Ray (302) 324-2500
PROD MGR-Distribution Center
News Journal, Wilmington, DE

McCanless, George (203) 789-5200
CFO, New Haven Register, New Haven, CT

McCann, Dennis (414) 224-2000
COL
Milwaukee Journal Sentinel, Milwaukee, WI

McCann, Gary (812) 332-4401
Sports ED
Herald-Times Inc, Bloomington, IN

McCann, Pat (904) 747-5000
Sports ED, News Herald, Panama City, FL

McCann, Tim (913) 367-0583
Sports ED
Atchison Daily Globe, Atchison, KS

McCanna, Rose (814) 723-8200
PROD FRM-Pre Press
Warren Times-Observer, Warren, PA

McCants, Randy (913) 899-2338
PUB, Goodland Daily News, Goodland, KS

McCargar, Victoria (213) 237-5000
Graphics ED
Los Angeles Times, Los Angeles, CA

McCarrick, Terry (704) 252-5611
CONT, Asheville Citizen-Times, Asheville, NC

McCarron, John (312) 222-3232
EDL Writer/COL
Chicago Tribune, Chicago, IL

McCarron, Tom (902) 564-5451
CIRC MGR, Cape Breton Post, Sydney, NS

McCart, Victor (316) 275-8500
PROD FRM-PR
Garden City Telegram, Garden City, KS

McCartan, Jerry (707) 546-2020
MGR-MKTG Services
Press Democrat, Santa Rosa, CA

McCarter, Jim (313) 961-4060
GM, Metro Times, Detroit, MI

McCarter, R Thomas (423) 428-0746
PROD DIR
Mountain Press, Sevierville, TN

McCarthey, Thomas K (801) 237-2031
VP-Kearns-Tribune Corp.,Deputy ED-ADM, Travel ED, Salt Lake Tribune, Salt Lake City, UT

McCarthy, A J (506) 546-4491
PUB, GM, Northern Light, Bathurst, NB

McCarthy, Brian (603) 536-1311
MAN ED, Record-Enterprise, Plymouth, NH

McCarthy, Dan (310) 540-5511
PROD SUPV-Production Control
Daily Breeze, Torrance, CA

McCarthy, Dan (602) 898-5680
ED, Tempe Daily News Tribune, Mesa, AZ

McCarthy, Darwin (913) 483-2116
PROD FRM, Russell Daily News, Russell, KS

McCarthy, Debbie (608) 252-6200
CIRC SUPV-Customer SRV
Madison Newspapers Inc., Madison, WI

McCarthy, Dennis (818) 713-3000
COL, Daily News, Woodland Hills, CA

McCarthy, Donald (319) 588-5611
PROD MGR-PR
Telegraph Herald, Dubuque, IA

McCarthy, Gene (519) 894-2231
Courts Reporter, Record, Kitchener, ON

McCarthy, Gerald (312) 222-3232
ADV DIR-GEN, Chicago Tribune, Chicago, IL

McCarthy, Heather (207) 784-5411
MAN ED-Graphics, Graphics ED/Art DIR, NTL ED, Sun-Journal, Lewiston, ME

McCarthy, Helen (312) 321-3000
ASST CONT, Chicago Sun-Times, Chicago, IL

McCarthy, James (207) 729-3311
BUS ED, News ED, SCI/Technology ED, Wire ED, Times Record, Brunswick, ME

McCarthy, John (918) 684-2828
PROD DIR, Muskogee Daily Phoenix & Times Democrat, Muskogee, OK

McCarthy, John P (914) 692-4572
ASSOC ED
Cineman Syndicate, Middletown, NY

McCarthy, Kerry (212) 736-7602
PRES, Photoreporters, Inc., New York, NY

McCarthy, Kevin (316) 694-5700
CIRC MGR, News, Hutchinson, KS

McCarthy, Lawrence V (330) 755-2155
PUB, Journal, Struthers, OH

McCarthy, Maureen (860) 225-4601
PROD SUPV-Dispatch
Herald, New Britain, CT

McCarthy, Michael J (214) 977-6606
Sr. VP/SEC/GEN Counsel
A H Belo Corp., Dallas, TX

McCarthy, Osler (512) 445-3500
State ED, American-Statesman, Austin, TX

McCarthy, Patrick (212) 630-4000
EXEC VP, Women's Wear Daily, New York, NY

McCarthy, Robert (207) 784-5411
PROD FRM-MR, Sun-Journal, Lewiston, ME

McCarthy, Robert (716) 849-3434
Political ED, Buffalo News, Buffalo, NY

McCarthy, Robert (319) 242-7101
CIRC DIR, Clinton Herald, Clinton, IA

McCarthy, Sharron (617) 786-7000
ADV MGR-RT/NTL
Patriot Ledger, Quincy, MA

McCarthy, Tim (603) 444-3927
ED, Courier, Littleton, NH

McCarthy, W Jack (317) 839-5129
PUB, Hendricks County Flyer, Plainfield, IN

McCartney, Jeanie (318) 255-4353
ADV DIR/MGR-CLASS, MGR-MKTG/PROM
Ruston Daily Leader, Ruston, LA

Mcc Who's Where-150

McCartney, Leslie .... (406) 657-1200
Health/Medical ED, Religion ED
Billings Gazette, Billings, MT
McCartney, Pat .... (916) 541-3880
Environmental Reporter
Tahoe Daily Tribune, South Lake Tahoe, CA
McCartney, William .... (216) 329-7000
PROD ASST SUPT
Chronicle-Telegram, Elyria, OH
McCarty, Dan .... (817) 897-2282
PUB, ED, Glen Rose Reporter, Glen Rose, TX
McCarty, Jason .... (405) 832-3333
ED, Cordell Beacon, Cordell, OK
McCarty, Merrill .... (619) 256-2257
MAN ED, Desert Dispatch, Barstow, CA
McCarty, Mike .... (918) 663-1414
ED, Collinsville News, Tulsa, OK
McCarty, Rex E .... (540) 386-7027
PUB, ED
Scott County Virginia Star, Gate City, VA
McCarty, Robert .... (423) 428-0746
News ED, Mountain Press, Sevierville, TN
McCarty, Thomas M .... (814) 532-5199
CIRC DIR, Tribune-Democrat, Johnstown, PA
McCarver, Chip .... (915) 682-5311
DIR-INFO SYS/Telecommunications
Midland Reporter-Telegram, Midland, TX
McCaskell, Don .... (306) 452-3363
PUB, GM, ED, MAN ED
Optimist, Redvers, SK
McCaskill, Barbara .... (615) 256-8288
ED, Nashville Record, Nashville, TN
McCaskill, Charlie .... (803) 771-6161
DP MGR, State, Columbia, SC
McCaslin, John .... (202) 636-3000
Inside the Beltway COL
Washington Times, Washington, DC
McCatherine, Tom .... (937) 328-0300
Wire ED, News-Sun, Springfield, OH
McCauley, Brian .... (617) 450-2000
DIR-Publishing
Christian Science Monitor, Boston, MA
McCauley, Russell L .... (304) 846-2029
PUB, ED
West Virginia Hillbilly, Richwood, WV
McCaulley, Glen L .... (330) 996-3000
VP-FIN/TREAS, ASST SEC
Akron Beacon Journal, Akron, OH
McCaulley, Jay .... (717) 248-6741
PROD FRM-COMP, PROD FRM-PR
Sentinel, Lewistown, PA
McCawley, Harry .... (812) 372-7811
ASSOC ED, Republic, Columbus, IN
McChesney, Charles .... (413) 772-0261
EDL Board, Recorder, Greenfield, MA
McChesney, Jane .... (413) 772-0261
Copy Desk Chief, Food/Home/Garden ED
Recorder, Greenfield, MA
McClain, Cindy .... (517) 772-2971
PROD MGR-COMP
Morning Sun, Mount Pleasant, MI
McClain, Clay .... (502) 247-5223
ADV DIR-NTL, Messenger, Mayfield, KY
McClain, David .... (970) 522-1990
PUB, Journal-Advocate, Sterling, CO
McClain, Martha .... (210) 399-2436
MAN ED, San Benito News, San Benito, TX
McClain, Peter W .... (416) 814-4239
Sr VP-Human Resources & Industrial Relations, Thomson Newspapers, Toronto, ON
McClanahan, Mike .... (615) 824-8480
ED, Hendersonville Star News, Hendersonville, TN
McClanahan, Tom .... (816) 234-4141
EDL Writer
Kansas City Star, Kansas City, MO
McClard, Bill .... (219) 933-3200
PROD FRM-Press, Times, Munster, IN
McClare, Tammy .... (405) 282-2222
ADV MGR, Guthrie News Leader, Guthrie, OK
McClarey, Robin .... (217) 465-6424
CIRC DIR, Paris Daily Beacon-News, Paris, IL
McClary, Kevin .... (518) 843-1100
GM, ADV DIR, Recorder, Amsterdam, NY
McClatchy, James B .... (916) 321-1855
PUB
McClatchy Newspapers, Sacramento, CA
McCleary, Louise .... (412) 224-4321
Librarian
Valley News Dispatch, Tarentum, PA
McCleary-La France, Kim .... (213) 237-5000
ADV DIR-Customer Service
Los Angeles Times, Los Angeles, CA
McCleerey, Ruth .... (701) 883-5393
PUB, ED, La Moure Chronicle, La Moure, ND
McCleery, Bill .... (317) 633-1240
EDL Writer
Indianapolis Star/News, Indianapolis, IN

McClellan, Bill .... (915) 573-5486
ED, Snyder Daily News, Snyder, TX
McClellan, Dee .... (915) 682-5311
Database MGR
Midland Reporter-Telegram, Midland, TX
McClellan, Gere .... (614) 773-2111
Local News ED
Chillicothe Gazette, Chillicothe, OH
McClellan, Randy .... (352) 374-5000
PROD MGR-PR
Gainesville Sun, Gainesville, FL
McClelland, Art .... (903) 597-8111
ADV MGR-RT
Tyler Morning Telegraph, Tyler, TX
McClelland, Harry .... (412) 439-7500
PROD SUPV-Page Makeup
Herald-Standard, Uniontown, PA
McClelland, M Dan .... (315) 287-2100
PUB, ED, Tribune-Press, Gouverneur, NY
McClennan, Jeanette .... (703) 471-2200
VP-Sales & MKTG, Reuters America Inc. (NewMedia), Reston, VA
McClennen, Barbara .... (215) 723-4801
ED, Souderton Independent, Souderton, PA
McClennen, Richard J .... (313) 222-6400
Senior VP-MKTG
Detroit Newspapers, Detroit, MI
McClintock, Gary .... (609) 272-7000
MGR-Telecommunications
Press of Atlantic City, Pleasantville, NJ
McClintock, Robert .... (914) 331-5000
CONT, Daily Freeman, Kingston, NY
McClintock, Sheri .... (618) 932-2146
CIRC MGR
Daily American, West Frankfort, IL
McCloat, Keith .... (212) 455-4000
VP/CONT, North America Syndicate, King Features Syndicate Inc., New York, NY
McClory, Daniel D .... (603) 298-8711
CONT, Valley News, White River Jct., VT
McCloskey, Robyn .... (219) 722-5000
ADV MGR-Sales
Pharos-Tribune, Logansport, IN
McCloskey, Tim .... (207) 784-5411
Action Line ED, Sun-Journal, Lewiston, ME
McCloud, Cheryl .... (561) 562-2315
Administrative ED
Vero Beach Press-Journal, Vero Beach, FL
McClughan, C F .... (817) 778-4444
ADV DIR-MKTG
Temple Daily Telegram, Temple, TX
McClure, Bob .... (813) 752-3113
ED, Plant City Courier, Plant City, FL
McClure, C Arnold .... (814) 447-5506
PUB, Valley Log, Orbisonia, PA
McClure, Duane .... (502) 769-2312
PROD Camera Team Leader
News Enterprise, Elizabethtown, KY
McClure, James .... (717) 771-2000
MAN ED, York Daily Record, York, PA
McClure, Jim .... (919) 829-4500
ADV DIR-Display
News & Observer, Raleigh, NC
McClure, John .... (219) 936-3101
ADV MGR, Pilot-News, Plymouth, IN
McClure, Mack .... (316) 431-4100
Sports ED, Chanute Tribune, Chanute, KS
McClure, Robert .... (954) 356-4000
Environmental ED
Sun-Sentinel, Fort Lauderdale, FL
McClure, Robin .... (703) 257-4600
ASSOC PUB
Prince William Journal, Manassas, VA
McClure, Rosemary .... (909) 889-9666
MAN ED-Night, Wire ED
Sun, San Bernardino, CA
McClure, Sue .... (615) 259-8800
Books ED, Nashville Banner, Nashville, TN
McClusky, Kathy .... (914) 694-9300
Entertainment ED, Travel ED
Reporter Dispatch, White Plains, NY
Gannett Co. Inc.
McCollough, Terry .... (218) 829-4705
PUB, Brainerd Daily Dispatch, Brainerd, MN
McCollum, Brian .... (313) 222-6400
Music Writer-Pop
Detroit Free Press, Detroit, MI
McCollum, Charles .... (408) 920-5000
EX News ED-PM
San Jose Mercury News, San Jose, CA
McCollum, Charles .... (801) 752-2121
MAN ED, Herald Journal, Logan, UT
McCollum, David .... (505) 523-4581
PUB, Las Cruces Sun-News, Las Cruces, NM
McCollum, David .... (501) 327-6621
Sports ED, Log Cabin Democrat, Conway, AR
McCollum, David .... (610) 867-5000
GM, Bethlehem Star, Bethlehem, PA
McCollum, Tina .... (509) 582-1500
DIR-FIN, Tri-City Herald, Tri-Cities, WA
McCollum, Trent Bonner .... (501) 633-3130
PUB, Times-Herald, Forrest City, AR
McComas, Frank .... (305) 376-3800
Sr VP-OPER, Knight-Ridder Inc., Miami, FL

McCombs, Allen P .... (909) 628-5501
PUB, ED, Chino Champion, Chino, CA
McCommons, Pete .... (706) 549-9523
ED, Flagpole Magazine, Athens, GA
McConachie, Bob .... (416) 947-2222
City ED, Toronto Sun, Toronto, ON
McConachie, Doug .... (306) 652-9200
Sports ED, StarPhoenix, Saskatoon, SK
McConal, Jon .... (817) 390-7400
COL
Fort Worth Star-Telegram, Fort Worth, TX
McConkey, Karen .... (910) 983-3109
ED, King Times-News, King, NC
McConnaughay, Dale .... (540) 574-6200
EPE, Daily News-Record, Harrisonburg, VA
McConnell, Darrell .... (317) 598-6397
PA, PROD MGR, Daily Ledger, Noblesville, IN
McConnell, Gregg .... (360) 675-6611
PUB, Whidbey News Times, Oak Harbor, WA
McConnell, Jim .... (804) 732-3456
Sports ED, Progress-Index, Petersburg, VA
McConnell, John T .... (309) 686-3000
PRES, PUB, Journal Star, Peoria, IL
Copley Press Inc.
McConnell, Johnny .... (901) 285-4091
ADV DIR, State Gazette, Dyersburg, TN
McConnell, Kim .... (405) 353-0620
EDU ED, Lawton Constitution, Lawton, OK
McConnell, Lawrence .... (804) 978-7200
PUB, Daily Progress, Charlottesville, VA
McConnell, Liz .... (612) 673-4000
Team Leader, Star Tribune, Minneapolis, MN
McCool, Elizabeth C .... (503) 382-1811
COB, Western Communications, Bend, OR
McCool, Glennys .... (605) 256-4555
ADV MGR-RT
Madison Daily Leader, Madison, SD
McCool, Lewis .... (970) 247-3504
News ED, Durango Herald, Durango, CO
McCord, Greg .... (334) 222-2402
MAN ED
Andalusia Star-News, Andalusia, AL
McCord, Mike .... (606) 231-3100
TREAS, CFO
Lexington Herald-Leader, Lexington, KY
McCorkindale, Douglas H .... (703) 284-6000
Vice Chairman/Chief Financial & Administrative OFF, Gannett Co. Inc., Arlington, VA
McCormac, Patty .... (602) 496-0665
MAN ED
Ahwatukee Weekly News, Phoenix, AZ
McCormack, Bruce E .... (307) 587-2231
PUB, ED, Cody Enterprise, Cody, WY
McCormack, Jerry .... (505) 622-7710
ED, Features ED, Graphics ED/Art DIR, NTL ED, Religion ED, SCI/Technology ED, Television/Film ED, Theater/Music ED, Travel ED, Roswell Daily Record, Roswell, NM
McCormack, Jim .... (562) 435-1161
EX ED-Sports
Press-Telegram, Long Beach, CA
McCormack, Jim .... (416) 947-2222
CIRC DIR, Toronto Sun, Toronto, ON
McCormack, Lee .... (510) 935-2525
Graphics ED
Contra Costa Times, Walnut Creek, CA
McCormick, Beecher .... (915) 573-5486
VP, Snyder Daily News, Snyder, TX
McCormick, Bill .... (302) 998-1650
GM, Motor Matters, Wilmington, DE
McCormick, Charles .... (405) 567-3933
PUB, ED, Times-Herald, Prague, OK
McCormick, Christy .... (514) 484-1107
ED, Suburban, Montreal, QC
McCormick, Doug .... (614) 461-5000
EDL Writer
Columbus Dispatch, Columbus, OH
McCormick, Gavin .... (508) 343-6911
BUS/FIN ED
Sentinel & Enterprise, Fitchburg, MA
McCormick, James .... (703) 560-4000
RE ED, Fairfax Journal, Fairfax, VA
Journal Newspapers Inc.
McCormick, James .... (301) 306-9500
ED, Prince George's Sentinel, Seabrook, MD
McCormick, James .... (518) 792-9914
VP-Information SYS
TV Data, Queensbury, NY
McCormick, Keith .... (817) 552-5454
TREAS, Vernon Daily Record, Vernon, TX
McCormick, Keith .... (615) 526-9715
CIRC MGR, Herald-Citizen, Cookeville, TN
McCormick, Mack .... (919) 829-4500
ADV MGR-Regional
News & Observer, Raleigh, NC
McCormick, Michael .... (313) 222-2300
Production ED, Detroit News, Detroit, MI
McCormick, Mike .... (405) 273-4200
MAN ED, Shawnee News-Star, Shawnee, OK
McCormick, Rob .... (705) 745-4641
Wire ED, Examiner, Peterborough, ON
McCormick, Robert M .... (609) 272-7000
EVP/COO, PUB
Press of Atlantic City, Pleasantville, NJ

McCormick, Robin .... (757) 247-4600
Opportunities ED
Daily Press, Newport News, VA
McCormick, Terry .... (901) 427-3333
Sports ED, Jackson Sun, Jackson, TN
McCormick, Timi .... (970) 867-5651
ADV DIR, MGR-PROM
Fort Morgan Times, Fort Morgan, CO
McCorstin, Darrell .... (903) 893-8181
News/Wire ED
Herald Democrat, Sherman, TX
McCoshen, Jeff .... (403) 532-1110
Sports ED
Daily Herald-Tribune, Grande Prairie, AB
McCouch, George .... (502) 886-4444
ADV DIR-Market RES, CIRC DIR
Kentucky New Era, Hopkinsville, KY
McCourt, Jeff .... (312) 397-0020
PUB, Windy City Times, Chicago, IL
McCowin, Gerald B .... (412) 775-3200
PROD MGR-Maintenance
Beaver County Times, Beaver, PA
McCoy, Ann .... (970) 884-2331
PUB, ED, Pine River Times, Bayfield, CO
McCoy, Belinda .... (903) 757-3311
Fashion/Style ED, Films/Theater ED, Food/Garden ED, Home Furnishings/Music ED, Women's/Clubs ED
Longview News-Journal, Longview, TX
McCoy, Benjamin .... (712) 246-3097
CIRC MGR
Valley News Today, Shenandoah, IA
McCoy, Bobbie .... (423) 981-1100
PROD FRM-COMP
Daily Times, Maryville, TN
McCoy, Brian .... (209) 943-6397
Drama ED, Music ED, Record, Stockton, CA
McCoy, Charles .... (212) 416-2000
BU Chief-San Francisco
Wall Street Journal, New York, NY
McCoy, David .... (706) 724-0851
PROD MGR-PR
Augusta Chronicle, Augusta, GA
McCoy, Dorothy .... (408) 423-4242
ADV MGR-Sales
Santa Cruz County Sentinel, Santa Cruz, CA
McCoy, Edwin L .... (540) 473-2741
GM, Fincastle Herald, Fincastle, VA
McCoy, Gloria .... (937) 773-2721
City ED, News ED
Piqua Daily Call, Piqua, OH
McCoy, John .... (607) 432-1000
PROD FRM-PR, Daily Star, Oneonta, NY
McCoy, Kathleen .... (907) 257-4200
Health/Medical ED, Lifestyle ED, Women's ED, Anchorage Daily News, Anchorage, AK
McCoy, Mike .... (501) 356-2111
GM, ED, Glenwood Herald, Glenwood, AR
McCoy, Richard .... (615) 296-2426
ED, News-Democrat, Waverly, TN
McCoy, Ruby .... (304) 938-2142
GM, MAN ED, Industrial News, Iaeger, WV
McCoy, Sheila .... (817) 647-1101
ED, Ranger Times, Ranger, TX
McCoy, Von .... (910) 786-4141
MGR-INFO Line
Mount Airy News, Mount Airy, NC
McCracken, Peggy .... (915) 445-5475
DP MGR, Pecos Enterprise, Pecos, TX
McCracken, Peggy .... (513) 863-8200
Religion ED, Journal-News, Hamilton, OH
McCraken, Anne W .... (307) 362-3736
DIR, Daily Rocket-Miner, Rock Springs, WY
McCraken, L Michael .... (307) 634-3361
PRES/PUB
Wyoming Tribune-Eagle, Cheyenne, WY
McCraken, William D .... (307) 347-3241
VP, Northern Wyoming Daily News, Worland, WY, McCraken Newspapers
McCrary, Karen G .... (210) 875-2116
PUB, ED
Luling Newsboy and Signal, Luling, TX
McCray, Robert D .... (412) 263-1100
ADV DIR
Pittsburgh Post-Gazette, Pittsburgh, PA
McCreary, Terri .... (903) 455-4220
ADV DIR
Greenville Herald-Banner, Greenville, TX
McCree, Alonda .... (708) 524-8300
ED, Wednesday Journal of Oak Park & River Forest, Oak Park, IL
McCrory, Sean .... (409) 833-3311
News ED
Beaumont Enterprise, Beaumont, TX
McCuaig, Paul .... (902) 629-6000
ADV DIR, Guardian, Charlottetown, PEI
McCuaig, Wayne .... (906) 632-2235
PROD MGR
Evening News, Sault Ste. Marie, MI
McCubbin, Patricia .... (216) 999-4500
ASSOC ED, Plain Dealer, Cleveland, OH
McCue, Danny .... (516) 747-8282
MAN ED
Port Washington News, Mineola, NY

Copyright ©1997 by the Editor & Publisher Co.

151-Who's Where **Mcg**

McCue, Janet .... (216) 999-4500
Fashion ED, Plain Dealer, Cleveland, OH
McCue, Marian L .... (207) 781-3661
PUB, Forecaster, Falmouth, ME
McCue, Pat .... (706) 724-0851
PROD ASST DIR
Augusta Chronicle, Augusta, GA
McCue, Tracy .... (316) 326-3326
Automotive ED, Radio/Television ED, Sports ED, Wellington Daily News, Wellington, KS
McCullers, Michael .... (405) 226-6397
MAN ED, Carter County Courier, Ardmore, OK
McCullers, Tim .... (405) 226-6397
PUB, Carter County Courier, Ardmore, OK
McCullick, Bill .... (614) 852-1616
ED, Tribune, London, OH
McCulloch, Joanne .... (213) 229-5300
ADV Representative
Daily Commerce, Los Angeles, CA
McCulloh, Burns .... (402) 336-1221
MAN ED
Holt County Independent, O'Neill, NE
McCullough, Dave .... (604) 273-7744
PUB, Richmond Review, Richmond, BC
McCullough, Jillyn .... (503) 399-6611
Garden ED, Statesman Journal, Salem, OR
McCullough, Joyce .... (815) 223-3200
VP/GM, PSL MGR
News-Tribune, La Salle, IL
McCullough, Mason .... (704) 873-1054
PUB, MAN ED
Iredell County News, Statesville, NC
McCullough, Melanie .... (219) 724-2121
EDU ED, Daily Democrat, Decatur, IN
McCullough, Michael .... (203) 964-2200
EX News ED
Stamford Advocate, Stamford, CT
McCullough, Richard A .... (412) 222-2200
CIRC DIR, ADTX MGR
Observer-Reporter, Washington, PA
McCullough, Ron .... (508) 458-7100
CIRC MGR-Home Delivery, Sun, Lowell, MA
McCully, Kim .... (417) 678-2115
ED, Aurora Advertiser, Aurora, MO
McCully, Sharon .... (819) 569-9526
EPE, Record, Sherbrooke, QC
McCune, Greg .... (202) 898-8300
Washington ED, Reuters, Washington, DC
McCune, Hal .... (541) 276-2211
News ED, East Oregonian, Pendleton, OR
McCurdy, Don .... (519) 894-2231
MAN ED, Record, Kitchener, ON
McCurley, Mary .... (209) 835-3030
Entertainment ED, Today's Living ED
Tracy Press, Tracy, CA
McCurry, Betty .... (704) 437-2161
DP MGR, News Herald, Morganton, NC
McCurry-Ross, Cindy .... (408) 424-2221
ED, Californian, Salinas, CA
McCusker, Tom .... (915) 673-4271
PROD FRM-Computers
Abilene Reporter-News, Abilene, TX
McCutchen, Glenn .... (409) 632-6631
PUB, Lufkin Daily News, Lufkin, TX
McCutcheon, Gene .... (901) 642-1162
News ED, Paris Post-Intelligencer, Paris, TN
McCutcheon, R L .... (705) 368-2744
PUB, Manitoulin Expositor, Little Current, ON
McCutcheon, Raymond .... (516) 843-2020
ADV DIR-Display, Newsday, Melville, NY
McDaniel, Bryan .... (913) 364-3141
PUB, Holton Recorder, Holton, KS
McDaniel, Deangelo .... (205) 974-1114
MAN ED, Moulton Advertiser, Moulton, AL
McDaniel, Debbie .... (815) 784-5138
ED
Genoa-Kingston-Kirkland News, Sycamore, IL
McDaniel, Earl .... (717) 771-2000
Automotive ED, BUS/FIN ED
York Daily Record, York, PA
McDaniel, George A .... (757) 247-4600
ADV VP/DIR, Daily Press, Newport News, VA
McDaniel, Greg .... (541) 926-2211
PROD ASST FRM-PR
Albany Democrat-Herald, Albany, OR
McDaniel, John M .... (607) 674-6071
PUB, ED, Sherburne News, Sherburne, NY
McDaniel, Kevin .... (573) 642-7272
ADV MGR, Fulton Sun, Fulton, MO
McDaniel, Leslie C .... (913) 364-3141
ED, Holton Recorder, Holton, KS
McDaniel, Lyn .... (502) 443-1771
Photo ED, Travel ED
Paducah Sun, Paducah, KY
McDaniel, Mike .... (713) 220-7171
Television ED
Houston Chronicle, Houston, TX
McDaniel, Renell .... (806) 762-8844
ADTX MGR, Avalanche-Journal, Lubbock, TX
McDaniel, Roberta .... (817) 883-2554
PUB, Marlin Democrat, Marlin, TX
McDaniel, Terry .... (301) 733-5131
VP, ADV DIR-Sales
Morning Herald, Hagerstown, MD

McDavid, G E .... (713) 220-7171
PRES, Houston Chronicle, Houston, TX
McDermond, David .... (409) 776-4444
Photo DEPT MGR, Eagle, Bryan, TX
McDermott, Alan .... (816) 932-6600
ASST VP/Senior ED
Universal Press Syndicate, Kansas City, MO
McDermott, Joe .... (520) 573-4220
ASST MAN ED-News Desk
Arizona Daily Star, Tucson, AZ
McDermott, Joe .... (515) 792-3121
PUB, Newton Daily News, Newton, IA
McDermott, Kathy .... (317) 736-7101
PROD MGR-Computer SYS
Daily Journal, Franklin, IN
McDermott, Larry A .... (413) 788-1000
EX ED, Union-News, Springfield, MA
McDermott, Michael .... (316) 775-2218
ED, Action Line ED, BUS/FIN ED, City/MET ED, EPE, News ED, SCI ED
Augusta Daily Gazette, Augusta, KS
McDermott, Susan .... (718) 981-1234
Graphic Arts ED
Staten Island Advance, Staten Island, NY
McDermott, Terry .... (206) 464-2111
COL, Seattle Times, Seattle, WA
McDevitt, Larry .... (610) 696-1775
Photo ED
Daily Local News, West Chester, PA
McDiarmid, Hugh .... (313) 222-6400
COL-News
Detroit Free Press, Detroit, MI
McDine, Lucretia .... (757) 247-4600
Amusements ED, Radio/Television ED
Daily Press, Newport News, VA
McDonagh, John .... (360) 694-3391
VP-MKTG/Advertising, ADV VP-MKTG
Columbian, Vancouver, WA
McDonald, DD, Most Rev A ...... (501)664-0125
PUB, Arkansas Catholic,, Little Rock, AR
McDonald, Archie .... (604) 732-2111
COL, Vancouver Sun, Vancouver, BC
McDonald, Barbara .... (503) 243-2122
GM, Willamette Week, Portland, OR
McDonald, Barry .... (619) 939-3354
ED, Rocketeer, Ridgecrest, CA
McDonald, Craig .... (614) 841-1781
MAN ED
Westerville This Week, Columbus, OH
McDonald, Dave .... (715) 842-2101
PROD MGR-PR
Wausau Daily Herald, Wausau, WI
McDonald, Frank .... (423) 756-6900
BC, PRES
Chattanooga Free Press, Chattanooga, TN
McDonald, Frank .... (804) 649-6000
VP/DIR-Human Relations
Richmond Times-Dispatch, Richmond, VA
McDonald, James .... (717) 622-3456
PA, PROD DIR-CORP SRV, Pottsville Republican & Evening Herald, Pottsville, PA
McDonald, James C .... (205) 532-4000
CIRC DIR, Huntsville Times, Huntsville, AL
McDonald, Jean .... (217) 351-5252
Sports ED, Online Contact
News-Gazette, Champaign, IL
McDonald, Joe .... (908) 722-8800
MET ED, Courier-News, Bridgewater, NJ
McDonald, Joyce .... (419) 394-7414
BM/PA, Evening Leader, St. Marys, OH
McDonald, Katherine .... (805) 736-2313
Health/Schools ED
Lompoc Record, Lompoc, CA
McDonald, Ken .... (815) 433-2000
CIRC ASST MGR, Daily Times, Ottawa, IL
McDonald, Kit .... (409) 776-4444
ADTX MGR-Sales, Eagle, Bryan, TX
McDonald, Legon .... (502) 754-3000
GM, Leader-News, Central City, KY
McDonald, Linda D .... (205) 396-5760
GM, Clay Times-Journal, Lineville, AL
McDonald, Mac .... (408) 372-3311
Music ED
Monterey County Herald, Monterey, CA
McDonald, Mark .... (515) 432-1234
CIRC MGR
Boone News-Republican, Boone, IA
McDonald, Michele .... (403) 235-7100
MGR-MKTG Resources
Calgary Herald, Calgary, AB
McDonald, Pete .... (912) 924-2751
CIRC MGR, Times-Recorder, Americus, GA
McDonald, Rick .... (309) 686-3000
PROD FRM-Transportation
Journal Star, Peoria, IL
McDonald, Robert .... (407) 242-3500
Photo DEPT MGR
Florida Today, Melbourne, FL
McDonald, Robert .... (301) 722-4600
PROD MGR-SYS
Cumberland Times-News, Cumberland, MD
McDonald, Robert .... (312) 222-3232
ADV MGR-Make-Up
Chicago Tribune, Chicago, IL

McDonald, Sean .... (541) 482-3456
ADV DIR, Daily Tidings, Ashland, OR
McDonald, Yolanda .... (915) 546-6100
CIRC MGR-Sales/MKTG
El Paso Times, El Paso, TX
McDonnell Jr, J P .... (612) 682-1221
PUB, ED
Wright County Journal-Press, Buffalo, MN
McDonough, Dina .... (218) 546-5029
ED, Crosby-Ironton Courier, Crosby, MN
McDonough, Doug .... (806) 296-1300
News ED/Wire ED
Plainview Daily Herald, Plainview, TX
McDonough, Jeffrey J .... (401) 423-3200
PUB, ED, Jamestown Press, Jamestown, RI
McDonough, John .... (312) 321-3000
ASST MAN ED-Production
Chicago Sun-Times, Chicago, IL
McDonough, Robert .... (413) 447-7311
Sports ED, Berkshire Eagle, Pittsfield, MA
McDonough, Tim .... (419) 784-5441
ASST Sports ED
Crescent-News, Defiance, OH
McDougal, John .... (817) 864-2686
PUB, Haskell Free Press, Haskell, TX
McDougal, R J .... (502) 753-1916
PROD FRM-PR
Murray Ledger & Times, Murray, KY
McDougall, Carole .... (902) 468-1222
MKTG DIR, Daily News, Halifax, NS
McDougall, Charlie .... (204) 687-7339
News ED, Reminder, Flin Flon, MB
McDougall, Robert .... (514) 521-4545
DP MGR
Le Journal de Montreal, Montreal, QC
McDougle, Mike .... (601) 798-4766
CIRC DIR, Picayune Item, Picayune, MS
McDowell, Bart .... (618) 443-2145
PUB, Sparta News-Plaindealer, Sparta, IL
McDowell, Bren .... (320) 365-3266
MAN ED, Bird Island Union, Bird Island, MN
McDowell, Charles .... (804) 649-6000
COL
Richmond Times-Dispatch, Richmond, VA
McDowell, Christine .... (904) 435-8500
Librarian
Pensacola News Journal, Pensacola, FL
McDowell, Greg .... (905) 433-5546
GM, Oshawa News, Courtice, ON
McDowell, Jerry .... (309) 686-3000
City ED-Day, SCI Technology ED
Journal Star, Peoria, IL
McDowell, Raymond .... (910) 727-7211
TREAS, CONT
Winston-Salem Journal, Winston-Salem, NC
McDowell, Richard .... (706) 682-3346
PUB, Bayonet, Columbus, GA
McDowell, Sandra .... (905) 433-5546
PUB, Oshawa News, Courtice, ON
McDowell, Teri .... (814) 274-8044
ED
Potter Leader-Enterprises, Coudersport, PA
McDowell, Thomas .... (313) 222-6400
PROD OPER DIR-Facilities
Detroit Newspapers, Detroit, MI
McDuffee, Susan L .... (616) 845-5181
TREAS, Daily News, Ludington, MI
McDuffie, Gary .... (912) 923-6432
PUB, Robins Rev-up, Warner Robins, GA
McDurmon, Cyndi .... (601) 842-2611
ADV MGR, Northeast Mississippi Daily Journal, Tupelo, MS
McDurmot, Don .... (937) 548-3151
Sports ED
Greenville Daily Advocate, Greenville, OH
McEachern, Bob .... (906) 228-2500
PROD MGR
Marquette Mining Journal, Marquette, MI
McEachran, Angus .... (901) 529-2211
PRES, ED/PRES
Commercial Appeal, Memphis, TN
Mc Elhaney, Jim .... (512) 364-1270
ED, Odem-Edroy Times, Sinton, TX
McElrath, Dwight .... (706) 278-1011
PROD FRM-PR
Daily Citizen-News, Dalton, GA
McElrath, Gary .... (502) 443-1771
PROD FRM-MR, Paducah Sun, Paducah, KY
McElrea, Kari .... (519) 354-2000
CIRC MGR
Chatham Daily News, Chatham, ON
McElroy, Edward J .... (800) 238-1133
SEC/TREAS, American Federation of Teachers, Washington, DC
McElroy, George .... (713) 527-8261
ED, Houston Informer & Texas Freeman, Houston, TX
McElroy, Jack .... (303) 892-5000
Deputy MAN ED
Rocky Mountain News, Denver, CO
McElroy, Ken .... (800) 835-7369
VP/NTL Sales, Thomson Newspapers Comic Group, Brookfield, WI

McElvaney, Lynn .... (505) 622-7710
SEC, Roswell Daily Record, Roswell, NM
McElwee, Sue .... (814) 643-4040
Books/EDU ED, COL, Features/Films ED, Radio/Television ED, Religion ED
Daily News, Huntingdon, PA
McEnery, Brian .... (914) 694-9300
CIRC MGR-OPER
Reporter Dispatch, White Plains, NY
Gannett Co. Inc.
McEnroe, Paul .... (612) 673-4000
GEN Assignment Reporter
Star Tribune, Minneapolis, MN
McEntee, Bruce .... (410) 332-6000
CIRC DIR-Distribution, Sun, Baltimore, MD
McEntee, Peg .... (801) 237-2031
EDU ED, Religion ED, School ED
Salt Lake Tribune, Salt Lake City, UT
McEntire, Tom .... (352) 394-2183
PUB, South Lake Press, Clermont, FL
McEvoy, Elaine .... (315) 823-3680
ADV MGR-CLASS
Evening Times, Little Falls, NY
McEvoy, Ted .... (501) 785-7700
ADV MGR-CLASS
Southwest Times Record, Fort Smith, AR
McEwan, Sally .... (941) 748-4140
GM, Weekly, Bradenton, FL
McEwen, Alvin .... (803) 799-5252
ED, South Carolina Black Media Group, Columbia, SC
McEwen, Andrew .... (609) 989-7800
Entertainment/Amusements ED, Health/Medical ED, Television/Film ED, Theater/Music ED, Trentonian, Trenton, NJ
McEwen, Craig .... (701) 253-7311
ED-Minnesota, Forum, Fargo, ND
McEwen, Don .... (406) 496-5500
PROD Printing Services Team Leader
Montana Standard, Butte, MT
McFadden, Alice .... (207) 596-0055
PUB, Free Press, Rockland, ME
McFadden, James .... (215) 536-6820
ED, Quakertown Free Press, Quakertown, PA
McFadden, Kay .... (704) 358-5000
Radio/Television Critic
Charlotte Observer, Charlotte, NC
McFadden, Miriam .... (423) 482-1021
CIRC MGR, Oak Ridger, Oak Ridge, TN
McFadden, Steven .... (509) 877-3322
ED, Wapato Independent, Wapato, WA
McFall, Cathleen .... (610) 588-2196
PUB, ED
Slate Belt Hometown News, Bangor, PA
McFall, Eunice .... (806) 455-1101
ED, Valley Tribune, Quitaque, TX
McFann, T Mark .... (970) 493-6397
CIRC DIR
Fort Collins Coloradoan, Fort Collins, CO
McFarland, Janice .... (507) 285-7600
Lifestyle ED, Post-Bulletin, Rochester, MN
McFarland, John .... (601) 896-2100
MGR-EDU SRV, DIR-MKTG SRV
Sun Herald, Biloxi, MS
McFarland, Tammy .... (617) 929-2000
MGR-Telecommunications
Boston Globe, Boston, MA
McFarlane, Clive .... (508) 793-9100
EDU ED, Telegram & Gazette, Worcester, MA
McFarlane, Gary L .... (605) 853-3575
PUB, ED, Miller Press, Miller, SD
McFarlane, Paula .... (605) 458-2253
PUB, ED, Times-Enterprise, Wessington, SD
McFarlin, Bob .... (417) 623-3480
PROD MGR-Pre Press
Joplin Globe, Joplin, MO
McFarlin, Diane H .... (941) 953-7755
EX ED, Sarasota Herald-Tribune, Sarasota, FL
McFate, Michael .... (520) 294-1200
CIRC MGR-Mailing SRV, Online MGR
Daily Territorial, Tucson, AZ
McFatridge, Kevin .... (315) 253-5311
ADV DIR-Creative, Citizen, Auburn, NY
McFeely, Robert W .... (412) 222-2200
DIR-Community Relations
Observer-Reporter, Washington, PA
McFerren, Robert .... (330) 747-1471
Graphics ED/Art DIR
Vindicator, Youngstown, OH
McFerrin, Clay .... (601) 647-8462
PUB, ED, Sun Sentinel, Charleston, MS
McGaha, Dayle E .... (405) 363-3370
PUB, GEN/PSL MGR, PA, ED, Books/Films ED, BUS ED/COL, EPE, Garden ED
Blackwell Journal-Tribune, Blackwell, OK
McGahan, Don .... (205) 766-3434
PROD DIR, Times Daily, Florence, AL
McGammon, Dave .... (317) 462-5528
ADV DIR, Daily Reporter, Greenfield, IN

Mcg Who's Where-152

McGann, Most Rev John R .... (516) 594-1000
PUB
Long Island Catholic, Rockville Center, NY

McGarry, Hugh .... (303) 892-5000
CIRC MGR-MET
Rocky Mountain News, Denver, CO

McGarry, Ron .... (309) 343-7181
PROD FRM-COMP
Register-Mail, Galesburg, IL

McGarvey, Jim .... (201) 428-6200
MET ED, Daily Record, Parsippany, NJ

McGaughey, Steve .... (918) 423-1700
Sports ED, McAlester News-Capital & Democrat, McAlester, OK

McGauley, James C .... (904) 259-2400
PUB, ED
Baker County Press, MacClenny, FL

McGawn, Matt .... (312) 644-4360
PRES, Derus Media Service Inc., Chicago, IL

McGeachie, Matt .... (250) 380-5211
CIRC MGR-Reader Services
Times Colonist, Victoria, BC

McGee, Dave .... (705) 268-5050
MAN ED, EPE, Daily Press, Timmins, ON

McGee, David .... (423) 323-5700
ED, Sullivan County News, Blountville, TN

McGee, David A .... (800) 749-1841
PRES, Tel-Aire Publications Inc., Dallas, TX

McGee, Doug .... (902) 564-5451
EPE, Cape Breton Post, Sydney, NS

McGee, Harvey C .... (209) 532-7151
PRES, PUB, ED, EPE
Union Democrat, Sonora, CA

McGee, Helen M .... (209) 532-7151
SEC/TREAS, CONT
Union Democrat, Sonora, CA

McGee, Linn .... (904) 682-6524
ED, North Okaloosa Bulletin, Crestview, FL

McGee, Mark .... (615) 684-1200
ED, EPE, Times-Gazette, Shelbyville, TN

McGee, Mary .... (315) 393-1000
ADV DIR, Courier-Observer Journal & The Advance-News, Ogdensburg, NY

McGee, Mike .... (615) 473-2191
ED, Warren County News, McMinnville, TN

McGee, Patricia K .... (410) 778-2011
ED, Kent County News, Chestertown, MD

McGee, Rhonda .... (614) 452-4561
Administrative MGR
Times Recorder, Zanesville, OH

McGee, Theresa .... (713) 266-3444
MAN ED
Highlands Star/Crosby Courier, Highlands, TX

McGeehan, Marc .... (508) 685-1000
Photo DEPT MGR
Eagle-Tribune, North Andover, MA

McGeehan, Thomas J .... (717) 255-8100
CIRC ASST DIR-Distribution/SRV
Patriot-News, Harrisburg, PA

McGeehee, Chris .... (502) 442-7380
PUB, West Kentucky News, Paducah, KY

McGehee, Ann .... (504) 643-4918
CONT, Slidell Sentry-News, Slidell, LA

McGehee, Chris .... (502) 628-5490
PUB, Carlisle County News, Bardwell, KY

McGehee, Kay .... (502) 422-2155
PUB
Meade County Messenger, Brandenburg, KY

McGehee, Mike .... (615) 259-8800
Graphics ED
Nashville Banner, Nashville, TN

McGehee, Scott .... (219) 461-8444
PRES/CEO
Fort Wayne Newspapers Inc., Fort Wayne, IN

McGervey, Prof John D .... (216) 932-5538
Co-Author, Numbers Game, Cleveland, OH

McGhee, Billy .... (205) 234-4281
ADV MGR
Alexander City Outlook, Alexander City, AL

McGhee, John .... (703) 276-3400
CIRC GM-Philadelphia
USA Today, Arlington, VA

McGhee, Steph .... (812) 268-6356
PROD SUPV
Sullivan Daily Times, Sullivan, IN

McGhie, John .... (905) 454-4344
MAN ED, Brampton Guardian, Brampton, ON

McGill, John .... (406) 338-2090
ED, Glacier Reporter, Browning, MT

McGill, Nicole .... (904) 359-4111
Call Box ED
Florida Times-Union, Jacksonville, FL

McGillivray, Tom .... (317) 747-5700
TREAS, Star Press, Muncie, IN

McGinley, John .... (717) 255-8100
Entertainment ED
Patriot-News, Harrisburg, PA

McGinley, Morgan .... (860) 442-2200
EPE, Day, New London, CT

McGinn, Barbro .... (608) 423-3213
ED, Cambridge News, Cambridge, WI

McGinnis, James M .... (218) 723-8000
PRES/CEO
Murphy McGinnis Media, Duluth, MN

McGinnis, Judith .... (817) 767-8341
Food ED, Wichita Falls Times Record News, Wichita Falls, TX

McGinnis, Mary Jane .... (860) 442-2200
DIR-Human Resources, Day, New London, CT

McGirr, Janice .... (605) 458-2253
GM, Times-Enterprise, Wessington, SD

McGivney, Betsy .... (518) 483-4700
BM, Malone Telegram, Malone, NY

McGlade, Keith .... (712) 563-2661
PUB, Audubon County Advocate Journal, Audubon, IA

McGlamery, Joe .... (912) 764-9031
PRES, Statesboro Herald, Statesboro, GA

McGlone, Arleen .... (508) 222-7000
CIRC MGR, Sun Chronicle, Attleboro, MA

McGlynn, Michael .... (717) 821-2091
Political ED
Citizens' Voice, Wilkes-Barre, PA

McGlynn, Timothy .... (609) 272-7000
Analyst-INFO SYS
Press of Atlantic City, Pleasantville, NJ

McGoldrick, Debbie .... (212) 684-3366
ED, Irish Voice, New York, NY

McGoldrick, James .... (304) 684-2424
PUB, ED, St. Marys Oracle, St. Marys, WV

McGonegal, Linda .... (715) 394-4411
Fashion ED, Food/Garden ED, Home Furnishings ED, Society/Women's ED
Daily Telegram, Superior, WI

McGonegal, Richard .... (573) 636-3131
MAN ED, News Tribune, Jefferson City, MO

McGoogan, K .... (403) 235-7100
Books ED, Calgary Herald, Calgary, AB

McGorman, Kelli .... (616) 796-4831
BM, Big Rapids Pioneer, Big Rapids, MI

McGough, Michael .... (412) 263-1100
EPE, Pittsburgh Post-Gazette, Pittsburgh, PA

McGovern, Judy .... (614) 283-4711
MAN ED, Herald-Star, Steubenville, OH

McGovern, Pat .... (803) 771-6161
Women's ED, State, Columbia, SC

McGovern, Robert .... (610) 323-3000
Graphics ED/Webmaster
Mercury, Pottstown, PA

McGowan, Cynthia .... (913) 295-1111
News ED
Topeka Capital-Journal, Topeka, KS

McGowan, Mike .... (330) 747-1471
Fashion/Food ED, Features ED, Health/Medical ED, Living/Lifestyle ED, SCI/Technology ED, Vindicator, Youngstown, OH

McGowen, Rebecca .... (305) 294-6641
Lifestyle ED, Key West Citizen, Key West, FL

McGrady, Tina .... (765) 762-2411
MAN ED
Fountain County Neighbor, Attica, IN

McGranahan, Ed .... (864) 298-4100
Sports ED, Greenville News, Greenville, SC

McGrath, Charles .... (212) 556-1234
Books Review ED
New York Times, New York, NY

McGrath, Debby .... (410) 228-3131
CIRC MGR, Daily Banner, Cambridge, MD

McGrath, Mary .... (402) 444-1000
Medical/SCI ED
Omaha World-Herald, Omaha, NE

McGrath, Paul .... (713) 220-7171
News ED, Houston Chronicle, Houston, TX

McGraw III, Harold W .... (212) 208-8369
PRES, Standard & Poor's Dividend Record, New York, NY, McGraw-Hill

McGraw, Kay .... (757) 446-2000
DIR-Human Resources
Virginian-Pilot, Norfolk, VA

McGraw, Scott D .... (616) 649-2333
PUB, ED
Vicksburg Commercial Express, Vicksburg, MI

McGraw, Tommy .... (205) 652-6100
PUB, ED, Sumter County Record-Journal, Livingston, AL

McGregor, Bryce .... (403) 627-3252
PUB, Pincher Creek Echo, Pincher Creek, AB

McGregor, James .... (903) 572-1705
CIRC MGR, Mount Pleasant Daily Tribune, Mount Pleasant, TX

McGregor, Jeremy .... (509) 325-0634
GM
Pacific Northwest Inlander, Spokane, WA

McGregor, Martha .... (903) 572-1705
ADV MGR, Mount Pleasant Daily Tribune, Mount Pleasant, TX

McGregor Jr, Ted S .... (509) 325-0634
PUB, ED
Pacific Northwest Inlander, Spokane, WA

McGrew, James B .... (717) 291-8811
MGR-PROM
Lancaster Intelligencer Journal/New Era/Sunday News, Lancaster, PA

McGrew, Lou .... (617) 284-2400
PUB, Revere Journal, Revere, MA

McGrew, Ray .... (309) 582-5112
GM, Times Record, Aledo, IL

McGrew, Sally .... (918) 663-1414
ED, Glenpool Post, Tulsa, OK

McGruder, Robert G .... (313) 222-6400
EX ED, Detroit Free Press, Detroit, MI

McGuerty III, B F .... (315) 497-1551
PUB, ED
Moravia Republican-Register, Moravia, NY

McGuigan, Pat .... (405) 475-3311
EDL Writer
Daily Oklahoman, Oklahoma City, OK

McGuiness, Jay .... (405) 255-5354
DP Manager, PROD MGR-SYS
Duncan Banner, Duncan, OK

McGuinness, Kathleen G .... (213) 237-3700
VP/GEN Counsel/SEC
Times Mirror Co., Los Angeles, CA

McGuire, Barb .... (520) 573-4400
CIRC MGR-Home Delivery, TNI Partners dba Tucson Newspapers, Tucson, AZ

McGuire, Bill .... (902) 893-9405
MAN ED, Daily News, Truro, NS

McGuire, Cecelia .... (514) 987-2222
Living ED, Gazette, Montreal, QC

McGuire, Dan .... (314) 340-8000
PROD ASST MGR-SYS
St. Louis Post-Dispatch, St. Louis, MO

McGuire, Jerry P .... (803) 547-2353
ED, Fort Mill Times, Fort Mill, SC

McGuire Sr, John J .... (518) 873-6368
GM, Times of Ti, Ticonderoga, NY

McGuire, Michael .... (209) 394-7939
ED, Chronicle, Livingston, CA

McGuire, Michael J .... (207) 621-6000
ED, Capital Weekly, Augusta, ME

McGuire, Nancy L .... (907) 443-5235
PUB, ED, Nome Nugget, Nome, AK

McGuire, Peter .... (506) 632-8888
Sports ED, Telegraph-Journal/Saint John Times Globe, Saint John, NB

McGuire, Tim J .... (612) 673-4000
Senior VP-Reader Customer Unit/ED, GM-Reader Customer Unit, ED-Reader Customer Unit, Star Tribune, Minneapolis, MN

McHale, SSgt Mary .... (609) 724-4091
ED, Airtides, Willingboro, NJ

McHaney, Catherine .... (512) 575-1451
SEC/TREAS, Victoria Advocate, Victoria, TX

McHarry, Elizabeth Poston .... (707) 786-4611
PUB, ED, Ferndale Enterprise, Ferndale, CA

McHenry, Steve .... (907) 456-6661
Religion ED
Fairbanks Daily News-Miner, Fairbanks, AK

McHugh, Most Rev James T .... (609) 756-7910
PUB, Catholic Star Herald, Camden, NJ

McHugh, Patrick .... (215) 854-2000
PROD VP, Philadelphia Inquirer, Philadelphia, PA, Knight-Ridder Inc.

McHugh, Paul .... (415) 777-1111
COL-Outdoors
San Francisco Chronicle, San Francisco, CA

McHugh, Susan .... (513) 459-1711
PUB, ED, Eastside Weekend, Mason, OH

McHughes, Pat .... (501) 879-5450
ED, Pine Bluff News, Pine Bluff, AR

McIlheran, Pat .... (218) 723-5281
EX ED-News
Duluth News-Tribune, Duluth, MN

McIlwain, Marvin .... (334) 897-2823
ED, Elba Clipper, Elba, AL

McIlyar, Christine .... (614) 373-2121
ADV MGR, Marietta Times, Marietta, OH

McInally, Michael .... (406) 523-5200
MAN ED, Missoulian, Missoula, MT

McInnes, Garry R .... (805) 229-1520
PUB, Marathon Mercury, Marathon, ON

McInnis, Andy .... (520) 445-3333
City ED, Daily Courier, Prescott, AZ

McInnis, Joan .... (717) 771-2000
Online MGR, York Daily Record, York, PA

McIntire, Carol .... (330) 627-5591
ED, Free Press Standard, Carrollton, OH

McIntosh, Barry .... (813) 893-8111
ADV MGR-Ad OPER
St. Petersburg Times, St. Petersburg, FL

McIntosh, Calvin .... (506) 357-3356
PUB, GM
Oromocto Post-Gazette, Oromocto, NB

McIntosh, Catherine .... (713) 220-7171
Picture ED, Houston Chronicle, Houston, TX

McIntosh, Ed .... (941) 629-2855
PROD MGR-Pre press
Sun Herald, Port Charlotte, FL

McIntosh, Jim .... (513) 721-2700
ADV MGR-CLASS/RE
Cincinnati Enquirer, Cincinnati, OH

McIntosh, Jim .... (573) 238-2821
ED, Banner-Press, Marble Hill, MO

McIntosh, Kevin .... (519) 255-5711
DIR-Manufacturing
Windsor Star, Windsor, ON

McIntosh, Tammie .... (330) 385-4545
ADV MGR, Review, East Liverpool, OH

McIntosh, Thane .... (619) 299-3131
Photo ADM
San Diego Union-Tribune, San Diego, CA

McIntosh, Tim .... (517) 787-2300
CONT, DP MGR
Jackson Citizen Patriot, Jackson, MI

McIntosh, Willie .... (864) 224-4321
Librarian, Independent-Mail, Anderson, SC

McIntyre, Bill .... (515) 573-2141
Outdoors ED, Sports ED
Messenger, Fort Dodge, IA

McIntyre, Garth .... (613) 732-3691
PROD FRM-COMP, Observer, Pembroke, ON

McIntyre, Janice .... (318) 927-3541
ED, Homer Guardian-Journal, Homer, LA

McIntyre, Ken .... (202) 636-3000
MET Times ED
Washington Times, Washington, DC

McIver, Jim .... (208) 743-9411
MGR-INFO SYS
Lewiston Morning Tribune, Lewiston, ID

McIver, Rose .... (609) 663-6000
MET ED, Political/Government ED
Courier-Post, Cherry Hill, NJ

McKain, Jon .... (412) 282-8000
ADV MGR-CLASS, Butler Eagle, Butler, PA

McKay, Amy .... (505) 887-5501
MGR-BUS, Current-Argus, Carlsbad, NM

McKay, Carol .... (916) 397-2601
PUB, Butte Valley-Lost River Star, Dorris, CA

McKay, Dan .... (802) 362-3535
PUB, GM
Vermont News Guide, Manchester Center, VT

McKay, Lani .... (707) 226-3711
ADV MGR-CLASS
Napa Valley Register, Napa, CA

McKeachie, Mel .... (419) 281-0581
MAN ED, Times-Gazette, Ashland, OH

McKeague, Paul .... (519) 255-5711
COL (Ottawa), Windsor Star, Windsor, ON

McKean, Kris .... (313) 222-6400
DIR-RES
Detroit Newspapers, Detroit, MI

McKean, Matthew T .... (205) 766-3434
Photo DEPT MGR, Times Daily, Florence, AL

McKeand, Bret .... (602) 972-6101
PUB, Sun Cities Independent, Sun City, AZ

McKechnie, Ed .... (316) 724-4426
PUB, Girard Press, Girard, KS

McKee, Beattie .... (910) 458-8156
PUB, Island Gazette, Carolina Beach, NC

McKee, Bill .... (540) 669-2181
Chief Photographer, Herald-Courier Virginia Tennessean, Bristol, VA

McKee, Caroline .... (206) 597-8742
MGR-MKTG/PROM
News Tribune, Tacoma, WA

McKee, George .... (717) 762-2151
BM, DP MGR
Record Herald, Waynesboro, PA

McKee, James S .... (912) 382-4321
PUB, PA, Tifton Gazette, Tifton, GA

McKee, Jim .... (912) 382-4321
PUB, Gazette Light, Tifton, GA

McKee, Jim .... (903) 887-4511
GM, Monitor/Leader, Mabank, TX

McKee, Katharine .... (313) 222-6400
Environmental Writer
Detroit Free Press, Detroit, MI

McKee, Rick .... (706) 724-0851
Graphics ED, Augusta Chronicle, Augusta, GA

McKee, Roger .... (910) 458-8156
PUB, ED, Island Gazette, Carolina Beach, NC

McKee, Sally .... (309) 686-3000
Fashion/Style ED, Living/Lifestyle ED
Journal Star, Peoria, IL

McKee, Tracy .... (318) 697-5521
GM, ED, Logansport Interstate-Progress, Logansport, LA

McKeeber, Lauren .... (208) 624-4455
ED, Fremont County Herald-Chronicle, St. Anthony, ID

McKeel, Jim .... (334) 433-1551
CIRC MGR-Single Copy
Mobile Press Register, Mobile, AL

McKeeman, James E .... (308) 772-3555
PUB, ED, Garden County News, Oshkosh, NE

McKeeman, Shelley .... (506) 466-3220
GM, Saint Croix Courier, St. Stephen, NB

McKeirnan, Kelly .... (619) 745-6611
PROD MGR-Press
North County Times, Escondido, CA

McKeithan, Ray .... (919) 243-5151
ADV DIR, Wilson Daily Times, Wilson, NC

McKeller, Mike .... (206) 597-8742
DIR-FIN, News Tribune, Tacoma, WA

McKelvey, Vince .... (937) 225-2000
Political/Government ED
Dayton Daily News, Dayton, OH

McKelvy, Billy Ray .... (501) 642-2111
ED, COL, DP MGR
De Queen Daily Citizen, De Queen, AR

153-Who's Where **Mcm**

McKenna, Anne .... (813) 963-1918
PUB, Laker, Tampa, FL
McKenna, John .... (860) 567-8766
MAN ED, Litchfield Enquirer, Litchfield, CT
McKenna, John .... (360) 378-4191
PUB, Journal of the San Juan Islands, Friday Harbor, WA
McKenna, Kevin .... (401) 277-7000
CIRC MGR-Sales Development
Providence Journal-Bulletin, Providence, RI
McKenna, Martin P .... (207) 729-3311
MAN ED, Times Record, Brunswick, ME
McKenna, Neil .... (516) 747-8282
ED, Levittown Tribune, Mineola, NY
McKenna, Patrick J .... (717) 348-9100
EPE
Tribune & Scranton Times, Scranton, PA
McKenzie, Arthur E .... (207) 990-8000
TREAS, Bangor Daily News, Bangor, ME
McKenzie, Bob .... (604) 562-2441
PUB
Prince George Citizen, Prince George, BC
McKenzie, Carole .... (509) 582-1500
ADV MGR-NTL
Tri-City Herald, Tri-Cities, WA
McKenzie, Gary .... (519) 738-2542
PUB, ED, Harrow News, Harrow, ON
McKenzie, Gary .... (608) 523-4284
MAN ED, Blade-Atlas, Blanchardville, WI
McKenzie, Hal .... (912) 924-2751
Reporter, Times-Recorder, Americus, GA
McKenzie, Jay .... (352) 867-4010
MAN ED, ADTX MGR (News)
Ocala Star-Banner, Ocala, FL
McKenzie, Laura J .... (803) 943-4645
ED, Hampton County Guardian, Hampton, SC
McKenzie, Louise .... (601) 225-4531
GM, Wilk-Amite Record, Gloster, MS
McKenzie, Madhu .... (508) 997-7411
ADV MGR
Standard Times, New Bedford, MA
McKenzie, Mark .... (408) 920-5000
MGR-I/S Development
San Jose Mercury News, San Jose, CA
McKenzie, Mitzi .... (717) 255-8100
ADV SUPV-RT, Patriot-News, Harrisburg, PA
McKenzie, Peggy .... (901) 529-2211
Families/Children ED
Commercial Appeal, Memphis, TN
McKenzie, Sophia .... (318) 487-6397
Religion ED, Alexandria Daily Town Talk, Alexandria, LA
McKenzie, William .... (214) 977-8222
EDL Writer, Dallas Morning News, Dallas, TX
McKeon, Chris .... (419) 475-6000
ED, Sylvania Herald, Toledo, OH
McKeon, John C .... (516) 843-2020
VP-Advertising, Newsday, Melville, NY
McKeown, Jim .... (803) 475-6095
PUB, ED, Kershaw News-Era, Kershaw, SC
McKeown, L D .... (803) 385-3177
ED, News & Reporter, Chester, SC
McKercher, Peter .... (608) 252-6200
PROD SUPT-PR
Madison Newspapers Inc., Madison, WI
McKernan, Heather .... (603) 924-7172
PUB, Monadnock Ledger, Peterborough, NH
McKernan, Kathleen .... (219) 235-6161
Travel ED
South Bend Tribune, South Bend, IN
McKey, Donna .... (601) 285-6248
ED, Choctaw Plaindealer, Ackerman, MS
McKibben, P Scott .... (913) 295-1111
ED/PUB, Topeka Capital-Journal, Topeka, KS
McKibben, Ryan .... (303) 820-1010
PRES/PUB, Denver Post, Denver, CO
McKie, Heather .... (416) 947-2222
ADV DIR, Toronto Sun, Toronto, ON
McKie, Paul .... (204) 697-7000
Films ED
Winnipeg Free Press, Winnipeg, MB
McKiernan, Jim .... (206) 888-2311
PUB
Snoqualmie Valley Record, Snoqualmie, WA
McKiernan, Karen .... (206) 888-2311
PUB
Snoqualmie Valley Record, Snoqualmie, WA
McKiernan, William .... (203) 789-5200
PROD MGR-Ad SRV
New Haven Register, New Haven, CT
McKillip, Michael .... (802) 863-3441
CIRC DIR
Burlington Free Press, Burlington, VT
McKillop, Dennis .... (916) 243-2424
PROD SUPT-Press
Record Searchlight, Redding, CA
McKim, Beverly .... (518) 584-4242
Features ED, Religion ED
Saratogian, Saratoga Springs, NY
McKinley, Brenda .... (616) 683-2100
PROD FRM-COMP
Niles Daily Star, Niles, MI
McKinley, Dan .... (520) 836-7461
CFO, Casa Grande Dispatch, Casa Grande, AZ
McKinney, Bill .... (814) 870-1600
Political ED, COL
Morning News/Erie Daily Times, Erie, PA
McKinney, Jan E .... (602) 977-8351
ADV MGR-RT
Sun City Daily News-Sun, Sun City, AZ
McKinney, Jim .... (317) 398-6631
EX ED, Shelbyville News, Shelbyville, IN
McKinney, John .... (503) 221-8327
PROD CNR-Quality
Oregonian, Portland, OR
McKinney, Kathy .... (309) 829-9411
BUS Writer
Bloomington Pantagraph, Bloomington, IL
McKinney, Kevin .... (317) 254-2400
PUB, NUVO, Indianapolis, IN
McKinney, Mike .... (501) 239-8562
Sports ED, Daily Press, Paragould, AR
McKinney, Mike .... (210) 682-2423
PUB, Valley Town Crier, McAllen, TX
McKinney, Norma .... (704) 464-0221
ADV MGR-CLASS
Observer-News-Enterprise, Newton, NC
McKinney, Robert .... (903) 572-1705
ADTX MGR, PROD MGR, Mount Pleasant Daily Tribune, Mount Pleasant, TX
McKinney, Robert M .... (505) 983-3303
BC, PUB, New Mexican, Santa Fe, NM
McKinney, Stan .... (502) 465-8111
ED, Central Kentucky News-Journal, Campbellsville, KY
McKinney, T Craig .... (914) 691-2000
PUB, ED, New Paltz News, Highland, NY
McKinney, Tessie .... (712) 662-7161
GM, ED, Sac Sun, Sac City, IA
McKinney, Walter V .... (503) 648-1131
PUB, Hillsboro Argus, Hillsboro, OR
McKinney, William .... (512) 445-3500
MGR-Cox Interactive Media MKTG
Austin American-Statesman, Austin, TX
McKinney, William C .... (419) 281-0581
GM, Ashland Times-Gazette, Ashland, OH
McKinney, Yvonne .... (209) 369-2761
City ED, Political/Government ED
Lodi News-Sentinel, Lodi, CA
McKinnis, Eldon .... (405) 336-2222
GM, Perry Daily Journal, Perry, OK
McKinnis, Vivian .... (405) 336-2222
CIRC MGR, Perry Daily Journal, Perry, OK
McKinnon, Mac B .... (915) 445-5475
PUB, EPE, Political ED
Pecos Enterprise, Pecos, TX
McKinnon, Michael P .... (807) 597-2731
ED, Atikokan Progress, Atikokan, ON
McKinnon, Mitch .... (954) 356-4000
ADV MGR-MKTG SRV/CLASS
Sun-Sentinel, Fort Lauderdale, FL
McKinnon, Nancy S .... (208) 377-6200
DIR-MKTG Services
Idaho Statesman, Boise, ID
McKirgan, Lowell .... (309) 932-2103
GM, Galva News, Galva, IL
McKnight, Cam .... (519) 688-6397
PUB, Tillsonburg News, Tillsonburg, ON
McKnight, Carol L .... (519) 389-4733
PUB, GM, ED
Shoreline News, Port Elgin, ON
McKnight, Jim .... (613) 829-9100
DP MGR, PROD MGR-Manufacturing-Pre Press, PROD MGR-Manufacturing-Computer Information Services
Ottawa Citizen, Ottawa, ON
McKnight, Paul D .... (203) 235-1661
SEC, Record-Journal, Meriden, CT
McKnight, Rene .... (604) 270-8031
ED, Richmond News, Richmond, BC
McKnight-Yeates, Lisa .... (604) 838-7229
ED, Enderby Commoner, Enderby, BC
McKown, Gene .... (864) 839-2621
PUB, ED, Blacksburg Times & Cherokee Tribune, Blacksburg, SC
McKula, Kathy .... (860) 241-6200
News Librarian
Hartford Courant, Hartford, CT
McLachlan, J H .... (204) 748-3931
PUB
Virden Empire-Advance, Virden, MB
McLachlan, Lloyd .... (519) 255-5711
COL-Sports, Windsor Star, Windsor, ON
McLachlin, Steve .... (904) 252-1511
Art DIR, Daytona Beach News-Journal, Daytona Beach, FL
McLain, Mike .... (810) 541-3000
PROD MGR-Pre Press
Daily Tribune, Royal Oak, MI
McLamb, Lynn .... (910) 862-4163
PUB, GM
Bladen Journal, Elizabethtown, NC
McLane, Bob .... (202) 334-6000
PROD MGR-NW Plant
Washington Post, Washington, DC
McLane, Lee .... (501) 882-5414
PUB, ED, Beebe News, Beebe, AR
McLaughlin, Arlena .... (409) 756-6671
VP-Gulf Coast Newspaper
Conroe Courier, Conroe, TX
McLaughlin, Ben .... (937) 592-3060
ASST ED, Wire ED
Bellefontaine Examiner, Bellefontaine, OH
McLaughlin, Betsy .... (860) 241-6200
MGR-Facilities Services
Hartford Courant, Hartford, CT
McLaughlin, Brett .... (517) 673-3181
PUB, Tuscola County Advertiser, Caro, MI
McLaughlin, Brian .... (515) 232-2160
Photo ED, Daily Tribune, Ames, IA
McLaughlin, Carol .... (419) 668-3771
DP MGR, PROD MGR-SYS
Norwalk Reflector, Norwalk, OH
McLaughlin, Deborah .... (316) 564-3116
ED, Ellinwood Leader, Ellinwood, KS
McLaughlin, Eloise .... (207) 990-8000
PSL MGR
Bangor Daily News, Bangor, ME
McLaughlin, Joanna .... (707) 884-3501
PUB
Independent Coast Observer, Gualala, CA
McLaughlin, Joe .... (403) 343-2400
MAN ED, Red Deer Advocate, Red Deer, AB
McLaughlin, John .... (201) 877-4141
COL, Star-Ledger, Newark, NJ
McLaughlin, Kirsten .... (319) 652-2441
ED
Maquoketa Sentinel-Press, Maquoketa, IA
McLaughlin, Phil .... (913) 294-2311
PUB, ED, Miami County Republic, Paola, KS
McLaughlin, Rick .... (915) 586-2561
PUB, ED, Winkler County News, Kermit, TX
McLaughlin, Stephen J .... (707) 884-3501
GM, ED
Independent Coast Observer, Gualala, CA
McLean, Allison .... (613) 236-0491
BM, Southam Syndicate, Ottawa, ON
McLean, Anna R .... (601) 842-2611
BC/CEO/PRES, Northeast Mississippi Daily Journal, Tupelo, MS
McLean, Chris .... (719) 544-3520
Photo DIR, Pueblo Chieftain, Pueblo, CO
McLean, Francis R .... (541) 889-5387
PUB, GM, Books ED, EDL Writer, Environmental/Ecology ED, Political ED
Argus Observer, Ontario, OR
McLean, Greg .... (306) 565-8211
ADV DIR, Leader-Post, Regina, SK
Hollinger Inc. (Sterling Newspapers)
McLean, Joy .... (541) 889-5387
Music ED, Argus Observer, Ontario, OR
McLean, Judith .... (810) 985-7171
ASST MAN ED, Times Herald, Port Huron, MI
McLean, Thomas N .... (803) 771-6161
EPE, State, Columbia, SC
McLean III, William L .... (610) 527-6330
PRES, Independent Publications Inc., Bryn Mawr, PA
McLellan, Bruce .... (205) 353-4612
Sports ED, Decatur Daily, Decatur, AL
McLellan, David .... (705) 472-3200
ED, COL, EDL Writer
North Bay Nugget, North Bay, ON
McLellan, Michele .... (503) 221-8327
Team Leader-Government
Oregonian, Portland, OR
McLelland, Dee .... (941) 463-4421
PUB, MAN ED, Fort Myers Beach Bulletin, Fort Myers Beach, FL
McLendon, Gerald .... (209) 722-1511
PROD MGR-PR
Merced Sun-Star, Merced, CA
McLendon-Carter, Sherri .... (770) 867-7557
ED, Winder News, Winder, GA
McLeod, Dan .... (604) 730-7000
PUB, ED, Georgia Straight, Vancouver, BC
McLeod, I .... (905) 526-3333
DIR-FIN, Spectator, Hamilton, ON
McLeod, John .... (902) 468-1222
BUS ED, Daily News, Halifax, NS
McLeod, Leanne .... (206) 339-3000
PA (Office), Herald, Everett, WA
McLeod, Philip R .... (519) 679-6666
ED, London Free Press, London, ON
McLeod, Scott .... (704) 648-2381
ED
Canton Enterprise Mountaineer, Canton, NC
McLeod, Stewart .... (910) 843-8171
PUB, Red Springs Citizen, Red Springs, NC
McLeod, Tommie Anne .... (813) 893-8111
CIRC DIR
St. Petersburg Times, St. Petersburg, FL
McLeod, Waldo L .... (912) 524-2343
PUB, ED
Donalsonville News, Donalsonville, GA
McLister, Steven K .... (605) 996-5514
PUB/GM
Mitchell Daily Republic, Mitchell, SD
McLoone, John E .... (414) 673-3500
PUB, ED, Hartford Times-Press, Hartford, WI
McLoone, Pat .... (215) 854-2000
Sports ED
Philadelphia Daily News, Philadelphia, PA
McLoud, Don .... (919) 778-2211
Political/Government ED
Goldsboro News-Argus, Goldsboro, NC
McLymont, Rosalind .... (212) 837-7000
MAN ED, Journal of Commerce & Commercial, New York, NY
McMacKen, Billy .... (605) 692-6271
Sports ED, Brookings Register, Brookings, SD
McMacken, Robin .... (605) 394-8300
Fashion/Garden ED
Rapid City Journal, Rapid City, SD
McMahan, Phil .... (619) 299-3131
Chief Photo ED
San Diego Union-Tribune, San Diego, CA
McMahon, Bryan T .... (504) 386-2877
PUB, ED
Ponchatoula Times, Ponchatoula, LA
McMahon, Chris .... (808) 235-5881
GM, Hawaii Navy News, Kaneohe, HI
McMahon, Cleon .... (515) 284-8000
PROD MGR-MR
Des Moines Register, Des Moines, IA
McMahon, Grace .... (413) 447-7311
Librarian, Berkshire Eagle, Pittsfield, MA
McMahon, Howard M .... (702) 623-5011
PRES, Humboldt Sun, Winnemucca, NV
McMahon, Jim .... (905) 358-5711
PROD FRM-PR
Niagara Falls Review, Niagara Falls, ON
McMahon, Jim .... (610) 696-1775
PROD DIR
Daily Local News, West Chester, PA
McMahon, Johnny .... (405) 256-2200
Sports ED
Woodward News, Woodward, OK
McMahon, Josh .... (201) 877-4141
ASST MET ED, Star-Ledger, Newark, NJ
McMahon, June M .... (702) 623-5011
SEC, Humboldt Sun, Winnemucca, NV
McMahon, Mike .... (518) 270-1200
Chief Photographer, Record, Troy, NY
McMahon, Patrick .... (213) 237-5000
Political ED-Calif/Deputy State/Specialist ED
Los Angeles Times, Los Angeles, CA
McMahon, Sean M .... (520) 753-6397
ED, Kingman Daily Miner, Kingman, AZ
McMahon, Stilla Janosa .... (812) 649-9196
PUB, ED, Journal-Democrat, Rockport, IN
McMahon, Terry Ann .... (504) 386-2877
PUB, Ponchatoula Times, Ponchatoula, LA
McMahon, Tom .... (519) 255-5711
ASST MET ED, Windsor Star, Windsor, ON
McManama, Tina .... (619) 322-8889
MGR-Communications
Desert Sun, Palm Springs, CA
McManigal, Marvin .... (402) 444-1000
PROD SUPT-Mechanical Maintenance
Omaha World-Herald, Omaha, NE
McManis Jr, Charles A .... (310) 540-5511
CIRC DIR, Daily Breeze, Torrance, CA
Copley Press Inc.
McManns, Katie .... (303) 820-1010
PROD MGR-Pre Press OPER
Denver Post, Denver, CO
McManus, Doyle .... (213) 237-5000
Washington DC BU
Los Angeles Times, Los Angeles, CA
McManus, Greg .... (207) 990-8000
Projects ED, Bangor Daily News, Bangor, ME
McManus, James A .... (416) 367-2000
ADV DIR-Group, Toronto Star, Toronto, ON
McManus, Jeanne .... (202) 334-6000
Sports Deputy ED
Washington Post, Washington, DC
McManus, Linda .... (219) 235-6161
Amusements ED
South Bend Tribune, South Bend, IN
McManus, Ted .... (504) 384-8370
MAN ED, Morgan City Newspapers Inc., Morgan City, LA
McMartin, Jeff .... (719) 544-3520
ADV MGR-GEN SRV
Pueblo Chieftain, Pueblo, CO
McMartin, Pete .... (604) 732-2111
COL, Vancouver Sun, Vancouver, BC
McMaster, David .... (44 171) 782-5000
Group Syndication MGR/News International Newspapers
News International Newspapers Ltd., London,
McMeel, John .... (816) 932-6600
PRES/CEO
Universal Press Syndicate, Kansas City, MO
McMenamy, David .... (701) 780-1100
PROD MGR-PR
Grand Forks Herald, Grand Forks, ND

Copyright ©1997 by the Editor & Publisher Co.

Mcm Who's Where-154

McMenemy, Cheryl .... (705) 653-3684
PUB
Campbellford Herald, Campbellford, ON
McMillan, Bob .... (615) 526-9715
Wire ED, Herald-Citizen, Cookeville, TN
McMillan, Brian M .... (704) 289-1541
PUB/GM, Enquirer-Journal, Monroe, NC
McMillan, Craig .... (402) 873-3334
Chairman
Nebraska City News-Press, Nebraska City, NE
McMillan, Gary .... (510) 661-2600
ED, Argus, Fremont, CA
McMillan, Janet .... (914) 694-9300
Senior MAN ED, Herald Statesman, Yonkers, NY, Gannett Co. Inc.
McMillan, Layune .... (800) 245-6536
Customer SRV CNR
US/Express, Chicago, IL
McMillan, M J .... (615) 289-3345
ED, Stewart-Houston Times, Erin, TN
McMillan, Matt .... (320) 587-5000
PUB, Hutchinson Leader, Hutchinson, MN
McMillan, Mike .... (704) 864-3291
PUB, Gaston Gazette, Gastonia, NC
McMillan, Richard .... (423) 523-3131
ADV MGR
Knoxville News-Sentinel, Knoxville, TN
McMillan, Steve .... (505) 823-7777
BUS/FIN ED
Albuquerque Journal, Albuquerque, NM
McMillen, Bill .... (316) 231-2600
Night ED, Morning Sun, Pittsburg, KS
McMillen, James J .... (765) 362-1200
PUB, Journal Review, Crawfordsville, IN
McMiller, Jim .... (517) 377-1000
City ED, Lansing State Journal, Lansing, MI
McMillian, Janet .... (609) 691-5000
EX ED, Daily Journal, Vineland, NJ
McMillian, Michelle .... (316) 241-2422
News ED
McPherson Sentinel, McPherson, KS
McMillian, William .... (313) 222-2300
News ED, Detroit News, Detroit, MI
McMinn, Ed .... (706) 549-0123
City ED (News), Athens Daily News/Banner-Herald, Athens, GA
McMinn, Judi .... (615) 824-8480
GM, Hendersonville Star News, Hendersonville, TN
McMorris, William J .... (217) 923-3704
PUB, ED, Greenup Press, Greenup, IL
McMorrow, Pat .... (612) 222-5011
Senior ED-Health & Religion
St. Paul Pioneer Press, St. Paul, MN
McMullen, Arthur .... (412) 834-1151
SEC, DIR-Employee Relations
Tribune-Review, Greensburg, PA
McMullen, Cary .... (912) 273-2277
Fashion/Food ED, Home/Garden ED, Women's/Society ED
Cordele Dispatch, Cordele, GA
McMullen, Fred .... (412) 834-1151
ADV MGR-NTL, ADV MGR-Key Accounts
Tribune-Review, Greensburg, PA
McMullen, Marianne .... (937) 275-8855
PUB, ED, Dayton Voice, Dayton, OH
McMullen, Polly .... (814) 643-4040
COL, Farm ED, News ED
Daily News, Huntingdon, PA
McMullen, Randy .... (510) 935-2525
ASST Features ED
Contra Costa Times, Walnut Creek, CA
McMullen, Samuel C .... (702) 738-3611
GM, Elko Independent, Elko, NV
McMullin, Craig S .... (515) 232-2160
EVP, TREAS, Daily Tribune, Ames, IA
McMullin, Michael .... (818) 713-3000
ADV MGR-RT
Daily News, Woodland Hills, CA
McMurdo, Doug .... (702) 727-5583
ED, Pahrump Valley Gazette, Pahrump, NV
McNab, Andrew .... (208) 983-1070
PUB
Idaho County Free Press, Grangeville, ID
McNabb, David .... (207) 791-6650
ASST MAN ED-Sports
Portland Press Herald, Portland, ME
Mc Nabb, Paul .... (509) 459-5000
MGR-Human Resources
Spokesman-Review, Spokane, WA
McNair, Billie .... (409) 828-3221
PUB, ED, Franklin News Weekly, Franklin, TX
McNair, Irene .... (416) 367-2000
MGR-Customer Accounts
Toronto Star, Toronto, ON
McNair, Mike .... (330) 743-2250
PUB, ED, Buckeye Review, Youngstown, OH
McNall, Cloann Wilkins .... (208) 476-4571
PUB, ED, Clearwater Tribune, Orofino, ID
McNall, John .... (209) 592-3171
GM, Sun, Exeter, CA
McNall, Mike .... (352) 374-5000
DIR-INFO Technology
Gainesville Sun, Gainesville, FL
McNally, James .... (413) 562-4181
MAN ED, Evening News, Westfield, MA
McNally, Pat .... (209) 722-1511
City ED, Merced Sun-Star, Merced, CA
McNamara, Connie .... (717) 255-8100
Travel ED, Patriot-News, Harrisburg, PA
McNamara, David .... (813) 879-7978
PUB, Florida Catholic, Tampa, FL
McNamara, Dennis .... (702) 788-6200
ADV MGR-CLASS, ADTX MGR
Reno Gazette-Journal, Reno, NV
McNamara, Harry .... (407) 242-3801
MAN ED, Tribune, Melbourne, FL
McNamara, John .... (704) 437-2161
News ED, News Herald, Morganton, NC
McNamara, Bishop Lawrence J (308) 382-4660
PUB
West Nebraska Register, Grand Island, NE
McNamara, Sean .... (518) 561-2300
ADV MGR-MKTG, ADTX MGR
Press-Republican, Plattsburgh, NY
McNamara, Steve .... (415) 383-4500
PUB, ED, Pacific Sun, Mill Valley, CA
McNamara, Tom .... (703) 276-3400
ASSOC ED, USA Today, Arlington, VA
McNamee, Carl .... (915) 653-1221
DP MGR, PROD SUPT-DP
Standard-Times, San Angelo, TX
McNamee, Kenneth W .... (901) 529-2211
CONT, Commercial Appeal, Memphis, TN
McNamee, Paul .... (309) 829-9411
CIRC MGR-Home Delivery
Pantagraph, Bloomington, IL
McNamee, Tom .... (312) 321-3000
Public Health/Medical Writer
Chicago Sun-Times, Chicago, IL
McNaughton, Burt .... (707) 425-4646
VP, SEC/TREAS, Daily Republic, Fairfield, CA
McNaughton Newspapers
McNaughton, Derek .... (604) 886-7077
ED, Gibsons Outlook, Gibsons, BC
McNaughton, Foy .... (916) 756-0800
PRES/CEO
McNaughton Newspapers, Davis, CA
McNaughton, Pat .... (605) 895-2505
GM, Lyman County Herald, Presho, SD
McNaughton, Tina .... (413) 283-8393
ED, Palmer Journal-Register, Palmer, MA
McNeal, Christine .... (309) 686-3000
ASST MAN ED-Photo/Graphic/Design
Journal Star, Peoria, IL
McNeal, Craig A .... (316) 767-5123
PUB/ED, MGR-MKTG/PROM
Council Grove Republican, Council Grove, KS
McNeal, Debby .... (304) 469-3373
GM, Fayette Tribune, Oak Hill, WV
McNeal, Don A .... (316) 767-5123
ADV MGR
Council Grove Republican, Council Grove, KS
McNeal, Stan .... (619) 299-3131
Sports ED-Day
San Diego Union-Tribune, San Diego, CA
McNeece, Mae .... (417) 876-2500
GM, Star, El Dorado Springs, MO
McNeel, William P .... (304) 799-4973
ED, Pocahontas Times, Marlinton, WV
McNeeley, Dave .... (512) 445-3500
Political ED
Austin American-Statesman, Austin, TX
McNeeley, Jack .... (201) 646-4000
Online ED, Record, Hackensack, NJ
McNeely, David .... (618) 734-4242
ED, Tri-State Advertiser, Cairo, IL
McNeely, Jack .... (304) 752-6950
MAN ED, EPE, Logan Banner, Logan, WV
McNees, Ronald .... (510) 465-3121
PROD Design
Inter-City Express, Oakland, CA
McNeil, Dave .... (902) 625-1900
ED, Scotia Sun, Port Hawkesbury, NS
McNeil, James S .... (207) 791-6650
ADV MGR-Group Sales
Portland Press Herald, Portland, ME
McNeil, John A .... (608) 328-4202
CIRC MGR, Monroe Times, Monroe, WI
McNeil, MaryAnn .... (702) 727-5583
PUB, Pahrump Valley Gazette, Pahrump, NV
McNeil, Peggy .... (304) 788-3333
CIRC DIR
Mineral Daily News-Tribune, Keyser, WV
McNeile, Jim .... (219) 294-1661
COL, Elkhart Truth, Elkhart, IN
McNeill, Betsy .... (903) 873-2525
GM, Wills Point Chronicle, Wills Point, TX
McNeill, Brian .... (503) 325-3211
Food ED, Daily Astorian, Astoria, OR
McNeill Jr, Glenn .... (903) 873-2525
PUB, MAN ED
Wills Point Chronicle, Wills Point, TX
McNeill, Mike .... (903) 935-7914
MAN ED, Fashion/Food ED, Women's ED
Marshall News Messenger, Marshall, TX
McNeill, Raymond .... (919) 708-9000
CIRC DIR, Sanford Herald, Sanford, NC
McNeill, Steve .... (905) 526-3333
BUS ED, Spectator, Hamilton, ON
McNell, Michael .... (614) 633-1131
Photo DEPT MGR
Times Leader, Martins Ferry, OH
McNell, Mike .... (352) 374-5000
ADTX MGR, Gainesville Sun, Gainesville, FL
McNelly, James .... (423) 756-6900
ADV MGR-CLASS
Chattanooga Free Press, Chattanooga, TN
McNerney, Maureen .... (502) 582-4011
Amusements ED, Arts/Entertainment ED
Courier-Journal, Louisville, KY
McNett, Roy C .... (210) 833-4812
PUB, ED, Blanco County News, Blanco, TX
McNiff, Nancy .... (508) 626-3800
PROD DIR-OPER
Middlesex News, Framingham, MA
McNiff, Tom .... (352) 867-4010
ASST City ED
Ocala Star-Banner, Ocala, FL
McNulti, Mike .... (330) 966-1121
MAN ED, Sun Journal, North Canton, OH
McNulty, Gord .... (905) 526-3333
EDL Writer, Spectator, Hamilton, ON
McNulty, James .... (604) 732-2222
EPE, Province, Vancouver, BC
McNulty, Mary .... (617) 245-0080
ADV MGR-CLASS
Wakefield Daily Item, Wakefield, MA
McNulty, Timothy J .... (312) 222-3232
Tempo ED, Chicago Tribune, Chicago, IL
McNutt, Byron .... (715) 479-4421
PUB
Vilas County News Review, Eagle River, WI
McNutt, James .... (412) 222-2200
Chief Photographer
Observer-Reporter, Washington, PA
McPherson, Beth .... (816) 238-3996
ED, Buchanan County News, Faucett, MO
McPherson, Jim .... (816) 238-3996
PUB, Buchanan County News, Faucett, MO
McPherson, Kenneth .... (402) 444-1000
PROD FRM-Platemaking
Omaha World-Herald, Omaha, NE
McPherson, Robert .... (717) 648-4641
CIRC DIR, News-Item, Shamokin, PA
McPhul, Steve F .... (334) 749-6271
PUB/GM, Opelika-Auburn News, Opelika, AL
McPoland, John .... (608) 754-3311
Asst Sports ED
Janesville Gazette, Janesville, WI
McQuaid, Carol .... (508) 458-7100
ASST MAN ED-Lifestyle, Food ED, Features ED, Living/Lifestyle ED, Radio/Television ED, Society ED, Women's ED, Sun, Lowell, MA
McQuaid, Joseph W .... (603) 668-4321
GM, EIC, Union Leader, Manchester, NH
McQueary, Kathleen .... (713) 220-7171
Online MGR, Houston Chronicle, Houston, TX
McQueen, Max .... (602) 898-6500
Films/Theater ED, Mesa Tribune, Mesa, AZ
Thomson Newspapers
McQueen, Roy .... (915) 573-5486
PRES, PUB, GM
Snyder Daily News, Snyder, TX
McQueen, Sam .... (512) 884-2011
CIRC MGR-Home Delivery, Corpus Christi Caller-Times, Corpus Christi, TX
McQuern, Marcia .... (909) 684-1200
CEO/PRES/PUB, ED
Press-Enterprise, Riverside, CA
McQuin, Robert L .... (316) 532-3151
PUB, ED
Kingman Leader-Courier, Kingman, KS
McQuinn, Tom .... (217) 379-4313
PA, Paxton Daily Record, Paxton, IL
McRae, Scott .... (704) 524-2010
ED, Franklin Press, Franklin, NC
McRae, Susan .... (704) 358-5000
PROD MGR-PR
Charlotte Observer, Charlotte, NC
McReady, Marcie .... (704) 484-7000
ADV MGR-RT, Shelby Star, Shelby, NC
McSain, Matt .... (716) 232-7100
PROD MGR-Advertising Production
Rochester Democrat and Chronicle; Rochester, NY Times-Union, Rochester, NY
McShane, Geri .... (507) 373-1411
Reporter
Albert Lea Tribune, Albert Lea, MN
McShane, Vern .... (319) 438-1313
PUB, ED, Linn News-Letter, Central City, IA
McSherry, John .... (617) 254-0334
GM
Allston-Brighton Citizen Journal, Boston, MA
McSwain, Larry .... (209) 578-2000
EPE, Modesto Bee, Modesto, CA
McSwain, Mary Jane .... (904) 252-1511
Garden ED, Daytona Beach News-Journal, Daytona Beach, FL
McSweegan, Frank J .... (603) 742-4455
DIR-Sales/MKTG
Foster's Democrat, Dover, NH
McSweeney Jr, William .... (816) 531-0538
PUB
National Catholic Reporter, Kansas City, MO
McSwords, Nancy .... (614) 633-1131
MGR-CR, Times Leader, Martins Ferry, OH
McTighe, Frank .... (403) 485-2036
PUB, ED, Advocate, Vulcan, AB
McTrocavage, Paul .... (717) 648-4641
ED, News-Item, Shamokin, PA
McTyre, Robert .... (313) 963-5522
ED, Michigan Chronicle, Detroit, MI
McVay, Bob .... (219) 362-2161
DP MGR, La Porte Herald-Argus, La Porte, IN
McVay, Charlotte .... (601) 423-2211
ED, Tishomingo County News, Iuka, MS
McVey, Bob .... (210) 765-6931
PUB, Zapata County News, Zapata, TX
McVey, Kate .... (210) 765-6931
ED, Zapata County News, Zapata, TX
McVey, Kathy .... (316) 355-6162
ED, Lakin Independent, Lakin, KS
McVey, Leigh .... (304) 327-2811
DP MGR, Daily Telegraph, Bluefield, WV
McVicar, D Morgan .... (401) 277-7000
EDU Writer, Journal-Bulletin, Providence, RI
McVoy, Michael .... (970) 925-3414
PRES, Co-PUB, Aspen Times, Aspen, CO
McWhinnie, Chuck .... (312) 321-3000
Obituaries, Chicago Sun-Times, Chicago, IL
McWhirter, Nickie .... (313) 222-2300
COL, Detroit News, Detroit, MI
McWhirter, Sam .... (281) 422-8302
PROD FRM-PR, Baytown Sun, Baytown, TX
McWhorter, Carol .... (806) 762-8844
MGR-MKTG
Lubbock Avalanche-Journal, Lubbock, TX
McWilliams, Michael .... (313) 222-2300
Television ED, Detroit News, Detroit, MI
Meacham, John .... (573) 547-8005
ED, Perryville Sun Times, Perryville, MO
Meachem, Matt .... (800) 424-4747
Sports ED, Tribune Media Services-Television Listings, Glens Falls, NY
Meachen, James .... (919) 778-2211
Automotive ED, BUS ED, Graphics ED, News ED, Goldsboro News-Argus, Goldsboro, NC
Mead, Christopher .... (814) 870-1600
MGR-MKTG SRV/PROM, ASST ADTX MGR
Morning News/Erie Daily Times, Erie, PA
Mead, Doug .... (910) 323-4848
Sports ED
Fayetteville Observer-Times, Fayetteville, NC
Mead, Edward M .... (814) 870-1600
COB, Times Publishing Inc., Erie, PA
Mead, Elizabeth .... (805) 822-6828
PUB, Tehachapi News, Tehachapi, CA
Mead, Jerry D .... (702) 884-2648
ED
Mead, Jerry D. Enterprises, Carson City, NV
Mead, John .... (609) 663-6000
DP MGR, Courier-Post, Cherry Hill, NJ
Mead, Kevin .... (814) 870-1600
VP/ASST SEC
Times Publishing Inc., Erie, PA
Mead, Kristi .... (701) 662-2127
Action Line ED, Society ED
Devils Lake Daily Journal, Devils Lake, ND
Mead, Michael .... (814) 870-1600
PRES/CEO/PUB
Times Publishing Inc., Erie, PA
Mead, Thom .... (310) 540-5511
Religion ED, Daily Breeze, Torrance, CA
Mead, William .... (805) 822-6828
PUB, Tehachapi News, Tehachapi, CA
Meade, Debra .... (540) 981-3100
DIR-Human Resources
Roanoke Times, Roanoke, VA
Meade, Henry .... (304) 327-2811
PROD MGR-OPER, PROD FRM-Camera
Bluefield Daily Telegraph, Bluefield, WV
Meade, Lois .... (408) 920-5000
MGR-INFO
San Jose Mercury News, San Jose, CA
Meade, W C .... (864) 847-7361
PUB, Journal, Williamston, SC
Meador, Ron .... (612) 673-4000
Projects Team Leader
Star Tribune, Minneapolis, MN
Meadows, Bill .... (817) 778-4444
PROD FRM-PR
Temple Daily Telegram, Temple, TX
Meadows, Brian .... (807) 274-5373
Sports ED
Fort Frances Daily Bulletin, Fort Frances, ON
Meadows, Cheryl .... (606) 528-2464
MAN ED, Living/Lifestyle ED, Society/Women's ED, Times-Tribune, Corbin, KY

Copyright ©1997 by the Editor & Publisher Co.

155-Who's Where **Men**

Meadows, David .... (912) 236-9511
PROD ASST DIR-Press/Pre-Press
Savannah Morning News, Savannah, GA
Meadows, Kathy .... (502) 827-2000
Graphics ED/Art DIR, Gleaner, Henderson, KY
Meadows, Steven .... (912) 226-2400
MAN ED, EPE, Thomasville Times-Enterprise, Thomasville, GA
Meahl, Joe .... (520) 466-7333
ED, Eloy Enterprise, Casa Grande, AZ
Meals, Pamela F .... (208) 377-6200
PRES, PUB, Idaho Statesman, Boise, ID
Means, Bill .... (404) 526-5151
MGR-CIRC SRV
Atlanta Journal-Constitution, Atlanta, GA
Means, Greg .... (616) 894-5356
ED, White Lake Beacon, Whitehall, MI
Mearns, Kirk .... (250) 372-2331
ADV DIR, DIR-MKTG/PROM
Kamloops Daily News, Kamloops, BC
Mears, Karen Kelley .... (717) 348-9100
Amusements ED, Features ED, Films/Theater ED, Home Furnishings ED, Northeast Woman ED, Performing Arts ED, Radio/Television ED, Teen-Age/Youth ED
Tribune & The Scranton Times, Scranton, PA
Measer, Trey .... (716) 632-4700
PUB, East Aurora Bee, Buffalo, NY
Mebane, William deB .... (703) 284-6000
Sr Group PRES-Piedmont Newspaper Group
Gannett Co. Inc., Arlington, VA
Mecak, Evan .... (702) 788-6200
Consumer MKTG
Reno Gazette-Journal, Reno, NV
Mechanic, Barry .... (212) 930-8000
VP-Technology, New York Post, New York, NY
Meche, John .... (318) 289-6300
ADV MGR, Advertiser, Lafayette, LA
Mechem, Allison .... (423) 246-8121
Amusements/Arts ED
Kingsport Times-News, Kingsport, TN
Mechler, Mary .... (618) 529-5454
ADV MGR-CLASS
Southern Illinoisan, Carbondale, IL
Mecklenburg, Merv .... (406) 365-3303
MAN ED
Glendive Ranger-Review, Glendive, MT
Mecklin, John .... (602) 271-0040
ED, New Times, Phoenix, AZ
Mecum, Gary .... (906) 932-2211
ADV DIR, Ironwood Daily Globe, Ironwood, MI
Medbery, Mary A .... (308) 245-4125
PUB, ED, Scotia Register, Scotia, NE
Medbery, Wilber D .... (308) 245-4125
PUB, ED, Scotia Register, Scotia, NE
Meddrens, Jo Ann .... (405) 225-3000
EDU ED, Television/Film ED
Elk City Daily News, Elk City, OK
Medeiros, Donna .... (619) 427-3000
PUB, Star-News, Chula Vista, CA
Medeiros Jr, Richard .... (860) 241-6200
ADV MGR-GEN
Hartford Courant, Hartford, CT
Medek, Gisela .... (401) 253-6000
ED, Bristol Phoenix, Bristol, RI
Medenica, Gordon .... (212) 556-1234
Senior VP/Group PUB
New York Times, New York, NY
Medhurst, Doris .... (309) 343-7181
ADV MGR-RT, Register-Mail, Galesburg, IL
Medias, Rive Nord .... (418) 589-5900
PUB, Objectif Plein Jour, Baie Comeau, QC
Medinger, Daniel .... (302) 573-3109
GM, Dialog, Wilmington, DE
Medley, Dianne .... (601) 328-2424
ADV DIR
Commercial Dispatch, Columbus, MS
Medley, Eddie .... (615) 967-2272
ED, Herald-Chronicle, Winchester, TN
Medrano, Linda .... (210) 423-5511
ADV MGR-CLASS
Valley Morning Star, Harlingen, TX
Medved, Michael .... (212) 930-8000
Films Critic ED
New York Post, New York, NY
Meece, Michael L .... (309) 829-9411
Human Resources DIR
Pantagraph, Bloomington, IL
Meecha, Tom .... (216) 329-7000
ADV MGR-Display
Chronicle-Telegram, Elyria, OH
Meegan, Elizabeth .... (309) 764-4344
Food ED, Dispatch, Moline, IL
Small Newspaper Group Inc.
Meehan, James J .... (330) 747-1471
CONT, Vindicator, Youngstown, OH
Meek, Phillip J .... (212) 456-7777
PRES-ABC Publishing Group
ABC Inc., New York, NY
Meek, Richard .... (304) 348-5140
PROD DIR
Charleston Newspapers, Charleston, WV
Meek, Richard .... (601) 467-5473
MAN ED, Sea Coast Echo, Bay St. Louis, MS
Meek, Tom .... (513) 761-1188
Contributing Critic
Critic's Choice Reviews, Cincinnati, OH
Meeker, Bill .... (605) 394-8300
CIRC MGR
Rapid City Journal, Rapid City, SD
Meeker, Frances .... (615) 259-8800
Religion ED, Nashville Banner, Nashville, TN
Meeker, Mike .... (970) 352-0211
PROD FRM-PR, Greeley Tribune, Greeley, CO
Meeker, Richard H .... (503) 243-2122
PUB, Willamette Week, Portland, OR
Meekins, Dennis .... (614) 397-5333
CIRC MGR
Mount Vernon News, Mount Vernon, OH
Meekins, Francis W .... (919) 473-2105
ED, Coastland Times, Manteo, NC
Meeks, David .... (504) 826-3279
Suburban ED
Times-Picayune, New Orleans, LA
Meers, Melinda .... (407) 242-3500
MAN ED, Florida Today, Melbourne, FL
Meers, Sandra .... (902) 532-2219
ED, Spectator, Annapolis Royal, NS
Mefford, Dave .... (308) 345-4500
PROD MGR-PR
McCook Daily Gazette, McCook, NE
Megerdichian, John .... (617) 926-3974
GM, Armenian Weekly, Watertown, MA
Meggitt, Art .... (612) 673-4000
CNR-Electronic Media
Star Tribune, Minneapolis, MN
Megill, Earl .... (908) 922-6000
PROD ASST MGR-PR
Asbury Park Press, Neptune, NJ
Megna, Alane .... (615) 552-1808
EPE, Leaf-Chronicle, Clarksville, TN
Megredy, Tod .... (316) 221-1050
MAN ED, Winfield Daily Courier, Winfield, KS
Mehalic, Leo .... (301) 921-2800
ED, Trident, Gaithersburg, MD
Mehdi, Dr M T .... (212) 972-0460
ED, Action, New York, NY
Mehegan, David .... (617) 929-2000
Books ED, Boston Globe, Boston, MA
Mehl, Gary .... (316) 241-2422
PUB, ADV DIR
McPherson Sentinel, McPherson, KS
Mehle, Michael .... (303) 892-5000
Music Critic-Popular
Rocky Mountain News, Denver, CO
Mehlhaff, Arlo C .... (605) 284-2631
PUB, GM, Northwest Blade, Eureka, SD
Mehlhaff, Bonnie L .... (605) 284-2631
ED, Northwest Blade, Eureka, SD
Mehlsak, Morris .... (207) 282-1535
BUS ED, Journal Tribune, Biddeford, ME
Meidell, James S .... (708) 755-6161
GM
Chicago Heights Star, Chicago Heights, IL
Meier, Al .... (217) 788-1300
PROD FRM-Press
State Journal-Register, Springfield, IL
Meier, Jill .... (605) 297-4419
GM, ED, New Era, Parker, SD
Meier, Lana .... (204) 347-8402
GM, Selkirk Journal, Stonewall, MB
Meier, Stephen C .... (213) 237-3700
VP-Public & Government Affairs
Times Mirror Co., Los Angeles, CA
Meier, Thomas P .... (614) 461-5000
CIRC MGR-State
Columbus Dispatch, Columbus, OH
Meierjurgen, Linda .... (541) 269-1222
Fashion/Food ED, World, Coos Bay, OR
Meikle, Ruth .... (616) 796-4831
DP MGR, Big Rapids Pioneer, Big Rapids, MI
Meiklejohn, Pat .... (519) 426-5710
EDU ED, Simcoe Reformer, Simcoe, ON
Meilach, Dona Z .... (619) 436-4395
PRES
Meilach, Dona Z. Features, Carlsbad, CA
Meilink, Linda .... (916) 877-4413
ED, Paradise Post, Paradise, CA
Meiliunas, Genevieve .... (212) 563-2210
GM, Tevyne, New York, NY
Meinert, Anthony .... (910) 343-2000
CIRC DIR, Morning Star/Sunday Star-News, Wilmington, NC
Meints, Larry U .... (712) 552-1051
PUB, ED, Independent, Hawarden, IA
Meirhaeghe, Judy .... (309) 764-4344
Religion ED, Dispatch, Moline, IL
Small Newspaper Group Inc.
Meis, Nancy .... (816) 932-6600
DIR-MKTG/New Media
Universal Press Syndicate, Kansas City, MO
Meisel, Thomas .... (212) 715-2100
VP/PROD, USA Weekend, New York, NY
Meislin, Richard .... (212) 556-1234
Technology ED
New York Times, New York, NY
Meisner, Beth .... (757) 898-7225
MAN ED, By The Bay, Yorktown, VA
Meisner, J D .... (505) 287-4411
ED, Cibola County Beacon, Grants, NM
Meissner, Bruce .... (916) 321-1000
PROD MGR-Press
Sacramento Bee, Sacramento, CA
Meister, Barb .... (712) 283-2500
ED, Bulletin Press, Sioux Rapids, IA
Meister, Tom .... (317) 622-1212
DIR-OPER, Herald Bulletin, Anderson, IN
Meitus, Marty .... (303) 892-5000
Food ED, Rocky Mountain News, Denver, CO
Meitzen, George .... (503) 864-2310
PUB, ED, Dayton Tribune, Dayton, OR
Meixner, Cristine Knapp .... (518) 548-6898
MAN ED
Hamilton County News, Speculator, NY
Mejia, Antonio .... (213) 622-8332
MAN ED-Entertainment
La Opinion, Los Angeles, CA
Mejia, Juan .... (541) 269-1222
ADV DIR, ADV MGR-South Coast Week, ADTX MGR, World, Coos Bay, OR
Mekeel, Peter C .... (717) 291-8811
News ED, Lancaster Intelligencer Journal/New Era/Sunday News, Lancaster, PA
Melamed, Carol D .... (202) 334-6000
VP-Government Affairs
Washington Post, Washington, DC
Melani, Deb .... (303) 776-2244
Special Sections ED
Daily Times-Call, Longmont, CO
Melbourne, Allan .... (403) 343-2400
CIRC MGR
Red Deer Advocate, Red Deer, AB
Melcher, Kay .... (205) 325-2222
Librarian, Post-Herald, Birmingham, AL
Melcher, Teresa .... (330) 833-2631
EDU ED, Independent, Massillon, OH
Melczek, Bishop Dale J .... (219) 769-9292
PUB
Northwest Indiana Catholic, Merrillville, IN
Meleady, Jane .... (302) 227-9466
GM
Delaware Beachcomber, Rehoboth Beach, DE
Melendes, Bill .... (414) 982-4321
PUB, ED, Press-Star, New London, WI
Melendez, Robin .... (912) 923-6432
DP MGR, Daily Sun, Warner Robins, GA
Melenesk, Betsy .... (210) 779-3751
PUB, ED, La Vernia News, La Vernia, TX
Melerine, Clarence .... (601) 798-4766
PROD FRM-PR
Picayune Item, Picayune, MS
Melhus, Troy .... (701) 223-2500
Voices/Online ED
Bismarck Tribune, Bismarck, ND
Meli, Mary Alice .... (412) 654-6651
Theater/Music ED
New Castle News, New Castle, PA
Melich, Nancy .... (801) 237-2031
Drama ED
Salt Lake Tribune, Salt Lake City, UT
Melin, Jon .... (309) 764-4344
ADV MGR-NTL, Dispatch, Moline, IL
Small Newspaper Group Inc.
Mell, Doug .... (715) 833-9200
City ED, Leader-Telegram, Eau Claire, WI
Mellao, Orlando .... (305) 633-3341
DP MGR, Diario Las Americas, Miami, FL
Mellema, Darryll .... (630) 232-9222
Sports ED
Kane County Chronicle, Geneva, IL
Mellen, Marni .... (515) 472-4129
City ED, Fairfield Ledger, Fairfield, IA
Mellenbruch, Joie .... (913) 371-4300
ADV DIR, ADV MGR-NTL
Kansas City Kansan, Kansas City, KS
Mellencamp, Tony .... (219) 589-2101
ED, Berne Tri Weekly News, Berne, IN
Mellman, Larry .... (219) 881-3000
DIR-Technology, Post-Tribune, Gary, IN
Mello, Joan .... (405) 353-0620
Librarian, Lawton Constitution, Lawton, OK
Mello, Paul .... (702) 882-2111
Sports ED, Nevada Appeal, Carson City, NV
Mello, Tim .... (316) 788-2835
CIRC MGR, Daily Reporter, Derby, KS
Mellon, Deborah .... (208) 783-1107
CLASS ED/Entertainment ED
Shoshone News-Press, Kellogg, ID
Mellott, Jeff .... (540) 574-6200
Political ED
Daily News-Record, Harrisonburg, VA
Mellott, John .... (404) 526-5151
VP/GM
Atlanta Journal-Constitution, Atlanta, GA
Mellott, Mark .... (403) 542-5380
ED, Western Review, Drayton Valley, AB
Melmer, David .... (703) 257-4600
DIR-Marketing/Promotion
Prince William Journal, Manassas, VA
Melnick, Dennis .... (717) 622-3456
PROD CNR-Pre Press, Pottsville Republican & Evening Herald, Pottsville, PA
Melnick, Michael G .... (613) 739-7000
DIR-Computer Services, DP MGR
Ottawa Sun, Ottawa, ON
Melnychuk, Jeff .... (506) 859-4900
ASST MAN ED
Times-Transcript, Moncton, NB
Melnykovych, Andrew .... (502) 582-4011
Environmental ED
Courier-Journal, Louisville, KY
Meloche, John .... (604) 382-6188
GM, Victoria's Monday Magazine, Victoria, BC
Melody, Mark .... (508) 793-9100
EDU ED, Telegram & Gazette, Worcester, MA
Melon, Mary .... (405) 235-3100
ADV MGR
Journal Record, Oklahoma City, OK
Melone, Mary Jo .... (813) 893-8111
COL
St. Petersburg Times, St. Petersburg, FL
Melot, Derek .... (918) 684-2828
EPE, Muskogee Daily Phoenix & Times Democrat, Muskogee, OK
Melton, Cathy .... (502) 582-4011
ADV DIR-CLASS
Courier-Journal, Louisville, KY
Melton, Floyd .... (423) 638-4181
PROD SUPV-Creative SRV
Greeneville Sun, Greeneville, TN
Melton, Greg .... (816) 827-2425
PUB, Central Missouri News, Sedalia, MO
Melton, Jan .... (912) 764-9031
ADV MGR-RT
Statesboro Herald, Statesboro, GA
Melton, Jean .... (417) 847-4475
PUB, Barry County Advertiser, Cassville, MO
Melton, Jeff .... (704) 484-7000
Photo ED, Shelby Star, Shelby, NC
Melton, Ken .... (352) 563-6363
ED, Citrus County Chronicle, Crystal River, FL
Melton, Randall .... (207) 729-3311
ED, Patroller, Brunswick, ME
Melton, Rollan D .... (702) 788-6200
COL, Reno Gazette-Journal, Reno, NV
Melton, Russ .... (417) 847-4475
GM, MAN ED
Barry County Advertiser, Cassville, MO
Melvin, Dick .... (218) 463-1521
ED, Roseau Times-Region, Roseau, MN
Melvin, Earl .... (904) 435-8500
Archives MGR
Pensacola News Journal, Pensacola, FL
Melvin, Gayle .... (510) 284-4444
ED, Contra Costa Sun, Lafayette, CA
Melvin, Greg .... (816) 932-6600
ASST ED
Universal Press Syndicate, Kansas City, MO
Melvin, Mary .... (701) 872-3755
GM, ED, Golden Valley News, Beach, ND
Melvold, Douglas D .... (319) 652-2441
PUB
Maquoketa Sentinel-Press, Maquoketa, IA
Memminger, Charles .... (808) 525-8000
COL, Honolulu Star-Bulletin, Honolulu, HI
Menard, Jeffrey R .... (805) 564-5200
DP MGR, PROD DIR-Publishing/Technological Services, Santa Barbara News-Press, Santa Barbara, CA
Menard, Mary .... (510) 208-6300
ADV MGR-NTL
Oakland Tribune, Oakland, CA
MediaNews Inc. (Alameda Newspapers)
Menard, Vicki .... (541) 672-3321
Food ED, News-Review, Roseburg, OR
Mencher, Brooks .... (916) 934-6805
ED, Willows Journal, Willows, CA
Mendelhallo, Mary .... (937) 328-0300
CONT
Springfield News-Sun, Springfield, OH
Mendell, Benita .... (512) 884-2011
ADV MGR-Specialty Products/Direct MKTG
Caller-Times, Corpus Christi, TX
Mendell, Fritz .... (913) 823-6363
Photo DEPT MGR, Salina Journal, Salina, KS
Menden, Joseph .... (419) 738-2128
Sports ED, Daily News, Wapakoneta, OH
Mendenhall, Doug .... (205) 353-4612
MAN ED, Automotive ED
Decatur Daily, Decatur, AL
Mendenhall, Thomas .... (703) 878-8000
CIRC DIR, Potomac News, Woodbridge, VA
Mendes, Andrea .... (508) 458-7100
ADV MGR-Sales Development
Sun, Lowell, MA
Mendez, Cruz Alberto .... (213) 622-8332
Special Sections ED
La Opinion, Los Angeles, CA
Mendiola, Mark .... (208) 232-4161
ASST MAN ED
Idaho State Journal, Pocatello, ID

Men Who's Where-156

Mendoza, Amando .... (415) 327-6397
CIRC MGR, Daily News, Palo Alto, CA
Mendoza, Cristina L .... (305) 376-3800
VP/GEN Counsel
Knight-Ridder Inc., Miami, FL
Mendyk, Lowell .... (502) 821-6833
Photo ED, Messenger, Madisonville, KY
Menees, Chris .... (901) 885-0744
Farm ED
Union City Daily Messenger, Union City, TN
Menees, Tim .... (412) 263-1100
Cartoonist
Pittsburgh Post-Gazette, Pittsburgh, PA
Menendez, Ronald L .... (712) 362-2622
GM/PUB, ADV DIR, MAN ED
Estherville Daily News, Estherville, IA
Mengel, Dave .... (412) 775-3200
PROD SUPV-Press
Beaver County Times, Beaver, PA
Menk, Kurt .... (507) 964-5547
ED, Arlington Enterprise, Arlington, MN
Menke, James A .... (402) 225-2301
PUB, ED, Nelson Gazette, Nelson, NE
Menscer, Dwaine .... (704) 873-1451
ADV DIR, Statesville Record & Landmark, Statesville, NC
Menser, Kelly .... (502) 484-3431
ED, News-Herald, Owenton, KY
Mento, Frank .... (412) 834-1151
PROD SUPT-Press
Tribune-Review, Greensburg, PA
Mentzer Sr, David M .... (814) 946-7411
PROD DIR, Altoona Mirror, Altoona, PA
Mentzer, Marie .... (407) 482-6271
Author-Health Care & Housing
Demko Publishing, Boca Raton, FL
Mentzer, Michael .... (414) 922-4600
City ED, Environmental ED, News ED, SCI/Technology ED
Reporter, Fond du Lac, WI
Mentzer, Mike .... (414) 922-4600
MAN ED, Reporter, Fond du Lac, WI
Menzer, Donald .... (203) 744-5100
PROD DIR, News-Times, Danbury, CT
Menzies, Peter .... (403) 235-7100
EPE, Calgary Herald, Calgary, AB
Meola, Patricia E .... (908) 464-1025
ED, Summit Herald, New Providence, NJ
Mercado, Nash .... (307) 347-3241
PROD SUPT
Northern Wyoming Daily News, Worland, WY
Mercaldo, Tony .... (717) 265-2151
ADV DIR, Daily Review, Towanda, PA
Mercanti, Michael .... (215) 854-2000
Photo ED
Philadelphia Daily News, Philadelphia, PA
Mercer, Bernice .... (715) 384-3131
CIRC MGR
Marshfield News-Herald, Marshfield, WI
Mercer, David .... (512) 884-2011
City ED-Night, Corpus Christi Caller-Times, Corpus Christi, TX
Mercer, Frank W .... (816) 542-0881
PUB, Carrollton Democrat, Carrollton, MO
Mercer, Jean H .... (514) 339-1292
PUB, Saint-Laurent News, Saint-Laurent, QC
Mercer, John .... (713) 220-7171
PROD MGR-Ads
Houston Chronicle, Houston, TX
Mercer, Peg .... (605) 352-6401
ADV DIR, Huron Plainsman, Huron, SD
Mercer, Robert .... (937) 328-0300
ADV DIR
Springfield News-Sun, Springfield, OH
Mercer, Steve .... (573) 785-1414
CIRC DIR
Daily American Republic, Poplar Bluff, MO
Mercer, Vivian .... (317) 636-0200
BM
Court & Commercial Record, Indianapolis, IN
Merchant, Brenda .... (318) 582-2000
ED, Iowa News, Iowa, LA
Mercier, David .... (619) 322-8889
ADV MGR-RT, Desert Sun, Palm Springs, CA
Mercier, Louis .... (514) 768-4777
ED
St. Henri La Voix Populaire, Montreal, QC
Mercier, Mike .... (205) 532-4000
Chief Photographer
Huntsville Times, Huntsville, AL
Meredith, Kathie .... (716) 394-0770
Entertainment/Amusements ED, Features ED, Films/Theater ED, Daily Messenger/The Sunday Messenger, Canandaigua, NY
Meredith, Rick .... (903) 794-3311
ADV MGR-RT
Texarkana Gazette, Texarkana, TX
Merenbloom, Paul .... (212) 535-6811
ASSOC ED, Megalo Media, Syosset, NY

Mergele, Fred .... (210) 225-7411
VP-FIN
San Antonio Express-News, San Antonio, TX
Mergerdichian, John .... (617) 926-3974
GM, Hairenik, Watertown, MA
Merino, Sonia .... (512) 884-2011
CIRC MGR-Subscriber SRV/Single Copy
Caller-Times, Corpus Christi, TX
Meriwether, Heath J .... (313) 222-6400
PUB, Detroit Free Press, Detroit, MI
Merkel, Lee .... (508) 793-9100
News ED
Telegram & Gazette, Worcester, MA
Merkle, Bryan .... (517) 625-3181
ED, Shiwassee County Journal, Perry, MI
Merkoski, Paul A .... (609) 272-7000
EX ED
Press of Atlantic City, Pleasantville, NJ
Merline, John .... (800) 223-2154
Washington BU Chief
Investor's Business Daily, Los Angeles, CA
Merrell, Gary D .... (614) 461-5000
ADV DIR
Columbus Dispatch, Columbus, OH
Merrell, Gerald .... (410) 332-6000
BUS ED, Sun, Baltimore, MD
Merrell, Jesse H .... (202) 265-1925
PRES, Merrell Enterprises, Washington, DC
Merriam, Jim .... (519) 376-2250
ED, Sun Times, Owen Sound, ON
Merrick, Sonja .... (915) 337-4661
Fashion/Food ED, Religion ED
Odessa American, Odessa, TX
Merrill, Barry W .... (919) 965-2033
PUB, ED, Johnstonian-Sun, Selma, NC
Merrill, Dorothy .... (612) 327-2216
ED, Silver Lake Leader, Silver Lake, MN
Merrill, Eleanor .... (410) 268-5000
ASSOC PUB, Capital, Annapolis, MD
Merrill, John R .... (206) 486-1231
ED, Northshore Citizen, Bothell, WA
Merrill, Kenneth .... (612) 327-2216
PUB, Silver Lake Leader, Silver Lake, MN
Merrill, Philip .... (410) 268-5000
PRES/PUB, Capital, Annapolis, MD
Merriman, Ann .... (804) 649-6000
Books ED, Commentary ED
Richmond Times-Dispatch, Richmond, VA
Merriman, Bruce .... (614) 461-5000
PROD MGR-Newsprint
Columbus Dispatch, Columbus, OH
Merriman, Dwight .... (406) 222-2000
News ED
Livingston Enterprise, Livingston, MT
Merriman, Todd .... (619) 299-3131
Senior ED-News
San Diego Union-Tribune, San Diego, CA
Merriman, Woodene .... (412) 263-1100
ASST to ED
Pittsburgh Post-Gazette, Pittsburgh, PA
Merritt, Christine .... (209) 634-9141
Farm ED, Turlock Journal, Turlock, CA
Merritt, Coralia S .... (508) 997-7411
ADV MGR
Standard Times, New Bedford, MA
Merritt Jr, Davis .... (316) 268-6000
Senior VP/ED, Wichita Eagle, Wichita, KS
Merritt, Eric J .... (408) 920-5000
MGR-Purchasing
San Jose Mercury News, San Jose, CA
Merritt, Gene .... (501) 862-6611
CIRC DIR
El Dorado News-Times, El Dorado, AR
Merritt, Greg .... (804) 787-1200
ED, Chincoteague Beachcomber, Onley, VA
Merritt, Harry .... (606) 231-3100
Story ED/Writing Coach
Lexington Herald-Leader, Lexington, KY
Merritt, Jeff .... (419) 668-3771
News ED, Norwalk Reflector, Norwalk, OH
Merritt, Jim .... (912) 384-2323
PUB, Douglas Enterprise, Douglas, GA
Merritt, Liz B .... (602) 898-6500
Fashion/Style ED, Features ED, Living/Lifestyle ED, Medical ED, SCI/Technology ED, Travel ED, Mesa Tribune, Mesa, AZ
Thomson Newspapers
Merritt, Patricia .... (941) 687-7000
Fashion ED, Ledger, Lakeland, FL
Merritt, Steve .... (208) 785-1100
ED, Morning News, Blackfoot, ID
Merriweather, Frank E .... (716) 882-9570
PUB, ED, Buffalo Criterion, Buffalo, NY
Merry, Robert .... (202) 887-8500
EX ED & VP, Congressional Quarterly Service, Washington, DC
Merryfield, Jerry .... (715) 833-9200
ADV DIR, Leader-Telegram, Eau Claire, WI
Mersch, Michael .... (941) 748-0411
EX Sports ED
Bradenton Herald, Bradenton, FL
Mersiel, Joyell .... (614) 574-8494
GM, Scioto Voice, Wheelersburg, OH

Mertens, Bill .... (319) 754-8461
PRES, PUB/GM, ED, EDL Writer
Hawk Eye, Burlington, IA
Mertens, Jerry .... (319) 689-3841
ED, Preston Times, Preston, IA
Mertens, Terry .... (319) 689-3841
PUB, Preston Times, Preston, IA
Mertes, Chris .... (608) 837-2521
ED, Star, Sun Prairie, WI
Mertz, Jennifer .... (219) 347-0400
ED, News-Sun Plus, Kendallville, IN
Mertz, Sharon .... (903) 872-3931
CIRC MGR
Corsicana Daily Sun, Corsicana, TX
Mervis, Scott .... (412) 263-1100
ED-Weekend
Pittsburgh Post-Gazette, Pittsburgh, PA
Merz, Thomas H .... (315) 337-4000
News ED, Daily Sentinel, Rome, NY
Mesalam, Mark .... (602) 271-8000
CIRC MGR-MET
Phoenix Newspapers Inc., Phoenix, AZ
Mescher, Lori .... (515) 232-2160
Community Life ED, Daily Tribune, Ames, IA
Meserve, Hamilton .... (914) 677-8241
PUB, Harlem Valley Times, Millbrook, NY
Meserve, Helen .... (914) 677-8241
PUB, Harlem Valley Times, Millbrook, NY
Mesh, John .... (316) 792-1211
Sports ED
Great Bend Tribune, Great Bend, KS
Meskauskas, Eric .... (212) 210-2100
DIR-Photography
New York Daily News, New York, NY
Mesler, Linda .... (817) 825-3201
PUB, ED, Nocona News, Nocona, TX
Mesler, Tracy .... (405) 757-2281
PUB, Ryan Leader, Ryan, OK
Mesler, Tracy .... (817) 825-3201
PUB, ED, Nocona News, Nocona, TX
Messenger, Tony .... (303) 933-2233
ED
Columbine Community Courier, Littleton, CO
Messer, Brad .... (602) 271-8000
MGR-Advertising Sales/PROM
Phoenix Newspapers Inc., Phoenix, AZ
Messer, Denise .... (904) 456-3121
MAN ED, Escambia Sun Press, Pensacola, FL
Messerschmidt, Lynn .... (613) 544-5000
MAN ED
Kingston Whig-Standard, Kingston, ON
Messersmith, Bea .... (515) 985-2142
ED, Riceville Recorder, Riceville, IA
Messersmith, M E .... (515) 985-2142
PUB, Riceville Recorder, Riceville, IA
Messersmith, Richard .... (517) 835-7171
PROD FRM-PR/Camera
Midland Daily News, Midland, MI
Messiah-Jiles, Sonceria .... (713) 663-6996
PUB, ED, Houston Defender, Houston, TX
Messick, Allen .... (503) 325-3211
Radio/Television ED
Daily Astorian, Astoria, OR
Messick, Steven R .... (612) 437-6153
PUB, Hastings Star Gazette, Hastings, MN
Messina, Louis A .... (405) 475-3311
PROD DIR
Daily Oklahoman, Oklahoma City, OK
Messing, Daniel .... (617) 426-3000
PROD SUPT-PR, Boston Herald, Boston, MA
Messinger, Lisa .... (310) 540-5511
Food ED, Daily Breeze, Torrance, CA
Copley Press Inc.
Messner, Gary .... (318) 942-4971
PROD MGR, Daily World, Opelousas, LA
Mestre, Ramon .... (305) 350-2111
Op-Ed ED-El Nuevo
Miami Herald, Miami, FL
Metcalf, D J .... (610) 696-1775
DIR-PROM
Daily Local News, West Chester, PA
Metcalf, Eric .... (864) 224-4321
Religion/Society ED
Anderson Independent-Mail, Anderson, SC
Metcalf, Kathy .... (618) 643-2387
GM
McLeansboro Times Leader, McLeansboro, IL
Metka, Philip E .... (815) 284-4000
CFO/SEC, Shaw Newspapers, Dixon, IL
Metoyer, Theodore .... (509) 459-5000
CIRC MGR-Home Delivery
Spokesman-Review, Spokane, WA
Metrejean, Ella .... (504) 473-3101
PUB, ED
Donaldsonville Chief, Donaldsonville, LA
Metz, Ken E .... (606) 674-2181
ED
Bath County News Outlook, Owingsville, KY
Metz, Linda .... (412) 523-6588
ASSOC ED
Standard Observer, Greensburg, PA
Metz, Margaret C .... (606) 674-2181
GM, MAN ED
Bath County News Outlook, Owingsville, KY

Metz, Michael .... (202) 334-6375
Sales Representative, Washington Post Writers Group, Washington, DC
Metz, Russell L .... (606) 674-2181
PUB
Bath County News Outlook, Owingsville, KY
Metzdorf, Ken .... (419) 625-5500
CIRC ASST MGR
Sandusky Register, Sandusky, OH
Metzger, Bernard .... (916) 243-2424
ADV MGR-RT
Record Searchlight, Redding, CA
Metzger, E S .... (412) 775-3200
CONT, Beaver County Times, Beaver, PA
Metzger, Juli .... (614) 373-2121
MAN ED, Marietta Times, Marietta, OH
Metzger, Roger .... (219) 356-1107
ED, Huntington County TAB, Huntington, IN
Metzler, John J .... (718) 591-7246
ED, World Watch/Foreign Affairs Syndicate, Kew Gardens Hills, NY
Metzler-Fitzgerald, Karma .... (208) 324-3391
ED, North Side News, Jerome, ID
Meunier, Robert L .... (508) 793-9100
MGR-CR, Telegram & Gazette, Worcester, MA
Meuser, Pamela .... (415) 588-5990
MAN ED, Yossarian Universal News Service, Millbrae, CA
Meyer, Anita .... (605) 225-4100
MAN ED-City, Sunday ED, Teen-Age/Youth ED, Aberdeen American News, Aberdeen, SD
Meyer, Annell .... (409) 836-7956
Office MGR, Banner-Press, Brenham, TX
Meyer, Bill .... (316) 382-2165
PUB, ED, Marion County Record, Marion, KS
Meyer, Bob .... (201) 646-4000
PROD MGR-MR, Record, Hackensack, NJ
Meyer, Bryce .... (812) 283-6636
Sports ED, Evening News, Jeffersonville, IN
Meyer, Debra .... (301) 722-4600
City ED
Cumberland Times-News, Cumberland, MD
Meyer, Donald .... (419) 784-5441
PROD MGR, PROD FRM-Engraving
Crescent-News, Defiance, OH
Meyer, Donald L .... (716) 487-1111
PUB, Post-Journal, Jamestown, NY
Meyer III, Herbert A .... (316) 331-3550
PRES, PUB, GM, PSL MGR, MGR-EDU SRV, BUS/FIN ED, EPE, Independence Daily Reporter, Independence, KS
Meyer, J Stryker .... (619) 745-6611
City ED-Oceanside
North County Times, Escondido, CA
Meyer, Jan .... (309) 343-7181
SEC, Register-Mail, Galesburg, IL
Meyer, Jane .... (206) 232-1215
GM, ED
Mercer Island Reporter, Mercer Island, WA
Meyer, Jeanne .... (816) 234-4141
Features ED
Kansas City Star, Kansas City, MO
Meyer, Jeff .... (507) 423-6239
PUB, Tri-County News, Cottonwood, MN
Meyer, Joe .... (614) 785-1212
MAN ED, Northland News, Columbus, OH
Meyer, John .... (910) 343-2000
MAN ED, Morning Star/Sunday Star-News, Wilmington, NC
Meyer, John .... (212) 450-7000
VP/Midwestern MGR/Newspaper Relations React, Parade Publications Inc., New York, NY
Meyer, John .... (203) 964-2200
PROD MGR-Packing, Stamford Advocate Stamford, CT, Times Mirror Co.
Meyer, Karin .... (970) 493-6397
News ED
Fort Collins Coloradoan, Fort Collins, CO
Meyer, Kristin .... (316) 331-3550
SEC/TREAS, Independence Daily Reporter, Independence, KS
Meyer, Larry .... (202) 334-6000
ASSOC ED
Washington Post, Washington, DC
Meyer, Marc .... (812) 283-6636
News ED, Wire ED
Evening News, Jeffersonville, IN
Meyer, Mary .... (614) 363-1161
Television ED
Delaware Gazette, Delaware, OH
Meyer, Nancy .... (607) 734-5151
ADV DIR, Star-Gazette, Elmira, NY
Meyer, Peter D .... (508) 775-1200
GM, Cape Cod Times, Hyannis, MA
Meyer, Sarah .... (505) 763-3431
Entertainment/Amusements ED
Clovis News Journal, Clovis, NM
Meyer, Sonja .... (717) 421-3000
Radio/Television ED, Sunday ED
Pocono Record, Stroudsburg, PA
Meyer, Suzy .... (970) 565-8527
ED
Cortez Montezuma Valley Journal, Cortez, CO

Copyright ©1997 by the Editor & Publisher Co.

157-Who's Where **Mil**

Meyer, Thomas .... (415) 777-1111
EDL Cartoonist
San Francisco Chronicle, San Francisco, CA
Meyer-Trigg, Lisa .... (317) 653-5151
COL, Family ED
Banner-Graphic, Greencastle, IN
Meyering, Carl .... (313) 886-2331
ED
Business Newsfeatures, Harper Woods, MI
Meyering, Robert H .... (313) 886-2331
OPER/MKTG
Business Newsfeatures, Harper Woods, MI
Meyers, Blair .... (507) 359-2911
Sports ED, Journal, New Ulm, MN
Meyers, Cesi .... (301) 459-3131
ASSOC PUB, ADV MGR
Prince George's Journal, Lanham, MD
Meyers, Christene .... (406) 657-1200
Entertainment/Amusements ED
Billings Gazette, Billings, MT
Meyers, Dave .... (310) 313-6727
MAN ED, Westchester News, Culver City, CA
Meyers, James K .... (414) 657-1000
EPE, Kenosha News, Kenosha, WI
Meyers, Karen .... (616) 527-2100
ADV MGR, Sentinel-Standard, Ionia, MI
Meyers, Larry .... (541) 889-5387
State/Wire ED, Argus Observer, Ontario, OR
Meyers, Lisa .... (507) 835-3380
MAN ED, Waseca County News, Waseca, MN
Meyers, Todd .... (717) 272-5611
BUS/FIN ED, Daily News, Lebanon, PA
Mezgar, Ann Sheldon .... (330) 996-3000
Features ED, Beacon Journal, Akron, OH
Mezick, Thomas .... (419) 929-3411
PUB, New London Record, New London, OH
Mezzacappa, Dale .... (215) 854-2000
EDU Writer
Philadelphia Inquirer, Philadelphia, PA
Mezzatesta, Jeff .... (410) 398-3311
GM, Cecil Whig, Elkton, MD
Mezzatesta, Jeff .... (610) 932-8886
GM, Oxford Tribune, Oxford, PA
Mezzeti, Jeff .... (916) 885-5656
CIRC DIR, Auburn Journal, Auburn, CA
Mial, Richard .... (608) 782-9710
EPE, La Crosse Tribune, La Crosse, WI
Micco, Lisa .... (412) 654-6651
Entertainment/Amusements ED, Lifestyle ED
New Castle News, New Castle, PA
Micek, Barb .... (308) 536-3100
MAN ED
Nance County Journal, Fullerton, NE
Michael, Clyde .... (417) 334-3161
CIRC DIR
Branson Tri-Lakes Daily News, Branson, MO
Michael, Graciela P .... (408) 295-4272
ED, El Observador, San Jose, CA
Michael, Lawrence J .... (516) 547-0668
PUB, ED, Halesite Gazette, Halesite, NY
Michael, Selvin .... (212) 932-7400
GM, Amsterdam News, New York, NY
Michaels, Arthur .... (212) 779-9200
PROD MGR
New York Law Journal, New York, NY
Michaels, Betty .... (601) 961-7000
CIRC MGR-Home Delivery
Clarion-Ledger, Jackson, MS
Michaels, Bruce .... (215) 942-7890
DIR-Technical OPER, Sports Network (Div. of Computer Info. Network), Southampton, PA
Michaels, Cash .... (919) 834-5558
MAN ED, Carolinian, Raleigh, NC
Michaels, Don .... (202) 797-7000
PUB, Washington Blade, Washington, DC
Michaels, John .... (717) 389-4825
ASSOC ED
Spectrum Features, Bloomsburg, PA
Michaels, Julie .... (617) 929-2000
Calendar ED, Boston Globe, Boston, MA
Michaels, Marion .... (715) 284-5638
PRES/ED
Michaels News, Black River Falls, WI
Michaels, Robert .... (212) 223-1821
Music Film ED, Entertainment News Syndicate, New York, NY
Michaelson, Judy .... (213) 237-5000
Radio Writer, Times, Los Angeles, CA
Michalowski, Jim .... (315) 253-5311
Photo ED, Citizen, Auburn, NY
Michaud, Charles .... (514) 436-5381
ED, L'Echo du Nord, Saint-Jerome, QC
Michaud, Joseph A .... (207) 791-6650
Online ED, Online MGR
Portland Press Herald, Portland, ME
Michel, Don .... (319) 398-8211
CIRC DIR, Gazette, Cedar Rapids, IA
Michel, Frank .... (713) 220-7171
Assoc ED, EDL Writer
Houston Chronicle, Houston, TX
Michel, Nancy .... (334) 793-9586
ED, Dothan Progress, Dothan, AL
Michel, Suzanne G .... (908) 531-6200
ED, Jewish Voice, Deal Park, NJ

Michele, Anthony .... (212) 930-8000
CIRC DIR-OPER (Day), PROD DIR (Day)
New York Post, New York, NY
Michelich, Joseph M .... (217) 438-6155
ED, Auburn Citizen, Auburn, IL
Michelich Jr, Joseph .... (217) 483-2614
PUB, Chatham Clarion, Chatham, IL
Michell, Nancy .... (908) 247-8700
ED, Somerset Spectator, Somerset, NJ
Michels, Jim .... (812) 424-7711
ASST Features ED
Evansville Courier, Evansville, IN
Michels, Stephen W .... (605) 624-2695
PUB, Plain Talk, Vermillion, SD
Michener, Pamela .... (303) 892-5000
MGR-RES
Rocky Mountain News, Denver, CO
Michlie, Jayne .... (414) 276-0273
PROD MGR, Daily Reporter, Milwaukee, WI
Mick, Andrew .... (703) 878-8000
PUB, Quantico Sentry, Woodbridge, VA
Mick, Nancy .... (502) 965-3191
PUB, Crittenden Press, Marion, KY
Mickelson, Chad .... (507) 962-3230
ED, Hills Cresent, Hills, MN
Mickens, Don .... (419) 943-2590
PUB, Leipsic Messenger, Leipsic, OH
Mickens, John .... (419) 278-2816
GM, Deshler Flag, Deshler, OH
Mickens, Keith .... (419) 943-2590
ED, Leipsic Messenger, Leipsic, OH
Mickey, William .... (216) 999-4500
CONT, Plain Dealer, Cleveland, OH
Mickler, Jeannettia .... (541) 926-2211
CIRC SUPV-Office
Albany Democrat-Herald, Albany, OR
Micklewright, Michelle .... (517) 265-5111
ADV MGR, MGR-MKTG & PROM, MGR-Telecommunications, Daily Telegram, Adrian, MI
Micklow, James T .... (717) 784-2121
TREAS, Press Enterprise, Bloomsburg, PA
Miclette, Nancy .... (860) 887-9211
DP MGR, Norwich Bulletin, Norwich, CT
Micozzi, Donald P .... (717) 286-5671
PRES, PUB, Daily Item, Sunbury, PA
Middlebrook, Mark .... (904) 359-4111
ASST MAN ED-Special Coverage
Florida Times-Union, Jacksonville, FL
Middlebrooks, Stephanie .... (334) 566-4270
CIRC MGR, Messenger, Troy, AL
Middlemas, Kendall .... (904) 747-5000
MAN ED, News Herald, Panama City, FL
Middleton, G A .... (905) 684-7251
DIR-OPER, Standard, St. Catharines, ON
Middleton, Ken .... (409) 833-3311
PROD SUPT-MR, Enterprise, Beaumont, TX
Middleton, Michael .... (419) 522-3311
CIRC MGR-Motor Route
News Journal, Mansfield, OH
Middleton, Stan .... (405) 223-2200
CIRC MGR-PROM, PROD FRM-MR
Daily Ardmoreite, Ardmore, OK
Midyette, Monty .... (904) 252-1511
Online MGR, Daytona Beach News-Journal, Daytona Beach, FL
Miedema, Laurence .... (208) 882-5561
Sports ED
Moscow-Pullman Daily News, Moscow, ID
Miel, Rhonda .... (517) 752-7171
Farm ED, Saginaw News, Saginaw, MI
Mielcarek, Kim .... (904) 435-8500
Entertainment/Amusements ED
Pensacola News Journal, Pensacola, FL
Miele, Donna C .... (212) 556-1234
VP-Human Resources
New York Times, New York, NY
Miele, Ward .... (201) 239-0900
ED, Verona-Cedar Grove Times, Verona, NJ
Miers, Barry L .... (610) 258-7171
PROD MGR-Plant OPER
Express-Times, Easton, PA
Miers, Tommy .... (903) 675-5626
PROD SUPT
Athens Daily Review, Athens, TX
Mies, Bob .... (215) 854-2000
VP-FIN
Philadelphia Inquirer, Philadelphia, PA
Mieth, Pamela .... (617) 933-3700
EDU ED, Daily Times Chronicle, Woburn, MA
Miezels, Stacey .... (518) 756-2030
ED, News-Herald, Ravena, NY
Mifflin, Jim .... (407) 420-5000
PROD MGR-OPER ADM
Orlando Sentinel, Orlando, FL
Miga, Andrew .... (617) 426-3000
Washington BU Chief
Boston Herald, Boston, MA
Migely, Jane .... (312) 222-3232
ADV DIR-Classified
Chicago Tribune, Chicago, IL
Migielicz, Geralyn .... (408) 920-5000
DIR-Photography
San Jose Mercury News, San Jose, CA

Migowsky, Duane .... (306) 662-2133
PUB, ED, MAN ED
Maple Creek News, Maple Creek, SK
Miguel, Dawne .... (808) 244-3981
ADV MGR, Maui News, Wailuku, HI
Miguel, Joe San .... (210) 775-1551
PUB, Del Rio News-Herald, Del Rio, TX
Mihalik, Pattie .... (610) 377-2051
Features ED, Times News, Lehighton, PA
Mihaly, Jim .... (403) 836-3588
PUB, ED, Banner Post, Manning, AB
Mihaly, Tom .... (403) 926-2000
PUB, ED, Echo, High Level, AB
Mihalyo, John .... (206) 622-8272
GM, ADV DIR, Seattle Daily Journal of Commerce, Seattle, WA
Mihaylo, John .... (805) 395-7500
CIRC MGR-County S/C
Bakersfield Californian, Bakersfield, CA
Mika, Michael J .... (904) 435-8500
Online DIR
Pensacola News Journal, Pensacola, FL
Mike, Ted .... (717) 888-9643
PUB, PA, Evening Times, Sayre, PA
Mike, Vickee .... (717) 888-9643
ADV MGR, Evening Times, Sayre, PA
Mikesell, Dave .... (937) 328-0300
Sports ED
Springfield News-Sun, Springfield, OH
Mikesell, Kelly .... (937) 225-2000
DIR-Consumer Sales & MKTG
Dayton Daily News, Dayton, OH
Mikinski, Rod .... (913) 776-2200
Photo ED
Manhattan Mercury, Manhattan, KS
Mikkelson, Cindy .... (702) 358-8061
DP MGR, Daily Sparks Tribune, Sparks, NV
Miko, Robert J .... (203) 378-2803
ED
Miko's Pacific News Service, Stratford, CT
Mikulenka, James .... (512) 445-3500
PROD MGR-MR
Austin American-Statesman, Austin, TX
Milam, Loy .... (502) 678-5171
Sports ED, Glasgow Daily Times, Glasgow, KY
Milbourne, Jim .... (909) 684-1200
ADV MGR-NTL
Press-Enterprise, Riverside, CA
Milburn, Robert .... (913) 738-3537
PROD FRM-Press
Beloit Daily Call, Beloit, KS
Miles, Bob .... (605) 665-7811
PROD SUPV
Yankton Daily Press & Dakotan, Yankton, SD
Miles Jr, Charles H .... (508) 222-7000
ADV MGR-CLASS
Sun Chronicle, Attleboro, MA
Miles, Chris .... (412) 664-9161
CFO, Daily News, McKeesport, PA
Miles, Cyndy .... (509) 582-1500
DIR-Human Resources
Tri-City Herald, Tri-Cities, WA
Miles, Dan .... (330) 364-5577
PROD ASST MGR
Times Reporter, New Philadelphia, OH
Miles Jr, Daniel B .... (816) 885-2281
GM, Clinton Daily Democrat, Clinton, MO
Miles, Duane .... (970) 522-1990
PROD SUPT, PROD SUPT-COMP
Journal-Advocate, Sterling, CO
Miles, George .... (506) 452-6671
PROD FRM-COMP
Daily Gleaner, Fredericton, NB
Miles, George A .... (402) 336-1221
PUB, ED
Holt County Independent, O'Neill, NE
Miles, Katherine .... (816) 885-2281
BM, ADV MGR
Clinton Daily Democrat, Clinton, MO
Miles, Kathleen White .... (816) 885-2281
PRES, PUB
Clinton Daily Democrat, Clinton, MO
Miles, Mahlon White .... (816) 885-2281
ED, EPE
Clinton Daily Democrat, Clinton, MO
Miles, Milton .... (803) 626-8555
DIR-MKTG SRV
Sun News, Myrtle Beach, SC
Miles, Susan .... (615) 552-1808
CIRC DIR
Leaf-Chronicle, Clarksville, TN
Miles, William C .... (812) 384-3501
PUB/GM, Evening World, Bloomfield, IN
Milhom, Cathy .... (302) 422-1200
ED, Milford Chronicle, Milford, DE
Miliani, Joanne .... (813) 259-7711
Arts Writer, Tribune and Times, Tampa, FL
Milicezic, Kelly .... (941) 983-9148
GM, Clewiston News, Clewiston, FL
Milks, Barbara .... (613) 342-4441
EDU SRV MGR, MGR-MKTG/PROM, Brockville Recorder and Times, Brockville, ON
Milks, Gary L .... (515) 448-4745
PUB, Eagle Grove Eagle, Eagle Grove, IA

Millar, Jeff .... (713) 220-7171
Films ED, Houston Chronicle, Houston, TX
Millard, Dave .... (909) 987-6397
PROD FRM-Press
Inland Valley Daily Bulletin, Ontario, CA
Millard, Jack .... (913) 743-2155
PUB, Western Kansas World, Wakeeney, KS
Millard, Jerry .... (913) 743-2155
PUB, ED
Western Kansas World, Wakeeney, KS
Millard, Stephen .... (303) 838-2108
ED, Park County Republican & Fairplay Flume, Bailey, CO
Millard, Steve .... (303) 442-1202
ASSOC ED, Daily Camera, Boulder, CO
Millay-Fullenlove, Kit .... (502) 222-7183
ED, Oldham Era, La Grange, KY
Miller, Ada .... (814) 643-4040
ADV MGR-CLASS
Daily News, Huntingdon, PA
Miller, Adrien .... (605) 331-2200
PROD MGR-Technical SRV
Argus Leader, Sioux Falls, SD
Miller, Alex .... (201) 877-4141
CONT, Star-Ledger, Newark, NJ
Miller, Allison E .... (717) 291-8811
ADTX CNR, Lancaster Intelligencer Journal/New Era/Sunday News, Lancaster, PA
Miller, Andy .... (206) 339-3000
CIRC CNR-Sales, Herald, Everett, WA
Miller, Anita .... (913) 295-1111
MAN ED-News
Topeka Capital-Journal, Topeka, KS
Miller, Ann .... (903) 893-8181
MGR-CR, Herald Democrat, Sherman, TX
Miller, Annette .... (805) 925-2691
ADV MGR-CLASS
Santa Maria Times, Santa Maria, CA
Miller, Antoinette .... (703) 276-3400
VP-BUS OPER, USA Today, Arlington, VA
Miller, Arnold .... (216) 329-7000
MAN ED, Chronicle-Telegram, Elyria, OH
Miller, Audrey J .... (406) 632-5633
PUB, Times Clarion, Harlowton, MT
Miller, August .... (801) 625-4200
Chief Photographer
Standard-Examiner, Ogden, UT
Miller, Barry .... (804) 458-8511
CIRC MGR, News, Hopewell, VA
Miller, Becky .... (309) 686-3000
ADV MGR-CLASS, Journal Star, Peoria, IL
Miller, Ben .... (303) 239-9890
ED, Jefferson Sentinel, Lakewood, CO
Miller, Bill .... (541) 485-1234
PROD FRM-COMP
Register-Guard, Eugene, OR
Miller, Bob .... (214) 977-8222
COL-BUS News
Dallas Morning News, Dallas, TX
Miller, Bonnie .... (970) 345-2296
PUB, Akron News-Reporter, Akron, CO
Miller, Bruce .... (712) 279-5019
Amusements ED, Films/Theater ED, Living ED, Music ED
Sioux City Journal, Sioux City, IA
Miller, C .... (204) 857-3427
CIRC SUPV
Daily Graphic, Portage la Prairie, MB
Miller, Carl .... (803) 626-8555
ADV MGR-GEN/Co-op
Sun News, Myrtle Beach, SC
Miller, Carolyn .... (217) 636-8453
ED, Menard County Review, Athens, IL
Miller, Charles .... (713) 220-7171
PROD MGR-Paperhandling/Newsprint
Houston Chronicle, Houston, TX
Miller, Chris .... (419) 352-4611
Automotive ED
Sentinel-Tribune, Bowling Green, OH
Miller, Chris .... (604) 567-9258
ED, Caledonia Courier, Fort St. James, BC
Miller, Chris .... (218) 723-5281
Deputy Sports ED
Duluth News-Tribune, Duluth, MN
Miller, Chris .... (301) 733-5131
CIRC MGR, Morning Herald, Hagerstown, MD
Miller, Clifford .... (414) 733-4411
EDL Writer, Post-Crescent, Appleton, WI
Miller, Connie .... (405) 922-4296
PUB, Vici Beacon News, Seiling, OK
Miller, Craig .... (910) 888-3500
EDU ED
High Point Enterprise, High Point, NC
Miller, Dan .... (216) 951-0000
ADV MGR-Co-op
News-Herald, Willoughby, OH
Miller, Darrel E .... (913) 282-3371
PUB, ED
Smith County Pioneer, Smith Center, KS

Mil Who's Where-158

Miller, Dave .... (412) 834-1151
News ED, Tribune-Review, Greensburg, PA
Miller, David .... (941) 335-0200
PROD ASST ENG-Plant
News-Press, Fort Myers, FL
Miller, David .... (207) 791-6650
PROD OPER MGR-Distribution (South Portland), Press Herald, Portland, ME
Miller, David .... (616) 946-2000
Local ED, Record-Eagle, Traverse City, MI
Miller, David C .... (419) 352-4611
ED, EPE, Features ED
Sentinel-Tribune, Bowling Green, OH
Miller, Dean S .... (208) 522-1800
MAN ED, Sunday ED
Post Register, Idaho Falls, ID
Miller, Debbie .... (704) 633-8950
Religion ED, Salisbury Post, Salisbury, NC
Miller, Debby .... (913) 734-2621
MAN ED, Bird City Times, Bird City, KS
Miller, Dennie .... (419) 522-3311
PROD MGR-Distribution Center
News Journal, Mansfield, OH
Miller, Dennis .... (510) 208-6300
Senior VP-Production, Oakland Tribune, Oakland, CA, MediaNews Inc.
Miller, Diane .... (847) 966-3900
ED, Bugle, Niles, IL
Miller, Don .... (313) 994-6989
PROD SUPV-Pre Press
Ann Arbor News, Ann Arbor, MI
Miller, Don .... (941) 335-0200
PROD VP-OPER, News-Press, Fort Myers, FL
Miller, Donald .... (412) 263-1100
Arts Critic
Pittsburgh Post-Gazette, Pittsburgh, PA
Miller, Donald .... (408) 423-4242
BUS ED
Santa Cruz County Sentinel, Santa Cruz, CA
Miller, Donna .... (318) 368-9732
ED, Farmerville Gazette, Farmerville, LA
Miller, Doris .... (817) 562-2868
CIRC MGR, Mexia Daily News, Mexia, TX
Miller, Doris Downing .... (913) 749-0006
PUB, Baldwin Ledger, Lawrence, KS
Miller, Dorothy L .... (904) 973-6397
PUB, ED
Madison County Press, Madison, FL
Miller, Douglas C .... (414) 435-4411
CONT
Green Bay Press-Gazette, Green Bay, WI
Miller, E J .... (614) 633-1131
CIRC DIR, Times Leader, Martins Ferry, OH
Miller, Edward .... (540) 574-6200
PROD SUPV-MR
Daily News-Record, Harrisonburg, VA
Miller, Edward .... (508) 456-8122
PUB, Harvard Post, Harvard, MA
Miller, Evan .... (360) 676-2600
MAN ED
Bellingham Herald, Bellingham, WA
Miller, Fort .... (815) 223-3200
MGR-MR, News-Tribune, La Salle, IL
Miller, Francine .... (316) 429-2773
CIRC MGR
Columbus Daily Advocate, Columbus, KS
Miller, Frederick C .... (815) 223-3200
SEC, News-Tribune, La Salle, IL
Miller, Frederick W .... (608) 252-6400
COB, Capital Times, Madison, WI
Miller, Gary .... (320) 235-1150
Food/Living ED, Women's ED
West Central Tribune, Willmar, MN
Miller, Gary .... (909) 889-9666
Photo DIR, Sun, San Bernardino, CA
Miller, Gene .... (305) 350-2111
ASSOC ED-Reporting
Miami Herald, Miami, FL
Miller, George .... (608) 252-6200
CIRC SUPV-Customer SRV
Madison Newspapers Inc., Madison, WI
Miller, Gerald H .... (406) 632-5633
PUB, ED, Times Clarion, Harlowton, MT
Miller, Grant .... (305) 669-7355
PUB
Kendall News-Gazette, South Miami, FL
Miller, Gregg .... (818) 713-3000
Art DIR, Daily News, Woodland Hills, CA
Miller, H Don .... (423) 753-3136
GM, Herald and Tribune, Jonesborough, TN
Miller, Harold E .... (717) 291-8811
ADV MGR-RT, Lancaster Intelligencer Journal/New Era/Sunday News, Lancaster, PA
Miller Jr, Harold E .... (717) 291-8811
VP-MKTG, Lancaster Intelligencer Journal/New Era/Sunday News, Lancaster, PA
Miller, Henry .... (803) 317-6397
Sports ED
Florence Morning News, Florence, SC
Miller, Herron .... (573) 815-1500
Wire ED, Daily Tribune, Columbia, MO
Miller, Hilda D .... (540) 967-0368
PUB, ED, Central Virginian, Louisa, VA
Miller, Jan .... (510) 428-2000
GM, Bay Area Press, Oakland, CA
Miller, Jason .... (703) 368-3101
Sports ED, Journal Messenger, Manassas, VA
Miller, Jean .... (806) 537-3634
PUB, Panhandle Herald, Panhandle, TX
Miller, Jeanne .... (606) 231-3100
ADV CNR-Co-op
Lexington Herald-Leader, Lexington, KY
Miller, Jeannette .... (817) 495-2149
PUB, ED, Electra Star-News, Electra, TX
Miller, Jeff .... (202) 408-2721
Night ED, Scripps-McClatchy Western Services, Washington, DC
Miller, Jeff .... (516) 298-3200
ED, Suffolk Times, Mattituck, NY
Miller, Jennifer .... (704) 464-0221
MAN ED, EDL Writer, Photo DEPT MGR
Observer-News-Enterprise, Newton, NC
Miller, Jerry .... (206) 597-8742
PROD MGR-PR/Plateroom
News Tribune, Tacoma, WA
Miller, Jim .... (405) 321-1800
PUB, Norman Transcript, Norman, OK
Miller, Jim .... (219) 294-1661
Religion ED, Elkhart Truth, Elkhart, IN
Miller, Jim .... (405) 332-4433
EDU ED, Entertainment/Amusements ED
Ada Evening News, Ada, OK
Miller, Jim .... (352) 374-5000
CIRC DIR, Gainesville Sun, Gainesville, FL
Miller, Jody .... (807) 274-5373
Government/Political ED
Fort Frances Daily Bulletin, Fort Frances, ON
Miller, Joe .... (919) 829-4500
Weekend/Entertainment ED
News & Observer, Raleigh, NC
Miller, Joe .... (573) 431-2010
Sports ED, Daily Journal, Park Hills, MO
Miller, John .... (904) 964-6305
PUB, Bradford County Telegraph, Starke, FL
Miller, John .... (607) 272-2321
ADV MGR-RT, Ithaca Journal, Ithaca, NY
Miller, John D .... (717) 326-1551
ADV MGR-CLASS
Williamsport Sun-Gazette, Williamsport, PA
Miller, John E .... (318) 289-6300
PUB, Advertiser, Lafayette, LA
Miller, John Winn .... (814) 238-5000
EX ED/VP
Centre Daily Times, State College, PA
Miller, John X .... (803) 626-8555
MAN ED, Sun News, Myrtle Beach, SC
Miller, Joseph J .... (806) 537-3634
PUB, Panhandle Herald, Panhandle, TX
Miller, Julian .... (706) 724-0851
GM, Augusta Chronicle, Augusta, GA
Miller, Karen .... (218) 246-8533
GM, Western Itasca Review, Deer River, MN
Miller, Kary .... (208) 436-4201
PUB, Minidoka County News, Rupert, ID
Miller, Kathy .... (913) 242-4700
DP MGR, Ottawa Herald, Ottawa, KS
Miller, Kenneth .... (817) 386-3145
PUB, ED, Herald News, Hamilton, TX
Miller, Kevin .... (541) 485-1234
ADTX MGR, Register-Guard, Eugene, OR
Miller, Larry .... (507) 477-2232
PUB, ED, Hayfield Herald, Hayfield, MN
Miller, Larry .... (816) 324-3149
PUB, Savannah Reporter and Andrew County Democrat, Savannah, MO
Miller, Larry .... (803) 726-6161
PUB, ED, Jasper County Sun, Ridgeland, SC
Miller, Larry .... (416) 367-2000
ASST CONT, Toronto Star, Toronto, ON
Miller, Larry F .... (317) 423-5511
VP/TREAS, Journal and Courier, Lafayette, IN
Gannett Co. Inc.
Miller, Linda .... (405) 475-3311
Fashion ED
Daily Oklahoman, Oklahoma City, OK
Miller, Lisa .... (405) 372-5000
Fashion/Style ED, Features ED, Living ED
News Press, Stillwater, OK
Miller, Lisa .... (573) 346-2132
ADV MGR, Lake Sun Leader, Camdenton, MO
Miller, Lisa .... (607) 432-1000
Community ED, Daily Star, Oneonta, NY
Miller, Lisa .... (520) 783-3333
DIR-Accounting, Yuma Daily Sun, Yuma, AZ
Miller, Lisa Barkley .... (360)676-2600
DIR-Market Development, Bellingham Herald, Bellingham, WA
Miller, Lynn S .... (717) 291-8811
Lifestyle ED, Lancaster Intelligencer Journal/New Era/Sunday News, Lancaster, PA
Miller, Lynne .... (507) 285-7600
DIR-Human Resources
Post-Bulletin, Rochester, MN
Miller, Mabel .... (405) 336-2222
ADV DIR, Perry Daily Journal, Perry, OK
Miller, Mack .... (405) 922-4296
PUB, Vici Beacon News, Seiling, OK
Miller, Margaret R .... (202) 265-1925
EVP, Merrell Enterprises, Washington, DC
Miller, Marjorie .... (213) 237-5000
Jerusalem BU
Los Angeles Times, Los Angeles, CA
Miller, Mark F .... (219) 724-2121
PUB, BM/PA, ED
Decatur Daily Democrat, Decatur, IN
Miller, Mark L .... (913) 527-2244
ED, Belleville Telescope, Belleville, KS
Miller, Marsha .... (405) 223-2200
Police, Daily Ardmoreite, Ardmore, OK
Miller, Mary .... (815) 223-3200
Co-PUB, News-Tribune, La Salle, IL
Miller, Mary .... (417) 836-1100
PROD MGR-MR
Springfield News-Leader, Springfield, MO
Miller, Mary Anne .... (212) 455-4000
International Sales MGR
North America Syndicate, King Features Syndicate Inc., New York, NY
Miller, Mary H .... (518) 584-4242
DIR-MKTG/PROM
Saratogian, Saratoga Springs, NY
Miller, Matt .... (619) 299-3131
Pacific Rim Writer
San Diego Union-Tribune, San Diego, CA
Miller, Max B .... (818) 508-6400
PUB, Fotos International, Studio City, CA
Miller, Melvin B .... (617) 357-4900
PUB, ED, Bay State Banner, Boston, MA
Miller, Merle M .... (913) 527-2224
PUB, ED, Farmer Stockman of the Midwest, Belleville, KS
Miller, Michael .... (423) 756-6900
PROD MGR-Engraving
Chattanooga Free Press, Chattanooga, TN
Miller, Michael .... (305) 669-7355
ED, Kendall News-Gazette, South Miami, FL
Miller, Michael .... (216) 951-0000
Films/Theater ED, News ED
News-Herald, Willoughby, OH
Miller, Michael D .... (541) 926-2211
CIRC MGR, Democrat-Herald, Albany, OR
Miller, Michael J .... (814) 946-7411
PUB, Altoona Mirror, Altoona, PA
Miller, Mike .... (309) 686-3000
Radio/Television ED, Religion ED
Journal Star, Peoria, IL
Miller, Monte .... (913) 749-0006
PUB, Baldwin Ledger, Lawrence, KS
Miller, Morgan .... (501) 378-3400
ADV MGR-CLASS, ADTX MGR
Arkansas Democrat-Gazette, Little Rock, AR
Miller, Nancy .... (918) 652-3311
PUB
Henryetta Daily Free-Lance, Henryetta, OK
Miller, Nancy .... (405) 864-7612
ED, Covington Record, Covington, OK
Miller, Neal R .... (517) 362-3456
ED
Iosco County News Herald, East Tawas, MI
Miller, Nelson L .... (605) 835-8089
PUB, ED, Times-Advocate, Gregory, SD
Miller, Norman C .... (213) 237-5000
NTL ED, Los Angeles Times, Los Angeles, CA
Miller, P .... (604) 562-2441
News ED
Prince George Citizen, Prince George, BC
Miller, Pam .... (419) 636-1111
DP MGR, Bryan Times, Bryan, OH
Miller, Paul .... (603) 352-1234
Sports ED, Keene Sentinel, Keene, NH
Miller, Paul .... (561) 820-4100
CIRC MGR-Distribution
Palm Beach Post, West Palm Beach, FL
Miller, Paul A .... (419) 592-5055
MAN ED, Northwest Signal, Napoleon, OH
Miller, Peg .... (540) 885-7281
DIR-MKTG/PROM
Daily News Leader, Staunton, VA
Miller, Peggy .... (317) 659-4622
Copy ED, Times, Frankfort, IN
Miller, Peter .... (815) 223-3200
PRES, TREAS, News-Tribune, La Salle, IL
Miller III, Peter .... (815) 223-3200
VP-OPER, ASST SEC, PUB
News-Tribune, La Salle, IL
Miller, Phil .... (919) 243-5151
CIRC MGR, Wilson Daily Times, Wilson, NC
Miller, Phil .... (317) 622-1212
City ED, Courts ED, Farm/Agriculture ED, Religion ED, Herald Bulletin, Anderson, IN
Miller, Phillip J .... (806) 779-2141
PUB, McLean News, McLean, TX
Miller, R B .... (317) 664-5111
EX BC, Chronicle-Tribune, Marion, IN
Miller Jr, R B .... (817) 386-3145
PUB, Herald News, Hamilton, TX
Miller, Rachel .... (605) 256-4555
Women's ED
Madison Daily Leader, Madison, SD
Miller, Ralph .... (317) 633-1240
PROD OPER FRM-COMP (Night)
Indianapolis Star/News, Indianapolis, IN
Miller, Randy N .... (616) 964-7161
PUB, Battle Creek Enquirer, Battle Creek, MI
Miller, Ray .... (334) 222-2402
PROD MGR
Andalusia Star-News, Andalusia, AL
Miller, Rebecca .... (412) 684-5200
City ED, News ED
Valley Independent, Monessen, PA
Miller, Renee .... (803) 726-6161
PUB, Jasper County Sun, Ridgeland, SC
Miller, Rick .... (419) 483-4190
GM, ADV MGR, CIRC MGR
Bellevue Gazette, Bellevue, OH
Miller, Rick .... (716) 372-3121
School ED, Olean Times-Herald, Olean, NY
Miller, Rita .... (515) 782-2141
Lifestyle ED, News-Advertiser, Creston, IA
Miller, Robert .... (540) 374-5000
ADV MGR-CLASS
Free Lance-Star, Fredericksburg, VA
Miller, Robert .... (415) 348-4321
ADV DIR-Sales
San Mateo County Times, San Mateo, CA
Miller, Robert .... (916) 885-5656
City/MET ED, Auburn Journal, Auburn, CA
Miller, Robert B .... (317) 423-5511
EX BC, Journal and Courier, Lafayette, IN
Miller, Robert C .... (607) 547-2545
PUB, Freeman's Journal, Cooperstown, NY
Miller, Robert G .... (802) 747-6121
GM/VP, ADTX MGR
Rutland Herald, Rutland, VT
Miller, Robert J .... (330) 454-5611
ADV DIR, Repository, Canton, OH
Miller, Robert L .... (712) 677-2438
PUB, Observer, Vail, IA
Miller, Roger G .... (413) 774-7226
PUB, Greenfield Town Crier, Greenfield, MA
Miller, Ron .... (910) 373-7000
Books ED, News & Record, Greensboro, NC
Miller, Roy .... (218) 829-4705
ED, Automotive ED, EPE
Brainerd Daily Dispatch, Brainerd, MN
Miller, Ruth .... (913) 282-3371
PUB
Smith County Pioneer, Smith Center, KS
Miller, Sally .... (605) 835-8089
GM, Times-Advocate, Gregory, SD
Miller, Sandra .... (562) 438-5641
ED, Reporter, Long Beach, CA
Miller, Sandra .... (318) 824-3011
CIRC MGR
Jennings Daily News, Jennings, LA
Miller, Sandy .... (606) 623-1669
Accountant
Richmond Register, Richmond, KY
Miller, Scott .... (319) 283-2144
Sports ED, Register, Oelwein, IA
Miller, Scott .... (410) 332-6000
Division MGR, ADV MGR-Division
Sun, Baltimore, MD
Miller, Shelby .... (405) 335-3893
PUB, Frederick Press, Frederick, OK
Miller, Steve .... (605) 394-8300
ED-City, Rapid City Journal, Rapid City, SD
Miller, Steve .... (406) 265-6795
MAN ED, EPE, News ED
Havre Daily News, Havre, MT
Miller, Steve .... (360) 377-3711
MGR-SYS, Sun, Bremerton, WA
Miller, Steve .... (916) 541-3880
Graphics ED/Art DIR
Tahoe Daily Tribune, South Lake Tahoe, CA
Miller, Steve .... (308) 632-0670
MAN ED, Star-Herald, Scottsbluff, NE
Miller, Susan K .... (818) 932-6161
PUB, Dodge Construction News Greensheet, Monrovia, CA
Miller, Susan H .... (408) 372-3311
PRES/PUB, ED
Monterey County Herald, Monterey, CA
Miller, T Alex .... (970) 668-0750
ED, Summit County Journal, Frisco, CO
Miller, Terry .... (610) 258-7171
BUS/FIN ED, Express-Times, Easton, PA
Miller, Thomas E .... (814) 781-1596
ADV MGR-NTL, Daily Press, St. Marys, PA
Miller, Thomas L .... (314) 239-7701
PUB
Washington Missourian, Washington, MO
Miller, Thomas R .... (315) 789-3333
ADV DIR, Finger Lakes Times, Geneva, NY
Miller, Thos C .... (715) 485-3121
PUB, County Ledger-Press, Balsam Lake, WI
Miller, Tim .... (937) 644-9111
Sports ED
Marysville Journal-Tribune, Marysville, OH

Copyright ©1997 by the Editor & Publisher Co.

159-Who's Where **Mit**

Miller, Tim .... (508) 775-1200
Entertainment ED
Cape Cod Times, Hyannis, MA
Miller, Tim .... (218) 751-3740
PROD FRM-Night Side
Daily Pioneer, Bemidji, MN
Miller, Todd E .... (607) 734-5151
CONT, Star-Gazette, Elmira, NY
Miller, Tom .... (812) 332-4401
PROD SUPT-PR
Herald-Times Inc, Bloomington, IN
Miller, Tommy .... (713) 220-7171
MGR-Purchasing, Deputy MAN ED
Houston Chronicle, Houston, TX
Miller, Tony .... (319) 754-8461
PROD MGR-SYS, Hawk Eye, Burlington, IA
Miller, Twila .... (816) 324-3149
PUB, ED, Savannah Reporter and Andrew County Democrat, Savannah, MO
Miller, Wes .... (716) 439-9222
PROD FRM-PR
Union-Sun & Journal, Lockport, NY
Miller, William .... (540) 465-5137
ADV DIR
Northern Virginia Daily, Strasburg, VA
Miller, William L .... (314) 239-7701
PUB, ED, MAN ED
Washington Missourian, Washington, MO
Millerick, William .... (860) 225-4601
EX ED, Books ED, Travel ED
Herald, New Britain, CT
Millet, Kristin .... (512) 884-2011
VP-Human Resources, Corpus Christi Caller-Times, Corpus Christi, TX
Millette, Lauren .... (520) 445-3333
Amusements/Books ED, Films/Theater ED, Food ED, Daily Courier, Prescott, AZ
Milley, Allan C .... (804) 793-2311
Sports ED, Register & Bee, Danville, VA
Millholland, David K .... (704) 322-4510
ADV DIR, Hickory Daily Record, Hickory, NC
Millholland, John G .... (704) 322-4510
SEC/TREAS, GM
Hickory Daily Record, Hickory, NC
Millholland, Kenneth .... (704) 322-4510
VP, Hickory Daily Record, Hickory, NC
Millholland, Suzanne G .... (704) 322-4510
PRES/PUB
Hickory Daily Record, Hickory, NC
Millhouse, Tom .... (937) 498-2111
Health/Medical ED, NTL ED, Political/Government ED
Sidney Daily News, Sidney, OH
Millians, Rick .... (513) 352-2000
Graphics ED, Cincinnati Post, Cincinnati, OH
Milligan, Annie .... (847) 382-1593
ED, Milligan Syndicate, Barrington, IL
Milligan, Brian .... (508) 626-3800
Regional ED-West
Middlesex News, Framingham, MA
Milligan, Delwin .... (941) 687-7000
Outdoors ED, Ledger, Lakeland, FL
Milligan, Lisa .... (415) 348-4321
Political/Government ED
San Mateo County Times, San Mateo, CA
Milligan, Michael .... (910) 276-2311
PUB, Exchange, Laurinburg, NC
Milligan, Molly .... (847) 382-1593
ED, Milligan Syndicate, Barrington, IL
Milligan, Tammy .... (316) 694-5700
ADV CNR-CLASS
Hutchinson News, Hutchinson, KS
Milligan, Ted .... (423) 523-3131
PROD DIR-OPER
Knoxville News-Sentinel, Knoxville, TN
Milligan, Valerie .... (515) 753-6611
BUS/FIN ED
Times-Republican, Marshalltown, IA
Milliken, Maureen .... (603) 668-4321
ED-Daily, Union Leader, Manchester, NH
Milliken, Michelle .... (941) 335-0200
ADV MGR-CLASS
News-Press, Fort Myers, FL
Milliman, Penelope Faber .... (616) 279-7488
PUB, Three Rivers Commercial-News, Three Rivers, MI
Milliman, Richard L .... (517) 676-9393
COB, Milliman Communications, Mason, MI
Milliman II, Richard .... (517) 676-9393
PRES, Milliman Communications, Mason, MI
Millington, Roland .... (309) 346-1111
Graphics ED/Art DIR
Pekin Daily Times, Pekin, IL
Millions, Rick .... (606) 292-2600
DIR-Photography
Kentucky Post, Covington, KY
Millizer, Steve .... (502) 443-1771
Sports ED, Paducah Sun, Paducah, KY
Millman, John .... (805) 395-7500
Sports ED
Bakersfield Californian, Bakersfield, CA
Millner, Gloria .... (216) 999-4500
ASSOC ED, Plain Dealer, Cleveland, OH
Mills, Andrea .... (815) 946-2364
ED, Tri-County Press, Polo, IL
Mills, Barbara .... (505) 523-4581
ADV MGR-CLASS
Las Cruces Sun-News, Las Cruces, NM
Mills, Beverly .... (919) 781-4622
PRES, Syndicated Features Inc., Raleigh, NC
Mills, Blair .... (250) 380-5211
Accounting MGR
Times Colonist, Victoria, BC
Mills, Deanna .... (717) 255-8100
Librarian, Patriot-News, Harrisburg, PA
Mills, Gene .... (915) 682-5311
MGR-INFO SYS
Midland Reporter-Telegram, Midland, TX
Mills, Glenda .... (806) 762-8844
MGR-Personnel
Lubbock Avalanche-Journal, Lubbock, TX
Mills, Jefferson D .... (314) 725-1515
ED
St. Louis Watchman Advocate, Clayton, MO
Mills, Kathy .... (540) 825-0771
ADV CLASS Phone Person
Culpeper Star-Exponent, Culpeper, VA
Mills, LaVale .... (205) 356-2148
PUB, Red Bay News, Red Bay, AL
Mills, Margie .... (209) 532-7151
Women's ED, Union Democrat, Sonora, CA
Mills, Molly .... (912) 923-6432
PA, Daily Sun, Warner Robins, GA
Mills, Mona .... (601) 842-2611
CONT, Northeast Mississippi Daily Journal, Tupelo, MS
Mills, Pat .... (916) 842-5777
Bookkeeper, PA
Siskiyou Daily News, Yreka, CA
Mills, Rick .... (517) 772-2971
ED, EPE, Morning Sun, Mount Pleasant, MI
Mills, Russ .... (613) 829-9100
PUB, Ottawa Citizen, Ottawa, ON
Mills, Shane .... (604) 564-0005
ED
Prince George Free Press, Prince George, BC
Mills, Steve .... (808) 525-8000
CIRC DIR
Hawaii Newspaper Agency Inc., Honolulu, HI
Mills, Tom .... (705) 759-3030
City/News ED
Sault Star, Sault Ste. Marie, ON
Millsap, David M .... (540) 669-2181
ADV MGR-CLASS, Herald-Courier Virginia Tennessean, Bristol, VA
Millsaps, Eric .... (704) 873-1451
MAN ED, EPE, Statesville Record & Landmark, Statesville, NC
Millsaps Jr, William H .... (804) 649-6000
Senior VP/EX ED
Richmond Times-Dispatch, Richmond, VA
Millson, Wendy .... (519) 822-4310
PROD FRM-MR, Daily Mercury, Guelph, ON
Millstein, Lincoln .... (617) 929-2000
VP-New Media, Boston Globe, Boston, MA
Millward, Deb .... (604) 732-2111
EDL Services, Vancouver Sun, Vancouver, BC
Milne, David .... (215) 854-2000
ASST MAN ED
Philadelphia Inquirer, Philadelphia, PA
Milne, Heather .... (619) 232-4381
MGR-MKTG/PROM
San Diego Daily Transcript, San Diego, CA
Milne, J P (Jamie) .... (506) 632-8888
PRES, New Brunswick Publishing Co. Ltd., Saint John, NB
Milne, James P .... (506) 632-8888
PRES, Telegraph-Journal/Saint John Times Globe, Saint John, NB
Milne, Les .... (902) 752-3000
CIRC Representative
Evening News, New Glasgow, NS
Milnes, Cal C .... (319) 578-3351
PUB, ED, Sumner Gazette, Sumner, IA
Milnes, Katy .... (319) 578-3351
PUB, Sumner Gazette, Sumner, IA
Milstead, Ken .... (972) 286-4000
PUB, ED
Suburban Tribune, Balch Springs, TX
Milton, Paul .... (410) 337-2400
ED, Towson Times, Towson, MD
Milversted, Mark .... (404) 526-5151
ADV MGR-Direct MKTG
Atlanta Journal-Constitution, Atlanta, GA
Milwee, Sam .... (606) 528-2464
CIRC MGR, Times-Tribune, Corbin, KY
Milza, Jane .... (718) 981-1234
Food ED
Staten Island Advance, Staten Island, NY
Mimoso, Michael .... (508) 880-9000
Sports ED
Taunton Daily Gazette, Taunton, MA
Mims, Steve .... (541) 265-7287
MAN ED, News Guard, Lincoln City, OR
Mims, William Walton .... (803) 637-3540
PUB, ED, Edgefield Advertiser, Edgefield, SC
Minassian, Mihran .... (617) 924-4420
GM
Armenian-Mirror Spector, Watertown, MA
Mincer, Kent .... (970) 945-8515
Sports ED, Post, Glenwood Springs, CO
Mincey, Allen .... (423) 472-5041
Fashion/Food ED
Cleveland Daily Banner, Cleveland, TN
Mincey, Lori .... (912) 374-0360
MAN ED, Dodge County News, Eastman, GA
Mindak, Denis L .... (612) 896-4700
PUB, Sun-Current, Bloomington, MN
Mindich, Stephen M .... (617) 536-5390
PUB, Boston Phoenix, Boston, MA
Minemyer, Chip .... (814) 532-5199
Sports ED, Tribune-Democrat, Johnstown, PA
Mineo, Tammye .... (915) 337-4661
ADV MGR-RT, Odessa American, Odessa, TX
Miner, Alan .... (212) 416-2000
PROD DIR-Publishing SYS
Wall Street Journal, New York, NY
Miner, John .... (519) 679-6666
BUS ED, London Free Press, London, ON
Miner, Laurie .... (607) 798-1234
Radio/Television ED
Press & Sun Bulletin, Binghamton, NY
Minervini, Rob .... (208) 743-9411
ADV DIR, ADV MGR-NTL
Lewiston Morning Tribune, Lewiston, ID
Minford, Chris .... (808) 244-3981
CIRC MGR-Distribution
Maui News, Wailuku, HI
Minge, Jim .... (402) 444-1000
Music ED (Pop), Radio/Television ED
Omaha World-Herald, Omaha, NE
Minichino, Adam .... (860) 347-3331
Sports ED
Middletown Press, Middletown, CT
Minick, William .... (609) 935-1500
BUS/FIN ED, Today's Sunbeam, Salem, NJ
Minister, Scott .... (614) 461-5000
DIR-Arts, Columbus Dispatch, Columbus, OH
Minjock, Vi .... (412) 684-5200
Accountant
Valley Independent, Monessen, PA
Mink, Kenneth P .... (540) 574-6200
MAN ED
Daily News-Record, Harrisonburg, VA
Minnich, David .... (352) 374-5000
ADV DIR, Gainesville Sun, Gainesville, FL
Minnick, Ben .... (206) 622-8272
Construction ED, Seattle Daily Journal of Commerce, Seattle, WA
Minning, Richard .... (937) 328-0300
News ED
Springfield News-Sun, Springfield, OH
Minnis, John .... (313) 882-0294
ED, Connection, Grosse Pointe, MI
Minnis, Raymond A .... (803) 577-7111
PROD MGR-Pre Press
Post and Courier, Charleston, SC
Minoque, James .... (212) 210-2100
PROD SUPT-Engraving
New York Daily News, New York, NY
Minor, Les .... (903) 794-3311
MAN ED, Texarkana Gazette, Texarkana, TX
Minor, Robyn .... (502) 781-1700
City ED, Daily News, Bowling Green, KY
Minor, Roger .... (816) 234-4141
CIRC MGR-Home Delivery
Kansas City Star, Kansas City, MO
Minosky, Frank .... (817) 634-2125
CIRC SUPV, Killeen Daily Herald, Killeen, TX
Minton, Freda .... (812) 283-6636
CIRC MGR, Evening News, Jeffersonville, IN
Minton, Meta .... (618) 656-4700
ASSOC PUB
Edwardsville Intelligencer, Edwardsville, IL
Mintz, Dan .... (908) 870-9338
ED, Atlanticville, Long Branch, NJ
Mintz, Gerald .... (212) 803-8200
PRES, American Banker, New York, NY
Thomson Financial Services
Minvielle, Paul .... (250) 380-5211
EDL Writer, Times Colonist, Victoria, BC
Mio, Peter L .... (706) 278-1011
ADV DIR, Daily Citizen-News, Dalton, GA
Miorelli, Michael M .... (610) 371-5000
Sports ED
Reading Times/Eagle, Reading, PA
Mirabella, Alan .... (212) 210-2100
BUS ED, New York Daily News, New York, NY
Miranda, Alice .... (315) 470-0011
CONT, Post-Standard/Syracuse Herald-Journal/American, Syracuse, NY
Miranda, Margaret .... (805) 736-2313
Family/Society ED, Women's ED
Lompoc Record, Lompoc, CA
Miranda-Jones, Carmen .... (609) 691-1148
PUB, ED, El Veterano, Vineland, NJ
Mirando, Lillian K .... (504) 345-2333
MAN ED, Daily Star, Hammond, LA
Mire, Judy T .... (318) 643-8002
ED, Kaplan Herald, Kaplan, LA
Mirecki, Peter .... (212) 837-7000
DP MGR, Journal of Commerce & Commercial, New York, NY
Mires, Butch .... (308) 345-4500
ADV DIR, McCook Daily Gazette, McCook, NE
Mirkovich, Paul .... (412) 946-3501
GM, Globe, New Wilmington, PA
Mirt, Kelly .... (803) 771-6161
ADV DIR, State, Columbia, SC
Mischner, Michael .... (803) 432-6157
PUB, Chronicle Independent, Camden, SC
Misfeldt, Jon .... (402) 564-2741
Sports ED
Columbus Telegram, Columbus, NE
Mishler, Todd .... (608) 754-3311
Features ED, Religion ED
Janesville Gazette, Janesville, WI
Misiak, Hank .... (203) 235-1661
ADV MGR-Sales
Record-Journal, Meriden, CT
Missett, Jim .... (619) 437-3024
PUB, Compass, San Diego, CA
Missett, Joan .... (619) 745-6611
ADV MGR-CLASS/Outside
North County Times, Escondido, CA
Missett, Thomas F .... (619) 745-6611
PUB-Oceanside
North County Times, Escondido, CA
Missler, Sherry .... (419) 238-2285
EDU ED, Entertainment/Amusements ED, Farm/Agriculture ED, Youth/Culture ED
Times-Bulletin, Van Wert, OH
Mister, Charlie .... (410) 535-1575
PUB
Calvert Independent, Prince Frederick, MD
Mistretta, Joe .... (209) 369-2761
PROD FRM-PR, Lodi News-Sentinel, Lodi, CA
Misureli, Frank M .... (414) 657-1000
VP/PUB (Zion Benton News/Bargaineer), ADV DIR, Kenosha News, Kenosha, WI
Mitchell, Bill .... (561) 461-2050
Photo ED, Tribune, Fort Pierce, FL
Mitchell, Bill .... (816) 932-6600
ED/DIR-Development/New Media
Universal Press Syndicate, Kansas City, MO
Mitchell, Bill .... (250) 380-5211
PROD FRM-COMP
Times Colonist, Victoria, BC
Mitchell, Bob .... (202) 628-2157
News Exchange ED
Thomson News Service, Washington, DC
Mitchell, Bruce .... (614) 594-8219
PUB, GM, Athens News, Athens, OH
Mitchell, Candy .... (713) 220-7171
ADV MGR-Sales
Houston Chronicle, Houston, TX
Mitchell, Catherine .... (601) 454-7196
ED, Belmont and Tishomingo Journal, Belmont, MS
Mitchell, Charles .... (203) 846-3281
Automotive ED, City ED, Hour, Norwalk, CT
Mitchell, Charles D .... (601) 636-4545
MAN ED, Vicksburg Post, Vicksburg, MS
Mitchell, Colleen .... (770) 478-5753
ADV DIR, Clayton News/Daily, Jonesboro, GA
Mitchell, Cynthia .... (515) 284-8000
Daily Features Section ED
Des Moines Register, Des Moines, IA
Mitchell, David C .... (970) 264-2101
PUB, ED
Pagosa Springs Sun, Pagosa Springs, CO
Mitchell, David J .... (519) 941-1350
PUB, Orangeville Banner, Orangeville, ON
Mitchell, David V .... (415) 663-8404
PUB, ED
Point Reyes Light, Pt. Reyes Station, CA
Mitchell, Denise .... (517) 752-7171
Religion ED, Saginaw News, Saginaw, MI
Mitchell, Dennis .... (970) 242-5050
ADV DIR, Daily Sentinel, Grand Junction, CO
Mitchell, Doug .... (605) 352-6401
Sports ED, Huron Plainsman, Huron, SD
Mitchell, Earl .... (334) 749-6271
CIRC MGR-Sales/Distribution
Opelika-Auburn News, Opelika, AL
Mitchell, Ellen .... (703) 878-8000
News ED, Potomac News, Woodbridge, VA
Mitchell, Dr Eugene .... (314) 531-1323
PUB, St. Louis Argus, St. Louis, MO
Mitchell, Gail .... (501) 642-2111
ADV MGR
De Queen Daily Citizen, De Queen, AR
Mitchell, Gary .... (505) 763-3431
Religion ED, Clovis News Journal, Clovis, NM
Mitchell, George S .... (201) 627-0400
PUB, ED
Citizen of Morris County, Denville, NJ
Mitchell, Glenn .... (604) 545-3322
MAN ED, Morning Star, Vernon, BC

Mit Who's Where-160

Mitchell, Glenn A .... (409) 379-2416
PUB, ED, Newton County News, Newton, TX
Mitchell, Gloria .... (912) 238-8010
GM, Freedom Journal, Savannah, GA
Mitchell, H T .... (604) 632-6144
PUB, News Advertiser, Kitimat, BC
Mitchell, Jack .... (817) 965-3124
ADV DIR, Stephenville Empire-Tribune, Stephenville, TX
Mitchell, Jackson C .... (316) 326-3326
PRES, PUB, EDL Writer
Wellington Daily News, Wellington, KS
Mitchell, Jeff .... (905) 985-7383
MAN ED
Port Perry Weekend Star, Port Perry, ON
Mitchell, Jim .... (541) 474-3700
News ED, Wire ED
Grants Pass Daily Courier, Grants Pass, OR
Mitchell, Jim .... (713) 220-7171
ADV DIR-GEN
Houston Chronicle, Houston, TX
Mitchell, Jim .... (408) 920-5000
BUS ED
San Jose Mercury News, San Jose, CA
Mitchell, Jim .... (318) 289-6300
Accountant, Advertiser, Lafayette, LA
Mitchell, Joseph E .... (616) 429-2400
BM, CONT, Herald-Palladium, St. Joseph, MI
Mitchell, Julie .... (208) 642-3357
ED, Independent Enterprise, Payette, ID
Mitchell, Karen .... (515) 284-8000
Photo ED
Des Moines Register, Des Moines, IA
Mitchell Jr, Kenneth B .... (617) 593-7700
PROD FRM-MR
Daily Evening Item, Lynn, MA
Mitchell, Lajune .... (205) 325-2222
PROD MGR-COMP
Birmingham News, Birmingham, AL
Mitchell, Larry .... (306) 873-4515
PUB, ED, Tisdale Recorder, Tisdale, SK
Mitchell, Lynda .... (416) 947-2222
CORP DIR-Human Resources
Toronto Sun, Toronto, ON
Mitchell, M Wayne .... (601) 454-7196
PUB, Belmont and Tishomingo Journal, Belmont, MS
Mitchell, Marie .... (501) 239-8562
Living/Lifestyle ED
Paragould Daily Press, Paragould, AR
Mitchell, Marilyn .... (601) 582-4321
EX ED
Hattiesburg American, Hattiesburg, MS
Mitchell, Mary .... (312) 321-3000
City Hall Reporter, COL
Chicago Sun-Times, Chicago, IL
Mitchell, Nelson .... (919) 778-2211
ADV DIR
Goldsboro News-Argus, Goldsboro, NC
Mitchell, Ophelia .... (706) 324-2404
PUB, Columbus Times, Columbus, GA
Mitchell, Pat .... (813) 259-7711
Graphics EDL Writer
Tampa Tribune and Times, Tampa, FL
Mitchell, R John .... (802) 747-6121
PRES, PUB, Rutland Herald, Rutland, VT
Mitchell, Randy .... (508) 374-0321
CIRC MGR, Haverhill Gazette, Haverhill, MA
Mitchell, Richard A .... (704) 758-7381
PUB, Lenoir News-Topic, Lenoir, NC
Mitchell, Rick .... (713) 220-7171
Music Critic, Houston Chronicle, Houston, TX
Mitchell, Rita .... (502) 472-1121
MAN ED, Fulton Leader, Fulton, KY
Mitchell, Steve .... (334) 433-1551
Regional News ED
Mobile Press Register, Mobile, AL
Mitchell, T Wayne .... (864) 224-4321
VP, ADTX MGR
Anderson Independent-Mail, Anderson, SC
Mitchell, Terrie .... (407) 420-5000
MGR-Consumer MKTG
Orlando Sentinel, Orlando, FL
Mitchell, Thomas .... (702) 383-0211
ED, Las Vegas Review-Journal, Las Vegas, NV
Mitchell, Tim .... (217) 485-4010
ED, County Star, Tolono, IL
Mitchell, Tom .... (414) 265-5300
MAN ED, Community Journal, Milwaukee, WI
Mitchell, William .... (217) 323-1010
PUB, Illinoian Star, Beardstown, IL
Mitchell, William .... (502) 472-1121
PUB, ED, Fulton Leader, Fulton, KY
Mitchell-Bray, Marsha .... (213) 299-3800
MAN ED
Los Angeles Sentinel, Los Angeles, CA
Mitich, Mary .... (360) 694-3391
ADV MGR-Display
Columbian, Vancouver, WA
Mitrowitz, Jim .... (607) 798-1234
PROD MGR-Pre Press
Press & Sun Bulletin, Binghamton, NY
Mitsoff, Chris .... (937) 426-5263
EDU ED, Entertainment/Amusements ED
Beavercreek News-Current, Beavercreek, OH
Mitsoff, Ruth .... (937) 426-5263
ADV MGR
Beavercreek News-Current, Beavercreek, OH
Mitsoff, Tom .... (937) 426-5263
ED, BUS/FIN ED, EPE
Beavercreek News-Current, Beavercreek, OH
Mittan, Charles .... (402) 746-3700
MAN ED, Red Cloud Chief, Red Cloud, NE
Mittelhanser, Milene .... (816) 826-1000
Librarian, Sedalia Democrat, Sedalia, MO
Mittelstaedt, Alan .... (207) 791-6650
Regional News ED
Portland Press Herald, Portland, ME
Mittlestadt, Mike .... (315) 782-1000
Farm ED, Daily Times, Watertown, NY
Miyagawa, Hajime .... (212) 603-6600
Correspondent
Kyodo News Service, New York, NY
Mizak Jr, Michael J .... (610) 371-5000
CFO/TREAS
Reading Times/Eagle, Reading, PA
Mize, Richard .... (817) 767-8341
Farm ED, Regional ED, Wichita Falls Times Record News, Wichita Falls, TX
Mladenich, Ronald .... (206) 597-8742
CIRC DIR, News Tribune, Tacoma, WA
Moak, Judith Fiske .... (202) 737-7377
VP-Development
Children's Express, Washington, DC
Moakley, Bill .... (405) 527-2126
MAN ED, Purcell Register, Purcell, OK
Moates, Cindy C .... (941) 687-7000
DIR-Human Resources, Ledger, Lakeland, FL
Moats, David .... (802) 747-6121
EPE, EDL Writer
Rutland Herald, Rutland, VT
Mobbs, John .... (501) 378-3400
ADV DIR
Arkansas Democrat-Gazette, Little Rock, AR
Moberg, Steve .... (360) 676-2600
PROD MGR-PR
Bellingham Herald, Bellingham, WA
Mobius, Ben .... (503) 873-8385
ED, Silverton Appeal Tribune/Mt. Angel News, Silverton, OR
Mobley, Kathy .... (304) 348-5140
Radio/Television ED, Charleston Gazette, Sunday Gazette-Mail, Charleston, WV
Mock, Van .... (912) 283-2244
PSL MGR
Waycross Journal-Herald, Waycross, GA
Moczygemba, Debbie .... (210) 383-2705
ADV MGR, DIR
Edinburg Daily Review, Edinburg, TX
Modderno, Francine .... (801) 355-3336
Washington BU Chief
FNA News, Salt Lake City, UT
Modestino, Lou .... (617) 344-2837
Author, International/New England Motorsports Syndication, Stoughton, MA
Modine, LeRoy .... (509) 582-1500
PROD MGR-Printing OPER
Tri-City Herald, Tri-Cities, WA
Modisett, Bill .... (915) 682-5311
EPE
Midland Reporter-Telegram, Midland, TX
Modlin, Margaret .... (515) 792-3121
BM, Newton Daily News, Newton, IA
Moehle, Dan .... (316) 268-6000
CFO, Wichita Eagle, Wichita, KS
Moehrke, Jim .... (707) 448-6401
Graphics ED/Art DIR, Online Contact Reporter, Vacaville, CA
Moeller, Bill .... (402) 553-3654
Author, Moeller, Jan & Bill, Omaha, NE
Moeller, Jan .... (402) 553-3654
Author, Moeller, Jan & Bill, Omaha, NE
Moeller, Lynne S .... (314) 340-8402
VP/DIR-MKTG
Pulitzer Publishing Co., St. Louis, MO
Moerle, Brenda .... (519) 894-2231
Assignment Desk, Record, Kitchener, ON
Moeur, John .... (520) 458-9440
MAN ED, Sierra Vista Herald, Sierra Vista, AZ
Wick Communications
Moffat, John .... (509) 663-5161
Wire ED, Wenatchee World, Wenatchee, WA
Moffat, Michael .... (415) 495-4200
Display Sales Representative
Daily Pacific Builder, San Francisco, CA
Moffeit, Miles .... (817) 695-0500
ED, Irving News, Arlington, TX
Moffeitt, Matt .... (212) 416-2000
Reporter-in-Charge (Rio de Janeiro)
Wall Street Journal, New York, NY
Moffett, Nancy .... (312) 321-3000
ASST MET ED
Chicago Sun-Times, Chicago, IL
Moffitt, Annie Laurie .... (304) 436-3144
TREAS, Welch Daily News, Welch, WV
Moffitt, Camille .... (615) 754-6397
ED, Mt. Juliet News, Mount Juliet, TN
Moffitt, Fred D .... (304) 436-3144
SEC, Welch Daily News, Welch, WV
Moffitt, John F .... (703) 344-2489
COB/CEO, Moffitt Newspapers, Roanoke, VA
Moffitt, Margret W .... (304) 645-1206
VP, West Virginia Daily News, Lewisburg, WV
Mogck, Patty .... (605) 583-4419
GM, ED, Scotland Journal, Scotland, SD
Mogensen, Mark .... (207) 784-5411
Assignment ED, Sun-Journal, Lewiston, ME
Mogielnicki, Wayne .... (804) 978-7200
ED, Daily Progress, Charlottesville, VA
Mogilefsky, David B .... (916) 546-5995
PUB, North Tahoe/Truckee Week Magazine, Tahoe Vista, CA
Mogle, Dan .... (903) 597-8111
Amusements ED, BUS ED
Tyler Morning Telegraph, Tyler, TX
Mohamed, Rozaan S .... (718) 264-1500
ED, New York Voice, Fresh Meadows, NY
Mohanna, Timothy J .... (308) 485-4284
PUB, Cairo Record, Cairo, NE
Mohl, Robert .... (919) 537-2505
News ED, Daily Herald, Roanoke Rapids, NC
Mohler, H H .... (304) 772-3016
PUB, ED, Monroe Watchman, Union, WV
Mohon, Wendy .... (409) 945-3441
City ED, Texas City Sun, Texas City, TX
Mohr, Jay .... (712) 754-2551
PUB, ED
Osceola County Gazette-Tribune, Sibley, IA
Mohr, Mike .... (618) 282-3803
GM, MAN ED
North County News, Red Bud, IL
Mohr, Thomas .... (612) 673-4000
VP-CLASS/Market Group Leader
Star Tribune, Minneapolis, MN
Mohr, Victor L .... (618) 282-3803
PUB, North County News, Red Bud, IL
Mohs, Randy .... (218) 631-2561
PUB, Wadena Pioneer Journal, Wadena, MN
Moiseeff, Dolly .... (810) 332-8181
Travel ED, Oakland Press, Pontiac, MI
Moissinac, Helen .... (609) 646-5843
GM, South Jersey Advisor, Cologne, NJ
Moissinac, Ronald G .... (609) 646-5843
PUB, South Jersey Advisor, Cologne, NJ
Mok, Andy .... (815) 459-4040
ADV MGR-CLASS
Northwest Herald, Crystal Lake, IL
Mokler, Don .... (501) 378-3400
PROD MGR-PR
Arkansas Democrat-Gazette, Little Rock, AR
Molchany, Rick .... (610) 820-6500
DIR-Manufacturing
Morning Call, Allentown, PA
Molde, Dawn .... (507) 285-7600
CIRC MGR-Customer SRV
Post-Bulletin, Rochester, MN
Molen, Logan .... (805) 395-7500
Features ED
Bakersfield Californian, Bakersfield, CA
Molenaar, Ruth .... (201) 863-3310
PUB, La Tribuna Publication, Union City, NJ
Molenaar, Soraya .... (201) 863-3310
GM, La Tribuna Publication, Union City, NJ
Molenda, Jules .... (802) 447-7567
PUB, Bennington Banner, Bennington, VT
Molick, Frank .... (218) 262-1011
PROD MGR, PROD MGR-Computer SYS
Daily Tribune, Hibbing, MN
Molina, Gerry .... (508) 685-1000
MAN ED, Eagle-Tribune, North Andover, MA
Molina, Roberto .... (212) 753-5572
Chief Correspondent
Prensa Latina, New York, NY
Molineux, Will .... (757) 247-4600
Books ED, EPE
Daily Press, Newport News, VA
Molle, Beth .... (715) 251-3638
MAN ED, Niagara Journal, Niagara, WI
Molle, Gary .... (715) 251-3638
PUB, ED, Niagara Journal, Niagara, WI
Moller, Dan .... (218) 723-5281
MGR-INFO SYS
Duluth News-Tribune, Duluth, MN
Moller, Dave .... (916) 257-5321
ED, Lassen County Times, Susanville, CA
Moller, Ed .... (403) 783-3074
PUB, Ponoka Herald, Ponoka, AB
Moller, Joyce .... (304) 275-8981
GM, ED, Wirt County Journal, Elizabeth, WV
Molley, John .... (540) 669-2181
EX ED, Herald-Courier Virginia Tennessean, Bristol, VA
Molloy, Joanna .... (212) 210-2100
Gossip COL
New York Daily News, New York, NY
Molloy, Kevin .... (516) 475-1000
ED, Long Island Advance, Patchogue, NY
Mollway, Paul .... (815) 987-1200
PROD DIR-OPER
Rockford Register Star, Rockford, IL
Moloney, Sharon .... (513) 352-2000
Political ED
Cincinnati Post, Cincinnati, OH
Molony, Staci .... (515) 284-8000
CIRC MGR-Home Delivery
Des Moines Register, Des Moines, IA
Molpus, Jim .... (615) 259-8800
Radio/Television ED
Nashville Banner, Nashville, TN
Molvar, Roger H .... (213) 237-3700
VP/CONT, Times Mirror Co., Los Angeles, CA
Molyneaux, David .... (216) 999-4500
Travel ED, Plain Dealer, Cleveland, OH
Mominee, Thomas .... (812) 424-7711
PSL DIR
Evansville Courier Co. Inc., Evansville, IN
Mon, Deborah .... (713) 529-8490
ED, Houston Voice, Houston, TX
Monaco, Janice .... (541) 523-3673
Bookkeeper
Baker City Herald, Baker City, OR
Monaco, Lou .... (201) 309-1200
DIR/MKTG Services
ESPN/SportsTicker, Jersey City, NJ
Monagan, Susan .... (212) 362-9256
Feature Sales, Cartoonists & Writers Syndicate, New York, NY
Monaghan, John J .... (401) 277-7000
MAN ED-ADM
Providence Journal-Bulletin, Providence, RI
Monaghan, Nancy .... (304) 526-4000
PRES, PUB, Herald-Dispatch, Huntington, WV, Gannett Co. Inc.
Monahan, Chris .... (212) 455-4000
TELEMKTG Sales Representative
North America Syndicate, King Features Syndicate Inc., New York, NY
Monahan, Iona .... (514) 987-2222
Fashion ED, Gazette, Montreal, QC
Monahan, John J .... (508) 793-9100
Environmental ED
Telegram & Gazette, Worcester, MA
Monahan, Kerri .... (508) 222-7000
Community ED, Sun Chronicle, Attleboro, MA
Monahan, Lesli .... (561) 395-8300
ADV DIR, News, Boca Raton, FL
Monchecourt, Joe .... (610) 622-8800
BUS/FIN ED
Delaware County Daily Times, Primos, PA
Moncivaiz, Lydia .... (562) 435-1161
PROD ASST MGR
Press-Telegram, Long Beach, CA
Moncrief, Jamie .... (910) 343-2000
Chief Photographer, Morning Star/Sunday Star-News, Wilmington, NC
Moncrief, Robert .... (308) 237-2152
SEC, BM, DP MGR
Kearney Hub, Kearney, NE
Monday, Jim .... (615) 552-1808
Religion ED, Leaf-Chronicle, Clarksville, TN
Mondesire, J Whyatt .... (215) 848-7864
PUB, ED
Philadelphia Sunday Sun, Philadelphia, PA
Mondragon, Diane .... (719) 589-2553
ADV MGR-CLASS
Valley Courier, Alamosa, CO
Monegain, Bernie .... (207) 729-3311
City ED, Times Record, Brunswick, ME
Moneo, Mitch .... (604) 642-5752
ED, Sooke Mirror, Sooke, BC
Monette, Gerard .... (514) 285-7272
Librarian, La Presse, Montreal, QC
Money, Jennifer .... (919) 419-6500
EDU ED, Herald-Sun, Durham, NC
Money, Mike .... (501) 271-3700
MGR-MKTG & PROM
Benton County Daily Record, Bentonville, AR
Money, Steve .... (404) 521-1227
CONT, Daily Report, Atlanta, GA
Monfort, Michelle .... (305) 294-6641
Entertainment/Amusements ED, Television/Film ED, Key West Citizen, Key West, FL
Mong, Robert W .... (502) 926-0123
PUB, Owensboro Messenger-Inquirer, Owensboro, KY
Mongelluzzo, Bill .... (212) 837-7000
BU Chief-Los Angeles/Long Beach, Journal of Commerce & Commercial, New York, NY
Mongenais, Jean .... (519) 948-4139
PUB, ED, Le Rempart, Tecumseh, ON
Monico, Nickolas .... (419) 522-3311
PUB, News Journal, Mansfield, OH
Monigan, Thomas J .... (707) 263-5636
MAN ED
Lake County Record-Bee, Lakeport, CA
Monihan, J Brian .... (503) 357-3181
PUB
Forest Grove News Times, Forest Grove, OR
Monk, Bob .... (318) 256-3495
ED, Sabine Index, Many, LA

Copyright ©1997 by the Editor & Publisher Co.

161-Who's Where **Moo**

Monk, Bobbe .... (909) 797-9101
ED, Yucaipa & Calimesa News-Mirror, Yucaipa, CA
Monk, Catherine .... (910) 997-3111
Society/Women's ED, Richmond County Daily Journal, Rockingham, NC
Monk, Katherine .... (604) 732-2111
Music Critic-Rock
Vancouver Sun, Vancouver, BC
Monmaney, Terence .... (213) 237-5000
Medical Writer
Los Angeles Times, Los Angeles, CA
Monopoli, Joy P .... (804) 978-7200
ADV MGR-Sales
Daily Progress, Charlottesville, VA
Monopoli, William V .... (810) 985-7171
PRES, PUB, Times Herald, Port Huron, MI
Monos, Jeannette .... (916) 885-5656
ADV MGR-CLASS
Auburn Journal, Auburn, CA
Monroe, Bryan .... (408) 920-5000
ASST MAN ED-Graphics
San Jose Mercury News, San Jose, CA
Monroe, Jim .... (903) 583-2124
SEC/TREAS, Favorite, Bonham, TX
Monroe, Jim .... (918) 696-2228
ED, Stilwell Democrat Journal, Stilwell, OK
Monroe, Linda .... (908) 722-8800
ASST MAN ED
Courier-News, Bridgewater, NJ
Monroe, Prentice .... (919) 834-5558
PUB, ED, Carolinian, Raleigh, NC
Monroe, Rick .... (619) 724-3075
PUB, ED, Good News Etc., Vista, CA
Monscour, Michael J .... (716) 232-7100
PROD VP, Rochester Democrat and Chronicle; Times-Union, Rochester, NY
Monson, Alvin L .... (320) 235-1150
PROD FRM-PR
West Central Tribune, Willmar, MN
Monsour, Paul .... (502) 333-5545
ED, Sturgis News, Sturgis, KY
Montague, Gary .... (509) 663-5161
ADV MGR-CLASS
Wenatchee World, Wenatchee, WA
Montaigne, Fen .... (215) 854-2000
Outdoors Writer
Philadelphia Inquirer, Philadelphia, PA
Montalbano, William D .... (213) 237-5000
London BU
Los Angeles Times, Los Angeles, CA
Montali Jr, Larry .... (619) 490-8266
ED, Southern Cross, San Diego, CA
Montana, Freddy .... (918) 256-6422
CIRC MGR, Daily Journal, Vinita, OK
Montavon, Bruce A .... (812) 275-3355
ADV MGR-CLASS, Times-Mail, Bedford, IN
Montclare, Louise .... (914) 965-4000
ED
Yonkers Home News & Times, Yonkers, NY
Monte, Richard Dal .... (604) 525-6397
ED, Sunday News, Port Coquitlam, BC
Montebello, George .... (516) 843-2020
PROD MGR-COMP/Platemaking
Newsday, Melville, NY
Monteiro, Liz .... (519) 894-2231
Multicultural Reporter
Record, Kitchener, ON
Monteleone, Patricia .... (913) 371-4300
CONT, Kansas City Kansan, Kansas City, KS
Montemurro, Ronald J .... (414) 657-1000
VP, ASST TREAS
Kenosha News, Kenosha, WI
Montes, Jennifer .... (770) 382-4545
ADV MGR-RT
Daily Tribune News, Cartersville, GA
Montes, Tamara M .... (505) 546-2611
PUB, Deming Headlight, Deming, NM
Montgomery, Adrianne .... (315) 470-0011
City ED, Post-Standard/Syracuse Herald-Journal/American, Syracuse, NY
Montgomery, Barb .... (313) 994-6989
ADV MGR-RT NTL/Co-op
Ann Arbor News, Ann Arbor, MI
Montgomery, Dan .... (757) 247-4600
State ED, Daily Press, Newport News, VA
Montgomery, Dave .... (817) 390-7400
Senior ED-News
Fort Worth Star-Telegram, Fort Worth, TX
Montgomery, Diana .... (617) 631-7701
ED, Marblehead Reporter, Marblehead, MA
Montgomery, Donna .... (770) 532-1234
ADV MGR-RT, Times, Gainesville, GA
Montgomery, Ed .... (405) 321-1800
EPE, Norman Transcript, Norman, OK
Montgomery, Grace E .... (405) 527-2126
GM, Purcell Register, Purcell, OK
Montgomery, Gregg .... (317) 598-6397
News ED, Daily Ledger, Noblesville, IN
Montgomery, Janet .... (307) 367-2123
ED, Pinedale Roundup, Pinedale, WY
Montgomery, John .... (419) 238-2285
PROD Computer SYS Administrator
Times-Bulletin, Van Wert, OH
Montgomery, John D .... (913) 242-4700
PRES, PUB, PA, ED, EPE
Ottawa Herald, Ottawa, KS
Montgomery Jr, John D .... (405) 527-2126
PUB, ED, Purcell Register, Purcell, OK
Montgomery, John Grey .... (913) 762-5000
PRES, PUB, ED
Daily Union, Junction City, KS
Montgomery, Marie .... (310) 540-5511
School/EDU ED, Daily Breeze, Torrance, CA
Montgomery, Mary .... (773) 252-3534
PUB, ED
Wicker Park/West Town Extra, Chicago, IL
Montgomery, Mary Lou .... (573) 221-2800
News ED, Courier-Post, Hannibal, MO
Montgomery, Mauri .... (806) 364-2030
ADV MGR, Hereford Brand, Hereford, TX
Montgomery, Melissa .... (419) 352-4611
PROD MGR-Computer SYS
Sentinel-Tribune, Bowling Green, OH
Montgomery, Patrick .... (800) 536-8442
PRES, Archive Photos, New York, NY
Montgomery, Steven .... (501) 338-9181
PROD MGR, Daily World, Helena, AR
Montgomery, Tiffany .... (562) 498-0707
MAN ED, Signal, Signal Hill, CA
Montgomery, Tom .... (517) 872-2010
ED, Cass City Chronicle, Cass City, MI
Montgomery, W Miller .... (803) 771-0219
PUB, Star-Reporter, Columbia, SC
Monti, Richard .... (412) 224-4321
MAN ED
Valley News Dispatch, Tarentum, PA
Montiel, Jennifer .... (409) 776-4444
Features ED, Eagle, Bryan, TX
Montini, E J .... (602) 271-8000
COL, Arizona Republic, Phoenix, AZ
Montorio, John .... (212) 556-1234
Style ED, New York Times, New York, NY
Montoya, Dolores .... (915) 445-5475
ADV MGR-CLASS
Pecos Enterprise, Pecos, TX
Montoya, Greg .... (303) 778-7900
PUB, ED, Out Front, Denver, CO
Montoya, Julio C .... (312) 522-0288
ED, Momento, Cicero, IL
Montoya, Ramiro .... (210) 728-2500
Lifestyle ED, Teen-Age/Youth ED
Laredo Morning Times, Laredo, TX
Montoya, Rudy .... (719) 846-3311
CIRC DIR, Chronicle-News, Trinidad, CO
Montoya, Sam .... (408) 842-6400
PROD MGR-PR, Dispatch, Gilroy, CA
USMedia Inc. (Central Valley Publishing)
Montri, Ron .... (313) 242-1100
Sports ED
Monroe Evening News, Monroe, MI
Monty, Paula .... (941) 262-3161
ADV MGR-Co-op
Naples Daily News, Naples, FL
Monych, Harry .... (409) 935-2431
PUB, ED, La Marque Times, La Marque, TX
Monzon, Zos .... (202) 636-3000
CIRC MGR
Washington Times, Washington, DC
Moody, B I .... (318) 783-3450
Co-owner, Crowley Post-Signal, Crowley, LA
Moody, Christian .... (540) 389-9355
ED, Salem Times Register, Salem, VA
Moody, James .... (817) 295-0486
PUB, ED, Burleson Star, Burleson, TX
Moody, John .... (903) 572-1705
ASST MAN ED, Mount Pleasant Daily Tribune, Mount Pleasant, TX
Moody, Linda .... (937) 548-3151
Lifestyle ED, Daily Advocate, Greenville, OH
Moody, Mary .... (713) 220-7171
Suburban ED
Houston Chronicle, Houston, TX
Moody, Richard M .... (307) 634-3361
PROD DIR
Wyoming Tribune-Eagle, Cheyenne, WY
Moody, Robert K .... (541) 382-1811
VP, Bulletin, Bend, OR
Western Communications Inc.
Moody, Walter T .... (401) 849-3300
Sports ED, Newport Daily News, Newport, RI
Moon, Craig .... (615) 259-8000
PRES/PUB, Tennessean, Nashville, TN
Moon, Don .... (519) 822-4310
PROD FRM-PR, Daily Mercury, Guelph, ON
Moon, Elane .... (937) 592-3060
ADV MGR-GEN
Bellefontaine Examiner, Bellefontaine, OH
Moon, Jean .... (410) 730-3620
GM, Columbia Flier, Columbia, MD
Moon, Linda .... (801) 237-2800
ADV MGR-CLASS/Inside Sales
Newspaper Agency Corp., Salt Lake City, UT
Moon, Roger .... (812) 275-3355
Farm ED, NTL ED, News ED
Times-Mail, Bedford, IN
Moon, Roxanne .... (409) 985-5541
BM, Port Arthur News, Port Arthur, TX
Moon, Tom .... (215) 854-2000
Music Critic-Popular
Philadelphia Inquirer, Philadelphia, PA
Mooney, Bill .... (610) 696-1775
News ED
Daily Local News, West Chester, PA
Mooney III, Burgett H .... (706) 629-2231
PUB, Calhoun Times and Gordon County News, Calhoun, GA
Mooney, Caroline Bodle .... (317) 742-2050
MAN ED, Catholic Moment, Lafayette, IN
Mooney, Charles .... (817) 840-2091
PUB, ED, McGregor Mirror & Crawford Sun, McGregor, TX
Mooney, Donna .... (501) 534-3400
Political/Government ED
Pine Bluff Commercial, Pine Bluff, AR
Mooney, Eileen W .... (413) 528-3020
ED, Berkshire Courier, Great Barrington, MA
Mooney, John W P .... (413) 528-3020
PUB, Berkshire Courier, Great Barrington, MA
Mooney, Randy .... (412) 224-4321
ADV DIR
Valley News Dispatch, Tarentum, PA
Mooney, Robert P .... (605) 886-6901
City ED
Watertown Public Opinion, Watertown, SD
Moore, Acel .... (215) 854-2000
ASSOC ED
Philadelphia Inquirer, Philadelphia, PA
Moore, Alexis .... (215) 854-2000
EDL Writer
Philadelphia Inquirer, Philadelphia, PA
Moore, Bill .... (817) 325-4465
ADV MGR-PROM
Mineral Wells Index, Mineral Wells, TX
Moore, Bill .... (916) 321-1000
Forum ED, Sacramento Bee, Sacramento, CA
Moore, Billy .... (919) 527-3191
ADV DIR, Free Press, Kinston, NC
Moore, Bob .... (423) 581-5630
Conservation ED, Farm ED, Health/Medical ED, Citizen Tribune, Morristown, TN
Moore, Bob .... (501) 836-8192
GM, Camden News, Camden, AR
Moore, Brian .... (601) 961-7000
Entertainment ED
Clarion-Ledger, Jackson, MS
Moore, C A .... (816) 679-6127
ED, News-Xpress, Butler, MO
Moore, Capri .... (541) 672-3321
Librarian, News-Review, Roseburg, OR
Moore, Carrie .... (801) 237-2188
Religion ED
Deseret News, Salt Lake City, UT
Moore, Catherine .... (518) 891-2600
PUB, ADV DIR, Adirondack Daily Enterprise, Saranac Lake, NY
Moore, Chris .... (541) 889-5387
EPE, EDL Writer, Political ED
Argus Observer, Ontario, OR
Moore, Christine .... (541) 276-2211
ADV MGR-Sales, ADV MGR-RT, ADV MGR-CLASS, East Oregonian, Pendleton, OR
Moore, Christine .... (619) 367-3577
GM, Desert Trail, Twenty-nine Palms, CA
Moore, Christopher .... (908) 464-1025
ED, Independent Press, New Providence, NJ
Moore, Christopher L .... (703) 437-5886
MAN ED, Observer, Herndon, VA
Moore, Christy .... (817) 325-4465
Lifestyle ED
Mineral Wells Index, Mineral Wells, TX
Moore, Cindy J .... (405) 247-3331
ADV MGR
Anadarko Daily News, Anadarko, OK
Moore, Colin .... (702) 882-2111
PROD SUPV-COMP
Nevada Appeal, Carson City, NV
Moore, Dan W .... (519) 762-2310
PUB, Dutton Advance, Dutton, ON
Moore, David .... (205) 586-3188
ED, Arab Tribune, Arab, AL
Moore, David .... (417) 652-3828
PUB, ED, Wheaton Journal, Wheaton, MO
Moore, Debra .... (213) 229-5300
CIRC MGR
Los Angeles Daily Journal, Los Angeles, CA
Daily Journal Corp.
Moore, Delores .... (408) 920-5000
ASST to PUB
San Jose Mercury News, San Jose, CA
Moore, Dennis .... (703) 276-3400
Television ED, USA Today, Arlington, VA
Moore, Diane .... (309) 833-2114
CIRC MGR, Macomb Journal, Macomb, IL
Moore, Dolores .... (419) 294-2332
Fashion/Style ED, Food/Home ED, Librarian, Radio/Television ED, Religion ED, Women's ED, Daily Chief-Union, Upper Sandusky, OH
Moore, Don .... (512) 258-4127
PUB, Hill Country News, Cedar Park, TX
Moore Sr, Earl F .... (614) 272-5422
PUB, Eastside Messenger, Columbus, OH
Moore, Emile .... (605) 542-4831
ED, Elkton Record, Elkton, SD
Moore, Erin .... (504) 732-2565
Teen-Age/Youth ED
Daily News, Bogalusa, LA
Moore, Ernest .... (715) 561-3405
PUB, ED, Iron County Miner, Hurley, WI
Moore, Felicia .... (816) 234-4141
Librarian, Kansas City Star, Kansas City, MO
Moore III, G B .... (912) 986-3929
PUB, Jones County News, Gray, GA
Moore, Gail .... (205) 325-2222
DIR-Human Resources
Birmingham News, Birmingham, AL
Moore, Gary .... (619) 299-3131
DIR-Advertising
San Diego Union-Tribune, San Diego, CA
Moore, Gary .... (412) 523-6588
PROD Press
Standard Observer, Greensburg, PA
Moore, Gary .... (408) 637-5566
DP MGR, Free Lance, Hollister, CA
Moore, Gary B .... (910) 888-3500
GM, High Point Enterprise, High Point, NC
Moore, George W .... (317) 482-4650
MAN ED, BUS/FIN ED, EPE
Reporter, Lebanon, IN
Moore, Glenn .... (614) 283-4711
PROD FRM-PR
Herald-Star, Steubenville, OH
Moore, Grace .... (606) 573-4510
Photo ED
Harlan Daily Enterprise, Harlan, KY
Moore, Grace .... (315) 789-3333
PROD FRM-COMP
Finger Lakes Times, Geneva, NY
Moore, Greg .... (210) 227-8300
MAN ED
San Antonio Informer, San Antonio, TX
Moore, Gregory L .... (617) 929-2000
MAN ED, Boston Globe, Boston, MA
Moore, H William .... (216) 999-4500
DIR-OPER, PROD DIR-OPER
Plain Dealer, Cleveland, OH
Moore, Harold .... (919) 419-6500
Photo DEPT MGR, Herald-Sun, Durham, NC
Moore, Heather .... (902) 838-2515
ED, Eastern Graphic, Montague, PEI
Moore, Horace .... (205) 921-3104
PUB, Journal Record, Hamilton, AL
Moore, James .... (541) 265-7287
PUB, ED, News Guard, Lincoln City, OR
Moore, James E .... (406) 322-5212
PUB, Stillwater County News, Columbus, MT
Moore, Jareta .... (501) 534-3400
BM, Pine Bluff Commercial, Pine Bluff, AR
Moore, Jean .... (505) 823-7777
Presentation (Design & Copydesk)
Albuquerque Tribune, Albuquerque, NM
Moore, Jeff .... (540) 523-1141
GM, MAN ED, Post, Big Stone Gap, VA
Moore, John .... (805) 781-7800
Online Contact
Telegram-Tribune, San Luis Obispo, CA
Moore, John L .... (717) 286-5671
EPE, Daily Item, Sunbury, PA
Moore, John S .... (915) 392-2551
PUB, Ozona Stockman, Ozona, TX
Moore, Kate .... (201) 646-4000
RE ED, Record, Hackensack, NJ
Moore, Kate .... (517) 629-3984
GM, ADV MGR, Albion Recorder, Albion, MI
Moore, Kathy .... (402) 475-4200
Features Reporter
Lincoln Journal Star, Lincoln, NE
Moore, Kay .... (208) 678-2201
Photo DEPT, PROD SUPT
South Idaho Press, Burley, ID
Moore, Keith .... (417) 683-4181
ED, Douglas County Herald, Ava, MO
Moore, Ken .... (941) 262-3161
Travel ED, Naples Daily News, Naples, FL
Moore, Kevin .... (312) 222-3232
Friday Section ED
Chicago Tribune, Chicago, IL
Moore, Kimberly .... (909) 889-9666
PROD MGR-Camera/Plate
Sun, San Bernardino, CA
Moore, Lauren .... (519) 255-5711
COL-Auto, Windsor Star, Windsor, ON
Moore, Lee .... (904) 252-1511
MAN ED-OPER, Daytona Beach News-Journal, Daytona Beach, FL
Moore, Lillie .... (423) 581-5630
Religion ED, Citizen Tribune, Morristown, TN
Moore, Linda .... (215) 854-2000
COL-Op-Ed, Daily News, Philadelphia, PA
Moore, Linda .... (915) 392-2551
ED, Ozona Stockman, Ozona, TX

Moo Who's Where-162

Moore, Rev John F (508) 675-7151
ED, Anchor, Fall River, MA

Moore, Mardy (816) 646-2411
BM, Constitution-Tribune, Chillicothe, MO

Moore, Marlene (519) 762-2310
ED, Dutton Advance, Dutton, ON

Moore, Michael (419) 294-2332
BUS/FIN ED, Features ED, Graphics ED/Art DIR, Daily Chief-Union, Upper Sandusky, OH

Moore, Michael D (218) 945-6120
PUB, ED, Fertile Journal, Fertile, MN

Moore, Michelle (919) 553-7234
ED, Clayton News-Star, Clayton, NC

Moore, Michelle A (219) 824-0224
CONT, News-Banner, Bluffton, IN

Moore, Milton (916) 891-1234
ADV DIR, Chico Enterprise-Record, Chico, CA
Donrey Media Group

Moore, Mona (609) 272-7000
Community ED
Press of Atlantic City, Pleasantville, NJ

Moore, Nancy (540) 374-5000
ASST MAN ED
Free Lance-Star, Fredericksburg, VA

Moore, Nancy (704) 864-3291
BUS ED, NTL ED, RE ED
Gaston Gazette, Gastonia, NC

Moore, Pat (312) 321-3000
Consumer Products/Labor
Chicago Sun-Times, Chicago, IL

Moore, Patty (606) 564-9091
ADV MGR
Ledger Independent, Maysville, KY

Moore, Paul (250) 762-4445
DIR-MKTG, Daily Courier, Kelowna, BC

Moore, Paul (410) 332-6000
Weekend ED, Sun, Baltimore, MD

Moore, Paula (915) 546-6100
MAN ED, El Paso Times, El Paso, TX

Moore, Rick (904) 312-5200
EX ED, Daily News, Palatka, FL

Moore, Robert (508) 458-7100
PROD MGR, Sun, Lowell, MA

Moore, Robert (214) 754-8710
PUB, Dallas Voice, Dallas, TX

Moore, Robert J (217) 446-1000
CONT, Commercial News, Danville, IL

Moore, Roger (910) 727-7211
Films/Theater ED
Winston-Salem Journal, Winston-Salem, NC

Moore, Roger K (518) 792-9914
VP-OPER/EX ED, TV Data, Queensbury, NY

Moore, Sandy (317) 529-1111
ADV MGR-CLASS
Courier-Times, New Castle, IN

Moore, Scott (909) 628-5501
MAN ED, Chino Champion, Chino, CA

Moore, Shirley (316) 421-2000
SEC/TREAS, Parsons Sun, Parsons, KS

Moore, Tasi (912) 986-3929
ED, Jones County News, Gray, GA

Moore, Terri (419) 784-5441
ADV MGR-CLASS
Crescent-News, Defiance, OH

Moore, Terry (310) 540-5511
Home Furnishings ED, Daily Breeze, Torrance, CA, Copley Press Inc.

Moore, Thomas J (606) 365-2104
PUB, ED, Interior Journal, Stanford, KY

Moore, Tina (417) 652-3828
PUB, Wheaton Journal, Wheaton, MO

Moore, Tom (704) 358-5000
CIRC MGR-Office
Charlotte Observer, Charlotte, NC

Moore, Tom (201) 383-1500
Friday/Day ED
New Jersey Herald, Newton, NJ

Moore, Tommy (210) 227-8300
PUB, San Antonio Informer, San Antonio, TX

Moore, Travis (503) 843-2312
MAN ED, Sun, Sheridan, OR

Moore, Troy (904) 252-1511
ASST MAN ED, Graphics ED/ASST MAN ED
Daytona Beach News-Journal, Daytona Beach, FL

Moore, Vicky (573) 624-4545
CIRC DIR, Daily Statesman, Dexter, MO

Moore III, Virgil E (817) 559-5412
PUB, American, Breckenridge, TX

Moore, Virginia (210) 227-8300
ED, San Antonio Informer, San Antonio, TX

Moore, William E (614) 472-1631
PUB, ED
Monroe County Sentinel, Woodsfield, OH

Moore-Yount, Jeanne (814) 724-6370
PUB/GM, Meadville Tribune, Meadville, PA

Moorehouse, Buddy (517) 548-2000
MAN ED
Livingston County Press, Howell, MI

Moorehouse, Melody A (501) 942-2142
PUB, ED, Sheridan Headlight, Sheridan, AR

Moore II, James E (406) 446-2222
PUB, Carbon County News, Red Lodge, MT

Moores, Anne (506) 452-6671
ASST MAN ED, Book Page ED, Front Page ED, Daily Gleaner, Fredericton, NB

Moores, John (709) 634-4348
ADV MGR, DIR-MKTG
Western Star, Corner Brook, NF

Moores, W Scott (410) 332-6000
CIRC ASST DIR-MKTG, Sun, Baltimore, MD

Moorhead, Cindy (419) 422-5151
Living/Lifestyle ED, Television/Film ED, Theater/Music ED, Travel ED
Courier, Findlay, OH

Moorhead, Ron C (707) 459-6027
GM
Glenmoor Enterprise Media Group, Willits, CA

Moorhead, Stacey (417) 256-9191
CIRC MGR
West Plains Daily Quill, West Plains, MO

Moorhouse, Virginia F (805) 395-7500
PUB/COB
Bakersfield Californian, Bakersfield, CA

Moorman, Carol (320) 352-6577
ED, Sauk Centre Herald, Sauk Centre, MN

Moormann, David D (616) 423-2411
PUB, ED, Decatur Republican, Decatur, MI

Moormann, Donald (616) 646-2101
PUB, ED, Marcellus News, Marcellus, MI

Moors, Nancy (408) 761-7300
ADV DIR
Register-Pajaronian, Watsonville, CA

Moos, Bob (214) 977-8222
Viewpoints Page ED
Dallas Morning News, Dallas, TX

Moosbrugger, Ed (310) 829-6811
BUS ED, RE ED, Outlook, Santa Monica, CA

Moose, Debbie (919) 829-4500
Food ED, News & Observer, Raleigh, NC

Moosman, Rosa S (208) 847-0552
GM, ED, News-Examiner, Montpelier, ID

Moote, Nancy (604) 886-7077
ED, Gibsons Coastlife, Gibsons, BC

Morabito, Jack (216) 999-4500
PROD FRM-MR, Plain Dealer, Cleveland, OH

Moraga, Frank (805) 650-2900
BUS/FIN ED
Ventura County Star, Ventura, CA

Morain, Frederick G (515) 386-4161
PUB, ED, Bee, Jefferson, IA

Morales, Angel (213) 881-6515
ED, Novedades, Los Angeles, CA

Morales, Betty (408) 295-4272
PUB, El Observador, San Jose, CA

Morales, Hilbert (408) 295-4272
PUB, El Observador, San Jose, CA

Morales, Reinaldo (703) 527-7860
GM, El Tiempo Latino, Arlington, VA

Moran, Dan (708) 336-7000
Television/Film ED, Theater/Music ED
News-Sun, Waukegan, IL

Moran, David (713) 477-0221
DP MGR, Pasadena Citizen, Pasadena, TX

Moran, Kay (413) 584-5000
EPE, Religion ED
Daily Hampshire Gazette, Northampton, MA

Moran, Kevin (518) 270-1200
Sports ED, Record, Troy, NY

Moran, Michael (617) 929-2000
PROD GEN FRM-PR (Billerica)
Boston Globe, Boston, MA

Moran, Patrick (315) 792-5000
DIR-Human Resources
Observer-Dispatch, Utica, NY

Moran, Robert (805) 781-7800
CIRC MGR-Zone
Telegram-Tribune, San Luis Obispo, CA

Moran, Shelly (501) 982-6506
PRES, ADV MGR, Patriot, Jacksonville, AR

Moran, Tim (209) 578-2000
Consumer Writer, Modesto Bee, Modesto, CA

Moran, Tom (201) 646-4000
EDU ED, Record, Hackensack, NJ

Morassut, Enrico (514) 328-2062
PUB, GM, Insieme, Montreal-North, QC

Morden, Beverley A (416) 445-6641
PRES-Southam Show Group (Southex Exhibitions), Southam Inc., Don Mills, ON

Moreau, Joanne (905) 358-5711
PROD DIR-Art, Review, Niagara Falls, ON

Moreau, Ron (401) 277-7000
ADV Sales DIR-RE
Providence Journal-Bulletin, Providence, RI

Morel, Nick (701) 225-8111
PROD FRM-PR
Dickinson Press, Dickinson, ND

Moreland, Pamela (415) 883-8600
Lifestyle ED
Marin Independent Journal, Novato, CA

Moreland, Scott (908) 349-3000
CIRC DIR
Ocean County Observer, Toms River, NJ

Morelli, Chris (814) 765-5581
Sports ED, Progress, Clearfield, PA

Morelli, Steve (607) 798-1234
Sunday ED
Press & Sun Bulletin, Binghamton, NY

Morena, Richard T (908) 922-6000
VP-FIN, New Jersey Press Inc., Neptune, NJ

Moreno, Cherie (415) 872-3000
MAN ED
Philippine News, South San Francisco, CA

Moreno, Joel (209) 634-9141
BUS/FIN ED, City ED
Turlock Journal, Turlock, CA

Moreno, Julie (505) 763-3431
PUB, Clovis News Journal, Clovis, NM

Moreno, T (209) 722-1511
PROD MGR-Pre Press
Merced Sun-Star, Merced, CA

Moreno, Tony (217) 235-5656
CIRC DIR
Mattoon Journal-Gazette, Mattoon, IL

Morenz, Delbert C (712) 688-2216
PUB, ED, Auburn Enterprise & Tri-County Special, Auburn, IA

Mores, Alan (712) 755-3111
PUB, News-Advertiser, Harlan, IA

Mores, Leo (712) 755-3111
PUB, News-Advertiser, Harlan, IA

Mores, Steven (712) 755-3111
PUB, News-Advertiser, Harlan, IA

Morey, Bill (219) 235-6161
PROD MGR-Facilities
South Bend Tribune, South Bend, IN

Morf, Marianne (515) 357-2131
ED, Clear Lake Reporter, Clear Lake, IA

Morford, Mary Ann (605) 852-2927
PUB, ED, Highmore Herald, Highmore, SD

Morgan, Arlane (215) 854-2000
ASST MAN ED
Philadelphia Inquirer, Philadelphia, PA

Morgan, Barbara (206) 455-2222
ED/VP-News, Eastside Journal, Bellevue, WA

Morgan, Bob (804) 385-5400
BUS ED, City ED, EDU ED
News & Advance, Lynchburg, VA

Morgan, Buddy (502) 827-2000
PROD MGR, Gleaner, Henderson, KY

Morgan, Cindy (515) 684-4611
ADV MGR-CLASS
Ottumwa Courier, Ottumwa, IA

Morgan, Colleen (316) 421-2000
EDU Reporter, Parsons Sun, Parsons, KS

Morgan, DeSales (304) 788-3333
PROD MGR-PR
Mineral Daily News-Tribune, Keyser, WV

Morgan, Diana (918) 825-3292
ADV DIR, Daily Times, Pryor, OK

Morgan, Donnie (301) 862-2111
MAN ED, Enterprise, Lexington Park, MD

Morgan, Duane (717) 637-3736
PROD SUPV-Post Press
Evening Sun, Hanover, PA

Morgan, Elaine (502) 926-0123
ADV MGR-Display
Messenger-Inquirer, Owensboro, KY

Morgan, Ione (412) 375-6611
ED, News, Aliquippa, PA

Morgan, James (334) 335-3541
GM, Luverne Journal, Luverne, AL

Morgan, Jan (573) 722-5322
ED, Advance Statesman, Advance, MO

Morgan, Janet Blackmon (919) 492-4001
Photo DEPT MGR
Henderson Daily Dispatch, Henderson, NC

Morgan, Jerry (304) 425-8191
GM, Princeton Times, Princeton, WV

Morgan, Jim (218) 736-7511
PUB
Fergus Falls Daily Journal, Fergus Falls, MN

Morgan, John (617) 482-9447
VP-News & Photo Services
BPI Entertainment News Wire, Boston, MA

Morgan, John (608) 221-1544
GM, Community Life, Monona, WI

Morgan, Judy (409) 564-8361
COL, Daily Sentinel, Nacogdoches, TX

Morgan, Laura (213) 237-5000
CIRC DIR-Communications
Los Angeles Times, Los Angeles, CA

Morgan, Lee (609) 663-6000
ADTX MGR, Courier-Post, Cherry Hill, NJ

Morgan, Lucy (813) 893-8111
ASSOC ED
St. Petersburg Times, St. Petersburg, FL

Morgan, Melissa (573) 336-3711
BM, Daily Guide, Waynesville, MO

Morgan, Miriam (415) 348-4321
Food ED
San Mateo County Times, San Mateo, CA

Morgan, Neil (619) 299-3131
ASSOC ED/Senior COL
San Diego Union-Tribune, San Diego, CA

Morgan, Neil (606) 248-1010
Sports ED, Daily News, Middlesboro, KY

Morgan, Pat (561) 820-4100
Features ED
Palm Beach Post, West Palm Beach, FL

Morgan, Pat (702) 383-0211
Food ED
Las Vegas Review-Journal, Las Vegas, NV

Morgan, Patricia (812) 268-6356
BM, Sullivan Daily Times, Sullivan, IN

Morgan, Paul (208) 467-9251
Sports ED, Idaho Press-Tribune, Nampa, ID

Morgan, Richard (412) 543-1303
PROD FRM-COMP
Leader Times, Kittanning, PA

Morgan Jr, Robert L (516) 294-8900
PUB, Garden City News, Garden City, NY

Morgan Jr, Robert (757) 446-2000
ADV MGR-Display, ADV MGR-Regional Sales
Virginian-Pilot, Norfolk, VA

Morgan, Ron (317) 633-1240
ADV DIR-OPER
Indianapolis Star/News, Indianapolis, IN

Morgan, Ron (615) 626-3222
ED, Claiborne Progress, Tazewell, TN

Morgan, Shannon (510) 339-4060
ED, Journal, El Cerrito, CA

Morgan, Shirley (813) 896-2922
ED, Weekly Challenger, St. Petersburg, FL

Morgan, Stanley (912) 283-2244
CIRC MGR
Waycross Journal-Herald, Waycross, GA

Morgan, Valerie H Y (404) 526-5151
City Life ED
Atlanta Journal-Constitution, Atlanta, GA

Morgan, Vicki (501) 378-3400
PROD MGR-COMP
Arkansas Democrat-Gazette, Little Rock, AR

Morgan, William (505) 437-7120
City ED
Alamogordo Daily News, Alamogordo, NM

Morgan, William A (405) 452-3294
PUB, ED
Hughes County Times, Wetumka, OK

Morgan, Willy (212) 837-7000
PUB, Journal of Commerce & Commercial, New York, NY

Morgan-Prager, Karole (916) 321-1855
SEC/GEN Counsel
McClatchy Newspapers, Sacramento, CA

Morganthaler, Jim (201) 309-1200
EX DIR/News
ESPN/SportsTicker, Jersey City, NJ

Morgenstern, Barbara G (716) 427-2434
PUB, ED, Jewish Ledger, Rochester, NY

Morgnanesi, Lanny (215) 345-3000
EX ED, Intelligencer/Record, Doylestown, PA

Moriarty, Dan (702) 788-6200
CIRC MGR-Sales/MKTG
Reno Gazette-Journal, Reno, NV

Moriarty, Jeff (707) 546-2020
Online Contact
Press Democrat, Santa Rosa, CA

Moriarty, Jo-Ann (413) 788-1000
Washington BU
Union-News, Springfield, MA

Moriarty, Mary Beth (616) 469-1100
PUB, ED
New Buffalo Times, New Buffalo, MI

Moriarty, Wayne (403) 429-5400
Sports ED, Edmonton Journal, Edmonton, AB

Moriguchi, Tomro (206) 624-4169
PUB, Northwest Nikkei, Seattle, WA

Morilak, Mark (216) 524-0830
ED, Sun Messenger, Cleveland, OH

Morimitsu, Art (773) 478-6170
ED, Chicago Shimpo, Chicago, IL

Morin Sr, Earl M (713) 869-5434
PUB Emeritus
Daily Court Review, Houston, TX

Morin Jr, Earl Milton (713) 869-5434
PUB/ED, Daily Court Review, Houston, TX

Morin, Jean (418) 723-4800
ED, Le Rimouskois, Rimouski, QC

Morin, Jim (305) 350-2111
Cartoonist, Miami Herald, Miami, FL

Morin, Richard R J (540) 574-6200
GM, PA, ED, Travel ED
Daily News-Record, Harrisonburg, VA

Morinville, Nancy (541) 296-2141
PROD SUPT
Dalles Daily Chronicle, The Dalles, OR

Morita, Lisa (213) 237-5000
ADV DIR-MKTG/Planning
Los Angeles Times, Los Angeles, CA

Moritsugu, John (212) 416-2000
BU MGR-Toronto
Wall Street Journal, New York, NY

Moritz, Bert (605) 532-3654
PUB, Clark County Courier, Clark, SD

Moritz, David (605) 532-3654
PUB, Clark County Courier, Clark, SD

Moritz, Jim (605) 598-6525
PUB, ED, Faulk County Record, Faulkton, SD

Moritz, Jody (605) 598-6525
PUB, Faulk County Record, Faulkton, SD

Copyright ©1997 by the Editor & Publisher Co.

163-Who's Where **Mos**

Mork, Karen ..... (419) 625-5500
Church ED, School ED
Sandusky Register, Sandusky, OH

Morlan, Frank ..... (515) 342-2131
PUB, ED, Sentinel-Tribune, Osceola, IA

Morlan, Michael ..... (515) 284-8000
PROD MGR-Pre Press
Des Moines Register, Des Moines, IA

Morlan, Sally T ..... (515) 342-2131
PUB, Osceola Sentinel-Tribune, Osceola, IA

Morley, Chuck ..... (912) 825-2432
GM, ED, Leader-Tribune, Fort Valley, GA

Morley, Cindy ..... (912) 825-2432
ED, Adel News-Tribune, Fort Valley, GA

Morlock, Jerry ..... (616) 722-3161
City ED, Muskegon Chronicle, Muskegon, MI

Moro, Eric ..... (805) 273-2700
Automotive ED
Antelope Valley Press, Palmdale, CA

Morozoff, Corrie ..... (604) 656-1151
PUB, Peninsula News Review, Sidney, BC

Morra, Bernadette ..... (416) 367-2000
Fashion ED, Toronto Star, Toronto, ON

Morrell, Gene ..... (540) 382-6171
ED, News Messenger, Christiansburg, VA

Morrell, Robert F ..... (912) 244-1880
PUB/GM, Valdosta Daily Times, Valdosta, GA

Morrelle, Bobbie ..... (806) 762-8844
Librarian
Lubbock Avalanche-Journal, Lubbock, TX

Morrill, Christopher ..... (860) 241-6200
Electronic News CNR
Hartford Courant, Hartford, CT

Morris, Amy ..... (507) 285-7600
News ED, Post-Bulletin, Rochester, MN

Morris, Ann ..... (404) 526-5151
Living/Lifestyle ED
Atlanta Journal-Constitution, Atlanta, GA

Morris, Carl R ..... (304) 354-6917
PUB, Calhoun Chronicle, Grantsville, WV

Morris, Charles E ..... (217) 446-1000
PRES, PUB, Commercial News, Danville, IL

Morris, Charles H ..... (912) 233-1281
PRES
Morris Newspaper Corp., Savannah, GA

Morris, Chris ..... (812) 944-6481
Sports ED
Tribune/Ledger & Tribune, New Albany, IN

Morris, Christine ..... (305) 350-2111
ASST MAN ED-Staff Development
Miami Herald, Miami, FL

Morris, Connie ..... (918) 689-5291
PUB, ED, Lake Eufaula World, Eufaula, OK

Morris, Dave ..... (319) 398-8211
Features ED, Food/Garden ED, Lifestyle ED, Youth Plus ED, Gazette, Cedar Rapids, IA

Morris, David ..... (613) 359-5544
PUB, ED, Rideau Review, Elgin, ON

Morris, Diana ..... (304) 348-5140
DP MGR, Charleston Gazette, Sunday Gazette-Mail, Charleston, WV

Morris, Doug ..... (423) 457-2515
PUB, ED, Courier-News, Clinton, TN

Morris, Edwin C ..... (803) 874-3137
PUB, ED, Calhoun Times, St. Matthews, SC

Morris, Gene O ..... (308) 345-4500
PUB, McCook Daily Gazette, McCook, NE

Morris, Greg ..... (317) 636-0200
ADV DIR
Court & Commercial Record, Indianapolis, IN

Morris, Gregg K ..... (315) 536-4422
PUB
Penn Yan Chronicle-Express, Penn Yan, NY

Morris, H Allen ..... (803) 761-6397
PUB, ED
Berkeley Independent, Moncks Corner, SC

Morris, J A H ..... (613) 774-2524
PUB, GM, Winchester Press, Winchester, ON

Morris, Jan ..... (904) 547-9414
ED, Holmes County Times, Bonifay, FL

Morris, Jeff ..... (515) 832-4350
PROD FRM-Press
Daily Freeman-Journal, Webster City, IA

Morris, Jerry ..... (617) 929-2000
Travel ED, Boston Globe, Boston, MA

Morris, Jim ..... (937) 225-2000
Outdoors ED, Dayton Daily News, Dayton, OH

Morris, Joel ..... (316) 345-6353
ED, Ledger, Moundridge, KS

Morris, John ..... (613) 925-4265
PUB, Prescott Journal, Prescott, ON

Morris, John Tyler ..... (706) 724-0851
DIR-Magazines & Specialized Publications
Morris Communications Corp., Augusta, GA

Morris, Jola ..... (907) 257-4200
CNR-Community Relations
Anchorage Daily News, Anchorage, AK

Morris, Julie ..... (904) 435-8500
MET ED-Day
Pensacola News Journal, Pensacola, FL

Morris, Kathy ..... (405) 922-4296
ED, Vici Beacon News, Seiling, OK

Morris, Kathy ..... (717) 297-3024
GM, Troy Gazette-Register, Troy, PA

Morris, Ken ..... (402) 371-1020
PROD MGR, Norfolk Daily News, Norfolk, NE

Morris, Kevin ..... (812) 231-4200
CIRC MGR-Target MKTG
Tribune-Star, Terre Haute, IN

Morris, Leo ..... (219) 461-8222
EPE, News-Sentinel, Fort Wayne, IN

Morris, Mark ..... (916) 321-1000
Photo DIR, Sacramento Bee, Sacramento, CA

Morris, Michelle ..... (805) 925-2691
Entertainment/Amusements ED, Living/Lifestyle ED, Society/Women's ED
Santa Maria Times, Santa Maria, CA

Morris, Mike ..... (304) 348-5140
ADV MGR-NTL, ADV MGR-Co-op
Charleston Newspapers, Charleston, WV

Morris, Mike ..... (803) 317-6397
Amusements ED, Fashion/Style ED, Lifestyle ED, Theater ED
Florence Morning News, Florence, SC

Morris, Pam ..... (208) 726-8060
PUB, Idaho Mountain Express, Ketchum, ID

Morris, Pancho ..... (915) 546-6100
Sports ED, El Paso Times, El Paso, TX

Morris, Paul ..... (519) 583-0112
GM, Port Dover Maple Leaf, Port Dover, ON

Morris, Phillip ..... (216) 999-4500
ASSOC ED, Plain Dealer, Cleveland, OH

Morris, Ralph W ..... (704) 526-4114
PUB, ED, Highlander, Highlands, NC

Morris, Richard ..... (419) 352-4611
VP, GM
Sentinel-Tribune, Bowling Green, OH

Morris, Robert ..... (501) 673-8533
CIRC MGR
Stuttgart Daily Leader, Stuttgart, AR

Morris, Robert ..... (502) 821-6833
PUB, Messenger, Madisonville, KY

Morris, Robin R ..... (613) 445-3805
PUB, Russell Villager, Russell, ON

Morris, Roger ..... (406) 293-4124
ED, Western News, Libby, MT

Morris, Ron ..... (540) 667-3200
MAN ED, Winchester Star, Winchester, VA

Morris, Scott ..... (205) 353-4612
City ED, Decatur Daily, Decatur, AL

Morris, Stan ..... (519) 583-0112
PUB, Port Dover Maple Leaf, Port Dover, ON

Morris, Susie B ..... (907) 283-7551
PUB, Clarion Dispatch, Kenai, AK

Morris, Terry ..... (937) 225-2000
Theater/Dance ED
Dayton Daily News, Dayton, OH

Morris, Tim ..... (504) 826-3279
Political/Government ED
Times-Picayune, New Orleans, LA

Morris, Tim ..... (309) 829-9411
PROD SUPV-COMP
Pantagraph, Bloomington, IL

Morris, Tom ..... (918) 581-8300
ADV MGR-RT, Tulsa World, Tulsa, OK

Morris, Tony ..... (512) 664-6588
PUB, Alice Echo-News, Alice, TX

Morris, Will ..... (308) 382-1000
PRES, Grand Island Independent, Grand Island, NE, Morris Communications Corp.

Morris III, William S ..... (706) 724-0851
COB/CEO
Morris Communications Corp., Augusta, GA

Morris IV, William S ..... (706) 724-0851
ASST to the PUB
Augusta Chronicle, Augusta, GA

Morris, Willy ..... (510) 758-8400
Environmental ED
West County Times, Pinole, CA

Morrison, Anne ..... (712) 943-4600
ED
Sergeant Bluff Advocate, Sergeant Bluff, IA

Morrison, Annette ..... (615) 259-8000
Librarian, Tennessean, Nashville, TN

Morrison, Ben ..... (717) 622-3456
Photo ED, Pottsville Republican & Evening Herald, Pottsville, PA

Morrison, Bruce ..... (712) 943-4600
PUB
Sergeant Bluff Advocate, Sergeant Bluff, IA

Morrison, Bruce ..... (423) 638-4181
Chief Operating OFF
Media Services Group, Greeneville, TN

Morrison, David ..... (304) 255-4400
Sports ED, Register Herald, Beckley, WV

Morrison, Emily ..... (914) 341-1100
Travel ED
Times Herald-Record, Middletown, NY

Morrison, Jack ..... (250) 762-4445
INFO SRV MGR, Daily Courier, Kelowna, BC

Morrison, James S ..... (320) 589-2525
GM, Morris Sun, Morris, MN

Morrison, Jean M ..... (613) 354-6641
PUB, Napanee Beaver, Napanee, ON

Morrison, Jim ..... (319) 283-2144
MAN ED, Register, Oelwein, IA

Morrison, Joan ..... (918) 684-2828
Farm/Agriculture Reporter, Muskogee Daily Phoenix & Times Democrat, Muskogee, OK

Morrison, Joy ..... (208) 232-4161
Food ED, Women's ED
Idaho State Journal, Pocatello, ID

Morrison, Mark ..... (540) 981-3100
Amusements ED, Features ED
Roanoke Times, Roanoke, VA

Morrison, Mike ..... (912) 265-8320
City ED, Brunswick News, Brunswick, GA

Morrison, Norman ..... (617) 321-8000
DIR, Daily News-Mercury, Malden, MA

Morrison, Pat ..... (812) 254-7322
MAN ED, Hoosier Express, Washington, IN

Morrison, Patricia Lynn ..... (419) 243-4178
GM, ED, Catholic Chronicle, Toledo, OH

Morrison, Patt ..... (213) 237-5000
COL-Local
Los Angeles Times, Los Angeles, CA

Morrison, Penny ..... (519) 376-2250
ADV MGR-CLASS
Sun Times, Owen Sound, ON

Morrison, Rick ..... (317) 342-3311
PA, PROD SUPT
Daily Reporter, Martinsville, IN

Morrison, Scott ..... (416) 947-2222
Sports ED, Toronto Sun, Toronto, ON

Morrison, Shauna ..... (212) 208-8000
EX ED-Market Scope/Daily News, Corporation Records, Daily News, New York, NY

Morrison, Susan ..... (706) 278-1011
Books/Lifestyle ED
Daily Citizen-News, Dalton, GA

Morrison, Teresa ..... (770) 306-2175
GM, Atlanta-News Leader, Union City, GA

Morrison, Warren ..... (903) 886-3196
ED, Commerce Journal, Commerce, TX

Morriss, Jim ..... (501) 751-6200
EX ED, Morning News of Northwest Arkansas, Springdale, AR

Morrissette, Robert A ..... (203) 235-1661
Sports ED, Record-Journal, Meriden, CT

Morrissey, Jake ..... (816) 932-6600
ASSOC ED
Universal Press Syndicate, Kansas City, MO

Morrissey, Paul J ..... (508) 222-7000
ADV DIR, Sun Chronicle, Attleboro, MA

Morrissey, Scot ..... (816) 254-8600
PROD SUPT, Examiner, Independence, MO

Morrissey, Wendy ..... (803) 626-8555
PROD DIR-OPER
Sun News, Myrtle Beach, SC

Morrow, Doug ..... (800) 223-2154
CIRC MGR-NTL Home Delivery
Investor's Business Daily, Los Angeles, CA

Morrow, Hilda ..... (864) 472-9548
ED, Inman Times, Inman, SC

Morrow, Jeff ..... (509) 582-1500
Sports ED, Tri-City Herald, Tri-Cities, WA

Morrow, Mike ..... (615) 259-8000
EDL Writer, Tennessean, Nashville, TN

Morrow, Ralph ..... (305) 294-6641
Sports ED, Key West Citizen, Key West, FL

Morrow, Shayne ..... (604) 723-8171
Sports ED
Alberni Valley Times, Port Alberni, BC

Morrow, Tammy ..... (614) 452-4561
CONT, Times Recorder, Zanesville, OH

Morrow, Terry ..... (423) 428-0746
Entertainment/Amusements ED, Television/Film ED, Theater/Music ED
Mountain Press, Sevierville, TN

Morsch, Mike ..... (217) 788-1300
Senior ED-News
State Journal-Register, Springfield, IL

Morse, David ..... (207) 621-6000
PUB, Capital Weekly, Augusta, ME

Morse, Donna ..... (360) 779-4464
GM, Kitsap County Herald, Poulsbo, WA

Morse, Emily ..... (606) 236-2551
Features ED
Advocate-Messenger, Danville, KY

Morse, Eric ..... (716) 343-8000
BUS/FIN ED, Wire ED
Daily News, Batavia, NY

Morse, Jay ..... (202) 334-6000
VP/CFO
Washington Post Co., Washington, DC

Morse, Joel ..... (414) 733-4411
ADV DIR, Post-Crescent, Appleton, WI

Morse, Kathy ..... (218) 723-5281
CIRC ASST DIR
Duluth News-Tribune, Duluth, MN

Morse, Rob ..... (415) 777-2424
COL
San Francisco Examiner, San Francisco, CA

Morse, Steve ..... (616) 964-7161
News ED
Battle Creek Enquirer, Battle Creek, MI

Morse, Steve ..... (617) 929-2000
Music ED-Contemporary
Boston Globe, Boston, MA

Mort, Denise ..... (406) 791-1444
Books ED
Great Falls Tribune, Great Falls, MT

Mort, Jane ..... (717) 248-6741
Features/Food ED, Sentinel, Lewistown, PA

Mortefolio, Steve ..... (518) 828-1616
ADV DIR, Register-Star, Hudson, NY

Morteith, Melissa ..... (937) 372-4444
ADV MGR, Xenia Daily Gazette, Xenia, OH

Mortensen, Lee ..... (847) 329-2000
PUB, Jefferson Park/Portage Park/Bel-Cragin Times, Lincolnwood, IL

Mortensen, Mike ..... (603) 524-3800
Regional ED, Citizen, Laconia, NH

Mortensen, Svend ..... (403) 250-4200
PROD MGR, Calgary Sun, Calgary, AB

Mortenson, Brian ..... (208) 678-2201
Sports ED, South Idaho Press, Burley, ID

Mortenson, Lee ..... (773) 281-7500
PUB, Lincoln Park/Lake View/Near North/Downtown Skyline, Chicago, IL

Mortimer, William James ..... (801) 237-2188
PRES, PUB/ED
Deseret News, Salt Lake City, UT

Mortimore, Gina ..... (308) 237-2152
ADV DIR, Kearney Hub, Kearney, NE

Morton, Betty ..... (704) 873-1451
ADV MGR-CLASS, Statesville Record & Landmark, Statesville, NC

Morton, Carol ..... (313) 222-6400
Deputy DIR-Free Press Plus-Web Page
Detroit Free Press, Detroit, MI

Morton, Dana ..... (903) 935-7914
BM, Marshall News Messenger, Marshall, TX

Morton, Douglas ..... (905) 468-3283
ED, Niagara Advance, Virgil, ON

Morton, Gary ..... (407) 660-9141
MAN ED, Florida Catholic, Orlando, FL

Morton, Glenn ..... (819) 825-3755
PUB, Val d'Or Star, Val d'Or, QC

Morton, Jeff ..... (330) 296-9657
PROD SUPT
Record-Courier, Kent-Ravenna, OH

Morton, Linda ..... (409) 945-3441
ADV MGR-CLASS
Texas City Sun, Texas City, TX

Morton, Marshall N ..... (804) 649-6000
Sr VP/CFO
Media General Inc., Richmond, VA

Morton, Norman L ..... (910) 739-4322
Political ED, Robesonian, Lumberton, NC

Morton, Randy ..... (912) 764-9031
PUB, Statesboro Herald, Statesboro, GA

Morton, Roger ..... (360) 452-2345
MAN ED, EPE
Peninsula Daily News, Port Angeles, WA

Morva, Abeiardo ..... (201) 864-9505
PUB, Continental Newspaper, Union City, NJ

Morway, Richard ..... (216) 999-4500
TREAS, Plain Dealer, Cleveland, OH

Mosberg, T M ..... (305) 674-9746
ASST ED
International News Agency, Miami Beach, FL

Mosby Jr, James R ..... (616) 345-3511
ED, Kalamazoo Gazette, Kalamazoo, MI

Mosby, Ray ..... (601) 873-4354
PUB, ED, Deer Creek Pilot, Rolling Fork, MS

Moscatelli, Liz ..... (703) 276-3400
CIRC GM-Minneapolis
USA Today, Arlington, VA

Mosco, E ..... (519) 255-5711
ADV MGR-CLASS, Windsor Star, Windsor, ON

Moscowitz, Raymond ..... (317) 473-6641
VP, PUB, Peru Tribune, Peru, IN

Mosel, Janice ..... (402) 893-2535
PUB, ED, Orchard News, Orchard, NE

Moseley, Carol ..... (919) 537-2505
CIRC DIR, Daily Herald, Roanoke Rapids, NC

Moseley, Earl ..... (806) 592-2141
ED, Denver City Press, Denver City, TX

Moseley, Jack ..... (501) 785-7700
ED, EPE, Political/Government ED
Southwest Times Record, Fort Smith, AR

Moseley, John ..... (915) 263-7331
News ED, Big Spring Herald, Big Spring, TX

Mosely, Charles ..... (316) 251-3300
SEC/TREAS
Coffeyville Journal, Coffeyville, KS

Moseman, Gary ..... (406) 791-1444
MAN ED, Great Falls Tribune, Great Falls, MT

Moser, Bob ..... (919) 286-1972
ED, Independent Weekly, Durham, NC

Moser, Charles ..... (409) 836-7956
PRES, PUB, ED, EPE, EDL Writer-Political
Brenham Banner-Press, Brenham, TX

Moser, Dan ..... (402) 475-4200
Entertainment/Features Reporter
Lincoln Journal Star, Lincoln, NE

Moser, Geoffrey L ..... (610) 272-2500
PUB, Times Herald, Norristown, PA

Moser, Gregg A ..... (319) 345-2031
ED, Reinbeck Courier, Reinbeck, IA

Moser, Jack ..... (610) 258-7171
PROD MGR-COMP
Express-Times, Easton, PA

Moser, Jim ..... (713) 232-3737
ADV DIR-RT/CLASS
Herald-Coaster, Rosenberg, TX

Moser, Leroy A ..... (319) 345-2031
PUB, Reinbeck Courier, Reinbeck, IA

Mos Who's Where-164

Moser, Mike (615) 484-5145
ED, Crossville Chronicle, Crossville, TN

Moses, Ellen (941) 748-0411
Schools/EDU ED
Bradenton Herald, Bradenton, FL

Moses, Karen (505) 823-7777
ASST MAN ED
Albuquerque Journal, Albuquerque, NM

Moses, Kaye (208) 785-1100
PUB, ADV DIR, Morning News, Blackfoot, ID

Moses, Michael (860) 225-4601
ADV DIR-MKTG, Herald, New Britain, CT

Moses, Monica (704) 358-5000
Design DIR
Charlotte Observer, Charlotte, NC

Mosesso, David (501) 268-8621
PUB, Daily Citizen, Searcy, AR

Mosher, Roger L (716) 343-8000
PUB, ED, Daily News, Batavia, NY

Mosher, Susan A (909) 338-1893
GM, Crestline Courier, Crestline, CA

Mosher, Terry (514) 987-2222
EDL Cartoonist, Gazette, Montreal, QC

Mosier, David L (419) 238-2285
ED, BUS/FIN ED, EPE
Times-Bulletin, Van Wert, OH

Mosier, Juanita (812) 849-2075
GM, MAN ED, Mitchell Tribune, Mitchell, IN

Mosier, Lynn (501) 785-9404
VP-Administrative Support Group
Donrey Media Group, Fort Smith, AR

Mosier, Lynn (405) 282-2222
VP-Administrative Support Group
Guthrie News Leader, Guthrie, OK

Mosier, Robert (410) 766-3700
ED, Maryland Gazette, Glen Burnie, MD

Mosier, Tami (317) 664-5111
CIRC CNR-Sales
Chronicle-Tribune, Marion, IN

Mosiman, Dean (360) 452-2345
EDU Writer
Peninsula Daily News, Port Angeles, WA

Moskal, Edward (312) 763-3343
PUB, Dziennik Zwaizkowy, Chicago, IL

Moskos, Harry (423) 523-3131
ED, Knoxville News-Sentinel, Knoxville, TN

Moskowitz, Gary (718) 263-8234
COL, Moskowitz, Gary, Flushing, NY

Mosley, Charles (316) 672-5511
SEC/TREAS, Pratt Tribune, Pratt, KS

Mosley, Jeff (601) 735-4341
PUB, Wayne County News, Waynesboro, MS

Mosmeyer, Chris (817) 387-3811
Political ED
Denton Record-Chronicle, Denton, TX

Mosqueda, Laura (207) 729-3311
Community SRV, Librarian
Times Record, Brunswick, ME

Moss, Bill (919) 537-2505
ED, Daily Herald, Roanoke Rapids, NC

Moss, Harvey (803) 782-2554
PUB, Fort Jackson Leader, Columbia, SC

Moss, Jack (616) 345-3511
Sports ED
Kalamazoo Gazette, Kalamazoo, MI

Moss, James (914) 341-1100
PUB, Times Herald-Record, Middletown, NY

Moss, Jim (210) 225-7411
EX ED/Senior VP-News
San Antonio Express-News, San Antonio, TX

Moss, Joe (219) 967-4135
PUB, Carroll County Comet, Flora, IN

Moss, Julie (601) 442-9101
ADV MGR-RT
Natchez Democrat, Natchez, MS

Moss, Paul (250) 380-5211
EDL Writer, Times Colonist, Victoria, BC

Moss, Rosanna (209) 441-6111
SEC, Fresno Bee, Fresno, CA

Moss, S M (203) 377-5525
SEC/TREAS
Metropolitan Press Syndicate, Stratford, CT

Moss, Steve (805) 546-8208
PUB, ED, New Times, San Luis Obispo, CA

Moss, Zoe Ann (904) 829-6562
MGR-Accounting
St. Augustine Record, St. Augustine, FL

Mossburger, Roger (502) 827-2000
Television/Film ED, Theater/Music ED
Gleaner, Henderson, KY

Mossman, James R (317) 482-4650
SEC/TREAS, Reporter, Lebanon, IN

Mossman, Michael D (317) 482-4650
PUB, GM, Reporter, Lebanon, IN

Mosso, Claudia (814) 833-7459
ED, Millcreek Sun, Erie, PA

Moster, Dennis (904) 252-1511
PROD FRM-COMP, Daytona Beach News-Journal, Daytona Beach, FL

Moszczynski, Joe (201) 383-1500
MAN ED, New Jersey Herald, Newton, NJ

Mote, Kimm (937) 866-3331
PUB, Miamisburg News, Miamisburg, OH

Motel, Robert L (904) 359-4111
CIRC DIR-Distribution Center
Florida Times-Union, Jacksonville, FL

Motes, Martha R (334) 246-4494
ED, South Alabamian, Jackson, AL

Moticha, Alysia (302) 378-9531
ED, Middletown Transcript, Middletown, DE

Motley, Albert (520) 783-3333
DIR-Technology & Commercial Print
Yuma Daily Sun, Yuma, AZ

Motley, Jeff (804) 385-5400
Sports ED, News & Advance, Lynchburg, VA

Motley, Peggy (972) 875-3801
CIRC MGR, Ennis Daily News, Ennis, TX

Motsch, Gunther (403) 468-0100
Chief Accountant
Edmonton Sun, Edmonton, AB

Motschenbacher, Brad (701) 253-7311
MGR-MIS, Forum, Fargo, ND

Mott, Bethany (800) 245-6536
GM-Sentinel Publishing
US/Express, Chicago, IL

Mott Jr, Frederick (803) 771-6161
PRES/PUB, State, Columbia, SC

Mott, Jan (607) 798-1234
ADV MGR-Account Development
Press & Sun Bulletin, Binghamton, NY

Motta, Joseph (401) 821-7400
MAN ED
Kent County Daily Times, West Warwick, RI

Motz, Gary (614) 363-1161
Entertainment ED, Wire ED
Delaware Gazette, Delaware, OH

Mouat, Trudy (519) 621-3810
ADV MGR
Cambridge Reporter, Cambridge, ON

Moulton, David (800) 561-8383
PRES, Constructive Ideas, Wilmington, DE

Moulton, David (800) 561-8383
MKTG
Syndication Associates Inc., Champlain, NY

Mount, Bonnie Jo (719) 632-5511
Photo DIR, Gazette, Colorado Springs, CO

Mount, Candice (618) 234-1000
News ED, News-Democrat, Belleville, IL

Mouser, James (405) 332-4433
PROD MGR, Ada Evening News, Ada, OK

Mouyiarist, Nick (718) 626-7676
PUB, Proini, Long Island City, NY

Movold, Margaret (604) 788-2246
PUB, ED, Chetwynd Echo, Chetwynd, BC

Movshovitz, Howie (303) 820-1010
Films Critic, Denver Post, Denver, CO

Mowbray, Kevin (402) 475-4200
ADV MGR-RT, Journal Star, Lincoln, NE

Mowbray, Mickey (519) 894-2231
Sports ED, Record, Kitchener, ON

Mowday, Bruce (610) 696-1775
MAN ED
Daily Local News, West Chester, PA

Mowers, Carolyn (207) 990-8000
VP/SEC, Bangor Daily News, Bangor, ME

Mowery, David P (817) 754-3511
GM, Waco Citizen, Waco, TX

Mowry, Ken (919) 829-4500
Graphics ED, News & Observer, Raleigh, NC

Mowry, Paul (602) 898-6500
PROD DIR-OPER, Mesa Tribune, Mesa, AZ
Thomson Newspapers

Moxam, Jean (816) 234-4141
DIR-Art, Kansas City Star, Kansas City, MO

Moy, Catherine (707) 425-4646
ASST City ED, Daily Republic, Fairfield, CA

Moyars, Karen (765) 884-1902
PUB, ED, Benton Review, Fowler, IN

Moye, Ollie (803) 276-0625
PUB, Newberry Observer & Herald & News, Newberry, SC

Moyer, Amy (717) 742-9671
GM, Milton Daily Standard, Milton, PA
Hollinger International Inc.

Moyer, J Keith (209) 441-6111
EX ED, Fresno Bee, Fresno, CA

Moyer, Michelle (814) 765-5581
ED, Progress, Clearfield, PA

Moyers, David (501) 853-2424
PUB, ED
Ashley County Ledger, Hamburg, AR

Moyers, Gary (606) 623-1669
ED, Richmond Register, Richmond, KY

Moynihan, Bishop James (315) 422-8153
PUB, Catholic Sun, Syracuse, NY

Mozer, Mindy (319) 337-3181
City ED, Iowa City Press-Citizen, Iowa City, IA

Mozley, C Dan (706) 291-6397
GM, PA, Rome News-Tribune, Rome, GA

Mpistolarides, Richard (312) 644-7800
PROD Plant MGR
Chicago Daily Law Bulletin, Chicago, IL

Mrachek, Don (701) 572-2165
PUB, Williston Daily Herald, Williston, ND

Mroz, Andrea (412) 834-1151
ADV MGR-CLASS
Tribune-Review, Greensburg, PA

Mubley, Murray (219) 456-2824
MAN ED, Todays Catholic, Fort Wayne, IN

Mucci, Paul (617) 433-6700
Acting PRES
Community Newspaper Co., Needham, MA

Muchin, Andy (414) 390-5888
ED
Wisconsin Jewish Chronicle, Milwaukee, WI

Muchler, Patricia (716) 232-7100
PROD MGR-Environmental Services
Rochester Democrat and Chronicle; Times-Union, Rochester, NY

Muchmore, Allan W (405) 765-3311
PUB, ED, Ponca City News, Ponca City, OK

Muchmore, Tom (405) 765-3311
BM, PA, Ponca City News, Ponca City, OK

Muchnic, Suzanne (213) 237-5000
Art Writer
Los Angeles Times, Los Angeles, CA

Muchnick, Laurie (516) 843-2020
Books ED, Newsday, Melville, NY

Muckelbauer, Dan (414) 338-0622
City ED, Daily News, West Bend, WI

Muckley, Paul K (419) 659-2173
GM, Putnam County Vidette/Pandora Times, Columbus Grove, OH

Mudd, Tom (216) 245-6901
BUS ED, Morning Journal, Lorain, OH

Muddiman, Harold (561) 461-2050
EX ED, Tribune, Fort Pierce, FL

Muder, Craig (216) 994-3241
Sports ED, Star-Beacon, Ashtabula, OH

Mudge, Angela (417) 532-9131
Photo ED, Daily Record, Lebanon, MO

Muehlbauer, Ed (414) 224-2000
PROD MGR-Night
Milwaukee Journal Sentinel, Milwaukee, WI

Mueller Jr, Arthur J (603) 893-4356
PUB, Salem Observer, Salem, NH

Mueller, B J (618) 423-2411
ED, Ramsey News-Journal, Ramsey, IL

Mueller, Charles (410) 235-3401
PUB, MAN ED
Baltimore Alternative, Baltimore, MD

Mueller, Clyde (505) 983-3303
Photo ED
Santa Fe New Mexican, Santa Fe, NM

Mueller, Donna (414) 457-7711
ADV ASST MGR
Sheboygan Press, Sheboygan, WI

Mueller, Edward C (908) 477-9110
PUB, ED, Brick Township Town News/Sampler, Brick, NJ

Mueller, Gene (414) 733-4411
PROD FRM-MR, Post-Crescent, Appleton, WI

Mueller, Monica (414) 542-2501
CIRC Sales, Waukesha County Freeman, Waukesha, WI

Mueller Sr, R J (618) 423-2411
PUB, Ramsey News-Journal, Ramsey, IL

Mueller, Robert (513) 721-2700
Telecommunications CNR
Cincinnati Enquirer, Cincinnati, OH

Mueller, Steven (562) 435-1161
PROD ASST MGR-Mailroom
Press-Telegram, Long Beach, CA

Muench, Joe (915) 546-6340
Sports ED, El Paso Herald-Post, El Paso, TX

Muessel, Tom (216) 245-6901
PROD DIR, Morning Journal, Lorain, OH

Muhlack, Jamie (860) 442-2200
ADV CNR-NTL, Day, New London, CT

Muhleman, Ron (360) 377-3711
GM, Sun, Bremerton, WA

Muhlstein, Jim (206) 339-3000
Communities ED, Public Life ED
Herald, Everett, WA

Muhlstein, Julie (206) 339-3000
Features ED, Food ED, Herald, Everett, WA

Muinzer, Andy S (317) 423-5511
MGR-CR, Journal and Courier, Lafayette, IN

Muir, Butch (504) 383-1111
Sports ED, Advocate, Baton Rouge, LA

Muir, Don (810) 985-7171
PROD MGR-Camera/Plate
Times Herald, Port Huron, MI

Muir, Ross (705) 368-2744
ED, Manitoulin Expositor, Little Current, ON

Muirtagh, Marie (516) 751-7744
ED, Times, Seatuket, NY

Mulcahy, James (814) 781-1596
City Sports ED, Daily Press, St. Marys, PA

Mulcahy, James (606) 564-9091
Design ED
Ledger Independent, Maysville, KY

Mulcahy-Reed, Lois (603) 742-4455
PROD MGR, Foster's Democrat, Dover, NH

Mulder, Donna (414) 722-4243
MAN ED, News-Record, Neenah, WI

Muldoon II, W H (970) 867-5651
PUB, Fort Morgan Times, Fort Morgan, CO

Muldron, Jim (704) 289-1541
News ED, Enquirer-Journal, Monroe, NC

Mulham, William (212) 210-2100
PROD MGR-MR
New York Daily News, New York, NY

Mulieri, Anthony (301) 733-5131
MAN ED (Mail)
Morning Herald, Hagerstown, MD

Mulkey, Pete (972) 542-2631
ADV MGR, Courier-Gazette, McKinney, TX

Mulkins, Phil (918) 581-8300
Action Line ED, Tulsa World, Tulsa, OK

Mullally, Beth (914) 341-1100
Medical/Health ED
Times Herald-Record, Middletown, NY

Mullan, Cecil (804) 385-5400
Fashion/Style ED, Features ED, Lifestyle ED
News & Advance, Lynchburg, VA

Mullay, Jim (717) 829-7100
MAN ED, Times Leader, Wilkes-Barre, PA

Mullen, Mike (717) 348-9100
Picture ED
Tribune & The Scranton Times, Scranton, PA

Mullen, Steve (601) 234-4331
News ED, Oxford Eagle, Oxford, MS

Mullen, Thomas J (419) 223-1010
PUB, Lima News, Lima, OH

Mullenary, Howard L (206) 455-2222
ADV EX VP, Eastside Journal, Bellevue, WA

Mullenix, Martha (512) 645-2330
PUB, ED, Texan Express, Goliad, TX

Mullens, Bonnie (817) 840-2091
PUB, McGregor Mirror & Crawford Sun, McGregor, TX

Mullens, Ron (304) 732-6060
ED, Independent Herald, Pineville, WV

Muller, Carol Doup (408) 920-5000
Books ED
San Jose Mercury News, San Jose, CA

Muller, Julia (912) 236-9511
Librarian
Savannah Morning News, Savannah, GA

Muller, Laurie (915) 546-6100
NTL ED, El Paso Times, El Paso, TX

Muller, Steven (210) 686-4343
DP MGR, Monitor, McAllen, TX

Muller, William (609) 272-7000
CIRC MGR-Sales
Press of Atlantic City, Pleasantville, NJ

Mullich, Joe (610) 279-5473
Owner/Writer
Mullich Communications, Norristown, PA

Mulligan, Carol (705) 673-5667
ED, Northern Life, Sudbury, ON

Mulligan, Gerard (352) 563-6363
PUB
Citrus County Chronicle, Crystal River, FL

Mulligan, Mike (312) 321-3000
Bears/NFL COL
Chicago Sun-Times, Chicago, IL

Mulligan, Tom (213) 237-5000
Wall Street
Los Angeles Times, Los Angeles, CA

Mullin, A C (606) 573-4510
Sports ED
Harlan Daily Enterprise, Harlan, KY

Mullin, Carolyn (905) 892-6022
ED, Pelham Herald, Fonthill, ON

Mullin, Jeff (405) 233-6600
News ED, Enid News & Eagle, Enid, OK

Mullin, Jim (305) 571-7699
ED, Miami New Times, Miami, FL

Mullin, Mitch (918) 567-2390
PUB, Talihina American, Wilburton, OK

Mullin, Sandy (918) 567-2390
PUB, Talihina American, Wilburton, OK

Mullinax, Shelia (770) 773-3754
ED, North Bartow News, Adairsville, GA

Mullings, David (970) 325-4412
PUB, ED
Ouray County Plaindealer, Ouray, CO

Mullins, Joyce (215) 790-1179
ED, Pride Weekly, Philadelphia, PA

Mullins, Mike (415) 777-5700
MGR-Labor Relations, San Francisco Newspaper Agency, San Francisco, CA

Mullins, Roger (540) 921-3434
ED, Virginian Leader, Pearisburg, VA

Mullins, Ronald (212) 837-7000
Insurance ED, Journal of Commerce & Commercial, New York, NY

Mullins, Steve (803) 577-7111
ASST MAN ED-Projects
Post and Courier, Charleston, SC

Mulock, Greg (506) 546-4491
MAN ED, Northern Light, Bathurst, NB

Mulvane, Sylvie (908) 722-3000
ED
South Plainfield Reporter, Sommerville, NJ

Mulvaney, Katie (404) 466-2222
MAN ED
Block Island Times, Block Island, RI

Mulvee, Most Rev Robert E (302) 573-3109
PUB, Dialog, Wilmington, DE

Mulvihill, Sandy (904) 264-3200
ED, Clay County Crescent, Orange Park, FL

Mulvoy Jr, Thomas F (617) 929-2000
MAN ED-News/OPER
Boston Globe, Boston, MA

Mumaw, Bill (213) 622-8332
PROD MGR, La Opinion, Los Angeles, CA

Copyright ©1997 by the Editor & Publisher Co.

165-Who's Where **Mus**

Mumford, Darrel .... (910) 623-2155
PROD MGR, Daily News, Eden, NC
Mumma, Madolyn .... (937) 225-2000
DIR-Human Resources
Dayton Daily News, Dayton, OH
Mummery, Bob .... (204) 867-3816
PUB, ED
Minnedosa Tribune, Minnedosa, MB
Muncaster, Richard .... (705) 949-6111
PUB, Sault Ste. Marie This Week, Sault Ste. Marie, ON
Munday, David .... (803) 577-7111
Automotive ED
Post and Courier, Charleston, SC
Munding, Elizabeth .... (615) 552-1808
Fashion/Features ED, Food/Home Furnishings ED, Leaf-Chronicle, Clarksville, TN
Mundrick, Robert .... (315) 792-5000
PROD MGR-Technical SRV
Observer-Dispatch, Utica, NY
Mundstock, Walter .... (605) 472-0822
PUB, Redfield Press, Redfield, SD
Mundy, Dave .... (713) 391-3141
ED, Katy Times, Katy, TX
Mundy, Eleanor M .... (864) 223-1411
PRES/TREAS/PUB
Index-Journal, Greenwood, SC
Mundy, Karen .... (330) 868-5222
ED, Press-News, Minerva, OH
Munford, Robert .... (206) 883-7187
GM, Redmond Sammamish Valley News, Redmond, WA
Munger, Charles T .... (213) 229-5300
COB
Los Angeles Daily Journal, Los Angeles, CA
Munger, Scott .... (605) 356-2632
PUB, ED, Leader-Courier, Elk Point, SD
Munkittrick, Arnold .... (802) 748-8121
GM, CIRC MGR
Caledonian-Record, St. Johnsbury, VT
Munn, Willie .... (803) 771-6161
Imaging Department MGR
State, Columbia, SC
Munoz Sr, Daniel L .... (619) 231-2873
PUB, La Prensa San Diego, San Diego, CA
Munoz Jr, Daniel H .... (619) 231-2873
ED, La Prensa San Diego, San Diego, CA
Munoz, Jesse .... (520) 783-3333
PROD FRM-MR, Yuma Daily Sun, Yuma, AZ
Munoz, Joe .... (409) 756-6671
PROD MGR, Conroe Courier, Conroe, TX
Munoz, Ron .... (909) 793-3221
PROD SUPV-PR
Redlands Daily Facts, Redlands, CA
Munoz, Sergio .... (213) 237-5000
EDL Writer
Los Angeles Times, Los Angeles, CA
Munro, Katherine .... (207) 743-7011
ED, Advertiser Democrat, Norway, ME
Munro, Kent .... (250) 352-3552
CIRC MGR, Nelson Daily News, Nelson, BC
Munro, Lynne .... (250) 380-5211
DIR-MKTG & Community Relations
Times Colonist, Victoria, BC
Munro, Neil J .... (810) 332-8181
ED, Oakland Press, Pontiac, MI
Munro, Scott .... (520) 573-4400
ADV MGR-CLASS, TNI Partners dba Tucson Newspapers, Tucson, AZ
Munroe, George .... (617) 929-2000
PROD MGR, Boston Globe, Boston, MA
Munroe, Lisa .... (416) 367-2000
ADV RE/New In Homes
Toronto Star, Toronto, ON
Munsey, Chris .... (410) 268-5000
Environmental ED, Capital, Annapolis, MD
Munsey, Linda .... (619) 775-4200
GM, Palm Desert Post, Indio, CA
Munson, Anita .... (317) 622-1212
BUS/Labor ED, Herald Bulletin, Anderson, IN
Munson, Anthony R .... (412) 271-0622
PUB, ED, Free Press, Braddock, PA
Munson, Jeff .... (916) 243-2424
EDU ED, Record Searchlight, Redding, CA
Munster, Gerhard J W .... (407) 628-8500
PUB, ED, Winter Park-Maitland Observer, Winter Park, FL
Munz, Carlos .... (718) 762-8833
MAN ED
De Norte A Sur, Fresh Meadows, NY
Munzell, Michael .... (415) 777-2424
PROD EX ED
San Francisco Examiner, San Francisco, CA
Murarka, Bina A .... (510) 652-3552
ED, India-West, Emeryville, CA
Murarka, Ramesh P .... (510) 652-3552
PUB, India-West, Emeryville, CA
Murchake, Richard P .... (410) 268-5000
PROD DIR-OPER, Capital, Annapolis, MD
Murchison, Bill .... (214) 977-8222
COL-EDL Page
Dallas Morning News, Dallas, TX
Murchison, Buddy .... (901) 386-3157
PUB, Cordova Beacon, Bartlett, TN
Murchison, Joe .... (301) 725-2000
ED, Laurel Leader, Laurel, MD
Murchison, John H .... (901) 388-1500
PUB, ED, Bartlett Express, Bartlett, TN
Murchison, Julie .... (207) 990-8000
Political ED, Bangor Daily News, Bangor, ME
Murdoch, Gail .... (501) 641-7161
MAN ED, Atkins Chronicle, Atkins, AR
Murdoch, Gilbert .... (212) 967-7313
GM, Jewish Post of New York, New York, NY
Murdoch, K Rupert .... (212) 930-8000
Chairman, New York Post, New York, NY
Murdoch, Sarah .... (416) 585-5000
ASSOC ED, Globe and Mail (Canada's National Newspaper), Toronto, ON
Murdoch, Scott .... (508) 586-7200
CIRC MGR, Enterprise, Brockton, MA
Murdock, Mark .... (219) 925-2611
Sports ED, Evening Star, Auburn, IN
Murfin, Gary .... (206) 455-2222
VP-MKTG/Interactive Technologies
Eastside Journal, Bellevue, WA
Muritech, James .... (403) 235-7100
Music Critic, Calgary Herald, Calgary, AB
Murphey, Deb .... (712) 279-5019
Librarian, Sioux City Journal, Sioux City, IA
Murphey, Marsha .... (509) 837-4500
CIRC DIR, Daily Sun News, Sunnyside, WA
Murphey III, Randolph C .... (540) 574-6200
Farm ED
Daily News-Record, Harrisonburg, VA
Murphey IV, Randolph C .... (540) 298-9444
GM, ED, Valley Banner, Elkton, VA
Murphy, Allan R .... (812) 332-4401
DIR-PSL/Community SRV, MGR-EDU SRV
Herald-Times Inc, Bloomington, IN
Murphy Jr, Andrew J .... (614) 461-5000
MAN ED-News
Columbus Dispatch, Columbus, OH
Murphy, Audie .... (407) 242-3500
EDL Writer, Florida Today, Melbourne, FL
Murphy, Bill .... (405) 338-3355
PUB, ED, Guymon Daily Herald, Guymon, OK
Murphy, Chris .... (613) 342-4441
ADV MGR, Brockville Recorder and Times, Brockville, ON
Murphy, Dan .... (916) 842-5777
Sports ED, Siskiyou Daily News, Yreka, CA
Murphy, David .... (312) 222-3232
ADV DIR-Sales, Chicago Tribune, Chicago, IL
Murphy, Dean E .... (213) 237-5000
Warsaw BU
Los Angeles Times, Los Angeles, CA
Murphy, Debra .... (306) 867-8262
ED, Outlook, Outlook, SK
Murphy, Deidre .... (201) 877-4141
ASST MAN ED, Star-Ledger, Newark, NJ
Murphy, Don .... (805) 564-5200
ASST City ED, Santa Barbara News-Press, Santa Barbara, CA
Murphy, Ed .... (860) 442-2200
ASST MAN ED-OPER, Automotive ED
Day, New London, CT
Murphy, Edward .... (313) 222-6400
ADV MGR-ADM Budgets
Detroit Newspapers, Detroit, MI
Murphy, Erich .... (815) 842-1153
Sports ED, Daily Leader, Pontiac, IL
Murphy, Gene .... (515) 672-2581
City ED, Oskaloosa Herald, Oskaloosa, IA
Murphy, Hank .... (806) 762-8844
City ED, Avalanche-Journal, Lubbock, TX
Murphy, J K .... (812) 372-7811
MAN ED, Republic, Columbus, IN
Murphy, Jane .... (603) 436-1800
MAN ED-Day
Portsmouth Herald, Portsmouth, NH
Murphy, Jim .... (216) 951-0000
Sports ED, News-Herald, Willoughby, OH
Murphy, John .... (717) 348-9100
Ecology/Enrivonment ED
Tribune & The Scranton Times, Scranton, PA
Murphy, John B .... (218) 723-8000
COB, Murphy McGinnis Media, Duluth, MN
Murphy, John H .... (403) 553-3391
PUB, GM, ED
Macleod Gazette, Fort Macleod, AB
Murphy, John J .... (301) 948-3120
ED, Gaithersburg Gazette, Gaithersburg, MD
Murphy, Kate .... (406) 266-3333
GM, Townsend Star, Townsend, MT
Murphy, Kim .... (213) 237-5000
Seattle BU
Los Angeles Times, Los Angeles, CA
Murphy, Larry .... (219) 294-1661
EPE, Elkhart Truth, Elkhart, IN
Murphy, Laurie .... (603) 224-5301
MGR-Human Resources
Concord Monitor, Concord, NH
Murphy, Linda .... (509) 663-5161
MGR-PROM/EDU SRV, CIRC DIR
Wenatchee World, Wenatchee, WA
Murphy, Linda .... (561) 820-4100
DIR-Human Resources
Palm Beach Post, West Palm Beach, FL
Murphy, Mark .... (412) 263-1100
ED-Sunday Magazine
Pittsburgh Post-Gazette, Pittsburgh, PA
Murphy, Mark .... (508) 626-3800
Sports ED
Middlesex News, Framingham, MA
Murphy, Mark .... (801) 625-4200
News ED, Standard-Examiner, Ogden, UT
Murphy, Michael .... (716) 247-9200
ED, Gates-Chili News, Rochester, NY
Murphy, Michael J .... (909) 889-9666
RE ED, Special Sections ED
Sun, San Bernardino, CA
Murphy, Mike .... (517) 479-3605
PUB, ED, Times, Harbor Beach, MI
Murphy, Patrick .... (307) 672-2431
Sports ED, Sheridan Press, Sheridan, WY
Murphy, Richard .... (907) 257-4200
Photo ED, Daily News, Anchorage, AK
Murphy, Robert T .... (617) 929-2000
VP-INFO Services, Boston Globe, Boston, MA
Murphy, Robert W .... (513) 863-8200
PUB, Journal-News, Hamilton, OH
Murphy, Rod .... (406) 523-5200
Local News ED, Missoulian, Missoula, MT
Murphy, Sean .... (617) 929-2000
City ED, Boston Globe, Boston, MA
Murphy, Shelba .... (423) 523-3131
DIR-MKTG, News-Sentinel, Knoxville, TN
Murphy, Sue .... (410) 268-5000
ADV MGR-RT, Capital, Annapolis, MD
Murphy, Suzanne .... (317) 482-4650
VP, Reporter, Lebanon, IN
Murphy, Ted .... (604) 946-4451
ED, Delta Optimist, Delta, BC
Murphy, Terry .... (404) 876-1819
ED, Southern Voice, Atlanta, GA
Murphy, Thomas .... (507) 724-3475
PUB, ED, Caledonia Argus, Caledonia, MN
Murphy, Tom .... (919) 446-5161
Farm ED
Rocky Mount Telegram, Rocky Mount, NC
Murphy, Tom .... (414) 435-4411
Farm ED
Green Bay Press-Gazette, Green Bay, WI
Murphy, Tom .... (864) 224-4321
DIR-Photography
Anderson Independent-Mail, Anderson, SC
Murphy, Tom .... (805) 925-2691
EDU ED
Santa Maria Times, Santa Maria, CA
Murphy, William .... (703) 878-8000
CONT, Potomac News, Woodbridge, VA
Murphy-Wright, Sheri .... (403) 527-1101
City ED
Medicine Hat News, Medicine Hat, AB
Murphy II, Francis L .... (202) 332-0080
PUB, Washington Afro-American and Tribune, Washington, DC
Murray, Alan .... (212) 416-2000
BU Chief-Washington
Wall Street Journal, New York, NY
Murray, Andrea .... (812) 332-4401
Features/Lifestyle ED
Herald-Times Inc, Bloomington, IN
Murray, Barry .... (202) 628-2300
PUB, ED, News Dimensions, Washington, DC
Murray, Betty J .... (540) 955-1111
GM, Clarke Courier, Berryville, VA
Murray, Bill .... (412) 342-5300
PRES
Minority Features Syndicate Inc., Farrel, PA
Murray, C Randall .... (561) 395-8300
EPE, News, Boca Raton, FL
Murray, Charles .... (601) 961-7000
PROD MGR-Building Maintenance
Clarion-Ledger, Jackson, MS
Murray, Clark O .... (913) 492-9050
COB/PRES
Inland Industries Inc., Lenexa, KS
Murray, Clem .... (215) 854-2000
Photo DIR
Philadelphia Inquirer, Philadelphia, PA
Murray, Clifford .... (319) 988-3855
PUB, ED, Hudson Herald, Hudson, IA
Murray, Craig .... (508) 586-7200
Photo ED, Enterprise, Brockton, MA
Murray, Dan .... (210) 686-4343
News ED, Monitor, McAllen, TX
Murray, Dan .... (914) 694-9300
ASST MAN ED-Nights
Reporter Dispatch, White Plains, NY
Gannett Co. Inc.
Murray, David .... (419) 245-6000
City ED, Blade, Toledo, OH
Murray, Deborah .... (770) 227-3276
ADV DIR, Griffin Daily News, Griffin, GA
Murray, Diane .... (915) 653-1221
Amusements/Books ED, Features ED, Films/Theater ED, Teen-Age/Youth ED
Standard-Times, San Angelo, TX
Murray, Dick .... (401) 277-7000
ADV Sales DIR-Automotive
Providence Journal-Bulletin, Providence, RI
Murray, Edward J .... (609) 845-3300
DP MGR, Gloucester County Times, Woodbury, NJ, MediaNews Inc.
Murray, Elisa .... (206) 623-0500
MAN ED, Eastsideweek, Seattle, WA
Murray, Ernie .... (409) 564-8361
MAN ED, Nacogdoches Daily Sentinel, Nacogdoches, TX
Murray, Ivan .... (520) 445-3333
MAN ED, Chino Valley Review, Prescott, AZ
Murray, Jack .... (415) 348-4321
PROD FRM-PR
San Mateo County Times, San Mateo, CA
Murray, Jack .... (708) 448-6161
ED, Reporter, Palos Heights, IL
Murray, John .... (219) 461-8444
CIRC DIR
Fort Wayne Newspapers Inc., Fort Wayne, IN
Murray, Ken .... (520) 458-9440
PROD MGR, PROD FRM-COMP, PROD FRM-Press/Camera, Sierra Vista Herald, Sierra Vista, AZ, Wick Communications
Murray, L Scott .... (801) 373-5050
ADV MGR-RT, Daily Herald, Provo, UT
Murray, Lance .... (817) 390-7400
Senior ED-OPER
Fort Worth Star-Telegram, Fort Worth, TX
Murray, Linda .... (318) 375-3294
PUB, ED, Caddo Citizen, Vivian, LA
Murray, Michael .... (908) 922-6000
CIRC DIR
New Jersey Press, Neptune, NJ
Murray, Mike .... (206) 339-3000
Entertainment/Film ED, Television ED, Travel ED, Herald, Everett, WA
Murray, Patsy .... (617) 837-3500
ED, Weymouth News, Weymouth, MA
Murray, Patsy .... (205) 549-2000
ADV SUPV-CLASS
Gadsden Times, Gadsden, AL
Murray, Robert .... (912) 924-2751
PROD FRM-PR
Americus Times-Recorder, Americus, GA
Murray, Sheila .... (405) 238-6464
MGR-Accounting/Office
Pauls Valley Daily Democrat, Pauls Valley, OK
Murray, Todd .... (919) 527-3191
Sports ED, Free Press, Kinston, NC
Murray, Tom .... (609) 845-3300
Sports ED
Gloucester County Times, Woodbury, NJ
Murray, Tom .... (417) 623-3480
MAN ED, Joplin Globe, Joplin, MO
Murray, William .... (212) 755-4363
Contributing Writer
Punch In Travel & Entertainment News Syndicate, New York, NY
Murray, William T .... (860) 489-3121
PUB, Register Citizen, Torrington, CT
Murrell, John .... (408) 920-5000
Senior Online ED
San Jose Mercury News, San Jose, CA
Murren, Wanda .... (717) 637-3736
Graphics ED, Online MGR
Evening Sun, Hanover, PA
Murri, Val .... (406) 265-6795
Office MGR, Havre Daily News, Havre, MT
Murry, Faye .... (812) 231-4200
ADV MGR
Terre Haute Tribune-Star, Terre Haute, IN
Murry, Terry .... (541) 276-2211
Teen-Age/Youth ED, Women's/Community ED
East Oregonian, Pendleton, OR
Murt, Mike .... (719) 634-1593
ADV MGR
Daily Transcript, Colorado Springs, CO
Murtha, Julie .... (902) 629-6000
CIRC MGR, Guardian, Charlottetown, PEI
Musall, Laura .... (317) 598-6397
Local ED
Noblesville Daily Ledger, Noblesville, IN
Muschi, Anthony .... (415) 362-8072
ED, Schweizer-Journal, San Francisco, CA
Muschi, Louis .... (415) 362-8072
ED, Schweizer-Journal, San Francisco, CA
Muschinsky, Alison W .... (203) 235-1661
VP, Record-Journal, Meriden, CT
Musco, Audrey .... (203) 333-0161
MGR-Human Resources
Connecticut Post, Bridgeport, CT
Muse, John .... (601) 774-9433
MAN ED, Union Appeal, Union, MS
Muse, Philip .... (405) 353-0620
Religion ED
Lawton Constitution, Lawton, OK
Musetto, Vincent .... (212) 930-8000
Entertainment/Amusements ED
New York Post, New York, NY
Musgrove, Dean .... (818) 713-3000
Photo DIR, Daily News, Woodland Hills, CA
Musgrove, Martha .... (305) 350-2111
ASSOC ED-EDL Page
Miami Herald, Miami, FL
Musgrove, Toni .... (800) 327-3378
GM, Press & Light, North Ridgeville, OH

Mus Who's Where-166

Musick, Earl T .... (419) 562-4778
MAN ED, Musick Toons, Bucyrus, OH
Musick, Jimmy .... (205) 532-4000
PROD SUPT-PR
Huntsville Times, Huntsville, AL
Musil, Ruthellyn .... (312) 222-3237
VP-CORP Relations, Tribune Co., Chicago, IL
Musser Jr, Dean .... (219) 461-8333
Chief Photographer
Journal Gazette, Fort Wayne, IN
Mussetter, Bill .... (217) 223-5100
BUS ED, Quincy Herald-Whig, Quincy, IL
Mustafaa, Ayesha K .... (312) 243-7600
PUB, ED, Muslim Journal, Chicago, IL
Muszak, John .... (519) 679-6666
DIR-Reader Sales/MKTG
London Free Press, London, ON
Mutter, Jeff .... (814) 946-7411
ADV DIR, Altoona Mirror, Altoona, PA
Mwanangombe, Lewis .... (416) 441-1405
Africa Journalist, Fotopress Independent News Service International, Toronto, ON
Mwansa, Andrew .... (416) 441-1405
Africa Journalist, Fotopress Independent News Service International, Toronto, ON
Myczkowiak, Mark A .... (517) 793-7661
GM, Catholic Weekly, Saginaw, MI
Myer, J Michael .... (304) 233-0100
EX ED, EPE, Intelligencer/Wheeling News-Register, Wheeling, WV
Myers, Aaron .... (614) 532-1441
CIRC MGR, Ironton Tribune, Ironton, OH
Myers, Albert .... (970) 963-8252
PUB, Family Times Magazine, Active Times Publications Inc., Carbondale, CO
Myers, Alyse .... (212) 556-1234
Group DIR-PROM
New York Times, New York, NY
Myers, Barry Lee .... (814) 234-9601
EVP, AccuWeather Inc., State College, PA
Myers, Bruce .... (360) 577-2500
PROD DIR, Daily News, Longview, WA
Myers, Bruce A .... (800) 939-6367
DIR-MKTG, National Financial News Service, West Chester, PA
Myers, Carole .... (619) 256-2257
BUS/FIN ED, Fashion/Style ED, Features ED, Living/Lifestyle ED, Religion ED, Women's ED, Desert Dispatch, Barstow, CA
Myers, Clay .... (509) 582-1500
DIR-Computer SRV, DP MGR
Tri-City Herald, Tri-Cities, WA
Myers, Cynthia .... (415) 777-2424
DIR-PROM
San Francisco Examiner, San Francisco, CA
Myers, Dave .... (310) 313-6733
MAN ED, Culver City News, Culver City, CA
Myers, Dave .... (717) 637-3736
PROD FRM-Press, Evening Sun, Hanover, PA
Myers, Debbie .... (616) 964-7161
Living/Lifestyle ED
Battle Creek Enquirer, Battle Creek, MI
Myers, Debra .... (419) 695-0015
CIRC MGR
Delphos Daily Herald, Delphos, OH
Myers, Diana Hunsaker .... (801) 257-5182
ED, Leader, Tremonton, UT
Myers, Elaine .... (313) 222-6400
ADV SALES DIR-RT
Detroit Newspapers, Detroit, MI
Myers, Evan A .... (814) 234-9601
Sr. VP, AccuWeather Inc., State College, PA
Myers, Frank .... (515) 421-0500
Lifestyle ED, Globe-Gazette, Mason City, IA
Myers, Frank .... (412) 834-1151
City ED, Tribune-Review, Greensburg, PA
Myers, Gary .... (601) 693-1551
News ED, Meridian Star, Meridian, MS
Myers, Gary .... (905) 526-3333
CIRC DIR-Distribution
Spectator, Hamilton, ON
Myers, Gene .... (313) 222-6400
Sports ED, Detroit Free Press, Detroit, MI
Myers Jr, George .... (614) 461-5000
Books ED, Dispatch, Columbus, OH
Myers, Jerry .... (217) 485-4010
GM, County Star, Tolono, IL
Myers, Jodi .... (419) 468-1117
MGR-Photo DEPT, Inquirer, Galion, OH
Myers, Dr Joel N .... (814) 234-9601
PRES, AccuWeather Inc., State College, PA
Myers, John .... (218) 723-5281
Environmental Writer
Duluth News-Tribune, Duluth, MN
Myers, John L .... (812) 636-7350
PUB, ED, Odon Journal, Odon, IN
Myers, Kim .... (410) 848-4400
MGR-MKTG/PROM, ADTX MGR
Carroll County Times, Westminster, MD
Myers, Lisa .... (219) 866-5111
BM, Republican, Rensselaer, IN
Myers, Max .... (864) 298-4100
PROD SUPT-PR
Greenville News, Greenville, SC
Myers, Nicola .... (719) 632-5511
ADV DIR-CLASS
Gazette, Colorado Springs, CO
Myers, Pat .... (360) 942-3466
PUB, Willapa Harbor Herald, Raymond, WA
Myers, Richard .... (209) 369-2761
Sports ED, Lodi News-Sentinel, Lodi, CA
Myers, Richard .... (616) 946-2000
PRES, Record-Eagle, Traverse City, MI
Myers, Rick .... (308) 632-0670
Photo, Star-Herald, Scottsbluff, NE
Myers, Robin L .... (610) 323-3000
CONT, Mercury, Pottstown, PA
Myers, Roger .... (913) 295-1111
Political ED, Capital-Journal, Topeka, KS
Myers, Stan .... (330) 454-5611
Photo ED, Repository, Canton, OH
Myers, Sue .... (812) 636-7350
GM, Odon Journal, Odon, IN
Myers, Terry .... (970) 723-4404
ED, Jackson County Star, Walden, CO
Myers, Terry .... (613) 735-3141
ED, Pembroke Daily News, Pembroke, ON
Myers, Tod .... (316) 268-6000
ADTX MGR, Wichita Eagle, Wichita, KS
Myers, Tom .... (304) 526-4000
CIRC MGR-Single Copy/Transportation
Herald-Dispatch, Huntington, WV
Myers, Valerie .... (814) 774-9648
ED, Cosmopolite Herald, Girard, PA
Myhre, Larry .... (712) 279-5019
ED, EPE, Sioux City Journal, Sioux City, IA
Myrick, Monte .... (918) 663-1414
ADV Sales Representative, Tulsa Daily Commerce & Legal News, Tulsa, OK
Myrkle, Bryan .... (517) 288-3164
ED, Durand Express, Durand, MI
Myrvall, Chris .... (808) 245-3681
ADV DIR, MGR-MKTG/PROM
Garden Island, Lihue, HI
Myrvold, Sylvia .... (408) 842-6400
PROD SUPV-COMP, Dispatch, Gilroy, CA
USMedia Inc. (Central Valley Publishing)
Myszkowski, Pete .... (218) 773-2808
ED, Exponent, East Grand Forks, MN

N

Nabors, Ginny .... (601) 627-2201
DP MGR, Press Register, Clarksdale, MS
Nacar, Terri .... (916) 832-4646
ED, Portola Reporter, Portola, CA
Nacchia, Joe .... (904) 863-1111
ADV MGR-CLASS, Northwest Florida Daily News, Fort Walton Beach, FL
Nachtigal, Ralph .... (605) 337-3101
PUB, ED, Platte Enterprise, Platte, SD
Nadeau, Andre .... (514) 755-4747
ED, Joliette Journal, Joliette, QC
Nadeau, Tom .... (916) 444-2355
Reporter, Daily Recorder, Sacramento, CA
Nadell, Lila .... (212) 861-3779
PRES, Fashion Sense, New York, NY
Naden, Kim L .... (308) 425-3481
PUB, ED, Franklin County Chronicle, Franklin, NE
Nadig, Brian .... (773) 286-6100
GM, Northwest Side Press, Chicago, IL
Nadig, Glenn .... (773) 286-6100
PUB, Northwest Side Press, Chicago, IL
Nadolski, Ed .... (414) 284-3494
MAN ED
Ozaukee Press, Port Washington, WI
Nadon, Jacques .... (819) 825-3755
ED, Val d'Or Star, Val d'Or, QC
Naegele, Tobias .... (703) 750-8636
ED, Navy Times, Springfield, VA
Naegele, Victoria .... (907) 376-5225
ED, Frontiersman, Wasilla, AK
Naess, Tommy .... (212) 768-8228
GM, Nordisk Tidende, New York, NY
Nafed, Emad .... (416) 362-0304
PUB, ED, Arc Arabic Journal, Toronto, ON
Naffah, Allen .... (508) 685-1000
MGR-CR, Eagle-Tribune, North Andover, MA
Nafsinger, Richard A .... (509) 837-4500
PRES, Daily Sun News, Sunnyside, WA
Nagel, Rick .... (630) 834-0900
ED, Lombard Spectator, Elmhurst, IL
Nagel, Roy .... (604) 562-2441
ED, EPE, Citizen, Prince George, BC
Nagen, James .... (402) 339-3331
PUB, Suburban Signal, Papillion, NE
Nagey, Richard .... (909) 987-6397
DP MGR
Inland Valley Daily Bulletin, Ontario, CA
Nagim, Kenny .... (504) 524-3785
PUB, Nolair News, New Orleans, LA
Nagle, Peter .... (617) 284-2400
ED, East Boston Sun Transcript, Revere, MA
Nagley, Shielia .... (813) 893-8111
CIRC MGR-MKTG
St. Petersburg Times, St. Petersburg, FL
Nagorka, Jennifer .... (214) 977-8222
EDL Writer, Dallas Morning News, Dallas, TX
Nahan, David .... (413) 663-3741
PUB, EPE
North Adams Transcript, North Adams, MA
Nahorney, Ramona .... (319) 752-8328
ED, Des Moines County News, West Burlington, IA
Nahriri, Sam .... (402) 444-1000
PROD MGR-MR, World-Herald, Omaha, NE
Nahshon, Gad .... (212) 967-7313
ED, Jewish Post of New York, New York, NY
Naidu, Venugopal .... (212) 889-6878
PUB, ED, India Monitor, New York, NY
Nail, Charles .... (601) 494-1422
PROD FRM-PR
Daily Times Leader, West Point, MS
Nailen, Laura A .... (203) 255-4561
MAN ED, Fairfield Citizen-News, Fairfield, CT
Najacht, Charles .... (308) 872-2471
PUB, Custer County Chief, Broken Bow, NE
Najera, Gloria .... (414) 224-2000
CIRC MGR-Consumer Services
Milwaukee Journal Sentinel, Milwaukee, WI
Nakaso, Dan .... (808) 525-8000
City ED, Religion ED
Honolulu Advertiser, Honolulu, HI
Nakowicz, Rev Stanley T .... (401) 272-1010
MAN ED, Providence Visitor, Providence, RI
Nakutin, Ethel .... (805) 259-1234
ADV DIR, ADTX MGR
Signal, Santa Clarita, CA
Nale, Dwight .... (414) 733-4411
Photo ED, Picture ED
Post-Crescent, Appleton, WI
Naman, Joseph .... (412) 465-5555
PROD FRM-PR, Indiana Gazette, Indiana, PA
Namanny, Beth .... (507) 376-9711
Lifestyle ED, Daily Globe, Worthington, MN
Namini, Yasmin .... (212) 556-1234
CIRC DIR-Home Delivery Expansion Team
New York Times, New York, NY
Namynanik, Kathy .... (716) 693-1000
CR MGR/Bookkeeper
Tonawanda News, North Tonawanda, NY
Nance, Alyson .... (910) 323-4848
ADTX MGR, Observer-Times, Fayetteville, NC
Nance, Dave .... (915) 546-6100
MGR-DP, DP MGR
El Paso Times, El Paso, TX
Nance, Patricia .... (208) 934-4449
PUB, Gooding County Leader, Gooding, ID
Naness, Barbara .... (718) 698-6979
Author/Owner
In A Nutshell, Staten Island, NY
Nangle, Hilary .... (207) 729-3311
Arts/Entertainment ED, Features ED, Living/Lifestyle ED, Radio/Television ED
Times Record, Brunswick, ME
Nangle, William .... (219) 933-3200
EX ED, Times, Munster, IN
Nanney, Dal .... (704) 652-3313
CIRC DIR, McDowell News, Marion, NC
Nanney Jr, Frank L .... (804) 447-3178
ED, South Hill Enterprise, South Hill, VA
Nanney, Shirley .... (901) 986-2253
ED
Carroll County News-Leader, Huntingdon, TN
Naquin, Gaston .... (504) 368-8900
PRES/TREAS, MGR
Daily Journal of Commerce, New Orleans, LA
Naquin, Robin .... (504) 447-4055
ADTX MGR, Daily Comet, Thibodaux, LA
Naranjo, Jaime .... (303) 442-1202
CIRC DIR, Daily Camera, Boulder, CO
Nardi, Glen E .... (803) 771-6161
VP-OPER, State, Columbia, SC
Nardini, Lynda .... (312) 762-2266
PUB, Lawndale News/Su Noticiero Bilingue, Chicago, IL
Nardini, Richard .... (312) 321-3000
ADV DIR-CLASS
Chicago Sun-Times, Chicago, IL
Nardini, Robert .... (312) 762-2266
GM, Lawndale News/Su Noticiero Bilingue, Chicago, IL
Nardo, Perry .... (304) 233-0100
ADV MGR-RT, Intelligencer/Wheeling News-Register, Wheeling, WV
Nardone, Phil .... (908) 766-3900
MAN ED
Bernardsville News, Bernardsville, NJ
Nardoza, Ed .... (212) 630-4000
VP/EXEC ED-WWD
Women's Wear Daily, New York, NY
Nartker, Dennis .... (219) 347-0400
Entertainment/Amusements ED
News-Sun, Kendallville, IN
Narum, Skip .... (712) 732-3130
ADV MGR, Pilot Tribune, Storm Lake, IA
Nasella, James .... (904) 359-4111
Sports ED
Florida Times-Union, Jacksonville, FL
Nash, Bill .... (613) 829-9100
PROD MGR-Manufacturing-Transportation
Ottawa Citizen, Ottawa, ON
Nash, Cyndi .... (206) 464-2111
ASSOC MAN ED, Seattle Times, Seattle, WA
Nash, Dave .... (630) 844-5844
ADV ASST MGR-Sales
Beacon-News, Aurora, IL
Nash, Larry .... (619) 442-4404
ADV DIR, ADV MGR-CLASS, MKTG & PROM DIR, Daily Californian, El Cajon, CA
Nash, Noel .... (352) 374-5000
Sports ED, Gainesville Sun, Gainesville, FL
Nash, Polly .... (203) 964-2200
ADV MGR-CLASS, Stamford Advocate, Stamford, CT, Times Mirror Co.
Nash, Ray .... (209) 441-6111
Automotive ED, Fresno Bee, Fresno, CA
Nash, Robert L .... (317) 552-3355
PUB, ADV DIR, Elwood Call-Leader, Elwood, IN, Ray Barnes Newspapers Inc.
Nash, Taneshia .... (908) 572-2120
DIR-Development, POSRO Media, Edison, NJ
Nash, Thomas B .... (203) 438-6544
PUB, Ridgefield Press, Ridgefield, CT
Nason, Janet .... (402) 873-3334
Comptroller
Nebraska City News-Press, Nebraska City, NE
Nass, Alisa .... (419) 522-3311
Features ED, News Journal, Mansfield, OH
Nasuti, Michael .... (413) 788-1000
Art DIR, Union-News, Springfield, MA
Natale, Carmen .... (415) 334-2061
MAN ED, El Latino, San Francisco, CA
Natale, Linda .... (401) 277-7000
PROD MGR-Pre-Publishing
Providence Journal-Bulletin, Providence, RI
Nath, Greg .... (712) 362-2622
Sports ED
Estherville Daily News, Estherville, IA
Nathan, David E .... (508) 793-9100
Sports ED
Telegram & Gazette, Worcester, MA
Natoli, Charles N .... (814) 765-5581
PROD SUPT-Plant, Progress, Clearfield, PA
Natoli, Joseph T .... (305) 350-2111
PRES, Miami Herald, Miami, FL
Natt, John J .... (360) 577-2500
VP, Daily News, Longview, WA
Natt, Ted M .... (360) 577-2500
PRES, PUB, ED, Daily News, Longview, WA
Nau, Michael C .... (616) 946-2000
CONT, DP MGR
Record-Eagle, Traverse City, MI
Naudin, Julio .... (915) 546-6100
CIRC DIR, El Paso Times, El Paso, TX
Nauman, Art .... (916) 321-1000
Ombudsman
Sacramento Bee, Sacramento, CA
Nauman, Barbara J .... (401) 277-7000
DIR-PROM
Providence Journal-Bulletin, Providence, RI
Nauman, Jane L .... (717) 291-8811
CONT, Lancaster Intelligencer Journal/New Era/Sunday News, Lancaster, PA
Nauman, Matthew .... (408) 920-5000
Automotive ED, Drive ED
San Jose Mercury News, San Jose, CA
Naumann, Karen .... (318) 289-6300
Teen-Age/Youth ED, Advertiser, Lafayette, LA
Nausley, Dan .... (423) 756-6900
ADV DIR, DIR-MKTG/PROM
Chattanooga Free Press, Chattanooga, TN
Nauss, Don .... (213) 237-5000
Auto Industry/Steel/Heavy Industry-Detroit
Los Angeles Times, Los Angeles, CA
Nauss, Pam .... (902) 426-2811
ADTX MGR, Chronicle-Herald, Halifax, NS
Nava, Heather .... (219) 722-5000
School Reporter
Pharos-Tribune, Logansport, IN
Navarro, Alma .... (210) 682-2423
ED, Valley Town Crier, McAllen, TX
Navarro, Barbara .... (510) 465-3121
Support Staff
Inter-City Express, Oakland, CA
Navarro, Ed .... (305) 294-6641
PROD FRM-Press
Key West Citizen, Key West, FL
Navarro, Irma .... (408) 842-6400
DP MGR, Dispatch, Gilroy, CA
Navarro, Rita .... (305) 633-3341
CIRC MGR, Diario Las Americas, Miami, FL
Nave, Sidney .... (423) 929-3111
PROD FRM-PR
Johnson City Press, Johnson City, TN
Nax, Sanford .... (209) 441-6111
RE Writer, Fresno Bee, Fresno, CA
Nay, Meta L .... (804) 293-4709
MKTG DIR, Keister-Williams Newspaper Services, Charlottesville, VA
Nayce, Linda .... (612) 689-1181
ED, Cambridge Star, Cambridge, MN
Naylor, Cindy .... (908) 359-0850
ED, Franklin News-Record, Princeton, NJ
Naylor, Dave .... (403) 250-4200
City ED, Calgary Sun, Calgary, AB
Naylor, Mitch .... (209) 826-3831
ED, Los Banos Enterprise, Los Banos, CA

Copyright ©1997 by the Editor & Publisher Co.

167-Who's Where **Nev**

Naylor, Wanda ... (601) 582-4321
ADV DIR-Human Resources
Hattiesburg American, Hattiesburg, MS

Nazario, Sonia ... (213) 237-5000
Urban Affairs Writer
Los Angeles Times, Los Angeles, CA

Nazzaro, Jeff ... (508) 658-2346
ED, Town Crier, Wilmington, MA

Neagle, Tim ... (415) 777-1111
NTL ED
San Francisco Chronicle, San Francisco, CA

Neal, Andrea ... (317) 633-1240
EDL Writer
Indianapolis Star/News, Indianapolis, IN

Neal, Clifton H ... (804) 649-6000
MGR-CR
Richmond Times-Dispatch, Richmond, VA

Neal, Gladys ... (317) 342-3311
Society ED, Daily Reporter, Martinsville, IN

Neal, Jeff ... (606) 678-8191
Sports ED
Commonwealth-Journal, Somerset, KY

Neal, Ken ... (918) 581-8300
EPE, EDL Writer, Tulsa World, Tulsa, OK

Neal, Maureen ... (604) 263-5643
ED, Vancouver Herald, Vancouver, BC

Neal, Paul ... (501) 425-3133
CIRC MGR
Baxter Bulletin, Mountain Home, AR

Neal, Robert ... (812) 275-3355
PROD FRM-Press, Times-Mail, Bedford, IN

Neal, Steve ... (312) 321-3000
Political COL
Chicago Sun-Times, Chicago, IL

Neal, Virginia ... (714) 835-1234
ADV DIR-New Media
Orange County Register, Santa Ana, CA

Neal, William ... (212) 989-3105
ED, Bootstraps Syndications, New York, NY

Neale, Lance ... (519) 255-5711
ADV DIR, Windsor Star, Windsor, ON

Nealy, Patrick ... (916) 541-3880
PROD MGR
Tahoe Daily Tribune, South Lake Tahoe, CA

Neary, James ... (915) 653-1221
DIR-FIN, Standard-Times, San Angelo, TX

Neary, Walter ... (360) 584-8080
ED, Lakewood Journal, Tacoma, WA

Neatherton, Dixie ... (937) 855-2300
GM, Germantown Press, Germantown, OH

Neaves, Jerry ... (305) 757-6333
GM, TWN News Magazine (The Weekly News), Miami, FL

Neavoll, George ... (207) 791-6650
EPE, Portland Press Herald, Portland, ME

Nee, Sherri ... (360) 694-3391
Political ED, Columbian, Vancouver, WA

Needham, John ... (213) 237-5000
EDL Writer
Los Angeles Times, Los Angeles, CA

Needham, Lorraine E ... (313) 222-2300
ASST to PUB, Detroit News, Detroit, MI

Needleman, Barbara ... (800) 245-6536
VP-Data Base & ADV
Tribune Media Services Inc., Chicago, IL

Needs, Mike ... (330) 996-3000
Deputy MAN ED-ADM
Akron Beacon Journal, Akron, OH

Neeleman, Gary ... (213) 237-5485
VP/DIR-Sales-LATSI, Los Angeles Times Syndicate, Los Angeles, CA

Neeley, Colleen M ... (607) 776-2122
PUB, Steuben Courier-Advocate, Bath, NY

Neely, Jack ... (412) 282-8000
Photo ED, Butler Eagle, Butler, PA

Neely, Larry ... (315) 823-3680
ED, Evening Times, Little Falls, NY

Neely, Paul ... (423) 756-1234
PUB, Chattanooga Times, Chattanooga, TN

Neely Jr, Richard A ... (804) 649-6000
CIRC MGR-MET
Richmond Times-Dispatch, Richmond, VA

Neer, Rod ... (701) 572-2165
ADV MGR-CLASS
Williston Daily Herald, Williston, ND

Neff, Erin ... (215) 855-8440
EDU ED, Reporter, Landsdale, PA

Neff Roth, Amy ... (215) 949-4000
Health/Medical Writer
Bucks County Courier Times, Levittown, PA

Neft, Sue ... (701) 572-2165
Lifestyle ED
Williston Daily Herald, Williston, ND

Negrete, Tom ... (916) 321-1000
Deputy Sports ED
Sacramento Bee, Sacramento, CA

Negroni, Andrea Lee ... (203) 637-1233
VP, Sisters Syndicate, Old Greenwich, CT

Negroni, Christine ... (203) 637-1233
PRES, Sisters Syndicate, Old Greenwich, CT

Neher, Megan ... (913) 843-1000
BUS ED, Journal-World, Lawrence, KS

Nehr, Tim ... (805) 763-3171
Sports ED, Daily Midway Driller, Taft, CA

Neice, Jack ... (606) 666-2451
ED, Jackson Times, Jackson, KY

Neidig, Brett ... (717) 286-5671
PROD SUPV-MR, Daily Item, Sunbury, PA

Neiers, Carl ... (319) 252-2421
GM, Guttenberg Press, Guttenberg, IA

Neighbors, Roy ... (918) 581-8300
PROD SUPT-PR, Tulsa World, Tulsa, OK

Neighbours, Jimmy ... (318) 559-2750
GM, Banner-Democrat, Lake Providence, LA

Neiheisel, Steven H ... (513) 721-2700
PROD MGR-MR
Cincinnati Enquirer, Cincinnati, OH

Neikirk, Mark ... (606) 292-2600
ASST MAN ED
Kentucky Post, Covington, KY

Neilan, Edward ... (81-3) 33063858
Asia & China COL, Neilan, Edward, Tokyo,

Neill, Kenneth ... (901) 521-9000
PUB, Memphis Flyer, Memphis, TN

Neill, Peter ... (773) 586-8800
EIC, Daily Southtown, Chicago, IL

Neill, Rolfe ... (704) 358-5000
Chairman, PUB, Observer, Charlotte, NC

Neilsen, Mark ... (604) 692-7526
ED, Lakes District News, Burns Lake, BC

Neilsen, Mike ... (303) 833-2331
PUB, ED
Frederick Farmer & Miner, Frederick, CO

Neilsen, Russ ... (503) 466-5311
PUB, ED, Times, Brownsville, OR

Neilson, Kathy ... (215) 854-2000
VP-Human Resources
Philadelphia Inquirer, Philadelphia, PA

Neilson, Larz D ... (508) 658-2346
PUB, Town Crier, Wilmington, MA

Neilson, Stu ... (508) 658-2346
GM, Town Crier, Wilmington, MA

Neiman, Kendall ... (308) 346-4504
PUB, ED, Burwell Tribune, Burwell, NE

Neira, Gail E ... (415) 821-4452
PUB, MAN ED
Tiempo Latino, San Francisco, CA

Neis, Keith ... (612) 459-3434
ED, Washington County Bulletin, Cottage Grove, MN

Neises, Craig ... (319) 465-3555
ED, Monticello Express, Monticello, IA

Neitz, Dean A ... (406) 563-5283
PUB, Anaconda Leader, Anaconda, MT

Nelander, Bob ... (847) 381-9200
MAN ED
Barrington Courier-Review, Barrington, IL

Nelms, Rosemary ... (901) 529-2211
Librarian, Commercial Appeal, Memphis, TN

Nelson, Alan ... (541) 382-1811
PROD SUPV-PR, Bulletin, Bend, OR

Nelson, Anne ... (910) 368-2222
GM, Pilot, Pilot Mountain, NC

Nelson, Chris ... (403) 250-4200
EIC, MAN ED, Calgary Sun, Calgary, AB

Nelson, Chuck ... (614) 224-4835
ED, Daily Reporter, Columbus, OH

Nelson, David ... (520) 364-3424
EPE, Daily Dispatch, Douglas, AZ

Nelson, David F ... (316) 783-5034
PUB, Galena Sentinel Times, Galena, KS

Nelson, Deanna ... (573) 471-1137
ADV MGR-GEN
Standard Democrat, Sikeston, MO

Nelson, Deb ... (913) 823-6363
ADTX MGR, Salina Journal, Salina, KS

Nelson, Don ... (706) 549-0123
BUS/FIN ED, RE ED, SCI/Tech ED, Athens Daily News/Banner-Herald, Athens, GA

Nelson, Don ... (806) 647-3123
PUB, ED, Castro County News, Dimmitt, TX

Nelson, Duwayne ... (412) 654-6651
CIRC MGR
New Castle News, New Castle, PA

Nelson, Gary ... (860) 646-0500
CIRC ASST DIR
Journal Inquirer, Manchester, CT

Nelson, Gary ... (541) 776-4411
Night ED, Mail Tribune, Medford, OR

Nelson, George ... (330) 629-6200
ED, Boardman Town Crier, Youngstown, OH

Nelson, Hulda ... (415) 777-1111
Art DIR
San Francisco Chronicle, San Francisco, CA

Nelson, J W ... (815) 625-3600
GM, Daily Gazette, Sterling, IL
Shaw Newspapers

Nelson, Jane ... (515) 421-0500
Regional ED, Globe-Gazette, Mason City, IA

Nelson, Janie ... (904) 599-2100
ASST MAN ED
Tallahassee Democrat, Tallahassee, FL

Nelson, Jeff ... (217) 732-2101
MAN ED, Courier, Lincoln, IL

Nelson, Jenny ... (409) 776-4444
EDU ED, Eagle, Bryan, TX

Nelson, Jim ... (605) 865-3546
PUB, ED
Timber Lake Topic, Timber Lake, SD

Nelson, John ... (414) 235-7700
ADV MGR-RT
Oshkosh Northwestern, Oshkosh, WI

Nelson, John ... (613) 445-3805
ED, Russell Villager, Russell, ON

Nelson, John A ... (606) 678-0161
PUB, Pulaski Week, Somerset, KY

Nelson, Judy ... (217) 223-5100
Librarian, Quincy Herald-Whig, Quincy, IL

Nelson, Kate ... (505) 823-7777
Breaking News ED, Politics
Albuquerque Tribune, Albuquerque, NM

Nelson, Kathleen ... (314) 340-8000
Travel ED, Post-Dispatch, St. Louis, MO

Nelson, Kathy ... (918) 825-3292
CIRC MGR, Daily Times, Pryor, OK

Nelson, Kathy Snyder ... (605) 865-3546
PUB, ED
Timber Lake Topic, Timber Lake, SD

Nelson, Kim ... (540) 980-5220
Sports ED, Southwest Times, Pulaski, VA

Nelson, Max ... (515) 753-6611
CIRC DIR
Times-Republican, Marshalltown, IA

Nelson, Michael ... (201) 646-4000
MGR-CR, Record, Hackensack, NJ

Nelson, Nancy ... (717) 767-6397
ADV MGR-CLASS
York Newspaper Company, York, PA

Nelson, Neil O ... (701) 524-1640
MAN ED, Steele County Press, Finley, ND

Nelson, Norrell ... (810) 332-8181
CIRC MGR-Sales, Oakland Press, Pontiac, MI

Nelson, Ralph ... (617) 593-7700
ASST MAN ED
Daily Evening Item, Lynn, MA

Nelson, Ralph ... (573) 759-2127
ED, Dixon Pilot, Dixon, MO

Nelson, Richard ... (814) 773-3161
PROD FRM, Ridgway Record, Ridgway, PA

Nelson, Rick ... (360) 795-3391
ED
Wahkiakum County Eagle, Cathlamet, WA

Nelson, Robert ... (203) 744-5100
PROD FRM-COMP, News-Times, Danbury, CT

Nelson, Robert ... (360) 795-3391
PUB, MAN ED
Wahkiakum County Eagle, Cathlamet, WA

Nelson, Roberta J ... (707) 545-1166
Filings, Sonoma County Daily Herald-Recorder, Santa Rosa, CA

Nelson, Roger ... (205) 325-2222
ADV MGR-RT
Birmingham Post-Herald, Birmingham, AL

Nelson, Stan ... (501) 442-1777
MGR-Computers/Technology
Northwest Arkansas Times, Fayetteville, AR

Nelson, Stephen C ... (904) 359-4111
Art DIR
Florida Times-Union, Jacksonville, FL

Nelson, Tammy ... (970) 867-5651
ADV MGR-CLASS, CIRC MGR
Fort Morgan Times, Fort Morgan, CO

Nelson, Terri ... (818) 713-3000
CONT, Daily News, Woodland Hills, CA

Nelson, Tina ... (512) 445-3500
MGR-Cox Interactive Media Content
Austin American-Statesman, Austin, TX

Nelson, Todd ... (402) 475-4200
ADV MGR-CLASS
Lincoln Journal Star, Lincoln, NE

Nelson, Tracey ... (334) 493-3595
ED, Opp News, Opp, AL

Nelson, William B ... (312) 222-3237
VP-Financial OPER
Tribune Co., Chicago, IL

Nelson III, William H M ... (910) 368-2222
PUB, ED, Pilot, Pilot Mountain, NC

Neman, Dan ... (804) 649-6000
Films Writer
Richmond Times-Dispatch, Richmond, VA

Nemec, John T ... (216) 541-7243
ED, Amerikanski Slovenec-Glasilo KSKJ, Cleveland, OH

Nemecek, Katherine M ... (716) 394-0770
ADV MGR-CLASS, Daily Messenger/The Sunday Messenger, Canandaigua, NY

Nemet, Charles ... (408) 761-7300
CIRC DIR
Register-Pajaronian, Watsonville, CA

Nemeth, Patrick ... (815) 223-3200
CIRC DIR, News-Tribune, La Salle, IL

Nemeth, Robert Z ... (508) 793-9100
EPE, Telegram & Gazette, Worcester, MA

Nemeti, Gay ... (305) 350-2111
Library MGR, Miami Herald, Miami, FL

Nemitz, Andrea ... (207) 791-6650
ASST MAN ED-Design
Portland Press Herald, Portland, ME

Nenni, Pete ... (847) 427-4300
ED-Lake County
Daily Herald, Arlington Heights, IL

Neral, Gene ... (814) 736-9666
GM, Portage Dispatch, Portage, PA

Nerber, Melinda ... (810) 756-8800
ED, Warren Weekly, Warren, MI

Neri, Al ... (814) 870-1600
Harrisburg BU, COL
Morning News/Erie Daily Times, Erie, PA

Neri, Thomas J ... (312) 321-3000
EVP/PUB (Pioneer Press)
Chicago Sun-Times, Chicago, IL

Nerney, Chris ... (508) 626-3800
BUS ED, Middlesex News, Framingham, MA

Neron, Carol ... (418) 545-4474
EDL, Le Quotidien, Chicoutimi, QC

Nesbit, John ... (614) 397-5333
ADV DIR, DP MGR
Mount Vernon News, Mount Vernon, OH

Nesbit, Mark ... (802) 362-2222
PUB, Manchester Journal, Manchester, VT

Nesbitt, Gregory ... (204) 759-2644
PUB, ED, Hamiota Echo, Shoal Lake, MB

Nesbitt, Jim L ... (403) 362-5571
PUB, Brooks Bulletin, Brooks, AB

Nesbitt Jr, Jim ... (403) 362-5571
ED, Brooks Bulletin, Brooks, AB

Nesbitt, Jon ... (403) 362-5571
GM, Brooks Bulletin, Brooks, AB

Neslin, Bud ... (801) 625-4200
CIRC MGR, Standard-Examiner, Ogden, UT

Nesmith, Alvin ... (408) 920-5000
PROD MGR-PR
San Jose Mercury News, San Jose, CA

Ness, Douglas ... (360) 694-3391
VP-FIN, Columbian, Vancouver, WA

Ness, Gunnard ... (701) 229-3641
PUB, Nelson County Arena, Fordville, ND

Ness, Truman ... (701) 229-3641
ED, Nelson County Arena, Fordville, ND

Nesseler, Marc ... (309) 764-4344
Sports ED, Dispatch, Moline, IL
Small Newspaper Group Inc.

Nesser, Janice ... (316) 283-1500
BM, DP MGR, Newton Kansan, Newton, KS

Nestler, Julia A ... (815) 454-2072
PUB, ED, Sheffield Bulletin, Sheffield, IL

Nethaway, Rowland ... (817) 757-5757
Senior ED, ADTX MGR
Waco Tribune-Herald, Waco, TX

Nethercutt, Judy ... (501) 378-3400
MGR-DP/BUS, DP MGR
Arkansas Democrat-Gazette, Little Rock, AR

Netherland, Debbie ... (504) 732-2565
ADV MGR-CLASS, Daily News, Bogalusa, LA

Netherton, Bob ... (602) 898-6500
Graphics ED/Art DIR, News ED
Mesa Tribune, Mesa, AZ
Thomson Newspapers

Neto, Julius ... (860) 241-6200
PROD MGR-Packaging & Transportation
Hartford Courant, Hartford, CT

Nettles, Randolph ... (912) 236-9511
PROD ASST SUPV-PR
Savannah Morning News, Savannah, GA

Neu, Margaret ... (512) 884-2011
Librarian, Corpus Christi Caller-Times, Corpus Christi, TX

Neubauer, Charles ... (312) 321-3000
Investigative Reporter
Chicago Sun-Times, Chicago, IL

Neuenschwander, Gary ... (608) 252-6400
Photo/Graphics ED
Capital Times, Madison, WI

Neuffer, Elizabeth ... (617) 929-2000
BU Chief-Berlin
Boston Globe, Boston, MA

Neugebauer, Mary ... (605) 946-5489
PUB, ED, Corsica Globe, Corsica, SD

Neuhauser, Ken ... (502) 582-4011
Action Line ED
Courier-Journal, Louisville, KY

Neuman, Johanna ... (703) 276-3400
Foreign ED, USA Today, Arlington, VA

Neumann, Brett ... (209) 734-5821
ADV MGR-CLASS
Visalia Times-Delta, Visalia, CA

Neumann, P ... (410) 752-3849
ADV Sales MGR
Daily Record, Baltimore, MD

Neumann, Roger ... (607) 734-5151
Sports ED, Star-Gazette, Elmira, NY

Neumeger, Paul ... (517) 752-7171
Sports ED, Saginaw News, Saginaw, MI

Neumueller, Anders ... (604) 731-6381
ED, Svenska Pressen, Blaine, WA

Neuwirth, Eric ... (608) 873-6671
ED, Stoughton Courier-Hub, Stoughton, WI

Nevan, Gary ... (503) 861-3331
PUB, ED, Columbia Press, Warrenton, OR

Nevan, Julia ... (503) 861-3331
PUB, Columbia Press, Warrenton, OR

Nevans, Lisa ... (301) 670-1400
EPE, Montgomery Journal, Rockville, MD

Nevarez, Manny ... (915) 546-6100
CIRC MGR-Single Copy Sales/Country
El Paso Times, El Paso, TX

Neve, Daryl ... (412) 654-6651
ADV MGR-RT
New Castle News, New Castle, PA

Nev Who's Where-168

Nevens, Tom ... (905) 684-7251
EPE, Standard, St. Catharines, ON

Neverman, Duane ... (603) 524-3800
PROD MGR, Citizen, Laconia, NH

Nevich, Dianne ... (518) 725-8616
BUS/FIN ED, Leader-Herald, Gloversville, NY

Nevich, Tom ... (518) 725-8616
ED, Books/Food ED, EPE
Leader-Herald, Gloversville, NY

Neville, John ... (716) 849-3434
News ED, Buffalo News, Buffalo, NY

Neville, Penn ... (281) 422-8302
ADV MGR-Display
Baytown Sun, Baytown, TX

Nevins, Gail ... (717) 421-3000
Action Line ED
Pocono Record, Stroudsburg, PA

Nevitt, Cindy ... (609) 272-7000
Food ED, Travel ED
Press of Atlantic City, Pleasantville, NJ

Nevius, C W ... (415) 777-1111
COL-Sports
San Francisco Chronicle, San Francisco, CA

Nevola, Robert ... (203) 789-5200
PROD MGR, Register, New Haven, CT

Newbart, Dave ... (608) 252-6400
Higher EDU ED, Capital Times, Madison, WI

Newbegin, William B ... (207) 873-3341
PROD DIR, Central Maine Morning Sentinel, Waterville, ME
Guy Gannett Communications

Newbury, Sally ... (908) 922-6000
ADV MGR-BUS Development
Asbury Park Press, Neptune, NJ

Newcom, Scot ... (205) 549-2000
CIRC DIR, Gadsden Times, Gadsden, AL

Newcombe, Richard S ... (310) 337-7003
PRES/CEO
Creators Syndicate, Los Angeles, CA

Newell, Cliff ... (915) 263-7331
Sports ED, Big Spring Herald, Big Spring, TX

Newell, Frank H ... (520) 625-5511
PUB
Green Valley News & Sun, Green Valley, AZ

Newell, Gary ... (218) 751-3740
CIRC DIR, Daily Pioneer, Bemidji, MN

Newell, Richard D ... (619) 433-5771
VP-ADM
Howard Publications, Oceanside, CA

Newfield, Jack ... (212) 930-8000
COL, New York Post, New York, NY

Newgate, J Baxter ... (212) 535-6811
PRES, Megalo Media, Syosset, NY

Newgren, Michael D ... (402) 341-7323
MAN ED, Reader, Omaha, NE

Newhall, Anthony ... (415) 777-1111
ASSOC PUB
San Francisco Chronicle, San Francisco, CA

Newhouse, Dave ... (510) 208-6300
Sports COL, Oakland Tribune, Oakland, CA
MediaNews Inc. (Alameda Newspapers)

Newhouse, Donald E ... (718) 981-1234
PRES
Advance Publications, Staten Island, NY

Newhouse, Eric ... (406) 791-1444
Opinion ED
Great Falls Tribune, Great Falls, MT

Newhouse II, John E ... (318) 487-6397
CEO, PUB
Alexandria Daily Town Talk, Alexandria, LA

Newhouse, Mark ... (201) 877-4141
VP, Star-Ledger, Newark, NJ

Newhouse, Michael ... (609) 989-5454
VP/SEC, GM, Times, Trenton, NJ

Newhouse, Nancy ... (212) 556-1234
Travel ED, New York Times, New York, NY

Newhouse, Robyn A ... (413) 788-1000
ASST to PUB, Union-News, Springfield, MA

Newhouse, S I ... (718) 981-1234
COB
Advance Publications, Staten Island, NY

Newhouse III, S I ... (503) 221-8327
TREAS, Oregonian, Portland, OR
Advance Publications

Newhouse, Steven ... (201) 653-1000
EIC, Jersey Journal, Jersey City, NJ

Newhouse, Theodore ... (503) 221-8327
VP, Oregonian, Portland, OR
Advance Publications

Newkirk, Jim ... (713) 220-7171
City ED-Day, Houston Chronicle, Houston, TX

Newland, Bill ... (316) 326-3326
ADV DIR
Wellington Daily News, Wellington, KS

Newland, Lafayette ... (817) 387-3811
PROD MGR
Denton Record-Chronicle, Denton, TX

Newlin, Paul ... (405) 372-5000
Agriculture ED, News Press, Stillwater, OK

Newlin, Tim ... (011) 45 31 863092
Self-Syndicator, Tim's Features, Denmark

Newman, Andy ... (412) 488-1212
ED
In Pittsburgh Newsweekly, Pittsburgh, PA

Newman, Brant ... (412) 222-2200
ED-Night
Observer-Reporter, Washington, PA

Newman, Denny ... (218) 829-4705
PROD MGR-Pre Press/SYS
Brainerd Daily Dispatch, Brainerd, MN

Newman, Deron ... (937) 456-5553
ED, County Register, Eaton, OH

Newman, Doris ... (903) 569-2442
ED, Mineola Monitor, Mineola, TX

Newman, Harry ... (330) 296-9657
CIRC DIR, PROD FRM-MR
Record-Courier, Kent-Ravenna, OH

Newman, Joe ... (561) 820-4100
BU Chief-Delray Beach
Palm Beach Post, West Palm Beach, FL

Newman, Launa Q ... (612) 827-4021
PUB
Minneapolis Spokesman, Minneapolis, MN

Newman, Linda ... (970) 879-1502
PROD MGR
Steamboat Today, Steamboat Springs, CO

Newman, Marvin ... (501) 315-8228
ADV DIR, Benton Courier, Benton, AR

Newman, Michael ... (604) 498-3711
PUB, MAN ED, Oliver Chronicle, Oliver, BC

Newman, Robin ... (406) 296-2514
PUB, Tobacco Valley News, Eureka, MT

Newman, Ruth ... (701) 572-2165
MAN ED
Williston Daily Herald, Williston, ND

Newman, Stanley ... (516) 795-8823
PRES/ED, American Crossword Federation, Massapequa Park, NY

Newman, Stephen ... (215) 557-2300
PROD MGR
Legal Intelligencer, Philadelphia, PA

Newman, Steve ... (406) 296-2514
PUB, ED, Tobacco Valley News, Eureka, MT

Newman, Sue ... (405) 223-2200
Religion ED, Daily Ardmoreite, Ardmore, OK

Newman, Susan ... (909) 684-1200
Art DIR, Press-Enterprise, Riverside, CA

Newman, Tina ... (707) 226-3711
CIRC DIR, Napa Valley Register, Napa, CA

Newman, Tom ... (215) 345-3000
PROD FRM-PR
Intelligencer/Record, Doylestown, PA

Newmark, Judy ... (314) 340-8000
Theater ED
St. Louis Post-Dispatch, St. Louis, MO

Newnes, Duane ... (216) 951-0000
CIRC DIR, News-Herald, Willoughby, OH

Newnham, Blaine ... (206) 464-2111
ASSOC ED-COL, Seattle Times, Seattle, WA

Newpher, Jan ... (802) 748-8121
City/MET ED
Caledonian-Record, St. Johnsbury, VT

Newquist, Lee ... (214) 757-9000
PUB, Dallas Observer, Dallas, TX

Newsom, Bill ... (501) 968-5252
EX ED, Courier, Russellville, AR

Newsom, Gary ... (915) 337-4661
ED, Odessa American, Odessa, TX

Newsome, Gail ... (904) 792-2487
ED, Jasper News, Jasper, FL

Newsome, Hal ... (904) 270-5226
ED, Mirror, Mayport, FL

Newsome, Michael ... (717) 771-2000
CONT, York Daily Record, York, PA

Newsome Sr, P Smythe ... (706) 678-2636
PUB, ED, News-Reporter, Washington, GA

Newsome, Sparky ... (706) 678-2636
GM, MAN ED
News-Reporter, Washington, GA

Newton, Jennifer ... (912) 625-7722
ED, News & Farmer & Wadely Herald, Louisville, GA

Newton, Kathleen ... (909) 684-1200
PUB-Temecula-Murrieta Edition
Press-Enterprise, Riverside, CA

Newton, Ken ... (816) 271-8500
City ED
St. Joseph News-Press, St. Joseph, MO

Newton, Kevin M ... (616) 722-3161
ADV DIR, Muskegon Chronicle, Muskegon, MI

Newton, Lauren P ... (202) 232-3060
GM, Washington New Observer, Washington, DC

Newton, Lena ... (609) 845-3300
PROD FRM-COMP
Gloucester County Times, Woodbury, NJ

Newton, P Carter ... (815) 777-0019
PUB, ED, Galena Gazette, Galena, IL

Newton, Robert B ... (202) 232-3060
PUB, ED
Washington New Observer, Washington, DC

Newton, Robert L ... (501) 226-5831
PUB, ED
Warren Eagle Democrat, Warren, AR

Newton, Russell ... (407) 420-5000
PROD MGR-Packaging/OPC
Orlando Sentinel, Orlando, FL

Newton, Tommy ... (502) 926-0123
Sunday ED
Messenger-Inquirer, Owensboro, KY

Ng, Assunta ... (206) 223-0623
PUB, MAN ED
Northwest Asian Weekly, Seattle, WA

Ng, Peter ... (306) 634-2654
PUB, Mercury, Estevan, SK

Nguyen, Co ... (714) 892-9414
ED
Nguoi Viet Daily News, Westminster, CA

Nguyen, Hoang ... (714) 892-9414
MAN ED
Nguoi Viet Daily News, Westminster, CA

Nianiatus, George ... (716) 372-3121
BUS ED, Olean Times-Herald, Olean, NY

Nibert, Brad ... (210) 383-2705
MAN ED, Society ED, PROD SUPV
Edinburg Daily Review, Edinburg, TX

Nibley, Andrew ... (202) 898-8300
Sr. VP-Sales & MKTG
Reuters, Washington, DC

Nicas, Leslie ... (402) 444-1000
CIRC CNR-EDU SRV
Omaha World-Herald, Omaha, NE

Nicastro, Joseph ... (201) 839-7200
PUB, ED
Independent News, Pompton Lakes, NJ

Nice, Shellie ... (219) 461-8444
CIRC MGR-Sales/PROM
Fort Wayne Newspapers Inc., Fort Wayne, IN

Nicewaner, Myron ... (937) 328-0300
PROD MGR, News-Sun, Springfield, OH

Nich, William ... (219) 255-4789
ED, Mishawaka Enterprise, Mishawaka, IN

Nichol, David ... (501) 238-2375
ED, East Arkansas News Leader, Wynne, AR

Nicholas, Jonathan ... (503) 221-8327
COL, Oregonian, Portland, OR

Nicholas, Wayne ... (601) 843-4241
MAN ED, Bolivar Commercial, Cleveland, MS

Nichols, Alan ... (415) 777-1111
COO
San Francisco Chronicle, San Francisco, CA

Nichols, Alan H ... (616) 845-5181
SEC, BM, Daily News, Ludington, MI

Nichols, Billy ... (601) 636-4545
DP MGR, Vicksburg Post, Vicksburg, MS

Nichols Jr, Carlos ... (915) 445-5475
PROD FRM-PR, Pecos Enterprise, Pecos, TX

Nichols, Cliff ... (304) 367-2500
Sports ED
Times-West Virginian, Fairmont, WV

Nichols, Clinton N ... (304) 587-4250
PUB, ED, Clay County Free Press, Clay, WV

Nichols, Dan ... (618) 532-5604
GM, ADV MGR
Centralia Sentinel, Centralia, IL

Nichols, Debi ... (814) 362-6563
ED, Bradford Journal-Miner, Bradford, PA

Nichols, Debra ... (316) 429-2773
VP/SEC
Columbus Daily Advocate, Columbus, KS

Nichols, Dennis ... (513) 863-8200
News ED, Journal-News, Hamilton, OH

Nichols Jr, Edward A ... (717) 821-2091
PRES, PUB
Citizens' Voice, Wilkes-Barre, PA

Nichols, Flora ... (805) 845-3704
ED, Lamont Reporter, Lamont, CA

Nichols, Grant ... (814) 362-6563
PUB, Bradford Journal-Miner, Bradford, PA

Nichols, Jeffrey L ... (316) 429-2773
PRES, PUB
Columbus Daily Advocate, Columbus, KS

Nichols, Jim ... (812) 283-6636
Fashion/Style ED, Lifestyle ED
Evening News, Jeffersonville, IN

Nichols, Joan L ... (419) 422-5151
ASST SEC, Courier, Findlay, OH

Nichols, John ... (608) 252-6400
Books ED, Political ED
Capital Times, Madison, WI

Nichols, Kent ... (360) 452-2345
BUS/FIN Writer
Peninsula Daily News, Port Angeles, WA

Nichols, Marita ... (903) 378-2396
ED
Honey Grove Signal Citizen, Honey Grove, TX

Nichols, Mark ... (501) 868-4400
VP, Daily Record, Little Rock, AR

Nichols, Nanalee ... (903) 632-5322
PUB, ED, Bogata News, Bogata, TX

Nichols, Newton ... (304) 354-6917
ED, Calhoun Chronicle, Grantsville, WV

Nichols, Paula ... (915) 558-3541
PUB, Crane County News, Crane, TX

Nichols, Rick ... (215) 854-2000
EDL Writer
Philadelphia Inquirer, Philadelphia, PA

Nichols, Skip ... (915) 558-3541
PUB, ED, Crane County News, Crane, TX

Nichols, Thomas ... (903) 652-4205
ED, Blossom Times, Blossom, TX

Nicholson, Ann ... (314) 426-2222
MAN ED
North County East Journal, St. Louis, MO

Nicholson, Jim ... (215) 854-2000
Obit Writer
Philadelphia Daily News, Philadelphia, PA

Nicholson, Jim ... (918) 297-2577
ED, Hartshorne Sun, Hartshorne, OK

Nicholson, Laura ... (916) 741-2345
Assignment ED
Appeal-Democrat, Marysville, CA

Nicholson, Virginia ... (304) 873-1600
PUB, ED, Herald Record, West Union, WV

Nichosia, Patsy ... (518) 234-2515
ED, Times-Journal, Cobleskill, NY

Nickel, David B ... (519) 271-2220
ADV MGR
Stratford Beacon-Herald, Stratford, ON

Nickel, Jackie ... (410) 687-7775
ED, Avenue News, Baltimore, MD

Nickel, Milo A ... (318) 783-3450
PUB, Crowley Post-Signal, Crowley, LA

Nicklaus, David ... (314) 340-8000
BUS/FIN ED
St. Louis Post-Dispatch, St. Louis, MO

Nicks, Nicholas ... (608) 782-9710
CIRC MGR, La Crosse Tribune, La Crosse, WI

Nicodemus, Charles ... (312) 321-3000
GEN Assignment
Chicago Sun-Times, Chicago, IL

Nicol, Richard ... (716) 232-7100
PROD MGR-Distribution, Rochester Democrat and Chronicle; Times-Union, Rochester, NY

Nicolette, David ... (616) 222-5400
Theater ED
Grand Rapids Press, Grand Rapids, MI

Nicoll, Ann ... (941) 763-3134
PROD DIR
Daily Okeechobee News, Okeechobee, FL

Nicolosi, Russell J ... (908) 922-6000
DIR-INFO Services
Asbury Park Press, Neptune, NJ

Nicoson, Don ... (602) 271-8000
EX News ED, Arizona Republic, Phoenix, AZ

Nicusanti, Diane ... (415) 777-5700
ADV MGR-Sales (SF Examiner Magazine)
San Francisco Newspaper Agency, San Francisco, CA

Niday, Troy ... (402) 444-1000
CIRC MGR-State
Omaha World-Herald, Omaha, NE

Nied, Thomas H ... (212) 556-1234
VP-Taxation
New York Times Co., New York, NY

Niederpruem, Kyle ... (317) 633-1240
Environmental Writer
Indianapolis Star/News, Indianapolis, IN

Niederquell, Jeri ... (517) 752-7171
ADV MGR-CLASS
Saginaw News, Saginaw, MI

Niehaus, Janet ... (313) 222-6400
MGR-SYS/Applications
Detroit Newspapers, Detroit, MI

Niehaus, Thomas E ... (513) 248-8600
PUB
Western Community Journal, Loveland, OH

Nielsen, David ... (916) 741-2345
Photo ED, Appeal-Democrat, Marysville, CA

Nielsen, Karol ... (914) 636-7400
ED, Parkchester News, Bronx, NY

Nielsen, M K ... (509) 459-5000
SEC/TREAS
Spokesman-Review, Spokane, WA

Nielsen, Melvin ... (309) 367-2335
PUB, ED, Metamora Herald, Metamora, IL

Nielsen, Nancy ... (212) 556-1234
VP-CORP Communications
New York Times Co., New York, NY

Nielsen, Randee ... (801) 625-4200
ADV MGR-RT
Standard-Examiner, Ogden, UT

Nielsen, Scott ... (916) 321-1000
PROD MGR-Post Press Op
Sacramento Bee, Sacramento, CA

Nielsen, Soren ... (319) 588-5611
MAN ED, Telegraph Herald, Dubuque, IA

Nielson, Alvin ... (307) 672-2431
PROD MGR-SYS
Sheridan Press, Sheridan, WY

Nielson, Donald L ... (712) 343-2154
PUB, ED, Avoca Journal-Herald, Avoca, IA

Nielson, Roger ... (706) 549-0123
Religion ED, Athens Daily News/Banner-Herald, Athens, GA

Nieman, Craig ... (806) 364-2030
CIRC MGR, Hereford Brand, Hereford, TX

Nieman, Jim ... (513) 422-3611
News ED
Middletown Journal, Middletown, OH

Nieman, Joy ... (414) 887-0321
DP MGR, Daily Citizen, Beaver Dam, WI

Nieman, O G ... (806) 364-2030
PRES, PUB, Hereford Brand, Hereford, TX

Nieman, Valerie ... (304) 367-2500
MAN ED
Times-West Virginian, Fairmont, WV

169-Who's Where **Nor**

Niemeyer, Diane .... (414) 563-5553
ADV MGR-CLASS, Daily Jefferson County Union, Fort Atkinson, WI
Nierling, Dan .... (319) 291-1400
Photo DEPT MGR
Waterloo Courier, Waterloo, IA
Nies, Christy .... (217) 245-6121
Farm ED, Journal-Courier, Jacksonville, IL
Niese, William A .... (213) 237-5000
Senior VP-Law/Human Resources
Los Angeles Times, Los Angeles, CA
Niesen, Bob .... (608) 252-6200
PROD SUPT-MR
Madison Newspapers Inc., Madison, WI
Niesen, Diana .... (801) 674-6200
CIRC MGR-Creative SRV
Spectrum, St. George, UT
Nieter, Gary .... (219) 267-3111
Photo DEPT MGR, Picture ED
Times-Union, Warsaw, IN
Nieto, Reynaldo .... (210) 775-1551
PROD SUPV-PR
Del Rio News-Herald, Del Rio, TX
Nikkel, Greg .... (306) 842-7487
ED, Weyburn Review, Weyburn, SK
Nikolich, Gojan .... (970) 328-6656
PUB, ED, Eagle Valley Enterprise, Eagle, CO
Nikolishen, Kathleen P .... (814) 472-8240
ED, Mountaineer-Herald, Ebensburg, PA
Nilles, Lori .... (515) 832-4350
ED, Daily Freeman-Journal, Webster City, IA
Nilsen, Richard .... (602) 271-8000
Fine Arts Writer
Arizona Republic, Phoenix, AZ
Nilson, Amy .... (209) 532-7151
BUS/FIN ED, Union Democrat, Sonora, CA
Nilson, Roy .... (508) 793-9100
Online MGR
Telegram & Gazette, Worcester, MA
Nilsson, Joel .... (602) 271-8000
EDL Writer, Arizona Republic, Phoenix, AZ
Nimocks, Amber .... (910) 323-4848
EDU ED
Fayetteville Observer-Times, Fayetteville, NC
Ninestine, Thomas J .... (717) 286-5671
Online Services ED, Daily Item, Sunbury, PA
Ninneman, Kathie .... (210) 379-5402
MAN ED
Seguin Gazette-Enterprise, Seguin, TX
Ninnemann, Gerald F .... (414) 533-8338
PUB, ED
Campbellsport News, Campbellsport, WI
Niquette, Mark .... (330) 747-1471
Political ED, Vindicator, Youngstown, OH
Niro, Leo .... (508) 343-6911
MGR-CR
Sentinel & Enterprise, Fitchburg, MA
Nisbet, Carolee .... (609) 724-4091
ED, Post, Willingboro, NJ
Nishida, Dorothy .... (503) 255-2142
ADV MGR-CLASS
Daily Shipping News, Portland, OR
Nishizaki, Bob .... (510) 935-2525
News ED
Contra Costa Times, Walnut Creek, CA
Niskanen, Chris .... (612) 222-5011
Outdoors ED
St. Paul Pioneer Press, St. Paul, MN
Nissen, Dale .... (713) 220-7171
PROD DIR-OPER/Technical SRV
Houston Chronicle, Houston, TX
Nistler, Joe .... (406) 765-2190
ED, Plentywood Herald, Plentywood, MT
Niswonger, Gary .... (937) 335-5634
PROD DIR, Troy Daily News/Miami Valley Sunday News, Troy, OH
Nitzel, Bob .... (614) 397-5333
MAN ED, EPE
Mount Vernon News, Mount Vernon, OH
Niven, Campbell B .... (207) 729-3311
PRES, PUB, Times Record, Brunswick, ME
Niven, Deuce .... (910) 653-3153
ED, Tabor City Tribune, Tabor City, NC
Niven, Douglas M .... (207) 729-3311
VP/ASST PUB, Times Record, Brunswick, ME
Nivens, Jackie .... (205) 325-2222
PROD MGR-Maintenance
Birmingham News, Birmingham, AL
Nix, Charles D .... (501) 483-6317
PUB, Trumann Democrat, Trumann, AR
Nix, John D .... (803) 577-7111
PROD MGR-Press Processing
Post and Courier, Charleston, SC
Nixon, Ann F .... (813) 942-2883
COB
Fackelman Newspapers, Tarpon Springs, FL
Nixon, Charles .... (712) 684-2821
PUB, ED
Coon Rapids Enterprise, Coon Rapids, IA
Nixon, Frank E .... (813) 942-2883
PRES
Fackelman Newspapers, Tarpon Springs, FL
Nixon, Gregory S .... (219) 563-2131
VP, Wabash Plain Dealer, Wabash, IN
Nixon, John R .... (317) 473-3091
PRES/CEO, Nixon Newspapers Inc., Peru, IN
Nixon, Mark .... (517) 377-1000
EPE, Lansing State Journal, Lansing, MI
Nixon, Treend Herington .... (505) 356-4481
Home Furnishings ED
Portales News-Tribune, Portales, NM
Noah, Douglas .... (507) 789-6161
ED, Kenyon Leader, Kenyon, MN
Noah, Jeanne .... (508) 685-1000
ADV MGR-RT
Eagle-Tribune, North Andover, MA
Noah, Robert D .... (507) 789-6161
PUB, Kenyon Leader, Kenyon, MN
Nobel, Carl .... (916) 891-1234
DP MGR, Chico Enterprise-Record, Chico, CA
Donrey Media Group
Nobel, Mary .... (541) 885-4410
Women's ED
Herald and News, Klamath Falls, OR
Nobile, Ricky .... (601) 843-4241
ADV MGR
Bolivar Commercial, Cleveland, MS
Noble Jr, Clifton J .... (413) 788-1000
Music Critic-Classical
Union-News, Springfield, MA
Noble, Edward R .... (810) 332-8181
Chief Photographer, Photo ED
Oakland Press, Pontiac, MI
Noble, Greg .... (513) 721-2700
Online ED
Cincinnati Enquirer, Cincinnati, OH
Noble, Jeff .... (806) 296-1300
ADV DIR-RT
Plainview Daily Herald, Plainview, TX
Noble, Richard .... (810) 766-6100
Automotive Writer, Flint Journal, Flint, MI
Noble, Robert W .... (518) 372-0785
MAN ED
Empire News Exchange, Schenectady, NY
Noble, Theresa .... (705) 282-2003
ED, Manitoulin Recorder, Gore Bay, ON
Nobles, Doug .... (318) 322-5161
PROD DIR, News-Star, Monroe, LA
Nobles, Fred .... (508) 586-7200
Books ED, Lifestyle ED, SCI/Technology ED, Travel ED, Enterprise, Brockton, MA
Noblitt, John F .... (812) 865-3242
PUB, ED, Progress Examiner, Orleans, IN
Nocera, Ray .... (212) 627-2120
GM, New York Native, New York, NY
Nock, Mary Ann .... (602) 271-8000
ASST MAN ED
Arizona Republic, Phoenix, AZ
Noden, Paul .... (619) 337-3400
Photo ED
Imperial Valley Press, El Centro, CA
Noe, Janet .... (707) 468-3500
ADV MGR-CLASS
Ukiah Daily Journal, Ukiah, CA
Noe, Shelly .... (719) 384-4475
ADV DIR
La Junta Tribune-Democrat, La Junta, CO
Noel, Anthony .... (215) 679-9561
ED, Town and Country, Pennsburg, PA
Noel, Don .... (860) 241-6200
COL-Political, Hartford Courant, Hartford, CT
Noel, Idella M .... (970) 356-7176
PUB, Voice, Kersey, CO
Noel, James P .... (970) 356-7176
PUB, Voice, Kersey, CO
Noel, Jon M .... (412) 439-7500
PROD DIR, Herald-Standard, Uniontown, PA
Noel, Pat .... (970) 963-3211
ED, Valley Journal, Carbondale, CO
Noem, Ruth .... (605) 628-2551
MAN ED, Bryant Dakotan, Bryant, SD
Noeth, Sheila Hoegl .... (516) 931-1400
ED, East Meadow Beacon, Hicksville, NY
Noffsinger, Rick L .... (601) 323-1642
PUB, Starkville Daily News, Starkville, MS
Hollinger International Inc.
Noffsinger, Tom .... (801) 654-1471
MAN ED, Wasatch Wave, Heber City, UT
Noftle, Randy .... (910) 727-7211
DIR-Human Resources
Winston-Salem Journal, Winston-Salem, NC
Nogle, Rick .... (716) 849-3434
PROD OPER FRM-Engraving
Buffalo News, Buffalo, NY
Noguchi, Sharon .... (408) 920-5000
EDL COL
San Jose Mercury News, San Jose, CA
Noguerus, Jose .... (419) 394-7414
MAN ED, Evening Leader, St. Marys, OH
Nola, Mike .... (504) 383-1111
ADV DIR-Display, Advocate, Baton Rouge, LA
Nola, Vicky .... (504) 383-1111
PROD Co-MGR-Creative SRV
Advocate, Baton Rouge, LA
Nolan, Beth .... (815) 842-1153
ADV DIR, Daily Leader, Pontiac, IL
Nolan, Bruce .... (504) 826-3279
Religion ED
Times-Picayune, New Orleans, LA
Nolan, Hazel .... (318) 783-3450
DP MGR, PROD FRM-COMP
Crowley Post-Signal, Crowley, LA
Nolan, Jack .... (334) 749-6271
ADV MGR, Opelika-Auburn News, Opelika, AL
Nolan, James F .... (212) 455-4000
Color Comics MGR, North America Syndicate, King Features Syndicate Inc., New York, NY
Nolan, Jim .... (303) 892-5000
PROD FRM-MR
Rocky Mountain News, Denver, CO
Nolan, John .... (603) 332-2300
ED, Rochester Times, Rochester, NH
Nolan, Kim .... (206) 883-7187
PUB, Redmond Sammamish Valley News, Redmond, WA
Nolan, Martin F .... (617) 929-2000
ASSOC ED, Boston Globe, Boston, MA
Nolan, MaryLou .... (816) 234-4141
Travel ED, Kansas City Star, Kansas City, MO
Nolan, Mason .... (360) 694-3391
SEC, Columbian, Vancouver, WA
Nolan, Mike .... (941) 629-2855
PROD MGR-Distribution
Sun Herald, Port Charlotte, FL
Nolan, Nell .... (504) 826-3279
COL, Times-Picayune, New Orleans, LA
Nolan, Paul .... (519) 853-5100
PUB, ED, Acton Tanner, Acton, ON
Nolan, Ron .... (203) 635-1819
PUB, ED, Cromwell Chronicle, Cromwell, CT
Noland, Kevin J .... (316) 886-5654
PUB, Gyp Hill Premiere, Medicine Lodge, KS
Noland, Ronda D .... (316) 886-5654
GM, Gyp Hill Premiere, Medicine Lodge, KS
Nolda, Harry L .... (319) 933-4370
PUB, ED, Strawberry Pt. Press Journal, Strawberry Point, IA
Nolen, Stan .... (409) 594-2126
ED, Trinity Standard, Trinity, TX
Noles Sr, James R .... (407) 366-9181
PUB, Oviedo Voice, Oviedo, FL
Noles, John C .... (407) 366-9181
GM, Oviedo Voice, Oviedo, FL
Noll, Frank K .... (814) 736-9666
PUB, Portage Dispatch, Portage, PA
Noll, Richard .... (717) 748-6791
ADV MGR, Express, Lock Haven, PA
Noller, Wayne .... (414) 922-4600
Automotive ED, State ED
Reporter, Fond du Lac, WI
Nolte, Ginger .... (304) 348-5140
CIRC DIR
Charleston Newspapers, Charleston, WV
Nolte, Rick .... (304) 526-4000
News ED, Herald-Dispatch, Huntington, WV
Nolte, Robert .... (352) 544-5200
MAN ED, Hernando Today, Brooksville, FL
Nolting, Ray .... (316) 421-2000
Farm/Regional ED, News ED, Television ED
Parsons Sun, Parsons, KS
Nomandin, James F .... (860) 289-6468
PUB
East Hartford Gazette, East Hartford, CT
Noon, Timothy .... (860) 646-0500
PROD FRM-PR
Journal Inquirer, Manchester, CT
Noonan, Frank .... (419) 695-0015
Sports ED
Delphos Daily Herald, Delphos, OH
Noonan, John C .... (708) 594-9340
PUB, ED
Des Plaines Valley News, Summit, IL
Noonan-Kaye, Grace .... (207) 791-6650
VP-Organization Development
Portland Press Herald, Portland, ME
Norais, David .... (507) 625-4451
PROD FRM-COMP, Free Press, Mankato, MN
Norbury, Keith .... (604) 478-9552
ED, Goldstream News Gazette, Victoria, BC
Nordby, Joy .... (218) 294-6220
GM, ED, Grygla Eagle, Grygla, MN
Nordhues, Angie .... (402) 337-0488
ED, Times, Randolph, NE
Nordin, Pam .... (501) 641-7161
GM, Atkins Chronicle, Atkins, AR
Nordine, Julie M .... (218) 436-2157
PUB, ED, North Star News, Karlstad, MN
Nordquist, Constance .... (306) 232-4865
PUB, ED
Saskatchewan Valley News, Rosthern, SK
Nordquist, Gordon .... (417) 468-2013
PUB, Marshfield Mail, Marshfield, MO
Nordstrom, Diane .... (508) 626-3800
ADV MGR-Print & Delivery
Middlesex News, Framingham, MA
Nordwind, Rich .... (714) 835-1234
Topics ED-Show
Orange County Register, Santa Ana, CA
Noren, Robert .... (219) 773-3127
ED, Nappanee Advance News, Nappanee, IN
Noren, Robert .... (616) 946-2000
ADV DIR, Record-Eagle, Traverse City, MI
Norland, Gail .... (218) 843-2868
GM, MAN ED
Kittson County Enterprise, Hallock, MN
Norlander, Richard .... (218) 927-3761
PUB, GM
Aitkin Independent Age, Aitkin, MN
Norlin, John E .... (405) 475-3311
CIRC MGR
Daily Oklahoman, Oklahoma City, OK
Norman, Charles .... (318) 352-5501
ADV MGR, MGR-MKTG/PROM, PROD MGR
Natchitoches Times, Natchitoches, LA
Norman, Chris .... (904) 599-2100
DIR-Technology
Tallahassee Democrat, Tallahassee, FL
Norman, Chris .... (615) 446-2811
ED, Dickson Herald, Dickson, TN
Norman, Dan .... (954) 356-4000
Deputy MAN ED/Sports & Features
Sun-Sentinel, Fort Lauderdale, FL
Norman, Dean .... (216) 251-1389
Artist/Owner
Beaver Creek Features, Cleveland, OH
Norman, Gerald .... (801) 237-2800
PROD FRM-COMP
Newspaper Agency Corp., Salt Lake City, UT
Norman, Nick .... (309) 764-4344
ADV DIR, Dispatch, Moline, IL
Small Newspaper Group Inc.
Norman, Tom .... (801) 373-5050
City ED, Daily Herald, Provo, UT
Normand, Greg .... (810) 651-4141
ED, Rochester Clarion, Rochester, MI
Normand, Juliet .... (403) 743-8186
CIRC MGR/SUPV
Fort McMurray Today, Fort McMurray, AB
Normand, Michel .... (613) 562-0111
ADTX MGR, PROD MGR
Le Droit, Ottawa, ON
Normandin, James F .... (860) 347-3331
PUB, Middlesex Express, Middletown, CT
Norment, Eric .... (617) 426-3000
Sunday ED, Boston Herald, Boston, MA
Norrie, Gordon .... (403) 250-4200
GM, Calgary Sun, Calgary, AB
Norris, David .... (705) 322-1871
ED, Creemore Star, Creemore, ON
Norris, Jan .... (561) 820-4100
Food ED
Palm Beach Post, West Palm Beach, FL
Norris, Jeff .... (501) 751-6200
PROD SUPT, Morning News of Northwest Arkansas, Springdale, AR
Norris, Jim .... (214) 977-8222
PROD Art DIR-Pre Press
Dallas Morning News, Dallas, TX
Norris, Jim .... (516) 843-2020
VP-OPER, PROD Senior VP/OPER DIR
Newsday, Melville, NY
Norris, Joe .... (301) 627-2833
ED
Maryland Independent, Upper Marlboro, MD
Norris, Judy .... (309) 764-4344
EDU ED, Dispatch, Moline, IL
Small Newspaper Group Inc.
Norris, Larry .... (704) 333-1718
ADV MGR
Independent Tribune, Concord, NC
Norris, Lynn E .... (804) 493-8096
GM, ED, Westmoreland News, Montross, VA
Norris, M .... (516) 746-0240
PUB, ED, New Hyde Park Herald Courier, Williston Park, NY
Norris, Meg .... (516) 294-8900
ED, Garden City News, Garden City, NY
Norris, Michael .... (918) 542-5533
PROD FRM-PR, CIRC DIR
Miami News-Record, Miami, OK
Norris, Tom .... (516) 843-2020
MGR-Publishing Data Center
Newsday, Melville, NY
Norstrud, Kim .... (515) 584-2770
ED, Thompson Courier, Thompson, IA
North, Eric .... (317) 462-5528
Religion ED, Daily Reporter, Greenfield, IN
North, Jack .... (519) 426-5710
PROD FRM-PR
Simcoe Reformer, Simcoe, ON
North, John E .... (540) 773-2222
PUB, ED, Declaration, Independence, VA
North, Kristin .... (970) 668-3998
ED, Summit Daily News, Frisco, CO
North, Marjorie .... (941) 953-7755
COL, Sarasota Herald-Tribune, Sarasota, FL
Northcott, Kaye .... (817) 390-7400
ASST Government Affairs ED
Fort Worth Star-Telegram, Fort Worth, TX
Northcott, Peggy .... (314) 432-3353
GM, Saint Louis Jewish Light, St. Louis, MO
Northcutt, Jerilyn .... (706) 724-0851
MGR-Personnel
Augusta Chronicle, Augusta, GA
Northington, Dickie .... (501) 534-3400
PROD FRM-COMP
Pine Bluff Commercial, Pine Bluff, AR
Northrop, Eliza A .... (412) 926-2111
PUB, ED, Record-Outlook, McDonald, PA

Nor Who's Where-170

Northrop, John L S .... (412) 222-2200
PRES, Co-PUB
Observer-Reporter, Washington, PA
Northrop, Thomas P .... (412) 222-2200
ASST VP, PA, PROD DIR-OPER
Observer-Reporter, Washington, PA
Northrop, William B .... (412) 222-2200
VP, Co-PUB
Observer-Reporter, Washington, PA
Northrop Jr, William B .... (412) 222-2200
ASST VP, DIR-MKTG
Observer-Reporter, Washington, PA
Northrup, Nancy .... (701) 873-4381
ED, Beulah Beacon, Beulah, ND
Northrup, Terry .... (801) 237-2800
PROD MGR
Newspaper Agency Corp., Salt Lake City, UT
Northsea, Michel .... (352) 489-2731
GM, Riverland News, Dunnellon, FL
Northy, Linda .... (864) 839-2621
GM, Blacksburg Times & Cherokee Tribune, Blacksburg, SC
Norton, John .... (719) 544-3520
BUS ED, Pueblo Chieftain, Pueblo, CO
Norton, John .... (517) 584-3967
GM, Carson City Gazette, Carson City, MI
Norton, John .... (914) 225-3633
PUB, Putnam Courier-Trader, Carmel, NY
Norton, Larry .... (330) 725-4166
Online MGR
Medina County Gazette, Medina, OH
Norton, Merle .... (706) 324-5526
ADV MGR-Ad Services
Columbus Ledger-Enquirer, Columbus, GA
Norton, Mindy .... (517) 772-2971
Sunday ED
Morning Sun, Mount Pleasant, MI
Norton, Paul .... (608) 252-6400
EDU ED, Capital Times, Madison, WI
Norton, Ross .... (770) 787-6397
MAN ED, Covington News, Covington, GA
Norton, Thomas G .... (618) 463-2500
CIRC DIR, Telegraph, Alton, IL
Norton, Thomas R .... (717) 767-6397
PROD VP-OPER
York Newspaper Company, York, PA
Norton, Wayne .... (408) 637-5566
MAN ED, Free Lance, Hollister, CA
Norton, William .... (603) 742-4455
PROD FRM-MR
Foster's Democrat, Dover, NH
Norwood, Doug .... (501) 751-6200
CIRC MGR, Morning News of Northwest Arkansas, Springdale, AR
Norwood, James .... (814) 371-4200
CIRC MGR, Courier-Express/Tri-County Sunday, Du Bois, PA
Norwood, Joy .... (814) 371-4200
Sunday ED, Courier-Express/Tri-County Sunday, Du Bois, PA
Norwood, Kim .... (913) 823-6363
ADV MGR-Sales, Salina Journal, Salina, KS
Nosel, Dennis M .... (814) 723-8200
CIRC MGR
Warren Times-Observer, Warren, PA
Noseworthy, Carl .... (709) 639-9203
GM, Humber Log, Corner Brook, NF
Nossaman, Larry .... (573) 581-1111
MAN ED, EPE, EDU ED, Farm/Agriculture ED, NTL ED, Political/Government ED, Religion ED, SCI ED
Mexico Ledger, Mexico, MO
Nostrand, Tim .... (201) 646-4000
Passaic ED, Record, Hackensack, NJ
Noto, Eileen .... (303) 820-1010
ADV MGR-NTL, Denver Post, Denver, CO
Nott, Gerry .... (519) 255-5711
ED, Windsor Star, Windsor, ON
Nottage, Samuel .... (904) 599-2100
TREAS, CFO
Tallahassee Democrat, Tallahassee, FL
Nottingham, Bill .... (213) 237-5000
ED-Orange County Edition
Los Angeles Times, Los Angeles, CA
Nottingham, Nancy .... (406) 657-1200
BUS/FIN ED, Billings Gazette, Billings, MT
Novak, Gerald .... (906) 774-2772
PROD FRM-COMP
Daily News, Iron Mountain, MI
Novak, Glenn .... (413) 447-7311
Wire ED, Berkshire Eagle, Pittsfield, MA
Novak, Jerry .... (906) 786-2021
PROD FRM-PR, Daily Press, Escanaba, MI
Novak, John .... (717) 348-9100
PROD FRM-COMP
Tribune & The Scranton Times, Scranton, PA
Novak, Joseph .... (203) 235-1661
DP MGR, Record-Journal, Meriden, CT
Novak, Kim .... (519) 426-5710
MAN ED, Amusements/Books ED, EPE, Farm ED, Simcoe Reformer, Simcoe, ON
Novak Jr, Mike .... (717) 272-5611
PROD FRM-Press, Daily News, Lebanon, PA
Novak, Nancy .... (218) 741-5544
BM, Mesabi Daily News, Virginia, MN
Novak, Scott .... (616) 782-2101
Sports/Films ED
Dowagiac Daily News, Dowagiac, MI
Novak, Theresa .... (503) 399-6611
Environmental ED
Statesman Journal, Salem, OR
Novel, Andrea .... (218) 723-5281
City ED, Duluth News-Tribune, Duluth, MN
Novosel, John .... (773) 586-8800
CIRC DIR, Daily Southtown, Chicago, IL
Novotney, Steve .... (304) 233-0100
Regional ED, Intelligencer/Wheeling News-Register, Wheeling, WV
Novotny, Joe .... (808) 525-8000
PROD MGR-News SYS
Hawaii Newspaper Agency Inc., Honolulu, HI
Novotny, Rose .... (212) 293-8500
MGR-International Syndication, United Media, United Feature Syndicate, Newspaper Enterprise Association, New York, NY
Nowack, Barbara Hill .... (217) 476-3332
PUB, ED, Ashland Sentinel, Ashland, IL
Nowak, Ron .... (914) 477-2575
ED, Greenwood Lake News and West Milford News, Greenwood Lake, NY
Nowicky, Bruno .... (313) 365-1990
PUB, Swiat Polski, Hamtramck, MI
Nowlan, Chuck .... (608) 845-9559
MAN ED, Fitchburg Star, Verona, WI
Nowlin, Gary L .... (610) 820-6500
CIRC MGR-Single Copy Sales
Morning Call, Allentown, PA
Noworyta, Linda .... (716) 282-2311
Features ED
Niagara Gazette, Niagara Falls, NY
Noyce, Robert .... (801) 237-2188
Graphics DIR
Deseret News, Salt Lake City, UT
Noyes, Philip .... (207) 791-6650
PROD OPER Page Build SUPV-Days
Portland Press Herald, Portland, ME
Nuckols, Pam .... (919) 946-2144
Lifestyle ED
Washington Daily News, Washington, NC
Nuel Cates Jr, E .... (214) 741-6366
PUB, ED
Daily Commercial Record, Dallas, TX
Nuese, Connie .... (507) 537-1551
ADV MGR, Independent, Marshall, MN
Nufer, Kathy .... (414) 733-4411
School ED, Post-Crescent, Appleton, WI
Nugent, Janice .... (309) 852-2181
ADV MGR-Sales, Star-Courier, Kewanee, IL
Nugent, Ken .... (905) 454-4344
PUB, Brampton Guardian, Brampton, ON
Nugent, Sue .... (702) 788-6200
ADV CNR-NTL
Reno Gazette-Journal, Reno, NV
Nugent, Wendy .... (316) 283-1500
Food/Lifestyle ED
Newton Kansan, Newton, KS
Nulph, Scott .... (701) 642-8585
Sports ED, Daily News, Wahpeton, ND
Nunes, Don .... (606) 231-3100
ADV DIR
Lexington Herald-Leader, Lexington, KY
Nunes, Janine .... (815) 877-4044
ED, Journal, Rockford, IL
Nunes, Teresa .... (914) 694-9300
CIRC MGR-ADM
Reporter Dispatch, White Plains, NY
Gannett Co. Inc.
Nunn, Bette .... (317) 342-3311
MAN ED, Daily Reporter, Martinsville, IN
Nunn, Charles .... (512) 445-3500
MGR-CR
Austin American-Statesman, Austin, TX
Nunn, Tom .... (519) 894-2231
FIN Reporter, Record, Kitchener, ON
Nunnelley, Carol .... (205) 325-2222
MAN ED
Birmingham News, Birmingham, AL
Nusbaum, Eliot .... (515) 284-8000
Art Critic
Des Moines Register, Des Moines, IA
Nusbaum, Mark .... (913) 295-1111
EX ED, Topeka Capital-Journal, Topeka, KS
Nusbaum, William T .... (414) 435-4411
PRES/PUB
Green Bay Press-Gazette, Green Bay, WI
Nussbaum, David .... (908) 531-6200
PUB, Jewish Voice, Deal Park, NJ
Nussbaum, Gene .... (212) 210-2100
PROD VP
New York Daily News, New York, NY
Nutt Jr, Charles W .... (607) 734-5151
ED, Star-Gazette, Elmira, NY
Nutting, G Ogden .... (304) 233-0100
PRES/PUB
Ogden Newspapers, Wheeling, WV
Nutting, Robert M .... (304) 233-0100
VP/GM, Ogden Newspapers, Wheeling, WV
Nutting, William C .... (304) 233-0100
VP, Ogden Newspapers, Wheeling, WV
Nutting, William D .... (518) 725-8616
SEC, Leader-Herald, Gloversville, NY
Nutting, William O .... (304) 233-0100
SEC/BUS MGR
Ogden Newspapers, Wheeling, WV
Nuzum, Scott .... (316) 223-1460
Sports ED, Fort Scott Tribune, Fort Scott, KS
Nyberg, Paul .... (415) 948-9000
PUB, Los Altos Town Crier, Los Altos, CA
Nyce, Henry H .... (717) 622-3456
ADV DIR, DIR-MKTG/Community SRV, Republican & Evening Herald, Pottsville, PA
Nydick, David .... (516) 921-4611
PRES, DANY News Service, Syosset, NY
Nye, Becky .... (417) 836-1100
ADV MGR-Sales
Springfield News-Leader, Springfield, MO
Nye, Charlie .... (317) 633-1240
ASST MAN ED-Photo/Graphics
Indianapolis Star/News, Indianapolis, IN
Nye, Kendall .... (508) 222-7000
PROD MGR, Sun Chronicle, Attleboro, MA
Nye, Paul .... (218) 547-1000
ED, Pilot-Independent, Walker, MN
Nyen, Bob .... (403) 743-8186
Sports ED
Fort McMurray Today, Fort McMurray, AB
Nygren, Herb .... (765) 362-1200
Photo ED, Journal Review, Crawfordsville, IN
Nyhan, David .... (617) 929-2000
ASSOC ED, Boston Globe, Boston, MA
Nylic, Catherine .... (413) 781-1900
PUB, Springfield Advocate, Springfield, MA
Nyquist, Jeff .... (701) 253-7311
CIRC DIR, CIRC MGR-OPER
Forum, Fargo, ND
Nyseth, Perry .... (715) 926-4970
PUB, Mondovi Herald-News, Mondovi, WI
Nystrom, Carol .... (201) 772-7003
MAN ED, Dateline Journal, Butler, NJ

O

Oakes, Alan .... (519) 756-2020
PROD ASST MGR, Expositor, Brantford, ON
Oakes, Sharon .... (413) 663-3741
ADV DIR, PROD FRM-COMP
North Adams Transcript, North Adams, MA
Oakland, Mike .... (360) 754-5400
EPE, Olympian, Olympia, WA
Oakley, Allen M .... (217) 223-5100
SEC, Quincy Newspapers Inc., Quincy, IL
Oakley, Bill .... (502) 443-1771
NTL ED, Paducah Sun, Paducah, KY
Oakley, David .... (201) 383-1500
CFO, New Jersey Herald, Newton, NJ
Oakley, Deborah .... (413) 584-5000
Sports ED
Daily Hampshire Gazette, Northampton, MA
Oakley, Jeff .... (712) 563-2661
ED, Audubon County Advocate Journal, Audubon, IA
Oakley, Meridith .... (501) 378-3400
COL
Arkansas Democrat-Gazette, Little Rock, AR
Oakley, Mitchell .... (919) 524-4376
PUB, ED, Times-Leader, Grifton, NC
Oakley, Peter A .... (217) 223-5100
ASST SEC/ASST TREAS
Quincy Newspapers Inc., Quincy, IL
Oakley, Ralph M .... (217) 223-5100
VP-ADM/ASST SEC, VP-Broadcast OPER
Quincy Newspapers Inc., Quincy, IL
Oakley, Thomas A .... (217) 223-5100
PRES/TREAS
Quincy Newspapers Inc., Quincy, IL
Oates, John .... (907) 257-4200
CIRC DIR
Anchorage Daily News, Anchorage, AK
Oathoudt, Frank .... (910) 373-7000
NTL ED, News & Record, Greensboro, NC
Oats, David .... (718) 357-7400
ED, Queens Tribune, Fresh Meadows, NY
Oben, Richard .... (202) 636-3000
DIR-Facilities
Washington Times, Washington, DC
Ober, David .... (909) 684-1200
ADTX MGR
Press-Enterprise, Riverside, CA
Ober, Dolores L .... (712) 434-2312
PUB, ED, Aurelia Sentinel, Aurelia, IA
Ober, Larry .... (712) 284-2300
PUB, Alta Advertiser, Alta, IA
Ober, Susan .... (408) 842-6400
PROD MGR-Pre Press, Dispatch, Gilroy, CA
USMedia Inc. (Central Valley Publishing)
Oberbroekling, Cathy .... (815) 459-4040
DIR-PROM
Northwest Herald, Crystal Lake, IL
Oberg, Diane .... (301) 474-4131
PUB, Greenbelt News Review, Greenbelt, MD
Oberheuser, Otto .... (314) 340-8000
PROD SUPT-Photomechanical
St. Louis Post-Dispatch, St. Louis, MO
Oberholzer, Zane .... (301) 733-5131
PROD FRM-Maintenance
Morning Herald, Hagerstown, MD
Oberjuerge, Paul R .... (909) 889-9666
Sports ED, Sun, San Bernardino, CA
Oberle, Marnie Mead .... (814) 870-1600
MAN ED-Sunday, Amusements ED, BUS ED, Sunday ED, Travel ED
Morning News/Erie Daily Times, Erie, PA
Oberle, Terry .... (910) 727-7211
Sports ED
Winston-Salem Journal, Winston-Salem, NC
Oberly, Beccy .... (406) 932-5299
ED, Big Timber Pioneer, Big Timber, MT
Oberly, Dale C .... (406) 932-5299
PUB, Big Timber Pioneer, Big Timber, MT
Obermaier, Dan .... (847) 866-5250
MAN ED, Skokie Review, Evanston, IL
Oberman, Martin .... (202) 334-6000
PROD SUPT-Engraving (SE)
Washington Post, Washington, DC
Obermark, Jerry .... (901) 529-2211
RE Reporter
Commercial Appeal, Memphis, TN
Obermeier, Ron .... (812) 424-7711
ADV MGR-Territory Sales
Evansville Courier Co. Inc., Evansville, IN
Obert, Jim .... (573) 887-3636
ED, Scott County Signal, Chaffee, MO
O'Blenis, Tara .... (902) 426-2811
ADV Sales MGR-CLASS
Chronicle-Herald, Halifax, NS
Obmascik, Mark .... (303) 820-1010
Environmental Reporter
Denver Post, Denver, CO
Obrecht, John .... (773) 586-8800
BUS/RE ED, Daily Southtown, Chicago, IL
O'Brian, Steve .... (972) 424-6565
BUS/FIN ED, Plano Star Courier, Plano, TX
O'Brien, Becky .... (816) 258-7237
ADV MGR-Display
Daily News-Bulletin, Brookfield, MO
O'Brien, Dan .... (309) 829-9411
PROD DIR, Pantagraph, Bloomington, IL
O'Brien, Dan .... (508) 997-7411
Theater/Music ED
Standard Times, New Bedford, MA
O'Brien, Dick .... (972) 542-2631
CIRC MGR
McKinney Courier-Gazette, McKinney, TX
O'Brien, Don .... (416) 367-2000
CIRC MGR-Distribution Services
Toronto Star, Toronto, ON
O'Brien, Eliot .... (505) 325-4545
BC/PRES, VBC, PUB, ED
Daily Times, Farmington, NM
O'Brien, Gerard .... (406) 657-1200
MAN ED, Billings Gazette, Billings, MT
O'Brien, Houston V .... (817) 629-1707
PUB, ED, Eastland Telegram, Eastland, TX
O'Brien, John .... (312) 222-5168
Sales Rep., Tribune TV Log, Chicago, IL
O'Brien, John J .... (908) 722-3000
PUB
Somerset Messenger-Gazette, Somerville, NJ
O'Brien, John M .... (212) 556-1234
Sr VP-OPER
New York Times Co., New York, NY
O'Brien, Kathy .... (518) 792-9914
NTL Accounts DIR, TV Data, Queensbury, NY
O'Brien, Ken .... (716) 328-2144
ASSOC ED
Syndicated News Service, Rochester, NY
O'Brien, Kevin .... (216) 999-4500
Chief EDL Writer
Plain Dealer, Cleveland, OH
O'Brien, Mary .... (510) 208-6300
CIRC MGR-OPER
Oakland Tribune, Oakland, CA
MediaNews Inc. (Alameda Newspapers)
O'Brien, Mike .... (541) 482-3456
PUB, Daily Tidings, Ashland, OR
O'Brien, Nancy .... (610) 828-4600
ED, Recorder, Conshohocken, PA
O'Brien, Patrick T .... (212) 621-1500
Senior VP/CFO/Dir of BUS Development
Associated Press, New York, NY
O'Brien, Paul .... (617) 929-2000
PROD SUPT-PR, Boston Globe, Boston, MA
O'Brien, Paul .... (905) 684-7251
Travel, Standard, St. Catharines, ON
O'Brien, Sue .... (303) 820-1010
EPE, Denver Post, Denver, CO
O'Brien, Tim .... (815) 284-2222
Wire ED, Telegraph, Dixon, IL
O'Brien, W .... (616) 256-9827
MAN ED
Leelanau Enterprise and Tribune, Leland, MI
O'Byrne, A .... (716) 243-2211
GM, Livonia Gazelle, Genesco, NY
O'Callaghan, Mike .... (702) 385-3111
COB, EX ED, Las Vegas Sun, Las Vegas, NV
O'Callaghan, Timothy .... (702) 293-2302
GM, Boulder City News, Boulder City, NV
O'Callahan, Patrick .... (206) 597-8742
Chief EDL Writer, News Tribune, Tacoma, WA

171-Who's Where **Oli**

Ocasek, Beverly .... (216) 232-4055
MAN ED
Bedford Times-Register, Bedford, OH
Occhipinti, John .... (561) 820-4100
MGR-DP, Palm Beach Post, West Palm Beach, FL, Cox Newspapers Inc.
Ochoa, Greg .... (314) 528-9550
ED, Troy Free Press, Troy, MO
Ochoa, Laurie .... (213) 237-5000
Food ED
Los Angeles Times, Los Angeles, CA
Ockert, Roy .... (501) 968-5252
MAN ED, Courier, Russellville, AR
Oclander, Jorge .... (312) 321-3000
Multicultural Affairs
Chicago Sun-Times, Chicago, IL
O'Connell, Jim .... (815) 987-1200
PROD MGR-Building SRV
Rockford Register Star, Rockford, IL
O'Connell, John .... (413) 788-1000
Boston BU, Union-News, Springfield, MA
O'Connell, Linda .... (203) 964-2200
Arts ED, Stamford Advocate, Stamford, CT
O'Connell, Maureen .... (520) 573-4220
EDU ED, Arizona Daily Star, Tucson, AZ
O'Connell, Sidnie .... (303) 239-9890
GM, Jefferson Sentinel, Lakewood, CO
O'Connor, C G .... (213) 525-2000
PROM MGR
Hollywood Reporter, Los Angeles, CA
O'Connor, Elizabeth .... (516) 594-1000
ED
Long Island Catholic, Rockville Center, NY
O'Connor, J P .... (816) 753-7880
PUB, ED
Kansas City New Times, Kansas City, MO
O'Connor, Justin .... (212) 803-8200
CIRC DIR, Bond Buyer, New York, NY
O'Connor, Kevin .... (518) 234-4368
ADV MGR, Daily Editor, Cobleskill, NY
O'Connor, Kyrie .... (860) 241-6200
Features ED, Hartford Courant, Hartford, CT
O'Connor, Larry .... (212) 268-2552
ED, Westsider, New York, NY
O'Connor, Linda .... (613) 962-9171
Women's ED, Intelligencer, Belleville, ON
O'Connor, Lona .... (561) 487-5104
Author, O'Connor, Lona, Boca Raton, FL
O'Connor, Lori Lee .... (317) 529-1111
ADTX MGR, Courier-Times, New Castle, IN
O'Connor, Michael .... (908) 859-4444
ED, Free Press, Phillipsburg, NJ
O'Connor, Patricia .... (508) 997-7411
BUS ED, Standard Times, New Bedford, MA
O'Connor, Phillip .... (312) 321-3000
GEN Assignment
Chicago Sun-Times, Chicago, IL
O'Connor, Robert .... (416) 441-1405
United Kingdom Reporter
Fotopress Independent News Service International (FPINS), Toronto, ON
O'Corozine, Julie .... (914) 255-7000
ED, Herald, New Paltz, NY
O'Crowley, Peggy .... (201) 646-4000
COL, Record, Hackensack, NJ
O'Day, James M .... (406) 873-4128
PUB, ED, Western Breeze, Cut Bank, MT
O'Day, L James .... (715) 536-7121
PUB, ED, Foto News, Merrill, WI
O'Day, Lauree .... (715) 536-7121
GM, MAN ED, Foto News, Merrill, WI
O'Dell, C J .... (804) 898-7225
ED, Flyer, Yorktown, VA
O'Dell, James .... (312) 222-3232
VP-OPER, PROD DIR
Chicago Tribune, Chicago, IL
O'Dell, Kathleen .... (417) 836-1100
BUS ED, RE ED
Springfield News-Leader, Springfield, MO
O'Dell, Nathan .... (423) 928-4151
BM, Elizabethton Star, Elizabethton, TN
O'Dell, Patrick .... (707) 725-6166
PUB, Humboldt Beacon, Fortuna, CA
O'Dell, William A .... (412) 775-3200
ADV MGR-SRV
Beaver County Times, Beaver, PA
Oden, Vicki .... (501) 337-7523
BM, Malvern Daily Record, Malvern, AR
Odette, Linda .... (616) 722-3161
Features ED
Muskegon Chronicle, Muskegon, MI
Odette, Pres .... (800) 544-4094
PUB, Clinton County News, St. Johns, MI
O'Doherty, Mary .... (606) 231-3100
City ED
Lexington Herald-Leader, Lexington, KY
Odom, Bob .... (512) 592-4304
PUB, ED, Kingsville Record and Bishop News, Kingsville, TX
Odom, Kyle .... (616) 345-3511
CIRC SUPV-Sales
Kalamazoo Gazette, Kalamazoo, MI
O'Donnell, Colin .... (847) 427-4300
MET ED, Daily Herald, Arlington Heights, IL
O'Donnell, Bishop Edward J ..... (314) 531-9700
PUB, St. Louis Review, St. Louis, MO
O'Donnell, Justin .... (717) 821-2091
ASST MAN ED
Citizens' Voice, Wilkes-Barre, PA
O'Donnell, Leslie .... (541) 265-8571
ED, News-Times, Newport, OR
O'Donnell, Marjorie .... (202) 636-3000
ADV ASST DIR
Washington Times, Washington, DC
O'Donnell, Maureen .... (312) 321-3000
GEN Assignment, Sun-Times, Chicago, IL
O'Donnell, Melita .... (814) 472-8240
GM, Mountaineer-Herald, Ebensburg, PA
O'Donnell, Michelle .... (415) 692-9406
ED, Foster City Progress, Burlingame, CA
O'Donnell, Paul .... (508) 943-8784
PUB, Patriot, Webster, MA
O'Donnell, Thomas P .... (954) 356-4000
Chairman, Sun-Sentinel, Fort Lauderdale, FL
O'Donnell, Timothy P .... (913) 764-2211
PRES/CEO, PUB, Daily News, Olathe, KS
O'Donoghue, Neal .... (519) 756-2020
ADV MGR-Sales, Expositor, Brantford, ON
O'Donovan, Pat .... (320) 384-6188
PUB, Hinckley News, Hinckley, MN
O'Donovan, William C .... (804) 220-1736
PUB, ED, Virginia Gazette, Williamsburg, VA
O'Dowd, Niall .... (212) 684-3366
PUB, Irish Voice, New York, NY
Oeding, Jill .... (812) 482-2424
MGR-OPER, Herald, Jasper, IN
Oehmke, Wayne .... (810) 731-1000
PUB, Source, Utica, MI
Oehrke, Galen .... (816) 826-1000
CONT/PA, Sedalia Democrat, Sedalia, MO
Oelke, Kimbel E .... (410) 288-6060
PUB, Dundalk Eagle, Dundalk, MD
Oelke, Mary G .... (410) 288-6060
GM, Dundalk Eagle, Dundalk, MD
Oeth, Annie .... (601) 961-7000
ASST MET ED, Clarion-Ledger, Jackson, MS
Oetting, Judy .... (714) 642-4321
ADV MGR-CLASS
Daily Pilot, Costa Mesa, CA
O'Farrell, Brenda .... (514) 630-6688
ED, Chronicle, Pointe Claire, QC
Offenburger, Chuck .... (515) 284-8000
Local COL
Des Moines Register, Des Moines, IA
Offer, David B .... (401) 849-3300
ED, Newport Daily News, Newport, RI
Offermann, Herb .... (208) 263-9534
ADV DIR
Bonner County Daily Bee, Sandpoint, ID
Offil, Bill .... (713) 220-7171
ADV MGR-CLASS
Houston Chronicle, Houston, TX
Offutt, Jason .... (816) 781-1044
ED, Northland News, Liberty, MO
O'Flannagan, Jerry .... (216) 999-4500
PROD SUPT-PR, Plain Dealer, Cleveland, OH
Ofobike, Laura .... (330) 996-3000
EDL Writer, Akron Beacon Journal, Akron, OH
Oftelie, Brian .... (218) 885-2100
PUB, Eastern Itascan, Nashwauk, MN
O'Gara, Patrick .... (419) 245-6000
Senior ED, Blade, Toledo, OH
O'Gorman, Christopher .... (415) 431-4792
GM
San Francisco Beacon, San Francisco, CA
Ogas, Billy .... (505) 388-1576
CIRC MGR, Silver City Daily Press & Independent, Silver City, NM
Ogata, Wendy .... (801) 625-4200
MET ED, Religion ED
Standard-Examiner, Ogden, UT
Ogburn, Thad .... (919) 829-4500
News ED, News & Observer, Raleigh, NC
Ogden, Marianne .... (802) 254-2311
Cuisine/Lifestyles ED
Brattleboro Reformer, Brattleboro, VT
Ogden, Victoria .... (508) 255-2121
PUB, Cape Codder, Orleans, MA
Ogilive, Glenn .... (519) 344-3641
Photo DEPT MGR, Observer, Sarnia, ON
Ogilvie, Amber .... (519) 631-2790
ASSOC PUB, ADV MGR
St. Thomas Times-Journal, St. Thomas, ON
Ogle, David L .... (219) 294-1661
GM, Elkhart Truth, Elkhart, IN
Ogle, Gary .... (405) 382-1100
PA, PROD MGR/FRM-COMP
Seminole Producer, Seminole, OK
Ogle, Mark .... (541) 485-1234
CIRC ASST MGR
Register-Guard, Eugene, OR
Oglesby, Joe .... (803) 771-6161
MAN ED, State, Columbia, SC
Oglesby, Rob .... (352) 374-5000
Online Contact
Gainesville Sun, Gainesville, FL
Oglesby, Roger D .... (610) 820-6500
ED/VP, Morning Call, Allentown, PA
O'Gorman, Kathy .... (313) 222-6400
EDU ED, Detroit Free Press, Detroit, MI
O'Grady, Dennis .... (712) 792-3573
Sports ED, Daily Times Herald, Caroll, IA
O'Grady, Joe .... (705) 567-5321
Farm ED
Northern Daily News, Kirkland Lake, ON
O'Grady, Patricia .... (614) 942-2118
PUB, Harrison News-Herald, Cadiz, OH
O'Grady, Patrick .... (602) 483-0977
ED, Town of Paradise Valley Independent, Scottsdale, AZ
O'Grady-Pyne, Katy .... (309) 827-8555
ED
Twin City Community News, Bloomington, IL
Ogurcak, Jan .... (717) 326-1551
Lifestyle ED, Sun-Gazette, Williamsport, PA
Oguro, Kuniji .... (212) 575-5830
PRES, Jiji Press America Ltd., New York, NY
O'Hagan, Arthur C .... (602) 263-0443
PUB, Irish Eyes, Phoenix, AZ
O'Halloran, Mary .... (602) 263-0443
ED, Irish Eyes, Phoenix, AZ
O'Hara, Delia .... (312) 321-3000
Features Reporter
Chicago Sun-Times, Chicago, IL
O'Hara, Dolly .... (614) 537-3776
ED, Citizen Tribune, Steubenville, OH
O'Hara, Donald .... (716) 849-3434
Automotive ED, Buffalo News, Buffalo, NY
O'Hara, James .... (706) 291-6397
Sports ED, Rome News-Tribune, Rome, GA
O'Hara, Jean .... (941) 748-0411
ADV MGR-CLASS
Bradenton Herald, Bradenton, FL
O'Hara, Jo Ellen .... (205) 325-2222
Food ED, Birmingham News, Birmingham, AL
O'Hara, Michael .... (609) 924-3244
GM, Princeton Packet, Princeton, NJ
O'Hara, Patrick J .... (614) 537-3776
PUB, ED, Citizen Tribune, Steubenville, OH
O'Hara, Tom .... (561) 820-4100
MAN ED, Palm Beach Post, West Palm Beach, FL
O'Hare, Kate .... (800) 424-4747
Features ED, Tribune Media Services-Television Listings, Glens Falls, NY
O'Hare, Kevin .... (413) 788-1000
Music Critic-Popular
Union-News, Springfield, MA
O'Hare, Michael .... (412) 543-1303
MAN ED, Leader Times, Kittanning, PA
O'Hearn, James I .... (508) 458-7100
ASST to PUB, Sun, Lowell, MA
O'Hern, Vincent P .... (608) 251-5627
PUB, Isthmus, Madison, WI
Ohlendorf, Jeff .... (815) 539-9396
GM, Mendota Reporter, Mendota, IL
Ohlinger, Royce .... (517) 265-5111
PROD SUPT-PR, Daily Telegram, Adrian, MI
Ohm, Andrew H .... (718) 482-1111
PUB, Korea Times, Long Island City, NY
Ohman, Jack .... (503) 221-8327
EDL Cartoonist, Oregonian, Portland, OR
Oi, Cynthia S .... (808) 525-8000
Books ED, Features ED, Films/Theater ED, Music/Women's ED, Radio/Television ED
Honolulu Star-Bulletin, Honolulu, HI
Oickle, Vernon .... (902) 543-2457
ED, Bulletin, Bridgewater, NS
Okada, K .... (415) 457-7141
Pacific Rim Report
Style International, San Francisco, CA
Okada, Mikio .... (415) 921-6820
Jpse. ED, Nichibet Times, San Francisco, CA
Okamoto, Sandra .... (706) 324-5526
Entertainment ED
Columbus Ledger-Enquirer, Columbus, GA
O'Keefe, Mark .... (412) 439-7500
ASSOC ED, Herald-Standard, Uniontown, PA
O'Keefe, Mark .... (757) 446-2000
Religion ED, Virginian-Pilot, Norfolk, VA
O'Keefe, Terry .... (605) 886-6901
Farm ED
Watertown Public Opinion, Watertown, SD
O'Kelley, Virginia .... (706) 783-2553
MAN ED, Comer News, Comer, GA
Okie, Susan .... (202) 334-6000
Staff Writer (Health)
Washington Post, Washington, DC
Okinga, Donna .... (916) 756-0800
ADV DIR, Davis Enterprise, Davis, CA
Okipniuk, W .... (416) 504-3443
PUB, Homin Ukrainy, Toronto, ON
Oksenhorn, Stewart .... (970) 925-3414
Entertainment/Amusements ED
Aspen Times, Aspen, CO
Okun, Janice .... (716) 849-3434
Food ED, Buffalo News, Buffalo, NY
Olaf, Wanda .... (701) 572-2165
PROD SUPV-COMP
Williston Daily Herald, Williston, ND
Olafson, Janice .... (701) 845-0463
ADV MGR
Valley City Times-Record, Valley City, ND
Oldaker, Wes .... (912) 265-8320
CIRC MGR, Brunswick News, Brunswick, GA
Oldani, Craig .... (810) 573-2755
Technology ED
Avanti NewsFeatures, Warren, MI
Oldani, Tony .... (810) 573-2755
Tools ED, Avanti NewsFeatures, Warren, MI
Oldenberg, Lu Ann .... (715) 723-5515
DP MGR
Chippewa Herald, Chippewa Falls, WI
Older, Mary .... (319) 372-6421
MGR-Accounting, DP MGR
Daily Democrat, Fort Madison, IA
Oldfield, Linda G .... (816) 297-2100
PUB, Adrian Journal, Adrian, MO
Oldfield, Stephen G .... (816) 297-2100
PUB, Archie News, Archie, MO
Oldfield, Stephen M .... (816) 297-2100
PUB, ED, Adrian Journal, Adrian, MO
Oldford, Dale .... (510) 935-2525
DP MGR, Contra Costa Times, Walnut Creek, CA, Knight-Ridder Inc.
Oldham, Lane .... (910) 888-3500
ADV MGR-GEN, Enterprise, High Point, NC
Olding, Steve .... (606) 781-4421
ED
Campbell County Recorder, Fort Thomas, KY
Olds, Ellen M .... (314) 522-1300
SEC/TREAS
Interstate News Services, St. Louis, MO
Olds, Michael J .... (314) 522-1300
PRES/MAN ED
Interstate News Services, St. Louis, MO
Olds, Sabrina J .... (502) 484-3431
GM, News-Herald, Owenton, KY
Olds, Susan .... (201) 877-4141
ASST MAN ED, Star-Ledger, Newark, NJ
O'Leary, Carol .... (715) 223-2342
GM, Tribune-Phonograph, Abbotsford, WI
O'Leary, Ed .... (519) 756-2020
Sports ED, Expositor, Brantford, ON
O'Leary, Fran .... (414) 922-4600
Farm ED, Features ED
Reporter, Fond du Lac, WI
O'Leary, J A .... (715) 748-2626
PUB, Star News, Medford, WI
O'Leary, Kevin .... (818) 962-8811
EPE, San Gabriel Valley Tribune, West Covina, CA, MediaNews Inc.
O'Leary, Kieran .... (212) 210-2100
News ED-Regional
New York Daily News, New York, NY
O'Leary, Linda .... (405) 338-3355
Society ED, Daily Herald, Guymon, OK
O'Leary, Peter .... (613) 829-9100
ADV MGR-Key Account
Ottawa Citizen, Ottawa, ON
O'Leary, Regina Clarkin .... (914) 737-7747
PUB, Peekskill Herald, Peekskill, NY
O'Leary, Timothy .... (214) 977-8222
EDL Writer, Dallas Morning News, Dallas, TX
O'Leary-Pickard, Maureen .... (519) 679-6666
MGR-Human Resources
London Free Press, London, ON
Olesak, Ken .... (860) 225-4601
Wire ED, Herald, New Britain, CT
Olesen, Doug .... (815) 732-2156
ED, Ogle County Life, Oregon, IL
Olesker, Michael .... (410) 332-6000
COL-Local, Sun, Baltimore, MD
Oleszczuk, Andrew J .... (312) 222-3237
VP-Development, Tribune Co., Chicago, IL
Olford, Dale .... (510) 462-4160
DP MGR, Valley Times, Pleasanton, CA
Olguin, Loretta .... (520) 294-1200
ADV MGR-Legal, Daily Territorial, Tucson, AZ
Olig, Linda .... (402) 475-4200
Features ED, Journal Star, Lincoln, NE
Olin, Dirk .... (415) 541-0700
ED, SF Weekly, San Francisco, CA
Olinek, Derek .... (403) 343-2400
PROD MGR, Advocate, Red Deer, AB
Olinger, David .... (813) 893-8111
Environmental ED
St. Petersburg Times, St. Petersburg, FL
Olinto, Deborah .... (619) 745-6611
ADV MGR-Major/NTL
North County Times, Escondido, CA
Oliva Jr, Frank .... (203) 333-0161
PROD DIR, Connecticut Post, Bridgeport, CT
Olivares, Jaime .... (213) 622-8332
State ED, La Opinion, Los Angeles, CA
Olive, Cornelia .... (919) 708-9000
ED, EPE, EDL Writer
Sanford Herald, Sanford, NC
Olive, David .... (416) 585-5000
ED (Report on BUS Magazine)
Globe and Mail, Toronto, ON
Olive, Donald .... (205) 766-3434
PROD MGR-PR, Times Daily, Florence, AL
Olive, Steve .... (941) 335-0200
PROD MGR-Camera
News-Press, Fort Myers, FL
Olive-Matthews, Carolyn .... (512) 445-3500
MGR-Cox Interactive Media Advertising
Austin American-Statesman, Austin, TX

Oliver, Alvin .... (405) 255-5354
PROD MGR, Duncan Banner, Duncan, OK
Oliver, Barbara R .... (518) 453-6688
GM, Evangelist, Albany, NY
Oliver, Carol .... (219) 583-5121
PROD MGR, Herald Journal, Monticello, IN
Oliver, Dotty .... (501) 372-4719
PUB, Little Rock Free Press, Little Rock, AR
Oliver, Erma .... (609) 935-1500
Sports ED, Today's Sunbeam, Salem, NJ
Oliver, Gerry .... (204) 697-7000
Garden ED, Free Press, Winnipeg, MB
Oliver, Ian .... (905) 632-4444
PUB, Burlington Post, Burlington, ON
Oliver, J T .... (910) 353-1171
SCI/Technology ED, Travel ED
Daily News, Jacksonville, NC
Oliver, James .... (814) 445-9621
ED, EPE, EDL Writer, ADTX MGR, PROD FRM-News DEPT
Daily American, Somerset, PA
Oliver Jr, John J .... (410) 554-8200
PUB
Baltimore Afro-American, Baltimore, MD
Oliver, Lee Ann .... (502) 827-2000
ADTX MGR, Gleaner, Henderson, KY
Oliver, Lela Ward .... (213) 291-9486
ED, Herald Dispatch, Los Angeles, CA
Oliver, Matthew .... (210) 225-7411
PROD SUPT-PR/ASST MGR
San Antonio Express-News, San Antonio, TX
Oliver, Myrna .... (213) 237-5000
Obituary Writer/ED
Los Angeles Times, Los Angeles, CA
Oliver, Neil .... (905) 632-4444
PUB, Burlington Post, Burlington, ON
Oliver, Stephanie .... (503) 221-8327
DIR-Public Affairs, Oregonian, Portland, OR
Oliver, Terence .... (330) 996-3000
Art DIR, Akron Beacon Journal, Akron, OH
Oliver, Thomas .... (404) 526-5151
ASST MAN ED-Projects
Atlanta Journal-Constitution, Atlanta, GA
Oliver, Wendy .... (910) 625-2101
PROD MGR-COMP
Courier-Tribune, Asheboro, NC
Olivetti, Jackie .... (803) 626-8555
DIR-Human Resources
Sun News, Myrtle Beach, SC
Olivia, Ric .... (203) 789-5200
CIRC MGR-Customer SRV
New Haven Register, New Haven, CT
Olivo, Pete .... (800) 223-2154
CIRC MGR-Fulfillment
Investor's Business Daily, Los Angeles, CA
Olkiewicz, Robert .... (712) 279-5019
PROD FRM-COMP Room
Sioux City Journal, Sioux City, IA
Oller, Joe Ben .... (813) 688-8500
PUB, Auburndale Star, Auburndale, FL
Ollove, Steve .... (508) 468-2632
ED, Sportsbuff Features, Hamilton, MA
Ollwerther, W Raymond .... (908) 922-6000
VP-News
New Jersey Press Inc., Neptune, NJ
Olmos, David .... (213) 237-5000
Health/Drugs
Los Angeles Times, Los Angeles, CA
Olmstead, Larry .... (305) 350-2111
MAN ED, Miami Herald, Miami, FL
Olmsted, Bill .... (608) 754-3311
Photo ED, Janesville Gazette, Janesville, WI
Olmsted, Richard .... (505) 622-7710
Area/Sunday ED, City/MET ED, News ED
Roswell Daily Record, Roswell, NM
Olsen, Brad .... (402) 371-1020
BM, DIR-MKTG/PROM
Norfolk Daily News, Norfolk, NE
Olsen, David A .... (717) 291-8811
ASST TREAS, Lancaster Intelligencer Journal/New Era/Sunday News, Lancaster, PA
Olsen, Jim .... (801) 528-3111
PUB, Gunnison Valley News, Gunnison, UT
Olsen, Jodi .... (906) 786-2021
ADV MGR, ADTX MGR
Daily Press, Escanaba, MI
Olsen, Joe .... (218) 685-5326
GM, Grant County Herald, Elbow Lake, MN
Olsen, Lawrence T .... (212) 455-4000
EVP & GM, North America Syndicate, King Features Syndicate Inc., New York, NY
Olsen, Lori .... (801) 528-3111
GM, ED
Gunnison Valley News, Gunnison, UT
Olsen, Maureen R .... (712) 485-2276
PUB, ED, Gazette, Neola, IA
Olsen, Ron .... (209) 943-6397
DIR-RES/PROM, Record, Stockton, CA
Olshan, Mort .... (310) 274-0848
ED/PUB, Olshan's, Mort Sports Features, Los Angeles, CA
Olson, Alice .... (605) 258-2604
PUB, ED, Onida Watchman, Onida, SD
Olson, Angie .... (815) 232-1171
MGR-BUS, PROD MGR-SYS
Journal-Standard, Freeport, IL
Olson, Arvid .... (317) 423-5511
DIR-Market Development, Online MGR
Journal and Courier, Lafayette, IN
Olson, Bart .... (608) 524-2115
PUB, Reedsburg Report, WI,
Olson, Carl .... (541) 271-3633
PUB, ED, Reedsport Courier, Reedsport, OR
Olson, Char .... (608) 524-2115
PUB, Reedsburg Report, WI,
Olson, Chris .... (617) 245-0080
Sports ED
Wakefield Daily Item, Wakefield, MA
Olson, Chris .... (402) 444-1000
RE ED, Omaha World-Herald, Omaha, NE
Olson, Craig .... (561) 820-4100
PROD SUPT-Camera/Platemaking
Palm Beach Post, West Palm Beach, FL
Olson, David .... (360) 754-5400
MGR-INFO SYS, Olympian, Olympia, WA
Olson, Diana Condon .... (402) 444-1000
ADV MGR-RT
Omaha World-Herald, Omaha, NE
Olson, Doug C .... (517) 741-8451
MAN ED, Register-Tribune, Union City, MI
Olson, Eric .... (612) 421-4444
GM, Anoka County Union, Coon Rapids, MN
Olson, Erik R .... (608) 647-6141
PUB, ED
Richland Observer, Richland Center, WI
Olson, Everett .... (206) 464-2111
PROD MGR-Electrical (Fairview)
Seattle Times, Seattle, WA
Olson, Glen .... (712) 279-5019
City ED, Sioux City Journal, Sioux City, IA
Olson, Hallie .... (206) 455-2222
ADV DIR-RT, Eastside Journal, Bellevue, WA
Olson, Harold .... (815) 673-3771
Sports ED, Streator Times-Press, Streator, IL
Olson, Howard .... (209) 578-2000
PROD MGR-COMP Room
Modesto Bee, Modesto, CA
Olson, Jason .... (801) 373-5050
Photo DEPT MGR, Daily Herald, Provo, UT
Olson, Jeff .... (701) 223-2500
Living/Lifestyle ED
Bismarck Tribune, Bismarck, ND
Olson, Jerry .... (406) 587-4491
CIRC MGR
Bozeman Daily Chronicle, Bozeman, MT
Olson, John J .... (320) 859-2143
PUB, Osakis Review, Osakis, MN
Olson, Jon .... (203) 235-1661
DIR-Photography
Record-Journal, Meriden, CT
Olson, Judy .... (605) 394-8300
CONT, Rapid City Journal, Rapid City, SD
Olson, Karen .... (715) 384-3131
ADV MGR, ADV MGR-NTL
Marshfield News-Herald, Marshfield, WI
Olson, Karen .... (312) 222-3232
Television ED, Chicago Tribune, Chicago, IL
Olson, Mark .... (507) 433-8851
Photo DEPT MGR
Austin Daily Herald, Austin, MN
Olson, Mark .... (408) 372-3311
CIRC DIR
Monterey County Herald, Monterey, CA
Olson, Michael .... (801) 465-9221
PUB, ED, Payson Chronicle, Payson, UT
Olson, Pamela .... (217) 245-6121
Fashion/Society ED, Food ED, Home Furnishings/Women's ED
Jacksonville Journal-Courier, Jacksonville, IL
Olson, Pat .... (403) 532-1110
PROD Office MGR
Daily Herald-Tribune, Grande Prairie, AB
Olson, Peter B .... (712) 859-3780
PUB, ED, Graettinger Times, Graettinger, IA
Olson, Roberta J .... (320) 859-2143
ED, Osakis Review, Osakis, MN
Olson, Ron .... (320) 235-1150
CIRC DIR
West Central Tribune, Willmar, MN
Olson, Scott J .... (360) 249-3311
PUB, ED, Montesano Vidette, Montesano, WA
Olson, Victor Woodrow .... (218) 652-3475
PUB, ED, Northwood Press, Nevis, MN
Olson, Walter .... (507) 249-3130
PUB, ED, Morgan Messenger, Morgan, MN
Olszak, Mitchel .... (412) 654-6651
EPE, EDL Writer
New Castle News, New Castle, PA
Olszewski, Jon .... (815) 933-1131
GM, Herald/Country Market, Bourbonnais, IL
Olszewski, Toby .... (815) 933-1131
PUB, ED
Herald/Country Market, Bourbonnais, IL
O'Malley, Robert .... (617) 426-9492
ED, Sampan, Boston, MA
O'Malley, Most Rev Sean P ..... (508) 675-7151
PUB, Anchor, Fall River, MA
O'Malley, Sheila .... (908) 899-1000
PUB, Leader, Pt. Pleasant Beach, NJ
O'Mara, Anne .... (402) 687-2616
ED, Lyons Mirror Sun, Lyons, NE
O'Mara, Cheryl M .... (210) 423-5511
MGR-CR, Valley Morning Star, Harlingen, TX
O'Mara, Marty .... (847) 888-7800
Copy Desk Chief, Courier-News, Elgin, IL
O'Mara, Tim .... (562) 435-1161
EX ED-News
Press-Telegram, Long Beach, CA
O'Marah, Robert .... (315) 778-3638
GM, Fort Drum Sentinel, Watertown, NY
Omdahl, Randy .... (541) 474-3700
PROD SUPT
Grants Pass Daily Courier, Grants Pass, OR
O'Meara, Brian .... (613) 962-9171
City ED, Intelligencer, Belleville, ON
O'Melia, Ted .... (307) 347-3241
VP
Northern Wyoming Daily News, Worland, WY
Omelus, Mike .... (416) 364-3172
GEN News DIR
Broadcast News Limited, Toronto, ON
Omernick, Gary .... (414) 684-4433
PUB/GM
Herald Times Reporter, Manitowoc, WI
O'Nan, Chris .... (770) 382-4545
Living/Lifestyle ED
Daily Tribune News, Cartersville, GA
O'Neal, Caroline .... (302) 856-0026
GM, Sussex Countian, Georgetown, DE
O'Neal, Denise .... (312) 321-3000
Guide Listings
Chicago Sun-Times, Chicago, IL
O'Neal, Dori .... (509) 925-1414
EDU/Features ED
Daily Record, Ellensburg, WA
O'Neal, Jim .... (314) 724-1111
ED, St. Peters Journal, St. Charles, MO
O'Neal, Ron .... (212) 450-7000
VP/Western Region MGR/Newspaper Relations, React, Parade Publications Inc., New York, NY
O'Neal, Sandra .... (770) 775-3107
GM, Jackson Progress-Argus, Jackson, GA
O'Neal, Sheri .... (903) 757-3311
MGR-MKTG/PROM
Longview News-Journal, Longview, TX
O'Neil, Bill .... (308) 237-2152
ADTX MGR, Kearney Hub, Kearney, NE
O'Neil, Charlotte .... (318) 377-1866
MGR-CR, Minden Press-Herald, Minden, LA
O'Neil, Daniel P .... (401) 596-7791
ADV MGR, Westerly Sun, Westerly, RI
O'Neil, Edward .... (316) 225-4151
PROD SUPT, PROD FRM-PR
Dodge City Daily Globe, Dodge City, KS
O'Neil, Kevin .... (201) 646-4000
Graphics ED, Record, Hackensack, NJ
O'Neil, Mark .... (508) 369-2800
PUB, Lexington Minuteman, Concord, MA
O'Neil, Melissa .... (509) 582-1500
RE ED, Tri-City Herald, Tri-Cities, WA
O'Neil, Owen .... (206) 622-8272
CIRC MGR, Seattle Daily Journal of Commerce, Seattle, WA
O'Neil, Robert .... (401) 277-7000
CIRC MGR-Single Copy Sales
Providence Journal-Bulletin, Providence, RI
O'Neil, Ronald .... (315) 337-4000
ADV DIR, Daily Sentinel, Rome, NY
O'Neil, T .... (902) 426-2811
Deputy MAN ED
Chronicle-Herald, Halifax, NS
O'Neil, Thomas .... (617) 929-2000
CIRC MGR-Sales, Boston Globe, Boston, MA
O'Neil, Tom .... (616) 429-2400
CIRC DIR, Herald-Palladium, St. Joseph, MI
O'Neil, W Scott .... (800) 223-2154
PUB
Investor's Business Daily, Los Angeles, CA
O'Neil, William J .... (800) 223-2154
Chairman
Investor's Business Daily, Los Angeles, CA
O'Neill, Alice .... (847) 446-4082
MAN ED
Los Angeles Features Syndicate, Winnetka, IL
O'Neill, Bernie .... (514) 484-7523
ED, Westmount Examiner, Westmount, QC
O'Neill, Brad .... (905) 684-7251
MGR-FIN, Standard, St. Catharines, ON
O'Neill, Brian .... (412) 263-1100
COL, Pittsburgh Post-Gazette, Pittsburgh, PA
O'Neill, Bryan .... (502) 753-1916
PROD FRM-COMP
Murray Ledger & Times, Murray, KY
O'Neill, Charles .... (616) 526-2191
GM, ED, Harbor Light, Harbor Springs, MI
O'Neill, David .... (210) 225-7411
PROD ASST MGR
San Antonio Express-News, San Antonio, TX
O'Neill, E B .... (306) 453-2525
PUB, ED, Carlyle Observer, Carlyle, SK
O'Neill, Gerard .... (617) 929-2000
Spotlight ED, Boston Globe, Boston, MA
O'Neill, Jim .... (616) 222-5400
News ED
Grand Rapids Press, Grand Rapids, MI
O'Neill, Kevin .... (616) 526-2191
PUB, Harbor Light, Harbor Springs, MI
O'Neill, Mike .... (219) 235-6161
CIRC MGR-Sales/PROM
South Bend Tribune, South Bend, IN
O'Neill, Pat .... (303) 820-1010
CIRC MGR-State, Denver Post, Denver, CO
O'Neill, Robert G .... (504) 826-3279
ADV DIR, Times-Picayune, New Orleans, LA
O'Neill, Sy .... (330) 688-0088
ED, Tallmadge Express, Stow, OH
Onestak, Thomas .... (412) 981-6100
CONT, Herald, Sharon, PA
Oney, Bob .... (919) 829-4500
ADV DIR-MKTG/RES
News & Observer, Raleigh, NC
Onley, Mary .... (912) 384-2323
GM, Douglas Enterprise, Douglas, GA
Onoda, Akihiro .... (212) 603-6600
Deputy BU Chief
Kyodo News Service, New York, NY
Onsgard, B A .... (507) 498-3868
PUB, Spring Grove Herald, Spring Grove, MN
Onsgard, F W .... (507) 498-3868
ED, Spring Grove Herald, Spring Grove, MN
Oordt, Darwin .... (507) 526-7324
PUB
Faribault County Register, Blue Earth, MN
Opatz, Jarred .... (419) 281-0581
Sports ED
Ashland Times-Gazette, Ashland, OH
Opavsky, Dave .... (705) 645-4463
ED, Muskoka Advance, Bracebridge, ON
Openshaw, Sean .... (520) 774-4545
Photo ED, Arizona Daily Sun, Flagstaff, AZ
Opotowsky, Mel .... (909) 684-1200
MAN ED, Press-Enterprise, Riverside, CA
Opp, Michael .... (605) 225-4100
MGR-MKTG/PROM
Aberdeen American News, Aberdeen, SD
Oppedahl, John F .... (602) 271-8000
PUB/CEO
Phoenix Newspapers Inc., Phoenix, AZ
Oppel, Rich .... (512) 445-3500
ED, Austin American-Statesman, Austin, TX
Oppman, Andrew .... (513) 721-2700
Kentucky ED
Cincinnati Enquirer, Cincinnati, OH
Oram, Rick .... (801) 625-4200
PROD MGR-PR
Standard-Examiner, Ogden, UT
Oravecz, Steve .... (330) 841-1600
EPE, Tribune Chronicle, Warren, OH
Oravelce, Jon .... (412) 834-1151
BUS ED, Tribune-Review, Greensburg, PA
Orazzi, Michael .... (609) 989-7800
Photo ED, Trentonian, Trenton, NJ
Orban, Jim .... (613) 829-9100
VP/MKTG/ASST to the PUB
Ottawa Citizen, Ottawa, ON
Orbanek, George .... (970) 242-5050
PRES, ED/PUB
Daily Sentinel, Grand Junction, CO
Orbaugh, Dave .... (704) 358-5000
DIR-Administrative SRV, DP MGR
Charlotte Observer, Charlotte, NC
Orben, Bill .... (407) 846-7600
ED, Osceola News-Gazette, Kissimmee, FL
Orcutt, Jamie .... (715) 842-2101
Features/Special Projects ED, Music/Radio ED, Television ED
Wausau Daily Herald, Wausau, WI
Ordway, R Chris .... (352) 563-6363
CIRC DIR
Citrus County Chronicle, Crystal River, FL
O'Rear, Bill .... (808) 935-6621
Sports ED, Hawaii Tribune-Herald, Hilo, HI
Orear, Gregory .... (816) 258-7237
ED, BUS/FIN ED, City/MET ED, EPE, Features ED, Graphics ED/Art DIR, News ED, Photo ED, Political/Government ED, Sports ED, Daily News-Bulletin, Brookfield, MO
Orechio, Frank A .... (201) 667-2100
PUB, Nutley Sun, Nutley, NJ
Ñredein, Obafimi .... (416) 441-1405
Africa Journalist
Fotopress Independent News Service International (FPINS), Toronto, ON
Oredson, Dean .... (408) 372-3311
PROD FRM-Camera
Monterey County Herald, Monterey, CA
Orehond, Shirley .... (757) 539-3437
CIRC MGR, Suffolk News-Herald, Suffolk, VA
O'Reilly, Brent .... (912) 923-6432
PROD FRM-PR
Daily Sun, Warner Robins, GA
O'Reilly, Buck .... (717) 923-1500
ED, Record, Renovo, PA
O'Reilly, Frank .... (717) 923-1500
PUB, Record, Renovo, PA
O'Reilly, Molly .... (614) 654-1321
EDU ED
Lancaster Eagle-Gazette, Lancaster, OH

173-Who's Where **Otu**

O'Reilly, Richard .... (213) 237-5000
COL-"Customer SRV"
Los Angeles Times, Los Angeles, CA

Oren, John C .... (218) 634-1722
PUB, ED, Baudette Region, Baudette, MN

Oren, Melanie A .... (806) 447-2559
MAN ED, Wellington Leader, Wellington, TX

Orenstein, Robert .... (610) 820-6500
Bethlehem ED, Morning Call, Allentown, PA

Oreskes, Michael .... (212) 556-1234
MET ED, New York Times, New York, NY

Organek, Ronald .... (201) 653-1000
CONT, Jersey Journal, Jersey City, NJ

Orgell, Judith A .... (847) 427-4300
VP-Human Resources
Daily Herald, Arlington Heights, IL

Orin, Deborah .... (212) 930-8000
Washington BU
New York Post, New York, NY

Orkus, Larry R .... (610) 371-5000
ASSOC PUB
Reading Times/Eagle, Reading, PA

Orlando, Chris .... (517) 835-7171
ADTX MGR
Midland Daily News, Midland, MI

Orlet, Chris .... (618) 337-7300
ED, Cahokia-Dupo Herald, Cahokia, IL

Orlinsky, S Zeke .... (410) 337-2400
PUB, Towson Times, Towson, MD

Orlowsky, Peter .... (310) 230-3400
BM (New York), Allsport Photography USA, Pacific Palisades, CA

Orme, Terry .... (801) 237-2031
Books ED, Entertainment ED, Fashion ED, Features ED
Salt Lake Tribune, Salt Lake City, UT

Orndoff, Bill .... (801) 394-9655
MAN ED, Hill Top Times, Roy, UT

Orndorff, Beverly .... (804) 649-6000
SCI/Medical Writer
Richmond Times-Dispatch, Richmond, VA

Orona, Manuel J .... (915) 570-0405
PUB, ED
El Editor Permian Basin, Midland, TX

Orosz, Lin .... (306) 728-5448
PUB, ED, MAN ED
Melville Advance, Melville, SK

Orosz, Mark .... (306) 728-5448
PUB, Melville Advance, Melville, SK

Orosz, Monica .... (304) 348-5140
Action Line/Hot Line ED
Charleston Daily Mail, Charleston, WV

O'Rourke, Barry .... (612) 222-5011
CIRC MGR-MET Sales
St. Paul Pioneer Press, St. Paul, MN

O'Rourke, Donna .... (508) 458-7100
Automotive ED, Sun, Lowell, MA

O'Rourke, Gerri .... (541) 895-2197
PUB, ED, Creswell Chronicle, Creswell, OR

O'Rourke, Gloria R .... (516) 922-4215
ED
Oyster Bay-Syosset Guardian, Oyster Bay, NY

O'Rourke, John .... (505) 823-7777
Sports ED
Albuquerque Tribune, Albuquerque, NM

O'Rourke, Maureen .... (510) 988-7800
ED, Rossmoor News, Walnut Creek, CA

O'Rourke, Mike .... (218) 829-4705
City ED
Brainerd Daily Dispatch, Brainerd, MN

O'Rourke, Tim .... (403) 743-8186
PUB/GM
Fort McMurray Today, Fort McMurray, AB

Orozco, Stella .... (210) 736-4450
Legal ED
Daily Commercial Recorder, San Antonio, TX

Orr, Betty .... (615) 359-1188
ED, Lewisburg Tribune, Lewisburg, TN

Orr, Bob .... (717) 854-1575
News ED
York Dispatch/York Sunday News, York, PA

Orr, J Scott .... (201) 877-4141
Washington BU, Star-Ledger, Newark, NJ

Orr, Jay .... (615) 259-8800
Music ED, Nashville Banner, Nashville, TN

Orr, Leith W .... (902) 893-9405
PUB/GM, Daily News, Truro, NS

Orr, Mary Ann .... (502) 753-1916
ADV MGR-RT
Murray Ledger & Times, Murray, KY

Orric, Phyllis .... (415) 541-0700
MAN ED, SF Weekly, San Francisco, CA

Orric, W .... (515) 435-4151
PUB, ED
Nashua Reporter & Weekly Post, Nashua, IA

Orrock, Ray .... (510) 783-6111
COL, Daily Review, Hayward, CA
MediaNews Inc. (Alameda Newspapers)

Orsborn, Harold .... (541) 753-2641
ADV MGR-CLASS
Corvallis Gazette-Times, Corvallis, OR

Orscheln, Harry .... (313) 242-1100
Wire ED, Monroe Evening News, Monroe, MI

Orsini, Pat .... (516) 843-2020
MGR-OPER BUS Data Center
Newsday, Melville, NY

Orso, Janet .... (206) 339-3000
PROD MGR-Color Separations
Herald, Everett, WA

Ortberg, Bart .... (805) 688-5522
MAN ED
Santa Ynez Valley News/Extra, Solvang, CA

Ortega, Claudia .... (912) 236-9511
Features Planning ED
Savannah Morning News, Savannah, GA

Ortega, Filemon .... (305) 551 3292
PUB, MAN ED
La Prensa Centroamericana, Miami, FL

Ortega, Francisco A .... (305) 551 3292
GM, La Prensa Centroamericana, Miami, FL

Ortego, David L .... (318) 363-3939
GM, Ville Platte Gazette, Ville Platte, LA

Ortegon, Janet .... (219) 874-7211
EDU/School ED
News Dispatch, Michigan City, IN

Ortez, Maria .... (209) 943-5143
PUB, La Nacion, Stockton, CA

Orth, Donald C .... (414) 657-1000
ADV MGR-CLASS
Kenosha News, Kenosha, WI

Orth, Mary .... (319) 398-8211
ADV MGR-CLASS, Gazette, Cedar Rapids, IA

Ortim, Melanie .... (210) 542-4301
ADV DIR, MGR-MKTG/PROM
Brownsville Herald, Brownsville, TX
Freedom Communications Inc.

Ortiz, Gus .... (909) 889-9666
DIR-MIS, Sun, San Bernardino, CA

Ortleb, Charles .... (212) 627-2120
PUB, ED, New York Native, New York, NY

Ortman, Loren .... (201) 428-6200
PROD FRM-Press
Daily Record, Parsippany, NJ

Orton, Judy .... (816) 263-4123
ADV DIR, MGR-MKTG/PROM, Living/Lifestyle ED, Moberly Monitor-Index & Democrat, Moberly, MO

Orvis, Althea .... (208) 377-6200
Librarian, Idaho Statesman, Boise, ID

Orwig, Christy .... (605) 665-7811
ADV MGR
Yankton Daily Press & Dakotan, Yankton, SD

Orwig, Tim .... (817) 778-4444
City ED, Temple Daily Telegram, Temple, TX

Osbon Jr, Charles .... (207) 282-1535
CIRC MGR, Journal Tribune, Biddeford, ME

Osborn, David A .... (501) 785-9404
VP-Western Newspaper Group
Donrey Media Group, Fort Smith, AR

Osborn, Douglas W .... (509) 459-5000
DIR-OPER, Spokesman-Review, Spokane, WA

Osborn, J D .... (903) 597-8111
GM, Tyler Morning Telegraph, Tyler, TX

Osborn, James J .... (541) 776-4411
GM, Mail Tribune, Medford, OR

Osborn, Kathy .... (515) 792-3121
PROD FRM-Engraving
Newton Daily News, Newton, IA

Osborn, Marlin M .... (904) 934-1200
PUB, Whiting Tower, Gulf Breeze, FL

Osborn, Rosemary .... (704) 624-5068
ED, Home News, Marshville, NC

Osborn, Steve .... (520) 763-2505
PROD MGR-Press/Post Press
Mohave Valley Daily News, Bullhead City, AZ

Osborne, Bill .... (604) 732-2222
PROD ASST DIR, Province, Vancouver, BC
Southam Inc.

Osborne, Burl .... (214) 977-6606
PRES-Publishing Division
A H Belo Corp., Dallas, TX

Osborne, Diana .... (907) 456-6661
MGR-CR, Daily News-Miner, Fairbanks, AK

Osborne, Jan .... (757) 446-2000
DP MGR, Virginian-Pilot, Norfolk, VA

Osborne, Janis .... (914) 856-5383
ED, Gazette, Port Jervis, NY

Osborne, Jeff .... (817) 965-3124
MAN ED, Stephenville Empire-Tribune, Stephenville, TX

Osborne, Jen .... (716) 366-3000
Features ED, Health/Medical ED, Living ED, Television/Music ED, Films/Theater ED
Evening Observer, Dunkirk, NY

Osborne, Mike .... (912) 744-4200
PROD MGR-Building SRV
Macon Telegraph, Macon, GA

Osborne, Paul .... (217) 422-9702
PUB, ED, Decatur Tribune, Decatur, IL

Osborne, Richard .... (304) 752-6950
PRES, PUB, PA, Logan Banner, Logan, WV

Osborne, Spencer .... (407) 242-3500
MGR-Purchasing
Florida Today, Melbourne, FL

Osborne, Tammy .... (606) 231-3100
CIRC MGR-Customer SRV
Lexington Herald-Leader, Lexington, KY

Osborne, Tom .... (206) 597-8742
Senior ED, News Tribune, Tacoma, WA

Osborne, William .... (619) 299-3131
News ED-Day
San Diego Union-Tribune, San Diego, CA

Osburn, Chaz .... (614) 773-2111
MAN ED, Chillicothe Gazette, Chillicothe, OH

Osenbaugh, Faye .... (316) 788-2835
ADV MGR, Daily Reporter, Derby, KS

Osenenko, Derek .... (914) 454-2000
EX ED
Poughkeepsie Journal, Poughkeepsie, NY

Oset, James .... (406) 657-1200
NTL ED, Billings Gazette, Billings, MT

O'Shaughnessy, Bud .... (908) 240-5330
VP
Urner Barry's Price-Current, Toms River, NJ

O'Shaughnessy, Michael .... (908) 240-5330
DIR
Urner Barry's Price-Current, Toms River, NJ

O'Shaughnessy, Tamara .... (309) 346-1111
MAN ED, Pekin Daily Times, Pekin, IL

O'Shaughnessy, Tracey .... (203) 574-3636
Accent ED, Travel ED, Waterbury Republican-American, Waterbury, CT

O'Shea, Brendan .... (810) 332-8181
PROD SUPT-MR, Oakland Press, Pontiac, MI

O'Shea, Dan .... (708) 336-7000
News ED, News-Sun, Waukegan, IL

O'Shea, James .... (312) 222-3232
Deputy MAN ED-News
Chicago Tribune, Chicago, IL

O'Shea, Mary .... (907) 456-6661
PA, Daily News-Miner, Fairbanks, AK

Osher, Barbro Sachs .... (415) 381-5149
PUB, Vestkusten, Mill Valley, CA

Oshiro, Sandra .... (808) 525-8000
Garden ED, Home Furnishings/Improvement ED, Honolulu Advertiser, Honolulu, HI

Oslund, Kevin .... (805) 650-2900
CIRC MGR-Distribution/MR
Ventura County Star, Ventura, CA

Osmond, Robert .... (510) 228-6400
ED, MAN ED
Martinez News-Gazette, Martinez, CA

Osmundson, Paul .... (803) 771-6161
EDU ED, State, Columbia, SC

Ossutt, Jason .... (816) 741-9530
MAN ED, Platte County Gazette, Liberty, MO

Osswald, Scott .... (518) 374-4141
ADV MGR-RT
Daily Gazette, Schenectady, NY

Ostby, Nancy .... (608) 543-3773
ED, Argyle Agenda, Argyle, WI

Ostdiek, Allen .... (402) 756-7284
PUB, ED
Lawrence Locomotive, Lawrence, NE

Ostdiek, Leland .... (402) 756-2077
PUB, ED, Blue Hill Leader, Blue Hill, NE

Osteen Jr, Hubert D .... (803) 775-6331
BC, PUB, ED, Item, Sumter, SC

Osteen II, Hubert Graham .... (803) 775-6331
VP, SEC, EX ED, EPE, Item, Sumter, SC

Osteen, Jim .... (352) 374-5000
EX ED, Gainesville Sun, Gainesville, FL

Osteen, Kyle Brown .... (803) 775-6331
VP, ADV DIR, Item, Sumter, SC

Osteen, Mike .... (813) 259-7711
ADV MGR-RT
Tampa Tribune and Times, Tampa, FL

Ostemiller, Marilyn .... (908) 722-8800
BUS ED, Courier-News, Bridgewater, NJ

Osten, Albert M .... (914) 297-3723
PUB, MAN ED, Southern Dutchess News, Wappingers Falls, NY

Ostendorf, William .... (401) 277-7000
MAN ED-Visuals
Providence Journal-Bulletin, Providence, RI

Oster, Rob .... (541) 258-3151
ED, Lebanon Express, Lebanon, OR

Osterbrock, Bill .... (408) 678-2660
ED, Soledad Bee, Soledad, CA

Osterhout, Marva .... (208) 678-2201
ADV MGR, South Idaho Press, Burley, ID

Ostermeier, Joseph .... (618) 234-1000
Sports ED
Belleville News-Democrat, Belleville, IL

Osterwald, Becky .... (719) 743-2371
PUB, ED
Eastern Colorado Plainsman, Hugo, CO

Ostler, Scott .... (415) 777-1111
COL-Sports
San Francisco Chronicle, San Francisco, CA

Ostlund, William .... (206) 863-8171
ED, News Review, Sumner, WA

Ostroff, Harold .... (212) 889-8200
GM, Jewish Forward, New York, NY

Ostrom, Gary W .... (616) 722-3161
PUB, Muskegon Chronicle, Muskegon, MI

Ostrom, Lee .... (320) 679-2661
ED, Kanabec County Times, Mora, MN

Ostrow, Joanne .... (303) 820-1010
Radio/Television COL
Denver Post, Denver, CO

Ostrowski, Bernard .... (212) 416-2000
PROD DIR-CORP DP
Wall Street Journal, New York, NY

Ostrowski, Darlene .... (630) 668-7957
ED, Wheaton Leader, Glen Ellyn, IL

Ostrum, Neenya .... (212) 627-2120
MAN ED, New York Native, New York, NY

Ostwald, Marvin .... (515) 228-3211
PROD FRM-Press
Charles City Press, Charles City, IA

O'Sullivan, Peter .... (416) 947-2222
EIC, Toronto Sun, Toronto, ON

O'Sullivan, Robert T .... (410) 332-6000
VP-Circulation, Sun, Baltimore, MD

O'Sullivan, Sean .... (905) 526-3333
DP MGR, Spectator, Hamilton, ON

O'Sullivan, Steve .... (818) 962-8811
OPER ED, San Gabriel Valley Tribune, West Covina, CA, MediaNews Inc.

Oswald, Bob .... (516) 843-2020
PROD MGR-Mechanical
Newsday, Melville, NY

Oswald, H L .... (910) 293-4534
PUB, Warsaw-Faison News, Warsaw, NC

Oswald III, H L .... (910) 285-2178
PUB, Wallace Enterprise, Wallace, NC

Oswald, John .... (201) 653-1000
City ED, Jersey Journal, Jersey City, NJ

Oswald, Nadine F .... (717) 622-3456
DIR-Human Resources, Pottsville Republican & Evening Herald, Pottsville, PA

Oszewski, Brian T .... (219) 769-9292
ED
Northwest Indiana Catholic, Merrillville, IN

Ota, Takeshi .... (213) 629-2231
ED, Rafu Shimpo, Los Angeles, CA

Otero, Salo .... (210) 728-2500
Sports ED, Laredo Morning Times, Laredo, TX

Otero-Vallejos, Liz .... (505) 823-7777
Radio/Television ED
Albuquerque Journal, Albuquerque, NM

Otey, Sara M .... (718) 238-6600
ED, Home Reporter and Sunset News, Brooklyn, NY

Othman, Sigamond .... (202) 898-8254
GEN MGR-Europe/Middle East
United Press International, Washington, DC

Otis, Al .... (408) 637-9795
Sales PROM
Post/Dispatch Features, Hollister, CA

Otis, George .... (517) 787-2300
ADV MGR-CLASS
Jackson Citizen Patriot, Jackson, MI

Otolski, C T .... (219) 362-2161
PUB, La Porte Herald-Argus, La Porte, IN

Otolski, Greg .... (502) 582-4011
Automotive ED, RE ED
Courier-Journal, Louisville, KY

O'Toole, Chris .... (805) 564-5200
PROD MGR-Pre Press, Santa Barbara News-Press, Santa Barbara, CA

O'Toole, Edward .... (402) 564-2741
BM, DP MGR
Columbus Telegram, Columbus, NE

O'Toole, Joanne R .... (216) 942-5455
Journalist, O'Toole Travel Journalist/Photographer, Tom & Joanne, Willoughby, OH

O' Toole, Joseph .... (301) 733-5131
TREAS, Morning Herald, Hagerstown, MD

O'Toole, Thomas .... (202) 408-1484
Sports ED, Scripps Howard News Service, Washington, DC

O'Toole, Thomas J .... (216) 942-5455
Journalist/Photographer
O'Toole Travel Journalist/Photographer, Tom & Joanne, Willoughby, OH

Ott, Eunice .... (937) 444-3441
ED, Brown County Press, Mt. Orab, OH

Ott, Gary .... (915) 682-5311
MAN ED, City/MET ED, NTL ED, Political/Government ED
Midland Reporter-Telegram, Midland, TX

Ott, Rick .... (619) 299-3131
DIR-MKTG
San Diego Union-Tribune, San Diego, CA

Ottaway Jr, James H .... (212) 416-2600
Sr VP/PRES-Magazines
Dow Jones & Co. Inc., New York, NY

Ottensmeyer, Richard .... (904) 435-8500
DIR-FIN, News Journal, Pensacola, FL

Otterbein, Jeff .... (860) 241-6200
Sports ED, Hartford Courant, Hartford, CT

Otterbourg, Ken .... (910) 727-7211
City ED
Winston-Salem Journal, Winston-Salem, NC

Ottey, Louis E .... (412) 775-3200
CIRC DIR, Beaver County Times, Beaver, PA

Ottinger, Jerry .... (423) 638-4181
PROD FRM-PR
Greeneville Sun, Greeneville, TN

Otto, Diana .... (712) 284-2300
GM, Alta Advertiser, Alta, IA

Otto, Mike .... (712) 448-3622
PUB, ED, Paullina Times, Paullina, IA

Otto, Steve .... (813) 259-7711
COL, Tampa Tribune and Times, Tampa, FL

Otu, Isaac .... (302) 324-2500
MGR-RES, News Journal, Wilmington, DE

Oue Who's Where-174

Ouellet, Gilles .... (418) 686-3233
City ED, Consumer Interest
Le Soleil, Quebec, QC

Ouellette, Marc .... (514) 581-5120
GM, L'Artisan, Repentigny, QC

Ouimet, Michele .... (514) 285-7272
EDU, La Presse, Montreal, QC

Ouimet, Polly .... (207) 784-5411
Entertainment/Amusements ED, Music ED
Sun-Journal, Lewiston, ME

Oulette, Phil .... (508) 744-0600
CIRC MGR
Salem Evening News, Beverly, MA

Ouroussoff, Nicolai .... (213) 237-5000
Architecture Critic
Los Angeles Times, Los Angeles, CA

Ousky, Rick .... (612) 345-3316
ED, Lake City Graphic, Lake City, MN

Outlaw, Billy .... (703) 368-3101
PROD MGR-PR
Journal Messenger, Manassas, VA

Outlaw, Cindy .... (817) 796-4325
PUB, Hico News-Review, Hico, TX

Ovalle, Juan Martine .... (972) 446-4346
ED, El Heraldo News, Carrollton, TX

Ovans, Susan .... (617) 925-9266
PUB, Hull Times, Hull, MA

Ovca, Michael S .... (217) 351-5252
SEC/TREAS, CFO, PA
News-Gazette, Champaign, IL

Over, John .... (709) 786-7014
PUB, Compass, Carbonear, NF

Overall, Mike .... (501) 935-5525
ASSOC ED, Films/Theater ED
Jonesboro Sun, Jonesboro, AR

Overcash, Bridgetta .... (716) 487-1111
Family ED, Magazine ED
Post-Journal, Jamestown, NY

Overeiner, Paul .... (517) 787-2300
BUS/FIN ED
Jackson Citizen Patriot, Jackson, MI

Overend, William .... (213) 237-5000
Ventura BU/City ED
Los Angeles Times, Los Angeles, CA

Overlie, B J .... (712) 722-0741
PUB, Sioux Center News, Sioux Center, IA

Overlie, Warren .... (712) 722-0741
PUB, Sioux Center News, Sioux Center, IA

Overly, Mettja .... (414) 435-4411
DIR-Human Resources
Green Bay Press-Gazette, Green Bay, WI

Overmann, Mike .... (402) 332-3232
ED, Gretna Guide, Gretna, NE

Overmann, Penny .... (402) 289-2329
PUB
Douglas County Post Gazette, Elkhorn, NE

Overmyer, Dave .... (419) 734-3141
CIRC MGR, News-Herald, Port Clinton, OH

Overmyer, Jack K .... (219) 223-2111
PRES, PUB-Emeritus
Rochester Sentinel, Rochester, IN

Overmyer, Margery H .... (219) 223-2111
VP/TREAS, Rochester Sentinel, Rochester, IN

Oversmith, Blake .... (619) 299-3131
CONT
San Diego Union-Tribune, San Diego, CA

Overton, Brian .... (203) 876-6800
ED, Post, Milford, CT

Overton, Jim .... (209) 578-2000
CIRC MGR-Home Delivery
Modesto Bee, Modesto, CA

Overton, Kelly .... (812) 254-0480
Photographer
Washington Times-Herald, Washington, IN

Overton, Thomas J .... (601) 287-6111
PUB, Daily Corinthian, Corinth, MS

Overturf, Betty .... (910) 628-7125
ED, Times-Messenger, Fairmont, NC

Overturf, Darrell .... (619) 322-8889
PROD MGR-Camera/Platemaking
Desert Sun, Palm Springs, CA

Owades, Mark .... (203) 255-8877
PUB, Fairfield Minuteman, Fairfield, CT

Owaisi, L .... (416) 493-4374
PUB, Al-Hilal, Willowdale, ON

Owden, Shirley-Anne .... (415) 348-4321
Radio/Television ED
San Mateo County Times, San Mateo, CA

Owen, B Ray .... (573) 335-6611
BUS ED
Southeast Missourian, Cape Girardeau, MO

Owen, Dave .... (304) 485-1891
ED, EPE, EDL Writer, Parkersburg News & Sentinel, Parkersburg, WV

Owen, Deb .... (319) 643-2131
PUB, West Branch Times, West Branch, IA

Owen, Howard .... (804) 649-6000
Deputy MAN ED-Flair/Sports
Richmond Times-Dispatch, Richmond, VA

Owen, Janet .... (209) 441-6111
PROD DIR, Fresno Bee, Fresno, CA

Owen, Jeff .... (317) 736-7101
ED, EPE, Daily Journal, Franklin, IN

Owen, Judy .... (937) 498-2111
City/MET ED, Travel ED
Sidney Daily News, Sidney, OH

Owen, Mike .... (319) 643-2131
PUB, ED
West Branch Times, West Branch, IA

Owen, Rhonda .... (501) 378-3400
ASST MAN ED-ADM
Arkansas Democrat-Gazette, Little Rock, AR

Owen, Rick .... (705) 567-5321
Photo ED
Northern Daily News, Kirkland Lake, ON

Owen, Rob .... (518) 454-5694
Television Writer, Times Union, Albany, NY

Owen, Vicki .... (501) 534-3400
Librarian
Pine Bluff Commercial, Pine Bluff, AR

Owen, W H .... (910) 323-4848
PROD MGR
Fayetteville Observer-Times, Fayetteville, NC

Owens, Amy .... (219) 933-3200
ADV DIR, Times, Munster, IN

Owens, Amy M .... (910) 323-4848
MGR-CR
Fayetteville Observer-Times, Fayetteville, NC

Owens, Carl .... (503) 221-8327
PA, Oregonian, Portland, OR

Owens, Cindy .... (812) 372-7811
BM, Republic, Columbus, IN

Owens, Claude .... (941) 687-7000
PROD MGR-MR, Ledger, Lakeland, FL

Owens, Diane .... (909) 684-1200
ADV MGR-RE
Press-Enterprise, Riverside, CA

Owens, Doris .... (803) 563-3121
PUB
Dorchester Eagle-Record, St. George, SC

Owens, Gene .... (334) 433-1551
Political ED
Mobile Press Register, Mobile, AL

Owens, Howard .... (909) 684-1200
DIR-OPER, PROD DIR-OPER
Press-Enterprise, Riverside, CA

Owens, J W .... (352) 567-5639
PUB, Pasco News, Dade City, FL

Owens, James .... (202) 636-3000
PROD MGR-Materials Handling
Washington Times, Washington, DC

Owens, Jennifer .... (216) 951-0000
EDU Writer, News-Herald, Willoughby, OH

Owens, Joseph .... (610) 258-7171
MAN ED, Express-Times, Easton, PA

Owens, Kay .... (903) 984-2593
PROD FRM-COMP
Kilgore News Herald, Kilgore, TX

Owens, Mark .... (216) 293-6097
ED, Pymatuning Area News, Andover, OH

Owens, Rita .... (317) 423-5511
Librarian, Journal and Courier, Lafayette, IN

Owens, William M .... (803) 563-3121
PUB, ED
Dorchester Eagle-Record, St. George, SC

Owens-Schiele, Elizabeth .... (800) 245-6536
Special Products CNR
US/Express, Chicago, IL

Owensby, John .... (910) 993-2161
PUB, Kernersville News, Kernersville, NC

Owensby, Mike .... (405) 353-0620
ADV MGR-RT
Lawton Constitution, Lawton, OK

Owney, William R .... (903) 796-7133
PUB, Atlanta Citizens Journal, Atlanta, TX

Owyer, Robert .... (617) 593-7700
PROD FRM-COMP
Daily Evening Item, Lynn, MA

Oxford, Earl .... (501) 785-7700
PROD SUPT-PR
Southwest Times Record, Fort Smith, AR

Oyadomari, James .... (808) 245-3681
PROD SUPT-Shop, Garden Island, Lihue, HI

Oyhamburu, Terry .... (406) 791-1444
Personnel DIR
Great Falls Tribune, Great Falls, MT

Oyler, Karen .... (804) 633-5005
GM, Caroline Progress, Bowling Green, VA

Ozaki, Hajime .... (212) 603-6600
Correspondent
Kyodo News Service, New York, NY

Ozawa, H .... (212) 575-5830
MAN ED
Jiji Press America Ltd., New York, NY

P

Paar, Thomas .... (219) 942-0521
PUB, Merrillville Herald, Merrillville, IN

Paben, Jean .... (970) 493-6397
PSL DIR
Fort Collins Coloradoan, Fort Collins, CO

Paccione, Don .... (212) 210-2100
PROD MGR-Building (Brooklyn)
New York Daily News, New York, NY

Pacciorini, Albert C .... (510) 237-0888
PUB, Jornal Portugues, San Pablo, CA

Pace, Christa .... (916) 444-2355
CIRC DIR-Sacramento Office
Daily Recorder, Sacramento, CA

Pace, Donna .... (510) 935-2525
Community ED
Contra Costa Times, Walnut Creek, CA

Pace, Edward M .... (334) 222-8541
PUB, Covington Times Courier, Andalusia, AL

Pace, Fred .... (304) 824-5465
ED, Weekly News Sentinel, Hamlin, WV

Pace III, J Malcolm .... (804) 798-9031
PUB, ED, Herald Progress, Ashland, VA

Pace, Jerry .... (405) 372-5000
CIRC MGR-PROM
News Press, Stillwater, OK

Pace, Kay .... (817) 645-2441
ADV MGR, Times-Review, Cleburne, TX

Pace, Len .... (902) 875-3244
ED, Coast Guard, Shelburne, NS

Pace, Lynn .... (817) 767-8341
CIRC MGR, Wichita Falls Times Record News, Wichita Falls, TX

Pace, Michael A .... (316) 356-1201
PUB, Ulysses News, Ulysses, KS

Pace, Russ .... (803) 558-3323
PUB, ED, Weekly Observer, Hemingway, SC

Pace, Shirley .... (316) 356-1201
ED, Ulysses News, Ulysses, KS

Pace, Stephen T .... (804) 798-9031
GM, Herald Progress, Ashland, VA

Pace, Sunie .... (417) 256-9191
ADV MGR
West Plains Daily Quill, West Plains, MO

Pace, Terry .... (205) 766-3434
Amusements/Books ED, Films/Theater ED, Music ED, Radio/Television ED
Times Daily, Florence, AL

Pacetti, Diane .... (419) 223-1010
City ED, Lima News, Lima, OH

Pach, Peter .... (860) 241-6200
EDL Writer, Hartford Courant, Hartford, CT

Pacheco, Robert .... (508) 676-8211
PROD FRM-MR, Herald News, Fall River, MA

Paci, Salvatore .... (201) 586-3012
PUB, Neighbor News, Denville, NJ

Pacitti, Bob .... (352) 489-2731
ED, Riverland News, Dunnellon, FL

Pack, Amy L .... (209) 734-5821
PRES, PUB, Visalia Times-Delta, Visalia, CA
Gannett Co. Inc.

Packard, Linda .... (405) 326-3311
ADV DIR, Hugo Daily News, Hugo, OK

Packo, Ed .... (203) 333-0161
ADV MGR-Art SRV
Connecticut Post, Bridgeport, CT

Paczak, Dave .... (518) 561-2300
Photo ED, Press-Republican, Plattsburgh, NY

Padavano, Dan .... (315) 470-0011
RE ED, Post-Standard/Syracuse Herald-Journal/American, Syracuse, NY

Padbury, Peter .... (613) 933-3160
ADV DIR, ADV MGR-CLASS
Standard-Freeholder, Cornwall, ON

Padden, Richard W .... (303) 776-2244
MGR-INFO SYS
Daily Times-Call, Longmont, CO

Paddock, Eric .... (814) 723-8200
City ED, EDL Writer, EDU ED
Warren Times-Observer, Warren, PA

Paddock, Laurence T .... (303) 442-1202
ED-Emeritus, Daily Camera, Boulder, CO

Paddock, Polly .... (704) 358-5000
Books ED, Charlotte Observer, Charlotte, NC

Paddock, Robert Y .... (847) 427-4300
Vice Chairman/EVP-ADM
Daily Herald, Arlington Heights, IL

Paddock Jr, Robert Y .... (847) 427-4300
ASST VP/MGR-ADM
Daily Herald, Arlington Heights, IL

Paddock Jr, Stuart R .... (847) 427-4300
BC/PUB/CEO
Daily Herald, Arlington Heights, IL

Paddock III, Stuart R .... (847) 427-4300
ASST VP/New Media MGR
Daily Herald, Arlington Heights, IL

Padecky, Bob .... (707) 546-2020
COL-Sports, Press Democrat, Santa Rosa, CA

Padelford, Jon .... (561) 461-2050
DP MGR, Tribune, Fort Pierce, FL

Paden, Kenneth S .... (607) 563-3526
PUB, Tri-Town News, Sidney, NY

Padgett, Beth .... (864) 298-4100
Deputy EPE, Greenville News, Greenville, SC

Padgett, Betsie .... (518) 792-3131
PROD FRM-COMP, Post-Star, Glens Falls, NY

Padilla, Billie .... (913) 295-1111
Television ED
Topeka Capital-Journal, Topeka, KS

Padilla, Manny .... (909) 487-2200
ADV DIR, Hemet News, Hemet, CA

Padilla, Molly .... (404) 526-5151
ADV MGR-Sports MKTG
Atlanta Journal-Constitution, Atlanta, GA

Padilla, Rosanna .... (316) 792-1211
Religion/Society ED
Great Bend Tribune, Great Bend, KS

Padilla, Steve .... (213) 237-5000
San Fernando Valley City ED
Los Angeles Times, Los Angeles, CA

Padilla, Wanda M .... (303) 936-8556
PUB, ED, La Voz Newspaper, Denver, CO

Padjen, Bill .... (773) 586-8800
Community News ED
Daily Southtown, Chicago, IL

Padovano, Dan .... (315) 470-0011
BUS/FIN ED, Post-Standard/Syracuse Herald-Journal/American, Syracuse, NY

Paduch, Margaretta L .... (717) 622-3456
SEC, Pottsville Republican & Evening Herald, Pottsville, PA

Padwin, David .... (515) 736-4541
PUB, ED, Enterprise Journal, St. Ansgar, IA

Paes, Helen .... (330) 747-1471
ADV DIR-Community Affairs
Vindicator, Youngstown, OH

Paeth, Greg .... (513) 352-2000
Radio/Television ED
Cincinnati Post, Cincinnati, OH

Paez, Marites .... (516) 378-3133
MAN ED, Leader, Freeport, NY

Paff, Bob .... (908) 722-8800
DP MGR, Courier-News, Bridgewater, NJ

Pagani, Ken .... (330) 821-1200
CIRC MGR, Alliance Review, Alliance, OH

Page, Candy .... (802) 863-3441
ASST MAN ED, Free Press, Burlington, VT

Page, Clarence .... (312) 222-3232
EDL Writer/COL
Chicago Tribune, Chicago, IL

Page, Clif .... (412) 775-3200
Graphics ED/Art DIR, Photo DEPT MGR
Beaver County Times, Beaver, PA

Page, Connie .... (617) 426-3000
State House BU Reporter
Boston Herald, Boston, MA

Page, Dan .... (306) 882-4202
PUB, GM, ED, MAN ED
Rosetown Eagle, Rosetown, SK

Page, Dan .... (304) 255-4400
EX ED, EPE, Register Herald, Beckley, WV

Page, David .... (405) 235-3100
MAN ED, Journal Record, Oklahoma City, OK

Page, Dian .... (414) 435-4411
Society/Women's ED
Green Bay Press-Gazette, Green Bay, WI

Page, Douglas .... (800) 245-6536
Sales MAN, News & Features
Tribune Media Services Inc., Chicago, IL

Page, Gary .... (509) 745-8313
PUB
Douglas County Empire Press, Waterville, WA

Page, James .... (615) 754-6397
PUB, Mt. Juliet News, Mount Juliet, TN

Page, Jeffrey .... (201) 646-4000
COL, Record, Hackensack, NJ

Page, JoAnn .... (903) 496-7297
GM, Wolfe City Mirror, Wolfe City, TX

Page, Lynda .... (313) 222-2300
Food ED, Detroit News, Detroit, MI

Page, Margi .... (509) 745-8313
PUB, ED
Douglas County Empire Press, Waterville, WA

Page, Psyche R .... (757) 247-4600
CIRC MGR-ADM SRV
Daily Press, Newport News, VA

Page, Robert .... (904) 252-1511
PROD MGR-Packing/Distribution
Daytona Beach News-Journal, Daytona Beach, FL

Page, Tom .... (804) 634-4153
GM, Independent-Messenger, Emporia, VA

Pagel, Julie .... (414) 435-4411
Weekend ED
Green Bay Press-Gazette, Green Bay, WI

Paglia, Tony .... (330) 747-1471
Senior Regional ED
Vindicator, Youngstown, OH

Pagliarini, Ed .... (908) 722-8800
Photo ED, Courier-News, Bridgewater, NJ

Pagones, Sara .... (504) 826-3279
EDL Writer
Times-Picayune, New Orleans, LA

Paige, Jane .... (919) 460-2600
ED, Cary News, Cary, NC

Paige, Philip .... (414) 375-5100
PUB, News Graphic, Cedarburg, WI

Paine, Kay .... (806) 376-4488
Oil ED, Amarillo Daily News/Globe Times, Amarillo, TX

Paine-Brooks, Lesia .... (423) 929-3111
Amusements ED, Films/Theater ED, Radio/Television ED
Johnson City Press, Johnson City, TN

Paino, Laura .... (201) 646-4000
Newsroom Administrator
Record, Hackensack, NJ

Painter, Kevin .... (903) 872-3931
Photo ED, Corsicana Daily Sun, Corsicana, TX

Painter, Len .... (616) 842-6400
News ED
Grand Haven Tribune, Grand Haven, MI

Copyright ©1997 by the Editor & Publisher Co.

175-Who's Where **Par**

Painter, Virginia .... (360) 754-5400
Amusements ED, ETO (Entertainment) ED, Films/Theater ED, Music ED, Radio/ Television ED, Olympian, Olympia, WA
Painting, Hollis .... (609) 758-2112
MAN ED, New Egypt Press, New Egypt, NJ
Paiva, Frank .... (206) 464-2111
VP-OPER, Seattle Times, Seattle, WA
Paiva, Richard .... (704) 758-7381
ADV DIR, Lenoir News-Topic, Lenoir, NC
Paiva, Tim .... (603) 742-4455
Sports ED, Foster's Democrat, Dover, NH
Pajak, Ronald .... (716) 849-3434
PROD OPER FRM-COMP/Ad OPER
Buffalo News, Buffalo, NY
Pakenham, Michael .... (410) 332-6000
Books ED, Sun, Baltimore, MD
Palace, Leslie .... (913) 295-1111
ADV MGR
Topeka Capital-Journal, Topeka, KS
Palacios, Ledis .... (813) 932-7181
MAN ED, Nuevo Siglo, Tampa, FL
Palacios, Neris Ramon .... (813) 932-7181
PUB, Nuevo Siglo, Tampa, FL
Palacios, Rosmeli .... (813) 932-7181
GM, Nuevo Siglo, Tampa, FL
Palange, Paul V .... (508) 676-8211
MAN ED, Herald News, Fall River, MA
Palangio, Michael .... (705) 272-4363
PUB, Northland Post, Cochrane, ON
Palazzo, Paul .... (206) 464-2111
Deputy Local ED, Seattle Times, Seattle, WA
Palella, John .... (518) 454-5694
PROD SUPT-COMP Room
Times Union, Albany, NY
Palen, Ann .... (307) 326-9852
Office MGR
Stampede Features, Saratoga, WY
Palen, Jerry .... (307) 326-9852
PRES, Stampede Features, Saratoga, WY
Palencia, Irene .... (210) 736-4450
Office MGR
Daily Commercial Recorder, San Antonio, TX
Palermini, Bob .... (954) 356-4000
DIR-Technology
Sun-Sentinel, Fort Lauderdale, FL
Palermo, Christopher M .... (315) 946-9701
PUB, Wayne County Star, Lyons, NY
Paley, Bernard .... (516) 265-2100
PUB, Smithtown News, Smithtown, NY
Palket, Raymond A .... (412) 375-6611
PUB, GM, News, Aliquippa, PA
Palkowetz, Bruce .... (212) 416-2000
PROD MGR (Seattle WA)
Wall Street Journal, New York, NY
Palladino Jr, Edward A .... (914) 331-5000
Sports ED, Daily Freeman, Kingston, NY
Palladino, Joseph .... (203) 729-2228
Sports ED
Naugatuck Daily News, Naugatuck, CT
Pallan, Rav .... (250) 380-5211
CIRC MGR-Distribution
Times Colonist, Victoria, BC
Pallares, Jan .... (219) 881-3000
DIR-FIN, Post-Tribune, Gary, IN
Palli, Randall J .... (605) 692-6271
PROD MGR
Brookings Register, Brookings, SD
Pallotto, Tony .... (619) 433-7333
PUB, Scout, Oceanside, CA
Palm, Mathew .... (607) 272-2321
Films/Theater ED, Ithaca Journal, Ithaca, NY
Palm, Rory .... (715) 425-1561
GM, River Falls Journal, River Falls, WI
Palmateer, Jim .... (902) 629-6000
EIC, Guardian, Charlottetown, PEI
Palmer, Barry .... (603) 668-4321
Entertainment ED, Religion ED
Union Leader, Manchester, NH
Palmer, Cheryl .... (909) 684-1200
MGR-INFO SYS
Press-Enterprise, Riverside, CA
Palmer, D W .... (503) 221-8327
ASST TREAS, CONT
Oregonian, Portland, OR
Palmer, Dave .... (301) 862-2111
GM, Enterprise, Lexington Park, MD
Palmer, David .... (205) 766-3434
Consumer Interest/Food ED, Features ED
Times Daily, Florence, AL
Palmer, Dean .... (910) 368-2222
MAN ED, Pilot, Pilot Mountain, NC
Palmer, Denise E .... (312) 222-3232
DIR-FIN, Chicago Tribune, Chicago, IL
Palmer, Dennis .... (601) 442-9101
CIRC DIR, Natchez Democrat, Natchez, MS
Palmer, Hal .... (704) 252-5611
PROD MGR-Distribution Center
Asheville Citizen-Times, Asheville, NC
Palmer, Jack .... (219) 933-3200
ASSOC PUB (Porter County)
Times, Munster, IN
Palmer, James .... (912) 744-4200
Content ED, Macon Telegraph, Macon, GA
Palmer, Jane .... (402) 444-1000
Food ED, Omaha World-Herald, Omaha, NE
Palmer, Jim .... (334) 262-1611
Cartoonist, Advertiser, Montgomery, AL
Palmer, Jodi White .... (912) 744-4200
Body & Soul ED, Telegraph, Macon, GA
Palmer, Jonna .... (510) 465-3121
Staff Writer, Inter-City Express, Oakland, CA
Palmer, Karen .... (419) 522-3311
Religion Writer, News Journal, Mansfield, OH
Palmer, Kay L .... (316) 733-2002
PUB, ED, Journal-Advocate, Andover, KS
Palmer, Mark .... (615) 388-6464
PUB, Daily Herald, Columbia, TN
Palmer, Molly .... (860) 887-9211
Features ED, Norwich Bulletin, Norwich, CT
Palmer, Nick .... (613) 962-9171
MAN ED, Intelligencer, Belleville, ON
Palmer, Nick .... (604) 732-2111
Chief News ED
Vancouver Sun, Vancouver, BC
Palmer, Peggy .... (507) 931-4520
PUB, ED, St. Peter Herald, St. Peter, MN
Palmer, R L .... (903) 572-1705
SEC/TREAS, PUB, ED, Mount Pleasant Daily Tribune, Mount Pleasant, TX
Palmer, Richard .... (805) 772-7346
GM, ED
Central Coast Sun-Bulletin, Morro Bay, CA
Palmer, Richard .... (315) 635-3921
ED, Camillus Advocate, Baldwinsville, NY
Palmer, Robert B .... (903) 572-1705
PRES, Mount Pleasant Daily Tribune, Mount Pleasant, TX
Palmer, Roger .... (605) 665-7811
CIRC MGR
Yankton Daily Press & Dakotan, Yankton, SD
Palmer, Steven J .... (507) 426-7235
ED, Fairfax Standard, Fairfax, MN
Palmer, Ted .... (501) 623-7711
CIRC DIR, Sentinel-Record, Hot Springs, AR
Palmer, Thomas .... (518) 454-5694
Art DIR, Times Union, Albany, NY
Palmer, Tim .... (314) 635-7931
MAN ED, Word and Way, Jefferson City, MO
Palmer, Vaughn .... (604) 732-2111
COL, Vancouver Sun, Vancouver, BC
Palmer, Vickie K .... (812) 886-9955
ADV MGR-RT
Vincennes Sun-Commercial, Vincennes, IN
Palmer, Wilma .... (505) 396-2844
CIRC MGR, Daily Leader, Lovington, NM
Palmertree, Gina .... (601) 453-5312
BM
Greenwood Commonwealth, Greenwood, MS
Palmisamo, Sharon .... (907) 257-4200
Librarian
Anchorage Daily News, Anchorage, AK
Palmisano, John .... (703) 276-3400
VP-INFO SYS, USA Today, Arlington, VA
Palmquist, Jay .... (408) 372-3311
ADV DIR
Monterey County Herald, Monterey, CA
Palmucci, Albert .... (203) 789-5200
PROD MGR-Vehicle Maintenance
New Haven Register, New Haven, CT
Palser, Lee .... (519) 255-5711
Op EDL Page ED, Windsor Star, Windsor, ON
Palsho, Dorothea Coccoli .... (212) 416-2000
PRES/BUS INFO Services
Dow Jones & Co. Inc., New York, NY
Paltrow, Scot .... (213) 237-5000
Securities-N.Y.
Los Angeles Times, Los Angeles, CA
Palya, William .... (412) 439-7500
DP MGR, Herald-Standard, Uniontown, PA
Pamley, Lorene .... (209) 582-0471
PA, Hanford Sentinel, Hanford, CA
Pamplin, Jim .... (305) 377-3721
COO/CFO
Miami Daily Business Review, Miami, FL
Pampo, Fidencio .... (619) 578-3547
ED, Kalayaan, San Diego, CA
Pamron, Charles .... (304) 824-5101
MAN ED, Lincoln Journal, Hamlin, WV
Panchak-Cohn, Pam .... (717) 771-2000
Graphics ED/Art DIR, Photo ED
York Daily Record, York, PA
Pandergrass, Darrell .... (715) 373-5500
ED, County Journal, Washburn, WI
Pando, Katy .... (912) 723-4376
ED, Early County News, Blakely, GA
Panek, Doug .... (715) 327-4236
PUB, Inter-County Leader, Frederic, WI
Panella, Joseph A .... (609) 654-5000
ED, Central Record, Medford, NJ
Panero, Joan .... (415) 777-5700
MGR-Circulation Accounts Receivable
San Francisco Newspaper Agency, San Francisco, CA
Panetta, Anthony .... (518) 943-2100
PUB, Daily Mail, Catskill, NY
Panetta, Gary .... (309) 686-3000
Arts Reporter, Films/Theater ED, Music ED
Journal Star, Peoria, IL
Paniagua, Joe .... (707) 226-3711
Photo DEPT MGR
Napa Valley Register, Napa, CA
Pankonin, Lori .... (308) 394-5389
PUB, ED, Wauneta Breeze, Wauneta, NE
Pankonin, Russ .... (308) 394-5389
PUB, ED, Wauneta Breeze, Wauneta, NE
Pankowski, Mark .... (904) 599-2100
Political ED
Tallahassee Democrat, Tallahassee, FL
Pankratz, Bruce .... (209) 386-9385
PUB, ED, Avenal Progress, Avenal, CA
Panlilio, Curtis .... (603) 298-8711
CIRC DIR, Valley News, White River Jct., VT
Pannell Jr, Creed W .... (770) 306-2175
PUB, Atlanta-News Leader, Union City, GA
Pannell, Karyn .... (409) 245-5555
MAN ED, Daily Tribune, Bay City, TX
Pannell, Rodger .... (540) 885-7281
CIRC ASST DIR
Daily News Leader, Staunton, VA
Panneton, Ginette .... (819) 376-2501
ADV DIR, Le Nouvelliste, Trois-Rivieres, QC
Panos, James .... (201) 843-5700
PUB, Our Town, Maywood, NJ
Panos, Katherine J .... (201) 843-5700
PUB, ED, Our Town, Maywood, NJ
Pantalone, John .... (401) 847-7766
ED, Newport This Week, Newport, RI
Pantel, Stan .... (404) 526-5151
VP-OPER, PROD VP
Atlanta Journal-Constitution, Atlanta, GA
Panteleeff, Judy .... (360) 736-3311
Women's ED (Living)
Chronicle, Centralia, WA
Pantenburg, Deborah .... (208) 377-6200
ADV DIR, Idaho Statesman, Boise, ID
Panzer, Mary .... (218) 829-4705
ADV ASST MGR
Brainerd Daily Dispatch, Brainerd, MN
Paoli, Richard .... (415) 777-2424
DIR-Photography
San Francisco Examiner, San Francisco, CA
Paolino, Charles .... (908) 246-5500
MET ED
Home News & Tribune, East Brunswick, NJ
Paparella, Donald A .... (315) 823-3680
PUB, Evening Times, Little Falls, NY
Paparone, Joe .... (330) 996-3000
PROD ASST MGR
Akron Beacon Journal, Akron, OH
Papatola, Dominic .... (218) 723-5281
Entertainment/Arts Writer
Duluth News-Tribune, Duluth, MN
Pape, Andrea .... (203) 574-3636
PROD DIR, Waterbury Republican-American, Waterbury, CT
Pape, Andrew J .... (203) 574-3636
ADV MGR-CLASS Display, Online MGR
Republican-American, Waterbury, CT
Pape II, William B .... (203) 574-3636
ASST TREAS/ASST SEC, BM, Republican-American, Waterbury, CT
Pape II, William J .... (203) 574-3636
PRES/TREAS, PUB, Republican-American, Waterbury, CT
Papendick, John .... (605) 225-4100
MAN ED-News, Sports ED
Aberdeen American News, Aberdeen, SD
Papert Jr, S W .... (214) 969-0000
Chairman
Texas Sunday Comic Section Inc., Dallas, TX
Papert III, S W .... (214) 969-0000
PRES
Texas Sunday Comic Section Inc., Dallas, TX
Papile, Cyndi .... (617) 786-7000
MGR-Human Resources
Patriot Ledger, Quincy, MA
Papinchak, Steve .... (702) 383-0211
City ED
Las Vegas Review-Journal, Las Vegas, NV
Papineau, Lou .... (401) 273-6397
ED, Providence Phoenix, Providence, RI
Papirno, Elissa .... (860) 241-6200
Reader Representative/ASSOC ED
Hartford Courant, Hartford, CT
Papp, Les .... (416) 367-2000
Medical Writer, Toronto Star, Toronto, ON
Pappalardo, Brian .... (607) 734-5151
News ED, Star-Gazette, Elmira, NY
Pappas, Carol .... (205) 362-1000
MAN ED, Daily Home, Talladega, AL
Pappas, Harold .... (941) 482-7111
PUB, Fort Myers Observer, Fort Myers, FL
Pappas, Nick .... (603) 882-2741
City ED, Telegraph, Nashua, NH
Pappas, Patricia .... (905) 294-2200
PUB
Markham Economist & Sun, Markham, ON
Paprochi, Sherry Bech .... (614) 587-3397
PUB, ED, Granville Sentinel, Granville, OH
Paproski, Bruce .... (306) 865-2771
ED, Post-Review, Hudson Bay, SK
Papson, Rick .... (910) 349-4331
Sports ED, Reidsville Review, Reidsville, NC
Paquette, Andre .... (514) 562-2494
PUB, ED, L'Argenteuil, Lachute, QC
Paquette, Dave .... (705) 674-5271
CIRC MGR, Sudbury Star, Sudbury, ON
Paquette, Denis P .... (518) 374-4141
GM, Daily Gazette, Schenectady, NY
Paquette, M A .... (613) 632-4155
PUB, ED, Le Carillon, Hawkesbury, ON
Parade, Jeryl .... (203) 789-5200
ADV MGR-CLASS
New Haven Register, New Haven, CT
Paradis, Hal J .... (619) 830-6213
PUB, Observation Post, Yucca Valley, CA
Paradis, Robert .... (514) 347-0323
ED, Le Canada Francais, Saint-Jean, QC
Paradis, Tom .... (714) 676-5247
GM, Rancho News, Temecula, CA
Paradise, Robert .... (212) 416-2600
VP-Barron's
Dow Jones & Co. Inc., New York, NY
Paramo, Fernando .... (213) 622-8332
Sports ED, La Opinion, Los Angeles, CA
Pardee, Diane B .... (609) 396-2200
VP-CORP Communications
Journal Register Co., Trenton, NJ
Pardo, Agatha .... (908) 922-6000
CIRC MGR-Sales
Asbury Park Press, Neptune, NJ
Pare, Steven .... (603) 882-2741
ADV MGR-Outside Sales
Telegraph, Nashua, NH
Parello, Jennifer .... (630) 969-0188
MAN ED
Downers Grove Reporter, Downers Grove, IL
Parent, Lynne .... (705) 272-4363
GM, Northland Post, Cochrane, ON
Parent, Maurice .... (603) 889-1590
PUB, 1590 Broadcaster, Nashua, NH
Parenteau, Connie A .... (715) 468-2314
PUB
Washburn County Register, Shell Lake, WI
Parenteau, Marc E .... (715) 468-2314
PUB, ED
Washburn County Register, Shell Lake, WI
Parfitt, Robert .... (610) 377-2051
ED, City/MET ED, News ED
Times News, Lehighton, PA
Pargh, Andy .... (615) 356-9595
PRES, Gadget Guru, Nashville, TN
Parham, Dash .... (703) 276-3400
Art DIR, USA Today, Arlington, VA
Parham, Maria .... (520) 573-4220
Fashion ED, Arizona Daily Star, Tucson, AZ
Parham, Robbie .... (706) 324-5526
CIRC MGR-Alternate Delivery
Columbus Ledger-Enquirer, Columbus, GA
Parham, Steven E .... (803) 279-1000
ED, Post, North Augusta, SC
Parichy, Jerry .... (215) 893-5700
GM, Jewish Exponent, Philadelphia, PA
Parillo, John .... (601) 798-4766
Photo DEPT MGR, PROD FRM-Camera
Picayune Item, Picayune, MS
Parillo, Rosemary .... (609) 663-6000
Living/Lifestyle ED
Courier-Post, Cherry Hill, NJ
Paris, Kevin .... (817) 767-8341
ADV MGR-RT, Wichita Falls Times Record News, Wichita Falls, TX
Paris, Linda .... (215) 854-2000
MGR-Telecommunications
Philadelphia Inquirer, Philadelphia, PA
Knight-Ridder Inc.
Paris, Ron .... (704) 245-6431
PRES, PUB, ED, Action Line/Hot Line ED, BUS/FIN ED, EPE, EDU ED, SCI ED
Daily Courier, Forest City, NC
Paris, Tony .... (404) 688-5623
ED, Creative Loafing, Atlanta, GA
Parise, Jim .... (508) 676-8211
ADV DIR, Herald News, Fall River, MA
Parish, Bertie G .... (334) 775-3254
PUB, ED, Clayton Record, Clayton, AL
Parish, John .... (503) 399-6611
DIR-MIS, Statesman Journal, Salem, OR
Parisi, Mark .... (617) 665-4442
PRES
Atlantic Feature Syndicate, Melrose, MA
Parizek, Starlene R .... (804) 857-1212
ED, Traveller, Norfolk, VA
Park, Bill .... (501) 673-8533
PUB, MGR MKTG/PROM
Stuttgart Daily Leader, Stuttgart, AR
Park, Eugene .... (757) 247-4600
VP/CFO, Daily Press, Newport News, VA
Park, Gary .... (403) 235-7100
ASST MAN ED, Calgary Herald, Calgary, AB
Park Jr, George A .... (315) 789-3333
PUB, Finger Lakes Times, Geneva, NY
Park, Mary Alice .... (219) 267-3111
Librarian, Times-Union, Warsaw, IN
Park, Mary Jane .... (813) 893-8111
Fashion ED, Times, St. Petersburg, FL
Park, Walter .... (508) 632-8000
CONT, Gardner News, Gardner, MA

Parke, James .... (214) 450-1717
Sr VP/CFO
Westward Communications Inc., Dallas, TX

Parker, Ana .... (510) 287-8200
ED, El Mundo, Oakland, CA

Parker, Andy .... (503) 221-8327
Team Leader-South
Oregonian, Portland, OR

Parker, Barbara .... (937) 328-0300
PROD MGR-MR, News-Sun, Springfield, OH

Parker, Bill .... (541) 474-3700
PA, Daily Courier, Grants Pass, OR

Parker, Bob .... (315) 792-5000
ADV DIR, Observer-Dispatch, Utica, NY

Parker, Bob .... (812) 944-6481
ADV MGR
Tribune/Ledger & Tribune, New Albany, IN

Parker, Brad .... (304) 292-6301
ADV MGR-CLASS
Dominion Post, Morgantown, WV

Parker, Cathie Lou .... (818) 962-8811
Entertainment ED, Television ED
San Gabriel Valley Tribune, West Covina, CA
MediaNews Inc.

Parker, Charles .... (941) 294-7731
City ED, News Chief, Winter Haven, FL

Parker, Chryl .... (704) 245-6431
ADV MGR-CLASS
Daily Courier, Forest City, NC

Parker, Constance .... (912) 764-9031
PROD FRM-COMP
Statesboro Herald, Statesboro, GA

Parker, Cortlandt .... (908) 766-3900
PUB, Bernardsville News, Bernardsville, NJ

Parker, David .... (860) 435-9873
ED, Lakeville Journal, Lakeville, CT

Parker, Doug .... (504) 826-3279
Photo ED, Times-Picayune, New Orleans, LA

Parker, Douglas .... (804) 649-6000
PROD MGR-MR
Richmond Times-Dispatch, Richmond, VA

Parker, Glen .... (902) 798-8371
ED, Hants Journal, Windsor, NS

Parker, J Michael .... (210) 225-7411
Religion Writer
San Antonio Express-News, San Antonio, TX

Parker, J S .... (770) 445-3379/5726
PUB, Dallas New Era, Dallas, GA

Parker, J T .... (770) 445-3379/5726
PUB, Dallas New Era, Dallas, GA

Parker, Jay .... (218) 262-1011
PROD FRM, Daily Tribune, Hibbing, MN

Parker, Jeanette .... (419) 562-3333
ADV MGR, Telegraph-Forum, Bucyrus, OH

Parker, Joe .... (912) 545-2103
ED, Ludowici News, Ludowici, GA

Parker, Jon .... (405) 226-6397
ED, Carter County Courier, Ardmore, OK

Parker, Karen .... (608) 337-4232
PUB, ED
County Line Connection, Ontario, WI

Parker, Karin .... (218) 835-4211
ED, American, Blackduck, MN

Parker, Kelvin .... (508) 458-7100
CIRC MGR-Single Copy, Sun, Lowell, MA

Parker, Kimberly J .... (317) 633-1240
ADV VP-MKTG
Indianapolis Star/News, Indianapolis, IN

Parker, Leewanna .... (205) 372-2232
ED, Greene County Independent, Eutaw, AL

Parker, Liz .... (908) 647-0412
ED, Echoes-Sentinel, Sterling, NJ

Parker, Mary Jo .... (541) 265-8571
PUB, News-Times, Newport, OR

Parker, Melody .... (319) 291-1400
Books ED, Fashion ED, Films ED, Home Furnishings ED, Music ED, Religion ED, Society/Women's ED, Travel ED
Waterloo Courier, Waterloo, IA

Parker, Michael .... (404) 526-5151
CIRC DIR-MKTG
Atlanta Journal-Constitution, Atlanta, GA

Parker, Michael A .... (401) 277-7000
DIR-Purchasing
Providence Journal-Bulletin, Providence, RI

Parker, Nancy .... (201) 770-1304
PUB, Roxbury Register, Landing, NJ

Parker, Randy .... (717) 771-2000
News ED, York Daily Record, York, PA

Parker, Sheila .... (508) 997-7411
DIR-Sales/MKTG
Standard Times, New Bedford, MA

Parker, Steve .... (502) 753-1916
Sports ED
Murray Ledger & Times, Murray, KY

Parker, Steve .... (314) 340-8000
News ED
St. Louis Post-Dispatch, St. Louis, MO

Parker, Sue Ellen .... (812) 385-2525
Living/Lifestyle ED, Women's ED
Princeton Daily Clarion, Princeton, IN

Parker, T E .... (770) 445-3379
ED, Dallas New Era, Dallas, GA

Parker, Tracy .... (508) 374-0321
BM, Haverhill Gazette, Haverhill, MA

Parker, Vern .... (202) 636-3000
Automotive ED
Washington Times, Washington, DC

Parker, Wallace .... (904) 359-4111
ADV MGR-MKTG Services
Florida Times-Union, Jacksonville, FL

Parker, Wayne .... (910) 353-1171
PROD FRM-PR, Daily News, Jacksonville, NC

Parker-McGhee, Audrey .... (901) 523-1818
ED, Tri State Defender, Memphis, TN

Parkins, Bob .... (901) 686-1632
PUB, ED, Milan Mirror-Exchange, Milan, TN

Parkinson, John .... (540) 667-3200
ADV MGR-RT, PROD MGR-COMP
Winchester Star, Winchester, VA

Parkinson, Kirk .... (801) 373-5050
PUB, Daily Herald, Provo, UT

Parkinson, Mary .... (541) 926-2211
Food, People ED
Albany Democrat-Herald, Albany, OR

Parkinson, Roger P .... (416) 814-4239
CEO/PUB-Globe & Mail
Thomson Newspapers, Toronto, ON

Parkman, Priscilla .... (770) 382-4545
Features ED
Daily Tribune News, Cartersville, GA

Parks, Chris .... (313) 961-3949
News ED, Detroit Legal News, Detroit, MI

Parks, Craig .... (517) 895-8551
PROD SUPV-Pre Press
Bay City Times, Bay City, MI

Parks, Greg .... (614) 439-3531
ED, EPE, Daily Jeffersonian, Cambridge, OH

Parks, Janet .... (541) 276-2211
ADV MGR-NTL
East Oregonian, Pendleton, OR

Parks, Kim .... (916) 243-2424
CONT, Record Searchlight, Redding, CA

Parks, Kyle .... (813) 893-8111
Automotive ED, RE/BUS ED
St. Petersburg Times, St. Petersburg, FL

Parks, Larry .... (303) 820-1010
PROD MGR-COMP, Denver Post, Denver, CO

Parks, Lisa .... (816) 234-4141
PROD MGR-MR
Kansas City Star, Kansas City, MO

Parks, Michael .... (213) 237-5000
Senior VP/MAN ED, MAN ED/Senior VP
Los Angeles Times, Los Angeles, CA

Parks, Peggy .... (208) 879-4445
PUB, ED, Challis Messenger, Challis, ID

Parks, Robert .... (606) 623-1669
CIRC MGR
Richmond Register, Richmond, KY

Parks, Robert W .... (203) 744-5100
GM, News-Times, Danbury, CT

Parks, Ruth .... (616) 964-7161
MGR-CR
Battle Creek Enquirer, Battle Creek, MI

Parks, Tim .... (405) 223-2200
ASST MAN ED, NTL ED
Daily Ardmoreite, Ardmore, OK

Parks, Will .... (608) 754-3311
ADV ASST MGR, Gazette, Janesville, WI

Parley, Graham .... (613) 829-9100
Chief News ED, Ottawa Citizen, Ottawa, ON

Parlin, Mary .... (308) 382-4660
ED
West Nebraska Register, Grand Island, NE

Parman, Michael J .... (707) 546-2020
VP, PUB, Press Democrat, Santa Rosa, CA

Parmelee, Scott K .... (860) 527-1175
GM, Catholic Transcript, Hartford, CT

Parmenter, Roger .... (320) 255-8700
MGR-Commercial
St. Cloud Times, St. Cloud, MN

Parmeter, John .... (218) 723-5281
ADV MGR-NTL
Duluth News-Tribune, Duluth, MN

Parmeter, Rich .... (708) 448-4000
MAN ED, Regional News, Palos Heights, IL

Parming, T .... (416) 466-0951
ED, Meie Elu, Toronto, ON

Parmley, JoAnn .... (309) 764-4344
Librarian, Dispatch, Moline, IL
Small Newspaper Group Inc.

Parnass, Larry .... (413) 584-5000
BUS ED, News ED
Daily Hampshire Gazette, Northampton, MA

Parnell, Samuel M .... (520) 364-3424
PUB, ED, Daily Dispatch, Douglas, AZ

Parnell, Susan .... (501) 836-8192
ADV DIR, Camden News, Camden, AR

Parnell, William .... (210) 625-9144
PROD MGR
New Braunfels Herald-Zeitung, New Braunfels, TX

Parnes, Francine .... (303) 820-1010
Fashion/Style Reporter
Denver Post, Denver, CO

Parodi, Oscar .... (408) 757-8118
PUB, ED, El Sol, Salinas, CA

Parr, Barry .... (408) 920-5000
Online Contact
San Jose Mercury News, San Jose, CA

Parr, Jane .... (609) 753-4500
PUB, Record-Breeze, Berlin, NJ

Parr, Marina .... (541) 276-2211
BUS/FIN ED, East Oregonian, Pendleton, OR

Parra, Steven .... (209) 441-6111
Art DIR, Fresno Bee, Fresno, CA

Parrack, Wayne .... (213) 237-5000
PROD DIR-Technology Resource Group
Los Angeles Times, Los Angeles, CA

Parrillo, Rosemary .... (609) 663-6000
Features ED, Courier-Post, Cherry Hill, NJ

Parris, John .... (704) 252-5611
Senior ED, Citizen-Times, Asheville, NC

Parris, Lou .... (864) 582-4511
COL, Herald-Journal, Spartanburg, SC

Parrish, George .... (507) 445-3400
PUB
Storden-Jeffers Times/Review, Storden, MN

Parrish, Marilyn .... (360) 452-2345
ADV SUPV-Ad Production
Peninsula Daily News, Port Angeles, WA

Parrish, Phil .... (918) 581-8300
Sports ED, Tulsa World, Tulsa, OK

Parrish, Will .... (803) 329-4000
Automotive ED, Herald, Rock Hill, SC

Parrott, Peter .... (905) 623-3303
ED, Bowmanville Canadian Statesman, Bowmanville, ON

Parrott, Rita .... (352) 374-5000
ADV MGR-CLASS
Gainesville Sun, Gainesville, FL

Parry, Dale .... (313) 222-6400
Features ED, Detroit Free Press, Detroit, MI

Parry, Kate .... (612) 222-5011
Senior ED-Public Interest
St. Paul Pioneer Press, St. Paul, MN

Parry, Merrie Jean .... (309) 329-2151
ED, Astoria South Fulton Argus, Astoria, IL

Parson, Paul .... (618) 529-5454
PROD MGR
Southern Illinoisan, Carbondale, IL

Parsons, Aaron .... (318) 942-4971
PRES, PUB, Daily World, Opelousas, LA

Parsons, Allen .... (805) 564-5200
EX ED, Santa Barbara News-Press, Santa Barbara, CA

Parsons, Bill .... (408) 385-4880
PUB, Rustler, King City, CA

Parsons, Bill .... (914) 297-3723
ED, Beacon Free Press, Wappingers Falls, NY

Parsons, David .... (315) 792-5000
ADV MGR-CLASS
Observer-Dispatch, Utica, NY

Parsons, Dorothy G .... (805) 763-3171
PUB, BM, Daily Midway Driller, Taft, CA

Parsons, Gail .... (913) 762-5000
Special Sections
Daily Union, Junction City, KS

Parsons, Ginna .... (601) 842-2611
City/MET ED, Northeast Mississippi Daily Journal, Tupelo, MS

Parsons, Gordon .... (709) 944-2957
ED, Aurora, Labrador City, NF

Parsons, Larry .... (408) 424-2221
City ED (interim), Californian, Salinas, CA

Parsons, Robby .... (405) 273-4200
PROD FRM-PR
Shawnee News-Star, Shawnee, OK

Parsons, Rodger .... (814) 870-1600
PROD GEN FRM-Press
Morning News/Erie Daily Times, Erie, PA

Parsons, Rose Ann .... (315) 963-7813
ED, Independent Mirror, Mexico, NY

Parsons, Steven .... (607) 936-4651
CIRC DIR, Leader, Corning, NY

Parta, Jennifer .... (218) 346-5900
GM, Enterprise-Bulletin, Perham, MN

Parta, Michael A .... (218) 385-2275
PUB, Contact, New York Mills, MN

Partain, Amy .... (501) 835-4875
ED, Sherwood Voice, Sherwood, AR

Partin, Molly .... (910) 997-3111
CIRC MGR, Richmond County Daily Journal, Rockingham, NC

Partington-Richer, Marilyn .... (403) 849-4380
ED, Lakeside Leader, Slave Lake, AB

Partlow, John .... (509) 525-3300
PROD MGR-PR
Walla Walla Union-Bulletin, Walla Walla, WA

Parton, Jodie .... (317) 675-2115
CIRC MGR
Tipton County Tribune, Tipton, IN

Parton, Linda .... (561) 746-7815
CIRC MGR
American Way Features, Jupiter, FL

Partridge, Marianne .... (805) 965-5205
ED, Santa Barbara Independent, Santa Barbara, CA

Partsch, Frank .... (402) 444-1000
EPE, Omaha World-Herald, Omaha, NE

Partusch, Bill .... (402) 444-1000
PROD MGR-COMP (Day)
Omaha World-Herald, Omaha, NE

Parvis, Byron .... (317) 423-5511
Religion ED
Journal and Courier, Lafayette, IN

Pascale, Neil .... (360) 532-4000
Wire ED, Daily World, Aberdeen, WA

Paschal, Barry .... (706) 724-0851
EDL Writer, Augusta Chronicle, Augusta, GA

Pascoe, Delma .... (573) 885-7460
PUB, Cuba Free Press, Cuba, MO

Pascoe, Percy .... (573) 885-7460
PUB, ED, Cuba Free Press, Cuba, MO

Paseman, Lloyd .... (541) 485-1234
Film ED, Register-Guard, Eugene, OR

Pasha, Ismat .... (416) 481-7793
MAN ED, New Canada, Toronto, Ontario

Pashley, Judy .... (805) 650-2900
CIRC MGR-Customer Service
Ventura County Star, Ventura, CA

Paskman, Ken .... (800) 245-6536
PROD/Graphics MGR
US/Express, Chicago, IL

Pasley, Erin .... (209) 943-6397
Lifestyle ED, Record, Stockton, CA

Pasmore, Elaine .... (954) 946-7277
MAN ED
Pompano Ledger, Pompano Beach, FL

Pasour, Melissa .... (704) 435-6752
MAN ED, Eagle, Cherryville, NC

Pasquale, Cynthia .... (303) 820-1010
Features ED, Living/Lifestyle ED
Denver Post, Denver, CO

Pasquale, Tony .... (814) 870-1600
MAN ED (Times)
Morning News/Erie Daily Times, Erie, PA

Passaro, Bob .... (208) 522-1800
News ED, Post Register, Idaho Falls, ID

Passell, Sarah .... (203) 744-5100
ASST MET ED, News-Times, Danbury, CT

Passey, Kristopher R .... (303) 756-9995
PUB/ED, Daily Journal, Denver, CO

Passifume, Marco .... (416) 947-2222
Sunday Showcase, Toronto Sun, Toronto, ON

Passon, Kevin .... (414) 324-5555
ED, Leader-News, Waupun, WI

Passy, Charles .... (561) 820-4100
Music ED-Classical
Palm Beach Post, West Palm Beach, FL

Pastin, Robert .... (304) 292-6301
Sports ED, Dominion Post, Morgantown, WV

Pastor, John .... (352) 365-8200
ED, Daily Commercial, Leesburg, FL

Pastor, Marc .... (619) 578-3547
PUB, Kalayaan, San Diego, CA

Pastorek, Monet .... (504) 392-1619
MAN ED
Placquemines Gazette, Belle Chasse, LA

Pastula, Gail .... (941) 335-0200
EPE, News-Press, Fort Myers, FL

Pastuszak, Barbara .... (410) 968-1188
ED, Crisfield Times, Crisfield, MD

Patafio, Ron .... (914) 694-9300
EPE, Reporter Dispatch, White Plains, NY
Gannett Co. Inc.

Patch, Deb .... (406) 232-0450
CIRC DIR, Miles City Star, Miles City, MT

Patchen, Susan A .... (410) 752-3504
PUB, Jewish Times, Baltimore, MD

Pate, Herb .... (910) 259-2504
MAN ED, Pender Chronicle, Burgaw, NC

Pate, J Michael .... (803) 626-8555
PRES, PUB, Sun News, Myrtle Beach, SC

Pate, Jack .... (812) 424-7711
ADV DIR, Evansville Courier Co., Evansville, IN

Pate, Susan .... (909) 987-6397
DIR-Creative SRV, PROD Creative Services
Inland Valley Daily Bulletin, Ontario, CA

Patel, Ron .... (215) 854-2000
Sunday ED
Philadelphia Inquirer, Philadelphia, PA

Patera, Paul .... (701) 223-2500
CONT, Bismarck Tribune, Bismarck, ND

Paternoster, Laurie .... (915) 546-6100
Action Line ED, Automotive ED, BUS ED
El Paso Times, El Paso, TX

Paterson, Barbara .... (713) 220-7171
PROD ASST MGR (Night)
Houston Chronicle, Houston, TX

Paterson, Jody .... (250) 380-5211
MAN ED, Times Colonist, Victoria, BC

Paterson, Steve .... (520) 763-2505
ADV DIR, DIR-MKTG/PROM
Mohave Valley Daily News, Bullhead City, AZ

Paterson, William H .... (320) 967-4244
PUB, ED, News, Raymond, MN

Pates, Mikkel .... (701) 253-7311
Farm ED, Forum, Fargo, ND

Patinella, John .... (410) 332-6000
PRES/CEO-Baltimore Community Newspapers/Homestead Publ. Co.
Sun, Baltimore, MD

Patino, Diana .... (516) 486-6457
GM
La Tribuna Hispana-NY/NJ, Westbury, NY

Patnaude, Philip .... (802) 863-3441
PROD Chief SYS Technician
Burlington Free Press, Burlington, VT

177-Who's Where **Pea**

Paton, John (613) 739-7000
PUB/CEO, Ottawa Sun, Ottawa, ON

Paton, Richard (419) 245-6000
EDL DIR, Blade, Toledo, OH

Patout, Michelle (318) 365-6773
ADTX MGR, Daily Iberian, New Iberia, LA

Patrick, Bernice (605) 629-8341
ED, Tri-City Star, White, SD

Patrick, Charles F (619) 454-0411
EVP/CFO, Copley Press Inc., La Jolla, CA

Patrick, David (601) 582-4321
PROD MGR, American, Hattiesburg, MS

Patrick, Dean (573) 581-1111
Photo DEPT MGR
Mexico Ledger, Mexico, MO

Patrick, Doug (502) 227-4556
CIRC MGR, State Journal, Frankfort, KY

Patrick, Edwin R (814) 755-4900
PUB, Forest Press, Tionesta, PA

Patrick, Jan (540) 669-2181
Radio/Television ED, Herald-Courier Virginia Tennessean, Bristol, VA

Patrick, Jim (705) 567-5321
MAN ED
Northern Daily News, Kirkland Lake, ON

Patrick, Michael (801) 373-5050
ED, Daily Herald, Provo, UT

Patrick, Nikki (316) 231-2600
Amusements/Books ED, Fashion/Food ED, Films/Theater ED, Radio/Television ED
Morning Sun, Pittsburg, KS

Patrick, Pauline (803) 635-4016
ED, Herald Independent, Winnsboro, SC

Patrick, Randy (606) 885-5381
ED, Jessamine Journal, Nicholasville, KY

Patrick, Roy (805) 399-5925
ED, Shafter Press, Shafter, CA

Patrick, Virginia (814) 755-4900
ED, Forest Press, Tionesta, PA

Patrick, Wayne T (903) 729-0281
VP, Palestine Herald-Press, Palestine, TX

Patrinos, Dan (414) 224-2000
Online MGR
Milwaukee Journal Sentinel, Milwaukee, WI

Patrone, Mary Jane (617) 929-2000
VP-Sales & MKTG, Boston Globe, Boston, MA

Patten, Marcia (603) 924-7172
ED, Monadnock Ledger, Peterborough, NH

Patten, Sharon (419) 636-1111
Women's ED, Bryan Times, Bryan, OH

Pattenaude, David (519) 882-1770
ED, Petrolia Topic, Petrolia, ON

Patterson, Bill (817) 387-3811
VP, GM
Denton Record-Chronicle, Denton, TX

Patterson, Bill (502) 821-6833
PROD MGR-COMP Room
Messenger, Madisonville, KY

Patterson, C K (541) 276-2211
CORP GM, East Oregonian, Pendleton, OR

Patterson, Charlotte (423) 482-1021
PROD FRM-COMP
Oak Ridger, Oak Ridge, TN

Patterson, Cindy (618) 438-5611
CIRC MGR
Benton Evening News, Benton, IL

Patterson, Daniel J (519) 376-2250
CIRC MGR, Sun Times, Owen Sound, ON

Patterson, Dee Ann (405) 353-0620
City ED, Food ED, Radio/Television ED
Lawton Constitution, Lawton, OK

Patterson Jr, Donald H (804) 446-2010
EVP/PRES-Landmark Broadcasting
Landmark Communications Inc., Norfolk, VA

Patterson, Fred (817) 387-3811
PRES, PUB
Denton Record-Chronicle, Denton, TX

Patterson, Jack (202) 334-6000
EX Consultant
Washington Post, Washington, DC

Patterson, James (317) 633-1240
EDL Writer
Indianapolis Star/News, Indianapolis, IN

Patterson, James (212) 556-1234
MAN ED-Times Online
New York Times, New York, NY

Patterson, Janet (810) 541-3000
ADV MGR-CLASS
Daily Tribune, Royal Oak, MI

Patterson, Jeffrey (612) 459-3434
GM, Washington County Bulletin, Cottage Grove, MN

Patterson, Ken (205) 236-1551
Sports ED, Anniston Star, Anniston, AL

Patterson, Kevin (206) 872-6600
Sports ED, South County Journal, Kent, WA

Patterson, Kim (208) 733-0931
ADV MGR-CLASS
Times-News, Twin Falls, ID

Patterson, Michael (330) 821-1200
News ED, Alliance Review, Alliance, OH

Patterson, Pat (717) 762-2151
PUB, Record Herald, Waynesboro, PA

Patterson, Patsy (817) 387-3811
SEC/TREAS
Denton Record-Chronicle, Denton, TX

Patterson, Paul (905) 835-2411
ED, Port Colborne News, Port Colborne, ON

Patterson, Peggy (765) 825-2496
PUB, Centerville Crusader, Centerville, IN

Patterson, Phillip (318) 281-4421
PROD SUPT
Bastrop Daily Enterprise, Bastrop, LA

Patterson, Sally (508) 943-8784
ED, Patriot, Webster, MA

Patterson, Scott (954) 698-6501
PUB, Sunrise Times, Deerfield Beach, FL

Patterson, Sherry (815) 433-2000
ADV MGR, Daily Times, Ottawa, IL

Patterson, Stu (416) 947-2222
PROD DIR, Toronto Sun, Toronto, ON

Patterson, Susan L (912) 452-0567
PUB/ED, Union-Recorder, Milledgeville, GA

Patterson, T J (806) 762-3612
PUB, ED, Southwest Digest, Lubbock, TX

Patterson, Tony (619) 457-5920
VP, Trade Service Corp., San Diego, CA

Patterson, Trudy (702) 383-0211
ADV MGR-NTL
Las Vegas Review-Journal, Las Vegas, NV

Patterson-Rabon, Ann (864) 582-4511
Radio/Television ED
Herald-Journal, Spartanburg, SC

Pattison, Howard (412) 222-2200
PROD GEN FRM
Observer-Reporter, Washington, PA

Pattison, Martha (352) 374-5000
MGR-BUS Office
Gainesville Sun, Gainesville, FL

Pattison, Neal (206) 448-8000
ASST MAN ED
Seattle Post-Intelligencer, Seattle, WA

Patton, Beth (803) 785-4293
MGR-MKTG/PROM
Island Packet, Hilton Head, SC

Patton, Janie (605) 225-4100
PROD CNR
Aberdeen American News, Aberdeen, SD

Patton, Joan (816) 637-6155
CIRC MGR
Daily Standard, Excelsior Springs, MO

Patton, John (805) 395-7500
ADTX MGR/Online Contact
Bakersfield Californian, Bakersfield, CA

Patton, Mark (805) 564-5200
Sports ED, Santa Barbara News-Press, Santa Barbara, CA

Patton, Paula (507) 334-1853
GM, ADV DIR, DIR-MKTG
Faribault Daily News, Faribault, MN

Patton, Price (561) 820-4100
State ED
Palm Beach Post, West Palm Beach, FL

Patton, Robert (515) 352-3325
PUB, Gowrie News, Gowrie, IA

Patton, Tyler (915) 337-4661
CIRC ASST DIR
Odessa American, Odessa, TX

Patton, Vickie (937) 382-2574
Food/Society ED, Music ED
Wilmington News Journal, Wilmington, OH

Paul, Alex (541) 367-2135
PUB, ED, New Era, Sweet Home, OR

Paul, April (608) 625-2451
PUB, ED, Epitaph-News, La Farge, WI

Paul, Debra (541) 367-2135
PUB, New Era, Sweet Home, OR

Paul, James C (716) 232-7100
CONT
Rochester Democrat and Chronicle; Rochester, NY Times-Union, Rochester, NY

Paul, Jenine (408) 424-2221
PSL DIR, Californian, Salinas, CA

Paul, Kenneth (203) 355-4141
ED, Litchfield County Times, New Milford, CT

Paul, Laurence (716) 849-3434
Deputy EPE, Buffalo News, Buffalo, NY

Paul, Marcia (320) 235-1150
ADV CNR-NTL
West Central Tribune, Willmar, MN

Paul, Robin (907) 586-3740
ADV MGR, Juneau Empire, Juneau, AK

Paul, Steve (816) 234-4141
Entertainment ED
Kansas City Star, Kansas City, MO

Paul-Martinez, Michelle (954) 356-4000
Charities CNR
Sun-Sentinel, Fort Lauderdale, FL

Pauley, Daniel R (914) 341-1100
ADV MGR-CLASS
Times Herald-Record, Middletown, NY

Pauley, Dennis (206) 461-1300
ED, Capitol Hill Times, Seattle, WA

Pauley, Peter (719) 632-5511
Art DIR, Gazette, Colorado Springs, CO

Paulissen, Timothy (713) 337-0009
PUB, Weekly News, Dickinson, TX

Paulsen, Ken (718) 981-1234
Lifestyle ED
Staten Island Advance, Staten Island, NY

Paulsen, Richard (515) 432-6694
PUB, Boone Today, Boone, IA

Paulsen, Sasha (508) 412-1500
ED
Hamilton-Wenham Chronicle, Ipswich, MA

Paulson, Carol (419) 278-2816
ED, Deshler Flag, Deshler, OH

Paulson, Charles B (507) 427-2725
PUB, ED, Mountain Lake Observer-Advocate, Mountain Lake, MN

Paulson, Joanne (306) 652-9200
BUS ED, StarPhoenix, Saskatoon, SK

Paulson, Kenneth A (914) 694-9300
VP/EX ED, Reporter Dispatch, White Plains, NY, Gannett Co. Inc.

Paulson, Marcia (507) 427-2725
PUB, Mountain Lake Observer-Advocate, Mountain Lake, MN

Paulus, Gordon (904) 435-8500
Sports ED
Pensacola News Journal, Pensacola, FL

Pauly, Michael (515) 284-8000
Senior ASST MAN ED
Des Moines Register, Des Moines, IA

Paupe, Christian M (416) 445-6641
Sr VP/CFO, Southam Inc., Don Mills, ON

Paustian, Jeanne (515) 473-2102
MAN ED, Northern-Sun Print, Gladbrook, IA

Pavan, Bruno (416) 441-1405
Southern Europe & Middle East Journalist
Fotopress Independent News Service International (FPINS), Toronto, ON

Pavelek, Machen (330) 424-9541
ADV MGR-RT, Morning Journal, Lisbon, OH

Pavelich, James S (415) 327-6397
Chairman, PUB
Palo Alto Daily News, Palo Alto, CA

Pavich, J Robert (217) 788-1300
PROD MGR
State Journal-Register, Springfield, IL

Pavich, Robert (313) 222-2300
Readers Representative
Detroit News, Detroit, MI

Pavilons, Mark (905) 857-6626
ED, Caledon Citizen, Bolton, ON

Pavison, Scott (250) 492-4002
Southern Exposure ED
Penticton Herald, Penticton, BC

Pavlick, Renee (201) 437-2460
GM, Bayonne Community News, Bayonne, NJ

Pavlin, Jill (250) 785-5631
MAN ED, Alaska Highway Daily News, Fort St. John, BC

Pavlovich, Jill (607) 798-1234
CIRC ASST to DIR
Press & Sun Bulletin, Binghamton, NY

Pavoncello, Bianca (508) 676-8211
ASST MAN ED, Herald News, Fall River, MA

Pawel, Miriam (516) 843-2020
ASST MAN ED-Long Island
Newsday, Melville, NY

Pawlak-Seaman, Sue (508) 997-7411
EDU ED, Standard Times, New Bedford, MA

Pawlow, Eric (617) 929-2000
PROD MGR-Imaging
Boston Globe, Boston, MA

Pawlowski, Stan (614) 633-1131
Telegraph ED, PROD CNR-SYS
Times Leader, Martins Ferry, OH

Pawula, Larissa (603) 436-1800
City ED
Portsmouth Herald, Portsmouth, NH

Paxson, Julia (610) 740-0944
ED, East Penn Press, Allentown, PA

Paxson, Richard (202) 334-6000
MET ED-Virginia
Washington Post, Washington, DC

Paxton, David A (515) 932-7121
PUB, ED, Albia Union-Republican, Albia, IA

Paxton, David M (502) 443-1771
Chief Financial OFF
Paxton Media Group Inc., Paducah, KY

Paxton, Fred (502) 443-1771
PRES/CEO
Paxton Media Group Inc., Paducah, KY

Paxton, Jim (502) 443-1771
VP/SEC, ED, Paducah Sun, Paducah, KY
Paxton Media

Paxton, Mark (408) 637-5566
EX ED, Free Lance, Hollister, CA

Paxton, Richard (502) 443-1771
VP/ASST SEC, Paducah Sun, Paducah, KY
Paxton Media

Paxton IV, M W (540) 463-3113
PUB, News-Gazette, Lexington, VA

Payment, Julie (616) 845-5181
CIRC MGR, Daily News, Ludington, MI

Payne, Alan (352) 365-8200
CONT, Daily Commercial, Leesburg, FL

Payne, Claudia (212) 556-1234
DIR-Fashion News
New York Times, New York, NY

Payne, David L (510) 228-6400
PUB, GM
Martinez News-Gazette, Martinez, CA

Payne, Donna (501) 785-7700
Television/Film ED, Theater/Music ED
Southwest Times Record, Fort Smith, AR

Payne, Elizabeth (405) 475-3311
PSL MGR
Daily Oklahoman, Oklahoma City, OK

Payne, Francie (520) 524-6203
GM, MAN ED
Holbrook Tribune-News, Holbrook, AZ

Payne, Jeanette (709) 364-6300
MGR-MKTG
Evening Telegram, St. John's, NF

Payne, Jeanne M (707) 643-1706
VP, Benicia Herald, Vallejo, CA

Payne, Jeff (810) 727-3745
ED, Chesterfield Review/Review/Independent Press, Richmond, MI

Payne, Joe (309) 764-4344
Consumer Affairs ED, Fashion/Style ED, Features ED, Women's ED, Dispatch, Moline, IL, Small Newspaper Group Inc.

Payne, John (712) 262-6610
ED, Daily Reporter, Spencer, IA

Payne, John W (202) 334-6173
VP/GM, Los Angeles Times-Washington Post News Service, Washington, DC

Payne, Les (516) 843-2020
ASST MAN ED-NTL/Foreign/State/Queens
Newsday, Melville, NY

Payne, Maria (910) 625-2101
Office MGR, Courier-Tribune, Asheboro, NC

Payne, Sandy (814) 938-8740
CIRC MGR, Spirit, Punxsutawney, PA

Paynic, Susan (507) 775-6180
PUB, ED, Byron Review, Byron, MN

Paynter, Marion (704) 358-5000
Librarian, Charlotte Observer, Charlotte, NC

Paynter, Rob (613) 739-7000
MAN ED, Ottawa Sun, Ottawa, ON

Paynter, Susan (206) 448-8000
COL-City
Seattle Post-Intelligencer, Seattle, WA

Paynter, Teddy (304) 327-2811
Sports ED
Bluefield Daily Telegraph, Bluefield, WV

Payntor, Scott (218) 741-5544
CIRC DIR-MKTG
Mesabi Daily News, Virginia, MN

Payson, Sandy (206) 455-2222
ADV EX DIR-RT
Eastside Journal, Bellevue, WA

Payton, Brenda (510) 208-6300
COL, Oakland Tribune, Oakland, CA

Payton, Dale (205) 532-4000
MGR-Telecommunications
Huntsville Times, Huntsville, AL

Payton, James (205) 325-2222
PROD DIR-OPER
Birmingham News, Birmingham, AL

Payton, John (416) 947-2222
PUB & CEO-Ottawa Sun
Sun Media Corp., Toronto, ON

Payton, Karen (505) 257-4001
GM, Ruidoso News, Ruidoso, NM

Payton, Laura (519) 284-2440
ED, Journal Argus, St. Marys, ON

Payton, Michael D (715) 394-4411
Farm ED, Daily Telegram, Superior, WI

Payton, Nick (505) 374-2587
PUB, ED, Union County Leader, Clayton, NM

Paz, Rob (717) 264-6161
ADV DIR, Public Opinion, Chambersburg, PA

Pea, John (910) 227-0131
MAN ED
Times News Publishing Co., Burlington, NC

Pea, Ricky (601) 961-7000
MGR-RES, Clarion-Ledger, Jackson, MS

Peabody, Alvin (202) 561-4100
MAN ED
Washington Informer, Washington, DC

Peabody, Denise (616) 527-2100
SUPV-BUS, PA, Sentinel-Standard, Ionia, MI

Peabody, Jane (812) 372-7811
Librarian, Republic, Columbus, IN

Peabody, Velton (716) 849-3434
Wire ED, Buffalo News, Buffalo, NY

Peace, Mitchell E (912) 739-2132
PUB, Claxton Enterprise, Claxton, GA

Peachey, J Lorne (412) 887-8500
PUB, Gospel Herald, Scottdale, PA

Peacock, Gordon (704) 633-8950
Wire ED, Salisbury Post, Salisbury, NC

Peacock, Joseph (517) 725-5136
MAN ED, City/MET ED, Films/Theater ED, Health/Medical ED, Radio/Television ED, Travel ED, Argus-Press, Owosso, MI

Peacock, Margaret (510) 465-3121
Support Staff
Inter-City Express, Oakland, CA

Peacock, Tonya (510) 465-3121
ADV MGR-Legal
Inter-City Express, Oakland, CA

Peak, Bill (309) 686-3000
City ED-Night, Journal Star, Peoria, IL

Pea Who's Where-178

Peak, Greg (409) 398-2535
ED, Corrigan Times, Corrigan, TX

Peak, Jim (541) 776-4411
News ED, Mail Tribune, Medford, OR

Peak, Jim (208) 377-6200
News ED, Idaho Statesman, Boise, ID

Peak, S Wade (504) 850-1100
CIRC MGR, Courier, Houma, LA

Peake, Lee Ann (317) 598-6397
MAN ED, Geist Gazette, Noblesville, IN

Pearce, Adrian (423) 523-3131
ADTX MGR, News-Sentinel, Knoxville, TN

Pearce, Bette (513) 863-8200
Health/Medical ED
Journal-News, Hamilton, OH

Pearce, Bob (403) 483-6000
PUB, GM, Examiner, Edmonton, AB

Pearce, David (812) 853-3366
ED, MAN ED
Newburgh-Chandler Register, Newburgh, IN

Pearce, Donna (918) 663-1414
ED, Skiatook Journal, Tulsa, OK

Pearce, Jeremy (313) 222-2300
Environment Writer, Detroit News, Detroit, MI

Pearce, Jon (907) 257-4200
PROD MGR-Packaging Center
Anchorage Daily News, Anchorage, AK

Pearce, Kelly (719) 632-5511
Military Reporter
Gazette, Colorado Springs, CO

Pearce, Raymond (212) 556-1234
CIRC DIR-Single Copy Expansion Team
New York Times, New York, NY

Pearce, Sara (513) 721-2700
Features ED, Enquirer, Cincinnati, OH

Pearl, Charlie (502) 692-6026
ED, Lebanon Enterprise, Lebanon, KY

Pearl, Rick (617) 933-3700
Sports ED, Daily Times Chronicle, Woburn, MA

Pearl, Terry (816) 449-2121
PUB
DeKalb County Record-Herald, Maysville, MO

Pearlman, Gene (562) 435-1161
ADV MGR-CLASS
Press-Telegram, Long Beach, CA

Pearse, Jo (804) 385-5400
ADV DIR, News & Advance, Lynchburg, VA

Pearson, A T (513) 761-1188
Contributing Critic
Critic's Choice Reviews, Cincinnati, OH

Pearson, Brian (817) 634-2125
MAN ED, Killeen Daily Herald, Killeen, TX

Pearson, Clarence (757) 247-4600
CIRC MGR-Transportation
Daily Press, Newport News, VA

Pearson, Dawn (209) 834-2535
MAN ED, Fowler Ensign, Fowler, CA

Pearson, Douglas (205) 221-2840
PUB, PA, ADV MGR-GEN, EPE
Daily Mountain Eagle, Jasper, AL

Pearson, Eric (803) 771-6161
ASST to MAN ED, State, Columbia, SC

Pearson, Eva Marie (501) 534-3400
Accent ED, Entertainment/Amusements ED, Fashion/Style ED, Films/Theater ED
Pine Bluff Commercial, Pine Bluff, AR

Pearson, Glenda (716) 945-1644
ADV MGR, Salamanca Press, Salamanca, NY

Pearson, J B (519) 679-6666
BC, London Free Press, London, ON

Pearson, Janet (918) 581-8300
EDL Writer, Tulsa World, Tulsa, OK

Pearson, Kay (814) 837-6000
PUB/GM, ADV DIR, Republican, Kane, PA

Pearson, Linda (701) 253-7311
MGR-EDU SRV, Forum, Fargo, ND

Pearson, Lori (513) 761-1188
Communications DIR
Critic's Choice Reviews, Cincinnati, OH

Pearson, Michael L (412) 263-1100
DIR-SYS & Technology
Pittsburgh Post-Gazette, Pittsburgh, PA

Pearson, Mike (518) 792-9914
Regional Sales DIR
TV Data, Queensbury, NY

Pearson, Mike (303) 892-5000
Entertainment ED
Rocky Mountain News, Denver, CO

Pearson, Myrna (970) 824-7031
MGR-MKTG/PROM
Northwest Colorado Daily Press, Craig, CO

Pearson, Phil (618) 438-5611
Reporter, Benton Evening News, Benton, IL

Pearson, Phyllis (605) 394-8300
Copy Desk Chief, Journal, Rapid City, SD

Pearson, Rand (702) 324-4440
GM, Reno News & Review, Reno, NV

Pearson, Rita (309) 764-4344
Automotive ED, BUS ED
Dispatch, Moline, IL
Small Newspaper Group Inc.

Pearson, Toby (205) 325-2222
CIRC DIR
Birmingham News, Birmingham, AL

Pease, Kip (806) 256-2131
PUB, ED, Shamrock Texan, Shamrock, TX

Peasley, Clyde (513) 863-8200
ADTX MGR, Journal-News, Hamilton, OH

Peaspanen, Michelle (419) 562-3333
Society ED, Telegraph-Forum, Bucyrus, OH

Peattie, Earl (714) 836-1177
PRES/Author
Mortgage News Company, Santa Ana, CA

Peaux, John (318) 365-6773
DP MGR, Daily Iberian, New Iberia, LA

Pebworth, Jim (405) 332-4433
CIRC MGR, Ada Evening News, Ada, OK

Pebworth, Randy (334) 493-3595
PUB, Opp News, Opp, AL

Pecht, Mary Margaret (717) 248-6741
Farm ED, Religion/Women's ED
Sentinel, Lewistown, PA

Peck, Anthony (805) 259-1234
Sports ED, Signal, Santa Clarita, CA

Peck, Barb (315) 782-1000
MGR-MKTG/PROM
Watertown Daily Times, Watertown, NY

Peck, Brenda (316) 431-4100
CIRC MGR, Chanute Tribune, Chanute, KS

Peck, Christopher (509) 459-5000
ED, Spokesman-Review, Spokane, WA

Peck, Claude (612) 321-7300
ED, Twin Cities Reader, Minneapolis, MN

Peck, David H (307) 548-2217
PUB, ED, Lovell Chronicle, Lovell, WY

Peck, Debbie (603) 356-3456
ADV MGR-CLASS
Conway Daily Sun, North Conway, NH

Peck, Dennis (503) 221-8327
Sports ED, Oregonian, Portland, OR

Peck, Greg (608) 754-3311
Sunday Gazette/Features ED
Janesville Gazette, Janesville, WI

Peck, Robert A (307) 856-2244
PRES, PUB, PA
Riverton Ranger, Riverton, WY

Peck, Steven R (307) 856-2244
VP, Co-PUB, Amusements/Automotive ED, COL, EPE, Photo DEPT MGR
Riverton Ranger, Riverton, WY

Peck, Thomas (212) 210-2100
CFO, New York Daily News, New York, NY

Peckham, Barry T (214) 977-8222
Senior VP-Circulation
Dallas Morning News, Dallas, TX

Peckham, Patrick (608) 847-6224
PUB, ED
Juneau County Star-Times, Mauston, WI

Peddicord, Terry (410) 398-3311
ED, Cecil Whig, Elkton, MD

Pedersen, Bruce (520) 753-6397
PROD DIR
Kingman Daily Miner, Kingman, AZ

Pedersen, Erik (714) 634-1567
ED, Cypress News, Anaheim, CA

Pedersen, Robert L (208) 377-6200
CIRC DIR, Idaho Statesman, Boise, ID

Pedersen, Tim (701) 572-2165
News ED
Williston Daily Herald, Williston, ND

Pederson, Dixie (712) 243-2624
CIRC DIR
Atlantic News-Telegraph, Atlantic, IA

Pederson, Lyle (701) 247-2482
PUB, ED, Lakota American, Lakota, ND

Pederson, Pamela (218) 386-1594
MAN ED, Warroad Pioneer, Warroad, MN

Pederson, Rena (214) 977-8222
VP/EPE, Dallas Morning News, Dallas, TX

Pederson, Rolf (519) 822-4310
EPE, EDL Writer, Daily Mercury, Guelph, ON

Pederson, Tony (713) 220-7171
VP-MAN ED, Houston Chronicle, Houston, TX

Pedigo, Wendell (615) 259-8000
ADV MGR-NTL, Tennessean, Nashville, TN

Pedlar, J Ken (306) 483-2323
PUB, ED, Oxbow Herald, Oxbow, SK

Pedley, Arlyn (712) 758-3140
GM, Ocheyedan Press-Melvin News, Ocheyedan, IA

Pedley, Jan Reiste (712) 758-3140
ED, Ocheyedan Press-Melvin News, Ocheyedan, IA

Pedroli, Rich (401) 762-3000
Sports ED, Call, Woonsocket, RI

Peebles, Carol Ann (330) 747-7777
Reporter, Daily Legal News, Youngstown, OH

Peek, Ralph (941) 574-1110
CIRC DIR
Cape Coral Daily Breeze, Cape Coral, FL

Peel, Bruce A (806) 385-6444
PUB, Amherst Press, Amherst, TX

Peel, John (970) 247-3504
Sports ED, Durango Herald, Durango, CO

Peele, Elwood (919) 752-6166
Senior Sports Writer/COL
Daily Reflector, Greenville, NC

Peeler, Jeannie (541) 672-3321
MGR-Office, News-Review, Roseburg, OR

Peeples, Gary (601) 693-1551
ADV DIR, MGR-MKTG/PROM, ADTX MGR
Meridian Star, Meridian, MS

Peery, David (Scoop) (816) 532-4444
PUB, Smithville Lake Democrat-Herald, Smithville, MO

Peery, John (407) 886-2777
ED, Planter, Apopka, FL

Peffer, John F (401) 277-7000
CIRC ASST DIR
Providence Journal-Bulletin, Providence, RI

Pegg, Maureen (613) 267-1100
ED, Perth Courier, Perth, ON

Peglow, Scott (317) 633-1240
MGR-Purchasing
Indianapolis Star/News, Indianapolis, IN

Pegram, Cynthia (804) 385-5400
Medical/SCI ED
News & Advance, Lynchburg, VA

Pegues, Joan (209) 582-0471
Fashion/Food ED, Lifestyle ED, Society/Women's ED, Hanford Sentinel, Hanford, CA

Pehr, Darrell J (505) 746-3524
ED, Artesia Daily Press, Artesia, NM

Peiker, Butch (813) 893-8111
ADV MGR-CLASS, Inside/Outside Sales
St. Petersburg Times, St. Petersburg, FL

Peil, Cyndee F (406) 791-1444
ADV MGR-CLASS
Great Falls Tribune, Great Falls, MT

Peipert, Jim (817) 390-7400
Foreign/NTL ED
Fort Worth Star-Telegram, Fort Worth, TX

Peirce, Larry (402) 475-4200
Regional Reporter, Journal Star, Lincoln, NE

Peirce, Nancy (319) 732-2029
GM, Wilton-Durant Advocate News, Wilton, IA

Peirce, Sandra (703) 878-8000
ADV DIR, Potomac News, Woodbridge, VA

Peiris, Sarath (306) 652-9200
EPE, StarPhoenix, Saskatoon, SK

Peitzsch, Gary (810) 469-4510
PROD FRM-MR, Macomb Daily, Mount Clemens, MI, Independent Newspapers Inc.

Peladeau, Pierre (514) 877-9777
COB/PRES/CEO, Quebecor Communications Inc., Montreal, QC

Pelak, Barbara (717) 821-2091
DP MGR, Citizens' Voice, Wilkes-Barre, PA

Pelascini, John (707) 441-0500
PROD FRM-PR, Times-Standard, Eureka, CA

Pelayo, Libertito (212) 967-5784
PUB, ED, Filipino Reporter, New York, NY

Pelchar, Joseph (610) 371-5000
CIRC MGR-Home Delivery
Reading Times/Eagle, Reading, PA

Pelchat, Martin (514) 285-7272
City ED, La Presse, Montreal, QC

Pelishek, Amy (414) 733-4411
Weekend ED, Post-Crescent, Appleton, WI

Pell, Robert W (614) 622-1122
BM, CIRC MGR
Coshocton Tribune, Coshocton, OH

Pelland, Wayne (401) 277-7000
PROD ASST to DIR of OPER
Providence Journal-Bulletin, Providence, RI

Pellant, Mike (604) 732-2111
CIRC VP-Reader Sales & SRV
Vancouver Sun, Vancouver, BC
Southam Inc.

Pellegrino, Robert (203) 625-4400
Features ED, Greenwich Time, Greenwich, CT

Pellek, John (419) 245-6000
PROD ASST MGR (Night), Blade, Toledo, OH

Pelletier, Phillip (508) 685-1000
ADV MGR-CLASS
Eagle-Tribune, North Andover, MA

Pellicelli, Laurier (418) 524-6400
GM, ED, L'Appel, Quebec, QC

Pelodeau, Pierre (819) 569-9526
PRES, Record, Sherbrooke, QC

Peloquin, Sharon (517) 895-8551
ADV MGR-NTL Representative
Bay City Times, Bay City, MI

Pelrine, Michael (302) 674-3600
News EX ED
Delaware State News, Dover, DE

Peltz, Jim (213) 237-5000
Aerospace/Defense/Transportation
Los Angeles Times, Los Angeles, CA

Pelusi, Rosemary (905) 358-5711
BM, Niagara Falls Review, Niagara Falls, ON

Pemberton, Charlene (918) 652-3311
CIRC MGR
Henryetta Daily Free-Lance, Henryetta, OK

Pemper, Suzanne (954) 698-6501
PUB, Tamarac/North Lauderdale Forum, Deerfield Beach, FL

Penalver, John (423) 756-6900
Photo DEPT MGR
Chattanooga Free Press, Chattanooga, TN

Penas, Lisa (609) 989-7800
ADV MGR-Art DEPT, Graphics ED/Art DIR
Trentonian, Trenton, NJ

Pence, Judy (505) 823-7777
Librarian
Albuquerque Journal, Albuquerque, NM

Penchoff, Jack (606) 792-2203
PUB, ED
Garrard County News, Lancaster, KY

Pendell, Teri (402) 335-3394
PUB, GM, Chieftain, Tecumseh, NE

Pendelton, Gail (201) 383-1500
Morning/Special Sections ED
New Jersey Herald, Newton, NJ

Pender, Kathleen (415) 777-1111
BUS/FIN ED
San Francisco Chronicle, San Francisco, CA

Pendergast, Karen W (903) 342-5247
MAN ED, Winnsboro News, Winnsboro, TX

Pendergast, Robert W (804) 649-6000
VP-CORP Communications
Media General Inc., Richmond, VA

Pendergast, Thomas F (903) 342-5247
PUB, ED, Winnsboro News, Winnsboro, TX

Pendery, Joann (912) 265-8320
Lifestyle ED, Brunswick News, Brunswick, GA

Pendleton, Nicki (615) 259-8800
Food ED, Nashville Banner, Nashville, TN

Pendleton, Robert (619) 241-7744
PROD DIR, Daily Press, Victorville, CA

Penfield, Fred (757) 247-4600
ADV MGR-Display
Daily Press, Newport News, VA

Penglase, Frank D (212) 208-8000
Senior VP Treasury OPER, Corporation Records, Daily News, New York, NY

Penick, Robert (317) 633-1240
CIRC MET Home Delivery
Indianapolis Star/News, Indianapolis, IN

Penikis, Maija (414) 733-4411
Health/Medical ED, Religion ED
Post-Crescent, Appleton, WI

Penko, Ron (216) 951-0000
PROD SUPT-Building
News-Herald, Willoughby, OH

Penley, Brenda (704) 758-7381
INFO Technologies
Lenoir News-Topic, Lenoir, NC

Penn, David H (817) 564-5558
PUB, ED, Olney Enterprise, Olney, TX

Pennekamp, Ted (414) 756-2222
MAN ED, Brillion News, Brillion, WI

Pennell, Paula (706) 283-3100
PUB, MAN ED, Elberton Star, Elberton, GA

Penner, Dixie (403) 872-2784
GM, Slave River Journal, Fort Smith, NT

Penner, Doug (204) 746-2868
PUB, ED, Scratching River Post, Morris, MB

Penner, Joyce (204) 746-2868
GM, Scratching River Post, Morris, MB

Penney, James (770) 748-1520
ED, Cedartown Standard, Cedartown, GA

Penney, John (518) 891-2600
ED, Adirondack Daily Enterprise, Saranac Lake, NY

Penniman IV, Nicholas G (314) 340-8402
Sr VP-Newspaper OPER
Pulitzer Publishing Co., St. Louis, MO

Pennington, Bill (201) 646-4000
COL, Record, Hackensack, NJ

Pennington, Brenda (618) 382-4176
CIRC MGR, Carmi Times, Carmi, IL

Pennington, Clarence (419) 435-6641
PRES, PUB, ED, EPE, Outdoors ED
Review Times, Fostoria, OH

Pennington, Gail (314) 340-8000
Radio/Television ED
St. Louis Post-Dispatch, St. Louis, MO

Pennington, Gary (715) 634-4881
PUB, Sawyer County Record, Hayward, WI

Pennington, J C (419) 435-6641
VP, Review Times, Fostoria, OH

Pennington, Jerry (606) 638-4581
ED, Big Sandy News, Louisa, KY

Pennington, Tonia (573) 471-1137
Food ED, Standard Democrat, Sikeston, MO

Pennington, Will (618) 532-5604
Photo DEPT MGR, Sentinel, Centralia, IL

Penny, Basil (205) 236-1551
NTL ED, News ED, Wire ED
Anniston Star, Anniston, AL

Penrod, Barbara (308) 995-4441
ADV MGR, MGR-MKTG/PROM
Holdrege Daily Citizen, Holdrege, NE

Penticuff, David (317) 747-5700
COL, Star Press, Muncie, IN

Penticuff, Donna (317) 747-5700
MET ED, Star Press, Muncie, IN

Penton, Bruce (306) 435-2445
PUB, GM, World-Spectator, Moosomin, SK

Pentt, Tom (360) 532-4000
PROD FRM-PR, Daily World, Aberdeen, WA

Pentz, Audrey M (360) 466-3315
PUB, Channel Town Press, LaConner, WA

Penuel, Glenn (919) 566-3028
PUB, ED, Weekly Gazette, LaGrange, NC

Peoples, Don (817) 645-2441
EDU ED, Photo Lab
Cleburne Times-Review, Cleburne, TX

Copyright ©1997 by the Editor & Publisher Co.

Peoples, Jackie .... (919) 492-4001
PROD FRM-PR
Henderson Daily Dispatch, Henderson, NC
Pepalis, Bob .... (803) 317-6397
City ED, Morning News, Florence, SC
Pepe, Joseph .... (219) 933-3200
Senior ASSOC PUB, Times, Munster, IN
Pepelnjak, James F .... (414) 224-2000
Labor Relations MGR
Milwaukee Journal Sentinel, Milwaukee, WI
Peper, Don .... (602) 271-8000
PROD Unit MGR-COMP
Phoenix Newspapers Inc., Phoenix, AZ
Peper, Doug .... (602) 271-8000
PROD Unit MGR-Packaging (Deer Valley, Mesa), Phoenix Newspapers Inc., Phoenix, AZ
Pepero, Marie .... (814) 367-2230
MAN ED, Free Press-Courier, Westfield, PA
Pepin, Matthew .... (860) 489-3121
Sports ED, Register Citizen, Torrington, CT
Pepin, Suzette .... (802) 257-7771
ED, Brattleboro Town Crier, Brattleboro, VT
Pepper, C J .... (306) 747-2442
PUB, Shellbrook Chronicle, Shellbrook, SK
Pepper, Jonathon .... (313) 222-2300
COL, Detroit News, Detroit, MI
Pepper, Linda .... (408) 424-2221
CIRC SUPV-Customer SRV
Californian, Salinas, CA
Pepper, Samuel J .... (520) 783-3333
PUB, Yuma Daily Sun, Yuma, AZ
Pepper, Suzanne .... (601) 961-7000
ADV MGR-RT, Clarion-Ledger, Jackson, MS
Pepple, Steve .... (616) 429-2400
MAN ED, Herald-Palladium, St. Joseph, MI
Peppler, Lonnie L .... (313) 242-1100
DIR-Sales & MKTG
Monroe Evening News, Monroe, MI
Pera, Jim .... (847) 475-0457
Artist/Owner
Second Ring Syndicate, Evanston, IL
Peragallo, Wayne .... (908) 922-6000
MGR-Computer Services
Asbury Park Press, Neptune, NJ
Perales, Christina .... (210) 686-4343
CIRC MGR-Customer SRV
Monitor, McAllen, TX
Percell, Chad .... (701) 228-2605
ED, Bottineau Courant, Bottineau, ND
Perch, Daryl .... (860) 241-6200
EDL Writer, Hartford Courant, Hartford, CT
Percival, Pam .... (915) 673-4271
Food ED, Abilene Reporter-News, Abilene, TX
Percival, Robert .... (801) 237-2800
PROD FRM-MR
Newspaper Agency Corp., Salt Lake City, UT
Percy, Suzanne .... (614) 224-4835
ADV Display, Daily Reporter, Columbus, OH
Perdomo, Araceli .... (305) 350-2111
ASSOC EPE-El Nuevo
Miami Herald, Miami, FL
Perdue, Andy .... (509) 582-1500
News ED, Tri-City Herald, Tri-Cities, WA
Peregrin, Isabelle .... (501) 623-7711
ASSOC ED, Features ED
Sentinel-Record, Hot Springs, AR
Peregrin, Patrick .... (513) 721-2700
ADV MGR-Sales
Cincinnati Enquirer, Cincinnati, OH
Pereira, Theresa .... (508) 997-7411
ADV MGR-Advertising Services
Standard Times, New Bedford, MA
Perella, John .... (212) 803-8200
CIRC DIR-Sales
American Banker, New York, NY
Perenboom, Jean .... (414) 435-4411
Books ED, Press-Gazette, Green Bay, WI
Perez, Abel .... (213) 483-4890
PUB, ED, 20 De Mayo, Los Angeles, CA
Perez, David .... (619) 442-4404
PROD MGR-Ad Composition
Daily Californian, El Cajon, CA
Perez, Demetrio .... (305) 643-4200
PUB, Libre Semanal, Miami, FL
Perez, Louis M .... (941) 687-7000
EX ED, Ledger, Lakeland, FL
Perez, Lupe .... (210) 876-2318
ED, Javelin, Carrizo Springs, TX
Perez, Marty .... (805) 925-2691
PROD FRM-Press
Santa Maria Times, Santa Maria, CA
Perez, Miguel .... (201) 646-4000
COL, Record, Hackensack, NJ
Perfater, Judith .... (540) 981-3100
ADV DIR/VP, Roanoke Times, Roanoke, VA
Perfette, John .... (330) 841-1600
GM, PROD MGR
Tribune Chronicle, Warren, OH
Perfontaine, Andre .... (514) 521-4545
VP, Le Journal de Montreal, Montreal, QC
Pergament, Alan .... (716) 849-3434
Radio/Television COL
Buffalo News, Buffalo, NY
Perillat, Danielle .... (914) 694-9300
Photo ED-Day, Reporter Dispatch, White Plains, NY, Gannett Co. Inc.

Perilloux, Gary .... (601) 627-2201
News ED, Press Register, Clarksdale, MS
Perini, Bob .... (770) 532-1234
PROD DIR, Times, Gainesville, GA
Perison, Kim .... (216) 376-0917
ADV MGR, Akron Legal News, Akron, OH
Peritano, John .... (203) 729-2228
MAN ED, Daily News, Naugatuck, CT
Perius, Rick .... (310) 540-5511
CIRC MGR-ADM, Daily Breeze, Torrance, CA
Copley Press Inc.
Perkes-Felcher, Allison .... (916) 622-1255
ADV MGR
Mountain Democrat, Placerville, CA
Perkins, Alice E .... (601) 684-2421
MGR-BUS Office
Enterprise-Journal, McComb, MS
Perkins, Andrew .... (509) 346-9723
PUB, ED, Royal Review, Royal City, WA
Perkins, Barbara .... (208) 726-8060
ED, Idaho Mountain Express, Ketchum, ID
Perkins, Betty .... (918) 825-3292
Features ED, Daily Times, Pryor, OK
Perkins, Broderick .... (408) 920-5000
RE ED
San Jose Mercury News, San Jose, CA
Perkins, Charles .... (603) 668-4321
News ED, Union Leader, Manchester, NH
Perkins III, Charles .... (603) 668-4321
EX ED, Union Leader, Manchester, NH
Perkins, Connie .... (318) 433-3000
ADV MGR-CLASS, Lake Charles American Press, Lake Charles, LA
Perkins, Cyndi .... (906) 482-1500
ED, Daily Mining Gazette, Houghton, MI
Perkins, Dave .... (414) 542-2501
ASSOC PUB, ADV DIR, MGR-MKTG/PROM
Waukesha County Freeman, Waukesha, WI
Perkins, Deborah .... (419) 422-5151
PROD MGR-Pre Press, Courier, Findlay, OH
Perkins, Gilda .... (504) 643-4918
COL, Slidell Sentry-News, Slidell, LA
Perkins, Jerry .... (603) 742-4455
CIRC DIR, Foster's Democrat, Dover, NH
Perkins, Jerry .... (515) 284-8000
Agribusiness/Farm ED
Des Moines Register, Des Moines, IA
Perkins, John .... (504) 643-4918
Amusements ED
Slidell Sentry-News, Slidell, LA
Perkins, Ken Parish .... (817) 390-7400
Television ED
Fort Worth Star-Telegram, Fort Worth, TX
Perkins, Mark .... (800) 267-8525
PRES
Consumer News Systems Ltd., Scottsdale, AZ
Perkins, Martha .... (705) 457-1037
ED, Haliburton County Echo, Haliburton, ON
Perkins, Mary .... (419) 332-5511
ADV MGR-Sales
News-Messenger, Fremont, OH
Perkins, Michael .... (219) 356-6700
ED, COL, EPE, EDL Writer, Features ED
Huntington Herald-Press, Huntington, IN
Perkins, Nena .... (330) 747-1471
ADV MGR-GEN/Co-op
Vindicator, Youngstown, OH
Perkins, Rachel .... (509) 346-9723
PUB, Royal Review, Royal City, WA
Perkins, Robert A .... (413) 788-1000
MAN ED-Sunday
Union-News, Springfield, MA
Perkins, Sue .... (201) 947-5000
MAN ED, Sun Bulletin, Palisades Park, NJ
Perkins, William .... (334) 792-3141
Senior ED, Dothan Eagle, Dothan, AL
Perlberg, Richard .... (517) 548-2000
GM, Livingston County Press, Howell, MI
Perlberg, Robert Edward ..... (517) 275-5100
PUB, Roscommon County Herald-News, Roscommon, MI
Perlenfein, Carol A .... (605) 654-2678
PUB, ED
Bonesteel Enterprise, Bonesteel, SD
Perlman, David .... (415) 777-1111
SCI ED
San Francisco Chronicle, San Francisco, CA
Perlman, Todd .... (916) 756-0800
Living/Lifestyle ED, Society/Women's ED
Davis Enterprise, Davis, CA
Permar, E J .... (912) 265-9654
PUB, Islander, St. Simons Island, GA
Permar, Matthew J .... (912) 265-9654
GM, ED, Islander, St. Simons Island, GA
Pero, Dave .... (409) 833-3311
ASST PUB
Beaumont Enterprise, Beaumont, TX
Perona, David W .... (716) 849-3434
VP, CIRC DIR, Buffalo News, Buffalo, NY
Perona, Jim .... (316) 724-4426
GM, Girard Press, Girard, KS
Perona, Robert .... (909) 684-1200
CIRC DIR, Press-Enterprise, Riverside, CA
Peronto, Linda .... (910) 888-3500
Librarian
High Point Enterprise, High Point, NC

Peroutek, Lesa .... (913) 378-3191
ED, Jewell County Post, Mankato, KS
Perreault, Luc .... (514) 285-7272
Cinema ED, La Presse, Montreal, QC
Perricone, Mike .... (404) 526-5151
VP-Advertising
Atlanta Journal-Constitution, Atlanta, GA
Perrien, Thomas .... (504) 826-3279
CNR-News Production
Times-Picayune, New Orleans, LA
Perrin, Joe W .... (205) 353-4612
CONT/PSL MGR, Decatur Daily, Decatur, AL
Perrin, Kim .... (801) 625-4200
Librarian, Standard-Examiner, Ogden, UT
Perrine, John .... (618) 532-5604
PRES/PUB, Centralia Sentinel, Centralia, IL
Perrine, William .... (618) 532-5604
SEC/TREAS, Centralia Sentinel, Centralia, IL
Perron, Maurice .... (613) 829-9100
ADV MGR-Sales Planning
Ottawa Citizen, Ottawa, ON
Perrott, Joann .... (416) 585-5000
CIRC Regional MGR-E Canada
Globe and Mail, Toronto, ON
Perrotto, Jody .... (319) 283-2144
PUB, Register, Oelwein, IA
Perrotto, Larry J .... (317) 584-4501
PRES, News-Gazette, Winchester, IN
Perrotto, Mark .... (319) 283-2144
GM, Register, Oelwein, IA
Perry, Allan .... (606) 638-4581
PUB, Big Sandy News, Louisa, KY
Perry, Beverly .... (815) 436-2431
PUB, Enterprise, Plainfield, IL
Perry, Bobby .... (903) 794-3311
CIRC DIR, Texarkana Gazette, Texarkana, TX
Perry, Carolyn .... (304) 348-5140
DIR-MKTG, Online MGR
Charleston Newspapers, Charleston, WV
Perry, Dave .... (303) 750-7555
MAN ED, Aurora Sentinel, Aurora, CO
Perry, Dave .... (307) 324-3411
PRES, TREAS, PUB, PA, MGR-PROM, ED
Rawlins Daily Times, Rawlins, WY
Perry, Donna .... (916) 741-2345
CIRC DIR, Appeal-Democrat, Marysville, CA
Perry, Gaither .... (757) 539-3437
PRES, PUB, News-Herald, Suffolk, VA
Perry, Harry .... (217) 465-6424
PROD FRM-Camera
Paris Daily Beacon-News, Paris, IL
Perry, Heidi .... (801) 237-2188
PROD DIR-Pagination
Deseret News, Salt Lake City, UT
Perry, Herb .... (317) 659-4622
Government ED, Times, Frankfort, IN
Perry, Jane .... (409) 632-6631
ADV DIR, Lufkin Daily News, Lufkin, TX
Cox Newspapers Inc.
Perry, Jim .... (352) 365-8200
PUB, DP MGR, PROD DIR
Daily Commercial, Leesburg, FL
Perry, Jim .... (918) 341-1101
Sports ED, Daily Progress, Claremore, OK
Perry, John .... (212) 455-4000
Southeast Sales, North America Syndicate,
King Features Syndicate Inc., New York, NY
Perry, John S .... (206) 872-6600
PUB, South County Journal, Kent, WA
Perry, Lynette .... (541) 523-3673
ADV MGR, MGR-MKTG/PROM
Baker City Herald, Baker City, OR
Perry, Mary .... (406) 353-2441
PUB, Harlem News, Harlem, MT
Perry, Michael .... (203) 964-2200
VP/ADV & MKTG, Stamford Advocate, Stamford, CT, Times Mirror Co.
Perry, Michael D .... (214) 977-6606
Sr. VP/CFO, A H Belo Corp., Dallas, TX
Perry, Michael D .... (406) 357-2680
PUB, ED, Chinook Opinion, Chinook, MT
Perry, Michael J .... (212) 450-7000
Northwestern MGR/Newspaper Relations,
VP/Northwestern MGR/Newspaper Relations
React, Parade Publications Inc., NY, NY
Perry, Mike .... (805) 395-7500
ASST MAN ED-Nights
Bakersfield Californian, Bakersfield, CA
Perry, Mike .... (616) 473-5421
PUB, Journal Era, Berrien Springs, MI
Perry, Rita .... (904) 634-1993
PUB
Jacksonville Free Press, Jacksonville, FL
Perry, Roger C .... (903) 852-7641
PUB, Chandler & Brownsboro Statesman, Brownsboro, TX
Perry, Russell M .... (405) 424-4695
PUB, ED
Black Chronicle, Oklahoma City, OK
Perry, Samantha .... (304) 327-2811
Entertainment/Amusements ED, Fashion/Style ED, Living/Lifestyle ED, Women's ED
Bluefield Daily Telegraph, Bluefield, WV
Perry, Scott .... (606) 886-8506
PUB, ED
Floyd County Times, Prestonsburg, KY

179-Who's Where **Pet**

Perry, Steve .... (612) 375-1015
ED, City Pages, Minneapolis, MN
Perry, Steve .... (360) 377-3711
ADV MGR-Major Accounts
Sun, Bremerton, WA
Perry, Sylvia .... (904) 634-1993
ED, Jacksonville Free Press, Jacksonville, FL
Perry, Tina .... (601) 328-2424
PROD DIR-Electronic SYS
Commercial Dispatch, Columbus, MS
Perry, Tom .... (908) 722-8800
COL/ASSOC ED
Courier-News, Bridgewater, NJ
Perry, Tony .... (213) 237-5000
San Diego BU
Los Angeles Times, Los Angeles, CA
Perry III, Victor A .... (213) 237-3700
VP-CORP Development
Times Mirror Co., Los Angeles, CA
Perry, Wayne .... (815) 436-2431
PUB, Enterprise, Plainfield, IL
Perry-Whittecar, Julie .... (913) 263-1000
Sports ED
Abilene Reflector-Chronicle, Abilene, KS
Persall, Steve .... (813) 893-8111
Films ED
St. Petersburg Times, St. Petersburg, FL
Perschau, Rob .... (816) 234-4141
SYS MGR, Kansas City Star, Kansas City, MO
Pershing, Anne .... (702) 423-6041
EVP, ED, Lahontan Valley News & Fallon Eagle Standard, Fallon, NV
Persiani, Daniel .... (303) 892-5000
VP-Technology INFO SRV
Rocky Mountain News, Denver, CO
Persinger, Joanne .... (812) 522-4871
News ED, Tribune, Seymour, IN
Persinger, Joseph F .... (812) 358-2111
PUB, ED
Jackson County Banner, Brownstown, IN
Perskie, James .... (609) 272-7000
ASSOC EPE
Press of Atlantic City, Pleasantville, NJ
Person, Karin W .... (415) 381-5149
ED, Vestkusten, Mill Valley, CA
Perszyk, Jinx M .... (717) 421-3000
ADV New Media Ventures, ADTX MGR
Pocono Record, Stroudsburg, PA
Perullo, Lou .... (212) 930-8000
VP-PROM, New York Post, New York, NY
Pescaia, Linn A .... (817) 826-3718
PUB, West News, West, TX
Pesch, Leo J .... (715) 582-4541
ED, Peshtigo Times, Peshtigo, WI
Pessetto, Amy .... (913) 628-1081
News ED, Hays Daily News, Hays, KS
Petak, Ron .... (402) 733-7300
ED, Bellevue Leader, Bellevue, NE
Peter, Steve .... (219) 874-7211
Chief Photographer
News Dispatch, Michigan City, IN
Peterlik, Pete .... (864) 298-4100
Automotive ED
Greenville News, Greenville, SC
Peters, Carol .... (304) 329-0090
MAN ED
Preston County Journal, Kingwood, WV
Peters, Charles .... (202) 462-0128
EIC, Washington Monthly Co., Washington, DC
Peters, Dale .... (616) 651-5407
PROD MGR, Sturgis Journal, Sturgis, MI
Peters, Dave .... (612) 222-5011
Senior ED-EDU & On-Line Newsroom Liason
St. Paul Pioneer Press, St. Paul, MN
Peters, Dennis .... (304) 329-0090
GM, Preston County Journal, Kingwood, WV
Peters, Dianne .... (506) 632-8888
CONT, Telegraph-Journal/Saint John Times Globe, Saint John, NB
Peters, Harvey B .... (401) 849-3300
News ED, Newport Daily News, Newport, RI
Peters, Jim .... (630) 844-5844
BUS/FIN ED, Beacon-News, Aurora, IL
Peters, Jim .... (816) 679-6127
PUB, News-Xpress, Butler, MO
Peters, John .... (306) 672-3373
PUB, ED
Gull Lake Advance, Gull Lake, SK
Peters, John .... (804) 333-3655
ED, Northern Neck News, Warsaw, VA
Peters, Keith E .... (207) 582-8486
PUB, ED
Community Advertiser, Farmingdale, ME
Peters, Kenn .... (315) 470-0011
Automotive ED, Post-Standard/Syracuse Herald-Journal/American, Syracuse, NY
Peters, Lenny .... (913) 682-0305
PROD FRM
Leavenworth Times, Leavenworth, KS

Pet Who's Where-180

Peters, Lesley .... (904) 473-2210
ED, Lake Region Monitor, Starke, FL
Peters, Mark .... (609) 228-7300
ED, News Report, Blackwood, NJ
Peters, Marveen .... (406) 822-3329
PUB, Mineral Independent, Superior, MT
Peters, Mike .... (937) 225-2000
Cartoonist, Dayton Daily News, Dayton, OH
Peters, Mike .... (970) 352-0211
Action Line ED, Greeley Tribune, Greeley, CO
Peters, Msgr R G .... (309) 673-3603
PUB, Catholic Post, Peoria, IL
Peters, Russ .... (403) 932-3500
ED, Rural Times, Cochrane, AB
Peters, Susan .... (415) 777-7212
ASSOC ED
Chronicle Features, San Francisco, CA
Peters, Susan .... (812) 663-3111
PROD MGR-COMP
Greensburg Daily News, Greensburg, IN
Peters, Vickie Canfield .... (814) 756-4133
ED, Albion News, Albion, PA
Petersen, Bernie .... (414) 733-4411
City ED, Post-Crescent, Appleton, WI
Petersen, Brenda .... (403) 328-4411
EDU SRV MGR
Lethbridge Herald, Lethbridge, AB
Petersen, Chris .... (800) 355-9500
PRES/COO, News USA Inc., Vienna, VA
Petersen, Jeff .... (541) 963-3161
Entertainment/Amusements ED, News ED, Television/Film ED, Theater/Music ED
Observer, La Grande, OR
Petersen, Nick .... (847) 888-7800
BUS ED, Courier-News, Elgin, IL
Petersen, Pamela .... (503) 397-0116
PUB
Chronicle and Sentinel-Mist, St. Helens, OR
Petersen, Rick .... (612) 673-4000
ADTX MGR, Star Tribune, Minneapolis, MN
Petersime, Alan .... (317) 664-5111
Photo ED, Chronicle-Tribune, Marion, IN
Petersohn, Matthew H .... (215) 675-6600
PUB, Progress of Montgomery County, Horsham, PA
Petersohn, Sandra L .... (215) 675-6600
ED, Progress of Montgomery County, Horsham, PA
Peterson, Beverly J .... (308) 745-1260
PUB, Sherman County Times, Loup City, NE
Peterson, Bill .... (330) 627-5591
GM, Free Press Standard, Carrollton, OH
Peterson, Bo .... (704) 864-3291
Environmental ED, SCI/Technology ED
Gaston Gazette, Gastonia, NC
Peterson, Brooks .... (512) 884-2011
EDL Writer, Corpus Christi Caller-Times, Corpus Christi, TX
Peterson, Charles .... (614) 942-2118
ED, Harrison News-Herald, Cadiz, OH
Peterson, Cheryl L .... (517) 724-6384
PUB, ED
Alcona County Review, Harrisville, MI
Peterson, Chuck .... (505) 983-3303
CIRC DIR
Santa Fe New Mexican, Santa Fe, NM
Peterson, Clay .... (408) 424-2221
Photo Chief, Californian, Salinas, CA
Peterson, Craig .... (306) 652-9200
CNR-PROM, ADTX MGR
StarPhoenix, Saskatoon, SK
Peterson, Curt .... (218) 723-5281
CIRC DIR, Duluth News-Tribune, Duluth, MN
Peterson, Dick .... (815) 459-4040
EPE, Northwest Herald, Crystal Lake, IL
Peterson, Eleanor .... (209) 736-2085
MAN ED
Calaveras Californian, Angels Camp, CA
Peterson, Eric .... (209) 736-2085
GM, Calaveras Californian, Angels Camp, CA
Peterson, Erik .... (714) 634-1567
ED, Buena Park News, Anaheim, CA
Peterson, Forrest .... (320) 235-1150
MAN ED, EPE
West Central Tribune, Willmar, MN
Peterson, Franklynn .... (608) 231-1003
DIR, P/K Associates Inc., Madison, WI
Peterson, Gary E .... (218) 863-1421
PUB, ED
Pelican Rapids Press, Pelican Rapids, MN
Peterson, George A .... (308) 452-3411
PUB, Ravenna News, Ravenna, NE
Peterson, Gil .... (415) 348-4321
PROD FRM-COMP
San Mateo County Times, San Mateo, CA
Peterson, Greg .... (909) 487-2200
DP MGR, Hemet News, Hemet, CA
Peterson, Janet S .... (309) 686-3000
MGR-MKTG, Journal Star, Peoria, IL
Peterson, Jeffrey .... (508) 543-4851
ED, Foxboro Reporter, Foxboro, MA
Peterson, Jill .... (309) 676-2511
MAN ED, East Peoria Courier, Morton, IL
Peterson, John .... (617) 933-3700
Picture ED
Daily Times Chronicle, Woburn, MA
Peterson, John .... (701) 223-2500
MET ED, Bismarck Tribune, Bismarck, ND
Peterson, John .... (618) 943-2331 ext. 100
ASSOC PUB, BUS ED, RE ED
Daily Record, Lawrenceville, IL
Peterson, John R .... (209) 736-2085
PUB, ED
Calaveras Californian, Angels Camp, CA
Peterson, Karen .... (317) 598-6397
MAN ED, Fishers Sun Herald, Noblesville, IN
Peterson, Kari .... (619) 745-6611
DIR-FIN, North County Times, Escondido, CA
Peterson, Larry .... (414) 235-7700
EPE, Oshkosh Northwestern, Oshkosh, WI
Peterson, Lee .... (310) 540-5511
Environmental/Ecology ED
Daily Breeze, Torrance, CA
Peterson, Linda .... (715) 485-3121
ED, County Ledger-Press, Balsam Lake, WI
Peterson, Lora .... (801) 529-7839
GM, Salina Sun, Salina, UT
Peterson, Mark .... (541) 926-2211
BUS, Albany Democrat-Herald, Albany, OR
Peterson, Mary .... (308) 995-4441
Society ED, Daily Citizen, Holdrege, NE
Peterson, Nick .... (541) 938-0702
ED, Valley Times, Milton-Freewater, OR
Peterson, Patti .... (715) 526-2121
ADV DIR, Shawano Leader, Shawano, WI
Peterson, Paul .... (208) 377-6200
CIRC MGR-Sales/PROM
Idaho Statesman, Boise, ID
Peterson, Paul L .... (541) 332-2361
ED, Port Orford News, Port Orford, OR
Peterson, Paul S .... (616) 845-5181
MAN ED, EPE, Radio/Television ED
Daily News, Ludington, MI
Peterson, Rich .... (619) 299-3131
DIR-New Ventures
San Diego Union-Tribune, San Diego, CA
Peterson, Richard .... (218) 863-1421
PUB
Pelican Rapids Press, Pelican Rapids, MN
Peterson, Richard M .... (701) 473-5436
PUB, ED, Benson County Farmers Press, Minnewaukan, ND
Peterson, Rick .... (507) 637-2929
PUB, ED, Gazette, Redwood Falls, MN
Peterson, Roland .... (517) 548-2000
PUB, Pinckney Post, Howell, MI
Peterson, Ronald C .... (406) 755-7000
PUB, PA, Daily Inter Lake, Kalispell, MT
Peterson, Roy .... (604) 732-2111
Cartoonist, Vancouver Sun, Vancouver, BC
Peterson, Scott .... (941) 953-7755
EX Sports ED
Sarasota Herald-Tribune, Sarasota, FL
Peterson, Scott .... (414) 367-3272
ED
Lake Country Reporter, Hartland Lake, WI
Peterson, Sharon .... (503) 226-1311
CIRC MGR
Daily Journal of Commerce, Portland, OR
Peterson, Stephen .... (717) 829-7100
CONT, Times Leader, Wilkes-Barre, PA
Peterson, Steve .... (209) 943-6397
SEC/TREAS, DIR-ADM SRV
Record, Stockton, CA
Peterson, Thomas F .... (908) 922-6000
DIR Facilities
Asbury Park Press, Neptune, NJ
Peterson, Vicki .... (507) 454-6500
ADV MGR-CLASS
Winona Daily News, Winona, MN
Peterson, Wayne .... (815) 987-1200
EPE, Rockford Register Star, Rockford, IL
Peterson, Wes .... (520) 445-3333
PROD MGR-MR, Daily Courier, Prescott, AZ
Peterson, Willie J .... (906) 228-2500
DIR-MKTG, Mining Journal, Marquette, MI
Petit, Diane .... (208) 743-9411
Features ED
Lewiston Morning Tribune, Lewiston, ID
Petrak, Michael R .... (816) 234-4141
VP-MKTG & Advertising
Kansas City Star, Kansas City, MO
Petranik, Steve .... (808) 525-8000
News ED, Wire ED
Honolulu Star-Bulletin, Honolulu, HI
Petras, George .... (702) 788-6200
News ED, Reno Gazette-Journal, Reno, NV
Petree, Denise Styers .... (910) 591-8191
ED, Danbury Reporter, Walnut Cove, NC
Petrena, George .... (904) 935-1427
ED, Branford News, Branford, FL
Petrey, Ronald K .... (904) 359-4111
PROD MGR-Technical SRV
Florida Times-Union, Jacksonville, FL
Petrich, Bernie .... (706) 549-0123
ADV DIR, Athens Daily News/Banner-Herald, Athens, GA
Petrie, Jay .... (201) 877-4141
ADV MGR-Sales Development
Star-Ledger, Newark, NJ
Petrik, Randall .... (630) 830-4145
PUB, Bartlett Examiner, Bartlett, IL
Petrino, Pat .... (203) 333-0161
PROD MGR-Plant
Connecticut Post, Bridgeport, CT
Petros, Liz .... (606) 231-3100
Regional ED
Lexington Herald-Leader, Lexington, KY
Petrowich, Tim .... (618) 542-2133
Sports ED, Online Contact
Du Quoin Evening Call, Du Quoin, IL
Petroziello, Guy .... (215) 949-4000
Government/Crime ED
Bucks County Courier Times, Levittown, PA
Petruno, Tom .... (213) 237-5000
COL-"Market Beat" (investment)
Los Angeles Times, Los Angeles, CA
Petrusaitis, Cindi .... (406) 363-3300
PUB, Ravalli Republic, Hamilton, MT
Petrusek, Wilma .... (409) 885-3562
ED, Sealy News, Sealy, TX
Petruska, Ed .... (520) 836-7461
Sports ED
Casa Grande Dispatch, Casa Grande, AZ
Petruska, Walt .... (919) 537-2505
Photo ED, Daily Herald, Roanoke Rapids, NC
Petry, Gail .... (301) 733-5131
ADV MGR-Territory Sales
Morning Herald, Hagerstown, MD
Petry, Gene .... (937) 225-2000
CIRC MGR, Dayton Daily News, Dayton, OH
Petryr, Diane .... (810) 643-9150
ED, St. Ignace News, St. Ignace, MI
Petsche, Jim .... (419) 294-2332
Action Line ED, City ED, Films/Theater ED
Daily Chief-Union, Upper Sandusky, OH
Pett, Joel .... (606) 231-3100
Cartoonist
Lexington Herald-Leader, Lexington, KY
Pett-Ridge, Christopher .... (412) 263-1100
ASST MAN ED-Graphics
Pittsburgh Post-Gazette, Pittsburgh, PA
Petterson, Karen .... (415) 348-4321
Films/Theater ED, NTL ED
San Mateo County Times, San Mateo, CA
Petterson, Mark .... (316) 364-5325
ED, Coffey County Today, Burlington, KS
Pettey, Carolyn .... (903) 626-4296
ED, Jewett Messenger, Jewett, TX
Pettey Jr, L D .... (903) 626-4296
PUB, Jewett Messenger, Jewett, TX
Petti, Joseph J .... (419) 683-3355
ED, Crestline Advocate, Crestline, OH
Pettigrew, Bill .... (604) 368-8551
ADV MGR, Trail Daily Times, Trail, BC
Pettis, Don .... (416) 441-1405
North America Journalist
Fotopress Independent News Service International (FPINS), Toronto, ON
Pettit, Bob .... (910) 373-7000
ASST MGR-Technology
News & Record, Greensboro, NC
Pettit, Burle .... (806) 762-8844
ED, Lubbock Avalanche-Journal, Lubbock, TX
Pettit, Diane .... (208) 743-9411
City ED, Health/Medical ED, SCI/Technology ED, Teen-Age/Youth ED
Lewiston Morning Tribune, Lewiston, ID
Pettit, Mike .... (505) 622-7710
Photo ED, Roswell Daily Record, Roswell, NM
Petty, Bill .... (801) 625-4200
PROD MGR-Technical SRV
Standard-Examiner, Ogden, UT
Petty, David B .... (601) 582-4321
PRES, PUB
Hattiesburg American, Hattiesburg, MS
Petty, Keith .... (316) 268-6000
CIRC MGR-MKTG & Distribution
Wichita Eagle, Wichita, KS
Petty, Marty .... (860) 241-6200
Senior VP/GM
Hartford Courant, Hartford, CT
Pettycrew, Janet .... (602) 898-6500
ASST to PUB, Mesa Tribune, Mesa, AZ
Thomson Newspapers
Petykiewicz, Ed .... (313) 994-6989
ED, Ann Arbor News, Ann Arbor, MI
Petykiewicz, Sandy .... (517) 787-2300
ED, Jackson Citizen Patriot, Jackson, MI
Petzer, Kristina C .... (313) 222-6400
ADV Senior Sales DIR-Major Accounts
Detroit Newspapers, Detroit, MI
Peura, Michael .... (630) 844-5844
CIRC MGR, Beacon-News, Aurora, IL
Peveto, Susane .... (318) 527-7075
ADV DIR, Southwest Daily News, Sulphur, LA
Pewters, Bill .... (970) 242-5050
DIR-MKTG/PROM
Daily Sentinel, Grand Junction, CO
Peyerley, Lance .... (604) 533-4157
ED, Langley Times, Langley, BC
Peyser, Andrea .... (212) 930-8000
COL, New York Post, New York, NY
Peyton, Paul J .... (908) 232-4407
ED, Westfield Leader, Westfield, NJ
Peyton, Tom .... (317) 633-1240
Art DIR
Indianapolis Star/News, Indianapolis, IN
Peyton, Vala .... (770) 428-9411
ED, Rockdale Neighbor, Marietta, GA
Pezley, Amy .... (319) 372-6421
Photographer
Daily Democrat, Fort Madison, IA
Pezzano, Jeff .... (317) 459-3121
ADV MGR-CLASS
Kokomo Tribune, Kokomo, IN
Pezzullo, Elizabeth .... (205) 236-1551
Farm/Agriculture ED, Health/Medical ED
Anniston Star, Anniston, AL
Pezzullo, Rick .... (914) 962-4748
MAN ED
North County News, Yorktown Heights, NY
Pfabe, Peter K .... (800) 223-2154
Senior ED
Investor's Business Daily, Los Angeles, CA
Pfaff, Mike .... (910) 727-7211
PROD MGR-Press
Winston-Salem Journal, Winston-Salem, NC
Pfaff, Steve .... (701) 223-2500
PROD MGR-PR, Tribune, Bismarck, ND
Pfanstiel, G B .... (562) 438-5641
PUB, Reporter, Long Beach, CA
Pfautz, Ann .... (814) 946-7411
MGR-MKTG/PROM/Co-op
Altoona Mirror, Altoona, PA
Pfeiffer, Denis .... (610) 323-3000
ADV DIR, Mercury, Pottstown, PA
Pfeiffer, John .... (716) 372-3121
PROD FRM-COMP
Olean Times-Herald, Olean, NY
Pfeiffer, Phyllis .... (415) 883-8600
PRES, PUB
Marin Independent Journal, Novato, CA
Pfeifle, David L .... (701) 587-6126
PUB, ED, Gleaner, Northwood, ND
Pfister, Darlene .... (612) 673-4000
DIR-Photography
Star Tribune, Minneapolis, MN
Pfisterer, Fred .... (540) 885-7281
Senior City ED
Daily News Leader, Staunton, VA
Pfluger, Peter .... (412) 263-1100
CIRC MGR-Sales
Pittsburgh Post-Gazette, Pittsburgh, PA
Pfohl, Richard .... (415) 777-5700
DIR-Financial Planning & Analysis
San Francisco Newspaper Agency, San Francisco, CA
Pfohman, Robert .... (503) 281-1191
ED, Catholic Sentinel, Portland, OR
Pfuehler, Phil .... (715) 425-1561
ED, River Falls Journal, River Falls, WI
Pfund, J R .... (218) 784-2541
PUB, Norman County Index, Ada, MN
Pfund, Ross D .... (218) 784-2541
ED, Norman County Index, Ada, MN
Phaneuf, Wayne E .... (413) 788-1000
MAN ED-News
Springfield Union-News, Springfield, MA
Phares, Cassandra .... (718) 981-1234
Special Projects ED
Staten Island Advance, Staten Island, NY
Phares, Doug .... (616) 683-2100
PUB/GM, Niles Daily Star, Niles, MI
Boone Newspapers Inc.
Phelan, Bryan .... (807) 737-2951
ED, Wawatay News, Sioux Lookout, ON
Phelon, Janett .... (913) 764-2211
DP MGR, Olathe Daily News, Olathe, KS
Phelphs, Gene .... (601) 842-2611
Sports ED, Northeast Mississippi Daily Journal, Tupelo, MS
Phelps, Art .... (619) 442-4404
ADV DIR-Major Accounts
Daily Californian, El Cajon, CA
Phelps Jr, Ashton .... (504) 826-3279
PRES, PUB
Times-Picayune, New Orleans, LA
Phelps, Candice .... (616) 651-5407
MAN ED, Sturgis Journal, Sturgis, MI
Phelps, Carlene .... (912) 384-9112
PUB, Coffee County News, Douglas, GA
Phelps, Christi .... (501) 378-3400
BUS Farm ED
Arkansas Democrat-Gazette, Little Rock, AR
Phelps, Dan .... (860) 423-8466
DP MGR/Online Contact
Chronicle, Willimantic, CT
Phelps, David .... (573) 642-7272
CIRC MGR, Fulton Sun, Fulton, MO
Phelps, Eulene .... (806) 249-4511
ADV MGR-CLASS, CIRC MGR
Dalhart Daily Texan, Dalhart, TX
Phelps, Melodie .... (606) 348-3338
ED, Wayne County Outlook, Monticello, KY
Phelps, Nathan .... (507) 359-2911
BUS/FIN ED, City Reporter, Political/Government ED, Journal, New Ulm, MN

181-Who's Where **Pik**

Phelps, Richard R (913) 427-2680
PUB, ED, Miltonvale Record, Miltonvale, KS

Phelps, Timothy (516) 843-2020
Foreign ED, Newsday, Melville, NY

Phialas, Mark (919) 419-6500
Amusements ED, Entertainment Preview ED
Herald-Sun, Durham, NC

Philip, Dawad (718) 636-9500
ED, New York Daily Challenge/Afro Times, Brooklyn, NY

Philipps, Carule (513) 352-2000
Features ED, Cincinnati Post, Cincinnati, OH

Philipps, Michael (513) 352-2000
MET ED, Cincinnati Post, Cincinnati, OH

Philippsen, Norman (519) 833-9603
PUB, ED, Erin Advocate, Erin, ON

Philips, Chuck (213) 237-5000
Entertainment Reporter-Music
Los Angeles Times, Los Angeles, CA

Philips, John R (805) 650-2900
DIR-MKTG, Ventura County Star, Ventura, CA

Phillips, Adam (918) 335-8200
CIRC Distribution Clerk
Examiner-Enterprise, Bartlesville, OK

Phillips, Andrew (412) 523-6588
ASST ED, Standard Observer, Greensburg, PA

Phillips, Arnold (204) 727-2451
PROD FRM-PR, Brandon Sun, Brandon, MB

Phillips, B J (215) 854-2000
COL-BUS
Philadelphia Inquirer, Philadelphia, PA

Phillips, Benny (910) 888-3500
Sports ED
High Point Enterprise, High Point, NC

Phillips, Bill (407) 420-5000
Newsphoto Chief
Orlando Sentinel, Orlando, FL

Phillips, Bob (415) 883-8600
PROD MGR-OPER
Marin Independent Journal, Novato, CA

Phillips, Bob (819) 986-8557
PUB, West-Quebec Post & Bulletin, Buckingham, QC

Phillips, Bruce (508) 343-6911
SCI/Technology ED
Sentinel & Enterprise, Fitchburg, MA

Phillips, Carolyn (212) 416-2000
ASST MAN ED
Wall Street Journal, New York, NY

Phillips, Carolyn (316) 421-2000
CIRC MGR, PROD MGR-SYS
Parsons Sun, Parsons, KS

Phillips, Charles (718) 526-9069
GM, Press Photo Service, Flushing, NY

Phillips, Clyde (417) 358-2191
CIRC MGR, Carthage Press, Carthage, MO

Phillips, Dan (601) 234-4331
ASST PUB, Oxford Eagle, Oxford, MS

Phillips, Darell (805) 259-1234
PUB, Signal, Santa Clarita, CA
Morris Newspaper Corp.

Phillips, Darlene (805) 273-2700
Fashion/Style ED
Antelope Valley Press, Palmdale, CA

Phillips, Darlos (217) 379-4313
SEC, Paxton Daily Record, Paxton, IL

Phillips, Dave (313) 222-2300
Automotive Writer, Detroit News, Detroit, MI
Gannett Co. Inc.

Phillips, David A (507) 346-7365
PUB
Spring Valley Tribune, Spring Valley, MN

Phillips, Deanita (618) 662-2108
CIRC MGR
Daily Clay County Advocate-Press, Flora, IL

Phillips, Deborah (802) 479-2582
PUB, World, Barre, VT

Phillips, Donald (908) 922-6000
ADV MGR-Sales Presentations
Asbury Park Press, Neptune, NJ

Phillips, Donna (912) 272-5522
ADV MGR-CLASS, Courier Herald, Dublin, GA

Phillips, Eleanore D (910) 326-5066
PUB, Tideland News, Swansboro, NC

Phillips, Glenna (719) 275-7565
PROD MGR-BUS
Daily Record, Canon City, CO

Phillips, Henry C (515) 284-8000
ADV VP, Des Moines Register, Des Moines, IA

Phillips, Howard (904) 698-1644
GM, ED, Putnam County Courier-Journal, Crescent City, FL

Phillips, Iris (902) 629-6000
Assignment ED
Guardian, Charlottetown, PEI

Phillips, Jan (864) 298-4100
Amusements/Books ED, Living/Lifestyle ED, Travel ED, Women's ED
Greenville News, Greenville, SC

Phillips, Jeff (918) 756-3600
Sports ED
Okmulgee Daily Times, Okmulgee, OK

Phillips, Jesse P (601) 234-4331
PUB, Oxford Eagle, Oxford, MS

Phillips, Jim (316) 672-5511
PUB, Pratt Tribune, Pratt, KS

Phillips, Joanne (520) 573-4400
CIRC MGR, Tucson Newspapers, Tucson, AZ

Phillips, John (412) 465-5555
ASST ED, Indiana Gazette, Indiana, PA

Phillips, Judy (910) 888-3500
Garden ED, Society/Women's ED
High Point Enterprise, High Point, NC

Phillips, Julien (250) 380-5211
PROD MGR, Times Colonist, Victoria, BC

Phillips, Karen (520) 783-3333
MGR-EDU SRV, Yuma Daily Sun, Yuma, AZ

Phillips, Ken (216) 245-6901
CONT, Morning Journal, Lorain, OH

Phillips, Lockwood (919) 726-7081
PUB, GM, Carteret County News-Times, Morehead City, NC

Phillips, Lorie (410) 749-7171
CONT, Daily Times, Salisbury, MD

Phillips, Lynne (419) 752-3854
MAN ED, Greenwich Enterprise Review, Greenwich, OH

Phillips, Melinda (919) 419-6500
ADV GM-Raleigh Extra
Herald-Sun, Durham, NC

Phillips, Michael (619) 299-3131
Theater Critic
San Diego Union-Tribune, San Diego, CA

Phillips, Mike (360) 377-3711
ED, Sun, Bremerton, WA

Phillips, Mike (602) 941-2300
City ED
Scottsdale Progress Tribune, Mesa, AZ

Phillips, Miles G (204) 534-6479
PUB, ED, Recorder, Boissevain, MB

Phillips, Nancy (405) 382-1100
SEC/TREAS, Books ED, Entertainment/Amusements ED, Travel ED
Seminole Producer, Seminole, OK

Phillips, Nancy K (716) 487-1111
ADV DIR, Post-Journal, Jamestown, NY

Phillips, Pam (360) 694-3391
CIRC MGR-Zone, Columbian, Vancouver, WA

Phillips, Ray (901) 529-2211
MGR-Office
Commercial Appeal, Memphis, TN

Phillips, Robert F (541) 926-2211
PROD MGR-OPER
Albany Democrat-Herald, Albany, OR

Phillips, Roger (805) 781-7800
CONT
Telegram-Tribune, San Luis Obispo, CA

Phillips, Ron D (306) 752-5737
ED, Melfort Journal, Melfort, SK

Phillips, Rupert E (703) 560-4000
Chairman, Journal Newspapers, Fairfax, VA

Phillips, Ryan E (703) 560-4000
PUB/CEO
Journal Newspapers Inc., Fairfax, VA

Phillips, Sandra F (501) 425-6301
Owner, Daily News, Mountain Home, AR

Phillips, Stacie M (904) 926-7102
ED, Wakulla News, Crawfordville, FL

Phillips, Steven (614) 387-7255
PUB, ED
Marion Newslife Advertiser, Marion, OH

Phillips, Stu (405) 382-1100
GM, CIRC DIR, Automotive ED, Graphics ED/Art DIR, Photo DEPT MGR, DIR-Telecommunications, DP MGR, PROD FRM-MR, Seminole Producer, Seminole, OK

Phillips, Ted M (405) 382-1100
PRES, Co-PUB, PSL MGR, Action Line ED, EPE, Environmental ED, NTL ED
Seminole Producer, Seminole, OK

Phillips, Teresa (910) 349-4331
ADV MGR-RT
Reidsville Review, Reidsville, NC

Phillips Jr, Thomas J (217) 562-2113
PUB, GM, Pana News-Palladium, Pana, IL

Phillips, Tim (601) 234-4331
ASST PUB, Oxford Eagle, Oxford, MS

Phillips, Todd (819) 979-5357
ED, Nunatsiaq News, Iqaluit, NT

Phillips, Tricia (817) 757-5757
DIR-ADV CLASS
Waco Tribune-Herald, Waco, TX

Phillips, Ty (916) 824-5464
ED, Corning Observer, Corning, CA

Phillips, Walter D (919) 726-7081
PUB, ED, Carteret County News-Times, Morehead City, NC

Phillips, Wayne (423) 638-4181
Sports ED, Greeneville Sun, Greeneville, TN

Phillips, William (904) 926-7102
GM, Wakulla News, Crawfordville, FL

Phillips, William (408) 920-5000
Central Coast ED
San Jose Mercury News, San Jose, CA

Phillips II, James K (316) 549-3201
PUB, St. John News, St. John, KS

Philp, Tom (916) 321-1000
Medical Writer
Sacramento Bee, Sacramento, CA

Philpot, Robert (817) 390-7400
Star Time ED
Fort Worth Star-Telegram, Fort Worth, TX

Philpott, Tom (703) 830-6863
Self-Syndicator
Military Update, Centreville, VA

Phinney, Bruce W (506) 632-8888
GM/EX VP, New Brunswick Publishing Co. Ltd., Saint John, NB

Phinney, Jack (303) 756-9995
Sr ED, Daily Journal, Denver, CO

Phinney, Susan (206) 448-8000
Fashion/Beauty ED
Seattle Post-Intelligencer, Seattle, WA

Phippen, Gary (509) 663-5161
ADV MGR-Display
Wenatchee World, Wenatchee, WA

Phipps, Curt (919) 829-4500
CIRC MGR-Home Delivery/Single Copy
News & Observer, Raleigh, NC

Phipps, Jack (306) 652-9200
CIRC MGR, StarPhoenix, Saskatoon, SK

Phipps, Marian (316) 488-2234
ED, Belle Plaine News, Belle Plaine, KS

Phipps, Peter (401) 277-7000
ASST MAN ED-MET
Providence Journal-Bulletin, Providence, RI

Phyrillas, Tony (610) 683-7343
ED, Patriot, Kutztown, PA

Piaggi, Claire (603) 863-1776
GM, Argus-Champion, Newport, NH

Piatt, Greg (517) 377-1000
Automotive ED
Lansing State Journal, Lansing, MI

Piatt, Richard (616) 651-5407
PUB, Sturgis Journal, Sturgis, MI

Piatt, Steve (717) 888-9643
MAN ED, City ED
Evening Times, Sayre, PA

Pic, Jan (316) 321-1120
Home Furnishings ED
El Dorado Times, El Dorado, KS

Pica, George M (206) 841-2481
ED, Pierce County Herald/Herald Sampler, Puyallup, WA

Picard, Jean-Claude (514) 899-5888
ED, Progres St-Leonard, St. Leonard, QC

Piccirillo, Joseph C (814) 773-3161
GM/PUB, Ridgway Record, Ridgway, PA

Picco, Raymon (604) 368-8551
PUB, Trail Daily Times, Trail, BC

Piccoli, Sean (954) 356-4000
Music Critic-Pop
Sun-Sentinel, Fort Lauderdale, FL

Picconi, Dottie (609) 691-5000
PROD MGR-COMP
Daily Journal, Vineland, NJ

Piche, Neil (613) 829-9100
PROD DIR-Manufacturing-Purchasing
Ottawa Citizen, Ottawa, ON

Piche, Rene (705) 335-2283
PUB, Northern Times, Kapuskasing, ON

Pickel, David (919) 829-4500
ASST MAN ED/Art DIR
News & Observer, Raleigh, NC

Pickens, Charles R (508) 793-9100
PROD MGR-Plant
Telegram & Gazette, Worcester, MA

Pickens, Daryl (808) 329-9311
CIRC MGR
West Hawaii Today, Kailua-Kona, HI

Pickering, Jane (309) 829-9411
BUS ED, Pantagraph, Bloomington, IL

Pickering, Jim (937) 866-3331
ED, Miamisburg News, Miamisburg, OH

Pickering, Mark (309) 829-9411
MET ED, Pantagraph, Bloomington, IL

Pickering, Mark (805) 650-2900
Chief Photographer
Ventura County Star, Ventura, CA

Pickett, Al (915) 673-4271
Sports ED
Abilene Reporter-News, Abilene, TX

Pickett, Connie (502) 678-5171
School/Women's ED
Glasgow Daily Times, Glasgow, KY

Pickle, Betsy (423) 523-3131
Films ED
Knoxville News-Sentinel, Knoxville, TN

Pickup, Chris (905) 765-4210
ED, Regional News This Week, Caledonia, ON

Pickup, Kevan S (905) 765-4210
PUB
Regional News This Week, Caledonia, ON

Pickup, Sandy (814) 724-6370
Lifestyle ED
Meadville Tribune, Meadville, PA

Picone, Linda (612) 673-4000
Deputy MAN ED-Human Resources
Star Tribune, Minneapolis, MN

Pidcock, Alan (205) 325-2222
PROD MGR-PR, PROD MGR-Newsprint
Birmingham News, Birmingham, AL

Pidgeon, Matt (518) 792-3131
PROD FRM-Distribution
Post-Star, Glens Falls, NY

Pidgeon, Tom (516) 843-2020
PROD DIR-Pre Press & Advertising
Newsday, Melville, NY

Pierce Jr, A Kenneth (614) 461-5000
VP/CFO, Columbus Dispatch, Columbus, OH

Pierce, April (501) 315-8228
CIRC DIR, Benton Courier, Benton, AR

Pierce, Barbara (309) 686-3000
CNR-NIE, Journal Star, Peoria, IL

Pierce, Charles (610) 323-3000
PROD MGR-Distribution
Mercury, Pottstown, PA

Pierce, Dann (212) 777-6200
MKTG DIR, Bettmann Archive/Bettman Newsphotos, New York, NY

Pierce, David C (716) 592-4550
ED, Springville Journal, Springville, NY

Pierce, Denise (515) 465-4666
MAN ED, Perry Chief, Perry, IA

Pierce, Donna (573) 815-1500
Features ED
Columbia Daily Tribune, Columbia, MO

Pierce, Jackie (403) 668-2063
SEC, GEN MGR
Whitehorse Star, Whitehorse, YT

Pierce, Joyce (601) 494-1422
ADV MGR-Local
Daily Times Leader, West Point, MS

Pierce, Kathleen (508) 793-9100
Special Sections ED
Telegram & Gazette, Worcester, MA

Pierce, Rebecca (616) 345-3511
MET ED
Kalamazoo Gazette, Kalamazoo, MI

Pierce, Robert (919) 829-4500
PROD MGR-OPER Support
News & Observer, Raleigh, NC

Pierce, Robert W (810) 766-6100
PROD DIR, Flint Journal, Flint, MI

Pierce, Scott (801) 237-2188
Television ED
Deseret News, Salt Lake City, UT

Pierce, Sterling (919) 658-9456
PUB
Mount Olive Tribune, Mount Olive, NC

Pierce, Steve (206) 464-2111
Environmental ED, ASST Regional ED
Seattle Times, Seattle, WA

Pierce, Susan (423) 756-6900
Society ED
Chattanooga Free Press, Chattanooga, TN

Pierce, Tom (414) 224-2000
VP-MKTG DIR
Milwaukee Journal Sentinel, Milwaukee, WI

Pierce, Victoria (309) 829-9411
EDU Writer, Pantagraph, Bloomington, IL

Pierce Geitz, Sarah (812) 268-6356
VP, Sullivan Daily Times, Sullivan, IN

Piercy, Janet (503) 620-4551
Self-Syndicator
Piercy & Barclay Designers Inc., Tigard, OR

Pieri, Leo (334) 262-1611
ADV VP
Montgomery Advertiser, Montgomery, AL

Piersa, Steve (914) 341-1100
CIRC MGR-MKTG
Times Herald-Record, Middletown, NY

Pierson, Chris (806) 667-3841
PUB, ED, Petersburg Post, Petersburg, TX

Pierson, Curt (352) 374-5000
MAN ED, Gainesville Sun, Gainesville, FL

Pierson, Eric J (412) 263-1100
Online Services MGR
Pittsburgh Post-Gazette, Pittsburgh, PA

Pierson-Solis, Leanoard (817) 387-3811
BUS ED, Record-Chronicle, Denton, TX

Piersons, Avery D (610) 562-7515
PUB, ED, Hamburg Item, Hamburg, PA

Pietro, Jackie (305) 377-3721
GEN MGR
Miami Daily Business Review, Miami, FL

Pietro, Richard (412) 775-3200
CIRC MGR, Beaver County Times, Beaver, PA

Pifarre, Juan J (415) 641-6051
PUB, Horizontes, San Francisco, CA

Pifer, Mark (540) 962-2121
Sports ED, Virginian Review, Covington, VA

Pifher, Maurice (905) 668-6111
ED, Whitby Free Press, Whitby, ON

Pigeon, Steve (800) 387-9010
PRES/GM, Masterfile (Stock Color Photo Library), Toronto, ON

Pihichyn, Paul (204) 697-7000
Design & Graphics ED
Winnipeg Free Press, Winnipeg, MB

Piimauna, Kathleen (808) 244-3981
CIRC MGR, Maui News, Wailuku, HI

Pike, B Ray (517) 772-2971
PRES, PUB
Morning Sun, Mount Pleasant, MI

Pike, Doug (215) 854-2000
EDL Writer
Philadelphia Inquirer, Philadelphia, PA

Pik Who's Where-182

Pike, Jagoda .... (416) 367-2000
VP-OPER/Human Resources
Toronto Star, Toronto, ON

Pilarczyk, Most Rev Daniel E .. (513) 421-3131
PUB, Catholic Telegraph, Cincinnati, OH

Pilcher, Lyle H .... (219) 696-7711
PUB, ED, Lowell Tribune/Cedar Lake Journal, Lowell, IN

Pilla, Bishop Anthony M .... (216) 696-6525
PUB
Catholic Universe Bulletin, Cleveland, OH

Pilla, Dave .... (908) 722-3000
ED, Metuchen/Edison Review, Somerville, NJ

Pillars, John .... (573) 471-1137
ED, News ED
Standard Democrat, Sikeston, MO

Piller, Frank .... (630) 232-9222
CIRC DIR
Kane County Chronicle, Geneva, IL

Pilmer, Sharon .... (515) 284-8000
MGR-RES
Des Moines Register, Des Moines, IA

Pilmore, John .... (517) 288-3164
GM, Durand Express, Durand, MI

Pilon, J P .... (514) 521-4545
PROD MGR
Le Journal de Montreal, Montreal, QC

Pimentel, Ricardo .... (520) 573-4561
MAN ED, Tucson Citizen, Tucson, AZ

Pimlatt, Terry .... (519) 344-3641
CIRC MGR, Observer, Sarnia, ON

Pinaire, Roland .... (812) 944-6481
PROD MGR-Commercial Printer
Tribune/Ledger & Tribune, New Albany, IN

Pinard, Guy .... (514) 285-7272
Features ED, Travel ED, Women's ED
La Presse, Montreal, QC

Pinchot, Joe .... (412) 981-6100
Television/Film ED, Theater/Music ED
Herald, Sharon, PA

Pinder, A J .... (515) 236-3113
PUB, ED, Herald-Register, Grinnell, IA

Pinder, Jeanne B .... (515) 236-3113
MAN ED, Herald-Register, Grinnell, IA

Pinder, Larry .... (515) 236-3113
MAN ED, Herald-Register, Grinnell, IA

Pine, Martin .... (718) 339-1417
DIR, Press News Syndicate, Brooklyn, NY

Pines, Bradley S .... (616) 345-3511
Photo ED
Kalamazoo Gazette, Kalamazoo, MI

Pines, Joyce .... (616) 345-3511
Features ED
Kalamazoo Gazette, Kalamazoo, MI

Pines, Larry .... (312) 407-0060
GM, Sentinel, Chicago, IL

Pineyro, Martin .... (212) 807-4600
CIRC MGR
El Diario La Prensa, New York, NY

Ping, Dan .... (423) 675-6397
ED, Press Enterprise, Knoxville, TN

Ping, Denice .... (712) 278-2092
PUB, Ireton Examiner, Ireton, IA

Pink, Dave .... (519) 894-2231
RE (Homes) ED, Record, Kitchener, ON

Pinkerton, Dave .... (541) 382-1811
ASST News ED, Bulletin, Bend, OR

Pinkerton, Sherry .... (308) 235-3631
PUB, GM
Western Nebraska Observer, Kimball, NE

Pinkham, Dave .... (360) 629-2155
PUB, ED
Stanwood/Camano News, Stanwood, WA

Pinkley, Sheila .... (205) 325-2222
Automotive/Aviation ED, BUS/FIN ED, RE ED
Birmingham Post-Herald, Birmingham, AL

Pinkoski, Darren .... (403) 826-3876
ED, Bonnyville Nouvelle, Bonnyville, AB

Pinkus, Susan H .... (213) 237-5000
Poll DIR (Acting)
Los Angeles Times, Los Angeles, CA

Pinnegar, Lynne .... (519) 323-1550
ED, Confederate, Mount Forest, ON

Pinnell, Gary .... (318) 487-6397
Automotive ED, BUS/FIN ED
Alexandria Daily Town Talk, Alexandria, LA

Pino, Ron .... (609) 272-7000
ADV MGR-Telesales
Press of Atlantic City, Pleasantville, NJ

Pinski, Jeff .... (814) 870-1600
MAN ED (News)
Morning News/Erie Daily Times, Erie, PA

Pinsky, Stephen .... (614) 337-2055
PUB, Ohio Jewish Chronicle, Columbus, OH

Pinsonnault, Jay .... (520) 753-6397
Sports ED, Daily Miner, Kingman, AZ

Pinto, Dolores .... (914) 454-2000
PSL DIR, Journal, Poughkeepsie, NY

Pinto, Linda .... (203) 333-0161
Fairfield County ED
Connecticut Post, Bridgeport, CT

Pinzino, Nadine .... (816) 271-8500
CIRC MGR-Customer SRV
St. Joseph News-Press, St. Joseph, MO

Piotrowski, Dennis .... (715) 365-6397
ADV MGR-RT, Daily News, Rhinelander, WI

Piper, Ann .... (604) 672-5611
ED
North Thompson Star/Journal, Barriere, BC

Piper, Cindy .... (219) 874-7211
ADV MGR-NTL Representative
News Dispatch, Michigan City, IN

Piper, George .... (608) 356-4808
ED, News-Republic/South Central Wisconsin News, Baraboo, WI

Piper, John .... (517) 787-2300
Features/Entertainment ED
Jackson Citizen Patriot, Jackson, MI

Piper, Ken .... (814) 736-9666
ED, Portage Dispatch, Portage, PA

Piper, Winnie .... (618) 544-2101
DP MGR, Robinson Daily News, Robinson, IL

Pipes, Donna .... (910) 343-2000
News ED, Morning Star/Sunday Star-News, Wilmington, NC

Pipkin, Ann .... (316) 231-2600
BM, Morning Sun, Pittsburg, KS

Pippen, Tony .... (405) 332-4433
BUS/FIN ED, Ada Evening News, Ada, OK

Pippin, David M (Mike) .... (864) 427-1234
PUB, Union Daily Times, Union, SC

Pippin, Nancy R .... (502) 827-2000
ADV DIR-Display, Gleaner, Henderson, KY

Pipps, Val .... (330) 996-3000
Weekend News ED
Akron Beacon Journal, Akron, OH

Pirtle, Mike .... (615) 893-5860
ED, BUS/FIN ED, COL, EDL Writer
Daily News Journal, Murfreesboro, TN

Pisani, Joseph .... (203) 625-4400
ED, Greenwich Time, Greenwich, CT

Pisapia, John .... (360) 577-2500
Sports ED, Daily News, Longview, WA

Pisarek, Bud .... (916) 652-7939
PUB, Loomis News, Loomis, CA

Piscopo, Nicole .... (561) 820-4100
Fashion ED
Palm Beach Post, West Palm Beach, FL

Pitcher, Ben .... (310) 322-1830
PUB, El Segundo Herald, El Segundo, CA

Pitcher, W Michael .... (516) 288-1100
ED, Hampton Chronicle-News, Westhampton Beach, NY

Pitchford, Peg .... (217) 446-1000
CIRC DIR, Commercial News, Danville, IL

Pitchford III, Robert B .... (502) 237-3441
ED, Citizen-Times, Scottsville, KY

Pitino, Yvonne .... (915) 445-5475
CIRC ASST MGR
Pecos Enterprise, Pecos, TX

Pitlo, Stan .... (907) 283-7551
GM, Peninsula Clarion, Kenai, AK

Pitlow, Stan .... (907) 283-7551
GM, Clarion Dispatch, Kenai, AK

Pitlyk, Ray .... (518) 454-5694
Religion ED, Times Union, Albany, NY

Pitocchelli, Steven .... (401) 722-4000
ADV DIR, Times, Pawtucket, RI

Pitre, Willie .... (318) 457-3061
PUB, Eunice News, Eunice, LA

Pitrone, Jim .... (215) 949-4000
Photo/Graphics ED
Bucks County Courier Times, Levittown, PA

Pitt, Ernest H .... (910) 722-8624
PUB, Winston Salem Chronicle, Winston-Salem, NC

Pitt, James .... (617) 929-2000
CIRC SUPT-Delivery
Boston Globe, Boston, MA

Pitt, Joe .... (206) 775-7521
GM, Enterprise, Lynnwood, WA

Pitt, Leon .... (312) 321-3000
GEN Assignment
Chicago Sun-Times, Chicago, IL

Pitt, Roger .... (414) 733-4411
Farm ED, Post-Crescent, Appleton, WI

Pitta, Julie .... (213) 237-5000
Technology-S.F.
Los Angeles Times, Los Angeles, CA

Pittman, Charles .... (704) 358-5000
Online MGR-Advertising, ADTX MGR
Charlotte Observer, Charlotte, NC

Pittman, Colleen .... (804) 446-2010
VP/CONT
Landmark Communications Inc., Norfolk, VA

Pittman, Jerry .... (405) 233-6600
MAN ED, Enid News & Eagle, Enid, OK

Pittman, John S .... (864) 298-4100
Senior VP/EX ED
Greenville News, Greenville, SC

Pittman, Tom .... (601) 842-2611
GM, Northeast Mississippi Daily Journal, Tupelo, MS

Pitts, Carter A .... (712) 568-2551
PUB, ED, Akron Register Tribune, Akron, IA

Pitts, Don .... (805) 259-1234
PROD DIR, Signal, Santa Clarita, CA

Pitts, Gary .... (916) 321-1000
CIRC MGR-OPER Service MGR
Sacramento Bee, Sacramento, CA

Pitts, Greg T .... (706) 356-8557
PUB, ED
Franklin County Citizen, Lavonia, GA

Pitts, John .... (800) 355-9500
Sr. ED, News USA Inc., Vienna, VA

Pitts, John P .... (915) 682-5311
BUS ED, Oil & Gas ED
Midland Reporter-Telegram, Midland, TX

Pitts, Leonard .... (305) 350-2111
Music Writer-Pop, Miami Herald, Miami, FL

Pitts, Susan .... (505) 437-5727
MAN ED, Sunburst, Alamogordo, NM

Pitts, Warren .... (804) 978-7200
PROD MGR-OPER
Daily Progress, Charlottesville, VA

Pitz, Peter E .... (316) 268-6000
PRES/PUB, Wichita Eagle, Wichita, KS

Pitz, Sandy .... (719) 336-2266
CIRC MGR, Lamar Daily News, Lamar, CO

Pitzen, Mel .... (515) 753-6611
City/MET ED, Farm/Agriculture ED, News ED
Times-Republican, Marshalltown, IA

Pitzer, Jack T .... (816) 726-3997
PUB, Albany Ledger, Albany, MO

Pitzer, Tanya L .... (816) 726-3997
PUB, Albany Ledger, Albany, MO

Pividal, Rebecca .... (813) 249-5603
ED, Town 'n Country News, Tampa, FL

Pizarro, Fernando .... (318) 459-3200
EDU/School ED, Religion ED, Teen-Age/Youth ED, Times, Shreveport, LA

Pizzaro, Cesar .... (305) 350-2111
ADV DIR-Display/Local
Miami Herald, Miami, FL

Pizzey, Len .... (705) 457-1037
PUB
Haliburton County Echo, Haliburton, ON

Pizzola, Carl .... (812) 231-4200
PROD FRM-MR
Tribune-Star, Terre Haute, IN

Placak, Marlene .... (909) 684-1200
ADV MGR-Regional
Press-Enterprise, Riverside, CA

Placements, Angele M .... (514) 455-6111
ED, L'Etoile de l'Outaouais-St-Laurent, Vandreuel-Dorian, QC

Plachecki, Laura .... (602) 271-8000
Teen-Age/Youth ED
Arizona Republic, Phoenix, AZ

Plackemeier, Gary .... (314) 340-8000
ADV MGR-NTL, Post-Dispatch, St. Louis, MO

Plageman, Mary Lynn .... (614) 461-5000
ASST MAN ED-Days
Columbus Dispatch, Columbus, OH

Plagens, Earl .... (915) 728-3413
PUB, Colorado City Record, Colorado City, TX

Plain, Steve .... (515) 753-6611
Graphics ED/Art DIR, PROD FRM-COMP
Times-Republican, Marshalltown, IA

Planck, Corri .... (619) 299-6397
ED, Gay & Lesbian Times, San Diego, CA

Plangere Jr, Jules L .... (908) 922-6000
COB, New Jersey Press Inc., Neptune, NJ

Plangere III, Jules L .... (908) 922-6000
EVP, New Jersey Press Inc., Neptune, NJ

Plank, Faye .... (806) 249-4511
Society ED, Dalhart Daily Texan, Dalhart, TX

Plank, JoAnne .... (206) 455-2222
City/MET ED, Eastside Journal, Bellevue, WA

Plank, Susan Patterson .... (320) 255-8700
DIR-MKTG Development
St. Cloud Times, St. Cloud, MN

Plaster, Bill .... (304) 348-5140
PROD MGR-Camera/Platemaking
Charleston Newspapers, Charleston, WV

Plath, Skip .... (616) 432-3488
PUB, ED, Colon Express, Colon, MI

Platsky, Jeffrey .... (607) 798-1234
BUS/FIN ED, RE ED
Press & Sun Bulletin, Binghamton, NY

Platt, Gordon .... (212) 837-7000
FIN ED, Journal of Commerce & Commercial, New York, NY

Platt, John .... (219) 294-1661
PROD MGR-PR, Elkhart Truth, Elkhart, IN

Platt, Ken .... (609) 646-5843
ED, South Jersey Advisor, Cologne, NJ

Platt, Pam .... (407) 242-3500
EPE, Florida Today, Melbourne, FL

Platt, Paul .... (214) 977-8222
PROD DIR-SYS
Dallas Morning News, Dallas, TX

Platt, Ron .... (219) 724-2121
ADV MGR, Daily Democrat, Decatur, IN

Platte, Cheryle .... (315) 792-5000
CIRC MGR-Transportation
Observer-Dispatch, Utica, NY

Platter, Jerry A .... (319) 267-2731
PUB, ED
Butler County Tribune Journal, Allison, IA

Plaxton, Joan .... (403) 524-3490
PUB, ED
Valleyview Valley Views, Valleyview, AB

Player, Alan .... (502) 582-4011
NTL ED, Courier-Journal, Louisville, KY

Pledger, Jackie .... (773) 283-7900
ED, Northwest Leader, Chicago, IL

Pledger-Skwerski, Jackie .... (312) 283-7900
ED, Spotlight Chicago, Chicago, IL

Plesa, Steve .... (714) 835-1234
Team Leader-Travel/Food
Orange County Register, Santa Ana, CA

Pletcher, James .... (412) 439-7500
BUS ED, EPE
Herald-Standard, Uniontown, PA

Pletsch, Lloyd .... (812) 886-9955
MAN ED
Vincennes Sun-Commercial, Vincennes, IN

Pletten, Christina .... (212) 768-8228
ED, Nordisk Tidende, New York, NY

Plevin, Nancy .... (505) 983-3303
Features ED
Santa Fe New Mexican, Santa Fe, NM

Plevka, John .... (815) 729-6161
MAN ED, Herald-News, Joliet, IL

Plitt, Loretta .... (717) 334-1131
PROD MGR
Gettysburg Times, Gettysburg, PA

Ploeger, Lois .... (320) 983-6111
GM, Mille Lacs County Times, Milaca, MN

Ploessl, Marty .... (319) 588-5611
PROD MGR-Pre Press
Telegraph Herald, Dubuque, IA

Plonka, Andrew .... (802) 254-2311
Wire ED
Brattleboro Reformer, Brattleboro, VT

Plotczyk, Michael .... (603) 352-1234
PROD CNR-SYS, Keene Sentinel, Keene, NH

Plothow, Roger .... (801) 674-6200
PUB, Spectrum, St. George, UT

Plotkin, Jay .... (804) 633-5005
ED, Caroline Progress, Bowling Green, VA

Plotkin, Ron .... (212) 208-8369
CIRC MGR, Standard & Poor's Dividend Record, New York, NY

Ploudre, Kurt E .... (602) 982-7799
PUB
East Mesa Independent, Apache Junction, AZ

Plourde, Marna .... (603) 882-2741
PSL MGR, Telegraph, Nashua, NH

Plowman, Gene .... (717) 637-3736
PROD MGR, Evening Sun, Hanover, PA

Plowman, John .... (219) 946-6628
ED, Pulaski County Journal, Winamac, IN

Plowman, Terry .... (302) 227-9466
ED, Delaware Beachcomber, Rehoboth Beach, DE

Plugh, James F .... (508) 586-7200
CEO, PUB, Enterprise, Brockton, MA

Pluim, Dale H .... (712) 737-4266
PUB, Sioux County Capital-Democrat, Orange City, IA

Plum, Dick .... (515) 295-3535
PUB, Algona Upper Des Moines, Algona, IA

Plumb, Charlie .... (509) 924-2440
ED, Valley Herald, Spokane, WA

Plumb, Terry C .... (803) 329-4000
ED, Herald, Rock Hill, SC

Plumley, William S .... (207) 791-6650
MGR-Non-Subscriber OPER
Portland Press Herald, Portland, ME

Plummer, Dennis .... (219) 267-3111
CONT, MGR-CR, Times-Union, Warsaw, IN

Plummer, Michael .... (219) 563-2131
PROD MGR
Wabash Plain Dealer, Wabash, IN

Plummer, Mike .... (406) 791-1444
PROD MGR-Press
Great Falls Tribune, Great Falls, MT

Plumridge, L .... (807) 274-5373
MGR
Fort Frances Daily Bulletin, Fort Frances, ON

Plunkett, Don .... (213) 633-1234
PUB, ED, Paramount Journal, Paramount, CA

Plunkett, Jim .... (912) 744-4200
PROD DIR, Macon Telegraph, Macon, GA

Pluto, Terry .... (330) 996-3000
COL-Sports
Akron Beacon Journal, Akron, OH

Ply, Michael P .... (616) 222-5400
CONT
Grand Rapids Press, Grand Rapids, MI

Plyler, Cecil .... (405) 924-6499
PUB, ED, Bryan County Star, Durant, OK

Plyler, Richard .... (215) 885-4111
GM, Leader, Philadelphia, PA

Poblete, Pati .... (707) 644-1141
Garden ED, Home ED
Vallejo Times-Herald, Vallejo, CA

Pochet, Richard .... (412) 537-3351
CIRC MGR, Latrobe Bulletin, Latrobe, PA

Pockrandt, Leah .... (507) 359-2911
Librarian, Religion ED
Journal, New Ulm, MN

Podashki, Karen .... (715) 833-9200
ADTX MGR, Leader-Telegram, Eau Claire, WI

Podd, Ann .... (212) 416-2000
ED-Spot News (New York)
Wall Street Journal, New York, NY

Copyright ©1997 by the Editor & Publisher Co.

183-Who's Where **Por**

Podey, Cleone ... (712) 677-2438
ED, Observer, Vail, IA
Podlak, Sam ... (603) 436-1800
ED, Portsmouth Herald, Portsmouth, NH
Podmolik, Mary Ellen ... (312) 321-3000
RT/Transportation
Chicago Sun-Times, Chicago, IL
Podolak, Janet ... (216) 951-0000
Food ED, Travel ED
News-Herald, Willoughby, OH
Poe, Christine ... (919) 537-2505
Reporter, Daily Herald, Roanoke Rapids, NC
Poe, David ... (304) 485-1891
Sports ED, News & Sentinel, Parkersburg, WV
Poe, Edgar ... (504) 826-3279
COL, Times-Picayune, New Orleans, LA
Poe, Janita ... (312) 222-3232
Urban Affairs Reporter
Chicago Tribune, Chicago, IL
Poe, Patty ... (207) 596-0055
ED, Free Press, Rockland, ME
Pogorzelski, Craig ... (915) 546-6340
CIRC MGR-City
El Paso Herald-Post, El Paso, TX
Pogue, George ... (417) 223-4377
PUB, ED, McDonald County News-Gazette, Pineville, MO
Pogue, Liz ... (250) 380-5211
Entertainment ED
Times Colonist, Victoria, BC
Pohl, Greg ... (402) 475-4200
CIRC MGR, Lincoln Journal Star, Lincoln, NE
Pohl, Jeanine ... (907) 586-3740
Health/Medical ED
Juneau Empire, Juneau, AK
Pohl, Susan ... (217) 446-1000
DP MGR, Commercial News, Danville, IL
Pohlman, Mary ... (608) 764-5515
ED, Independent, Deerfield, WI
Pohly, George ... (810) 469-4510
Sports ED
Macomb Daily, Mount Clemens, MI
Poignant, Gary ... (403) 468-0100
Wire ED, Edmonton Sun, Edmonton, AB
Poindexter, Kim ... (918) 456-8833
MAN ED, COL-Features, EPE, Features ED, Wire/Women's ED
Tahlequah Daily Press, Tahlequah, OK
Point, Flora ... (601) 896-2100
CFO, Sun Herald, Biloxi, MS
Poirier, Diane ... (413) 772-0261
Librarian, Recorder, Greenfield, MA
Poirier, John ... (318) 942-4971
CIRC MGR, Daily World, Opelousas, LA
Poirier, Mario ... (819) 376-2501
CIRC MGR, Le Nouvelliste, Trois-Rivieres, QC
Poirier, Michel ... (418) 683-1573
City ED, FIN ED, Religion ED, SCI/Technology ED
Le Journal de Quebec, Ville Vanier, QC
Poitras, Andre ... (819) 376-2501
News ED, Le Nouvelliste, Trois-Rivieres, QC
Pokas, Betty ... (614) 633-1131
EDU ED, Times Leader, Martins Ferry, OH
Pokorny, Bob ... (541) 276-2211
ADV MGR-Major Accounts
East Oregonian, Pendleton, OR
Pokrandt, Jim ... (970) 923-5829
PUB, ED
Snowmass Sun, Snowmass Village, CO
Pokress, Jackson B ... (516) 679-9888
PUB, ED
Seaford/Wantagh Observer, Bellmore, NY
Poland, Matthew K ... (860) 241-6200
VP-Employee Services & Community Affairs
Hartford Courant, Hartford, CT
Polaske, Dianna ... (512) 596-4871
ED, Moulton Eagle, Moulton, TX
Pole, Jeffrey ... (315) 470-0011
MGR-CR, Post-Standard/Syracuse Herald-Journal/American, Syracuse, NY
Polen, Bruce ... (330) 264-1125
ADV MGR-CLASS, Daily Record, Wooster, OH
Polen, Richard ... (417) 623-3480
BUS ED, RE ED, Joplin Globe, Joplin, MO
Poletti, Ed ... (215) 854-2000
PROD DIR-Facilities
Philadelphia Inquirer, Philadelphia, PA
Knight-Ridder Inc.
Poley, Marcia ... (615) 444-3952
Books/Features ED, Food/Women's ED
Lebanon Democrat, Lebanon, TN
Polhemus, David ... (808) 525-8000
EDL Writer
Honolulu Advertiser, Honolulu, HI
Policinski, Mark R ... (513) 489-7227
PRES/CEO
Brown Publishing Co., Cincinnati, OH
Polin, Andrew ... (954) 698-6501
MAN ED
Miami Hi-Riser, Deerfield Beach, FL
Poling, Jerry ... (715) 833-9200
Wire ED, Leader-Telegram, Eau Claire, WI
Poling, Jim ... (416) 364-0321
GM, Canadian Press & Broadcast News, Toronto, ON

Politano, Anthony ... (705) 759-3030
PROD FRM-PR
Sault Star, Sault Ste. Marie, ON
Polito, Joseph M ... (216) 696-6525
GM
Catholic Universe Bulletin, Cleveland, OH
Polizano, John ... (212) 210-2100
ADV VP/Group Sales DIR
New York Daily News, New York, NY
Polk, Gerald H ... (408) 920-5000
VP-OPER, PROD VP-OPER
San Jose Mercury News, San Jose, CA
Polk, Tim ... (406) 765-2190
PUB, Plentywood Herald, Plentywood, MT
Pollace, Judi ... (707) 263-5636
PUB, Lake County Record-Bee, Lakeport, CA
Pollak, Peter G ... (518) 372-0785
PRES, Empire News Exchange, Empire Information Services, Schenectady, NY
Pollak, William L ... (212) 556-1234
CIRC EVP, New York Times, New York, NY
Pollard, Gayle ... (213) 237-5000
EDL Writer
Los Angeles Times, Los Angeles, CA
Pollard, Jeff ... (614) 335-3611
PUB
Record Herald, Washington Court House, OH
Pollard, Jim ... (713) 220-7171
ADV DIR, Houston Chronicle, Houston, TX
Pollard, Kim ... (813) 259-7711
SYS ED
Tampa Tribune and Times, Tampa, FL
Pollard, Mike ... (910) 227-0131
Accent ED
Times News Publishing Co., Burlington, NC
Pollard, Norval ... (806) 762-8844
ASST MAN ED-Sports/Features
Lubbock Avalanche-Journal, Lubbock, TX
Pollard, Valerie ... (706) 324-5526
Librarian
Columbus Ledger-Enquirer, Columbus, GA
Pollard, Wes ... (201) 365-3000
BUS ED
North Jersey Herald & News, Passaic, NJ
Pollett, Chuck ... (806) 376-4488
Artist, Daily News/Globe Times, Amarillo, TX
Pollick, Steve ... (419) 245-6000
Outdoors ED, Blade, Toledo, OH
Pollina, Ronald ... (508) 685-1000
CONT, Eagle-Tribune, North Andover, MA
Polliver, Heidi ... (816) 438-6312
GM, Benton County Enterprise, Warsaw, MO
Pollock, Audrey ... (412) 794-6857
PUB, Tri-County News, Slippery Rock, PA
Pollock, Bart ... (315) 470-0011
MAN ED-Shared DEPT, Post-Standard/Syracuse Herald-Journal/American, Syracuse, NY
Pollock, Ben ... (501) 378-3400
Wire ED
Arkansas Democrat-Gazette, Little Rock, AR
Pollock, Chuck ... (716) 372-3121
Sports ED, Olean Times-Herald, Olean, NY
Pollock, Colleen A ... (412) 872-6800
ED, Times-Sun, West Newton, PA
Pollock, Jack ... (308) 284-4046
PUB, ED, Keith County News, Ogallala, NE
Pollock, Jerome ... (609) 989-5454
CIRC ASST DIR, Times, Trenton, NJ
Pollock, Kent ... (907) 257-4200
ED, Anchorage Daily News, Anchorage, AK
Pollock, Susan H ... (617) 361-6500
PUB, Hyde Park Tribune, Hyde Park, MA
Polly, Debbie ... (502) 358-3118
PUB, ED
LaRue County Herald News, Hodgenville, KY
Polovich, Ralph W ... (810) 985-7171
Photo DEPT MGR
Times Herald, Port Huron, MI
Polzin, Kevin ... (815) 459-4040
BUS ED, Northwest Herald, Crystal Lake, IL
Pomana, Peggy ... (716) 849-3434
CIRC MGR-Customer SRV
Buffalo News, Buffalo, NY
Pomcey, Temple ... (903) 757-3311
Sports ED
Longview News-Journal, Longview, TX
Pomerantz, Bruce ... (212) 736-7602
PRES, Photoreporters, Inc., New York, NY
Pomeroy, Bert ... (709) 896-3341
ED, Labradorian, Happy Valley, NF
Pomeroy, Tim ... (410) 332-6000
ADV MGR-Division, Sun, Baltimore, MD
Pomfret, Bruce ... (617) 979-5670
ED, Stoneham Sun, Melrose, MA
Pomichter, Jennifer ... (203) 789-5200
DIR-PROM
New Haven Register, New Haven, CT
Pommer, Matt ... (608) 252-6400
Capitol BU ED, Capital Times, Madison, WI
Pompei, Dan ... (312) 321-3000
Bears/NFL COL
Chicago Sun-Times, Chicago, IL
Pomper, Mike ... (806) 481-3681
PUB, ED, State Line Tribune, Farwell, TX
Pompia, Jon ... (719) 846-3311
News ED, Chronicle-News, Trinidad, CO

Pomponio, Ken C ... (307) 634-3361
ED-Sports
Wyoming Tribune-Eagle, Cheyenne, WY
Ponath, Todd ... (414) 542-2501
Photo ED
Waukesha County Freeman, Waukesha, WI
Pond, Bill ... (612) 388-8235
Photo ED, Republican Eagle, Red Wing, MN
Pond, Jerry ... (616) 627-7144
PROD MGR, Daily Tribune, Cheboygan, MI
Ponder, Brian ... (410) 749-7171
Local News ED, Daily Times, Salisbury, MD
Ponder, Keith ... (515) 672-2581
PUB, Oskaloosa Herald, Oskaloosa, IA
Ponder, Nicole ... (409) 756-6671
Films/Theater ED, Food ED
Conroe Courier, Conroe, TX
Ponder, Randy ... (601) 467-5473
GM, Sea Coast Echo, Bay St. Louis, MS
Ponds, Eddie ... (504) 386-6537
PUB, ED, Drum, Ponchatoula, LA
Poniers, David T ... (810) 766-6100
Sports ED, Flint Journal, Flint, MI
Ponikvar, Veda ... (218) 254-4432
PUB, ED
Tribune Press-Free Press, Chisholm, MN
Ponnikas, Mali ... (614) 773-2111
DIR-Market Development
Chillicothe Gazette, Chillicothe, OH
Pontari, Frank ... (817) 390-7400
Graphics DIR
Fort Worth Star-Telegram, Fort Worth, TX
Pontelandolfo, Jennifer ... (203) 406-2406
MAN ED
Fairfield County Weekly, Stamford, CT
Pontius, Dana ... (619) 241-7744
Religion ED, Daily Press, Victorville, CA
Pool, John R ... (706) 692-2457
PUB, Pickens County Progress, Jasper, GA
Pool, Martha E ... (706) 692-2457
ED, Pickens County Progress, Jasper, GA
Pool, Ronald ... (419) 294-2332
PROD MGR
Daily Chief-Union, Upper Sandusky, OH
Pool, William E ... (706) 692-2457
MAN ED
Pickens County Progress, Jasper, GA
Poole, Bob ... (972) 782-6171
ED, Farmersville Times, Farmersville, TX
Poole, James ... (518) 234-2515
PUB, Times-Journal, Cobleskill, NY
Poole, Jeff ... (540) 672-1266
ED, Orange County Review, Orange, VA
Poole, Kevin ... (817) 325-4465
PROD MGR-COMP
Mineral Wells Index, Mineral Wells, TX
Poole, Marcia ... (712) 279-5019
Fashion ED, Food ED, Society/Women's ED
Sioux City Journal, Sioux City, IA
Poole, Monte ... (510) 208-6300
Sports COL, Oakland Tribune, Oakland, CA
MediaNews Inc. (Alameda Newspapers)
Poole, Murray ... (912) 265-8320
Sports ED, Brunswick News, Brunswick, GA
Pooley, J D ... (419) 352-4611
MGR-Photo DEPT
Sentinel-Tribune, Bowling Green, OH
Poon, Albert ... (408) 920-5000
ED-Multimedia Design
San Jose Mercury News, San Jose, CA
Poon, Cheryl ... (510) 783-6111
ADV MGR-Legal, Daily Review, Hayward, CA
Poore, Becky ... (208) 377-6200
ADV MGR-CLASS
Idaho Statesman, Boise, ID
Poore, Ralph ... (208) 377-6200
BUS ED, RE ED, Idaho Statesman, Boise, ID
Poorman, Kyle ... (812) 231-4200
CIRC MGR-Single Copy
Tribune-Star, Terre Haute, IN
Poorman, Michelle ... (812) 231-4200
CIRC MGR-ADM
Tribune-Star, Terre Haute, IN
Popa, Gregory J ... (802) 253-2101
ED, MAN ED, Stowe Reporter, Stowe, VT
Pope, Carla ... (903) 628-2329
PUB, Red River Review, New Boston, TX
Pope, Edwin ... (305) 350-2111
Sports ED, Miami Herald, Miami, FL
Pope, Eric ... (313) 961-3949
ED, Detroit Legal News, Detroit, MI
Pope, Harold R ... (214) 667-2509
PUB, ED, De Kalb News, De Kalb, TX
Pope, John ... (504) 826-3279
Health/Medical Writer
Times-Picayune, New Orleans, LA
Pope, Kathy ... (770) 468-6511
ED, Monticello News, Monticello, GA
Pope, Larry ... (903) 757-3311
PROD FRM-PR
Longview News-Journal, Longview, TX
Pope, Larry ... (704) 252-5611
VP/EX ED
Asheville Citizen-Times, Asheville, NC
Pope, Leilani ... (601) 469-2561
MAN ED, Scott County Times, Forest, MS

Pope, Mary Ann ... (903) 628-5801
PUB, Bowie County Citizens Tribune, New Boston, TX
Pope, Robert ... (217) 788-1300
DIR-Photography
State Journal-Register, Springfield, IL
Pope, Roger ... (214) 667-2509
ED, De Kalb News, De Kalb, TX
Pope, Steven ... (313) 459-2700
GM, Livonia Observer, Plymouth, MI
Pope-Johnson, Cathie ... (904) 224-3805
ED, Tallahassean, Tallahassee, FL
Popiel, David ... (423) 623-6171
PUB, ED, Newport Plain Talk, Newport, TN
Popielski, Mike ... (219) 235-6161
PROD MGR-Quality
South Bend Tribune, South Bend, IN
Popkey, Dan ... (208) 377-6200
COL, Idaho Statesman, Boise, ID
Popkins, Ned ... (407) 420-5000
BUS ED, Orlando Sentinel, Orlando, FL
Poplin, Kyle ... (912) 236-9511
South Carolina ED
Savannah Morning News, Savannah, GA
Popp, David ... (407) 242-3500
CIRC MGR-Budget/SYS
Florida Today, Melbourne, FL
Popp, Debbie ... (412) 561-0700
ED, Almanac, McMurray, PA
Popp, Milo ... (319) 337-3181
PROD MGR-PR
Iowa City Press-Citizen, Iowa City, IA
Poppe, Pam ... (707) 643-1706
ADV MGR, Benicia Herald, Vallejo, CA
Poppenhagen, Ronald W ... (414) 432-2941
GM, ED
Green Bay News-Chronicle, Green Bay, WI
Popyk, Lisa ... (513) 352-2000
Courts/Law ED
Cincinnati Post, Cincinnati, OH
Pore, Bette ... (605) 352-6401
MAN ED, Huron Plainsman, Huron, SD
Pore, Robert ... (605) 352-6401
Agriculture ED, Huron Plainsman, Huron, SD
Portantino, Michael G ... (619) 299-6397
PUB, Gay & Lesbian Times, San Diego, CA
Portell, Mark ... (913) 456-7838
PUB, ED, Wamego Times, Wamego, KS
Portelli, Maggy ... (519) 621-3810
Accountant
Cambridge Reporter, Cambridge, ON
Porter, Andy ... (505) 863-6811
EDU ED, Gallup Independent, Gallup, NM
Porter, Andy ... (201) 383-1500
PROD SUPT, New Jersey Herald, Newton, NJ
Porter, Carol Ann ... (302) 398-3206
ED, Harrington Journal, Harrington, DE
Porter, Charles W ... (334) 602-0210
PUB, ED, National Inner City, Mobile, AL
Porter, David ... (407) 420-5000
Chief EDL Writer
Orlando Sentinel, Orlando, FL
Porter, Deborrah ... (508) 249-3535
Society ED, Athol Daily News, Athol, MA
Porter, Diana ... (541) 276-2211
CONT, East Oregonian, Pendleton, OR
Porter, Don ... (801) 625-4200
EPE, Standard-Examiner, Ogden, UT
Porter, DuBose ... (912) 272-5522
SEC/TREAS, ED, Courier Herald, Dublin, GA
Porter Jr, Francis ... (606) 329-1717
PROD MGR-PR
Daily Independent, Ashland, KY
Porter, George ... (250) 380-5211
PROD MGR-Maintenance
Times Colonist, Victoria, BC
Porter, Glen ... (205) 549-2000
ADV MGR-Display
Gadsden Times, Gadsden, AL
Porter, Janet ... (212) 837-7000
Chief European Correspondent (London)
Journal of Commerce & Commercial, New York, NY
Porter, Jeff ... (501) 793-2383
EPE, Photo DEPT MGR
Batesville Guard, Batesville, AR
Porter, Jill ... (215) 854-2000
COL-News, Daily News, Philadelphia, PA
Porter, Judson D ... (805) 466-2585
PUB, Atascadero News, Atascadero, CA
Porter, Julie ... (209) 441-6111
MGR-Human Resources
Fresno Bee, Fresno, CA
Porter, Larry ... (402) 444-1000
Outdoors ED
Omaha World-Herald, Omaha, NE
Porter, Nancy L ... (508) 880-9000
PROD MGR, Daily Gazette, Taunton, MA
Porter, Phil ... (614) 461-5000
EDL Writer
Columbus Dispatch, Columbus, OH

Por Who's Where-184

Porter, Philip .... (803) 785-4293
ADV DIR, Island Packet, Hilton Head, SC
Porter, Phyllis J .... (360) 289-2441
PUB, North Coast News, Ocean Shores, WA
Porter, Roger O .... (208) 356-5441
PUB, ED
Rexburg Standard-Journal, Rexburg, ID
Porter, Ross .... (519) 631-2790
MAN ED, Books
St. Thomas Times-Journal, St. Thomas, ON
Porter, Scott .... (602) 898-6500
PROD DIR, Mesa Tribune, Mesa, AZ
Thomson Newspapers
Porter, Susan .... (318) 255-4353
Photo ED, Ruston Daily Leader, Ruston, LA
Porter, Tim .... (415) 777-2424
ASST MAN ED-News
San Francisco Examiner, San Francisco, CA
Porter, Tom .... (919) 527-3191
VP, PUB, Free Press, Kinston, NC
Freedom Communications Inc.
Porter, Tom .... (316) 221-1050
PROD ASST MGR
Winfield Daily Courier, Winfield, KS
Porter, Vikki .... (619) 322-8889
EX ED, Desert Sun, Palm Springs, CA
Porter-Nichols, Stephanie .... (800) 655-1406
ED
Southwest Virginia Enterprise, Wytheville, VA
Porterfield, Don .... (540) 981-3100
ADV MGR-RT, Roanoke Times, Roanoke, VA
Portmann, Charles .... (502) 586-4481
ED, Franklin Favorite, Franklin, KY
Portner, Allan .... (209) 722-1511
VP-US Media Group Inc., PUB, ED
Merced Sun-Star, Merced, CA
Portnoy, Irene .... (517) 895-8551
EPE, Bay City Times, Bay City, MI
Portwood, Aaron .... (904) 584-5513
ED, Taco Times, Perry, FL
Posavetz, Dave .... (810) 469-4510
Photo DEPT MGR
Macomb Daily, Mount Clemens, MI
Posey, William .... (216) 329-7000
MGR-CR, ADV DIR
Chronicle-Telegram, Elyria, OH
Poskey, Rachelle .... (501) 523-5855
BM
Newport Daily Independent, Newport, AR
Poss, Mark .... (612) 388-8235
GM/PA, PROD MGR
Republican Eagle, Red Wing, MN
Post, Audrey .... (912) 744-4200
Region/State ED
Macon Telegraph, Macon, GA
Post, Ben .... (502) 582-4011
ASST MAN ED-OPER
Courier-Journal, Louisville, KY
Post, Hyde .... (404) 526-5151
ASST MAN ED-Innovation Team
Atlanta Journal-Constitution, Atlanta, GA
Post, Jerry .... (707) 441-0500
EDL Writer, Times-Standard, Eureka, CA
Post, Kevin .... (609) 272-7000
Automotive ED, BUS/FIN ED, Consumer ED, RE ED
Press of Atlantic City, Pleasantville, NJ
Post, Mary .... (609) 272-7000
ASST to ED
Press of Atlantic City, Pleasantville, NJ
Poster, Helen .... (516) 223-6514
GM, Polish American World, Baldwin, NY
Postin, Matthew .... (409) 598-3377
ED, Light and Champion, Center, TX
Poston, Wayne H .... (941) 748-0411
VP, EX ED, Bradenton Herald, Bradenton, FL
Potash, Mark .... (312) 321-3000
High School, Chicago Sun-Times, Chicago, IL
Poteat, Bill .... (704) 437-2161
ED, COL, EPE, News Herald, Morganton, NC
Pothier, Chisholm .... (709) 643-4531
ED, Georgian, Stephenville, NF
Pothier, Mark .... (508) 746-5555
ED, Old Colony Memorial, Plymouth, MA
Pothier, Sam .... (209) 532-7151
CIRC DIR, Union Democrat, Sonora, CA
Pothoven, Christopher .... (319) 538-4665
ED, Allamakee Journal, Lansing, IA
Potie, Francis .... (306) 347-0481
GM, Journal L'eau Vive, Regina, SK
Potter, Dan .... (816) 254-8600
ADTX MGR, Examiner, Independence, MO
Morris Communications Corp.
Potter, Dave .... (905) 526-3333
PROD MGR-Pressroom
Spectator, Hamilton, ON
Potter, Donald I .... (419) 237-2591
ED, Fayette Review, Fayette, OH
Potter, Elliott .... (910) 353-1171
ED, EPE, NTL ED, Political/Government ED
Daily News, Jacksonville, NC
Potter, George .... (503) 325-3211
GM, Daily Astorian, Astoria, OR
Potter, Jim .... (319) 291-1400
EPE, EDL Writer
Waterloo Courier, Waterloo, IA
Potter, Joe .... (219) 347-0400
BUS/FIN ED, News-Sun, Kendallville, IN
Potter, Jon .... (802) 447-7567
Sports ED
Bennington Banner, Bennington, VT
Potter, Karen .... (518) 454-5694
MAN ED-Features, Books ED, Food ED
Times Union, Albany, NY
Potter, Kathy .... (715) 284-4304
GM, Banner Journal, Black River Falls, WI
Potter, Lana .... (802) 479-0191
CIRC DIR, Times Argus, Barre, VT
Potter, Lori .... (308) 237-2152
Regional ED, Kearney Hub, Kearney, NE
Potter, Melanie .... (619) 232-4381
PSL MGR
San Diego Daily Transcript, San Diego, CA
Potter, Miriam .... (912) 233-1281
VP, Morris Newspaper Corp., Savannah, GA
Potter, Rob .... (519) 599-3760
ED, Thornbury Courier-Herald, Thornbury, ON
Potter, Robert .... (813) 894-2411
PUB, ED, Pinellas News, St. Petersburg, FL
Potter, Yvonne J .... (419) 237-2591
PUB, Fayette Review, Fayette, OH
Potters, Gloria .... (317) 825-0581
PROD Pre Press
Connersville News-Examiner, Connersville, IN
Pottorff, Tom .... (313) 242-1100
CIRC DIR
Monroe Evening News, Monroe, MI
Potts, Debra .... (405) 542-6644
MAN ED, Hinton Record, Hinton, OK
Potts, Erwin .... (916) 321-1855
COB
McClatchy Newspapers, Sacramento, CA
Potts, Joan .... (309) 343-7181
BM, Register-Mail, Galesburg, IL
Potts, Joe .... (405) 924-4388
CIRC MGR-Sales
Durant Daily Democrat, Durant, OK
Potts, Jon-Paul .... (617) 444-1706
ED, Needham Times, Needham, MA
Potts, Mark .... (502) 827-2000
CIRC MGR, Gleaner, Henderson, KY
Potts, Rex .... (202) 334-6000
PROD MGR-Newsprint
Washington Post, Washington, DC
Poulin, Gaetan .... (819) 583-1630
PUB, ED, L'Echo de Frontenac, Lac Megantic, Cte. Megantic, QC
Poulin, Michelle .... (416) 364-3172
BM, Broadcast News Limited, Toronto, ON
Poulin, Norman .... (310) 540-5511
PROD FRM-Color DEPT
Daily Breeze, Torrance, CA
Poulin, Normand .... (819) 362-7049
ED, La Feuille d'Erable, Plessisville, QC
Pouliri, Ginette .... (819) 845-2705
ED, L'Etincelle, Windsor, QC
Poulos, Stavros .... (718) 784-5255
MAN ED
National Herald, Long Island City, NY
Poulson, Sandy .... (907) 747-3219
SEC, Co-PUB, BM, MAN ED, Society ED, Women's ED, Daily Sitka Sentinel, Sitka, AK
Poulson, Thad .... (907) 747-3219
PRES, Co-PUB, EX ED
Daily Sitka Sentinel, Sitka, AK
Pouncey, Tim .... (316) 542-3111
ED, Times Sentinel, Cheney, KS
Pounds, Thomas F .... (412) 263-1100
CIRC DIR
Pittsburgh Post-Gazette, Pittsburgh, PA
Povse, Paul .... (217) 788-1300
Features ED
State Journal-Register, Springfield, IL
Pow, Ewan .... (204) 476-2309
PUB, GM, Neepawa Press, Neepawa, MB
Powell, Bill .... (541) 776-4411
Wire ED, Mail Tribune, Medford, OR
Powell, Chris .... (860) 646-0500
MAN ED/VP-News
Journal Inquirer, Manchester, CT
Powell, Chuck .... (317) 633-1240
CIRC MGR-Fleet & Distribution OPER
Indianapolis Star/News, Indianapolis, IN
Powell, Donald .... (541) 963-3161
GM, ADV MGR, Observer, La Grande, OR
Powell, Doyle .... (706) 549-0123
CONT-Division, Athens Daily News/Banner-Herald, Athens, GA
Powell, Dwane .... (919) 829-4500
Cartoonist, News & Observer, Raleigh, NC
Powell, F Kirk .... (816) 987-2138
PUB, ED
Pleasant Hill Times, Pleasant Hill, MO
Powell, Gary .... (402) 475-4200
CONT, Lincoln Journal Star, Lincoln, NE
Powell, Jan .... (816) 987-2138
GM, Pleasant Hill Times, Pleasant Hill, MO
Powell, Mrs Jeree .... (409) 883-3571
DP MGR, Orange Leader, Orange, TX
Powell, Julie .... (970) 533-7766
ED, Mancos Times-Tribune, Mancos, CO
Powell, June D .... (704) 377-6221
GM, Mecklenburg Times, Charlotte, NC
Powell, Kathryn .... (810) 985-7171
ADV DIR, Times Herald, Port Huron, MI
Powell, Larry .... (214) 977-8222
COL-MET, Dallas Morning News, Dallas, TX
Powell, Larry .... (919) 527-3191
PROD MGR, Free Press, Kinston, NC
Powell, Linda .... (405) 282-2222
PROD SUPT-COMP
Guthrie News Leader, Guthrie, OK
Powell, Mark .... (605) 394-8300
EPE, Rapid City Journal, Rapid City, SD
Powell, Mary .... (405) 235-3100
PROD MGR
Journal Record, Oklahoma City, OK
Powell, Michael S .... (301) 662-1177
MAN ED
Frederick Post/The News, Frederick, MD
Powell, Mickey .... (910) 623-2155
Religion ED, Daily News, Eden, NC
Powell, Mike .... (310) 230-3400
DIR-Photography, Allsport Photography USA, Pacific Palisades, CA
Powell, Mike .... (334) 262-1611
VP-BUS & Administration
Montgomery Advertiser, Montgomery, AL
Powell, Nic .... (561) 589-4566
ED, Vero Beach Sun, Vero Beach, FL
Powell, Roger .... (419) 422-5151
MGR-EDU SRV, ADV DIR-Market Development, Courier, Findlay, OH
Powell, Rusty .... (770) 428-9411
CIRC DIR
Marietta Daily Journal, Marietta, GA
Powell, Sammy .... (512) 445-3500
PROD DIR-Transportation
Austin American-Statesman, Austin, TX
Powell, Sandy .... (970) 493-6397
ADV MGR-Outside Sales
Fort Collins Coloradoan, Fort Collins, CO
Powell, Steve .... (310) 230-3400
PRES, Allsport Photography USA, Pacific Palisades, CA
Powell, Steve .... (360) 452-2345
News ED
Peninsula Daily News, Port Angeles, WA
Powell, Thomas .... (937) 644-9111
Photo ED
Marysville Journal-Tribune, Marysville, OH
Powell, Wayne .... (334) 262-1611
PROD SUPT-PR
Montgomery Advertiser, Montgomery, AL
Powell, Wayne .... (717) 243-2611
PUB, Sentinel, Carlisle, PA
Powell, Wickliff R .... (606) 329-1717
ED, Daily Independent, Ashland, KY
Powell, Wilson .... (501) 793-2383
BM, Books ED, Historian
Batesville Guard, Batesville, AR
Power, Edward .... (757) 446-2000
Deputy MAN ED-Military/Virginia BUS, Military ED, Virginian-Pilot, Norfolk, VA
Power, John R .... (217) 245-6121
PUB/GM
Jacksonville Journal-Courier, Jacksonville, IL
Power, Larry .... (713) 479-2760
PUB, Deer Park Progress/Deer Park Broadcaster, Deer Park, TX
Power, Phil .... (313) 459-2700
PUB, Livonia Observer, Plymouth, MI
Power, Ted .... (615) 259-8000
GM/ED-Williamson, Days
Tennessean, Nashville, TN
Powers, Andy .... (619) 745-6611
PROD MGR-Press
North County Times, Escondido, CA
Powers, Arthur S .... (540) 669-2181
VP, PUB, Herald-Courier Virginia Tennessean, Bristol, VA
Powers, Bob .... (517) 377-1000
ADV MGR-NTL/Co-op
Lansing State Journal, Lansing, MI
Powers, Jim .... (815) 459-4040
DIR-MKTG
Northwest Herald, Crystal Lake, IL
Powers, Lenita .... (702) 788-6200
COL, Reno Gazette-Journal, Reno, NV
Powers, Mary .... (901) 529-2211
Medical Reporter
Commercial Appeal, Memphis, TN
Powers, Mary Caroline .... (518) 584-4242
CNR-Special Projects, EPE
Saratogian, Saratoga Springs, NY
Powers, Nancy .... (613) 472-2431
ED, Havelock Citizen, Marmora, ON
Powers, Patricia .... (607) 739-3001
PUB
Chemung Valley Reporter, Horseheads, NY
Powers, Robert L .... (317) 825-0581
MAN ED, Amusements ED, Automotive ED, EPE, News-Examiner, Connersville, IN
Powers, Scott .... (617) 929-2000
Arts ED, Boston Globe, Boston, MA
Powers, Shad .... (517) 437-7351
Sports ED, Daily News, Hillsdale, MI
Powls, David .... (913) 242-4700
BUS/FIN ED, Ottawa Herald, Ottawa, KS
Pownall, Jeff .... (409) 632-6631
News ED, Lufkin Daily News, Lufkin, TX
Poyen, Jennifer .... (619) 270-3103
MAN ED
La Jolla Village News, San Diego, CA
Poynor, David .... (205) 734-2131
MAN ED, Cullman Times, Cullman, AL
Poynor, Jay .... (212) 327-0998
PRES, Animagic Syndication, New York, NY
Prada, Angel M .... (213) 388-4639
PUB, ED, LA Voz Libre, Los Angeles, CA
Pradarelli, Steve .... (414) 235-7700
City ED, Oshkosh Northwestern, Oshkosh, WI
Prah-Perochon, Anne .... (415) 921-5100
ED, Journal Francais, San Francisco, CA
Prahl, Jack .... (816) 932-6600
Sales MGR/Southeast Div.
Universal Press Syndicate, Kansas City, MO
Praiss, Joan .... (215) 854-2000
DIR-MKTG
Philadelphia Inquirer, Philadelphia, PA
Knight-Ridder Inc.
Prall, Shirley .... (616) 347-2544
Librarian, Religion ED
Petoskey News-Review, Petoskey, MI
Pranger, Ken .... (810) 469-4510
CONT, Macomb Daily, Mount Clemens, MI
Independent Newspapers Inc. (MI)
Prater, Michael .... (513) 863-8200
DP MGR, Journal-News, Hamilton, OH
Prater, Nancy .... (317) 622-1212
ADTX MGR, Herald Bulletin, Anderson, IN
Prather, David .... (205) 532-4000
City ED, Huntsville Times, Huntsville, AL
Prather, E Waid .... (601) 267-4501
MAN ED, Carthaginian, Carthage, MS
Prather, Jean .... (937) 222-6000
Office MGR
Daily Court Reporter, Dayton, OH
Pratt, Adrian .... (706) 549-0123
EX ED, Athens Daily News/Banner-Herald, Athens, GA
Pratt, Beth .... (806) 762-8844
Religion ED
Lubbock Avalanche-Journal, Lubbock, TX
Pratt, Brad .... (308) 237-2152
SYS SUPT, Kearney Hub, Kearney, NE
Pratt, Brian T .... (413) 447-7311
CIRC MGR-Home Delivery
Berkshire Eagle, Pittsfield, MA
Pratt, Colin .... (415) 692-9406
PUB, San Mateo Weekly, Burlingame, CA
Pratt, Ernie .... (816) 882-5335
CIRC DIR,
Boonville Daily News, Boonville, MO
Pratt, Roger .... (812) 254-0480
PROD FRM-COMP
Washington Times-Herald, Washington, IN
Pratt, Sheila .... (403) 429-5400
MAN ED, Edmonton Journal, Edmonton, AB
Pratt, Sue .... (715) 833-9200
CIRC MGR-Leader Telegram OPER
Leader-Telegram, Eau Claire, WI
Pratt, Todd .... (941) 992-2110
ED, Bonita Banner, Bonita Springs, FL
Pratt, Tom .... (903) 597-8111
NTL ED, Political/Government ED, Religion ED, Tyler Morning Telegraph, Tyler, TX
Prauner, Jay .... (402) 371-1020
Sports ED, Norfolk Daily News, Norfolk, NE
Prause, Diane .... (409) 743-3450
ED, Schulenburg Sticker, Schulenburg, TX
Prause, Paul .... (512) 865-3510
PUB, Flatonia Argus, Flatonia, TX
Pravata, Renn .... (504) 643-4918
Sports ED, Slidell Sentry-News, Slidell, LA
Pray, Van M .... (619) 373-4812
PUB, Mojave Desert News, California City, CA
Praytor, Steve .... (417) 451-1520
ADV MGR, Neosho Daily News, Neosho, MO
Praytor, Valerie .... (417) 451-1520
PUB, Neosho Daily News, Neosho, MO
Prazma, Michael .... (414) 435-4411
CIRC DIR
Green Bay Press-Gazette, Green Bay, WI
Preece, Gordon .... (204) 697-7000
Art DIR, Winnipeg Free Press, Winnipeg, MB
Preiser, Jerry .... (212) 755-4363
MAN ED, Punch In Travel & Entertainment News Syndicate, New York, NY
Preiser, Nancy .... (212) 755-4363
MAN ED, Punch In Travel & Entertainment News Syndicate, New York, NY
Preisser, Dave .... (407) 242-3500
PROD DIR, Florida Today, Melbourne, FL
Preisser, David E .... (513) 721-2700
VP-Production, PROD VP
Cincinnati Enquirer, Cincinnati, OH
Preive, Judith .... (510) 757-2525
Lifestyle ED, Ledger Dispatch, Antioch, CA

Copyright ©1997 by the Editor & Publisher Co.

185-Who's Where **Pro**

Prejean, Lisa .... (301) 733-5131
Food/Women's ED, Lifestyle ED, Theater/Music ED, Morning Herald, Hagerstown, MD

Prell, Marla .... (406) 232-0450
MAN ED, Miles City Star, Miles City, MT

Prendergast, Robin .... (561) 395-8300
ADV MGR-RT, News, Boca Raton, FL

Prendergrist, Pat .... (606) 236-2551
CIRC MGR
Advocate-Messenger, Danville, KY

Prendimano, Andrew .... (908) 922-6000
Design DIR, Asbury Park Press, Neptune, NJ

Prentice, Donna .... (770) 532-1234
CIRC DIR, Times, Gainesville, GA

Prentice, James .... (403) 562-8884
PUB, Crowsnest Pass Promoter, Blairmore, AB

Prentice, Sheryl .... (219) 925-2611
Women's ED, Evening Star, Auburn, IN

Prentiss, Tom .... (847) 427-4300
Weekend ED
Daily Herald, Arlington Heights, IL

Presas, Renet .... (512) 445-3500
ASST DIR-MKTG
Austin American-Statesman, Austin, TX

Presby, Daniel .... (207) 791-6650
PROD OPER Page Build SUPV-Nights
Portland Press Herald, Portland, ME

Prescott, Jean .... (601) 896-2100
Entertainment ED, Sun Herald, Biloxi, MS

Presler, A Frederick .... (216) 245-6901
CIRC DIR, Morning Journal, Lorain, OH

Presley, Fran .... (903) 794-3311
Religion ED
Texarkana Gazette, Texarkana, TX

Presley, Gary L .... (513) 248-8600
ED
Western Community Journal, Loveland, OH

Presley, Velma .... (423) 638-4181
Lifestyle ED
Greeneville Sun, Greeneville, TN

Pressler, Dan .... (765) 362-1200
BUS ED, Journal Review, Crawfordsville, IN

Pressley, Linda .... (360) 676-2600
ADV MGR-RT
Bellingham Herald, Bellingham, WA

Pressnall, Randy .... (208) 882-5561
ADV DIR-MKTG, ADV MGR-Sales, DP MGR
Moscow-Pullman Daily News, Moscow, ID

Presson, Tracy .... (704) 633-8950
EDU ED, Salisbury Post, Salisbury, NC

Prestel, Donald .... (317) 633-1240
PROD OPER DP MGR
Indianapolis Star/News, Indianapolis, IN

Prestera, Lauretta .... (212) 556-1234
CIRC VP-Home Delivery/Customer SRV
New York Times, New York, NY

Presto, Mike .... (212) 210-2100
Senior VP-MKTG
New York Daily News, New York, NY

Preston, Candy .... (615) 259-8000
BUS News ED, Tennessean, Nashville, TN

Preston, Dick .... (202) 334-6173
VP/Comm. DIR
Los Angeles Times-Washington Post News Service, Washington, DC

Preston, Jim .... (410) 332-6000
Photo DIR, Sun, Baltimore, MD

Preston, Kay .... (502) 628-5490
ED, Carlisle County News, Bardwell, KY

Preston, Russ .... (204) 345-8611
PUB, ED, Leader, Lac du Bonnet, MB

Prestopine, B .... (412) 758-5573
CIRC ASST MGR
Ellwood City Ledger, Ellwood City, PA

Pretorius, Richard .... (202) 408-2721
Night ED, Scripps-McClatchy Western Services, Washington, DC

Preuss III, L M (Buddy) .... (409) 542-2222
PUB, ED
Giddings Times & News, Giddings, TX

Preuss, Sam .... (409) 567-3286
PUB, ED, Burleson County Citizen Tribune, Caldwell, TX

Prevento, Kay .... (304) 436-3144
CIRC MGR, Welch Daily News, Welch, WV

Previte, Mike .... (210) 896-7000
Sports ED, Kerrville Daily Times, Kerrville, TX

Previtire, Chuck .... (818) 962-8811
PROD MGR
San Gabriel Valley Tribune, West Covina, CA
MediaNews Inc.

Previty, Joseph .... (508) 222-7000
PROD MGR-SYS
Sun Chronicle, Attleboro, MA

Prewitt, Bill .... (713) 220-7171
System ED, Houston Chronicle, Houston, TX

Pribble, Randall J .... (573) 547-4567
PUB, ED, Republic-Monitor, Perryville, MO

Pricco, Ernie .... (415) 777-5700
ADV MGR-NTL Sales, San Francisco Newspaper Agency, San Francisco, CA

Price, Angie .... (410) 643-7770
ED, Kent Island Bay Times Extra, Stephensville, MD

Price, Bill .... (908) 722-8800
Sports ED, Courier-News, Bridgewater, NJ

Price, Brenda .... (704) 289-1541
PROD ASST MGR-COMP
Enquirer-Journal, Monroe, NC

Price, Charlie .... (704) 484-7000
ADV DIR, Shelby Star, Shelby, NC

Price, Chris .... (617) 254-0334
ED
Allston-Brighton Citizen Journal, Boston, MA

Price, David .... (520) 474-5251
PUB, Payson Roundup, Payson, AZ

Price, David .... (216) 245-6901
City ED, Morning Journal, Lorain, OH

Price, David E .... (415) 327-6397
Chief Trustee, EX ED
Palo Alto Daily News, Palo Alto, CA

Price, Debra Z .... (803) 648-2311
ADV MGR-NTL/RT/Co-op
Aiken Standard, Aiken, SC

Price, Donna .... (308) 762-3060
MAN ED, Books ED, EPE, Features ED
Alliance Times-Herald, Alliance, NE

Price, Elton .... (719) 634-1593
ED, Space Observer, Colorado Springs, CO

Price, Eugene .... (919) 778-2211
VP, Aviation/Books ED, EPE
Goldsboro News-Argus, Goldsboro, NC

Price, G Jefferson .... (410) 332-6000
Foreign ED, Sun, Baltimore, MD

Price, Hollis .... (713) 220-7171
CIRC DIR, Houston Chronicle, Houston, TX

Price, Hugh .... (202) 334-6000
PROD MGR-Planning
Washington Post, Washington, DC

Price, J Michael .... (915) 546-6100
ADV DIR, El Paso Times, El Paso, TX

Price, Jack .... (403) 328-4411
PROD FRM-COMP Room
Lethbridge Herald, Lethbridge, AB

Price, Jean .... (918) 696-2228
GM, MAN ED
Stilwell Democrat Journal, Stilwell, OK

Price, Jeffrey .... (215) 854-2000
ASST MAN ED
Philadelphia Inquirer, Philadelphia, PA

Price, Jerry .... (407) 420-5000
CIRC MGR-OPER
Orlando Sentinel, Orlando, FL

Price, Julian .... (407) 242-3500
ADV MGR-RT, Florida Today, Melbourne, FL

Price, Kim N .... (205) 669-3131
PUB, ED
Shelby County Reporter, Columbiana, AL

Price, Mary .... (908) 246-5500
ASST Features ED
Home News & Tribune, East Brunswick, NJ

Price, Michael D .... (817) 390-7400
VP/Chief INFO SYS Officer, VP-INFO SRV
Fort Worth Star-Telegram, Fort Worth, TX

Price, Michael H .... (817) 390-7400
Films ED
Fort Worth Star-Telegram, Fort Worth, TX

Price, Niki .... (520) 474-5251
ED, Payson Roundup, Payson, AZ

Price, Peggy .... (618) 463-2500
ADV MGR-CLASS, Telegraph, Alton, IL

Price, Ray .... (618) 945-2111
ED, Bridgeport Leader-Times, Bridgeport, IL

Price, Rich .... (712) 343-2154
MAN ED, Avoca Journal-Herald, Avoca, IA

Price, Rob .... (607) 324-1425
Sunday ED, Evening Tribune, Hornell, NY

Price, Roger .... (907) 456-6661
Online Contact
Fairbanks Daily News-Miner, Fairbanks, AK

Price, Thomas I .... (540) 374-5000
Photo DEPT MGR
Free Lance-Star, Fredericksburg, VA

Price, Tunney .... (308) 995-4441
ED, SCI ED
Holdrege Daily Citizen, Holdrege, NE

Prichard, Harvey .... (423) 928-4151
ASSOC PUB, ADV DIR
Elizabethton Star, Elizabethton, TN

Prichard, Kerry .... (501) 785-7700
Farm/Agriculture ED, Health/Medical ED
Southwest Times Record, Fort Smith, AR

Prichard, Phil .... (319) 629-5207
PUB, Reporter, Lone Tree, IA

Prickett, Jerry .... (817) 665-5511
MAN ED
Gainesville Daily Register, Gainesville, TX

Priddy, Tommy .... (901) 642-1162
Sports ED, Paris Post-Intelligencer, Paris, TN

Pride, Ellen .... (812) 254-0480
Librarian
Washington Times-Herald, Washington, IN

Pride, Linwood .... (912) 236-9511
CIRC DIR
Savannah Morning News, Savannah, GA

Pride, Michael .... (603) 224-5301
ED, Concord Monitor, Concord, NH

Pride Jr, R W .... (334) 376-2325
PUB, ED, Butler County News, Georgiana, AL

Pridgen, Denise .... (803) 317-6397
EDU ED
Florence Morning News, Florence, SC

Pridham, Karen .... (519) 376-2250
News ED, Sports ED
Sun Times, Owen Sound, ON

Priest, Ellen C .... (803) 648-2311
BM, Aiken Standard, Aiken, SC

Priest, Lisa .... (416) 367-2000
Health Writer, Toronto Star, Toronto, ON

Priester, Brian .... (605) 331-2200
DIR-MKTG Development
Argus Leader, Sioux Falls, SD

Priestman, Gordon .... (604) 832-2131
ED
Shuswap Market News, Salmon Arm, BC

Prieto, Joey .... (505) 546-2611
CIRC DIR, Deming Headlight, Deming, NM

Priewe, Rob .... (541) 753-2641
City ED-Night
Corvallis Gazette-Times, Corvallis, OR

Prillhart, Ken .... (601) 736-2611
PUB, ED, Columbian-Progress, Columbia, MS

Prim, Eugene .... (218) 483-3306
PUB, Hawley Herald, Hawley, MN

Prim, Marilyn .... (515) 432-1234
Bookkeeper
Boone News-Republican, Boone, IA

Primmer, John .... (802) 748-8121
Clerk, Caledonian-Record, St. Johnsbury, VT

Prince, Carolyn .... (219) 235-6161
PROD MGR-MR
South Bend Tribune, South Bend, IN

Prince, Ed .... (908) 349-3000
Automotive ED, BUS/FIN ED
Ocean County Observer, Toms River, NJ

Prince, James .... (504) 383-1111
CIRC MGR, Advocate, Baton Rouge, LA

Prince III, James E .... (601) 853-4222
PUB, ED
Madison County Journal, Ridgeland, MS

Prince, Lisette .... (401) 847-7766
PUB, Newport This Week, Newport, RI

Prince, Lucille .... (205) 766-3434
Religion ED, Times Daily, Florence, AL

Prince, Ron .... (864) 427-1234
ADV DIR, MGR-MKTG/PROM
Union Daily Times, Union, SC

Prince, Ronald H .... (601) 837-8111
PUB, ED, Southern Sentinel, Ripley, MS

Prince, Sandra .... (704) 692-0505
DP MGR, PROD MGR-SYS/DP
Times-News, Hendersonville, NC

Prindable, Dennis .... (314) 340-8000
PROD ASST MGR-Northwest Plant
St. Louis Post-Dispatch, St. Louis, MO

Prins, Ron .... (613) 962-9171
CIRC MGR, Intelligencer, Belleville, ON

Prins, Todd .... (515) 232-2160
DP MGR, Daily Tribune, Ames, IA

Prinsen, Steven .... (320) 398-5000
PUB, Tri-County News, Kimball, MN

Prinsky, Robert .... (212) 416-2414
MAN ED, Dow Jones Financial News Services, New York, NY

Printing, Heritage .... (502) 223-1736
Owner
Community Press Service, Frankfort, KY

Prior, Kevin .... (517) 835-7171
ADV MGR-New Projects Development
Midland Daily News, Midland, MI

Prior, Richard .... (540) 574-6200
EDU ED
Daily News-Record, Harrisonburg, VA

Prisco, Edward K .... (210) 225-7411
VP-Advertising/MKTG, Senior VP-Sales & MKTG
San Antonio Express-News, San Antonio, TX

Prisendorf, Anthony .... (413) 528-5380
PUB, Berkshire Record, Great Barrington, MA

Prisendorf, Donna .... (413) 528-5380
ED, Berkshire Record, Great Barrington, MA

Pristawa, Walter .... (401) 762-3000
PROD FRM-COMP, Call, Woonsocket, RI

Pritchard, Catherine .... (910) 323-4848
BUS ED
Fayetteville Observer-Times, Fayetteville, NC

Pritchard, Dean .... (204) 734-3858
ED, Star & Times, Swan River, MB

Pritchard, Joann .... (817) 683-4021
ED, Bridgeport Index, Bridgeport, TX

Pritchard, Patty .... (304) 824-5101
GM, Lincoln Journal, Hamlin, WV

Pritchard, William .... (301) 662-1177
EDL/Op-Ed Pages
Frederick Post/The News, Frederick, MD

Pritchartt, Van .... (901) 853-2241
PUB, ED, Collierville Herald, Collierville, TN

Pritchett, Cyndi .... (502) 864-3891
ED
Cumberland County News, Burkesville, KY

Pritchett, John W .... (707) 464-2141
MAN ED, Triplicate, Crescent City, CA

Pritchett, Kimberly Cassel .... (912) 923-6432
Health/Medical Writer, NTL Writer, Political/Government Writer, Religion Writer
Daily Sun, Warner Robins, GA

Pritchett, Leigh .... (205) 549-2000
Amusements ED, Films/Theater ED, Music ED, Radio/Television ED
Gadsden Times, Gadsden, AL

Pritchett, Lloyd .... (360) 377-3711
Military Writer, Sun, Bremerton, WA

Pritchett, Vanessa .... (318) 828-3706
MAN ED
Franklin Banner-Tribune, Franklin, LA

Pritt, Pamela E .... (304) 799-4973
MAN ED, Pocahontas Times, Marlinton, WV

Pritts, Ronald .... (814) 445-9621
Sports ED, Daily American, Somerset, PA

Privett, Tom .... (904) 599-2100
VP-MKTG, ADV VP-MKTG
Tallahassee Democrat, Tallahassee, FL

Privette, Annette .... (704) 664-5554
MAN ED
Mooresville Tribune, Mooresville, NC

Privette, Barbara .... (803) 775-6331
MGR-CR, Item, Sumter, SC

Probst, Joyce .... (217) 857-3116
GM, MAN ED, Teutopolis Press-Dieterich Special Gazette, Teutopolis, IL

Prochaska, Dick .... (614) 654-1321
Photo ED
Lancaster Eagle-Gazette, Lancaster, OH

Procopio, David .... (617) 284-2400
ED, Revere Journal, Revere, MA

Proctor, Colleen .... (860) 442-2200
PROD SUPV-MR, Day, New London, CT

Proctor, David .... (205) 396-5760
PUB, ED, Clay Times-Journal, Lineville, AL

Proctor, Glenn .... (201) 877-4141
ASST MAN ED, Star-Ledger, Newark, NJ

Proctor, Steve .... (410) 332-6000
ASST MAN ED-Features, Sun, Baltimore, MD

Prodan, John .... (403) 865-3115
PUB, Parklander, Hinton, AB

Proeber, David .... (309) 829-9411
Photo ED, Pantagraph, Bloomington, IL

Proebstle, Mike .... (619) 299-3131
CIRC DIR
San Diego Union-Tribune, San Diego, CA

Proffitt Jr, Waldo .... (941) 953-7755
ED, Sarasota Herald-Tribune, Sarasota, FL

Profit, Carrie .... (615) 552-1808
ADV MGR-CLASS/Consumer
Leaf-Chronicle, Clarksville, TN

Prohaska, Louis .... (402) 296-2141
PUB, Plattsmouth Journal, Plattsmouth, NE

Proietti, Matt .... (909) 336-3555
ED, Mountain News & Mountaineer, Lake Arrowhead, CA

Pronko, Matthew J .... (716) 849-3434
ADV MGR-NTL, Buffalo News, Buffalo, NY

Pronovost, Jacques .... (819) 564-5450
ED, EPE, Photo DEPT MGR
La Tribune, Sherbrooke, QC

Pronovost, Marc .... (819) 376-2501
PROD MGR
Le Nouvelliste, Trois-Rivieres, QC

Pronovost, Paul .... (508) 668-0243
ED, Walpole Times, Walpole, MA

Prop, Lyn .... (403) 429-5400
ADV MGR-Services
Edmonton Journal, Edmonton, AB

Propernick, Ron .... (310) 540-5511
PROD SUPV-Camera Platemaking
Daily Breeze, Torrance, CA

Propp, Jon .... (218) 741-5544
MGR-OPER, Mesabi Daily News, Virginia, MN

Propp, Sheila .... (334) 947-7318
MAN ED, Independent, Robertsdale, AL

Proselandis, Gerald .... (604) 732-2111
BUS ED, Vancouver Sun, Vancouver, BC

Prosinski, Steve .... (619) 299-3131
Senior ED-BUS & Sports
San Diego Union-Tribune, San Diego, CA

Prosser, Iona .... (419) 468-1117
ADV MGR-NTL, Galion Inquirer, Galion, OH

Proulx, John .... (603) 752-1200
MAN ED, Berlin Reporter, Berlin, NH

Proulx, Roger .... (603) 224-5301
ADV DIR, Concord Monitor, Concord, NH

Prouty, Judy .... (213) 237-5000
Style/Fashion ED
Los Angeles Times, Los Angeles, CA

Provan, Sandra .... (219) 362-2161
Features ED, Films/Theater ED, Food/Home Furnishings ED, Teen-Age/Youth ED
La Porte Herald-Argus, La Porte, IN

Provano, Mark .... (502) 582-4011
Regional ED, Courier-Journal, Louisville, KY

Provant, Kelly .... (208) 377-6200
MGR-CR, Idaho Statesman, Boise, ID

Provencal, Randy .... (403) 743-8186
City ED, Today, Fort McMurray, AB

Provence, Van .... (501) 523-5855
Sports ED
Newport Daily Independent, Newport, AR

Pro Who's Where-186

Provencher, Norman (613) 829-9100
Music/Dance ED, Ottawa Citizen, Ottawa, ON
Provencher, Normand (418) 686-3233
Films/Theater ED, Le Soleil, Quebec, QC
Provencher, Ron (708) 846-3188
ED, Patriot Citizen, Buena Vista, GA
Provenza, Nick (206) 464-2111
ASST Local ED, Seattle Times, Seattle, WA
Provine, Joyce (601) 226-4321
DP MGR, Daily Sentinel-Star, Grenada, MS
Provost, Christine (504) 384-8370
Photo ED, Daily Review, Morgan City, LA
Provost, Robert (518) 454-5694
DIR-MKTG, Times Union, Albany, NY
Provost, Roger (817) 390-7400
CONT, Star-Telegram, Fort Worth, TX
Provost, Steve (209) 734-5821
News ED, Visalia Times-Delta, Visalia, CA
Provst, Mike (512) 729-9900
PUB, Rockport Pilot, Rockport, TX
Pruden, Jennifer (517) 752-7171
Automotive ED, BUS/FIN ED, RE ED
Saginaw News, Saginaw, MI
Pruden, Wesley (202) 636-3000
EIC, Washington Times, Washington, DC
Prue, Lisa (402) 444-1000
Youth ED, Omaha World-Herald, Omaha, NE
Prufer, Mona (803) 626-8555
Features ED, Sun News, Myrtle Beach, SC
Prugh, Jeff (415) 883-8600
EPE, Marin Independent Journal, Novato, CA
Pruitt, Gary B (916) 321-1855
PRES/CEO
McClatchy Newspapers, Sacramento, CA
Pruitt, Phil (703) 276-5800
Regional ED/East
Gannett News Service, Arlington, VA
Prusi, Renee (906) 228-2500
Lifestyle ED, Mining Journal, Marquette, MI
Prusia, Roxanne (602) 458-3340
PUB, Huachuca Scout, Sierra Vista, AZ
Prutsok, Andy (804) 458-8511
PUB, News, Hopewell, VA
Pryde, Jo-Anne (818) 713-3000
ADV MGR-NTL
Daily News, Woodland Hills, CA
Prye, John (540) 949-8213
PROD MGR-PRESS
News Virginian, Waynesboro, VA
Pryke, Raymond (619) 247-6700
PUB, Apple Valley News, Apple Valley, CA
Pryor, Bruce (415) 588-5990
ASSOC ED, Yossarian Universal News Service, Millbrae, CA
Pryor, Cheryl (301) 662-1177
PA, Frederick Post/The News, Frederick, MD
Pryor, Gerald W (912) 423-9331
PUB, ED, Herald-Leader, Fitzgerald, GA
Pryor, Gibson (706) 682-3346
GM, Bayonet, Columbus, GA
Pryor, Patty (816) 645-2217
ED, Braymer Bee, Braymer, MO
Pryor, Renita (703) 878-8000
PROD MGR, Potomac News, Woodbridge, VA
Pryor, Travis (303) 776-2244
News ED, Daily Times-Call, Longmont, CO
Przybylek, Francis X (410) 332-6000
PROD MGR-Pre Press OPER
Sun, Baltimore, MD
Przybys, John (702) 383-0211
Religion ED
Las Vegas Review-Journal, Las Vegas, NV
Przystas, Ronald A (517) 426-9411
PUB, ED
Gladwin County Record, Gladwin, MI
Ptacin, Gregory (614) 654-1321
PUB/GM
Lancaster Eagle-Gazette, Lancaster, OH
Ptak, Kathy (602) 977-8351
PROD MGR-COMP
Daily News-Sun, Sun City, AZ
Ptolemy, Pat (719) 384-8121
GM, Arkansas Valley Journal, La Junta, CO
Pucci, Carol (206) 464-2111
ASST BUS ED, Seattle Times, Seattle, WA
Puchalski, R Vincent (717) 348-9100
DIR-MKTG/PROM
Tribune & The Scranton Times, Scranton, PA
Puchalski, Renee (717) 348-9100
ADV MGR-NTL
Tribune & The Scranton Times, Scranton, PA
Puchek, Joe (219) 933-3200
MAN ED-Westlake, Times, Munster, IN
Pucin, Diane (215) 854-2000
COL-Sports
Philadelphia Inquirer, Philadelphia, PA
Pucket, Frank (915) 676-6765
PUB, Dyess Peacemaker, Abilene, TX
Pucket, Susan (404) 526-5151
Food ED
Atlanta Journal-Constitution, Atlanta, GA
Puckett, Ann (501) 338-9181
ADV MGR, Daily World, Helena, AR
Puckett, Danny (816) 562-2424
PROD MGR
Maryville Daily Forum, Maryville, MO
Puckett, DuAnne (502) 633-2526
ED, Sentinel-News, Shelbyville, KY
Puckett Jr, Frank (210) 829-9000
VP, Harte-Hanks Communications Inc., San Antonio, TX
Puckett, Jeffrey (502) 582-4011
Music ED, Courier-Journal, Louisville, KY
Puckett, R G (919) 847-2127
ED, Biblical Recorder, Raleigh, NC
Puente, Dr Jose Enrique (305) 530-8787
MAN ED, El Nuevo Patria, Miami, FL
Puerner, John P (312) 222-3237
PRES/PUB/CEO-Sentinel Communications Co., Tribune Co., Chicago, IL
Pufahl, Ron (509) 765-4561
CIRC MGR
Columbia Basin Herald, Moses Lake, WA
Puffer, Ed (508) 922-1234
City ED, Gloucester Times, Beverly, MA
Puffer, Evelyn (612) 689-1981
ED, Isanti County News, Cambridge, MN
Pugh, Christy (540) 468-2147
PUB, ED, Recorder, Monterey, VA
Pugh, Ken (919) 492-4001
CIRC MGR
Henderson Daily Dispatch, Henderson, NC
Pugh, Odessa (407) 322-2611
BM, Sanford Herald, Sanford, FL
Pugh, Roger (405) 373-1616
PUB, ED, Oklahoma City Northwest News, Piedmont, OK
Pugsley, Crystal (605) 352-6401
Regional ED, Huron Plainsman, Huron, SD
Puhalla, Beverly J (402) 852-2575
PUB, ED
Pawnee Republican, Pawnee City, NE
Puhalla, Ronald J (402) 852-2575
PUB, Pawnee Republican, Pawnee City, NE
Puig, Claudia (213) 237-5000
Movie Industry Writer
Los Angeles Times, Los Angeles, CA
Pujol Jr, Maurice (904) 638-0212
PUB, ED
Washington County News, Chipley, FL
Pujol, Moe (334) 684-2280
PUB, Geneva County Reaper, Geneva, AL
Pukanecz, Charles S (609) 396-2200
CORP EDL DIR
Journal Register Co., Trenton, NJ
Pulcrano, Dan (408) 298-8000
ED, Metro, San Jose, CA
Pulfer, Bob (416) 947-2222
PROD SUPV-PR, Toronto Sun, Toronto, ON
Pulitzer, Michael E (314) 340-8402
COB/PRES/CEO
Pulitzer Publishing Co., St. Louis, MO
Pullano, Kathy (616) 473-5421
ED, Journal Era, Berrien Springs, MI
Pullen, Doug (810) 766-6100
Music ED, Flint Journal, Flint, MI
Pullen, Ken (519) 822-4310
PROD FRM-COMP
Daily Mercury, Guelph, ON
Pulley, Paula (804) 649-6000
ADTX MKTG
Richmond Times-Dispatch, Richmond, VA
Pulliam, Eugene S (317) 231-9200
EVP
Central Newspapers Inc., Indianapolis, IN
Pulliam, John (309) 343-7181
City/MET ED, Register-Mail, Galesburg, IL
Pulliam, Myrta (317) 633-1240
DIR-Electronic News/INFO
Indianapolis Star/News, Indianapolis, IN
Pulliam, Patricia (616) 245-8737
PUB, ED
Grand Rapids Times, Grand Rapids, MI
Pulliam, Russel B (317) 633-1240
News ED, EPE
Indianapolis Star/News, Indianapolis, IN
Pulliam, Yergan (616) 245-8737
MAN ED
Grand Rapids Times, Grand Rapids, MI
Pullins, Chuck (501) 425-6301
PUB, ADV MGR
Daily News, Mountain Home, AR
Pulse, Sheryn (307) 742-2176
ADV DIR
Laramie Daily Boomerang, Laramie, WY
Pulson, Amy (405) 256-2200
ADV DIR, Woodward News, Woodward, OK
Pumarlo, Jim (612) 388-8235
ED, Arts/Entertainment ED, Automotive ED, BUS/FIN ED, EPE, EDU/School ED, Farm/RE ED, Fashion ED, Food/Home ED, Picture ED
Republican Eagle, Red Wing, MN
Pummer, C (410) 752-3849
MAN ED, Daily Record, Baltimore, MD
Pummill, Bill (937) 335-5634
PROD MGR-PR, Troy Daily News/Miami Valley Sunday News, Troy, OH
Punneo, Jackie (423) 756-6900
Librarian, Free Press, Chattanooga, TN
Punzel, Dennis (608) 252-6400
BUS ED, Consumer Interest ED, RE ED
Capital Times, Madison, WI
Pupillo, Eric (219) 722-5000
Sports ED, Pharos-Tribune, Logansport, IN
Puppel, Doug (702) 383-0211
BUS ED
Las Vegas Review-Journal, Las Vegas, NV
Puravs, John A (517) 752-7171
EPE, Saginaw News, Saginaw, MI
Purcel, Robert (610) 258-7171
Circulation SYS MGR
Express-Times, Easton, PA
Purcell, Darryle (520) 763-2505
MAN ED, EPE
Mohave Valley Daily News, Bullhead City, AZ
Purcell, Pam (706) 857-5433
ED, Chattooga Press, Summerville, GA
Purcell, Patrick J (617) 426-3000
Owner/PUB, Boston Herald, Boston, MA
Purcell, Rick M (616) 429-2400
ADV MGR-RT
Herald-Palladium, St. Joseph, MI
Purcell, William (704) 437-2161
Religion ED, News Herald, Morganton, NC
Purcell-Guerra, Beverly (210) 225-7411
Images ED
San Antonio Express-News, San Antonio, TX
Purdom, David (561) 820-4100
CONT
Palm Beach Post, West Palm Beach, FL
Purdon, Jim (912) 764-9031
CIRC MGR
Statesboro Herald, Statesboro, GA
Purdue, Lars (812) 254-0480
PUB/GM
Washington Times-Herald, Washington, IN
Purdy, Jill (704) 377-6221
ED, Mecklenburg Times, Charlotte, NC
Purdy, Mark (408) 920-5000
Sports COL
San Jose Mercury News, San Jose, CA
Purdy, Martha (815) 937-3300
Food ED, Daily Journal, Kankakee, IL
Puri, Promod (604) 876-9300
PUB, Link, Vancouver, BC
Puri, Shamlal (0171) 411-3111
MAN ED, Newslink Africa Ltd., London,
Purifoy, Cindy (501) 836-8192
CIRC MGR, Camden News, Camden, AR
Purin, John (801) 625-4200
Online MGR, Standard-Examiner, Ogden, UT
Purnell, Ross (403) 562-8884
ED, Crowsnest Pass Promoter, Blairmore, AB
Pursell, Elaine (573) 624-4545
ADV MGR, Daily Statesman, Dexter, MO
Pursell, Linda (502) 582-4011
VP-Market Development, DIR-Market Development, Courier-Journal, Louisville, KY
Purser, Thomas H (912) 375-4225
PUB, ED
Jeff Davis County Ledger, Hazlehurst, GA
Purvas, Grace (313) 994-6989
Librarian, Ann Arbor News, Ann Arbor, MI
Purves, J S (902) 426-2811
MAN ED, Chronicle-Herald, Halifax, NS
Purvis, Cal (803) 577-7111
MGR-CR, Post and Courier, Charleston, SC
Purvis, Kathi (704) 358-5000
Food ED, Charlotte Observer, Charlotte, NC
Puryear, Jack (512) 445-3500
ADV MGR-NTL
Austin American-Statesman, Austin, TX
Puskar, Susan (412) 263-1100
ASST MAN ED-Features
Pittsburgh Post-Gazette, Pittsburgh, PA
Pustaver, Jennifer (540) 885-7281
CONT, Daily News Leader, Staunton, VA
Puterbaugh, Jay (317) 675-2115
ADV MGR-RT
Tipton County Tribune, Tipton, IN
Putka, Gary (212) 416-2000
BU Chief-Boston
Wall Street Journal, New York, NY
Putnam, C J (307) 634-3361
ED-Features
Wyoming Tribune-Eagle, Cheyenne, WY
Putnam, Judy (305) 674-9746
Travel
International News Agency, Miami Beach, FL
Putnicki, Scott (619) 745-6611
ADV DIR
North County Times, Escondido, CA
Putt, Judy (601) 842-2611
Radio/Television ED, Northeast Mississippi Daily Journal, Tupelo, MS
Putzer Jr, Anton (414) 235-7700
PROD MGR
Oshkosh Northwestern, Oshkosh, WI
Pye, Douglas (864) 582-4511
PROD MGR-Pre Press
Herald-Journal, Spartanburg, SC
Pye, Jerry (816) 562-2424
PUB, Maryville Daily Forum, Maryville, MO
Pyette, Lester (416) 947-2222
PUB & CEO-Calgary Sun/VP-Western Pub
Sun Media Corp., Toronto, ON
Pyke, Bonnie Ewen (519) 822-4310
Assignment ED-News
Daily Mercury, Guelph, ON
Pylant, Sue (615) 684-1200
ADV MGR-CLASS
Shelbyville Times-Gazette, Shelbyville, TN
Pyle, Amy (213) 237-5000
EDU Writer (K-12)
Los Angeles Times, Los Angeles, CA
Pyle, George (913) 823-6363
SEC/TREAS, EPE, Salina Journal, Salina, KS
Pyle, Nancy (941) 382-1164
ED, Highlands Today, Sebring, FL
Pyle, Natalie (606) 528-2464
Accountant, PA, DP MGR
Times-Tribune, Corbin, KY
Pyne, Derek (403) 723-3301
PUB, Edson Leader, Edson, AB
Pyne, Mark (707) 425-4646
Photo DEPT MGR
Daily Republic, Fairfield, CA
Pynn, Manning (407) 420-5000
EPE, Orlando Sentinel, Orlando, FL
Pyykola, Dean (218) 723-5281
PROD MGR-SYS & Services
Duluth News-Tribune, Duluth, MN

Q

Quaal, Debra (612) 333-4244
PUB
Finance and Commerce, Minneapolis, MN
Quackenbush, Rich (713) 220-7171
Weekend ED
Houston Chronicle, Houston, TX
Quaid, Juanita (504) 473-3101
MAN ED
Donaldsonville Chief, Donaldsonville, LA
Quale, Alan (415) 348-4321
News ED
San Mateo County Times, San Mateo, CA
Qualls, Bob R (501) 425-3133
ED, Baxter Bulletin, Mountain Home, AR
Qualls, Chris (501) 862-6611
News ED
El Dorado News-Times, El Dorado, AR
Qualls, Lori (517) 835-7171
Entertainment/Amusements ED, Fashion/Style ED, Living/Lifestyle ED, Women's ED
Midland Daily News, Midland, MI
Quan, Millie A (206) 464-2111
ASST MAN ED-ADM
Seattle Times, Seattle, WA
Quarles, Billy (803) 775-6331
BUS ED, News ED, Item, Sumter, SC
Quarles III, Orage (209) 578-2000
PUB, Modesto Bee, Modesto, CA
Quast, Lanae (208) 882-5561
PROD FRM-Computers
Moscow-Pullman Daily News, Moscow, ID
Quattlebaum, Howard (334) 393-2969
PUB, Southeast Sun, Enterprise, AL
Quattro, James (607) 756-5665
CIRC MGR, Cortland Standard, Cortland, NY
Quayle, Corinne (219) 356-6700
SEC/TREAS
Huntington Herald-Press, Huntington, IN
Quayle, James C (219) 356-6700
PRES/PUB
Huntington Herald-Press, Huntington, IN
Quayle, Michael E (812) 886-9955
PUB
Vincennes Sun-Commercial, Vincennes, IN
Queen, Alice (770) 483-7108
ED, Rockdale Citizen, Conyers, GA
Queen, Cynthia (619) 459-4201
ED, La Jolla Light, La Jolla, CA
Queen, Linda (614) 384-6102
GM, Wellston Telegram, Wellston, OH
Queen, Mike (304) 592-1030
PUB, ED, Shinnston News & Harrison County Journal, Shinnston, WV
Quellette, Marc (514) 667-4360
GM, Contact Laval, Laval Des Rapides, QC
Querin-Andre, Joanne (360) 785-0345
PUB, Ledger, Winlock, WA
Query, Howard (515) 421-0500
PUB, Globe-Gazette, Mason City, IA
Questel, Brian (330) 264-1125
Sports ED, Daily Record, Wooster, OH
Quick, Bob (505) 983-3303
BUS/FIN ED
Santa Fe New Mexican, Santa Fe, NM
Quick, Nancy (518) 843-1100
News ED, Recorder, Amsterdam, NY
Quick, Nancy (715) 423-7200
Food ED, Living/Lifestyle ED, Religion ED
Daily Tribune, Wisconsin Rapids, WI
Quick, Shirley Ann (618) 245-6216
PUB, ED, Farina News, Farina, IL
Quick, Wade (501) 239-8562
Features ED
Paragould Daily Press, Paragould, AR

Copyright ©1997 by the Editor & Publisher Co.

187-Who's Where **Ram**

Quickel, Beth S .... (610) 371-5000
CIRC MGR-Database/MKTG
Reading Times/Eagle, Reading, PA
Quier, Myrtle B .... (610) 371-5000
BC, Reading Times/Eagle, Reading, PA
Quiggle, Lynn .... (916) 243-2424
DP MGR
Record Searchlight, Redding, CA
Quigley, David .... (403) 468-0100
City ED, Edmonton Sun, Edmonton, AB
Quigley, Linda .... (615) 259-8000
Books ED, Tennessean, Nashville, TN
Quigley, Mike .... (541) 885-4410
Sports ED
Herald and News, Klamath Falls, OR
Quigley, Paul .... (717) 253-3055
MAN ED, Wayne Independent, Honesdale, PA
Quigley, Peter .... (212) 450-7000
VP/DIR of ADV
Parade Publications Inc., New York, NY
Quigley, Stephen .... (617) 284-2400
GM, Revere Journal, Revere, MA
Quigley, Sue .... (352) 544-5200
Design ED, Hernando Today, Brooksville, FL
Quill, Greg .... (416) 367-2000
Radio/Television Writer
Toronto Star, Toronto, ON
Quillen, Terry .... (615) 259-8000
Op-Ed ED, Tennessean, Nashville, TN
Quillon, Robin L .... (540) 825-0771
PUB, PA
Culpeper Star-Exponent, Culpeper, VA
Quimby, Bonnie .... (715) 344-6100
ADV MGR-CLASS
Stevens Point Journal, Stevens Point, WI
Quimby, Kathy .... (412) 654-6651
EDU ED, New Castle News, New Castle, PA
Quimet, Polly .... (207) 784-5411
Television ED, Sun-Journal, Lewiston, ME
Quinelly, Lorie .... (918) 224-5185
News ED, Sapulpa Daily Herald, Sapulpa, OK
Quinlan, Tom E .... (847) 427-4300
Sports ED
Daily Herald, Arlington Heights, IL
Quinly, Pat .... (816) 385-3121
GM, ADV DIR, MGR-MKTG/PROM
Macon Chronicle-Herald, Macon, MO
Quinn, Carroll .... (412) 834-1151
CIRC DIR-Pittsburgh
Tribune-Review, Greensburg, PA
Quinn, Charles .... (912) 759-2413
ED, Lee County Ledger, Leesburg, GA
Quinn, Derryl .... (912) 759-2413
PUB, Lee County Ledger, Leesburg, GA
Quinn, Don .... (619) 337-3400
Films/Theater ED, Radio/Television ED, Wire ED, Imperial Valley Press, El Centro, CA
Quinn, Gary S .... (815) 232-1171
PUB, Journal-Standard, Freeport, IL
Quinn, Jerry .... (918) 756-3600
PUB, Okmulgee Daily Times, Okmulgee, OK
Quinn, Jerry .... (503) 399-6611
PROD DIR, Statesman Journal, Salem, OR
Quinn, John .... (908) 922-6000
MAN ED-Sports
Asbury Park Press, Neptune, NJ
Quinn, Kelly .... (401) 821-7400
ADV MGR
Kent County Daily Times, West Warwick, RI
Quinn, Martin .... (202) 334-6000
PROD SUPT-Engraving (VA)
Washington Post, Washington, DC
Quinn, Mary Alice .... (901) 529-2211
ASST MAN ED-Community Affairs
Commercial Appeal, Memphis, TN
Quinn, Michael .... (909) 684-1200
MGR-New Media/PE.net
Press-Enterprise, Riverside, CA
Quinn, Michael F .... (313) 222-6400
VP-OPER, Detroit Newspapers, Detroit, MI
Quinn, Mike .... (520) 453-4237
PRES, PUB, ED
Today's News-Herald, Lake Havasu City, AZ
Quinn, Roger .... (205) 549-2000
ADV DIR, Gadsden Times, Gadsden, AL
Quinn, Sara .... (316) 268-6000
Presentation ED, Wichita Eagle, Wichita, KS
Quinn, Tom .... (806) 273-5611
PUB, Borger News-Herald, Borger, TX
Quinn, Tomari .... (316) 275-8500
Society ED, Teen-Age/Youth ED, Women's ED
Garden City Telegram, Garden City, KS
Quinn, Valecia .... (614) 773-2111
CIRC DIR
Chillicothe Gazette, Chillicothe, OH
Quinnett, Jim .... (915) 673-4271
Cartoonist
Abilene Reporter-News, Abilene, TX
Quintana, Hugo .... (213) 622-8332
Entertainment ED
La Opinion, Los Angeles, CA
Quirindongo, Rafael .... (212) 930-8000
MGR-Technical Support
New York Post, New York, NY
Quirk, Susan .... (860) 241-6200
Creative DIR, Hartford Courant, Hartford, CT
Quirt, Aaron .... (218) 445-5779
ED, Verndale Sun, Verndale, MN
Quirt, Peter .... (320) 594-2911
PUB, Browerville Blade, Browerville, MN
Quirt, Theresa .... (320) 594-2911
ED, Browerville Blade, Browerville, MN
Quissell, Delores .... (507) 348-4176
GM, Jasper Journal, Jasper, MN
Quist, Rick .... (818) 713-3000
News ED
Los Angeles Daily News, Woodland Hills, CA

R

Raabe, Steve .... (303) 820-1010
RE Reporter, Denver Post, Denver, CO
Raasch, Janet .... (414) 938-5000
GM, Whitefish Bay Herald, New Berlin, WI
Rabe, Alma .... (219) 926-1131
CIRC MGR
Chesterton Tribune, Chesterton, IN
Raber, Martha .... (508) 586-7200
Films/Theater ED, Music ED, Radio/Television ED, Enterprise, Brockton, MA
Raber, Rick .... (302) 324-2500
BUS ED, News Journal, Wilmington, DE
Rabidoux, Michelle .... (517) 627-6085
ED, Independent, Grand Ledge, MI
Rabin, Katie .... (415) 777-2424
BUS ED
San Francisco Examiner, San Francisco, CA
Rabon, Linda .... (405) 326-8353
PUB, MAN ED
Choctaw County Times, Hugo, OK
Rabon, Neill .... (916) 662-5421
ADV DIR, Daily Democrat, Woodland, CA
Rabon, Terri .... (910) 888-3500
PROD MGR-Dispatch
High Point Enterprise, High Point, NC
Racette, Felix A .... (616) 657-3072
PUB, ED, Courier-Leader, Paw Paw, MI
Racette, Steven A .... (616) 657-3072
GM, Courier-Leader, Paw Paw, MI
Racher, Dave .... (215) 854-2000
Courts Reporter
Philadelphia Daily News, Philadelphia, PA
Racher, Randy .... (519) 344-3641
CR MGR/PA, Observer, Sarnia, ON
Rachey, Julian .... (204) 697-7000
Sports ED
Winnipeg Free Press, Winnipeg, MB
Rachlis, Eric .... (800) 536-8442
VP-Sales, Archive Photos, New York, NY
Rachlis, Mr Kit .... (213) 237-5000
Los Angeles Times Magazine Senior ED/So Socal ED
Los Angeles Times, Los Angeles, CA
Rachuba, Gary .... (601) 896-2100
PROD MGR-COMP, Sun Herald, Biloxi, MS
Racicot, Rita .... (613) 623-6571
ED, Arnprior Chronicle-Guide, Arnprior, ON
Racinowski, Janice .... (312) 842-5883
ED, Bridgeport News, Chicago, IL
Rackers, Tom .... (573) 636-3131
Sports ED, News Tribune, Jefferson City, MO
Rackley, Andy .... (910) 592-8137
Sports ED, Sunday ED
Sampson Independent, Clinton, NC
Radcliffe, Jim .... (310) 540-5511
Transportation ED
Daily Breeze, Torrance, CA
Radcliffe, Sandra .... (401) 277-7000
VP-FIN
Providence Journal-Bulletin, Providence, RI
Radde, T C .... (608) 269-3186
PUB, ED, Sparta Herald, Sparta, WI
Radel, Marie .... (317) 473-6641
ADV DIR, Peru Tribune, Peru, IN
Rademacher, Patricia M .... (406) 547-3831
PUB, Meagher County News, White Sulphur Springs, MT
Rademacher, Tom .... (616) 222-5400
COL, Grand Rapids Press, Grand Rapids, MI
Rademacher, Verle L .... (406) 547-3831
PUB, ED, Meagher County News, White Sulphur Springs, MT
Rademaekers, Ed .... (210) 225-7411
New Media MGR
San Antonio Express-News, San Antonio, TX
Rader, Bo .... (316) 268-6000
Photo ED, Wichita Eagle, Wichita, KS
Radford, Darrel K .... (317) 529-1111
MAN ED
New Castle Courier-Times, New Castle, IN
Radford, Debbie .... (803) 524-3183
Neighbors ED
Beaufort Gazette, Beaufort, SC
Radford, Don .... (204) 325-4772
ED, Winkler Times, Winkler, MB
Radford, Drema .... (304) 255-4400
BM, DP MGR
Beckley Register Herald, Beckley, WV
Radford, Larry .... (616) 781-3943
CIRC MGR, Marshall Chronicle, Marshall, MI
Radler, F David .... (416) 363-8721
PRES/CEO, Hollinger Inc., Toronto, ON
Radmacher, Dan .... (304) 348-5140
EPE, Charleston Gazette, Sunday Gazette-Mail, Charleston, WV
Radoff, Mike .... (417) 836-1100
CIRC MGR-Home Delivery
Springfield News-Leader, Springfield, MO
Raduechel, Ken .... (805) 650-2900
ADTX MGR
Ventura County Star, Ventura, CA
Rae, Cindy .... (904) 264-3200
CIRC MGR, Clay Today, Orange Park, FL
Rae, Richard P .... (508) 473-1111
ADV DIR/ASST PUB
Milford Daily News, Milford, MA
Rae, Richard T .... (770) 963-9205
PRES, PUB, Gwinnett Daily Post, Lawrenceville, GA, Gray Communications
Rae, Richard T .... (412) 523-6588
PUB, Community News, Irwin, PA
Raese, David A .... (304) 292-6301
PRES, PUB, Dominion Post, Morgantown, WV
Raese, John R .... (304) 292-6301
VP, Dominion Post, Morgantown, WV
Raese, Kathleen A .... (304) 292-6301
ASSOC PUB
Dominion Post, Morgantown, WV
Raeside, John .... (510) 540-7400
ED, East Bay Express, Berkeley, CA
Raess, John .... (408) 920-5000
Bay Area ED, Suburban ED
San Jose Mercury News, San Jose, CA
Raether, Helmut .... (212) 355-0318
Chief Correspondent
German Press Agency, New York, NY
Rafael, Lynne .... (201) 437-2460
ED, Bayonne Community News, Bayonne, NJ
Rafal, Alan .... (800) 223-2154
CIRC MGR-NTL Single Copy
Investor's Business Daily, Los Angeles, CA
Rafferty, Brian .... (757) 899-3551
ED, Sussex-Surry Dispatch, Wakefield, VA
Rafferty Jr, Raymond R .... (215) 557-2300
COB/PUB
Legal Intelligencer, Philadelphia, PA
Raffety, Michael .... (916) 622-1255
ED, Mountain Democrat, Placerville, CA
Rafter, Michael .... (508) 676-8211
CIRC DIR
Fall River Herald News, Fall River, MA
Raftis, Connie .... (352) 543-5701
GM, MAN ED
Cedar Key Beacon, Cedar Key, FL
Raftis, Mike .... (352) 543-5701
PUB, Cedar Key Beacon, Cedar Key, FL
Raftis, Patrick .... (519) 236-4312
GM, ED, Lakeshore Advance, Zurich, ON
Rafuse, Sgt Michelle .... (913) 762-5000
ED, Fort Riley Post, Junction City, KS
Ragan, Larry G .... (208) 344-2055
PUB, Boise Weekly, Boise, ID
Ragan, Ron .... (205) 532-4000
ADV MGR-Services
Huntsville Times, Huntsville, AL
Raggio, Maria Marta .... (56-2) 235-2902
ED
Europa Press News Service, Santiago, Chile
Ragin, Karen .... (317) 398-6631
ADV MGR-RT
Shelbyville News, Shelbyville, IN
Ragland, Janet .... (903) 882-3232
ED, Lindale News, Lindale, TX
Raglin, Rod .... (604) 327-0221
PUB, ED, East Side, Vancouver, BC
Rago, John .... (212) 779-9200
CONT, New York Law Journal, New York, NY
Ragovin, Helene .... (908) 329-0260
ED, Central Post, Dayton, NJ
Ragsdale, Betty .... (501) 887-2002
PUB, Nevada County Picayune, Prescott, AR
Ragsdale, John R .... (501) 887-2002
PUB, ED
Nevada County Picayune, Prescott, AR
Ragsdale, Shirley .... (317) 423-5511
EPE, Journal and Courier, Lafayette, IN
Ragusa, Carlo .... (504) 368-8900
PUB, ED
Daily Journal of Commerce, New Orleans, LA
Rahlf, Rona .... (406) 657-1200
ADV DIR
Montana Newspaper Group, Billings, MT
Rahme, Mike .... (401) 277-7000
CIRC MGR-OPER
Providence Journal-Bulletin, Providence, RI
Raia, James .... (916) 448-5122
Self-Syndicator
Raia, James, Sacramento, CA
Raihala, Nancy J .... (218) 476-2232
PUB, ED, Forum, Floodwood, MN
Rail, William J .... (901) 645-5346
PUB, Independent Appeal, Selmer, TN
Rainer, Dave .... (334) 433-1551
Outdoors ED
Mobile Press Register, Mobile, AL
Raines, Alice .... (501) 735-1010
MGR-Office, MGR-CR
Evening Times, West Memphis, AR
Raines, Elaine .... (520) 573-4220
Librarian, Arizona Daily Star, Tucson, AZ
Raines, Howell .... (212) 556-1234
EPE, New York Times, New York, NY
Raines, Jennie .... (304) 636-2121
ADV MGR-Production
Inter-Mountain, Elkins, WV
Raines, Jimmy .... (606) 432-0148
MAN ED
Appalachian News-Express, Pikeville, KY
Rainey, Jimmy .... (817) 627-5987
ED, Wise County Messenger, Decatur, TX
Rains, Ed .... (901) 523-1561
BM, Daily News, Memphis, TN
Rains Jr, Ellsworth .... (405) 765-3311
ASST to PUB, ADV DIR
Ponca City News, Ponca City, OK
Rains, John .... (910) 323-4848
News ED
Fayetteville Observer-Times, Fayetteville, NC
Rainsford, Bettis C .... (803) 279-1000
PUB, Post, North Augusta, SC
Rainsford, Joanne .... (803) 279-1000
GM, Post, North Augusta, SC
Rainwater, Joe .... (903) 935-7914
ADV DIR, News Messenger, Marshall, TX
Rainwater, Mark .... (318) 322-3161
ED, Ouachita Citizen, West Monroe, LA
Rainwater, Rex .... (205) 695-7029
PUB, Lamar Democrat, Vernon, AL
Raison, Barry .... (613) 342-4441
ASST City ED, Brockville Recorder and Times, Brockville, ON
Raison, Bob .... (209) 591-4632
PUB, ED, Dinuba Sentinel, Dinuba, CA
Raison, Diane .... (209) 591-4632
PUB, Dinuba Sentinel, Dinuba, CA
Raitano, Barbara A .... (412) 684-5200
PUB, Valley Independent, Monessen, PA
Rajala, Shirley .... (508) 586-7200
Religion ED, Enterprise, Brockton, MA
Raju, Gopal .... (212) 929-1727
PUB, ED, India Abroad, New York, NY
Rakes, Kenneth .... (540) 921-3434
PUB, Virginian Leader, Pearisburg, VA
Rakes, Rick .... (606) 329-1717
CONT, Daily Independent, Ashland, KY
Rakestraw, Regina .... (219) 235-6161
MGR-Human Resources
South Bend Tribune, South Bend, IN
Raksin, Alex .... (213) 237-5000
EDL Writer
Los Angeles Times, Los Angeles, CA
Raleigh, John .... (405) 772-3301
PROD MGR, PROD FRM-COMP
Weatherford Daily News, Weatherford, OK
Raleigh, Kathie .... (401) 762-3000
Fashion/Women's ED, Garden ED
Call, Woonsocket, RI
Ralls, Barbara .... (812) 332-4401
News ED, Herald-Times Inc, Bloomington, IN
Ralls, Bill .... (713) 220-7171
DIR-ADM SRV
Houston Chronicle, Houston, TX
Ralph, Marvin .... (216) 994-3241
PROD FRM-PR, Star-Beacon, Ashtabula, OH
Ralph, Msgr Thomas J .... (319) 588-0556
GM, MAN ED, Witness, Dubuque, IA
Ralph, William .... (212) 837-7000
Online MGR, Journal of Commerce & Commercial, New York, NY
Ralston, Rich .... (814) 623-1151
MAN ED, Bedford Gazette, Bedford, PA
Ramage, Trilla .... (215) 345-3000
Entertainment/Amusements ED
Intelligencer/Record, Doylestown, PA
Ramait, Philip .... (704) 322-4510
Sports ED, Hickory Daily Record, Hickory, NC
Rambo, Beverly .... (501) 382-4925
MAN ED, Dumas Clarion, Dumas, AR
Ramer, Nancy .... (717) 264-6161
CIRC DIR-Customer SRV
Public Opinion, Chambersburg, PA
Rames, Diane .... (408) 920-5000
ADV MGR-RT/Local Accounts
San Jose Mercury News, San Jose, CA
Ramey, John .... (573) 335-6611
News ED
Southeast Missourian, Cape Girardeau, MO
Ramey, Judi .... (713) 869-5434
Display ADV DIR
Daily Court Review, Houston, TX
Ramey, Michael .... (903) 757-3311
ED-Night/News
Longview News-Journal, Longview, TX

Copyright ©1997 by the Editor & Publisher Co.

Ram Who's Where-188

Rami, Debra (615) 526-9715
Women's ED, Herald-Citizen, Cookeville, TN

Ramie, Laurie (914) 887-5200
ED, Sullivan County Democrat, Callicoon, NY

Ramige, William C (320) 864-5518
PUB
McLeod County Chronicle, Glencoe, MN

Ramirez, Carlos D (212) 807-4600
PUB, El Diario La Prensa, New York, NY

Ramirez, Cindy (915) 546-6100
EDU ED, El Paso Times, El Paso, TX

Ramirez, Katia (213) 622-8332
Food ED, La Opinion, Los Angeles, CA

Ramirez, Mario (619) 428-2277
ED, Ahora Now, San Diego, CA

Ramirez, Michael (901) 529-2211
EDL Cartoonist
Commercial Appeal, Memphis, TN

Ramirez, Orlando (909) 684-1200
Food ED, Press-Enterprise, Riverside, CA

Ramirez, Ruben R (915) 546-6340
Photo ED, El Paso Herald-Post, El Paso, TX

Ramon, Joe (210) 225-7411
CIRC MGR-MR
San Antonio Express-News, San Antonio, TX

Ramos, Ana (210) 423-5511
DIR-MKTG
Valley Morning Star, Harlingen, TX

Ramos, Connie (707) 644-1141
Librarian, Vallejo Times-Herald, Vallejo, CA

Ramos, Debra (916) 795-4551
ED, Winters Express, Winters, CA

Ramos, George (210) 225-7411
CIRC MGR-PROM
San Antonio Express-News, San Antonio, TX

Ramos, Mary (214) 977-8222
ED-Texas Almanac
Dallas Morning News, Dallas, TX

Ramsay, Paul (902) 893-9405
ADV MGR, MGR-MKTG/PROM
Daily News, Truro, NS

Ramsdall, Tammy (601) 961-7000
MET ED, Clarion-Ledger, Jackson, MS

Ramsdell, Becky (520) 774-4545
Books Review ED, Entertainment/Amusements ED, Music ED
Arizona Daily Sun, Flagstaff, AZ

Ramsey, Charles (218) 741-5544
Regional ED
Mesabi Daily News, Virginia, MN

Ramsey, Kent (913) 242-9200
GM, Ottawa Times, Ottawa, KS

Ramsey, Lynn (903) 893-8181
Sports ED, Herald Democrat, Sherman, TX

Ramsey, Marshall (601) 961-7000
EDL Cartoonist, Clarion-Ledger, Jackson, MS

Ramsey, Mathew (317) 423-5511
CONT, Journal and Courier, Lafayette, IN

Ramsey, Rebecca (520) 458-3340
PUB, Huachuca Scout, Sierra Vista, AZ

Ramsey, Stan (904) 663-2255
PUB, ED, Twin City News, Chattahoochee, FL

Ramsey, Wesley R (904) 227-1278
PUB, ED, Star, Port St. Joe, FL

Ramsey, William (360) 779-4464
ED, Kitsap County Herald, Poulsbo, WA

Ramstetter, Michele (716) 773-7676
ED, Island Dispatch, Grand Island, NY

Ranard, Chris (812) 829-3936
GM, Owen Leader, Spencer, IN

Rand, Ed (704) 333-1718
BUS MGR
Independent Tribune, Concord, NC

Rand, Michael (815) 562-2061
SEC, News Media Corp., Rochelle, IL

Rand, Mike (217) 935-3171
CONT, Clinton Daily Journal, Clinton, IL

Rand, Wes (860) 887-9211
Graphics ED, Online Contact
Norwich Bulletin, Norwich, CT

Randa, Larry (708) 242-1234
GM, Cicero-Berwyn-Stickney Forest View Life, Berwyn, IL

Randall, Carol (410) 332-6000
PA, Sun, Baltimore, MD

Randall, Christine (803) 577-7111
Amusements ED
Post and Courier, Charleston, SC

Randall, Colleen (801) 237-2188
Librarian, Deseret News, Salt Lake City, UT

Randall Esq, George E (301) 662-1177
VP, GEN Counsel, GM
Frederick Post/The News, Frederick, MD

Randall, Judy (718) 981-1234
Political ED
Staten Island Advance, Staten Island, NY

Randall, Ron (209) 634-9141
PROD SUPT, Turlock Journal, Turlock, CA

Randall-Grier, Carol (317) 633-1240
CIRC MGR-Customer SRV/Quality Assurance
Indianapolis Star/News, Indianapolis, IN

Randazzo, Gary (713) 220-7171
VP-Sales, Houston Chronicle, Houston, TX

Randle, Judy (918) 581-8300
Books ED, Tulsa World, Tulsa, OK

Randolph, Bill (606) 734-2726
PUB, ED
Harrodsburg Herald, Harrodsburg, KY

Randolph, Irving (215) 893-4050
ED, Philadelphia Tribune, Philadelphia, PA

Randolph, Lynn (805) 564-5200
ADV DIR-RT, Santa Barbara News-Press, Santa Barbara, CA

Randolph, Pat (704) 682-2120
GM, Times Journal, Burnsville, NC

Randolph, Victor (913) 877-3361
ADV MGR
Norton Daily Telegram, Norton, KS

Ranes, Doug (206) 464-2111
PROD MGR-Plant (Fairview)
Seattle Times, Seattle, WA

Raney, Jim (903) 893-8181
PROD MGR-COMP
Herald Democrat, Sherman, TX

Raney, Mark (505) 622-7710
CIRC MGR
Roswell Daily Record, Roswell, NM

Rang, Terry (717) 622-3456
News ED, Pottsville Republican & Evening Herald, Pottsville, PA

Ranga, Srinivas (212) 481-3110
MAN ED, News India-Times, New York, NY

Rank, Dave (414) 938-5000
ED, Wauwatosa News-Time, New Berlin, WI

Rankin, Don (217) 268-4959
PUB, ED, Arcola Record-Herald, Arcola, IL

Rankin, Doug (414) 922-4600
ADV CNR-NTL, Reporter, Fond du Lac, WI

Rankin, Jerry (209) 966-2500
MAN ED, Mountain Life, Mariposa, CA

Rankin, Jim (765) 362-1200
PROD MGR-COMP Room
Journal Review, Crawfordsville, IN

Rankin, John (713) 220-7171
PROD MGR-Page Assembly/Platemaking
Houston Chronicle, Houston, TX

Rankin, Nancy K (314) 340-8402
ASST SEC
Pulitzer Publishing Co., St. Louis, MO

Rankin, Robert (209) 582-0471
ADV DIR, Hanford Sentinel, Hanford, CA

Rankin, Terry (304) 292-6301
PROD FRM-Building & Maintenance
Dominion Post, Morgantown, WV

Rann, Carol (618) 273-3379
Office MGR
Eldorado Daily Journal, Eldorado, IL

Ranney, Cecil (907) 486-3227
ED, Kodiak Daily Mirror, Kodiak, AK

Ranney, William A (518) 792-9914
Regional Sales DIR
TV Data, Queensbury, NY

Rannochio, Susan (703) 276-3400
ADV DIR-CLASS, USA Today, Arlington, VA

Ransburg, Eleanor (318) 459-3200
ASST MAN ED, Times, Shreveport, LA

Ransdell, Ty (208) 733-0931
CIRC MGR, Times-News, Twin Falls, ID

Ranson, Pat (910) 727-7211
ADV MGR-CLASS
Winston-Salem Journal, Winston-Salem, NC

Ranson, Terry (304) 272-3433
MAN ED, Wayne County News, Wayne, WV

Ranten, Kari (360) 424-3251
Farm/Agriculture ED
Skagit Valley Herald, Mount Vernon, WA

Ranze, Tony (941) 687-7000
Photo ED, Ledger, Lakeland, FL

Ranzenberger, Mark (517) 835-7171
NTL Writer, Political/Government Writer, ADTX MGR
Midland Daily News, Midland, MI

Ranzer, Stephen N (803) 648-2311
ADV DIR, Aiken Standard, Aiken, SC

Raper, Dudley (501) 673-8533
PROD SUPT
Stuttgart Daily Leader, Stuttgart, AR

Rapier, Joe L (406) 822-3329
ED, Mineral Independent, Superior, MT

Rapinchuk, Bruce (204) 694-2022
Photo ED, Winnipeg Sun, Winnipeg, MB

Rapoport, Roger (510) 595-0595
Chairman, RDR Books, Oakland, CA

Raposa, Laura (617) 426-3000
The Inside Track COL
Boston Herald, Boston, MA

Raposo, Fernando (416) 868-6621
ED, Journal Acoriano, Toronto, ON

Rappaport, Louis (518) 374-4141
Wire ED, Daily Gazette, Schenectady, NY

Rappaport, Mike (909) 987-6397
COL, Inland Valley Daily Bulletin, Ontario, CA

Rapsavage, Doug (701) 843-7567
PUB, New Salem Journal, New Salem, ND

Rapsavage, Rocky (701) 843-7567
PUB, ED
New Salem Journal, New Salem, ND

Rapsis, Jeffrey A (603) 427-6500
GM, ED
Bedford-Merrimack Bulletin, Bedford, NH

Rardon, J R (907) 283-7551
Sports ED, Peninsula Clarion, Kenai, AK

Rasberry, Sherry (903) 657-2501
Accountant
Henderson Daily News, Henderson, TX

Rasche, Mike (812) 753-3553
ED
South Gibson Star Times, Fort Branch, IN

Raschke, Steve (616) 345-3511
CIRC MGR-Distribution
Kalamazoo Gazette, Kalamazoo, MI

Rascovar, Barry (410) 332-6000
EDL Page DIR, Sun, Baltimore, MD

Raskert, Gary (601) 896-2100
CIRC DIR, Sun Herald, Biloxi, MS

Rasmussen, Alan (414) 432-2941
VP-Publications
Green Bay News-Chronicle, Green Bay, WI

Rasmussen, Eric N (406) 323-1105
PUB, Roundup Record-Tribune/Winnett Times, Roundup, MT

Rasmussen, Jeannie (702) 788-6200
ASST Librarian
Reno Gazette-Journal, Reno, NV

Rasmussen, Jim (206) 872-6600
PROD MGR, South County Journal, Kent, WA

Rasmussen, Louise G (406) 323-1105
ED, Roundup Record-Tribune/Winnett Times, Roundup, MT

Rasmussen, Pat (913) 524-4200
PUB
Lincoln Sentinel-Republican, Lincoln, KS

Rasmussen, Patti (414) 432-2941
Weekend ED
Green Bay News-Chronicle, Green Bay, WI

Rasmussen, Ray (913) 524-4200
PUB, ED
Lincoln Sentinel-Republican, Lincoln, KS

Rasnic, Nikki (301) 670-1400
ADV MGR
Montgomery Journal, Rockville, MD

Rasor, Rob (405) 224-2600
PROD FRM-PR
Chickasha Daily Express, Chickasha, OK

Raspberry, Bill (202) 334-6000
COL, Washington Post, Washington, DC

Rassfensterger, Nancy (319) 291-1400
City ED, Waterloo Courier, Waterloo, IA

Rassmann, Rich (803) 329-4000
City ED, Herald, Rock Hill, SC

Ratcliff, Genevieve (817) 926-5351
PUB, Commercial Recorder, Fort Worth, TX

Ratcliff, Richard (817) 926-5351
VP, MGR
Commercial Recorder, Fort Worth, TX

Ratcliffe, Jerry (804) 978-7200
Sports ED, Daily Progress, Charlottesville, VA

Ratcliffe, Ken (330) 424-9541
CIRC DIR, Morning Journal, Lisbon, OH

Rath, James M (307) 634-3361
ADV MGR-RT
Wyoming Tribune-Eagle, Cheyenne, WY

Rathbun, Chuck (818) 962-8811
PUB
West Covina Highlander, West Covina, CA

Rathbun, Jon (315) 823-3680
Sports ED, Evening Times, Little Falls, NY

Rathbun, Kate (607) 734-5151
DP MGR, Star-Gazette, Elmira, NY

Rathbun, Mark (509) 459-5000
CIRC CNR-NIE/Single Copy
Spokesman-Review, Spokane, WA

Rathburn, Flora (216) 999-4500
MET ED, Plain Dealer, Cleveland, OH

Rathell, James (970) 963-8252
PRES, Family Times Magazine, Active Times Publications Inc., Carbondale, CO

Rathet, Mike (215) 854-2000
EX Sports ED
Philadelphia Daily News, Philadelphia, PA

Rathke, Eric (316) 283-1500
Photographer, Newton Kansan, Newton, KS

Ratliff, Broward E (813) 942-2883
TREAS, Fackelman Newspapers, Tarpon Springs, FL

Ratliff, Gregg (919) 335-0841
ADV DIR, Daily Advance, Elizabeth City, NC

Ratliff, Kathryne (402) 371-1020
Teen-Age/Youth ED
Norfolk Daily News, Norfolk, NE

Ratliff, Larry (210) 225-7411
Films/Theater ED
San Antonio Express-News, San Antonio, TX

Ratliff, Tonya (210) 423-5511
Amusements ED, Fashion/Food ED, Society/Women's ED, Television/Film ED
Valley Morning Star, Harlingen, TX

Rattenbury, Thomas J (616) 445-2656
PUB, Cassopolis Vigilant, Cassopolis, MI

Ratterman Jr, Robert A (513) 523-4139
ED, Oxford Press, Oxford, OH

Rattican, Neal (910) 599-0162
ED, Courier-Times, Roxboro, NC

Ratto, Ray (415) 777-2424
Sports COL
San Francisco Examiner, San Francisco, CA

Rattray, Helen S (516) 324-0002
ED, East Hampton Star, East Hampton, NY

Ratts, Deanna (812) 886-9955
Religion ED
Vincennes Sun-Commercial, Vincennes, IN

Ratzky, Harlan B (800) 223-2154
MGR-MKTG, Online Contact
Investor's Business Daily, Los Angeles, CA

Rau, Alice W (801) 625-4200
VP/TREAS, Standard-Examiner, Ogden, UT
Sandusky-Norwalk Newspapers

Rau, David A (423) 392-0295
COB/PRES, Sandusky-Norwalk Newspapers, Kingsport, TN

Rau, Elizabeth (401) 277-7000
EDU Writer, Journal-Bulletin, Providence, RI

Rau, Gretchen (517) 652-3246
GM, Frankenmuth News, Frankenmuth, MI

Rau, Jes (212) 875-8914
PUB
Staats-Zeitung Und Herold, New York, NY

Rau, Paul (517) 752-7171
EDU ED, Saginaw News, Saginaw, MI

Rauch, Doni Mae B (906) 774-2772
Outdoors ED, Daily News, Iron Mountain, MI

Raupp, Paul (502) 926-0123
ED-City, Messenger-Inquirer, Owensboro, KY

Rausch, Brian (708) 381-9200
ED, Schaumburg Review, Barrington, IL

Rausch, Brooke (810) 766-6100
ASSOC ED, Flint Journal, Flint, MI

Rausch, Conrad (212) 210-2100
PROD DIR-Engineering
New York Daily News, New York, NY

Rausch, William (419) 468-1117
PROD FRM-PR, Galion Inquirer, Galion, OH

Rauscher, Penny (319) 728-2413
GM, Columbus Gazette, Columbus Jct., IA

Rauson, Randy (519) 354-2000
CR MGR, Chatham Daily News, Chatham, ON

Rausten, Shirley (208) 783-1107
ADV MGR-NTL
Shoshone News-Press, Kellogg, ID

Rauzi, David (541) 782-4241
ED, Dead Mountain Echo, Oakridge, OR

Rave, Ed (606) 292-2600
CIRC MGR, Kentucky Post, Covington, KY

Raveane, Michael (313) 676-0515
ED, Ile Camera, Grosse Ile, MI

Ravellette, Belle (605) 279-2565
GM, Pennington County Courant, Wall, SD

Ravellette, Don (605) 859-2516
PUB, Pioneer-Review, Philip, SD

Raven, Kymberlee (818) 713-3000
MGR-MKTG RES/Development
Daily News, Woodland Hills, CA

Raven, Mark (607) 776-2122
ED, Steuben Courier-Advocate, Bath, NY

Ravick, Rhonda (419) 562-3333
News ED, Telegraph-Forum, Bucyrus, OH

Raville, Sheila (209) 358-5311
ED, Hughson Chronicle, Hughson, CA

Rawers, Mindy (619) 299-3131
MGR-MKTG SRV
San Diego Union-Tribune, San Diego, CA

Rawley Jr, David A (910) 888-3500
VP, High Point Enterprise, High Point, NC

Rawley, Joseph P (910) 888-3500
VP/SEC/TREAS
High Point Enterprise, High Point, NC

Rawlings, Bruce (603) 543-3100
Financial MGR, Eagle Times, Claremont, NH

Rawlings, Jane (719) 544-3520
Online MGR, Pueblo Chieftain, Pueblo, CO

Rawlings, Mary G (719) 544-3520
VP, SEC, Pueblo Chieftain, Pueblo, CO

Rawlings, Nancy Ann (800) 760-3100
SEC/TREAS
Williams Syndications Inc., Holiday, FL

Rawlings, Robert H (719) 544-3520
PRES, TREAS, PUB, ED
Pueblo Chieftain, Pueblo, CO

Rawlins, Tom (813) 893-8111
Senior ED
St. Petersburg Times, St. Petersburg, FL

Rawls, Linda (561) 820-3800
ED, Palm Beach Daily News, Palm Beach, FL

Rawn, Gary B (715) 262-5454
PUB, ED, Prescott Journal, Prescott, WI

Rawson, Christopher (412) 263-1100
Films/Theater ED
Pittsburgh Post-Gazette, Pittsburgh, PA

Rawson, Davis (207) 623-3811
ASSOC ED, Kennebec Journal, Augusta, ME

Rawson, Joel P (401) 277-7000
Senior VP/EX ED
Providence Journal-Bulletin, Providence, RI

Rawson, Nyla (913) 546-2266
ED, Marquette Tribune, Marquette, KS

Ray, Beth (918) 387-2125
PUB, ED, Yale News, Yale, OK

Ray, Christopher A (218) 685-5326
ED, Grant County Herald, Elbow Lake, MN

189-Who's Where **Ree**

Ray, David .... (219) 235-6161
VP, VP-Development & Planning
South Bend Tribune, South Bend, IN
Ray, Dennis .... (812) 424-7711
PROD DIR-OPER, Evansville Courier, Evansville, IN, Scripps Howard
Ray, Doug .... (615) 552-1808
ED, Leaf-Chronicle, Clarksville, TN
Ray, Douglas K .... (847) 427-4300
VP/ED, Daily Herald, Arlington Heights, IL
Ray, Evan .... (702) 788-6200
CONT, Reno Gazette-Journal, Reno, NV
Ray, Gary .... (517) 772-2971
PROD MGR-PR
Morning Sun, Mount Pleasant, MI
Ray, Gretchen .... (512) 884-2011
Weekend Magazine ED, Corpus Christi Caller-Times, Corpus Christi, TX
Ray, Homer .... (918) 387-2125
PUB, ED, Yale News, Yale, OK
Ray, Isolde .... (615) 552-1808
Photo/Graphics CNR
Leaf-Chronicle, Clarksville, TN
Ray, Karen .... (512) 392-2458
PROD MGR
San Marcos Daily Record, San Marcos, TX
Ray, Nancye .... (305) 361-3333
PUB, ED, Islander News, Key Biscayne, FL
Ray, Pat .... (405) 326-8353
ED, Choctaw County Times, Hugo, OK
Ray, Rhonda .... (419) 522-3311
CIRC MGR-Single Copy Sales
News Journal, Mansfield, OH
Ray, Rowe .... (512) 392-2458
MAN ED, Action/Hot Line ED, EPE
San Marcos Daily Record, San Marcos, TX
Ray, Steve .... (608) 252-6400
News ED, Capital Times, Madison, WI
Ray, Sue .... (904) 599-2100
Automotive ED
Tallahassee Democrat, Tallahassee, FL
Raybon Jr, Otis .... (770) 227-3276
PUB, PA, GM, Griffin Daily News, Griffin, GA
Rayburn, Ronald .... (317) 462-5528
CIRC MGR, Daily Reporter, Greenfield, IN
Rayburn, Ted .... (615) 259-8000
News ED, Tennessean, Nashville, TN
Raykie Jr, James A .... (412) 981-6100
ED, Herald, Sharon, PA
Raykie, Jim .... (412) 981-6100
ED, Herald Plus, Sharon, PA
Rayl, Harris .... (913) 823-6363
PRES, PUB, Salina Journal, Salina, KS
Raymaker, Derek .... (613) 237-8226
MAN ED, Ottawa XPress, Ottawa, ON
Raymer, Jackie .... (219) 223-2111
Living/Lifestyle ED
Rochester Sentinel, Rochester, IN
Raymer, John .... (413) 584-5000
PROD MGR-PR
Daily Hampshire Gazette, Northampton, MA
Raymond, Art .... (518) 454-5694
DIR-Technology, Times Union, Albany, NY
Raymond, Carol A .... (207) 990-8000
MGR-Computer SRV
Bangor Daily News, Bangor, ME
Raymond, L .... (203) 622-1547
VP In Charge of Sales
Cartoonews Inc., Greenwich, CT
Raymond, Mark E .... (937) 878-3993
PUB, Fairborn Daily Herald, Fairborn, OH
Amos Press
Raymond, Steve .... (618) 393-2931
PUB, Olney Daily Mail, Olney, IL
Raymond, Terrence J .... (506) 753-4413
PUB, Tribune, Campbellton, NB
Raymond, Willard .... (217) 226-3721
PUB, ED
Golden Prairie News, Assumption, IL
Raymond, Yvonne .... (412) 588-5000
Society ED, Record-Argus, Greenville, PA
Raymus, Antone E .... (209) 599-2194
PUB, Ripon Record, Ripon, CA
Raymus, Toni M .... (209) 599-2194
MAN ED, Ripon Record, Ripon, CA
Raynaldo, Gary .... (415) 931-5778
ED, California Voice, San Francisco, CA
Raynard, Faye .... (508) 887-2727
ED, Tri-Town Transcript, Topsfield, MA
Rayner, Bob .... (804) 746-1235
MAN ED
Mechanicsville Local, Mechanicsville, VA
Rayner, Polly .... (610) 820-6500
EX Women's ED, Morning Call, Allentown, PA
Raynes, Diane .... (816) 359-2212
News ED, Republican-Times, Trenton, MO
Raynes, Jim T .... (972) 563-6476
Aviation/Books ED, City ED, COL, EDL Writer, Farm/Food ED, Lifestyle ED, PROD MGR-COMP, Terrell Tribune, Terrell, TX
Raytis, John B .... (614) 452-4561
Publisher, Times Recorder, Zanesville, OH
Raz, Michael .... (541) 485-1234
ADV DIR, Register-Guard, Eugene, OR
Rea, Del .... (618) 724-9423
ED, Progress, Christopher, IL
Rea, Glenn .... (512) 275-3464
PUB, ED, Cuero Record, Cuero, TX
Rea, Larry .... (901) 529-2211
Outdoors Reporter
Commercial Appeal, Memphis, TN
Rea, Mary .... (509) 997-7011
ED, Methow Valley News, Methow Valley, WA
Rea, Michael F .... (402) 352-2424
ED, Schuyler Sun, Schuyler, NE
Rea, Steven .... (215) 854-2000
Films Critic
Philadelphia Inquirer, Philadelphia, PA
Rea, Tom .... (307) 266-0500
City ED, Star-Tribune, Casper, WY
Read, Kay .... (912) 888-9300
ED, Albany Herald, Albany, GA
Read, Lynda .... (401) 762-3000
Photo DEPT MGR, Call, Woonsocket, RI
Read, Marvin .... (719) 544-3520
City ED, Pueblo Chieftain, Pueblo, CO
Read, Phil .... (201) 646-4000
BUS ED, Consumer Affairs ED, Personal FIN ED, Record, Hackensack, NJ
Reade, Robert .... (613) 829-9100
EDL Writer/Opinions ED
Ottawa Citizen, Ottawa, ON
Readel, Harry .... (505) 622-7710
Sports ED
Roswell Daily Record, Roswell, NM
Readman, Mary K .... (403) 577-3611
GM, ED, Consort Enterprise, Consort, AB
Readman, William J .... (403) 577-3611
PUB, Consort Enterprise, Consort, AB
Reagan, Bill .... (334) 262-1611
DP MGR
Montgomery Advertiser, Montgomery, AL
Reagan, Danny .... (915) 673-4271
ADTX MGR
Abilene Reporter-News, Abilene, TX
Reagan, Gail .... (214) 902-0942
COL, Have Fun at the Movies, Dallas, TX
Reagen, James E .... (315) 393-1000
MAN ED (Journal/Advance News)
Courier-Observer Journal & The Advance-News, Ogdensburg, NY
Reager, Skip .... (916) 891-1234
Sports ED
Chico Enterprise-Record, Chico, CA
Reagor, Catherine .... (602) 271-8000
RE Writer, Arizona Republic, Phoenix, AZ
Real-McKeighan, Tammy .... (402) 721-5000
City/Regional ED
Fremont Tribune, Fremont, NE
Reaney, James .... (519) 679-6666
Sports ED, London Free Press, London, ON
Reape, Lisa .... (315) 778-3638
ED, Fort Drum Sentinel, Watertown, NY
Reasner, Pamela .... (415) 777-1111
ASST MAN ED-Page One
San Francisco Chronicle, San Francisco, CA
Reason, Betsy .... (317) 598-6397
Women's ED, Daily Ledger, Noblesville, IN
Reaves, Ron .... (205) 549-2000
EX ED, Gadsden Times, Gadsden, AL
Reaves, Roy .... (817) 767-8341
DP MGR, Wichita Falls Times Record News, Wichita Falls, TX
Reavis, Chuck .... (910) 227-0131
DP MGR, PROD MGR-SYS
Times News Publishing Co., Burlington, NC
Reavis, Joe .... (903) 389-3334
PUB, ED, Fairfield Recorder, Fairfield, TX
Rebar, Keith .... (304) 752-6950
CIRC MGR, Logan Banner, Logan, WV
Rebbeck, Dick .... (605) 394-8300
Farm ED, Outdoors ED
Rapid City Journal, Rapid City, SD
Rebchook, John .... (303) 892-5000
RE Writer, Rocky Mountain News, Denver, CO
Rebello, Judy .... (508) 676-8211
Librarian, Herald News, Fall River, MA
Reber, Dan .... (612) 222-5011
PROD MGR-Platemaking
St. Paul Pioneer Press, St. Paul, MN
Reber, Gary .... (316) 225-4151
MAN ED, Automotive/Books ED, BUS/FIN ED, EPE, EDL Writer/EDU ED, News ED
Dodge City Daily Globe, Dodge City, KS
Reber, Grata .... (806) 385-6444
ED, Amherst Press, Amherst, TX
Reber, Jack .... (619) 299-3131
SYS/Facilities ED
San Diego Union-Tribune, San Diego, CA
Rebibo, Joel .... (212) 599-3666
ED, Jerusalem Post International Edition, New York, NY
Rebuck, Leon .... (410) 822-1500
CIRC MGR, Star-Democrat, Easton, MD
Rebuffoni, Dean .... (612) 673-4000
Natural Resources Reporter
Star Tribune, Minneapolis, MN
Recchi, Ray .... (954) 356-4000
COL, Sun-Sentinel, Fort Lauderdale, FL
Recchi, Sal .... (407) 420-5000
NTL ED, State ED
Orlando Sentinel, Orlando, FL
Rech, Marilyn .... (318) 459-3200
ADV MGR-TELEMKTG, Times, Shreveport, LA
Rechtenbach, Marc .... (712) 343-2154
GM, Avoca Journal-Herald, Avoca, IA
Reconnu, Carole C .... (847) 427-4300
SEC, Daily Herald, Arlington Heights, IL
Record, Phil J .... (817) 390-7400
Ombudsman/Special ASST to PUB
Fort Worth Star-Telegram, Fort Worth, TX
Recore, Kathi .... (518) 454-5694
ADV MGR-Display, Times Union, Albany, NY
Recore, Robert N .... (508) 793-9100
ADV DIR, Telegram & Gazette, Worcester, MA
Rectanus, Danielle .... (330) 364-5577
ADV MGR-NTL
Times Reporter, New Philadelphia, OH
Rector, Jerry .... (704) 322-4510
PROD FRM-COMP
Hickory Daily Record, Hickory, NC
Rector, Linda .... (423) 942-2433
ED, Jasper Journal, Jasper, TN
Rector, Peggy .... (970) 675-5033
GM, Rangely Times, Rangely, CO
Rector, Roger D .... (712) 364-3131
PUB, Ida County Courier, Ida Grove, IA
Rector, Sylvia .... (313) 222-6400
Food ED, Detroit Free Press, Detroit, MI
Rector Jr, W F .... (501) 868-4400
PUB, Daily Record, Little Rock, AR
Rector, William F .... (501) 868-4400
PRES, Daily Record, Little Rock, AR
Redd, Nicole .... (614) 439-3531
Women's ED
Daily Jeffersonian, Cambridge, OH
Reddell, Mike .... (210) 257-3300
MAN ED, Mountain Sun, Kerrville, TX
Redden, Mike .... (615) 754-6397
PUB, Mt. Juliet News, Mount Juliet, TN
Redden, Oran .... (405) 794-5555
PUB, Moore American, Moore, OK
Redder, Carl .... (616) 347-2544
CIRC MGR
Petoskey News-Review, Petoskey, MI
Reddick, Bill .... (519) 354-2000
BUS/FIN ED, Fashion/Society ED, Food ED
Chatham Daily News, Chatham, ON
Reddick, Richard D .... (805) 238-6500
PUB, North County Journal, Paso Robles, CA
Redding, Alesia .... (219) 235-6161
Radio/Television Writer
South Bend Tribune, South Bend, IN
Redding, Michael .... (417) 451-1520
CIRC MGR, Neosho Daily News, Neosho, MO
Redding, Richard .... (310) 832-0221
EDU ED, News-Pilot, San Pedro, CA
Redding, William R .... (423) 523-3131
DIR-Human Resources
Knoxville News-Sentinel, Knoxville, TN
Reddington, Rosanne .... (401) 277-7000
ADTX MGR
Providence Journal-Bulletin, Providence, RI
Redditt, Sophie .... (214) 902-0942
ED/Computer Layout
Have Fun at the Movies, Dallas, TX
Reddy, Taurun .... (501) 442-1777
BUS ED
Northwest Arkansas Times, Fayetteville, AR
Rede, George .... (503) 221-8327
Recruiting DIR, Oregonian, Portland, OR
Redecker, Jerre .... (360) 754-5400
Features ED, Teen-Age/Youth ED, Women's/Food ED, Olympian, Olympia, WA
Redekop, H R .... (204) 697-7000
PUB, Winnipeg Free Press, Winnipeg, MB
Redfeam, Kelly .... (541) 485-1234
ADV MGR-CLASS
Register-Guard, Eugene, OR
Redfern, Ron .... (714) 835-1234
ADV Senior VP-Advertising/MKTG
Orange County Register, Santa Ana, CA
Redfield, Anne .... (412) 981-6100
Photo ED, Herald, Sharon, PA
Redfield, Joye .... (509) 248-1251
Features ED, Women's ED
Yakima Herald-Republic, Yakima, WA
Redman, Robert C .... (616) 839-4315
PUB, ED, Waterfront of Missaukee County, Lake City, MI
Redmann, Paula .... (701) 223-2500
MGR-MKTG/PROM
Bismarck Tribune, Bismarck, ND
Redmond, Don .... (905) 827-2244 ext. 244
ED, Oakville Free Press Journal, Oakville, ON
Redmond, Tim .... (415) 255-3100
MAN ED, San Francisco Bay Guardian, San Francisco, CA
Reed, Alan .... (701) 463-2201
ED
McLean County Independent, Garrison, ND
Reed, Alan .... (614) 892-2771
ED, Utica Herald, Utica, OH
Reed, Ann .... (206) 339-3000
DIR-Human Resources, Herald, Everett, WA
Reed, Bill .... (212) 416-2000
PROD Senior MGR (Chicopee MA)
Wall Street Journal, New York, NY
Reed, Brian .... (360) 676-2600
CIRC ASST DIR
Bellingham Herald, Bellingham, WA
Reed, Chris .... (909) 987-6397
COL, Inland Valley Daily Bulletin, Ontario, CA
Reed, Cindy .... (913) 483-2116
BM, Russell Daily News, Russell, KS
Reed, Craig .... (541) 672-3321
Sports ED, News-Review, Roseburg, OR
Reed, Dana .... (206) 464-2111
PROD MGR-Electrical (North Creek)
Seattle Times, Seattle, WA
Reed, David .... (912) 888-9300
PROD SUPV-MR, Albany Herald, Albany, GA
Reed, Debbie .... (608) 252-6100
DIR-Human Resources
Wisconsin State Journal, Madison, WI
Reed, Donald L .... (805) 845-3704
PUB, Lamont Reporter, Lamont, CA
Reed, Donna .... (813) 259-7711
Deputy MAN ED
Tampa Tribune and Times, Tampa, FL
Reed, Douglas H .... (508) 699-6755
PUB, ED, Free Press, North Attleborough, MA
Reed, Edwin H .... (205) 586-3188
PUB, Arab Tribune, Arab, AL
Reed, Ernest S .... (610) 258-7171
ADV DIR, Express-Times, Easton, PA
Reed, Frank W .... (805) 845-3704
PUB, Lamont Reporter, Lamont, CA
Reed, Gerald .... (508) 793-9100
PROD SUPV-Alternate Delivery
Telegram & Gazette, Worcester, MA
Reed III, Howard .... (770) 963-9205
MAN ED
Gwinnett Daily Post, Lawrenceville, GA
Reed, Jan .... (818) 355-3324
PUB, ED
Sierra Madre News, Sierra Madre, CA
Reed, Jane .... (314) 340-8000
Books ED
St. Louis Post-Dispatch, St. Louis, MO
Reed, Jay .... (414) 224-2000
COL, Outdoors Writer
Milwaukee Journal Sentinel, Milwaukee, WI
Reed, Jeremy .... (802) 524-9771
ADV DIR
St. Albans Messenger, St. Albans, VT
Reed, JoAnn F .... (716) 232-7100
CIRC MGR
Rochester Democrat and Chronicle; Rochester, NY Times-Union, Rochester, NY
Reed, Ken .... (405) 336-2222
Co-Owner, Perry Daily Journal, Perry, OK
Reed, Lauren .... (414) 684-4433
MGR-MKTG/PROM
Herald Times Reporter, Manitowoc, WI
Reed, Len .... (503) 221-8327
Team Leader-Environment
Oregonian, Portland, OR
Reed, Marcia .... (207) 472-3111
ED, Fort Fairfield Review, Fort Fairfield, ME
Reed, Mark .... (706) 324-5526
MGR-Programming
Columbus Ledger-Enquirer, Columbus, GA
Reed, Mike .... (901) 968-6397
GM, ED, Lexington Progress, Lexington, TN
Reed, Nerwin O .... (307) 436-2211
PUB, Glenrock Independent, Glenrock, WY
Reed, Olga .... (903) 657-2501
CIRC MGR
Henderson Daily News, Henderson, TX
Reed, Phyllis .... (405) 336-2222
Co-Owner, PUB
Perry Daily Journal, Perry, OK
Reed, Rick .... (317) 584-4501
PROD MGR, News-Gazette, Winchester, IN
Reed, Sarah .... (330) 868-5222
GM, ED, Minerva Leader, Minerva, OH
Reed, Sgt .... (301) 921-2800
ED, Henderson Hall News, Gaithersburg, MD
Reed, Sheila .... (606) 231-3100
Features ED, Herald-Leader, Lexington, KY
Reed, Steve .... (515) 684-4611
PROD FRM-Press
Ottumwa Courier, Ottumwa, IA
Reed, Steve .... (970) 641-1414
ED, Gunnison Country Times, Gunnison, CO
Reed, Steve .... (202) 334-6000
CIRC DIR-Home Delivery
Washington Post, Washington, DC
Reed, Susanne .... (501) 362-2425
PUB, Cleburne County Sun-Times, Heber Springs, AR
Reed, Tom .... (770) 532-1234
Photo ED, Times, Gainesville, GA
Reed, Vester .... (316) 431-4100
PROD FRM-PR, Tribune, Chanute, KS
Reed, Vincent .... (202) 334-6000
VP-Communications
Washington Post, Washington, DC

Ree Who's Where-190

Reed, Warren .... (212) 416-2000
PROD MGR (Palo Alto CA)
Wall Street Journal, New York, NY
Reeder, Mike .... (610) 377-2051
DP MGR, Times News, Lehighton, PA
Reeder, Paige .... (318) 624-1212
ED, Claiborne Banner, Homer, LA
Reeder, Pat .... (918) 341-1101
MAN ED, Action Line ED (U-Ask-It), City ED
Claremore Daily Progress, Claremore, OK
Reedy, Jeffrey .... (409) 833-3311
CIRC DIR-OPER
Beaumont Enterprise, Beaumont, TX
Reedy, Vincent .... (512) 575-1451
ASSOC ED, Victoria Advocate, Victoria, TX
Reems, June .... (970) 242-5050
EX SEC, Daily Sentinel, Grand Junction, CO
Reen, Michelle .... (517) 278-2318
ED, EPE, Daily Reporter, Coldwater, MI
Rees, Dixie .... (816) 886-2233
ADV MGR
Marshall Democrat-News, Marshall, MO
Rees, Francis .... (618) 548-3330
PUB, Salem Times-Commoner, Salem, IL
Rees, Jennifer .... (503) 325-3211
ADV DIR, Daily Astorian, Astoria, OR
Rees, Judy .... (905) 684-7251
CIRC MGR- City
Standard, St. Catharines, ON
Rees, Michael W .... (219) 563-8326
GM, Paper, Wabash, IN
Rees, Thomas L .... (314) 340-8402
VP/DIR-ADV
Pulitzer Publishing Co., St. Louis, MO
Rees, Wayne W .... (219) 563-8326
PUB, Paper, Wabash, IN
Reese, Brian .... (540) 669-2181
MAN ED, Herald-Courier Virginia Tennessean, Bristol, VA
Reese, Charlie .... (813) 963-1918
ED, Laker, Tampa, FL
Reese, Dave .... (916) 985-2581
PUB, Folsom Telegraph, Folsom, CA
Reese, Donald .... (610) 377-2051
ADV DIR-MKTG, Times News, Lehighton, PA
Reese, Kelly .... (817) 387-3811
EDU ED
Denton Record-Chronicle, Denton, TX
Reese, Kenneth .... (205) 734-2131
PROD MGR, Cullman Times, Cullman, AL
Reese, Robert .... (317) 747-5700
DIR-INFO Services, Star Press, Muncie, IN
Reese, Robert .... (312) 222-3232
ADV MGR-Supplements
Chicago Tribune, Chicago, IL
Reesing, Brad .... (405) 286-3321
Sports ED
McCurtain Daily Gazette, Idabel, OK
Reetz, Brian .... (316) 225-4151
Sports ED
Dodge City Daily Globe, Dodge City, KS
Reetz, John .... (404) 526-5151
ASST MGR-News OPER
Atlanta Journal-Constitution, Atlanta, GA
Reeve, Tad .... (715) 833-9200
Sports ED, Leader-Telegram, Eau Claire, WI
Reeves, Bob .... (402) 475-4200
Religion/Values Reporter
Lincoln Journal Star, Lincoln, NE
Reeves, Duane .... (618) 664-3144
PUB, ED, Greenville Advocate, Greenville, IL
Reeves, Earl .... (405) 464-2410
PUB, ED, Cyril News, Cyril, OK
Reeves, Fiona .... (360) 458-2681
ED, Nisqually Valley News, Yelm, WA
Reeves, Frank .... (412) 263-1100
Harrisburg BU
Pittsburgh Post-Gazette, Pittsburgh, PA
Reeves, Garland .... (205) 325-2222
Travel ED
Birmingham News, Birmingham, AL
Reeves, Howard L .... (205) 695-7029
ED, Lamar Democrat, Vernon, AL
Reeves Jr, J Doug .... (307) 634-3361
VP, Wyoming Tribune-Eagle, Cheyenne, WY
Reeves, Janet .... (303) 892-5000
Photo ED, Rocky Mountain News, Denver, CO
Reeves, Jeffrey .... (800) 828-2453
Features ED
U-Bild Newspaper Features, Van Nuys, CA
Reeves, Jim .... (703) 560-4000
DP MGR, DIR-Telecommunications, PROD DIR-OPER, Fairfax Journal, Fairfax, VA
Journal Newspapers Inc.
Reeves, Lloyd .... (402) 826-2147
PUB, ED, Crete News, Crete, NE
Reeves, Pat .... (515) 628-3882
GM, Pella Chronicle, Pella, IA
Reeves, Peggie .... (770) 428-9411
ED
Alpharetta-Roswell Neighbor, Marietta, GA
Reeves, Rachel J .... (305) 757-1147
PUB, Miami Times, Miami, FL
Reeves, Randy .... (812) 372-7811
PROD MGR, Republic, Columbus, IN
Reeves, Richard .... (813) 893-8111
ADV DIR, St. Petersburg Times, St. Petersburg, FL
Reeves, Rick .... (303) 776-2244
CIRC MGR-District
Daily Times-Call, Longmont, CO
Reeves, Sharon .... (619) 299-3131
Library MGR
San Diego Union-Tribune, San Diego, CA
Reeves, Shawn .... (704) 484-7000
Theater/Music ED, Shelby Star, Shelby, NC
Reeves, Thomas W .... (505) 437-7120
PUB/PA, Daily News, Alamogordo, NM
Reeves, Trudy .... (402) 826-2147
PUB, Crete News, Crete, NE
Reeves, William .... (607) 432-1000
ADV MGR, Daily Star, Oneonta, NY
Reevs, James A .... (906) 228-2500
PUB, Mining Journal, Marquette, MI
Regan, Bill .... (603) 668-4321
BUS/FIN ED, Union Leader, Manchester, NH
Regan, Claire .... (718) 981-1234
ASST News ED
Staten Island Advance, Staten Island, NY
Regan, David B .... (408) 423-4242
PRES, PUB
Santa Cruz County Sentinel, Santa Cruz, CA
Regan, James .... (617) 929-2000
DIR-Sales PROM/Public Relations
Boston Globe, Boston, MA
Regan, Michael .... (860) 241-6200
ASST MAN ED-Connecticut
Hartford Courant, Hartford, CT
Regan, Ronald T .... (205) 764-4268
GM, Courier Journal, Florence, AL
Regentin, Douglas .... (810) 376-3805
PUB, ED
Deckerville Recorder, Deckerville, MI
Reger, J Kevin .... (416) 814-4239
Sr VP-Planning
Thomson Newspapers, Toronto, ON
Regier, Jackie .... (402) 564-2741
CIRC MGR
Columbus Telegram, Columbus, NE
Regier, Kristi .... (405) 772-3301
ADV MGR-Display
Weatherford Daily News, Weatherford, OK
Regier, Virginia .... (913) 742-2111
ED, Everest World, Hiawatha, KS
Regnier, Jonie .... (913) 243-2424
ADV MGR, Blade-Empire, Concordia, KS
Rego, Nancy .... (508) 880-9000
PROD SUPV-COMP Room
Taunton Daily Gazette, Taunton, MA
Regulski, Frank .... (607) 798-1234
CIRC MGR-MET East
Press & Sun Bulletin, Binghamton, NY
Rehbein, Joe .... (360) 694-3391
CIRC MGR-TMC/Alternate Delivery/Motor Route, Columbian, Vancouver, WA
Rehberg, Charles .... (509) 459-5000
ASSOC ED
Spokesman-Review, Spokane, WA
Rehberg, Michael .... (618) 529-5454
CIRC MGR
Southern Illinoisan, Carbondale, IL
Rehbinder, Henrik .... (213) 622-8332
NTL ED, La Opinion, Los Angeles, CA
Rehlander, Robert .... (219) 362-2161
BM, PA, La Porte Herald-Argus, La Porte, IN
Rehm, John .... (617) 433-6700
CFO
Community Newspaper Co., Needham, MA
Reiber, Marjorie .... (970) 669-5050
PSL SEC
Loveland Daily Reporter-Herald, Loveland, CO
Reibold, Carl .... (561) 287-1550
PROD MGR-MR, Stuart News, Stuart, FL
Reibsane, June B .... (717) 647-2191
ED, West Schuylkill Herald, Tower City, PA
Reichard, Craig .... (301) 733-5131
ADV MGR-Territory Sales
Morning Herald, Hagerstown, MD
Reichard, John .... (520) 458-9440
CIRC DIR
Sierra Vista Herald, Sierra Vista, AZ
Wick Communications
Reichart, Paul .... (814) 368-3173
MAN ED, Bradford Era, Bradford, PA
Reichert, Barb .... (719) 632-5511
Sports ED, Gazette, Colorado Springs, CO
Reichert, George .... (207) 729-3311
CIRC MGR, Times Record, Brunswick, ME
Reichley, Charley Ann .... (334) 683-6318
ED, Marion Times-Standard, Marion, AL
Reichman, Bob .... (352) 793-2161
GM, ED, Sumter County Times, Bushnell, FL
Reichold, Martha .... (205) 532-4000
PROD DIR, Huntsville Times, Huntsville, AL
Reicks, Bonnie J .... (847) 427-4300
ADV MGR-Co-op
Daily Herald, Arlington Heights, IL
Reid, Aleksei .... (704) 358-5000
CIRC DIR-MKTG
Charlotte Observer, Charlotte, NC
Reid, Andy .... (615) 444-3952
Sports ED, Lebanon Democrat, Lebanon, TN
Reid, Barry .... (905) 526-3333
ADV MGR-Sales Planning
Spectator, Hamilton, ON
Reid, Brenda .... (404) 526-5151
MGR-MKTG Communications
Atlanta Journal-Constitution, Atlanta, GA
Reid, Dave .... (401) 277-7000
ASST MAN ED (Journal-Bulletin)
Providence Journal-Bulletin, Providence, RI
Reid, David W .... (918) 225-3333
PUB, Cushing Daily Citizen, Cushing, OK
Reid, Don .... (902) 468-1222
PROD Consultant, Daily News, Halifax, NS
Reid, Gary .... (405) 375-3220
PUB, ED, Times & Free Press, Kingfisher, OK
Reid, Jeanne Ann .... (405) 772-3301
SEC/TREAS
Weatherford Daily News, Weatherford, OK
Reid, John .... (541) 776-4411
EX ED, Mail Tribune, Medford, OR
Reid, John W .... (212) 621-1500
VP/DIR of Communications & Technology
Associated Press, New York, NY
Reid III, John .... (918) 253-4322
ED, Delaware County Journal, Jay, OK
Reid, Ken .... (405) 772-3301
COL
Weatherford Daily News, Weatherford, OK
Reid, Michael D .... (250) 380-5211
Arts/Entertainment Reporter
Times Colonist, Victoria, BC
Reid, Myra .... (918) 225-3333
SEC, Cushing Daily Citizen, Cushing, OK
Reid, Phillip R .... (405) 772-3301
PRES, PUB/GM, MGR-CR/PA, MGR-MKTG/PROM, COL
Weatherford Daily News, Weatherford, OK
Reid, Wanda S .... (717) 533-2900
PUB, Hershey Chronicle, Hershey, PA
Reid, Wayne .... (334) 433-1551
DP MGR, Mobile Press Register, Mobile, AL
Reidie, Dave .... (403) 429-5400
CIRC VP-Reader Sales & SRV
Edmonton Journal, Edmonton, AB
Reigel, Becky .... (410) 398-3311
Features ED, Cecil Whig, Elkton, MD
Reigler, Hunter .... (502) 926-0123
News ED
Messenger-Inquirer, Owensboro, KY
Reik, Lynn .... (517) 377-1000
MGR-CR, Lansing State Journal, Lansing, MI
Reiland, Catherine .... (714) 835-1234
DIR-ADM
Orange County Register, Santa Ana, CA
Reiley, Betty Homes .... (814) 445-9621
PRES, Daily American, Somerset, PA
Reiley, David H .... (814) 445-9621
TREAS, PUB, Daily American, Somerset, PA
Reiley, Ronnie G .... (814) 445-9621
VP, Travel ED, Daily American, Somerset, PA
Reilly, Brian .... (209) 887-3112
PUB, ED, Linden Herald, Linden, CA
Reilly, Helen .... (908) 247-8700
PUB, Somerset Spectator, Somerset, NJ
Reilly, J Patrick .... (608) 935-2331
PUB, ED
Dodgeville Chronicle, Dodgeville, WI
Reilly, John P .... (203) 846-3281
EX ED, EPE, Hour, Norwalk, CT
Reilly, John P .... (608) 523-4284
PUB, ED, Blade-Atlas, Blanchardville, WI
Reilly, Joseph .... (312) 782-8100
ED/GM
City News Bureau of Chicago, Chicago, IL
Reilly, Larry .... (212) 807-6622
Billing & Returns, Impact Visuals Photo & Graphics Inc., New York, NY
Reilly, Mike .... (402) 444-1000
Enterprise/Public Affairs ED
Omaha World-Herald, Omaha, NE
Reilly, T Michael .... (608) 935-2331
PUB, ED
Dodgeville Chronicle, Dodgeville, WI
Reilly, Tom .... (516) 843-2020
PROD GEN FRM-Newsprint
Newsday, Melville, NY
Reilly, Wayne .... (207) 990-8000
Projects ED, Bangor Daily News, Bangor, ME
Reily, DD, Most Rev Daniel P .. (508) 757-6387
PUB, Catholic Free Press, Worcester, MA
Reily, Jerry .... (716) 366-3000
Sports ED, Evening Observer, Dunkirk, NY
Reimer, Luci .... (719) 775-2064
ED, Limon Leader, Limon, CO
Reimer, Susan .... (410) 332-6000
COL-Features, Sun, Baltimore, MD
Reinart, Richard .... (918) 581-8300
PROD SUPT-Mechanical Maintenance
Tulsa World, Tulsa, OK
Reinert, Connie .... (712) 272-4417
GM, Buena Vista County Journal, Newell, IA
Reinhard, David .... (503) 221-8327
EDL Writer, Oregonian, Portland, OR
Reinhard, Paul .... (610) 820-6500
Sports ED, Morning Call, Allentown, PA
Reinhardt, Robert P .... (402) 586-2661
PUB, ED, Wausa Gazette, Wausa, NE
Reinhold, Dorothy .... (818) 962-8811
MAN ED, San Gabriel Valley Tribune, West Covina, CA, MediaNews Inc.
Reinholt, Tracy .... (610) 323-3000
PSL DIR, Mercury, Pottstown, PA
Reiniger, John W .... (419) 695-0015
VP-FIN, Delphos Daily Herald, Delphos, OH
Reinken, Charles .... (910) 323-4848
EPE, Observer-Times, Fayetteville, NC
Reinmart, Tony .... (519) 894-2231
Police, Record, Kitchener, ON
Reinschmidt, Paul C .... (605) 886-6901
CIRC MGR
Watertown Public Opinion, Watertown, SD
Reinwald, Pete .... (904) 599-2100
Sports ED
Tallahassee Democrat, Tallahassee, FL
Reisinger, Sue .... (305) 350-2111
ASST MAN ED-News
Miami Herald, Miami, FL
Reiskind, Steven .... (954) 698-6397
ED, Eastsider, Deerfield Beach, FL
Reisman, Larry .... (561) 562-2315
ED
Vero Beach Press-Journal, Vero Beach, FL
Reisman III, Phil .... (914) 694-9300
ASST MAN ED
Reporter Dispatch, White Plains, NY
Gannett Co. Inc.
Reiss, Al .... (541) 776-4411
COL, Films/Theater ED
Mail Tribune, Medford, OR
Reiss, Cory .... (804) 295-0124
MAN ED, Charlottesville Albemarle Observer, Charlottesville, VA
Reiss JCD, Most Rev John C .... (609) 586-7400
PUB, Monitor, Trenton, NJ
Reist, Margaret .... (402) 475-4200
Police Reporter
Lincoln Journal Star, Lincoln, NE
Reiste, Bob .... (712) 758-3140
PUB, Ocheyedan Press-Melvin News, Ocheyedan, IA
Reitan, Lester R .... (503) 981-3441
PUB, Woodburn Independent, Woodburn, OR
Reiter, Jay .... (503) 399-6611
Photo ED, Statesman Journal, Salem, OR
Reiter, Jess .... (916) 756-0800
CIRC MGR, Davis Enterprise, Davis, CA
Reiter, John .... (812) 424-7711
Features ED
Evansville Courier, Evansville, IN
Reiterman, Tim .... (213) 237-5000
State Projects ED
Los Angeles Times, Los Angeles, CA
Reithmiller, Patricia .... (517) 787-0450
ED, News, Jackson, MI
Reitz, Bob .... (360) 754-5400
DIR-MKTG SRV, Olympian, Olympia, WA
Reitz, Rick .... (717) 626-2191
ED, Lititz Record Express, Lititz, PA
Reitzel, Lisa .... (310) 540-5511
ASST MAN ED, Daily Breeze, Torrance, CA
Reiz, Paul .... (313) 222-6400
PROD OPER MGR-Strategic Planning
Detroit Newspapers, Detroit, MI
Relph, Joseph .... (316) 378-4415
PUB, ED
Wilson County Citizen, Fredonia, KS
Relph, Rita .... (316) 378-4415
PUB, ED
Wilson County Citizen, Fredonia, KS
Remenick, Lori .... (301) 334-9172
GM, Garrett County Weekender, Oakland, MD
Remensky, Carl .... (412) 263-1100
ASSOC ED-News
Pittsburgh Post-Gazette, Pittsburgh, PA
Remer, Donna .... (810) 949-7900
ED, Bay Voice, New Baltimore, MI
Remington, Bob .... (403) 429-5400
Leisure/Entertainment ED, Radio/Television ED, Edmonton Journal, Edmonton, AB
Remley, Steve .... (319) 383-2200
PROD MGR-PR
Quad-City Times, Davenport, IA
Remmert, Richard H .... (901) 529-2211
VP, GM, Commercial Appeal, Memphis, TN
Rems, Janet .... (703) 437-5400
MAN ED
Springfield Times Courier, Reston, VA
Remsburg, Craig .... (906) 228-2500
Sports ED, Mining Journal, Marquette, MI
Remsen, Nancy .... (802) 863-3441
ASST MET ED
Burlington Free Press, Burlington, VT
Remy, Bill .... (419) 522-3311
PROD MGR-Plate COMP
News Journal, Mansfield, OH
Renander, Jan Castle .... (712) 623-2566
ED, Red Oak Express, Red Oak, IA

191-Who's Where **Ric**

Renaud, John (573) 335-6611
PROD MGR
Southeast Missourian, Cape Girardeau, MO
Renault, Dennis (916) 321-1000
Cartoonist, Sacramento Bee, Sacramento, CA
Renberg, Werner (914) 241-2038
Self-Syndicator
Renberg, Werner, Chappaqua, NY
Rene, Janet (603) 742-4455
PSL MGR, Foster's Democrat, Dover, NH
Reneau, Danny (409) 385-5278
PUB, ED, Silsbee Bee, Silsbee, TX
Reneau, Janet (409) 385-5278
GM, Silsbee Bee, Silsbee, TX
Renfro, David (910) 625-2101
PUB, Courier-Tribune, Asheboro, NC
Renfro, Newton E (417) 472-3100
PUB, ED, Newton County News, Granby, MO
Renfroe, Brenda (614) 532-1441
ADV Representative
Ironton Tribune, Ironton, OH
Renkes, Jim (319) 383-2200
Features ED, Quad-City Times, Davenport, IA
Renkes, Mike (815) 625-3600
Sports ED, Daily Gazette, Sterling, IL
Renneau, Lani (701) 223-2500
ADV DIR, Bismarck Tribune, Bismarck, ND
Renneisen, Beth (415) 883-8600
Graphics Design ED
Marin Independent Journal, Novato, CA
Renner, Delinda (318) 322-5161
CONT, News-Star, Monroe, LA
Renner, Gerald (860) 241-6200
Religion Writer
Hartford Courant, Hartford, CT
Renner, Howard F (610) 820-6500
ADV DIR, Morning Call, Allentown, PA
Renner, Maxene (608) 782-9710
BUS ED, La Crosse Tribune, La Crosse, WI
Rennie, Gary (519) 255-5711
Labor ED, Windsor Star, Windsor, ON
Rennie, George (416) 947-2222
PROD DIR-Pre Press OPER
Toronto Sun, Toronto, ON
Renninger, Richard (610) 272-2500
PROD FRM-COMP
Times Herald, Norristown, PA
Reno, David (910) 373-7000
PROD DIR, News & Record, Greensboro, NC
Reno, John M (314) 421-1880
PROD MGR
St. Louis Countain, St. Louis, MO
ABC Inc. (Legal Communications Corp.)
Renshaw, Michael (416) 367-2000
System Administrator
Toronto Star, Toronto, ON
Renshaw, Timothy (604) 985-2131
ED, North Shore News, North Vancouver, BC
Renteria, Fred (619) 256-2257
CIRC MGR-Home Delivery
Desert Dispatch, Barstow, CA
Rentsch, Bill (515) 573-2141
Farm ED, Messenger, Fort Dodge, IA
Renzhofer, Marty (801) 237-2031
Music ED-Pop
Salt Lake Tribune, Salt Lake City, UT
Repentigny, Alain De (514) 285-7272
Amusements ED, La Presse, Montreal, QC
Reppert, Jerry L (618) 734-4242
PUB, Tri-State Advertiser, Cairo, IL
Resch, Alan D (919) 663-3232
PUB, ED, Chatham News, Siler City, NC
Resenbrink, Jane (212) 529-2255
PUB, Downtown, New York, NY
Resler, Pete C (815) 942-3221
MAN ED, City ED, Daily Herald, Morris, IL
Resneder, James (405) 343-2513
PUB, Washita County Enterprise, Corn, OK
Reso, Renee (517) 835-7171
News ED, Midland Daily News, Midland, MI
Respondek, Janice (519) 894-2231
RES MGR, Record, Kitchener, ON
Restauri, Denise (703) 276-3400
CIRC VP-NTL Circulation Sales
USA Today, Arlington, VA
Restell, Lonnie (250) 380-5211
PROD FRM-MR, Times Colonist, Victoria, BC
Rester, Michelle (209) 562-2585
ED, Lindsay Gazette, Lindsay, CA
Restivo, Joseph F (419) 245-6000
ASST SEC/ASST TREAS, Blade, Toledo, OH
Reston, Mary Jo (508) 627-4311
PUB, GM, Vineyard Gazette, Edgartown, MA
Reston, Richard F (508) 627-4311
PUB, ED, Vineyard Gazette, Edgartown, MA
Reswow, Olga (330) 996-3000
NTL ED, Akron Beacon Journal, Akron, OH
Retherford, Bill R (918) 258-7171
PUB
Broken Arrow Ledger, Broken Arrow, OK
Retherford, Ken (205) 353-4612
Health/Medical ED
Decatur Daily, Decatur, AL
Retherford, Tim R (918) 663-1414
ASSOC PUB, Tulsa Daily Commerce & Legal News, Tulsa, OK

Rethi, Donna (412) 465-5555
PROD MGR-OPER
Indiana Gazette, Indiana, PA
Retigg, Gregg (614) 875-2307
MAN ED, Grove City Record, Grove City, OH
Retit, Bill (210) 896-7000
Magazine ED, Daily Times, Kerrville, TX
Rettig, James L (406) 378-2176
PUB, ED, Mountaineer, Big Sandy, MT
Retzlaff, Gene (402) 475-4200
MGR-OPER
Lincoln Journal Star, Lincoln, NE
Reuper, Werner (510) 935-2525
PROD MGR-PR, Contra Costa Times, Walnut Creek, CA, Knight-Ridder Inc.
Reuter, Heidi (414) 224-2000
Senior ED-Features
Milwaukee Journal Sentinel, Milwaukee, WI
Reuter, Lisa (614) 461-5000
Travel ED
Columbus Dispatch, Columbus, OH
Revelant, Mary (317) 473-6641
Librarian, Peru Tribune, Peru, IN
Revelle-Eckls, Ellen (619) 232-4381
PUB
San Diego Daily Transcript, San Diego, CA
Revells, Sonja (904) 526-3614
Photo ED
Jackson County Floridan, Marianna, FL
Revenaugh, Lois (810) 766-6100
ADV MGR-Sales/Development/NTL/Co-op
Flint Journal, Flint, MI
Revis, Amy (704) 245-6431
Art DIR, City ED, Environmental/Ecology ED, Graphics ED, Health/Medical ED, News ED
Daily Courier, Forest City, NC
Revlett, Teresa (502) 273-3287
GM, McLean County News, Calhoun, KY
Rexford, Peter (314) 727-5850
PRES, Rexford Group, St. Louis, MO
Rexroad, Carl (618) 529-5454
ED, Southern Illinoisan, Carbondale, IL
Reyer, A L (910) 285-2178
GM, Richlands-Beulaville Advertiser News, Wallace, NC
Reyes, Bleu (915) 236-6677
PROD FRM-PR
Sweetwater Reporter, Sweetwater, TX
Reyes, Ernesto (415) 883-8600
PROD DIR
Marin Independent Journal, Novato, CA
Reyes, Lupe (505) 437-7120
PROD SUPV-Press
Alamogordo Daily News, Alamogordo, NM
Reyes, Oscar (301) 853-4504
ED, El Pregonero, Washington, DC
Reyes, Raul (210) 225-7411
ASST MAN ED
San Antonio Express-News, San Antonio, TX
Reyes, Sylvia (512) 884-2011
EDL Writer, Corpus Christi Caller-Times, Corpus Christi, TX
Reynaud, Wilbur (504) 869-5784
PUB, News-Examiner, Lutcher, LA
Reynolds, Andy (610) 622-8800
ED, EPE, NTL ED, Political/Government ED, SCI/Technology ED, Television/Film ED
Delaware County Daily Times, Primos, PA
Reynolds, David (707) 441-0500
Books ED, Times-Standard, Eureka, CA
Reynolds, David L (314) 839-1111
PUB, ED
Florissant Valley Reporter, Florissant, MO
Reynolds, Donald W (702) 383-0211
Founder
Las Vegas Review-Journal, Las Vegas, NV
Donrey Media Group
Reynolds, Geri (309) 343-7181
EDU ED, Register-Mail, Galesburg, IL
Reynolds, Hugh (914) 331-5000
EPE, Political ED
Daily Freeman, Kingston, NY
Reynolds, Jeff (518) 792-3131
Office MGR, Post-Star, Glens Falls, NY
Reynolds, Jim (305) 294-6641
CIRC MGR, Key West Citizen, Key West, FL
Reynolds, John (501) 523-5855
PUB/GM, ADV DIR
Newport Daily Independent, Newport, AR
Reynolds, Josh (508) 922-1234
Photo ED, Gloucester Times, Beverly, MA
Reynolds, Larry (210) 379-5402
PUB, Seguin Gazette-Enterprise, Seguin, TX
Reynolds, Laura (518) 270-1200
CONT, Record, Troy, NY
Reynolds, Lawrence D (513) 721-2700
PROD MGR-Pre Press
Cincinnati Enquirer, Cincinnati, OH
Reynolds, Lisa (510) 758-8400
EDU ED, West County Times, Pinole, CA
Reynolds, Michael (915) 546-6100
CIRC MGR-OPER
El Paso Times, El Paso, TX
Reynolds, Neil (506) 632-8888
PUB/EIC, EIC/PUB, Telegraph-Journal/Saint John Times Globe, Saint John, NB

Reynolds, Neil (613) 829-9100
ED, Ottawa Citizen, Ottawa, ON
Reynolds, Nikki (208) 377-6200
ADV MGR-NTL/Major
Idaho Statesman, Boise, ID
Reynolds, Paula J (406) 265-6795
ADV MGR, Havre Daily News, Havre, MT
Reynolds, Peg (815) 692-2366
ED, Blade, Fairbury, IL
Reynolds, Peggy (401) 277-7000
DIR-Database MKTG
Providence Journal-Bulletin, Providence, RI
Reynolds, R Vincent (540) 981-3100
PROD MGR, Roanoke Times, Roanoke, VA
Reynolds, Richard W (416) 413-4900
EX ED, INSIGHT News, Toronto, ON
Reynolds, Rick (334) 566-4270
PRES, PUB, Messenger, Troy, AL
Reynolds, Stephen B (614) 373-2121
PRES, PUB, Marietta Times, Marietta, OH
Reynolds, Steve (702) 882-2111
ADV DIR, Nevada Appeal, Carson City, NV
Reynolds, Theresa (540) 949-8213
Health/Medical ED, Music/Arts ED
News Virginian, Waynesboro, VA
Reynolds, Tim (518) 891-2600
Sports ED, Adirondack Daily Enterprise, Saranac Lake, NY
Reynolds, Timothy (207) 990-8000
CONT, Bangor Daily News, Bangor, ME
Reynolds, Vicki (402) 475-4200
Book Review ED, Journal Star, Lincoln, NE
Reynolds, Vicki (800) 424-4747
Customer Support MGR, Tribune Media Services-Television Listings, Glens Falls, NY
Reynose, Raymundo (213) 622-8332
Latin America ED
La Opinion, Los Angeles, CA
Reynozo, Alfonso (408) 372-3311
MGR-INFO SRV
Monterey County Herald, Monterey, CA
Reza, Cindy (419) 734-3141
News ED, News-Herald, Port Clinton, OH
Reza, Jesus (915) 546-6100
PROD MGR-Building Maintenance
El Paso Times, El Paso, TX
Rezaie, Virginia (405) 482-1221
ADV DIR, Altus Times, Altus, OK
Reznick, Lynn (617) 665-4442
MKTG DIR
Atlantic Feature Syndicate, Melrose, MA
Rhea, Butch (901) 465-3567
GM, ED, Fayette Falcon, Somerville, TN
Rhea, Ron (707) 644-1141
PUB, Grapevine, Vallejo, CA
Rhein, David (515) 284-8000
Deputy MAN ED
Des Moines Register, Des Moines, IA
Rhine, Mae (609) 466-1190
ED, Beacon, Hopewell, NJ
Rhinehart, Eugene (208) 642-3357
PUB, Independent Enterprise, Payette, ID
Rhinehart, Gene (541) 889-5387
ASST PUB, PROD MGR/FRM
Argus Observer, Ontario, OR
Rhoades, Jeff (806) 376-4488
Amusements/Music ED, Films/Theater ED, Travel ED, Amarillo Daily News/Globe Times, Amarillo, TX
Rhoades, John (303) 756-9995
CIRC MGR, Daily Journal, Denver, CO
Rhoades, Kenneth H (402) 426-2121
PUB, Blair Enterprise, Blair, NE
Rhoades, Mark (402) 426-2121
PUB, Blair Enterprise, Blair, NE
Rhoades, Mark A (712) 642-2791
PUB, Valley Times-News, Missouri Valley, IA
Rhoades, Rex (419) 625-5500
MAN ED, Sandusky Register, Sandusky, OH
Rhoades, Rich (814) 371-4200
Sports ED, Courier-Express/Tri-County Sunday, Du Bois, PA
Rhoades, Robert (317) 664-5111
PROD MGR-PR
Chronicle-Tribune, Marion, IN
Rhoades, Virginia (402) 332-3232
PUB, Gretna Guide, Gretna, NE
Rhoads, S Keating (213) 237-5000
Senior VP-OPER/Technology, PROD Senior VP-OPER/Technology
Los Angeles Times, Los Angeles, CA
Rhoden, Russell B (912) 557-6761
PUB, ED, Tattnall Journal, Reidsville, GA
Rhoden, Wilton R (912) 557-6761
MAN ED, Tattnall Journal, Reidsville, GA
Rhodes, Barbara (910) 843-8171
ED, Red Springs Citizen, Red Springs, NC
Rhodes, Bob (501) 442-1777
COL, EPE, EDL Writer
Northwest Arkansas Times, Fayetteville, AR
Rhodes, C Adrienne (212) 210-2100
DIR-Communications & Media Relations
New York Daily News, New York, NY
Rhodes, Carrol (901) 529-2211
PROD MGR-COMP
Commercial Appeal, Memphis, TN

Rhodes, Ellison (518) 584-4242
CIRC DIR, Saratogian, Saratoga Springs, NY
Rhodes, Guy (334) 727-3020
ED, Tuskegee News, Tuskegee, AL
Rhodes, Harry D (814) 870-1600
PROD SYS MGR
Morning News/Erie Daily Times, Erie, PA
Rhodes, John (918) 581-8300
MGR-Creative SRV, Tulsa World, Tulsa, OK
Rhodes, Mel (817) 325-4465
ED, Mineral Wells Index, Mineral Wells, TX
Rhodes, Melinda (316) 223-1460
MAN ED, BUS/FIN ED, City/MET ED, EPE
Fort Scott Tribune, Fort Scott, KS
Rhodes, Michael C (603) 668-4321
CIRC DIR, Union Leader, Manchester, NH
Rhodes, Mike (918) 756-3600
PROD FRM-PR
Okmulgee Daily Times, Okmulgee, OK
Rhodes, Nancy (413) 584-5000
Librarian
Daily Hampshire Gazette, Northampton, MA
Rhodes, Paul (316) 542-3111
PUB, Times Sentinel, Cheney, KS
Rhodes, Ralph (702) 788-6200
PROD MGR, Reno Gazette-Journal, Reno, NV
Rhodes, Stephen (519) 822-4310
PUB/GM, Daily Mercury, Guelph, ON
Rhodes, Wright (813) 259-7711
CIRC MGR-Customer Relations
Tampa Tribune and Times, Tampa, FL
Rhodin, Tony (610) 258-7171
ASSOC ED-Graphics
Express-Times, Easton, PA
Rhoten, Larry (717) 334-1131
DIR-News OPER/PUB
Gettysburg Times, Gettysburg, PA
Rhoten, Lisa (970) 249-3444
ADV MGR-CLASS
Montrose Daily Press, Montrose, CO
Rhymer, Sharon (704) 464-0221
ADV DIR
Observer-News-Enterprise, Newton, NC
Rian, Russell (214) 977-8222
EPE, Dallas Morning News, Dallas, TX
A H Belo Corp.
Ribadeneira, Diego F (617) 929-2000
Religion ED, Boston Globe, Boston, MA
Ribet, James (919) 419-6500
PROD MGR-Dayside Press
Herald-Sun, Durham, NC
Rible, Gail (908) 922-6000
ADV MGR-Direct MKTG
Asbury Park Press, Neptune, NJ
Ricardo, Larry (401) 277-7000
ADV Sales DIR-GEN CLASS
Providence Journal-Bulletin, Providence, RI
Riccelli, Christine (515) 284-8000
Lifestyle ED
Des Moines Register, Des Moines, IA
Ricci, James (203) 235-1661
CIRC ASST DIR, Record-Journal, Meriden, CT
Ricci, Thomas M (616) 964-7161
CONT, PA
Battle Creek Enquirer, Battle Creek, MI
Riccioli, Jim (612) 447-6669
ED, Prior Lake American, Prior Lake, MN
Rice, Belinda (606) 329-1717
PROD MGR-COMP
Daily Independent, Ashland, KY
Rice, Betsy (605) 225-4100
EPE
Aberdeen American News, Aberdeen, SD
Rice, Bill (817) 645-2441
PUB, Cleburne Times-Review, Cleburne, TX
Rice, Brian (816) 637-6155
ADV MGR, MGR-MKTG/PROM
Daily Standard, Excelsior Springs, MO
Rice, Darrell (405) 623-4922
ED, Watonga Republican, Watonga, OK
Rice, David C (937) 392-4321
GM, Ripley Bee, Ripley, OH
Rice, Delbert L (918) 581-8300
DIR-Human Resources
Tulsa World, Tulsa, OK
Rice, Don (806) 273-5611
Photo DEPT MGR, Picture ED
Borger News-Herald, Borger, TX
Rice, Jackie (406) 791-1444
Food ED, Great Falls Tribune, Great Falls, MT
Rice, James W (250) 758-4917
PUB/GM, Daily Free Press, Nanaimo, BC
Rice, Jeff (970) 522-1990
ED, Journal-Advocate, Sterling, CO
Rice, John (713) 220-7171
News ED, Houston Chronicle, Houston, TX
Rice, Kay (504) 383-1111
MGR-CR, Advocate, Baton Rouge, LA
Rice, Michelle (512) 445-3500
News ED
Austin American-Statesman, Austin, TX

Ric Who's Where-192

Rice, Mick .... (701) 252-3120
PROD FRM, Jamestown Sun, Jamestown, ND
Rice, Pat .... (314) 340-8000
Religion ED, Post-Dispatch, St. Louis, MO
Rice, Peter .... (619) 299-3131
ADV MGR-Sales NTL
San Diego Union-Tribune, San Diego, CA
Rice, Shauna .... (913) 899-2338
BM, Goodland Daily News, Goodland, KS
Rice, Teresa .... (502) 348-9003
MAN ED, Kentucky Standard, Bardstown, KY
Rice, Thomas E .... (618) 463-2500
PUB, Telegraph, Alton, IL
Rice, William .... (312) 222-3232
COL, Food/Wine COL
Chicago Tribune, Chicago, IL
Rich, Andrea .... (719) 456-1333
MAN ED
Bent County Democrat, Las Animas, CO
Rich, Charles .... (618) 529-5454
DP MGR, Southern Illinoisan, Carbondale, IL
Rich, Fred J .... (816) 747-3135
GM, Standard-Herald, Warrensburg, MO
Rich, John .... (209) 441-6111
Sports Writer, Fresno Bee, Fresno, CA
Rich, Macon .... (864) 298-4100
PROD MGR-Mailroom
Greenville News, Greenville, SC
Rich, Michael .... (205) 532-4000
Fashion ED, Life ED
Huntsville Times, Huntsville, AL
Rich, Pat .... (412) 465-5555
Religion ED, Indiana Gazette, Indiana, PA
Rich, Ron .... (904) 863-1111
PROD FRM-PR, Northwest Florida Daily News, Fort Walton Beach, FL
Rich, Sandy .... (810) 766-6100
PROD MGR-Pre Press Ad SRV
Flint Journal, Flint, MI
Rich, Sherry .... (910) 343-2000
PROD FRM-COMP (Day), Morning Star/ Sunday Star-News, Wilmington, NC
Rich, Steve .... (502) 443-1771
MGR-PROM, Paducah Sun, Paducah, KY
Richard, Amy .... (541) 482-3456
Entertainment/Amusements ED, Television/ Film ED, Theater/Music ED
Daily Tidings, Ashland, OR
Richard, Cody .... (318) 377-1866
PROD FRM
Minden Press-Herald, Minden, LA
Richard, Lourdes .... (506) 536-2500
ED, Sackville Tribune Post, Sackville, NB
Richard, Marc A .... (813) 942-2883
VP-OPER
Fackelman Newspapers, Tarpon Springs, FL
Richard, Nolin .... (418) 683-1573
PROD MGR
Le Journal de Quebec, Ville Vanier, QC
Richard, Paul .... (202) 334-6000
Arts Critic-Style
Washington Post, Washington, DC
Richard, Paula .... (316) 725-3176
ED, Sedan Times-Star, Sedan, KS
Richard, Philippe-Denis .... (514) 285-7272
ASST to PRES/Legal Counsel
La Presse, Montreal, QC
Richard, Sheila .... (847) 317-0500
MAN ED
Libertyville Review, Bannockburn, IL
Richard, Stephanie .... (903) 757-3311
Graphics ED
Longview News-Journal, Longview, TX
Richard, Susan .... (314) 421-1880
ADV MGR, Courier Post, St. Charles, MO
Richards, Amy .... (216) 329-7000
Accent EX ED
Chronicle-Telegram, Elyria, OH
Richards, Bob .... (312) 321-3000
Sports Active Page
Chicago Sun-Times, Chicago, IL
Richards, Charles .... (708) 448-6161
PUB, Reporter, Palos Heights, IL
Richards, Cindy .... (312) 321-3000
EDL Board Member/EDL Writer
Chicago Sun-Times, Chicago, IL
Richards, Cloy A .... (915) 928-5712
PUB, ED, Merkel Mail, Merkel, TX
Richards, Corrine J .... (218) 487-5225
ED, Leader Record, Gonvick, MN
Richards, Dargan .... (803) 771-6161
Librarian, State, Columbia, SC
Richards, Dave .... (814) 870-1600
COL, Music ED
Morning News/Erie Daily Times, Erie, PA
Richards, Florence .... (415) 777-5700
ADTX MGR, San Francisco Newspaper Agency, San Francisco, CA
Richards, Fred .... (217) 351-5252
PROD MGR, PROD FRM-PR
News-Gazette, Champaign, IL
Richards, Harley .... (403) 345-3081
ED, Sunny South News, Coaldale, AB
Richards, Helen .... (318) 627-3737
ED, Colfax Chronicle, Colfax, LA
Richards, Jeff .... (607) 734-5151
Photo ED, Star-Gazette, Elmira, NY
Richards, Jim .... (970) 858-3924
ED, Fruita Times, Fruita, CO
Richards, John .... (615) 259-8000
ED-Night/Weekend
Tennessean, Nashville, TN
Richards, Louis .... (919) 419-6500
PROD MGR-Nightside Distribution Center
Herald-Sun, Durham, NC
Richards, Melanie .... (915) 928-5712
PUB, Merkel Mail, Merkel, TX
Richards, Neil .... (573) 438-5141
PUB, ED, Independent-Journal, Potosi, MO
Richards, Richard D .... (218) 487-5225
PUB, Leader Record, Gonvick, MN
Richards, Richard P .... (512) 758-5391
PUB, Progress, Aransas Pass, TX
Richards, Robert .... (508) 586-7200
Suburban ED, Enterprise, Brockton, MA
Richards, Robin .... (619) 326-2222
GM, ED, Needles Desert Star, Needles, CA
Richards, Ruby .... (573) 438-5141
PUB, Independent-Journal, Potosi, MO
Richards, Terry L .... (616) 345-3511
PROD FRM-PR
Kalamazoo Gazette, Kalamazoo, MI
Richards, Tom .... (414) 733-4411
Radio/Television ED
Post-Crescent, Appleton, WI
Richards, Tony .... (604) 537-9933
PUB, ED, Gulf Islands Driftwood, Salt Spring Island, BC
Richards, W Dru .... (318) 627-3737
PUB, MAN ED, Colfax Chronicle, Colfax, LA
Richardson, Al .... (360) 484-7722
PRES, Tiptoe Literary Service, Naselle, WA
Richardson, Annetta .... (304) 485-1891
MAN ED, City ED, Films/Theater ED, Parkersburg News & Sentinel, Parkersburg, WV
Richardson, Cathy .... (520) 783-3333
BUS ED, Special Sections ED, Travel ED
Yuma Daily Sun, Yuma, AZ
Richardson, Charles .... (912) 744-4200
Perspective ED
Macon Telegraph, Macon, GA
Richardson, Charles E .... (307) 362-3736
PRES, PUB, PSL MGR, PA, Amusements ED, BUS/FIN ED, Consumer Interest/EDU ED, EPE, Environmental/Food ED, State ED
Daily Rocket-Miner, Rock Springs, WY
Richardson, Clem .... (212) 210-2100
Deputy MAN ED
New York Daily News, New York, NY
Richardson, Darrell .... (423) 376-3481
ED, Roane County News, Kingston, TN
Richardson, Dave .... (330) 753-1068
PUB, ED, Barberton Herald, Barberton, OH
Richardson, Dennis .... (954) 356-4000
ADV MGR-Special Sections
Sun-Sentinel, Fort Lauderdale, FL
Richardson, Dennis M .... (901) 986-2253
PUB
Carroll County News-Leader, Huntingdon, TN
Richardson, Ed .... (217) 732-2101
Online MGR, PROD FRM-COMP
Courier, Lincoln, IL
Richardson, Eddie P .... (806) 762-3612
PUB, ED, Southwest Digest, Lubbock, TX
Richardson, Elouise .... (702) 358-8061
ADV MGR-CLASS
Daily Sparks Tribune, Sparks, NV
Richardson, Flo .... (405) 343-2513
ED, Washita County Enterprise, Corn, OK
Richardson, Frank .... (508) 586-7200
Chairman, Enterprise, Brockton, MA
Richardson, Gerry .... (317) 962-1575
CIRC MGR-Customer SRV
Palladium-Item, Richmond, IN
Richardson, J .... (604) 723-8171
CIRC MGR
Alberni Valley Times, Port Alberni, BC
Richardson, Jack .... (508) 586-7200
PROD FRM-COMP Room
Enterprise, Brockton, MA
Richardson, Jenn .... (518) 584-4242
News ED, Wire ED
Saratogian, Saratoga Springs, NY
Richardson, Jim .... (916) 321-1000
EDU Writer
Sacramento Bee, Sacramento, CA
Richardson, John .... (413) 447-7311
DIR-OPER/Facilities
Berkshire Eagle, Pittsfield, MA
Richardson, Joyce .... (202) 334-6000
ADV DIR-CLASS
Washington Post, Washington, DC
Richardson, Ken .... (501) 474-5215
PUB, Press Argus-Courier, Van Buren, AR
Richardson, Lee .... (317) 633-1240
CIRC MGR-Sales & MKTG
Indianapolis Star/News, Indianapolis, IN
Richardson, Lisa .... (901) 584-7200
PUB, Camden Chronicle, Camden, TN
Richardson, Lynn .... (423) 929-3111
MGR-EDU SRV
Johnson City Press, Johnson City, TN
Richardson, M B .... (910) 372-5490
PUB, ED, Blue Ridge Sun, Sparta, NC
Richardson, Margaret E .... (307) 362-3736
TREAS
Daily Rocket-Miner, Rock Springs, WY
Richardson, Marion .... (301) 722-4600
ADV MGR-CLASS
Cumberland Times-News, Cumberland, MD
Richardson, Mark .... (902) 468-1222
PRES/PUB, Daily News, Halifax, NS
Richardson, Michael .... (201) 798-7800
ED, North Bergen/North Hudson Reporter, Hoboken, NJ
Richardson, Robert .... (705) 759-3030
PRES/PUB, Sault Star, Sault Ste. Marie, ON
Richardson, Ron .... (817) 757-5757
PROD MGR-SYS
Waco Tribune-Herald, Waco, TX
Richardson, Steve .... (423) 756-6900
PROD MGR-MR
Chattanooga Free Press, Chattanooga, TN
Richardson, Terri .... (304) 235-4242
EPE, SCI ED
Williamson Daily News, Williamson, WV
Richardson, Toni .... (561) 820-3800
ADV DIR
Palm Beach Daily News, Palm Beach, FL
Richardson, Wayne .... (609) 871-8000
Sports ED
Burlington County Times, Willingboro, NJ
Richelderfer, Robert .... (610) 820-6500
ADV MGR-NTL, Morning Call, Allentown, PA
Richenberg, Bob .... (352) 242-9819
PUB, News Leader, Clermont, FL
Richendrfer, Heather .... (360) 676-2600
PSL DIR
Bellingham Herald, Bellingham, WA
Richeson, David .... (561) 395-8300
CIRC DIR, News, Boca Raton, FL
Richey, Gary .... (419) 784-5441
PROD FRM-PR
Crescent-News, Defiance, OH
Richey, Mike .... (904) 359-4111
ASST MAN ED-News
Florida Times-Union, Jacksonville, FL
Richie, Tom .... (414) 634-3322
PROD SUPV-MR, Journal Times, Racine, WI
Richman, Chris .... (419) 294-2332
Automotive/Aviation ED, Sports ED
Daily Chief-Union, Upper Sandusky, OH
Richman, Elizabeth .... (304) 348-5140
VP, Charleston Gazette, Sunday Gazette-Mail, Charleston, WV
Richmond, Bill .... (317) 584-4501
Report Photographer
News-Gazette, Winchester, IN
Richmond, Della .... (913) 885-4582
PUB, ED, Independent Record, Natoma, KS
Richmond, Dionne .... (508) 758-9055
ED, Wanderer, Mattapoisett, MA
Richmond, Julie .... (937) 378-6161
GM
Georgetown News Democrat, Georgetown, OH
Richmond, Mable .... (502) 255-3205
GM, Trimble Banner-Democrat, Bedford, KY
Richmond, Mark D .... (614) 345-4053
PUB/GM, Advocate, Newark, OH
Richmond, Randy .... (705) 325-1355
Automotive ED, BUS ED, Environmental ED, Farm ED, News ED, Political ED
Packet & Times, Orillia, ON
Richmond, Stan .... (937) 225-2000
PROD VP-OPER
Dayton Daily News, Dayton, OH
Richner, Clifford .... (516) 569-4000
PUB, Nassau Herald, Lawrence, NY
Richner, Stuart .... (516) 569-4000
PUB, Nassau Herald, Lawrence, NY
Richter, Betty .... (912) 226-2400
PROD FRM-COMP, Thomasville Times-Enterprise, Thomasville, GA
Richter, Denise .... (217) 446-1000
MAN ED, Commercial News, Danville, IL
Richter, Ed .... (513) 746-3691
MAN ED, Franklin Chronicle, Franklin, OH
Richter, G P .... (507) 877-2281
PUB, ED, Comfrey Times, Comfrey, MN
Richter, Glenn .... (203) 235-1661
ASST MAN ED-Sunday
Record-Journal, Meriden, CT
Richter, Joe .... (616) 946-2000
Senior VP, Record-Eagle, Traverse City, MI
Richter, Judy .... (415) 348-4321
Films/Theater ED, Garden ED, Music ED
San Mateo County Times, San Mateo, CA
Richter, Martin .... (618) 277-7000
ED, Belleville Journal, Belleville, IL
Richter, Richard .... (717) 286-5671
CIRC MGR, Daily Item, Sunbury, PA
Richter, Tammie .... (218) 751-3740
BM, MGR-MIS, Daily Pioneer, Bemidji, MN
Rickard, Brian .... (502) 227-4556
Sports ED, State Journal, Frankfort, KY
Rickard, Cindy .... (330) 747-1471
Regional ED-Mahoning & Pennsylvania
Vindicator, Youngstown, OH
Rickard, Mark .... (506) 273-2285
ED
Victoria County Record, Perth-Andover, NB
Rickard, Victor .... (309) 392-2414
PUB, ED, Olympia Review, Minier, IL
Rickel, Cleon .... (316) 792-1211
MAN ED
Great Bend Tribune, Great Bend, KS
Rickelman, Sam .... (217) 347-7151
Sports ED
Effingham Daily News, Effingham, IL
Ricken, Carol .... (518) 589-7007
PUB, Mountain Eagle, Tannersville, NY
Ricken, Mike .... (802) 863-3441
ADV DIR
Burlington Free Press, Burlington, VT
Ricker, Fred E .... (414) 657-1000
CONT, Kenosha News, Kenosha, WI
Ricker, Jane .... (419) 695-0015
ADV DIR, Delphos Daily Herald, Delphos, OH
Ricker, Peter .... (605) 331-2200
ADV DIR, Argus Leader, Sioux Falls, SD
Ricker, Peter W .... (908) 722-8800
ADV DIR, Courier-News, Bridgewater, NJ
Rickert, Meredith .... (715) 266-2511
PUB, ED, Sawyer County Gazette, Winter, WI
Rickert, Rock .... (818) 932-6161
Sr News MGR, Dodge Construction News Greensheet, Monrovia, CA
Ricketson, J Thomas .... (501) 735-1010
SEC/TREAS
Evening Times, West Memphis, AR
Ricketson, John E .... (407) 886-2777
PUB, Planter, Apopka, FL
Ricketson, Lynette .... (501) 735-1010
PRES, Evening Times, West Memphis, AR
Ricketts, James B .... (601) 875-2791
PUB, ED
Ocean Springs Record, Ocean Springs, MS
Rickey, Carrie .... (215) 854-2000
Films Critic
Philadelphia Inquirer, Philadelphia, PA
Rickey, Regina P .... (314) 327-6279
GM, Wentzville Union and St. Charles County Record, St. Charles, MO
Rickley, Diane .... (913) 632-2127
Fashion/Home Furnishings ED, Society ED
Clay Center Dispatch, Clay Center, KS
Rickman, Dick .... (503) 221-8327
MGR-Production SYS
Oregonian, Portland, OR
Rickman, Jim .... (406) 523-5200
CIRC DIR, Missoulian, Missoula, MT
Rickman, Paul .... (217) 429-5151
PROD MGR-Commercial Printing
Herald & Review, Decatur, IL
Rickman, Ron L .... (319) 383-2100
VP-Newspaper
Lee Enterprises Inc., Davenport, IA
Rico, Richard .... (707) 448-6401
PUB, ED, Reporter, Vacaville, CA
Riddell, Robert A .... (313) 943-4250
PUB
Press & Guide Newspapers, Dearborn, MI
Ridden, Bill .... (207) 791-6650
DP MGR-Software
Portland Press Herald, Portland, ME
Ridder, Lynn .... (815) 223-3200
PROD MGR, News-Tribune, La Salle, IL
Ridder, P Anthony .... (305) 376-3800
COB/CEO, Knight-Ridder Inc., Miami, FL
Ridder, Peter B .... (612) 222-5011
PRES, PUB
St. Paul Pioneer Press, St. Paul, MN
Ridder, Rick .... (408) 920-5000
DIR-FIN
San Jose Mercury News, San Jose, CA
Riddick, Cathy .... (209) 441-6111
MET ED, Fresno Bee, Fresno, CA
Riddle, Bill .... (501) 731-2561
ED, Woodruff Monitor-Leader-Advocate, McCrory, AR
Riddle, Curtis W .... (703) 284-6000
Sr Group PRES-East Newspaper Group
Gannett Co. Inc., Arlington, VA
Riddle, Jill .... (313) 222-6400
MGR-Event MKTG
Detroit Newspapers, Detroit, MI
Riddle, Robin .... (409) 564-8361
DP MGR, Daily Sentinel, Nacogdoches, TX
Riddle, W Curtis .... (302) 324-2500
PRES, PUB, News Journal, Wilmington, DE
Ridenour, Chuck .... (419) 342-4276
Sports ED, Daily Globe, Shelby, OH
Ridenour, Shelley .... (307) 856-2244
PROD MGR-Commercial Printing
Riverton Ranger, Riverton, WY
Rideout, Dale .... (903) 532-6012
PUB, Howe Enterprise, Howe, TX
Rideout, Lana .... (903) 532-6012
ED, Howe Enterprise, Howe, TX

Copyright ©1997 by the Editor & Publisher Co.

HEAVY-WEIGHT

**FIRST ANNUAL EDITION ...
THE 1997 U.S. MARKET
FORECASTS. ECONOMIC
AND DEMOGRAPHIC PROFILES
OF 14,639 U.S. MARKETS.**

✓ Easier to use, less expensive than comparable data sources.

✓ Extensive, sensible and usable market data on over 11,000 towns and cities.

✓ Reliable 1997 state by state forecasts including population and age, ethnicity, household, education, money, income, employment and retail sales (9 categories).

✓ 100% Money-Back Guarantee. Return it within 15 days if you are not satisfied and receive a full refund of your payment.

♻ RECYCLED PAPER

Payment must accompany all orders. California, District of Columbia, New York and Ohio residents must add applicable tax. Canada residents please add GST. MFB7Y

☑ **YES!** Please send me a copy of the 1997 <u>U.S. MARKET FORECASTS</u>. My payment of $269 is enclosed.

Name_____
Company_____
Address_____
(Sorry, no deliveries to P.O. boxes)
City_____State_____Zip_____
Phone_____Fax_____
(In case we have questions about your order.)

❑ My check is enclosed (payable to Editor & Publisher Company). Payment must be in US Dollars drawn on a US bank.

❑ Charge my ❑ MC ❑ VISA ❑ AMEX

#_____

Exp. Date_____Signature_____

Your Business (Check one Category Only)
1. ❑ Newspaper
2. ❑ Newspaper Equip. Mfr.
3. ❑ Syndicate/News Service
4. ❑ Advertising Agency
5. ❑ Public Relations Firm
6. ❑ Legal Firm
7. ❑ Government
8. ❑ Manufacturer – General
9. ❑ Manufacturer – Auto & Truck
10. ❑ Manufacturer – Food
11. ❑ Service Industry
12. ❑ University/Public Library
13. ❑ Financial
14. ❑ Retail
15. ❑ Public Transportation
16. ❑ Individual
17. ❑ Publishing Other Than Newspaper
18. ❑ Real Estate
19. ❑ Other_____

FREE PAPER PUBLISHER

FPP

Now Published by The Editor & Publisher Co.!

The **ONLY** magazine exclusively serving the free paper industry! Only $24 for 12 monthly issues. Subscribe today!

Name_____
Company_____
Address_____
City_____State____Zip_____

District of Columbia residents please add applicable sales tax. Canada residents please add GST.
Your subscription is tax deductible.   FPB7Y

EDITOR&PUBLISHER

❑ **YES!** Please rush me the latest issue of Editor & Publisher and enter a one-year subscription (52 Issues for $65) in my name.

Name_____
Company_____
Address_____
City_____State____Zip_____

A. Your Business (Check Only **One** Category)
1. ❑ Daily Newspaper
2. ❑ Weekly Newspaper
3. ❑ Corp./Ind./Assn. Buying Advertising Space
4. ❑ Advertising Agency
5. ❑ Newspaper Rep.
6. ❑ Magazine/Other Publication
7. ❑ Graphic Arts / Printing Service / Newspaper Supplier
8. ❑ News Service / Feature Syndicate
9. ❑ Publicity and Public Relations
10. ❑ Library / Federal / State and Local Governments
11. ❑ Education: Students / Teachers

Other (Please specify)_____

B. Your Occupation (Check Only **One** Category)
A. ❑ Publisher
B. ❑ President
C. ❑ V. President
D. ❑ Editor
E. ❑ General Mgr.
F. ❑ Business Mgr.
G. ❑ Controller
H. ❑ Advertising Mgr.
I. ❑ Sales Mgr.
J. ❑ Class. Mgr.
K. ❑ Research Mgr.
L. ❑ Promo. Mgr
M. ❑ PR Mgr.
O. ❑ Prod. Mgr.
P. ❑ Composing Mgr.
Q. ❑ Circulation Mgr.
R. ❑ Editorial Dept.
S. ❑ Advertising Dept.
T. ❑ Circulation Dept.
V. ❑ Production Dept.
W. ❑ Promotion Dept.
X. ❑ Freelance Artist / Writer
Y. ❑ Newspaper Dealer / Distributor
Z. ❑ Retired
AA. ❑ MIS Mgr.
BB. ❑ Prepress Mgr.
CC. ❑ Mailroom Mgr.

Other (Please specify)_____

District of Columbia residents please add applicable sales tax. Canada residents please add GST.
Your subscription is tax deductible.   EPB7Y

BUSINESS REPLY MAIL
FIRST-CLASS MAIL   PERMIT NO.20   NEW YORK, NY

POSTAGE WILL BE PAID BY ADDRESSEE

Editor&Publisher
U.S. Market Forecasts
CIRCULATION DEPARTMENT
11 W 19TH ST
NEW YORK NY 10114-0111

NO POSTAGE NECESSARY IF MAILED IN THE UNITED STATES

RUSH: NEW SUBSCRIBER ORDER

BUSINESS REPLY MAIL
FIRST-CLASS MAIL   PERMIT NO.20   NEW YORK, NY

POSTAGE WILL BE PAID BY ADDRESSEE

Editor & Publisher
CIRCULATION DEPARTMENT
11 W 19TH ST
NEW YORK NY 10114 - 0741

NO POSTAGE NECESSARY IF MAILED IN THE UNITED STATES

RUSH: NEW SUBSCRIBER ORDER

BUSINESS REPLY MAIL
FIRST-CLASS MAIL   PERMIT NO.20   NEW YORK, NY

POSTAGE WILL BE PAID BY ADDRESSEE

Free Paper Publisher
EDITOR & PUBLISHER
CIRCULATION DEPARTMENT
11 W 19TH ST
NEW YORK NY 10114 - 0741

NO POSTAGE NECESSARY IF MAILED IN THE UNITED STATES

193-Who's Where **Rit**

Rideout, Roy P (902) 468-7557
PRES/COO
Newfoundland Capital Corp., Dartmouth, NS
Rider, Robert (803) 423-2050
PUB
Marion Star & Mullins Enterprise, Marion, SC
Ridge, Randall (312) 321-3000
PROD MGR, Chicago Sun-Times, Chicago, IL
Ridgway, Art (423) 523-3131
DIR-SYS, News-Sentinel, Knoxville, TN
Ridgway, Rick (404) 526-5151
PROD ASST MGR-Gwinnett Printing Facility
Atlanta Journal-Constitution, Atlanta, GA
Ridgway, Ronald H (314) 340-8402
Sr VP-FIN
Pulitzer Publishing Co., St. Louis, MO
Ridgway, Scott (310) 230-3400
Darkroom MGR, Allsport Photography USA, Pacific Palisades, CA
Riding, Beth (423) 986-6581
MAN ED, News-Herald, Lenoir City, TN
Ridings, Bill (615) 296-2426
PUB, News-Democrat, Waverly, TN
Ridings, H Dean (704) 739-7496
PUB
Kings Mountain Herald, Kings Mountain, NC
Ridley, Cliff (215) 854-2000
Theater Critic
Philadelphia Inquirer, Philadelphia, PA
Ridolfi, Mark (319) 383-2200
City ED, Quad-City Times, Davenport, IA
Ridosh, Margaret (607) 734-5151
Librarian, Star-Gazette, Elmira, NY
Rieb, Jeanette B (970) 332-4846
PUB, Wray Gazette, Wray, CO
Rieb, Ronald C (970) 332-4846
PUB, Wray Gazette, Wray, CO
Riebe, Rae (319) 398-8211
News ED, Gazette, Cedar Rapids, IA
Riebe, Randy (715) 842-2101
Fashion ED, Films/Theater ED, Teen-Age/Youth ED
Wausau Daily Herald, Wausau, WI
Riebel, Charles (404) 526-5151
MGR-Creative SRV
Atlanta Journal-Constitution, Atlanta, GA
Riebel, Chic (757) 446-2000
Sports ED, Virginian-Pilot, Norfolk, VA
Rieckman, Stewart (414) 235-7700
MAN ED
Oshkosh Northwestern, Oshkosh, WI
Ried, Rob (519) 894-2231
Art/Theatre ED, Record, Kitchener, ON
Riedel, Charlie (913) 628-1081
Photo ED, Hays Daily News, Hays, KS
Riedel, K (204) 748-3931
GM, Virden Empire-Advance, Virden, MB
Riedel, Mary (954) 356-4000
MGR-Database MKTG
Sun-Sentinel, Fort Lauderdale, FL
Riedemann, Fred (712) 328-1811
CIRC MGR
Daily Nonpareil, Council Bluffs, IA
Riedl, Marion (616) 845-5181
Religion ED, Women's
Daily News, Ludington, MI
Riedy, Linda (913) 282-3371
MAN ED
Smith County Pioneer, Smith Center, KS
Rief, Jeanne (904) 863-1111
MKTG DIR, Northwest Florida Daily News, Fort Walton Beach, FL
Riefstall, Gina (937) 652-1331
CIRC MGR
Urbana Daily Citizen, Urbana, OH
Riefterer, Ron (510) 208-6300
DIR-Photo/Graphics
Oakland Tribune, Oakland, CA
Rieger, Andy (405) 321-1800
MAN ED, Norman Transcript, Norman, OK
Riegle, Richard J (915) 646-2541
ASSOC PUB
Brownwood Bulletin, Brownwood, TX
Riegle, Rick (206) 872-6600
ADV DIR-RT
South County Journal, Kent, WA
Riehle, Joette (330) 996-3000
ASST to PUB
Akron Beacon Journal, Akron, OH
Riemann, Robert (914) 341-1100
BUS ED
Times Herald-Record, Middletown, NY
Ries, Ted (403) 235-7100
PROD MGR-MR, Calgary Herald, Calgary, AB
Riesau, Sue Ellen (360) 683-3311
GM, Sequim Gazette, Sequim, WA
Riesel, Annette (303) 659-1141
PUB, Brighton Standard Blade, Brighton, CO
Riese Willy, Scott (512) 664-6588
ED, Alice Echo-News, Alice, TX
Riesner, Karen Pike (802) 863-3441
Photo ED
Burlington Free Press, Burlington, VT
Riesz Jr, Charles W (910) 343-2000
EPE, Morning Star/Sunday Star-News, Wilmington, NC

Rieth, Mary Jo (816) 886-2233
MAN ED, Democrat-News, Marshall, MO
Rife, James M (904) 435-8500
PROD DIR, News Journal, Pensacola, FL
Rife, Judy (914) 341-1100
Economic Development ED
Times Herald-Record, Middletown, NY
Rife, Tom (941) 262-3161
Sports ED, Naples Daily News, Naples, FL
Rifenberg, Vicky (937) 773-2721
GM/PUB, Piqua Daily Call, Piqua, OH
Thomson Newspapers
Rifkin, Ira (202) 463-8777
NTL Correspondent
Religion News Service, Washington, DC
Rigali, Romola Mimi (413) 788-1000
MAN ED-Features
Union-News, Springfield, MA
Rigas, David A (716) 326-3163
PUB, Westfield Republican, Westfield, NY
Rigby, Jill (416) 947-2222
Travel ED, Toronto Sun, Toronto, ON
Rigby, Paul (212) 210-2100
EDL Cartoonist
New York Daily News, New York, NY
Rigdon, Terri (606) 796-6182/2331
MAN ED
Lewis County Herald, Vanceburg, KY
Riggenbach, Don (712) 527-9517
MGR, Jandon Features, Glenwood, IA
Riggins, Ron (904) 359-4111
CIRC MGR-PROM
Florida Times-Union, Jacksonville, FL
Riggle, Rhonda G (812) 939-2163
PUB, ED, News, Clay City, IN
Riggle, Terry (616) 696-3655
ED, Cedar Springs Post, Cedar Springs, MI
Riggs, Andy (212) 210-2100
PROD VP
New York Daily News, New York, NY
Riggs, Bill (505) 393-2123
Photo DEPT MGR
Hobbs Daily News-Sun, Hobbs, NM
Riggs, Brett (316) 275-8500
Sports ED
Garden City Telegram, Garden City, KS
Riggs, Dee (509) 663-5161
Consumer Interest ED, Society/Women's ED
Wenatchee World, Wenatchee, WA
Riggs, George E (510) 935-2525
PUB/CEO
Contra Costa Times, Walnut Creek, CA
Knight-Ridder Inc.
Riggs, Ginger (941) 494-2434
ED, Arcadian, Arcadia, FL
Riggs, James H (716) 487-1111
Sports ED, Post-Journal, Jamestown, NY
Riggs, Robert (717) 532-4101
GM, News-Chronicle, Shippensburg, PA
Righi, Jane (419) 625-5500
MGR-CR, Sandusky Register, Sandusky, OH
Rigler, Judyth (210) 225-7411
Books ED
San Antonio Express-News, San Antonio, TX
Rigney, Pat (606) 573-4510
EDU ED, Fashion/Style ED, Living/Lifestyle ED, Religion ED, Women's ED
Harlan Daily Enterprise, Harlan, KY
Riha, Michael (810) 766-6100
MET ED-AM, Flint Journal, Flint, MI
Riippi, Reino (815) 756-4841
ADV ASST MGR, Daily Chronicle, De Kalb, IL
Rilea, Ted (312) 321-3000
VP-Labor Relations (Chicago Sun-Times/Chicago Group)
Chicago Sun-Times, Chicago, IL
Riley, Charlotte (414) 657-1000
ADV CNR-NTL, Kenosha News, Kenosha, WI
Riley, Cindy (502) 388-2269
PUB, ED, Herald-Ledger, Eddyville, KY
Riley, Darrell (352) 867-4010
Researcher, Ocala Star-Banner, Ocala, FL
Riley, David (502) 886-4444
DIR-INFO Services
Kentucky New Era, Hopkinsville, KY
Riley, Denise (410) 822-1500
ED, Star-Democrat, Easton, MD
Riley, Diane (603) 352-1234
ED-Special Sections
Keene Sentinel, Keene, NH
Riley, Eleanor McGraw (319) 924-2361
PUB, ED, Lamont Leader, Lamont, IA
Riley, Gerry W (601) 961-7000
PROD DIR-OPER
Clarion-Ledger, Jackson, MS
Riley, Kevin (937) 225-2000
News ED, EX Sports ED
Dayton Daily News, Dayton, OH
Riley, Larry (805) 395-7500
CIRC MGR
Bakersfield Californian, Bakersfield, CA
Riley, Liz (509) 935-8422
ED, Chewelah Independent, Chewelah, WA
Riley, Pat (714) 835-1234
Ombudsman
Orange County Register, Santa Ana, CA

Riley, Rochelle (502) 582-4011
ASSOC ED, Courier-Journal, Louisville, KY
Riley, Steve (319) 337-3181
Sports ED
Iowa City Press-Citizen, Iowa City, IA
Riley, Steve (919) 829-4500
Sports ED, News & Observer, Raleigh, NC
Riley, Susan (613) 829-9100
COL, Ottawa Citizen, Ottawa, ON
Riley, Walter (860) 423-8466
ADV DIR, Chronicle, Willimantic, CT
Riley, William J (614) 353-3101
PUB
Portsmouth Daily Times, Portsmouth, OH
Rimbey, H Michael (602) 271-8000
PROD CNR-Products
Phoenix Newspapers Inc., Phoenix, AZ
Rimel, Chris (901) 627-3247
GM, ED
Dyer County Tennessean, Dyersburg, TN
Rimelspach, Rick (219) 461-8222
Copy Desk Chief
News-Sentinel, Fort Wayne, IN
Rimer, Skip (310) 829-6811
EX ED/ASST to PUB
Outlook, Santa Monica, CA
Rimmer, Addie (303) 442-1202
EX ED, Daily Camera, Boulder, CO
Rinaldi, Joe (202) 334-6000
PROD ASST MGR-Project (SE)
Washington Post, Washington, DC
Rincones, Ramiro (210) 423-5511
PROD FRM-PR
Valley Morning Star, Harlingen, TX
Rindfleisch, Terry (608) 782-9710
SCI/Technology ED
La Crosse Tribune, La Crosse, WI
Rinehart, Charles (937) 225-2000
CFO, Dayton Daily News, Dayton, OH
Rinehart, Harold (716) 282-2311
PROD MGR-Technical SRV
Niagara Gazette, Niagara Falls, NY
Rinehart, Nilla (615) 459-3868
GM, Rutherford Courier, Smyrna, TN
Rinehart, Richard (317) 633-1240
PROD OPER MGR/ENG
Indianapolis Star/News, Indianapolis, IN
Riney, T Edward (502) 926-0123
GM, Messenger-Inquirer, Owensboro, KY
Rinfret, Alex (604) 559-4680
ED, Islands Observer, Queen Charlotte, BC
Ring, David (216) 999-4500
PROD MGR, Plain Dealer, Cleveland, OH
Ring, Scott (201) 653-1000
PUB, Jersey Journal, Jersey City, NJ
Ring, Twyla L (612) 674-7025
ED, ECM Post Review, North Branch, MN
Ringel, Eleanor (404) 526-5151
Films ED
Atlanta Journal-Constitution, Atlanta, GA
Ringenberg, John (419) 668-3771
ADV MGR, Norwalk Reflector, Norwalk, OH
Ringer, Jon (815) 942-3221
ADV MGR, Daily Herald, Morris, IL
Ringgold, John (903) 984-2593
Sports ED, Kilgore News Herald, Kilgore, TX
Ringhand, Eugene (715) 833-9200
ED, EPE, EDL Writer
Leader-Telegram, Eau Claire, WI
Ringkdist, Mathew (517) 265-5111
PROD FRM-COMP
Daily Telegram, Adrian, MI
Ringler, Larry (330) 841-1600
BUS ED, Tribune Chronicle, Warren, OH
Ringo, Gary (212) 416-2000
PROD MGR (Riverside CA)
Wall Street Journal, New York, NY
Ringwood, Jon L (801) 237-2188
News ED, Deseret News, Salt Lake City, UT
Rini, Alan (504) 447-4055
ADV DIR, Daily Comet, Thibodaux, LA
Rink, Ellen (805) 395-7500
ADV MGR-Inside Sales
Bakersfield Californian, Bakersfield, CA
Rink, John (704) 633-8950
GM, BM/PA, Salisbury Post, Salisbury, NC
Rinne, Fred (807) 468-5555
ED, Daily Miner & News, Kenora, ON
Rintoul, Mary (316) 694-5700
City ED, Hutchinson News, Hutchinson, KS
Rio, Raul (407) 659-1833
PUB, La Voz Hispana, West Palm Beach, FL
Riojas-Aguero, Olga (806) 763-3841
GM, MAN ED, El Editor-Lubbock, Lubbock, TX
Riordan, Ginger (316) 792-1211
CIRC MGR
Great Bend Tribune, Great Bend, KS
Rios, Jimmie (210) 896-7000
PROD SUPT
Kerrville Daily Times, Kerrville, TX
Rios, Mavis (615) 552-1808
Librarian, Leaf-Chronicle, Clarksville, TN
Riotto, James (717) 622-3456
ADV MGR-CLASS, Pottsville Republican & Evening Herald, Pottsville, PA

Ripley, A J (902) 426-2811
VP/GM, Chronicle-Herald, Halifax, NS
Ripley, James (512) 445-3500
VP/CFO
Austin American-Statesman, Austin, TX
Ripley, Jim (602) 898-6500
MAN ED, Mesa Tribune, Mesa, AZ
Thomson Newspapers
Ripley, Ken (919) 478-3651
PUB, ED, Spring Hope Enterprise & The Bailey News, Spring Hope, NC
Ripley, Robert E (816) 446-3331
ED, Times Observer, Oregon, MO
Ripley, Wilma J (816) 446-3331
PUB, Times Observer, Oregon, MO
Ripperger, Nick (320) 589-2525
ED, Morris Sun, Morris, MN
Rips, Geoff (512) 477-0746
PUB, Texas Observer, Austin, TX
Ripsom, Cathy T (916) 541-3880
CONT
Tahoe Daily Tribune, South Lake Tahoe, CA
Risch, Carla S (317) 825-0581
MGR-BUS Office
Connersville News-Examiner, Connersville, IN
Risch, Vivian (765) 458-5114
ED, Union County Review, Liberty, IN
Rischmueller, Linda H (402) 287-2323
PUB, ED
Wakefield Republican, Wakefield, NE
Rischmueller, William H (402) 287-2323
PUB, ED
Wakefield Republican, Wakefield, NE
Rising, Evelyn (505) 393-2123
Women's ED
Hobbs Daily News-Sun, Hobbs, NM
Riskedahl, Reed (515) 753-6611
ADV DIR, ADV MGR-CLASS
Times-Republican, Marshalltown, IA
Risley, Allyson (815) 433-2000
MGR-Human Resources
Daily Times, Ottawa, IL
Risling, Greg (415) 289-4040
ED, Newspointer, Sausalito, CA
Risser, Larry (916) 885-5656
MGR-Telecommunications, PROD MGR-SYS
Auburn Journal, Auburn, CA
Rissover, B Jean (573) 883-2222
MAN ED, Herald, Ste. Genevieve, MO
Ristine, Jeff (619) 299-3131
EDU Writer (Colleges/Universities)
San Diego Union-Tribune, San Diego, CA
Ristow, Bill (206) 464-2111
EDU ED, Seattle Times, Seattle, WA
Ristow, James L (402) 444-1000
CIRC DIR, Omaha World-Herald, Omaha, NE
Ritch, James S (410) 228-3131
VP, Daily Banner, Cambridge, MD
Ritchey, Mike (970) 728-9788
PUB, DP News LLC, Telluride, CO
Ritchie, Bruce (352) 374-5000
Environmental Writer, Scene Magazine ED
Gainesville Sun, Gainesville, FL
Ritchie, Chris (717) 829-7100
Features ED, Times Leader, Wilkes-Barre, PA
Ritchie, Dave (506) 452-6671
Sports ED, Daily Gleaner, Fredericton, NB
Ritchie, Lauren (407) 420-5000
ED-Lake County
Orlando Sentinel, Orlando, FL
Ritchie, Robert (604) 624-6781
ADV MGR, Daily News, Prince Rupert, BC
Ritchot, Georges (403) 235-7100
CIRC VP-Reader Sales & SRV
Calgary Herald, Calgary, AB
Ritscher, Charles W (908) 922-6000
VP-Sales & MKTG
New Jersey Press Inc., Neptune, NJ
Ritt, Glenn H (201) 646-4000
VP-ED, Record, Hackensack, NJ
Ritter, Alfred F (804) 446-2010
EVP
Landmark Communications Inc., Norfolk, VA
Ritter, Byron (910) 373-7000
CIRC MGR-Distribution/Single Copy/TMC
News & Record, Greensboro, NC
Ritter, C D (619) 934-3929
ED, Mammoth Times Weekly, Mammoth Lakes, CA
Ritter, Hal (703) 276-3400
MAN ED-News, USA Today, Arlington, VA
Ritter, Jim (312) 321-3000
Environmental/SCI Writer
Chicago Sun-Times, Chicago, IL
Ritter, John (305) 372-0933
PRES/Writer, Legal & Word Briefs, Miami, FL
Ritter, Laura (717) 272-5611
Entertainment/Amusements ED
Daily News, Lebanon, PA
Ritter, Robert W (703) 276-5800
ED, Gannett News Service, Arlington, VA

Rit Who's Where-194

Rittinger, Carolyne .... (519) 894-2231
ED, Record, Kitchener, ON
Ritz, Don .... (214) 754-8710
GM, Dallas Voice, Dallas, TX
Ritz, Kathrine .... (610) 367-6041
ED, News of Southern Berks, Boyertown, PA
Ritzer, Linda .... (412) 222-2200
ASST News ED
Observer-Reporter, Washington, PA
Ritzler, Karl .... (404) 526-5151
Automotive ED, RE ED
Atlanta Journal-Constitution, Atlanta, GA
Rivais, Larry .... (413) 788-1000
City ED-Day
Springfield Union-News, Springfield, MA
Rivard, Bob .... (210) 225-7411
MAN ED, Express-News, San Antonio, TX
Rivard, Ray .... (715) 339-3036
ED, Bee, Phillips, WI
Rivard, Richard .... (802) 334-6568
PUB, Newport Daily Express, Newport, VT
Rivas, Josue R .... (212) 807-4600
Entertainment ED
El Diario La Prensa, New York, NY
Rivedall, Karen .... (815) 459-4040
Political Reporter
Northwest Herald, Crystal Lake, IL
Rivenbark, Celia .... (910) 343-2000
COL, Morning Star/Sunday Star-News, Wilmington, NC
Rivera, Ray .... (505) 983-3303
Sports ED
Santa Fe New Mexican, Santa Fe, NM
Rivera-Brooks, Nancy .... (213) 237-5000
Regional Issues/S California Small BUS/Travel/Tourism
Los Angeles Times, Los Angeles, CA
Rivero, Ivonne .... (503) 736-9878
ED, El Hispanic News, Portland, OR
Rivero, Roger .... (213) 622-8332
BUS ED, La Opinion, Los Angeles, CA
Rivers, Jeff .... (517) 377-1000
Sports ED
Lansing State Journal, Lansing, MI
Rivers, Jeff .... (860) 241-6200
ASSOC ED-Recruiting, COL-Lifestyle
Hartford Courant, Hartford, CT
Rives, Jerry .... (903) 597-8111
CIRC DIR, Tyler Morning Telegraph, Tyler, TX
Rivet, Wayne E .... (207) 647-2851
ED, Bridgton News, Bridgton, ME
Rixon, Paul A .... (508) 222-7000
VP, PUB
Attleboro Sun Chronicle, Attleboro, MA
Rizzi, Jim .... (415) 541-0700
PUB, SF Weekly, San Francisco, CA
Rizzo, Angelyn R .... (317) 423-5511
Human Resources DIR
Journal and Courier, Lafayette, IN
Rizzo, Karen .... (630) 834-0900
ED, Roselle Press, Elmhurst, IL
Roach, Donna .... (909) 684-1200
CIRC MGR-Sales Development
Press-Enterprise, Riverside, CA
Roach, Gerald .... (716) 849-3434
PROD OPER MGR-Distribution
Buffalo News, Buffalo, NY
Roach, Jamie .... (506) 433-1070
ED, MAN ED
Kings County Record, Sussex, NB
Roach, Rick .... (707) 448-6401
Photo ED, Reporter, Vacaville, CA
Roads, Darlene .... (405) 336-2222
DIR-Accounts
Perry Daily Journal, Perry, OK
Roales, Judith .... (813) 893-8111
EX VP, GM
St. Petersburg Times, St. Petersburg, FL
Roan, Joni .... (818) 713-3000
CIRC MGR-NIE
Daily News, Woodland Hills, CA
Roan, Shari .... (213) 237-5000
Health Writer, Medical Reporter
Los Angeles Times, Los Angeles, CA
Roark, Shelly .... (903) 597-8111
Food ED, Travel ED
Tyler Morning Telegraph, Tyler, TX
Roath, Gwen .... (505) 835-0520
PUB, ED, Defensor Chieftain, Socorro, NM
Robanske, Eric .... (805) 273-2700
CIRC DIR
Antelope Valley Press, Palmdale, CA
Robards, Richard .... (502) 465-8111
PUB, Central Kentucky News-Journal, Campbellsville, KY
Robb, Ann .... (803) 524-3183
ADV DIR, Beaufort Gazette, Beaufort, SC
Robb, Diane .... (414) 435-4411
Librarian
Green Bay Press-Gazette, Green Bay, WI
Robb, Edith .... (506) 859-4900
News ED, Times-Transcript, Moncton, NB
Robb, Gary .... (805) 564-5200
Lifestyle Production ED, Santa Barbara News-Press, Santa Barbara, CA
Robb, Jack .... (412) 772-3900
ADV DIR
North Hills News Record, Warrendale, PA
Robb, John .... (414) 435-4411
Photo ED
Green Bay Press-Gazette, Green Bay, WI
Robb, Kathy .... (614) 592-6612
Community ED
Athens Messenger, Athens, OH
Robb, Michael .... (810) 766-6100
Graphics ED, Flint Journal, Flint, MI
Robb, Peter .... (613) 829-9100
ASST City ED, Ottawa Citizen, Ottawa, ON
Robb, Rich .... (909) 889-9666
CIRC MGR-Home Delivery
Sun, San Bernardino, CA
Robb, Rick .... (954) 356-4000
NTL/State/Foreign ED
Sun-Sentinel, Fort Lauderdale, FL
Robbennolt, Jola .... (719) 632-5511
PROD OPER FRM-Composing
Gazette, Colorado Springs, CO
Robbins, Arnie .... (612) 673-4000
Change ED, Star Tribune, Minneapolis, MN
Robbins, Carolyn .... (413) 788-1000
BUS ED, Union-News, Springfield, MA
Robbins, Chrys .... (334) 262-1611
Society/Women's ED
Montgomery Advertiser, Montgomery, AL
Robbins, Dana .... (905) 526-3333
MET ED, Spectator, Hamilton, ON
Robbins, Gene .... (201) 635-0639
MAN ED, Chatham Courier, Chatham, NJ
Robbins, Jamie .... (702) 788-6200
Online MGR
Reno Gazette-Journal, Reno, NV
Robbins, Keith .... (212) 416-2000
PROD MGR (Des Moines IA)
Wall Street Journal, New York, NY
Robbins, Kimberly .... (804) 295-0124
GM, Charlottesville Albemarle Observer, Charlottesville, VA
Robbins, Len .... (912) 487-5337
ED, Clinch County News, Homerville, GA
Robbins, Robert E .... (360) 676-2600
PUB, Bellingham Herald, Bellingham, WA
Robbins, Walt .... (916) 885-5656
PROD DIR, Auburn Journal, Auburn, CA
Roberge, Huguette .... (514) 285-7272
Cinema ED, La Presse, Montreal, QC
Roberson, Dale .... (512) 858-7893
PUB, ED, Dripping Springs Dispatch, Dripping Springs, TX
Roberto, Philomena .... (610) 272-2500
Lifestyle ED, Times Herald, Norristown, PA
Roberts, Alfred G .... (610) 820-6500
Deputy MAN ED
Allentown Morning Call, Allentown, PA
Roberts, Amy .... (209) 582-0471
Religion ED, Hanford Sentinel, Hanford, CA
Roberts, Armida .... (209) 674-2424
ADV MGR-RT, Madera Tribune, Madera, CA
Roberts, Bill .... (970) 247-3504
EPE, Durango Herald, Durango, CO
Roberts, Bill .... (208) 377-6200
Religion ED, Idaho Statesman, Boise, ID
Roberts, Bill .... (918) 663-1414
Mechanical SUPT, OPER DIR, Tulsa Daily Commerce & Legal News, Tulsa, OK
Roberts, Bill .... (602) 898-6500
DIR-Multimedia Services
Mesa Tribune, Mesa, AZ
Thomson Newspapers
Roberts, Bruce .... (417) 679-4641
ED, Ozark County Times, Gainesville, MO
Roberts, Byron K .... (302) 324-2500
MGR-Strategic MKTG
News Journal, Wilmington, DE
Roberts, C Frank .... (212) 556-1234
VP-Broadcasting
New York Times Co., New York, NY
Roberts, Chad .... (217) 446-1000
Sports ED, Commercial News, Danville, IL
Roberts, Charles .... (515) 672-2581
PROD MGR, Oskaloosa Herald, Oskaloosa, IA
Roberts, Chris .... (303) 442-1202
Environmental ED
Daily Camera, Boulder, CO
Roberts, Christopher .... (207) 563-3171
PUB
Lincoln County News, Damariscotta, ME
Roberts, Clara .... (216) 999-4500
Deputy MET ED, Plain Dealer, Cleveland, OH
Roberts, Collette Kaercher ...... (612) 633-3434
GM, Focus News, Roseville, MN
Roberts, David .... (708) 345-1750
PUB, ED
Proviso Star-Sentinel, Melrose Park, IL
Roberts, David O .... (864) 582-4511
PUB, Herald-Journal, Spartanburg, SC
Roberts, Dennis .... (209) 578-2000
Religion Writer, Modesto Bee, Modesto, CA
Roberts, Diane .... (319) 342-2429
ED, Progress-Review, La Porte City, IA
Roberts, Donnie .... (704) 249-3981
Photo DEPT MGR, Dispatch, Lexington, NC
Roberts, Edwin A .... (813) 259-7711
EPE, Tampa Tribune and Times, Tampa, FL
Roberts, Elise B .... (615) 268-9725
ED, Jackson County Sentinel, Gainesboro, TN
Roberts, Gene .... (212) 556-1234
MAN ED, New York Times, New York, NY
Roberts, Greg .... (206) 448-8000
Food ED
Seattle Post-Intelligencer, Seattle, WA
Roberts, Jack .... (504) 683-5195
PUB, Watchman, Clinton, LA
Roberts, James .... (817) 552-5454
VP, Vernon Daily Record, Vernon, TX
Roberts, Janes .... (903) 872-3931
PROD FRM-PR
Corsicana Daily Sun, Corsicana, TX
Roberts, Jerry .... (415) 777-1111
City ED
San Francisco Chronicle, San Francisco, CA
Roberts, Jim .... (919) 335-0841
Fashion/Women's ED, SCI ED
Daily Advance, Elizabeth City, NC
Roberts, John .... (360) 694-3391
PROD MGR-Camera Room
Columbian, Vancouver, WA
Roberts, John .... (403) 843-2231
ED, Rimbey Record, Rimbey, AB
Roberts, John .... (816) 748-3266
PUB, Post-Telegraph, Princeton, MO
Roberts, John .... (519) 843-1310
PUB, Fergus-Elora News Express, Fergus, ON
Roberts III, John (Trey) .... (817) 390-7400
PROD MGR-Packaging/Distribution
Fort Worth Star-Telegram, Fort Worth, TX
Roberts, John M .... (512) 575-1451
PRES, PUB, Victoria Advocate, Victoria, TX
Roberts, Kate .... (209) 578-2000
Librarian, Modesto Bee, Modesto, CA
Roberts, Katherine J .... (212) 556-1234
Op-Ed ED, New York Times, New York, NY
Roberts, Kathy .... (517) 895-8551
Entertainment/Amusements ED, Fashion/Style ED, Features ED, Lifestyle ED, Religion ED, Bay City Times, Bay City, MI
Roberts, Kelly .... (713) 446-3733
PUB, Humble Echo, Humble, TX
Roberts, Kenneth .... (210) 487-2819
ED, Rio Grande Herald, Rio Grande, TX
Roberts, Kenneth W .... (609) 854-1400
PUB, ED, Retrospect, Collingswood, NJ
Roberts, Laren .... (208) 888-1941
ED, Valley News, Meridian, ID
Roberts, Larry .... (806) 762-8844
CIRC MGR-State
Lubbock Avalanche-Journal, Lubbock, TX
Roberts, Larry D .... (541) 782-4241
PUB, Dead Mountain Echo, Oakridge, OR
Roberts, SSgt Lee .... (919) 736-5170
ED, Scope, Goldsboro, NC
Roberts, Leslie .... (417) 667-3344
COL, Nevada Daily Mail, Nevada, MO
Roberts, Lewis F .... (607) 798-1234
ADV DIR
Press & Sun Bulletin, Binghamton, NY
Roberts, London .... (916) 885-5656
Entertainment/Amusements ED
Auburn Journal, Auburn, CA
Roberts, Mana .... (913) 243-2424
BM, Blade-Empire, Concordia, KS
Roberts, Michael .... (513) 721-2700
Training ED
Cincinnati Enquirer, Cincinnati, OH
Roberts, Mrs Morris .... (512) 575-1451
VP, Victoria Advocate, Victoria, TX
Roberts, Odell .... (941) 748-0411
PROD MGR-PR/OPER
Bradenton Herald, Bradenton, FL
Roberts, Phillip A .... (937) 393-3456
PUB, Press Gazette, Hillsboro, OH
Roberts, Randall .... (505) 823-7777
ASST MAN ED-Visuals/Technology
Albuquerque Tribune, Albuquerque, NM
Roberts, Randy .... (816) 776-5454
ED, Daily News, Richmond, MO
Roberts, Randy .... (419) 448-3200
Photo ED, Advertiser-Tribune, Tiffin, OH
Roberts, Renae .... (304) 348-5140
ADV MGR-CLASS
Charleston Newspapers, Charleston, WV
Roberts, Richard .... (612) 633-3434
PUB, Focus News, Roseville, MN
Roberts, Rob .... (913) 762-5000
News ED, Daily Union, Junction City, KS
Roberts, Russell .... (507) 235-3303
ED, EDL Writer, DP MGR
Sentinel, Fairmont, MN
Roberts, Sandra .... (615) 259-8000
MAN ED-Opinion, Tennessean, Nashville, TN
Roberts, Sandy .... (208) 467-9251
Religion ED, Idaho Press-Tribune, Nampa, ID
Roberts, Sharon .... (707) 546-2020
ASST MAN ED-Design
Press Democrat, Santa Rosa, CA
Roberts, Sherry A .... (317) 825-0581
PROD MGR
Connersville News-Examiner, Connersville, IN
Roberts, Sherry J .... (317) 825-0581
CNR-Plant
Connersville News-Examiner, Connersville, IN
Roberts, Steven .... (819) 979-5357
PUB, Nunatsiaq News, Iqaluit, NT
Roberts, Sue .... (208) 743-9411
CIRC MGR-OPER
Lewiston Morning Tribune, Lewiston, ID
Roberts, Tim .... (972) 392-0888
VP-SYS
Wieck Photo DataBase Inc., Dallas, TX
Roberts, Toby .... (312) 321-3000
EDL Art DIR-Nights
Chicago Sun-Times, Chicago, IL
Roberts, Valeria .... (904) 526-3614
ADV DIR
Jackson County Floridan, Marianna, FL
Roberts, Vida .... (410) 332-6000
Fashion ED, Sun, Baltimore, MD
Roberts, William G .... (702) 482-3365
PUB, ED
Times-Bonanza/Goldfield News, Tonopah, NV
Robertson, Andrew .... (902) 485-8014
GM, Pictou Advocate, Pictou, NS
Robertson, Angus .... (202) 383-6150
EX VP/News, Bridge News, Washington, DC
Robertson, Charles E .... (513) 721-2700
PROD MGR-PR
Cincinnati Enquirer, Cincinnati, OH
Robertson, Clint .... (804) 458-8511
ADV DIR, News, Hopewell, VA
Robertson, Ed .... (913) 295-1111
PROD ASST MGR
Topeka Capital-Journal, Topeka, KS
Robertson, George .... (503) 843-2312
PUB, ED, Sun, Sheridan, OR
Robertson, Irving .... (718) 946-4949
COL, Independent Cartoonist Freelance, Brooklyn, NY
Robertson, Jeff .... (815) 562-4171
ED, Rochelle News-Leader, Rochelle, IL
Robertson, Jim .... (573) 815-1500
MAN ED, EPE
Columbia Daily Tribune, Columbia, MO
Robertson, Jim .... (815) 987-1200
CIRC MGR, Register Star, Rockford, IL
Robertson, Jim .... (972) 542-2631
PUB, ED, Courier-Gazette, McKinney, TX
Robertson, Jimmy .... (501) 623-7711
PROD MGR
Sentinel-Record, Hot Springs, AR
Robertson, John .... (505) 823-7777
Political ED
Albuquerque Journal, Albuquerque, NM
Robertson, Ken .... (509) 582-1500
MAN ED, Tri-City Herald, Tri-Cities, WA
Robertson, Larry .... (310) 540-5511
PROD FRM-COMP, Daily Breeze, Torrance, CA, Copley Press Inc.
Robertson, Lisa .... (502) 769-2312
MGR-MKTG, ADTX MGR
News Enterprise, Elizabethtown, KY
Robertson, Martha .... (806) 396-5885
PUB, ED, Stratford Star, Stratford, TX
Robertson, Maureen .... (619) 789-1350
ED, Ramona Sentinel, Ramona, CA
Robertson, Nancy .... (919) 419-6500
DIR-FIN, Herald-Sun, Durham, NC
Robertson, Robbie .... (601) 762-1111
News ED, Mississippi Press, Pascagoula, MS
Robertson, Stephanie .... (602) 271-8000
Perspective ED
Arizona Republic, Phoenix, AZ
Robertson, Stephen .... (403) 667-6285
GM, MAN ED, Yukon News, Whitehorse, YT
Robertson, Steve .... (405) 353-0620
ASST MAN ED, BUS/FIN ED
Lawton Constitution, Lawton, OK
Robertson, Steve .... (803) 248-6671
PUB, Horry Independent, Conway, SC
Robertson, Terry .... (415) 348-4321
EPE
San Mateo County Times, San Mateo, CA
Robey, Virginia .... (806) 447-2559
ED, Wellington Leader, Wellington, TX
Robidoux, Joe .... (818) 962-8811
CIRC MGR-Home Delivery, San Gabriel Valley Tribune, West Covina, CA, MediaNews Inc.
Robillard, Ron .... (860) 423-8466
EDL DIR, BUS/FIN ED, EDL Writer
Chronicle, Willimantic, CT
Robin, Laura .... (613) 829-9100
Food ED, Ottawa Citizen, Ottawa, ON
Robinet, Karen .... (519) 785-2455
ED, Chronicle, Rodney, ON
Robinette, Eddie .... (941) 953-7755
Regional ED, Herald-Tribune, Sarasota, FL
Robinette, Gale .... (206) 841-2481
PUB, Pierce County Herald/Herald Sampler, Puyallup, WA

Copyright ©1997 by the Editor & Publisher Co.

195-Who's Where **Roe**

Robinette, George L .... (804) 793-2311
ADV DIR, ADV MGR-Co-op/Insert
Danville Register & Bee, Danville, VA

Robinette, Holly .... (304) 788-3333
ADV MGR-Sales
Mineral Daily News-Tribune, Keyser, WV

Robinette, Judy D .... (941) 385-6155
PUB, News-Sun, Sebring, FL

Robins, Marjorie Kaplan .... (516) 843-2020
Travel, Newsday, Melville, NY

Robinson, Barry .... (210) 225-7411
Sports ED
San Antonio Express-News, San Antonio, TX

Robinson, Bill .... (405) 379-5411
PRES
Robinson-Pettis Publishing, Holdenville, OK

Robinson, Billie S .... (712) 728-2223
PUB, Hartley Sentinel, Hartley, IA

Robinson, Charles .... (212) 556-1234
DIR-News INFO SRV
New York Times, New York, NY

Robinson, Charles I .... (423) 928-4151
PRES, PUB
Elizabethton Star, Elizabethton, TN

Robinson, Christopher .... (617) 426-8246
PUB, In Newsweekly, Boston, MA

Robinson, Chuck .... (913) 631-2550
PUB, ED
Shawnee Journal Herald, Shawnee, KS

Robinson, Dan .... (419) 674-4066
PROD FRM-PR, Kenton Times, Kenton, OH

Robinson, Dave .... (313) 222-6400
Deputy MAN ED
Detroit Free Press, Detroit, MI

Robinson, David .... (716) 849-3434
RE ED, Buffalo News, Buffalo, NY

Robinson, David .... (207) 873-3341
PROD DIR-Post Press, Central Maine Morning Sentinel, Waterville, ME
Guy Gannett Communications

Robinson, Dayna .... (405) 927-2355
PUB, Coalgate Record-Register, Coalgate, OK

Robinson, Dean .... (219) 461-8333
Television ED
Journal Gazette, Fort Wayne, IN

Robinson, Delmer .... (304) 348-5140
Food ED, Charleston Gazette, Sunday Gazette-Mail, Charleston, WV

Robinson, Dennis .... (219) 461-8444
ADV MGR-Strategic Initiatives
Fort Wayne Newspapers Inc., Fort Wayne, IN

Robinson, Dennis .... (416) 585-5000
Picture ED, Globe and Mail, Toronto, ON

Robinson, Diane .... (417) 836-1100
Fashion ED, Home Furnishings ED, Life/Times ED, Weekend/Entertainment ED
Springfield News-Leader, Springfield, MO

Robinson, Don W .... (541) 485-1234
EPE, Register-Guard, Eugene, OR

Robinson, Doug .... (502) 926-0123
CONT, Owensboro Messenger-Inquirer, Owensboro, KY

Robinson, Doug .... (215) 854-2000
State ED
Philadelphia Inquirer, Philadelphia, PA

Robinson, Edward .... (712) 728-2223
PUB, Hartley Sentinel, Hartley, IA

Robinson, Frank .... (304) 636-2121
ED, News ED, Inter-Mountain, Elkins, WV

Robinson, Fred .... (704) 437-2161
PROD SUPT, News Herald, Morganton, NC

Robinson, Gail .... (708) 336-7000
ADV MGR-CLASS, News-Sun, Waukegan, IL

Robinson, Gail .... (212) 889-5155
MAN ED, World Press Review, New York, NY

Robinson, Gene .... (202) 334-6000
Foreign ED
Washington Post, Washington, DC

Robinson, Greg .... (406) 791-1444
CONT, Great Falls Tribune, Great Falls, MT

Robinson, Henry .... (704) 252-5611
Religion ED
Asheville Citizen-Times, Asheville, NC

Robinson, J Mack .... (912) 888-9390
CEO, Gray Communications, Albany, GA

Robinson, Janet .... (320) 398-5000
ED, Tri-County News, Kimball, MN

Robinson, Janet L .... (212) 556-1234
PRES/GM
New York Times Co., New York, NY

Robinson, Jeff .... (704) 321-4271
ED, Andrews Journal, Andrews, NC

Robinson, Jeff .... (406) 587-4491
Sports ED
Bozeman Daily Chronicle, Bozeman, MT

Robinson, Jennifer .... (514) 987-2222
EPE, Gazette, Montreal, QC

Robinson, Jens .... (212) 362-9256
VP/ED, Cartoonists & Writers Syndicate, New York, NY

Robinson, Jerry .... (212) 362-9256
PRES/EDL DIR, Cartoonists & Writers Syndicate, New York, NY

Robinson, Jerry .... (206) 932-0300
PUB, West Seattle Herald, Seattle, WA

Robinson, Jim .... (562) 435-1161
EX City ED, Press-Telegram, Long Beach, CA

Robinson, Jody .... (815) 537-5107
MAN ED
Prophetstown Echo, Prophetstown, IL

Robinson, John .... (801) 237-2188
Sports ED
Deseret News, Salt Lake City, UT

Robinson, Johnnie .... (501) 338-9181
Sports Writer, Daily World, Helena, AR

Robinson, Joleen .... (308) 382-1000
ADTX MGR
Grand Island Independent, Grand Island, NE

Robinson, Keith .... (310) 379-5337
Cartoonist/Owner
Making It Productions, Manhattan Beach, CA

Robinson, Ken .... (712) 651-2321
PUB, ED, News Gazette, Bayard, IA

Robinson, Ken .... (360) 794-7116
PUB, ED
Monroe Monitor/Valley News, Monroe, WA

Robinson, Kenneth .... (317) 747-5700
PROD MGR-COMP, Star Press, Muncie, IN

Robinson III, Kenneth H .... (203) 235-1661
ASST MAN ED
Meriden Record-Journal, Meriden, CT

Robinson, Lonell .... (713) 524-4474
PUB, GM, Houston Sun, Houston, TX

Robinson, Max .... (813) 688-8500
ED, Auburndale Star, Auburndale, FL

Robinson, Michael .... (316) 777-4233
PUB, ED, Mulvane News, Mulvane, KS

Robinson, Mike .... (905) 871-3100
ED, Fort Erie Times, Fort Erie, ON

Robinson, Neil .... (815) 537-5107
PUB, ED
Prophetstown Echo, Prophetstown, IL

Robinson, Pat .... (903) 583-2124
PROD MGR, Favorite, Bonham, TX

Robinson, Peggy .... (918) 663-1414
ED, Owasso Reporter, Tulsa, OK

Robinson, Ray L .... (540) 473-2741
PUB, Fincastle Herald, Fincastle, VA

Robinson, Robert J .... (619) 299-3131
DIR-Project MGT
San Diego Union-Tribune, San Diego, CA

Robinson, Rodney .... (916) 321-1000
MGR-Networks ENG
Sacramento Bee, Sacramento, CA

Robinson, Rosemary .... (315) 470-0011
MAN ED, Post-Standard/Syracuse Herald-Journal/American, Syracuse, NY

Robinson, Roy .... (303) 426-6000
PUB, Lowry Airman, Westminster, CO

Robinson, Shuronda .... (512) 467-2881
ED, Austin Sun, Austin, TX

Robinson, Steve .... (206) 597-8742
ADM DIR, News Tribune, Tacoma, WA

Robinson, Sue .... (757) 446-2000
ED-Virginia, Political ED
Virginian-Pilot, Norfolk, VA

Robinson, Susan .... (508) 626-3800
ADV DIR (Acting)
Middlesex News, Framingham, MA

Robinson, Ted .... (630) 232-9222
PROD MGR-Plant
Kane County Chronicle, Geneva, IL

Robinson, Terry .... (509) 582-1500
PROD DIR, Tri-City Herald, Tri-Cities, WA

Robinson, Terry .... (516) 747-8282
ED, Massapequan Observer, Mineola, NY

Robinson, Thomas A .... (304) 824-5101
PUB, Lincoln Journal, Hamlin, WV

Robinson, Tim .... (417) 623-3480
CONT, Joplin Globe, Joplin, MO

Robinson, Tom .... (717) 348-9100
Sports ED
Tribune & Scranton Times, Scranton, PA

Robinson, Walter V .... (617) 929-2000
ASST MAN ED, Boston Globe, Boston, MA

Robinson, Will .... (712) 834-2388
ED, Everly-Royal News, Everly, IA

Robinson, Willa .... (818) 241-4141
ADV DIR, Glendale News-Press, Glendale, CA

Robinson, William .... (315) 470-0011
Administrative ED, Books ED, Post-Standard/Herald-Journal/American, Syracuse, NY

Robinson, William O .... (304) 743-1222
PUB, ED, Cabell Record, Culloden, WV

Robison, James .... (212) 556-1927
EX ED
New York Times News Service, New York, NY

Robison, Pete .... (406) 348-2649
PUB, Yellowstone County News, Huntley, MT

Robison, Rebecca Tescher ..... (406) 348-2649
PUB, GM, ED
Yellowstone County News, Huntley, MT

Robison, Susie .... (501) 763-4461
PA, PROD FRM-PR
Blytheville Courier News, Blytheville, AR

Robledo, Roberto .... (408) 424-2221
EPE, Californian, Salinas, CA

Robling, Mary Anne .... (812) 853-3366
GM
Newburgh-Chandler Register, Newburgh, IN

Robson, Dale .... (204) 727-2451
CIRC MGR, Brandon Sun, Brandon, MB

Robson, James .... (508) 685-1000
PROD SUPT-COMP
Eagle-Tribune, North Andover, MA

Robustelli, Peter .... (860) 489-3121
PROD FRM-PR
Register Citizen, Torrington, CT

Roby, Mark .... (319) 383-2200
DIR-MKTG, Quad-City Times, Davenport, IA

Roby, Ray .... (615) 552-1808
ADV MGR-NTL/Co-Op
Leaf-Chronicle, Clarksville, TN

Roby, Shelby .... (317) 664-5111
Features ED, Chronicle-Tribune, Marion, IN

Roca, Karen .... (501) 855-3724
ED, Weekly Vista, Bella Vista, AR

Rocconi, Rosemary .... (215) 345-3000
ADV DIR
Intelligencer/Record, Doylestown, PA

Rocha, Julie J .... (619) 233-8496
PUB, ED
El Sol de San Diego, San Diego, CA

Roche, Kevin J .... (212) 416-2600
VP/CFO
Dow Jones & Co. Inc., New York, NY

Roche, Walter .... (617) 426-3000
Investigative/Politics ED
Boston Herald, Boston, MA

Rochelle, Anna .... (812) 875-2141
PUB, ED
Worthington Times, Worthington, IN

Rocher, Alain .... (819) 376-2501
MGR-PSL, DIR-FIN
Le Nouvelliste, Trois-Rivieres, QC

Rochester, Mark .... (317) 633-1240
ASST MAN ED-Projects
Indianapolis Star/News, Indianapolis, IN

Rochon, Daniel .... (514) 285-7272
VP Finance/ADM, La Presse, Montreal, QC

Rochon, Joel .... (520) 573-4561
Art DIR, Tucson Citizen, Tucson, AZ

Rock, Dean .... (801) 674-6200
Sports ED, Spectrum, St. George, UT

Rock, George .... (518) 561-2300
ADV MGR-RT
Press-Republican, Plattsburgh, NY

Rock, Steve .... (605) 331-2200
PROD MGR-PR
Argus Leader, Sioux Falls, SD

Rocker, A V .... (912) 236-9511
MGR-CR
Savannah Morning News, Savannah, GA

Rockey, Travis O .... (803) 577-7111
VP
Evening Post Publishing Co., Charleston, SC

Rockley, Paul W .... (403) 938-6397
PUB, Okotoks Western Wheel, Okotoks, AB

Rockmore, Milton .... (203) 377-5525
PRES
Metropolitan Press Syndicate, Stratford, CT

Rockmore, Sylvia .... (203) 377-5525
GM
Metropolitan Press Syndicate, Stratford, CT

Rockowicz, John J .... (610) 371-5000
DP MGR, PROD DIR-Electronic SYS
Reading Times/Eagle, Reading, PA

Rockwell, Carla .... (813) 689-7764
GM, Brandon News, Brandon, FL

Rockwell, Curtis .... (601) 762-1111
Sports ED, Mississippi Press, Pascagoula, MS

Rockwell, Jan V .... (501) 892-4451
PUB
Pocahontas Star Herald, Pocahontas, AR

Rockwell, Keith M .... (212) 837-7000
BU Chief-Washington, Journal of Commerce & Commercial, New York, NY

Roda, Barbara Hough .... (717) 291-8811
Style ED, Lancaster Intelligencer Journal/New Era/Sunday News, Lancaster, PA

Rodak, Peter .... (416) 255-8604
PUB, Moloda Ukraina, Toronto, ON

Rodak, Walentina .... (416) 255-8604
ED, Moloda Ukraina, Toronto, ON

Roddy, Beth .... (972) 424-6565
ADV DIR-MKTG
Plano Star Courier, Plano, TX

Roddy, Daniel L .... (541) 926-2211
DIR-MIS
Albany Democrat-Herald, Albany, OR

Roddy, Donald .... (419) 332-5511
PROD MGR-PR
News-Messenger, Fremont, OH

Rode, Nancy .... (604) 368-8551
Home Furnishings ED, Women's ED
Trail Daily Times, Trail, BC

Rodeffer, Dessa L .... (309) 924-1871
PUB, ED
Henderson County Quill, Stronghurst, IL

Rodeffer, Lucille .... (217) 659-3316
GM, Hancock County Quill, La Harpe, IL

Rodenfels, Dan .... (614) 385-2107
PUB, Logan Daily News, Logan, OH

Roderick, Anne .... (419) 668-3771
ADV MGR-CLASS
Norwalk Reflector, Norwalk, OH

Rodewalt, Vance .... (403) 235-7100
Cartoonist, Calgary Herald, Calgary, AB

Rodgers, Bruce .... (816) 561-6061
ED, PitchWeekly, Kansas City, MO

Rodgers, Charlotte .... (423) 929-3111
Librarian
Johnson City Press, Johnson City, TN

Rodgers, Jack .... (618) 262-5144
PRES, PUB
Daily Republican Register, Mount Carmel, IL

Rodgers, Joy .... (206) 339-3000
Public Life ED-Night, Herald, Everett, WA

Rodgers, Marc E .... (514) 630-6688
PUB, Chronicle, Pointe Claire, QC

Rodgers, Max .... (405) 372-5000
Housing/Home Furnishings ED
News Press, Stillwater, OK

Rodgers, Vernor .... (818) 962-8811
Automotive ED
San Gabriel Valley Tribune, West Covina, CA
MediaNews Inc.

Rodi, Bob .... (330) 264-1125
Mechanical SUPT, PROD SUPT-Mechanical
Daily Record, Wooster, OH

Rodimer, Bishop Frank J .... (201) 279-8845
PUB, Beacon, Clifton, NJ

Rodis-Brown, Estelle .... (219) 982-6383
ED, News-Journal, North Manchester, IN

Rodney, John R .... (609) 272-7000
DIR-Production, DP MGR, PROD DIR
Press of Atlantic City, Pleasantville, NJ

Rodney, Rod .... (603) 742-4455
EX ED, Foster's Democrat, Dover, NH

Rodricks, Dan .... (410) 332-6000
COL-Local, Sun, Baltimore, MD

Rodrigues, Lorraine .... (508) 458-7100
DP MGR, Sun, Lowell, MA

Rodrigues, Rod .... (201) 646-4000
ADV MGR-NTL Sales
Record, Hackensack, NJ

Rodriguez, Carlos .... (210) 686-4343
EPE, Monitor, McAllen, TX

Rodriguez, Estella .... (210) 728-2500
News ED, Laredo Morning Times, Laredo, TX

Rodriguez Jr, Joseph .... (408) 920-5000
EDL Writer
San Jose Mercury News, San Jose, CA

Rodriguez, Julian .... (210) 728-2500
PROD FRM-PR
Laredo Morning Times, Laredo, TX

Rodriguez, Lori .... (713) 220-7171
Minority Affairs
Houston Chronicle, Houston, TX

Rodriguez, Manuel .... (334) 433-1551
PROD ASST DIR
Mobile Press Register, Mobile, AL

Rodriguez, Medwviges .... (520) 783-3333
MAN ED, Bajo El Sol, Yuma, AZ

Rodriguez, Richard .... (415) 243-4364
ASSOC ED
Pacific News Service, San Francisco, CA

Rodriguez, Rick .... (916) 321-1000
MAN ED, Sacramento Bee, Sacramento, CA

Rodriguez, Robert .... (914) 694-9300
Photo DIR, Reporter Dispatch, White Plains, NY, Gannett Co. Inc.

Rodriguez, Robert R .... (541) 592-2541
PUB, ED
Illinois Valley News, Cave Junction, OR

Rodriguez, Tim .... (608) 252-6400
ADV DIR, Capital Times, Madison, WI

Rodriguez, Vicente P .... (305) 687-5555
PUB, GM, ED
La Voz de la Calle, Hialeah, FL

Rodriguez, Virginia .... (202) 334-6000
DIR-Public Relations
Washington Post, Washington, DC

Rodriquez, Alex .... (312) 321-3000
Suburban Writer
Chicago Sun-Times, Chicago, IL

Rodriquez, Lionel .... (201) 863-3310
ED, La Tribuna Publication, Union City, NJ

Rodriquez, Suzette .... (919) 552-5675
ED, Fuquay-Varina Independent, Fuquay-Varina, NC

Roe, Dave .... (919) 446-5161
CIRC DIR, Telegram, Rocky Mount, NC

Roe, Jim .... (602) 898-6500
DIR-Computer Services, Mesa Tribune, Mesa, AZ, Thomson Newspapers

Roe, John .... (519) 894-2231
Environment Reporter
Record, Kitchener, ON

Roe, Tim .... (707) 448-6401
Sports ED, Reporter, Vacaville, CA

Roeder, Kent .... (201) 383-1500
PUB, ED, New Jersey Herald, Newton, NJ

Roehm, Ollie .... (513) 367-4582
ED, Harrison Press, Harrison, OH

Roenigk, Ronald .... (773) 878-7333
PUB, Inside Publications, Chicago, IL

Copyright ©1997 by the Editor & Publisher Co.

Roe Who's Where-196

Roeper, Richard .... (312) 321-3000
COL-GEN, Chicago Sun-Times, Chicago, IL
Roeser, Bob .... (805) 925-2691
CIRC DIR
Santa Maria Times, Santa Maria, CA
Roeser, Stan .... (320) 693-3266
PUB, ED
Independent Review, Litchfield, MN
Roesslein, Kenneth P .... (414) 224-2000
EPE, Journal Sentinel, Milwaukee, WI
Roessner, Frank .... (607) 798-1234
EPE, Press & Sun Bulletin, Binghamton, NY
Rogahn, Kurt .... (319) 398-8211
EDL Writer, Gazette, Cedar Rapids, IA
Rogala, Diane .... (908) 922-6000
ADV MGR-NTL
Asbury Park Press, Neptune, NJ
Rogalski, James .... (802) 447-7567
MAN ED
Bennington Banner, Bennington, VT
Rogell, Pat .... (561) 820-4100
ADV MGR-Major Accounts
Palm Beach Post, West Palm Beach, FL
Roger, Andy .... (901) 427-3333
CONT, Jackson Sun, Jackson, TN
Rogers, Benny .... (903) 675-5626
Sports ED, Athens Daily Review, Athens, TX
Rogers, Bonnie .... (214) 977-8222
PROD ASST MGR
Dallas Morning News, Dallas, TX
Rogers, Charles .... (315) 470-0011
PROD ASST MGR (Night)
Post-Standard/Syracuse Herald-Journal/American, Syracuse, NY
Rogers, Charles .... (718) 257-0600
ED, Canarsie Courier, Brooklyn, NY
Rogers, Cheryl .... (610) 272-2500
City ED, Times Herald, Norristown, PA
Rogers, Chip .... (508) 685-1000
VP, GM, Eagle-Tribune, North Andover, MA
Rogers, Debbie .... (419) 352-4611
Films/Theater ED, Radio/Television ED
Sentinel-Tribune, Bowling Green, OH
Rogers, Deborah .... (334) 262-1611
CIRC MGR
Montgomery Advertiser, Montgomery, AL
Rogers, Dennis .... (919) 829-4500
COL/EDL Writer
News & Observer, Raleigh, NC
Rogers, Dinah .... (504) 826-3279
Photo ED, Times-Picayune, New Orleans, LA
Rogers, Don .... (915) 236-6677
MAN ED
Sweetwater Reporter, Sweetwater, TX
Rogers, Don .... (315) 253-5311
MAN ED, EPE, Citizen, Auburn, NY
Rogers, Elizabeth .... (412) 222-2200
City/MET ED, News ED
Observer-Reporter, Washington, PA
Rogers, Forrest .... (404) 526-5151
MGR-Events
Atlanta Journal-Constitution, Atlanta, GA
Rogers, Holly .... (803) 771-6161
DIR-Human Resources, State, Columbia, SC
Rogers, Holly H .... (972) 322-4248
PUB, Buffalo Press, Buffalo, TX
Rogers Jr, Irving E .... (508) 685-1000
PRES/TREAS, PUB
Eagle-Tribune, North Andover, MA
Rogers III, Irving E .... (508) 475-5731
PUB, Andover Townsman, Andover, MA
Rogers, J U .... (502) 384-6471
GM, Adair Progress, Columbia, KY
Rogers, Janice .... (918) 647-3188
CIRC MGR, Poteau News & Sun, Poteau, OK
Rogers, Jeff .... (815) 232-1171
ED, Journal-Standard, Freeport, IL
Rogers, Jeffery B .... (317) 633-1240
BM, Indianapolis Star/News, Indianapolis, IN
Rogers, Jerry W .... (757) 857-1212
ED, Wheel, Norfolk, VA
Rogers, John A .... (414) 582-4541
PUB, Winneconne News, Winneconne, WI
Rogers, Ken .... (701) 223-2500
Innovations ED
Bismarck Tribune, Bismarck, ND
Rogers, Larry .... (913) 295-1111
PROD DIR
Topeka Capital-Journal, Topeka, KS
Rogers, Laurie .... (408) 920-5000
PROD MGR-MR
San Jose Mercury News, San Jose, CA
Rogers, Linda Faye .... (423) 949-2505
ED, Dunlap Tribune, Dunlap, TN
Rogers, Lou .... (604) 489-3455
GM, Kootenay Advertiser, Cranbrook, BC
Rogers, M L (Tex) .... (409) 732-2304
PUB, ED
Colorado County Citizen, Columbus, TX
Rogers, Margaret E .... (414) 582-4541
ED, Winneconne News, Winneconne, WI
Rogers, Mark .... (704) 252-5611
DP MGR, Citizen-Times, Asheville, NC
Rogers, Mary .... (817) 390-7400
Society ED
Fort Worth Star-Telegram, Fort Worth, TX
Rogers, Mike .... (409) 883-3571
Sports ED, Orange Leader, Orange, TX
Rogers, Patsy .... (817) 743-3322
PUB, ED, Twin Cities News, Rochester, TX
Rogers, Peter D .... (701) 225-8111
PUB, PA, MGR-PROM
Dickinson Press, Dickinson, ND
Rogers, Ric .... (219) 982-6383
GM, News-Journal, North Manchester, IN
Rogers, Rick .... (405) 475-3311
Music ED
Daily Oklahoman, Oklahoma City, OK
Rogers, Rob .... (412) 263-1100
Cartoonist, Post-Gazette, Pittsburgh, PA
Rogers, Ron .... (360) 452-2345
PROD SUPV-PR
Peninsula Daily News, Port Angeles, WA
Rogers, Stephen A .... (315) 470-0011
PRES, PUB, Post-Standard/Syracuse Herald-Journal/American, Syracuse, NY
Rogers, Steve .... (615) 452-2561
ED, News-Examiner, Gallatin, TN
Rogers, Virginia .... (860) 584-0501
Librarian, Bristol Press, Bristol, CT
Rogers, Wanda .... (615) 325-9241
PUB, Portland Leader, Portland, TN
Rogers, Warren .... (406) 657-1200
Sports ED, Billings Gazette, Billings, MT
Rogers, Warren .... (703) 764-0496
Washington Correspondent
Associated Features Inc., Burke, VA
Rogers Jr, William C .... (912) 237-9971
PUB, Blade, Swainsboro, GA
Roghaar, Bradley N .... (801) 625-4200
ADV DIR, Standard-Examiner, Ogden, UT
Roghair, Clarice .... (605) 669-2529
PUB, ED, Murdo Coyote, Murdo, SD
Roghair, Melvin .... (605) 669-2529
PUB, Murdo Coyote, Murdo, SD
Rohan, Ginny .... (201) 646-4000
Television Reviewer, Record, Hackensack, NJ
Rohde, Darleen .... (419) 734-3141
MGR-Office, News-Herald, Port Clinton, OH
Roherty, Dan .... (414) 733-4411
Copy Desk Chief, Post-Crescent, Appleton, WI
Rohloff, Greg .... (806) 376-4488
Radio/Television ED, Amarillo Daily News/Globe Times, Amarillo, TX
Rohn, David .... (317) 633-1240
EDL Writer
Indianapolis Star/News, Indianapolis, IN
Rohrig, Byron .... (812) 424-7711
EDU Reporter
Evansville Courier, Evansville, IN
Rohrs, Jeremy J .... (419) 445-9456
ED, Archbold Farmland News, Archbold, OH
Rohwer, Maggie .... (315) 253-5311
Fashion/Style ED, Television/Music ED, Films/Theater ED, Citizen, Auburn, NY
Rojas, Alida .... (212) 930-8000
MGR-BUS SYS
New York Post, New York, NY
Rojas, Fernando F .... (718) 899-8603
PUB, Resumen Newspaper, Woodside, NY
Rojas, Fernando J .... (718) 899-8603
ED, Resumen Newspaper, Woodside, NY
Rojas, Gaspar .... (312) 768-1622
PUB, ED, El Observador, Chicago, IL
Rojas-Burke, Joe .... (541) 485-1234
Health/Medical ED
Register-Guard, Eugene, OR
Roknick, Michael .... (412) 981-6100
BUS ED, Herald, Sharon, PA
Roler, Dennis .... (541) 474-3700
ED, EPE
Grants Pass Daily Courier, Grants Pass, OR
Roley, Terry .... (309) 833-2114
PROD FRM-PR
Macomb Journal, Macomb, IL
Rolfe, Bruce .... (616) 746-4331
PUB, ED, Climax Crescent, Climax, MI
Rolfe, Glenn .... (717) 888-9643
Sports ED, Evening Times, Sayre, PA
Rolfes, Terri .... (712) 262-6610
DP MGR, Daily Reporter, Spencer, IA
Rolfsrud, Stan .... (612) 447-6669
GM, Prior Lake American, Prior Lake, MN
Roline, Tim .... (218) 751-3740
PROD SUPT-Plant
Daily Pioneer, Bemidji, MN
Roll, Pat .... (402) 444-1000
CIRC MGR-Single Copy
Omaha World-Herald, Omaha, NE
Roller, Howard .... (502) 582-4011
PROD GEN SUPV-COMP
Courier-Journal, Louisville, KY
Roller, Vera M .... (416) 439-9117
ED, Novy Domov, Scarborough, ON
Rolley, Robert .... (717) 326-1551
BUS ED, News ED
Williamsport Sun-Gazette, Williamsport, PA
Rollin, Ann .... (707) 425-4646
ADV DIR, Daily Republic, Fairfield, CA
Rollings, Lynn .... (334) 262-1611
Fashion ED
Montgomery Advertiser, Montgomery, AL
Rollins Jr, E T .... (919) 419-6500
COB, Herald-Sun, Durham, NC
Rollins, Heather .... (520) 783-3333
ADV CNR-Co-op, Yuma Daily Sun, Yuma, AZ
Rollins, Judy B .... (801) 237-2031
Deputy ED-Features
Salt Lake Tribune, Salt Lake City, UT
Rollins, Maggie .... (502) 926-0123
ADV MGR-CLASS
Messenger-Inquirer, Owensboro, KY
Rollins, Michael .... (503) 221-8327
Team Leader-Living, Oregonian, Portland, OR
Rollins, Paul .... (910) 323-4848
CIRC MGR-Packaging
Fayetteville Observer-Times, Fayetteville, NC
Rollins, Ron .... (937) 225-2000
Living/Lifestyle ED
Dayton Daily News, Dayton, OH
Rollison, Fred .... (864) 298-4100
Photo ED, Greenville News, Greenville, SC
Rolnick, Jody .... (541) 942-3325
PUB, Sentinel, Cottage Grove, OR
Rom, Louis .... (813) 472-5185
ED
Sanibel-Captiva Islander, Sanibel Island, FL
Roma, Jim .... (817) 965-3124
CIRC DIR, Stephenville Empire-Tribune, Stephenville, TX
Romalewski, Linda .... (516) 223-6514
ED, Polish American World, Baldwin, NY
Roman, Jennifer .... (407) 420-5000
ADV MGR-Advertising Development
Orlando Sentinel, Orlando, FL
Roman, Marnie .... (309) 944-2119
GM, Geneseo Republic, Geneseo, IL
Romanelli, Jack .... (514) 987-2222
ASST MAN ED, Gazette, Montreal, QC
Romano, Carlin .... (215) 854-2000
Books Critic
Philadelphia Inquirer, Philadelphia, PA
Romano, Marilyn .... (907) 456-6661
ADV DIR
Fairbanks Daily News-Miner, Fairbanks, AK
Romanow, Marc .... (401) 789-9744
PUB, Narragansett Times, Wakefield, RI
Romanowsky, Bernardo .... (619) 565-9135
PUB, ED
San Diego Weekly News, San Diego, CA
Romanska, Anna .... (203) 744-5100
MGR-CR, News-Times, Danbury, CT
Romantic, Bob .... (520) 783-3333
Sports ED, Yuma Daily Sun, Yuma, AZ
Romanus, Michelle .... (217) 324-2121
MAN ED, Wire ED
News-Herald, Litchfield, IL
Romanyshyn, O .... (416) 504-3443
ED, Homin Ukrainy, Toronto, ON
Rombach, Klaus .... (909) 684-1200
MGR-Purchasing
Press-Enterprise, Riverside, CA
Rombouts, Christina .... (805) 822-6828
ED, Tehachapi News, Tehachapi, CA
Romeo, Robert .... (217) 223-5100
PROD FRM-Press
Quincy Herald-Whig, Quincy, IL
Romere, Carla .... (501) 442-1777
PROD FRM-COMP
Northwest Arkansas Times, Fayetteville, AR
Romero, Baldemar .... (210) 686-4343
PROD MGR-Press, Monitor, McAllen, TX
Romero Jr, Jose .... (718) 899-8603
MAN ED
Resumen Newspaper, Woodside, NY
Romero, Lorenzo .... (408) 920-5000
First Editions ED
San Jose Mercury News, San Jose, CA
Romero, Margie .... (412) 488-1212
MAN ED
In Pittsburgh Newsweekly, Pittsburgh, PA
Romero, Michael .... (602) 898-6500
CIRC DIR, Mesa Tribune, Mesa, AZ
Thomson Newspapers
Romero, Reg .... (604) 467-1122
PUB, ED
Maple Ridge News, Maple Ridge, BC
Romero, Rolando .... (210) 242-7900
MAN ED
La Prensa De San Antonio, San Antonio, TX
Romero, Ron .... (318) 824-3011
PROD FRM-PR
Jennings Daily News, Jennings, LA
Romero, Veronica .... (201) 864-9505
MAN ED
Continental Newspaper, Union City, NJ
Romig, Rob .... (541) 746-1671
MAN ED, Springfield News, Springfield, OR
Romine, Robert .... (970) 493-6397
PROD MGR-Technical SRV
Fort Collins Coloradoan, Fort Collins, CO
Romkey, Mike .... (319) 326-5848
ED, Leader, Davenport, IA
Romme, Carol .... (201) 383-1500
DP MGR, New Jersey Herald, Newton, NJ
Rommelmeyer, Karen .... (864) 224-4321
ADV MGR-Display
Anderson Independent-Mail, Anderson, SC
Romujue, Barb .... (719) 384-4475
CIRC MGR, Tribune-Democrat, La Junta, CO
Ron, Ricardo .... (415) 334-2061
PUB, El Latino, San Francisco, CA
Ronald, John C .... (219) 726-8141
BC, PRES, PUB
Commercial Review, Portland, IN
Ronald, Steve .... (612) 673-4000
Production ED
Star Tribune, Minneapolis, MN
Ronaldson, Tonia .... (208) 467-9251
DIR-MKTG/PROM
Idaho Press-Tribune, Nampa, ID
Ronalter, Jane .... (910) 888-3500
Fashion ED, Food ED
High Point Enterprise, High Point, NC
Ronconi, Robin .... (315) 253-5311
EDU ED, Citizen, Auburn, NY
Rondarte, Armando .... (520) 445-3333
PROD MGR, Daily Courier, Prescott, AZ
Rondeau, Mark .... (413) 458-9000
ED
Advocate/South Advocate, Williamstown, MA
Rondeau, Rob .... (403) 578-4111
MAN ED, Coronation Review, Coronation, AB
Rondeau-Bassett, Cheryl .... (605) 938-4651
PUB, ED, Wilmot Enterprise, Wilmot, SD
Rongo, Steve .... (401) 277-7000
ADV Sales DIR-Food & Drug
Providence Journal-Bulletin, Providence, RI
Rood, Edwin W .... (515) 685-3412
PUB, ED, Tri-County Times, Slater, IA
Rood, John .... (402) 475-4200
Online MGR, Journal Star, Lincoln, NE
Rood, Lee .... (320) 255-8700
Topics ED, St. Cloud Times, St. Cloud, MN
Rood, Owen A .... (517) 288-3164
PUB, Durand Express, Durand, MI
Rood, Sharon .... (515) 685-3412
MAN ED, Tri-County Times, Slater, IA
Rook, Chris .... (901) 427-3333
City ED, Jackson Sun, Jackson, TN
Rooke, Lisa .... (501) 425-6301
Society/Food ED
Daily News, Mountain Home, AR
Rooker, D Gregory .... (800) 655-1406
PUB
Southwest Virginia Enterprise, Wytheville, VA
Rooney, Brian .... (212) 318-2300
New York BU Chief
Bloomberg Business News, New York, NY
Rooney, Darrell .... (612) 222-5011
ADV MGR-CLASS
St. Paul Pioneer Press, St. Paul, MN
Rooney, David .... (403) 762-2453
ED, Banff Crag & Canyon, Banff, AB
Rooney, Pete .... (217) 788-1300
PROD FRM-COMP
State Journal-Register, Springfield, IL
Roop, Roy .... (918) 224-5185
CIRC DIR
Sapulpa Daily Herald, Sapulpa, OK
Roos, Frits .... (519) 894-2231
EPE, Record, Kitchener, ON
Roos, Jim .... (305) 350-2111
Music Writer-Classical
Miami Herald, Miami, FL
Roosenboom, D .... (613) 933-3160
PROD FRM-PR/Stereo
Standard-Freeholder, Cornwall, ON
Roosevelt, Phil .... (212) 803-8200
ED, American Banker, New York, NY
Root, Jay .... (817) 390-7400
BU Chief-Austin
Fort Worth Star-Telegram, Fort Worth, TX
Root, Joanne G .... (508) 829-5981
PUB, MAN ED, Landmark, Holden, MA
Roper, Joseph S .... (513) 721-2700
CIRC MGR-Single Copy
Cincinnati Enquirer, Cincinnati, OH
Ropp, Kathy .... (803) 248-6671
ED, Horry Independent, Conway, SC
Ropp, Thomas .... (602) 271-8000
Garden Writer, Arizona Republic, Phoenix, AZ
Rorick, George .... (202) 383-6080
DIR-Graphic SRV & News in Motion
Knight-Ridder/Tribune Information Services, Washington, DC
Rosa, Gina .... (800) 828-2453
GM
U-Bild Newspaper Features, Van Nuys, CA
Rosa, Michelle .... (201) 933-1166
MAN ED, South Bergenite, Rutherford, NJ
Rosado, Fernando .... (415) 647-1924
PUB, ED
El Bohemio News, San Francisco, CA
Rosado, Rossana .... (212) 807-4600
ED, El Diario La Prensa, New York, NY
Rosales, Agustine .... (213) 622-8332
PROD ASST MGR
La Opinion, Los Angeles, CA

Copyright ©1997 by the Editor & Publisher Co.

197-Who's Where **Rot**

Rosales, Guy .... (915) 546-6100
CIRC MGR-Customer SRV
El Paso Times, El Paso, TX
Rosario, Annie Del .... (407) 878-4365
PUB, ED, Alma Latina, Port St. Lucie, FL
Rosch, Ray .... (208) 743-9411
BM, Lewiston Morning Tribune, Lewiston, ID
Roschke, Joan .... (716) 343-8000
ADV MGR-CLASS
Batavia Daily News, Batavia, NY
Rosckes, Jared .... (214) 757-9000
GM, Dallas Observer, Dallas, TX
Roscouius, Scott .... (414) 432-2941
Sports ED, News-Chronicle, Green Bay, WI
Rose, Barry .... (812) 424-7711
ASST MET ED-City
Evansville Courier, Evansville, IN
Rose, Chris .... (804) 443-2200
ED, Rappahannock Times, Tappahannock, VA
Rose, Connie .... (805) 650-2900
CIRC MGR-Office OPER
Ventura County Star, Ventura, CA
Rose, Dallas .... (423) 581-5630
PROD MGR, Citizen Tribune, Morristown, TN
Rose, Doug .... (607) 432-1000
PROD FRM-COMP (Night)
Daily Star, Oneonta, NY
Rose, Ed .... (412) 775-3200
Sports ED, Beaver County Times, Beaver, PA
Rose, Elizabeth .... (619) 299-3131
CIRC MGR-OPER
San Diego Union-Tribune, San Diego, CA
Rose, Harold .... (502) 886-4444
PROD FRM-PR
Kentucky New Era, Hopkinsville, KY
Rose, John .... (540) 574-6200
Graphics ED/Art DIR
Daily News-Record, Harrisonburg, VA
Rose, John .... (205) 236-1551
CIRC DIR, Anniston Star, Anniston, AL
Rose, Joyce .... (606) 623-1669
PROD MGR
Richmond Register, Richmond, KY
Rose, Judy .... (313) 222-6400
RE Writer, Detroit Free Press, Detroit, MI
Rose, Karla .... (218) 736-7511
EDU ED, Daily Journal, Fergus Falls, MN
Rose, Kay .... (615) 684-1200
Society ED
Shelbyville Times-Gazette, Shelbyville, TN
Rose, Kelly .... (504) 826-3279
ADV MGR-RT
Times-Picayune, New Orleans, LA
Rose, Larry L .... (512) 884-2011
EVP/GM, Corpus Christi Caller-Times, Corpus Christi, TX
Rose, Lloyd .... (202) 334-6000
Theater Critic (Style)
Washington Post, Washington, DC
Rose, Lori .... (906) 786-2021
Librarian, Music ED, School ED, Teen-Age/Youth ED, Daily Press, Escanaba, MI
Rose, Mark .... (504) 826-3279
ADV MGR-RT
Times-Picayune, New Orleans, LA
Rose, Stan .... (913) 381-1010
PUB, Sun Newspapers, Overland Park, KS
Rose, Steve .... (913) 381-1010
PUB, Sun Newspapers, Overland Park, KS
Rose, Thomas .... (412) 222-2200
Sports ED
Observer-Reporter, Washington, PA
Rose, Tom .... (617) 643-7900
ED, Arlington Advocate, Arlington, MA
Rose, Valerie .... (906) 632-2235
BM, Evening News, Sault Ste. Marie, MI
Roseberry, Donald .... (610) 258-7171
MGR-Accounting
Easton Express-Times, Easton, PA
Roseberry, Lisa .... (812) 663-3111
BM, Greensburg Daily News, Greensburg, IN
Rosebery, Jim .... (405) 544-2222
PUB, ED, Boise City News, Boise City, OK
Rosebrock, Eric .... (206) 464-2111
PROD MGR-Mechanical (North CreeK)
Seattle Times, Seattle, WA
Roselle, John .... (302) 324-2500
DP MGR, News Journal, Wilmington, DE
Rosen, David A .... (516) 795-8823
VP/Senior ED, American Crossword Federation, Massapequa Park, NY
Rosen, Howard .... (619) 235-3000
GM, San Diego Reader, San Diego, CA
Rosen, Jeffrey S .... (212) 456-7777
VP-Human Resources
ABC Inc., New York, NY
Rosen, Richard .... (212) 210-2100
Deputy MAN ED
New York Daily News, New York, NY
Rosenbaum, Keith .... (410) 752-3849
CIRC MGR
Baltimore Daily Record, Baltimore, MD
Rosenbaum, William .... (208) 733-0931
PROD FRM-COMP
Times-News, Twin Falls, ID
Rosenberg, Alan .... (401) 277-7000
Entertainment/Amusements ED
Providence Journal-Bulletin, Providence, RI
Rosenberg, Alec .... (619) 337-3400
BUS ED, Imperial Valley Press, El Centro, CA
Rosenberg, Carol A .... (619) 463-5515
ED, San Diego Jewish Times, La Mesa, CA
Rosenberg, David .... (618) 234-1000
DIR-INFO Services Pre-Press PROD
Belleville News-Democrat, Belleville, IL
Rosenberg, Donald .... (216) 999-4500
Music ED-Classical
Plain Dealer, Cleveland, OH
Rosenberg, Garry L .... (619) 463-5515
PUB, San Diego Jewish Times, La Mesa, CA
Rosenberg, Howard .... (213) 237-5000
Television Critic
Los Angeles Times, Los Angeles, CA
Rosenberg, J Ivanhoe .... (303) 936-7776
PUB, ED, Herald Dispatch, Denver, CO
Rosenberg, Madelyn .... (540) 981-3100
Music ED, Roanoke Times, Roanoke, VA
Rosenberg, Steve .... (770) 454-9388
ED, South De Kalb Neighbor, Atlanta, GA
Rosenberg, Wolf .... (209) 826-3831
PUB, Los Banos Enterprise, Los Banos, CA
Rosenberger, Barb .... (320) 255-8700
PROD MGR-Packaging/Distribution Center
St. Cloud Times, St. Cloud, MN
Rosenberger, Deborah .... (913) 742-2111
MAN ED
Hiawatha Daily World, Hiawatha, KS
Rosenberger, Gene .... (215) 949-4000
PROD DIR
Bucks County Courier Times, Levittown, PA
Rosenberger, James .... (717) 622-3456
PROD SUPV-Ad-Tech DEPT, Pottsville Republican & Evening Herald, Pottsville, PA
Rosenberry, Dena .... (909) 987-6397
Lifestyle/Community News ED
Inland Valley Daily Bulletin, Ontario, CA
Rosenblatt, Gary .... (212) 921-7822
PUB, ED, Jewish Week, New York, NY
Rosenblatt, Robert .... (213) 237-5000
Economy-D.C.
Los Angeles Times, Los Angeles, CA
Rosenblum, Connie .... (212) 556-1234
Arts/Leisure ED
New York Times, New York, NY
Rosenbluth, Susan L .... (201) 569-2845
PUB
Jewish Voice and Opinion, Englewood, NJ
Rosenburg, Steve .... (770) 428-9411
ED, Dunwoody/Chamblee/Doraville/De Kalb Neighbor, Marietta, GA
Rosenburgh, Carleton .... (703) 284-6000
Sr VP-Newspaper Division
Gannett Co. Inc., Arlington, VA
Rosencrans, Joyce .... (513) 352-2000
Food ED, Cincinnati Post, Cincinnati, OH
Rosencrans, Kendra .... (218) 723-5281
Health Writer
Duluth News-Tribune, Duluth, MN
Rosendale, Charles .... (412) 439-7500
Chief Photographer
Herald-Standard, Uniontown, PA
Rosendall, Ken .... (517) 752-7171
PROD FRM-PR, Saginaw News, Saginaw, MI
Rosener, Daven .... (206) 883-7187
MAN ED, Redmond Sammamish Valley News, Redmond, WA
Rosenfeld, Arnold S .... (404) 843-5000
Sr VP/EIC, Cox Newspapers Inc., Atlanta, GA
Rosenfeld, Harry M .... (518) 454-5694
ED-at-Large, Times Union, Albany, NY
Rosenfeld, Ira .... (212) 837-7000
MGR-Transportation, Journal of Commerce & Commercial, New York, NY
Rosenfeld, Stephen .... (202) 334-6000
Deputy EPE
Washington Post, Washington, DC
Rosenfield, George .... (617) 786-7000
CIRC MGR, Patriot Ledger, Quincy, MA
Rosenfield, Gregg R .... (210) 736-4450
ASSOC PUB
Daily Commercial Recorder, San Antonio, TX
Rosenhause, Sharon .... (415) 777-2424
MAN ED-News
San Francisco Examiner, San Francisco, CA
Rosenheim, Daniel .... (415) 777-1111
MAN ED
San Francisco Chronicle, San Francisco, CA
Rosenheim, Jacob .... (216) 999-4500
MGR-VIS, Plain Dealer, Cleveland, OH
Rosenstern, Peter .... (808) 329-9311
PROD MGR-System/COMP
West Hawaii Today, Kailua-Kona, HI
Rosenthal, Andrew .... (212) 556-1234
Washington ED
New York Times, New York, NY
Rosenthal, David .... (410) 332-6000
ED-Baltimore County Sun
Sun, Baltimore, MD
Rosenthal, Faigi .... (212) 210-2100
Librarian
New York Daily News, New York, NY
Rosenthal, Ira .... (619) 745-6611
PUB-Solana Beach
North County Times, Escondido, CA
Rosenthal, Jack .... (212) 556-1234
ASST MAN ED/Magazine ED
New York Times, New York, NY
Rosenthal, Robert J .... (215) 854-2000
EX ED
Philadelphia Inquirer, Philadelphia, PA
Rosenthal, Traja .... (916) 786-6500
ED, Press-Tribune, Roseville, CA
Rosenwinkle, Wendy .... (607) 936-4651
Office MGR, DP MGR, Leader, Corning, NY
Rosenzweig, Sid .... (716) 328-2144
ASSOC ED
Syndicated News Service, Rochester, NY
Roser, Roger .... (216) 647-3171
MAN ED, Enterprise, Wellington, OH
Rosevear, Jerry .... (616) 347-2544
Sports ED
Petoskey News-Review, Petoskey, MI
Roshka, Osip .... (215) 627-0233
ED, America Ukrainian Catholic Daily, Philadelphia, PA
Rosiek, Susan .... (313) 459-2700
ED, Livonia Observer, Plymouth, MI
Rosinski, Norman A .... (312) 321-3000
EVP/PUB (Daily Southtown & Star Newspapers), Chicago Sun-Times, Chicago, IL
Hollinger International Inc.
Rosman, Mark R .... (908) 972-6740
MAN ED, News Transcript, Morganville, NJ
Roso, Jane .... (860) 489-3121
ADV MGR-CLASS
Register Citizen, Torrington, CT
Ross, Alicia .... (919) 781-4622
SEC, Syndicated Features Inc., Raleigh, NC
Ross, Bill .... (416) 367-2000
PROD Chief Machinist
Toronto Star, Toronto, ON
Ross, Bob .... (520) 573-4400
PROD MGR-Physical Resources, TNI Partners dba Tucson Newspapers, Tucson, AZ
Ross, Bob .... (415) 861-5019
PUB, Bay Area Reporter, San Francisco, CA
Ross, Bob .... (813) 259-7711
Films ED
Tampa Tribune and Times, Tampa, FL
Ross, Bonnie .... (315) 470-0011
Librarian, Post-Standard/Syracuse Herald-Journal/American, Syracuse, NY
Ross, Brenda .... (219) 356-6700
ADV MGR-CLASS
Huntington Herald-Press, Huntington, IN
Ross, Catriona .... (613) 544-5000
BM, Kingston Whig-Standard, Kingston, ON
Ross, Cecil (Bud) .... (618) 632-3643
PUB, Base News, O'Fallon, IL
Ross, Christine .... (619) 299-3131
Graphics ED
San Diego Union-Tribune, San Diego, CA
Ross, Danielle .... (303) 442-1202
PSL DIR, Daily Camera, Boulder, CO
Ross, David .... (619) 749-1112
ED, Valley Roadrunner, Valley Center, CA
Ross, Diane .... (314) 522-1300
ASST MAN ED
Interstate News Services, St. Louis, MO
Ross, Don .... (604) 732-2944
VP-FIN, Pacific Press Limited, Vancouver, BC
Ross, Don .... (508) 222-7000
Area ED, Sun Chronicle, Attleboro, MA
Ross, Donald J .... (401) 277-7000
ADV VP
Providence Journal-Bulletin, Providence, RI
Ross, Elizabeth .... (617) 450-2000
Travel ED
Christian Science Monitor, Boston, MA
Ross, Elizabeth G .... (510) 944-1344
SEC
Law Education Institute, Walnut Creek, CA
Ross, Gail .... (508) 458-7100
BUS ED, Sun, Lowell, MA
Ross, Gerard .... (209) 578-2000
MGR-BUS SYS, Modesto Bee, Modesto, CA
Ross, Glen .... (519) 255-5711
CIRC DIR, Windsor Star, Windsor, ON
Ross, J Walter .... (208) 847-0552
PUB, News-Examiner, Montpelier, ID
Ross, Jeffrey S .... (510) 944-1344
ASST ED
Law Education Institute, Walnut Creek, CA
Ross, Jenny .... (303) 442-1202
DIR-INFO SRV/Technical SRV
Daily Camera, Boulder, CO
Ross, John .... (204) 694-2022
ADV DIR-Sales, Winnipeg Sun, Winnipeg, MB
Ross, John .... (506) 859-4900
PROD MGR, Times-Transcript, Moncton, NB
Ross, Julie .... (773) 586-8800
ADV MGR, Daily Southtown, Chicago, IL
Ross, Kaye .... (408) 920-5000
City ED (Night)
San Jose Mercury News, San Jose, CA
Ross, Ken .... (508) 222-7000
Sunday ED, Sun Chronicle, Attleboro, MA
Ross, Lilla .... (904) 359-4111
Religion ED
Florida Times-Union, Jacksonville, FL
Ross, Madelyn .... (412) 263-1100
MAN ED
Pittsburgh Post-Gazette, Pittsburgh, PA
Ross, Martin J .... (510) 944-1344
ED/Owner
Law Education Institute, Walnut Creek, CA
Ross Jr, Morgan .... (937) 392-4321
PUB, ED, Ripley Bee, Ripley, OH
Ross, Peggy .... (334) 262-1611
Librarian
Montgomery Advertiser, Montgomery, AL
Ross, Percy .... (612) 835-2400
PRES
Thanks A Million Inc., Minneapolis, MN
Ross, Robert .... (313) 222-6400
MGR-SYS Applications
Detroit Newspapers, Detroit, MI
Ross, Scott .... (406) 228-9301
ED, Glasgow Courier, Glasgow, MT
Ross, Shane .... (902) 468-1222
Sunday ED, Daily News, Halifax, NS
Ross, Sharon .... (219) 933-3200
MAN ED-Eastlake, Times, Munster, IN
Ross, Shelley .... (204) 483-2070
PUB, ED, Souris Plaindealer, Souris, MB
Ross, Terry L .... (520) 783-3333
ED, EPE, Health/Medical ED, SCI/Technology ED, Yuma Daily Sun, Yuma, AZ
Ross, Tim B .... (314) 340-8000
Illinois ED
St. Louis Post-Dispatch, St. Louis, MO
Ross, Tom .... (970) 879-1502
MAN ED
Steamboat Today, Steamboat Springs, CO
Ross, Walter .... (208) 852-0155
PUB, Preston Citizen, Preston, ID
Ross, Wendy .... (202) 334-6000
ASST MAN ED-News
Washington Post, Washington, DC
Ross, William .... (810) 766-6100
PROD MGR-MR, Flint Journal, Flint, MI
Ross-White, Elizabeth .... (617) 450-2000
Environmental ED
Christian Science Monitor, Boston, MA
Rosse, James N .... (714) 553-9292
PRES/CEO
Freedom Communications Inc., Irvine, CA
Rossello, Larry .... (609) 691-5000
MGR-CR, Daily Journal, Vineland, NJ
Rossi, Christina .... (201) 368-0100
MAN ED, Ridgewood News, Paramus, NJ
Rossi, K .... (801) 355-3336
Energy ED/Acting BU Chief-Houston
FNA News, Salt Lake City, UT
Rossi, Luis .... (312) 525-6285/9400
PUB, La Raza Newspaper, Chicago, IL
Rossi, Peter .... (617) 245-0080
ED, Wakefield Daily Item, Wakefield, MA
Rossi, Rosalind .... (312) 321-3000
EDU Writer, Chicago Sun-Times, Chicago, IL
Rossi, Steven B .... (215) 854-2000
EVP/GM
Philadelphia Inquirer, Philadelphia, PA
Rossi, Tony .... (310) 337-7003
Sales EX
Creators Syndicate, Los Angeles, CA
Rossie, Dave .... (607) 798-1234
COL-Outdoors
Press & Sun Bulletin, Binghamton, NY
Rossiter, David .... (403) 328-4411
Photo DEPT MGR
Lethbridge Herald, Lethbridge, AB
Rossiter, Donald J .... (402) 362-4478
PROD MGR, York News-Times, York, NE
Rossiter, Maggie .... (517) 752-7171
COL, Saginaw News, Saginaw, MI
Rossman, Jeanie .... (913) 242-4700
PROD FRM-COMP
Ottawa Herald, Ottawa, KS
Rossman, John .... (317) 633-1240
PROD OPER FRM-MR
Indianapolis Star/News, Indianapolis, IN
Rossow, Jim .... (217) 351-5252
EX Sports ED, News-Gazette, Champaign, IL
Rost, Joan .... (515) 232-2160
CONT, Daily Tribune, Ames, IA
Roston, Margo .... (613) 829-9100
Fashion ED, Ottawa Citizen, Ottawa, ON
Roszczyk, Stephen .... (330) 841-1600
PUB, Tribune Chronicle, Warren, OH
Roszkiewicz, Carolyn .... (562) 435-1161
ASST MAN ED
Press-Telegram, Long Beach, CA
Rotella, Sebastian .... (213) 237-5000
Buenos Aires BU
Los Angeles Times, Los Angeles, CA
Roteman, Joel .... (412) 687-1000
ED, Jewish Chronicle, Pittsburgh, PA

Rot Who's Where-198

Roten, Robert .... (307) 742-2176
Environmental ED
Laramie Daily Boomerang, Laramie, WY
Rotenberk, Lori .... (312) 321-3000
GEN Assignment
Chicago Sun-Times, Chicago, IL
Roth, Charlie .... (717) 648-4641
Sports ED, News-Item, Shamokin, PA
Roth, Jean .... (608) 735-4413
GM, Crawford County Independent Kickapoo Scout, Gays Mills, WI
Roth, Joseph P .... (515) 456-2585
PUB, Hampton Times, Hampton, IA
Roth, Kathy .... (707) 838-9211
GM, Times, Windsor, CA
Roth, Kelly .... (306) 232-4865
GM
Saskatchewan Valley News, Rosthern, SK
Roth, Maria .... (319) 337-3181
DIR-Human Resources
Iowa City Press-Citizen, Iowa City, IA
Roth, Marilyn .... (541) 298-8545
PUB, Dalles Reminder, The Dalles, OR
Roth, Mark .... (412) 263-1100
ASST MAN ED-Projects
Pittsburgh Post-Gazette, Pittsburgh, PA
Roth, Mary Kay .... (402) 475-4200
Kids/Features Reporter
Lincoln Journal Star, Lincoln, NE
Roth, Mona .... (715) 842-2101
ADV DIR, Wausau Daily Herald, Wausau, WI
Roth, Robert .... (705) 949-6111
MAN ED, Sault Ste. Marie This Week, Sault Ste. Marie, ON
Roth, Steve .... (573) 237-3222
ED, New Haven Leader, New Haven, MO
Roth, Ted .... (217) 245-6121
ED, Books ED, EPE
Jacksonville Journal-Courier, Jacksonville, IL
Roth, Thomas .... (215) 854-2000
PROD DIR-Planning & Environmental
Philadelphia Inquirer, Philadelphia, PA
Knight-Ridder Inc.
Roth, Valarie .... (203) 744-5100
MET ED, News-Times, Danbury, CT
Roth, William A .... (208) 289-5731
PUB, ED, Kendrick Gazette, Kendrick, ID
Rothacker, Robert .... (610) 272-2500
CIRC DIR, Times Herald, Norristown, PA
Rothbauer, Larry .... (512) 798-2481
PUB, Lavaca County Tribune-Herald, Hallettsville, TX
Rothenberg, Alex .... (518) 270-1200
News ED, Record, Troy, NY
Rothenburger, M G .... (250) 372-2331
ED, Kamloops Daily News, Kamloops, BC
Rothfeder, Jeff .... (212) 318-2300
NTL News ED/Princeton BU Chief
Bloomberg Business News, New York, NY
Rothfeld, Barry .... (607) 798-1234
ED, Press & Sun Bulletin, Binghamton, NY
Rothgeb, Jim .... (360) 377-3711
COL, Sun, Bremerton, WA
Rothman, Marshall .... (215) 885-4111
ED, Leader, Philadelphia, PA
Rothovius, Anita Valkama .... (718) 237-9396
ED, New Yorkin Uutiset, Brooklyn, NY
Rothrock, Neil .... (910) 373-7000
DP MGR, News & Record, Greensboro, NC
Rothschild, Mary .... (206) 464-2111
ASST Suburban ED
Seattle Times, Seattle, WA
Rothschild, Scott .... (512) 884-2011
MET ED, Caller-Times, Corpus Christi, TX
Rothschild, Trip .... (860) 354-2261
PUB, New Milford Times, New Milford, CT
Rothschild, Walter N .... (860) 567-8766
PUB, Litchfield Enquirer, Litchfield, CT
Rotter, John .... (805) 650-2900
CIRC MGR-Home Delivery
Ventura County Star, Ventura, CA
Rotzell, Brenda .... (312) 321-3000
Travel Writer
Chicago Sun-Times, Chicago, IL
Rotzetter, Eva .... (204) 774-1883
GM, Kanada Kurier, Winnipeg, MB
Rotzien, Rick .... (612) 633-3434
MAN ED, Focus News, Roseville, MN
Rouch, Helen .... (219) 726-8141
ADV MGR-CLASS
Commercial Review, Portland, IN
Rough, Ervin .... (717) 784-2121
PROD SUPT-Press
Press Enterprise, Bloomsburg, PA
Roule, Bob .... (919) 708-9000
Features ED, Sanford Herald, Sanford, NC
Rouleau, Marcel .... (418) 862-1774
GM, Le Saint-Laurent Echo du Grand-Po, Riviere-du-Loup, QC
Rounce, Robert R .... (860) 241-6200
CONT, Hartford Courant, Hartford, CT
Rounds, David .... (510) 462-4160
GM, Valley Times, Pleasanton, CA
Knight-Ridder Inc.
Rounds, Edward J .... (607) 756-5665
GM, ADV MGR-GEN, ADV MGR-RT
Cortland Standard, Cortland, NY
Rounds, Rick .... (201) 646-4000
DIR-MIS, Record, Hackensack, NJ
Roundtree, Pat .... (912) 283-2244
ADV MGR-CLASS
Waycross Journal-Herald, Waycross, GA
Rounsavall, Ann .... (903) 432-3132
GM, Cedar Creek Pilot, Seven Points, TX
Rountree, Ginger .... (904) 359-4111
ADV MGR-MKTG/PROM
Florida Times-Union, Jacksonville, FL
Rountree, Mark .... (405) 233-6600
Sports ED, Enid News & Eagle, Enid, OK
Rountree, Tommy .... (912) 995-2175
PUB, ED, Dawson News, Dawson, GA
Rourke, Cathy Barringer .... (810) 724-2615
ED, Tri-City Times, Imlay City, MI
Rouse, Alice .... (502) 753-1916
GM, Murray Ledger & Times, Murray, KY
Rouse, David .... (919) 778-2211
SYS ED, News-Argus, Goldsboro, NC
Rouse, Harlan .... (712) 752-8401
PUB, ED, Siouxland Press, Hospers, IA
Rouse, John L .... (301) 262-3700
GM, ED, Bowie Blade-News, Bowie, MD
Rouse, Katie .... (712) 752-8401
PUB, ED, Siouxland Press, Hospers, IA
Rouse, Mike .... (919) 778-2211
ED, Goldsboro News-Argus, Goldsboro, NC
Rouse, Sheila .... (573) 333-4336
GM
Tuesday Democrat-Argus, Caruthersville, MO
Rousey, Mike .... (912) 382-4321
PROD FRM-PR/Camera
Tifton Gazette, Tifton, GA
Roush, Deborah .... (614) 773-2111
CIRC MGR-Sales
Chillicothe Gazette, Chillicothe, OH
Roush, Sue .... (816) 932-6600
MAN ED
Universal Press Syndicate, Kansas City, MO
Rousmaniere Jr, James A .... (603) 352-1234
PRES, ED, Keene Sentinel, Keene, NH
Rousseau, Claude .... (418) 587-2090
MAN ED
Journal Haute Cote-Nord, Forestville, QC
Rousseau, David M .... (603) 668-4321
ADV MGR-RT
Union Leader, Manchester, NH
Rousseau, Terry .... (603) 524-3800
ADV DIR, Citizen, Laconia, NH
Roux, Ray .... (207) 892-1166
PUB, Suburban News, Windham, ME
Rove, Olaf .... (360) 694-3391
MGR-INFO Systems
Columbian, Vancouver, WA
Rovner, Michael .... (808) 525-8000
ASST MAN ED
Honolulu Star-Bulletin, Honolulu, HI
Rowan, Beth .... (207) 594-4401
MAN ED, Midcoast Encore, Rockland, ME
Rowan, Phyllis .... (610) 696-1775
ED, Village News, West Chester, PA
Rowe, Charles .... (803) 577-7111
ASST ED, Post and Courier, Charleston, SC
Rowe, Charles S .... (540) 374-5000
SEC, TREAS, Co-PUB, ED
Free Lance-Star, Fredericksburg, VA
Rowe, Constance D .... (352) 377-2444
PUB, Record/Farm d'Ranch, Gainesville, FL
Rowe, David .... (603) 882-2741
CIRC MGR, Telegraph, Nashua, NH
Rowe, Frank .... (903) 984-2593
PUB, EPE, Kilgore News Herald, Kilgore, TX
Rowe III, J B .... (352) 377-2444
GM, Record/Farm d'Ranch, Gainesville, FL
Rowe Jr, J Wesley .... (317) 529-1111
PUB, Courier-Times, New Castle, IN
Rowe III, Josiah P .... (540) 374-5000
PRES, Co-PUB, GM
Free Lance-Star, Fredericksburg, VA
Rowe, Kermit .... (216) 245-6901
Sports ED, Morning Journal, Lorain, OH
Rowe, Mary .... (215) 855-8440
Fashion/Women's ED, Films/Theater ED, Home Furnishings/Music ED
Reporter, Landsdale, PA
Rowe, Peter .... (619) 299-3131
COL-Lifestyle
San Diego Union-Tribune, San Diego, CA
Rowe, Ramona .... (201) 428-6200
DIR-Public Affairs
Daily Record, Parsippany, NJ
Rowe, Rena .... (520) 753-6397
PROD SUPV-COMP Room
Kingman Daily Miner, Kingman, AZ
Rowe, Sandra Mims .... (503) 221-8327
ED, Oregonian, Portland, OR
Rowe, Tom .... (216) 999-4500
PROD ASST MGR
Plain Dealer, Cleveland, OH
Rowe, William J .... (213) 237-3700
PUB-Hartford Courant & Stamford Advocate
Times Mirror Co., Los Angeles, CA
Rowell, Brian .... (906) 786-2021
Automotive/Aviation ED, Health/Medical ED, SCI/Technology ED
Daily Press, Escanaba, MI
Rowell, Kathie .... (318) 459-3200
Features ED, Food/Garden ED, Leisure/ Culture ED, Society/Women's ED, Travel ED
Times, Shreveport, LA
Rowell, Melissa C .... (607) 865-4131
PUB, Reporter, Walton, NY
Rowell, Robert R .... (207) 791-6650
VP-OPER, Press Herald, Portland, ME
Rowell, Van .... (704) 289-1541
CIRC MGR, Enquirer-Journal, Monroe, NC
Rowen, LaWanda .... (520) 753-6397
ADV MGR-TMC
Kingman Daily Miner, Kingman, AZ
Rowland, Bruce .... (518) 561-2300
Regional ED
Press-Republican, Plattsburgh, NY
Rowland, Dean .... (201) 877-4141
Special Sections ED
Star-Ledger, Newark, NJ
Rowland, Gary .... (203) 789-5200
ADV MGR-Preprint
New Haven Register, New Haven, CT
Rowland, Hank .... (912) 265-8320
MAN ED, Brunswick News, Brunswick, GA
Rowland, Jeremi .... (417) 532-9131
DP MGR, PROD MGR-COMP
Lebanon Daily Record, Lebanon, MO
Rowland, Mary Pat .... (603) 742-4455
MAN ED, Foster's Democrat, Dover, NH
Rowland, Norm .... (713) 446-3733
ED, Humble Echo, Humble, TX
Rowlee, Linda .... (805) 273-2700
ADV DIR-RT
Antelope Valley Press, Palmdale, CA
Rowlett, Brad .... (615) 754-6397
PUB, GM, Mt. Juliet News, Mount Juliet, TN
Rowley, Don G .... (520) 774-4545
PUB/PSL MGR, PA, MGR-PROM
Arizona Daily Sun, Flagstaff, AZ
Rowley, James P .... (302) 324-2500
DIR-Market Development, ADTX MGR
News Journal, Wilmington, DE
Rowley, Robert .... (607) 324-1425
CONT, DP MGR
Evening Tribune, Hornell, NY
Rowsome, John .... (613) 739-7000
GM, Ottawa Sun, Ottawa, ON
Roy, Brenda .... (409) 756-6671
ADV DIR, ADV DIR-Creative
Conroe Courier, Conroe, TX
Roy, Brent .... (504) 638-7155
PUB, Pointe Coupee Banner, New Roads, LA
Roy, Carolyn .... (318) 352-5501
ED, Natchitoches Times, Natchitoches, LA
Roy, Francois .... (613) 562-0111
MAN ED, News DIR, Le Droit, Ottawa, ON
Roy, Gaetan .... (514) 375-4555
Leisure/Sports, La Voix de l'Est, Granby, QC
Roy, Guy .... (514) 774-5375
PUB, Le Clairon, Saint-Hyacinthe, QC
Roy, Mario .... (514) 285-7272
Books ED, La Presse, Montreal, QC
Roy, Paul .... (423) 569-6343
PUB, ED, Independent Herald, Oneida, TN
Roy, Pierrette .... (819) 564-5450
Amusements/Books ED, Radio/Television ED
La Tribune, Sherbrooke, QC
Roy, Raymond U .... (203) 235-1661
ADV DIR, Automotive ED, RE ED
Record-Journal, Meriden, CT
Roy, Viviane .... (514) 285-7272
Fashion ED, La Presse, Montreal, QC
Roy, Wayne .... (915) 673-4271
ADV DIR, Abilene Reporter-News, Abilene, TX
Roy, Yvon .... (418) 228-8858
ED, Beauce Nouvelle/L'Eclaireur-Progres, Saint-Georges, QC
Royalty, O J .... (502) 351-4407
PUB, ED, Sentinel, Radcliff, KY
Royhab, Ron .... (419) 245-6000
MAN ED, Blade, Toledo, OH
Royko, Mike .... (312) 222-3232
COL, Chicago Tribune, Chicago, IL
Roysdon, Robin .... (317) 747-5700
Films/Theater ED, Star Press, Muncie, IN
Royse, Bruce A .... (316) 431-4100
SEC/TREAS, DP MGR
Chanute Tribune, Chanute, KS
Royse, John .... (606) 231-3100
PROD MGR-PR
Lexington Herald-Leader, Lexington, KY
Royston, Tamrus .... (717) 334-1131
CIRC DIR, Gettysburg Times, Gettysburg, PA
Rozell, Susan .... (605) 225-4100
MGR-Human Resources
Aberdeen American News, Aberdeen, SD
Rozen, Lee .... (206) 448-8000
New Media MGR
Seattle Post-Intelligencer, Seattle, WA
Rozenman, Martin M .... (614) 785-1212
ED, Northland News, Columbus, OH
Rozgonyi, Timothy .... (412) 263-1100
DIR-INFO SRV
Pittsburgh Post-Gazette, Pittsburgh, PA
Roznovsky, Ann .... (817) 757-5757
DIR-MKTG, Waco Tribune-Herald, Waco, TX
Ruark, Pat .... (606) 796-6182/2331
ED, Lewis County Herald, Vanceburg, KY
Ruben, Mike .... (304) 372-2421
MAN ED, Jackson Herald, Ripley, WV
Rubich, Chris .... (406) 657-1200
Special Projects ED, Travel ED, Women's ED
Billings Gazette, Billings, MT
Rubin, Carol .... (954) 356-4000
MGR-Community Relations (Palm Beach)
Sun-Sentinel, Fort Lauderdale, FL
Rubin, Debra .... (201) 887-3900
MAN ED
Metrowest Jewish News, Whippany, NJ
Rubin, Linda .... (860) 887-9211
CONT, Norwich Bulletin, Norwich, CT
Rubin, Michelle .... (319) 351-1531
ED, Icon, Iowa City, IA
Rubin, Neil .... (404) 352-2400
ED, Atlanta Jewish Times, Atlanta, GA
Rubin, Trudy .... (215) 854-2000
EDL Writer
Philadelphia Inquirer, Philadelphia, PA
Rubinkowski, Rob .... (412) 628-2000
Sports ED, Daily Courier, Connellsville, PA
Rubino, James C .... (305) 852-3216
ED, Reporter, Tavernier, FL
Rubino, Marty .... (415) 883-8600
ADV DIR
Marin Independent Journal, Novato, CA
Rubino, Mike .... (812) 482-2424
Sports ED, Herald, Jasper, IN
Rubinoff, Joel .... (519) 894-2231
Humor/Youth Beat Reporter
Record, Kitchener, ON
Rubinote, Mildred .... (717) 455-3636
Lifestyle ED, Standard-Speaker, Hazleton, PA
Rubinton, Noel .... (516) 843-2020
Viewpoints ED, Newsday, Melville, NY
Ruble, Dick .... (612) 673-4000
PROD MGR, Star Tribune, Minneapolis, MN
Ruble, Gary .... (609) 272-7000
CIRC MGR-Single Copy Sales
Press of Atlantic City, Pleasantville, NJ
Ruble, Melinda .... (419) 448-3200
Farm/Agriculture ED
Advertiser-Tribune, Tiffin, OH
Ruble, Tony .... (614) 283-4711
PROD DIR, Herald-Star, Steubenville, OH
Ruchalski, Sharon .... (617) 593-7700
ADV MGR-CLASS
Daily Evening Item, Lynn, MA
Ruck, Randy .... (717) 854-1575
BM
York Dispatch/York Sunday News, York, PA
Rucker, Bob .... (707) 527-1200
PUB
Sonoma County Independent, Santa Rosa, CA
Rucker, Virginia .... (704) 245-6431
Books ED, Fashion/Food ED, Librarian, Travel ED, Daily Courier, Forest City, NC
Ruckman, Andrew .... (216) 329-7000
EPE, Chronicle-Telegram, Elyria, OH
Rud, Jeff .... (250) 380-5211
Sports COL, Times Colonist, Victoria, BC
Rudat, Peter .... (519) 894-2231
PROD MGR-Press, Record, Kitchener, ON
Rudd, Shirley .... (904) 997-3568
GM, Monticello News, Monticello, FL
Rudden, Anne .... (212) 777-6200
ASSOC DIR, Bettmann Archive/Bettman Newsphotos, New York, NY
Rudden, Rick .... (906) 786-2021
ED, EPE, NTL ED, News ED, Political/ Government ED
Daily Press, Escanaba, MI
Rudderow, Kay .... (609) 451-1000
Food ED, Librarian, Religion ED, Women's ED, Bridgeton Evening News, Bridgeton, NJ
Ruddiman, Susan .... (601) 762-1111
Food ED, Women's ED
Mississippi Press, Pascagoula, MS
Ruddle, Harold .... (214) 450-1717
Sr VP-OPER
Westward Communications Inc., Dallas, TX
Rudewicz, Walter .... (860) 646-0500
VP-FIN, Journal Inquirer, Manchester, CT
Rudicel, Keith .... (316) 321-1120
CIRC MGR, El Dorado Times, El Dorado, KS
Rudiger, Edward .... (718) 981-1234
ADV MGR-Co-op
Staten Island Advance, Staten Island, NY
Rudis, Al .... (562) 435-1161
Restaurant Reviews ED
Press-Telegram, Long Beach, CA
Rudloff, Jim .... (614) 452-4561
Design DIR, Times Recorder, Zanesville, OH
Rudolf, Geri .... (517) 752-7171
Environmental ED
Saginaw News, Saginaw, MI

199-Who's Where **Rut**

Rudolfsen, Bev ... (403) 782-3498
ED, Lacombe Globe, Lacombe, AB
Rudolph, Jean L ... (847) 427-4300
Features ED
Daily Herald, Arlington Heights, IL
Rudolph, Joyce ... (818) 241-4141
Living/Lifestyle ED, Religion ED
Glendale News-Press, Glendale, CA
Rudy, Gary ... (609) 886-8600
GM, Herald Newspapers, Rio Grande, NJ
Rudy, Robert ... (415) 348-4321
City ED
San Mateo County Times, San Mateo, CA
Ruef, Randy ... (815) 987-1200
Sports ED, Register Star, Rockford, IL
Ruegg, Phil ... (719) 544-3520
MGR-INFO SRV
Pueblo Chieftain, Pueblo, CO
Ruehl, Larry ... (513) 863-8200
CONT, Journal-News, Hamilton, OH
Ruemenapp, Dirk F ... (603) 668-4321
VP-OPER, Online MGR, PROD VP
Union Leader, Manchester, NH
Rueter, Mary ... (319) 659-3121
GM, ED, DeWitt Observer, DeWitt, IA
Ruff, Dale ... (413) 788-1000
Photo ED, Union-News, Springfield, MA
Ruff, Denette ... (204) 694-2022
Librarian, Winnipeg Sun, Winnipeg, MB
Ruff, Jerry ... (608) 788-1524
ED, Times Review, La Crosse, WI
Ruff, Jimmy ... (334) 875-2110
PROD MGR, Selma Times-Journal, Selma, AL
Ruff, Scott ... (216) 951-0000
ADV DIR, News-Herald, Willoughby, OH
Ruff, Wilson ... (414) 457-7711
Wire ED, Sheboygan Press, Sheboygan, WI
Ruffin, Jane ... (919) 829-4500
EDL Writer, News & Observer, Raleigh, NC
Ruffin, Nate ... (601) 961-7000
DIR-Human Resources
Clarion-Ledger, Jackson, MS
Ruffner, Larry ... (814) 765-5581
PROD FRM-PR, Progress, Clearfield, PA
Rufty, Bill ... (941) 687-7000
Political/Government ED
Ledger, Lakeland, FL
Rugaber, Walter ... (804) 446-2010
EVP/PRES-Landmark Publishing Group
Landmark Communications Inc., Norfolk, VA
Ruggles, Rick ... (402) 444-1000
EDU (Higher)
Omaha World-Herald, Omaha, NE
Ruhl, Bill ... (319) 398-8211
CIRC MGR-Country
Gazette, Cedar Rapids, IA
Ruhlman, Bill ... (308) 345-4500
VP/SEC/TREAS
McCook Daily Gazette, McCook, NE
Ruhlman, William J ... (314) 937-5200
VP/SEC/TREAS
USMedia Group Inc., Crystal City, MO
Ruhnke, Tim ... (613) 584-4161
ED, North Renfrew Times, Deep River, ON
Ruinsky, Steve ... (516) 843-2020
ASST MAN ED-Sports, Newsday, Melville, NY
Ruis, Betty ... (912) 273-2277
PROD Compositor
Cordele Dispatch, Cordele, GA
Ruis, Tom ... (212) 210-2100
Deputy MAN ED-Graphics
New York Daily News, New York, NY
Ruiter, M A ... (604) 845-2890
PUB, ED
Houston Today Newspaper, Houston, BC
Ruiz, Carlos ... (520) 763-2505
PROD MGR-Camera/Stripping
Mohave Valley Daily News, Bullhead City, AZ
Ruiz, Don ... (206) 597-8742
Books ED, Entertainment ED, Fashion/Style ED, Radio/Television Reporter, Travel ED
News Tribune, Tacoma, WA
Ruiz, Emilio A ... (516) 486-6457
PUB
La Tribuna Hispana-NY/NJ, Westbury, NY
Ruiz, Marji ... (206) 464-2111
VP-Strategic MKTG
Seattle Times, Seattle, WA
Ruka, Frances ... (909) 684-1200
ADV MGR-RT
Press-Enterprise, Riverside, CA
Rule, Gwen ... (501) 442-1777
COL
Northwest Arkansas Times, Fayetteville, AR
Rule, James E ... (818) 706-0266
PUB, Acorn, Agoura Hills, CA
Rule, Lisa ... (818) 706-0266
GM, Acorn, Agoura Hills, CA
Rumbach, Dan E ... (812) 482-2424
Co-PRES, TREAS, Co-PUB
Herald, Jasper, IN
Rumbach, Edwin J ... (812) 482-2424
VP, ADV DIR, Herald, Jasper, IN
Rumbach, John A ... (812) 482-2424
Co-PRES, SEC, Co-PUB, EPE, ED
Herald, Jasper, IN
Rumbler, Bill ... (312) 321-3000
RE Writer, Chicago Sun-Times, Chicago, IL
Rummel, Mark ... (906) 774-2772
Photo ED, Daily News, Iron Mountain, MI
Rummel, Mark W ... (517) 453-3100
PUB, ED, Newsweekly, Pigeon, MI
Rummel, Robert B ... (970) 669-5050
EDL Writer, GM
Loveland Daily Reporter-Herald, Loveland, CO
Rumpf, Chuck ... (954) 356-4000
CIRC MGR-Palm Beach County
Sun-Sentinel, Fort Lauderdale, FL
Rundle, Sandy ... (902) 752-3000
ADV MGR, Evening News, New Glasgow, NS
Rung, John ... (815) 625-3600
DIR-MKTG, Daily Gazette, Sterling, IL
Shaw Newspapers
Runge, Bill ... (912) 273-2277
MAN ED, Cordele Dispatch, Cordele, GA
Runge, Fred ... (613) 591-3060
GM, Kanata Kourier-Standard, Kanata, ON
Runge, Mel ... (812) 424-7711
Automotive/Aviation ED, BUS/FIN ED, RE ED
Evansville Press, Evansville, IN
Runge, Patricia A ... (513) 721-2700
DIR-Purchasing
Cincinnati Enquirer, Cincinnati, OH
Runions, Rollie ... (501) 855-3724
GM, Weekly Vista, Bella Vista, AR
Runkle, Sue ... (419) 826-3580
MAN ED, Swanton Enterprise, Swanton, OH
Runkle, Todd ... (704) 437-2161
Sports ED, News Herald, Morganton, NC
Runnels, Sheila ... (918) 684-2828
ADV DIR, Muskogee Daily Phoenix & Times Democrat, Muskogee, OK
Runnoe, Chuck ... (715) 223-2342
ED, Tribune-Phonograph, Abbotsford, WI
Runser, Karl ... (614) 592-6612
MAN ED, Athens Messenger, Athens, OH
Runyon, Keith ... (502) 582-4011
Books ED, Opinion Page ED
Courier-Journal, Louisville, KY
Runyon, Ruth ... (614) 773-2111
Opinion ED, Gazette, Chillicothe, OH
Ruoho, Bob ... (906) 482-1500
CIRC MGR
Daily Mining Gazette, Houghton, MI
Rupert, Larry ... (717) 748-6791
CIRC DIR, Express, Lock Haven, PA
Rupert, Shirley ... (814) 238-5000
CIRC MGR-Home Delivery, CIRC MGR-Customer SRV
Centre Daily Times, State College, PA
Rupich, Elizabeth ... (407) 482-6271
Author-Arts & Entertainment
Demko Publishing, Boca Raton, FL
Rupnik, Frank ... (519) 344-3641
MAN ED, EPE, Observer, Sarnia, ON
Rupp, Steve ... (360) 676-2600
Sports ED
Bellingham Herald, Bellingham, WA
Rupp, William ... (401) 245-6002
PUB, ED, Warren Times-Gazette, Warren, RI
Ruppart, Karen ... (907) 486-3227
MGR-Office, Kodiak Daily Mirror, Kodiak, AK
Ruppert, Chris ... (504) 826-3279
DP MGR, Times-Picayune, New Orleans, LA
Ruppert, Jim ... (217) 788-1300
Sports ED
State Journal-Register, Springfield, IL
Ruse, Tim ... (317) 633-1240
PROD OPER ASST
Indianapolis Star/News, Indianapolis, IN
Ruser, Dee ... (509) 659-1020
PUB
Ritzville Adams County Journal, Ritzville, WA
Ruser, Duane W ... (509) 234-3181
PUB, ED
Franklin County Graphic, Connell, WA
Rush, Chris ... (918) 542-5533
ADV MGR-Display
Miami News-Record, Miami, OK
Rush, Debbie ... (757) 446-2000
CIRC MGR-PROM
Virginian-Pilot, Norfolk, VA
Rush, Don ... (810) 628-4801
GM, Oxford Leader, Oxford, MI
Rush, Doris G ... (315) 253-5311
PUB, Citizen, Auburn, NY
Rush, Earl ... (360) 377-3711
ADV DIR, Sun, Bremerton, WA
Rush, George ... (212) 210-2100
Gossip COL
New York Daily News, New York, NY
Rush, William J ... (609) 396-2200
VP, Journal Register Co., Trenton, NJ
Rushing, Bill ... (806) 296-1300
PROD ASST MGR, PROD FRM-PR
Plainview Daily Herald, Plainview, TX
Rusincovitch, James ... (419) 625-5500
ADV MGR-CLASS
Sandusky Register, Sandusky, OH
Russ, Bill ... (510) 935-0809
ED, Syndicated Automotive News, Walnut Creek, CA
Russ, Bob ... (419) 625-5500
Boating ED, City ED, Farm ED, Outdoors/Sports ED
Sandusky Register, Sandusky, OH
Russ, Carey ... (510) 935-0809
ASST ED, Syndicated Automotive News, Walnut Creek, CA
Russell, Bill ... (619) 299-3131
PROD MGR-ADM
San Diego Union-Tribune, San Diego, CA
Russell, Bud ... (417) 623-3480
PROD FRM-COMP (Night)
Joplin Globe, Joplin, MO
Russell, Carl ... (803) 626-8555
CIRC MGR-Home Delivery
Sun News, Myrtle Beach, SC
Russell, Charles F ... (212) 416-2000
PROD VP-Technology
Wall Street Journal, New York, NY
Russell, Charlotte ... (316) 275-8500
ADTX MGR
Garden City Telegram, Garden City, KS
Russell, Chris ... (708) 258-3473
GM, Peotone Vedette, Peotone, IL
Russell, Daniel ... (505) 393-2123
BUS/FIN Writer, Environmental ED, Farm/Agriculture ED
Hobbs Daily News-Sun, Hobbs, NM
Russell, Danny ... (614) 847-3800
ED, Other Paper, Columbus, OH
Russell, David ... (970) 728-9788
CIRC MGR
Telluride Daily Planet, Telluride, CO
Russell, David ... (915) 653-1221
PROD SUPT-MR
Standard-Times, San Angelo, TX
Russell, Dennis ... (503) 221-8327
PROD SUPT-PR, Oregonian, Portland, OR
Russell, Don ... (909) 987-6397
GM, Inland Valley Daily Bulletin, Ontario, CA
Russell, Donald L ... (402) 773-5576
PUB, Clay County News, Sutton, NE
Russell, Donald S ... (916) 289-3262
PUB, ED
Mountain Messenger, Downieville, CA
Russell, Edwin F ... (717) 255-8100
PRES, Patriot-News, Harrisburg, PA
Russell, Frances ... (520) 367-6877
GM, White Mountain Weekly, Lakeside, AZ
Russell, Frank E ... (317) 633-1240
SEC/TREAS, Indianapolis Star/News, Indianapolis, IN, Central Newspapers Inc.
Russell, Gilbert L ... (708) 258-3473
PUB, Peotone Vedette, Peotone, IL
Russell, Glenda J ... (317) 636-0200
PUB
Court & Commercial Record, Indianapolis, IN
Russell, Gloria ... (413) 788-1000
Arts Critic, Union-News, Springfield, MA
Russell, Guy P ... (316) 321-1120
PUB, El Dorado Times, El Dorado, KS
Russell, Inez ... (505) 983-3303
City ED
Santa Fe New Mexican, Santa Fe, NM
Russell, James ... (815) 673-3771
MAN ED, EPE
Streator Times-Press, Streator, IL
Russell, John ... (630) 844-5844
City ED, EDU ED, Farm/Agriculture ED
Beacon-News, Aurora, IL
Russell, Kathleen ... (912) 437-4251
ED, Darien News, Darien, GA
Russell, Keith ... (219) 235-6161
VP-OPER
South Bend Tribune, South Bend, IN
Russell, Ms Larry G ... (405) 665-4333
PUB, ED
Wynnewood Gazette, Wynnewood, OK
Russell, Linda ... (501) 642-2111
Society ED
De Queen Daily Citizen, De Queen, AR
Russell, Linda A ... (402) 773-5576
PUB, Clay County News, Sutton, NE
Russell, Loren ... (541) 575-0710
ED, Blue Mountain Eagle, John Day, OR
Russell, Margaret Hough ... (508) 548-4700
PUB, ED, Enterprise, Falmouth, MA
Russell, Mark ... (216) 999-4500
BUS/FIN ED, Plain Dealer, Cleveland, OH
Russell, Marlene L ... (301) 733-5131
CONT, Morning Herald, Hagerstown, MD
Russell, Mike ... (415) 348-4321
Photo ED
San Mateo County Times, San Mateo, CA
Russell, Nelson ... (814) 368-3173
PSL MGR, PA, Bradford Era, Bradford, PA
Russell, Nick ... (520) 367-6877
PUB, ED, MAN ED
White Mountain Weekly, Lakeside, AZ
Russell, Patrick ... (315) 369-3747
ED, Adirondack Echo, Old Forge, NY
Russell, Paul ... (905) 660-9556
ED, King Vaughan Weekly, Concord, ON
Russell, Pru ... (603) 543-3100
PROD FRM-COMP
Eagle Times, Claremont, NH
Russell, Renee ... (414) 922-4600
Family ED, Fashion/Style ED, Health/Medical ED, Living/Lifestyle ED, Women's ED
Reporter, Fond du Lac, WI
Russell, Richard M ... (506) 632-8888
CIRC DIR-Reader Services, Telegraph-Journal/Saint John Times Globe, Saint John, NB
Russell, Rick ... (604) 732-2111
CIRC MGR-Customer SRV, Vancouver Sun, Vancouver, BC, Southam Inc.
Russell, Sharon ... (201) 877-4141
Picture ED, Star-Ledger, Newark, NJ
Russell, Steve ... (501) 265-2071
PUB, ED, Chicot Spectator, Lake Village, AR
Russell, Steve ... (818) 892-9433
ED
Science Features Service, North Hills, CA
Russell, Susan S ... (719) 267-3576
ED, Ordway New Era, Ordway, CO
Russell, Thomas ... (910) 888-3500
BUS/FIN ED
High Point Enterprise, High Point, NC
Russell, Thomas A ... (317) 742-2050
ED, Catholic Moment, Lafayette, IN
Russell, Todd ... (419) 223-1010
CIRC DIR, Lima News, Lima, OH
Russell, Walt ... (757) 247-4600
ADV MGR-Production/Pre Press
Daily Press, Newport News, VA
Russell Jr, William C ... (303) 582-5333
PUB, Weekly Register-Call, Central City, CO
Russett, Chris ... (806) 995-3535
PUB, ED, Tulia Herald, Tulia, TX
Russiff, Diana ... (406) 657-1200
Nat'l. ADV Coord.
Montana Newspaper Group, Billings, MT
Russo, Ed ... (402) 475-4200
BUS Reporter
Lincoln Journal Star, Lincoln, NE
Russo, Joe ... (212) 210-2100
PROD MGR-Plateroom
New York Daily News, New York, NY
Russo, John ... (904) 747-5000
Graphics ED/Art DIR
News Herald, Panama City, FL
Russo, Lorie ... (908) 722-3000
ED, Franklin Focus, Somerville, NJ
Russo, Maryl ... (209) 734-5821
DIR-MKTG, Visalia Times-Delta, Visalia, CA
Russo, Pat ... (203) 729-2228
MGR-CR, MGR-Purchasing
Naugatuck Daily News, Naugatuck, CT
Rust, Gary W ... (573) 335-6611
PRES
Rust Communications, Cape Girardeau, MO
Rust, John ... (573) 333-4336
PUB
Tuesday Democrat-Argus, Caruthersville, MO
Rust, Jon K ... (901) 627-3247
PUB
Dyer County Tennessean, Dyersburg, TN
Rust, Mike ... (909) 793-3221
CIRC SUPV-Distribution
Redlands Daily Facts, Redlands, CA
Rust, Tom ... (864) 298-4100
PROD FRM-COMP (Day)
Greenville News, Greenville, SC
Rustad, Cindy ... (406) 791-1444
DP MGR, Great Falls Tribune, Great Falls, MT
Ruszkiewicz, Rob ... (412) 588-5000
CIRC MGR, Record-Argus, Greenville, PA
Rutar, Eric ... (801) 373-5050
EPE, Religion ED, Daily Herald, Provo, UT
Ruth, Art ... (614) 363-1161
GM, Delaware Gazette, Delaware, OH
Ruth, Brian ... (903) 455-4220
PROD FRM-COMP
Greenville Herald-Banner, Greenville, TX
Ruth, Dan ... (813) 259-7711
COL, Tampa Tribune and Times, Tampa, FL
Ruth, James R ... (717) 291-8811
Entertainment ED
Lancaster Intelligencer Journal/New Era/Sunday News, Lancaster, PA
Ruth, Ray ... (803) 577-7111
DP MGR, Post and Courier, Charleston, SC
Ruth, Rob ... (208) 549-1717
ED, Weiser Signal American, Weiser, ID
Ruth, Terry ... (515) 684-4611
PROD FRM-MR
Ottumwa Courier, Ottumwa, IA
Ruther, Leigh ... (505) 523-4581
DP MGR
Las Cruces Sun-News, Las Cruces, NM
Rutherford, Bill ... (501) 255-4538
ED, Grand Prairie Herald, Hazen, AR
Rutherford, Bonnie ... (501) 523-5855
CIRC MGR
Newport Daily Independent, Newport, AR
Rutherford, Jeff ... (409) 756-6671
CIRC DIR, Conroe Courier, Conroe, TX

Rut Who's Where-200

Rutherford, Joe (601) 842-2611
EPE, EDL Writer, Northeast Mississippi Daily Journal, Tupelo, MS
Rutherford, Jon C (847) 427-4300
ADV MGR-Division Sales, ADV MGR-NTL
Daily Herald, Arlington Heights, IL
Rutherford, Lenore (209) 532-7151
Fashion/Style ED, Religion ED
Union Democrat, Sonora, CA
Ruthhart, Roger (309) 786-6441
MAN ED, Rock Island Argus, Rock Island, IL
Ruthig, Donald P (410) 332-6000
DIR-INFO SYS, Sun, Baltimore, MD
Ruthizer, Jeffrey (212) 456-7777
VP-Labor Relations, ABC Inc., New York, NY
Ruthman, Brigitte (203) 574-3636
Environmental Writer, Waterbury Republican-American, Waterbury, CT
Rutkin, Bill (817) 634-2125
Sports ED, Killeen Daily Herald, Killeen, TX
Rutkowski, Gary (802) 524-9771
GM, MAN ED
St. Albans Messenger, St. Albans, VT
Rutledge, Craig (910) 679-2341
PUB, Yadkin Ripple, Yadkinville, NC
Rutledge, Cynthia (804) 376-2795
GM, Union Star, Brookneal, VA
Rutledge, David T (561) 461-2050
PUB, Tribune, Fort Pierce, FL
Rutledge, Don (330) 627-5591
MAN ED, Free Press Standard, Carrollton, OH
Rutledge, Kathleen (402) 475-4200
City ED, Lincoln Journal Star, Lincoln, NE
Rutledge, Peter (908) 922-6000
MGR-CR, Asbury Park Press, Neptune, NJ
Rutledge, Randy (918) 581-8300
DP MGR-Production SYS
Tulsa World, Tulsa, OK
Rutman, Ken (213) 229-5300
Open Forum ED
Los Angeles Daily Journal, Los Angeles, CA
Rutowski, Gary (802) 524-9771
BUS ED
St. Albans Messenger, St. Albans, VT
Ruttan, Beth (705) 567-5321
BM/PA
Northern Daily News, Kirkland Lake, ON
Ruwart, Sharon (408) 920-5000
ADV MGR-Employment
San Jose Mercury News, San Jose, CA
Ruxton, Jeanette (715) 284-4304
ED, Banner Journal, Black River Falls, WI
Ruyle, Darlene (970) 483-7460
ED, Wiggins Courier, Wiggins, CO
Ryall, Zach (512) 445-3500
Photo DIR
Austin American-Statesman, Austin, TX
Ryan, Carolyn (506) 632-8888
MAN ED (Saint John Times Globe)
Telegraph-Journal/Saint John Times Globe, Saint John, NB
Ryan, Carolyn (617) 786-7000
NTL ED, Political/Government ED
Patriot Ledger, Quincy, MA
Ryan, Charles (617) 933-3700
Librarian, Religion/School ED
Daily Times Chronicle, Woburn, MA
Ryan, Charles R (717) 748-6791
PUB, GM, Express, Lock Haven, PA
Ryan, Cherie (618) 487-5634
MAN ED
Beecher City Journal, Beecher City, IL
Ryan, Bishop Daniel L (217) 698-8500
PUB, Catholic Times, Springfield, IL
Ryan, David (403) 328-4411
CFO, CR MGR
Lethbridge Herald, Lethbridge, AB
Ryan, Desmond (215) 854-2000
Films Critic
Philadelphia Inquirer, Philadelphia, PA
Ryan, Dianne (201) 383-1500
ADV DIR, New Jersey Herald, Newton, NJ
Ryan, Evelyn (304) 292-6301
BUS ED, Dominion Post, Morgantown, WV
Ryan, Frank (403) 442-2711
PUB, ED, Highway 21 News, Trocho, AB
Ryan, Fred (819) 684-4755
PUB, Aylmer Bulletin D'Alymer, Aylmer, QC
Ryan, J Austin (515) 284-8000
PROD VP
Des Moines Register, Des Moines, IA
Ryan, Jack (601) 684-2421
MAN ED, Books ED
Enterprise-Journal, McComb, MS
Ryan, Jerry (402) 947-2391
PUB, Sentinel, Friend, NE
Ryan, Jim (714) 835-1234
ADV DIR-Display
Orange County Register, Santa Ana, CA
Ryan, Jim (402) 947-2391
PUB, Sentinel, Friend, NE
Ryan, Joyce (616) 965-3955
ED, Shopper News, Battle Creek, MI
Ryan, Keith A (716) 352-3411
PUB, Suburban News, Spencerport, NY
Ryan, Kevin (914) 454-2000
PROD MGR-MR
Poughkeepsie Journal, Poughkeepsie, NY
Ryan, Kimberly Potter (860) 388-3441
MAN ED
Pictorial Gazette, Old Saybrook, CT
Ryan, Linda (403) 932-3500
PUB, Rural Times, Cochrane, AB
Ryan, Lisa (205) 625-3231
MAN ED, Blount Countian, Oneonta, AL
Ryan, Louis F (804) 446-2010
EVP/GEN Counsel
Landmark Communications Inc., Norfolk, VA
Ryan, Mark (401) 277-7000
VP-Legal/ADM
Providence Journal-Bulletin, Providence, RI
Ryan, Mark (419) 784-5441
ADV MGR-RT
Defiance Crescent-News, Defiance, OH
Ryan, Michael (904) 435-8500
MAN ED
Pensacola News Journal, Pensacola, FL
Ryan, Michael J (505) 892-8080
PUB, ED, Observer, Rio Rancho, NM
Ryan, Mike (913) 295-1111
EDL Page Writer
Topeka Capital-Journal, Topeka, KS
Ryan, Mike (508) 374-0321
Sports ED, Haverhill Gazette, Haverhill, MA
Ryan, Molly Howard (205) 625-3231
PUB, ED, Blount Countian, Oneonta, AL
Ryan, P J (618) 487-5634
PUB, ED
Beecher City Journal, Beecher City, IL
Ryan, Pat (406) 447-4000
Sports/Outdoors ED
Helena Independent Record, Helena, MT
Ryan, Paul (508) 374-0321
GM, ADV MGR, MGR-MKTG/PROM
Haverhill Gazette, Haverhill, MA
Ryan, Richard (718) 981-1234
Entertainment/Amusements ED
Staten Island Advance, Staten Island, NY
Ryan, Robert J (408) 920-5000
DIR-Mercury Center
San Jose Mercury News, San Jose, CA
Ryan, Rory (937) 393-3456
ED, Times-Gazette, Hillsboro, OH
Ryan, Sharon (402) 947-2391
ED, Sentinel, Friend, NE
Ryan, Shaun (412) 588-5000
City ED, Record-Argus, Greenville, PA
Ryan, Steve (619) 241-7744
MGR-SYS, Daily Press, Victorville, CA
Freedom Communications Inc.
Ryan, Suzanne C (617) 929-2000
Fashion ED, Boston Globe, Boston, MA
Ryan, Terry (617) 786-7000
MAN ED, Patriot Ledger, Quincy, MA
Ryan, Tim (715) 526-2121
Political/Government ED
Shawano Leader, Shawano, WI
Ryan, Timothy (203) 235-1661
VP, CIRC DIR, Record-Journal, Meriden, CT
Ryan, Timothy E (215) 854-2000
VP-Subscriber MKTG & Services
Philadelphia Inquirer, Philadelphia, PA
Rybak, R T (612) 321-7300
PUB, Twin Cities Reader, Minneapolis, MN
Rybinski, Joe (810) 985-7171
PROD MGR-MR
Times Herald, Port Huron, MI
Rychetnik, Tammy (907) 257-4200
Radio/Television ED
Anchorage Daily News, Anchorage, AK
Rychlik, Michael (903) 885-8663
Sports ED, Sulphur Springs News-Telegram, Sulphur Springs, TX
Ryder, Bob (516) 843-2020
PROD GEN FRM-Mechanical Shop
Newsday, Melville, NY
Ryder, Thomas (812) 424-7711
ASST MAN ED-Sunday
Evansville Courier, Evansville, IN
Rydzaj, T (212) 594-2266
GM, Nowy Dziennik, New York, NY
Ryen, Sally (916) 756-0800
EDU/Schools ED, Davis Enterprise, Davis, CA
Ryerson, Dennis (515) 284-8000
ED, Des Moines Register, Des Moines, IA
Rykert, Ellen S (904) 389-4293
PUB, Kings Bay Periscope, Jacksonville, FL
Rykken, Rolf (513) 761-1188
Contributing Critic
Critic's Choice Reviews, Cincinnati, OH
Ryland, Gloria (412) 439-7500
ADV CNR-NTL
Herald-Standard, Uniontown, PA
Rylander-Davis, Karen (218) 723-5281
DIR-Human Resources
Duluth News-Tribune, Duluth, MN
Ryle, Sherry (513) 721-2700
ADV MGR-Kentucky
Cincinnati Enquirer, Cincinnati, OH
Ryle, Sherry (606) 292-2600
ADV MGR-Sales
Kentucky Post, Covington, KY
Ryll, Tom (360) 694-3391
Automotive/Aviation ED
Columbian, Vancouver, WA
Ryman, Anne (602) 483-0977
ED
Paradise Valley Independent, Scottsdale, AZ
Ryon, Sue (414) 224-2000
Deputy EPE
Milwaukee Journal Sentinel, Milwaukee, WI
Ryono, Debi (805) 650-2900
ED-Moorpark Edition
Ventura County Star, Ventura, CA
Ryser, Betty (903) 378-2396
GM, MAN ED, Signal Citizen, Honey Grove, TX
Ryser, Carl (903) 378-2396
PUB, Signal Citizen, Honey Grove, TX
Ryshkus, Les (414) 657-1000
Wire ED, Kenosha News, Kenosha, WI
Rysz, Bishop Anthony M (717) 346-9131
ED, Rola Boza, Scranton, PA
Ryzewicz, Carol (203) 762-0400
ED, Wilton Villager, Wilton, CT

S

Saad, Nabil (416) 787-8815
PUB, El Expresso, Toronto, ON
Saatmann, Kristi (505) 461-1952
MAN ED, Quay County Sun, Tucumcari, NM
Saba, Joe (317) 736-7101
PROD MGR, Daily Journal, Franklin, IN
Sabatini, Lou (504) 643-4918
CIRC DIR, Slidell Sentry-News, Slidell, LA
Sabatino, Louis W (215) 854-2000
Senior VP-Employee Relations
Philadelphia Inquirer, Philadelphia, PA
Sabba, Joseph (718) 729-3444
PUB, ED, Woodside Herald, Sunnyside, NY
Sabbadini, Annarosa (514) 393-1010
ED, Montreal Mirror, Montreal, QC
Sabella, Connie (412) 537-3351
ADV MGR-CLASS
Latrobe Bulletin, Latrobe, PA
Sabo, Bill (303) 442-1202
ADV DIR, Daily Camera, Boulder, CO
Sabo, Dennis (419) 483-4190
MAN ED, Bellevue Gazette, Bellevue, OH
Sabo, Linda (302) 674-3600
ADTX MGR, Delaware State News, Dover, DE
Sabo, Lynda (507) 834-6966
ED, Gibbon Gazette, Gibbon, MN
Sabo, Tim (919) 752-6166
PROD MGR, Daily Reflector, Greenville, NC
Sabocinski, Kathy (716) 893-5771
GM, Polish-American Journal, Buffalo, NY
Sabolowsky, Rob (212) 210-2100
PROD MGR-Technical Training
New York Daily News, New York, NY
Sabulis, Jill (404) 526-5151
Home/Garden ED
Atlanta Journal-Constitution, Atlanta, GA
Sabulis, Tom (404) 526-5151
Entertainment/Amusements ED, Music ED
Atlanta Journal-Constitution, Atlanta, GA
Saccoman, John (218) 262-1011
City ED, Daily Tribune, Hibbing, MN
Sachetti, James (717) 784-2121
ED, EPE, Press Enterprise, Bloomsburg, PA
Sachs, Lloyd (312) 321-3000
Music ED-Jazz, Sun-Times, Chicago, IL
Sacks, Gordon (518) 792-9914
ED-Entertainment Features Syndicate
TV Data, Queensbury, NY
Sacks, Mike (954) 356-4000
PROD MGR
Sun-Sentinel, Fort Lauderdale, FL
Saddler, Lyle E (608) 782-9710
PROD MGR-Press/Plate
La Crosse Tribune, La Crosse, WI
Sade, Charles (217) 223-5100
PROD SUPT-MR, Herald-Whig, Quincy, IL
Sadek, Barbara (312) 321-3000
Food ED, Chicago Sun-Times, Chicago, IL
Sadler, Stan M (501) 325-6412
PUB, ED
Cleveland County Herald, Rison, AR
Sadock, Popsy (412) 834-1151
Action ED, Tribune-Review, Greensburg, PA
Sadowski, Ervin (414) 224-2000
PROD FRM-Paper/Ink
Milwaukee Journal Sentinel, Milwaukee, WI
Sadowski, Larry (316) 283-1500
CIRC MGR, Newton Kansan, Newton, KS
Sadowski, Richard J (562) 435-1161
PRES, PUB, Press-Telegram, Long Beach, CA
Sadowski, Vivien L (913) 263-1000
PRES, PUB, Reflector-Chronicle, Abilene, KS
Saferite, Sylvia (205) 845-2550
PROD FRM-COMP
Times Journal, Fort Payne, AL
Saffron, Inga (215) 854-2000
Moscow BU, Inquirer, Philadelphia, PA
Sagan, Bruce (773) 643-8533
PUB, Hyde Park Herald, Chicago, IL
Sage, T Don (318) 322-5161
CIRC DIR, News-Star, Monroe, LA
Sager, Martin (201) 342-2985
BM, Newsportraits Syndicate, Hackensack, NJ
Sagermann, Lewis (330) 454-5611
Design ED, Repository, Canton, OH
Sahagun, Louis (213) 237-5000
Denver BU, Times, Los Angeles, CA
Sahlberg, Bert (208) 743-9411
Sports ED, Morning Tribune, Lewiston, ID
Sailer, Linda (701) 225-8111
Books ED, Entertainment ED, Librarian
Dickinson Press, Dickinson, ND
Sailor, Craig (360) 754-5400
Photo ED, Olympian, Olympia, WA
Sailor, Jody (507) 359-2911
EDU/Women's ED, Journal, New Ulm, MN
Sailor, Shelley (209) 784-5000
DP MGR, Recorder, Porterville, CA
Sailus, Charles (717) 821-2091
PROD FRM-COMP
Citizens' Voice, Wilkes-Barre, PA
Saine, Deb (219) 722-5000
Lifestyle ED, Pharos-Tribune, Logansport, IN
Saint, Marion (505) 622-7710
ADV DIR/MGR-MIS, Daily Record, Roswell, NM
Saint, Steve (619) 469-0101
PUB, ED
Spring Valley Bulletin, Lemon Grove, CA
St. Amand, Charles (508) 458-7100
MET ED, Sun, Lowell, MA
St. Amour, Chuck (619) 469-0101
CIRC MGR, Press, Grand Rapid, MI
St. Amant, Michael (819) 376-2501
News ED-Night
Le Nonvelliste, Trois-Rivieres, QC
St. Clair, Billy (912) 888-9300
CIRC DIR, Albany Herald, Albany, GA
St. Clair, Cathy (540) 935-2123
MAN ED, Virginia Mountaineer, Grundy, VA
St. Clair, Tina Corey (812) 424-7711
ADV MGR-Territory Sales
Evansville Courier Co. Inc., Evansville, IN
St. Claire, Allison (303) 355-3882
PUB/ED, Senior Wire News Service, Denver, CO
St. Cyr, Larry (615) 259-8000
DIR-FIN, Tennessean, Nashville, TN
St-Jean, Luce (819) 326-1844
GM, Information Bu Nordi, Le Sommet, Saint-Jovite, QC
St. John, Abigal (515) 842-2155
ED, Knoxville Journal-Express, Knoxville, IA
St. John, Bill (303) 892-5000
DiningWine ED
Rocky Mountain News, Denver, CO
St. John, Bob (214) 977-8222
COL-MET, Dallas Morning News, Dallas, TX
St. John, Edward F (508) 676-8211
PUB-Emeritus, Herald News, Fall River, MA
St. Louis, Patty (719) 382-5611
MAN ED, El Paso County Advertiser & News, Fountain, CO
St. Martin, Barbara (612) 222-0059
BM, St. Paul Legal Ledger, St. Paul, MN
St. Mary, David (617) 426-3000
VP-Human Resources
Boston Herald, Herald, MA
St. Peter, Jeff (208) 935-0838
ED, Clearwater Progress, Kamiah, ID
Sakson, Anthony (609) 272-7000
ADV MGR-Ad Production
Press of Atlantic City, Pleasantville, NJ
Salamon, Milt (407) 242-3500
COL, Florida Today, Melbourne, FL
Salamone, Anthony (610) 258-7171
Action Line ED (Action Express)
Express-Times, Easton, PA
Salamone, Gary P (619) 492-8696
Syndicate ED, Continental Features/Continental News Service, San Diego, CA
Salantai, Gail L (618) 656-4700
ASST TREAS, CONT
Edwardsville Intelligencer, Edwardsville, IL
Salazar, Christina (360) 577-2500
MGR-EDU SRV, Daily News, Longview, WA
Salazar, Hector (800) 995-8626
MAN ED, El Popular, Bakersfield, CA
Salazar, Herb (818) 566-4388
GM, Entertainment Today, Burbank, CA
Salazar, John (818) 566-4388
PUB, Entertainment Today, Burbank, CA
Salazar, Lupe (213) 237-5485
Reprints & Permissions, Los Angeles Times Syndicate, Los Angeles, CA
Salazar, Veronica (210) 225-7411
VP-Community Relations
San Antonio Express-News, San Antonio, TX
Salazar, Vivian (806) 376-4488
Fashion/Style ED, Features ED, Amarillo Daily News/Globe Times, Amarillo, TX
Salcedo, Juan (800) 223-2154
MGR/CONT
Investor's Business Daily, Los Angeles, CA

201-Who's Where **San**

Salcedo, Myra .... (915) 682-5311
EDU ED, Reporter-Telegram, Midland, TX
Saldivar, Olga .... (210) 542-4301
MGR-CR, Brownsville Herald, Brownsville, TX
Saldivar, Roberta J .... (210) 542-4301
PROD MGR-SYS, Brownsville Herald, Brownsville, TX, Freedom Communications
Sale, John .... (509) 459-5000
Photo ED, Spokesman-Review, Spokane, WA
Salem, Lee .... (816) 932-6600
VP/EDL DIR
Universal Press Syndicate, Kansas City, MO
Salemme, William .... (908) 922-6000
PROD Manufacturing Administrator
Asbury Park Press, Neptune, NJ
Salerno, Richard .... (718) 981-1234
CIRC MGR, Advance, Staten Island, NY
Sales, Jack .... (317) 633-1240
ASST MAN ED-PM Cycle
Indianapolis Star/News, Indianapolis, IN
Sales, Morgan .... (714) 492-5121
ED, Sun Post News, San Clemente, CA
Salesman, Marilyn .... (812) 231-4200
BUS ED, Tribune-Star, Terre Haute, IN
Salfrank, Terry .... (605) 225-4100
PROD MGR-Press
Aberdeen American News, Aberdeen, SD
Salgado, Teresa .... (915) 729-4342
MAN ED, Big Bend Sentinel, Marfa, TX
Salgado-Halpern, Rosario .... (915) 229-3877
GM, MAN ED
International Presidio Paper, Presidio, TX
Salinas, Connie .... (512) 445-3500
DIR-InfoVENTURES
Austin American-Statesman, Austin, TX
Salinas, Michael .... (415) 861-5019
ED, Bay Area Reporter, San Francisco, CA
Salinas, Tony .... (512) 527-3261
PUB, ED
Hebbronville Enterprise, Hebbronville, TX
Salisbury, Catherine .... (514) 393-1010
PUB, Montreal Mirror, Montreal, QC
Salisbury, Thom .... (909) 889-9666
ADV MGR-Creative SRV
Sun, San Bernardino, CA
Sall, Judy .... (214) 977-8222
Reference ED, Morning News, Dallas, TX
Salladay, Robert .... (510) 661-2600
Sacramento BU ED
Fremont Argus, Fremont, CA
Sallinas, Sergio H .... (214) 977-8222
VP-Advertising, Morning News, Dallas, TX
Sallinger, David .... (412) 664-9161
Entertainment/Amusements ED
Daily News, McKeesport, PA
Sallo, Stewart .... (303) 494-5511
PUB, Boulder Weekly, Boulder, CO
Salm, Pete .... (510) 208-6300
PROD MGR-Pre Press
Oakland Tribune, Oakland, CA
MediaNews Inc. (Alameda Newspapers)
Salman, Carroll .... (847) 696-3133
ED, Herald-Advocate, Park Ridge, IL
Salmon, David B...................... (908) 992-6000
MGR-Accounting
Asbury Park Press, Neptune, NJ
Salmon, Donna .... (707) 552-1699
ED/PROM, Salmon Syndication, Vallejo, CA
Salmon, Patrick J .... (312) 927-7200
PUB, Back of the Yards Journal/El Periodico, Chicago, IL
Salmon, Ray .... (707) 552-1699
Author, Salmon Syndication, Vallejo, CA
Salmon, Stephen .... (707) 552-1699
PROD, Salmon Syndication, Vallejo, CA
Salow, Beth .... (313) 242-1100
ADV MGR-CLASS
Monroe Evening News, Monroe, MI
Saloway, Tony .... (403) 468-0100
News ED, Edmonton Sun, Edmonton, AB
Salsburg, Mike .... (208) 733-0931
Photo DEPT MGR, Times-News, Twin Falls, ID
Salster, Ann .... (804) 561-3655
PUB, Amelia Bulletin Monitor, Amelia, VA
Salster, Michael D .... (804) 561-3655
ED, Amelia Bulletin Monitor, Amelia, VA
Saltas, John .... (801) 575-7003
PUB, Private Eye Weekly, Salt Lake City, UT
Salter, Bill .... (915) 337-4661
PUB, Odessa American, Odessa, TX
Salter, Peter .... (701) 223-2500
State ED, Bismarck Tribune, Bismarck, ND
Salter, Sidney L .... (601) 469-2561
PUB, ED, Scott County Times, Forest, MS
Salter, Stephanie .... (415) 777-2424
COL
San Francisco Examiner, San Francisco, CA
Salters, Paul .... (508) 586-7200
Farm/Agriculture ED
Enterprise, Brockton, MA
Salthammer, Sharon .... (204) 687-7339
ADV MGR, Reminder, Flin Flon, MB
Saltisiak, John .... (757) 446-2000
PROD DIR-Engineering
Virginian-Pilot, Norfolk, VA

Saltz, Donald .... (202) 966-0025
Author, Quiz Features, Washington, DC
Saltz, Mozelle .... (202) 966-0025
RES DIR, Quiz Features, Washington, DC
Saltzman, Mort .... (916) 321-1000
ASST MAN ED-Sports/BUS/Photo/Art
Sacramento Bee, Sacramento, CA
Salustro, John .... (941) 574-1110
PROD MGR-COMP
Cape Coral Daily Breeze, Cape Coral, FL
Salvante, Gloria J M .... (510) 748-1666
ED, Alameda Journal, Alameda, CA
Salvatore, Terri .... (914) 478-2787
ED, Enterprise, Hastings-on-Hudson, NY
Salvoni, Paul .... (408) 920-5000
Online ED
San Jose Mercury News, San Jose, CA
Salyers, Debbie .... (423) 246-8121
MGR-Office, Times-News, Kingsport, TN
Salyers, Jeff .... (812) 268-6356
News ED, Sullivan Daily Times, Sullivan, IN
Salzer, Nancy .... (513) 352-2000
CIRC DIR-Home Delivery
Cincinnati Post, Cincinnati, OH
Salzman, Dorothy .... (916) 444-2355
Personnel DIR
Daily Recorder, Sacramento, CA
Salzman, Gerald .... (213) 229-5300
PUB, Daily Journal, Los Angeles, CA
Salzman, Jerry .... (916) 444-2355
PRES, Daily Recorder, Sacramento, CA
Salzmann, Kathy .... (334) 433-1551
ADV ASST MGR-RT
Mobile Press Register, Mobile, AL
Sama, Anita .... (703) 276-3400
Health/Medical ED, USA Today, Arlington, VA
Samblin, Evelyn .... (205) 221-2840
MGR-PROM
Daily Mountain Eagle, Jasper, AL
Samek, Gary .... (860) 887-9211
Sports ED, Norwich Bulletin, Norwich, CT
Samer, Yuri .... (503) 344-3416
Author/Owner
Krebbs Cycle Productions, Eugene, OR
Sames, Dave .... (513) 863-8200
PROD FRM-COMP
Journal-News, Hamilton, OH
Samitz, Mary .... (718) 257-0600
PUB, Canarsie Courier, Brooklyn, NY
Sammons, Janet .... (919) 419-6500
Librarian, Herald-Sun, Durham, NC
Samoniantz, Serge .... (818) 409-0949
ED, California Courier, Glendale, CA
Sample, George R .... (618) 937-6411
Vice Chairman, Hollinger International Inc., West Frankfort, IL
Sample III, George .... (814) 643-4040
PRES, Daily News, Huntingdon, PA
Sample, Michael D .... (814) 827-3634
PUB, ADV DIR, ADV MGR-NTL
Titusville Herald, Titusville, PA
Samples, Henry .... (423) 929-3111
MAN ED, Automotive ED, News ED, Religion ED, Johnson City Press, Johnson City, TN
Sampson, Ron .... (515) 964-9375
GM, Ankeny Today, Ankeny, IA
Sampson, Stanley .... (617) 426-3000
PROD SUPT-Engraving
Boston Herald, Boston, MA
Sams, Parker .... (419) 422-5151
ASSOC ED, EPE
Findlay Courier, Findlay, OH
Samsell, John .... (304) 292-6301
Special Sections ED
Dominion Post, Morgantown, WV
Samson, Chris .... (707) 762-4541
ED, Argus-Courier, Petaluma, CA
Samson, Iris .... (412) 687-1000
MAN ED, Jewish Chronicle, Pittsburgh, PA
Samson, J Jacques .... (418) 686-3233
EPE, Le Soleil, Quebec, QC
Samson, Steve .... (219) 294-1661
PROD MGR-COMP, Truth, Elkhart, IN
Samuel, Roger D .... (810) 766-6100
PUB, Flint Journal, Flint, MI
Samuels, Jeanne F .... (713) 630-0391
ED, Jewish Herald-Voice, Houston, TX
Samuels, Jeff .... (215) 854-2000
Sportsweek ED
Philadelphia Daily News, Philadelphia, PA
Samuels, Joseph W .... (713) 630-0391
PUB, Jewish Herald-Voice, Houston, TX
Samuels, Lennox .... (214) 977-8222
ASST MAN ED-NTL/International
Dallas Morning News, Dallas, TX
Samuels, Stuart .... (410) 268-5000
City ED, Political/Government ED
Capital, Annapolis, MD
Samuelson, Julie .... (913) 852-4900
GM, Western Times, Sharon Springs, KS
Sanata, Larry .... (412) 981-6100
Automotive ED, Health/Medical ED, SCI/Technology ED, Herald, Sharon, PA
Sanchez, Dolores .... (213) 263-5743
PUB, Eastern Group, Los Angeles, CA

Sanchez, Dolores .... (313) 841-0100
PUB, El Central, Detroit, MI
Sanchez, Gonzalo .... (312) 455-0300
ED, El Heraldo, Chicago, IL
Sanchez, Jesus .... (213) 237-5000
RE/Hotels/Gambling/Insurance ED
Los Angeles Times, Los Angeles, CA
Sanchez, John .... (213) 263-5743
ED, Wyvernwood Chronicle, Los Angeles, CA
Sanchez, Jonathan .... (213) 263-5743
GM, ED, Eastern Group, Los Angeles, CA
Sanchez, Kathy .... (407) 242-3500
CIRC MGR-Customer SRV
Florida Today, Melbourne, FL
Sanchez, Lora .... (718) 639-7000
GM, Long Island City/Astoria Journal, Maspeth, NY
Sanchez, Phillip .... (212) 684-5656
PUB, Noticias del Mundo, New York, NY
Sanchez, Robert .... (210) 242-7900
GM
La Prensa De San Antonio, San Antonio, TX
Sanchez, Walter H .... (718) 639-7000
PUB, ED, Long Island City/Astoria Journal, Maspeth, NY
Sanchioni, Paul .... (705) 674-5271
PROD FRM-PR, Sudbury Star, Sudbury, ON
Sand, Dora .... (913) 337-2242
PUB, Hanover News, Hanover, KS
Sand, R L .... (913) 337-2242
PUB, ED, Hanover News, Hanover, KS
Sandberg, Doug .... (403) 328-4411
PROD MGR, Herald, Lethbridge, AB
Sandberg, Steve .... (414) 338-0622
MAN ED, Daily News, West Bend, WI
Sandbulte, Jane .... (316) 221-1050
News ED, Daily Courier, Winfield, KS
Sandell, David .... (608) 252-6400
Chief Photographer
Capital Times, Madison, WI
Sandella, Richard .... (203) 789-5200
Fashion/Style ED, Features ED, Living ED
New Haven Register, New Haven, CT
Sander, Carol .... (405) 323-5151
VP, Clinton Daily News, Clinton, OK
Sander, Pam .... (910) 343-2000
Fashion/Food ED, Features ED, Home Furnishings ED, Lifestyle ED, Travel ED
Morning Star, Wilmington, NC
Sanderlin, Brant .... (919) 752-6166
Photo ED, Daily Reflector, Greenville, NC
Sanders, Anthony L .... (314) 535-4033
GM, ED, Evening Whirl, St. Louis, MO
Sanders, C G .... (318) 574-1404
PUB, Madison Journal, Tallulah, LA
Sanders, Carl P .... (307) 672-2431
EVP, PUB, Sheridan Press, Sheridan, WY
Sanders, Carla .... (818) 962-8811
Fashion/Style ED, San Gabriel Valley Tribune, West Covina, CA, MediaNews Inc.
Sanders, Carol .... (807) 343-6200
Assignment ED
Chronicle-Journal, Thunder Bay, ON
Sanders, Connie .... (717) 966-2255
ED, Mifflinburg Telegraph, Mifflinburg, PA
Sanders, Darla .... (719) 336-2266
ADV MGR-CLASS, Daily News, Lamar, CO
Sanders, David .... (402) 444-1000
MKTG MGR-Advertising/MKTG
Omaha World-Herald, Omaha, NE
Sanders, Don .... (618) 658-4321
PUB, ED, Vienna Times, Vienna, IL
Sanders Jr, Douglas .... (205) 367-2217
ED, Pickens County Herald, Carrollton, AL
Sanders, Duane .... (817) 594-7447
CIRC ASST MGR, Democrat, Weatherford, TX
Sanders, Gary .... (812) 275-3355
PROD FRM-MR
Bedford Times-Mail, Bedford, IN
Sanders Jr, J H (Sandy) .... (912) 427-3757
PUB, Press-Sentinel, Jesup, GA
Sanders, Jack .... (203) 438-6544
ED, Ridgefield Press, Ridgefield, CT
Sanders, Jacquin .... (813) 893-8111
COL
St. Petersburg Times, St. Petersburg, FL
Sanders, Larry .... (423) 756-6900
CIRC MGR-Single Copy Sales
Chattanooga Free Press, Chattanooga, TN
Sanders, Lowell .... (501) 836-8192
Sports ED, Camden News, Camden, AR
Sanders, Matt .... (502) 443-1771
SCI/Technology ED
Paducah Sun, Paducah, KY
Sanders, Paul .... (318) 487-6397
CIRC DIR, Daily Town Talk, Alexandria, LA
Sanders, Randy .... (806) 762-8844
EX ED, Radio/Television ED
Lubbock Avalanche-Journal, Lubbock, TX
Sanders, Ray .... (719) 336-2266
PROD SUPT, Lamar Daily News, Lamar, CO
Sanders, Rhonda .... (810) 766-6100
COL, Flint Journal, Flint, MI
Sanders, Steve .... (501) 364-5186
ED, Ashley News Observer, Crossett, AR

Sanders, Sue-Ellen .... (561) 461-2050
MGR-Community Relations
Tribune, Fort Pierce, FL
Sanders, Susan .... (803) 577-7111
MGR-PROM
Post and Courier, Charleston, SC
Sanders, Teresa .... (707) 987-3602
PUB, ED, Times Star, Middletown, CA
Sanders, Thomas .... (219) 881-3000
ADV Deputy DIR-CLASS/NTL
Post-Tribune, Gary, IN
Sanders, Walt .... (417) 679-4641
PUB, Ozark County Times, Gainesville, MO
Sanders, Wilene M .... (615) 684-1200
ASSOC PUB, MGR-Office
Shelbyville Times-Gazette, Shelbyville, TN
Sanders, Mrs Wilene M .... (615) 684-1200
DP MGR, Times-Gazette, Shelbyville, TN
Sanders, William E .... (614) 461-5000
CIRC MGR-City
Columbus Dispatch, Columbus, OH
Sanderson, Blake L .... (717) 272-5611
PUB, GM, Daily News, Lebanon, PA
Sanderson, Gary .... (413) 772-0261
Sports ED, Recorder, Greenfield, MA
Sanderson, Lorry .... (507) 658-3919
MAN ED
Buffalo Ridge Gazette, Ruthton, MN
Sanderson, Margaret .... (705) 282-2003
PUB, Manitoulin Recorder, Gore Bay, ON
Sanderson, Shirley .... (307) 455-2525
PUB, Dubois Frontier, Dubois, WY
Sandigo, Henry .... (415) 777-5700
MGR-Telecom, San Francisco Newspaper Agency, San Francisco, CA
Sandin, Jo .... (414) 224-2000
Religion Reporter
Milwaukee Journal Sentinel, Milwaukee, WI
Sandlin, Bill .... (405) 475-3311
Art DIR
Daily Oklahoman, Oklahoma City, OK
Sandlin, Darrell .... (412) 224-4321
PROD DIR, Valley News Dispatch, Tarentum, PA, Gannett Co. Inc.
Sandmeier, Bryan .... (913) 823-6363
CIRC MGR, Salina Journal, Salina, KS
Sandmeyer, Duane .... (217) 446-1000
PROD FRM-COMP
Commercial News, Danville, IL
Sandoval, Ricardo .... (408) 920-5000
General Assignment Reporter/ED
San Jose Mercury News, San Jose, CA
Sands, David .... (604) 426-5201
ED, Daily Townsman, Cranbrook, BC
Sands, Deanna .... (402) 444-1000
MAN ED, Omaha World-Herald, Omaha, NE
Sandstrom, Eve .... (405) 353-0620
Wire ED, Lawton Constitution, Lawton, OK
Sandstrom, Karen .... (216) 999-4500
Home ED, Plain Dealer, Cleveland, OH
Sandvig, David .... (360) 694-3391
ADV MGR-Customer SRV
Columbian, Vancouver, WA
Sandy, Robert .... (941) 262-3161
ADV MGR-NTL/Major
Naples Daily News, Naples, FL
Sandy, Robert .... (860) 241-6200
Deputy DIR-OPER/Telecommunications
Hartford Courant, Hartford, CT
Sanen, Maria .... (415) 749-5400
ADV Display MGR
Recorder, San Francisco, CA
Sanfield, Phillip F .... (310) 832-0221
MAN ED, EPE, News-Pilot, San Pedro, CA
Sanford, Billy .... (706) 278-1011
CIRC MGR, Daily Citizen-News, Dalton, GA
Sanford, Bob .... (702) 463-4242/2856
PUB, Mason Valley News, Yerington, NV
Sanford, Christopher .... (518) 861-6641
ED, Altamont Enterprise and Albany County Post, Altamont, NY
Sanford, David .... (702) 463-4242/2856
PUB, ED, Mason Valley News, Yerington, NV
Sanford, Diana .... (419) 332-5511
PROD MGR-SYS/Imaging
News-Messenger, Fremont, OH
Sanford, Jim .... (702) 463-4242
PUB, GM, Mason Valley News, Yerington, NV
Sanford, Keith .... (501) 751-6200
CIRC DIR, Morning News of Northwest Arkansas, Springdale, AR
Sanford, Larry .... (601) 794-2765
PUB, Lamar County News, Purvis, MS
Sanford, Mary .... (616) 873-5620
ED, Oceana's Herald Journal, Hart, MI
Sanford, Otis .... (901) 529-2211
Deputy MAN ED
Commercial Appeal, Memphis, TN
Sanford, Richard D .... (914) 586-2601
PUB
Catskill Mountain News, Margaretville, NY

San Who's Where-202

Sanft, Marshall .... (508) 764-4325
CIRC MGR, News, Southbridge, MA
Sanger, Randy .... (304) 327-2811
DIR-MKTG/PROM
Bluefield Daily Telegraph, Bluefield, WV
Sanguinetti, Phillip A .... (205) 236-1551
PRES
Consolidated Publishing Co., Anniston, AL
San Miguel, Joe .... (512) 775-1551
PUB, Border Eagle, Del Rio, TX
Sannes, Randy .... (303) 776-2244
PROD MGR-Distribution
Daily Times-Call, Longmont, CO
Sannes, Robert .... (507) 285-7600
PROD MGR-Pre Press/Quality
Post-Bulletin, Rochester, MN
Sanow, Troy .... (507) 537-1551
PROD MGR, Independent, Marshall, MN
San Pedro, Patricia .... (305) 350-2111
VP-Community Relations
Miami Herald, Miami, FL
Sansfacon, Jean-Robert .... (514) 985-3333
ASST EIC, Le Devoir, Montreal, QC
Santamour, Bill .... (847) 329-2000
ED, Lerner News Star, Lincolnwood, IL
Santamour, William .... (773) 281-7500
ED, Lincoln Park/Lake View/Near North/Downtown Skyline, Chicago, IL
Santarelli, Denny .... (217) 351-5252
ADV MGR-NTL
News-Gazette, Champaign, IL
Santarpio, Marcia .... (617) 933-3700
ADV MGR-NTL
Daily Times Chronicle, Woburn, MA
Santarris, Ben .... (360) 676-2600
Living/Lifestyle ED
Bellingham Herald, Bellingham, WA
Santelices, Alicia C .... (708) 484-1188
PUB, ED, El Imparcial, Chicago, IL
Santiago, Alex .... (941) 294-7731
CIRC DIR, News Chief, Winter Haven, FL
Santiago, Mike .... (310) 337-7003
EVP, Creators Syndicate, Los Angeles, CA
Santillan, Rogelio .... (972) 386-9120
PUB, El Sol de Texas, Dallas, TX
Santine, Karen .... (313) 222-6400
MGR-Training & Development
Detroit Newspapers, Detroit, MI
Santistevan, Jan .... (970) 824-7031
CIRC MGR
Northwest Colorado Daily Press, Craig, CO
Santopatre, Jean .... (203) 333-0161
Photo/Graphics ED
Connecticut Post, Bridgeport, CT
Santora, James .... (212) 581-4640
GM, America, New York, NY
Santori, Jim P .... (608) 782-9710
PUB, La Crosse Tribune, La Crosse, WI
Santos, Bonnie .... (216) 329-7000
Religion ED, Chronicle-Telegram, Elyria, OH
Santos, Ricardo .... (210) 728-2500
Photo DEPT MGR
Laredo Morning Times, Laredo, TX
Santoyo, Gus .... (714) 634-1567
ED, Yorba Linda Star, Anaheim, CA
Santy, Allen .... (316) 225-4151
Picture ED
Dodge City Daily Globe, Dodge City, KS
Sanville, Connie .... (802) 222-5281
GM, Journal Opinion, Bradford, VT
Sapatkin, Don .... (215) 854-2000
Weekend Section ED
Philadelphia Inquirer, Philadelphia, PA
Sapio, Bob .... (212) 210-2100
Deputy MAN ED-News
New York Daily News, New York, NY
Sapiro, Adam .... (203) 574-3636
Suburban ED, Waterbury Republican-American, Waterbury, CT
Sapp, Perry .... (404) 526-5151
CIRC MGR-SYS OPER
Atlanta Journal-Constitution, Atlanta, GA
Sapp, Vicki .... (413) 562-4181
TREAS
Westfield Evening News, Westfield, MA
Sappell, Joel .... (213) 237-5000
MET Projects ED
Los Angeles Times, Los Angeles, CA
Saputo, Vince .... (630) 739-2300
GM, Darien Metropolitan, Lemont, IL
Sar, Ali .... (818) 962-8811
BUS ED, SCI/Technology ED
San Gabriel Valley Tribune, West Covina, CA
MediaNews Inc.
Sara, Bill .... (518) 792-3131
CIRC MGR, Post-Star, Glens Falls, NY
Sarantitis, Anthony .... (415) 777-5700
CIRC MGR-OPER, San Francisco Newspaper Agency, San Francisco, CA
Sarasohn, David .... (503) 221-8327
EDL Writer, Oregonian, Portland, OR
Sarchuk, David .... (306) 764-4276
PROD FRM-COMP
Prince Albert Daily Herald, Prince Albert, SK
Sardinia, Michele .... (607) 272-2321
MKTG DIR-Market Development
Ithaca Journal, Ithaca, NY
Sargent, Bill .... (407) 242-3500
Outdoors ED, Florida Today, Melbourne, FL
Sargent, Ed .... (405) 475-3311
News ED
Daily Oklahoman, Oklahoma City, OK
Sargent, Edward D .... (202) 269-3311
PUB, Sunday Morning Glory, Washington, DC
Sargent, Tim .... (330) 264-1125
PROD FRM-PR, Daily Record, Wooster, OH
Sarins, Laura .... (217) 837-2414
PUB, ED, Newman Independent, Newman, IL
Sarno, William .... (860) 584-0501
Books ED, EPE, Religion ED
Bristol Press, Bristol, CT
Sarris, Eve .... (516) 843-2020
LI Sports ED, Newsday, Melville, NY
Sartain, Father J Peter .... (901) 722-4770
PUB, Common Sense, Memphis, TN
Sartori, Larry .... (314) 340-8000
PROD GEN FRM-MR
St. Louis Post-Dispatch, St. Louis, MO
Sarubbi, Wendy Spirduso .... (407) 420-5000
ED-Florida Magazine
Orlando Sentinel, Orlando, FL
Sarver, Janet .... (318) 783-3450
Fashion ED, Society ED
Crowley Post-Signal, Crowley, LA
Sas, Paul .... (860) 442-2200
ADV MGR-CLASS, Day, New London, CT
Sass, Carrie .... (209) 943-6397
Community Relations
Record, Stockton, CA
Sass, Jerry .... (503) 221-8327
Copy Desk Chief, Oregonian, Portland, OR
Sass, Rick .... (703) 276-3400
CIRC GM-Kansas City
USA Today, Arlington, VA
Sasser, Donna .... (305) 350-2111
ADV DIR-Target Marketing
Miami Herald, Miami, FL
Sasser, Ray .... (214) 977-8222
Outdoors Writer
Dallas Morning News, Dallas, TX
Sassman, David C .... (317) 632-1984
ED/PUB, Pro-Am Sports Service/Mile Square Publisher, Indianapolis, IN
Sassman, Robert J .... (319) 882-4207
PUB, ED, Tripoli Leader, Tripoli, IA
Sassong, Paul .... (847) 317-0500
GM, Review, Bannockburn, IL
Sassounian, Harut .... (818) 409-0949
PUB, California Courier, Glendale, CA
Sataloff, Ronald A .... (609) 468-1099
PRES
World Features Syndicate, La Jolla, CA
Satchfield, Dan .... (417) 836-1100
CONT
Springfield News-Leader, Springfield, MO
Sater, Lori .... (612) 777-8800
ED, South-West Review, North St. Paul, MN
Saternow, Lynn .... (412) 981-6100
Sports ED, Herald, Sharon, PA
Satnan, Bob .... (815) 987-1200
News ED
Rockford Register Star, Rockford, IL
Sato, Kii .... (334) 433-1551
Photo ED, Mobile Press Register, Mobile, AL
Satran Jr, Dan .... (608) 643-3444
ED, Sauk Prairie Star, Sauk City, WI
Sattely, Terry .... (201) 383-1500
CIRC MGR, New Jersey Herald, Newton, NJ
Satterfield, Bill .... (813) 893-8111
PROD MGR-COMP
St. Petersburg Times, St. Petersburg, FL
Satterfield, Dave .... (305) 350-2111
City ED, Miami Herald, Miami, FL
Satterly, Eric .... (409) 744-3611
PROD FRM-COMP
Galveston County Daily News, Galveston, TX
Satterwhite, John H .... (618) 937-6411
EVP, Hollinger International Inc., West Frankfort, IL
Satullo, Chris .... (215) 854-2000
Deputy EPE
Philadelphia Inquirer, Philadelphia, PA
Saturn, Lionel .... (212) 930-8000
ADV DIR-OPER
New York Post, New York, NY
Saucier, Mike .... (508) 764-4325
MAN ED, News, Southbridge, MA
Sauder, Steven .... (717) 348-9100
ADV MGR
Tribune & The Scranton Times, Scranton, PA
Sauer, Andy .... (203) 574-3636
Design ED, Pagination ED, Waterbury Republican-American, Waterbury, CT
Sauer, Don .... (208) 783-1107
City ED, Shoshone News-Press, Kellogg, ID
Sauer, Georgia .... (412) 263-1100
Fashion ED, Post-Gazette, Pittsburgh, PA
Sauer, Mark .... (815) 284-2222
Photo ED, Telegraph, Dixon, IL
Saul, Bob .... (717) 485-4513
ED
Fulton County News, McConnellsburg, PA
Saul, Deborah .... (313) 242-1100
MAN ED, Monroe Evening News, Monroe, MI
Saul, John .... (206) 464-2111
Deputy News ED, Seattle Times, Seattle, WA
Saul, Nancy .... (217) 732-2101
Lifestyle ED, Courier, Lincoln, IL
Saul, Ray .... (717) 455-3636
MAN ED, Standard-Speaker, Hazleton, PA
Saul, Robin A .... (410) 848-4400
PUB, Carroll County Times, Westminster, MD
Sauls, Kevin .... (209) 532-7151
Sports ED, Union Democrat, Sonora, CA
Saunders, Ailiene .... (614) 335-3611
CIRC MGR
Record Herald, Washington Court House, OH
Saunders, Barry .... (919) 829-4500
COL/EDL Writer
News & Observer, Raleigh, NC
Saunders, Charles .... (804) 649-6000
Librarian, Times-Dispatch, Richmond, VA
Saunders, David .... (562) 430-0534
MAN ED, Leisure World Golden Rain News, Seal Beach, CA
Saunders, Debra .... (415) 777-1111
COL
San Francisco Chronicle, San Francisco, CA
Saunders, Dusty .... (303) 892-5000
Radio/Television ED
Rocky Mountain News, Denver, CO
Saunders, Jack .... (914) 341-1100
CIRC MGR
Times Herald-Record, Middletown, NY
Saunders, Janet .... (309) 343-7181
Fashion/Style ED, Features ED, Living/Lifestyle ED, Women's ED
Register-Mail, Galesburg, IL
Saunders, Janice W .... (803) 394-3571
PUB, News & Post, Lake City, SC
Saunders, Jim .... (904) 359-4111
EDU ED
Florida Times-Union, Jacksonville, FL
Saunders, Mark .... (912) 764-9031
PROD MGR-Pre Press
Statesboro Herald, Statesboro, GA
Saunders, Mary V .... (512) 847-2202
PUB, Wimberley View, Wimberley, TX
Saunders, Mike .... (208) 664-8176
Cartoonist, Press, Coeur d'Alene, ID
Saunders, Patrick .... (303) 776-2244
Sports ED, Daily Times-Call, Longmont, CO
Saunders, Robert .... (207) 282-1535
MAN ED, Journal Tribune, Biddeford, ME
Saunders, Rosemary .... (937) 335-5634
PROD MGR-COMP, Troy Daily News/Miami Valley Sunday News, Troy, OH
Saunders, Seanne Gillen .... (907) 874-2301
PUB, Wrangell Sentinel, Wrangell, AK
Saunders, SSgt Tom .... (316) 942-5010
ED, Contrails, Wichita, KS
Sauve, Ann .... (517) 895-8551
Librarian, Bay City Times, Bay City, MI
Sauve, Paul .... (514) 644-8484
ED, Journal L'Avenir de l'Est, Pointe-aux-Trembles, QC
Savage, Alicia .... (705) 428-2638
ED, Stayner Sun, Stayner, ON
Savage, Dan .... (817) 757-5757
PUB, Waco Tribune-Herald, Waco, TX
Savage, Jim .... (305) 350-2111
ASSOC ED-Investigations
Miami Herald, Miami, FL
Savage, Julie .... (415) 348-4321
MGR-MKTG SRV
San Mateo County Times, San Mateo, CA
Savage, Larry .... (352) 867-4010
Sports ED, Ocala Star-Banner, Ocala, FL
Savage, Mark .... (414) 224-2000
Automotive Reporter
Milwaukee Journal Sentinel, Milwaukee, WI
Savage, Nancy Agris .... (508) 820-9700
ED, Hellenic Chronicle, Framingham, MA
Savage, Robert .... (812) 424-7711
ADV MGR-Display
Evansville Courier Co. Inc., Evansville, IN
Savage, Stuart .... (919) 752-6166
BUS ED, Daily Reflector, Greenville, NC
Savard, Mario .... (514) 285-7272
VP-MKTG, La Presse, Montreal, QC
Savastano, David .... (201) 784-0266
ED, Suburbanite, Closter, NJ
Savelle, Jon .... (206) 622-8272
RE ED, Seattle Daily Journal of Commerce, Seattle, WA
Savercool, Erlyne .... (916) 527-2151
PROD SUPV-COMP
Daily News, Red Bluff, CA
Saville, Jaqueline .... (807) 223-2390
PUB, Dryden Observer, Dryden, ON
Savino, John .... (201) 438-8700
PUB, Commercial Leader, Lyndhurst, NJ
Savoy, Ramon .... (702) 380-8100
PUB, ED
Las Vegas Sentinel-Voice, Las Vegas, NV
Sawatzky, Pete .... (405) 323-5151
PROD SUPT, Clinton Daily News, Clinton, OK
Sawchuk, Bill .... (905) 732-2411
Sports ED, Tribune, Welland, ON
Sawyer, Ben .... (508) 458-7100
CIRC ASST DIR, Sun, Lowell, MA
Sawyer, Gary .... (515) 421-0500
ED, EPE, Globe-Gazette, Mason City, IA
Sawyer, John .... (716) 232-7100
PROD FRM-PR (Democrat and Chronicle)
Rochester Democrat and Chronicle; Rochester, NY Times-Union, Rochester, NY
Sawyer, Jon .... (314) 340-8000
Washington BU Chief
St. Louis Post-Dispatch, St. Louis, MO
Sawyer, Lee .... (816) 271-8500
CIRC DIR
St. Joseph News-Press, St. Joseph, MO
Sawyer, Roger .... (205) 236-1551
BM, DP MGR, DIR-INFO SYS, PROD SUPT
Anniston Star, Anniston, AL
Consolidated Publishing Co.
Sawyer, Ron .... (205) 345-0505
PUB, Tuscaloosa News, Tuscaloosa, AL
Sawyer, Steve .... (334) 285-6000
ED, Community Press, Millbrook, AL
Sawyer Sr, Thomas C .... (508) 473-1111
PUB, Milford Daily News, Milford, MA
Sawyer, Todd C .... (508) 473-1111
MGR-INFO SYS
Milford Daily News, Milford, MA
Sawyer, Tom .... (510) 208-6300
City ED, Oakland Tribune, Oakland, CA
Sawyer, Verlee .... (712) 423-2021
PUB, ED, Onawa Sentinel, Onawa, IA
Sax, Bob .... (618) 234-1000
PROD FRM-COMP
Belleville News-Democrat, Belleville, IL
Saxberg, Lois .... (701) 797-3331
ED, Griggs County Sentinel-Courier, Cooperstown, ND
Saye, Wade .... (423) 523-3131
ED-Special Publications
Knoxville News-Sentinel, Knoxville, TN
Sayer, Marilyn .... (705) 567-5321
ADV MGR
Northern Daily News, Kirkland Lake, ON
Sayers, Rick .... (203) 333-0161
ED, Connecticut Post, Bridgeport, CT
Sayler, John .... (316) 257-2368
ED, Sports ED, Lyons Daily News, Lyons, KS
Sayler, Mrs John .... (316) 257-2368
Wire ED, Lyons Daily News, Lyons, KS
Sayles Jr, Frank .... (803) 317-6397
MAN ED
Florence Morning News, Florence, SC
Saylor, Mark .... (213) 237-5000
Records/Radio
Los Angeles Times, Los Angeles, CA
Saylor, Pam .... (717) 854-1575
Sunday ED
York Dispatch/York Sunday News, York, PA
Sbranti, J N .... (209) 578-2000
Technology Writer
Modesto Bee, Modesto, CA
Scadding, Anne .... (617) 979-5670
ED, Wakefield Observer, Melrose, MA
Scaduto, James .... (212) 416-2600
VP-Employee Relations
Dow Jones & Co. Inc., New York, NY
Scaggs, Brentron .... (817) 883-2554
ED, Marlin Democrat, Marlin, TX
Scaglione, Cecil .... (619) 483-3412
EIC/Financial ED
Mature Life Features, San Diego, CA
Scaglione, Ralph .... (813) 893-8111
ADV MGR-RT
St. Petersburg Times, St. Petersburg, FL
Scaife, Richard M .... (412) 834-1151
COB, Tribune-Review Publishing Co., Greensburg, PA
Scala, Nick .... (304) 485-1891
Sports ED, Parkersburg News & Sentinel, Parkersburg, WV
Scaletta, Sue Ellyn .... (701) 780-1100
Environmental Reporter, Health ED
Grand Forks Herald, Grand Forks, ND
Scalf, Delaney .... (423) 928-4151
GM, PROD SUPT
Elizabethton Star, Elizabethton, TN
Scallon, Sean .... (715) 526-2121
Outdoors ED, Photo ED
Shawano Leader, Shawano, WI
Scamihorn, Mike .... (219) 933-3200
MGR-PROM, Times, Munster, IN
Scandale, Frank .... (303) 820-1010
MET ED, Denver Post, Denver, CO
Scanlan, Connie .... (814) 948-6210
ED, Barnesboro Star, Barnesboro, PA
Scanlon, John .... (215) 355-9009
ED, Northeast Times, Trevose, PA
Scanlon, Leslie .... (502) 582-4011
Religion ED, Courier-Journal, Louisville, KY

Copyright ©1997 by the Editor & Publisher Co.

203-Who's Where **Sch**

Scarboro, Augustine .... (912) 236-9511
Division CONT
Savannah Morning News, Savannah, GA

Scarborough, Jean .... (508) 880-9000
PUB, Taunton Daily Gazette, Taunton, MA

Scarbrough, Linda .... (512) 930-4824
ED, Sunday Sun, Georgetown, TX

Scarbrough, Neal .... (303) 820-1010
Sports ED, Denver Post, Denver, CO

Scarbrough, Virginia .... (308) 334-5226
GM, Hitchcock County News, Trenton, NE

Scaring, Jennifer .... (219) 362-2161
Librarian
La Porte Herald-Argus, La Porte, IN

Scarlett, Fran .... (216) 999-4500
ADV MGR-Planning & ADM
Plain Dealer, Cleveland, OH

Scarpone, Carol Smith .... (618) 544-2174
PUB, Robinson Argus, Robinson, IL

Scarpone, Sam .... (618) 544-2174
ED, Robinson Argus, Robinson, IL

Scarritt, Tom .... (205) 325-2222
EX ED, Birmingham News, Birmingham, AL

Scartland, Judy .... (615) 893-5860
ADV MGR-CLASS
Daily News Journal, Murfreesboro, TN

Scauzillo, Steve .... (818) 962-8811
Environmental Reporter
San Gabriel Valley Tribune, West Covina, CA

Scavotto, Deborah .... (617) 450-2000
PROD MGR-Distribution
Christian Science Monitor, Boston, MA

Scenters, Teresa .... (606) 623-1669
ADV DIR, Richmond Register, Richmond, KY

Schaab, David .... (315) 782-1000
ADV MGR-CLASS
Watertown Daily Times, Watertown, NY

Schaad, Robert J .... (908) 922-6000
ADV DIR-Pre Press Services & Technology
Asbury Park Press, Neptune, NJ

Schaaf, Judy .... (573) 546-3917
PUB, Mountain Echo, Ironton, MO

Schaber, Rick .... (715) 842-2101
BUS ED, RE ED
Wausau Daily Herald, Wausau, WI

Schad, Anthony E .... (513) 923-3111
PUB, Western Hills Press, Cincinnati, OH

Schad, Clayton .... (602) 496-0665
PUB, ED
Ahwatukee Weekly News, Phoenix, AZ

Schadenberg, Mark .... (519) 537-2341
Sports ED, Sentinel-Review, Woodstock, ON

Schadewald, H Robert .... (716) 394-0770
ADV VP-MKTG, Daily Messenger/The Sunday Messenger, Canandaigua, NY

Schaefer, Mari .... (520) 573-4220
Photo ED, Arizona Daily Star, Tucson, AZ

Schaefer, Ralph .... (918) 663-1414
ED/MAN ED, Tulsa Daily Commerce & Legal News, Tulsa, OK

Schaefer, Rene .... (512) 575-1451
ADV MGR-RT, Victoria Advocate, Victoria, TX

Schaefer, Robert .... (319) 242-7101
PROD MGR-SYS, PROD FRM-COMP
Clinton Herald, Clinton, IA

Schaefer, Roy .... (206) 464-2111
ADV MGR-CLASS, Seattle Times, Seattle, WA

Schaefer, Tom .... (316) 268-6000
Body and Soul ED
Wichita Eagle, Wichita, KS

Schaefers, Allison .... (912) 882-4927
ED, Camden County Tribune, St. Marys, GA

Schaeffer, Gussie .... (360) 377-3711
DIR-MKTG, Sun, Bremerton, WA

Schaeffer, Karl .... (215) 854-2000
Television Magazine ED
Philadelphia Inquirer, Philadelphia, PA

Schaeffer, Paula .... (717) 345-4455
ED, Press-Herald, Pine Grove, PA

Schafer, A J .... (515) 858-5051
PUB, Eldora Herald-Ledger, Eldora, IA

Schafer, Dennis .... (909) 684-1200
CIRC MGR, Press-Enterprise, Riverside, CA

Schafer, James H .... (206) 464-2111
Senior VP-Employee Resources Group
Seattle Times, Seattle, WA

Schafer, Paul .... (509) 459-5000
PROD MGR
Spokesman-Review, Spokane, WA

Schaffer, Barbara .... (541) 923-3936
ED, Auto Digest, Prineville, OR

Schaffer, Bill .... (541) 447-6205
GM
Prineville Central Oregonian, Prineville, OR

Schaffer, Harwood .... (507) 764-6681
PUB, ED
West Martin Weekly News, Sherburn, MN

Schaffer, Mike .... (215) 854-2000
Books ED
Philadelphia Inquirer, Philadelphia, PA

Schaffer, Paul .... (212) 837-7000
Senior News ED-Statistics, Journal of Commerce & Commercial, New York, NY

Schaffer, Polly Anna .... (507) 764-6681
PUB
West Martin Weekly News, Sherburn, MN

Schaffer, Suzy .... (310) 230-3400
RES, Allsport Photography USA, Pacific Palisades, CA

Schaffner, John .... (419) 732-2154
PUB, ED
Port Clinton Beacon, Port Clinton, OH

Schaidle, Catherine .... (317) 459-3121
City ED, Kokomo Tribune, Kokomo, IN

Schaife, Richard M .... (412) 523-6588
PUB, Standard Observer, Greensburg, PA

Schain, Dennis .... (860) 241-6200
MGR-Public Relations
Hartford Courant, Hartford, CT

Schaller, Bob .... (308) 632-0670
Sports ED, Star-Herald, Scottsbluff, NE

Schaller, Charmian .... (505) 662-4185
MAN ED, Monitor, Los Alamos, NM

Schaller, John .... (616) 347-2544
SEC, Petoskey News-Review, Petoskey, MI

Schaller, Kirk .... (616) 347-2544
PRES, PUB
Petoskey News-Review, Petoskey, MI

Schaller, Pat .... (219) 223-2111
CIRC DIR, Rochester Sentinel, Rochester, IN

Schallert, Katie .... (309) 786-6441
Environmental Writer
Rock Island Argus, Rock Island, IL

Schamberry, Jeff .... (516) 843-2020
Deputy Picture ED, Newsday, Melville, NY

Schanche Jr, Don .... (912) 452-0567
City ED, Union-Recorder, Milledgeville, GA

Schanen III, William F .... (414) 284-3494
PUB, ED
Ozaukee Press, Port Washington, WI

Schanen IV, Bill .... (414) 284-3494
MAN ED
Ozaukee Press, Port Washington, WI

Schanhals, Mark .... (517) 893-6507
ED, Valley Farmer, Bay City, MI

Schanus, Chris .... (320) 543-2131
ED, Howard Lake Herald, Howard Lake, MN

Schardt, Jeff .... (619) 337-3400
PROD FRM-COMP
Imperial Valley Press, El Centro, CA

Scharf, Harry .... (216) 991-8300
PUB, Cleveland Jewish News, Cleveland, OH

Scharfeld, Jeff .... (703) 276-3400
CIRC GM-Washington/Baltimore
USA Today, Arlington, VA

Scharnberg, Terry .... (218) 736-7511
PROD FRM-PR
Fergus Falls Daily Journal, Fergus Falls, MN

Scharnow, Michael .... (602) 837-1931
ED
Times of Fountain Hills, Fountain Hills, AZ

Scharow, Stephanie .... (617) 426-3000
Lifestyle ED, Sunday Magazine
Boston Herald, Boston, MA

Scharrer, Gary .... (915) 546-6100
Political/Government ED
El Paso Times, El Paso, TX

Schatt, Paul .... (602) 271-8000
EPE, Arizona Republic, Phoenix, AZ

Schatz, Duane .... (701) 584-2900
PUB, ED, Grant County News, Elgin, ND

Schatz, Gail .... (701) 584-2900
PUB, Grant County News, Elgin, ND

Schatz, R Allen .... (412) 222-2200
CFO/TREAS
Observer-Reporter, Washington, PA

Schatzman, George .... (513) 761-1188
Contributing Critic
Critic's Choice Reviews, Cincinnati, OH

Schaub, Jeannine .... (515) 432-1234
SEC, Boone News-Republican, Boone, IA

Schaub, Robert C .... (515) 432-1234
PRES, PUB
Boone News-Republican, Boone, IA

Schauppner, Kurt .... (916) 458-2121
ED, Colusa County Sun-Herald, Colusa, CA

Schechtman, Cliff .... (508) 775-1200
ED, Cape Cod Times, Hyannis, MA

Scheel, Pat .... (414) 542-2501
ADV SUPV-Creative Services
Waukesha County Freeman, Waukesha, WI

Scheer, Bill .... (802) 878-5282
PUB, ED, Essex Reporter, Essex Junction, VT

Scheer, Peter E .... (415) 749-5400
PUB, ED, Recorder, San Francisco, CA

Schefer, Michael .... (215) 854-2000
ASST MAN ED
Philadelphia Daily News, Philadelphia, PA

Scheiber, Dave .... (813) 893-8111
Amusements ED, Music ED-Pop, Performing Arts ED
St. Petersburg Times, St. Petersburg, FL

Scheideman, Inez .... (403) 963-2291
PUB, Stony Plain Reporter, Stony Plain, AB

Scheihing, Will .... (610) 258-7171
Area ED (PA), Express-Times, Easton, PA

Scheinin, Rich .... (408) 920-5000
Religion/Ethics ED
San Jose Mercury News, San Jose, CA

Schelke, Larry .... (517) 269-6461
PROD MGR
Huron Daily Tribune, Bad Axe, MI

Schell, Gary .... (414) 224-2000
PROD MGR-Night
Milwaukee Journal Sentinel, Milwaukee, WI

Schell, Jeff .... (414) 634-3322
CIRC MGR
Racine Journal Times, Racine, WI

Schell, Kris .... (415) 243-4364
Publications MGR
Pacific News Service, San Francisco, CA

Schellenberg, Rob .... (403) 545-2258
PUB, ED, 40-Mile County Commentator, Bow Island, AB

Scheller, Annette .... (806) 227-2183
ED, Sudan Beacon News, Sudan, TX

Schellhardt, Timothy D .... (312) 750-4000
News BU Chief, Wall Street Journal-Central Edition, Chicago, IL

Schelske, Don .... (810) 653-3511
ED, Davison Index, Davison, MI

Scheltema, Will .... (703) 560-4000
News ED, Fairfax Journal, Fairfax, VA
Journal Newspapers Inc.

Schemm, Leo .... (316) 257-2368
PROD MGR, Lyons Daily News, Lyons, KS

Schemmer, Clint .... (703) 878-8000
EDL Writer
Potomac News, Woodbridge, VA

Schenden, Laurie .... (213) 237-5000
Writer-54 Hours
Los Angeles Times, Los Angeles, CA

Schenet, Bob .... (206) 448-8000
NTL/Foreign ED
Seattle Post-Intelligencer, Seattle, WA

Schenk, Charles .... (610) 838-2066
ED, Valley Voice, Hellertown, PA

Schenkler, Michael .... (718) 357-7400
PUB, Queens Tribune, Fresh Meadows, NY

Schensul, Jill .... (201) 646-4000
Travel ED, Record, Hackensack, NJ

Schepeler, Matt .... (517) 592-2122
PUB, Exponent, Brooklyn, MI

Scheppers, Lillian .... (405) 226-6397
GM, Carter County Courier, Ardmore, OK

Scher, Valerie .... (619) 299-3131
Music Writer-Classical
San Diego Union-Tribune, San Diego, CA

Scherb, Jeff R .... (312) 222-3237
Sr VP/Chief Technology OFF
Tribune Co., Chicago, IL

Scherer, Alan R .... (218) 723-5281
DIR-FIN, Duluth News-Tribune, Duluth, MN

Scherer, Robert F .... (541) 863-5233
PUB, ED
Umpqua Free Press, Myrtle Creek, OR

Scherer, Sally .... (912) 744-4200
Lifestyle ED, Macon Telegraph, Macon, GA

Scherer, Sharon W .... (541) 863-5233
PUB, Umpqua Free Press, Myrtle Creek, OR

Scherf, Scott .... (419) 422-5151
Photo ED, Courier, Findlay, OH

Schermann, B J .... (807) 826-3788
PUB, Echo, Manitouwadge, ON

Schermer, Lloyd G .... (319) 383-2100
COB, Lee Enterprises Inc., Davenport, IA

Schettler, Bob .... (805) 725-0600
ED, Delano Record, Delano, CA

Scheuer, Joe .... (215) 854-2000
PROD ASST DIR-Facilities
Philadelphia Daily News, Philadelphia, PA

Scheuerman, Rick .... (813) 259-7711
Tampa Bay Online ED
Tampa Tribune and Times, Tampa, FL

Scheuermann, Kim .... (412) 981-6100
MGR-Human Resources, Herald, Sharon, PA

Scheurer, Joe .... (215) 854-2000
PROD ASST DIR-Facilities
Philadelphia Inquirer, Philadelphia, PA

Scheurich, Wendy .... (419) 784-5441
Fashion/Style ED, Lifestyle ED, Religion ED
Crescent-News, Defiance, OH

Schewel, Steve .... (919) 286-1972
PUB, Independent Weekly, Durham, NC

Schexnayder, Charlotte .... (501) 382-4925
PUB, Dumas Clarion, Dumas, AR

Schiavone, Deanna .... (716) 693-1000
PROD FRM-COMP
Tonawanda News, North Tonawanda, NY

Schiefelbein, Kathleen .... (352) 544-5200
ADV MGR-CLASS
Hernando Today, Brooksville, FL

Schiefelbein, Lynn .... (605) 331-2200
Graphics ED
Sioux Falls Argus Leader, Sioux Falls, SD

Schieffer, Gary .... (217) 788-1300
ASST City ED
State Journal-Register, Springfield, IL

Schiele, Mark .... (610) 272-2500
Sports ED
Norristown Times Herald, Norristown, PA

Schierbeck, Peter K .... (403) 765-3604
PUB
Rycroft Central Peace Signal, Rycroft, AB

Schiff, Margaret .... (202) 334-6000
VP/CONT/PSL ADM
Washington Post, Washington, DC

Schiffer, Theresa .... (414) 634-3322
Graphics DIR, Journal Times, Racine, WI

Schiffman, Robert .... (517) 377-1000
PROD MGR-MR
Lansing State Journal, Lansing, MI

Schiffres, Jeremy .... (914) 331-5000
BUS/FIN ED, City ED, EDU ED, News ED, Photo ED, Daily Freeman, Kingston, NY

Schilbe, Orval .... (519) 692-3825
PUB, ED, Herald, Thamesville, ON

Schile, Wayne .... (406) 657-1200
PUB
Montana Newspaper Group, Billings, MT

Schilero, Frank .... (212) 210-2100
VP-Technical
New York Daily News, New York, NY

Schiller, Alexander .... (608) 222-5522
Office MGR
Shetland Productions, Madison, WI

Schiller, Donald .... (203) 235-1661
MAN ED, Record-Journal, Meriden, CT

Schiller, Marie .... (813) 788-1998
Owner, Smith, Al Feature Service Inc., Zephyrhills, FL

Schilling, Allan .... (561) 287-1550
News ED, Stuart News, Stuart, FL

Schilling, Richard .... (319) 568-3431
ED, Waukon Standard, Waukon, IA

Schimps, Sheila .... (517) 377-1000
Religion ED
Lansing State Journal, Lansing, MI

Schinkel, Doug .... (605) 225-4100
CIRC MGR-Office
Aberdeen American News, Aberdeen, SD

Schinske, Don .... (415) 663-8404
GM, Point Reyes Light, Pt. Reyes Station, CA

Schipper, Lionel H .... (403) 468-0100
BC, Edmonton Sun, Edmonton, AB

Schisles, Earl .... (412) 834-1151
ADTX MGR, Tribune-Review, Greensburg, PA

Schlabaugh, Bruce .... (719) 687-3006
PUB, Ute Pass Courier, Woodland Park, CO

Schleier, Curt .... (201) 391-7135
PRES, Schleier, Curt Reviews, River Vale, NJ

Schleihs, Janice .... (715) 735-6611
BM, DP MGR, EagleHerald, Marinette, WI

Schleis, Paula .... (330) 996-3000
EDU Writer
Akron Beacon Journal, Akron, OH

Schlenker, David .... (352) 867-4010
Entertainment ED
Ocala Star-Banner, Ocala, FL

Schleper, Anne .... (812) 424-7711
Food ED, Evansville Courier, Evansville, IN

Schlepper, Sam .... (218) 624-3349
PUB, Proctor Journal, Proctor, MN

Schlereth, Abby .... (419) 522-3311
CIRC MGR-OPER/Home Delivery
News Journal, Mansfield, OH

Schlesinger, D Michael .... (515) 484-2841
PUB, Toledo Chronicle, Tama, IA

Schlesinger, Emily .... (703) 522-9898
PUB, Arlington Courier, Arlington, VA

Schlesinger, Mike .... (515) 753-6611
PUB, Times-Republican, Marshalltown, IA

Schlicht, Miriam .... (203) 263-2116
ED, Voices, Southbury, CT

Schlichtman, Lisa .... (417) 847-2610
PUB, ED, Cassville Democrat, Cassville, MO

Schlichtman, Mike .... (417) 847-2610
PUB, Cassville Democrat, Cassville, MO

Schlosberg, Drew .... (619) 299-3131
MGR-MKTG-Community Relations
San Diego Union-Tribune, San Diego, CA

Schlosberg III, Richard T .... (213) 237-3700
EX VP/PUB & CEO-Los Angeles Times
Times Mirror Co., Los Angeles, CA

Schlossenberg, William .... (301) 948-3120
PUB
Gaithersburg Gazette, Gaithersburg, MD

Schlosser, Brian .... (717) 265-2151
PROD FRM-PR (Night)
Daily Review, Towanda, PA

Schlotterbeck, Rob .... (816) 254-8600
News ED
Independence Examiner, Independence, MO

Schlotthauer, Mike .... (707) 448-6401
PROD MGR, Reporter, Vacaville, CA

Schlottman, Kristi .... (208) 743-9411
ADV MGR-Sales
Lewiston Morning Tribune, Lewiston, ID

Schludecker, Lorri .... (805) 736-2313
PROD SUPV-COMP Room
Lompoc Record, Lompoc, CA

Schmadeke, Gary .... (319) 337-3181
CIRC DIR
Iowa City Press-Citizen, Iowa City, IA

Schmanske, Ronald .... (219) 294-1661
DIR-Community Relations
Elkhart Truth, Elkhart, IN

Sch Who's Where-204

Schmersahl, Mark J .... (618) 337-7300
PUB, Cahokia-Dupo Herald, Cahokia, IL
Schmich, Bill .... (970) 669-5050
PROD CNR-Copy Flow
Loveland Daily Reporter-Herald, Loveland, CO
Schmick III, William F .... (202) 828-3390
BU Chief
Ottaway News Service, Washington, DC
Schmickle, Sharon .... (612) 673-4000
Congressional ED
Star Tribune, Minneapolis, MN
Schmid, Bette D .... (217) 283-5111
PUB, Chronicle, Hoopeston, IL
Schmid, John .... (505) 763-3431
Picture ED, Clovis News Journal, Clovis, NM
Schmidt, Angela .... (515) 887-4141
PUB, ED, West Bend Journal, West Bend, IA
Schmidt, Ann .... (608) 527-5252
ED, New Glarus Post, New Glarus, WI
Schmidt, Art .... (516) 843-2020
MGR-INFO SYS, Newsday, Melville, NY
Schmidt, Charles .... (718) 981-1234
Sunday ED
Staten Island Advance, Staten Island, NY
Schmidt, Cheryl .... (813) 259-7711
EDU ED
Tampa Tribune and Times, Tampa, FL
Schmidt, Chris .... (937) 222-6000
ED, Daily Court Reporter, Dayton, OH
Schmidt, D J .... (915) 337-4661
MGR-MKTG, Odessa American, Odessa, TX
Schmidt, Doris .... (413) 788-1000
Entertainment/Arts ED
Union-News, Springfield, MA
Schmidt, Elizabeth .... (312) 625-8774
ED
Amerikai-Kanadai Magyar Elet, Akron, OH
Schmidt, James W .... (519) 632-7432
PUB, Ayr News, Ayr, ON
Schmidt, John .... (203) 622-1547
Accountant/CPA
Cartoonews Inc., Greenwich, CT
Schmidt, John .... (712) 852-2323
PUB, Democrat, Emmetsburg, IA
Schmidt, John P .... (519) 632-7432
ED, Ayr News, Ayr, ON
Schmidt, Keith .... (414) 338-0622
Sports ED, Daily News, West Bend, WI
Schmidt, Larry .... (615) 552-1808
Sports ED, Leaf-Chronicle, Clarksville, TN
Schmidt, Margaret .... (201) 653-1000
Lifestyle ED, Jersey Journal, Jersey City, NJ
Schmidt, Mike .... (913) 462-3963
MAN ED, Colby Free Press, Colby, KS
Schmidt, Neal .... (515) 887-4141
PUB, ED, West Bend Journal, West Bend, IA
Schmidt, Norma .... (406) 496-5500
PROD Software/SYS Specialist
Montana Standard, Butte, MT
Schmidt, Patrick A .... (320) 269-2156
ED
Montevideo American-News, Montevideo, MN
Schmidt, Patrick H .... (307) 864-2328
PUB, ED, Thermopolis Independent Record, Thermopolis, WY
Schmidt, Paul .... (360) 825-2555
ED, Enumclaw Courier-Herald/Buckley News Banner, Enumclaw, WA
Schmidt, Richard .... (307) 672-2431
PROD FRM-PR
Sheridan Press, Sheridan, WY
Schmidt, Rick .... (812) 231-4200
ADV DIR, Tribune-Star, Terre Haute, IN
Schmidt, Robyn Adams .... (817) 237-1184
MAN ED, Azle News, Azle, TX
Schmidt, Roger .... (308) 345-4500
PROD MGR
McCook Daily Gazette, McCook, NE
Schmidt, Seth .... (507) 629-4300
PUB, ED, Tracy Headlight-Herald, Tracy, MN
Schmidt, Stephen P .... (716) 591-3010
PRES, Schmidt Services Inc., Attica, NY
Schmidt, Steve .... (619) 299-3131
EDU Writer (Colleges/Universities)
San Diego Union-Tribune, San Diego, CA
Schmidt, Steve .... (701) 780-1100
EDU ED
Grand Forks Herald, Grand Forks, ND
Schmidt, Steve .... (941) 687-7000
ADV DIR, Ledger, Lakeland, FL
Schmidt, Thomas H .... (301) 853-4599
GM, Catholic Standard, Washington, DC
Schmidt, Tina .... (310) 230-3400
RES ASST, Allsport Photography USA, Pacific Palisades, CA
Schmidt, Todd .... (715) 568-3100
ED, Bloomer Advance, Bloomer, WI
Schmidt, Tom .... (314) 937-5200
VP, USMedia Group Inc., Crystal City, MO
Schmidt-McKeon, Kim .... (308) 237-2152
EDU ED, Kearney Hub, Kearney, NE
Schmit, Boni L .... (406) 566-2471
ED, Judith Basin Press, Stanford, MT
Schmitt, Most Rev Bernard W . (304) 233-0880
PUB, Catholic Spirit, Wheeling, WV
Schmitt, Bernie .... (812) 886-9955
Radio/Television ED
Vincennes Sun-Commercial, Vincennes, IN
Schmitt, Bill .... (212) 887-8550
News ED
American Metal Market, New York, NY
Schmitt, Charles .... (914) 694-9300
VP-FIN, Reporter Dispatch, White Plains, NY
Gannett Co. Inc.
Schmitt, Chris .... (217) 854-2534
PUB, ED
Macoupin County Enquirer, Carlinville, IL
Schmitt, Chris .... (408) 920-5000
Writer Telecommunications ED
San Jose Mercury News, San Jose, CA
Schmitt, R Barrie .... (401) 277-7000
DIR-Human Resources
Providence Journal-Bulletin, Providence, RI
Schmitt, Tom .... (712) 546-7031
PUB, Le Mars Daily Sentinel, Le Mars, IA
Schmitz, Greg .... (319) 291-1400
PROD FRM-MR
Waterloo Courier, Waterloo, IA
Schmitz, James J .... (612) 689-1181
PUB, Cambridge Star, Cambridge, MN
Schmitz, Janine .... (701) 324-4646
GM, Herald-Press, Harvey, ND
Schmitz, Jerry .... (308) 237-2152
PROD FRM-Press, Kearney Hub, Kearney, NE
Schmitz, Mark .... (916) 527-2151
PROD SUPV-Press
Daily News, Red Bluff, CA
Schmitz, Mary .... (701) 742-2361
ED, Oakes Times, Oakes, ND
Schmitz, Peg .... (319) 398-8211
PROD MGR-Pre Press
Gazette, Cedar Rapids, IA
Schmitz, Sheila .... (805) 650-2900
ASST MAN ED-Photo/Graphics
Ventura County Star, Ventura, CA
Schmoldt, Pam .... (608) 754-3311
DP MGR, Janesville Gazette, Janesville, WI
Schmoll, Donna .... (507) 451-2840
CIRC ASSOC MGR-Delivery
Owatonna People's Press, Owatonna, MN
Schmucker, Jane .... (419) 245-6000
Farm/Agriculture Reporter, Blade, Toledo, OH
Schmunk, Harold .... (701) 253-7311
PROD DIR, Forum, Fargo, ND
Schnabel, Keith .... (407) 242-3500
PROD MGR-Building
Florida Today, Melbourne, FL
Schnabel, Mark .... (316) 283-1500
Sports ED, ADTX MGR
Newton Kansan, Newton, KS
Schnabel, Megan .... (540) 981-3100
Home Furnishings ED
Roanoke Times, Roanoke, VA
Schnaitmann, Peter .... (310) 230-3400
Art DIR, Allsport Photography USA, Pacific Palisades, CA
Schnare, Dale .... (518) 943-2100
PROD FRM-Press, Daily Mail, Catskill, NY
Schnase, John .... (406) 883-4343
PUB, Lake County Leader, Polson, MT
Schnedler, Jack .... (501) 378-3400
Features ED
Arkansas Democrat-Gazette, Little Rock, AR
Schneideau, Amy .... (765) 362-1200
Fashion/Style ED, Food ED, Health/Medical ED, Living/Lifestyle ED, Religion ED, Women's ED, Journal Review, Crawfordsville, IN
Schneider, Arlene .... (908) 922-6000
Deputy MAN ED-Weekend
Asbury Park Press, Neptune, NJ
Schneider, Brad .... (502) 821-6833
Sports ED, Messenger, Madisonville, KY
Schneider, Don .... (501) 785-9404
VP-Eastern Newspaper Group
Donrey Media Group, Fort Smith, AR
Schneider, Donald S .... (212) 556-1234
Sr VP-Human Resources
New York Times Co., New York, NY
Schneider, Ed .... (612) 222-5011
DP MGR, Pioneer Press, St. Paul, MN
Schneider, Frosty .... (614) 373-2121
PROD MGR-MR
Marietta Times, Marietta, OH
Schneider, Gail .... (816) 826-1000
News ED, Sedalia Democrat, Sedalia, MO
Schneider, Gary .... (805) 273-2700
DP MGR
Antelope Valley Press, Palmdale, CA
Schneider, Heather .... (812) 847-4487
MAN ED, Linton Daily Citizen, Linton, IN
Schneider, Hilary .... (410) 332-6000
VP/DIR-Sales, Sun, Baltimore, MD
Schneider, Howard .... (516) 843-2020
MAN ED-News, Newsday, Melville, NY
Schneider, Jack .... (408) 920-5000
DIR-INFO SYS, PROD DIR-INFO SYS
San Jose Mercury News, San Jose, CA
Schneider, Jay .... (507) 362-4495
PUB, ED, Lake Region Life, Waterville, MN
Schneider, Kathy .... (315) 470-0011
Features ED, Post-Standard/Syracuse Herald-Journal/American, Syracuse, NY
Schneider, Kathy .... (414) 922-4600
ADV MGR-CLASS, Reporter, Fond du Lac, WI
Schneider, Mark .... (502) 582-4011
MGR-RES, Courier-Journal, Louisville, KY
Schneider, Morris .... (504) 826-3279
CIRC DIR, Times-Picayune, New Orleans, LA
Schneider, Richard .... (406) 482-2403
PUB, Sidney Herald, Sidney, MT
Schneider, Richard A .... (901) 427-3333
EX ED, Jackson Sun, Jackson, TN
Schneider, Robert .... (414) 657-1000
PROD SUPV-Distribution Center
Kenosha News, Kenosha, WI
Schneider, Roger .... (219) 533-2151
City ED, Goshen News, Goshen, IN
Schneider, Roger .... (414) 435-4411
Consumer Interest ED
Green Bay Press-Gazette, Green Bay, WI
Schneider, Shirley .... (605) 448-2281
ED, Langford Bugle, Langford, SD
Schneider, Skip .... (801) 674-6200
CIRC DIR-Newspaper Sales/PROM
Spectrum, St. George, UT
Schneider, Tracy .... (407) 322-2611
ADV DIR, CIRC ASST MGR
Sanford Herald, Sanford, FL
Schneiderman, David .... (212) 475-3333
PUB, Village Voice, New York, NY
Schnell, Judy .... (414) 563-5553
CIRC MGR, Daily Jefferson County Union, Fort Atkinson, WI
Schnell, Linda .... (541) 459-2261
ED, Sun Tribune, Sutherlin, OR
Schnelle, James .... (219) 866-5111
PROD FRM-Press
Republican, Rensselaer, IN
Schneller, John .... (573) 815-1500
City ED, Daily Tribune, Columbia, MO
Schnepf, Kevin .... (701) 253-7311
Sports ED, Forum, Fargo, ND
Schneps, Victoria .... (718) 224-5863
PUB, MAN ED, Queen Courier, Bayside, NY
Schnitter, Marilyn .... (914) 225-7735
VP-MKTG
All-Sports Publications, Carmel, NY
Schnoebelen, Tim .... (405) 994-5410
PUB, ED, Mooreland Leader, Mooreland, OK
Schnorous, Paula .... (212) 208-8000
ASSOC ED, Corporation Records, Daily News, New York, NY
Schnurmacher, Tom .... (514) 987-2222
Society COL, Gazette, Montreal, QC
Schober, Darlene J .... (507) 864-7700
PUB, ED, Tri-County Record, Rushford, MN
Schober, James R .... (408) 920-5000
DIR-Human Resources
San Jose Mercury News, San Jose, CA
Schober, Myron J .... (507) 864-7700
PUB, ED, Tri-County Record, Rushford, MN
Schoch, Eric .... (317) 633-1240
Medical Writer
Indianapolis Star/News, Indianapolis, IN
Schoch, Stephen J .... (213) 237-3700
VP/TREAS, Times Mirror Co., Los Angeles, CA
Schock, Bill .... (402) 245-2431
ED, Journal, Fall City, NE
Schock, George W .... (402) 245-2431
PUB, Journal, Fall City, NE
Schock, Rob .... (416) 585-5000
Online MGR, Globe and Mail, Toronto, ON
Schock, Scott .... (402) 245-2431
MAN ED, Journal, Fall City, NE
Schoebel, Barbara S .... (717) 421-3000
ADV Telephone Sales (CLASS)
Pocono Record, Stroudsburg, PA
Schoeberl, Marcia .... (605) 256-4555
MAN ED, Wire ED
Madison Daily Leader, Madison, SD
Schoedler, Randy .... (414) 634-3322
PROD SUPV-Electronic Copy Processing
Journal Times, Racine, WI
Schoelles, Marjorie .... (616) 964-7161
PROD MGR-Commericial Printing
Battle Creek Enquirer, Battle Creek, MI
Schoen, Kevin F .... (401) 849-3300
PROD MGR-Mail/Distribution
Newport Daily News, Newport, RI
Schoen, Matthew .... (310) 230-3400
SYS ADM, Allsport Photography USA, Pacific Palisades, CA
Schoening, Gary .... (908) 922-6000
MAN ED-Projects & Technology
Asbury Park Press, Neptune, NJ
Schoepke, Michael P .... (847) 427-4300
ASST VP/DP MGR
Daily Herald, Arlington Heights, IL
Schoepke, William F .... (847) 427-4300
VP-Production, PROD DIR
Daily Herald, Arlington Heights, IL
Schofer, Laura .... (516) 378-3133
MAN ED, Leader, Freeport, NY
Scholl, Larry .... (414) 224-2000
PROD FRM-Camera/Platemaking
Milwaukee Journal Sentinel, Milwaukee, WI
Scholl, Peggy .... (713) 232-3737
PROD MGR, Herald-Coaster, Rosenberg, TX
Scholl, Susan .... (219) 967-4135
PUB, ED, Carroll County Comet, Flora, IN
Scholler, Ray .... (414) 994-9244
PUB, Sounder, Random Lake, WI
Scholtz, Dana .... (508) 685-1000
PROD ENG-Plant
Eagle-Tribune, North Andover, MA
Scholz, Anne .... (715) 833-9200
PROD Electronic Composition
Leader-Telegram, Eau Claire, WI
Scholz, Frank .... (717) 348-9100
Farm ED
Tribune & Scranton Times, Scranton, PA
Scholz, Jane .... (202) 383-6080
ED, Knight-Ridder/Tribune Information Services, Washington, DC
Schonwetter, Norma .... (810) 547-7056
PRES, Nasco Products Co., Oak Park, MI
Schoolcraft, Laurie .... (819) 569-9526
CIRC MGR, Record, Sherbrooke, QC
Schooley, Elizabeth .... (317) 398-6631
ADV MGR-CLASS
Shelbyville News, Shelbyville, IN
Schooley, Kay .... (605) 326-5212
ED, Viborg Enterprise, Viborg, SD
Schooley, Loretta .... (907) 895-5115
GM, MAN ED
Delta Wind, Delta Junction, AK
Schoolfield, Robert M .... (910) 472-9500
PUB, Thomasville Times, Thomasville, NC
Schoolmeester, Ron .... (703) 276-3400
Leisure/Travel ED, USA Today, Arlington, VA
Schoonejongen, John .... (609) 845-3300
EPE, Gloucester County Times, Woodbury, NJ
Schoonmaker, Emma .... (405) 393-4348
MAN ED, Sentinel Leader, Sentinel, OK
Schoonmaker, Mark .... (405) 393-4348
PUB, ED, Sentinel Leader, Sentinel, OK
Schoonover, Steve .... (916) 891-1234
Wire ED, Chico Enterprise-Record, Chico, CA
Schorman, Rob .... (812) 332-4401
MAN ED, Herald-Times Inc, Bloomington, IN
Schossou-Halter, Susan .... (507) 523-2119
ED, Lewiston Journal, Lewiston, MN
Schott, Mark .... (330) 833-2631
BM, Independent, Massillon, OH
Schrader, Ann .... (303) 820-1010
SCI Reporter, Denver Post, Denver, CO
Schrader, Bud .... (816) 665-2808
Sports ED, Kirksville Daily Express & News, Kirksville, MO
Schrader, Gordon .... (217) 429-5151
ADV MGR-CLASS
Herald & Review, Decatur, IL
Schrader, Kathleen .... (417) 673-2421
MAN ED, Webb City Sentinel/Wise Buyer, Webb City, MO
Schrader, William F .... (515) 923-2684
PUB, Garner Leader/Signal, Hancock, IA
Schrag, Jeff .... (417) 866-1401
PUB, Daily Events, Springfield, MO
Schrag, John .... (503) 243-2122
MAN ED, Willamette Week, Portland, OR
Schrank, Dale .... (608) 524-2115
PUB, Reedsburg Report, WI,
Schrank, Karen .... (608) 524-2115
PUB, Reedsburg Report, WI,
Schratz, Joe .... (609) 871-8000
ASST News ED
Burlington County Times, Willingboro, NJ
Schratz, Paul .... (604) 732-2222
EDL Writer, Province, Vancouver, BC
Schreiber, Carol .... (507) 793-2327
ED, Tri-County News, Heron Lake, MN
Schreiber, Glenn C .... (712) 335-3553
PUB, ED, Pocahontas Record-Democrat, Pocahontas, IA
Schreiber, Wanda .... (712) 272-4417
PUB, Buena Vista County Journal, Newell, IA
Schreiner, Mark .... (507) 454-6500
CIRC MGR, Winona Daily News, Winona, MN
Schrepf, Robert .... (860) 241-6200
Deputy EPE, Hartford Courant, Hartford, CT
Schreppel, Ed .... (717) 622-3456
ASST News ED, Pottsville Republican & Evening Herald, Pottsville, PA
Schretzmann, Stephen .... (706) 724-0851
Photo ED, Augusta Chronicle, Augusta, GA
Schrieber, Don .... (573) 785-1414
PUB
Daily American Republic, Poplar Bluff, MO
Schroder, Sue .... (616) 222-5400
Features ED
Grand Rapids Press, Grand Rapids, MI
Schrodt, Alice .... (815) 937-3300
CIRC Office MGR
Daily Journal, Kankakee, IL

205-Who's Where **Sco**

Schroeder, Charles (919) 335-0841
Sports ED, Daily Advance, Elizabeth City, NC
Schroeder, Christopher (202) 334-6000
TREAS
Washington Post Co., Washington, DC
Schroeder, Clint (210) 896-7000
MAN ED, DP MGR
Kerrville Daily Times, Kerrville, TX
Schroeder, Debbie (706) 846-3188
ED
Stewart-Webster Journal, Manchester, GA
Schroeder, Donna (520) 453-4237
DP MGR
Today's News-Herald, Lake Havasu City, AZ
Schroeder, Henry W (608) 845-9559
PUB, Verona Press, Verona, WI
Schroeder, Lynn (701) 265-8844
PUB, ED, Cavalier Chronicle, Cavalier, ND
Schroeder, Mylan (605) 842-1481
PUB, Winner Advocate, Winner, SD
Schroeder, Stephen (509) 663-5161
PROD DIR-Technology/Pre Press
Wenatchee World, Wenatchee, WA
Schroeder, William H (847) 223-8161
PUB, Great Lakes Bulletin, Grayslake, IL
Schrum, Jim (910) 373-7000
PROD ASST DIR
News & Record, Greensboro, NC
Schubert, Linda (703) 560-4000
Tempo ED, Fairfax Journal, Fairfax, VA
Journal Newspapers Inc.
Schubert, Suzanne (910) 323-4848
Graphics DIR
Fayetteville Observer-Times, Fayetteville, NC
Schubring, Joyce (414) 766-4651
ED, Kaukauna Times, Kaukauna, WI
Schuchmann, Mark (414) 938-5000
ED, Whitefish Bay Herald, New Berlin, WI
Schuchmann, Mary (414) 938-5000
ED, Shorewood Herald, New Berlin, WI
Schueler, John R (714) 835-1234
PRES/COO
Orange County Register, Santa Ana, CA
Schueller, Debbie (306) 287-4388
PUB, East Central Connection, Watson, SK
Schuerger, Fred (814) 870-1600
PROD GEN FRM-Distribution
Morning News/Erie Daily Times, Erie, PA
Schuerman, Michael (909) 684-1200
MKTG RES MGR
Press-Enterprise, Riverside, CA
Schuette, David (910) 343-2000
ADV DIR, Morning Star, Wilmington, NC
Schuetz, Barbara A (414) 634-3322
Features ED, Journal Times, Racine, WI
Schuler, Barbara (516) 843-2020
Fashion/Lifestyle ED, Home Living ED
Newsday, Melville, NY
Schuler, Lewis (Woody) (504) 826-3279
PROD MGR-MR
Times-Picayune, New Orleans, LA
Schulken, Mary C (919) 752-6166
EPE, Daily Reflector, Greenville, NC
Schuller, Constance (416) 585-5000
Fashion & Design ED, Globe and Mail (Canada's National Newspaper), Toronto, ON
Schuller, Fritz (705) 428-2638
PUB, Stayner Sun, Stayner, ON
Schulman, Paul (201) 646-4000
Library MGR, MGR-EDL INFO Services
Record, Hackensack, NJ
Schulte, Eugene W (414) 657-1000
Sr VP, United Communications Corp., Wilmington, DE
Schultes, Tom (520) 537-5721
ED
White Mountain Independent, Show Low, AZ
Schultheis, Rob (970) 949-0555
MGR-BUS Office, Vail Daily News, Vail, CO
Schulty, David L (919) 473-2105
MAN ED, Coastland Times, Manteo, NC
Schultz, Betty J (412) 981-6100
MGR-BUS Office, Herald, Sharon, PA
Schultz, Beverly A (812) 934-4343
PUB, Herald Tribune, Batesville, IN
Schultz, Carolyn (913) 525-6355
ED, Lucas-Sylvan News, Lucas, KS
Schultz, Catherine (510) 783-6111
Food ED, Daily Review, Hayward, CA
Schultz, Dave (941) 687-7000
EPE, Ledger, Lakeland, FL
Schultz, David (519) 756-2020
MAN ED, EPE, Expositor, Brantford, ON
Schultz, Don (608) 943-6553
ED, Rural Register, Montfort, WI
Schultz, Doug (612) 437-6153
ED, Hastings Star Gazette, Hastings, MN
Schultz, Frank (608) 754-3311
EDU ED, Janesville Gazette, Janesville, WI
Schultz, Karen (503) 399-6611
ADV MGR-CLASS
Statesman Journal, Salem, OR
Schultz, Kirby (910) 349-4331
CIRC MGR, Reidsville Review, Reidsville, NC
Schultz, Mark (919) 419-6500
Chapel Hill Herald ED
Herald-Sun, Durham, NC
Schultz, Paul (212) 210-2100
Lifestyle ED
New York Daily News, New York, NY
Schultz, Randy (561) 820-4100
EPE, Palm Beach Post, West Palm Beach, FL
Schultz, Richard (203) 744-5100
CONT, News-Times, Danbury, CT
Schultz, Susy (312) 321-3000
Features Reporter
Chicago Sun-Times, Chicago, IL
Schultz, Tawny (250) 785-5631
CIRC MGR, Alaska Highway Daily News, Fort St. John, BC
Schultz, Ted (319) 242-7101
Sports ED, Clinton Herald, Clinton, IA
Schultz, Thomas L (414) 261-4949
MAN ED, EPE
Watertown Daily Times, Watertown, WI
Schultz, Tom (814) 723-8200
ED-Night, Radio/Television ED
Warren Times-Observer, Warren, PA
Schulz, Hans (603) 224-5301
Sunday ED, Concord Monitor, Concord, NH
Schulz, Jeff (540) 374-5000
Automotive ED
Free Lance-Star, Fredericksburg, VA
Schulz, John (219) 362-2161
CIRC MGR
La Porte Herald-Argus, La Porte, IN
Schumacher, Chris (605) 627-9471
PUB, Volga Tribune, Volga, SD
Schumacher, D G (708) 336-7000
Opinion Page ED, News-Sun, Waukegan, IL
Schumacher, Dennis (612) 345-3316
PUB, Lake City Graphic, Lake City, MN
Schumacher, Geoff (702) 385-3111
City ED, Las Vegas Sun, Las Vegas, NV
Schumacher, Jeff (701) 579-4530
PUB, Herald, New England, ND
Schumacher, Mary Jeanne (812) 547-3424
ED, Perry County News, Tell City, IN
Schumacher, Robert L (414) 457-7711
ED, Sheboygan Press, Sheboygan, WI
Schumacher, Sharon (320) 398-5000
PUB, Tri-County News, Kimball, MN
Schumaker, Amanda (207) 791-6650
ADV DIR
Portland Press Herald, Portland, ME
Schumaker, Tom (305) 743-5551
PUB, Florida Keys Keynoter, Marathon, FL
Schuman, Karen (317) 747-5700
ADV DIR, Star Press, Muncie, IN
Schuman, Matthew (215) 893-5700
ED, Jewish Exponent, Philadelphia, PA
Schuman, Tom (317) 622-1212
MAN ED, Herald Bulletin, Anderson, IN
Schumann, Mark (561) 589-4566
PUB, Vero Beach Sun, Vero Beach, FL
Schumway, Lee (208) 522-1800
CONT, BM, Post Register, Idaho Falls, ID
Schur, Jerome A (847) 427-4300
PROD MGR/ASST VP
Daily Herald, Arlington Heights, IL
Schurig, Lynn (616) 964-7161
PROD MGR-PR
Battle Creek Enquirer, Battle Creek, MI
Schurkey, Steve (360) 694-3391
CIRC MGR-Single Copy Sales/Motor Route
Columbian, Vancouver, WA
Schurmann, Franz (415) 243-4364
ASSOC ED
Pacific News Service, San Francisco, CA
Schurz Jr, Franklin D (219) 287-1001
PRES
Schurz Communications Inc., South Bend, IN
Schurz, James S (219) 287-1001
VP
Schurz Communications Inc., South Bend, IN
Schurz, Mary (219) 287-1001
VP/SEC
Schurz Communications Inc., South Bend, IN
Schurz, Scott C (219) 287-1001
VP
Schurz Communications Inc., South Bend, IN
Schurz, Todd (219) 235-6161
PRES, PUB, ED
South Bend Tribune, South Bend, IN
Schuster, Bob (602) 898-6500
EPE, Mesa Tribune, Mesa, AZ
Thomson Newspapers
Schuster, Doris (937) 225-2000
Garden ED, Dayton Daily News, Dayton, OH
Schuster, Karla (203) 789-5200
EDU ED
New Haven Register, New Haven, CT
Schuster, Larry (202) 898-8254
SCI ED
United Press International, Washington, DC
Schuster, Margo (800) 223-2154
VP
Investor's Business Daily, Los Angeles, CA
Schutt Jr, L Peter (901) 523-1561
COB/PUB, Daily News, Memphis, TN
Schuttrow, Charles (815) 432-5227
News ED, Iroquois County's Times-Republic, Watseka, IL
Schutz, Bernie (619) 322-8889
ADV MGR-CLASS
Desert Sun, Palm Springs, CA
Schutz, Gayle Gill (308) 962-7261
GM, Arapahoe Public Mirror, Arapahoe, NE
Schuver, Michael F (205) 543-3417
VP
Lancaster Management Inc., Gadsden, AL
Schwab, Cathy (330) 454-5611
DP MGR, Repository, Canton, OH
Schwab, Gary (704) 358-5000
EX Sports ED
Charlotte Observer, Charlotte, NC
Schwab, Richard P (412) 238-2111
ED, Ligonier Echo, Ligonier, PA
Schwabe, Paul A (508) 458-7100
ADV DIR-Sales/MKTG, ADTX MGR
Sun, Lowell, MA
Schwadron, Harley (313) 426-8433
ED, Schwadron Cartoon & Illustration Service, Ann Arbor, MI
Schwadron, Terry (213) 237-5000
Deputy MAN ED, Online Services ED
Los Angeles Times, Los Angeles, CA
Schwalbach, Paul (520) 573-4561
Design ED, Tucson Citizen, Tucson, AZ
Schwalbert, Nancy (617) 729-6100
ED, Winchester Star, Winchester, MA
Schwalenberg, Lois (410) 939-4040
MAN ED, Record, Havre De Grace, MD
Schwalm, Lynda (416) 947-2222
DIR-MKTG, Toronto Sun, Toronto, ON
Schwan, Gary (561) 820-4100
Arts/Architecture ED
Palm Beach Post, West Palm Beach, FL
Schwanke, Bruce H (204) 522-3491
PUB, GM, ED, Melita New Era, Melita, MB
Schwanke, James (608) 588-2508
PUB, Weekly Home News, Spring Green, WI
Schwanke, Linda (608) 588-2508
PUB, Weekly Home News, Spring Green, WI
Schwans, Danny (605) 772-5644
PUB, ED, Miner County Pioneer, Howard, SD
Schwans, Troy (605) 425-2361
PUB, ED, Salem Special, Salem, SD
Schwantes, Jon (317) 633-1240
City ED
Indianapolis Star/News, Indianapolis, IN
Schwartz, Amy (419) 332-5511
CONT, News-Messenger, Fremont, OH
Schwartz, Ann (218) 927-3761
ED, Aitkin Independent Age, Aitkin, MN
Schwartz, Bob (304) 348-5140
Religion ED, Charleston Gazette, Sunday Gazette-Mail, Charleston, WV
Schwartz, Carl (414) 224-2000
Senior ED-Weekend
Milwaukee Journal Sentinel, Milwaukee, WI
Schwartz, Craig (610) 622-8800
ADV ASST MGR-RT
Delaware County Daily Times, Primos, PA
Schwartz, Gary (206) 464-2111
ASST Sports ED, Seattle Times, Seattle, WA
Schwartz, Gary (206) 348-5598
Self-Syndicator
Schwartz, Gary, Mukilteo, WA
Schwartz III, H L (Sandy) (609) 989-7800
PUB, Trentonian, Trenton, NJ
Schwartz, James (612) 633-2777
ED, Shoreview/Arden Hills Bulletin, New Brighton, MN
Schwartz, Jerry (404) 875-6572
MAN ED, Atlanta Bureau, Atlanta, GA
Schwartz, Kathy (402) 426-2121
ED, Blair Enterprise, Blair, NE
Schwartz, Leland (202) 628-3100
ED, States News Service (NY Times Subscriber Service), Washington, DC
Schwartz, March (310) 278-1322
PUB, ED
Beverly Hills Courier, Beverly Hills, CA
Schwartz, Maryln (214) 977-8222
COL-Today, Dallas Morning News, Dallas, TX
Schwartz, Michael (909) 684-1200
Health ED, Press-Enterprise, Riverside, CA
Schwartz, Mike (404) 526-5151
MGR-News ADM & Training
Atlanta Journal-Constitution, Atlanta, GA
Schwartz, Robert (414) 224-2000
ADV MGR-NTL
Milwaukee Journal Sentinel, Milwaukee, WI
Schwartz, Sanford (602) 898-6500
PRES, PUB, Mesa Tribune, Mesa, AZ
Thomson Newspapers
Schwartz, William A (908) 531-6200
PUB, Jewish Voice, Deal Park, NJ
Schwartz-Barker, Lynn (304) 348-5140
Garden ED, Charleston Gazette, Sunday Gazette-Mail, Charleston, WV
Schwartzberg, Florence B (516) 374-9200
PUB, South Shore Record, Woodmere, NY
Schwartzenberger, Jerome (701) 754-2212
PUB, Napoleon Homestead, Napoleon, ND
Schwartzenberger, Terry (701) 754-2212
ED, Napoleon Homestead, Napoleon, ND
Schwarz, Dave (406) 637-5513
ED, Terry Tribune, Terry, MT
Schwarz, Glenn (415) 777-2424
Sports ED
San Francisco Examiner, San Francisco, CA
Schwarz, Lisa (507) 334-1853
MAN ED
Faribault Daily News, Faribault, MN
Schwarzentraub, Betsy (916) 756-0800
Religion ED, Davis Enterprise, Davis, CA
Schwarzentraub, Maggie (217) 762-2511
ED, Piatt County Journal-Republican, Monticello, IL
Schwebs, David (414) 733-4411
CIRC DIR, Post-Crescent, Appleton, WI
Schwed, Craig (703) 276-5800
BUS ED
Gannett News Service, Arlington, VA
Schweit, Ernie (847) 427-4300
Time Out! ED
Daily Herald, Arlington Heights, IL
Schweizer, Eberhard (908) 245-7995
PUB, ED, Freie Zeitung, Kenilworth, NJ
Schwenk, Robert J (610) 258-7171
CIRC DIR, Express-Times, Easton, PA
Schwerzler, Nancy (202) 898-2300
VP/ED, Legi-Slate, Washington, DC
Schwilling, Jerry (316) 273-6391
PUB, ED, Chase County Leader-News, Cottonwood Falls, KS
Schwind, Jim (713) 331-4421
PUB, ED, Sun, Alvin, TX
Schwindt, Troy (719) 275-7565
MAN ED, EPE, Daily Record, Canon City, CO
Schwing, John (203) 255-8877
ED, Fairfield Minuteman, Fairfield, CT
Schwinghamer, Gord (403) 468-0100
ADV MGR-CLASS
Edmonton Sun, Edmonton, AB
Schwinke, Del (314) 340-8000
ADV MGR
St. Louis Post-Dispatch, St. Louis, MO
Sciacca, Joe (617) 426-3000
ED/COL, Boston Herald, Boston, MA
Sciarini, Edmund P (209) 722-1511
Graphics ED, Merced Sun-Star, Merced, CA
Scibona, Renie (602) 483-0977
GM
Paradise Valley Independent, Scottsdale, AZ
Scilley, Claude (613) 544-5000
City/Regional ED
Kingston Whig-Standard, Kingston, ON
Sclafani, Diane (718) 447-4700
MAN ED
Staten Island Register, Staten Island, NY
Scobey, Michael S (715) 842-2101
PRES/PUB, Daily Herald, Wausau, WI
Scobie, Jerry (360) 694-3391
CONT, Columbian, Vancouver, WA
Scofield, Bill (206) 339-3000
PROD MGR-Pagination/Special Projects
Herald, Everett, WA
Scoggins, Jim (509) 248-1251
Sports ED, Herald-Republic, Yakima, WA
Scogin, Mike (502) 863-1111
PUB, News-Graphic, Georgetown, KY
Scoles, Ron (406) 657-1200
ADV MGR-Co-op/Direct MKTG, ADV MGR-Commercial Print
Billings Gazette, Billings, MT
Scollan, Tom (212) 930-8000
PROD FRM-Paperhandler
New York Post, New York, NY
Scopin, Joseph W (202) 636-3000
ASST MAN ED
Washington Times, Washington, DC
Scotchie, Joseph (516) 747-8282
ED, Roslyn News, Mineola, NY
Scott III, Albert W (217) 942-3626
ED, Gazette-Patriot, Carrollton, IL
Scott, Angus (905) 774-7632
ED, Dunnville Chronicle, Dunnville, ON
Scott, Bill (403) 532-1110
ED, Automotive ED, Lifestyle ED, News ED
Daily Herald-Tribune, Grande Prairie, AB
Scott, Bob (315) 792-5000
CIRC DIR, Observer-Dispatch, Utica, NY
Scott, Bob (902) 468-1222
ADV MGR-CLASS, Daily News, Halifax, NS
Scott, C A (404) 659-1110
PUB, ED, Atlanta Daily World, Atlanta, GA
Scott, Clay (502) 432-3291
PUB, ED, Herald-News, Edmonton, KY

Copyright ©1997 by the Editor & Publisher Co.

Sco Who's Where-206

Scott, Cliff .... (805) 781-7800
PROD FRM-COMP
Telegram-Tribune, San Luis Obispo, CA
Scott, Dan .... (304) 752-6950
Sports ED, Logan Banner, Logan, WV
Scott, Daniel .... (505) 268-8111
GM, Weekly Alibi, Albuquerque, NM
Scott, Danny .... (505) 746-3524
CIRC MGR, PROD SUPT, PROD FRM-PR
Artesia Daily Press, Artesia, NM
Scott, Dave .... (317) 462-5528
ED, EPE, Entertainment ED, Photo ED, Travel ED, Daily Reporter, Greenfield, IN
Scott, David .... (404) 526-5151
PUB-Electronic INFO SRV
Atlanta Journal-Constitution, Atlanta, GA
Scott, David .... (817) 665-5511
PUB, Daily Register, Gainesville, TX
Scott, David .... (219) 356-8400
ED, Our Sunday Visitor, Huntington, IN
Scott, David .... (704) 358-5000
DIR-Newsroom ADM
Charlotte Observer, Charlotte, NC
Scott, Debbie .... (210) 625-9144
ADV DIR, New Braunfels Herald-Zeitung, New Braunfels, TX
Scott, Diana .... (508) 793-9100
Travel ED
Telegram & Gazette, Worcester, MA
Scott, Duncan .... (216) 951-0000
Photo DEPT MGR
News-Herald, Willoughby, OH
Scott, Eugene .... (312) 225-2400
GM, Chicago Daily Defender, Chicago, IL
Scott, Frances .... (212) 666-2300
ASST to the PUB/Women's ED, Basch, Buddy Feature Syndicate, New York, NY
Scott, Frank C .... (617) 367-9100
MAN ED, Jewish Advocate, Boston, MA
Scott, Fred .... (334) 875-2110
PROD FRM-MR
Selma Times-Journal, Selma, AL
Scott, Gail .... (201) 877-4141
Medical ED, Star-Ledger, Newark, NJ
Scott, Gary .... (505) 746-3524
PUB/BM/PA, ADV MGR, ADV MGR-PROM
Artesia Daily Press, Artesia, NM
Scott, Gordon .... (403) 625-4474
PUB, ED
Claresholm Local Press, Claresholm, AB
Scott Jr, J W (Dick) .... (803) 484-9431
PUB, Lee County Observer, Bishopville, SC
Scott, Jack L .... (304) 255-4400
ADV DIR-OPER
Register Herald, Beckley, WV
Scott, Jacque .... (303) 279-5541
ED, Golden Transcript, Golden, CO
Scott, Jason .... (904) 829-6562
Entertainment/Amusements ED
St. Augustine Record, St. Augustine, FL
Scott, Jeff .... (502) 443-1771
CIRC DIR, Paducah Sun, Paducah, KY
Scott, Jerry .... (817) 390-7400
VP-MKTG
Fort Worth Star-Telegram, Fort Worth, TX
Scott, Joe .... (817) 757-5757
ADV MGR-CLASS
Waco Tribune-Herald, Waco, TX
Scott, Kelly .... (213) 237-5000
Sunday Calendar ED
Los Angeles Times, Los Angeles, CA
Scott, Kevin .... (506) 452-6671
PROD FRM-PR
Daily Gleaner, Fredericton, NB
Scott, Laura .... (816) 234-4141
ASST EPE
Kansas City Star, Kansas City, MO
Scott, Linda McGregor .... (901) 853-7060
MAN ED, Independent, Collierville, TN
Scott, Lynn .... (412) 465-5555
ASST EX ED, EDL, Family/Fashion ED, Home Furnishings ED, Indiana Gazette, Indiana, PA
Scott, Lynnette .... (918) 581-8300
ADV DIR, Tulsa World, Tulsa, OK
Scott, Mae .... (970) 945-8515
DP MGR
Glenwood Post, Glenwood Springs, CO
Scott, Mark .... (913) 776-2200
Religion ED
Manhattan Mercury, Manhattan, KS
Scott, Mary Ann .... (815) 457-2245
ED, Rankin Independent, Cissna Park, IL
Scott, Maude .... (206) 622-8272
ED, Seattle Daily Journal of Commerce, Seattle, WA
Scott, Michael .... (403) 873-4031
GM, News/North, Yellowknife, NT
Scott, Michael .... (807) 824-2021
ED, Schreiber News, Terrace Bay, ON
Scott, Michael .... (604) 732-2111
Music Critic-Classical
Vancouver Sun, Vancouver, BC
Scott, Pamela Brunger .... (415) 777-2424
MAN ED-OPER
San Francisco Examiner, San Francisco, CA
Scott, Pat .... (913) 243-2424
CIRC DIR, Blade-Empire, Concordia, KS
Scott, Patrick .... (916) 527-2151
CIRC MGR, Daily News, Red Bluff, CA
Scott, Paul .... (914) 246-4985
MAN ED
Old Dutch Post Star, Saugerties, NY
Scott, Paul G .... (613) 382-2156
PUB, Reporter, Gananoque, ON
Scott, Portia A .... (404) 659-1110
MAN ED, Atlanta Daily World, Atlanta, GA
Scott, Robert .... (864) 298-4100
BUS/FIN ED
Greenville News, Greenville, SC
Scott, Ronda .... (405) 323-5151
CIRC MGR, Clinton Daily News, Clinton, OK
Scott, Ross .... (910) 323-4848
Copy Desk Chief
Fayetteville Observer-Times, Fayetteville, NC
Scott, Russell A .... (309) 764-4344
MAN ED, Dispatch, Moline, IL
Scott, Sharon .... (800) 223-2154
ADV VP-East Coast
Investor's Business Daily, Los Angeles, CA
Scott, Sharon .... (202) 334-6000
Deputy ED
Washington Post, Washington, DC
Scott, Steven .... (214) 428-8958
GM, Dallas Weekly, Dallas, TX
Scott, Taylor .... (561) 395-8300
Sports ED, News, Boca Raton, FL
Scott, Terry .... (416) 364-3172
GEN EX-Client Liaison
Broadcast News Limited, Toronto, ON
Scott, Tom .... (847) 381-9200
MAN ED, Lake Zurich Courier, Barrington, IL
Scott-Bertling, Terry .... (210) 225-7411
ASST MAN ED
San Antonio Express-News, San Antonio, TX
Scott II, Albert W .... (217) 942-3626
PUB, Gazette-Patriot, Carrollton, IL
Scotto, Michael L .... (203) 235-1661
PROD DIR-Graphic SRV
Record-Journal, Meriden, CT
Scourtis, Marilyn .... (904) 599-2100
PROD MGR-Materials & Distribution
Tallahassee Democrat, Tallahassee, FL
Scoville, Jennifer .... (512) 454-5766
MAN ED, Austin Chronicle, Austin, TX
Scrader, J R .... (540) 980-5220
EDL Writer, Southwest Times, Pulaski, VA
Scribner, David .... (413) 447-7311
ED, Berkshire Eagle, Pittsfield, MA
Scripps, Barry H .... (541) 296-2141
PRES, Dalles Daily Chronicle, The Dalles, OR
Scripps, Betty Knight .... (541) 296-2141
Vice Chairman/CORP SEC
Dalles Daily Chronicle, The Dalles, OR
Scripps Jr, Charles E .... (561) 746-5111
GM, Jupiter Courier, Jupiter, FL
Scripps, E W .... (541) 296-2141
BC/TREAS, Daily Chronicle, The Dalles, OR
Scripps, J P .... (360) 377-3711
PUB, Sun, Bremerton, WA
Scripps, Paul K .... (360) 377-3711
BC (John P Scripps Newspapers)
Sun, Bremerton, WA, Scripps Howard
Scriven, Bill .... (519) 537-2341
Entertainment ED
Sentinel-Review, Woodstock, ON
Scroggins, Howard .... (419) 625-5500
PROD FRM-PR
Sandusky Register, Sandusky, OH
Scruggs, Afi-Odelia E .... (216) 999-4500
COL, Plain Dealer, Cleveland, OH
Scruggs, John .... (915) 653-1221
ADTX MGR, Standard-Times, San Angelo, TX
Scudamore, Richard .... (203) 425-2500
Sr VP-OPER South
Thomson Newspapers, Stamford, CT
Scudder, Richard B .... (303) 820-1952
COB, MediaNews Group Inc., Denver, CO
Scully, Bob .... (616) 845-5181
COL, Daily News, Ludington, MI
Scully, Janene .... (805) 925-2691
Missiles/Space ED, Times, Santa Maria, CA
Scully, Susan .... (508) 685-1000
Women's ED
Eagle-Tribune, North Andover, MA
Scwwein, Rick .... (215) 854-2000
Senior ED-SYS
Philadelphia Inquirer, Philadelphia, PA
Seabaugh, Lisa .... (573) 471-1137
Accountant
Standard Democrat, Sikeston, MO
Seabrook, Don .... (509) 663-5161
Photographer
Wenatchee World, Wenatchee, WA
Seaburg, Michele .... (209) 582-0471
Military ED, Hanford Sentinel, Hanford, CA
Seacrest, Eric R .... (308) 532-6783
EVP/CEO
Western Publishing Co., North Platte, NE
Seacrest, Gary .... (308) 632-0670
SEC/TREAS, Star-Herald, Scottsbluff, NE
Seacrest, James C .... (308) 532-6783
COB/PRES
Western Publishing Co., North Platte, NE
Seady, Tom .... (314) 340-8000
PROD CNR-Newsprint
St. Louis Post-Dispatch, St. Louis, MO
Seagle, Tim .... (419) 522-3311
EDU ED, News Journal, Mansfield, OH
Seago, David .... (206) 597-8742
EPE, News Tribune, Tacoma, WA
Seagrave, Jane .... (215) 557-2300
PRES/COO
Legal Intelligencer, Philadelphia, PA
Seal, Sandy .... (504) 732-2565
MAN ED, Daily News, Bogalusa, LA
Sealover, Robin .... (410) 848-4400
Librarian
Carroll County Times, Westminster, MD
Seals, Louise .... (804) 649-6000
MAN ED
Richmond Times-Dispatch, Richmond, VA
Sealy, Robert .... (717) 748-6791
MAN ED, EPE, Express, Lock Haven, PA
Seaman, Laurin .... (610) 933-8926
PROD FRM-COMP Room
Phoenix, Phoenixville, PA
Seaman, Patricia .... (717) 272-5611
Fashion/Style ED, Women's ED
Daily News, Lebanon, PA
Seamons, Necia .... (208) 852-0155
ED, Preston Citizen, Preston, ID
Searcy, Katherine .... (310) 337-7003
VP/EDL DIR
Creators Syndicate, Los Angeles, CA
Searl, Char .... (312) 321-3000
EDL Art DIR-Days
Chicago Sun-Times, Chicago, IL
Searles, Art .... (912) 436-2156
PUB, ED
Albany Southwest Georgian, Albany, GA
Sears, Bill .... (301) 722-4600
Graphics ED/Art DIR
Cumberland Times-News, Cumberland, MD
Sears, Broc .... (817) 390-7400
Senior ED-Design/Graphics
Fort Worth Star-Telegram, Fort Worth, TX
Sears, Edward M .... (561) 820-4100
ED, Palm Beach Post, West Palm Beach, FL
Sears, Ron .... (209) 582-0471
CIRC DIR, Hanford Sentinel, Hanford, CA
Sease, Cindy .... (712) 279-5019
ADV MGR-CLASS
Sioux City Journal, Sioux City, IA
Sease, Linda .... (303) 892-5000
VP-MKTG/Sales, VP-MKTG/Public Relations, Online Contact
Rocky Mountain News, Denver, CO
Seaton, Donald R .... (402) 462-2131
PRES, PUB
Hastings Tribune, Hastings, NE, Seaton
Seaton, Edward L .... (402) 462-2131
VP, Hastings Tribune, Hastings, NE
Seaton
Seaton, Frederick D .... (316) 221-1050
PRES, SEC/TREAS, PUB, ED, EDL Writer, ADTX MGR
Winfield Daily Courier, Winfield, KS
Seaton, Martin .... (416) 947-2222
CONT, Toronto Sun, Toronto, ON
Seaton, Richard M .... (316) 251-2900
COB, Seaton Group, Coffeyville, KS
Seaton, William A .... (519) 652-3421
PUB, ED, News-Star, Lambeth, ON
Seaward, Greg .... (709) 256-4371
ED, Gander Beacon, Gander, NF
Seay, Susan B .... (502) 247-5223
ADV DIR, Mayfield Messenger, Mayfield, KY
Sebastian, Anthony .... (412) 263-1100
PROD MGR-Pre Press
Pittsburgh Post-Gazette, Pittsburgh, PA
Sebastiani, Mario .... (815) 937-3300
VP-OPER/GM, Daily Journal, Kankakee, IL
Sechowski, Kathleen .... (219) 235-6161
Fashion ED
South Bend Tribune, South Bend, IN
Seckar, John .... (613) 395-3015
PUB, Community Press, Stirling, ON
Secor, John .... (815) 756-4841
MAN ED, Daily Chronicle, De Kalb, IL
Secord, Stan .... (419) 245-6000
CIRC MGR-Zone North, Blade, Toledo, OH
Secrist, Frances C .... (316) 783-5034
ED, Galena Sentinel Times, Galena, KS
Seddon, Bill .... (516) 843-2020
Long Island Night ED, Newsday, Melville, NY
Sedeno, David .... (214) 977-8222
EDU ED, Dallas Morning News, Dallas, TX
Sedeno, Edna .... (915) 653-1221
Librarian
San Angelo Standard-Times, San Angelo, TX
Sederberg, Deborah .... (219) 874-7211
COL, News Dispatch, Michigan City, IN
Sedgwick, Dallas .... (316) 342-4800
PROD MGR, Emporia Gazette, Emporia, KS
Sedgwick, Katherine .... (905) 885-2471
GEN MGR, Evening Guide, Port Hope, ON
Sedjo, Anntovza .... (907) 581-2092
MAN ED
Dutch Harbor Fisherman, Dutch Harbor, AK
Sedlmeyer, Agnes .... (512) 594-3346
MAN ED, Shiner Gazette, Shiner, TX
Sedmak, Jay .... (412) 695-1100
ED, Prosveta, Imperial, PA
See, Bill .... (410) 749-7171
Sports ED, Daily Times, Salisbury, MD
See, Charles .... (304) 822-3871
ED, Hampshire Review, Romney, WV
Seebach, Linda .... (510) 462-4160
EPE, Valley Times, Pleasanton, CA
Seeber, Glen .... (405) 255-5354
BUS ED, Duncan Banner, Duncan, OK
Seeber, Michael .... (815) 987-1200
CONT, Rockford Register Star, Rockford, IL
Seed, Colin .... (250) 352-3552
ADV MGR, Nelson Daily News, Nelson, BC
Seed, Donald R .... (810) 651-4141
PUB, Rochester Clarion, Rochester, MI
Seed, Shawna .... (214) 977-8222
Sunday ED, Dallas Morning News, Dallas, TX
Seeger, Bill .... (302) 324-2500
ADV MGR-RT, News Journal, Wilmington, DE
Seeger, Mel .... (860) 442-2200
PA, Day, New London, CT
Seeley, Frances .... (402) 761-2911
PUB, ED, Milford Times, Milford, NE
Seeley, George R .... (402) 761-2911
PUB, Milford Times, Milford, NE
Seeley, Sue .... (712) 225-5111
PROD SUPT
Cherokee County's Daily Times, Cherokee, IA
Seeley, Thomas .... (315) 253-5311
BUS/FIN ED, Citizen, Auburn, NY
Seeling, Michael .... (847) 427-4300
DIR-Photo
Daily Herald, Arlington Heights, IL
Seelman, Nan .... (616) 964-7161
EX ED
Battle Creek Enquirer, Battle Creek, MI
Seelmeyer, John .... (916) 273-9561
MAN ED, Union, Grass Valley, CA
Seely, Jeri .... (219) 658-4111
ED, Paper, Milford, IN
Seely, Ralph .... (506) 859-4900
CONT, Times-Transcript, Moncton, NB
Seelye, Tracy .... (508) 343-6911
EPE, EDU ED, Political/Government ED
Sentinel & Enterprise, Fitchburg, MA
Seeman, Steve .... (800) 222-5551
SRV MGR, North American Precis Syndicate Inc., New York, NY
Seering, Jeff .... (608) 524-2115
GM, ED, Reedsburg Report, WI,
Seffrin, Mike .... (937) 498-2111
EDU ED, Farm/Agriculture ED, Home Furnishings ED
Sidney Daily News, Sidney, OH
Segal, Cheryl .... (757) 247-4600
EDU ED, Religion ED
Daily Press, Newport News, VA
Segal, D R .... (714) 553-9292
PRES Emeritus
Freedom Communications Inc., Irvine, CA
Segal, Jonathan M .... (714) 553-9292
Sr VP/PRES-Eastern Newspaper Division
Freedom Communications Inc., Irvine, CA
Segal, Lewis .... (213) 237-5000
Dance Critic
Los Angeles Times, Los Angeles, CA
Segal, Mark A .... (215) 625-8501
PUB
Philadelphia Gay News, Philadelphia, PA
Segal, S Damien .... (513) 761-1188
Senior Critic
Critic's Choice Reviews, Cincinnati, OH
Segall, Lynne .... (213) 525-2000
ASSOC PUB
Hollywood Reporter, Los Angeles, CA
Segall, Vivian .... (860) 442-2200
EDU ED, Fashion/Style ED, Food ED
Day, New London, CT
Segelke, Verna .... (970) 483-7460
PUB, Wiggins Courier, Wiggins, CO
Segraves, Hope .... (501) 886-2464
GM, Times Dispatch, Walnut Ridge, AR
Segrest, Melissa .... (561) 820-4100
ASST MAN ED-Features
Palm Beach Post, West Palm Beach, FL
Segroves, David .... (615) 684-1200
PUB, Photo DEPT MGR, PROD MGR
Shelbyville Times-Gazette, Shelbyville, TN

Copyright ©1997 by the Editor & Publisher Co.

207-Who's Where **Sgr**

Segroves, Mrs Nina Gay .... (615) 684-1200
SEC, Times-Gazette, Shelbyville, TN
Seguin, Ken .... (705) 674-5271
PUB/GM, Sudbury Star, Sudbury, ON
Seguin, Maurice .... (514) 987-2222
PROD MGR-MR, Gazette, Montreal, QC
Seib, Randy .... (601) 896-2100
PROD MGR-Distribution
Sun Herald, Biloxi, MS
Seibel, Chris .... (414) 457-7711
CIRC ASST DIR-Sales & MKTG
Sheboygan Press, Sheboygan, WI
Seibel, Mark .... (305) 350-2111
ADV DIR-International
Miami Herald, Miami, FL
Seiber, Cliff .... (318) 436-0583
ED, Moss Bluff News, Sulphur, LA
Seibert, Barbara .... (606) 292-2600
Librarian, Kentucky Post, Covington, KY
Seibert, Mark .... (515) 284-8000
EDU Reporter-College
Des Moines Register, Des Moines, IA
Seibert, Richard R .... (402) 444-1000
VP, Omaha World-Herald Co., Omaha, NE
Seid, Dennis .... (601) 636-4545
Sports ED, Vicksburg Post, Vicksburg, MS
Seid, Marvin .... (213) 237-5000
EDL Writer
Los Angeles Times, Los Angeles, CA
Seidel, Andrea .... (715) 365-6397
PROD FRM-COMP
Daily News, Rhinelander, WI
Seidel, Barbara .... (908) 349-3000
Entertainment/Amusements ED, Fashion/Style ED, Living/Lifestyle ED, Religion ED
Ocean County Observer, Toms River, NJ
Seidl, Frank .... (612) 222-5011
MGR-CR
St. Paul Pioneer Press, St. Paul, MN
Seidman, Eric .... (757) 446-2000
Creative DIR, Virginian-Pilot, Norfolk, VA
Seifer, Trenda .... (308) 386-4617
PUB, ED, Courier-Times, Sutherland, NE
Seifferlein, Carol .... (810) 679-4500
ED, Sanilac Jeffersonian, Croswell, MI
Seiger, Jennifer .... (502) 756-2109
ED, Breckinridge County Herald-News, Hardinsburg, KY
Seiler, Fanny .... (304) 348-5140
COL, Charleston Gazette, Sunday Gazette-Mail, Charleston, WV
Seiler, Leroy .... (941) 262-3161
DP MGR, PROD MGR-Pre Press
Naples Daily News, Naples, FL
Seip, Doug .... (514) 484-1107
GM, Suburban, Montreal, QC
Seirer, Scott .... (913) 823-6363
EX ED, Automotive ED
Salina Journal, Salina, KS
Seis, Peggy .... (505) 823-7777
CONT, Albuquerque Publishing Co., Albuquerque, NM
Seisser, Jeff .... (414) 563-5553
Sports ED, Daily Jefferson County Union, Fort Atkinson, WI
Seitel, Nelson .... (212) 779-9200
SEC/ASSOC PUB
New York Law Journal, New York, NY
Seits, L D .... (812) 424-7711
News ED, Evansville Courier, Evansville, IN
Seitz, Karl .... (205) 325-2222
EPE
Birmingham Post-Herald, Birmingham, AL
Seitz, Matt Zoller .... (201) 877-4141
COL, Star-Ledger, Newark, NJ
Seitzinger, Rob .... (609) 522-3423
ED, Cape May County Gazette Leader, Wildwood, NJ
Sejeck, Ana .... (562) 435-1161
ASST SEC, Press-Telegram, Long Beach, CA
Knight-Ridder Inc.
Sekella, Richard M .... (330) 296-9657
GM, Record-Courier, Kent-Ravenna, OH
Sekiya, Baron .... (808) 329-9311
Online Contact
West Hawaii Today, Kailua-Kona, HI
Selby, Craig .... (304) 348-5140
PUB, Charleston Gazette, Sunday Gazette-Mail, Charleston, WV
Selby, Jolene .... (406) 447-4000
CONT
Helena Independent Record, Helena, MT
Selby, Sally Ann .... (805) 395-7500
MGR-PROM/Community Services
Bakersfield Californian, Bakersfield, CA
Selch, R Kay .... (317) 342-3311
PUB, ADV DIR
Daily Reporter, Martinsville, IN
Self, Carol .... (937) 225-2000
DIR-Purchasing
Dayton Daily News, Dayton, OH
Self, Jane .... (912) 744-4200
Religion Writer
Macon Telegraph, Macon, GA
Self, Tom .... (205) 325-2222
Photo Chief
Birmingham News, Birmingham, AL
Selfridge, Jeannine .... (814) 765-5581
ADV MGR-Display, Progress, Clearfield, PA
Seligman, Pat .... (505) 823-7777
Librarian
Albuquerque Tribune, Albuquerque, NM
Seligson, Linda .... (717) 771-2000
EPE, York Daily Record, York, PA
Seline, Rex .... (817) 390-7400
Senior ED-BUS
Fort Worth Star-Telegram, Fort Worth, TX
Selingo, Jeff .... (910) 343-2000
Environmental ED, Morning Star/Sunday Star-News, Wilmington, NC
Selkowe, Peter .... (414) 634-3322
PUB, Journal Times, Racine, WI
Sell, John .... (404) 292-3536
ED, Decatur-De Kalb News/Era, Decatur, GA
Sell, Steve .... (316) 241-2422
Sports ED
McPherson Sentinel, McPherson, KS
Sellar, Don .... (416) 367-2000
Ombudsman, Toronto Star, Toronto, ON
Sellars, Becky .... (816) 532-4444
MAN ED, Smithville Lake Democrat-Herald, Smithville, MO
Sellars, Ron .... (713) 220-7171
ADV DIR-OPER
Houston Chronicle, Houston, TX
Selle, Charles .... (708) 336-7000
Opinion Page ED, News-Sun, Waukegan, IL
Sellers, Dana .... (803) 317-6397
Librarian
Florence Morning News, Florence, SC
Sellers, David .... (405) 232-4151
PUB, ED
Capitol Hill Beacon, Oklahoma City, OK
Sellers, John .... (334) 433-1551
SYS ED, Mobile Press Register, Mobile, AL
Sellers, Michael C .... (717) 742-9671
PROD DIR, Milton Daily Standard, Milton, PA
Hollinger International Inc.
Sellers, O G .... (601) 947-2967
PUB, ED
George County Times, Lucedale, MS
Sellers, Troy .... (717) 742-9671
MAN ED, Milton Daily Standard, Milton, PA
Hollinger International Inc.
Sellers, William .... (406) 755-7000
ADTX MGR, PROD SUPT
Daily Inter Lake, Kalispell, MT
Sellers-Earl, Laura .... (503) 325-3211
MAN ED, Amusements ED, Wire ED
Daily Astorian, Astoria, OR
Sellett, Michael .... (307) 733-2047
PUB, Jackson Hole News, Jackson, WY
Sellman, Collis D .... (512) 786-3022
PUB, ED, Progress, Three Rivers, TX
Sellstrom, Lori .... (916) 842-5777
GEN Reporting
Siskiyou Daily News, Yreka, CA
Selph, Carol .... (941) 687-7000
ADTX MGR, Ledger, Lakeland, FL
Selsor, Jeff .... (205) 549-2000
CONT, Gadsden Times, Gadsden, AL
Selvin, Molly .... (213) 237-5000
EDL Writer
Los Angeles Times, Los Angeles, CA
Selvy, Arlean .... (614) 472-0734
ED, Monroe County Beacon, Woodsfield, OH
Selwa, Bob .... (810) 469-4510
Farm/Agriculture ED
Macomb Daily, Mount Clemens, MI
Selweski, Chad .... (810) 469-4510
Political/Government ED
Macomb Daily, Mount Clemens, MI
Seman, Paul E .... (517) 793-7661
ED, Catholic Weekly, Saginaw, MI
Semel, Mike .... (201) 646-4000
ASST MAN ED-Assignment CNR
Record, Hackensack, NJ
Semerad, Tony .... (801) 237-2031
Online MGR
Salt Lake Tribune, Salt Lake City, UT
Seminario, Walter .... (416) 531-2495
ED, El Popular, Toronto, ON
Semion, Kay .... (313) 994-6989
EPE, EDL Writer
Ann Arbor News, Ann Arbor, MI
Semo, John .... (716) 282-2311
PROD DIR
Niagara Gazette, Niagara Falls, NY
Semple, Bill .... (902) 436-2121
Sports ED, Journal-Pioneer, Summerside, PEI
Semple, Paul E .... (217) 347-7151
GM, ED, DP MGR
Effingham Daily News, Effingham, IL
Senchyne, William .... (716) 849-3434
PROD OPER FRM-Electrician
Buffalo News, Buffalo, NY
Sender, Chuck .... (206) 464-2111
PA, Seattle Times, Seattle, WA
Sendle, Virginia M .... (507) 527-2492
PUB, ED
West Concord Enterprise, West Concord, MN
Senechal, France .... (506) 753-7637
GM, Journal L'Aviron, Campbellton, NB
Senft, Paul .... (815) 756-4841
PUB, Daily Chronicle, De Kalb, IL
Senften, Rick .... (330) 454-5611
City ED, Repository, Canton, OH
Senger, Frank B .... (616) 946-2000
PUB, Record-Eagle, Traverse City, MI
Senger, John .... (517) 629-3984
CIRC MGR, Albion Recorder, Albion, MI
Sengstacke, Frederick D .... (312) 225-2400
PRES, PUB, Chicago Defender, Chicago, IL
Sengstacke, John H .... (412) 481-8302
PUB
New Pittsburgh Courier, Pittsburgh, PA
Sengstacke, John H .... (901) 523-1818
PUB, Tri State Defender, Memphis, TN
Sengstacke, Robert .... (312) 225-2400
SEC, Chicago Defender, Chicago, IL
Senick, David .... (250) 380-5211
Sports ED, Times Colonist, Victoria, BC
Senison, Brad .... (503) 873-8385
PUB, Silverton Appeal Tribune/Mt. Angel News, Silverton, OR
Sennett, Frank .... (312) 243-8786
MAN ED, New City, Chicago, IL
Sennott, Anne G .... (508) 771-1427
PUB, Barnstable Patriot, Hyannis, MA
Sennott, Robert F .... (508) 771-1427
PUB, Barnstable Patriot, Hyannis, MA
Sensenig, Terry .... (301) 662-1177
MGR-Credit
Frederick Post/News, Frederick, MD
Senti, Richard .... (520) 432-7254
ED, Bisbee Observer, Bisbee, AZ
Seppala, Joan Kinney .... (510) 447-8700
PUB, Independent, Livermore, CA
Sepulveda, Sylvia P .... (210) 736-4450
PROD MGR
Daily Commercial Recorder, San Antonio, TX
Sequeira, Eddie .... (707) 468-3500
ADV MGR-Local/Display
Ukiah Daily Journal, Ukiah, CA
Serafin, Susan .... (616) 429-2400
MGR-Accounting
Herald-Palladium, St. Joseph, MI
Serafini, Alfred H .... (412) 263-1100
PROD MGR-North Plant
Pittsburgh Post-Gazette, Pittsburgh, PA
Serafino, Angelo .... (518) 454-5694
PROD SUPT-Press, Times Union, Albany, NY
Seraile, Brian .... (318) 459-3200
Music ED, Times, Shreveport, LA
Sercombe, Charles .... (313) 365-9500
ED, Citizen, Hamtramck, MI
Seremet, Ken .... (412) 537-3351
ADV MGR, Latrobe Bulletin, Latrobe, PA
Sereno, Jennifer .... (608) 252-6100
Automotive ED, Farm ED, FIN ED
Wisconsin State Journal, Madison, WI
Sereno, Julian .... (919) 419-6500
Hometown ED, Herald-Sun, Durham, NC
Serfass, Ron .... (610) 820-6500
PROD FRM-Inserting
Morning Call, Allentown, PA
Serfoss, Rod .... (405) 323-5151
GM/ASSOC PUB, Daily News, Clinton, OK
Sernett, Rebecca .... (315) 635-3921
ED, Messenger, Baldwinsville, NY
Serota, Kenneth .... (312) 321-3000
VP/GEN Counsel
Chicago Sun-Times, Chicago, IL
Serpas, Paul .... (504) 368-8900
ADV DIR, Features ED
Daily Journal of Commerce, New Orleans, LA
Serra, Robert .... (541) 997-3441
ED, Siuslaw News, Florence, OR
Serraglio, Mike .... (606) 231-3100
PROD MGR-BUS SYS
Lexington Herald-Leader, Lexington, KY
Servatius, Jim .... (915) 682-5311
ED, Midland Reporter-Telegram, Midland, TX
Serwacki, Frank .... (406) 363-3300
PROD MGR, Ravalli Republic, Hamilton, MT
Sesker, Craig .... (319) 754-8461
Sports ED, Hawk Eye, Burlington, IA
Sessa, Cammy .... (757) 446-2000
Women's/Fashion ED
Virginian-Pilot, Norfolk, VA
Sessoms, Hettie .... (970) 493-6397
CIRC MGR-Home Delivery
Fort Collins Coloradoan, Fort Collins, CO
Sestak, Elaine .... (507) 348-4176
ED, Jasper Journal, Jasper, MN
Seth, Dale .... (315) 363-5100
ASSOC ED
Oneida Daily Dispatch, Oneida, NY
Setner, Tracy .... (906) 774-2772
CIRC MGR
Iron Mountain Daily News, Iron Mountain, MI
Setser, Jerilyn L .... (704) 735-3031
GM, Lincoln Times-News, Lincolnton, NC
Setter, Dennis .... (810) 733-2239
ED, Suburban News, Flint, MI
Settino, Carol .... (603) 437-7000
MAN ED, Derry News, Derry, NH
Settle, David .... (405) 381-3173
ED, Tuttle Times, Tuttle, OK
Settle, Gary .... (206) 464-2111
Photo Coach, Seattle Times, Seattle, WA
Settle, Jimmy .... (615) 552-1808
BUS/FIN ED, Leaf-Chronicle, Clarksville, TN
Settle, John M .... (316) 564-3116
PUB, Ellinwood Leader, Ellinwood, KS
Settle, Marshall .... (316) 285-3111
PRES, PUB, Tiller & Toiler, Larned, KS
Setzer, David .... (704) 652-3313
GM, ED, McDowell News, Marion, NC
Seubert, Helen .... (405) 363-3370
Amusements ED, City ED, Consumer Interest/Food ED, EDU/Religion ED
Blackwell Journal-Tribune, Blackwell, OK
Seubold, Linda .... (501) 785-7700
COL
Southwest Times Record, Fort Smith, AR
Sevag, Aris .... (718) 380-1200
MAN ED, Armenian Reporter International, Fresh Meadows, NY
Sevart, Paul .... (414) 224-2000
Senior ED-Copy Desk
Milwaukee Journal Sentinel, Milwaukee, WI
Sevaska, Paul .... (334) 821-7150
PUB, Auburn Bulletin-Eagle, Auburn, AL
Severn, Ron .... (510) 935-2525
PROD MGR-Centralized Maintenance
Contra Costa Times, Walnut Creek, CA
Severns, Amber .... (417) 623-3480
MGR-CR, Joplin Globe, Joplin, MO
Severns, Joseph .... (918) 335-8200
CIRC Distribution Clerk
Examiner-Enterprise, Bartlesville, OK
Severson, Jack .... (215) 854-2000
EX Travel ED
Philadelphia Inquirer, Philadelphia, PA
Severson, Sandra .... (507) 285-7600
BM, DIR-MIS, Post-Bulletin, Rochester, MN
Sevilla, Susan .... (707) 875-3574
PUB, ED, Navigator, Bodega Bay, CA
Sevrens, James .... (415) 777-2424
GM
San Francisco Examiner, San Francisco, CA
Sewall, Thomas .... (616) 345-3511
PROD MGR
Kalamazoo Gazette, Kalamazoo, MI
Seward, Jeff .... (417) 623-3480
PROD FRM-MR
Joplin Globe, Joplin, MO
Sewell, Donnie .... (501) 268-8621
EDU ED, Entertainment/Amusements ED, Television/Film ED, Theater/Music ED, Travel ED, Daily Citizen, Searcy, AR
Sewell, Ray .... (801) 674-6200
Cedar City BU ED, Spectrum, St. George, UT
Sewell, Rhonda B .... (419) 245-6000
Fashion Reporter, Blade, Toledo, OH
Sexton, C Reece .... (423) 581-5630
ADV DIR, Citizen Tribune, Morristown, TN
Sexton, Denzil .... (304) 624-6411
PROD FRM-MR, Clarksburg Exponent/Telegram, Clarksburg, WV
Sexton, Dick .... (707) 644-1141
PROD FRM-Page Production
Vallejo Times-Herald, Vallejo, CA
Sexton, Jimmy .... (972) 937-3310
PUB, Daily Light, Waxahachie, TX
Sexton, Megon .... (803) 771-6161
News ED, State, Columbia, SC
Sexton, Michael J .... (207) 873-3341
PRES/Central Maine Newspapers
Central Maine Morning Sentinel, Waterville, ME, Guy Gannett Communications
Sexton, R D .... (606) 231-3100
PROD MGR-Plant OPER
Lexington Herald-Leader, Lexington, KY
Seyer, Loretta G .... (203) 288-5600
ED, Catholic Twin Circle, Hamden, CT
Seymour, Judy .... (719) 275-7565
CIRC MGR, Daily Record, Canon City, CO
Sferrazza, Steve .... (617) 929-2000
PROD SUPT-Engraving
Boston Globe, Boston, MA
Sforza, Kevin .... (301) 921-2800
ED, Journal, Gaithersburg, MD
Sgambati, Fred .... (902) 681-2121
ED, Advertiser, Kentville, NS
Sgro, Joseph .... (860) 241-6200
PROD MGR-Press (Days)
Hartford Courant, Hartford, CT

Copyright ©1997 by the Editor & Publisher Co.

Sgr Who's Where-208

Sgro, Joseph E .... (508) 793-9100
CONT, Telegram & Gazette, Worcester, MA
Shabazz, Estella .... (912) 238-8010
PUB, MAN ED
Freedom Journal, Savannah, GA
Shabazz, Yusuf .... (912) 238-8010
PUB, ED, Freedom Journal, Savannah, GA
Shackelford, Laurel .... (502) 582-4011
EDL Writer, Courier-Journal, Louisville, KY
Shackelford, Nancy .... (517) 772-2971
ADV MGR-CLASS
Morning Sun, Mount Pleasant, MI
Shade, Jason .... (717) 682-9081
MAN ED, Citizen-Standard, Valley View, PA
Shadrick, Robert A .... (401) 277-7000
VP-OPER, PROD DIR-OPER
Providence Journal-Bulletin, Providence, RI
Shaffer, Barbara .... (330) 747-1471
Society/Women's ED
Vindicator, Youngstown, OH
Shaffer, Cathie .... (606) 329-1717
Living/Leisure ED, Women's News ED
Daily Independent, Ashland, KY
Shaffer, Gary .... (405) 475-3311
ADV CNR-Co-op
Daily Oklahoman, Oklahoma City, OK
Shaffer, James B .... (207) 828-8100
PRES/CEO
Guy Gannett Communications, Portland, ME
Shaffer, James R .... (814) 275-3131
PUB, Leader-Vindicator, New Bethlehem, PA
Shaffer, Joe .... (316) 268-6000
PROD OPER MGR-PR
Wichita Eagle, Wichita, KS
Shaffer, John .... (717) 673-5151
PUB
Canton Independent Sentinel, Canton, PA
Shaffer, Kelly .... (814) 938-8740
Sports ED, Spirit, Punxsutawney, PA
Shaffer, Linda .... (503) 842-7535
PUB, Headlight-Herald, Tillamook, OR
Shaffer, Mary Ann .... (330) 747-7777
Office MGR, CIRC MGR
Daily Legal News, Youngstown, OH
Shaffer, Robert C .... (330) 821-1200
GM, Alliance Review, Alliance, OH
Shaffer, Thomas .... (814) 532-5199
DP MGR, Tribune-Democrat, Johnstown, PA
Shah, Pramond .... (818) 241-4141
TREAS, Glendale News-Press, Glendale, CA
Shah, Yatin .... (707) 938-2111
GM, Sonoma Index-Tribune, Sonoma, CA
Shaheen, Joe .... (330) 833-2631
Sports ED, Independent, Massillon, OH
Shaib, Diane .... (212) 293-8500
Sr. VP-US Licensing
United Media, New York, NY
Shalaway PhD, Scott .... (304) 686-3541
Nature Writer, Wild Side, Cameron, WV
Shales, Tom .... (202) 334-6000
Television Critic (Style)
Washington Post, Washington, DC
Shaller, Kirk .... (616) 547-6558
PUB, Charlevoix Courier, Charlevoix, MI
Shallit, Bob .... (916) 321-1000
BUS ED, Sacramento Bee, Sacramento, CA
Shambarger, Craig .... (219) 223-2111
PROD MGR-Press
Rochester Sentinel, Rochester, IN
Shamir, Shlomo .... (212) 629-9443
ED, Haddoar (Post), New York, NY
Shanahan, Deb .... (402) 444-1000
State ED, Omaha World-Herald, Omaha, NE
Shanahan, Patricia .... (609) 989-7800
Librarian, Trentonian, Trenton, NJ
Shanahan, Tom .... (208) 377-6200
Photographer, Idaho Statesman, Boise, ID
Shandy, Gwen .... (918) 756-3600
Office MGR
Okmulgee Daily Times, Okmulgee, OK
Shaner, Steve .... (937) 335-5634
Photo DEPT MGR, Troy Daily News/Miami Valley Sunday News, Troy, OH
Shank, Alinda .... (413) 447-7311
MGR-Human Resources
Berkshire Eagle, Pittsfield, MA
Shank, Janice .... (207) 924-7402
PUB, Eastern Gazette, Dexter, ME
Shank, John .... (815) 732-2156
GM, Ogle County Life, Oregon, IL
Shank, Robert H .... (207) 924-7402
PUB, ED, Eastern Gazette, Dexter, ME
Shank, Robin .... (305) 350-2111
PROD MGR-Printing
Miami Herald, Miami, FL
Shank, Steve .... (309) 647-5100
Sports ED, Daily Ledger, Canton, IL
Shanker, Albert .... (800) 238-1133
PRES, American Federation of Teachers, Washington, DC
Shankland, Mark A .... (207) 729-3311
Automotive ED, EPE
Times Record, Brunswick, ME
Shanklin, Sherry .... (901) 885-0744
BM, Daily Messenger, Union City, TN
Shanks, Jim .... (423) 837-6312
PUB, ED
South Pittsburg Hustler, South Pittsburg, TN
Shanley, Jean .... (814) 724-6370
Community ED
Meadville Tribune, Meadville, PA
Shannon, Bernie .... (209) 369-2761
PROD FRM-COMP
Lodi News-Sentinel, Lodi, CA
Shannon, Brian .... (360) 424-3251
MGR-INFO SYS
Skagit Valley Herald, Mount Vernon, WA
Shannon, C George .... (419) 422-5151
VP, ADV MGR-Market, DIR-MKTG
Courier, Findlay, OH
Shannon, Ed .... (405) 278-6005
MAN ED, Tinker Take-Off, Oklahoma City, OK
Shannon, Mike .... (405) 475-3311
Senior ASST MAN ED
Daily Oklahoman, Oklahoma City, OK
Shannon, Mona .... (847) 746-9000
ED, Zion Benton News, Zion, IL
Shannon, Murray .... (908) 922-6000
MGR-Design
Asbury Park Press, Neptune, NJ
Shannon, Ron .... (915) 673-4271
PROD FRM-PR
Abilene Reporter-News, Abilene, TX
Shannon, Tracy .... (714) 835-1234
CIRC DIR-Consumer Sales
Orange County Register, Santa Ana, CA
Shannon, William F .... (360) 736-3311
CIRC DIR, Chronicle, Centralia, WA
Shannonhouse, Rebecca .... (212) 293-8500
MAN ED-UFS & NEA, United Media, United Feature Syndicate, Newspaper Enterprise Association, New York, NY
Shao, Ben .... (212) 373-1800
Senior Information OFF
Taipei Economic & Cultural Office, Information Division, New York, NY
Shapcott, Carol .... (215) 949-4000
MGR-PROM, ADTX MGR
Bucks County Courier Times, Levittown, PA
Shapiro, Barry .... (770) 428-9411
Photo DEPT MGR
Marietta Daily Journal, Marietta, GA
Shapiro, David .... (808) 525-8000
MAN ED, Online Contact
Honolulu Star-Bulletin, Honolulu, HI
Shapiro, Elliott .... (716) 849-3434
Librarian, Buffalo News, Buffalo, NY
Shapiro, Howie .... (215) 854-2000
Fine Arts ED
Philadelphia Inquirer, Philadelphia, PA
Shapiro, Michael P .... (908) 432-7711
PUB, Jewish Star, South River, NJ
Shapiro, Michelle .... (805) 564-5200
Graphics ED, Santa Barbara News-Press, Santa Barbara, CA
Shapiro, Sandra .... (508) 752-2512
ED, Jewish Chronicle, Worcester, MA
Shapiro, Saul .... (319) 291-1400
ED, Waterloo Courier, Waterloo, IA
Shapiro, Stuart .... (608) 424-3232
PUB, MAN ED
Belleville Recorder, Belleville, WI
Shareef, Alvein .... (601) 582-4321
MGR-BUS SYS
Hattiesburg American, Hattiesburg, MS
Sharif, Ayman .... (402) 444-1000
CIRC MGR-ADM
Omaha World-Herald, Omaha, NE
Sharif, Roshan .... (715) 833-9200
PROD MGR-SYS
Leader-Telegram, Eau Claire, WI
Sharkey, Nancy .... (212) 556-1234
EDU ED, New York Times, New York, NY
Sharma, Babita .... (419) 238-2285
City ED, News ED
Times-Bulletin, Van Wert, OH
Sharon, D'Anna .... (615) 259-8000
Art DIR, Tennessean, Nashville, TN
Sharp, Andrew .... (908) 922-6000
EPE, Asbury Park Press, Neptune, NJ
Sharp, Bob .... (609) 871-8000
PROD MGR-SYS
Burlington County Times, Willingboro, NJ
Sharp, Chris .... (816) 776-5454
PUB, SEC, ADV MGR, MGR-MKTG/PROM, Aviation/Books ED, COL, EPE, EDU ED, Features ED, Health/Lifestyle ED, Librarian
Daily News, Richmond, MO
Sharp, David .... (910) 888-3500
ADV MGR-RT
High Point Enterprise, High Point, NC
Sharp, David C .... (806) 762-8844
PUB, Avalanche-Journal, Lubbock, TX
Sharp, Dennis .... (408) 372-3311
EPE, Monterey County Herald, Monterey, CA
Sharp, Jane .... (910) 373-7000
MGR-Human Resources
News & Record, Greensboro, NC
Sharp, Janie .... (210) 775-1551
ADV MGR, Del Rio News-Herald, Del Rio, TX
Sharp, Jeanny .... (913) 823-6363
ADV DIR, Salina Journal, Salina, KS
Sharp, Jennifer .... (414) 542-2501
BUS ED
Waukesha County Freeman, Waukesha, WI
Sharp, John .... (562) 435-1161
PROD MGR-Printing/Packaging
Press-Telegram, Long Beach, CA
Sharp, Mary .... (319) 398-8211
MET ED, Gazette, Cedar Rapids, IA
Sharp, Mike .... (916) 662-5421
PROD FRM-PR
Daily Democrat, Woodland, CA
Sharp, Robert .... (515) 284-8000
CIRC MGR-State
Des Moines Register, Des Moines, IA
Sharp, Steve .... (508) 586-7200
Librarian, Enterprise, Brockton, MA
Sharpe, Amy .... (218) 546-5029
MAN ED, Crosby-Ironton Courier, Crosby, MN
Sharpe, Amy .... (508) 775-1200
Cape Week ED
Cape Cod Times, Hyannis, MA
Sharpe, Hal C .... (919) 586-6397
PUB, Littleton Observer, Littleton, NC
Sharpe, Lee .... (704) 632-2532
PUB, Taylorsville Times, Taylorsville, NC
Sharpf, Pat .... (804) 732-3456
ED, Progress-Index, Petersburg, VA
Sharples, Bob .... (814) 870-1600
PROD GEN FRM-COMP
Morning News/Erie Daily Times, Erie, PA
Sharrah, Alan .... (206) 464-2111
PROD MGR-Packaging
Seattle Times, Seattle, WA
Sharrieff, Ibn .... (312) 346-8123
PUB, ED, Tri-City Journal, Chicago, IL
Sharry, Paul M .... (803) 577-7111
PSL MGR, Post and Courier, Charleston, SC
Shasteen, Jerry .... (614) 474-3131
ADV DIR, Herald, Circleville, OH
Shatrau, Patricia .... (315) 343-3800
PROD MGR-COMP
Palladium-Times, Oswego, NY
Shatterly, Eddie .... (910) 227-0131
ADV MGR-Sales
Times News Publishing Co., Burlington, NC
Shatto, Ron .... (619) 442-4404
CONT, MGR-Human Resources
Daily Californian, El Cajon, CA
Shattuck, Harry .... (713) 220-7171
Travel ED, Houston Chronicle, Houston, TX
Shaughnessy, Greg .... (619) 299-3131
ADV MGR-Sales Major Accounts
San Diego Union-Tribune, San Diego, CA
Shaughnessy, John .... (317) 633-1240
COL
Indianapolis Star/News, Indianapolis, IN
Shaulis, Debra .... (330) 747-1471
Films/Theater ED, Music ED, Radio/Television ED, Vindicator, Youngstown, OH
Shaull, L R (Verne) .... (519) 621-3810
PUB/GM
Cambridge Reporter, Cambridge, ON
Shaver, Carl .... (916) 786-6500
GM, Press-Tribune, Roseville, CA
Shaver, Gary .... (607) 324-1425
CIRC MGR, Evening Tribune, Hornell, NY
Hollinger International Inc.
Shaver, John .... (503) 382-1811
VP-FIN
Western Communications Inc., Bend, OR
Shaver, Linda .... (204) 694-2022
ADV MGR-CLASS Sales
Winnipeg Sun, Winnipeg, MB
Shaw, Andrea .... (504) 826-3279
MET ED-Night
Times-Picayune, New Orleans, LA
Shaw, Arthur .... (205) 549-2000
BUS/FIN ED, EPE, EDL Writer
Gadsden Times, Gadsden, AL
Shaw, Bill .... (206) 455-2222
ADV MGR-NTL
Eastside Journal, Bellevue, WA
Shaw, Bob .... (612) 222-5011
Senior ED-Arts & Entertainment
St. Paul Pioneer Press, St. Paul, MN
Knight-Ridder Inc.
Shaw, Charles R .... (717) 291-8811
News ED, Lancaster Intelligencer Journal/New Era/Sunday News, Lancaster, PA
Shaw, Dan .... (614) 283-4711
EX ED, Herald-Star, Steubenville, OH
Shaw, David .... (213) 237-5000
Media Critic
Los Angeles Times, Los Angeles, CA
Shaw, Deborah .... (610) 446-8700
PUB
News of Delaware County, Havertown, PA
Shaw, Donald .... (606) 329-1717
CIRC MGR, Daily Independent, Ashland, KY
Shaw, Donna .... (305) 674-9746
Arts DEPT
International News Agency, Miami Beach, FL
Shaw, E K .... (815) 284-4000
COB, Shaw Newspapers, Dixon, IL
Shaw, Eleanor .... (916) 321-1000
State ED, Sacramento Bee, Sacramento, CA
Shaw, James D .... (516) 843-2020
Senior VP-Finance/CFO
Newsday, Melville, NY
Shaw, Joe .... (814) 275-3131
ED, Leader-Vindicator, New Bethlehem, PA
Shaw, John .... (508) 343-6911
Online MGR
Sentinel & Enterprise, Fitchburg, MA
Shaw, John K .... (904) 252-1511
CIRC MGR-PROM/TELEMKTG/Customer Relations/TMC, Daytona Beach News-Journal, Daytona Beach, FL
Shaw, Kevin .... (219) 235-6161
CIRC ASST DIR, CIRC MGR-Alternate Delivery
South Bend Tribune, South Bend, IN
Shaw, Mark .... (614) 345-4053
BUS ED, Advocate, Newark, OH
Shaw, Matt .... (910) 576-6051
MAN ED, Montgomery Herald, Troy, NC
Shaw, Michele .... (412) 224-4321
DIR-Human Resources
Valley News Dispatch, Tarentum, PA
Shaw, Mike .... (317) 473-6641
Lifestyle ED, Peru Tribune, Peru, IN
Shaw, Paul .... (916) 842-5777
CIRC MGR, Siskiyou Daily News, Yreka, CA
Shaw, Robert A .... (815) 284-4000
VP, TREAS, Shaw Newspapers, Dixon, IL
Shaw, Rodney .... (806) 762-8844
PROD SUPT-PR
Lubbock Avalanche-Journal, Lubbock, TX
Shaw, Ron .... (616) 722-3161
PROD SUPT-MR
Muskegon Chronicle, Muskegon, MI
Shaw, Stanley .... (706) 884-7311
CIRC MGR, Daily News, La Grange, GA
Shaw, Stephen T .... (804) 649-6000
DIR-RES
Media General Inc., Richmond, VA
Shaw, Terry .... (716) 693-1000
ED, EPE
Tonawanda News, North Tonawanda, NY
Shaw, Thomas D .... (815) 284-4000
PRES/CEO, Shaw Newspapers, Dixon, IL
Shaw, Tom .... (304) 624-6411
PROD FRM-COMP (Exponent), Clarksburg Exponent/Telegram, Clarksburg, WV
Shaw, William E .... (815) 284-4000
VP, Shaw Newspapers, Dixon, IL
Shawgo, Carla .... (309) 647-5100
BM, DP MGR, Daily Ledger, Canton, IL
Shawl, Sherry .... (601) 287-6111
Society ED, Daily Corinthian, Corinth, MS
Shawrer, Sam .... (304) 788-3333
News ED, Wire ED
Mineral Daily News-Tribune, Keyser, WV
Shay, James .... (203) 333-0161
Norwalk/Westport ED
Connecticut Post, Bridgeport, CT
Shea, Bill .... (913) 762-5000
Political/Government
Daily Union, Junction City, KS
Shea, Dan .... (504) 826-3279
EX ED-News
Times-Picayune, New Orleans, LA
Shea, Darlene .... (902) 436-2121
MAN ED, Journal-Pioneer, Summerside, PEI
Shea, David .... (315) 393-1000
Sports ED, Courier-Observer Journal & The Advance-News, Ogdensburg, NY
Shea, Jeffrey L .... (412) 775-3200
PROD SUPV-Insert
Beaver County Times, Beaver, PA
Shea, Joe .... (513) 241-1450
PRES, Cincinnati Court Index, Cincinnati, OH
Shea, John .... (315) 393-1000
PROD FRM-MR, Courier-Observer Journal & The Advance-News, Ogdensburg, NY
Shea, Sandra .... (215) 854-2000
ASST MAN ED
Philadelphia Daily News, Philadelphia, PA
Shea, Tom .... (413) 788-1000
COL, Union-News, Springfield, MA
Sheaffer, Liz .... (330) 725-4166
MAN ED
Medina County Gazette, Medina, OH
Shealy, Ralph B .... (864) 445-2527
PUB, ED, Standard Sentinel, Saluda, SC
Shear, Irving .... (805) 238-6500
ED, North County Journal, Paso Robles, CA
Shear, Michael .... (213) 229-5300
CIRC MGR
Daily Commerce, Los Angeles, CA
Shearer, Alan .... (202) 334-6375
EDL DIR/GM, Washington Post Writers Group, Washington, DC

Copyright ©1997 by the Editor & Publisher Co.

209-Who's Where **She**

Shearer, Betty .... (601) 473-1473
GM
North Mississippi Herald, Water Valley, MS

Shearer, Connie .... (304) 348-5140
Fashion ED, Home Furnishings ED
Charleston Gazette, Charleston, WV

Shearer III, Ed .... (601) 473-1473
PUB, ED
North Mississippi Herald, Water Valley, MS

Shearer, Larry .... (308) 532-6000
PUB, Telegraph, North Platte, NE

Shearer, Lee .... (706) 549-0123
Environmental ED, Athens Daily News/Banner-Herald, Athens, GA

Shearer, Michael .... (513) 422-3611
City ED
Middletown Journal, Middletown, OH

Shearer, Richard .... (215) 855-8440
EPE, Reporter, Landsdale, PA

Shearlaw, Timothy .... (403) 443-5133
PUB, ED, Three Hills Capital, Three Hills, AB

Shearman Jr, Thomas B .... (318) 433-3000
VP, Shearman Newspapers, Lake Charles, LA

Shearman III, Thomas B .... (318) 433-3000
PRES
Shearman Newspapers, Lake Charles, LA

Shearn, Ian .... (201) 365-3000
VP/ED
North Jersey Herald & News, Passaic, NJ

Shearon, Robert .... (501) 295-2521
ED, Courier Index, Marianna, AR

Shearron, Betsy .... (706) 549-0123
MET ED, Athens Daily News/Banner-Herald, Athens, GA

Shears, Mary Deanne .... (416) 367-2000
Deputy MAN ED-News
Toronto Star, Toronto, ON

Sheasly, Barbara J .... (412) 543-1303
ADV DIR, Leader Times, Kittanning, PA

Sheau, Phil .... (215) 855-8440
DIR-PSL, Reporter, Landsdale, PA

Shebshaivitz, Marilyn .... (914) 423-5009
ED, Jewish Chronicle, Yonkers, NY

Shects, Pam .... (219) 533-2151
BM, Goshen News, Goshen, IN

Shedd, Aileen .... (517) 269-6461
Online/New Media MGR, ADTX MGR
Huron Daily Tribune, Bad Axe, MI

Sheddy, O R .... (403) 823-2580
PUB, ED, Drumheller Mail, Drumheller, AB

Sheedy, Kevin .... (316) 268-6000
Leisure ED, Wichita Eagle, Wichita, KS

Sheedy Jr, William E .... (860) 241-6200
ASSOC PUB-Middlesex County
Hartford Courant, Hartford, CT

Sheehan, Kevin .... (908) 775-0007
GM, Ocean Grove & Neptune Times, Ocean Grove, NJ

Sheehan, Michael S .... (860) 225-4601
CIRC DIR, Herald, New Britain, CT

Sheehan, Robert .... (617) 426-3000
ADV MGR-RT, Boston Herald, Boston, MA

Sheehan, Shaun M .... (312) 222-3237
VP-Washington, Tribune Co., Chicago, IL

Sheehan, Tim .... (209) 896-1976
ED, Selma Enterprise, Selma, CA

Sheehan, Tom .... (414) 728-3411
ED, Delavan Enterprise, Delavan, WI

Sheehy, Bill .... (541) 447-6205
MAN ED
Prineville Central Oregonian, Prineville, OR

Sheehy, Mike .... (513) 863-8200
City ED, Journal-News, Hamilton, OH

Sheely, Dennis .... (717) 829-7100
ADV VP/DIR, Times Leader, Wilkes-Barre, PA

Sheenan, Mark .... (816) 271-8500
EPE, St. Joseph News-Press, St. Joseph, MO

Sheer, Jonathan R .... (416) 814-4239
VP-Electronic Products
Thomson Newspapers, Toronto, ON

Sheeran, Owen .... (909) 889-9666
Travel ED, Sun, San Bernardino, CA

Sheeran, Patrick C .... (603) 668-4321
City ED, Union Leader, Manchester, NH

Sheets, Christopher .... (912) 924-2751
Reporter
Americus Times-Recorder, Americus, GA

Sheets, Jocelyn .... (316) 365-2111
Photo ED, Sports ED
Iola Register, Iola, KS

Sheets, Les .... (817) 387-3811
PROD FRM-COMP
Denton Record-Chronicle, Denton, TX

Sheil, Tim .... (773) 586-8800
News ED, Daily Southtown, Chicago, IL

Shelburne, Anita .... (804) 978-7200
EPE, Daily Progress, Charlottesville, VA

Shelby, Barry .... (212) 889-5155
Senior ED
World Press Review, New York, NY

Shelby, Ken .... (614) 345-4053
PROD MGR, Advocate, Newark, OH

Sheldon, Janice .... (310) 540-5511
ADV MGR-RT, Daily Breeze, Torrance, CA
Copley Press Inc.

Sheldon, Keith .... (716) 366-3000
ED, MAN ED, EDU ED, Regional ED
Evening Observer, Dunkirk, NY

Sheldon, Kenneth .... (814) 723-8200
PROD FRM-PR
Warren Times-Observer, Warren, PA

Sheldon, Richard .... (918) 786-9002
CIRC MGR, Grove Daily News, Grove, OK

Shelds, Rose .... (609) 871-8000
Photo Chief
Burlington County Times, Willingboro, NJ

Sheley, Gene .... (916) 842-5777
GEN Reporting
Siskiyou Daily News, Yreka, CA

Sheley, John .... (618) 357-2811
ED, Pinckneyville Democrat, Pinckneyville, IL

Shell, Don .... (616) 842-6400
Sports ED, Tribune, Grand Haven, MI

Shell, Henrietta Hayward .... (615) 256-8288
GM, Nashville Record, Nashville, TN

Shell, Laura .... (716) 232-6920
ADV MGR, Daily Record, Rochester, NY

Shellborn, Daryl .... (604) 489-3455
ED, MAN ED
Kootenay Advertiser, Cranbrook, BC

Shelledy, James E .... (801) 237-2031
ED, Salt Lake Tribune, Salt Lake City, UT

Shellenberger, Janice B .... (610) 820-6500
Neighbors CNR, Morning Call, Allentown, PA

Shelley, David .... (910) 353-1171
Entertainment/Amusements ED, Home Furnishings ED, Television ED
Daily News, Jacksonville, NC

Shelley, Susan .... (818) 884-7137
Self-Syndicator, tidbits, Woodland Hills, CA

Shelline, Stewart .... (801) 237-2188
DIR-INFO SRV
Deseret News, Salt Lake City, UT

Shelling, Dave .... (619) 299-3131
SYS ED
San Diego Union-Tribune, San Diego, CA

Shellman, Roger F .... (414) 846-3427
PUB, ED, Oconto County Times-Herald, Oconto Falls, WI

Shellock, Marie .... (330) 747-1471
Religion ED, Vindicator, Youngstown, OH

Shelly, Peter .... (412) 263-1100
Harrisburg BU, Post-Gazette, Pittsburgh, PA

Shelton, A B .... (915) 673-4271
COB, Abilene Reporter-News, Abilene, TX

Shelton Jr, Barrett C .... (205) 353-4612
PRES/PUB, Decatur Daily, Decatur, AL

Shelton, Brenda .... (573) 765-3391
GM, Richland Mirror, Richland, MO

Shelton, Charles E .... (212) 556-1234
CIRC VP-Distribution
New York Times, New York, NY

Shelton, Clint .... (205) 353-4612
ADTX MGR, PROD MGR
Decatur Daily, Decatur, AL

Shelton, David .... (706) 695-4646
PUB, ED
Chatsworth Times, Chatsworth, GA

Shelton, Don .... (206) 464-2111
ASST Sports ED, Seattle Times, Seattle, WA

Shelton, Georgia T .... (205) 353-4612
SEC/TREAS, Decatur Daily, Decatur, AL

Shelton, J Kay .... (765) 362-1200
BM, Journal Review, Crawfordsville, IN

Shelton, Joe .... (573) 364-2468
CIRC SUPV, Rolla Daily News, Rolla, MO

Shelton Jr, Joe W .... (219) 868-5501
PUB, ED, Butler Bulletin, Butler, IN

Shelton, Keith A .... (804) 572-3945
PUB, ED, South Boston Gazette-Virginian, South Boston, VA

Shelton, Norm .... (204) 694-2022
CONT, Winnipeg Sun, Winnipeg, MB

Shelton, Sam .... (618) 993-2626
PUB, Marion Daily Republican, Marion, IL

Shelton, Scott .... (618) 993-2626
CIRC MGR
Marion Daily Republican, Marion, IL

Shelton, Shelley .... (501) 741-2325
Entertainment/Amusements ED, Television/Film ED, Theater/Music ED
Harrison Daily Times, Harrison, AR

Shelton, Steve .... (618) 993-2626
PROD MGR
Marion Daily Republican, Marion, IL

Shelton, Tony .... (219) 461-8333
ADTX MGR, Journal Gazette, Fort Wayne, IN

Shelton, Tony .... (309) 764-4344
ADV DIR-Sales, Dispatch, Moline, IL
Small Newspaper Group Inc.

Shemanske, Susan .... (414) 634-3322
Sports ED, Journal Times, Racine, WI

Shemely, Larry .... (970) 247-3504
CIRC MGR, Durango Herald, Durango, CO

Shen, Catherine .... (206) 872-6600
ED/VP-News
South County Journal, Kent, WA

Shenefelt, Mark .... (801) 625-4200
ASST MAN ED
Standard-Examiner, Ogden, UT

Shenk, Willis W .... (717) 291-8811
BC, Lancaster Intelligencer Journal/New Era/Sunday News, Lancaster, PA

Shenkman, Jennifer .... (941) 294-7731
Food ED, Lifestyle ED
News Chief, Winter Haven, FL

Shennan, George .... (803) 771-6161
ADV MGR-NTL, State, Columbia, SC

Shepard, Charles B .... (601) 786-3661
ED, Fayette Chronicle, Fayette, MS

Shepard, Charles K .... (601) 786-3661
PUB, Fayette Chronicle, Fayette, MS

Shepard, Donald D .... (513) 721-2700
ADV MGR-SRV
Cincinnati Enquirer, Cincinnati, OH

Shepard, Jan .... (307) 362-3736
CIRC MGR
Daily Rocket-Miner, Rock Springs, WY

Shepard, Kathy .... (864) 582-4511
ADV MGR-CLASS
Herald-Journal, Spartanburg, SC

Shepard, Michael .... (360) 308-9161
PUB, Central Kitsap Reporter, Silverdale, WA

Shepard, Terence .... (561) 395-8300
Local ED, News, Boca Raton, FL

Shepard, Wayne .... (508) 793-9100
PROD MGR-MR
Telegram & Gazette, Worcester, MA

Shephard, Doug .... (419) 886-2291
MAN ED
Bellville Star & Tri-Forks Press, Bellville, OH

Shepherd, Angie .... (613) 591-3060
PUB, Kanata Kourier-Standard, Kanata, ON

Shepherd, Barb .... (904) 734-4622
ED, DeLand Beacon/West Volusia Beacon, DeLand, FL

Shepherd, Dan .... (301) 670-1400
Sports ED
Montgomery Journal, Rockville, MD

Shepherd, Edith .... (307) 756-3371
PUB, ED, Moorcroft Leader, Moorcroft, WY

Shepherd, Harvey .... (514) 987-2222
Religion Reporter, Gazette, Montreal, QC

Shepherd, Janice .... (606) 886-8506
MAN ED
Floyd County Times, Prestonsburg, KY

Shepherd, Lee .... (607) 798-1234
Fashion ED
Press & Sun Bulletin, Binghamton, NY

Shepherd, Leslie .... (306) 692-6441
City ED
Moose Jaw Times-Herald, Moose Jaw, SK

Shepherd, Mike .... (609) 272-7000
Sports ED
Press of Atlantic City, Pleasantville, NJ

Shepherd, Patt .... (815) 273-2277
GM, Savanna Times-Journal, Savanna, IL

Shepherd, Richard .... (502) 886-4444
PROD SUPT
Kentucky New Era, Hopkinsville, KY

Shepherd, Steve .... (617) 786-7000
News ED-Night, Patriot Ledger, Quincy, MA

Sheppard, Andy .... (813) 259-7711
PROD MGR-Night
Tampa Tribune and Times, Tampa, FL

Sheppard, David .... (915) 546-6100
Environmental ED, SCI/Technology ED
El Paso Times, El Paso, TX

Sheppard, Jack .... (813) 893-8111
ASST MAN ED-Sports
St. Petersburg Times, St. Petersburg, FL

Sheppard, Mike .... (906) 774-2772
PRES/CEO (Great Lakes Group)
Daily News, Iron Mountain, MI

Sheppard, Roy .... (404) 526-5151
ADV MGR-RT/Major Account Sales
Atlanta Journal-Constitution, Atlanta, GA

Sheppard, Tom .... (404) 526-5151
CIRC MGR-State
Atlanta Journal-Constitution, Atlanta, GA

Sheppard-Borton, Corrine .... (609) 691-5000
Living ED, Daily Journal, Vineland, NJ

Shepperd, Wayne J .... (203) 744-5100
PUB, News-Times, Danbury, CT

Sher, Gerald .... (617) 426-3000
CIRC MGR-Home Delivery
Boston Herald, Boston, MA

Sher, Louis Y .... (972) 234-6161
Owner/PRES, Witzzle Co., Richardson, TX

Sherbo, Jo .... (402) 564-2741
ADV DIR, Columbus Telegram, Columbus, NE

Sherborne, Robert .... (615) 259-8000
Regional ED-Day, Tennessean, Nashville, TN

Sherer, Valerie .... (205) 766-3434
Librarian, Times Daily, Florence, AL

Sheridan, Christianne .... (216) 999-4500
ASSOC ED, Plain Dealer, Cleveland, OH

Sheridan, Dan .... (607) 547-2545
ED, Freeman's Journal, Cooperstown, NY

Sheridan, Martha .... (214) 977-8222
Home/Garden ED
Dallas Morning News, Dallas, TX

Sheridan, Tom .... (312) 321-3000
EDL Board Member/EDL Writer
Chicago Sun-Times, Chicago, IL

Sheriff, Gary .... (717) 648-4641
PROD FRM-PR, News-Item, Shamokin, PA

Sheriff, Stephen H .... (330) 996-3000
ASST TREAS
Akron Beacon Journal, Akron, OH
Knight-Ridder Inc.

Sherker, RJ .... (305) 674-9746
EX ED
International News Agency, Miami Beach, FL

Sherle, Pat .... (406) 265-6795
ADV Representative-NTL/Regional
Havre Daily News, Havre, MT

Sherlock, Donald J .... (201) 646-4000
VP-Product SRV, Record, Hackensack, NJ

Sherlock, Gary F .... (703) 284-6000
Group PRES-Atlantic Newspaper Group
Gannett Co. Inc., Arlington, VA

Sherlock, John .... (215) 854-2000
Graphics ED
Philadelphia Daily News, Philadelphia, PA

Sherlock, Mark .... (308) 762-3060
PROD MGR
Alliance Times-Herald, Alliance, NE

Sherman Jr, Albert K .... (401) 849-3300
PRES, PUB
Newport Daily News, Newport, RI

Sherman, Bruce H .... (401) 849-3300
SEC, Newport Daily News, Newport, RI

Sherman, Charles .... (608) 252-6400
City ED, Capital Times, Madison, WI

Sherman, Chris .... (813) 893-8111
Food ED
St. Petersburg Times, St. Petersburg, FL

Sherman, Dale .... (540) 574-6200
PROD SUPV-PR
Daily News-Record, Harrisonburg, VA

Sherman, Dale .... (518) 584-4242
PROD FRM-PR
Saratogian, Saratoga Springs, NY

Sherman, Darwin K .... (319) 653-2191
PRES, PUB/GM, PA
Washington Evening Journal, Washington, IA
Inland Industries Inc.

Sherman, Dave .... (716) 632-4700
MAN ED, East Aurora Bee, Buffalo, NY

Sherman, Debra A .... (914) 341-1100
DIR-Human Resources
Times Herald-Record, Middletown, NY

Sherman Jr, James A .... (810) 653-3511
PUB, Davison Index, Davison, MI

Sherman, Joseph .... (312) 321-3000
ASST PUB
Chicago Sun-Times, Chicago, IL

Sherman, Joseph .... (508) 586-7200
Amusements ED, Features ED, Sunday ED
Enterprise, Brockton, MA

Sherman, Joseph R .... (218) 547-1000
PUB, Pilot-Independent, Walker, MN

Sherman, Mike .... (315) 792-5000
Sports ED, Observer-Dispatch, Utica, NY

Sherman, Paula .... (815) 284-2222
Fashion/Women's ED, Food/Home Furnishings ED, Living/Lifestyle ED, Society ED, Travel ED, Telegraph, Dixon, IL

Sherman, Randy .... (619) 922-3181
ED, Palo Verde Valley Times, Blythe, CA

Sherman, Richard M .... (612) 469-2181
PUB, ED
Lakeville Life & Times, Lakeville, MN

Sherman, Sharon .... (610) 696-1775
ADV MGR-RT
Daily Local News, West Chester, PA

Sherman, William E .... (401) 596-7791
PUB, Westerly Sun, Westerly, RI

Sheroan, Ben .... (304) 485-1891
ED, Parkersburg News & Sentinel, Parkersburg, WV

Sherrer, Pauline D .... (615) 484-5145
PUB, Crossville Chronicle, Crossville, TN

Sherrill, Thomas B .... (614) 461-5000
VP-MKTG
Columbus Dispatch, Columbus, OH

Sherrington, Al .... (206) 464-2111
PROD MGR-PR, Seattle Times, Seattle, WA

Sherrington, Kevin .... (214) 977-8222
COL-SportsDay
Dallas Morning News, Dallas, TX

Sherrod, Blackie .... (214) 977-8222
COL-SportsDay
Dallas Morning News, Dallas, TX

Sherrod, James .... (405) 363-3370
CIRC MGR, Journal-Tribune, Blackwell, OK

Sherrow, Rita .... (918) 581-8300
Radio/Television ED, Tulsa World, Tulsa, OK

Sherry, Lowell .... (902) 893-9405
CIRC MGR, Daily News, Truro, NS

Sherry, Mark .... (414) 898-4276
PUB, ED
New Holstein Reporter, New Holstein, WI

She Who's Where-210

Sherry, Mike .... (414) 235-7700
Sports ED
Oshkosh Northwestern, Oshkosh, WI
Sherwood, Joan .... (404) 876-1819
MAN ED, Southern Voice, Atlanta, GA
Sherwood, John .... (616) 964-7161
EPE, Battle Creek Enquirer, Battle Creek, MI
Sherwood, Rick .... (406) 265-6795
CIRC DIR, Havre Daily News, Havre, MT
Sheth, Priyanka .... (501) 534-3400
Features ED, Religion ED
Pine Bluff Commercial, Pine Bluff, AR
Sheue, Bob .... (303) 820-1010
Travel ED, Denver Post, Denver, CO
Shewnarain, Manita .... (416) 494-4990
ADV Inside Sales MGR, Daily Commercial News and Construction Record, N. York, ON
Shidemantle, Dale .... (814) 870-1600
BUS ED
Morning News/Erie Daily Times, Erie, PA
Shiel, Thomas .... (860) 347-3331
ED, Middlesex Express, Middletown, CT
Shields, Jan .... (518) 270-1200
City ED (Night), Record, Troy, NY
Shields, Jim .... (707) 984-6223
PUB, ED
Mendocino County Observer, Laytonville, CA
Shields, John .... (805) 925-2691
PUB, Santa Maria Times, Santa Maria, CA
Shields, Mitchell .... (713) 624-1400
MAN ED, Houston Press, Houston, TX
Shields, Robert .... (609) 989-7800
News ED, Trentonian, Trenton, NJ
Shiemo, John .... (517) 265-5111
Farm/County ED, Daily Telegram, Adrian, MI
Shikoski, Dick .... (414) 733-4411
CONT, Post-Crescent, Appleton, WI
Shilling, Don .... (330) 747-1471
Farm/Agriculture ED
Vindicator, Youngstown, OH
Shillingburg, Dan L .... (614) 224-4835
VP/GM, Daily Reporter, Columbus, OH
Shillington, Doug .... (250) 380-5211
PROD FRM-PR, Times Colonist, Victoria, BC
Shima, Jolene .... (406) 862-3505
GM, Whitefish Pilot, Whitefish, MT
Shimono, Larry .... (715) 229-2103
PUB, ED, O-W Enterprise, Withee, WI
Shina, Merrie .... (616) 964-7161
CIRC MGR-Home Delivery
Battle Creek Enquirer, Battle Creek, MI
Shinaut, Jerry .... (602) 271-8000
PROD CNR-Quality Assurance
Phoenix Newspapers Inc., Phoenix, AZ
Shine, Eve .... (807) 597-2731
PUB, Atikokan Progress, Atikokan, ON
Shine, James .... (419) 223-1010
ADV DIR, Lima News, Lima, OH
Shine, Tom .... (316) 268-6000
Sports ED, Wichita Eagle, Wichita, KS
Shiner, Josette .... (202) 636-3000
MAN ED, Washington Times, Washington, DC
Shingler, Judy .... (414) 235-7700
ADV MGR-PROM
Oshkosh Northwestern, Oshkosh, WI
Shingler, Mark .... (414) 235-7700
ADV MGR-CLASS
Oshkosh Northwestern, Oshkosh, WI
Shinneman, Sue .... (520) 645-8888
PUB, Lake Powell Chronicle, Page, AZ
Shinohara, Rosemary .... (907) 257-4200
EDU Reporter
Anchorage Daily News, Anchorage, AK
Shinske, Stuart .... (914) 454-2000
News ED-Night
Poughkeepsie Journal, Poughkeepsie, NY
Shintaku, Howard .... (916) 321-1000
Art DIR, Sacramento Bee, Sacramento, CA
Shiplett Jr, David H .... (540) 574-6200
PROD DIR
Daily News-Record, Harrisonburg, VA
Shipman, Neal A .... (701) 842-2351
PUB, ED
McKenzie County Farmer, Watford City, ND
Shippee, Jeff .... (603) 863-1776
ED, Argus-Champion, Newport, NH
Shipps, Jean .... (402) 873-3334
PROD SUPT
Nebraska City News-Press, Nebraska City, NE
Shiraishi, Al .... (250) 380-5211
DIR-FIN, Times Colonist, Victoria, BC
Shirk, Steve .... (816) 234-4141
Weekend ED
Kansas City Star, Kansas City, MO
Shirley, Andy .... (504) 384-8370
GM/ADV DIR, Morgan City Newspapers Inc., Morgan City, LA
Shirley, Doyle E .... (504) 384-8370
Owner/PRES/PUB, Morgan City Newspapers Inc., Morgan City, LA
Shirley, Julie .... (916) 741-2345
ED, EPE, Appeal-Democrat, Marysville, CA
Shirley, Red .... (504) 384-8370
MGR-MKTG/PROM
Daily Review, Morgan City, LA
Shirley, Steve .... (406) 791-1444
Projects ED, Tribune, Great Falls, MT
Shirley, Steve .... (504) 384-8370
ED/ASSOC PUB, Morgan City Newspapers Inc., Morgan City, LA
Shitut, Prashant B .... (717) 829-7100
VP-INFO SYS & Technology
Times Leader, Wilkes-Barre, PA
Shively, Chris .... (713) 220-7171
International ED
Houston Chronicle, Houston, TX
Shiver Jr, Jube .... (213) 237-5000
Telecommunications/Regulation & Policy-D.C., Los Angeles Times, Los Angeles, CA
Shiver, Leo .... (706) 324-5526
PROD MGR, Ledger-Enquirer, Columbus, GA
Shiver, William .... (212) 450-7000
Southeastern MGR/Newspaper Relations
Parade Publications Inc., New York, NY
Shiverdecker, Jerry .... (601) 773-6241
PUB, ED
Winston County Journal, Louisville, MS
Shivers, Gary .... (609) 272-7000
Photo ED
Press of Atlantic City, Pleasantville, NJ
Shmidheiser, Ken .... (606) 376-5356/5357
ED
McCreary County Record, Whitley City, KY
Shockey, Dennis .... (717) 762-2151
MGR-EDU SRV, ADV MGR
Record Herald, Waynesboro, PA
Shockley, Martha .... (402) 993-2205
GM, Genoa Leader-Times, Genoa, NE
Shockley, Shelley .... (216) 791-7600
ED, Call and Post, Cleveland, OH
Shockman, Luke .... (507) 285-7600
Medical/SCI ED
Post-Bulletin, Rochester, MN
Shoemaker, Darrell .... (541) 474-3700
PROD FRM-PR
Grants Pass Daily Courier, Grants Pass, OR
Shoemaker, Dixon .... (509) 582-1500
ADV MGR-Sales
Tri-City Herald, Tri-Cities, WA
Shoemaker, Nancy .... (816) 258-7237
CIRC MGR
Daily News-Bulletin, Brookfield, MO
Shoemaker, Stefana H .... (717) 928-8136
PUB, ED, Sullivan Review, Dushore, PA
Shoemaker, Steve .... (205) 345-0505
CONT, Tuscaloosa News, Tuscaloosa, AL
Shoemaker, T W .... (717) 928-8136
PUB, Sullivan Review, Dushore, PA
Shoenfeld, Ed .... (907) 586-3740
News ED, Juneau Empire, Juneau, AK
Shogan, Robert .... (213) 237-5000
Political Writer-D.C.
Los Angeles Times, Los Angeles, CA
Shokrian, Michael .... (415) 465-3121
ED, Inter-City Express, Oakland, CA
Sholar, Larry .... (502) 443-1771
PROD MGR, Paducah Sun, Paducah, KY
Sholes, Carol .... (315) 470-0011
DIR-INFO SYS, Post-Standard/Syracuse Herald-Journal/American, Syracuse, NY
Sholette, Robert .... (315) 782-1000
ADV MGR-NTL/Co-op
Watertown Daily Times, Watertown, NY
Sholin, Roz .... (305) 674-9746
Food
International News Agency, Miami Beach, FL
Sholin, Terry .... (505) 393-2123
COL, News ED, News/Regional ED
Hobbs Daily News-Sun, Hobbs, NM
Sholly, Gene .... (717) 272-5611
Art DIR, Graphics ED
Daily News, Lebanon, PA
Shonce, Glen .... (330) 332-4601
PROD FRM-PR, Salem News, Salem, OH
Shook, Dean .... (216) 329-7000
PROD SUPT-PR
Chronicle-Telegram, Elyria, OH
Shook, Melvin K .... (216) 329-7000
PROD SUPT, Chronicle-Telegram, Elyria, OH
Shook, Sandra .... (704) 264-3612
MAN ED, Watauga Democrat, Boone, NC
Shook, Ted .... (317) 664-5111
PROD MGR-Distribution
Chronicle-Tribune, Marion, IN
Shoopman, Don .... (318) 365-6773
News ED, Wire ED
Daily Iberian, New Iberia, LA
Shope, Don .... (803) 775-6331
PROD FRM-PR, Item, Sumter, SC
Shor, Gal .... (818) 783-3090
MAN ED, Shalom L.A., Van Nuys, CA
Shore, Donna .... (212) 755-4363
Contributing Writer
Punch In Travel & Entertainment News Syndicate, New York, NY
Shore, Randy .... (604) 437-7030
MAN ED, Vancouver Echo, Vancouver, BC
Shores, Jack D .... (330) 833-2631
PUB, Independent, Massillon, OH
Shores, Larry .... (317) 747-5700
COL, EPE, EDL Writer
Star Press, Muncie, IN
Shorey III, H A .... (207) 647-2851
PUB, Bridgton News, Bridgton, ME
Shorey, Stephen E .... (207) 647-2851
GM, Bridgton News, Bridgton, ME
Shors, David .... (406) 447-4000
City ED
Helena Independent Record, Helena, MT
Short, Alice .... (213) 237-5000
Life/Style ED
Los Angeles Times, Los Angeles, CA
Short, Chris .... (515) 782-2141
Sports ED, News-Advertiser, Creston, IA
Short, Gina .... (606) 248-1010
Bookkeeper, Daily News, Middlesboro, KY
Short, Joseph .... (401) 277-7000
PROD MGR-Properties
Providence Journal-Bulletin, Providence, RI
Short, Lisa L .... (614) 435-3531
ED
New Concord Area Leader, Cambridge, OH
Short, Raymond .... (606) 248-1010
MAN ED
Middlesboro Daily News, Middlesboro, KY
Short, Robin .... (709) 364-6300
Sports ED, Evening Telegram, St. John's, NF
Shorter, Dan .... (561) 820-4100
DIR-New Ventures
Palm Beach Post, West Palm Beach, FL
Shorts, Gary F .... (213) 237-3700
PUB/CEO-Morning Call
Times Mirror Co., Los Angeles, CA
Shorts, T Mark .... (614) 592-6612
CIRC MGR, Athens Messenger, Athens, OH
Shoup, Michael .... (201) 877-4141
Travel ED, Star-Ledger, Newark, NJ
Shover, William R .... (602) 271-8000
DIR-Public Affairs
Phoenix Newspapers Inc., Phoenix, AZ
Showalter, Doug .... (812) 372-7811
Regional ED, Republic, Columbus, IN
Showalter, Nelson H .... (319) 754-8461
SEC, ADV DIR, Hawk Eye, Burlington, IA
Showell, Philip .... (908) 722-8800
EPE, Courier-News, Bridgewater, NJ
Showers, Dean .... (715) 356-5236
ED, Lakeland Times, Minocqua, WI
Showley, Ryan N .... (219) 223-2111
ADV DIR, Rochester Sentinel, Rochester, IN
Shown, George .... (219) 881-3000
PROD DIR, Post-Tribune, Gary, IN
Shows, Susan .... (713) 220-7171
DIR-INFO/Technology Resources, PROD DIR-INFO/Technology Resources
Houston Chronicle, Houston, TX
Shows, Thurman .... (601) 582-4321
PROD MGR-PR
Hattiesburg American, Hattiesburg, MS
Shprintz, Janet .... (213) 229-5300
ED
Los Angeles Daily Journal, Los Angeles, CA
Shrader, Greg .... (210) 896-7000
ED/PUB, Kerrville Daily Times, Kerrville, TX
Shrader, James .... (330) 364-5577
PRES/PUB
Times Reporter, New Philadelphia, OH
Shraluka, Robert W .... (219) 724-2121
MAN ED
Decatur Daily Democrat, Decatur, IN
Shreeves, Susan .... (803) 785-4293
BM, Island Packet, Hilton Head, SC
Shreve, Donald L .... (812) 482-2424
ADV MGR, Herald, Jasper, IN
Shrewsbury, Danny .... (715) 842-2101
CIRC MGR
Wausau Daily Herald, Wausau, WI
Shrewsbury, Jeff .... (803) 524-3183
Sports ED, Beaufort Gazette, Beaufort, SC
Shrewsbury, Walt .... (803) 626-8555
PROD MGR-Packaging
Sun News, Myrtle Beach, SC
Shribman, David .... (617) 929-2000
BU Chief-Washington
Boston Globe, Boston, MA
Shrimpton, Helen L .... (516) 739-6400
ED
Rockville Centre News & Owl, Mineola, NY
Shriner, Lori .... (402) 643-3676
GM, ED
Seward County Independent, Seward, NE
Shriver, Greg .... (414) 922-4600
Sports ED, Reporter, Fond du Lac, WI
Shriver, Stephen .... (319) 878-4111
PUB, GM, ED, Van Buren County Leader-Record, Farmington, IA
Shriver, William .... (212) 450-7000
VP/Southeastern MGR/Newspaper Relations
React, New York, NY
Shrock, Dan .... (503) 472-5114
MAN ED
McMinnville News-Register, McMinnville, OR
Shroder, Tom .... (305) 350-2111
Sunday Magazine (Tropic) ED
Miami Herald, Miami, FL
Shubert, Dave .... (614) 342-4121
GM
Perry County Tribune, New Lexington, OH
Shubert, Frank .... (817) 697-6671
PUB, ED, Cameron Herald, Cameron, TX
Shuchman, Lisa .... (561) 820-4100
Farm/Agriculture ED
Palm Beach Post, West Palm Beach, FL
Shuck, W Ferrell .... (816) 524-2345
PUB
Lee's Summit Journal, Lee's Summit, MO
Shuckhart, Bob .... (206) 597-8742
ADV MGR-NTL, News Tribune, Tacoma, WA
Shue, Hal .... (616) 683-2100
ADV MGR-CLASS
Niles Daily Star, Niles, MI
Shuemake, Jim .... (501) 378-3400
PROD MGR-Technical Support
Arkansas Democrat-Gazette, Little Rock, AR
Shuftan, Frank S .... (708) 755-6161
MAN ED
Chicago Heights Star, Chicago Heights, IL
Shula, Jeff .... (207) 942-2913
ED, Weekly, Bangor, ME
Shuler, Al .... (614) 461-5000
PROD MGR-Color
Columbus Dispatch, Columbus, OH
Shulgasser, Barbara .... (415) 777-2424
Movie Critic
San Francisco Examiner, San Francisco, CA
Shulgold, Mark .... (303) 892-5000
Music Critic
Rocky Mountain News, Denver, CO
Shull, Mickey .... (803) 771-6161
CIRC DIR, State, Columbia, SC
Shulman, Rich .... (206) 339-3000
Photo ED, Herald, Everett, WA
Shulman, Stan .... (602) 468-6565
VP-Printing, Daily Racing Form, Phoenix, AZ
Shult, Eric .... (360) 424-3251
PROD MGR
Skagit Valley Herald, Mount Vernon, WA
Shults, J W .... (309) 432-2505
ED, Minonk News-Dispatch, Minonk, IL
Shultz, Anette .... (405) 824-2171
ED, Woods County Enterprise, Waynoka, OK
Shultz, Beverly .... (317) 932-2222
PUB, Rushville Republican, Rushville, IN
Shultz, Charles R .... (405) 526-3392
PUB, ED
Beckham County Democrat, Erick, OK
Shultz, Craig .... (909) 487-2200
ED, Hemet News, Hemet, CA
Shultz, Dave .... (815) 987-1200
Neighbors ED
Rockford Register Star, Rockford, IL
Shultz, Helen .... (405) 526-3392
PUB, ED
Beckham County Democrat, Erick, OK
Shultz, Jeff .... (405) 824-2171
PUB
Woods County Enterprise, Waynoka, OK
Shultz, Joe .... (319) 588-5611
CIRC DIR, PROD MGR-MR
Telegraph Herald, Dubuque, IA
Shultz, Lea .... (606) 623-1669
ASST ED, Richmond Register, Richmond, KY
Shultz, Michael .... (410) 332-6000
MGR-Communication/RES
Sun, Baltimore, MD
Shuma, Michael .... (814) 948-6210
GM, Barnesboro Star, Barnesboro, PA
Shumake, Rodney .... (770) 428-9411
ED, East Cobb Neighbor, Marietta, GA
Shumaker, Scott .... (814) 634-8321
ED, New Republic, Meyersdale, PA
Shuman, Eric L .... (416) 814-4239
Sr VP/CFO
Thomson Newspapers, Toronto, ON
Shumate, Rodney .... (770) 428-9411
Online MGR, Daily Journal, Marietta, GA
Shumway, Bill .... (315) 265-2068
PUB, North Country This Week, Potsdam, NY
Shupe, Andy .... (501) 442-1777
Photo DEPT MGR
Northwest Arkansas Times, Fayetteville, AR
Shur, Ed .... (702) 788-6200
Sunday ED, Reno Gazette-Journal, Reno, NV
Shur, Ronald S .... (800) 939-NFNS (6367)
CEO, National Financial News Service, West Chester, PA
Shurett, Ben .... (205) 845-2550
PUB, Times Journal, Fort Payne, AL
Shurley, Richard .... (504) 383-1111
DIR-INFO, Advocate, Baton Rouge, LA
Shustak, Bernadette .... (914) 855-1100
MAN ED, News-Chronicle, Pawling, NY
Shuster, Bill .... (615) 526-9715
PUB, Herald-Citizen, Cookeville, TN

211-Who's Where **Sim**

Shuster, Larry (412) 543-1303
DIR-MKTG/PROM
Leader Times, Kittanning, PA
Shutt, Linda (905) 684-7251
EDU, Standard, St. Catharines, ON
Sias, John B (415) 777-7444
PRES/CEO
Chronicle Publishing Co., San Francisco, CA
Siba, Tom (604) 946-4451
PUB, Delta Optimist, Delta, BC
Sibley, Celestine (404) 526-5151
COL, Journal-Constitution, Atlanta, GA
Siburt, Debrah (715) 842-2101
Librarian, Wausau Daily Herald, Wausau, WI
Sicard, Pam (802) 863-3441
ADV MGR-CLASS
Burlington Free Press, Burlington, VT
Siccardi, Joseph L (315) 568-6400
PUB
Reveille/Between the Lakes, Seneca Falls, NY
Siceloff, Bruce (919) 829-4500
New Media ED
News & Observer, Raleigh, NC
Siciliano, Michael D (413) 788-1000
PROD MGR-SYS, PROD SUPV-COMP
Union-News, Springfield, MA
Siciliano, Sam (908) 922-6000
ADV MGR-Local
Asbury Park Press, Neptune, NJ
Sickafus, Karl (610) 696-1775
DP MGR, PROD MGR-COMP
Daily Local News, West Chester, PA
Sickels, Daniel L (614) 461-5000
DIR-Maintenance/Engineering
Columbus Dispatch, Columbus, OH
Sickle, Kenneth H (304) 455-3300
PUB, Wetzel Chronicle, New Martinsville, WV
Sickler, Dale A (308) 237-2152
PROD MGR, Kearney Hub, Kearney, NE
Sickler, Linda (618) 529-5454
Entertainment/Amusements ED, Television/Film ED, Theater/Music ED
Southern Illinoisan, Carbondale, IL
Sicola, Michelle (304) 292-6301
CIRC MGR-PROM
Dominion Post, Morgantown, WV
Sidbury, Dan (310) 829-6811
CIRC MGR, Outlook, Santa Monica, CA
Siddiqui, Haroon (416) 367-2000
EPE, Toronto Star, Toronto, ON
Siddons, Brad (717) 248-6741
MAN ED, COL, EPE, Sentinel, Lewistown, PA
Sidey, Kenneth H (515) 743-6121
PUB, ED
Adair County Free Press, Greenfield, IA
Sidhu, Joella (705) 325-1355
Food/Garden ED, Home ED, Medical/Health ED, Teenage Youth/Women's ED, Travel ED
Packet & Times, Orillia, ON
Sidlo, Steve (937) 225-2000
MAN ED, Dayton Daily News, Dayton, OH
Siebeneck, Rob (573) 636-3131
CIRC MGR, News Tribune, Jefferson City, MO
Siedlik, Lawrence E (561) 820-4100
VP/TREAS
Palm Beach Post, West Palm Beach, FL
Sieg, Pam (541) 776-4411
Librarian, Mail Tribune, Medford, OR
Siegal, Allan M (212) 556-1234
ASST MAN ED
New York Times, New York, NY
Siegel, Edward (617) 929-2000
Drama ED, Boston Globe, Boston, MA
Siegel, Gary (707) 441-0500
ADV MGR, Times-Standard, Eureka, CA
Siegel, Harris (908) 922-6000
MAN ED-Design
Asbury Park Press, Neptune, NJ
Siegel, Irwin (954) 356-4000
ADV MGR-Sales Training/Development
Sun-Sentinel, Fort Lauderdale, FL
Siegel, Lee (801) 237-2031
SCI ED
Salt Lake Tribune, Salt Lake City, UT
Siegel, Randy (310) 540-5511
CONT, Daily Breeze, Torrance, CA
Siegel, Randy (216) 321-2300
PUB, Cleveland Free Times, Cleveland, OH
Siegfried, Paul (219) 356-6700
Sports ED, Herald-Press, Huntington, IN
Siegfried, Tom (214) 977-8222
SCI ED, Dallas Morning News, Dallas, TX
Siekman, Mark (712) 624-8512
PUB, ED, Malvern Leader, Malvern, IA
Sieleman, Greg (319) 283-2144
BUS ED, Register, Oelwein, IA
Siemering, Ron (607) 272-2321
MGR-INFO SRV, Ithaca Journal, Ithaca, NY
Siemers, Edward J (617) 786-7000
ADV MGR-OPER/RT
Patriot Ledger, Quincy, MA
Siemers, Linda (617) 786-7000
ADV MGR-CLASS, ADTX MGR
Patriot Ledger, Quincy, MA
Sienkiewizz, Joe (414) 235-7700
Chief Photographer
Oshkosh Northwestern, Oshkosh, WI
Sierra, Ric (813) 259-7711
MGR-Communications
Tampa Tribune and Times, Tampa, FL
Siers, James J (517) 752-7171
CIRC MGR, Saginaw News, Saginaw, MI
Sieve, G Alan (319) 642-5506
MAN ED
Marengo Pioneer-Republican, Marengo, IA
Sievers, Linda (907) 257-4200
Fashion/Food ED
Anchorage Daily News, Anchorage, AK
Sievers, Lisa (319) 263-2331
CONT, Muscatine Journal, Muscatine, IA
Siewert, Susan (616) 637-1104
DP MGR
South Haven Daily Tribune, South Haven, MI
Sifton, Michael (705) 745-4641
PRES/COO, Examiner, Peterborough, ON
Sigafoose, Steve (712) 328-1811
Sports ED
Daily Nonpareil, Council Bluffs, IA
Sigal, Peter (408) 372-3311
News ED, RE/Sunday ED, Wire ED
Monterey County Herald, Monterey, CA
Sigal, Phyllis (614) 633-1131
MAN ED, Amusements ED, Fashion/Food ED, Home Furnishings/Women's ED, Music ED, Society ED, Times Leader, Martins Ferry, OH
Sigler, Linda (405) 223-2200
PROD MGR, Daily Ardmoreite, Ardmore, OK
Sigler, Rob (601) 798-4766
Sports ED, Picayune Item, Picayune, MS
Sigman, Michael (213) 465-9909
PUB, LA Weekly, Los Angeles, CA
Sigman, Robert P (816) 234-4141
EDL Writer
Kansas City Star, Kansas City, MO
Sigmon, Caroline (803) 775-6331
DIR-MKTG, Item, Sumter, SC
Sigmon, Debora (803) 775-6331
ADV MGR-RT/Display, Item, Sumter, SC
Signs, Charles (800) 657-5889
ED, Denison Review, Denison, IA
Sigvaldason, J W (403) 873-4031
PUB, ED, News/North, Yellowknife, NT
Sikes, Don (409) 833-3311
PROD DIR
Beaumont Enterprise, Beaumont, TX
Sikop, David A (413) 584-5000
ADV MGR-CLASS
Daily Hampshire Gazette, Northampton, MA
Sikora, Anthony (218) 753-3170
PUB, Tower News, Tower, MN
Sikora, Frank (205) 325-2222
Farm ED
Birmingham News, Birmingham, AL
Silberkleit, Tom (707) 585-0328
PRES, T.A.S. Syndicate, Sonoma, CA
Silberman, Jean (507) 895-2940
PUB, ED
Houston County News, La Crescent, MN
Silberman, Steve (714) 768-3631
ED, Dana Point News, Lake Forest, CA
Silbernagel, Bob (970) 242-5050
EPE, Daily Sentinel, Grand Junction, CO
Silbernagel, Diane (218) 756-2131
PUB, ED
Independent News Herald, Clarissa, MN
Silbernagel, Ernie (218) 756-2131
PUB, ED
Independent News Herald, Clarissa, MN
Siler, Melvin (810) 332-8181
DIR-MKTG, Oakland Press, Pontiac, MI
Silkowski, Joseph (315) 337-4000
Sports ED, Daily Sentinel, Rome, NY
Sill, Melanie (919) 829-4500
ASST MAN ED/Special Projects ED
News & Observer, Raleigh, NC
Sillanpaa, Ted (707) 441-0500
Sports ED, Times-Standard, Eureka, CA
Sillers, John (415) 777-2424
CONT-Resident
San Francisco Examiner, San Francisco, CA
Silliman, Hal (209) 369-2761
BUS/FIN ED, Farm ED
Lodi News-Sentinel, Lodi, CA
Sills, Joanne (215) 854-2000
ASST City ED
Philadelphia Daily News, Philadelphia, PA
Silva, Emmy (214) 309-0990
PUB, ED, El Extra, Dallas, TX
Silva, Ernie (512) 445-3500
CIRC MGR
Austin American-Statesman, Austin, TX
Silva, George (508) 744-0600
PROD SYS MGR-MR
Salem Evening News, Beverly, MA
Silva, Jill (816) 234-4141
Food ED, Kansas City Star, Kansas City, MO
Silva, Joanne (610) 932-2444
ED, Chester County Press, Oxford, PA
Silva, John A (702) 882-2111
PROD MGR-PR
Nevada Appeal, Carson City, NV
Silva, John P C (520) 573-4220
ASST MAN ED-MET/State
Arizona Daily Star, Tucson, AZ
Silva, Juan J (214) 309-0990
GM, El Extra, Dallas, TX
Silva, Marcelo (512) 325-2200
PUB, ED, Falfurrias Facts, Falfurrias, TX
Silva, Michael (508) 676-8211
EX Sports ED, Herald News, Fall River, MA
Silva, Mike (901) 427-3333
DIR-Photography, Jackson Sun, Jackson, TN
Silva, Scott (508) 458-7100
Online MGR, Sun, Lowell, MA
Silvas, Frank (806) 296-1300
CIRC DIR
Plainview Daily Herald, Plainview, TX
Silvassy, Kathleen (202) 898-8254
Washington BU MGR
United Press International, Washington, DC
Silver, Allison (213) 237-5000
Opinion Section ED
Los Angeles Times, Los Angeles, CA
Silver, Deborah (304) 263-8931
Travel/Television, Journal, Martinsburg, WV
Silver, Donna (918) 335-8200
ADV DIR
Examiner-Enterprise, Bartlesville, OK
Silver, John (612) 257-5115
PUB, ED
Chicago County Press, Lindstrom, MN
Silver, Michael A (800) 245-6536
VP-Electronic Information Services
Tribune Media Services Inc., Chicago, IL
Silver, Sheryl (202) 334-5353
Owner/Author
Career Source/Column, Washington, DC
Silverberg, Kathy (205) 766-3434
EX ED, Times Daily, Florence, AL
Silverio, Manolo (305) 350-2111
News ED-El Nuevo, Miami Herald, Miami, FL
Silverman, Gene (707) 644-1141
Food ED, Vallejo Times-Herald, Vallejo, CA
Silverman, Leslie (860) 225-4601
Fashion/Style ED, Women's ED
Herald, New Britain, CT
Silverman, Mark (502) 582-4011
VP/EX ED, EX ED/VP-News
Courier-Journal, Louisville, KY
Silvernail, Dan (616) 222-5400
PROD FRM-PR
Grand Rapids Press, Grand Rapids, MI
Silvers, Gary (215) 949-4000
Sports ED
Bucks County Courier Times, Levittown, PA
Silvers, Gerald T (513) 721-2700
VP-Market Development
Cincinnati Enquirer, Cincinnati, OH
Silverstein, Arthur (718) 981-1234
CONT
Staten Island Advance, Staten Island, NY
Silverstein, Ed (203) 255-8877
MAN ED, Fairfield Minuteman, Fairfield, CT
Silverstein, Joni (419) 245-6000
DIR-MKTG & New BUS Development
Blade, Toledo, OH
Silverstein, Lenore (212) 643-1890
GM, Jewish Telegraphic Agency Daily News Bulletin, New York, NY
Silverstein, Stuart (213) 237-5000
Workplace Issues
Los Angeles Times, Los Angeles, CA
Silvestri, Tom (804) 649-6000
Deputy MAN ED-Weekend OPER
Richmond Times-Dispatch, Richmond, VA
Silvia, Robert (508) 880-9000
PROD SUPV-PR
Taunton Daily Gazette, Taunton, MA
Simard, Jean (418) 545-4474
PROD MGR, Le Quotidien, Chicoutimi, QC
Simavi, Erol (212) 921-8880
PUB, Hurriyet, New York, NY
Simborski, Rosanne (860) 442-2200
City ED, Day, New London, CT
Simbro, William C (515) 284-8000
Religion ED
Des Moines Register, Des Moines, IA
Simes, Libby (701) 223-2500
MGR-Human Resources
Bismarck Tribune, Bismarck, ND
Siminatis, Dave (702) 383-0211
ADV MGR-RT
Las Vegas Review-Journal, Las Vegas, NV
Simini, Joseph Peter (415) 282-1950
Self-Syndicator
Simini, Joseph Peter, San Francisco, CA
Simison, Robert (212) 416-2000
BU Chief-Detroit
Wall Street Journal, New York, NY
Simkins, Connie (702) 726-3333
PUB, ED
Lincoln County Record, Caliente, NV
Simkovic, Sue (412) 664-9161
BUS ED, Daily News, McKeesport, PA
Simmers, Craig (202) 636-3000
CIRC DIR
Washington Times, Washington, DC
Simmon, Jim (713) 624-1400
ED, Houston Press, Houston, TX
Simmonds, Glenn (416) 367-2000
DIR-Production, PROD DIR
Toronto Star, Toronto, ON
Simmons, Anthony M (609) 396-2200
CORP CIRC DIR
Journal Register Co., Trenton, NJ
Simmons, Arlecia (910) 623-2155
Entertainment ED, Daily News, Eden, NC
Simmons, Barb (309) 734-3176
PROD MGR
Daily Review Atlas, Monmouth, IL
Simmons, Becky (423) 523-3131
Religion ED
Knoxville News-Sentinel, Knoxville, TN
Simmons, Bill (501) 378-3400
Political ED
Arkansas Democrat-Gazette, Little Rock, AR
Simmons, Chellette (601) 783-2441
ED, Magnolia Gazette, Magnolia, MS
Simmons, Chris (540) 574-6200
Sports ED
Daily News-Record, Harrisonburg, VA
Simmons, Danny (404) 526-5151
PROD ASST MGR
Atlanta Journal-Constitution, Atlanta, GA
Simmons, David (409) 883-3571
CIRC DIR, Orange Leader, Orange, TX
Simmons, Debbie (504) 643-4918
ADV MGR-CLASS, RE ED
Slidell Sentry-News, Slidell, LA
Simmons, Denny (816) 271-8500
Photo ED
St. Joseph News-Press, St. Joseph, MO
Simmons, Doug (212) 475-3333
MAN ED, Village Voice, New York, NY
Simmons, Ethie (561) 622-7567
VP, Simmons Touch, North Palm Beach, FL
Simmons, Geitner (704) 633-8950
EPE, Salisbury Post, Salisbury, NC
Simmons, Jewel B (617) 450-2000
Graphics ED/Art DIR
Christian Science Monitor, Boston, MA
Simmons, Sgt Kim (206) 584-5818
ED, Northwest Guardian, Tacoma, WA
Simmons, Lewis (817) 549-7800
ED, Graham Leader, Graham, TX
Simmons, Martha (334) 433-1551
EDU Reporter
Mobile Press Register, Mobile, AL
Simmons, Michael R (910) 862-4163
MAN ED, Bladen Journal, Elizabethtown, NC
Simmons, Michael T (319) 642-5506
PUB
Marengo Pioneer-Republican, Marengo, IA
Simmons, Ray (616) 222-5400
PROD FRM-Plate/Camera
Grand Rapids Press, Grand Rapids, MI
Simmons, Richard B (303) 776-2244
VP-FIN, Daily Times-Call, Longmont, CO
Lehman Communications Corp.
Simmons, Ross (561) 622-7567
PRES
Simmons Touch, North Palm Beach, FL
Simmons, Tony (904) 747-5000
EDU ED, News Herald, Panama City, FL
Simmons IV, W E (504) 732-2565
SCI/Sunday ED, Daily News, Bogalusa, LA
Simmons, William (505) 983-3303
TREAS
Santa Fe New Mexican, Santa Fe, NM
Simms, Jimmy (205) 734-2131
News ED, Farm ED, Special Sections ED, Women's ED, Cullman Times, Cullman, AL
Simms, Nancee (812) 424-7711
ADTX MGR, Evansville Courier, Evansville, IN
Simollardes, Anthony J (508) 793-9100
ADV MGR-OPER
Telegram & Gazette, Worcester, MA
Simon, Amy (402) 564-2741
BUS/FIN Reporter, Farm/Agriculture ED
Columbus Telegram, Columbus, NE
Simon, Celeste P (320) 255-8700
ADV MGR-Sales, Times, St. Cloud, MN
Simon, David (504) 447-4055
CIRC DIR, Daily Comet, Thibodaux, LA
Simon, Elly (770) 478-5753
BM, Clayton News/Daily, Jonesboro, GA
Simon, Helen (802) 863-3441
ASST MET ED, Free Press, Burlington, VT
Simon, Jeanneane (614) 461-5000
PROD SUPV-Make-up
Columbus Dispatch, Columbus, OH

Sim Who's Where-212

Simon, Jeff (716) 849-3434
Books ED, Films/Theater ED
Buffalo News, Buffalo, NY

Simon, Karen (320) 364-8601
ED
Montgomery Messenger, Montgomery, MN

Simon, Michelle (954) 356-4000
ADV MGR (South Broward)
Sun-Sentinel, Fort Lauderdale, FL

Simon, Neal (716) 593-5300
News ED, Reporter
Wellsville Daily Reporter, Wellsville, NY

Simon, Paul S (913) 295-1111
PRES, Topeka Capital-Journal, Topeka, KS
Morris Communications Corp.

Simon, Raymond (201) 877-4141
ADV MGR-MKTG, Star-Ledger, Newark, NJ

Simone, Rose (519) 894-2231
Gender Issues Reporter
Record, Kitchener, ON

Simoneau, Denys (418) 728-2131
GM, ED
Peuple de Lotbiniere, Laurier-Station, QC

Simoneau, Louis (613) 562-0111
DP MGR, PROD MGR-Computer SYS
Le Droit, Ottawa, ON

Simonet, Stacy (907) 694-2727
MAN ED, Chugiak-Eagle River Alaska Star, Eagle River, AK

Simonetti, Marie Claire (519) 255-5711
Features Saturday
Windsor Star, Windsor, ON

Simons, Dan (913) 843-1000
New Ventures, Online MGR, ADTX MGR
Journal-World, Lawrence, KS

Simons, Dan C (505) 546-2611
Owner, Deming Headlight, Deming, NM

Simons Jr, Dolph C (913) 843-1000
PRES, PUB, ED
Journal-World, Lawrence, KS

Simons III, Dolph C (913) 843-1000
MGR-OPER, Journal-World, Lawrence, KS

Simons, Ken (316) 231-2600
COL, Morning Sun, Pittsburg, KS

Simons, Marie N (913) 843-1000
SEC/TREAS, Journal-World, Lawrence, KS

Simons, Nan (800) 646-6397
ED
Portland Review and Observer, Portland, MI

Simons, Patricia (803) 329-4000
PROD DIR, Herald, Rock Hill, SC

Simons, Vicki (518) 325-4400
ED, Independent, Hillsdale, NY

Simonson, Dick (941) 953-7755
PROD MGR-Packaging/Distribution
Sarasota Herald-Tribune, Sarasota, FL

Simpkins, David (320) 352-6577
PUB, MAN ED
Sauk Centre Herald, Sauk Centre, MN

Simpkins, Gerald (413) 447-7311
PROD MGR-Press
Berkshire Eagle, Pittsfield, MA

Simpkins Jr, Irby C (615) 259-8800
PUB/CEO, Nashville Banner, Nashville, TN

Simpkins, Joe (317) 529-1111
PROD FRM-PR
Courier-Times, New Castle, IN

Simpson, Andrew (908) 722-3000
MAN ED
Somerset Messenger-Gazette, Somerville, NJ

Simpson, Charles (770) 382-4545
PROD SUPT-PR
Daily Tribune News, Cartersville, GA

Simpson, Chuck (503) 363-0006
PUB, Community News, Salem, OR

Simpson, Claudia (508) 997-7411
Action Line ED
Standard Times, New Bedford, MA

Simpson, David C (309) 346-1111
PUB, PROD MGR-Plant
Pekin Daily Times, Pekin, IL

Simpson, Dawn (915) 283-2003
GM, MAN ED
Van Horn Advocate, Van Horn, TX

Simpson, Doug (903) 893-8181
MGR-MKTG/PROM
Herald Democrat, Sherman, TX

Simpson, Ed (330) 841-1600
MET ED, Tribune Chronicle, Warren, OH

Simpson, Harriet (941) 335-0200
BUS ED, News-Press, Fort Myers, FL

Simpson, Harvey (912) 273-2277
COL, Sports ED
Cordele Dispatch, Cordele, GA

Simpson, James A (619) 457-5920
Chairman/CEO
Trade Service Corp., San Diego, CA

Simpson, James R (208) 549-1717
PUB, Weiser Signal American, Weiser, ID

Simpson, James R (213) 237-3700
Sr VP-Human Resources
Times Mirror Co., Los Angeles, CA

Simpson, Jane L (508) 793-9100
MGR-Purchasing
Telegram & Gazette, Worcester, MA

Simpson, Joan (209) 943-6397
Fashion ED, Food ED, Lifestyle ED
Record, Stockton, CA

Simpson, John (703) 276-3400
MAN ED-International Edition
USA Today, Arlington, VA

Simpson, Larry (502) 781-1700
PROD MGR, Daily News, Bowling Green, KY

Simpson, Larry (915) 283-2003
PUB, ED, Van Horn Advocate, Van Horn, TX

Simpson, Les (409) 833-3311
CIRC MGR-City
Beaumont Enterprise, Beaumont, TX

Simpson, Les (706) 549-0123
News ED, Athens Daily News/Banner-Herald, Athens, GA

Simpson, Lewis (Sandy) (907) 257-4200
PROD DIR-Newspaper SYS
Anchorage Daily News, Anchorage, AK

Simpson, Mary W (904) 766-8834
PUB, Florida Star, Jacksonville, FL

Simpson, Melissa (757) 247-4600
Librarian, Daily Press, Newport News, VA

Simpson, P Erica (904) 766-8834
MAN ED, Florida Star, Jacksonville, FL

Simpson, Pat (305) 674-9746
Sports
International News Agency, Miami Beach, FL

Simpson, Robert (816) 271-8500
PROD SUPT-MR
St. Joseph News-Press, St. Joseph, MO

Simpson, Robert (601) 896-2100
CONT, Sun Herald, Biloxi, MS

Simpson, Shannon (807) 343-6200
CIRC MGR
Chronicle-Journal, Thunder Bay, ON

Simpson, Stan (860) 241-6200
COL, Hartford Courant, Hartford, CT

Simpson, Stuart (606) 678-0161
ED, Pulaski Week, Somerset, KY

Simross, Lynn (213) 237-5000
COL-Consumer (freelance contributor)
Los Angeles Times, Los Angeles, CA

Sims, Anne (205) 345-0505
ADV MGR-TELEMKTG
Tuscaloosa News, Tuscaloosa, AL

Sims, Bill (410) 398-3311
CIRC DIR, Cecil Whig, Elkton, MD

Sims, Bob (941) 294-7731
MAN ED, News Chief, Winter Haven, FL

Sims, Dave (601) 798-4766
PUB, ED, EDL Writer
Picayune Item, Picayune, MS

Sims, Edward H (941) 366-2169
ED/PUB
Editor's Copy Syndicate, Sarasota, FL

Sims, Floyd (409) 945-3441
PROD MGR, Texas City Sun, Texas City, TX

Sims, Frederik (941) 366-2169
CIRC MGR
Editor's Copy Syndicate, Sarasota, FL

Sims, Greg (519) 733-2211
ED, Kingsville Reporter, Kingsville, ON

Sims, Juanita (519) 679-6666
Art DIR, London Free Press, London, ON

Sims, Nancy (618) 993-2626
GM, Marion Daily Republican, Marion, IL

Sims, Pam (609) 989-0285
ED, Nubian News, Trenton, NJ

Sims, Patricia (901) 696-4558
ED, Crockett Times, Alamo, TN

Sims, Robert (954) 698-6501
ED, Miami Hi-Riser, Deerfield Beach, FL

Sims, Robert B (901) 696-4558
PUB, Crockett Times, Alamo, TN

Sims, Rosemary (804) 843-2282
GM, Tidewater Review, West Point, VA

Sims, Tom (215) 854-2000
VP-SYS/Technology, DP MGR, Philadelphia Inquirer, Philadelphia, PA, Knight-Ridder

Sims, Wendy (970) 249-3444
ADV DIR, Daily Press, Montrose, CO

Sinasac, Joe (519) 894-2231
Books ED, Record, Kitchener, ON

Sincell, Donald W (301) 334-3963
ED, Republican, Oakland, MD

Sincell, Robert B (301) 334-3963
PUB, GM, Republican, Oakland, MD

Sinclair, Janis (316) 374-2101
ED, Elk County Citizen-Advance News, Howard, KS

Sinclair, John (403) 468-0100
Librarian, Edmonton Sun, Edmonton, AB

Sinclair, Steve (402) 444-1000
Sports ED, Omaha World-Herald, Omaha, NE

Sinclair, Wayland (802) 748-8121
Picture ED
Caledonian-Record, St. Johnsbury, VT

Sinding, Peter (970) 963-8252
DIR Newspaper Relations
Family Times Magazine, Active Times Publications Inc., Carbondale, CO

Sines, Scott (509) 459-5000
MAN ED-Presentation & Opinion
Spokesman-Review, Spokane, WA

Sing, Bill (213) 237-5000
BUS ED, Los Angeles Times, Los Angeles, CA

Singer, Dale (314) 340-8000
ASST EPE
St. Louis Post-Dispatch, St. Louis, MO

Singer, Harold (516) 561-6900
PUB, Jewish Journal, Valley Stream, NY

Singer, Marylou (315) 472-7825
ED, Onondaga Valley News, Syracuse, NY

Singer, Paul (814) 946-7411
Picture Desk ED, Altoona Mirror, Altoona, PA

Singer, Phyllis (516) 843-2020
ASST MAN ED-Features
Newsday, Melville, NY

Singer, Phyllis R (513) 621-3145
ED, American Israelite, Cincinnati, OH

Singer, Stephen (601) 842-2611
BUS/FIN ED, Northeast Mississippi Daily Journal, Tupelo, MS

Singerman, Martin (212) 930-8000
PUB, New York Post, New York, NY

Singes, David (802) 254-2311
CIRC MGR
Brattleboro Reformer, Brattleboro, VT

Singleton, Belinda (601) 785-6525
ED, Smith County Reformer, Taylorsville, MS

Singleton, Mary (803) 648-2311
CIRC CNR, Aiken Standard, Aiken, SC

Singleton, Norm (330) 364-5577
BUS ED, Religion ED
Times Reporter, New Philadelphia, OH

Singleton, Robert F (706) 324-5526
VP, Columbus Ledger-Enquirer, Columbus, GA, Knight-Ridder Inc.

Singleton, Tina (718) 636-9500
GM, New York Daily Challenge/Afro Times, Brooklyn, NY

Singleton, William Dean (303) 820-1952
VBC/PRES/CEO
MediaNews Group Inc., Denver, CO

Sink Jr, Joe S (704) 249-3981
PUB, PA, Dispatch, Lexington, NC

Sink, Steve (516) 843-2020
BUS ED, Newsday, Melville, NY

Sinkclear, Jill (573) 221-2800
CIRC MGR, ADTX MGR
Hannibal Courier-Post, Hannibal, MO

Sinkewicz, Lyle (306) 652-9200
PUB/EX VP, StarPhoenix, Saskatoon, SK

Sinks, James (541) 672-3321
BUS ED, News-Review, Roseburg, OR

Sinn, Charlene (219) 235-6161
PROD ASST DIR
South Bend Tribune, South Bend, IN

Sinnard, Carolyn J (208) 467-9251
ADV DIR, Idaho Press-Tribune, Nampa, ID

Sinsel, Donean (509) 248-1251
Librarian
Yakima Herald-Republic, Yakima, WA

Sipes, Karen (913) 295-1111
Features Page
Topeka Capital-Journal, Topeka, KS

Siporen, Wendy (541) 482-3456
City/MET ED, EPE
Daily Tidings, Ashland, OR

Sipper, Kimberly M (210) 658-7424
GM, Herald, Universal City, TX

Sipple, Candy (915) 236-6677
Fashion/Women's ED, Home Furnishings ED
Sweetwater Reporter, Sweetwater, TX

Sipress, Alan (215) 854-2000
Cairo BU
Philadelphia Inquirer, Philadelphia, PA

Siress, Hap (502) 443-1771
PROD FRM-PR, PROD FRM-Camera
Paducah Sun, Paducah, KY

Sirmans, Ron (770) 532-1234
News ED, Times, Gainesville, GA

Sirmon, Charity (806) 226-2008
ED, Claude News, Claude, TX

Sirmon, Steve (806) 226-2008
PUB, Claude News, Claude, TX

Sirmons, Susan (601) 961-7000
DIR-Market Development
Clarion-Ledger, Jackson, MS

Sisco, Michael (304) 824-5101
ED, Lincoln Journal, Hamlin, WV

Sisk, Jan (417) 264-3085
MAN ED
South Missourian-News, Thayer, MO

Sisk, Linda D (701) 245-6461
PUB, ED, Standard, Westhope, ND

Siskel, Gene (312) 222-3232
Movie COL, Chicago Tribune, Chicago, IL

Siskin, Diane (423) 756-6900
Fashion ED, Travel ED
Chattanooga Free Press, Chattanooga, TN

Sisko, Eileen (616) 845-5181
COL, Daily News, Ludington, MI

Sisler, Bev (614) 387-0400
ADV MGR-NTL, Marion Star, Marion, OH

Sison, Cathy (616) 637-1104
ED
South Haven Daily Tribune, South Haven, MI

Sisson, Bob (360) 694-3391
Health/Medical ED
Columbian, Vancouver, WA

Sisson, Ed (417) 532-9131
City ED, EPE
Lebanon Daily Record, Lebanon, MO

Sistek, Joan (562) 435-1161
PROD MGR-Ad SRV/Make-Up
Press-Telegram, Long Beach, CA

Sisto, Jean (514) 285-7272
VP/GM-J.T.C., La Presse, Montreal, QC
Les Journaux Trans-Canada (JTC)

Sitarz, Joe (864) 223-1411
BUS/FIN ED, Graphics ED/Art DIR
Index-Journal, Greenwood, SC

Sitler, Tom (717) 784-2121
PROD MGR-OPER
Press Enterprise, Bloomsburg, PA

Sito, Louis (516) 843-2020
VP-Distribution, CIRC VP-Distribution
Newsday, Melville, NY

Sitrin, Gregg (212) 688-7557
Staff, World Union Press, New York, NY

Sitter, Pat (701) 223-2500
PROD MGR-MR
Bismarck Tribune, Bismarck, ND

Sivesind, Cam (541) 266-6831
ED, Canby Herald/Wilsonville Spokesman, Canby, OR

Sivret, Tom (802) 479-0191
News ED, Times Argus, Barre, VT

Sivric, Rev Ivo (312) 373-3463
ED, Nasa Nada, Chicago, IL

Six, Allan (209) 578-2000
DIR-MIS, PROD DIR
Modesto Bee, Modesto, CA

Six, Jim (609) 845-3300
Travel ED
Gloucester County Times, Woodbury, NJ

Sizemore, H Mason (206) 464-2329
PRES/COO, Seattle Times Co., Seattle, WA

Sizer, Karen A (308) 764-2402
ED, Arthur Enterprise, Arthur, NE

Sjostrom, Jan (561) 820-3800
Entertainment ED
Palm Beach Daily News, Palm Beach, FL

Sjuts, David H (402) 362-4478
ADV MGR, York News-Times, York, NE

Skaggs, Donald R (508) 793-9100
PRES/Massachusetts OPER
Telegram & Gazette, Worcester, MA
Chronicle Publishing Co.

Skaggs, Steve (352) 544-5200
ADV MGR-RT
Hernando Today, Brooksville, FL

Skala, Mark (508) 255-2121
ED, Cape Codder, Orleans, MA

Skala, Mary Jane (216) 524-0830
ED, Sun Press, Valley View, OH

Skally, Francis (716) 693-1000
ADV DIR
Tonawanda News, North Tonawanda, NY

Skantzos, Joanne (416) 367-2000
DIR-CORP Systems
Toronto Star, Toronto, ON

Skapley, Rosemary (516) 843-2020
Kidsday ED, Newsday, Melville, NY

Skattum, Donna (319) 928-6876
PUB, Reminder, Edgewood, IA

Skattum, Roger (319) 928-6876
PUB, ED, Reminder, Edgewood, IA

Skayhan, Richard (503) 786-1996
PUB, Clackamas Review, Milwaukie, OR

Skazyk, Bob (204) 697-7000
PROD FRM-PR
Winnipeg Free Press, Winnipeg, MB

Skeen, Jimmy (318) 322-5161
ADV MGR-RT, News-Star, Monroe, LA

Skelley, Jack (213) 481-1448
MAN ED, Los Angeles Downtown News, Los Angeles, CA

Skelley, Spencer (409) 744-3611
County News ED
Galveston County Daily News, Galveston, TX

Skelton, George (213) 237-5000
COL-State/Political
Los Angeles Times, Los Angeles, CA

Skelton, Mark (905) 476-7753
PUB
Keswick Georgina Advocate, Keswick, ON

Skemp, William (319) 588-5611
PRES, Telegraph Herald, Dubuque, IA

Skene, Neil (202) 887-8500
PUB/PRES, Congressional Quarterly Service, Washington, DC

Skertchly, Mario A (203) 288-5600
GM, Catholic Twin Circle, Hamden, CT

Copyright ©1997 by the Editor & Publisher Co.

213-Who's Where **Smi**

Skewis, Pat (412) 523-6588
PROD MR/Distribution
Standard Observer, Greensburg, PA

Skidmore, Bill (406) 447-4000
EPE, Political ED
Helena Independent Record, Helena, MT

Skidmore, Linda (304) 636-2121
City ED, Inter-Mountain, Elkins, WV

Skidmore, Marshall B (206) 627-4853
PUB/ED, Tacoma Daily Index, Tacoma, WA

Skidnuk, Darrell (403) 743-8186
MAN ED
Fort McMurray Today, Fort McMurray, AB

Skiles, Russel (806) 872-2177
PUB, ED, Press-Reporter, Lamesa, TX

Skiles, Sharyn (308) 345-4500
BM, McCook Daily Gazette, McCook, NE

Skillings, Wesley (717) 746-1217
ED, Rocket-Courier, Wyalusing, PA

Skillingstad, Kyle (602) 271-8000
PROD Unit MGR-Newsprint (Deer Valley, Mesa)
Phoenix Newspapers Inc., Phoenix, AZ

Skillman, Brad (508) 369-2800
ED, Lincoln Journal, Concord, MA

Skilton, Mary (312) 321-3000
Television Prevue
Chicago Sun-Times, Chicago, IL

Skinner, Aaron (501) 785-7700
Photo ED
Southwest Times Record, Fort Smith, AR

Skinner, Cheryl (713) 242-9104
ED, Fort Bend Mirror, Sugarland, TX

Skinner, Dan (317) 552-3355
GM, Elwood Call-Leader, Elwood, IN

Skinner, Edward B (706) 724-0851
VP-Newspapers
Morris Communications Corp., Augusta, GA

Skinner, Geof (618) 833-2158
ED, Monday's Pub, Anna, IL

Skinner, John (604) 732-2111
Saturday Review ED
Vancouver Sun, Vancouver, BC

Skinner, Mary Ann (516) 843-2020
DIR-INFO Technology, Newsday, Melville, NY

Skinner, Peter G (212) 416-2600
Sr VP/GEN Counsel/SEC
Dow Jones & Co. Inc., New York, NY

Skinner, Scott (715) 423-7200
CIRC MGR
Daily Tribune, Wisconsin Rapids, WI

Skinner, Wendell E (614) 353-3101
PROD FRM-Press Stereo
Portsmouth Daily Times, Portsmouth, OH

Skipper, Deborah (601) 961-7000
ASST MET ED, Clarion-Ledger, Jackson, MS

Skipper, Mike (910) 739-4322
PROD MGR-PR, Robesonian, Lumberton, NC

Skipworth, Joe (205) 532-4000
ADV MGR-Co-op
Huntsville Times, Huntsville, AL

Skirvin, Howard (408) 424-2221
PROD DIR, Californian, Salinas, CA

Sklar, Robert (313) 459-2700
MAN ED, Livonia Observer, Plymouth, MI

Skoch, Larry (405) 475-3311
ADV MGR-Display
Daily Oklahoman, Oklahoma City, OK

Skoch, Tom (216) 245-6901
MAN ED, Morning Journal, Lorain, OH

Skoglund, Dennis (413) 584-5000
CIRC MGR
Daily Hampshire Gazette, Northampton, MA

Skoglund, Lori (860) 241-6200
News ADM MGR
Hartford Courant, Hartford, CT

Skoglund, Robert (207) 372-8052
COL, Skoglund Features, St. George, ME

Skoloda, David (608) 781-6700
ED, Onalaska Community Life, Onalaska, WI

Skoloda, Gretchen (608) 781-6700
PUB
Onalaska Community Life, Onalaska, WI

Skonberg, Laura (907) 486-3227
ADV MGR-Display
Kodiak Daily Mirror, Kodiak, AK

Skovgaard, Alex (402) 444-1000
CIRC MGR-Alternate Delivery
Omaha World-Herald, Omaha, NE

Skowronski, Larry (814) 870-1600
PROD MGR-Technical Services
Morning News/Erie Daily Times, Erie, PA

Skrivan, Joseph M (402) 373-2332
PUB, ED
Bloomfield Monitor, Bloomfield, NE

Skrivan, Mary Ellen (402) 373-2332
GM, Bloomfield Monitor, Bloomfield, NE

Skube, Michael (404) 526-5151
Books ED
Atlanta Journal-Constitution, Atlanta, GA

Skubek, Randy (412) 537-3351
Sports ED, Latrobe Bulletin, Latrobe, PA

Skuce, Marsha (613) 829-9100
ADV MGR-PROM, Ottawa Citizen, Ottawa, ON

Skufca, Sherry (219) 461-8333
MAN ED, Journal Gazette, Fort Wayne, IN

Skutt, Bill (813) 259-7711
ASST MAN ED
Tampa Tribune and Times, Tampa, FL

Skvarenina, Joe (317) 787-3291
ED, Christian Advocate, Beech Grove, IN

Skwar, Don (617) 929-2000
EX ED-Sports, Boston Globe, Boston, MA

Skyberg, Carol (423) 482-1021
BM, Oak Ridger, Oak Ridge, TN

Skyles, Lyman (573) 888-4505
ASSOC ED
Daily Dunklin Democrat, Kennett, MO

Slaats, Shirley (519) 785-2455
PUB, Chronicle, Rodney, ON

Slabaugh, Randy J (304) 485-1891
CIRC DIR, News & Sentinel, Parkersburg, WV

Slacian, Joe (219) 563-2131
MAN ED, Wabash Plain Dealer, Wabash, IN

Slack, Anne L (715) 986-4675
ED, Turtle Lake Times, Turtle Lake, WI

Slack, Chris (217) 732-2101
CIRC MGR, Courier, Lincoln, IL

Slack, Chris (217) 892-9613
ED, Rantoul Press, Rantoul, IL

Slack, James P (715) 986-4675
PUB, Turtle Lake Times, Turtle Lake, WI

Slack, Jeff (212) 416-2000
PROD MGR (Naperville IL)
Wall Street Journal, New York, NY

Slack, Ron (408) 394-5656
GM, Coast Weekly, Seaside, CA

Slade, Daniel B (508) 526-7131
ED, Manchester Cricket, Manchester, MA

Slade, Ernest E (810) 664-0811
PUB, County Press, Lapeer, MI

Slade, Kathy (804) 458-8511
Religion ED, Society ED, News, Hopewell, VA

Slade Jr., Harry B (508) 526-7131
GM, Manchester Cricket, Manchester, MA

Slagle, Kerry (212) 563-2252
PRES/CEO
Editors Press Service Inc., New York, NY

Slagle, LuAnne (202) 887-8500
DIR-MKTG, Congressional Quarterly Service, Washington, DC

Slaight, Shelley (605) 847-4421
ED, Lake Preston Times, Lake Preston, SD

Slaimaker, Joy (903) 657-2501
PROD SUPT/FRM-COMP
Henderson Daily News, Henderson, TX

Slama, Mary (216) 871-5797
MAN ED, West Life, Westlake, OH

Slane, Judith (618) 547-3111
ED, Kinmundy Express, Kinmundy, IL

Slane, Rudolph D (618) 547-3111
PUB, Kinmundy Express, Kinmundy, IL

Slapak, Trevor (403) 562-2248
ED, Pass Herald, Blairmore, AB

Slat, Charles (313) 242-1100
BUS ED, Monroe Evening News, Monroe, MI

Slate, Charles (803) 626-8555
Photo ED, Sun News, Myrtle Beach, SC

Slater, Brad (605) 394-8300
ADV MGR-CLASS
Rapid City Journal, Rapid City, SD

Slater, Jim (412) 224-4321
PROD ASST DIR
Valley News Dispatch, Tarentum, PA

Slater, Paul A (573) 897-2109
ED, Unterrified Democrat, Linn, MO

Slater, Richard N (219) 785-2234
PUB, Regional News, La Crosse, IN

Slaton, Luke (205) 974-1114
PUB, ED, Moulton Advertiser, Moulton, AL

Slator, Roger (717) 821-2091
PROD MGR, Citizens' Voice, Wilkes-Barre, PA

Slator, Susanna (717) 821-2091
CIRC DIR, Citizens' Voice, Wilkes-Barre, PA

Slattery, Diann (954) 356-4000
Health/Medical ED
Sun-Sentinel, Fort Lauderdale, FL

Slattery, Patrick (802) 287-2043
MAN ED, Poultney News, E. Poultney, VT

Slaughter, Essie (601) 961-7000
MGR-CR, Clarion-Ledger, Jackson, MS

Slaughter, Ken (319) 398-8211
VP, TREAS, Gazette, Cedar Rapids, IA

Slaughter, Mike M (504) 850-1100
EX ED, Courier, Houma, LA

Slaughter, Thomas E (212) 621-1500
DIR-Strategic Planning
Associated Press, New York, NY

Slaughter, Warren (806) 249-4511
SCI ED, Dalhart Daily Texan, Dalhart, TX

Slaven, Shirley (606) 436-5771
GM, Herald Voice, Hazard, KY

Slaven, Theresa (812) 847-4487
CIRC MGR, Linton Daily Citizen, Linton, IN

Slavin, David (914) 782-4000
PUB, ED, Sparta Independent, Monroe, NY

Slayton, Jack (423) 745-5664
Sports ED, Daily Post-Athenian, Athens, TN

Slechta, Ronald C (319) 656-2273
PUB, ED, Kalona News, Kalona, IA

Sledge Jr, James L (601) 743-5760
PUB
Kemper County Messenger, De Kalb, MS

Sledge, Sarah (618) 242-0117
ADV MGR, Register-News, Mount Vernon, IL

Sleeper, Jerry (970) 925-2220
CIRC MGR, PROD MGR-PR
Aspen Daily News, Aspen, CO

Sleet, Phyllis (405) 353-0620
Librarian, Lawton Constitution, Lawton, OK

Sleeth, Amy (509) 582-1500
Films/Theater ED
Tri-City Herald, Tri-Cities, WA

Sleight, Kari (541) 889-5387
ADV MGR-CLASS, RE ED
Argus Observer, Ontario, OR

Slenning, Glenna (541) 926-2211
ADV CNR-NTL, Democrat-Herald, Albany, OR

Slep, Dan (814) 946-7411
CIRC DIR, Altoona Mirror, Altoona, PA

Slepicka, Lon (301) 459-3131
MAN ED
Prince George's Journal, Lanham, MD

Slepicka, Nancy (217) 532-3929
PUB, Montgomery County News, Hillsboro, IL

Slepicka, Richard (217) 532-3929
ED, Montgomery County News, Hillsboro, IL

Slinger, Elsie (507) 583-4431
PUB, ED
Prairie Times, Blooming Prairie, MN

Slipper, Fred (360) 855-1641
GM, Courier Times, Sedro-Woolley, WA

Sloan, Bob (910) 739-4322
Sports ED, Robesonian, Lumberton, NC

Sloan, Denise (916) 541-3880
Entertainment/Amusements ED, Tahoe Action ED, Theater/Music ED
Tahoe Daily Tribune, South Lake Tahoe, CA

Sloan, Donald (915) 372-5115
PUB, San Saba News & Star, San Saba, TX

Sloan, Greg B (217) 429-5151
CIRC MGR, Herald & Review, Decatur, IL

Sloan, James (702) 788-6200
Films/Theater ED, Lifestyle, Radio/Television ED, Reno Gazette-Journal, Reno, NV

Sloan, Kenny (423) 756-6900
City ED, Free Press, Chattanooga, TN

Sloan, Pat (402) 475-4200
Librarian, Lincoln Journal Star, Lincoln, NE

Sloan, Pete (614) 654-1321
News ED
Lancaster Eagle-Gazette, Lancaster, OH

Sloan, Richard (817) 634-2125
GM, Killeen Daily Herald, Killeen, TX

Sloane, Nancy (410) 752-3849
ASSOC PUB, Daily Record, Baltimore, MD

Slobodian, Linda (403) 468-0100
COL, Edmonton Sun, Edmonton, AB

Sloca, John (319) 385-3131
News ED
Mt. Pleasant News, Mount Pleasant, IA

Slocum, Cindy (504) 732-2565
PROD MGR, Daily News, Bogalusa, LA

Sloggatt, Peter (516) 427-7000
ED, Long-Islander, Huntington, NY

Slone, Diana (304) 255-4400
ADV MGR-CLASS
Register Herald, Beckley, WV

Sloninger, Gene (318) 878-2444
PUB, ED, Delhi Dispatch, Delhi, LA

Slonoff, James E (630) 887-0600
GM, Doings, Hinsdale, IL

Slother, Len (814) 684-4000
Sports ED, Daily Herald, Tyrone, PA

Slovut, Gordon (612) 673-4000
Medical Issues/RES Reporter
Star Tribune, Minneapolis, MN

Slugett, Rodney (604) 949-6225
PUB, North Island Gazette, Port Hardy, BC

Slusher, James E (847) 427-4300
ASSOC ED
Daily Herald, Arlington Heights, IL

Slusser, Richard (202) 636-3000
Food/Travel ED
Washington Times, Washington, DC

Sly, Judy (209) 578-2000
ASST MAN ED, Modesto Bee, Modesto, CA

Sly, Julie (916) 452-3344
ED, Catholic Herald, Sacramento, CA

Slykhuis, John (905) 476-7753
ED, Keswick Georgina Advocate, Keswick, ON

Smaglinski, Carol (405) 341-2121
Food ED, Edmond Evening Sun, Edmond, OK

Smale, James S (919) 772-8747
PUB, Garner News, Garner, NC

Small, David (207) 990-8000
MGR-CR, Bangor Daily News, Bangor, ME

Small, James S (608) 375-4458
PUB, Boscobel Dial, Boscobel, WI

Small, Jason (605) 352-6401
PROD FRM-PR, PROD MGR-Pre Press
Huron Plainsman, Huron, SD

Small, Jay (317) 633-1240
Online ED
Indianapolis Star/News, Indianapolis, IN

Small, Jean Alice (815) 937-3300
COB
Small Newspaper Group Inc., Kankakee, IL

Small, Jim (812) 372-7811
Sports ED, Republic, Columbus, IN

Small, Jim (919) 362-8356
PUB, Apex Herald, Apex, NC

Small, John A (405) 924-4388
News ED, Durant Daily Democrat, Durant, OK

Small, Karen (615) 259-8000
World News Extra ED
Tennessean, Nashville, TN

Small, Len Robert (815) 937-3300
PRES
Small Newspaper Group Inc., Kankakee, IL

Small, Robert J (717) 334-1131
DIR-MKTG/PROM
Gettysburg Times, Gettysburg, PA

Small, Thomas P (815) 937-3300
Sr VP/SEC
Small Newspaper Group Inc., Kankakee, IL

Smallacombe, Dusty (912) 985-4545
CIRC DIR, Observer, Moultrie, GA

Smalley Jr, Garrett L (816) 931-2002
Co-PUB, Daily Record, Kansas City, MO

Smalley, John (608) 782-9710
City ED, La Crosse Tribune, La Crosse, WI

Smalley, Robert W (816) 931-2002
SEC, Daily Record, Kansas City, MO

Smalls, Connie (804) 857-1212
ED, Casemate, Norfolk, VA

Smallwood, John (215) 854-2000
Sports COL
Philadelphia Daily News, Philadelphia, PA

Smallwood, Phyllis (501) 785-7700
MGR-CR
Southwest Times Record, Fort Smith, AR

Smart, Joe (218) 829-4705
ADV MGR
Brainerd Daily Dispatch, Brainerd, MN

Smart, Karen (414) 542-2501
Librarian
Waukesha County Freeman, Waukesha, WI

Smart, Paul (518) 589-7007
ED, Mountain Eagle, Tannersville, NY

Smart, Tom (801) 237-2188
Photo ED, Deseret News, Salt Lake City, UT

Smart, Wayland (409) 265-7411
Graphics ED/Art DIR
Brazosport Facts, Clute, TX

Smaus, Robert (213) 237-5000
Gardening ED
Los Angeles Times, Los Angeles, CA

Smed, Roger (515) 964-0639
PUB, Ankeny Press Citizen, Ankeny, IA

Smedes, Steve (707) 546-2020
PROD MGR-Pre Press
Press Democrat, Santa Rosa, CA

Smedley, Ann Marie (502) 781-1700
Religion ED, Daily News, Bowling Green, KY

Smekens, Joel (219) 824-0224
MAN ED, News ED
News-Banner, Bluffton, IN

Smelley, Mike (334) 727-3020
GM, Tuskegee News, Tuskegee, AL

Smelser, Emmett K (317) 962-1575
PRES, PUB, Palladium-Item, Richmond, IN

Smelser, Erik (601) 582-4321
DIR-Market Development
Hattiesburg American, Hattiesburg, MS

Smelser, Larry (419) 586-2371
PROD SUPT, Daily Standard, Celina, OH

Smeraglia, Traci (205) 252-3672
MAN ED
Alabama Messenger, Birmingham, AL

Smetanka, Mary Jane (612) 673-4000
EDU Reporter-Trends
Star Tribune, Minneapolis, MN

Smetzer, MaryBeth (907) 456-6661
Librarian/Northland News ED/Reporter
Fairbanks Daily News-Miner, Fairbanks, AK

Smiddy, Debbie (423) 523-3131
ADV DIR
Knoxville News-Sentinel, Knoxville, TN

Smidt, Mark (515) 573-2141
ED, Books/Travel ED, City/MET ED, EPE, Environmental ED, Features ED, NTL ED, News ED, Political/Government ED
Messenger, Fort Dodge, IA

Smiley, Frank D (316) 234-5241
PUB, Stafford Courier, Stafford, KS

Smiley, Greg (541) 474-3700
BUS ED, RE ED
Grants Pass Daily Courier, Grants Pass, OR

Smiley, Marilyn A (316) 234-5241
PUB, Stafford Courier, Stafford, KS

Smi Who's Where-214

Smilie, Jim (318) 487-6397
MGR-Cityline, ADTX MGR
Alexandria Daily Town Talk, Alexandria, LA
Sminton, Val (816) 263-4123
Features ED, Moberly Monitor-Index & Democrat, Moberly, MO
Smit, Marcella (418) 650-1764
GM, Quebec Chronicle Telegraph, Ste-Foy, QC
Smit, Mike (406) 587-4491
ADV DIR, Daily Chronicle, Bozeman, MT
Smit, Rick (807) 727-2618
PUB, ED, District News, Red Lake, ON
Smith, Abby (312) 397-0020
GM, Windy City Times, Chicago, IL
Smith, Al (419) 784-5441
NTL ED, News ED, Wire ED
Crescent-News, Defiance, OH
Smith, Al (206) 872-6600
ADV DIR-NTL
South County Journal, Kent, WA
Smith, Albert (Bo) (815) 385-2231
GM, McHenry Star, McHenry, IL
Smith, Alice (618) 393-2931
MGR-Composition
Olney Daily Mail, Olney, IL
Smith, Alison (401) 724-0200
ED
Rhode Island Jewish Herald, Providence, RI
Smith, Allan (800) 245-6536
MAN ED-Sentinel Publishing
US/Express, Chicago, IL
Smith, Allen (318) 377-1866
MAN ED, Action Line ED, Automotive/Travel ED, BUS/FIN ED, City ED, Environmental ED, NTL ED, News ED, Photo ED, Political/ Government ED, SCI/Technology ED
Minden Press-Herald, Minden, LA
Smith, Allen W (217) 345-5592
Self-Syndicator
Ironwood Publications, Charleston, IL
Smith, Amy (423) 523-3131
Higher EDU ED
Knoxville News-Sentinel, Knoxville, TN
Smith, Andy (401) 277-7000
Music Writer-Pop
Providence Journal-Bulletin, Providence, RI
Smith, Andy (604) 732-2944
VP-Human Resources/ASST PUB
Pacific Press Limited, Vancouver, BC
Smith, Ann (508) 775-1200
Action Line ED (Write to Know)
Cape Cod Times, Hyannis, MA
Smith, Arlinda (304) 526-4000
Features ED
Herald-Dispatch, Huntington, WV
Smith, Arnold (319) 653-2191
ADV MGR, ADV MGR-CLASS
Washington Evening Journal, Washington, IA
Smith, Art (614) 373-2121
Presentation ED
Marietta Times, Marietta, OH
Smith, Austin L (937) 225-2000
CIRC VP, Dayton Daily News, Dayton, OH
Smith, B N (615) 552-1808
SEC, CONT, Leaf-Chronicle, Clarksville, TN
Smith, Barbara (802) 748-8121
TREAS, Books/Food ED, Women's ED
Caledonian-Record, St. Johnsbury, VT
Smith, Barry (704) 864-3291
EPE, EDL Writer
Gaston Gazette, Gastonia, NC
Smith, Barry (702) 882-2111
ED, City ED, EPE
Nevada Appeal, Carson City, NV
Smith, Barry A (519) 271-2220
SEC-TREAS, PA, CR MGR
Stratford Beacon-Herald, Stratford, ON
Smith, Bart (541) 672-3321
ED, EDL Writer, News-Review, Roseburg, OR
Smith, Mrs. Battle (706) 485-3501
PUB, Eatonton Messenger, Eatonton, GA
Smith, Becky (757) 363-2400
PUB, Port Folio, Virginia Beach, VA
Smith, Ben M (304) 752-6950
VP, Logan Banner, Logan, WV
Smith, Betty (606) 744-3123
Food ED, Women's ED
Winchester Sun, Winchester, KY
Smith, Betty Barker (501) 425-3133
PUB, Baxter Bulletin, Mountain Home, AR
Smith, Bill (608) 462-8224
ED, Wonewoc Reporter, Wonewoc, WI
Smith, Billie (605) 225-4100
PRES, PUB
Aberdeen American News, Aberdeen, SD
Smith, Billy R (901) 285-4091
PUB, State Gazette, Dyersburg, TN
Smith, Brent A (765) 534-4900
PUB, Lapel Post, Lapel, IN
Smith, Brian Woodley (800) 747-1429
ED, Craft Patterns Inc., St. Charles, IL
Smith, Bruce (503) 226-1311
PROD FRM-PR
Daily Journal of Commerce, Portland, OR
Smith, Bruce K (801) 752-2121
PRES/PUB, Herald Journal, Logan, UT
Smith, Bruce P (508) 586-7200
EX ED, Enterprise, Brockton, MA
Smith, C Fraser (410) 332-6000
COL-Political, Sun, Baltimore, MD
Smith, C P (714) 835-1234
Topics ED-Courts/Cops/Social Issues
Orange County Register, Santa Ana, CA
Smith, C T (901) 772-1172
PUB, ED, States-Graphic, Brownsville, TN
Smith, Carol (219) 235-6161
ADV DIR
South Bend Tribune, South Bend, IN
Smith, Carolyn C (215) 949-4000
VP
Bucks County Courier Times, Levittown, PA
Calkins Newspapers
Smith, Cathy (519) 631-2790
MGR-MKTG & PROM, CIRC MGR
St. Thomas Times-Journal, St. Thomas, ON
Smith, Cecil J (812) 883-3281
MAN ED, Your Advantage, Salem, IN
Smith, Ceil (609) 935-1500
ADV MGR, Today's Sunbeam, Salem, NJ
Smith, Chad (318) 942-4971
PROD FRM-MR, Daily World, Opelousas, LA
Smith, Chard (970) 723-4404
PUB, Jackson County Star, Walden, CO
Smith, Charles (817) 390-7400
CIRC MGR-Single Copy
Fort Worth Star-Telegram, Fort Worth, TX
Smith, Charles (610) 258-7171
PROD MGR-PR, Express-Times, Easton, PA
Smith, Charles P (412) 775-3200
EVP, Beaver County Times, Beaver, PA
Calkins Newspapers
Smith, Charlotte (219) 235-6161
Food ED
South Bend Tribune, South Bend, IN
Smith, Cheryl (561) 461-2050
City ED, Tribune, Fort Pierce, FL
Smith, Cheryl (317) 423-5511
ADV MGR-CLASS, ADTX MGR
Journal and Courier, Lafayette, IN
Smith, Cheryl I (714) 835-1234
Deputy ED-Nights
Orange County Register, Santa Ana, CA
Smith, Chris (706) 647-5414
PUB, ED, Thomaston Times, Thomaston, GA
Smith, Chuck (316) 792-1211
News ED
Great Bend Tribune, Great Bend, KS
Smith, Chuck (717) 748-6791
PROD MGR, Express, Lock Haven, PA
Smith, Cindy (615) 259-8000
ASST MAN ED-Planning
Tennessean, Nashville, TN
Smith, Cindy W (804) 352-8215
GM, Times-Virginian, Appomattox, VA
Smith, Clausie W (913) 422-4048
PUB, ED, Bonner Springs-Edwardsville Chieftain, Bonner Springs, KS
Smith, Clifford B (816) 931-2002
PRES, Daily Record, Kansas City, MO
Smith Jr, Clifton S (818) 282-5707
PUB, San Marino Tribune, San Marino, CA
Smith, Cort (908) 219-5788
ED, Two River Times, Red Bank, NJ
Smith, Craig A (304) 765-5555
PUB, MAN ED
Braxton Democrat-Central, Sutton, WV
Smith, Craig J (412) 523-6588
EX ED, Standard Observer, Greensburg, PA
Smith, Cynthia (914) 962-4748
PUB
North County News, Yorktown Heights, NY
Smith, Dan (216) 245-6901
Sunday ED, Television ED
Morning Journal, Lorain, OH
Smith, Dan P (816) 254-8600
VP-Community Newspapers
Examiner, Independence, MO
Smith, Danny (334) 289-4017
PUB, ED, Demopolis Times, Demopolis, AL
Smith, Darin (309) 647-5100
PROD MGR, Daily Ledger, Canton, IL
Smith, Darren (908) 254-7000
MAN ED, Sentinel, East Brunswick, NJ
Smith, Daryl C (519) 344-3641
PUB, Observer, Sarnia, ON
Smith, Dave (214) 977-8222
Deputy MAN ED/EX Sports ED
Dallas Morning News, Dallas, TX
Smith, Dave (515) 228-3211
Sports ED
Charles City Press, Charles City, IA
Smith, Dave (219) 933-3200
PROD FRM-MR, Times, Munster, IN
Smith, Dave (805) 650-2900
ED-Camarillo Edition
Ventura County Star, Ventura, CA
Smith, David (216) 999-4500
INFO SYS MGR-Publishing
Plain Dealer, Cleveland, OH
Smith, David (317) 622-1212
PUB, Herald Bulletin, Anderson, IN
Smith, David D (401) 596-7791
News ED, Westerly Sun, Westerly, RI
Smith, David L (205) 845-5510
COB, Smith Newspapers Inc., Fort Payne, AL
Smith, Dean (407) 322-2611
Sports ED, Sanford Herald, Sanford, FL
Smith, Deb (360) 377-3711
Librarian, Sun, Bremerton, WA
Smith, Debbie (618) 443-2145
GM, Sparta News-Plaindealer, Sparta, IL
Smith, Debbie (307) 787-3229
PUB, Uinta County Pioneer, Lyman, WY
Smith, Deborah L (765) 534-4900
PUB, ED, Lapel Post, Lapel, IN
Smith, Deidra J (423) 727-6121
ED, Tomahawk, Mountain City, TN
Smith, Deirdre Parker (704) 633-8950
Books ED, Teen-Age/Youth ED
Salisbury Post, Salisbury, NC
Smith, Denise (217) 675-2461
MAN ED, Franklin Times, Franklin, IL
Smith, Dennis (509) 837-4500
BC, Daily Sun News, Sunnyside, WA
Smith, Don (214) 977-8222
ASST MAN ED
Dallas Morning News, Dallas, TX
Smith, Don (206) 448-8000
BUS ED
Seattle Post-Intelligencer, Seattle, WA
Smith, Don (605) 665-7811
PUB
Yankton Daily Press & Dakotan, Yankton, SD
Smith, Don (705) 645-4463
PUB, Muskoka Advance, Bracebridge, ON
Smith, Don (803) 423-2050
MAN ED
Marion Star & Mullins Enterprise, Marion, SC
Smith, Don (304) 455-3300
ED, Wetzel Chronicle, New Martinsville, WV
Smith, Dona (318) 824-3011
GM, ADV DIR
Jennings Daily News, Jennings, LA
Smith, Donald (603) 882-2741
MGR-Accounting, Telegraph, Nashua, NH
Smith, Donald Q (612) 295-3131
PUB, ED, Monticello Times, Monticello, MN
Smith, Donna (423) 482-1021
News ED, Oak Ridger, Oak Ridge, TN
Smith, Dorothy Haugsten (503) 226-1311
PUB/SEC/TREAS
Daily Journal of Commerce, Portland, OR
Smith, Dorsey (912) 985-4545
PROD DIR, PROD FRM/MGR-PR
Observer, Moultrie, GA
Smith, Duane (512) 258-4127
MAN ED, Hill Country News, Cedar Park, TX
Smith, Dusty (970) 723-4404
PUB, Jackson County Star, Walden, CO
Smith, E Berry (219) 287-1001
VP
Schurz Communications Inc., South Bend, IN
Smith, Edith (409) 336-6416
ED, Liberty Gazette, Liberty, TX
Smith, Edna M (219) 745-0552
ED
Ft. Wayne Frost Illustrated, Ft. Wayne, IN
Smith, Edward (303) 820-1010
"Empire" Magazine ED
Denver Post, Denver, CO
Smith, Edward N (219) 745-0552
PUB
Ft. Wayne Frost Illustrated, Ft. Wayne, IN
Smith, Ellen (419) 522-3311
Librarian, News Journal, Mansfield, OH
Smith, Elmer (215) 854-2000
COL-News
Philadelphia Daily News, Philadelphia, PA
Smith, Emilie (519) 679-6666
ASSOC ED, London Free Press, London, ON
Smith, Erik (509) 582-1500
Political ED, Tri-City Herald, Tri-Cities, WA
Smith, Eugene R (212) 580-8559
ED, Journal Press Syndicate, New York, NY
Smith, Eva E (304) 294-4144
GM, MAN ED
Mullens Advocate, Mullens, WV
Smith, Everett W (914) 562-1218
PUB, ED, Sentinel, Vails Gate, NY
Smith, Frances (540) 825-0771
CIRC MGR
Culpeper Star-Exponent, Culpeper, VA
Smith, Francine (408) 920-5000
West Magazine ED
San Jose Mercury News, San Jose, CA
Smith, Francis J (860) 887-9211
CIRC DIR, Norwich Bulletin, Norwich, CT
Smith, Franklyn (519) 863-2334
ED, Norwich Gazette, Norwich, ON
Smith, Fred (812) 482-2424
City ED, Herald, Jasper, IN
Smith, Fred W (812) 254-0480
Chairman (MGT Committee/Senior Consultant), Times-Herald, Washington, IN
Smith, Gary (423) 581-5630
Chief Photographer, Photo ED
Citizen Tribune, Morristown, TN
Smith, Gary (206) 597-8742
Electronic MKTG MGR, ADTX/Online MGR
News Tribune, Tacoma, WA
Smith, Gary (617) 786-7000
DP MGR, Patriot Ledger, Quincy, MA
Smith, Gayle (704) 358-5000
ADV MGR-Display
Charlotte Observer, Charlotte, NC
Smith, George (205) 236-1551
COL, Anniston Star, Anniston, AL
Smith, George (605) 996-5514
PROD FRM-COMP
Daily Republic, Mitchell, SD
Smith, George (330) 852-4634
ED, Budget, Sugarcreek, OH
Smith, George (304) 478-3533
PUB, Parsons Advocate, Parsons, WV
Smith, Gerald (773) 586-8800
VP-Production/GM
Daily Southtown, Chicago, IL
Smith, Ginny (334) 262-1611
Living/Lifestyle ED, Women's ED
Montgomery Advertiser, Montgomery, AL
Smith, Glen (972) 722-5191
PUB, Journal-Success, Rockwall, TX
Smith, Gordon (619) 299-3131
COL-News
San Diego Union-Tribune, San Diego, CA
Smith Jr, Grady (205) 345-0505
ADV DIR, ADTX MGR
Tuscaloosa News, Tuscaloosa, AL
Smith, Greig (504) 826-3279
ADV MGR-Sales & Development
Times-Picayune, New Orleans, LA
Smith, Gretchen (814) 674-3666
ED, Union Press Courier, Patton, PA
Smith Jr, Griffin (501) 378-3400
EX ED
Arkansas Democrat-Gazette, Little Rock, AR
Smith, H Alan (515) 464-2440
PUB, ED
Mount Ayr Record-News, Mount Ayr, IA
Smith, H G (802) 748-8121
PRES, Caledonian-Record, St. Johnsbury, VT
Smith, Hal (305) 571-7699
PUB, Miami New Times, Miami, FL
Smith, Harley L (508) 249-3535
PROD SUPT, Athol Daily News, Athol, MA
Smith, Hazel Bledsoe (816) 727-3395
PUB, ED, Media, Kahoka, MO
Smith, Henrietta (713) 526-4727
GM, Houston Metro, Houston, TX
Smith, Herb (501) 763-4461
ADV MGR
Blytheville Courier News, Blytheville, AR
Smith, Howard (716) 849-3434
EX Sports ED, Buffalo News, Buffalo, NY
Smith, J Berkeley (517) 739-2054
PUB, Oscoda Press, Oscoda, MI
Smith, J T (915) 673-4271
Farm ED, Abilene Reporter-News, Abilene, TX
Smith, Jack (334) 687-3506
GM, Eufaula Tribune, Eufaula, AL
Smith, Jack H (505) 522-1277
COL, Smith, Jack H., Las Cruces, NM
Smith, Jack L (304) 624-6411
ADV MGR-Display, Clarksburg Exponent/ Telegram, Clarksburg, WV
Smith, James (412) 439-7500
ASSOC ED, Herald-Standard, Uniontown, PA
Smith, James (513) 721-2700
MET ED, Cincinnati Enquirer, Cincinnati, OH
Smith, James (518) 270-1200
BUS/FIN ED, Record, Troy, NY
Smith, James (208) 232-4161
CIRC DIR, Idaho State Journal, Pocatello, ID
Smith, James C (330) 454-5611
PUB, Repository, Canton, OH
Smith, James C (318) 365-6773
ED, EPE, Daily Iberian, New Iberia, LA
Smith, James E (954) 356-4000
VP-MKTG, VP/DIR-MKTG/PROM
Sun-Sentinel, Fort Lauderdale, FL
Smith, James H (203) 235-1661
VP, EX ED, Record-Journal, Meriden, CT
Smith III, James I (412) 261-6255
MAN ED
Pittsburgh Legal Journal, Pittsburgh, PA
Smith, James O (541) 447-6205
PUB
Prineville Central Oregonian, Prineville, OR
Smith, James P (916) 321-1855
VP-FIN
McClatchy Newspapers, Sacramento, CA

Copyright ©1997 by the Editor & Publisher Co.

215-Who's Where **Smi**

Smith, James W (817) 675-3336
PUB, Clifton Record, Clifton, TX
Smith, Jamie (904) 427-1000
ADV DIR, Observer, New Smyrna Beach, FL
Smith, Jane A (509) 337-6631
PUB, Times, Waitsburg, WA
Smith, Janell (309) 852-2181
PROD FRM-COMP, Star-Courier, Kewanee, IL
Smith, Janet (703) 276-3400
ADV VP-Travel/Related Sales
USA Today, Arlington, VA
Smith, Janet (803) 785-4293
MAN ED, Island Packet, Hilton Head, SC
Smith, Janet (405) 864-7612
ED, Covington Record, Covington, OK
Smith, Jason (541) 926-2211
CIRC CNR-TMC
Albany Democrat-Herald, Albany, OR
Smith, Jason (918) 423-1700
MAN ED, City ED, McAlester News-Capital & Democrat, McAlester, OK
Smith, Jay R (404) 843-5000
PRES, Cox Newspapers Inc., Atlanta, GA
Smith, Jeff (607) 334-3276
PROD MGR, Evening Sun, Norwich, NY
Smith, Jeff (360) 754-5400
BUS ED, Olympian, Olympia, WA
Smith, Jim (916) 662-5421
ED, Daily Democrat, Woodland, CA
Smith, Jim (215) 854-2000
Courts Reporter
Philadelphia Daily News, Philadelphia, PA
Smith, Jim (203) 425-2500
Sr VP-OPER Central
Thomson Newspapers, Stamford, CT
Smith, Jo Anne (903) 597-8111
ADV MGR-NTL
Tyler Morning Telegraph, Tyler, TX
Smith, Joel P (334) 687-3506
PUB, ED, Eufaula Tribune, Eufaula, AL
Smith, John (606) 231-3100
CIRC MGR-State
Lexington Herald-Leader, Lexington, KY
Smith, John (301) 722-4600
Copy Desk Chief
Cumberland Times-News, Cumberland, MD
Smith, John A (604) 442-2191
PUB, Gazette, Grand Forks, BC
Smith, John B (404) 523-6086
PUB, Atlanta Inquirer, Atlanta, GA
Smith, John L (312) 752-2500
GM, Chicago Crusader, Chicago, IL
Smith, Bishop John M (904) 432-5215
PUB, Florida Catholic, Pensacola, FL
Smith, Judith Zelmer (541) 469-3123
PUB, Curry Coastal Pilot, Brookings, OR
Smith, Julie (507) 932-3663
ED, St. Charles Press, St. Charles, MN
Smith, Karen (802) 748-8121
EDU ED
Caledonian-Record, St. Johnsbury, VT
Smith, Karen (602) 898-6500
ADV MGR-RT, Mesa Tribune, Mesa, AZ
Thomson Newspapers
Smith, Kathleen (215) 355-9009
ED, Bucks County Midweek, Trevose, PA
Smith, Kathryn (864) 224-4321
Books ED
Anderson Independent-Mail, Anderson, SC
Smith, Kathy (518) 725-8616
Fashion/Style ED, Home Furnishings ED, Living/Lifestyle ED, Women's ED
Leader-Herald, Gloversville, NY
Smith, Kemp (815) 223-3200
Picture ED, News-Tribune, La Salle, IL
Smith, Ken (864) 582-4511
CIRC DIR, Herald-Journal, Spartanburg, SC
Smith, Kenneth (909) 849-4586
PUB, Record-Gazette, Banning, CA
Smith, Kenneth (201) 383-1500
ASSOC ED, New Jersey Herald, Newton, NJ
Smith, Kenneth J (814) 643-4040
DIR-OPER, PA, Daily News, Huntingdon, PA
Smith, Kenneth W (909) 845-9564
PUB, Community Adviser, Beaumont, CA
Smith, Kerri (303) 820-1010
Farm/Agriculture Reporter
Denver Post, Denver, CO
Smith, Kevin (816) 271-8500
CIRC MGR
St. Joseph News-Press, St. Joseph, MO
Smith, Kevin (412) 224-4321
Sports ED
Valley News Dispatch, Tarentum, PA
Smith, Kris (815) 987-1200
PROD MGR-Pre Press
Rockford Register Star, Rockford, IL
Smith, Kurt (201) 383-1500
PROD FRM-PR
New Jersey Herald, Newton, NJ
Smith, L Melissa (704) 636-8932
PUB, ED, Piedmont Sun, Statesville, NC
Smith, LaDeanne (409) 544-2238
ED, Houston County Courier, Crockett, TX

Smith, Lalla (812) 829-2255
MGR-Office
Spencer Evening World, Spencer, IN
Smith, Larry (217) 446-1000
EPE, Commercial News, Danville, IL
Smith, Larry (219) 244-5153
CIRC MGR, Post & Mail, Columbia City, IN
Smith, Larry (806) 376-4488
CONT-Division, DP MGR, Amarillo Daily News/Globe Times, Amarillo, TX
Smith, Larry B (915) 597-2959
PUB, ED, Brady Standard, Brady, TX
Smith, Larry K (423) 562-8468
PUB, La Follette Press, La Follette, TN
Smith, Laurell (812) 944-6481
Society ED
Tribune/Ledger & Tribune, New Albany, IN
Smith, Lawrence (219) 881-3000
CIRC MGR-Home Delivery
Post-Tribune, Gary, IN
Smith, Lawrence M (503) 226-1311
PRES
Daily Journal of Commerce, Portland, OR
Smith, Layne (915) 673-4271
Graphics ED/Art DIR
Abilene Reporter-News, Abilene, TX
Smith, Lee (618) 253-7146
ED, Daily Register, Harrisburg, IL
Smith, LeRoy (937) 225-2000
ADV MGR-RT
Dayton Daily News, Dayton, OH
Smith, Les (517) 377-1000
BUS ED, SCI/Technology ED
Lansing State Journal, Lansing, MI
Smith, Leslie (213) 622-8332
CIRC DIR, La Opinion, Los Angeles, CA
Smith, Libby (501) 378-3400
Travel ED
Arkansas Democrat-Gazette, Little Rock, AR
Smith, Linda (919) 537-2505
Office MGR
Daily Herald, Roanoke Rapids, NC
Smith, Linda L (814) 371-4200
ADV DIR
Courier-Express/Tri-County Sunday, Du Bois, PA
Smith, Lindell (618) 662-2108
Sports ED
Daily Clay County Advocate-Press, Flora, IL
Smith, Lori (609) 871-8000
ADV MGR-PROM
Burlington County Times, Willingboro, NJ
Smith, Lori Klinger (614) 373-2121
ADV DIR, Marietta Times, Marietta, OH
Smith, Lorne (604) 732-2222
BUS/FIN ED, Province, Vancouver, BC
Smith, Lorrie (757) 899-3551
GM, MAN ED
Sussex-Surry Dispatch, Wakefield, VA
Smith, Lucinda (201) 746-1100
ED, Montclair Times, Montclair, NJ
Smith, Lynn H (219) 933-3200
MGR-NTL RT, Times, Munster, IN
Smith, Lytton (206) 448-8000
Librarian
Seattle Post-Intelligencer, Seattle, WA
Smith, M J (808) 525-8000
MAN ED-News Presentation/OPER
Honolulu Advertiser, Honolulu, HI
Smith, Maralee (410) 332-6000
CIRC ASST DIR-RT Sales
Sun, Baltimore, MD
Smith, Marci (919) 708-9000
Food ED, Lifestyle ED, Television ED
Sanford Herald, Sanford, NC
Smith, Marcia (360) 424-3251
ADV MGR-Sales
Skagit Valley Herald, Mount Vernon, WA
Smith, Mariwyn M (304) 478-3533
PUB, ED, Parsons Advocate, Parsons, WV
Smith, Marjorie (618) 656-4700
ADV MGR
Edwardsville Intelligencer, Edwardsville, IL
Smith, Mark (802) 748-8121
VP, PUB, PA
Caledonian-Record, St. Johnsbury, VT
Smith, Mark (603) 569-6550
ED, Lakes Region Courier, Wolfeboro, NH
Smith, Meceal Hollier (318) 536-6016
PUB, ED, Gueydan Journal, Gueydan, LA
Smith, Melanie (205) 353-4612
Religion ED, Decatur Daily, Decatur, AL
Smith, Melissa (205) 234-4281
BUS MGR
Alexander City Outlook, Alexander City, AL
Smith, Merle (705) 674-5271
PROD FRM-COMP
Sudbury Star, Sudbury, ON
Smith, Miatta (212) 213-8585
ED, New York Beacon, New York, NY
Smith, Michael (217) 223-5100
CIRC MGR, Quincy Herald-Whig, Quincy, IL
Smith, Michael (713) 485-2785
ED, Friendswood Journal, Friendswood, TX

Smith, Michelle (510) 783-6111
Sports COL, Daily Review, Hayward, CA
Smith, Mike (540) 638-8801
Sports ED
Martinsville Bulletin, Martinsville, VA
Smith, Mike (847) 888-7800
News ED, Courier-News, Elgin, IL
Smith, Mike (909) 987-6397
PROD SUPV-Press
Inland Valley Daily Bulletin, Ontario, CA
Smith, Mike (704) 864-3291
Sports ED, Gaston Gazette, Gastonia, NC
Smith, Mike (313) 222-6400
DIR-Photography, Free Press, Detroit, MI
Smith, Mike (864) 582-4511
EPE, Herald-Journal, Spartanburg, SC
Smith, Mike (504) 345-2333
ADV MGR-CLASS, Daily Star, Hammond, LA
Smith, Mike (314) 340-8000
Sports ED, Post-Dispatch, St. Louis, MO
Smith, Mike (604) 732-2222
COL, Province, Vancouver, BC
Smith, Mikel (803) 771-6161
PROD MGR-OPER, State, Columbia, SC
Smith, Milton C (864) 476-3513
PUB, ED, Woodruff News, Woodruff, SC
Smith, Nancy (609) 871-8000
ADV MGR-CLASS
Burlington County Times, Willingboro, NJ
Smith, Nancy B (561) 287-1550
MAN ED, Stuart News, Stuart, FL
Smith, Nelson A (614) 892-2771
PUB, On Target, Utica, OH
Smith, P T (304) 348-5140
SEC, Charleston Gazette, Sunday Gazette-Mail, Charleston, WV
Smith, Pat (712) 328-1811
PROD FRM-MR
Daily Nonpareil, Council Bluffs, IA
Smith, Patricia M (716) 247-9200
PUB, Gates-Chili News, Rochester, NY
Smith, Patrick (616) 723-3592
DP MGR
Manistee News-Advocate, Manistee, MI
Smith, Paul (501) 378-3400
VP/GM
Arkansas Democrat-Gazette, Little Rock, AR
Smith, Paul C (813) 259-7711
EX Sports ED
Tampa Tribune and Times, Tampa, FL
Smith, Peter (503) 226-1311
VP, CIRC MGR-Commercial Sales
Daily Journal of Commerce, Portland, OR
Smith, Phil (219) 267-3111
CIRC MGR, Times-Union, Warsaw, IN
Smith, Quinton (503) 221-8327
Suburban ED, Oregonian, Portland, OR
Smith, R Scudder (203) 426-3141
PUB, ED, Newtown Bee, Newtown, CT
Smith, Ramona (215) 854-2000
Environmental ED
Philadelphia Daily News, Philadelphia, PA
Smith, Randall (816) 234-4141
MET ED, Kansas City Star, Kansas City, MO
Smith, Randi (715) 394-4411
ADV MGR, Daily Telegram, Superior, WI
Smith, Randy (860) 646-0500
Sports ED, Journal Inquirer, Manchester, CT
Smith, Randy (501) 268-8621
CIRC DIR, Daily Citizen, Searcy, AR
Smith, Rebecca (408) 481-0174
ED, Sunnyvale Sun, Sunnyvale, CA
Smith, Rebecca (817) 995-2586
PUB, Saint Jo Tribune, Saint Jo, TX
Smith, Rex (518) 454-5694
MAN ED-News, Times Union, Albany, NY
Smith, Richard (717) 326-1551
PROD SUPT-PR
Williamsport Sun-Gazette, Williamsport, PA
Smith, Richard D (800) 355-9500
Chairman/CEO, News USA Inc., Vienna, VA
Smith, Richard E (913) 457-3411
PUB
Westmoreland Recorder, Westmoreland, KS
Smith, Richard J (512) 467-2881
MAN ED, Austin Sun, Austin, TX
Smith, Rick (915) 653-1221
COL, Standard-Times, San Angelo, TX
Smith, Rick (905) 684-7251
CIRC DIR-Reader, Sales & SRV
Standard, St. Catharines, ON
Smith, Rick (801) 575-7003
GM, Private Eye Weekly, Salt Lake City, UT
Smith, Ricky (410) 228-3131
PROD Cameraman
Daily Banner, Cambridge, MD
Smith, Rob (206) 242-0100
ED
Highline News/Des Moines News, Burien, WA
Smith, Robert (405) 372-5000
RE ED, News Press, Stillwater, OK
Smith, Robert (402) 444-1000
City ED-Day
Omaha World-Herald, Omaha, NE

Smith, Robert B (816) 462-3848
PUB, La Belle Star, La Belle, MO
Smith, Robert C (941) 262-3161
ADV ASST DIR
Naples Daily News, Naples, FL
Smith, Robin (802) 447-7567
Wire ED, Bennington Banner, Bennington, VT
Smith, Roger (501) 963-2901
ED, Paris Express-Progress, Paris, AR
Smith, Roger (606) 298-7570
GM, Mountain Citizen, Inez, KY
Smith, Roger (213) 237-5000
Deputy NTL ED
Los Angeles Times, Los Angeles, CA
Smith, Ron (941) 629-2855
ADV MGR-CLASS
Sun Herald, Port Charlotte, FL
Smith, Ron (704) 464-0221
PROD FRM-PR
Observer-News-Enterprise, Newton, NC
Smith, Ron (573) 785-1414
Outdoors ED, Sports ED
Daily American Republic, Poplar Bluff, MO
Smith, Ron (316) 221-1050
PROD MGR
Winfield Daily Courier, Winfield, KS
Smith, Ron (812) 231-4200
CIRC DIR, Tribune-Star, Terre Haute, IN
Smith, Ron D (509) 337-6631
PUB, ED, Times, Waitsburg, WA
Smith, Ronald C (423) 756-1234
MAN ED
Chattanooga Times, Chattanooga, TN
Smith, Ronn (505) 763-3431
City/MET ED
Clovis News Journal, Clovis, NM
Smith, Russ (618) 463-2500
Photo DEPT MGR, Telegraph, Alton, IL
Smith, Russ (212) 941-1130
ED, New York Press, New York, NY
Smith, Sam (918) 581-8300
MGR-CR, Tulsa World, Tulsa, OK
Smith, Sandra (603) 224-5301
Sports ED, Concord Monitor, Concord, NH
Smith, Scott (501) 642-2111
Sports ED
De Queen Daily Citizen, De Queen, AR
Smith, Scott (913) 764-2211
GM, Olathe Daily News, Olathe, KS
Smith, Scott (312) 222-3237
PRES/PUB/CEO-Sun Sentinel Co.
Tribune Co., Chicago, IL
Smith, Scott W (307) 634-3361
EPE, Wyoming Tribune-Eagle, Cheyenne, WY
Smith, Sharon E (717) 622-3456
DIR-Sales & MKTG, Pottsville Republican & Evening Herald, Pottsville, PA
Smith, Sheila (913) 899-2338
CIRC MGR, DP MGR
Goodland Daily News, Goodland, KS
Smith, Shelby (513) 721-2700
ADV CNR-Preprint
Cincinnati Enquirer, Cincinnati, OH
Smith, Shirley (818) 932-6161
PROD MGR, Dodge Construction News Greensheet, Monrovia, CA
Smith, Shirley (205) 539-9828
GM, Redstone Rocket, Huntsville, AL
Smith, Shirley (606) 784-4116
ED, Morehead News, Morehead, KY
Smith, Si (847) 329-2000
GM, Lerner News Star, Lincolnwood, IL
Smith, Sid (312) 222-3232
Arts Critic, Chicago Tribune, Chicago, IL
Smith, Slim (707) 546-2020
Sports ED, Press Democrat, Santa Rosa, CA
Smith, Stanford (541) 926-2211
Photo ED, Democrat-Herald, Albany, OR
Smith, Starley (805) 650-2900
Life ED, Ventura County Star, Ventura, CA
Smith, Steve (503) 226-1311
ADV MGR-Display
Daily Journal of Commerce, Portland, OR
Smith, Steve (609) 663-6000
PROD MGR-Technical SRV, PROD SUPT-Building, Courier-Post, Cherry Hill, NJ
Smith, Steve (316) 321-1120
SCI ED, El Dorado Times, El Dorado, KS
Smith, Steve (816) 858-5154
ED, Platte County Citizen, Platte City, MO
Smith, Steve (317) 459-3121
DP MGR, Kokomo Tribune, Kokomo, IN
Thomson Newspapers
Smith, Steve (304) 425-8191
PUB, Princeton Times, Princeton, WV
Smith, Steven (360) 496-5993
ED, Morton Journal, Morton, WA
Smith, Steven A (719) 632-5511
ED, Gazette, Colorado Springs, CO

Smi Who's Where-216

Smith, Steven A .... (805) 650-2900
CIRC DIR, Ventura County Star, Ventura, CA
Smith, Steven D .... (413) 788-1000
City ED-Night, Union-News, Springfield, MA
Smith, Steven L .... (717) 326-1551
CONT, Sun-Gazette, Williamsport, PA
Smith, Stuart .... (941) 953-7755
ADV MGR-MKTG
Sarasota Herald-Tribune, Sarasota, FL
Smith, Sue .... (203) 661-3386
SEC/TREAS, Newspaper Features Council Inc., Greenwich, CT
Smith, Sue .... (214) 977-8222
ASST MAN ED-Lifestyles
Dallas Morning News, Dallas, TX
Smith, Sue .... (716) 232-7100
Health ED, Rochester Democrat and Chronicle; Times-Union, Rochester, NY
Smith, Sue .... (217) 935-3171
CIRC DIR, Clinton Daily Journal, Clinton, IL
Smith, Susan A .... (515) 284-8000
VP-FIN, Des Moines Register, Des Moines, IA
Smith, Susan White .... (801) 625-4200
SEC, Standard-Examiner, Ogden, UT
Smith, Sylvia .... (407) 242-3500
PROD MGR-Pre Press
Florida Today, Melbourne, FL
Smith, Tanny .... (318) 783-3450
Photo DEPT MGR
Crowley Post-Signal, Crowley, LA
Smith, Taylor .... (803) 549-2586
PUB, Press & Standard, Walterboro, SC
Smith, Terry .... (770) 428-9411
EVP, Marietta Daily Journal, Marietta, GA
Smith, Terry .... (614) 594-8219
ED, MAN ED, Athens News, Athens, OH
Smith, Thomas C .... (804) 649-6000
CIRC MGR-MET
Richmond Times-Dispatch, Richmond, VA
Smith, Thomas R .... (419) 483-4190
PRES, Bellevue Gazette, Bellevue, OH
Smith, Tim .... (954) 356-4000
Music Critic-Classical
Sun-Sentinel, Fort Lauderdale, FL
Smith, Tom .... (513) 721-2700
ADV MGR-CLASS/Automotive
Cincinnati Enquirer, Cincinnati, OH
Smith, Tom .... (816) 932-6600
Sales MGR/Northeast Div.
Universal Press Syndicate, Kansas City, MO
Smith, Tom .... (216) 647-3171
PUB, Wellington Enterprise, Wellington, OH
Smith, Tom .... (403) 235-7100
PROD FRM-Distribution Center
Calgary Herald, Calgary, AB
Smith, Tori .... (212) 621-1500
DIR-CORP Communications
Associated Press, New York, NY
Smith, Traci .... (205) 232-2720
Women's ED, News Courier, Athens, AL
Smith, Valerie .... (970) 949-0555
ADV DIR, Vail Daily News, Vail, CO
Smith, Venetta .... (212) 455-4000
MGR-Wire Services, North America Syndicate, King Features Syndicate, NY, NY
Smith, Vera .... (606) 744-3123
TREAS, Winchester Sun, Winchester, KY
Smith, Vernon .... (214) 977-8222
ASST MAN ED-Recruiting
Dallas Morning News, Dallas, TX
Smith, Virgil .... (704) 252-5611
PRES, PUB
Asheville Citizen-Times, Asheville, NC
Smith, W Leon .... (817) 675-3336
PUB, ED, Clifton Record, Clifton, TX
Smith, W Terry .... (540) 949-8213
MAN ED, Amusements/Travel ED, Radio/Television ED, News Virginian, Waynesboro, VA
Smith Jr, Walter .... (212) 213-8585
PUB, New York Beacon, New York, NY
Smith, Wayne .... (205) 766-3434
Political ED, Times Daily, Florence, AL
Smith, Wayne .... (502) 821-6833
CONT, CNR-SYS
Messenger, Madisonville, KY
Smith, Wayne .... (804) 732-3456
CIRC DIR, Progress-Index, Petersburg, VA
Smith, Wendell .... (806) 376-4488
CIRC MGR-Country, Amarillo Daily News/Globe Times, Amarillo, TX
Smith, Whit .... (901) 529-2211
Theater Reporter
Commercial Appeal, Memphis, TN
Smith, William .... (615) 552-1808
CONT, Leaf-Chronicle, Clarksville, TN
Smith, William .... (312) 321-3000
RE Markets, Chicago Sun-Times, Chicago, IL
Smith, William .... (508) 775-1200
EPE, Cape Cod Times, Hyannis, MA
Smith, William .... (520) 774-4545
PROD MGR-PR
Arizona Daily Sun, Flagstaff, AZ
Pulitzer Publishing Co.
Smith, William B .... (317) 284-2528
PUB, Advertiser, Muncie, IN
Smitherman, Lamar .... (334) 262-1611
VP-Specialty Products
Montgomery Advertiser, Montgomery, AL
Smithers, James .... (561) 287-1550
PROD MGR-Camera/Plateroom
Stuart News, Stuart, FL
Smithers, Stacy .... (916) 645-7733
PUB, Lincoln News Messenger, Lincoln, CA
Smith II, Abb Jacson .... (912) 732-2731
GM, Cuthbert Times and News Record, Cuthbert, GA
Smithson, Steve .... (519) 426-5710
CIRC MGR, Simcoe Reformer, Simcoe, ON
Smits, Mike .... (414) 435-4411
Computer Technician
Green Bay Press-Gazette, Green Bay, WI
Smizik, Robert .... (412) 263-1100
Sports COL
Pittsburgh Post-Gazette, Pittsburgh, PA
Smokler, Charlotte .... (303) 442-1202
Librarian, Daily Camera, Boulder, CO
Smolinski, Jim .... (916) 541-3880
ADV MGR-RT
Tahoe Daily Tribune, South Lake Tahoe, CA
Smoljo, Joseph A .... (402) 462-2131
CIRC MGR, Hastings Tribune, Hastings, NE
Smollon, Chris .... (908) 722-8800
CIRC MGR-Home Delivery
Courier-News, Bridgewater, NJ
Smoragiewicz, Margaret .... (617) 749-0031
PUB, Hingham Journal, Hingham, MA
Smotherman, Charles .... (615) 893-5860
PROD SUPV
Daily News Journal, Murfreesboro, TN
Smothers, Jimmy .... (205) 549-2000
Sports ED, Gadsden Times, Gadsden, AL
Smothers, William .... (205) 551-1020
PUB, ED, Speakin' Out Weekly, Huntsville, AL
Smylie, Robert T .... (215) 355-9009
PUB, Bucks County Midweek, Trevose, PA
Smyntek, John .... (313) 222-6400
Special Features/Syndicate ED
Detroit Free Press, Detroit, MI
Smyser, A A (Bud) .... (808) 525-8000
Contributing ED
Honolulu Star-Bulletin, Honolulu, HI
Smyth, Joe .... (800) 426-4192
COB/CEO, Independent Newspapers Inc. (DE), Dover, DE
Smyth, Mitch .... (416) 367-2000
Travel ED, Toronto Star, Toronto, ON
Smyth, Russell .... (970) 728-4488
ED, Telluride Times-Journal, Telluride, CO
Smythe, Dan .... (613) 236-0491
EDL CNR, Southam Syndicate, Ottawa, ON
Snapp, Cathy .... (510) 935-2525
MET ED
Contra Costa Times, Walnut Creek, CA
Snapp, Dan .... (802) 748-8121
Sports ED
Caledonian-Record, St. Johnsbury, VT
Snarr, L Glen .... (801) 237-2188
COB, Deseret News, Salt Lake City, UT
Snavely, Celeste .... (301) 733-5131
CIRC DIR, Morning Herald, Hagerstown, MD
Snead, Bill .... (913) 843-1000
Deputy ED, Journal-World, Lawrence, KS
Snead, Elizabeth .... (703) 276-3400
Fashion/Style Reporter
USA Today, Arlington, VA
Sneddon, James D .... (717) 854-1575
PUB, ED, York Dispatch, York, PA
Sneddon, Steve .... (702) 788-6200
COL, Reno Gazette-Journal, Reno, NV
Sneed, Michael .... (312) 321-3000
COL-GEN, Chicago Sun-Times, Chicago, IL
Snell, Bob .... (904) 260-9770
ED, Folio Weekly, Jacksonville, FL
Snell, Carvy .... (912) 685-6566
PUB, ED, Metter Advertiser, Metter, GA
Snellings, Thomas L .... (540) 374-5000
CIRC MGR
Free Lance-Star, Fredericksburg, VA
Snezrud, Bill .... (316) 241-2422
CIRC MGR
McPherson Sentinel, McPherson, KS
Snider, Betty .... (501) 642-2111
CIRC MGR
De Queen Daily Citizen, De Queen, AR
Snider, Marie .... (316) 283-2309
Self-Syndicator
This Side of 60, North Newton, KS
Snider, Steve .... (716) 232-7100
Graphics ED, Rochester Democrat and Chronicle; Times-Union, Rochester, NY
Snider, Tina .... (417) 532-9131
ADTX MGR
Lebanon Daily Record, Lebanon, MO
Sniffen, Bill .... (215) 854-2000
News ED
Philadelphia Inquirer, Philadelphia, PA
Sniffin, William C .... (307) 332-2323
PUB, Wyoming State Journal, Lander, WY
Snipes, David .... (910) 893-5121
ED, Harnett County News, Lillington, NC
Snoddy, Fran .... (504) 222-4541
MAN ED, St. Helena Echo, Greensburg, LA
Snodgrass, Patti .... (703) 777-1111
MAN ED
Loudoun Times-Mirror, Leesburg, VA
Snodgress, David .... (812) 332-4401
Photo DEPT MGR
Herald-Times Inc, Bloomington, IN
Snook, Edward M .... (207) 784-5411
TREAS, Sun-Journal, Lewiston, ME
Snook, Steve .... (712) 328-1811
PROD FRM-COMP
Daily Nonpareil, Council Bluffs, IA
Snortland, Ann .... (406) 791-1444
DIR-MKTG
Great Falls Tribune, Great Falls, MT
Snow, A C .... (919) 829-4500
COL, News & Observer, Raleigh, NC
Snow, Craig .... (802) 747-6121
PROD FRM-PR/Pre Press
Rutland Herald, Rutland, VT
Snow, Daniel A .... (414) 275-2166
GM, Times, Walworth, WI
Snow, Daniel H .... (207) 729-3311
VP/GM, Times Record, Brunswick, ME
Snow, Gary A .... (610) 258-7171
CONT, Express-Times, Easton, PA
Snow, Jane .... (330) 996-3000
Food Writer, Beacon Journal, Akron, OH
Snow, Jeanne R .... (315) 482-2581
ED
Thousand Islands Sun, Alexandria Bay, NY
Snow, Mark .... (816) 385-3121
ED, Macon Chronicle-Herald, Macon, MO
Snow, Marvin .... (408) 637-6300
ED, Pinnacle, Hollister, CA
Snow, Mary .... (970) 669-5050
Design ED, News ED, Wire ED
Loveland Daily Reporter-Herald, Loveland, CO
Snow, Shauna .... (213) 237-5000
"Morning Report" Column
Los Angeles Times, Los Angeles, CA
Snow, Tony .... (313) 222-2300
EDL Writer, Detroit News, Detroit, MI
Snow, Wayne .... (913) 242-4700
PROD FRM-PR, Ottawa Herald, Ottawa, KS
Snowert, Glenn .... (314) 340-8000
PROD SUPT-SYS SRV
St. Louis Post-Dispatch, St. Louis, MO
Snuffer, Evangelina .... (209) 578-2000
Chief Copy Clerk, Modesto Bee, Modesto, CA
Snure, Melody L .... (330) 264-1125
MAN ED, EPE, Special Edition ED
Daily Record, Wooster, OH
Snyder, Bette .... (419) 294-2332
MGR-EDU SRV, EPE, EDU ED, Entertainment ED, Features ED, Health/Medical ED, NTL ED, News ED, SCI/Technology ED
Daily Chief-Union, Upper Sandusky, OH
Snyder, Bill .... (615) 259-8800
Medical ED, Nashville Banner, Nashville, TN
Snyder, Bonnie .... (360) 577-2500
TREAS, BM, DP MGR
Daily News, Longview, WA
Snyder, Carolyn .... (408) 920-5000
Special Sections ED
San Jose Mercury News, San Jose, CA
Snyder, Darrell .... (808) 935-6621
CIRC MGR-Subscriber SRV
Hawaii Tribune-Herald, Hilo, HI
Snyder, David L .... (814) 793-2144
PUB, ED
Morrisons Cove Herald, Martinsburg, PA
Snyder, Diana .... (614) 474-3131
CIRC MGR, Herald, Circleville, OH
Snyder, Elizabeth .... (414) 657-1000
ED-Kenosha Life, Fashion/Women's ED, Food ED, Home Furnishings ED, Religion/Society ED, Kenosha News, Kenosha, WI
Snyder, Eric .... (520) 294-1200
Desk ED, Daily Territorial, Tucson, AZ
Snyder, Frank M .... (419) 586-2371
PUB, Daily Standard, Celina, OH
Snyder, Gene .... (806) 592-2141
PUB, Denver City Press, Denver City, TX
Snyder, Howard .... (606) 231-3100
Radio/Television Writer
Lexington Herald-Leader, Lexington, KY
Snyder, Jack .... (617) 929-2000
PROD GEN FRM (Westwood)
Boston Globe, Boston, MA
Snyder, Jodie .... (602) 271-8000
Health/Medical Writer
Arizona Republic, Phoenix, AZ
Snyder, Joe .... (319) 291-1400
PROD FRM-Press
Waterloo Courier, Waterloo, IA
Snyder, John .... (518) 234-4368
GM, Daily Editor, Cobleskill, NY
Snyder, John .... (517) 368-0365
ED, Camden Publications, Camden, MI
Snyder, John P .... (315) 866-2220
ADV MGR, Evening Telegram, Herkimer, NY
Snyder, Jud .... (707) 584-2222
ED, Community Voice, Rohnert Park, CA
Snyder, Karen .... (614) 474-3131
PROD SUPV-COMP, Herald, Circleville, OH
Snyder, Kenneth C .... (610) 258-7171
MGR-CR, Express-Times, Easton, PA
Snyder, Melissa .... (703) 276-3400
VP-MKTG/PROM, CIRC VP-MKTG
USA Today, Arlington, VA
Snyder, Mike .... (717) 264-6161
CIRC MGR-Home Delivery
Public Opinion, Chambersburg, PA
Snyder, Mike .... (713) 220-7171
ASST City ED
Houston Chronicle, Houston, TX
Snyder, Ralph .... (314) 340-8000
PROD ASST MGR-Color Quality Control
St. Louis Post-Dispatch, St. Louis, MO
Snyder, Richard .... (607) 334-3276
PRES, PUB, Evening Sun, Norwich, NY
Snyder, Robert T .... (207) 784-5411
CIRC DIR, Sun-Journal, Lewiston, ME
Snyder, Sara .... (412) 222-2200
EDU ED, Observer-Reporter, Washington, PA
Snyder, Sherry .... (618) 393-2931
ADV MGR-CLASS, Olney Daily Mail, Olney, IL
Snyder, Sonja .... (503) 484-0519
PUB, Eugene Weekly, Eugene, OR
Snyder, Thomas .... (301) 722-4600
MGR-FIN
Cumberland Times-News, Cumberland, MD
Snyder, Tim .... (602) 496-0665
GM, Ahwatukee Weekly News, Phoenix, AZ
Snylyk, Zenon .... (201) 434-0237
ED, Svoboda Ukrainian Daily, Jersey City, NJ
So, Angela .... (630) 627-7010
ED, Villa Park Review, Lombard, IL
Sobczyk, Mike .... (419) 422-5151
BUS/FIN Reporter, Farm/Agriculture Reporter
Courier, Findlay, OH
Sobel, Joseph P .... (814) 234-9601
Sr. VP, AccuWeather Inc., State College, PA
Sobie, Tim .... (414) 473-3363
ED, Whitewater Register, Whitewater, WI
Sobiloff, James .... (401) 762-3000
ADV DIR-MKTG, Call, Woonsocket, RI
Soble, Anne .... (310) 457-2112
PUB, ED, Malibu Surfside News, Malibu, CA
Sobota, Lenore .... (309) 829-9411
Chief EDL Writer
Pantagraph, Bloomington, IL
Socha, Edward .... (717) 455-3636
ED-Night, Standard-Speaker, Hazleton, PA
Socha, Gary .... (301) 948-3120
PUB, Rockville Gazette, Gaithersburg, MD
Socha, Miles .... (519) 894-2231
Fashion/General Reporter
Record, Kitchener, ON
Sodoma, Bill .... (607) 432-1000
Sports ED, Daily Star, Oneonta, NY
Sodomka, Dennis .... (706) 724-0851
EX ED, Augusta Chronicle, Augusta, GA
Soens, Most Rev Lawrence D .. (712) 255-2550
PUB, Globe, Sioux City, IA
Soergel, Brian .... (909) 987-6397
Entertainment ED
Inland Valley Daily Bulletin, Ontario, CA
Soergel, Matt .... (904) 359-4111
Films/Theater ED
Florida Times-Union, Jacksonville, FL
Soesbee, Gilbert .... (423) 623-6171
MAN ED, Newport Plain Talk, Newport, TN
Soeteber, Ellen .... (954) 356-4000
MAN ED, Sun-Sentinel, Fort Lauderdale, FL
Sofi, Al .... (617) 269-5192
GM, Liria, South Boston, MA
Soforic, Joseph F .... (412) 547-5722
GM
Mount Pleasant Journal, Mount Pleasant, PA
Soga, Aki .... (802) 863-3441
BUS ED
Burlington Free Press, Burlington, VT
Sohl, Ron .... (903) 455-4220
PUB
Greenville Herald-Banner, Greenville, TX
Sohlstrom, John .... (802) 479-0191
PROD FRM-PR/MR, Times Argus, Barre, VT
Sohn-Shahi, Virginia .... (505) 983-3303
ADV DIR
Santa Fe New Mexican, Santa Fe, NM
Sokol, Fred .... (413) 788-1000
Theater Critic, Union-News, Springfield, MA
Sokolov, Ray .... (212) 416-2000
Entertainment/Amusements ED
Wall Street Journal, New York, NY
Sokolsky, Bob .... (909) 684-1200
Radio/Television ED
Press-Enterprise, Riverside, CA

Copyright ©1997 by the Editor & Publisher Co.

217-Who's Where **Spa**

Sola, Mike ... (714) 888-6511
Self-Syndicator
Sola, Mike, San Bernadino, CA
Solander, O J ... (209) 369-2761
Environmental ED, News-Sentinel, Lodi, CA
Solari, Jan ... (614) 299-7764
ED, Stonewall Journal, Columbus, OH
Soldier, Kay ... (207) 892-1166
ED, Suburban News, Windham, ME
Soldwedel, Donald N ... (520) 783-3311
COB, Western Newspapers Inc., Yuma, AZ
Soldwedel, Joseph E ... (520) 783-3311
PRES, Western Newspapers Inc., Yuma, AZ
Soldwedel, Lou Edith ... (520) 445-3333
SEC, Daily Courier, Prescott, AZ
Soles, Jody ... (915) 546-6100
Librarian, El Paso Times, El Paso, TX
Soles, Walter ... (330) 747-1471
PROD FRM-PR, Vindicator, Youngstown, OH
Solesbee, John D ... (706) 778-2400
PUB, Northeast Georgian, Cornelia, GA
Soliman, Michael ... (520) 573-4400
VP-Market Development, TNI Partners dba Tucson Newspapers, Tucson, AZ
Solinsky, Matt ... (317) 664-5111
Sports ED, Chronicle-Tribune, Marion, IN
Solis, Rebecca ... (210) 542-4301
CIRC MGR, Brownsville Herald, Brownsville, TX, Freedom Communications Inc.
Solis, Sandy ... (912) 888-9300
ADV MGR-CLASS/Telemarketing
Albany Herald, Albany, GA
Solley, Frances ... (501) 534-3400
Graphics ED/Art DIR
Pine Bluff Commercial, Pine Bluff, AR
Solley, Joseph ... (915) 653-1221
CIRC MGR, Standard-Times, San Angelo, TX
Solloway, Christine ... (207) 873-3341
DP MGR, Central Maine Morning Sentinel, Waterville, ME, Guy Gannett Communications
Soloman, Alan ... (312) 222-3232
Travel ED, Chicago Tribune, Chicago, IL
Solomon, Buddy ... (404) 843-5000
CONT, Cox Newspapers Inc., Atlanta, GA
Solomon, David ... (603) 882-2741
MAN ED, Telegraph, Nashua, NH
Solomon, Digby ... (757) 247-4600
GM-Digital City Hampton Roads
Daily Press, Newport News, VA
Solomon, Fran ... (813) 259-7711
ASST DIR-PROM
Tampa Tribune and Times, Tampa, FL
Solomon, George ... (202) 334-6000
ASST MAN ED-Sports
Washington Post, Washington, DC
Solomon, Goody L ... (202) 723-2477
Author/Owner, Food Nutrition Health News Service, Washington, DC
Solomon, Michele ... (518) 454-5694
Entertainment ED, Times Union, Albany, NY
Solomon, Raymond Reuven ... (212) 688-7557
Staff, World Union Press, New York, NY
Solomon, Sam ... (508) 685-1000
PROD FRM-PR
Eagle-Tribune, North Andover, MA
Soltys, Judie ... (705) 759-3030
CR MGR, Sault Star, Sault Ste. Marie, ON
Somaini, Roy ... (802) 479-0191
BM, DP MGR, Times Argus, Barre, VT
Somerville, John R ... (707) 569-9893
PRES, Asterisk Features, Santa Rosa, CA
Somerville, Sonja ... (815) 232-1171
City ED, Journal-Standard, Freeport, IL
Sommer, Bredgit ... (915) 673-4271
ADV MGR-MKTG SRV, MGR-MKTG/PROM
Abilene Reporter-News, Abilene, TX
Sommer, Shirley ... (507) 647-5357
ED, Winthrop News, Winthrop, MN
Sommerdorf, Scott ... (415) 777-1111
Photo DIR
San Francisco Chronicle, San Francisco, CA
Sommerhof, John ... (618) 656-4700
News ED
Edwardsville Intelligencer, Edwardsville, IL
Sommers, Edith ... (517) 752-7171
PROD MGR-Pre Press
Saginaw News, Saginaw, MI
Sommers, Michael ... (201) 877-4141
Drama Critic (New York)
Star-Ledger, Newark, NJ
Somorjai, Agnes ... (416) 221-6195
PUB, Magyar Elet, Willowdale, ON
Sondag, William H ... (309) 246-2865
PUB, ED, Lacon Home Journal, Lacon, IL
Sondej, Lydia ... (609) 989-7800
ADV MGR-CLASS, Trentonian, Trenton, NJ
Sonderegger, Leo ... (520) 325-9501
Contact, Alburn Bureau, Tucson, AZ
Sondreal, Jerry ... (715) 268-8101
ED, Amery Free Press, Amery, WI
Sondreal, Palmer H ... (715) 268-8101
PUB, Amery Free Press, Amery, WI
Sondreal, Steve ... (715) 268-8101
GM, Amery Free Press, Amery, WI

Sones, Bill ... (216) 932-5538
Co-Author, Numbers Game, Cleveland, OH
Song, Frank ... (206) 223-0623
ED, Seattle Chinese Post, Seattle, WA
Songe, Alex ... (504) 447-4055
Sports ED, Daily Comet, Thibodaux, LA
Songer, Kris ... (319) 523-4631
ED, Wapello Republican, Wapello, IA
Songini, Marc ... (617) 878-5100
MAN ED, South Shore News, Rockland, MA
Sonia III, Joe ... (619) 372-4747
PUB, Trona Argonaut, Trona, CA
Sonnenberg, Jim ... (217) 446-1000
BUS ED, Commercial News, Danville, IL
Sonnenfelt, David ... (402) 358-5220
ED, Creighton News, Creighton, NE
Sonnenreich, Sharon E ... (801) 237-2800
GEN Counsel
Newspaper Agency Corp., Salt Lake City, UT
Sonnenschein, Bruno ... (401) 821-7400
PROD FRM-PR
Kent County Daily Times, West Warwick, RI
Sonnichsen, David P ... (206) 284-4424
CONT, Pioneer Newspapers, Seattle, WA
Sonnie, David ... (609) 272-7000
CIRC MGR-Transportation
Press of Atlantic City, Pleasantville, NJ
Sons, Beverly ... (815) 223-3200
Society/Women's ED
News-Tribune, La Salle, IL
Sons, Charles ... (615) 967-2272
PUB, Herald-Chronicle, Winchester, TN
Sons, Davis ... (615) 967-2272
GM, Herald-Chronicle, Winchester, TN
Sons, Lester ... (708) 755-6161
ED
Chicago Heights Star, Chicago Heights, IL
Soper, Susan ... (404) 526-5151
ASST MAN ED-Features
Atlanta Journal-Constitution, Atlanta, GA
Sopinsky, Jordan ... (302) 427-2100
ED, Jewish Voice, Wilmington, DE
Sopkow, Ken ... (306) 563-5131
PUB, ED, Norquay North Star, Canora, SK
Sopoci, Anna L ... (201) 676-0280
ED, Sokol Times, East Orange, NJ
Sora, Joe ... (307) 856-2244
Sports ED, Riverton Ranger, Riverton, WY
SoRelle, Ruth ... (713) 220-7171
Medical ED, Houston Chronicle, Houston, TX
Sorensen, Alan ... (540) 981-3100
EPE, Roanoke Times, Roanoke, VA
Sorensen, Alan ... (406) 265-6795
EDU ED, Religion ED
Havre Daily News, Havre, MT
Sorensen, Bob ... (562) 435-1161
PROD MGR-Pre Press
Press-Telegram, Long Beach, CA
Sorensen, Chris ... (719) 438-5352
PUB, ED, Kiowa County Press, Eads, CO
Sorensen, John ... (414) 657-1000
Photo DEPT MGR
Kenosha News, Kenosha, WI
Sorensen, Robert B ... (914) 939-1164
PUB, Port Chester Guide, Port Chester, NY
Sorenson, Edith ... (520) 573-4220
Films ED, Arizona Daily Star, Tucson, AZ
Sorenson, Kirsten ... (801) 625-4200
Health/Medical ED
Standard-Examiner, Ogden, UT
Sorlie, Devon Hubbard ... (406) 388-6762
PUB, ED, High Country Independent Press, Belgrade, MT
Soroka, Gerald E ... (604) 287-9227
PUB
Campbell River Mirror, Campbell River, BC
Sorrells, Charles ... (507) 235-3303
Sports ED, Sentinel, Fairmont, MN
Sosinski, Stephan J ... (707) 441-0500
PUB, Times-Standard, Eureka, CA
Sosniecki, Gary ... (417) 935-2257
PUB, ED
Webster County Citizen, Seymour, MO
Sosniecki, Helen ... (417) 935-2257
PUB, ED
Webster County Citizen, Seymour, MO
Sosnowski, Vivienne ... (604) 732-2222
MAN ED, Province, Vancouver, BC
Soso, Hector ... (702) 649-8553
MAN ED, El Mundo, Las Vegas, NV
Sossamon, Cody ... (864) 489-1131
ED, Gaffney Ledger, Gaffney, SC
Sossamon, Louis C ... (864) 489-1131
PUB, GM, Gaffney Ledger, Gaffney, SC
Soto, Cesar ... (619) 356-2995
ED, Imperial Valley Weekly, Holtville, CA
Soto, Lucia ... (708) 484-1188
GM, El Imparcial, Chicago, IL
Soto, Mildred Torres ... (860) 241-6200
MGR-Community Affairs
Hartford Courant, Hartford, CT
Soto, Robert ... (512) 884-2011
PROD MGR-Distribution Center, Corpus Christi Caller-Times, Corpus Christi, TX

Sotomayor, Ernie ... (516) 843-2020
Regional ED, Newsday, Melville, NY
Soucheray, Joe ... (612) 222-5011
COL, St. Paul Pioneer Press, St. Paul, MN
Soucie, Christine ... (902) 426-2811
Books ED, Chronicle-Herald, Halifax, NS
Soucy, Magella ... (418) 686-3233
Features ED, Teen-age/Youth, Travel ED
Le Soleil, Quebec, QC
Soudre, Rene ... (514) 276-9615
PUB, L 'Express d 'Outremont, Montreal, QC
Soule, Brian ... (804) 732-3456
Photo DEPT MGR
Progress-Index, Petersburg, VA
Soule, Dorothy ... (307) 742-2176
ADV MGR-RT, Daily Boomerang, Laramie, WY
Soulen, Ric ... (303) 820-1010
PROD MGR-Pre Press
Denver Post, Denver, CO
Soult, Terry ... (412) 588-5000
PROD MGR, Record-Argus, Greenville, PA
Sousa, Frank ... (413) 788-1000
Outdoors ED, Union-News, Springfield, MA
Sousa, Richard ... (619) 745-6611
PROD MGR-Pre Press
North County Times, Escondido, CA
Souser, Mark ... (303) 820-1010
PROD MGR-Digital Services
Denver Post, Denver, CO
Sousley, Will ... (503) 221-8327
PROD ASST SUPT-MR
Oregonian, Portland, OR
Souslin, Karla ... (419) 752-3854
GM
Greenwich Enterprise Review, Greenwich, OH
South, Bob ... (519) 894-2231
Online MGR, Record, Kitchener, ON
Southard, Christina Cronin ... (516) 747-8282
ED, Port Washington News, Mineola, NY
Southard, Donna L ... (703) 922-1712
Photo ED
World Images News Service, Alexandria, VA
Southerland, Bill ... (203) 574-3636
VP/ASST TREAS, EX ED, Waterbury Republican-American, Waterbury, CT
Southerland, Charlie C ... (912) 783-1291
PUB, Hawkinsville Dispatch and News, Hawkinsville, GA
Southern, William A ... (312) 321-3000
ADV DIR-Planning & Strategy
Chicago Sun-Times, Chicago, IL
Southwick, Peter A ... (617) 929-2000
DIR-Photography, Boston Globe, Boston, MA
Southwick, Ron ... (609) 845-3300
EDU ED
Gloucester County Times, Woodbury, NJ
Southworth, Ginny ... (803) 648-2311
Photo ED, Aiken Standard, Aiken, SC
Souza, Chip ... (903) 432-3132
ED, Cedar Creek Pilot, Seven Points, TX
Souza, Dawn ... (617) 979-5670
ED, Saugus Advertiser, Melrose, MA
Souza, Joe ... (603) 524-3800
Sports ED, Citizen, Laconia, NH
Souza, John ... (909) 987-6397
ADV DIR-Display
Inland Valley Daily Bulletin, Ontario, CA
Souza, Kenneth J ... (508) 758-9055
ED, Harborview, Mattapoisett, MA
Sova, Rod ... (301) 733-5131
CIRC MGR-PROM
Morning Herald, Hagerstown, MD
Sovde, Roger L ... (803) 329-4000
GM, Herald, Rock Hill, SC
Sovell, Jane ... (507) 537-1551
BM, Independent, Marshall, MN
Sovik, John W ... (330) 747-1471
ADV MGR-CLASS
Vindicator, Youngstown, OH
Sowecke, Timothy M ... (610) 258-7171
PUB, Express-Times, Easton, PA
Sowel, Susan ... (912) 294-3661
GM, Pelham Journal, Pelham, GA
Sowers, Craig ... (517) 278-2318
PROD MGR, Daily Reporter, Coldwater, MI
Sowers, Gene ... (316) 775-2218
PROD MGR-Commercial Printing
Augusta Daily Gazette, Augusta, KS
Sowers, Richard ... (508) 343-6911
Photo ED
Sentinel & Enterprise, Fitchburg, MA
Sowers, Stephen E ... (573) 364-2468
PUB, ED, Rolla Daily News, Rolla, MO
Sozanski, Ed ... (215) 854-2000
Art Critic
Philadelphia Inquirer, Philadelphia, PA
Spaar, Betty S ... (573) 882-5700
PRES, Columbia Missourian, Columbia, MO
Spacek, Robert ... (608) 782-9710
PROD MGR-SYS
La Crosse Tribune, La Crosse, WI
Spach, Jay J ... (203) 425-2500
Sr VP-Organization & MGT Development
Thomson Newspapers, Stamford, CT

Spader, Tom ... (908) 349-3000
Photo ED
Ocean County Observer, Toms River, NJ
Spafford, Horace W ... (201) 384-0998
PUB, Twin-Boro News, Bergenfield, NJ
Spahr, Steve ... (501) 751-6200
DP MGR, Morning News of Northwest Arkansas, Springdale, AR
Spain, Amber ... (315) 685-8338
ED, Skaneateles Press, Skaneateles, NY
Spain, Hal ... (915) 453-2433
PUB, Observer Enterprise, Robert Lee, TX
Spain, Karl ... (703) 560-4000
PRES/COO
Journal Newspapers Inc., Fairfax, VA
Spain, Michael V ... (518) 454-5694
ASST MAN ED, Times Union, Albany, NY
Spain, Tom ... (803) 577-7111
DIR-Photography
Post and Courier, Charleston, SC
Spain, Tom ... (901) 853-2241
GM, Collierville Herald, Collierville, TN
Spaite, Karen S ... (330) 755-2155
ED, Journal, Struthers, OH
Spalding, Dan ... (219) 267-3111
Entertainment/Amusements ED, NTL ED, Political/Government ED
Times-Union, Warsaw, IN
Spalding, Steve ... (810) 332-8181
BUS ED, Oakland Press, Pontiac, MI
Spalvieri, Dennis ... (330) 424-9541
Amusements/Books ED
Morning Journal, Lisbon, OH
Spander, Art ... (510) 783-6111
Sports COL, Daily Review, Hayward, CA
Spang, Karen ... (313) 365-9500
PUB, Citizen, Hamtramck, MI
Spangler, Christine ... (414) 563-5553
ED, EPE, Farm ED, Fashion/Society ED, News ED, Daily Jefferson County Union, Fort Atkinson, WI
Spangler, Eric ... (513) 923-3111
ED, Hilltop News-Press, Cincinnati, OH
Spangler, James ... (316) 268-6000
DIR-Employee Relations
Wichita Eagle, Wichita, KS
Spangler, Keith ... (903) 785-8744
CIRC MGR, Paris News, Paris, TX
Spangler, Wayne ... (717) 767-6397
PROD MGR-Pre Press
York Newspaper Company, York, PA
Spanier, Carolyn ... (541) 926-2211
Regional
Albany Democrat-Herald, Albany, OR
Spano, Andrew ... (508) 685-1000
EPE, Eagle-Tribune, North Andover, MA
Sparber, Gordon ... (910) 727-7211
Music ED
Winston-Salem Journal, Winston-Salem, NC
Spargur, Thomas E ... (216) 966-1121
PUB, Sun Journal, North Canton, OH
Sparkes, Paul ... (709) 364-6300
MAN ED, Evening Telegram, St. John's, NF
Sparkes, Tabitha ... (205) 325-2222
Amusements ED, Fashion ED, Features ED, Women's ED
Birmingham Post-Herald, Birmingham, AL
Sparkman, Melanie ... (501) 561-4634
MAN ED
Northeast Arkansas Town Crier, Manila, AR
Sparks, Cody ... (915) 653-1221
CNR-MKTG, Standard-Times, San Angelo, TX
Sparks, Dwight ... (704) 634-2129
PUB, ED, Davie County Enterprise Record, Mocksville, NC
Sparks, James ... (405) 321-1800
PROD MGR, Norman Transcript, Norman, OK
Sparks, Jeff ... (918) 652-3311
Sports ED, Daily Free-Lance, Henryetta, OK
Sparks, Jon ... (901) 529-2211
Amusements/Arts ED, Entertainment ED
Commercial Appeal, Memphis, TN
Sparks, Kenneth M ... (217) 897-1525
PUB, ED, Fisher Reporter, Fisher, IL
Sparks, Kyle E ... (317) 825-0581
CIRC MGR, News-Examiner, Connersville, IN
Sparks, Robert ... (217) 897-1525
PUB, Fisher Reporter, Fisher, IL
Sparks, Rodney ... (817) 634-2125
Accountant, Killeen Daily Herald, Killeen, TX
Sparks, Stephen R ... (206) 464-2111
VP-Circulation,
Seattle Times, Seattle, WA
Sparrow, Cynthia R ... (410) 442-1638
ASSOC ED/COL
Main Street Features, Ellicott City, MD
Sparrow, J D ... (410) 442-1638
ASSOC ED/Special Feature
Main Street Features, Ellicott City, MD

Spa Who's Where-218

Spates, David (615) 484-5145
MAN ED, Crossville Chronicle, Crossville, TN
Spatz, Dan (541) 298-8545
ED, Dalles Reminder, The Dalles, OR
Spatz, Tom (312) 321-3000
CIRC MGR-OPER
Chicago Sun-Times, Chicago, IL
Spaulding, Richard (619) 232-4381
RE ED, Daily Transcript, San Diego, CA
Spear, Glen (502) 781-1700
PROD FRM-PR
Daily News, Bowling Green, KY
Spear, Harold (502) 678-5171
ADV DIR, Glasgow Daily Times, Glasgow, KY
Spear, James (941) 953-7755
PROD MGR-PR
Sarasota Herald-Tribune, Sarasota, FL
Spear, Joe (507) 625-4451
News DIR-Content/Reporting
Free Press, Mankato, MN
Spear, John M (914) 496-3611
PUB, ED
Orange County Post, Washingtonville, NY
Spears, Bob (309) 734-3176
CIRC MGR
Daily Review Atlas, Monmouth, IL
Spears, Cate (319) 629-5207
ED, Reporter, Lone Tree, IA
Spears, Donna (501) 327-6621
ADV MGR, Log Cabin Democrat, Conway, AR
Spears, Lawanza (202) 332-0080
ED, Washington Afro-American and Tribune, Washington, DC
Spears, Louis F (757) 446-2000
SEC, Virginian-Pilot, Norfolk, VA
Spears, Richard F (757) 446-2000
VP, Virginian-Pilot, Norfolk, VA
Specht, Art (619) 295-5432
PUB
Uptown San Diego Examiner, San Diego, CA
Specht, Carl (218) 829-4705
ADTX MGR
Brainerd Daily Dispatch, Brainerd, MN
Specht, David A (318) 377-1866
PRES, Minden Press-Herald, Minden, LA
Specht Jr, David (318) 377-1866
VP, ASST PUB, Graphics ED/Art DIR
Minden Press-Herald, Minden, LA
Specht, J (619) 295-5432
ED
Uptown San Diego Examiner, San Diego, CA
Specht, James A (334) 847-2599
PUB, Washington County News, Chatom, AL
Specht, Tina (318) 377-1866
CIRC DIR, Minden Press-Herald, Minden, LA
Speck, John (707) 468-3500
ADV DIR, Ukiah Daily Journal, Ukiah, CA
Speck, Peter (604) 985-2131
PUB
North Shore News, North Vancouver, BC
Spector, Albert (330) 852-4634
PUB, Budget, Sugarcreek, OH
Speed, James T (601) 776-3726
PUB, Clarke Co. Tribune, Quitman, MS
Speed, Mary C (601) 776-3726
GM, Clarke Co. Tribune, Quitman, MS
Speelman, Patty (937) 773-2721
MAN ED, Piqua Daily Call, Piqua, OH
Speer, Bill (517) 354-3111
PUB, PSL MGR, GEN MGR, ED
Alpena News, Alpena, MI
Speer, Claude (501) 337-7523
PROD FRM-COMP
Malvern Daily Record, Malvern, AR
Speer, Diane (517) 354-3111
Entertainment/Amusements ED, Fashion/Style ED, Lifestyle ED, Television/Film ED, Travel ED, Alpena News, Alpena, MI
Speer, Ronald L (757) 446-2000
GM-North Carolina
Virginian-Pilot, Norfolk, VA
Speer, Sean (913) 632-2127
PROD SUPT/FRM-COMP
Clay Center Dispatch, Clay Center, KS
Speer, William (941) 953-7755
Photo ED
Sarasota Herald-Tribune, Sarasota, FL
Speicher, Melanie (419) 738-2128
Women's/Society ED
Wapakoneta Daily News, Wapakoneta, OH
Speights, Patsy (601) 792-4221
ED, Prentiss Headlight, Prentiss, MS
Speirs, Julie (402) 564-2741
PUB, Columbus Telegram, Columbus, NE
Speizer, Jayne (803) 329-4000
PUB, Herald, Rock Hill, SC
Spellman, Kent (304) 643-2221
ED, Ritchie Gazette & The Cairo Standard, Harrisville, WV

Spence, Anthony J (615) 383-6393
GM, ED, Tennessee Register, Nashville, TN
Spence, Blake (612) 673-4000
PROD MGR-PR
Star Tribune, Minneapolis, MN
Spence, Boyd (919) 829-4500
ADV MGR-NTL
News & Observer, Raleigh, NC
Spence, Charles A (915) 682-5311
PUB
Midland Reporter-Telegram, Midland, TX
Spence, Joedie (919) 829-4500
CIRC MGR-Distribution
News & Observer, Raleigh, NC
Spence, Sharon (209) 943-6397
Radio/Television ED, Record, Stockton, CA
Spence, Steve (573) 431-2010
ADV MGR-CLASS, ADV MGR-Display
Daily Journal, Park Hills, MO
Spencer, Anne (904) 526-3614
Entertainment/Amusements ED, Lifestyle ED
Jackson County Floridan, Marianna, FL
Spencer, Christopher (308) 432-5511
PUB, ED, Chadron Record, Chadron, NE
Spencer, Clara (601) 948-4122
GM, Jackson Advocate, Jackson, MS
Spencer, Cynthia (616) 964-7161
DIR-Human Resources
Battle Creek Enquirer, Battle Creek, MI
Spencer, Ed (503) 221-8327
PROD SUPT-MR, Oregonian, Portland, OR
Spencer, Eric (419) 281-0581
PROD FRM-COMP
Ashland Times-Gazette, Ashland, OH
Spencer, Fern H (970) 867-5651
Books ED, Fashion/Food ED, Home Furnishings ED, Living/Lifestyle ED, Music ED, Fort Morgan Times, Fort Morgan, CO
Spencer, Foster L (716) 849-3434
MAN ED, Buffalo News, Buffalo, NY
Spencer, Gil (610) 622-8800
COL
Delaware County Daily Times, Primos, PA
Spencer, Marilyn (617) 433-7825
ED
Wayland-Weston Town Crier, Needham, MA
Spencer, Mark (416) 367-2000
ADV MGR-National
Toronto Star, Toronto, ON
Spencer, Paul (860) 241-6200
ASST MAN ED-Nights
Hartford Courant, Hartford, CT
Spencer, Rob (970) 949-0555
ED, Vail Daily News, Vail, CO
Spencer, Robert W (970) 867-5651
GM, MAN ED
Fort Morgan Times, Fort Morgan, CO
Spencer Jr, Robert W (970) 867-5651
ED, EPE, News ED
Fort Morgan Times, Fort Morgan, CO
Spencer, Sarah (405) 341-2121
SEC, Edmond Evening Sun, Edmond, OK
Spencer, T Floyd (804) 649-6000
ADV MGR-MKTG SRV
Richmond Times-Dispatch, Richmond, VA
Spencer, Tina (613) 829-9100
City ED, Lifestyle ED, Society ED
Ottawa Citizen, Ottawa, ON
Spencer, Tom (205) 236-1551
Political/Government ED
Anniston Star, Anniston, AL
Spencer, William (302) 856-0026
MAN ED, Sussex Countian, Georgetown, DE
Spencer, William (970) 867-5651
NTL ED, Fort Morgan Times, Fort Morgan, CO
Spera, Keith (504) 826-3279
Music Writer-Pop
Times-Picayune, New Orleans, LA
Spero, Steve (607) 798-1234
ASST MAN ED
Press & Sun Bulletin, Binghamton, NY
Sperry, Loren (715) 258-5546
ED, Waupaca County Post, Waupaca, WI
Sperry, Rob (916) 541-3880
MGR-MIS
Tahoe Daily Tribune, South Lake Tahoe, CA
Speth, Brenda (605) 394-8300
ADV MGR-RT
Rapid City Journal, Rapid City, SD
Spevak, Jeff (716) 232-7100
Pop Music/Nite Scene Reporter
Rochester Democrat and Chronicle; Rochester, NY Times-Union, Rochester, NY
Spice, Byron (412) 263-1100
SCI ED
Pittsburgh Post-Gazette, Pittsburgh, PA
Spicer, Al (910) 373-7000
DIR-Photography
News & Record, Greensboro, NC
Spicer, Frank L (703) 344-2489
VP, Moffitt Newspapers, Roanoke, VA
Spicer, Gerry (804) 649-6000
CIRC MGR-Single Copy
Richmond Times-Dispatch, Richmond, VA

Spicer, Richard (902) 667-5102
ADV MGR, Amherst Daily News, Amherst, NS
Spiece, Kathy (317) 462-5528
Administrative MGR, DP MGR
Daily Reporter, Greenfield, IN
Spiegel, Jan (719) 632-5511
Food ED, Gazette, Colorado Springs, CO
Spiegel, Kevin (215) 942-7890
Media Sales, Sports Network (Div. of Computer Info. Network), Southampton, PA
Spielman, Fran (312) 321-3000
City Hall Reporter
Chicago Sun-Times, Chicago, IL
Spielvogel, Gerald A (412) 775-3200
PROD DIR, Beaver County Times, Beaver, PA
Spielvogel, Lee (419) 924-2382
ED, Advance Reporter, West Unity, OH
Spielvogel, Regis L (419) 924-2382
PUB, Advance Reporter, West Unity, OH
Spiers, Paul (614) 363-1161
ADTX MGR, Delaware Gazette, Delaware, OH
Spies, Dennis (806) 376-4488
MAN ED, Amarillo Daily News/Globe Times, Amarillo, TX
Spigolon, Tom (615) 893-5860
MAN ED
Daily News Journal, Murfreesboro, TN
Spilak, Brent (403) 875-3362
PUB, Lloydminster Meridian Booster, Lloydminster, AB
Spillers, Hilda H (318) 927-3541
GM, Homer Guardian-Journal, Homer, LA
Spinks, Bruce (713) 220-7171
News ED, Houston Chronicle, Houston, TX
Spira, Paul (608) 252-6100
DIR-MKTG/PROM
Wisconsin State Journal, Madison, WI
Spirey, Christopher (717) 255-8100
DP MGR, Patriot-News, Harrisburg, PA
Spitler, Denise (817) 390-7400
VP/CFO, Star-Telegram, Fort Worth, TX
Spitz, Sherwood L (201) 664-2501
PUB, Community Life, Westwood, NJ
Spitza, Anne (602) 271-8000
Fashion Writer
Arizona Republic, Phoenix, AZ
Spitzer, Brad (405) 928-5540
PUB, Sayre Record, Sayre, OK
Spitzer, Dayva (405) 928-5540
ED, Sayre Record, Sayre, OK
Spitzer, George (719) 544-3520
PROD FRM-COMP
Pueblo Chieftain, Pueblo, CO
Spitzer, Helene (719) 544-3520
Librarian, Pueblo Chieftain, Pueblo, CO
Splittgerber, James (414) 457-7711
PROD FRM-COMP
Sheboygan Press, Sheboygan, WI
Spofford, Kristen (508) 297-0050
ED, Winchendon Courier, Winchendon, MA
Spohn, Larry (505) 823-7777
SCI/Technology
Albuquerque Tribune, Albuquerque, NM
Sponder, Sheri (605) 394-8300
Librarian
Rapid City Journal, Rapid City, SD
Sponseller, Barbara (419) 342-4276
ADV DIR, Daily Globe, Shelby, OH
Sponsler, Virginia (515) 877-3951
GM, ED, Humeston New Era, Humeston, IA
Spoon, Alan G (202) 334-6000
PRES/COO
Washington Post Co., Washington, DC
Spoor, Pam (616) 723-3592
Entertainment/Amusements ED, Films/Theater ED, Religion ED
Manistee News-Advocate, Manistee, MI
Spore, Keith (414) 224-2000
PRES/PUB
Milwaukee Journal Sentinel, Milwaukee, WI
Sportelli, Albina (201) 772-7003
ED, Dateline Journal, Butler, NJ
Spotleson, Bruce (520) 458-3973
PUB, Wick Communications, Sierra Vista, AZ
Spox, James M (207) 990-8000
MGR-MKTG ADM, CIRC MGR
Bangor Daily News, Bangor, ME
Spracklen, Jeff (817) 461-6397
CIRC MGR-Zone
Arlington Morning News, Arlington, TX
Spradlin, Melissa (615) 259-8000
NIE MGR, Tennessean, Nashville, TN
Sprague, Dennis (941) 262-3161
ADV MGR-CLASS
Naples Daily News, Naples, FL
Sprague, Gary (603) 224-5301
CIRC DIR, Concord Monitor, Concord, NH
Sprague, Randy (415) 777-5700
MGR-Publishing SYS, San Francisco Newspaper Agency, San Francisco, CA
Sprague, Seth (800) 286-6601
PUB, Casco Bay Weekly, Portland, ME
Spraw, Jan (419) 468-1117
State ED, Galion Inquirer, Galion, OH

Sprayberry, Noble (423) 756-1234
Leisure ED
Chattanooga Times, Chattanooga, TN
Sprayberry, Stephanie (704) 249-3981
CONT-BUS Office, Dispatch, Lexington, NC
Sprehe, Gary E (618) 532-5604
PA, PROD MGR
Centralia Sentinel, Centralia, IL
Sprenger, Pat (218) 829-4705
PROD FRM-PR
Brainerd Daily Dispatch, Brainerd, MN
Sprepski, Ellen (812) 424-7711
Librarian, Evansville Press, Evansville, IN
Sprick, Dennis (914) 341-1100
Arts/Entertainment ED, Entertainment/Amusements ED, Television/Film ED
Times Herald-Record, Middletown, NY
Springer, Daintry (416) 864-4262
MKTG & RES
Thomson Comics Group, Toronto, ON
Springer, David (707) 546-2020
PROD MGR-Packaging/Distribution
Press Democrat, Santa Rosa, CA
Springer, Julie A (217) 435-9221
GM, ED, Waverly Journal, Waverly, IL
Springer, Liz (334) 937-2511
MAN ED, Baldwin Times, Bay Minette, AL
Springer, Nancy P (217) 435-9221
PUB, Waverly Journal, Waverly, IL
Springston, Mike (618) 443-2145
ED, Sparta News-Plaindealer, Sparta, IL
Sprinkle, Virginia (803) 532-6203
ED, Twin City-News, Batesburg, SC
Sprong, Deb (219) 267-3111
EDU ED, Times-Union, Warsaw, IN
Sproul, Don (818) 962-8811
Graphics ED
San Gabriel Valley Tribune, West Covina, CA
MediaNews Inc.
Sproule, Louise (613) 678-3327
PUB, GM, ED, Review, Vankleek Hill, ON
Sproule, Robert (416) 947-2222
CIRC MGR-Home Delivery
Toronto Sun, Toronto, ON
Sprout, Greg (608) 252-6100
Sports ED
Wisconsin State Journal, Madison, WI
Sprung, Dan (219) 663-4212
GM, Lake County Star, Crown Point, IN
Sprung, James C (414) 235-7700
ADV DIR/VP-MKTG
Oshkosh Northwestern, Oshkosh, WI
Sprung, Russell F (414) 235-7700
PRES, PUB
Oshkosh Northwestern, Oshkosh, WI
Spry, Harvey (705) 749-3383
ED
Peterborough This Week, Peterborough, ON
Spry, Pamela J (315) 376-3525
PUB, Journal and Republican, Lowville, NY
Spurgeon, C Gary (515) 664-2334
PUB, ED
Bloomfield Democrat, Bloomfield, IA
Spurgeon, Thomas J (215) 949-4000
GM
Bucks County Courier Times, Levittown, PA
Spurlock, Delbert (212) 210-2100
EVP/ASSOC PUB
New York Daily News, New York, NY
Spurlock, Kathy (318) 322-5161
ED, News-Star, Monroe, LA
Spurr, Kim (919) 419-6500
Films/Theater ED, Food ED, Life ED, Music ED, Radio/Television ED
Herald-Sun, Durham, NC
Spyers, Bill (404) 526-5151
CIRC DIR-Distribution
Atlanta Journal-Constitution, Atlanta, GA
Squibb, Karen (219) 235-6161
PROD DIR
South Bend Tribune, South Bend, IN
Squiers, Randy (309) 343-7181
Photo DEPT MGR
Register-Mail, Galesburg, IL
Squires, David (912) 744-4200
BUS/Goverment ED
Macon Telegraph, Macon, GA
Squires, Susan (715) 526-2121
Farm/Agriculture ED
Shawano Leader, Shawano, WI
Squires, Tom (407) 242-3500
Sports ED, Florida Today, Melbourne, FL
Sradromski, Ann Marie (717) 264-6161
Lifestyle ED
Public Opinion, Chambersburg, PA
Srathdee, Mike (519) 894-2231
BUS Reporter, Record, Kitchener, ON
Staab, Belinda J (412) 867-1112
ED, Progress News, Emlenton, PA
Staab, David J (412) 867-1112
PUB, ED, Progress News, Emlenton, PA
Staab, Mike (316) 792-1211
PROD FRM-MR
Great Bend Tribune, Great Bend, KS

Copyright ©1997 by the Editor & Publisher Co.

219-Who's Where **Sta**

Staats, David .... (505) 823-7777
RE ED
Albuquerque Journal, Albuquerque, NM
Stabbert Jr, Fred W .... (914) 887-5200
PUB
Sullivan County Democrat, Callicoon, NY
Stabell, Shawn .... (305) 350-2111
PROD ASST MGR-Imaging
Miami Herald, Miami, FL
Stabile, Joe .... (810) 949-7900
GM, Downriver Voice, Marine City, MI
Stabile, Robert .... (508) 374-0321
PROD SUPT-COMP
Haverhill Gazette, Haverhill, MA
Stachiew, Mark .... (514) 987-2222
ADTX MGR, Gazette, Montreal, QC
Stachnik, Mary .... (518) 843-1100
BM, Recorder, Amsterdam, NY
Stachokas, George .... (603) 668-4321
ADV MGR-CLASS
Union Leader, Manchester, NH
Stack, Kathleen .... (860) 633-4691
ED, Glastonbury Citizen, Glastonbury, CT
Stack, Peter .... (415) 777-1111
Films ED
San Francisco Chronicle, San Francisco, CA
Stackhouse, Ben .... (207) 784-5411
Community News, EPE, Political/Government ED, Sun-Journal, Lewiston, ME
Stackhouse, John W .... (317) 473-3091
VP-FIN/CFO, Nixon Newspapers, Peru, IN
Stackhouse, Mary A .... (316) 234-5241
ED, Stafford Courier, Stafford, KS
Stacks, David .... (616) 392-2311
MAN ED, Suburban Review, Holland, MI
Stacy, Cindy .... (301) 334-9172
MAN ED
Garrett County Weekender, Oakland, MD
Stacy, Mark .... (304) 292-6301
News ED, Dominion Post, Morgantown, WV
Stacy, Mitch .... (352) 374-5000
ASST MET ED
Gainesville Sun, Gainesville, FL
Stadelman, Chris .... (304) 348-5140
Automotive ED, BUS/FIN ED, Farm/Agriculture ED, SCI ED
Charleston Daily Mail, Charleston, WV
Stadler, Angela .... (910) 623-2155
Agriculture ED, BUS/FIN ED, EDU ED, Farm/Agriculture ED, Health/Medical ED
Daily News, Eden, NC
Stadnick, Sue .... (306) 869-2202
ED, Radville Star, Radville, SK
Staebler, James .... (203) 574-3636
Photo ED, Waterbury Republican-American, Waterbury, CT
Staebner, Leanda .... (605) 649-7866
GM, Selby Record, Selby, SD
Staffa, Mary .... (213) 481-1448
GM, Los Angeles Downtown News, Los Angeles, CA
Stafford, Chuck .... (616) 845-5181
COL, Daily News, Ludington, MI
Stafford, Elaine .... (616) 345-3511
ADV SUPV-CLASS
Kalamazoo Gazette, Kalamazoo, MI
Stafford, Most Rev J Francis .... (303) 388-4411
PUB, Denver Catholic Register, Denver, CO
Stafford, Jim D .... (317) 423-5511
ASST Sports ED
Journal and Courier, Lafayette, IN
Stafford, John .... (616) 754-9301
COB/PUB, Daily News, Greenville, MI
Stafford, Linda .... (616) 754-9301
SEC, Daily News, Greenville, MI
Stafford, Lorna .... (318) 459-3200
This Week ED, Times, Shreveport, LA
Stafford, Ray M .... (210) 423-5511
PUB, Rio Grande Valley Group, Harlingen, TX
Stafford, Sandie .... (618) 943-2331 ext. 100
ADV DIR, Daily Record, Lawrenceville, IL
Stafford, Tom .... (937) 328-0300
Food ED, Women's ED
Springfield News-Sun, Springfield, OH
Stagar, Lee .... (423) 727-6121
GM, Tomahawk, Mountain City, TN
Stagen, Randy .... (214) 696-2900
PUB, Met, Dallas, TX
Stagg, Bill .... (919) 419-6500
City ED, Herald-Sun, Durham, NC
Stahl, Fran .... (813) 394-7592
MAN ED
Marco Island Eagle, Marco Island, FL
Stahl, Gerald .... (517) 846-4531
GM
Arenac County Independent, Standish, MI
Stahl, Matt .... (606) 564-9091
ED, Ledger Independent, Maysville, KY
Stahl, Michael .... (507) 359-2911
ADV DIR, Journal, New Ulm, MN
Stahl, Robin .... (412) 834-1151
Focus ED, Tribune-Review, Greensburg, PA
Stahlberg, Mike .... (541) 485-1234
Outdoors ED, Register-Guard, Eugene, OR
Stahle, J Howard .... (801) 250-5656
PUB, ED, Magna Times, Magna, UT
Stahle, R Gail .... (801) 547-9800
PUB, ED, Kaysville Today, Layton, UT
Stahle, Shaun .... (801) 674-6200
Religion ED, Spectrum, St. George, UT
Staik, Paul .... (941) 953-7755
CIRC MGR-Sales/PROM
Sarasota Herald-Tribune, Sarasota, FL
Stair, Randolph N .... (716) 439-9222
TREAS, Union-Sun & Journal, Lockport, NY
Stairs, Jonna .... (412) 547-5722
ED, Adviser, Scottdale, PA
Stairs, Robert W .... (207) 990-8000
VP-ADM, Bangor Daily News, Bangor, ME
Stalberg, Zachary (Zack) .... (215) 854-2000
EVP/ED (Daily News), Philadelphia Inquirer, Philadelphia, PA, Knight-Ridder Inc.
Stalcup, Jeff .... (206) 597-8742
PROD DIR-OPER
News Tribune, Tacoma, WA
Stalder, Merle .... (910) 891-1234
Aviation ED, Daily Record, Dunn, NC
Stalder, Rick .... (816) 259-2266
ED, News, Lexington, MO
Stalker, Randy D .... (307) 436-2211
MAN ED
Glenrock Independent, Glenrock, WY
Stall, Bill .... (213) 237-5000
EDL Writer
Los Angeles Times, Los Angeles, CA
Stall, Bob .... (604) 732-2222
COL, Province, Vancouver, BC
Stallard, Jack .... (409) 632-6631
Sports ED, Lufkin Daily News, Lufkin, TX
Stallbaumer, Beverly .... (316) 326-3326
MGR-Office, CIRC MGR-Subscriptions
Wellington Daily News, Wellington, KS
Stallbaumer, Tom .... (501) 751-6200
PUB, Morning News of Northwest Arkansas, Springdale, AR
Stallcop, Brian .... (360) 377-3711
MAN ED, Sun, Bremerton, WA
Stallings, Wahnee .... (915) 372-5115
ED, San Saba News & Star, San Saba, TX
Stallings, Walt .... (214) 977-8222
ASST MAN ED-MET, MET ED
Dallas Morning News, Dallas, TX
Stalls, Sonny H .... (941) 657-6000
PUB, Caloosa Belle, La Belle, FL
Stallwitz, Steve .... (913) 776-2200
ADV MGR-NTL
Manhattan Mercury, Manhattan, KS
Stalnaker, Jack .... (713) 869-5434
ASST ED, Daily Court Review, Houston, TX
Staloch, Stephen P .... (815) 432-6066
VP
Independent Media Group Inc., Watseka, IL
Stalvig, Finley .... (715) 394-4411
Amusements/Aviation ED, Films/Theater ED, Librarian/Music ED, Radio/Television ED, RE ED, Travel ED, Daily Telegram, Superior, WI
Stamm, John .... (717) 966-2255
PUB, Mifflinburg Telegraph, Mifflinburg, PA
Stamm, John .... (901) 529-2211
EX Sports ED
Commercial Appeal, Memphis, TN
Stamm, Mrs Laurin .... (601) 636-4545
Food ED, Vicksburg Post, Vicksburg, MS
Stamm Jr, Robert J .... (412) 263-1100
DIR-FIN
Pittsburgh Post-Gazette, Pittsburgh, PA
Stammer, Larry .... (213) 237-5000
Religion Writer
Los Angeles Times, Los Angeles, CA
Stamp, Chris .... (770) 483-7108
News ED, Rockdale Citizen, Conyers, GA
Stamper, Don .... (773) 586-8800
PROD MGR-Post Press
Daily Southtown, Chicago, IL
Stamper, J B .... (606) 662-3595
ED, Wolfe County News, Campton, KY
Stamper, Judy .... (405) 326-3311
VP/SEC/TREAS, Hugo Daily News, Hugo, OK
Stamper, Stan .... (405) 326-3311
PRES, PUB/GM, Hugo Daily News, Hugo, OK
Stamper, Tom .... (214) 977-8222
PROD MGR-Distribution
Dallas Morning News, Dallas, TX
Stamps, David M .... (815) 385-2231
PUB, McHenry Star, McHenry, IL
Stancampiano, Lou .... (201) 646-4000
ADV MGR-Display, Record, Hackensack, NJ
Stancavage, John .... (918) 581-8300
BUS/FIN ED, Tulsa World, Tulsa, OK
Stancil, John .... (606) 528-2464
Sports ED, Times-Tribune, Corbin, KY
Stanczyk, Alaine .... (609) 663-6000
MGR-PROM, Courier-Post, Cherry Hill, NJ
Standaert, Jeff .... (206) 339-3000
Economy ED, RE ED, Herald, Everett, WA
Standen, Craig C .... (513) 977-3000
Sr VP-CORP Development
E W Scripps Co., Cincinnati, OH
Standley, Bess .... (918) 652-3311
ADV MGR-RT, DIR-MKTG/PROM
Henryetta Daily Free-Lance, Henryetta, OK
Standley, Frank D .... (508) 458-7100
ADV MGR-NTL, Sun, Lowell, MA
Standring, Chris .... (403) 429-5400
Fashion ED
Edmonton Journal, Edmonton, AB
Stanfield, Brian .... (316) 321-1120
ADV MGR, El Dorado Times, El Dorado, KS
Stanfilo, Joe .... (501) 239-8562
CIRC MGR, Daily Press, Paragould, AR
Stanford, Debbie .... (504) 643-4918
Books/EDU ED, Fashion/Food ED, Religion ED, Society/Women's ED
Slidell Sentry-News, Slidell, LA
Stanford, Judith .... (704) 249-3981
PROD FRM-COMP, Dispatch, Lexington, NC
Stanford, Larry .... (770) 775-3107
ED, Jackson Progress-Argus, Jackson, GA
Stanford, Tom .... (615) 259-8000
Picture ED, Tennessean, Nashville, TN
Stang, John .... (509) 582-1500
SCI/Technology ED
Tri-City Herald, Tri-Cities, WA
Stanger, Sandra .... (617) 593-7700
Radio/Television
Daily Evening Item, Lynn, MA
Stangl, Tom .... (712) 378-2770
PUB, ED, Kingsley News-Times, Kingsley, IA
Stangle, Mark .... (937) 225-2000
ADV VP, Dayton Daily News, Dayton, OH
Stangroom, Diane .... (603) 882-2741
PROD FRM-COMP, Telegraph, Nashua, NH
Stanhope, Brad .... (707) 425-4646
Sports ED, Daily Republic, Fairfield, CA
Stanislaw, John .... (406) 228-9301
PUB, Glasgow Courier, Glasgow, MT
Stankiewicz, Robert .... (717) 821-2091
PROD FRM-PR
Citizens' Voice, Wilkes-Barre, PA
Stankovich, Kaine .... (937) 225-2000
Automotive ED, Aviation ED, BUS/FIN ED
Dayton Daily News, Dayton, OH
Stanley, Anne .... (707) 226-3711
EDU ED, Napa Valley Register, Napa, CA
Stanley, Chris .... (702) 383-0211
Television ED, Review-Journal, Las Vegas, NV
Stanley, D .... (604) 265-4215
PUB, ED, Arrow Lakes News, Nakusp, BC
Stanley, David L .... (404) 523-6086
ED, Atlanta Inquirer, Atlanta, GA
Stanley, Dennis .... (615) 597-5485
GM, ED, Smithville Review, Smithville, TN
Stanley, Edna .... (405) 353-0620
ADV MGR-CLASS, Constitution, Lawton, OK
Stanley, George .... (414) 224-2000
Senior ED-BUS
Milwaukee Journal Sentinel, Milwaukee, WI
Stanley, Jack .... (713) 220-7171
VP-OPER, Houston Chronicle, Houston, TX
Stanley, James .... (573) 581-1111
Sports ED, Mexico Ledger, Mexico, MO
Stanley, Ken .... (616) 347-2544
MAN ED, Films/Theater ED, Music ED
Petoskey News-Review, Petoskey, MI
Stanley, Kirsten .... (970) 641-1414
PROD MGR
Gunnison Country Times, Gunnison, CO
Stanley, Michael G .... (901) 529-2211
ADV MGR-CLASS
Commercial Appeal, Memphis, TN
Stanley, Rosiland .... (304) 235-4242
BU Chief-Pikeville
Williamson Daily News, Williamson, WV
Stansfield, Mike .... (801) 373-5050
ADV MGR-GEN, Daily Herald, Provo, UT
Stantis, Scott .... (205) 325-2222
Cartoonist
Birmingham News, Birmingham, AL
Stanton, Cathy .... (954) 356-4000
MGR-Sales/MKTG
Sun-Sentinel, Fort Lauderdale, FL
Stanton, Fred .... (914) 454-2000
PROD MGR-Press
Poughkeepsie Journal, Poughkeepsie, NY
Stanton, Jeff .... (317) 462-5528
Agriculture ED, Daily Reporter, Greenfield, IN
Stanton, Jim .... (319) 291-1400
EDU ED, School ED
Waterloo Courier, Waterloo, IA
Stanton, Marcie .... (208) 476-4571
MAN ED, Clearwater Tribune, Orofino, ID
Stanton, Mathew .... (715) 823-3151
MAN ED, Tribune-Gazette, Clintonville, WI
Stanton, Mike .... (206) 464-2111
News ED, Seattle Times, Seattle, WA
Stanton, Russ .... (714) 835-1234
Team Leader-BUS
Orange County Register, Santa Ana, CA
Stanton, Wayne .... (408) 423-4242
PROD FRM-COMP
Santa Cruz County Sentinel, Santa Cruz, CA
Stanway, Eric .... (508) 343-6911
Food ED
Sentinel & Enterprise, Fitchburg, MA
Stanway, Paul .... (403) 468-0100
EIC, Edmonton Sun, Edmonton, AB
Stanz, Beth .... (919) 938-7467
ED, Globe, Jacksonville, NC
Staples, Barbara .... (513) 422-3611
ADV DIR
Middletown Journal, Middletown, OH
Staples, Gloria .... (804) 385-5400
Librarian, News & Advance, Lynchburg, VA
Staples, John .... (910) 993-2161
ED, Kernersville News, Kernersville, NC
Staples, Michael .... (506) 357-3356
ED, Oromocto Post-Gazette, Oromocto, NB
Stapleton, Becky .... (318) 649-7136
GM, News Journal, Columbia, LA
Stapleton, F .... (808) 935-6621
SCI ED, Hawaii Tribune-Herald, Hilo, HI
Stapley, Charles .... (613) 739-7000
PROD DIR, Ottawa Sun, Ottawa, ON
Starbuck, Barb .... (614) 452-4561
PROD MGR-Ad Graphics
Times Recorder, Zanesville, OH
Starchman, David .... (417) 623-3480
PROD MGR-Press, Joplin Globe, Joplin, MO
Stark, Andrew .... (305) 538-6077
PUB, SunPost, Miami Beach, FL
Stark, Jeanette .... (305) 538-6077
ED, SunPost, Miami Beach, FL
Stark, Joe .... (816) 799-3735/3162
PUB, ED, Quad River News, Sheridan, MO
Stark, Joel N .... (401) 277-7000
Senior VP-MKTG & Development
Providence Journal-Bulletin, Providence, RI
Stark, Judy .... (813) 893-8111
Home Furnishings ED, RE/At Home ED
St. Petersburg Times, St. Petersburg, FL
Stark, Kate .... (805) 781-7800
Graphics ED
Telegram-Tribune, San Luis Obispo, CA
Stark, Susan .... (313) 222-2300
Films Writer, Detroit News, Detroit, MI
Starkey, Barbara .... (502) 389-1833
GM, Union County Advocate, Morganfield, KY
Starkey, Jim .... (616) 222-5400
Photo ED
Grand Rapids Press, Grand Rapids, MI
Starkey, Rodger .... (520) 763-2505
CIRC DIR
Mohave Valley Daily News, Bullhead City, AZ
Starkey, Shawn .... (412) 981-6100
Religion ED, Herald, Sharon, PA
Starks, Richard .... (214) 977-8222
Senior VP-Sales/MKTG
Dallas Morning News, Dallas, TX
Starling, Claude .... (919) 243-5151
Features ED, Wilson Daily Times, Wilson, NC
Starling, Jim .... (757) 857-1212
MAN ED, Booster, Norfolk, VA
Starn, Jon G .... (814) 445-9621
GM, PA, MGR-PROM
Daily American, Somerset, PA
Starn, Michael B .... (610) 696-1775
CIRC DIR
Daily Local News, West Chester, PA
Starnes, Amy .... (317) 622-1212
Special Projects Reporter
Herald Bulletin, Anderson, IN
Starnes, Andy .... (412) 263-1100
Picture ED, Post-Gazette, Pittsburgh, PA
Starnes, Judy .... (409) 265-7411
GM, Brazosport Facts, Clute, TX
Starr, Bill .... (803) 771-6161
Amusements/Arts ED, Books ED
State, Columbia, SC
Starr, Bonnie .... (406) 654-2020
PUB, Phillips County News, Malta, MT
Starr, Curtis H .... (406) 654-2020
PUB, ED, Phillips County News, Malta, MT
Starr, David .... (413) 788-1000
PRES, PUB, Union-News, Springfield, MA
Starr, George .... (423) 472-5041
EX ED, News ED
Cleveland Daily Banner, Cleveland, TN
Starr, John Robert .... (501) 378-3400
COL
Arkansas Democrat-Gazette, Little Rock, AR
Starr, Robert .... (904) 312-5200
PUB, Daily News, Palatka, FL
Starr, Tena .... (802) 525-3531
ED, Chronicle, Barton, VT
Starren, Peter O .... (207) 791-6650
CIRC DIR, Press Herald, Portland, ME
Starzynski, Nancy .... (716) 849-3434
ADV MGR-MKTG RES
Buffalo News, Buffalo, NY
Stas, Louis C .... (806) 826-3123
PUB, ED, Wheeler Times, Wheeler, TX
Stash, Richard .... (770) 834-6631
PROD SUPT-Press
Times-Georgian, Carrollton, GA

Sta Who's Where-220

Stasi, Linda .... (212) 210-2100
COL, New York Daily News, New York, NY
Stasney, Ted .... (813) 259-7711
DIR-RES
Tampa Tribune and Times, Tampa, FL
Stastny, Tony .... (912) 236-9511
Sports ED
Savannah Morning News, Savannah, GA
Stasulis, Larry .... (802) 863-3441
PROD DIR, Free Press, Burlington, VT
Staszak, Ted .... (603) 436-1800
GM, PROD FRM-PR
Portsmouth Herald, Portsmouth, NH
Stateler, Jim .... (800) 223-2154
MGR-MIS
Investor's Business Daily, Los Angeles, CA
Stateler, Nyle .... (419) 596-3897
PUB, ED, News Review, Continental, OH
Staten, Andy .... (520) 537-5721
ED
White Mountain Independent, Show Low, AZ
Statler, Gene .... (619) 934-8544
GM, Review Herald, Mammoth Lakes, CA
Staton, Charley .... (918) 423-1700
CIRC MGR, McAlester News-Capital & Democrat, McAlester, OK
Staton, Marianne .... (508) 228-0001
PUB, ED
Inquirer and Mirror, Nantucket, MA
Staton, Tracy .... (817) 461-6397
City ED
Arlington Morning News, Arlington, TX
Statti, Larry .... (909) 987-6397
ADTX MGR
Inland Valley Daily Bulletin, Ontario, CA
Stattman, Ed .... (317) 972-7800
MAN ED, National Jewish Post & Opinion, Indianapolis, IN
Stauffer, Bill .... (405) 223-2200
PUB, GM/PA
Daily Ardmoreite, Ardmore, OK
Stauffer, L W .... (717) 275-3235
PRES, Danville News, Danville, PA
Stauton, Peter .... (508) 799-0511
PUB, Worcester Magazine, Worcester, MA
Stavakas, Scott .... (815) 284-2222
ADV MGR-CLASS, Telegraph, Dixon, IL
Stave, Dave .... (541) 963-3161
EX ED, EDL Writer
Observer, La Grande, OR
Staver, Dave .... (812) 886-9955
Sports ED
Vincennes Sun-Commercial, Vincennes, IN
Staver, Wallace .... (414) 224-2000
PROD FRM-COMP
Milwaukee Journal Sentinel, Milwaukee, WI
Stavola, Joanne .... (773) 586-8800
PROD MGR-Pre Press
Daily Southtown, Chicago, IL
Stayton, Lisa .... (606) 298-7570
PUB, MAN ED, Mountain Citizen, Inez, KY
Stazak, Ted .... (410) 749-7171
CIRC DIR, Daily Times, Salisbury, MD
Stead, Maureen .... (412) 222-2200
ASST MAN ED-Graphics/PROD, Graphics ED/Art DIR, Photo ED
Observer-Reporter, Washington, PA
Stead, Sylvia .... (416) 585-5000
Deputy MAN ED, Globe and Mail (Canada's National Newspaper), Toronto, ON
Stealey, Amy .... (813) 635-2171
ED, Frostproof News, Frostproof, FL
Stealey, Robert .... (304) 624-6411
ED-Telegraph, Clarksburg Exponent/Telegram, Clarksburg, WV
Stearns, Claude .... (618) 529-5454
PROD SUPV-Press
Southern Illinoisan, Carbondale, IL
Stearns, Debbie .... (334) 433-1551
Librarian, Mobile Press Register, Mobile, AL
Stearns, Kathi .... (404) 888-7832
MAN ED, Georgia Bulletin, Atlanta, GA
Stearns, Patty LaNove .... (313) 222-6400
Restaurant Critic, Free Press, Detroit, MI
Stebbins, Rodney .... (716) 593-5300
Sports ED, Daily Reporter, Wellsville, NY
Steck, Jodie .... (714) 835-1234
News ED-Photos
Orange County Register, Santa Ana, CA
Steck, Sharon .... (716) 849-3434
ADV MGR-New BUS Development
Buffalo News, Buffalo, NY
Steckel, James R .... (212) 837-7000
VP-OPER, Journal of Commerce & Commercial, New York, NY
Steckles, Garry .... (604) 732-2222
News ED-Features, Province, Vancouver, BC
Stedham, Michael .... (205) 236-1551
Amusements ED, Radio/Television ED
Anniston Star, Anniston, AL

Stedl, Jane .... (414) 432-2941
BM, News-Chronicle, Green Bay, WI
Stedman, Bill .... (508) 222-7000
Sports ED, Sun Chronicle, Attleboro, MA
Stedman, Frank .... (509) 647-5551
PUB, ED, Wilbur Register, Wilbur, WA
Steed, Kathy .... (208) 365-6066
GM, Messenger-Index, Emmett, ID
Steedman, Lonnie .... (916) 533-3131
ADV MGR-RT
Oroville Mercury Register, Oroville, CA
Steel, Arlet .... (715) 478-3315
GM, Forest Republican, Crandon, WI
Steel, Nancy .... (501) 785-7700
Fashion/Style ED, Features ED, Lifestyle ED, Travel ED
Southwest Times Record, Fort Smith, AR
Steel, Russell H .... (715) 478-3315
PUB, ED, Forest Republican, Crandon, WI
Steel, Susan .... (212) 715-2100
West Coast MGR
USA Weekend, New York, NY
Steele, Brian .... (847) 329-2000
ED, Harlem-Irving Times, Lincolnwood, IL
Steele, Don .... (210) 896-7000
ADV DIR, Kerrville Daily Times, Kerrville, TX
Steele, Georgia .... (212) 887-8550
BM, American Metal Market, New York, NY
Steele, Gerry .... (541) 523-3673
BUS/FIN ED, Farm/Agriculture ED, Sports ED
Baker City Herald, Baker City, OR
Steele, Greg .... (813) 893-8111
PROD MGR-Production News
St. Petersburg Times, St. Petersburg, FL
Steele, Harry .... (902) 468-7557
COB/CEO
Newfoundland Capital Corp., Dartmouth, NS
Steele, Jon F .... (908) 359-0850
ED, Hillsborough Beacon, Hillsborough, NJ
Steele, Lori .... (913) 371-4300
PROD MGR
Kansas City Kansan, Kansas City, KS
Steele, Mark .... (208) 547-3260
PUB, ED
Caribou County Sun, Soda Springs, ID
Steele, Michael .... (612) 673-4000
Theater/Dance Reporter
Star Tribune, Minneapolis, MN
Steele, Michael .... (804) 649-6000
DIR-Electronic Publishing
Richmond Times-Dispatch, Richmond, VA
Steele, Peter .... (508) 487-1170
PUB, ED, Advocate, Provincetown, MA
Steele, Ray .... (916) 321-1855
DIR-Community Publications
McClatchy Newspapers, Sacramento, CA
Steele, Steve .... (801) 373-5050
PROD FRM-PR, Daily Herald, Provo, UT
Steelhammer, Rick .... (304) 348-5140
COL, Charleston Gazette, Sunday Gazette-Mail, Charleston, WV
Steelman, Ben .... (910) 343-2000
Books ED, Morning Star/Sunday Star-News, Wilmington, NC
Steely, Lynn .... (215) 854-2000
PROD DIR-Packaging & Distribution
Philadelphia Inquirer, Philadelphia, PA
Knight-Ridder Inc.
Steen, Sheryl .... (319) 398-8211
CIRC MGR-SRV, Gazette, Cedar Rapids, IA
Steenslang, Craig .... (605) 326-5212
PUB, Viborg Enterprise, Viborg, SD
Steenson, Bob .... (515) 421-0500
City ED, Globe-Gazette, Mason City, IA
Steeves, Michelle .... (905) 526-3333
Life ED, Spectator, Hamilton, ON
Stefaniak, Rich .... (217) 446-1000
Graphics ED, Photo ED
Commercial News, Danville, IL
Stefanucci, Jim .... (814) 724-6370
Photo ED, Meadville Tribune, Meadville, PA
Steffens, Martha .... (607) 798-1234
MAN ED
Press & Sun Bulletin, Binghamton, NY
Steffensen, Chris .... (847) 882-2552
PUB, ED
Den Danske Pioneer, Hoffman Estates, IL
Stegall, Veronica .... (504) 926-8882
ED, PROD MGR, Baton Rouge Daily Legal News, Baton Rouge, LA
Steger, Ken .... (713) 391-3141
PUB, Katy Times, Katy, TX
Steger, Pat .... (415) 777-1111
Society ED
San Francisco Chronicle, San Francisco, CA
Steiden, Bill .... (941) 953-7755
Features ED
Sarasota Herald-Tribune, Sarasota, FL
Steidle, LaJeune .... (717) 385-3120
ED, Call, Schuylkill Haven, PA
Steidtmann, Nancy .... (415) 457-7141
PRES, Style International, San Francisco, CA
Steigel, Bob .... (408) 761-7300
MAN ED, EPE
Register-Pajaronian, Watsonville, CA

Steiger, Paul E .... (212) 416-2600
VP/MAN ED-WSJ, Dow Jones & Co., NY, NY
Steiger, William E .... (407) 420-5000
VP/DIR-ADV
Orlando Sentinel, Orlando, FL
Steigerwald, William .... (910) 323-4848
DP MGR, Observer-Times, Fayetteville, NC
Steigmeyer, Rick .... (509) 663-5161
Farm ED, SCI/Technology ED
Wenatchee World, Wenatchee, WA
Stein, Bernard L .... (718) 543-6065
PUB, ED, Riverdale Press, Bronx, NY
Stein, Beth .... (615) 259-8800
Senior ED, Nashville Banner, Nashville, TN
Stein, C R .... (601) 392-3307
PUB, Biloxi-D'Iberville Press, Biloxi, MS
Stein, Dick .... (516) 843-2020
MGR-Network MGT, Newsday, Melville, NY
Stein, Ed .... (303) 892-5000
EDL Cartoonist
Rocky Mountain News, Denver, CO
Stein, Huey .... (504) 869-5784
GM, ED, News-Examiner, Lutcher, LA
Stein, Jeannine .... (213) 237-5000
Society Writer
Los Angeles Times, Los Angeles, CA
Stein, Richard .... (800) 749-1841
NTL Sales MGR
Tel-Aire Publications Inc., Dallas, TX
Stein, Richard L .... (718) 543-6065
PUB, GM, Riverdale Press, Bronx, NY
Stein, Steve .... (210) 686-4343
ASST MET ED, Monitor, McAllen, TX
Steinauer, Bill .... (215) 949-4000
EX ED
Bucks County Courier Times, Levittown, PA
Steinbach, Alice .... (410) 332-6000
COL-Features, Sun, Baltimore, MD
Steinbach, Chris .... (402) 475-4200
BUS Reporter
Lincoln Journal Star, Lincoln, NE
Steinbacher, William .... (315) 470-0011
PROD MGR-MR, Post-Standard/Syracuse Herald-Journal/American, Syracuse, NY
Steinback, Bob .... (305) 350-2111
COL, Miami Herald, Miami, FL
Steinbeck, Daniel .... (573) 288-5668
ED, Canton Press-News Journal, Canton, MO
Steinbeck, David .... (573) 288-5668
PUB
Canton Press-News Journal, Canton, MO
Steinberg, David .... (505) 823-7777
Books ED
Albuquerque Journal, Albuquerque, NM
Steinberg, Michael A .... (814) 234-9601
Sr. VP, AccuWeather Inc., State College, PA
Steinberg, Neil .... (312) 321-3000
GEN Assignment
Chicago Sun-Times, Chicago, IL
Steiner, Fred .... (419) 358-8010
ED, Bluffton News, Bluffton, OH
Steiner, Lora D .... (573) 594-2222/3322
PUB, Vandalia Leader-Press, Vandalia, MO
Steiner, Mary K .... (573) 594-2222/3322
ED, Vandalia Leader-Press, Vandalia, MO
Steiner, William C .... (573) 594-2222
ED, Vandalia Leader-Press, Vandalia, MO
Steinfeldt, Joel .... (309) 346-1111
City ED, Pekin Daily Times, Pekin, IL
Steinhauer, Jack .... (609) 272-7000
PROD MGR-Maintenance
Press of Atlantic City, Pleasantville, NJ
Steinhoff, Ken .... (561) 820-4100
MGR-Telecommunications
Palm Beach Post, West Palm Beach, FL
Steininger, Harold .... (541) 296-2141
PUB, PA, CIRC MGR
Dalles Daily Chronicle, The Dalles, OR
Steinke, Steven .... (815) 544-9811
GM, PROD MGR
Belvidere Daily Republican, Belvidere, IL
Steinlechner, Norma .... (412) 946-3501
ED, Globe, New Wilmington, PA
Steinlechner, Richard .... (412) 946-3501
PUB, Globe, New Wilmington, PA
Steinley, Jerry .... (605) 347-2503
ED
Meade County Times-Tribune, Sturgis, SD
Steinmetz, Greg .... (212) 416-2000
BU Chief-Berlin
Wall Street Journal, New York, NY
Steinmetz Jr, Paul .... (203) 744-5100
ED, News-Times, Danbury, CT
Steinmetz, Robert .... (416) 814-4239
VP-Procurement
Thomson Newspapers, Toronto, ON
Steinruck, Mark .... (717) 389-4825
PROD DIR
Spectrum Features, Bloomsburg, PA
Steitz, Marjorie .... (202) 882-8882
MAN ED, Artists and Writers Syndicate, Washington, DC
Steitz, Philip .... (202) 882-8882
PRES/EX ED, Artists and Writers Syndicate, Washington, DC

Stella, Charles .... (614) 461-5000
EDL Writer
Columbus Dispatch, Columbus, OH
Stelling, Linda .... (320) 243-3772
ED, Paynesville Press, Paynesville, MN
Stellrecht, Fritz .... (703) 276-3400
CIRC GM-Los Angeles
USA Today, Arlington, VA
Stelter, Corinne F .... (507) 485-3141
PUB, ED, Wood Lake News, Wood Lake, MN
Stelzner, Linda .... (206) 464-2111
ADTX MGR, Seattle Times, Seattle, WA
Stemen, Marlanea .... (517) 437-7351
ADV CNR, Hillsdale Daily News, Hillsdale, MI
Stengel, Carl .... (937) 592-3060
PROD FRM-COMP
Bellefontaine Examiner, Bellefontaine, OH
Stengel, Norvell .... (314) 340-8000
PROD FRM-Loading Dock
St. Louis Post-Dispatch, St. Louis, MO
Stenger, Jenny .... (301) 662-1177
SUPV-Accounting
Frederick Post/The News, Frederick, MD
Stenger, Richard T .... (610) 696-1775
PUB, Daily Local News, West Chester, PA
Steninger, Dan .... (702) 738-3119
SEC, Co-PUB, Opinion ED
Elko Daily Free Press, Elko, NV
Steninger, Kim .... (702) 738-3119
PRES, Co-PUB
Elko Daily Free Press, Elko, NV
Steninger, Rex .... (702) 738-3119
TREAS, Co-PUB, ED
Elko Daily Free Press, Elko, NV
Stennes, John .... (701) 780-1100
Photo ED
Grand Forks Herald, Grand Forks, ND
Stenneski, Dion .... (812) 546-6113
PUB, Hope Star-Journal, Hope, IN
Stenseng, Rusty .... (316) 947-3975
MAN ED
Hillsboro Star-Journal, Hillsboro, KS
Stenseng, Stacy .... (316) 947-3975
PUB, ED
Hillsboro Star-Journal, Hillsboro, KS
Stenseth, Jackie .... (605) 331-2200
CONT, Argus Leader, Sioux Falls, SD
Stenuis, Babette .... (616) 347-2544
Family/Food ED, People ED
Petoskey News-Review, Petoskey, MI
Stenvall, Karen .... (303) 776-2244
ADV MGR-Display
Daily Times-Call, Longmont, CO
Steo, Joseph .... (212) 930-8000
CIRC DIR-OPER (Night), PROD DIR (Night)
New York Post, New York, NY
Stepanich, Greg .... (561) 287-1550
ASST City ED, Stuart News, Stuart, FL
Stepankowsky, Andre .... (360) 577-2500
Environmental ED, Daily News, Longview, WA
Stepankowsky, Paula .... (360) 577-2500
BUS/FIN ED, RE ED
Daily News, Longview, WA
Stepanovich, Mike .... (805) 395-7500
BUS/Industry ED
Bakersfield Californian, Bakersfield, CA
Stepenski, Ron .... (201) 428-6200
BUS ED, Daily Record, Parsippany, NJ
Stephan, Hope .... (814) 724-6370
ED, Meadville Tribune, Meadville, PA
Stephan, Paul M .... (941) 262-3161
DIR-FIN, Naples Daily News, Naples, FL
Stephanak, James J .... (717) 255-8100
ADV DIR, Patriot-News, Harrisburg, PA
Stephani, Will .... (403) 468-0100
PROD MGR-Pre Press
Edmonton Sun, Edmonton, AB
Stephens, Barbara .... (216) 329-7000
MGR-EDU SRV
Chronicle-Telegram, Elyria, OH
Stephens, Bryan .... (904) 252-1511
ADV MGR-CLASS, Daytona Beach News-Journal, Daytona Beach, FL
Stephens, Frank .... (916) 622-2280
PUB, ED, Reporter, Placerville, CA
Stephens, Glenn .... (205) 325-2222
Political/Government ED, State ED
Birmingham News, Birmingham, AL
Stephens, Jackson T .... (501) 785-9404
COB, Donrey Media Group, Fort Smith, AR
Stephens, Jim .... (703) 276-3400
CIRC GM-Carolinas
USA Today, Arlington, VA
Stephens, Jodi .... (907) 874-2301
ED, Wrangell Sentinel, Wrangell, AK
Stephens, Larry .... (801) 625-4200
Art DIR, Standard-Examiner, Ogden, UT
Stephens, Linda .... (605) 375-3228
PUB, Nation's Center News, Buffalo, SD
Stephens, Mike .... (503) 399-6611
Entertainment/Amusements ED, Features ED
Statesman Journal, Salem, OR
Stephens, Monica .... (334) 262-1611
MGR-RES
Montgomery Advertiser, Montgomery, AL

Copyright ©1997 by the Editor & Publisher Co.

221-Who's Where **Sti**

Stephens, Nelson .... (814) 946-7411
PROD FRM-PR, Altoona Mirror, Altoona, PA
Stephens, Robert A .... (919) 753-4126
PUB, ED, Farmville Enterprise, Farmville, NC
Stephens, Stephanie .... (806) 428-3591
PUB, ED
O'Donnell Index-Press, O'Donnell, TX
Stephens, Thomas .... (212) 930-8000
PROD FRM-PR
New York Post, New York, NY
Stephens, Wally .... (605) 375-3228
PUB, ED, Nation's Center News, Buffalo, SD
Stephens, Wendy .... (219) 722-5000
CIRC MGR, Pharos-Tribune, Logansport, IN
Stephenson, Arni .... (403) 778-3977
PUB, Whitecourt Star, Whitecourt, AB
Stephenson, David .... (630) 844-5844
Photo ED, Beacon-News, Aurora, IL
Stephenson, Jim .... (316) 788-2835
PUB, Daily Reporter, Derby, KS
Stephenson, Lonna .... (573) 364-2468
ADV MGR, Rolla Daily News, Rolla, MO
Stephenson, Thomas A .... (612) 222-5011
Senior VP-ADM
St. Paul Pioneer Press, St. Paul, MN
Stepleton, Jon .... (719) 632-5511
Public ED, Gazette, Colorado Springs, CO
Stepp, Gene .... (814) 749-8631
GM, Nanty Glo Journal, Nanty Glo, PA
Stepro, Keith .... (805) 273-2700
Religion ED
Antelope Valley Press, Palmdale, CA
Sterbakov, Hugh .... (513) 761-1188
Contributing Critic
Critic's Choice Reviews, Cincinnati, OH
Sterbenc, Kathy .... (815) 544-9811
MAN ED, EDL Writer
Belvidere Daily Republican, Belvidere, IL
Sterkel, Laurel .... (915) 337-4661
MGR/CNR-PROM
Odessa American, Odessa, TX
Sterling, Bill .... (804) 787-1200
GM, Chincoteague Beachcomber, Onley, VA
Sterling, Brad .... (315) 343-3800
ADV MGR, Palladium-Times, Oswego, NY
Sterling, Bradford D .... (609) 845-3300
CIRC DIR
Gloucester County Times, Woodbury, NJ
MediaNews Inc. (Garden State Newspapers)
Sterling, Dana .... (918) 581-8300
State ED, Tulsa World, Tulsa, OK
Sterling, Robert .... (541) 776-4411
Reporter Team ED
Mail Tribune, Medford, OR
Stern, Dennis Lee .... (212) 556-1234
ASSOC MAN ED-PSL/ADM
New York Times, New York, NY
Stern, Douglas R .... (212) 293-8500
PRES/CEO, United Media, United Feature Syndicate, Newspaper Enterprise Association, New York, NY
Stern, Earle .... (617) 593-7700
City ED, Daily Evening Item, Lynn, MA
Stern, Jim .... (515) 753-6611
MAN ED, EPE, NTL ED, Political/Government ED, Times-Republican, Marshalltown, IA
Stern, Michael .... (315) 470-0011
MGR-Production, Post-Standard/Syracuse Herald-Journal/American, Syracuse, NY
Stern, Paul .... (860) 241-6200
Deputy CT ED
Hartford Courant, Hartford, CT
Stern, Sherry .... (213) 237-5000
Deputy Calendar ED
Los Angeles Times, Los Angeles, CA
Sternberg, Bill .... (202) 628-2157
BU Chief
Thomson News Service, Washington, DC
Sternberg, Mike .... (704) 692-0505
ADV DIR, ADTX MGR
Times-News, Hendersonville, NC
Sterne, Joseph R L .... (410) 332-6000
EPE, Sun, Baltimore, MD
Sternickel, Sgt J W .... (912) 368-0526
ED, Patriot, Hinesville, GA
Stersic, Thomas .... (616) 345-3511
Religion ED
Kalamazoo Gazette, Kalamazoo, MI
Sterton, Stephen C .... (619) 565-9135
MAN ED
San Diego Weekly News, San Diego, CA
Stertz, Bradley .... (313) 222-2300
Automotive ED, Detroit News, Detroit, MI
Sterzel, Maryann .... (904) 359-4111
Librarian
Florida Times-Union, Jacksonville, FL
Sterzuk, Kathy .... (306) 692-6441
CIRC MGR
Moose Jaw Times-Herald, Moose Jaw, SK
Steuerman, Rina .... (416) 364-3172
Satellite Services MGR
Broadcast News Limited, Toronto, ON
Steve, Tom .... (320) 255-8700
CIRC MGR-Motor Route/Single Copy
St. Cloud Times, St. Cloud, MN

Stevens, Amy .... (423) 246-8121
BUS/FIN ED, RE ED
Kingsport Times-News, Kingsport, TN
Stevens, Anne .... (815) 732-6166
ED, Oregon Republican-Reporter, Oregon, IL
Stevens, Carol .... (914) 428-6200
VP, Stevens Features/Mark Stevens & Co., White Plains, NY
Stevens, Cindy .... (207) 873-3341
DIR-PROM, Central Maine Morning Sentinel, Waterville, ME
Guy Gannett Communications
Stevens, Clifford .... (212) 416-2000
Reporter-in-Charge (Vienna)
Wall Street Journal, New York, NY
Stevens, Dan .... (208) 377-6200
DP MGR, Idaho Statesman, Boise, ID
Stevens, Dave .... (817) 778-4444
News ED, Daily Telegram, Temple, TX
Stevens, Gary .... (212) 265-8054
PRES
Stevens, Gary Associates, New York, NY
Stevens, Harold .... (614) 272-5422
ED, Southwest Messenger, Columbus, OH
Stevens, Jan .... (520) 774-4545
Women's ED
Arizona Daily Sun, Flagstaff, AZ
Stevens, Janet .... (541) 382-1811
VP, Deputy ED, Bulletin, Bend, OR
Western Communications Inc.
Stevens, Joan H .... (601) 627-2201
ADV MGR, Press Register, Clarksdale, MS
Stevens, Kenneth .... (317) 747-5700
PROD MGR-PR, Star Press, Muncie, IN
Stevens, Lainey .... (903) 757-3311
ADV MGR-CLASS
Longview News-Journal, Longview, TX
Stevens, Lori L .... (814) 643-4040
CIRC MGR, Daily News, Huntingdon, PA
Stevens, Mark .... (423) 929-3111
Fashion/Women's ED, Food/Garden ED, Home Furnishings ED, Lifestyle ED, Ski ED, Teen-Age/Youth ED, Travel ED
Johnson City Press, Johnson City, TN
Stevens, Mark .... (914) 428-6200
PRES, Stevens Features/Mark Stevens & Co., White Plains, NY
Stevens, Mark .... (416) 947-2222
GEN MGR, Toronto Sun, Toronto, ON
Stevens, Michelle .... (312) 321-3000
EPE, EDL Board Member/EDL Writer
Chicago Sun-Times, Chicago, IL
Stevens, Mike .... (206) 872-6600
ADV VP-Sales
South County Journal, Kent, WA
Stevens, Patricia Watts .... (204) 694-2022
DIR-Communications
Winnipeg Sun, Winnipeg, MB
Stevens, Paula .... (602) 271-8000
Librarian, Arizona Republic, Phoenix, AZ
Stevens, Randy .... (512) 392-2458
Sports ED
San Marcos Daily Record, San Marcos, TX
Stevens, Richard .... (615) 259-8000
ASST MAN ED, Tennessean, Nashville, TN
Stevens, Richard .... (505) 823-7777
COL-Sports
Albuquerque Tribune, Albuquerque, NM
Stevens, Rik .... (518) 584-4242
Sports ED, Saratogian, Saratoga Springs, NY
Stevens, Robin .... (502) 522-6605
ED, Cadiz Record, Cadiz, KY
Stevens, Ron .... (302) 674-3600
SEC, Delaware State News, Dover, DE
Stevens, Selena .... (913) 682-0305
Family Page ED
Leavenworth Times, Leavenworth, KS
Stevens, Steve .... (913) 762-5000
ADV MGR, Daily Union, Junction City, KS
Stevens, Steve .... (603) 437-7000
ED, Derry News, Derry, NH
Stevens, Susan .... (817) 757-5757
Radio/Television ED
Waco Tribune-Herald, Waco, TX
Stevens, Susan .... (312) 782-8100
Broadcast ED
City News Bureau of Chicago, Chicago, IL
Stevens, Tala .... (512) 884-2011
PROD MGR-Creative Resources (Ad Production), Corpus Christi Caller-Times, Corpus Christi, TX
Stevens, Thomas B .... (309) 329-2151
PUB, Astoria South Fulton Argus, Astoria, IL
Stevens, Walter B .... (515) 573-2141
ED-Emeritus, Messenger, Fort Dodge, IA
Stevenson, Audrey .... (318) 322-5161
DIR-Market Development
News-Star, Monroe, LA
Stevenson, Bill .... (705) 848-7195
ED, Standard, Elliot Lake, ON
Stevenson, Bruce .... (514) 484-7523
PUB, Westmount Examiner, Westmount, QC
Stevenson, Gary W .... (406) 646-9719
PUB, West Yellowstone News, West Yellowstone, MT

Stevenson, George W .... (215) 949-4000
CIRC DIR
Bucks County Courier Times, Levittown, PA
Stevenson, Gwen .... (813) 849-7500
ED, Suncoast News, New Port Richey, FL
Stevenson, Jim .... (616) 683-2100
ADV MGR, Niles Daily Star, Niles, MI
Stevenson, Jimmy .... (915) 247-4433
GM, Llano News, Llano, TX
Stevenson, Jo Ann .... (905) 294-2200
ED
Markham Economist & Sun, Markham, ON
Stevenson, John W .... (334) 863-2819
PUB, ED, Randolph Leader, Roanoke, AL
Stevenson, Morris .... (903) 455-4220
PROD FRM-PR
Greenville Herald-Banner, Greenville, TX
Stevenson, Scott .... (819) 986-8557
PUB, West-Quebec Post & Bulletin, Buckingham, QC
Stevenson, Susan .... (404) 526-5151
ASST MAN ED-Opinion
Atlanta Journal-Constitution, Atlanta, GA
Stevenson, Tom .... (541) 296-2141
ED, MAN ED
Dalles Daily Chronicle, The Dalles, OR
Steves, Renie .... (817) 732-4758
Writer, Cuisine Concepts, Fort Worth, TX
Steves, Sterling .... (817) 732-4758
Writer, Cuisine Concepts, Fort Worth, TX
Steward, Carl .... (510) 208-6300
Sports COL, Oakland Tribune, Oakland, CA
MediaNews Inc. (Alameda Newspapers)
Steward, Hartley .... (416) 947-2222
PUB & CEO-Toronto Sun
Sun Media Corp., Toronto, ON
Steward, Mike .... (916) 321-1000
CIRC MGR-City Single Copy
Sacramento Bee, Sacramento, CA
Steward, Peggy .... (509) 925-1414
MAN ED, Films/Theater ED, Home Furnishings ED, Women's ED
Daily Record, Ellensburg, WA
Stewart, Barbara J .... (201) 664-2501
ED, Community Life, Westwood, NJ
Stewart, Belinda .... (815) 987-1200
City ED, Rockford Register Star, Rockford, IL
Stewart, Betty .... (615) 388-6464
MGR-CR, Daily Herald, Columbia, TN
Stewart, Betty .... (813) 254-5888
ED, Free Press, Tampa, FL
Stewart, Betty .... (608) 879-2211
MAN ED
Journal & Footville News, Orfordville, WI
Stewart, Betty Jo .... (601) 534-6321
ED, New Albany Gazette, New Albany, MS
Stewart, Bill .... (706) 549-0123
Automotive ED, Athens Daily News/Banner-Herald, Athens, GA
Stewart, Bob .... (807) 468-5555
CIRC MGR, Daily Miner & News, Kenora, ON
Stewart, Carl .... (510) 734-8600
Sports COL, Tri-Valley Herald, Pleasanton, CA
Stewart, Carole C .... (412) 787-2881
VP
Home Improvement Time Inc., Oakdale, PA
Stewart, Charles .... (304) 624-6411
PROD FRM-COMP (Telegram), Clarksburg Exponent/Telegram, Clarksburg, WV
Stewart, Colin .... (617) 786-7000
Automotive ED, BUS/FIN ED
Patriot Ledger, Quincy, MA
Stewart, D L .... (937) 225-2000
COL, Dayton Daily News, Dayton, OH
Stewart, Dale .... (208) 733-0931
News ED, Times-News, Twin Falls, ID
Stewart, David .... (416) 367-2000
MGR-MKTG SYS/ACM
Toronto Star, Toronto, ON
Stewart, Dianne .... (706) 547-6629
GM, Jefferson Reporter, Wrens, GA
Stewart, Don .... (504) 383-1111
ADV DIR, Advocate, Baton Rouge, LA
Stewart, Don .... (250) 380-5211
BUS SYS MGR, Times Colonist, Victoria, BC
Stewart, Donna F .... (816) 842-3804
MAN ED, Call, Kansas City, MO
Stewart, Gary .... (607) 272-2321
EPE, Ithaca Journal, Ithaca, NY
Stewart, Gary .... (704) 739-7496
ED
Kings Mountain Herald, Kings Mountain, NC
Stewart, George E .... (608) 879-2211
PUB, ED
Journal & Footville News, Orfordville, WI
Stewart, Greg .... (813) 259-7711
PROD DIR
Tampa Tribune and Times, Tampa, FL
Stewart, Itzel .... (316) 275-8500
ED, La Semana en el suroeste de Kansas, Garden City, KS
Stewart, James .... (717) 784-2121
Entertainment/Amusements ED, Television/Film ED, Theater/Music ED
Press Enterprise, Bloomsburg, PA

Stewart, James .... (610) 489-3001
ED, Independent, Collegeville, PA
Stewart, James A .... (412) 787-2881
PUB, Home Improvement Time, Oakdale, PA
Stewart, Jeffrey .... (501) 315-8228
Sports ED, Benton Courier, Benton, AR
Stewart, Joanne .... (402) 444-1000
MET ED, Omaha World-Herald, Omaha, NE
Stewart, John .... (803) 533-5500
CIRC MGR
Times and Democrat, Orangeburg, SC
Stewart, John .... (610) 489-3001
PUB, Independent, Collegeville, PA
Stewart, John .... (815) 937-3300
Theater/Music ED, Daily Journal, Kankakee, IL
Stewart, Karen .... (719) 384-8121
ED, Arkansas Valley Journal, La Junta, CO
Stewart, Kathie .... (352) 746-4292
GM, Beverly Hills Visitor, Beverly Hills, FL
Stewart, Lalena .... (702) 298-6090
PUB, Laughlin Nevada Times, Laughlin, NV
Stewart, Linda .... (360) 736-3311
Librarian, Chronicle, Centralia, WA
Stewart, Lize-Anne .... (860) 442-2200
PROD CNR, Day, New London, CT
Stewart, Mark .... (334) 792-3141
EPE, Dothan Eagle, Dothan, AL
Stewart, Martin .... (609) 989-5454
VP/TREAS, CONT, Times, Trenton, NJ
Stewart, Mike .... (717) 784-2121
MAN ED-Sports/Features
Press Enterprise, Bloomsburg, PA
Stewart, Mike .... (907) 586-3740
Sports ED, Juneau Empire, Juneau, AK
Stewart III, Mitzell .... (330) 996-3000
MET ED, Akron Beacon Journal, Akron, OH
Stewart, Myron A .... (419) 472-4521
ED, Toledo Journal, Toledo, OH
Stewart, Perry .... (817) 390-7400
Theater ED
Fort Worth Star-Telegram, Fort Worth, TX
Stewart, Peter .... (707) 546-2020
PROD MGR-Building SRV (Santa Rosa/Rohnert Park)
Press Democrat, Santa Rosa, CA
Stewart, Phyllis .... (518) 483-4700
MAN ED, Malone Telegram, Malone, NY
Stewart, Richard D .... (919) 284-2295
PUB, ED, Kenly News, Kenly, NC
Stewart, Robert .... (512) 445-3500
CONT, American-Statesman, Austin, TX
Stewart, Robert .... (330) 454-5611
Sports ED, Repository, Canton, OH
Stewart, Robert .... (210) 907-3882
MAN ED
Times Guardian/Chronicle, Canyon Lake, TX
Stewart, Ronald J .... (541) 672-3321
PUB, News-Review, Roseburg, OR
Stewart, Rose Russell .... (419) 245-6000
ASSOC ED, Blade, Toledo, OH
Stewart, Russell .... (909) 487-2200
ADV MGR-CLASS
Hemet News, Hemet, CA
Stewart, Sandra S .... (419) 472-4521
PUB, Toledo Journal, Toledo, OH
Stewart, Sandy .... (330) 364-5577
MAN ED
Times Reporter, New Philadelphia, OH
Stewart, Steve .... (515) 753-6611
Photo ED
Times-Republican, Marshalltown, IA
Stewart, Susan .... (219) 563-8326
MAN ED, Paper, Wabash, IN
Stewart, Tom .... (412) 834-1151
News ED, Sunday ED
Tribune-Review, Greensburg, PA
Stewart, Trudy .... (715) 344-6100
Women's ED
Stevens Point Journal, Stevens Point, WI
Stewart, Victoria .... (360) 740-0445
ED, Lewis County News, Chehalis, WA
Stewart, Wayne .... (719) 632-5511
ASST ED, Colorado Springs Gazette, Colorado Springs, CO
Sthare, Conrad .... (610) 377-2051
ASST GM, Times News, Lehighton, PA
Stickel, Fred A .... (503) 221-8327
PRES, PUB, Oregonian, Portland, OR
Stickel Jr, Fred .... (717) 255-8100
PROD MGR, Patriot-News, Harrisburg, PA
Stickel, Patrick F .... (503) 221-8327
PRES, Oregonian, Portland, OR
Stickland, Kari .... (405) 772-3301
ADV MGR-CLASS
Weatherford Daily News, Weatherford, OK
Stickney, Ken .... (205) 345-0505
EPE, Tuscaloosa News, Tuscaloosa, AL
Stidham, Rochelle .... (606) 528-2464
PUB, Times-Tribune, Corbin, KY

Sti Who's Where-222

Stidom, Dolan ... (817) 390-7400
CIRC MGR-Arlington
Fort Worth Star-Telegram, Fort Worth, TX

Stienstra, Tom ... (415) 777-2424
Sports COL
San Francisco Examiner, San Francisco, CA

Stier, Mary P ... (703) 284-6000
Group PRES-Midwest Newspaper Group
Gannett Co. Inc., Arlington, VA

Stierly, Elizabeth ... (814) 367-2230
ED, Free Press-Courier, Westfield, PA

Stiff, Burl ... (619) 299-3131
Society Writer
San Diego Union-Tribune, San Diego, CA

Stiff, Cary ... (303) 567-4491
PUB, ED
Clear Creek Courant, Idaho Springs, CO

Stiff, Robert ... (704) 249-3981
EX ED, Dispatch, Lexington, NC

Stifflemire, Glenn ... (409) 297-6512
GM, Brazorian News, Lake Jackson, TX

Stiles, Bryan ... (864) 582-4511
Photo ED, Herald-Journal, Spartanburg, SC

Stiles, Carrie ... (616) 627-7144
ED, Cheboygan Daily Tribune, Cheboygan, MI

Stiles, Gordon ... (902) 485-8014
ED, Pictou Advocate, Pictou, NS

Stiles, John ... (309) 734-3176
ED, Daily Review Atlas, Monmouth, IL

Stiles, Roxanne ... (616) 527-2100
CIRC MGR, Sentinel-Standard, Ionia, MI

Stiles, Virginia ... (515) 858-5051
ED, Eldora Herald-Ledger, Eldora, IA

Still II, David B ... (508) 771-1427
ED, Barnstable Patriot, Hyannis, MA

Still, Eugene ... (204) 745-2051
ED, Valley Leader, Carman, MB

Still, Thomas ... (608) 252-6100
ASSOC ED
Wisconsin State Journal, Madison, WI

Stiller, Don ... (704) 633-8950
MGR-MKTG/PROM
Salisbury Post, Salisbury, NC

Stillwell, Dan ... (304) 436-3144
Sports ED, Welch Daily News, Welch, WV

Stillwell, Mary ... (304) 436-3144
MAN ED, Welch Daily News, Welch, WV

Stillwell, Vic ... (316) 421-2000
BUS ED, Parsons Sun, Parsons, KS

Stilwell, Don ... (706) 638-1859
ED, Walker County Messenger, LaFayette, GA

Stilwell, John ... (901) 454-1411
ED, Triangle Journal News, Memphis, TN

Stimmel, Gord ... (416) 947-2222
Television Guide, Toronto Sun, Toronto, ON

Stimson, Cinthia ... (907) 424-7181
MAN ED, Cordova Times, Cordova, AK

Stinchcomb, Lex ... (561) 820-4100
PROD SUPT-Building
Palm Beach Post, West Palm Beach, FL

Stinchfield, Janet L ... (541) 384-2421
PUB, Times-Journal, Condon, OR

Stinchfield, McLaren E ... (541) 384-2421
PUB, ED, Times-Journal, Condon, OR

Stingley, Herb ... (405) 356-2478
PUB, Wellston News, Wellston, OK

Stingley, Jean ... (405) 356-2478
ED, Wellston News, Wellston, OK

Stinnett, Chuck ... (502) 827-2000
Automotive ED, BUS/FIN ED, Environmental ED, Farm/Agriculture ED, SCI/Technology ED
Gleaner, Henderson, KY

Stinnett, Donna ... (502) 827-2000
Entertainment/Amusements ED, Fashions/Style ED, Features ED, Lifestyle ED, Travel ED, Gleaner, Henderson, KY

Stinnett, Joe ... (804) 385-5400
MAN ED, News & Advance, Lynchburg, VA

Stinnett, Linda ... (316) 326-3326
City ED, EDU ED, Features ED
Wellington Daily News, Wellington, KS

Stinnett, Lisa ... (806) 272-4536
GM, Bailey County Journal, Muleshoe, TX

Stinnett, Marshall ... (505) 356-4481
PUB, Mach Meter, Portales, NM

Stinnett, Peggy ... (510) 208-6300
EPE, Oakland Tribune, Oakland, CA

Stinnett, Scot ... (806) 272-4536
PUB, Bailey County Journal, Muleshoe, TX

Stinnett, Tony ... (615) 459-3868
ED, Rutherford Courier, Smyrna, TN

Stinson, Barbara ... (912) 744-4200
Development/Support ED
Macon Telegraph, Macon, GA

Stinson, Barrett ... (308) 382-1000
Photo ED
Grand Island Independent, Grand Island, NE

Stinson, Darlene ... (713) 220-7171
News SRV ED
Houston Chronicle, Houston, TX

Stinson, Donald M ... (703) 284-6000
VP-ADV, Gannett Co. Inc., Arlington, VA

Stinson, Douglas ... (403) 672-4421
ED, Camrose Canadian, Camrose, AB

Stinson, Jefferey ... (703) 276-5800
Regional ED
Gannett News Service, Arlington, VA

Stinson, Roddy ... (210) 225-7411
COL
San Antonio Express-News, San Antonio, TX

Stinson, Sharlene ... (610) 696-1775
City ED, Daily Local News, West Chester, PA

Stinson, Steve ... (540) 981-3100
Graphics DIR, Roanoke Times, Roanoke, VA

Stipe, Francis D ... (918) 456-8833
PRES/Owner, Daily Press, Tahlequah, OK

Stipp, Anna ... (606) 231-3100
ADV ASST MGR-Display
Lexington Herald-Leader, Lexington, KY

Stipsits, Bill ... (904) 252-1511
ADTX MGR-SRV, Daytona Beach News-Journal, Daytona Beach, FL

Stith, Pat ... (919) 829-4500
Computer-aided ED
News & Observer, Raleigh, NC

Stiver, Wendy ... (717) 748-6791
Lifestyle ED, Express, Lock Haven, PA

Stivers, Mary B ... (573) 223-7122
PUB
Wayne County Journal-Banner, Piedmont, MO

Stobbe, Mike ... (904) 359-4111
Medical ED
Florida Times-Union, Jacksonville, FL

Stock, Gregory L ... (412) 527-2868
ED, Jeannette Spirit, Jeannette, PA

Stockdale, Christie ... (605) 665-7811
ED
Town & Country Weekly News, Yankton, SD

Stocker, Carol ... (617) 929-2000
Garden ED, Boston Globe, Boston, MA

Stockinger, Jake ... (608) 252-6400
Films/Theater ED
Capital Times, Madison, WI

Stockland, Peter ... (403) 235-7100
EDL Writer, Calgary Herald, Calgary, AB

Stockman, Jay ... (812) 424-7711
ASST Sports ED
Evansville Courier, Evansville, IN

Stocks, David ... (616) 392-2311
MAN ED, Holland Sentinel, Holland, MI

Stockstill, Denise ... (513) 721-2700
RE ED, Cincinnati Enquirer, Cincinnati, OH

Stockton, Dennis ... (770) 887-3126
PUB, Forsyth County News, Cumming, GA

Stockton, Terry ... (318) 649-6411
PUB
Caldwell Watchman Progress, Columbia, LA

Stockwell, Junior ... (208) 743-9411
PROD MGR-PR
Lewiston Morning Tribune, Lewiston, ID

Stockwell-Rushton, Gwen ... (215) 340-9811
ED, Doylestown Patriot, Doylestown, PA

Stoddard, Carl ... (810) 766-6100
BUS ED, Flint Journal, Flint, MI

Stoddard, Martha ... (402) 475-4200
Environmental Reporter, State Government Reporter, Lincoln Journal Star, Lincoln, NE

Stoddard, Phil ... (608) 252-6200
CIRC DIR-Customer SRV
Madison Newspapers Inc., Madison, WI

Stodder, Mark ... (414) 276-0273
VP/PUB, Daily Reporter, Milwaukee, WI

Stodola, Chris ... (604) 495-7225
PUB, GM, Osoyoos Times, Osoyoos, BC

Stoeckle, Jan ... (517) 269-6461
CIRC MGR
Huron Daily Tribune, Bad Axe, MI

Stoeffler, David ... (608) 782-9710
ED, La Crosse Tribune, La Crosse, WI

Stoetzel, Teresa ... (615) 563-2512
GM, Cannon Courier, Woodbury, TN

Stoffer, Gary ... (317) 664-5111
DIR-SYS & Technology
Chronicle-Tribune, Marion, IN

Stoffer, Jeff ... (406) 266-3333
PUB, ED, Townsend Star, Townsend, MT

Stoffman, Judy ... (416) 367-2000
Book ED, Toronto Star, Toronto, ON

Stofft, Lori ... (520) 783-3333
MGR-MKTG, Yuma Daily Sun, Yuma, AZ

Stogsdill, Carol ... (213) 237-5000
VP-Senior ED, Senior ED/VP
Los Angeles Times, Los Angeles, CA

Stohlberg, Douglas W ... (715) 386-9333
ED, Hudson Star-Observer, Hudson, WI

Stohs, Nancy ... (414) 224-2000
Food ED
Milwaukee Journal Sentinel, Milwaukee, WI

Stoiber, Raymond ... (414) 224-2000
PROD MGR-Post Press
Milwaukee Journal Sentinel, Milwaukee, WI

Stokes, Barry A ... (913) 742-2111
PUB, Everest World, Hiawatha, KS

Stokes, Henry A ... (901) 529-2211
MAN ED, Commercial Appeal, Memphis, TN

Stokes, Ron ... (770) 787-6397
PUB, ED, Covington News, Covington, GA

Stokes, Sandi ... (410) 228-3131
Office MGR
Cambridge Daily Banner, Cambridge, MD

Stolar, David M ... (412) 263-1100
CIRC MGR-Single Copy
Pittsburgh Post-Gazette, Pittsburgh, PA

Stoler, David ... (520) 294-1200
ADV MGR, Daily Territorial, Tucson, AZ

Stolk, Dale ... (519) 679-6666
News Design ED
London Free Press, London, ON

Stoller, Stuart ... (212) 556-1234
VP/CORP CONT
New York Times Co., New York, NY

Stolns, Carol ... (970) 249-3444
Regional ED
Montrose Daily Press, Montrose, CO

Stoltler, David ... (562) 435-1161
VP, Press-Telegram, Long Beach, CA

Stoltz, David L ... (605) 239-4521
PUB, ED
Alexandria Herald, Alexandria, SD

Stoltz, Tom ... (912) 888-9390
VP-Publishing Division
Gray Communications, Albany, GA

Stone, Allen ... (815) 433-2000
PROD FRM-COMP, Daily Times, Ottawa, IL

Stone, Andy ... (970) 925-3414
PUB, ED, Aspen Times, Aspen, CO

Stone, Bill ... (808) 235-5881
ED, Windward Sun Press, Kaneohe, HI

Stone, Calvin ... (405) 225-3000
CIRC MGR, PROD MGR
Elk City Daily News, Elk City, OK

Stone, Danny ... (912) 283-2244
PROD FRM-PR, PROD SUPT-Press/Plateroom
Waycross Journal-Herald, Waycross, GA

Stone, David ... (606) 231-3100
PROD DIR-OPER
Lexington Herald-Leader, Lexington, KY

Stone, Dean ... (423) 981-1100
ED, EPE, Daily Times, Maryville, TN

Stone, Del ... (904) 863-1111
Wire ED, Northwest Florida Daily News, Fort Walton Beach, FL

Stone, Ethel ... (915) 337-4661
ADV MGR-NTL
Odessa American, Odessa, TX

Stone, Freeman ... (912) 236-9511
PROD SUPT-MR
Savannah Morning News, Savannah, GA

Stone, Greg ... (304) 348-5140
Health/Medical ED, Charleston Gazette, Sunday Gazette-Mail, Charleston, WV

Stone, Gregory N ... (860) 442-2200
Deputy EPE, Day, New London, CT

Stone, Henry D ... (502) 586-4481
PUB, Franklin Favorite, Franklin, KY

Stone, J Timothy ... (503) 399-6611
CIRC DIR, Statesman Journal, Salem, OR

Stone, Jack ... (405) 247-3331
ED, Features ED
Anadarko Daily News, Anadarko, OK

Stone, John R ... (320) 634-4571
PUB, ED
Pope County Tribune, Glenwood, MN

Stone, Kay ... (704) 484-7000
CIRC MGR, Shelby Star, Shelby, NC

Stone, Kelly ... (403) 542-5380
PUB, Western Review, Drayton Valley, AB

Stone, Ken ... (606) 824-3343
PUB
Grant County Express, Williamstown, KY

Stone, Larry ... (515) 284-8000
Outdoors ED
Des Moines Register, Des Moines, IA

Stone, Leigh ... (606) 878-7400
MAN ED, Sentinel-Echo, London, KY

Stone, M Gerald ... (918) 786-9051
PUB, ED, Grove Sun, Grove, OK

Stone, Mark ... (502) 754-2331
PUB, ED, Times-Argus, Central City, KY

Stone, Molly ... (716) 663-0068
ED, AdNet Community News, Rochester, NY

Stone, Phyllis ... (817) 390-7400
BUS ED-Tarrant
Fort Worth Star-Telegram, Fort Worth, TX

Stone, R Dwayne ... (306) 697-2722
PUB, Grenfell Sun, Grenfell, SK

Stone, Rex ... (401) 277-7000
PROD MGR-OPER Engineering
Providence Journal-Bulletin, Providence, RI

Stone, Richard ... (601) 961-7000
CIRC DIR, Clarion-Ledger, Jackson, MS

Stone, Robert Rade ... (412) 612-6600
ED, American Srbobran, Pittsburgh, PA

Stone, Sam ... (513) 931-4050
ED, Christian Standard, Cincinnati, OH

Stone, Scott ... (847) 888-7800
Assignment ED, Courier-News, Elgin, IL

Stone, Stuart S ... (630) 469-0100
PUB, Glen Ellyn News, Glen Ellyn, IL

Stone, Sue ... (903) 872-3931
PROD MGR-COMP
Corsicana Daily Sun, Corsicana, TX

Stone, Todd ... (318) 459-3200
News ED, Times, Shreveport, LA

Stone-Heyen, Melanie ... (318) 255-4353
ED, BUS/FIN ED, EDU ED, News ED
Ruston Daily Leader, Ruston, LA

Stoneback, Diane ... (610) 820-6500
Home/Food ED, Morning Call, Allentown, PA

Stoneberg, David D ... (707) 994-6444
ED
Clear Lake Observer-American, Clearlake, CA

Stoneburner, Mary Lou ... (860) 241-6200
ADV MGR-CLASS
Hartford Courant, Hartford, CT

Stoneman, Susan ... (360) 452-2345
ADV SUPV-Inside Sales
Peninsula Daily News, Port Angeles, WA

Stoner, Don ... (715) 246-6881
ED, News, New Richmond, WI

Stoner, Jack L ... (605) 765-2464
PUB, Potter County News, Gettysburg, SD

Stoner, James C ... (717) 622-3456
BUS/FIN ED, RE ED, Religion/School ED
Pottsville Republican & Evening Herald, Pottsville, PA

Stoner, Jane F ... (712) 295-7711
ED, Peterson Patriot, Peterson, IA

Stoner, Joan ... (313) 242-1100
SEC, BM, Monroe Evening News, Monroe, MI

Stoner, Roger E ... (712) 295-7711
PUB, Peterson Patriot, Peterson, IA

Stones, Marlon U ... (801) 355-3336
Technology ED
FNA News, Salt Lake City, UT

Stong, Marilyn ... (604) 365-5266
PUB, Castlegar Sun, Castlegar, BC

Stong, Sue Dixon ... (808) 245-8825
MAN ED, Kauai Times, Lihue, Kauai, HI

Stophel, Tony O ... (804) 978-7200
CIRC DIR, Daily Progress, Charlottesville, VA

Storey, Alan ... (316) 429-2773
ED, Wire ED
Columbus Daily Advocate, Columbus, KS

Storey, David ... (319) 398-8211
ADV DIR, Gazette, Cedar Rapids, IA

Storey, Deborah ... (205) 532-4000
Travel ED, Huntsville Times, Huntsville, AL

Storey, Jeff ... (914) 341-1100
MAN ED
Times Herald-Record, Middletown, NY

Storey, Michael ... (501) 378-3400
Television/Film ED
Arkansas Democrat-Gazette, Little Rock, AR

Storey, Stephanie ... (309) 833-2114
ADTX MGR, Macomb Journal, Macomb, IL

Storin, Matthew V ... (617) 929-2000
ED, Boston Globe, Boston, MA

Storm, Sheila ... (414) 235-7700
BUS ED, Oshkosh Northwestern, Oshkosh, WI

Stormont, David ... (617) 450-2000
PROD DIR-OPER
Christian Science Monitor, Boston, MA

Storring, Dwight ... (519) 894-2231
ADTX MGR, Record, Kitchener, ON

Stortz, Cathy ... (816) 646-2411
ED, BUS/FIN ED, City ED, EPE, Features ED, Graphics ED/Art DIR, News ED, Photo ED, Political/Government ED
Constitution-Tribune, Chillicothe, MO

Story, Brenda ... (309) 686-3000
Action Line ED, Journal Star, Peoria, IL

Story, Dave ... (918) 341-1101
PUB/PA, ED, EPE, Political/Government ED
Claremore Daily Progress, Claremore, OK

Story, David ... (405) 475-3311
SEC/TREAS
Daily Oklahoman, Oklahoma City, OK

Story, Frank ... (619) 299-3131
PROD MGR-Maintenance
San Diego Union-Tribune, San Diego, CA

Story, Shawn ... (712) 328-1811
PROD FRM-Press
Daily Nonpareil, Council Bluffs, IA

Stotler, David ... (562) 435-1161
VP-Circulation, CIRC VP
Press-Telegram, Long Beach, CA

Stott, Jason ... (904) 829-6562
Theater/Music ED
St. Augustine Record, St. Augustine, FL

Stottlemyer, Woody ... (301) 662-1177
MGR-Infor Services, PROD SUPV-COMP (Day & Night)
Frederick Post/The News, Frederick, MD

Stouffer, Steve ... (301) 722-4600
ADV DIR
Cumberland Times-News, Cumberland, MD

Stout, Bradley L ... (212) 837-7000
CIRC MGR-Distribution, Journal of Commerce & Commercial, New York, NY

Stout, Byron ... (941) 335-0200
Outdoors Writer, News-Press, Fort Myers, FL

Stout, Charles J ... (352) 867-4010
VP, PUB, Ocala Star-Banner, Ocala, FL

Copyright ©1997 by the Editor & Publisher Co.

223-Who's Where **Stu**

Stout, David .... (704) 531-9988
ED, Q Notes, Charlotte, NC
Stout, Gene .... (206) 448-8000
Music Editor-Popular/Jazz
Seattle Post-Intelligencer, Seattle, WA
Stout, Harold .... (205) 345-0505
Sports ED, Tuscaloosa News, Tuscaloosa, AL
Stout, Jill .... (210) 423-5511
BM, Valley Morning Star, Harlingen, TX
Stout, Lyndall .... (918) 793-3841
ED, Shidler Review, Shidler, OK
Stout, Mary Charlotte .... (307) 324-3411
SEC, Rawlins Daily Times, Rawlins, WY
Stout, Michael .... (504) 652-9545
MAN ED, LaPlace L'Observateur, LaPlace, LA
Stout, Michael W .... (208) 467-9251
PROD MGR, Idaho Press-Tribune, Nampa, ID
Stout, Robert .... (417) 223-4377/4675
GM, McDonald County News-Gazette, Pineville, MO
Stout, Steve .... (937) 652-1331
Sports ED, Urbana Daily Citizen, Urbana, OH
Stout, Steve .... (970) 242-5050
News ED, Daily Sentinel, Grand Junction, CO
Stouwie, Guillermina .... (213) 622-8332
ADV DIR-CLASS
La Opinion, Los Angeles, CA
Stouwie, Marie .... (213) 622-8332
ADTX MGR, La Opinion, Los Angeles, CA
Stover, Bob .... (407) 242-3500
MET ED, Florida Today, Melbourne, FL
Stover, Jeff .... (304) 255-4400
SYS MGR, Register Herald, Beckley, WV
Stover, Mike .... (805) 781-7800
City ED
Telegram-Tribune, San Luis Obispo, CA
Stover, Nello C .... (717) 767-6397
CIRC DIR, York Newspaper Co., York, PA
Stowe, Michael .... (540) 981-3100
MET ED, Roanoke Times, Roanoke, VA
Stowell, Francis E .... (816) 234-4141
VP-Human Resources
Kansas City Star, Kansas City, MO
Stowell Jr, Roger .... (208) 377-6200
PROD DIR, Idaho Statesman, Boise, ID
Strabala, Robert W .... (217) 429-5151
PROD MGR-Product SRV
Herald & Review, Decatur, IL
Stracener, Jane .... (915) 653-1221
Oil ED, Standard-Times, San Angelo, TX
Strachan, Eric .... (941) 262-3161
Photo ED, Naples Daily News, Naples, FL
Strachan, Jane .... (216) 951-0000
Librarian, News-Herald, Willoughby, OH
Strader, Jerry J .... (618) 937-6411
PRES/CEO, Hollinger International Inc., West Frankfort, IL
Strader, Leslie .... (915) 673-4271
EDU ED-Lower
Abilene Reporter-News, Abilene, TX
Stradling, Mark .... (609) 989-7800
EPE, Trentonian, Trenton, NJ
Stradling, Richard .... (757) 247-4600
Environmental ED, SCI/Technology ED
Daily Press, Newport News, VA
Strahl, Tony .... (812) 275-3355
PROD MGR, Times-Mail, Bedford, IN
Straight, Cathy .... (615) 259-8000
Special Projects ED
Tennessean, Nashville, TN
Straka, Fredrick .... (802) 674-2975
PUB, ED, Windsor Chronicle, Windsor, VT
Straka, Olga .... (802) 674-2975
PUB, Windsor Chronicle, Windsor, VT
Strand, Bruce .... (320) 235-1150
Sports ED
West Central Tribune, Willmar, MN
Strand, Jody .... (406) 778-3344
ED, Fallon County Times, Baker, MT
Strand, John A .... (701) 352-0640
ED, Walsh County Record, Grafton, ND
Strand, Michael .... (405) 223-2200
City ED, Environmental ED
Daily Ardmoreite, Ardmore, OK
Strandberg, Diane .... (604) 531-1711
ED, Peace Arch News, White Rock, BC
Strandburg, Chuck .... (814) 723-8200
PROD FRM-COMP
Warren Times-Observer, Warren, PA
Strang, James .... (216) 999-4500
Foreign/NTL ED, Plain Dealer, Cleveland, OH
Strange, J E .... (601) 683-2001
PUB, ED, Newton Record, Newton, MS
Strange, Michelle .... (423) 581-5630
Features ED, Citizen Tribune, Morristown, TN
Strantz, Anne G .... (219) 287-1001
ASST SEC/TREAS
Schurz Communications Inc., South Bend, IN
Strasser, Robert C .... (847) 427-4300
ADV MGR-Division Sales
Daily Herald, Arlington Heights, IL
Strate, Jack .... (423) 581-5630
SEC/TREAS, Citizen Tribune, Morristown, TN
Strate, L D .... (806) 669-2525
Sports ED, Pampa News, Pampa, TX
Strathder, Mike .... (519) 894-2231
Agriculture ED, Record, Kitchener, ON
Strattan, Lisa .... (508) 676-8211
EPE, Herald News, Fall River, MA
Stratton, J T .... (606) 376-5356/5357
GM
McCreary County Record, Whitley City, KY
Stratton, Richard H .... (601) 657-4818
PUB, ED, Southern Herald, Liberty, MS
Stratton, Tim .... (606) 678-8191
GM, ED
Commonwealth-Journal, Somerset, KY
Straub, Charles .... (860) 423-8466
PROD MGR-Distribution Center
Chronicle, Willimantic, CT
Straughn, Lynn .... (520) 573-4400
PROD MGR-Environmental, TNI Partners dba Tucson Newspapers, Tucson, AZ
Strauss, Bob .... (818) 713-3000
Films Critic, Daily News, Woodland Hills, CA
Strauss, Jim .... (406) 791-1444
EX ED, Great Falls Tribune, Great Falls, MT
Strauss, Michael .... (561) 820-3800
Sports ED
Palm Beach Daily News, Palm Beach, FL
Strauss, Pat .... (512) 575-1451
MGR-BUS Office
Victoria Advocate, Victoria, TX
Straw, Ronald .... (301) 722-4600
PROD FRM-COMP
Cumberland Times-News, Cumberland, MD
Strawn, Charlotte .... (573) 815-1500
CIRC MGR, Daily Tribune, Columbia, MO
Strawn II, John C .... (515) 483-2120
PUB, ED, Enterprise-Record, State Center, IA
Strecker, Paul .... (860) 442-2200
CIRC MGR-Distribution
Day, New London, CT
Streeby, Michelle Martin .... (915) 546-6340
DIR-Public SRV
El Paso Herald-Post, El Paso, TX
Street, Bernard .... (919) 708-9000
PROD FRM-PR, Sanford Herald, Sanford, NC
Street, C Murphy .... (540) 374-5000
ADV DIR
Free Lance-Star, Fredericksburg, VA
Street, Cheryl .... (864) 298-4100
Food ED, Greenville News, Greenville, SC
Street, Chris .... (706) 549-0123
Online MGR, Athens Daily News/Banner-Herald, Athens, GA
Street, Edra .... (912) 764-9031
DP MGR, Statesboro Herald, Statesboro, GA
Streeter, Leslie .... (209) 578-2000
MGR-PROM, Modesto Bee, Modesto, CA
Streets, Nancy .... (702) 358-8061
ADV MGR-Display
Daily Sparks Tribune, Sparks, NV
Streeval, Maleena .... (606) 787-7171
ED, Casey County News, Liberty, KY
Streim, Karen .... (707) 263-5636
BM, Lake County Record-Bee, Lakeport, CA
Streit Jr, James B .... (302) 737-0724
PUB, ED, Newark Post, Newark, DE
Streitenberger, Becky .... (712) 246-3097
ADV MGR-CLASS
Valley News Today, Shenandoah, IA
Streng, Aileen .... (910) 353-1171
City ED, Food ED
Daily News, Jacksonville, NC
Streng, Donald .... (937) 644-9111
PROD MGR
Marysville Journal-Tribune, Marysville, OH
Strenger, Scott .... (402) 721-5000
Sports ED, Fremont Tribune, Fremont, NE
Stretch, Kelvin .... (250) 372-2331
MGR-FIN, Daily News, Kamloops, BC
Strettell, David .... (212) 929-6000
EDL DIR
Magnum Photos Inc., New York, NY
Strick, Stan .... (206) 339-3000
EX ED, Herald, Everett, WA
Stricker, Debby .... (618) 243-5563
ED, Okawville Times, Okawville, IL
Stricker, Gary W .... (618) 243-5563
PUB, Okawville Times, Okawville, IL
Stricker, Pam .... (513) 721-2700
ADV MGR-NTL
Cincinnati Enquirer, Cincinnati, OH
Strickland, Bill .... (912) 888-9300
PROD MGR-INFO SYS
Albany Herald, Albany, GA
Strickland, Cheryl .... (916) 441-6397
GM, Mom Guess What Newspaper, Sacramento, CA
Strickland, Dee-Dee .... (612) 222-5011
Senior ED-Presentation Hub
St. Paul Pioneer Press, St. Paul, MN
Strickland, Gene .... (903) 597-8111
City ED, Tyler Morning Telegraph, Tyler, TX
Strickland, Kimi .... (405) 335-2188
CIRC MGR, Frederick Leader, Frederick, OK
Strickland, Terrell .... (501) 378-3400
MGR-Accounting
Arkansas Democrat-Gazette, Little Rock, AR
Strickland, Walt .... (423) 756-1234
Graphics DIR
Chattanooga Times, Chattanooga, TN
Strickler, Dan .... (423) 246-8121
DP MGR, Times-News, Kingsport, TN
Strickler, Jeff .... (612) 673-4000
Movie Critic, Star Tribune, Minneapolis, MN
Strickler, John W .... (610) 323-3000
Photo DEPT MGR, Mercury, Pottstown, PA
Striegel, Colleen .... (509) 459-5000
ADTX MGR
Spokesman-Review, Spokane, WA
Striessky, Patricia M .... (717) 785-3800
ED, Forest City News, Forest City, PA
Strigler, Mordecai .... (212) 889-8200
ED, Jewish Forward, New York, NY
Stringer, David R .... (707) 644-1141
PUB, Vallejo Times-Herald, Vallejo, CA
Stringer, Don .... (502) 781-1700
EPE, Daily News, Bowling Green, KY
Stringer, Larry .... (601) 795-2247
ED, Poplarville Democrat, Poplarville, MS
Stringer, Patsy .... (704) 358-5000
ADV MGR-Production SRV
Charlotte Observer, Charlotte, NC
Stringfellow, Eric .... (601) 961-7000
ASST MET ED, Clarion-Ledger, Jackson, MS
Stringfellow, Lee .... (334) 433-1551
DIR-Human Resources
Mobile Press Register, Mobile, AL
Stripling, Gerald .... (501) 898-3462
PUB, Little River News, Ashdown, AR
Stripp, Rich .... (406) 883-4343
ED, Lake County Leader, Polson, MT
Strobel, John .... (808) 525-8000
News ED, Honolulu Advertiser, Honolulu, HI
Strobel, Mike .... (416) 947-2222
MAN ED, Toronto Sun, Toronto, ON
Stroble, David .... (910) 373-7000
ADTX MGR, News & Record, Greensboro, NC
Strode, Dale .... (970) 925-3414
Sports ED, Aspen Times, Aspen, CO
Strode, George .... (614) 461-5000
Sports ED
Columbus Dispatch, Columbus, OH
Strogoff, Jody Hope .... (303) 837-8600
PUB, ED, Colorado Statesman, Denver, CO
Stroh, Don .... (314) 340-8000
PROD GEN FRM-Paperhandling
St. Louis Post-Dispatch, St. Louis, MO
Strohmeyer, Joseph E .... (540) 465-5137
MAN ED
Northern Virginia Daily, Strasburg, VA
Strom, Thai .... (209) 943-6397
Librarian, Record, Stockton, CA
Stromberg-Brink, Bridget .... (415) 381-5149
MAN ED, Vestkusten, Mill Valley, CA
Stromme, Tom .... (701) 223-2500
Photographer
Bismarck Tribune, Bismarck, ND
Strong, Corrin .... (716) 243-3530
PUB, ED, Lake & Valley Clarion, Geneseo, NY
Strong, Gary .... (213) 237-5000
DIR-Accounting OPER
Los Angeles Times, Los Angeles, CA
Strong, Kim .... (717) 771-2000
Entertainment ED, Features ED, Living ED
York Daily Record, York, PA
Strong, Martha .... (601) 562-4414
MAN ED, Democrat, Senatobia, MS
Strosnider, Ann .... (360) 377-3711
Community ED, Sun, Bremerton, WA
Strother, Jeff .... (860) 442-2200
PROD MGR-Receiving, Day, New London, CT
Strother, William .... (812) 332-4401
City ED, Herald-Times Inc, Bloomington, IN
Strothers, Annette F .... (717) 291-8811
MGR-MKTG/Advertising
Lancaster Intelligencer Journal/New Era/Sunday News, Lancaster, PA
Stroud, Donald .... (216) 999-4500
MIS DIR, Plain Dealer, Cleveland, OH
Stroud, Jerry .... (915) 546-6100
PROD MGR-COMP
El Paso Times, El Paso, TX
Stroud, Joseph H .... (313) 222-6400
ED, EPE, Detroit Free Press, Detroit, MI
Stroup, Sheila .... (504) 826-3279
COL, Times-Picayune, New Orleans, LA
Strout, Bill .... (910) 227-0131
PROD ASST FRM-PR
Times News Publishing Co., Burlington, NC
Strout, Jeff .... (207) 990-8000
Maine Style ED
Bangor Daily News, Bangor, ME
Strout, Steven B .... (416) 814-4239
VP-Information Technology
Thomson Newspapers, Toronto, ON
Strowd, Larry .... (501) 793-2383
Travel ED, Batesville Guard, Batesville, AR
Strub, Denise .... (601) 843-4241
Society ED
Bolivar Commercial, Cleveland, MS
Struck, Myron .... (703) 368-3101
MAN ED, Journal Messenger, Manassas, VA
Strumold, Al .... (401) 277-7000
ADV Sales DIR-NTL Chains
Providence Journal-Bulletin, Providence, RI
Strunk, Chris .... (316) 775-2218
Photo ED, Religion ED, Sports ED
Augusta Daily Gazette, Augusta, KS
Struth, Garry .... (204) 523-4611
PUB, ED, Killarney Guide, Killarney, MB
Struthers, Gord .... (306) 652-9200
City ED, StarPhoenix, Saskatoon, SK
Strutton, Larry D .... (303) 892-5000
PRES/CEO, PUB
Rocky Mountain News, Denver, CO
Struve, Harold W .... (402) 365-7221
PUB, ED, Deshler Rustler, Deshler, NE
Stryker, Mark .... (313) 222-6400
Music Writer-Classical
Detroit Free Press, Detroit, MI
Stuart, Cynthia L .... (217) 692-2323
PUB, ED
Blue Mound Leader, Blue Mound, IL
Stuart III, Donald C .... (609) 924-2200
PUB, ED, Town Topics, Princeton, NJ
Stuart, Laurie .... (914) 252-7414
GM, River Reporter, Narrowsburg, NY
Stuart, Len .... (603) 668-4321
Photo ED, Union Leader, Manchester, NH
Stuart, Maria .... (517) 548-2000
ED, Livingston County Press, Howell, MI
Stuart, Paul .... (412) 772-3900
Sports ED
North Hills News Record, Warrendale, PA
Stuart, Paulette .... (719) 544-3520
ADV MGR-PROM
Pueblo Chieftain, Pueblo, CO
Stubbe, Glen .... (202) 636-3000
Photo DIR
Washington Times, Washington, DC
Stubbe, Lori .... (414) 235-7700
ADV MGR-NTL
Oshkosh Northwestern, Oshkosh, WI
Stubbe, Richard .... (614) 452-4561
MAN ED, EPE
Times Recorder, Zanesville, OH
Stubbendieck, Alison .... (330) 725-4166
ADV DIR-Sales
Medina County Gazette, Medina, OH
Stubblefield, Brenda .... (901) 642-1162
ADV MGR, Paris Post-Intelligencer, Paris, TN
Stubbs, Angela .... (403) 527-1101
Society ED
Medicine Hat News, Medicine Hat, AB
Stubbs, Dave .... (514) 987-2222
Sports ED, Gazette, Montreal, QC
Stubbs, Mike .... (417) 235-3135
ADV MGR-RT, Times, Monett, MO
Stubbs, Pat .... (706) 324-5526
PROD DIR
Columbus Ledger-Enquirer, Columbus, GA
Stubler, Paul .... (614) 622-1122
ADV MGR
Coshocton Tribune, Coshocton, OH
Stuck, Cliff .... (219) 294-1661
PROD DIR, Elkhart Truth, Elkhart, IN
Stuck, Nelda .... (909) 793-3221
Community ED
Redlands Daily Facts, Redlands, CA
Stuckey, Andrew .... (403) 932-3500
MAN ED, Rural Times, Cochrane, AB
Stuckey, Anita .... (316) 694-5700
ADV CNR-NTL
Hutchinson News, Hutchinson, KS
Stuckey, John .... (403) 668-2063
CIRC MGR, Whitehorse Star, Whitehorse, YT
Stuckey, Sharon .... (205) 372-2232
GM, Greene County Independent, Eutaw, AL
Studer, Wayne A .... (609) 935-1500
PUB, Record, Salem, NJ
Studt, Gary .... (914) 331-5000
CIRC DIR, Daily Freeman, Kingston, NY
Studt, William E .... (914) 331-5000
PROD MGR, PROD FRM-PR
Daily Freeman, Kingston, NY
Studwell, John .... (904) 829-6562
Photo DEPT MGR
St. Augustine Record, St. Augustine, FL
Stuewe, Ervan D .... (913) 765-3327
PUB, ED, Signal Enterprise, Alma, KS
Stuewe, Pamela K .... (913) 765-3327
PUB, Signal Enterprise, Alma, KS
Stufflebeam, Jim .... (941) 748-0411
PROD MGR-Pre Press/MR/Bindery OPER, Bradenton Herald, Bradenton, FL
Stults, Bill .... (206) 448-8000
MGR-Technology
Seattle Post-Intelligencer, Seattle, WA
Stultz, Kristy .... (317) 348-0110
Sports ED, News-Times, Hartford City, IN
Stumb, Jett .... (901) 872-2286
PUB, Millington Star, Millington, TN

Stu Who's Where-224

Stumb, Patricia (901) 872-2286
PUB, Millington Star, Millington, TN

Stumbo, Betty E (419) 529-2847
MAN ED, Tribune Courier & Madison Tribune, Ontario, OH

Stumbo, Frank (419) 529-2847
PUB, Tribune Courier & Madison Tribune, Ontario, OH

Stumfall, Derek (202) 898-8254
GEN MGR-Asia/Pacific
United Press International, Washington, DC

Stump, Dave (804) 857-1212
ED, Soundings, Norfolk, VA

Stump, David (609) 691-5000
ASSOC ED, Daily Journal, Vineland, NJ

Stump, John M (312) 321-3000
ADV DIR-VIS, ADTX MGR
Chicago Sun-Times, Chicago, IL

Stumpf, Michael (715) 672-4252
PUB, Courier-Wedge, Durand, WI

Stumpf, Rebecca (512) 884-2011
Sunday ED, Corpus Christi Caller-Times, Corpus Christi, TX

Sturgeon, Bryan (317) 633-1240
CIRC MGR-Single Copy
Indianapolis Star/News, Indianapolis, IN

Sturgeon, Terry E (616) 345-3511
ASST to PUB
Kalamazoo Gazette, Kalamazoo, MI

Sturges, R G (605) 983-5491
PUB, Arlington Sun, Arlington, SD

Sturges, Tim (605) 983-5491
ED, Arlington Sun, Arlington, SD

Sturgill, Larry E (410) 442-1638
MAN ED-COL
Main Street Features, Ellicott City, MD

Sturgis, Ron (712) 469-3381
ED, Manson Journal, Manson, IA

Sturkel, Scott (800) 365-3020
MAN ED, Gunfighter, Boise, ID

Sturmon-Dale, Sarah (513) 352-2000
Local Government ED
Cincinnati Post, Cincinnati, OH

Sturms, Bob (303) 892-5000
PROD MGR-Platemaking
Rocky Mountain News, Denver, CO

Sturrock, Staci (864) 298-4100
Theater ED, Greenville News, Greenville, SC

Sturrup, John (705) 749-3383
PUB
Peterborough This Week, Peterborough, ON

Stuski, Nancy (215) 854-2000
ADV DIR-Daily News ADV & Sales Development, Philadelphia Inquirer, Philadelphia, PA

Stutes, Troy (409) 985-5541
PROD ASST MGR
Port Arthur News, Port Arthur, TX

Stutler, Bill (513) 422-3611
CIRC MGR
Middletown Journal, Middletown, OH

Stutsman, Colin (403) 328-4411
PROD FRM-MR
Lethbridge Herald, Lethbridge, AB

Stutzin, Leo (209) 578-2000
Arts/Theater ED, Theater/Music Writer
Modesto Bee, Modesto, CA

Stutzman, Rosalie (308) 485-4284
ED, Cairo Record, Cairo, NE

Styer, James (616) 964-7161
Television ED
Battle Creek Enquirer, Battle Creek, MI

Styles, George (519) 894-2231
PROD MGR-SYS, Record, Kitchener, ON

Styron, Emery A (319) 385-3131
PUB, Mt. Pleasant News, Mount Pleasant, IA

Su, Chi (213) 782-8770
PUB, Free China Journal, Los Angeles, CA

Suarez, Amancio (305) 856-5664
PUB, Viva Semanal, Miami, FL

Subber, Richard (610) 820-6500
ADV MGR-ADM SRV
Morning Call, Allentown, PA

Suber, Jim (913) 295-1111
Farm ED, Topeka Capital-Journal, Topeka, KS

Suber, Lou Anne (903) 665-2462
ED, Jefferson Jimplecute, Jefferson, TX

Sublett, Barry H (205) 353-4612
Entertainment/Amusements ED, Fashion/Style ED, Features/Travel ED, Films/Television ED, Food/Home Furnishings ED, Living Today/Society ED, Decatur Daily, Decatur, AL

Such, Frank (312) 321-3000
MGR-Market RES
Chicago Sun-Times, Chicago, IL

Sucha, Kathleen (517) 793-7661
ED, Catholic Weekly, Saginaw, MI

Sudbrook, Jeff (216) 951-0000
ADV MGR-RT, News-Herald, Willoughby, OH

Sudol, Valerie (201) 877-4141
Dance Critic, Star-Ledger, Newark, NJ

Sue, Deborah (817) 292-1855
VP/Special Projects, A & A, Ft. Worth, TX

Suelean, Beverly (317) 622-1212
Librarian, Herald Bulletin, Anderson, IN

Suellentrop, Paul (816) 271-8500
Sports ED, News-Press, St. Joseph, MO

Suenaga, Richard (213) 725-0083
ED, Pacific Citizen, Monterey Park, CA

Suffolk, Ted E (330) 747-1471
ASST GM, Vindicator, Youngstown, OH

Sugamele, Michael (619) 427-3000
GM, Star-News, Chula Vista, CA

Sugano, Akiko F (773) 478-6170
PUB, Chicago Shimpo, Chicago, IL

Sugg, Brad (918) 456-8833
PUB, EIC
Tahlequah Daily Press, Tahlequah, OK

Sugg, Marvine (615) 388-6464
Religion ED, Society ED
Daily Herald, Columbia, TN

Suggett, Mary (816) 932-6600
Permissions DIR
Universal Press Syndicate, Kansas City, MO

Suggs, Donald (314) 533-8000
PUB, St. Louis American, St. Louis, MO

Suggs, Sherry (520) 763-2505
ADV MGR-RT
Mohave Valley Daily News, Bullhead City, AZ

Sugrue, Margo (310) 337-7003
Sales EX
Creators Syndicate, Los Angeles, CA

Suisman, Gary M (517) 377-1000
PRES, PUB
Lansing State Journal, Lansing, MI

Suk, John (616) 246-0732
ED, Banner, Grand Rapids, MI

Sukle Jr, Joseph C (717) 944-4628
PUB, ED, Press and Journal, Middletown, PA

Suklis, Glenda (541) 926-2211
Librarian
Albany Democrat-Herald, Albany, OR

Sullens, David (601) 693-1551
MAN ED, Automotive ED, EPE, EDL Writer
Meridian Star, Meridian, MS

Sulliman, George (860) 489-3121
CIRC DIR, Register Citizen, Torrington, CT

Sullivan, A Dent (704) 758-7381
CONT, Lenoir News-Topic, Lenoir, NC

Sullivan, Beth (317) 241-4345
PUB, ED, Northwest Press, Speedway, IN

Sullivan, Brian (413) 447-7311
ASST News ED
Berkshire Eagle, Pittsfield, MA

Sullivan, Charles E (512) 547-3274
ED, Mathis News, Mathis, TX

Sullivan, Dan (704) 692-0505
News ED, Times-News, Hendersonville, NC

Sullivan, Gary (619) 745-6611
PROD MGR-QA
North County Times, Escondido, CA

Sullivan, Jerry (716) 849-3434
COL-Sports, Buffalo News, Buffalo, NY

Sullivan, Joe (423) 522-5399
PUB, Metro Pulse, Knoxville, TN

Sullivan, John (312) 321-3000
ADV DIR-ADM
Chicago Sun-Times, Chicago, IL

Sullivan, John (204) 697-7000
ASST MAN ED
Winnipeg Free Press, Winnipeg, MB
Thomson Newspapers

Sullivan, John (406) 222-2000
PRES/GM
Yellowstone Newspapers, Livingston, MT

Sullivan III, John (912) 924-2751
Sports ED, Times-Recorder, Americus, GA

Sullivan III, John A (201) 226-8900
PUB, Progress, Caldwell, NJ

Sullivan, John F J (603) 742-7209
ED, Dover Times, Dover, NH

Sullivan, John L .... (937) 592-3060, Examiner, Bellefontaine, OH

Sullivan, Kathy (313) 222-6400
MGR-ADM SRV
Detroit Newspapers, Detroit, MI

Sullivan, Ken (319) 398-8211
EDL Writer, Political ED
Gazette, Cedar Rapids, IA

Sullivan, Lisa (803) 329-4000
DIR-PROM, Herald, Rock Hill, SC

Sullivan, Margaret (716) 849-3434
ASST MAN ED-Features, Features ED, Lifestyle Pages ED
Buffalo News, Buffalo, NY

Sullivan, Mark (202) 797-7000
MAN ED, Washington Blade, Washington, DC

Sullivan, Marty (601) 494-1422
CIRC MGR
Daily Times Leader, West Point, MS

Sullivan, Maureen (508) 947-1111
PUB, Capeway News, Middleboro, MA

Sullivan, Michele (540) 635-4174
ED, Warren Sentinel, Front Royal, VA

Sullivan, Pat (403) 328-4411
Entertainment ED
Lethbridge Herald, Lethbridge, AB

Sullivan, Patricia (408) 920-5000
Online ED
San Jose Mercury News, San Jose, CA

Sullivan, Paul (604) 732-2111
MAN ED, Vancouver Sun, Vancouver, BC

Sullivan, R Joe (573) 335-6611
ED
Southeast Missourian, Cape Girardeau, MO

Sullivan, Ray (419) 223-1010
ED, Lima News, Lima, OH

Sullivan, Rich (315) 470-0011
Regional ED, Post-Standard/Syracuse Herald-Journal/American, Syracuse, NY

Sullivan, Robert (317) 825-0581
Sports ED
Connersville News-Examiner, Connersville, IN

Sullivan, Stephen W (210) 829-9000
Sr VP/PRES-Harte-Hanks Newspapers, PRES/PUB-Caller Times, Corpus Christi, TX
Harte-Hanks Communications Inc., San Antonio, TX

Sullivan, Teresa (502) 665-9492
ED, Advance-Yeoman, Wickliffe, KY

Sullivan, Terry (510) 935-2525
ADV MGR-CLASS
Contra Costa Times, Walnut Creek, CA

Sullivan, Terry T (703) 276-3400
VP-Human Resources
USA Today, Arlington, VA

Sullivan, Tim (208) 882-5561
Sports Writer
Moscow-Pullman Daily News, Moscow, ID

Sullivan, Will (601) 798-4766
MAN ED, Picayune Item, Picayune, MS

Sullivan, William (617) 933-3700
Automotive/Aviation ED, EDL Writer
Daily Times Chronicle, Woburn, MA

Sulliven, Lynn (919) 752-6166
MGR-PROM, Daily Reflector, Greenville, NC

Sulzberger, Arthur Ochs (212) 556-1234
COB/CEO
New York Times Co., New York, NY

Sulzberger Jr, Arthur (212) 556-1234
PUB, New York Times Co., New York, NY

Summar, Polly (505) 823-7777
Women's Magazine ED
Albuquerque Journal, Albuquerque, NM

Summer, Donna (713) 220-7171
MGR-New Business Development
Houston Chronicle, Houston, TX

Summer, Jane (214) 977-8222
Films Critic, Dallas Morning News, Dallas, TX

Summerford, Garry (901) 755-7386
PUB, Shelby Sun Times, Germantown, TN

Summerlin, Anthony (910) 786-4141
ADV MGR, Mount Airy News, Mount Airy, NC

Summerlin, George W (910) 786-4141
PUB, Mount Airy News, Mount Airy, NC

Summers, Barbara (614) 384-6102
MAN ED, Wellston Telegram, Wellston, OH

Summers, Lloyd (217) 245-6121
PROD SUPT, Journal-Courier, Jacksonville, IL

Summers, Pam (334) 262-1611
ADV MGR-ADTX, ADTX MGR
Montgomery Advertiser, Montgomery, AL

Summers, Phil (812) 385-2525
GM, ADV DIR, Daily Clarion, Princeton, IN

Summers, Roger (817) 390-7400
Obit ED
Fort Worth Star-Telegram, Fort Worth, TX

Summers, Rose Marie (217) 374-2871
GM, Greene Prairie Press, White Hall, IL

Summers, Stephanie (860) 241-6200
Lifestyles/Specialities ED
Hartford Courant, Hartford, CT

Summers, Susan G (301) 662-1177
Farm/Agriculture ED
Frederick Post/The News, Frederick, MD

Sumner, Brent R (801) 225-1340
PUB, Orem-Geneva Times, Orem, UT

Sumner, Darren (417) 732-2525
PUB, Republic Monitor, Republic, MO

Sumner, Dorothy (540) 745-2127
PUB, GM, Floyd Press, Floyd, VA

Sumner, Marian A (912) 776-7713
PUB, ED
Sylvester Local News, Sylvester, GA

Sumner, Teresa (915) 337-4661
CIRC MGR-OPER
Odessa American, Odessa, TX

Sumney, Mark (219) 461-8444
ADV MGR-Sales
Fort Wayne Newspapers Inc., Fort Wayne, IN

Sumperer, Janet (617) 527-1549
CEO, Twenty First Century Family Syndicate, Newton, MA

Sumpter, Brian (707) 263-5636
Sports ED
Lake County Record-Bee, Lakeport, CA

Sumrall, Bill (318) 365-6773
EDU ED, Religion ED
Daily Iberian, New Iberia, LA

Sumrell, Doug (316) 268-6000
VP-Circulation, CIRC DIR
Wichita Eagle, Wichita, KS

Sunberg, Dawn (501) 777-8841
CIRC DIR, Hope Star, Hope, AR

Sunderland, Donald (907) 456-6661
PROD SUPT-PR
Fairbanks Daily News-Miner, Fairbanks, AK

Sunderland, Gladys (970) 874-4421
PUB, Delta County Independent, Delta, CO

Sunderland, John (303) 820-1010
Photo Assignment ED
Denver Post, Denver, CO

Sunderland, Mike (402) 386-5384
PUB, Petersburg Press, Petersburg, NE

Sunderland, Norman (970) 874-4421
PUB, Delta County Independent, Delta, CO

Sunderland, Pat (970) 874-4421
ED, Delta County Independent, Delta, CO

Sunderland, Randy (970) 874-4421
GM, Delta County Independent, Delta, CO

Sundstrom, Allen (714) 835-1234
PROD VP-Customer Fulfillment
Orange County Register, Santa Ana, CA

Sundstrom, M Jill (605) 763-2006
PUB, ED, Beresford Republic, Beresford, SD

Sundstrom, Penny (609) 871-8000
Features ED, Travel ED
Burlington County Times, Willingboro, NJ

Sundstrom-Lundegaard, Ingrid (612) 673-4000
Home/Garden ED
Star Tribune, Minneapolis, MN

Sundvor, John (701) 253-7311
Political ED (MN), Forum, Fargo, ND

Sung, David (212) 362-9256
ASST ED, Cartoonists & Writers Syndicate, New York, NY

Sunkes, Jack (213) 857-6600
CIRC Distribution MGR
Daily Variety, Los Angeles, CA

Supplee, Vinton (602) 271-8000
News ED, Arizona Republic, Phoenix, AZ

Suprenant, Jean-Claude (613) 562-0111
Books ED, Food ED, Radio/Television ED
Le Droit, Ottawa, ON

Suprynowicz, Vin (702) 870-3515
PRES, Mountain Media, Las Vegas, NV

Surace, Philip (315) 792-5000
PROD MGR-PR
Observer-Dispatch, Utica, NY

Suraci, Frank (310) 540-5511
City ED, Daily Breeze, Torrance, CA

Surber, Jim (817) 552-5454
ADV DIR, Vernon Daily Record, Vernon, TX

Surbrugg, Mike (417) 623-3480
Farm ED, Joplin Globe, Joplin, MO

Surenkanp, Gregg (812) 522-4871
PROD FRM-Photo, Tribune, Seymour, IN

Surkamer, Rick (312) 222-3232
CIRC DIR-MET
Chicago Tribune, Chicago, IL

Surrat, Larry (213) 237-5000
PROD DIR-Pre Press OPER, PROD DIR-Technology Resource Group
Los Angeles Times, Los Angeles, CA

Surso, Virginia (219) 422-5900
ED, Macedonian Tribune, Fort Wayne, IN

Sury, Ken (409) 883-3571
EX ED, EPE, Orange Leader, Orange, TX

Sussman, Paul (203) 333-0161
State ED, Connecticut Post, Bridgeport, CT

Sutcliffe, Neil (403) 986-2271
PUB, Leduc Representative, Leduc, AB

Suther, Betty (913) 292-4726
PUB, ED, Frankfort Area News, Frankfort, KS

Sutherland, Barbara (517) 584-3967
ED, Carson City Gazette, Carson City, MI

Sutherland, Frank (615) 259-8000
VP-News/ED, Tennessean, Nashville, TN

Sutherland, Glenn (913) 442-3791
PUB, ED, Highland Vidette, Highland, KS

Sutherland, Jeannise (250) 380-5211
ADV MGR-CLASS
Times Colonist, Victoria, BC

Sutherland, Lynn (812) 522-4871
PROD FRM-PR, Tribune, Seymour, IN

Sutherland, Lynn (415) 495-4200
BM, Daily Pacific Builder, San Francisco, CA

Sutherland, Pat (616) 964-7161
Sports ED, Enquirer, Battle Creek, MI

Sutherland, Randy (914) 454-2000
CONT, Journal, Poughkeepsie, NY

Sutherland, Whitney (860) 646-0500
PROD VP, Journal Inquirer, Manchester, CT

Sutherlin, Denise (406) 225-3821
ED, Boulder Monitor, Boulder, MT

Sutherlin, Vernon A (406) 225-3821
PUB, Boulder Monitor, Boulder, MT

Sutliff, Chris (208) 678-2201
CIRC MGR, South Idaho Press, Burley, ID

Sutphin, Ray (304) 327-2811
PROD FRM-MR
Bluefield Daily Telegraph, Bluefield, WV

Sutter, Harris (718) 526-9069
PRES/ED, Press Photo Service, Flushing, NY

Sutter, Judith (207) 633-4620
ED
Wiscasset Newspaper, Boothbay Harbor, ME

Copyright ©1997 by the Editor & Publisher Co.

225-Who's Where **Swo**

Sutter, Mark .... (910) 373-7000
BUS/FIN ED
News & Record, Greensboro, NC

Sutterby, Spring .... (316) 365-2111
CIRC MGR, Iola Register, Iola, KS

Suttles, Karla .... (618) 463-2500
PROD MGR, Telegraph, Alton, IL

Sutton, Andrea .... (717) 673-5151
ED
Canton Independent Sentinel, Canton, PA

Sutton, Becky .... (716) 593-5300
Reporter
Wellsville Daily Reporter, Wellsville, NY

Sutton, Bob .... (910) 227-0131
Sports ED
Times News Publishing Co., Burlington, NC

Sutton, Carol .... (516) 569-4000
ED, Valley Stream Herald, Lawrence, NY

Sutton, Frank .... (704) 289-1541
PROD FRM-PR (Night)
Enquirer-Journal, Monroe, NC

Sutton, Goodloe .... (334) 295-5224
PUB, ED, Democrat-Reporter, Linden, AL

Sutton, Howard .... (401) 277-7000
PRES/GM
Providence Journal-Bulletin, Providence, RI

Sutton, James K .... (912) 744-4200
PROD MGR-MR
Macon Telegraph, Macon, GA

Sutton, Jim .... (904) 829-6562
ED, EPE
St. Augustine Record, St. Augustine, FL

Sutton, Kim .... (812) 332-4401
ADV MGR-RT
Herald-Times Inc, Bloomington, IN

Sutton, Ned .... (719) 544-3520
PROD MGR, Pueblo Chieftain, Pueblo, CO

Sutton, Ron .... (309) 764-4344
MET ED, Dispatch, Moline, IL
Small Newspaper Group Inc.

Sutton, Sandra T .... (517) 269-6461
ED, Huron Daily Tribune, Bad Axe, MI

Sutton, Will .... (919) 829-4500
MAN ED, News & Observer, Raleigh, NC

Suwanski, Rich .... (502) 926-0123
Sports ED
Messenger-Inquirer, Owensboro, KY

Suwyn, Dan .... (912) 236-9511
MAN ED
Savannah Morning News, Savannah, GA

Suzuki, Kunihiko .... (212) 603-6600
NY BU Chief
Kyodo News Service, New York, NY

Svanum, Ken .... (707) 546-2020
ADV DIR, Press Democrat, Santa Rosa, CA

Svec, Kyle .... (402) 462-2131
Sports ED, Hastings Tribune, Hastings, NE

Svec, Teresa .... (412) 523-6588
MGR-BUS Office
Standard Observer, Greensburg, PA

Svee, Gary .... (406) 657-1200
EPE, Billings Gazette, Billings, MT

Sveikauskas, Geddy .... (914) 255-7000
PUB, Herald, New Paltz, NY

Sveinson, Pam .... (612) 673-4000
VP-Human Resources (Cowles Media Co.)
Star Tribune, Minneapolis, MN

Svela, Kris .... (519) 369-2504
GM, ED, Durham Chronicle, Durham, ON

Svenning, Tore Eide .... (416) 441-1405
Europe Photographer
Fotopress Independent News Service International (FPINS), Toronto, ON

Svidal, Kathy .... (701) 662-2127
GM, ADV MGR-RT
Devils Lake Daily Journal, Devils Lake, ND

Svihlik, Susan Jessup .... (330) 841-1600
EX ED, Tribune Chronicle, Warren, OH

Svihovec, Steve .... (715) 833-9200
CIRC DIR, Leader-Telegram, Eau Claire, WI

Svihovec, Travis .... (605) 845-3646
MAN ED, Mobridge Tribune, Mobridge, SD

Svoboda, Francis C .... (402) 352-2424
PUB, Schuyler Sun, Schuyler, NE

Swafford, Johnnie .... (205) 734-2131
PROD MGR-Camera Room
Cullman Times, Cullman, AL

Swafford, Joyce .... (319) 394-3174
GM, Mediapolis News, Mediapolis, IA

Swails, Steve .... (608) 252-6400
CIRC DIR, Capital Times, Madison, WI

Swaim, Will .... (714) 708-8400
ED, OC Weekly, Costa Mesa, CA

Swaim, William R .... (937) 328-0300
PUB, Springfield News-Sun, Springfield, OH

Swain, Lecia D .... (405) 525-9885
PUB, ED, Ebony Tribune, Oklahoma City, OK

Swain, Tony .... (816) 665-2808
PROD SUPT, Kirksville Daily Express & News, Kirksville, MO

Swalboski, Craig .... (507) 285-7600
Sports ED, Post-Bulletin, Rochester, MN

Swan, Barbara .... (414) 338-0622
ADV MGR, ADTX MGR
Daily News, West Bend, WI

Swan, John .... (306) 565-8211
ASSOC ED, Leader-Post, Regina, SK

Swan, Paul .... (203) 235-1661
Lifestyle ED, Record-Journal, Meriden, CT

Swan, Toni .... (217) 379-4313
VP, ADV MGR, Daily Record, Paxton, IL

Swan, Vic .... (604) 847-3266
PUB, Interior News, Smithers, BC

Swander, Jim .... (812) 231-4200
ADV MGR, Tribune-Star, Terre Haute, IN

Swaney, Garry .... (317) 423-5511
PROD MGR
Journal and Courier, Lafayette, IN

Swanger, Michael .... (515) 792-3121
Living/Lifestyle ED, Women's ED
Newton Daily News, Newton, IA

Swanke, James .... (414) 235-7700
PROD MGR-Camera
Oshkosh Northwestern, Oshkosh, WI

Swanson, Chris .... (712) 262-6610
ADV DIR, Daily Reporter, Spencer, IA

Swanson, Chris .... (812) 331-0963
GM, Bloomington Voice, Bloomington, IN

Swanson, Craig .... (414) 657-1000
ED, Kenosha News, Kenosha, WI

Swanson, Dan .... (402) 873-3334
ED
Nebraska City News-Press, Nebraska City, NE

Swanson, David .... (402) 269-2135
ED, Journal-Democrat, Syracuse, NE

Swanson, David C .... (315) 337-4000
MAN ED, Daily Sentinel, Rome, NY

Swanson, Jack .... (206) 842-6613
ED, Bainbridge Review, Bainbridge Isle, WA

Swanson, Janet .... (913) 856-7615
ED, Spring Hill New Era, Gardner, KS

Swanson, John .... (714) 634-1567
ED, Anaheim Bulletin, Anaheim, CA

Swanson, John .... (503) 399-6611
CONT, Statesman Journal, Salem, OR

Swanson, Katherine .... (805) 650-2900
MGR-SYS OPER
Ventura County Star, Ventura, CA

Swanson, Ken .... (517) 377-1000
PROD DIR
Lansing State Journal, Lansing, MI

Swanson, Patricia ....
EDU ED, Religion/School ED
Evansville Press, Evansville, IN

Swanson, Pete .... (812) 385-2525
Sports ED
Princeton Daily Clarion, Princeton, IN

Swanson, R A .... (320) 235-1150
PROD MGR-Pre Press
West Central Tribune, Willmar, MN

Swanson, Roger .... (520) 763-2505
City ED
Mohave Valley Daily News, Bullhead City, AZ

Swanson, Scott .... (216) 647-3171
GM, Wellington Enterprise, Wellington, OH

Swanson, Stevenson .... (312) 222-3232
Environmental Writer
Chicago Tribune, Chicago, IL

Swanson, Thomas B .... (301) 662-1177
PROD ASST MGR-Art
Frederick Post/The News, Frederick, MD

Swant, Jacqueline .... (206) 597-8742
ADV MGR-CLASS
News Tribune, Tacoma, WA

Swantek, Most Rev John F ...... (717) 346-9131
GM, MAN ED, Rola Boza, Scranton, PA

Swanton, Andrew .... (607) 734-5151
PROD DIR, Star-Gazette, Elmira, NY

Swarner, Ken .... (206) 584-1212
ED, Ranger, Tacoma, WA

Swarner, Tom .... (206) 584-1212
PUB, Ranger, Tacoma, WA

Swart, Donald L .... (541) 426-4567
PUB
Wallowa County Chieftain, Enterprise, OR

Swart, Richard W .... (541) 426-4567
ED, Wallowa County Chieftain, Enterprise, OR

Swartley, John .... (408) 920-5000
Letters ED
San Jose Mercury News, San Jose, CA

Swartz, Dale .... (616) 722-3161
PROD MGR
Muskegon Chronicle, Muskegon, MI

Swartz, David .... (712) 362-2622
EPE, Estherville Daily News, Estherville, IA

Swartz, Don .... (423) 428-0746
ADV DIR-MKTG
Mountain Press, Sevierville, TN

Swartz, Jack .... (573) 882-5700
ADV DIR
Columbia Missourian, Columbia, MO

Swartz, Mim .... (303) 892-5000
Travel ED
Rocky Mountain News, Denver, CO

Swartz, Steve .... (913) 295-1111
State ED
Topeka Capital-Journal, Topeka, KS

Swartzlander, David .... (402) 475-4200
Health/Fitness Reporter, Neighbors Reporter
Lincoln Journal Star, Lincoln, NE

Swasy, Alecia .... (813) 893-8111
BUS ED
St. Petersburg Times, St. Petersburg, FL

Swauger, Troy .... (916) 645-7733
ED, Lincoln News Messenger, Lincoln, CA

Swayne, Don .... (613) 342-4441
City ED, Recorder and Times, Brockville, ON

Swayne, Matt .... (814) 684-4000
ED, Daily Herald, Tyrone, PA

Swearingen, David H .... (901) 529-2211
DIR-MKTG
Commercial Appeal, Memphis, TN

Swearingen, Roger .... (815) 842-1153
CIRC MGR, Daily Leader, Pontiac, IL

Sweat, Jimmye .... (601) 957-1122
ED, Northside Sun, Jackson, MS

Sweatt, Carolyn H .... (910) 754-6890
PUB, Brunswick Beacon, Shallotte, NC

Sweatt, Edward M .... (910) 754-6890
PUB, Brunswick Beacon, Shallotte, NC

Swecker, Linda .... (540) 574-6200
ADV DIR
Daily News-Record, Harrisonburg, VA

Swed, Mark .... (213) 237-5000
Music Critic
Los Angeles Times, Los Angeles, CA

Swedberg, Claire .... (201) 895-2601
ED, Randolph Reporter, Randolph, NJ

Sweeney, Annie .... (773) 586-8800
EDU Writer, Daily Southtown, Chicago, IL

Sweeney, Edwin .... (304) 624-6411
ED-Exponent, Clarksburg Exponent/Telegram, Clarksburg, WV

Sweeney, Gerri .... (303) 773-8313
PUB, ED, Villager, Greenwood Village, CO

Sweeney, Jack .... (713) 220-7171
VP/GM, Houston Chronicle, Houston, TX

Sweeney, John .... (302) 324-2500
Public ED, News Journal, Wilmington, DE

Sweeney, Kevin .... (507) 359-2911
ED, COL, EPE, EDL Writer
Journal, New Ulm, MN

Sweeney, Mike .... (203) 625-4400
EPE, Greenwich Time, Greenwich, CT

Sweeney, Mike .... (330) 424-9541
PROD MGR-Press
Morning Journal, Lisbon, OH

Sweeney, Robert F .... (970) 464-5614
PUB, Palisade Tribune, Palisade, CO

Sweeney, Sid .... (716) 487-1111
PROD FRM-COMP
Post-Journal, Jamestown, NY

Sweep, Laura .... (970) 352-0211
MGR-MKTG, CIRC DIR
Greeley Tribune, Greeley, CO

Sweet, Brenda .... (800) 424-4747
PROD MGR, Tribune Media Services-Television Listings, Glens Falls, NY

Sweet, Lynn .... (312) 321-3000
Washington BU Chief
Chicago Sun-Times, Chicago, IL

Sweet, Richard .... (330) 296-9657
MGR-Photo DEPT
Record-Courier, Kent-Ravenna, OH

Sweet, Sheril .... (903) 729-0281
Community ED
Palestine Herald-Press, Palestine, TX

Sweetapple, Ray .... (709) 634-4348
EPE, Western Star, Corner Brook, NF

Sweetman, Dave .... (618) 463-2500
PROD FRM-PR, Telegraph, Alton, IL

Sweetman, Jennie .... (914) 986-2216
GM, MAN ED
Warwick Valley Dispatch, Warwick, NY

Sweetwood, Mark M .... (815) 459-4040
ED, Northwest Herald, Crystal Lake, IL

Sweigart, Ann .... (816) 886-2233
BM, Marshall Democrat-News, Marshall, MO

Swendra, Mark .... (912) 236-9511
Community News ED
Savannah Morning News, Savannah, GA

Swendsen, Harry .... (218) 285-7411
ADV MGR
Daily Journal, International Falls, MN

Swensen, Rich .... (800) 365-3020
GM, Gunfighter, Boise, ID

Swensen, T M .... (218) 546-5029
PUB, Crosby-Ironton Courier, Crosby, MN

Swenson, Brad .... (218) 751-3740
MAN ED, EPE, Features ED, News ED, NTL ED, Political/Government ED
Daily Pioneer, Bemidji, MN

Swenson, Charles R .... (803) 237-8438
PUB, ED
Coastal Observer, Pawleys Island, SC

Swenson, Coleen .... (208) 587-3331
PUB
Mountain Home News, Mountain Home, ID

Swenson, Jim .... (319) 588-5611
Features ED, Telegraph Herald, Dubuque, IA

Swenson, Steve .... (320) 453-2460
PUB, ED
Eden Valley Journal Patriot, Eden Valley, MN

Swenson, Steve .... (330) 454-5611
PROD MGR-PR, Repository, Canton, OH

Swenson, Tom .... (317) 633-1240
News ED-PM
Indianapolis Star/News, Indianapolis, IN

Swerens, Jon .... (716) 366-3000
ASST MAN ED, EPE, Religion ED
Evening Observer, Dunkirk, NY

Swettman Jr, Al .... (217) 626-1711
PUB, ED
New Berlin Bee, Pleasant Plains, IL

Swibold, Denise .... (818) 962-8811
ASST City ED
San Gabriel Valley Tribune, West Covina, CA

Swick, Tom .... (954) 356-4000
Travel ED, Sun-Sentinel, Fort Lauderdale, FL

Swickard, Jack M .... (505) 622-7710
GM, Roswell Daily Record, Roswell, NM

Swickerath, Mary Anne .... (407) 656-2121
ED, West Orange Times, Winter Garden, FL

Swidey, Neil .... (508) 626-3800
Regional ED-Central
Middlesex News, Framingham, MA

Swiech, Paul .... (309) 829-9411
BUS Writer, Pantagraph, Bloomington, IL

Swiercz, Greg .... (219) 235-6161
City ED
South Bend Tribune, South Bend, IN

Swiergosz, Rick .... (204) 694-2022
CIRC DIR, Winnipeg Sun, Winnipeg, MB

Swietek, Wes .... (770) 267-8371
MAN ED, Walton Tribune, Monroe, GA

Swift, Daniel B .... (518) 561-2300
GM, Press-Republican, Plattsburgh, NY

Swift, Debra .... (703) 276-3400
CIRC GM-Western New York
USA Today, Arlington, VA

Swift, Katherine M .... (507) 734-5421
PUB, ED
Balaton Press Tribune, Balaton, MN

Swift, Philip E .... (916) 273-9561
Chairman, Union, Grass Valley, CA
Swift Newspapers

Swift, Phillip .... (520) 684-5454
ED, Wickenburg Sun, Wickenburg, AZ

Swift, Ronald .... (209) 892-6187
PUB, ED, Patterson Irrigator, Patterson, CA

Swihart, Ric .... (403) 328-4411
Agriculture ED, BUS ED
Lethbridge Herald, Lethbridge, AB

Swil, Warren .... (818) 241-4141
EPE, News ED
Glendale News-Press, Glendale, CA

Swincher, Ty .... (765) 345-2111
PUB, Tri-County Banner, Knightstown, IN

Swindell, Jennifer .... (208) 377-6200
Sports ED, Idaho Statesman, Boise, ID

Swindell, Larry .... (817) 390-7400
Books ED
Fort Worth Star-Telegram, Fort Worth, TX

Swindle, Howard .... (214) 977-8222
ASST MAN ED-Projects
Dallas Morning News, Dallas, TX

Swindler, DeEllda .... (309) 742-2521
PUB, Tri-County News, Elmwood, IL

Swindler, Linda S .... (309) 742-2521
ED, Tri-County News, Elmwood, IL

Swinford, Kay .... (806) 273-5611
MGR-Office, Borger News-Herald, Borger, TX

Swing Jr, Ted .... (352) 544-5200
Sports ED, Hernando Today, Brooksville, FL

Swing, Virgil .... (218) 723-5281
EPE, Duluth News-Tribune, Duluth, MN

Swingle, John J .... (309) 686-3000
PSL MGR, Journal Star, Peoria, IL

Swingle, Pam .... (614) 452-4561
BUS/FIN ED, City/News ED, EDU ED, Entertainment/Amusements ED, Fashion/Style ED, Features ED, Lifestyle ED
Times Recorder, Zanesville, OH

Swingler, Maryann .... (206) 622-8272
PROD MGR, Seattle Daily Journal of Commerce, Seattle, WA

Swinson, Ginny .... (704) 358-5000
MGR-EDU SRV
Charlotte Observer, Charlotte, NC

Swirks, Cindy .... (352) 374-5000
EDU Writer, Gainesville Sun, Gainesville, FL

Swisher, Amelia .... (612) 777-8800
ED, Roseville Review, N. St. Paul, MN

Swisher, Peggy .... (304) 263-8931
Family ED, Farm/Food ED, Living/Lifestyle ED, Women's ED, Journal, Martinsburg, WV

Swiston, Jeff .... (715) 682-2313
ADV DIR, Daily Press, Ashland, WI

Switzer, Marlene .... (508) 369-2800
MAN ED, Concord Journal, Concord, MA

Switzer, Michael .... (510) 758-8400
CIRC MGR, West County Times, Pinole, CA

Swoboda, Bob .... (217) 788-1300
PROD FRM-MR
State Journal-Register, Springfield, IL

Swo Who's Where-226

Swofford, Robert .... (707) 546-2020
MAN ED, Press Democrat, Santa Rosa, CA

Swogetinsky, Steve .... (601) 693-1551
Sports ED, Meridian Star, Meridian, MS

Swonke, Robert .... (512) 352-8535
VP, PUB, PROD MGR-PR
Taylor Daily Press, Taylor, TX

Swope, Burton .... (805) 650-2900
County ED, Ventura County Star, Ventura, CA

Swor, Jeffery W .... (218) 624-3665
GM, Budgeteer Press, Duluth, MN

Sword, Al .... (610) 377-2051
Automotive ED, Times News, Lehighton, PA

Sword, Jeanne .... (540) 574-6200
Fashion ED, Films/Theater ED, Food/Fashion ED, Women's ED
Daily News-Record, Harrisonburg, VA

Sword, Lewis .... (540) 574-6200
Wire ED
Daily News-Record, Harrisonburg, VA

Sword, Steve .... (614) 335-3611
PROD MGR
Record Herald, Washington Court House, OH

Swyers, Vicki .... (314) 340-8000
Production ED
St. Louis Post-Dispatch, St. Louis, MO

Swygart, J .... (419) 738-2128
MAN ED, Local News ED
Wapakoneta Daily News, Wapakoneta, OH

Sybert, William K .... (860) 646-0500
ADV VP, Journal Inquirer, Manchester, CT

Sygutek, Gail .... (403) 562-2248
PUB, Pass Herald, Blairmore, AB

Sykes, April .... (541) 676-9228
PUB, ED, Gazette Times, Heppner, OR

Sykes, Dave .... (519) 524-2614
GM, ED, Goderich Signal-Star, Goderich, ON

Sykes, David .... (541) 676-9228
PUB, Heppner Gazette Times, Heppner, OR

Sykes, Deirdre .... (201) 646-4000
ASST MAN ED-News CNR
Record, Hackensack, NJ

Sykes, Jack W .... (703) 922-1712
CEO/Chief Photographer
World Images News Service, Alexandria, VA

Sykes, Leonard .... (414) 224-2000
Public Affairs ED
Milwaukee Journal Sentinel, Milwaukee, WI

Sykes, Shinika .... (801) 237-2031
Ombudsman
Salt Lake Tribune, Salt Lake City, UT

Sylvester, Edwin .... (218) 281-2730
CIRC DIR
Crookston Daily Times, Crookston, MN

Sylvester, Robert D .... (617) 929-2000
ASST DIR-INFO Services
Boston Globe, Boston, MA

Sylvia, Albert E .... (617) 334-6319
PUB, Lynnfield Villager, Lynnfield, MA

Sylvia Jr, Albert E .... (508) 664-4761
PUB
North Reading Transcript, North Reading, MA

Sylvie, Coty .... (819) 752-6718
ED, La Nouvelle, Victoriaville, QC

Sylvis, Alice .... (814) 371-4200
Farm/Agriculture ED, Courier-Express/Tri-County Sunday, Du Bois, PA

Symes, Bruce .... (316) 365-2111
Action Line ED, Environmental ED, Farm/Agriculture ED, Features ED, SCI/Technology ED, Iola Register, Iola, KS

Symons, Most Rev J Keith .... (407) 775-9527
PUB
Florida Catholic, Palm Beach Gardens, FL

Sypek, Robert .... (203) 744-5100
CIRC DIR, News-Times, Danbury, CT

Syphen, Mike .... (860) 423-8466
Sports ED, Chronicle, Willimantic, CT

Syrek, Tim .... (616) 796-4831
Sports ED
Big Rapids Pioneer, Big Rapids, MI

Syse, Scarlett .... (317) 398-6631
ED, Radio/Television ED
Shelbyville News, Shelbyville, IN

Szabo, Jane .... (907) 257-4200
Religion EDL ASST
Anchorage Daily News, Anchorage, AK

Szabo, Rae .... (216) 696-3322
ADV Display, Daily Legal News and Cleveland Recorder, Cleveland, OH

Szachara, Bernard A .... (607) 798-1234
PROD DIR
Press & Sun Bulletin, Binghamton, NY

Szal, Lisa A .... (215) 949-4011
DIR-ADV & MKTG
Calkins Newspapers, Levittown, PA

Szaloczi, Linda .... (303) 776-2244
ADV DIR, Daily Times-Call, Longmont, CO

Szapko, Sheila .... (204) 328-7494
GM, MAN ED, Rivers Banner, Rivers, MB

Szarka, George .... (216) 951-0000
PROD MGR-MR
News-Herald, Willoughby, OH

Szasz, Christina .... (818) 707-1548
PUB
Magyarok Vasarnapja, Thousand Oaks, CA

Szasz, Elizabeth .... (818) 707-1548
GM
Magyarok Vasarnapja, Thousand Oaks, CA

Szasz, Lorant .... (818) 707-1548
ED
Magyarok Vasarnapja, Thousand Oaks, CA

Szczesny, Joseph .... (810) 332-8181
Automotive ED, Oakland Press, Pontiac, MI

Szkatulski, Anthony .... (716) 849-3434
ADV MGR-Sunday Magazine Sales
Buffalo News, Buffalo, NY

Szorek, Gerald .... (814) 870-1600
ADV MGR-NTL, ADV MGR-RES
Morning News/Erie Daily Times, Erie, PA

Szozda, John .... (419) 836-2221
GM
Suburban Press & Metro Press, Millbury, OH

Szudlo, Betty .... (330) 725-4166
ASSOC ED
Medina County Gazette, Medina, OH

Szumski, Jerry .... (515) 284-8000
Automotive ED
Des Moines Register, Des Moines, IA

Szymanski, Jim .... (206) 597-8742
RE Reporter, News Tribune, Tacoma, WA

Szymanski, Lillian F .... (313) 365-1990
GM, MAN ED, Swiat Polski, Hamtramck, MI

T

Taba, Harry .... (416) 593-6953
PUB, ED, Canada Times, Toronto, ON

Tabacsko, Ken .... (517) 752-7171
Features ED, Garden/Home Furnishings ED, Health/Medical ED, SCI/Technology ED
Saginaw News, Saginaw, MI

Taber, Tony .... (904) 359-4111
PROD CNR-Newsprint
Florida Times-Union, Jacksonville, FL

Tabor, Daniel .... (915) 893-4244
ED, Clyde Journal, Clyde, TX

Tabor, Don .... (915) 893-4244
PUB, Clyde Journal, Clyde, TX

Tabor, Glen .... (334) 433-1551
CIRC MGR, Press Register, Mobile, AL

Tabor, John .... (603) 772-6000
PUB, Exeter News-Letter, Exeter, NH

Tabor, Mike .... (352) 357-3199
PUB, Eustis News, Mount Dora, FL

Taborski, Michael C .... (916) 257-5321
PUB, Lassen County Times, Susanville, CA

Tabuchi, Miho .... (212) 603-6600
Correspondent
Kyodo News Service, New York, NY

Tacheny, Maggie .... (612) 777-8800
ED, East Side Review, North St. Paul, MN

Tachney, Neal .... (919) 778-2211
CIRC DIR
Goldsboro News-Argus, Goldsboro, NC

Tackett, Dan .... (217) 732-2101
City ED, Courier, Lincoln, IL

Tackett, Debbie .... (972) 727-3352
GM, Allen American, Allen, TX

Tackett, Ron .... (209) 578-2000
CIRC MGR-Home Delivery/State
Modesto Bee, Modesto, CA

Taffet, Saul .... (941) 574-1110
Photo DEPT MGR, Picture ED
Cape Coral Daily Breeze, Cape Coral, FL

Tafoya, Bill .... (505) 823-7777
ADV MGR-CLASS, Albuquerque Publishing Co., Albuquerque, NM

Tafoya, Diane .... (719) 544-3520
MGR-BUS Office, PA
Pueblo Chieftain, Pueblo, CO

Taft, Susan .... (903) 856-6629
ED, Pittsburg Gazette, Pittsburg, TX

Taggart, Karen .... (904) 747-5000
BM, News Herald, Panama City, FL

Tagle, Gilbert .... (210) 383-2705
EX ED, Edinburg Daily Review, Edinburg, TX

Taguma (Eng), Kenji .... (415) 921-6820
ED, Nichibet Times, San Francisco, CA

Taiclet, Rea .... (330) 747-1471
Regional ED-City Edition
Vindicator, Youngstown, OH

Taira, Lana .... (808) 329-9311
DP MGR
West Hawaii Today, Kailua-Kona, HI

Tait, Barry .... (604) 453-2261
ED, Ashcroft Journal, Ashcroft, BC

Tait, Elaine .... (215) 854-2000
Food COL
Philadelphia Inquirer, Philadelphia, PA

Tait, Tom .... (619) 322-8889
ASST MAN ED
Desert Sun, Palm Springs, CA

Takacs, Steve .... (864) 224-4321
CIRC MGR
Anderson Independent-Mail, Anderson, SC

Takahashi, Peggy .... (209) 943-6397
MGR-Office, Record, Stockton, CA

Takiff, Jonathan .... (215) 854-2000
Music ED, News ED-Day
Philadelphia Daily News, Philadelphia, PA

Talarico, Tom .... (203) 574-3636
Sports ED, Waterbury Republican-American, Waterbury, CT

Talbert, Bob .... (313) 222-6400
COL-Features, Detroit Free Press, Detroit, MI

Talbert, Jim .... (540) 963-1081
MAN ED
Clinch Valley News, Richlands, VA

Talbert, Lee .... (423) 929-3111
Photo DEPT MGR
Johnson City Press, Johnson City, TN

Talbot, Roger .... (603) 668-4321
EDU ED, Union Leader, Manchester, NH

Talbot, Warren .... (617) 786-7000
Senior News ED, Patriot Ledger, Quincy, MA

Talbott, Basil .... (312) 321-3000
Washington BU
Chicago Sun-Times, Chicago, IL

Talbott, Michael .... (308) 874-2207
PUB, ED, Chappell Register, Chappell, NE

Talbutt, Brad .... (702) 385-3111
Photo ED, Las Vegas Sun, Las Vegas, NV

Talcott, Richard .... (603) 882-2741
PROD FRM-Press, Telegraph, Nashua, NH

Talent, Britt .... (501) 534-3400
BUS/FIN ED, Environmental ED, Farm ED, Regional ED, SCI/Technology ED
Pine Bluff Commercial, Pine Bluff, AR

Tallackson, Andrew .... (317) 473-6641
MAN ED, Peru Tribune, Peru, IN

Talley, Carol .... (717) 243-2611
ED, Sentinel, Carlisle, PA

Talley, Keith .... (615) 388-6464
Farm ED, News ED
Daily Herald, Columbia, TN

Talley, Laurel .... (405) 424-4695
GM, Black Chronicle, Oklahoma City, OK

Talley, Lucy C .... (803) 577-7111
ADV DIR-Sales
Post and Courier, Charleston, SC

Talley, Mitch .... (706) 629-2231
ED, MAN ED, Calhoun Times and Gordon County News, Calhoun, GA

Talley, Nick .... (706) 884-7311
ADV MGR-CLASS
La Grange Daily News, La Grange, GA

Talley, Tommy .... (334) 262-1611
PROD SUPT-MR
Montgomery Advertiser, Montgomery, AL

Tallmadge, David .... (813) 893-8111
PROD MGR-Press
St. Petersburg Times, St. Petersburg, FL

Tallman, Brenda J .... (518) 561-2300
PUB, Press-Republican, Plattsburgh, NY

Tallman, Chuck .... (334) 433-1551
ADV MGR-Zoned Editions
Mobile Press Register, Mobile, AL

Tallman, Doug .... (301) 662-1177
EDU ED, Frederick Post/News, Frederick, MD

Talton, Jon .... (704) 358-5000
BUS/FIN ED
Charlotte Observer, Charlotte, NC

Tambini, Walter .... (718) 981-1234
PROD FRM-PR
Staten Island Advance, Staten Island, NY

Tambling, Richard .... (860) 646-0500
Living Section ED
Journal Inquirer, Manchester, CT

Tamboer, Andrea .... (616) 222-5400
Travel ED
Grand Rapids Press, Grand Rapids, MI

Tamez, Betty .... (210) 686-4343
ADV MGR-RT, Monitor, McAllen, TX

Tamke, Jon .... (218) 864-5952
PUB, ED
Battle Lake Review, Battle Lake, MN

Tamkin, Samuel J .... (847) 835-3450
ED
Real Estate Matters Syndicate, Glencoe, IL

Tammeus, Bill .... (816) 234-4141
Humor COL
Kansas City Star, Kansas City, MO

Tamraz, Cathy Baron .... (415) 986-4422
Senior VP, Business Wire, San Francisco, CA

Tancrede, Jeanne .... (603) 668-4321
MGR-EDU/Youth SRV
Union Leader, Manchester, NH

Tandy, Katheleen Q .... (805) 395-7500
DIR-Human & Organizational Development
Bakersfield Californian, Bakersfield, CA

Tandy, Mary .... (317) 923-8291
PUB, ED, Indiana Herald, Indianapolis, IN

Tandy, Mike .... (701) 223-2500
PROD MGR
Bismarck Tribune, Bismarck, ND

Tanfield, Suzan .... (307) 324-3411
PROD Graphics Artist
Rawlins Daily Times, Rawlins, WY

Tani, Betty .... (914) 855-1100
MAN ED, News-Chronicle, Pawling, NY

Taniguchi, S .... (206) 624-4169
ED, Northwest Nikkei, Seattle, WA

Tanious, Marilyn .... (602) 271-8000
ADV MGR-CLASS
Phoenix Newspapers Inc., Phoenix, AZ

Tankersely, Tawanda .... (601) 563-4591
PUB, ED, Panolian, Batesville, MS

Tann, Dr Marie P .... (704) 377-4329
MAN ED, Star of Zion, Charlotte, NC

Tann, Dr Morgan W .... (704) 377-4329
ED, Star of Zion, Charlotte, NC

Tannehill, Jack R .... (601) 774-9433
PUB, ED, Union Appeal, Union, MS

Tanner, David .... (912) 283-2244
ADV MGR, ADV MGR-NTL
Waycross Journal-Herald, Waycross, GA

Tanner, Donna .... (501) 338-9181
CIRC DIR, Daily World, Helena, AR

Tanner Jr, Hal .... (919) 778-2211
PRES, PUB, News-Argus, Goldsboro, NC

Tanner III, Hal .... (864) 298-4100
CIRC VP/DIR, Greenville News, Greenville, SC

Tanner, Kenneth .... (941) 262-3161
CIRC DIR, Naples Daily News, Naples, FL

Tanner, Robert C .... (334) 875-2110
VP, Selma Times-Journal, Selma, AL

Tannler, Michael J .... (609) 895-2600
VP-Labor
Goodson Newspaper Group, Lawrenceville, NJ

Tansey, David .... (319) 291-1400
ASST to PUB, ADV DIR, ADV MGR-GEN
Waterloo Courier, Waterloo, IA

Tanton, Tim .... (615) 259-8800
BUS ED, Nashville Banner, Nashville, TN

Tanzone, Daniel F .... (201) 777-4010
ED, Katolicky Sokol/Slovak Catholic Falcon, Passaic, NJ

Tao, Eugene .... (808) 935-6621
ED, Hawaii Tribune-Herald, Hilo, HI

Tapp, Dave .... (319) 394-3174
PUB, Mediapolis News, Mediapolis, IA

Tapp, Phyllis .... (319) 394-3174
PUB, Mediapolis News, Mediapolis, IA

Tapp, Susan .... (217) 824-2233
DIR-MKTG/PROM, Taylorville Daily Breeze-Courier, Taylorville, IL

Tappy, Dave .... (219) 461-8444
PROD MGR-COMP
Fort Wayne Newspapers Inc., Fort Wayne, IN

Tapscott, Mark .... (301) 670-1400
MAN ED, Montgomery Journal, Rockville, MD
Journal Newspapers Inc.

Tardani, Phil .... (970) 669-5050
Regional ED
Loveland Daily Reporter-Herald, Loveland, CO

Tardif, Raymond .... (819) 564-5450
PRES, PUB/GM, La Tribune, Sherbrooke, QC

Targe, Mark .... (907) 257-4200
ADV DIR-Sales, Daily News, Anchorage, AK

Tarkany, John .... (805) 650-2900
CIRC MGR-Star in EDU
Ventura County Star, Ventura, CA

Tarle, Patti .... (310) 540-5511
MGR-Credit, Daily Breeze, Torrance, CA

Tarleton, Harold V .... (919) 243-5151
ED, EPE, Wilson Daily Times, Wilson, NC

Tarleton, Larry W .... (803) 577-7111
EX ED, Post and Courier, Charleston, SC

Tarney, Margaret .... (219) 347-0400
COL, Food ED, Women's ED
News-Sun, Kendallville, IN

Tarpley, Cassie .... (704) 484-7000
EDU ED, Religion ED
Shelby Star, Shelby, NC

Tarrant, John G .... (616) 533-8523
PUB, Antrim County News, Bellaire, MI

Tarry, Lisa .... (816) 932-6600
ASSOC ED
Universal Press Syndicate, Kansas City, MO

Tartaglia, Robert .... (914) 454-2000
PROD MGR-Pre Press
Poughkeepsie Journal, Poughkeepsie, NY

Tartt, Murray .... (601) 428-0551
EDU ED, Fashion/Food ED, Garden/Home Furnishings ED, Music ED, Society ED
Laurel Leader-Call, Laurel, MS

Taschinger, Tom .... (409) 833-3311
EPE, Beaumont Enterprise, Beaumont, TX

Taschler, Joe .... (913) 295-1111
BUS ED, Topeka Capital-Journal, Topeka, KS

Tash, Paul .... (813) 893-8111
VP, EX ED
St. Petersburg Times, St. Petersburg, FL

Tashjian, John .... (610) 622-8800
CONT
Delaware County Daily Times, Primos, PA

Tataren, Nick .... (604) 732-2111
CIRC MGR-ADM SYS, Vancouver Sun, Vancouver, BC, Southam Inc.

Tate, Byron .... (501) 534-3400
ED, EPE
Pine Bluff Commercial, Pine Bluff, AR

Tate, Casandra .... (202) 462-0128
PUB
Washington Monthly Co., Washington, DC

Copyright ©1997 by the Editor & Publisher Co.

227-Who's Where **Tea**

Tate Sr, Hugh C (304) 564-3131
PUB, ED, Hancock County Courier, New Cumberland, WV

Tate, Jenay (540) 679-1101
ED, Coalfield Progress, Norton, VA

Tate, Jim (507) 537-1551
ED, Independent, Marshall, MN

Tate, Lisa (707) 644-1141
DIR-MIS, Vallejo Times-Herald, Vallejo, CA

Tate, Lisa (409) 245-5555
Society/Women's ED
Daily Tribune, Bay City, TX

Tate, Michael (540) 926-8816
MAN ED, Dickenson Star, Clintwood, VA

Tate, Mike (615) 259-8000
Copy Desk Chief, Tennessean, Nashville, TN

Tate, Nick (404) 526-5151
SCI/Medical ED
Atlanta Journal-Constitution, Atlanta, GA

Tate, Robbie G (540) 679-1101
PUB, Coalfield Progress, Norton, VA

Tate, Russ (205) 325-2222
Wire ED, Birmingham News, Birmingham, AL

Tate, Tom (417) 836-1100
PROD MGR-Pre Press
Springfield News-Leader, Springfield, MO

Tatko, Mike (208) 743-9411
Online ED, Morning Tribune, Lewiston, ID

Tatman Jr, George S (606) 744-3123
PRES, Winchester Sun, Winchester, KY

Tatro, George (913) 568-2565
ED, Glasco Sun, Glasco, KS

Tatro, Royanne (913) 568-2565
PUB, ED, Glasco Sun, Glasco, KS

Tattum, Dennis (414) 435-4411
ADV MGR-NTL
Green Bay Press-Gazette, Green Bay, WI

Tatum, Wilbert A (212) 932-7400
PUB, ED
New York Amsterdam News, New York, NY

Taulman, Julie N (315) 253-5311
ADV DIR, Citizen, Auburn, NY

Taunehill, Judy (601) 693-1551
ADV MGR-CLASS
Meridian Star, Meridian, MS

Tausky, Ed (603) 882-2741
ADV MGR-Major Accounts
Telegraph, Nashua, NH

Tave, Kate (541) 269-1222
City ED, World, Coos Bay, OR

Tavey, Debi (707) 448-6401
ADV MGR-RT, Reporter, Vacaville, CA

Tawasha, Mary (704) 249-3981
EDU ED, Television ED
Dispatch, Lexington, NC

Taylor, Alan (515) 523-1010
PUB, GM, Stuart Herald, Stuart, IA

Taylor, Alistair (604) 287-9227
ED
Campbell River Mirror, Campbell River, BC

Taylor, Alvin (919) 752-6166
Senior ASSOC ED
Daily Reflector, Greenville, NC

Taylor, Andrew (804) 649-6000
City ED
Richmond Times-Dispatch, Richmond, VA

Taylor, Andy (316) 336-2100
ED, Cherryvale Chronicle, Cherryvale, KS

Taylor, Art (304) 263-8931
PROD FRM-PR, Journal, Martinsburg, WV

Taylor, Barbara (202) 636-3000
ASST MAN ED
Washington Times, Washington, DC

Taylor, Barbara (904) 252-1511
Regional ED, Daytona Beach News-Journal, Daytona Beach, FL

Taylor, Benjamin B (617) 929-2000
PRES, COO, Boston Globe, Boston, MA

Taylor, Bill (904) 599-2100
PROD MGR-Pre Press
Tallahassee Democrat, Tallahassee, FL

Taylor, Bonnie (250) 762-4445
Accountant, Daily Courier, Kelowna, BC

Taylor, Bonnie K (706) 724-2122
GM, Fort Gordon Signal, Waynesboro, GA

Taylor, Brent (915) 573-5486
Sports ED, Snyder Daily News, Snyder, TX

Taylor, Brooks (319) 653-2191
City ED, EPE, Chief Photographer
Washington Evening Journal, Washington, IA

Taylor, Brooks N (601) 363-1511
PUB, ED, Tunica Times, Tunica, MS

Taylor, Charles (505) 425-6796
SEC, TREAS, GEN MGR
Las Vegas Optic, Las Vegas, NM

Taylor, Charlotte (303) 582-5333
ED, Weekly Register-Call, Central City, CO

Taylor, Chris (913) 367-0583
Photo DEPT MGR
Atchison Daily Globe, Atchison, KS

Taylor, Christine H (603) 882-2741
PROD MGR, Telegraph, Nashua, NH

Taylor, Chuck (206) 464-2111
Media Reporter, Seattle Times, Seattle, WA

Taylor, Dan (707) 546-2020
Films/Theater ED, Music ED, Radio/Television ED, Press Democrat, Santa Rosa, CA

Taylor, Darlene (304) 624-6411
Society ED-Exponent, Clarksburg Exponent/Telegram, Clarksburg, WV

Taylor, Dave (905) 526-3333
ADV MGR-Local Accounts
Spectator, Hamilton, ON

Taylor, David (215) 854-2000
ASST to ED
Philadelphia Inquirer, Philadelphia, PA

Taylor, Dawn (308) 324-4060
PUB, ED, El Hispano, Lexington, NE

Taylor, Deborah (606) 231-3100
PROD MGR-Environmental/Safety
Lexington Herald-Leader, Lexington, KY

Taylor, Dennis (403) 935-4221
PUB, 5 Village Weekly, Irricana, AB

Taylor, Diane (515) 967-4224
ED, Altoona Herald-Mitchellville Index, Altoona, IA

Taylor, Don (414) 235-7700
PROD MGR-PR
Oshkosh Northwestern, Oshkosh, WI

Taylor, Dorothy (541) 396-3191
GM, Coquille Valley Sentinel, Coquille, OR

Taylor, Douglas S (606) 498-2222
PUB, Mt. Sterling Advocate, Mt. Sterling, KY

Taylor, Duff (501) 785-7700
CNR-PROM
Southwest Times Record, Fort Smith, AR

Taylor Jr, Edward A (618) 745-6267
PUB, Pulaski Enterprise, Mounds, IL

Taylor, Edwin (540) 473-2741
ED, Fincastle Herald, Fincastle, VA

Taylor, Elizabeth (Boots) (717) 278-6397
PUB, Susquehanna County Independent, Montrose, PA

Taylor, Elvin (937) 225-2000
MGR-PSL, Dayton Daily News, Dayton, OH

Taylor, Everett (903) 597-8111
EIC, Books ED, COL, EDL Writer
Tyler Morning Telegraph, Tyler, TX

Taylor, Faye (601) 896-2100
CNR-CR, Sun Herald, Biloxi, MS

Taylor, Frank (919) 823-3106
ED, County ED
Daily Southerner, Tarboro, NC

Taylor, Frederick (541) 396-3191
PUB, ED
Coquille Valley Sentinel, Coquille, OR

Taylor, G L (Don) (619) 745-6611
PUB-Fallbrook
North County Times, Escondido, CA

Taylor, Gail (937) 328-0300
Health/Medical ED
Springfield News-Sun, Springfield, OH

Taylor, Gary (847) 866-6501
ED, Evanston Review, Evanston, IL

Taylor, George (610) 377-2051
EDU ED, Graphics ED/Art DIR
Times News, Lehighton, PA

Taylor, Gerald J (309) 764-4344
PUB, ED, Dispatch, Moline, IL
Small Newspaper Group Inc.

Taylor, Gladys (403) 935-4221
ED, 5 Village Weekly, Irricana, AB

Taylor, Graham (812) 265-3641
MAN ED, Madison Courier, Madison, IN

Taylor, Gregory H (541) 776-4411
PUB, Mail Tribune, Medford, OR

Taylor, Heber (409) 744-3611
MAN ED, EPE
Galveston County Daily News, Galveston, TX

Taylor, Helen (937) 498-2111
Entertainment/Amusements ED
Sidney Daily News, Sidney, OH

Taylor, Helen (617) 786-7000
ADV MGR-OPER/CLASS
Patriot Ledger, Quincy, MA

Taylor Jr, Henry (561) 820-4100
PROD SUPT-Press
Palm Beach Post, West Palm Beach, FL

Taylor, Holly (518) 454-5694
Medical Writer, Times Union, Albany, NY

Taylor, James (419) 674-4066
PROD SUPT, PROD FRM-COMP
Kenton Times, Kenton, OH

Taylor, James (306) 783-7355
ED, News, Yorkton, SK

Taylor, James L (217) 936-2295
PUB, ED, Dispatch-Times, Camp Point, IL

Taylor, Janet (406) 523-5200
ADV MGR-CLASS, Missoulian, Missoula, MT

Taylor, Jean (800) 760-3100
Medicare & S.S. ED/Tampa
Williams Syndications Inc., Holiday, FL

Taylor, Jeff (301) 670-1400
Chief Photographer/Graphics ED
Montgomery Journal, Rockville, MD

Taylor, Jeff (904) 829-6562
PROD FRM-Camera/Platemaking
St. Augustine Record, St. Augustine, FL

Taylor, Jennifer (417) 836-1100
DIR-Human Resources
Springfield News-Leader, Springfield, MO

Taylor, Jerry (970) 240-4900
ED, Morning Sun, Montrose, CO

Taylor, Jill (612) 222-5011
VP/DIR-Employee Relations
St. Paul Pioneer Press, St. Paul, MN

Taylor, Jim (317) 342-3311
CIRC DIR, Daily Reporter, Martinsville, IN

Taylor, Jimmye C (806) 492-3585
PUB, ED, Paducah Post, Paducah, TX

Taylor, Jody (602) 898-6500
DIR-MKTG/PROM, Mesa Tribune, Mesa, AZ
Thomson Newspapers

Taylor, Joe (360) 676-2600
PROD MGR-MR
Bellingham Herald, Bellingham, WA

Taylor, John (913) 843-1000
News ED, Journal-World, Lawrence, KS

Taylor, John (209) 441-6111
Religion Writer, Fresno Bee, Fresno, CA

Taylor, John A (313) 222-6400
DIR-Labor Relations/Senior Legal Counsel
Detroit Newspapers, Detroit, MI

Taylor, Jonathan (213) 857-6600
ED, Daily Variety, Los Angeles, CA

Taylor, Joyce (423) 472-5041
CONT, MGR-CR, Daily Banner, Cleveland, TN

Taylor, Judith (514) 264-5364
ED, Gleaner, Huntingdon, QC

Taylor, Keith (606) 623-1669
Sports ED
Richmond Register, Richmond, KY

Taylor, Kenny (501) 785-7700
PROD MGR
Southwest Times Record, Fort Smith, AR

Taylor, Kerry (306) 825-5522
ADV DIR
Lloydminster Times, Lloydminster, SK

Taylor, Kevin (800) 828-2453
PRES
U-Bild Newspaper Features, Van Nuys, CA

Taylor, Larry (803) 648-2311
Sports ED, Aiken Standard, Aiken, SC

Taylor, Lee Ann (703) 276-3400
Political/Government ED
USA Today, Arlington, VA

Taylor, Liggett (509) 248-1251
Radio/Television ED
Yakima Herald-Republic, Yakima, WA

Taylor, Lottie M (618) 745-6267
ED, Pulaski Enterprise, Mounds, IL

Taylor, Madison (910) 353-1171
MAN ED, Environmental ED, News ED
Daily News, Jacksonville, NC

Taylor, Maria (818) 932-6161
ED, Dodge Construction News Greensheet, Monrovia, CA

Taylor, Marianne (810) 354-6060
GM, Detroit Jewish News, Southfield, MI

Taylor, Mark A (513) 931-4050
PUB, Christian Standard, Cincinnati, OH

Taylor, Martha (904) 294-1210
GM, Mayo Free Press, Mayo, FL

Taylor, Mary (919) 419-6500
DIR-INFO SYS, Herald-Sun, Durham, NC

Taylor, Mary Jane (508) 775-1200
MGR-CR, Cape Cod Times, Hyannis, MA

Taylor, Matt (509) 582-1500
Aviation ED, Books ED, EPE
Tri-City Herald, Tri-Cities, WA

Taylor, Mike K (517) 352-6026
ED, Lakeview Enterprise, Lakeview, MI

Taylor, Mynette (817) 840-2091
PUB, McGregor Mirror & Crawford Sun, McGregor, TX

Taylor, Norman G (308) 987-2451
PUB, ED, Beacon-Observer, Overton, NE

Taylor, O Roger (419) 445-9456
PUB
Archbold Farmland News, Archbold, OH

Taylor, Pat (205) 236-1551
GM, DIR-MKTG, Anniston Star, Anniston, AL

Taylor, Peter W (416) 869-4991
MGR, Toronto Star Syndicate, Toronto, ON

Taylor, Polly A (308) 987-2451
PUB, Beacon-Observer, Overton, NE

Taylor, Quincy (806) 267-2230
PUB, ED, Vega Enterprise, Vega, TX

Taylor, Randall (604) 792-9117
PUB, Chilliwack Times, Chilliwack, BC

Taylor, Ray (618) 529-5454
PROD SUPV-Pre Press
Southern Illinoisan, Carbondale, IL

Taylor, Rebecca (205) 325-2222
Food ED
Birmingham Post-Herald, Birmingham, AL

Taylor, Rick (360) 694-3391
ADV MGR-CLASS
Columbian, Vancouver, WA

Taylor, Robert (505) 983-3303
MGR-SYS, DP MGR
Santa Fe New Mexican, Santa Fe, NM

Taylor, Robert (510) 208-6300
Books ED, Oakland Tribune, Oakland, CA
MediaNews Inc. (Alameda Newspapers)

Taylor, Robert (403) 468-0100
PROD FRM-PR
Edmonton Sun, Edmonton, AB

Taylor, Roger (902) 426-2811
BUS ED, Chronicle-Herald, Halifax, NS

Taylor, Ron (615) 794-2555
ED, Review Appeal, Franklin, TN

Taylor, Ross William (419) 445-4466
PUB, Archbold Buckeye, Archbold, OH

Taylor, Rudy M (316) 879-2156
PUB, ED, Caney Chronicle, Caney, KS

Taylor, Sally (916) 541-3880
Religion ED
Tahoe Daily Tribune, South Lake Tahoe, CA

Taylor, Sally I (319) 886-2131
MAN ED, Tipton Conservative and Advertiser, Tipton, IA

Taylor, Sam (904) 260-9770
PUB, Folio Weekly, Jacksonville, FL

Taylor, Sam (919) 459-7101
GM, Nashville Graphic, Nashville, NC

Taylor, Sandra N (602) 977-8351
ADV MGR-CLASS
Daily News-Sun, Sun City, AZ

Taylor, Sharon (904) 263-6015
ED, Graceville News, Graceville, FL

Taylor, Sharon (803) 259-3501
ED, People-Sentinel, Barnwell, SC

Taylor, Sharon S (419) 445-4466
GM, Archbold Buckeye, Archbold, OH

Taylor, Sherly (704) 464-0221
BM, Observer-News-Enterprise, Newton, NC

Taylor, Stephen E (617) 929-2000
EVP, Boston Globe, Boston, MA

Taylor, Steve (512) 321-2557
PUB, Bastrop Advertiser & County News, Bastrop, TX

Taylor, Sue (512) 445-3500
Travel ED
Austin American-Statesman, Austin, TX

Taylor, Suzi (408) 385-4880
MAN ED, Rustler, King City, CA

Taylor, Ted (317) 423-5511
ADV DIR, Journal and Courier, Lafayette, IN

Taylor, Teresa (803) 577-7111
EX BUS ED, Post and Courier, Charleston, SC

Taylor, Thomas C (206) 851-9921
PUB, Peninsula Gateway, Gig Harbor, WA

Taylor, Tony (504) 758-2795
PUB, St. Charles Herald-Guide, Boutte, LA

Taylor, Velma (505) 395-2516
ED, Jal Record, Jal, NM

Taylor, Vicki (515) 523-1010
ED, Stuart Herald, Stuart, IA

Taylor, Vickie (417) 256-9191
Arts/Theater ED, Entertainment ED, Health/Medical ED, Theater/Music ED
West Plains Daily Quill, West Plains, MO

Taylor, W R (910) 353-1171
ADV MGR, Daily News, Jacksonville, NC

Taylor, William O (617) 929-2000
COB/CEO, PUB, Boston Globe, Boston, MA

Taylor-Wells, Sheila (817) 390-7400
COL
Fort Worth Star-Telegram, Fort Worth, TX

Tazioli, Terry (206) 464-2111
Lifestyle/Scene ED
Seattle Times, Seattle, WA

Teaff, Rick (212) 887-8550
News ED
American Metal Market, New York, NY

Teagan, Jerry (313) 222-6400
BM, Detroit Free Press, Detroit, MI

Teagarden, Douglas R (412) 663-7742
PUB, ED, Weekly Recorder, Claysville, PA

Teague, Jerry (541) 469-3123
ED, Curry Coastal Pilot, Brookings, OR

Teague Jr, Jim (847) 317-0500
MAN ED, Review, Bannockburn, IL

Teague, Paul (704) 758-7381
Sports ED, Lenoir News-Topic, Lenoir, NC

Teague, Willie (803) 786-9486
PUB, South Carolina United Methodist Advocate, Columbia, SC

Teahen, Paul (519) 291-1660
PUB, Listowel Banner, Listowel, ON

Teal, Marilyn (912) 923-6432
Fashion/Style ED, Living/Lifestyle ED, Women's ED, Daily Sun, Warner Robins, GA

Teal, Myra (812) 897-2330
PUB, Boonville Standard, Boonville, IN

Teall-Trudeau, Pat (519) 679-6666
ADV MGR-Sales Planning
London Free Press, London, ON

Tearney, Pat (414) 457-7711
BUS ED, Sheboygan Press, Sheboygan, WI

Teb Who's Where-228

Tebbe, Jay .... (618) 234-1000
CIRC DIR, News-Democrat, Belleville, IL
Tebben, Jerry .... (614) 461-5000
BUS ED, Columbus Dispatch, Columbus, OH
Techel, Doug .... (515) 684-4611
CIRC MGR, Ottumwa Courier, Ottumwa, IA
Tecklanberg, Jeff .... (319) 263-2331
MAN ED, EPE, Photo DEPT MGR
Muscatine Journal, Muscatine, IA
Tedesco, Sara Sue .... (314) 421-1880
PUB, St. Louis Countain, St. Louis, MO
ABC Inc. (Legal Communications Corp.)
Tedquest, Steven .... (716) 487-1111
PROD FRM-PR, Post-Journal, Jamestown, NY
Teeboom, Leon .... (714) 564-7072
MAN ED, Tustin News, Santa Ana, CA
Teegarden, Jack .... (317) 664-5111
CIRC MGR-Home Delivery
Chronicle-Tribune, Marion, IN
Tefft, Culver S .... (518) 692-2266
GM, Journal-Press, Greenwich, NY
Tefft, Sally B .... (518) 692-2266
PUB, MAN ED, Journal-Press, Greenwich, NY
Teglas, Johnny .... (540) 679-1101
GM, Coalfield Progress, Norton, VA
Teichmann, Stephanie .... (213) 413-5500
PUB
California-Staats Zeitung, Los Angeles, CA
Teitgen, Robert .... (716) 232-7100
ADV MGR-RT, Rochester Democrat and Chronicle; Times-Union, Rochester, NY
Telander, Rick .... (312) 321-3000
COL-Sports, Chicago Sun-Times, Chicago, IL
Telesnick, Jill .... (212) 930-8000
ADV MGR-RT, New York Post, New York, NY
Telfer II, John H .... (517) 835-7171
ED, Midland Daily News, Midland, MI
Telford, Eddie J .... (501) 623-7711
VP, Sentinel-Record, Hot Springs, AR
Wehco Media Inc.
Telford, Tracy .... (803) 423-2050
ED
Marion Star & Mullins Enterprise, Marion, SC
Tell, Bea .... (702) 876-1255
GM, Las Vegas Israelite, Las Vegas, NV
Tell, Judy Nies .... (313) 994-6989
Photo ED, Ann Arbor News, Ann Arbor, MI
Tell, Michael .... (702) 876-1255
PUB, ED, Las Vegas Israelite, Las Vegas, NV
Telle, Sheila .... (310) 337-7003
Sales Administrator
Creators Syndicate, Los Angeles, CA
Tellefsen, Cindy .... (805) 781-7800
DP MGR
Telegram-Tribune, San Luis Obispo, CA
Teller, Woolsey .... (317) 633-1240
EDL Writer
Indianapolis Star/News, Indianapolis, IN
Tellez, Mila .... (312) 252-3534
PUB, Extra Bilingual Community Newspapers, Chicago, IL
Telli, Andy .... (615) 259-8800
EDU ED, Nashville Banner, Nashville, TN
Temby, Mabel .... (414) 388-3175
ED, Kewaunee Enterprise, Kewaunee, WI
Temby, Pam .... (510) 634-2125
ED, Brentwood News, Brentwood, CA
Temelini, Walter .... (519) 253-8883
PUB, ED, La Gazzetta, Windsor, ON
Tempelmayr, Manfred .... (604) 746-4451
PUB, Pictorial, Duncan, BC
Tempero, Sue .... (317) 633-1240
PSL DIR
Indianapolis Star/News, Indianapolis, IN
Tempero, Sue .... (515) 284-8000
VP-Human Resources
Des Moines Register, Des Moines, IA
Tempest, Jeanne B .... (603) 569-3126
ED, Granite State News, Wolfeboro, NH
Tempest, Kristen .... (412) 537-3351
MGR-Office, Latrobe Bulletin, Latrobe, PA
Tempest, Rone .... (213) 237-5000
Beijing BU
Los Angeles Times, Los Angeles, CA
Tempesta, Mike .... (508) 685-1000
COL, Eagle-Tribune, North Andover, MA
Temple, Bob .... (612) 894-1111
GM, Dakota County Tribune, Burnsville, MN
Temple, Bruce Gregory .... (812) 988-2221
PUB, Brown County Democrat, Nashville, IN
Temple, Georgia .... (915) 682-5311
Entertainment/Amusements ED, Religion ED
Midland Reporter-Telegram, Midland, TX
Temple, James S .... (419) 258-8161
PUB, Antwerp Bee-Argus, Antwerp, OH
Temple, John .... (303) 892-5000
MAN ED, Rocky Mountain News, Denver, CO
Temple, June L .... (419) 258-8161
GM, Antwerp Bee-Argus, Antwerp, OH
Temple, Richard .... (941) 262-3161
PROD MGR-Press, Daily News, Naples, FL
Temple, Rodger S .... (419) 258-8161
MAN ED, Antwerp Bee-Argus, Antwerp, OH
Temple, Sandra K .... (419) 258-8161
ED, Antwerp Bee-Argus, Antwerp, OH
Temple, Susan .... (616) 392-2311
ADV MGR, Holland Sentinel, Holland, MI
Temple, Wick .... (212) 621-1500
VP/DIR of Newspaper Membership
Associated Press, New York, NY
Templett, Don .... (713) 220-7171
ADTX MGR, Houston Chronicle, Houston, TX
Templin, Norman .... (815) 369-2811
ED, Northwestern Illinois Farmer, Lena, IL
Tempus, Kent .... (715) 526-2121
MAN ED, EPE, NTL ED, News ED
Shawano Leader, Shawano, WI
Tenggren, Kevin .... (207) 794-6532
MAN ED, Lincoln News, Lincoln, ME
Tenggren, M Sheila .... (207) 794-6532
PUB, ED, Lincoln News, Lincoln, ME
Tennant, Bob .... (610) 622-8800
Sports ED
Delaware County Daily Times, Primos, PA
Tennant, Diane .... (941) 953-7755
Living/Health ED, Travel ED
Sarasota Herald-Tribune, Sarasota, FL
Tennant, Jack .... (403) 227-3612
PUB, ED, Innisfail Province, Innisfail, AB
Tennant, Larry .... (304) 292-6301
ADV MGR-RT
Dominion Post, Morgantown, WV
Tennant, Laura .... (702) 463-4242
ED
Fernley Leader/Dayton Courier, Yerington, NV
Tennant, Rich .... (508) 546-2448
Cartoonist, 5th Wave, Rockport, MA
Tennant, Ron .... (706) 724-0851
ADV DIR, Augusta Chronicle, Augusta, GA
Tennent, Kris .... (212) 556-1234
DIR-Publishing SYS
New York Times, New York, NY
Tenney, Robert W .... (315) 824-2150
PUB, Mid-York Weekly, Hamilton, NY
Tennis, Kamie .... (608) 356-4808
PROD MGR-Press, News-Republic/South Central Wisconsin News, Baraboo, WI
Tennyson, David .... (501) 763-4461
PRES, PUB, Courier News, Blytheville, AR
Tennyson, Karen .... (573) 695-3415
ED, Steele Enterprise, Steele, MO
Tennyson, Sandra .... (501) 763-4461
ED, Features/Travel ED
Blytheville Courier News, Blytheville, AR
Tenreiro, Jesus M .... (908) 355-8835
ED, Mensaje, Elizabeth, NJ
Tenszen, Tom .... (204) 857-3427
PUB, Daily Graphic, Portage la Prairie, MB
Teplick, Pamela .... (801) 355-3336
Society ED, FNA News, Salt Lake City, UT
Teplitz, Ben .... (212) 887-8550
EX ED
American Metal Market, New York, NY
Tepps, David .... (408) 920-5000
EX Sports ED
San Jose Mercury News, San Jose, CA
Terceno, Jack .... (203) 268-6234
ED, Stratford Star, Trumbull, CT
Terentiew, Malgorzata .... (715) 345-0744
GM, ED, Gwiazda Polarna, Stevens Point, WI
Tergliafera, Turk .... (910) 679-4900
PUB, Enterprise, Yadkinville, NC
Terhaar, Joyce .... (916) 321-1000
City ED, Sacramento Bee, Sacramento, CA
TerHorst, Cheryl A .... (847) 427-4300
Fashion ED
Daily Herald, Arlington Heights, IL
Terhune, Jim .... (765) 948-4164
PUB, ED, News-Sun, Fairmount, IN
Terilli Jr, Samuel A .... (305) 350-2111
GEN Counsel, Miami Herald, Miami, FL
Ternet, Lois .... (219) 623-3316
ED, Monroeville News, Monroeville, IN
Ternosky, Betty .... (216) 376-0917
CIRC MGR, Akron Legal News, Akron, OH
Ternus, Anne Marie .... (916) 444-2355
Reporter, Daily Recorder, Sacramento, CA
Terrell, Jamie .... (573) 471-1137
Sports ED, Standard Democrat, Sikeston, MO
Terrell, Jim .... (512) 664-6588
News ED, Alice Echo-News, Alice, TX
Terrell, Len .... (941) 629-2855
CIRC DIR, Sun Herald, Port Charlotte, FL
Terrell, Lisa .... (717) 255-8100
ADV CNR-NTL, Patriot-News, Harrisburg, PA
Terrell, Pam .... (605) 331-2200
EPE, Argus Leader, Sioux Falls, SD
Terrell, Scott .... (360) 424-3251
Photo DEPT MGR
Skagit Valley Herald, Mount Vernon, WA
Terrien, Martin D .... (413) 447-7311
VP/CFO, Berkshire Eagle, Pittsfield, MA
MediaNews Inc. (New England Newspapers)
Terrill, James .... (212) 556-1234
CONT, New York Times, New York, NY
Terrill, John .... (715) 532-5591
ED, Ladysmith News, Ladysmith, WI
Terrill, Marge .... (319) 242-7101
MGR-Office, Clinton Herald, Clinton, IA
Terry, Connie .... (801) 355-3336
Health ED/Acting BU Chief-Los Angeles
FNA News, Salt Lake City, UT
Terry, Craig .... (904) 863-1111
Artist, Northwest Florida Daily News, Fort Walton Beach, FL
Terry, Janet .... (915) 337-4661
Graphics ED/Art DIR
Odessa American, Odessa, TX
Terry, Jim .... (304) 327-2811
Special Projects ED
Bluefield Daily Telegraph, Bluefield, WV
Terry, John .... (800) 245-6536
ED, US/Express, Chicago, IL
Terry, Leslie .... (508) 775-1200
MGR-Human Resources
Cape Cod Times, Hyannis, MA
Terry, Mark .... (817) 767-8341
ADTX MGR, Wichita Falls Times Record News, Wichita Falls, TX
Terry, Michele .... (910) 227-0131
MGR-MKTG/PROM
Times News Publishing Co., Burlington, NC
Terry, Pat .... (713) 220-7171
News ED, Houston Chronicle, Houston, TX
Terry, Paul .... (910) 865-4179
ED, St. Pauls Review, St. Pauls, NC
Terry Jr, Randall B .... (910) 888-3500
PRES, High Point Enterprise, High Point, NC
Terry, Sandra .... (716) 487-1111
Librarian, Post-Journal, Jamestown, NY
Terry, Sue .... (501) 921-5711
ED
Lafayette County Democrat, Lewisville, AR
Terry, Thomas C .... (309) 944-2119
PUB, Geneseo Republic, Geneseo, IL
Tervo, Donald .... (906) 482-1500
PROD MGR
Daily Mining Gazette, Houghton, MI
Terzian, Philip .... (401) 277-7000
COL, Journal-Bulletin, Providence, RI
Teschner, J Peter .... (630) 887-0600
PUB, ED, Doings, Hinsdale, IL
Tesconi, Tim .... (707) 546-2020
Agriculture ED
Press Democrat, Santa Rosa, CA
Teskey, Frank .... (604) 572-0064
PUB, Surrey/North Delta Now, Surrey, BC
Tesmer, David .... (937) 372-4444
CIRC MGR, Xenia Daily Gazette, Xenia, OH
Teter, Herb .... (308) 345-4500
Sports ED
McCook Daily Gazette, McCook, NE
Tetlow, Ranae .... (913) 985-2456
GM, MAN ED, Kansas Chief, Troy, KS
Tetlow, Steven C .... (913) 985-2456
PUB, ED, Kansas Chief, Troy, KS
Tetreault, Alain .... (819) 569-9526
ADV DIR, MGR-MKTG/PROM
Record, Sherbrooke, QC
Tetreault, Philip .... (506) 632-8888
PROD MGR, Telegraph-Journal/Saint John Times Globe, Saint John, NB
Tetreault, Richard .... (401) 762-3000
PROD SUPT-MR, Call, Woonsocket, RI
Tetrick, James L .... (304) 788-3333
PRES/Co-PUB, BM, PROD SUPT
Mineral Daily News-Tribune, Keyser, WV
Tetrick, Kathy .... (304) 788-3333
ADV MGR-Sales
Mineral Daily News-Tribune, Keyser, WV
Tetrick, Robert G .... (304) 788-3333
VP/Co-PUB, ADV MGR
Mineral Daily News-Tribune, Keyser, WV
Teut, Elaine .... (712) 676-3414
GM, Schleswig Leader, Schleswig, IA
Teutsch, Clifford L .... (860) 241-6200
MAN ED, Hartford Courant, Hartford, CT
Tew, Nancy .... (213) 237-5000
Comics ED
Los Angeles Times, Los Angeles, CA
Tezak, James J .... (630) 355-0063
PUB, GM, Naperville Sun, Naperville, IL
Tezak, John J .... (630) 759-9169
GM, Bolingbrook Sun, Bolingbrook, IL
Tezon, Anne L .... (816) 583-2116
PUB, ED, Hamilton Advocate, Hamilton, MO
Thacker, Cleo E .... (217) 824-2233
MGR-CR, Taylorville Daily Breeze-Courier, Taylorville, IL
Thacker, Harry .... (206) 597-8742
Administrative Services MGR
News Tribune, Tacoma, WA
Thacker, Leigh .... (304) 526-4000
CONT, Herald-Dispatch, Huntington, WV
Thacker, Richard .... (816) 271-8500
ADV MGR-NTL
St. Joseph News-Press, St. Joseph, MO
Thacker, Susan .... (316) 792-1211
Farm ED
Great Bend Tribune, Great Bend, KS
Thackeray, Fred W .... (217) 388-7721
PUB, ED, Ford County Press, Melvin, IL
Thackeray, Jonathan E .... (212) 649-2000
VP/GEN Counsel
Hearst Newspapers, New York, NY
Thakery, Jane .... (317) 932-2222
ADV MGR-CLASS
Rushville Republican, Rushville, IN
Thalasinos, George .... (610) 446-1463
ED, Hellenic News of America, Havertown, PA
Thaler, David .... (908) 246-5500
GM
Home News & Tribune, East Brunswick, NJ
Thall, Burnett M .... (416) 367-2000
VP, Toronto Star, Toronto, ON
Thames, Beth .... (216) 329-7000
Health/Medical ED, MET ED
Chronicle-Telegram, Elyria, OH
Thames, Rick .... (704) 358-5000
Public ED, Charlotte Observer, Charlotte, NC
Tharp, Patty .... (209) 578-2000
CIRC MGR-Sales Development
Modesto Bee, Modesto, CA
Thatch, Mary J .... (910) 765-5502
ED, Wilmington Journal, Wilmington, NC
Thatcher, Bonnie .... (618) 662-2108
PROD MGR
Daily Clay County Advocate-Press, Flora, IL
Thatcher, Gary .... (205) 766-3434
MAN ED, Online Contact
Times Daily, Florence, AL
Thatcher, Jack L .... (618) 662-2108
GM, ED
Daily Clay County Advocate-Press, Flora, IL
Thatcher, Rex H .... (517) 752-7171
PUB, Saginaw News, Saginaw, MI
Thate, Lisa .... (507) 235-3303
PROD SUPT, Sentinel, Fairmont, MN
Thaxton, Earl .... (334) 262-1611
State ED
Montgomery Advertiser, Montgomery, AL
Thaxton, James A .... (770) 684-7811
ED, Rockmart Journal, Rockmart, GA
Thayer, Brian C .... (617) 593-7700
PUB, Daily Evening Item, Lynn, MA
Thayer, Daniel .... (518) 561-2300
PROD MGR
Press-Republican, Plattsburgh, NY
Thayer, Delbert .... (304) 765-5193
ED, Braxton Citizens' News, Sutton, WV
Thayer, Janet .... (970) 669-5050
Political ED
Loveland Daily Reporter-Herald, Loveland, CO
Thayne, Jared .... (801) 752-2121
Features ED, Herald Journal, Logan, UT
Thein, Irene P .... (307) 634-3361
ADV MGR-CLASS/ADTX
Wyoming Tribune-Eagle, Cheyenne, WY
Theis, Bill .... (209) 582-0471
PROD SUPT, Hanford Sentinel, Hanford, CA
Theis, Bruce .... (360) 754-5400
CONT, Olympian, Olympia, WA
Theis, Charles .... (502) 781-1700
CIRC MGR, Daily News, Bowling Green, KY
Theiss, Evelyn .... (216) 999-4500
Political Writer, Plain Dealer, Cleveland, OH
Theiss, Roy .... (702) 293-2302
ED, Boulder City News, Boulder City, NV
Thelen, Gil .... (803) 771-6161
EX ED, State, Columbia, SC
Themelis, William J .... (508) 957-0007
PUB, Dracut Dispatch, Dracut, MA
Themer, Bob .... (815) 937-3300
Agriculture ED, Environmental ED
Daily Journal, Kankakee, IL
Theno, Meg .... (608) 252-6100
Photo Dept ED
Wisconsin State Journal, Madison, WI
Theo, Tracy .... (864) 427-1234
Sports ED, Union Daily Times, Union, SC
Theodore, John .... (800) 760-3100
Features ED/Chicago
Williams Syndications Inc., Holiday, FL
Theophilakos, Jonathan J .... (201) 646-4000
ADV GM-Passaic/Morris
Record, Hackensack, NJ
Theriault, Johny .... (819) 770-2205
GM, ED, Bonjour Dimanche, Hull, QC
Theriault, Normand .... (514) 985-3333
Art ED, Literary Pages
Le Devoir, Montreal, QC
Theriot, Ecton .... (813) 259-7711
Home ED, Tribune and Times, Tampa, FL
Theroux, Lance .... (914) 341-1100
ASST MAN ED
Times Herald-Record, Middletown, NY
Thibault, Francine .... (819) 569-9526
PROD MGR-COMP, Record, Sherbrooke, QC
Thibault, Michel .... (514) 692-8552
ED
Le Soleil du St-Laurent, Chateauguay, QC

Copyright ©1997 by the Editor & Publisher Co.

229-Who's Where **Tho**

Thibeault, Cheryl .... (203) 789-5200
CONT, New Haven Register, New Haven, CT

Thibeault, Denise .... (519) 882-1770
PUB, Petrolia Topic, Petrolia, ON

Thibo, Martine .... (317) 633-1240
PROD OPER MGR-Building Maintenance
Indianapolis Star/News, Indianapolis, IN

Thibodeau, Mike .... (519) 326-4434
ED, Leamington Post, Leamington, ON

Thibodeau, Patrick .... (860) 225-4601
EPE, Herald, New Britain, CT

Thibodeaux, Anna .... (205) 345-0505
EDU ED, Environmental ED
Tuscaloosa News, Tuscaloosa, AL

Thiboult, Art .... (716) 282-2311
PROD FRM-PR
Niagara Gazette, Niagara Falls, NY

Thiboutot, Phyllis A .... (207) 729-3311
VP-Human Resources
Times Record, Brunswick, ME

Thiel, Art .... (206) 448-8000
COL-Sports, Post-Intelligencer, Seattle, WA

Thiel, Paul .... (313) 222-6400
CIRC DIR-New Sales/Media
Detroit Newspapers, Detroit, MI

Thiel, Polly .... (515) 989-0525
ED, Carlisle Citizen, Carlisle, IA

Thiele, Alicia P .... (605) 582-6025
ED, Brandon Valley Challenger, Brandon, SD

Thiele, Bonnie .... (403) 343-2400
CONT, Red Deer Advocate, Red Deer, AB

Thieme, Rita K .... (508) 997-7411
DIR-PROM
Standard Times, New Bedford, MA

Thiesen, Bob .... (402) 444-1000
Training MGR
Omaha World-Herald, Omaha, NE

Thiessen, Mark .... (402) 289-2329
ED
Douglas County Post Gazette, Elkhorn, NE

Thigpen, Ron .... (941) 687-7000
PROD DIR, Ledger, Lakeland, FL

Thilgen, Jeffrey A .... (630) 844-5844
ADV MGR-Sales, Beacon-News, Aurora, IL

Thistle, Jan .... (613) 965-7248
MAN ED, Contact, Astra, ON

Thoele, Carl .... (217) 347-7151
ADV DIR
Effingham Daily News, Effingham, IL

Thoemke, Grace .... (701) 347-4493
GM, Cass County Reporter, Casselton, ND

Thokey, Thomas E .... (937) 335-5634
EVP, SEC, GM, Troy Daily News/Miami Valley Sunday News, Troy, OH

Thom, Neil .... (306) 782-2465
PUB, GM
Yorkton This Week & Enterprise, Yorkton, SK

Thoma, Tom .... (515) 421-0500
Sports ED, Globe-Gazette, Mason City, IA

Thomalla, Gail .... (715) 384-3131
Sports ED
Marshfield News-Herald, Marshfield, WI

Thomas, Alfred .... (501) 378-3400
Librarian
Arkansas Democrat-Gazette, Little Rock, AR

Thomas, Barry R .... (314) 535-4033
PUB, Evening Whirl, St. Louis, MO

Thomas, Bill .... (540) 628-7101
PUB
Washington County News, Abingdon, VA

Thomas, Bob .... (815) 937-3300
EPE, Daily Journal, Kankakee, IL

Thomas, Bob .... (312) 222-3232
CIRC MGR-Single Copy
Chicago Tribune, Chicago, IL

Thomas, Bruce .... (403) 849-4350
PUB, Scope, Slave Lake, AB

Thomas, Catriena .... (716) 282-2311
DP MGR, Niagara Gazette, Niagara Falls, NY

Thomas, Chris .... (408) 991-1873
PUB, ED, OutNOW!, San Jose, CA

Thomas, David .... (610) 444-6590
ED, Kennett Paper, Kennett Square, PA

Thomas, Dick .... (604) 732-2944
MGR-INFO SYS
Pacific Press Limited, Vancouver, BC

Thomas, Donna S .... (941) 494-7600
PUB, DeSoto Sun-Herald, Arcadia, FL

Thomas, Edward R .... (717) 286-5671
PROD DIR, Daily Item, Sunbury, PA

Thomas, Eric .... (360) 676-2600
EPE, Bellingham Herald, Bellingham, WA

Thomas, Eugene .... (970) 858-3924
PUB, GM, Fruita Times, Fruita, CO

Thomas, Frank .... (406) 755-6767
ED, Kalispell News, Kalispell, MT

Thomas, Gary .... (717) 582-4305
MAN ED
Perry County Times, New Bloomfield, PA

Thomas, Gloria M .... (510) 757-2525
GM, Ledger Dispatch, Antioch, CA

Thomas, Greg .... (504) 826-3279
RE ED, Times-Picayune, New Orleans, LA

Thomas, Helen .... (601) 226-4321
Living/Lifestyle ED
Daily Sentinel-Star, Grenada, MS

Thomas, Helen .... (202) 898-8254
UPI White House BU MGR
United Press International, Washington, DC

Thomas, Helen .... (806) 273-5611
ADV DIR, Borger News-Herald, Borger, TX

Thomas, Jack G .... (606) 436-5771
PUB, ED, Herald Voice, Hazard, KY

Thomas, Jacqueline .... (313) 222-2300
BU Chief-Washington
Detroit News, Detroit, MI

Thomas, Jason .... (317) 659-4622
Sports ED, Times, Frankfort, IN

Thomas, Jean .... (614) 633-1131
Librarian, Radio/Television ED, Religion ED
Times Leader, Martins Ferry, OH

Thomas, Jeffrey .... (408) 920-5000
EX News ED-AM
San Jose Mercury News, San Jose, CA

Thomas, Jerry .... (619) 299-3131
PROD DIR
San Diego Union-Tribune, San Diego, CA

Thomas, James L .... (615) 259-8000
TREAS, Tennessean, Nashville, TN
Gannett Co. Inc.

Thomas, Jim .... (916) 741-2345
PROD FRM-PR
Appeal-Democrat, Marysville, CA

Thomas, Jim .... (317) 462-7368
PUB, ED, Indy East News, Greenfield, IN

Thomas, Jim .... (314) 664-6411
PUB, ED, News Telegraph, St. Louis, MO

Thomas, Jim .... (509) 248-1251
CIRC DIR
Yakima Herald-Republic, Yakima, WA

Thomas, Joe .... (334) 296-3491
ED, Tri-City Ledger, Flomaton, AL

Thomas, Joe .... (317) 653-5151
Political/Religion ED, Wire ED
Banner-Graphic, Greencastle, IN

Thomas, John N .... (719) 775-2064
PUB, Limon Leader, Limon, CO

Thomas, Kathy .... (616) 866-4465
GM, Rockford Squire, Rockford, MI

Thomas, Katie .... (801) 679-8730
PUB, Garfield County News, Tropic, UT

Thomas, Ken .... (414) 387-2211
ED, Mayville News, Mayville, WI

Thomas, Kenneth .... (213) 299-3800
PUB, Los Angeles Sentinel, Los Angeles, CA

Thomas, Lancie M .... (334) 479-0629
PUB, Mobile Beacon and Alabama Citizen, Mobile, AL

Thomas, Larry .... (208) 377-6200
ADV MGR-RT, Idaho Statesman, Boise, ID

Thomas, Larry .... (510) 757-2525
PROD MGR-PR
Ledger Dispatch, Antioch, CA

Thomas, Laurie .... (914) 694-9300
VP-Human Resources, Reporter Dispatch, White Plains, NY, Gannett Co. Inc.

Thomas, Laurie .... (316) 268-6000
MGR-PROM, Wichita Eagle, Wichita, KS

Thomas, Lee .... (606) 371-6177
PUB, ED, Dixie News, Florence, KY

Thomas, Lloyd W .... (714) 893-4501
PUB, ED
Westminster Herald, Westminster, CA

Thomas, Lois .... (423) 523-3131
BUS/FIN ED, RE ED
Knoxville News-Sentinel, Knoxville, TN

Thomas, Lovan .... (318) 352-5501
PRES, PUB
Natchitoches Times, Natchitoches, LA

Thomas, Marjean .... (406) 755-6767
PUB, Kalispell News, Kalispell, MT

Thomas, Mark .... (414) 224-2000
VP-Circulation MKTG, CIRC VP-MKTG
Milwaukee Journal Sentinel, Milwaukee, WI

Thomas, Mark .... (312) 222-3232
PROD MGR-COMP SRV
Chicago Tribune, Chicago, IL

Thomas, Martha .... (502) 678-5171
PROD SUPT, PROD SUPV-COMP
Glasgow Daily Times, Glasgow, KY

Thomas, Mary Lou .... (619) 241-7744
Features ED, Daily Press, Victorville, CA

Thomas, Mia .... (604) 442-2191
ED, Boundary Bulletin, Grand Forks, BC

Thomas, Michael .... (410) 332-6000
MGR-Telecommunications
Sun, Baltimore, MD

Thomas, Michele .... (541) 474-3700
ADV DIR, Daily Courier, Grants Pass, OR

Thomas, Michele .... (815) 877-4044
ED
Northern Ogle County Tempo, Loves Park, IL

Thomas, Miles .... (403) 429-5400
ADV MGR-NTL Sales/Key Accounts
Edmonton Journal, Edmonton, AB

Thomas, Mitch .... (207) 897-4321
ED, Livermore Falls Advertiser, Livermore Falls, ME

Thomas Jr, Morrell L .... (803) 393-3811
PUB, News and Press, Darlington, SC

Thomas, Nancie .... (218) 723-5281
ADV MGR-RT, News-Tribune, Duluth, MN

Thomas, Nancy G .... (812) 883-3281
GM, Your Advantage, Salem, IN

Thomas, Patricia .... (619) 244-0021
GM, Hesperia Resorter, Hesperia, CA

Thomas, Patricia O .... (414) 265-5300
PUB, Community Journal, Milwaukee, WI

Thomas, Patrick A .... (910) 259-9111
PUB, ED, Pender Post, Burgaw, NC

Thomas, Patty .... (412) 439-7500
PROD MGR-MR
Herald-Standard, Uniontown, PA

Thomas, Richard G .... (212) 556-1234
TREAS, New York Times Co., New York, NY

Thomas, Richard G .... (202) 737-1888
PUB/ED, Roll Call Report Syndicate (Thomas Reports Inc.), Washington, DC

Thomas, Robert .... (509) 459-5000
CIRC MGR
Spokesman-Review, Spokane, WA

Thomas, Robert .... (510) 540-7400
GM, East Bay Express, Berkeley, CA

Thomas, Robert .... (414) 265-5300
GM, Community Journal, Milwaukee, WI

Thomas, Roy .... (601) 746-4911
PUB, ED, Yazoo Herald, Yazoo City, MS

Thomas, Steve .... (816) 882-5335
ED, Boonville Daily News, Boonville, MO

Thomas, Steve .... (912) 236-9511
BUS ED/Public Affairs ED
Savannah Morning News, Savannah, GA

Thomas, Timothy .... (419) 674-4066
ED, Radio/Television ED, Wire ED
Kenton Times, Kenton, OH

Thomas, Tommy .... (208) 678-2201
PRES, South Idaho Press, Burley, ID

Thomas, Troy .... (317) 462-7368
GM, Indy East News, Greenfield, IN

Thomas, Wade .... (814) 445-9621
ED-City, Daily American, Somerset, PA

Thomas, Will .... (415) 348-4321
RE ED
San Mateo County Times, San Mateo, CA

Thomas, William M .... (517) 278-2318
SEC, Daily Reporter, Coldwater, MI

Thomas Jr, William O .... (810) 332-8181
EX ED, Oakland Press, Pontiac, MI

Thomas, Wright M .... (315) 393-1000
PRES, Courier-Observer Journal & Advance-News, Ogdensburg, NY
Park Communications Inc.

Thomas, Wyland .... (806) 669-2525
PUB, Pampa News, Pampa, TX

Thomas-Rico, Kathy .... (707) 448-6401
Entertainment/Amusements ED
Reporter, Vacaville, CA

Thomason, Jo .... (770) 532-1234
CNR-INFO SYS, Times, Gainesville, GA

Thomason, Rick .... (919) 527-3191
ED, Free Press, Kinston, NC

Thomasson, Dan .... (202) 408-1484
BU Chief/ED, Scripps Howard News Service, Washington, DC

Thomasson, Jana .... (502) 443-1771
ASST GM, ADV DIR-CLASS, ADV MGR-RT
Paducah Sun, Paducah, KY

Thomasson, Marianne C .... (770) 253-1576
ED, Newnan Times-Herald, Newnan, GA

Thomasson, William .... (770) 253-1576
PUB, Newnan Times-Herald, Newnan, GA

Thomer, Richard .... (715) 384-3131
PROD MGR
Marshfield News-Herald, Marshfield, WI

Thompkins, John .... (719) 589-2553
PRES, Valley Courier, Alamosa, CO

Thompkins, Kevin .... (317) 482-4650
Sports ED, Reporter, Lebanon, IN

Thompkins, Mike .... (719) 589-2553
VP, Valley Courier, Alamosa, CO

Thompson, Albert .... (615) 526-9715
ADV MGR, Herald-Citizen, Cookeville, TN

Thompson, Andy .... (607) 324-1425
ED, Evening Tribune, Hornell, NY

Thompson, Ann .... (817) 390-7400
Asst City ED
Fort Worth Star-Telegram, Fort Worth, TX

Thompson, Anne .... (719) 254-3351
PRES, PUB
Rocky Ford Daily Gazette, Rocky Ford, CO

Thompson, Art .... (215) 483-7300
MAN ED, Review, Philadelphia, PA

Thompson, Barbara .... (717) 776-3197
ED, Valley Times-Star, Newville, PA

Thompson, Ben .... (806) 296-1300
PROD MGR
Plainview Daily Herald, Plainview, TX

Thompson, Bev .... (705) 745-4641
EPE, Examiner, Peterborough, ON

Thompson, Bill .... (817) 390-7400
COL-Star
Fort Worth Star-Telegram, Fort Worth, TX

Thompson, Bill .... (803) 577-7111
Books ED, Films/Theater ED
Post and Courier, Charleston, SC

Thompson, Bob .... (416) 947-2222
EX Entertainment ED
Toronto Sun, Toronto, ON

Thompson, Bob .... (202) 334-6000
Washington Post Magazine Senior ED
Washington Post, Washington, DC

Thompson, Bradley L .... (313) 961-3949
PUB, Detroit Legal News, Detroit, MI

Thompson, Carol .... (614) 773-2111
ADV MGR-Creative SRV
Chillicothe Gazette, Chillicothe, OH

Thompson, Carolyn .... (912) 375-4225
GM
Jeff Davis County Ledger, Hazlehurst, GA

Thompson, Carolyn .... (612) 421-4444
ED, Blaine-Spring Lake Park Life, Coon Rapids, MN

Thompson, Catherine .... (519) 894-2231
Kitchener & Regional Gov't
Record, Kitchener, ON

Thompson, Connie M .... (308) 754-4401
ED, Phonograph-Herald, St. Paul, NE

Thompson, D B .... (250) 380-5211
ADV MGR-RT, Times Colonist, Victoria, BC

Thompson, Darla .... (816) 778-3205
ED, Hopkins Journal, Hopkins, MO

Thompson, Most Rev David B .. (803) 724-8375
PUB
New Catholic Miscellany, Charleston, SC

Thompson, David E .... (814) 472-8240
PUB, Mountaineer-Herald, Ebensburg, PA

Thompson, David L .... (405) 475-3311
ADV DIR
Daily Oklahoman, Oklahoma City, OK

Thompson, David L .... (912) 496-3585
PUB, ED
Charlton County Herald, Folkston, GA

Thompson, David L .... (913) 682-1334
PUB, GM
Lansing Chronicle, Leavenworth, KS

Thompson, Debbie .... (501) 731-2561
GM, Woodruff Monitor-Leader-Advocate, McCrory, AR

Thompson, Denise .... (310) 337-7003
Sales Administrator
Creators Syndicate, Los Angeles, CA

Thompson, Dennis .... (603) 436-1800
CIRC DIR
Portsmouth Herald, Portsmouth, NH

Thompson, Don .... (319) 398-8211
NTL/Foreign ED, Gazette, Cedar Rapids, IA

Thompson, Donald .... (314) 531-1323
ED, St. Louis Argus, St. Louis, MO

Thompson, Donna .... (315) 866-2220
EDU ED, Features ED
Evening Telegram, Herkimer, NY

Thompson, Dorothy .... (601) 693-1551
Entertainment/Amusements ED, Fashion/Style ED, Religion ED, Society/Women's ED
Meridian Star, Meridian, MS

Thompson, Doug .... (408) 624-0162
ED, Carmel Pine Cone, Carmel, CA

Thompson, Doug .... (501) 378-3400
Farm ED
Arkansas Democrat-Gazette, Little Rock, AR

Thompson, Ed .... (505) 325-4545
Sports ED, Daily Times, Farmington, NM

Thompson, F Clair .... (814) 765-5581
TREAS/CONT, Progress, Clearfield, PA

Thompson, Fritz .... (505) 823-7777
Farm ED
Albuquerque Journal, Albuquerque, NM

Thompson, Gail .... (203) 789-0010
PUB, New Haven Advocate, New Haven, CT

Thompson, Gina .... (519) 376-2250
BM, Sun Times, Owen Sound, ON

Thompson, Gus .... (916) 885-5656
BUS/FIN ED, Auburn Journal, Auburn, CA

Thompson, Guy .... (219) 463-2166
ED, LaGrange Standard, LaGrange, IN

Thompson, Gwen .... (250) 352-3552
Office MGR, Nelson Daily News, Nelson, BC

Thompson, H M .... (312) 616-3282
Art DIR, Dodge Construction News Chicago, Chicago, IL

Thompson, Herbert .... (207) 729-3311
PROD MGR-Pre Press
Times Record, Brunswick, ME

Thompson, Herman L .... (918) 733-4898
PUB, ED, Morris News, Morris, OK

Thompson, J B .... (561) 791-7790
ED, Wellington/Royal Palm Beach Forum, Wellington, FL

Thompson, J R .... (719) 254-3351
SEC/TREAS, BM, MAN ED
Rocky Ford Daily Gazette, Rocky Ford, CO

Copyright ©1997 by the Editor & Publisher Co.

Tho Who's Where-230

Thompson, Jackie L .... (701) 352-0640
PUB, Walsh County Record, Grafton, ND
Thompson, James .... (208) 664-8176
PUB, Coeur d'Alene Press, Coeur d'Alene, ID
Thompson, James .... (719) 275-7565
PROD SUPT, PROD Sales-Commercial Printing, Daily Record, Canon City, CO
Thompson, Jan .... (308) 237-2152
Farm/Agriculture ED
Kearney Hub, Kearney, NE
Thompson, Jay .... (805) 927-8652
ED, Cambrian, Cambria, CA
Thompson, Jay .... (507) 625-4451
ADV DIR-MKTG, Free Press, Mankato, MN
Thompson, Jim .... (541) 753-2641
CIRC MGR
Corvallis Gazette-Times, Corvallis, OR
Thompson, Jim .... (814) 870-1600
Political ED
Morning News/Erie Daily Times, Erie, PA
Thompson, Jim .... (901) 925-6397
ED, Courier, Savannah, TN
Thompson, Jim .... (360) 785-0345
ED, Ledger, Winlock, WA
Thompson, Joe .... (817) 573-7066
GM, Hood County News, Granbury, TX
Thompson, Joey .... (604) 732-2222
COL, Province, Vancouver, BC
Thompson, John .... (904) 438-5421
PUB, Gosport, Pensacola, FL
Thompson, John .... (502) 582-4011
DP MGR, Courier-Journal, Louisville, KY
Thompson, John W .... (705) 673-5667
PUB, Northern Life, Sudbury, ON
Thompson, Joyce .... (702) 423-6041
ADV MGR, Lahontan Valley News & Fallon Eagle Standard, Fallon, NV
Thompson, Judi .... (604) 248-4341
PUB, News, Parksville, BC
Thompson, Kathleen .... (910) 739-4322
MAN ED, Robesonian, Lumberton, NC
Thompson, Kay McMullen .... (702) 738-3611
PUB, ED, Elko Independent, Elko, NV
Thompson, Laura .... (719) 254-3351
ADV MGR
Rocky Ford Daily Gazette, Rocky Ford, CO
Thompson, Leanna .... (816) 230-5311
GM, Odessan, Odessa, MO
Thompson, Lee .... (912) 564-2045
MAN ED, Sylvania Telephone, Sylvania, GA
Thompson, Linda .... (616) 722-3161
Librarian
Muskegon Chronicle, Muskegon, MI
Thompson, Lou .... (609) 691-5000
CIRC DIR, Daily Journal, Vineland, NJ
Thompson, Marie .... (317) 962-1575
PSL DIR, Palladium-Item, Richmond, IN
Thompson, Mark .... (808) 525-8000
CIRC MGR-OPER
Hawaii Newspaper Agency Inc., Honolulu, HI
Thompson, Marlin .... (507) 368-4214
PUB, ED, Lincoln County Valley Journal, Lake Benton, MN
Thompson, Martha J .... (818) 713-3000
CIRC DIR, Daily News, Woodland Hills, CA
Thompson, Martin C .... (212) 621-1500
DIR-State News
Associated Press, New York, NY
Thompson, Mildred I .... (308) 754-4401
PUB, Phonograph-Herald, St. Paul, NE
Thompson, Morris .... (215) 854-2000
EPE
Philadelphia Daily News, Philadelphia, PA
Thompson, Neil .... (812) 372-7811
PROD DIR, Republic, Columbus, IN
Thompson, Olivia .... (212) 630-4000
VP, Women's Wear Daily, New York, NY
Thompson, Patricia Camp .... (408) 920-5000
ASST MAN ED-Development
San Jose Mercury News, San Jose, CA
Thompson, Paul .... (937) 328-0300
PROD SUPT-PR
Springfield News-Sun, Springfield, OH
Thompson, Paul E .... (816) 778-3205
PUB, Hopkins Journal, Hopkins, MO
Thompson, Richard .... (334) 262-1611
Automotive ED, BUS/FIN ED
Montgomery Advertiser, Montgomery, AL
Gannett Co. Inc.
Thompson, Robert .... (330) 364-5577
PROD FRM-PR
Times Reporter, New Philadelphia, OH
Thompson, Rose .... (617) 944-4444
ED, Suburban News, Reading, MA
Thompson, Roy .... (970) 522-1990
Sports ED, Journal-Advocate, Sterling, CO
Thompson, Roy .... (212) 686-6850
ED
Black Press Service Inc. (BPS), New York, NY
Thompson, Sally .... (701) 780-1100
Cultural Issues ED, Entertainment ED
Grand Forks Herald, Grand Forks, ND
Thompson, Sandra .... (702) 385-3111
MAN ED, Las Vegas Sun, Las Vegas, NV
Thompson, Sandra .... (501) 442-1777
MGR-CR
Northwest Arkansas Times, Fayetteville, AR
Thompson, Scott .... (305) 441-2526
PRES, SATCO Marketing & Promotional Printing, Coral Gables, FL
Thompson, Sean S .... (702) 738-3611
MAN ED, Elko Independent, Elko, NV
Thompson, Stacy Angle .... (817) 658-3142
PUB, ED, Knox County News, Knox City, TX
Thompson, Tara .... (918) 652-3311
Features ED
Henryetta Daily Free-Lance, Henryetta, OK
Thompson, Terrance .... (816) 234-4141
DIR-ADM, Kansas City Star, Kansas City, MO
Thompson, Terry .... (515) 284-8000
CIRC VP
Des Moines Register, Des Moines, IA
Thompson, Tim .... (205) 766-3434
ADV DIR, Times Daily, Florence, AL
Thompson, Tom .... (502) 582-4011
DIR-Procurement
Courier-Journal, Louisville, KY
Thompson, Tom .... (360) 452-2345
Photo Chief
Peninsula Daily News, Port Angeles, WA
Thompson, Tuck .... (912) 236-9511
State ED
Savannah Morning News, Savannah, GA
Thompson, Verna D .... (306) 962-3221
PUB, ED, Press Review, Eston, SK
Thompson, Wayne .... (503) 221-8327
EDL Writer, Oregonian, Portland, OR
Thompson, William H .... (308) 536-3100
PUB, ED
Nance County Journal, Fullerton, NE
Thoms, Diane .... (603) 880-1516
ED, MAN ED
Hudson-Litchfield News, Hudson, NH
Thoms, Sue .... (616) 222-5400
Books ED
Grand Rapids Press, Grand Rapids, MI
Thomsen, Brian D .... (414) 775-4431
ED, Valders Journal, Valders, WI
Thomsen, David .... (360) 676-2600
DP MGR
Bellingham Herald, Bellingham, WA
Thomsen, Debra .... (307) 742-2176
Entertainment/Amusements ED, Television/Film ED, Theater/Music ED
Laramie Daily Boomerang, Laramie, WY
Thomson, Candy .... (410) 332-6000
ED-Arundel Sun, Sun, Baltimore, MD
Thomson III, H C .... (614) 363-1161
SEC, CIRC MGR
Delaware Gazette, Delaware, OH
Thomson, Helen U .... (614) 363-1161
VP, Delaware Gazette, Delaware, OH
Thomson, John .... (937) 225-2000
Deputy MAN ED
Dayton Daily News, Dayton, OH
Thomson Jr, John .... (203) 387-0354
PUB, Inner-City, New Haven, CT
Thomson, Ken R .... (416) 585-5000
BC, Globe and Mail (Canada's National Newspaper), Toronto, ON
Thomson, Linda .... (801) 237-2188
Farm/Agriculture Writer
Deseret News, Salt Lake City, UT
Thomson, Lori .... (907) 586-3740
BUS/FIN ED, Juneau Empire, Juneau, AK
Thomson, Max .... (412) 654-6651
PUB/GM, New Castle News, New Castle, PA
Thomson, Mike .... (515) 522-7155
ED, Free Press, Brooklyn, IA
Thomson, Robert .... (218) 723-5281
ADV MGR-Major Accounts
Duluth News-Tribune, Duluth, MN
Thomson, Scott Bruce .... (715) 538-4765
ED, Whitehall Times, Whitehall, WI
Thomson, Stephanie .... (360) 694-3391
Music/Theater ED
Columbian, Vancouver, WA
Thomson, Thomas T .... (614) 363-1161
TREAS, PROD MGR
Delaware Gazette, Delaware, OH
Thomson II, W D .... (614) 363-1161
PRES/CEO, PUB
Delaware Gazette, Delaware, OH
Thoreson, Kerri .... (208) 773-7502
PUB, ED, Post Falls Tribune, Post Falls, ID
Thoreson, Rod .... (218) 584-5195
PUB, MAN ED, Twin Valley Times/Gary Graphic, Twin Valley, MN
Thorn-Levitt, Capt P .... (613) 965-7248
ED, Contact, Astra, ON
Thornberg, Cheryl .... (505) 523-4581
Amusements/Films ED, Features ED
Las Cruces Sun-News, Las Cruces, NM
Thornberry, David .... (606) 474-5101
PUB, Grayson Journal-Enquirer, Grayson, KY
Thornberry, Mike .... (316) 251-3300
PUB, Coffeyville Journal, Coffeyville, KS
Thornberry, Rob .... (208) 522-1800
Hunting & Fishing ED, Sports ED
Post Register, Idaho Falls, ID
Thornburg, Ron .... (801) 625-4200
MAN ED, Standard-Examiner, Ogden, UT
Thorndyke, Eddie .... (919) 934-2176
PUB, Smithfield Herald, Smithfield, NC
Thorne, David M .... (310) 540-5511
BM, Daily Breeze, Torrance, CA
Copley Press Inc.
Thorne, Leon M .... (319) 346-1461
PUB, ED, Parkersburg Eclipse-News-Review, Parkersburg, IA
Thornewell, Michelle L .... (704) 322-4510
Wire ED, Hickory Daily Record, Hickory, NC
Thornjon, Larry .... (405) 964-2920
PUB, ED, McLoud News, McLoud, OK
Thornley, Bill .... (715) 635-2181
ED, Spooner Advocate, Spooner, WI
Thornton, Almus J .... (205) 236-1551
SEC/TREAS, Anniston Star, Anniston, AL
Consolidated Publishing Co.
Thornton, Andrea .... (810) 766-6100
Television ED, Flint Journal, Flint, MI
Thornton, Gail .... (817) 562-2868
Bookkeeper, ADV MGR-CLASS
Mexia Daily News, Mexia, TX
Thornton, Gregory L .... (617) 929-2000
VP-Employee Relations
Boston Globe, Boston, MA
Thornton, James A .... (207) 784-5411
CONT, Sun-Journal, Lewiston, ME
Thornton, Jerry .... (205) 236-1551
PROD FRM-COMP
Anniston Star, Anniston, AL
Thornton, Joy .... (540) 980-5220
PROD SUPT-COMP
Southwest Times, Pulaski, VA
Thornton, Ken .... (205) 221-2840
PROD SUPT
Daily Mountain Eagle, Jasper, AL
Thornton, Penny .... (501) 623-7711
ADV MGR-RT
Sentinel-Record, Hot Springs, AR
Thornton, Thomas .... (816) 932-6600
VP
Universal Press Syndicate, Kansas City, MO
Thornton, Tim .... (540) 783-5121
ED
Smyth County News & Messenger, Marion, VA
Thornton, Tom .... (904) 359-4111
PA/DIR-SRV
Florida Times-Union, Jacksonville, FL
Thorntorn, Tami .... (602) 271-8000
Entertainment ED
Arizona Republic, Phoenix, AZ
Thorp, Susan Adler .... (901) 529-2211
Political COL
Commercial Appeal, Memphis, TN
Thorpe, Maureen .... (413) 788-1000
ADV MGR-CLASS
Union-News, Springfield, MA
Thorpe, Mike .... (541) 382-1811
ADV DIR-MKTG, Bulletin, Bend, OR
Thorsell, William .... (416) 585-5000
EIC, Globe and Mail (Canada's National Newspaper), Toronto, ON
Thorson, Alice .... (816) 234-4141
Arts ED, Kansas City Star, Kansas City, MO
Thorson, Jared .... (701) 780-1100
CIRC MGR-City Zone
Grand Forks Herald, Grand Forks, ND
Thorson, Todd .... (515) 733-4318
PUB, ED, Story City Herald, Story City, IA
Thorton, Lorrenda D .... (813) 689-7764
ED, Thunderbolt, Brandon, FL
Thouin, Francois .... (514) 985-3333
VP-BUS/FIN, Le Devoir, Montreal, QC
Thouvenel, David .... (503) 538-2181
PUB, ED, Newberg Graphic, Newberg, OR
Threde, Jill .... (510) 935-2525
ADV MGR-Major
Contra Costa Times, Walnut Creek, CA
Thren, Tom .... (608) 754-3311
PROD MGR-SYS
Janesville Gazette, Janesville, WI
Threshie Jr, R David .... (714) 553-9292
Sr VP-Orange County Newspapers
Freedom Communications Inc., Irvine, CA
Throne, Tom .... (913) 682-0305
PUB/GM
Leavenworth Times, Leavenworth, KS
Throop, Regina .... (409) 722-0479
ED, Mid County Chronicle, Nederland, TX
Thuermer Jr, Angus .... (307) 733-2047
ED, Jackson Hole News, Jackson, WY
Thul, Daryl .... (507) 665-3332
ED, News-Herald, Le Sueur, MN
Thunemann, Karl .... (206) 455-2222
BUS/FIN ED, Eastside Journal, Bellevue, WA
Thurber, Jon .... (213) 237-5000
News ED, Jazz ED
Los Angeles Times, Los Angeles, CA
Thurlow, George .... (805) 965-5205
PUB, Santa Barbara Independent, Santa Barbara, CA
Thurlow, Rich .... (702) 727-5102
PUB, ED
Pahrump Valley Times, Pahrump, NV
Thurm, David A .... (212) 556-1234
PROD VP, New York Times, New York, NY
Thurman, Chuck .... (408) 394-5656
MAN ED, Coast Weekly, Seaside, CA
Thurman, Jim .... (408) 920-5000
PROD MGR-Facilities
San Jose Mercury News, San Jose, CA
Thurman, Norma .... (515) 523-1010
MAN ED, Stuart Herald, Stuart, IA
Thurman, Susan .... (615) 388-6464
Photo DEPT MGR
Daily Herald, Columbia, TN
Thurmond, Chuck .... (423) 472-5041
Sports ED
Cleveland Daily Banner, Cleveland, TN
Thurmond, Clark .... (512) 930-4824
PUB, Sunday Sun, Georgetown, TX
Thurmond, Patricia .... (210) 232-5204
PUB, ED, Real American, Leakey, TX
Thwaite, Jay .... (419) 668-3771
MAN ED, Norwalk Reflector, Norwalk, OH
Thwaites, Bob .... (905) 358-5711
CIRC MGR
Niagara Falls Review, Niagara Falls, ON
Tiajcliff, Y L .... (201) 342-2985
EX ED
Newsportraits Syndicate, Hackensack, NJ
Tiano, Rev Christopher .... (860) 527-1175
ED, Catholic Transcript, Hartford, CT
Tibado, Maryl .... (941) 294-7731
BM, News Chief, Winter Haven, FL
Tibbels, Cathy .... (402) 339-3331
ED, Suburban Signal, Papillion, NE
Tibbets, Earl .... (512) 575-1451
PROD SUPV-MR
Victoria Advocate, Victoria, TX
Tibbetts, Donn .... (603) 668-4321
COL, Union Leader, Manchester, NH
Tibbits, Susan Dix .... (813) 286-1600
MAN ED, Weekly Planet, Tampa, FL
Tibbles, Isabelle .... (604) 485-5313
ED, Powell River Peak, Powell River, BC
Tice, Doug .... (612) 222-5011
EDL Writer
St. Paul Pioneer Press, St. Paul, MN
Tichenor, Esther .... (406) 622-3311
PUB, River Press, Fort Benton, MT
Tichenor, Stan .... (406) 622-3311
PUB, River Press, Fort Benton, MT
Tidrick, Dennis .... (203) 964-2200
PROD MGR-Pre Press, Stamford Advocate, Stamford, CT, Times Mirror Co.
Tidwell, David .... (501) 565-4601
ED, Baptist Trumpet, Little Rock, AR
Tidwell, Janet .... (414) 634-3322
MGR-Human Resources
Journal Times, Racine, WI
Tidwell, Jerry .... (817) 573-7066
PUB, Hood County News, Granbury, TX
Tidwell, Cpl Lisa .... (520) 783-3333
ED, Cactus Comet, Yuma, AZ
Tidwell, Wendell .... (912) 263-4615
PUB, ED, Quitman Free Press, Quitman, GA
Tidwell, William .... (912) 764-9031
PROD FRM-MR
Statesboro Herald, Statesboro, GA
Tiedemann, J B .... (515) 993-4233
PUB
Dallas County News & Roundup, Adel, IA
Tiedemann, Paul .... (505) 763-3431
PA, PROD SUPT
Clovis News Journal, Clovis, NM
Tiedemann, Wally .... (510) 734-8600
CIRC DIR, Tri-Valley Herald, Pleasanton, CA
MediaNews Inc. (Alameda Newspapers)
Tieman, Mike .... (409) 833-3311
ADV DIR
Beaumont Enterprise, Beaumont, TX
Tieman, Mike .... (210) 379-5402
CIRC DIR
Seguin Gazette-Enterprise, Seguin, TX
Tiernan, Tom .... (618) 684-5833
PUB, ED
Murphysboro American, Murphysboro, IL
Tierney, Catherine .... (330) 996-3000
Chief Librarian
Akron Beacon Journal, Akron, OH
Tierno, Anthony F .... (717) 854-1575
EVP/COO, York Dispatch/York Sunday News, York, PA, MediaNews Inc.
Tiffany, Jim .... (509) 663-5737
PUB, GM, ED, El Mundo, Wenatchee, WA
Tiffany, Lynn .... (619) 241-7744
MGR-PROM, Auto ED, Daily Press, Victorville, CA, Freedom Communications Inc.

Copyright ©1997 by the Editor & Publisher Co.

231-Who's Where **Ton**

Tiffin, Jim .... (520) 384-3571
MAN ED, Arizona Range News, Willcox, AZ
Tift, Mary E .... (616) 345-3511
EPE, EDL Writer
Kalamazoo Gazette, Kalamazoo, MI
Tigani, Christina .... (814) 837-6000
News Reporter, Kane Republican, Kane, PA
Tigelman, Robert J .... (330) 996-3000
VP-INFO Technology
Akron Beacon Journal, Akron, OH
Tigerman, Lawrence .... (816) 234-4141
MGR-CR, Kansas City Star, Kansas City, MO
Tigges, Daniel .... (712) 792-3573
CIRC MGR, Daily Times Herald, Caroll, IA
Tighe, Charlie .... (516) 843-2020
PROD GEN FRM-Daily Inserting
Newsday, Melville, NY
Tighe, Timothy .... (860) 225-4601
PROD SUPV-PR, Herald, New Britain, CT
Tigner, Jill .... (334) 298-0679
PUB, Phenix Citizen, Phenix City, AL
Tihey, Patti .... (215) 625-8501
ED, Philadelphia Gay News, Philadelphia, PA
Tijerina, Richard .... (210) 625-9144
Sports ED, New Braunfels Herald-Zeitung, New Braunfels, TX
Tilis, Jerome S .... (305) 376-3800
VP-MKTG, Knight-Ridder Inc., Miami, FL
Tiller, Jim .... (904) 252-1511
Photo DEPT MGR, Daytona Beach News-Journal, Daytona Beach, FL
Tiller, Martha .... (541) 382-1811
ADV MGR-Display, ADTX MGR
Bulletin, Bend, OR
Tilley, Jim .... (501) 448-3321
PUB, Marshall Mountain Wave, Marshall, AR
Tilley, Shannon .... (912) 888-9300
ADTX MGR, Albany Herald, Albany, GA
Tillis, Dale .... (813) 893-8111
PROD ENG-Staff
St. Petersburg Times, St. Petersburg, FL
Tillotson, Dolph .... (409) 744-3611
PUB, ED
Galveston County Daily News, Galveston, TX
Tillson, J Bradford .... (937) 225-2000
PUB, Dayton Daily News, Dayton, OH
Tilson, Bettina .... (540) 574-6200
BUS ED
Daily News-Record, Harrisonburg, VA
Tilson, Kerrene .... (705) 368-2744
GM, Manitoulin Expositor, Little Current, ON
Tilson, Ron .... (707) 644-1141
PROD FRM-PR
Vallejo Times-Herald, Vallejo, CA
Tilton, David V .... (941) 656-0225
Self-Syndicator/Owner/Writer
Tilton, David V., North Fort Myers, FL
Tim West .... (630) 355-0063
ED, Naperville Sun, Naperville, IL
Timbers, Howard .... (706) 724-0851
CIRC MGR-PROM
Augusta Chronicle, Augusta, GA
Timko, Steve .... (702) 788-6200
Courts ED, Reno Gazette-Journal, Reno, NV
Timm, Lori .... (309) 686-3000
Entertainment/Amusements ED
Journal Star, Peoria, IL
Timme, Greg .... (314) 340-8000
PROD ASST MGR-Purchased Supplements
St. Louis Post-Dispatch, St. Louis, MO
Timmerman, Gayle .... (503) 221-8327
ADV MGR-CLASS, Oregonian, Portland, OR
Timmermann, Jim .... (616) 392-2311
City ED, News ED
Holland Sentinel, Holland, MI
Timmons, Emily .... (904) 765-8982
GM
Northeast Florida Advocate, Jacksonville, FL
Timmons, Karen .... (202) 408-2721
ED, Scripps-McClatchy Western Services, Washington, DC
Timmons, Richard .... (715) 365-6397
PUB/ED, ADV MGR-NTL
Daily News, Rhinelander, WI
Timmons, Tim .... (812) 522-4871
PUB, Tribune, Seymour, IN
Tindal, Debbie .... (613) 544-5000
ADV SUPV-Special Sections
Kingston Whig-Standard, Kingston, ON
Tindel, Joe W .... (903) 876-2218
PUB, ED, Frankston Citizen, Frankston, TX
Tiner, Stan .... (334) 433-1551
ED/VP-News
Mobile Press Register, Mobile, AL
Tingle, Bobby .... (409) 632-6631
CIRC DIR, Lufkin Daily News, Lufkin, TX
Cox Newspapers Inc.
Tingley, Ken .... (518) 792-3131
Sports ED, Post-Star, Glens Falls, NY
Tingwall, John .... (313) 222-6400
ADV Sales DIR/ASST to VP
Detroit Newspapers, Detroit, MI
Tinkel, Janice .... (913) 628-1081
BM, Hays Daily News, Hays, KS
Tinkey, Duane .... (505) 393-2123
Photo DEPT MGR
Hobbs Daily News-Sun, Hobbs, NM
Tinkler, John .... (504) 383-1111
PROD SUPT-MR, Advocate, Baton Rouge, LA
Tinnen, J W .... (816) 539-2111
PUB, ED
Clinton County Leader, Plattsburg, MO
Tino, Martin .... (418) 962-9441
PUB, ED
Nordest/Nordest Plus, Sept-Isles, QC
Tinsley, Anita .... (318) 433-3000
MGR-CR, Lake Charles American Press, Lake Charles, LA
Tinsley, Jack B .... (817) 390-7400
VP/EDL Chairman
Fort Worth Star-Telegram, Fort Worth, TX
Tinsley, William J .... (502) 678-5171
PUB, PA, Glasgow Daily Times, Glasgow, KY
Tippet, Ron .... (518) 234-4368
CIRC MGR, Daily Editor, Cobleskill, NY
Tippett, Janet A .... (717) 286-5671
GM, Weekender, Sunbury, PA
Tippett, Janet Mittelstadt .... (717) 286-5671
GM, Daily Item, Sunbury, PA
Tippett, Rick .... (202) 334-6000
ADV DIR-NTL
Washington Post, Washington, DC
Tippie, Steve .... (800) 245-6536
DIR-MKTG
Tribune Media Services Inc., Chicago, IL
Tippin, Steve .... (541) 885-4410
CIRC MGR
Herald and News, Klamath Falls, OR
Tipton, Fred .... (423) 981-1100
PROD MGR, Daily Times, Maryville, TN
Tipton, Virgil .... (314) 340-8000
Online MGR, Post-Dispatch, St. Louis, MO
Tirschwell, Peter .... (212) 837-7000
ED-West Coast, BU Chief-San Francisco
Journal of Commerce & Commercial, NY, NY
Tisdale, Charles W .... (601) 948-4122
PUB, ED, Jackson Advocate, Jackson, MS
Tisue, Kaarin .... (312) 321-3000
WeekendPlus ED
Chicago Sun-Times, Chicago, IL
Titcombe, David .... (416) 442-3444
Sales DIR, Southam TV Times, Don Mills, ON
Titone, Robert .... (217) 788-1300
CIRC MGR
State Journal-Register, Springfield, IL
Tittle, Mel .... (806) 762-8844
ASST MAN ED-News
Lubbock Avalanche-Journal, Lubbock, TX
Tittley, Alain .... (514) 276-9615
PUB, ED
L'Express d'Outremont, Montreal, QC
Titus, Cathleen .... (212) 455-4000
DIR-International Licensing
North America Syndicate, King Features Syndicate Inc., New York, NY
Toal, Margaret .... (409) 883-3571
ED, Opportunity Valley News, Orange, TX
Toale, Owen P .... (716) 798-1400
PUB, GM, Journal-Register, Medina, NY
Tobar, Alfonso .... (416) 441-1405
South America Photographer
Fotopress Independent News Service International (FPINS), Toronto, ON
Tobek, Wayne .... (217) 446-1000
MGR-CR, Commercial News, Danville, IL
Tobener, Mike .... (707) 546-2020
PROD DIR-OPER
Press Democrat, Santa Rosa, CA
Tobey, Charles .... (518) 843-1100
CONT, Recorder, Amsterdam, NY
Tobias, Anita .... (310) 337-7003
EVP, Creators Syndicate, Los Angeles, CA
Tobias, Jack .... (610) 820-6500
Easton ED, Morning Call, Allentown, PA
Tobias, Manuel .... (209) 943-5143
ED, La Nacion, Stockton, CA
Tobias, Suzanne Perez .... (316) 268-6000
Learning ED, Wichita Eagle, Wichita, KS
Tobiason, Carol .... (317) 348-0110
CEO, News-Times, Hartford City, IN
Tobin, Donna .... (505) 325-4545
PROD SUPT-PR
Daily Times, Farmington, NM
Tobin, James .... (313) 222-2300
Medical ED, Detroit News, Detroit, MI
Tobin, Joanna .... (818) 706-0266
ED, Acorn, Agoura Hills, CA
Tobin, Jonathan S .... (860) 231-2424
ED, Connecticut Jewish Ledger, West Hartford, CT
Tobin, Kathleen A .... (715) 453-2151
PUB, ED, Tomahawk Leader, Tomahawk, WI
Tobin, Larry M .... (715) 453-2151
PUB, Tomahawk Leader, Tomahawk, WI
Tocco, Paul .... (810) 751-2855
ED, Italian American, Warren, MI
Tock, Greg .... (520) 537-5721
PUB
White Mountain Independent, Show Low, AZ
Todaro, Tim .... (904) 359-4111
MGR-CR
Florida Times-Union, Jacksonville, FL
Todd, Anita .... (417) 276-4211
ED, Cedar County Republican/Stockton Journal, Stockton, MO
Todd, Chris .... (601) 961-7000
DIR-Photography
Clarion-Ledger, Jackson, MS
Todd, Chris .... (218) 285-7411
Sports ED
Daily Journal, International Falls, MN
Todd, Doug .... (416) 227-1141
ED, Thorold News, Thorold, ON
Todd, Ed .... (915) 682-5311
Farm/Agriculture ED, Health/Medical ED
Midland Reporter-Telegram, Midland, TX
Todd, Jack .... (514) 987-2222
COL, Gazette, Montreal, QC
Todd, Jeanette .... (209) 992-3115
ED, Corcoran Journal, Corcoran, CA
Todd, Kenneth R .... (317) 633-1240
DIR-Safety
Indianapolis Star/News, Indianapolis, IN
Todd, Lori .... (210) 761-9341
ED, Coastal Current, South Padre Island, TX
Todd, Lynda .... (705) 932-3001
PUB, ED, Millbrook Times, Millbrook, ON
Todd, Marion .... (215) 854-2000
PROD ASST DIR-Packaging & Distribution
Philadelphia Inquirer, Philadelphia, PA
Knight-Ridder Inc.
Todd, Mark .... (919) 362-8356
ED, Apex Herald, Apex, NC
Todd, Michael .... (805) 925-2691
BUS ED, City ED, News ED
Santa Maria Times, Santa Maria, CA
Todd, Randa .... (702) 383-0211
ADV MGR-CLASS
Las Vegas Review-Journal, Las Vegas, NV
Todd, Richard .... (815) 433-2000
PROD FRM-Press, Daily Times, Ottawa, IL
Todd, Robert .... (806) 376-4488
PROD DIR, Amarillo Daily News/Globe Times, Amarillo, TX
Todd, Steve .... (908) 922-6000
CIRC MGR-Home Delivery
Asbury Park Press, Neptune, NJ
Todd, Wendy .... (309) 734-3176
ADV MGR, Daily Review Atlas, Monmouth, IL
Todd, William J .... (708) 336-7000
PUB, News-Sun, Waukegan, IL
Toedtman, Jim .... (516) 843-2020
Washington BU Chief
Newsday, Melville, NY
Toenniessen, Joan Connor ...... (610) 446-8700
MAN ED
News of Delaware County, Havertown, PA
Tofani, A Philip .... (619) 451-6200
GM, Brehm Communication, San Diego, CA
Tokarz, Wally .... (312) 782-8100
Overnight ED
City News Bureau of Chicago, Chicago, IL
Tokiwa, Noriko .... (416) 593-1583
MAN ED, New Canadian, Toronto, ON
Tolan, Mary .... (520) 774-4545
EDU ED, Arizona Daily Sun, Flagstaff, AZ
Tolan, Susan E .... (515) 432-1234
ADV MGR
Boone News-Republican, Boone, IA
Tolarchynk, John .... (515) 573-2141
Online Contact, Messenger, Fort Dodge, IA
Tolbert, Art .... (609) 989-0285
GM, Nubian News, Trenton, NJ
Tolbert, Edwin .... (616) 222-5400
CIRC MGR-City
Grand Rapids Press, Grand Rapids, MI
Tolbert, James .... (313) 994-6989
MGR-Telecommunications
Ann Arbor News, Ann Arbor, MI
Toler, John T .... (540) 347-4222
GM
Fauquier Times-Democrat, Warrenton, VA
Toler Jr, James E .... (800) 424-4747
Regional Accounts MGR, Tribune Media Services-Television Listings, Glens Falls, NY
Toles, Thomas .... (706) 291-6397
ED, Rome News-Tribune, Rome, GA
Toles, Tom .... (716) 849-3434
Cartoonist, Buffalo News, Buffalo, NY
Toliver, Patricia .... (510) 935-2525
ADV MGR-CLASS
Contra Costa Times, Walnut Creek, CA
Tollefson, Roger .... (308) 632-0670
CIRC DIR, PROD DIR
Star-Herald, Scottsbluff, NE
Tollefson, Roger S .... (507) 283-2333
PUB, Rock County Star Herald, Luverne, MN
Tollett, Brenda .... (405) 332-4433
Fashion/Style ED, Living/Lifestyle ED, Travel ED, Ada Evening News, Ada, OK
Tolley, Grant .... (501) 785-7700
Sports ED
Southwest Times Record, Fort Smith, AR
Tolley, Laura .... (210) 225-7411
Austin BU Chief
San Antonio Express-News, San Antonio, TX
Tolson, Dorma .... (330) 424-9541
ED, Morning Journal, Lisbon, OH
Tolson, Kyn .... (860) 442-2200
ASST MAN ED-Reporting/Sunday, Features ED, Leisure ED, Living/Lifestyle ED, Religion ED, Day, New London, CT
Tolson, Terry L .... (412) 775-3200
ADV DIR, Beaver County Times, Beaver, PA
Tom, Christina .... (415) 457-7141
MAN ED
Style International, San Francisco, CA
Tom, Michael .... (509) 843-1313
PUB, ED, East Washingtonian, Pomeroy, WA
Tom, Teresa M .... (509) 843-1313
PUB, East Washingtonian, Pomeroy, WA
Tomaro, David .... (765) 362-1200
City/MET ED, Features ED, Graphics ED, News ED, Journal Review, Crawfordsville, IN
Tomaselli, Jeannie .... (908) 899-1000
ED, Leader, Pt. Pleasant Beach, NJ
Tomaselli, Ralph .... (203) 235-1661
GEN Assignment MGR
Record-Journal, Meriden, CT
Tomasello, Mary .... (847) 427-4300
Librarian, Daily Herald, Arlington Heights, IL
Tomasi, Tom .... (904) 599-2100
ADV MGR-MKTG
Tallahassee Democrat, Tallahassee, FL
Tomasik, Mark .... (513) 352-2000
Sports ED, Cincinnati Post, Cincinnati, OH
Scripps Howard
Tomaszewski, Mark .... (714) 835-1234
Sports ED
Orange County Register, Santa Ana, CA
Tomaszewski, Richard .... (618) 327-3411
PUB, ED, Nashville News, Nashville, IL
Tomb, Steve .... (212) 416-2000
PROD Senior MGR (South Brunswick NJ)
Wall Street Journal, New York, NY
Tombarge, Chuck .... (507) 433-8851
BUS/FIN ED
Austin Daily Herald, Austin, MN
Tomczyk, Mary .... (810) 227-7866
Author, Learning and Loving It, Brighton, MI
Tomino, Steve .... (808) 525-8000
CIRC MGR-Suburban Home Delivery
Hawaii Newspaper Agency Inc., Honolulu, HI
Tomion, Mary Geo .... (607) 243-7600
PUB, ED, Dundee Observer, Dundee, NY
Tomlin, Jimmy .... (910) 888-3500
COL, High Point Enterprise, High Point, NC
Tomlinson, Bruce .... (217) 223-5100
RES MGR, Quincy Herald-Whig, Quincy, IL
Tomlinson, Christopher .... (970) 242-5050
Photo ED, Grand Junction Daily Sentinel, Grand Junction, CO
Tomlinson, Harley .... (219) 866-5111
Sports ED
Rensselaer Republican, Rensselaer, IN
Tomlinson, Jean .... (713) 220-7171
ADV MGR-Sales
Houston Chronicle, Houston, TX
Tomolonis, Andrew .... (617) 426-3000
Deputy MAN ED-News
Boston Herald, Boston, MA
Tompkin, Elliot .... (317) 622-1212
ED, Herald Bulletin, Anderson, IN
Tompkins, John C .... (815) 562-2061
PRES, News Media Corp., Rochelle, IL
Tompkins, Michael .... (815) 562-2061
VP, News Media Corp., Rochelle, IL
Tompkins Jr, William .... (202) 334-6000
VP-MKTG/ADM
Washington Post, Washington, DC
Tompt, Brenda .... (701) 845-0463
CIRC MGR
Valley City Times-Record, Valley City, ND
Toms, James A .... (614) 785-1212
PUB, New Albany News, Columbus, OH
Tonder, Johan Van .... (416) 441-1405
Africa Journalist, Fotopress Independent News Service International, Toronto, ON
Tonello, John .... (607) 734-5151
Online Services MGR
Star-Gazette, Elmira, NY
Toner, Ann .... (402) 444-1000
Farm Writer, World-Herald, Omaha, NE
Toner, Frank .... (516) 843-2020
VP-INFO SYS & Engineering Services
Newsday, Melville, NY
Toner, Jim .... (407) 420-5000
Deputy MAN ED-Local/State
Orlando Sentinel, Orlando, FL
Toney, Carlene .... (409) 793-6560
PUB, Gulf Coast Tribune, Needville, TX

Copyright ©1997 by the Editor & Publisher Co.

Ton Who's Where-232

Toney, David E .... (409) 345-3127
PUB, ED
Brazoria County News, West Columbia, TX

Toney, Doug .... (210) 625-9144
PUB/ED, New Braunfels Herald-Zeitung, New Braunfels, TX

Toney III, Julian .... (601) 247-3373
GM, Belzoni Banner, Belzoni, MS

Toney, Mary W .... (601) 247-3373
PUB, ED, Belzoni Banner, Belzoni, MS

Toney, Michele .... (614) 461-5000
Entertainment ED
Columbus Dispatch, Columbus, OH

Tong, Hoang .... (714) 892-9414
GM, Nguoi Viet Daily News, Westminster, CA

Tong, Jance .... (208) 983-1070
ED, Idaho County Free Press, Grangeville, ID

Tonkyn, Laura .... (605) 394-8300
Special Sections ED
Rapid City Journal, Rapid City, SD

Tonner, Erica .... (404) 466-2222
GM, Block Island Times, Block Island, RI

Tonos, Mike .... (601) 896-2100
EX ED, Sun Herald, Biloxi, MS

Tonsing, Julie .... (970) 522-1990
BM, Journal-Advocate, Sterling, CO

Tooker, Eric S .... (317) 231-9200
SEC, Central Newspapers, Indianapolis, IN

Tookey, Michael A .... (317) 633-1240
ADV MGR-RT
Indianapolis Star/News, Indianapolis, IN

Toole, Betty Jo .... (912) 758-5549
GM, Miller County Liberal, Colquitt, GA

Toole, Mike .... (757) 247-4600
Automotive ED, BUS ED, Farm/Agriculture ED, Daily Press, Newport News, VA

Toole, Scott .... (610) 258-7171
Copy Desk Chief, NTL ED, News ED
Express-Times, Easton, PA

Toole, Terry .... (912) 758-5549
PUB, ED, Miller County Liberal, Colquitt, GA

Tooley, Bob .... (505) 894-2143
PUB, Herald, Truth or Consequences, NM

Tooley, Brad .... (806) 655-7121
PUB, Canyon News, Canyon, TX

Tooley, Hugh .... (317) 342-3311
ASST Sports ED
Daily Reporter, Martinsville, IN

Tooley, Mike .... (505) 894-2143
PUB, Herald, Truth or Consequences, NM

Tooley, Shawn .... (910) 323-4848
Online ED, Observer-Times, Fayetteville, NC

Toops, Darlene M .... (602) 842-6000
PUB, Glendale Star, Glendale, AZ

Toops, William E .... (602) 842-6000
GM, Tallyho, Glendale, AZ

Toops, William V .... (602) 842-6000
PUB, Glendale Star, Glendale, AZ

Toothaker, Keith .... (207) 791-6650
PROD OPER SUPV-PR/Platemaking
Portland Press Herald, Portland, ME

Tope, Lindsey .... (614) 363-1161
DP MGR, Delaware Gazette, Delaware, OH

Topham, Renee .... (204) 774-1883
PUB, Kanada Kurier, Winnipeg, MB

Topp, Angie .... (419) 586-2371
BM, Daily Standard, Celina, OH

Topp, Walter .... (216) 329-7000
Environmental ED
Chronicle-Telegram, Elyria, OH

Toppel, Ann .... (409) 756-6671
BM, DP MGR, Conroe Courier, Conroe, TX

Topping, Julie .... (313) 222-6400
Reader Representative
Detroit Free Press, Detroit, MI

Toppins, John .... (614) 353-3101
CIRC MGR
Portsmouth Daily Times, Portsmouth, OH

Toppman, Larry .... (704) 358-5000
Films ED, Charlotte Observer, Charlotte, NC

Torbett, Alice J .... (423) 929-3111
VP
Carl A Jones Newspapers, Johnson City, TN

Torey, Jack .... (412) 263-1100
Washington BU
Pittsburgh Post-Gazette, Pittsburgh, PA

Torgerson, Lois .... (320) 325-5152
ED, Northern Star, Ortonville, MN

Torgerson, Stan .... (601) 693-1551
BUS/FIN ED, Meridian Star, Meridian, MS

Torgulson, Leann .... (604) 566-4425
ED, Valley Sentinel, Valemount, BC

Toriski, John .... (814) 827-3634
PROD MGR, Titusville Herald, Titusville, PA

Torizuka, Sakura .... (416) 593-1583
ED, New Canadian, Toronto, ON

Torkelson, Jean .... (303) 892-5000
Religion Writer
Rocky Mountain News, Denver, CO

Tormeno, Mark .... (937) 225-2000
CIRC MGR, Dayton Daily News, Dayton, OH

Tormey, Norma .... (212) 755-4363
Contributing Writer, Punch In Travel & Entertainment News Syndicate, NY, NY

Tornielli, Charles P .... (610) 371-5000
CIRC SUPV-MR, Times/Eagle, Reading, PA

Toro, Manuel A .... (407) 767-0070
PUB, GM, La Prensa, Longwood, FL

Torpey, Mark .... (617) 426-3000
Sports ED, Boston Herald, Boston, MA

Torpey, William F .... (203) 846-3281
Entertainment/Amusements ED, NTL/State ED, Hour, Norwalk, CT

Torraca, Elizabeth .... (207) 791-6650
PROD OPER SUPV-ADV Graphics
Portland Press Herald, Portland, ME

Torralva, Maria Elena .... (212) 649-2000
DIR of Profession Development & Diversity
Hearst Newspapers, New York, NY

Torrance, Kim .... (403) 468-0100
CIRC MGR-PROM
Edmonton Sun, Edmonton, AB

Torreano, Tony .... (616) 222-5400
MGR-INFO SYS
Grand Rapids Press, Grand Rapids, MI

Torres, Anibal .... (407) 420-5000
ADV MGR (Regional Division)
Orlando Sentinel, Orlando, FL

Torres, Consuelo .... (972) 446-4346
GM, El Heraldo News, Carrollton, TX

Torres, Craig .... (212) 416-2000
Reporter-in-Charge (Mexico)
Wall Street Journal, New York, NY

Torres, Dezi .... (806) 659-3434
PUB, ED, Hansford County Reporter-Statesman, Spearman, TX

Torres, Dorothy .... (203) 235-1661
ASST MAN ED-Design/Graphics
Record-Journal, Meriden, CT

Torres, Eddie .... (317) 664-5111
PROD MGR-Pre Press
Chronicle-Tribune, Marion, IN

Torres, Eliseo .... (806) 762-8844
CIRC MGR-City
Lubbock Avalanche-Journal, Lubbock, TX

Torres Jr, Jose .... (972) 446-4346
PUB, El Heraldo News, Carrollton, TX

Torres, Laydra .... (210) 383-2705
ADV MGR-CLASS
Edinburg Daily Review, Edinburg, TX

Torres, Vicki .... (213) 237-5000
Small BUS
Los Angeles Times, Los Angeles, CA

Torrey, Allen .... (919) 829-4500
EDL Writer, News & Observer, Raleigh, NC

Torrez Jr, Antonio .... (210) 727-8507
MAN ED, El Clamor, Laredo, TX

Tortora, Dean M .... (508) 586-7200
CIRC DIR, Enterprise, Brockton, MA

Tortorano, David .... (334) 433-1551
BUS/FIN ED
Mobile Press Register, Mobile, AL

Toscano, Linda Laursen .... (516) 378-5320
PUB, Merrick Life, Merrick, NY

Tosches, Nicholas J .... (508) 473-1111
ED, SCI ED, Milford Daily News, Milford, MA

Tosches, Peter J .... (508) 473-1111
BUS ED, Wire ED
Milford Daily News, Milford, MA

Tosonotti, William .... (718) 981-1234
MGR-CR
Staten Island Advance, Staten Island, NY

Toth, John .... (415) 726-4424
PUB, ED
Half Moon Bay Review, Half Moon Bay, CA

Toth, John .... (409) 849-5407
PUB, GM, ED
Bulletin of Brazoria County, Angleton, TX

Toth, Sharon .... (409) 849-5407
PUB, MAN ED
Bulletin of Brazoria County, Angleton, TX

Toth, Terri .... (304) 526-4000
CIRC MGR-Customer SRV
Herald-Dispatch, Huntington, WV

Totoraitis, John .... (313) 222-6400
VP-INFO SYS
Detroit Newspapers, Detroit, MI

Totten, Shay .... (802) 985-2400
ED, Vermont Times, Shelburne, VT

Touchberry, Bobby .... (803) 775-6331
ADV MGR-CLASS, Item, Sumter, SC

Touchet, Judith .... (318) 828-3706
DP MGR
Franklin Banner-Tribune, Franklin, LA

Touchstone, Gayle .... (706) 291-6397
ADV DIR, Rome News-Tribune, Rome, GA

Touchstone, Tonya .... (806) 762-8844
CIRC MGR-ADM
Lubbock Avalanche-Journal, Lubbock, TX

Tougas, Maurice .... (403) 483-6000
ED, Edmonton Examiner, Edmonton, AB

Touney, Jan .... (217) 429-5151
City ED, Herald & Review, Decatur, IL

Toups, Vivian .... (607) 798-1234
ADV MGR-Display
Press & Sun Bulletin, Binghamton, NY

Tousignant, Jacques .... (514) 285-7272
VP-PSL/Labor Relations
La Presse, Montreal, QC

Touzalin, Jane .... (703) 560-4000
Sr ED, Journal Newspapers Inc., Fairfax, VA

Toward, Trisha .... (419) 522-3311
ADV CNR-NTL, News Journal, Mansfield, OH

Towata, Lillian .... (808) 329-9311
Club News ED
West Hawaii Today, Kailua-Kona, HI

Towery, Mike .... (864) 582-4511
PROD MGR-PR
Herald-Journal, Spartanburg, SC

Towler, Mary Anna .... (716) 244-3329
PUB, ED, City Newspaper, Rochester, NY

Towler, Rita .... (706) 324-5526
CFO, Ledger-Enquirer, Columbus, GA

Towler, William .... (716) 244-3329
PUB, City Newspaper, Rochester, NY

Town, Lynn .... (602) 271-8000
MGR-MKTG Services
Phoenix Newspapers Inc., Phoenix, AZ

Towne, Jon .... (508) 485-7830
ED, Marlboro Enterprise, Marlboro, MA

Towner, James E .... (717) 265-2151
VP, PUB, PA, Daily Review, Towanda, PA

Townsend, Brian .... (909) 889-0597
PUB, ED
Precinct Reporter, San Bernardino, CA

Townsend, Dara L .... (815) 453-2551
ED, Ashton Gazette, Ashton, IL

Townsend, David W .... (815) 453-2551
PUB, Ashton Gazette, Ashton, IL

Townsend, Denny .... (800) 355-9500
ED DIR, News USA Inc., Vienna, VA

Townsend, Eugene M .... (207) 255-6561
ED
Machias Valley News Observer, Machias, ME

Townsend, Georgie .... (915) 673-4271
ADV MGR-RT Sales
Abilene Reporter-News, Abilene, TX

Townsend III, H Guy .... (816) 454-9660
PUB, Dispatch-Tribune/Press Dispatch, Kansas City, MO

Townsend, Margaret .... (561) 461-2050
PROD FRM-MR, Tribune, Fort Pierce, FL

Townsend, Mike .... (415) 883-8600
ED
Marin Independent Journal, Novato, CA

Townshend, Cathy .... (613) 829-9100
ADV MGR-Inside Sales
Ottawa Citizen, Ottawa, ON

Toy, Bruce .... (919) 829-4500
PROD MGR-Printed Quality
News & Observer, Raleigh, NC

Tozner, Tom .... (704) 358-5000
Deputy MAN ED-Presentation & Change
Charlotte Observer, Charlotte, NC

Tracewski, Rick .... (603) 224-5301
News ED, Concord Monitor, Concord, NH

Tracey, Gerald J .... (613) 628-2332
PUB, ED, Eganville Leader, Eganville, ON

Tracey, Ron R .... (613) 628-2332
PUB, Eganville Leader, Eganville, ON

Trachtman, Joe .... (215) 563-7400
PUB, Philadelphia Weekly, Philadelphia, PA

Tracy, Belinda .... (512) 528-2515
ED, Taft Tribune, Taft, TX

Tracy, Byron .... (618) 544-2101
MAN ED, Picture ED
Robinson Daily News, Robinson, IL

Tracy, Dick .... (916) 321-1000
Garden ED
Sacramento Bee, Sacramento, CA

Tracy, Doug .... (214) 977-8222
MGR-Communications
Dallas Morning News, Dallas, TX

Tracy, Dwight .... (541) 885-4410
PRES, PUB/ED
Herald and News, Klamath Falls, OR

Tracy, Elizabeth .... (304) 847-5828
MAN ED
Webster Echo, Webster Springs, WV

Tracy, James .... (903) 893-8181
ADV MGR-RT
Herald Democrat, Sherman, TX

Tracy Jr, James F .... (512) 643-1566
Co-PUB, Portland News, Portland, TX

Tracy, Jim .... (406) 859-3223
PUB, ED, Philipsburg Mail, Philipsburg, MT

Tracy, John H .... (512) 643-1566
Co-PUB, Portland News, Portland, TX

Tracy, Lee .... (406) 859-3223
PUB, GM, Philipsburg Mail, Philipsburg, MT

Tracy, Lisa .... (215) 854-2000
RE Writer
Philadelphia Inquirer, Philadelphia, PA

Tracy, Pat .... (604) 525-6306
ED
Royal City Record/Now, New Westminster, BC

Traczyk-Thomas, Terri .... (609) 272-7000
MGR-Public Relations
Press of Atlantic City, Pleasantville, NJ

Traeger, Tim .... (916) 541-3880
ASST MAN ED
Tahoe Daily Tribune, South Lake Tahoe, CA

Trafford, Abigail .... (202) 334-6000
Health ED
Washington Post, Washington, DC

Trafford, Dan .... (401) 821-7400
Deputy MAN ED
Kent County Daily Times, West Warwick, RI

Trager, Jane .... (216) 329-7000
BUS/FIN ED, Chronicle-Telegram, Elyria, OH

Trahan, Brian .... (318) 824-3011
Sports ED, Daily News, Jennings, LA

Trahan, Lucien G .... (603) 668-4321
CIRC MGR, Union Leader, Manchester, NH

Trahan, Randy .... (504) 826-3279
ADV ASST DIR
Times-Picayune, New Orleans, LA

Trahan II, Roy S .... (616) 627-7144
PUB, ADV MGR
Cheboygan Daily Tribune, Cheboygan, MI

Trahan, Sherman .... (318) 289-6300
PROD SUPT, Advertiser, Lafayette, LA

Trahant, Mark N .... (208) 882-5561
PUB, ED, EPE, Online Contact
Moscow-Pullman Daily News, Moscow, ID

Trail, Maurice G .... (304) 348-5140
PROD MGR-Ad SRV
Charleston Newspapers, Charleston, WV

Trail, Sandra A .... (913) 346-5424
ED, Osborne County Farmer, Osborne, KS

Trainer, Frank .... (919) 829-4500
PROD CNR-Material Safety
News & Observer, Raleigh, NC

Trainer-Stutts, Donna .... (305) 377-3721
PUB, Daily Business Review, Miami, FL

Trainor, Ed .... (501) 338-9181
PUB, Daily World, Helena, AR

Trainor, Jack .... (419) 547-9194
GM, Clyde Enterprise, Clyde, OH

Trainor, Michael .... (209) 578-2000
CIRC DIR, Modesto Bee, Modesto, CA

Trakas, Tom .... (219) 881-3000
PROD MGR-MR, Post-Tribune, Gary, IN

Trambley, Jerry .... (814) 870-1600
Automotive ED, Religion ED, SCI/Technology ED, Morning News/Erie Daily Times, Erie, PA

Trammell, Vance .... (405) 233-6600
PROD SUPT-PR
Enid News & Eagle, Enid, OK

Trammer, Monte I .... (518) 584-4242
PUB, Saratogian, Saratoga Springs, NY

Tramo, Charles .... (215) 854-2000
VP-Single Copy Sales
Philadelphia Inquirer, Philadelphia, PA

Tran, Nam .... (909) 889-9666
CIRC MGR-Division
Sun, San Bernardino, CA

Transmondi, Lori .... (609) 663-6000
DIR-Human Resources
Courier-Post, Cherry Hill, NJ

Tranter, John David .... (219) 723-4771
PUB, Tribune-News, South Whitley, IN

Tranter, Linda .... (219) 723-4771
ED, Tribune-News, South Whitley, IN

Tranum, Brian .... (601) 323-1642
ADV MGR
Starkville Daily News, Starkville, MS

Trapnell, Tom .... (213) 237-5000
EDL Design DIR
Los Angeles Times, Los Angeles, CA

Trapp, Robert B .... (505) 753-2126
MAN ED, Rio Grande Sun, Espanola, NM

Trapp, Robert E .... (505) 753-2126
PUB, Rio Grande Sun, Espanola, NM

Trapp, Stella A .... (704) 883-8156
PUB, GM, ED
Transylvania Times, Brevard, NC

Trappe, Kathy .... (602) 898-6500
PROD MGR-Distribution/Packaging, Mesa Tribune, Mesa, AZ, Thomson Newspapers

Trappe, Renee C .... (847) 427-4300
City ED, Daily Herald, Arlington Heights, IL

Trask-Elliott, Catherine .... (705) 745-4641
CONT, Examiner, Peterborough, ON

Trastan, Margee .... (506) 653-6806
GM, New Freeman Catholic, Saint John, NB

Traughber, Clarence .... (806) 868-2521
PUB, Miami Chief, Miami, TX

Traughber, Valda .... (806) 868-2521
PUB, ED, Miami Chief, Miami, TX

Trauner, Scott .... (219) 356-1107
PUB, MAN ED
Huntington County TAB, Huntington, IN

Trauth, Thomas .... (412) 834-1151
PROD MGR, Tribune-Review, Greensburg, PA

Trautman, Donald W .... (814) 824-1160
PUB, Lake Shore Visitor, Erie, PA

Trautman, Linda .... (330) 296-9657
PROD FRM-COMP
Record-Courier, Kent-Ravenna, OH

233-Who's Where **Tuc**

Trautner, Laurie .... (319) 754-8461
ADV MGR-CLASS, ADV MGR-PROM
Hawk Eye, Burlington, IA
Trautwein, Sue .... (502) 926-0123
DIR-Human Resources
Messenger-Inquirer, Owensboro, KY
Travelstead, Coleman .... (305) 442-2462
ASSOC PUB, Vista - The Hispanic Magazine, Coral Gables, FL
Traven, Tony .... (915) 337-4661
CIRC DIR, Odessa American, Odessa, TX
Travin, Michael .... (212) 679-1850
PUB, Upper West Side Resident, New York City, NY
Travis, Greg .... (502) 527-3162
ED, Tribune-Courier, Benton, KY
Travis, Herb .... (504) 732-2565
PROD FRM-PR, Daily News, Bogalusa, LA
Travis, James I .... (913) 457-3411
ED
Westmoreland Recorder, Westmoreland, KS
Travis, Mark .... (603) 224-5301
MAN ED, Online MGR
Concord Monitor, Concord, NH
Travis, Patricia G .... (307) 362-3736
BM/CR MGR
Daily Rocket-Miner, Rock Springs, WY
Travis, Patrick C .... (406) 468-9231
PUB, ED, Cascade Courier, Cascade, MT
Travis, Rick .... (609) 522-3423
PUB, Cape May County Gazette Leader, Wildwood, NJ
Travis, Tom .... (612) 222-5011
PROD DIR, Pioneer Press, St. Paul, MN
Travnicek, Jan J .... (416) 439-9117
GM, Novy Domov, Scarborough, ON
Traxler, Buck .... (406) 278-5561
ED, Independent Observer, Conrad, MT
Traynham, Gary .... (916) 662-5421
Sports ED, Daily Democrat, Woodland, CA
Traynor, Michael .... (912) 236-9511
PROD DIR
Savannah Morning News, Savannah, GA
Treadway, Chris .... (510) 339-8777
ED, Montclarion, Oakland, CA
Treat, Karen .... (405) 223-2200
EDU ED, Daily Ardmoreite, Ardmore, OK
Treat, Shon .... (918) 225-3333
PROD MGR, Daily Citizen, Cushing, OK
Trebilcock, Leanne C .... (906) 341-5200
PUB, ED, Pioneer-Tribune, Manistique, MI
Trebish, Loren .... (406) 523-5200
Online MGR, Missoulian, Missoula, MT
Tredway, Joyce .... (618) 943-2331 ext. 100
CIRC MGR, Daily Record, Lawrenceville, IL
Treeten, Jim .... (612) 673-4000
PROD MGR-Machine Shop
Star Tribune, Minneapolis, MN
Tregaskis, Brian .... (801) 373-5050
PROD FRM-COMP, Daily Herald, Provo, UT
Trei, Faye .... (712) 475-3351
PUB, MAN ED
Lyon County News, George, IA
Treinen, Mark .... (715) 842-2101
EDU ED, Entertainment/Amusements ED, Travel ED, Wausau Daily Herald, Wausau, WI
Treloar, Sharon .... (319) 476-3550
ED, Dysart Reporter, Dysart, IA
Tremblay, Brian .... (519) 354-2000
PROD FRM-PR
Chatham Daily News, Chatham, ON
Tremblay, Claude .... (613) 562-0111
ADV DIR, DIR-Sales/PROM, MKTG DIR
Le Droit, Ottawa, ON
Tremblay, Denis .... (416) 364-0321
VP-French Services, Canadian Press & Broadcast News, Toronto, ON
Tremblay, Guy .... (418) 748-6406
PUB, La Sentinelle de Chibougamau-chapais, Chibougamau, QC
Tremblay, Jean .... (418) 545-4474
ADV MGR (Progres-Dimanche), MGR-MKTG/PROM, Le Quotidien, Chicoutimi, QC
Tremblay, Jean-Pierre .... (514) 987-2222
DIR-Human Resources
Gazette, Montreal, QC
Tremblay, Mark .... (403) 235-7100
Sports ED, Calgary Herald, Calgary, AB
Tremblay, Roger .... (207) 942-2913
GM, Weekly, Bangor, ME
Trenado, Cilla .... (318) 459-3200
DP MGR, Times, Shreveport, LA
Trenholn, Ed .... (423) 428-0746
CIRC MGR, Mountain Press, Sevierville, TN
Trensdell, Deb .... (509) 248-1251
MGR-MKTG/PROM
Yakima Herald-Republic, Yakima, WA
Trent, Chuck .... (618) 542-2133
ED, Ashley News, Du Quion, IL
Trepanier, Francois .... (514) 285-7272
Desk ED (Day), La Presse, Montreal, QC
Tresnei, Les .... (316) 225-4151
CIRC MGR
Dodge City Daily Globe, Dodge City, KS

Tretter, Kathy .... (812) 367-2041
PUB, Ferdinand News, Ferdinand, IN
Tretter, Richard .... (812) 367-2041
PUB, ED, Ferdinand News, Ferdinand, IN
Trettin, Mary .... (715) 672-4252
ED, Courier-Wedge, Durand, WI
Trever, John .... (505) 823-7777
EDL Cartoonist
Albuquerque Journal, Albuquerque, NM
Trewin, A David .... (313) 242-1100
ADV DIR, Monroe Evening News, Monroe, MI
Trexler, Frank .... (423) 981-1100
MAN ED, Daily Times, Maryville, TN
Tribble, Bob .... (912) 934-6303
PUB, Cochran Journal, Cochran, GA
Tribble, John .... (202) 636-3000
CIRC ASSOC DIR
Washington Times, Washington, DC
Tribble, Mitch .... (864) 638-5856
GM, Keowee Courier, Walhalla, SC
Tribble, Robert E .... (770) 461-6317
PUB, Fayette County News, Fayetteville, GA
Triblehorn, Chuck .... (908) 349-3000
ED, Ocean County Observer, Toms River, NJ
Trick, Marlon .... (970) 723-4404
MAN ED, Jackson County Star, Walden, CO
Tridenti, Frank .... (508) 685-1000
PROD FRM-MR
Eagle-Tribune, North Andover, MA
Triest, Steve .... (618) 932-2146
PROD MGR
Daily American, West Frankfort, IL
Trigg, Peter .... (212) 499-3334
DIR-Communications & Technology, New York Times Syndication Sales Corp., NY, NY
Trillhaase, Marty .... (208) 522-1800
EPE, Post Register, Idaho Falls, ID
Trimble, Blanche B .... (502) 487-5576
PUB, MAN ED
Tompkinsville News, Tompkinsville, KY
Trimble, Guy .... (512) 392-2458
PUB, Daily Record, San Marcos, TX
Trimble, Jane Ramos .... (817) 594-7447
PUB, Weatherford Democrat, Weatherford, TX
Trimble, Linda .... (904) 252-1511
EDU ED, Daytona Beach News-Journal, Daytona Beach, FL
Trimble, Richard .... (606) 546-9225
ED, Mountain Advocate, Barbourville, KY
Trimble, Robert .... (713) 869-5434
PROD DIR, Daily Court Review, Houston, TX
Trimble, Sheila .... (509) 663-5161
Fashion ED
Wenatchee World, Wenatchee, WA
Trinka, David .... (616) 673-5534
ED, Allegan County News, Allegan, MI
Triplett, Gene .... (405) 475-3311
City ED
Daily Oklahoman, Oklahoma City, OK
Triplett, John .... (512) 445-3500
GM-Cox Interactive Media
Austin American-Statesman, Austin, TX
Tripp, Lori .... (607) 798-1234
Society ED
Press & Sun Bulletin, Binghamton, NY
Tripp, Mary K .... (806) 376-4488
Books ED, Amarillo Daily News/Globe Times, Amarillo, TX
Tripp, Pat .... (604) 886-2622
PUB, Sunshine Coast News, Gibsons, BC
Tripp, Ricky .... (817) 390-7400
CIRC MGR-ADM
Fort Worth Star-Telegram, Fort Worth, TX
Trippiedi, Sue .... (217) 351-5252
ADV DIR, ADV MGR-CLASS
News-Gazette, Champaign, IL
Trippler, Dean .... (612) 934-5045
ED, Chanhassen Villager, Chanhassen, MN
Trisel, Vickie .... (419) 238-2285
Office MGR, Times-Bulletin, Van Wert, OH
Tritt, Abner .... (504) 895-8784
PUB, Jewish Voice, New Orleans, LA
Tritt, Claire .... (504) 895-8784
ED, Jewish Voice, New Orleans, LA
Trittschuh, Dan .... (614) 272-5422
ED, Westside Messenger, Columbus, OH
Tritz, Judy .... (816) 665-2808
ED, Kirksville Daily Express & News, Kirksville, MO
Trivett, Jama .... (606) 298-4612
MAN ED, Martin County Sun, Inez, KY
Trivett, Phil .... (502) 926-0123
PROD Ad/Imaging Leader
Messenger-Inquirer, Owensboro, KY
Trivett, Terri .... (904) 435-8500
DP MGR
Pensacola News Journal, Pensacola, FL
Troester, Donna L .... (970) 878-4017
GM, Meeker Herald, Meeker, CO
Troester, Glenn R .... (970) 878-4017
PUB, ED, Meeker Herald, Meeker, CO
Troger, Stacey .... (607) 936-4651
ADV MGR-Creative Services
Leader, Corning, NY

Troianello, Karen .... (509) 248-1251
Fashion/Style ED, Living/Lifestyle ED
Yakima Herald-Republic, Yakima, WA
Troill, Riley .... (912) 783-1291
ED, Dispatch and News, Hawkinsville, GA
Troisi, David F .... (717) 326-1551
ED, Sun-Gazette, Williamsport, PA
Trolinger, Steve .... (501) 271-3700
PRES
Benton County Daily Record, Bentonville, AR
Trollinger, Gary .... (610) 371-5000
EPE, Reading Times/Eagle, Reading, PA
Trongaard, Craig .... (319) 588-5611
Senior VP, Telegraph Herald, Dubuque, IA
Troost, Cheryl .... (608) 356-4808
CONT, News-Republic/South Central Wisconsin News, Baraboo, WI
Tropea, Vincent .... (716) 282-2311
CIRC DIR, Niagara Gazette, Niagara Falls, NY
Troppens, Dave .... (616) 781-3943
ED, Marshall Chronicle, Marshall, MI
Trosky, Pat .... (717) 821-2091
Women's ED
Citizens' Voice, Wilkes-Barre, PA
Trosley, Stephen .... (909) 987-6397
ED, Inland Valley Daily Bulletin, Ontario, CA
Trotant, Allan D .... (615) 526-9715
DIR-MKTG, Herald-Citizen, Cookeville, TN
Trotman, Rosalie .... (919) 752-6166
Lifestyle ED, Daily Reflector, Greenville, NC
Trotta, James .... (201) 653-1000
MGR-CR, Jersey Journal, Jersey City, NJ
Trotta, Liz .... (202) 636-3000
New York BU Chief
Washington Times, Washington, DC
Trotter, Gloria .... (405) 275-3121
MAN ED, How-Ni-Kan, Shawnee, OK
Trotter, Herman .... (716) 849-3434
Music ED, Buffalo News, Buffalo, NY
Trotter, Joe .... (606) 663-5540
MAN ED, Clay City Times, Stanton, KY
Trotter, Wayne .... (405) 275-3891
PUB, ED, Shawnee Sun, Shawnee, OK
Trotz, Joseph .... (706) 724-0851
Online Contact
Augusta Chronicle, Augusta, GA
Trounstine, Phil .... (408) 920-5000
Political ED
San Jose Mercury News, San Jose, CA
Troup, Penny .... (714) 553-9292
VP-Risk MGT
Freedom Communications Inc., Irvine, CA
Trout, Steve .... (317) 633-1240
PROD OPER SUPT-PR (Night)
Indianapolis Star/News, Indianapolis, IN
Troutman, John .... (717) 255-8100
City ED (Day), Patriot-News, Harrisburg, PA
Troutt, John Ed .... (501) 935-5525
ASST PUB, Jonesboro Sun, Jonesboro, AR
Troutt Jr, John W .... (501) 935-5525
PUB, ED, EPE
Jonesboro Sun, Jonesboro, AR
Troutt, Robert W .... (501) 935-5525
ASST PUB, Jonesboro Sun, Jonesboro, AR
Trow, Lisa .... (409) 295-5407
ED, Huntsville Item, Huntsville, TX
Trowbridge, Caroline .... (913) 843-1000
EDU ED, Journal-World, Lawrence, KS
Trowbridge, Cathy .... (913) 682-0305
ED, Sunday ED
Leavenworth Times, Leavenworth, KS
Troxler, Howard .... (813) 893-8111
Political ED
St. Petersburg Times, St. Petersburg, FL
Troy, Barbara .... (415) 327-6397
ADV MGR-City, Daily News, Palo Alto, CA
Troy, Bishop J Edward .... (506) 653-6806
PUB, New Freeman Catholic, Saint John, NB
Troy, James M .... (304) 292-6301
VP-SEC/TREAS
Dominion Post, Morgantown, WV
Trozzo, Sandy .... (412) 222-2200
Health/Medical ED
Observer-Reporter, Washington, PA
Truax, Alan .... (209) 441-6111
ADV DIR, Fresno Bee, Fresno, CA
Truax, Jon .... (419) 994-4166
PUB, Loudonville Times, Loudonville, OH
Trubiano, Patrick .... (603) 352-1234
CIRC MGR, Keene Sentinel, Keene, NH
Trubisky, Ronald J .... (614) 461-5000
DIR-Information/Planning, DP MGR
Columbus Dispatch, Columbus, OH
Truby, Ted .... (417) 334-3161
MAN ED
Branson Tri-Lakes Daily News, Branson, MO
Truchard, Liam .... (619) 792-3820
ED, Del Mar/Solana Beach/Carmel Valley/ Rancho Santa Fe Sun, Del Mar, CA
Truchot, Jeff .... (307) 324-3411
Sports ED, Rawlins Daily Times, Rawlins, WY
Trudeau, Michael .... (416) 367-2000
ADV MGR-MKTG RES/INFO
Toronto Star, Toronto, ON

Trudeau, Susan .... (816) 468-5999
ED, Sun Chronicle, Kansas City, MO.
True, Alison .... (312) 828-0350
ED, Chicago Reader, Chicago, IL
True, David .... (409) 542-2222
MAN ED
Giddings Times & News, Giddings, TX
Trueblood, David .... (617) 433-8200
MAN ED, Boston TAB, Needham, MA
Trueblood, Mike .... (309) 343-7181
Sports ED, Register-Mail, Galesburg, IL
Trueblood, Nancy .... (309) 686-3000
Sunday ED, Journal Star, Peoria, IL
Truesdale, Dennie .... (803) 332-6545
ED, Hartsville Messenger, Hartsville, SC
Truesdell, Jeff .... (407) 645-5888
ED, Weekly, Winter Park, FL
Truesdell, Wally .... (518) 725-8616
Automotive ED
Leader-Herald, Gloversville, NY
Truffa, John .... (813) 259-7711
DP/INFO Services DIR
Tampa Tribune and Times, Tampa, FL
Truitt, John .... (302) 324-2500
CIRC DIR, News Journal, Wilmington, DE
Truitt, Krishna .... (609) 989-0285
MAN ED, Nubian News, Trenton, NJ
Trujillo, Berna .... (505) 425-6796
ADV MGR-CLASS
Las Vegas Optic, Las Vegas, NM
Trujillo, Guillermo .... (56-2) 235-2902
MGR, Europa Press News Service, Santiago,
Trujillo, Vernon .... (719) 589-2553
PROD MGR, PROD FRM-PR
Valley Courier, Alamosa, CO
Truly, Pat .... (817) 390-7400
EDL Writer
Fort Worth Star-Telegram, Fort Worth, TX
Truman, Betty .... (540) 638-8801
ADV MGR-GEN
Martinsville Bulletin, Martinsville, VA
Truman, Cheryl .... (606) 231-3100
BUS ED
Lexington Herald-Leader, Lexington, KY
Trumbull, Kathy .... (954) 356-4000
Deputy MAN ED/News
Sun-Sentinel, Fort Lauderdale, FL
Trump, Charles .... (219) 244-5153
ASSOC ED, Post & Mail, Columbia City, IN
Trump, John .... (919) 492-4001
Regional ED
Henderson Daily Dispatch, Henderson, NC
Trump, Lawrence .... (937) 328-0300
Music ED
Springfield News-Sun, Springfield, OH
Trundle, W Scott .... (801) 625-4200
VP, PUB, Standard-Examiner, Ogden, UT
Trussell, David G .... (970) 352-0211
PUB, Greeley Tribune, Greeley, CO
Trussow, Ausra .... (905) 275-4672
GM, Teviskes Ziburiai, Mississauga, ON
Trust, B Cooper Walls .... (713) 266-5481
Owner-Review (NC)
Southern Newspapers Inc., Houston, TX
Trust, Lissa W Walls .... (713) 266-5481
Owner-Review (NC)
Southern Newspapers Inc., Houston, TX
Try, Linda .... (330) 296-9657
DP MGR, Record-Courier, Kent-Ravenna, OH
Trybus, Steve .... (406) 523-5200
ADV MGR-RT, Missoulian, Missoula, MT
Tryon, Thomas Lee .... (941) 953-7755
EPE, Sarasota Herald-Tribune, Sarasota, FL
Tschanz, Skip .... (541) 296-2141
ADV DIR, ADV MGR-CLASS
Dalles Daily Chronicle, The Dalles, OR
Tschorn, Adam R .... (802) 362-2222
MAN ED
Manchester Journal, Manchester, VT
Tsuha, Art .... (808) 245-3681
PROD SUPT-Mechanical
Garden Island, Lihue, HI
Tsukamoto, Dennis .... (808) 525-8000
PROD MGR-MR
Hawaii Newspaper Agency Inc., Honolulu, HI
Tubbs, William F .... (319) 285-8111
PUB, North Scott Press, Eldridge, IA
Tuccillo, Frederick J .... (516) 843-2020
DIR-New Media & Products
Newsday, Melville, NY
Tuchler, Amy .... (219) 933-3200
ASSOC PUB (East Lake), Times, Munster, IN
Tuchler, Jim .... (219) 933-3200
Online MGR, Times, Munster, IN
Tuck, Deborah .... (919) 492-4001
ADV DIR
Henderson Daily Dispatch, Henderson, NC
Tuck, Kenneth .... (334) 347-9533
News ED, Enterprise Ledger, Enterprise, AL

Tuc Who's Where-234

Tuck, Raymond K .... (423) 981-1100
ADV DIR, Daily Times, Maryville, TN
Tuck, Steve .... (912) 236-9511
ADV MGR-CLASS
Savannah Morning News, Savannah, GA
Tucker, Angela .... (404) 526-5151
MGR-News Personnel
Atlanta Journal-Constitution, Atlanta, GA
Tucker, Avis G .... (816) 747-8123
PRES, PUB, BM, ED, EPE
Daily Star-Journal, Warrensburg, MO
Tucker, Barbara .... (405) 335-2188
GM, MGR-PROM
Frederick Leader, Frederick, OK
Tucker, Barbara .... (317) 861-4242
ED, New Palestine Press, New Palestine, IN
Tucker, Bill .... (618) 656-4700
Sports ED, Intelligencer, Edwardsville, IL
Tucker, Carll .... (914) 763-3200
PUB, ED, Patent Trader, Cross River, NY
Tucker, Carol .... (815) 947-2311
GM, Stockton/Warren Gazette, Stockton, IL
Tucker, Connie .... (205) 232-2720
MGR-Office, News Courier, Athens, AL
Tucker, Cynthia .... (404) 526-5151
EPE (Constitution)
Atlanta Journal-Constitution, Atlanta, GA
Tucker, Dan .... (503) 221-8327
PROD SUPT-Platemaking
Oregonian, Portland, OR
Tucker, David .... (215) 854-2000
City ED
Philadelphia Inquirer, Philadelphia, PA
Tucker, Donald C .... (937) 372-4444
PROD FRM-PR
Xenia Daily Gazette, Xenia, OH
Tucker, Dorothy C .... (804) 696-5550
PUB, ED
Kenbridge-Victoria Dispatch, Victoria, VA
Tucker, Doug .... (910) 727-7211
DP MGR
Winston-Salem Journal, Winston-Salem, NC
Tucker, Glenn .... (803) 432-6157
PUB, ED
Chronicle Independent, Camden, SC
Tucker, Janet .... (405) 475-3311
Purchasing Administrator
Daily Oklahoman, Oklahoma City, OK
Tucker, John .... (208) 377-6200
Farm/Agriculture ED
Idaho Statesman, Boise, ID
Tucker, John .... (316) 624-2541
CIRC MGR
Southwest Daily Times, Liberal, KS
Tucker, John L .... (405) 273-4200
PUB, ED, EPE
Shawnee News-Star, Shawnee, OK
Tucker, Kevin .... (937) 335-5634
Arts ED, Entertainment/Amusements ED
Troy Daily News/Miami Valley Sunday News, Troy, OH
Tucker, Larry .... (904) 752-1293
PROD DIR, Lake City Reporter, Lake City, FL
Tucker, Laura .... (419) 422-5151
Family ED, Courier, Findlay, OH
Tucker, Lynn .... (616) 392-2311
ADTX MGR, Holland Sentinel, Holland, MI
Tucker, Marilyn .... (573) 624-4545
PROD FRM-COMP
Daily Statesman, Dexter, MO
Tucker, Melanie .... (423) 981-1100
Entertainment/Amusements ED, Fashion/Style ED, Living/Lifestyle ED, Women's ED
Daily Times, Maryville, TN
Tucker III, Otis O .... (804) 568-3341
ED, Charlotte Gazette, Drakes Branch, VA
Tucker, R D .... (209) 966-2500
GM, Mountain Life, Mariposa, CA
Tucker, Rebecca .... (913) 823-6363
CIRC Customer SRV
Salina Journal, Salina, KS
Tucker, Robert .... (540) 962-2121
ADV DIR, DIR-MKTG/PROM
Virginian Review, Covington, VA
Tucker, Robert L .... (614) 461-5000
PROD DIR
Columbus Dispatch, Columbus, OH
Tucker, Robert M .... (205) 755-0110
PUB, ED, Chilton County News, Clanton, AL
Tucker, Stacy B .... (215) 942-7890
DIR-MKTG, Sports Network (Div. of Computer Info. Network), Southampton, PA
Tucker, Steve .... (312) 321-3000
High School, Chicago Sun-Times, Chicago, IL
Tucker, Victor L .... (317) 861-4242
PUB, New Palestine Press, New Palestine, IN
Tuckwood, Jan .... (561) 820-4100
ASSOC ED
Palm Beach Post, West Palm Beach, FL
Tudhope, Annamarie .... (320) 864-4715
PUB, ED, Glencoe Enterprise, Glencoe, MN
Tudino, Denise .... (401) 722-4000
ADV MGR-CLASS, Times, Pawtucket, RI
Tudor, Don .... (419) 562-3333
MAN ED, Telegraph-Forum, Bucyrus, OH
Tudor, Julene .... (801) 625-4200
ADV SUPV-CLASS Telephone Sales
Standard-Examiner, Ogden, UT
Tuell, Tom .... (305) 743-5551
ED, Florida Keys Keynoter, Marathon, FL
Tuff, Kaydee .... (941) 353-0444
ED, Golden Gate Gazette, Naples, FL
Tuff, Maria .... (941) 353-0444
GM, Golden Gate Gazette, Naples, FL
Tuff, Roy .... (941) 353-0444
PUB, Golden Gate Gazette, Naples, FL
Tuff, Russell .... (941) 353-0444
PUB, Golden Gate Gazette, Naples, FL
Tufte, Angela .... (602) 271-8000
CONT, Phoenix Newspapers Inc., Phoenix, AZ
Tuggle, Donna .... (206) 464-2111
ADV MGR-NTL, Seattle Times, Seattle, WA
Tuggle, Terri .... (605) 673-2217
PUB, Custer County Chronicle, Custer, SD
Tuite, Elizabeth D .... (617) 929-2000
Librarian, Boston Globe, Boston, MA
Tulgan, Carol .... (330) 452-6444
ED, Stark Jewish News, Canton, OH
Tulis, Spencer .... (518) 725-8616
Photo ED, Leader-Herald, Gloversville, NY
Tuller, Carol .... (619) 232-4381
BM
San Diego Daily Transcript, San Diego, CA
Tulley, Marilee .... (707) 226-3711
Environmental ED, Graphics ED/Art DIR, MAN ED, Napa Valley Register, Napa, CA
Tullos, Jesse .... (803) 546-4148
ED, Georgetown Times, Georgetown, SC
Tully, Mac .... (817) 390-7400
PUB (Arlington Star-Telegram), Senior VP-ADV, Fort Worth Star-Telegram, Fort Worth, TX
Tulumello, Kathy .... (602) 271-8000
Sports ED, Arizona Republic, Phoenix, AZ
Tuma, David .... (210) 672-2861
PUB, Gonzales Inquirer, Gonzales, TX
Tumbull, Shannon .... (904) 926-7102
MAN ED, Wakulla News, Crawfordville, FL
Tumin, Marc-Yves .... (212) 684-3366
MAN ED, Irish Voice, New York, NY
Tuminski, Sharon .... (606) 744-3123
SEC, MGR-FIN
Winchester Sun, Winchester, KY
Tune, Gary .... (209) 532-7151
ADV MGR-CLASS
Union Democrat, Sonora, CA
Tune, John .... (616) 946-2000
ED, EPE, Record-Eagle, Traverse City, MI
Tunison, Michael .... (818) 566-4388
ED, Entertainment Today, Burbank, CA
Tunney, Kelly Smith .... (212) 621-1500
ASST to the PRES
Associated Press, New York, NY
Tupa, Mike .... (918) 335-8200
Sports ED
Examiner-Enterprise, Bartlesville, OK
Tupper, Mark .... (217) 429-5151
Sports ED, Herald & Review, Decatur, IL
Turan, Kenneth .... (213) 237-5000
Movie Critic
Los Angeles Times, Los Angeles, CA
Turbeville, Kevin .... (501) 935-5525
Sports ED, Jonesboro Sun, Jonesboro, AR
Turcotte, Elise .... (613) 735-3141
CIRC MGR
Pembroke Daily News, Pembroke, ON
Turcotte, Steve .... (613) 732-3691
PROD FRM-PR, Observer, Pembroke, ON
Turczyn, Coury .... (423) 522-5399
MAN ED, Metro Pulse, Knoxville, TN
Turek, Sonia .... (617) 426-3000
Deputy MAN ED-Arts/Lifestyle
Boston Herald, Boston, MA
Turgeon, Kathleen .... (406) 447-4000
ADV MGR-CLASS
Helena Independent Record, Helena, MT
Turick, Scott .... (305) 253-4339
ED, Cutler Courier, Miami, FL
Turley, Alan .... (573) 323-4515
PUB, Current Local, Van Buren, MO
Turley, Marjorie .... (573) 323-4515
PUB, Current Local, Van Buren, MO
Turley, Michael E .... (502) 247-5223
ED, Mayfield Messenger, Mayfield, KY
Turley, Patrick H .... (413) 283-8393
PUB, Palmer Journal-Register, Palmer, MA
Turley, Steve .... (573) 323-4515
ED, Current Local, Van Buren, MO
Turley, Thomas A .... (413) 323-5999
PUB, Sentinel, Belchertown, MA
Turlin, Jean-Louis .... (212) 221-6700
GM, ED, France-Amerique, New York, NY
Turman, Chuck .... (405) 372-5000
DP MGR, News Press, Stillwater, OK
Turmel, Dennis .... (508) 685-1000
PROD MGR
Eagle-Tribune, North Andover, MA
Turnage, Neal H .... (601) 289-2251
PUB, Star-Herald, Kosciusko, MS
Turnbach, Ann .... (713) 220-7171
VP-Human Resources, DIR-Human Resources
Houston Chronicle, Houston, TX
Turnbaugh Jr, James .... (816) 761-6200
PUB, ED
Jackson County Advocate, Grandview, MO
Turnbaugh, Kay .... (303) 258-7075
PUB, ED, Mountain-Ear, Nederland, CO
Turnbull, Bill .... (212) 889-6633
PRES, New York Press Photographers Association, New York, NY
Turnbull, Sam .... (301) 733-5131
PROD FRM-COMP
Morning Herald, Hagerstown, MD
Turnbull, Thomas .... (716) 343-8000
ASST PUB, ADV DIR, DIR-MKTG/PROM
Daily News, Batavia, NY
Turner, Barbara .... (561) 791-7790
PUB, Wellington/Royal Palm Beach Forum, Wellington, FL
Turner, Bo .... (904) 454-1297
ED, High Springs Herald, High Springs, FL
Turner, Bridge .... (334) 644-1101
ADV DIR, Valley Times-News, Lanett, AL
Turner, Chip .... (601) 335-1155
ADTX MGR
Delta Democrat Times, Greenville, MS
Turner, Craig .... (716) 873-2594
ED, West Side Times, Buffalo, NY
Turner, Craig .... (213) 237-5000
Toronto BU
Los Angeles Times, Los Angeles, CA
Turner, Dan .... (318) 459-3200
Political/Government ED
Times, Shreveport, LA
Turner, David .... (518) 843-1100
City ED, Recorder, Amsterdam, NY
Turner, Denise .... (770) 258-2838
ED, Bowdon Bulletin, Bowdon, GA
Turner, Fred .... (954) 356-4000
Sports ED, Sun-Sentinel, Fort Lauderdale, FL
Turner, Gloria .... (417) 623-3480
People/Lifestyle ED, Joplin Globe, Joplin, MO
Turner, Jack .... (541) 523-3673
PUB, Baker City Herald, Baker City, OR
Turner, James .... (502) 726-8394
MAN ED
News Democrat & Leader, Russellville, KY
Turner, Jamie .... (808) 525-8000
Sports ED, Honolulu Advertiser, Honolulu, HI
Turner, Jim .... (414) 684-4433
PROD FRM-PR
Herald Times Reporter, Manitowoc, WI
Turner, John F .... (601) 394-5070
PUB, Greene County Herald, Leakesville, MS
Turner, Johney S .... (318) 428-3207
ED, West Carroll Gazette, Oak Grove, LA
Turner, Joyce .... (903) 597-8111
Fashion ED, Living/ Lifestyle ED, Women's ED, Tyler Morning Telegraph, Tyler, TX
Turner, K A .... (205) 234-4281
ED, EPE, Outlook, Alexander City, AL
Turner, Leola .... (601) 394-5070
ED, Greene County Herald, Leakesville, MS
Turner, Mark .... (907) 235-7767
GM, ED, Homer News, Homer, AK
Turner, Mary Ellison .... (919) 527-3191
Community News ED
Free Press, Kinston, NC
Turner, Melanie .... (916) 756-0800
Features ED, Davis Enterprise, Davis, CA
Turner, Mike .... (250) 492-4002
MAN ED, Penticton Herald, Penticton, BC
Turner, Patrick .... (604) 495-7225
PUB, ED, Osoyoos Times, Osoyoos, BC
Turner, Randy .... (417) 358-2191
MAN ED, Carthage Press, Carthage, MO
Turner Jr, Robert G .... (941) 748-0411
VP, GM, Bradenton Herald, Bradenton, FL
Turner, Ron .... (208) 743-9411
PROD MGR-Wet Commercial Painting
Lewiston Morning Tribune, Lewiston, ID
Turner, Ron .... (403) 527-1101
BM, Medicine Hat News, Medicine Hat, AB
Turner, Rusty .... (501) 751-6200
MAN ED, Morning News of Northwest Arkansas, Springdale, AR
Turner, Sandy .... (816) 254-8600
PROD MGR-SYS
Examiner, Independence, MO
Turner, Scott .... (205) 734-2131
Sports ED, Cullman Times, Cullman, AL
Turner, Scott B .... (715) 258-5546
PUB, Wisconsin State Farmer, Waupaca, WI
Turner, Sonny .... (205) 232-2720
ED, EPE, News ED, Political ED
News Courier, Athens, AL
Turner, Ted .... (519) 376-2250
PROD MGR, Sun Times, Owen Sound, ON
Turner, Tom .... (423) 756-6900
State ED
Chattanooga Free Press, Chattanooga, TN
Turner, Tom .... (573) 346-2132
GM, Lake Sun Leader, Camdenton, MO
Turner, Tom .... (520) 573-4220
Travel ED, Arizona Daily Star, Tucson, AZ
Turner, Troy .... (970) 669-5050
ASST MAN ED
Loveland Daily Reporter-Herald, Loveland, CO
Turner, Wendy L .... (540) 728-7311
ED, Carroll News, Hillsville, VA
Turner, Wesley R .... (816) 234-4141
EVP/GM, Kansas City Star, Kansas City, MO
Turner, William .... (517) 437-7351
PUB, Hillsdale Daily News, Hillsdale, MI
Turner-Collins, Richelle .... (901) 427-3333
Religion ED, Jackson Sun, Jackson, TN
Turnpenny, Michael .... (604) 642-5752
PUB, Sooke Mirror, Sooke, BC
Turosz, Robert .... (508) 664-4761
ED
North Reading Transcript, North Reading, MA
Turpin, Bill .... (902) 468-1222
MAN ED, Daily News, Halifax, NS
Turpin, Carmel .... (709) 639-9203
ED, Humber Log, Corner Brook, NF
Turzer, Donna .... (903) 597-8111
ADV MGR-Ad Production
Tyler Morning Telegraph, Tyler, TX
Tush, Terry .... (405) 341-2121
Sports ED
Edmond Evening Sun, Edmond, OK
Tuskan, Beverly .... (601) 762-1111
Librarian, Mississippi Press, Pascagoula, MS
Tuss, Vince .... (208) 377-6200
Wire ED, Idaho Statesman, Boise, ID
Tussing, Kathy .... (206) 339-3000
Religion ED, Herald, Everett, WA
Tustin, Steve .... (416) 367-2000
Sports ED, Toronto Star, Toronto, ON
Tuthill, John T .... (516) 475-1000
PUB, Long Island Advance, Patchogue, NY
Tutor, Laura .... (205) 236-1551
Religion ED, Anniston Star, Anniston, AL
Tutt, Christine .... (514) 987-2222
EDU SRV MGR, MGR-MKTG
Gazette, Montreal, QC
Tuttell, Richard .... (704) 758-7381
ED, Lenoir News-Topic, Lenoir, NC
Tuttle, Al .... (508) 343-6911
Automotive ED
Sentinel & Enterprise, Fitchburg, MA
Tuttle, Ray .... (918) 581-8300
Oil ED, Tulsa World, Tulsa, OK
Tutty, Sheila .... (604) 342-9216
PUB, Valley Echo, Invermere, BC
Tuzon, Brandy .... (408) 424-2221
BUS Writer, Californian, Salinas, CA
Tvedte, Jim .... (319) 337-3181
DP MGR
Iowa City Press-Citizen, Iowa City, IA
Tveiten, Rodger .... (515) 762-3994
PUB, ED, Kanawha Reporter, Kanawha, IA
Tweedy, James .... (405) 353-0620
PROD FRM-PR (Night)
Lawton Constitution, Lawton, OK
Twersky, David .... (201) 887-3900
ED, Metrowest Jewish News, Whippany, NJ
Twesten, Robert .... (914) 694-9300
ADV DIR-Display, Reporter Dispatch, White Plains, NY, Gannett Co. Inc.
Twichell, Allen .... (316) 251-3300
Sports ED
Coffeyville Journal, Coffeyville, KS
Twigg, Rick .... (301) 722-4600
Automotive ED
Cumberland Times-News, Cumberland, MD
Twitchell, Cleve .... (541) 776-4411
COL, Food/Garden ED, Radio/Television ED
Mail Tribune, Medford, OR
Twitchell, Nancy .... (801) 679-8730
ED, Garfield County News, Tropic, UT
Twohey, John .... (312) 222-3232
Senior ED, Chicago Tribune, Chicago, IL
Twombly, Angus H .... (207) 791-6650
VP-MKTG
Portland Press Herald, Portland, ME
Twyman, Carla .... (540) 669-2181
Community ED, Teen-Age/Youth ED, Herald-Courier Virginia Tennessean, Bristol, VA
Tycz, Becky .... (605) 589-3242
ED, Tribune & Register, Tyndall, SD
Tyer, Cal .... (515) 782-2141
CIRC DIR
Creston News-Advertiser, Creston, IA
Tyers, William .... (603) 882-2741
PROD MGR-Distribution
Telegraph, Nashua, NH
Tyger, Frank .... (609) 989-5454
DIR-MKTG SRV, Times, Trenton, NJ
Tyler, Carl .... (509) 525-3300
ADV MGR
Walla Walla Union-Bulletin, Walla Walla, WA

Copyright ©1997 by the Editor & Publisher Co.

235-Who's Where **Val**

Tyler, Carolyn B .... (307) 856-2244
COL, Riverton Ranger, Riverton, WY
Tyler, Debbie .... (615) 446-2811
GM, Dickson Herald, Dickson, TN
Tyler, Edward .... (212) 779-9200
ADV VP/DIR
New York Law Journal, New York, NY
Tyler, Frank .... (214) 977-8222
PROD DIR
Dallas Morning News, Dallas, TX
Tyler, Jana Reed .... (307) 436-2211
GM, Glenrock Independent, Glenrock, WY
Tyler, Ken .... (803) 533-5500
Photographer
Times and Democrat, Orangeburg, SC
Tyler, Robert H .... (307) 856-2244
MGR-CR, Riverton Ranger, Riverton, WY
Tymula, Frank .... (203) 964-2200
PROD SUPT-COMP, Stamford Advocate, Stamford, CT, Times Mirror Co.
Tyne, Victor .... (508) 922-1234
City ED
Daily News of Newburyport, Beverly, MA
Tyner, Howard A .... (312) 222-3232
VP/ED, Chicago Tribune, Chicago, IL
Tynes, Scott A .... (601) 736-2611
MAN ED, Columbian-Progress, Columbia, MS
Tyo Esq, David .... (513) 489-7227
VP, Brown Publishing Co., Cincinnati, OH
Tyra, Ty .... (205) 221-2840
Sports ED, Daily Mountain Eagle, Jasper, AL
Tyson, Ginnie .... (501) 641-7161
PUB, Atkins Chronicle, Atkins, AR
Tyson, Rae .... (703) 276-3400
Environmental ED, USA Today, Arlington, VA
Tyson, Van A .... (501) 641-7161
PUB, ED, Atkins Chronicle, Atkins, AR
Tyssen, Linda .... (218) 741-5544
News ED, Mesabi Daily News, Virginia, MN
Tysver, Jay .... (205) 549-2000
ADV Creative Services
Gadsden Times, Gadsden, AL
Tyus, Bill .... (217) 429-5151
PROD SUPV-Press
Herald & Review, Decatur, IL

U

Uebelacker, Barbara .... (414) 435-4411
Topics ED-MET, Green Bay Press-Gazette, Green Bay, WI
Uecker, Ronald .... (209) 722-1511
ADV MGR-Display
Merced Sun-Star, Merced, CA
Uffelman, Fred .... (717) 767-6397
ADV MGR-RT, York Newspaper Co., York, PA
Uhall Sr, Ted .... (318) 365-6773
PROD MGR, Daily Iberian, New Iberia, LA
Uhl, Christopher .... (716) 232-7100
PROD Building Services Plant ENG
Rochester Democrat and Chronicle; Times-Union, Rochester, NY
Uhler, Tom .... (817) 390-7400
ASST NTL ED
Fort Worth Star-Telegram, Fort Worth, TX
Uhlmann, Carol A .... (309) 343-7181
ADV MGR-CLASS
Register-Mail, Galesburg, IL
Uhlmann, Rick .... (608) 252-6100
ASST City ED
Wisconsin State Journal, Madison, WI
Uhls, C Duane .... (423) 638-4181
CIRC DIR, Greeneville Sun, Greeneville, TN
Uhrig, Bruce .... (605) 394-8300
PROD FRM-COMP
Rapid City Journal, Rapid City, SD
Uhriniak, Robert .... (412) 775-3200
EPE, Beaver County Times, Beaver, PA
Uhrmann, Linda .... (609) 272-7000
Librarian
Press of Atlantic City, Pleasantville, NJ
Ulerich, William K .... (814) 765-5581
BC, PUB, Progress, Clearfield, PA
Ulhs, Amy .... (317) 787-3291
ED
Perry Township Weekly, Beech Grove, IN
Ulin, Trisha .... (319) 456-6641
ED, Plainsman-Clarion, Richland, IA
Ulku, Jay .... (701) 253-7311
Copy Chief, Forum, Fargo, ND
Ullmann, Caroline .... (206) 597-8742
Health/Medical Reporter
News Tribune, Tacoma, WA
Ullmann, Harrison .... (317) 254-2400
ED, NUVO, Indianapolis, IN
Ulloa, Sylvia .... (408) 424-2221
Features ED, Living ED
Californian, Salinas, CA
Ullom, Bruce .... (719) 632-5511
CIRC MGR-Home Delivery
Gazette, Colorado Springs, CO
Ullrih, Brian .... (605) 642-2761
CIRC MGR
Black Hills Pioneer, Spearfish, SD
Ulm, Gerry .... (916) 622-1255
CIRC MGR
Mountain Democrat, Placerville, CA
Ulmer, Tracy .... (303) 820-1010
MGR-PROM, Denver Post, Denver, CO
Ulrich, Allan .... (415) 777-2424
Dance Critic
San Francisco Examiner, San Francisco, CA
Ulrich, Ronald G .... (219) 362-2161
PROD FRM-PR
La Porte Herald-Argus, La Porte, IN
Ulrich, Roy .... (408) 372-3311
CIRC MGR-OPER
Monterey County Herald, Monterey, CA
Ulrich, Yolanda .... (305) 245-2311
MAN ED
South Dade News Leader, Homestead, FL
Ulry, Tom .... (614) 387-0400
CONT, Marion Star, Marion, OH
Ultang, James .... (414) 733-4411
ADV MGR-NTL/Regional Sales
Post-Crescent, Appleton, WI
Ultee, John .... (860) 633-4691
GM, Glastonbury Citizen, Glastonbury, CT
Uluc, Dogan .... (212) 921-8880
ED, Hurriyet, New York, NY
Umbaugh, Bernard (Bud) .... (215) 949-4000
DIR-PROM
Bucks County Courier Times, Levittown, PA
Umphress, Jon .... (419) 634-6055
ED, Ada Herald, Ada, OH
Umphrey, Mike .... (705) 472-3200
COL, North Bay Nugget, North Bay, ON
Underdonk, Carol .... (502) 769-2312
CIRC Sales Team Leader
News Enterprise, Elizabethtown, KY
Underhill, L A .... (906) 563-5212
PUB, Norway Current, Norway, MI
Underhill, Vicki .... (906) 563-5212
ED, Norway Current, Norway, MI
Underwood, Evelyn .... (615) 646-6131
PUB, Westview, Nashville, TN
Underwood, Janice .... (817) 246-2473
PUB, ED, White Settlement Bomber News, Fort Worth, TX
Underwood, Jerald .... (713) 220-7171
PROD ASST DIR
Houston Chronicle, Houston, TX
Underwood, Judy .... (423) 346-6225
ED
Morgan County News & Times, Wartburg, TN
Underwood, Masie .... (770) 386-0872
ED, Bartow Neighbor, Carterville, GA
Underwood, Rick .... (618) 529-5454
Sports ED
Southern Illinoisan, Carbondale, IL
Underwood, Roger .... (334) 792-3141
CIRC DIR, Dothan Eagle, Dothan, AL
Thomson Newspapers
Underwood, Scott .... (317) 747-5700
Sports ED, Star Press, Muncie, IN
Underwood, Zilpha .... (904) 599-2100
Features ED, Living/Lifestyle ED,Tallahassee Democrat, Tallahassee, FL
Ung, Trudy .... (818) 932-6161
Graphic Artist, Dodge Construction News Greensheet, Monrovia, CA
Ungard, Mike .... (937) 426-5263
Sports ED
Beavercreek News-Current, Beavercreek, OH
Unger, Bert .... (910) 997-3111
News ED, Richmond County Daily Journal, Rockingham, NC
Unger, Robert .... (816) 271-8500
EX ED
St. Joseph News-Press, St. Joseph, MO
Ungos, Peggy .... (561) 562-2315
MGR-Techinal Services
Vero Beach Press-Journal, Vero Beach, FL
Unisowicz, Stan .... (520) 453-4237
MAN ED
Today's News-Herald, Lake Havasu City, AZ
Unkart, Carla .... (410) 848-4400
CIRC DIR
Carroll County Times, Westminster, MD
Unterman, Thomas .... (213) 237-3700
Sr VP/CFO
Times Mirror Co., Los Angeles, CA
Unzicker, Tim .... (630) 232-2324
MAN ED, Geneva Republican, Geneva, IL
Updike, Robin .... (206) 464-2111
Arts Critic, Seattle Times, Seattle, WA
Upstrom, Teri .... (319) 588-5611
ADV MGR-RT
Telegraph Herald, Dubuque, IA
Upton, Chris .... (423) 992-3392
PUB, Union News Leader, Maynardville, TN
Upton, Janet .... (802) 228-8817
ED, Black River Tribune, Ludlow, VT
Upton, Lee .... (812) 522-4871
CIRC DIR, Tribune, Seymour, IN
Urban, Robert .... (610) 377-2051
MAN ED, BUS/FIN ED, EPE, EDL Writer
Times News, Lehighton, PA
Urbanczyk, Barbara A .... (716) 849-3434
SEC, Buffalo News, Buffalo, NY
Urbanek, Debbie .... (409) 945-3441
SEC/TREAS, CONT
Texas City Sun, Texas City, TX
Urbanek, Laura .... (515) 733-4318
PUB, ED, Story City Herald, Story City, IA
Urbin, Susan .... (219) 586-3139
PUB, ED, Independent News, Walkerton, IN
Urbon, Stephen F .... (508) 997-7411
EPE, Standard Times, New Bedford, MA
Urguhart, John .... (212) 416-2000
BU MGR-Ottawa
Wall Street Journal, New York, NY
Uribe, Abel .... (217) 245-6121
Photo DEPT MGR
Jacksonville Journal-Courier, Jacksonville, IL
Urillo, Anthony L .... (860) 621-6751
PUB, Observer, Southington, CT
Urillo, Robert .... (860) 241-6200
PROD MGR, Hartford Courant, Hartford, CT
Urlacher, Joanne .... (306) 228-2267
PUB, ED, Northwest Herald, Unity, SK
Urlacher, Mark .... (306) 228-2267
GM, Northwest Herald, Unity, SK
Urlaub, Mike .... (307) 682-9306
PROD MGR, News-Record, Gillette, WY
Urquhart, Janet .... (970) 925-3414
BUS/FIN ED, Aspen Times, Aspen, CO
Urrutia, Larry .... (702) 788-6200
PROD DIR, Reno Gazette-Journal, Reno, NV
Urseny, Laura .... (916) 891-1234
BUS ED, Chico Enterprise-Record, Chico, CA
Urseth, Mark .... (520) 836-7461
PROD DIR
Casa Grande Dispatch, Casa Grande, AZ
Uruena, Eduardo .... (416) 531-2495
PUB, El Popular, Toronto, ON
Usher, Bill .... (561) 562-2315
PROD MGR-COMP
Vero Beach Press-Journal, Vero Beach, FL
Ussery, Guy C .... (607) 756-5665
CIRC CNR-MKTG/PROM
Cortland Standard, Cortland, NY
Ustaszewski, Laura .... (614) 387-0400
ASST MAN ED, City ED
Marion Star, Marion, OH
Uthoff, Renee .... (319) 337-3181
ADV MGR-RT
Iowa City Press-Citizen, Iowa City, IA
Utley, Michael .... (212) 803-8200
MAN ED, Bond Buyer, New York, NY
Utley, Rae .... (541) 926-2211
PROD SUPV-MR
Albany Democrat-Herald, Albany, OR
Utnik, David .... (540) 825-0771
Sports ED
Culpeper Star-Exponent, Culpeper, VA
Utt, Michael L .... (701) 347-4493
ED, Cass County Reporter, Casselton, ND
Utter, Cindy .... (805) 736-2313
Aviation/Space ED
Lompoc Record, Lompoc, CA
Utter, Marlo .... (605) 823-4490
GM, Corson County News, McLaughlin, SD
Utter, Nicholas C .... (401) 596-7791
TREAS, Westerly Sun, Westerly, RI
Utter, Robert D .... (401) 596-7791
SEC, CIRC MGR, Westerly Sun, Westerly, RI

V

Vacar, Vaughn .... (412) 775-3200
CIRC MGR-MKTG
Beaver County Times, Beaver, PA
Vacek, Rick .... (209) 441-6111
ASST MAN ED-Sports
Fresno Bee, Fresno, CA
Vaden, Ted .... (919) 932-2000
PUB, ED, Chapel Hill News, Chapel Hill, NC
Vader, Rick .... (519) 537-2341
PROD FRM-COMP
Sentinel-Review, Woodstock, ON
Vadnais, Ed .... (401) 821-7400
GM
Kent County Daily Times, West Warwick, RI
Vaga, Airi .... (212) 689-2939
ED, Vaba Eesti Sona, New York, NY
Vahidi, Ellen M .... (212) 476-0802
PRES, International BusinessMan News Bureau, New York, NY
Vahldiek, Lissa Walls .... (713) 266-5481
VP/SEC/COO, Owner-Times-Journal (AL)
Southern Newspapers Inc., Houston, TX
Vail, Dorothy .... (902) 742-7111
GM, Vanguard, Yarmouth, NS
Vaillancourt, Alain .... (514) 273-2525
ED
Hebdo Journal de Rosemont, Montreal, QC
Vaillancourt, Gerald .... (207) 791-6650
PROD OPER Page Ad Build SUPV-Nights
Portland Press Herald, Portland, ME
Vainer, George .... (212) 387-0299
ED, Novoye Russkoye Slovo, New York, NY
Vala, Vince .... (540) 825-3232
ED, Culpeper News, Culpeper, VA
Valadez, Eloise .... (773) 586-8800
Food/Society Writer
Daily Southtown, Chicago, IL
Valbert, Charlotte .... (618) 945-2111
PUB
Bridgeport Leader-Times, Bridgeport, IL
Valbert, Louis H .... (618) 945-2111
PUB
Bridgeport Leader-Times, Bridgeport, IL
Valdes, Lesley .... (215) 854-2000
Music Critic-Classical
Philadelphia Inquirer, Philadelphia, PA
Valdez, Kathy .... (509) 234-3181
GM, MAN ED
Franklin County Graphic, Connell, WA
Valdez, Linda .... (602) 271-8000
EDL Writer, Arizona Republic, Phoenix, AZ
Valdez, Marie .... (415) 777-5700
MGR-Purchasing, San Francisco Newspaper Agency, San Francisco, CA
Valencia, Sylvia .... (713) 869-5434
PROD DIR, Daily Court Review, Houston, TX
Valenta, Anthony .... (607) 798-1234
MGR-RES
Press & Sun Bulletin, Binghamton, NY
Valenta, Peter .... (416) 947-2222
PROD SUPV-Maintenance
Toronto Sun, Toronto, ON
Valenti, Carl .... (212) 416-2000
PRES/PUB-News Services
Wall Street Journal, New York, NY
Valenti, Carl M .... (212) 416-2600
Sr VP/PRES & PUB-Dow Jones News Services
Dow Jones & Co. Inc., New York, NY
Valenti, Joe .... (717) 654-1260
PUB, ED
Greater Pittston Gazette, Pittston, PA
Valenti, Michael J .... (213) 237-5000
DIR-Human Resources
Los Angeles Times, Los Angeles, CA
Valenti, Mickie .... (813) 259-7711
COL, Tampa Tribune and Times, Tampa, FL
Valenti, Philip A .... (757) 247-4600
CIRC VP/DIR, Daily Press, Newport News, VA
Valentine, Carla .... (413) 525-6661
MAN ED, Reminder, East Longmeadow, MA
Valentine, Gwen .... (916) 891-1234
ADV MGR-CLASS
Chico Enterprise-Record, Chico, CA
Valentine Jr, H E .... (913) 632-2127
PRES/TREAS, PUB/GM, PA/BM, COL, EPE
Clay Center Dispatch, Clay Center, KS
Valentine, Terry .... (517) 787-2300
ADTX MGR
Jackson Citizen Patriot, Jackson, MI
Valentine, Virginia .... (860) 225-4601
Regional MGR-CR, Herald, New Britain, CT
Valeo, Thomas A .... (847) 427-4300
Theater ED
Daily Herald, Arlington Heights, IL
Valerino, John .... (941) 687-7000
Sports ED, Ledger, Lakeland, FL
Valeton Jr, O J .... (504) 826-3279
News ED, Times-Picayune, New Orleans, LA
Valiante, Chet .... (201) 365-3000
CIRC DIR
North Jersey Herald & News, Passaic, NJ
Valicente, Hugo .... (213) 622-8332
Copy ED, La Opinion, Los Angeles, CA
Valiquette, Paul .... (613) 739-7000
PROD SUPT-PR, Ottawa Sun, Ottawa, ON
Vallance, Ike .... (509) 689-2507
PUB, ED
Brewster Quad City Herald, Brewster, WA
Vallatini, Lynda .... (508) 458-7100
ADV MGR-Major Accounts, Sun, Lowell, MA
Vallatini, Roy .... (508) 586-7200
ADV DIR, ADV MGR-CLASS
Enterprise, Brockton, MA
Valleau, Brenda .... (306) 652-9200
TV Times ED, StarPhoenix, Saskatoon, SK
Vallee, Jacques .... (514) 285-7272
PROD VP, La Presse, Montreal, QC
Vallely, Joseph .... (516) 795-8823
VP/DIR-Sales, American Crossword Federation, Massapequa Park, NY
Vallery, Janet .... (419) 448-3200
PROD SUPT, Advertiser-Tribune, Tiffin, OH
Vallier, Keith .... (423) 756-1234
News ED
Chattanooga Times, Chattanooga, TN
Vallillee, Wendy .... (613) 259-2220
PUB, ED, Era, Lanark, ON
Valois, Renee .... (206) 455-2222
Librarian, Eastside Journal, Bellevue, WA
Valpy, Amanda .... (416) 585-5000
Librarian, Globe and Mail (Canada's National Newspaper), Toronto, ON
Valpy, Bruce .... (403) 873-4031
MAN ED, News/North, Yellowknife, NT

Val Who's Where-236

Valuckas, Tommy .... (860) 274-8851
ED, Town Times, Watertown, CT
Valunas, Walter T .... (203) 235-1661
PROD FRM-PR, Record-Journal, Meriden, CT
Vanacore, Michael .... (860) 283-4355
GM, Thomaston Express, Thomaston, CT
Vanacore, Michael R .... (860) 584-0501
PUB, Bristol Press, Bristol, CT
Van Allen, Judy .... (604) 453-2261
PUB, Ashcroft Journal, Ashcroft, BC
Van Anglen, James B .... (603) 427-6500
MAN ED
Bedford-Merrimack Bulletin, Bedford, NH
Van Asselt Karl A.....................(609)468-1099
Assoc ED, World Feature
Syndicate, La Jolla, CA
Van Atten, Suzanne .... (770) 428-9411
Entertainment/Amusements ED, Television/Film ED, Daily Journal, Marietta, GA
Vanaver, Elissa .... (305) 350-2111
Features ED, Miami Herald, Miami, FL
Van Bridger, Allan .... (613) 774-2524
MAN ED, Winchester Press, Winchester, ON
Van Buren, Tony .... (616) 651-5407
PRES, ADV DIR, Sturgis Journal, Sturgis, MI
VanCamp, Lyle .... (701) 454-6333
PUB, ED, Valley News & Views, Drayton, ND
Van Camp, Rikki .... (716) 394-0770
Photo ED, Daily Messenger/Sunday Messenger, Canandaigua, NY
VanCamp, Roberta .... (701) 454-6333
GM, Valley News & Views, Drayton, ND
Vance, Carolyn .... (217) 351-5252
Librarian, News-Gazette, Champaign, IL
Vance, Debra .... (606) 292-2600
EDU ED, Kentucky Post, Covington, KY
Vance, Loretta .... (309) 829-9411
ADV MGR-ADV OPER
Pantagraph, Bloomington, IL
Vance, Moss .... (606) 873-4131
ED, Woodford Sun, Versailles, KY
Vance, Patrick .... (212) 499-3334
DIR-Special Projects, New York Times Syndication Sales Corp., New York, NY
Vance, Sharon .... (217) 774-2161
ED, Daily Union, Shelbyville, IL
Vance, Trisha .... (910) 343-2000
Health/Medical ED, Morning Star/Sunday Star-News, Wilmington, NC
Vancel, Ingraham .... (317) 482-4650
PROD MGR, Reporter, Lebanon, IN
Vanchure, Carlon .... (937) 335-5634
PROD MGR-MR, Troy Daily News/Miami Valley Sunday News, Troy, OH
Vandeboon, Ron .... (406) 265-6795
BUS/FIN ED, Havre Daily News, Havre, MT
Van DeMark, Bonnie J .... (418) 678-2324
PUB, ED
Mercer County Chronicle, Coldwater, OH
VanDemark, Steve .... (419) 784-5441
GM, Crescent-News, Defiance, OH
VandenBosh, Mike .... (209) 599-2194
GM, ED, Ripon Record, Ripon, CA
VandenBrand, Fred .... (616) 842-6400
MAN ED
Grand Haven Tribune, Grand Haven, MI
Van Den Branden, Michael J ... (906) 439-5111
PUB, ED, Porcupine Press, Chatham, MI
Vanden Brook, Tom .... (414) 224-2000
EDU Reporter
Milwaukee Journal Sentinel, Milwaukee, WI
Vandenburg, Doyle .... (409) 295-5407
PROD MGR, Huntsville Item, Huntsville, TX
Vandenheede, John .... (616) 429-2400
Sports ED, Herald-Palladium, St. Joseph, MI
Van Den Henvel, Kirk D .... (715) 842-2101
CONT, Wausau Daily Herald, Wausau, WI
VanDerburgh, William .... (941) 335-0200
PROD MGR-PR, News-Press, Fort Myers, FL
Vanderels, Leigh .... (404) 876-1819
PUB, Southern Voice, Atlanta, GA
Vanderford, Diane .... (502) 448-4581
PUB, ED, Southwest Newsweek, Shively, KY
Vander Goore, Peter .... (208) 743-9411
PROD MGR-Electronic Processing
Lewiston Morning Tribune, Lewiston, ID
Vandergrift, Patty .... (304) 348-5140
City ED, Charleston Gazette, Sunday Gazette-Mail, Charleston, WV
Van der Heide, A A .... (604) 532-1733
PUB, Windmill Herald, Lynden, WA
Vanderhoof, E Joe .... (507) 625-4451
PRES/PUB, Free Press, Mankato, MN
Vanderlin, Geoff .... (815) 625-3600
CIRC MGR, Daily Gazette, Sterling, IL
Shaw Newspapers
Van Der Linden, Dirk J .... (515) 444-3333
PUB, Belmond Independent, Belmond, IA
Van Der Linden, Lee H .... (515) 444-3333
PUB, Belmond Independent, Belmond, IA
van der Linden, Tom .... (507) 895-2940
PUB, ED
Houston County News, La Crescent, MN
VanderMalle, Rebecca .... (716) 232-7100
MGR-Computer OPER, Rochester Democrat and Chronicle; Times-Union, Rochester, NY
Van Der Meulen, Fred .... (601) 961-7000
PROD MGR-Distribution Center
Clarion-Ledger, Jackson, MS
Vander Plas, Melissa .... (507) 493-5204
ED, News Record, Mabel, MN
Vanderpool, Jennifer .... (515) 284-8000
ADV MGR-RT, Register, Des Moines, IA
VanderStucken, Ed .... (409) 245-5555
Sports ED, Daily Tribune, Bay City, TX
Van Veen, Hank .... (209) 578-2000
CIRC MGR-Packaging/Distribution
Modesto Bee, CA
VanderVelden, Grant .... (608) 754-3311
MAN ED, Janesville Gazette, Janesville, WI
Vandervielt, Brian .... (919) 335-0841
Photo DEPT MGR
Daily Advance, Elizabeth City, NC
Vanderwaak, Walter .... (519) 287-2615
PUB, ED
Transcript & Free Press, Glencoe, ON
Vanderweide, Doug .... (207) 873-3341
EDL DIR, Central Maine Morning Sentinel, Waterville, ME
Van Der Werff, Renee .... (605) 724-2747
PUB, ED, Armour Chronicle, Armour, SD
Vanderwoude, Kari .... (712) 732-3130
BM, Pilot Tribune, Storm Lake, IA
Vanderzee, Karin .... (905) 732-2411
CIRC MGR, Tribune, Welland, ON
Van Dettey, Lisa .... (916) 846-3661
GM, Gridley Herald, Gridley, CA
Van Deventer, Betty .... (402) 475-4200
EDU Reporter (Lower), Police Reporter
Lincoln Journal Star, Lincoln, NE
Van Deventer, Dale .... (405) 372-5000
PROD SUPT, News Press, Stillwater, OK
Van de Voorde, Andy .... (303) 296-7744
MAN ED, Denver Westword, Denver, CO
van de Water, Ava .... (561) 820-4100
Home/Society ED
Palm Beach Post, West Palm Beach, FL
VandeWater, John .... (201) 877-4141
Garden ED, Star-Ledger, Newark, NJ
Vandewiele, Barb .... (309) 764-4344
Helping Hand ED, Dispatch, Moline, IL
Small Newspaper Group Inc.
Van DeWiele, Daniel .... (308) 235-3631
ED, Western Nebraska Observer, Kimball, NE
VanDeWoestyne, Jerilyn .... (309) 936-7215
ED, Atkinson Annawan News, Atkinson, IL
VanDien, Roark .... (800) 424-4747
TELEMKTG Sales Representative
Tribune Media Services-Television Listings, Glens Falls, NY
Van Doren, Mary .... (508) 528-2600
ED, Country Gazette, Franklin, MA
Van Dorn, Michael .... (618) 943-2331
MAN ED, Action Line ED, City ED, EPE, SCI/Technology ED, MGR-MIS
Daily Record, Lawrenceville, IL
Van Dusen, John H .... (315) 331-1000
PUB, Courier-Gazette, Newark, NY
Van Duuren, Ev .... (705) 789-5541
ED, Huntsville Forester, Huntsville, ON
Van Duyne, Richard .... (619) 337-3400
CIRC MGR
Imperial Valley Press, El Centro, CA
Van Dyck, Dave .... (312) 321-3000
Baseball Writer
Chicago Sun-Times, Chicago, IL
Van Dyke, Carol .... (913) 434-4525
PUB, ED, Plainville Times, Plainville, KS
Van Ee, Marty .... (319) 334-2557
PUB, Independence Bulletin-Journal, Independence, IA
VanEkeren, R A .... (307) 742-2176
PRES, TREAS, PUB
Laramie Daily Boomerang, Laramie, WY
Van Engelenhoven, Deb .... (515) 672-2581
ADV DIR, Oskaloosa Herald, Oskaloosa, IA
Van Enkenvoort, Bob .... (507) 376-9711
MAN ED, EPE, Daily Globe, Worthington, MN
Van Fossen, Drew .... (406) 496-5500
MAN ED, Reader Acquisition & Retention
Montana Standard, Butte, MT
Vangelos, Nick .... (216) 999-4500
PROD Chief ENG
Plain Dealer, Cleveland, OH
Van Genderen, Adeline E .... (605) 942-7770
PUB, ED, South Dakota Mail, Plankinton, SD
Van Halsema, Dick .... (704) 358-5000
DIR-Newsroom SYS, Online MGR-Technical
Charlotte Observer, Charlotte, NC
Van Harten, Peter .... (905) 526-3333
EDL Writer, Spectator, Hamilton, ON
Van Hine, Michael .... (810) 766-6100
DP MGR, Flint Journal, Flint, MI
VanHoesen, John .... (802) 747-6121
MAN ED, Rutland Herald, Rutland, VT
Van Hook, William B .... (601) 762-1111
CIRC DIR, Mississippi Press, Pascagoula, MS
VanHoose, Evelyn .... (816) 263-4123
CIRC MGR-CLASS, Moberly Monitor-Index & Democrat, Moberly, MO
Van Houten, George .... (607) 734-5151
PROD MGR-PR, Star-Gazette, Elmira, NY
Van Huffel, Jim .... (616) 429-2400
PROD MGR-Distribution
Herald-Palladium, St. Joseph, MI
Van Hulle, Phil .... (810) 469-4510
ED, EDU ED
Macomb Daily, Mount Clemens, MI
Van Hyning, Jim .... (217) 245-6121
PROD FRM-MR
Jacksonville Journal-Courier, Jacksonville, IL
Van Koevering, Kurtis .... (616) 772-2131
ED, Zeeland Record, Zeeland, MI
Van Koevering, Paul .... (616) 772-2131
PUB, Zeeland Record, Zeeland, MI
Van Kooten, Dennis .... (219) 838-0717
GM, Calumet Press, Highland, IN
Van Kooten, John .... (905) 358-5711
PUB, Niagara Falls Review, Niagara Falls, ON
Van Kuren, Paula .... (607) 734-5151
ADV MGR-CLASS, Star-Gazette, Elmira, NY
Vanlandingham, Gary .... (616) 429-2400
PROD MGR-Press
Herald-Palladium, St. Joseph, MI
Vanlaningham, Bill .... (818) 713-3000
MGR-Public Relations, DIR-MKTG
Daily News, Woodland Hills, CA
VanLaningham, Kelly .... (309) 686-3000
News ED, Journal Star, Peoria, IL
Vanlaningham, Stephanie .... (309) 367-2335
GM, MAN ED
Metamora Herald, Metamora, IL
Van Leer, Betty .... (541) 247-6643
PUB, ED
Curry County Reporter, Gold Beach, OR
Van Leer, Robert .... (541) 247-6643
PUB, Curry County Reporter, Gold Beach, OR
van Leerdam, Tammy .... (208) 354-8101
GM, Teton Valley News, Driggs, ID
VanLeeuwen, Karen .... (316) 231-2600
ADV MGR, Morning Sun, Pittsburg, KS
Van Liew, Norman C .... (601) 843-4241
VP, PUB/GM, ED
Bolivar Commercial, Cleveland, MS
Van Meter, Mike .... (541) 382-1811
EDU ED, Bulletin, Bend, OR
Van Meter, Val .... (540) 955-1111
ED, Clarke Courier, Berryville, VA
Van Moorlehem, Tracey .... (313) 222-6400
EDU Writer, Detroit Free Press, Detroit, MI
Vann, David .... (501) 623-7711
Photo ED, Sentinel-Record, Hot Springs, AR
Vann, Larry .... (601) 762-1111
PROD ASST SUPT
Mississippi Press, Pascagoula, MS
Van Namee, Joanne J .... (207) 990-8000
Chairman, Bangor Daily News, Bangor, ME
Van Nie, Rob .... (519) 255-5711
Sports ED, Windsor Star, Windsor, ON
Van Noord, Roger .... (810) 766-6100
MAN ED, Flint Journal, Flint, MI
Van Noppen, Rebecca .... (613) 652-4395
ED, Chieftain, Iroquois, ON
Van Orden, Dell .... (801) 237-2188
Church News
Deseret News, Salt Lake City, UT
Van Ormer, Alan .... (605) 256-4555
City ED, Madison Daily Leader, Madison, SD
VanOrmer, Chris .... (352) 544-5200
News ED, Hernando Today, Brooksville, FL
Vanover, Billy .... (202) 334-6000
PROD MGR-MR (NW)
Washington Post, Washington, DC
Van Patten, Mark .... (502) 781-1700
GM, MGR-PROM
Daily News, Bowling Green, KY
Van Patton, Mary Jan .... (913) 877-3361
CIRC MGR-Carrier
Norton Daily Telegram, Norton, KS
Pelt, Barbara .... (214) 977-8222
VP-MKTG, Dallas Morning News, Dallas, TX
Van Pelt, Bernadette .... (302) 674-3600
VP, CIRC MGR, Delaware State News, Dover, DE, Independent Newspapers Inc. (DE)
Van Ryswyck, Helen .... (803) 329-4000
DIR-Human Resources, Herald, Rock Hill, SC
Van Schouwen, Daryl .... (312) 321-3000
GEN Assignment
Chicago Sun-Times, Chicago, IL
Van Scoder, Dennis .... (419) 784-5441
BUS/FIN ED, Crescent-News, Defiance, OH
VanSickle, Richard .... (613) 739-7000
EIC, Ottawa Sun, Ottawa, ON
Van Slambrouck, Paul .... (408) 920-5000
ASST MAN ED-News
San Jose Mercury News, San Jose, CA
Van Strien, Leslie .... (573) 581-1111
MGR-MIS, Mexico Ledger, Mexico, MO
VanStry, Michael .... (805) 684-4428
PUB, Coastal View, Carpinteria, CA
VanStrydonck, John .... (605) 394-8300
PUB, Rapid City Journal, Rapid City, SD
Van Susteren, Dirk .... (802) 479-0191
Sunday ED, Times Argus, Barre, VT
Van Tighem, Greg .... (541) 963-3161
Health/Medical ED, Religion ED
Observer, La Grande, OR
Vantosky, Kurt M .... (207) 873-3341
ADV DIR, Central Maine Morning Sentinel, Waterville, ME, Guy Gannett Communications
Vantran, Kathy .... (410) 730-3620
ED, Soundoff!, Columbia, MD
Vantrease, David .... (706) 738-1142
PUB, ED, Metropolitan Spirit, Augusta, GA
Van Treese, Donna .... (405) 255-5354
Women's ED, Duncan Banner, Duncan, OK
Van Valkenburg, Mal .... (716) 282-2311
Sports ED
Niagara Gazette, Niagara Falls, NY
Van Valkenburg, Nancy .... (203) 574-3636
Entertainment/Amusements ED, Waterbury Republican-American, Waterbury, CT
VanVeghten, Rudy .... (603) 279-4516
ED, Meredith News, Meredith, NH
Van Wagenen, Chris .... (806) 762-8844
BUS/FIN ED, Oil/RE ED
Lubbock Avalanche-Journal, Lubbock, TX
Van Wagoner, Carol .... (801) 237-2031
EDL PROM MGR
Salt Lake Tribune, Salt Lake City, UT
Vanway, David .... (501) 839-2771
GM, MAN ED
Washington County Observer, West Fork, AR
Vanzee, Kris .... (605) 647-2284
PUB, ED, Lennox Independent, Lennox, SD
Van Zomeren, Valerie .... (616) 222-5400
CIRC MGR-MET South
Grand Rapids Press, Grand Rapids, MI
Vanzuro, Carl .... (706) 896-4454
ED, Towns County Herald, Hiawassee, GA
Varas, Feli .... (514) 987-2222
DP MGR, Gazette, Montreal, QC
Varble, Bill .... (541) 776-4411
Books ED, Music ED
Mail Tribune, Medford, OR
Vardaman, Didi .... (205) 766-3434
Teen-Age/Youth ED
Times Daily, Florence, AL
Vardeman, Johnny .... (770) 532-1234
ED, Times, Gainesville, GA
Varelli, Jerri T .... (908) 657-8936
PUB, Advance News, Lakehurst, NJ
Varga, George .... (619) 299-3131
Music Writer-Pop/Jazz
San Diego Union-Tribune, San Diego, CA
Varga, Victoria .... (716) 328-2144
Correspondent
Syndicated News Service, Rochester, NY
Vargas, Larry .... (909) 684-1200
ADV MGR-Ad SRV
Press-Enterprise, Riverside, CA
Vargo, Kathi .... (520) 753-6397
ADV DIR, Kingman Daily Miner, Kingman, AZ
Vargo, Norman .... (412) 664-9161
Sports ED, Daily News, McKeesport, PA
Varkonyi, Charlyne .... (954) 356-4000
Garden ED
Sun-Sentinel, Fort Lauderdale, FL
Varney, Del .... (614) 461-5000
PROD ASST DIR-Press
Columbus Dispatch, Columbus, OH
Varno, William .... (518) 374-4141
PROD FRM-PR
Daily Gazette, Schenectady, NY
Varosh, Lori .... (206) 455-2222
Special Sections ED
Eastside Journal, Bellevue, WA
Vartabedian, Ralph .... (213) 237-5000
Aerospace/Defense/Transportation-D.C.
Los Angeles Times, Los Angeles, CA
Vasallo, Alberto .... (617) 876-4293
PUB, ED, El Mundo, Cambridge, MA
Vasche, Mark .... (209) 578-2000
MAN ED, Modesto Bee, Modesto, CA
Vase, Nancy .... (307) 362-3736
Fashion/Society ED, Religion ED
Daily Rocket-Miner, Rock Springs, WY
Vasilyev, Rita .... (601) 234-4331
ASST PUB, Oxford Eagle, Oxford, MS
Vasquez, Jesus A .... (915) 673-4271
DIR-FIN, Abilene Reporter-News, Abilene, TX
Vasquez, Ricardo .... (313) 222-6400
MGR-Electronic Services
Detroit Newspapers, Detroit, MI
Vasquez, Rick .... (210) 423-5511
Photo DEPT MGR
Valley Morning Star, Harlingen, TX
Vasquez, Tina .... (512) 884-2011
Television ED, Caller-Times, Corpus Christi, TX
Vasquez MD, Erwin M .... (954) 527-0627
PUB, ED
El Heraldo de Broward, Ft. Lauderdale, FL
Vass, John .... (423) 756-6900
BUS ED
Chattanooga Free Press, Chattanooga, TN

237-Who's Where **Vin**

Vaughan, Albert ... (903) 886-3196
PUB, Commerce Journal, Commerce, TX

Vaughan, Brian ... (610) 933-8926
CIRC DIR, Phoenix, Phoenixville, PA

Vaughan, Dorothy ... (903) 785-8744
Society ED, Paris News, Paris, TX

Vaughan, Earl ... (910) 323-4848
Religion ED
Fayetteville Observer-Times, Fayetteville, NC

Vaughan, Joseph N ... (919) 332-2123
PUB, ED, News Herald, Ahoskie, NC

Vaughan, Peter ... (612) 673-4000
Theater Reporter
Star Tribune, Minneapolis, MN

Vaughan, Steve ... (804) 385-5400
Political ED, News & Advance, Lynchburg, VA

Vaughn, Alan ... (315) 253-5311
News ED, Wire ED, Citizen, Auburn, NY

Vaughn, Ed ... (704) 289-1541
CIRC FRM-MR
Enquirer-Journal, Monroe, NC

Vaughn, Jackie ... (330) 877-9345
MAN ED, Hartville News, Hartville, OH

Vaughn, John ... (520) 783-3333
City ED, EDU ED, Environmental ED, Features ED, Yuma Daily Sun, Yuma, AZ

Vaughn, Laura ... (914) 341-1100
ADV MGR-Niche Pubs
Times Herald-Record, Middletown, NY

Vaughn, Lucy ... (816) 388-6131
ED, Salisbury Press-Spectator, Salisbury, MO

Vaughn, Michael ... (630) 469-0100
ED, Glen Ellyn News, Glen Ellyn, IL

Vaughn, Robin ... (502) 667-2068
ED, Journal Enterprise, Providence, KY

Vaughn, Skip ... (205) 539-9828
ED, Redstone Rocket, Huntsville, AL

Vaughn, Tommy ... (615) 684-1200
CIRC MGR
Shelbyville Times-Gazette, Shelbyville, TN

Vaught, Larry ... (606) 236-2551
Sports ED, Advocate-Messenger, Danville, KY

Vaught, Randall ... (606) 787-7171
PUB, Casey County News, Liberty, KY

Vautour, Cindy ... (416) 463-3824
Syndication Representative
Graphics Syndicate, Toronto, ON

Vawter, Vince ... (812) 424-7711
PUB, ED, Evansville Courier, Evansville, IN
Scripps Howard

Vazquez, Rey Guevara ... (210) 542-4301
EPE, Brownsville Herald, Brownsville, TX

Veach, Morris ... (334) 875-2110
PROD FRM-COMP
Selma Times-Journal, Selma, AL

Veal, Sylvia ... (807) 223-2390
ED, Dryden Observer, Dryden, ON

Vealey, Randy ... (304) 292-6301
Wire ED, Dominion Post, Morgantown, WV

Veatch, Carol A ... (702) 333-7676
CORP DIR-PSL, Swift Newspapers, Reno, NV

Veatty, Mark ... (513) 241-1450
PUB
Cincinnati Court Index, Cincinnati, OH

Veazey, Doug ... (505) 863-6811
ADV MGR, Gallup Independent, Gallup, NM

Veazey, Walter ... (202) 408-1484
ASST MAN ED-Features, Scripps Howard News Service, Washington, DC

Vecchio, Pat ... (716) 372-3121
Automotive ED, Films/Theater ED
Olean Times-Herald, Olean, NY

Vecchio, Toni ... (719) 852-3531
ED, Monte Vista Journal, Monte Vista, CO

Vecsey, Laura ... (206) 448-8000
COL-Sports
Seattle Post-Intelligencer, Seattle, WA

Vedder, Bob ... (941) 484-2611
PUB, Venice Gondolier, Venice, FL

Vedvei, Jerrie ... (605) 352-6401
ADV MGR-CLASS Display
Huron Plainsman, Huron, SD

Veenbaaf, Jim ... (403) 349-3033
ED, Westlock News, Westlock, AB

Vega, Enedina ... (914) 358-2200
ADV DIR
Rockland Journal-News, West Nyack, NY

Vega, Frank J ... (313) 222-6400
PRES/CEO, Detroit Newspapers, Detroit, MI

Vega, Martin ... (212) 807-6622
EX DIR, Impact Visuals Photo & Graphics Inc., New York, NY

Vega, Philip ... (520) 458-9440
GM, Bravo, Sierra Vista, AZ

Vega, Philip ... (919) 537-2505
EDU ED, Features ED, NTL ED, Political/Government ED, Daily Herald, Roanoke Rapids, NC, Wick Communications

Vega, Victor M ... (305) 633-3341
BM, CONT, Diario Las Americas, Miami, FL

Vega-Lloyd, Miltie ... (360) 694-3391
MGR-Human Resources
Columbian, Vancouver, WA

Veigle, Ann ... (202) 636-3000
BUS ED, Washington Times, Washington, DC

Veillette, Bob ... (203) 574-3636
MAN ED, Waterbury Republican-American, Waterbury, CT

Veirs, Carlton ... (901) 772-1172
GM, States-Graphic, Brownsville, TN

Veitch, Arthur B ... (403) 827-3539
ED, Grande Cache Mountaineer, Grande Cache, AB

Veitz, Wendy ... (814) 938-8740
Fashion/Food ED, Home Furnishings ED, Society/Women's ED, Youth ED
Spirit, Punxsutawney, PA

Vela, Ricardo ... (312) 252-3534
ED, Northeast Extra, Chicago, IL

Velder, Tim ... (605) 456-2585
PUB, ED, Valley Irrigator, Newell, SD

Veldkamp, Brad ... (703) 276-3400
CIRC GM-Cincinnati
USA Today, Arlington, VA

Veldman, Mary Ann ... (310) 337-7003
Sales EX
Creators Syndicate, Los Angeles, CA

Veley, Cathy ... (805) 781-7800
CIRC MGR-Zone
Telegram-Tribune, San Luis Obispo, CA

Vellani, John ... (614) 224-5195
GM, Catholic Times, Columbus, OH

Vellardita, Mary ... (810) 541-3000
GM, Daily Tribune, Royal Oak, MI

Velotta, Rick ... (702) 385-3111
BUS ED, Las Vegas Sun, Las Vegas, NV

Veltri, Debbie ... (304) 624-6411
ADV MGR-CLASS, Clarksburg Exponent/Telegram, Clarksburg, WV

Venable, Chris ... (501) 751-6200
Online Contact, Morning News of Northwest Arkansas, Springdale, AR

Venable, Jack B ... (334) 283-6568
PUB, ED, Tallassee Tribune, Tallassee, AL

Venable, Mike ... (334) 298-0679
PUB, ED, Phenix Citizen, Phenix City, AL

Venable, Sam ... (423) 523-3131
COL, Knoxville News-Sentinel, Knoxville, TN

Vendemark, Larry ... (916) 842-5777
PROD SUPT, Siskiyou Daily News, Yreka, CA

Venetian, Charles S ... (513) 721-2700
CIRC DIR-Home Delivery
Cincinnati Enquirer, Cincinnati, OH

Vennels, Bill ... (604) 732-2222
PROD DIR, Province, Vancouver, BC
Southam Inc.

Venouziou, Ester ... (703) 257-4600
News ED
Prince William Journal, Manassas, VA

Venslovaitis, Al ... (416) 585-5000
VP-Information Technology, Globe and Mail (Canada's National Newspaper), Toronto, ON

Venter, Harry L ... (303) 769-4646
PUB, Tri-County Tribune, Deer Trail, CO

Venturella, Robert ... (814) 676-7444
News ED, News-Herald, Oil City, PA

Venus, Larry ... (909) 242-7614
ED, Valley Times, Moreno Valley, CA

Vera, Monica ... (915) 236-6677
PROD SUPT
Sweetwater Reporter, Sweetwater, TX

Verbyla, Elsa C ... (804) 693-3101
ED, Gloucester Mathews Gazette-Journal, Gloucester, VA

Vercauteren, Gary ... (414) 849-7036
PUB, Chilton Times-Journal, Chilton, WI

Vercher, Dennis ... (214) 754-8710
ED, Dallas Voice, Dallas, TX

Verdel, Frank ... (941) 953-7755
GM/News DIR-News Channel
Sarasota Herald-Tribune, Sarasota, FL

Verdi, Bob ... (312) 222-3232
COL, Chicago Tribune, Chicago, IL

Verdon, Roger ... (913) 843-1000
MAN ED, Journal-World, Lawrence, KS

Verdun, Bob ... (519) 669-5155
PUB, ED, Elmira Independent, Elmira, ON

Veres, Louise ... (519) 255-5711
PSL MGR, Windsor Star, Windsor, ON

Vergara, Carmelo ... (305) 858-9613
ASST DIR
Colombian Comics Syndicate, Miami, FL

Verghese, Sally ... (215) 855-8440
DP MGR, Reporter, Landsdale, PA

Verlich, Edward J ... (412) 351-3909
ED, Zajednicar, Pittsburgh, PA

Ver Meer, Preston ... (507) 962-3230
PUB, Hills Cresent, Hills, MN

Vermillion, John F ... (316) 331-4950
PUB, ED
Independence News, Independence, KS

Verniere, Jim ... (617) 426-3000
Films Critic ED, Boston Herald, Boston, MA

Vernon, Dane ... (573) 392-5658
PUB, Eldon Advertiser, Eldon, MO

Vernon, Dennis ... (701) 857-1900
CIRC DIR, Minot Daily News, Minot, ND

Vernon, Jerry ... (703) 838-0302
PUB
Alexandria Gazette Packet, Alexandria, VA

Vernon, Michelle ... (215) 855-8440
ADV MGR-RT, Reporter, Landsdale, PA

Verrasso, Vernetta ... (505) 622-7710
ADV SUPV-CLASS
Roswell Daily Record, Roswell, NM

Verrella, Marlo ... (304) 367-2500
Women's ED
Times-West Virginian, Fairmont, WV

Verrengia, Joseph ... (303) 892-5000
SCI Writer
Rocky Mountain News, Denver, CO

Ver Steeg, Jane ... (712) 753-2258
ED, West Lyon Herald, Inwood, IA

Vertrees, Carl ... (541) 548-2184
PUB, Redmond Spokesman, Redmond, OR

Veselenak, Joe ... (616) 754-9301
Chief Photographer
Daily News, Greenville, MI

Vesely, Jim ... (206) 464-2111
ASSOC EPE, Seattle Times, Seattle, WA

Vesper, Carolyn ... (703) 276-3400
ADV Senior VP/ASSOC PUB
USA Today, Arlington, VA

Vespi, Peggy ... (315) 823-3680
ADV MGR-PROM
Evening Times, Little Falls, NY

Vess, Todd ... (970) 686-9646
ED, Windsor Beacon, Windsor, CO

Vest, Stephen ... (803) 329-4000
Sports ED, Herald, Rock Hill, SC

Vestal, Shawn ... (406) 587-4491
City ED, Daily Chronicle, Bozeman, MT

Vetroczky, Mike ... (309) 346-1111
DP MGR, Pekin Daily Times, Pekin, IL

Vettel, Phil ... (312) 222-3232
Restaurant Critic
Chicago Tribune, Chicago, IL

Vetter, Kathy ... (817) 390-7400
MAN ED-MET, State, NTL, Foreign, Photo, Copy Desk
Fort Worth Star-Telegram, Fort Worth, TX

Veuger, Jules ... (619) 299-3131
CIRC MGR-Delivery Operations
San Diego Union-Tribune, San Diego, CA

Vevoda, Jodi ... (212) 715-2100
DIR/Midwest Sales
USA Weekend, New York, NY

Vezina, Doris ... (712) 728-2223
ED, Hartley Sentinel, Hartley, IA

Vezina Jr, W R ... (712) 728-2223
ED, Hartley Sentinel, Hartley, IA

Vezza, Richard J ... (201) 365-3000
PRES, PUB
North Jersey Herald & News, Passaic, NJ

Vial, Jose J Rios ... (56-2) 235-2902
DIR, Europa Press News Service, Santiago

Vibrock, Connie ... (573) 377-4616
ED, Morgan County Press, Stover, MO

Vicarro, Roxanne ... (540) 949-8213
ADV DIR, News Virginian, Waynesboro, VA

Vicars, Dan ... (814) 946-7411
DP MGR, Altoona Mirror, Altoona, PA

Vicars, Diane ... (402) 223-5233
MAN ED, Amusements ED, EPE/Writer, News ED, State ED
Beatrice Daily Sun, Beatrice, NE

Viccari, Dom A ... (412) 758-5573
ADV DIR
Ellwood City Ledger, Ellwood City, PA

Viccaro, Roxanne ... (307) 682-9306
ADV MGR, News-Record, Gillette, WY

Vick, Glen ... (317) 423-5511
CIRC MGR-Home Delivery
Journal and Courier, Lafayette, IN

Vickery, Jerry ... (864) 855-0355
PUB, Easley Progress, Easley, SC

Vickery, June ... (573) 729-4126
PUB, Salem News, Salem, MO

Vickery, Kathleen ... (804) 625-0700
ED, Our Own Community Press, Norfolk, VA

Vickery, Peggy ... (706) 376-8025
PUB, Hartwell Sun, Hartwell, GA

Vickery, W Ray ... (573) 729-4126
PUB, Salem News, Salem, MO

Vickery, Wassie ... (706) 376-8025
ED, Hartwell Sun, Hartwell, GA

Vickrey, Robert ... (815) 223-3200
ADV VP, MGR-MKTG/Sales
News-Tribune, La Salle, IL

Vico, Ray ... (954) 356-4000
ADV MGR-Display
Sun-Sentinel, Fort Lauderdale, FL

Victor, Beaux ... (318) 462-0616
ADV MGR
Beauregard Daily News, De Ridder, LA

Victor Dix, Robert ... (419) 784-5441
VP, Crescent-News, Defiance, OH

Victory, Hershel ... (205) 236-1551
ADV MGR-NTL, Anniston Star, Anniston, AL

Victory, Mark ... (972) 298-4211
MAN ED, Lancaster Today, Duncanville, TX

Vida, Vera ... (617) 786-7000
Travel ED, Patriot Ledger, Quincy, MA

Vidal, Josephina ... (213) 622-8332
Features ED, La Opinion, Los Angeles, CA

Vied, Joe ... (210) 728-2500
CONT, Laredo Morning Times, Laredo, TX

Viehman, Ava ... (573) 775-5454
ED
Steelville Star-Crawford Mirror, Steelville, MO

Vieira, Ginger ... (508) 880-9000
ADV MGR
Taunton Daily Gazette, Taunton, MA

Vienneau, Hermel ... (506) 727-4444
ED, MAN ED
L'Acadie Nouvelle, Caraquet, NB

Viera, James J ... (612) 673-4000
VP/CFO, Star Tribune, Minneapolis, MN

Viereck, Darla J ... (605) 778-6253
ED, Brule County News, Kimball, SD

Viergutz, Greg ... (308) 537-3636
PUB, Gothenburg Times, Gothenburg, NE

Viergutz, Kathi ... (308) 537-3636
PUB, Gothenburg Times, Gothenburg, NE

Vierthaler, L A ... (316) 385-2200
PUB, ED, Spearville News, Spearville, KS

Viggiano, Anthony ... (201) 365-3000
ADV DIR, ADV DIR-NTL
North Jersey Herald & News, Passaic, NJ

Viggiano, Jay ... (218) 723-5281
CIRC MGR-OPER
Duluth News-Tribune, Duluth, MN

Vigil, Evelyn ... (505) 662-4185
ED/PUB
Los Alamos Monitor, Los Alamos, NM

Vigil, Joseph ... (505) 983-3303
ADV MGR-RT
Santa Fe New Mexican, Santa Fe, NM

Vigil, Vicki ... (719) 539-6691
ADV MGR, Mountain Mail, Salida, CO

Vigilante, Ellen ... (908) 574-1200
PUB, ED, Atom Tabloid, Rahway, NJ

Vigliante, Lorenzo ... (409) 776-4444
CIRC DIR, Eagle, Bryan, TX

Viglione, Barb ... (814) 773-3161
CIRC DIR, Ridgway Record, Ridgway, PA

Vigliotti, Carole A ... (216) 247-5335
GM, Chagrin Valley Times, Chagrin Falls, OH

Vigna, Paul ... (717) 771-2000
Sports ED, York Daily Record, York, PA

Vignali, Sharon ... (919) 829-4500
PROD MGR-PR
News & Observer, Raleigh, NC

Vigneault, Francois ... (506) 753-7637
ED, Journal L'Aviron, Campbellton, NB

Vigneault, Jean ... (514) 773-6028
ED, Le Courrier de Saint-Hyacinthe, Saint-Hyacinthe, QC

Viklund, Sakri ... (807) 344-1611
ED, Canadan Uutiset, Thunder Bay, ON

Viksna, Ingida ... (416) 465-7902
ED, Latvija-Amerika, Toronto, ON

Vilchis, Eric ... (909) 987-6397
SYS ED
Inland Valley Daily Bulletin, Ontario, CA

Villa, Mary Jo ... (608) 754-3311
Human Resources DIR
Bliss Communications Inc., Janesville, WI

Villacres, Elsie ... (718) 507-0832
GM, El Tiempo de Nueva York, New York, NY

Villalobos, George ... (408) 272-9394
PUB, GM
Alianza Metropolitan News, San Jose, CA

Villalobos, Michael ... (408) 272-9394
PUB
Alianza Metropolitan News, San Jose, CA

Villalpando, Karen ... (213) 933-5518
PUB, Beverly Press/Park LaBrea News, Los Angeles, CA

Villalpando, Michael ... (213) 933-5518
PUB, Beverly Press/Park LaBrea News, Los Angeles, CA

Villard, Charles E ... (207) 990-8000
PROD FRM-PR, Daily News, Bangor, ME

Villarreal, Gene ... (219) 461-8444
ADV MGR-Sales
Fort Wayne Newspapers Inc., Fort Wayne, IN

Villilobos, Christi ... (941) 748-0411
Women's/Society ED
Bradenton Herald, Bradenton, FL

Vincent, Charlie ... (313) 222-6400
COL-Sports, Detroit Free Press, Detroit, MI

Vincent, Chuck ... (603) 224-5301
GM, Concord Monitor, Concord, NH

Vincent, David ... (901) 529-2211
EPE, Commercial Appeal, Memphis, TN

Vincent, Gordon ... (617) 933-3700
Environmental ED, Farm ED
Daily Times Chronicle, Woburn, MA

Vincent, Jennifer ... (800) 544-4094
ED, Clinton County News, St. Johns, MI

Vincent, Jim ... (508) 997-7411
RE ED, Standard Times, New Bedford, MA

Vincent, John ... (401) 722-4000
City ED, Times, Pawtucket, RI

Vin Who's Where-238

Vincent, Kathleen .... (214) 977-8222
Art DIR-News
Dallas Morning News, Dallas, TX

Vincent, Kevin .... (705) 268-6252
PUB, GM, Timmins Times, Timmins, ON

Vincent, Louise .... (514) 987-2222
Graphics ED, Gazette, Montreal, QC

Vincent, Mal .... (757) 446-2000
Films/Theater ED, Radio/Television ED
Virginian-Pilot, Norfolk, VA

Vincent, Thomas .... (407) 322-2611
Chief Photographer
Sanford Herald, Sanford, FL

Vincent, W Curt .... (812) 944-6481
MAN ED
Tribune/Ledger & Tribune, New Albany, IN

Vincent, Wendy .... (508) 764-4325
PROD MGR, News, Southbridge, MA

Vineberg, Tammy .... (403) 849-4350
ED, Scope, Slave Lake, AB

Vines, Georgiana .... (915) 546-6340
PRES, PUB, ED
El Paso Herald-Post, El Paso, TX

Vineyard, Kristina .... (614) 472-0734
PUB
Monroe County Beacon, Woodsfield, OH

Vingle, Mitch .... (304) 348-5140
Sports ED, Charleston Gazette, Sunday Gazette-Mail, Charleston, WV

Vinson, Ben .... (717) 243-2611
CIRC DIR, Sentinel, Carlisle, PA

Viola, Richard .... (516) 843-2020
ADV New BUS/OPER, Newsday, Melville, NY

Virbila, S Irene .... (213) 237-5000
Restaurant Critic
Los Angeles Times, Los Angeles, CA

Vircoe, Jeff .... (604) 248-4341
ED, News, Parksville, BC

Virgin, Bruce .... (903) 893-8181
PROD MGR-Distribution
Herald Democrat, Sherman, TX

Virtanen, Michael .... (518) 454-5694
Travel ED, Times Union, Albany, NY

Virtue, Anna .... (213) 237-5000
Miami BU
Los Angeles Times, Los Angeles, CA

Virzi, Ann Maria .... (203) 333-0161
ASST MAN ED-News
Connecticut Post, Bridgeport, CT

Vise, Tammy .... (505) 763-3431
ADV MGR-CLASS
Clovis News Journal, Clovis, NM

Visser, Nancy .... (904) 359-4111
Features ED
Florida Times-Union, Jacksonville, FL

Visser, Robert .... (202) 234-8787
DIR-Photography
Photopress Washington, Washington, DC

Vissing, John .... (812) 283-6636
PROD FRM-Press
Evening News, Jeffersonville, IN

Vit, Bruno .... (705) 759-3030
PROD MGR-Manufacturing
Sault Star, Sault Ste. Marie, ON

Vitale, James M .... (717) 622-3456
ADV MGR-RT, Pottsville Republican & Evening Herald, Pottsville, PA

Vitale, Phil .... (219) 235-6161
Automotive ED, Building ED, Garden ED
South Bend Tribune, South Bend, IN

Vito, Marie .... (609) 845-3300
ADV MGR-CLASS/MKTG Services
Gloucester County Times, Woodbury, NJ

Vitolo, Rino .... (508) 744-0600
CIRC DIR, Salem Evening News, Beverly, MA
Ottaway Newspapers Inc.

Vitorelo, Terry .... (415) 986-4422
VP-OPER, Business Wire, San Francisco, CA

Vitt, Shawn .... (503) 221-8327
Graphics ED, Oregonian, Portland, OR

Vittorini, Carlo .... (212) 450-7000
Chairman/PUB, React, Parade Publications Inc., New York, NY

Vives, Lisa .... (212) 286-0123
DIR, OPECNA, Inter Press Service, Africa Information Afrique, New York, NY

Vivion, Mike .... (573) 636-3131
BM, DP MGR
News Tribune, Jefferson City, MO

Vivona, John .... (816) 932-6600
Sales MGR/Midwest Div.
Universal Press Syndicate, Kansas City, MO

Vizard, David .... (517) 895-8551
NTL ED, News ED
Bay City Times, Bay City, MI

Vizer, Tim .... (618) 234-1000
Chief Photographer
Belleville News-Democrat, Belleville, IL

Vizzini, John .... (605) 331-2200
CIRC DIR, Argus Leader, Sioux Falls, SD

Vlha, Scott .... (510) 935-2525
Photo ED
Contra Costa Times, Walnut Creek, CA

Vlossak, Dan .... (207) 778-2075
MAN ED, Franklin Journal & Farmington Chronicle, Farmington, ME

Voas, Jeremy .... (602) 271-0040
MAN ED, New Times, Phoenix, AZ

Vodenichar, Ronald A .... (412) 282-8000
GM, DIR-MKTG/PROM
Butler Eagle, Butler, PA

Vodusek, Joe .... (705) 268-5050
PROD MGR-PR, Daily Press, Timmins, ON

Voelker, Gary .... (314) 340-8000
MGR-CR, Post-Dispatch, St. Louis, MO

Voelker, N Jean .... (217) 347-7151
ADV MGR-CLASS, Daily News, Effingham, IL

Voell, Paula .... (716) 849-3434
Home Furnishings ED
Buffalo News, Buffalo, NY

Vogel, Art .... (614) 461-5000
PROD MGR-Pre Press
Columbus Dispatch, Columbus, OH

Vogel, Bruce (Bud) .... (209) 532-7151
ADV MGR-Display
Union Democrat, Sonora, CA

Vogel, David .... (414) 224-2000
Senior ED-Night News
Milwaukee Journal Sentinel, Milwaukee, WI

Vogel, Josie .... (416) 494-4990
CIRC MGR, Daily Commercial News and Construction Record, N. York, ON

Vogel, Michael .... (716) 849-3434
Environmental ED, SCI/Technology ED
Buffalo News, Buffalo, NY

Vogelpohl, James M .... (314) 340-8402
TREAS, Pulitzer Publishing, St. Louis, MO

Vogl, Twila .... (308) 665-2310
PUB, ED
Crawford Clipper/Harrison Sun, Crawford, NE

Vogler, Mark E .... (508) 228-8455
ED, Nantucket Beacon, Nantucket, MA

Vogt, John .... (518) 828-1616
CIRC MGR, Register-Star, Hudson, NY

Vogt, Nancy .... (515) 352-3325
ED, Gowrie News, Gowrie, IA

Vogt, Peter .... (423) 392-0295
VP/GEN Counsel/CFO, Sandusky-Norwalk Newspapers, Kingsport, TN

Vogt, Tom .... (360) 694-3391
EDU ED, Columbian, Vancouver, WA

Voiers, Kelly .... (606) 329-1717
ADV DIR, Daily Independent, Ashland, KY

Voigt, Craig .... (701) 947-2417
PUB
New Rockford Transcript, New Rockford, ND

Voigt, Sally .... (618) 262-5144
ADV DIR
Daily Republican Register, Mount Carmel, IL

Voigt, Tom .... (419) 636-1111
GM, ADV MGR, MGR-MKTG/PROM, Online MGR, Bryan Times, Bryan, OH

Voisin, Paul .... (504) 826-3279
PROD MGR-Mechanical/Building Maintenance, Times-Picayune, New Orleans, LA

Voit, Stan .... (334) 821-7150
GM, ED, Auburn Bulletin-Eagle, Auburn, AL

Voitavitch, Cindy .... (203) 729-2228
ADV MGR, Daily News, Naugatuck, CT

Voket, John .... (203) 926-2080
ED, Monroe Courier, Monroe, CT

Volcek, Joe .... (308) 532-6000
MKTG INFO MGR-New BUS Development, CIRC MGR, ADTX MGR, Online MGR
North Platte Telegraph, North Platte, NE

Volesky, Richard .... (701) 225-8111
BUS/FIN ED, Dickinson Press, Dickinson, ND

Voleta, George .... (773) 586-8800
Administrative OPER MGR
Daily Southtown, Chicago, IL

Volgenau, Gerry .... (313) 222-6400
Travel Writer
Detroit Free Press, Detroit, MI

Volkman, Richard D .... (402) 755-2204
PUB, ED
Nebraska Journal-Leader, Ponca, NE

Vollmer, Becky .... (607) 432-1000
Wire ED, Daily Star, Oneonta, NY

Vollmer, Frank .... (716) 849-3434
MGR-CR, Buffalo News, Buffalo, NY

Vollmer, Ted .... (608) 782-9710
News ED, La Crosse Tribune, La Crosse, WI

Volovski, Steven .... (203) 574-3636
DP MGR, Waterbury Republican-American, Waterbury, CT

Volpe, Mike .... (416) 585-5000
CIRC Regional MGR-Prairies, Globe and Mail (Canada's National Newspaper), Toronto, ON

Volpe, Stephen P .... (401) 277-7000
CIRC MGR-Budgets
Providence Journal-Bulletin, Providence, RI

Voltoline, Frank .... (407) 322-2611
PROD MGR, Sanford Herald, Sanford, FL

Voltz, Edith .... (219) 724-2121
BUS/FIN ED
Decatur Daily Democrat, Decatur, IN

Vonderhaar, Larry .... (502) 582-4011
VP-Labor, Courier-Journal, Louisville, KY

Vondracek, Sue .... (205) 236-1551
Action Line ED, Anniston Star, Anniston, AL

Vondrak, James .... (773) 476-4800
PUB, Southwest News-Herald, Chicago, IL

von Drehle, David .... (202) 334-6000
ASST MAN ED-Style, Entertainment/Amusements ED, Washington Post, Washington, DC

Von Esslyn, Drew .... (757) 539-3437
Sports ED, Suffolk News-Herald, Suffolk, VA

vonKaenel, Jeff .... (916) 498-1234
PUB
Sacramento News & Review, Sacramento, CA

von Kampen, Joan .... (308) 532-6000
News ED
North Platte Telegraph, North Platte, NE

von Netzer, Garet .... (806) 376-4488
PUB, Amarillo Daily News/Globe Times, Amarillo, TX

Von Rhein, John .... (312) 222-3232
Music Critic-Classical
Chicago Tribune, Chicago, IL

Vonthron, Deborah .... (419) 625-5500
Librarian, Sandusky Register, Sandusky, OH

Von Werder, Allan .... (318) 828-3706
PUB, Online MGR
Franklin Banner-Tribune, Franklin, LA

Von Werder, Debbie .... (318) 828-3706
ADV MGR
Franklin Banner-Tribune, Franklin, LA

Voorhies, John E .... (541) 474-3700
PRES
Grants Pass Daily Courier, Grants Pass, OR

Vopelak, Judith .... (518) 454-5694
ADTX MGR, Times Union, Albany, NY

Vorosvary, Irene .... (416) 233-3131
PUB, MAN ED
Kanadai Magyarsag, Etobicoke, ON

Vorous, Richard .... (408) 920-5000
CIRC MGR-Budget/Technology
San Jose Mercury News, San Jose, CA

Vorpahl, Doug .... (408) 920-5000
PROD MGR-COMP
San Jose Mercury News, San Jose, CA

Vortherms, Rebecca J .... (413) 772-0261
CONT, Recorder, Greenfield, MA

Vos, Ady .... (613) 962-9171
Sports ED, Intelligencer, Belleville, ON

Vos, Kathy .... (507) 625-4451
News DIR-Content/Editing
Free Press, Mankato, MN

Vosburgh, Catherine .... (802) 447-7567
MGR-Office
Bennington Banner, Bennington, VT

Voskuhl, John .... (606) 231-3100
State ED
Lexington Herald-Leader, Lexington, KY

Vosmeier, Chris .... (219) 461-8444
ADV MGR-Specialty Publications
Fort Wayne Newspapers Inc., Fort Wayne, IN

Voss, Charlotte .... (205) 345-0505
Religion ED
Tuscaloosa News, Tuscaloosa, AL

Voss, Jerrilynn S .... (573) 897-2109
PUB, Unterrified Democrat, Linn, MO

Vosskuehler, Charles .... (937) 236-4990
ED, Huber Heights Courier, Dayton, OH

Votaw, Parke .... (216) 951-0000
CIRC MGR, News-Herald, Willoughby, OH

Votel, Jay .... (410) 268-5000
NTL ED, Capital, Annapolis, MD

Vowell, Roberta .... (757) 446-2000
Entertainment ED, Music ED
Virginian-Pilot, Norfolk, VA

Vrabel, Joe D .... (512) 859-2238
PUB, ED, Nasinec, Granger, TX

Vradenburg, Sarah .... (330) 996-3000
EDL Writer, Akron Beacon Journal, Akron, OH

Vrana, Debora .... (213) 237-5000
Personal FIN
Los Angeles Times, Los Angeles, CA

Vrazo, Fawn .... (215) 854-2000
London BU
Philadelphia Inquirer, Philadelphia, PA

Vroman, Barbara .... (408) 920-5000
ASSOC EPE
San Jose Mercury News, San Jose, CA

Vroom, Richard .... (800) 388-1356
PRES
Liberty Features Syndicate, Lewistown, NY

Vucic, Bob .... (717) 255-8100
EX News ED, Patriot-News, Harrisburg, PA

Vukelich, Dan .... (505) 823-7777
BUS ED
Albuquerque Tribune, Albuquerque, NM

Vuletich, Matthew .... (303) 688-3128
MAN ED, Elbert County News, Kiowa, CO

Vurpillat, Glenda .... (904) 747-5000
ADV SUPV-CLASS
News Herald, Panama City, FL

Vyeda, Ed .... (408) 423-4242
Fashion ED, Features ED, Food ED, Living ED, Television ED
Santa Cruz County Sentinel, Santa Cruz, CA

Vyhnak, Carola .... (416) 367-2000
Fashion/Life ED, Toronto Star, Toronto, ON

Vyvjala, Darrell .... (409) 743-3450
MAN ED
Schulenburg Sticker, Schulenburg, TX

Vyvjala, Maxine .... (409) 743-3450
PUB, Schulenburg Sticker, Schulenburg, TX

W

Wablay, John .... (501) 785-7700
NTL ED
Southwest Times Record, Fort Smith, AR

Wachowicz, David .... (517) 895-8551
CIRC MGR, Bay City Times, Bay City, MI

Wachs, Derrick M .... (219) 866-5111
PROD MGR, Republican, Rensselaer, IN

Wachsman, Doris .... (520) 458-3340
ED, Huachuca Scout, Sierra Vista, AZ

Wachsmuth, William .... (412) 775-3200
PROD SUPV-Plate
Beaver County Times, Beaver, PA

Wachter, Blythe .... (715) 833-9200
Food ED, Religion ED
Leader-Telegram, Eau Claire, WI

Wachtler, George .... (308) 237-2152
TREAS, Kearney Hub, Kearney, NE

Wack, Craig .... (217) 245-6121
Sports ED
Jacksonville Journal-Courier, Jacksonville, IL

Wacker, Wayne .... (970) 867-5651
PROD FRM-PR
Fort Morgan Times, Fort Morgan, CO

Waclawek, Nancy .... (813) 893-8111
ASST MAN ED-Features
St. Petersburg Times, St. Petersburg, FL

Wada, Karen .... (213) 237-5000
Deputy MAN ED-Times Poll/Column One/Special Projects
Los Angeles Times, Los Angeles, CA

Waddell, Alex .... (317) 633-1240
News ED-AM
Indianapolis Star/News, Indianapolis, IN

Waddell, Eileen .... (803) 775-6331
City/MET ED, Political/Government ED
Item, Sumter, SC

Waddell, Ken .... (204) 328-7494
PUB, ED, Rivers Banner, Rivers, MB

Wadden, Ron .... (613) 544-5000
News ED
Kingston Whig-Standard, Kingston, ON

Waddington, Bret .... (217) 429-5151
PROD SUPV-Press
Herald & Review, Decatur, IL

Waddle, Chris .... (205) 236-1551
Deputy ED, EPE, Anniston Star, Anniston, AL

Waddle, Ray .... (615) 259-8000
Religion ED, Tennessean, Nashville, TN

Wade, Ben .... (517) 787-0450
PUB, ED, News, Jackson, MI

Wade, David E .... (717) 527-2213
PUB, ED, Times, Port Royal, PA

Wade, Gerald .... (402) 444-1000
Consumer Interest ED
Omaha World-Herald, Omaha, NE

Wade, Jim .... (501) 968-5252
CIRC MGR, Courier, Russellville, AR

Wade, Judy .... (813) 949-9310
ED, Lake Area News, Lutz, FL

Wade, LaDonna J .... (757) 247-4600
VP/DIR-Human Resources
Daily Press, Newport News, VA

Wade, Larry R .... (405) 225-3000
PRES, PUB, BUS/FIN ED, EPE, NTL ED, Political/Government ED
Elk City Daily News, Elk City, OK

Wade, Margaret .... (701) 223-2500
PUB, Bismarck Tribune, Bismarck, ND

Wade, Mary Jane .... (405) 225-3000
SEC/TREAS
Elk City Daily News, Elk City, OK

Wade, Nicholas .... (212) 556-1234
Health/SCI ED
New York Times, New York, NY

Wade, Nigel .... (312) 321-3000
EIC (Chicago Sun Times)
Chicago Sun-Times, Chicago, IL

Wade, Ron .... (612) 673-4000
ASST MAN ED-Production
Star Tribune, Minneapolis, MN

Wade, Stephen .... (913) 295-1111
DP MGR, Topeka Capital-Journal, Topeka, KS

Wadkins, Bill .... (309) 389-2811
PUB, ED, Glasford Gazette, Glasford, IL

Wadley, Carma .... (801) 237-2188
Features ED, Living/Lifestyle ED, Society ED
Deseret News, Salt Lake City, UT

Wadsworth, Ted .... (508) 412-1500
ED, Georgetown Record, Ipswich, MA

Waechter, Carla .... (316) 356-1201
GM, Ulysses News, Ulysses, KS

Waechter, Marlin G .... (402) 439-2173
PUB, ED, Stanton Register, Stanton, NE

Waechter, Roland E .... (913) 762-5000
VP/SEC, GM, PA
Daily Union, Junction City, KS

239-Who's Where **Wal**

Waer, Ronald R .... (203) 729-2228
PUB, Naugatuck Daily News, Naugatuck, CT
Wafer Jr, Thomas J .... (619) 454-0411
VP, Copley Press Inc., La Jolla, CA
Wagar, Michael .... (360) 308-9161
ED, Central Kitsap Reporter, Silverdale, WA
Wager, Leona C .... (605) 948-2110
PUB, ED, Hoven Review, Hoven, SD
Wager, Richard K .... (914) 454-2000
PUB, Journal, Poughkeepsie, NY
Wages, Jena .... (706) 549-0123
ADV MGR-Sales, Athens Daily News/Banner-Herald, Athens, GA
Waggoner, Doug .... (573) 636-3131
EX ED, News Tribune, Jefferson City, MO
Waggoner, J LaJeune .... (704) 982-2121
PUB, Stanly News and Press, Albemarle, NC
Waggoner, Judy .... (616) 698-3209
MAN ED, Zondervan Press Syndicate, Grand Rapids, MI
Waggoner, Michael L .... (817) 422-4314
PUB, Munday Courier, Munday, TX
Wagler, Robert J .... (423) 638-4181
CONT, Greeneville Sun, Greeneville, TN
Wagnaar, Norm .... (705) 887-2940
ED, Fenelon Falls Gazette, Fenelon Falls, ON
Wagner, Barbara .... (914) 694-9300
CIRC DIR-Customer SRV, Reporter Dispatch, White Plains, NY, Gannett Co. Inc.
Wagner, Charles .... (419) 625-5500
Sports ED, Sandusky Register, Sandusky, OH
Wagner, Dave .... (316) 331-3550
Aviation ED, COL, Sports ED, Independence Daily Reporter, Independence, KS
Wagner, Dave .... (602) 271-8000
Political ED, Arizona Republic, Phoenix, AZ
Wagner, Dave .... (206) 464-2111
Seattle Times, Seattle, WA
Wagner, David .... (937) 592-3060
ED, EPE, Features ED, News ED, Political ED Bellefontaine Examiner, Bellefontaine, OH
Wagner, Dennis .... (909) 987-6397
CIRC DIR
Inland Valley Daily Bulletin, Ontario, CA
Wagner, Don .... (540) 885-7281
ADV MGR-CLASS
Daily News Leader, Staunton, VA
Wagner, Eugene .... (712) 792-3573
PROD FRM-COMP
Daily Times Herald, Caroll, IA
Wagner, Fred .... (608) 752-0777
ED
Sunday Janesville Messenger, Janesville, WI
Wagner, Greg .... (409) 632-6631
CONT, DP MGR, Lufkin Daily News, Lufkin, TX, Cox Newspapers Inc.
Wagner, Holly .... (217) 223-5100
Amusements ED, Films/Theater ED, Radio/ Television ED
Quincy Herald-Whig, Quincy, IL
Wagner, James D .... (757) 446-2000
VP/TREAS, Virginian-Pilot, Norfolk, VA
Wagner, Jeff .... (712) 324-5347
GM, N'West Iowa Review, Sheldon, IA
Wagner, Jim .... (312) 321-3000
Television Prevue
Chicago Sun-Times, Chicago, IL
Wagner, Jim .... (505) 823-7777
Breaking News ED
Albuquerque Tribune, Albuquerque, NM
Wagner, Joe .... (907) 456-6661
MGR-EDU SRV (NIE)
Fairbanks Daily News-Miner, Fairbanks, AK
Wagner, Karen .... (860) 241-6200
EDL Writer, Hartford Courant, Hartford, CT
Wagner, Kathleen .... (812) 424-7711
ASST MAN ED-News
Evansville Courier, Evansville, IN
Wagner, Ken .... (508) 468-2632
ASSOC ED
Sportsbuff Features, Hamilton, MA
Wagner, Kimberly .... (918) 256-6422
ADV MGR-CLASS
Vinita Daily Journal, Vinita, OK
Wagner, Leroy .... (847) 888-7800
CIRC MGR-Transportation
Courier-News, Elgin, IL
Wagner, Margo A .... (508) 922-1234
ADV MGR-CLASS
Gloucester Times, Beverly, MA
Wagner, Mel .... (916) 527-2151
PUB, Daily News, Red Bluff, CA
Wagner, Peter .... (808) 525-8000
ASST City ED
Honolulu Star-Bulletin, Honolulu, HI
Wagner, Peter W .... (712) 324-5347
PUB, N'West Iowa Review, Sheldon, IA
Wagner, Rob .... (909) 987-6397
MAN ED-MET
Inland Valley Daily Bulletin, Ontario, CA
Wagner, Robert J .... (319) 342-2429
PUB, Progress-Review, La Porte City, IA
Wagner, Rodd .... (207) 791-6650
DIR-RES & Market INFO
Portland Press Herald, Portland, ME
Wagner, Susan .... (804) 978-7200
ADTX MGR
Daily Progress, Charlottesville, VA
Wagner, William A .... (916) 243-2424
PROD DIR-Technical Services
Record Searchlight, Redding, CA
Wagner, William R .... (406) 265-6795
PROD SUPT, Havre Daily News, Havre, MT
Wagniere, Frederic .... (514) 285-7272
EDL Writer, La Presse, Montreal, QC
Wahl, Andrew .... (800) 760-3100
Cartoonist/Everett, WA
Williams Syndications Inc., Holiday, FL
Wahl, Paul .... (612) 429-7781
MAN ED
White Bear Press, White Bear Lake, MN
Wahl, Tim .... (716) 366-3000
PROD MGR-Press
Evening Observer, Dunkirk, NY
Wahl-Justesen, DeAnn .... (805) 650-2900
ED-Thousand Oaks Edition
Ventura County Star, Ventura, CA
Wahlheim, Daniel .... (309) 764-4344
PROD DIR, Dispatch, Moline, IL
Small Newspaper Group Inc.
Wahpepah, Wilda .... (503) 221-8327
Team Leader-Crime, Oregonian, Portland, OR
Wahrman, Paul .... (909) 684-1200
PROD MGR-PR
Press-Enterprise, Riverside, CA
Wahto, Kathy .... (360) 452-2345
BM, Peninsula Daily News, Port Angeles, WA
Waidelich, Martin .... (360) 676-2600
Photo ED
Bellingham Herald, Bellingham, WA
Waigand, Lee .... (937) 225-2000
Graphics ED/Art DIR
Dayton Daily News, Dayton, OH
Wainer, Minnie L .... (914) 647-7222
PUB, ED, Ellenville Press, Ellenville, NY
Wainwright, Albert .... (716) 849-3434
PROD OPER MGR
Buffalo News, Buffalo, NY
Wainwright, Joanne .... (250) 380-5211
CR MGR, Times Colonist, Victoria, BC
Waite, Ron .... (330) 296-9657
ADV DIR, DIR-MKTG
Record-Courier, Kent-Ravenna, OH
Waite, Stephanie .... (412) 775-3200
BUS ED, RE ED
Beaver County Times, Beaver, PA
Waite, Steve .... (616) 964-7161
DP MGR, PROD MGR-Technical Services/SYS
Battle Creek Enquirer, Battle Creek, MI
Waits, Tim .... (817) 778-4444
Sports ED
Temple Daily Telegram, Temple, TX
Waitt, Dan .... (630) 844-5844
Religion ED, Beacon-News, Aurora, IL
Waitt, Robert .... (908) 922-6000
ADV MGR-CLASS Display
Asbury Park Press, Neptune, NJ
Waixel, Vivian .... (201) 646-4000
MAN ED, Record, Hackensack, NJ
Wakefield, Chet .... (816) 234-4141
VP-Production/INFO MGT, DP MGR, PROD DIR-OPER
Kansas City Star, Kansas City, MO
Wakefield, Ellen .... (541) 776-4411
ASST News ED, Mail Tribune, Medford, OR
Wakefield, Jerry .... (606) 231-3100
ASST MAN ED-News
Lexington Herald-Leader, Lexington, KY
Wakefield, Judy .... (508) 685-1000
Amusements ED, Films/Theater ED, Radio/ Television ED
Eagle-Tribune, North Andover, MA
Wakefield, Larry R .... (916) 243-2424
GM/PUB, Record Searchlight, Redding, CA
Wakely, Rick .... (207) 791-6650
Graphics ED
Portland Press Herald, Portland, ME
Waker, Morley .... (204) 697-7000
Book ED
Winnipeg Free Press, Winnipeg, MB
Wakley, Ralph .... (801) 625-4200
Military ED, Standard-Examiner, Ogden, UT
Walbaum, Sharon J .... (515) 852-3640
PUB, ED, Dows Advocate, Dows, IA
Walblay, Marsha .... (501) 785-7700
PROD SUPV-COMP
Southwest Times Record, Fort Smith, AR
Walbley, John .... (501) 785-7700
News ED
Southwest Times Record, Fort Smith, AR
Walburn, Erich J .... (614) 773-2111
CONT, DP MGR, Gazette, Chillicothe, OH
Walbye, Phillis .... (970) 669-5050
Valley Window ED
Loveland Daily Reporter-Herald, Loveland, CO
Wald, David .... (201) 877-4141
Political ED, Star-Ledger, Newark, NJ
Walda, Julie Inskeep .... (219) 461-8333
VP, ASST PUB
Journal Gazette, Fort Wayne, IN
Walden, Cynthia .... (541) 485-1234
PSL/Human Resources MGR
Register-Guard, Eugene, OR
Walden, Dwain .... (912) 985-4545
ED, Observer, Moultrie, GA
Walden, Kim .... (816) 234-4141
ADV DIR-RES
Kansas City Star, Kansas City, MO
Walden, Michael .... (503) 221-8327
Team Leader-Family/EDU
Oregonian, Portland, OR
Waldman, Amy .... (202) 462-0128
ED
Washington Monthly Co., Washington, DC
Waldman, Loretta .... (860) 584-0501
EDU ED, Bristol Press, Bristol, CT
Waldmeir, Pete .... (313) 222-2300
COL, Detroit News, Detroit, MI
Waldo, Luann .... (712) 651-2321
MAN ED, News Gazette, Bayard, IA
Waldon, Mitchel .... (601) 833-6961
CIRC DIR, Daily Leader, Brookhaven, MS
Waldorf, Jacqueline .... (604) 932-5131
ED, Whistler Question, Whistler, BC
Waldrip, Chyrl .... (706) 265-2345
ED, Dawson County Advertiser & News, Dawsonville, GA
Waldrip, Don .... (706) 265-2345
PUB, Dawson County Advertiser & News, Dawsonville, GA
Waldroff, Wayne .... (416) 364-0321
VP-Broadcasting, Canadian Press & Broadcast News, Toronto, ON
Waldron, Alan .... (801) 625-4200
PROD DIR-OPER
Standard-Examiner, Ogden, UT
Waldron, Jim .... (352) 245-3161
PUB, Voice of South Marion, Belleview, FL
Waldron, Kathy .... (609) 272-7000
ADV MGR-Phone Room
Press of Atlantic City, Pleasantville, NJ
Waldron, Sandy .... (352) 245-3161
ED, Voice of South Marion, Belleview, FL
Walentis, Albert W .... (610) 371-5000
Design ED
Reading Times/Eagle, Reading, PA
Walery, Debi .... (503) 221-8327
ADV MGR-GEN, Oregonian, Portland, OR
Wales, Ruth J .... (617) 450-2000
Page One ED
Christian Science Monitor, Boston, MA
Waleski Jr, Walter L .... (804) 649-6000
DIR-Information Services
Media General Inc., Richmond, VA
Walford, Janice .... (508) 548-4700
MAN ED, Enterprise, Falmouth, MA
Waligore, Mark .... (609) 989-7800
ED, Trentonian, Trenton, NJ
Walker, Alvin .... (302) 324-2500
PROD ASST DIR
News Journal, Wilmington, DE
Walker, Ana Pecina .... (903) 757-3311
MAN ED, EDU ED
Longview News-Journal, Longview, TX
Walker, Anthony S .... (616) 796-4831
CIRC MGR
Big Rapids Pioneer, Big Rapids, MI
Walker, Barbara White .... (316) 342-4800
VP, ED, Travel ED
Emporia Gazette, Emporia, KS
Walker, Barry .... (913) 852-4900
ED, Western Times, Sharon Springs, KS
Walker, Bill .... (503) 399-6611
PROD MGR-PR
Statesman Journal, Salem, OR
Walker, Brian .... (317) 747-5700
MAN ED, Star Press, Muncie, IN
Walker, Carl .... (212) 210-2100
EDL Art DIR
New York Daily News, New York, NY
Walker, Cecil .... (518) 374-4141
Sports ED, Daily Gazette, Schenectady, NY
Walker, Charles .... (914) 331-5000
ADV MGR-RT, Daily Freeman, Kingston, NY
Walker, Charles .... (712) 643-5380
ED, Dunlap Reporter, Dunlap, IA
Walker, Christopher White ...... (316) 342-4800
SEC, TREAS, ASST PUB
Emporia Gazette, Emporia, KS
Walker, Craig .... (413) 447-7311
Photo ED, Berkshire Eagle, Pittsfield, MA
Walker, Danny .... (901) 427-3333
PROD MGR-DP, Jackson Sun, Jackson, TN
Walker, Dave .... (602) 271-8000
Radio/Television ED
Arizona Republic, Phoenix, AZ
Walker, David .... (514) 987-2222
Foreign ED, Gazette, Montreal, QC
Walker, Diana .... (403) 664-3622
ED, Oyen Echo, Oyen, AB
Walker, Dianne .... (712) 643-5380
PUB, Dunlap Reporter, Dunlap, IA
Walker, Don .... (414) 224-2000
Senior ED-Enterprise
Milwaukee Journal Sentinel, Milwaukee, WI
Walker, Donald .... (715) 356-5236
PUB, Lakeland Times, Minocqua, WI
Walker, Donna .... (864) 298-4100
Films ED, Greenville News, Greenville, SC
Walker, Douglas .... (540) 465-5137
PROD FRM-PR
Northern Virginia Daily, Strasburg, VA
Walker, Ed .... (307) 324-3411
ADV DIR
Rawlins Daily Times, Rawlins, WY
Walker, Edward .... (416) 441-1405
North America Journalist
Fotopress Independent News Service International (FPINS), Toronto, ON
Walker, Eric .... (352) 394-2183
ED, South Lake Press, Clermont, FL
Walker, Geri Sue .... (317) 664-5111
ADV SUPV-CLASS Phone Sales
Chronicle-Tribune, Marion, IN
Walker, Gordon .... (405) 755-3311
MAN ED, Friday, Oklahoma City, OK
Walker, Greg .... (310) 230-3400
VP/GM, Allsport Photography USA, Pacific Palisades, CA
Walker, Gregory .... (603) 352-1234
PROD FRM-PR
Keene Sentinel, Keene, NH
Walker, Helen .... (918) 256-6422
ADV MGR, Vinita Daily Journal, Vinita, OK
Walker, Helen .... (301) 459-3131
CIRC SUPV
Prince George's Journal, Lanham, MD
Walker, Jackie .... (913) 852-4900
PUB, Western Times, Sharon Springs, KS
Walker, James .... (614) 532-1441
Sports ED, Ironton Tribune, Ironton, OH
Walker, Jana .... (308) 647-5158
GM, Shelton Clipper, Shelton, NE
Walker, Jeffrey .... (704) 464-0221
Sports ED
Observer-News-Enterprise, Newton, NC
Walker, Jennifer .... (913) 462-3963
CIRC MGR, Colby Free Press, Colby, KS
Walker, Jim .... (317) 462-5528
BUS/FIN ED, Daily Reporter, Greenfield, IN
Walker, Joel H .... (937) 335-5634
PRES/CEO, PUB, ED, Troy Daily News/Miami Valley Sunday News, Troy, OH
Walker, John .... (619) 299-3131
PROD MGR-PR/Postpress
San Diego Union-Tribune, San Diego, CA
Walker, John .... (908) 922-6000
PROD ASST MGR-PR
Asbury Park Press, Neptune, NJ
Walker, John .... (916) 273-9561
PUB, Union, Grass Valley, CA
Walker, John H .... (915) 263-7331
ED, Big Spring Herald, Big Spring, TX
Walker, Jon .... (605) 331-2200
Features ED, Argus Leader, Sioux Falls, SD
Walker, Judy .... (602) 271-8000
Food Writer, Arizona Republic, Phoenix, AZ
Walker, Karen .... (512) 445-3500
ADV MGR-RT
Austin American-Statesman, Austin, TX
Walker, Ken .... (904) 359-4111
Photo Chief
Florida Times-Union, Jacksonville, FL
Walker, Kimberly .... (515) 672-2581
ED, Oskaloosa Herald, Oskaloosa, IA
Walker, Larry .... (907) 257-4200
PROD MGR-Commercial Printing
Anchorage Daily News, Anchorage, AK
Walker, Leeanna .... (501) 751-6200
MET ED, Morning News of Northwest Arkansas, Springdale, AR
Walker, Leslie .... (202) 334-6000
MET ED-Maryland
Washington Post, Washington, DC
Walker, Linda .... (910) 353-1171
PROD MGR, Daily News, Jacksonville, NC
Walker, Marcella .... (801) 756-7669
ED
Pleasant Grove Review, American Fork, UT
Walker, Mark .... (604) 437-7030
GM, Vancouver Echo, Vancouver, BC
Walker, Michael W .... (937) 335-5634
DIR-Community Relations, Troy Daily News/ Miami Valley Sunday News, Troy, OH
Walker, Mike .... (423) 581-5630
ADTX MGR, Citizen Tribune, Morristown, TN
Walker, Missy .... (606) 598-2319
GM, Manchester Enterprise, Manchester, KY
Walker, Molly .... (541) 247-6643
MAN ED
Curry County Reporter, Gold Beach, OR
Walker, Morley .... (204) 697-7000
Tempo ED
Winnipeg Free Press, Winnipeg, MB

Wal Who's Where-240

Walker, Nancy (219) 461-8444
PROD SUPV-Electronic Imaging
Fort Wayne Newspapers Inc., Fort Wayne, IN
Walker, Pat (215) 949-4000
Night ED
Bucks County Courier Times, Levittown, PA
Walker, Pat (414) 567-5511
ED
Oconomowoc Enterprise, Oconomowoc, WI
Walker, Paul David (316) 342-4800
PRES, PUB
Emporia Gazette, Emporia, KS
Walker, Prescilla (864) 298-4100
Books/Women's ED, Fashion/Style ED, Features/Food ED, Teen-Age/Youth ED, Theater ED, Greenville News, Greenville, SC
Walker, Ray (919) 446-5161
PROD FRM-PR
Rocky Mount Telegram, Rocky Mount, NC
Walker, Relan (903) 785-8744
PA, Paris News, Paris, TX
Walker, Robert (918) 581-8300
CIRC DIR, Tulsa World, Tulsa, OK
Walker, Sandy (517) 823-8579
ED, Vassar Pioneer Times, Vassar, MI
Walker, Sandy (520) 445-3333
RE ED, Religion ED
Daily Courier, Prescott, AZ
Walker, Scott (512) 575-1451
ASST MAN ED, News ED
Victoria Advocate, Victoria, TX
Walker, Scott (307) 634-3361
ADV DIR
Wyoming Tribune-Eagle, Cheyenne, WY
Walker, Sherri (310) 510-0500
PUB, ED, Catalina Islander, Avalon, CA
Walker, Steve (360) 736-3311
TREAS, CONT
Centralia Chronicle, Centralia, WA
Walker, Susan (409) 985-5541
City ED, EDU ED, Fashion/Food ED, Political ED, Port Arthur News, Port Arthur, TX
Walker, Susan J (773) 643-8533
GM, Hyde Park Herald, Chicago, IL
Walker, Terry (615) 259-8000
CONT, Tennessean, Nashville, TN
Walker, Thom (520) 573-4220
Home Furnishings ED
Arizona Daily Star, Tucson, AZ
Walker, Tom (810) 985-7171
EPE, Times Herald, Port Huron, MI
Walker, Tom (303) 820-1010
Weekend ED, Denver Post, Denver, CO
Walker, Tony (616) 796-4831
CIRC DIR, Pioneer Group, Big Rapids, MI
Walker Jr, W Lawrence (210) 225-7411
PRES/CEO, PUB
San Antonio Express-News, San Antonio, TX
Walker, William (901) 427-3333
CIRC MGR-MKTG/Sales
Jackson Sun, Jackson, TN
Walkling, Jennifer (810) 766-6100
Home Section ED, Flint Journal, Flint, MI
Walkowski, Walt (517) 486-2400
ED, Blissfield Advance, Blissfield, MI
Wall, J C (313) 928-2955
PUB, ED, Ecorse Telegram, Ecorse, MI
Wall, James (413) 447-7311
PRES/CEO, Berkshire Eagle, Pittsfield, MA
Wall, Kathie (904) 456-3121
GM, Escambia Sun Press, Pensacola, FL
Wall, Steven E (804) 392-4151
PUB, Farmville Herald, Farmville, VA
Wallace, Amy (213) 237-5000
EDU Writer-Higher EDU
Los Angeles Times, Los Angeles, CA
Wallace, Ann (423) 337-7101
ED, Monroe County Advocate/Democrat, Sweetwater, TN
Wallace, Bill (405) 475-3311
MAN-CR
Daily Oklahoman, Oklahoma City, OK
Wallace, Bill (318) 433-3000
ADV DIR, Lake Charles American Press, Lake Charles, LA
Wallace, Brian (907) 586-3740
Photo ED, Juneau Empire, Juneau, AK
Wallace, Bruce (205) 234-4281
PUB
Alexander City Outlook, Alexander City, AL
Wallace, Catherine (514) 987-2222
City ED, Gazette, Montreal, QC
Wallace, Charles R (916) 795-4551
PUB, Winters Express, Winters, CA
Wallace, Dave (912) 744-4200
DIR-MKTG, Macon Telegraph, Macon, GA
Wallace, Dean (864) 224-4321
BUS SYS Analyst, DP DIR
Anderson Independent-Mail, Anderson, SC
Wallace, Don (903) 586-2236
Sports ED/ASSOC ED
Jacksonville Daily Progress, Jacksonville, TX
Wallace, Don (209) 578-2000
DIR-Community Affairs
Modesto Bee, Modesto, CA
Wallace, Frank (501) 793-2383
BUS/FIN ED, Farm ED
Batesville Guard, Batesville, AR
Wallace, George (516) 427-7000
ED, Northport Journal, Huntington, NY
Wallace, J W George (304) 737-0946
PUB, ED
Brooke County Review, Wellsburg, WV
Wallace, Jay D (616) 722-3161
CIRC DIR
Muskegon Chronicle, Muskegon, MI
Wallace, Jeffrey B (803) 648-2311
MAN ED, Aiken Standard, Aiken, SC
Wallace, Jim (705) 325-1355
PROD FRM-PR, Packet & Times, Orillia, ON
Wallace, John (423) 581-5630
VP, Citizen Tribune, Morristown, TN
Wallace, John (334) 222-2402
Sports ED, Star-News, Andalusia, AL
Wallace, Julia (503) 399-6611
EX ED, Statesman Journal, Salem, OR
Wallace, Kathy (217) 453-6771
ED, Nauvoo News Independent, Nauvoo, IL
Wallace, Kendall M (508) 458-7100
SEC/TREAS, GM, Sun, Lowell, MA
Wallace, Kim (614) 335-3611
ADV MGR
Record Herald, Washington Court House, OH
Wallace, Lloyd (616) 845-5181
Sports ED, Daily News, Ludington, MI
Wallace, Mark (704) 289-1541
City/MET ED, Enquirer-Journal, Monroe, NC
Wallace, Melissa (360) 577-2500
Garden ED, Daily News, Longview, WA
Wallace, Mike (817) 757-5757
EDU ED, Waco Tribune-Herald, Waco, TX
Wallace, Paulette (802) 888-2212
ED, News & Citizen, Morrisville, VT
Wallace, Richard (603) 298-8711
ADV MGR, Valley News, White River Jct., VT
Wallace, Richard A (714) 553-9292
VP-CORP Affairs/SEC
Freedom Communications Inc., Irvine, CA
Wallace, Rick (801) 752-2121
ADTX MGR, Herald Journal, Logan, UT
Wallace, Robert J (715) 394-4411
CFO/SEC/TREAS, Daily Telegram, Superior, WI
Murphy McGinnis Media
Wallace, Ron (616) 392-2311
PUB, Holland Sentinel, Holland, MI
Wallace, Shiela (502) 451-8840
ED, Community, Louisville, KY
Wallace, Stanley (212) 582-2300
TREAS, Whitcom Partners, New York, NY
Wallace, Sue (616) 222-5400
Entertainment ED
Grand Rapids Press, Grand Rapids, MI
Wallace, Susan (817) 390-7400
MGR-EDU SRV
Fort Worth Star-Telegram, Fort Worth, TX
Wallace, Wendy W (813) 893-8111
DIR-Internal Services
St. Petersburg Times, St. Petersburg, FL
Wallace, Yvonne (615) 444-3952
CEO, DIR-FIN, GM
Lebanon Democrat, Lebanon, TN
Wallach, Rachel (410) 337-2400
ED, Baltimore Messenger, Towson, MD
Wallen, Ardell (707) 464-2141
MGR-Office, DP MGR
Triplicate, Crescent City, CA
Waller, Caroline (919) 527-3191
MAN ED, Free Press, Kinston, NC
Waller, Dennis R (360) 736-3311
VP, PUB, Chronicle, Centralia, WA
Waller, Denny (360) 458-2681
PUB, Nisqually Valley News, Yelm, WA
Waller, James (501) 836-8192
ED, Camden News, Camden, AR
Waller, Michael E (213) 237-3700
VP/PUB & CEO-The Hartford Courant
Times Mirror Co., Los Angeles, CA
Waller, Steve (218) 829-4705
Entertainment/Lifestyle ED, Television/Film ED, Brainerd Daily Dispatch, Brainerd, MN
Wallhausen, Mildred (573) 683-3351
PUB, Enterprise-Courier, Charleston, MO
Wallick, George (508) 374-0321
PROD FRM-PR
Haverhill Gazette, Haverhill, MA
Wallick, Steve (701) 223-2500
News ED, Bismarck Tribune, Bismarck, ND
Walling, Bonnie (908) 957-0070
ED, Courier, Middletown, NJ
Wallingford, Linda (216) 999-4500
CIRC MGR-MKTG
Plain Dealer, Cleveland, OH
Wallingford, Margaret F (606) 564-9091
BM, Ledger Independent, Maysville, KY
Wallis Jr, Don R (812) 427-2311
PUB, ED, Reveille-Enterprise, Vevay, IN
Wallis, Jack R (801) 789-3511
PUB, Vernal Express, Vernal, UT
Wallis, Jerry (847) 317-0500
MAN ED, Gurnee Review, Bannockburn, IL
Wallis, Steven R (801) 789-3511
ED, Vernal Express, Vernal, UT
Walls, B Cooper (713) 266-5481
VP/TREAS/CIO, Owner-Tribune (TX)
Southern Newspapers Inc., Houston, TX
Walls Sr, C Lee (205) 870-1684
PRES
Cleveland Newspapers Inc., Birmingham, AL
Walls, Carmage (713) 266-5481
Owner, Walls Investment Co., Houston, TX
Walls, Cathy (519) 923-2203
ED, Herald, Dundalk, ON
Walls, Cooper (910) 349-4331
VP, Reidsville Review, Reidsville, NC
Southern Newspapers Inc.
Walls, Cynthia (601) 961-7000
Features ED, Clarion-Ledger, Jackson, MS
Walls, Dean L (501) 256-4254
PUB, ED, White River Journal, Des Arc, AR
Walls, Freeda (412) 439-7500
ADV MGR-CLASS
Herald-Standard, Uniontown, PA
Walls, Jeanne (409) 833-3311
Librarian, Enterprise, Beaumont, TX
Walls, Lissa W (910) 349-4331
VP, Reidsville Review, Reidsville, NC
Walls, Martha Ann (713) 266-5481
COB/PRES/CEO
Southern Newspapers Inc., Houston, TX
Walls, Matthew (519) 923-2203
PUB, Herald, Dundalk, ON
Walls, Peggy (601) 494-1422
BUS MGR
Daily Times Leader, West Point, MS
Walls, Yvonne (601) 843-4241
SEC/TREAS, Bolivar Commercial, Cleveland, MS, Cleveland Newspapers Inc.
Walls-Cowart, Nell D (334) 644-1101
PRES, Valley Times-News, Lanett, AL
Walman, J (212) 755-4363
PRES, Punch In Travel & Entertainment News Syndicate, New York, NY
Waln, Missy (402) 376-2833
MAN ED, Midland News, Valentine, NE
Waloff, Richard (212) 921-7822
GM, Long Island Jewish Week, New York, NY
Walser, Bill (704) 249-3981
CIRC DIR, Dispatch, Lexington, NC
Walser, Jane N (717) 455-3636
PRES, PUB
Standard-Speaker, Hazleton, PA
Walser, Jim (704) 358-5000
Senior ED-Recruiting & Staff Development
Charlotte Observer, Charlotte, NC
Walser, Paul N (717) 455-3636
VP, PUB, Standard-Speaker, Hazleton, PA
Walser, Steven (717) 455-3636
CIRC MGR-CR
Standard-Speaker, Hazleton, PA
Walsey, Scott (404) 688-5623
PUB, Creative Loafing, Atlanta, GA
Walsh, Dennis (910) 727-7211
PA
Winston-Salem Journal, Winston-Salem, NC
Walsh, Ellen (201) 612-5200
ED, Sunday News, Ridgewood, NJ
Walsh, Ellin (330) 688-0088
ED, Cuyahoga Falls News-Press, Stow, OH
Walsh, Jack (212) 455-4000
DIR-Print Sales, North America Syndicate, King Features Syndicate Inc., New York, NY
Walsh, Jackie (902) 863-4370
ED, Casket, Antigonish, NS
Walsh, James F (847) 427-4300
VP-Advertising, ADV DIR
Daily Herald, Arlington Heights, IL
Walsh, Jeffrey (508) 458-7100
Graphics ED, Sun, Lowell, MA
Walsh, John (714) 835-1234
CIRC VP-Consumer MKTG
Orange County Register, Santa Ana, CA
Walsh, John (408) 761-7300
Sports ED
Register-Pajaronian, Watsonville, CA
Walsh, Juliann (201) 667-2100
ED, Nutley Sun, Nutley, NJ
Walsh, Kevin F (216) 245-6901
PUB, Morning Journal, Lorain, OH
Walsh, Lawrence (603) 543-3100
Sports ED, Eagle Times, Claremont, NH
Walsh, Lawrence M (508) 667-2156
ED
Tewksbury Advertiser, North Billerica, MA
Walsh, Mary Williams (213) 237-5000
Berlin BU
Los Angeles Times, Los Angeles, CA
Walsh, Matthew G (813) 383-5509
PUB, ED
Longboat Observer, Longboat Key, FL
Walsh, Michael (705) 445-4611
PUB, GM
Enterprise-Bulletin, Collingwood, ON
Walsh, Mick (706) 324-5526
Radio/Television ED
Columbus Ledger-Enquirer, Columbus, GA
Walsh, Ray (212) 210-2100
PROD MGR-Press (Brooklyn)
New York Daily News, New York, NY
Walsh, Robert (203) 333-0161
DIR-SYS, Connecticut Post, Bridgeport, CT
Walsh, Robert A (804) 649-6000
Flair (Features) ED
Richmond Times-Dispatch, Richmond, VA
Walsh, Steven (401) 277-7000
PROD GEN FRM of Support Services
Providence Journal-Bulletin, Providence, RI
Walsh, Tom (313) 222-6400
BUS ED, Detroit Free Press, Detroit, MI
Walsh-Sarnecki, Peggy (313) 222-6400
EDU Writer, Detroit Free Press, Detroit, MI
Walston, Janet R (919) 778-2211
SEC/TREAS, BM, MGR-CR, PA
Goldsboro News-Argus, Goldsboro, NC
Walston, Ken (505) 823-7777
Auto/Aviation ED, Deputy News ED, Wire ED
Albuquerque Journal, Albuquerque, NM
Walter, Barbara A (405) 853-4888
ED, Hennessey Clipper, Hennessey, OK
Walter, Brent (913) 823-6363
CIRC MGR-State, Salina Journal, Salina, KS
Walter, Brian (913) 823-6363
CIRC MGR-City, Salina Journal, Salina, KS
Walter, Carolyn (423) 581-5630
Fashion/Food ED, Lifestyle ED, Women's ED
Citizen Tribune, Morristown, TN
Walter, Connie (402) 475-4200
Focus/TV Week ED
Lincoln Journal Star, Lincoln, NE
Walter, Darious (717) 762-2151
PROD FRM-PR
Record Herald, Waynesboro, PA
Walter, Donald E (509) 982-2632
PUB, ED, Odessa Record, Odessa, WA
Walter, Jeff (805) 273-2700
PROD MGR-OPER
Antelope Valley Press, Palmdale, CA
Walter, John (404) 526-5151
MAN ED, Journal-Constitution, Atlanta, GA
Walter, Linda (218) 483-3306
GM, ED, Hawley Herald, Hawley, MN
Walter, Margaret (603) 882-2741
Sunday ED, Telegraph, Nashua, NH
Walter, Michael (414) 733-4411
EPE, EDL Writer
Post-Crescent, Appleton, WI
Walter, Ron (306) 692-2325
ED, Moose Jaw This Week, Moose Jaw, SK
Walter, Tom (901) 529-2211
Radio/Television ED
Commercial Appeal, Memphis, TN
Walter, William B (405) 853-4888
PUB, Hennessey Clipper, Hennessey, OK
Walters, Allen (303) 820-1010
VP Advertising, ADV VP
Denver Post, Denver, CO
Walters, Aubrey (519) 894-2231
Community Relations MGR
Record, Kitchener, ON
Walters, Barry (415) 777-2424
Pop Music Critic
San Francisco Examiner, San Francisco, CA
Walters, Beth (601) 896-2100
NIE CNR, Sun Herald, Biloxi, MS
Walters, Dan (916) 321-1000
COL, Sacramento Bee, Sacramento, CA
Walters, Dave (501) 378-3400
ADV MGR-RT Sales
Arkansas Democrat-Gazette, Little Rock, AR
Walters, David (813) 782-1558
ED, Zephyrhills News, Zephyrhills, FL
Walters, David (812) 372-7811
CIRC DIR, Republic, Columbus, IN
Walters, Helen (219) 724-2121
Living/Lifestyle ED, Women's ED
Decatur Daily Democrat, Decatur, IN
Walters, Keith (205) 251-5158
ED, Birmingham Times, Birmingham, AL
Walters, Ken (561) 820-4100
DIR-MKTG
Palm Beach Post, West Palm Beach, FL
Walters, Kirk (419) 245-6000
EDL Cartoonist, Blade, Toledo, OH
Walters, Les (205) 921-3104
GM, MAN ED, Journal Record, Hamilton, AL
Walters, Linda M (605) 947-4501
PUB, ED, Waubay Clipper, Waubay, SD
Walters, Malea (501) 664-0125
ED, Arkansas Catholic, Little Rock, AR
Walters, R Keith (704) 484-7000
PUB, Shelby Star, Shelby, NC
Walters, Randy (606) 439-4953
ED, Perry County News, Hazard, KY
Walters, Robert (937) 328-0300
PROD MGR-Electronic SYS
Springfield News-Sun, Springfield, OH

241-Who's Where **War**

Walters, Steve .... (817) 778-4444
MAN ED, Temple Daily Telegram, Temple, TX
Walther, Keith .... (937) 878-3993
Sports ED
Fairborn Daily Herald, Fairborn, OH
Walthers, Maureen E .... (718) 821-7500
PUB, ED, Times Newsweekly, Ridgewood, NY
Walthes, Diann .... (618) 932-2146
ADV MGR, Daily American, West Frankfort, IL
Waltman, Mike .... (541) 885-4410
ADV DIR, ADTX MGR
Herald and News, Klamath Falls, OR
Waltner, Tim .... (605) 925-7033
PUB, ED, Freeman Courier, Freeman, SD
Walton, Allan .... (412) 263-1100
ASSOC ED-Features
Pittsburgh Post-Gazette, Pittsburgh, PA
Walton, Allen .... (804) 649-6000
CIRC DIR/VP
Richmond Times-Dispatch, Richmond, VA
Walton, Bob .... (210) 828-7660
PUB, San Antonio Current, San Antonio, TX
Walton, Charlie .... (304) 845-2660
Owner, PUB, PA, Sports ED
Moundsville Daily Echo, Moundsville, WV
Walton, Don .... (402) 475-4200
Politics/People Reporter
Lincoln Journal Star, Lincoln, NE
Walton, Georgianne .... (803) 533-5500
MGR-Office, DP MGR
Times and Democrat, Orangeburg, SC
Walton, Judy .... (423) 756-1234
Regional ED
Chattanooga Times, Chattanooga, TN
Walton, Marian .... (304) 845-2660
ADV MGR-RT/NTL
Moundsville Daily Echo, Moundsville, WV
Walton, Mike .... (540) 885-7281
City ED, Daily News Leader, Staunton, VA
Walton, Nancy .... (405) 233-6600
ADV DIR, Enid News & Eagle, Enid, OK
Walton, Narva Christopher .... (360) 754-5400
ADV DIR, Olympian, Olympia, WA
Walton, Shane .... (417) 334-3161
ADV DIR
Branson Tri-Lakes Daily News, Branson, MO
Walton, Thomas .... (419) 245-6000
ED, EPE, Blade, Toledo, OH
Walts, Loren .... (315) 782-1000
CFO, Watertown Daily Times, Watertown, NY
Waltz, Christopher .... (816) 741-9530
ED, Platte County Gazette, Liberty, MO
Waltz, Kathleen M .... (312) 222-3232
VP-Developing BUS
Chicago Tribune, Chicago, IL
Waltz, Linda .... (803) 771-6161
ADV MGR-Augmentation
State, Columbia, SC
Walworth, Clark .... (208) 733-0931
MAN ED, EDL Writer
Times-News, Twin Falls, ID
Walz, Kent .... (505) 823-7777
ED, Albuquerque Journal, Albuquerque, NM
Walz, Mary .... (605) 352-6401
BM, Huron Plainsman, Huron, SD
Walz, Mel .... (716) 849-3434
PROD OPER ASST MGR
Buffalo News, Buffalo, NY
Walzer, Allison .... (717) 829-7100
Senior VP & ED
Times Leader, Wilkes-Barre, PA
Wamack, Larry .... (916) 541-3880
ADV DIR
Tahoe Daily Tribune, South Lake Tahoe, CA
Wamen, Charles .... (418) 665-6121
MAN ED
Plein Jour de Charlevoix, La Malbaie, QC
Wampler, Wesley B .... (540) 885-7281
PUB, Daily News Leader, Staunton, VA
Wamsley, Gary .... (517) 835-7171
CIRC MGR, Midland Daily News, Midland, MI
Wamsley, H Allen .... (517) 269-6461
PUB, Huron Daily Tribune, Bad Axe, MI
Wanamaker, Ralph .... (573) 335-6611
Regional ED
Southeast Missourian, Cape Girardeau, MO
Wancewicz, Robert .... (518) 843-1100
PROD FRM-PR, Recorder, Amsterdam, NY
Wandell, Fritz .... (813) 248-3921
MAN ED
Community Connections, Tampa, FL
Wanfried, Kurt .... (717) 243-2611
MAN ED, Sentinel, Carlisle, PA
Wang, David Yin-Chi .... (212) 643-9332
New York BU Chief
Central News Agency Inc., New York, NY
Wang, Dr K C .... (718) 461-7668
ED, Pacific Times, Flushing, NY
Wang, Frank .... (416) 585-5000
CIRC Regional MGR-British Columbia
Globe and Mail, Toronto, ON
Wang, Yuk Tsun .... (212) 513-1440
GM, ED, United Journal, New York, NY
Wann, E Charles .... (612) 758-4435
PUB, New Prague Times, New Prague, MN
Wann, Lois Suel .... (612) 758-4435
ED, New Prague Times, New Prague, MN
Wanner, Marilyn .... (701) 225-8111
Office MGR, Dickinson Press, Dickinson, ND
Wanninger, Charles T .... (319) 337-3181
PRES/PUB, Press-Citizen, Iowa City, IA
Wansley, Shawn .... (601) 428-0551
Sports ED, Laurel Leader-Call, Laurel, MS
Wanstrath, George R .... (501) 921-5711
PUB
Lafayette County Democrat, Lewisville, AR
Wantland, Joseph .... (502) 582-4011
PROD GEN SUPV-Engraving
Courier-Journal, Louisville, KY
Wantuch, Brian .... (219) 223-2111
Sports ED, Rochester Sentinel, Rochester, IN
Wanzek, Carol .... (818) 762-1707
Contact, Family Matters Publications, North Hollywood, CA
Warbelow, Kathy .... (512) 445-3500
MAN ED
Austin American-Statesman, Austin, TX
Warburton, Bob .... (607) 936-4651
Sports ED, Leader, Corning, NY
Warchol, Glen .... (214) 757-9000
MAN ED, Dallas Observer, Dallas, TX
Warcup, Bob .... (562) 435-1161
BUS ED, Press-Telegram, Long Beach, CA
Ward, Barbara .... (209) 722-1511
ADV MGR-CLASS
Merced Sun-Star, Merced, CA
Ward, Bill .... (509) 582-1500
Wire ED, Tri-City Herald, Tri-Cities, WA
Ward, Butch .... (215) 854-2000
MAN ED
Philadelphia Inquirer, Philadelphia, PA
Ward, Chad .... (316) 326-3326
Bookkeeper, ADV MGR-CLASS
Wellington Daily News, Wellington, KS
Ward, Charles M .... (716) 372-3121
PUB, Olean Times-Herald, Olean, NY
Ward, Cliff .... (815) 459-4040
MAN ED, Northwest Herald, Crystal Lake, IL
Ward, Darryl .... (306) 842-7487
PUB, Weyburn Review, Weyburn, SK
Ward, David M .... (508) 528-6211
Auto News Writer
Kruza Kaleidoscopix Inc., Franklin, MA
Ward, Debbie .... (808) 329-9311
ADV MGR
West Hawaii Today, Kailua-Kona, HI
Ward, Earlene .... (209) 683-4464
ED, Sierra Star, Oakhurst, CA
Ward, Fred .... (212) 930-8000
CIRC MGR-Sales
New York Post, New York, NY
Ward, Fred .... (209) 674-2424
PUB, Madera Tribune, Madera, CA
Ward, Greg .... (704) 358-5000
ADV MGR-Display
Charlotte Observer, Charlotte, NC
Ward, Hal .... (520) 865-3162
ED, Copper Era, Clifton, AZ
Ward, Jeff .... (317) 473-6641
Electronic Media MGR, EPE, ADTX MGR
Peru Tribune, Peru, IN
Ward, Jerry .... (800) 678-8135
VP-Publishing Group, Better Homes & Gardens Features Syndicate, Des Moines, IA
Ward, Jim .... (573) 636-3131
ADV DIR, News Tribune, Jefferson City, MO
Ward, Joanne .... (518) 792-9914
MAN, Newspaper Services
TV Data, Queensbury, NY
Ward, John W .... (209) 441-6111
GM, Fresno Bee, Fresno, CA
Ward, Ken .... (818) 713-3000
BUS ED, Daily News, Woodland Hills, CA
Ward, Leslie .... (213) 237-5000
Travel ED
Los Angeles Times, Los Angeles, CA
Ward, Mark .... (414) 224-2000
SCI Reporter
Milwaukee Journal Sentinel, Milwaukee, WI
Ward, Mike .... (813) 893-8111
MGR-CR
St. Petersburg Times, St. Petersburg, FL
Ward, Mike .... (309) 764-4344
ADV CNR-CLASS, Dispatch, Moline, IL
Ward, Patricia .... (306) 842-7487
MAN ED, Weyburn Review, Weyburn, SK
Ward, Paul J .... (203) 333-0161
ADV MGR-NTL/Major Accounts
Connecticut Post, Bridgeport, CT
Ward, Phil .... (954) 356-4000
Deputy MAN ED/Sunday & Projects
Sun-Sentinel, Fort Lauderdale, FL
Ward Jr, R J (Bob) .... (205) 532-4000
ASST to PUB
Huntsville Times, Huntsville, AL
Ward, Rose .... (607) 798-1234
DP MGR, PROD MGR-SYS
Press & Sun Bulletin, Binghamton, NY
Ward, Ted .... (707) 644-1141
Sports ED, Vallejo Times-Herald, Vallejo, CA
Ward, Terry .... (405) 238-6464
CIRC DIR
Pauls Valley Daily Democrat, Pauls Valley, OK
Ward, Thomas V .... (401) 658-1234
PUB, Valley Breeze, Cumberland, RI
Warde, Robert .... (414) 276-0273
ED, Daily Reporter, Milwaukee, WI
Wardell, Teresa .... (405) 772-3301
Bookkeeper
Weatherford Daily News, Weatherford, OK
Warden, Christopher T .... (800) 223-2154
Senior ED
Investor's Business Daily, Los Angeles, CA
Warden, Dierdre .... (614) 363-1161
ADV MGR, Delaware Gazette, Delaware, OH
Warden, Don .... (573) 437-2323
PUB, Gasconade County Republican, Owensville, MO
Warden, Mary .... (573) 732-4410
PUB, ED, Bourbon Beacon, Bourbon, MO
Warden, Patrick .... (806) 249-4511
ADV MGR, Dalhart Daily Texan, Dalhart, TX
Warden, Thomas C .... (573) 437-2323
PUB, ED, Gasconade County Republican, Owensville, MO
Warden, Tom .... (520) 836-7461
CIRC DIR
Casa Grande Dispatch, Casa Grande, AZ
Wardlaw, Bob .... (904) 599-2100
CIRC MGR-Home Delivery
Tallahassee Democrat, Tallahassee, FL
Wardlaw, Jack .... (504) 826-3279
COL, Times-Picayune, New Orleans, LA
Wardle, Lance .... (801) 625-4200
PROD FRM-Plate/Camera
Standard-Examiner, Ogden, UT
Wardrip, James .... (414) 634-3322
MGR-MKTG/Shoppers
Journal Times, Racine, WI
Ware, Ellen .... (812) 275-3355
ADV DIR, ADV MGR-RT, ADTX MGR
Times-Mail, Bedford, IN
Ware, Janis .... (404) 524-6426
PUB, Atlanta Voice, Atlanta, GA
Ware, Joyce .... (716) 849-3434
Garden ED, Travel ED
Buffalo News, Buffalo, NY
Ware, Ron .... (937) 328-0300
Automotive ED
Springfield News-Sun, Springfield, OH
Ware, Scott .... (505) 823-7777
ED, Albuquerque Tribune, Albuquerque, NM
Warfel, Regina .... (219) 866-5111
CIRC MGR, Republican, Rensselaer, IN
Warfel, Susan .... (800) 223-2154
MAN ED
Investor's Business Daily, Los Angeles, CA
Wark, Lois .... (215) 854-2000
ASST MAN ED
Philadelphia Inquirer, Philadelphia, PA
Warkentin, Abe .... (204) 326-6790
PUB, Mennonitische Post, Steinbach, MB
Warkins, Roger N .... (541) 296-2141
EVP, Dalles Daily Chronicle, The Dalles, OR
Warman, Kerry .... (816) 987-2138
MAN ED
Pleasant Hill Times, Pleasant Hill, MO
Warmath, J Frank .... (901) 855-1711
PUB, Herald Gazette, Trenton, TN
Warmouth, Lee .... (810) 985-7171
CIRC DIR, Times Herald, Port Huron, MI
Warneke, Kent .... (402) 371-1020
ED, Norfolk Daily News, Norfolk, NE
Warneke, Leonald J .... (402) 582-4921
PUB, Plainview News, Plainview, NE
Warner, Amy Lynn .... (717) 637-3736
DIR-MKTG/PROM, Evening Sun, Hanover, PA
Warner, Bill .... (318) 281-4421
MAN ED
Bastrop Daily Enterprise, Bastrop, LA
Warner, Bill .... (717) 272-5611
Sports ED, Daily News, Lebanon, PA
Warner, Carlos .... (352) 544-5200
CIRC MGR, Hernando Today, Brooksville, FL
Warner, Charles H .... (507) 426-7235
PUB, Fairfax Standard, Fairfax, MN
Warner, Cromwell .... (509) 663-5161
EPE, Wenatchee World, Wenatchee, WA
Warner, Daniel .... (508) 685-1000
ED, Action Line ED, Books ED
Eagle-Tribune, North Andover, MA
Warner, David .... (215) 854-2000
City/News ED
Philadelphia Daily News, Philadelphia, PA
Warner, Dean .... (250) 762-4445
CIRC DIR, Daily Courier, Kelowna, BC
Warner, Gary D .... (316) 342-4800
CIRC MGR, Emporia Gazette, Emporia, KS
Warner, Janet K .... (207) 778-2075
PUB, Franklin Journal & Farmington Chronicle, Farmington, ME
Warner, Jim .... (304) 472-2800
MAN ED, Record Delta, Buckhannon, WV
Warner, Joe .... (810) 731-1000
ED, Source, Utica, MI
Warner, Judy .... (352) 544-5200
MGR-Special Sections/PROM, PROD MGR-Creative & Ad Services
Hernando Today, Brooksville, FL
Warner, Julie .... (417) 256-9191
Amusements ED, Food ED
West Plains Daily Quill, West Plains, MO
Warner, Kenneth .... (507) 524-3212
PUB, Maple River Messenger, Mapleton, MN
Warner, Mark .... (604) 567-9258
PUB, Omineca Express, Vanderhoof, BC
Warner, Melinda .... (209) 674-2424
EDU/School ED, Madera Tribune, Madera, CA
Warner, Mike .... (517) 568-4646
PUB, ED, Homer Index, Homer, MI
Warner, Paul .... (912) 888-9300
PROD SUPV-Camera
Albany Herald, Albany, GA
Warner, Sharon .... (517) 568-4646
PUB, GM, Homer Index, Homer, MI
Warner, Sherida .... (913) 823-6363
Fashion/Food ED, Home Furnishings ED, Society ED, Salina Journal, Salina, KS
Warner, Stuart .... (330) 996-3000
ASSOC MAN ED-News
Akron Beacon Journal, Akron, OH
Warner, Tracy .... (219) 461-8333
MET ED, Journal Gazette, Fort Wayne, IN
Warnick, Denny K .... (606) 567-5051
PUB, Gallatin County News, Warsaw, KY
Warnick, Gene .... (315) 782-1000
Sports ED
Watertown Daily Times, Watertown, NY
Warnick, Kelley .... (606) 567-5051
GM, ED, Gallatin County News, Warsaw, KY
Warning, Helen .... (217) 223-5100
Home Section/Food ED, Women's ED, Youth Page ED, Quincy Herald-Whig, Quincy, IL
Warnock, Lamon .... (803) 635-4016
PUB, Herald Independent, Winnsboro, SC
Warnock, Polly .... (915) 348-3545
PUB, ED, Santa Anna News, Santa Anna, TX
Warnock, William R .... (614) 353-1151
PUB, Community Common, Portsmouth, OH
Warren, Anita .... (317) 482-4650
MGR-CR, ADV MGR-CR
Reporter, Lebanon, IN
Warren, Cheryl .... (402) 944-3397
ED, Ashland Gazette, Ashland, NE
Warren, Clif .... (405) 341-2121
Films/Theater ED
Edmond Evening Sun, Edmond, OK
Warren, Dennis .... (409) 985-5541
ADV MGR-RT
Port Arthur News, Port Arthur, TX
Warren, Douglas M .... (617) 929-2000
Night ED, Boston Globe, Boston, MA
Warren, Iris .... (709) 256-4371
GM, Gander Beacon, Gander, NF
Warren III, J H .... (215) 665-8400
PUB, ED
Philadelphia New Observer, Philadelphia, PA
Warren, James E .... (715) 735-6611
SEC, EagleHerald, Marinette, WI
Bliss Communications Inc.
Warren, John .... (619) 266-2233
PUB, ED
Voice & Viewpoint, San Diego, CA
Warren, John .... (540) 343-0720
ED, Vinton Messenger, Vinton, VA
Warren, Julie .... (816) 327-4192
MAN ED, Monroe Co. Appeal, Paris, MO
Warren, Ken .... (205) 236-1551
ADV MGR-RT, Anniston Star, Anniston, AL
Warren, Ken .... (910) 727-7211
ADV MGR-RT
Winston-Salem Journal, Winston-Salem, NC
Warren, Lara .... (334) 875-2110
Society ED, Selma Times-Journal, Selma, AL
Warren, Linda .... (541) 889-5387
ADV DIR, Argus Observer, Ontario, OR
Warren, Lisa .... (513) 352-2000
ASST MET ED
Cincinnati Post, Cincinnati, OH
Warren, Lisa .... (407) 420-5000
MGR-Community Relations
Orlando Sentinel, Orlando, FL
Warren, Mike .... (812) 838-4811
GM, ED
Mount Vernon Democrat, Mount Vernon, IN
Warren, Nancy .... (330) 841-1600
PROD FRM-COMP
Tribune Chronicle, Warren, OH
Warren, Richard J .... (207) 990-8000
PRES, PUB, ED, Chairman-EX Committee
Daily News, Bangor, ME
Warren, Stanley .... (334) 792-3141
PUB, Dothan Eagle, Dothan, AL
Thomson Newspapers

Copyright ©1997 by the Editor & Publisher Co.

War Who's Where-242

Warren, Steven .... (609) 272-7000
Deputy MAN ED
Press of Atlantic City, Pleasantville, NJ
Warren, Tim .... (561) 461-2050
PROD FRM-COMP (Night)
Tribune, Fort Pierce, FL
Warrington, Clyde .... (519) 621-3810
MAN ED (Acting)
Cambridge Reporter, Cambridge, ON
Warrum, Dallas M .... (217) 754-3369
PUB, ED, Triopia Tribune, Bluffs, IL
Warrum, Elaine J .... (217) 754-3369
GM, Triopia Tribune, Bluffs, IL
Warshal, Rabbi Bruce S .... (954) 698-6397
PUB, Boca Monday, Deerfield Beach, FL
Warshaw, Donald .... (201) 877-4141
Labor ED, Star-Ledger, Newark, NJ
Warshaw, Holly .... (617) 786-7000
ADV MGR-SYS/CLASS
Patriot Ledger, Quincy, MA
Warszawski, Marek .... (916) 756-0800
Sports ED, Davis Enterprise, Davis, CA
Wartes, Sara .... (210) 693-7152
MAN ED, Picayune, Marble Falls, TX
Warthen, Brad .... (803) 771-6161
ASSOC ED, State, Columbia, SC
Wartinger, John .... (360) 754-5400
PROD DIR, Olympian, Olympia, WA
Wartzman, Rick .... (212) 416-2000
BU Chief-Houston
Wall Street Journal, New York, NY
Warwick, Julie .... (802) 863-3441
Features ED, Living ED
Burlington Free Press, Burlington, VT
Wasburn, Drew .... (315) 363-5100
Features ED, Daily Dispatch, Oneida, NY
Wascak, Carl .... (814) 665-8291
PROD FRM
Corry Evening Journal, Corry, PA
Wascha, Cookie .... (810) 766-6100
Features ED, Flint Journal, Flint, MI
Waseleski, Tom .... (412) 263-1100
ASSOC ED
Pittsburgh Post-Gazette, Pittsburgh, PA
Wasenius, Brent .... (402) 721-5000
MAN ED, Fremont Tribune, Fremont, NE
Wash, Barbara Aston .... (423) 523-3131
Home Furnishings ED
Knoxville News-Sentinel, Knoxville, TN
Washburn, Carolyn K .... (716) 232-7100
MAN ED, Rochester Democrat and Chronicle; Times-Union, Rochester, NY
Washburn, Gary .... (312) 222-3232
Transportation Writer
Chicago Tribune, Chicago, IL
Washburn, Jeff .... (901) 364-2234
GM, ED, Dresden Enterprise and Sharon Tribune, Dresden, TN
Washburn, Joel T .... (901) 352-3323
ED, McKenzie Banner, McKenzie, TN
Washburn, Mark .... (305) 350-2111
State/Environmental ED
Miami Herald, Miami, FL
Washburn, Ramona .... (901) 352-3323
PUB, McKenzie Banner, McKenzie, TN
Washer, F Gene .... (615) 552-1808
PUB, Leaf-Chronicle, Clarksville, TN
Washington, Chuck .... (503) 288-0033
PUB, ED, Portland Observer, Portland, OR
Washington, Isaac .... (803) 799-5252
PUB, South Carolina Black Media Group, Columbia, SC
Washington, Jim .... (214) 428-8958
PUB, ED, Dallas Weekly, Dallas, TX
Washington, Joe .... (512) 499-8713
MAN ED, Nokoa-The Observer, Austin, TX
Washington, John .... (904) 432-8410
GM, ED
New American Press, Pensacola, FL
Washington, Joyce .... (503) 288-0033
PUB, Portland Observer, Portland, OR
Washington, Mark .... (405) 336-2222
DP MGR, PROD MGR
Perry Daily Journal, Perry, OK
Washington, Ray .... (352) 374-5000
EDU Writer-Higher
Gainesville Sun, Gainesville, FL
Washington, Robin .... (617) 357-4900
MAN ED, Bay State Banner, Boston, MA
Washington, Stan .... (404) 524-6426
ED, Atlanta Voice, Atlanta, GA
Washner, Romayne .... (717) 348-9100
MGR-CR
Tribune & Scranton Times, Scranton, PA
Wasiak, Kathy .... (306) 773-9321
ED, Southwest Booster, Swift Current, SK
Wasielewski, Ron .... (814) 870-1600
City ED
Morning News/Erie Daily Times, Erie, PA

Wasik, John .... (847) 526-0522
Environment, BUS & Technology COL
New Consumer Institute, Wauconda, IL
Wasinger, Bob .... (214) 977-8222
MGR-PROM
Dallas Morning News, Dallas, TX
Wasko, Richard .... (412) 775-3200
MAN ED, Beaver County Times, Beaver, PA
Wasniewski, Mary Beth .... (860) 347-3331
City ED, Middletown Press, Middletown, CT
Wason, Tom .... (941) 369-2191
ED
Lehigh Acres News-Star, Lehigh Acres, FL
Wass, Jerry .... (616) 222-5400
PROD SUPT-Maintenance
Grand Rapids Press, Grand Rapids, MI
Wasser, Scott .... (717) 829-7100
Sports ED, Times Leader, Wilkes-Barre, PA
Wasserman, Edward .... (305) 377-3721
COB, EIC
Miami Daily Business Review, Miami, FL
Wasserman, Steve .... (213) 237-5000
Books ED
Los Angeles Times, Los Angeles, CA
Wassermann, Vic .... (308) 536-3100
GM, Nance County Journal, Fullerton, NE
Wassink, Ronald .... (519) 881-1600
ED, Herald-Times, Walkerton, ON
Wasson, Teresa .... (904) 435-8500
EX ED
Pensacola News Journal, Pensacola, FL
Wastler, Allen .... (212) 837-7000
Maritime ED, Journal of Commerce & Commercial, New York, NY
Waszak, Dennis .... (718) 845-3221
ED, Forum of Queens, Ozone Park, NY
Watanabe, Mark .... (206) 464-2111
ASST Regional ED, SCI/High Tech ED
Seattle Times, Seattle, WA
Watanabe, Teresa .... (213) 237-5000
Tokyo BU
Los Angeles Times, Los Angeles, CA
Waterbury, Kathie .... (209) 532-7151
Travel ED, Union Democrat, Sonora, CA
Waterhouse, Steve .... (510) 734-8600
City ED, Tri-Valley Herald, Pleasanton, CA
Waterman, Brian .... (913) 845-2222
MAN ED, Tonganoxie Mirror, Tonganoxie, KS
Waterman, Don .... (913) 845-2222
PUB, ED, Tonganoxie Mirror, Tonganoxie, KS
Waterman, Donald A .... (508) 775-1200
CIRC DIR, Cape Cod Times, Hyannis, MA
Waterman, Glenn .... (860) 646-0500
Photo ED, Journal Inquirer, Manchester, CT
Waterman, Mary .... (913) 845-2222
PUB, Tonganoxie Mirror, Tonganoxie, KS
Waterman, Tina .... (937) 498-2111
CIRC MGR, Sidney Daily News, Sidney, OH
Waters, Barbara M .... (207) 723-8118
ED, Katahdin Times, Millinocket, ME
Waters, Betty .... (903) 597-8111
EDU ED, Tyler Morning Telegraph, Tyler, TX
Waters, Bill .... (505) 983-3303
EPE, Santa Fe New Mexican, Santa Fe, NM
Waters, Bob .... (603) 356-3456
ADV MGR-Sales
Conway Daily Sun, North Conway, NH
Waters, Carla .... (815) 432-5227
ED, Iroquois County's Times-Republic, Watseka, IL
Waters, David .... (901) 529-2211
Religion Reporter
Commercial Appeal, Memphis, TN
Waters Jr, Ed .... (301) 662-1177
BUS ED, RE ED
Frederick Post/News, Frederick, MD
Waters, Gene .... (407) 242-3500
ADV MGR-NTL, Florida Today, Melbourne, FL
Waters, George B .... (315) 337-4000
PRES, ED, Daily Sentinel, Rome, NY
Waters III, Henry J .... (573) 815-1500
PRES/TREAS, PUB, ED, EDL Writer
Columbia Daily Tribune, Columbia, MO
Waters, Jack .... (573) 815-1500
VP/SEC, GM
Columbia Daily Tribune, Columbia, MO
Waters Jr, John .... (619) 329-1411
ED, Desert Sentinel, Desert Hot Springs, CA
Waters, Margaret .... (501) 297-8300
MAN ED
White River Current, Calico Rock, AR
Waters, Marjorie B .... (214) 369-7570
PUB, ED, Park Cities News, Dallas, TX
Waters, Michael .... (773) 586-8800
Sports ED, Daily Southtown, Chicago, IL
Waters, Pam S .... (912) 654-2515
PUB, ED, Glennville Sentinel, Glennville, GA
Waters, Patricia .... (402) 444-1000
Features ED, Living ED
Omaha World-Herald, Omaha, NE
Waters, Peter H .... (214) 369-7570
MAN ED, Park Cities News, Dallas, TX
Waters, Randy .... (816) 234-4141
PROD MGR-OPER
Kansas City Star, Kansas City, MO

Waters, Rob .... (919) 829-4500
North Carolina ED
News & Observer, Raleigh, NC
Waters, Roni Rucker .... (517) 377-1000
MAN ED, Lansing State Journal, Lansing, MI
Waters, Shirley B .... (315) 337-4000
VP, SEC, Daily Sentinel, Rome, NY
Waters, Stephen B .... (315) 337-4000
VP, PUB, Daily Sentinel, Rome, NY
Waters, Steve .... (954) 356-4000
Outdoors ED
Sun-Sentinel, Fort Lauderdale, FL
Waters, Susan .... (573) 815-1500
PROD MGR, Daily Tribune, Columbia, MO
Waters, Sylvia .... (903) 675-5626
Amusements ED, Books ED
Athens Daily Review, Athens, TX
Waters, Thomas R .... (214) 369-7570
GM, Park Cities News, Dallas, TX
Waterson, Tim .... (972) 436-3566
ED, Market, Lewisville, TX
Waterton, Willy .... (519) 376-2250
Photo DEPT MGR
Sun Times, Owen Sound, ON
Wateski, Colleen .... (717) 829-7100
PSL DIR, Times Leader, Wilkes-Barre, PA
Wathen, George .... (502) 582-4011
PROD GEN SUPV-Transportation
Courier-Journal, Louisville, KY
Watherby, Dawn .... (770) 942-6571
PUB
Douglas County Sentinel, Douglasville, GA
Watkins, Craig .... (816) 632-6543
PUB, ED, Citizen Observer, Cameron, MO
Watkins, Ed .... (205) 345-0505
Farm ED, Tuscaloosa News, Tuscaloosa, AL
Watkins, Eileen .... (201) 877-4141
Arts Critic, Star-Ledger, Newark, NJ
Watkins, Gordon .... (818) 932-6161
Group OPER MGR, Dodge Construction News Greensheet, Monrovia, CA
Watkins, Jamie .... (405) 338-3355
Sports ED, Daily Herald, Guymon, OK
Watkins, Linda .... (573) 815-1500
PROD MGR-COMP
Columbia Daily Tribune, Columbia, MO
Watkins, O Ray .... (310) 635-6776
PUB, Compton Bulletin, Compton, CA
Watkins, Pat .... (912) 876-00156
ED, Coastal Courier, Hinesville, GA
Watkins, Pat .... (419) 874-4491
ED, Perrysburg Messenger-Journal, Perrysburg, OH
Watkins, Stephen E .... (505) 983-3303
PRES, Santa Fe New Mexican, Santa Fe, NM
Watkins, T J .... (718) 643-1162
ASSOC PUB, Daily Challenge, Brooklyn, NY
Watkins Jr, Thomas .... (718) 643-1162
PUB, Daily Challenge, Brooklyn, NY
Watkins, Virginia .... (316) 672-5511
CONT, Pratt Tribune, Pratt, KS
Watkins, William .... (304) 367-2500
ADV DIR, DIR-MKTG/PROM
Times-West Virginian, Fairmont, WV
Watness, Philip .... (360) 754-5400
RE ED, Olympian, Olympia, WA
Watral, Janet M .... (314) 421-1880
INFO Services MGR
St. Louis Countain, St. Louis, MO
ABC Inc. (Legal Communications Corp.)
Watson, Adrienne .... (616) 927-1527
MAN ED, Citizen, Benton Harbor, MI
Watson, Aleta .... (408) 920-5000
EDU ED
San Jose Mercury News, San Jose, CA
Watson, Bill .... (305) 757-6333
PUB, TWN News Magazine (The Weekly News), Miami, FL
Watson, Bill .... (910) 835-1513
ED, Tribune, Elkin, NC
Watson III, Bill .... (717) 655-1418
GM, Sunday Dispatch, Pittston, PA
Watson, Catherine .... (612) 673-4000
Travel ED, Star Tribune, Minneapolis, MN
Watson, Chris .... (408) 423-4242
Books ED
Santa Cruz County Sentinel, Santa Cruz, CA
Watson, Danny .... (304) 526-4000
PROD MGR-Distribution Center
Herald-Dispatch, Huntington, WV
Watson, Darryll .... (904) 863-1111
CIRC DIR, Northwest Florida Daily News, Fort Walton Beach, FL
Watson, Dave .... (416) 494-4990
ADV Sales MGR-Display, Daily Commercial News and Construction Record, N. York, ON
Watson, David .... (405) 273-4200
PROD MGR
Shawnee News-Star, Shawnee, OK
Watson, Diane .... (609) 845-3300
Environmental ED
Gloucester County Times, Woodbury, NJ
Watson, Don .... (330) 821-1200
ADV DIR, ADTX MGR
Alliance Review, Alliance, OH

Watson, Donald R .... (540) 546-1210
PUB, ED
Powell Valley News, Pennington Gap, VA
Watson, Donna .... (508) 632-8000
ADV MGR, Gardner News, Gardner, MA
Watson, Douglas .... (423) 638-4181
MAN ED, Greeneville Sun, Greeneville, TN
Watson, Gary L .... (703) 284-6000
PRES-Newspaper Division
Gannett Co. Inc., Arlington, VA
Watson III, Gilbert L .... (410) 332-6000
ASST MAN ED-MET, Sun, Baltimore, MD
Watson, Jennifer .... (610) 258-7171
Area ED (Bethlehem)
Express-Times, Easton, PA
Watson, Jennifer .... (609) 845-3300
Arts/Music ED, City/MET ED, Entertainment/Amusements ED, Fashion/Style ED, Features ED, Films/Theater ED, Food ED
Gloucester County Times, Woodbury, NJ
Watson, John .... (201) 653-1000
News ED, Jersey Journal, Jersey City, NJ
Watson, John .... (717) 655-1418
PUB, Sunday Dispatch, Pittston, PA
Watson, John .... (406) 232-0450
PUB/GM, Miles City Star, Miles City, MT
Watson, Lynn .... (704) 245-6431
DP MGR, Daily Courier, Forest City, NC
Watson, Margie .... (706) 324-5526
PSL MGR
Columbus Ledger-Enquirer, Columbus, GA
Watson, Maurice .... (805) 781-7800
SEC, Telegram-Tribune, San Luis Obispo, CA
Watson, Michelle .... (615) 243-2235
ED, Citizen-Statesman, Celina, TN
Watson, Neal .... (403) 468-0100
Television ED, Edmonton Sun, Edmonton, AB
Watson, Peter .... (508) 744-0600
GM, Salem Evening News, Beverly, MA
Ottaway Newspapers Inc.
Watson, Phil .... (616) 796-4831
ED-Night, Big Rapids Pioneer, Big Rapids, MI, Pioneer
Watson, Randi .... (360) 377-3711
PROD MGR-Ad Services
Sun, Bremerton, WA
Watson, Rick L .... (540) 546-1210
GM, Powell Valley News, Pennington Gap, VA
Watson, Robert .... (219) 294-1661
TREAS, Federated Media Corp., Elkhart, IN
Watson, Robert W .... (815) 273-2277
PUB, ED
Savanna Times-Journal, Savanna, IL
Watson, Rod .... (716) 849-3434
EDL Writer, Buffalo News, Buffalo, NY
Watson, Sam .... (423) 929-3111
EDU/School ED
Johnson City Press, Johnson City, TN
Watson IV, Solomon B .... (212) 556-1234
Sr VP/GEN Counsel
New York Times Co., New York, NY
Watson, T J .... (316) 836-3152
PUB, ED, Gridley Gleam, Gridley, KS
Watson, Teresa .... (412) 222-2200
ADV MGR-Special Sections
Observer-Reporter, Washington, PA
Watson, Tom .... (423) 482-1021
PROD MGR, Oak Ridger, Oak Ridge, TN
Watson, Warren .... (207) 873-3341
EX ED, Central Maine Morning Sentinel, Waterville, ME
Watson, William H .... (800) 355-9500
EX VP/PUB, News USA Inc., Vienna, VA
Watt, Earl .... (316) 624-2541
PROD SUPT
Southwest Daily Times, Liberal, KS
Wattenbarger, Pledger L .... (423) 472-5041
PUB, PSL MGR, ED, EPE
Cleveland Daily Banner, Cleveland, TN
Watters, Christa .... (703) 838-0302
ED
Alexandria Gazette Packet, Alexandria, VA
Watters, Jim .... (305) 350-2111
BUS Monday News ED
Miami Herald, Miami, FL
Watters, Pete .... (602) 271-8000
Visual ED, Arizona Republic, Phoenix, AZ
Watters, Sadie .... (802) 334-6568
CIRC MGR, Daily Express, Newport, VT
Watterson, Tim .... (972) 424-6565
ED, News ED, Plano Star Courier, Plano, TX
Watts, C D .... (606) 638-9957
PUB, ED, Tri-Rivers Advertiser, Louisa, KY
Watts, Mary Lou .... (415) 495-4200
ED, Daily Pacific Builder, San Francisco, CA
Watts, Patricia .... (907) 456-6661
Books ED, Entertainment/Amusements ED, Features ED, Food ED, Women's ED
Fairbanks Daily News-Miner, Fairbanks, AK
Watts, Randy .... (334) 433-1551
CIRC MGR-State
Mobile Press Register, Mobile, AL
Watts, Ron .... (910) 323-4848
ADV DIR, ADV DIR-MKTG
Fayetteville Observer-Times, Fayetteville, NC

243-Who's Where **Weh**

Watts, Sandra .... (604) 442-2191
PUB, Boundary Bulletin, Grand Forks, BC

Waugaman, Randy K .... (412) 263-1100
CIRC MGR-Home Delivery
Pittsburgh Post-Gazette, Pittsburgh, PA

Waugh, Diane E .... (317) 832-2443
SEC/TREAS, Daily Clintonian, Clinton, IN

Waugh, Neil .... (403) 468-0100
COL, Edmonton Sun, Edmonton, AB

Waughtel, Vicky .... (309) 647-5100
PROD MGR-COMP, Daily Ledger, Canton, IL

Way, Betty .... (717) 255-8100
CIRC DIR, Patriot-News, Harrisburg, PA

Way, Dan .... (601) 335-1155
ED, Delta Democrat Times, Greenville, MS

Way, Kenneth B .... (605) 886-6901
PRES
Watertown Public Opinion, Watertown, SD

Waybright, Brenda .... (606) 231-3100
ADV MGR-CLASS
Lexington Herald-Leader, Lexington, KY

Wayland, Barbara C .... (540) 675-3349
GM, Rappahannock News, Washington, VA

Waymire, Tim .... (317) 552-3355
Photo DEPT MGR
Elwood Call-Leader, Elwood, IN

Wayne, Robert N .... (813) 259-7711
ASST CONT
Tampa Tribune and Times, Tampa, FL

Wayne, Ron .... (770) 227-3276
MAN ED, Griffin Daily News, Griffin, GA

Wayne Mitchell, T .... (864) 224-4321
ED
Anderson Independent-Mail, Anderson, SC

Wazney, Edward L .... (803) 775-6331
GM, BM, PSL MGR, DP MGR, PROD SUPT
Item, Sumter, SC

Wazney, Robert .... (803) 775-6331
CIRC MGR-Distribution, Item, Sumter, SC

Weafer, Mike .... (502) 926-0123
PROD MGR
Messenger-Inquirer, Owensboro, KY

Weakland, Archbsp Rembert G . (414) 769-3500
PUB, Catholic Herald, Milwaukee, WI

Weaks, James .... (205) 236-1551
PROD FRM-PR, Anniston Star, Anniston, AL

Wear, Jay .... (615) 552-1808
CIRC MGR-Mail
Leaf-Chronicle, Clarksville, TN

Wearing, Ben .... (913) 823-6363
Deputy ED, Salina Journal, Salina, KS

Weatherbee, Lane .... (205) 447-2837
PUB, ED, Piedmont Journal-Independent, Piedmont, AL

Weatherby, Dawn .... (770) 834-6631
PUB, Times-Georgian, Carrollton, GA

Weatherly, Brenda .... (408) 637-5566
ADV DIR/BM, DIR-MKTG/PROM
Free Lance, Hollister, CA

Weatherly, Bud .... (714) 835-1234
PROD MGR-Production ADM
Orange County Register, Santa Ana, CA

Weatherly, Jack .... (601) 289-2251
ED, Star-Herald, Kosciusko, MS

Weathersbee, Avis .... (312) 321-3000
ASST Weekend Plus ED
Chicago Sun-Times, Chicago, IL

Weatherwax, Wendell .... (808) 525-8000
PROD MGR-Press
Hawaii Newspaper Agency Inc., Honolulu, HI

Weaver, Bill .... (912) 744-4200
RES ED, Macon Telegraph, Macon, GA

Weaver, Brett .... (808) 245-3681
CIRC MGR, Garden Island, Lihue, HI

Weaver, Brian .... (717) 275-3235
CIRC MGR-Distribution
Danville News, Danville, PA

Weaver, Bryan .... (618) 382-4176
Sports ED, Carmi Times, Carmi, IL

Weaver, Charles .... (941) 337-4444
PUB, ED, Community Voice, Fort Myers, FL

Weaver, Coary .... (910) 259-2504
GM, Pender Chronicle, Burgaw, NC

Weaver, Curt .... (509) 765-4561
PROD SUPT
Columbia Basin Herald, Moses Lake, WA

Weaver, Darvin E .... (417) 843-5315
PUB, ED, Liberal News, Liberal, MO

Weaver, Doug .... (816) 234-4141
BUS ED, Kansas City Star, Kansas City, MO

Weaver, F T .... (517) 787-2300
PUB, Jackson Citizen Patriot, Jackson, MI

Weaver, Franklin .... (517) 787-2300
PUB, News Advertiser, Jackson, MI

Weaver, Gary .... (910) 285-2178
GM, Wallace Enterprise, Wallace, NC

Weaver, Greg .... (508) 626-3800
CFO, Middlesex News, Framingham, MA

Weaver, Howard .... (916) 321-1855
Asst to the Pres-New Media Strategies
McClatchy Newspapers, Sacramento, CA

Weaver, Janet .... (316) 268-6000
MAN ED, Wichita Eagle, Wichita, KS

Weaver, Joel .... (605) 348-9150
PUB, Plainsman, Ellsworth, SD

Weaver, Joyce .... (704) 249-3981
Family ED, Food ED
Dispatch, Lexington, NC

Weaver, M Steven .... (717) 291-8811
PSL MGR, Lancaster Intelligencer Journal/New Era/Sunday News, Lancaster, PA

Weaver, Marion .... (316) 273-6391
MAN ED, Chase County Leader-News, Cottonwood Falls, KS

Weaver, Mark .... (316) 268-6000
Money & BUS ED
Wichita Eagle, Wichita, KS

Weaver, Mike .... (352) 563-6363
PROD MGR
Citrus County Chronicle, Crystal River, FL

Weaver, Pamela .... (816) 931-2002
GM/TREAS, ADV Legal
Daily Record, Kansas City, MO

Weaver, Rick V .... (406) 265-6795
PUB, Havre Daily News, Havre, MT

Weaver, Rob .... (419) 448-3200
City ED, Graphics ED/Art DIR, News ED
Advertiser-Tribune, Tiffin, OH

Weaver, Ruth Ann .... (417) 843-5315
PUB, ED, Liberal News, Liberal, MO

Weaver, Scott .... (717) 762-2151
Sports ED, Record Herald, Waynesboro, PA

Weaver, Scott .... (816) 254-8600
Photo DEPT MGR
Examiner, Independence, MO

Weaver, Steve .... (408) 920-5000
ADV DIR
San Jose Mercury News, San Jose, CA

Weaver, Terry .... (219) 881-3000
ADV MGR-Inside Sales
Post-Tribune, Gary, IN

Weaver, Timothy J .... (215) 345-3000
CONT, Intelligencer/Record, Doylestown, PA

Weaver, Virginia .... (918) 569-4741
GM, ED, Clayton Today, Clayton, OK

Weaver, William .... (423) 472-5041
CIRC MGR
Cleveland Daily Banner, Cleveland, TN

Webb, Aubrey .... (304) 526-4000
PROD MGR-PR
Herald-Dispatch, Huntington, WV

Webb, Aubrey L .... (409) 833-3311
PUB, Beaumont Enterprise, Beaumont, TX

Webb, Betty .... (602) 898-6500
Books ED, Music ED, Mesa Tribune, Mesa, AZ, Thomson Newspapers

Webb, Brenda .... (616) 627-7144
Specialty Page ED
Cheboygan Daily Tribune, Cheboygan, MI

Webb, Bruce .... (910) 548-6047
PUB, ED, Messenger, Madison, NC

Webb, Carol .... (520) 364-3424
CIRC MGR, Daily Dispatch, Douglas, AZ

Webb, Coley .... (716) 343-8000
PROD MGR, Daily News, Batavia, NY

Webb, Dan .... (715) 723-5515
PROD MGR
Chippewa Herald, Chippewa Falls, WI

Webb, David .... (601) 384-2484
PUB, ED, Franklin Advocate, Meadville, MS

Webb, Dennis .... (216) 999-4500
News SYS DIR, Plain Dealer, Cleveland, OH

Webb, Dennis .... (970) 945-8515
MAN ED
Glenwood Post, Glenwood Springs, CO

Webb, Dick .... (412) 834-1151
PROD ASST MGR
Tribune-Review, Greensburg, PA

Webb, Don .... (804) 793-2311
ADTX MGR, PROD DIR-ADTX
Danville Register & Bee, Danville, VA

Webb, Dwain .... (417) 334-3161
PROD MGR
Branson Tri-Lakes Daily News, Branson, MO

Webb, Gary .... (423) 756-6900
PROD ASST MGR
Chattanooga Free Press, Chattanooga, TN

Webb, Gordon .... (916) 741-2345
PROD FRM-Pre Press
Appeal-Democrat, Marysville, CA

Webb, James C .... (916) 622-1255
PUB, Mountain Democrat, Placerville, CA

Webb, James C .... (610) 367-6041
PUB, Boyertown Area Times, Boyertown, PA

Webb, Jeff .... (405) 335-2188
Sports ED, Frederick Leader, Frederick, OK

Webb, Jeri .... (501) 246-5525
CIRC MGR
Arkadelphia Siftings Herald, Arkadelphia, AR

Webb, John .... (818) 713-3000
PROD DIR, Daily News, Woodland Hills, CA

Webb, Jonell .... (209) 784-5000
ADV DIR, Recorder, Porterville, CA

Webb, Judy .... (617) 482-9447
Sales MGR
BPI Entertainment News Wire, Boston, MA

Webb, Judy .... (405) 688-9271/3376
GM, ED, Hollis News, Hollis, OK

Webb, Mary Ellen .... (703) 560-4000
Entertainment/Amusements ED, Fairfax Journal, Fairfax, VA, Journal Newspapers Inc.

Webb, Patrick .... (219) 881-3000
Porter County ED, Post-Tribune, Gary, IN

Webb, Paul .... (214) 977-8222
PROD MGR-OPER
Dallas Morning News, Dallas, TX

Webb, Pauline .... (605) 964-2100
ED, Eagle Butte News, Eagle Butte, SD

Webb, Rondee .... (913) 823-6363
PROD SUPV-Pre Press
Salina Journal, Salina, KS

Webb, Sally .... (412) 224-4321
Lifestyle ED, Valley News Dispatch, Tarentum, PA, Gannett Co. Inc.

Webb, Terry .... (402) 444-1000
INFO Services MGR-SYS
Omaha World-Herald, Omaha, NE

Webb, Walter W .... (601) 252-4261
PUB, ED, South Reporter, Holly Springs, MS

Webb, Willis .... (409) 384-3441
PUB, Jasper News-Boy, Jasper, TX

Webber, Don .... (704) 873-1451
PROD FRM-COMP, Statesville Record & Landmark, Statesville, NC

Webber, Jeff .... (703) 276-3400
CIRC VP, USA Today, Arlington, VA

Webber, Karen .... (508) 793-9100
ASST Features ED
Telegram & Gazette, Worcester, MA

Weber, Allen B .... (515) 232-2160
PRES, GM, PROD Commercial Printing
Daily Tribune, Ames, IA

Weber, Andrew G .... (614) 397-5333
VP, Mount Vernon News, Mount Vernon, OH

Weber, Bernie .... (612) 673-4000
PROD MGR-Platemaking
Star Tribune, Minneapolis, MN

Weber, Bill .... (617) 426-3000
ASST MAN ED-Arts/Entertainment
Boston Herald, Boston, MA

Weber, Bonnie .... (301) 662-1177
ADV MGR-CLASS
Frederick Post/News, Frederick, MD

Weber, Christine .... (630) 844-5844
MGR-PROM, Beacon-News, Aurora, IL

Weber, Christine .... (307) 347-3241
People Page ED
Northern Wyoming Daily News, Worland, WY

Weber, Damon F .... (316) 845-2320
PUB, ED, Caldwell Messenger, Caldwell, KS

Weber, Donna .... (507) 359-2911
News ED, Journal, New Ulm, MN

Weber, Doris M .... (507) 723-4225
ED
Springfield Advance-Press, Springfield, MN

Weber, Doug .... (212) 837-7000
ADV VP/Deputy DIR, Journal of Commerce & Commercial, New York, NY

Weber, Duane L .... (402) 337-0488
PUB, Times, Randolph, NE

Weber, Eugene T .... (419) 422-5151
ADV MGR-Sales, Courier, Findlay, OH

Weber II, Fred W .... (614) 592-6612
GM, Athens Messenger, Athens, OH

Weber, Greg .... (914) 358-2200
Entertainment/Amusements ED, Fashion/Style ED, Features ED
Rockland Journal-News, West Nyack, NY

Weber, Jackie .... (616) 264-9711
GM, Town Meeting, Elk Rapids, MI

Weber, James .... (330) 454-5611
ED-at-Large, Repository, Canton, OH

Weber, Jonathan .... (213) 237-5000
"Cutting Edge"/Multimedia
Los Angeles Times, Los Angeles, CA

Weber, Kenda .... (608) 754-3311
CIRC CNR-NIE
Janesville Gazette, Janesville, WI

Weber, Mark .... (612) 829-0265
PUB, ED
Eden Prairie News, Eden Prairie, MN

Weber, Mary Ann .... (703) 838-0302
MAN ED
Alexandria Gazette Packet, Alexandria, VA

Weber, Michele L .... (614) 397-5333
VP, Mount Vernon News, Mount Vernon, OH

Weber, Mike .... (718) 526-9069
VP, Press Photo Service, Flushing, NY

Weber, Robert .... (561) 820-4100
CIRC MGR-Single Copy
Palm Beach Post, West Palm Beach, FL

Weber, S .... (519) 679-6666
ADV DIR-Sales
London Free Press, London, ON

Weber, Tad .... (805) 564-5200
ASST City ED, Santa Barbara News-Press, Santa Barbara, CA

Weber Jr, Thomas E .... (561) 287-1550
PRES/PUB, ED, Stuart News, Stuart, FL

Weber, Todd .... (414) 849-4773
ED, Chilton Spirit, Chilton, WI

Weber, Wade .... (320) 679-2661
PUB, Kanabec County Times, Mora, MN

Weber, Wendy Fox .... (708) 336-7000
Entertainment/Amusements ED, Fashion/Style ED, Features ED, Living/Lifestyle ED, Women's ED, News-Sun, Waukegan, IL

Webster, Bette .... (909) 676-4315
CIRC MGR, Californian, Temecula, CA

Webster, Brian .... (907) 456-6661
SYS MGR
Fairbanks Daily News-Miner, Fairbanks, AK

Webster, Carol .... (403) 333-2100
PUB, ED, Grizzly Gazette, Swan Hills, AB

Webster, Clent H .... (618) 965-3417
PUB, ED, Steeleville Ledger, Steeleville, IL

Webster, Daniel .... (215) 854-2000
Music Critic-Classical
Philadelphia Inquirer, Philadelphia, PA

Webster, Gary .... (517) 725-5136
Sports ED, Argus-Press, Owosso, MI

Webster, John .... (509) 459-5000
Opinion ED
Spokesman-Review, Spokane, WA

Webster, Joyce .... (403) 578-4111
PUB, ED
Coronation Review, Coronation, AB

Webster, Lori .... (907) 225-3157
ADV MGR
Ketchikan Daily News, Ketchikan, AK

Webster, Mark .... (803) 626-8555
DP MGR, PROD MGR-INFO SYS & Technology, Sun News, Myrtle Beach, SC

Webster, Robert A .... (613) 342-4441
PROD FRM-PR, Brockville Recorder and Times, Brockville, ON

Webster, Robin .... (330) 385-4545
City ED, Review, East Liverpool, OH

Webster, Russell F .... (518) 483-4700
PUB, ADV DIR
Malone Telegram, Malone, NY

Webster, Virginia .... (916) 865-4433
ED, Orland Press-Register, Orland, CA

Wechsler, Beth .... (802) 479-0191
ADV MGR-Sales, Times Argus, Barre, VT

Wecker, David .... (513) 352-2000
COL, Cincinnati Post, Cincinnati, OH

Weddell, Kristie .... (317) 584-4501
CIRC MGR, News-Gazette, Winchester, IN

Weddell, Leslie .... (719) 632-5511
Home ED, Gazette, Colorado Springs, CO

Weddle, Tim .... (816) 271-8500
ADV MGR-RT
St. Joseph News-Press, St. Joseph, MO

Wedel, David T .... (915) 682-5311
CONT, Reporter-Telegram, Midland, TX

Wedeward, David .... (608) 754-3311
Sports ED, Janesville Gazette, Janesville, WI

Weed, Dorothy .... (203) 846-3281
TREAS, Hour, Norwalk, CT

Weedmark, Kevin .... (306) 435-2445
ED, World-Spectator, Moosomin, SK

Weekley, Pat .... (612) 673-4000
PROD MGR-Pre Press
Star Tribune, Minneapolis, MN

Weeks, Charles .... (902) 447-2051
ED, Oxford Journal, Oxford, NS

Weeks, Everton J .... (716) 232-7100
ADV VP, Rochester Democrat and Chronicle; Rochester, NY Times-Union, Rochester, NY

Weeks, George .... (313) 222-2300
COL, Detroit News, Detroit, MI

Weeks, James C .... (212) 556-1234
PRES/COO-Regional Newspaper Group
New York Times, New York, NY
New York Times Co.

Weeks, Joanna McQuillen .... (508) 997-7411
Food ED, Standard Times, New Bedford, MA

Weeks, John .... (909) 889-9666
Features ED, Sun, San Bernardino, CA

Weeks, Kirk .... (706) 724-0851
EDL Writer, Augusta Chronicle, Augusta, GA

Weeks, Laura .... (518) 584-4242
CONT, Saratogian, Saratoga Springs, NY

Weeks, Lisa .... (315) 253-5311
ADV MGR-CLASS, Citizen, Auburn, NY

Weeks Jr, Roland .... (601) 896-2100
PUB/PRES, Sun Herald, Biloxi, MS

Weems, Christopher .... (404) 523-6086
MAN ED, Atlanta Inquirer, Atlanta, GA

Weerheim, Joni .... (712) 262-6610
PUB, Daily Reporter, Spencer, IA

Weese, Buford .... (405) 256-2200
PROD MGR-PR, News, Woodward, OK

Weese, Douglas .... (360) 779-4464
PUB, Kitsap County Herald, Poulsbo, WA

Weese, John .... (519) 336-1100
PUB, Gazette, Sarnia, ON

Weesner, Betty Jean .... (765) 745-2777
PUB, ED, Republican, Danville, IN

Wegars, Don .... (707) 963-2731
ED, St. Helena Star, St. Helena, CA

Wehenkel, Arthur D .... (423) 638-4181
ADV MGR, Greeneville Sun, Greeneville, TN

Wehinger, Frank .... (610) 258-7171
CIRC MGR-Home Delivery
Express-Times, Easton, PA

Weh Who's Where-244

Wehle, Greg .... (800) 657-5889
GM, Denison Review, Denison, IA
Wehner, Ron .... (812) 265-3641
ADV MGR, Madison Courier, Madison, IN
Wehner, Thomas .... (414) 922-4600
PROD SUPT-PR
Fond du Lac Reporter, Fond du Lac, WI
Wehrenberg, Michael .... (405) 341-2121
PROD FRM-COMP
Edmond Evening Sun, Edmond, OK
Wehrle, Bruce .... (704) 249-3981
Sports ED, Dispatch, Lexington, NC
Wehrle, Cathy .... (814) 938-8740
Radio/Television ED, PROD FRM-COMP
Spirit, Punxsutawney, PA
Wehrs, Marc .... (608) 782-9710
Sports ED
La Crosse Tribune, La Crosse, WI
Weible, Susanne .... (517) 787-2300
Librarian, Citizen Patriot, Jackson, MI
Weidenbacher, John .... (604) 732-2944
PROD ASST MGR
Pacific Press Limited, Vancouver, BC
Weidig, David .... (614) 452-4561
Sports ED
Zanesville Times Recorder, Zanesville, OH
Weiermiller, Kathy .... (714) 835-1234
VP/CFO-FIN
Orange County Register, Santa Ana, CA
Weiers, Larry .... (605) 642-2761
EX ED, Black Hills Pioneer, Spearfish, SD
Weige, Deb .... (414) 849-7036
ED, Chilton Times-Journal, Chilton, WI
Weigel, Bob .... (913) 628-1081
CIRC MGR, Hays Daily News, Hays, KS
Weightman, Barbara .... (905) 372-0131
CIRC MGR
Cobourg Daily Star, Cobourg, ON
Weikal, Thad .... (417) 235-3135
PROD MGR, Times, Monett, MO
Weikoff, Dave .... (937) 592-3060
PROD FRM-PR
Bellefontaine Examiner, Bellefontaine, OH
Weil III, Louis A .... (317) 231-9200
PRES/CEO
Central Newspapers Inc., Indianapolis, IN
Weil, Richard K .... (314) 340-8000
MAN ED
St. Louis Post-Dispatch, St. Louis, MO
Weil, Robert J .... (209) 441-6111
PUB, Fresno Bee, Fresno, CA
Weiland, Keith .... (517) 354-3111
PROD FRM-PR, Alpena News, Alpena, MI
Weiland, Patti .... (334) 393-2969
ED, Southeast Sun, Enterprise, AL
Weiler, Joe .... (219) 461-8222
EX ED, News-Sentinel, Fort Wayne, IN
Weiler, Joseph .... (419) 562-3333
PROD FRM-PR
Telegraph-Forum, Bucyrus, OH
Weiler, Sherry .... (815) 937-3300
Religion ED, Teen-Age/Youth ED, Television/Film ED, Daily Journal, Kankakee, IL
Weimar, James (Jay) .... (904) 359-4111
ADV MGR-Display
Florida Times-Union, Jacksonville, FL
Weimer, Fred .... (504) 383-1111
PROD DIR
Baton Rouge Advocate, Baton Rouge, LA
Weimer, Steve .... (312) 252-3534
GM, Extra Bilingual Community Newspapers, Chicago, IL
Weinand, Shawn .... (218) 262-1011
CIRC MGR, Daily Tribune, Hibbing, MN
Weinberg, Anna C .... (607) 798-1234
DIR-Human Resources
Press & Sun Bulletin, Binghamton, NY
Weinberg, Gloria .... (561) 461-2050
Life ED, Tribune, Fort Pierce, FL
Weinberg, Jeff .... (516) 843-2020
Night Sports ED, Newsday, Melville, NY
Weinberg, Lawrence .... (212) 387-0299
PUB, Novoye Russkoye Slovo, New York, NY
Weinberg, Mark .... (214) 977-8222
ASST MAN ED-Lifestyles
Dallas Morning News, Dallas, TX
Weinberg, Marshall M .... (330) 833-2631
ADV MGR-Sales
Independent, Massillon, OH
Weinberger, Martin .... (909) 621-4761
PUB, ED, Claremont Courier, Claremont, CA
Weinberger, Peter .... (612) 222-5011
Senior ED-Visuals
St. Paul Pioneer Press, St. Paul, MN
Weiner, Becky .... (608) 222-5522
ASSOC ED
Shetland Productions, Madison, WI
Weiner, Judy .... (402) 444-1000
Action Line ED
Omaha World-Herald, Omaha, NE
Weiner, Margaret .... (310) 230-3400
Senior MGR/Human Resources, Allsport Photography USA, Pacific Palisades, CA
Weingand, Bishop William ...... (916) 452-3344
PUB, Catholic Herald, Sacramento, CA
Weingarten, Sherwood .... (415) 263-7200
MAN ED, Jewish Bulletin of Northern California, San Francisco, CA
Weingrad, Jeff .... (212) 210-2100
Television ED
New York Daily News, New York, NY
Weinrauch, Jonas .... (306) 634-2654
ED, Mercury, Estevan, SK
Weinreich, Judi .... (319) 754-8461
ADV CNR-Co-op, Hawk Eye, Burlington, IA
Weinschenk, Peter .... (715) 223-2342
ED, Record Review, Abbotsford, WI
Weinstein, Henry .... (213) 237-5000
Legal Affairs Writer
Los Angeles Times, Los Angeles, CA
Weinstein, Howard G .... (410) 332-6000
VP-Employee/Labor Relations
Sun, Baltimore, MD
Weinstein, Stacey .... (212) 803-8200
PROD MGR-SRV
American Banker, New York, NY
Weintraub, Joanne .... (414) 224-2000
Radio/Television Reporter
Milwaukee Journal Sentinel, Milwaukee, WI
Weintrob, Ed .... (718) 834-9161
PUB, Brooklyn Paper, Brooklyn, NY
Weir Jr, Ben F .... (816) 254-8600
PUB, Examiner, Independence, MO
Weir, Ron .... (573) 431-2010
PUB/GM, Daily Journal, Park Hills, MO
Weir, William .... (816) 932-6600
Sales MGR/Western Div.
Universal Press Syndicate, Kansas City, MO
Weis, P K .... (520) 573-4561
Photo ED, Tucson Citizen, Tucson, AZ
Weisbeck Sr, Leonard A .... (716) 937-9226
ED, Alden Advertiser, Alden, NY
Weisbeck Jr, Leonard A .... (716) 937-9226
GM, Alden Advertiser, Alden, NY
Weisberg, John .... (715) 842-2101
PROD DIR
Wausau Daily Herald, Wausau, WI
Weisfeld, Martha M .... (540) 628-2962
PUB, ED, Abingdon Virginian, Abingdon, VA
Weishaar, Marilyn .... (605) 225-4100
Features ED, Food/Garden ED, Women's ED
Aberdeen American News, Aberdeen, SD
Weisman, Robert .... (206) 464-2111
BUS ED, Seattle Times, Seattle, WA
Weisman, Seena .... (516) 569-4000
ED, Rockaway Journal, Lawrence, NY
Weismann, Randall .... (312) 222-3232
ASSOC MAN ED-News Editing
Chicago Tribune, Chicago, IL
Weiss, Arnold .... (716) 854-2192
PUB, Buffalo Jewish Review, Buffalo, NY
Weiss, Carol S .... (414) 273-8696
PUB, City Edition, Milwaukee, WI
Weiss, Hedy .... (312) 321-3000
Theater Critic
Chicago Sun-Times, Chicago, IL
Weiss, John .... (719) 577-4545
PUB, Colorado Springs Independent, Colorado Springs, CO
Weiss, John .... (507) 285-7600
Environmental/Ecology ED
Post-Bulletin, Rochester, MN
Weiss, Kris .... (419) 625-5500
Industry/Labor ED
Sandusky Register, Sandusky, OH
Weiss, Margi .... (712) 279-5019
DIR-MKTG/PROM
Sioux City Journal, Sioux City, IA
Weiss, Richard .... (314) 340-8000
Features DIR
St. Louis Post-Dispatch, St. Louis, MO
Weiss, Steven .... (718) 853-5435
PRES, Rothco Cartoons, Brooklyn, NY
Weiss, Susan .... (703) 276-3400
MAN ED-Life, USA Today, Arlington, VA
Weiss, Ted .... (807) 468-5555
ADV MGR, Daily Miner & News, Kenora, ON
Weiss, Todd .... (805) 273-2700
Entertainment/Amusements ED, Television/Film ED, Theater/Music ED
Antelope Valley Press, Palmdale, CA
Weisser, Steve .... (312) 222-3232
PROD MGR-Packaging
Chicago Tribune, Chicago, IL
Weissert, Judie .... (541) 926-2211
ADV MGR-RT
Albany Democrat-Herald, Albany, OR
Weissman, Art .... (908) 922-6000
State House ED
Asbury Park Press, Neptune, NJ
Weitzel, Harry .... (800) 223-2154
PROD MGR
Investor's Business Daily, Los Angeles, CA
Weitzel, Wendy .... (916) 741-2345
Entertainment/Amusements ED, Features ED
Appeal-Democrat, Marysville, CA
Welborn, James .... (702) 385-3111
Online Publishing Webmaster
Las Vegas Sun, Las Vegas, NV
Welborn, Jim .... (803) 771-6161
PROD MGR-Maintenance
State, Columbia, SC
Welborn, Vickie .... (318) 872-4120
ED, Mansfield Enterprise, Mansfield, LA
Welbro, Terry .... (817) 387-3811
News ED, Wire ED
Denton Record-Chronicle, Denton, TX
Welby, Ron .... (401) 277-7000
ADV Sales DIR-EDU/Employment
Providence Journal-Bulletin, Providence, RI
Welch, Bill .... (814) 870-1600
Amusements ED, City ED, SCI/Technology ED
Morning News/Erie Daily Times, Erie, PA
Welch, Chris .... (205) 532-4000
EX Sports ED
Huntsville Times, Huntsville, AL
Welch, David .... (507) 645-5615
ED, Northfield News, Northfield, MN
Welch, Dean .... (404) 526-5151
DIR-CLASS Advertising
Atlanta Journal-Constitution, Atlanta, GA
Welch, Dominic .... (801) 237-2031
PRES/PUB
Kearns-Tribune Corp., Salt Lake City, UT
Welch, Doug .... (608) 868-2442
ED, Milton Courier, Milton, WI
Welch, Nancy .... (912) 764-9031
Women's ED
Statesboro Herald, Statesboro, GA
Welch, Noble .... (903) 657-2501
PRES, PUB, ED, Daily News, Henderson, TX
Welch, Paul .... (705) 526-5431
ED, Free Press, Midland, ON
Welch, Richard .... (203) 574-3636
ADV MGR-NTL, Waterbury Republican-American, Waterbury, CT
Welch, Rick .... (219) 563-2131
ADV MGR, Wabash Plain Dealer, Wabash, IN
Welch, Robert C .... (419) 874-4491
PUB, Messenger-Journal, Perrysburg, OH
Welch, Robt .... (541) 485-1234
Features ED, Living/Lifestyle ED, Travel ED, Women's ED, Register-Guard, Eugene, OR
Welchlin, Brenda .... (972) 727-3352
MAN ED, Allen American, Allen, TX
Welden, Beth .... (218) 262-1011
Family ED, Daily Tribune, Hibbing, MN
Weldon, Jeremy .... (601) 686-4081
PUB, ED, Leland Progress, Leland, MS
Weldon, Tom .... (415) 348-4321
CIRC DIR
San Mateo County Times, San Mateo, CA
Weldon, Mrs William H .... (573) 636-3131
Owner/PUB
News Tribune, Jefferson City, MO
Weleschuk, Damian .... (416) 234-1212
GM, Svitlo, Etobicoke, ON
Welin, Joel .... (941) 953-7755
Radio/Television ED
Sarasota Herald-Tribune, Sarasota, FL
Welker, Harold .... (301) 722-4600
ADV MGR-RT
Cumberland Times-News, Cumberland, MD
Welker, Steve .... (515) 684-4611
SYS Specialist
Ottumwa Courier, Ottumwa, IA
Welkos, Robert .... (213) 237-5000
Movie Industry Writer
Los Angeles Times, Los Angeles, CA
Wellborn, David .... (501) 425-6301
Sports ED, Daily News, Mountain Home, AR
Welle, Doris .... (712) 338-4712
ED, Milford Mail, Milford, IA
Wellendorf, Kirk .... (919) 419-6500
PROD MGR-Dayside Distribution Center
Herald-Sun, Durham, NC
Wellendorf, Meredith .... (919) 419-6500
MGR-Community Relations
Herald-Sun, Durham, NC
Wellenkamp, Pat .... (217) 323-1010
GM, Illinoian Star, Beardstown, IL
Weller, Ben .... (516) 843-2020
Political ED, Sunday ED
Newsday, Melville, NY
Weller, Doug .... (913) 628-1081
ASST MAN ED, Hays Daily News, Hays, KS
Weller, Linda .... (618) 463-2500
EDU/Schools ED, Telegraph, Alton, IL
Weller, Rusty .... (512) 643-1566
ED, Portland News, Portland, TX
Weller, Worth .... (219) 982-6383
PUB, News-Journal, North Manchester, IN
Wellman, Curt .... (317) 633-1240
ASST MAN ED-AM Cycle
Indianapolis Star/News, Indianapolis, IN
Wellman, Darrell .... (402) 274-3185
ED, Auburn Press-Tribune, Auburn, NE
Wellman, Dave .... (304) 526-4000
Sports ED, Herald-Dispatch, Huntington, WV
Wellman, Roy C .... (608) 365-8811
PRES, Beloit Daily News, Beloit, WI
Hagadone Corp.
Wellman, Ruth .... (517) 851-7833
ED, Town Crier, Stockbridge, MI
Wellman, Shirley .... (330) 725-4166
PROD SUPT
Medina County Gazette, Medina, OH
Wellman, Thomas .... (419) 245-6000
ASSOC ED, Blade, Toledo, OH
Wells, Adrienne S .... (810) 766-6100
ASST to PUB, Flint Journal, Flint, MI
Wells, Ann .... (616) 222-5400
Food ED
Grand Rapids Press, Grand Rapids, MI
Wells, Barbara .... (214) 977-8222
DIR-RES, Dallas Morning News, Dallas, TX
Wells, Cindy .... (501) 996-4494
PUB, Greenwood Democrat, Greenwood, AR
Wells, Clifton .... (501) 354-2451
PUB, ED, Conway County Petit Jean Country Headlight, Morrillton, AR
Wells, Clyde .... (706) 724-0851
Cartoonist, Augusta Chronicle, Augusta, GA
Wells, Craig .... (941) 748-0411
PRES/PUB, Bradenton Herald, Bradenton, FL
Wells, Danny .... (304) 348-5140
COL, Charleston Gazette, Sunday Gazette-Mail, Charleston, WV
Wells, Dean .... (410) 228-3131
Sports ED, Daily Banner, Cambridge, MD
Wells, Debra .... (806) 857-2123
PUB, ED, Eagle Press, Fritch, TX
Wells, Derrol .... (806) 857-2123
PUB, Eagle Press, Fritch, TX
Wells, Don .... (408) 372-3311
PROD FRM-PR/Plate
Monterey County Herald, Monterey, CA
Wells, Douglas F .... (520) 635-4426
PUB, Williams-Grand Canyon News Inc., Williams, AZ
Wells, Greg .... (903) 873-2525
ED, Van Zandt News, Wills Point, TX
Wells, Hal .... (562) 435-1161
Photo DIR, Press-Telegram, Long Beach, CA
Wells, Harold .... (423) 523-3131
PROD OPER SUPT-PR
Knoxville News-Sentinel, Knoxville, TN
Wells, Henry W .... (806) 447-2559
PUB, GM, Wellington Leader, Wellington, TX
Wells, James A .... (717) 784-2121
VP, GM, Press Enterprise, Bloomsburg, PA
Wells, John .... (805) 395-7500
ADV DIR
Bakersfield Californian, Bakersfield, CA
Wells, Leon O .... (402) 589-1010
PUB, ED, Spencer Advocate, Spencer, NE
Wells, Marie .... (505) 437-7120
CIRC DIR
Alamogordo Daily News, Alamogordo, NM
Wells, Martha .... (515) 684-4611
PUB, Ottumwa Courier, Ottumwa, IA
Wells, Mary Kaye .... (904) 312-5200
ADV MGR-CLASS, Daily News, Palatka, FL
Wells, Pamela .... (608) 252-6100
CONT, Wisconsin State Journal, Madison, WI
Wells, Paul .... (403) 948-7280
ED, Airdrie Echo, Airdrie, AB
Wells, Susan .... (404) 526-5151
ASST MAN ED-BUS
Atlanta Journal-Constitution, Atlanta, GA
Wells, Sybil Andrews .... (813) 248-1921
PUB, Florida Sentinel-Bulletin, Tampa, FL
Wells, Tommy .... (817) 325-4465
Sports ED
Mineral Wells Index, Mineral Wells, TX
Wells, Vinde .... (815) 732-6166
ED, Mount Morris Times, Oregon, IL
Wells, Virginia .... (913) 263-1000
PROD SUPV-CR
Abilene Reflector-Chronicle, Abilene, KS
Wells-Lego, Pamela .... (812) 372-7811
ADV DIR, ADTX MGR
Republic, Columbus, IN
Welmers, Ben .... (517) 846-4531
ED
Arenac County Independent, Standish, MI
Welna, Jane .... (212) 807-6622
Sales MGR, Impact Visuals Photo & Graphics Inc., New York, NY
Welsch, Jeff .... (541) 753-2641
Sports ED
Corvallis Gazette-Times, Corvallis, OR
Welsh, Anne Marie .... (619) 299-3131
Dance ED
San Diego Union-Tribune, San Diego, CA
Welsh, Candice .... (970) 925-3414
ADV DIR, Aspen Times, Aspen, CO
Welsh, John .... (818) 241-4141
City ED, Glendale News-Press, Glendale, CA
Welsh, Melinda .... (916) 498-1234
ED
Sacramento News & Review, Sacramento, CA
Welsh, Mickey .... (334) 262-1611
Photo MGR
Montgomery Advertiser, Montgomery, AL
Welsh, Mike .... (520) 573-4400
CIRC MGR-OPER, TNI Partners dba Tucson Newspapers, Tucson, AZ

245-Who's Where **Wha**

Welsh, William R .... (402) 269-2135
PUB
Syracuse Journal-Democrat, Syracuse, NE
Welty, George .... (410) 848-4400
Photo/Production ED
Carroll County Times, Westminster, MD
Welty, Kimberly .... (410) 268-5000
ADV MGR-CLASS, Capital, Annapolis, MD
Welty, Terry .... (309) 343-7181
CIRC MGR, Register-Mail, Galesburg, IL
Weltz, Hugh .... (519) 669-5155
GM, Elmira Independent, Elmira, ON
Wemple, Erik .... (202) 332-2100
MAN ED
Washington City Paper, Washington, DC
Wenaus, Susie .... (541) 776-4411
ADV CNR-CLASS Phone Sales
Mail Tribune, Medford, OR
Wenchell, Wally .... (516) 843-2020
PROD MGR-OPER, Newsday, Melville, NY
Wendel, Dorothy .... (319) 252-2421
ED, Guttenberg Press, Guttenberg, IA
Wendel, Thomas E .... (541) 296-2141
VP-FIN
Dalles Daily Chronicle, The Dalles, OR
Wendell, Mary Lou .... (207) 784-5411
EDU ED, Sun-Journal, Lewiston, ME
Wendland, Leslie .... (512) 884-2011
ADV VP, Corpus Christi Caller-Times, Corpus Christi, TX
Wendorf, Greg .... (210) 783-0036
PUB, ED, Advance News, Pharr, TX
Wendorf, Mike .... (712) 642-2791
GM, Valley Times-News, Missouri Valley, IA
Wendorff, Michael .... (308) 836-2200
PUB, ED, Callaway Courier, Callaway, NE
Wendover, W Edward .... (313) 453-6900
PUB, Community Crier, Plymouth, MI
Wenger, Linda .... (319) 728-2413
ED, Columbus Gazette, Columbus Jct., IA
Wenk, William .... (810) 469-4510
CFO, Macomb Daily, Mount Clemens, MI
Independent Newspapers Inc. (MI)
Wenner, Susan .... (407) 322-2611
Religion ED, Sanford Herald, Sanford, FL
Wenner, Virginia L .... (716) 232-7100
MGR-Telecommunications
Rochester Democrat and Chronicle; Times-Union, Rochester, NY
Wenninger, Michael .... (916) 623-2055
ED, Trinity Journal, Weaverville, CA
Wenninger, Sarah .... (916) 623-2055
PUB, Trinity Journal, Weaverville, CA
Wenrich, Jay H .... (717) 291-8811
TREAS, BM, Lancaster Intelligencer Journal/New Era/Sunday News, Lancaster, PA
Wensits, James .... (219) 235-6161
ASSOC ED
South Bend Tribune, South Bend, IN
Wente, Margaret .... (416) 585-5000
BUS/FIN ED, Globe and Mail (Canada's National Newspaper), Toronto, ON
Wentworth, Slade .... (360) 377-3711
PROD MGR-INFO Services
Sun, Bremerton, WA
Wentz, Sharon .... (610) 377-2051
CIRC MGR, Times News, Lehighton, PA
Wenzel, Dennis P .... (605) 539-1281
PUB, ED, True Dakotan/Alpena Journal, Wessington Springs, SD
Wenzel, Holly .... (612) 777-8800
ED
Ramsey County Review, North St. Paul, MN
Wenzel, J Craig .... (605) 539-1281
PUB, ED, True Dakotan/Alpena Journal, Wessington Springs, SD
Wenzel, Korrie .... (605) 996-5514
Sports ED, Daily Republic, Mitchell, SD
Wenzel, Scott .... (517) 652-3246
ED, Frankenmuth News, Frankenmuth, MI
Wenzelburger, Bill .... (813) 893-8111
PROD MGR-Maintenance
St. Petersburg Times, St. Petersburg, FL
Wenzl, Roy .... (316) 268-6000
Crime/Safety ED, Wichita Eagle, Wichita, KS
Wenzl, Tim .... (316) 227-1500
PUB, ED
Southwest Kansas Register, Dodge City, KS
Werblo, Terry .... (817) 387-3811
EPE, Denton Record-Chronicle, Denton, TX
Werder, Claude J .... (414) 435-4411
ED, Green Bay Press-Gazette, Green Bay, WI
Werder, Nicholas .... (304) 263-8931
PROD FRM-COMP, Journal, Martinsburg, WV
Werkman, Deb .... (319) 824-6958
ED, Grundy Register, Grundy Center, IA
Werley, Bob .... (520) 783-3333
Foothill's News ED
Yuma Daily Sun, Yuma, AZ
Werley, Lenora .... (520) 783-3333
Fashion/Style ED, Home Furnishings/Garden ED, Living/Lifestyle ED, Religion ED, Women's ED, Yuma Daily Sun, Yuma, AZ
Werling, Ericka .... (913) 263-1000
City/County ED
Abilene Reflector-Chronicle, Abilene, KS

Wern, Kathleen F .... (518) 792-9914
VP-Sales, TV Data, Queensbury, NY
Werner, Al .... (615) 893-5860
ADV MGR-NTL
Daily News Journal, Murfreesboro, TN
Werner, Barry .... (212) 210-2100
Deputy Sports ED
New York Daily News, New York, NY
Werner, Jeff .... (215) 493-2794
ED, Yardley News, Yardley, PA
Werner, Larry .... (612) 673-4000
Projects Team Leader
Star Tribune, Minneapolis, MN
Werner, Mary Ann .... (202) 334-6000
VP/Counsel
Washington Post, Washington, DC
Werner, R Wesley .... (412) 775-3200
DP MGR, PROD MGR-Computer SYS
Beaver County Times, Beaver, PA
Werner, Thomas .... (815) 747-3171
PUB
East Dubuque Register, East Dubuque, IL
Werner, Troy .... (216) 245-6901
PROD DIR-DP
Lorain Morning Journal, Lorain, OH
Werrell, James .... (803) 329-4000
EPE, Herald, Rock Hill, SC
Wersich, Carol .... (812) 424-7711
DIR-Community SRV
Evansville Courier, Evansville, IN
Werst, David L .... (915) 884-2215
ED, Big Lake Wildcat, Big Lake, TX
Werst Jr, J L .... (915) 884-2215
PUB, Big Lake Wildcat, Big Lake, TX
Wert, David .... (909) 987-6397
MET ED-San Bernadino Co.
Inland Valley Daily Bulletin, Ontario, CA
Werth, Bill .... (414) 634-3322
ADV MGR-CLASS, Online MGR
Journal Times, Racine, WI
Werth, Brian .... (812) 332-4401
BUS ED, Herald-Times Inc, Bloomington, IN
Werth, Roger .... (360) 577-2500
Photo ED, Daily News, Longview, WA
Wertman, Michael .... (716) 798-1400
MAN ED, Sports ED
Journal-Register, Medina, NY
Wertz, Bob .... (412) 856-7400
ED, Woodland Area Progress, Monroeville, PA
Wertz, Jean .... (203) 235-1661
News ED, Record-Journal, Meriden, CT
Wertz, Jerry .... (419) 422-5151
PROD FRM-PR, Courier, Findlay, OH
Wescott, Scott .... (814) 870-1600
EDU ED
Morning News/Erie Daily Times, Erie, PA
Weseloh, Harold .... (612) 523-2032
ED, Olivia Times-Journal, Olivia, MN
Wesley, Pattie .... (203) 263-2116
ED, Voices, Southbury, CT
Wesner, Ken .... (405) 832-3333
PUB, Cordell Beacon, Cordell, OK
Wesner, Scott .... (405) 875-3326
PUB, ED, Walters Herald, Walters, OK
Wesnick, Richard .... (406) 657-1200
ED, Montana Newspaper Group, Billings, MT
Wesolowski, Monica .... (954) 356-4000
CIRC MGR-Customer Relations
Sun-Sentinel, Fort Lauderdale, FL
Wessel, Tom .... (409) 883-3571
PROD MGR, Orange Leader, Orange, TX
Wesselhoff, Bill .... (815) 756-4841
Sports ED, Daily Chronicle, De Kalb, IL
Wessell Sr, Richard C .... (847) 299-5511
PUB, Des Plaines Journal, Des Plaines, IL
Wessell, Todd C .... (847) 299-5511
ED, Des Plaines Journal, Des Plaines, IL
Wessing, James .... (315) 792-5000
PROD DIR, Observer-Dispatch, Utica, NY
Wessler, Kirk .... (309) 686-3000
Sports ED, Journal Star, Peoria, IL
Wessling, Dianne .... (712) 243-2624
ADV MGR-CLASS
Atlantic News-Telegraph, Atlantic, IA
Wessman, Lois L .... (218) 741-5544
TREAS, Mesabi Daily News, Virginia, MN
Wessol, Shay .... (618) 656-4700
MAN ED
Edwardsville Intelligencer, Edwardsville, IL
West, Andrew .... (302) 934-9261
ED, Sussex Post, Lewes, DE
West, Annette .... (515) 792-3121
ADV MGR
Newton Daily News, Newton, IA
West, Bert C .... (512) 782-3547
PUB, ED
Jackson County Herald/Tribune, Edna, TX
West, Bob .... (409) 985-5541
COL, Sports ED
Port Arthur News, Port Arthur, TX
West, Carl .... (502) 227-4556
ED, News ED, State Journal, Frankfort, KY
West, Dan .... (713) 220-7171
PROD MGR-PR
Houston Chronicle, Houston, TX

West, Dennis .... (704) 358-5000
ADV MGR-Sales
Charlotte Observer, Charlotte, NC
West, Don .... (864) 582-4511
PROD MGR-MR
Herald-Journal, Spartanburg, SC
West, Eddie .... (615) 735-1110
ED, Carthage Courier, Carthage, TN
West, Ernest .... (304) 292-6301
PROD DIR, Dominion Post, Morgantown, WV
West, Ernie .... (860) 241-6200
MGR-Training, Hartford Courant, Hartford, CT
West, Gary .... (619) 241-7744
MAN ED-MET, Daily Press, Victorville, CA
West Jr, James .... (618) 833-2158
GM, Monday's Pub, Anna, IL
West, Jeff .... (517) 437-7351
PROD CNR-OPER
Hillsdale Daily News, Hillsdale, MI
West, Jim .... (618) 734-4242
GM, Tri-State Advertiser, Cairo, IL
West, John R .... (864) 459-5461
ED, Press & Banner, Abbeville, SC
West, Judy .... (541) 889-5387
MGR-CR, Argus Observer, Ontario, OR
West, Kenneth .... (706) 745-6343
ED, North Georgia News, Blairsville, GA
West, Larry .... (609) 272-7000
ADV MGR-At The Shore BUS
Press of Atlantic City, Pleasantville, NJ
West, Lee .... (706) 884-7311
GM, La Grange Daily News, La Grange, GA
West, Lora .... (616) 796-4831
PROD MGR
Big Rapids Pioneer, Big Rapids, MI
West, Luke .... (703) 878-8000
ED, Potomac News, Woodbridge, VA
West, Marvin .... (202) 408-1484
MAN ED, Scripps Howard News Service, Washington, DC
West, Mike .... (205) 325-2222
ADV MGR-SRV
Birmingham News, Birmingham, AL
West, Nicholas M .... (512) 972-3009
PUB, ED, Palacios Beacon, Palacios, TX
West, Paul .... (410) 332-6000
Washington BU Chief, Sun, Baltimore, MD
West, Randy .... (812) 738-2211
ED, Corydon Democrat, Corydon, IN
West, Ray .... (910) 323-4848
ADV MGR
Fayetteville Observer-Times, Fayetteville, NC
West, Richard (Woody) .... (202) 636-3000
ASSOC ED
Washington Times, Washington, DC
West, Robert .... (205) 325-2222
ADV MGR-RES/BUS Development
Birmingham News, Birmingham, AL
West, Roland B .... (310) 540-5511
MGR-INFO SYS, Daily Breeze, Torrance, CA
Copley Press Inc.
West, Ronald .... (908) 922-6000
PROD MGR-Transportation
Asbury Park Press, Neptune, NJ
West, Steven .... (802) 864-6399
MAN ED
Out in the Mountains, Burlington, VT
West, Sue .... (509) 284-5782
PUB, Standard-Register, Tekoa, WA
West, Tammy .... (540) 635-4174
GM, Warren Sentinel, Front Royal, VA
West, Timothy J .... (815) 942-3221
PUB, ED, Daily Herald, Morris, IL
West, Tina .... (317) 529-1111
ADV DIR, Courier-Times, New Castle, IN
West, Tom .... (507) 835-3380
PUB, ED, Waseca County News, Waseca, MN
West, Virginia .... (816) 263-4123
BUS/FIN ED, Moberly Monitor-Index & Democrat, Moberly, MO
West, Wanda R .... (706) 745-6343
PUB, North Georgia News, Blairsville, GA
West, Wendy .... (304) 292-6301
PROD MGR-Pre Press/SYS
Dominion Post, Morgantown, WV
Westberry, Henry .... (912) 764-9031
PROD SUPV-Press
Statesboro Herald, Statesboro, GA
Westbrook, Bruce .... (713) 220-7171
Radio/Video ED
Houston Chronicle, Houston, TX
Westbrook, Eugene .... (919) 778-2211
PROD MGR
Goldsboro News-Argus, Goldsboro, NC
Westbrook, Sarah .... (915) 337-4661
EDU ED, Odessa American, Odessa, TX
Westby, Jeanne .... (914) 694-9300
ADV MGR-Display, Reporter Dispatch, White Plains, NY, Gannett Co. Inc.
Westby, Kelli Maria .... (707) 527-1200
GM
Sonoma County Independent, Santa Rosa, CA
Westen, Joan .... (902) 468-1222
News ED, Daily News, Halifax, NS
Wester, Milton .... (406) 628-4412
PUB, Laurel Outlook, Laurel, MT

Westerbeck, David .... (913) 764-2211
CIRC DIR, Olathe Daily News, Olathe, KS
Westercamp, Holly .... (507) 451-2840
ADV MGR
Owatonna People's Press, Owatonna, MN
Westerfield, Jay .... (812) 332-4401
CIRC MGR
Herald-Times Inc, Bloomington, IN
Westerfield, Richard A .... (815) 842-1153
PUB, Daily Leader, Pontiac, IL
Westergaard, Leslie .... (916) 756-0800
PROD FRM-COMP
Davis Enterprise, Davis, CA
Westerman, Jolene .... (414) 733-4411
Automotive ED, Garden ED, Home Furnishings ED, Post-Crescent, Appleton, WI
Westfall, Allison .... (208) 467-9251
City ED, Recreation/Entertainment ED
Idaho Press-Tribune, Nampa, ID
Westfall, Jennifer .... (304) 788-3333
Society ED, Teen-Age/Youth ED
Mineral Daily News-Tribune, Keyser, WV
Westling, Mark .... (714) 835-1234
VP-INFO Services, DP MGR
Orange County Register, Santa Ana, CA
Westlund, Robert .... (309) 852-2181
Sports ED, Star-Courier, Kewanee, IL
Westman, Roy H .... (218) 741-5544
SEC, Mesabi Daily News, Virginia, MN
Westmoreland, Mark A .... (404) 659-8809
ED
Wesleyan Christian Advocate, Atlanta, GA
Weston, Butch .... (919) 946-2144
MGR-MKTG/PROM, CIRC DIR, ADTX MGR, PROD FRM-MR
Washington Daily News, Washington, NC
Weston, Chris .... (864) 298-4100
MAN ED-Local News
Greenville News, Greenville, SC
Weston, Tom .... (212) 755-4363
Contributing Writer, Punch In Travel & Entertainment News Syndicate, NY, NY
Westphal, Al .... (319) 242-7101
PROD MGR, Clinton Herald, Clinton, IA
Westphal, Allyce .... (906) 774-2772
Women's ED, Daily News, Iron Mountain, MI
Westphal, Stephen .... (616) 222-5400
ADV DIR
Grand Rapids Press, Grand Rapids, MI
Westphelling Jr, Paul .... (502) 236-2726
PUB, Hickman Courier, Hickman, KY
Wetak, Nancy .... (414) 733-4411
Librarian, Post-Crescent, Appleton, WI
Wethington, Jerry D .... (316) 251-3300
Chairman, Coffeyville Journal, Coffeyville, KS
Hometown Communications
Wetjen, Andre .... (250) 762-4445
Entertainment ED
Daily Courier, Kelowna, BC
Wetmore, Pete .... (217) 351-5252
Television ED, News-Gazette, Champaign, IL
Wetnight, Denise .... (408) 761-7300
ADV MGR-CLASS
Register-Pajaronian, Watsonville, CA
Wetz, Larry .... (330) 264-1125
PROD FRM-Plate Room
Daily Record, Wooster, OH
Wetzel, Paul .... (801) 237-2031
EDL Writer
Salt Lake Tribune, Salt Lake City, UT
Weve, Delores A .... (316) 667-2697
ED, Mount Hope Clarion, Mount Hope, KS
Wexeil, Gordon .... (701) 662-2127
MAN ED
Devils Lake Daily Journal, Devils Lake, ND
Wexell, Jim .... (412) 523-6588
Sports ED
Standard Observer, Greensburg, PA
Weyant, Linda .... (914) 341-1100
ADM ASST
Times Herald-Record, Middletown, NY
Weybret, Fred .... (209) 369-2761
Chairman, EPE
Lodi News-Sentinel, Lodi, CA
Weybret, Jim .... (209) 369-2761
SEC/TREAS, Co-PUB, BM
Lodi News-Sentinel, Lodi, CA
Weybret, Marty .... (209) 369-2761
PRES, Co-PUB/ED
Lodi News-Sentinel, Lodi, CA
Weydert, Debra .... (816) 932-6600
Special Sales/TELEMKTG
Universal Press Syndicate, Kansas City, MO
Whack, Mike .... (813) 893-8111
CIRC MGR-Home Delivery
St. Petersburg Times, St. Petersburg, FL
Whalen, Christine .... (808) 528-1475
MAN ED, Honolulu Weekly, Honolulu, HI
Whalen, Michael J .... (507) 642-3636
PUB
Madelia Times-Messenger, Madelia, MN

Wha Who's Where-246

Whalen, Richard .... (507) 454-6500
CONT, Winona Daily News, Winona, MN
Whalen, Valerie .... (401) 722-4000
MGR-BUS Office, Times, Pawtucket, RI
Whaley, Daniel .... (716) 232-6920
GM, Daily Record, Rochester, NY
Whaley, John .... (904) 359-4111
CIRC DIR
Florida Times-Union, Jacksonville, FL
Whaley, Kevin .... (770) 428-9411
Sports ED
Marietta Daily Journal, Marietta, GA
Whaley, Rhonda .... (423) 745-5664
BM, DP MGR
Daily Post-Athenian, Athens, TN
Whaley, Scott .... (901) 989-4624
PUB, ED
Chester County Independent, Henderson, TN
Whall, Louise .... (417) 836-1100
Projects ED
Springfield News-Leader, Springfield, MO
Whanger, Russell .... (573) 642-7272
Photo ED, Fulton Sun, Fulton, MO
Whatley, Harold .... (334) 541-3902
PUB, Eclectic Observer, Eclectic, AL
Whatley, Charlotte .... (806) 779-2141
ED, McLean News, McLean, TX
Wheat, Dan .... (509) 663-5161
EDU ED, Political ED
Wenatchee World, Wenatchee, WA
Wheat, Lynda .... (601) 833-6961
ADV MGR-CLASS
Daily Leader, Brookhaven, MS
Wheater, Richard C .... (616) 924-4400
PUB, ED
Fremont Times-Indicator, Fremont, MI
Wheatley, Brenda .... (518) 792-9914
DIR-Client & Technical Services
TV Data, Queensbury, NY
Wheatley, Guy .... (903) 794-3311
Graphics ED/Art DIR
Texarkana Gazette, Texarkana, TX
Wheatley, Linda .... (519) 679-6666
ADV MGR-Local RT Sales
London Free Press, London, ON
Wheeland, Christi .... (918) 486-4444
ED, Coweta American, Coweta, OK
Wheeler, Carla .... (909) 889-9666
Religion ED, Sun, San Bernardino, CA
Wheeler, Dan .... (203) 744-5100
Online MGR, News-Times, Danbury, CT
Wheeler, Glenn .... (416) 461-0871
MAN ED, NOW, Toronto, ON
Wheeler, M M .... (405) 255-5354
VP, Duncan Banner, Duncan, OK
Wheeler, Richard M .... (219) 279-2167
PUB, ED
New Wolcott Enterprise, Wolcott, IN
Wheeler, Sandy .... (916) 662-5421
PROD SUPV-COMP Room
Daily Democrat, Woodland, CA
Wheeler, Scott .... (704) 873-1451
CIRC MGR, Statesville Record & Landmark, Statesville, NC
Wheeler, Tammy .... (614) 353-3101
PROD MGR
Portsmouth Daily Times, Portsmouth, OH
Wheeler, Tim .... (212) 924-2523
ED, People's Weekly World, New York, NY
Wheeler, Vince .... (910) 888-3500
Sunday ED
High Point Enterprise, High Point, NC
Wheeler, Virginia .... (716) 232-7100
Library MGR
Rochester Democrat and Chronicle; Rochester, NY Times-Union, Rochester, NY
Wheelock, Sharon M .... (308) 458-2425
PUB, ED, Grant County News, Hyannis, NE
Whelan, George .... (304) 269-1600
ED, Weston Democrat, Weston, WV
Whelan, James .... (818) 282-5707
ED, San Marino Tribune, San Marino, CA
Whelan, Mary Beth .... (212) 689-1340
PRES, Globe Photos Inc., New York, NY
Whelchel, Mary .... (757) 446-2000
CIRC MGR-Single Copy
Virginian-Pilot, Norfolk, VA
Whellan, Floyd .... (319) 383-2100
VP-Human Resources
Lee Enterprises Inc., Davenport, IA
Whelton, Suzanne .... (202) 334-6375
OPER MGR/Comics ED, Washington Post Writers Group, Washington, DC
Whepley, Brian .... (316) 268-6000
Presentation ED, Wichita Eagle, Wichita, KS
Wherry, Greg A .... (208) 962-3851
ED, Cottonwood Chronicle, Cottonwood, ID
Wherry, Patricia E .... (208) 937-2671
PUB, Lewis County Herald, Nezperce, ID
Wherry, Robert E .... (208) 937-2671
ED, Lewis County Herald, Nezperce, ID
Whetstone, Peggy .... (812) 749-3913
ED, Oakland City Journal, Oakland City, IN
Whetten, Bruce .... (520) 364-3424
Sports ED, Daily Dispatch, Douglas, AZ
Whichard III, David Jordan .... (919) 752-6166
PUB, Daily Reflector, Greenville, NC
Whipple, Andy .... (541) 382-1811
Entertainment ED, Features ED, Television/Film ED, Theater ED, Bulletin, Bend, OR
Whipple, Dale E .... (801) 743-6983
PUB, ED
Millard County Gazette, Fillmore, UT
Whipple, Harry M .... (513) 721-2700
PRES/PUB
Cincinnati Enquirer, Cincinnati, OH
Whipple, Kathy .... (816) 628-6010
GM, Kearney Courier, Kearney, MO
Whipple, Richard N .... (816) 628-6010
PUB, ED, Kearney Courier, Kearney, MO
Whirsl, Tracy .... (941) 983-9148
ED, Clewiston News, Clewiston, FL
Whisnand, Charles .... (209) 784-5000
Sports ED, Recorder, Porterville, CA
Whisnant, Scott .... (910) 343-2000
Farm ED, Morning Star/Sunday Star-News, Wilmington, NC
Whitacre, Ann .... (540) 667-3200
ADV MGR-CLASS
Winchester Star, Winchester, VA
Whitaker, Amy .... (616) 264-9711
ED, Town Meeting, Elk Rapids, MI
Whitaker, Belinda .... (540) 669-2181
DP MGR, Herald-Courier Virginia Tennessean, Bristol, VA
Whitaker, Charles W .... (606) 855-4541
PUB, ED, Letcher County Community Press, Cromona, KY
Whitaker, Charlotte .... (903) 887-4511
PUB, Monitor/Leader, Mabank, TX
Whitaker, David .... (817) 390-7400
PROD DIR-OPER
Fort Worth Star-Telegram, Fort Worth, TX
Whitaker, Harbour .... (405) 658-6657
PUB, ED, Marlow Review, Marlow, OK
Whitaker, Jack .... (806) 762-8844
CIRC DIR
Lubbock Avalanche-Journal, Lubbock, TX
Whitaker, Jim .... (573) 221-2800
News ED, Hannibal Courier-Post, Hannibal, MO, Morris Communications Corp.
Whitaker, Joan .... (219) 987-5111
GM, ED
Kankakee Valley Post-News, Demotte, IN
Whitaker, Larry .... (417) 836-1100
ADV DIR
Springfield News-Leader, Springfield, MO
Whitaker, Stanley .... (770) 428-9411
VP, Marietta Daily Journal, Marietta, GA
Whitaker, Tim .... (215) 563-7400
ED, Philadelphia Weekly, Philadelphia, PA
Whitaker, William M .... (606) 855-4541
MAN ED, Letcher County Community Press, Cromona, KY
Whitbread, William .... (905) 857-3433
ED, Bolton Enterprise, Bolton, ON
Whitcomb, Robert .... (401) 277-7000
EPE
Providence Journal-Bulletin, Providence, RI
Whitcomb, Thea J .... (802) 524-9771
CIRC MGR
St. Albans Messenger, St. Albans, VT
White, Agnes .... (804) 979-0373
PUB, ED
Albermarle Tribune, Charlottesville, VA
White, Allen .... (508) 685-1000
City ED, MET ED
Eagle-Tribune, North Andover, MA
White, B J .... (812) 268-6356
ADV MGR-RT
Sullivan Daily Times, Sullivan, IN
White, Barbara .... (409) 327-4357
ED, Polk County Enterprise, Livingston, TX
White, Barbara C .... (203) 235-1661
Vice COB, EDL BC
Record-Journal, Meriden, CT
White, Barney .... (501) 394-1900
PUB, Mena Star, Mena, AR
White, Bettina .... (502) 845-2858
ED, Henry County Local, New Castle, KY
White, Betty .... (804) 649-6000
MGR-EDU SRV
Richmond Times-Dispatch, Richmond, VA
White, Bettye .... (318) 368-9732
GM, Farmerville Gazette, Farmerville, LA
White, Bill .... (907) 257-4200
BUS ED, RE ED
Anchorage Daily News, Anchorage, AK
White, Bill .... (941) 382-1164
Sports ED, Highlands Today, Sebring, FL
White, Byron .... (312) 222-3232
Urban Affairs Reporter
Chicago Tribune, Chicago, IL
White, Carlton .... (318) 368-9732
PUB, Farmerville Gazette, Farmerville, LA
White, Carter H .... (203) 235-1661
COB, Record-Journal, Meriden, CT
White, Cecile Holmes .... (713) 220-7171
Religion ED, Houston Chronicle, Houston, TX
White, Cheryl .... (802) 388-6366
PUB, Valley Voice, Middlebury, VT
White, Chris .... (417) 256-9191
BUS/FIN ED, Fashion ED, Home Furnishings ED, Religion ED, Teen-Age/Youth ED
West Plains Daily Quill, West Plains, MO
White, Clifford .... (918) 663-1414
Legal News MGR, Tulsa Daily Commerce & Legal News, Tulsa, OK
White, Connie .... (316) 283-1500
MAN ED, Newton Kansan, Newton, KS
White, Connie .... (212) 499-3334
Sales EX-North America, New York Times Syndication Sales Corp., New York, NY
White, Connie .... (515) 782-2141
Office MGR, DP MGR
Creston News-Advertiser, Creston, IA
White, Cynthia .... (817) 422-4314
ED, Munday Courier, Munday, TX
White, D'Ann .... (813) 689-7764
ED, Brandon News, Brandon, FL
White, Dan .... (608) 754-3311
ADV MGR, ADTX MGR
Janesville Gazette, Janesville, WI
White, David .... (518) 454-5694
ADV DIR, Times Union, Albany, NY
White, Deborah G .... (914) 725-2500
PUB, Scarsdale Inquirer, Scarsdale, NY
White, Denise .... (406) 363-3300
BM, Ravalli Republic, Hamilton, MT
White, Diana .... (319) 337-3181
ADV DIR, Press-Citizen, Iowa City, IA
White, Diane .... (716) 394-0770
CONT, Daily Messenger/Sunday Messenger, Canandaigua, NY
White, Dianne .... (540) 297-1222
GM, Smith Mountain Eagle, Moneta, VA
White, Don .... (502) 839-6906
PUB, ED, Anderson News, Lawrenceburg, KY
White, Doug .... (502) 827-2000
City ED, News ED, Gleaner, Henderson, KY
White, Dudley A .... (616) 842-6400
BC, Grand Haven Tribune, Grand Haven, MI
White, E M .... (504) 638-7155
PUB, Pointe Coupee Banner, New Roads, LA
White, Eliot C .... (203) 235-1661
PRES, TREAS, PUB, ED
Record-Journal, Meriden, CT
White, Ervin .... (910) 323-4848
PROD MGR-PR
Fayetteville Observer-Times, Fayetteville, NC
White, Gail Glickman .... (413) 582-9870
PUB, Jewish News of Western Massachusetts, Northampton, MA
White, Geoffrey T .... (707) 464-2141
PUB, Triplicate, Crescent City, CA
White, George .... (213) 237-5000
RT, Los Angeles Times, Los Angeles, CA
White, Geraldine .... (407) 420-5000
VP/DIR-Human Resources
Orlando Sentinel, Orlando, FL
White, Helena .... (604) 428-2266
PUB, Creston Valley Advance, Creston, BC
White, Herb .... (704) 376-0496
ED, Charlotte Post, Charlotte, NC
White, Herbert .... (804) 649-6000
PROD MGR-Advertising/News
Richmond Times-Dispatch, Richmond, VA
White, Ian R .... (204) 857-3427
ED
Herald Leader Press, Portage La Prairie, MB
White, Jack N .... (765) 354-2221
PUB, Middletown News, Middletown, IN
White, Jacqueline .... (816) 234-4141
Fashion ED
Kansas City Star, Kansas City, MO
White, James R .... (915) 263-7331
ADV DIR, Big Spring Herald, Big Spring, TX
White, James S .... (501) 741-2325
BUS/FIN ED
Harrison Daily Times, Harrison, AR
White Jr, James .... (501) 222-3922
PUB
McGehee-Dermott Times/News, McGehee, AR
White, Jane .... (402) 223-5233
Sports ED
Beatrice Daily Sun, Beatrice, NE
White, Jane See .... (602) 271-8000
Staff Development & Training ED
Arizona Republic, Phoenix, AZ
White, Janice .... (513) 721-2700
ADV MGR-Sales
Cincinnati Enquirer, Cincinnati, OH
White, Jay .... (509) 663-5161
ADV DIR
Wenatchee World, Wenatchee, WA
White, Jeff .... (303) 239-9890
ED, Arvada Jefferson Sentinel, Arvada, CO
White, Jeff .... (414) 273-8696
ED, City Edition, Milwaukee, WI
White, Jennifer .... (516) 569-4000
ED
Oceanside/Island Park Herald, Lawrence, NY
White, Jerry .... (512) 445-3500
MET ED
Austin American-Statesman, Austin, TX
White, Jerry .... (360) 452-2345
PROD SUPV-MR
Peninsula Daily News, Port Angeles, WA
White, Jim .... (518) 792-3131
News ED, Post-Star, Glens Falls, NY
White, John .... (617) 933-3700
News ED
Daily Times Chronicle, Woburn, MA
White, John .... (617) 929-2000
Automotive ED, Boston Globe, Boston, MA
White, John .... (814) 723-8200
Sports ED
Warren Times-Observer, Warren, PA
White, John .... (501) 378-3400
ADV MGR-RT
Arkansas Democrat-Gazette, Little Rock, AR
White, John G .... (320) 847-3130
ED, Clara City Herald, Clara City, MN
White, John K .... (403) 723-3301
ED, Edson Leader, Edson, AB
White, Katherine .... (910) 727-7406
ED, SpotLight, Winston-Salem, NC
White, Kathryn Williams .... (907) 225-3157
PUB/BM/CORP SEC
Ketchikan Daily News, Ketchikan, AK
White, Kenneth Glickman .... (413) 582-9870
PUB, Jewish News of Western Massachusetts, Northampton, MA
White, Kim .... (306) 463-4611
ED, Leader News, Kindersley, SK
White, Lance .... (301) 722-4600
MAN ED
Cumberland Times-News, Cumberland, MD
White, Larry .... (800) 322-5101
DIR, Time Data Syndicate, Manchester, NH
White, Laura .... (330) 626-5558
ED, Gateway Press, Streetsboro, OH
White, Leo .... (617) 326-9240
PRES
White, Leo Productions, Westwood, MA
White, Linda .... (814) 946-7411
EX ED, Altoona Mirror, Altoona, PA
White, Lydia .... (816) 885-2281
SEC, Clinton Daily Democrat, Clinton, MO
White, Mahlon K .... (816) 438-6312
PUB, ED
Benton County Enterprise, Warsaw, MO
White, Marcia .... (800) 322-5101
TREAS
Time Data Syndicate, Manchester, NH
White, Marcy .... (505) 863-6753
GM, Gallup Weekly Paper, Gallup, NM
White, Mark .... (606) 528-9767
ED, News Journal, Corbin, KY
White, Marty .... (540) 885-7281
ADV DIR, Daily News Leader, Staunton, VA
White, Mary V .... (617) 326-9240
ED, White, Leo Productions, Westwood, MA
White, Melissa .... (800) 424-4747
Software DEPT MGR, Tribune Media Services-Television Listings, Glens Falls, NY
White, Meredith .... (334) 928-2321
PUB, Fairhope Courier, Fairhope, AL
White, Meredith .... (410) 749-7171
ADV DIR, Daily Times, Salisbury, MD
White, Michael .... (814) 946-7411
CFO, Altoona Mirror, Altoona, PA
White, Neal .... (608) 365-8811
City ED, Beloit Daily News, Beloit, WI
White Jr, Norman S .... (817) 896-2311
ED, Riesel Rustler, Riesel, TX
White, Patricia .... (317) 598-6397
MAN ED
Carmel News Tribune, Noblesville, IN
White, Randy .... (716) 237-2212
PUB, Perry Herald, Perry, NY
White, Randy .... (812) 275-3355
PROD FRM-COMP, Times-Mail, Bedford, IN
White, Richard .... (916) 756-0800
PROD FRM-PR, Davis Enterprise, Davis, CA
White, Rick .... (717) 582-4305
PUB
Perry County Times, New Bloomfield, PA
White, Rick .... (806) 272-4536
ED, Bailey County Journal, Muleshoe, TX
White, Robert .... (517) 752-7171
PROD MGR, Saginaw News, Saginaw, MI
White, Robert .... (513) 352-2000
EPE, Cincinnati Post, Cincinnati, OH
White, Robert M .... (215) 949-4000
CONT
Bucks County Courier Times, Levittown, PA
White, Ronald .... (213) 237-5000
EDL Writer
Los Angeles Times, Los Angeles, CA
White, Roslyn .... (408) 372-3311
Amusements ED, Features ED, Food ED, Garden ED, Religion ED, Travel ED, Women's ED, Monterey County Herald, Monterey, CA
White, Sara .... (902) 538-3180
ED, Register, Berwick, NS
White, Stefka .... (970) 824-7031
ED, Hayden Valley Press, Hayden, CO

247-Who's Where **Wie**

White, Susan .... (316) 285-3111
ADV Representative
Tiller & Toiler, Larned, KS
White, Susan .... (402) 564-2741
Features ED, NTL ED
Columbus Telegram, Columbus, NE
White, Susan Cady .... (716) 237-2212
ED, Perry Herald, Perry, NY
White, Susan E .... (419) 625-5500
SEC, Sandusky Register, Sandusky, OH
Sandusky-Norwalk Newspapers
White, Timothy .... (508) 775-1200
MAN ED, Cape Cod Times, Hyannis, MA
White, Timothy O .... (518) 454-5694
PUB, Times Union, Albany, NY
White, Tom .... (501) 367-5325
PUB
Advance-Monticellonian, Monticello, AR
White, Tom .... (402) 475-4200
ED, Lincoln Journal Star, Lincoln, NE
White, Vera .... (208) 882-5561
BUS/FIN ED, Films/Music ED, Health ED
Moscow-Pullman Daily News, Moscow, ID
White, Virginia .... (413) 562-4181
SEC, Westfield Evening News, Westfield, MA
White, W M .... (804) 649-6000
CIRC MGR-State
Richmond Times-Dispatch, Richmond, VA
White, William .... (334) 749-6271
Food ED, Society ED
Opelika-Auburn News, Opelika, AL
White, William A .... (508) 343-6911
PUB/GM
Sentinel & Enterprise, Fitchburg, MA
White, Yvonne .... (205) 532-4000
Religion ED, Huntsville Times, Huntsville, AL
White-Arsenault, Saundi .... (905) 358-5711
PROD FRM-COMP
Niagara Falls Review, Niagara Falls, ON
Whited, Rod .... (205) 532-4000
Photo ED, Huntsville Times, Huntsville, AL
Whitefield, Paul .... (213) 237-5000
Washington Edition ED
Los Angeles Times, Los Angeles, CA
Whitehair, Jennifer .... (702) 385-3111
Online Publshing News ED
Las Vegas Sun, Las Vegas, NV
Whitehead, Andrew .... (212) 286-0123
News ED, Inter Press Service (Distributed by Global Info. Network), New York, NY
Whitehead, Charles .... (201) 646-4000
PROD MGR-SYS Support
Record, Hackensack, NJ
Whitehead, David A .... (860) 887-9211
PRES, PUB, Norwich Bulletin, Norwich, CT
Whitehead, Donna .... (508) 339-8977
ED, Mansfield News, Mansfield, MA
Whitehead, E H .... (903) 683-2257
PUB, Cherokeean/Herald, Rusk, TX
Whitehead, Gord .... (519) 294-6264
ED, Parkhill Gazette, Parkhill, ON
Whitehead, Kim .... (519) 537-2341
ADV MGR, Sentinel-Review, Woodstock, ON
Whitehead, Marie .... (903) 683-2257
ED, Cherokeean/Herald, Rusk, TX
Whitehead, Mike .... (318) 459-3200
ED, Times, Shreveport, LA
Whitehead, Nancy .... (330) 996-3000
ADV MGR-OPER
Akron Beacon Journal, Akron, OH
Whitehead, Stephen R .... (515) 465-4666
PUB, Perry Chief, Perry, IA
Whitehead, Vicky .... (912) 739-2132
GM, ED, Claxton Enterprise, Claxton, GA
Whitehead Jr, W R .... (501) 352-3144
PUB, ED
Fordyce News-Advocate, Fordyce, AR
Whitehorn, Dave .... (516) 843-2020
Sunday Sports ED, Newsday, Melville, NY
Whitehouse, Tom .... (503) 221-8327
MGR-Human Resources
Oregonian, Portland, OR
Whitehurst, Tom .... (512) 884-2011
MET ED-Weekends, Corpus Christi Caller-Times, Corpus Christi, TX
Whitelaw, Bill .... (403) 328-4411
MAN ED, Books ED, EPE, Travel ED
Lethbridge Herald, Lethbridge, AB
Whitely, Margaret .... (516) 747-8282
ED, New Hyde Park Illustrated, Mineola, NY
Whiteman, Hazel D .... (412) 537-3351
VP, Latrobe Bulletin, Latrobe, PA
Whiteman, John .... (603) 436-1800
MAN ED-Night
Portsmouth Herald, Portsmouth, NH
Whiteman, Susan .... (518) 374-4141
Librarian, Daily Gazette, Schenectady, NY
Whiteman, Thomas M .... (412) 537-3351
CEO/PUB, Latrobe Bulletin, Latrobe, PA
Whiteman, Weldon .... (817) 390-7400
VP-Circulation, CIRC DIR
Fort Worth Star-Telegram, Fort Worth, TX
Whiteside, Andrea .... (607) 432-1000
Librarian, Daily Star, Oneonta, NY
Whiteside, John .... (815) 729-6161
City ED, Herald-News, Joliet, IL
Whiteside, Pat .... (314) 528-9550
PUB, Troy Free Press, Troy, MO
Whitfield, Dick .... (630) 553-7431
PUB, ED
Fox Valley Shopping News, Yorkville, IL
Whitfield, Jeff .... (770) 478-5753
BUS/FIN ED, COL, Religion ED
Clayton News/Daily, Jonesboro, GA
Whitfield, Joe .... (912) 934-6303
GM, MAN ED, Cochran Journal, Cochran, GA
Whitfield, Johnny .... (919) 693-2646
ED, Oxford Public Ledger, Oxford, NC
Whitin, Harry T .... (508) 793-9100
ED, Telegram & Gazette, Worcester, MA
Whiting, Ann .... (617) 266-3900
ED, Zion's Herald, Boston, MA
Whiting, Bill .... (305) 350-2111
INFO SRV ED, Miami Herald, Miami, FL
Whiting, Bruce .... (208) 733-0931
BUS ED, Times-News, Twin Falls, ID
Whiting, Charles .... (609) 871-8000
CIRC MGR-Sales
Burlington County Times, Willingboro, NJ
Whiting, Don .... (250) 762-4445
PROD FRM, Daily Courier, Kelowna, BC
Whiting, Jim .... (619) 944-4530
Cartoonist
Whiting, Jim Cartoons, Encinitas, CA
Whiting, Lezlee .... (801) 722-5131
ED, Uintah Basin Standard, Roosevelt, UT
Whiting, Richard .... (803) 317-6397
EPE, Florence Morning News, Florence, SC
Whitley, Alice .... (910) 891-1234
ADV MGR-CLASS, Daily Record, Dunn, NC
Whitley, Fred .... (904) 829-6562
Farm/Agriculture ED
St. Augustine Record, St. Augustine, FL
Whitley, George T .... (901) 476-7116
PUB, MAN ED, Leader, Covington, TN
Whitley, Jerry C .... (803) 771-6161
BM, State, Columbia, SC
Whitley, Lenore .... (770) 394-4147
ED, Dunwoody Crier, Dunwoody, GA
Whitley, Maggie .... (516) 747-8282
ED, Mineola American, Mineola, NY
Whitley, Robert .... (310) 540-5511
Sports ED, Daily Breeze, Torrance, CA
Copley Press Inc.
Whitley, Scott .... (916) 321-1000
ADV MGR-CLASS
Sacramento Bee, Sacramento, CA
Whitley, Ty .... (504) 383-1111
ADTX MGR, Advocate, Baton Rouge, LA
Whitlock, Becky .... (423) 246-8121
Features ED, Radio/Television ED, Theater/Music ED, Times-News, Kingsport, TN
Whitlock, Jason .... (816) 234-4141
Sports COL
Kansas City Star, Kansas City, MO
Whitlock, John T .... (606) 528-2464
City/MET ED, Times-Tribune, Corbin, KY
Whitlock, Stanley W .... (423) 246-8121
ASST MAN ED-News
Kingsport Times-News, Kingsport, TN
Whitman, Victor .... (501) 623-7711
Political ED
Sentinel-Record, Hot Springs, AR
Whitmer, Dave .... (330) 364-5577
Sports ED
Times Reporter, New Philadelphia, OH
Whitmer, Kevin .... (201) 877-4141
Sports ED, Star-Ledger, Newark, NJ
Whitmire, Carol .... (817) 663-5333
ED, Tribune-Chief, Quanah, TX
Whitmore, Jane .... (712) 852-2323
ED, Democrat, Emmetsburg, IA
Whitmore, Kathy .... (216) 329-7000
ADV MGR-SRV
Chronicle-Telegram, Elyria, OH
Whitmore, Steve .... (316) 694-5700
MAN ED, BUS/FIN ED, EPE, EDL Writer/Travel ED, Oil & Gas/Political ED
Hutchinson News, Hutchinson, KS
Whitner, Calvin .... (409) 744-3611
Librarian
Galveston County Daily News, Galveston, TX
Whitney, Joe .... (214) 943-7755
PUB, Oak Cliff Tribune, Dallas, TX
Whitney, Jonathan K .... (815) 259-2131
PUB, Carroll County Review, Thomson, IL
Whitney, Linda .... (602) 271-8000
MGR-Client Support
Phoenix Newspapers Inc., Phoenix, AZ
Whitney, Mary .... (716) 328-2144
ASSOC PUB/Art DIR
Syndicated News Service, Rochester, NY
Whitney, Terry .... (908) 922-6000
VP-Manufacturing & Distribution
New Jersey Press Inc., Neptune, NJ
Whitney, William .... (413) 788-1000
MET ED, Union-News, Springfield, MA
Whitt, Alan .... (313) 222-2300
Sports ED, Detroit News, Detroit, MI
Whittaker, Anne .... (816) 932-6600
Sales Administrator/New Media
Universal Press Syndicate, Kansas City, MO
Whittaker, Cathleen .... (201) 586-3012
ED, Neighbor News, Denville, NJ
Whittaker, Dala .... (417) 962-4411
ED, Cabool Enterprise, Cabool, MO
Whittaker, Frank R J .... (916) 321-1000
PRES/GM, Sacramento Bee, Sacramento, CA
Whittaker, Marguerite W .... (606) 792-2831
ED, Lancaster Central Record, Lancaster, KY
Whittaker, Mark .... (412) 772-3900
EPE
North Hills News Record, Warrendale, PA
Whittaker, Timothy .... (905) 373-7355
PUB, Northumberland News, Cobourg, ON
Whittemore, Bennie .... (202) 334-6000
CIRC DIR-OPER
Washington Post, Washington, DC
Whitten, Clark J .... (409) 825-6484
PUB, GM, ED, Examiner, Navasota, TX
Whitten, Debbie .... (415) 692-9406
GM, Foster City Progress, Burlingame, CA
Whitten, Don .... (601) 234-4331
Sports ED, Oxford Eagle, Oxford, MS
Whitten, Grace .... (319) 242-7101
Telegraph ED, Clinton Herald, Clinton, IA
Whitten, John .... (903) 572-1705
Sports ED, Mount Pleasant Daily Tribune, Mount Pleasant, TX
Whitten, Robert H .... (409) 825-6484
PUB, Navasota Examiner, Navasota, TX
Whittenberg, Bruce .... (406) 447-4000
PUB
Helena Independent Record, Helena, MT
Whittinghill, Thom .... (812) 283-6636
Photo ED, Evening News, Jeffersonville, IN
Whittington, Mark .... (408) 372-3311
City ED
Monterey County Herald, Monterey, CA
Whittington, Tom .... (216) 245-6901
Chief Photographer
Morning Journal, Lorain, OH
Whittle, Donna .... (901) 285-4091
City ED, State Gazette, Dyersburg, TN
Whittlesey, Kristin .... (615) 259-8800
Wire ED, Nashville Banner, Nashville, TN
Whitton, Brett .... (203) 846-3281
EVP/GM, Hour, Norwalk, CT
Whitton, Dennis .... (508) 458-7100
Sports ED, Sun, Lowell, MA
Whitton, Jack H .... (203) 846-3281
PRES, ADV MGR-RT, Hour, Norwalk, CT
Whitton, Jeff .... (714) 553-9292
VP/CONT
Freedom Communications Inc., Irvine, CA
Whitton, Walter E .... (203) 846-3281
Chairman/FIN OFF, Hour, Norwalk, CT
Whittum, Jim .... (504) 383-1111
MAN ED, Advocate, Baton Rouge, LA
Whitty, Stanly P .... (941) 953-7755
CIRC DIR-OPER/Distribution, PROD DIR-OPER/Distribution
Sarasota Herald-Tribune, Sarasota, FL
Whitworth, Bruce .... (209) 592-3171
ED, Sun, Exeter, CA
Whitworth, Claudia A .... (540) 343-0326
PUB, ED, Roanoke Tribune, Roanoke, VA
Whitworth, Don R .... (941) 687-7000
PUB/PRES, Ledger, Lakeland, FL
Whitworth, Edie .... (210) 689-2421
GM, Raymondville Chronicle & Willacy County News, Raymondville, TX
Whitworth, Mark .... (210) 689-2421
MAN ED, Raymondville Chronicle & Willacy County News, Raymondville, TX
Whitworth, Mike .... (903) 729-0281
ADV DIR
Palestine Herald-Press, Palestine, TX
Whitworth, Paul E .... (210) 689-2421
PUB, ED, Raymondville Chronicle & Willacy County News, Raymondville, TX
Whobrey, Fred W .... (217) 429-5151
ADV MGR-NTL/Major Accounts
Herald & Review, Decatur, IL
Whorton, Jay .... (770) 428-9411
ASSOC PUB
Marietta Daily Journal, Marietta, GA
Whymer, Jim .... (810) 985-7171
Sports ED, Times Herald, Port Huron, MI
Whynacht, Dave .... (902) 468-1222
Sports ED, Daily News, Halifax, NS
Whysall, Steve .... (604) 732-2111
New Homes ED
Vancouver Sun, Vancouver, BC
Whyte, Marilyn .... (218) 796-5181
ED, Oklee Herald, Oklee, MN
Whyte, Tim .... (805) 259-1234
MAN ED, EPE, Signal, Santa Clarita, CA
Wible, Arthur E .... (815) 439-5300
PRES/Pub, Copley Press Inc., La Jolla, CA
Wichman, Julie .... (414) 276-2222
MAN ED, Shepherd Express Weekly News, Milwaukee, WI
Wichner, David .... (602) 271-8000
Farm/Agriculture Writer
Arizona Republic, Phoenix, AZ
Wick, Lane .... (616) 345-3511
News ED, Kalamazoo Gazette, Kalamazoo, MI
Wick, Leroy .... (916) 243-2424
CIRC MGR
Record Searchlight, Redding, CA
Wick, Rob .... (618) 382-4176
City News ED, Carmi Times, Carmi, IL
Wick, Robert J .... (520) 458-3973
VP/SEC
Wick Communications, Sierra Vista, AZ
Wick, Walter M .... (520) 458-3973
PRES/TREAS
Wick Communications, Sierra Vista, AZ
Wickenberg, Ken .... (403) 429-5400
VP-Human Resources, VP-Manufacturing (acting), Edmonton Journal, Edmonton, AB
Wickenhauser, David .... (209) 358-6431
PUB, ED, Atwater Signal, Atwater, CA
Wicker, Sherril .... (405) 338-3355
CIRC MGR
Guymon Daily Herald, Guymon, OK
Wicker, Wayne .... (352) 365-8200
PROD MGR-PR
Daily Commercial, Leesburg, FL
Wickett, Ann .... (402) 335-3394
ED, Tecumseh Chieftain, Tecumseh, NE
Wickline, Mike .... (208) 743-9411
Political ED
Lewiston Morning Tribune, Lewiston, ID
Wicklund, Pete .... (414) 763-3511
ED
Burlington Standard Press, Burlington, WI
Wickman, Dennis .... (212) 930-8000
Graphics ED/Art DIR
New York Post, New York, NY
Wicks, Clyde .... (519) 376-2250
PRES, PUB, Sun Times, Owen Sound, ON
Wicks, Kathy .... (701) 252-3120
ED, EPE, EDU ED, Sports ED
Jamestown Sun, Jamestown, ND
Wicks, Mark .... (515) 228-3211
MAN ED, EPE, NTL ED, News ED, Photo ED, Political/Government ED, Weekend ED
Charles City Press, Charles City, IA
Widder, Pat .... (312) 222-3232
ASSOC MAN ED-Financial News, FIN ED
Chicago Tribune, Chicago, IL
Widdison, Kevin .... (541) 474-3700
City ED
Grants Pass Daily Courier, Grants Pass, OR
Widelka, Ken .... (312) 222-3232
Photo/Graphic Sales
Chicago Tribune, Chicago, IL
Wideman, Charlie .... (214) 977-8222
PROD DIR-Imaging
Dallas Morning News, Dallas, TX
Widener, Lynda .... (423) 929-3111
ADV MGR-CLASS
Johnson City Press, Johnson City, TN
Widmyer, Ralph .... (864) 582-4511
PROD MGR-Electronical/Mechanical
Herald-Journal, Spartanburg, SC
Widner, Ellis .... (501) 378-3400
Theater/Music ED
Arkansas Democrat-Gazette, Little Rock, AR
Widner, James L .... (219) 563-2131
PUB, Wabash Plain Dealer, Wabash, IN
Widner SV, Rev Thomas C ...... (312) 243-1300
ED, New World, Chicago, IL
Widner, Tracy .... (541) 889-5387
Religion ED, Argus Observer, Ontario, OR
Wieber, Michael .... (517) 377-1000
CONT, Lansing State Journal, Lansing, MI
Wieck, Jim .... (972) 392-0888
PRES/COO, Wieck Photo DataBase, Dallas, TX
Wiedmaien, Linda .... (816) 271-8500
Features ED, Radio/Televison ED
St. Joseph News-Press, St. Joseph, MO
Wiedman, Brian .... (815) 284-2222
Sports ED, Telegraph, Dixon, IL
Wieland, Jeannie .... (414) 938-5000
MAN ED
Whitefish Bay Herald, New Berlin, WI
Wieler, Liz .... (204) 324-5001
PUB, ED, Red River Valley Echo, Altona, MB
Wienandt, Linda .... (805) 395-7500
ASST MAN ED-Days
Bakersfield Californian, Bakersfield, CA
Wieneke, Misti .... (812) 522-4871
Home Furnishings ED, Society ED
Tribune, Seymour, IN
Wiercinski, Joe .... (412) 981-6100
EDU ED, Political/Government ED
Herald, Sharon, PA
Wierman, David D .... (313) 994-6989
PUB, Ann Arbor News, Ann Arbor, MI
Wiernik, Julie .... (313) 994-6989
Connection ED, Features ED, Health/Medical ED, Living/Lifestyle ED, SCI ED, Women's ED
Ann Arbor News, Ann Arbor, MI
Wiersma, John .... (414) 326-5151
ED, Advance, Randolph, WI

Wie Who's Where-248

Wierzba, Julie .... (715) 842-2101
News ED, Wausau Daily Herald, Wausau, WI
Wierzbianski, B .... (212) 594-2266
PUB, ED, Nowy Dziennik, New York, NY
Wierzewski PhD, Wojciech A .. (312) 286-0500
ED, Zgoda, Chicago, IL
Wiese, Kathryn .... (719) 382-5611
PUB, GM, El Paso County Advertiser & News, Fountain, CO
Wiese, Virginia .... (212) 803-8200
ADV DIR-MKTG
American Banker, New York, NY
Wieser, Charles .... (402) 345-1303
News EX, Daily Record, Omaha, NE
Wiesner, Penny .... (608) 837-2521
GM, Star, Sun Prairie, WI
Wiest, Geraldine .... (717) 255-8100
PA, Patriot-News, Harrisburg, PA
Wiggins, James Russell .... (207) 667-2576
ED, Ellsworth American, Ellsworth, ME
Wiggins, Keith (Tony) .... (860) 241-6200
PROD MGR-Distribution
Hartford Courant, Hartford, CT
Wiggins, Shanna .... (541) 889-5387
Fashion/Home Improvement ED, Society/Women's ED, Argus Observer, Ontario, OR
Wigginton, Mark .... (503) 221-8327
Senior ED-Features, Oregonian, Portland, OR
Wigglesworth, Zeke .... (408) 920-5000
Travel ED
San Jose Mercury News, San Jose, CA
Wiggonton, Pat .... (205) 549-2000
Fashion/Food ED, Garden/Home Furnishings ED, Society ED, Travel/Women's ED
Gadsden Times, Gadsden, AL
Wight, Scott .... (207) 729-3311
PROD MGR-Maintenance
Times Record, Brunswick, ME
Wihtol, Christian .... (541) 485-1234
Automotive ED, BUS/FIN ED
Register-Guard, Eugene, OR
Wikle, Jim .... (712) 732-3130
CIRC MGR, Pilot Tribune, Storm Lake, IA
Wikstrom, Elaine .... (409) 833-3311
Food ED
Beaumont Enterprise, Beaumont, TX
Wilary, Stephen .... (518) 374-4141
CIRC MGR, Daily Gazette, Schenectady, NY
Wilbanks, Beth .... (509) 248-1251
ADTX MGR, Herald-Republic, Yakima, WA
Wilbanks, Ken .... (601) 859-1221
ED, Madison County Herald, Canton, MS
Wilber, James .... (605) 428-5441
PUB, Dell Rapids Tribune, Dell Rapids, SD
Wilburn, Bob .... (913) 776-2200
PROD CNR-Quality
Manhattan Mercury, Manhattan, KS
Wilburn, Carol .... (303) 838-2108
MAN ED, Park County Republican & Fairplay Flume, Bailey, CO
Wilcher, Larry .... (540) 885-7281
PROD SUPV-Camera Room
Daily News Leader, Staunton, VA
Wilcott, Curt .... (915) 682-5311
Photo ED, Reporter-Telegram, Midland, TX
Wilcox, A M .... (803) 577-7111
SEC
Evening Post Publishing Co., Charleston, SC
Wilcox, Barbara .... (408) 298-8000
ED, San Jose City Times, San Jose, CA
Wilcox, Carol .... (303) 567-4491
PUB, ED
Clear Creek Courant, Idaho Springs, CO
Wilcox, Cheryl .... (614) 387-0400
ADV MGR-CLASS, Marion Star, Marion, OH
Wilcox, Dennis W .... (515) 795-2730
PUB, ED, Madrid Register-News, Madrid, IA
Wilcox, Don .... (705) 726-6537
City ED, Examiner, Barrie, ON
Wilcox, Ed .... (910) 739-4322
City ED, Robesonian, Lumberton, NC
Wilcox, Elizabeth .... (912) 468-5433
GM, MAN ED, Ocilla Star, Ocilla, GA
Wilcox, Joe .... (508) 744-0600
PROD SYS MGR-PR
Salem Evening News, Beverly, MA
Wilcox, John N .... (508) 775-1200
PRES/PUB, Cape Cod Times, Hyannis, MA
Wilcox, John P .... (805) 650-2900
VP, PUB, Ventura County Star, Ventura, CA
Wilcox, Mike .... (313) 729-4000
PUB, Westland Eagle, Wayne, MI
Wilcox, Rhonda .... (706) 865-4718
PUB, White County News, Cleveland, GA
Wilcox, Ronald A .... (217) 351-5252
ADV VP-MKTG, News-Gazette, Champaign, IL
Wilcox, Tom .... (805) 736-2313
CIRC MGR, Lompoc Record, Lompoc, CA
Wild, Gary L .... (808) 525-8000
VP-SYS, PROD VP-SYS
Hawaii Newspaper Agency Inc., Honolulu, HI
Wilde, Marc .... (805) 643-5952
PUB, Ventura Independent, Ventura, CA
Wilder, Marty Robacker .... (814) 368-3173
City ED, Bradford Era, Bradford, PA
Wilder, Paul J .... (606) 589-2588
PUB, ED, Tri-City News, Cumberland, KY
Wilderman, Greg .... (515) 421-0500
ADV MGR-CLASS
Globe-Gazette, Mason City, IA
Wildermuth, Todd .... (505) 445-2721
MAN ED, Raton Range, Raton, NM
Wildes, Alston .... (207) 990-8000
PROD FRM-COMP, Daily News, Bangor, ME
Wilding, Don .... (508) 222-7000
Entertainment ED
Sun Chronicle, Attleboro, MA
Wildsmith, Steve .... (615) 473-2191
ED, Southern Standard, McMinnville, TN
Wiles, John .... (317) 459-3121
ED, EPE, Kokomo Tribune, Kokomo, IN
Wiles, Mary Lou .... (909) 889-9666
ADV MGR-CLASS
San Bernardino Sun, San Bernardino, CA
Wiley, Donna .... (913) 843-1000
CONT, Journal-World, Lawrence, KS
Wiley, Jack .... (307) 682-9306
BM, News-Record, Gillette, WY
Wiley, Joan .... (905) 684-7251
Religion, Standard, St. Catharines, ON
Wiley, Rick .... (602) 898-6500
Photo ED, Mesa Tribune, Mesa, AZ
Thomson Newspapers
Wiley, Verlin .... (312) 321-3000
DP MGR, Chicago Sun-Times, Chicago, IL
Wilfahrt, Gerri .... (507) 359-2911
PROD SUPT, Journal, New Ulm, MN
Wilfley, Mark .... (704) 358-5000
VP, CIRC DIR
Charlotte Observer, Charlotte, NC
Wilhelm, Roy .... (419) 332-5511
ASSOC ED, News-Messenger, Fremont, OH
Wilhoite, Marion .... (615) 388-6464
Sports ED, Daily Herald, Columbia, TN
Wilk, Stuart .... (214) 977-8222
MAN ED, Dallas Morning News, Dallas, TX
Wilke, Beverly .... (806) 762-8844
MGR-Accounting
Lubbock Avalanche-Journal, Lubbock, TX
Wilke, Bill .... (406) 587-4491
ED, Books ED
Bozeman Daily Chronicle, Bozeman, MT
Wilken, Larry .... (414) 487-2222
GM, Algoma Record-Herald, Algoma, WI
Wilkerson, April .... (405) 273-4200
Sunday Escort Magazine ED
Shawnee News-Star, Shawnee, OK
Wilkerson, Bill .... (210) 569-2341
PUB, Pleasanton Express, Pleasanton, TX
Wilkerson, Cathy .... (803) 546-4148
PUB, Georgetown Times, Georgetown, SC
Wilkerson, David .... (210) 569-2341
MAN ED, Pleasanton Express, Pleasanton, TX
Wilkerson, Gray .... (919) 492-4001
Sports ED
Henderson Daily Dispatch, Henderson, NC
Wilkerson, Jeanette .... (712) 764-4818
PUB, ED
Elk Horn Kimballton Review, Elk Horn, IA
Wilkerson, Judy .... (210) 569-2341
PUB, Pleasanton Express, Pleasanton, TX
Wilkerson, M P .... (334) 262-1611
Theater/Music ED, Travel ED
Montgomery Advertiser, Montgomery, AL
Wilkerson, Raymond .... (214) 739-2244
PUB, ED, Park Cities People, Dallas, TX
Wilkerson, Roland .... (616) 222-5400
EDU ED
Grand Rapids Press, Grand Rapids, MI
Wilkerson, Van .... (803) 577-7111
ADV MGR-CLASS
Post and Courier, Charleston, SC
Wilkins, Dave .... (313) 994-6989
Environmental ED
Ann Arbor News, Ann Arbor, MI
Wilkins, Debra .... (915) 263-7331
MGR-BUS Office
Big Spring Herald, Big Spring, TX
Wilkins, Ron .... (317) 622-1212
Police, Herald Bulletin, Anderson, IN
Wilkins, Sherry J .... (405) 273-4200
ADV DIR, Shawnee News-Star, Shawnee, OK
Wilkins, Woodrow .... (601) 335-1155
City ED
Delta Democrat Times, Greenville, MS
Wilkinson, Ann .... (616) 627-7144
BM, Daily Tribune, Cheboygan, MI
Wilkinson, Barbara .... (219) 726-8141
News ED, Commercial Review, Portland, IN
Wilkinson, Darryl .... (816) 663-2154
PUB, ED
Gallatin North Missourian, Gallatin, MO
Wilkinson, David .... (606) 231-3100
DIR-PROM, Herald-Leader, Lexington, KY
Wilkinson, Dennis .... (941) 294-7731
CIRC MGR-OPER, PROD MGR
News Chief, Winter Haven, FL
Wilkinson, Jeff .... (705) 567-5321
Sports ED
Northern Daily News, Kirkland Lake, ON
Wilkinson, Mary Jane .... (617) 929-2000
ASST MAN ED-Features
Boston Globe, Boston, MA
Wilkinson, Sandy .... (417) 334-3161
GM
Branson Tri-Lakes Daily News, Branson, MO
Wilkinson, Signe .... (215) 854-2000
Cartoonist
Philadelphia Daily News, Philadelphia, PA
Wilkinson, Tom .... (202) 334-6000
ASST MAN ED
Washington Post, Washington, DC
Wilkinson, Tracy .... (213) 237-5000
Vienna BU
Los Angeles Times, Los Angeles, CA
Wilks, Art .... (204) 694-2022
PROD MGR, Winnipeg Sun, Winnipeg, MB
Wilks, Doug .... (415) 883-8600
City BUS ED
Marin Independent Journal, Novato, CA
Wilks, Glenn .... (919) 829-4500
PROD MGR-Computer OPER
News & Observer, Raleigh, NC
Willard, H Eugene .... (704) 437-2161
PUB, ED, Valdese News, Morgantown, NC
Willard, Ken .... (316) 694-5700
ADTX MGR
Hutchinson News, Hutchinson, KS
Willard, Scotty .... (502) 227-4556
PROD FRM-PR, State Journal, Frankfort, KY
Willcox, Suzanne .... (561) 820-4100
MGR-RES
Palm Beach Post, West Palm Beach, FL
Willems, George .... (210) 876-2318
PUB, Javelin, Carrizo Springs, TX
Willems, John .... (210) 876-2318
ED
Carrizo Springs Javelin, Carrizo Springs, TX
Willenbrink, Jack .... (502) 582-4011
DIR-FIN, Courier-Journal, Louisville, KY
Willenbrock, Fred J .... (509) 447-2433
PUB, ED, Newport Miner, Newport, WA
Willes, Mark H .... (213) 237-3700
COB/PRES/CEO
Times Mirror Co., Los Angeles, CA
Willett, Janet .... (573) 221-2800
BM, Hannibal Courier-Post, Hannibal, MO
Willey, Keven .... (602) 271-8000
Political COL, Arizona Republic, Phoenix, AZ
Willhide, Ed .... (209) 578-2000
NTL ED, News ED
Modesto Bee, Modesto, CA
Willhoit, Lisa .... (918) 341-1101
City ED, EDU ED
Claremore Daily Progress, Claremore, OK
Williams, Addie .... (405) 757-2281
ED, Ryan Leader, Ryan, OK
Williams, Anne C .... (901) 642-1162
SEC, Paris Post-Intelligencer, Paris, TN
Williams, Barbara S .... (803) 577-7111
ED, EPE, Post and Courier, Charleston, SC
Williams, Bart .... (405) 475-3311
PROD MGR-Pre Press SRV
Daily Oklahoman, Oklahoma City, OK
Williams, Bess E .... (352) 528-6397
PUB, Williston Sun-Suwanee Valley News, Williston, FL
Williams, Bill .... (901) 642-1162
PRES/TREAS, PUB
Paris Post-Intelligencer, Paris, TN
Williams, Bill .... (860) 241-6200
Letters ED, Hartford Courant, Hartford, CT
Williams, Bob .... (215) 345-3000
PROD FRM-COMP
Intelligencer/Record, Doylestown, PA
Williams, Bob .... (405) 282-2222
ED, Guthrie News Leader, Guthrie, OK
Williams, Bob .... (205) 549-2000
News ED, RE ED
Gadsden Times, Gadsden, AL
Williams, Bob .... (212) 416-2414
DIR-ADM, Dow Jones Financial News Services, New York, NY
Williams, Bobby .... (910) 353-1171
CIRC MGR, Daily News, Jacksonville, NC
Williams, Bobby .... (573) 624-4545
PROD FRM-PR, Daily Statesman, Dexter, MO
Williams, C B .... (519) 848-2410
PUB, Arthur Enterprise News, Arthur, ON
Williams, C M .... (219) 267-3111
PSL MGR, Times-Union, Warsaw, IN
Williams Jr, Carey .... (706) 453-7988
PUB, ED, Herald Journal, Greensboro, GA
Williams, Carol J .... (213) 237-5000
Moscow BU
Los Angeles Times, Los Angeles, CA
Williams, Carolyn .... (502) 247-5223
SEC/TREAS, BM
Mayfield Messenger, Mayfield, KY
Williams, Charles .... (910) 838-4117
ED, Journal-Patriot, North Wilkesboro, NC
Williams, Charles C .... (915) 263-7331
PUB, Big Spring Herald, Big Spring, TX
Williams, Charles deV .... (803) 577-7111
BUS ED, Post and Courier, Charleston, SC
Williams, Cheryl .... (912) 449-6693
GM, Blackshear Times, Blackshear, GA
Williams, Cheryl .... (706) 724-0851
ADV MGR-BUS Development
Augusta Chronicle, Augusta, GA
Williams, Christine .... (402) 324-5764
GM, ED, Chester Herald, Chester, NE
Williams, Chuck .... (706) 324-5526
Sports ED, Ledger-Enquirer, Columbus, GA
Williams, Cindi .... (903) 572-1705
DP MGR, Mount Pleasant Daily Tribune, Mount Pleasant, TX
Williams, Cindy .... (501) 534-3400
Food ED, Commercial, Pine Bluff, AR
Williams, Cindy R .... (816) 529-2888
MAN ED, Slater News-Rustler, Slater, MO
Williams, Clive .... (519) 338-2341
PUB, ED, Harriston Review, Harriston, ON
Williams, Corey .... (313) 222-2300
City ED-Night
Detroit News, Detroit, MI
Williams, Cristal .... (330) 996-3000
Deputy MET ED
Akron Beacon Journal, Akron, OH
Williams, Curtis .... (505) 445-2721
PUB, Raton Range, Raton, NM
Williams, Dave .... (209) 943-6397
VP-Circulation, Record, Stockton, CA
Williams, David .... (217) 774-2161
PROD MGR, Daily Union, Shelbyville, IL
Williams, David .... (716) 328-2144
Features ED
Syndicated News Service, Rochester, NY
Williams, David D .... (800) 245-6536
PRES/CEO
Tribune Media Services Inc., Chicago, IL
Williams, David G .... (209) 943-6397
CIRC DIR, Record, Stockton, CA
Williams, Debbie .... (903) 757-3311
PROD FRM-COMP
Longview News-Journal, Longview, TX
Williams, Debby .... (501) 327-6621
PROD SUPV
Log Cabin Democrat, Conway, AR
Williams, Dennis .... (816) 699-2344
PUB, ED, Clarence Courier, Clarence, MO
Williams, Diane .... (904) 312-5200
Lifestyle ED, Daily News, Palatka, FL
Williams, Dick .... (770) 394-4147
PUB, Dunwoody Crier, Dunwoody, GA
Williams, Donna P .... (904) 359-4111
PSL DIR
Florida Times-Union, Jacksonville, FL
Williams, Doug .... (619) 299-3131
Sports ED-Night
San Diego Union-Tribune, San Diego, CA
Williams, Douglas R .... (773) 586-8800
MET ED, Daily Southtown, Chicago, IL
Williams, Earl .... (423) 892-1336
PUB, ED
Hamilton County Herald, Chattanooga, TN
Williams, Ed .... (704) 358-5000
EPE, Charlotte Observer, Charlotte, NC
Williams, Ed .... (910) 373-7000
Life ED, News & Record, Greensboro, NC
Williams, Ed .... (717) 248-6741
CIRC MGR, Sentinel, Lewistown, PA
Williams, Eleanor .... (608) 222-5522
ED, Shetland Productions, Madison, WI
Williams, Elizabeth A .... (513) 721-2700
VP-Human Resources
Cincinnati Enquirer, Cincinnati, OH
Williams, Ellen T .... (334) 567-7811
PUB, Wetumpka Herald, Wetumpka, AL
Williams, Fred .... (717) 455-3636
PROD FRM-COMP (Night)
Standard-Speaker, Hazleton, PA
Williams, Gayle T .... (914) 694-9300
ED-Reader SRV, Reporter Dispatch, White Plains, NY, Gannett Co. Inc.
Williams, Gene .... (704) 358-5000
EVP, Charlotte Observer, Charlotte, NC
Knight-Ridder Inc.
Williams, George .... (218) 834-2141
PUB, Lake County News-Chronicle, Two Harbors, MN
Williams Sr, Gerald M .... (334) 567-7811
ED, Wetumpka Herald, Wetumpka, AL
Williams, Geri .... (318) 828-3706
ADV MGR-CLASS
Franklin Banner-Tribune, Franklin, LA
Williams, Glenn .... (941) 262-3161
PROD MGR-MR, Daily News, Naples, FL
Williams, Graham .... (864) 427-1234
ED, EPE, Union Daily Times, Union, SC
Williams, Irene .... (405) 323-5151
PROD FRM-COMP, Daily News, Clinton, OK
Williams III, Isiah J .... (904) 765-8982
PUB, ED
Northeast Florida Advocate, Jacksonville, FL
Williams, J R .... (317) 584-4501
EVP/SEC, News-Gazette, Winchester, IN
Williams Jr, J Sharpe .... (910) 326-5066
ED, Tideland News, Swansboro, NC

249-Who's Where **Wil**

Williams, Jack .... (509) 382-2221
PUB, ED, Dayton Chronicle, Dayton, WA
Williams III, Jack .... (912) 283-2244
ED, Books ED, EPE, Farm/Picture ED
Waycross Journal-Herald, Waycross, GA
Williams, Jake .... (510) 935-2525
EPE, Contra Costa Times, Walnut Creek, CA
Williams Jr, James L .... (800) 760-3100
PRES
Williams Syndications Inc., Holiday, FL
Williams, James M .... (402) 324-5764
PUB, Chester Herald, Chester, NE
Williams, James R .... (212) 621-1500
VP/DIR of Broadcast SRV
Associated Press, New York, NY
Williams, Jean .... (801) 237-2188
Food ED, Deseret News, Salt Lake City, UT
Williams, Jeff .... (719) 589-2553
Sports, Valley Courier, Alamosa, CO
Williams, Jennifer .... (319) 385-3131
ADV MGR-CLASS
Mt. Pleasant News, Mount Pleasant, IA
Williams, Jennifer .... (804) 978-7200
News ED, Daily Progress, Charlottesville, VA
Williams, Jerry .... (804) 649-6000
Garden Writer
Richmond Times-Dispatch, Richmond, VA
Williams, Jill .... (215) 854-2000
Entertainment/Amusements ED, Deputy Features ED
Philadelphia Daily News, Philadelphia, PA
Williams, Jim .... (972) 875-3801
Sports ED, Ennis Daily News, Ennis, TX
Williams Jr, Jim .... (330) 332-4601
ADV DIR, Salem News, Salem, OH
Williams, Jimmy .... (901) 642-1162
PA, PROD SUPT
Paris Post-Intelligencer, Paris, TN
Williams, Jobe .... (902) 564-5451
BM, Cape Breton Post, Sydney, NS
Williams, Joe .... (415) 883-8600
CONT
Marin Independent Journal, Novato, CA
Williams, Joe .... (614) 345-4053
Entertainment/Amusements ED
Advocate, Newark, OH
Williams, John .... (937) 225-2000
CIRC MGR-Single Copy
Dayton Daily News, Dayton, OH
Williams, John .... (810) 387-3282
PUB, Munising News, Munising, MI
Williams, John .... (800) 832-5522
Senior VP, PR Newswire, New York, NY
Williams, Judy .... (414) 733-4411
Political COL, Post-Crescent, Appleton, WI
Williams, Julia S .... (901) 642-1162
VP, Paris Post-Intelligencer, Paris, TN
Williams, K .... (817) 872-2247
GM, Bowie News, Bowie, TX
Williams, Karen .... (717) 272-5611
ADV MGR-RT, DP MGR
Daily News, Lebanon, PA
Williams, Karen .... (501) 862-6611
ADV DIR
El Dorado News-Times, El Dorado, AR
Williams, Kathleen .... (909) 657-1967
PUB, Perris Valley News, Sun City, CA
Williams, Kathleen Burke ....(510) 935-2525
Features/Lifestyle ED
Contra Cost Times, Walnut Creek, CA
Williams, Kathy .... (903) 893-8181
City ED, Herald Democrat, Sherman, TX
Williams, Ken .... (205) 325-2222
MGR-Purchasing
Birmingham News, Birmingham, AL
Williams, Kitty .... (804) 784-5025
EDL DIR
Hope Springs Press, Manakin-Sabot, VA
Williams, Laurie .... (509) 582-1500
City ED, Religion ED
Tri-City Herald, Tri-Cities, WA
Williams, Laurie A .... (213) 469-2333
MAN ED
World News Syndicate Ltd., Hollywood, CA
Williams, Leigh .... (905) 358-5711
Living ED, Sports ED
Niagara Falls Review, Niagara Falls, ON
Williams, Leslie .... (504) 826-3279
EDU ED, Times-Picayune, New Orleans, LA
Williams III, Lew .... (907) 225-3157
PRES, PUB
Ketchikan Daily News, Ketchikan, AK
Williams, Linda .... (205) 232-2720
ADV DIR, News Courier, Athens, AL
Williams, Linda .... (219) 881-3000
ASST MAN ED, Post-Tribune, Gary, IN
Williams, Linus G .... (918) 967-4655
PUB, Stigler News-Sentinel, Stigler, OK
Williams, Lisa .... (301) 662-1177
ADV MGR-Display
Frederick Post/News, Frederick, MD
Williams, Lori .... (713) 488-1108
ED, Citizen, Webster, TX
Williams, Luanne .... (704) 289-1541
EX ED, Enquirer-Journal, Monroe, NC

Williams, Lucille .... (408) 920-5000
Photo ED
San Jose Mercury News, San Jose, CA
Williams, Luis M .... (334) 433-1551
EVP/TREAS, Comptroller, Mobile Press Register, Mobile, AL, Advance Publications
Williams, M R .... (219) 267-3111
PRES, SEC/TREAS, PUB, PA
Times-Union, Warsaw, IN
Williams, Maridee .... (706) 769-5175
GM, Oconee Enterprise, Watkinsville, GA
Williams, Marilyn .... (516) 826-0333
GM, Bellmore Life, Bellmore, NY
Williams, Mark .... (601) 843-4241
CIRC MGR
Bolivar Commercial, Cleveland, MS
Williams, Mark .... (941) 687-7000
Art DIR, Ledger, Lakeland, FL
Williams, Mark T .... (520) 573-4400
DIR-MIS, TNI Partners dba Tucson Newspapers, Tucson, AZ
Williams, Melinda .... (540) 483-5113
ED
Franklin News-Post, Rocky Mount, VA
Williams, Melvin W .... (717) 291-8811
ADV MGR-NTL, Lancaster Intelligencer Journal/New Era/Sunday News, Lancaster, PA
Williams, Melvyn J .... (912) 746-5605
PUB, ED, Macon Courier, Macon, GA
Williams, Michael .... (901) 642-1162
ED, Paris Post-Intelligencer, Paris, TN
Williams, Michael .... (209) 727-5776
ED
Lockeford-Clements News, Lockeford, CA
Williams, Michael .... (513) 422-3611
MAN ED
Middletown Journal, Middletown, OH
Williams, Michael C .... (314) 531-2101
PUB, ED, Metro Sentinel, St. Louis, MO
Williams, Michelle .... (304) 327-2811
PROD FRM-COMP
Bluefield Daily Telegraph, Bluefield, WV
Williams, Michelle .... (213) 237-5000
Health/Fitness ED, Deputy Life/Style ED
Los Angeles Times, Los Angeles, CA
Williams, Mike .... (540) 980-5220
ED, Southwest Times, Pulaski, VA
Williams, Naomi .... (352) 374-5000
ADV ASST MGR-CLASS
Gainesville Sun, Gainesville, FL
Williams, Neil D .... (209) 582-0471
PUB, ED, Hanford Sentinel, Hanford, CA
Williams, Neoma Wall .... (806) 938-2640
PUB, GM, ED, Hart Beat, Hart, TX
Williams, Nick .... (352) 528-6397
ED, Williston Sun-Suwanee Valley News, Williston, FL
Williams Jr, Nick .... (213) 237-5000
Deputy EPE
Los Angeles Times, Los Angeles, CA
Williams, Norma .... (612) 827-4021
ED
Minneapolis Spokesman, Minneapolis, MN
Williams, Patrick .... (216) 593-6030
ED, Courier, Conneaut, OH
Williams, Paul .... (902) 426-2811
DP MGR, Chronicle-Herald, Halifax, NS
Williams, Paul .... (617) 786-7000
SYS ED, Patriot Ledger, Quincy, MA
Williams, Peggy .... (402) 494-4264
ED
South Sioux City Star, South Sioux City, NE
Williams, Peter .... (910) 786-4141
ED, Mount Airy News, Mount Airy, NC
Williams, R .... (709) 634-4348
MAN ED
Western Star, Corner Brook, NF
Williams, Randy .... (517) 875-4151
ED, Gratiot County Herald, Ithaca, MI
Williams, Rich .... (719) 632-5511
CIRC DIR-Subscriber Sales
Gazette, Colorado Springs, CO
Williams, Rob .... (520) 836-7461
DP MGR
Casa Grande Dispatch, Casa Grande, AZ
Williams, Robert .... (704) 252-5611
ADV DIR
Asheville Citizen-Times, Asheville, NC
Williams, Robert E .... (601) 693-2372
PUB, ED
Mississippi Memo Digest, Meridian, MS
Williams, Robert H .... (703) 922-1712
News ED
World Images News Service, Alexandria, VA
Williams Jr, Robert M .... (912) 449-6693
PUB, ED
Blackshear Times, Blackshear, GA
Williams, Roberta A .... (918) 367-2282
GM, Bristow News, Bristow, OK
Williams, Roger L .... (912) 283-2244
PRES, PUB
Waycross Journal-Herald, Waycross, GA
Williams, Ron .... (313) 961-4060
PUB, Metro Times, Detroit, MI

Williams, Sandy .... (501) 968-5252
BUS MGR
Russellville Courier, Russellville, AR
Williams, Sarah H .... (601) 675-2446
MAN ED
Coffeeville Courier, Coffeeville, MS
Williams, Scott .... (916) 846-3661
ED, Gridley Herald, Gridley, CA
Williams, Sherry .... (972) 875-9015
PUB, ED, Press, Ennis, TX
Williams, Stacey .... (970) 249-3444
PROD MGR, Daily Press, Montrose, CO
Williams, Stephen M .... (619) 241-7744
EPE, Daily Press, Victorville, CA
Williams, Tena .... (907) 225-3157
PRES, PUB
Ketchikan Daily News, Ketchikan, AK
Williams, Terrence L .... (603) 882-2741
PUB, Telegraph, Nashua, NH
Williams, Todd .... (605) 642-2761
City ED, Black Hills Pioneer, Spearfish, SD
Williams, Tom .... (414) 542-2501
PROD FRM-Press
Waukesha County Freeman, Waukesha, WI
Williams, Troi .... (307) 876-2627
PUB, ED
Shoshoni Pioneer, Shoshoni, WY
Williams, Vern .... (203) 789-5200
ASST MAN ED-Design, Photo ED
New Haven Register, New Haven, CT
Williams, Vern .... (209) 722-1511
Sports ED, Merced Sun-Star, Merced, CA
Williams, Veronica .... (250) 380-5211
ADV DIR, Times Colonist, Victoria, BC
Williams, Vinnie .... (706) 769-5175
PUB, Oconee Enterprise, Watkinsville, GA
Williams, Walt .... (209) 578-2000
Fashion/Style Writer, Travel Writer
Modesto Bee, Modesto, CA
Williams, Will .... (607) 798-1234
CIRC MGR-MET West
Press & Sun Bulletin, Binghamton, NY
Williams-Tracy, Laura .... (704) 864-3291
EDU ED, Gaston Gazette, Gastonia, NC
Williamson, Bill .... (805) 650-2900
PROD DIR-OPER
Ventura County Star, Ventura, CA
Williamson, Bonnie .... (912) 529-6624
GM, Montgomery Monitor, Ailey, GA
Williamson Jr, Mr Charles M ... (912) 437-4251
PUB, Darien News, Darien, GA
Williamson Jr, Mrs Charles M . (912) 437-4251
PUB, Darien News, Darien, GA
Williamson, Dick .... (303) 892-5000
Automotive ED
Rocky Mountain News, Denver, CO
Williamson, Doug .... (915) 673-4271
BUS ED, Abilene Reporter-News, Abilene, TX
Williamson, Doug .... (519) 255-5711
Entertainment ED, ASST MET ED
Windsor Star, Windsor, ON
Williamson, Ernie .... (713) 220-7171
Art DIR, Houston Chronicle, Houston, TX
Williamson, Harry .... (303) 726-5721
ED, Winter Park Manifest, Winter Park, CO
Williamson, James .... (501) 898-3462
PUB, ED, Little River News, Ashdown, AR
Williamson, Jim .... (407) 242-3500
Group CONT, Florida Today, Melbourne, FL
Williamson, Kevin .... (601) 764-3104
ED, Jasper County News, Bay Springs, MS
Williamson, Mary Lou .... (301) 474-4131
ED, Greenbelt News Review, Greenbelt, MD
Williamson, Terry .... (915) 682-5311
Sports ED
Midland Reporter-Telegram, Midland, TX
Williford, Joy L .... (318) 487-6397
DIR-PSL
Alexandria Daily Town Talk, Alexandria, LA
Willig, Blaise .... (410) 337-2400
ED, Northeast Times Booster, Towson, MD
Willingham, Bruce .... (405) 286-3321
PRES, PUB, ED
McCurtain Daily Gazette, Idabel, OK
Willingham, Gwen .... (405) 286-3321
VP, McCurtain Daily Gazette, Idabel, OK
Willingham, Haskell .... (405) 286-3321
SEC/TREAS
McCurtain Daily Gazette, Idabel, OK
Willis, Alan R .... (403) 742-2395
PUB, Stettler Independent, Stettler, AB
Willis, Edward .... (910) 343-2000
DP MGR, DIR-INFO SYS, Morning Star/ Sunday Star-News, Wilmington, NC
Willis, Gerald .... (618) 497-8273
PUB, ED, County Journal, Percy, IL
Willis, Henny .... (541) 485-1234
EDL Writer
Eugene Register-Guard, Eugene, OR
Willis, James D .... (205) 325-2222
MAN ED
Birmingham Post-Herald, Birmingham, AL
Willis, Jerry .... (918) 684-2828
Photo DEPT MGR, Muskogee Daily Phoenix & Times Democrat, Muskogee, OK

Willis, Ken .... (904) 252-1511
Sports ED, Daytona Beach News-Journal, Daytona Beach, FL
Willis, L Clayton .... (202) 333-3007
PRES/White House Correspondent/Photojournalist/Critic, Evening News Broadcasting & Willis News Service, Collector Watch Ltd., Washington, DC
Willis, Larry .... (618) 497-8273
PUB, ED, County Journal, Percy, IL
Willis, R C .... (403) 742-2395
PUB, Stettler Independent, Stettler, AB
Willis, Richard .... (860) 442-2200
DIR-FIN, Day, New London, CT
Willis, Scott .... (408) 920-5000
EDL Cartoonist
San Jose Mercury News, San Jose, CA
Willison, Joan .... (613) 544-5000
PROM/Community SRV
Kingston Whig-Standard, Kingston, ON
Willistein, Paul .... (610) 820-6500
Features ED, Morning Call, Allentown, PA
Willits, Michelle .... (970) 242-5050
Entertainment/Amusements ED, Fashion/Style ED, Features ED, Living/Lifestyle ED, Religion ED, Television/Film ED
Daily Sentinel, Grand Junction, CO
Willman, Dorothy .... (918) 341-1101
Environmental ED, Farm/Agriculture ED, Features ED, Lifestyle ED, Religion ED
Claremore Daily Progress, Claremore, OK
Willmann, Theresa .... (417) 836-1100
ADV SUPV-Tele Sales
Springfield News-Leader, Springfield, MO
Willmon, Gary .... (409) 829-1801
ED, Free Press, Diboll, TX
Willmott Sr, David J .... (516) 369-0800
PUB, ED
Suffolk Life Newspapers, Riverhead, NY
Willmott Jr, David J .... (516) 369-0800
GM, Suffolk Life Newspapers, Riverhead, NY
Willnow, Ronald .... (314) 340-8000
Deputy MAN ED
St. Louis Post-Dispatch, St. Louis, MO
Willoughby, Brian .... (360) 694-3391
Religion ED, Columbian, Vancouver, WA
Willows, Terry .... (905) 526-3333
CIRC DIR-Reader Sales & SRV
Spectator, Hamilton, ON
Willroth IV, William .... (605) 624-2695
PUB, Wakonda Times, Vermillion, SD
Wills, Bill .... (309) 829-9411
MAN ED-EDL, Pantagraph, Bloomington, IL
Wills, Clyde .... (618) 524-2141
PUB, ED, Metropolis Planet, Metropolis, IL
Wills, Jim .... (606) 231-3100
PROD MGR-Pre Press
Lexington Herald-Leader, Lexington, KY
Wills, John .... (516) 843-2020
DIR-OPER ADM, PROD DIR-Management
Newsday, Melville, NY
Wills, Larry .... (909) 684-1200
CIRC MGR-Insert & Packaging
Press-Enterprise, Riverside, CA
Wills, Leslie .... (502) 583-4471
MAN ED, Daily Record, Louisville, KY
Wills, Newman .... (910) 888-3500
PROD DIR
High Point Enterprise, High Point, NC
Wills, Richard .... (819) 647-2204
ED, Equity, Shawville, QC
Wills, Todd .... (817) 461-6397
Sports ED, Morning News, Arlington, TX
Willse, James .... (201) 877-4141
ED, Star-Ledger, Newark, NJ
Willy, John .... (573) 785-1414
BUS ED, News ED
Daily American Republic, Poplar Bluff, MO
Wilmington, Michael .... (312) 222-3232
Movie Critic, Chicago Tribune, Chicago, IL
Wilmore, Sharon .... (219) 881-3000
Daily Magazine ED, Post-Tribune, Gary, IN
Wilmot, Ron .... (505) 461-1952
PUB, ED, Quay County Sun, Tucumcari, NM
Wilmot, Ron .... (757) 562-3187
GM, Tidewater News, Franklin, VA
Wilner, Paul .... (415) 777-2424
ASST MAN ED-Features, Sunday Magazine ED, San Francisco Examiner, San Fran., CA
Wilpers, John .... (617) 969-0340
ED, Newton TAB, Newton, MA
Wilson, Allen .... (208) 733-0931
BM, Times-News, Twin Falls, ID
Wilson, Anita .... (704) 649-2741
GM, News-Record, Marshall, NC
Wilson, Ann .... (712) 792-3573
VP/SEC, Daily Times Herald, Caroll, IA
Wilson, Anna .... (704) 437-2161
Amusements ED, BUS/FIN ED, Features ED, Radio/Television ED, RE ED, Wire ED
News Herald, Morganton, NC

Wil Who's Where-250

Wilson, Anne ... (801) 237-2031
Medical ED
Salt Lake Tribune, Salt Lake City, UT
Wilson, Aubrey C ... (502) 773-3401
PUB, Progress, Cave City, KY
Wilson Jr, Aubrey C ... (502) 773-3401
MAN ED, Progress, Cave City, KY
Wilson, Beryl ... (912) 265-8320
PROD FRM-PR
Brunswick News, Brunswick, GA
Wilson, Betty ... (310) 635-6776
ED, Compton Bulletin, Compton, CA
Wilson, Betty ... (309) 968-6705
GM, Manito Review, Manito, IL
Wilson, Bill ... (316) 283-1500
News ED, Newton Kansan, Newton, KS
Wilson, Brad ... (610) 688-3000
ED, Suburban Advertiser, Wayne, PA
Wilson, C Z ... (213) 290-3000
PUB
Central-News Wave Group, Los Angeles, CA
Wilson, Carey ... (919) 894-3331
ED, Four Oaks-Benson News in Review, Benson, NC
Wilson, Carroll ... (817) 767-8341
ED, Wichita Falls Times Record News, Wichita Falls, TX
Wilson, Cathy ... (904) 681-1852
GM, Capitol Outlook, Tallahassee, FL
Wilson, Cecil H ... (606) 546-9225
PUB, Mountain Advocate, Barbourville, KY
Wilson, Charles ... (707) 448-6401
News ED, Reporter, Vacaville, CA
Wilson, Charles ... (813) 259-7711
MGR-CR, Tribune and Times, Tampa, FL
Wilson, Charlie ... (317) 932-2222
ED, Food/Society ED
Rushville Republican, Rushville, IN
Wilson, Chris ... (417) 468-2013
ED, Marshfield Mail, Marshfield, MO
Wilson, Chris ... (601) 256-5647
ED, Amory Advertiser, Amory, MS
Wilson, Christopher ... (352) 493-1553
PUB, Chiefland Citizen, Chiefland, FL
Wilson, Christy ... (808) 244-3981
City ED, Maui News, Wailuku, HI
Wilson, Dale ... (812) 265-3641
PROD MGR, Madison Courier, Madison, IN
Wilson, Dave ... (216) 951-0000
DP MGR, PROD DIR-SYS
News-Herald, Willoughby, OH
Wilson, Dave ... (305) 350-2111
EX Sports ED, Miami Herald, Miami, FL
Wilson, Dean ... (601) 788-6031
GM, Richton Dispatch, Richton, MS
Wilson, Dee ... (515) 284-8000
MGR-INFO Services
Des Moines Register, Des Moines, IA
Wilson, Dennis ... (707) 468-3500
PUB, Ukiah Daily Journal, Ukiah, CA
Wilson, Dewayne ... (615) 552-1808
Copy Desk Chief, PROD Copy Desk Chief
Leaf-Chronicle, Clarksville, TN
Wilson, Don ... (972) 937-3310
ADV MGR
Waxahachie Daily Light, Waxahachie, TX
Wilson, Donald ... (910) 888-3500
CIRC DIR
High Point Enterprise, High Point, NC
Wilson, Dorothy ... (803) 771-6161
News ED-Presentation, State, Columbia, SC
Wilson, Dorothy D ... (502) 773-3401
PUB, ED, Progress, Cave City, KY
Wilson, Dorris ... (502) 886-4444
CIRC SUPV-MR
Kentucky New Era, Hopkinsville, KY
Wilson, Doug ... (219) 874-7211
CIRC MGR, PROD MGR
News Dispatch, Michigan City, IN
Wilson, Doug ... (217) 223-5100
Political (Senior Writer, EDL ASST)
Quincy Herald-Whig, Quincy, IL
Wilson Jr, Edward G ... (717) 291-8811
Librarian, Lancaster Intelligencer Journal/New Era/Sunday News, Lancaster, PA
Wilson, Ella ... (203) 789-5200
PROD MGR-MR
New Haven Register, New Haven, CT
Wilson, Ellen Silva ... (214) 977-8222
VP-Human Resources
Dallas Morning News, Dallas, TX
Wilson, Frank W ... (306) 946-3343
PUB, ED, Watrous Manitou, Watrous, SK
Wilson, Fred ... (210) 225-7411
DIR-Photography
San Antonio Express-News, San Antonio, TX
Wilson, Gail ... (609) 272-7000
Entertainment ED, Fashion ED
Press of Atlantic City, Pleasantville, NJ
Wilson, Geordie ... (603) 224-5301
City ED, Concord Monitor, Concord, NH
Wilson, George ... (405) 475-3311
Photo Chief
Daily Oklahoman, Oklahoma City, OK
Wilson, George ... (601) 627-2201
PROD MGR, Press Register, Clarksdale, MS
Wilson, George Q ... (618) 253-7146
PUB, Online Contact, Daily Register, Harrisburg, IL, Hollinger International Inc.
Wilson, George W ... (603) 224-5301
PRES/TREAS
Newspapers of New England, Concord, NH
Wilson, Henry (Hank) L ... (561) 287-1550
Deputy MAN ED, Stuart News, Stuart, FL
Wilson Jr, Hobart ... (614) 446-2342
ED, Gallipolis Daily Tribune/Sunday Times-Sentinel, Gallipolis, OH
Wilson, Ingrid M ... (802) 485-3681
PUB, ED, Northfield News, Northfield, VT
Wilson, Jack ... (562) 435-1161
VP-Human Resources
Press-Telegram, Long Beach, CA
Wilson, Jackman ... (541) 485-1234
EDL Writer, Register-Guard, Eugene, OR
Wilson, James ... (605) 648-3821
PUB, ED, Marion Record, Marion, SD
Wilson, James B ... (712) 792-3573
PRES, TREAS, PUB, BM, MAN ED
Daily Times Herald, Carroll, IA
Wilson, James L ... (802) 485-3681
PUB, Northfield News, Northfield, VT
Wilson, James R ... (919) 419-6500
EPE, Herald-Sun, Durham, NC
Wilson, Jay ... (601) 287-6111
CIRC MGR, Daily Corinthian, Corinth, MS
Wilson, Jean ... (612) 439-3130
ADV MGR-CLASS
Stillwater Evening Gazette, Stillwater, MN
Wilson, Jeff ... (515) 472-4129
PUB, Fairfield Ledger, Fairfield, IA
Wilson, Jeff ... (613) 472-2431
ED, Stirling News-Argus, Marmora, ON
Wilson, Jeffrey A ... (706) 549-0123
PUB, Athens Daily News/Banner-Herald, Athens, GA
Wilson, Jim ... (208) 522-1800
VP, VP-MKTG/Development
Post Register, Idaho Falls, ID
Wilson, Jim D ... (808) 935-6621
PUB, Hawaii Tribune-Herald, Hilo, HI
Wilson, Joe ... (502) 886-4444
Sports ED
Kentucky New Era, Hopkinsville, KY
Wilson, Joel ... (502) 678-5171
MAN ED, EPE
Glasgow Daily Times, Glasgow, KY
Wilson, Joey ... (912) 272-5522
Photo ED, Courier Herald, Dublin, GA
Wilson, John ... (209) 835-3030
PROD FRM-PR, Tracy Press, Tracy, CA
Wilson, John ... (913) 392-2129
PUB, ED
Minneapolis Messenger, Minneapolis, KS
Wilson, John C ... (804) 435-1701
ED, Rappahannock Record, Kilmarnock, VA
Wilson, John F ... (614) 224-4835
PROD MGR, Daily Reporter, Columbus, OH
Wilson, Judith V ... (954) 428-9045
MAN ED, Deerfield Beach-Lighthouse Point Observer, Deerfield Beach, FL
Wilson, Judy ... (616) 754-9301
PROD MGR-COMP
Daily News, Greenville, MI
Wilson, Julia ... (501) 442-1777
County ED
Northwest Arkansas Times, Fayetteville, AR
Wilson, Julie ... (213) 237-5000
ED-Ventura County Edition, Ventura County Edition ED
Los Angeles Times, Los Angeles, CA
Wilson, Keith D ... (423) 246-8121
PUB, Kingsport Times-News, Kingsport, TN
Wilson, Kelly ... (217) 223-5100
Health/Medical ED
Quincy Herald-Whig, Quincy, IL
Wilson, Ken E ... (409) 849-8581
PUB, Angleton Times, Angleton, TX
Wilson, Kenneth F ... (704) 648-2381
PUB, Enterprise Mountaineer, Canton, NC
Wilson, Kim ... (304) 526-4000
ADV MGR-RT
Herald-Dispatch, Huntington, WV
Wilson, Larry ... (503) 221-8327
PROD MGR-Ad SRV, Oregonian, Portland, OR
Wilson, Larry A ... (601) 788-6031
PUB, ED, Richton Dispatch, Richton, MS
Wilson, Laura ... (405) 372-5000
BUS ED, News Press, Stillwater, OK
Wilson, Laura ... (605) 648-3821
GM, Marion Record, Marion, SD
Wilson, Lawrence ... (818) 578-6300
ED, Star-News, Pasadena, CA
Wilson, Lee ... (319) 337-3181
PROD DIR
Iowa City Press-Citizen, Iowa City, IA
Wilson, LeRoy ... (806) 266-5576
PUB, ED, Morton Tribune, Morton, TX
Wilson, Linda ... (360) 577-2500
Entertainment/Amusements ED
Daily News, Longview, WA
Wilson, Lisa Klem ... (212) 293-8500
VP-Sales & MKTG, United Media, United Feature Syndicate, Newspaper Enterprise Association, New York, NY
Wilson, Mabel ... (209) 441-6111
Librarian, Fresno Bee, Fresno, CA
Wilson, Marc ... (406) 837-5131
PUB, ED, Bigfork Eagle, Bigfork, MT
Wilson, Mark ... (919) 269-6101
PUB, Zebulon Record, Zebulon, NC
Wilson, Martha W ... (561) 287-1550
Entertainment/Amusements ED, Health/Medical ED, Religion ED, SCI/Technology ED, Travel ED, Stuart News, Stuart, FL
Wilson, Mary Ellen ... (713) 479-2760
MAN ED, Deer Park Progress/Deer Park Broadcaster, Deer Park, TX
Wilson, Mary Lou ... (707) 448-6401
Features ED, Reporter, Vacaville, CA
Wilson, Matthew ... (415) 777-1111
EX ED
San Francisco Chronicle, San Francisco, CA
Wilson, Melody K ... (501) 325-6412
GM, Cleveland County Herald, Rison, AR
Wilson, Michael ... (212) 416-2000
ADV DIR-CLASS
Wall Street Journal, New York, NY
Wilson, Mike ... (813) 893-8111
Religion ED
St. Petersburg Times, St. Petersburg, FL
Wilson, Paul ... (801) 625-4200
PROD MGR-Network
Standard-Examiner, Ogden, UT
Wilson, Peter A ... (405) 933-4579
PUB, ED, Valliant Leader, Valliant, OK
Wilson, Phil ... (412) 523-6588
Chief Photographer
Standard Observer, Greensburg, PA
Wilson, Randy ... (330) 264-1125
ADV MGR-NTL, Daily Record, Wooster, OH
Wilson, Randy ... (207) 828-5432
ED, Maine Times, Portland, ME
Wilson, Randy ... (520) 774-4545
BUS/FIN ED, City/MET ED, News ED
Arizona Daily Sun, Flagstaff, AZ
Wilson, Ray C ... (407) 393-4777
PRES/PUB, Wilson, Ray C., Boca Raton, FL
Wilson, Rex ... (707) 441-0500
MAN ED, Times-Standard, Eureka, CA
Wilson, Richard ... (212) 455-4000
Weekly SRV NTL Sales DIR, North America Syndicate, King Features Syndicate, NY, NY
Wilson, Robert ... (918) 756-3600
CIRC MGR-Subscriber SRV
Okmulgee Daily Times, Okmulgee, OK
Wilson, Robert ... (307) 742-2176
MAN ED, Boomerang Bonus
Laramie Daily Boomerang, Laramie, WY
Wilson, Robert L ... (423) 523-3131
ASST MAN ED-Graphics
Knoxville News-Sentinel, Knoxville, TN
Wilson, Robert S ... (518) 454-5694
GM, Times Union, Albany, NY
Wilson, Robert W ... (816) 265-4244
PUB, GM, ED, Milan Standard, Milan, MO
Wilson, Roosevelt ... (904) 681-1852
PUB, ED, Capitol Outlook, Tallahassee, FL
Wilson, Roy ... (419) 332-5511
EPE, News-Messenger, Fremont, OH
Wilson, Ruth Ann ... (501) 446-2645
ED, Newton County Times, Jasper, AR
Wilson, S K ... (802) 747-6121
CIRC MGR, Rutland Herald, Rutland, VT
Wilson, Sarah O ... (219) 223-2111
PUB, Compass, Rochester, IN
Wilson, Sarah Overmyer ... (219) 223-2111
SEC, PUB, Rochester Sentinel, Rochester, IN
Wilson, Scott ... (360) 385-2900
PUB, Port Townsend Jefferson County Leader, Port Townsend, WA
Wilson, Shea ... (501) 862-6611
Features ED
El Dorado News-Times, El Dorado, AR
Wilson, Sim ... (360) 659-1300
PUB, Globe, Marysville, WA
Wilson, Stan ... (913) 367-0583
PUB, ADV MGR
Atchison Daily Globe, Atchison, KS
Wilson, Steve ... (602) 271-8000
COL, Arizona Republic, Phoenix, AZ
Wilson, Steve ... (205) 532-4000
ADV MGR-RT
Huntsville Times, Huntsville, AL
Wilson, Susie ... (402) 873-3334
CIRC MGR
Nebraska City News-Press, Nebraska City, NE
Wilson, Terry ... (419) 929-3411
ED, New London Record, New London, OH
Wilson III, Thomas G ... (423) 337-7101
PUB, Monroe County Advocate/Democrat, Sweetwater, TN
Wilson, Tom ... (614) 397-5333
Sports ED
Mount Vernon News, Mount Vernon, OH
Wilson, Tom ... (717) 326-1551
City ED, Entertainment ED
Williamsport Sun-Gazette, Williamsport, PA
Wilson, Tom ... (250) 762-4445
EPE, Daily Courier, Kelowna, BC
Wilson, Trish ... (919) 829-4500
Specialties ED
News & Observer, Raleigh, NC
Wilson, Verl Dan ... (810) 387-3282
ED, Munising News, Munising, MI
Wilson, Virginia ... (406) 837-5131
MAN ED, Bigfork Eagle, Bigfork, MT
Wilson, William S ... (219) 223-2111
ED, EPE/Writer, Farm ED
Rochester Sentinel, Rochester, IN
Wilson, Wihlena V ... (352) 493-1553
GM, ED, Chiefland Citizen, Chiefland, FL
Wilson, William ... (219) 294-1661
News ED, Elkhart Truth, Elkhart, IN
Wilson, William ... (213) 237-5000
Art Critic
Los Angeles Times, Los Angeles, CA
Wilson-Renner, Polly ... (414)922-4600
Entertaiment/Amusments ED, Religion ED, Reporter, Fond du Lac, WI
Wiltz, Teresa ... (312) 222-3232
Fashion Writer, Chicago Tribune, Chicago, IL
Wimberly, Alex ... (504) 826-3279
ADV MGR-NTL
Times-Picayune, New Orleans, LA
Wimborne, Margaret ... (208) 522-1800
Features ED, Food/Community ED
Post Register, Idaho Falls, ID
Wimer, Connie ... (515) 288-3336
PUB, Cityview, Des Moines, IA
Wimer, Robert C ... (804) 385-5400
EPE, News & Advance, Lynchburg, VA
Wimmer, Donn K ... (502) 927-6945
PUB, ED, Hancock Clarion, Hawesville, KY
Winas, Charles ... (501) 735-1010
CIRC MGR
Evening Times, West Memphis, AR
Winburne, Peggy Reisser ... (901) 529-2211
Living/Lifestyle ED
Commercial Appeal, Memphis, TN
Wincewicz, Theresa ... (360) 532-4000
ADV DIR, Daily World, Aberdeen, WA
Wind, Andrew ... (507) 359-2911
County Reporter, Journal, New Ulm, MN
Windels, Paul ... (218) 829-4705
EDU ED
Brainerd Daily Dispatch, Brainerd, MN
Windemuth, Susan ... (209) 578-2000
ASST MAN ED, Modesto Bee, Modesto, CA
Winders, Glenda ... (619) 293-1818
EDL MGR
Copley News Service, San Diego, CA
Windham, Ben ... (205) 345-0505
MAN ED, Tuscaloosa News, Tuscaloosa, AL
Windham, Bob ... (409) 598-3377
PUB, Light and Champion, Center, TX
Windham, Gene ... (601) 582-4321
PROD DIR
Hattiesburg American, Hattiesburg, MS
Windholz, Glen ... (913) 628-1081
PROD FRM-PR, Hays Daily News, Hays, KS
Windishar, Anne ... (509) 459-5000
Youth Page ED
Spokesman-Review, Spokane, WA
Windom, Kathy ... (612) 425-3323
PUB, Rockford News Leader, Rockford, MN
Windom, Larry ... (612) 425-3323
PUB, Rockford News Leader, Rockford, MN
Windslow, Bud ... (970) 242-5050
CIRC MGR
Daily Sentinel, Grand Junction, CO
Windsor, Bill ... (703) 276-3400
CIRC GM-Boston, USA Today, Arlington, VA
Windsor, Brad ... (941) 335-0200
News ED, News-Press, Fort Myers, FL
Windsor, James T ... (912) 529-6624
PUB, ED, Soperton News, Soperton, GA
Windsor, Shawn ... (205) 532-4000
Health ED, Huntsville Times, Huntsville, AL
Winegarden, Dave ... (209) 943-6397
VP-Advertising, ADV DIR
Record, Stockton, CA
Winegarden, Richard ... (713) 220-7171
VP/CFO, Houston Chronicle, Houston, TX
Wineka, Mark ... (704) 633-8950
Political ED, Sports ED
Salisbury Post, Salisbury, NC
Wineman, Rick ... (330) 833-2631
PROD FRM-PR, Independent, Massillon, OH
Winer, Laurie ... (213) 237-5000
Theater Critic
Los Angeles Times, Los Angeles, CA
Winer, Valerie ... (508) 793-9100
MGR-INFO SYS
Telegram & Gazette, Worcester, MA
Wines, Les ... (903) 893-8181
PROD MGR-PR
Herald Democrat, Sherman, TX

251-Who's Where **Wol**

Winey, Leslie (219) 235-6161
PA, South Bend Tribune, South Bend, IN

Winfield, Bruce (604) 338-5811
ED, Comox Valley Record, Courtenay, BC

Winfree, Scott (615) 735-1110
PUB, Carthage Courier, Carthage, TN

Winfrey, Carlton (810) 766-6100
EPE, Flint Journal, Flint, MI

Winfrey, Charles (423) 562-8468
ED, La Follette Press, La Follette, TN

Winfrey, Henry G (919) 249-1555
PUB, Pamlico News, Oriental, NC

Wingard, Laura (909) 684-1200
Deputy MET ED
Press-Enterprise, Riverside, CA

Wingate, John (608) 365-8811
ADV DIR, Beloit Daily News, Beloit, WI

Winge, Vicki (612) 388-8235
ADV DIR, Republican Eagle, Red Wing, MN

Wingelaar, Roger (810) 332-8181
ASST MAN ED, Oakland Press, Pontiac, MI

Winger, Barry (412) 981-6100
PROD MGR-SYS & COMP
Herald, Sharon, PA

Winger, Bruce (330) 996-3000
ASST MAN ED-Technology/Nights
Akron Beacon Journal, Akron, OH

Winger, Don (517) 835-7171
Sports ED, Midland Daily News, Midland, MI

Wingert, Bridget (215) 862-9415
ED, New Hope Gazette, New Hope, PA

Wingert, Stephen (210) 686-4343
PROD DIR, Monitor, McAllen, TX

Wingett, Robert L (614) 446-2342
PUB, Gallipolis Daily Tribune/Sunday Times-Sentinel, Gallipolis, OH, Gannett Co. Inc.

Wingfield, James (618) 242-0117
CIRC MGR, Register-News, Mount Vernon, IL

Wingfield, Mark (502) 244-6470
MAN ED, Western Recorder, Louisville, KY

Wingo, Mike (405) 332-4433
Sports ED, Ada Evening News, Ada, OK

Winick, Norm (309) 342-2010
PUB, ED, Zephyr, Galesburg, IL

Winjum, Kimberlly (360) 384-1411
GM, Record-Journal, Ferndale, WA

Winkelman, Gary (810) 731-1000
MAN ED, Source, Utica, MI

Winkleman, John (314) 937-9811
ED, News Democrat Journal, Festus, MO

Winklemann, John (505) 393-5141
MAN ED, Hobbs Flare, Hobbs, NM

Winkler, Barbara (405) 223-2200
ADV MGR, MGR-PROM
Daily Ardmoreite, Ardmore, OK

Winkler, Charles (707) 441-0500
BUS ED, City ED
Times-Standard, Eureka, CA

Winkler, Dolores E (513) 294-2662
PUB, Oakwood Register, Dayton, OH

Winkler, Herbert (202) 783-5097
BU Chief, Deutsche Presse-Agentur (dpa), Washington, DC

Winkler, Matt (212) 318-2300
EIC
Bloomberg Business News, New York, NY

Winkley, Jim (317) 633-1240
PROD OPER FRM-COMP (Day)
Indianapolis Star/News, Indianapolis, IN

Winmill, Tina (410) 398-3311
ADV DIR, Cecil Whig, Elkton, MD

Winn, Ann B (540) 638-8801
SEC, CONT, Bulletin, Martinsville, VA

Winn, Billy (706) 324-5526
EPE, Ledger-Enquirer, Columbus, GA

Winn, John (818) 962-8811
CIRC MGR-Single Copy, San Gabriel Valley Tribune, West Covina, CA, MediaNews Inc.

Winn, Michael (615) 552-1808
ASST TREAS, Leaf-Chronicle, Clarksville, TN

Winn, Steve (816) 234-4141
Deputy EPE
Kansas City Star, Kansas City, MO

Winn, Steven (415) 777-1111
Theater ED
San Francisco Chronicle, San Francisco, CA

Winnecke, Joyce (312) 321-3000
EX News ED
Chicago Sun-Times, Chicago, IL

Winner, Karin (619) 299-3131
ED
San Diego Union-Tribune, San Diego, CA

Winning, Jack (916) 891-1234
ED, Chico Enterprise-Record, Chico, CA

Winsberg, Elana (206) 448-8000
Photo/Graphics ED
Seattle Post-Intelligencer, Seattle, WA

Winsby, Bryden (604) 763-3212
MAN ED
Kelowna Capital News, Kelowna, BC

Winship, George (916) 243-2424
BUS/FIN ED
Record Searchlight, Redding, CA

Winskowski, Dennis (218) 732-9242
PUB
Park Rapids Enterprise, Park Rapids, MN

Winslow, Carmen (406) 496-5500
News ED, Montana Standard, Butte, MT

Winson, Diana (618) 438-5611
Sports ED, Benton Evening News, Benton, IL

Winsor, Deborah (941) 953-7755
Charlotte County BU Chief
Sarasota Herald-Tribune, Sarasota, FL

Wintel, Donna (916) 321-1000
ADV MGR-RT
Sacramento Bee, Sacramento, CA

Winter, Abe (701) 223-2500
Sports ED, Bismarck Tribune, Bismarck, ND

Winter, C J (630) 969-0188
PUB, ED
Downers Grove Reporter, Downers Grove, IL

Winter, Christopher (609) 845-3300
Health/Medical ED
Gloucester County Times, Woodbury, NJ

Winter, Don (212) 679-1850
PUB, Upper West Side Resident, New York City, NY

Winter, Jim (817) 872-2247
PUB, Bowie News, Bowie, TX

Winter, Judy A (507) 234-6651
PUB, ED
Janesville Argus, Janesville, MN

Winter, Ken (616) 347-2544
VP, GM, CIRC MGR-PROM, ED, EPE
Petoskey News-Review, Petoskey, MI

Winter, Ken (910) 727-7406
ED, Star Watch, Winston-Salem, NC

Winter, Mary (303) 892-5000
Lifestyle ED
Rocky Mountain News, Denver, CO

Winter, Michelle (864) 224-4321
Fashion/Travel ED, Features ED, Food ED, Garden ED, Music ED
Anderson Independent-Mail, Anderson, SC

Winter, P K (630) 969-0188
PUB
Downers Grove Reporter, Downers Grove, IL

Winter, Reni (601) 798-4766
Fashion ED, Society/Women's ED
Picayune Item, Picayune, MS

Winterhalt, Elaine (306) 825-5522
CIRC DIR
Lloydminster Times, Lloydminster, SK

Winterland, Barry L (309) 829-9411
DIR-FIN, FIN DIR
Pantagraph, Bloomington, IL

Winters, Edward (203) 574-3636
CIRC DIR, Waterbury Republican-American, Waterbury, CT

Winters, Gordon (402) 475-4200
Sports ED, Lincoln Journal Star, Lincoln, NE

Winters, John A (907) 586-3740
PUB, Juneau Empire, Juneau, AK

Winters, Mary (217) 223-5100
ADV MGR-RT
Quincy Herald-Whig, Quincy, IL

Winters, Matt (360) 642-8181
ED, Chinook Observer, Long Beach, WA

Winters, Paula Underwood (615) 646-6131
ED, Westview, Nashville, TN

Winters, Phillip (770) 532-1234
PROD SUPT-MR, Times, Gainesville, GA

Winters, Stephen J (203) 333-0161
EPE, Connecticut Post, Bridgeport, CT

Winters, Terry (209) 578-2000
MGR-Technical SRV
Modesto Bee, Modesto, CA

Winton, Ben (602) 271-8000
Religion Writer
Arizona Republic, Phoenix, AZ

Winton, Jerry (405) 223-2200
ADV MGR-Sales
Daily Ardmoreite, Ardmore, OK

Wirski, Jim (501) 633-3130
ADV DIR, Times-Herald, Forrest City, AR

Wirta, Connie (218) 723-5281
City ED, Duluth News-Tribune, Duluth, MN

Wirtz, Ralph (517) 835-7171
MAN ED, EPE, SCI/Technology ED
Midland Daily News, Midland, MI

Wisch, Jimmy (817) 927-2831
PUB, ED, Texas Jewish Post, Dallas, TX

Wischnowski, Stan (716) 232-7100
News ED-Democrat and Chronicle
Rochester Democrat and Chronicle; Times-Union, Rochester, NY

Wisdom, Nancy (816) 259-2266
GM, News, Lexington, MO

Wise, Christina (419) 448-3200
EDU ED, Advertiser-Tribune, Tiffin, OH

Wise, Erbon W (318) 527-7075
COB, PUB, Southwest Daily News, Sulphur, LA, News Leader Inc.

Wise, Howard (217) 824-2233
PROD MGR, Taylorville Daily Breeze-Courier, Taylorville, IL

Wise, Jennifer (904) 879-2727
PUB, Nassau County Record, Callahan, FL

Wise, Jerry (318) 786-8004
PUB, ED, DeQuincy News, DeQuincy, LA

Wise, Jim (919) 419-6500
COL, Herald-Sun, Durham, NC

Wise III, John Laing (412) 282-8000
VP/SEC, ED, Butler Eagle, Butler, PA

Wise, Joy (318) 786-8004
PUB, DeQuincy News, DeQuincy, LA

Wise, Keith (408) 372-3311
PROD MGR-Packaging Center
Monterey County Herald, Monterey, CA

Wise, Maureen (914) 267-4114
ED
Rockland Jewish Reporter, Valley Cottage, NY

Wise Jr, Vernon L (412) 282-8000
PRES/PUB, Butler Eagle, Butler, PA

Wise III, Vernon L (412) 282-8000
VP/TREAS, Butler Eagle, Butler, PA

Wise, Warren (864) 855-0355
MAN ED, Easley Progress, Easley, SC

Wisecaver, Sandra (208) 543-4335
ED, Buhl Herald, Buhl, ID

Wiseman, Clayton (713) 220-7171
DP MGR, Houston Chronicle, Houston, TX

Wiseman, Erin (916) 541-3880
BM
Tahoe Daily Tribune, South Lake Tahoe, CA

Wiseman, Jerry D (515) 885-2531
PUB, Bancroft Register, Bancroft, IA

Wiseman, Robert (330) 747-1471
PSL MGR/Labor Relations
Vindicator, Youngstown, OH

Wiseman, Sylvia (704) 633-8950
Features ED, Women's ED
Salisbury Post, Salisbury, NC

Wisemiller, Gerald W (614) 461-5000
CIRC MGR-ADM
Columbus Dispatch, Columbus, OH

Wisener, Robert (501) 623-7711
Sports ED
Sentinel-Record, Hot Springs, AR

Wishard, Dell (605) 244-7199
PUB, GM, ED, Bison Courier, Prairie City, SD

Wishard, Glenn (605) 244-7199
PUB, GM, ED, Bison Courier, Prairie City, SD

Wishart, Bruce (604) 627-8482
PUB
Prince Rupert This Week, Prince Rupert, BC

Wishart, Ron (212) 210-2100
PROD MGR-Engineering (Kearny)
New York Daily News, New York, NY

Wiskow, Jodi (218) 463-1521
GM, Roseau Times-Region, Roseau, MN

Wisniewski, Bernard (715) 344-6100
PROD SUPT-PR
Stevens Point Journal, Stevens Point, WI

Wissinger, Bruce (814) 532-5199
EPE, Tribune-Democrat, Johnstown, PA

Witcofski, Paul (717) 455-3636
CIRC MGR-Distribution
Standard-Speaker, Hazleton, PA

Witcomb, Bill (506) 452-6671
MAN ED, Daily Gleaner, Fredericton, NB

Witham, Donovan C (701) 282-2443
PUB, West Fargo Pioneer, West Fargo, ND

Witherall, Graham (310) 540-5511
Aviation ED, Daily Breeze, Torrance, CA

Withers, John (507) 285-7600
SUPT-Building, DIR-PROM
Post-Bulletin, Rochester, MN

Witherspoon, Agnes (204) 827-2343
GM, Gazette, Glenboro, MB

Witherspoon, J H (910) 727-7211
PRES, PUB, Journal, Winston-Salem, NC

Witherspoon, Mary Jo (816) 885-2281
ADV MGR-CLASS, CIRC MGR
Clinton Daily Democrat, Clinton, MO

Witke, David (515) 284-8000
EX Sports ED
Des Moines Register, Des Moines, IA

Witmar, Nick (717) 888-9643
PROD MGR, Evening Times, Sayre, PA

Witmer, Keith (716) 343-8000
CIRC DIR, Daily News, Batavia, NY

Witmyer, Christine (201) 473-5414
MAN ED, Post Eagle, Clifton, NJ

Witt, Brian (415) 749-5400
ADV CLASS DIR
Recorder, San Francisco, CA

Witt, Jim (817) 390-7400
VP/EX ED, Star-Telegram, Fort Worth, TX

Witt, Linda (423) 828-5254
PUB, Grainger County News, Rutledge, TN

Witt, Marianne (352) 357-3199
GM, Eustis News, Mount Dora, FL

Witt, Richard (602) 468-6565
National ADV DIR
Daily Racing Form, Phoenix, AZ

Witt, Robert (219) 235-6161
MGR-RES
South Bend Tribune, South Bend, IN

Wittchow, Scott (414) 922-8640
MAN ED, Action Advertiser/Action Sunday, Fond du Lac, WI

Witte, Daniel (608) 297-2424
PUB
Marquette County Tribune, Montello, WI

Witte, Mark (608) 297-2424
PUB
Marquette County Tribune, Montello, WI

Wittell, Fern (573) 468-6511
MAN ED, Independent News, Sullivan, MO

Witten, Debbie (415) 692-9406
GM, Redwood City Tribune, Burlingame, CA

Witten, Scott (910) 739-4322
BUS ED, Robesonian, Lumberton, NC

Wittenmyer, Mike (417) 623-3480
CIRC DIR, Joplin Globe, Joplin, MO

Witter, Jim (206) 597-8742
PROD MGR-COMP Room
News Tribune, Tacoma, WA

Wittler, Ruth Ann (419) 695-0015
PA, Delphos Daily Herald, Delphos, OH

Wittman, Duane D (304) 233-0100
TREAS/CONT
Ogden Newspapers, Wheeling, WV

Wittman, Kevin L (908) 254-7000
PUB, Sentinel, East Brunswick, NJ

Witty, Jan (502) 522-6605
GM, Cadiz Record, Cadiz, KY

Witty, Robert M (619) 293-1818
EVP/ED, Copley News Service, San Diego, CA

Witvoet, Bert (905) 682-8311
ED, Christian Courier, St. Catharines, ON

Witwer, Bruce (813) 259-7711
MAN ED, Tribune and Times, Tampa, FL

Witwer, George B (219) 347-0400
VP, News-Sun, Kendallville, IN
Witwer Newspapers

Witwer, George O (219) 347-0400
Chairman
Witwer Newspapers, Kendallville, IN

Witzel, John C (614) 461-5000
CONT, Columbus Dispatch, Columbus, OH

Wixon, Matt (520) 774-4545
Sports ED, Arizona Daily Sun, Flagstaff, AZ

Woare, Karen (217) 429-5151
DP SUPV, Herald & Review, Decatur, IL

Woehler, Bob (509) 582-1500
Wine COL, Tri-City Herald, Tri-Cities, WA

Woelfel, Robert W (412) 775-3200
ADV MGR-Sales
Beaver County Times, Beaver, PA

Woellert, Larry K (319) 927-2020
PUB, ED, Manchester Press, Manchester, IA

Woerpel, Craig (906) 786-2021
Travel ED, Daily Press, Escanaba, MI

Woerpel, Don (715) 748-2626
ED, Star News, Medford, WI

Woesman, Frank H (513) 721-2700
PROD MGR-Building SRV/Newsprint
Cincinnati Enquirer, Cincinnati, OH

Woessner, Bob (414) 435-4411
Opinion Page ED
Green Bay Press-Gazette, Green Bay, WI

Wofford, Sally (618) 253-7146
ADV DIR, Daily Register, Harrisburg, IL
Hollinger International Inc.

Wogan, David (412) 282-8000
PROD FRM-PR, Butler Eagle, Butler, PA

Wognum, Anne (218) 365-3141
PUB, Ely Echo, Ely, MN

Wognum, Nick (218) 365-3141
GM, Ely Echo, Ely, MN

Wohl, Karen (215) 345-3000
ADV MGR-CLASS
Intelligencer/Record, Doylestown, PA

Wohler, Jeff (503) 221-8327
ADTX ED, Oregonian, Portland, OR

Wohlful, Laurie (719) 634-1593
ED, Falcon Flyer, Colorado Springs, CO

Wohlgemuth, Barbara (512) 476-0576
GM, Texas Triangle, Austin, TX

Woishwill, Craig (305) 350-2111
PROD MGR-Packaging
Miami Herald, Miami, FL

Woit, Marian (609) 691-5000
MGR-MKTG SRV, Daily Journal, Vineland, NJ

Woitte, Laurie (503) 255-2142
Vessel Movements ED
Daily Shipping News, Portland, OR

Wojciak, Glenn (216) 524-0830
ED, Medina Sun, Cleveland, OH

Wojciechowski, Don (847) 888-7800
Sports ED, Courier-News, Elgin, IL

Wojcik, Joe (814) 870-1600
ADV MGR-Creative SRV
Morning News/Erie Daily Times, Erie, PA

Wojonowski, Bob (313) 222-2300
COL, Detroit News, Detroit, MI

Wolcott, Mike (510) 935-2525
ASST Sports ED
Contra Costa Times, Walnut Creek, CA

Woldenberg, John F (773) 665-1231
PRES, M.C.E. Media Syndicate, Chicago, IL

Woldmoe, Bob (415) 883-8600
ADV MGR-NTL
Marin Independent Journal, Novato, CA

Woldt Jr, Harold F (212) 556-1234
CIRC VP-Sales/MKTG
New York Times, New York, NY

Wol Who's Where-252

Wolf, Andrew .... (718) 543-5200
PUB, Bronx Press-Review, Bronx, NY
Wolf, Carol .... (603) 298-8711
ADV SUPV-CLASS
Valley News, White River Jct., VT
Wolf, Frank .... (303) 892-5000
PROD MGR-Publishing SYS, PROD FRM-COMP, Rocky Mountain News, Denver, CO
Wolf, Gary L .... (765) 458-5114
PUB, Union County Review, Liberty, IN
Wolf, Gordon .... (712) 722-0741
ED, Sioux Center News, Sioux Center, IA
Wolf, Jeff .... (915) 673-4271
EPE, Abilene Reporter-News, Abilene, TX
Wolf, John .... (214) 450-1717
Sr VP-MKTG
Westward Communications Inc., Dallas, TX
Wolf, Linda .... (812) 231-4200
Features ED, Tribune-Star, Terre Haute, IN
Wolf, Mark .... (303) 892-5000
Sports COL
Rocky Mountain News, Denver, CO
Wolf, Marlin E .... (610) 264-9451
PUB, ED
Catasauqua Dispatch, Catasauqua, PA
Wolf, Michael .... (301) 722-4600
PROD FRM-MR
Cumberland Times-News, Cumberland, MD
Wolf, Patti .... (310) 829-6811
City ED, Outlook, Santa Monica, CA
Wolfe, Aaron .... (319) 351-1531
PUB, Icon, Iowa City, IA
Wolfe, Al .... (610) 820-6500
PROD MGR-Pre Press
Morning Call, Allentown, PA
Wolfe, Bill .... (502) 582-4011
Consumer ED, Courier-Journal, Louisville, KY
Wolfe, Billy .... (509) 248-1251
PROD FRM-PR
Yakima Herald-Republic, Yakima, WA
Wolfe, Buster .... (318) 322-5161
BUS ED, News-Star, Monroe, LA
Wolfe, Charlotte .... (601) 842-2611
MAN ED, Northeast Mississippi Daily Journal, Tupelo, MS
Wolfe, Cheryl .... (309) 923-5841
ED, Roanoke Review, Roanoke, IL
Wolfe, Ed .... (312) 222-3232
CIRC MGR-SYS
Chicago Tribune, Chicago, IL
Wolfe, John .... (602) 972-6101
ED, Sun Cities Independent, Sun City, AZ
Wolfe, John F .... (614) 461-5000
BC, PUB/PRES/CEO
Columbus Dispatch, Columbus, OH
Wolfe, John S .... (716) 924-4040
GM, Brighton-Pittsford Post, Victor, NY
Wolfe, Lisa .... (608) 323-3366
GM, Arcadia News-Leader, Arcadia, WI
Wolfe, Mitch .... (807) 468-5555
PUB, Daily Miner & News, Kenora, ON
Wolfe, Phyllis .... (515) 284-8000
Librarian, Register, Des Moines, IA
Wolfe, Tom .... (206) 455-2222
MAN ED, Eastside Journal, Bellevue, WA
Wolfe, Tom .... (618) 529-5454
BUS/FIN ED, City/MET ED, Features ED
Southern Illinoisan, Carbondale, IL
Wolfe Jr, William C .... (614) 461-5000
VP-Community Affairs
Columbus Dispatch, Columbus, OH
Wolfenbarger, Rick .... (423) 523-3131
PROD OPER SUPT-Imaging
Knoxville News-Sentinel, Knoxville, TN
Wolff, Cindy .... (901) 529-2211
RE Reporter
Commercial Appeal, Memphis, TN
Wolff, Dagny .... (305) 852-3216
PUB, Reporter, Tavernier, FL
Wolff, James L .... (414) 361-1515
ED, Berlin Journal, Berlin, WI
Wolff, Jeff .... (319) 398-8211
MGR-MKTG RES, Gazette, Cedar Rapids, IA
Wolff, Kathy .... (617) 536-5390
GM, Boston Phoenix, Boston, MA
Wolfford, George .... (606) 329-1717
EDU ED, Daily Independent, Ashland, KY
Wolfgram, Fred .... (414) 224-2000
PROD MGR-Advertising Services
Milwaukee Journal Sentinel, Milwaukee, WI
Wolfram, Jerry .... (614) 498-7117
PUB
Newcomerstown News, Newcomerstown, OH
Wolfram, Reinhold .... (508) 793-9100
ADV MGR-Zone Sales Division
Telegram & Gazette, Worcester, MA
Wolfrom, Kenneth E .... (717) 532-4101
PUB, News-Chronicle, Shippensburg, PA
Wolfzorn, E John .... (205) 325-2222
TREAS, Birmingham Post-Herald, Birmingham, AL, Scripps Howard
Wolgamott, L Kent .... (402) 475-4200
Entertainment Reporter
Lincoln Journal Star, Lincoln, NE
Wolgast, Steve .... (307) 266-0500
Books/BUS ED, News ED
Star-Tribune, Casper, WY
Wolgemuth, Samuel .... (714) 553-9292
VP/PRES-Freedom Magazines Inc.
Freedom Communications Inc., Irvine, CA
Wolinsky, Leo .... (213) 237-5000
MET ED, Los Angeles Times, Los Angeles, CA
Wolk, Ray .... (206) 455-2222
VP-FIN, Eastside Journal, Bellevue, WA
Wolken, Sandra .... (414) 367-3272
ED, Sussex Sun, Hartland, WI
Wollard, Charan .... (408) 920-5000
News ED, Mercury News, San Jose, CA
Wollfolk, Steve .... (816) 562-2424
MAN ED, Sports ED
Maryville Daily Forum, Maryville, MO
Wollstadt, David C .... (207) 827-4451
PUB, ED, Penobscot Times, Old Town, ME
Wolman, J Martin .... (608) 252-6100
Asst SEC/TREAS
Wisconsin State Journal, Madison, WI
Woloszyn, Tony .... (412) 758-5573
PROD FRM-PR
Ellwood City Ledger, Ellwood City, PA
Wolter, Doug .... (507) 376-9711
Sports ED, Daily Globe, Worthington, MN
Wolterman, Beth .... (712) 364-3131
ED, Ida County Courier, Ida Grove, IA
Woltman, Wayne G .... (630) 231-0500
PUB, ED
West Chicago Press, West Chicago, IL
Woltz, Missy .... (614) 385-2107
ADV MGR-CLASS
Logan Daily News, Logan, OH
Wolverton, Alison .... (307) 733-2430
GM, Jackson Hole Guide, Jackson, WY
Wolverton, L .... (412) 758-5573
ED, Action Line ED
Ellwood City Ledger, Ellwood City, PA
Womack, Bill .... (970) 240-4900
CIRC DIR, Morning Sun, Montrose, CO
Womack, Brian .... (208) 467-9251
BUS ED, Idaho Press-Tribune, Nampa, ID
Womack, Cathy .... (912) 273-2277
ADV MGR-CLASS
Cordele Dispatch, Cordele, GA
Womack Jr, Charles A .... (804) 432-2791
PUB, Star-Tribune, Chatham, VA
Womack III, Charles A .... (910) 841-4933
PUB, ED, Jamestown News, Jamestown, NC
Womack, Clydette .... (405) 475-3311
ADV MGR-Market RES, DIR-MKTG
Daily Oklahoman, Oklahoma City, OK
Womack, Jerry P .... (417) 256-9191
GM, MAN ED
West Plains Daily Quill, West Plains, MO
Womack, Sharon .... (205) 259-1020
ADV MGR-RT, Daily Sentinel, Scottsboro, AL
Womack, Zan .... (804) 352-8215
PUB, Times-Virginian, Appomattox, VA
Womble, Charles .... (501) 268-8621
PROD MGR, Daily Citizen, Searcy, AR
Womble, Sharon .... (504) 822-4433
ED, New Orleans Data News Weekly, New Orleans, LA
Womick, Chip .... (910) 824-2231
PUB, ED, Bulletin, Ramseur, NC
Won, Marilyn .... (617) 929-2000
ADV MGR-CLASS, Boston Globe, Boston, MA
Wonder, William A .... (712) 423-2411
PUB, ED, Onawa Democrat, Onawa, IA
Wonder II, Fredrick W .... (712) 423-2411
PUB, ED, Onawa Democrat, Onawa, IA
Wong, Derrick .... (902) 468-1222
DP MGR, Daily News, Halifax, NS
Wong, Peter .... (541) 776-4411
Political ED, Mail Tribune, Medford, OR
Wong, Vino .... (316) 342-4800
Photo DEPT MGR
Emporia Gazette, Emporia, KS
Wonham, Lincoln .... (609) 691-5000
Sports ED, Daily Journal, Vineland, NJ
Wonsey, Sheron .... (616) 743-2481
GM, Marion Press, Marion, MI
Woo, Chin Fu .... (212) 513-1440
PUB, United Journal, New York, NY
Woo, Elaine .... (213) 237-5000
EDU Writer (K-12)
Los Angeles Times, Los Angeles, CA
Wood, Bruce M .... (909) 628-5501
GM, Chino Champion, Chino, CA
Wood, C Russell .... (417) 962-4411
PUB, Cabool Enterprise, Cabool, MO
Wood, Cameron J .... (519) 357-2320
ED, Wingham Advance-Times, Wingham, ON
Wood, Charles .... (406) 447-4000
ED, Helena Independent Record, Helena, MT
Wood, Charles .... (210) 672-2861
ED, Gonzales Inquirer, Gonzales, TX
Wood, Charles A .... (402) 444-1000
MKTG MGR-Public Affairs
Omaha World-Herald, Omaha, NE
Wood, Chris .... (414) 743-3321
GM, Door County Advocate, Sturgeon Bay, WI
Wood, Christina .... (541) 523-3673
Fashion/ Style ED, Religion ED, Women's ED
Baker City Herald, Baker City, OR
Wood, Cy .... (334) 644-1101
VP, PUB, MAN ED
Valley Times-News, Lanett, AL
Wood, Dave .... (414) 432-2941
CIRC DIR
Green Bay News-Chronicle, Green Bay, WI
Wood, Dave .... (612) 673-4000
Books Reporter
Star Tribune, Minneapolis, MN
Wood, Dave .... (317) 659-4622
ADV MGR-CLASS, Times, Frankfort, IN
Wood, David .... (937) 378-6161
ED
Georgetown News Democrat, Georgetown, OH
Wood, David J .... (801) 625-4200
DIR-MIS, Standard-Examiner, Ogden, UT
Wood, Debi .... (805) 781-7800
CIRC MGR-Single Copy Transportation
Telegram-Tribune, San Luis Obispo, CA
Wood, Diane .... (519) 894-2231
EDU, Record, Kitchener, ON
Wood, Ed .... (608) 754-3311
Benefits MGR
Bliss Communications Inc., Janesville, WI
Wood, Ed .... (703) 276-3400
CIRC GM-Houston, USA Today, Arlington, VA
Wood Jr, Ellis .... (901) 427-3333
PROD MGR-Camera/Plate/Press
Jackson Sun, Jackson, TN
Wood, Fran .... (212) 210-2100
Deputy MAN ED-Features
New York Daily News, New York, NY
Wood Jr, Frank A .... (414) 432-2941
PRES, PUB
Green Bay News-Chronicle, Green Bay, WI
Wood, Frank D .... (304) 367-2500
PUB, Times-West Virginian, Fairmont, WV
Wood, Giff .... (406) 232-0450
ADV DIR, Miles City Star, Miles City, MT
Wood, Greg .... (304) 348-5140
News ED
Charleston Daily Mail, Charleston, WV
Wood, Guy H .... (505) 377-2358
PUB
Sangre de Cristo Chronicle, Angel Fire, NM
Wood, Henry .... (919) 419-6500
DIR-Human Resources
Herald-Sun, Durham, NC
Wood, Jim .... (307) 632-5666
PUB, Sentinel, Cheyenne, WY
Wood, Joan R .... (937) 378-6161
PUB
Georgetown News Democrat, Georgetown, OH
Wood, Joanne M .... (417) 962-4411
PUB, Cabool Enterprise, Cabool, MO
Wood, Katherine .... (316) 342-4800
Wire ED, Emporia Gazette, Emporia, KS
Wood, Kenneth R .... (405) 867-4457
PUB, ED, Maysville News, Maysville, OK
Wood, Kevin .... (613) 476-3201
ED, Picton Gazette Regional, Picton, ON
Wood, L Stedem .... (360) 424-3251
PUB
Skagit Valley Herald, Mount Vernon, WA
Wood, Laurie .... (501) 425-6301
ASSOC ED, BUS ED
Daily News, Mountain Home, AR
Wood, Lee .... (202) 737-7377
Acting EX DIR, VP-MKTG & Communications
Children's Express, Washington, DC
Wood, Leighton P .... (360) 424-3251
BC, PRES/Owner
Skagit Valley Herald, Mount Vernon, WA
Wood, Len .... (805) 564-5200
Photo DEPT MGR/Photo ED, Santa Barbara News-Press, Santa Barbara, CA
Wood, Lewis .... (804) 352-8215
ED, Times-Virginian, Appomattox, VA
Wood, Lon .... (250) 380-5211
COL, Times Colonist, Victoria, BC
Wood, Marcia T .... (505) 377-2358
PUB, MAN ED
Sangre de Cristo Chronicle, Angel Fire, NM
Wood, Margie .... (719) 544-3520
Lifestyle ED, Religion ED
Pueblo Chieftain, Pueblo, CO
Wood, Marion .... (918) 581-8300
PROD SUPT-COMP, Tulsa World, Tulsa, OK
Wood, Nora Ann .... (334) 792-3141
MGR-MKTG, Dothan Eagle, Dothan, AL
Wood, Pat .... (414) 432-2941
ASSOC PUB
Green Bay News-Chronicle, Green Bay, WI
Wood, Paul A .... (360) 424-3251
ADV DIR
Skagit Valley Herald, Mount Vernon, WA
Wood, Peter .... (404) 466-2222
PUB, ED
Block Island Times, Block Island, RI
Wood, Presnall H .... (214) 630-4571
PUB, Baptist Standard, Dallas, TX
Wood, Robert .... (719) 784-6383
ED, Florence Citizen, Florence, CO
Wood, Ron L .... (818) 962-8811
CIRC DIR, San Gabriel Valley Tribune, West Covina, CA, MediaNews Inc.
Wood, Ronald .... (810) 332-8181
CIRC DIR, Oakland Press, Pontiac, MI
Wood, Roy .... (403) 429-5400
ASST MAN ED
Edmonton Journal, Edmonton, AB
Wood, Sandy .... (215) 854-2000
ASSOC MAN ED
Philadelphia Inquirer, Philadelphia, PA
Wood, Sheila .... (816) 637-6155
Artist SUPV, PROD MGR-COMP
Daily Standard, Excelsior Springs, MO
Wood, Stella .... (518) 642-1234
ED, North Country Free Press, Granville, NY
Wood, Sue .... (519) 621-3810
CIRC MGR
Cambridge Reporter, Cambridge, ON
Wood, Thomas H .... (904) 249-9033
PUB
Beaches Leader, Jacksonville Beach, FL
Wood, Tim .... (615) 388-6464
ED, Daily Herald, Columbia, TN
Woodall, Bill .... (903) 569-2442
PUB, Mineola Monitor, Mineola, TX
Woodall Jr, Howard (Bill) .... (503) 769-6338
PUB, ED, Stayton Mail, Stayton, OR
Woodard, Clarence .... (307) 468-2642
PUB, ED, Weston County Gazette, Upton, WY
Woodard, Connie .... (316) 431-4100
Fashion/School ED, Teen-Age/Youth ED
Chanute Tribune, Chanute, KS
Woodard, Stephanie .... (619) 745-6611
PROD MGR-Packaging
North County Times, Escondido, CA
Woodard, Stewart A .... (616) 964-7161
PROD DIR
Battle Creek Enquirer, Battle Creek, MI
Woodbury, John .... (907) 543-3500
ED, Tundra Drums, Bethel, AK
Woodford, Marie .... (937) 644-9111
ADV MGR
Marysville Journal-Tribune, Marysville, OH
Woodford, Riley .... (907) 789-4144
GM, Capital City Weekly, Juneau, AK
Woodgeard, Ron .... (912) 744-4200
Projects/Perspectives Writer
Macon Telegraph, Macon, GA
Woodham, Gary .... (904) 234-6990
PUB
Beach-Bay News, Panama City Beach, FL
Woodham, Merl .... (334) 858-3342
MAN ED, Florala News, Florala, AL
Woodhatch, Maynard .... (318) 433-3000
SEC/TREAS, Lake Charles American Press, Lake Charles, LA
Woodhouse, Scott .... (519) 538-1421
ED, Express, Meaford, ON
Woodhull, Paula .... (617) 837-3500
ED, Kingston Mariner, Marshfield, MA
Woodka, Chris .... (719) 544-3520
City ED, Pueblo Chieftain, Pueblo, CO
Woodleif, Wayne .... (617) 426-3000
Political COL, Boston Herald, Boston, MA
Woodley, Fleet .... (919) 829-4500
PROD MGR, News & Observer, Raleigh, NC
Woodley III, J K .... (804) 392-4151
ED, Farmville Herald, Farmville, VA
Woodlief, H Graham .... (804) 649-6000
VP, Media General Inc., Richmond, VA
Woodling, Chuck .... (913) 843-1000
Sports ED, Journal-World, Lawrence, KS
Woodman, Thomas .... (518) 374-4141
MAN ED, Daily Gazette, Schenectady, NY
Woodring, C J .... (352) 357-3199
ED, Eustis News, Mount Dora, FL
Woodring, Miriam L .... (803) 279-2793
PUB, ED, Star, North Augusta, SC
Woodring, Twyla .... (806) 257-3314
ED, Earth Weekly News, Earth, TX
Woodrome, Bill .... (910) 227-0131
CIRC DIR
Times News Publishing Co., Burlington, NC
Woodrow, Randy .... (520) 573-4400
PROD MGR-SRV, TNI Partners dba Tucson Newspapers, Tucson, AZ
Woodruff, Amber .... (316) 635-2312
PUB, ED, Clark County Clipper, Ashland, KS
Woodruff, Cosby .... (912) 985-4545
Sports ED, Observer, Moultrie, GA
Woodruff, Francis .... (330) 828-8401
PUB, ED
Dalton Gazette & Kidron News, Dalton, OH
Woodruff, H L .... (814) 368-3173
GM, ADV MGR, ADV MGR-CLASS
Bradford Era, Bradford, PA
Woodruff, Steve .... (406) 523-5200
Opinion Page ED, Missoulian, Missoula, MT
Woodruff, Virginia .... (507) 285-7750
VP, Fischer Production, Ed, Rochester, MN
Woods, Aubrey .... (812) 522-4871
EDU/Police ED, Farm ED
Tribune, Seymour, IN

Copyright ©1997 by the Editor & Publisher Co.

253-Who's Where **Wri**

Woods, Betty L .... (501) 255-4538
PUB, Grand Prairie Herald, Hazen, AR
Woods, Curt .... (319) 398-8211
ADV MGR-NTL, Gazette, Cedar Rapids, IA
Woods, Katherine T .... (509) 663-5161
VP, Wenatchee World, Wenatchee, WA
Woods, Kathleen K .... (509) 663-5161
SEC, Wenatchee World, Wenatchee, WA
Woods, Kristin .... (916) 258-3115
ED, Chester Progressive, Chester, CA
Woods, Linda .... (309) 647-5100
ED, Daily Ledger, Canton, IL
Woods, Lloyd .... (503) 665-2181
ED, Gresham Outlook, Gresham, OR
Woods, Lou .... (816) 254-8600
ADV MGR-Legal
Examiner, Independence, MO
Woods, Malcolm McDowell .... (414) 273-8132
MAN ED, Irish American Post, Milwaukee, WI
Woods, Michael .... (419) 245-6000
Health/Medical ED, Blade, Toledo, OH
Woods, Orian .... (515) 994-2349
PUB, ED, Prairie City News, Prairie City, IA
Woods, Paul .... (416) 364-0321
Chief-Ontario SRV, Canadian Press & Broadcast News, Toronto, ON
Woods, Peggy .... (419) 592-5055
ADV MGR-Legal; MGR-CR
Northwest Signal, Napoleon, OH
Woods, Robert W .... (509) 663-5161
TREAS, ASSOC PUB
Wenatchee World, Wenatchee, WA
Woods, Rufus .... (509) 663-5161
ED, Travel ED
Wenatchee World, Wenatchee, WA
Woods, Steven .... (801) 752-2121
MGR-MKTG/PROM, CIRC MGR
Herald Journal, Logan, UT
Woods, Terri Hayes .... (914) 694-9300
CIRC DIR-Sales/MKTG, Reporter Dispatch, White Plains, NY, Gannett Co. Inc.
Woods, Wilfred R .... (509) 663-5161
PRES, PUB
Wenatchee World, Wenatchee, WA
Woodside, Gary .... (209) 734-5821
MGR-SYS, Visalia Times-Delta, Visalia, CA
Gannett Co. Inc.
Woodson, Charles .... (510) 643-6614
Author, Woodson, Charles, Berkeley, CA
Woodson, Darryl .... (540) 463-3113
ED, News-Gazette, Lexington, VA
Woodward, A Mark .... (207) 990-8000
EPE, Bangor Daily News, Bangor, ME
Woodward, Bob .... (202) 334-6000
ASST MAN ED-Investigative
Washington Post, Washington, DC
Woodward, Dennis .... (607) 756-5665
PROD FRM-PR, Standard, Cortland, NY
Woodward, Don .... (801) 237-2188
MAN ED, Deseret News, Salt Lake City, UT
Woodward, Don .... (205) 582-3232
PUB, GM, Advertiser-Gleam, Guntersville, AL
Woodward, Earle .... (803) 775-6331
CIRC DIR, Item, Sumter, SC
Woodward Jr, F Robert .... (319) 588-5611
BC, Telegraph Herald, Dubuque, IA
Woodward, Nance .... (717) 255-8100
Living ED, Patriot-News, Harrisburg, PA
Woodward, Paul .... (910) 353-1171
Graphics ED/Art DIR
Daily News, Jacksonville, NC
Woodworth, Jim .... (617) 828-0006
ED, Canton Journal, Canton, MA
Woodworth, Robert C .... (816) 234-4141
PUB, Kansas City Star, Kansas City, MO
Woody, Frances .... (910) 227-0131
ASST MAN ED
Times News Publishing Co., Burlington, NC
Woody, Laura .... (561) 287-1550
ASST City ED, Stuart News, Stuart, FL
Woody, Stephen .... (919) 537-2505
PUB, PA, EPE
Daily Herald, Roanoke Rapids, NC
Wooge, Karen .... (913) 242-4700
ADV MGR-CLASS, Ottawa Herald, Ottawa, KS
Woolard, Cathy .... (316) 659-2080
PUB, ED
Edwards County Sentinel, Kinsley, KS
Woolard, Holly .... (415) 883-8600
Sports ED
Marin Independent Journal, Novato, CA
Woolard Jr, William G .... (937) 549-2800
PUB, ED, Signal, Manchester, OH
Woolbright, Richard R .... (703) 368-3101
CIRC DIR, Journal Messenger, Manassas, VA
Woolcock, Mary Sue .... (717) 784-2121
ADV MGR-CLASS
Press Enterprise, Bloomsburg, PA
Woolen, Terri .... (812) 424-7711
ADTX MGR
Evansville Courier Co., Evansville, IN
Wooley, Larry .... (334) 433-1551
SEC, ADV DIR, Press Register, Mobile, AL
Woolf, Gwen .... (540) 374-5000
Books ED
Free Lance-Star, Fredericksburg, VA
Woolf, R Lee .... (540) 374-5000
Sports ED
Free Lance-Star, Fredericksburg, VA
Woolley, Brian .... (608) 252-6100
DP MGR
Wisconsin State Journal, Madison, WI
Woolman, Ron .... (417) 256-9191
EDU ED
West Plains Daily Quill, West Plains, MO
Woolsey, Leonard .... (770) 942-6571
GM, Tri-County News, Douglasville, GA
Woolsey, Mary K .... (307) 634-3361
MAN ED
Wyoming Tribune-Eagle, Cheyenne, WY
Woolsey, Peter .... (403) 532-1110
PUB/BM
Daily Herald-Tribune, Grande Prairie, AB
Woolston, Deborah .... (360) 377-3711
Entertainment/Amusements Writer
Sun, Bremerton, WA
Woolum, Darlene .... (304) 235-4242
CIRC MGR
Williamson Daily News, Williamson, WV
Woolwine, Sam .... (423) 756-6900
ASST Sports ED
Chattanooga Free Press, Chattanooga, TN
Woolwine, Walter W .... (610) 371-5000
ADV DIR, Reading Times/Eagle, Reading, PA
Wooten, Alan .... (910) 353-1171
Sports ED, Daily News, Jacksonville, NC
Wooten, Frank .... (803) 577-7111
Radio/Television ED
Post and Courier, Charleston, SC
Wooten, Irene .... (304) 436-3144
PA, Welch Daily News, Welch, WV
Wooten, James .... (404) 526-5151
EPE (Journal)
Atlanta Journal-Constitution, Atlanta, GA
Wooten, Ken .... (904) 252-1511
CONT, Daytona Beach News-Journal, Daytona Beach, FL
Worcester, Adam .... (206) 932-0300
ED, West Seattle Herald, Seattle, WA
Word, Dave .... (757) 446-2000
DIR-Newsroom Staff Development
Virginian-Pilot, Norfolk, VA
Woreham, Fraser .... (306) 692-6441
PROD FRM-PR
Moose Jaw Times-Herald, Moose Jaw, SK
Work, Bob .... (610) 562-7515
MAN ED, Hamburg Item, Hamburg, PA
Work, Wayne .... (306) 764-4276
Rural Roots (Agriculture) ED
Prince Albert Daily Herald, Prince Albert, SK
Working, Russell .... (206) 597-8742
EDU Reporter (Education K-12)
News Tribune, Tacoma, WA
Workman, Beth .... (417) 843-5315
GM, Liberal News, Liberal, MO
Workman, Harold .... (717) 622-3456
PROD MGR-Electronic SYS,
Pottsville Republican & Evening Herald, Pottsville, PA
Workman, Jean .... (941) 335-0200
PROD MGR, News-Press, Fort Myers, FL
Workman, Tammy .... (334) 262-1611
ADV MGR-RT
Montgomery Advertiser, Montgomery, AL
Workman, Titus L .... (304) 292-6301
ADV DIR, Dominion Post, Morgantown, WV
Workman, Wayne .... (330) 725-4166
CIRC MGR
Medina County Gazette, Medina, OH
Worley, Dale .... (913) 346-5424
PUB, Osborne County Farmer, Osborne, KS
Worley, Joe .... (918) 581-8300
EX ED, Tulsa World, Tulsa, OK
Worley, Kathy .... (405) 223-2200
BM, CONT/CR MGR, PSL MGR, DP MGR
Daily Ardmoreite, Ardmore, OK
Worley, Ray .... (540) 962-2121
CIRC DIR, Virginian Review, Covington, VA
Worley, Tara .... (515) 472-4129
ADV MGR-CLASS
Fairfield Ledger, Fairfield, IA
Wornham, Traci .... (215) 536-6820
GM, Quakertown Free Press, Quakertown, PA
Woronchak, Gary .... (313) 943-4250
MAN ED
Press & Guide Newspapers, Dearborn, MI
Woronoff, Bob .... (919) 829-4500
TREAS, News & Observer, Raleigh, NC
Woronoff, David .... (910) 692-7271
PUB, ED, Pilot, Southern Pines, NC
Worrall, David .... (908) 686-7700
PUB, News-Record of Maplewood & South Orange, Maplewood, NJ
Worrall, Kent .... (813) 893-8111
PROD MGR-Facilities
St. Petersburg Times, St. Petersburg, FL
Worrall, Robyn .... (605) 352-6401
PROD MGR-MR
Huron Plainsman, Huron, SD
Worrell, Anne .... (540) 669-2181
PRES, Fashion ED, Herald-Courier Virginia Tennessean, Bristol, VA
Worrell, Bradley .... (303) 857-4440
ED, Fort Lupton Press, Brighton, CO
Worrell, Kathy S .... (402) 387-2844
PUB, Ainsworth Star-Journal, Ainsworth, NE
Worrell, Paul .... (919) 778-2211
ADV MGR-CLASS
Goldsboro News-Argus, Goldsboro, NC
Worrell, Rodney B .... (402) 387-2844
PUB, ED, Star-Journal, Ainsworth, NE
Worrell Jr, Thomas Eugene ..... (540) 669-2181
BC, Herald-Courier Virginia Tennessean, Bristol, VA
Wortel, Gary .... (615) 259-8000
ADV MGR-Display
Tennessean, Nashville, TN
Worth, Lynn .... (910) 372-8999
ED, Alleghany News, Sparta, NC
Worthington, Frances .... (864) 298-4100
Gardening ED
Greenville News, Greenville, SC
Worthington, John .... (609) 753-4500
MAN ED, Record-Breeze, Berlin, NJ
Worthington IV, John D .... (410) 838-4400
PUB, Weekender, Bel Air, MD
Woughter, Ron .... (412) 588-5000
ED, Record-Argus, Greenville, PA
Woutat, Don .... (213) 237-5000
Health/Drugs
Los Angeles Times, Los Angeles, CA
Wozney, Gilbert .... (307) 856-2244
PROD FRM-PR
Riverton Ranger, Riverton, WY
Wozniak, Mark P .... (812) 332-4401
TREAS/SEC, CONT, Herald-Times Inc, Bloomington, IN, Schurz Communications
Wozniak, Monica .... (412) 775-3200
PROD SUPV-COMP
Beaver County Times, Beaver, PA
Wray, Charles .... (609) 272-7000
City ED
Press of Atlantic City, Pleasantville, NJ
Wray, Dawn .... (205) 259-1020
CIRC MGR, Daily Sentinel, Scottsboro, AL
Wray, Ginny .... (540) 638-8801
ED, EDL Writer
Martinsville Bulletin, Martinsville, VA
Wray, Ralph L .... (716) 849-3434
Senior VP-Employee Relations
Buffalo News, Buffalo, NY
Wren, David .... (803) 626-8555
BUS ED, Sun News, Myrtle Beach, SC
Wrench, Morris .... (816) 234-4141
PROD MGR-Quality Assurance
Kansas City Star, Kansas City, MO
Wright, Andree .... (819) 362-7049
PUB, La Feuille d'Erable, Plessisville, QC
Wright, April L .... (205) 251-5158
GM, Birmingham Times, Birmingham, AL
Wright, Bart .... (360) 377-3711
Sports ED, Sun, Bremerton, WA
Wright, Ben .... (706) 324-5526
Fashion/Style ED, Features ED
Columbus Ledger-Enquirer, Columbus, GA
Wright, Ben .... (616) 279-7488
PROD SUPV-PR, Three Rivers Commercial-News, Three Rivers, MI
Wright, Betty Jane .... (914) 294-6111
PUB, Independent Republican, Goshen, NY
Wright, Bob .... (505) 763-3431
MAN ED
Clovis News Journal, Clovis, NM
Wright, Brent .... (204) 638-4420
PUB, GM, Dauphin Herald, Dauphin, MB
Wright, Carl L .... (540) 981-3100
TREAS, PA, Roanoke Times, Roanoke, VA
Wright, Carol .... (561) 820-3800
BUS ED
Palm Beach Daily News, Palm Beach, FL
Wright, Cindy .... (330) 332-4601
PROD FRM-COMP, Salem News, Salem, OH
Wright, Colleen .... (815) 432-5227
ADV DIR, Iroquois County's Times-Republic, Watseka, IL
Wright, Dalton C .... (417) 532-9131
PRES, Lebanon Daily Record, Lebanon, MO
Wright, Debra .... (910) 323-4848
CIRC MGR
Fayetteville Observer-Times, Fayetteville, NC
Wright, Diane .... (206) 339-3000
Books ED, Herald, Everett, WA
Wright, Dianne .... (313) 222-6400
DIR-Creative SRV
Detroit Newspapers, Detroit, MI
Wright, Dick .... (614) 461-5000
Cartoonist
Columbus Dispatch, Columbus, OH
Wright, Don .... (561) 820-4100
EDL Cartoonist
Palm Beach Post, West Palm Beach, FL
Wright, Donald F .... (213) 237-3700
Sr VP-Eastern Newspapers
Times Mirror Co., Los Angeles, CA
Wright, Dru .... (803) 771-6161
MGR-CR, State, Columbia, SC
Wright Jr, Earl .... (209) 298-8081
PUB, ED, Clovis Independent, Clovis, CA
Wright, Fred .... (250) 758-4917
PROD FRM-Composing
Nanaimo Daily Free Press, Nanaimo, BC
Wright, Gail .... (573) 765-3391
PUB, ED, Richland Mirror, Richland, MO
Wright, George .... (402) 475-4200
ASST News ED
Lincoln Journal Star, Lincoln, NE
Wright, Gordon .... (403) 527-1101
MAN ED, Photo DEPT MGR
Medicine Hat News, Medicine Hat, AB
Wright, Grant .... (204) 677-4534
ED, Nickel Belt News, Thompson, MB
Wright, Heidi .... (406) 496-5500
CONT/Distribution, DP MGR
Montana Standard, Butte, MT
Wright, Jaye .... (407) 242-3500
Action Line/Help ED
Florida Today, Melbourne, FL
Wright, Jeff .... (415) 777-5700
CONT, San Francisco Newspaper Agency, San Francisco, CA
Wright, Jerry M .... (619) 248-7878
PUB, Lucerne Leader, Lucerne Valley, CA
Wright, Jim .... (214) 977-8222
COL-EDL Page
Dallas Morning News, Dallas, TX
Wright, Jim .... (801) 625-4200
Outdoors ED, Standard-Examiner, Ogden, UT
Wright, Joan .... (204) 677-4534
PUB, Nickel Belt News, Thompson, MB
Wright, Joe .... (330) 364-5577
Wire ED
Times Reporter, New Philadelphia, OH
Wright III, John P .... (903) 893-8181
PUB, PA, Herald Democrat, Sherman, TX
Wright, Joye .... (405) 588-3862
ED, Apache News, Apache, OK
Wright, Julie .... (316) 268-6000
Public Life ED
Wichita Eagle, Wichita, KS
Wright, Larry .... (313) 222-2300
Cartoonist, Detroit News, Detroit, MI
Wright, Margaret .... (804) 979-0373
GM, Albermarle Tribune, Charlottesville, VA
Wright, Mary Ellen .... (717) 291-8811
BUS ED, Lancaster Intelligencer Journal/New Era/Sunday News, Lancaster, PA
Wright, Michael .... (806) 273-5611
Sports ED, Borger News-Herald, Borger, TX
Wright, Mike .... (352) 563-6363
News ED
Citrus County Chronicle, Crystal River, FL
Wright, Nancy .... (812) 865-3242
MAN ED, Progress Examiner, Orleans, IN
Wright, Pam .... (205) 362-1000
ADV DIR, Daily Home, Talladega, AL
Wright, Pat .... (903) 537-2228
MAN ED
Mt. Vernon Optic-Herald, Mount Vernon, TX
Wright, Peg Churchill .... (518) 374-4141
Entertainment/Amusements ED
Daily Gazette, Schenectady, NY
Wright, Peter .... (502) 886-4444
Photo DEPT MGR
Kentucky New Era, Hopkinsville, KY
Wright, Polly .... (209) 943-6397
ADV MGR-CLASS, Record, Stockton, CA
Wright, R .... (205) 353-4612
Farm/Agriculture ED
Decatur Daily, Decatur, AL
Wright, Randy .... (208) 377-6200
Graphics ED/Art DIR
Idaho Statesman, Boise, ID
Wright, Robert .... (320) 632-2345
GM, Morrison County Record, Little Falls, MN
Wright, Robert E .... (817) 562-2868
ED, Mexia Daily News, Mexia, TX
Wright, Robert W .... (903) 537-2228
PUB
Mt. Vernon Optic-Herald, Mount Vernon, TX
Wright, Roosevelt .... (318) 388-1310
PUB, ED, Monroe Free Press, Monroe, LA
Wright, Sarah .... (617) 426-3000
Fashion ED, Sunday Magazine
Boston Herald, Boston, MA
Wright, Scott .... (417) 623-3480
ADV MGR-RT, Joplin Globe, Joplin, MO
Wright, Sharon .... (502) 827-2000
EDU ED, Gleaner, Henderson, KY
Wright, Stan .... (405) 588-3862
PUB, Apache News, Apache, OK
Wright, Steve .... (706) 278-1011
CONT, Daily Citizen-News, Dalton, GA
Wright, Susan .... (614) 965-3891
ED, Sunbury News, Sunbury, OH
Wright, Susan Slater .... (219) 785-2234
ED, Regional News, La Crosse, IN
Wright, Susann .... (817) 645-2441
ASSOC ED
Cleburne Times-Review, Cleburne, TX

Wri Who's Where-254

Wright, Suzannah .... (217) 465-6424
School ED
Paris Daily Beacon-News, Paris, IL
Wright, Terry .... (517) 348-6811
ED, Crawford County Avalanche, Grayling, MI
Wright, Tom .... (205) 353-4612
ED, EPE, Decatur Daily, Decatur, AL
Wright, Warren .... (719) 634-1593
ED, Daily Transcript, Colorado Springs, CO
Wright, Wilbur .... (912) 744-4200
PROD ASST DIR
Macon Telegraph, Macon, GA
Wright, Zeb .... (304) 348-5140
Garden ED, Daily Mail, Charleston, WV
Wrighthouse, Randy .... (541) 482-3456
Picture ED, Daily Tidings, Ashland, OR
Wrightson, Kathy .... (408) 255-7500
GM, Cupertino Courier, Cupertino, CA
Wrinkle, Chris .... (417) 581-3541
ED
Christian County Headliner News, Ozark, MO
Wrinkle, Jim .... (419) 636-1111
Sports ED, Bryan Times, Bryan, OH
Wroblewski, Dan .... (817) 387-3811
CIRC DIR
Denton Record-Chronicle, Denton, TX
Wroblewski, Larry .... (716) 893-5771
MAN ED
Polish-American Journal, Buffalo, NY
Wroblewski, Mike .... (414) 542-2501
Graphics ED
Waukesha County Freeman, Waukesha, WI
Wrolstad, Jay .... (607) 277-7000
MAN ED, Ithaca Times, Ithaca, NY
Wuchner, James .... (812) 482-2424
CIRC MGR, Herald, Jasper, IN
Wuebker, Margie .... (937) 498-2111
Features ED, Living/ Lifestyle ED,
Sidney Daily News, Sidney, OH
Wuennenberg, Eric .... (608) 634-4317
ED, Times, Westby, WI
Wujcik, Steve .... (609) 871-8000
News ED
Burlington County Times, Willingboro, NJ
Wunderle, Angela .... (913) 455-3466
MAN ED, Clifton News-Tribune, Clifton, KS
Wunderlich, Linda .... (909) 676-4315
PUB, ADV MGR, MGR-MKTG/PROM
Californian, Temecula, CA
Wundram, William .... (319) 383-2200
ASSOC ED, Quad-City Times, Davenport, IA
Wunstel, Linda .... (504) 383-1111
DIR-MKTG/PROM
Advocate, Baton Rouge, LA
Wuntch, Philip .... (214) 977-8222
Films Critic, Dallas Morning News, Dallas, TX
Wurth, Julie .... (217) 351-5252
EDU ED, News-Gazette, Champaign, IL
Wurth, Julie .... (541) 776-4411
Features ED, Sunday ED
Mail Tribune, Medford, OR
Wurzbach, Karl .... (717) 829-7100
CIRC DIR, Times Leader, Wilkes-Barre, PA
Wurzer, Buzz .... (212) 649-2000
MKTG Development MGR
Hearst Newspapers, New York, NY
Wurzer, Mark .... (213) 237-5000
ADV DIR-NTL
Los Angeles Times, Los Angeles, CA
Wyan, Roger .... (209) 722-1511
Chief Photographer
Merced Sun-Star, Merced, CA
Wyand, Doug .... (209) 582-0471
PROD FRM-PR
Hanford Sentinel, Hanford, CA
Wyant, Corbin A .... (941) 262-3161
PRES, PUB, Naples Daily News, Naples, FL
Wyatt, Charles W .... (864) 488-1016
ED, Cherokee Chronicle, Gaffney, SC
Wyatt, Don .... (612) 222-5011
Senior ED-Minneapolis & Suburbs
St. Paul Pioneer Press, St. Paul, MN
Wyatt, Doug .... (912) 236-9511
Arts/Books ED, Television ED
Savannah Morning News, Savannah, GA
Wyatt, Elizabeth .... (616) 964-7161
EDU ED
Battle Creek Enquirer, Battle Creek, MI
Wyatt, James .... (609) 234-0200
GM, Record-Breeze, Blackwood, NJ
Wyatt, Ken .... (517) 787-2300
EDL Writer
Jackson Citizen Patriot, Jackson, MI
Wyatt, Louis .... (501) 763-4461
PROD MGR, PROD FRM-COMP
Blytheville Courier News, Blytheville, AR
Wyatt, T L .... (512) 476-0082
PUB, ED, Villager, Austin, TX
Wyche, Fred .... (505) 823-7777
PROD DIR, Albuquerque Publishing Co.,
Albuquerque, NM
Wyckoff, Edith Hay .... (516) 676-1434
PUB, ED, Leader, Locust Valley, NY
Wyckoff, Richard .... (814) 532-5199
PROD DIR-OPER
Tribune-Democrat, Johnstown, PA
Wycliff, Don .... (312) 222-3232
EPE, Chicago Tribune, Chicago, IL
Wyke, Paul .... (604) 656-1151
ED, Peninsula News Review, Sidney, BC
Wykle, Nancy .... (301) 459-3131
News ED
Prince George's Journal, Lanham, MD
Wylie, Faith .... (918) 443-2428
PUB, Oologah Lake Leader, Oologah, OK
Wylie, Margaret .... (501) 754-2005
ED, Johnson County Graphic, Clarksville, AR
Wylie, Nancy .... (541) 776-4411
PROD MGR-Creative Services
Mail Tribune, Medford, OR
Wylie, Ron .... (501) 754-2005
GM, Johnson County Graphic, Clarksville, AR
Wylie II, John .... (918) 443-2428
PUB, ED, Oologah Lake Leader, Oologah, OK
Wyman, Max .... (604) 732-2111
Books ED, Vancouver Sun, Vancouver, BC
Wymer, Cathy .... (618) 234-1000
ADV MGR-CLASS
Belleville News-Democrat, Belleville, IL
Wyne, Mike .... (206) 464-2111
ASST Suburban ED
Seattle Times, Seattle, WA
Wyngarden, Mike .... (616) 669-2700
MAN ED, Westside Advance, Jenison, MI
Wynn, Dennis .... (210) 686-4343
CIRC MGR-Single Copy, Monitor, McAllen, TX
Wynn, Eric .... (214) 977-8222
CIRC MGR-Single Copy
Dallas Morning News, Dallas, TX
Wynn, Larry .... (305) 350-2111
VP-Advertising, Miami Herald, Miami, FL
Wynn, Liz .... (317) 584-4501
Features/Lifestyle ED, Women's ED
News-Gazette, Winchester, IN
Wynn, Randall .... (205) 232-2720
CIRC MGR, News Courier, Athens, AL
Wynn, Randy .... (202) 628-2157
News ED
Thomson News Service, Washington, DC
Wynn, Wycliff .... (904) 362-1734
GM, Suwannee Democrat, Live Oak, FL
Wynne, John O .... (757) 446-2010
PRES/CEO
Landmark Communications Inc., Norfolk, VA
Wynns, Patsy .... (615) 444-3952
ADV MGR-CLASS, Democrat, Lebanon, TN
Wysocki, Gail .... (313) 222-6400
Sales DIR-ADV Development
Detroit Newspapers, Detroit, MI
Wysocki, Jim .... (405) 235-3100
CIRC MGR
Journal Record, Oklahoma City, OK
Wysong, Breena .... (317) 747-5700
Librarian, Star Press, Muncie, IN
Wysong, Pippa B .... (416) 463-0257
PRES/Children's SCI COL
Ask Pippa, Toronto, ON
Wyss, Cyndi .... (815) 459-4040
ED-McHenry
Northwest Herald, Crystal Lake, IL
Wyss, Jack .... (719) 544-3520
ADV DIR-MKTG, DIR-MKTG/PROM
Pueblo Chieftain, Pueblo, CO

X

Xiques, Linda .... (415) 383-4500
MAN ED, Pacific Sun, Mill Valley, CA
Xu, Chao .... (312) 222-3232
Webmaster, Chicago Tribune, Chicago, IL

Y

Yablonski, Steve .... (315) 343-3800
City ED, Palladium-Times, Oswego, NY
Yack, Patrick A .... (910) 373-7000
ED, News & Record, Greensboro, NC
Yackamouih, Nick .... (941) 763-3134
CIRC DIR
Daily Okeechobee News, Okeechobee, FL
Yackley, Kris .... (320) 255-8700
ADV CNR-NTL, Times, St. Cloud, MN
Yacoe, Don .... (212) 803-8200
EIC, Bond Buyer, New York, NY
Yacubeck, Gary .... (717) 455-3636
ADV DIR, Standard-Speaker, Hazleton, PA
Yadamec, Jerry .... (320) 255-8700
SYS ED, St. Cloud Times, St. Cloud, MN
Yaeger, Bernard .... (970) 675-5033
PUB, Rangely Times, Rangely, CO
Yaeger, Geary J .... (320) 255-8700
CIRC DIR, St. Cloud Times, St. Cloud, MN
Yahner, John .... (717) 326-1551
ADV DIR, Sun-Gazette, Williamsport, PA
Yakata, Sharon .... (212) 556-1234
Group DIR-Community Affairs
New York Times, New York, NY
Yakola, Kenneth P .... (508) 775-1200
Building MGR, Cape Cod Times, Hyannis, MA
Yaltiera, Eloy .... (416) 441-1405
North America Photographer
Fotopress Independent News Service International (FPINS), Toronto, ON
Yamada, Ted .... (310) 540-5511
Buyer, Daily Breeze, Torrance, CA
Copley Press Inc.
Yamamoto, Robert S .... (217) 235-5656
ADV DIR, PROD MGR, Mattoon Journal-Gazette, Mattoon, IL, Howard Publications
Yamashita, Michael .... (415) 861-5019
GM, Bay Area Reporter, San Francisco, CA
Yance, Eric .... (334) 433-1551
ADV MGR-CLASS
Mobile Press Register, Mobile, AL
Yancey, Jim .... (501) 327-6621
CONT, Log Cabin Democrat, Conway, AR
Yancey, Kitty .... (703) 276-3400
Entertainment ED, Trends ED
USA Today, Arlington, VA
Yancey, Lisa .... (573) 546-3917
GM, Mountain Echo, Ironton, MO
Yandle, Carlyn .... (604) 273-7744
ED, Richmond Review, Richmond, BC
Yandle, Pam .... (918) 335-8200
CIRC DIR
Examiner-Enterprise, Bartlesville, OK
Yang, Dr Cliff .... (718) 461-7668
PUB, Pacific Times, Flushing, NY
Yang, Wei .... (212) 343-9717
GM, New Jersey China Times, Edison, NJ
Yanick, Randy .... (603) 298-8711
CIRC MGR, Valley News, White River Jct., VT
Yanish, Donna .... (408) 920-5000
Senior Online ED
San Jose Mercury News, San Jose, CA
Yankun, Richard .... (617) 929-2000
CIRC MGR-Transportation/Distribution
Boston Globe, Boston, MA
Yanni, John .... (619) 337-3400
ADV MGR-Display
Imperial Valley Press, El Centro, CA
Yanos, Larry .... (301) 733-5131
Sports ED, Morning Herald, Hagerstown, MD
Yanoshik, David .... (610) 258-7171
ADV MGR-RT, Express-Times, Easton, PA
Yarber, Danny .... (601) 428-0551
CIRC MGR, Laurel Leader-Call, Laurel, MS
Yarber, Richard .... (423) 472-5041
PROD FRM-PR, Daily Banner, Cleveland, TN
Yarborough, J R .... (706) 724-0851
CIRC MGR-City/County
Augusta Chronicle, Augusta, GA
Yarborough, Leigh M .... (601) 328-2424
Fashion/Society ED
Commercial Dispatch, Columbus, MS
Yarborough, Patricia .... (909) 621-4761
MAN ED, Claremont Courier, Claremont, CA
Yarborough, Ramon L .... (910) 323-4848
PRES, PUB
Fayetteville Observer-Times, Fayetteville, NC
Yarbro, Kathryn .... (704) 735-3031
MAN ED, Times-News, Lincolnton, NC
Yarbrough, Charlotte .... (419) 435-6641
PROD MGR, Review Times, Fostoria, OH
Yarbrough, Ernest .... (770) 483-7108
ADV MGR, Rockdale Citizen, Conyers, GA
Yarbrough, Jim .... (704) 531-9988
PUB, Q Notes, Charlotte, NC
Yarbrough, Paul .... (805) 564-5200
Copy Desk Chief, Santa Barbara News-Press, Santa Barbara, CA
Yarbrough, Ron .... (209) 634-9141
CIRC DIR, Turlock Journal, Turlock, CA
Yardley, Donna .... (360) 577-2500
Librarian, Daily News, Longview, WA
Yarley, Pam .... (205) 325-2222
PROD MGR-Dispatch
Birmingham News, Birmingham, AL
Yarnell, A Bruce .... (614) 439-3531
Sunday CNR
Daily Jeffersonian, Cambridge, OH
Yarnold, David .... (408) 920-5000
MAN ED
San Jose Mercury News, San Jose, CA
Yasick, Ed .... (412) 465-5555
PROD MGR-SYS, PROD SUPT-Mechanical
Indiana Gazette, Indiana, PA
Yasuda, Midori .... (310) 832-0221
Librarian, News-Pilot, San Pedro, CA
Yataco, Johnny .... (202) 667-8881
PUB, Washington Hispanic, Washington, DC
Yates, Bob .... (214) 977-8222
Sports ED, Dallas Morning News, Dallas, TX
Yates, David .... (514) 987-2222
Senior BUS ED, Gazette, Montreal, QC
Yates, Franklin .... (615) 684-1200
PRES
Shelbyville Times-Gazette, Shelbyville, TN
Yates, Mrs. Franklin ....(615) 684-1200
VP, Times-GAzette, Shelbyville, TN
Yates, John .... (716) 232-7100
PROD MGR, Rochester Democrat and Chronicle; Times-Union, Rochester, NY
Yates, Mrs Johnaie .... (615) 684-1200
TREAS, Times-Gazette, Shelbyville, TN
Yates, Lauren .... (502) 255-3205
ED, Trimble Banner-Democrat, Bedford, KY
Yates, Peter S .... (804) 793-2311
PUB, Danville Register & Bee, Danville, VA
Yates, Phil .... (219) 347-0400
PROD FRM-PR, News-Sun, Kendallville, IN
Yates, Sarah .... (801) 723-3471
ED
Box Elder News Journal, Brigham City, UT
Yates, Scott .... (970) 669-5050
EDU ED, Daily Reporter-Herald, Loveland, CO
Yawger, Doane .... (209) 634-9141
ED, EPE, Turlock Journal, Turlock, CA
Yazbec, Val .... (309) 764-4344
ADV MGR-Inside Sales, Dispatch, Moline, IL
Small Newspaper Group Inc.
Yeager, Janet .... (304) 369-5175
PUB, ED, Hometown News, Madison, WV
Yeager, Melanie .... (806) 376-4488
EDU ED, Amarillo Daily News/Globe Times, Amarillo, TX
Yeaman, Kevin .... (303) 820-1010
MGR-Purchasing, Denver Post, Denver, CO
Year, Peggy .... (402) 254-3997
PUB, Cedar County News, Hartington, NE
Yearty, James C (Kit) .... (903) 757-3311
PROD DIR, News-Journal, Longview, TX
Yeates, Andrew J K .... (604) 838-7229
PUB, Enderby Commoner, Enderby, BC
Yee, Laura .... (216) 999-4500
Food ED, Plain Dealer, Cleveland, OH
Yee, Margie .... (217) 446-1000
Food ED, Health ED
Commercial News, Danville, IL
Yeger, Andrea .... (601) 896-2100
MAN ED, Sun Herald, Biloxi, MS
Yelaja, Priti .... (519) 894-2231
EDU, Record, Kitchener, ON
Yelland, David .... (212) 930-8000
FIN ED, New York Post, New York, NY
Yelton, Karen .... (916) 321-1000
ED-Neighbors
Sacramento Bee, Sacramento, CA
Yempuku, Paul S .... (808) 845-2255
PUB, ED, Hawaii Hochi, Honolulu, HI
Yeninas, Joseph .... (212) 837-7000
Graphics ED, Journal of Commerce & Commercial, New York, NY
Yenkel, Penny .... (308) 635-2045
PUB, ED
Business Farmer-Stockman, Scottsbluff, NE
Yepsen, David .... (515) 284-8000
Political ED
Des Moines Register, Des Moines, IA
Yetter, Frank E .... (617) 937-8000
PUB, Cambridge Chronicle, Woburn, MA
Yetter, Vicki .... (937) 335-5634
ADV DIR, Troy Daily News/Miami Valley Sunday News, Troy, OH
Yezak, Betty .... (817) 746-7033
PUB, ED, Bremond Press, Bremond, TX
Yim, Jenny .... (206) 461-1300
ED, Beacon Hill News/The South District Journal, Seattle, WA
Yinghuang, Zhu .... (212) 488-9677
ED, China Daily, New York, NY
Yingling, Steve .... (916) 541-3880
Sports ED
Tahoe Daily Tribune, South Lake Tahoe, CA
Yoachum, Susan .... (415) 777-1111
Political ED
San Francisco Chronicle, San Francisco, CA
Yoakum, Lois .... (606) 348-3338
PUB, Wayne County Outlook, Monticello, KY
Yoakum, Ron .... (217) 824-2233
Sports ED, Taylorville Daily Breeze-Courier, Taylorville, IL
Yocun, Mark .... (814) 724-6370
ADV DIR, Meadville Tribune, Meadville, PA
Yoder, Bob .... (219) 874-7211
PROD MGR-Press
News Dispatch, Michigan City, IN
Yoder, Bruce .... (307) 362-3736
MAN ED, News ED, Picture ED
Daily Rocket-Miner, Rock Springs, WY
Yoder, Mike .... (913) 843-1000
Photo DEPT MGR
Journal-World, Lawrence, KS
Yoder, Shannon .... (812) 254-0480
EDU ED
Washington Times-Herald, Washington, IN
Yoder, Sheri .... (864) 582-4511
DIR-Human Resources
Herald-Journal, Spartanburg, SC
Yoder, Steve .... (212) 416-2000
BU Chief-Tokyo
Wall Street Journal, New York, NY
Yoder, Tammy .... (717) 637-3736
CIRC MGR, Evening Sun, Hanover, PA
Yoder, Thomas K .... (202) 332-2100
PUB, Washington City Paper, Washington, DC
Yoh, Kim .... (419) 238-2285
PROD FRM-PR
Times-Bulletin, Van Wert, OH

Copyright ©1997 by the Editor & Publisher Co.

255-Who's Where **Zav**

Yoho, Steve .... (219) 461-8444
PROD MGR-Technology
Fort Wayne Newspapers Inc., Fort Wayne, IN
Yong, Aries .... (415) 826-1100
GM, San Francisco Independent, San Francisco, CA
Yook, Kil Won .... (312) 463-1050
ED, Korea Times, Chicago, IL
Yoon, Hyun-Jae .... (416) 537-3474
ED, Minjoong Shinmoon, Toronto, ON
Yopp, Mike .... (919) 829-4500
MAN ED-Daily
News & Observer, Raleigh, NC
York, Arnold G .... (310) 456-5507
PUB, ED, Malibu Times, Malibu, CA
York, Bob .... (413) 772-0261
BUS ED, Recorder, Greenfield, MA
York, Cheryl .... (419) 562-3333
CONT, Telegraph-Forum, Bucyrus, OH
York, Dale .... (317) 529-1111
PROD MGR-SYS
Courier-Times, New Castle, IN
York, Emily .... (513) 829-7900
ED, Fairfield Echo, Fairfield, OH
York, Gary .... (508) 744-0600
CONT, Salem Evening News, Beverly, MA
York, Janie .... (512) 392-2458
CIRC MGR
San Marcos Daily Record, San Marcos, TX
York, Peter .... (208) 733-0931
ADV DIR, ADTX MGR
Times-News, Twin Falls, ID
York, Robert .... (310) 540-5511
Photo ED, Daily Breeze, Torrance, CA
York, William .... (603) 536-1311
GM, ED, Record-Enterprise, Plymouth, NH
Yosay, Bob .... (330) 747-1471
Photo ED, Vindicator, Youngstown, OH
Yoset, Jack .... (814) 724-6370
EPE, Meadville Tribune, Meadville, PA
Yoshida, Stanley N .... (716) 232-7100
CIRC VP, Rochester Democrat and Chronicle; Rochester, NY Times-Union, Rochester, NY
Yoshihara, Nancy .... (213) 237-5000
EDL Writer
Los Angeles Times, Los Angeles, CA
Yost, Aaron .... (541) 926-2211
ASST Sports ED
Albany Democrat-Herald, Albany, OR
Yost, Dana .... (320) 235-1150
Regional ED
West Central Tribune, Willmar, MN
Yost, Elizabeth .... (402) 283-4267
PUB, ED, Coleridge Blade, Coleridge, NE
Yost, Julie .... (618) 463-2500
CONT, Telegraph, Alton, IL
Yost, Nicholas S .... (610) 371-5000
News ED, Reading Times/Eagle, Reading, PA
Yost, Patricia .... (508) 997-7411
Controller, Standard Times, New Bedford, MA
Yost, Patrick .... (706) 342-2424
MAN ED, Madisonian, Madison, GA
Yost, Philip .... (408) 920-5000
Chief EDL Writer
San Jose Mercury News, San Jose, CA
Yost, Rae .... (507) 423-6239
ED, Tri-County News, Cottonwood, MN
Yost, Robert .... (317) 423-5511
PROD DIR, Journal and Courier, Lafayette, IN
Yost, Robert .... (402) 283-4267
PUB, ED, Coleridge Blade, Coleridge, NE
Yostt, Tim .... (937) 878-3993
CIRC DIR
Fairborn Daily Herald, Fairborn, OH
Youmans, Fred .... (209) 578-2000
ASSOC ED, Modesto Bee, Modesto, CA
Young, Andrew R .... (216) 329-7000
EX ED, Chronicle-Telegram, Elyria, OH
Young, Ann .... (815) 232-1171
ADV MGR-CLASS
Journal-Standard, Freeport, IL
Young, Brenda .... (419) 468-1117
MGR-EDU SRV, BUS/FIN ED, EDL Writer, Historical ED, News ED, School ED
Galion Inquirer, Galion, OH
Young, Bruce .... (518) 891-2600
DP MGR, Adirondack Daily Enterprise, Saranac Lake, NY
Young, Carol .... (401) 277-7000
Deputy EX ED
Providence Journal-Bulletin, Providence, RI
Young, Chris .... (508) 685-1000
EDU ED, Eagle-Tribune, North Andover, MA
Young, Clifford .... (213) 291-9486
PUB, Herald Dispatch, Los Angeles, CA
Young, David T .... (616) 945-9554
ED, Sun & News, Hastings, MI
Young, Denise .... (716) 693-1000
City ED
Tonawanda News, North Tonawanda, NY
Young, Elizabeth .... (203) 453-2711
ED, Shore Line Times, Guilford, CT
Young, Ellen .... (319) 478-2323
ED, Traer Star-Clipper, Traer, IA
Young, Eric .... (937) 225-2000
CONT, Dayton Daily News, Dayton, OH
Young, Frances .... (818) 854-8700
ED, San Dimas/La Verne Highlander, West Covina, CA
Young, Gary .... (520) 634-2241
GM, Verde Independent, Cottonwood, AZ
Young, Gary .... (704) 758-7381
PROD MGR-PR
Lenoir News-Topic, Lenoir, NC
Young, Gene .... (717) 767-6397
PROD MGR-Plant
York Newspaper Company, York, PA
Young, Gwen .... (516) 843-2020
Criminal Justice ED
Newsday, Melville, NY
Young, Hal .... (405) 475-3311
CIRC MGR-EDU
Daily Oklahoman, Oklahoma City, OK
Young, J Alan .... (803) 435-8422
PUB, ED, Manning Times, Manning, SC
Young, James A .... (219) 533-2151
ADV DIR, Goshen News, Goshen, IN
Young, James .... (609) 272-7000
MGR-MIS
Press of Atlantic City, Pleasantville, NJ
Young Jr, James G .... (219) 287-1001
Chief Financial EX/TREAS
Schurz Communications Inc., South Bend, IN
Young, Jean .... (803) 626-8555
MGR-FIN, Sun News, Myrtle Beach, SC
Young, Jeff .... (515) 782-2141
MAN ED
Creston News-Advertiser, Creston, IA
Young, Jeffrey A .... (717) 291-8811
Sports ED, Lancaster Intelligencer Journal/ New Era/Sunday News, Lancaster, PA
Young, JoAnne .... (402) 475-4200
ASST City ED, Health Policy Reporter
Lincoln Journal Star, Lincoln, NE
Young, John .... (604) 847-3266
ED, Interior News, Smithers, BC
Young, John .... (817) 757-5757
Opinion Page ED
Waco Tribune-Herald, Waco, TX
Young, John .... (905) 523-5800
PUB
Hamilton Mountain News, Stoney Creek, ON
Young, John .... (306) 747-2442
ED, Shellbrook Chronicle, Shellbrook, SK
Young, Joseph O .... (816) 338-2195
PUB, ED, Glasgow Missourian, Glasgow, MO
Young, Julia .... (800) 424-4747
Database OPER MGR, Tribune Media Services-Television Listings, Glens Falls, NY
Young, Karen .... (515) 898-7554
PUB, ED, Seymour Herald, Seymour, IA
Young, Karinne .... (919) 778-2211
Environmental ED
Goldsboro News-Argus, Goldsboro, NC
Young, Kay .... (501) 534-3400
EDU/School ED
Pine Bluff Commercial, Pine Bluff, AR
Young, Kay Lyn .... (806) 684-2637
PUB, Kress Chronicle, Kress, TX
Young, Kerry .... (510) 757-2525
Sports ED, Ledger Dispatch, Antioch, CA
Young, Lawrence .... (817) 461-6397
MAN ED
Arlington Morning News, Arlington, TX
Young, Linda .... (318) 433-3000
Photo ED, State ED, Lake Charles American Press, Lake Charles, LA
Young, Lisa .... (941) 748-0411
Graphics ED
Bradenton Herald, Bradenton, FL
Young, Malie K .... (808) 528-1475
GM, Honolulu Weekly, Honolulu, HI
Young, Marilyn .... (317) 622-1212
Automotive ED, Books/Music ED, Entertainment/Amusements ED, Features ED
Herald Bulletin, Anderson, IN
Young, Marlene B .... (301) 662-1177
SEC, Frederick Post/News, Frederick, MD
Young, Neely .... (770) 478-5753
PUB, ED, Clayton News/Daily, Jonesboro, GA
Young, Paul .... (808) 329-9311
Outdoors/ Sports ED
West Hawaii Today, Kailua-Kona, HI
Young, Paul .... (408) 372-3311
ADV MGR-NTL/Co-op
Monterey County Herald, Monterey, CA
Young, Rich .... (518) 792-9914
TransEdit Product MGR
TV Data, Queensbury, NY
Young, Richard .... (412) 981-6100
Travel ED, Herald, Sharon, PA
Young, Rob .... (414) 684-4433
Political/RE ED
Herald Times Reporter, Manitowoc, WI
Young, Ruth .... (816) 338-2195
ED, Glasgow Missourian, Glasgow, MO
Young Jr, Sam .... (602) 271-8000
DIR-SRV
Phoenix Newspapers Inc., Phoenix, AZ
Young, Sarah .... (318) 433-3000
DP MGR, Lake Charles American Press, Lake Charles, LA
Young, Susan .... (510) 208-6300
Television ED, Oakland Tribune, Oakland, CA
MediaNews Inc. (Alameda Newspapers)
Young, Thomas C .... (517) 785-4214
PUB, ED
Montmorency County Tribune, Atlanta, MI
Young, Troy .... (519) 983-5301
PUB, ED, Weekly Times, Orono, ON
Young-Oda, Lucy .... (808) 525-8000
City ED, Honolulu Star-Bulletin, Honolulu, HI
Youngblood, R W .... (713) 220-7171
TREAS, Houston Chronicle, Houston, TX
Youngblood, Richard .... (612) 673-4000
COL-BUS, Star Tribune, Minneapolis, MN
Younger, June .... (303) 288-7987
ED
Commerce City Express, Commerce City, CO
Younger, Willa .... (417) 623-3480
Food ED, Joplin Globe, Joplin, MO
Youngerberg, Lon .... (507) 625-4451
PROD FRM-PR, Free Press, Mankato, MN
Younghaus, Paul .... (803) 551-1551
ED, Lake Edition, Irmo, SC
Youngman, Dan .... (903) 675-5626
ADV MGR-CLASS, ADV CNR-RT Sales
Athens Daily Review, Athens, TX
Youngman, Owen .... (312) 222-3232
DIR-Interactive Media
Chicago Tribune, Chicago, IL
Youngquist, Jeff .... (203) 876-6800
ED, Hamden Chronicle, Milford, CT
Younker, Cathy .... (217) 379-4313
CIRC MGR, Paxton Daily Record, Paxton, IL
Younkin, Linda .... (502) 227-4556
Sports ED, State Journal, Frankfort, KY
Yourse, Denyse .... (412) 775-3200
Religion E
Beaver County Times, Beaver, PA
Youso, Ronald .... (320) 968-7220
PUB, ED, Benton County News, Foley, MN
Youst, Roy .... (614) 654-1321
ED, Automotive ED, EPE
Lancaster Eagle-Gazette, Lancaster, OH
Yowitz, Mike .... (406) 587-4491
News ED, Daily Chronicle, Bozeman, MT
Yowts, Maj James R .... (334) 347-9533
ED, Army Flier, Enterprise, AL
Yozwiak, Steve .... (602) 271-8000
EDU/Environment Writer
Arizona Republic, Phoenix, AZ
Yu, Sam .... (301) 662-1177
Chief Photographer, Photo ED
Frederick Post/The News, Frederick, MD
Yucha, M Philip .... (717) 648-4641
PUB/GM, PA, News-Item, Shamokin, PA
Yucis, Edward .... (609) 691-5000
CONT, Daily Journal, Vineland, NJ
Yuen, Mike .... (808) 525-8000
Political Reporter
Honolulu Star-Bulletin, Honolulu, HI
Yules, Susan Chrein .... (416) 814-4239
VP-Financial Planning & BUS Development
Thomson Newspapers, Toronto, ON
Yung, Cameron .... (518) 792-9914
Regional Sales DIR
TV Data, Queensbury, NY
Yung, Katherine .... (313) 222-2300
Automotive Writer
Detroit News, Detroit, MI
Yunt, Thomas A .... (319) 588-5611
VP/PUB, Telegraph Herald, Dubuque, IA
Yuste, Jose A .... (305) 633-3341
ADV MGR-CLASS
Diario Las Americas, Miami, FL
Yznaga, Bob .... (805) 564-5200
PROD MGR-PR, Santa Barbara News-Press, Santa Barbara, CA

Z

Zabrodsky, Michael .... (716) 487-1111
Television ED, Post-Journal, Jamestown, NY
Zaccamundeo, A .... (515) 653-2344
GM, Hedrick Journal, Hedrick, IA
Zaccaria, Judy .... (316) 221-1050
Lifestyle ED
Winfield Daily Courier, Winfield, KS
Zacchino, Narda .... (213) 237-5000
VP-ASSOC ED, ASSOC ED/VP
Los Angeles Times, Los Angeles, CA
Zachariah, Holly .... (937) 644-9111
MAN ED
Marysville Journal-Tribune, Marysville, OH
Zacharias, Pat .... (313) 222-2300
Librarian, Detroit News, Detroit, MI
Zacharias, Steven R .... (804) 649-6000
TREAS, Media General Inc., Richmond, VA
Zaemisch, Peg .... (715) 235-3411
ED, Dunn County News, Menomonie, WI
Zaffarano, Steve .... (718) 981-1234
Photo DEPT MGR
Staten Island Advance, Staten Island, NY
Zagone, J C .... (318) 459-3200
PROD DIR, Times, Shreveport, LA
Zagorski III, Edward J .... (414) 485-2016
ED, Horicon Reporter, Horicon, WI
Zagrzecki, Richard .... (713) 232-3737
City ED, Herald-Coaster, Rosenberg, TX
Zahara, Dan .... (403) 765-3604
ED, Rycroft Central Peace Signal, Rycroft, AB
Zainey, Joseph E .... (317) 542-8149
PUB
Lawrence Township Journal, Lawrence, IN
Zainey, Shelly .... (317) 542-8149
GM, ED
Lawrence Township Journal, Lawrence, IN
Zaiser, Catherine .... (701) 253-7311
Entertainment ED, Fashion ED, Lifestyle ED
Forum, Fargo, ND
Zajac, Ken .... (215) 942-7890
NTL Sales MGR, Sports Network (Div. of Computer Info. Network), Southampton, PA
Zajakowski, Michael .... (219) 933-3200
Photo ED, Times, Munster, IN
Zakarian, John J .... (860) 241-6200
EPE, Hartford Courant, Hartford, CT
Zakes, Jerry .... (317) 633-1240
CIRC ASST DIR
Indianapolis Star/News, Indianapolis, IN
Zales, Joan .... (719) 632-5511
Features ED, Gazette, Colorado Springs, CO
Zaleski, Jack .... (701) 253-7311
EPE, Forum, Fargo, ND
Zalewski, Dale .... (605) 225-4100
DIR-INFO SYS
Aberdeen American News, Aberdeen, SD
Zaltsberg, Robert .... (812) 332-4401
ED, EPE, Herald-Times Inc, Bloomington, IN
Zambiasi, Donna .... (972) 377-2141
ED, Frisco Enterprise, Frisco, TX
Zandbergen, Yvette .... (519) 344-3641
Fashion/Society ED, Observer, Sarnia, ON
Zander, Jerry .... (406) 365-3303
PUB, Glendive Ranger-Review, Glendive, MT
Zander, Larry .... (360) 736-3311
EPE, Chronicle, Centralia, WA
Zander, Noel .... (414) 756-2222
PUB, Brillion News, Brillion, WI
Zander, Robert .... (616) 527-2100
PROD MGR, Sentinel-Standard, Ionia, MI
Zander, Zane C .... (414) 756-2222
PUB, ED, Brillion News, Brillion, WI
Zane, Peder .... (919) 829-4500
Books ED, News & Observer, Raleigh, NC
Zanella, Bob .... (970) 945-8515
ADV MGR, ADTX MGR
Glenwood Post, Glenwood Springs, CO
Zanetos, Carla .... (419) 352-4611
EDU ED
Sentinel-Tribune, Bowling Green, OH
Zanghi, Domenic .... (609) 663-6000
ADV MGR-CLASS
Courier-Post, Cherry Hill, NJ
Zankowski, Francis J .... (860) 548-9300
PUB, Hartford Advocate, Hartford, CT
Zanmiller, Pete .... (810) 985-7171
PROD DIR-OPER
Times Herald, Port Huron, MI
Zanon, Geri .... (360) 452-2345
Librarian
Peninsula Daily News, Port Angeles, WA
Zanotelli, Cheri .... (719) 544-3520
Design ED, Pueblo Chieftain, Pueblo, CO
Zant, John .... (805) 564-5200
Sports COL, Santa Barbara News-Press, Santa Barbara, CA
Zapcic, William .... (908) 246-5500
Night ED
Home News & Tribune, East Brunswick, NJ
Zappe, John .... (562) 435-1161
State/Web ED
Press-Telegram, Long Beach, CA
Zasada, Cathy .... (602) 271-8000
ADV MGR-GEN (N.R.S.D.)
Phoenix Newspapers Inc., Phoenix, AZ
Zaslow, Jeffrey .... (312) 321-3000
COL-Advice, Chicago Sun-Times, Chicago, IL
Zastrow, Marilyn .... (308) 382-4660
ED
West Nebraska Register, Grand Island, NE
Zautyk, Karen .... (212) 210-2100
EDL Writer, Daily News, New York, NY
Zavadil, Christopher J .... (402) 454-3818
PUB, ED, Madison Star-Mail, Madison, NE
Zavala, Elizabeth .... (817) 390-7400
ED-La Estrella, Star-Telegram, Fort Worth, TX
Zavala, Richard .... (520) 783-3333
PROD FRM-PR, Yuma Daily Sun, Yuma, AZ
Zavalick, Charles T .... (908) 766-3900
ED, Bernardsville News, Bernardsville, NJ
Zavarise, Dean .... (416) 367-2000
PROD ASST DIR, Toronto Star, Toronto, ON
Zavinski, John .... (412) 981-6100
Graphics ED/Art DIR, Herald, Sharon, PA
Zavoral, Linda .... (408) 920-5000
Getting Ahead ED
San Jose Mercury News, San Jose, CA

Copyright ©1997 by the Editor & Publisher Co.

Zaw   Who's Where-256

Zawacki, Kay .... (901) 658-3691
GM, Bolivar Bulletin-Times, Bolivar, TN
Zawacki, Mark .... (602) 898-6500
PROD MGR-Pre Press, Mesa Tribune, Mesa,
AZ, Thomson Newspapers
Zawislak, Jim .... (218) 723-5281
PROD FRM-Ad Composition
Duluth News-Tribune, Duluth, MN
Zbick, Jim .... (610) 377-2051
ASSOC ED, NTL ED, Political/Government
ED, Wire ED, Times News, Lehighton, PA
Zebora, James .... (203) 235-1661
BUS ED, Record-Journal, Meriden, CT
Zebora, Jim .... (203) 235-1758
Self-Syndicator, What's Brewing, Meriden, CT
Zebrun-Gero, Tom .... (406) 447-4000
ADV MGR-RT
Helena Independent Record, Helena, MT
Zechman, Pat .... (615) 473-2191
GM, Southern Standard, McMinnville, TN
Zeeck, David A .... (206) 597-8742
EX ED, News Tribune, Tacoma, WA
Zeeman, Diane S .... (914) 696-8245
ED, Bronxville Review-Press Reporter,
Yonk-ers, NY
Zegers, Sally .... (607) 637-3591
ED, Hancock Herald, Hancock, NY
Zeggert, Dave .... (607) 798-1234
Photo/Graphics ED
Press & Sun Bulletin, Binghamton, NY
Zehner, Gary .... (800) 583-6056
EX DIR, Name Game Co. Inc., Plantation, FL
Zehr, Jeff .... (864) 582-4511
Graphics ED, Herald-Journal, Spartanburg, SC
Zeiger, Dinah .... (303) 820-1010
Technology ED, Denver Post, Denver, CO
Zeigler, Clay .... (904) 599-2100
News ED, Democrat, Tallahassee, FL
Zeiglex, Gordon .... (806) 296-1300
Online MGR
Plainview Daily Herald, Plainview, TX
Zeimen, Nancy .... (517) 627-6085
ED
Delta-Waverly News Herald, Grand Ledge, MI
Zeiner, Jerald W .... (319) 291-1400
BM, Waterloo Courier, Waterloo, IA
Zeisman, Derek .... (604) 365-5266
ED, Castlegar Sun, Castlegar, BC
Zeiss, Timothy P .... (908) 922-6000
MGR-CORP Communications
Asbury Park Press, Neptune, NJ
Zelisko, Larry .... (915) 673-4271
News ED, Reporter-News, Abilene, TX
Zell, Joy .... (403) 742-2395
ED, Stettler Independent, Stettler, AB
Zellars, Todd .... (317) 653-5151
COL/Sports Writer
Banner-Graphic, Greencastle, IN
Zellers, Terry .... (717) 767-6397
PROD MGR-Transportation
York Newspaper Company, York, PA
Zellman, Ande .... (617) 929-2000
ASSOC ED-New Media
Boston Globe, Boston, MA
Zellmer, Doug .... (414) 235-7700
Farm/Agriculture ED
Oshkosh Northwestern, Oshkosh, WI
Zellmer, Pat .... (573) 335-6611
ADV MGR-Sales
Southeast Missourian, Cape Girardeau, MO
Zelnik, Joseph R .... (609) 886-8600
ED, Herald Newspapers, Rio Grande, NJ
Zelz, Eric .... (207) 990-8000
Graphics/Design DIR
Bangor Daily News, Bangor, ME
Zeman, Lori .... (618) 542-2133
MAN ED, Ashley News, Du Quion, IL
Zeman, Tammy .... (405) 363-3370
ADV DIR
Blackwell Journal-Tribune, Blackwell, OK
Zemnickas, Karen .... (313) 222-6400
PROD OPER MGR-Administrative
Detroit Newspapers, Detroit, MI
Zemrak, Gary .... (207) 873-3341
BM, Central Maine Morning Sentinel, Waterville, ME, Guy Gannett Communications
Zender, Stephen C .... (419) 396-7567
PUB, ED, Mohawk Leader, Sycamore, OH
Zenick, Gerald .... (817) 390-7400
VP-OPER
Fort Worth Star-Telegram, Fort Worth, TX
Zenor, Mary Lou .... (319) 398-8211
ASSOC-CR, Gazette, Cedar Rapids, IA
Zentz, Rachel .... (408) 424-2221
Graphics ED (interim)
Californian, Salinas, CA
Zentz, Renny .... (319) 588-5611
Sports ED, Telegraph Herald, Dubuque, IA
Zepeda-Liberman, Angela .... (408) 920-5000
MGR-Hispanic MKTG
San Jose Mercury News, San Jose, CA

Zepp, George .... (615) 259-8000
ED-Night/Weekend
Tennessean, Nashville, TN
Zepp, Ken .... (215) 855-8440
Photo DEPT MGR, Reporter, Landsdale, PA
Zerbe, Carter .... (316) 775-2218
PUB, Augusta Daily Gazette, Augusta, KS
Zerbey IV, Joseph H .... (717) 767-6397
PRES, York Newspaper Company, York, PA
Zerbisias, Antonia .... (416) 367-2000
Radio/Television Writer
Toronto Star, Toronto, ON
Zerilli, Joseph R .... (810) 296-6007
PUB, Detroit Monitor, Fraser, MI
Zeringue, Jeff .... (318) 942-4971
COL, Fashion/Society ED, Films/Theater ED,
Food/Garden ED, Women's ED
Daily World, Opelousas, LA
Zerrer, Brian .... (330) 264-1125
PROD MGR-Typesetting/Ad Composition
Daily Record, Wooster, OH
Zessimopoulos, Thanasis .... (718) 626-7676
GM, Proini, Long Island City, NY
Zettler, Linda .... (904) 435-8500
Health/Medical ED
Pensacola News Journal, Pensacola, FL
Zettler, Marie .... (613) 646-2380
ED, Cobden Sun, Cobden, ON
Zettler, Phyllis .... (601) 862-3141
GM, Itawamba County Times, Fulton, MS
Zeve, Bradley .... (408) 394-5656
PUB, Coast Weekly, Seaside, CA
Zey, Chris .... (816) 271-8500
CIRC MGR-Regional Sales
St. Joseph News-Press, St. Joseph, MO
Zhu, Louise .... (617) 426-9492
ED-Chinese, Sampan, Boston, MA
Zickafoose, Sherri .... (403) 627-3252
ED, Pincher Creek Echo, Pincher Creek, AB
Zidich, John .... (702) 788-6200
ADV DIR, Reno Gazette-Journal, Reno, NV
Ziebell, Bob .... (714) 634-1567
ED, Fullerton News-Tribune, Anaheim, CA
Ziegler, Darlene .... (205) 353-4612
ADV MGR-CLASS, Decatur Daily, Decatur, AL
Ziegler, George .... (309) 364-3250
PUB, Henry News Republican, Henry, IL
Ziegler, Harry .... (908) 922-6000
MAN ED-Lifestyles
Asbury Park Press, Neptune, NJ
Ziegler, Joe .... (605) 331-2200
PROD MGR-Pre Press
Argus Leader, Sioux Falls, SD
Ziegler, Lou .... (318) 289-6300
MAN ED, Advertiser, Lafayette, LA
Ziegler, Monika .... (212) 873-7400
ED, Aufbau, New York, NY
Ziegler, Robert .... (412) 775-3200
PROD SUPV-Computer SYS
Beaver County Times, Beaver, PA
Ziegler, Wayne .... (610) 622-8800
CIRC DIR
Delaware County Daily Times, Primos, PA
Ziehm, Len .... (312) 321-3000
Sports Active Page-Golf/Tennis
Chicago Sun-Times, Chicago, IL
Zielinski, Leszek .... (813) 525-2100
ED, Horyzonty, Sheboygan, WI
Zielinski, Michael C .... (610) 371-5000
MET ED, Reading Times/Eagle, Reading, PA
Zieman, Mark .... (816) 234-4141
MAN ED-News, Star, Kansas City, MO
Zientara, Bob .... (715) 386-9333
MAN ED, Hudson Star-Observer, Hudson, WI
Zientarski, Carol .... (216) 245-6901
Home Furnishings ED, Living ED
Morning Journal, Lorain, OH
Zientek, M P .... (713) 659-5461
ED, Texas Catholic Herald, Houston, TX
Zieralski, Ed .... (619) 299-3131
Outdoors Writer
San Diego Union-Tribune, San Diego, CA
Zieschang, Ernie E .... (409) 336-3611
PUB, ED, Liberty Vindicator, Liberty, TX
Zikias, Robert .... (203) 964-2200
VP/CFO, VP/CONT/DIR of Systems, Stamford
Advocate, Stamford, CT, Times Mirror Co.
Zima, Jim .... (414) 435-4411
SYS ED, Press-Gazette, Green Bay, WI
Zimbalist III, Efrem .... (213) 237-3700
VP/PRES & CEO-Times Mirror Magazines
Times Mirror Co., Los Angeles, CA
Zimbrakos, Paul .... (312) 782-8100
MAN ED
City News Bureau of Chicago, Chicago, IL
Zimerle, Ronnie .... (912) 923-6432
PROD MGR, Daily Sun, Warner Robins, GA
Ziminsky, Geoffrey .... (603) 882-2741
MIS MGR, Telegraph, Nashua, NH
Zimmer, Arthur .... (315) 422-7011
PUB, Syracuse New Times, Syracuse, NY
Zimmer, Bill .... (320) 235-1150
Photo DEPT MGR
West Central Tribune, Willmar, MN
Zimmer, Jeff .... (919) 419-6500
Medical Reporter, Herald-Sun, Durham, NC

Zimmer, Teresa .... (619) 337-3400
TREAS, CONT
Imperial Valley Press, El Centro, CA
Zimmer, Vanessa .... (801) 625-4200
Entertainment/Amusements ED,
Standard-Examiner, Ogden, UT
Zimmerman, Bill .... (601) 924-7142
ED, Clinton News, Clinton, MS
Zimmerman, Brad .... (770) 532-1234
CONT, Times, Gainesville, GA
Zimmerman, Carl .... (808) 525-8000
EDL Writer
Honolulu Star-Bulletin, Honolulu, HI
Zimmerman, Carol .... (770) 532-1234
ADV MGR-CLASS, Times, Gainesville, GA
Zimmerman, Cathy .... (360) 577-2500
Food/Women's ED, Lifestyle ED
Daily News, Longview, WA
Zimmerman, Chris .... (316) 251-3300
ADV DIR, Coffeyville Journal, Coffeyville, KS
Zimmerman, Dan .... (707) 762-4541
PUB, Argus-Courier, Petaluma, CA
Zimmerman, Hank .... (540) 465-5137
Consultant
Northern Virginia Daily, Strasburg, VA
Zimmerman, Harvey .... (209) 441-6111
MGR-Community Relations
Fresno Bee, Fresno, CA
Zimmerman, Jackie .... (409) 632-6631
City ED, Lufkin Daily News, Lufkin, TX
Zimmerman, Josephine .... (801) 373-5050
Farm/Garden ED, Daily Herald, Provo, UT
Zimmerman, Molly .... (903) 834-6178
PUB, ED, Overton Press, Overton, TX
Zimmerman, Rebecca .... (505) 821-3214
ED
New Mexico Jewish Link, Albuquerque, NM
Zimmerman, Rex .... (316) 825-4229
PUB, ED, Kiowa News, Kiowa, KS
Zimmerman, William .... (601) 961-7000
Community ED
Jackson Clarion-Ledger, Jackson, MS
Zimmermann, Mark V .... (301) 853-4599
ED, Catholic Standard, Hyattsville, MD
Zink, Brian .... (317) 659-4622
News ED, Times, Frankfort, IN
Zink, Joe .... (402) 374-2225
PUB, Burt County Plaindealer, Tekamah, NE
Zink, Roger .... (715) 735-6611
PROD MGR-Press
EagleHerald, Marinette, WI
Zinke, Karl .... (816) 826-1000
Sports ED, Sedalia Democrat, Sedalia, MO
Zinn, David W .... (304) 348-5140
VP/TREAS
Charleston Newspapers, Charleston, WV
Zinn, Rhonda .... (316) 775-2218
Graphics ED/Art DIR
Augusta Daily Gazette, Augusta, KS
Zinselmeier, Rich .... (414) 634-3322
ADV MGR-RT, Journal Times, Racine, WI
Ziomek, John E .... (609) 663-6000
ADV DIR, Courier-Post, Cherry Hill, NJ
Ziomek, Karl .... (313) 246-0828
ED, News-Herald Newspapers, Southgate, MI
Zipp, Fred .... (561) 820-4100
MET ED
Palm Beach Post, West Palm Beach, FL
Zipp, Judith .... (210) 225-7411
Librarian
San Antonio Express-News, San Antonio, TX
Zipperer, Joanne .... (414) 435-4411
State ED
Green Bay Press-Gazette, Green Bay, WI
Zipperlen, Gene .... (817) 390-7400
Copy Desk Chief
Fort Worth Star-Telegram, Fort Worth, TX
Zippert, Carol .... (205) 372-3373
PUB, Greene County Democrat, Eutaw, AL
Zippert, John .... (205) 372-3373
PUB, ED
Greene County Democrat, Eutaw, AL
Zirkel, Mary Jane .... (415) 348-4321
TREAS
San Mateo County Times, San Mateo, CA
Zisko, Allison .... (516) 569-4000
ED, Baldwin Herald, Lawrence, NY
Zisman, Lawrence H .... (609) 443-4012
Author, MarketPlace Project, Princeton, NJ
Zitko, Don .... (314) 340-8000
VP-CONT, Post-Dispatch, St. Louis, MO
Zitko, Donald J .... (314) 340-8402
VP, Pulitzer Publishing Co., St. Louis, MO
Zito, Casper M .... (203) 333-0161
MGR-BUS, Connecticut Post, Bridgeport, CT
Zitrin, Richard .... (716) 394-0770
EPE, Daily Messenger/Sunday Messenger,
Canandaigua, NY
Zivitz, Marvin .... (514) 987-2222
ASST MAN ED, Gazette, Montreal, QC
Zizza, Susan .... (603) 237-5501
MAN ED, News and Sentinel, Colebrook, NH
Zlotky, Alan .... (202) 636-3000
Deputy DIR-Photography
Washington Times, Washington, DC

Zloza, Marlene .... (219) 696-7711
ED, Lowell Tribune/Cedar Lake Journal,
Lowell, IN
Zmijewski, Richard .... (201) 365-3000
City ED
North Jersey Herald & News, Passaic, NJ
Zobell, Charles .... (702) 383-0211
MAN ED, Review-Journal, Las Vegas, NV
Zoeckler, Eric L .... (206) 284-9566
COL, Taming The Workplace, Seattle, WA
Zoeller, David .... (309) 692-4910
GM, Observer, Peoria, IL
Zoghby, J C .... (334) 433-1551
Health/Medical Reporter
Mobile Press Register, Mobile, AL
Zohner-Maxwell, Anne .... (316) 225-4151
Society/ Women's ED
Dodge City Daily Globe, Dodge City, KS
Zoldan, Denise .... (941) 262-3161
EDU ED, Naples Daily News, Naples, FL
Zollinger, Jan .... (609) 597-3211
ED, Beacon Mailbag, Manahawkin, NJ
Zollinger, John K .... (505) 863-6811
Chairman, Gallup Independent, Gallup, NM
Zollinger, Robert C .... (505) 863-6811
VP, PUB, Gallup Independent, Gallup, NM
Zollman, Joseph .... (516) 431-6697
Author/Owner
Stamping Grounds, Long Beach, NY
Zomparelli, Wendy .... (540) 981-3100
ED, Roanoke Times, Roanoke, VA
Zon, Karl .... (415) 431-4792
PUB, Beacon, San Francisco, CA
Zopatti, Steve .... (508) 586-7200
PROD FRM-PR, Enterprise, Brockton, MA
Zorc, Frank .... (708) 336-7000
PROD MGR-Pre Press
News-Sun, Waukegan, IL
Zorichak, Maureen M .... (412) 439-7500
ADV DIR, MGR-MKTG
Herald-Standard, Uniontown, PA
Zorn, Eric .... (312) 222-3232
COL-MET, Chicago Tribune, Chicago, IL
Zorzi, Bill .... (410) 332-6000
COL-Political, Sun, Baltimore, MD
Zoucha, Pam .... (402) 721-5000
ADV DIR, Fremont Tribune, Fremont, NE
Zsenai, John .... (510) 935-2525
DIR-FIN/ADM
Contra Costa Times, Walnut Creek, CA
Zuber, Constance Haas .... (219) 461-8222
Neighbors ED, News-Sentinel, Fort Wayne, IN
Zucca, John .... (212) 210-2100
PROD MGR-Plant (Kearny)
New York Daily News, New York, NY
Zucchino, David .... (215) 854-2000
Foreign ED, Inquirer, Philadelphia, PA
Zucker, Diane .... (914) 677-8241
ED, Gazette Advertiser, Millbrook, NY
Zucker, Harvey .... (201) 653-1000
Sports ED, Jersey Journal, Jersey City, NJ
Zuckerman, Mortimer B .... (212) 210-2100
Chairman/Co-PUB
New York Daily News, New York, NY
Zuelke, Lauren .... (205) 766-3434
News ED, Times Daily, Florence, AL
Zuhl, Joanne .... (765) 362-1200
Civic Affairs ED, Political ED
Journal Review, Crawfordsville, IN
Zuhl, Kris .... (616) 222-5400
ADV MGR-Major Accounts
Grand Rapids Press, Grand Rapids, MI
Zummo, Sandra .... (718) 981-1234
Home Furnishings ED
Staten Island Advance, Staten Island, NY
Zuppa, Thomas .... (508) 458-7100
Suburban ED, Sun, Lowell, MA
Zurbrick, Kristy .... (614) 852-0809
ED, Madison Messenger, London, OH
Zusman, Mark L .... (503) 243-2122
ED, Willamette Week, Portland, OR
Zutaut, R E (Bob) .... (304) 255-4400
DIR-OPER, PROD MGR
Register Herald, Beckley, WV
Zuzel, Mike .... (360) 694-3391
EDL Writer, Columbian, Vancouver, WA
Zwahlen, Cyndia .... (213) 237-5000
Banking, Los Angeles Times, Los Angeles, CA
Zwaniga, David .... (519) 894-2231
PROD MGR, Record, Kitchener, ON
Zwecker, Bill .... (312) 321-3000
COL-Celebrities, Sun-Times, Chicago, IL
Zweifel, Dave .... (608) 252-6400
VP-EDL, Capital Times, Madison, WI
Zwick, Ray .... (513) 721-2700
Librarian, Enquirer, Cincinnati, OH
Zwierzchowski, Constance ...... (313) 961-3949
ASST Legal ED
Detroit Legal News, Detroit, MI
Zwingli, John C .... (212) 208-8000
Group VP Equity Services, Corporation
Records, Daily News, New York, NY
Zwolakski, Robert .... (313) 841-0100
GM, El Central, Detroit, MI
Zyla, Gregory J .... (717) 682-9081
PUB, ED, Citizen-Standard, Valley View, PA

Copyright ©1997 by the Editor & Publisher Co.